SAN JOAQUIN VALLEY LIBRARY SYSTEM

W9-BGG-788

R 973 DIC sup. 7   cop 1
Dictionary of American
 Biography, sup. 7
                          $50.00

1 9 JAN 1982

Tulare County Free Library
THIS BOOK DOES NOT CIRCULATE
FOR REFERENCE USE ONLY

DICTIONARY
OF
AMERICAN BIOGRAPHY

PUBLISHED UNDER THE AUSPICES OF
THE AMERICAN COUNCIL OF LEARNED SOCIETIES

The American Council of Learned Societies, organized in 1919 for the purpose of advancing the study of the humanities and of the humanistic aspects of the social sciences, is a nonprofit federation comprising forty-three national scholarly groups. The Council represents the humanities in the United States in the International Union of Academies, provides fellowships and grants-in-aid, supports research-and-planning conferences and symposia, and sponsors special projects and scholarly publications.

MEMBER ORGANIZATIONS
AMERICAN PHILOSOPHICAL SOCIETY, 1743
AMERICAN ACADEMY OF ARTS AND SCIENCES, 1780
AMERICAN ANTIQUARIAN SOCIETY, 1812
AMERICAN ORIENTAL SOCIETY, 1842
AMERICAN NUMISMATIC SOCIETY, 1858
AMERICAN PHILOLOGICAL ASSOCIATION, 1869
ARCHAEOLOGICAL INSTITUTE OF AMERICA, 1879
SOCIETY OF BIBLICAL LITERATURE, 1880
MODERN LANGUAGE ASSOCIATION OF AMERICA, 1883
AMERICAN HISTORICAL ASSOCIATION, 1884
AMERICAN ECONOMIC ASSOCIATION, 1885
AMERICAN FOLKLORE SOCIETY, 1888
AMERICAN DIALECT SOCIETY, 1889
AMERICAN PSYCHOLOGICAL ASSOCIATION, 1892
ASSOCIATION OF AMERICAN LAW SCHOOLS, 1900
AMERICAN PHILOSOPHICAL ASSOCIATION, 1901
AMERICAN ANTHROPOLOGICAL ASSOCIATION, 1902
AMERICAN POLITICAL SCIENCE ASSOCIATION, 1903
BIBLIOGRAPHICAL SOCIETY OF AMERICA, 1904
ASSOCIATION OF AMERICAN GEOGRAPHERS, 1904
HISPANIC SOCIETY OF AMERICA, 1904
AMERICAN SOCIOLOGICAL ASSOCIATION, 1905
AMERICAN SOCIETY OF INTERNATIONAL LAW, 1906
ORGANIZATION OF AMERICAN HISTORIANS, 1907
COLLEGE ART ASSOCIATION OF AMERICA, 1912
HISTORY OF SCIENCE SOCIETY, 1924
LINGUISTIC SOCIETY OF AMERICA, 1924
MEDIAEVAL ACADEMY OF AMERICA, 1925
AMERICAN MUSICOLOGICAL SOCIETY, 1934
SOCIETY OF ARCHITECTURAL HISTORIANS, 1940
ECONOMIC HISTORY ASSOCIATION, 1940
ASSOCIATION FOR ASIAN STUDIES, 1941
AMERICAN SOCIETY FOR AESTHETICS, 1942
METAPHYSICAL SOCIETY OF AMERICA, 1950
AMERICAN STUDIES ASSOCIATION, 1950
RENAISSANCE SOCIETY OF AMERICA, 1954
SOCIETY FOR ETHNOMUSICOLOGY, 1955
AMERICAN SOCIETY FOR LEGAL HISTORY, 1956
AMERICAN SOCIETY FOR THEATRE RESEARCH, 1956
SOCIETY FOR THE HISTORY OF TECHNOLOGY, 1958
AMERICAN COMPARATIVE LITERATURE ASSOCIATION, 1960
AMERICAN ACADEMY OF RELIGION, 1963
AMERICAN SOCIETY FOR EIGHTEENTH-CENTURY STUDIES, 1969

DICTIONARY
OF
American Biography

Supplement Seven

1961–1965

John A. Garraty, *Editor*

WITH AN INDEX GUIDE TO THE SUPPLEMENTS

Charles Scribner's Sons

NEW YORK

cop 1

The preparation of the original twenty volumes of the Dictionary was made possible by the public-spirited action of the New York Times Company and its president, the late Adolph S. Ochs, in furnishing a large subvention. The preparation and publication of Supplement 7 have been supported by the sale of those volumes and the preceding Supplements. Entire responsibility for the contents of the Dictionary and its Supplements rests with the American Council of Learned Societies.

COPYRIGHT © 1981 AMERICAN COUNCIL OF LEARNED SOCIETIES

Library of Congress Cataloging in Publication Data (Revised)
Main entry under title:

Dictionary of American biography.

Includes index.
Supplements 1–2 comprise v. 11 of the main work.
CONTENTS: 3. 1941–1945.—4. 1946–1950—
5. 1951–1955.   —7. 1961–1965.
1. United States—Biography. I. Garraty, John
Arthur, 1920–
E176.D563 suppl. 2   920'.073   77–2942
ISBN 0–684–16794–8 (Suppl. 7)   AACR1

This book published simultaneously in the
United States of America and in Canada–
Copyright under the Berne Convention

All rights reserved. No part of this book
may be reproduced in any form without the
permission of Charles Scribner's Sons.

1 3 5 7 9 11 13 15 17 19   V/C   20 18 16 14 12 10 8 6 4 2

Printed in the United States of America

The paper in this book meets the guidelines for
permanence and durability of the Committee on
Production Guidelines for Book Longevity of the
Council on Library Resources.

American Council of Learned Societies Committee on the
Dictionary of American Biography

ROBERT M. LUMIANSKY, *Chairman*

FREDERICK BURKHARDT

ALFRED D. CHANDLER, JR.

GEORGE W. CORNER

IRVING DILLIARD

WENDELL D. GARRETT

PETER J. GOMES

CARYL P. HASKINS

DAVID McCORD

DUMAS MALONE

JOAN HOFF WILSON

LEONARD G. WILSON

HARRIET A. ZUCKERMAN

Editorial Staff

DAVID WILLIAM VOORHEES, *MANAGING EDITOR*

CHRISTIANE L. DESCHAMPS, *Assistant Managing Editor*

G. MICHAEL McGINLEY, *Associate Editor*

JAMES F. MAURER, *Assistant Editor*

CAROLYN PATTON, *Assistant Editor*

MARYLOU H. MANTLO, *Editorial Assistant*

JOEL HONIG, *Associate Editor*

ELIZABETH I. WILSON, *Associate Editor*

JOHN F. FITZPATRICK, *Copy Editor*

INA JAEGER, *Copy Editor*

LELAND S. LOWTHER, *Copy Editor*

IRINA RYBACEK, *Copy Editor*

JANET HORNBERGER, *Production Supervisor*

MARSHALL DE BRUHL, *DIRECTOR, REFERENCE BOOK DIVISION*

PREFACE

With this supplement, which contains biographies of 572 persons, written by more than 400 authors, the *Dictionary of American Biography* extends its coverage through December 31, 1965, and reaches a total of 17,656 sketches. As with earlier volumes, this one could not have been completed without the generous and unpaid cooperation of dozens of experts in various fields. These scholars have assisted both in deciding which persons to include in the supplement and in locating authors for the biographies. I wish to thank them most sincerely for their help.

As was the case with *Supplements Five* and *Six*, the authors of the sketches have been asked to fill out data sheets for their subjects covering the following information: Section I: full date of birth and death; place of birth; full name of father; full name of mother; father's occupation; economic and social position of the family at the time of the subject's birth; education; institutions attended, dates, degrees earned; full name of spouse, or if never married mention of this fact; date of marriage; number of children, names of any of apparent historical importance; place of death. Section II: number of siblings, number of each sex; order of birth of subject, order among those of same sex; economic and social position of mother's family; names of close relatives who achieved distinction; nationality and time of migration to the United States of ancestors; religious affiliation of subject; religious affiliations of father and mother; religious affiliation of spouse; economic and social position of spouse at time of marriage; highest education of spouse; names and dates of birth of children; cause of subject's death; place of burial; date of spouse's death.

Authors were asked to include in their essays all the facts in Section I, but only such details from Section II as seemed relevant. The purpose was to gather the material in a form convenient for researchers, but to keep most of it out of the biographies themselves. The data sheets will be placed on file along with other *DAB* papers in the Library of Congress, so that sociologists, psychologists, and other researchers interested in collective biography can have access to them.

As with past volumes, we are much indebted to individuals and institutions that have provided help with our editorial task, particularly Elizabeth Mason and the late Louis Starr of the Oral History Collection, Columbia University; Susan O. Thompson of Columbia University; Walter C. Allen and Rolland E. Stevens of the University of Illinois; Haynes McMullen of the University of North Carolina; Ronald Blazek and Charles William Conway of Florida State University; Linda Lucas of the University of South Carolina; Robert D. Harlan of the University of California, Berkeley; Julia Emmons of Emory University; Mary Lee Bundy of the University of Maryland; and Gordon Eriksen of Western Michigan University. We are most grateful for the assistance of all these persons.

I wish also once again to thank the American Council of Learned Societies, its president, Robert Lumiansky, and the members of the council's board for the *DAB* for their many kindnesses and wise guidance.

JOHN A. GARRATY

DICTIONARY

OF

AMERICAN BIOGRAPHY

ADAMS, FRANK RAMSAY (July 7, 1883–
Oct. 8, 1963), novelist, lyricist, playwright, and
screenwriter, was born in Morrison, Ill., the son
of George Bradford Adams, an editor, and Lucy
E. Ramsay. Adams graduated from Hyde Park
High School in Chicago in 1900. Four years
later he received a Ph.B. from the University of
Chicago, where earlier he and Will M. Hough
had begun collaborating with Joseph Edgar
("Joe") Howard, the well-known composer,
singer, director, and producer. During his career, Adams wrote lyrics for over 200 songs.

Howard, Adams, and Hough dominated the
Chicago musical stage for almost a decade.
Some of their works appeared on Broadway, although with far less popular and critical appeal.
Their first success was *His Highness, the Bey*,
which began a three-month run on Nov. 21,
1904, at the La Salle Theatre. *The Isle of Bong-
Bong* premiered on Mar. 14, 1905, and starred
Howard, with Cecil Lean and Florence Holbrook, who would appear in other works by the
trio and become Chicago's most popular stage
stars of the day. *The Umpire*, opened on Dec.
2, 1905, and ran for 300 performances.

During the 1906–1907 Chicago season *The
Girl Question* and *The Time, the Place, and
the Girl* were long-running triumphs. The
latter contained the popular songs "Blow
the Smoke Away" and "Waning Honeymoon,"
and its 400-plus performances remained unsurpassed in Chicago for years. On July 23, 1907,
Adams married Hazel Leslie Judd; they had no
children.

The 1908 season saw the trio's *Honeymoon
Trail* at the La Salle and also *A Stubborn Cinderella*, which inaugurated the Princess Theater, enjoyed 300 performances, and included the
song "When You First Kiss the Last Girl You

Love." Despite the good notices for the young
John Barrymore, *Cinderella* was less successful
in New York in 1909. Howard, Hough, and
Adams offered *The Prince of Tonight, The
Golden Girl, The Flirting Princess*, and *The
Goddess of Liberty* in 1909. The first of these
musicals presented the song "I Wonder Who's
Kissing Her Now," the music of which was com-
posed by Harold Orlob.

Miss Nobody from Starland (1910) ran for
only fifteen weeks and marked the end of the
trio's collaboration. Hough and Adams created
The Heart-Breakers in 1911, with a score by
Orlob and Melville J. Gideon, but this too did
not achieve the popularity of their earlier works.

Adams then turned to fictional and journalis-
tic writing. He was a reporter for the *Chicago
Tribune, Daily News*, and *Chicago Herald and
Examiner*. He also published two novels: *Five
Fridays* (1915) and *Molly and I, or the Silver
Ring* (1915). Both of these light and witty
works were made into musicals. George Broad-
hurst wrote *Fast and Grow Fat* (1916), based on
Five Fridays, and Adams worked with Louis
Hirsch on the musical *Molly and I* (1915).

After serving as a first lieutenant in the
Coast Artillery Corps during World War I,
Adams returned to fiction writing. His many
light-hearted romances (sometimes tinged
with intrigues of murder) included *Stage-
struck* (1924), *Peter and Mrs. Pan* (1929),
Help Yourself to Happiness (1929), *Long
Night* (1929), *King's Crew* (1929), *Secret
Attic* (1930), *Gangway* (1931), *For Valor*
(1931), *Happiness Preferred* (1936), *She Said
I Do* (1937), *Men on Foot* (1937), *Gunsight
Ranch* (1939), *Fathers of Madelon* (1939),
Arizona Feud (1941), *When I Come Back*
(1943), *The Hearse at the Wedding* (1945),

1

Nothing to Lose (1946), and *Thirteen Lucky Guys* (1951). After his first marriage ended in divorce in 1927, Adams married Lorna D. Margrave on Dec. 1, 1931; they had one daughter.

As a staff scenario writer and screenwriter in Hollywood, Adams collaborated on scripts for some twenty-five movies, including *The Cowboy and the Lady* (1938), with Gary Cooper and Merle Oberon, and *Trade Winds* (1938), with Fredric March and Joan Bennett. He worked for Metro-Goldwyn-Mayer (1932–1933); Paramount (1934–1936); and Columbia (1937). Several of his stories were made into such films as *The Marriage Cheat* (1924), with Adolphe Menjou; *Stage Struck* (1925), with Gloria Swanson; *Love in Bloom* (1935), with George Burns and Gracie Allen; and *Outcast* (1937).

Adams maintained residences in San Diego, Calif., and Whitehall, on White Lake, Mich. He died at Whitehall.

Adams' lengthy career engaged different writing forms. His role as librettist helped establish a spirited center in the Chicago theater. His journalistic endeavors, his novels, and his film scripts, although frequently as lighthearted as his lyrics, could also project stories of crime and political clashes. His main value now seems to be as a figure representative of a certain style and formation of ideas associated with American literature during the first half of the twentieth century. Yet the concise and direct narrative of his prose can still create a lasting sensitive impression upon the reader.

[The Billy Rose Theatre Collection of the New York Public Library has three unpublished works: "A Wrong-Angled Triangle," "The Haunted Hats," and "Tea For Two or Two For Tea." In addition to works mentioned in the text, Adams wrote short stories: "Love *and* Life *and* Epigrams" (Feb. 1915), "The Balcony Spot" (Mar. 1915), and "Nora" (Oct. 1915), in *Green Book Magazine;* "The Golden Nuisance" (June 1916) and "Spare Parts" (Mar. 1925), both in *American Magazine;* "Double Quits," *Good Housekeeping,* June 1923; "Sally Comes Back," *Collier's,* Dec. 26, 1925; and "Three Thousand Miles Away," *Reader's Digest,"* Nov. 1942. His novel *Haunts of Men* appeared in *Woman's Home Companion,* Feb.–July 1932.

Reviews of his work are in the *New York Times:* July 4, 1915; Apr. 30, 1939; Sept. 14, 1941; Oct. 22, 1942. See also *Life,* Sept. 14, 1916, and Nov. 21, 1938; *Newsweek,* Nov. 28, 1938, and Jan. 2, 1939; *Time,* Nov. 21, 1938, and Dec. 26, 1938. See also Gerald Bordman, *The American Musical Theatre* (1978). Adams' obituary appeared in the *New York Times,* Oct. 9, 1963.]

MADELINE SAPIENZA

ADLER, ELMER (July 22, 1884–Jan. 11, 1962), collector, printer, publisher, and bibliophile, was born in Rochester, N.Y., the son of Abram Adler and Ella Stern. His father managed the clothing firm of Rochester-Adler, one of the largest in the city. Comfortably established, socially and financially, the Adlers sent their children to private schools. Adler later alleged that he had been dismissed from at least four of them; he recorded only the two years at Powder Point, Duxbury, Mass. (1899–1901), and a final year at Phillips Academy, Andover, Mass. (1903).

About 1904 Adler began to work for the family firm, gravitating to sales promotion and advertising. In 1922 he resigned his $15,000-a-year job and moved to New York City to make a vocation of an increasingly absorbing avocation —the collecting of books and fine prints. He had started collecting as a defense, he said, against his inadequacies as a student. He bought his first piece of incunabula, a fifteenth-century book, sometime in 1909. Curiosity about the provenance of items that fell into his hands led to absorption in the history of the printed word. He had shared and promoted these interests with others in Rochester. In 1915 he organized for the Rochester Memorial Art Gallery an exhibit of James McNeill Whistler's portraiture; in 1920 he prepared an exhibit on the history of the art of printing. The success of the latter, rippling far beyond Rochester, won him recognition as an authority on the printed word.

In New York City in 1922 Adler founded Pynson Printers, named after the sixteenth-century printer Richard Pynson. Adler's primary commitment was to quality and to the belief that, in his words, "the printer should be primarily an artist—a designer and a creator rather than mere manufacturer." The firm's first significant commission came from the young publisher Alfred A. Knopf, for whom Pynson designed and printed in 1923 a limited edition of Willa Cather's 1903 book of poems, *April Twilights.*

In 1924 Pynson Printers moved into the annex of the *New York Times* building on West 43rd Street, remaining there until 1940. The establishment was noted for its handsome exhibition area and growing library that spanned five centuries of work by master printers. Equally noted were the informal seminars on prints and printmaking that Adler conducted around a wide oval table in the library.

Adler served as consultant on typography for the *New York Times,* and in 1925 for Harold Ross of the *New Yorker.* In 1924 he designed the cover for the *American Mercury,* a magazine newly launched by H. L. Mencken and George Jean Nathan. In 1938 Adler established at Pynson a permanent exhibit and center for study of the history of the printed word. Pynson placed its imprint on nearly 10,000 jobs ranging from small special printings of personal bookplates and commercial announcements to sumptuous limited editions such as the twelve volumes of *The Work of Stephen Crane* (1925–1927) for Knopf. In 1927 Adler joined with Bennett Cerf and Donald Klopfer to found Random House publishers; Pynson produced the new firm's first book, Voltaire's *Candide.*

Adler left Random House in 1932 to devote full time to Pynson and to the *Colophon: A Book Collector's Quarterly,* a venture he began in 1930. Others shared the editorial masthead, but the *Colophon* (1930–1940) was essentially Adler's show as chief editor, designer, and producer, and so, too, was the revived *New Colophon* (1948–1950). From 1930, to 1935 the *Colophon* appeared in five volumes totaling twenty parts, with each part made up of sections produced by printers other than Pynson. From 1935 to 1938 it appeared as the *New Series,* twelve numbers in three volumes, and was wholly the work of Pynson. From 1939 through 1940 it appeared as the *New Graphic Series* (subtitled *The Quarterly for Bookmen*) in four volumes, returning to the original assemblage of sections by different printers. Of the *Colophon* Edward Naumberg wrote: "It is not critical appraisal but mere statement of fact to say that a complete run is a necessity to everyone interested in books and their making." *Breaking into Print* (1937), published by Simon and Schuster, edited and designed by Adler, reproduced several accounts by writers that had originally appeared in one of the regular features of the *Colophon.*

In 1940 Adler closed down Pynson and moved with his vast library and the oval table to Princeton, N.J. He established a department of graphic arts at Princeton University, led informal seminars as a research associate, and in 1946 was named assistant professor and curator of the Department of Graphic Arts.

Retired from Princeton in June 1952, Adler retreated briefly to his Bucks County home in Erwinna, Pa., before continuing the teaching experiment begun at Princeton. In 1952–1953 he toured the South, Southwest, and California, giving informal talks on book collecting at colleges and universities. Touring again in 1953–1954, under the auspices of the American Federation of Arts, he offered joint seminars with

Dard Hunter on the graphic arts and papermaking. In March 1955 Adler's two-week vacation in Puerto Rico led to an invitation to establish an art-of-the-book project, and in September he returned for a two-year commitment to oversee the restoration of a dilapidated eighteenth-century building that was to house the project. In July 1956, this job completed, he moved in as curator of La Casa del Libro, a museum and design center. It opened on October 12 with an exhibit based on materials related to Christopher Columbus. His two-year stay extended, Adler continued his collecting and informal teaching. In 1958 an official Puerto Rico "Operation Bootstrap" advertisement appeared in several magazines featuring a full-page portrait of Adler standing before some of La Casa del Libro's new treasures and captioned "Puerto Rico and the Princeton Professor." Adler died in San Juan.

Adler's achievement is most evident in the many works of printing art that Pynson Printers and others issued under his guiding hand. All who were associated with him, while they often expressed gently ironic reservations about his business acumen, judged his influence as decisive. Some judged him dictatorial, but he exercised his authority benignly. His lifelong aim at perfection, precision, simplicity, and quality earned him the sobriquet "Squire" from undergraduates at Princeton. Somewhere in the affectionately respectful mantle of that title lies a fuller, if subtler, measure of his influence as teacher and apostle of good taste in art and life joined.

[Adler's papers and the archives of the Pynson Printers and the *Colophon* are in the Manuscript Division of Firestone Library, Princeton University.

The best single biographical source is *Elmer Adler in the World of Books* (1964), edited by Paul A. Bennett; this contains reminiscences by friends and associates, a chronological checklist, examples of Adler's typography, and a reprinting of his "Informal Talk," originally published in 1954. See also interviews in the *New Yorker*: "Adler-Pynson," Nov. 12, 1932; "Expatriate," Sept. 19, 1959. From 1940 on, both the *Princeton University Library Chronicle* and the *Princeton Alumni Weekly* published a number of short notes and articles; few books on the history of bookmaking and printing published after the 1920's are without some reference to Adler, Pynson Printers, or the *Colophon.*]

James R. Vitelli

ADLER, POLLY (Apr. 16, 1900–June 9, 1962), madam and author, was born Pearl Adler in Ivanovo, White Russia, the daughter of Isidore Adler, a tailor, and Sarah Adler. Restless, inquisitive, and ambitious, she was tutored by the village rabbi in preparation for the female gymnasium at Pinsk. She entered a scholarship competition, but before the results were known, her father decided in 1912 that she should be the first member of the family to go to the United States. When the cousin who was to accompany her turned back at Bremen, Germany, Adler embarked by herself on the *Naftar.*

While living with friends of the family in Holyoke, Mass., Adler helped with household chores and attended local schools. The outbreak of World War I prevented her family from joining her as planned, or sending further funds. She therefore had to quit school and go to work in a paper factory. Two years later she was living with relatives in Brooklyn, where she worked in a corset factory and then a shirt factory while attending night school.

In 1920, hoping to find her more remunerative work, a friend introduced Adler to a clothing manufacturer. Through an actress friend of the manufacturer, Adler was introduced to a world of fast-moving, opium-smoking theater people and "kept" women. A bootlegger-gambler who was having an affair with a married woman asked Adler to keep an apartment for them. Since this seemed an improvement over factory work, she agreed to accept payment for this arrangement.

Established in a Manhattan pied-à-terre, Adler was launched on a new career, frequenting dance halls and speakeasies to find more clients and "girls." But after her first arrest on the charge of being a procuress she decided to start a legitimate business. In 1922, having saved $6,000, she and a friend opened a lingerie shop (it was at this time that she changed her name to Polly). She was arrested again soon afterward—she claimed that the charges were trumped up.

When her shop became insolvent within a year, Adler resumed work as a madam, serving a clientele that included gangsters and hoodlums. At their suggestion she began selling liquor as well. She paid off policemen, made deals with rival madams, and stayed in apartments "hardly long enough to powder my nose." The decor of her bordellos was eclectic—Louis XV and XVI, which she claimed were "sort of traditional for a house," contrasted with rooms furnished with Egyptian or Chinese pieces. When the police went to raid one of her Saratoga Springs, N.Y., parties, where she had taken her "best girls" for the social season, the prohibition agent Moe Smith, a guest, talked the police out

of arresting her. Thereafter, as Adler's social contacts expanded, her New York "house" also became a "salon" where prominent people drank, played cards, and arranged business deals.

Despite several more arrests, by 1929 Adler was making a great deal of money from her business and the stock market. She had a joint stock account with Irwin O'Leary, a vice squad officer and friend who was dismissed from the force in 1931 because of his association with her. On May 20, 1929, Adler became a United States citizen. Although she lost a lot of money in the stock market crash later that year, her in-house business, especially at the bar, picked up.

In November 1930 Adler learned that she was about to be subpoenaed by the Seabury Committee, which was investigating corruption in the New York City criminal justice system. Anxious not to disclose her role in buying judicial favors, she fled to Miami while the press speculated on her whereabouts and hinted at her links with Vivian Gordon, a prostitute who was murdered after agreeing to testify before the committee. While Adler was in hiding, John C. Weston, who had been a special prosecutor in the Women's Court for eight years, told of taking some $20,000 in bribes in exchange for dismissing 600 cases. As part of his defense, Weston claimed that he had feared Adler's "influence." After this testimony she was especially sought as a witness. In eleven previous appearances in the court she had never been convicted; moreover, she had not even been fingerprinted.

Thinking that the focus of the investigation had shifted to those higher up in the judicial and political system, Adler returned to New York. Subpoenaed on May 6, 1931, she refused to reveal any information, alleging that "two magistrates and a Supreme Court Justice are on my string." The press, though, reported that she told a "tale of millions in graft, of gilded palaces of shame run in connivance of the Vice Squad, of the most sordid depths of New York, and of gangsters harbored in the scented boudoirs of 'Polly Adler's girls.'"

Samuel Seabury questioned Adler about her financial association with O'Leary, and asked if there was truth to the rumor that Mayor James Walker had attended one of her parties, which she denied. The climax of the investigation occurred on May 23, 1932, when Seabury confronted Walker, bringing about the mayor's resignation in September.

In some respects the Seabury investigation was actually advantageous for Adler. While attention focused on those who failed to enforce the law, those who were breaking it enjoyed a reprieve—there were very few arrests for prostitution in 1931, with policemen asking not to be assigned to the stigmatized vice squad. And it had become harder to stage frame-up arrests or to ask for payoffs.

In the early 1930's, Adler also had to contend with Arthur ("Dutch Schultz") Flegenheimer and his entourage. He was a dangerous, capricious, and unruly patron, but she had no choice but to keep a large apartment for his convenience. Since he was hiding from his archrival, Vincent ("Mad Dog") Coll, Adler lived in terror of being caught in the crossfire of gang warfare. The problem was resolved when Schultz left town shortly before Coll's murder in February 1932.

In October 1934, Adler rented an entire floor at 30 East 55th Street, Manhattan, with a staff that included two cooks, two maids, and four "girls." Tipped off that the police knew about her gambling operation, she promised to close. When she returned from vacation, she found another cleanup campaign, this time under Mayor Fiorello La Guardia, in progress. Her place was raided in March 1935, three women were charged with vagrancy, and Adler was charged with operating a disorderly house and possessing obscene films. The attendant publicity turned the spotlight on her swank "silk stocking bordello," a plushly furnished apartment with a game room, bar, and contents valued at $35,000.

After many postponements Adler stood trial. The film possession charge was dropped, but on May 10 she was sentenced to thirty days in the Women's House of Detention and fined $500 for being a procuress. Released six days early for good behavior, Adler again considered pursuing a more respectable career. But she felt permanently tagged as a madam and eventually reopened a "house." She avoided questioning during Thomas E. Dewey's 1936 vice investigation by vacationing on the West Coast.

In the early 1940's Adler claimed that she did as much social greeting as Grover A. Whalen, New York City's official greeter; those welcomed at her house, she said, included people listed in Who's Who, the Social Register, and Burke's Peerage. On Jan. 13, 1943, while she was ill with pleurisy, her place was again raided. She was taken to a prison ward of Bellevue Hospital. When her case was dismissed about two weeks later, she finally decided to retire.

On her attorney's suggestion Adler began her autobiography in June 1945. She later moved to Los Angeles, where she completed her high school education and attended college. Her autobiography, A House Is Not a Home (1953), was a best-seller, although some reviewers insinuated that it had been ghostwritten. (A film based on the book was released in 1964.) Adler subsequently moved to Burbank, Calif. She never completed her second book, which was to have been about her New York City customers. She died in Hollywood.

Four feet, eleven inches tall and stocky, Adler was described as crude and tough but endowed with great natural intelligence. Her personal life was subservient to her goal of becoming "the best goddamn madam in all America." She never married.

A rags-to-riches immigrant who prospered in a climate of hypocrisy, Adler thrived by collaborating with the very officials who outwardly most condemned her life-style. She was able to remain in business despite her arrests and notoriety partly because of the renown of many of her guests. Her connections to those in power—and especially in the underworld—were also a factor.

Adler was not concerned with the moral or feminist issues of prostitution: to her it was a business like any other, contingent on the law of supply and demand. "Prostitution exists because men will pay for sexual gratification," she wrote, "and whatever men are willing to pay for, someone will provide."

[Despite the use of pseudonyms and the lack of specific dates, Adler's autobiography provides a good overview. Conflicting information appears on her death certificate; her parents' names are listed as Morris Adler and Gertrude Koval, her birth date as Apr. 16, 1899. Also see the Adler clipping file from the New York Sun morgue at the New York Public Library Newspaper Annex, which includes articles for the years 1931–1943. "Vice in New York," Fortune, July 1939, p. 48, also mentions her. On Adler and other well-known American madams, see Harry Benjamin and R. E. L. Masters, Prostitution and Morality (1964). Her autobiography is reviewed in "Pollyadlery," Newsweek, June 8, 1953, and Lee Rogow, "The Wayside Sin," Saturday Review, June 27, 1953. There are obituaries in the Los Angeles Times, June 10, 1962; and the New York Times, June 10 and 11, 1962.]

CHRISTIANE L. DESCHAMPS

ALEXANDER, FRANZ GABRIEL (Jan. 22, 1891–Mar. 8, 1964), psychoanalyst, was born in Budapest, Austria-Hungary, the son of Bernard Alexander, a professor of philosophy at Budapest University, and of Regina Brössler. He was privately educated during his grammar school years, took violin lessons from the concertmaster of the Budapest Opera, and generally enjoyed the intellectual and cultural privileges of an upper-class child of that time. He graduated from the Humanistic Gymnasium and at his father's suggestion began to study archaeology at the University of Budapest. His interest soon shifted to philosophy and science and gradually to medicine. He spent some time in Göttingen, where he took courses at the university and was exposed to theoretical mathematicians, physicists, and philosophers such as Edmund Husserl and Martin Heidegger. Alexander received the M.D. from the University of Budapest in 1913. He was serving his compulsory year in the military when war broke out. He joined the Austro-Hungarian Army and served in a medical unit until the defeat of the Central Powers. After the war he became a research associate in bacteriology at the University of Budapest's Institute for Hygiene. His growing interest in Sigmund Freud's theories prompted a move to Berlin, where he was the first training candidate accepted by the Institute for Psychoanalysis.

Alexander's introduction to psychoanalytic thinking had come as an undergraduate, when his father asked him to review Freud's *Interpretation of Dreams.* In Göttingen and Berlin he was exposed to Freud's theory of the unconscious but turned from this approach to a study of neurophysiology. It was not until after his war experience with patients that he was convinced of the validity of the unconscious and became directly involved in psychoanalytic studies.

In Berlin, Alexander came under Freud's immediate influence, and in 1921 he was awarded the Freud Prize for the best clinical essay of the year: "Castration Complex in the Formation of Character." Alexander was considered one of the best of Freud's pupils, and after the completion of his analysis by Hans Sachs in 1921, he was appointed assistant at the Institute of Psychoanalysis. There he became increasingly involved in the analysis and training of the American physicians who flocked to Berlin. Their interest lay primarily in therapy, as opposed to the Europeans' more theoretical emphasis on the nature and structure of personality. On Mar. 7, 1921, he married Anita Venier; they had two daughters.

On his first trip to America in 1930, Alexander became professor of psychoanalysis in the Department of Medicine of the University of Chicago. In 1932 he was in the forefront of the exodus of anti-Nazi psychoanalysts to America. Freud, who disapproved of the move, "hoped that America will leave intact something of the real Franz Alexander." Settling first in Boston, Alexander did research in criminology at the Judge Baker Foundation and acted as training analyst at the new Boston Psychoanalytic Institute.

Later in 1932, Alexander returned to Chicago, where he founded the Chicago Institute for Psychoanalysis, modeled on that in Berlin. Karen Horney was associate director at the Institute from 1932 to 1934, and it was said that the interaction of these two vivid personalities was not always smooth. Alexander became a naturalized citizen in 1938. He remained director at the Chicago Institute for twenty-five years, attracting many first-rate European and American analysts, including Bruno Bettelheim, Therese Benedict, Carl Becker, and Flanders Dunbar. He initiated research in developing variations in therapeutic techniques and was especially interested in briefer methods or irregular sessions. But the main thrust of his work at Chicago lay in exploring the relationship between specific psychic conflicts and psychosomatic dysfunction, and distinguishing between hysterical conversion and psychosomatic disorders. As innovator and organizer, he must be credited with launching the psychosomatic movement.

In 1956 Alexander moved to Los Angeles as director of psychiatric and psychosomatic research at Mt. Sinai Hospital. There his principal research involved patient-therapist interaction and a study of transference phenomena in the therapeutic process. From 1957 to 1963 he was clinical professor of psychiatry at the University of Southern California School of Medicine. He died in Palm Springs, Calif., shortly before he was to assume the newly established Franz Alexander chair in psychophysiology and psychosomatic medicine.

Alexander was a creative and charismatic personality with a broad range of interests and intellectual pursuits. His heritage and life experience, spanning two continents in a time of profound social change, fitted him to apply his psychoanalytic insights to art, culture, politics, and philosophy, as well as his own profession. He moved from the stable humanist tradition of prewar, upper-class Austria-Hungary, with its clearly defined values and commitments, to the chaos, social and cultural upheaval, changing moods, and relativist values of postwar Europe and America. To a degree shared by only a few other psychoanalysts, among them Karen Horney, he was always aware of the importance of the cultural setting, as well as early life experience, in the development of personality. He was often prescient in his interests, at the growing edge of psychoanalytic theory—for example, in a paper, published in the early years in Berlin, that first articulated the ideas of the new ego psychology.

Alexander was a leader, active in the institutional organizations of the psychoanalytic community, and always on guard against the stultifying effects of intellectual conformity. He was able to attract excellent colleagues and to work productively with them. He could deviate from or disagree with orthodox views without stirring up animosity or personalizing disputed issues. In the early days, when one of his articles questioned a position of Freud's, he had anxiously written to explain himself, only to be told by Freud that he was "too resigned and unassuming." More characteristically, as he matured, he persistently presented new or critical views, seeking always to promote psychoanalysis as a science, to subject its tenets and procedures to objective report, review, and evaluation. Friends and colleagues wondered whether he repressed the impact of the controversies he often precipitated, or merely deemed it politically expedient to ignore them. In any event, he usually stayed above the factionalism he deplored and remained in good standing with the community and on good terms with Freud.

Alexander was in the best sense antiauthoritarian. He believed in autonomy for the individual psychoanalytic institutes and thought that an overemphasis on uniformity was achieved at the expense of genuine growth. Certainly in his life and work he exemplified the questioning spirit he theoretically endorsed.

[Alexander's writings include *Man's Supreme Inheritance* (1920); *The Medical Value of Psychoanalysis* (1932; rev. and enl. ed., 1936); *Roots of Crime* (1935), with William Healy; *Our Age of Unreason* (1942; rev. and enl. ed., 1951); *Psychoanalytic Therapy* (1946) and *Studies in Psychosomatic Medicine* (1948), with Thomas Morton French; *Fundamentals of Psychoanalysis* (1948); *Psychosomatic Medicine* (1950); *Dynamic Psychiatry* (1952), edited with Helen Ross; *The Criminal, the Judge, and the Public* (rev. ed., 1956), with Hugo Staub; *Psychoanalysis and Psychotherapy* (1956); *The Western Mind in Transition* (1960); *The Scope of Psychoanalysis, 1921–1961* (1961); *The Impact of Freudian Psychiatry* (1961), edited with Helen Ross; *Psychosomatic Medicine* (1965); and *Psychoanalytic Pioneers* (1966), edited with S. Eisenstein and M. Grotjahn.]

EDNA A. LERNER

ALLEN, ARTHUR AUGUSTUS (Dec. 28, 1885–Jan. 17, 1964), ornithologist, was born in Buffalo, N.Y., the son of Daniel Williams Allen and Anna Moore. He grew up in nearby Hamburg, N.Y., where his father was a businessman active in railroading and land development. Following graduation from Buffalo High School, Allen entered Cornell University in the fall of 1904, earning his A.B. (1907), M.A. (1908), and Ph.D. (1911). His dissertation, *The Red Winged Blackbird: A Study in the Ecology of a Cattail Marsh* (1914), combined the life history of this species with a detailed analysis of its relationship with the environment. Many subsequent researchers structured their studies in a similar fashion. One reviewer called the work "one of the finest ecologic studies that has yet appeared"; another claimed it was "the best, most significant biography which has thus far been prepared of any American bird."

Allen began working at Cornell as an assistant in ornithology during his senior year in college. Frank M. Chapman, chairman of the Department of Ornithology at the American Museum of Natural History in New York City, invited him to head a museum expedition to Colombia in the late summer of 1911. Suffering from malaria, Allen was compelled to return to Ithaca in the spring of 1912. That fall he began his duties as instructor in zoology at Cornell. He was made assistant professor of ornithology in 1915, and full professor in 1925. Allen married Elsa Guerdrum on Aug. 17, 1913. They had five children.

Allen made ornithological expeditions to Labrador (1918), Hudson Bay (1934), and Europe (1938). He returned to Hudson Bay in 1944 and to Labrador a year later. During the latter stages of World War II, he spent some months in Panama researching jungle acoustics for the War Department. Later expeditions were made to Mexico in 1946 and Alaska in 1948.

During the 1920's Allen spent considerable time studying the diseases of the ruffed grouse and successfully devised methods for raising this species in captivity, a challenging task. Later, he did pioneering research on the sex rhythm in this bird and other species, including cowbirds, house wrens, Canadian geese, yellow warblers, and song sparrows.

Allen was an excellent teacher who attracted substantial numbers of undergraduates and graduates to his ornithology courses. He created the first American course in wildlife conservation. His *Laboratory Notebook* (1927) went through five editions and a textbook, *The Book of Bird Life* (1930), was reprinted a dozen times and revised in 1961.

By the 1930's, "Doc," as Allen was familiarly known, had a nationwide reputation. Until the early 1940's, Cornell was the only institution offering a doctorate in ornithology. An important feature of Allen's "Grad Lab" was the weekly evening seminar at which speakers—usually Cornell faculty or students, although occasionally distinguished visitors—held forth. Invariably, those in attendance would be expected to compare notes on birds observed during the week. The camaraderie among students and faculty during the Allen era was an important element in his program's success. This program, known unofficially as the "Laboratory of Ornithology" for many years, did not become a formal element in the university structure until 1955. In 1957 the laboratory was finally given its own building, which flanked a ten-acre pond and faced Sapsucker Woods, an excellent place for birdwatching.

Allen soon took an interest in photography and quickly incorporated both still pictures and movies in his lectures. Many of his observations were not written up for scientific journals but rather provided grist for his lectures and popular articles. These were necessary sources of additional income for his growing family. He gradually gave up most research work for a successful career of writing and lecturing, which he found more challenging and rewarding. His film commentaries were fascinating, his lecture voice excellent, and his sense of humor pervasive.

In 1929 a group of filmmakers went to Ithaca to make sound movies of singing wild birds. Allen and an associate, Peter Paul Kellogg, were inspired to produce a library of sound recordings of various species in their natural settings. With the aid of Albert Rich Brand, the first phonograph recording was produced by Allen and Kellogg in 1932; and the Laboratory of Ornithology eventually housed one of the most extensive collections of bird vocalizations in the world.

As early as 1912, Chapman, whose own role in popularizing bird study had been notable, urged Allen to contribute to *Bird-Lore*, Chapman's magazine of popular ornithology. From 1919 until 1934 Allen edited the School Department of this publication. This led to his series of bird "autobiographies," in which he had each species discuss its life history. Although these were technically accurate, informative, and well written, some critics deprecated what they considered to be Allen's misleading anthropomorphic approach. Yet the articles were well received by teachers. Nearly fifty were published in *American Bird Biographies* (1934) and *The Golden Plover and Other Birds* (1939). With these and other publications, Allen had clearly inherited Chapman's mantle as the nation's preeminent popularizer of ornithology. At

no time did Allen take any liberties with the facts of bird life. Konrad Lorenz considered Allen one of the first great students of bird behavior long before that term became well known.

When Allen retired in 1953, he had reached well over 10,000 individuals through his courses at Cornell, and he had directed the efforts of more than a hundred holders of graduate degrees. Many of the latter achieved eminence in their own right. At meetings of the American Ornithologists' Union, about a third of the papers read were by Allen's students.

Allen died in Ithaca, N.Y.

[Allen's papers, including correspondence, field notebooks, and originals of his published articles, are in the Ornithological Archives at the Cornell University Library: see *Laboratory of Ornithology Newsletter*, Summer 1978. His correspondence may also be found in the papers of Brand, Kellogg, and William Irving Myers, also at Cornell. A taped interview with Allen, made in 1963, is in the Carolynne H. Cline Papers at Cornell.

Allen's other publications include: "Ornithological Education in America," *Fifty Years' Progress of American Ornithology* (1933); with Henry Kyllingstad, "The Eggs and Young of the Bristle-thighed Curlew," *Auk* (1949); and with others, *Stalking Birds with Color Camera* (1951). Allen describes the creation of the building for the Laboratory of Ornithology in "Cornell's Laboratory of Ornithology," *The Living Bird* (1962). An excellent sketch by former student Olin Sewall Pettingill, Jr., is "In Memoriam: Arthur A. Allen," *Auk* (1968). A brief but good description of graduate student life during Allen's tenure is found in George Miksch Sutton, *Bird Student: An Autobiography* (1980). Much personal data was supplied by a former associate of Allen's, Dr. Sally Spofford.]

KEIR B. STERLING

ALLEN, GRACIE (July 26, 1905–Aug. 27, 1964), entertainer, was born Grace Ethel Cecile Rosalie Allen in San Francisco, Calif., the daughter of Edward Allen, an entertainer, and Margaret Darragh. When only three years old, Gracie made her stage debut with her father, a local entertainer. She was educated at the Star of the Sea Convent, a Catholic girls' school, but left school at the age of fourteen to permanently join her father and three older sisters on the stage. Soon, the Allen sisters signed with the Larry Reilly Company, which began to feature Gracie's Irish songs and dancing. After several seasons of touring, she quit the troupe in a dispute over billing. Unhappy with her stage career, she enrolled in a secretarial school.

While attending school in 1922, Allen visited backstage at the Union Theater in Union Hill,

N.J. She had learned from friends that the comedy team of George Burns and William Lorraine would soon break up, and Lorraine would need another partner. Mistaking Burns for Lorraine, she inquired about forming a team. After three days Burns confessed his true identity, but Gracie vowed to give the act a chance.

The new team of Burns and Allen opened at the Hill Street Theater in Newark, N.J. Recognizing that Allen was a natural comedienne, Burns rewrote their sketches to give her the witty lines and assumed for himself a secondary role. The performances relied heavily on Allen's singing and dancing talents and always concluded with Allen dancing an exuberant Irish jig. After three years of traveling together, the couple married on Jan. 7, 1926, in Cleveland, Ohio.

In 1926 Burns developed a routine entitled *Lamb Chops*, which played at the Jefferson Theater in New York City. Then the Keith Theater chain signed them to a five-year contract: Burns and Allen had reached top billing in vaudeville. While performing on European stages for Keith, the couple made their radio debut over the British Broadcasting Corporation's network. The new medium seemed tailored to their intimate style of comedy.

By the late 1920's, Burns and Allen were one of the most popular acts in the United States. Toward the end of 1930, they appeared for nine weeks at New York's Palace Theater, headlining a program billed as marking vaudeville's end. Several weeks later, Eddie Cantor asked Allen to be a guest on his radio program. Her popularity with listeners prompted invitations from other radio shows, and soon the Columbia Broadcasting System (CBS) offered Burns and Allen a contract. On the night of Feb. 15, 1932, they joined Guy Lombardo's musical variety show. Within a year, Lombardo had been reduced to a supporting role on the Burns and Allen Comedy Show.

The switch to radio required major changes in the Burns and Allen style. Dialogue assumed primary importance, which lessened the emphasis on Allen's singing and dancing. Burns suggested they pretend to play themselves and give the audience a glimpse of their private lives—a milestone in the development of the domestic situation comedy. In the future, the Burns and Allen formula would spawn many imitators.

In the late 1930's their radio program was ranked as one of the top three shows in the United States; an estimated 45 million people listened to their show each week. Burns and Allen were always affiliated with CBS, except in 1937 when they moved to NBC. Over the years, the show was sponsored by a number of companies: Robert Burns Cigars, Lever Brothers, Maxwell House Coffee, Campbell Soup, Grape Nuts, General Foods, and Swan Soap.

Domestic humor was the staple of Burns and Allen. A typical example was the search in 1933 for Gracie's "lost brother." During the hunt, she visited all major radio programs and urged the public to help seek out her elusive relative. Gracie's real brother, George Allen, a San Francisco accountant, was forced to go into seclusion until the gag was terminated.

Occasionally Burns and Allen departed from their usual format. In 1940, for instance, Allen decided to run for president as the candidate of the Surprise party. She declared her political philosophy to be the avoidance of overconfidence. "I realize," she said, "that the President of today is merely the postage stamp of tomorrow."

Early in the 1930's, Burns and Allen took up residence in Beverly Hills, Calif. Their domestic life was happy and tranquil. In the middle of the decade, they adopted two children. During these years, they also starred in a number of feature films for Paramount Studios, including *The Big Broadcast* (1932), *Six of a Kind* (1934), and *College Holiday* (1936). But motion pictures were a distant second to their weekly radio program.

In October 1950, Burns and Allen moved to television. Their popularity continued but Allen began to tire of the character she had played for so many years. In 1958 she retired from show business, while Burns pursued an independent career. She died in Los Angeles.

From the 1920's to the 1950's, Allen stood at center stage as one of America's favorite female entertainers. She and Burns pioneered in the development of the domestic situation comedy. She always played the role of a zany woman who had found happiness through pleasant insanity. Her appeal rested upon an ability to convince an audience that in reality she was indeed the scatterbrained character she portrayed.

[The George Burns and Gracie Allen Papers are at the Doheny Library, University of Southern California, Los Angeles. For biographical information see Gracie Allen, *How to Become President* (1940); George Burns, *I Love Her, That's Why!* (1955), and *Living It Up: or, They Still Love Me in Altoona!* (1976); John Dunning, *Tune in Yesterday* (1976); and the obituary in the *New York Times*, Aug. 29, 1964.]

GERALD THOMPSON

ALLISON, SAMUEL KING (Nov. 13, 1900–Sept. 15, 1965), physicist, was born in Chicago, Ill., the son of Samuel Buell Allison and Caroline King. He attended public schools in Chicago, where his father was a high school principal. He received the B.S. degree from the University of Chicago in 1921 and the Ph.D. there in 1923, working with W. D. Harkins. His research interests developed in precision X-ray spectroscopy, which he pursued as a National Research Council Fellow at Harvard in 1923–1925, and as a Carnegie Foundation Fellow at the Carnegie Institution of Washington during 1925–1926.

In William Duane's laboratory at Harvard, Allison became involved in the controversy between Duane and Arthur H. Compton on the validity of the X-ray scattering experiments that were basic for the "Compton effect." Compton's now classic experiments, crucial for the support of the photon theory of radiation, were conducted at Washington University in St. Louis and had been challenged by several X-ray physicists, including Nobel laureate C. G. Barkla at Edinburgh and Bergen Davis at Columbia, but especially by Duane, for they were in direct conflict with J. J. Thomson's accepted theory of X-ray scattering. Duane had interpreted his own experiments, carried on in collaboration with students at Harvard, as being adequately explained as "tertiary radiation" of the bremsstrahlung type, produced from carbon and oxygen in the box enclosing the X-ray tube, by impact of photoelectrons ejected by the primary X-rays. Compton had explained his results by the quantum theory and the photon hypothesis —not generally accepted at that time. Duane's opposition to Compton's discovery is curious, for his own earlier X-ray work, leading to the basic Duane-Hunt law, had given important support for the photon theory of radiation.

After Allison joined Duane's group at Harvard, the experiments were repeated with greater care and precision. The earlier results were shown to be due to secondary X rays produced through scattering of the primary beam by the walls of the box housing the apparatus. When these results were known, Duane immediately withdrew his objections and supported Compton's work in a memorable session at the next meeting of the American Physical Society. The lifelong friendship of Allison and Arthur Compton began at this time.

Allison was a member of the physics faculty of the University of California at Berkeley from 1926 until 1930. During this period he continued his X-ray research, which included precise determinations of the widths and relative intensities of X-ray lines. These gave experimental confirmation of the dynamical theory of X-ray diffraction of P. P. Ewald and C. G. Darwin. For this work he made basic improvements in the design and extended the use of the double-crystal X-ray spectrometer (invented by Compton) in collaboration with John H. Williams.

Allison married Helen Catherine Campbell on May 28, 1928. They had two children. In 1930 he was persuaded by Compton to return to the University of Chicago. Until 1935 he continued his X-ray researches, which culminated in the treatise *X-rays in Theory and Experiment* (1935), prepared in collaboration with Compton. This work continues to be an authoritative reference.

From 1935 until World War II, Allison developed the first laboratory for nuclear physics in the University of Chicago physics department. W. D. Harkins had already begun work with neutrons in the Chicago chemistry department. Allison began by spending six months in Ernest Rutherford's laboratory at Cambridge, working with the Cockcroft-Walton apparatus. On his return to Chicago he and his students built (with a grant of $3,000) a nuclear accelerator of this type. This apparatus, used by Allison with a succession of graduate students, produced much valuable research. Their results included precise measurements of the energy released in proton-induced nuclear transformations, and later in reactions induced by heavier ions. These gave precise values for the masses and energy content of a series of light elements and also confirmed the relativistic mass-energy changes in the reactions with a high degree of accuracy.

When Compton organized the "metallurgical laboratory" at the University of Chicago for work on the atomic bomb, he invited Allison to return to Chicago from Washington, where he was already engaged in rocket research. Allison organized a group and began work on the use of beryllium in nuclear energy. An important peacetime application of this effort was the use of beryllium as a reflector in the materials testing reactor (M.T.R.) built at the National Reactor Testing Station in Idaho.

Allison was an important member of Enrico Fermi's group that built the historic natural uranium-graphite chain-reacting "pile" that went critical on Dec. 2, 1942. He was responsible for the last-ditch safety measures for this test, which fortunately were not needed.

Compton appointed Allison director of the chemical division, and later overall coordinator of all scientific work, at the "Met Lab" when Compton himself became deeply involved with the Oak Ridge reactor and the reactors for producing plutonium at Hanford, Wash. Later in 1943–1944, Allison was director of the "Met Lab" until he transferred to Los Alamos, N.M., in November 1944. During his final period at Chicago, Allison spent much time conferring with the Du Pont Company engineers and the Du Pont management on the engineering aspects of the design and construction of the Hanford reactors.

At Los Alamos, Allison was chairman of the Technical and Scheduling Committee that brought work on the atomic bomb to a successful conclusion. He took part in the test of the first atomic bomb at Alamogordo, N.M., on July 16, 1945, and "called the countdown" across the desert for the first nuclear explosion. For his war work he was awarded the Medal for Merit with a special citation from President Harry Truman.

After the war Allison returned to the University of Chicago, where he served as director of the Enrico Fermi Institute for Nuclear Studies from 1945 to 1958, and from 1963 until his death. This laboratory, with its distinguished staff, had a major influence under Fermi and Allison in reestablishing nuclear research in American universities after the war. Allison was a strong advocate of civilian control of nuclear energy and its development for peaceful purposes. At the time of his death in Oxford, England, he was official observer of the Atomic Energy Commission at the International Conference on Thermonuclear Programs. He was a member of the National Academy of Sciences.

[Allison's papers are still classified information with the Manhattan District. Biographical data and a list of his principal writings are at the archives of the National Academy of Sciences, Washington, D.C. An obituary appeared in the *Washington Star*, Sept. 16, 1965.]

R. S. SHANKLAND

AMMANN, OTHMAR HERMANN (Mar. 26, 1879–Sept. 22, 1965), civil engineer, was born in Schaffhausen, Switzerland, the son of Emanuel Christian Ammann, hat manufacturer, and Emilie Rosa Labhardt, the daughter of the landscape painter Emanuel Labhardt. He attended the Industrial School and the Swiss Federal Polytechnic Institute in Zurich, studying at the latter under Wilhelm Ritter, an authority on suspension bridges. After graduating in 1902, he was employed by the construction firm of Wartmann and Valette, in Brugg. Later

he moved to Frankfurt-am-Main to work for Buchheim and Heister.

Hoping to gain experience in American bridge-building techniques, Ammann came to the United States in 1904 (he became a naturalized citizen in 1924). He became associated with the engineering firm of Joseph Mayer in New York, where he worked on problems related to railroad bridges. A year later, he took a position with the Pennsylvania Steel Company, investigating the causes of the collapse of the Quebec Bridge over the St. Lawrence River. His report is still regarded as a model in the field.

From 1909 to 1912 Ammann was associated with the firm of F. C. Kunz and C. C. Schneider in the designing of steel bridges. Moving in 1912 to the firm of Gustav Lindenthal, one of the leading bridge builders in America, he served as chief engineer on the building of the Hell Gate Bridge over the East River, which had the longest span (977.5 feet) of any arched bridge in the world at that time.

Ammann secured his place as a leading designer of bridges through his work on the George Washington Bridge. The construction of a bridge over the Hudson River had been considered too costly by most experts. But the rapid increase in the number of automobiles in New York City and the movement of the population northward convinced him of the urgent need for a means of rapid communication between northern Manhattan and New Jersey. Determined to solve the problem, Ammann left Lindenthal in 1923 to work on the design for such a bridge. Under the auspices of the Port of New York Authority, construction on the bridge was begun in 1927 and completed in 1931, a time considered very short by most experts of the day.

The bridge was remarkable for the absence of the stiffening trusses normally used to prevent vibration and swaying. Ammann's use of the weight and inertia of the bridge to stabilize the structure represented an important step in bridge design. It significantly reduced the cost of the bridge and at the same time enhanced its grace and beauty. With its towers rising 595 feet and its clear span of 3,500 feet, the longest in the world at that time, the bridge quickly became a New York landmark and a model for bridge builders. During this same period, Ammann planned the Kill Van Kull Bridge at Bayonne, N.J., which, when it was completed in 1931, was the longest arched bridge in the world.

While continuing his association with the Port of New York Authority throughout the

1930's, Ammann also became involved with the Triborough Bridge Authority in the construction of the Triborough and Bronx-Whitestone bridges. The latter bridge, which spanned 2,300 feet, was regarded as one of the most graceful and elegant bridges in America. In 1946 Ammann entered into partnership with Charles S. Whitney to form Ammann and Whitney, consultants in engineering.

Other major accomplishments of Ammann's career, which spanned more than half a century in America, included the building of the Lincoln Tunnel under the Hudson River, the Throgs Neck Bridge, the Walt Whitman Bridge in Philadelphia, Lincoln Center in Manhattan, and Dulles International Airport in Washington, D.C. He also served as a member of the board of engineers that built the Golden Gate Bridge at San Francisco. His last major project was the design and construction of the Verrazano-Narrows Bridge, which links Brooklyn and Staten Island and spans 4,260 feet, the longest clear span in the world.

Ammann stated that the bridge designer "must be capable of bringing into order the skills and techniques of many varied and highly specialized fields," and his long apprenticeship in the steel and bridge-building industries provided a sound and comprehensive background for his career. His work was known for its technical brilliance and economy of construction. But his bridges were more than marvels of functional engineering; they were characterized by grace and classic beauty as well. Ammann maintained that "a great bridge . . . although primarily utilitarian in its purpose, should nevertheless be a work of art to which Science lends its aid." In recognition of his contributions to science and engineering, Ammann was awarded the National Medal of Science by President Lyndon Johnson in 1965.

Ammann and his first wife, Lilly Selma Wehrli, whom he married on July 24, 1905, had three children. She died in 1933, and he married Kläry Vogt Nötzli on Mar. 2, 1935. Ammann died at Rye, N.Y.

[Representative of the numerous publications of Ammann in the field of engineering are "George Washington Bridge, General Conception and Development of Design," *Transactions of the American Society of Civil Engineers*, May 1933; "Planning the Lincoln Tunnel Under the Hudson," *Civil Engineering*, June 1937; "Present Status of Design of Suspension Bridges with Respect to Dynamic Wind Action," *Journal of the Boston Society of Civil Engineers*, July 1953; and "Planning and Design of the Verrazano-Narrows Bridge," *Transactions of New York Academy of Sciences*, April 1963. Fritz Stüssi, *Othmar H. Ammann: Sein Beitrag zur Entwicklung des Brückenbaus* (1974), discusses Ammann's work in detail. Henry Billings, *Bridges* (1956), and H. Shirley Smith, *The World's Great Bridges* (1953), contain more general descriptions of his work.]

KEITH M. HEIM

ANDERSON, MARY (Aug. 27, 1872–Jan. 29, 1964), labor organizer and public official, was born in Lidköping, Sweden, the daughter of Magnus Anderson and Matilda Johnson, who were farmers. She attended grammar school in Sweden before immigrating to the United States at the age of sixteen to join an older sister who had settled in Ludington, Mich. During her first year in America, Anderson worked as a dishwasher and cook in a lumber camp and learned English. About 1890, she moved to West Pullman, Ill., with her now-married sister and held a variety of unskilled jobs until she went to work as a stitcher in a shoe factory around 1891. She never married.

Working as a stitcher for Schwab's in Chicago, Anderson joined the International Boot and Shoe Workers' Union in 1894. The following year she became president of Stitchers Local 94 and retained that position until 1910; she also represented the union to the Chicago Federation of Labor and for eleven years was the only woman on the parent union's executive board.

When the Women's Trade Union League (WTUL) was established in 1903, Anderson joined the Chicago branch. By 1910 she was representing the Chicago WTUL to the United Garment Workers. She participated in the Hart, Schaffner, and Marx clothing workers' strike during the winter of 1911. From 1910 to 1913 she served as an investigator to insure compliance with the agreement that had ended this confrontation. A full-time organizer for the National WTUL from 1913 to 1920, she was involved in investigations of the 1913 copper miners' strike in Calumet, Mich., and the 1916 spar miners' strike in Rosiclare, Ill. She became a United States citizen in 1915.

Following the American entry into World War I, Anderson served in the Women in Industry Section of both the Advisory Committee of the Council of National Defense and the Ordnance Department. Increased employment of women during the war as well as arguments by reformers for more than ten years finally resulted in the establishment of a Women in Industry Service in the United States Department of Labor. Anderson was appointed its assistant director in 1918 and succeeded Mary Van Kleeck as director in 1919.

In 1920 Anderson headed the newly created Women's Bureau of the United States Department of Labor, a post she retained until 1944. In both the Women in Industry Service and the Women's Bureau, she emphasized the importance of investigating the working conditions of employed women and establishing firm standards of safety and efficiency. In her writings as well as in testimonies before congressional and industrial bodies, she particularly emphasized equal pay for equal work.

Because Anderson believed that concrete evidence and effective publicity would elicit support for such standards, during her tenure as director, the Women's Bureau issued more than one hundred and fifty bulletins. Topics covered in these bulletins were federal and state legislation affecting wages, hours, and conditions of work; hazardous industries employing women; arguments against homework and in favor of the shorter workday; analyses of specific industries and the industries of particular states; and attacks on the "pin money theory" of why women sought employment. During World War II the Women's Bureau emphasized adequate training for newly recruited women war workers and strongly advocated equal pay.

Between the world wars, Anderson maintained contacts with national and international labor organizations. She attended the labor conferences at the Paris Peace Conference of 1919 as a representative of the WTUL, as well as the First and Third International Congresses of Working Women in 1919 and 1923, and the 1928 Pan-Pacific Union Conference in Honolulu. She was the United States' unofficial delegate to the International Labor Organization Conference in Geneva in 1931. President Franklin D. Roosevelt named her adviser to the American delegation to the Technical Tripartite Conference on the Textile Industry in Washington, D.C., in 1937.

Anderson resigned her official positions in 1944. In retirement she continued to testify on the equal rights and equal pay issues before political conventions and congressional committees and wrote *Woman at Work: The Autobiography of Mary Anderson As Told to Mary N. Winslow* (1951). This book contains an extensive discussion of the Women's Bureau during the years Anderson served as director. She died in Washington, D.C.

[Anderson's manuscripts and taped and transcribed materials are housed in the Schlesinger Library at Radcliffe College; additional manuscript sources are included in the papers of the National Women's Trade Union League at the Library of Congress and in the Women's Bureau records at the National Archives.

In addition to her autobiography, Anderson wrote many articles on women and employment, including "Working-Woman's Views," *Harper's Bazaar,* May 1911; "Wages for Women Workers," *Annals of the American Academy of Political and Social Science,* Jan. 1919; and "What Use Is the Women's Bureau to the Woman Worker?" *American Federationist,* Aug. 1929.

See also the *New York Times* obituary, Jan. 30, 1964; and Sister John Marie Daly, "Mary Anderson, Pioneer Labor Leader" (Ph.D. diss., Georgetown University, 1968).]

SUSAN ESTABROOK KENNEDY

ANTHONY, KATHARINE SUSAN (Nov. 27, 1877–Nov. 20, 1965), writer, biographer, and women's rights advocate, was born in Roseville, Ark., the daughter of Ernest Augustus Anthony and Susan Jane Cathey, a pioneer suffragette. Following a public school education in Fort Smith, Ark., she attended Peabody Normal College, Nashville, Tenn., from 1895 to 1897 on a scholarship. She taught briefly in the public schools of Fort Smith before resuming education at the universities of Heidelberg and Freiburg, where she took additional courses in German, psychology, and philosophy (1901–1902). She completed her formal education at the University of Chicago, earning a Ph.B. in 1905.

From 1907 to 1908, Anthony taught English at Wellesley College. Subsequently she settled in New York City, where she combined social service work with writing. While working for the Russell Sage Foundation (1909–1913), as well as other social service organizations, she did economic research, analyzing statistics, drawing up reports, and preparing various studies.

Anthony's first major book, *Mothers Who Must Earn* (1914), funded by the Russell Sage Foundation, was a detailed study of 370 tenement mothers who had to work to support their families. She interviewed many women in their homes to glean human insights as well as the economic and sociological data. The result was a perceptive and sympathetic portrait of bleak and difficult lives.

This deep interest in women's issues and the women's movement came naturally. Anthony's mother had been a pioneer worker for women's suffrage. In 1915 Anthony published *Feminism in Germany and Scandinavia,* a study of women's education, employment, and political status. The work also discussed illegitimacy and the new area of state maternity insurance and support of women in that part of Europe. In 1917, Anthony compiled *Labor Laws of New York: A Handbook* for the Consumers' League.

Anthony then turned from such social topics to the field of biography, specializing almost exclusively in women. Her admiration of Sigmund Freud's theories and writings influenced her choice of subjects as well as her treatment of them. *Margaret Fuller: A Psychological Biography* (1920); *Catherine the Great* (1925); *Queen Elizabeth* (1929); *Marie Antoinette* (1933); *Louisa May Alcott* (1938); and *The Lambs* (1945) clearly reveal this predisposition. Anthony also wrote *Dolly Madison: Her Life and Times* (1949); *Susan B. Anthony: Her Personal History and Her Era* (1954); and *First Lady of the Revolution: The Life of Mercy Otis Warren* (1958).

Although Anthony's biographies were based on extensive historical research and reading, their reviews were mixed. Some critics considered her Freudian interpretations simplistic. This was particularly true of studies of Fuller, Catherine the Great, Alcott, and the Lambs. In portraying the troubled life of Fuller, Anthony explained her personality in terms of childhood hysteria and later neuroticism. Alcott is described as a psychically wounded, sex-starved spinster possessing little humor and affection. In *The Lambs,* Anthony theorized that in addition to Mary's insanity and Charles's drinking, they suffered from an Electra and Orestes complex, respectively. Their writing, she said, was a sublimation of incestuous love. Anthony's popular biography of Catherine, a Literary Guild selection in 1925, was written after a trip to the Soviet Union in 1923. Subsequently she translated Catherine's letters and diaries as *Memoirs of Catherine the Great* (1927). The biography of Queen Elizabeth, which was less psychoanalytical, was among the most popular books of 1929. A Literary Guild selection, it was translated into French.

Anthony traveled widely in the United States and Europe, doing research and gathering historical background for her writing. She was fluent in German and French and also knew Russian.

Anthony contributed to many periodicals, including *Reader's Digest, Good Housekeeping, Woman's Home Companion,* and the *New Republic.* One series of articles in the *Woman's Home Companion* (July, August, and September 1926) is a charming vignette of a camping trip she took with a friend and her dog back to the South. She also contributed an essay on the American family in *Civilization in the United States: An Inquiry by Thirty Americans* (1922), edited by Harold E. Stearns.

Anthony never married. She lived simply in a Greenwich Village apartment and at her farmhouse in Connecticut during the summers. Although never active in politics, she closely watched current events. In 1917 she campaigned against conscription, and in 1932 she rode in a Chicago peace parade. She was also very much interested in the emerging power and evolving status of the Soviet Union. Among the public figures that she most admired were Fiorello La Guardia, Franklin and Eleanor Roosevelt, and George Bernard Shaw. She died in New York City.

[Anthony's papers are in the Schlesinger Library at Radcliffe. *The Writer's Book* (1950), edited by Helen R. Hull, contains an essay by Anthony on "Writing Biography." See also Stanley J. Kunitz: *Authors Today and Yesterday* (1933), *Twentieth Century Authors* (1942), and its *First Supplement* (1955). Obituaries appeared in the *New York Times,* Nov. 22, 1965, and in *Publishers Weekly,* Nov. 29, 1965.]

MARY SUE DILLIARD SCHUSKY

ARCHIPENKO, ALEXANDER (May 30, 1887–Feb. 25, 1964), sculptor, painter, and graphic artist, was born in Kiev, Ukraine, now the Soviet Union, the son of Porfiry Antonovich Archipenko and Poroskovia Wassilievna Machova. His paternal grandfather was said to have been a church icon painter; his father was an engineer, inventor, and professor at the University of Kiev. As a child, Archipenko was first taught by a tutor, and then studied at the Kiev Gymnasium. Between 1902 and 1905 he studied painting and sculpture at the Kiev Art Institute but was expelled for criticizing the Institute's traditional teaching methods.

After two years in Moscow, Archipenko went to Paris in 1908, where he studied briefly at the École des Beaux-Arts. He then opened a studio in Montparnasse. Among his acquaintances were Henri Gaudier-Brzeska and Amadeo Modigliani. This period saw Archipenko's first significant contributions to modern sculpture. He belonged to the avant-garde cubist-abstract movement, and his innovations included a new attitude toward space: usual convex curves found in nature were replaced by concave penetrations. "Those parts which are absent have the form of the absent object which I want to present. I draw a parallel between space problems and the pause in music, which has as much meaning as sound itself," he explained.

Archipenko also stressed the importance of color in sculpture (as in his "sculpto-paintings")

14

and the multiple combination of materials, such as metal, wood, plastic, glass, stone, plaster, terra-cotta, and cement, with opaque or sometimes transparent effects. Examples of such amalgamated pieces are *Carrousel Pierrot* (1913) and *Medrano II* (1913), both in the Solomon R. Guggenheim Museum, New York City. Archipenko exhibited with other cubists in the Salon de la Société des Artistes Indépendants (1910), the Salon d'Automne (1911), and with the 1912 Salon de "La Section d'Or" group, which included Pablo Picasso, Georges Braque, Juan Gris, Francis Picabia, Raymond Duchamp-Villon, and Fernand Léger. After his exhibition with Henri Le Fauconnier at the Folkwang Museum, Hagen, Germany (1912), and his one-man show at the Galerie Der Sturm, Berlin (1913), Guillaume Apollinaire praised Archipenko's work.

In Paris, Archipenko opened an art school in 1912. Four of his sculptures and five drawings were selected by Walter Pach for inclusion in the 1913 Armory Show in New York City. The largest piece, a forceful six-foot plaster work of intertwined figures entitled *La vie familiale* (1912), was later destroyed during World War I. The others were two cement figures, *Négresse* (1910–1911) and *Salomé* (1910), and *Le repos* (1911–1912), probably plaster. As a graphic artist, Archipenko produced his first works in 1913 for a futurist publication (*Lacerba*, 1914). He continued to work in this field throughout his life, particularly in lithography and serigraphy.

Archipenko spent the war years in southern France near Nice, and then traveled and exhibited throughout Europe. In 1921 he married Angelica Bruno-Schmitz, a sculptor. While living in Berlin (1921–1923), he opened an art school. A marked stylistic change occurred at this time. He shifted from the daring innovations of his earlier Paris period to a more naturalistic, lyrical manner, particularly in his execution of elongated female forms.

Disillusioned by conditions in postwar Europe and encouraged by the reaction to his first one-man exhibition in the United States (a 1921 exhibit by the Société Anonyme), Archipenko and his wife emigrated from Germany. They arrived in New York City on Oct. 16, 1923. A New York newspaper noted Archipenko's plans to exhibit and open "the only modern art school in the world" in New York. He was optimistic about the direction of art in America; because the country appeared fresh and vital, he felt that it would be the place to look for the great art of the future. Approaching Broadway for the first time, he remarked: "But it is beautiful! Why

doesn't everyone talk of it as a beautiful place?" In May of 1929 Archipenko became an American citizen.

In 1923 Archipenko opened a school in New York City and, in 1924, a summer art school in Woodstock, N.Y., which he eventually enlarged with additional buildings, including his own studio. The same year he developed a technique of mobile sculpture-painting called "Archipentura" or "Peinture Changeante" by which motorized canvas slats described his interpretation of the female form. This work anticipated later kinetic sculpture. He taught at Mills College and the Chouinard School, both in California (1933), the University of Washington (1935–1936), and the New Bauhaus School of Industrial Arts, Chicago, opening another school there in 1937. He reopened his New York City and Woodstock art schools in 1939; later he taught at the Chicago Institute of Design (1946), the University of Kansas City (1950), and in 1951 at the Carmel Institute of Art, California, the University of Oregon, and the University of Washington. In 1952, he taught at the University of Delaware and in 1956 the University of British Columbia. His wife died on Dec. 5, 1957, and on Aug. 1, 1960, Archipenko married a former student and sculptor, Frances Gray. He died in New York City.

In addition to a number of group shows, Archipenko had over one hundred one-man exhibitions. Three retrospective shows were held after his death, including one at the Museum of Modern Art, New York City, in 1970. Examples of Archipenko's work are in collections throughout the world. During the Nazi attack on modern art in the 1930's, most of his sculptures and paintings in German museums were confiscated as "decadent." He is represented in many American collections, and the largest number of his works are in the Hirshhorn Museum, Washington, D.C., and in his widow's possession in Woodstock, N.Y.

[Microfilm of Archipenko's papers is in the Archives of American Art branches in Washington, D.C., Detroit, and New York City. See Archipenko et al., *Archipenko: Fifty Creative Years, 1908–1958* (1960).

Donald H. Karshan, the leading authority on Archipenko, edited the Smithsonian Institution exhibition catalogue, *Archipenko, International Visionary* (1969); and wrote, *Archipenko: The Sculpture and Graphic Art* (Germany, 1974; United States, 1975), which contains good photographs, a detailed biographical chronology, and a catalogue raisonné of prints. See also the University of California at Los Angeles Art Galleries, *Alexander Archipenko: A Me-*

morial Exhibition, 1967–1969 (1967); Cynthia Jaffee McCabe, *The Golden Door: Artist-Immigrants of America 1876–1976* (1976), with photographs and data on the artist's immigration; and Katherine Jánszky Michaelsen, *Archipenko: A Study of the Early Works, 1908–1920* (1977). His obituary is in the *New York Times*, Feb. 26, 1964.]

FRANCIS S. GRUBAR

ARNOLD, LESLIE PHILIP (Aug. 28, 1893–Mar. 21, 1961), pioneer aviator and airline executive, was born in New Haven, Conn., the son of Frank Leslie Arnold, a railroad worker, and of Cora Fiske. Following graduation from high school in New London, he worked as a tobacco salesman and, for four years, on the construction of submarines. He enlisted in the Army Air Service in 1917, after the United States entered World War I. Following flight training at Waco, Tex., and Issoudun, France, he was assigned to the First Aero Squadron shortly before the armistice.

After the war Arnold gained experience in various aspects of aeronautics, serving tours of duty at the Aberdeen Proving Ground in 1920 and at the Air Service Photographic School in 1922. He also participated in bombing experiments conducted by General William Mitchell off the Virginia Capes in 1921 and off Cape Hatteras in 1923.

The Air Service sponsored numerous long-distance flights during the 1920's, intended to test and develop technology, train personnel, and generate favorable publicity. By far the most ambitious project called for a round-the-world flight by four Douglas single-engine biplanes. Arnold flew in one of these planes as copilot to Lowell H. Smith. They took off from Seattle, Wash., on Apr. 6, 1924.

Only two of the four aircraft completed the flight. Smith and Arnold, in World Cruiser *Chicago*, narrowly escaped disaster while attempting to cover the 560 miles from Ivigtut, Greenland, to Icy Tickle on the coast of Labrador. Some 200 miles from land, over the forbidding Davis Strait, their fuel pump failed. When the backup unit also broke down, Arnold had to operate an emergency wobble pump by hand. It took nearly three hours of exhausting effort to reach Labrador.

Smith and Arnold arrived back in Seattle on Sept. 26, 1924, having flown 26,345 miles in 363 hours and 7 minutes. The list of records established attests to the state of aviation in 1924 and the magnitude of their accomplishment. Foremost among their feats were the first aerial crossing of the Pacific Ocean and the first west-to-east crossing of the Atlantic. Arnold was the only member of the group to keep a complete log of the journey.

Arnold left the Air Service in 1928 to become assistant to Jack L. Maddux, an automobile dealer from Los Angeles and pioneer of scheduled air passenger service on the West Coast. When Transcontinental Air Transport, an early aeronautical conglomerate, absorbed Maddux Air Lines in 1929, Arnold became an executive with the merged carrier. Arnold had married Mildred Avery on Aug. 13, 1917, but the couple separated on their wedding day. He married Priscilla Dean, a film actress, on Oct. 6, 1928. When his 1926 divorce was declared invalid, he sought a second divorce. This divorce was granted, and Arnold remarried Dean. They had no children.

In 1936, Arnold became vice-president of the newly formed Pennsylvania Central Airlines. Four years later, after supervising the rapid expansion of the airline's routes, he joined Eastern Airlines as assistant to President Edward V. Rickenbacker, a close friend. Following American entry into World War II, Rickenbacker offered Arnold the senior position in Eastern's Military Transport Division. But Arnold declined, preferring to return to active duty with the Air Corps. During the war he organized military air transportation. At one point he commanded the Ferry and Transport Services of the Air Service Command in Europe, a unit that played an important role in supplying the Normandy beachhead in 1944. He retired at the end of the war with the rank of colonel.

Arnold rejoined Eastern in 1946 as vice-president for leases and properties. He was responsible to Rickenbacker for all matters pertaining to the airline's use of airports, terminals, and hangar facilities in the ninety-odd cities served by Eastern and also advised airport committees on the design of facilities. Maurice Lethbridge, a close associate, characterized Arnold in his dealings with various airport bodies as "a shrewd negotiator but very fair."

Arnold's influence on Eastern's development also was felt in a less direct manner. Rickenbacker, whose office adjoined Arnold's, frequently consulted his longtime friend and associate on matters far afield from properties and leases.

Eight months after retiring from Eastern, Arnold died in Leonia, N.J.

[Arnold's log of the round-the-world flight is at the Smithsonian Institution's National Air and Space Museum, as is the Douglas World Cruiser *Chicago*. The best account of the flight, with liberal quotations from Arnold's log, is Lowell Thomas, *The First World Flight* (1925). R. E. G. Davies, *Airlines of the United States Since 1914* (1972), and Robert J. Serling, *From the Captain to the Colonel* (1980), provide background for Arnold's career as an airline executive. An obituary is in the *New York Times,* Mar. 22, 1961.]

WILLIAM M. LEARY

ARTZYBASHEFF, BORIS (May 25, 1899–July 16, 1965), artist, illustrator, and author, was born in the Ukrainian city of Kharkov, the son of Mikhail Petrovich Artsybashev, a novelist and poet, and of Anna Vassilievna Koboushko. Artzybasheff grew up in affluent circumstances. After his parents separated in 1900, he went with his mother to St. Petersburg; thereafter he saw his father only infrequently. At age eight he entered the Prince Tenishev school in St. Petersburg, where he soon displayed artistic talent. Despite the outbreak of the Russian Revolution in 1917, he graduated in 1918 and was admitted to law school at the University of Kiev.

Shortly after commencing his collegiate studies, Artzybasheff was drafted into the German-supported army that was attempting to establish an independent Ukrainian republic. Having no sympathy with this cause, he escaped to the Black Sea, where he signed on as a seaman aboard a vessel that he thought was bound for Ceylon, but whose destination turned out to be the United States.

Arriving in New York City in 1919 with no knowledge of English and no money, Artzybasheff was detained at Ellis Island for nearly a month. Eventually an immigration officer found work for him drawing letters and ornamental borders for a local engraver. He proved himself to be an able illustrator and soon managed to publish a series of caricatures in the *New York World.*

After working again as a seaman, this time aboard an oil tanker bound for South America, Artzybasheff saved enough money to open his own New York studio in 1921, barely sustaining himself as a decorator of classic Russian interiors. His first book illustration was for John Peale Bishop's *The Undertaker's Garland,* published by Knopf in 1922. But it was the innovative motif he created for the murals of a new Russian restaurant in 1922 that brought him to the attention of the E. P. Dutton publishing house, which subsequently commissioned him to illustrate Mamin Siberiak's *Verotchka's Tales* (1922). With the success of this work, Artzybasheff found himself in demand to illustrate children's books with foreign settings, including Harriet Martineau's Norwegian *Feats on the Fiord* (1924), Ella Young's Celtic *The Wonder Smith and His Son* (1927), and Dhan Gopal Mukerji's Indian story *Ghond the Hunter* (1928). For Padraic Colum's *The Forge in the Forest* (1925) he used an art nouveau style that was widely acclaimed for its innovative use of color; this was the first of Artzybasheff's two dozen book designs. For Colum's *Creatures* (1927), he used black and white ink on scratchboard to develop a unique style of decorative curves, a design that inspired many imitators.

Although he became an American citizen in 1926, Artzybasheff spent much of the next four years in Paris, where his four one-man exhibitions received unqualified praise. Upon returning to America, he married Elisabeth Southard Snyder of Melrose, N.Y., on Feb. 22, 1930; they had no children.

Despite the general constrictions placed on publishers by the Great Depression, Artzybasheff created some of his best illustrative work during the 1930's. In 1931 he produced *Poor Shaydullah,* his first book of prose and his only original story. His edition of *Aesop's Fables* (1933) was highly acclaimed, and his *Seven Simeons* (1937) won several design awards, including the *Herald Tribune* Spring Book Festival Prize of 1937. The bizarre style he used to illustrate Charles Grandison Finney's *The Circus of Dr. Lao* (1935) was termed "surrealism" by critic Clifton Fadiman, a label that Artzybasheff greatly resented, claiming that he had developed this style long before Salvador Dali.

Determined not to be typed as a children's illustrator, Artzybasheff began his long association with Time Inc. in 1934, drawing statistical charts, maps, and graphs for *Fortune.* In 1941 he began his series of illustrations for *Life,* depicting war machines with human attributes. These macabre drawings caught the fancy of the public, as did the similar "Axis in Agony" advertising series, which was published by the Wickwire Spencer Steel Company in 1944. The artist's humanoid drawings and paintings, which best expressed his wry and sardonic wit, reached their peak with the publication of *As I See It* (1954), a satirical view of the machine age.

In 1941, when *Time* began to use portraits instead of photographs for its covers, Artzybasheff was one of the first artists featured. He proved to be a serious and sensitive portraitist who skillfully employed expressive backgrounds to highlight his subjects. During the next twenty-four years he created 219 cover portraits for *Time,* including likenesses of Harry S. Truman, T. S. Eliot, and George S. Patton.

Artzybasheff died in Old-Lyme, Conn.

[Many of Artzybasheff's portraits for *Time* are part of the permanent collection of the Smithsonian Institution's National Portrait Gallery, Washington, D.C. Other works are exhibited at Harvard University and the Massachusetts Institute of Technology. His book illustrations are discussed in Barbara Bader, *American Picturebooks from Noah's Ark to the Beast Within* (1976), and *The Illustrator in America, 1900–1960's* (1966), edited by Walt Reed. See also *Life,* Nov. 3, 1941; *American Artist,* Dec. 1941; and *Time,* July 3, 1944, June 25, 1945, Nov. 22, 1954, and June 6, 1960.

Obituaries are in the *New York Times, New York Herald-Tribune,* and *Washington Post,* July 18, 1965.]

MICHAEL L. LAWSON

ARVIN, NEWTON (Aug. 23, 1900–Mar. 21, 1963), literary critic and teacher, was born Frederick Newton Arvin, Jr., in Valparaiso, Ind., the son of Frederick Arvin, an insurance salesman, and Jessie Hawkins. By 1906 Arvin's father and older brother were spending little time at home, so he grew up in Valparaiso among women: his mother, grandmother, and four sisters. "I was certainly a girlish small boy," he wrote later; "I was timid, shrinking, weak, and unadventuresome." He became close friends with a neighbor, David Lilienthal, and in a few years they were discussing literature and national issues, and writing a magazine together. After graduating from Valparaiso High School, Arvin entered Harvard, where his older brother had done graduate work and at which Lilienthal had enrolled the year before. Despite periods of ill health, he was an outstanding student. In 1920 he sent one of his essays to Van Wyck Brooks, associate editor of the *Freeman,* who immediately recognized him as "a critic by nature" and assigned him book reviews.

Arvin graduated with a B.A. summa cum laude from Harvard in 1921 and taught at Detroit Country Day School before accepting an instructorship in English at Smith College in 1922. He remained at Smith throughout his teaching career, except for occasional visiting lectureships and a year as coeditor of the *Living Age* in New York (1925–1926). Under the continuing encouragement of Brooks, Arvin published reviews and essays—chiefly about American writers—in the *Freeman* as well as in the *New York Herald Tribune,* the *Independent,* and the *Atlantic Monthly.* Brooks wrote to him in 1922, "You are a born critic and you will be a distinguished one." The remark was prescient.

Promoted to assistant professor, Arvin traveled in Europe in the summer of 1929 and that year published *The Heart of Hawthorne's Journals,* an anthology of which he was editor, and *Hawthorne,* a landmark biographical and critical interpretation of the writer's obsession with guilt. During the Great Depression Arvin became increasingly concerned with social and political questions: he worked for a local American Federation of Teachers union, published essays on "Literature and Social Change" and "The Writer as Partisan," spoke on "Literature and Propaganda," and joined the National Committee for the Defense of Political Prisoners. He received national attention when, on Sept. 11, 1932, he pledged to vote Communist along with such other writers as Lincoln Steffens, John Dos Passos, Sherwood Anderson, and Theodore Dreiser. Promoted to associate professor in 1933, Arvin received a Guggenheim fellowship for 1935–1936 and began a study of Walt Whitman's social thought. His *Whitman* (1938) was generally thought to have transcended the socialist ideology that inspired it.

Meanwhile Arvin had begun in 1930 a long association with Yaddo, the writer's colony near Saratoga Springs, N.Y., where he met such lifelong friends as Louis Kronenberger, Granville Hicks, William Maxwell, and Malcolm Cowley. Also at Yaddo, Arvin married a former Smith College student, Mary Jordan Garrison, on Aug. 12, 1932, but the marriage proved unhappy. His wife suffered a nervous collapse in 1938 and entered a sanitarium the next year. They had no children and were divorced in 1940. Never in strong physical or emotional health himself, Arvin had a nervous breakdown in the fall of 1940 and underwent treatment in sanitariums the following spring. He became a professor, with tenure, in 1941.

Arvin's literary life gradually resumed with all its intensity. Having been elected to the Yaddo board of directors in 1939, he now befriended such younger writers as Carson McCullers and Truman Capote. His reviews and essays appeared frequently in the *New Republic,* the *Nation,* and the *Partisan Review.* He edited *Hawthorne's Short Stories* (1946) and *Moby Dick* (1948). *Herman Melville* (1950), a critical biography and perhaps his finest work, won a National Book Award. In his acceptance speech Arvin celebrated both Melville, who "spoke out for the 'august dignity' of the democratic man," and Ralph Waldo Emerson, "who cried out, again and again, on behalf of the free spirit of man and against the brutal, power-hungry and inhumane forces that would enslave that spirit." Arvin was elected to the National Institute of Arts and Letters in February 1952.

He next undertook a book-length study of Emerson but was plagued by illnesses for several years. To a friend he wrote of the "recurrent sickness (of the mind, that is) that took me to hospitals . . . some four or five times and involved me in 'treatments' that were sometimes worse than the sickness itself." Despite his celebrations of democracy and the free spirit of man, Arvin was one of several Smith College professors accused of "un-American activities" in 1954. He abandoned his Emerson book but published one of his finest essays, "The House of Pain: Emerson and the Tragic Sense," in the *Hudson Review* in 1959 and became Mary Augusta Jordan Professor at Smith in February 1960.

Arvin was subjected to a police raid on suspicion of homosexuality and was subsequently arrested with two other Smith College professors on obscenity and lewdness charges in September 1960. Despite protests and letters from nationally known scholars and colleagues, Arvin was convicted, fined, and given a suspended sentence. He was retired from Smith in 1961. Although suffering repeatedly from ill health, he managed to complete and publish *Longfellow: His Life and Work* (1963) shortly before his death, in Northampton, Mass.

Arvin was respected by most of the prominent literary scholars, critics, and editors of his time. He corresponded with such scholars as Austin Warren, Lewis Mumford, Lionel Trilling, and Merle Curti. His friendships with Brooks, Kronenberger, and Hicks remained close; and he came to know many younger critics, such as Alfred Kazin, Irving Howe, and R. W. B. Lewis. Edmund Wilson wrote that Arvin was "one of the two or three best contemporary writers on American classical literature." Brooks described him as a "quiet man with a violent mind," who "would gladly have stood against a wall and faced a fusillade for his convictions." Daniel Aaron praised him for his "range of comprehension, richness in reference and analogy, quiet responsibility, and justice." Although he was temperamentally shy and reserved, Arvin's innumerable friends knew him as witty, amusing, affectionate, and formidably learned. Despite the repeated torments of his personal life, he continued to affirm with Emerson and Melville "the free spirit of man." He was hard at work editing a four-volume history of American literature and writing a new book on Hawthorne when he died.

[Arvin's correspondence, miscellaneous writings, and academic records are at the Neilson Library of Smith College. His letters to David Lilienthal (1913–1963) are at the Princeton University Library; his letters to Van Wyck Brooks are at the University of Pennsylvania Library. An unpublished autobiography, diaries, and lecture notes—a prime source—are in private hands. A selection of his best reviews and essays is *American Pantheon,* Daniel Aaron and Sylvan Schendler, eds., with a memoir by Louis Kronenberger (1966). Arvin also edited Hawthorne's *The Scarlet Letter* (1950); *Selected Letters of Henry Adams* (1951); and George W. Cable's *The Grandissimes* (1957). See also *Twentieth Century Authors,* Stanley J. Kunitz and Howard Haycraft, eds. (1942); Jonathan Katz, *Gay American History* (1976); and James Hoopes, *Van Wyck Brooks* (1977).]

DEAN FLOWER

ASBURY, HERBERT (Sept. 1, 1891–Feb. 24, 1963), newspaperman and historian, was born in Farmington, Mo., the son of Samuel Lester Asbury, surveyor of St. Francois County and city clerk of Farmington, and of Ellen N. Prichard. Asbury was educated at Elmwood Seminary, Baptist College, and Carleton College, all in Farmington. He worked on the Farmington *Times* during a summer and after graduation took a full-time job with the paper. He did every type of work: printing, reporting, editing. He was fired, however, when he extended a vacation. Asbury then worked briefly in a lumberyard but, as he later explained in his characteristic style: " . . . I concluded that the lumber business held out no glowing promise for a young man who wished to retain his health and have leisure for a reasonable amount of traffic with Satan."

Asbury returned to journalism by getting a job on the Quincy, Ill., *Journal* (1910–1912). He then moved to the Peoria *Journal* (1912–1913) and on to William Randolph Hearst's Atlanta *Georgian* (1913–1915). While working as a reporter for the *Georgian,* Asbury played an important part in getting a child labor law through the Georgia legislature in 1914. He left Atlanta for the New York *Press* in 1915. In 1916 he switched to the New York *Tribune* and later that year to the New York *Sun.*

Asbury enlisted in the army on Dec. 8, 1917. He was made a second lieutenant, infantry, in July 1918. He was wounded and gassed in France and, in January 1919, honorably discharged. He returned to the New York *Sun,* but left in 1920 to work for the New York *Herald,* and, after 1924 for the new *Herald Tribune.* One of the fastest rewrite men, he was considered an excellent journalist by others in the field.

Asbury became known nationally when H. L. Mencken published Asbury's article, "Hatrack," in the April 1926 issue of the *American Mercury*. The article was about a prostitute in Asbury's hometown who worked at a cemetery. Asbury later said the article " . . . was somewhat critical of the attitude of the churches and the virtuous people of Farmington toward their fallen sisters . . . ." In Boston, the Watch and Ward Society succeeded in getting the issue banned. Mencken, who wanted a test case, was arrested on the Boston Common for selling allegedly obscene material. The post office barred the issue from the mails. Although Mencken later won the case, the *New York Herald Tribune* editorialized (Apr. 7, 1926): "In our judgment the article does not deserve suppression on the ground of obscenity. There are, however, substantial grounds for suppression on the score of sacrilege. . . ."

In 1926 Asbury published his autobiographical *Up From Methodism*, which covers the events up to 1910. The next year his biography of Bishop Francis Asbury, *A Methodist Saint,* appeared. Asbury married Helen Hahn, who also worked at the *Herald Tribune,* on Aug. 31, 1928. They had no children. He left the newspaper the same year to devote full time to writing. He published *The Gangs of New York* (1928), *The Life of Carry Nation* (1929), and *The Barbary Coast: An Informal History of the San Francisco Underworld* (1933). Asbury also wrote histories of the underworlds of New Orleans and Chicago. He was skeptical of any attempt to control morality by law, and very skeptical of the reformers themselves.

Sucker's Progress: An Informal History of Gambling in America from the Colonies to Canfield was published in 1938. A reviewer in the *New Yorker* (Nov. 12, 1938), said: "Mr. Asbury, who has made all American sinfulness his province, apparently has no feelings about his subject. Coldly, soberly, industriously he records the facts . . . he lacks either moral indignation or that spontaneous admiration for rascality. . . ."

Asbury had a wide readership. His articles appeared in the *New Yorker, Cosmopolitan,* and other magazines. He also did screenwriting. During World War II he wrote articles about military equipment and strategy for *Popular Science.* His writings provoked comment and controversy, both for their subject matter—histories of vice, crime, and self-indulgence—and for his uninvolved, nonjudgmental attitude toward what he portrayed.

From 1942 to 1948 Asbury was an editor at *Collier's Weekly.* His first marriage had ended in divorce in 1944, and on Mar. 29, 1945, he married Edith S. Evans, a journalist who later worked for the *New York Times.* This marriage ended in separation. His last book was *The Great Illusion: An Informal History of Prohibition* (1950). The July 1951 issue of the *American Historical Review* called it a fascinating and significant study. Asbury challenged many accepted myths, and his newspaperman's experience helped him analyze the propaganda of both sides—in this case the wets and drys—just as it had in his earlier books on crime and corruption. He continued writing until his death in New York City.

[Asbury's papers are in private hands. Two articles Asbury wrote for the *American Mercury* deal with important periods in his journalistic career: "Hearst Comes to Atlanta" (Jan. 1926), and "The Day Mencken Broke the Law" (Oct. 1951). Asbury's other books include *The Devil of Pei-Ling* (1927), *Ye Olde Fire Laddies* (1930), *All Around the Town* (1934), *The French Quarter: An Informal History of the New Orleans Underworld* (1936), *Gem of the Prairie: An Informal History of the Chicago Underworld* (1940), and *The Golden Flood: An Informal History of America's First Oil Field* (1942). Also see the *New York Times,* Apr. 9, 1926, and the obituary, Feb. 25, 1963.]

RALPH KIRSHNER

ASHURST, HENRY FOUNTAIN (Sept. 13, 1874–May 31, 1962), U. S. senator, was born in Winnemucca, Nev., the son of William Henry Ashurst and Sarah Elizabeth Bogard. His father, a sheep rancher, and his mother had been brought as children to California following the Gold Rush. In 1875 the family migrated south in a covered wagon and settled nine miles south of what now is Williams, Ariz. Drought in 1877 devastated Ashurst's stock and forced the family to move to a ranch near Mormon Lake, southeast of present-day Flagstaff. In this rugged and scenic country Ashurst grew to manhood.

His father served as a representative in the Fourteenth Territorial Legislature (1887). Supporting a family of ten children placed a severe strain on him, and because ranching proved unprofitable, he began mining a claim in the Grand Canyon. He died in an accident there in 1901. To better educate her children and to avoid another harsh winter on the ranch, Sarah Ashurst moved the family into Flagstaff.

Ashurst received, at best, the rudiments of an education. He learned much from ranch hands, working as a range rider both on the home and on nearby ranches. When he was nineteen, Sheriff J. J. ("Sandy") Donahue hired him as turnkey in the county jail at Flagstaff. Shortly thereafter Ashurst took a job in a lumber yard and started to study law at night. In 1895 he went to California, where he worked as a lumberjack in the Los Angeles area and as a hod carrier in San Francisco. In 1895 he resumed work briefly in the Flagstaff lumber yard, but returned to California in the fall to enroll in Stockton Business College. He worked as a newspaper reporter in his spare time. Graduating at the end of the term, he returned to Arizona and secured a job as a stenographer in Williams. Shortly thereafter he was appointed justice of the peace.

In November 1896, Ashurst was elected as a Democrat to the Territorial House of Representatives. He was elected to a second term and was chosen speaker, reportedly the youngest person ever to hold that position. As speaker he sponsored a bill establishing the Northern Arizona Normal School (today Northern Arizona University). In 1897, Ashurst was admitted to the bar and started his law practice in Williams. He was elected to the Territorial Senate in 1902, served a term, and then spent a year (1903–1904) at the University of Michigan Law School, completing his formal education.

His early training enamored Ashurst with the joys of public speaking. He practiced extensively, sometimes bellowing his remarks in the open country while riding the range, or even while running, to expand his lung capacity. He continually improved his vocabulary and throughout his life devoted considerable time to studying the classics. He gained an ever-expanding reputation and skill as an orator, which afforded him a great advantage in launching his legal and political career. It also brought him considerable public attention in later years and, indeed, was his chief claim to fame. Ashurst, reviewing his career, estimated that he had delivered 5,000 speeches.

On Mar. 2, 1904, after his return from Ann Arbor, Ashurst married Elizabeth McEvoy Renoe, a widow with four children, who had come from Baltimore in 1898 to establish, and then manage, a United States weather station. They had no children. She became his constant companion and political confidante.

Ashurst's first post after his marriage was that of district attorney of Coconino County, an office he held until 1908. The following year he moved to Prescott, where he maintained a residence for the rest of his career, and quickly established himself as the most prominent lawyer in northern Arizona. He was a patient, fair prosecutor, and a sympathetic pleader.

Ashurst was one of five Democratic candidates for the Arizona senatorial seats in 1911.

Of the primary campaign he wrote in his diary: "I have travelled by automobile, by steamers, buckboard, stagecoach and on horseback and have been a peripatetic bifurcated volcano in eruption. I quoted poetry, good and bad, I hurled tropes, metaphors, and similes." He and Marcus A. Smith were chosen the Democratic nominees. At the general election in December, both of them were elected. The following March, by the unanimous vote of both houses of the first legislature of the new state of Arizona, Ashurst and Smith were elected United States senators.

Ashurst was handily reelected to four successive terms in the Senate, garnering 72 percent of the votes in 1934 and never receiving less than 54 percent. In the Senate he was a devoted Wilsonian. From May 1914 to March 1921, he chaired the Indian Affairs Committee. During the 1920's he was a consistent critic of the Republican administrations: their programs, their policies, and their presidential appointments. By 1933 he had gained enough seniority to chair the Judiciary Committee, a post he filled for the remainder of his career in the Senate. At first a reluctant, critical New Dealer, he eventually supported its measures. Although he served almost forty years on Capitol Hill, Ashurst's name is associated with no significant measure or cause. He gained a widespread reputation for three related reasons.

Two were suggested by Senator Lawrence Y. Sherman in 1919, during the debate on the Versailles Peace Treaty, when the Illinois senator, an irreconcilable opponent of the treaty, called Ashurst, a treaty supporter, "the Chesterfield in charge of Senatorial behavior and . . . the Beau Brummel of forensic taste." Sherman's barbed remarks called attention to Ashurst's sartorial splendor and eloquent oratory. The other characteristic in which Ashurst also delighted was inconsistency. He made a virtue of it and relished in being known as the "Dean of Inconsistency."

Throughout his career Ashurst often appeared on the Senate floor, and elsewhere, in a black-braided coat, striped trousers, wing collar, and corded eyeglasses. Tall and with the manner of a Shakespearean actor, Ashurst matched his florid oratory to his attire. His speeches were models of polysyllabic splendor. Although he was not a Latin scholar, he memorized innumerable Latin quotations. His speeches were rich in literary references, and he spent part of every morning reading from the classics and ransacking the dictionary to expand his vocabulary. Ashurst used his oratory to defend and support the best interests of his constituents, once stating at a luncheon in his honor that he served in Washington "as a very well-paid messenger boy doing your errands. My chief occupation is going around with a forked stick, picking up little fragments of patronage for my constituents." Throughout the 1920's he championed the cause of Arizona in fighting for a greater share of the water of the Colorado River, which he believed was threatened chiefly by California.

Possibly the highlight of Ashurst's Senate career came on June 15, 1935, when he attacked Huey Long in what *Time* (Aug. 7, 1939) called "one of the most comprehensive dressing downs administered in the Senate chamber in modern history," politely and neatly executed, brimming with classical allusions and historical references. More often, though, observers noted his shifting views on important issues. Ashurst made a virtue of what others usually considered a vice, claiming that the first law of politics is "Rise above your principles."

Although his name came first in the roll call, Ashurst usually voted after the initial calling of the roll. Elected as a "dry," he voted both for the Eighteenth Amendment and for its repeal. Of his four votes on a bonus for veterans, two were for and two against. In 1937, when a woman wrote applauding his stand during the Supreme Court fight, he replied, "Dear Madame: Which stand?" Despite his concern for Arizona, Ashurst was honest and courageous in denouncing the "pork barrel" and the spoils system. He attacked the Ku Klux Klan at the height of its political power in the 1920's. He also argued that "constitutional amendments should be ratified by the qualified electors in each state, and not by the legislatures of the states."

From June 1910 to July 27, 1937, Ashurst kept a diary. The last sentence, indicative of its contents, reads, "It is comforting assurance that nothing in this diary will cause pain to any living person or bring reproach to the memory of anyone who is dead." Although pleasant reading, it offers little or no comment, and few insights, on the important issues of the day. It does contain fascinating pen portraits of several senators. The diary, edited by George F. Sparks and entitled *A Many Colored Toga*, was published in 1962.

In 1940, when Ashurst sought his sixth term in the Senate, at the age of sixty-six, he was sad and weary. His wife had died the previous year, after a lengthy illness. He did not campaign in the primary. His opponent, Ernest W. McFarland, made much of Ashurst's long absences from the Senate and of his vote against conscription. McFarland won the primary and Ashurst withdrew from the race.

Although he talked about returning to Arizona, Ashurst stayed on in Washington. He served for two years (1941–1943) as a member of the Board of Immigration Appeals of the Department of Justice. Thereafter, the traits that made him attractive as a political figure— his humor, kindliness, "old-school" courtesy, and his verbal pyrotechnics—brought him twice again to public attention. He appeared on the television quiz program "The $64,000 Question," winning $16,000. In 1959, after fraud by the producers of the program had been revealed, Ashurst said he had received no assistance with his questions and answers and found nothing irregular with the show. In 1961 he went to Hollywood to appear in the movie version of Allen Drury's novel *Advise and Consent* as Senator McCafferty, who dozed throughout most of the film except for intermittent eruptions of flowery rhetoric. Ashurst died in Washington, D.C.

Ashurst's life fulfilled the response he offered to reporters and others who asked him, in various ways, "What is the greatest thing in your public life?" His invariable reply was: "Ability to control my temper and the realization that this is a comic world."

[Ashurst's papers are at the University of Arizona and the Arizona Historical Society. Barry Goldwater collected and published *Speeches of Henry Fountain Ashurst of Arizona* (1953). Ashurst wrote "Making Amendments," *Saturday Evening Post*, Apr. 25, 1925. Scholarly works on Ashurst are George F. Sparks, "The Speaking of Henry Fountain Ashurst" (Ph.D. diss., University of Utah, 1952); Robert E. Cogmac, "The Senatorial Career of Henry Fountain Ashurst" (M.A. thesis, Arizona State University, 1953). Jay J. Wagoner, *Arizona Territory 1863–1912* (1970), provides information on Ashurst's early political career. Articles include George Creel, "Coconino Cloudburst," *Collier's*, Nov. 13, 1937; Alva Johnston, "The Dean of Inconsistency," *Saturday Evening Post*, Dec. 25, 1937; *Time*, Sept. 23, 1940, and June 8, 1962. An obituary is in the *New York Times*, June 1, 1962.]

RICHARD LOWITT

AUSTIN, WARREN ROBINSON (Nov. 12, 1877–Dec. 25, 1962), U.S. senator and ambassador to the United Nations, was born in Highgate Center, Vt., the son of Chauncey Goodrich Austin, a lawyer, and of Anne Mathilda Robinson. Austin grew up in a typical small-town, middle-class environment and attended the Highgate public school and Brigham Academy in nearby Bakersfield (1891–1895). In 1899 he graduated from the University of Vermont with a Ph.B. While at the university, Austin met Mildred Marie Lucas, the daughter of a trainmaster. They were married on June 26, 1901, and had two children.

Austin read law in his father's office and was admitted to the Vermont bar in 1902. He joined his father's legal practice in St. Albans, where over the next few years his two brothers also became partners. Austin joined the Republican party and in 1904 was elected state's attorney for Franklin County for a two-year term. In 1906, the Second Circuit of the United States Court admitted him to practice, and in 1907 he was named a United States commissioner. His political reputation grew with his election as chairman of the Republican State Convention in 1908 and as mayor of St. Albans in 1909. In 1912, following his losing bid for the Republican nomination for Congress, he turned his attention back to law. He was admitted to practice before the Supreme Court in 1914.

In 1916, Austin accepted a position with the American International Corporation, a new venture backed by the National City Bank of New York. He represented the company in Peking, China, where he negotiated loans with the Chinese government for railroad and canal-engineering projects. Austin remained in China until mid-1917, when he severed connections with the New York-based business and returned to Vermont.

Ambitious and hardworking, Austin settled in Burlington, the state's largest city, rather than in St. Albans. For the next twelve years, he successfully built his legal business while concurrently pursuing an active life in community affairs and Republican state politics. He did not run for an elective office again until 1930, by which time he had become one of Vermont's best-known attorneys and Republican workers.

In December 1930, U.S. Senator Frank L. Greene died with four years left in his term of office. Austin decided to run for the vacant seat in a special election held in March 1931. He defeated Frank C. Partridge in a close, hard-fought primary election and handily won over Democrat Stephen M. Driscoll in the general election.

Austin's fifteen-year senatorial career was characterized by an anti-New Deal stance in domestic affairs and a bipartisan, internationalist position in foreign relations. As a senator from a rock-ribbed Republican and conservative state, he served his constituency well. His voting record reflected his frugal, honest, individualistic

political position, and he opposed nearly every New Deal measure. No major piece of permanent legislation bears his name, nor was he significantly involved in providing leadership on major domestic issues. He was a follower in the Republican Senate establishment, overshadowed by William Borah, Arthur Vandenberg, Charles McNary, and Robert Taft.

It is Austin's record as an internationalist that makes him notable. He believed that America had a democratic, moralistic, capitalistic mission to the world. A flexible foreign policy should be followed; independence did not mean isolation. This attitude placed him in a tiny minority in the isolationist, Republican side of the Senate in the 1930's. He voted against the neutrality laws of that era and advocated a buildup of the nation's defenses.

After America's entry into World War II, Austin called for planning for the postwar world. The Roosevelt administration sought his support in its bipartisan approach to postwar planning. Secretary of State Cordell Hull asked Austin to become a charter member of the State Department's congressional foreign policy advisory group when it was formed in 1942; he later was a key member of the Committee of Eight, composed of prominent senators who favored some form of postwar international organization.

In 1943, Austin played an important role in directing the Republican party toward acceptance of an international organization plank in its 1944 platform. In addition, he supported administration internationalist actions that included the United Nations Relief and Rehabilitation Administration, the Dumbarton Oaks recommendation for a postwar international organization, and the 1946 British loan.

In spite of staunch membership in the conservative coalition, Austin's bipartisan internationalist position brought him into conflict with the Senate Republican isolationist bloc. In December 1942, that group purged him from the informal assistant minority leader's position he had held since 1933, and he did not receive the Senate Foreign Relations Committee assignment he wished until February 1944.

On June 5, 1946, President Harry S. Truman selected Austin as the first United States ambassador to the United Nations. The nomination was the capstone of Austin's career. He carried into the position his moralistic and idealistic premises of how the world organization could be used in the conduct of foreign relations. He assumed the United Nations was an arena for the dissemination of truth. He saw nationalistic views brought together there under a system of moral and legal rules and restraints where world public opinion scrutinized each nation's foreign policy.

Often, however, the United Nations mission was bypassed in major administration policy decisions. These events placed Austin's universal, idealistic views in an awkward position. Yet he accepted the American hard-line stance by rationalizing the tactics of containment as a series of short-range alternatives that supported the long-range goals of the United Nations.

Through the turbulent events of the cold-war years—the Greek-Turkish crisis and European economic situation that led to the Truman Doctrine and the Marshall Plan, the Palestine imbroglio of 1947 and 1948, the 1948 Berlin blockade, and the Korean War of 1950–1953—Austin spoke for American policy at the United Nations but had little influence on policy decisions.

While ambassador, Austin never had a close working relationship with the secretaries of state who served in the Truman administration: James F. Byrnes, George C. Marshall, and Dean G. Acheson. Yet all three appreciated the important relationship between America's continued support (although it was at times only rhetorical) for the United Nations as a part of the nation's foreign policy. They also appreciated Austin as an important link between the United States and the United Nations. With his sincere, cooperationist outlook, he eloquently carried out the role of American spokesman.

Between 1946 and 1953, Austin hardened his attitude toward the Soviet Union and its allies. His contact through the United Nations with the continued intransigence of the Soviets coupled with the administration's hard-line attitude brought him to this view. The early months of the Korean conflict were particularly influential. Both the Soviet Union and the People's Republic of China sorely taxed Austin. After early 1951, he appeared quite pessimistic regarding any modus vivendi with the Communists. Yet he never lost faith in the importance and goals of the United Nations.

At the close of the Truman administration in January 1953, Austin retired to Burlington, where he spent many hours pursuing his lifelong leisure-time activity as an amateur aboriculturist. His backyard was filled with various strains of apple trees. He also retained his interest in foreign affairs. As a symbol of his conversion to hard-line anti-Communism, he accepted the position of honorary chairman of the Committee of One Million, organized to keep the People's Republic of China out of the United Nations. He died in Burlington.

[The Austin papers are at the University of Vermont in Burlington. Yale University has a small collection of constituent correspondence to Austin on the question of the reorganization of the federal judiciary in 1937. For the United Nations years, the Austin papers must be supplemented by State Department records at the National Archives.

Articles by Austin include "United We Stand," *Foreign Policy Reports*, Oct. 1, 1944; "The Policy of War and Peace in the Platform of the Republican Party," *American Peace Society Bulletin*, Oct. 1944; "A Pincer Movement for Peace," *American Foreign Service Journal*, Jan. 1948; and "A Warning on World Government," *Harper's Magazine*, May 1948.

See Beverly Smith, "A Yankee Meets the World," *Saturday Evening Post*, Aug. 24, 1946, and *Time*, cover story, Feb. 5, 1951. George T. Mazuzan wrote the first scholarly work in "Warren R. Austin: Republican Internationalist and United States Foreign Policy" (Ph.D. diss., Kent State University, 1969). Henry W. Berger covered the China venture in "Warren R. Austin in China, 1916–1917," *Vermont History*, Autumn 1971. Austin's role is viewed in a larger context in Mazuzan, " 'Our New Gold Goes Adventuring': The American International Corporation in China," *Pacific Historical Review*, May 1974. David Porter analyzed Austin's role in congressional foreign policymaking in "Senator Warren R. Austin and the Neutrality Act of 1939," *Vermont History*, Summer 1974. The most complete account is Mazuzan, *Warren R. Austin at the U.N., 1946–1953* (1977).]

GEORGE T. MAZUZAN

AVERY, MILTON CLARK (Mar. 7, 1893– Jan. 3, 1965), artist, was born in Altmar, N.Y., the son of Russell Eugene Avery, a tanner, and Esther March. In 1905 the family moved to Hartford, Conn., where Avery graduated from Hartford High School in 1911. At the age of eighteen, he took a correspondence course in lettering, intending to become a commercial artist. Later he enrolled at the Connecticut League of Art Students, but when he found the class in lettering filled, he joined the life drawing class. Although Avery found the training inadequate under Charles Noel Flagg, he was inspired to become a painter. In order to paint during the day, he took a night job with the Travelers Insurance Company. He continued this arrangement for a number of years.

In the summer of 1925, Avery went to Gloucester, Mass., to join the artists' colony. While there he met Sally Michel, who had come from Brooklyn for a summer of painting.

He followed her to New York City and on May 1, 1926, they were married. Avery was able to devote his full time to painting because his wife obtained illustrating assignments that provided a decent living even during the Great Depression. In 1932, their daughter, March, was born. She became his constant model, and his family life provided most of his subjects other than landscapes, seascapes, and a few portraits of friends.

Primarily, Avery was a painter of nature with very finely attuned sensibilities. He loved the light and the colors of the beach, glorying in the subtle, closely related color harmonies he found there. He simplified forms and flattened masses, attaining a vision all his own, regardless of prevailing fashions in art. His art throughout his career remained firmly attached to his own temperament. Gentleness and quiet humor added grace to the boldness of his simplification of objects. Avery was a quiet person. When friends gathered in his studio–living room, Sally Avery showed them what Milton had been painting while Milton sat in a big rocking chair, occasionally interjecting a humerous quip or a few words concerning one or another of his paintings. For the most part, he let Sally speak for him. "Why talk when you can paint," he would say. He was wholly content with his lot in life, devoted to his wife and daughter. His painting advanced steadily, and many of his best works date from his later years, those from the early 1960's being among his finest.

During the summer months the family usually went to Gloucester, Cape Ann, or even as far north as the Gaspé peninsula. He filled notebooks with sketches and color notations. From them, he developed larger watercolors and then oil paintings that were completed in his studio. With each of these steps, his work became more refined and more sensitively structured. It was in his landscapes and seascapes that he verged closest to the frontier of abstraction. Perhaps, for that reason, they have exercised a special fascination for such artists as Mark Rothko and Adolph Gottlieb, who painted nonobjectively.

Throughout his career, Avery continued to draw from life. Once a week, until a serious illness in 1960 interrupted the habit, he attended a sketch class, drawing from the model. One is constantly aware of his expert draftsmanship as he set down the gesture and feeling of the pose in as truthful and economical a statement as possible. As Hilton Kramer has written: "The degree of individual identity that Avery is able to confer on these figures, despite the severe abstraction to which they are subjected, is

one of the marvels of his art." This abstracting is even more apparent in his landscapes and seascapes, which became increasingly simple and monumental. The dominant horizontal of the horizon line often gives them a sense of quietude. In some, though, a contrasting movement is introduced by patterns of zigzags or scumbled paint in ripples or dashes.

Avery's color sense and his whole attitude to art were closer to those of Henri Matisse than those of any other American artist of his time. Like Matisse, he felt that art "should have the lightness and joyousness of a springtime which never lets anyone suspect the labors it has cost." To both artists, composition meant the placing of the various elements to express feeling in a decorative arrangement in which color was always predominantly expressive. Avery learned to know the paintings of Matisse through visits to American museums; he was actually almost sixty years old before he went to Europe. Indeed, Avery's methods were entirely his own. He was unhurried, patient, and thoroughly satisfied to pursue his course of continued study alone. Acknowledgement of his achievement has continued to grow in the years since his death in New York City. At a memorial service for Avery, his friend and fellow artist Rothko said:

The instruction, the example, the nearness in the flesh of this marvelous man—all this was a significant fact—one which I shall never forget. Avery was first a great poet. His is the poetry of sheer loveliness, of sheer beauty. Thanks to him this kind of poetry has been able to survive in our time.

[Hilton Kramer, *Milton Avery Paintings, 1930–1960* (1960), is the closest thing to a biography. Other biographical material can be found in Maude Riley, "Milton Avery Fills a Gap," *Art Digest*, Jan. 15, 1945; and May Swenson, "Milton Avery," *Arts Yearbook* (1959). Important paintings are *Seated Blonde*, Walker Art Center, Minneapolis; *Breaking Sea*, Baltimore Museum of Art; *Sea Grasses and Blue Sea*, Museum of Modern Art, New York; *Spring Orchard*, National Museum of American Art, Washington, D.C.; *Black Sea*, Philips Collection, Washington, D.C.]

ADELYN D. BREESKIN

BACHRACH, LOUIS FABIAN (July 16, 1881–July 24, 1963), portrait photographer, essayist, and connoisseur, was born in Baltimore, Md., the son of David Bachrach, Jr., a pioneering photographer, and Frances Keyser. Bachrach's formal education scarcely extended beyond the elite Baltimore Polytechnic Institute, from which he graduated with honors in 1897. Presumably he was to become an engineer, but reacting to the rigors and monotony of his first jobs in industry, he persuaded his father, in 1900, to accept him as an apprentice in his Baltimore studio. Two years later, he toured some of the better New York studios, while furthering his training in drawing at the Art Students League. He became manager of his father's Washington, D.C., studio when he was twenty-one.

Chafing under his father's direction and longing to escape Washington and Baltimore summers, Bachrach borrowed $2,300 from his father and a family friend to purchase a small studio in Worcester, Mass., in March 1904. For four years he worked with some success. Then, about 1908, he began to offer sittings in homes in and near Worcester at no additional cost, an innovation made possible by the automobile. This device was to set him apart from his competitors and soon "Photos by Bachrach" became available to well-to-do families throughout New England. On June 29, 1909, Bachrach married Dorothy Deland Keyes. They had three children, of whom two sons, Bradford Keyser and Louis Fabian, Jr., were to play significant roles in the firm.

Achieving a growing mastery of group portraits in relaxed domestic settings, in 1913 Bachrach began concentrating on the more lucrative Boston market. That year he established his first central processing plant in Boston, settling permanently in Newtonville, Mass. By 1917 he owned four thriving studios and held another one jointly with his brother, Walter, on Fifth Avenue in New York City. (Walter had discontinued an engineering career to enter into partnership with his father and, upon David Bachrach's retirement in 1913, continued to operate the "southern" Bachrach organization, headquartered in Baltimore.) In 1925 Walter sold out to Louis, who now headed a chain of some twenty studios with sales exceeding $1.5 million dollars. Reluctantly going along with the tide of big business, Bachrach expanded his studios to forty-eight and employed some six hundred people by 1929. His operations extended from Portland, Maine, to Indianapolis, Ind.

Even during the bullish 1920's, when photography came of age in America, many Bachrach studios were losing money. Labor costs, high rents, and advertising costs outstripped sales. The Depression and demands of creditors forced Bachrach to cut back the number of his studios to eight and to trim the staff to some two hundred by 1935. He thus improved communi-

cation among staff and restored quality control. From 1932 to 1960, when he delegated this responsibility to his sons, he insisted upon examining daily every proof submitted for client approval. Encouraged by annual sales that once again exceeded a million dollars, Bachrach opened a ninth studio, in Chicago, in 1944. In 1955 Bachrach relinquished the presidency to his elder son, Bradford, continuing as chairman of the board until his death.

"Louis Bachrach's principal contribution to photography," Bradford Bachrach wrote in 1971, "was his devotion to high standards of portraiture and the merchandising thereof, and his ability to inspire his associates to work within these standards." More than half of Bachrach's employees in the late 1950's had been with the firm for twenty-five to thirty years or more. It is evident he inspired considerable loyalty despite his reputation as a severe taskmaster. The distinguishing feature marking his enduring merchandising success was Bachrach's early and persistent application of sound business principles to the operation of portrait studios—measures that ranged from maximizing modest talent by training employees for specialized duties to maintaining a central processing plant distinct from the studios to ensure quality and cost control. The equally enduring success of the Bachrach style was founded less upon creative or experimental impulses than upon a mastery of a proven technique, for which Bachrach was indebted to Ira Hill, Pirie MacDonald, and a number of fashion photographers, as well as his own unflagging enthusiasm for life and understanding of human nature.

In Bachrach's view, most subjects wished to be idealized rather than being given mere maps of their faces and these wishes should be respected: all men should be portrayed as "virile, intelligent and handsome," and all women as either beautiful or having a "charming, graceful . . . and aristocratic bearing." Since photographing men and women posed different technical and psychological demands, Bachrach and his sons adopted the novel but effective practice of dividing their main branches into separate studios with separate staffs for male and female portraits.

In the tradition established by his father, Bachrach photographed many famous personages, including American presidents from Taft to Kennedy. But he eschewed the professional limelight and cultivated both a rugged and refined individualism; he never lost the common touch. Bachrach was a slight, wiry, intensely animated man with rapidly blinking gray eyes.

He spoke quickly but precisely and enjoyed telling colorful stories drawn from an ever-present pocket notebook. Like his father, he contributed to magazines and newspapers; his subjects ranged from photography to horticulture. Bachrach was a connoisseur and collector of art and historic objects and was an active outdoorsman, playing golf in the low 90's. His greatest pleasure, characteristically, was in confounding experts by growing certain flowers and shrubs in supposedly inhospitable New England soil.

On Nov. 9, 1957, the year following his wife's death, Bachrach married Marjorie Whitney Callard. He died in Boston.

[Bradford K. Bachrach very generously provided much testimony from memory and family documents for this article. Manuscripts of Bachrach's articles, speeches, interviews, and certain letters as well as some two hundred photographs by three generations of Bachrachs were donated to George Arents Library, Syracuse University; see Bradford Bachrach, "Four Bachrachs," *Syracuse University Library Associates Courier*, Jan. 1972. Bachrach was interviewed in *Boston Herald*, Aug. 10–12, 1949, and he traced his own career in *Christian Science Monitor*, Jan. 16–19, 1957. See also Evan Hill, "The Flattering Camera," *Saturday Evening Post*, Aug. 19, 1961, which is anecdotal but accurate. His own writings are too numerous to list, as are his obituaries; the best of the latter appeared in *New York Times*, July 26, 1963, and *Popular Photography*, Nov. 1963.]

PAUL CHRISTOPHER

BAKER, JOHN FRANKLIN (Mar. 13, 1886–June 28, 1963), baseball player best known as "Home Run" Baker, was born in Trappe, Talbot County, Md., the son of Franklin Adams Baker, a farmer and butcher, and Mary Catherine Rust. He grew up on the farm, attended grade school, played baseball, hunted and fished, and developed a deep attachment to the life of the Eastern Shore, where his family had lived for at least five generations. After some semipro and minor-league play at Reading, Pa., Baker signed a contract in 1908 with Connie Mack, manager of the Philadelphia Athletics. He played nine games for the Athletics that year. In 1909 he became the regular third baseman. On Nov. 12, 1909, he married Ottilie Rosa Tschantre; they had two daughters.

A left-handed batter, Baker had a free swing, and with his heavy (fifty-two-ounce) bat he quickly established himself as one of the game's leading power hitters in the "dead-ball" era. In the six full years that he played for Philadelphia, he averaged more than 100 runs batted in, leading the American League in 1912 and 1913. He

also led the league in home runs for four years (1911–1914), with twelve his highest total. In four World Series (1910, 1911, 1913, 1914) he batted .378, one of the highest World Series averages ever achieved. The Athletics won the first three but lost the last series to the "Miracle" Boston Braves.

Baker's sobriquet was the result of his feats in the 1911 World Series against the New York Giants. In the second game his two-run homer in the sixth inning helped the Athletics to a 3–1 victory. The next day his home run in the top of the ninth inning tied the game 1–1 and his single kept the winning rally going in the eleventh. A *New York Times* writer referred to him then as "Home Run" Baker, a nickname that caught on and became part of baseball lore and legend. So, too, did the inspiration of another sportswriter, who referred to the great Athletics' infield of Stuffy McInnis, Eddie Collins, Jack Barry, and Baker as the "$100,000 infield."

Because of a contract dispute with Connie Mack, Baker sat out the 1915 season. Mack vowed that Baker would never play in the majors again, but relented and sold his contract to the New York Yankees for $37,500. He played for six years with the Yankees. The first four (1916–1919) were productive but not on a level with his years at Philadelphia.

On Feb. 12, 1920, Ottilie Baker died unexpectedly. Baker announced his retirement and did not play during 1920, the year that Babe Ruth joined the Yankees. He returned to the Yankees in 1921 and hit nine home runs, although he played in fewer than 100 games. He was used only part-time in 1922, and he retired before the start of the 1923 season.

On Jan. 16, 1922, Baker married Margaret Elizabeth Mitchell. They had two children. The remainder of his life was devoted to his farm in Trappe, where he died.

In his playing days Baker was a trim six-footer who weighed 175 pounds. He was not a colorful personality. Sportswriters and fellow players regarded him as a cool, steady player who apparently felt no tension and who was at his best in crucial games. They emphasized, too, his solid, dependable, rural virtues: his love of farming and hard work; his devotion to his family; his sense of loyalty and responsibility to his team and to baseball. Characteristically, Baker remarked that he would have retired in 1919 except that he felt that the Yankees had not received due return on their investment in him, and he felt a duty to help both baseball and the country return to normal after the war. It may be that his lack of color denied him the attention received by some of his more flamboyant contemporaries.

As a player, Baker clearly ranks at a level immediately below the outstanding stars of the game. Ironically, given his nickname, his ninety-three career home runs are among his least impressive statistics. They have been used as a bench mark by which to measure Ruth's achievements and the differences between the "dead ball" and "live ball" eras. Yet Baker's name appears frequently in the record books for both offensive and, occasionally, defensive achievements. He played on two of baseball's greatest teams; he played with or against many of the greatest players of his era; and in his best years (1911–1914) he was their peer. But he did not sustain that level over a long enough period. His .307 lifetime batting average, for instance, is good but not outstanding.

In 1955 the Committee on Veterans elected Baker to the Baseball Hall of Fame, a belated but not undeserved honor. Like most Hall of Fame nominees, he made intangible contributions beyond those that show in the record books.

[There is no biography of Baker. A clipping file in the National Baseball Library has material on Baker from the *Sporting News,* various New York papers, and other sources. Statistical data are in *Ronald's Encyclopedia of Baseball* (1962) and *The Baseball Encyclopedia* (1969), but one should be aware that early record keeping was more casual than it is now. References to Baker and the "flavor" of the era are in Lee Allen, *100 Years of Baseball* (1950), and *The American League Story* (1962); Frederick G. Lieb, *The Baseball Story* (1950); Harold Seymour, *Baseball: The Golden Age* (1971); David Voigt, *American Baseball* (1970). Lawrence Ritter, *The Glory of Their Times* (1966), contains interviews with some of Baker's contemporaries. An obituary appeared in the *New York Times,* June 29, 1963.]

HORTON W. EMERSON, JR.

BALCH, EMILY GREENE (Jan. 8, 1867– Jan. 9, 1961), social worker and peace activist, was born in Jamaica Plain, Mass., the daughter of Francis Vergnies Balch, a lawyer, and Ellen Maria Noyes. She attended private schools in Boston. In 1889 she received her B.A. at Bryn Mawr College, where she was a member of the first graduating class. After a year of private study with sociologist Franklin H. Giddings, she won a Bryn Mawr European Fellowship, which she used to study the French system of poor relief in Paris. In 1893 the American Economic Association published her monograph *Public Assistance of the Poor in France.*

On her return from France in 1891, Balch became involved in social work in Boston. One of her projects was to gather information on laws and agencies related to juvenile delinquency. Her *Manual for Use in Cases of Juvenile Offenders and Other Minors* was published in 1895, and revised in 1903 and 1908. In December 1892 she became a founder and temporary first head of a social settlement, Denison House. The following year she joined the Federal Labor Union, which was part of the American Federation of Labor, and attended one state labor meeting as a representative of the Cigar Makers Union.

In 1895, in order to prepare for teaching, Balch studied for a semester at Harvard Annex (now Radcliffe), and for a quarter at the University of Chicago. She then studied at the University of Berlin for a year. On her return, she joined the faculty of Wellesley College as an assistant in economics. She was promoted to instructor in 1897, associate professor in 1903, and professor in 1913.

While teaching courses on the labor movement, socialism, and immigration, Balch remained active in social causes. In 1903 she helped found the Women's Trade Union League. Later she worked on drafting a Massachusetts minimum wage bill (which failed to be enacted) and was among the organizers of the first State Conference of Charities in Massachusetts. She served on the Municipal Board of Trustees in charge of delinquent and neglected children in Boston (1897–1898); the Massachusetts State Commission on Industrial Education (1908–1909); the Progressive party's committee on immigration (1912); the Massachusetts State Commission on Immigration (1913–1914); and the Boston City Planning Board (1914–1917).

Balch combined a settlement worker's interest in immigrants with academic discipline. She used a sabbatical leave (1904–1905) and a leave without pay (1905–1906) to spend almost a year in Austria-Hungary studying emigration. For the remaining time she visited Slavic communities around the United States. This resulted in the publication of *Our Slavic Fellow Citizens* (1910), one of the more frequently cited books on histories of immigration.

After the outbreak of World War I, Balch began her career as a peace activist. In 1915 she accompanied Jane Addams and forty-two other American women to the International Congress of Women at The Hague. The congress sent delegations to neutral countries with the aim of convincing those governments to mediate the war. Balch was one of four delegates to visit

Scandinavian and Russian governments. With Jane Addams and Alice Hamilton, she wrote *Women at The Hague* (1915), and the following year she participated in an unofficial Neutral Conference for Continuous Mediation, backed by Henry Ford. Balch used a sabbatical in 1916 to participate in the Committee Against Militarism, the Collegiate Anti-Militarism League, and the Fellowship of Reconciliation. When the United States entered the war, Balch requested and received an extension of her leave. In 1918, despite student and faculty protest, the Wellesley College trustees decided not to reappoint her because of her social and pacifist views. In that year her *Approaches to the Great Settlement*, regarding the impending peace negotiations, was published.

Balch worked for a year on the editorial staff of the *Nation* and continued to devote herself to the peace movement. In 1919 the Women's International League for Peace and Freedom established its headquarters in Geneva with Balch as secretary-treasurer. She ran the international office until 1922, a year after formally adopting the Quaker faith. (She had been brought up a Unitarian.) In 1927 Balch was one of the League's representatives investigating conditions in Haiti. The resulting report, *Occupied Haiti* (1927), advocated an end to American intervention on the island. She also worked with the League of Nations on drug control, international aviation, Albania's admission to the league, and disarmament. From the spring of 1934 to the fall of 1935 she resumed her position as international secretary of the Women's International League; due to a financial crisis she worked without pay.

World War II strained Balch's pacifism; she could not reconcile her beliefs with her concern for the victims of fascist aggression. She attacked the policy of unconditional surrender as unnecessarily prolonging the war but reluctantly supported the war. She helped European refugees settle in the United States, worked to get the interned Japanese-Americans out of relocation camps, and made proposals for international cooperation in such areas as the polar regions and aircraft. In 1946 the Nobel Peace Prize was jointly awarded to Balch and international YMCA leader John R. Mott. She donated her $17,000 prize to the Women's International League for Peace and Freedom and related causes.

Balch never married. Her hobbies were sketching and writing. She wrote *The Miracle of Living* (1941), her only published book of poems, and *Vignettes in Prose* (1952). Although she moved into a nursing home in December 1956, she remained active in league affairs. In 1959 she co-chaired the celebration of the hundredth anniversary of the birth of former league president Jane Addams. Balch died in Cambridge, Mass.

[The Swarthmore College Peace Collection houses Balch's papers. Manuscript sources may also be found in the archives of the Geneva Office of the Women's International League for Peace and Freedom at the University of Colorado, Boulder; and some items relating to Balch's academic career are in the Wellesley College Archives.

The only book-length biography is Mercedes M. Randall, *Improper Bostonian: Emily Greene Balch* (1964). Biographical sketches include John Herman Randall, Jr., *Emily Greene Balch of New England* (1946), a pamphlet of Women's International League for Peace and Freedom; *Beyond Nationalism: The Social Thought of Emily Greene Balch* (1972), edited by Mercedes M. Randall; and Olga S. Opfell, *Lady Laureates* (1978). Her obituary appeared in the *New York Times*, Jan. 11, 1961.]

JUDITH ANN TROLANDER

BARNARD, CHESTER IRVING (Nov. 7, 1886–June 7, 1961), telephone executive and foundation trustee, was born in Malden, Mass., the son of Charles H. Barnard, a mechanic, and of Mary E. Putnam, who died when young Barnard was five. He worked his way through Mt. Hermon Academy in Northfield, Mass. Next he supported himself by tuning pianos. In 1906, Barnard obtained a scholarship to Harvard University, where he led a dance orchestra, typed student papers, and operated a translation service. He left Harvard in 1909 without completing the requirements for a bachelor's degree. Immediately thereafter he obtained a job at the American Telephone and Telegraph Company (AT and T) in Boston, working in the foreign statistical section as a translator of German, French, and Italian, languages he learned while attending Harvard. On Dec. 6, 1911, he married Grace Frances Noera; they had one daughter.

After becoming a commercial engineer with AT and T in 1915, Barnard revised the general commercial practices of the Bell system for greater efficiency. He served as technical adviser on rates to the Rate Commission and Operating Board of the U.S. Telephone Administration during World War I. In 1922 he was appointed assistant vice-president and general manager of the Bell Telephone Company of Pennsylvania. In 1925 he was made vice-president; in 1926, vice-president in charge of operations; and in 1927, president of the newly organized New

Jersey Bell Telephone Company. He remained in the last position until his retirement in 1948.

Active in many other fields, Barnard served on numerous civic and welfare boards at the local, state, and national levels. He organized the New Jersey State Emergency Relief Administration in 1931, directing it until 1933 and again in 1935. In November and December 1937 he lectured on "The Functions of the Executive" at Harvard University. The lectures were published as *The Functions of the Executive* (1938). The book was an outcome of Barnard's failure to find an adequate explanation of his own executive experience in classic organization or economic theory. Frequently reprinted, and translated into Spanish, Turkish, Arabic, and Japanese, the book has become a classic of organization theory. In the less well-known *Organization and Management* (1948), Barnard presents a basically sociological analysis. While he sought to construct a theoretical framework of organization and the executive function, he recognized the importance of habitual experience, which led to intuitive understanding.

In 1941 Barnard was appointed special assistant secretary of the treasury. In April 1942 he became president of the United Service Organizations for National Defense (USO), the leading agency providing recreational facilities for armed forces personnel during World War II. Under Barnard's leadership (1942–1945), the USO grew from 692 units to 2,723. Barnard described his work with this agency as "the most difficult single organization and management task" in his experience. For his work with the USO and for his directorship of the National War Fund (1943–1946), he received the Presidential Medal for Merit in 1946.

Following the war Barnard was appointed a consultant to the United States representative on the United Nations Atomic Energy Committee, and was a coauthor of *A Report on the International Control of Atomic Energy* (1946), which formed the basis for the policy of the United States on atomic energy. Having been a member of the board of trustees and the executive committee of the Rockefeller Foundation since 1940, he was elected president of the latter and of its General Education Board in 1948. He served until 1952. From 1950 to 1956, Barnard was also chairman of the National Science Board and from 1952 to 1954, he served as chairman of the National Science Foundation.

Barnard enjoyed golf and swimming. His hobby was music, and he was among the founders of the Bach Society of New Jersey and the Newark Art Theatre. Until his death

in New York City, he continued to advise many civic, business, public service, and educational organizations.

[Barnard's manuscripts and copies of his published and unpublished articles, addresses, and letters are in the Barnard Collection, Baker Library, Harvard University. In addition to books, he wrote "An Analysis of a Speech of the Hon. D. J. Lewis Comparing Governmental and Private Telegraph and Telephone Utilities," *Commercial Bulletin* (AT and T Commercial Engineers' Office, Mar. 2, 1914); and "Arms Race v. Control," *Scientific American*, Nov. 1949. Also see William B. Wolf's *Conversations with Chester I. Barnard* (1973) and *The Basic Barnard* (1974); L. M. Wells, "Limits of Formal Authority," *Public Administration Review*, Sept. 1963; David Arthur, "Chester I. Barnard and Educational Administration" (Ph.D. diss., University of Chicago, 1969); Daniel G. Donnelly, "The Basic Theoretical Contribution of Chester I. Barnard to Contemporary Administrative Thought" (Ed.D. diss., University of Massachusetts, 1966); and James A. Gazell, "Authority-Flow Theory and the Impact of Chester Barnard," *California Management Review*, Fall 1970. An obituary is in the *New York Times*, June 8, 1961.]

SONDRA VAN METER

BARRETT, FRANK ALOYSIUS (Nov. 10, 1892–May 30, 1962), Wyoming congressman, governor, and U.S. senator, was born near Omaha, Nebr., the son of Patrick J. Barrett and Elizabeth A. Curran. Both parents were schoolteachers, and Patrick Barrett also worked as a mortician and court bailiff. Barrett attended public schools and Creighton University, Omaha, earning an A.B. in 1913 and an LL.B. in 1916. During World War I he served seventeen months in the Army Balloon Corps. Discharged in January 1919, he married Alice Catherine Donoghue in Omaha on May 21 of that year. They had three children.

Barrett then moved to the eastern Wyoming oil boom town of Lusk, where he established his legal practice. As his practice thrived, Barrett, a Catholic, joined a variety of civic organizations and developed an interest in business and in Republican politics. In 1924 he acquired a substantial sheep and cattle ranch near Lusk and became active in the Wyoming Stock Growers Association, the Wyoming Wool Growers Association, and the Rocky Mountain Oil and Gas Association—all organizations of significant influence in the state. He served as Niobrara County attorney (1923–1932), as state senator (1933–1935), and as a trustee of the University of Wyoming (1939–1943).

Barrett lost his initial race for the United States Congress in 1936, but in 1942 he was elected. A folksy, energetic politician and campaigner, he paid exceptional attention to constituent concerns during his eight years in the House. He opposed proposals to deepen the Missouri River channel for fear that it would endanger the water supply of the upper Missouri basin states. He called for higher wool tariffs and for protection of the western livestock industry. In 1943 President Franklin Roosevelt created Jackson Hole National Monument in northwestern Wyoming by executive order; and Barrett, like most Wyoming politicians of both parties, strenuously objected on the grounds that the move threatened existing grazing, hunting, and fishing privileges and violated states' rights. Barrett drafted a bill to abolish the controversial monument that passed Congress in 1944 only to be pocket vetoed by the president.

After the war, Congressman Barrett emerged as a leader of western interests, demanding greater local control over grazing and mineral rights on the public domain. Appealing to a general antagonism among stockmen toward tightened federal grazing regulations, he chaired a series of highly publicized hearings in 1947 condemning the Forest Service and other federal agencies. The hearings brought down on Barrett the wrath of conservationist groups but probably strengthened him at home. On the national level, the conservative Barrett voted to override President Harry S. Truman's veto of the Taft-Hartley Act and supported the House Un-American Activities Committee and the Mundt-Nixon Communist-control bill of 1948.

In 1950 Barrett was elected governor of Wyoming. There he sidetracked proposals for a severance tax on the oil industry and imposed stringent economies on the state government. Again responsive to local economic interests, he advocated higher price supports for the Wyoming dairy and sugar beet industries, pushed for industrial and mineral development, and solicited defense installations for the state.

Barrett capitalized on Dwight D. Eisenhower's popularity, growing public frustration with the Korean War, and discontent over scandals and alleged Communist influence in the Truman administration to unseat veteran Senator Joseph C. O'Mahoney in the 1952 election. In the Senate Barrett was identified with the Republican right wing, voting for balanced budgets, the Bricker Amendment (intended to curtail presidential power to conclude international agreements), and the exemption of interstate natural-gas pipelines from federal regulation. He voted against the censure of Joseph R. McCarthy (who had campaigned for him in

1952). As a member of the Armed Services Committee, he worked to expand Warren Air Force Base in Cheyenne. But he devoted most of his energies to the Interior and Insular Affairs Committee, laboring to promote Wyoming economic growth and curtail federal regulation over the extensive public lands in the state.

Following the passage of the Submerged Lands Act of 1953, which gave the states control over offshore oil, Barrett pushed for legislation that would transfer control over federal grazing lands to the states and private ranchers. Conservation forces labeled his proposal a "land grab," and the administration rejected it as excessive. Undeterred, Barrett offered legislation to vest control of water rights in the West in the states, to return 90 percent of oil royalties from the public domain to the western states, and to permit Wyoming to levy property taxes on the large federal parks in its boundaries. None of these proposals was accepted. He encouraged exploitation of oil, gas, and uranium deposits on the federal domain and the development of reclamation and hydroelectric projects in the region—including a proposed dam at Echo Park in Colorado that many believed would endanger Dinosaur National Monument. While opposing high farm price supports, he urged import tariffs on foreign wools and expanded exports and school lunch programs to aid the livestock industry. Barrett's political career reflected the West's hunger for economic development, frequently through federal stimulation, and simultaneously its hostility to federal control and regulation.

A liberal Democratic trend, the recession, and charges (later retracted) by columnist Drew Pearson that Barrett had improperly interceded in a tax case for another Wyoming Republican contributed to his defeat by Gale McGee in 1958. President Eisenhower named him general counsel for the Department of Agriculture and member of the board of directors of the Commodity Credit Corporation in 1959. But in 1960 Barrett resigned both positions in an unsuccessful attempt to regain a United States Senate seat.

Barrett's wife died in 1956. On Apr. 4, 1959, he married Augusta K. Hogan. He died in Cheyenne, Wyo.

[The senatorial papers of Frank A. Barrett and a valuable biographical clipping file are in the Western History Research Center at the University of Wyoming in Laramie. Other useful sources are T. A. Larson, *History of Wyoming* (2nd ed., 1978); and Elmo R. Richardson, *Dams, Parks and Politics* (1973). An obituary appeared in the *New York Times,* May 31, 1962.]

WILLIAM HOWARD MOORE

BARTHELMESS, RICHARD (May 9, 1895– Aug. 17, 1963), motion picture actor, was born in New York City, the son of Caroline Harris, a stage and screen actress. He graduated from the Hudson River Academy at Nyack, N.Y., in 1913, and studied at Trinity College, Hartford, Conn., for a year. As a child he worked in theaters between schooling.

Barthelmess first appeared in films as an extra. His earliest important role was in *War Brides* (1916) with the Russian-born actress Alla Nazimova, whom his mother had befriended. He subsequently was the leading man in a number of films starring Marguerite Clark, the leading rival of Mary Pickford in screen popularity. An association soon followed with the Gish sisters and their mentor, D. W. Griffith. In 1919, Barthelmess starred with Lillian Gish in *Broken Blossoms,* the story of a young Chinese who befriends a slum girl. The film received international critical praise, was a financial success, and proved to be the vehicle that launched Barthelmess' cinematic career. Dorothy Gish, a frequent costar with Barthelmess, called his face the "most beautiful of any man who ever went before a camera."

At the premiere of *Broken Blossoms,* Barthelmess met Mary Hay, a Ziegfeld girl; they were married in June 1920. The couple appeared together in *Way Down East* (1920), a horse-and-buggy melodrama. A year later he starred in *Tol'able David,* the story of a southern mountain boy who sees to it that the mail gets through. The film met with great critical acclaim and financial success, enabling Barthelmess to buy the rights from D. W. Griffith and form Inspiration Pictures. He appeared in *Enchanted Cottage* in 1924, playing the role of a World War I veteran who finds happiness in the love of a plain woman.

In 1926, Barthelmess was divorced. He also decided to terminate his financial interest in Inspiration Pictures in order to accept a three-film-per-year contract with First National Pictures, at an estimated $375,000 a year. During his affiliation with Inspiration Pictures he had produced twelve box-office hits.

Barthelmess' first film for First National was *Patent Leather Kid* (1927), the story of a prizefighter. It was followed closely by *The Noose* (1928), the tale of a man imprisoned for a murder he did not commit. In 1927, Barthelmess served on a committee that formulated plans for an award program for the motion picture industry, thus becoming one of the founders of the Academy of Motion Picture Arts and Sciences. At the first presentation ceremony for the Academy Awards, held in 1928, Barthelmess was a nominee for best actor. He was not voted best actor, but he did receive a special award for distinguished achievement, on the basis of his work in *Patent Leather Kid* and *The Noose.* On Apr. 20, 1928, Barthelmess married Jessica Stewart Sargeant. He adopted her son, Stewart.

These successes of the late 1920's reestablished Barthelmess as one of the screen's leading actors. His first talkie was *Weary River* (1929), in which he played the part of a bootlegger who had been framed. The film was soon followed by the Howard Hawks production of *The Dawn Patrol* (1930), a war movie with a strong pacifist message, which received the 1930 Academy Award for the best original story.

In the 1930's Barthelmess began to travel a great deal and continued to make pictures for First National, now Warner Brothers. The films, which included *Alias the Doctor* (1932), *Heroes for Sale* (1933), and *Massacre* (1934), experienced limited popularity. In 1935, Barthelmess began to free-lance. Perhaps his most memorable performance in the later 1930's came in *Only Angels Have Wings* (1939), in which he portrayed Rita Hayworth's cowardly husband. His last motion picture performance was *The Spoilers* (1942).

During his nearly three decades in motion pictures, Barthelmess appeared in seventy-six films. At the peak of his career he received nearly 6,000 pieces of fan mail per month. He left films feeling "the fun had gone out of picture making." In 1942 he joined the U.S. Navy as a lieutenant commander. After the war Barthelmess retired from the motion picture industry to lead the life of a socialite. Moving to Long Island, N.Y., he acquired substantial real estate holdings. In 1955 he sold his fifty-acre beachfront estate at Southampton, N.Y., to Henry Ford II. He died in Southampton, N.Y.

[The *New York Times* obituary, Aug. 18, 1963, provides a relatively full account of Barthelmess' life. Also see Mrs. D. W. Griffith, *When the Movies Were Young* (1925); and Lillian Gish, *Lillian Gish: The Movies, Mr. Griffith and Me* (1969).]

FRANK R. LEVSTIK

BARTLETT, FRANCIS ALONZO (Nov. 13, 1882–Nov. 21, 1963), tree-care expert, was born on a farm near Belchertown, Mass. His early interest in trees led him to major in horticulture and natural science at Boston University and Massachusetts Agricultural College; he graduated from the latter institution in 1905 with a B.S. degree. Shortly after graduation Bartlett moved to Virginia, where he taught agriculture and horticulture at Hampton Institute for two years. He also began the research in shade-tree care that led him, in 1907, to buy a farm in Stamford, Conn., and to begin a private practice of caring for shade trees. He built a laboratory on his farm and began developing tools, products, and practices used in this field. Bartlett married Myrtle Kezar; they had two children.

Bartlett soon founded the Bartlett Shade Tree Experts Company. Continuing his research in methods and materials as his company grew, he and his associates introduced the use of chemotherapy in fighting vascular disease in trees, produced a new filling for tree cavities, and experimented with feeding practices. The material devised as cavity filler supplanted cement, which was commonly used, but was too rigid. The other innovation developed by the Bartlett organization in its early years involved the use of a strong steel cable, rather than chain, to support physically weak trees.

Bartlett's Stamford farm supported many other experiments related to tree care: the life cycles and life patterns of numerous insects were tracked, nonnative and native plants were examined, and various diseases were investigated. Bartlett was instrumental in saving the chestnut tree from extinction in the United States. By 1916 the species had been nearly eradicated by the chestnut blight. The U.S. Bureau of Plant Industry at Chico, Calif., sent hybrid seedlings to twenty tree experts for testing; Bartlett's was the only sample to grow successfully, hence the name Bartlett chestnut. Seedlings from his trees were distributed throughout the United States. At first Bartlett's company awarded fellowships for the study of trees at educational institutions around the country. Then, in 1923, he started the Bartlett School of Tree Surgery to train dendricians. A year later he gathered experts in entomology, pathology, physiology, and horticulture to form a research staff for the newly created Bartlett Tree Research Laboratories; the profits of the tree-care company supported the laboratories' efforts. That same year he initiated a meeting of tree specialists to found the National Shade Tree Conference, later renamed the International Shade Tree Conference.

While in Europe in 1927, Bartlett investigated a disease afflicting Dutch elms. He published his results upon returning to the United States, predicting the appearance of the blight on American elm stands. When the Dutch elm disease was noticed in the United States, Bartlett recommended ridding the elms of the elm bark beetle, carrier of the fungus responsible for the blight. His efforts at least slowed transmission of Dutch elm disease.

Bartlett's tract on Dutch elm disease was one of his numerous efforts to educate the public about caring for shade trees. During 1929–1930 his organization sponsored, and subsequently published, a series of fifteen-minute radio broadcasts titled "Radio Tree Talks." Each of these related to some aspect of shade-tree care. The introduction to one such text, published by the laboratories' public relations bureau, called the broadcasts an attempt "to stimulate interest in the improvement of shade tree growth through scientific methods."

As urban areas grew, Bartlett expanded his company's activities to deal with the problems created in that environment. Tree ailments studied by Bartlett's staff included those caused by air pollution, drought, and the growing network of highways. The company developed methods for regulating woody plants along utility rights of way and was the first to use helicopters to spray herbicides, a practice that grew controversial with the increased concern over the dispersal of unknown quantities of pesticides to outlying areas.

Bartlett retired as president of the shade-tree company in 1936 and was succeeded by his son, Robert A. Bartlett. He remained chairman of the board until his death in Stamford, Conn.

Bartlett's early research and organizational efforts led to widespread interest in and understanding of shade trees and their care. The laboratories he founded continue to add significant research to support the care provided by his now-national company.

[Bartlett's papers are at the Bartlett Tree Research Laboratories in Stamford, Conn. He also wrote *The Tree Expert* (1956). See obituaries in the *New York Times*, Nov. 22, 1963, and *Connecticut Woodlands*, Jan. 1964.]

RACHEL BURD

BARTON, JAMES EDWARD (Nov. 1, 1890–Feb. 19, 1962), comedian, dancer, and singer, was born in Gloucester, N.J., the son of James Charles Barton, an interlocutor with the West and Primrose Minstrels, and Clara Anderson, a dancer and singer. Barton made his first stage appearance at the age of two in *The Silver King*, and by the age of four he was playing Topsy in *Uncle Tom's Cabin*. From 1897 until

1903, the Bartons had a family act in which James was billed as "the boy comedian." During those years of touring, Barton picked up schooling wherever he could; his formal education ended with the sixth grade in Camden, N.J.

As a young man, Barton worked in stock companies and vaudeville shows, and in 1915 he signed on as a dancing comedian in *Twentieth Century Maids,* a production of the Columbia burlesque chain. His first big break came in 1919, when he was to play in *The Passing Show of 1919,* a Broadway revue. But before the show opened, Actors Equity Association called a strike. A benefit was planned for the strikers, and Barton was scheduled to make a minor appearance. His dancing stopped the show. And when *The Passing Show of 1919* finally opened, he again was a hit.

Over the next fifteen years Barton became known as a top hoofer on the stage. He compiled an impressive list of Broadway credits, including *The Last Waltz* (1921), *The Rose of Stamboul* (1922), *Dew Drop Inn* (1923), *The Passing Show of 1924* (1924), *Artists and Models* (1925), *Palm Beach Nights* (1926), and *No Foolin'* (1926). In 1928 and 1929 he was on the road with *Burlesque.* He returned to Broadway in 1930 and appeared in *Moonshine* and *Sweet and Low.* Between 1928 and 1932 he also made numerous appearances as a headliner at the Palace Theater.

In 1912, Barton married Ottilie Regina Kleinert. The couple, who had no children, separated in 1926. Three years later Barton sustained injuries in an accident that forced him to use considerable makeup to hide facial scars and to reshape his nose. In 1933, the Bartons were divorced, and he married Kathryn Penman, a former Ziegfeld girl.

In 1934, Barton, who had been called "the man with the laughing feet" and who had entertained audiences by dancing, singing, and imitating drunks, replaced Henry Hull as Jeeter Lester in the play *Tobacco Road.* Over the next five years he played that role 1,899 times, and his earthy portrayal of the crude, degenerate Lester won him not only plaudits but also recognition as a genuinely versatile performer.

Barton's success in *Tobacco Road* led to motion picture contracts. (He earlier had made a few two-reelers in which he mostly danced.) He played in *Captain Hurricane* and *His Family Tree* (1935). The latter film especially allowed him to exhibit his repertoire of Irish brogue, dancing, and comedy. Barton also played a character role in *The Shepherd of the Hills* (1941).

Back on the stage, Barton appeared in *Free and Equal* (1942), *Bright Lights of 1944* (1943), and *The Girl from Nantucket* (1945). In 1946 he was cast as Hickey in Eugene O'Neill's *The Iceman Cometh.* His portrayal of the loquacious salesman—a role that entailed delivering an eighteen-minute soliloquy—won Barton more critical acclaim.

In 1948, Barton played the boozy, bragging old Indian scout in the screen version of William Saroyan's *The Time of Your Life.* He also appeared in *Yellow Sky,* a western in which he played a clever, whiskey-drinking old prospector. In the following two years he was in two lighthearted Hollywood productions, *The Daughter of Rosie O'Grady* (1949) and *Wabash Avenue* (1950). He made three more movies in 1951: *Here Comes the Groom, Golden Girl,* and *The Scarf,* the last a drama that featured Barton as a salty old turkey rancher who befriends an accused murderer.

Typecast in Hollywood as a supporting actor in musicals and westerns, Barton returned to Broadway in 1951 to star in the musical *Paint Your Wagon.* Again he had the role of a hard-drinking old westerner, Ben Rumson. Barton subsequently appeared in a few more movies and in several television plays, including *The Iceman Cometh.* He also starred in a short-lived Broadway drama, *The Sin of Pat Muldoon* (1956). He made his last screen appearance in *The Misfits* (1961).

Barton died in Mineola, N.Y. A trouper of the old school, often noted for his coarse mannerisms and tough temperament, he spent his entire life in show business. An accomplished performer, he was equally polished and confident in vaudeville, on the legitimate stage, or in front of the camera.

[Material on Barton and his career is in the Billy Rose Theatre Collection in the Library and Museum of the Performing Arts, the New York Public Library at Lincoln Center. See John B. Kennedy, "The Bouncing Barton," *Collier's,* Aug. 11, 1928; *Time,* Sept. 30, 1935; Richard Gehman, "James Barton," *Theatre Arts,* February 1952; and Marshall and Jean Stearns, *Jazz Dance: The Story of American Vernacular Dance* (1968). Obituaries are in the *New York Times,* Feb. 20, 1962; and *Variety,* Feb. 21, 1962.]

THOMAS BURNELL COLBERT

BARUCH, BERNARD MANNES (Aug. 19, 1870–June 20, 1965), financier and public adviser, was born in Camden, S.C., the son of Simon Baruch, a Jewish immigrant who fled East Prussia in 1855, and Belle Wolfe, the daughter of an established southern Jewish family. Baruch admired his father's struggle to become a physician, revered his enlistment with the Confederacy during the Civil War, and generously supported his medical causes in later years. Throughout his life Baruch identified his father with the ideal of public service.

At his wife's urging, Simon Baruch moved the family in 1881 to New York, where Bernard attended public school. In 1884, although only fourteen, Baruch registered at the College of the City of New York. He preferred social and athletic activities to intellectual achievement and was graduated in 1889 with indifferent grades. He flirted briefly with the idea of a medical career, but the life-style of his father's wealthy clientele proved more attractive than his father's profession.

In 1891 Baruch joined the brokerage firm of A. A. Housman and Company as a bond salesman and customers' man. After some initial setbacks his personal speculations resulted in a series of successful plunges in sugar, tobacco, and railroad stocks. Baruch played a lone hand, followed his hunches, and achieved his greatest triumphs during bear markets, selling short as stock prices tumbled. His flamboyance did not gain him respectability among the Morgans, Warburgs, and other pillars of New York's financial establishment, but he was a millionaire at thirty. In 1903 Baruch left Housman to establish his own firm. In frequent alliance with the Guggenheim brothers he speculated in copper, sulfur, gold, rubber, tungsten, zinc, and iron investments in the United States and abroad. Baruch did not organize or manage business institutions, but he accumulated a great deal of knowledge about men and markets in the raw material industries.

During these years Baruch began to put his wealth to use in politics and public affairs. He responded to the rising civic consciousness of the Progressive era. He took an interest in New York City politics and became a friend and admirer of Woodrow Wilson. Baruch and Wilson shared a number of values; both sought a place in the lineage of great American patriots. It is significant that Baruch did not believe that his Jewishness barred him from this opportunity; he regarded himself as an assimilated Jew. He married an Episcopalian, Annie Griffen, on Oct. 20, 1897, and their three children were raised as Christians. Wilson and Baruch also saw themselves as independent, autonomous individuals outside the established centers of political and financial power. Their southern backgrounds offered further grounds for empathy. (In 1905 Baruch

acquired a South Carolina estate, the Hobcaw Barony, where he lavishly entertained visiting politicians in subsequent years.)

Above all, Wilson valued that rarity, a Democrat on Wall Street. After 1915, as the United States edged closer to war, Baruch, a preparedness advocate, received a series of appointive posts in the government's fitful mobilization program. In the summer of 1916 President Wilson appointed him to the seven-man Advisory Commission of the Council for National Defense, a cabinet committee responsible for national mobilization. In the spring of 1917 Baruch enlisted former business contacts to negotiate and administer informally a series of raw material purchases for the military. Later that summer he became commissioner for raw materials in the newly formed War Industries Board (WIB).

Domestic mobilization ground to a halt in the winter of 1917–1918. In March, Wilson elevated Baruch to the WIB chairmanship and designated the board the major civilian agency for industrial mobilization. Baruch did not acquire sole decision-making authority for industrial mobilization; for example, he did not displace military prerogatives in contracting. Yet his position as chairman, combined with membership in the president's war council, gave him a strategic position at the heart of the government's competing mobilization agencies.

Baruch's was one of the outstanding success stories of World War I. He entered Washington a private speculator and emerged a public statesman. Rapid recruitment of an expert, knowledgeable staff; a sure grasp of power politics; sensitivity to the uses of private dealings and public relations; and loyalty and sensitivity to presidential wishes contributed to the transformation. Wilson's decision to take him to the postwar peace conference also helped. In Paris, in 1919, Baruch became chairman of the raw materials section of the Supreme Economic Council and a delegate to the committees on economic and reparation clauses, where he fought a losing battle against British and French demands for greater German reparations. With the assistance of John Foster Dulles, a fellow delegate, he recorded his experiences in *The Making of the Reparation and Economic Sections of the Treaty* (1920).

Baruch remained loyal to Wilson's memory for the rest of his life. Although self-taught in business, he learned his political philosophy from Wilson. He shared the view of Wilsonians and corporate spokesmen that social stability and economic prosperity in the postwar world required newer forms of cooperative institutions among business, labor, and agriculture, and between business and government. The virtues of private enterprise and the law of supply and demand remained central values, but he believed that historical changes had made conventional laissez-faire impractical. His acceptance in October 1919 of a place on the National Industrial Conference Board, which was charged with finding a way through the postwar epidemic of labor strikes, was consistent with this view. So were his postwar recommendations for antitrust revision. Baruch offered the same kind of advice during the New Deal experimentations with business cartelization under the National Recovery Administration (NRA).

During the Republican ascendancy after World War I, a beleaguered Senate Democratic leadership proved particularly receptive to Baruch's generous campaign contributions. It was partly because of Baruch's advice that in 1933 President Franklin D. Roosevelt appointed Hugh S. Johnson, a Baruch protégé, head of the NRA, and George N. Peek, another Baruch associate, head of the Agricultural Adjustment Administration.

Baruch shrewdly employed the power of publicity in his interwar campaign for industrial preparedness. He commissioned Grosvenor B. Clarkson's portrait of the WIB, *Industrial America in the World War* (1923), and he championed such postwar experiments in industrial-military planning as the Army Industrial College, founded in 1924. He also participated in the compilation and subsequent revisions of the War Department's Industrial Mobilization Plan of 1930 in hopes of persuading military officers to accept civilian business planning for war under a reconstituted WIB.

Baruch preached a message of total mobilization of population and resources and complete economic stabilization through comprehensive price and wage controls in the event of war. He made his case before the War Policies Commission in 1931 and the Nye Committee in 1935; in 1941 he capped his prewar sermons with the reissue of the WIB's final report of March 1921, *American Industry in the War.*

By the late 1930's, Baruch had come to symbolize the lessons of World War I. Roosevelt frequently and publicly consulted him on defense matters. But three factors barred Baruch's path to supreme authority in defense organization. Before Pearl Harbor and a declaration of war, the public would not countenance the creation of the post Baruch coveted. Liberal New Dealers mistrusted Baruch as a stalking-horse

for conservative business and military interests. And Roosevelt, ever jealous of his own prerogatives, opposed a WIB beyond White House control. As a result, Roosevelt excluded Baruch from the War Resources Board established in 1939, and he resisted the concepts of one-man emergency control and comprehensive price controls throughout 1940–1941.

After Pearl Harbor political and economic conditions favored Baruch's recommendations, although he never became the mobilization czar of World War II. He possessed political influence, but not administrative power. Friendships with key war administrators provided a major source of Baruch's wartime influence. James V. Forrestal, undersecretary and then secretary of the navy; Robert P. Patterson, undersecretary of war; Ferdinand E. Eberstadt, chairman of the Army-Navy Munitions Board; and James F. Byrnes, chief of the Office of War Mobilization in 1943, were all receptive to his advice. And Baruch gave it: a consistent plea for one-man administrative control.

In early 1943 Roosevelt, at Byrnes's request, offered Baruch the chairmanship of the War Production Board, the World War II equivalent of the WIB. When Baruch procrastinated, Roosevelt changed his mind. Later that year Baruch turned down Byrnes's offer of the directorship of the Office of Economic Stabilization. In addition to concern about his age and health, Baruch enjoyed the play of politics behind the scenes.

Yet Baruch did not forgo formal appointments altogether. In 1942 Roosevelt appointed him, along with James B. Conant and Karl T. Compton, to the Rubber Survey Committee to investigate the nation's rubber shortage. In 1943 Byrnes asked Baruch and John M. Hancock, then of Lehman Brothers, to submit a reconversion program. The White House intended to use Baruch's prestige to make difficult political choices more acceptable to Congress. First, the Baruch Committee called for nationwide gasoline rationing, expanded production of synthetic rubber, and appointment of a rubber administrator; Congress approved rationing, and Roosevelt appointed a rubber administrator. Second, the "Baruch-Hancock Report on War and Postwar Adjustment Policies" (Feb. 18, 1944) was intended to head off proponents of public works and government planning in favor of a disposal of surplus property and job creation through private enterprise. Congress established the Surplus Property Administration, and Roosevelt appointed William L. Clayton, a Texas cotton broker, administrator.

By the end of World War II Baruch had become firmly established as an American folk hero. President Harry S. Truman, like Roosevelt before him, attempted to capitalize on the mystique by appointing Baruch ambassador to the United Nations Atomic Energy Commission in 1946. "We will sleep more comfortably in our beds," one newspaper noted, "because clear-eyed Barney Baruch is on guard."

The Baruch Plan, presented to the Atomic Energy Commission on June 14, 1946, did guard America's atomic secrets. American production of atomic bombs would cease only after implementation of a system of controls, including full managerial control of manufacturing plants by the World Atomic Authority and a strict limitation on the use of the Security Council veto. Soviet representatives balked at Baruch's insistence that they waive the Security Council veto. Most Americans, however, regarded the Baruch Plan as exceptionally generous. If nothing else, it provided a propaganda victory for the United States and a personal triumph for Baruch.

Baruch's role in atomic diplomacy was his last opportunity to directly influence the nature of major government policy during the Truman administration. Baruch had already differed with Truman. He supported Henry Morgenthau's plan to strip postwar Germany of her industrial base; Truman did not. He lobbied against the administration's postwar loan to a British Labour government that in his view threatened private enterprise. And in the immediate postwar period Baruch recommended a more conciliatory attitude toward the Soviet Union than the administration was prepared to accept.

When the Korean conflict broke out in June 1950, Baruch was far more eager than Truman for all-out economic controls. Left out of the inner circle, he made known his views in public testimony and in private correspondence with influential congressmen such as Carl Vinson, chairman of the House Armed Services Committee, and Lyndon B. Johnson of the Senate's Armed Services Committee. "We face a double threat," Baruch wrote Johnson in the fall of 1950, "one from outside and the other from inside. Wisdom would direct us to arm against a possible invasion, and in doing so to make sure we do not destroy ourselves economically, as we are doing now through the inflationary measures which the government itself is causing." Baruch participated vigorously in the public debate over price and wage controls, and his prestige gave added weight to arguments for tougher measures. But his influence with both the White House and significant congressmen had greatly waned.

Baruch was eighty-three when the Korean conflict ended, and he spent much of his remaining years extending and shaping his public reputation. Impressed with Margaret L. Coit's Pulitzer prize–winning biography, *John C. Calhoun* (1950), Baruch suggested that the author do his biography. *Mr. Baruch* appeared in 1957. Baruch, unhappy with Coit's work, wrote *Baruch: My Own Story* (1957) and *Baruch: The Public Years* (1960). Both reveal the enduring impact of Wilson and World War I on Baruch's conception of his country and himself. They also reveal that he self-consciously pursued the heady ambition of having the history of his age recorded through his public career. He died in New York City.

[The Bernard Baruch papers, a large collection including bound copies of his major addresses and articles, are at the Seeley G. Mudd Manuscript Library, Princeton University. Baruch's far-flung political correspondence leads to many collections, including the Woodrow Wilson and Eugene Meyer, Jr., papers at the Library of Congress, Washington, D.C.; the James V. Forrestal and Arthur Krock papers at Princeton; and the Roosevelt papers at the Franklin D. Roosevelt Library, Hyde Park, N.Y.

Baruch hired several writers who prepared works such as *Taking the Profits out of War* (1926), *Preventing Inflation* (1942), and *A Philosophy for Our Time* (1954).

Baruch's own memoirs and the Coit biography provide the best starting point for understanding Baruch's career. For additional information, see Robert D. Cuff, "Bernard Baruch: Symbol and Myth in Industrial Mobilization," *Business History Review*, Summer 1969; Paul A. C. Koistinen, "The 'Industrial-Military Complex' in Historical Perspective: The Interwar Years," *Journal of American History*, Mar. 1970; Jordan A. Schwarz, *The Interregnum of Despair: Hoover, Congress, and the Depression* (1970); Richard Polenberg, *War and Society* (1972); Frank B. Freidel, *Franklin D. Roosevelt: Launching the New Deal* (1973); and Barton J. Bernstein, "The Quest for Security: American Foreign Policy and International Control of Atomic Energy, 1942–1946," *Journal of American History*, Mar. 1974.]

ROBERT D. CUFF

BASSO, (JOSEPH) HAMILTON (Sept. 5, 1904–May 13, 1964), novelist, was born in New Orleans, La., the son of Dominick Basso and Louise Calamari. His paternal grandfather, Joseph Basso, had emigrated from Genoa, and in the 1880's opened a small shoe factory and shoe store in the French Quarter of New Orleans. The family lived above the store until Basso was seven; then they moved "uptown." After graduating from Easton High School, Basso entered Tulane University in 1922. He was enrolled in the law course but was attracted chiefly to literature and history. He left Tulane in 1926, a few months short of graduation, determined to be a writer.

After a disappointing year in New York, Basso returned to New Orleans as reporter on, successively, the *Tribune,* the *Item,* and the *Times-Picayune.* He was a junior in the group of Sherwood Anderson, William Faulkner, Oliver La Farge, and others who contributed to the *Double-Dealer* and frequented the Pelican Bookshop in the French Quarter, managed by Etolia Moore Simmons. "It was during prohibition," she recorded. "Ham had the water-front beat, and frequently persuaded the captains to part with a bottle of real stuff which he would share with the others. We would lock the doors at five o'clock and open the bottle," usually wine.

Basso's first novel, *Relics and Angels* (1929), was autobiographical, on the theme he would often repeat: a young man's return from the North to his home in the South. Basso married Etolia Simmons, a graduate of Newcomb College, June 2, 1930; they had one son. For a time the Bassos lived in a mountain cabin near Brevard, N.C. There he completed the biography *Beauregard: The Great Creole* (1933). The work combined the historian's research and the novelist's perception, and was playful about the idolatry of his general. The book had the misfortune to appear on the day President Franklin D. Roosevelt closed all the banks.

Cinnamon Seed (1934), a story of the Civil War and Reconstruction in Louisiana, introduced a figure that was to reappear in some of Basso's later novels: the person of mixed blood in southern society. Basso spent the winter of 1934 in Aiken, S.C. The resort town offered the contrast between wealthy northern vacationers and local folk of humbler stripe that Basso depicted in *In Their Own Image* (1935).

Basso was always a journalist as well as a novelist, to the benefit of both callings. As associate editor of the *New Republic* in 1935–1937, he reported the presidential race, the Scottsboro case, and strikes in cotton mills of the South. Returning to the North Carolina mountains, Basso renewed his close friendship with Thomas Wolfe. In 1938 the Bassos traveled in Italy and lived briefly in the south of France. *Days Before Lent* received the Southern Authors Award in 1939. The winter of 1941–1942, spent in South Hadley, Mass., furnished acquaintance with

New England academic communities that Basso compared with southern coastal towns of less learning in *Wine of the Country* (1941). *Sun in Capricorn* (1942) pictured the prototype of Huey Long, whose demagoguery Basso knew inside out.

Writing in the special style of *Time* magazine, Basso applied for a position on its staff and was a contributing editor in 1942–1943. Next he was associate editor of the *New Yorker* from 1944 to 1962. From his country home in Weston, Conn., in the midst of stimulating friends (Malcolm Cowley, Van Wyck Brooks, Matthew Josephson, John Hersey, Peter De Vries) Basso contributed regularly to the *New Yorker:* short fiction pieces, factual articles, profiles of celebrities, book reviews. Notable among the profiles were lengthy interviews with Somerset Maugham (1944) and Eugene O'Neill (1948).

Basso broke the intensity of his book writing by travel to out-of-the-way places, including a sultry port in Honduras; the Maroon country in Jamaica, an area settled by the offspring of Confederate expatriates; and Robert Louis Stevenson's retreat in Samoa. All his travel reports appeared in the *New Yorker* and later were collected in *A Quota of Seaweed* (1960). These essays illustrated Basso's gift for instant communication with the most varied characters, no matter how alien in locale and culture.

Basso supplied lively introductions to his wife's *The World from Jackson Square* (1948), a collection of writings about New Orleans, and to his own edition of W. L. Herndon's *Exploration of the Valley of the Amazon* (1952). His special success among his eleven novels was *The View from Pompey's Head* (1954), a best seller that was made into a motion picture (1955). It is the story of a southerner exiled in New York who briefly relives the scenes of his youth.

Basso was too intelligent and informed to subscribe to the myth of the Old South that more romantic novelists espoused. He valued the South for quite other qualities—love of place, emotions lying near the surface, easy person-to-person relationships—and pitied it for certain regional disabilities. He was elected to the National Institute of Arts and Letters in 1955.

Basso was trim, had dark eyes and hair, and was apt to wear a smile. His last book, *A Touch of the Dragon* (1964), was completed while he was suffering from cancer. He died in New Haven, Conn.

[Basso's manuscripts and correspondence are in the Beinecke Library, Yale University. See also Malcolm

Cowley, "The Writer as Craftsman: The Literary Heroism of Hamilton Basso," *Saturday Review of Literature*, June 27, 1964; Rose B. Green, *The Italian American Novel* (1973); and Joseph R. Millichap, *Hamilton Basso* (1979). Obituaries are in the *New York Times*, May 14, 1964; and the *Illustrated London News*, May 23, 1964.

BROADUS MITCHELL

BAZIOTES, WILLIAM (June 11, 1912–June 5, 1963), artist, was born in Pittsburgh, Pa., the son of Frank Angelus Baziotes and Stella Eliopoulos. In 1913 his family moved to Reading, Pa., where his father opened a restaurant. Fire destroyed the family business in 1919 and hard times followed. In 1921 Frank Baziotes opened a bakery. Baziotes attended high school in Reading. In 1931 he was employed by the Kase Glass Company, and inspired by the stained glass artists, he enrolled in a sketching class. In 1933 he moved to New York City and studied art at the National Academy of Design under artists such as Charles Curran, Ivan Olinsky, Gifford Beal, and Leon Kroll.

Fascinated by the history of art, Baziotes haunted the museums and libraries, making copies and reading. In his work he rejected the social realism of the day, which dwelt on the expression of political and economic theories. Instead, he turned to aristocratic values found in the classics. Baziotes' art of the 1930's represents a search for a personal style in which he drew upon a number of influences. His nudes and Minotaur series, for example, reflect his studied interest in Picasso's work. His handling of color is reminiscent of Cézanne. Baziotes was drawn to Amerind art and primitive African art as well. With Ezio Martinelli he developed a credo of line, consisting of a sculpturelike outlining of figures that owed much to Rodin, Ingres, and Picasso. His mastery of quick sketching techniques was noted by fellow artists of the time. Baziotes' fascination with the poetry of Baudelaire lent a sinister and dark element to his pictures. During the 1930's he refined his belief that paintings should reveal stored-up memories, often those of childhood. These subconscious forms he held to be universal, timeless, and abstract.

Baziotes first showed in 1936 at the Municipal Art Gallery in New York City. That same year he was hired by the Works Progress Administration (WPA) as a teacher at Queen's Museum. Two years later he was placed on the WPA Easel Painting Project. A turning point was his introduction to surrealists such as Gordon Onslow Ford and Roberto Matta Echaurren in the early 1940's. He began using an auto-matic approach. Later labeled abstract expressionism, this intuitive and reflexive style called for deep trancelike concentration during the painting of the picture. In the 1940's he did a series of mirrorlike pictures of subconscious forms, but there is also an effort to reveal the skeletal structure, and in this Matta's influence is clearly discernible.

On Apr. 12, 1941, Baziotes married Ethel Copstein. In December 1942 he exhibited "First Papers of Surrealism" with Robert Motherwell, Max Ernst, and David Hare. In 1943 he showed at Peggy Guggenheim's Art of This Century Gallery in New York City, and the following year he had his first one-man show there. Thereafter, he showed his work at the Sidney Janis Gallery, the Kootz Gallery, the Museum of Modern Art, the Whitney Museum, the Metropolitan Museum of Art, and elsewhere on a regular basis. The Art Institute of Chicago awarded Baziotes the Walter M. Campana Memorial Purchase Prize for his painting *Cyclops* in 1947 and the Frank Logan Medal for *The Sea* in 1961.

In 1948 Baziotes helped found, and taught at, the Subject of the Artist art school in New York City. Between 1949 and 1952 he taught painting at the Brooklyn Museum Art School and New York University. From 1950 to 1952 he also taught at the People's Art Center for the Museum of Modern Art. From 1952 until his death he was an associate professor of art at Hunter College.

By the 1950's Baziotes' work had become more refined and calmer, and was characterized by a watery quality. He read occult and mystical works and was preoccupied by death and evil. Prompted by a growing interest in the primeval, he and his wife spent long hours studying fossils in the American Museum of Natural History. His pictures from this period are noted for prehistoric themes. His *Dwarf* (1947), Baziotes said, depicted the eyes and teeth of prehistoric animals, while representing a childhood fear of the dark.

Thus, as a mature painter, Baziotes had settled upon a style that showed a variety of influences: surrealism, classicism, and primitivism were coupled with a regard for science, mysticism, and poetry. Mona Hadler has written of his work: "His later paintings are never nonobjective; their translucent backgrounds and elegant understated forms articulate with great economy of means a variety of poetic moods ranging from the macabre to tender sadness."

Although sensitive and shy, Baziotes could be entertaining and colorful. Friends compared him to Humphrey Bogart. (He loved gangsters and gangster movies.) He and his wife led a secluded life, rarely traveling, except to visit in Reading. He was perhaps best described by his wife, who called him "a darkling poet." Baziotes died in New York City.

[On Baziotes and his work, see Irving Sandler, "Baziotes: Modern Mythologist," *Art News*, Feb. 1965; Lawrence Alloway, *William Baziotes: A Memorial Exhibition*, Exhibition Catalog of the Solomon R. Guggenheim Museum (1965); Melinda Lorenz, "William Baziotes" (M.A. thesis, University of Maryland, 1972); Mona Hadler, "The Art of William Baziotes" (Ph.D. diss., Columbia University, 1977); "William Baziotes: A Retrospective Exhibition," Newport Harbor Art Museum (1978); and Milton W. Brown et al., *American Art* (1979). An obituary appeared in the *New York Times*, June 7, 1963.]

SPENCER J. MAXCY

BEACH, SYLVIA WOODBRIDGE (Mar. 14, 1887–Oct. 4 or 5, 1962), bookseller and publisher, was born Nancy Woodbridge Beach in Baltimore, Md., the daughter of Sylvester Woodbridge Beach, a Presbyterian minister, and Eleanor Orbison, a painter and musician whose father had been a medical missionary in India. Until the age of fifteen Beach lived in Bridgeton, N.J., where her father was the minister of the First Presbyterian Church. From 1902 to 1905 she was in Paris, where her father was assistant to the pastor of the American Church and in charge of Students' Atelier Reunions. It was at this time that Beach acquired her love for France and the French. She briefly attended a private school for girls in Lausanne, receiving her only formal education other than that acquired in the Bridgeton public schools. Her true and lifelong education was provided by reading, travel, and friendships with writers.

In 1905 Sylvester Beach became the pastor of the First Presbyterian Church in Princeton, N.J., and the family moved there. They visited France frequently, and as a young woman Beach traveled independently there and in other countries, including Italy and Spain. She spent World War I in Europe, moving to Paris in 1917. In her autobiography she wrote: "For some time, I had had a particular interest in contemporary French writing. Now I wanted to pursue my studies at the source."

In Paris, Beach met Adrienne Monnier, the writer, bookseller, and publisher, who was to become her closest friend as well as her literary adviser. Monnier, the owner of La Maison des Amis des Livres, a bookshop on the Left Bank, did not just sell and lend books. She also sponsored readings by writers who were among her friends and patrons, and published small editions of works by Paul Valéry, Paul Claudel, and others. Beach, who "had long wanted a bookshop" of her own, was inspired by Monnier's example. In 1919, after working for several months with the American Red Cross in Belgrade, she set about realizing her ambition. At first she considered running a French bookshop in New York but then decided to start an English-language bookshop in Paris, where costs were much lower. The shop, called Shakespeare and Company, opened on Nov. 19, 1919, on the rue Dupuytren, near the rue de l'Odéon. In 1921, Beach moved to larger premises at 12 rue de l'Odéon, across the street from La Maison des Amis des Livres.

The bookshop, which included a lending library, soon became the most important center in Paris for disseminating literature in the English language. As such, it was irreplaceable not only for the English-speaking expatriate community but also for interested French readers and writers. Among the regular patrons were André Gide and Valéry.

Although devoted to the classics, Beach above all promoted the new writing that was being published by small presses and magazines. Shakespeare and Company became an informal gathering place where writers could meet to exchange ideas and establish friendships under the aegis of its generous hostess. Among those who frequented the shop over the years were Ernest Hemingway, Archibald MacLeish, F. Scott Fitzgerald, Sherwood Anderson, Katherine Anne Porter, William Carlos Williams, Ezra Pound, T. S. Eliot, and James Joyce.

Beach took the greatest pride in her association with Joyce, whom she met in 1920 and whose *Ulysses* she published courageously and with limited financial means in 1922, despite charges of obscenity brought against the portions of the novel that had appeared in *Little Review*. She issued eleven printings of *Ulysses*. Following a court decision that it was not obscene, she relinquished her rights to the work, without remuneration by Joyce, so that it might be published to his greater advantage by Random House (1934). Her only other publishing ventures were Joyce's *Pomes Penyeach* (1927) and *Our Exagmination Round His Factification for Incamination of Work in Progress* by Samuel Beckett and others (1929), a collection of articles on *Finnegans Wake*.

With much difficulty Beach kept Shakespeare and Company open through the Great Depression and the early days of the German occupation of Paris, where she chose to live during the war rather than return to the United States. She never gave up her American citizenship. After American entry into World War II, her shop was closed by the Germans, and from August 1942 until March 1943, she was interned as an enemy alien. After the war, declining strength and lack of funds prevented her from reopening Shakespeare and Company, but she remained in Paris, surrounded by friends and much honored, until her death there by a heart attack. Her body was discovered on Oct. 6, 1962.

Beach, who never married, was a slightly built but vigorous woman, with "a lively, sharply sculptured face, brown eyes that were as alive as a young animal's and as gay as a young girl's," in the words of her friend Ernest Hemingway. For Adrienne Monnier she was "American by her nature—'young, friendly, fresh, heroic . . . electric' (I borrow the adjectives from [Walt] Whitman speaking of his fellow citizens). French through her passionate attachment to our country, through her desire to embrace its slightest nuances."

[Beach's papers are at Princeton University. Her James Joyce collection is at the State University of New York at Buffalo. Her autobiography, *Shakespeare and Company* (1959), is the only full-length book about her and her bookshop. The *Mercure de France*, Aug.–Sept. 1963, is a memorial issue containing numerous memoirs in French and English by her friends and her own account of her wartime internment. In the same year the issue was reprinted, with photographs added, as *Sylvia Beach (1887–1962)*. Articles include Jackson Mathews, "Conversation with Sylvia Beach and Company," *Kenyon Review*, Winter 1960; and Noel Fitch, "Sylvia Beach's Shakespeare and Company: Port of Call for American Expatriates," *Research Studies*, Dec. 1965. Appraisals of Beach and her work appear in Hugh Ford, *Published in Paris* (1975); and Richard McDougall, *The Very Rich Hours of Adrienne Monnier* (1976). An obituary appeared in the *New York Times*, Oct. 10, 1962.]

RICHARD MCDOUGALL

BEATTY, CLYDE RAYMOND (June 10, 1903–July 19, 1965), wild animal trainer, was born near Chillicothe, Ohio, the son of James Edward Beatty, a farmer, and of Margaret Everhart. After finishing Bainbridge Elementary School in 1917, he left home at age 15 to join Howe's Great London Circus, one of the dozens of circuses then flourishing under the shadow of the Ringling Brothers-Barnum and Bailey organization. Beatty worked briefly as an acrobat and cage boy for $3 a week. Within three years he completed apprenticeship as a trainer for the wild animal acts that had become popular around the turn of the century. His first solo act was with polar bears for the Gollmar Circus in 1922; two years later he had the largest bear act in America and worked with leopards and other large cats as well. By 1926, Beatty had moved to the Hagenbeck-Wallace show, where he remained until the Great Depression. He handled lions and tigers, a combination he used for the rest of his life. He steadily built a reputation for big-cat training and showmanship despite a declining demand for wild animal acts in the late 1920's. In 1930, Beatty married Harriett Evans, a circus aerialist. They had one daughter.

Perhaps because of the onset of the Great Depression, the public showed a rekindled interest in such "uncivilized" cultural phenomena as the film *King Kong* (1933), tough-talking actors such as James Cagney, and the animal collector "Bring 'Em Back Alive" Frank Buck. Beatty exploded into prominence as part of this trend. His style fit its temper perfectly. Short and stocky, with a gravelly voice, unpolished grammar, and rustic pronunciation, he appeared to have a "primitive, almost Neanderthal" relation to his animals. Carrying a whip, a chair, and a .38-caliber blank pistol, he presented what another trainer called "the purest version of the all-American 'fighting-act,' " an aggressive display abhorred by the gentler European school of training, but capable of producing a sensational spectacle.

The costs to Beatty in raked, clawed flesh were substantial. So were the rewards. As chief attraction for the Ringling Brothers' organization, which had absorbed Hagenbeck-Wallace and most other small shows, Beatty earned $250 per week. In 1936, one year after starting his own circus, he netted $40,000 plus additional fees from vaudeville appearances, two movies, and a book, *The Big Cage* (1933), written with Edward Anthony. His fans included celebrities as varied as Jack Dempsey, Ernest Hemingway, and Dale Carnegie. In 1937, Beatty appeared on the cover of *Time* magazine, which found social significance in his views on the virtues of wildness: "Our civilization places too high a valuation on the cute and the cunning. There is nothing more characterless than a spoiled lion or tiger cub."

Beatty's successful challenge to Ringling Brothers' monopoly prompted numerous similar ventures. Few of these had Beatty's drawing power, his contacts with zookeepers willing to sell animals cheaply in order to save on food bills, or a financial "angel" such as the Texas oilman Frank Walters, who invested heavily out of friendship and love of animals.

After difficulties in 1938 and during World War II, Beatty organized a lucrative tour of western Canada, one of the most profitable for any circus since the 1920's. He appeared in two movies and starred on a network radio program, and he issued two more books. After the death of his second wife in 1950, Beatty married Jane Abel in 1951; they had one son.

By the early 1950's, Beatty's circus employed 500 people. It moved from city to city in fifteen railroad cars, the only large railroad circus besides Ringling Brothers then in existence. But Beatty, along with the Ringlings, faced formidable problems: deteriorating rail service, a lack of good open-air urban locations, a paucity of animals born in the wild, the desire of crowds for air conditioning. The Beatty show, traveling by motor vehicle and appearing indoors, had to close in 1956 and again in 1963, by which time Beatty himself had relinquished personal control. His eighteen-minute act—performed twice a day forty weeks a year—could still generate an occasional good season. Even so, the end of the age of the American circus—and hence of Beatty's fame—was in sight.

Beatty reigned virtually unchallenged as the foremost American handler of big cats. Over a forty-year period he trained some 2,000 lions and tigers to pyramid, spin, roll, jump hurdles, move globes, dive through hoops, and "fight" with him and his wooden chair. He also trained, besides several bears, perhaps a hundred leopards, pumas, and jaguars; but he always preferred the mixture of lions and tigers, whose hostility to each other he used for his own protection. At one time he worked with forty of these big cats in the giant center cage. As a modern circus showman he was unrivaled, traveling a million miles and performing before 40 million people. Probably typical was the fan who declared, "After ye seen Beatty the rest of them stinks." Hemingway once said that Beatty used his chair in the cage as a matador used his cape and that he was "smooth, graceful, forceful—like a ballet dancer."

Despite his "tough-guy" Great Depression image, Beatty never hunted. He disliked the idea of hurting animals or humiliating them. He studied them closely and well, augmenting his understanding by reading Charles Darwin and T. H. Huxley. A leading zoo curator called him an "intuitive naturalist." Beatty died in Ventura, Calif.

[Beatty's books include *Jungle Performers* (1941), written with Earl Wilson, and *Facing the Big Cats* (1965), written with Edward Anthony. For details on his career, see "Cat Man," *Time*, Mar. 29, 1937; Collie Small, "Lions 'n' Tigers 'n' Clyde Beatty," *Collier's*, Apr. 7, 1951; and Charles P. Fox and Tom Parkinson, *The Circus in America* (1969). An obituary is in the *New York Times*, July 20, 1965.]

RONALD STORY

BEATTY, WILLARD WALCOTT (Sept. 17, 1891–Sept. 29, 1961), educator, was born in Berkeley, Calif., the son of William Adam Beatty and Mabel Walcott. After being awarded a B.S. degree by the School of Mechanical Arts of the University of California in 1913, he was hired as a teacher of drawing at Oakland Technical High School. On Dec. 13, 1913, he married Elise Hersey Biedenbach; they had two children.

Beatty's collaboration with two progressive educators, Frederic Burk and Carleton Washburne, shaped his views on education. From 1915 to 1920, while serving as head of the arithmetic, civics, and history departments and as director of teacher training at San Francisco State Normal School, he worked closely with Burk, who had developed the concept of "motivated individual instruction." After two years at the Presidio Open Air School in San Francisco, Beatty was hired as the principal of Skokie Junior High School and assistant superintendent of schools at Winnetka, Ill., a wealthy Chicago suburb, under the leadership of Washburne.

Both Beatty and Washburne were educational disciples of Burk, and further developed their mentor's child-centered approach in an experiment that became nationally acclaimed as the "Winnetka technique." Each child was encouraged to advance at his or her own pace and each teacher was responsible for helping and supervising on an individual basis.

Because of the success of the Winnetka technique, Beatty was appointed superintendent of the school system of Bronxville, N.Y., a wealthy suburb of New York City, in 1926. Besides his continued emphasis on individualized instruction, he developed units to foster racial tolerance; wrote a curriculum for the seventh and eighth grades that related mathematics to real, not abstract, situations in the pupils' own lives; introduced sex education as early as the seventh grade; stressed civics education to promote a better understanding of the American political system; and redesigned the physical environment of the classroom to promote learning.

This "Bronxville experiment" aroused considerable attention, and the General Education

Board in 1931 appointed Beatty to undertake a survey of all progressive schools. His appointment, his writings on educational reform, and his conducting of summer institutes made Beatty a political force in the Progressive Educational Association. As president of the organization from 1933 to 1937, he faced the crisis in education caused by the Great Depression. It was also a time when the association was strongly divided into radical and "child-centered" factions.

In January 1936, Beatty left Bronxville to become director of education in the Bureau of Indian Affairs. In sharp contrast with his earlier experiences, he had to administer a much-maligned agency responsible for the educational needs of more than 80,000 poor Indian children. During his most innovative years as director, from 1936 to the outbreak of World War II, he established more day schools, in place of boarding schools, on reservations; began in-service summer teaching programs to inculcate Bureau of Indian Affairs teachers with a common progressive educational approach; held curriculum planning conferences on reservations for teachers and administrators; decentralized educational administration by setting up regional staffs in order to attempt to satisfy individualized Indian and tribal needs; and launched *Indian Education*, a newsletter.

Working closely with anthropologists, educators, and linguists, Beatty encouraged the development of a new curriculum, some of it bilingual, for Indian schools. Special pamphlets on tribal cultures, the Indian Life series, were written by Bureau of Indian Affairs personnel, translated and illustrated by Indians, and employed to meet the special needs of students. Beatty's attempt at bilingualism proved ahead of its time, largely because there were too few teachers capable of Indian-language instruction.

World War II and its aftermath virtually wiped out Beatty's prewar innovations. In the cost-conscious era bilingual experiments ended; boarding schools were resurrected; in-service training disappeared; and cultural relativism and cross-cultural educational ideas were abandoned, replaced by a philosophy of assimilating Indians into the mainstream of white culture. Beatty was also faced with overcrowded schools, the deterioration of school facilities, the loss of most of his innovative personnel, and an educational crisis situation among the Navajo, a tribe that had only one-third of its children in school in 1945.

Despite the significant accomplishments of his Navajo Special Education Program, begun in 1946, which attempted to provide the equivalent of twelve years of education in five, Beatty's contribution to Indian educational improvement was largely over by the end of the war. Faced with new political and economic realities, he increasingly emphasized that Indian schools should be vehicles for cultural change and integration into off-reservation life.

In 1951, after the powers of the director were further curtailed in a reorganization of the Bureau of Indian Affairs, Beatty resigned to become the deputy director of education of the United Nations Educational, Scientific and Cultural Organization, a post he held until 1953. In the last years of his life, he served as executive vice-president of Save the Children Federation and, in 1959, was appointed a member of the Bureau of Indian Affairs' Indian Arts and Crafts Board. He died in Washington, D.C.

Although Beatty can be criticized for not including Indians in his decision making and for abandoning his progressive ideals in the last years of his directorship of the Office of Indian Education, he represented an important voice of the progressive education movement and was a significant transition figure in the evolution of a contemporary, more sensitive approach to the educational needs of American Indians.

[Beatty's official correspondence, 1936–1951, is in Record Group 75, National Archives. His writings include "Creative Living in the Bronxville Schools," *Progressive Education*, Sept.–Nov. 1929; "Progressive Education in the Public Schools," *Progressive Education*, Nov. 1932; "Planning Indian Education in Terms of Pupil and Community Needs," *Indians at Work*, Sept. 1, 1936; *Education for Action* (1944); *Education for Cultural Change* (1953); and "Twenty Years of Indian Education," in David A. Baerreis, ed., *The Indian in Modern America* (1956). Also see Lawrence A. Cremin, *The Transformation of the School* (1961); C. A. Bowers, *The Progressive Educator and the Depression* (1969); George A. Boyce, *When Navajos Had Too Many Sheep* (1974); and Margaret Szasz, *Education and the American Indian* (1974).]

LAURENCE M. HAUPTMAN

BEAVERS, LOUISE (Mar. 8, 1902–Oct. 26, 1962), film actress who was typecast as a maid or "Mammy" in dozens of Hollywood films, was born in Cincinnati, Ohio, the daughter of William Beavers. She moved with her parents to Pasadena, Calif., in 1913 and graduated from Pasadena High School in 1918. Beavers considered a career in nursing because she "liked the uniform" but quickly changed her mind. Between 1920 and 1926 she worked as a dressing room attendant for a photographer and then as the personal maid to actress Leatrice Joy. Beavers enjoyed singing and joined a minstrel show with an amateur cast of sixteen women in Los Angeles. She had been with the group for about a year when she was spotted by movie scouts and selected to play a role in *Uncle Tom's Cabin* (1927). This began her thirty-year film career, in which she alternated roles as a maid or cook with actual jobs as maid (during the early years) to such stars as Mae West and Jean Harlow.

Beavers worked hard to maintain the contemporary Hollywood image that black domestics were all fat and happy. She was stocky but by no means fat; her high-calorie diet was often supplemented by heavy padding and several wide petticoats. She also took voice lessons to transform her typical Californian speech pattern to a more acceptable "Southern" drawl.

Beavers had acted in over twenty-five films, silents and talkies, among them *Coquette* (1929), *Up for Murder* (1931), *Ladies of the Big House* (1932), *What Price Innocence?* (1933), *Bombshell* (1933), *She Done Him Wrong* (1933), and *Pick Up* (1933), before she won the biggest role in her career, Aunt Delilah in *Imitation of Life* (1934) with Claudette Colbert. In her role as Colbert's housekeeper, she appeared to create delicious flapjacks that Colbert was able to promote into a million-dollar business. Since Beavers actually could not cook, experts worked with her for days helping her create the illusion of making flapjacks. Her warm, sympathetic characterization of the cook troubled by her confused daughter was considered worthy of an Oscar nomination. Beavers was the first black to achieve stardom in Hollywood.

Although she was then considered for a role in *Gone with the Wind* and scheduled to star as Aunt Jemima in a film by Sol Lesser (1936), the high salary Beavers could now demand would have priced her out of the only roles Hollywood would offer her, the stereotyped domestic. She acted in over forty more films as Ophelia, Ruby, or Mammy Lou. Ramon Romero wrote: "Whenever they need a big round colored gal in Hollywood to play a maid, they always send for Louise." Even in her last film, *The Facts of Life* (1961), she was cast as a maid, placed last in the billing and not even mentioned in the *New York Times* review. Hollywood's failure to make full use of her talents was a tragic waste.

In *Rainbow on the River* (1936) Beavers did have an important featured role as Toinette, an ex-slave, a portrayal made "totally believable by the strength of her performance," wrote Eileen Landay. In another departure from the usual stereotype, she gave a fine performance as

the baseball star's mother in *The Jackie Robinson Story* (1950). Beavers was also a pioneer in the all-black-cast films produced by Million Dollar Productions, *Life Goes On* (1938) and *Reform School* (1939). In the former film she played the distraught mother of two sons on opposite sides of the law, and in the latter she played a probation officer determined to alter the terrible conditions at a badly administered institution.

Beavers appeared in such popular films as *Holiday Inn* (1942), *DuBarry Was a Lady* (1943), *Lover Come Back* (1946), *Mr. Blandings Builds His Dream House* (1948), *Good Sam* (1948), *My Blue Heaven* (1950), *Never Wave at a WAC* (1953), *The Goddess* (1958), and *All the Fine Young Cannibals* (1960). She also made personal appearances. In February 1935 she sang at the Roxy Theater in New York City, and at the State in New York in 1944, she gave a six-minute performance, singing "in a pleasing contralto" and presenting a scene from the movie *Belle Star* (1941), which *Variety* reviewed as a show-stopper. She toured with Mae West in 1954.

In 1946 Beavers joined two other prominent black entertainers, Hattie McDaniel and Ethel Waters (along with thirty other black property owners), in an effort to win the right to live in an "exclusive" district, West Adams. When the case was appealed in the California Supreme Court, their attorneys cited the United Nations Charter as their protection from racial discrimination.

During the 1950's Beavers launched her television career. In 1952 she followed Waters and McDaniel as "Beulah," a warm-hearted maid who guided her bumbling employers through various domestic crises. The show had a good rating but ended the next year when Beavers declined to continue in the role. She also appeared in "The Hostess with the Mostest" on "Playhouse 90" (1957) and in the "Swamp Fox" segment of "Walt Disney Presents" (1959).

Although Beavers once told an interviewer she would never marry ("another mouth to feed") and was content to live with her mother, she married LeRoy Moore. They had no children. She died in Los Angeles.

[For further information, see clippings in the Academy of Motion Picture Arts and Sciences National Film Information Service Library, Los Angeles; New York Public Library Theater Collection, Lincoln Center; Peter Noble, *The Negro in Films* (1948); Eileen Landay, *Black Film Stars* (1973); Donald Bogle, *Toms, Coons, Mulattoes, Mammies, and Bucks: An Interpretive History of Blacks in American Films* (1973); Thomas Cripps, *Slow Fade to Black: The Negro in American Film, 1900–1942* (1977); Henry T. Sampson, *Blacks in Black and White* (1977); and *The Complete Directory to Prime Time Network TV Shows 1946–Present*, edited by Tim Brooks and Earle Marsh (1979). Obituaries appeared in the *New York Times, New York Herald-Tribune, New York World Telegram and Sun*, Oct. 27; *Variety*, Oct. 31 and *Time*, Nov. 2, all in 1962.]

ELIZABETH R. NELSON

BEEBE, (CHARLES) WILLIAM (July 29, 1877–June 4, 1962), naturalist and oceanographer, was born in Brooklyn, N.Y., the son of Charles Beebe and Henrietta Marie Younglove. The elder Beebe was employed in his father's paper business in New York City. In the mid-1880's the family moved to East Orange, N.J. Beebe's childhood was a happy one. Curious about most aspects of natural history, he concentrated on birds from an early age, his first publication being a letter to the editor of *Harper's Young People* early in 1895.

Henrietta Beebe was a determined and ambitious woman who was anxious that her son should succeed in the profession of his choice. Once his predilection for natural history became apparent, many prominent naturalists in New York City encountered in her a forceful personality, for she made certain that her son became acquainted with the leaders in the field.

Following Beebe's graduation from East Orange High School (1896), where he completed a number of extra science courses, Beebe entered Columbia University as a special student in zoology. Although he later claimed that he received a B.S. from Columbia, he was never a degree candidate. The professor who most influenced him was Henry Fairfield Osborn.

In 1899, when the New York Zoological Society, of which Osborn was vice-president, was seeking an assistant curator of birds for its zoological park, Beebe was appointed at Osborn's suggestion. He became curator of birds three years later. On Aug. 2, 1902, he married Mary Blair; they had no children and were divorced in 1913.

Beebe was not happy being curator, which was a relatively sedentary assignment dealing mainly with caged birds. He was strongly oriented toward field research, and this he began with trips in the eastern United States and Canada in 1900. He was backed by Osborn, but William Temple Hornaday, the zoo director, objected to Beebe's absence for all or part of every year. An able surrogate was found, though, and Beebe was freed to do the work for which

he was best suited. His first book, *Two Bird Lovers in Mexico*, written with his wife, appeared in 1905, and his first scientific volume, *The Bird, Its Form and Function*, in 1906. Twenty-two other volumes, some scientific and some for a popular audience, appeared between 1906 and 1955. Many were later translated into foreign languages.

In 1909, Beebe was commissioned to write a monograph on the pheasants of the world by a New Jersey utilities magnate, Anthony R. Kuser. Several years were consumed in field research, principally in Southeast Asia. World War I delayed publication, but *A Monograph of the Pheasants* was issued in four volumes between 1918 and 1922. One authority has termed this "perhaps the greatest ornithological monograph of the present century."

In 1916, following expeditions to Trinidad, Venezuela, Brazil, and British Guiana, Beebe established the New York Zoological Society's department of tropical research at Bartica, British Guiana. He became director of this operation and honorary curator of birds at the New York City Zoological Park. The tropical research program was later transferred to Kartabo, where it continued operations off and on until 1926.

Beebe's jungle work was briefly interrupted by enlistment in the French Aviation Service in 1917–1918. A wrist injury sustained in a fall kept him on the ground for some months, during which he went back to British Guiana to capture native mammals for the New York Zoological Park. Several years later he took time from his Guianan efforts to visit the Galapagos Islands. On these trips, financed by Harrison Williams and others, Beebe used the steam yachts *Noma* in 1923 and *Arcturus* in 1925, with the latter also exploring the Sargasso Sea. Although he had studied ocean life prior to 1925, the *Arcturus* trip marked the first time that Beebe had undertaken helmet diving to study marine species at first hand. In 1927, aboard the schooner *Lieutenant*, chartered by the New York Zoological Society, he studied fish and coral life in Haitian waters. On Sept. 22, 1927, he married Elswyth Thane Ricker, a writer who was almost a quarter-century his junior. They had no children.

Beginning in 1928, Beebe set up the tropical research program on the Bermudan island of Nonsuch. There, in 1930, he made the first of more than thirty descents in a spherical diving device, the bathysphere, with Otis Barton, who had developed it and financed its construction. Four years later they achieved their record dive of 3,028 feet, a depth that was not exceeded until 1949. These descents permitted Beebe to make detailed observations of previously unrecorded species of deep-sea life. He also studied color changes in the water as surface light became diffused in the course of his descents.

Most of Beebe's diving thereafter was confined to shallower depths. He carried on other oceanographic research, off Baja California in 1936 and the Pacific coast of Central America in 1937 and 1938, aboard Templeton Crocker's yacht *Zaca*.

The tropical research unit of the New York Zoological Society was reestablished in Venezuela in 1942, the work being done at several locations until 1948. In 1949, Beebe purchased land at Simla, in the Arima Valley of Trinidad, and established a research station there that he later presented to the Zoological Society. He continued working there for part of every year until his death, despite his official retirement as director of tropical research in 1952.

Beebe expected his subordinates to adhere to his high standards, but balanced this with a good sense of humor. He wrote some 800 articles and many books on both technical and popular subjects, but despite his prodigious efforts he was not considered a major scientific figure by most professional biologists. Doubtless many were reluctant to accord serious standing to a successful popularizer.

Beebe named eighty-seven species of fish and one bird form, but his systematic work has been largely superseded. Perhaps his youthful disinclination for the rigors of formal training and the fact that his busy later career precluded any comprehensive study of the fields in which he was active were contributing factors.

Beebe's major contributions lay in the breadth and detail of his field observations, his emphasis upon the interrelationships of living forms, his abiding concern with conservation, and the felicity with which he expressed himself in his writings. He did much to close the gap between the world of science and the general public, one oceanographer terming him "the Captain Cousteau of my generation." Theodore Roosevelt wrote of Beebe's book *Jungle Peace* (1919): ". . . it will stand on the shelves of cultivated people, of people whose taste in reading is both wide and good, as long as men and women appreciate charm of form in the writing of men. . . ." Beebe died at Simla, Trinidad.

[Some of Beebe's letters are in the Alpheus Hyatt Correspondence at the Princeton University Library. Among his many books are *Tropical Wildlife in British Guiana,* of which only vol. I (1917), written with

C. I. Hartley and P. G. Howes, was published; *Edge of the Jungle* (1921); *Beneath Tropic Seas* (1928); *Nonsuch: Land of Water* (1932); *Field Book of the Shore Fishes of Bermuda* (1933); *Half Mile Down* (1934); *Zaca Adventure* (1938); *High Jungle* (1949); and *Unseen Life of New York* (1953). Also see Lee S. Crandall, in *Auk,* Jan. 1964; William Bridges, *Gathering of Animals* (1974); Robert Henry Welker, *Natural Man: The Life of William Beebe* (1975); and Tim M. Berra, *William Beebe: An Annotated Bibliography* (1977). An obituary is in the *New York Times,* June 6, 1962.]

KEIR B. STERLING

BELL, JAMES FORD (Aug. 16, 1879–May 7, 1961), industrialist and first president of General Mills, was born in Philadelphia, Pa., the son of James Stroud Bell, an executive in the milling industry, and Sallie Montgomery Ford. The family had been active in the flour-milling business in southeastern Pennsylvania since the eighteenth century. The Bells moved to Minneapolis, where James Ford attended the public schools. He later attended the Lawrenceville School and the University of Minnesota. He was graduated with a B.S. in chemistry in 1901. On Dec. 10, 1902, he married Louise Heffelfinger of Minneapolis; they had four children.

Bell went to work for the Washburn Crosby Company, a merchant-milling firm in Minneapolis headed by his father, and gained familiarity with all aspects of milling. He became a director of the company in 1909, and a vice-president upon the death of his father in 1915. Bell directed the Milling Division of the United States Food Administration during World War I. He accompanied Herbert Hoover on the European Food Mission following the Armistice, and at Hoover's instigation became treasurer and general manager of the Sugar Equalization Board during 1918–1919.

In 1925 Bell was elected president of Washburn Crosby. He turned his attention to reorganizing the milling industry. After winning over skeptics on his own board, Bell persuaded the Red Star Milling Company of Wichita, the Kell group of mills in Texas and Oklahoma, and the Sperry Flour Company of California to merge with Washburn Crosby. The outcome of his efforts was the formation of General Mills Company in 1928. In 1929 the Larrowe Milling Company of Michigan, a major formula-feed business, and other smaller firms joined General Mills. By the late 1930's the company was the largest flour-milling enterprise in the world, but it remained decentralized until Bell introduced consolidation and tighter central control in 1937.

The formation of General Mills was part of a general pattern of consolidation in American industry in the late 1920's. But specific developments in the flour-milling business also encouraged consolidation. Milling was highly competitive, with low profit margins on each barrel of flour sold. Because of the steady decline in per capita flour consumption, many mills encountered financial difficulties in the 1920's. With 75 percent of its flour mills centered in the upper Midwest, in areas that made up only a quarter of the national market, Washburn Crosby was particularly vulnerable. Furthermore, bakers shifted their preference from spring wheat, grown in the upper Midwest, to winter wheat, grown farther south.

Under Bell's leadership, first as president and after 1934 as chairman of the board, General Mills met these problems. Between 1928 and 1947 it never failed to make a profit or pay dividends on common stock, of which Bell was the largest holder. In 1947, the last year of Bell's administration, General Mills netted a record $9.2 million on $371 million in sales. In this period, the company grew to be twice as large as its nearest competitor, Pillsbury Flour Mills.

Some of this success came from Bell's enlargement of his regional firm, Washburn Crosby, into a national one, General Mills. Transport costs were so high that a large market could be reached only by a firm with mills in all parts of the country. Furthermore, only a nationwide company could take advantage of the advertising possibilities offered by the development of radio and television networks. Advertising was crucial to success in the business because there was little difference in quality between one company's flour and another's.

Bell encouraged an aggressive advertising campaign for General Mills. The imaginary Betty Crocker encouraged the American homemaker to use General Mills products. Sports enthusiasts heard the General Mills breakfast cereal Wheaties promoted as "The Breakfast of Champions" during the first televised professional baseball game, in 1939.

Bell also pushed for diversification. New packaged foods, most notably Bisquick, were major successes. In the late 1930's and early 1940's, non-flour-related items, including vitamins, chemical products, and home appliances, were produced. This diversification was aided by the emphasis Bell placed on research.

Bell was a Republican. In the early years of the New Deal, General Mills opposed the Agricultural Adjustment Administration, and Bell was among the Republican businessmen who

resigned from the Commerce Department's Business Advisory Council in July 1935. Government policies made it impossible for management to guarantee profitable operations, he claimed. Later in the 1930's, however, Bell began to accept government direction of basic industrial activity and emphasized that private industry should concentrate on merchandising and public-relations activities.

Even after his retirement, Bell remained head of the company's committee on financial and technological progress. He was also active in civic affairs in Minneapolis. Among his pastimes was the collection of books on the early history of commerce and exploration, which formed the basis of the James Ford Bell Library at the University of Minnesota. He died in Minneapolis.

[Bell's papers, 1917–1928, are located at the Hoover Institution, Stanford University. Considerable correspondence is in the University of Minnesota Library and the Minnesota Historical Society. Bell wrote "Public Attitude Toward Agriculture," *Saturday Evening Post,* Dec. 5, 1931; and "Can We Finance the Future?," *Atlantic Monthly,* July 1943. Excerpts from a Bell address on modern corporate management are in the *New York Times,* June 19, 1938. Bell is the central figure in James Gray, *Business Without Boundary* (1954). The best sources for biographical information are Val Björnson, *The History of Minnesota,* III (1969); and obituaries in the *New York Times* and the *Minneapolis Tribune,* both May 8, 1961.]

ROBERT GOUGH

BEMELMANS, LUDWIG (Apr. 27, 1898–Oct. 1, 1962), writer and artist, was born in Meran, in the Austrian Tyrol (now Merano, Italy), the son of Lambert Bemelmans, a Belgian painter and member of a family that had invested early in the European Ritz hotel chain, and Frances Fischer, the daughter of a prosperous Bavarian brewer. His earliest memories were of living with his father and a pantheistic French governess who taught him that church attendance was unnecessary because God was everywhere. In 1904 his father left with the governess, and his mother divorced him and took Ludwig to her family in Regensburg, Germany.

Bemelmans's antagonism to authoritarians and his sympathy for rebels derived from his experiences in the Regensburg schools. After successfully negotiating the four lower grades, he attended the Königliche Realschule (1908–1911), where he was forced to repeat a year and finally failed altogether. Another unsuccessful year at a private academy in Rothenburg and six months with a tutor, who finally gave up on him, constituted the rest of his formal education.

In 1912 he was apprenticed to an uncle who owned a number of hotels in the Tyrol. Although he later wrote of his many failures and dismissals, he acquired useful experience there. Unfortunately, his career was interrupted in late 1914 when he shot and almost killed a vicious headwaiter who had struck him with a heavy whip. His family was given a choice: he could be sent to a kind of reform school on a German merchant marine training ship, or he could go to America.

On Christmas Eve in 1914 Bemelmans arrived at Ellis Island armed only with letters of introduction to his uncle's hotel friends. Eventually he found a place as a waiter's "runner" at the Ritz-Carlton. At this time the great New York hotels were European islands, full of interesting characters who provided subjects for the sketches that Bemelmans included in *Life Class* (1938) and *Hotel Splendide* (1941).

In June 1917 Bemelmans enlisted in the United States Army and for seventeen months kept a diary, which was later published as *My War with the United States* (1937). He spent much of the time working in the wards of a hospital for the criminally insane, most of them shell-shock victims. His descriptions of primitive psychiatric methods, of guards cracking under the strain, and of his own doubts about his sanity clearly explain why he wrote years later that his life was deeply colored by this experience. At that time he learned to discipline his mind and emotions and never forget that "the key to happiness" is "to forget the 'I.'"

In June 1918 Bemelmans became an American citizen. At the end of the war he was a graduate of Officers' Training School, with a second lieutenant's commission. In 1919 he returned to the Ritz-Carlton, where he worked off and on until 1932. In 1933 he headed a group that opened Hapsburg House in New York City, which was successful in its cuisine and art—the walls were decorated with Bemelmans's drawings and watercolors. Unfortunately, the restaurant was a financial failure and was sold in 1935. But by that time Bemelmans had launched his literary career. In 1934 he published *Hansi*, a juvenile book that, like most of his forty volumes, includes drawings that seem to be part of the story rather than mere "illustrations." Bemelmans married Madeline Freund on Nov. 23, 1935; they had one daughter.

In the years before World War II he began traveling, writing, and illustrating, a pattern he followed for the rest of his life. In 1937 and again in 1940 he traveled extensively in Ecuador, gathering the material for *The Donkey Inside* (1941), a remarkable combination of ebullient good humor and vignettes that are stunning in their horror and violence. The work of this period reflects his loathing of Nazism, no doubt affected by his overnight imprisonment by the gestapo in Munich in 1935 for a satiric speech about Hitler that he had made in an inn in Berchtesgaden. But his horrifying description in *The Best of Times* (1948) of a postwar visit to Dachau also includes an affirmation of his faith in "the small bourgeoisie" and in civilization's power to survive.

In 1947 he published *Dirty Eddie*, a funny by-product of his experience in Hollywood, where he had coauthored *Yolanda and the Thief* (1945) and met Lady Elsie Mendl, to whose vitality, courage, and gospel of beauty he paid homage in *To the One I Love Best* (1955).

Bemelmans considered himself an artist to whom writing was only an economic necessity. His art, too, was always for a "purpose" until 1953, when he began to paint seriously. The characteristic works reproduced in *My Life in Art* (1958) are reminiscent of Chagall in mood and of the fauvists in method. In these years he also produced several novels that are among his best work—particularly *Are You Hungry, Are You Cold* (1960)—and a number of well-received children's books.

Just three days before his death in New York City, Bemelmans began writing the story of his childhood. The juxtaposition of these events is suggestive. Like many comic writers he felt deeply the tragedy of human existence. But he also saw the world as a place of miracles and great rewards and wrote, "I just can't seem to hate the people I write about." If only a minor novelist, he was also a painter of great verve and excitement, a brilliant creator of children's books, and one of the most distinguished figures in the long line of American humorists.

[Bemelmans's papers are in the possession of Madeline Freund Bemelmans; they have been promised to the Library of Congress. His own writings, although they must be used with caution, are the primary published source of information about his life.

His other works include the novels *Now I Lay Me Down to Sleep* (1943), *The Blue Danube* (1945), *The Eye of God* (1949), *The Woman of My Life* (1957), and *The Street Where the Heart Lies* (1963); the volumes of sketches and travel books *Small Beer* (1939), *I Love You, I Love You, I Love You* (1942), *How to Travel Incognito* (1952), *Father, Dear Father* (1953), and *On Board Noah's Ark* (1962); and the juveniles *Madeline* (1939), *Madeline's Rescue* (1953), *The High World* (1954), *Madeline and the Bad Hat* (1956), *Madeline and the Gypsies* (1959), and *Madeline in London* (1961). Collected writings include *Hotel Bemelmans* (1946), *The World of Bemelmans* (1955), and a posthumous volume, edited by Donald and Eleanor Friede, *La Bonne Table* (1964). See also Robert van Gelder, "An Interview with Ludwig Bemelmans," *New York Times Book Review,* Jan. 26, 1941; and the obituary, *New York Times,* Oct. 2, 1962.]

ROBERT L. BERNER

BENDER, GEORGE HARRISON (Sept. 29, 1896–June 17 or 18, 1961), U.S. congressman and senator, was born in Cleveland, Ohio, the son of Joseph Bender, an employee of the General Electric Company, and of Anna Sir. He was educated in the Cleveland public schools, graduating in 1914 from West Commerce High School.

Possessed of an outgoing personality, Bender directed his energies to politics, even as a teenager. When he was fifteen, he met former President Theodore Roosevelt and later, backed by the reputed 10,000 signatures he had collected, he urged Roosevelt to run in 1912. Roosevelt informed Bender of his intention to do so in a letter sent shortly before the public announcement of his candidacy. Bender was still too young to vote when he served as a delegate to the 1916 Progressive Party Convention, while continuing campaign activities on behalf of Republican candidates in Cleveland. Characteristic of his efforts was his flair for independence within a framework of rigid party regularity. Bender defended his maverick actions as a fulfillment of his mother's advice never to cease being a disturbing element within the community.

Bender's various business connections as advertising manager of a department store, manager of the Cleveland Stadium, and owner of the Bender Insurance Company financed a political career and the life-style he felt went with it. Yet politics remained foremost: "I have always worked for a living in order to keep myself in politics." In 1920, Bender became the youngest person to be elected to the Ohio senate up to that time. On June 2, 1920, he married Edna Eckhardt; they had two daughters.

In the Ohio senate, Bender was a leader in several areas, among them the unsuccessful attempt to establish teacher tenure. One dramatic event changed him from an ardent "dry" to a vocal critic of Prohibition. Enforcement authorities, acting on an anonymous tip, launched a surprise raid on his home. They found no

alcohol, and Bender won a lawsuit over the incident.

Beginning in 1930, Bender sought election to the United States House of Representatives. He finally succeeded in 1938 and, with the exception of a defeat in 1948, he retained his seat until 1954. From 1936 until 1954, he was also chairman of the Cuyahoga County Republican Central Committee, a post he held in spite of opposition from Republican authorities in the city of Cleveland and the state. In 1934, Bender began publishing two newspapers for party workers, the *Ohio Republican* and the *National Republican.* He worked closely in Ohio Republican circles with U.S. Senator Robert A. Taft.

In Congress, Bender vigorously criticized the foreign and domestic policies of President Franklin D. Roosevelt, although he supported some New Deal measures of a humanitarian nature, such as the Works Progress Administration (WPA), but only as a temporary expedient. He brought together his indictment of the Roosevelt administration in *The Challenge of 1940* (1940), a book that served as an extended brief for Wendell Willkie's presidential campaign.

Bender's career after World War II is chiefly remembered for his having championed measures to abolish poll taxes and having denounced the Truman Doctrine and the Marshall Plan. Although he favored humanitarian assistance to Greece and Turkey, he insisted that it be channeled through the United Nations. As for the Marshall Plan, he preferred the use of private relief agencies. Direct government aid to Greece and Turkey, Bender told Congress in 1947, showed that President Truman was accommodating the "needs of a collapsing British Empire" that sought to transfer its liabilities to the United States while keeping its assets.

Bender's love for all aspects of politics resulted in his being placed in charge of publicity and promotion for the Taft forces at the Republican conventions of 1948 and 1952. In this capacity he led demonstrations, conducted singing, provided bands, and personally undertook the ringing of a cowbell. The bell ringing and the other devices he employed to focus attention caused Bender to be ridiculed, especially within the anti-Taft segment of the Republican party, as the "Clown Prince," an aspersion that unjustly cast him as a comic rather than serious figure in public affairs.

After Dwight D. Eisenhower won the 1952 presidential nomination, Bender transferred his loyalty to him. Following the death of Senator Taft in 1953, Bender gave up his safe

House seat to run for Taft's unexpired Senate term, this time with the ardent endorsement of Eisenhower Republicans. He won that race by a narrow margin and entered the Senate to give two years of solid support to the Eisenhower program. The term "isolationist," hurled at Bender earlier in his career, whether appropriately or not, now unquestionably applied no longer. He even reversed his views on America's relationship to Britain, seeing it as salutary that the United States had assumed the obligations once borne by the British.

In 1956, when Bender sought reelection against Governor Frank J. Lausche, he did so, paradoxically, as the comparatively more liberal candidate. He was defeated. His last government post was as special assistant to the secretary of the interior (June 1957 to May 1958). While in office he lobbied for Alaskan statehood, which was achieved in 1959.

In August 1958, Bender was hired by Teamsters Union president James R. Hoffa to investigate corruption in the union. His acceptance, coupled with charges that he had benefited from Teamsters contributions in the past, caused a cloud of doubt to descend over Bender. He held the Teamsters post for a year and a half. Although he vigorously denied any impropriety, and although none has ever been established, Bender was defeated in his effort to be a delegate to the 1960 Republican Convention and again in 1961, when he sought the post of committeeman for Precinct E in Chagrin Falls, a suburb of Cleveland. He was found dead of a heart attack at his home there.

[Bender's papers are at the Western Reserve Historical Society in Cleveland. His articles and speeches include "The Poll Tax Disgrace," *Christian Century,* July 23, 1947; "Should the Voice of America Project Be Established by Congress?" *Congressional Digest,* Feb. 1948; "A Faith for Fifty-One," *Vital Speeches,* July 1, 1951. Also see Paul F. Healy, "Noisiest Man on Capitol Hill," *Saturday Evening Post,* Aug. 7, 1954; "The Man with the Bell," *Newsweek,* Sept. 13, 1954; Robert F. Kennedy, *The Enemy Within* (1960); and Ronald Radosh, *Prophets on the Right* (1975). An obituary is in the *New York Times,* June 19, 1961.]

JOSEPH MAY

BENNETT, CONSTANCE CAMPBELL (Oct. 22, 1904–July 25, 1965), actress, was born in New York City, the daughter of Richard Bennett and Mabel Adrienne Morrison, both actors. The theatrical tradition of the Bennett family dated back several generations and was carried on not only by Constance but also by her two sisters, Barbara and Joan. Bennett attended schools in New York City and graduated from Miss Merrill's School in Mamaroneck, N.Y. She also attended finishing schools in Switzerland and Paris.

Bennett's earliest theatrical experiences were the result of her family associations. She appeared with her parents in the film *Valley of Decision* (1916) and with her mother in a production of *Everyman* (1918). Although she enjoyed theatrical life, Bennett did not have an overwhelming ambition to become an actress. She equally enjoyed being a debutante, and her private life throughout the 1920's exemplified the flapper image she would project on screen. On June 6, 1921, Bennett eloped with Chester Hirst Moorehead, a University of Virginia law student. Their parents quickly separated the couple, and the marriage was annulled in 1923.

In the early 1920's Bennett had several small parts in feature films made in New York City. In 1924 she was brought to Hollywood for a screen test by Samuel Goldwyn, who had met her at an Actors' Equity Ball. She was assigned a supporting role in *Cytherea* (1924), a major production that led to her first critical recognition. She then returned to New York to act in a Pathé serial titled *Into the Net* (1924).

Bennett made several more films in Hollywood before retiring to marry Philip Morgan Plant, son of a wealthy industrialist, on Nov. 23, 1925. They had one son. The family spent the next four years in Europe, living the life of wealthy expatriates. In 1929 Bennett returned to the United States and was divorced that December.

Bennett signed a contract with Pathé and made her first sound film, *This Thing Called Love,* in 1929. This well-received film was followed by five others released in 1930. All were successful at the box office. *Common Clay,* made for Fox, established Bennett's screen image: a woman of easy virtue, tempted by the fast life of the idle rich, who ultimately finds redemption in a good marriage to a man with more stable values. This formula, which was to make Bennett one of the highest-paid stars in Hollywood (she reportedly made $35,000 per week at the height of her career), served her in such films as *The Easiest Way, Born to Love, Common Law,* and *Bought* (all 1931), the last also starring her father, Richard Bennett.

On Nov. 22, 1931, Bennett married Henri de la Falaise, marquis de la Coudraye, who had been a Pathé executive and was the former husband of Bennett's rival, Gloria Swanson. The couple lived lavishly in Hollywood. Bennett was reputed to be an excellent business-woman who invested one-third of her salary and soon became a multimillionaire. These precautions were well-advised, for her career faltered quickly. In 1933, RKO refused to renew her contract, and from then on, her salary decreased along with her box-office potential.

Shortly before this downturn, Bennett made her best-known and most respected film of the period, George Cukor's *What Price Hollywood* (1932), in which she played a rising actress linked to a director in decline, a story that would be refilmed three times as *A Star Is Born*. Her subsequent films were less noteworthy, and by the early 1940's she was playing supporting roles (notably to Greta Garbo in *Two-Faced Woman*, 1941). Except for the popular and well-received *Topper* in 1937, in which she costarred with Cary Grant as a mischievous ghost, Bennett's days as a front-ranking star were over.

In 1940, Bennett divorced Henri de la Falaise, and on Apr. 20, 1941, she married actor Gilbert Roland. They had two daughters. While continuing to appear in films, Bennett broadened her career to include the stage (she debuted in the touring company of Noel Coward's *Easy Virtue* in 1939) and business activities (a successful cosmetics company and an endorsement for a firm that sold clothing door to door). She also was active in organizing benefits for the war effort. In 1945 she took on a weekday radio show called "Constance Bennett Calls on You," and in 1946 she produced the film *Paris Underground*.

The Rolands were divorced in 1945, and on June 22, 1946, Bennett married John Theron Coulter, an Air Force colonel. After Coulter was assigned to the Berlin Airlift in 1948, Bennett organized stage productions for military bases in Europe.

In the 1950's Bennett rarely appeared in films, but continued her career in radio, television, and the theater. In 1965 she returned to Hollywood to appear in *Madame X* (1966). She and her husband, then a brigadier general and commander of the New York Air Defense Sector, lived at McGuire Air Force Base. She died at Fort Dix, N.J.

[The most complete accounts of Bennett's career are in Gene Ringgold, "Constance Bennett," *Films in Review*, Oct. 1965; James Robert Parish, "Constance Bennett," in *The RKO Gals* (1974). Also see Joan Bennett and Lois Kibbee, *The Bennett Playbill* (1970). An obituary is in the *New York Times*, July 26, 1965.]

EVELYN EHRLICH

BENTLEY, ELIZABETH TERRILL (Jan. 1, 1908–Dec. 3, 1963), Soviet agent and FBI informer, was born in New Milford, Conn., the daughter of Charles Prentiss Bentley, a newspaper editor and department store manager, and of Mary Burrill, a schoolteacher.

Claiming descent from Roger Sherman, a signer of the Declaration of Independence and one of the creators of the Constitution, Bentley described her childhood as "an overly stern, old-fashioned New England upbringing." The family moved frequently, and Bentley attended public schools in New Milford, Ithaca, N.Y., Poughkeepsie, N.Y., McKeesport, Pa., and Rochester, N.Y., where she graduated from high school. She graduated from Vassar College with an A.B. in English in 1930. After brief service (1930–1932) as a teacher at the Foxcroft School, she entered a master's degree program in languages at Columbia University in the fall of 1932; she received an M.A. in 1935. A fellowship enabled her to spend the 1933–1934 academic year at the University of Florence. Returning to New York City in July 1934, but unable to find work as a teacher, she enrolled in a secretarial training program.

In March 1935, Bentley was hired as a caseworker by the Home Relief Bureau of New York City. That same month, she reluctantly joined the Communist party in response to the urging of a woman who had befriended her at Columbia. Bentley left the bureau in July 1935 and held a succession of temporary jobs until June 1938, when she was hired as a secretary by the Italian Library of Information in New York. She rationalized working for an agency of the Mussolini government by viewing it as a useful source of information for the Communist party in its campaign against fascism. She tells of receiving encouragement in this from Jacob Golos, a party officer and Soviet secret-police agent, who was soon to become her lover. At their first meeting, Bentley later asserted, he made her a member of a secret underground cut off from everyone in the Communist party but him.

Bentley claimed that by the summer of 1941 she had become the regular courier between a group of Communist agents employed in the federal bureaucracy in Washington and Golos in New York. She made regular trips to the capital to relay instructions about what information Moscow wanted, and in turn received copies of the material taken from government offices, collected the spies' party dues, and delivered the latest Communist publications. According to Bentley, the operation was so successful that she usually returned to New York with nearly forty rolls of microfilm made of documents containing information from the White House; the Pentagon; the Office of Strategic Services; the Departments of State, the Treasury, and Justice; and other agencies.

Bentley portrayed herself as taking a larger role in espionage and Communist party work after the death of Golos in November 1943, but her autobiography reveals a remarkable ignorance of the critical events in the party's tumultuous history from the end of 1943 through 1945. Alone and alienated, Bentley turned to the Federal Bureau of Investigation (FBI) in August 1945 and offered to tell her story. She later agreed to serve the FBI as its agent within the Communist party. With her appearance before a grand jury in New York during the last weeks of 1946, her career as a double agent ended.

The anti-Communist tide was running powerfully in the summer of 1948. Twelve leaders of the American Communist party were indicted in late July for conspiring to teach and advocate the overthrow of the government by force and violence. Early in August, Bentley testified before the House of Representatives Committee on Un-American Activities about her life in espionage, naming over three dozen people who, she alleged, supplied her with secret military and political information. Several of them, including Assistant Secretary of the Treasury Harry Dexter White, later denied the accusation under oath before the committee or in statements to the press. Others exercised their constitutional right not to answer questions the committee asked them. None of the people Bentley named were ever indicted for espionage.

Nevertheless, Bentley's testimony at the two trials of William W. Remington, an economist in the Department of Commerce, helped to convict him of perjury. She settled out of court a lawsuit he brought against her for statements she had made about him during a radio broadcast. The legal process was corrupted by the fact that the foreman of the grand jury that indicted Remington had earlier contracted with Bentley to ready her autobiography for publication. Sentenced to three years, Remington was murdered by another prisoner in 1954. Her testimony also helped convict Morton Sobell and Julius and Ethel Rosenberg of spying for the Soviet Union.

Like several other well-publicized ex-Communists, Bentley converted to Catholicism in November 1948 through the ministrations of Monsignor Fulton J. Sheen. She earned her living for a time as a consultant and lecturer on Communism, eventually joining the faculty of a Catholic college in Louisiana. From 1958 until her death in New Haven, Conn., she taught at the Long Lane School for Girls, a state correctional institute, in Middletown, Conn.

By 1956 Bentley had disappeared from the news. But in the summer of 1948 and during the months that followed, Bentley played a leading role as the "blond Spy Queen" in the cold-war theatrics of anti-Communism.

[All information originating with Bentley must be used with caution. This includes her autobiography, *Out of Bondage* (1951), the relevant files of the Federal Bureau of Investigation, her statements before the House Committee on Un-American Activities and the Senate Internal Security Subcommittee, her testimony in *United States* v. *William Remington, United States* v. *Abraham Brothman and Miriam Moskowitz*, and *United States* v. *Julius and Ethel Rosenberg and Morton Sobell.* See also Fred J. Cook, *The FBI Nobody Knows* (1964); Walter and Miriam Schneir, *Invitation to an Inquest* (1965); and David Caute, *The Great Fear* (1978). An obituary appeared in the *New York Times,* Dec. 4, 1963.]

"THE EDITORS"

BIDDLE, ANTHONY JOSEPH DREXEL, JR. (Dec. 17, 1896–Nov. 13, 1961), diplomat and sports enthusiast, was born in Philadelphia, Pa., the son of Anthony Joseph Drexel Biddle and Cordelia Rundell Bradley. The family was part of the wealthy Drexel-Biddle complex that was prominent in the pages of the *Social Register* no less than in industry and banking. Biddle's father, who was at home in the boxing ring, where he was known as "Tim O'Biddle," brought pugilism into association with religion through a movement that he called Athletic Christianity. A humorous, highly individualistic man, he was the subject of Kyle Crichton's Broadway play *The Happiest Millionaire* in 1956–1957.

Young Biddle was senior class president and captain of both the football team and the crew at St. Paul's School, Concord, N.H. He did not go to college. In 1915 he married Mary L. Duke, heiress to a tobacco fortune. They had two children and were divorced in 1931. Volunteering for military service in 1917, Biddle was assigned to the Squadron A Cavalry, in which he attained the rank of captain.

During the 1920's and early 1930's, Biddle combined shipping and mining businesses with various sports and society activities. He emulated his father in boxing and relished polo, skiing, fencing, and his special interest, tennis. In the last he was skilled enough to be on the American teams that competed in England for the Bathurst Cup in 1932–1934, and to win the French court championship in 1933. His business ventures included the Central Park Casino in New York City, criticized as a private club on public property. For a time he contended with legal proceedings after the bankruptcy of the Sonora Products Company, of which he was a director. In 1931, Biddle married Margaret Thompson Schulze, heiress to a Montana copper fortune. They had no children and were divorced.

In the early 1930's Biddle entered Democratic politics, campaigning in Pennsylvania for George H. Earle for governor and nationally for Franklin D. Roosevelt. The latter appointed Biddle minister to Norway in 1935 and two years later named him ambassador to Poland. Biddle's tenure in Norway was uneventful, and in 1936 he was back in Philadelphia serving as assistant secretary at the Democratic National Convention that renominated Roosevelt. But his Warsaw post soon caught him up in the maneuvers of Hitler that led to the German invasion of Poland and to World War II. In 1939, after the invasion, Biddle followed the fleeing Polish government to a succession of temporary capitals. Holding on as long as he could, he barely escaped with his wife to Bucharest, Rumania. His next base was at Angers, France. In 1940 he was named deputy ambassador to France, based at Tours and later at Bordeaux.

By 1941, European governments in exile were numerous. One after another they became Biddle's diplomatic responsibility. From 1941 to 1944 he served, chiefly in London, as the United States ambassador extraordinary and minister plenipotentiary to the refugee governments of Poland, Belgium, the Netherlands, Norway, Greece, Yugoslavia, and Czechoslovakia. He was also minister to Luxembourg.

Biddle combined gracious hospitality, reassuring counsel, and skill at handling many of the wants of dispossessed royalty in a way that made him ideal for his many-sided, difficult task. He was of inestimable help to General Dwight D. Eisenhower in the crucial months leading to the invasion of Normandy.

In 1944, Biddle went on active duty with the army as a lieutenant colonel. He served as deputy chief of the European Allied Contact Section of Supreme Headquarters, Allied Expeditionary Force, moving after the German surrender in 1945 to U.S. Forces, European Theater, where he was chief of the Allied Contact Division. He continued on European assignment until 1948. In July 1946 Biddle married Margaret Atkinson Loughborough, a Canadian on General Eisenhower's staff. They had two children.

After returning to the United States, Biddle was foreign liaison officer in the Department of the Army from 1950 to 1951. This post brought him the rank of brigadier general in 1951. His experience in diplomatic and military matters won him an influential place as special assistant to the army's chief of staff, General Matthew B. Ridgway (1953–1955).

After going on inactive army status in 1955, Biddle was appointed adjutant general of Pennsylvania, with the rank of major general. Concurrently he was chairman of the Pennsylvania Aeronautics Commission and of the State Governmental Reorganization Commission. He was president of the Association of the United States army in 1958–1959. In July of 1961, when seriously ill, he was promoted to lieutenant general in the Pennsylvania National Guard, his highest rank.

Biddle returned to diplomacy in March 1961, when he accepted appointment by President John F. Kennedy as ambassador to Spain, a post he held until being stricken by lung cancer. He died in Washington, D.C. In a message of sympathy, President Kennedy said: "As soldier and diplomat in two wars and in other times of crisis, he won the affection and admiration of the international community of free men."

[A library of Biddle's books, letters, papers, and records is at Duke University. See *Literary Digest*, July 27, 1935; *Nation*, Aug. 7, 1935; *New York Sun*, June 24, 1940; *New York Times*, June 25 and June 30, 1940, Aug. 11, 1940; *New York Post*, Oct. 22, 1940; *New York World-Telegram*, Feb. 22, 1941; *Time*, Aug. 5, 1941. Obituaries are in *Philadelphia Inquirer* and *New York Times*, Nov. 14, 1961.]

IRVING DILLIARD

BINKLEY, WILFRED ELLSWORTH (July 29, 1883–Dec. 8, 1965), educator and author, was born in Lafayette, Ohio, the son of George Washington Binkley, a carpenter who was active in local politics, and of Nancy Jane Desenberg. He was educated in the Lafayette public schools and then taught in a one-room school (1900–1903) before entering Ohio Northern University. After graduating with the B.S. in 1907, he again taught school (1907–1909) at Lafayette and served as a superintendent. In 1910 Binkley took a B.A. degree at Antioch College, whereupon he was granted a university scholarship to attend Harvard for the academic year 1910–1911. On Aug. 14, 1911, he married Dora Nancy Stotts; they had four sons. From 1911 to 1921 he was part of the faculty of Lima (Ohio) Central High School.

In 1921 Binkley began his long career at Ohio Northern University as assistant professor of political science and history, remaining there until his death. While at Ohio Northern he earned the M.A. (1926) and the Ph.D. (1936) at Ohio State University. His first scholarly book, *Problems in American Government*, appeared in 1926. He held visiting professorships at the American University Center at Biarritz, France (1945–1946), the University of Oxford (Fulbright lecturer, 1949–1950 and 1953), and Columbia University (summers, 1947–1952).

Binkley's two most important books, *President and Congress* (1943) and *American Political Parties* (1949), were characterized by a consistent concern for analysis shaped by the force of historical events. A historian and political scientist, Binkley thus wed political analysis and historical causation.

President and Congress was a revised and updated version of his *The Powers of the President* (1937). Admitting that the president's relationship with the Congress was perplexing when viewed historically, Binkley insisted that the study of events, and not theory, was the only feasible approach to an understanding of the problem. He traced the concept of a chief executive back to the office of the colonial governor. By recounting the vicissitudes of the presidents from George Washington to Franklin D. Roosevelt, Binkley intended to demonstrate that the relationship was largely experiential. If there was any theory to it, it was embedded in the history of the relationship. To those dissatisfied with the inefficiency of a government of divided and sometimes contending powers, Binkley pointed out that the American constitutional system was no less a product of the American society and environment than the parliamentary system was an outgrowth of English experience.

The same combination of analysis and history was evident in *American Political Parties*, subtitled *Their Natural History*. In attempting to ascertain and account for the social or group composition of American political parties and how these parties were galvanized to act by party leadership, Binkley tended to deemphasize explicit economic influences. Instead, he found that the "climate of opinion" and the "social environment" were major factors in bringing together effective political combinations. As for leadership, "expediency" had been the key to party leadership. For example, expedi-

ency rather than an adherence to strict (as distinguished from loose) construction of the Constitution was the better clue to why presidents acted as they had in the early years of the Republic. Practical judgments, not ideological commitments, explained Abraham Lincoln's conduct of the Civil War. Binkley followed in the tradition of Charles A. Beard because he was willing to take a hard look at the heroes of the past.

Critics found *American Political Parties* both useful and sagacious. The book appeared in Spanish, German, and Russian translations. *President and Congress* was praised for insights and analytical worth. Although he was a lifelong Republican, bred in the heart of Taft country, in his writings Binkley showed a preference for presidential powers broadly interpreted, as required by the exigencies of history. His other books included *The Man in the White House* (1959) and *A Grammar of American Politics* (1949), a standard text in political science written with Malcolm Moos.

Among his many honors the one Binkley greatly prized was the appointment by President Dwight D. Eisenhower to membership on the National Historical Publications Commission in 1954. Although Binkley received offers from larger and better-known institutions, he said he preferred the charm and quiet of rural Ohio. His attachment to Ada, Ohio, where the university was located, was very strong. He was on the town council from 1936 to 1949 and served a term as mayor (1952–1953). He was working on a new book, a study of the Republican presidency from Lincoln to Eisenhower, when he died at Ada.

[The files of the Alumni Office of Ohio Northern University contain useful information. An obituary is in the *New York Times*, Dec. 10, 1965.]

DAVID H. BURTON

BLACKMUR, RICHARD PALMER (Jan. 21, 1904–Feb. 2, 1965), literary critic, author, and teacher, was born in Springfield, Mass., the son of George Edward Blackmur, variously a stockbroker, woolbroker, and self-employed businessman, and Helen Palmer, a physical therapist whose father and grandfather were celebrated preachers. This evangelical strain was pronounced in the career of Blackmur, over whom his mother exerted a powerful influence until her death in 1963. With his father, a dignified and reclusive failure, Blackmur quarreled early, and their relationship remained embittered. His childhood and adolescent life were troubled by poverty and the rancorous marriage of his parents. About 1905 the family moved to New York City, where George Blackmur worked as a broker on Wall Street. This move turned out badly, and within five years Blackmur's mother was supporting the family by operating a boardinghouse in Cambridge, Mass., near the Harvard Yard. Until Blackmur was almost nine he remained at home, tutored by his mother. He then enrolled in the fourth grade at Peabody Grammar School. In 1916 he went to his mother's old school, Cambridge High and Latin, from which he was expelled two years later for arguing with the headmaster. He was failing all of his subjects at the time of his expulsion, and his formal education ended at this point.

From 1918 to 1925 Blackmur lived at home, keeping himself in pocket money by jerking sodas and clerking for bookstores in Cambridge and for the Widener Library at Harvard. He assuaged his loneliness by writing poetry and stories, by courting Tessa Gilbert (the daughter of the composer Henry Gilbert), to whom he made an unsuccessful proposal of marriage, and by friendship with his cousin by adoption, George A. Palmer. In 1922 Blackmur's favorite uncle, George M. Palmer, killed himself. This catastrophic event seems an appropriate emblem for the frustration and despair that characterized his young manhood.

Blackmur's fortunes turned upward in 1925. With his future brother-in-law, Wallace Dickson, he opened a bookstore in Cambridge. The partnership lasted only a year but introduced Blackmur to Maurice Firuski, the proprietor of the Dunster House Book Shop in Cambridge. For two years he clerked for Firuski and served as his secretary. He also developed his taste in music under the tutelage of Robert Donaldson Darrell, the creator of the *Phonograph Monthly Review*, to which Blackmur contributed essays. In 1928 his friends Lincoln Kirstein and Bernard Bandler appointed him editor of the *Hound and Horn*, the most successful and prestigious of the little magazines. Blackmur lost this job in 1930 when the magazine moved to New York, but he continued to publish in it until its demise in 1934. His literary essays—notably on T. S. Eliot, Wallace Stevens, e. e. cummings, and Henry James—established his reputation as one of the foremost American critics. On June 14, 1930, he married the painter Helen Dickson; they had no children. For most of the next ten years they lived in the West End of Boston and summered in the Dickson farmhouse near Harrington, Maine. Maine changed

Blackmur; he became an expert gardener and subsisted largely on his garden and what he took from the sea. He cultivated an ear for country speech and an eye for country pieties, which shows profoundly in his poetry, fiction, and critical prose of this period.

Twelve critical essays, mostly on modern poets, were published in 1935 as *The Double Agent*. With this book, said Allen Tate, Blackmur "invented" the New Criticism. The New Critical method meant approaching a text with absolute patience and humility, so encouraging the words to give up their sense. Biographical and cultural considerations were not exactly scanted—the ideal New Critic was a committed scholar—but the work itself got primary attention. Few critics have scrutinized their material so acutely as Blackmur in this collection or in *The Expense of Greatness* (1940). An unremitting concern with language is equally the hallmark of his first book of poetry, *From Jordan's Delight* (1937), whose title refers to an island off the coast of Maine. In his earliest poetry Blackmur slavishly imitated such masters as Eliot and Ezra Pound, but in the poems of *From Jordan's Delight* he speaks in his own voice, producing, said one reviewer, "the best American poetry of the decade." This seems a tenable judgment. In the 1920's and 1930's Blackmur also worked on short stories, novels, and plays. He was disappointed in his hopes that two of his plays might be produced on Broadway. His first novel, "King Pandar," was rejected by fifteen publishers before he ceased submitting it. His second, *The Greater Torment*, he broke off, having completed the first of three planned books. Blackmur's chief labor of the 1930's was his projected life of Henry Adams, for which he received a Guggenheim Fellowship in 1936–1937, subsequently renewed for a second year. For more than half of his life, he strove to complete this book; at his death, he left a torso of more than 600 pages. Although it lacks a chronological beginning and the coda Blackmur intended, it can stand as a satisfying, complete work. Only a little less ambitious was Blackmur's endeavor to write the definitive study of Henry James, the novelist for whom he cared most. In 1940 he signed a contract for the James book but only discrete essays were written. The fragmentary nature of this study is like Blackmur's achievement as a whole. His work and his life were a series of approaches or essays, in the sense that his hero Montaigne used the word.

Blackmur's years as free-lance critic and poet, living—often barely—by his wits, ended in 1940 when he accepted an appointment at

Princeton University. He took the job as assistant to Allen Tate in a newly constituted program in creative arts only to secure "the minimum necessities"; he expected to move on within a year. Blackmur remained at Princeton for the rest of his life, although he traveled abroad in 1952–1953 and 1956–1957 and held the Pitt Professorship in American History and Institutions at Cambridge University in 1961–1962. At first Blackmur found life in Princeton antipathetic. He had no degrees, the English department seemed hostile, and he shuttled between the department and the Institute for Advanced Study while looking for a permanent home. The strain on his marriage, which had been faltering for years, was aggravated by academic life; in 1951 he and his wife were divorced. Nonetheless, tenure and a full professorship came the same year.

Eventually Blackmur became a powerful presence in the American literary establishment, partly because he directed the Christian Gauss Seminars in Criticism, beginning in 1956. His students knew him as a great if often enigmatic teacher, his colleagues as a fascinating conversationalist whose conversation became monologues as he got older.

Blackmur paid a price for success; his literary career changed direction. Although for some years he continued to write poetry—*The Second World* (1942) and his last volume, *The Good European* (1947)—his poetic inspiration gradually dried up. The concreteness that marks the poems of the 1930's was displaced by a growing dependence upon abstraction and a presumption that ideas can carry the burden of poetry. Attention to ideas is conspicuous in his later criticism as well. *Eleven Essays in the European Novel* (1964)—"fragments of an unfinished ruin," as he called it—was based on translations. Inevitably, his practice of close reading of texts was a casualty of this reading at a remove. In *The Lion and the Honeycomb* (1955), *Anni Mirabiles* (1956), and *A Primer of Ignorance* (1967), the process of attenuation carries further. These books contain plenty of luminous writing, but by and large meticulous analysis has given way to the prophetic and evangelizing mode.

The major work of Blackmur's life was *Language As Gesture* (1952), arguably the finest criticism ever published in America, but for the most part a pulling together of earlier essays. The same holds true of *Form and Value in Modern Poetry* (1957), a felicitous plundering of previously published work. But if Blackmur's career describes a downward curve, this does not diminish the magnitude of his achievement. He made a small body of permanent poetry and a larger body of immaculate criticism. On a generation of students, his impact as a man of letters is impossible to exaggerate. He thought that "when the language of words most succeeds it *becomes* gesture in its words." In his own art he managed this. Blackmur died in Princeton.

[The most important collections of Blackmur's papers are at Firestone Library, Princeton University; the *Hound and Horn* Archive of Yale University; Harvard University; and *Poetry Magazine* Archive of the University of Chicago. Other collections are listed in *American Literary Manuscripts.*
The most nearly complete bibliography is Gerald J. Pannick, "R. P. Blackmur: A Bibliography," *Bulletin of Bibliography*, Oct. 1974, which supplements Carlos Baker, "R. P. Blackmur: A Checklist," *Princeton University Library Chronicle*, Apr. 1942, and Allen Tate, *Sixty American Poets* (1954). An annotated bibliography with introductory essay is being prepared by Harry Thomas. In addition to the works mentioned in the text, Blackmur wrote *New Criticism in the United States* (1959); and *Henry Adams* (1980), edited by Veronica Makowsky. His poetry was republished, as *Poems of R. P. Blackmur* (1977), with an introduction by Denis Donoghue.
Writings about Blackmur include a biography in preparation by Russell Fraser; Stanley E. Hyman, *The Armed Vision* (1948); Randall Jarrell, *Poetry and the Age* (1953); Hugh Kenner, *Gnomon* (1958); Robert Foster, *The New Romantics* (1962); Joseph Frank, *The Widening Gyre* (1963); John Wain, *Essays on Literature and Ideas* (1963); Walter Sutton, *Modern American Criticism* (1963); Leonard Greenbaum, *The Hound and Horn* (1966); William H. Pritchard, "R. P. Blackmur and the Criticism of Poetry," *Massachusetts Review*, Fall 1967; Delmore Schwartz, *Selected Essays*, edited by Donald A. Dike and David H. Zucker (1970); Rene Wellek, "R. P. Blackmur Re-Examined," *Southern Review* (1971); Grant Webster, *The Republic of Letters: A History of Postwar American Literary Opinion* (1979); Russell Fraser, "R. P. Blackmur: The Politics of a New Critic," *Sewanee Review*, Fall 1979; and Robert Boyers, *R. P. Blackmur: Poet-Critic* (1980).]

RUSSELL FRASER

BLACKSTONE, HARRY (Sept. 27, 1885– Nov. 16, 1965), magician, was born Henry Boughton in Chicago, Ill., the son of Alfred Boughton and Barbara Degan. His father was a florist who had tried many jobs and was often away from his family for long periods. The man who became the Great Blackstone began his many name changes by calling himself Harry Bouton. Blackstone saw his first magician, Harry Kellar, in 1897. The Great Kellar put him under a spell at McVicker's Theatre, and his life went in one direction after that, although

Blackstone often told the story in different ways.

Blackstone studied magic at the public library. But it was not his only interest. According to Robert Parrish, he told a reporter, "If I was not born with a wand in my hand, I may have been clutching a tiny chisel. I was inclined toward woodworking at a very early age. . . ." He took a job as assistant cabinetmaker and built trick boxes and instruments that were sold to magicians.

In 1904 Blackstone began his career with his brother Peter. Their act was called "Harry Bouton & Co., Straight and Crooked Magic." Blackstone was the conjurer, and wore a white tie and tails. Peter Bouton dressed in a clown costume. The name of the act was later changed to "The Bouton Brothers." After Blackstone was able to buy a huge supply of playbills printed for a magician named Fredrik, he toured as Fredrik the Great. But World War I made that name a box office liability and he chose the name Blackstone—according to one story, from the Chicago hotel.

Blackstone did many performances in vaudeville. His show had something for everyone. His wife, Inez Norse ("The Little Banjo Fiend"), did a musical number. There were flags and patriotic music and beautiful women (who would sometimes "be cut in half" with a buzz saw). There were animals (a donkey or elephant) that Blackstone made disappear in a puff of smoke. Sid Lorraine, a magician who saw him in 1920, at the Grand Opera House in Toronto, later wrote: "The Blackstone show was different from any magic show I'd seen. He didn't act sinister or too mysterious. He had a warm personality, a sly chuckle, an impressive voice and, most of all, a great sense of fun."

Blackstone was an expert at sleight of hand and card tricks. In the popular how-to books on magic that he wrote, he emphasized that anyone can learn some tricks. Blackstone did not need to cultivate the magician's mystique. His presence alone sufficed. He was an impressive figure with a large head and—in later years—a striking mane of white hair.

The dancing handkerchief became one of Blackstone's most famous acts. He would borrow a handkerchief and give it life. The handkerchief would dance and talk: it had a personality of its own. Blackstone's feats were generally illusions. He considered magic "the art of misdirecting thoughts." The audience believed that they had seen things that actually had not happened. He could seem to make a light bulb—and even a young woman—float in the air. His shows had the quality of dreams.

Blackstone was invited to perform at the White House for President Calvin Coolidge. He "stole" the president's pen and the wallet belonging to Secretary of State Frank B. Kellogg. The president's Secret Service bodyguard did not notice this or the disappearance of his handgun. Out of the pocket of Treasury Secretary Andrew W. Mellon, Blackstone pulled a rabbit. The president's laconic comment was, "This man's a magician."

In 1926 Blackstone bought more than 200 acres in Colon, Mich., and started a farm and a magic factory. On the farm he raised the animals for his show. The Blackstone Magic Company built equipment used by magicians.

After a divorce from his first wife, Blackstone married Mildred Irene Phinney, who had worked in his show; they had one son. Blackstone's son, also a magician, continued his father's tradition of giving away a rabbit at each performance.

Blackstone was also an entrepreneur, selling animals raised on his farm to other magicians; and in addition to doing commercials for candy companies, he was often hired by manufacturers (particularly of business machines or other new products) to advise their salesmen.

During World War II, Blackstone worked with the USO and entertained at 165 military bases in the United States. After a severe attack of asthma in March 1945, his doctors urged him to be less active. Blackstone did the opposite. In 1946–1947 he did a nine-month transcontinental tour. The late 1940's was a time of great success for Blackstone's *Show of 1001 Wonders.* He also had a radio series. Blackstone had been long divorced when he married his third wife, Elizabeth Ross, in November 1950.

Blackstone stopped giving stage shows in 1955, but still made television appearances. In 1960 he moved to Hollywood, where he often spent his evenings at a magicians' club called the Magic Castle. Blackstone was liked and admired by his colleagues, who considered him the greatest living magician. He died in Hollywood.

[There is a large collection of Blackstone's letters at the American Museum of Magic, Marshall, Mich. He wrote *Blackstone's Secrets of Magic* (1929), *Blackstone's Modern Card Tricks* (1929), and *Blackstone's Tricks Anyone Can Do* (1948). *Genii: The Conjurors' Magazine* devoted its Sept. 1965 issue to Blackstone. Also see Milbourne Christopher, *Illustrated History of Magic* (1973); and Daniel Waldron, "Blackstone: A Biographical Sketch," in *Great Lakes Informant,* Apr. 1978. There is an extensive clipping file on Blackstone at the Theatre Collection, New York Public Library, at Lincoln Center. Obituaries are in the *New Tops*, Dec. 1965, and *New York Times* and *New York Herald Tribune*, Nov. 18, 1965.]

RALPH KIRSHNER

BLAIR, WILLIAM RICHARDS (Nov. 7, 1874–Sept. 2, 1962), physicist and inventor, was born near Coleraine, County Derry, Ireland, the son of Thomas Wray Blair and Mary Richards. The family immigrated in 1884 to the United States, where his father engaged in farming near Emporia, Kans. Blair graduated from the State Normal School at Emporia in 1895 with a teaching certificate. After serving as principal of Pittsburg (Kans.) High School and as an instructor in mathematics at the Wisconsin State Normal School at Oshkosh (1897–1902), he entered the University of Chicago, from which he received the B.S. in 1904 and the Ph.D. in 1906.

In 1906, Blair began service in the U.S. Weather Bureau as a meteorologist. While director of upper-air research at the Mount Weather Observatory, Bluemont, Va. (1907–1910), he married Florence Lyon Smith on Oct. 10, 1909; they had three sons. In 1917, Blair joined the army and served with the Allied Expeditionary Force in France, as head of the meteorological section.

Blair remained in the army after the war. In 1919 he was a member of the Interallied Committee for Aerial Navigation and of the International Wireless Commission. His interest in meteorology led naturally to an interest in better means of atmospheric detection and navigation. This meshed well with the need of the military for better means of detecting the approach of enemy aircraft.

Blair later stated that the concept that became pulse-echo radar came to him as early as 1926 (an important date, in light of later charges that others had preceded him in the development of radar) at the Army Command and General Staff School at Fort Leavenworth, Kans. The idea arose from class discussions on how to track and direct antiaircraft fire to fast-moving enemy aircraft. Blair worked on the concept while in charge of the research and engineering division of the Office of the Chief Signal Officer at Washington, D.C., in the late 1920's. As director of the Signal Corps Laboratories at Fort Monmouth, N.J. (1930–1938), he brought his work in pulse-echo radar to fruition.

Blair was dissatisfied with detection by sound, then the chief means, and thought that high-frequency radio or thermal detection would be more successful. In 1931 he brought all army experiments in detection together in Project 88,

"Position Finding by Means of Light." Blair sustained the Signal Corps interest in radiowave detection, and supported radio pulse-echo over radio beat because the former could differentiate targets. He kept open other avenues of detecting, such as thermal and sound, but he held firmly to his belief that the only feasible plan lay in pulse-echo detection, and he clearly stated this in his 1935 report to the chief signal officer. In spite of work by the Naval Research Laboratories with radio detection, Blair remained strong in his objections to this method. He was encouraged when thermal detection was declared ineffective by researchers in the Signal Corps and the Corps of Engineers.

Although little funding was forthcoming, research in pulse-echo detection received high priority from the War Department. In May 1937 the first U.S. Army radar was successfully demonstrated to influential military and government officials. This radar, to be known as SCR-268, was a short-range radio locator for controlling searchlights. The army pronounced it to be "as important and far reaching in its military applications as the first United States patent on the telephone was to commercial applications." All further development—such as radar countermeasures, airborne radar, and microwave early warning—were based on the SCR-268, which was the backbone of the military detection as late as 1944.

As a result of the secrecy surrounding SCR-268, Blair did not apply for a patent until 1945. Twelve years later he was awarded U.S. Patent 2,808,819. There was controversy over the invention. Some claimed that the navy had developed the fundamental system before 1930. Others credited Sir Watson Watt of Britain with the invention. But Blair's system utilized pulse-echo, and that of the navy did not. Watt's system needed two receivers, and Blair's did not. In addition, Blair's unit was mobile, and the other two systems were not.

Although the army considered Blair the "father of radar," some commercial users did not recognize his patent and refused to pay him royalties. Dr. Robert Morris Page, former director of research at the U.S. Naval Laboratory, makes no mention of Blair in his *Origin of Radar* (1962).

Blair retired from the army in 1938 because of ill health, but continued as a technical adviser to the Signal Corps. He died in Fair Haven, N.J.

[See Dulany Terrett, *The Signal Corps: The Emergency* (1956). An obituary is in the *New York Times*, Sept. 3, 1962.]

RONALD H. RIDGLEY

BLALOCK, ALFRED (Apr. 5, 1899–Sept. 15, 1964), surgeon and educator, was born in Culloden, Ga., the son of George Z. Blalock, a merchant, and Martha Davis. He completed the ninth grade at Jonesboro, Ga., and then studied at Georgia Military College at Milledgeville. He received his B.A. from the University of Georgia in 1918 and his M.D. from the Johns Hopkins University School of Medicine in 1922. Blalock credited his interest in medical research to a classmate at Johns Hopkins, Tinsley R. Harrison.

After graduation from medical school, Blalock was appointed house medical officer in urology under Hugh H. Young. Despite illness during his intern year, Blalock gained an assistant residency on the general surgical service the following year. In July 1924 he began a year as extern in otolaryngology under Samuel J. Crowe. With Harrison, Blalock published "The Effects of Changes in Hydrogen Ion Concentration on the Blood Flow of Morphinized Dogs" (*Journal of Clinical Investigation*, 1925) and "Partial Tracheal Obstruction: An Experimental Study on the Effects on the Circulation and Respiration of Morphinized Dogs" (*Archives of Surgery*, 1926).

In 1925 Blalock became the chief resident in surgery at the newly reorganized school of medicine at Vanderbilt University. His friend Harrison was the chief resident in medicine; they continued their investigative work, studying the influence of various factors on the output of the heart. Over the next few years, Blalock's interest shifted more toward problems of cardiac output that had some direct application to the clinical problems of surgery. He began his work on shock. In 1928 he initiated studies in which the oxygen content of blood withdrawn from veins in various parts of the body was determined in shock produced by different methods, including trauma and the injection of histamine. He concluded that the local accumulation of blood at the site of trauma to a large area, such as the intestinal tract or an extremity, was evidence against the systemic action of a histaminelike substance. In "Experimental Shock: The Cause of Low Blood Pressure Produced by Muscle Injury to Dogs" (*Archives of Surgery*, 1930), he wrote: "The experiments presented in this paper offer no evidence that trauma to an extremity produced a toxin that caused a general dilatation of capillaries with an increase in capillary permeability and a general loss of fluid from the blood stream."

Blalock and his group explored every facet of the problem; they gathered overwhelming evidence that shock was caused by the loss of fluid outside the vascular bed with resulting decrease in blood volume. Blalock's recognition of the need for volume replacement was corroborated during World War II. Large quantities of blood, blood substitutes, and plasma expanders were used in treating the wounded, which resulted in the saving of many lives. Clearly, Blalock's most important scientific work was that on traumatic and hemorrhagic shock. On Oct. 25, 1930, Blalock married Mary O'Bryan. They had three children.

In 1941 Blalock became professor of surgery and chairman of the Department of Surgery at the Johns Hopkins University School of Medicine and surgeon-in-chief of Johns Hopkins Hospital. Soon thereafter he collaborated with A. McGehee Harvey and Joseph L. Lilienthal, Jr., in performing, for the first time, total removal of the thymus gland in patients with myasthenia gravis. This operation is still utilized in the treatment of this disease.

At the suggestion of Helen B. Taussig, a dedicated pediatric cardiologist, Blalock devised subclavian-pulmonary artery anastomosis, an operation for improving pulmonary circulation in children with pulmonic stenosis. After thorough study of this procedure in experimental animals, the first operation on a patient with the tetralogy of Fallot ("blue baby" syndrome in children) was done on Nov. 29, 1944. The operation, on a two-year-old, was successful at the initial attempt. This monumental accomplishment brought fame to both Blalock and Taussig and ushered in the modern era of cardiac surgery. On Nov. 12, 1959, after his first wife died, Blalock married Alice S. Waters.

No other surgeon of Blalock's era trained so many residents for important academic appointments. He gave his best energies to the development of a children's surgical unit at Johns Hopkins. The effort culminated in the great Children's Medical and Surgical Center in Baltimore, dedicated in the year of Blalock's retirement. Because of Blalock's accomplishments and contributions to Johns Hopkins, the trustees changed the name of the clinical science building to the Alfred Blalock Building. He died in Baltimore.

[A more extensive biographical sketch of Blalock and a complete bibliography are in *The Papers of Alfred Blalock*, II (1966), edited by Mark N. Ravitch; A. McGehee Harvey, "Alfred Blalock" *Biographies of Members of the National Academy of Sciences*, (forthcoming). See also the obituary in the *New York Times*, Sept. 16, 1964.]

A. McGehee Harvey

BLISS, ROBERT WOODS (Aug. 5, 1875–Apr. 19, 1962), diplomat, was born in St. Louis, Mo., the son of William Henry Bliss, an attorney, and of Annie-Louise Woods. He attended preparatory schools in Virginia, Minnesota, and Massachusetts and then graduated from Harvard University with a B.A. in 1900. Bliss entered the diplomatic service upon graduation and worked first in the office of the secretary of the United States civil government in Puerto Rico. From 1901 to 1903 he was private secretary to the governor of the island.

After passing the State Department qualifying examination in 1903, Bliss was assigned to Venice as United States consul. The following year he was appointed second secretary to the United States embassy in St. Petersburg, where he remained until January 1907. On Apr. 14, 1908, he married Mildred Barnes, daughter of United States Congressman Demas Barnes of Ohio; they had no children. In 1907, Bliss had been named secretary of the legation in Brussels, and the following year he served as a delegate to the international conference that considered the revision of the arms and ammunition regulations of the General Act of Brussels of 1890.

From 1909 to 1912 Bliss served in Buenos Aires as secretary of the legation. In June 1912 he attended the international conference at Paris that met to consider the relief of aliens. From 1912 to 1916 Bliss was secretary of the Paris embassy; from 1916 to 1920 he held the rank of counselor of the embassy. In 1918 he was temporarily assigned to serve as chargé d'affaires at the United States legation in The Hague.

Bliss was recalled to Washington in 1920 and became chief of the Division of Western European Affairs at the Department of State. He was in charge of protocol and ceremonies during the 1921–1922 Washington Conference on Limitation of Armaments. Simultaneously he served as chairman of the diplomatic service board of examiners.

A lifelong Republican, Bliss was appointed by President Warren Harding as envoy extraordinary and minister plenipotentiary to Sweden in 1923. He served there until 1927, when he was named ambassador to Argentina by President Calvin Coolidge. Bliss's career was typical of many foreign service officers. Having paid his dues in relatively minor posts during three decades of dedicated service, he was rewarded by promotion to ambassador in his final years. Bliss retired in July 1933, perhaps in reaction to the election of the Democrat Franklin D. Roosevelt as president.

After American entry into World War II, Bliss was called out of retirement. He served as a consultant to the State Department in 1942 and 1943, as a special assistant to Secretary of State Cordell Hull beginning in February 1944, and as a consultant to Secretary of State Edward Stettinius beginning in December 1944. He again retired in November 1945.

Bliss and his wife collected pre-Columbian, medieval, and Byzantine art. Many of their Byzantine pieces were acquired during extensive travels in Greece and Turkey. In 1940 the Blisses donated Dumbarton Oaks, their Georgian estate in Washington, D.C., together with a specialized art research library of 50,000 volumes and a collection of medieval and Byzantine art, to Harvard University. They later established endowments for the maintenance of the estate as a museum of Byzantine art and library. Bliss was cofounder of the Dumbarton Oaks Research Library and Collection. In 1944 the estate was the scene of an international conference that worked out details for the creation of the United Nations.

In his retirement years Bliss engaged in many cultural and civic pursuits. He was president of the American Federation of Arts and the American Foreign Service Association. He was vice-chairman of the Smithsonian Art Commission and the board of the National Trust for Historic Preservation. He served as a director and first vice-president of the Washington Criminal Justice Association and was on the Board of Overseers of Harvard University (1939–1945).

Through his many years of collecting, Bliss had become a highly regarded authority on pre-Columbian art, and wrote *The Indigenous Art of the Americas* (1947; reissued as *Pre-Columbian Art* in 1957). He died at Washington, D.C.

[Department of State, Foreign Relations of the United States series, provides communications to and from Bliss in his various diplomatic posts. An obituary is in the *New York Times*, Apr. 20, 1962.]

STEPHEN D. BODAYLA

BLITZSTEIN, MARC (Mar. 2, 1905–Jan. 22, 1964), composer and playwright, was born in Philadelphia, Pa., the son of Samuel Marcus Blitzstein, a banker, and Anna Esther Levitt. He was a musical prodigy, and after studying at the University of Pennsylvania and the Curtis Institute (1923–1925) and then with Nadia Boulanger in Paris (1926) and Arnold Schönberg in Berlin (1927), he embarked on a career as a serious composer. In the 1920's he worked mostly in the style of the Austrian composer Ernst Krenek, but by the early 1930's he found himself disillusioned with scholastic composition, which seemed to him irrelevant to the real world. A turning point came with his composition of *Triple Sec* (1928), a brief operatic farce that appeared in the musical revue *Garrick Gaieties* (1930). Blitzstein felt more at home in the musical theater, which directly reflected the everyday world. On Mar. 2, 1933, Blitzstein married Eva Goldbeck; she died three years later. They had no children.

The major turning point in Blitzstein's development was the composition, in 1936, of *The Cradle Will Rock*. Partly opera, partly musical comedy, partly revue, this play—which he conceived and for which he created script, lyrics, and music—was a cruelly ironic assault on those who sell out their convictions to the establishment (specifically doctors, clergymen, artists, and professors, all of whom are servants of "Mr. Mister" and his family) and simultaneously made an inspiring proclamation of a healthy future brought forth by the labor movement.

Opinions today differ on whether *The Cradle* is merely a curiosity of the 1930's or a truly provocative piece of musical drama, but there is no question that its initial performance was unparalleled in American theater history. The work had originally been a part of the Works Progress Administration's Federal Theater Project, but by 1937 the project was being regarded suspiciously in Washington. Before *The Cradle* could open in New York City, the authorities ordered the Maxine Elliott Theatre padlocked. Undaunted, Blitzstein, with his colleagues John Houseman and Orson Welles, led the audience up Broadway to the vacant Venice Theatre for *The Cradle*'s premiere. Musicians were forbidden by their union to perform, so Blitzstein played the score alone on a hastily rented piano, while the cast (similarly forbidden to appear onstage) rose from their seats to perform their parts; ever since, *The Cradle* is often performed without scenery and with solo piano accompaniment as a homage to the initial performance. The work has proved tough and honest and witty enough to survive the vicissitudes of changing times, but it is as a remarkable piece of theater lore that its immortality is assured.

Blitzstein continued in this vein with *I've Got the Tune* (1937), a one-act radio musical that focused on a composer's gradual coming to political awareness; it is, arguably, Blitzstein's most purely personal work. From 1938 to 1949 Blitzstein was a member of the Communist party. The musical drama *No for an Answer* (1941), more of a conventional agitprop political play than *The Cradle*, treated the struggles of some restaurant workers and the attempt of a wealthy liberal to find his natural allies.

Blitzstein was committed early to the struggle against fascism. He wrote scores for *The Spanish Earth* (1937) and other documentary films before enlisting in the Army Air Force. While serving in Great Britain, he wrote *Freedom Morning* (1943), a symphonic poem for black troops, and the *Airborne Symphony* (completed 1946), his most famous work for the concert stage. This massive composition for male soloist, chorus, orchestra, and narrator depicts the story of man's early attempts at flight and then the collapse of human inventiveness in bloody air warfare. Today the music seems bombastic and the text banal, but the work is nevertheless full of impassioned concern.

The late 1940's saw what may be remembered as Blitzstein's major achievement: *Regina* (1949), an operatic treatment of Lillian Hellman's searing indictment of capitalistic greed, *The Little Foxes*. Blitzstein's leftist predilections naturally drew him to the Hellman play, but what he produced was no didactic argument; it was a visceral musical transcription of the original work. In incorporating spirituals and folk idioms into the opera, Blitzstein contributed, along with Kurt Weill in *Street Scene* (1947) and Gian-Carlo Menotti in *The Consul* (1950), to the impulse to merge the best of operatic and musical comedy traditions.

Other operatic and film-music compositions followed. Blitzstein continually sought new ways to merge music and drama. He made a brilliant adaptation of Bertolt Brecht's lyrics for *The Three-Penny Opera*. The production, which ran for six years at the Theatre De Lys in New York City, was in large part responsible for the resurgent American interest in Brecht. Blitzstein made a single foray into the conventional musical theater with *Juno* (1959), an adaptation of Sean O'Casey's play *Juno and the Paycock*, for which he wrote music and lyrics for Joseph Stein's book. The show was vague and uncertain whether it wanted to be political or charmingly ethnic. It had a run of only two weeks, but some of the score is remarkable. Finally, Blitzstein worked off and on for ten years on an opera treating the trials of Nicola Sacco and Bartolomeo Vanzetti. This was to be his major work. It was commissioned by the Metropolitan Opera, which was to give its first production. Enough of it survives in manuscript to indicate how powerful an opera it might have been. Unfortunately, the complexity of the story, the composer's uncertainty about the nature of the heroes, and his qualms over accepting foundation money for what he saw as an antiestablishment project led him down one blind alley after another. It was still in sketch form when Blitzstein died in Fort-de-France, Martinique, the victim of assault and robbery. Also left unfinished were operatic versions of two Bernard Malamud stories, "Idiots First" and "The Magic Barrel."

Blitzstein is seldom regarded as an important figure in the evolution of contemporary classical music, and if he is mentioned at all today in music criticism, it is usually only as an imitator of Aaron Copland or Paul Hindemith. In the limited terms of pure music this estimate may be accurate, but in the ongoing search for new ways to blend music and drama and to break down the subtle barriers between the "classical" and the "popular," his contributions have been considerable and underrated. And regardless of his influence, his works remain exciting by themselves.

On the strength of *The Cradle Will Rock, Regina*, the adaptation of *The Three-Penny Opera*, and occasional moments from *No for an Answer, Juno*, and *Sacco and Vanzetti*, Blitzstein can be called a major figure in contemporary American music. He may have done little that is innovative in purely musicological terms, but he brought contemporary idioms—the verbal language of the street and the musical language of jazz and the blues—to the sanctified regions of opera. In this respect his music is a true forerunner of such works as *West Side Story*, which make up much of contemporary musical theater. And what he wrote was heartfelt. As long ago as 1941, Copland wrote that Blitzstein proved a simple truth: "Every artist has the right to make his art out of an emotion that really moves him. If Blitzstein, like many other artists in every field, was moved to expression by the plight of the less privileged in their struggle for a fuller life, that was entirely his right."

[The best collection of materials on Blitzstein is the manuscript collection at the Wisconsin Center for Theater Research. It includes microfilms of all sketches for *Sacco and Vanzetti* and full scores of *The Cradle Will Rock, No for an Answer*, and the opera *Parabola and Circula*. Additional Blitzstein material is held by the New York Public Library, the Federal Theater Project Archive in Fairfax, Va., the National Archives, and the Nathan Pusey Library at Harvard. *The Cradle Will Rock* was published in 1937. The *Schwann Record and Tape Guide* lists recordings of *The Cradle Will Rock* and *Regina*, the latter containing a libretto. Recordings of the *Airborne Symphony, Freedom Morning, No for an Answer*, and *Juno* are available at the Rodgers and Hammerstein

Library of Recorded Sound (New York Public Library of the Performing Arts). Also available (although deleted from the catalog) is the recording *Marc Blitzstein Discusses His Theater Compositions*, Spoken Arts 717 (1956). John Houseman, *Run-Through* (1972), provides the most thorough description of the opening of *The Cradle Will Rock*. An article by Eric Gordon, "Of the People," appeared in *Opera News*, Apr. 12, 1980. The obituary is in the *New York Times*, Jan. 24, 1964.]

JOHN D. SHOUT

BLUE, GERALD MONTGOMERY ("MONTE") (Jan. 11, 1887[?]–Feb. 18, 1963), motion picture actor, was born in Indianapolis, Ind., the son of Lousetta and William Blue, a Civil War veteran. Many sources give Blue's date of birth as Jan. 11, 1890; but records at the Indiana children's home where he lived indicate that he was born on that date in 1887. He was part Cherokee Indian. After his father's death in 1895 Blue went to the Indiana Soldiers' and Sailors' Children's Home in Knightstown, Ind. In January 1903 he was discharged from the home to his mother, who was living in Indianapolis.

Following high school, Blue worked as a newspaper reporter, miner, seaman, cowhand, and circus bareback performer before going to California. There he got his start in motion pictures as a ditchdigger for $1.50 a day on the D. W. Griffith lot. In 1914 Griffith hired him as an actor, scriptwriter, and stunt man. Blue appeared as an extra in *Birth of a Nation* (1915) and played a strike leader in Griffith's *Intolerance*, which was released the following year.

After supporting such stars as Mary Pickford and Douglas Fairbanks in a variety of pictures, Blue attracted attention in Cecil B. DeMille's *The Affairs of Anatol* (1921). Director Robert Z. Leonard cast him as Mae Murray's leading man in both *Peacock Alley* (1921) and *Broadway Rose* (1922). In 1922 Blue appeared as Danton in Griffith's *Orphans of the Storm*, a role many critics consider his best. During the early 1920's he was placed under contract by Warner Brothers, where he remained a popular player for the remainder of the decade. He became a top silent star in three of Ernst Lubitsch's most popular comedies: *The Marriage Circle* (1924), with Adolphe Menjou and Florence Vidor; *Kiss Me Again* (1925), with Clara Bow and Marie Prevost; and *So This Is Paris* (1926), with Patsy Ruth Miller. On Nov. 1, 1924, Blue married Tove Janson, a former Ziegfeld Follies girl; they had two children.

Among the many other films Blue appeared in during the 1920's are *Main Street* (1923),

The Lover of Camille (1924), *Hogan's Alley* (1925), *Other Women's Husbands* (1926), *Wolf's Clothing* (1927), *Across the Atlantic* (1928), and *Conquest* (1929).

Blue was in Tahiti making *White Shadows of the South Seas* (1928) when sound was introduced to the movie industry. The picture was released with music and a voice dubbed in for Blue's. The sound quality was so poor that Blue subsequently found it increasingly difficult to get parts; many believed that his voice was unsuitable for sound films. Ironically, his role as Dr. Matthew Lloyd in *White Shadows* is perhaps his best known. Taking a world cruise in the early 1930's, Blue returned to find that the savings he had invested were gone. He later told a reporter: "I decided to build my new magic on rock instead of sand. So I started out at the bottom as an extra. I was in the awkward stage between stardom and character parts."

After a short stint in the theater, Blue began a comeback in Hollywood as a bit player. During the 1930's, it was not uncommon for "Poverty Row" producers to hire silent film stars who had not made it in the talkies, give them bit parts, and then advertise them as the stars. Blue's appearance in such films as *Trails of the Wild* (1935) and *Social Error* (1937) were the results of such practices. He played small roles, frequently as a villain, in such serials as *The Undersea Kingdom* (1936), *Secret Agent X-9* (1937), and *The Great Adventures of Wild Bill Hickok* (1938). His better-known films of the 1930's include *Lives of a Bengal Lancer* (1935), *G-Men* (1935), *The Outcasts of Poker Flat* (1937), *Dodge City* (1939), and *Juarez* (1939).

By 1940, Blue had established himself in what amounted to a new career as one of Hollywood's more capable character actors, and as such appeared in a wide variety of films, many of them westerns. He had sizable roles in *Law of the Timber* (1941), *Silver River* (1948), *The Iroquois Trail* (1950), *Three Desperate Men* (1951), and *Hangman's Knot* (1952). During the same period, Blue also appeared in *The Road to Morocco* (1942), *Mission to Moscow* (1943), *The Adventures of Mark Twain* (1944), *San Antonio* (1945), *Cinderella Jones* (1946), *Life with Father* (1947), *Key Largo* (1948), *Johnny Belinda* (1948), *The Younger Brothers* (1949), *Dallas* (1950), *Warpath* (1951), *Rose of Cimarron* (1952), *The Last Posse* (1953), and *Apache* (1954).

In the 1950's, Blue appeared in supporting roles in a number of filmed television series, playing Indian chiefs, sheriffs, and small-town shopkeepers. He was in one or more episodes of "The Adventures of Rin-Tin-Tin," "Jim Bowie," "The Lone Ranger," "Mark Saber," "Racket Squad," "Rawhide," "Sky King," "Wagon Train," and "Wild Bill Hickok." Tove Blue died in 1956; and on Oct. 4, 1959, Blue married Betty Munson Mess. At the time of his death in Milwaukee, Wis., he was a publicity agent for the Hamid-Morton Circus.

In spite of the suave parts he played in the 1920's, Blue was primarily associated with outdoor roles. Taking the fluctuations of his career in stride, he said in the early 1940's, "I know it is a mistake to live in the past, I am now getting a foothold in the present." By 1954, when he made his last motion picture appearance in Robert Aldrich's *Apache*, Blue was well known to many moviegoers—especially western fans—as one of Hollywood's top character actors.

[See *Photoplay*, Mar. 1919, May 1926, and Oct. 1930; Hal C. Herman, ed., *How I Broke into the Movies* (1928); Harry T. Brundidge, *Twinkle, Twinkle Movie Star!* (1930); *New York Times*, Apr. 25, 1943, and Mar. 24, 1956; Bert Gray, "Monte Blue," *Films in Review*, May 1963; Kenneth W. Scott, "Monte Blue," *Films in Review*, Oct. 1963; Ray Stuart, comp., *Immortals of the Screen* (1965), with photographs; and Alfred E. Twomey and Arthur F. McClure, *The Versatiles* (1969), with photographs. Obituaries appeared in the *New York Times* and the *Times* (London), both on Feb. 19, 1963.]

L. MOODY SIMMS, JR.

BOISEN, ANTON THEOPHILUS (Oct. 29, 1876–Oct. 1, 1965), theologian, psychologist, and founder of the movement for clinical pastoral education, was born in Bloomington, Ind., the son of Hermann Balthazar Boisen and Louise Wylie. His father taught modern languages and botany at Indiana University, later moving, with his family, to Williams College, Mass., and to the Lawrenceville School in New Jersey. Contemporary accounts speak of his father as "eccentric" and "a mental enthusiast with a surprising genius." Boisen's mother was one of the first women to enroll at Indiana University.

Boisen lived an energetic yet structured childhood, spurred on by his father's enthusiasms. But his father's death when he was seven was soon followed by an accident in which he lost the sight in his left eye. Henceforth he felt overwhelmed at times by shyness and insecurity. In 1897 Boisen graduated from Indiana University, but while he was pursuing further studies there in modern languages, his inner tensions reached a peak and he was overcome by despair. Fortunately, he was able to share this experience with his mother and a respected professor. The disturbance subsided, but it presaged the course of his later life.

We know more about Boisen than about most men of his time and circumstance because he left "My Own Case Record" (1928), later revised and published as *Out of the Depths: An Autobiographical Study of Mental Disorder and Religious Experience* (1960)—a documented account of his "valid religious experience which was at the same time madness of the most profound and unmistakable variety." During his life Boisen experienced at least five "major decisions" (1898, 1902, 1904, 1905, 1919) "marked by deviation from the normal," as well as at least six psychotic episodes (1908, 1920, 1921, 1928, 1930, 1935). His lifework, from 1920 on, was to focus on how such crises represent the mind's attempts toward cure.

Having decided that modern languages were too stimulating, Boisen resolved in 1902 to become a forester, in honor of his father's interest in botany. This decision came to him "automatically," just as three years later, while studying forestry at Yale, there came "surging" into his mind words that he took to be his call to the ministry. It also reflected Boisen's complex relationship with Alice L. Batchelder, whom he courted over the thirty-three years between their meeting in 1902 and her death. The vicissitudes of Boisen's relationship with her accounted directly for two of his six psychotic episodes (1930, 1935), and indirectly for a third (1928). The "surging" words, with reference to Alice, led him to realize that his was "an appeal to a beloved person stronger" than himself, and "for her sake" he was thus "led into the Christian ministry."

Boisen entered Union Theological Seminary in New York City in 1908, concentrating on "scientific," as opposed to "scholastic," theology, under the tutelage of psychologist of religion George Albert Coe. In 1911 he was ordained in the Presbyterian Church. He then spent two years (1911–1912) doing rural survey work in Missouri and Tennessee for the Presbyterian Board of Home Missions; five years as a pastor in rural Iowa, Kansas, and Maine; almost two years with the Overseas YMCA in France; and about a year directing a rural survey in North Dakota for the Interchurch World Movement. He was forty-four years old, and his lifework had not yet begun.

On Oct. 11, 1920, Boisen's role in life suddenly became clear to him. That evening he discovered a "process of regeneration which could be used to save other people"; he found that he had "broken an opening in the wall which separated religion and medicine." These thoughts were patently delusional; after twenty years of lesser emotional problems Boisen was finally suffering his first episode of "dementia praecox, catatonic type," a form of schizophrenia. When the disturbed condition cleared, he pondered the meaning of the episode. In view of the extremely productive course his life now took, there may be some justification for agreeing with his belief that "the cure has lain in the faithful carrying through of the delusion itself." Boisen concluded that "in many of its forms, insanity . . . is a religious rather than a medical problem," and a later delusion prompted him to outline a definite "plan of cooperation between medical and religious workers."

After his release from a fifteen-month confinement at Westboro (Mass.) State Hospital in January 1922, Boisen lived and studied at the Episcopal Theological Seminary and took additional courses at Andover Theological Seminary. He entered the Harvard School of Graduate Studies as a student of Richard C. Cabot (social ethics) and William McDougall (abnormal psychology). He also joined a seminar on the psychology of delusion and belief taught by C. Macfie Campbell, the psychiatrist who had earlier examined him. Campbell later allowed him to do social work with those cases at Boston Psychopathic Hospital "in which the religious factors were in evidence." Boisen persuaded Worcester (Mass.) State Hospital to take him on as chaplain in July 1924. A year later, when he offered his first summer program of "clinical experience" for seminarians, he had already published several studies on the relationship between mental disorder and religious experience.

Boisen's program at Worcester was incorporated in January 1930 as the Council for the Clinical Training of Theological Students, and soon grew to embrace chaplaincy training programs nationwide. In June 1928, and especially in November 1930, Boisen suffered relapses that ultimately necessitated his giving up the chaplaincy at Worcester. Since 1925 he had been spending part of each year as lecturer and research associate at Chicago Theological Seminary, so with minimal difficulty he transferred his chaplaincy to Elgin (Ill.) State Hospital in 1932. A final relapse in 1935 sent Boisen to Sheppard and Enoch Pratt Hospital, Baltimore, but otherwise this was a very productive period. Between 1925 and 1938 he published *Lift Up Your Hearts* (1926; later revised as *Hymns of Hope and Courage*) and *Exploration of the Inner World: A Study of Mental Disorder and*

Religious Experience (1936), as well as four scientific articles and fifteen religious articles focusing on discovering the "laws of spiritual life" as revealed at times of crisis.

From 1938 to 1942, Boisen was in residence at Chicago Theological Seminary. In this period he wrote fourteen articles—four for psychiatric journals—and dozens of book reviews. World War II brought him back to Elgin as chaplain in 1942, despite his age. He retired in 1945, continuing to live at Elgin, but from 1947 to 1950 and again from 1951 to 1954, he was pressed into service. During these later years he published *Problems in Religion and Life: A Manual for Pastors* (1946), *Religion in Crisis and Custom: A Sociological and Psychological Study* (1955), and thirty-four articles, six in scientific journals. Boisen died at Elgin.

[The Boisen Files, in the Boisen Room of Chicago Theological Seminary Library, contain most of Boisen's manuscripts and personal correspondence, case history, and photographic negative files. Some additional items are with the Boisen Papers in the Menninger Foundation Archives, Topeka, Kans. The most comprehensive studies of Boisen's life and work are Henri J. M. Nouwen, "Anton T. Boisen and the Study of Theology Through 'Living Human Documents,' " *Pastoral Psychology,* Sept. 1968; Robert C. Powell, *Anton T. Boisen: "Breaking an Opening in the Wall Between Religion and Medicine"* (1976), and "Anton T. Boisen's 'Psychiatric Examination: Content of Thought' (c.1925–31): An Attempt to Grasp the Meaning of Mental Disorder," *Psychiatry,* Nov. 1977.]

ROBERT CHARLES POWELL

BORZAGE, FRANK (Apr. 23, 1893–June 19, 1962), motion picture director and producer, was born in Salt Lake City, Utah, the son of Lewis Borzage and Mari Reich. Lacking interest in his father's successful cattle ranch, he quit school at age thirteen. After working in a silver mine to pay for a correspondence school course in drama, he drifted about the country for three years as a character actor, living in boxcars and tents. He reached Hollywood in 1913, ambitious to further his modest acting career.

In Hollywood, Borzage became part of Thomas H. Ince's production company, playing romantic leads and stock villains in westerns for $5 a day and carfare. In 1916 he began directing short films in which he frequently starred. In the same year he married Rena Rogers, a vaudeville performer and actress. By 1920, when *Humoresque,* his first major production, was released, Borzage had nearly three dozen short films to his credit.

The appearance of *Humoresque,* which many critics considered one of the finest films of the year, earned Borzage a reputation for excellence that was considerably enhanced seven years later when he won, for *Seventh Heaven,* the first Academy Award for direction. The film also established the unknown Janet Gaynor and Charles Farrell as stars who appeared in subsequent Borzage productions.

Within two years of directing his first sound film, *They Had to See Paris* (1929), starring Will Rogers, Borzage won his second Oscar for *Bad Girl* (1931). During the 1930's, the most productive and artistically important decade of his career, he directed many romantic classics. Among the most acclaimed films were *A Farewell to Arms* (1932), *Man's Castle* (1933), *Little Man, What Now?* (1934), *Desire* (1936), *History Is Made at Night* (1937), and *Three Comrades* (1938).

Borzage preferred above all to underscore the power and purity of love in the face of adversity. His best films depended for their success on the creation of a pair of screen lovers. Optimistic and tender, his romantic films became more religious by the end of the 1930's. In *The Shining Hour* (1938), *Disputed Passage* (1939), and *Strange Cargo* (1940), he displayed sensitivity in the handling of his cast and in his visual style. Critics began to notice the "spiritual" qualities of his cinematography. Borzage also started producing films at this time, although it was not until the 1940's that he became heavily involved with production. Even so, he limited himself to directing duties for the most part. It may not be entirely coincidental that in none of his finest films was he both producer and director.

Borzage, who free-lanced after leaving the Fox studios in the early 1930's, departed to a degree from melodrama during World War II, in order to undertake a greater variety of scripts. Some were on wartime themes (the best being *The Mortal Storm* in 1940), and he also managed a comedy and a musical. Few rose above the mediocre, and *Moonrise* (1949), the most critically praised and ambitious, was a failure at the box office. In 1940 he and his wife were divorced. On Nov. 25, 1945, Borzage married Edna Stilwell Skelton, former wife of comedian Red Skelton; they were divorced in 1949. He married Juanita Scott on June 16, 1953. All his marriages were childless.

For a filmmaker who at the height of his career had frequently directed three films a year, the 1950's were an unusually fallow period. A nine-year interval separated *Moonrise* from *China Doll,* a World War II melodrama released in 1958. Borzage's last film, and his longest one, was *The Big Fisherman,* a three-hour biblical spectacular (1959). He died at Los Angeles, Calif.

As a director Borzage (or Mr. Frank, as he was frequently called) insisted on spontaneity, and he held rehearsal time to a minimum. Repetition, he believed, destroyed naturalness, "the primary requisite of good acting." He was even-tempered and good-natured in his handling of cast and crew, and his views on filmmaking were simple and basic. "The first duty of a director is to tell a story," he liked to say. The finished film should show "no sign of effort" on the part of cast or director.

Borzage excelled in golf and polo, and enjoyed horseback riding, yachting, and piloting his own plane. Shortly before his death he received from the Directors Guild of America the D. W. Griffith Award for special achievement in filmmaking. His work was, as one critic has observed, "imbued with a warmth, a humanity, that often carried it over the line between delicacy and preciousness, between compassion and sentimentality, but which never failed to stir the passions of his audience."

[Borzage's views on directing are in Richard Koszarski, *Hollywood Directors: 1914–1940* (1976). Also see John Belton, *The Hollywood Professionals,* III˙ (1974), and "Souls Made Great by Adversity: The Romantic Cinema of Frank Borzage," *L.A. Film Calendar,* Dec. 1976; Robert A. Juran, "A Frank Borzage Filmography," *L.A. Film Calendar,* Feb. 1977, and "Frank Borzage," *National Film Theatre* (London), May–Aug. 1975; Steven C. Earley, *An Introduction to American Movies* (1978); and William K. Everson, *American Silent Film* (1978). The Academy of Motion Picture Arts and Sciences has a clipping file on Borzage. An obituary is in the *New York Times,* June 20, 1962.]

JACK L. HAMMERSMITH

BOUCHÉ, RENÉ ROBERT (Sept. 20, 1905–July 3, 1963), fashion and advertising illustrator and painter, was born Robert August Buchstein in Prague, Austria-Hungary, the son of Siegfried Buchstein, a German-Jewish itinerant laborer who abandoned his family when young Buchstein was an infant. He began painting at the age of five and "never did anything else." When he was fifteen, Buchstein set out for Munich to fend for himself as an illustrator; there he studied art history briefly under Heinrich Wölfflin and began a lifelong friendship with Richard Lindner, a promising painter. In 1927–1928 he moved to Berlin, where he worked as an advertising illustrator and sought

a new persona by adopting the name René Robert Bouché. It was there that he met his future wife, Margot ("Pony") Beate Schoenlank, also an advertising artist.

Increasingly uncomfortable with events in Berlin, Bouché and Schoenlank moved to Paris shortly before Adolf Hitler became chancellor of Germany in 1933. In Paris Bouché received his first significant formal training in oil painting, studying under Amédée Ozenfant at the Académie Ozenfant during 1933 and 1934. By the late 1930's he had established himself as an art director and advertising and fashion illustrator in Paris.

Shortly after the birth of a son, Bouché and Schoenlank finally overcame a passport obstacle and were married on Jan. 12, 1935. They legally remained refugees, however, and were separated for six years following the outbreak of war in September 1939. Bouché was placed in a French detention camp, but he escaped before advancing German forces arrived and made his way to Biarritz, where he stayed for a year before managing to reach Lisbon. With timely funds from New York *Vogue,* he then secured passage on one of the last American ships to sail from Europe before the United States entered World War II. His wife and son remained in Paris for the duration of the war.

Scarcely settled in America, Bouché was drafted into the United States Army early in 1942, only to suffer severe head injuries in an accident immediately before he was to report for active duty. Following hospitalization he was given an honorable discharge in 1943. He became a naturalized citizen and soon resumed in New York his career as an advertising and fashion illustrator. Beginning with an assignment of fashion drawings for Paris *Vogue* in 1938, Bouché maintained a more or less uninterrupted relationship with *Vogue* enterprises for the rest of his life. In addition to his regular contributions to *Vogue,* during the 1940's he made advertising sketches for Saks Fifth Avenue and handled most of Elizabeth Arden's advertising campaigns. In 1944 he taught at the Art Students League. His wife and son arrived in the United States in February 1946. The couple separated in 1949 and were divorced in 1954.

Except for an earlier flirtation with neocubism, Bouché's painting until the late 1940's was basically figurative, realistic, and clearly overshadowed by his magnificently free yet incisive drawings and fashion sketches. In 1949, however, he became absorbed in abstract expressionism, after becoming a member of the Eighth Street Avant-Garde Painters' Club. Although his later portraits were to benefit from this transitional period, he soon lost interest in the abstractionist style. By 1953 he was concentrating on what was to become almost a mission: to restore portraiture to its pride of place in art.

Bouché continued to exhibit his remarkable flair for advertising illustrations, as shown in his commissions for Schweppes and Jaguar in the mid-1950's. He also designed stage sets and costumes for the play *Child of Fortune* (1954) and the ballet *Offenbach in the Underworld* (1956). Well before his first major show of portrait oils in December 1955, he had begun making portrait sketches of radio and television personalities for the Columbia Broadcasting System that became media trademarks. Indeed, the volume of portrait drawings he produced during the last ten years of his life may ultimately represent the most important testimony to his skills and talents as an artist, despite the attention he drew to his portrait oils.

In his canvases Bouché usually combined "a free brush line drawn dynamically through thin washes of color and areas of empty canvas with details closely observed and precisely transposed in faces." Poised against criticisms of his "soupy washes" and likenesses that were "caricatural, somewhat superficial and often cruel" were praises for his "lightly limned tonal style," "quick, intuitive, and penetrating" insights into character, and evocative bodily gestures and original arrangements that lent an air of vivacity and "engaging informality" to his sitters.

During the winter following his second marriage, to a former *Vogue* editor, Denise Lawson-Johnston, on June 28, 1962, Bouché embarked, with seeming urgency, upon two departures from his style. Absent entirely in the first was any suggestion of drawing or use of the strong black line characteristic of his work; large patterns of color defined forms, sometimes with vivid hues. Then, during the two weeks before his death at East Grinsted in Sussex, England, Bouché began making charcoal drawings in which features emerged through agitated patterns of hatchings.

Depicted as a "slight, wiry cosmopolite" and a "smiling Mephistopheles in spats," Bouché moved easily between New York, London, and Paris, and was an occasional guest on television shows. He usually enjoyed portraying the famous and fashionable with, in his words, "a kind of loving criticism." Many of his best drawings and oils appear to have been inspired by subjects, often friends, in the arts: Jacques Lipchitz, Igor Stravinsky, Frederick Kiesler, Georges Braque, Truman Capote, Willem and Elaine de Kooning.

[Michel Bouché, Pembroke Lakes, Fla., has preserved much of the existing manuscript material on his father's life, including his notebooks. No manuscript nor published biography of the artist appears to exist, and no catalogue raisonné of his works has been produced. The pages of New York *Vogue* offer the most accessible source of reproductions of his drawings and paintings. Reviews of his exhibits during the 1950's are in *Arts* and *Art News*. See also *Time,* Nov. 9, 1959; *Life,* May 19, 1961; *Newsweek,* July 22, 1963; *Vogue,* Sept. 1, 1963. An obituary is in the *New York Times,* July 7, 1963.]

PAUL CHRISTOPHER

BOW, CLARA GORDON (July 29, 1905–Sept. 26, 1965), actress, was born in Brooklyn, N.Y., the daughter of Robert Bow and Sarah Gordon. The family was poor, her father working at such jobs as waiter and handyman. Her mother was a nervous semi-invalid. Bow later recalled that because of her shabby clothing she was the "worst looking kid on the street." Keenly aware of her family's poverty, she avoided the better-dressed girls and played boys' games like baseball and football, and even boxed. Some writers have speculated that this early companionship with males helped to account for her essentially boyish approach to life. Never a good student, she quit school after the eighth grade and began working as a receptionist in a physician's office.

In November 1921, Bow won a national beauty contest. Among the prizes she received was the chance to appear in a motion picture. Good looks were extremely important in silent films, and any young woman with a beautiful face and figure had a chance to get into movies. Bow made her film debut in 1922, in *Beyond the Rainbow,* but her scenes were cut before the release. Her photograph in *Motion Picture* caught the eye of director Elmer Clifton. He put Bow in one of his productions, a whaling story entitled *Down to the Sea in Ships* (1922). In this movie Bow, playing a young woman who disguises herself as a boy to go along on the voyage, received some very good comments from the reviewers. A short time later she was signed by Preferred Pictures.

During the next few years there followed a series of unexceptional roles in ordinary films such as *Maytime* (1923), *The Daring Years* (1923), *Grit* (1924), *Daughters of Pleasure* (1924), *Wine* (1924), *Black Lightning* (1924), *Capital Punishment* (1925), *Parisian Lovers* (1925), *Eve's Lover* (1925), *Kiss Me Again* (1925), and *The Primrose Path* (1925). Although these films were far from great, the plump, vivacious, little redheaded flapper with the wide brown eyes was gaining recognition in the film industry. In 1925, *The Plastic Age*, a romantic story about youth and morality in the Jazz Age, provided the ideal vehicle for Bow's vivacity and zest for life. After this movie she was touted as "the hottest jazz baby in films."

Late in 1925, Bow's contract was purchased by Paramount for $25,000. The first picture she made for Paramount was *Dancing Mothers* (1926). This was followed the same year by *The Runaway, Kid Boots*, and *Mantrap*. In *Mantrap*, directed by Victor Fleming, she gave one of her best performances; the film did very well at the box office. By late 1926 she was receiving 40,000 fan letters each week.

In 1927 came the turning point in Bow's career. She was chosen to play the lead in the screen version of Elinor Glyn's book *It*. "It" was supposedly the quality possessed by rare individuals to attract members of the opposite sex, and Bow became the personification of that quality. She was now the "It Girl" of the movies, the actress who symbolized the 1920's flapper on the screen. *It* made her a major star.

Bow is in many respects the perfect representative figure of Hollywood during the 1920's. Movies had become a part of high finance, and it was important for the studios to find performers with personalities that could attract millions of paying customers. The star system, with much publicity involved, became standard. Bow was also representative of the general relaxing of moral standards that occurred right after World War I. Her style of sophisticated sexuality enjoyed wide appeal.

In the next few years Bow's film credits included *Children of Divorce* (1927), *Rough House Rosie* (1927), *Wings* (1927), *Hula* (1927), *Red Hair* (1928), and *The Fleet's In* (1928). But almost as sudden as her rise to stardom was her decline. In the 1920's cheap tabloids played up the vice and sin in Hollywood. Bow was one of the many young stars who had become rich and famous almost overnight, and like many others she could not handle the money or the fame. Her excesses, like those of Hollywood in general, were legendary. She would cruise down the boulevards in a convertible, surrounded with seven red chow dogs who matched her hair. She got headlines by running up large gambling debts in Reno. She had a scandalous affair with her physician, Dr. William Earl Pearson. Her private secretary, Daisy Devoe, made lurid disclosures about her love life. Although she married western actor Rex Bell on Dec. 4, 1931, the marriage did not change her reputation. Another factor that

damaged her career was the advent of sound in movies. Like many other silent film stars, she had trouble adjusting to talkies. And the Great Depression put an end to the appeal of the carefree screen flapper. Whatever the case, Paramount did not renew her contract when it expired.

Although Bow tried a movie comeback in *Call Her Savage* (1932) and in *Hoopla* (1933), it did not work out. She settled on her husband's Nevada ranch, and later had two sons. Her later years were marked by nervous breakdowns and long stays in sanitariums. She died in Culver City, Calif.

Although the critics were never greatly impressed with Bow's acting ability, she remains a legend in the history of movies because she epitomized the era of the Roaring Twenties, the flapper, the jazz baby, and flaming youth. Her films were not great, but they were not intended to be. They were made primarily to display her body and personality.

[On Bow's life and career, see Alexander Walker, *The Celluloid Sacrifice* (1966); James R. Parish, *The Paramount Pretties* (1972); and Marjorie Rosen, *Popcorn Venus* (1973). Background material is in Gilbert Seldes, *The Movies Come from America* (1937); Arthur Knight, *The Liveliest Art* (1957); Edward C. Wagenknecht, *The Movies in the Age of Innocence* (1962); Paul Rotha, *The Film Till Now* (1967); John Baxter, *Hollywood in the Thirties* (1968); David Robinson, *Hollywood in the Twenties* (1968); and Kenneth Anger, *Hollywood Babylon* (1975). Obituaries are in the *New York Times*, Sept. 28, 1965; *Time* and *Life*, Oct. 8, 1965.]

J. MICHAEL QUILL

BRADY, MILDRED ALICE EDIE (June 3, 1906–July 27, 1965), reporter, editor, and consumer advocate, was born in Little Rock, Ark., the daughter of Stewart Carson Edie, a pharmacist, and Maude Alice White, a telegraph operator. The family moved often because the father managed a succession of restaurants and drugstores. In 1920 they settled in Kansas City, Mo., where he became manager and druggist for Katz drugstores.

Edie graduated from Northeast High School in Kansas City in 1923. She then entered Kansas City Junior College (now Kansas City University), but was expelled for her involvement in the publication of a radical student newspaper called the *Sacred Cow*. She next went to the University of Missouri, from which she was expelled for failure in classes and for helping publish the mildly left-wing magazine the *Dove*. She then enrolled at the University of

Kansas, but left a few weeks short of graduation in 1929 and went to New York City. There Edie got a job in Brentano's bookstore and also became an associate editor of *Theatre Arts Monthly*. She met and married Gerald Fling in that year, but divorced him in 1931; they had no children. In 1930 she was hired as chief staff writer and chief reporter for *Tide* magazine, for which she covered the advertising and marketing business.

About 1932 Edie met Arthur KaNet and Fred Schlink of Consumers Research in Washington, N.J., and became very interested in consumer affairs. In 1935 she wrote an investigative report on the strike and breakup of Consumers Research, which stemmed from a disagreement (one of many) between Schlink and KaNet over unionization of Consumers Research staff. While conducting interviews for that project she met Robert Alexander Brady, a professor of economics at the University of California at Berkeley who had just returned from Germany. When Consumers Union was founded in 1936, Dexter Masters, the editor of *Tide*, encouraged Edie to become involved in its work. She and Brady went to Berkeley together and in 1938 established the Western Consumers Union, he as president and she as director. They began to live together and had two daughters. Although not married, Edie began to use Brady as her surname at this time.

In 1940, Western Consumers Union closed, and Brady and Edie returned to New York City. There, she edited a periodical called *Friday*, and she edited *Bread and Butter* for Consumers Union during 1941. From 1942 to 1944 she worked as a specialist on consumer education for the Consumer Division of the Office of Price Administration in Washington, D.C. Brady also worked there, as economic consultant to the Consumer Division.

After World War II, Edie edited a column for *McCall's*. She also did some writing, including an article in *Harper's* (April 1947), "The New Cult of Sex and Anarchy." After a year in England with Brady, she returned to work for Consumers Union in 1950, writing and editing a column for *Consumer Reports* called "Economics for Consumers." In 1956, after a common-law marriage of twenty years, she and Brady were married in Berkeley. He suffered a paralyzing stroke in 1958, and she moved the family from Berkeley back to New York, where she became the editorial director of *Consumer Reports*, a position she held until 1964, when she became senior editor. During these years she testified before the Federal Trade Commission

and various Senate subcommittees on such subjects as administered prices in the drug industry (1960), truth in packaging (1963 and 1965), and regulation of cigarette advertising (1964). She also investigated and reported on these and other topics for *Consumer Reports*. Her work for Consumers Union took her to Japan, the Netherlands, and Norway.

After the death of her husband in 1963, she moved to Harrison, N.Y., where she died two years later. Senator Philip Hart of Michigan said of Brady: "[She was] a lady who pulled no punches when criticizing the shenanigans which consumers too often today face in the marketplace." She was a pioneer in consumer affairs and the driving spirit behind the consumer movement in California.

[There is a small amount of Brady's correspondence in the collections of Dr. Colston Warne and the Consumers Union, Inc., at the Center for the Study of Consumer Affairs in Mt. Vernon, N.Y. Her writings include "A Western CU," *Consumer Reports*, Apr. 1938; "Let 'Em Eat Ice Cream," *New Republic*, Oct. 13, 1947; "The Case of the Stubborn Grocer," *Consumer Reports*, May 1950; "The Great Ham Robbery," *Consumer Reports*, Mar. 1961; "American Family and Consumer Economics," *Marriage and Family Living*, Nov. 1963; and "Let the Reader Beware," *Consumer Reports*, Oct. 1965. See also Norman D. Katz, "Consumers Union: The Movement and the Magazine, 1936–1957" (Ph.D. diss., Rutgers University, 1977). Obituaries are in the *New York Times*, July 29, 1965; and *Consumer Reports*, Sept. and Oct. 1965.]

PATRICIA PAINTER

BRECKINRIDGE, AIDA DE ACOSTA (July 28, 1884–May 27, 1962), organization executive and philanthropist, was born in Elberon, N.J., the daughter of Ricardo de Acosta, a merchant, and Micaela Hernández de Alba. Of Spanish-Cuban ancestry, she was educated at the Sacred Heart Convent in Paris. On June 29, 1903, she became the first woman to solo in a dirigible: under the instruction of Alberto Santos-Dumont, a Brazilian air navigator, she made a five-mile flight over Paris. Upon hearing the news, her parents ordered her home.

De Acosta married Oren Root, the nephew of United States Secretary of State Elihu Root, on Nov. 5, 1908. Root was a director, and later president, of the Hudson and Manhattan Railroad Company. They had two children. The marriage ended in divorce in 1923. On Aug. 5, 1927, Aida de Acosta Root married Henry S. Breckinridge, a lawyer and former assistant secretary of war (1913–1916). The Breckinridges were divorced in 1947.

Breckinridge's career interests spanned the fields of child health, welfare, and aid to the handicapped. During World War I she sold Liberty Bonds valued at a record $2 million, and after the war she worked abroad with the American Committee for Devastated France. Upon returning home she became director of the department of publications and promotion of the American Child Health Association, serving in that capacity from 1923 to 1932. As promotion director, Breckinridge's major accomplishment was the designation of May 1 as Child Health Day, proclaimed nationally by President Calvin Coolidge in 1928. She served as assistant director for public relations of the 1929 White House Conference on Child Health and Protection. Breckinridge also worked with the American Red Cross, the Association for Improving the Condition of the Poor, and the Commission for the Prevention and Relief of Tuberculosis.

In 1935, Mayor Fiorello H. La Guardia named Breckinridge head of the Municipal Art Committee for New York City, the purpose of which was to promote La Guardia's plans for a municipal art center. The committee was unable to realize this goal, but it promoted exhibits in a municipal art gallery, operas in city schools, song contests, and publication of the magazine *Exhibition*, edited by Breckinridge. She resigned this post in 1939. She also served as chairman of the advisory committee on fine arts of the New York World's Fair of 1939–1940, and she headed the women's division of the Associated Willkie Clubs of America during the 1940 presidential campaign.

Breckinridge's major public activity was her work in aiding the blind. She first became interested in eye diseases in 1922, when both her eyes became inflamed during a holiday in Southampton, N.Y. The infection led to glaucoma. After visiting a number of physicians, none of whom was able to diagnose the problem, Breckinridge was referred to Dr. William Holland Wilmer of Washington, D.C. Wilmer performed several operations, but he was able to save only a small amount of the vision in her left eye—less than 20 percent. After the operation Breckinridge began a fund-raising effort to build a hospital where Wilmer might pursue research on restoring sight and instruct other doctors in his surgical techniques. With foundation support she raised more than $5 million to establish the Wilmer Ophthalmological Institute at Johns Hopkins University in 1929. It was the first eye institute of its kind in the United States.

In 1944 one of Wilmer's former students, Dr. R. Townley Paton, approached Breckinridge to suggest the founding of an eye bank. Research had established the effectiveness of corneal tissue transplants in restoring sight when human eyes could be obtained and utilized within seventy-two hours after removal from the body. Paton proposed to establish a facility for eye donations, and he asked Breckinridge to head the fund-raising, educational, and organizational effort. Within a short time she had established an office and raised $50,000. The Eye-Bank for Sight Restoration was incorporated in February 1945, with headquarters at the Manhattan Eye, Ear and Throat Hospital.

The major organizational difficulties related to locating and transporting corneas within the time limit. Ample publicity, the use of donation forms, and the enlistment of the airlines and the Red Cross for transportation arrangements were Breckinridge's solutions. She continued to serve as executive director during the first ten years of the Eye Bank's operation. At the time of her retirement in 1955, the organization had trained more than seventy doctors in the corneal graft technique, 4,500 corneas had been transplanted, five affiliated eye banks had been established, and more than 175 hospitals had joined in the work. For her work in aiding the blind, Breckinridge received the Migel Medal, the highest award of the American Foundation for the Blind, in October 1956. She died in Bedford, N.Y.

[Breckinridge's life and career are discussed in Daniel Schwarz, "Builder of the Eye Bank," *New York Times Magazine*, Nov. 2, 1947. On her work with the Eye Bank, see *New York Times Magazine*, Apr. 28, 1946; Lois Mattox Miller, "She Deals in Human Eyes," *Reader's Digest*, Aug. 1948; *New York Times*, Dec. 13, 1951, and Oct. 31, 1955; and Joseph A. Spalding, "Americans Not Everybody Knows," *PTA* magazine, June 1966. An obituary is in the *New York Times*, May 29, 1962.]

JANE A. BENSON

BREEN, JOSEPH IGNATIUS (Oct. 14, 1890–Dec. 7, 1965), Hollywood film censor, was born in Philadelphia, Pa., the son of Joseph Breen, an Irish immigrant whose chief bequests to him were ambition, "street" wisdom, and Catholic piety. He attended parochial schools and St. Joseph's College in Philadelphia, from which he received the B.A. After working for several years as a journalist in Philadelphia and spending four years in the U.S. Consular Service, Breen joined the immigration bureau of the National Catholic Welfare Conference. In

1926 he directed publicity for the International Eucharistic Congress in Chicago. He married Mary Derin, a childhood playmate; they had six children.

Breen moved to Hollywood in 1930 to help implement a "production code" drafted by Martin Quigley, editor of the *Motion Picture Herald,* and Father Daniel Lord of St. Louis University. As early as 1922 the leading Hollywood producers had appointed Will Hays, a former Harding cabinet member, to help the film industry, recently rocked by scandal and a sensationalist image, regulate itself. The "Hays Office" checked scripts and circulated a list of "Don'ts and Be Carefuls" that warned against profanity, nudity, drugs, perversion, miscegenation, blasphemy, and violence.

The list was advisory only, and producers commonly disregarded it. The 1930 production code made the proscriptions more precise and looked to stricter enforcement. The industry was responding partly to the self-regulatory model of professional baseball under Commissioner Kenesaw Mountain Landis, partly to a wave of local censorship, and especially to a drive by Roman Catholics for higher moral standards in movies. A papal representative called American movies an "incalculable" source of evil. Denis Cardinal Dougherty enjoined Philadelphia's Catholics from seeing any films. Other American Catholic leaders organized the Legion of Decency, with authority to rate films for Catholic viewing.

In 1934 Breen, a friend of both Hays and Dougherty, became head of the Production Code Administration. His impact on American film making was enormous. He reduced the tide of Depression-era gangster movies, with their violence and disrespect for law and order. He eliminated the screen sexuality made famous by Jean Harlow and Mae West, and excised what he considered excessively "crude" or "suggestive" dialogue. He advised Louis B. Mayer, for example, to eliminate the word "floozy" from a picture, to avoid having the heroine kissed "savagely," and even not to allow her to apply perfume "behind her ears." In scripts dealing with crime or extramarital sex, the wrongdoer had to suffer in the end. Nudity was forbidden.

To a lesser extent Breen watched out for religioethnic stereotyping. Jews hardly appeared at all in American movies; Catholics invariably appeared in a favorable light. Blacks fared less well, although they could not be brutalized; Breen forbade brutality if not racism. The Production Code Administration also censored some political material, warning Samuel Gold-

wyn to be "less emphatic" in contrasting "the poor in tenements and the rich in apartment houses," and telling Jack Warner to delete "Robin Hood kicking the sheriff in the stomach." But the code's enforcers concerned themselves mainly with sex and obscenity. "I don't interpret the code," said Breen, "I make it."

Some of Breen's influence came from his city-bred capacity to match studio heads expletive for expletive and from the assertiveness of his young staff of fellow Catholics. All scripts had to receive a Breen "Purity Seal." Producers releasing a movie without the seal could be fined $25,000 and prevented from distributing it through studio-owned theater chains. The fine was inconsequential, but access to the theaters in that monopolistic era was crucial. By 1940 over 95 percent of American theaters showed only "seal" movies. Sometimes Breen could even persuade bankers to refuse to finance productions he deemed inappropriate. Most important, he worked closely with the Legion of Decency, whose ratings usually matched those of the Breen office.

Except for a stint as general manager of RKO Pictures in 1941–1942, Breen exercised authority in Hollywood for twenty years. Toward the end, however, his troubles mounted. Foreign films appeared that treated sex more candidly and played without the Purity Seal. Rebel Hollywood directors such as Howard Hughes and Otto Preminger refused to censor material from *The Outlaw* and *The Moon Is Blue,* and the films were box-office hits without the seal. Public opinion was growing more tolerant in sexual matters. Moreover, since the studios no longer controlled the theaters and thus had less direct influence over what was shown, they could not enforce the code as strictly as before. With the rise of television as the main form of American family entertainment, movie producers competed for a more "adult" audience by producing more "adult" films with more and more sex and violence.

Breen retired in 1954, ostensibly for reasons of health. Although he had called his a "controversial and thankless" job for which he was "too fat and too genial," he nonetheless received a special Oscar from the Motion Picture Academy in 1953. In retirement he devoted himself mainly to his family and, as a member of the Orders of St. Stephen and St. Gregory and a regent of Loyola University, to church affairs. He died in Hollywood, Calif.

Breen's influence on American movies may be variously assessed. Screenwriters found it stultifying. "I spent most of my time," said one, "pulling punches." Producers, although grateful for the seal, were irked by having to cover women's navels, make them not give a "darn," and change (as David Selznick had in *Gone with the Wind*) "Lawd" to "Lawsy."

Actually, Breen approved some films that included antilabor violence, bank villainy, and the "seamy side" of life. For Breen himself the record was clear. He freed the screen of its "whorehouse crap" so that "decent people could enjoy themselves in a theater without blushing."

[The obituaries in the *New York Times* and *Los Angeles Times*, Dec. 8, 1965, provide an overview of Breen's life and career. The best ongoing record of his activities is in the files of the trade paper *Variety*. For the indispensable inside view, see J. P. McEvoy, "The Back of Me Hand to You," *Saturday Evening Post*, Dec. 24, 1938; Raymond Moley, *The Hays Office* (1945); Murray Schumach, *The Face on the Cutting Room Floor* (1964); and especially Jack Vizzard, *See No Evil* (1970).]

                                    RONALD STORY

BREWSTER, RALPH OWEN (Feb. 22, 1888–Dec. 25, 1961), lawyer, governor of Maine, and U.S. senator, was born in Dexter, Maine, the son of William E. Brewster and Carrie S. Bridges. He graduated from Bowdoin College with the A.B. in 1909. After serving as a high school principal for one year, Brewster enrolled in Harvard Law School, where he earned money by waiting on tables and tutoring other students. He also found time to serve with future Ohio Senator Robert A. Taft on the editorial board of the *Harvard Law Review*.

After receiving the LL.B. from Harvard in 1913, Brewster began practicing law in Portland, Maine. On Apr. 20, 1915, he married Dorothy Foss; they had two sons. In Portland he soon entered Republican party politics, winning election to the lower house of the Maine legislature in 1916. Two years later he resigned to enter the army. When the armistice was signed, Brewster was in the officers' candidate school at Camp Zachary Taylor, Ky. He was reelected to the Maine House of Representatives that year, and in 1922 he was elected to the Maine Senate. As a member of the legislature he introduced resolutions for two amendments to the state constitution—to permit absentee voting and to limit the total municipal representation in the state house of representatives—that were later ratified. He also wrote the city charter that Portland adopted in 1923.

Brewster was elected governor of Maine in 1924 and 1926. As governor he set up the Maine Development Commission to attract tourism and industry and introduced a pay-as-you-go program for the state. In 1925 he helped found the New England Council for regional development and cooperation.

After his second term as governor, Brewster returned to private law practice. Over the next few years he suffered successive political setbacks. Twice he was defeated for the Republican nomination as candidate for the United States Senate. He then moved from Portland to Dexter, hoping to win a seat in Congress from Maine's Third District. In 1932 he lost a close congressional election to Democrat John G. Utterback, but in 1934 he defeated Utterback, partly because of his support for the Townsend Pension Plan, which was popular in Maine.

Brewster's three terms in the House and his later career in the Senate were stormy. He opposed most of Franklin D. Roosevelt's New Deal, particularly the Supreme Court "packing" plan and the bill to abolish public-utility holding companies. The latter bill embroiled him in a controversy with Thomas G. Corcoran, one of the president's advisers. Brewster accused Corcoran of threatening to stop construction on the Passamaquoddy Bay tidal power project in Maine unless Brewster voted for the "death sentence clause" of the public-utility holding company act. Corcoran vigorously denied the charges. Subsequently the "Quoddy" project was abandoned.

In 1940, after winning a bitter fight for the Republican senatorial nomination over Governor Lewis O. Barrows, Brewster defeated his Democratic opponent, former Governor Louis J. Brann. He became a member of the Senate Naval Affairs Committee, and after American entry into World War II, he was named to the War Investigating Committee, headed by Harry Truman. He was one of five committee members who made a world tour in 1943 to study military installations and lend-lease administration. Despite partisan differences, Brewster and Truman became close friends.

Brewster also served on the Joint Congressional Committee of Inquiry formed in 1946 to investigate the attack on Pearl Harbor. The majority report placed the blame for this disaster solely on the military in Hawaii and Washington. Brewster and Republican Senator Homer Ferguson of Michigan contended in a minority report that the president shared responsibility with the military for American unpreparedness.

In August 1947, Brewster, as chairman of the Senate War Investigating Committee, launched a subcommittee investigation into the $40 million in contracts awarded to the Hughes Aircraft Company during the war. Howard Hughes charged that Brewster had attempted to "blackmail" him into merging his Trans World Airlines with Pan American Airways by offering to quash the inquiry. In an unprecedented move, Brewster appeared as a witness before his own committee and denied the accusation under oath. The inquiry eventually came to nothing.

In 1952, Brewster testified before the House Ways and Means Committee concerning a $10,000 check he had given in 1950 to Henry W. Grunewald, a one-time Washington influence peddler. Denying any wrongdoing, he testified that the money was designated for the primary campaigns of Senator Milton R. Young of North Dakota and Richard M. Nixon of California. (Nixon was running for the Senate for the first time.) As chairman of the Republican Senate Campaign Committee, Brewster stated, he could not openly contribute, so he had used Grunewald as a "conduit" to transfer the money to the two candidates as a loan.

Brewster became a member of the Senate Foreign Relations Committee in 1951. The following year, in his bid for reelection, he lost the primary to Governor Frederick G. Payne in a campaign focusing on a liquor scandal in which both candidates were accused of graft. Both denied the charges.

In retirement Brewster played an active role in Americans for Constitutional Action, a conservative organization. A Christian Scientist, he was president of the First Church of Christ, Scientist, in Boston in 1932–1933. He died in Brookline, Mass.

[There is no collection of Brewster's personal papers available to researchers. For his early career, see *Lewiston Journal*, Feb. 18, 1928. Magazines mentioning him include *Newsweek*, Mar. 31, 1952; *Time*, Mar. 31, 1952; and *New Republic*, June 30, 1952. Bowdoin College Library has a copy of President James S. Cole's address given at the Bowdoin memorial service for Brewster on Jan. 3, 1962. For Brewster's activities in the McCarthy era, see Robert Griffith, *The Politics of Fear* (1970), and Fred J. Cook, *The Nightmare Decade* (1971). There are a few references to Brewster in Allen Drury, *A Senate Journal* (1963). An obituary is in the *New York Times*, Dec. 26, 1961.]

MELBA PORTER HAY

BRIDGES, (HENRY) STYLES (Sept. 9, 1898–Nov. 26, 1961), governor of New Hampshire and U.S. senator, was born in West Pembroke, Maine, the son of Earl Leopold Bridges, a farmer, and Alina Roxana Fisher. His father

died when Bridges was nine, and his mother, to provide for her young family, taught in the local school. Bridges assumed responsibility for the family farm and continued his schooling. He graduated from Pembroke High School in 1914 and from the University of Maine, where he majored in agriculture, in 1918.

After graduation Bridges became an agriculture instructor at Sanderson Academy in Ashfield, Mass. He returned to Maine as Hancock County agricultural agent in 1920 and the next year moved to the University of New Hampshire as a member of the agricultural extension staff. He became executive secretary of the New Hampshire Farm Bureau Federation in 1922. From 1924 to 1926 he edited *Granite Monthly*, and from 1924 until 1929 he also served as director and secretary of the New Hampshire Investment Company.

Bridges entered politics in 1930, when Republican Governor Charles W. Tobey appointed him to the New Hampshire Public Service Commission. In 1934, Bridges was elected governor, at thirty-six the youngest chief executive in the history of New Hampshire and the youngest in the nation at the time. During his two years in office, Bridges balanced the state budget, initiated a new agricultural standards act, and sponsored state unemployment compensation and old age benefits. Under his leadership, New Hampshire became the first state to qualify for the new federal Social Security Act.

After a bitter Republican primary campaign against former Senator George H. Moses, Bridges was elected to the United States Senate in 1936. He represented New Hampshire in the Senate until his death—easily winning reelections in 1942, 1948, 1954, and 1960. Known as the Gray Eminence of the Republican Party, he was sometimes referred to as an authentic American Tory. He used his influence in the party in an attempt to preserve it as he had known it earlier—before, in his terms, it became dominated by "liberals, moderates and moderns."

Bridges wanted everyone to recognize his conservatism. He even stopped using his first name, it was said, when the left-leaning West Coast union leader Harry Bridges became a controversial figure in the late 1930's. He wanted no public confusion about which Bridges was which.

In the Senate, Bridges served on the Appropriations and Military Affairs committees, and in 1945 was appointed to the Foreign Relations Committee. During the long years of Democratic control of the Congress, he consistently criticized Democratic acts and admi nis'tration policies. In 1937 he denounced President Franklin D. Roosevelt's Supreme Court reorganization plan and voted against all the later New Deal measures. After the out' break of war in Europe in 1939, he supported efforts to extend aid to victims of Nazi aggres sion. He supported Wendell Willkie for pres ident in 1940, particularly backing his refusal t o take an isolationist position. Yet Bridges can not be classified as either an interventionist or an internationalist. In the postwar period he did not support bipartisanship in foreign poli cy.

Bridges was strongly ant i-Communist. He railed against postwar contin uation of lend-lease to Russia, and in March 195 0 he attacked Secretary of State Dean Ache son's defense of Alger Hiss. He also was a leading supporter of General Douglas MacArthur at t he congressional hearings after President Har ry S. Truman dismissed the general in 1951. In 1955, when the Yalta papers were released to the public, Bridges called the agreements "one of the sad lessons of history." He oppose d President Dwight D. Eisenhower's willingn ess to negotiate with the Soviet Union and Co mmunist China. Toward the end of Senator Jos eph McCarthy's vitriolic anti-Communist care er, Bridges led a move to save his colleague fr om a Senate censure vote. He claimed partial victory when the word "censure" was drop ped from the Senate action condemning the Wisconsin Republican.

His strong stand against Communism was in part related to his fiscal conservatism. In the Republican -controlled Eightieth Congress, Bridges be came chairman of the Appropriations Committ ee (1947). He immediately pressed for a $6 bill ion cut in the budget, with a hefty part of the reduction to be in foreign aid. After Eisenho wer was elected in 1952, Bridges again head ed the Appropriations Committee. This tim e he found an ally in the White House who sup ported his attempt to balance the budget. As p art of this effort he again opposed extensive f oreign aid, particularly to Communist countries. For example, he denounced a $75 million item that would provide surplus commodities and loans for farm machinery to Poland. He also attempted to restrict aid to Yugoslavia.

Consistency marked Bridges's Senate career. Anti-New Deal, anti-Communist, and fiscal and political conservative are labels that fit him throughout his tenure. Elected to a fifth term in 1960, he had seniority that made him a potentially powerful figure in the Eighty-seventh Congress (he had already served as Republican floor leader in 1952–1953 and had been president pro tem in 1953–1955). He died at Concord, N.H.

Bridges had married early but that marriage, a well-kept secret, ended in divorce. In 1928 he married Sally Clement; they had three sons. Sally Bridges died in 1938, and in 1944 Bridges married Doloris Thauwald.

[Bridges's papers are at New England College, Henniker, N.H. Little has been written about Bridges, and no scholarly study has appeared. But see Stephen Horn, *Unused Power: The Work of the Senate Committee on Appropriations* (1970). An obituary is in the *New York Times,* Nov. 27, 1961.]

GEORGE T. MAZUZAN

BRIDGMAN, PERCY WILLIAMS (Apr. 21, 1882–Aug. 20, 1961), physicist and philosopher of science, was born in Cambridge, Mass., the son of Raymond Landon Bridgman, a journalist and author, and of Mary Ann Maria Williams. After attending public schools in Newton, Mass., he enrolled at Harvard College in 1900, beginning a lifelong affiliation with that institution. He studied physics, chemistry, and mathematics and graduated in 1904 with a B.A. Continuing at Harvard as a graduate student in physics, Bridgman obtained the M.A. in 1905 and the Ph.D. in 1908. After two years as a research fellow in the Department of Physics, he was appointed instructor in 1910. This was followed by promotion to assistant professor in 1913, professor in 1919, and Hollis professor of mathematics and natural philosophy in 1926. He married Olive Ware on July 16, 1912; they had two children.

It was during his early decades on the staff at Harvard, from about 1910 to 1930, that Bridgman took his biggest steps in physics and philosophy of science. He gained prominence in physics through experimental investigations of high-pressure phenomena. His advances in this field grew out of design changes he introduced into laboratory apparatus. While attempting to improve methods of measuring high pressures, he devised a new type of pressure seal or "packing" that became more leakproof with increasing pressure. This self-sealing packing, when used with such other innovations as an accurate pressure gauge (a manganin wire device) and an efficient compressor (a hydraulic press), enabled Bridgman to subject test materials to pressures reaching 20,000 atmospheres. (Previous experimenters were limited to pressures of about 3,000 atmospheres.) Bridgman thus was able to break new ground in the study of the mechanical, electrical, and thermal properties of materials under high pressures.

He proceeded to expose an increasingly broad range of materials to an increasingly high range of pressures. This research program involved the investigation of such specific properties as compressibility, electrical resistance, elasticity, fracturing, melting, thermoelectricity, and thermal conductivity. His research on high-pressure transitions in the physical makeup of minerals (polymorphism) had special relevance to geologists. During World War I, Bridgman developed a high-pressure process for prestraining one-piece gun barrels. (This was in addition to his wartime research at New London, Conn., on submarine sound-detection systems.) In 1931 he summarized his findings of the prior two decades and pointed the way to future research with the publication of his definitive text, *The Physics of High Pressure.*

It was also between 1910 and 1930 that Bridgman began delving into the philosophy of science and evolved his influential "operational" perspective on science, particularly physics. He began to consider the logical foundations of physics in 1914 when he was unexpectedly required to teach advanced courses on modern electrodynamic theory, a field in conceptual disarray. His thoughts on the foundations of physics continued to develop when around 1920 he clarified the principles of dimensional analysis—a shortcut method of discerning the functional relations between measurable quantities. Finally, in 1926, during a sabbatical, he formulated the seminal statement of his operational philosophy, published the following year as *The Logic of Modern Physics.*

Implicitly drawing on an often tacit tradition of empiricism and positivism in science, as well as on his personal laboratory experiences, Bridgman sought in *The Logic* to reevaluate the entire conceptual structure of physics and to bring understanding especially to the new and confusing fields of relativity and quantum theory. At the heart of this reevaluation was his insistence that all physical and mental concepts be definable in terms of actual, explicit operations. "In general," he wrote, "we mean by any concept nothing more than a set of operations; *the concept is synonymous with the corresponding set of operations.*" This operational attitude was intended, above all, to eradicate meaningless concepts that might be inhibiting the growth of science. Bridgman's central example of the operational attitude at work was what he perceived to be Albert Einstein's revolutionary critique of Isaac Newton's empirically vacuous notions of absolute space and time.

In 1931, Bridgman moved from his old research quarters in the basement of the Jefferson Physical Laboratory to modern facilities in the new Lyman Laboratory of Physics. This move coincided with the beginning of a thirty-year period of elaborating his earlier achievements in both high-pressure physics and operational philosophy. Continuing to work with only modest equipment and two technical assistants, he extended his experiments to higher and higher pressures, at first 30,000 and eventually to about 400,000 atmospheres.

In 1939, prior to the onset of World War II, Bridgman caused a stir by announcing that he would henceforth withhold his research findings from scientists of any totalitarian state. During the war he again used his expertise with high pressures to solve military problems, examining both the design of armor plate and the compressibility of uranium and plutonium. In recognition of his contributions to the science of high pressures, he received the 1946 Nobel Prize for physics.

Bridgman also elaborated his operational philosophy during these later decades. Through a number of books, articles, and lectures, he refined his analyses of specific areas of physics, such as thermodynamics. In addition he extended his operational critique from the physical domain to include social, political, psychological, religious, and philosophical issues. *The Intelligent Individual and Society* (1938) marked his first comprehensive attempt to bring "operational meaning" to such "fuzzy" concepts as "duty," "freedom," and "right." Bridgman's work led to an increased interaction with philosophers and psychologists—a sometimes quarrelsome interaction that caused him further to sharpen and reappraise his operational outlook.

In 1950, Bridgman was named Higgins university professor at Harvard. He retired four years later. Suffering from incurable and increasingly debilitating cancer, he chose, while at his summer home in Randolph, N.H., to end his life.

[Although Bridgman reportedly destroyed part of his correspondence before he died, about thirty linear feet of his unpublished papers have survived and are shelved at the University Archives, Harvard University Library. The collection includes professional correspondence, research notebooks, lecture notes, and materials from the memorial meeting at Harvard for Bridgman in October 1961. The Smithsonian Institution and the Harvard Collection of Historical Scientific Instruments have apparatus and specimens from his laboratory. Bridgman's published writings include thirteen books and about 260 papers, most of which are listed in the bibliography of Edwin C. Kemble and Francis Birch, "Percy Williams Bridgman," *Biographical Memoirs, National Academy of Sciences* (1970). Most of his technical papers are reprinted in his *Collected Experimental Papers*, 7 vols. (1964). Most of his nontechnical writings are in his *Reflections of a Physicist* (1950; 2nd ed., 1955). An overview of Bridgman's career appears in Edwin C. Kemble, Francis Birch, and Gerald Holton, "Bridgman, Percy Williams," *Dictionary of Scientific Biography* (1970). An obituary is in the *New York Times,* Aug. 21, 1961.]

ALBERT E. MOYER

BRIGGS, LYMAN JAMES (May 7, 1874– Mar. 25, 1963,), physicist, was born in Assyria, Mich., the son of Chauncey Lewis Briggs, a farmer, and Isabella McKelvey. He received his early education at the Briggs District School, so named because it stood on land donated by his father. From there he went directly to State Agricultural College (now Michigan State University) in East Lansing, where he received the B.S. in 1893. He earned the M.S. at the University of Michigan in 1895 and the Ph.D. at Johns Hopkins University in 1901. Briggs married Katharine Elizabeth Cook, a fellow graduate of State Agricultural College, on Dec. 23, 1896. They had two children.

In 1896, Briggs joined the staff of the U.S. Department of Agriculture, the start of nearly fifty years in government service. During his time at the department, he established the science of soil physics. His research dealt particularly with the effect of climate on the quantity of water required for a crop, the relative water retentivity of soil, and the lower limit of water in soil available to plants. In 1906 he organized the biophysical laboratory in the Bureau of Plant Industry, where he carried out basic studies of environmental factors in water requirements of plants. Working at the Department of Agriculture until 1920, Briggs made important contributions in the application of physics to agriculture.

In 1917 he was assigned to the National Bureau of Standards for research on a stable zenith instrument for the U.S. Navy. Three years later he became chief of the Mechanics and Sound Division. Here he and Paul Heyl invented the earth inductor compass, an instrument that solved perplexing navigational problems. For this invention the American Philosophical Society awarded them the Magellan Medal in 1922.

At Mechanics and Sound, Briggs gave special attention to research in air flow. Working with Hugh L. Dryden, he made pioneer measurements of flow around airfoils at speeds up to and beyond that of sound. His findings were applied in the designing of the blade form of airplane propellers.

Briggs's interest in the problems of designing apparatus resulted in the creation of specialized equipment at the National Bureau of Standards, including a machine for floating specimens to be tested for metal fatigue on a layer of compressed air and another for measuring forces exerted on an elastic ball when it is struck. He also planned and designed the instruments carried on two stratospheric balloon flights sponsored by the National Geographic Society and the U.S. Army Air Corps in 1934 and 1935.

In 1932, Briggs was nominated director of the National Bureau of Standards by President Herbert Hoover, but the administration changed before the Senate took action. President Franklin Roosevelt repeated the nomination, explaining, "I haven't the slightest idea whether Dr. Briggs is a Republican or a Democrat; all I know is that he is the best qualified man for the job." Briggs served as director until his retirement in 1945. He was also active in professional organizations, serving as president of the American Physical Society in 1938.

In October 1939, Roosevelt asked Briggs to organize and chair the first government committee to investigate possible military use of atomic energy. This secret advisory committee on uranium reported the possibility of producing an atomic bomb. In 1940 the group became a subcommittee of the National Defense Research Committee. Late in 1941, Briggs's subcommittee was made part of the Office of Scientific Research and Development. In 1948, President Harry Truman awarded Briggs the Medal of Merit for his work relating to atomic fission.

Briggs's scientific interests were far-reaching. From 1933, when he joined the board of trustees of the National Geographic Society, he was involved in diverse projects of the society. As chairman of its research committee (1934–1960), he helped to formulate plans for expeditions in many parts of the world. He was active in directing National Geographic Society studies of solar eclipses, including an expedition to Siberia in 1936 and two to Brazil in 1940 and 1947. During the 1947 field trip Briggs measured temperature changes of air near the surface of the earth at the time of eclipse. Cosmic-ray research, a continuing project of the society, was also one of his interests.

Briggs was due to retire from the Bureau of Standards during World War II but was asked to remain at his post until the end of the war. After retirement he retained a laboratory and continued research until his death in Washington, D.C. Briggs published more than sixty articles in scientific, government, and popular publications. In tribute to his accomplishments, the May 1954 issue of *Scientific Monthly* was devoted to his work as an eightieth-birthday present.

[Briggs's principal publications from 1900 to 1953 are listed in Wallace R. Brode, "Lyman J. Briggs: Recognition of His Eightieth Birthday, May 7, 1954," *Scientific Monthly*, May 1954. Later articles include "Gallium: Thermal Conductivity; Supercooling; Negative Pressure," *Science*, Apr. 20, 1956; and "When Mt. Mazama Lost Its Top," *National Geographic*, July 1962. See also *Scientific American*, July 1933; Gilbert Grosvenor, "Earth, Sea, and Sky: Twenty Years of Exploration by the National Geographic Society," *Scientific Monthly*, May 1954; L. A. Richards, "The Measurement of Soil Water in Relation to Plant Requirements," ibid., and "Perfect Curve," *Scientific American*, May 1959. An obituary is in the *New York Times*, Mar. 27, 1963.]

ADELE HAST

BROKENSHIRE, NORMAN ERNEST (June 10, 1898–May 4, 1965), radio announcer, commentator, and newspaper editor, was born in Murcheson, Ontario, Canada, the son of William Henry Brokenshire, an itinerant minister, and Georgina Jones, a daughter of a missionary. The father served Presbyterian, Congregational, and Methodist churches in remote areas of Canada and in the eastern United States. The family moved from town to town, never spending more than a few years in one place. After the family established a semipermanent residence in Cambridge, Mass., Brokenshire graduated from a Boston high school in 1915. He held various odd jobs until 1918, when he served in the U. S. Army.

Brokenshire's parents had hoped that he would become a minister. For a short time after the war he worked for the Near East Relief campaign and then became a secretary for the Young Men's Christian Association in Fort Totten, Queens, N.Y. He attended Syracuse University on a scholarship, receiving an A.B. in 1924 and an A.M. in 1925. He visited New York City in 1924 and worked as an announcer for radio station WJZ, inaugurating a career that lasted for about forty years. He became one of radio's first personalities because of his keen ad-lib skills and his rolling, resonant, and deliberate voice, a voice that fitted well with his appearance; he was stocky and about six feet tall. Brokenshire was one of the first announcers to use his full name instead of initials on the air, and he fashioned a verbal trademark ("How do you do, ladies and gentlemen, how *do* you *do!*") that set him apart in the highly competitive field of radio announcing.

Brokenshire broadcast many of the major news events of the 1920's, including the 1924 Democratic National Convention in Madison Square Garden, the inauguration of President Calvin Coolidge in 1925 (as well as all presidential inaugurals for the next three decades), the funeral of William Jennings Bryan, and the New York City reception for Charles A. Lindbergh. He did the first broadcast of the Miss America beauty contest, and in 1929 he interviewed Hugo Eckener, commander of the German dirigible *Graf Zeppelin*, on its second visit to New York.

Brokenshire left radio briefly in 1926 and invested his savings in an amusement park. When that failed, he was hired by Atlantic City to promote its attractions. *Time* called him "the highest paid press agent in America." In 1928 he joined the staff of WCAU in Philadelphia. On Dec. 12, 1928, he married Eunice S. Schmidt. They had no children.

In the 1930's Brokenshire's career turned from news to entertainment, and he became the announcer for several highly popular radio programs, including "The Chesterfield Hour," "Eddie Cantor's Radio Follies," "Major Bowes' Original Amateur Hour," "The Good Gulf Show," and "The Children's Hour." Brokenshire developed a style of announcing that propelled him into the spotlight, and he often received more fan mail than the stars of the programs. In 1932 he was voted "King of the Announcers" in a *New York Mirror* contest, topping a field that included Graham McNamee and Jimmy Wallington. His salary was unofficially reported as $60,000 to $100,000 a year, making him one of radio's highest-paid personalities.

Within a few years drinking became a problem, and his career plummeted. He lost his job and then applied for a job as a day laborer with the Works Progress Administration. Brokenshire maintained, in later years, that his departure from radio was the result of a nervous breakdown. By the 1940's he had joined Alcoholics Anonymous and his career took an upward turn. He did commentaries for films and narrations for documentaries, and his return to prominence was cheered by colleagues in the industry, critics, and loyal fans. In 1945 he was the announcer for "Theatre Guild on the Air," also known as the "United States Steel Hour," and in 1947 he hosted WNBC's popular "Take It Easy Time." During his comeback he also was the announcer for the CBS program "Hollywood Star Playhouse," and reportedly his salary was in the five- to six-figure range.

In the 1950's Brokenshire left big-time radio but continued to host programs on stations on Long Island, including "The Brokenshire Show" on WKIT in Garden City after 1957. From 1958 to 1961 Brokenshire was the editor of the *Port Jefferson Record*, a Long Island weekly newspaper, and in his last years he worked part-time announcing for several stations near Hauppauge, N.Y., where he lived. He died in Smithtown, N.Y.

Brokenshire's career was a Horatio Alger story several times over. Called "the pioneer radio announcer," he was a dean of American announcers whose highly successful style set standards for those who followed him.

[On Brokenshire and his career, see his *This Is Norman Brokenshire* (1954); Erik Barnouw, *A History of Broadcasting in the United States*, I (1966); and obituaries in the *New York Times* and the *New York Herald Tribune*, both May 5, 1965. For information on Brokenshire's popular radio programs, see Frank Buxton and Bill Owen, *The Big Broadcast* (1972).]

JOSEPH P. McKERNS

BROOKS, OVERTON (Dec. 21, 1897–Sept. 16, 1961), congressman, was born in East Baton Rouge Parish, La., the son of Claude M. Brooks and Penelope Overton. He graduated from the parish high school and in 1918 enlisted in the Sixth Field Artillery of the First Regular Army Division. After only a month's basic training he was sent overseas as a private. In France he won two battle stars and promotion to sergeant. Brooks entered Louisiana State University law school in 1919 and received the LL.B. degree in 1923. He then passed the bar examination and entered practice in Shreveport, La. For a decade beginning in 1925, Brooks served as United States commissioner in Louisiana. On June 1, 1933, he married Mollie Meriwether; they had one daughter.

An admirer of Senator Huey P. Long, Brooks entered the 1936 Democratic primary for the Fourth Louisiana Congressional District seat formerly occupied by John N. Sandlin, who sought to fill the Senate seat left vacant by Long's assassination in 1935. He served in Congress for twenty-six years. His first assignment was to the House Military Affairs Committee (later the Armed Services Committee), on which he served for the rest of his life.

Brooks was ambivalent with regard to American neutrality before the nation's entry into World War II. He maintained in October 1939 that Americans should not travel on belligerent ships, yet a month later he voted against the continuance of the embargo on the shipment of arms on American vessels. He also supported the lend-lease bill (1941).

Brooks's voting record was decidedly antilabor. In 1940 he favored drastic amendments to the National Labor Relations Act. He voted for the Smith antistrike bill in 1941 and to override President Franklin D. Roosevelt's veto of a modified Smith bill in 1943. In 1947 he voted to override President Harry S. Truman's veto of the Taft-Hartley Act and in 1952 voted in favor of invoking that act to halt the steel strike. In 1950 he opposed the voluntary fair employment practices bill.

Brooks was best known for his interest in military reserve affairs and was dubbed "Mr. Reserve" by Carl Vinson, chairman of the House Armed Services Committee. After a visit to France in 1944, Brooks declared that Congress must soon take up the question of training reserves for postwar police duty. He supported compulsory military training and in 1946 introduced a universal military training bill that failed but was reintroduced in 1947 after President Truman advocated a similar plan. Always a friend of the military, Brooks persuaded the House in 1950 to remove limitations on Defense Department expenditures for the construction of armories and training facilities for the National Guard and the army reserve. In 1951 he introduced a bill creating within each of the services the categories of "ready, standby, and retired reserve," subject to recall to duty in that order. The following year he urged retroactive extra combat pay for ground troops in Korea.

In 1955 Brooks chaired an armed services subcommittee that studied and approved an administration bill to provide a military reserve of 2.9 million men by 1960, manned partly by volunteers and partly by draftees.

The question of the reserves arose again in 1957, when Secretary of Defense Charles E. Wilson charged that the National Guard had been a "haven for draft dodgers" during the Korean War and the army announced that beginning on April 1 of that year, persons joining the National Guard would be required to undergo the six-month training required of the army reserve recruits. The guard contended that compulsory six-month basic training would reduce enlistments and argued for an eleven-week summer training program instead. Brooks personally negotiated a compromise. The army agreed to postpone its mandatory six-month training order until Jan. 1, 1958, for National Guard recruits aged seventeen to eighteen and a half. This allowed the guard to recruit men under eighteen and a half for eleven weeks of summer training.

Brooks chaired the House Committee on Science and Astronautics from its formation in 1959 and became one of the leading proponents of an enlarged space program and a manned space satellite. He voted for the tidelands oil bills of 1948 and 1951. In 1956 he supported the upper Colorado River development project and urged federal appropriations for rainmaking experiments and the conversion of seawater to fresh water. From 1954 until his death, Brooks was president of the National Rivers and Harbors Congress, composed of federal, state, and local leaders devoted to the development of the nation's water resources.

Following the death of his uncle, Senator John Holmes Overton, in 1948, Brooks briefly became a candidate to complete the unexpired term. He withdrew when Russell Long announced his interest in the position.

A staunch advocate of federal assistance to farmers, Brooks suggested, after a 1947 visit to Europe, that the United States "lend" cotton and wool to European nations for the rehabilitation of their textile industries. In 1956 he was the only House Democrat to support a Republican-sponsored amendment to the omnibus farm bill that allowed prepayment to farmers in connection with the proposed soil bank.

Brooks was a typical southern conservative in his voting as well as in his dress and demeanor. He rarely spoke on the floor of Congress. His manner was quiet and sincere, and he impressed observers with his industry and knowledge of his specialty areas. He died at Bethesda, Md.

[Brooks's papers are at Louisiana State University, Baton Rouge. A profile is in *New York Times*, Feb. 27, 1957. His congressional activities can be found in the *Congressional Record*. An obituary is in the *New York Times*, Sept. 17, 1961.]

STEPHEN D. BODAYLA

BROOKS, VAN WYCK (Feb. 16, 1886–May 2, 1963), critic, biographer, and literary historian, was born in Plainfield, N.J., the son of Charles Edward Brooks, a stockbroker, and Sarah Bailey Ames. He was conservatively reared in that New York City suburb of "not fewer than 100 millionaires." At age twelve Brooks spent a year abroad, mainly in Germany,

France, and England, on a journey portentous in that Europe was thereafter to preoccupy him. He was torn between the impulse to expatriate and a determined will to conduct an American life in art and letters.

Brooks entered Harvard in 1903. In his sophomore year he and John Hall Wheelock assembled their apprentice poetry in a privately printed volume, *Verses by Two Undergraduates* (1905). Completing his studies for the A.B. a year early, in 1907 Brooks went abroad, chiefly to England, for a period of eighteen months. During that time he wrote his first study of America as a civilization, *The Wine of the Puritans* (1908). He supported himself in England by free-lance journalism, and on his return to New York he did hack chores for the *Standard Dictionary* and *Collier's Encyclopedia*. This led to a post as editorial assistant on *The World's Work* under Walter Hines Page. In addition he wrote and had privately printed *The Soul: An Essay Towards a Point of View* (1910).

Brooks was appointed instructor of English at Stanford University in 1911. On Apr. 26, 1911, he married Eleanor Kenyon Stimson, daughter of the artist John Ward Stimson. They had two sons. In 1913, having in manuscript books on Mark Twain and Henry James, he left Stanford to again settle in England. He taught as an extension lecturer of the University of London for the Workers' Educational Association, wrote his landmark book *America's Coming-of-Age*, and published *The Malady of the Ideal* (1913). He also completed two biographies, *John Addington Symonds* (1914) and *The World of H. G. Wells* (1915).

Three months after the outbreak of World War I Brooks returned to New York and once again took up diverse literary labors, particularly the translation of French texts. After publication of *America's Coming-of-Age* in 1915 he became celebrated as the most audacious and articulate member of the Young Generation, a group of literary radicals chiefly associated with the short-lived journal *Seven Arts*. In that journal and elsewhere, Brooks attacked elder critics of lofty status but of old-fashioned and unenlightened taste. (One of these, William C. Brownell, an adviser to Scribners, had rejected *America's Coming-of-Age* because, as Edmund Wilson wrote many years later, "it was still 'too early' to call attention to the weakness of our supposed classics.") Introducing the terms "highbrow" and "lowbrow" into American literary and social discourse, Brooks railed against his countrymen for attempting to conduct a society in which the life of art and imagination is divorced from the practical conduct of affairs. A society so misled, he contended, so consumed by acquisitiveness that it holds all other energies and values in contempt, cannot conceivably fulfill, but must in the end destroy, the promise of American life.

Famed among resurgent writers as their most eloquent advocate, as a partisan and fractious critic of wide learning, hard to rebut, Brooks next published *Letters and Leadership* (1918), a collection of papers written mainly for *Seven Arts,* and an edition of Randolph Bourne's *The History of a Literary Radical* (1920).

As a regular contributor to, and literary editor of, the *Freeman* from 1920 to 1924, Brooks—now settled in Westport, Conn.—was in the vanguard of American literary men and women of the 1920's. Although in the long run he found the role awkward to maintain and discomfiting, it seemed at the time well-suited to his disputatious nature. In 1920 he published *The Ordeal of Mark Twain,* which both consolidated and undermined his reputation as a man of letters gifted with responsible judgment and a venturesome mind. In this unprecedented work, groundbreaking in its use of psychoanalytic and other kinds of psychiatric opinion, Brooks indicted Twain for acquiescing in a national style of betrayal. Victim of the genteel tradition in nineteenth-century American writing, Twain was presented as a case study of a failed artist, an American writer compromised by rewards and riches won for submission to philistine rule.

Recognized in its day as criticism of the first order of interest despite its thesis and the author's bias, it remains a major text for students both of Twain's temperament and Brooks's sensibility. Although unquestionably flawed and vulnerable on many grounds, this pioneer effort in psychobiography is a seminal document. It also became a main source of embarrassment to the author. Bernard De Voto's *Mark Twain's America* (1932), a fierce and ill-natured defense of the American West and of Mark Twain as a frontier humorist, attacked Brooks's interpretation with devastating force. Brooks then published a revised 1933 edition in which he modified his argument. Eventually he repudiated central aspects of his thesis.

The *Dial* Award for 1923—as well as an offer to edit that distinguished and powerful magazine—and the publication of *The Pilgrimage of Henry James* (1925) concluded the first major period of Brooks's work. In 1925 he experienced an emotional breakdown from which he did not recover until 1931. Unable to work *(Emerson and Others,* 1927, came from a backlog that included papers written for the *Freeman),* Brooks was hospitalized in institutions in the United States and Great Britain. A main element of his illness was intense anxiety about money. After family arrangements brought relief—and when Lewis Mumford and Maxwell Perkins got into print his stalled manuscript, *The Life of Emerson* (1932)—Brooks emerged from his "season in hell." He prepared *Sketches in Criticism* (1932) and edited *The Journal of Gamaliel Bradford* (1933). *Three Essays on America* (1934) came next.

But it was *The Flowering of New England, 1815–1865* (1936), first of five volumes collectively called *Makers and Finders,* a major venture in American literary and intellectual history, on which his second career was founded. The first half of Brooks's life was spent in demonstrating the ulcerous effects of America on the creative spirit; the second half in maintaining that "America," the word in its root meaning, signified the very spirit of health. Renewing his search for what he now called a "usable" past in national life and letters, during the 1930's and 1940's, he discovered what he had earlier despaired of finding. This was an American "collective literary mind" that "fertilizes the living mind and gives it the sense of a base on which to live." Revived, this "special kind of memory" enables society to recover and preserve and revere its "dream of Utopia."

Beginning with his receipt of the Pulitzer Prize for history in 1937, Brooks acquired unrivaled favor with that large general audience to which the remaining volumes—*New England: Indian Summer, 1865–1915* (1940), *The World of Washington Irving* (1944), *The Times of Melville and Whitman* (1947), and *The Confident Years: 1885–1915* (1952)—were in part addressed. Mumford observed that the public's "undiscriminating praise" contrasted with his former colleagues' "undiscriminating blame," especially in regard to Brooks's *Opinions of Oliver Allston* (1941), which flaunted an attack on modernism. As a member of the League of American writers and of the American Academy of Arts and Letters, Brooks became a forceful figure in the literary establishment. Although politically a socialist, Brooks found himself engaged in a battle of the books with writers of the Left. He was a traditionalist and antimodernist in literary matters. Dwight Macdonald and others associated with the *Partisan Review* passionately resented, as Daniel Aaron later wrote, "what they considered his parochialism and his celebration of books and writers and literary tendencies he had once condemned." They attacked him for having embraced a nationalism so coarse-grained that it was barely distinct from the totalitarianism it was supposed to repel.

Despite Brooks's serious decline of standing among literary intellectuals in the postwar era, he held to his course. Following his wife's death in 1946, he married Gladys Rice Billings in 1948. On completing *Makers and Finders* he wrote *John Sloan* (1955); *Helen Keller* (1956); *Howells: His Life and World* (1959); *A Chilmark Miscellany* (1948); *The Writer in America* (1953); *From a Writer's Notebook* (1958); *Fenollosa and His Circle* (1962); *Scenes and Portraits* (1954); *Days of the Phoenix* (1957); *From the Shadow of the Mountain* (1961); *The Dream of Arcadia* (1958); and many commissioned articles. His eclipse of fame by the late 1950's was in part compensated for by his private life. He retained old ties and affections and never lost what Wheelock called the look of "austere concentration and intelligence." Brooks died in Bridgewater, Conn.

Although it is no longer possible to endorse the claim that Brooks ranks with the critics Edgar Allan Poe, T. S. Eliot, and Edmund Wilson, he belongs nonetheless in the company of all those American writers who hoped to negotiate an uncharted wilderness. In his own tormented person he exemplifies the exquisite power and fragility of a purely literary mind and remains a sovereign figure in any inquiry into the creative life of his age.

[The Van Wyck Brooks papers are held at the University of Pennsylvania library. Other significant holdings are in private hands or in various university collections, particularly Harvard's. Van Wyck Brooks's autobiography appeared as *An Autobiography* (1965). Aside from Robert E. Spiller, ed., *The Van Wyck Brooks–Lewis Mumford Letters* (1970), only small segments of his correspondence have appeared in print. See also Dwight Macdonald, "Kulturbolshewismus and Mr. Van Wyck Brooks," *Partisan Review* (Nov.–Dec. 1941); the *New York Times* obituary, May 3, 1963; Susan J. Turner, *A History of The Freeman* (1963); William Wasserstrom, *The Time of The Dial* (1963); Newton Arvin, *American Pantheon* (1966), edited by Daniel Aaron and Sylvan Schendler; Gladys Brooks, *If Strangers Meet* (1967); Edmund Wilson, *New Yorker*, May 31, 1969; James R. Vitelli, *Van Wyck Brooks* (1969); William Wasserstrom, *The Legacy of Van Wyck Brooks* (1971); James Hoopes, *Van Wyck Brooks* (1977); and William Wasserstrom, *Van Wyck Brooks* (1979).]
WILLIAM WASSERSTROM

BROPHY, JOHN (Nov. 6, 1883–Feb. 19, 1963), labor leader, was born in St. Helens, Lancashire, England, the son of Patrick Brophy, a coal miner, and of Mary Dagnall. In 1892 the family immigrated to the bituminous coal fields of Pennsylvania, where they endured the hard times of the 1890's. Brophy supplemented the third-grade education he had received in English Catholic schools with a few years of public schooling in Pennsylvania. Although his self-education continued through a lifetime of assiduous reading, his formal learning ended at the age of twelve, when he joined his father in the mines.

Under the pressure of unemployment as well as the coal operators' blacklist, Brophy spent the next twenty-one years seeking steady work in numerous coal towns, primarily in Pennsylvania, but also in Iowa, Illinois, and Michigan. Having joined the United Mine Workers Union (UMW) in 1899, he won his first union office (secretary of the Greenwich, Pa., local) in 1904. His growing prominence as a union activist led to the offer of a paid position as an organizer attached to the national office in 1908, but Brophy preferred to remain a rank-and-filer and an official of his local in Nanty Glo, Pa. Besides tenaciously fighting the coal operators, Brophy challenged the district union leaders whenever he felt they were following an insufficiently militant policy. As a result he increasingly spoke for the insurgent forces within Central Pennsylvania's District 2 and in 1916 was narrowly elected its president. On Aug. 13, 1918, Brophy married Anita Anstead; they had two children.

Although he was the leader of 40,000 Pennsylvania bituminous miners, Brophy continued to clash with the union leadership. Now, though, his conflicts were also with John L. Lewis, who became national president of the UMW in 1920. The two men contrasted sharply in appearance and style: Lewis was big, burly, and brash, while Brophy was short, slender, and soft-spoken. Friends and acquaintances invariably described Brophy as gentle, kindly, unassuming, and good-humored.

Lewis and Brophy differed in trade union policy as well as personality. In 1922, when Brophy brought out 20,000 formerly nonunion miners in Somerset County, Pa., in support of a nationwide strike, he insisted that they be included in any settlement. But Lewis signed an agreement covering only the traditional union properties, and Brophy blamed him for the failure of the newly unionized miners to win a contract after their seventeen-month strike. Lewis further angered Brophy by refusing to give more than token support to the drive for nationalization of the mines, which Brophy saw as the fundamental solution to the problems of the coal miners.

These and other conflicts led Brophy to challenge Lewis for the UMW presidency in 1926. He called for organization of nonunion coal fields, nationalization of the mines, and support for a labor party. Brophy's "Save the Union" movement attracted the support of progressives, socialists, and Communists. Although he shared some of the ideals of reformist socialism, Brophy apparently never joined the Socialist party. He was a devout Catholic and his guiding ideology centered more on the Catholic social activism embodied in Leo XIII's papal encyclical *Rerum Novarum* of 1891.

Brophy was defeated by Lewis, 170,000 to 60,000, but vote stealing probably exaggerated the margin of victory. For the next six years Brophy remained active in the opposition to Lewis, even though Lewis had him expelled from the union and the operators' blacklist kept him from working in the mines. Initially his wife supported the family, but later he spent three years as a salesman for the Columbia Conserve Company in Indianapolis, Ind.

The revival of the UMW in the summer of 1933 with the help of New Deal legislation and depression-sparked militancy put the job of organizing the unorganized, which Brophy had always advocated, on the agenda. Lewis decided to welcome his old enemy back into the fold to help with that task. At first this meant organizing and lobbying for the UMW, but by 1935, Lewis and Brophy were looking beyond the coal fields to the millions of unorganized industrial workers.

After the 1935 American Federation of Labor convention defeated a resolution backing industrial unionism, dissident unionists under Lewis' leadership formed the Committee for Industrial Organization (CIO), in Washington, D.C., with Brophy as the director of organization. Serving as the "detail man" under Lewis' direction, he played a crucial role in the organizing drives that tripled the size of the labor movement in the 1930's. In a wide range of industries —auto, rubber, steel, electrical products, maritime, shoes, lumber—Brophy's long trade union experience proved invaluable to workers struggling for union recognition. "In most cases," Brophy recalled in his autobiography, "it was an undramatic routine of meetings, letters, and occasional personal contacts, with me in the role of adviser—arguing, persuading, or just giving encouragement to the men in the field."

Despite Brophy's success as labor organizer and administrator, his prominence within the CIO declined in the late 1930's. In 1938, Lewis passed over him for the crucial post of

CIO secretary and the following year demoted him from national director to director of local industrial unions. Moreover, in 1940, while Brophy was bedridden for several months with a heart ailment, Lewis had his desk removed from the CIO office. While Brophy attributed his fall from grace to his vigorous opposition to Lewis' isolationism in late 1939 and early 1940, it also seems likely that Lewis was trying to eliminate a possible rival for power and to reduce the influence of leftist sympathizers like Brophy within the CIO.

By the time Brophy was able to return to work, Lewis had resigned the CIO presidency after workers refused to follow his lead in supporting Wendell Willkie for president in the 1940 election. Philip Murray, who replaced Lewis, restored Brophy's office and gave him the more important job of director of industrial union councils. During the war, though, Brophy devoted much of his time to service on the War Labor Board. After the war he became a key figure in the fight against Communists in the CIO. Although Brophy had himself been the victim of "Red baiting" and had worked with Communists in the 1920's and 1930's, he joined with surprising vigor in the anti-Communist hysteria that gripped the labor movement and the general population in the late 1940's and 1950's.

In declining health, Brophy retired from the CIO in 1961. He died in Falls Church, Va. For most of his life Brophy had fought for progressive trade unionism, and on balance he was, as labor historian Philip Taft wrote shortly after his death, "a representative of the best type of unionist of the last generation."

[Brophy's papers are at Catholic University, Washington, D.C. His autobiography, *A Miner's Life* (1964), edited and supplemented by John P. Hall, draws on his oral history memoir at Columbia University. His relationship with John L. Lewis is documented in Melvyn Dubofsky and Warren Van Tine, *John L. Lewis* (1977). Also see McAlister Coleman, *Men and Coal* (1943); Philip Taft, *The AFL in the Time of Gompers* (1957); Len De Caux, *Labor Radical* (1970); Irving Bernstein, *The Turbulent Years* (1970); and Bert Cochran, *Labor and Communism* (1977). Obituaries are in the *AFL-CIO News*, Feb. 23, 1963; *UMW Journal*, Mar. 1, 1963; and *New York Times*, Apr. 1, 1963 (delayed by newspaper strike).]

Roy Rosenzweig

BROWN, CHARLOTTE HAWKINS (June 11, 1883–Jan. 11, 1961), educator, was born in Henderson, N.C., on land that was formerly part of the Hawkins plantation. Her father, Edmund H. Hight, from whom she was separated after birth, belonged to a family that had grown up as slaves on the adjoining plantation. Her mother, Caroline F. Hawkins, was the twelfth child of Mingo and Rebecca, slaves on the Hawkins plantation. When Lottie, as Charlotte was called, was about six, she moved with her mother; her stepfather, a Mr. Willis; and sixteen other members of her family to Cambridge, Mass.

Although Lottie was expected to help with her mother's hand laundry enterprise, she also attended Allston Grammar School and Cambridge English High and Latin School, from which she graduated in 1900. Her mother thought this was sufficient education, but Lottie displayed the pragmatism, assertiveness, and determination that were to mark her later endeavors. She convinced her mother that a two-year normal-school course would improve her chances of obtaining a teaching job. While looking through school catalogs she spied the name of Alice F. Palmer, who was on the board of education in Massachusetts and a former president of Wellesley College. During the previous spring, Palmer had observed Lottie in a Cambridge park wheeling the baby for whom she was caring and reading from her high school Virgil text. Lottie was later flattered to learn that the lady, who had stopped briefly to chat with her, was Alice Palmer and that she had called her high school principal to learn her name. Recalling this expression of interest, Lottie wrote Palmer about her desire to attend normal school. Palmer promptly volunteered to pay her expenses, and Lottie began at State Normal School in Salem, Mass., that fall.

In October of Brown's second year at Salem, a field secretary for the American Missionary Association (AMA) offered her a teaching job in the South, where the demand for teachers was great. With the completion of disenfranchisement by the 1890's, education had emerged in the minds of many blacks as being the only route toward an improved status in society. At the same time, southern school boards denied blacks a fair portion of tax money for their schools. Private schools, supported by agencies like the Baptist AMA, seemed the only hope for education for blacks. Within days Brown had arranged for a leave from her school and was on a train bound for McLeansville, a whistle-stop eight miles from Greensboro, N.C., near the one-room schoolhouse of Sedalia where she was to teach. Salem agreed to her leaving with the understanding that she would return the follow-

ing summer to complete the two-year course. Although she never returned, a diploma was eventually awarded on the basis of evaluation of her teaching. The First Grade Certificate for which she qualified was signed Nov. 1, 1901.

Brown never abandoned the task she so resolutely began the morning of Oct. 12, 1901, when she met the fifteen children who straggled into the unkempt building housing Sedalia Institute. A year later, when the AMA moved to close all of its one- and two-room schools, she decided to found her own school at Sedalia. The summer of 1902 found her back in Massachusetts, raising funds for the new venture. Although only nineteen, she approached persons in Boston recommended to her by Palmer and solicited money in the resort hotels of Gloucester where she had once held summer jobs. Back in Sedalia with nearly $400, fifteen acres donated by friends, and the loan of an old blacksmith shop, she inaugurated Palmer Memorial Institute.

The school, named after her benefactress, was an industrial institute modeled after Hampton and Tuskegee. By the mid-1930's it had nearly 300 students. Four hundred acres of land and fourteen buildings, valued at over $1 million, attested to Brown's untiring efforts to develop the school. It became a leader among the fifteen private educational enterprises for blacks that emerged in North Carolina between 1870 and 1910. President Charles W. Eliot of Harvard headed its first board of trustees. The school attracted significant contributions from the North as well as the South and made a remarkable contribution to the education of the southern blacks. It filled a gap in a state that had no accredited teacher-training facilities for blacks until the 1930's and in a community where no tax-supported public school was open to blacks until 1937. In that year a public school for blacks was finally opened. This and financial problems forced the institute to merge with Bennett College in Greensboro in 1971.

In a sense, Palmer Memorial Institute was Brown's life; her home was the residence of pupils too young for the dormitory and those who were unable to return home summers. Edward S. Brown, whom she married on June 12, 1911, taught and had charge of the boys' dormitory for several years until he accepted a teaching position elsewhere. Divorce followed; they had no children. But the school did not absorb all of Brown's energies. She was also interested in the improvement of prison conditions and the education of inmates' children, sponsorship of local health clinics and child care centers, voter registration campaigns, and furtherance of the family-owned farm concept. She was in great demand as a speaker. A gradualist in racial matters, Brown succeeded in effecting marked integration in her local community. She worked for equal rights by concrete actions in the coffee shops of Greensboro and in the larger arenas of the state and nation. Gaining several firsts for black women, she was appointed to the State Council of Defense in North Carolina in 1940 and to the national board of the Young Women's Christian Association. Although Brown retired as president of Palmer in 1952, she remained director of finance until 1955. She died in Greensboro, N.C.

[Brown wrote a short autobiographical piece, "A Biography," and brief notes on public speaking, "Formal Training (An Explanation)" and "My Theory of Public Speaking." These undated papers and others are in the Schlesinger Library of Women in America, Radcliffe College. Published works are a fictional indictment of slavery, *Mammy* (1919); a book of manners, *The Correct Thing to Do, to Say, to Wear* (1941); and a chapter in *Rhetoric of Racial Revolt* (1964), edited by Roy L. Hill.
See also Constance H. Marteena, *Lengthening Shadow of a Woman* (1977); Sadie I. Daniel, *Women Builders* (1931); Benjamin Brawley, *Negro Builders and Heroes* (1937); Wilhelmina S. Robinson, "Historical Negro Biographies," in *International Library of Negro Life and History* (1967); and an obituary in the *New York Times*, Jan. 12, 1961.]
KAREN KENNELLY, C. S. J.

BROWN, CLARENCE JAMES (July 14, 1893–Aug. 23, 1965), congressman, was born in Blanchester, Ohio, the son of Owen Brown and Ellen Barerre McCoppin. He graduated from Blanchester High School in 1912. From 1913 to 1915 he studied law at Washington and Lee University but never practiced law.

In 1915 Brown was appointed to his first public office, state statistician and election supervisor in the office of the Ohio secretary of state. On July 15, 1916, he married Ethel McKinney; they had three children. The following year he purchased his first newspaper. The Brown Publishing Company eventually grew to own a number of newspapers and commercial printing shops in southwestern Ohio. He was its president for the rest of his life.

In 1918, as a Republican, Brown was elected lieutenant governor of Ohio, reportedly the youngest person to hold that position in Ohio history. He was reelected in 1920. In 1926 Brown was elected to the first of three terms as Ohio secretary of state. While in that post he removed from office the entire Cuyahoga and

Mahoning County Boards of Elections—in 1928 and 1930, respectively—after investigations of election fraud in those counties.

Brown entered the gubernatorial primary in 1932, but was narrowly defeated. Two years later he was nominated for governor, but was defeated by a small margin in the November election. In 1936 he was a delegate to the Republican National Convention and headed Frank Knox's campaign for the presidential nomination. Brown was elected to the House of Representatives from the Seventh Ohio Congressional District in 1938. He was reelected every two years for the rest of his life.

Brown opposed all legislation that might involve the United States in the growing conflicts in Europe and Asia. He opposed the repeal of the arms embargo, conscription, and lend-lease. After Pearl Harbor, however, he supported the war effort. By 1943 he endorsed postwar United States international collaboration. That year he became a member of the Republican steering committee.

In 1940, 1948, and 1952 Brown supported Senator Robert A. Taft's attempts to secure the Republican presidential nomination and was his floor manager at the 1940 Republican National Convention. Four years later he was floor manager for John W. Bricker at the Republican Convention. During the campaign he served on the executive committee of the Republican National Committee.

On domestic issues Brown was decidedly conservative. He opposed the New Deal job creation programs. In 1943 he voted for the liquidation of the Home Owners Loan Corporation and against increased funds for the Rural Electrification Administration program. The following year he called for an investigation intended to curb "the dissemination of New Deal and fourth-term political propaganda" to American forces abroad.

A defender of civil rights, Brown voted with the Republican majority for the abolition of poll taxes and unsuccessfully sponsored an amendment that would have prohibited discrimination on the basis of race, creed, or color in the recruitment of nurses for the armed services.

While asserting his belief in labor's right to organize, bargain collectively, and strike, Brown was a consistent opponent of what he deemed to be labor's excesses. In 1946 he supported the Case antistrike bill, and in 1947 he was a proponent of the Taft-Hartley bill. He opposed the continuance of the draft in peacetime and civilian control of atomic energy. In 1947 Brown supported the proposed constitutional amendment that limited a president to two terms in office.

In the postwar period Brown favored creation of a permanent House Committee on Un-American Activities. While directing the Republican national campaign in 1946, he denounced the Democratic party as tending toward socialism and called the Congress of Industrial Organizations Political Action Committee a "conduit of communism." He interpreted his reelection and the landslide Republican victory in the 1946 congressional elections as signaling the "beginning of the end of an era" of presidential power. Soon thereafter he sponsored a resolution that would officially declare the war to be ended in order to remove wartime controls.

Brown called for decreased federal spending and blamed the federal deficit on the $420 million contributed to the World Bank, the World Stabilization Fund, and the loan to Great Britain. He opposed that loan and aid to Greece and Turkey, arguing that if there was not to be tax relief in the United States, then there should be no European relief. He suggested that the United States could be a good neighbor without being a soft touch.

With Senator Taft, Brown sponsored a bill that would streamline the executive branch by eliminating overlapping functions. Two Commissions on Organization of the Executive Branch of Government were created in 1947 and were chaired by Herbert Hoover. Brown was appointed to the commissions.

Brown served for many years on the House Rules Committee and was the ranking Republican member at the time of his death. The committee was often regarded during these years as a bottleneck for progressive legislation. In 1961 and 1964 the Democratic House stripped the committee of much of its power. In 1964 Brown was forced out as Ohio's Republican national committeeman by the state Republican chairman, Ray Bliss. He died at Bethesda, Md.

[Brown's papers are at the Ohio Historical Society, Columbus. See *Everybody's Business,* Feb. 1946; *U.S. News and World Report,* Nov. 22, 1946; *New York Times Magazine,* Dec. 29, 1946. His congressional activities can be found in the *Congressional Record.* An obituary is in the *New York Times,* Aug. 24, 1965.]

STEPHEN D. BODAYLA

BROWN, WALTER FOLGER (May 31, 1869–Jan. 26, 1961), lawyer, politician, and postmaster general, was born in Massillon,

Ohio, the son of James Marshall Brown and Lavinia Folger. Shortly after his birth the family moved to Toledo, where James Brown became a lawyer. A Republican, he served as postmaster of Toledo from 1890 to 1894. Walter graduated from Western Reserve Academy in 1888 and received the A.B. from Harvard in 1892. During the summer of 1891 he had campaigned for William McKinley for governor of Ohio. He also was a reporter for the *Toledo Blade* and became city editor shortly after graduation. But Brown's father persuaded him to attend Harvard Law School. In 1894, after about two years at Harvard, Brown was admitted to the Ohio bar. He remained a partner in his father's firm until 1905, when he founded Brown, Hahn and Sanger. On Sept. 10, 1903, he married Katherine Hafer; they had no children.

Politics was always Brown's main interest. Beginning as a precinct worker, he was elected chairman of the Toledo Republican Central Committee in 1897. That year he was instrumental in the election of reformer Samuel "Golden Rule" Jones as mayor. But Jones's independence caused a party split in Toledo. Jones temporarily joined Senator Joseph Foraker, while Brown allied with Senator Mark Hanna. In 1899, Brown's opposition forced Jones to seek reelection as a nonpartisan. The two fought until Jones's death in 1904. By then Brown's machine dominated Toledo politics. Brown was the attorney for the local traction company and also represented the utilities, breweries, and other corporations needing assistance. Despite his silky manner and polished speech, he was as much a political boss as the crude, unlettered George Cox of Cincinnati.

Brown also played a significant part in state politics. In 1899 he became a member of the Ohio Republican Central Committee. In 1906 he became its chairman, and working with the conservatives, he stemmed the progressive insurgency of that year. He remained chairman until 1912. In 1908 he backed the presidency of William Howard Taft. At the Ohio Republican convention two years later, Brown worked with other standpatters to defend the Taft administration against the progressive Republican groundswell. In the fall of 1911, Brown proclaimed himself a progressive. He was elected a delegate to the Ohio Constitutional Convention of 1912, where he introduced progressive amendments to the state constitution. He also supported Theodore Roosevelt's unsuccessful fight for the Republican presidential nomination in 1912. When Roosevelt formed the Progressive party that June, Brown directed his campaign in Ohio. Brown claimed that he had acted for the Republican party's welfare in supporting Roosevelt; more likely he became a Progressive to survive politically. But Taft had not always consulted him on local appointments, nor had he accommodated Brown when he sought a reconsideration of an antitrust indictment involving a client.

After Roosevelt's defeat Brown continued as Progressive party state chairman. In 1916 he returned to the Republican party despite strong conservative opposition. Out of this turmoil emerged the presidential candidacy of Warren G. Harding in 1920. Harding won Brown's support, and Brown contributed significantly to Harding's preconvention campaign, eventually serving as Harding's floor manager at the national convention. Consequently Harding favored Brown as his Senate replacement. But Brown, in the only elective office he sought, lost to Frank B. Willis in the primary. Harding then appointed Brown chairman of the Joint Congressional Reorganization Committee. Under Brown's leadership (1921–1924) the committee recommended sweeping changes, many of which were later adopted, including the combining of the War and Navy Departments into the Department of Defense and the consolidation of related services into the Department of Health, Education and Welfare. Brown so impressed Secretary of Commerce Herbert Hoover that he became his assistant secretary in 1927. During the 1928 presidential campaign Hoover relied extensively on Brown, particularly in Ohio. After the election he appointed Brown postmaster general.

At age sixty the bespectacled and scholarly-appearing Brown had reached the pinnacle of his career. The press described him as self-effacing, soft-spoken, and low-key. Nevertheless, he attracted national attention by requesting $3,500 for a new official vehicle because a low car roof had crushed the silk hat he wore to Hoover's inauguration. As postmaster general he improved the efficiency of the national post office. He also expanded the air transport of mail by negotiating favorable contracts with large aviation companies. In 1934 a Senate investigation revealed that the Post Office Department had not held competitive bidding, which hurt the small independent lines, and had subsidized several aviation holding companies. Brown apparently sought to use airmail contracts to encourage major airlines to expand passenger service. Nonetheless, enough irregularities existed to cause the Roosevelt administration to cancel the contracts.

Brown played a leading part in Hoover's 1932 campaign for reelection. He remained as Republican national committeeman until 1936 and was a delegate to the next three Republican national conventions. In 1933 he was board chairman, and from 1934 to 1946 he was president, of the Hudson and Manhattan Railroad Company. He then returned to Toledo, Ohio, where, after a long retirement, he died.

Brown was one of the most durable politicians of the twentieth century. He served three presidents and helped to elect several others. Herbert Hoover once said that Brown possessed "a greater knowledge of the federal machinery than any other man in the United States." Yet historians have ignored Brown largely because of his unobtrusive personality and his failure to accomplish the dramatic.

[The Walter F. Brown Papers, Ohio Historical Society, Columbus, are incomplete but still the best primary source; Brown's correspondence is also in the Arthur Garford and Warren G. Harding Papers (Ohio Historical Society), Herbert Hoover Papers (Herbert Hoover Presidential Library, West Branch, Iowa), and the Charles Dewey Hilles Papers (Yale University Library). The best published material on Brown includes Harvey Ford, "Walter Folger Brown," *Northwest Ohio Quarterly*, Summer 1954; and Theodore G. Joslin, "Postmaster General Brown: His Past and Yours," *World's Work*, Aug. 1930. Obituaries are in the *New York Times* and *Toledo Blade*, Jan. 27, 1961.]

JAMES N. GIGLIO

BROWNING, TOD (July 12, 1880–Oct. 6, 1962), film director, writer, and actor, was born Charles A. Browning in Louisville, Ky., the son of Charles Avery Browning, a prosperous cabinetmaker, and Lydia J. Browning. He attended Louisville Male High School; but at sixteen, moved by desire for adventure, he joined a traveling circus, the Manhattan Fair and Carnival Company. He served as boy-of-all-work and was introduced to sideshow grotesquerie and deception, which figured prominently in his films. At eighteen Browning became a jockey, but within three years he was a singer and dancer with river shows on the Ohio and Missouri.

In 1905 Browning teamed with Roy C. Jones to form "Lizard and Coon," a popular comedy-contortion act, and he played in other acts and in musical comedy. In 1910 he joined a vaudeville-burlesque troop, "World of Mirth," for three seasons as principal comic. In the company was Alice L. Houghton Wilson, whom he married in 1916. They had no children.

While touring in Los Angeles in 1913, Browning visited the vaudevillian Charlie Murray, then working at the Mack Sennett studio. Murray persuaded him to try motion pictures, and in October 1913 Browning appeared in his first film, *Scenting a Terrible Crime*. This one-reel Biograph comedy foreshadowed his later work: in the film neighbors mistake the smell of sauerkraut for the odor of a corpse, but they are set right by a German coroner.

In the same month Browning moved with the D. W. Griffith organization from Biograph to Mutual, where he appeared in a series of one-reel comedies released by Komic (1914–1915); most were directed by Eddie Dillon and co-starred Fay Tincher. Browning also directed some twenty-five two-reel comedies (released by Reliance-Majestic) and obtained his first credit as scenarist of a Dorothy Gish film, *Atta Boy's Last Race* (1916), for Fine Arts/Triangle. He appeared as a crook and a race driver (and possibly other roles) in Griffith's *Intolerance* (1916). He was also one of Griffith's numerous assistants.

In 1917 Browning made his first feature, *Jim Bludso* (Fine Arts/Triangle), with Wilfrid Lucas. He made two more features with Lucas before moving to Metro Pictures to direct five suspense melodramas (1917–1918). After the war, Browning joined Universal Pictures for ten features with Priscilla Dean (1918–1923). These films marked his emergence as a major director, and the stories reflected his taste for underworld settings and low-life characters. *Outside the Law* (1921), featuring Lon Chaney, and *The White Tiger* (1923) were adapted by Browning from his own stories. In these years he also made two features starring Edith Roberts and three with Mary MacLaren, all of them at Universal.

Browning was among that studio's most successful directors, enjoying the support of production chief Irving Thalberg. But from 1923 to 1925, he suffered severe alcoholism. He left Universal and made *The Day of Faith* (1923) for Goldwyn Picture Corporation and two minor Evelyn Brent romances for Film Booking Offices (1924).

Recovering in 1925, Browning went to Thalberg, who was then at Metro-Goldwyn-Mayer (MGM). Browning was to direct films for Chaney, whose popularity had increased with *The Hunchback of Notre Dame* (1923) and *The Phantom of the Opera* (1925). Some believe Chaney personally requested Browning. MGM was seeking a vehicle to equal Chaney's earlier successes, and Browning suggested a bizarre crime story, *The Unholy Three*. Filmed in 1925, it gained great popularity and became the first of eight grotesque fantasies by Chaney and Browning at MGM: *The Black Bird* (1926), *The Road to Mandalay* (1926), *London After Midnight* (1927), *The Unknown* (1927), *The Big City* (1928), *West of Zanzibar* (1928), and *Where East Is East* (1929). The films portrayed fake vampirism, transvestite disguise, and other aberrations. All but two had stories by Browning. In this period he also directed MGM features starring John Gilbert, Conrad Nagel, Aileen Pringle, and Edward G. Robinson.

With the coming of sound, Browning directed three pictures for Universal, of which *Dracula* (1931) became his most popular film. Cold and atmospheric, its romantic treatment of the vampire is not typical of the seediness Browning usually found in depravity. *Dracula* began a vogue of horror films. Back at MGM Browning directed *Freaks* (1932), widely considered his finest work and one that best exemplifies his use of the grotesque. It presents real circus freaks as selfless members of a loyal community; the "normal" characters are greedy and dehumanized. The film's financial failure (and the enmity it aroused between Browning and Louis B. Mayer) undermined Browning's independence at MGM. In his last seven years before retirement, complaining of front office interference, he made only four films.

In 1939 Browning retired to his Malibu cottage. He traveled, tended his ranch, added to his occult and mystery library, and wrote stories. One of these, *Inside Job*, was filmed by Universal in 1946. Studios sometimes called on him to rework problem scripts. After the death of his wife in 1944, Browning lived in seclusion. He died in Santa Monica.

Browning's reputation remains controversial. Raoul Walsh places him "around the first ten" American directors who began in the silent era; others dismiss him as a conscientious craftsman or even as a hack. He is generally more appreciated in Europe than in America. His forty-eight films, preoccupied with grotesque motifs drawn from the circus and underworld, encourage viewers almost cynically to distrust complacent, corrupt appearances; they also show a rare sympathy for characters ostracized by society and victimized by their own obsessions.

[The Academy of Motion Picture Arts and Sciences, Beverly Hills, Calif., maintains a file on Browning. Articles appear in *Motion Picture News*, Dec. 25, 1920; *Motion Picture Classic*, Mar. 1928; *Films in Review*, Oct. 1953; Louisville *Courier-Jour-*

nal, Apr. 2, 1978. See also I. G. Edmonds, *The Big U: Universal in the Silent Days* (1977); Stuart Rosenthal and Judith M. Kass, *Tod Browning, Don Siegel* (1975); and *Motion Picture Studio Directory,* 1916–1918.]

ALAN BUSTER

BUCHMAN, FRANK NATHAN DANIEL (June 4, 1878–Aug. 7, 1961), founder and guiding light of the controversial religious movement known successively as the First Century Christian Fellowship, the Oxford Group, and Moral Re-Armament, was born at Pennsburg, Pa., the son of Frank Buchman, a hotel owner, and Sarah Greenawalt. When he was fifteen, the family moved to Allentown, Pa. Buchman's parents trained him in a theologically conservative brand of German Lutheran Pietism. After graduating from Allentown High School and Muhlenberg College (1899), he completed the course at the Mt. Airy Lutheran Theological Seminary and was ordained in 1902. In 1902–1903 he studied at Westminster College, Cambridge, England, and at Inner-Mission in Germany.

For the next five years Buchman served as minister at the Overbrook Church of the Good Shepherd, in an impoverished section of West Philadelphia, and founded and administered settlement house centers in Philadelphia and other cities. In 1908 he ceased his involvement with the settlement centers because of a financial dispute with the governing trustees. He then went to England to attend the "deeper-life" Keswick Convention. While there he became convinced of the "selfishness, pride and ill-will" in his life and confessed the same in letters to the trustees with whom he had quarreled. The experience, he said, changed his life.

After returning to the United States, Buchman spent the years from 1909 to 1915 as the leader of the Pennsylvania State University YMCA chapter. Here he gained valuable experience in fund raising, recruiting members (the membership doubled during his tenure), and developing a dynamic organization.

After a year with evangelist Sherwood Eddy in the Orient, Buchman in 1916 accepted the position of "extension lecturer" in evangelism at Hartford Seminary. The seminary allowed him to spend much time off campus in evangelistic work. Accordingly, he again traveled in the Far East in 1917–1919.

While on campus Buchman received a mixed reception from students and faculty. His emphasis was always practical rather than intellectual, and some thought that his group sessions

diverted too much attention from scholarly pursuits. His off-campus activities, by contrast, met with increasing success; consequently, in 1921 he chose to pursue his religious endeavors independent of any institutional connection.

This independent movement initially assumed the name First Century Christian Fellowship. During the early 1920's Buchman worked primarily through "house parties" on prestigious eastern college campuses, where he sought to lead the students to changed lives through public confession of their sins. These confessions often centered on sexual matters, with resultant public disapproval. (President John Grier Hibbin banned him from Princeton in 1924 after he refused to delete sexual discussions from the meetings.)

After the mid-1920's Buchman worked with people of all ages, and increasingly he concentrated his efforts and experienced his greatest satisfaction outside the United States. When a team of his disciples, composed mostly of Oxford students, visited South Africa in 1928 to seek to ease the racial problems of that country through evangelism, the *Cape Times* referred to them as "the Oxford Group." To the pleasure of Buchman, who always enjoyed identification with prestigious organizations and people, the name gained acceptance as a label for the movement as a whole.

Buchmanism was a movement outside the established churches that sought to bring individuals to dynamic spiritual earnestness within the framework of their own religious traditions. What theology it had was drawn from the common elements of the major world religions. As Buchman stated: "Catholic, Jew and Protestant, Hindu, Buddhist and Confucianist—all find they can change where needed and travel along this good road together."

The "good road" was a changed world order that was to be brought about by individuals who had confessed their sins, committed themselves to God absolutely, and regularly sought God's guidance through meditation. The confessions took place at house parties (often held in luxurious settings) in front of caring support groups that were led by Buchman and his staff of "life-changers." Recruits—especially from the upper class—were attracted to the meetings by lists of prominent sponsors (statesmen, generals, entrepreneurs, the social elite, theologians, and even labor leaders) whose backing Buchman actively solicited. By the mid-1930's Henry P. Van Dusen, a student of the movement, could describe it as "the most striking spiritual phenomenon of our time."

In 1938, as the nations rearmed preparatory to World War II, Buchman changed the name of his organization to Moral Re-Armament (MRA) to dramatize its new specific goal of "preventing war by a moral and spiritual awakening." In contrast with his earlier small-group techniques, his effort to prevent the war involved mass rallies and mass advertising campaigns. It also brought him great attention and acclaim, especially in an England that was ill prepared and panicky in the face of the mounting Nazi military power.

The coming of World War II brought a sharp decline in the influence of the movement, which many associated with the discredited appeasement policy of Prime Minister Neville Chamberlain. Buchman's chief American sponsor, Samuel Shoemaker, whose Manhattan Calvary Episcopal Church had served as movement headquarters, broke with Buchman.

Although the movement never again realized the degree of influence that it knew in the 1930's, it did rally somewhat after the war. Buchman's efforts in postwar reconciliation and international goodwill resulted in his receiving citations from the governments of France, West Germany, Japan, Greece, the Philippines, Thailand, and Iran. A plush conference center at Caux, Switzerland, became the world headquarters, and Buchman spent part of his later years there. A lifelong bachelor, he died at Freudenstadt, Germany.

Buchman combined an unusual commitment to doing the will of God, as he understood it, with brilliant organizational and promotional skills, energy and self-assurance almost without limit, and a near-psychic ability to diagnose quickly and accurately the problems of the people he counseled.

[Buchman's books include *For Sinners Only* (1932); *I Was a Pagan* (1934); *Life Began Yesterday* (1935); *How Do I Begin?* (1937); *Remaking the World* (1949); and *Frank Buchman, Eighty* (1959). Books on Buchman and his movement include Walter H. Clark, *The Oxford Group: Its History and Significance* (1951); Allan W. Eister, *Drawing Room Conversion* (1950); Basil Entwistle and John McCook Roots, *Moral Re-armament: What Is It?* (1967); and Peter Howard, *That Man Frank Buchman* (1946). Articles include Stanley High, "What Is Moral Rearmament?," *Saturday Evening Post*, Aug. 12, 1939; Reinhold Niebuhr, "Hitler and Buchman," *Christian Century*, Oct. 7, 1936; John McCook Roots, "Frank M. Buchman: An Apostle to Youth," *Atlantic Monthly*, Dec. 1928; Henry P. Van Dusen, "Apostle to the Twentieth Century," *Atlantic Monthly*, July 1934, and "The Oxford Group Movement," *Atlantic Monthly*, Aug. 1934. See also the editorial, "Moral Rearmament," *Christian Century*, May 31, 1939.

An obituary is in the *New York Times*, Aug. 9, 1961.]

WILLIAM C. RINGENBERG

BUDD, RALPH (Aug. 20, 1879–Feb. 2, 1962), railroad executive, was born on a farm near Washburn, Iowa, the son of Charles Wesley Budd, a farmer, and of Mary Ann Warner. As a child, because of his patience with animals, Ralph's job was to coax the heifers into being milked. In 1893 the family moved to Des Moines, Iowa, where he completed high school and college in six years, graduating from Highland Park College in 1899 with a degree in civil engineering.

Budd's first railway job was as a draftsman with the Chicago Great Western Railroad at Des Moines late in 1899. The next summer he went out on the line as an assistant engineer. He married Georgia A. Marshall on Dec. 25, 1900; they had three children. Meanwhile, having secured A. N. Talbot's revolutionary work on locating track, *Talbot's Railway Transition Spiral* (1909), Budd proceeded to study and to apply the new techniques. His work brought steady advancement.

In 1902, Budd accepted an offer to work on the Rock Island's St. Louis–Kansas City line. There he met John F. Stevens, who in 1906, as chief engineer of the Panama Canal, brought Budd down to relocate, and eventually extend, the Panama Railroad. Although the line was often through tangled jungle, Budd pushed the project through ahead of schedule. One result was another call from Stevens, who by this time (1909) was in the Pacific Northwest, where James J. Hill, head of the Great Northern and Northern Pacific railroads, was planning to build a line south from the Columbia River toward California. Budd surveyed a line from Bend, Oreg., to Bieber, Calif., and on to Keddie, a station on the newly formed Western Pacific. Hill was greatly impressed, and promptly named Budd chief engineer of his Oregon lines: the Oregon Trunk, the Spokane and Inland Empire, and the Spokane, Portland and Seattle. In January 1913 he called Budd to St. Paul, Minn., obviously to groom Budd for the presidency of the Great Northern. Budd was elected to the post in 1919.

As president, Budd vigorously carried on Hill's constant search for direct lines, low grades, easy curves, balanced traffic, modern equipment, efficient motive power, and meticulous maintenance. But Budd was also an innovator. In 1926 he began the New Cascade Tunnel in central Washington; the 7.79-mile bore was completed in 1929. He then turned to the construction of the Bend-Bieber line he had surveyed almost twenty years earlier; its completion in 1931 created a heavy-duty alternative to the coastal route between Seattle and San Francisco. Meanwhile, in 1929, Budd put the *Empire Builder* on a schedule that saved an entire day on the scenic run between Chicago and the West Coast via Glacier National Park. As always, however, revenues from freight far exceeded those from passengers; hence Budd saw to it that, for example, the standard ore-carrying cars of fifty tons were replaced by new ones of seventy tons or more. Budd's ideas on railroading found a new audience when, in 1930, he headed a five-man mission to inspect the Soviet railway system. Their 376-page report urged the Russians to adopt American rather than European techniques.

Budd's seventeen years as president of the Chicago, Burlington, and Quincy (1932–1949) marked the culmination of his career. Having been a director since 1916, he was thoroughly acquainted with the property that since 1901 had been owned jointly by the Great Northern and Northern Pacific railroads. In 1932, however, the Burlington accounted for more ton-miles than the two "Northern" lines combined. Thus the Burlington, considerably longer than either of its owners, deserved and enjoyed a great measure of autonomy.

Budd's accomplishments were legion: to fight the Great Depression he simplified the divisional structure, introduced the nation's first streamlined train to enter regular service (the *Pioneer Zephyr*, in 1934), and actively supported the Dotsero Cutoff, which chopped 175 miles from the Denver and Rio Grande's Denver–Salt Lake City run and led to a quadrupling of the Burlington's transcontinental business. He also carried out a debt reduction plan that cut the Burlington's charges for fixed interest by more than 37 percent between 1940 and the end of 1945. In the latter year Budd gained another first for his road by introducing the dome car. In 1949, the *California Zephyr*, with five dome cars, began its twenty-one-year tour of duty on the San Francisco run.

Beyond these developments Budd served from May 1940 to December 1941 as transportation commissioner for President Franklin D. Roosevelt. His ticklish task was to coordinate shippers' demands with available transport of every type. So well did he succeed that the

threat of a government take-over of the railroads (as in World War I) was effectively quashed.

Two important projects long championed by Budd were completed only after his retirement from the Burlington presidency in 1949. One was the improvement of the Burlington's roundabout line between Chicago and Kansas City. A new route, opened in 1952, was fully competitive. The other project was the long-sought merger of the Burlington and the two "Northern" lines; this was finally achieved in 1970.

After his retirement Budd became chairman of the Chicago Transit Authority. Until 1954 he brought operating and financial order out of near chaos. In 1954 Budd and his wife moved to Santa Barbara, Calif., but until 1958 he continued to serve as a Burlington director. During his last years he brilliantly annotated a 2,375-page manuscript history of the Burlington. He died at Santa Barbara.

Budd possessed both intelligence and a strong character. His keen perception and mental energy go far to explain his success as a railroader. But it was his consideration for others and his innate humility that enabled him to exert effective leadership and brought him a wide and devoted circle of friends.

[As of 1979, Budd's papers had not been collected or cataloged, although there are some 100 speeches and articles for 1923–1949 and about 50 letters written 1954–1962, mostly concerning Burlington history. See John F. Stevens, *An Engineer's Recollections* (1936); *Railway Age*, Feb. 5, 1949; Richard C. Overton, "Ralph Budd, Railroad Entrepreneur," *Palimpsest*, Nov. 1955; Chicago, Burlington, and Quincy, *Annual Report for 1958* (1959); Richard C. Overton, *Burlington Route* (1965); Albro Martin, *James J. Hill and the Opening of the Northwest* (1976). Two sources pertaining to Budd are forthcoming: Ralph and Muriel Hidy, *History of the Great Northern;* and Richard C. Overton, *Perkins/Budd: Railway Statesmen of the Burlington*. An obituary appeared in the *New York Times*, Feb. 3, 1962.]
                                    RICHARD C. OVERTON

BUNDY, HARVEY HOLLISTER (Mar. 30, 1888–Oct. 7, 1963), lawyer, assistant secretary of state, and special assistant to the secretary of war, was born in Grand Rapids, Mich., the son of McGeorge Bundy, a lawyer, and Mary Goodhue Hollister. His family was socially prominent. Bundy attended the Hackley School in Tarrytown, N.Y., and Yale University, from which he was graduated in 1909. He taught briefly at St. Mark's School in Southboro, Mass., and worked as a traveling companion (1910–1911) before entering Harvard University Law

School. He received his law degree in 1914 and became a secretary to U.S. Supreme Court Justice Oliver Wendell Holmes.

Bundy was admitted to the Massachusetts bar in 1915. On Apr. 17, 1915, he married Katherine L. Putnam. They had five children; two of their sons, William Putnam and McGeorge, also had careers in government service and foreign affairs. Urbane, scholarly, and erudite, Bundy began a successful legal practice that was interrupted frequently by calls to government service. After less than a year as a clerk with the firm of Hale and Grinell, he joined the firm of Putnam, Putnam and Bell, where his father-in-law was a senior partner.

In 1917 Bundy served as assistant counsel for the U.S. Food Administration. He was secretary of the U.S. Sugar Equalization Board from 1919 to 1925. Bundy earned a reputation for quiet, intelligent, and adroit administration, and he became familiar with complex economic matters. After several years of private legal practice in Boston, Bundy's qualifications brought him to the attention of Secretary of State Henry L. Stimson, who was anxious to have on his staff a reliable senior officer with a solid background in finance. Stimson appointed Bundy assistant secretary of state in July 1931. Although Bundy served less than two years, he and Stimson developed a close and lasting relationship. Bundy helped organize the Foreign Bond Holders Protective Council. He also served as a State Department liaison with President-elect Franklin D. Roosevelt during the final months of the Hoover administration.

Leaving the State Department in 1933, Bundy returned to the Boston legal firm of Choate, Hall and Stewart. He had joined this firm as a partner in 1929 and remained affiliated with it throughout the remainder of his career. In April 1941, Stimson, now secretary of war, called upon Bundy to be his special assistant. When the United States entered World War II, Stimson relied heavily on Bundy for advice on the most urgent administrative, personnel, and policy matters. He regarded him as his "closest personal assistant." Throughout the war Bundy traveled widely, attending conferences in Europe and touring front lines. Although his position in the War Department was never precisely defined, he exerted considerable influence through his involvement in sensitive matters and his closeness to the secretary.

An especially critical area with which Bundy was entrusted concerned liaison work between scientists and educators. With Vannevar Bush and representatives of the army and navy,

Bundy set up a committee to educate the Joint Chiefs of Staff on scientific problems. Upon the recommendation of Bundy and Bush, the new-weapons section of the General Staff was made independent in 1942. Within the War Department Bundy became a prime mover in coordinating the rapid development of scientific projects, in particular, the atom bomb. Bundy communicated with General Leslie R. Groves, director of the secret Manhattan Project, during the critical months of the weapon's development and deployment, and he briefed Stimson almost daily on the project's progress. Bundy also sat on the secretary's Interim Committee (which met to determine recommendations for the military use of atomic weapons) during the weeks prior to the explosion of the atom bombs over Japan in August 1945. In the summer of 1945 Bundy accompanied Stimson to the Potsdam Conference, where he joined in talks with Prime Minister Winston Churchill concerning the strategic use of atomic energy.

Bundy returned to private life following the war, but he remained interested in international affairs. In January 1948, he accepted an appointment from President Harry S. Truman to serve on a task force with the former deputy director of the Office of Strategic Services, James Grafton Rogers, a close friend and colleague. They headed a study of the conduct of American foreign policy and prepared a report for the Congressional Commission on the Organization of the Executive Branch of the Government. Their study was completed in January 1949. In 1952 Bundy succeeded John Foster Dulles as chairman of the Carnegie Endowment for International Peace.

Bundy spent his final years in Boston, where he died.

[Manuscripts include a 319-page transcript, Oral History Project, Columbia University; correspondence (1942–1963) is in the James Grafton Rogers Papers, Colorado Historical Society, Denver.

See also Henry L. Stimson and McGeorge Bundy, *On Active Service in Peace and War* (1947); Harvey H. Bundy and James G. Rogers, *Task Force Report on Foreign Affairs* (1949); Elting E. Morison, *Turmoil and Tradition: A Study of the Life and Times of Henry L. Stimson* (1960); Herbet Feis, *1933: Characters in Crisis* (1966); and obituaries in the *New York Times*, Oct. 8, 1963, and the *Boston Herald*, Oct. 8, 1963.]

MICHAEL J. DEVINE

BUNKER, ARTHUR HUGH (July 29, 1895–May 19, 1964), corporation executive and World War II mobilization administrator, was born in Yonkers, N.Y., the son of George Raymond Bunker, founder and president of the National Sugar Refining Company, and Jeanie Polhemus Cobb. Following education at the Taft School and Yale University (from which he graduated in 1916), Bunker served during World War I with the Navy's Bureau of Aeronautics. He then entered the minerals business in Denver, Colo., as president of the Radium Company of Colorado. The company mined uranium to extract radium for medical uses, a successful enterprise until richer uranium ores were discovered in the Belgian Congo. In 1925, Bunker developed a new process for extracting vanadium, a metal used to toughen steel and put the snap in springs, from Colorado ores. He sold his company, United States Vanadium, to Union Carbide and Carbon Corporation in 1927 for a handsome profit.

Bunker briefly engaged in developing petroleum in South America and quickly disposed of oil leases for sizable gains. He then took an option on a New Jersey nursery specializing in orchids and turned it into the world's largest producer of the exotic plant. Just eight days before the crash of 1929, Bunker became executive vice-president of the Lehman Corporation, an investment trust organized by Lehman Brothers, who were Wall Street bankers. Judging by his later involvements, Bunker remained active in the development of metal ore extraction. Bunker married Antoinette Marie Blache on May 9, 1933. They had three children.

During World War II, Bunker joined other major corporation executives who organized and administered war production. On June 10, 1941, he was appointed to the Office of Production Management as the acting deputy chief of the materials and metals division, becoming chief of the aluminum and magnesium unit in December. With the creation of the War Production Board (WPB) in 1942, Bunker became director of its aluminum and magnesium division, then vice-chairman for metals and minerals. He played an important role in the vital production of light metals for aircraft. In the words of Donald M. Nelson, chairman of the WPB, Bunker "was more nearly right in his predictions of what was needed, and when it was needed, than anyone else in WPB. Certainly, the fact that the aluminum problem was solved was due in no small degree to Arthur Bunker."

As war production and reconversion to peacetime production issues came to a head in June 1944, Bunker's authority was enhanced by his appointment as vice-chairman of the Production Executive Committee and director of its staff, and then as deputy executive vice-chairman of the WPB.

In 1943–1944 a controversy developed that involved liberals who wanted reconversion to commence before the war ended, in order to give civilian production advantages to small business while minimizing worker joblessness, and the military and big businessmen who argued that a delayed reconversion would assure the armed forces of supplies needed to win the war and would discourage workers from abandoning war-related jobs for those in civilian production. Bunker's rise in the WPB hierarchy was seen as a triumph for the latter group.

Bunker did not disappoint his business admirers. The only cutbacks in war production made in mid-1944 were to free labor for more essential production of planes and tires. In September, Bunker was elevated to WPB chief of staff in a reorganization that practically eliminated liberals. Following his efforts to sustain output of metals through long-term contracts that included government subsidies, Bunker resigned from the WPB on Dec. 19, 1944, and became a general partner in Lehman Brothers in 1945.

Tall and spare with silvery hair, Bunker presented the image of a successful engineer-financier. Like many of the top wartime administrators, he eschewed a production man's perspective for a financier's broader view of the economy. He used technicians shrewdly, worked long hours, and delayed tough decisions but, once having made them, had them implemented with a firmness that brooked no opposition.

Bunker's interest in development of metals persisted, and four years after he joined Lehman Brothers he left for the presidency of Climax Molybdenum Company, the world's largest producer of molybdenum, a metal mostly used to harden and toughen steel and increasingly used in manufacturing jet engines and gas turbines because of its durability at high temperatures. Bunker diversified the company into uranium and oil production. In 1951, President Harry Truman appointed him a member of the Materials Policy Commission, the purpose of which was to study long-range national needs for development of metals. Its advocacy of expansion led to Bunker's inclusion on a permanent advisory panel on mineral discovery and development created by the National Science Foundation. On July 31, 1959, he married Isabel Leighton.

Through his ties to Wall Street (he was a director of the Lehman Corporation and several others) and Washington, Bunker appears to have played a significant but unobtrusive role in policy planning for the American political economy following World War II. He died in New York City.

[On Bunker's role in the WPB, see U. S. Civilian Production Administration, *Minutes of the War Production Board* (1946) and *Industrial Mobilization for War* (1947); Donald M. Nelson, *Arsenal of Democracy* (1946); Jack W. Peltason, "The Reconversion Controversy," in Harold Stein, ed., *Public Administration and Policy Development* (1948); and Barton J. Bernstein, "The Debate on Industrial Reconversion: The Protection of Oligopoly and Military Control of the Economy," *American Journal of Economics and Sociology*, Apr. 1967. Additional biographical information is in *Business Week*, July 1, 1944, and the *New York Times*, May 29, 1955. Bunker's obituary is in the *New York Times*, May 20, 1964.]

JORDAN A. SCHWARZ

BURDICK, EUGENE LEONARD (Dec. 12, 1918–July 26, 1965), political theorist and writer, was born in Sheldon, Iowa, the son of John ("Jack") D. Burdick, a house painter, and Marie Ellerbroek. When Burdick was four, his father died. When he was seven, his mother married Fritz Gaillard, a Dutch immigrant, who later became a cellist with the Los Angeles Philharmonic. The family settled permanently in Los Angeles. Burdick, an accomplished athlete, attended Santa Monica Junior College and Santa Barbara Junior College before transferring to Stanford as a sophomore. A scholarship student, he distinguished himself academically, receiving a degree in psychology in 1941.

Burdick married Carol Warren on July 3, 1942. They had three children. In 1942 he was commissioned an ensign in the navy. He was decorated for bravery in the battle of Guadalcanal, where he was captain of an amphibious personnel carrier. Assigned to navy schools in Miami and Washington, he became a destroyer gunnery officer. In 1945 Burdick wrote his first short story. Two years later, upon his return to civilian life, he attended graduate school at Stanford, incidentally studying writing under Wallace Stegner. This led to a Breadloaf Writer's Fellowship for 1948 and then to a major short story prize.

Burdick went to England as a Rhodes scholar in 1948 and completed his Oxford University D.Phil. in political science in 1950. Then, as a lieutenant commander in the Naval Reserve, he taught for two years at the Naval War College at Newport, R.I. In 1952 he became an assistant professor of political science at the University of California at Berkeley.

Burdick's first book, *The Ninth Wave* (1956), was a political, semiautobiographical novel adumbrating all of his interests and later themes. It was a best-seller and a Book-of-the-Month-Club selection. But *The Ugly American* (1958), written with William J. Lederer, made him famous. He visited Vietnam with Lederer, a Vietnamese-speaking, navy-loving writer, before collaborating on the novel. Its events occur in the fictitious Sarkhan and deal with the administration of American foreign aid in Southeast Asia. A best seller, the book was made into a successful movie, and its title became a term of opprobrium, although the Ugly American in the book was actually the hero.

In 1959 Burdick coedited with Arthur J. Brodbeck *American Voting Behavior*, an important anthology. He also suffered his first heart attack in that year. The *New York Times* praised his next book, *The Blue of Capricorn* (1961). "Readers will share his fascination for the emptiness, silence, vastness and passion of the South Pacific," the reviewer wrote. Perhaps his best-written work, it mixed short fiction with travel essays.

Fail-Safe (1962), written with Harvey Wheeler, was his most spectacular and controversial work, a political novel treating the terrifying unreliability of devices designed to prevent accidental thermonuclear war. Criticism ranged from Sidney Hook's "sensational hysteria-mongering science fiction" to Norman Cousins' "an essay on the end of man, swiftly paced, ingeniously constructed, a glimpse of reality in our time, a precious commodity." It too was a best seller, a Book-of-the-Month-Club selection, and a highly successful film.

Next Burdick wrote *The 480* (1964), a tale suggesting that computers and polling might eventuate in the nomination of a presidential candidate who could not lose. Reviewers took their usual ambivalent view of Burdick's work— "a gimmick kind of novel," but "a strong sense of foreboding lingers in the mind."

In 1965 two novels appeared: *Nina's Book* and *Sarkhan*, written with Lederer. In his last years Burdick had visited India on a corporate writing assignment and Australia on a University of Chicago writing commission. He often returned to the South Pacific, sometimes with his friend the actor Marlon Brando, who had starred in the movie version of *The Ugly American*. The visits usually centered on his cottage near Tahiti.

Burdick had an almost archetypal professorial career; his teaching and writing informed each other. He was a popular lecturer and a respected political theorist. Yet he found time to write his novels, working every night and taking an occasional school quarter off. Apparently he overextended himself. Often he said (according to his family) that he had "so much to do in such a short time." He died in San Diego, Calif.

It is easy to fault Burdick for the flamboyance of *Fail-Safe* or to damn him with the faint praise of "popular." But creative imagination combined with rigorous insight and a powerful morality produced *The 480, Fail-Safe,* and *The Ugly American. Fail-Safe's* expansion of awareness helped arouse America to an ever-present danger. *The Ugly American* enlarged the national consciousness and marked a coming of age and a new national maturity.

[There are some 150 cartons of Burdick's manuscripts including notes and unfinished pieces of work, at the Boston University library. A collection of his adventure stories is *A Role in Manila* (1966). In addition to titles listed in the text, Burdick contributed articles and stories to a number of journals, including *Argosy, Collier's, Esquire, Harper's,* and the *New Yorker.* See also Sidney Hook, *The Fail-Safe Fallacy* (1963); and the *New York Times* obituary, July 27, 1965.]

DONALD D. WILSON

BURGESS, THORNTON WALDO (Jan. 14, 1874–June 5, 1965), author of children's stories, was born in Sandwich, Mass., the son of Thornton Waldo Burgess and Caroline F. Hayward. His father died when he was nine months old. From the time he was six, he worked at odd jobs—picking cranberries, herding cows, selling his semi-invalid mother's homemade candy. Despite this relative penury, Burgess always maintained that he had had an idyllic childhood. His chores kept him continually outdoor amid the ponds, meadows, and marshes of rural Cape Cod. His early experience of nature and the Protestant work ethic of his mother are incorporated into his stories.

In 1891, Burgess graduated from Sandwich High School. Too poor to attend college, he accepted financial aid from his uncle to enter a business school in Boston. He left that school after one term to work as an assistant bookkeeper for a Boston shoe factory. His letters to his mother during this period recorded his resolve to remain cheerful despite the poverty, his dislike of the job, and also his efforts to launch a career as a writer of verse and copy for various commercial concerns, including a water company and a cereal manufacturer.

In 1895, Burgess got a job as office boy for the Phelps Company in Springfield, Mass., publishers of *Good Housekeeping* magazine and an illustrated weekly, the *Springfield Homestead.* Within a year he was a reporter and editorial "utility man" for the *Homestead.* From 1901 to 1911 he served as literary and household editor for the Orange Judd weeklies, a group of agricultural papers published in association with Phelps. From 1904 to 1911, he was also an associate editor of *Good Housekeeping.* Under the pseudonym W. B. Thornton he wrote a sports and nature calendar for *Country Life in America* magazine. In 1905, Phelps published his first book, *Bride's Primer,* a collection of pieces first published in *Good Housekeeping.* On June 30, 1905, Burgess married Nina E. Osborne. A son was born in 1906, but Nina Burgess died in childbirth.

Burgess' career as a children's story writer began in 1910. While his son was visiting relatives in Chicago, he included in each of his fourteen letters to the boy a bedtime story concerning the adventures of semianthropomorphized animals who lived in the Green Meadow. The editors at Little, Brown in Boston liked the stories, commissioned two more, and published all sixteen under the title *Old Mother West Wind* (1910). The book was an immediate success and continued to earn royalties throughout Burgess' life.

On Apr. 30, 1911, Burgess married Fannie P. Johnson, mother of two teen-age children. The same year Phelps, after selling *Good Housekeeping,* fired Burgess, who then turned to writing full time, producing *Mother West Wind's Children* (1911). From 1910 to 1965, Little, Brown published some fifty-four volumes of children's stories by Burgess, plus his autobiography. It was one of the longest continuous associations in publishing history. In addition Burgess marketed thirty-two books through other publishers. After 1913 the majority of his stories were illustrated by Harrison Cady.

Most of Burgess' books were collections of stories written for newspaper syndication. In 1912 he signed a contract with the Associated Newspaper Syndicate to provide a "Little Stories for Bedtime" feature six days a week. In 1918, after a dispute over serial rights, Burgess moved to the New York Tribune Syndicate (later the Herald Tribune), for which he provided a similar daily feature. This association lasted thirty-six years.

Burgess' writing increasingly reflected his belief that animal stories were the most effective means of instilling good moral values and a reverence for nature in children. He inaugurated a series of conservationist clubs, complete with buttons and certificates. During World War I he used his daily column to encourage children to buy war savings stamps. From 1924 to 1934, Burgess was also host of "Radio Nature League," a weekly half-hour radio show on WBZ, Springfield, Mass. (later WBZ, Boston), in which he promoted wildlife conservation.

Self-conscious about his lack of formal education, Burgess sought the friendship and endorsement of eminent professional naturalists, such as William T. Hornaday of the New York Zoological Society. He cherished awards given to him for his efforts as a conservationist. In the subtitle of his autobiography, *Now I Remember* (1960), he pointedly identified himself as an "amateur naturalist."

Although praised for having created a fictional world as complete in its proprietary idiosyncrasy as William Faulkner's Yoknapatawpha County or Lewis Carroll's Wonderland, Burgess was pursued by the charge that the name of his most famous character, Peter Rabbit, had been pilfered from the British author Beatrix Potter. Burgess responded that although "Miss Potter gave Peter a name known the world over, . . . I perhaps made him a character."

By 1960, Burgess had retired from writing. He died in Hampden, Mass.

[In addition to the works cited in the text, Burgess' publications include Old Mother West Wind series, 7 vols. (1910–1918); Boy Scouts series, 4 vols. (1912–1915); Bedtime Story-Book series, 20 vols. (1913–1919); Green Meadow series, 4 vols. (1918–1920); Nature Stories series, 13 vols. (1919–1965); *Animal Stories* (1920); Green Forest series, 4 vols. (1921–1923); Smiling Pool series, 4 vols. (1924–1927); Tales from the Storyteller's House series, 2 vols. (1937–1939); Little Color Classics series, 3 vols. (1941–1942). Also see Paul O'Neil, "Fifty Years in the Green Meadow," *Life*, Nov. 14, 1960. An obituary is in the *New York Times*, May 6, 1965.]

NANCY L. STEFFEN

BURTON, HAROLD HITZ (June 22, 1888– Oct. 28, 1964), associate justice of the Supreme Court, was born in Jamaica Plain, Mass., the son of Alfred Edgar Burton, a professor of civil engineering at the Massachusetts Institute of Technology, and of Gertrude Hitz. Burton spent much of his early life in Switzerland with his terminally ill mother. There he learned French and was strongly influenced by his grandfather, John Hitz, the first Swiss consul general to the United States. Burton returned to the United States in 1895. He graduated in 1909 from Bow-

doin College, where he was a quarterback and a pole vaulter.

Burton graduated from Harvard Law School in 1912, and on June 15 of that year married Selma Florence Smith; they had four children. The Burtons moved to Cleveland, where he joined her uncle's law firm, Gage, Wilbur and Wachner. In 1914 they moved to Salt Lake City, Utah, and in 1916 to Boise, Idaho, where he became head of the legal department of the Idaho Power Company. Serving in the army from 1917 to 1919, Burton received the Belgian Croix de Guerre, the Meritorious Service Citation, and the Purple Heart.

Burton returned to Cleveland and practiced law with the firm of Day, Day and Wilkin from 1919 to 1925, and in 1925 joined the firm of Cull, Burton and Laughlin. He quickly established himself as a capable attorney and civic activist. He was elected to the East Cleveland Board of Education (1928–1929) and served as a commander of the local American Legion post. In establishing a strong political base, Burton was greatly aided by his wife, an avid political campaigner.

Burton unsuccessfully sought a district judgeship in the late 1920's. In 1929 he became both a member of the Ohio House of Representatives and director of law for the city of Cleveland. He held the latter post until 1932. In 1934 he was elected mayor of Cleveland. In office, the public viewed him as hardworking, capable, and moral—the "Boy Scout Mayor." Burton reduced the city debt by $15.6 million, developed a low-cost transit system, waged an effective war on organized crime, and averted laying off 75,000 WPA recipients by borrowing on anticipated revenues. He was reelected in 1937 and 1939 by the largest majorities in Cleveland's history, drawing support from both parties and from blacks.

Elected to the United States Senate in 1940, Burton quickly established himself as a moderate Republican with a conservative but nondoctrinaire slant, a man who on most issues voted strictly on the merits. He was appointed to the War Investigating Committee, headed by Harry Truman, which exposed wartime profiteering and reformed the government contract system. In addition Burton sponsored the Hill-Burton Hospital Construction Act, which made hospital facilities available to 15 million people under a $105 million federal grant; the Ball-Burton-Hill-Hatch Resolution (B_2H_2), which later was superseded by the Connally Act, calling for United States leadership in the United Nations; and the Ball-Burton-Hatch Act, which anticipated the Taft-Hartley Act.

In 1945, Burton became the first Truman appointee to the Supreme Court. He quickly joined the Frankfurter, self-restraint wing of the Court. His behavior as a justice was cautious, at times ambivalent, and generally conservative. He tended to uphold government power, especially when the issue was one of balancing individual liberty against national security. In one of his first dissents, *Duncan* v. *Kahanamoku* (327 U.S. 304 [1946]), he argued for the use of military courts for civilian matters in wartime, even when this meant the suspension of civil law with the normal courts open. In the economic area he was concerned about the growth of union power, feeling labor had to be reined in. But he did not shrink from government regulation of business as well. In the civil rights field, after a dissent in the desegregation case of *Morgan* v. *Virginia* (328 U.S. 373 [1946]), he consistently voted to extend the constitutional rights of blacks. In *Henderson* v. *United States* (339 U.S. 816 [1950]) he wrote the majority opinion, which held that separate dining cars were illegal in interstate commerce.

Burton's more important opinions were variations on these themes. In June 1946 he wrote a landmark opinion in an antitrust case against three major tobacco companies (*American Tobacco Co.* v. *United States* [328 U.S. 781]), establishing that a combination or conspiracy creating the power to exclude competition or to raise prices violated the Sherman Antitrust Act, even if the power had never been exercised. In *United States* v. *National Lead* (332 U.S. 319 [1947]), Burton held that a titanium cartel should be broken up and patents forced onto the open market. Such views may well have emerged from his Truman Committee disillusionment with big business, a position reiterated in his opinion in *Lichter* v. *United States* (334 U.S. 742 [1948]), in which he upheld in strong terms a wartime act providing for renegotiation of wartime contracts to prevent gouging.

On the other hand, Burton voted against the Truman administration in 1952, supporting the Supreme Court's action in holding the president's seizure of the steel industry illegal (*Youngstown Sheet and Tube* v. *Sawyer* [343 U.S. 579]), and dissented in the 1957 case of *United States* v. *Du Pont* (335 U.S. 586), expressing opposition to applying the antitrust laws to vertical acquisitions and to stock transactions that had occurred years before.

In nonsecurity-oriented civil liberties situations, Burton was fairly pragmatic. He dissented when the Supreme Court upheld the right of Jehovah's Witnesses to distribute literature in a company town (*Marsh* v. *Alabama* [326 U.S. 501 (1946)]), and when the majority overturned a local ordinance that banned the use of sound trucks without a police permit (*Saia* v. *New York* [334 U.S. 558 (1948)]). On the other hand, he deplored a second attempt to execute a black man, Willie Francis, because the electric chair had malfunctioned, asserting that this surely constituted cruel and unusual punishment (*Louisiana ex rel Francis* v. *Resweber* [329 U.S. 459 (1947)]). But shortly thereafter he spoke for the Supreme Court in holding that counsel was not a constitutional guarantee and was not needed for a fair trial (*Bute* v. *Illinois* [333 U.S. 640 (1948)]).

In the loyalty-security area Burton had little time for those who opposed government loyalty policies. In the vital cases of *American Communications Association* v. *Douds* (339 U.S. 382 [1950]) and *Dennis* v. *United States* (341 U.S. 494 [1951]), Burton voted with the government to sustain the non-Communist affidavit provision of the Taft-Hartley Act and the conviction of the eleven leaders of the American Communist party. Subsequently he wrote an opinion in *Joint Anti-Fascist Refugee Committee* v. *McGrath* (341 U.S. 123 [1951]) holding that the Justice Department could have lists of subversives but that the lists could not be used arbitrarily. In *Bailey* v. *Richardson* he voted to support the operations of the loyalty program, including its use of evidence obtained from unnamed informants (341 U.S. 918 [1951]), but in *Bridges* v. *United States* (346 U.S. 209 [1953]) he set aside the perjury conviction of the West Coast longshoremen's leader Harry Bridges, accused of having sworn falsely at his 1945 naturalization hearing that he was not a Communist, on the ground that the statute of limitations had run out before Bridges was indicted.

As the 1950's proceeded and the Warren Court majority took shape, Burton found himself more and more with the conservative dissenters. He dissented in *Pennsylvania* v. *Nelson* (350 U.S. 497 [1956]) from the majority's holding that the Smith Act (1940) superseded the Pennsylvania state sedition law and, by inference, similar statutes in forty-two other states. He did vote to reverse the conviction of state Communist leaders in *Yates* v. *United States* (354 U.S. 298 [1957]), but disagreed that the California anti-Communist law was unconstitutional, and wrote an opinion in *Beilan* v. *Board of Education* (357 U.S. 399 [1957]) upholding the dismissal of a public school teacher for "incompetency" after he had refused to tell school officials whether he had served as an official of the Communist Political Association. He also voted to approve the dismissal of a New York City subway conductor for invoking the Fifth Amendment when city authorities asked about his Communist party membership (*Lerner* v. *Casey* [357 U.S. 468 (1958)]).

By the late 1950's Burton was in increasingly poor health. He announced his retirement in 1958. The Parkinson's disease from which he suffered intensified over the next six years, eventually leading to his death at Washington, D.C.

Although Burton was not an outstanding Supreme Court figure and has been rated one of the eight failures in Albert Blaustein and R. M. Minsky, *The First One Hundred Justices* (1978), he was affable, honest, hardworking, courteous, and a unifying influence at a time when the Supreme Court was often bitterly divided. He wrote his own opinions, answered all personal inquiries, and used his law clerks only in limited, supporting ways. Well liked by justices and clerks alike, Burton promoted cooperation among the justices and was respected for not expressing his personal philosophy in opinions. His opinions were unimaginative and frequently tedious, tending to find narrow grounds for decision, but improved in clarity with time, especially in their introductory statements of issues and results.

Burton, a Unitarian, did not smoke or swear, and never drank more than one martini. He enjoyed bird watching, daily exercise, and tracing the history of the Supreme Court. His social life was indifferent at best; he attended parties mainly because his wife enjoyed them. Noted for his independence and open-mindedness, Burton won the respect of his contemporaries for his diligence, objectivity, and strong sense of moderation. As Chief Justice Earl Warren said at the time of his death, "His one overwhelming desire was to be helpful to everyone, on and off the Court."

[Burton's personal papers are in the Manuscript Division of the Library of Congress. Edward G. Hudon, ed., *The Occasional Papers of Harold Burton* (1969), contains a collection of Burton's writings in legal history. Detailed biographies focusing on his Supreme Court career are in Catherine Barness, *Men of the Supreme Court* (1978); and Leon Friedman and Fred L. Israel, eds., *The Justices of the United States Supreme Court,* 4 vols. (1969). A comprehensive analysis of Burton's Supreme Court career is in Mary F. Berry, *Stability, Security and Continuity* (1978). His viewpoints on specific areas are dealt with in David W. Atkinson, "American Constitutionalism Under Stress: Mr. Justice Burton's Response to National Security Issues," *Houston Law Review,* Nov. 1971, and C. Herman Pritchett, *Civil Liberties and the Vinson Court* (1954). Doris M. Provine, *Case Selection in the U.S. Supreme Court* (1980), contains an analysis of Burton's docket books and other papers.]

PAUL L. MURPHY
CYNTHIA S. KORHONEN

CABOT, GODFREY LOWELL (Feb. 26, 1861–Nov. 2, 1962), industrialist and philanthropist, was born in Boston, Mass., the son of Samuel Cabot, a physician, and Hannah Lowell Jackson. The "runt" of a family of six boys and two girls, he adopted a vigorous regimen for building himself up physically, walking long distances daily—a practice he continued until halted by his doctors when in his nineties. Cabot was educated at the Brimmer, Boston Latin, and Hopkinson schools, and attended the Massachusetts Institute of Technology (MIT) for one year before entering Harvard College in 1878. He graduated magna cum laude in 1882 with a B.A. in chemistry.

Upon graduation Cabot was hired by his older brother Samuel, a chemist who, among other things, manufactured lampblack. The soot from burning kerosene, lampblack was a coloring agent in inks, paint, and stove polish. The Cabot brothers, in search of a blacker carbon and a cheaper source of fuel for making it, began experiments with carbon black, the soot of burning natural gas. Samuel built a small carbon black plant at Worthington, Pa., in 1882, and Godfrey worked there in 1883 before leaving for eighteen months of travel and study in Europe. He studied chemistry at the Zurich Polytechnicum and the University of Zurich in 1883–1884.

Upon returning home, Cabot went into partnership with his brother and then educated himself in the natural gas business by tramping the oil fields of western Pennsylvania, where the gas was often burned off just to be gotten rid of. He bought out Samuel's interest in the Worthington plant in 1887, acquired natural-gas rights in the area, and began making carbon black on a large scale. On June 23, 1890, he married Maria Buckminster Moors; they had five children.

In 1891, Cabot returned to Harvard for graduate work in chemistry and geology, but his business travels precluded regular attendance. Both Cabot's business and the demand for carbon black increased. He built the Grantsville Carbon Works in West Virginia in 1899 and purchased the Pennsylvania and West Virginia Carbon companies in 1911 and 1913, respectively. Eventually controlling eleven plants, he became the nation's leading producer of carbon black and an important figure in the chemical industry. Meanwhile, new uses for carbon black developed: as coating for carbon paper and as an ingredient in fertilizers, batteries, insulating materials, and plastics. It also became important in such processes as the hardening of steel and the toughening of the rubber used for automobile tires.

As Cabot acquired natural gas for making carbon black, he branched out into the production and distribution of gas for lighting and heating. In time he became a producer of oil field equipment, crude oil, gasoline, and industrial chemicals. Through the firm of Godfrey L. Cabot, Inc. (and its successor, the Cabot Corporation), his industrial empire came to include not only carbon black plants but also tens of thousands of acres of land rich in gas, oil, and other minerals, 1,000 miles of pipeline, seven corporations with worldwide operations, three facilities for converting natural gas into gasoline, and a number of research laboratories.

"If you haven't a zest for living," Cabot declared, "you weren't brought up right. . . ." He traveled frequently to all corners of the world, crossing the Atlantic by steamer forty-four times prior to World War II, and became an early enthusiast of flying. Only four days after the flight at Kitty Hawk, N.C., in December 1903, Cabot congratulated the Wright brothers on their success, and within the month he had proposed to Senator Henry Cabot Lodge that the government take an interest in aircraft for defense purposes. At fifty-four he learned to fly.

In March 1917, Cabot became a lieutenant in the Naval Reserve Flying Corps and at his own expense and in his own plane patrolled Boston Harbor and the New England coastline, looking for German submarines. On May 3, 1918, he conducted the first successful pickup of a package from the ocean surface by an aircraft in full flight. In 1922 he patented a system for refueling planes in the air. Following World War I he established the Wright Brothers Memorial Trophy and served as president of the National Aeronautic Association.

Solar energy was another forward-looking interest of Cabot's. His gift of $647,700 to MIT in 1930 to support solar research resulted in important discoveries in photochemistry and thermal electricity and in the construction of experimental solar houses. Other Cabot philanthropies included $615,773 to Harvard to establish the Maria Moors Cabot Foundation for Botanical Research and funding for the annual Maria Moors Cabot prizes awarded by the Columbia School of Journalism to newspaper editors and writers who most advance international friendship in the western hemisphere.

In spite of the breadth of his interests, Cabot's views on morality were narrow. He completely abstained from alcoholic beverages and drank neither coffee nor tea. He devoted much money and effort to the suppression of vice and corruption in Boston. In 1900 he joined the Watch and Ward Society, became a member of its board in 1908, and served as treasurer from 1915 until 1940. Under his direction in the 1920's and 1930's, the society's work made Boston synonymous with blue-nosed puritanism. Showing little sensitivity for the constitutional rights of their quarry, Cabot and his associates used economic, social, and legal pressures and harassing techniques to block the sale and distribution of books of which they disapproved. Among their victims were many of the foremost writers of the era: Conrad Aiken, Sherwood Anderson, John Dos Passos, Theodore Dreiser, William Faulkner, Ernest Hemingway, Aldous Huxley, James Joyce, Sinclair Lewis, Bertrand Russell, Upton Sinclair, and H. G. Wells. The society also forced changes in, or the omission of "offensive" parts from, plays and moving pictures; waged war on saloons and alcohol; and attacked prostitution, gambling, narcotics dealing, and other vices.

Almost single-handedly Cabot brought about the disbarment of Joseph C. Pelletier, district attorney of Suffolk County, Mass., for failing to prosecute criminals and for accepting bribes to drop pending cases. Yet during the era of Senator Joseph McCarthy, he spoke out in defense of professors and others accused of Communist sympathies. He died in Boston at the age of 101.

[There are sixty boxes of Cabot's papers at the Massachusetts Historical Society in Boston, and a considerable correspondence between Cabot and Karl Taylor Compton in the Office of the President Records, 1930–1958, Institute Archives and Special Collections, MIT. The MIT Historical Collections have a biographical sketch of Cabot by the MIT News Office, Jan. 1953, and notices of Cabot's death that include biographical information from Randolph Antonsen, Andrew D. Fuller, and William S. Edgerly for the Alumni Association and from MIT President Julius A. Stratton. Also see A. S. Plotkin, biographical sketch, *Boston Sunday Globe*, Nov. 4, 1962; and Leon Harris, *Only to God: The Extraordinary Life of Godfrey Lowell Cabot* (1967). Obituaries are in the *New York Times* and *New York Herald Tribune*,

Nov. 3, 1962; *Time,* Nov. 9, 1962; and *Rubber Age,* Dec. 1962.]

GERALD G. EGGERT

CAHN, EDMOND NATHANIEL (Jan. 17, 1906–Aug. 9, 1964), lawyer and legal philosopher, was born in New Orleans, La., the son of Edgar Mayer Cahn, a lawyer, and Minnie Sarah Cohen. After attending public schools in New Orleans, he enrolled at Tulane University, from which he received the B.A. in 1925, and the J.D. degree in 1927, ranking first in his class.

In part because of his distaste for racial segregation, after graduation Cahn practiced law in New York City. Specializing in trusts and estates, and later in taxation, he practiced there until 1950, when he became a full-time member of the faculty of the New York University School of Law. On Mar. 18, 1930, he married Lenore Lebach; they had two children.

As a legal philosopher Cahn dealt mainly with the ethical and moral insights that law encompasses. His basic thoughts were conceptual statements of the elements of Jewish belief. His first book, *The Sense of Injustice* (1949), which propelled him to public attention, can be regarded as a philosophical treatment of the Hebrew prophets' war on individual and social injustice. Cahn challenged the prevailing legal formalism with a frankly anthropocentric system of juridical theory: Law exists to serve the citizens, to minister to their everyday needs; it is in this sense a malleable tool to be molded as they see fit. According to Cahn, justice consists not in natural-law principles nor in the acceptance of legalized power, but in "the *active process* of remedying or preventing what would arouse the sense of injustice." The sense of injustice is an "indissociable blend of reason and empathy" and in many demonstrable ways is "a real causal factor in the daily operation of law."

After the publication of *The Sense of Injustice,* the American Law Institute asked Cahn to prepare a survey of morals as revealed in court opinions. When he submitted the first section of his report, the institute criticized it as "controversial." Because he wanted "perfect freedom of expression" and feared being a "kept scholar," Cahn decided to go ahead with the study at his own expense.

The result was *The Moral Decision* (1955). The Hebraic and Hellenic ideal that the law should serve as "a lamp unto the feet and a light unto the path" inspired him. Seeking guides for daily behavior and private moral judgments, Cahn critically evaluated the moral precepts found in society in the light of American law

and illustrated the extent to which judges, in deciding cases, actually reflect those precepts.

Writing the section on death while he was ill with tuberculosis, and with his survival in doubt, Cahn employed the lawyer's technique of working from concrete cases. In extracting moral issues from reported decisions, he showed, in opposition to the traditional philosophical method, how the particular can illuminate the general. Since moral values exist both inside and outside the law, "the only practical difference between them is in the respective *methods* by which they are *enforced.*" He scrupulously respected the line between morals and ethics. Morals are a species of the generic term "ethics" and are concerned with the relative contextual correctness of specific judgments. Cahn found the basis for moral decisions in a dynamic human nature achieving active adjustment in a complex and fluid community.

Cahn next wrote *The Predicament of Democratic Man* (1961), which develops the biblical insight that a people is accountable for the moral quality of its law. His thesis revolved around the political-ethical quandary whether it is possible to live under a democratic government without becoming morally contaminated. He confronted this issue by explaining the nature and background of our moral involvement in governmental wrongs and by providing the criteria for determining individual and collective guilt. The citizen, he felt, must accept individual responsibility for the transgressions of the government. Cahn rejected such traditional philosophical queries as whether life has any meaning because they leave the ethical individual in a state of passive contemplation. The central ethical question to him was how we can infuse meaning into life by the ways in which we behave toward ourselves and others.

Throughout the corpus of Cahn's writing fact-skepticism is especially prominent. As developed by Jerome Frank, this approach aims to rid the judicial process of the cloak of certainty and to expose its realities by the continual questioning of factual assumptions. This method emphasizes the difficulty of re-creating the past or predicting the future and stresses the importance of the personal element in choice and decision. It is "vitalistic, pluralistic, and above all, personalistic."

Cahn expanded upon Frank's approach, applying it in divers areas. The "insight of irreversibility" helped him to believe that the death penalty should be abolished. Among all forms of punishment, "it alone is irreversible" and "completely irremediable." A mistake-laden legal system imposes a final result on the basis of necessarily incomplete facts about the past and without knowing what relevant data will turn up in the future. Likewise, overreliance on the findings of disputing experts in other disciplines can lead judges to abdicate their responsibility in the search for justice.

Cahn skirted nominalism. His focus on the person on trial left him open to charges that he cared more about the fate of the individual than about the legal principles involved. Law, said Cahn, must be viewed from the vantage point of those who use it; he labeled this idea the "consumer perspective." He evolved the theory of "graded pragmatism," in which limits are imposed on physical and psychological experiments on human beings to verify scientific hypotheses. Assaults on the inviolability of the human personality he regarded as ethically pernicious; the individual must possess the freedom to refine his principles progressively through constant usage. Actions must be judged in light of their consequences on those affected.

Cahn viewed his task as furnishing the theoretical underpinnings of a philosophy of action to provide a more just society. Despite his aversion to joining groups whose positions might threaten his intellectual independence, he was no closet philosopher. As a member of the board of the Union for Democratic Action, the predecessor of the Americans for Democratic Action, he was "the only one who," according to its secretary, Joseph P. Lash, "made an intellectual contribution." Later he was active in the New York League to Abolish Capital Punishment. Many judges at all levels were among his friends, and he was in the forefront of those who lauded the efforts of the Supreme Court in extending protection of individual rights. At times he felt the Court did not go far enough in enforcing constitutional guarantees. His philosophical skepticism did not prevent Cahn from advocating an "absolute" concept of the First Amendment. The Bill of Rights, he told his students, is "our most solemnly declared public policy. . . ." It is "our way, with it we stand or fail."

Cahn was a tall, courtly man whose subtle mind, intensity, and passionate spirit often hid a ready wit. His Reform Judaism infused his inspirational writings; the moral ideal permeated his thoughts and actions. He strove to demonstrate the relevance of legal and moral theory to contemporary concerns. Cahn's significance lay partly in the fact that he was able to step outside the milieu of professional discourse and convey his ideas to the general public. He was an easy conversationalist and accomplished public speaker, and made an especial effort to befriend judges in hope of influencing their thoughts.

In 1955 the American Philosophical Society awarded Cahn its Phillips Prize in Jurisprudence, which had been bestowed only eight times since its inception in 1888. Three years later he was the first guest lecturer in philosophy of law at the Hebrew University in Jerusalem. Shortly before his death he was elected to the national board of the American Civil Liberties Union. He also edited and contributed to *The Great Rights* (1963), a collection of speeches about the primary safeguards of American freedom delivered at his urging by Supreme Court Justices Hugo L. Black (whose mutuality of views with Cahn's led to a warm and enduring intellectual and personal bond), William J. Brennan, Jr., William O. Douglas, and Chief Justice Earl Warren.

After Cahn's death in New York City, Justice Black wrote that Cahn's writings "will live for a long time to give hope and courage to many people who want to see this troubled world one in which a sense of justice is a more widespread and abiding faith."

[Cahn's correspondence and personal papers are in private possession. Large collections of his correspondence are in the Jerome Frank MSS (Yale University Library), Irving Brant MSS (Library of Congress), Huntington Cairns MSS (Library of Congress), and, especially, Hugo Black MSS (Library of Congress). His teaching notebooks and part of his library are at the New York University School of Law. Lenore L. Cahn, ed., *Confronting Injustice* (1966), is a thorough selection of his writings almost exclusively from sources other than his books; it contains an essentially complete bibliography. Memorials and insightful analyses are in the *New York University Law Review*, Apr. 1965. Aspects of his life and thought are considered in Paul Ramsey, *Nine Modern Moralists* (1962); Thomas A. Cowan, "A Report on the Status of the Philosophy of Law in the United States," *Columbia Law Review*, Dec. 1950; Edward F. McClain, "A Law from the Burning Bush: The Moral Foundations of the Legal Philosophy of Edmond Cahn," M.A. thesis, Southern Illinois University, 1963; Roger K. Newman, "Hugo Black and Edmond Cahn: A Philosophical Friendship" (M.A. thesis, University of Virginia, 1976); and Jay A. Sigler, "Edmond Cahn and the Search for Empirical Justice," *Villanova Law Review*, Winter 1967. Obituaries are in the *New York Times* and *New York Herald Tribune*, Aug. 10, 1964.]

ROGER K. NEWMAN

CALKINS, EARNEST ELMO (Mar. 25, 1868–Oct. 4, 1964), advertising executive and author, was born at Geneseo, Ill., the son of

William Clinton Calkins and Mary Harriet Manville. His first name was suggested by a sentimental aunt to signify that he was a pledge or "earnest" of others to come; his middle name recalled the hero of a romantic best seller of the post–Civil War period, *St. Elmo.*

Shortly after Calkins was born, the family moved to Galesburg, Ill., a country town then emerging from its pioneer state. Calkins' father entered the practice of law and became city attorney, but was chiefly remembered by Earnest for his skill at pinochle and billiards, his frequent absences, and his somewhat uncertain provision for the family's needs.

When Earnest was six he was deafened by an attack of measles and an inherited tendency. This handicap, which soon became severe, shaped the rest of his life. He attended public school in Galesburg and graduated with the B.A. from Knox College in 1891, but profited little from his formal education because he could not hear his teachers, participate in classroom work, or enter into extracurricular student activities. Reading omnivorously, Calkins in effect educated himself.

Since he had manual dexterity and bookish interests, he acquired a small foot-powered press and some battered type and then taught himself to use a composing stick and kick a press. Finding employment in a local newspaper office, he set up advertisements, as well as personals, verse, and high school and college news, these latter items directly in type.

When he was twenty-three, Calkins made an unsuccessful effort to establish himself in New York City. There he edited, briefly, a trade paper entitled the *Butchers' Gazette and Sausage Journal,* owned by a piratical publisher who might well have stepped out of the pages of Charles Dickens. When Calkins applied for another position through a "blind" ad, he turned out to be asking for his own job. His departure was automatic.

Calkins returned to Galesburg, where it was assumed that he would "soon return," as he later wrote of the episode, "to big affairs that engaged me." This belief was not shared by his father. A friend accosted the latter, saying, "I want to see Earnest before he goes back. How long will he be here?" "All his life, I am afraid," was the reply.

Calkins became a columnist for the *Galesburg Evening Mail,* started a copywriting service for local advertisers, and won a national contest for the best advertisement for a carpet sweeper. This encouragement determined his future vocation. In 1894, Calkins became advertising manager for a department store in Peoria, Ill. Before his contract expired, he sent samples of his work to Charles Austin Bates, whose advertising agency in New York City was one of the first to supply advertisers with copy as well as space. Bates offered a job. "He was," Calkins wrote, "to be the last employer I was ever to have—except myself."

Important writing assignments followed. Meanwhile Calkins studied art at the Pratt School of Design. As his responsibilities increased, he added an art department to the agency and induced artists with established reputations to undertake commissions for national advertisers. A friendship with Ralph Holden, a colleague at the Bates firm, resulted in the establishment in 1902 of Calkins and Holden, often described as the pattern for the modern advertising agency. Holden supplied the business judgment and handled outside contacts; Calkins contributed what he called "the red fire." On May 5, 1904, he married Angie Cushman Higgins. They had no children.

Calkins and Holden attracted attention because of its emphasis upon strong copy and good artwork, tasteful layouts and typography, new concepts in packaging, and integrated plans for advertising campaigns. The firm prospered accordingly. In 1905, with Holden, Calkins published *Modern Advertising,* the first textbook describing modern advertising procedures, and in 1908 he organized the first exhibition of advertising art, held at the National Arts Club in New York City. Recognized as an authority, Calkins wrote and lectured extensively on business and advertising topics. In 1925 he received the Edward W. Bok gold medal for his pioneering efforts in raising the standards of advertising.

Holden died in 1926, and five years later Calkins resigned as president of Calkins and Holden. The agency was merged into the Interpublic Group of Companies, Inc., in 1963. Essentially a writer, Calkins in his later years widened his range of subjects to include books and magazine articles (with some fifty pieces in the *Atlantic Monthly* alone) on American food, European travel, small-town life, fine printing, creative hobbies, Middle West social history, and especially the problems of the deaf. His shrewd and often whimsical observations of the contemporary scene frequently appeared in the letter columns of the *New York Times* on such disparate themes as panhandling, dining car service, investment strategies, beating traffic lights, and square pies. It was a way for a deaf man to keep in touch.

Calkins was a handsome man of dignified bearing. Outgoing by nature, he was barred by his deafness from the easy social intercourse he greatly desired, but he reached out through correspondence and his writings to those who shared his interests and to those who shared his handicap. He died in New York City.

[Calkins' papers, manuscripts, and correspondence are in the Henry W. Seymour Library of Knox College, Galesburg, Ill. Autobiographical writings include *Louder, Please!* (1924) and *And Hearing Not—* (1946), which reprints much of the earlier book with a substantial amount of new material. Books, include on business, *The Advertising Man* (1922) and *Business the Civilizer* (1927); and on Middle West history, *They Broke the Prairie* (1937). See also the *New York Times*, Feb. 23, 1926, and Sept. 15, 1931; "St. Elmo," *Saturday Review of Literature*, Dec. 16, 1939; and the obituary in the *New York Times*, Oct. 6, 1964.]

GERALD CARSON

CALLIMACHOS, PANOS DEMETRIOS (Dec. 4, 1879–Oct. 13, 1963), Greek Orthodox priest, journalist, author, and advocate of Hellenism, was born Demetrios Paximadas in Madytos, Dardanelles, Turkey, the son of Panagiotis Paximadas, a public employee in Madytos, and Grammatiki Paximadas. He was educated in Constantinople, Smyrna, and Athens. While a divinity student at the University of Athens, he joined Hellenismos, a society dedicated to the fulfillment of Greek territorial aspirations. After receiving the D.D. degree in 1902, he became the managing editor of the society's official organ and also worked for *Akropolis*, an Athens newspaper. Later, as a lecturer for Regeneration, a society devoted to the moral and cultural advancement of the Greek people, he traveled throughout Greece and visited Greek-speaking communities in Asia Minor, the Holy Land, Egypt, and the Sudan.

While secretary of the Patriarchate of Alexandria (1906–1914), Callimachos was granted leave to study the manuscripts in the monasteries of the island of Patmos and published *The Patriarchate of Alexandria in Abyssinia*. On July 24, 1908, in Cairo, he married Olga Andres; they had two sons. As a volunteer chaplain in the Balkan Wars of 1912–1913, he took part in a number of battles. His war dispatches appeared in the Athens press, and his wartime memoirs were published in two small pamphlets: *The Giganto Macheia of Kikis* and *Immortal Greece*.

Callimachos arrived in the United States late in 1914 with his wife and his surviving son to help revitalize the Panhellenic Union, the purpose of which was to keep the spirit of Hellenism alive among the Greeks in America. In 1915 he became the editor of the newly founded Greek-language daily *National Herald*, established in New York City to combat the proroyalist policies of its rival, *Atlantis*.

Callimachos espoused the cause of Greek liberalism and argued that Greece had to throw its lot in with the Allies during World War I if it hoped to fulfill its territorial aspirations. He resigned as editor of *National Herald* in 1918 because of differences with the publisher. He served as priest of St. Constantine's Church in Brooklyn; temporarily managed and edited *National Renaissance*, a monthly magazine devoted to Hellenic topics; and was a part-time professor at the short-lived St. Athanasius Seminary in Astoria, Queens, before returning to his former position with the *Herald* in 1922. That same year, Callimachos was among those who accompanied Meletios Metaxakis, the deposed head of the church of Greece, to Constantinople for his enthronement as patriarch.

He retained his liberal affiliations and concern with Greek-American affairs after the heat of the partisan battles began to wane, kept in close touch with developments within the Greek Orthodox Church in America, resisted the spirit of assimilation that swept the country in the 1920's, and joined the Greek-American Progressive Association, which advocated the preservation and perpetuation of Greek language, customs, and traditions.

Callimachos was among the first Greek-American journalists to endorse Franklin D. Roosevelt for the presidency in 1932. He opposed the restoration of the Greek monarchy in 1935 and the regime of John Metaxas (who seized power in Greece in 1936), but later conceded that the Metaxas government was preferable to Communist rule.

Callimachos retained his strong attachment to the Greek Orthodox Church in America. He welcomed the truce that had been reached by the contending factions in 1931 and became a warm admirer of Archbishop Athenagoras, who was elevated in 1947 to the patriarchate. His relations with the new archbishop, Michael, were friendly, and both Patriarch Athenagoras and Michael sought his opinions on matters relating to the church in the United States.

During World War II, Callimachos was active as a speaker, journalist, clergyman, and relief worker. Changes in the ownership of the *Herald* and differences with the new publisher again caused him to resign, and in 1944 he became the editor of *Eleutheros Typos* ("Free Press"), a Greek-language weekly. In the closing stages of World War II he bitterly denounced the Greek Left and those who aided it in the United States. This, combined with his interest in current events and the writing of articles on the history of the more important Greek Orthodox church parishes in New York City, absorbed his interests until 1947, when he was recalled by the new publisher of the *Herald* to become emeritus editor. His last work, *How and Why Americans Succeed,* was aimed at a Greek audience inspired by the postwar influence of the United States.

Callimachos was among the last of the Panhellenists who continued to write about Hellenic causes in the spirit of the pre– and post–World War I eras. He was honored by the Greek government and the Greek Orthodox Church for his many services; among the honors was the ecclesiastical title master of the ecumenical throne. He died in New York City.

[Callimachos' surviving correspondence and papers, mostly in Greek, are in the possession of Theodore Saloutos, and eventually will be turned over to the Special Collections Section, University of California at Los Angeles Library. On his early years, see *Monthly Illustrated National Herald,* Apr. 1925, in Greek; scattered references in Theodore Saloutos, *The Greeks in the United States* (1964), and "Demetrios Callimachos," English supp. to *Krikos* (London), July–Aug. 1964.]

THEODORE SALOUTOS

CANBY, HENRY SEIDEL (Sept. 6, 1878–Apr. 5, 1961), editor, literary critic, and educator, was born in Wilmington, Del., the son of Edward Tatnall Canby, a founder and president of the Delaware Trust Company, and Ella Augusta Seidel. Although the family's fortunes declined somewhat in the 1890's, Canby's childhood was a comfortable one. He attended the Friends School, and his Quaker background, he was convinced, shaped his temperament and made him emotionally reticent, tolerant of others, and concerned with seeking "quality in everything." As a boy, he collected minerals and developed a love of nature and books.

After a year of work following graduation from high school, Canby enrolled in 1896 in the Sheffield Scientific School at Yale University, where he edited two undergraduate publications. He received the Ph.B. degree in 1899 and, dreading the alternative of a business career, stayed at Yale for graduate study in English. He completed the Ph.D. in 1905 and remained at

Yale as a faculty member. He was an assistant (1900–1903), an instructor (1903–1908), and an assistant professor (1908–1916). An idealistic teacher, Canby introduced his students to nonutilitarian values.

On June 15, 1907, Canby married Marion Ponsonby Gause, the sister of his Yale roommate. They had two sons. "Lady" Canby, as she was known, eventually published several volumes of poetry. But it was Canby's writing career that grew rapidly. Canby wrote *The Short Story* (1902), *The Short Story in English* (1909), and *A Study of the Short Story* (1913)—as well as a number of fictional and critical magazine pieces.

In 1911 Wilbur Cross founded the *Yale Review* and invited Canby to become assistant editor, a position he held until 1920. Canby and Cross believed in the importance of a journal that could address both scholarly and general audiences; they sought serious contributions that were not too technical or too journalistic. The assumption that scholarship should not be remote from a commercially oriented society, but should instead enrich it and be responsive to its needs, pervaded Canby's *College Sons and College Fathers* (1915), a collection of articles.

During World War I Canby went to Europe under the auspices of the British Ministry of Information, as part of a mission to promote "mutual understanding." He wrote of his experiences in *Education by Violence* (1919). That year he also published his only novel, *Our House.* After the war Canby returned to Yale, where he gave one of the first courses on American literature in its social context. But he grew increasingly dissatisfied with his prospects as an academic. In 1920 he eagerly accepted the opportunity to become the first editor of a weekly supplement to the *New York Evening Post,* the *Literary Review.* He maintained his affiliation with the university by teaching occasional courses in criticism and writing. Along with staff members William Rose Benét, Amy Loveman, and Christopher Morley, Canby strove to make the *Literary Review* a publication that would, as he wrote, "bring to the interpretation of new books for the intelligent reader the trained thinking and real erudition of the universities." This sort of literary journalism, he explained in *Everyday Americans* (1920), was necessary to prevent the debilitating standardization of culture threatened by widespread postwar prosperity. Canby retained this outlook when he and his staff resigned from the *Evening Post* in 1924 to found the *Saturday Review of Literature.* "I wanted to go in for adult education in the value of books. I wished to make criticism first of all a teaching job . . . I recognized the value of speculation . . . but left that to different minds and temperaments."

Under Canby's editorship, which lasted until 1936, the *Saturday Review* became America's most influential journal of liberal criticism. Wary of modernism and experimentation, neutral and balanced in tone, it tried to reaffirm supposedly timeless aesthetic standards while responding to the needs of a middle class eager to acquire culture along with consumer goods.

Unlike many of his literary contemporaries, Canby saw the 1920's as a time of opportunity, not of cultural bankruptcy. His other efforts to shape American taste reflect his willingness to meet the middle class halfway: he lectured to women's groups, wrote a popular writers' manual (*Better Writing*, 1926), and, most important, in 1926 became the first chairman of the Board of Judges of the Book-of-the-Month Club. Although the club was attacked as an instrument of standardization, Canby's view of the enterprise was the opposite. He felt that distributing books to a large number of subscribers would cultivate a widespread demand for better reading and so safeguard culture. At this time, Canby also brought out two collections of his previously published essays, *Definitions* (1922, 1924) and *American Estimates* (1929).

The Depression brought an end to Canby's sense of a golden age in American letters. He suffered a minor breakdown in 1930 and slipped into a mood of nostalgia for the security of the 1890's, an era he described in *The Age of Confidence* (1934) and *Alma Mater* (1936). Finding respite from violence, Marxism, fascism, and economic distress in literary history, Canby stepped down from his *Saturday Review* editorship. As a contributing editor he devoted himself to studies of nineteenth-century American writers, a subject he had begun exploring in his survey *Classic Americans* (1931). He published *Seven Years' Harvest* (1936), a compendium of *Saturday Review* essays; *Thoreau* (1939); and *Walt Whitman* (1943). These years he lived at Killingworth, Clinton, Conn.

In 1941 Canby contributed a volume titled *The Brandywine* to the Rivers of America series. After the outbreak of World War II, he became a consultant to the Office of War Information. He lectured in Australia and New Zealand in 1945 on the importance of a national literature. His last work, *Turn West, Turn East,* a study of Mark Twain and Henry James, appeared in 1951. In 1955, after twenty-nine

years, he retired from the Book-of-the-Month Club board. He died in Ossining, N.Y.

Robert Spiller, with whom Canby collaborated on *A Literary History of America* (1948), once described him as "the complete product of nineteenth-century liberalism." Aware that he was living in an age of transition, Canby typified the American intellectual of the post–World War I era who tried to adjust those older values to twentieth-century realities. Although his gentlemanly restraint and allegiance to convention incurred the disfavor of the avant-garde, Canby's career as literary expert for what the Book-of-the-Month Club called the "average intelligent reader" earned him a permanent place in American cultural history.

[The principal collection of Canby's papers is at the Beinecke Rare Book and Manuscript Library, Yale University. An interview with Canby about the Book-of-the-Month Club is part of the Columbia Oral History Project. The best single source on Canby's life is his *American Memoir* (1947), which incorporates revised versions of *The Age of Confidence* and *Alma Mater*. See also "The Literary Spotlight," *Bookman*, September 1924; Henry Seidel Canby, "Henry Seidel Canby," *Nation*, Oct. 8, 1924; H. L. Mencken, "Light and Leading," *Saturday Review of Literature*, Apr. 6, 1929; Norman Foerster, "The Literary Historians," *Bookman*, July 1930; Allan Nevins, "Henry Seidel Canby: SRL Founder and Editor," *Saturday Review of Literature*, Apr. 22, 1961; and Malcolm Cowley, "Dr. Canby and His Team," *Saturday Review of Literature*, Aug. 29, 1964. The obituary appeared in the *New York Times* on Apr. 6, 1961.]

JOAN SHELLEY RUBIN

CANNON, CLARENCE (Apr. 11, 1879–May 12, 1964), congressman, was born in Elsberry, Mo., the son of John Randolph Cannon, a prosperous merchant, and Ida Glovina Whiteside. He attended La Grange College (now Hannibal-La Grange College), and earned the B.A. (1903) and M.A. (1904) from William Jewell College. He next studied law at the University of Missouri, and received the LL.B. in 1908. A quiet and industrious young man, Cannon worked while obtaining his education as a teacher and principal in public schools and later as a teacher of history at Stephens College (1904–1908). On Aug. 30, 1906, he married Ida Dawson Wigginton; they had two daughters.

After practicing law for three years, Cannon moved to Washington, D.C. He worked first as confidential secretary for his congressman, Champ Clark, who was then the Speaker of the House. Cannon later became journal clerk and parliamentarian. In 1920 he was appointed parliamentarian of the Democratic National Convention, a post he held until 1960.

Cannon took a scholarly approach to his duties. Beginning in 1918, he published several books and articles concerned with the business of the House, its procedures and rules, and parliamentary law. These works sharply reduced the time Congress spent debating parliamentary questions, and guided speakers and others on ways of behaving and deciding matters in the House. Cannon was a storehouse of information on House rules, and he knew how to put them to good use.

In 1922 Cannon was elected to the House of Representatives, beginning a career there that lasted more than forty years. He won election after election by developing and maintaining close ties with his constituents and serving their interests. He delivered the public works desired by the district, battled for veterans of World Wars I and II, and paid careful attention to the wants of commercial farmers. Legislative proposals he favored provided veterans with a variety of benefits, combatted flooding along the Mississippi and Missouri rivers, and raised farm prices.

Cannon had a large nose and ears; he usually wore a black suit, a black tie, and a dour expression on his lined face. When accused of being two-faced, he snapped: "If I had another face, don't you think I'd use it?" When relaxed, he could tell good stories; but on Capitol Hill he seldom relaxed. Cannon was extremely stubborn, quick-tempered, and combative, even resorting to physical force on occasion. He had a sharp, sarcastic tongue, and became increasingly impatient and irascible with age. He abstained from alcohol, tobacco, and small talk, lived a quiet life, and seldom attended parties.

Support from his constituents, hard work, and ability, not charm, made Cannon a power in Washington. In 1941 he became chairman of the powerful Committee on Appropriations, and he held the post for all but four of the next twenty-three years. Since money bills originated in Appropriations, congressmen depended on it for the funds needed for their pet projects. Cannon did not have the power of appointment to the committee, but he did distribute assignments within it, creating and dissolving subcommittees, defining their jurisdictions, changing their sizes, selecting their Democratic members, and appointing their chairmen when the Democrats controlled the House. Much of the time he served on all subcommittees and chaired the one concerned with public works.

Cannon used his power to affect the level of federal appropriations. He supported President Franklin D. Roosevelt's requests for the funds required to fight and win World War II, including the money for the atomic bomb project. At the same time he worked to cut spending on nonwar programs. After the war, while talking economy and reduction of the national debt, he supported the defense and foreign programs of President Harry Truman, including the European Recovery Program. He also worked for passage of the spending proposals of the Air Force.

During his last years Cannon was often at odds with the executive branch and the House leadership. Frequently resisting pressure, he emphasized the value of his committee as the guardian of the national treasury and sought to guarantee that programs cost no more than he regarded as necessary. He became especially critical of foreign aid, and he called the program to land a man on the moon a "moondoggle."

Cannon also clashed frequently with the Senate. He regarded senators as wasteful, and fought against their restoration of cuts his committee had made. A major battle in 1962 pitted Cannon against the chairman of the Senate Appropriations Committee, Carl Hayden, also an octogenarian. It involved the authority of the appropriations committees and the control of the House-Senate conferences designed to iron out disagreements on money bills.

Cannon died in Washington, D.C.

[There is a small collection of Cannon papers in the Western Historical Manuscripts Collection of the University of Missouri, Columbia. His most important publications are *Cannon's Precedents of the House of Representatives* (1935–1941) and *Procedure in the House of Representatives* (1920, 1928, 1939, 1945, and 1963). See Richard F. Fenno, Jr., *The Power of the Purse* (1966); P. F. Healy, "Nobody Loves Clarence," *Saturday Evening Post*, Mar. 25, 1950; Neil McNeil, *Forge of Democracy* (1963); and C. Herschel Schooley, *Missouri's Cannon in the House* (1977). Obituaries are in the *St. Louis Post-Dispatch*, May 12, 1964; *New York Times*, May 13, 1964; *Time*, May 22, 1964; and *Newsweek*, May 25, 1964.]

RICHARD S. KIRKENDALL

CANTOR, EDDIE (Jan. 31, 1892–Oct. 10, 1964), comedian, was born in New York City, the son of Michael Iskowitz and Maite Kantrowitz, impoverished Russian Jewish immigrants who had settled on the Lower East Side. Cantor's mother died in childbirth in 1893; and his father, an unemployed violinist, died a year later. His maternal grandmother, Esther Kantrowitz, raised him and was the dominant influence of his childhood, which was scarred by hardship. Cantor, an indifferent student, never finished elementary school. He was able to transcend so unpromising an upbringing through a natural and irrepressible capacity for performance, beginning with inaccurate but comic impersonations.

Cantor, shortening his grandmother's surname, made his vaudeville debut in 1907 at the Clinton Music Hall in his neighborhood; he and a friend formed a song-and-dance team. The following year Cantor's professional career was inaugurated when he won $5 in an amateur contest at Miner's Theatre on the Bowery. That success led to a job with a touring vaudeville company, in which he assumed the blackface role with which he was to be associated. The eyeglasses he put on along with the burnt cork were a special touch. When the tour folded, he became a singing waiter in a Coney Island saloon in which the pianist was Jimmy Durante. There Cantor came to the attention of Marcus Loew and Adolph Zukor, who booked him on their small vaudeville circuit in 1909. His appearances were noted for the repetitions of the same act in different ethnic accents, as well as in blackface, which provoked laughs because of the very familiarity of the lines. From 1910 to 1912, Cantor, as the Black Face Stooge, shared the bill with the comedy juggling team of Bedini and Arthur. Beginning as their valet, and then as their assistant, he gradually enlarged his role.

Another break came in 1912 with *Kid Kabaret*, a showcase for talented children. Along with George Jessel, who became perhaps his closest friend in show business, Cantor remained in the show for two years. On June 9, 1914, he wed Ida Tobias; their marriage was considered one of the most harmonious in show business. It was certainly among the best-known, since Cantor incorporated anecdotes about his wife and their five daughters into his routines. "Ida" became the theme song by which he was instantly recognized. Cantor's wholesome presentation of himself as a family man was undoubtedly important to his popularity.

Cantor's extraordinary comic impact upon audiences in such musicals as *Canary Cottage* (1916) attracted the interest of producer Florenz Ziegfeld, who put him in *Midnight Frolic* (1917) and in the *Ziegfeld's Follies* of 1917, 1918, and 1919. But the impresario canceled plans to star Cantor in his next show when the comedian helped lead a strike of the Actors'

Equity Association that briefly shut down Broadway in 1919. When the Schubert brothers cast Cantor in their *Midnight Rounders* in 1920, his name was for the first time displayed above the name of the show on the marquee.

After the Schuberts' *Make It Snappy* (1922), Ziegfeld persuaded Cantor to star in *Kid Boots* (1923), a musical comedy in which Cantor wrote most of his own material; it ran for three years. With *Ziegfeld's Follies* of 1927, Cantor broke precedent by being designated the star of the revue. He won equivalent billing for Ziegfeld's *Whoopee* (1928–1930). At $5,000 a week, he was probably the highest-salaried comedian in history up to that time.

Much of his wealth evaporated in the Great Depression, but Cantor was resilient. He capitalized on the general failure with a successful 1929 joke book about the stock market crash, *Caught Short!* And when the talkies helped doom vaudeville, he adapted himself to the movies, earning $450,000 a year by 1930. For Samuel Goldwyn in particular, Cantor starred in a string of musical comedies, such as *Palmy Days* (1931), *The Kid from Spain* (1932), *Roman Scandals* (1933), *Kid Millions* (1934), *Strike Me Pink* (1936), and *Forty Little Mothers* (1940). Such frothy entertainment enhanced Cantor's popularity without accelerating the aesthetic development of the American cinema.

His radio career was more impressive. Pop-eyed wonder had been Cantor's stage trademark, along with his dancing and the relentless energy that animated his every movement and gesture. He nevertheless made an easy transition to radio, where he satisfied the craving for comedy that Depression audiences apparently required. His insistence on having studio audiences, rather than an empty chamber, also helped to account for his triumphant radio career, which began in 1931 with "The Chase and Sanborn Hour." By 1933 Cantor's show headed the National Broadcasting Company's "red" comedy roster and was topping even "Amos 'n' Andy" in the ratings.

Unexcelled vigor and unabashed sentimentality contributed to Cantor's status as a radio star for two decades. But he also made the move to television, appearing in several comedy and variety shows, including "The Eddie Cantor Comedy Theatre" (1955). A dramatic role on "Playhouse 90" in "Seidman and Son" (1956) won him critical acclaim as well. His last film was a brief appearance at the conclusion of Warner Brothers' *The Eddie Cantor Story* (1953), starring Keefe Brasselle. The movie was released a year after a heart attack forced Cantor into semiretirement. He died in Hollywood, Calif.

Cantor's popularity can be attributed to his dignified yet boyish charm and to his irresistible human warmth. He was frequently occupied with charitable activities, especially bond drives during both world wars, the March of Dimes, and Zionism. His devotion to such causes probably enlarged his appeal. Cantor was not a satirist, and he was neither profound nor original. Yet his friend Jessel may have been right to call him "the most resourceful comic figure that there ever was in America."

[The basic sources of information on Cantor's life are his autobiographies: *My Life Is in Your Hands*, as told to David Freedman (1928), and *Take My Life*, with Jane Kesner Ardmore (1957). These books can be supplemented with his recollections in *Between the Acts* (1930) and *As I Remember Them* (1963). Cantor's radio career is briefly discussed in Erik Barnouw, *The Golden Web*, II (1968). George Jessel's comments can be found in Larry Wilde, *The Great Comedians* (1973). An obituary is in the *New York Times*, Oct. 11, 1964.]

STEPHEN J. WHITFIELD

CARRORA, JOSEPH. See DUNDEE, JOHNNY.

CARSON, JACK (Oct. 27, 1910–Jan. 2, 1963), comedian and actor, was born John Elmer Carson in Carman, Manitoba, Canada, the son of Elmer Llewellyn Carson, a salesman, and of Elsa Brunke. When he was a small child, the family moved to Milwaukee, Wis., where Elmer Carson became the district manager of an insurance company. Jack—as he was called—did not become a United States citizen until 1949.

Carson attended Milwaukee public schools before studying at St. John's Military Academy, Delafield, Wis., from 1923 to 1928. He was a popular cadet and participated in many athletic and musical activities. In the fall of 1928 he enrolled in Illinois College, Jacksonville, Ill., but did poorly in his studies and left before the end of the term. The following semester he entered Carleton College, Northfield, Minn., where he remained for two years. Although he played in college drama productions, he was best known on campus for his accomplishments as a varsity football player and swimmer. But because of his propensity to play pranks, he was asked not to reenroll after the fall semester of 1930.

After selling insurance for a few months, Carson got his start in show business when Dave Willock, a fellow Milwaukeean and fledgling vaudeville comedian, invited him to become his stage partner. In the fall of 1931, Willock and Carson played the midwestern vaudeville cir-

cuit, featuring an act burlesquing movie newsreels in which they did impersonations and exchanged humorous comments about current topics. They later toured California and the East Coast, where they played the Roxy in New York City. With the demise of vaudeville, the act broke up in the spring of 1935. For a few months Carson was master of ceremonies at the Tower Theatre in Kansas City, Mo. In 1936 he set out for Hollywood, to try his luck in motion pictures.

In Hollywood, Carson managed to secure some work as an extra while studying at the Ben Bard School of Drama. His performances there won the favorable attention of Frank Stempel, an agent with whom he formed a lifelong association. He soon began to obtain bit roles. His first speaking part—one line—was in *You Only Live Once*, released by United Artists in 1937. A few months later he signed a contract with Radio-Keith-Orpheum (RKO), for which he played in several undistinguished gangster and comedy pictures in 1937 and 1938. In comedies he usually played the brash, blustering "smart guy" type who eventually lost the girl. With the expiration of his contract with RKO, he played better roles in more substantial movies, such as *Destry Rides Again* (Universal) and *Mr. Smith Goes to Washington* (Columbia), both in 1939. He also became a popular radio performer as master of ceremonies for the "Signal Caravan" program on the National Broadcasting Company's (NBC) Pacific Coast network.

In 1941, following his appearance in *The Strawberry Blonde*, Carson signed a long-term contract with Warner Brothers. For Warner's he generally played supporting comedy roles, although he occasionally had leading parts. He made nine movies with Dennis Morgan, a former Milwaukee resident who became one of his closest friends in Hollywood. But Carson enjoyed best those infrequent roles that enabled him to depart from the wisecracking comedy parts he was usually assigned. His favorite movie role was that of the ineffectual salesman in *Roughly Speaking* (1945). His radio career continued to prosper; in 1943 he began a half-hour national show on the Columbia Broadcasting System (CBS), and in 1947 he signed a five-year contract with NBC.

Carson's contract with Warner Brothers expired in 1950. Thereafter he appeared less frequently in movies. Two of his later roles were the cynical press agent in *A Star Is Born* (1954) and Big Daddy's grasping older son in *Cat on a Hot Tin Roof* (1958). He was one of the first movie stars to recognize the potential of television, serving as one of the original hosts of NBC's "All Star Revue" (1950–1952). Between 1950 and 1962 he made more than thirty appearances in television plays, principally in dramatic roles. In 1952 he starred in a short-lived revival of *Of Thee I Sing* on Broadway, and he frequently toured the country in road companies. In August 1962 he collapsed while rehearsing a play in Andover, N.J. A little more than four months later he died of cancer at his home in Encino, Calif.

Carson's first three marriages ended in divorce. The first (1934–1937) was to Betty Alice Linde, a dancer whom he met on the vaudeville circuit. His second marriage, to Kay St. Germaine, a singer on his radio show, lasted from 1940 to 1950; they had two children. Actress Lola Albright was his third wife (1952–1958). His fourth wife was Sandra Tucker, whom he married in 1961.

A tall man (six feet, two inches) who needed to watch his diet, Carson was affable and bighearted but loved a good argument. He was an outdoorsman who particularly enjoyed playing golf. Although best remembered for his early comedy roles that tended to typecast him as an unsympathetic loudmouth, he preferred to be called an actor rather than a comedian, and demonstrated in some of his later performances that he was an actor of considerable talent.

[See James R. Parish and Lennard De Carl, *Hollywood Players: The Forties* (1976); David Shipman, *The Great Movie Stars: The International Years* (1973). Also see the clipping files of the Academy of Motion Picture Arts and Sciences; Milwaukee Public Library; Kansas City (Mo.) Public Library; and Carleton College Archives. A list of articles on Carson is in Mel Shuster, comp., *Motion Picture Performers* (1971) and supplement (1976).

Obituaries are in the *Los Angeles Herald-Examiner*, *Los Angeles Times*, *New York Times* (West Coast ed.), Jan. 3, 1963. Dave Willock of North Hollywood, Calif., provided information about Carson's vaudeville career.]

EDWIN A. MILES

CARSON, RACHEL LOUISE (May 27, 1907–Apr. 14, 1964), marine biologist, ecologist, and writer, was born in Springdale, Pa. Her father, Robert Warden Carson, had moved his family from nearby Pittsburgh to a sixty-five-acre farm in 1900, and it was in this setting, close to nature, that Rachel Carson spent her childhood. Her mother, Maria Frazier McLean, was influential in molding her early interest in, and love of, the natural environment. They remained close throughout her life.

After graduating from high school in Parnassus, Pa., Carson attended the Pennsylvania College for Women (now Chatham College) in Pittsburgh, with the intention of becoming a writer. She had early shown talent for writing, and had won an award from *St. Nicholas* magazine at the age of ten. But a course in biology redirected her interest to science, and she graduated with a degree in zoology in 1929. She later admitted that she had, for a time, felt that writing and science were in some way mutually exclusive, but in her 1952 National Book Award acceptance speech, she said, "The aim of science is to discover and illuminate truth. And that, I take it, is the aim of literature, whether biography or history or fiction; it seems to me, then, that there can be no separate literature of science."

Graduate work at Johns Hopkins University led to the M.A. in 1932. Carson had, a year earlier, joined the zoology department at the University of Maryland. In addition she spent several summers at the Marine Biological Laboratory, Woods Hole, Mass., and taught summer courses at Johns Hopkins. During this period she wrote feature articles on scientific topics for the *Baltimore Sunday Sun*. In 1936, Carson joined the Bureau of Fisheries (later the Fish and Wildlife Service) as a writer for a series of radio broadcasts it sponsored. Subsequently she was appointed a staff biologist and progressed steadily in the organization until she became editor in chief in 1949.

At the suggestion of a supervisor, Carson reworked a rejected script into an article and submitted it to the *Atlantic Monthly*. "Undersea" appeared in the September 1937 issue, and soon thereafter Quincy Howe of Simon and Schuster asked her to write a full-length book on the sea. *Under the Sea-Wind* was published in 1941. Although critically and scientifically praised, the book sold only about 1,400 copies in its first year.

During the 1940's Carson remained in her government post, but financial obligations plagued her. She was caring for her mother and her late sister's two daughters. This devotion to family was a strong characteristic throughout Carson's life. She never married. When she was in her fifties, she adopted a niece's son when he was left an orphan. She brought in extra money by writing magazine pieces, and at one time applied for a job as an editor with *Reader's Digest*. But she never gave up the idea of doing more substantial work, and *Under the Sea-Wind* proved to be a rehearsal for *The Sea Around Us*, published by Oxford University Press in 1951.

Carson was a slow writer and felt that she had had a good day if she wrote 500 words. The writing of the book took three years, but in preparation she learned deep-sea diving (admittedly to only a very shallow depth) and went on a ten-day voyage on a research ship to the Georges Bank.

The Sea Around Us was an immediate best seller. There was great prepublication interest aroused by a three-part serialization in the *New Yorker*, but the book succeeded because Carson combined scrupulous scientific research with genuine literary art. The book stresses the geologic processes that formed the earth and produced its oceans, at the same time conveying the mystery of the sea and its eternal fascination for land dwellers. In a chapter entitled "The Long Snowfall," Carson discusses the process of sedimentation: "I see always the steady, unremitting, downward drift of materials from above, flake upon flake, layer upon layer—a drift that has continued for hundreds of millions of years, that will go on as long as there are seas and continents. . . . It is interesting to think that even now, in our own lifetime, the flakes of a new snow storm are falling, falling, one by one, out there on the ocean floor. The billions of Globigerina are drifting down, writing their unequivocal record that this, our present world, is on the whole a world of mild and temperate climate. Who will read their record, ten thousand years from now?"

The book was on the *New York Times* best-seller list for eighty-six weeks, thirty-nine in first place. Meanwhile, rights to *Under the Sea-Wind* were bought by Oxford and it was rereleased, soon joining *The Sea Around Us* on the best-seller list. Carson was at first uncomfortable with her celebrity, but she grew accustomed to it. The money enabled her to buy property on the Maine coast, at West Southport, and freed her from worry about properly supporting her family. She was also able to resign from the Fish and Wildlife Service in 1952 and devote herself to writing full time.

Carson's next book, *The Edge of the Sea* (1956), was a disappointment to some of her admirers but a best seller nonetheless. Jacquetta Hawkes, writing in the *New Republic*, said: "I think Miss Carson has succeeded again, although with enough weakening and diminishment for even this success to appear a little sad. The truth is expressed in the title: Miss Carson, having exhausted the heart of her subject, has been forced to move out to gather what was left round the periphery."

Whether or not she had exhausted the sea as a subject, Carson at this time turned to a new one that was to make her name a household word and set in motion one of the great movements of the century—environmentalism. When *Silent Spring* appeared in 1962, the controversy was already building. (Indeed, in her preface to a new edition of *The Sea Around Us* [1961] Carson had already warned of polluting the oceans with atomic wastes.) Again the new book had been partly serialized in the *New Yorker*, and her detractors—and her partisans—were gathering.

Silent Spring was instrumental in bringing about public awareness of the dangers of pesticides and herbicides—which Carson termed "biocides," in that they can kill all life. Not surprisingly the chemical industry rose to the attack. W. J. Darby, in a review entitled "Silence, Miss Carson," in *Chemical and Engineering News*, typified the opposition: "Miss Carson's book adds no new factual material not already known to such serious scientists as those concerned with these developments nor does it include information essential for the reader to interpret the knowledge. It does confuse the information and so mix it with her opinions that the uninitiated reader is unable to sort fact from fancy. . . . In view of her scientific qualifications in contrast to those of our distinguished scientific leaders and statesmen, this book should be ignored." Darby did feel that the "responsible scientist should read this book to understand the ignorance of those writing on the subject and the educational task which lies ahead."

The attacks on *Silent Spring* reflected the alliance that had developed between science and industry. Even the government regulatory agencies relied on the companies they were supposed to be regulating to set the allowable tolerances for pesticides. This symbiotic relationship between science, government, and industry was the central problem in awakening the public to the danger posed by pesticides and herbicides. One respected science newsletter advised its readers to order a report setting forth the horrors of a pesticide-free world—a report prepared by the Monsanto Chemical Company.

But the public outcry could not be ignored. A special presidential advisory committee was appointed to look into the problem. The committee called for more research into the possible health hazards of pesticides and warned against their indiscriminate use. Eventually many pesticides—in particular, DDT—were banned outright or brought under stringent control. These were but the first victories in a continuing war.

In an editorial the *New York Times* declared that if Rachel Carson "did arouse the public to immunize government agencies against the blandishments of the hucksters and cause enforcement of adequate controls then she deserved the Nobel Prize as much as the inventor of DDT."

Carson understood and practiced Albert Schweitzer's "reverence for life"; indeed, *Silent Spring* was dedicated to him. Her editor, friend, and biographer, Paul Brooks, tells of studying microscopic marine animals with Carson at her Maine cottage. Afterward she carefully returned the tiny creatures to the sea outside her door.

She was a warm person who inspired affection in her friends and colleagues but, by her own admission, "had no small talk." She did have a fine sense of humor. During a discussion on evolution, her mother reminded her that, according to the Bible, God had created the world. Carson agreed that that was true, but she added that General Motors had created her Oldsmobile—the question was how.

Fifteen years after her death, of cancer, in Silver Spring, Md., all of Rachel Carson's books were still in print. Her syntheses of science and literature have continued to gain new audiences each year. While new discoveries in oceanography, marine biology, and other sciences have made some of her views obsolete, her philosophical outlook toward nature and the environment has, in large part, become the accepted view.

[Paul Brooks, *The House of Life: Rachel Carson at Work* (1972), is an affectionate and indispensable biography by her editor at Houghton Mifflin. The book has a complete bibliography. Also see Frank Graham, Jr., *Since Silent Spring* (1970), and Philip Sterling, *Sea and Earth* (1970). An obituary is in the *New York Times*, Apr. 15, 1964.]

MARSHALL DE BRUHL

CASE, FRANCIS HIGBEE (Dec. 9, 1896–June 22, 1962), journalist and U.S. congressman and senator, was born in Everly, Iowa, the son of the Reverend Herbert Llywellan Case, a Methodist minister, and of Mary Ellen Grannis. He attended high school in Sturgis (where his father's circuit was based) and Hot Springs, S.D., graduating from the latter in 1914. That fall he entered Dakota Wesleyan University at Mitchell, S.D., where he worked on the newspaper and gained recognition as an orator. Following graduation, Case enlisted in 1918 as a private in the Marine Corps, serving for eight months and never getting beyond boot camp at Mare Island, Calif. He later held reserve commissions in both the army (1924–1931) and the Marine Corps (from 1937).

After the war Case resumed his education, receiving an M.A. in 1920 from Northwestern University at Evanston, Ill. From 1920 to 1922, while continuing his studies at Northwestern, he was assistant editor of the *Epworth Herald*, published in Chicago by the Young People's League of the Northern Methodist Church. He also prepared two volumes devoted to church advertising (1921, 1925). In 1922 he returned to South Dakota as telegraph editor and editorial writer of the *Rapid City Daily Journal.* He and his brother Leland sold their interest in the paper in 1925, and thereafter purchased and sold several other newspapers.

On Aug. 19, 1926, Case married Myrle Lucile Graves; they had two children. In 1928, while editing a newspaper in Hot Springs, Case successfully promoted the idea of inviting President Calvin Coolidge to vacation in the Black Hills. The president eventually did visit.

After moving to Custer, S.D., in 1931, Case edited and published the *Custer Chronicle,* and invested in ranch lands in the surrounding Black Hills. At that time he also entered public life, serving as a state regent of education (1931–1933). In 1934 he was an unsuccessful Republican candidate for election to Congress, but in 1936 he defeated the Democratic incumbent, T. B. Werner, by 2,263 votes. He served seven terms in the House of Representatives. Case's district encompassed the western half of South Dakota. Although largely rural and inhabited by more than 20,000 Indians, it was dominated politically as well as economically by the Homestake Mining Company.

In the House, Case served on the Appropriations Committee, proving himself a diligent, effective, and (until 1946) relatively obscure member. He received little credit, for example, for his 1942 amendment calling for the renegotiation of war contracts, an approach that became standard practice and by June 1946 had returned more than $9 billion to the United States treasury. Case's voting record, typical of midwestern Republicans, was largely isolationist. Three weeks before Pearl Harbor, for example, he voted against amendments to the Neutrality Act permitting American merchant ships to be armed and to carry supplies to belligerents. In July 1946, though, he did not follow the majority of his party when he voted for the $3.75 billion loan to Great Britain.

It was in this year that Case emerged from obscurity by drafting a bill seeking tighter control of labor, the most far-reaching such measure that Congress had approved since the passage of the Wagner Act in 1935. Case claimed he introduced the bill largely because of constituents' demands that he do something about the rash of postwar strikes that were upsetting war-weary citizens throughout the country. His measure, which was modified in its passage through the Congress, called for a five-member labor-management mediation board, a sixty-day cooling-off period, and provisions for holding unions, employees, and employers accountable for infringement of contracts or restraint of trade.

The bill was backed in the House by the Rules Committee, controlled by a coalition of conservative southern Democrats and Republicans; this allowed it to bypass the Labor Committee, which had given it no previous consideration. Case declared that the bill was planned to overcome alleged injustices in the National Labor Relations Act and "bring about mutuality of contract obligations and restrictions on the use of force and violence." President Harry Truman, questioning the measure on constitutional grounds and contending that the instrumentalities provided could not achieve their goals, vetoed it on June 11. The veto was sustained in the House by 255 to 135, five votes less than the two-thirds necessary to override. The measure presaged the Taft-Hartley Act, approved over the president's veto in 1947.

In 1950, Case was elected to the Senate, and was reelected in 1956. Although he captured 63.9 percent of the vote in 1950, he ran the closest race of his public life in 1956, winning only 50.8 percent.

In the Senate, Case served on the Armed Services and Public Works committees, chairing a subcommittee on each. He continued his diligent, unobtrusive service, introducing measures of importance to his constituents, favoring self-government for the city of Washington, serving on the committee investigating the conduct of Wisconsin Senator Joseph R. McCarthy, and sitting as an ex officio member of the Appropriations Committee when it considered funding measures for rivers and harbors and for the Department of Defense. Continuing a pattern evident during his tenure in the House of Representatives, Case became known to his colleagues as "the amendingest senator" because of his attention to details and his close scrutiny of proposed laws.

In 1956, Case again came to national attention, sparking one of the great uproars of the Eighty-fourth Congress. On February 10, during the debate on a bill removing controls over producers' prices of natural gas, he disclosed his refusal to accept a $2,500 "campaign contribution" from a lawyer serving as an oil company lobbyist. He said an envelope containing twenty-five $100 bills was given to a South Dakota friend with the explanation that it was a campaign contribution. It was given before Case announced his candidacy for a second Senate term.

Prior to December 1955, when the money was offered, Case said he favored the bill. As a result of the offer he changed his mind. The Congress nevertheless approved the bill, but President Dwight D. Eisenhower vetoed it. Case meanwhile asked his South Dakota friend either to return the money or to give it to an orphanage. At no time in the course of his remarks did he reveal the lawyer's name. Majority leader Lyndon B. Johnson, disturbed by Case's charge, said it reflected "upon the integrity of the Senate itself" and endorsed the appointment of a bipartisan committee to determine if bribery was involved. The committee learned that John M. Neff, a Lexington, Neb., lawyer, had received the $2,500 he contributed to Case's campaign from the Superior Oil Company of Los Angeles and that Neff had received further funds for political gift giving. Despite these and other disclosures, the committee, fearful of the repercussions in an election year, did not pursue the matter.

Once the furor unleashed by his remarks abated, Case resumed his unobtrusive role in the Senate and continued to promote regional interests. He favored, for example, continuing federal construction of big multipurpose dams, including the development of the Missouri River Basin program. He voted against the construction of the Hell's Canyon dam on the Snake River in Idaho because he thought the fiscal arrangements were unduly favorable to the Idaho Power Company. On the other hand, in the Public Works Committee and on the Senate floor he endorsed bills allowing the Tennessee Valley Authority to issue its own bonds and the state of New York to develop the hydroelectric potential of the Niagara River. In each instance his vote was based on the premise that "much power development for a growing United States without any demands on the Federal Treasury" could be achieved, especially if a large multipurpose dam at Hell's Canyon could be constructed by a private power company.

Case's chief contribution in the Senate, as in the House, was in clarifying provisions of bills and proposing amendments that would make measures more precise or trim out unnecessary federal spending. Early in 1962 he was named to the Senate Committee on Preparedness, service on which would have considerably enhanced his chances of success in his reelection campaign. But on June 21 he suffered a heart attack in his office. He died the following day in Bethesda, Md.

In 1962, Congress authorized the naming of the new $7 million span across the Washington channel of the Potomac River in his honor. In the following year the Fort Randall Reservoir in South Dakota was renamed Lake Francis Case.

Like many midwestern Republicans, Case throughout his years in Congress followed the ritual of curbing the expansion of federal power and bureaucracy except when it benefited his constituents.

[Case's papers are at Dakota Wesleyan University. A biography by Richard R. Chenoweth is in South Dakota Historical Collections, vol. 39 (1979). An obituary appeared in the New York Times, June 23, 1962.]

RICHARD LOWITT

CASTLE, WILLIAM RICHARDS, JR. (June 19, 1878–Oct. 13, 1963), diplomat and author, was born in Honolulu, Hawaii, the son of William Richards Castle, a prominent entrepreneur, and Ida Beatrice Lowrey. He attended Harvard, receiving an A.B. degree in 1900. On June 3, 1902, he married Margaret Farlow. They had one daughter.

From 1906 to 1913, Castle was assistant dean of Harvard College; in 1913 he was promoted to dean. During these years he began a writing career, publishing two melodramatic novels (The Green Vase, 1912; The Pillar of Sand, 1914), a descriptive volume (Hawaii, Past and Present, 1913), and a nonfiction work pleading for military preparedness (Wake Up, America, 1916). In 1915, Castle left the deanship to become editor of the Harvard Graduates' Magazine. Two years later, he was appointed director of the Bureau of Communications of the National American Red Cross.

Castle's State Department career began in 1919, when he became a special assistant attached to the Division of West European Affairs. In 1921 Castle became chief of that division, serving in that post until February 1927, when he was promoted to assistant secretary of state, overseeing West European, East European, and Near Eastern affairs. Castle was one of the first career diplomats to become an assistant secretary of state, which was normally a political appointment. As a neighbor and friend of Secretary of State Frank B. Kellogg,

Castle played an important role as his listening post and helped moderate the high-strung secretary's foreign policy thinking. By this time, Castle had begun to develop his beliefs in realism and noninterventionism in foreign policy. He had scant use for the World Court and saw little practical value in conciliation and arbitration treaties. He thought the Kellogg-Briand Pact (1928) was futile as anything but a public relations device and was concerned that Kellogg took the pact seriously.

In December 1929, Castle was named ambassador to Japan, an appointment designed solely to give the United States an ambassador there during the 1930 London Naval Conference. While in Tokyo, Castle developed a sympathetic position toward Japan. He saw that country's position in the Far East as comparable to that of the United States in the western hemisphere.

President Herbert Hoover named Castle undersecretary of state in April 1931, an appointment, as it turned out, that substantially exacerbated the tension between the president and his secretary of state, Henry L. Stimson. As Hoover's more pacific views gradually diverged from Stimson's more activist ones, Stimson came to resent Castle, who personally and philosophically was closer to Hoover. The climax of this strained relationship came in May 1932, when, while Stimson was in Europe, Castle gave a speech, authorized by Hoover, stating that United States policy toward Japan during the Manchurian crisis would go no further than a declaration of nonrecognition. It would not involve economic sanctions, such as boycotts. This speech, taken as official United States policy, undercut any efforts Stimson might have had in mind to employ a more assertive policy toward Japan. The secretary was furious, all the more so when Castle referred to the doctrine of nonrecognition as the Hoover Doctrine rather than the Stimson Doctrine, as it is commonly known.

The Manchurian crisis was the major diplomatic event during Castle's years as undersecretary of state. In this crisis, Castle's generally pro-Japanese views stood as a counterpoint to those of Stanley K. Hornbeck, chief of the Division of Far Eastern Affairs, who was the State Department's leading advocate of economic sanctions against Japan. Castle's objections to sanctions were based on the damage they might do to the depression-ridden world economy as well as on his belief, firm by this time, that Japan could be a "useful friend in the Orient" and the keystone to the maintenance of Far Eastern stability, if dealt with properly. In the end, Castle gave his support to the idea of nonrecognition and its linkage to the Nine-Power Treaty (1922) and the Kellogg-Briand Pact, quite possibly because of his belief that such statements had little practical value and would not deter Japan in her effort, as he saw it, to bring stability to the Far East.

As late as October 1940, Castle's sympathy toward Japan still ran deep. In an article in the *Atlantic Monthly* he urged that the United States accept a Japanese Monroe Doctrine, prohibiting any nation from acquiring or transferring territory in the Far East. This, he asserted, would cement United States–Japanese friendship and help Japan cope with the threat of German military adventurism. This attitude toward Japan stemmed as much from Castle's general belief in isolationism as from his pro-Japanese sympathies.

Although Castle had left the State Department in 1933 after Franklin D. Roosevelt became president, Castle nonetheless remained in the public eye as a frequent speaker and author of magazine articles on current events. He opposed the New Deal on constitutional and monetary grounds, deplored the renunciation of intervention in Latin America, and urged the administration to stay out of the developing problems in Europe by refusing all aid to Great Britain. Castle also opposed the recognition of Soviet Russia until he satisfied himself that formal diplomatic recognition did not necessarily imply endorsement of the government being recognized.

Castle served as president of the Garfield Memorial Hospital in Washington, D.C., from 1945 to 1952. He died in Washington, D.C.

Castle's mark in American diplomacy came not from innovative policymaking but rather from his reputation as a thorough student of foreign affairs and his ability to make the most of his personal relationships within the State Department and White House bureaucracies. Although Stimson lost confidence in him, this was more than offset by the widely recognized influence he had with Kellogg and, later, Hoover. His diary is a major source for the diplomatic history of the times.

[Castle's papers are at the Hoover Library, West Branch, Iowa. A typescript of an unpublished diary of Castle's is at Harvard. See also L. Ethan Ellis, *Republican Foreign Policy, 1921–33* (1968); Robert H. Ferrell, *American Diplomacy in the Great Depression* (1957); and obituary in the *New York Times*, Oct. 14, 1963.]

JOHN E. FINDLING

CHAMBERS, WHITTAKER (Apr. 1, 1901–July 9, 1961), journalist, writer, Soviet agent, and witness for the U.S. government, was born Jay Vivian Chambers in Philadelphia, Pa., the son of Jay Chambers, a commercial artist, and of Laha Whittaker, a former actress. He grew up in Lynbrook, N.Y. After his parents separated, he took the name David Whittaker Chambers (he would also assume nearly a dozen aliases in his lifetime for literary and political reasons). After graduating from high school in 1919, Chambers did construction work in Washington, D.C., then lived for several months in New Orleans. He then returned home and worked for the Frank Seaman Company, an advertising firm in New York City.

Chambers enrolled at Columbia College in the fall of 1920. His fervent conservatism soon withered under the influence of Professor Mark Van Doren and of such friends as Meyer Schapiro, Louis Zukovsky, Clifton Fadiman, Langston Hughes, and Lionel Trilling. His poetry, drama, and stories convinced Columbia literary circles that he could become a major American writer—even a great poet.

In January 1923 Chambers left Columbia after unfavorable administration reaction to his *A Play for Puppets,* a "blasphemous" play about the Crucifixion, that had appeared in the student literary magazine, *Morningside* (of which he was editor). After spending the summer in Europe, he worked part-time in the New York Public Library. He was readmitted to Columbia in 1924, but the decision to join the Communist party in the early spring of 1925 led him to drop out at that time.

Soon after joining the Communist party Chambers began organizing and teaching for the party and writing for the *Daily Worker.* Soviet praise of his work led to his promotion to foreign news writer and to editor of the paper. A two-year break with the party, over political strategy, followed the take-over of the American Communist party in 1929 by the Stalinists William Z. Foster and Earl Browder. Chambers had already established a reputation as the gifted translator of Felix Salten's *Bambi,* and of novels by Heinrich Mann (*Mother Mary*) and Franz Werfel (*Class Reunion*). (Later, in 1938–1939, he translated Gustav Regler's novel of the Spanish Civil War, *The Great Crusade.*) He mastered twelve languages, including Russian and Hungarian, and translated works from German and French.

Several short stories published in *New Masses* brought Chambers renown as a proletarian artist. His "Can You Hear Their Voices?" was adapted for the stage by Hallie Flanagan, and became a staple of the radical theater. These successes brought favorable reaction from Moscow. In 1931, Chambers returned to the Communist party. On April 15 of that year he married Esther Shemitz, a socialist artist; they had two children. He also was named editor of *New Masses.* An official Soviet critic praised his work: "For the first time [in American writing], it raises the image of the Bolshevik."

Chambers was tapped for underground work in 1932, and by 1934 he was working in Washington, D.C., where he became an important and (exceptional for an American) respected functionary. He started out as liaison between the American Communist party underground and the Russian espionage network in New York City. Beginning in 1934 he nurtured a "leading group" of influential Soviet agents in Washington and recruited new ones. Chambers acted as courier of classified government information that the Washington group was passing to Moscow. He helped organize worldwide networks for Soviet military intelligence, traveled to Russia for training, and was decorated as an officer in the Red Army.

Stalin's purges of the Red Army, reaching deep into the foreign intelligence branches by mid-1937, provoked Chambers' disillusionment with international Communism. With the disappearance and assassination of other underground figures in Europe and America and himself facing recall to Moscow (and likely death), Chambers broke with the underground in April 1938. He took his family into hiding until he could establish a new identity a year later as a writer for *Time* magazine.

Chambers rose swiftly from book reviewer to become a senior editor. During this period he embraced the values of family (after having experimented with homosexuality), the land, and religion (Episcopalian, then Quaker), on which he based an anti-Communism as absolute as had been his Leninism.

An extremely controversial figure at *Time,* Chambers had the backing and friendship of publisher Henry Luce and managing editor T. S. Matthews. By 1944 he was editing *Time's* foreign news section, provoking the wrath of overseas correspondents John Hersey, Theodore White, and John Osborne for the unyielding anti-Communist slant of his editorial pencil. A particularly acrimonious dispute over Chambers' assessment of Soviet aims in Eastern Europe was quelled by his recurrent heart trouble. Thereafter the special projects department was created for Chambers and his friend James Agee. There the two men Luce considered his most gifted writers produced many *Time* cover stories and *Life* articles on cultural, political, and religious subjects.

The emerging cold war forced Chambers to face a different destruction than the one he had feared from Russian assassins. A series of postwar espionage cases (Igor Gouzenko in Canada, *Amerasia* and Elizabeth Bentley in the United States) inevitably brought journalists and government investigators to interview him. Chambers was reluctant, with no apparent effect, to testify to the story of Soviet spy rings in Washington that he had told to Adolf Berle, President Franklin Roosevelt's assistant secretary of state in charge of security, after the 1939 Hitler-Stalin pact. He was subpoenaed to appear before the House Committee on Un-American Activities in August 1948, setting off the most dramatic and divisive United States court case since the trial of Sacco and Vanzetti.

Chambers alleged that dozens of officials in the executive branch had been, and possibly still were, Communists or party sympathizers, working for the interests of the Soviet Union. One of those named was Alger Hiss, a brilliant young New Dealer who had risen to high rank in the State Department and in 1948 was president of the Carnegie Endowment for World Peace. He denied the charges, and sued Chambers for libel. The case became the contest of two men and escalated until espionage was alleged against Hiss by the self-implicated Chambers. Chambers produced a cache of confidential State Department documents and microfilm—the celebrated "pumpkin papers"—many written in Hiss's hand or copied on his Woodstock typewriter and allegedly given to Chambers to be passed to Moscow. Chambers claimed he had hidden the material as a "life preserver" against Soviet retribution for his defection. Hiss was indicted by a federal grand jury, but at his first trial (May 31–July 7, 1949) the jury could not reach a verdict. At the second trial (Nov. 17, 1949–Jan. 21, 1950) he was convicted of perjury (the statute of limitations on espionage had elapsed) and sentenced to five years in prison (he served less than four years).

Chambers' critics charged that his pathological lying had unleashed a wave of anti-Communist hysteria that terrorized American society. His defenders believed that his patriotic self-sacrifice had aroused the moral strength of the nation to fight Communist subversion at home and a growing Soviet menace abroad. One's views on the case became a shorthand for one's position on internal security, Stalinism, and the response of radical intellectuals to their past.

Vindicated, but physically and emotionally broken, Chambers retired to his Westminster, Md., farm, where he wrote his autobiography. Considered by many critics a classic of confessional literature, *Witness* (1952) enjoyed a favorable critical and popular reception. The book was Chambers' fullest statement of the psychological appeal and ideological imperatives of the Communist movement.

Anathematized by the "anti-anti-Communists" and by many establishment conservatives, and kept at a distance by old colleagues who now belonged to the anti-Stalinist left, Chambers became a hero to the emerging intellectual right. Befriended by Arthur Koestler, William F. Buckley, Jr., Ralph de Toledano, and others, he was an editor of Buckley's *National Review* from August 1957 to November 1959. He was also the confidant of Richard Nixon, whose political future was secured by his key role in convicting Hiss. Chambers died at Westminster, Md.

Meyer Schapiro, a comrade from the radical days, recalled that in his last years Chambers saw himself in the tradition of Hildebrand, a "farmer monk who restored civilization"; but he also believed this restoration, as he wrote to Buckley, to be a labor of Sisyphus. In his lifelong struggle to change and understand the history in which he had so large a part, Chambers found only partial success. If only finally out of weariness, over the ideologue the poet did prevail.

[Chambers' writings include *Cold Friday*, edited by Duncan Norton-Taylor (1964); and *Odyssey of a Friend*, edited by William F. Buckley, Jr. (1969). Biographical material is in Ralph de Toledano, *Lament for a Generation* (1960); William F. Buckley, Jr., *Rumbles Left and Right* (1963); Murray Kempton, *Part of Our Time* (1967); Robert T. Elson, *The World of Time, Inc.*, II (1973); Lionel Trilling, "Whittaker Chambers and The Middle of the Journey," *New York Review of Books*, Apr. 17, 1975; Sidney Hook, "The Strange Case of Whittaker Chambers," *Encounter*, Jan. 1976; Allen Weinstein, *Perjury* (1978). On the Hiss Case, see Ralph de Toledano and Victor Lasky, *Seeds of Treason* (1950; rev. ed., 1962); Leslie Fiedler, *An End to Innocence* (1952); Arthur Koestler, *The Trail of the Dinosaur* (1955); Bert and Peter Andrews, *A Tragedy of History* (1962); Diana Trilling, *Claremont Essays* (1964); Meyer A. Zeligs, *Friendship and Fratricide* (1967); John Chabot Smith, *Alger Hiss: The True Story* (1976). Also see Alistair Cooke, *A Generation on Trial* (1950), and John Strachey, *The Strangled Cry* (1962). An obituary is in the *New York Times*, July 12, 1961.]

JOHN DAVID FOX

CHAPELLE, DICKEY (Mar. 14, 1918–Nov. 4, 1965), photojournalist and war correspondent, was born Georgette Louise Meyer in Shorewood, Wis., a Milwaukee suburb, the daughter of Paul Gerhart Meyer, a salesman of construction materials, and Edna Francisca Engelhardt, an interior designer. She grew up in a permissive, pacifist household consisting of her parents, brother, grandparents, and several other adult relatives. Her aunts were to have much influence over Georgette, who thought of herself as a tomboy during her high school years. While friends had movie stars as heroes, she so idolized Admiral Richard E. Byrd that after seeing a film about his South Pole expedition that sparked her interest in aviation, and later meeting him after a lecture in Milwaukee, she began to use a form of his name, Dickey, as her pen name.

She graduated as valedictorian from Shorewood High School in 1935 and went to the Massachusetts Institute of Technology to study aeronautical engineering on a scholarship that fall. Because she spent so much time writing news stories for the *Boston Traveler* and exploring the Boston Navy Yard, she did poorly in her classes and did not return after her sophomore year. Instead she took flying lessons and attended air shows in Milwaukee. When she accompanied her grandparents to their winter home in Florida, she took a job as a publicist for a Miami air show and also reported on aviation. In early 1938 she went to New York City to become director of publicity for Trans World Airlines (then Transcontinental and Western Airlines).

Chapelle had been with TWA for about two years when she began to study photography with the airline's publicity photographer, Tony Chapelle. She married him in October 1940; they had no children. During the next year she worked to build a reputation as a free-lance journalist by shooting photo essays, especially on aviation.

When the United States entered World War II in December 1941, her husband volunteered for naval service and was sent to Panama. Dickey followed in June 1942 on assignment for *Look* magazine. After returning to New York in 1943, she wrote and contributed to several books on aviation. In January 1945 she was sent to the Pacific by Fawcett Publications. On Iwo Jima she photographed the transfer of wounded marines to a Red Cross hospital ship. By Apr. 1, 1945, she had arrived on Okinawa, where she continued to photograph casualties, asking to be taken "as far forward as you'll let me go," a request she was to repeat throughout her career.

During 1946 and 1947, Chapelle served as associate editor of *Seventeen* magazine, traveling to thirty countries. During the next six years she worked with her husband to document the war devastation in Europe and the Middle East for the American Friends Service Committee, CARE, UNICEF, Save the Children, *National Geographic*, and the U.S. State Department. In 1949 they founded AVISO (the American Volunteer Information Services Overseas), which remained active for only one year.

Shortly after her divorce in 1956, while she was director of public information for the Research Institute of America, Chapelle was asked to photograph Hungarian refugees for the International Rescue Committee and *Life* magazine. She worked for ten days at Andau with James Michener and others, documenting the flight of the refugees across the frozen fields to the Austrian border. On December 5, accompanying two Hungarians attempting to bring penicillin into their homeland, she was captured. She spent the next five weeks alone in a cell at Fo Street Prison in Budapest. She engaged in what she later described as a "battle of the wills" against cold, hunger, lengthy interrogations, and uncertainty by exercising, memorizing poetry, and reviewing a mental balance sheet each day. On Jan. 14, 1957, she was transferred to the Marco Street jail, where she shared a cell with eight Hungarian women until her trial and release thirteen days later.

In July 1957, Chapelle again traveled to a combat zone by having herself smuggled in and out of Algeria to photograph the Scorpion Battalion of the Algerian Federation of National Liberation. She then went to the Mediterranean to document the activities of the U.S. Sixth Fleet, and from there to cover marines at the front lines in Lebanon. She entered Cuba as a tourist in November 1958 and spent the following nine weeks photographing Fidel Castro's revolution, for which he awarded her a medal in April 1959. It was during 1959 that she learned parachuting and jumped with an army airborne division into Korea.

In 1962, Chapelle received the Overseas Press Club's highest honor, the George Polk Memorial Award, for her courageous coverage of the Vietnam War. That year her autobiography, *What's a Woman Doing Here?*, was published. She continued to photograph combat in Vietnam for such publications as *Reader's Digest* and *National Geographic*, and to speak about the conflict to groups in the United

States. In the field she dressed in fatigues and carried only her two cameras and a small combat pack. She was respected by the marines she photographed for her courage and her attitude, which was exemplified by her comment, "I lug my own stuff and I take no favors."

On Nov. 4, 1965, Chapelle was with two companies of marines near Chulai, Vietnam. At dawn she was moving toward the village with the troops when a mine exploded. She was one of four killed by the blast. Her last article, "Water War in Vietnam," published in *National Geographic* in February 1966, described the dangers of Vietcong mortar fire and mine explosions.

[There is an unpublished guide to the Dickey Chapelle Papers at the State Historical Society of Wisconsin. Chapelle's autobiography, *What's a Woman Doing Here?* (1962), is an important source for information. Her writings include "New Life for India's Villagers," *National Geographic*, Apr. 1956, with Tony Chapelle; and "The Fighting Priest of South Vietnam," *Reader's Digest*, July 1963. Obituaries are in the *New York Times*, Nov. 4, 1965; *National Observer*, Nov. 8, 1965; and *Overseas Press Bulletin*, Nov. 13, 1965.]

PATRICIA SCOLLARD PAINTER

CHAPIN, JAMES PAUL (July 9, 1889–Apr. 5, 1964), ornithologist, was born in New York City, the son of Gilbert Granger Chapin, a greengrocer, and Nano Eagle. His boyhood was spent on Staten Island, where he first learned and became enthusiastic about natural history. He was helped by William T. Davis, who had been largely responsible for the creation of the Natural Science Association of Staten Island. Chapin was made a member of this group at age fifteen and read his first scientific paper before it in October 1905; the paper dealt with the behavior of jumping mice in captivity.

On graduating from high school in 1905 Chapin took a position with the department responsible for preparing exhibits at the American Museum of Natural History in New York, because he felt that he should wait for a year before entering college. In 1906 he entered Columbia University, where he concentrated on biology. After completing his sophomore year, Chapin was invited to join the American Museum's Belgian Congo Expedition, headed by Herbert Lang of the museum's preparation department. It was understood that he might have to interrupt his education for several years.

Chapin accepted the offer, and was in Africa from 1909 until 1915. His work proved to be a major element in the expedition's success, despite his youth and inexperience. He frequently worked by himself for periods of up to a year. The expedition brought back more than 126,-000 specimens, thousands of photographs, and some paintings, all the product of some 15,000 miles of foot travel. Upon his return to New York, Chapin was made a full-time assistant in the museum's department of ornithology by its chairman, Frank M. Chapman.

Chapin completed the requirements for the B.A. and M.A. at Columbia in 1916 and 1917, but his further studies were interrupted by military service in World War I. Fluent in French, he was assigned duty as a billeting officer in France with the rank of first lieutenant in the Allied Expeditionary Force (AEF).

When Chapin returned to the museum in 1919, he was made an assistant curator of ornithology. He was promoted in 1923 to associate curator, the rank he held until his retirement in 1948. The bulk of his time was taken up with the study of the Belgian Congo bird materials brought back in 1915. The dissertation for his doctorate, received from Columbia in 1932, was based upon his African research and a biological assessment of the ornithology of the Belgian Congo. This material also served, in somewhat different form, as a major portion of the first volume of Chapin's *Birds of the Belgian Congo* (1932–1954). This four-volume work of more than 3,000 pages and 400 illustrations is considered the foremost contribution to African ornithology by an American, and one of the best regional studies done on any part of Africa.

Chapin married Suzanne Drouël on Oct. 31, 1921; they had four children. They were divorced in 1939, and on Sept. 5, 1940, he married Ruth Trimble, who had been an assistant curator of birds at the Carnegie Museum in Pittsburgh.

Chapin did further research in the Congo in 1926–1927, 1930, 1937, and 1942, the last in connection with wartime work for the Office of Strategic Services in Africa and on Ascension Island. Chapin also made short expeditions to the Canadian Rockies in 1915, to Panama in 1923, to the Galapagos in 1930, and to Polynesia in 1934–1935. This last trip resulted in the collection of some of the specimens later mounted in the museum's Hall of Oceanic Birds. His final expedition, made with his second wife following his retirement, lasted from April 1953 to February 1958. He carried on research under the aegis of L'Institut pour la Recherche Scientifique en Afrique Centrale.

Chapin was frequently consulted by other ornithologists studying African birds. A man of integrity, tact, and good humor, he was unfailingly helpful and did much to prod other workers into becoming productive researchers. He was an indefatigable worker. For example, the entire day (a Saturday) preceding his death was spent at the museum.

Chapin's attention to detail and his powers of observation are exemplified by the story, frequently recounted by his colleagues, of an unusual wing feather from a then unknown bird that was given to him at Avakubi, in the northeastern Belgian Congo, in 1913. It had been part of a costume, and Chapin had expressed interest in it. Twenty-three years later, while doing research at the Congo Museum in Tervuren, Belgium, he spotted two unfamiliar mounted birds that previous workers had assumed were immature domestic peacocks. Chapin quickly realized that his lone feather was from the same species. These birds were Congo peacocks, a new species. This was a major ornithological discovery, for it had long been supposed that the avian fauna of the Congo had been thoroughly cataloged.

Some of Chapin's colleagues were distressed because the first two volumes of the Congo work (1932, 1938) were followed at such a lengthy remove by the remaining two in 1953 and 1954. Chapin was involuntarily retired from the American Museum staff and made curator emeritus at the end of 1948, six months before his sixtieth birthday. Funds raised by his department colleague Robert Cushman Murphy enabled him to complete the Congo bird manuscript as research associate in African ornithology after 1949, and he spent much time in his museum office on other projects in later years.

From his student days Chapin maintained meticulous notes embellished with clear drawings and other illustrations. Bird skins prepared by him were described by one associate as being superior in appearance to the living birds themselves. Another colleague described Chapin as "the best loved and also one of the most scholarly of American naturalists." Chapin died in New York City.

[Chapin's field notes and much of his professional correspondence are at the American Museum of Natural History, New York City. Autobiographical notes are in the files of the Department of Ornithology at the American Museum. Appreciations of his life and work are in *Natural History*, Jan. 1942; *Audubon* magazine, July 1946; *Auk*, Apr. 1966. Additional information was provided by Dean Amadon and Mary Le Croy of the American Museum of Natural History. An obituary is in the *New York Times*, Apr. 7, 1964.]

KEIR B. STERLING

CHAPLIN, RALPH HOSEA (Aug. 30, 1887–Mar. 23, 1961), radical editor, poet, songwriter, and commercial artist, was born in Ames, Kans., the son of Edgar Chaplin and Clara Bradford. His father operated a prosperous grain and livestock farm until ruined by drought and depression in 1886–1887. Subsequently the family moved to Chicago, where Chaplin's father worked as a railroad employee until the Pullman boycott of 1894.

Chaplin grew up in the slums of the South Side of Chicago and attended a neighborhood elementary school, an experience that indelibly impressed on him the class divisions in American society. The defeat of the American Railway·Union in 1894 and his father's blacklisting by the railroads further impressed Chaplin with the intensity of labor-capital conflict. Unable to find work in Chicago during the depression of the 1890's, the elder Chaplin tried farming in 1895–1896 near Panora, Iowa, but failed. A year later the family moved to Dodge City, Kans., at the invitation of relatives, but there, too, success eluded them. By the end of the 1890's they were back in Chicago. The depression over, Edgar Chaplin found steady work and Ralph attended grammar school through the seventh grade.

As a teenager, Chaplin became a socialist and served as a "soldier-salesman" for the *Appeal to Reason*. He also worked as an apprentice commercial artist at the American Art School and attended evening classes at the Chicago Art Institute. He immersed himself in the intellectual and cultural life of Chicago, becoming a regular at the Hull House evening lectures and seminars. In the summer of 1905, Chaplin married Edith Medin, also a commercial artist. Working together, both of them were active in socialist circles. Chaplin became an illustrator for the *International Socialist Review* and a member of the board of directors (1908–1913) of the Charles H. Kerr Publishing Company, for which he illustrated Jack London's *Dream of Debs*.

A restless young man, Chaplin spent a year (about 1909–1910) in Mexico City as an artist. There he observed the revolutionary ferment in the country, and met and talked with other radical émigré Americans. Just before Porfirio Díaz fell from power in 1911; the Chaplins returned to Chicago, where their only child, a son, was born. Soon they moved to Huntington, W.Va., where Chaplin worked as a commercial artist,

edited a local labor paper, involved himself in the violent Paint Creek–Cabin Creek coal strikes of 1912–1913, and composed poetry about the miners (published in 1917 as *When the Leaves Come Out*). By late 1913 he was in Cleveland, where he joined the Industrial Workers of the World (IWW) and contributed regularly to its paper, *Solidarity*.

From Cleveland, Chaplin moved to Montreal in 1914, then back to Chicago in 1915. During his involvement with the IWW in Chicago he became a close friend of William D. ("Big Bill") Haywood, the dominant figure in the organization from 1916 through 1919. At that time Chaplin wrote the words to the most famous of all American labor songs, "Solidarity Forever" (1915).

In 1917, Haywood appointed Chaplin editor of *Solidarity*. As its editor during World War I, Chaplin favored the militant antiwar, anticonscription element among Wobblies and published antiwar propaganda. He was arrested, together with more than 100 other IWW leaders, by the federal government in September 1917, and was convicted in 1918 of conspiracy to violate the wartime espionage and sedition acts. Judge Kenesaw M. Landis sentenced him to twenty years in the federal prison at Leavenworth, Kans.

While out on bail pending an appeal, Chaplin made a national lecture tour to raise funds for other convicted Wobblies and wrote *The Centralia Conspiracy* (1920), a defense of the IWW role in the violence in Centralia, Wash., on Armistice Day, 1919. Chaplin joined the newly formed American Communist party in 1919.

After the Supreme Court rejected his appeal on Apr. 11, 1921, Chaplin began serving his prison term. In prison he continued to write poetry (a collection of his prison poems was published as *Bars and Shadows*, 1922), and steadily drifted away from the IWW and toward religion. In 1922, a year before President Warren G. Harding commuted his sentence, Chaplin informed his father, "I have quit the I.W.W. and quit for good." Yet after his release from prison, as much from habit as from conviction, he returned to work for the IWW as a writer-editor and rejoined the Communist party. Nevertheless, while he toiled publicly for radicalism, he was becoming increasingly more religious, conservative, and even "bourgeois" in his values.

In 1928, Chaplin broke with communism. Later, during the New Deal era, he criticized both President Franklin D. Roosevelt and the Congress of Industrial Organizations (CIO) as forerunners of state socialism or communism. In 1937 he moved to the West Coast to work as a writer for groups in the labor movement opposed to Harry Bridges and the CIO. Unable to defeat Bridges within the International Longshoreman and Warehouseman's Union, Chaplin next served Dave Beck of the International Brotherhood of Teamsters in combating alleged communism in the CIO.

After a brief return to Chicago late in 1940, Chaplin settled in Tacoma, Wash., in the summer of 1941. There he continued as an American Federation of Labor (AFL) editor. He became an ardent advocate of the American role in World War II, though still a bitter critic of the Soviet Union. Together with his wife he joined the First Congregational Church of Tacoma and started to work on an autobiography, *Wobbly: The Rough and Tumble Story of an American Radical* (1948). The book describes exceedingly well the circumstances that made a midwestern American of New England colonial stock into a militant radical, and the subsequent intellectual journey that brought him back to his roots. The book also foreshadowed the anticommunist hysteria that was soon to plague the nation in the era of McCarthyism. In his final years Chaplin served as a curator at the Washington State Historical Society. He died at Tacoma, Wash.

[Manuscripts and personal material are at the Joseph Labadie Collection, University of Michigan, Ann Arbor; the Washington State Historical Society, Olympia; and the Archives of Labor History and Urban Affairs, Walter Reuther Library, Wayne State University, Detroit. Publications by Chaplin not cited in the article include *Somewhat Barbaric* (1944) and *American Labor's Case Against Communism* (1947).

For information about Chaplin and the IWW, see William D. Haywood, *Bill Haywood's Book* (1929); Patrick Renshaw, *The Wobblies* (1967); Joseph R. Conlin, *Bread and Roses Too* (1969); Melvin Dubofsky, *We Shall Be All: A History of the IWW* (1969).

A brief obituary is in *New York Times*, Mar. 28, 1961.]

MELVYN DUBOFSKY

CHASE, (MARY) AGNES MERRILL (Apr. 20, 1869–Sept. 24, 1963), systematic botanist and agrostologist, was born in Iroquois County, Ill., the daughter of Martin John Merrill and Mary Cassidy. She attended public and private schools in Chicago, and developed an interest in botany, especially grasses, during her youth. On Jan. 21, 1888, she married William Ingraham

Chase, who died almost a year later. They had no children.

During the 1890's Chase worked evenings as a proofreader for the *Inter-Ocean Newspaper*, while she botanized and took extension courses at the Lewis Institute and University of Chicago during the day. In 1901 she was appointed assistant in botany at the Field Museum of Natural History in Chicago, where she did line drawings for *Plantae Yucatanae* (published in 1903–1904) for her mentor, Charles Frederick Millspaugh. A job in Washington, D.C., as a botanical illustrator for the U.S. Department of Agriculture (USDA) followed in 1903. Chase worked after hours in the USDA Herbarium, studying grasses, and in 1906 published the first of her scientific papers on the genera of the Paniceae. The following year she was appointed scientific assistant in systematic agrostology, working with Albert S. Hitchcock.

Chase started her field collections for the USDA with trips to the southeastern United States. These led to publication, with Hitchcock, of *The North American Species of Panicum* (1910), considered a standard reference, and of *Tropical North American Species of Panicum* (1915). In 1913 she collected in Puerto Rico, and in 1917 she and Hitchcock published *Grasses of the West Indies*. As an agrostologist, or grass culture expert, Chase's responsibilities included determination of varieties of commercial grasses in order to expose many of the fraudulent claims for common grasses made by seed sellers, and to recommend the best species of grasses for livestock.

Chase was also involved in the women's suffrage movement. In January 1915 she was among those arrested for maintaining a continuous fire fed by copies of all of President Woodrow Wilson's speeches that referred to liberty or freedom. She was jailed again in August 1918 for picketing the White House.

Chase's *First Book of Grasses, the Structure of Grasses Explained for Beginners* was published in 1922. That year she traveled to European cities to study botanical collections. The following year she became an assistant botanist with the USDA. During this period she also was assistant custodian of the Grass Herbarium, which was transferred from the USDA to the United States National Museum (USNM) in 1912.

In November 1924, Chase began her major field explorations of South America with a trip through eastern Brazil. She was no "closet botanist," but enjoyed traveling on her own to remote regions of Brazil and Venezuela by train, donkey, and foot to collect specimens. Upon her return in

1925, she was promoted to associate botanist with the USDA. She returned to Brazil during 1929–1930 for another collecting expedition.

Chase substantially assisted Hitchcock in his work on *Manual of the Grasses of the United States* (1935). After he died in December 1935, Chase was appointed senior botanist in charge of all systematic agrostology for the Bureau of Plant Industry of the USDA in 1936, and custodian of the Section of Grasses of the USNM, with responsibility for the Grass Herbarium in 1937.

Chase retired from the USDA in April 1939, but she continued her scientific work. She was appointed research associate in the Division of Plants of the USNM and custodian of grasses for the National Herbarium. In 1940 she went to Venezuela, at the request of that government, to conduct a survey and recommend an agrostological program. Despite her age she amassed a substantial field collection for the National Herbarium.

In 1951, Chase published a revised edition of Hitchcock's *Manual of the Grasses of the United States*. At the fiftieth anniversary of the Botanical Society of America in 1956, she was one of fifty botanists to be presented with a certificate of merit, as "one of the world's outstanding agrostologists and preeminent among American students in this field." In 1958 she was awarded an honorary D.Sc. by the University of Illinois, her only college degree. Chase died in Bethesda, Md.

Chase's life was single-mindedly devoted to the study of grasses. Reputedly her first question when meeting someone was, "And what grasses do you work on?" If the new acquaintance did not study grasses, she walked away, bored. She often remarked that grasses are what hold the earth together, and believed that civilization was based upon them. Chase amassed thousands of specimens for the Grass Herbarium, and she described and classified a substantial portion of the grasses of America, leaving a bibliography of more than seventy publications. She completely revised the annotated index to grass species of more than 80,000 cards, published in three volumes in 1962. This index and the revised *Manual of the Grasses of the United States* were her crowning achievements.

[See Department of Botany records, Smithsonian Institution Archives; biographical file, New York Botanical Garden Library; "Agnes Chase," *Taxon*, June 1959, which includes a bibliography of her work; and the obituary in the *New York Times*, Sept. 26, 1963.]

PAMELA M. HENSON

CHATTERTON, RUTH (Dec. 24, 1893–Nov. 24, 1961), actress and novelist, was born in New York City, the daughter of William Chatterton, an architect, and Lillian Reed. She attended Pelham School for Girls at Pelham Manor, N.Y. At the age of fourteen she attended a stock company's performance in Washington, D.C., with a number of her school friends. Her criticism of the leading lady's performance led one of her friends to dare Ruth to do better. She accepted the challenge, and a few days later joined the chorus of that company in the play *Merely Mary Ann*. Her first New York stage appearance was as Isolde Brand in James Clarence Harvey's comedy *The Great Name* (1911). Later that year she appeared in Chicago in *Standing Pat*. When she returned to Broadway in 1912, she played the lead with Henry Miller in *The Rainbow*.

In 1914, Chatterton's career made a major advance when she accepted the starring role in *Daddy Long-Legs*. Her success led to a number of Broadway appearances, including parts in *Frederic Lemaitre* (1916), *Come out of the Kitchen* (1917), *A Bit o' Love* (1918), and *Perkins* (1918). In 1918 she re-created her starring role in a revival of *Daddy Long-Legs*, to great critical acclaim. One reviewer described her as an "artist of extraordinary subtlety and authenticity of charm." She appeared in *Moonlight and Honeysuckle* (1919) and *Mary Rose* (1920). She also starred in two plays she had adapted from the French, *La Tendresse* (1922) and *The Man in Evening Clothes* (1924). In 1923 she appeared in *The Changelings*.

After her next success, *The Magnolia Lady*, opened, Chatterton married her costar, English actor Ralph Forbes, on Dec. 20, 1924. In 1925 she and Forbes appeared in *The Little Minister*, and later that year she had a role in *The Man with the Load of Mischief*.

Chatterton made her first film, *Sins of the Father*, in 1928. She remained in Hollywood for eight years, appearing, under contract to Paramount, in *The Doctor's Secret* (1929) and *The Dummy* (1929). Later that year she achieved her first major film success in Metro-Goldwyn-Mayer's (MGM) *Madame X*. Chatterton next made *Charming Sinners* (1929), *The Laughing Lady* (1929), *Sarah and Son* (1930), and *Anybody's Woman* (1930), usually portraying a worldly and even tragic character. But after she made *Unfaithful* (1931), *The Magnificent Lie* (1931), *Once a Lady* (1931), and *Tomorrow and Tomorrow* (1932), her Paramount contract was terminated. As film historian Leslie Halliwell noted, "Her style was too intense for the more sophisticated later dramas."

In August 1932, Chatterton divorced Forbes and, a few days later, on August 12, married actor George Brent. She appeared in five films: *The Crash* (1932), *Frisco Jenny* (1933), *Lilly Turner* (1933), *Female* (1933), and *Journal of a Crime* (1934). In *The Crash, Lilly Turner,* and *Female* she appeared with Brent, although often in a supporting role. The Brents were divorced in October 1934.

In 1936, Chatterton ended her American film career with *Lady of Secrets, Girls' Dormitory,* and *Dodsworth.* She then moved to England, where she starred in the play *The Constant Wife* (1937), then two films, *The Rat* (1937) and *A Royal Divorce* (1938). The following year she returned to New York and appeared in the plays *West of Broadway* (1939), *The Affairs of Anatol* (1940), and *Leave Her to Heaven* (1940). Chatterton next toured the country playing Eliza in a stock company production of *Pygmalion* (1940–1941). Also in that production was the Australian actor John Barry Thomson, whom she married in 1941. Through 1942, Chatterton and Thomson played in road company productions of *Private Lives* and *Caprice.* In 1946 she returned to the Broadway stage to costar with Thomson in *Second Best Bed.* Later that year she narrated the production of *A Flag Is Born.*

Apart from her interest in acting, Chatterton devoted herself to humanitarian work. With the creation of the state of Israel in 1948, she served on the Committee to Save the Middle East from Communism and worked with the American League for a Free Palestine. She also lobbied to relieve the food shortages in Israel in the early years of its creation. For her efforts she received the Woman of Achievement Award from the Federation of Jewish Women's Organizations in 1951. That year marked her last appearance on Broadway, in a revival of *Idiot's Delight.* She made her last stage appearance in 1956, as Mrs. St. Maugham in *The Chalk Garden,* in St. Louis.

Chatterton was also a novelist. In 1950 she published *Homeward Borne,* a novel about an American couple's adoption of a child who had lived in a concentration camp during World War II. It was a widely praised best-seller. *The Betrayers* (1953) was a novel set in Washington, D.C., during the McCarthy witch-hunt days. This effort was less successful. According to many reviewers, it was too close to the news of the day, and tended to confuse real with fictitious events. In 1954, Chatterton published

Pride of the Peacock, which focused on average people with ordinary problems. This book was well received for its warmth and understanding. Her fourth and last novel, *The Southern Wild* (1958), was criticized for its melodramatic flourishes and stereotypical portrayal of race relations in the modern South. Despite Chatterton's extensive research one reviewer felt that "her effort to see the situation from every angle . . . militates against the book as novel."

Chatterton spent her last years in Redding, Conn. She died in Norwalk, Conn.

[Obituary notices are in *New York Times* and *New York Herald Tribune,* Nov. 25, 1961; *London Times,* Nov. 27, 1961. Also see *Time,* Dec. 1, 1961; *Newsweek,* Dec. 4, 1961; *Films in Review,* Jan. 1962.]

FRANCIS J. BOSHA

CHAVEZ, DENNIS (Apr. 8, 1888–Nov. 18, 1962), lawyer and U.S. Senator, was born at Los Chavez, Valencia County, N.M., the son of David Chavez, an impoverished farmer-laborer, and of Paz Sanchez. He was baptized Dionisio, but his name was changed to Dennis at school. The family soon moved to Albuquerque, where at thirteen Chavez dropped out of the eighth grade and took a job as a grocery delivery boy. In 1911 he married Imelda Espinosa; they had three children.

For a time Chavez worked for the Albuquerque Engineering Department, but in 1916 he obtained temporary employment as a Spanish interpreter for Senator A. A. Jones's reelection campaign. He was rewarded with a clerkship in the U.S. Senate (1918–1919). Although he had never completed high school, Chavez passed a special examination and was admitted to Georgetown University Law School. At the age of thirty-two he obtained the LL.B. and immediately returned to Albuquerque.

A Democrat, Chavez was more interested in politics than law, and embarked on an ambitious political career. After serving in the New Mexico House of Representatives (1923–1924), Chavez was elected to the U.S. House of Representatives in 1930. During his second term he decided to challenge Bronson F. Cutting, the Democratic incumbent, for the Senate nomination. The 1934 election was both bitter and close. Chavez lost and charged the opposition with fraud. Early in 1935, Cutting was killed in an airplane crash and Governor Clyde Tingley, influenced by the Democratic National Committee, appointed Chavez to the seat. When Chavez was being sworn in, five New Deal liberal senators, friends of Cutting, walked out in protest.

Chavez was elected senator in his own right in 1936, and reelected in 1940, 1946, 1952, and 1958. Only the 1952 election was close. In 1946 he defeated Patrick Hurley, Herbert Hoover's secretary of war and Franklin D. Roosevelt's ambassador to China. Hurley challenged him again in 1952. When the vote count indicated a narrow Chavez victory, Hurley charged "error, fraud, and violations of the election law." Two Senate committees recommended that Chavez be unseated, but the full Senate voted by a narrow margin that his election should stand.

Chavez was known as a quiet member of the Senate. He spoke little, but worked hard on committees and for legislation he supported. He was basically liberal in his approach to national problems. In 1952 the Congress of Industrial Organizations listed him as one of only eight senators who voted "right" on labor-related issues.

Chavez's Spanish heritage led him to be concerned about the status of Puerto Rico, especially during World War II, when unemployment was high and poverty rampant on the island. Chavez was an advocate of the Good Neighbor Policy toward Latin America. He favored normalization of relations with Spain in 1939 and urged the inclusion of Spain in the NATO treaty a decade later.

During the New Deal, Chavez opposed Commissioner of Indian Affairs John Collier's program of assisting American Indians to restore their culture and regain some of their land. For example, when Collier proposed to cut Navajo grazing stock as a conservation measure, Chavez and the Navajos objected. After a number of confrontations, Chavez tried to get Collier fired and demanded an investigation of Collier's goal of making Indian tribes self-sustaining. Chavez believed that the road to success for Indians, Puerto Ricans, or any other minority was through integration into the larger society. That is one reason why he opposed Indian autonomy and proposed making English the language of Puerto Rico.

Chavez earned some degree of national reputation for his long and sustained battle to establish a permanent Fair Employment Practices Commission (FEPC). He argued that racial discrimination must be eliminated from all areas of federal employment. Chavez succeeded in getting a temporary FEPC during the war, but he persisted in seeking a permanent commission. He also wanted to extend its jurisdiction beyond federal employment to encompass all aspects of employment. The bill was filibustered to death in 1946 by southern Democrats and conservative Republicans. President Harry Truman was able to enact some parts of the FEPC legislation by executive order, and the remaining provisions were included in the civil rights laws of the 1960's.

During Dwight D. Eisenhower's administration Chavez scrambled to maintain his position and to survive McCarthyism. He called the McCarthy era "a period when we quietly shackled men's minds." He became chairman of the Senate Appropriations Subcommittee for Defense and was beginning to take an interest in that area when he was found to be suffering from cancer in early 1961. He died at Washington, D.C. At the graveside service Vice-President Lyndon B. Johnson referred to Chavez as a man "who recognized that there must be champions for the least among us."

[As of this writing, the Chavez papers have not been deposited. The presidential libraries of Franklin D. Roosevelt, Harry Truman, Dwight D. Eisenhower, John F. Kennedy, and Lyndon B. Johnson contain holdings of Chavez material. Perhaps the best clipping file is at the AFL-CIO Library in Washington, D.C. An obituary is in the *New York Times*, Nov. 19, 1962.]

F. ROSS PETERSON

CHESTER, COLBY MITCHELL (July 23, 1877–Sept. 26, 1965), lawyer and corporation officer, was born at the U.S. Naval Academy, Annapolis, Md., the son of Colby M. Chester, then a lieutenant commander, who later served as commandant of the Naval Academy, and of Malancia Antoinette Tremaine. He attended schools in Annapolis and in the District of Columbia, and the Mohegan Lake Academy at Peekskill, N.Y. From 1891 to 1894, Chester studied at St. John's College in Annapolis; then he entered Yale College, from which he received the Ph.B. in 1897 and the B.A. in 1898.

Chester next enrolled at the New York Law School, which awarded him the LL.B. in 1900. After being admitted to the New York bar, he worked briefly for the firm of Carter, Hughes, and Dwight, and then for a year with the firm of Rich, Woodford, Bovee, and Butcher. In 1902 he and two classmates established the firm of Ely, Billings, and Chester.

On Apr. 20, 1904, Chester married Jessie Campbell Moore; they had three children. Also in 1904 he left his law partnership to become treasurer of Manning, Maxwell, and Moore, an industrial supply firm located in Bridgeport, Conn., of which his father-in-law was a partner.

Chester resumed his law practice in New York City in 1911, specializing in corporate law. In 1917, as a National Guard lieutenant, he was called to active duty and was commissioned a major in the infantry. After serving at Camp Meade, Md., Camp MacArthur, Tex., and Camp Mills, S.C., he was assigned to the Inspector General Corps. He was discharged Dec. 27, 1918.

In 1919 Chester entered the food industry as assistant treasurer of the Postum Cereal Company of Battle Creek, Mich. During the next five years he served as treasurer, vice-president, and, in 1924, president. The Postum Company moved to New York City, and in 1929 merged with fifteen other food manufacturers to form the General Foods Corporation, of which Chester was the first president.

During his presidency, which continued until 1935, General Foods acquired the Cheek-Neal Company, manufacturer of Maxwell House Coffee, the Certo Corporation, Frosted Foods, Inc., the Dunlap Milling Company, the Bennett Day Importing Company, and the Franklin Baker Company. Sales increased from $25 million to $120 million. In 1935, Chester became chairman of the board and from 1943 to 1946 he was chairman of the executive committee.

Chester was also chairman of the boards of Manning, Maxwell, and Moore, the Zonite Products Corporation, and the Lehigh Valley Railroad, and director of the New Jersey, Indiana, and Illinois Railroad Company, of Twentieth Century-Fox Film Corporation, of Chase Manhattan Bank, and of Manufacturers Hanover Trust Company.

Civic and philanthropic affairs were also among Chester's activities. He was chairman of the New York chapter of the American Red Cross and of the Red Cross War Fund of Greater New York (1943–1952); member of the Yale University Development Committee and of the St. John's College Advisory Board; and president of the National Institute of Social Sciences from 1942 to 1945. He was prominent in the affairs of the National Association of Manufacturers (NAM) during the mid-1930's, and became its president in 1936. During this period he made a number of speeches in which he advocated better employee and community relations for corporate management, in order to meet what he termed "public distrust and misunderstanding of big corporations."

Chester's management style was reflected in his description, in early 1939, of a business executive's responsibilities in the Great Depression: ". . . to fill the weekly pay envelope; to see that

local, state, and national government is supplied with the wherewithal; to provide the consumer with goods honestly made and reasonably priced; to get out of the difference between the price and the cost a return to the investor that will induce him to entrust his money to us, for without his capital there could be no plant and no production."

Chester died in Greenwich, Conn.

[A number of Chester's speeches as president and board chairman of the NAM were published in *Vital Speeches of the Day*. They include "Business, the Guinea Pig" (June 17, 1935); "Industry and Recovery" (Apr. 6, 1936); "Money Is not Enough" (Aug. 1, 1936). He also opposed American entry into the war in 1939 in "Industry's Stand Against the War," *Vital Speeches* (Nov. 1, 1939). Yale University has a portrait of Chester in the Yale Picture Collection.]

DAVID W. HERON

CHOTZINOFF, SAMUEL (July 4, 1889–Feb. 9, 1964), pianist and music critic, was born in Vitebsk, Russia, the first of three children born to Mayshe Baer Chatianov, a schoolteacher, and Rachel Treskanoff. Since his parents had previous marriages, Samuel had four half-brothers and four half-sisters. The large Chatianov family was extremely poor and left Vitebsk in 1895. After spending a difficult year in London, they immigrated to the United States, settling on New York's Lower East Side in August 1896.

Chotzinoff was enrolled in the second grade in Public School No. 2 and took his first piano lessons when he was ten years old. His formal training was interrupted in 1901 when the family moved to Waterbury, Conn., where two of Samuel's half-brothers had settled. There Chotzinoff attended the Webster Grammar School, finishing in 1904, shortly before the family returned to New York City. That year Chotzinoff resumed his piano lessons and studied with Jeanne Franko. He made his public debut as soloist in the Mozart Piano Concerto in D minor, K. 466, with the Educational Alliance Orchestra, in the fall of 1905.

Although Chotzinoff did not attend high school, he passed the entrance examinations for Columbia University in 1908. He was not a music major but he took classes taught by Daniel Gregory Mason. He left Columbia in 1911 without graduating and became the accompanist for the Russian violinist Efrem Zimbalist, with whom he remained until 1918. Chotzinoff became an American citizen in 1918. During his years with Zimbalist, he also accompanied the sopranos Alma Gluck and Frieda Hempel.

In 1919 he supplanted André Benoist as Jascha Heifetz's accompanist, and worked with him until 1922. On Dec. 10, 1925, Chotzinoff married Pauline Heifetz, sister of the violinist; they had two children.

Chotzinoff's first published music criticism, in the magazine *Vanity Fair*, reviewed the famous Feb. 12, 1924, concert in which George Gershwin introduced his *Rhapsody in Blue*. This review so impressed Deems Taylor, then music critic of the *New York World*, that, upon his resignation the following year, he recommended that Chotzinoff succeed him. Chotzinoff wrote for the *World* until its demise in 1931. When Oscar L. Thompson left the *Evening Post* in 1934, Chotzinoff stepped in, remaining with that newspaper until 1941.

In 1936 Chotzinoff was engaged as a music consultant to the NBC radio network by David Sarnoff. His first assignment was to lure Arturo Toscanini back to the United States, a mission he accomplished by assembling the NBC Symphony Orchestra for the conductor. The orchestra played its first concert under Toscanini for a vast radio audience on Dec. 25, 1937. Chotzinoff was known throughout the country as the commentator for the orchestra's regular Saturday night broadcasts. He then commissioned for NBC the first opera composed specifically for radio—Gian-Carlo Menotti's *The Old Maid and the Thief*, first broadcast on Apr. 22, 1939.

Connections with RCA allowed Chotzinoff in 1939 to mastermind a promotion stunt for the *New York Post* that was widely imitated. RCA's studio made a special series of recordings by prominent orchestras that were not identified; these were sold at cost by the *Post*. The *Washington Star* took up the scheme, organized a national music appreciation committee, and began distributing the records at an unprecedented $1.39 per set. Many Americans were introduced to classical music by this scheme.

In January 1949 Chotzinoff was appointed general music director for NBC radio and television. He organized the NBC Television Opera Theater and commissioned the first television opera, Menotti's *Amahl and the Night Visitors*, first seen on Christmas Eve in 1951.

Chotzinoff's last, and perhaps most impressive, writings were *Toscanini: An Intimate Portrait* (1956) and *A Little Nightmusic* (1964). He was not a giant figure in American music criticism, and it is doubtful that his writings will endure. But he left a permanent mark on American culture through his work for NBC radio and television. Chotzinoff died in New York City.

[Published biographical material is scant and untrustworthy; even the *New York Times* obituary, Feb. 11, 1964, is highly inaccurate. The most reliable sources of information are Chotzinoff's two memoirs, *A Lost Paradise* (1955), which covers the years through 1905, and *Day's at the Morn* (1964), which ends in 1911. Information about his years with Heifetz, as well as some of his reviews, may be found in *Heifetz* (1976), edited by Herbert R. Axelrod. His relationship with Menotti is discussed in John Gruen, *Menotti* (1978). Both *Fortune*, January 1938, and *Time*, July 3, 1939, have articles about his Toscanini coup.]

IRVING LOWENS

CLARK, JOHN MAURICE (Nov. 30, 1884–June 27, 1963), economist, was born at Northampton, Mass., the son of John Bates Clark and Myra Almeda Smith. Following graduation from Amherst (1905) and from Columbia (Ph.D. 1910), he taught at Colorado College, then Amherst. After a decade at the University of Chicago he returned to Columbia as professor (1926–1953). He married Winifred Fiske Miller on June 17, 1921; they had two sons.

Clark liked to think of himself as the lengthened shadow of his father. His father was his teacher; they collaborated on the revision of his father's *The Control of Trusts* (1912); he succeeded to his father's chair at Columbia University; and each, in semiretirement, devoted himself to world peace. They also were alike in meticulous scholarship. In the substance of their work they differed. John Bates Clark, while fully aware of interferences with laissez-faire, concentrated on theory in an economy of equilibrium, which was expected to keep itself in balance automatically. By the time of the son's entrance into the field, departures from competition were so prominent and proliferating as to claim major attention.

Clark sought to make the most of freedom in economic life, even at the expense of losing something of efficiency. He sought to minimize controls with a consistency that betrayed an emotional as well as a rational objection. His father had the same stance, as shown in *Social Justice Without Socialism* (1914); the son entitled a series of lectures *Alternative to Serfdom* (1947).

At the same time there was a progressive erosion of a freely acting American economy. Growth in size and scope of some business enterprises damaged or extinguished smaller rivals, monopolies multiplied, government intervened with both subsidies and preventives. World War I spread national management to areas of the economy hitherto the preserves of private initiative. The Great Depression demanded unexampled governmental intervention to salvage enterprise, encourage labor organization, and feed and house large sections of the population. America's entrance into World War II weakened old inhibitions to governmental responsibility and ushered in fresh controls of production, consumption, prices, and wages.

By the 1940's it was generally accepted that the American economy that Clark depicted was a far cry from the pure competition his father had analyzed; it was a mix of private capitalism and governmental responsibility. The question was how best to adjust interaction of those two forces so as to preserve both elasticity and security. In addition to the increase of public commitment, combination advanced in the private sector. "Big labor" began to be coupled with "big business."

"The continued existence of effective competitive forces," Clark wrote, "is not to be too easily taken for granted. One cannot ignore the question whether such forces have ceased to have a role of any importance under the conditions modern industrialism imposes." Although he dealt with most aspects of the economy, it was on the mechanics of disappearing competition that he focused. In examining the overhead or fixed costs of large-scale business—and of quite limited agricultural production—he found rigidities in exchange. If demand for certain products is imperious, as in wartime, an industry may shift to supply the need if its equipment is adaptable. An automobile manufacturer may turn out tanks, molders of radiators may cast cannon, the machinery that made collapsible fishing rods may furnish tall poles for aerials— Clark cited many more ingenious conversions. But lacking such incentive, the plant with a large, specialized investment may seek to preserve its prices by curtailing production if demand falls off.

Clark stressed, in season and out, the economic loss from chronically idle capital. Capital was no longer the protean instrument envisaged by classical theory, but of permanent form and, if unused, liable to rapid obsolescence. Neither can a farmer change his cash crop short of the natural season for growing and harvesting. These are crude examples; in his elaborate inspection of overhead costs, Clark discussed every aspect of this maladjustment in the economy. If the resulting loss is large and persistent, some sort of public assistance is called for; it may take the form of subsidy or of price maintenance with production control. In his writings looms the prospect of public subventions to those, including workers, who produce the necessities of life.

In Clark's hands economic theory—he called himself a theorist—became largely a description of potent institutions, or habits, that profoundly modify free conduct. A familiar illustration is the behavior of consumers conditioned by mass advertising. Joseph Dorfman has summarized his work thus: "The great value of his contribution lies in its synthesis of neo-classical economics and institutionalism, its presentation as an integrated whole." Clark was not content to let ills go untreated. His "social liberal" planning, he wrote, contemplated "a unified program via general controls that keep within the limits consistent with a healthy private enterprise, more complete controls being limited to certain strategic factors which condition private economic enterprise . . . such as a 'liberal' government may administer."

Some of Clark's most influential works are *Studies in the Economics of Overhead Costs* (1923), *Social Control of Business* (1926), *Strategic Factors in Business Cycles* (1934), and *The Costs of the* [First] *World War to the American People* (1931). These and his many publications over a period of more than fifty years are sparing of mathematical expressions.

Clark served on and reported for numerous official commissions, including regulative bodies. He was president of the American Economic Association in 1935 and was awarded its Walker Medal in 1952. He retired from Columbia as professor in 1953, continuing as special lecturer until shortly before his death. Clark died at Westport, Conn.

[Among numerous appraisals of Clark are Joseph Dorfman, *The Economic Mind in American Civilization*, V (1959), pp. 438–463; Allan G. Gruchy, *Modern Economic Thought: The American Contribution* (1947; repr. 1966), pp. 337–402; Ben B. Seligman, *Main Currents in Modern Economics* (1962), pp. 200–221. C. Addison Hickman, *J. M. Clark*, (1975), quotes Clark's views of some of his peers, and has a full bibliography of his works. An obituary is in *New York Times*, June 28, 1963.]

BROADUS MITCHELL

CLARK, JOSHUA REUBEN, JR. (Sept. 1, 1871–Oct. 6, 1961), lawyer, diplomat, and churchman, was born near Grantsville, Utah, the son of Joshua Reuben Clark, a Union soldier in the Civil War and a Montana miner, and of Mary Louisa Woolley. He was tutored by his mother until the age of ten, then completed the eight grades of public school available in Grantsville. Next he became curator of the Deseret Museum in Salt Lake City. Clark enrolled in the University of Utah in 1894, finishing high school and college in four years and graduating with the B.S. as valedictorian and secretary to the president of the university. In 1898 he married Luacine Annetta Savage in the Salt Lake City Temple; they had four children. He was a teacher in several Utah localities until 1903, when he took his family to New York City. He entered Columbia University Law School, where he received the LL.B. in 1906.

At Columbia, Clark came to the attention of James Brown Scott, professor of international law. When Scott became solicitor of the Department of State in 1906, he appointed Clark assistant solicitor. Clark soon prepared the monograph *Judicial Determination of Questions of Citizenship*, which became an authoritative text for immigration cases. On July 1, 1910, President William H. Taft appointed Clark solicitor of the Department of State. Shortly afterward Clark finished a massive documentation for the American case in the Alsop Arbitration with Chile, involving Chilean expropriation of several American companies. The king of England was the "amiable compositeur," and as arbitrator awarded the United States $905,000, one of the largest awards made up to that time. Another of Clark's activities as solicitor was preparation of *Memorandum on the Right to Protect Citizens in Foreign Countries by Landing Forces*, a useful document for the United States government in its relations with Caribbean and Central American nations.

Leaving the State Department in 1913, Clark opened a law office in Washington, with branches in New York and Salt Lake City. During World War I he was a major on the Army Judge Advocate General's staff and helped draft the Selective Service regulations.

In 1928, Clark was appointed undersecretary of state, an office similar to that of solicitor, which it had superseded. In this capacity he helped draw up the "Clark Memorandum" on the Monroe Doctrine. The memorandum seemed to say that the Roosevelt Corollary of 1904 was not properly a part of the Monroe Doctrine. It was a long document of 238 printed pages, with a prolix covering letter of seventeen pages to Secretary of State Frank B. Kellogg. Although it was published by the Government Printing Office in 1930, the memorandum was not officially sanctioned by the Department of State and has taken on importance only in the writings of historians and international lawyers who have seen it as definitive.

Clark left the State Department in 1929 to become aide to Dwight Morrow, ambassador to Mexico, and in 1930 succeeded Morrow in Mexico, where he remained until March 1933. If his Mexican years did not see any notable achievements, neither were there notable failures. His stay there was marked by the exercise of good sense; at one juncture he said, thoughtfully, "Mexican ethical, moral, and legal standards are different from those in the United States, but not necessarily lower, and at any rate are controlling here."

In 1933, Clark commenced a virtually new career as a high official of the Church of Jesus Christ of Latter-Day Saints, with appointment as second counselor to President Heber J. Grant. He became first counselor in 1934, and served as an apostle from that year until his death at Salt Lake City.

Clark's legal and diplomatic ideas were considered noteworthy in their day. He possessed a sense of humor, and in his old age, when he still held to his ideas of years before, remarked: "Many think me just a doddering old fogy. I admit the age, but deny the rest of the allegation—the doddering and fogyness." He shared his church's feeling for the divine mission of America: "Believing as we do that America is Zion, we shall then see the beginning of the fulfillment of the prophecy of Isaiah of old 'for out of Zion shall go forth the law.' . . ." Nothing, he thought, should subtract from American sovereignty and from American moral force, the force that came from divine mission. The country, he sometimes said, had gone through three epochs: the first from the Revolution until 1800, when American separateness from Europe was achieved; the second during the nineteenth century, when a marvelous perfection—that is, separateness—was confirmed; and the third beginning with World War I, when tragedy followed tragedy. He supported American participation in both world wars, but opposed the League of Nations and the United Nations because they subtracted from American sovereignty, and hence from America's mission.

[The Clark papers, a collection of 140,000 items, are at Brigham Young University Library, Provo, Utah. Besides Clark's speeches and legal writings, see especially his *Memorandum on the Monroe Doctrine* (1930); Robert H. Ferrell, "Repudiation of a Repudiation," *Journal of American History*, 1964–1965; Ray C. Hillam, ed., *J. Reuben Clark, Jr.: Diplomat and Statesman* (1973). An obituary is in the *New York Times*, Oct. 7, 1961.]

ROBERT H. FERRELL

CLOTHIER, WILLIAM JACKSON (Sept. 27, 1881–Sept. 4, 1962), coal merchant and athlete, was born at Sharon Hill, Pa., the ninth (and last) child of Mary Clapp Jackson and Isaac Hallowell Clothier, a founder of the Strawbridge and Clothier department store in Philadelphia. He was educated at Haverford School and Swarthmore College, of which his father was a trustee. After two years at Swarthmore, Clothier transferred to Harvard, from which he graduated in 1904.

In college Clothier played football, ice hockey, and tennis. As early as 1899 he had been a finalist in the Pennsylvania State Tennis Championship. He won the title in 1901, 1902, and 1903. In 1902 he won the National Intercollegiate Championships in both singles and doubles, and in 1903 and 1904 he was the runner-up in the National Singles Championship.

In 1905, Clothier was a member of the first American Davis Cup team to go abroad, and he also played on the Davis Cup team in 1906. In the latter year he won the National Singles Championship at Newport, R.I. From 1901 through 1914, Clothier was nationally ranked among the top ten American tennis players eleven times. Many years later, Clothier and his son, William Jackson II, won the National Father and Son title in 1935 and 1936. They were runners-up in 1937 and 1941.

After graduation from Harvard, Clothier worked briefly for Edward B. Smith and Company in Philadelphia. In 1905 he became the Philadelphia representative of Wrenn Brothers and Company, bankers of New York and Boston. From 1907 to 1921 he was partner in the banking house of Montgomery, Clothier, and Tyler.

Meanwhile, in 1911, Clothier organized, and in 1915 became president of, Boone County Coal Corporation of Sharples, W.Va. Also in 1911 he began to purchase land in the Pickering Valley near Valley Forge, Pa. Eventually his Valley Hill Farm covered almost 1,000 acres. He joined his pack of hounds with those of the recently founded Pickering Hunt Club, and was master of the hounds at Pickering from 1911 until 1951.

Clothier married Anita Porter on Feb. 21, 1906. The wedding took place in the groom's bedroom because he had broken his pelvis in a riding accident two weeks earlier. Neither he nor the bride seemed daunted by the medical prognosis that Clothier might never again play tennis or ride to hounds. Their faith in his recuperative powers was sustained—Clothier recovered and won the National Singles Tennis Championship that summer and the Radnor point-to-point race in the fall.

The Clothiers had five children. Anita Clothier shared her husband's interest in tennis, hunting, horses, and dogs. Together they made Valley Hill Farm a spectacular recreational center. Every year from 1913 until 1950, when the mansion burned down, the farm was the site of the annual Pickering Race Meet and Farmers' Day in November, and competitors and spectators came from the surrounding area to take part. The Clothiers also bred and trained horses and hounds.

Clothier was instrumental in establishing the International Tennis Hall of Fame at Newport, R.I., in 1954, serving as its president from 1954 to 1957. He kept it going largely with his own funds, and acquired a sizable collection of tennis memorabilia for its museum. He was himself inducted into the International Tennis Hall of Fame in 1956.

Clothier was a prototype of the early twentieth-century country gentleman. *Country Life* described him as "purposeful in all things, correct, unostentatious, enthusiastic, thorough." "Hunting with Clothier," the article continued, "is stout and straight . . . not meant to be fun." The reader can almost see him riding in a point-to-point race or leading a bucket brigade of local children as they iced the half-mile toboggan run at Valley Hill Farm or presiding graciously over the trophy table at race meet day.

Clothier retired from his coal corporation in 1957. He spent the rest of his life at Valley Hill Farm, where he also died.

[See Harvard University Alumni Association, *25th Anniversary Report of the Class of 1904* (1929) and *50th Anniversary Report of the Class of 1904* (1954); Sophia Yarnall, "Full Length Portrait of a Country Gentleman, VII, William J. Clothier," *Country Life* (October 1934); Dirk Van Ingen, "Master of the Pickering," *Country Life* (January 1940). An obituary is in *New York Times*, Sept. 6, 1962.]

JOANNE F. McADAM

COBB, TYRUS RAYMOND ("TY") (Dec. 18, 1886–July 17, 1961), baseball player, was born in Narrows, Banks County, Ga., the son of William Herschel Cobb and Amanda Chitwood. His father was a school principal who served in the Georgia Senate, where he helped to establish the county school system. The family moved to Royston, Ga., when Tyrus (he answered to the nickname "Ty" only after he became a big leaguer) was very young. There he attended school and grew up playing and dreaming baseball. Despite his father's hope that he would become a medical doctor or a lawyer, he eventually won parental approval of his choice of profession.

Cobb honed his skills playing town ball, an older form of baseball. In town ball a team could have an unlimited number of players, and a base runner could be put out only when a fielder hit him with a thrown ball. Winning therefore required precise place hitting and nimble baserunning—and Cobb came to excel at both.

When Cobb was only nine years old, he was a star player on a local sandlot team. He signed with Augusta of the South Atlantic League in April 1904, to fill in for the regular center fielder, then under suspension. When the regular returned, Cobb was released. He caught on briefly with Anniston (Alabama) in the Southeastern League and then, after twenty-two games, returned to Augusta in May. The following year, he hit .326. Late in the 1905 season the Detroit Tigers bought his contract for $750, then regarded as a substantial price. The sportswriter Grantland Rice, who saw him playing for Augusta, dubbed him the "Georgia Peach," a sobriquet Cobb wore with pride for the rest of his life.

Cobb hit only .240 in his first year with the Tigers, handicapped in adjusting to major-league play by a brash manner, a thin skin, and a trigger-quick temper that antagonized teammates as well as opponents, umpires, and sometimes fans. He became for a time a lone wolf, rooming and taking his meals by himself.

But the brilliance of Cobb's performance as the Tigers' center fielder won the admiration of all baseball devotees. Weighing about 175 pounds and standing just over six feet tall, he cut a lithe and graceful figure. Cobb batted .320 in 1906, the first of twenty-three straight years in which he hit .300 or better. In that period he led the league twelve times, nine in a row. The first time, in 1907, he was only twenty years old. Three times he hit more than .400 in a season, a feat equaled by only two other players. His highest average—in 1911—was .420. That year he struck out swinging only twice.

Cobb's style of batting was unorthodox. A left-hander at the plate (he threw right-handed), he hunched himself in a knock-kneed crouch with his feet close together; he grasped the thick-handled bat with his right hand about three inches from the knob and placed his left hand about six inches above the right. The control this sliding grip gave him enabled him to poke the ball through the infield, deliberately foul it off, hit to any field, bunt precisely, or even swing from the heels without telegraphing his intention.

As a competitor Cobb was unsurpassed, regarding all rival pitchers and infielders as his natural enemies. He always denied that he filed his spikes to razor sharpness or that he deliberately spiked an opponent. Still, his own legs bore the scars of spike wounds suffered in encounters with players who were repaying him in kind. His brawls with other ballplayers—and once with an umpire—were legion, taking place on the field, in hotel rooms, and under grandstands. In 1912 the American League president, Ban Johnson, suspended him for jumping into the bleachers to strike a crippled fan who had heckled him.

Besides being able to hit with utter confidence, Cobb was a wizard on the base paths. In his career he stole 892 bases, a record that stood for half a century. Several times he stole second, third, and home in succession. He was not the fleetest runner, but he combined with his considerable speed immense guile, an uncanny knowledge of his opponents, and not a little terror and cruelty, both physical and psychological. His ability to execute the fall-away or hook slide—which he perfected—made him a constant menace on the base paths as well as a stirring personification of energy and determination. A 1909 photograph of Cobb hook-sliding into third base with teeth gritted, eyes narrowed, and one arm off the ground to balance himself while the baseman, poised on one leg, awaits the throw, is widely regarded as the best action picture ever taken on a baseball field. The picture fits with the legend about a manager who asked a rookie catcher: "What will you do if Cobb breaks from first base to steal?" "Why," the young man replied, "I'll fake a throw to second and try to nail him at third."

Cobb's playing was consistently outstanding, for he entered every game as if his life depended on the outcome. Again and again he rose to remarkable heights under pressure. At the time of his suspension in 1912, his teammates went on strike in support of him when the Tigers reached Philadelphia. The Athletics proceeded to pulverize the team of second-stringers that the Tigers fielded. Cobb was outraged at what he regarded as "laying it on," and he spoke his mind in the newspapers. When the schedule again brought the Tigers to Philadelphia, he was under such physical and verbal threat from the local fans that the mayor felt obliged to send heavy police reinforcements to the ball park for the three doubleheaders in a row that the Tigers and Athletics would be playing. In those six games—against some of the best pitchers in baseball, including Eddie Plank, Chief Bender, and Herb Pennock—Cobb collected eighteen hits in twenty-eight times at bat. He considered this series the best he ever played.

During World War I, Cobb served briefly in the Chemical Warfare Division of the army, rising to the rank of captain. Nevertheless, he did not miss a playing season, and his athletic gifts remained undiminished. In late 1920, Frank Navin, the Tigers' owner, signed Cobb to manage the team. As player-manager Cobb brought the club in second in the pennant race of 1923, the best finish he was to achieve. His abrasive personality, combined with his unquenchable perfectionism, limited his effectiveness as a leader. But being manager did not hurt his own playing. In 1922, his eighteenth year in the majors, he hit .401. He resigned as manager at the end of the 1926 season.

Shortly afterward, Cobb and Tris Speaker of the Cleveland Indians, another all-time great center fielder, were accused by Dutch Leonard, a former Tiger pitcher, of having helped throw a game in 1919. The accusation became a topic of national conversation. After a personal investigation, Judge Kenesaw Mountain Landis, the commissioner of baseball, exonerated both men.

Cobb, who by now had given thought to retiring, signed with the Philadelphia Athletics in 1927 for a reported $60,000. Connie Mack, the long-time manager of the team, had persuaded Cobb that with him in the lineup, a pennant would be sure. Although Cobb hit .357 that year, the club came in second. Cobb's last season was 1928, when the Athletics again were runners-up. As a Tiger, Cobb had participated in three consecutive World Series, those of 1907, 1908, and 1909—each time on the losing side.

Research published in 1981 based on a reexamination of American League records showed that in 1910 Cobb actually hit .382, not .385, and thus had been nosed out for the batting championship by Napoleon Lajoie who hit .383. The corrections give Cobb 4,190 hits in his career, and a lifetime average of .366. The baseball commissioner and the league presidents did not dispute the findings but insisted on retaining the existing statistics as official.

Off the field Cobb, an ardent hunter and a lusty drinker, was a shrewd businessman. Wise investments in real estate and cotton paid off for him, as did his purchases of Coca-Cola and General Motors stocks. He had become a millionaire long before he retired from baseball.

After he left the game, Cobb moved restlessly from Georgia to California to Nevada and then back to Georgia. In 1953 he created the Cobb Educational Foundation to provide scholarships for needy Georgia college students. In memory of his parents he built and furnished a hospital for his hometown of Royston. When he died in an Atlanta hospital, he had brought with him $1 million in negotiable securities, which he laid on his bedside table and covered with a pistol.

Cobb married Charlotte Marion Lombard on Aug. 8, 1908; they had five children. They were divorced in 1947. He married Frances Cass on Sept. 24, 1949; they were divorced in 1955.

The "Georgia Peach" is generally acknowledged to have been the greatest all-around player in baseball. In 1936, when the Baseball Hall of Fame was established at Cooperstown, N.Y., he was the first man elected, in a select group that included Honus Wagner, Babe Ruth, Christy Mathewson, and Walter Johnson. As he grew older Cobb mellowed—he could even admit that he had been mean and difficult in his younger days. In a fiercely competitive society where winning was everything, he had shown how being number one could be a thrilling obsession.

[Memorabilia and newspaper clippings are in the National Baseball Hall of Fame, Cooperstown, N.Y. Cobb's autobiography, prepared with the assistance of Al Stump, is *My Life in Baseball: The True Record* (1961). The statistics of Cobb's career are in *The Baseball Encyclopedia* (1969). See also John McCallum, *The Tiger Wore Spikes* (1956); Gene Schoor, *The Story of Ty Cobb* (1952); and Paul MacFarlane, "Why Was Cobb Awarded 1910 Bat Title?" *Sporting News,* Apr. 18, 1981.

Obituaries are in the *New York Times* and the *New York Herald Tribune,* July 18, 1961, and a tribute, in *Time,* July 28, 1961. The picture referred to is reproduced in the *Times* story.]

HENRY F. GRAFF

COCHRANE, GORDON STANLEY ("MICKEY") (Apr. 6, 1903–June 28, 1962), baseball player, was born in Bridgewater, Mass., the son of John Cochrane and Sarah Campbell. His father, an Irish immigrant, was a laborer at the time of his birth and later became part owner of a local movie theater.

After graduating from Bridgewater High School in 1921, Cochrane attended Boston University for three years. There the 5-foot-10½-inch, 180-pounder won ten varsity athletic letters in football, baseball, basketball, and hockey, and was also on the boxing team. He was a star left halfback and kicker for the football team, and once drop-kicked a record forty-eight-yard field goal in a game against Brown University.

While at Boston University, Cochrane played semiprofessional baseball during the summer for the Saranac Lake, N.Y., club. In 1923 he broke into professional baseball as an outfielder with the Dover, Del., team of the Eastern Shore League. Throughout his career Cochrane batted left-handed but threw with his right. On Mar. 25, 1924, he married Mary Bohr. They had three children.

Cochrane left college in 1924 and was signed by the Portland (Oreg.) Beavers of the Pacific Coast League, for whom he played catcher. Later in 1924 the Philadelphia Athletics of the American League purchased the Portland club, partly in order to obtain Cochrane. The following year Cochrane began a long and happy association with Connie Mack, owner and manager of the team. During his nine-year reign as Mack's regular catcher, "Black Mike" (as Cochrane was called because of his fiery, competitive spirit) hit over .300 in six seasons. He struck out an average of only seventeen times per season. On defense Cochrane's skills were such that he has been described as a "master of the mechanics of catching." He caught the best pitchers of his era, including Eddie Rommel, Rube Walburg, George Earnshaw, and Lefty Grove.

In 1925, 1929, 1930, and 1932, Cochrane had the highest fielding average of any catcher in the league. From 1926 through 1930, and again in 1932, he led the league in putouts by a catcher. In 1928 he was chosen the most valuable player in the American League, and the next three seasons he helped the A's capture the league pennant. The team won the World Series in 1929 and 1930.

In 1933, desperate for capital, Mack reluctantly began to dispose of his high-salaried stars. He accepted $100,000 and a player from the Detroit Tigers in exchange for Cochrane, who immediately was named player-manager of Detroit.

The Tigers had not won a pennant since 1909, but Cochrane led them into the World Series in both 1934 and 1935, winning the series in the latter year. His $30,000 salary was second in the major leagues only to that of Babe Ruth. In 1934 he batted .320 and again was selected the most valuable player in the league. That year Cochrane caught Schoolboy Rowe's sixteen consecutive victories.

Midway through the 1936 season, Cochrane suffered a nervous breakdown. After returning from a rest period at a Wyoming ranch, he led the Tigers in a race that fell just short of the pennant. In 1937, while batting in a game against the New York Yankees, Cochrane was hit in the head by a pitch. His skull was frac-tured in three places. For several days his life was in danger, and the injury ended his career as a player. He finished with a lifetime batting average of .320. In the 1938 season he was non-playing manager until August, when he was replaced by Del Baker.

After the outbreak of World War II, Cochrane was commissioned a lieutenant in the physical education branch of the U.S. Navy, where he served under Lieutenant Commander Gene Tunney, the boxer. He saw duty in the South Pacific and also managed the Great Lakes Naval Training Station baseball team, which included many major leaguers. He was discharged as a lieutenant commander in 1945. During the war his son, Gordon Stanley Cochrane, Jr., was killed in the Netherlands.

After the war Cochrane was a partner in a cattle and dude ranch operation at Nye, Mont., and a partner in an automobile dealership in Billings, Mont. In 1949 he rejoined Mack (then in his fifty-second year as a major-league manager) as a coach with the Athletics. The following year he served as general manager in charge of the farm system of the Athletics, but resigned after a few months, when Mack's sons bought out their father's share of the team.

In 1947, Cochrane was elected to the Baseball Hall of Fame. Five years later he and Bill Dickey of the New York Yankees were named the best catchers of the half-century by the All-American Board of Baseball.

In his last years Cochrane served as a scout and training camp coach for the Yankees (1955), and as a Chicago area scout for the Tigers (1960). He also did some public relations work. He died at Lake Forest, Ill.

As a catcher Cochrane displayed uncommon durability, playing in 100 or more games for eleven successive seasons. His skill with the bat is emphasized by the fact that he batted third in a lineup composed of excellent hitters that featured two other future Hall of Fame members, Jimmy Foxx and Al Simmons, known for their hitting proficiency. In an era of colorful athletes, Cochrane stood out for his peppery personality and his ability to instill a fighting spirit in his players and teammates.

[See Frederick G. Lieb, *Connie Mack* (1945); Harold Seymour, *Baseball: The Golden Age* (1971); *The Baseball Encyclopedia* (1974); and Marshall Smelser, *The Life That Ruth Built* (1975). The Baseball Hall of Fame, Cooperstown, N.Y., holds memorabilia of Cochrane's career. Obituaries appeared in the June 29, 1962, editions of *New York Times, Chicago Tribune,* and *Washington Post.*]

STEPHEN D. BODAYLA

COLE, NAT ("KING") (Mar. 17, 1919–Feb. 15, 1965), pianist and singer, was born Nathaniel Adams Coles in Montgomery, Ala., the son of the Reverend Edward James Coles, a Baptist minister, and of Perlina Adams. When he was four years old, his father became minister of the True Light Church in Chicago. Cole began playing the organ and the piano in his father's church at the age of twelve, and he was privately tutored on those instruments. He soon organized a band that played for $1.50 a night.

Cole graduated from Phillips High School in Chicago in 1936. He made his first recordings at the age of nineteen, with the Rogues of Rhythm, a group led by his bass-playing brother Eddie, for Decca Records. He then joined a black revue, *Shuffle Along,* as pianist, touring with the show until it closed in Long Beach, Calif. He then worked in small nightclubs, forming a trio with Oscar Moore on guitar and Wesley Prince on string bass; this group was eventually known as the King Cole Trio. They quickly attracted the attention of jazz fans, especially after they recorded with the popular vibraphone player Lionel Hampton in 1940. After an eight-month stay in New York, Cole hired Carlos Gastel as his manager and began recording for the fledgling Capitol Records Company, later becoming its most successful recording artist.

Between 1941 and 1947, Cole recorded nearly all his important work as a pianist and received numerous awards from *Esquire, Metronome,* and *Down Beat* magazines. Strongly influenced by Earl Hines, and to a lesser extent by Art Tatum, he played in a manner at once rhapsodic and heavily rhythmic, creating a style strongly punctuated with arabesques. Many jazz enthusiasts maintain that had Cole pursued his career as an instrumentalist, he would have been acclaimed as on a par with any jazz keyboard artist. His virtual abandonment of the piano for vocalizing occasioned not a few accusations of pandering to popular taste. Cole cited financial necessity as the reason for switching almost exclusively to popular singing.

From the early years of the trio, the group featured novelty unison vocals, with an occasional vocal solo from Cole (whose early feature number was "Sweet Lorraine"). In November 1943 they recorded their first national hit, "Straighten Up and Fly Right," Cole's composition. (The words were derived from one of his father's sermons.) Cole often denigrated his voice, once saying it "is nothing to be proud of. It runs maybe two octaves in range. I guess it's the hoarse, breathy noise that some like—that's

why they call me The Sound." On the other hand, one jazz critic remarked, "He is more gifted with jazz wisdom than with a voice, but his ingenuity and sure beat give added distinction to his songs." Above all, his voice was both husky and gentle, paradoxically nasal and soothing.

Among Cole's best-selling records were "It's Only a Paper Moon," "Get Your Kicks on Route 66," "I Love You for Sentimental Reasons," "The Christmas Song," "Nature Boy," "Mona Lisa," "Answer Me, My Love," "Too Young," "Walking My Baby Back Home," "Somewhere Along the Way," and "Smile."

After recording "The Christmas Song" in 1946, Cole augmented the trio with a string section and various other arranged settings. By 1949 he was an international show-business personality, appearing at such exclusive supper clubs as the Trocadero in Hollywood, which went so far as to name a room in his honor. Occasionally he made concert tours that took him throughout the world. Cole also appeared in seven feature films: *The Blue Gardenia* (1953), *Small Town Girl* (1953), *Istanbul* (1957), *China Gate* (1957), *St. Louis Blues* (1958), playing the leading role of W.C. Handy, *Night of the Quarter Moon* (1959), and *Cat Ballou* (1965).

In 1937, Cole married Nadine Robinson, a dancer; they had no children. They were divorced in 1946. Two years later he married Marie Antoinette Ellington, a singer with the Duke Ellington (no relation) orchestra. They had five children, two of whom were adopted.

Cole, who was black, bought a house in the fashionable Los Angeles suburb of Hancock Park in 1948. Some of his neighbors protested the sale of the property to him because of his race. In 1951 the government seized the house for alleged nonpayment of $146,000 in income taxes; the claim was settled and Cole kept the house, after having weathered a number of incidents of vandalism on his property.

Cole was the first black musical artist to have a sponsored radio series. In 1953 he collapsed while performing at Carnegie Hall in New York City and underwent a serious operation for stomach ulcers.

For many years Cole was active in the movement for racial equality. While performing in Birmingham, Ala., on Apr. 11, 1956, he was attacked by six white men and received a slight back injury. In 1956–1957 he became the first black to have a weekly series on national television; because it was then deemed too "controversial" to sponsor a black, the show was soon canceled despite its popularity. A heavy smoker, Cole died of lung cancer at Santa Monica, Calif.

[See *Newsweek*, Aug. 12, 1946; *Time*, July 30, 1951; *Saturday Evening Post*, July 17, 1954; *Look*, Apr. 19, 1955. Obituaries are in the *New York Times* and the *Chicago Tribune*, Feb. 16, 1965]

ARTHUR PAUL LIVINGSTON

COMPTON, ARTHUR HOLLY (Sept. 10, 1892–Mar. 15, 1962), physicist, was born in Wooster, Ohio, the son of Elias Compton, a Presbyterian minister who was professor of philosophy at the University (now College) of Wooster; and of Otelia Catherine Augspurger. His eldest brother, Karl Taylor, had an outstanding career as a physicist, president of the Massachusetts Institute of Technology, and as an influential figure in American higher education and government. The parents and their four children accumulated more than seventy earned and honorary degrees.

Compton grew up in a family in which parental love and guidance, self-education and self-discipline, and religious training permeated the children's lives. Both parents had a deep understanding of child psychology. They knew how to temper freedom with restraint, to instill mental and physical discipline, and to focus their children's ambitions on service to their fellow human beings. These influences were the soil in which the remarkable achievements and dedicated lives of the children were rooted.

Compton attended the Wooster Elementary and Grammar School (1898–1905) and Wooster Preparatory School (1905–1909). His interest in science, first centered on paleontology, fully awakened during this period. He vividly recalled how on a cold evening in February 1905, he observed the gradual appearance of what his father told him was the constellation Orion and the Dog Star Sirius in the winter sky; how his brother Karl suggested that he read Agnes Giberne's popular book on astronomy; how he secured his parents' permission to purchase a telescope; and how he eagerly awaited the appearance of Halley's Comet, photographing it with considerable difficulty in 1910. At the same time, during his second year at the Wooster Preparatory School, he became fascinated with airplanes and constructed a huge number of models. Ultimately he built a triplane glider with a twenty-seven-foot wingspan and, after testing it in 1909, he successfully flew it for about 185 feet on Apr. 3, 1910. These early excursions into astronomy and aeronautics displayed Compton's enormous patience, love of observation, craftsmanship, dedication, and physical stamina.

In the fall of 1909 Compton entered the College of Wooster and soon confronted a crucial decision: whether to devote his life to science or to the ministry. Two factors most influenced his choice: his father's recognition of his inclination toward science and encouragement to pursue it; and his brother Karl's earlier decision to become an experimental physicist. Compton received the B.S. degree in 1913.

Karl's choice of Princeton for graduate study in physics led Arthur Compton to follow him there. He studied briefly with Karl's dissertation adviser, O. W. Richardson, who was primarily responsible for making Princeton a leading institution in physics at the time. Richardson recognized Compton's exceptional abilities and made the extraordinary gesture of turning over his own X-ray equipment to Compton for his graduate studies. Compton had intended to leave physics for engineering after his first year, because he felt engineering offered more possibilities for bettering the human condition. But he became captivated with physics, recognizing its fundamental importance for achieving the same end.

Compton entered Princeton at the time when W. H. Bragg and W. L. Bragg, father and son, were opening up the field of X-ray spectroscopy following Max Laue's discovery of the crystal diffraction of X rays in 1912. This work permitted Compton to put Richardson's X-ray equipment to good use in his doctoral research. He completed his Ph.D. degree in 1916 under H. L. Cooke. His dissertation research determined the distribution of electrons in crystals by studying the intensity of X rays reflected from them as a function of angle of reflection. Along the way he developed a two-crystal version of the Bragg spectrometer, and with his brother Karl (who in 1915 had returned to Princeton as assistant professor) developed an improved quadrant electrometer that was the most sensitive current-measuring instrument of its type for many years.

Compton held the Porter Ogden Jacobus fellowship, then Princeton's most distinguished fellowship, during his final year of graduate study (1915–1916). After receiving the Ph.D. he accepted a position at the University of Minnesota as instructor in physics. On June 28, 1916, Compton married Betty Charity McCloskey, a former classmate at Wooster. They had two sons.

Compton's most important researches at Minnesota, in part carried out with the help of Oswald Rognley, involved studying the reflection of X rays from a magnetic crystal, first in a magnetized and then in an unmagnetized state. The absence of any detectable change in the reflected intensity distribution led Compton to conclude in 1920 that magnetism is not an atomic effect, and that the electron itself must be the "ultimate magnetic particle." Six years later G. E. Uhlenbeck and S. Goudsmit, without being aware of Compton's work, started from very different considerations and published the electron spin hypothesis in its modern form.

Compton left Minnesota in 1917 to accept a position as research engineer in the Westinghouse Lamp Company in East Pittsburgh, Pa., at double his Minnesota salary. At Westinghouse he was drawn into the development of aircraft instrumentation for the U.S. Signal Corps and, after the end of World War I, into the development of the sodium vapor lamp. He found this work challenging, but he continued to be attracted to the fundamental physical problem of understanding how X rays interact with matter. Gradually he came to realize that it was in such basic research that his true interests lay. In 1919 he received a National Research Council fellowship—one of the first since their establishment after the war—for a year's study with Ernest Rutherford at the Cavendish Laboratory in Cambridge, England.

Compton, who regarded Rutherford as the greatest experimentalist of the day, was thoroughly stimulated by his experience with Rutherford and Rutherford's predecessor as Cavendish professor of physics, J. J. Thomson. He remained in Cambridge until late summer 1920, when he was appointed Wayman Crow Professor and head of the Department of Physics at Washington University in St. Louis.

During his years at Westinghouse, the Cavendish Laboratory, and Washington University, Compton's theoretical and experimental researches gradually evolved. They culminated in his most important contribution, the discovery of the Compton effect, for which he shared the Nobel Prize of 1927 with C. T. R. Wilson. Compton proved that X rays exhibit particle characteristics. To appreciate the historical significance of the discovery, it is necessary to examine in more detail the situation in physics at the time.

Although Albert Einstein, in advancing his light quantum hypothesis, had suggested as early as 1905 that high-frequency radiation can exhibit particle characteristics, in 1917 there was still almost universal skepticism about it among physicists. R. A. Millikan in 1915–1917 explicitly eschewed Einstein's light quantum hypothesis as an interpretation of Millikan's recent and classic photoelectric effect experiments. Compton himself, following O. W. Richardson, was initially antagonistic toward Einstein's quantum ideas. In 1917, when he learned of a puzzling result found by C. G. Barkla in X-ray absorption experiments, he accounted for it along strictly classical lines. He concluded that the X rays incident on the absorbing material consisted of ordinary electromagnetic waves that were being diffracted in the material by electrons—eventually he took them to be ring-shaped electrons—that were some thousand times larger than had been previously assumed.

Shortly thereafter, at the Cavendish Laboratory, Compton found experimentally that gamma rays incident on matter give rise to secondary gamma rays, the penetrating power of which decreases with increasing scattering angle, a phenomenon he interpreted as evidence for the existence of a new type of fluorescent radiation. Only after conducting entirely new X-ray scattering experiments at Washington University, in which he examined the scattered rays spectroscopically, did he reject both his large electron theory and his fluorescent radiation hypothesis and arrive at the true interpretation: When X rays or gamma rays are incident on matter, they behave like particles or quanta of radiation that collide with single electrons, lose energy, and as a result undergo a discrete increase in wavelength. These longer-wavelength scattered rays were the rays that he had previously interpreted as diffracted or fluorescent rays.

Compton published his discovery of the Compton effect in 1923. It provided the first conclusive experimental proof of Einstein's light quantum hypothesis, and it exerted a decisive influence on Niels Bohr, Werner Heisenberg, and others who created modern quantum theory in the period 1924–1927. Compton himself, though, was not directly influenced by Einstein's publications. His discovery grew out of his own hard-won theoretical and experimental insights. This was in sharp contrast with Peter Debye, who independently arrived at the identical theory of scattering several months after Compton by basing his ideas directly on Einstein's, and without carrying out any experiments.

Compton's goal was to understand the scattering of X rays as thoroughly as possible, and to achieve it he carried out other experiments at Washington University. In early 1921, for example, he and C. F. Hagenow conducted important X-ray polarization experiments, and one year later Compton proved that X rays can be totally reflected from glass and silver surfaces. This result led to the extraordinary situation that, at the end of 1922, Compton reported conclusive experimental evidence for both the wave and the particle behavior of X rays—an apparent contradiction that may be regarded as symbolic of the conceptual upheaval occurring in physics at the time.

In 1923 Compton became professor of physics at the University of Chicago. Throughout his career he was an inspiring teacher, both in the classroom and in the laboratory. He and his students at Chicago carried out a variety of experiments related to the Compton effect. One stimulus was an experimental challenge offered by William Duane and his group at Harvard, who could not obtain the Compton effect. This lively scientific controversy was not resolved in Compton's favor until the end of 1924. Another stimulus was a theoretical challenge offered by Bohr, H. A. Kramers, and J. C. Slater in Copenhagen, who presented a statistical interpretation of the Compton effect. This question was settled, again in Compton's favor, first by the experiments of Walter Bothe and Hans Geiger, and then by Compton himself and A. W. Simon. Other important work consisted of R. L. Doan's ruled grating experiments, which allowed the determination of absolute X-ray wavelengths and ultimately led to J. A. Bearden's revision of the accepted value of the electronic charge.

In 1927, in addition to sharing the Nobel Prize for Physics, Compton was elected to the National Academy of Sciences. Two years later he was appointed Charles H. Swift Distinguished Service Professor at Chicago. By age thirty-seven Compton had reached the apex of his profession.

In December 1930, Compton's researches took a new turn when, stimulated by R. A. Millikan's address to the American Association for the Advancement of Science, he became interested in the nature of the highly penetrating rays impinging upon the earth from outer space. These rays were variously called "Hess-rays," after V. F. Hess, who discovered them in 1911–1912, "ultra-gamma radiation," *Höhenstrahlung,* or "cosmic rays," which was Millikan's term and the one generally adopted. Compton immediately recognized that to understand cosmological processes, it was of fundamental importance to determine the nature and origin of these rays. He obtained financial support from the Carnegie Institution to conduct a world survey of cosmic rays, and between 1931 and 1934 he sent out nine different expeditions, each armed with identical detectors that he had developed. Compton, his wife, and elder son constituted one of the expeditions, traveling more than 40,000 miles, from Switzerland to New Zealand and Australia, and from Peru to northern Canada.

Compton's world survey proved that the cosmic ray intensity steadily decreases as one moves from the poles to the equator. This "latitude effect" had been observed in 1927 by the Dutch physicist Jakob Clay, but Clay's evidence was both unknown to Compton and inconclusive. Compton's results left no doubt as to the validity of the effect, which implied that at least a substantial fraction of the primary cosmic rays must be charged particles, since they could be deflected by the earth's magnetic field. Others, such as Bothe and Werner Kolhörster, had reached this same conclusion in the late 1920's on other grounds; nevertheless it was vigorously disputed by R. A. Millikan, who argued that the primary cosmic rays consisted of high-energy electromagnetic radiation, or photons. Millikan's debates with Compton made headlines, attracting widespread attention among scientists and nonscientists alike. Ultimately Millikan's position could not be maintained—the primary cosmic rays consist mostly of positively charged hydrogen and helium nuclei.

Compton's numerous X-ray and cosmic-ray researches established his reputation as a leading American physicist. In addition to his academic work at Chicago, he was a valued consultant for the General Electric Company from 1926 to 1945. He was George Eastman Visiting Professor and fellow of Balliol College, Oxford, in 1934–1935.

A year in India on a Guggenheim fellowship in 1926–1927 had made a deep impression on Compton, enabling him to see his own cultural heritage in broad perspective, and stimulating a renewed and deeper insight into his personal religious, philosophical, and human values—a common theme in his lectures in the 1930's.

Compton's ultimate goal was to illuminate such ancient questions as human free will and man's relationship to God through historical and philosophical reflection, taking into account the profound scientific insights gained from modern quantum theory and the theory of relativity. Thus it was entirely fitting that Compton should dedicate his Terry lectures at Yale (1931) to his father, "philosopher and friend," who taught "a rational and satisfying Christian philosophy" that he "found for himself by careful study, constructive imagination, and keen appreciation of the values of life." Compton left no doubt that he was adopting his father's approach to these questions.

The outbreak of war in Europe in 1939 brought awesome new responsibilities to Compton. The discovery of nuclear fission in Germany, widespread recognition of the enormous energy released when a single atom of uranium fissions, speculations and calculations on the possibility of a chain reaction, and other momentous developments in nuclear physics prompted Frank B. Jewett, president of the National Academy of Sciences, to ask Compton to chair a committee to assess the prospects for developing atomic energy for military purposes. Compton's conclusions, which were transmitted to President Franklin D. Roosevelt in November 1941, constituted one of the decisive steps leading to a full-scale effort to develop the atomic bomb in the United States.

At the same time Compton, despite the pacifism of his mother and others close to him, concluded that to survive, it was essential that the United States have possession of this fearsome weapon before Nazi Germany did. He therefore accepted the directorship of the Metallurgical Laboratory of the Manhattan Project in 1942. It was he who brought Enrico Fermi to Chicago, where on Dec. 2, 1942, Fermi succeeded in producing the first manmade nuclear chain reaction. It was he who oversaw the enormous expansion of the plutonium program. And it was he who, on the interim committee appointed by President Harry Truman, voted with the majority, recommending the military use of the weapon against Japan.

At war's end Compton returned to academic life as chancellor of Washington University, on condition that he could remain president of the Board of Trustees of Wooster College. He served as chancellor from 1945 to 1953, and as distinguished service professor of natural philosophy from 1954 to 1961. As chancellor he led Washington University into an influential position in American higher education. He dedicated himself to the cause of world peace and religious brotherhood, lecturing and consulting widely, and serving on many national and international bodies. Appointed professor at large in 1961, he intended to divide his time among Washington University, the College of Wooster, and the University of California at Berkeley. By this time he was a senior statesman

of science, having been elected to more than thirty foreign and domestic professional societies and academies. He was awarded the U.S. Government Medal for Merit in 1946. Compton died at Berkeley, Calif.

[Compton's research notebooks (1919–1941) and other unpublished materials are in the Washington University Archives; duplicate copies of the notebooks are in the American Institute of Physics Center for History of Physics, New York City. A substantial fraction of Compton's papers are collected in the Robert S. Shankland ed., *Scientific Papers of Arthur Holly Compton* (1973); papers not included are listed in the bibliography at the end of that work. His books include *X-Rays and Electrons* (1926), 2nd ed. rev. and enl. with Samuel K. Allison, *X-Rays in Theory and Experiment* (1935); *The Freedom of Man* (1935); *The Human Meaning of Science* (1940); *Atomic Quest: A Personal Narrative* (1956); *The Cosmos of Arthur Holly Compton* (1967), edited by Marjorie Johnston. Also see Samuel K. Allison, "Arthur Holly Compton," *Biographical Memoirs. National Academy of Sciences* (1965); James R. Blackwood, *The House on College Avenue: The Comptons at Wooster* (1968); Robert S. Shankland, "Compton, Arthur Holly," *Dictionary of Scientific Biography* (1970), and his introduction to Compton's *Scientific Papers*; Roger H. Stuewer, *The Compton Effect* (1975); Roger H. Stuewer and M. J. Cooper, introduction to Brian Williams, ed., *Compton Scattering* (1977); Daniel J. Kevles, *The Physicists* (1978). The obituary is in *New York Times*, Mar. 16, 1962.]

ROGER H. STUEWER

CONE, RUSSELL GLENN (Mar. 22, 1896–Jan. 21, 1961), civil engineer, was born in Ottumwa, Iowa, the son of Frank Cone and Alice Haddon. His father was a superintendent for the Chicago, Burlington and Quincy Railroad. It was with this firm that Cone began his career in 1915 as a rodman on the construction of the Metropolis Bridge across the Ohio River near Paducah, Ky. In 1916 he enrolled at the University of Illinois at Urbana to study civil engineering. When the United States entered World War I in 1917, Cone enlisted in the army and served eighteen months in Europe with the 149th Field Artillery, 42nd Division. After his discharge in May 1919, he completed the B.S. in civil engineering. On June 10, 1922, he married Izetta Lucas; they had one son.

Cone first worked in Philadelphia, where he was a junior engineer on the construction of the 1,750-foot Delaware River (Philadelphia-Camden) Bridge, then the longest suspension bridge in the world. He was quickly promoted to assistant engineer, and then to resident engineer in charge of central span construction. With the completion of the Delaware River

Bridge in 1926, Cone moved in 1927 to Detroit, where he was made resident engineer in charge of all construction on the Ambassador Bridge. Linking Detroit with Windsor, Ontario, across the Detroit River, the 1,850-foot Ambassador Bridge superseded the Delaware River Bridge as the world's longest suspended span. Although the Ambassador Bridge opened in November 1929, Cone remained with the bridge until early 1930 when he became general manager of the Tacony-Palmyra Toll Bridge at Palmyra, N.J.

Cone's preeminence as an authority on suspension bridge construction soon led Joseph B. Strauss, chief engineer of the Golden Gate Bridge, to seek his assistance. Although Strauss was an internationally renowned bridge engineer, he had had no experience with suspension structures. Cone would provide that needed experience. Work commenced on the 4,200-foot structure in February 1933, with Cone as resident engineer in charge of construction. He continued to direct the engineers and inspectors until the bridge was opened in 1937.

Cone succeeded Strauss as engineer in charge of maintenance for the Golden Gate Bridge and Highway District. He served in that position from 1937 to 1941, introducing several novel procedures in the maintenance of the bridge. In recognition of this work, the American Society of Civil Engineers awarded him its Construction Engineering Prize in 1940.

Following a divorce from his first wife in 1938, Cone married Jeanne Fozard Hamilton on Jan. 6, 1939. When he left the employ of the Golden Gate Bridge and Highway District in 1941, he undertook the engineering study for the passenger tramway at Mt. San Jacinto near Palm Springs, Calif. In that year he was also appointed a member of the board of investigation of the Tacoma Narrows Bridge collapse by the Washington State Toll Bridge Authority.

Later in 1941, Cone became associated with the Silas Mason Company of New York, which had received a large government contract to build the Louisiana Ordnance Plant near Shreveport, La. He began as assistant general manager with that project. Throughout World War II he directed construction of other large ordnance plants for the company, including the Iowa Ordnance Plant at Burlington, the Cornhusker Ordnance Plant at Grand Island, Nebr., and the Green River Ordnance Plant at Dixon, Ill. Cone continued working for the Silas Mason Company after the war as general manager, helping the firm enter the field of atomic weapons design and production for the Department

of Defense. In 1950 the firm took over the architectural-engineering responsibilities for the first atomic tests in Nevada. Cone served as the site project manager for the atomic tests staged between 1950 and 1953 by the Atomic Energy Commission at Frenchman's Flat and Yucca Flats. He also directed construction of the Pantex Implosion Plant at Amarillo, Tex.

In 1956 Cone was drawn back to large-scale bridge construction as vice-president and general manager of the Mason Hanger–Silas Mason Company, which had a contract to build the foundations for the Carquinez Strait Bridge at Crockett, Calif. This was the biggest pier project since the foundations for the San Francisco–Oakland Bay Bridge were erected in the 1930's. The Carquinez project proved to be a particularly difficult engineering task, and it was finally completed at a substantial financial loss.

After a divorce from his second wife, Cone married Pearl Janet Bloomquist on Feb. 3, 1957. In the year prior to his death at Vallejo, Calif., he was negotiating with the directors of the Bay Area Rapid Transit District to become the district's general manager and chief engineer.

Cone's forty-year career as a civil engineer centered on large and challenging projects. He was one of the nation's preeminent bridge engineers and one of the leading civil engineers involved in the early stages of nuclear development.

[Cone's technical articles include "The Erection of the Suspended Structure of the Delaware River Bridge," *Journal of the Franklin Institute,* June 1926; "Construction of the Ambassador Bridge," *Canadian Engineer,* Dec. 10, 1929; "Battling Storm and Tide in Founding Golden Gate Pier," *Engineering News-Record,* Aug. 22, 1935; "Permanent Painting Scaffolds for the Golden Gate Bridge," *Engineering News-Record,* Apr. 25, 1940; "Field Practice with Special Reference to Golden Gate Bridge," *Civil Engineering,* July 1940. See also Allen Brown, *Golden Gate* (1965), for material on Cone. Obituaries are in *San Francisco Examiner* and *New York Times,* Jan. 22, 1961; *Engineering News-Record,* Jan. 26, 1961; *Civil Engineering,* Mar. 1961.]

JEFFREY K. STINE

CONNALLY, THOMAS TERRY ("TOM") (Aug. 19, 1877–Oct. 28, 1963), lawyer and U.S. congressman and senator, was born on a farm near Hewitt in McLennan County, Tex., the son of Jones Connally and Mary Ellen Terry. His father, a prosperous farmer, moved the family to Falls County when Connally was five. He entered Baylor University at the age of fourteen, received a B.A. in 1896, and attended the University of Texas Law School, which awarded him the LL.B. in absentia in 1898. During the Spanish-American War, Connally served in the Second Texas Infantry Volunteers. The war ended before he saw action, and he survived a severe case of jaundice contracted while at camp in Florida.

Connally opened a law practice at Marlin in 1899, and was elected to the Texas House of Representatives in 1900, serving two terms. He opposed the reelection of U.S. Senator Joseph Weldon Bailey in 1901 and sponsored antitrust legislation in 1903. Elected Falls County prosecuting attorney in 1906 and serving until 1910, he gained a reputation for being severe with hostile witnesses and for making dramatic speeches to juries. In 1916, Connally defeated two opponents in the Democratic primary to represent the Eleventh District in the U.S. House of Representatives, and thus was assured victory in the general election.

Connally arrived in Washington in time to vote for the declaration of war against Germany in April 1917. He supported the Wilson administration faithfully in his first year, won reelection, and then enlisted in the army, with the rank of captain, in September 1918. Illness prevented him from accompanying his brigade, and the war ended before he could leave for France. "I have been in more wars and done less fighting than any other American," he wrote of his military service.

Over the next decade Connally opposed Republican tariff policy and, like other Democrats, evidenced a deep concern for southern agriculture. In 1928 he concluded that the incumbent Texas senator, Earle B. Mayfield, could be defeated. Mayfield had been elected in 1922, with the support of the Ku Klux Klan, but the power of the hooded order had faded in Texas when Connally announced his candidacy on Jan. 24, 1928. He labeled Mayfield the "bedsheet and mask candidate," and accused him of having shaken down oilmen in his earlier Senate race. Connally ran second in a field of six in the Democratic primary, and thus earned the right to oppose Mayfield in the runoff a month later. He easily defeated the incumbent, then won the general election, and took his seat in the Senate in March 1929.

Connally cut an impressive figure. More than six feet tall and weighing 200 pounds, he dressed in the manner of William Jennings Bryan— white shirt, black string tie, black suit in winter and white in summer. He wore his hair long. A Texas politician called Connally "the only man in the United States Senate who could wear a Roman Toga and not look like a fat man in a nightgown." In debate he could be cutting. To a legislative enemy he said, "We'd make a lot more progress if you approached this subject with an open mind instead of an open mouth."

In 1932–1933, Connally urged President Franklin D. Roosevelt to reduce taxes drastically and to inaugurate federal borrowing for direct relief. He asked the new president, "If it was constitutional to spend forty billion dollars in a war, isn't it just as constitutional to spend a little money to relieve the hunger and misery of our citizens?" This penchant for bold innovation waned as Connally saw the New Deal in practice. He opposed the National Recovery Act in 1933, and led the fight against reorganization of the Supreme Court in 1937.

For Connally the sensibilities of his white constituents outweighed any claims of racial justice for black Americans. He directed the Senate filibuster against antilynching legislation in the 1930's and 1940's. "I am against the lynching of any man. It is murder," he contended. "But I am also against a lynching of the Constitution of the United States."

Connally assiduously defended his state's interests in Congress. The Jones-Connally Act (1934) addressed the problems of the cattle industry through direct federal relief for ranchers. An amendment to the Agriculture Adjustment Act gave assistance to cotton growers through bounties for the export of their crop. The Connally "Hot Oil" Act responded to the glutted market for petroleum that arose with the discovery of the East Texas oil field. Low-cost Texas oil was sold illegally outside the state, and Connally proposed to give the president the authority to bar the interstate or foreign movement of oil produced in violation of a state law. An amendment to the National Industrial Recovery Act (NIRA) in 1933 accomplished his purpose. After the Supreme Court declared the NIRA unconstitutional in 1935, a revised bill provided for a government oil administrator to enforce the prohibition against interstate shipment of "hot oil."

When he entered the Senate, Connally was assigned to the Foreign Relations Committee. He supported the administration on reciprocal trade, worked for naval appropriations, and gradually moved closer to Roosevelt's policies as the world situation worsened at the end of the 1930's. Despite his relatively low seniority on the committee, Connally gained influence as the chairman, Key Pittman of Nevada, lost power because of illness and alcoholism. He piloted repeal of the arms embargo through the

Senate in 1939, an achievement that Roosevelt called "the most important action that has taken place in our foreign policy during my administration."

Connally became increasingly important to the White House as war approached. He spoke effectively for the Selective Service Act in 1940, and he was the Senate manager of the Lend-Lease Act in 1941. That July, after the deaths of Pittman and Senator Pat Harrison of Mississippi, who had been next in seniority, Connally became chairman of the Foreign Relations Committee.

During and after the war Connally remained conservative on domestic issues. He filibustered against legislation to eliminate the poll tax, introduced a bill to grant the president the power to take over a war plant that unions had struck (1943), and he voted for the Taft-Hartley Law.

Connally's central role was in foreign affairs. In the shaping of the United Nations and the evolution of American policy for the postwar world, he acted as an intermediary between the White House, the Department of State, and the Senate. He believed in 1943 that an international agency should be set up to prevent aggression and to preserve the peace of the world, and that its decisions and actions should be enforced by military and naval forces whenever necessary to preserve the peace of the world. He worked closely with Senator Arthur H. Vandenberg and other Republicans to construct a bipartisan consensus on foreign policy, and wished to insure congressional approval of whatever treaties came out of World War II. The Connally Resolution, passed by the Senate in November 1943, endorsed an international organization in accordance with the Moscow Declaration of that month, but also emphasized the importance of normal constitutional methods in the formulation and approval of treaties and postwar agreements.

Connally was vice-chairman of the American delegation to the United Nations conference at San Francisco in 1945, and led the Senate in ratifying the United Nations Charter and the law that authorized the nation's participation in the United Nations. He was a member of the United States delegation at the first General Assembly, and had an advisory role at the Council of Foreign Ministers in 1946. The Connally Amendment of 1946 limited the jurisdiction of the World Court in cases involving the United States to those that the government itself decided were not domestic in nature.

Republican control of Congress after the elections of 1946 deprived Connally of his com-

mittee chairmanship, but he continued to cooperate with Vandenberg, the new chairman, on such issues as aid to Greece and Turkey and the Marshall Plan. After the Democrats regained the majority in 1948, he worked for approval of the North Atlantic Treaty, although insisting on language that seemed to him to preserve the right of Congress to declare war.

As he approached the end of his fourth Senate term, Connally faced political difficulties in Texas. Attorney General Price Daniel was preparing to challenge him, with lavish financial support from the oil industry. Connally's interest in foreign policy had left him little time to attend to the concerns of oilmen about interstate oil shipments and the tidelands oil controversy. Coupled with intense Texas animosity against President Harry S. Truman and the Fair Deal, the defection of Connally's monetary support made the outcome in the Democratic primary highly doubtful. One source reports that oil industry agents actually showed him the war chest they had amassed for Daniel, and thus secured his withdrawal from the race.

In retirement Connally practiced law in Washington and compiled his memoirs. The volumes have numerous quotations from his speeches and a few illuminating anecdotes, but offer little insight into the nuances of the legislative process. His papers went to the Library of Congress, but one of his staff removed many of the substantive items and sold them. What remains, most scholars agree, is a disappointment.

Connally married Louise Clarkson on Nov. 16, 1904; they had one son. Louise Connally died in 1935, and on Apr. 25, 1942, Connally married Lucille Sanderson Sheppard, the widow of Senator Morris Sheppard. Connally died in Washington, D.C.

Estimates of Connally's ability and character range from derision to respect. His appearance and style led Henry Wallace to call him "essentially a demagogue with no depth of perception, no sense of the general welfare, and no interest in it." Historians have generally reached a similar judgment. Yet Dean Acheson said of Connally: "Behind the black clothes, the black bow string tie, the white curls over the collar, were irony and sarcasm. Under the irony and sarcasm were perceptions of the great issues to be decided in the war and postwar years, and strong unfailing support for the measures to deal with them."

[There is no full-length biography of Connally. Despite their gaps the Connally Papers, at the Library of Congress, contain indispensable material.

Also see the files on Connally at the Franklin D. Roosevelt Library, Hyde Park, N.Y.; letters from Connally in the J. C. Granbery Papers, University of Texas Archives; Senate Foreign Relations Committee's Historical Series; the relevant volumes of the State Department's Foreign Relations Series. *My Name is Tom Connally* (1954), as told to Alfred Steinberg, is his autobiography. Helpful articles are "The Senate and the Peace," *Time*, Mar. 13, 1944; Otis Miller and Anita F. Alpern, "Tom Connally: 'One of the Senate Gallery's Favorites,' " in J. T. Salter, ed., *Public Men in and out of Office* (1946; repr. 1972).

Other accounts are Robert A. Divine, *Second Chance* (1967); Lionel V. Patenaude, "Garner, Sumners and Connally: The Defeat of the Roosevelt Court Bill in 1937," *Southwestern Historical Quarterly*, July 1970; John M. Blum, ed., *The Price of Vision: The Diary of Henry Wallace, 1942–1946* (1973); George N. Green, *The Establishment in Texas Politics* (1979). An obituary is in the *New York Times*, Oct. 29, 1963.]

Lewis L. Gould

CONNOLLY, THOMAS H. (Dec. 31, 1870–Apr. 28, 1961), baseball umpire, was born in Manchester, England. At the age of thirteen he immigrated to America with his family and settled in Natick, Mass. Soon he became interested in baseball, but he never amounted to much as a player. He therefore read every baseball book he could find and eventually became an expert on its rules. At fifteen Connolly began umpiring local YMCA games as well as school and sandlot contests. In 1894 he obtained his first professional job, in the New England League.

Connolly moved in 1898 to the National League, where he worked two and a half seasons before quitting because he felt that club owners did not offer umpires firm enough support when disputes arose with players. This issue was of special importance to Connolly, who at five feet, six inches, and 130 pounds could ill afford to stand alone in confrontations with angry athletes.

In 1901 the American League was formed, and Connolly accepted Ban Johnson's offer of a job. Of four games scheduled on opening day, three were rained out. Only the game between Chicago and Cleveland, the contest that Connolly was working, was played. Consequently, Connolly enjoyed the distinction of umpiring the first American League game. That the American League offered more support and protection to its umpires than the National League did is testified to by his ejection of ten players from games in his first season, without being injured.

In 1902, Connolly married Margaret L. Davis; they had ten children. As his career developed, Connolly added other "firsts" to that of single-handedly umpiring the first American League game. He umpired the first game at Shibe Park, Philadelphia, at Fenway Park in Boston, at the old New York Highlanders' field, and, almost a quarter-century later, at Yankee Stadium in New York City. In addition he and Hank O'Day officiated in the first modern World Series, played in 1903 between Boston and Pittsburgh. (Eventually Connolly umpired a total of eight World Series—1903, 1908, 1910, 1911, 1913, 1916, 1920, and 1924.) The Boston-Pittsburgh game was Connolly's first experience working with another umpire, for until 1909 umpires almost always operated alone. Connolly said, "It was really lonely when I broke in in '96. The umpire worked all alone. That's why we got mobbed so often. Was I ever mobbed? Plenty of times. . . ."

One call that almost got Connolly mobbed took place in Detroit during a tight pennant race. Ty Cobb was at bat, with the Tigers one run behind in the ninth inning. He hit a triple, but stepped across the plate as he did so, and Connolly had to call him out. He attributed his safe exit from the park that day to the fact that there were plenty of police present.

Another notable call came in 1922, at the Polo Grounds in New York City. Babe Ruth, in one of his "bad boy" outbursts, headed for the stands in pursuit of a fan who had been heckling him. Connolly stopped the Babe by blocking his way, then threw him out of the game. The star reacted with a barrage of what was later officially labeled in a suspension notice as "vulgar and vicious" language. This incident was both the last time Babe Ruth was ejected from a game and the final time Connolly ejected a player. Connolly's authority on the field enabled him to spend his last decade as an umpire without removing a player from a contest.

When he retired from active officiating in 1931, Connolly accepted the position of chief of staff of American League umpires. He attended major league games to review the umpires' performance. He retired from this post in January 1954, after fifty-six years in professional baseball. Connolly left his mark behind home plate, for he was largely responsible for the retention of the inflated chest protector worn for many years by American League umpires.

Even after his retirement Connolly continued to serve baseball as a member of the Rules Committee. In 1953 he and Bill Klem were elected to the Baseball Hall of Fame, the first umpires honored in such a manner. He died at Natick, Mass.

[See James Kahn, *The Umpire Story* (1953); and Martin Appel and Burt Goldblatt, *Baseball's Best: The Hall of Fame Gallery* (1977). An obituary is in the *New York Times*, Apr. 29, 1961.]

MICHAEL DAHER

CONOVER, HARRY SAYLES (Aug. 29, 1911–July 21, 1965), founder of the Harry Conover Modeling Agency, was born in Chicago, Ill., the son of Harry Conover, Jr., a washing machine salesman, and Claire Byrnes. He was the grandson of Harry Conover, the supposed inventor of the washing machine (the invention did not lead to wealth because a large company began to manufacture it before Conover's idea was patented). Shortly after Conover's birth, his parents were divorced. Conover and his mother moved in with her parents; her father, John Byrnes, was a well-known Chicago lawyer. When Conover was nine, his mother remarried; her second husband was Harold B. Griffen, the owner of the Griffen Tool and Die Company. They moved to Brooklyn, N.Y.

Conover attended Culver Military Academy in Culver, Ind., from 1923 to 1928, taking frequent vacations to Palm Beach. After completing military school, he rebelled against his mother's plans for him to become a priest. He left Notre Dame University on the day of his arrival in 1930.

During the next five years Conover held department store jobs in New York City, performed in a radio soap opera, and then became what he claimed was the first radio disc jockey in the United States in Royal Oak, Mich. In 1935, the tall, dark-haired, green-eyed Conover went to work as a model for the John Robert Powers Modeling Agency, the foremost agency of the day. Despite success as a model, Conover soon became more interested in management. With a $1,000 loan from Gerald Ford (later president of the United States) and with some former Powers models as employees, Conover opened an office in New York City in 1939.

Ford, then a Yale Law School student, did part-time modeling and was introduced by his girl friend to Harry Conover, a full-time Powers model. His "silent partner" association with Conover ended early in 1942 but they remained friends. By that time, the Harry Conover Modeling Agency was serving as agent for about 200 models and grossing $750,000 annually. In 1943, the agency made approximately $100,000 profit.

Ever conscious of trends and utilizing the knowledge gained from his exposure to advertisers and photographers, Conover saw the need for the fresh-faced, natural look in modeling, as opposed to the nameless show girls, "Long Stemmed American Beauty Roses," popularized by Powers. In the 1940's photographs were rapidly replacing artists' sketches on magazine covers. These covers needed women with personality and appearance with whom ordinary women could identify. American GI's in World War II intensified the need for a curvaceous "girl next door" image. Conover provided it with his "Conover Cover Girls," many of whom were coeds that he and his talent scouts found on college campuses.

The "Conover Girls" participated in United Service Organizations (USO) trips during the war and Conover, who was exempted from active duty due to hypertension, worked at home in the United Youth for Defense. These activities, coupled with the appearance of "Conover Girls" on the covers of the leading magazines of the day—*Mademoiselle, Glamour, Life, Harper's Bazaar, Cosmopolitan, Vogue*—gave the Conover modeling agency a national and international reputation.

Conover's message as a recruiter of "intelligent" models on campuses and elsewhere was that ". . . the modeling profession is one of the choicest vocations today the American girl can select. In addition to being a profitable profession, it is one of the few vocations that leads to other fields." These remarks, made in 1941, proved prophetic. His models included movie stars Shelley Winters, Joan Caulfield, Nina Foch, and Anita Colby, and radio personality Jinx Falkenburg.

Conover's primary talent lay in promotion technique. He brought out the individuality of a model and used it to his or her advantage. Frequently he rechristened models with names that were highly effective in gaining publicity—Lassie, Dusty, Choo-Choo, Chili, and Candy. He published an annual *Who Is She?*, which provided pertinent information on each model in his employ. The successful Paramount movie *Cover Girl* (1944) starring Rita Hayworth and Gene Kelly, gave the Conover model agency added prestige. Conover served as a technical adviser and provided both the name and the background models, and Anita Colby, a former Conover model and Conover's friend, assisted in producing the film and also appeared in it.

On Feb. 17, 1940, Conover married Gloria Dalton, a Conover model. They were divorced in 1946 after the birth of two daughters. On July

4, 1946, Conover married Candy Jones, the former Jessica Wilcox, whom he had discovered at the Miss Atlantic City Beauty Pageant in 1941. She was a highly successful "Conover Cover Girl," and in 1947 became Conover's business partner as head of the Candy Jones Career Girl School. This was a separate business from the modeling agency. Conover and Candy Jones had three sons.

Conover established a special television department in 1949 that booked models exclusively for television. It, too, was successful, grossing one million dollars in 1954. As the agency became more financially complex, however, Conover's attention and daily presence at the office began to decrease. He indulged in lavish living and wild spending and the agency began to lose ground. The exclusivity of the model-agent relationship, which had sustained Conover's business, waned in the 1950's because of pressure from advertisers and photographers, and the predictability of receipts declined. Trouble came to the agency in May 1959 when Conover was unable to pay child models within a reasonable period of time. The parents of the children demanded an investigation of the agency's books and records and, as a result, its license could not be renewed. On May 28, 1959, the *New York Times* reported that Candy Jones had been running the business at her own expense since Conover deserted her in 1958. They were divorced in 1959. Warrants of arrest were eventually issued for both Conover and his ex-wife concerning the reported sum of $125,283 owed to more than 200 models. Conover claimed the amount was closer to $25,000. The case was eventually resolved out of court but it dealt a fatal blow to Conover's reputation. In August 1959 new regulations required that all modeling agencies keep a separate account for client fees.

After the dissolution of the Conover Modeling Agency (the Candy Jones Career Girl School survived), Conover attempted to franchise his name for charm schools on the West Coast but without success. In the early 1960's he worked at a hotel in New Jersey. In 1964, dependent on the financial support of his mother, Conover was arrested for nonpayment of alimony and child support. He suffered a heart attack upon arrival at Hart's Island for a two-year prison sentence, and was released within a week after the intercession of his mother. He died of a second heart attack in Elmhurst, Queens, N.Y.

Conover's business failure and untimely death has prohibited any positive evaluation of him as a trend-setter in the modeling industry. However, his undeniable influence is seen in the high-visibility models of the 1970's who with their memorable names and individuality became television and movie stars. Conover would not be surprised at this development.

[Conover's biography by his daughter Carole Conover, *Cover Girls* (1978), is a slightly biased but indispensable account. Candy Jones has written prolifically but not on her former husband; *More Than Beauty* (1970) provides some information. Conover wrote a short pamphlet, "Modeling," published by his agency in 1941. See also *New York Times*, May 27–28, 1959; June 26, 1959; July 11, 25, 1959; August 14, 1959; and his obituary, July 25, 1965.]

BARBARA McCARTHY CROFTON

COOKE, SAMUEL (Dec. 29, 1898–May 22, 1965), businessman, was born in the Ukraine, Russia, the son of Kalman Cooke, a tailor, and of Ethel Winokur. The family immigrated to the United States and settled in Philadelphia in 1908. Cooke became a citizen upon his father's naturalization in 1913.

Cooke's life was a typical immigrant success story. After completing grammar school in 1910, he began selling vegetables door to door, first from a basket and later from a pushcart. As he prospered, he acquired a horse and wagon and, finally, a truck. Cooke was a food speculator from 1920 to 1927. In the latter year, with two partners, Morris and Isaac Kaplan, he founded the Penn Fruit Company, serving as its president until 1960. (At about the same time, in Memphis, Tenn., Clarence Saunders opened the first store in what became the Piggly Wiggly chain; Saunders and Cooke are considered the originators of the self-service supermarket.) He married Doris Beyer on Jan. 1, 1938. They had two daughters.

Cooke believed that for the supermarket, volume and variety were related factors, and that the automobile was the key to that relation. In 1955 he explained the concept thus: "Variety attracts thousands of customers. These customers assure a turnover of merchandise high enough to justify diversity." The advent of the automobile made possible large stores strategically located to draw on more than one neighborhood.

The Penn Fruit specialty was fresh fruit and vegetables, which, because of their perishability, other grocers regarded as marginal. Cooke was a pioneer in techniques of getting these goods from the farm to the store quickly, without loss of freshness. For example, in order to market corn before the heat of the day caused its sugar content to turn to starch, Penn Fruit arranged with Bucks County farmers to pick their corn in the cool hours after midnight; eggs were purchased, candled, and put on sale in less than twenty-four hours. Techniques such as these made possible the quality perishables that assured Penn Fruit's success.

With thirty employees in 1927, Penn Fruit grossed $213,102; when Cooke retired as president in 1960 the company had 5,000 employees and grossed $167 million. By that time the company was operating eighty supermarkets in Pennsylvania, Maryland, Delaware, New Jersey, and New York. It had a huge food distribution center in Philadelphia, as well as bakery, greenhouse, candy kitchen, and seafood subsidiaries. Sales in Penn Fruit stores were consistently double those of the average American supermarket.

A characteristic example of Cooke's unorthodox methods was the huge store, probably the largest of its type in the world at that time (46,700 square feet of floor space), that Penn Fruit built in downtown Philadelphia in 1946. Assuming that the store would attract many of the trolley, subway, automobile, and suburban train passengers who passed through the area each day, as well as many movie patrons, the company built a store specializing in perishables and providing many conveniences, including a refrigerator in which customers could check purchases while they attended a movie or shopped elsewhere. In the first week the store registered 50,000 sales.

Cooke was involved in a number of other business enterprises. He was president of Hanna Realty Company from 1927 until his death, and a member of the board of the Camden Cold Storage Company and the Crown Cork and Seal Company. In 1942 he helped found Topco Associates to centralize the buying power of twenty-seven food chains, so that they could compete with larger chains.

Cooke served from 1948 to 1952 on the U.S. Department of Agriculture's deciduous fruit committee, and in 1954 he prepared the comprehensive plan for the Food Distribution Center, Philadelphia's wholesale fruit and produce distributing facility. In 1953 he advised Swedish cooperatives on the conversion of their markets to self-service stores, and his advice was sought in the establishment of the first Australian and Yugoslav supermarkets. Cooke also was influential in the development of the Delaware Valley College of Science and Agriculture in Doylestown, Pa. (founded in 1896 as the National Agricultural College), and provided internships for its students in his stores.

Cooke showed great regard for the rights of his employees, and was a leader in the adoption of fair employment practices in Philadelphia. Turnover of company personnel was very low, and 98 percent of the employees who served in World War II returned to the company after the war.

Cooke was an innovator whose understanding of the limitations and the possibilities of the grocery business enabled him to succeed by methods that his competitors considered excessively risky. He died in Cheltenham, Pa.

[See "Unorthodox Giant," *Business Week,* Apr. 20, 1946; "Penn Fruit Expands Its Orbit," *Business Week,* Dec. 24, 1955. An obituary is in *New York Times,* May 23, 1965.]

ROBERT L. BERNER

COOPER, GARY (May 7, 1901–May 13, 1961), was christened Frank James Cooper in Helena, Mont., the son of Charles Henry Cooper, a lawyer, and Alice Louise Brazier, both English immigrants. Charles Cooper, as a lawyer, assistant U.S. attorney, and State Supreme Court justice, was grimly determined to bring order to Helena, which still honored the vigilante tradition. His wife was equally fixed upon providing her two sons with a proper education, removed from the crudeness of a small western community. For four years Cooper attended Dunstable Public School in England. Totally unprepared for the rigor and snobbery of English secondary education, he found the experience sufficiently painful to become permanently shy and withdrawn.

Cooper worked on his father's ranch in 1918 and 1919, then enrolled in Wesleyan College at Bozeman, Mont., in 1920. After a serious automobile accident, which left him with a broken hip (and a characteristic gait), Cooper transferred to Grinnell College, in Grinell, Iowa, in 1921. At Grinnell he proved an indifferent student. Art ranked as his sole passion, but he displayed little talent as an illustrator. Quitting Grinnell in 1924, Cooper went to Los Angeles. There he unsuccessfully sought work as a political cartoonist or artist for an advertising agency. He had to become a door-to-door salesman of discount coupons for a photography studio in order to earn a living.

In desperation, Cooper took the advice of two Montana friends who were former rodeo stars, and joined them as an extra in motion picture westerns in 1925. Soon realizing how much leading cowboy players earned, he decided to be an actor. He took the name Gary to distinguish himself from an abundance of Frank Coopers then in Hollywood. But not until *The Winning of Barbara Worth* (1926) did he secure a key supporting role. Although the film received mixed notices, Cooper won much praise. Paramount Pictures soon signed a contract with him.

Cooper possessed a natural, understated capacity to project himself before a camera. In *Wings* (1927), a World War I epic, he appeared for only 127 seconds, yet his portrayal of a doomed flyer stole the film. Somehow, Cooper bridged the gap between the male acting styles of the 1920's. Neither completely the child-boy of Buddy Rogers, nor the hardened warrior of William S. Hart, he managed to combine a measure of innocence about women and ideas with a knowingness about the ways of the West and its traditions.

Cooper was soon starring in films and, with the aid of skilled sound engineers, easily shifted his talents and light baritone voice to talking pictures. One of his first, *The Virginian* (1929), helped to stereotype him as the classic cinema man of the West (even though fewer than one-fourth of all his feature films were horse operas). In *Morocco* (1930) Cooper played a narcissistic cad in the Foreign Legion, while in *A Farewell to Arms* (1932) he sensitively portrayed the suffering protagonist of Ernest Hemingway's novel. His critical notices tended to improve, though some reviewers dismissed him as a mere matinee idol.

Cooper married Veronica Balfe, an aspiring actress, on Dec. 15, 1933; they had one daughter. The marriage supposedly indicated Cooper's inclination to settle down after a series of torrid love affairs with such actresses as Clara Bow and Lupe Velez. But Cooper proved an unfaithful husband. He frequently had affairs with female costars and briefly separated from his wife in 1951–1952.

Part of Cooper's success on screen was due to his capacity to appeal to both women and men. Women found his boyishness and good looks irresistible. Men regarded his unassuming, polite manner less threatening than the style of such other love idols as Clark Gable.

Between 1936 and 1943, Cooper's career took a new direction. He enjoyed a succession of box office and critical triumphs that transformed his screen image from the young (sometime) roué to an inherently good Mr. Everyman. For director Frank Capra, Cooper starred in *Mr. Deeds Goes to Town* (1936) and *Meet John Doe* (1941). An Academy Award and New York Film Critics Prize for best actor resulted from his portrayal of the title character in *Sergeant*

York (1941). A year later he gave what some critics held to be an even finer performance as Lou Gehrig, in *The Pride of the Yankees*. In 1943 he again starred as a Hemingway hero in *For Whom the Bell Tolls*, which, while drained of its leftist political material, proved a box office hit because of the romantic pairing of Cooper and Ingrid Bergman. Most of these films cast him as a noble hero. "Whatever the deep psychological or physiological roots of his fascination," wrote the *New York Times*'s Frank Nugent in 1942, "the simple fact is that to a large bloc of the population, Mr. Cooper has come to represent the All-American man."

That image was hard to maintain between 1943 and 1952, as Cooper groped for good vehicles. Such attempts at self-parody as *Casanova Brown* (1944) and *Good Sam* (1948) served him ill, and potboilers like *Dallas* (1950) were best forgotten. His boyish thinness turned to middle-aged gauntness, and improper lighting often caused him to appear far older than his years. Furthermore, into the 1950's he was wracked by an unhappy personal life and ill health (a painful back and ulcers), which often prevented him from selecting good scripts and delivering able performances. His lack of self-confidence caused Cooper to rely for career advice on such middle-brow taste makers as director Cecil B. De Mille and gossip columnist Hedda Hopper. They encouraged him to protect his screen image by choosing "safe" stories.

The influence of De Mille and Hopper showed in other ways. In 1944 they persuaded Cooper to deliver a radio talk opposing President Franklin Roosevelt's bid for reelection. Cooper referred to Roosevelt's "foreign notions," adding, "I don't like the company he's keeping." Some construed such references as aimed at the president's Jewish counselors.

Two years later Cooper testified as a "friendly" witness before the House Un-American Activities Committee (HUAC), which was investigating Communism in the film industry. He vaguely described Communist infiltration at social gatherings and story conferences while demonstrating his total ignorance of Karl Marx. "From what I hear, I don't like it [Communism] because it isn't on the level," he said.

Ironically, in the years after his HUAC testimony, Cooper's greatest critical success came with a film scripted by Carl Foreman, a writer accused of Communist biases. In *High Noon* (1952), a western, Cooper played Will Kane, a retiring town marshal. On his wedding day Kane has to defend himself against an old nemesis— arriving on the midday train—who intends to

kill him. As noon approaches, both the towns-
people he has served and his bride desert him.
Cooper masterfully played the tortured marshal,
whom he admiringly identified with his father.
His physical maladies and weariness, which so
hampered his later performances, worked to his
advantage in *High Noon.* So did close editing,
skillful direction, and an evocative musical
score. The film brought Cooper a second Academy Award for best actor.

Cooper's subsequent roles drew mixed notices. Occasionally critics underrated good films
such as *Vera Cruz* (1954), directed by Robert
Aldrich, and *Man of the West* (1958), directed
by Anthony Mann. Most hailed his portrayal of
a Quaker father in *Friendly Persuasion* (1956).
Otherwise he remained subject to miscasting or
indifferent work and inept direction, problems
he eventually recognized.

By 1960, Cooper had decided to alter the
direction of his career. Entering television, he
narrated a widely hailed documentary, "The
Real West" (1961), which tried to separate the
frontier realities from the images in the television westerns he had come to detest. Cooper
also planned to play more morally ambivalent
characters, beginning with *The Naked Edge*
(1961), in which he portrayed a mercurial businessman suspected of murder by his wife.

As Cooper lay dying of cancer, Pope John
XXIII, President John F. Kennedy, and Queen
Elizabeth II sent get-well messages, which
demonstrated Cooper's position as a beloved
modern folk hero, and also the industry's myth-
making capacity. He died at Los Angeles. His
death, which followed Gable's by about six
months, seemed to many to signal the end of an
era in Hollywood.

Like many American movie stars, Cooper was
not a great actor. Yet he possessed a distinctive
screen image that mirrored much that was worthy in the American character. By box office
figures, Cooper was the most popular male film
star of the 1930's, 1940's, and 1950's. Although
he had great limitations—ones he perhaps too
willingly accepted—such accomplished performers as Charles Laughton, John Barrymore,
and Charles Chaplin considered him America's
most skilled film actor. On stage or live television, Cooper was usually a disaster. But before
a camera he could evoke the most favorable
image of the wholly decent and innocent American. He epitomized what one writer called "our
pioneer belief in the triumph of good over evil."

[There is considerable Cooper material in the
Hedda Hopper Papers, Academy of Motion Picture

Arts and Sciences Library, Los Angeles; the Daniel
Blum Collection, Wisconsin Center for Film and
Theater Research, State Historical Society of Wisconsin; items filed under "Cooper" in the Performing
Arts Library of the New York Public Library, Lincoln
Center. Cooper published a series of memoirs in *Sat-
urday Evening Post,* Feb. 18–Apr. 7, 1956. *McCall's*
ran a partial reminiscence in Jan. 1961. Biographical
studies include Lucien Escoubé, *Gary Cooper, le cav-
alier de l'Ouest* (1965); George Carpozi, *The Gary
Cooper Story* (1970); Rene Jordan, *Gary Cooper*
(1974); Hector Arce, *Gary Cooper* (1979). Also see
Kenneth Anger, *Hollywood Babylon* (1965); Homer
Dickens, *The Films of Gary Cooper* (1970). Contem-
porary analyses of Cooper include Jim Tully, "He
'Stole the Picture,' " *This Week Magazine,* Aug. 23,
1936; *Time's* cover story, Mar. 3, 1941; Frank S.
Nugent, "The All American Man," *New York Times
Magazine,* July 5, 1942; Thomas B. Morgan, "The
American Hero Grows Older," *Esquire,* May 1961.
Russell L. Merritt, "The Bashful Hero in American
Film of the Nineteen Forties," *Quarterly Journal of
Speech,* Apr. 1975, provides a good analysis of
Cooper's image on the screen. An obituary appeared
in the *New York Times* on May 14, 1961.]

JAMES L. BAUGHMAN

COOPER, KENT (Mar. 22, 1880–Jan. 31,
1965), journalist, was born in Columbus, Ind.,
the son of George William Cooper, a lawyer,
and Sina Green. He spent occasional winters in
Washington, D.C., where his father served in
the United States House of Representatives
from 1889 to 1895. Upon his father's death in
1899, Cooper had to leave Indiana University in
his sophomore year. He took a job as a reporter
on the *Indianapolis Press,* and when the *Press*
ceased publication eighteen months later, he
was hired by the *Indianapolis Sun.* In 1903 he
became an Indianapolis correspondent for the
Scripps-McRae Press Association (SMPA). In
this post he developed a network of small newspapers as clients for a SMPA "pony" (abbreviated) news service.

On May 29, 1905, Cooper married Daisy
McBride; they had one daughter. When SMPA
refused to give him a raise, he resigned and
formed his own agency in 1905. He pioneered
in the use of telephone circuits rather than
leased wires to disseminate his pony service.
SMPA bought out Cooper in 1906, and he
again worked as their Indianapolis bureau chief.
In 1907 SMPA was absorbed by the United
Press (UP). Cooper became a traveling agent for
UP, using the advantages of the telephone circuit to lure small papers away from the older and
more powerful Associated Press (AP).

Ambitious and restless, Cooper went to New
York in 1910 to discuss with the American Tele-

phone and Telegraph Company (AT and T) his ideas for forming his own news transmission company. AT and T officials were not interested but encouraged Cooper to see Melville E. Stone, general manager of AP. Stone promptly offered him a job as traveling inspector at $65 a week. Cooper hesitated, then accepted because "I thought I might go further . . . than I could at UP where there were several competent young men with high ambitions . . . AP's men were elderly."

In the next two years Cooper traveled to every AP bureau and member office collecting information and making contacts. He developed plans to restructure AP and renegotiate wire leasing agreements. When Stone failed to act on his recommendations, Cooper went directly to board members Adolph S. Ochs and Valentine S. McClatchy. With their backing, he put his plans into effect, saving AP $100,000 in one year.

At the age of thirty-two Cooper was made chief of AP's newly created Traffic Department. In 1914 he introduced the first teletype machines, and in 1918 he put into effect the first employee pension plan of the news industry. Cooper also began to articulate his central vision: the creation of a worldwide AP. AP's role in the world was circumscribed by a set of exclusive contracts with the big three European news agencies—Reuter's of Great Britain, Havas of France, and Wolff of Germany (Reuter's being the most dominant)—who virtually controlled news dissemination throughout the world. These contracts gave AP the exclusive right to "exploit" North America but prevented it from operating independently anywhere else. AP had a decided advantage because its competitors, UP and Hearst's International News Service (INS), were denied access to Reuter's dispatches. But the agreement left AP dependent upon these European dispatches (which Cooper regarded as unreliable and propagandistic) and prevented AP's expansion. Although Stone resolutely backed the AP-Reuter's pact, Cooper, for idealistic and pragmatic reasons, worked steadfastly throughout his career so that AP could compete internationally. He began in 1918 by negotiating with Havas a "free hand" for AP in South America.

In 1920, shortly after the death of his wife, Cooper was named assistant general manager. He married Marian Rothwell on Sept. 27, 1920, and spent much of the next four years traveling and talking to AP members. In April 1925 he was elected general manager and immediately began to make sweeping changes in AP's rather staid image. Whereas Stone had regarded human interest stories as "mayflies in the world of news," Cooper believed that "there is nothing so important . . . as the true day-by-day story of humanity." Accordingly, he inaugurated an AP feature service, expanded over the years to include Hollywood gossip and cartoons. He lifted a ban on the use of slang, ran interviews, awarded by-lines, and hired special writers to cover science and medicine. In 1927 he established an AP mail photo service and developed the idea of sending pictures directly over the wires. (The AP Wirephoto was first used in 1935.)

Cooper was also laying the groundwork for AP's eventual break with Reuter's and the Europen cartel. As he explained in his *Barriers Down* (1942), the chance came in 1933 when he negotiated a nonexclusive contract with Rengo News Association of Japan, formerly allied with Reuter's. When Reuter's chief, Sir Roderick Jones, heard of the AP-Rengo agreement, he was incensed and terminated the AP-Reuter's contract. Cooper consolidated his position by making a five-year pact with UP in which they agreed not to negotiate exclusive contracts with any European agency. The new AP-Reuters agreement signed in February 1934 gave AP freedom to expand throughout the world—which it did rapidly under Cooper's aggressive leadership.

Divorced in 1940, Cooper was married on Feb. 28, 1942, to Sarah A. Gibbs, his executive secretary for many years. In 1943, he became AP's executive director. He retired as general manager in 1948 but remained executive director until 1951. He wrote *The Right to Know* (1956), an informal history of press censorship, and his autobiography, *Kent Cooper and the Associated Press* (1959).

In estimating his own achievements, Cooper was proudest of his crusade against cartel control of international news. Most of his contemporaries agreed with him, although some argued that this and other of Cooper's innovations resulted less from his personal foresight than from competitive pressures on AP from rival press associations. Whatever his motivations, Cooper's energetic and single-minded devotion to AP transformed it in forty-one years from the most parochial of American news agencies into a dominant international force. "He was a tradition-smasher and an applecartupsetter," said long-time AP colleague Hal Boyle. "He swept through the stodgy newspaper atmosphere of his day like a polar wind." Cooper died in West Palm Beach, Fla.

[In addition to the books cited in the text, Cooper wrote *Anna Zenger: Mother of Freedom* (1946), a novelized biography. The best source on Cooper is his own autobiography, but the following works are also useful: Oliver Gramling, *AP: The Story of the News* (1940); Sidney Kobre, *Development of American Journalism* (1969); Edwin Emery, *The Press and America* (1972). Obituaries appeared in the *New York Times*, Jan. 31, 1965, and *Newsweek*, Feb. 15, 1965.]

NANCY L. STEFFEN

CORWIN, EDWARD SAMUEL (Jan. 19, 1878–Apr. 29, 1963), historian and political scientist, was born on a farm near Plymouth, Mich., the son of Frank Adelbert Corwin and Cora C. Lyndon. His scholarly bent manifested itself early in life. After graduating from Plymouth High School, Corwin entered the University of Michigan, where Andrew C. McLaughlin stirred his interest in constitutional law. He graduated with the Ph.B. in 1900, a member of Phi Beta Kappa and president of his class. For graduate work he went to the University of Pennsylvania, completing his doctoral dissertation in 1905 under the guidance of John Bach McMaster.

While discussing his "approaching jobless condition" with the McMasters in June 1905, his mentor suggested he "run over to Princeton and apply to Woodrow Wilson for one of those preceptorships they're handing out over there." A letter of introduction from McMasters led to interviews, and to Corwin's appointment as a preceptor. That fall, in Wilson's original group of preceptors (assistant professors for small student discussion groups), Corwin began an association that was to last almost sixty years.

Although Corwin considered Wilson "the most impressive human being" he had ever met, he did not hesitate to challenge some of Wilson's more conservative views. In 1908, Wilson selected Corwin to update his book *Division and Reunion.* Corwin wrote Part VI, published in 1909. On June 28, 1909, he married Mildred Sutcliffe Smith. They had no children, but over the years developed warm relationships with many students and younger colleagues. A man of rare charm and broad culture, Corwin was widely read in many fields, a connoisseur of music, especially opera, and an inveterate gardener.

Promoted to professor in 1911, Corwin was appointed seven years later to the chair first occupied by Woodrow Wilson, McCormick Professor of Jurisprudence, which he held until retirement in 1946. When a separate depart-

ment of politics was formed in 1924, he became its first chairman.

Corwin's performance as a teacher led seniors repeatedly to vote his course on constitutional interpretation both the "most difficult" and the "most valuable." Because of his staccato speech and military bearing, he was affectionately dubbed "the General." Corwin had a special gift for reaching each student, discovering and eliciting something worthwhile, and encouraging him to follow his own bent. Rare sensitivity enabled him to judge young men not by what they were but by what they might become.

Corwin's first book, *National Supremacy—Treaty Power vs. State Power* (1913) indicated interest in the intricate relationship between federal and state powers in foreign affairs. A year later *The Doctrine of Judicial Review* appeared. *French Policy and the American Alliance* (1916), *The President's Control of Foreign Relations* (1917), and *John Marshall and the Constitution* (1919) followed in rapid succession, establishing Corwin as an authority on the Constitution. Chief Justice John Marshall was his hero. He believed with Justice Oliver Wendell Holmes that "if American law were to be represented by a single figure, that figure could be one alone, John Marshall."

Corwin's most successful and widely read book was written at the suggestion of his companions in the Snuff Club, an elite cross-departmental group of Princeton scholars. After hearing one of his papers, Christian Gauss urged him to write an exposition of the Constitution for the general reader. *The Constitution and What It Means Today* (1920) continues in print after thirteen revised editions and numerous translations.

During the 1930's and 1940's, Corwin continued to enhance his reputation with a number of penetrating studies on the Supreme Court, the presidency, and the Constitution. "By and large," he concluded, "the history of the Presidency has been the history of aggrandizement." When a revised fourth edition appeared in 1958, *The President: Office and Powers* was still considered the bible in its field.

A distinctive characteristic of Corwin's literary style was his penchant for arresting comment, graphic illustrations, and devastating wit. His mind was sharp, penetrating, and sometimes astringent. The imaginative and original flavor of his style was illustrated in *Twilight of the Supreme Court* (1934). Corwin characterized the supremacy clause (Article VI, section 2) as the "linchpin of the Constitution," and judicial review as "American democracy's way of covering its bet."

Corwin served as visiting professor and held prestigious lectureships at Johns Hopkins, New York University, Boston University, Louisiana State, Yale, and many other universities. In 1928–1929 he was visiting professor at Yenching University, Peiping (Peking), China. He was president of the American Political Science Association (1931), and winner of the American Philosophical Society's Franklin Medal (1940) and the Henry M. Phillips Prize in the Science and Philosophy of Jurisprudence (1942).

Corwin's expertise and influence eventually extended to the federal government, which he served in 1935 as adviser to the Public Works Administration, and in 1936 and 1937 as special assistant and consultant to the attorney general on constitutional issues. In 1937, Corwin supported President Franklin D. Roosevelt's plan to enlarge the Supreme Court, but he opposed Roosevelt's breach of the third-term tradition.

Corwin's retirement in 1946 ended neither his academic career nor his public service. During the academic year 1947–1948 he was visiting professor at Columbia. From 1949 to 1952 he served as editor for the Legislative Reference Section, Library of Congress, directing a research project that produced the massive volumes of *The Constitution Annotated: Analysis and Interpretation.* In 1954 he became chairman of a national committee opposed to the Bricker amendment to restrict the president's treaty-making power.

Although Corwin carried on an active and fruitful career to an advanced age, the latter part of his life was plagued by declining health due to the onset of cancer. He died at Princeton.

Although he never wrote the single monumental work he had planned, Corwin's writings embrace every significant aspect of his subject. He stands among the giants of American constitutional commentators—James Kent, Joseph Story, and Thomas Cooley. He was the only nonlawyer among the ten legal writers most frequently cited by the Supreme Court. Corwin justified and illustrated the truth of his incisive observation: "If judges make law, so do commentators."

[The Corwin papers are in the Firestone Library, Princeton University. His scholarly contributions are in Richard Loss, ed., *Presidential Power and the Constitution: Essays by Edward S. Corwin* (1976), and in Alpheus Thomas Mason and Gerald Garvey, eds., *American Constitutional History: Essays by Edward S. Corwin*, 2 vols. (1964). See also William Starr Myers, ed., *Woodrow Wilson, Some Princeton Memories by Edward S. Corwin and Others* (1946). For material about Corwin see Gerald Garvey, "Corwin on the Constitution: the Content and Context of Modern American Constitutional Theory" (Ph.D. diss., Princeton University, 1962); Alexander Leitch, *A Princeton Companion* (1978); A. T. Mason, "Edward S. Corwin," *Princeton Alumni Weekly*, Oct. 22, 1963. Obituaries are in the *New York Times*, Apr. 30, 1963, and *American Political Science Review*, Sept. 1963.]

ALPHEUS THOMAS MASON

COSTAIN, THOMAS BERTRAM (May 8, 1885–Oct. 8, 1965), editor and novelist, was born in Brantford, Ontario, Canada, the son of John Herbert Costain, a carpenter and building contractor, and of Mary Schultz. He was educated in the Brantford public schools, where he showed an early interest in history and biography. He always wanted to be a writer, and before graduating from high school he completed four novels. None brought him more than a letter of rejection. One of these early efforts was a 70,000-word romance about Maurice of Nassau.

Costain's writing career began in 1902, when, having had a mystery story accepted by the *Brantford Courier*, he was offered a $5-a-week job as a reporter on the newspaper: "I think I was a good one. I still think of myself as a reporter in the sense that a reporter tries to be accurate and interesting . . . a writer has no right to be dull." After his job with the Brantford paper, Costain went to work for the *Guelph* (Ontario) *Daily Mercury* (1908). On Jan. 12, 1910, he married Ida Randolph Spragge; they had two daughters. Also in 1910 he joined the Maclean Publishing Company, editing three trade journals: *Plumber and Steamfitter*, *Hardware and Metal*, and *Milliner and Drygoods*. Soon thereafter he became editor of *Maclean's Magazine*, a position he held until 1920.

Costain went to the United States in 1920 as chief associate editor of the *Saturday Evening Post*. After being naturalized as a United States citizen later that year, he spent fourteen years with the *Post*, contacting and working with new writers. In 1934 he became eastern story editor for Twentieth Century-Fox Film Corporation. From 1937 to 1939, with E. H. Ellis and P. Hal Sims, Costain put out a small literary magazine, *American Cavalcade*, which in his later years he described as "a promising infant, but it died young." From 1939 to 1946 Costain was a part-time advisory editor for Doubleday.

In 1940, Costain's interest in history, coupled with a less time-consuming schedule, led to his first serious fictional efforts. Yet his first start was a false one. He began work on four short novels, but was "enough of an editor not to send them out."

Costain found his métier by turning to what he knew best—history and biography. He conceived a six-part series, "The Stepchildren of History," in which he intended to sketch the lives of six interesting but unknown historical figures. On the advice of his editor, Costain turned each sketch into a book. The first, *For My Great Folly* (1942), depicts the life of John Ward, a seventeenth-century English pirate. It is based on the Free Rovers, sailors who fought the Spanish but were alienated from their homeland.

In *The Black Rose* (1945) Costain describes the life and times of the Mongolian warrior Bayan of the Hundred Eyes. It sold about 1 million copies in six months. Like his later novel *The Silver Chalice* (1952), it was made into a movie.

Costain's historical novels were based on extensive research. For *The Silver Chalice* he consulted more than 1,000 sources on biblical culture in order to tell the story of the young artisan who later made the chalice to hold the sacred cup that Christ had used at the Last Supper. Much like well-detailed social histories, Costain's novels show what people wore, what they ate and drank, and how they spoke (including slang and dialects, which he managed to represent in English).

Costain's nonfiction historical series "Pageant of England" and his books on Canadian history have been praised by experts. The historian Geoffrey Bruun said of *The Conquerers* (1949), Costain's history of England in the Middle Ages: "Thomas Costain belongs to the school of Michelet in his conviction that history ought to be a resurrection of the flesh, and he is in the great tradition of Scott and Dumas in his ability to make it fascinating."

A prolific writer who produced an average of more than 3,000 words a day, Costain is best known for his historical novels. He was a masterful storyteller. With fast-moving adventure plots, intriguing characters, and vivid descriptions of past times and places, Costain's novels represent a notable achievement. But he should also be recognized as a successful editor and literary scout during his years with the *Saturday Evening Post*. Costain died in New York City.

[Works by Costain not mentioned in the text include *The Tontine* (1955), *Below the Salt* (1957), and *The Last Plantagenets* (1962). An informative interview is in the *New York Times Book Review*, Aug. 17, 1952. An obituary is in the *New York Times*, intl. ed., Oct. 9–10, 1965.]

PHILIP LUTHER

COVICI, PASCAL ("PAT") (Nov. 4, 1885– Oct. 14, 1964), book publisher and editor, was born in Botosani, Rumania, the son of Wolf Covici and Schfra Barish. He came to the United States in 1898 with his parents and sister to join his brothers in Chicago. Covici attended the University of Michigan, Ann Arbor, and the University of Chicago, studying literature. He left college without a degree and for a time managed six five-and-ten stores owned by his brothers. On Aug. 1, 1915, he married Dorothy Soll; they had one son.

From 1918 to 1922, Covici worked for Waterbury Grapefruit Groves, Bradenton, Fla., publishing a monthly newspaper, managing a nursery, and supervising workers. He returned to Chicago in 1922. There he and a partner, Billy McGee, a former priest, opened a bookstore. They became publishers the following year. Ben Hecht, whose *1001 Afternoons in Chicago* was one of Covici-McGee's first publications, wrote that their cluttered shop quickly became a "Mecca of the arts." He described Covici as "a tall shapely man with a Punchinello handsomeness," who was always excited about books and was ever solicitous of the needs of both his customers and the artists who gathered in his shop.

Covici-McGee's small list consisted largely of "lush and unusual books" that were meant for limited-edition collectors. One of these books, Hecht's *Fantazius Mallare* (1922), got the publishers into legal trouble; it was seized by postal authorities as obscene, and the publishers, author, and illustrator were arrested. Covici reluctantly pleaded nolo contendere and paid a $1,000 fine. In 1924 McGee left the business because of illness, and the following year the publishing firm became Pascal Covici, Inc.

Covici and Donald Friede formed a New York publishing house in 1928, with a staff of seven (including themselves and their wives). During the next half-dozen years Covici-Friede was regarded as one of the most exciting publishing firms in America. It continued and expanded Covici's practice of specializing in lavishly illustrated limited editions, and published such authors as Wyndham Lewis, Clifford Odets, Gene Fowler, and Nathanael West. One of its successes was the Hecht and Charles MacArthur play *The Front Page* (1928). Another was Dr. T. H. van de Velde's sex manual *Ideal Marriage* (1930). Friede described his partner as a "flamboyant Rumanian with the shock of white hair on a poet's head, which in turn was set on a football player's . . . body."

Covici-Friede's unconventional and unorthodox practices brought it almost immediately both legal and financial difficulties. In 1928 it published Radclyffe Hall's *The Well of Loneliness*, a novel about lesbianism that outraged the Society for the Suppression of Vice. The book was seized as obscene in January 1929. The publishers were convicted in magistrate's court, but a higher court reversed their convictions and dismissed the case. The decision was important because of its finding that a book could not be declared obscene simply because of its subject.

Friede sold his share of the business in 1935, and three years later the firm was liquidated in order to pay its debts. Before its dissolution Covici-Friede had added to its list of authors John Steinbeck, whose three previously published novels had been commercial failures and whose fourth had been rejected by several publishers. Covici had come across Steinbeck's *The Pastures of Heaven* (1932) on a remainder table in a friend's Chicago bookshop in 1934. He read it and wrote to Steinbeck that he would like to be his publisher. Covici-Friede brought out Steinbeck's *Tortilla Flat* in 1935. It was a success for both author and publisher. Four other Steinbeck works were published in 1936 and 1937, and Covici bought the rights to Steinbeck's earlier works and reissued them. "I have the best publisher in the world," Steinbeck wrote in 1937.

In 1938, after Covici-Friede was dissolved, Covici became a senior editor at the Viking Press. He gave his birth year as 1888, so that he would not appear to be older than fifty. In his career at Viking, Covici, in addition to bringing Steinbeck to the firm and being his editor, was responsible for overall editing of the Viking Portable Library and also was editor for other writers, including Saul Bellow and Arthur Miller. Bellow's *Herzog* (1964) was dedicated to Covici. Writers and associates valued his editorial skills and his ability to motivate writers to their best effort. Miller described him as "a mixture of slave-driver and very caring father." More than thirty authors dedicated books to him.

Covici's relationship with Steinbeck was an extraordinary one. They conducted a voluminous correspondence. Steinbeck's *Journal of a Novel: The East of Eden Letters* (1969) consisted of a journal prepared for his editor in 1951

as he was writing the novel. Steinbeck dedicated the novel to Covici and presented the manuscript to him in a mahogany box he had carved while writing the novel.

After Covici's death in New York City, Steinbeck said: "For nearly forty years Pat was my collaborator and my conscience. He demanded of me more than I had and thereby caused me to be more than I should have been without him."

[The Covici-Steinbeck correspondence is in the John Steinbeck Collection, University of Texas, Austin. See Donald Friede, *The Mechanical Angel* (1948); Ben Hecht, *A Child of the Century* (1954); Morris Ernst and Alan U. Schwartz, *Censorship* (1964); Charles Madison, *Book Publishing in America* (1966), and *Irving to Irving* (1974); Elaine Steinbeck and Robert Wallsten, eds., *Steinbeck: A Life in Letters* (1975); Thomas Fensch, *Steinbeck and Covici* (1979). Obituaries are in the *New York Times*, Oct. 15, 1964, and *Publishers Weekly*, Oct. 26, 1964. A memorial, limited, not-for-sale volume is *Pascal Covici, 1888–1964*, published by Viking in 1964.]

RONALD S. MARMARELLI

COWEN, JOSHUA LIONEL (Aug. 25, 1880–Sept. 8, 1965), inventor and manufacturer, was born in New York City, the son of Haymen Cowen, a real estate dealer. Repelled by the efforts of teachers to guide him in uninteresting directions, he began experimenting at home with various explosive mixtures. This dangerous situation led his father to enroll him in supervised laboratory classes at Cooper Union. He later attended classes at the City College of New York and, at sixteen, entered Columbia University's engineering school. One semester of studying bridges and dams was enough because, as Cowen liked to recall, his interest lay in smaller things. After leaving Columbia he worked at various jobs, staying after hours to tinker with his own projects.

The first fruit of Cowen's efforts was a fuse to ignite the magnesium powder used in flash photography. The Navy Department saw merit in this device as a fuse to detonate submarine mines. Cowen, only eighteen, was called to Washington, where he presented his idea with such skill and confidence that he won a contract to supply fuses that netted him and his one assistant a profit of $12,000.

Cowen's next idea was an early version of the battery-powered flashlight. Bemused by its novelty applications (an illuminated flowerpot was one), he failed to see that the real value of his invention was as a practical hand torch. When the first design failed to work as well as it should, he lost interest and gave the entire rights to his partner, Conrad Hubert, who went on to found the Eveready Flashlight Company.

Cowen next fashioned a miniature electric motor that he fastened to a fan blade, but lost interest when the weather turned cool. Always fascinated with miniaturization, he decided to see if he could capture some of the excitement of railroading in a tiny train. In 1901 he built a "locomotive" (hardly more than a wooden flatcar with motor and battery), another flatcar, and a caboose of sorts, all running on a circle of handmade brass track. He took the novelty to a local toy store, the proprietor of which was so delighted with it that he ordered a half dozen more.

Nationally, the railroads had captured the public's imagination. They were in their most vigorous era, before their strength was sapped by government intervention. "Lionel Lines" trains soon became as much a symbol of Christmas as Santa Claus or the Christmas tree around which the little trains chugged. Little girls continued to hug a new doll on Christmas morning, but boys forsook toy drums to kneel on the floor (often alongside their equally entranced fathers) and operate the new electric train. Cowen married Cecilia Liberman on Feb. 25, 1904; they had two children.

In 1907, Cowen introduced a model of the locomotive that the Baltimore and Ohio Railroad had placed in operation in its Baltimore tunnel, starting a craze for models of electrically propelled locomotives that paralleled the short-lived era of electrification of American railroads. Intelligent product innovation was Cowen's strongest point. In the following years came the transformer (about 1910), which made batteries unnecessary; the sequence switch (1926), which permitted remote control of switch positions and locomotive direction; specialized freight cars, such as cranes, milk cars, and log cars, that actually performed their functions, often by remote control; a completely separate line of two-rail "HO" gauge equipment for the "full scalers," or serious hobbyists, who promised to become as important as the "high railers" (mostly youngsters, who were the backbone of the "O" gauge, or toy market). After the war, during which Lionel put toy trains aside for war production contracts including radar equipment, the company moved toward electronic remote-control devices. Founded as a proprietorship in 1901, the company was incorporated as Lionel Manufacturing Company in New Jersey in 1906, and reorganized under New York laws in 1918 as Lionel Corporation.

Cowen's other strong point was his thirst for realism in the modeling of toy trains. The anecdotes are endless of how the exact number of rivets in a locomotive tender was determined, how smoke could be made to come from the stack of an engine, and what was involved in duplicating the chugging, puffing noise of a highballing locomotive. While not losing sight of the fact that the trains had to be durable, simple, and safe for their juvenile operators, Cowen never forgot the deep yearning to recreate the real world in miniature that he had known as a boy, and that he knew lay deep in the psyche of all youngsters.

The Great Depression years were lean ones for all toy manufacturers, but Lionel, which had built a large 450,000-square-foot factory in Irvington, N.J., just before World War I, came through safely, while its major competitors, Ives and American Flyer, fell on hard times. In 1934, Cowen eliminated spring-wound trains, which he had always hated, from his line; and when the Ives Company, whose carelessly designed equipment he considered "inartistic," fell into bankruptcy the same year, he bought its assets and dropped all its dies into the Connecticut River. In 1941, Lionel had sales of $4.25 million, but its great growth came with the population boom of the postwar years.

Cowen's wife died in 1946, and he married Lillian Herman in November 1949. By 1954, several years after Cowen's son, Lawrence, had taken over management of Lionel, annual sales reached $33 million as the American birthrate continued to soar. According to the company, Lionel Lines had laid more than 25,000 miles of track by 1960, more than any single real railroad.

Cowen was a short, peppery man who seldom contained his impatience with stodginess, even while attending the board meetings of more staid companies of which he was a director. Even when his work force had grown to 3,000, his constant physical presence greatly helped labor relations. But as business became more "professionalized," formal labor relations became a necessity; and when the rising tide of conglomerate mergers washed over American business in the early 1960's, the Cowens lost control of the company. Cowen died at Palm Beach, Fla.

[See "Profiles: High Railers and Full Scalers," *New Yorker*, Dec. 13, 1947; "He Put Tracks Beneath the Christmas Tree," *Reader's Digest*, Jan. 1954. An obituary is in *New York Times*, Sept. 9, 1965.]

ALBRO MARTIN

COYLE

COYLE, GRACE LONGWELL (Mar. 22, 1892–Mar. 8, 1962), social worker and social work theorist, was born in North Adams, Mass., the daughter of John Patterson Coyle, a Congregationalist minister, and Mary Allerton Cushman. Inspired as a young girl by the writings of Jane Addams, she volunteered at a Boston settlement house while earning a B.A. at Wellesley College (1914). At the New York School of Social Work, where she received a certificate in 1915, Coyle took courses from Edward T. Devine and Mary Van Kleeck.

After three years as a settlement worker in the coal region of Wilkes-Barre, Pa., Coyle returned to New York City to work in the Industrial Women's Department of the Young Women's Christian Association (YWCA). Here she designed leadership training courses and nourished an interest in adult education and recreation. Resuming her schooling in 1926, she earned an M.A. in economics (1928) and a Ph.D. in sociology (1931), both from Columbia University. She also held a part-time position on the staff of The Inquiry, a New York City–based organization that sought to reduce conflict between races and nationalities through the methodology of group discussions. Those who participated in the investigations of The Inquiry included William H. Kilpatrick, John Dewey, Harrison Elliott, Alfred Sheffield, Herbert Croly, and the recreational theorist Eduard C. Lindeman. All were influential in Coyle's intellectual development. Her dissertation, *Social Process in Organized Groups,* was published in 1930, the year she rejoined the YWCA as director of the laboratory division of the national board.

In 1934, Coyle joined the group work faculty of the School of Applied Social Sciences at Western Reserve University, where she remained, except for a two-year term on the staff of the War Relocation Authority during World War II, until her death. She used her influence as perhaps the leading social group work educator in the decade after 1935 to encourage the development of a group (as opposed to an individual, or casework) approach to social work, and to stimulate the training of professionals in group leadership. Coyle's success in these undertakings is reflected in her service as president of the National Conference of Social Work (1940), the American Association of Social Workers (1942–1944), and the Council on Social Work Education (1958–1960). She never married.

Coyle's lifelong advocacy of group work involved an entirely original way of conceptualizing and managing social relationships, built on a foundation of history and social theory. With Mary Parker Follett, Elton Mayo, Kilpatrick, and others, Coyle believed that science, technology, and urbanization had destroyed traditional sources of social cohesion, such as the neighborhood, and were threatening democracy itself. For Coyle, neither the thousands of functional groups that served the specific interests of their members nor existing ways of eliminating differences between them ensured a sufficient degree of social unity. Conflict between classes, races, and ethnic groups seemed to be the rule, and although some conflicts were based on virtually irreconcilable points of view, many, Coyle argued, were caused by excessive emotion that interfered with rational problem solving. She found the solution within the structure and process of the group. Consensus could be achieved through informal, cooperative group discussion, guided by a leader trained in "collective thinking" and the art of persuasion. Because it was participatory, the process itself would teach the habits of democracy and the meaning of life.

Coyle's most important contribution was to articulate a body of existing social theory. Although she did not often participate in the creation of working groups, her theoretical perspective and world view were of enormous influence in the half-century after World War I. For example, in the strained climate of labor relations created by the war, employers in Dayton, Ohio, brought the city's foremen into the first of many clubs designed to convince these supervisors that their primary loyalty resided with capital rather than with labor. Christian associations, settlement houses, and recreation centers formed hundreds of clubs as forums for applying group process concepts. Several major New Deal agencies, including the Works Progress Administration, utilized the techniques of group process. Even Dr. Benjamin Spock, in *The Common Sense Book of Baby and Child Care* (1945), conceptualized the family as a small group and the parents as group leaders.

In the late 1930's, Coyle joined the social welfare agencies and philanthropic foundations of Cleveland in creating the Golden Age Clubs, in part to provide the elderly with a healthy and democratic organizational alternative to the pension clubs of Francis Townsend. And in the mid-1940's she endorsed self-governing teenage canteens as a means of achieving attitudinal changes in juvenile delinquents.

Coyle appreciated the dangers inherent in her brand of social engineering. Guided discussion could easily degenerate into manipulation. She believed that voluntarism would prevent manipulation, and she had a profound faith in the power of reason and reflection to overcome irrational prejudices, habits, and emotions. Like so many others who had grown to maturity in the age of organization and who had, at the same time, come to question the ability of representative democracy to hold the society together, she could see no alternative. Coyle died in Cleveland.

[Coyle's papers are in the University Archives, Case Western Reserve University, Cleveland. Her published works include "Group Work and Social Change," *Proceedings of the National Conference of Social Work, 1935* (1935); "What Is This Social Group Work?" *The Survey,* May 1935; "Social Group Work," *Social Work Year Book, 1937* (1937); *Group Experience and Democratic Values* (1947); she also edited *Studies in Group Behavior* (1937). See also John Dewey, *Democracy and Education* (1916); Mary Parker Follett, *Creative Experience* (1924); William H. Kilpatrick, ed., *The Educational Frontier* (1933); Bruno Lasker, *Democracy Through Discussion* (1949), Bruno Lasker Papers, Columbia University Archives, Division of Special Collections, Butler Library; Elton Mayo, *The Social Problems of an Industrial Civilization* (1945); Ben Zion Shapiro, "Grace Longwell Coyle: Contributions to the Philosophy and Practice of Social Work" (seminar paper, 1965, School of Applied Social Sciences Library, Case Western Reserve University); Alfred Sheffield, *Creative Discussion* (1933).
Obituaries are in the *New York Times,* Mar. 10, 1962, and *Social Science Review,* June 1962.]

WILLIAM GRAEBNER

CROMWELL, DEAN BARTLETT (Sept. 20, 1879–Aug. 3, 1962), track and field coach, was born in Turner, Oreg., where his father operated a sawmill and owned a small ranch. The family moved to southern California before Cromwell entered Occidental College Prep School in 1896. An excellent athlete, he played on several Occidental College teams. (At the time prep school athletes were allowed to compete on college teams.) In 1898, Cromwell enrolled at Occidental College, where he played right halfback on the football team, first base on the baseball team, and participated in eight different events at track meets. In 1901 he was recognized as the outstanding athlete in southern California when he received the Helms Athletic Award. After graduating in 1902 he represented the Los Angeles YMCA at track meets throughout the nation.

For a time Cromwell worked in the contracts department of the telephone company in southern California. Hired in 1908 by the University of Southern California, Cromwell began coach-

ing track and football in 1909. He coached football through the 1914 season, compiling a record of twenty-one wins, eight losses, and six ties. Although relieved of football responsibilities, his tenure as track coach continued through the 1948 season.

Because of his coaching success Cromwell became known as "the Dean" or, more expressively, as "the Maker of Champions." Between 1912 and 1948 eight of his athletes won a total of twelve Olympic gold medals, at least one in each Olympiad. At one time or another trackmen coached by Cromwell held thirteen individual world records and three relay-team world records.

During his tenure at Southern California, Cromwell's team dominated intercollegiate track and field, winning nine championships of the Intercollegiate Association of Amateur Athletes of America (seven in a row between 1933 and 1939), as well as twelve National Collegiate Athletic Association championships (nine in a row between 1935 and 1943). He was named head track and field coach for the 1948 United States Olympic team.

Cromwell was not a specialist whose teams concentrated on one phase of track and field. Champions and world record setters came from many events in both running and field events. His athletes won Olympic gold medals in seven different events.

Cromwell's success did not depend on any particular style or philosophy of coaching. He tried to find the best athletes and then to observe their styles and methods closely. He had lesser athletes emulate the methods of those who were faster or stronger. Cromwell also stressed motivation, always referring to his charges individually as "champ." He believed that a coach should never speak negatively to his team, but should assure them that they were capable, and able to defeat any challenger.

Perhaps because of his success, Cromwell had a long-running feud with Robert L. "Dink" Templeton, the track coach at Stanford University. The rivalry consisted largely of good-natured spoofing and highly competitive meets between their teams, which were generally the best on the West Coast. Ironically, the two rivals died within four days of each other.

Despite his record, Cromwell's appointment as Olympic track coach met with some opposition from reporters in the East. They charged that his success came from being in southern California, where it was easy to recruit quality athletes, and not from his coaching abilities.

Cromwell retired from active coaching in 1949. His salary of $1,500 in 1909 rose to $6,500 in the mid-1930's, when the school won the string of national championships, and finally reached $8,500 when he retired. He had invested in southern California real estate over the years, and owned apartment houses, bungalows, and business properties as well as recreation property and an orchard in Oregon.

Cromwell was elected to the Helms Foundation Hall of Fame in 1948 and to the National Track and Field Hall of Fame in 1974, as one of its initial inductees. In retirement he served as adviser for track programs throughout the world. He was an active and highly visible figure in all areas of sport in southern California until he died at Los Angeles.

[Information on Cromwell is in the clipping files of the athletic department of the University of Southern California and the Helms Foundation Library in Los Angeles. Also see Quentin Reynolds, "The Perfect Track Man," *Collier's,* Jan. 12, 1935; Pete Martin, "Wizard of the Cinders," *Saturday Evening Post,* Mar. 20, 1948; and *Track and Field News,* Aug. 1962. An obituary is in the *New York Times,* Aug. 4, 1962.]

HARRY JEBSEN, JR.

CROSBY, PERCY LEE (Dec. 8, 1891–Dec. 8, 1964), cartoonist and artist, was born in Brooklyn, N.Y., the son of Thomas Francis Crosby and Frances Greene. His father was a dealer in art materials and painted as an avocation. Percy attended public schools in Queens, N.Y. He left high school in his sophomore year and found a job in the art department of the *Delineator* (edited by Theodore Dreiser). Subsequently he worked for the *New York Call* and at the age of seventeen for the New York *Globe,* where he was a sports and political cartoonist, court sketcher, and comic artist. While with the *Globe* he received first prize in a cartoonist contest, which helped him obtain a position with the New York *World.* At this time he also attended Pratt Institute in Brooklyn and the Art Students League in Manhattan.

Between 1915 and 1917 Crosby drew a comic strip called "The Clancy Kids," distributed by the McClure Syndicate, which reflected his fascination with the antics of children, a lifelong obsession. On July 7, 1917, Crosby married Gertrude Volz; they had one daughter.

During World War I Crosby served overseas in the infantry with the 77th Division and achieved the rank of first lieutenant. He became a captain in 1919. While a soldier, he published two books of war cartoons, *Between Shots*

(1919) and *That Rooky of the 13th Squad* (1919).

After the war Crosby's cartoons began appearing in the humor magazine *Life,* for which, in 1923, he introduced a "Skippy" series. In 1925 "Skippy" became a daily comic strip distributed by Hearst's King Features, although Crosby owned the copyright. The pranks, philosophy, and boyhood nonsense of this cartoon imp found a wide audience among both youngsters and adults in the United States and later abroad. In 1926 the artist Charles Dana Gibson wrote: "Skippy is one of the truest and most thoroughly sympathetic characters that I have ever known. He deserves to be placed with Kim, Huck Finn, and Penrod in the gallery of real boys." Skippy's escapades were featured in the motion pictures *Skippy* (1931), starring Jackie Cooper, and *Sookey* (1932).

By the early 1930's, Crosby's considerable income from "Skippy" enabled him to live on a large farm in McLean, Va., employ two secretaries, keep racing horses, and use five rooms of a large house as studios. One contemporary described him in 1931 as "a solidly built young man, thirty-nine years old of medium height, with thick blond hair and a stout jaw. He is constantly on the hop, like Douglas Fairbanks." Crosby divorced his first wife in 1927 and on Apr. 4, 1929, he married Agnes Dale Locke. They had four children.

Besides cartoons, Crosby did drawings, lithographs, etchings, watercolors, and oils. He achieved an international reputation as an artist. His first exhibition was in New York in February 1928 and included some 300 works prepared over the preceding ten years. According to a *New York Times* art critic, the works covered "an astonishing range of subjects and techniques. But more significant than the versatility they reveal, is the faculty here attested for catching life in motion."

Crosby proceeded to perfect his talent for reproducing motion. At the International Art Competition in Los Angeles in 1932, he won an Olympic Silver Medal for a drawing entitled *Jack Knife,* a simple picture of a few lines embodying the essence of a figure executing this dive. Two other New York shows occurred—in January 1931, at the Anderson Galleries, and in November 1933 at the Macbeth Annex. A reviewer of the latter cited "motion" as Crosby's "big act" and noted that his "black and white" drawings and lithographs were his "best mediums," while most of the watercolors were "superficial and crude." From the summer of 1934 to the summer of 1935 Crosby's works were exhibited in Europe—Paris, London, and Rome. Pictures were purchased by the Luxembourg Museum, by the Italian government, and by Lord Duveen for the British Museum.

Crosby also wrote over sixteen books and pamphlets. His books about Skippy and his associates, either cartoons or fiction, were best received. He also wrote on controversial, contemporary, and patriotic subjects, such as Prohibition (in his personal life he was a dry but politically he was a wet) and Communism, which he opposed. Failing to find a commercial publisher, he brought out most of these opinionated works himself. On occasion he would purchase newspaper space and advertise his views; in the Dec. 8, 1931, edition of the *New York Times*, he placed an advertisement entitled "A Letter to George Bernard Shaw and His Brother Communists Who Are Now Guests of the Nation's Capital."

Crosby and his second wife separated in 1939 and were divorced in the spring of 1940. On May 17 of that year he married Carolyn E. Soper. Crosby retired about 1952 because of ill health. He died in New York City.

[Books written by Crosby include *Skippy* (1925), cartoons from the pages of *Life; Skippy* (1929), a novel; *Always Belittlin'* (1933), cartoons and prose. *A Cartoonist's Philosophy* (1931) and *Would Communism Work Out in America?* (1938) present Crosby's views on religion, art, Prohibition, and Communism. *Sport Drawings* (1933) and *Skippy: A Complete Compilation: 1925–1926* (1977) contain reproductions of his work.
See also the *American Magazine*, Nov. 1931; the *New York Times*, Feb. 12, 1928; Nov. 17, 1933; July 27, 1934; Jan. 22, 1935; July 11, 1935; Dec. 14, 1964; *Literary Digest*, Sept. 8, 1934; and *Newsweek*, Aug. 4, 1934.]

ALLAN NELSON

CROSLEY, POWEL, JR. (Sept. 18, 1886– Mar. 28, 1961), manufacturer and baseball club owner, was born in Cincinnati, Ohio, the son of Powel Crosley, a prominent local attorney, and Charlotte W. Utz. Taking only odd jobs, he claimed he never earned more than $20 a week until he was thirty years old. He graduated from College Hill Public School in 1901 and the Ohio Military Institute four years later. At the University of Cincinnati he studied engineering (1906) and law (1906–1907), but he never received a degree. His mechanical gadgets and business attracted him more than education.

Crosley's father, who regarded autos as a passing fancy, bet him $10 that he could not build a car that would run from Cincinnati's Presbyte-

rian church to the Post Office. Crosley won the money with a contraption that attained a speed of five miles an hour. He later worked as a chauffeur to learn more about automobiles. In 1907 he entered manufacturing. Borrowing $10,000, he organized a company to produce the Marathon Six, an inexpensive six-cylinder automobile. He planned to sell it for $300 less than other cars on the market. But the panic of 1907 cut short his plans.

Crosley tried twice more to produce automobiles, but both efforts failed. He finally succeeded in 1916 when he established a mail-order business, the American Automobile Accessory Company, that marketed various gadgets, mostly of Crosley's invention. Within two years, Crosley bought out his partner, and the company boasted a $2 million-a-year business. In 1910, Crosley married Gwendolyn Badewell Aiken. They had two children.

While looking for a radio for his son, Crosley was astounded at the high prices. He then bought some diagrams, crystal-set parts, and began experimenting. He soon began manufacturing cheap tubes and parts and, with the help of two university engineering students, designed a cheap radio receiver that could be marketed for less than $20. They produced the Harko, Jr., a crystal set powered by a flashlight battery, and the Harko, Sr., a vacuum tube set. By the spring of 1922 the Crosley Radio Corporation was the largest radio manufacturer in the world. That year Crosley began operating Station WLW, Cincinnati.

When demand for his receivers began to decline, Crosley added refrigerators and other electrical appliances to his line of products. His success with the Shelvador refrigerator (with shelves on the door) resulted from competitive marketing; it sold for $50 less than other models. The company also produced air-conditioning equipment, a scalp exerciser, and a portable refrigerator. All were priced for the mass market.

In 1939 Crosley first produced a small, two-cylinder lightweight automobile. In June 1945 he sold most of his interests in the Crosley Corporation—including the manufacturing plant and WLW—to the Aviation Corporation (AVCO). But he maintained control of his automobile company and devoted himself to producing a low-cost compact car. By 1947 he had a station wagon, a truck, and a sports car on the market. His goal was to produce the first $500 car; but production never reached beyond 28,000 a year and the price never dipped below $800. In 1952 he sold his automobile interests, and the Crosley, one of the nation's first compact cars, soon passed from the scene.

In 1934 Crosley had invested in the Cincinnati Reds baseball team, becoming president of the organization. In 1936 he bought the controlling interest. In his will, he left the ownership of the franchise to a charitable foundation under his family's direction—with the proviso that the Reds must remain in Cincinnati. Profits from the team were left to the city's charitable, scientific, and educational organizations.

Crosley's first wife died in 1939. He married Marrianne Richards in 1943, but they were divorced the following year. In 1952 he married Eva Brokaw. After her death in 1955, he married Charlotte K. Wilson in 1956. They were divorced in 1960.

Crosley died in Cincinnati.

[For more information on Crosley, see Gerard Piel, *Life*, Feb. 17, 1947. Obituaries are in the *Cincinnati Enquirer*, Mar. 29, 1961; *Cincinnati Post-Times-Star*, Mar. 28, 1961; *New York Times*, Mar. 29, 1961; and *Sports Illustrated*, Apr. 10, 1961.]

WILLIAM H. BREEZLEY

CROSSWAITH, FRANK RUDOLPH (July 16, 1892–June 17, 1965), labor organizer, was born in Frederiksted, St. Croix, Virgin Islands, the son of William Ignatius Crosswaith, a painter, and Anne Eliza. He began working at age thirteen, came to the United States in 1910, and spent several years in the navy as a messboy. In January 1915 he married Alma E. Besard of Charleston, S.C.; they had three children. While working as an elevator operator in New York City, he attended night schools. In 1918 he was graduated from the Rand School of Social Science, and he taught there part-time for many years.

Crosswaith claimed that he had always been interested in the downtrodden of the world because of the plight of his people in the Virgin Islands. The Rand School, founded in 1906 as a socialist institution, provided nurture and focus for his radicalism; he was also inspired by the idealism of Eugene V. Debs. In Harlem at that time there was a group of radical blacks, many of them socialists, who styled themselves as the vanguard of the "New Negro"—a black who no longer tolerated capitalist exploitation of black workers and the old, accommodating black leadership. It was within this milieu that Crosswaith came to political maturity, attaining considerable organizational skills. He developed an enduring belief that racism was primarily the result of job competition and would be elimi-

nated only when all workers joined unions able to protect their common interests.

In 1920 Crosswaith joined A. Philip Randolph and other radicals in the Friends of Negro Freedom (FNF), an all-black civil rights organization more militant than other existing ones; they hoped to educate blacks in union principles and organize independent black unions where white exclusion made it necessary. Except for its role in organizing attacks on Marcus Garvey in the early 1920's, the FNF was little more than an intellectual forum for New York's black socialists. By 1925, Crosswaith had helped organize tenants and elevator operators and constructors. He also lectured for the Socialist party and the League for Industrial Democracy, traveling widely and earning the reputation as the "Negro Debs" because of his fiery speeches in behalf of the rights of workers. He was the unsuccessful Socialist party candidate for several offices.

In mid-1925, with the encouragement of the Urban League, socialist unions, and the American Fund for Public Service, Crosswaith created the Trade Union Committee for Organizing Negro Workers (TUCONW). Its aim was to bring about unionization of unorganized black workers in New York City and to encourage white-dominated unions to accept them. As the executive secretary of TUCONW, the task of overcoming black indifference, white animosity, and inadequate funds fell to Crosswaith. He made a few black placements in exclusionary unions, but an attempt to organize exploited laundry workers failed. The organization died out within a year, partly because white unions failed to provide promised support.

In 1925 Randolph founded the Brotherhood of Sleeping Car Porters (BSCP), and while Crosswaith was still serving as executive secretary of TUCONW, he became a special assistant to the BSCP; in 1926 he was appointed its first professional organizer. But Crosswaith became the victim of rank-and-file resentment of New Yorkers' domination of the headquarters. In addition, he came under fire from those who thought he spent too much time on public relations and too little time organizing porters. The feuding finally resulted in his being fired in late 1928.

After leaving the BSCP, Crosswaith became a general organizer for the International Ladies' Garment Workers' Union (ILGWU), a position he held for the rest of his career. During the 1930's he continued to be a candidate for various offices on the Socialist party ticket. In 1935, with the aid of the ILGWU and the encouragement of the American Federation of Labor, he created the Negro Labor Committee (NLC) to carry on the task of organizing black workers into established trade unions. He was chairman of the committee for many years to come. Unlike the earlier TUCONW, the NLC endured in Harlem because the Great Depression and the National Industrial Recovery Act created an atmosphere in which union officials became more committed to organizing black workers. It was as head of the NLC that Crosswaith joined with Randolph in the March on Washington Committee in 1941. In 1946 the NLC claimed that it had changed Harlem "from a community of scabs to a community of labor conscious workers."

In the late 1930's Crosswaith joined the American Labor party (ALP). He remained in the Socialist party until 1941, when he left the party over its stand against American involvement in the European war. In 1941 he became a founding member of the anti-Communist Union for Democratic Action and was a leader of the liberal right wing of the ALP. In 1944 he joined the anti-Communist exodus from the ALP to create the Liberal party, becoming a member of its state executive board. Mayor Fiorello La Guardia appointed him to the New York City Housing Authority in 1942, a post he held for many years.

Crosswaith's anti-Communism became even more strident as the cold war developed. In 1952 representatives from seventy-five trade unions met to expand the NLC into a national organization, the Negro Labor Committee, U.S.A., with Crosswaith as chairman. The committee pledged to combat Communist efforts among blacks and to continue the unionization of black workers. Long before his death Crosswaith had become part of the liberal and labor establishments; yet he never stopped demanding equal rights and opportunities for blacks. He died in New York City.

[Manuscript sources pertaining to Crosswaith's career include: Negro Labor Committee Papers, 1925–1969 (Schomburg Branch, New York Public Library); Socialist Party of America Papers (Microfilming Corporation of America, Sanford, N.C.).

Some of Crosswaith's writings include: "The Trade Union Committee for Organizing Negro Workers," *The Messenger*, August 1925; "Sound Principle and Unsound Policy," *Opportunity*, February 1934; with Alfred B. Lewis, *Negro and White Labor Unite for True Freedom* (1942); Negro Labor Committee, *1936–1946: Negro Labor Committee; Ten Years of Struggle* (1946). An enlightening contemporary newspaper account of his work is "How Is

the Race Faring in Union Organizations," *Chicago Defender*, Sept. 30, 1939.

See also Sterling D. Spero and Abram L. Harris, *The Black Worker* (1931); Charles L. Franklin, *The Negro Labor Unionist of New York* (1936); Philip S. Foner, *Organized Labor and the Black Worker, 1619–1973* (1974); Jervis Anderson, *A. Philip Randolph* (1973); Theodore Kornweibel, Jr., *No Crystal Stair* (1975); William H. Harris, *Keeping the Faith* (1977). For more specific information see Irwin M. Marcus, "Frank Crosswaith," *Negro History Bulletin*, August–September 1974; and the *New York Times* obituary, June 18, 1965.]

                                    RICHARD M. DALFIUME

CROY, HOMER (Mar. 11, 1883–May 24, 1965), journalist and novelist, was born near Maryville, Mo., the son of Amos J. Croy, a farmer, and Susan Sewell. His parents had come to Missouri from Indiana in a covered wagon after the Civil War. Croy began to do farm chores at an early age; and although he later traveled widely, mentally he never left the rural world of his youth. And, like so many farm boys, he learned to hate hard physical labor.

Early intrigued with words, Croy studied a pocket dictionary, memorizing words and learning to use them. At fourteen he sold an article to *Puck*, astonishing his father when he produced a check for eight dollars. While in Maryville High School he continued to sell articles to farm journals. For a time he was employed by the *Maryville Tribune* (1900–1901) at a salary of $3 per week.

Enrolling at the University of Missouri in 1901, Croy earned his way by writing and editing. Later he claimed to have been "the first student in the first school of journalism." He did not graduate because he failed a senior course in English (in 1954 his alma mater awarded him an honorary LL.D. degree).

Croy worked briefly for the *St. Louis Post-Dispatch* in 1907, after which he moved to New York City. There he was hired by Butterick Publications to assist Theodore Dreiser, who then was editing three magazines. "I had never had the slighted interest in baseball and had never attended a big league game," Croy later recalled, "but by a twist of circumstance I became editor of *Baseball Magazine*. A few weeks after I had been made editor, I went to a game and found it much as I had expected."

In 1914, Croy was assigned to travel around the world, writing magazine articles for Butterick Publications, and he persuaded Universal Film Company to send a cameraman with him to make travelogues. The outbreak of World War I stranded him in Calcutta. A friend, Mae

Belle Savell, cabled him funds with which to return home; and on Feb. 7, 1915, after his return, they were married. They had three children.

Croy's world trip led in 1918 to the publication of his first book, *How Motion Pictures Are Made*, by Harper. The same publishing house also brought out Croy's first novel, *Boone Stop* (1918). Like most of his novels, it was set in small-town Missouri. Several other books followed, but it was *West of the Water Tower* (1923) that brought him to national attention. Because the reviewers had not been extremely kind to his earlier books, this work was issued anonymously. Ironically, it won critical acclaim.

There followed a highly productive and lucrative period. Croy became a bread-and-butter writer for the *Saturday Evening Post* while turning out almost a book a year for the next two decades. Among his better-known novels were *They Had to See Paris* (1926), which subsequently became the basis of Will Rogers' first talking picture (later he wrote the scripts for several of Rogers's movies); *Sixteen Hands* (1938), made into the motion picture *I'm from Missouri; Family Honeymoon* (1941), turned into a stage play and a movie; and *The Lady from Colorado* (1957), converted into an opera in 1964. In addition he published an autobiography, *Country Cured* (1943), and a volume of reminiscences, *Wonderful Neighbor* (1945). Late in his career Croy began writing serious nonfiction: *Jesse James Was My Neighbor* (1949), *He Hanged Them High* (1952), *Our Will Rogers* (1953), *Wheels West* (1955), *Trigger Marshal* (1957), and *Star Maker: The Story of D. W. Griffith* (1959).

The critics rarely were kind to Croy, seeing him only as a writer of rural and small-town midwestern humor stories. But underneath the surface in these books were a directness and strength that they mistook for crudity.

Croy liked to write letters on the back of letters he had received from others, and these he signed "Two Gun Croy, the Law North of 125th Street" or "Homer Croy, Enemy of Sin and Dutch Elm Disease." He died in New York City.

[Manuscript materials concerning Croy can be found at the University of Missouri, Columbia. In addition to his autobiography and volume of reminiscences, see Charles A. O'Dell, "Homer Croy, Maryville Writer: The First Forty Years, 1883–1923," *Bulletin of Northwest Missouri State University*, Aug. 1973. An obituary is in *New York Times*, May 25, 1965.]

ODIE B. FAULK

CUMMINGS, E E (Oct. 14, 1894–Sept. 3, 1962), poet, was born Edward Estlin Cummings in Cambridge, Mass., the son of the Reverend Edward Cummings, a Unitarian minister, and Rebecca Haswell Clarke. His father taught sociology at Harvard and in 1900 became minister of the South Congregational Church in Boston. His idealism had a formative effect on Cummings, who wrote: "My father gave me Plato's metaphor of the cave with my mother's milk." The family lived in a large and pleasant house in Cambridge. As a child, Cummings read and told stories enthusiastically and wrote poetry. Josiah Royce, a neighbor, introduced him to the sonnet. Following the example of his father, Cummings also drew, and eventually considered himself a painter as well as a poet.

After attending public schools in Cambridge, Cummings entered Harvard in 1911, receiving the B.A. in 1915 and the M.A. in 1916. He contributed poems to the *Harvard Monthly*, and his classmate S. Foster Damon introduced him to the modernist poetry of Ezra Pound. In a commencement address, Cummings aligned himself with "The New Art," exemplified by Henri Matisse, Constantin Brancusi, Marcel Duchamp, and Gertrude Stein. His good friends at Harvard included Scofield Thayer, James Sibley Watson, and John Dos Passos.

In 1917, after working three months for the mail-order bookseller P. F. Collier and Son in New York, Cummings joined the Norton Harjes Ambulance Corps of the American Red Cross in order to avoid the draft. He became close friends with another volunteer, William Slater Brown, with whom he spent a joyful month in Paris before their assignment to the Noyon sector of the front. By September, they were in trouble with French authorities. Unlike the other Americans, they had fraternized with French soldiers, and Brown, who had attended the Columbia School of Journalism, wrote letters home and to his German professor at Columbia in which he freely reported their speculations. French censors imagined they had detected a traitor, and Brown and Cummings were interrogated and then imprisoned in a concentration camp at La Ferté Macé in Orne— Cummings solely because he refused to dissociate himself from his friend.

Cummings described this experience in *The Enormous Room* (1922), a prose work modeled on *The Pilgrim's Progress*. The book's philosophical center is Cummings' discovery of what John Bunyan called the "Delectable Mountains," four men "who are so integrated within their own personalities that prison cannot touch them." Despite this revelation of Emersonian self-reliant individuality, Cummings found himself mentally and physically broken by three months of prison brutality. He did not recover until his return to the United States. His father had worked unceasingly through the Red Cross and the State Department for his son's release. Ironically, Cummings was drafted in 1918, although the armistice prevented his being sent back to France.

During the 1920's Cummings developed rapidly as a poet. He began publishing in *The Dial*, which had been purchased by Thayer and Watson, and in 1923 his first collection of poems appeared, *Tulips and Chimneys*. A good example of his poetry of this period is "in Just-," a transparent lyric that evokes the memory of childhood sexual play. From the beginning Cummings was famous or infamous for his deliberate and experimental use of typography; his poetry has an important visual dimension. In extreme instances the words in his poems become as refracted as images in a Cubist painting, and they cannot be read out loud. He once characterized himself as "an author of pictures, a draughtsman of words."

Cummings published four volumes of poetry in the 1920's. Although he continued to write poetry for the next forty years, he did not appreciably change his style or his themes. He had found his poetic voice. In 1926 he described his technique as that of a burlesque comedian; and certainly this is true of his many satires on the evils of the contemporary world. A widely anthologized sonnet begins, "next to of course god america i/love you land of the pilgrims' and so forth oh/say can you see. . . ." Here Cummings mimics and mocks the tone of the cynical manipulative self-styled patriot conning a generation of young men to join the "heroic happy dead." Other antiwar satires based on Cummings' World War I experiences include "my sweet old etcetera," "look at this)," and "i sing of Olaf glad and big." Following the outbreak of World War II he applied the same satiric techniques in "plato told," "ygUDuh," and "why must itself up every of a park."

In addition to this articulation of his hatred, Cummings is equally well known for his love poetry, which is both deeply rooted in tradition and surprisingly new. The poem that begins, "since feeling is first/ who pays any attention/ to the syntax of things/ will never wholly kiss you," concludes with the theme of carpe diem (expressed definitively by Catullus, John Donne, and Andrew Marvell): "laugh, leaning back in my arms/ for life's not a paragraph/ And death

i think is no parenthesis." Another poem with the same theme but with a more colloquial tone begins, "(ponder, darling, these busted statues."

Many of Cummings' love poems are addressed to his "lady," as in the Provençal tradition and in Dante. The last poem in his collection of 1926, a sonnet, contrasts her inexpressible beauty with his poor verses: "if i have made,my lady,intricate/ imperfect various things chiefly which wrong/ your eyes. . . ." He also wrote frankly erotic love poems, such as "my girl's tall with hard long eyes," and "i like my body when it is with your."

The common basis of Cummings' poems of hate and love is a unified poetic vision, a philosophy so intensely felt that it must be expressed in the highly charged language of poetry, rather than in the remote and analytic abstractions of philosophy per se. The heart of his vision is a mystical reverence for the wholeness and immediacy of life. He seeks to open the eternal dimension in the present moment—"to see a World in a Grain of Sand and a Heaven in a Wild Flower," as William Blake said. This would be our natural mode of life except that we are mentally conditioned into ·accepting an inauthentic reality; instead of a world, we habitually haunt an "unworld," a "colossal hoax of clocks and calendars." Cummings' anger at the perpetrators of this unworld is expressed in his satirical poems; and his celebration of love is a way of self-transcendence. His poems also celebrate moments of full awareness, when he feels wholly alive to the world, as in these lines: "the hours rise up putting off stars and it is/ dawn/ into the street of the sky light walks scattering poems." Since ordinary language belongs to the one-dimensional unworld, Cummings seeks to renew language by the discovery of new meanings and usages for old words. In *The Enormous Room* (1922) he speaks of a fully alive individual as an "IS"; and a well known early poem begins, "Spring is like a perhaps hand."

From 1921 to 1923 Cummings lived in Europe, mostly in Paris, painting by day and writing by night. In 1923 he moved to 4 Patchin Place in Greenwich Village, which remained his home for the rest of his life. Cummings married Elaine Orr, on Mar. 17, 1924, but they were divorced in December of the same year. She had previously been the wife of his friend Scofield Thayer. She and Cummings had one child, Nancy. On May 1, 1929, Cummings married Anne Barton. In 1927 he had published a play, *Him*, which he dedicated to her and had as its subject the problematical identity of the artist. Its production in 1928 at the Provincetown

Playhouse included a bewildering blend of burlesque and circus spectacles (to which Cummings was always attracted), surrealistically mixed with the story of two lovers, Him and Me. Him conceives of himself as "an artist, a man, a failure."

In the spring of 1931 Cummings spent a month in the Soviet Union. He studied that communist society from an emotional, not ideological, standpoint, which he recorded in a travel diary that he smuggled out of the country. Within this text Cummings built up a philosophical conception of the individual that could exist despite the atmosphere of shabbiness, collectivism, tension, and fear. Published in 1933, the journal was called *Eimi* (I Am). Like *The Enormous Room*, it analyzed a situation of world-historical importance in a highly personal way. He took the organizing metaphor from Dante: the human soul journeying through hell. The style was experimental and obscure, an attempt to capture experiences impinging directly on the author's sensibility. It clearly grew out of Cummings' famous kaleidoscopic conversational style, which so often became a rapid monologue several hours long. However, the political implications of *Eimi* drove a wedge between Cummings and the increasingly leftist intelligentsia of the 1930's.

In 1931 Cummings exhibited his paintings for the first time in New York, at the Society of Painters, Sculptors, and Gravers, and published *CIOPW*, a book of pictures in charcoal, ink, oil, pencil, and watercolor. Although he exhibited through the 1940's, his genius was for poetry. In 1932 Cummings was divorced and married Marion Morehouse, a well-known fashion model, photographer, and actress. The marriage was a success.

During the 1930's Cummings pushed typographical experimentation to its limit, as with "r-p-o-p-h-e-s-s-a-g-r," a poem about the leap of the grasshopper. Norman Friedman claimed that his love poems became "less erotic and more transcendental": for example, "somewhere i have never travelled,gladly beyond." Most significantly, he began to evolve capable and heroic images of the self: "conceive a man, should he have anything," and the great elegy, "my father moved through dooms of love." These later developments continued although he soon relaxed the typographical distortions.

In 1938 Cummings published *Collected Poems*, a comprehensive selection. By 1940 his poetic development was complete, and signs of decline began to appear. The neologisms he had created over twenty years seemed fossilized by

repetition and became a kind of philosophical shorthand. Even good poems such as "one's not half two. It's two are halves of one" and "all ignorance toboggans into know" began to show the abstract complacency of sermons.

Yet during the 1940's and 1950's Cummings received increasing recognition; in 1952 he was appointed Charles Eliot Norton Professor of Poetry at Harvard for one year. He delivered lectures about himself—published as *I: Six Nonlectures* (1953)—which were followed by poetry readings. He interpreted works by himself and others most effectively in a high, clear, incantatory voice. In 1954 his complete poems were published as *Poems 1923–1954*. He died in North Conway, N.H., near Joy Farm, the boyhood summer home that he inherited from his mother.

[Cummings' papers are in the Houghton Library at Harvard University. All of his poetry can be found in E. E. Cummings, *Complete Poetry* (1968). Full descriptive bibliographies of Cummings' writings can be found in George J. Firmage, *E. E. Cummings: A Bibliography* (1960); and Guy L. Rotella, *E. E. Cummings, A Reference Guide* (1979).

Among the many critical writings on Cummings, see Patricia Buchanan Tal-Mason Cline, "The Whole E. E. Cummings," *Twentieth Century Literature*, July 1968; F. W. Dupee and George Stade, eds., *Selected Letters of E. E. Cummings* (1969); Irene Fairley, *E. E. Cummings and Ungrammar: A Study of Syntactic Deviance in His Poems* (1975); and Norman Friedman, *E. E. Cummings: The Art of His Poetry* (1960), and, as ed., *E. E. Cummings: A Collection of Critical Essays* (1972).

Biographical material may be found in Norman Friedman, *E. E. Cummings: The Growth of a Writer* (1964); Richard S. Kennedy, *Dreams in the Mirror* (1979); and Charles Norman, *E. E. Cummings: The Magic-Maker* (1958, rev. 1964). An obituary appeared in the *New York Times*, Sept. 4, 1962.]

PETER MOTT

CURTIZ, MICHAEL (Dec. 24, 1888–Apr. 11, 1962), film director, was born Mihály Kertész in Budapest, Hungary, the son of Ignatz Kertész, a carpenter, and Aranka Kertész, an opera singer. The family was, in Curtiz's words, "very poor" when he was a child. In 1899 Curtiz made his acting debut, playing a bit part in an opera in which his mother also appeared.

Curtiz graduated from Markoczy School in Budapest in 1906, then spent several years with a traveling circus, doing acrobatics, mime, and juggling. In 1910 he enrolled in Budapest's Royal Academy of Theater and Art, where he studied acting, languages, and stage production, completing his work two years later.

After leaving the academy, Curtiz became involved as actor and director in Hungary's nascent film industry. Reliable sources suggest that he directed the first Hungarian feature film, *Ma és holnap* (*Today and Tomorrow*, 1912). In 1913, Curtiz studied the filmmaking methods of the prominent Nordisk Studios in Denmark. After serving briefly in the Austrian artillery early in World War I, he married actress Lucy Doraine (Ilonka Kovács Perényi) in 1915. They had one daughter. Doraine starred in many of the thirty-eight feature films Curtiz directed between 1912 and 1919. The marriage ended in divorce in 1923.

In April 1919, when Béla Kun's government created the world's first nationalized film industry—four months before the Soviet Union— Curtiz was named to the Arts Council, a five-member body that read scripts and decided on the film production schedule. After the Kun regime toppled in August, Curtiz, who had signed a contract in 1918 with a Viennese film company, left Hungary. Between 1919 and 1926, he directed films for Sascha Studios in Austria, one of which, *Die Sklavenkönigin* (1924), released in the United States as *Moon of Israel* (1927), caught the eye of a producer at Warner Brothers, who induced Curtiz to come to the United States and direct.

Going to Hollywood in 1926, Curtiz was part of a great migration of successful and talented European filmmakers—like F. W. Murnau, Ernst Lubitsch, Victor Sjöström, and Mauritz Stiller—who in varying degrees enriched the American film industry. He arrived about a year before Warner Brothers led the industry's transformation to sound films, and his first four films were silent. Six part-talkies and talkies followed between 1927 and 1929. On Dec. 7, 1929, Curtiz married screenwriter Bess Meredyth. They had no children. In 1937 he became an American citizen.

Working for a company famed for its heavy demands on employees, Curtiz was a tyrant on the set and obsessively dedicated to his work. In the 1930's he directed no less than forty-four features. His work in the same decade reveals his versatility: among other genres he made musicals (*Mammy*, 1930), horror films (*Dr. X*, 1932), prison films (*20,000 Years in Sing-Sing*, 1933), detective films (*The Kennel Murder Case*, 1933), social melodramas (*Black Fury*, 1935), newspaper films (*Front Page Woman*, 1935), gangster films (*Angels with Dirty Faces*, 1938), and westerns (*Dodge City*, 1939). To all his projects he brought an energetic film style, commonly characterized by a moving camera, rapid

pace, and, when appropriate, expressionistic lighting, as with the shadow of a condemned man's hand in the final scene of *Angels with Dirty Faces*. Curtiz's most popular movies in the 1930's were his series of films starring Errol Flynn, including *Captain Blood* (1935) and *The Adventures of Robin Hood* (1938).

During the 1940's Curtiz directed several of the films for which he is best remembered: *Yankee Doodle Dandy* (1942), *Casablanca* (1942), and *Mildred Pierce* (1945). The first is a patriotic musical biography of composer George M. Cohan, dominated by the Oscar-winning performance by James Cagney. *Casablanca*, the classic portrayal of romantic renunciation and patriotism during wartime, won four Oscars, including that for best film and Curtiz's one Oscar for best director. *Mildred Pierce* starred Joan Crawford and used a murder-mystery frame to present a woman's climb to financial success and simultaneous failure to win the love of her spoiled daughter. Crawford won an Oscar for her performance.

Curtiz continued his hectic working pace, making twenty-eight more films for Warner Brothers between 1940 and 1954, among them the fascinating, pro-Soviet propaganda film, *Mission to Moscow* (1943), and the evocative re-creation of family life in the 1880's, *Life with Father* (1947).

From 1954 on, Curtiz worked for several studios. Although his second film after leaving Warner Brothers was the popular *White Christmas* (1954), these later years were generally unexceptional ones for Curtiz. As audiences and the studio system itself began to decline, so did Curtiz's career. Nevertheless, he continued directing, completing *The Comancheros* (1961), with John Wayne, only a few months before his death in Los Angeles.

Curtiz never mastered English and was famous in Hollywood for his malapropisms and general misuse of the English language. Once, after failing a second time to receive an Oscar for which he had been nominated, Curtiz lamented being "always a bridesmaid and never a mother." Another time, he told producer Jack Warner he hoped to reach the "pinochle of success" as a director.

Judged from a broad perspective, Curtiz never reached the depth and unity of vision achieved by directors like D. W. Griffith, John Ford, Frank Capra, and Orson Welles. He worked too fast and had too little control over what scripts he would film to reach such unity of vision. He was an archetypal Hollywood professional during the studio era, able to function and thrive within the limitations of that system.

[There is at present no full-length biography of Curtiz. Besides obituaries and sketches in film reference works (many of which are inaccurate or vague about Curtiz's life before 1926), two books are most helpful. István Nemeskürty, *Word and Image: History of the Hungarian Cinema* (1968), provides the most detailed information about Curtiz's place in the Hungarian cinema. Kingsley Canham, *The Hollywood Professionals; Michael Curtiz, Raoul Walsh, Henry Hathaway,* I (1973), although incomplete on Curtiz's pre-Hollywood career, gives a brief survey and a complete, relatively accurate filmography of his American films.]

CHARLES MALAND

DALE, CHESTER (May 3, 1883–Dec. 16, 1962), investment banker and art collector, was born in New York City, the son of Thomas W. Dale, a department store salesman, and Jane Roberts. He grew up in modest but comfortable circumstances. He briefly attended Peekskill (N.Y.) Military Academy but left before graduating. Still in his mid-teens, Dale got a job as an office boy on Wall Street, working twelve hours a day for five dollars a week. Eventually, he became a runner for the firm of F. J. Lisman, which specialized in railroad securities and other corporate bonds. Dale studied intricate mortgage situations and tried his hand in the market. By about 1904, he was trading on his own with a desk at Pollock and Vaughan. In 1909 he went into business with a friend, William C. Langley, specializing in railroad mortgages and utilities. In 1918 he became a member of the New York Stock Exchange. He consolidated power companies and sold their stocks and bonds to the public. These utilities made him wealthy. Dale retired from W. C. Langley and Company in 1935. Dale married Maud Murray on Apr. 28, 1911, a few weeks after her divorce from his friend Frederick M. Thompson. The Dales had no children and led an active social life, which was recorded in detail by the New York press.

Maud Dale had studied painting and, at her suggestion, they began to collect American paintings. Among others, they enjoyed the work of Benjamin West, Mary Cassatt, and Guy Pène du Bois. A favorite painter at this time was their neighbor George Bellows. After World War I the Dales traveled regularly to Europe, and their collection began to include earlier European artists, impressionists, and contemporary French painters. In the early 1930's Dale became a partner in the Galerie Georges Petit in Paris, thus gaining the advantage of being able to bid on paintings before their availability became generally known. Although guided to some extent by Parisian art dealers, the Dales usually bought paintings selected by Maud Dale. Dale frequently remarked that she had the knowledge and he the acquisitiveness. He enjoyed bargaining for the works and was proud of their increasing market value; but he also loved the paintings as if they were his children.

Dale was a peppery, ebullient, and impetuous person. He was a heavy drinker and astonished friends and acquaintances with his rough vocabulary. He was a sports enthusiast (having at one time been a welterweight boxer) and an avid fire buff, proud of his honorary membership in a local hook-and-ladder company of the New York City Fire Department. The Dales lived apart for some years before Maud's death in 1953. On May 27, 1954, at the age of seventy-one, Dale married Mary Towar Bullard, who had been Maud Dale's secretary for almost a quarter of a century.

"Chesterdale," as both wives referred to him, was a trustee of numerous museums, including the Metropolitan Museum of Art (1952–1962), the Museum of Modern Art in New York (1929–1931), the Art Institute of Chicago (1943–1952), the Philadelphia Museum of Art (1943–1956), and the National Gallery of Art in Washington, D.C. (1943–1955). Of the last named, he was president of the board from 1955 until his death. He lent large portions of his collection to the Art Institute of Chicago and the Philadelphia Museum of Art in the 1940's— with the apparent understanding that the museums would eventually receive the art by bequest. But in 1951 he suddenly withdrew the paintings from both institutions and lent them to the National Gallery, although even then he constantly threatened to donate the works elsewhere. Only after Dale's death in New York City was it known that the National Gallery would be the repository of the bulk of his vast collection.

A highly personal collection somewhat uneven in quality, the Dale Collection contains many superb examples of art, including works by the old masters (Tintoretto, El Greco, Rubens), bought partly to explain later works. The Dales' American paintings, on the whole, do not measure up to the extraordinary quality of the works by impressionists, postimpressionists, and the so-called School of Paris. Two outstanding works are Manet's *Old Musician* (1862) and Picasso's *Family of Saltimbanques* (1905). These two paintings, the largest in the collection, bear an artistic relationship as well as a psychological affinity to each other.

The nine rooms devoted to the Chester Dale Collection at the National Gallery contain works by Corot, Cézanne, Degas, Monet, Renoir, Toulouse-Lautrec, and van Gogh. Works by twentieth-century artists such as Braque, Matisse, Modigliani, and Picasso are on view in the modern East Wing. Salvador Dali's *The Sacrament of the Last Supper* (1955) was among the first paintings by a living artist to be hung in the museum, and Renoir's *Girl with a Watering Can* (1870) is one of the most popular paintings in the National Gallery.

[A collection of unpublished correspondence, scrapbooks, and other memorabilia of Chester Dale is stored in the Archives of American Art in Washington, D.C. Dale wrote "The Golden Century of French Art," *New York Times Magazine*, May 17, 1942.

Articles about Dale and his collection are Henry McBride, "The Chester Dale Collection at New York," *Formes*, April 1931; Murdock Pendleton, "Ambassador to Art," *Esquire*, February 1938; "French Impressionists in America," *Life*, Oct. 10, 1938; Henry McBride, "Chesterdale's Way," *Art News*, December 1952; Aline B. Saarinen, "New Regime at the National Gallery," *New York Times Magazine*, May 6, 1956; Geoffrey T. Hellman, "Custodian," *New Yorker*, Oct. 25, 1958; obituary, *New York Times*, Dec. 18, 1962; Neil MacNeil, "Chester Dale," *McCall's*, November 1963; H. Lester Cooke, "A Plunger in the Market," *Art in America*, April 1965; "For the People," *Newsweek*, May 10, 1965; John Walker, "The Most Unlikely Collector," *Self-Portrait with Donors* (1969); and John Walker, *National Gallery of Art, Washington, D.C.* (1963, revised 1976).

The most comprehensive publications specifically about the collection are Maud Dale's *Before Manet to Modigliani in the Chester Dale Collection* (1929) and "French Art in the Chester Dale Collection," *Art News*, Apr. 27, 1929; *Eighteenth and Nineteenth Century Paintings and Sculpture of the French School in the Chester Dale Collection* (1953, revised 1965), *Twentieth Century Paintings and Sculpture of the French School in the Chester Dale Collection* (1953, revised 1965), and *Paintings Other than French in the Chester Dale Collection* (1965)—all from the National Gallery. One of the few reserved evaluations of the collection is by Alfred Frankfurter, "How Great Is the Dale Collection?" *Art News*, May 1965.

Portraits of Chester Dale by George Bellows (1924), Jean Lurçat (1938), and Diego Rivera (1945) are in the National Gallery. The Metropolitan Museum owns Guy Pène du Bois's double portrait, *Mr. and Mrs. Chester Dale Dining Out*, of the mid-1920's.]

ELLEN B. HIRSCHLAND

DANDRIDGE, DOROTHY JEAN (Nov. 9, 1922–Sept. 8, 1965), singer and actress, was born in Cleveland, Ohio, the daughter of Cyril Dandridge, a laborer, and Ruby Butler. She was black-African and white-English on her father's side and Jamaican and Mexican on her mother's side—a mixture to which she attributed both her alluring looks and her somewhat schizoid black-white identity. Barely knowing her father, she was raised by her mother, a minor stage, film, and television actress. At an early age Dorothy appeared with her older sister Vivian as "The Wonder Kids," singing and dancing at Baptist gatherings around the country. Eventually they reached Los Angeles, where Dorothy had a few years of schooling. She appeared as an extra in her first film, *A Day at the Races*, with the Marx Brothers, in 1937. The sisters preferred live performance, and with Etta Jones they appeared as the Dandridge Sisters, both on Broadway, in *Swingin' the Dream* (1939), and in nightclubs, with Jimmy Lunceford's band. The Dandridge Sisters also appeared at the Cotton Club in Harlem, billed with such notables as Duke Ellington and Bill Robinson. They often performed with the Nicholas Brothers, a highly acclaimed dance duo. When in 1944, Dandridge married Harold Nicholas, she abandoned show business.

A year later, their only child, Harolyn, was born; had she been healthy Dandridge's career might have ended. But the little girl was severely retarded, a condition with which Dandridge was never entirely reconciled and which contributed to the Nicholases' divorce in 1950 or 1951. Dandridge then resumed her career, taking acting lessons and accepting a sequence of increasingly lucrative nightclub engagements. With the help of her teacher and arranger, Phil Moore, and her agent, Earl Mills, she exploited her sultry glamour and her melodious singing voice to become more and more of a sensation on the nightclub circuit. Her success led to a renewal of her film career.

Dandridge's most important film was Otto Preminger's *Carmen Jones* (1954), a close copy of Oscar Hammerstein's Broadway success of the previous decade—a resetting of Bizet's *Carmen* in black America. Although the film now seems like a tawdry exploitation of black stereotypes, it was a great success. Dandridge's Carmen was a special sensation, winning her an Academy Award nomination for best actress. Although she lost the award to Grace Kelly, she was the third black actress—after Hattie McDaniel and Ethel Waters—to win a nomination and the first to be cited for a leading role.

But Dandridge soon found that there were strict limits to her success. Roles for black actresses in the 1950's were still more or less confined to tramps, maids, or exotic island goddesses. The all-black film aimed at the all-black film house was a thing of the past, yet depiction of black-white relationships remained a strained and questionable matter. In Dandridge's later films—many of them made in England—she appeared frequently as a temptress vaguely involved with a white man (the association always carefully underplayed). Only in *Island in the Sun* (1957) was her interracial romance allowed a happy ending, and that film is a sorry exercise in Hollywood timidity. *Porgy and Bess* (1959), Samuel Goldwyn's bungled filming of the Gershwin-Heyward folk opera, was denounced as exploitive by the black community. Dandridge was criticized for appearing as Bess, still another role that confined her to the stereotype. Ironically, her singing voice—a large part of her appeal—was replaced by dubbing, as it had been in *Carmen Jones.*

With no challenging roles, Dandridge found her career virtually at a dead end. Simultaneously in private life she seemed to be playing out the very role she had been confined to in films. Never fully accepted by the white film establishment, having been relegated to "tragic mulatto" roles (a theatrical stereotype dating from the nineteenth century), she tried unsuccessfully to live the life of a white star. Her second marriage, on June 22, 1959, to Jack Denison, a white nightclub owner, ended in divorce in 1963. Professionally, Dandridge was less and less sought after, and bad investments plunged her into debt. Although she was planning a nightclub tour that might have brought her back to public attention just as interest in black artists was surging, her debts, declining career, failed marriages, and the steady deterioration of her daughter deepened her depression. She was found dead in her apartment in West Hollywood, Calif. The cause of death was originally reported to be an embolism; later it was found to be an overdose of Tofranil, presumed deliberate.

Upon viewing Dandridge's movies today, one is not likely to acclaim her as an actress; but the insipidity of her roles must be taken into consideration. Her singing voice was rarely recorded, and her voice alone, in any case, cannot convey her allure. Rather, Dandridge's significance is symbolic. A victim of Hollywood's narrow conceptions of black people, she was confined most rigidly to stereotypes and, tragically, came to embody one of them herself. In the 1950's, when a handful of performers struggled against stereotypes imposed on blacks

by the film studios, Dandridge symbolized the costs of that struggle. Whatever her stature as an artist, her importance as a symbol is unquestioned.

[Dandridge's autobiography, *Everything and Nothing* (1970), was coauthored with Earl Conrad, who claimed to have taken Dandridge's own words on tapes. The best clipping file is in the Billy Rose Theatre Collection of the New York Public Library at Lincoln Center. A full list of screen credits for Dandridge can be found in John T. Weaver's *Forty Years of Screen Credits, 1929–1969,* I (1970). Mel Schuster's *Motion Picture Performers* (1971) lists periodical articles of the years up to 1969. Eileen Landay's *Black Film Stars* (1973) contains excellent still photographs from the films. The Rodgers and Hammerstein Library of Recorded Sound, Lincoln Center, New York, has one Dandridge recording.]

JOHN D. SHOUT

DARLING, JAY NORWOOD ("DING") (Oct. 21, 1876–Feb. 12, 1962), cartoonist and conservationist, was born in Norwood, Mich., the son of the Reverend Marcellus Warner Darling, a Civil War veteran and Methodist minister, and of Clara Woolson. The family moved about in Michigan and Indiana, and in 1886 from Elkhart, Ind., to Sioux City, Iowa.

As a schoolboy Darling carried a sketch pad and pencil even though in the strict Darling home drawing was considered a sinful waste of time. During summers he worked as a farmhand and sometimes explored the Missouri River country. The abundant vegetation and diverse wildlife of the region led to his early interest in the protection of natural resources. He also herded cattle, often sleeping under the stars.

At Yankton College in Yankton, S.D., which he entered in 1894, Darling assembled, played on, and captained the first football team. But a prank involving the college president's horse and buggy resulted in his expulsion after one year. In 1896 he enrolled at Beloit College in Beloit, Wis., with the intention of becoming a doctor. His musical talent, both vocal and instrumental, enabled him to meet most of his college costs. Indeed, Darling's extracurricular activities were so all-encompassing that he was suspended for failing grades. In his junior year (1897–1898), as yearbook art director, he lampooned the dignified faculty as a line of chorus girls. According to college records he was again suspended, this time for a year, "on account of irregularities in attendance and poor scholarship." He had signed the "chorus line" drawings "Ding," the name by which he was known for the rest of his life.

Prior to his return to Beloit in 1899 for graduation in 1900, Darling sang on a Chautauqua circuit, traversed the wilds of Florida, worked as a cowhand, and was briefly a reporter on the *Sioux City Tribune*. To accumulate funds for medical school, he returned to Sioux City as a reporter for the *Journal* in 1900, a job that exposed him to the violence of river life in the raw. When he was prevented from photographing a newsworthy lawyer, Darling produced a sketch that was used with the article. The reaction was so favorable that he was assigned to draw a series called "Local Snapshots," depicting Sioux City notables.

For six years Darling combined drawing with reporting. His first conservation sketch supported the proposal for a forestry service advanced by President Theodore Roosevelt. By now his talents were being noticed throughout Iowa. On Oct. 31, 1906, he married Genevieve Pendleton; they had two children. While on his honeymoon Darling received a telegram inviting him to be the cartoonist of the *Register and Leader* in Des Moines. He survived heavy criticism of his first *Register* cartoon, which inappropriately made a monk smoking a "soft coal" pipe responsible for Des Moines's polluted air. He created two widely popular characters, the Iowa farmer Uncle John Iowa and the collegian Alonzo Applegate.

Aside from 1911–1913, when Darling moved to New York City to work for the *New York Globe* syndicate, Des Moines was his home. He found the Atlantic coast too far from the heartland that was his inspiration.

After a serious illness he lost the use of his right arm in 1914–1916, but he taught himself to draw with his left hand. The nerve problem was then surgically corrected.

In 1917 the *New York Tribune* syndicate began to distribute Darling's work nationally, with the result that his frequently humorous, often amazingly detailed, always unmistakable work eventually appeared in some 130 newspapers. Darling also drew for *Collier's Weekly*. National syndication made him both a millionaire and the foremost political cartoonist of his time, as a poll in *Editor and Publisher* proclaimed. In politics he was generally conservative, and attended the Republican National Convention in 1932 as a Platform Committee delegate. A strong admirer of Herbert Hoover, Darling defended him against his critics. Hoover was depicted as an orphan who overcame that handicap in Darling's first Pulitzer Prize cartoon, which appeared May 6, 1923. His second Pulitzer Prize, awarded in 1943, was for

a cartoon showing the national capitol covered by mountains of paperwork. Ding believed the latter choice a poor one and said so.

His most famous drawings, somewhat similar, were "Gone to Join the Mysterious Caravan" (Jan. 11, 1917), which marked the death of Iowa native Buffalo Bill Cody, and "The Long, Long Trail" (Jan. 7, 1919), which showed his friend Rough Rider Teddy Roosevelt waving farewell. The latter cartoon, a favorite of the Roosevelt family, was issued in millions of copies, and reproduced in bronze for the Hotel Roosevelt in New York City.

Darling was proud that his work appeared on the *Register*'s front page. His freedom at the daily was virtually unlimited—he might draw on almost any subject and take any position. Sometimes, however, he was in conflict with the policy of the *Register*, of which he became a director. He campaigned for preparedness in 1916, backed the League of Nations, disdained the short workweek, and scourged industrial polluters of streams, eroders of land, and unrestrained hunters and fishermen.

A trip to the Soviet Union, in 1931, at Joseph Stalin's invitation, was recounted in a book of friendly comment and sketches, *Ding Goes to Russia* (1932). He also produced a "trailer travelogue," *The Cruise of the Bouncing Betsy* (1937).

In the preservation of land and wildlife, Darling was an out-in-front activist. His official participation in conservation began when he was appointed to the Iowa Fish and Game Commission, which developed a twenty-five-year state park and lake improvement program. In Des Moines he served on the city park board and helped create the city's art center. Darling opposed Franklin D. Roosevelt in 1932 and caricatured the New Deal, yet in January 1934, Roosevelt appointed him to a committee to propose a migratory waterfowl plan. Later that year Darling was invited by Secretary of Agriculture Henry A. Wallace to be chief of the U.S. Bureau of Biological Survey. He accepted, exchanging an income of $100,000 per year for an $8,000 salary. For twenty months he worked for the nation's wildlife as no one in Washington before him. He compiled and distributed the facts about waterfowl decline, and crusaded for funds to enlarge and increase game refuges. Called the "best friend ducks ever had," Darling designed the first waterfowl postage stamp and promoted its sale. He campaigned for a federation of the many small conservation groups; this led to his election as the first president of the National Wildlife Federation in

1936. He gave special attention to Captiva Island, Fla., where he maintained a winter home, and to adjacent Sanibel Island. After his death the Sanibel Wildlife Refuge was renamed in his honor (1967).

In his conservation work Darling insisted on the application of scientific methods whether dealing with Congress, the bureaucracy, or the White House. Feeling that he had accomplished as much as he could, he resigned in November 1935 and resumed daily cartooning. Darling also wrote, collected his cartoons, and became involved in such conservation efforts as the designation and protection of campsites on the Lewis and Clark Trail. He was awarded the Audubon Medal in 1960.

Darling resigned from the *Register* in 1949. His last years were so clouded by sickness (he suffered from arthritis, cataracts, and deafness) that he wished "the Great Referee would blow the whistle on me." Through secretarial help he kept up with his reading and correspondence until a series of strokes in 1961 and 1962. He died in Des Moines.

Darling's last cartoon appeared on the *Register*'s front page the morning after his death. Drawn in 1958, when he was alarmed into being "prepared," it showed his littered studio, empty chair and drawing board, fishing rods and decoy ducks, the hazy cartoonist waving farewell at the door. His caption was " 'Bye Now—It's Been Wonderful Knowing You."

Darling gave his cartoon collection to the University of Iowa, although he believed that "yesterday's cartoons" were "cold potatoes." He knew the shortcomings of his profession. Seeking to establish a news bureau for the conservation movement, he said that most of the press preferred "Hollywood and glamour girls. Don't expect too much from newspapers, although I say it with shame." Nor was he reassured by the rank and file: "I shudder when I recall how the long-eared, sleep-walking public has disregarded the screeching siren's warning of dangers ahead, while inflationary policies, political debauchery and smothering taxation carry our beloved country to the brink of national bankruptcy just as sure as God made little red apples."

[Collections of Darling's cartoons are at the University of Iowa, Iowa State University, and Drake University. Biographies are John Henry, *Ding's Half Century* (1962); and David L. Lendt, *Ding: The Life of Jay Norwood Darling* (1979). Also see William Murrell, *A History of American Graphic Humor* (1938); Tom Mahoney, "How to Be a Cartoonist," *Saturday Evening Post,* Oct. 19, 1940, repr. in J. E. Drewry, ed., *More Post Biographies* (1947); Stephen Hess and Milton Kaplan, *The Ungentlemanly Art* (1968); and George Mills, Des Moines *Register,* Apr. 22, 1979. Obituaries are in the *Des Moines Tribune,* Feb. 12, 1962; and the Des Moines *Register* and the *New York Times,* Feb. 13, 1962.]

                                    IRVING DILLIARD

DAVIES, MARION CECILIA (Jan. 3, 1897–Sept. 22, 1961), stage and film actress, was born in Brooklyn, N.Y., the daughter of Bernard J. Douras, a lawyer, and Rose Reilly. She attended Public School 93 and Convent of the Sacred Heart at Hastings-on-Hudson, N.Y., before following her three older sisters onto the stage. Blonde, graceful, and beautiful, with an intriguing stutter, she changed her name from Douras to Davies. She was a chorus girl in the revue *Stop! Look! Listen!* (1915) when she met the publishing magnate William Randolph Hearst. The story that he attended the 1916 *Ziegfeld Follies,* in which she also appeared, every night for eight weeks just to gaze at her may be apocryphal, but he was verifiably smitten for the rest of his life.

Hearst was thirty-four years Davies' senior. His wife, the former showgirl Millicent Willson, refused him a divorce. Davies, however, was then not averse to an arrangement without marriage. Hearst planned to make her the nation's leading screen actress and himself the foremost impresario. He had her trained by experts in poise and expression, and starred her in films shot at his upper Manhattan lot. The appointment of her father as a city magistrate was arranged through Hearst's influence with the mayor, and Hearst often aided the entire Douras family.

Davies' first feature picture, *Cecilia of the Pink Roses* (1918), was a teary triviality hailed in headlines by the Hearst press but dismissed by other critics. She scored a success in the movie *When Knighthood Was in Flower* (1922) and again in *Little Old New York* (1923) and *Janice Meredith* (1924). Louella Parsons led the Hearst writers in the required adulation, but independent reviewers recognized Davies' talent. She also appeared in many expensive failures. To a friend who remarked, "There's money in the movies," Hearst joked, "Yes, mine." The skilled scenarist Frances Marion, lured by a $2,000-a-week salary, urged that Davies' gift for light comedy be exploited, but Hearst felt this an underestimation of her talents. Indeed, he saw her as Mary Pickford's successor.

Hearst had established a modus vivendi with his wife, continuing to act the paterfamilias as he vainly sought political office. In 1924 he moved his film operations to Culver City, Calif., in a deal with Metro-Goldwyn-Mayer (MGM). Davies became chatelaine of his vast, twin-towered castle at San Simeon. Guests there included reigning screen idols, politicians, film executives, and other personages ranging from Calvin Coolidge to Winston Churchill and George Bernard Shaw. The abstemious Hearst kept his parties temperate, although the fun-loving Davies, who liked a nip, kept gin in the ladies' room. Thirty-five cars were at her disposal, and it cost $6,000 a day to run the castle when it was filled with guests. The grandeur there was unparalleled. But a Los Angeles evangelist kept assailing the Hearst-Davies relationship, a few of the straitlaced refused to visit San Simeon, and occasionally Davies grew bitter over her irregular status.

A hard worker who was paid $10,000 a week, Davies served champagne between takes in her fourteen-room "bungalow" on the MGM lot. Hearst also built her the fifty-five-room Ocean House on the beach at Santa Monica, where twelve Hearst-commissioned portraits of Davies in the foremost of her roles in more than forty films were hung. Comparisons with such women as Madame de Pompadour missed the mark, since no mistress in history had enjoyed such splendor.

When Davies failed to get the coveted lead role in *The Barretts of Wimpole Street*, Norma Shearer, who won the part, was banished from mention in all Hearst publications. Among Davies' later pictures were *Lights of Old Broadway* (1925), *Zander the Great* (1925), *Beverly of Graustark* (1926), *The Red Mill* (1927), and *Quality Street* (1927). Although some were highly praised, none were of lasting distinction. Most were money-losers.

Shrewdly investing in real estate, Davies was rich when Hearst neared financial ruin in the late 1930's. She lent him $1 million. Neither was pleased by Orson Welles's *Citizen Kane* (1941), a wounding parody of her life with Hearst. Because of its scornful characterization of Susan Alexander (supposed to represent Davies), it fed the fiction that she was merely the talentless plaything of a newspaper mogul. The Hearst press refused to review the film, but it went on to the cinema glory denied Davies.

Davies sustained Hearst in his last, failing years and was with him when he died in her Beverly Hills home in 1951. She was not invited to his funeral. Millicent Hearst, still bearing the name Davies had hoped to take, was there. Perhaps resentment hastened Davies' marriage on Oct. 31, 1951, to Captain Horace G. Brown, Jr., a merchant marine officer. The marriage was stormy. Her weakness for liquor occasionally worsted her.

Davies was applauded for her long service as president of the Motion Picture Relief Fund and many other charities. In 1957 she donated $1.5 million for a children's hospital in Los Angeles. She died in Hollywood.

[The only full-length biography is Fred Lawrence Guiles, *Marion Davies* (1972). Some details of her life can be found in her *The Times We Had* (1975). Also see Bosley Crowther, *Hollywood Rajah* (1960); and W. A. Swanberg, *Citizen Hearst* (1961). An obituary is in the *New York Times*, Sept. 24, 1961.]
                                          W. A. SWANBERG

DAVIS, ARTHUR VINING (May 30, 1867– Nov. 17, 1962), industrialist and philanthropist, was born in Sharon, Mass., the son of Perley B. Davis, a Congregational minister, and Mary Frances. After attending school at Hyde Park, Mass., and Roxbury Latin School in Boston, Davis entered Amherst College, graduating in 1888. As a result of his father's friendship with a former parishioner, Alfred E. Hunt, founder of the Pittsburgh Reduction Company that made aluminum, Davis obtained a job with that company. Although aluminum's favorable characteristics as an industrial metal had been known for several decades, it was expensive to manufacture; Hunt's company hoped to capitalize on Charles Martin Hall's experiments to produce the metal at low cost. Davis thus joined a firm that was adventurous. The work required a handyman's disposition—overalls and a twelve-hour day—for the manufacturing process was a continuous one. Davis and Hall became close associates during the experimental phase, and on Thanksgiving Day of 1888 they poured the first commercial aluminum.

Davis soon became general manager of the firm and a director in 1892. He continued as general manager when the firm became the Aluminum Company of America (Alcoa) in 1907; he became president in 1910 and chairman of the board in 1928. Although by this time aluminum was more widely known, it was by no means a household word. Davis' major responsibility was to promote the manufacturing and selling of quality aluminum products: Alcoa's Wear-Ever line of cookware was sold by college students recruited each spring; Alcoa made aluminum wire as an electrical conductor when copper-wire producers refused to do so; and aluminum horseshoes, bicycles, covers for bottles, canteens, and ships, and the Wright Brothers' airplane engine were evidence of the metal's versatility.

But these years were also highlighted by confrontations with the government over antitrust issues. In 1912 the Justice Department charged Alcoa with three counts of violation of the antitrust laws; within a few weeks the company signed a consent decree. In 1922 the company underwent investigation by the Federal Trade Commission, but the case was dismissed in 1930. In 1937 the Justice Department began an extensive antitrust case against Alcoa. This one was conspicuous for its duration and for Davis' extraordinary performance on the witness stand. Davis was the star witness, testifying for six weeks and contributing over two thousand pages of testimony. In dismissing the petition of the Justice Department, the trial judge praised Davis, who also drew accolades from his Alcoa colleagues for having personally won the company's case.

Awarded the Presidential Certificate of Merit for ensuring that the government had adequate supplies of aluminum in World War II, Davis built Alcoa into an industrial giant. He also amassed great wealth as the company's largest stockholder, thereby provoking continued personal confrontation with Washington. At the time of his retirement from Alcoa in 1957, he was listed as the third-richest individual in the world.

Because Davis cherished privacy, his personal success was not accompanied by much exposure to the media about his business or private life. He did not usually fare well in his rare interviews. "I've had to work hard all my life," he asserted to a reporter. "I've had to work sixteen hours a day to make a good living. Do you work sixteen hours a day?" *Time* magazine referred to Davis as a "terrible-tempered tycoon . . . ruling [Alcoa] with desk-thumping autocracy," a view that was not atypical in the press at large.

Davis married Florence Holmes in 1896. She died in 1908. In March 1912 he married Elizabeth Hawkins Weiman, who died in 1933. He had no children. Before retiring from Alcoa, Davis began a second career by investing primarily in the Bahamas and Florida. The investments included extensive real estate holdings in the Miami area (estimated at one-eighth of Dade County) and on Cuba's Isle of Pines, as well as ownership or control of some thirty Florida enterprises ranging from dairy farms to resort hotels. The flurry and size of the investments resulted in considerable publicity and additional controversy with the government, this time with the Securities and Exchange Commission.

Davis died in Miami, leaving a $400-million estate. Only a small portion of his wealth went to individuals. The majority went to a trust he had established in 1952 and to Arvida, a North Canadian model town he had founded for working families. The Davis foundations provide financial assistance to educational, religious, cultural, and scientific institutions.

[There is no standard work on Davis, but information can be gleaned from Charles C. Carr, *Alcoa: An American Enterprise* (1952); Junius D. Edwards, *The Immortal Woodshed* (1955); and Charlotte F. Muller, *Light Metals Monopoly* (1968). See also *Architectural Forum*, November 1958; *Fortune*, September 1956; *Look*, Aug. 7, 1956, and *Time*, Nov. 23, 1962. In the *New York Times* see Oct. 28, 1957; Nov. 27, 1962; and especially the obituary, Nov. 18, 1962.]

THOMAS V. DiBACCO

DAVIS, ERNEST R. ("ERNIE") (Dec. 14, 1939–May 18, 1963), first black football player to be awarded the Heisman Trophy, was born in New Salem, Pa. An only child, he said later that he never knew his father, who was separated from his family and died in an accident. Davis lived for his first eleven years with his grandmother in Uniontown, Pa. He then moved to Elmira, N.Y., to rejoin his mother, who had remarried.

Davis was drawn to sports early. He played some baseball and was considered a good basketball player at Elmira Free Academy and later in college. But it was as a football player that he was to achieve fame. On the sandlots and for three years in high school, he played end and running back, setting school records for rushing and points scored, and gaining recognition as a regional and national all-star.

Recruited by many universities, Davis finally chose to attend Syracuse, a ranking football power. Visits from the legendary Jim Brown, the proximity of Syracuse to his home, and the friendship of his high school coach with the Syracuse coach, Ben Schwartzwalder, all played a role in his choice.

After playing on an undefeated freshman team, Davis starred on the 1959 national championship Syracuse varsity and went on to establish school records: total yards gained (3,414), touchdowns (35), points scored (220), and total offense average per play (6.8 yards). He eventually surpassed many of the records of Jim Brown, with whom he was often compared.

At six feet, two inches, and about 210 pounds, Davis was regarded as the complete football player. While best known as a runner (he ran for more than 100 yards a game eleven times), he was also an effective pass receiver, a good blocker, a fine option-play passer (until he injured a shoulder) and, in the absence of the free substitution rule, a good defensive back. He also kicked extra points for the team. A quiet but inspirational leader, he worked tirelessly to improve his skills.

Syracuse ran from a winged-T and an unbalanced line and Davis played either tailback or wingback. From these positions he ran off tackle with the option pitchout, around end on the power sweep, on a reverse from the wing, or received a pass. He had great ability to "cut" up the field and the speed to outdistance the defense.

In the 1961 Liberty Bowl, Davis gained 140 yards and led his team back from a halftime deficit to a 17–14 victory over Miami of Florida. But it was the Syracuse win over Texas in the 1960 Cotton Bowl that best typified his talents. Although injured, he scored two touchdowns, broke open the game early with an improvised eighty-seven-yard run with a pass, and contributed a third-quarter interception that led to another score. He was voted the outstanding back in the game.

The Cotton Bowl game also brought racial issues to the fore. There were claims (and denials) that racial slurs had been aimed at several of Davis's black teammates, charges Davis was to repeat in a television interview. He said at that time that he had not given much thought to the racial problems. Consequently, some saw Davis as a symbol of black passivity. However, others found new appreciation for the black athlete in his dignified and restrained response.

Davis's receipt of the 1961 Heisman Trophy, which is granted to the outstanding college football player in the United States, marked the height of his career. Already selected for All-American honors, he was the recipient of numerous other awards and he became the first black athlete to receive the coveted Heisman award. His close competition with Bob Ferguson of Ohio State, another outstanding black running back, seemed to signal a lifting of the barriers and to make possible similar recognition for other black players.

After receiving the Heisman, Davis was the subject of spirited bidding between the rival professional football leagues. Selected by the Buffalo Bills of the American Football League and recruited by the Canadian League, he was also the first player chosen in the National Football League draft. This latter choice, by the Washington Redskins, caused comment because that team had never before drafted a black player. It was later revealed that there had been a prior agreement whereby Washington traded its rights to Davis to the Cleveland Browns, the team with which he ultimately signed a contract for a reported $80,000.

But Davis never played professional football. He became ill with leukemia in the summer of 1962, while preparing to play in the College All-Star game. Later, after treatment in Cleveland and Bethesda, Md., and with the disease said to be in "a perfect state of remission," he resumed training. This decision, criticized by some doctors, apparently reflected a dispute between the Browns' management and the team coach, Paul Brown, who later said that he had never intended to let Davis play.

The confusion may have developed because the management chose not to make public the full extent of Davis's illness. Davis was finally told he had leukemia in early October. He discussed the situation frankly in a national magazine later that winter. Yet it is uncertain that he ever knew the grim prognosis, for he often told friends that he was planning to resume his football career. He continued to work that winter on a film project for the team and as a salesman for a soft drink firm. After one last trip back East, he reentered Lakeside Hospital, Cleveland, where he died.

Davis, who never married, was by all accounts a cheerful, friendly, and gentle man with great affection for children. He was also noted for his grace and dignity in handling the public attention given a great athlete. Not a gifted student, he worked hard in his studies and graduated from Syracuse in 1962 with a better-than-average academic record. He was well liked on campus and chosen as a senior marshal at the time of his graduation.

Davis may come to be known best as a symbol of the acceptance of the black athlete in intercollegiate sports. But this should not obscure his brilliant record as an athlete or the genuine affection people felt for this good man who tragically died young.

[Most of the limited material on Davis is in the newspapers and magazines. See *New York Times*, Jan. 2, 12, 1960; Nov. 29, Dec. 3, 5, 6, 1961; and Oct. 6, 7, 1962. The obituary and comment appeared in *New York Times* on May 19 and 22, 1963. See also articles in *Ebony*, December 1961; *Saturday Evening Post*, Mar. 30, 1963; and *Sports Illustrated*, May 27, 1963.]

DANIEL R. GILBERT

DAVIS, FRANCIS BREESE, JR. (Sept. 16, 1883–Dec. 22, 1962), business executive, was born at Fort Edward, N.Y., the son of Francis Breese Davis, a farmer, and of Julia Underwood. He graduated from the Academy of Glens Falls (N.Y.) and then worked his way through the Sheffield Scientific School at Yale University by selling supplies to incoming engineering students. He graduated in 1906 with a Ph.B. in engineering. Davis worked briefly in the office of the New Haven, Conn., city engineer at $40 per month and next was employed by the Empire Engineering Corporation on the construction of a portion of the Erie Barge Canal near Fort Edward.

In 1907 Davis joined the maintenance-of-way department of the Philadelphia, Baltimore, and Washington Railroad (controlled by the Pennsylvania Central Railroad). His first job, in Washington, D.C., involved the removal of the old tracks at the Broad Street Station and the transfer of passenger activities to Union Station. Later he was assigned to do sketches of locations where accidents had occurred.

Davis joined the construction engineering department of E. I. du Pont de Nemours and Company in 1909 at its Belin black powder plant near Noosic, Pa. Two years later he was transferred to Du Pont's Wilmington, Del., headquarters as a division engineer in charge of black powder engineering. He also played a role in the construction of plants at Du Pont, Wash., and Augusta, Colo. Davis married Jean Reybold on Apr. 16, 1913; they had one daughter. That same year he was appointed superintendent of the sporting powder division of the black powder operating department. With the outbreak of World War I, Davis directed the building of a guncotton plant at Hopewell, N.J., and for several months was in charge of its operations. He next operated a smokeless powder factory at Carney's Point, N.J. Later he was an assistant to the engineer in charge of the construction of a munitions plant at Old Hickory, Tenn.

After the war Davis was promoted to vice-president of the Du Pont Chemical Company and put in charge of the disposal of surplus materials and factories that had been built during the war to meet specific military requirements. In 1920 he served briefly with the plastics manufacturing Pyralin division.

In 1918 the Du Ponts acquired a controlling interest in the General Motors Corporation (GM), and Pierre S. du Pont became its president in 1920. The following year Davis was made assistant general manager in charge of manufacture and sales of products at the GM

Saginaw, Mich., plant. In 1923 he returned to the Pyralin division as general manager, and in 1925 was named president of the recently acquired Viscoloid Company (now Du Pont Viscoloid Company). While continuing as president of this subsidiary, Davis also served as president of Celastic Corporation, another Du Pont subsidiary. In 1928, under Davis' direction, Du Pont Viscoloid joined with Pittsburgh Plate Glass Company to form Pittsburgh Safety Glass Corporation, which manufactured safety glass for automobile windows. Davis was the first chairman of the board of directors of the new company.

It was common for well-regarded Du Pont executives to be moved to companies in which Du Pont had investments. In January 1929, Davis was elected president and chairman of the board of United States Rubber Company, controlled since 1927 by Du Pont. The company was on the verge of bankruptcy when Davis took the helm. He immediately installed the Du Pont form of decentralized operating structure and Du Pont-like centralized financial and statistical control. He disposed of unprofitable plants and product lines, increased productivity, and modernized operating techniques. Despite the Great Depression, in three years he reduced the company's funded debt from $130 million to $90 million. By 1935 the company showed a profit, the first in seven years.

Davis placed a high priority on the development of new products. He authorized a sizable increase in research expenditures that resulted in the development of foam rubber cushioning material in 1934, the manufacture of elastic fiber (with the trade name Lastex), and the development of rayon cord used to manufacture stronger and more durable tires in 1938. Experimentation with synthetic rubber enabled the company to begin construction of synthetic rubber plants immediately after the Japanese invasion of Indonesia cut off America's primary source of natural rubber. Soon U.S. Rubber had three synthetic rubber plants in operation.

In 1942 Davis resigned as president but remained chairman of the board and chief executive officer. By 1949, when he retired as chairman, net sales topped $500 million and the company was manufacturing more than 30,000 products ranging from automobile tires to footwear, golf balls, yarns, conveyor belts, hoses, adhesives, and myriad specialized chemicals, rubbers, plastics, and resins.

Davis continued to serve on the finance committee of the board of directors until 1959, and thereafter was an advisory director until his death. In his retirement years he raised cattle and ponies in South Carolina and owned three GM automobile dealerships in that state. He died at Savannah, Ga.

[See Glenn D. Babcock, *History of the United States Rubber Co.* (1966); Alfred D. Chandler and Stephen Salsbury, *Pierre S. Du Pont and the Making of the Modern Corporation* (1971); Gerald C. Zilg, *Du Pont: Behind the Nylon Curtain* (1974). Also see "U.S. Rubber, I, The Corporate State," *Fortune,* Feb. 1934. An obituary is in the *Washington Post,* Dec. 23, 1962.]

STEPHEN D. BODAYLA

DAVIS, STUART (Dec. 7, 1894–June 24, 1964), artist, was born in Philadelphia, Pa., the son of Edward Wyatt Davis, an artist who was art editor of the *Philadelphia Press,* and of Helen Stuart Foulke, a sculptor. Both his parents had studied under Thomas Anschutz at the Pennsylvania Academy of Fine Arts.

In 1901 the family moved to East Orange, N.J., because Edward Davis had joined the *Newark Evening News* as art editor and cartoonist. When young Davis was sixteen, he began to commute to New York City to study with the painter Robert Henri. At Henri's school he formed a close friendship with Glenn O. Coleman. Together they followed Henri's encouragement to get out in the streets and paint the life of the city. In sharp contrast with the usual academic studio training of the time, this requirement led to direct observation of the world of forms and colors. In Davis' case it also led to an appreciation of the jazz that he heard in the honky-tonks of Manhattan and Hoboken and that became a lifelong passion reflected in certain staccato rhythms in his later painting.

From 1912 to 1916, Davis produced covers and drawings for the leftist magazine *The Masses.* The political nature of this work was balanced by his profound dedication to the principles of art and art's demands. Although he was only nineteen at the time of the Armory Show of 1913, five of his watercolors were exhibited beside the best of the European masters of impressionism and cubism as well as with the most well established American artists. The art of the European postimpressionists and cubists in the Armory Show became a challenge to Davis. "I was," he wrote in his autobiography in 1945, "enormously excited by the show." He "responded particularly to Gauguin, van Gogh and Matisse, because the broad generalization of form and the non-imitative use of color were already practices within my own experience

. . . and I resolved that I would quite definitely have to become a *modern* artist."

By the early 1920's Davis had begun to work the principles of cubism into a personal style that he developed during the rest of his life. He committed himself to the study of pictorial structure and to the definition of what he called "color-shapes." Although he never entirely abandoned inspirational sources in his visual experiences of landscape and real objects, his art from this time forward became increasingly abstract. In 1928, for example, Davis nailed an eggbeater, a fan, and a glove to a table and proceeded doggedly to draw and paint this still life over and over again. The resulting cubist-influenced *Eggbeater* series is witness to his determination to make a work of art rather than a mere representation of nature as it appears.

Later that year, having sold a number of paintings to the Whitney Studio Club (the forerunner of the Whitney Museum of American Art), Davis went to Paris. The paintings produced during this year-long sabbatical—such as *Place Pasdeloup, Place de Vosges,* and *Rue Vercingetorix*—were primarily abstract urban landscapes. In these charming pictures he translated streets and architecture into flat planes of bright, textured color and symbolically simplified indications of doors, windows, shutters, paving stones, and street lamps. His sojourn in Paris affected him deeply, and there are many references to it in his later paintings. In 1929 he married Bessie Chosak, who died about three years later.

Davis' works of the 1930's are mostly landscapes created by a virtual montage of "color-shapes" and linear suggestions of architectural and natural elements derived in large part from the scenes around Gloucester, Mass., where he spent his summers. His color became more brilliant and cheerful; and while the glistening light and openness of the seacoast undoubtedly were the stimuli, Davis' success in imparting these qualities to his work came from his increasing knowledge of color. He wrote that in his earlier development in the 1920's he had "learned to think of color more or less objectively so that [he] could paint a green tree red without batting an eye. Purple or green faces didn't bother [him] at all. . . . But the ability to think about positional relationships objectively in terms of what they represented [pictorially] took many years." By the end of the 1930's Davis had become a master at composing a painting almost entirely with color alone. In this accomplishment he shares a key place in twentieth-century art with Henri Matisse and Piet Mondrian.

On Oct. 12, 1936, Davis married Roselle Springer, an art student; they had one son. Like many American artists working in the 1930's, Davis was aroused to political activism by the Great Depression and its accompanying social tensions. He helped organize the leftist-oriented Artists' Union in 1934 and the American Artists' Congress in 1936, and edited *ART FRONT.* He also painted two murals for the Works Progress Administration. Ultimately Davis came into ideological conflict with the extreme leftists over the abstractness of his art and his unwillingness to make it serve political rather than aesthetic ends.

Throughout the 1940's and 1950's Davis found an analogy for his art in the emotional clarity and purity of sound in jazz. The paintings of this period are syncopations of color. He had achieved his goal, the creation of a sensuous, rhythmical space through color and shape alone. As his paintings became ostensibly simpler in composition and form, they became more monumental and profound in terms of aesthetic experience. They also became more influential among younger painters, especially the generation that followed the abstract expressionists. One finds traces of Davis in the work of Frank Stella, Robert Indiana, and Ellsworth Kelly. And his "all-over" compositions for the huge mural for the Hall of Communications at the New York World's Fair of 1939, an earlier one (1938) for a Brooklyn housing project (now at Indiana University), and the *Allée* mural at Drake University (1955) influenced the large poured canvases by Jackson Pollock in the early 1950's.

From 1927 to 1962, Davis' one-man shows were held at the Downtown Gallery in New York City. In 1952 he was honored by an exhibition in the American Pavilion at the Venice Biennale. His numerous awards included a John Simon Guggenheim Memorial Foundation fellowship in 1958 and renewed in 1960.

Plagued by cataracts and general ill health during his last decade, Davis nevertheless continued to work in his New York City studio until his death. On Dec. 2, 1964, a postage stamp of his design was issued by the United States Postal Service. The following year a major memorial exhibition was organized and shown by the Smithsonian Institution in Washington, D.C., the Art Institute of Chicago, the Whitney Museum of American Art in New York City, and the University of California at Los Angeles. Davis holds a major position in the history of twentieth-century art.

[Nine microfilmed volumes of Davis' personal scrapbooks and a taped interview are on deposit with the Archives of American Art of the Smithsonian Institution, Washington, D.C., and New York. His autobiography is *Stuart Davis* (1945). Also see James Johnson Sweeney, *Stuart Davis* (1945); H. H. Arnason, *Stuart Davis* (1957), an exhibition catalog; E. C. Goossen, *Stuart Davis* (1959); Smithsonian Institution, *Stuart Davis Memorial Exhibition* (1965); Diane Kelder, ed., *Stuart Davis* (1971); John R. Lane, *Stuart Davis* (1978). An obituary is in the *New York Times,* June 26, 1964.]

E. C. GOOSSEN

DAVIS, WILLIAM HAMMATT (Aug. 29, 1879–Aug. 13, 1964), patent attorney and labor mediator, was born in Bangor, Me., the son of Owen Warren Davis, an engineer and businessman, and of Abigail Gould. He graduated from high school in Bangor in 1896 and then worked for his brother, A. G. Davis, who headed the patent department of General Electric in the District of Columbia. There Davis attended the Corcoran Scientific School and the George Washington University Law School, from which he graduated in 1901. After a year as an examiner in the U.S. Patent Office (1902–1903), Davis joined Betts, Betts, Sheffield and Betts, the premier patent law firm in New York City. He remained there until 1906, when he joined Pennie and Goldsborough (later Pennie, Davis, Marvin and Edmonds), with which he remained affiliated for thirty-nine years, becoming a senior partner responsible for many large corporate accounts. On June 23, 1906, he married Grace Greenwood Colyer; they had three children. Davis was elected president of the New York Patent Law Association in 1932.

Davis entered government service in World War I as head of the contract section of the War Department's Planning Division of Purchase, Storage, and Traffic (1917). In 1918–1919 he was legal adviser to the War Department's Claims Board. In these posts Davis, a Democrat, came to know many of the administrative liberals with whom he would be closely associated in the New Deal era. He became a close personal friend of Frances Perkins in the late 1920's and developed a warm regard for labor leader Sidney Hillman in the early 1930's. After Franklin Roosevelt's election as president, Davis returned to Washington as deputy administrator for the National Recovery Administration (NRA), where he helped write the shipbuilding and retail coal codes, and then as NRA compliance director (1933–1934). Although he found NRA work administratively frustrating, the experience reinforced his belief that the government could play an active role in resolving social conflict through mechanisms involving labor, management, and public representatives. He thought strong, stable trade unions essential to this process.

From 1937 to 1940, Davis chaired the New York State Mediation Board, on which he won the confidence of important sections of the union movement and built a national reputation as a resourceful labor mediator. After the National Labor Relations Board came under attack by conservative forces in 1938, President Roosevelt appointed Davis to the commission of business, civic, and labor leaders who investigated industrial conditions in Great Britain and Sweden, where unions were well established. He chaired the Twentieth Century Fund's Labor Committee, which in the late 1930's and early 1940's backed the Wagner Act.

Davis played his most important public role as a key figure in the government's effort to maintain social peace on the home front during World War II. In March 1941, at Sidney Hillman's suggestion, Roosevelt appointed Davis a member of the National Defense Mediation Board (NDMB). Militant unions, many affiliated with the aggressive Congress of Industrial Organizations (CIO), were conducting organizing campaigns that threatened to slow defense production. Davis used his considerable personal prestige and that of the government to end several work stoppages in April and May.

A turning point came in early June 1941, by which time Davis had become chairman of the NDMB, when a United Automobile Workers local in southern California struck North American Aviation in defiance of the NDMB's authority. Davis persuaded the Army to delay the deployment of troops to break the strike until CIO leaders declared the walkout an unauthorized wildcat strike instigated by Communists. After the Army moved in on June 9, Davis cooperated closely with Hillman and the CIO to assure that a reorganized "responsible" UAW local at North American would win favorable NDMB adjudication of its bargaining demands. His deft handling of this difficult situation transformed the NDMB into a virtual arbitrator of industrial relations, while retaining the cooperation of most trade unionists with the government's growing system of economic controls.

After Pearl Harbor, Davis faced a new challenge as chairman of the National War Labor Board (NWLB). A series of mine strikes over the union shop had virtually destroyed the effectiveness of the old NDMB in late 1941. Under the leadership of John L. Lewis, the United Mine Workers of America had made the union shop a major industrial relations issue in the months immediately preceding Pearl Harbor, and Davis found the problem a "crying baby on the doorstep" when the new NWLB began work in January 1942. Union leaders feared that the traditional web of loyalties that bound workers to their unions might unravel when labor ceased to exercise the strike weapon and when wages were held in check by government fiat. They therefore demanded "union security" for the duration of the war. Davis steered the NWLB toward implementation of a modified union shop—maintenance of membership—that allayed business fears of "compulsory union membership" while assuring union leaders of organizational stability and membership growth in the booming wartime industries.

A short, sloppily dressed man with a wild mop of sandy hair, Davis enjoyed the confidence of George Meany, Philip Murray, and other trade-union leaders. He favored a flexible interpretation of the NWLB's "Little Steel" wage formula (July 1942) that would boost substandard and inequitable rates of pay. (The "Little Steel" guidelines provided for a wage increase not to exceed 15 percent of the level of Jan. 1, 1941.) Davis battled within the Roosevelt administration against a hard wage line while resisting the pressures generated by wildcat strikers and combating the 1943 campaign by United Mine Workers' President John L. Lewis to destroy the NWLB's authority to set a general pay standard. During this era he helped set the pattern for postwar collective bargaining by encouraging labor unions to seek nonmonetary fringe benefits as a means of leasing some of the pressure for direct wage increases that the NWLB could not allow.

This task was made more difficult by the NWLB's gradual loss of authority in the latter half of the war; in March 1945, President Roosevelt averted serious labor disaffection only by appointing Davis to the more powerful Office of Economic Stabilization. As the war came to an end, Davis favored a reformulation of government wage-price guidelines that would assure workers a substantial increase in real pay, but his efforts to implement a smooth postwar transition were undercut by the rapid dismantling of the wartime controls.

Davis founded the New York City law firm of Davis, Hoxie, Faithfull and Hapgood in 1945, after failing to reach a financial agreement with his former associates over the basis on which he would resume an active part in the affairs of the firm. During the next decade he took on a number of public service assignments. As a commissioner of the New York City Board of Transportation in 1946 and 1947, he helped resolve difficult labor relations problems of the subway system. In the late 1940's and early 1950's he was a member of the patent advisory panel of the Atomic Energy Commission (1947–1957), and chairman of the President's Commission on Labor Relations in Atomic Installations (1948–1949) and of the Atomic Energy Labor Relations Panel (1949–1953). Davis was chairman of the board of trustees of the New School for Social Research from 1950 to 1957. He died in Southwest Harbor, Me.

[Davis' chairmanship of the NDMB and NWLB is chronicled in the papers of these agencies on deposit at the National Archives. Twenty-six boxes of additional material are at the Wisconsin Historical Society. Information on the politics of the NWLB is in U.S. Department of Labor, *Problems and Policies of Dispute Settlement and Wage Stabilization During World War II* (1950); Nelson Lichtenstein, *Worker Insurgency, Union Security* (forthcoming). The Columbia Oral History Collection contains a 1958 memoir. An obituary is in the *New York Times,* Aug. 15, 1964.]

NELSON LICHTENSTEIN

DE CUEVAS, MARQUIS (May 26, 1885–Feb. 22, 1961), ballet impresario and patron of the arts, was born Jorge de Cuevas in Santiago, Chile, the son of Eduardo de las Cuevas, a banker who had immigrated to Chile from Spain, and of Manuela Bartholin. When he was seven, the family moved to Europe, eventually settling in Paris. De Cuevas later returned to Chile, where he earned a bachelor's degree from the Catholic University of Santiago, but then resumed residence in Europe. He was probably in his mid-twenties when he attended his first ballet performance in Paris, where Serge Diaghilev's Ballets Russes was presenting annual seasons. In 1912, de Cuevas published a novel, *El amigo Jacques,* which he reportedly wrote in three days simply to prove that one could do so.

During this period the socially ambitious de Cuevas paid a fee to reinstate the hereditary Spanish title of marqués de Piedrablanca de Guana, to which he laid claim through his father. According to a story he later told, this title, though genuine, seemed cumbersome for an artist, in the view of Alfonso XIII, exiled king of Spain. The monarch proposed dubbing his friend "marqués de Cuevas" instead. Although the title was never actually created, de Cuevas adopted it as a way of paying homage to the king.

Multilingual, witty, fond of pomp but also possessing a spirit of buffoonery, de Cuevas established himself in Paris as a fashionable dress designer. On Aug. 3, 1927, he married Margaret Strong, a granddaughter of John D. Rockefeller. They had two children. The couple divided their time between Europe and America. In 1937, Rockefeller left his granddaughter a fortune estimated at $25 million.

Two years later, at the New York World's Fair, de Cuevas first tried his hand at large-scale showmanship. He and his wife sponsored an exhibition of old master and French modern paintings valued at $30 million. But at the same time that he was beginning his career as a latter-day Medici, the paradoxical de Cuevas renounced his title, and in July 1940 became an American citizen, declaring, "Mister is good enough for me." (He nevertheless continued to employ the title socially and professionally until his death.)

In 1944 de Cuevas launched his first company, Ballet International, in New York City. Unlike other dance troupes of the time, Ballet International was to be a resident company, housed in its own theater, and so spared the grueling routine of extended tours. De Cuevas engaged Bronislava Nijinska and Léonide Massine to head his choreographers and commissioned Salvador Dali, his favorite artist, to design the décor and costumes for two productions. Despite these lavish efforts the eight-week season, which opened on October 30, was a critical and financial failure. Although principal dancers such as André Eglevsky and Marie-Jeanne were praised, the company as a whole was criticized for its weak ensemble dancing and mediocre repertory. More crucially, Ballet International lacked a clear personality that would distinguish it from America's other leading companies, Ballet Theatre and the Ballet Russe de Monte Carlo. The company disbanded the following year.

When in 1947 de Cuevas assumed the management of the Nouveau Ballet de Monte Carlo, he asked several dancers from the defunct Ballet International to accompany him. De Cuevas renamed his new company the Grand Ballet de Monte Carlo. Its fall season at the Alhambra Theater, a popular music hall in Paris, was a triumph. The repertory, combining traditional works with new ballets by the young American choreographers William Dollar and Edward Caton, was well-liked, and the American style of classical dancing, as exemplified by Rosella Hightower, Marjorie Tallchief, and much of the corps de ballet, proved to be influential on the

French school. Throughout the company's subsequent seasons in Paris, and on successful tours in Europe, South America, and northern Africa, de Cuevas emphasized the simple American roots of his Monaco-based company. At the same time he sought to create a glamorous, courtly milieu for himself and the ballet. Surrounded by his Pekingese dogs, he would receive the press sitting up in bed, as at a royal levee. He called his dancers his children; they in turn addressed him as Marquis. The European ballet world delighted in his role of a grand seigneur, which de Cuevas, with his genius for publicity, played to the full.

In 1950 he relocated his company to Paris and changed its name to Grand Ballet du Marquis de Cuevas. When he brought the troupe to New York that autumn, he characterized the season as one of a native company returning home after three years abroad as ambassadors of American culture. Much to his disappointment the Grand Ballet played to mixed notices. As had been the case with Ballet International, most critics cited a lack of firm artistic direction as the company's major flaw. No de Cuevas troupe danced in the United States again. In France, though, the Grand Ballet was continually acclaimed. At its height during the mid-1950's, it developed a large popular audience that was slowly acquiring a taste for classical dancing. The company's daily performances in Paris completely overshadowed the weekly ballet evening at the Opera. Regrettably, the Grand Ballet's emphasis was usually on extravagant production rather than on memorable choreography. Although de Cuevas featured most of the leading dancers of the day, either as guest artists or as members of his company, none of the ballets created for it survives in repertory today.

Typical of the grand gesture of which he was so fond was the elaborate costume ball de Cuevas hosted at Biarritz in September 1953. Two thousand guests frolicked at what was said to be Europe's largest postwar party. The Vatican newspaper, *L'osservatore romano*, denounced the masquerade as "an immoral, pagan, barbarous orgy, . . . an abuse of money gained one does not know how. . . ." De Cuevas sued, declaring this an insult to his wife's family, and asked one franc in damages.

Under circumstances that provoked almost as much publicity, de Cuevas fought a duel in March 1958 with Serge Lifar, ballet master of the Paris Opera, after the latter allegedly insulted Hightower's performance in his ballet *Noir et Blanc*. Tremendous public interest centered on this rivalry, much magnified by the press, between the two most powerful forces in the Paris ballet world. Armed with an épée, the seventy-three-year-old de Cuevas managed to scratch Lifar, twenty years his junior, lightly on the arm. Both men burst into tears, embraced, and were immediately reconciled.

Earlier that year de Cuevas changed his company's name for the third time, calling it the International Ballet of the Marquis de Cuevas. Its greatest success was *The Sleeping Beauty*, which it first presented in 1960. The following year Rudolf Nureyev made his Western company debut in this production immediately after his defection from the Soviet Union. Mounted with sumptuous decor and costumes, the exorbitant cost of which forced de Cuevas to sell his Quai Voltaire apartment and part of his art collection, this ballet was de Cuevas' final extravagance. In February he died at his villa, Les Delices, in Cannes, the night before the Riviera premiere of *The Sleeping Beauty*. The company cancelled the performance as a sign of mourning.

Although possessed of a deep passion for the ballet, de Cuevas was no Diaghilev. With his wife's fortune this "Alice-in-Wonderland King," as his daughter called him, supported various companies as frames for superb soloists, but he never introduced a single ballet of enduring value. The International Ballet gave its last performances in 1962.

[For de Cuevas' views on his work, see "Why I Am in Ballet—and What My Dancers Say of My Being There," *Ballet Today*, Mar. 1954; and Pierre Daguerre's *Le marquis de Cuevas* (1954). Isobel Joy Aronin, "The Marquis Is a Showman," *Dance Magazine*, May 1955, gives a good idea of how de Cuevas lived, as does José Javier Alexandre's "El marqués de Cuevas: Empresario de 'ballet' y hombre decadente," *La actualidad española*, Aug. 4, 1955. Obituaries are in the *New York Times*, Feb. 23, 1961; *Ballet Today*, Apr. 1961; *Ballet Annual*, 1962. The New York Public Library's Dance Collection at Lincoln Center has clipping files on de Cuevas and his companies.]

GARY PARKS

DE FOREST, LEE (Aug. 26, 1873–June 30, 1961), inventor, was born in Council Bluffs, Iowa, the son of Henry Swift de Forest, a Congregational minister, and of Anna Margaret Robbins. In 1879 the family moved to Talladega, Ala., where Henry de Forest assumed the presidency of Talladega College, a school for blacks. In that impoverished rural community Lee de Forest spent his formative years. His self-reliance and inventiveness date from that time, during which his fascination with machinery manifested itself. He made minor inventions and constructed models of such technological marvels as steam locomotives and blast furnaces.

In 1891, de Forest was sent to Mount Hermon School to prepare for Yale, at which an ancestor had established a de Forest scholarship. After completing three years' work in two, he worked for part of the summer of 1893 as a chair boy at the World's Columbian Exposition in Chicago, where he spent as much time as possible in the Hall of Machines. That fall, de Forest matriculated at Yale's Sheffield Scientific School, where he was enrolled in one of the first courses solely on the subject of electricity ever offered in an American university.

Too poor to engage in social activities, de Forest immersed himself in his studies and continued to invent. After receiving the Ph.B. in 1896, he continued at Yale, where he obtained the Ph.D. in 1899, despite having spent seven months in the Yale Battery during the Spanish-American War (1898). He specialized in theoretical mathematical physics and electricity. His dissertation was on the reflection of Hertzian (radio) waves.

After graduation de Forest went to Chicago, where he secured a job with Western Electric. The following year he moved to the American Wireless Telegraph Company in Milwaukee, but was fired when he refused to share the results of his independent electrical investigations. After returning to Chicago, he devoted himself to research full time, except for a weekly lecture at the Armour Institute, which provided him with support and laboratory space.

De Forest's first major invention, the responder, was made in Milwaukee. These were the early days of wireless telegraphy, and others, particularly Guglielmo Marconi, had been making rapid progress in the transmission and reception of radio waves. De Forest set out to improve the sensitivity and efficiency of the most common detector then in use, the coherer, which consisted of a tube filled with metal filings. Placed in a circuit with headphones, the filings cohered under the influence of a radio wave, suddenly lowering the circuit's resistance and thereby allowing a burst of current to flow, causing the operator to hear a buzz (a dot or dash). The coherer's chief defect lay in its inability to maintain its sensitivity; the filings tended to stay packed together, preventing a return to their original resistance. That restoration had to be accomplished by shaking the tube.

De Forest's extensive reading in scientific and technical journals helped him envisage a solution to the coherer restoration problem. Following some accounts of German research, he succeeded, after nearly a year of trial and error, in constructing his "sponder," a detector in which a liquid electrolyte substituted for the metal filings. The original idea was that the naturally continual motion of the molecules of a liquid would automatically return to its initial resistance following the removal of an external influence. In a later version of his device, gas bubbles on the electrodes maintained a high resistance in the receiver circuit. The bubbles dissipated on arrival of radio waves, but immediately reappeared in their absence, thus making the device "self-restoring."

De Forest's earnings from the sponder enabled him to secure the capital necessary to form the American De Forest Wireless Telegraph Company to compete with Marconi. Although his detector was no better than his competitors', de Forest used newspaper publicity to great advantage. The award of the gold medal at the Louisiana Purchase Exposition at St. Louis in 1904, and the highly publicized use of de Forest's equipment in reporting the early days of the Russo-Japanese War in 1904, helped his company gain contracts, particularly from the U.S. Navy.

In 1903 de Forest began to use a new version of his sponder, more sensitive than the original, that bore a remarkable similarity to the detector patented by Reginald A. Fessenden, whose laboratories de Forest had visited early in 1903. In 1905 court injunctions were issued against his company's use of the detector, on the ground that it constituted a patent infringement.

Discharged by the company's directors, de Forest concentrated on wireless telephony instead of telegraphy. In 1906 he began applying for patents on the triode (three-element vacuum tube) Audion, one of the most important and fundamental inventions of the twentieth century. The triode began the age of electronics, which has transformed the technology of communication and the processing of information. Contemporary transistors can be seen as smaller, more efficient forms of vacuum tubes; integrated circuits and microchips, as miniature combinations of them with other components.

What led de Forest to the invention of the triode remains obscure. He claims in his autobiography that his inspiration came from observations he made in 1900, while investigating the sensitivity of a gas flame to electromagnetic radiation. At the time it appeared that sound, rather than radio, waves explained the apparent responses of the flame, but de Forest maintained that he had never felt fully satisfied with the explanation. Thus, he was later led to attempt to develop a gas detector in place of an electrolytic one.

De Forest began working with a gas-filled diode (a two-electrode vacuum tube). The English inventor John Ambrose Fleming, a consultant to Marconi, had developed the diode for use as a spark detector. De Forest began his research in an attempt to improve upon it for use as a detector in wireless telegraphy. The diode, or "valve," as it was called, acted as a rectifier of alternating currents because it permitted current to flow in only one direction. The filament, when hot, continuously emitted electrons, which were alternately attracted and repelled by the plate electrode (connected to an alternating-current voltage) as its charge alternated between positive and negative. Current flowed between the electrodes from filament to plate, but only when the plate was positive.

De Forest's key contribution, the addition of a third electrode to the tube, clearly did not result from theoretical insight. In a series of developments between 1905 and 1907, de Forest and his assistant H. W. Babcock (who suggested the name Audion) tried out a number of configurations of the three elements. Eventually they achieved what became the conventional placement of the third electrode, the grid, between the filament and the plate. Signals received by an antenna connected to the grid produced variations in the grid's voltage, which in turn were superimposed on the larger filament-plate current. Thus, the Audion not only could serve as a spark detector but also could detect and reproduce continuously varying signals, such as voice transmissions, with some small amplification. De Forest patented various types of Audion, the most significant one in 1907. But the early tubes did not work well as spark detectors in wireless telegraphy; until after 1912 only 200 to 300 were made annually.

In retrospect it is clear that de Forest neither fully understood nor appreciated his invention, despite his training in theoretical science. His account of what he thought he was doing is self-contradictory, and it was not until 1912 that he realized the triode's most significant features, its oscillating and amplifying capabilities.

Meanwhile, the promise of the Audion enabled de Forest to raise capital to form a new company and to begin the process of transmitting and receiving voice. During this period of development and securing contracts, he met Nora Stanton Blatch, a civil engineer, whom he married Feb. 14, 1908. They had one daughter.

(His 1906 marriage to Lucille Sheardown had been annulled in 1907.) The de Forests toured Europe that summer, demonstrating and installing radiotelephones and obtaining contracts. But the marriage could not withstand two professional careers, and the couple separated in 1909. They were divorced in 1911.

One of de Forest's lifelong loves was fine music; on Jan. 20, 1910, in New York City, in order to demonstrate his new technology, he chose to broadcast live opera featuring Enrico Caruso. Radio had begun; its subsequent commercialization, which he despised, led him to later ask, "What have you gentlemen done with my child?" Later in 1910 he moved to California, where he worked for the Federal Telegraph Company in Palo Alto. In 1912 he and his coworkers discovered that if the output of one triode was connected to the input of another and a chain was formed, the triodes could be used to amplify and repeat weak voice-frequency signals. This made intercontinental telephony possible. By feeding back a triode's output to its input, one could use it as a powerful generator or transmitter of high-frequency radio signals.

Once that recognition had dawned upon the American Telephone and Telegraph Company, it managed by indirect means to buy the long-distance telephony rights from de Forest in 1913, for a fraction of their worth. In 1914 American Telephone acquired the radio signaling rights to the Audion; therafter, industrial research laboratories became the principal sites of further development of vacuum-tube technology.

De Forest married Mary Mayo on Dec. 23, 1912; they had two daughters. The couple separated about 1930. De Forest's next major project was to investigate the possibility of talking motion pictures. By the early 1920's he had succeeded in devising an electrical-optical method of recording sound waves on film so that they could be rebroadcast in synchronization with pictures. In principle the solution was simple; in practice, difficult. Patterns of varying sound waves converted to electricity and amplified were in turn converted to patterns of light intensity and recorded on film alongside the frames of the action. The photoelectric effect—the ability of light falling on sensitive metallic surfaces to produce electricity—enabled the reconversion from light to electricity; the conversion from electricity to sound was easy. On Apr. 12, 1923, de Forest presented the first commercial talking picture, at the Rivoli Theater in New York City. For several years the major movie studios failed to take much notice of his Phonovision Company's process. Finally, in 1926, Warner Brothers, Fox, and other film companies began to use it, and the era of sound motion pictures was launched.

Although de Forest pioneered in wireless telegraphy, telephony, and sound motion pictures, in each case he was beset with financial and legal problems connected with the business side of development. In each area, he was involved by others in lengthy patent litigation; the Marconi Company suit over the Fleming valve lasted from 1914 to 1943. Having made fortunes through invention and lost them through development, de Forest changed his strategy in his fifties and began to devote himself primarily to invention, selling the rights to his discoveries to others. New technology had become the preserve of big business and team research; individual inventors were increasingly at a competitive disadvantage.

In 1930, shortly after his divorce from Mary Mayo, de Forest married Marie Mosquini, a motion picture actress. He continued to experiment for nearly thirty more years, devoting considerable time to diathermy and color television. The last of de Forest's more than 300 patents was issued when he was eighty-three; even after a heart attack in 1957, he continued to work. De Forest's indefatigable service earned him many honors and much recognition, including the title "Father of Radio." His death in Hollywood, Calif., marked the passing of the last of the colorful, almost mythical, individualistic figures of the heroic age of American invention.

[De Forest's papers are at the Foothills Electronics Museum, Los Altos Hills, Calif. His autobiography is *Father of Radio* (1950). Also see the biography by I. E. Levine, *Electronics Pioneer, Lee deForest* (1964); and a more critical evaluation of deForest and the triode-work in Robert A. Chipman, "DeForest and the Triode Detector," *Scientific American,* Mar. 1965. Obituaries are in the *New York Times,* July 2, 1961; and *Proceedings of the Institute of Radio Engineers,* Oct. 1961.]

DONALD deB. BEAVER

DEL RUTH, ROY (Oct. 18, 1895–Apr. 27, 1961), motion picture director, was born in Philadelphia, Pa., the son of Alfred and Theresa Del Ruth. Educated in public schools in Philadelphia and Williamsport, Pa., and Brooklyn, N.Y., he filled his textbook margins with sketches, revealing an early interest in art. After a stay in London, Del Ruth returned to Philadelphia, where he worked as a sketch artist and then as a reporter, first for the *Philadelphia North American* and later for the *Philadelphia Inquirer.* Varied assignments, usually in sports, provided an outlet for his restless nature and artistic talent. Del Ruth reported and illustrated prizefights, World Series games, polo matches, and tennis tournaments. He attained a pinnacle of sorts when he covered the Jack Johnson–Jess Willard championship fight at Havana in 1915 for the Curtis Publishing Company.

But a journalistic career was not satisfying. In 1915, Del Ruth's brother Hampton, already working as a director and "gag man" for Mack Sennett's Keystone Film Company, got him a job as a scenarist. Del Ruth moved to Hollywood and spent the next two years writing slapstick comedy scripts for the Keystone stable of stars, which included Mabel Normand, Wallace Beery, Roscoe "Fatty" Arbuckle, Gloria Swanson, and Ben Turpin. In 1917 Del Ruth advanced to the direction of shorts starring Turpin. After brief military service during World War I, Del Ruth joined William Fox and the Fox Film Corporation in 1918 as a writer and director of two-reel comedies, then the staple of the film industry. During the next few years he wrote and directed 150 of these. On Mar. 14, 1921, Del Ruth married Olive Simons; they had one son.

In 1925, Warner Brothers, then a second-rate production facility, hired Del Ruth to direct feature-length films. It was an apparent stroke of good fortune for him. Within five years, Warner Brothers' promotion of the Vitaphone sound process and close identification with sound films through the release of *The Jazz Singer* (1927) made it one of the major motion picture studios. Almost as quickly, under the close supervision of Jack L. Warner, vice-president in charge of production, and Darryl F. Zanuck, head of production until 1933, Warner Brothers' films developed a distinctive "look." Fast-paced, action-packed crime melodramas and musical extravaganzas, characterized by medium shots, low-key lighting to add atmosphere and hide shabby sets, and raucous dialogue, were turned out by the score for a mass audience. If a film achieved commercial success, its formula was repeated, often with the same plot and actors. Production resembled a factory assembly line: directors were foremen who took the scripts, cameramen, and actors assigned them, shot the film entirely in first takes (if possible), and completed it under budget and within a rigid production schedule. Studio technicians cut the film to a maximum of seventy minutes, and editing insured a distinctive "look." The final print was approved by Warner and Zanuck before being released.

Since most Warner Brothers' films were the creation of many hands, it is not easy to pinpoint the director's contribution or discuss his artistic vision. Without doubt the studio's assembly line production and forced "style" diminished Del Ruth's directorial imprint, but his technical virtuosity and ability to work with actors shine through, distinguishing his films from those of other directors. Both abilities helped to give the studio a more reputable image and to assist its leading contract players in giving strong, highly characteristic performances. For example, Del Ruth's direction helped James Cagney project a pugnacious screen image in *Blonde Crazy* (1931); *Taxi* (1932), a typical Warner's working-class melodrama and one of Cagney's best early screen performances; and *Lady Killer* (1933), a satire on the movie industry. Above all, Del Ruth was efficient. Although he is not generally regarded as one of Warner Brothers' top-ranking directors, he directed thirty-seven feature films there —comedies, mysteries, melodramas, and musicals—between 1925 and 1934. In some years he was pushed to turn out as many as six.

After 1934, Del Ruth did not direct another film for Warner Brothers until 1949. Perhaps he was no longer willing to accept the studio's excessive demands for output, but Zanuck's resignation in 1933 and Jack Warner's decision to cut all salaries by 50 percent to compensate for the fall in business caused by the Great Depression in that year may also have been factors. Del Ruth already had a reputation as a director of musicals and comedies, and for the next twenty years he made two or three films a year for Metro-Goldwyn-Mayer (MGM), Twentieth Century–Fox, and Paramount, many of them vehicles for screen or show-business personalities. Among his best films were three starring Eleanor Powell, *Broadway Melody of 1936* (MGM, 1935), *Born to Dance* (MGM, 1936), and *Broadway Melody of 1938* (MGM, 1937). Other films included Sonja Henie's *Happy Landing* (1938) and *My Lucky Star* (1938), both for Twentieth Century–Fox; the delightful *Du Barry Was a Lady* (MGM, 1943) with Red Skelton, Gene Kelly, and Lucille Ball; *Always Leave Them Laughing* (Warner Brothers, 1949), starring Milton Berle; and four Gordon MacRae vehicles for Warner Brothers, *On Moonlight Bay* (1951), *Starlift* (1951), *About Face* (1952), and *Three Sailors and a Girl* (1953). While many of these films contain charming episodes and are not completely overshadowed by the best musicals of these years, it is clear that Del Ruth was faltering. After his

first marriage ended in divorce in 1947, on Aug. 6, 1947, Del Ruth married Winifred Reeves Lightner, a musical comedy star whom he had directed in four musicals for Warner Brothers in the late 1920's and early 1930's. They had one son.

Del Ruth's last feature film, *Why Must I Die* (1960), an embarrassingly executed diatribe against capital punishment, was a sad conclusion to a forty-year career that had produced approximately 100 feature films. In the last years before his death in Sherman Oaks, Calif., Del Ruth moved into television, directing episodes of "Warner Brothers Hour," "Four Star Theatre," and "Adventures in Paradise."

Despite his productivity, technical proficiency, and association with some of Hollywood's most appealing personalities, some critics regard Del Ruth as little more than a Warner Brothers' hack. But such a dismissal ignores the characteristic style of the American cinema from 1930 to 1940 and the demands the studio system made upon directors. Certainly it disregards the intelligence and charm of many of his films. If not an artist, Del Ruth was a diligent and skilled craftsman created by the studio system of the 1930's.

[See a Warner Brothers' studio biography (1951), in the possession of the American Film Institute; John Baxter, *Hollywood in the Thirties* (1968); James R. Parish and Michael R. Pitts, *Film Directors* (1974); and Mario Salmi, "Roy Del Ruth," *Film Dope*, Sept. 1976. An obituary is in the *New York Times*, Apr. 28, 1961.]

G. F. GOODWIN

DE PAOLIS, ALESSIO (Mar. 5, 1893–Mar. 9, 1964), opera singer, was born in Rome, Italy, the son of Rodolfo De Paolis and Bianca Lovatti. His father was a well-to-do civil servant; his mother, a noblewoman. The family derived its substantial wealth from investments, land development, and real estate holdings.

De Paolis commenced musical studies at the age of seven, and within a few years had become an accomplished violinist. In his early teens he began voice lessons at Santa Cecilia Academy in Rome, where his principal teacher was Alberto de Pietro. In 1913, having completed his secondary-school education, De Paolis enlisted in the Italian army. Because of World War I, he remained in uniform for six years, serving a portion of that time as a dirigible crew member.

In 1919, De Paolis made his professional operatic debut in Bologna as the Duke in *Rigoletto*. Two years later he sang the role of Fenton in

Falstaff, at Arturo Toscanini's historic reopening of Milan's La Scala opera house. During the 1920's De Paolis sang leading lyric tenor roles with the major opera companies of Italy, in addition to performing in Berlin, Barcelona, Lisbon, and other European cities. He achieved his greatest success as Rodolfo in *La Boheme* and Alfredo in *La Traviata,* his two favorite roles.

On Oct. 3, 1930, De Paolis married Ines Maggiori Schileo, an artist and dress designer who later opened a couturier shop in New York City; they had two children. About this time he began to take "character" roles. He was so successful ("It must have come naturally for me") that during the 1931–1932 opera season the management of the Teatro dell'Opera in Rome persuaded him to devote himself exclusively to key supporting (comprimario) roles.

"Since I had never had a large voice," De Paolis said in *Opera News* (1959), "I had no regrets about making the transition." He set out to become "the best character actor in the world." Furthermore, as a comprimario he anticipated more operatic engagements and a prolonged professional life. De Paolis soon became a master of his craft. A detailed study of the opera libretto, together with a natural stage presence, an expressive face, and a careful attention to costume and makeup, enabled him to immerse himself in any role. "When I am on stage," he said, "I no longer realize just what I do to 'create' the part. I enter wholly into the personage . . . I simply forget that De Paolis ever existed" (*Musical America,* November 1963).

By the late 1930's De Paolis had appeared in more than 150 roles, many in seldom-performed operas or newly composed works. Especially notable were his characterizations in the premiere performances of Alfredo Casella's *La Donna Serpente* and *La Favola d'Orfeo* (1932), and Franco Alfano's *Cirano di Bergerac* (1936).

In the fall of 1938, De Paolis began a twenty-six-season association with the Metropolitan Opera Company. He made his debut on December 3 as Cassio in an *Otello* cast that starred Giovanni Martinelli and Lawrence Tibbett. Altogether, he sang forty-eight roles in 1,192 performances of forty operas at the Met, appearing as Remandado in *Carmen* 112 times, as Goro in *Madame Butterfly* 93 times, and as Spoletta in *Tosca* 85 times. He is perhaps best remembered for such comic roles as Alcindoro in *La Boheme,* the Old Prisoner in *La Périchole,* and Don Basilio in *The Marriage of Figaro.*

During his American career De Paolis also sang with the Cincinnati Summer Opera (1948, 1952–1955), and with the San Francisco Opera (1940, 1942–1956), and in Los Angeles. In addition, during the 1930's he sang at the Teatro Colón in Buenos Aires, as well as in Brazil, Cuba, and Mexico.

The dual facets of De Paolis' career are preserved on records. While singing leading roles in Europe, he made a number of solo disks for Polydor. Some twenty-five years later he recorded a number of his principal comprimario roles for Columbia and RCA Victor.

World War II temporarily separated De Paolis from his wife and children, who were unable to obtain passage on the last ships from Italy to America. They rejoined him in 1946, the year he became a naturalized American citizen.

De Paolis was described as "a short, round man with a warm face and hearty laugh." Congenial and witty, he enjoyed all forms of comedy, especially slapstick humor. A close personal friend was Salvatore Baccaloni, the celebrated basso buffo at the Metropolitan opera. De Paolis died in New York City from injuries sustained in an automobile accident while en route to his home.

[De Paolis wrote no memoirs, nor has a biography of him been published. Useful information may be found in *New York Times,* Nov. 17, 1957; *Opera News,* Feb. 2, 1959; and *Musical America,* Nov. 1963. *Opera News,* Mar. 14, 1964, contains photographs of De Paolis in a variety of moods and roles. An obituary is in *New York Times,* Mar. 10, 1964.]

LOUIS R. THOMAS

DENNIS, EUGENE (Aug. 10, 1905–Jan. 31, 1961), labor organizer and Communist functionary, was born Francis Xavier Waldron, Jr., in Seattle, Wash., the son of Francis Xavier Waldron and Nora Vieg. His mother was the daughter of Norwegian immigrants; his father, of Irish descent, had come to Washington around 1900, attracted by the lure of financial success. He never realized this dream, and his bitterness and economic failures influenced his son's life.

Having to work to help support the family, young Waldron (he assumed the name Eugene Dennis in 1935) was attracted to labor radicalism and in 1926 joined the Communist party. While an instructor at a Communist summer camp in Woodland, Wash., in June 1928, Dennis met the recently married Regina (Peggy) Karasick Schneiderman. They fell in love and, upon completion of the camp session, Peggy left her husband amicably (they filed for divorce in 1936). Never legally married, Peggy and Dennis lived together until his death; they had two children.

Active in Communist party work in Los Angeles and head of the party's Trade Union Unity League, Dennis personally experienced the antiradicalism and bitter antiunionism of Los Angeles employers and political leaders. He was frequently arrested for leading demonstrations among the unemployed, organizing migrant farm workers and longshoremen, or recruiting members to the Communist party. Between Nov. 29, 1929, and Mar. 8, 1930, Dennis was arrested, released, and rearrested six times. He was eventually tried and convicted, on Apr. 14, 1930, on the charge of attempting to riot, fined $500, and sentenced to 180 days in prison. In June 1930, Dennis went underground rather than serve this sentence, leaving Peggy and his infant son Tim and traveling to New York. In January 1931, he advised Peggy of his imminent departure for the Soviet Union, and she and Tim joined him for the move. Owing to his fugitive status, Dennis took out a passport under the name of Paul Walsh.

Dennis attended the Lenin School in Moscow. He was soon assigned to the Comintern's Far Eastern Section and for the next four years was engaged in covert revolutionary activities in the Philippines, South Africa, and China. In January 1935 the Dennises returned to the United States without their son, fearing that his fluency in Russian might attract undesired attention. (Tim eventually became a Soviet citizen and a prominent Soviet Communist party official.) Upon returning to the United States, Dennis was assigned as state secretary of the Wisconsin Communist party and, from 1935 to 1937, helped promote good relations with other progressive labor and political groups. Dennis next served as the U.S. Communist party's representative to the Comintern in 1937. He returned to the United States in January 1938 and was appointed the Communist party's national secretary for political and legislative affairs. In 1941 he again served as the U.S. Communist party's Comintern representative but returned after the German invasion of the Soviet Union on June 22.

With the end of World War II, and the demotion of Earl Browder as Communist party leader in April 1945, followed by Browder's expulsion, Dennis aligned with William Z. Foster and in February 1946 became the party's general secretary. In conjunction with Foster, Dennis assumed a crucial role in the U.S. Communist party's adoption of an increasingly more sectarian strategy of militant radicalism and abject pro-Sovietism—a strategy, given the prevailing climate of opinion, that isolated American Communists and increased their vulnerability to efforts by the FBI, the Truman administration, and the McCarthyites to link Communism with treason.

Ironically, and inadvertently, Dennis helped to popularize the U.S. Communist party's subversive character. Requesting the opportunity to testify in opposition to legislation that the House Committee on Un-American Activities had drafted to outlaw the Communist party, he appeared before the committee on Mar. 26, 1947. Never permitted to read his prepared statement, Dennis was questioned instead about his personal background. Refusing to answer these questions, he was served with a subpoena and was ordered to appear on April 9. Dennis instead sent a lawyer to challenge the committee's authority. As a result, on June 27, 1947, he was sentenced to one year in prison for contempt of Congress.

Before Dennis could serve his sentence, he was indicted on July 20, 1948, along with eleven other Communist party leaders, for violation of the Smith Act by conspiring, teaching, and advocating the forcible overthrow of the U.S. government. The trial, which began on Jan. 17, 1949, and lasted until Oct. 21, 1949, posed complex procedural issues, the more so because the indictment focused on the political activities of the Communist party. Dennis' dismissal of his attorneys so that he could act as his own counsel symbolized the Communists' strategy. Rather than focusing on First Amendment principles, the defense sought to portray the various cited activities of the party leadership as intended to create a better society. These efforts to justify the party's history were frustrated by Judge Harold Medina's rulings of relevance, which the defense bitterly challenged and for which they received contempt citations after the completion of the trial. Dennis was convicted, fined $10,000, and given a five-year prison sentence. On Aug. 1, 1950, the U.S. Court of Appeals upheld this ruling, as did the U.S. Supreme Court on June 4, 1951, in *Dennis* v. *United States* (341 U.S. 494).

Dennis began serving his sentence for his contempt-of-Congress conviction on May 12, 1950, during the lengthy appeal process. In the interim, fearing the imminence of war and "fascist" repression, the Communist leadership decided to go underground. Pursuant to this decision, five of the eleven convicted Communist leaders would not report on July 2, 1951, to begin serving their prison sentences. Dennis was to have been among them, but his inability to make an arranged contact led to his imprisonment.

While in prison, Dennis maintained contact with Communist activities through personal meetings and correspondence with Peggy. Protesting the censorship of his mail, he won permission to comment on current events. Subject to the terms of his parole upon his release in March 1955, he did not resume an active leadership role in the party until 1956.

By going underground the party leaders had denied themselves martyrdom for First Amendment rights and had become further isolated from the political mainstream. The years 1956–1957, accordingly, became crucial for the party's future with Dennis' and other Communist leaders' return to active participation. International developments further complicated this internal crisis—notably, Soviet Premier Nikita Khrushchev's denunciation of Stalin's "crimes" and the "cult of personality," and the outbreak in October 1956 of the Hungarian Revolution and its suppression by Soviet tanks.

These developments deeply divided the party. In this internal conflict Dennis advocated the need for reexamination, for adopting a strategy based on the principle of "American Communism," but also hesitated to adopt an independent line toward the Soviet Union. Ultimately he sided with William Foster's "left" faction, but his ambivalent reformism contributed to the party's further isolation and to defections of many members. Although national chairman at the time of his death in New York City, Dennis presided over a virtually defunct organization.

Dennis' career partially explains the decline of American Communism. Owing to his ideological and organizational identification with the Soviet Union, he was incapable of intelligently confronting the complex problems besetting American Communism during the cold war years. Instead, his personal history unwittingly served to confirm the subservience of the American Communist party to Moscow.

[Primary source material detailing Dennis' career is not accessible because relevant files are closed. Researchers can consult back issues of U.S. Communist party publications and the court transcripts and rulings pertaining to Dennis' contempt-of-Congress and Smith Act trials. Biographical material is in U.S. House Committee on Un-American Activities, *Hearings on Investigation of Un-American Propaganda Activities in the United States (Regarding Eugene Dennis)* (1947); *Time*, Apr. 25, 1949; obituary in *New York Times*, Feb. 1, 1961; Peggy Dennis, *The Autobiography of an American Communist* (1977). Also see John Gates, *The Story of an American Communist* (1958); David Shannon, *The Decline of American Communism* (1959); Theodore Draper, *American Communism and Soviet Russia* (1960); George Charney, *A Long Journey* (1968); Joseph Starobin, *American Communism in Crisis* (1972); and Michal Belknap, *Cold War Political Justice* (1977).]

ATHAN THEOHARIS

DICKINSON, EDWIN DE WITT (May 19, 1887–Mar. 26, 1961), professor of international law, was born in Bradford, Iowa, the son of William Elihu Dickinson, a farmer, and Edna Jessie Hickock. "Ned" graduated in 1904 from Cedar Valley Seminary in Osage, Iowa, and then attended Carleton College in Northfield, Minn., where he was a classmate of Herbert Goodrich, later an outstanding federal appellate judge. Dickinson engaged in college debates and also played football. After graduating in 1909, he taught history at Dartmouth University, from which he received an M.A. in 1911. On Aug. 30, 1913, he married his college classmate and "loyal companion in research," May Luella Hall. They had no children.

In 1918 Dickinson received a Ph.D. from Harvard; his dissertation was his first book, *The Equality of States in International Law* (1920). In it he argued (somewhat contrary to the apparent meaning of the title) that equal sovereignty of states was no more than a theoretical ideal. It was more useful to examine the practice of states, geography, and social distinctions in molding the law into a vital force in international relations. Dickinson thus allied himself with the philosophical pragmatists, then at the height of their influence, rather than with the early American school of jurisprudence, which held that law was a natural force, the same in all times and places, that had merely to be discovered by the judiciary.

Dickinson received his law degree from the University of Michigan in 1919 and soon assumed a full-time position on the University of Michigan Law School faculty. Although a Democrat, he spoke out against the Wilsonian argument that the invention of the submarine should not change standards relating to the conduct of belligerents upon the open seas; against Wilson's notion that a League of Nations with one vote per state would be an effective deterrent to international strife; and against the refusal of the United States to recognize communist Russia.

In 1933 Dickinson left Michigan to become professor of international law at the University of California at Berkeley. In 1936 he became dean of that law school, and in 1938 President

Franklin D. Roosevelt named him United States Commissioner on the Permanent Commission of Investigation under the Montevideo Protocol. Dickinson's service was interrupted in 1941 when he took a leave of absence. He moved to Washington, D.C., where until 1944 he served for brief periods as a special assistant attorney general and as general counsel to the Mexican-American Claims Commission. While in the Justice Department, Dickinson was instrumental in clearing certain federal employees accused of disloyalty by the Martin Dies Committee on Un-American Activities. In 1944 Dickinson became assistant diplomatic adviser to the United Nations' Relief and Rehabilitation Association and soon afterward became chairman of the United States Alien Enemy Repatriation Hearing Board for Japanese aliens.

Dickinson then returned to the University of California, where he oversaw the planning for a new law school building and supervised a faculty of notable legal scholars. In 1948 he joined the faculty of the University of Pennsylvania Law School in Philadelphia.

In 1949 Dickinson became president of the Association of American Law Schools. The following year the United States State Department named him to a commission that was to have been established jointly with Hungary and other nations to investigate asserted violations of human rights by the communist regime in Budapest. But the Hungarians refused to name a member to the tribunal and the matter died there. In 1951 Dickinson was named to the Permanent Court of Arbitration—in effect an honorary position, as the court handled very few cases.

Also in 1951 Dickinson published *Law and Peace*, which displays a mastery of law, political science, and history. When read in connection with his other articles of the time, this work summarizes Dickinson's mature views as a legal scholar. He had three basic principles. First, international law must take cognizance of the divergent geographical and cultural factors of each nation. For example, a landlocked nation can hardly be expected to comply with the rules of law designed for maritime powers. Second, there is a pragmatically arranged set of rules that are applicable between nations and have full standing as rules of law in the courts of the United States. Third, nations, including the United States, must not neglect their ability and duty to use the treaty power and international law. Thus, Dickinson encouraged American participation in international tribunals and agencies. Otherwise, he argued, the United States

would surrender a valuable tool in obtaining the resolution of disputes in a manner favorable to American interests.

Dickinson's book, which was an indirect attack on the so-called Bricker amendment (proposed to limit federal power over foreign affairs), apparently received wide favor from legal scholars. In 1952 he was elected president of the American Society of International Law at a time when the society included such diverse figures as John Foster Dulles, Dean Acheson, and Walter Lippmann.

In 1956 Dickinson returned to California, where he taught for a time at Hastings College of Law. Dickinson wrote to an editor concerning further research on the day he died at his retirement home in St. Helena, Calif.

Dickinson closed *Law and Peace* with some lines from Walt Whitman that summarize his personal philosophy:

I see Freedom, completely arm'd and victorious and very Haughty, with Law on one side and Peace on the other
A stupendous trio. . . .

[Dickinson's early approach to legal and political problems is revealed in "The Lusitania—Destruction of Enemy Merchant Ships Without Warning," *Michigan Law Review* (1918) and "Recognition of Russia," *ibid.* (1930). "L'Interprétation et l'Application du Droit International dans les Pays Anglo-Américains," 40 *Recueil des Cours* 305 (1932, II), is an example of his deep understanding of legal history. Some commentators believe that *What is Wrong with International Law?* (1947) is Dickinson's best work. "The Law of Nations as National Law of the United States," *University of Pennsylvania Law Review* (1952, 1953) and "The Law of Nations as National Law: Political Questions," *ibid.* (1956), are good surveys aimed at a general legal audience. The *New York Times* and the *San Francisco Examiner* carried obituaries on Mar. 27, 1961. Judge Herbert Goodrich published a valuable memoriam in *University of Pennsylvania Law Review* (1961).]

JOHN DAVID HEALY

DICKSON, EARLE ENSIGN (Oct. 10, 1892–Sept. 21, 1961), inventor of the adhesive bandage, was born in Grandview, Tenn., the son of Richard Ensign Dickson, a physician, and Mary Augusta Hester. He graduated from Yale University in 1913 and the Lowell Textile Institute in 1914; two years later he became a cotton buyer for a subsidiary of Johnson and Johnson, which was already one of the largest producers of surgical bandages and gauze in the United States. On Dec. 6, 1917, Dickson married Josephine Frances Knight. They had two sons.

By 1920 Josephine Dickson's proclivity for accidents around the house apparently kept Dickson busy applying gauze and surgical tape to her hands. Unfortunately, such bandages were clumsy to apply and easily lost. Dickson later recalled: "I was determined to devise some manner of bandage that would stay in place, be easily applied, and still retain its sterility." After some reflection, he laid gauze pads on strips of surgical tape and covered both with strips of crinoline. Whenever his wife required first aid, she needed only to cut off a bandage from the handy roll. Now she could treat her cuts and burns without assistance.

When Dickson mentioned his innovation to a fellow employee, he was encouraged to seek a hearing from his superiors within the organization. The company's president, James W. Johnson, saw the potential in Dickson's idea and decided to manufacture the item under the now famous trademark of "Band-Aid." The name was suggested by W. Johnson Kenyon, at that time superintendent of the mill at the Johnson and Johnson plant.

The first adhesive bandages were produced in long sections that allowed the user to cut off the desired amount. They were produced by hand, and initially sales were not especially large. Gradually the product caught the attention of the public. In 1924 machinery was developed to precut three-inch by three-quarter-inch bandages, and business increased by 50 percent.

As a direct result of Dickson's invention, he was named manager of the hospital sales division, which he played a major role in organizing, in 1925, and was named to the board of directors in 1929. From that time he ascended in the corporate structure until his retirement as a vice-president in 1957. He died at New Brunswick, N.J., having produced one of the most widely used products of the twentieth century. Nevertheless, despite the popularity of the adhesive bandage and the entrance into the popular culture of the brand name as a generic label, Dickson remains largely unknown. In a culture that reveres knowing how in preference to knowing why, such anonymity is not surprising.

[For further information see the obituary in the *New York Times*, Sept. 22, 1961; and "The Story Behind the Band-Aid Brand Adhesive Bandage" (Johnson and Johnson, 1961).]

J. K. SWEENEY

DILLER, BURGOYNE (Jan. 13, 1906–Jan. 30, 1965), abstract painter and sculptor, was born in New York City, the son of Andrew Diller, a concert violinist, and May Burgoyne. His father died when he was very young, and Diller spent his childhood and youth in Battle Creek, Mich., living with his mother and her second husband, Adrian Adney, an industrial draftsman. He began to sketch and paint at the age of fourteen, and the yearbook from his senior year of high school characterized him as preoccupied chiefly with "drawing." In the fall of 1925, intent on a career in art, he entered Michigan State College on a track scholarship. On free weekends Diller often hitchhiked to Chicago to tour the galleries of the Art Institute, where he discovered the works of Paul Cézanne, a primary inspiration in his own early painting.

After two years Diller dropped out of Michigan State. Shortly thereafter he married Sally Conboy and moved to New York City, where from 1928 to about 1932 he studied at the Art Students League under William von Schlegell. Throughout this period Diller experimented primarily in cubism. He was among the first American-born artists to adopt a purely abstract style. In 1932 his paintings and those of three other young artists made up an exhibition at the Art Students League that is reputed to have been the first show in the United States devoted entirely to abstract art. A year later his one-man show at the Contemporary Arts Gallery in New York prompted German émigré artist Hans Hofmann to proclaim Diller one of the most promising young American painters.

Over the next few years, Diller abandoned cubism for "neoplasticism," a theory of esthetics set forth by Dutch modernist Piet Mondrian in about 1920. Mondrian's personal interpretation of the "de Stijl" movement, this new doctrine called for rejection of representational art in all its forms and urged artists to explore the "universal" truths of pure geometric form and color. In carrying out this mandate, Mondrian claimed, the artist would become part of a vanguard that promised to cleanse the social environment of divisive differences and so raise mankind to levels of greater harmony. By the mid-1930's, Diller had embraced neoplasticism in total and his art now consisted of studies in rectangular shape and line. Adhering further to the principles of his European mentor, he limited the color range in his work to red, yellow, and blue.

Although Diller never deviated from the commitment to neoplasticism, the character of his work altered substantially over the years. A painfully meticulous craftsman, he was constantly changing the tones of the black and white grounds in his canvases and searching for new variations in his three primary colors. In terms of composition, his art can be divided into what he later defined as three themes. The first theme consisted of rectangles and lines floating against monochromatic planes. The shapes in his second-theme works lost their independence as they crisscrossed and extended to the edges of the picture. His third-theme paintings were in some respects his most dynamic, with complex line patterns and overlapping geometric forms. In his last years, during which he divided his creative energies between sculpture and painting, Diller became almost totally absorbed in exploring the potentials of his first theme. Critics agree that the output of this final phase is his finest and most mature.

Diller did not sell a single work in the 1930's. From 1935 to 1942 he earned his livelihood working for the Works Progress Administration (WPA), first as director of the Mural Division of the New York City Federal Art Project and later as assistant technical director for the city's Federal Art Project as a whole. In addition to allocating work to other artists, he did several public murals, none of which survive. Following America's entry into World War II, Diller was appointed New York City director of art of the WPA's War Service Section, a post he held until inducted into the navy as a lieutenant. In the navy he designed a signal system for ship-to-ship communication.

After the war Diller joined the art department of Brooklyn College, where he taught until his death. In 1956, two years after the death of his first wife, he married Grace Kelso.

During the last fifteen years of his career, Diller became increasingly reclusive and periodically engaged in bouts of heavy drinking. When not teaching, he retreated to the solitude of the one-room studio he had built in Atlantic Highlands, N.J. A founding member of American Abstract Artists, he was eventually dropped from its membership for failure to participate in its exhibitions, and from 1951 to 1961 he did not enter his work in any major show. Within this self-chosen isolation, Diller's creative powers grew. By the early 1960's, as his painting reached new levels of originality, he was simultaneously engaged in devising painted and formica-sheathed wooden sculptures which in effect became three-dimensional renderings of the geometric forms found in his canvases.

The last decade of of his life brought increasing recognition of his pioneering contribution to the American abstract movement. A hero to the new generation of avant-garde artists, he was honored in 1954 with an invitation from the Yale School of Art and Architecture to serve as visiting critic. By the time of his death in New York City, observers of his career began to realize that Diller, though a follower of Mondrian, was by no means a mere imitator. Summarizing Diller's accomplishments after his death, critic Hilton Kramer claimed that Diller had employed the concepts of neo-plasticism as if they "were his own invention." In the process he became "one of the few American artists . . . to find a kind of artistic freedom . . . in self-abnegation."

[Diller's canvases and sculptures can be found in many public institutions including the Museum of Modern Art and the Whitney Museum of American Art, both in New York City; the Newark Museum, Newark, N.J.; and the Yale University Art Gallery, New Haven, Conn. See Elaine de Kooning, "Diller Paints a Picture," *Art News*, Jan. 1953; and Lawrence Campbell, "Diller: The Ruling Passion," *Art News*, Oct. 1968. Useful exhibition catalogs include Galerie Challette (New York), *Diller* (1961); New Jersey State Museum (Trenton), *Burgoyne Diller* (1966); Meredith Long Contemporary (New York), *Burgoyne Diller* (1980). A good source of information on Diller's work for the WPA is his interview with Ruth Bowman, Mar. 3, 1964, in Archives of American Art, Smithsonian Institution, Washington, D.C. An obituary is in the *New York Times*, Jan. 31, 1965.]

FREDERICK VOSS

DILLINGHAM, WALTER FRANCIS (Apr. 5, 1875–Oct. 22, 1963), business executive, was born in Honolulu, Hawaii, the son of Benjamin Franklin Dillingham, the operator of a railway and land company, and Emma Louise Smith. After preparatory education at Punahou School, Honolulu, and a public high school in Newton, Mass., he entered Harvard University in 1898. Two years later he returned home to help his father operate the financially troubled Oahu Railway and Land Company. The company had been dubbed "Dillingham's Folly" when Benjamin Dillingham founded it in 1889, but the skeptics were proved wrong. The enterprise succeeded in opening up hitherto unused land for the production of sugarcane. By 1900, however, the road was $4 million in debt. Walter Dillingham brought stability to the business and was named president of Oahu Railways and associated companies in 1904, when ill health forced his father to retire. On May 2, 1910, Dillingham married Louise Olga Gaylord; they had four children.

In 1902, Dillingham and several associates formed the Hawaiian Dredging Company (later the Hawaiian Dredging and Construction Company), which grew to be one of the most powerful and influential enterprises in Hawaii. The company was responsible for the dredging operations that made possible the development of Pearl Harbor as a great harbor and naval station, and for the reclamation of thousands of acres of land in Hawaii and on other islands in the Pacific. Waikiki Beach was made possible by the work done by Hawaiian Dredging, and much of the military construction work done in the Pacific Theater before, during, and after World War II was done by the company. In 1961, Hawaian Dredging merged with the Oahu Railway and Land Company to form the Dillingham Corporation.

Although he never held political office, Dillingham was a Republican of great influence. The Dillingham company was not one of the "Big Five," the group of family firms that dominated Hawaii's economic and political life until World War II, but it was known as the "Big Sixth." Dillingham was considered by some to be the single most powerful businessman in the territory. The six families involved were related directly or by marriage to the island's first missionary families.

At one time Dillingham was an officer or director of twenty corporations, and he served in an advisory capacity to presidents Franklin D. Roosevelt and Dwight Eisenhower, territorial governors, and state governors. During World War I he was a major in the Army Motor Transport Corps in Washington, D.C. In World War II he worked with both the Army and the Navy, as well as with civilian agencies, in handling construction, shipping, and food production problems. Dillingham opposed statehood for Hawaii on the grounds that the time was not right for such a move and that it would put Hawaii under the control of Communists in the labor movement.

Dillingham, an avid polo player, was active in the sport until his mid sixties. He was a founder of the Hawaii Polo and Racing Club, and served as Hawaiian delegate to the United States Polo Association. He died in Honolulu.

[There are significant passages concerning Dillingham in John Hungerford, *Hawaiian Railroads* (1963); Gavan Daws, *Shoal of Time* (1968); and Francine du Plessix Gray, *Hawaii: The Sugar Coated Fortress* (1972); *Time*, Nov. 1, 1963, contains a profile of him, and more information on him is in an article on his son, Lowell Dillingham, *Time*, Aug. 16, 1963. An obituary is in the *New York Times*, Oct. 23, 1963.]

ROBERT L. HUNGARLAND

DINGMAN, MARY AGNES (Apr. 9, 1864– Mar. 21, 1961), disarmament and peace activist, was born in Newark, N.J., the daughter of James Alva Dingman, a physician, and of Nettie Clyde Beveridge. She attended Northfield Seminary, Northfield, Mass. (1893–1895), graduated from the New Paltz (N.Y.) Normal School in 1899, and received the B.S. degree from Teachers College, Columbia University, in 1910. Dingman's teaching career began in the elementary schools of Spring Valley and Brooklyn, N.Y. Between 1910 and 1914 she taught history and economics at Dana Hall, a girls' boarding school in Wellesley, Mass.

Dingman abandoned teaching in 1914 because, she later explained, she disagreed with her superiors regarding "certain principles involved in the work." She became a traveling secretary for the Young Women's Christian Association (YWCA), and worked with Florence Simms in the relatively new industrial program that adapted the philosophy of the Social Gospel movement to YWCA work. Preceding the 1910 convention of the world YWCA, Simms had chaired a commission to study the possibilities for YWCA work among working women. The resolutions adopted by the international convention served as the basis for the national YWCA's interest in industrial work. Self-governing clubs were introduced as a means of extending YWCA activity to working women in the United States. This extension work was Dingman's major concern for three years.

In 1917 she was one of three American women selected by the YWCA national board to travel to France to survey conditions among women munitions workers. In cooperation with the French War Department, they were to formulate plans to assist the women. When the war ended, Dingman was given responsibility for all YWCA work in France and Belgium. By 1921 she had opened working women's clubs in more than twenty cities and towns with a total of 10,000 members. For this service she received two decorations from the French government in 1919.

Dingman was called to London in 1921 to join the world YWCA headquarters as social and industrial secretary of the World Committee. She served in that capacity for fourteen years, visiting more than forty countries in Europe and Asia in the course of compiling information on industrial conditions and organizing programs to assist working women. The headquarters organization sent her to the Far East in 1923 as industrial secretary for the Far Eastern Region, primarily to aid the China Na-

185

tional Committee. During two years in China, she served on a multinational Commission on Child Labor appointed by the Shanghai Municipal Council. The committee's child labor code, intended for approval in June 1925, was never adopted because of the clashes of Chinese Nationalists with the authorities in Shanghai.

In addition to her YWCA work, Dingman served as a delegate to the first meeting of the Institute of Pacific Relations at Honolulu in 1925. In 1928 she was an industrial adviser to the Missionary Conference in Jerusalem, where she worked with Richard H. Tawney and Harold Grimshaw, among others, to establish the Social and Industrial Research Bureau of the International Missionary Council. Dingman was a delegate to the World Churches Conference at Oxford in 1937. In 1938 she visited India for three months and attended the All-India Women's Conference in New Delhi.

In the spring of 1930, the YWCA transferred its headquarters from London to Geneva, Switzerland, the headquarters city of the League of Nations and the focal point of the work of a number of international organizations. For Dingman the move heralded a second major career transition. In 1931 fourteen women's peace organizations united their efforts through the formation of the Peace and Disarmament Committee, Women's International Organizations, which claimed a membership of 45 million women in more than fifty countries. Representatives of the member organizations chose Dingman as president of the committee. In that post she led the effort to focus public opinion on the disarmament problem, and served as the main advocate for member organizations before the League of Nations.

One of Dingman's first tasks was to present petitions bearing the signatures of more than 8 million women to the World Disarmament Conference of 1932. In 1936 she again spoke for women when the seventeenth session of the Assembly of the League of Nations received an international delegation. When she was re-elected to the presidency in 1935, Dingman resigned her YWCA post and devoted all her efforts to promoting international cooperation. One result of her work was her detention in Italy in 1939. Fascist authorities offered no explanation, but Dingman had encouraged League of Nations sanctions against Italy in the Ethiopian war. Intervention by the U.S. State Department led to her release within twenty-four hours.

Soon after returning to the United States, Dingman retired as president of the Peace and Disarmament Committee (January 1940). She retained the title of honorary president and continued her work in the peace movement as a lecturer on international affairs. She became associated with efforts of the Women's Action Committee for Lasting Peace to mobilize public opinion to secure favorable congressional action on the United Nations. Dingman attended the first conference of the World Federation of United Nations Associations as an American delegate in 1946, and during that year and again in 1948 she lectured abroad for the British United Nations Association. The United Nations recognized her long-time interest in child welfare by naming her as consultant for the International Union for Child Welfare in 1948. She served as the union's representative to the United Nations until 1954, at which time she retired. She died in Berea, Ky.

[The Mary Dingman Papers, including the papers of the Peace and Disarmament Committee, Women's International Organizations, are at the Schlesinger Library, Radcliffe College. See her article, "Missionaries and Christian Social Service," *International Review of Missions*, Apr. 1927.

On her YWCA work see the *New York Times*, Aug. 4 and 16, 1925, and Dec. 10, 1925; Anna V. Rice, *A History of the World's Young Women's Christian Association* (1947). On her peace and disarmament work see Phyllis M. Lovell, "Mary Dingman: Disciple of Right," *Christian Science Monitor Weekly Magazine*, Sept. 23, 1936; and the *New York Times*, Dec. 24, 1939, and Jan. 7, 1940. An obituary is in the *New York Times*, Mar. 22, 1961.]

JANE A. BENSON

DIVINE, FATHER (*ca.* 1878/1880–Sept. 10, 1965), black religious leader, was born George Baker in rural Georgia, probably on a rice plantation situated on Hutchinson's Island in the Savannah River. Further details about his early life are unclear.

Around 1900, Baker moved to Baltimore, where he worked as a gardener. His religious interests led him to become a part-time Baptist minister. In 1907 he met Samuel Morris, an itinerant mulatto preacher who called himself "Father Jehoviah." Morris established a church of his own and designated Baker his "Messenger." A third leader, John (St. John the Vine) Hickerson, joined the group in 1908. Quarrels fragmented the church in 1912, and Baker went south.

By 1914, Baker had attracted a religious following in Valdosta, Ga., but he was arrested as a public nuisance. Given the choice of being sent to an asylum or of leaving the state, he moved north again, first to Brooklyn, N.Y., and then to Sayville, N.Y., on Long Island. Now using the name Reverend Major J. Devine, he organized a religious group that came to be known as the Peace Mission Movement. Its center was an eight-room house, apparently purchased with the earnings of his wife, Peninah, who had become Baker's disciple in Valdosta.

Numerous adherents were being attracted to Devine by 1919. Some sought his spiritual counsel; others found that he offered food and help in securing jobs. Some of his followers began to call him "Father," and Devine did not protest. Indeed, in 1930 he reported his rebirth and formally adopted the name Father Divine. In November 1931 he was arrested when the crowd at his house disturbed the peace. He spent several weeks in jail.

Divine lacked formal education, and he was not ordained by any established religion. Nonetheless this short, squat man had charisma. In 1933, when the Great Depression was at its worst, he moved the Peace Mission to Harlem. A decade of rapid expansion ensued. Although property disputes led to legal difficulties, prompting Divine to move his headquarters to Philadelphia in 1942, growth continued.

The Peace Mission kept no official membership records, but Divine could count thousands of followers, whites as well as blacks. Eventually there were nearly 200 major centers—or "Heavens," as they were called—most of them in New York City and Philadelphia. Although in theory no hierarchical distinctions stratified the membership, in practice Divine's disciples were of two kinds. The majority retained their usual occupations, but there also emerged an inner circle who gave all their worldly resources to the Peace Mission, lived communally, and worked full-time for the cause. Also noteworthy is the fact that Divine regarded property ownership as a mark of spiritual success. The holdings amassed under his leadership—including the huge Woodmont estate in suburban Philadelphia, which became his home—were worth millions of dollars.

After Divine's first wife had died, even though his teachings rejected matrimony and urged celibacy and segregation of the sexes, on Apr. 28, 1946, he secretly married Edna Rose Ritchings. Known as "Sweet Angel," this attractive white woman had joined his entourage while still in her teens and had become his personal stenographer. The announcement of their wedding in August 1946 was controversial and sensationalized by the press. Divine convinced his followers that the marriage was a spiritual matter, and "Sweet Angel" emerged as Mother Divine. She succeeded her husband as the movement's leader.

Divine emphasized equality among races—even the words "white" and "Negro" were forbidden—and it is likely that his strict teachings on celibacy were intended to reduce the hostility that he could expect his racial philosophy to draw. More of his convictions are reflected in a summary of Peace Mission tenets printed after Divine's death in the Mar. 8, 1967, issue of *New Day*, the movement's official (even canonical) publication. That statement cites the following beliefs as fundamental: Father Divine's "International Modest Code" is to be obeyed. Tobacco, liquor, and profanity are ruled out. Public education is affirmed; it should be open and free, with advancement to its highest levels determined by ability. Furthermore, English is called the "Universal Language," and it ought to be "compulsory in the educational institutions of all nations." The statement goes on to underscore the Peace Mission's commitment to full employment, mass production as the best means of eliminating poverty and want universally, business transactions by "cash on the spot," and cooperation among members "to purchase, own and manage all our possessions in the best interest of humanity generally." None of Father Divine's genuine disciples shall be on relief. Social Security will be unnecessary when people express "their individual independence as true Americans." In fact, the United States is to be "the Birth Place of the Kingdom of God on earth," and that kingdom is coming in accordance with the King James version of the Bible.

Although Father Divine never explicitly identified himself as God, it is unlikely that he would have disavowed the 1967 statement's assertion that he "fulfills the Scriptural Prophecy of the Second Coming of Christ for the Christian world and the Coming of the Messiah for the Jewish world." Nor is it probable that he would have denied the proposition that his adherents have "One Father and One Mother—God—Personified in Father Divine and His Spotless Virgin Bride—Mother Divine."

In appraising Father Divine and his work, it is helpful to differentiate a sect from a cult. A sect is a movement that restores or intensifies basic emphases in an established tradition, whereas a cult originates a new religion based on novel revelations, doctrines, or messianic claims. Father Divine's Peace Mission falls between the two. Many of his teachings about moral perfection, the kingdom of God, and even economics link him to a long history of spin-offs from mainstream Protestant Christianity in America. But the centrality of Divine, the charismatic, messianic leader who enjoined obedience and claimed to control powers of retribution, is sufficient to qualify the Peace Mission as a new religion. As such it has been branded escapist, opportunistic, and worse; but it also worked to reduce racial conflict, and one can hardly deny that Father Divine helped many persons to add meaning and integrity to their lives. He died in Lower Merion Township, Pa.

[See Sara Harris, *Father Divine* (1971); Sydney E. Ahlstrom, *A Religious History of the American People* (1972); Kenneth E. Burnham, *God Comes to America* (1979). An obituary is in *New York Times*, Sept. 11, 1965.]

JOHN K. ROTH

DOBIE, J(AMES) FRANK (Sept. 26, 1888–Sept. 18, 1964), writer and folklorist, was born in a ranch house on Ramirenia Creek in Live Oak County, Tex., the son of Richard Jonathan Dobie, a cattleman, community leader, and county commissioner, and of Ella Byler, a former schoolteacher. His mother compiled "recommended reading" lists for her son and supplemented his meager education until he was sixteen. Then he was sent to high school in Alice, Tex., where he lived with his maternal grandparents.

In 1906 Dobie enrolled at Southwestern University in Georgetown, Tex., a small, Methodist, liberal arts institution. After graduating in 1910 he worked as a journalist and taught school and served as principal in Alpine, Tex., before enrolling at Columbia University in 1913. He received a master's degree the following year. He then began teaching English at the University of Texas at Austin, an association frequently strained and periodically broken by teaching stints elsewhere and by leaves of absence. On Sept. 20, 1916, Dobie married Bertha McKee, a former college classmate; they had no children. Bertha Dobie became—in the words of Francis E. Abernethy—her husband's "chief editor and assistant, a contributor to some of the volumes he edited, and his substitute in class when he was off on the trail of some story." Also in 1916 Dobie joined the Texas Folklore Society. Six years later he was elected secretary-editor, thus beginning a twenty-one-year editorship of the society's annual publications.

Dobie served in France with the 116th Field Artillery as first lieutenant in 1917–1919. After another year's break from teaching while he managed a 250,000-acre ranch for an uncle, James Dobie, Dobie settled down seriously to

writing, his real passion for the next forty years, and gave up for good any notion of writing a dissertation. *A Vaquero of the Brush Country* (1929) and *Coronado's Children* (1930) established him as a master of the story form, one of the primary genres of folklore. *Coronado's Children* won the Literary Guild Award for 1931 and secured a Guggenheim grant (1932–1933) for Dobie. Four more books of collected folktales followed, and in 1939 he published *Apache Gold and Yaqui Silver*, a sequel in some ways to the treasure-hunting stories of *Coronado's Children*.

Dobie averaged a volume every year and a half, and produced, among other works, a series of books on animals of the Southwest—*The Longhorns* (1941), *The Voice of the Coyote* (1949), and *The Mustangs* (1952)—conveying a strong sense of nature and the interrelatedness of all living things. A posthumous volume, *The Rattlesnakes*, edited by Bertha McKee Dobie, was published in 1965. Dobie's books brought him national recognition and substantial income that gradually enabled him to become independent of his teaching at the University of Texas, where he had become full professor in 1933, the first native Texan to secure that rank in its English department.

During World War II, Dobie was visiting professor of American history at Cambridge University (1943–1944). He recounted his experiences in *A Texan in England* (1944). After the war (1945–1946) he went back to Europe under the auspices of the War Department (Intelligence and Education Division) to lecture to American servicemen in England, Germany, and Austria. These visits, which brought Dobie face to face with issues of the modern world and aesthetic considerations far more encompassing than the smaller dragons he had fought in Texas, profoundly changed him. Happiest when combatting narrow-mindedness, pedantry, or bigotry, Dobie took on the University of Texas regents during a purge of liberals on the faculty, lashed out at McCarthyism, and became even more outspoken in his demands for desegregation of higher education. In 1947 he was dismissed from the university when he refused to accept curtailment of his numerous leaves of absence.

Dobie thereafter published seven books. At his death he left manuscripts for seven more volumes. His *Guide to the Life and Literature of the Southwest* (1943; rev. and enl. ed., 1952), contains a prefatory "Declaration" in which he describes his eclectic sense of values in literature. *The Mustangs* is a tribute to the freedom and nobility of the mind, and *Cow People* (1964) is a retrospective volume that contains some of Dobie's most technically perfect writing. He died at Austin, Tex.

Dobie was probably the most significant writer in Texas and the most ardent interpreter of southwestern culture between the late 1920's and mid-1960's. He belonged to a group of regionally based liberals, predominantly Texans, that included the folklorists John Avery Lomax and Stith Thompson, and the historian Walter Prescott Webb, at a time when grass-roots agrarianism, collectivism, and national consensus dominated American culture. An avowed realist, yet in many respects much more a local colorist than a serious artist, Dobie fell short of such contemporaries as Robert Frost, Carl Sandburg, Grant Wood, John Steuart Curry, Thomas Hart Benton, and Georgia O'Keeffe, all of whom had similar but broader aesthetics than he.

[Collections of Dobieana are at the University of Texas at Austin, Texas A&M University at College Station, Southwestern University at Georgetown, and Baylor University at Waco.

See Bertha McKee Dobie, ed., *Some Part of Myself,* (1967); Lon Tinkle, *An American Original: The Life of J. Frank Dobie* (1978). Also see Francis Edward Abernethy, *J. Frank Dobie* (1967); and Winston Bode, *Portrait of Pancho* (1965). An obituary is in the *New York Times,* Sept. 19, 1964.]

GLEN E. LICH

DODGE, JOSEPH MORRELL (Nov. 18, 1890–Dec. 2, 1964), banking executive and government official, was born in Detroit, Mich., the son of Joseph Cheeseman Dodge, an artist, and Gertrude Hester Crow. After graduation from Detroit Central High School (1908), he worked briefly as a glue salesman and bank messenger, and in clerical and bookkeeping positions. From 1911 to 1916 he worked for the Michigan State Banking Department and the Michigan Securities Commission as an examiner. On June 28, 1916, he married Julia Jane Jeffers. They had one son. From 1917 to 1932, Dodge was vice-president and general manager of the Thomas J. Doyle Company, an automotive concern, and in 1933 he began a twenty-year presidency of the Detroit Bank. In 1947–1948 he was president of the American Bankers Association.

In 1941 Dodge was director of a headquarters staff division of Army Service Forces. In 1942 Dodge's government career began when he was a price adjuster for the Army Air Force Price Adjustment Board for the Central Procurement District, making sure that the government did not pay excessive prices to private contractors. In September 1943 he became chairman of the War Department's Price Adjustment Board in Washington; and by October he was chairman of the Joint Price Adjustment Board and the War Contracts Price Adjustment Board, with broad powers to settle problems previously under the jurisdiction of six separate federal agencies. At the end of the war, during 1945–1946, Dodge served under General Dwight D. Eisenhower as financial adviser of the Office of Military Government in Berlin and later as finance director for American forces in Germany under General Lucius D. Clay. For this work Dodge was awarded the Medal for Merit in 1946.

When the Big Four foreign ministers convened for the Austrian peace treaty, they authorized establishment of an advisory commission to confront the thorny issues of reparations, frontiers, and the disposition of German assets in Austria. In May 1947, President Harry S. Truman appointed Dodge to head the American delegation to that commission, with the rank of minister. Later that year Dodge attended a Big Four foreign ministers' meeting in London as Secretary of State George C. Marshall's deputy for Austrian affairs. He resigned this post in January 1948. From 1948 to 1951, Dodge served as a member of the advisory committee on fiscal and monetary problems of the Economic Cooperation Administration, which directed the original Marshall Plan.

In 1949, Dodge was sent to Japan as chief financial and economic adviser, with the rank of minister, to General Douglas MacArthur. In effect, Dodge became the principal American architect of the postwar industrial rehabilitation of Japan and exercised the final decision over its economic policies. His efforts to balance the Japanese budget by reducing government subsidies, by insisting that management dismiss surplus workers, and by imposing a single exchange rate for the yen aroused opposition among trade unions and liberal industrialists. But his "Dodge line" held fast against inflationary pressures, and in 1950 the Japanese Diet approved an austere budget that decreased the costs of the occupation by 18 billion yen and decreased Japanese government spending by 80 billion yen. It was the first balanced Japanese budget in almost twenty years. In 1950 the Department of the Army awarded Dodge its Exceptional Civilian Service Medal for his Japanese economic stabilization program, and on Apr. 28, 1962, the tenth anniversary of the postwar independence of the nation, the Japanese cabinet bestowed upon him the Grand Cordon Order of the Rising Sun.

In November 1952, President-elect Eisenhower asked Dodge to become director of the Bureau of the Budget, with cabinet-level status. An avowed enemy of inflation, Dodge found a deficit of almost $10 billion in the federal budget. During his fifteen months in office, the deficit was cut in half. At the outset he forbade all departments and agencies to fill any personnel vacancies unless absolutely necessary and to put off all but the most urgent construction projects. Ultimately Dodge "squeezed" more than $12 billion out of government spending programs, but he found his goal of a balanced budget hampered by several obstacles: the large national security programs—the Defense Department, the mutual security pacts, and atomic energy—accounted for nearly 70 percent of total outlays; an additional 20 percent was protected by existing legislation; and the interest on the national debt accounted for 8 percent. Still, Dodge's efforts convinced many in the business and financial community that he had recaptured control over the federal budget. Dodge compared being budget director to "being taken by the scruff of the neck and thrown into a basket of snakes."

In September 1954, Dodge was back in Washington, reviewing long-range plans for American foreign economic aid programs. Three months later Eisenhower appointed him special assistant to the president and created for him a new cabinet-level post, chairman of the Council on Foreign Economic Policy. Dodge coordinated the policies of the various government entities in the field of foreign aid and analyzed the Soviet economic offensive in underdeveloped countries. In June 1956, Dodge's Detroit Bank merged with three other local financial institutions. He left government service to become chairman of the new Detroit Bank and Trust Company, the assets of which exceeded $1 billion. He died in Detroit.

Among his banking and government colleagues, Dodge had a reputation for candor and a willingness to let the facts overrule his preconceptions. He was a "complete rationalist," who seemed never to be influenced by accident or emotion. Dodge had a "congenital" distaste for publicity and flamboyant behavior and regularly advised banking subordinates to avoid "excessive" entertainment and "undue cordiality." This no-nonsense attitude kept his bank operating smoothly during his frequent absences. But Washington was not Detroit. In reflecting on his term as budget director, Dodge confessed that in government he found "always an opposition . . . either in some element of the public or in Congress, and this opposition is a highly vocal one."

[Dodge presented some of his banking and economic views in *An Introduction to the Business of Management* (1939); *Editorials on Our Changing Banking* (1941); and two speeches to the Economic Club of Detroit: "Price Adjustments of War Contracts" (1943) and "Problems of European Aid and Reconstruction" (1947). The most complete account of Dodge's life is the obituary in the *New York Times*, Dec. 3, 1964. See also Duncan Norton-Taylor, "The Banker in the Budget Bureau," *Fortune*, Mar. 1953; and "Meet Vice-President Dodge," *Banking*, Nov. 1946.]

IRVING KATZ

DOOLEY, THOMAS ANTHONY, III (Jan. 17, 1927–Jan. 18, 1961), physician, was born in St. Louis, Mo., the son of Thomas A. Dooley, Jr., and Agnes Wise Manzelman. The elder Dooley was an executive with American Car and Foundry Company, and Dooley was thus raised in a home of comfortable wealth. He attended Catholic grade school, completed an accelerated program at St. Louis University High School, and began his premedical studies at the University of Notre Dame in March 1944. He withdrew in October 1944 to enlist as a medical corpsman in the U.S. Navy, serving in military hospitals in New York and California. Dooley returned to Notre Dame in 1946, spent the summer of 1948 studying French in Europe, and enrolled in St. Louis University Medical School that fall. He received the M.D. degree in 1953.

Reenlisting in the navy, Dooley served for sixteen months as a medical intern at Camp Pendleton, Calif., and in Japan, and was assigned to the cargo attack ship *Montague* in the summer of 1954. This ship, converted to passenger use, was assisting refugees leaving North Vietnam for South Vietnam according to the terms of the Geneva accords signed earlier that year and Dooley served as the ship's medical officer and occasionally as interpreter for French and American officials. He established a refugee camp near Haiphong to treat evacuees before they boarded the ship, and he and his team of corpsmen were soon processing 2,000 refugees daily. He remarked later: "I was crowding more practice in malaria, yaws, beri-beri, leprosy and cholera into a month than most doctors see in a long lifetime." He was also exposed to Communist and anti-Western atrocities—"things . . . I didn't think human beings were capable

190

of doing," he wrote in 1954. By the following May more than 600,000 refugees had been treated and transferred. Dooley was decorated by the South Vietnamese government, and at twenty-eight he became the youngest medical officer in the U.S. Navy to receive the Legion of Merit.

After a three-month lecture tour of the United States in early 1956, Dooley resigned from the navy and, with three of his former corpsmen, returned to Southeast Asia, this time to Laos. Supported by private gifts, donations of medicines and equipment from American manufacturers, and proceeds from the best-selling account of his work in Vietnam, *Deliver Us from Evil* (1956), he set up clinics at Vang Vieng and at Nam Tha, five miles from the Chinese border. He spent much of each day in his dispensary or in surgery, promoted higher standards of cleanliness and personal hygiene, and trained teams of native assistants to whom he could entrust his clinics when he moved on to found others. "In Asia," he stated, "I run a nineteenth-century hospital. Upon my departure the hospital may drop to the eighteenth century. That is fine, because previously the tribes in the high valleys lived, medically speaking, in the fifteenth century." He was an unabashed propagandist, reminding each patient that he was an American doctor and that it was American aid he was dispensing.

Dooley returned to the United States in late 1957, and recorded his Laotian experiences in a second best-seller, *The Edge of Tomorrow* (1958). With Dr. Peter Comanduras, a Washington physician, he founded MEDICO (Medical International Corporation Organization) to bring medical assistance to the peoples of less-developed countries. Leaving the administration of MEDICO to others, Dooley returned to Laos and opened a third clinic at Muong Sing. He described this work in *The Night They Burned the Mountain* (1960). While on a routine visit to neighboring villages in early 1959, he lost his footing and tumbled down a twenty-foot embankment, injuring his chest. A tumor that developed proved to be malignant, and he underwent surgery in New York City later that year. Dooley returned to Muong Sing to continue his work in December, but the cancer was spreading. Twelve months later he reentered the hospital in New York City, where he died.

Dooley, who never married, was controversial both during and after his brief life. He was undeniably talented—an accomplished pianist, swimmer, and horseman. He also had a boyish charm and sense of humor that attracted others instantly. He was an effective public speaker, a tireless worker, and a demanding administrator. Deeply religious, Dooley sought to begin each day with mass. Yet he could also be brash, impatient with authority, and even egotistical. He was probably too blatant in his political propagandizing and too ready to ascribe atrocities and organized opposition to Communism. His reputation suffered in the late 1970's, when an association with the Central Intelligence Agency was revealed; but this may have been nothing more than a willingness to share with government officials at home information he gathered in normal conversations with villagers. To the allegation that his procedures were too hurried, he countered that long lines of patients precluded more leisurely practice and that most native ills were common and uncomplicated.

Dooley's detractors, however, were a minority. A 1959 Gallup poll listed him as one of the ten most admired men in the world. Honored by countless civic and private organizations, he was revered throughout the world as a dedicated young doctor impatient to serve others in a life he knew was too short. Dooley's favorite quotation from Robert Frost seemed fitting:

The woods are lovely, dark and deep.
But I have promises to keep,
And miles to go before I sleep.

[Most of Dooley's correspondence remains in private hands, although a small portion is preserved in the Archives of St. Louis University. Transcripts and tape recordings of broadcasts sent by Dooley from Asia (1956–1960) and aired over radio station KMOX in St. Louis are in the Library of the University of Missouri, St. Louis. Works about Dooley include Norman Cousins, "Tom Dooley and His Mission," *Saturday Review*, Feb. 4, 1961; Agnes Wise Dooley, *Promises to Keep: The Life of Doctor Thomas A. Dooley* (1962); Teresa Gallagher, *Give Joy to My Youth: A Memoir of Dr. Tom Dooley* (1965); Boniface Hanley, O.F.M., "A Sense of Urgency," *The Anthonian*, 2nd Quarter, 1978; Scot Leavitt, "Tom Dooley at Work: Dissent on Him and His Medicine," *Life*, Apr. 18, 1960; and Jim Winters, "Tom Dooley: The Forgotten Hero," *Notre Dame Magazine*, May 1979.]

THOMAS E. BLANTZ

DORN, HAROLD FRED (July 30, 1906– May 9, 1963), medical statistician and government administrator, was born near Ithaca, N.Y., the son of Fred E. Dorn and Minnie Elizabeth Miller, prosperous dairy farmers. After completing high school in Ithaca, he worked on the family farm for two years before entering Cornell University. He majored in rural sociology, receiving the B.S. in 1929 and the M.S. in 1930.

Dorn developed an interest in statistics during his graduate studies at the University of Wisconsin. While on a rural sociology fellowship in 1931–1932, he studied with Warren S. Thompson, director of the Scripps Foundation for Research in Population Problems at Miami University in Ohio. He received the Ph.D. in sociology from the University of Wisconsin in 1933. A Social Science Research Council fellowship followed in 1933–1934 for studies on the application of recently developed statistical techniques to social data under Egon S. Pearson of the Galton Laboratory at University College, London.

Upon his return to the United States in 1934, Dorn was appointed a research analyst in the Federal Emergency Relief Administration of the Works Progress Administration. In 1936 he served as a staff member on the Committee on Population Problems of the National Resources Committee, and began his lifelong career as a statistician with the U.S. Public Health Service. Dorn was assigned to the National Institutes of Health to initiate application of statistical methods to their research, and became especially involved in problems of demography, epidemiology, mortality, and vital statistics. He married Celia Camine on June 25, 1932; they had two daughters.

From 1943 to 1946, Dorn served as a lieutenant colonel and director of the Medical Statistics Division of the Office of the Surgeon General of the U.S. Army, for which work he was awarded the Legion of Merit. After the war he returned to the National Institutes of Health, where he played an important role in the growth and staffing of a program in medical statistics. As chief of the Biometrics Research Branch of the National Heart Institute, Dorn was considered the "de facto if not de jure Chief Statistician of the National Institutes of Health." Although he did not consider himself a mathematical statistician, he was interested in the application of new methodology. In 1961 he received a Distinguished Service Award from the Department of Health, Education and Welfare.

Dorn was influential in the development of international programs of health and population statistics as an American representative to the conferences on revision of the International Lists of Diseases, Injuries and Causes, as a member of the World Health Organization Expert Committee on Health Statistics, and as a member of the U.S. National Committee on Vital and Health Statistics. He sought revision of re-

porting practices of the International Statistical Classification of the World Health Organization to include multiple causes of death.

Dorn is probably best known for his development of statistical methodology for large-scale epidemiological studies of cardiorespiratory diseases. In 1938 and 1948 he conducted surveys in ten major cities, and with Sidney J. Cutler published the results in *Morbidity from Cancer in the United States, Parts I and II* (1955, 1959). In 1954, Dorn surveyed approximately 250,000 World War I veterans to determine the relationship between smoking and health. In his findings, "Tobacco Consumption and Mortality from Cancer and Other Diseases," presented to the Seventh International Cancer Congress (1958), he found a significant link between early mortality from lung cancer and other cardiorespiratory diseases and a high rate of tobacco consumption.

Dorn's study of veterans was a major piece of evidence leading to the announcement in 1959 by U.S. Surgeon General Leroy E. Burney of a significant relationship between smoking and lung cancer. The Dorn study was also relied upon extensively in the 1964 *Report of the Surgeon General's Advisory Committee on Smoking and Health.* Initially this correlation of smoking and lung cancer provoked a storm of controversy and rebuttal from the tobacco industry and segments of the medical community, but subsequent studies proved the link to be valid.

In 1959, Dorn was designated the Cutter Lecturer in Preventive Medicine at Harvard University, in recognition of his outstanding epidemiological research. As general secretary of the International Union against Cancer from 1953 on, he was involved in its expansion and in coordination of international studies. He was a member of the scientific advisory council of the American Cancer Society, and of the Joint U.S.–U.K. Board on Cardio-Respiratory Diseases.

Dorn published extensively on demography, and in the January 1962 issue of *Science* he presented an invited essay, "World Population Growth: An International Dilemma." He was a member of the Population Association, the American Eugenics Society, and the American Society for Human Genetics.

A hard and steady worker, Dorn possessed a keen sense of humor and skill as a raconteur. His early farm influence was reflected in the extensive garden at his home. He was also an avid amateur photographer and a devotee of classical music. Dorn died of bone cancer in Washington, D.C.

[The Harold Fred Dorn Papers are Manuscript Collection 235 in the National Library of Medicine, Bethesda, Md. See Jerome Cornfield, "Harold Fred Dorn," *American Statistician,* June 1963; Celia C. Dorn, "Harold F. Dorn, 1906–1963: Reminiscences," *ibid.* For a bibliography see William Haenszel, ed., *Epidemiological Approaches to the Study of Cancer and Other Chronic Diseases,* National Cancer Institute Monograph 19 (1966). Obituaries appeared in the *New York Times,* the *Washington Post,* and the *Washington Evening Star* on May 10, 1963.]

PAMELA M. HENSON

DOUGLASS, ANDREW ELLICOTT (July 5, 1867–Mar. 20, 1962), astronomer and dendrochronologist, was born in Windsor, Vt., the son of the Reverend Malcolm Douglass and Sarah Hale. Spending his childhood in the comfortable surroundings of Episcopalian rectories in Vermont and Massachusetts, Douglass excelled in high school science and math courses and displayed an early interest in astronomy. He entered Trinity College (Hartford, Conn.) in 1885, securing a student assistantship at the campus observatory a few months after his arrival. He graduated with a B.A. in 1889.

Although Douglass had hoped to undertake graduate study, his father's death in 1887 made this a financial impossibility. He therefore accepted a position as an assistant at the Harvard College Observatory in the fall of 1889. In late 1890 Douglass was chosen to accompany a Harvard expedition to Arequipa, Peru, to establish an observatory in the Southern Hemisphere. He remained there for the next three years.

A few months after his return in the fall of 1893, Douglass accepted the position of principal assistant at the planned Lowell Observatory. Percival Lowell, a wealthy Boston financier and astronomer, decided to erect an observatory in the American Southwest to investigate the planet Mars, and sent Douglass to Arizona to survey potential sites for the installation. Early in 1894 Douglass forwarded his findings to Boston, where Lowell in April selected a mesa west of Flagstaff as the site of the observatory.

Subsequently, Douglass assumed the duties of acting director at Flagstaff almost from the beginning, because Lowell spent relatively little time there. Over the next seven years Douglass directed an intensive study of Mars, the results of which Lowell used to support his theory of an intelligent Martian civilization. Lowell's forceful advocacy of this theory disturbed Douglass, who suggested that his employer restrict his writing to popularized science, which was clearly Lowell's greatest talent. In consequence

of his challenges to Lowell's theory Douglass was dismissed from the observatory in July 1901.

Responding to the pleas of his many friends, Douglass remained in Flagstaff for the next five years, teaching Spanish and history at Northern Arizona Normal School and working as a mineral assayer. He also served two terms as probate judge of Coconino County. On Aug. 3, 1905, he married Ida Whittington, a music teacher. The added responsibility of marriage (although the couple remained childless) led Douglass to increase his efforts to secure academic employment, but he had no success until 1906, when he joined the University of Arizona faculty as assistant professor of physics. He later served as professor and chairman of physics and astronomy (1906–1937), acting president (1910–1911), and dean of the College of Letters, Arts and Sciences (1915–1918).

Douglass was enthusiastic about his new position, but he felt disappointed that the university in Tucson lacked the basic equipment for astronomical research. Over the next decade he drafted various plans for a suitable observatory and attempted to secure funding for the proposed facility. In 1916 he finally obtained a $60,000 gift from Lavinia Steward. The construction of the 36-inch reflecting telescope was completed in the late summer of 1922. It was named Steward Observatory and Douglass became its director.

Shortly after his dismissal from the Lowell Observatory, Douglass had begun to study tree rings. Believing that sunspots influenced terrestrial weather, Douglass examined northern Arizona pines for variations in tree-ring width. By 1909 he found a clear relation between rainfall and tree growth, and discovered a cyclical variation of slightly more than eleven years, the same period displayed by sunspot cycles. Although he spent the rest of his long life searching for a definitive relation between sunspots and weather, his work proved suggestive but inconclusive.

In his attempt to obtain extensive tree-ring records, Douglass was limited by the absence of very old trees with the proper ring characteristics. Sequoias and redwoods, although quite old, did not display the patterned variation in tree-ring width between wet and dry years, which was the basis for Douglass's dating method. With the assistance of archaeologists, Douglass therefore began examining beams and other wood artifacts from ancient ruins in the Southwest. By late July 1929 he had gathered and analyzed sufficient wood and charcoal specimens to construct a tree-ring record beginning in A.D. 700. Within five years, he extended the chronology back to A.D. 11, and thus provided his archaeological colleagues with a valuable tool for dating prehistoric ruins.

Douglass retired from the directorship of Steward Observatory in late 1937 (although he returned as acting director from 1942 to 1946), but quickly took on similar duties as director of the newly established Laboratory of Tree-Ring Research at the University of Arizona, a post he held until 1958. The two decades of his leadership established the facility as the center of dendrochronological research. Douglass's health failed rapidly after retirement in 1958. He died in Tucson.

[The A. E. Douglass Papers are at the University of Arizona, Tucson, and in the Lowell Observatory Archives, Flagstaff. Douglass's most important work is *Climatic Cycles and Tree Growth* (3 vols., 1919, 1928, 1936). Some of the numerous articles he wrote appeared in *Popular Astronomy* (Feb. 1899); *Popular Science Monthly* (May 1907); *Monthly Weather Review* (June 1909); and *National Geographic* (Dec. 1929). See also George E. Webb, "Scientific Career of A. E. Douglass, 1894–1962" (Ph.D. diss., University of Arizona, 1978). Obituaries are found in *New York Times*, Mar. 21, 1962; *Arizona Daily Star*, Mar. 21, 1962; *Trinity College Alumni Magazine*, May 1962.]

GEORGE ERNEST WEBB

DOULL, JAMES ANGUS (Sept. 8, 1889– Apr. 6, 1963), epidemiologist, was born in New Glasgow, Nova Scotia, the son of James Forbes Doull, a wholesale and retail grocer, and Mary Chisholm. After receiving his secondary education at New Glasgow High School, he entered Dalhousie University in Halifax, Nova Scotia, where he was awarded a B.A. in 1911 and an M.D., C.M., in 1914. He interned for a year (1913–1914) at the Nova Scotia Hospital before beginning to practice medicine at Glace Bay, Nova Scotia, in 1914. The following year Doull was commissioned a lieutenant in the British Royal Army Medical Corps. He spent the next three and a half years serving on the front lines in France, often performing emergency surgery on the battlefield. For his efforts, particularly in the battle of the Somme in 1916 and at Passchendaele in 1917, he received the Military Cross (Great Britain) and the Croix de Guerre.

Largely as a result of his experience in the war, Doull decided to pursue a career in public health. While earning a D.P.H. at Cambridge University, he interned at the Brompton Hospital in London. In 1919 he returned to Canada and served briefly as provincial health inspector for Nova Scotia.

In 1920 Doull entered the newly established Johns Hopkins School of Hygiene and Public Health, the first such institution in the United States. Modeled on the German institutes of hygiene, it reflected the latest developments in public health with its emphasis on biological sciences, infectious disease, bacteriology, and statistics. Doull, appointed a Rockefeller Fellow, came under the tutelage of the noted epidemiologist Wade Hampton Frost, serving as his assistant. Frost argued that biological findings should be integrated with rigorous demographic studies in epidemiological research, a theme that Doull applied to his work throughout his career.

After he earned a D.P.H. in 1921, the School of Hygiene appointed Doull associate in epidemiology and, in 1924, associate professor. During his tenure at Johns Hopkins, he conducted a comprehensive survey of the epidemiology of diphtheria in Baltimore and published a series of important papers concerning the prevalence, distribution, and transmission of the disease. He advocated the prophylactic use of diphtheria antitoxin at a time when many public health officials were questioning its value.

While at Johns Hopkins, Doull was director of the John J. Abel Fund for Research on the Common Cold (1928–1930). In this capacity he published a series of reports of investigations relating to susceptibility to, and transmission of, upper respiratory infections. Through experiments with filterable viruses, he concluded that common colds could be caused only by infection, and not, as previously assumed, by dressing inadequately in cold weather or by sitting in a draft.

Doull left Johns Hopkins in 1930 to become professor of hygiene and public health at Western Reserve University in Cleveland, a position he held for the next fifteen years. During this period he conducted epidemiological investigations of such infectious diseases as typhoid fever, tuberculosis, and syphilis. At the frequent request of Surgeon General Thomas Parran, Doull would travel to the scene of an epidemic to determine its cause and prescribe measures for its control. In 1936 he helped to found the Cleveland Health Museum, a facility dedicated to public education in preventive medicine.

World War II drew Doull into world health politics, and he became a leading proponent of the creation of an international health organization. In 1943 he traveled to Australia and New Zealand for the Lend-Lease Administration, to assist those countries in securing badly needed medical supplies.

As a medical consultant to the United Nations Rehabilitation and Relief Administration in 1944, Doull helped to draft international sanitary conventions for maritime and aerial commerce, in an attempt to avert serious epidemics. In 1945 and 1946 he served as a United States delegate to the international meetings that led to the establishment of the World Health Organization (WHO). In that year he resigned from Western Reserve University to become the first chief of the Office of International Health Relations of the U.S. Public Health Service, which was created to coordinate American health activities overseas.

Doull left the Public Health Service in 1948 to become medical director of the Leonard Wood Memorial (American Leprosy Foundation), a position he held until his death. In 1933, Doull had traveled to the Philippines to survey health conditions; tropical medicine, particularly the problem of leprosy, had remained a central interest. As director of the Leonard Wood Memorial, he initiated a series of important double-blind clinical studies to test the efficacy of several therapies for leprosy. Under Doull's guidance the American Leprosy Foundation dramatically expanded both its research and its clinical facilities. Although his career in epidemiology and public health was multifaceted, it was for his work on leprosy that he was most often recognized.

Throughout his life Doull maintained an interest in the history of medicine. While at Johns Hopkins he collected the papers of William Budd, an early British epidemiologist, and often exchanged notes regarding the early history of bacteriology with the renowned pathologist William Henry Welch. In 1952, Doull contributed the section "Bacteriological Era (1879–1920)" to *History of American Epidemiology*, a standard text.

On Dec. 16, 1919, Doull married Ethel MacQuarrie; they had two children. In 1931, he became an American citizen. He died in Baltimore.

[A small collection of Doull's personal papers, including a complete bibliography of his writings, is at the National Library of Medicine, Bethesda, Md. On his life, see *Leprosy Review*, July 1963; *International Journal of Leprosy*, April–June 1963; and the obituary notice, *New York Times*, Apr. 9, 1963.]

ALLAN M. BRANDT

DOWNEY, SHERIDAN (Mar. 9, 1884–Oct. 25, 1961), U.S. senator, was born in Laramie, Wyoming Territory, the son of Stephen Wheeler Downey and Evangeline Victoria Owen. His father was an attorney and one of the territory's first delegates to the U.S. Congress. Downey attended public schools and the University of Wyoming, and in 1907 received an LL.B. from the University of Michigan Law School. That year he was admitted to the Wyoming bar and began practicing law in Laramie. In 1908, as a Republican, he was elected district attorney of Albany County on a reform ticket. Reportedly he angered wealthy cattlemen by refusing to accept their bribes during disputes with homesteaders. On Nov. 15, 1910, he married Helen Symons; they had five children.

In 1912, Downey split the Wyoming Republican party by leading a faction in support of Theodore Roosevelt's "Bull Moose" movement. As a result the state went Democratic. But when the Democrats offered Downey a patronage position, he rejected it. He then moved to Sacramento, Calif., where he formed a law partnership with his brother Stephen. For several years he remained out of politics, devoting himself to the law practice and to real estate development.

In 1924, Downey supported the third-party effort of Progressive Robert La Follette, and by 1932 he had become a Democrat. In 1934 he ran unsuccessfully for lieutenant governor of California on the same slate with Upton Sinclair. Soon thereafter Downey became an attorney for Dr. Francis Townsend, who was capturing national attention with his $200 per month pension proposal for citizens aged sixty or over who agreed to spend the money within one month. The pension program was to be financed by a 2 percent federal sales tax. Downey's enthusiasm for the program led him to write *Why I Believe in the Townsend Plan* (1936).

Downey ran unsuccessfully as a Townsendite candidate for Congress in 1936, but two years later was elected to the U.S. Senate, running on a "$30 Every Thursday" (for unemployed citizens over fifty) platform. He had the support of several pro-pension groups, liberals, and organized labor. He served two terms in the Senate. As he had promised during his campaign, Downey introduced a series of pension bills beginning in early 1940. In 1941 he chaired a special Senate committee on old age insurance that recommended increasing monthly pension benefits to a minimum of $30.

While serving on the Senate Military Affairs Committee, Downey supported a limited draft and limited industrialization for war. But in 1941 he opposed granting the administration authority to requisition industrial plants and machinery. He supported draft deferment for fathers, opposed the movement of agricultural workers into war industry, and suggested that Mexican workers be brought to California in order to maintain agricultural production. On several occasions he proposed saturation bombing attacks on Germany as a substitute for an invasion of Europe.

After the war Downey opposed the continuation of the draft, charged that the army was "hoarding" doctors badly needed by civilian communities, and called for the cancellation of all lend-lease obligations in the interest of peace. He favored international control of atomic energy under United Nations auspices, the sharing of atomic secrets in order to prevent a nuclear arms race, and the development of industrial uses of atomic energy. As chairman of the Senate Civil Service Committee he sponsored legislation to increase salaries and improve working conditions for federal employees.

In 1944, always concerned with California-related issues, Downey launched a campaign for the California Central Valley project. He introduced an amendment, never passed, to a rivers and harbors bill that would have exempted the project from limitations preventing farms larger than 160 acres from receiving irrigation from federally financed projects. He wrote *They Would Rule the Valley* (1948), condemning the Bureau of Reclamation for its role in applying the legislation to the Central Valley project.

Downey supported the tidelands oil bill, which established state rather than federal ownership of oil-rich underwater marginal land. After his retirement from Congress in 1950, because of ill health, Downey remained briefly in Washington in order to represent the city of Long Beach, Calif., in its controversy with the federal government over ownership of offshore oil lands. California Governor Earl Warren appointed Senator-elect Richard M. Nixon to fill Downey's unexpired term.

Downey died at San Francisco.

[Downey also wrote *Onward America* (1933), *Pensions or Penury?* (1939), and *Highways to Prosperity* (1940). Profiles of Downey are in the *New Republic*, Feb. 15, 1939; and *Nation*, Mar. 13, 1948. Also see Abraham Holtzman, *The Townsend Movement* (1963); and Jackson K. Putnam, *Old-Age Politics in California* (1970). An obituary is in the *New York Times*, Oct. 27, 1961.

STEPHEN D. BODAYLA

DREIER, MARY ELISABETH (Sept. 26, 1875–Aug. 15, 1963), reformer and philanthropist, was born in Brooklyn, N.Y., the daughter of Theodor Dreier, a businessman, and Doro-

thea Adelheid. Her parents had emigrated from Bremen, Germany. She was educated by private tutors and then attended the School of Philanthropy in New York City.

Dreier's major personal and philanthropic activities focused on working women, woman suffrage, and social and civic improvement. In 1906 she became president of the New York branch of the National Women's Trade Union League (WTUL), an association of employed working-class women and middle- and upper-class "allies" devoted to the organization of working women into trade unions. She retained that post until 1915; she again served as acting president in 1935. During her presidency the New York group was particularly active among garment workers, supporting their organization into the International Ladies Garment Workers Union and assisting them in strike activities.

Dreier wrote articles for the WTUL's journal, *Life and Labor*, to encourage unionization. In addition, the NYWTUL worked to educate working women to their work and civic opportunities, and pressed for legislation aimed at protecting employed women and children. Dreier, who remained on the national board of the WTUL until 1950, worked closely with her sister, Margaret Dreier Robins, who was active in the Chicago branch and who served as president of the national organization.

From 1911 to 1915, Dreier served on the New York State Factory Investigating Commission, which carried out a massive survey of industrial working conditions that provided evidence for the passage of factory reform legislation. In 1915, Mayor John Mitchell appointed her to the New York City Board of Education.

Dreier resigned all of these posts in spring 1915, in order to participate completely in the final drive to achieve the vote for women. She chaired the Industrial Section of the New York State Woman's Suffrage Party, the Americanization Committee for New York State, and the New York City Woman's Suffrage Party.

In 1917, Dreier became chairman of the New York State Committee on Women in Industry of the Advisory Commission of the Council of National Defense. After the war she was a member of the executive committee of the New York Council for Limitation of Armaments (1921–1927) and headed the Committee for the Outlawry of War of the WTUL.

Dreier's activities on behalf of labor, civic, and social improvement and of the disadvantaged continued with service on the national board of the Young Women's Christian Association, the New York Commission for Law Enforcement, the Ellis Island Committee, the Regional Labor Board in New York, and the Federal Advisory Council of the U.S. Employment Service. She was also head of the Women's Joint Legislative Conference, secretary of the New York Conference for Unemployment Insurance Legislation, head of the New York State Conference for Ratification of the Child Labor Amendment (1937), and frequent consultant to New York City and New York State officials regarding social and industrial matters of concern to women.

Prior to American entry into World War II, Dreier was a member of the women's division of the Committee to Defend America by Aiding the Allies. After Pearl Harbor she chaired the War Labor Standards Committee and was appointed by the labor commissioner to serve on the Women's Commission in 1942. She also continued her peace activities as a member of Promoting Enduring Peace.

In 1950 she published a biography of her sister, *Margaret Dreier Robins: Her Life, Letters and Work.* Dreier, who never married, died at her summer residence in Bar Harbor, Maine.

Mary Elisabeth Dreier represents the involved philanthropist of the early twentieth century. From a financially secure family, she constantly contributed time, funds, and organizing talents to a variety of feminist causes, most notably women workers and the suffrage movement. Her social prominence and social commitments led to her service on local and regional boards and commissions, particularly those dealing with labor and with penal reform.

[Dreier's manuscripts are housed in the Schlesinger Library at Radcliffe College; additional manuscript materials are in the Leonora O'Reilly papers at the Schlesinger Library, the Margaret Dreier Robins Collection at the University of Florida, the New York WTUL papers at the New York State Labor Library at Cornell University, and the papers of the WTUL at the Library of Congress. Her writings include contributions to *Reports of the Factory Investigating Commission* (1912–1915); "To Wash or Not to Wash: Aye, There's the Rub," *Life and Labor,* Mar. 1912; and "The Neckwear Workers and Their Strike," *Life and Labor,* Dec. 1912. Also see Judith O'Sullivan and Rosemary Gallick, *Workers and Allies* (1975). An obituary is in the *New York Times,* Aug. 17, 1963.]

SUSAN ESTABROOK KENNEDY

DRESSER, LOUISE KERLIN (Oct. 5, 1882–Apr. 24, 1965), actress, was born in Evansville, Ind., the daughter of William and Ida Kerlin. Upon the death of her father, a railroad engineer, she was obliged to cut short her education at the eighth grade and find a job. Equipped with a railroad pass, she traveled to Boston with the promise of a singing engagement. The job turned out to be in a burlesque house. Despite misgivings, she donned tights and performed, often supplementing her income by singing sentimental songs at a local wax museum. While on tour in vaudeville in Chicago, she sought out songwriter Paul Dresser (brother of the novelist Theodore Dreiser and composer of "On the Banks of the Wabash") to ask for a special orchestration. As she often recounted to interviewers, Paul Dresser, who admired William Kerlin, was delighted to meet the daughter of one of his heroes and immediately called a stage manager to find a part for his "sister." On the basis of this connection, she adopted the name Dresser, although she never acknowledged rumors that she had been legally adopted by Dresser.

Described as "the girl with the pleasing contralto voice" and regarded as one of the most beautiful actresses on Broadway, Dresser made her musical comedy debut in Lew Fields's *About Town* (1906). She may have been added to the cast at the suggestion of Jack Norworth, a popular young leading man and author of "Shine On Harvest Moon." Her marriage in 1906 to Norworth ended in divorce in 1908 because of his relationship with actress Trixie Friganza. In May of that year Dresser married Jack Gardner, a singer and later casting director at Fox. They had no children.

Despite Fields's introduction, Dresser credits Charles Frohman with giving her the finest stage opportunity of her career when he cast her in his *The Girls of Gottenburg* (1909). This placed her, according to reviewers, in the "foremost ranks of musical comedy favorites." Thereafter she was always considered for parts requiring a beautiful blonde or talented comedienne, or when a "snappy new song" was to be introduced. Dresser appeared in *The Girl Behind the Counter* (1907), *Candy Shop* (1909), and *Matinee Idol* (1910); she toured in *The Golden Widow* (1909) and *A Lovely Liar* (1911). She returned to New York in *Broadway to Paris* (1912) and *Potash and Perlmutter* (1913), reviewed as the best work of her career. She played Patsy Pygmalion in George M. Cohan's *Hello, Broadway!* (1914) and appeared in *Cordelia Blossom* (1917) and in the Jerome Kern musicals *Have A Heart* (1917) and *Rock-a-bye, Baby* (1918).

Between musical comedies Dresser continued to tour in vaudeville, often billed as the "Girl from the Wabash." Her status as reigning Broadway beauty also won her lecture engagements (often delivered in the morning before performances). Magazines and newspapers featured articles in which she gave beauty advice and hints on controlling weight (a perennial problem for her). Dresser was frequently photographed for fashion pages.

In the *Have A Heart* production Dresser tripped over a loose carpet on stage and broke her wrist in February 1917; she later sued the Liberty Theatre owners for $50,000. Despite some work in vaudeville, her career ebbed at this point; *Variety* reported that she had been inactive for the year of 1919. Lured by Pauline Frederick's suggestion that she join the cast of *The Glory of Clementina* (1922), Dresser moved to Glendale, Calif. Her film career began with roles as a much-put-upon mother or a patient wife in *Prodigal Daughters* (1923); *The City That Never Sleeps* (1924); *The Third Degree*, *White Flannels*, and *Mr. Wu* (1927); *The Air Circus* (1928); *Not Quite Decent* (1929); *Mammy* (1930); and *A Girl of the Limberlost* (1934). She was featured in Fox's first "talking drama," playing the mother in *Mother Knows Best* (1928). In 1927 the Flint (Mich.) *Journal* reported that "few other screen actresses of the day can so authentically portray the maternal." Dresser also created a "nicely costumed" Catherine the Great in *The Eagle* (1925), with Rudolf Valentino; an accused murderer in *Blind Goddess* (1926); a leather-lunged Calamity Jane in 1931; a prioress in *Cradle Song* (1933); and Empress Elizabeth in *The Scarlet Empress* (1934). Richard Watts, Jr., named Dresser one of the ten best actresses of 1926; the *Pittsburgh Post* described her as "the female Lon Chaney"; and Louella Parsons commented that she illustrated the importance of gifted character actresses.

While Dresser's role as the immigrant mother in *A Ship Comes In* (1928) won her a "Citation of Merit" at the first Academy Awards presentations, she was most widely praised for a performance that "electrified moviegoers with the reality of the characterization" when she played the drunken ex-star in *The Goose Woman* (1925). After successes as Will Rogers's foil in films such as *Lightnin'* (1930), *State Fair* (1933), *David Harum* (1934), and *The Country Chairman* (1935), she made her last film appearance in *Maid of Salem* (1937). In retirement she lived quietly in Glendale until her death in Woodland Hills, Calif.

[For more information on Dresser, see clippings and scrapbooks in the New York Public Library Theater Collection at Lincoln Center. Interviews and sketches of Dresser appear in *Theater*, July 1912; *Green Book*, Oct. 1912 and Jan. 1916; *Cosmopolitan*, June 1914; *Motion Picture*, Aug. 1926, Nov. 1929, and Oct. 1933; *Motion Picture Classic*, Sept. 1928; and *Photoplay*, May 1925 and Mar. 1930. Obituaries are found in the *New York Times*, Apr. 25, 1965; *Time*, Apr. 30, 1965; and *Screen World* (1966).]

ELIZABETH R. NELSON

DREYFUS, MAX (Apr. 1, 1874–May 12, 1964), music publisher, was born in Kuppenheim, Germany, the son of Elias Dreyfus, a farmer, and of Amelia Esther Hertz. At the age of fourteen, he immigrated to New York City, hoping to become a composer. He had little success but found intermittent work as a pianist. He also arranged songs for his friend Paul Dresser, who helped him establish contacts with *Ev'ry Month*, a music-publishing magazine edited by Dresser's brother, the novelist Theodore Dreiser. In 1895 Dreyfus took his compositions to M. Witmark and Sons, a New York City music-publishing house. Witmark rejected his music but hired him as a demonstration pianist. On Oct. 18, 1897, Dreyfus married Victoria Brill; they had no children.

In 1900, under the pseudonym "Max Eugene," Dreyfus published a wordless ballad, "Cupid's Garden," which was popular briefly as background music for silent films. But by this time he had largely abandoned his ambitions as a composer, concentrating instead on becoming a music publisher. In 1901 he purchased a 25 percent interest in T. B. Harms, Inc., a Witmark rival, and over the next few years achieved managerial and financial control of the company.

Dreyfus met the aspiring composer Jerome Kern in 1904 and promptly hired him to sell music for Harms in the Hudson Valley region, which he later called "the toughest job I know." Kern succeeded as a salesman, and Dreyfus retained him as a rehearsal pianist and arranger. In 1905 he engineered Kern's first big break, a song-writing credit ("Howd You Like to Spoon with Me?") in Ivan Caryll's *The Earl and the Girl*. In 1912 Dreyfus gave the composer Charles Rudolph Friml an entrée into musical theater by recommending him to replace Victor Herbert in Arthur Hammerstein's production of *The Firefly*. In 1914 Dreyfus helped to found the American Society of Composers, Authors and Publishers

(ASCAP), on whose board of directors he served until his death.

In 1917 a young rehearsal pianist, George Gershwin, showed several of his songs to Dreyfus ("You-oo, Just You" and "There's More to a Kiss Than XXX"). Dreyfus gave Gershwin a $35-a-week retainer. Dreyfus' faith in Gershwin was rewarded; Dreyfus-controlled firms published all of Gershwin's subsequent work beginning in 1918 with "Some Wondeful Sort of Someone." During this period, Dreyfus wooed such established composers as Herbert from Witmark to Harms and inaugurated a retainer system to support the development of beginning composers.

In succeeding years, Dreyfus-controlled companies published the work of virtually every major musical theater composer and lyricist except Irving Berlin. Among these, besides Kern and George and Ira Gershwin, were Richard Rodgers, Oscar Hammerstein II, Sigmund Romberg, Cole Porter, Vincent Youmans, Kurt Weill, Alan Jay Lerner, Frederick Loewe, Stephen Sondheim, Adolph Green, and Johnny Mercer. With several of these talents, Dreyfus pioneered partnership agreements. In 1929 Dreyfus sold his interest in Harms to the Music Publishing Holding Corporation, a subsidiary of Warner Brothers Pictures, Inc., for a reported $8 million to $10 million. Warners retained Dreyfus as president and director until 1935, but it was essentially a consultant's role. He described the job frankly as "all hooey. Picture people don't take advice. They give orders."

Dreyfus acquired control of the British music publishing concern Chappell and Company, Inc., in 1935. His younger brother, Louis, became president, while Max Dreyfus assumed control of its New York City branch. The two dominated the music publishing industry in the western hemisphere.

In 1945 Warner Brothers produced a film biography of George Gershwin, *Rhapsody in Blue*, in which Dreyfus was portrayed by the rotund and expansive actor Charles Coburn. In reality, Dreyfus was "a soft-spoken, slightly-built man who was reserved almost to a fault." "He betrayed little elation when he heard a tune he liked," said Richard Rodgers. "He was not very enthusiastic, but his work was. . . . He knew how and where to promote a song."

On May 6, 1964, the London offices of Chappell were destroyed by fire. Many precious musical manuscripts were lost. Six days later Dreyfus died at his 700-acre estate near Brewster, N.Y. Upon his death, Irving Caesar remarked that "Max Dreyfus did not build a

publishing company. He forged an empire that is as big abroad as it is in this country. The shape of the new music business will make it impossible for anyone else to duplicate Dreyfus' achievement."

[See Stanley Green, *The World of Musical Comedy* (1960); and obituaries in the *New York Times* and *New York Herald Tribune*, both May 16, 1964; and Herm Schoenfeld, in *Variety*, May 20, 1964.]

NANCY L. STEFFEN

DRYFOOS, ORVIL E. (Nov. 8, 1912–May 25, 1963), newspaper executive, was born in New York City, the son of Jack A. Dryfoos, a textile merchant, and of Florence Levi. He attended the Horace Mann School and was a sociology major at Dartmouth College, from which he graduated with the B.A. in 1934. Soon thereafter he joined Asiel and Company, a Wall Street brokerage firm. Dryfoos remained on Wall Street until after his marriage to Marian Effie Sulzberger on July 8, 1941; they had three children. His wife was the eldest daughter of Arthur Hays Sulzberger and Iphigene Ochs, who held a controlling interest in the *New York Times*. Despite his ownership of a seat on the New York Stock Exchange, Dryfoos was persuaded to give up his career on Wall Street. On Jan. 2, 1942, he began working as a cub reporter on the *Times*. An attempt to enter the armed services after the outbreak of World War II was thwarted when his physical examination revealed a heart defect (he had suffered from rheumatic fever as a child).

Thereafter Dryfoos dedicated himself to newspaper publishing. Guided by the counsel of his father-in-law, he served an apprenticeship in the newsroom as both a legman for more experienced reporters and as a makeup editor. Sulzberger himself had been brought to the *Times* as a son-in-law of Adolph S. Ochs and was determined that Dryfoos would not undergo the humiliation he had experienced as a stern father-in-law's understudy. Dryfoos understood the relationship and sought to imitate Sulzberger's fair-mindedness by insisting that he be treated as a *Times* employee rather than a member of the Ochs-Sulzberger dynasty.

In 1943, Dryfoos left the newsroom to become assistant to the publisher. He learned all phases of the growing publishing empire, which included paper mills, a radio station, and subsidiary activities that made use of his knowledge of financial dealings. His associates remarked upon his informal approach, an unpretentious eagerness to absorb information, and his unfailing kindness toward subordinates. "I was sensible enough to marry the boss's daughter," Sulzberger once said to Dryfoos, "and you were, too." Staff members who worked closely with Dryfoos found that he was acutely conscious of his circumstances, and thus often deferred to others even though his own judgment was valid.

From 1944 to 1960, Dryfoos maintained his interest in political affairs and attended every major national convention. He also had an abiding devotion to the New York Yankees baseball team. His other outside interests were trout fishing, tennis, and golf. He was a fierce competitor until advised by doctors to lessen his participation in games involving intense physical exercise.

In 1955, Dryfoos succeeded Julius Ochs Adler as vice-president of the *Times* and became a member of the board of directors. Three years later he was elevated to the presidency of the *Times*. During this period Sulzberger called Dryfoos into the decision-making process at the newspaper, and some important matters were left to his judgment. At the retirement of Sulzberger on Apr. 25, 1961, Dryfoos succeeded him as publisher of the *Times*. Dryfoos sought to maintain Adolph Ochs's general rules stressing news coverage, accurate reporting, and sound fiscal policies. A feature of the latter policy was the continued plowing back of profits into the *Times* even as labor, paper, and circulation costs rose.

The news staff under Dryfoos was headed by Turner Catledge, and included a galaxy of reporters, critics, and reviewers with national reputations. Dryfoos made the decision to publish a western edition of the *Times*, which first appeared on Oct. 1, 1962. Meanwhile, negotiations with the New York printers' union were under way, and there was talk of the first strike by the shop workers since 1883. After a series of fruitless contract discussions, the strike began on Dec. 8, 1962. It continued for 114 days. Dryfoos left the principal task of bargaining to his general manager, Amory Bradford. He was under great personal strain as the staff at the *Times* was reduced from nearly 5,000 to a token force of 900.

Dismayed by the events that halted production on the *Times* and six other New York daily newspapers, Dryfoos directed the *Times*-owned radio station, WQXR, to double its newscast time. He stayed in the background during contract negotiations (the printers feared automation and wanted considerably more than the $141 average weekly wage), but went to his office every day and wrote personal letters to employees in a show of concern over their morale. He ordered a syndicated column by columnist James Reston killed because of its attack on the union president. He urged the negotiators to stay at the bargaining table, despite the apparent hostility between the union executives and the representatives of the *Times*.

When the strike finally ended on Mar. 31, 1963, a story was prepared that was somewhat critical of the negotiating team of the *Times*. Bradford asked that the story be altered, but Dryfoos backed his reporter and the story was printed. Fatigued by the strike, Dryfoos soon left for a vacation in Puerto Rico. There he became ill and was flown back to New York City, where he died.

James Reston delivered the eulogy at Dryfoos' funeral: "He wore his life away . . . worrying about other people."

[The best accounts of Dryfoos' life and career are in the *New York Times*, Apr. 26, 1961, and May 26–29, 1963. See also Gay Talese, *The Kingdom and the Power* (1969). Personal letters from Hugh Dryfoos, Ivan Veit, and Turner Catledge concerning Dryfoos' life, sent to the author, are in the University of Virginia Library.]

ROBERT A. RUTLAND

DU BOIS, WILLIAM EDWARD BURGHARDT (Feb. 23, 1868–Aug. 27, 1963), Afro-American historian, sociologist, crusading editor, and political activist, was born in Great Barrington, Mass., the son of Alfred Du Bois, who was of French and African descent, and of Mary Sylvina Burghardt. His father deserted his mother soon after their marriage. The Burghardts formed part of a stable but impoverished group of about fifty blacks in the Great Barrington population of some 5,000. Du Bois attended the town's Congregational Church and Sunday school; there, as in his classes in elementary and high school, he was usually the only black child. He eagerly absorbed the values of discipline, hard work, and thrift: "in general thought and conduct I became quite thoroughly New England." His racial identification developed slowly, but at fifteen, as a correspondent for the *New York Globe*, a progressive black paper, he commenced a lifelong career of service to his fellow blacks.

Supported by his headmaster and members of the Congregational Church, Du Bois set out in 1885 for Fisk University at Nashville, Tenn., one of the colleges founded after the Civil War by the American Missionary Association to educate blacks. His initial exposure to southern racism was devastating. "No one but a Negro," he wrote, "going into the South without previous experience of color caste can have any conception of its barbarism." At Fisk, though, Du Bois was happy under the tutelage of its dedicated faculty (almost all white) and as a member of a student body that was his first sustained encounter with the variety of his race. He was also moved by the experience of teaching school during the summers in rural Tennessee.

Du Bois excelled as a student, especially in philosophy, and was editor-in-chief of the monthly *Fisk Herald* in his last year. Graduating in 1888, he declined the offer of a scholarship to study for the ministry, preferring to enter Harvard as a junior, to continue his study of philosophy. His experience of southern segregation had altered his attitude to whites; at Harvard he shunned the company of his fellow students even as he craved the attention of the faculty, especially the historian Albert Bushnell Hart and the psychologist and philosopher William James. He later ranked James with his mother as the greatest influences on his life. As a frequent visitor in James's house, he was exposed to a range of secular liberal opinion that contrasted sharply with the pieties of his Fisk instructors; he later claimed that James turned him away from the study of philosophy and toward history and social problems. In 1890, Du Bois delivered a well-received but immature commencement oration, "Jefferson Davis as a Representative of Civilization," in which he contrasted Teutonic force of will with the more "submissive" quality of blacks and urged the blending of these qualities in American life.

In the fall of 1890, Du Bois began graduate study in history at Harvard under Hart. In 1892, with all but his thesis completed for the doctoral degree, he enrolled as a special student at the University of Berlin. Again he found brilliant teachers, the most important of whom were the economists Gustav Schmoller and Adolf Wagner and the historian Heinrich von Treitschke. Europe deeply affected Du Bois. "The unity beneath all life clutched me," he wrote; "I was not less fanatically a Negro, but 'Negro' meant a greater, broader sense of humanity and world fellowship."

In 1894 Du Bois "dropped suddenly back into 'nigger'-hating America!" At Wilberforce University, an African Methodist Episcopal school in Ohio, he found himself improbably appointed professor of Latin and Greek. He found the college generally lethargic except for its obsession with religion and quickly offended his superiors by bluntly refusing to lead spontaneous public prayer.

By this time certain aspects of Du Bois' appearance and manner were set. Of less than medium height, bald, handsome, with a neatly trimmed Vandyke that set off patrician features, he dressed as formally as any occasion permitted. Although James Weldon Johnson noted that among his friends he was "the most jovial and fun-loving of men," at times Du Bois was so sensitive to the possibility of insult that some thought him nearly paranoid and vindictive. Characteristically tactless, Du Bois seldom backed away from controversy. He himself admitted only that "with all my belligerency I was in reality unreasonably shy."

In 1895, Du Bois received the doctorate from Harvard, which inaugurated its Historical Studies series the following year with his dissertation, *The Suppression of the African Slave-Trade to the United States.* Scrupulously documented, the work argues that moral weakness in the face of economic opportunity prolonged the slave trade after it was legally abolished; conversely, economic dictates, not moral suasion, ended the trade. On May 12, 1896, Du Bois married Nina Gomer, a Wilberforce student of German and Afro-American parentage; they had two children. Resigning from Wilberforce, he then accepted a one-year assignment at the University of Pennsylvania as an "assistant instructor" to produce a study of blacks in Philadelphia. Living amid "dirt, drunkenness, poverty, and crime," he interviewed some 5,000 persons in the course of writing *The Philadelphia Negro* (1899). Relatively novel in its statistical and empirical component, this much-acclaimed work sought to locate the black population, "their occupations and daily life, their homes, their organizations, and, above all, their relation to their million white fellow citizens." Du Bois' emphasis on environmental and historical rather than on genetic explanations of black behavior set new standards for the study of Afro-Americans.

Submersion in a black urban population further released Du Bois's creativity. In August 1897 the *Atlantic Monthly* published "Strivings of the Negro People," which included his historic formulation of Afro-American identity; the black American was "a sort of seventh son, born with a veil, and gifted with second-sight in this American world—a world which yields him no true self-consciousness, but only lets him see himself through the revelation of the other world. It is a peculiar sensation, this double-consciousness. . . . One ever feels his twoness—an American, a Negro; two souls, two thoughts, two unreconciled strivings; two warring ideals in one dark body, whose dogged strength alone keeps it from being torn asunder." The same year he spoke to the American Negro Academy in Washington, D.C., on "The Conservation of Races," proclaiming black Americans to be members of a "vast historic race" whose destiny was neither absorption into nor a "servile imitation of Anglo-Saxon culture, but a stalwart originality which shall unswervingly follow Negro ideals." At the Pan-African Conference in London in 1900, he warned the world: "The problem of the twentieth century is the problem of the color line."

In the fall of 1897, Du Bois moved to Atlanta University to teach economics, history, and sociology, and to take charge of the annual Atlanta University Conference for the Study of the Negro Problems and to edit and publish its proceedings. Uneven in quality, the studies supervised by Du Bois (1898–1914) testify to his great faith in remedial social science. From the outset, though, his faith was tested by the raw racism of the South. The lynching of a black laborer in 1897 while Du Bois was preparing an objective study of the charge against him was deeply disturbing; he also blamed the death of his son on inadequate medical facilities for blacks in the South. He began to agonize over the limits of scholarship and the need for action. He grew to resent the leadership of the most influential black in America, Booker T. Washington, who argued that vocational education was the key to black progress.

Du Bois' 1902 review of Washington's autobiography, *Up from Slavery*, was included in his greatest work, *The Souls of Black Folk* (1903), which established him as Washington's main ideological rival. A hauntingly complex portrait of the Afro-American people, *Souls of Black Folk* blended history, sociology, memoir, biography, and fiction so effectively that it became perhaps the most influential work on blacks in America since *Uncle Tom's Cabin*. The brief "Credo," Du Bois's most widely republished piece, appeared in 1904.

Drawn deeper into the struggle for equality for blacks by the jailing in 1903 of William Monroe Trotter, radical editor of the *Boston Guardian*, for disrupting a speech by Booker T. Washington in Boston, Du Bois organized the Niagara Movement, named after the site of its first meeting in July 1905. The movement called for agitation against all forms of segregation and other injustice. In April 1906, Du Bois led a barefoot march at Harpers Ferry, W. Va., drawing on the memory of John Brown's defiance

and demanding "manhood rights" for blacks: "we are men, we will be treated as men. On this rock we have planted our banners." The Niagara Movement, however, made little headway against the entrenched power of Booker T. Washington, and even less against segregation.

Du Bois tried unsuccessfully to increase his influence by founding two magazines of news, opinion, and essays, the weekly *Moon* (1905–1906) and the monthly *Horizon* (1907–1910). His position at Atlanta University, which depended for financial aid on philanthropists generally loyal to Booker T. Washington, became more difficult, but Du Bois did not retreat. A commencement speech at Atlanta by Franz Boas on the glories of African culture and its relevance to black Americans led Du Bois to deeper reading on the subject; the African perspective entered his work to stay. The Atlanta Riots of 1906 further darkened his spirit, as his prose poem "A Litany at Atlanta" (1906) attests. His brooding resulted in a biography of *John Brown* (1909), with its reiterated theme: "the cost of liberty is less than the price of repression."

The opportunity to act in a way consonant with his scholarly training came in 1909 with the planning of the National Association for the Advancement of Colored People (NAACP) by liberal whites determined to end segregation and improve the general situation of Afro-Americans. Resigning from Atlanta, Du Bois brought to the NAACP his considerable personal and intellectual knowledge—but also his radical reputation. He was installed as director of publications and research in 1910; more significantly, with neither capital nor the assurance of constant financial support, he founded *Crisis*, the monthly organ of the NAACP. Du Bois clashed repeatedly over the years with leaders of the NAACP over control of the magazine, which was of incalculable value to the organization. Arthur B. Spingarn stated that without it the NAACP could not have been "what it was and is."

For most of the twenty-four years of his editorship, *Crisis* remained the most important magazine aimed primarily at black Americans; in its pages Du Bois thundered against lynching and other outrages, proclaimed the achievements of prominent and obscure blacks, reviewed works of significance to the cause, stimulated pride in and knowledge of the African cultures, and encouraged literary and other intellectual and social achievement. From a first printing of 1,000 copies the magazine rose to a peak circulation of just over 100,000 in 1919.

In 1911, perhaps influenced by the leftist element among the NAACP founders, Du Bois joined the American Socialist Party, but soon withdrew in protest against its softness on the issue of race. Also that year he attended the Universal Races Congress in London and was elected joint secretary of the American delegation. In addition he published a novel, *The Quest of the Silver Fleece,* a tale of cotton (perhaps patterned on Frank Norris' proposed trilogy of wheat) in which romantic elements and a cold exposure of the economics of the industry are not always smoothly blended. His reading in African history culminated in *The Negro* (1915), which became a kind of Bible of Pan-Africanism.

In May 1915 the *Atlantic Monthly* published Du Bois' essay "African Roots of the War," a brilliant blending of Marxism with an African point of.view in relating World War I to colonialism and imperialism. Nevertheless, Du Bois strongly supported the Allied cause against Germany; his editorial "Close Ranks" (July 1918), in which he urged blacks to "forget our special grievances and close our ranks" with whites, provoked a storm of criticism from *Crisis* readers.

Following the end of the war, Du Bois moved to capitalize on the Allied victory through the Pan-African congresses that met in Europe in 1919, 1921, and 1923, and in New York in 1927. At the first congress he urged the seizure of the German territories in Africa as the nucleus of an international but African-controlled free state. This plan foundered on the intransigence of the colonial powers and the factionalism and suspicion of African leaders.

Du Bois believed that the congresses influenced the League of Nations to some extent, but by 1923 the Pan-African Congress was essentially moribund. In the meantime he had clashed openly with the leader of the mass back-to-Africa movement in the United States, Marcus Garvey. To Du Bois, Garvey was an almost criminally misguided and disorganized demogogue; Garvey declared that Du Bois was a fake aristocrat ashamed of his race: "If there is a man who is most dissatisfied with himself, it is Dr. Du Bois" (*Negro World,* Jan. 8, 1921).

Crisis undoubtedly encouraged the outpouring of arts and letters in the 1920's known as the Harlem Renaissance. Du Bois himself wrote *Darkwater: Voices from Within the Veil* (1920), a combination of pieces not unlike *The Souls of Black Folk* but far less lyrical and more polemical in tone. Some aspects of the new literary movement distressed Du Bois, though, especially the antipolitical calls for artistic freedom

and the frequent depiction of Harlem lowlife and sexuality. In "Criteria of Negro Art" (1926) he argued that art and propaganda are basically the same. *Crisis* launched severe attacks on the major white champion of the new writers, the novelist Carl Van Vechten (*Nigger Heaven,* 1926), as well as on Langston Hughes, Claude McKay, Arna Bontemps, and other black writers. Du Bois tried to show the way himself in *Dark Princess* (1928), a novel he called "my favorite book." The novel dealt with a plot among the darker races of the world to overthrow white domination; but its epic scale and some brilliant scenes do not make up for its instability of language and tone and its absurdities of plot.

Unable to influence the thinking of many of the younger writers, Du Bois stressed the dangers of dependence on white patronage. The virtual disappearance of the Harlem Renaissance following the onset of the Great Depression seemed to him to prove his point.

A visit to the Soviet Union in 1926 had brought the power of socialism home to Du Bois: "if what I have seen with my eyes and heard with my ears in Russia is Bolshevism, I am a Bolshevik," he wrote in *Crisis* (November 1926). The dismal Afro-American situation forced him to argue for voluntary segregation for black business, education, and other activities. This point of view proved extremely unpopular with the NAACP leadership, which was committed to interracial liberalism and capitalism. Nonetheless, Du Bois pushed his program. Finally, in 1934 he resigned from the organization when it moved to curb his power as editor. In its farewell the NAACP noted: "He created, what never existed before, a Negro intelligentsia, and many who have never read a word of his writings are his spiritual disciples and descendants."

In 1934, Du Bois returned to Atlanta University. The following year he published *Black Reconstruction in America,* a monumental revaluation of the often maligned role of blacks in the Civil War and the years following. Using a great quantity of hitherto ignored monographs, and applying Marxist terminology if not Marxist method, Du Bois argued that the revolt of the black workers was the cause of the war and a prime factor in the victory of the Union, and that black leadership in the Reconstruction governments was generally honest and farsighted.

In February 1936, Du Bois began a weekly column in black newspapers that kept his name alive even as his influence generally diminished;

he published pieces in the *Pittsburgh Courier,* then from 1939 in the New York *Amsterdam News,* and between 1945 and 1948 in the *Chicago Tribune.* The book *Black Folk: Then and Now* (1939) contained large portions of *The Negro,* augmented by new material, but did not repeat the use of Marxist terms in *Black Reconstruction;* neither did it raise much immediate hope for the end of colonialism. At Atlanta University, Du Bois busied himself with a grand scheme in sociology, convincing the presidents of twenty black land-grant colleges in 1940 to cooperate to upgrade the study of black America and to pool their results for practical application to the needs of the race. The same year he published the first of two autobiographies, *Dusk of Dawn: An Autobiography of a Concept of Race,* in which he traced the evolution of modern racial theory and practice against the background of his life.

In 1944, Du Bois was suddenly retired from his Atlanta position because, in his opinion, of the egotism and envy of his superiors; certainly his aggressive socialist and Pan-African newspaper writing offended conservative sensibilities. The NAACP returned him to New York as director of special research, perhaps intending it as an honorary position for one presumably near the end of a distinguished life. In his four years there he published a vigorous critique of capitalism and colonialism, *Color and Democracy: Colonies and Peace* (1945)—which designated as colonies not only Africa but every country not in command of its own resources—and *The World and Africa* (1947), a study of the continent from the vantage point of a Europe ruined by World War II. In 1945, at the Fifth Pan-African Congress in Manchester, England, Du Bois was hailed as the "father of Pan-Africanism." Working within the NAACP, he produced the pamphlet "An Appeal to the World," submitting it in 1946 on behalf of black Americans to the United Nations Commission on Human Rights. The following year he openly endorsed the presidential candidacy of Henry Wallace and the Progressive party, whereas the NAACP leadership preferred Harry Truman. This difference of opinion—but ultimately of ideology—led to his dismissal by the NAACP in 1948.

Du Bois then moved steadily toward Communism. He accepted office space and an unpaid position with the radical Council on African Affairs, led by Paul Robeson and Alphaeus Hunton, undismayed at its designation as "subversive" by the attorney general. In 1949 he addressed the mass rally in New York City of the much-criticized Conference for World Peace organized by the National Council of the Arts, Sciences, and Professions. Next he headed the American delegation to the World Congress of the Defenders of Peace in Paris. In 1950 he became chairman of the Peace Information Center, formed to circulate the Stockholm Peace Appeal against the spread of nuclear weapons. Later that year Du Bois ran in Harlem for the United States Senate on the American Labor party ticket; he was soundly defeated, gaining less than 15 percent of the Harlem vote.

Early in 1951, Du Bois and four other members of the Peace Information Center were indicted as unregistered agents of a foreign power. He was arraigned in February, in Washington, and released on bail. On Feb. 27, 1951, he married Shirley Lola Graham, a long-time friend and an advocate of socialism, his first wife having died in 1950. In November, Du Bois came to trial; after testimony was heard, a motion of the defense for a directed acquittal was granted by the presiding judge. "Blessed are the Peacemakers," he wrote shortly afterward, "for they shall be called Communists."

Du Bois' radical activities continued. His passport was revoked to prevent him from traveling, but he was not silent. In 1953, at the funeral service for the executed spies Julius and Ethel Rosenberg, he recited the Twenty-Third Psalm. That same year he mourned the passing of Josef Stalin as a "simple, calm and courageous" man. The most bitter price Du Bois paid for his radical politics was ostracism by certain black leaders. Invitations to speak at black colleges and elsewhere dropped dramatically in number. "The colored children," he lamented, "ceased to hear my name."

Du Bois turned to fiction. Between 1955 and 1957 he wrote the first draft of a trilogy, *The Black Flame* (*The Ordeal of Mansart,* 1957; *Mansart Builds a School,* 1959; *Worlds of Color,* 1961), the story of a black man born in 1876 who rises, more by patience and hard work than by great intelligence, to the leadership of a small Southern school. Du Bois traces the fortunes of Emmanuel Mansart and his family down through the generations to his death in 1954; equally important in this unpolished work is the dramatization of concurrent national and world history by which Du Bois explains the forces that Mansart himself could never fully understand.

When the State Department lifted its ban on his travel in 1958, Du Bois set out almost at once on a tour that took him to Britain, France, Czechoslovakia, the German Democratic Republic, the Soviet Union, and China. In Prague and Berlin he received honorary doctorates; in China he celebrated his ninety-first birthday with a radio broadcast from Peking; in Moscow, on May Day 1959, he received the Lenin Peace Prize.

The next year Du Bois went to Ghana for the inauguration of Kwame Nkrumah as its first president; Nkrumah invited him to return to Ghana permanently and begin work on the *Encyclopedia Africana*, in which he had long been interested. Du Bois accepted this invitation. His final act before leaving the United States was to apply for membership in the Communist Party of the United States. He was admitted on Oct. 13, 1961, a week after he left for Ghana.

In 1962 ill health took Du Bois to Rumania for treatment and to London for an abdominal operation. He returned via Cairo, and later that year visited Peking and Moscow. In February 1963 he renounced his American citizenship and took that of Ghana. He died in Accra, Ghana, where he is buried. His death came in the same year as the largest gathering in the history of the American civil rights movement, the march on Washington, D.C.

In his combination of excellent academic training and political activism on behalf of blacks, Du Bois had virtually no superior among his fellow Americans. His importance lies in this application of knowledge, especially in history and sociology, to the historic struggle of his race in the twentieth century. A well developed poetic sense gave him extraordinary insight into the American dilemma, as well as real distinction as a writer. His great energy and his longevity enabled him to maximize his effectiveness. His scholarly standards undoubtedly suffered because of his political zeal, but in his best work, such as *The Souls of Black Folk*, Du Bois established himself firmly among the major interpreters of American history and culture and at the very center of the Afro-American intellectual tradition.

[Du Bois' papers can be found at the University of Massachusetts, Amherst. Additional books by him include *In Battle for Peace* (1952) and *The Autobiography of W. E. B. Du Bois* (1968). Collections are Herbert Aptheker, ed., *The Correspondence of W. E. B. Du Bois*, 3 vols. (1973–1978); and Philip S. Foner, ed., *W. E. B. Du Bois Speaks . . . 1890–1919* (1970). For bibliographical information see Herbert Aptheker, *Annotated Bibliography of the Published Writings of W. E. B. Du Bois* (1973); and Paul G. Partington, *W. E. B. Du Bois: A Bibliography of His Published Writings* (1977). Biographies are Francis L. Broderick, *W. E. B. Du Bois* (1959); Elliott M. Rudwick, *W. E. B. Du Bois* (1968); and Arnold Rampersad, *The Art and Imagination of W. E. B. Du Bois* (1976). An obituary is in the *New York Times*, Aug. 25, 1963.]

ARNOLD RAMPERSAD

DUFFY, EDMUND (Mar. 1, 1899–Sept. 13, 1962), cartoonist, was born in Jersey City, N.J., the son of John Joseph Duffy, a policeman, and Anna Hughes. He attended elementary school in Jersey City and in 1914 enrolled at New York's Art Students' League, where he studied under George Bridgman, Boardman Robinson, and John Sloan. He graduated in 1919.

Duffy's first major contribution to a newspaper was a sketch of the Armistice Day festivities of World War I for the Sunday magazine of the *New York Tribune*. He also submitted his work to the weekend magazines and sports pages of the *New York Herald, New York Evening Post*, and *Scribner's* and *Century* magazines.

In 1920 Duffy withdrew his entire savings of $150 and sailed to Europe. He sketched briefly for the *London Evening News* before moving on to Paris. There he studied art, reveled in the city's nightlife, and dispatched his sketches to the *New York Herald*.

Upon his return to the United States in 1922, Duffy illustrated for the Sunday magazine and theater section of the *Brooklyn Daily Eagle*, the *New York Leader*, and *Collier's* and *Century* magazines.

On Nov. 26, 1924, he married Anne Rector, a painter; they had one daughter. Also in 1924, Duffy became editorial cartoonist for the *Baltimore Sun*, where he developed a national reputation and won three Pulitzer Prizes. His political cartoons were notable for their bold line, stark realism, and blunt condemnation of injustice and hypocrisy. They were stylistically simple and often bore short captions that drove home the point. Duffy drew from deep conviction. As one colleague put it succinctly: "If Duffy don't believe it, Duffy don't draw it."

He won his first Pulitzer Prize in 1931 for "An Old Struggle Still Going On." A denunciation of religious persecution in the Soviet Union, it depicted a martial figure, labeled "Russia," straining to break off a cross from atop a church dome. Domestic injustice was the subject of his 1934 Pulitzer-Prize cartoon, "California Points with Pride," a slap at California's Governor James Rolph, Jr., for condoning the lynching of two men in San Jose. At the bottom of the panel stands a portly, content Rolph who "points with pride" to the two lifeless bodies dangling from a tree limb.

Duffy won a third Pulitzer Prize in 1940 for "The Outstretched Hand," generally regarded as his most powerful statement. A condemnation of German duplicity and a warning against future appeasement, the cartoon appeared in the *Baltimore Sun* on Oct. 7, 1939, shortly after Hitler's invasion of Poland and its division between Germany and Russia. The illustration is dominated by a huge Adolf Hitler in full Nazi regalia. Figures labeled "minorities" cower about his feet and smoldering ruins fill the background. In his left hand, Hitler clutches ragged sheets of paper, one marked "broken promises," another "treaty," and a third "no more territorial demands." His outstretched right hand bears the words "peace offer" and drips with blood.

Occasionally Duffy wrote book reviews and other features for the *Baltimore Sun.* In a front-page story in August 1935, he covered in moving detail the funeral of humorist Will Rogers. He resigned from the *Sun* in 1948 and joined the *Saturday Evening Post* as editorial cartoonist in early 1949.

Duffy retired in 1957, having drawn some 8,000 cartoons during a career that spanned nearly four decades. His work has been exhibited at various institutions around the country, including the Whitney Museum of American Art in New York City and the Henry E. Huntington Library and Art Gallery in San Marino, Calif.

Of slender build, Duffy was careful about his dress and was amiable and easygoing. He was a regular attendant at the racetracks. He died in New York City.

[Duffy's prizewinning cartoons appear with explanatory text in Richard Spencer, *Pulitzer Prize Cartoons* (1951). "The Outstretched Hand" was reprinted in the *New York Times,* May 7, 1940, along with coverage of Pulitzer awards of that year. See also "Idea Man," *Time,* May 24, 1948, "Pinch Hitter," *Time,* Nov. 2, 1959; "Duffy Don't Draw It," *Saturday Evening Post,* Jan. 15, 1949; and Duffy's obituary in the *New York Times,* Sept. 13, 1962.]

WILLIAM A. DEGREGORIO

DUMONT, ALLEN BALCOM (Jan. 29, 1901–Nov. 15, 1965), electrical engineer and manufacturer, was born in Brooklyn, N.Y., the son of William Henry Beaman Dumont, an executive with the Saterbury Clock Company, and Lillian Felton Balcom. When he was eleven, Dumont contracted polio, which left him with a permanent limp. While recuperating, he became an amateur radio enthusiast and at the age of fourteen acquired a first-class commercial li-

cense. For eight summers he worked as a wireless operator on ships. He received a degree in electrical engineering from Rensselaer Polytechnic Institute in 1924.

From 1924 to 1928, Dumont was a development and production engineer for the Westinghouse Lamp Company in Bloomfield, N.J. He invented and patented high-speed manufacturing and testing equipment that resulted in dramatic increases in receiving tube production. On Oct. 19, 1926, he married Ethel Martha Steadman; they had two children.

In 1928, Dumont became chief engineer of the De Forest Radio Company in Passaic, N.J. He designed improved transmitting and receiving tubes, production facilities, and a line of radio transmitters ranging in capacity from fifty watts to ten kilowatts. In 1930 he worked with Lee de Forest on the design of an experimental television station (W2XCD) that employed mechanical disk scanning to broadcast programs.

When the De Forest Radio Company was acquired by the Radio Corporation of America (RCA) in 1931, Dumont found himself unemployed. He established a small laboratory in the basement of his home in Upper Montclair, N.J., and hired several glassblowers to help him begin development of cathode-ray tubes for possible use in television receivers. At the start he supplemented his income by serving as an expert witness in patent litigation and by taking consulting jobs.

In 1932 Dumont invented the "Magic Eye," a cathode-ray tube that could be used as a visual tuning aid in radio receivers. He sold the rights to the invention to RCA for $20,000, which he used as capital for expansion. He developed a long-persistence coating for cathode-ray tubes used with the "cathautograph" or electronic pencil, a device permitting remote-controlled writing on a screen. In 1933, Dumont proposed a radio-detection system, but was asked by the Army Signal Corps not to obtain patents because of its military significance. The following year his laboratory was incorporated as the Allen B. Dumont Laboratories and moved to a former pickle factory in Passaic.

When the television market for cathode-ray tubes was slow to develop, Dumont turned to the manufacture of cathode-ray oscilloscopes for use as research and test instruments. One of his best customers during the 1930's was Ernest O. Lawrence of the University of California, who used oscilloscopes in atomic research. Dumont promoted the use of oscilloscopes in engineering schools, where many new applications were discovered. Sales increased steadily from about

$1,200 in 1932 to more than $100,000 in 1937.

In the late 1930's Dumont traveled to Europe to study the latest developments in television in England, France, and Germany. After his return he developed an all-electronic television receiver that was ready to be marketed by 1938. In 1939 Dumont criticized the television standards proposed by the Radio Manufacturers Association and proposed alternatives that would be more compatible with future innovations. He became an influential member of the National Television Systems Committee, which formulated the standards ultimately adopted. In 1941 he initiated experimental telecasts over W2XWV (later WABD) in New York City. He was the first president of the Television Broadcasters Association in 1943.

During World War II the Dumont Laboratories manufactured instruments, radar, and navigational systems for the navy and Signal Corps. It also participated in the Manhattan Project. Television experiments were continued on a reduced scale. In 1944, Dumont delivered the speech "Television Now and Tomorrow," and commented that TNT would be an apt title for a communications technology with such explosive potential. Noting that the war had held back television development, he asserted that "brakes can be a good thing." Having to operate with shortages of materials and personnel had caused the evolution of a "molehill concept" from what had been a "mountain concept." His implication was that instead of a few television stations costing millions of dollars, it would probably be feasible to establish many stations throughout the country. He stated that the Dumont station W2XWV had served as a "television kindergarten" for experiments in programming and advertising that were "bringing about a new industry, a new means of entertainment, a new marketing medium, a new age."

After the war the Dumont television network was established. Initially it linked WABD in New York with WTTG in Washington, D.C. It soon expanded to serve approximately 200 affiliated stations and was incorporated as Metropolitan Broadcasting Company in 1955 (later Metromedia).

Dumont established assembly plants for television receivers in Clifton, N.J., in 1947 and in East Paterson, N.J., in 1949. The receiver manufacturing business was sold to the Emerson Radio and Phonograph Company in 1958. Dumont also established the Allen B. Dumont Foundation that supported educational television development at Montclair State Teachers College beginning in 1952.

In 1960 the Dumont Laboratories were merged with the Fairchild Camera and Instrument Company. Dumont served as senior technical consultant until his death. He was a powerboating enthusiast and used his avocation to conduct experiments on multipath propagation of television and radar. His associate Mortimer Loewi once stated that Dumont had been the "only inventor in history, who has made more money than his promoters." Dumont died in New York City.

[An important body of manuscript sources is the Allen B. Dumont Laboratories collection in the Library of Congress. Dumont's publications include "Making the A-C Heater Tube Noiseless," *Radio Engineering*, Apr. 1929; "An Investigation of Various Electrode Structures of Cathode Ray Tubes Suitable for Television Reception," *Proceedings of the Institute of Radio Engineers*, Dec. 1932; "The Cathautograph: An Electronic Pencil," *Electronics*, Jan. 1933; "Design Problems for Television Systems and Receivers," *Journal of the Society of Motion Picture Engineers*, July 1939. Obituaries are in *New York Times*, Nov. 16, 1965, and *IEEE Spectrum*, Jan. 1966.]

JAMES E. BRITTAIN

DUMONT, MARGARET (Oct. 20, 1889–Mar. 6, 1965), actress, best known for her portrayal of a dignified dowager whose aplomb was threatened but never shattered by the Marx Brothers, was born Marguerite Baker in Brooklyn, N.Y., the only child of William Lawrence Baker and Lillian Harvey Dumont. Thought to be delicate, she was educated by private tutors and raised mainly in Europe. Her mother, whose maiden name she assumed for the stage, wanted her to become an opera singer; but her voice, although opera-trained, proved better suited to musical revues and comedies. Having served an apprenticeship in the music halls of England and France, she made her debut as a featured singer at the Casino de Paris in Paris. J. J. Shubert saw her there and signed her for a part in a Broadway show, *The Girl Behind the Counter* (1907), starring Lew Fields. Roles in other Broadway musicals and comedies followed, but her performances generally passed unnoticed by critics.

Dumont's statuesque beauty and dignified bearing did attract the attention of John Moller, Jr., a New York socialite. After Moller's divorce and her final appearance in another Fields vehicle, *The Summer Widowers* (1910), she married Moller and retired from the stage. For the next few years she lived the life of a society matron —an experience that was later to prove useful.

Moller was financially dependent on his elderly father, and when the senior Moller remarried in 1917, he ceased paying his son an allowance. A lawsuit to require its payment proved unsuccessful and made any reconciliation between father and son impossible.

After her husband's death in 1918, Dumont was forced to return to the stage to earn a living. Although she gained parts in two George M. Cohan shows, *Mary* (1920) and *Rise of Rosie O'Reilly* (1923), among others, she did not set the theatrical world afire. But George S. Kaufman saw her performance as a social climber in *The Four-Flusher* (1925) and suggested her for the part of Mrs. Potter, a society grande dame, in *The Cocoanuts*, the comedy he was then writing for the Marx Brothers. *The Cocoanuts* opened on Broadway in December 1925. In it, and as Mrs. Rittenhouse in *Animal Crackers* (1928), written by Kaufman and Morrie Ryskind, Dumont created the character of the stately, dignified, stuffy, and unflappable society woman that she was to play, with few exceptions, for the rest of her show business career.

When *The Cocoanuts* (1929) and *Animal Crackers* (1930) were filmed in Paramount's Astoria Studios in New York City, Dumont played the same roles. But she did not accompany the Marx Brothers to Hollywood to appear in their next two films, *Monkey Business* (1931) and *Horse Feathers* (1932). It was clear that they did not regard her as a permanent fixture. But the dowagers she played were popular, and critics considered the later films inferior to *The Cocoanuts* and *Animal Crackers*. The Marx Brothers came to regard her as a good luck charm. At their request she moved to California to appear in five of the remaining nine Marx Brothers films: *Duck Soup* (1933), *A Night at the Opera* (1935), *A Day at the Races* (1937), *At the Circus* (1939), and *The Big Store* (1941). She won the Screen Actors Guild Award for best supporting actress in 1937, for her portrayal of Mrs. Emily Upjohn in *A Day at the Races*.

Although Dumont remained active in show business for the next two decades, her association with the Marx Brothers marked the high point of her career. She wanted to move beyond these comic parts to more serious roles, but not surprisingly her desire was not to be realized. Having seen Dumont as a comic foil of the Marx Brothers, no one could accept her playing serious roles. Everyone would have been waiting for Groucho or Harpo Marx to dash from the wings. While the Marx Brothers had lifted her

out of obscurity, they had limited her to a career in slapstick comedy.

But in this role Dumont found a niche, albeit a small one. She appeared in *Never Give a Sucker an Even Break* (1941) as W. C. Fields's wife, in *The Dancing Masters* (1943) with Stan Laurel and Oliver Hardy, and in *The Horn Blows at Midnight* (1945) with Jack Benny. In the 1950's she played small parts in a few films and appeared frequently in television sketches with such comedians as Bob Hope, Dean Martin, and Jerry Lewis. Eventually, out of financial necessity, Dumont was reduced to brief appearances on situation comedies such as "The Donna Reed Show." Shortly before her death in Los Angeles, she gave an appropriate final performance—a re-creation with Groucho Marx of the arrival of Captain Spaulding in *Animal Crackers*—on the television variety show "The Hollywood Palace."

Of handsome if formidable appearance, Dumont was much the same character offscreen as she tried to be onscreen: a woman of elegance, dignity, fastidiousness, and graciousness. Offscreen as well, she was the victim of the Marx Brothers' pranks. When the Broadway shows went on the road or tours were made to test gags that were to be used in their films, their assaults on her dignity ranged from removal of her wig and clothes to attempts to get her arrested as a prostitute. Shocked and confused, Dumont quit again and again. But since her association with them had brought her both fame and financial security, she could not leave. In any case, Groucho would assure her that they meant no real harm, and coax her back.

Although Dumont was a talented comedienne, the Marx Brothers insisted that she play her roles in a serious manner. Her demeanor was in such contrast with theirs that she often appeared to have wandered into their films from a drawing room comedy being shot on an adjoining studio lot. According to Groucho, she was able to give this impression because she did not understand most of the jokes, even when he explained them to her. While this explanation may account for her response to double entendres, she acted exactly as she knew a straight woman should.

Dignified and impervious, Dumont was the eye of the hurricane that was the Marx Brothers. She provided a solid wall off which their zany antics, outrageous puns, and nonsensical routines could bounce. When Groucho described her in later years as "practically the fifth Marx Brother," he recognized her contribution to their comic genius.

[See Kyle Crichton, "Don't Call Me a Stooge," *Collier's*, May 15, 1937; and John Springer and Jack Hamilton, *They Had Faces Then: . . . the Superstars, Stars, and Starlets of the 1930s* (1974). Moller's difficulties are mentioned in the *New York Times*, July 22, 1917, and May 30, 1924. See also Groucho Marx and Richard J. Anobile, *The Marx Brothers Scrapbook* (1973); Allen Eyles, *The Marx Brothers: Their World of Comedy* (1966); and Hector Arce, *Groucho* (1979). An accurate checklist of her film roles is in *Monthly Film Bulletin*, June 1971. Charlotte Chandler, *Hello, I Must Be Going* (1978), states that Dumont was born in Atlanta, Ga., and raised in the home of her godfather, Joel Chandler Harris, both of which would appear to be erroneous.]

G. F. GOODWIN

DUNDEE, JOHNNY (Nov. 22, 1893–Apr. 22, 1965), featherweight boxing champion, was born Giuseppe Carrora in Sciacca, Sicily. The family immigrated to the United States shortly after his birth. He was raised in Manhattan's Hell's Kitchen section, where his parents ran a fish market. As a youth he frequently fought in smokers, fights at which the hat was passed to raise a purse for the combatants.

At the age of seventeen, Carrora became a professional boxer under the tutelage of Scottie Montieth. Montieth reported that "I liked everything about the kid except his name," and encouraged Carrora to change his name. As Johnny Dundee, Carrora became one of the first prominent immigrant fighters to use an anglicized name in the belief that fighters with more traditional names had greater opportunities.

Dundee attracted national attention when, at nineteen, he fought a stirring twenty-round draw with featherweight champion Johnny Kilbane at Vernon, Calif. Much to Dundee's displeasure, Kilbane refused to give him another chance at the title. Dundee, nicknamed the "Little Bar of Iron" or the "Scotch-Wop," developed into one of New York City's favorite boxers. He trained at Stillman's Gym on Eighth Avenue, and achieved a certain notoriety for superstitiously wearing the same ring robe for many years and attending the theater the night before a fight. Among his most notable non-championship matches were eight no-decision fights with lightweight Benny Leonard. "I taught him Italian, and he taught me Jewish," reported Dundee of these contests.

In 1921, Dundee won the junior lightweight title, defeating George Chaney. He successfully defended this title several times, finally relinquishing it to Kid Sullivan in 1924. But Dundee was most celebrated as a featherweight. He won the featherweight title from

Eugene Criqui at the Polo Grounds on July 26, 1923. Dundee, who was noted for his agility and stamina, won an easy fifteen-round decision. Yet his share of the $185,514 purse was only 12.5 percent. As Criqui reached the ring, he was greeted by sustained jeering, due primarily to Dundee's popularity. This rudeness to the champion, a war hero who had been wounded at Verdun, caused strong negative comment in the national press.

Dundee held the featherweight title for two years, relinquishing it voluntarily because he had great difficulty making the weight limit. In 1927 he fought Tony Canzoneri for the lightweight title, but was soundly defeated. His career declined quickly thereafter, but like many boxers he continued to fight well past his prime. His last fight was in 1932. Of his 321 matches he won 113, drew 18, and lost 31. He also had 159 no-decision fights.

Dundee remained active in New York City fight circles and was a frequent spectator at major bouts. Although he held titles only briefly, he was one of the most highly regarded fighters of his day, and was inducted into the Boxing Hall of Fame in 1957. Ring authority Nat Fleischer rated him the fourth-best featherweight of all time. Dundee played an important role in glamorizing the lighter boxing divisions. More important, he symbolized the rise of the Italian-American to athletic prominence. Thus his life illustrates the tendency of ethnic groups recently arrived in America to achieve fame and fortune through professional sports.

Dundee married once and had one daughter. He died at East Orange, N.J.

[Dundee's obituary in the *New York Times*, Apr. 23, 1965, is the fullest treatment of his life in print. Lester Bromberg, *Boxing's Unforgettable Fights* (1962), includes some useful material on Dundee and an excellent photograph of him just prior to the Canzoneri fight.]

WILLIAM DONN ROGOSIN

DU PONT, IRÉNÉE (Dec. 21, 1876–Dec. 19, 1963), industrialist, was born at Nemours, near Wilmington, Del., the son of Lammot du Pont and Mary Belin. In 1881 the family moved to Philadelphia, and Lammot du Pont built and operated a plant to make dynamite across the river in New Jersey.

Du Pont attended the Penn Charter School in Philadelphia, graduating at the age of fifteen. After a year at Phillips Andover, he entered the Massachusetts Institute of Technology (MIT), receiving the B.S. degree in chemistry in 1897 and the M.A. in chemical engineering a year later. After a few unrewarding months as an apprentice in the paper-making shops of Pusey and Jones, he joined William H. Fenn of the Manufacturers Contracting Company in Newark, N.J., as a partner and secretary-treasurer. On Feb. 1, 1900, Du Pont married Irene Sophie du Pont, a second cousin; they had nine children.

From the start, Du Pont's career was guided by his older brother Pierre, who had taken charge of the family affairs after the death of their father in an explosion in 1884 and who was always called "Dad" by his younger brothers and sisters. Pierre encouraged Irénée to enroll at MIT; he was responsible for the partnership with Fenn, and gave that partnership contracts for the building of street railways he was financing in Dallas. After Pierre and his cousins, Alfred Irénée and Thomas Coleman Du Pont, acquired the family enterprise on the death of the senior partner in 1902, completely reorganized it, and acquired through merger 70 percent of the nation's explosives industry, Irénée Du Pont's firm received the contracts to build the new company's offices.

Late in 1903, Du Pont joined the new E. I. du Pont de Nemours Powder Company. His first job was to appraise the assets of all the firms involved in the merger. After serving for two years in the construction division of the black powder operating department, he joined the treasurer's department. There he was responsible for carrying out the procedures devised by Pierre to coordinate, and to assure a continuous review of, long-term capital appropriations, which is a most critical task for the continuing health and growth of a large industrial enterprise. At the same time Du Pont became the chairman of the new operative committee, which consisted of department directors, and was responsible for the day-to-day operations of the company.

After a three-year stint as the head of the development department, Du Pont became assistant general manager. When Pierre du Pont took command of the company in 1914, Irénée was named chairman of the executive committee, the company's top decision-making body. A few months later he joined with his brothers and three other close associates to purchase T. Coleman's shares—a purchase that assured their branch of the family complete control of the company. As chairman of the Executive Committee until 1919, Du Pont was responsible for carrying out the massive expansion of plant and facilities in order to meet the war orders.

In April 1919, Du Pont took Pierre's place as president. One major achievement of his administration was the successful diversification into chemical products other than explosives, including paints, dyes, film, Fabrikoid, cellophane, and rayon—a strategy devised to make use of the managerial staff and physical facilities expanded by wartime demands. The complicated administrative needs created by diversification led to another achievement for which his presidency is remembered—the adoption in 1921 of a new multidivision form of organization. This institutional invention became the standard for the management of large industrial enterprises throughout the world. Yet, Du Pont himself played only a small part in these two developments. He opposed the introduction of a multidivision form, a creation of younger managers, until the depression of 1920–1921 made the need for organizational change clear. His contribution to the family empire was that of a manager who handled often rapidly changing operational problems with great skill, but had neither the organizational nor the entrepreneurial talents of his brother Pierre or his cousin Coleman, the men who built the modern E. I. du Pont de Nemours and Company.

After he turned the presidency over to his brother Lammot in 1926, Du Pont spent relatively little time on business or industrial activities, except to keep a close watch on the family investments. He remained vice-chairman of the Board of Directors until becoming honorary chairman in 1940, and he continued to serve on the Du Pont Finance Committee and the Finance Committee of the General Motors Corporation, in which the Du Pont Company had made a substantial investment in 1917. He joined the Association Against the Prohibition Amendment in 1926, and in 1934 was a founder and funder of the American Liberty League. More outgoing and gregarious than his brother, Du Pont played a larger part in the affairs of both these associations than did Pierre. But much of his time was spent enlarging his valuable mineral collection, expanding his estate in Cuba, Xanadu, and enjoying the great house at Granouge in the rolling Delaware countryside, where he died.

[The collection of Du Pont's papers, housed in the Eleutherian Mills Historical Library in Greenville, Del., is indexed in John B. Riggs, *A Guide to the Manuscripts in the Eleutherian Mills Historical Library* (1970). Also see John K. Winkler, *The Du Pont Dynasty* (1935); William S. Dutton, *Du Pont 140 Years* (1949); William H. A. Carr, *The Du Ponts of Delaware* (1964); Alfred D. Chandler, Jr., and Stephen Salsbury, *Pierre S. Du Pont and the Making of the Modern Corporation* (1971). An obituary is in *New York Times*, Dec. 20, 1963.]

ALFRED D. CHANDLER, JR.

DURSTINE, ROY SARLES (Dec. 13, 1886– Nov. 28, 1962), advertising executive, was born in Jamestown, N.D., the son of Lee Brenton Durstine and Kathrine Sarles. His father was with the New York Life Insurance Company, and the family moved several times during Durstine's childhood. He graduated from the Lawrenceville, N.J., School in 1904 and received a B.A. from Princeton in 1908. His first job was with the *New York Sun*, where he worked as a reporter. He had a wide range of assignments, including coverage of President William Howard Taft during his 1909 summer vacation in Massachusetts.

Although he enjoyed journalism and looked back on the *Sun* as a great newspaper, Durstine resigned in 1912 and became a copywriter for the Street Railways Advertising Company. The initial exposure to the advertising business was brief. He recalled later that he had hated the work and had taken it only to make more money because he was engaged. He married Harriet H. Hutchins on Nov. 12, 1912; they had three daughters.

In the summer of 1912, Durstine received an invitation from George W. Perkins, manager of Theodore Roosevelt's "Bull Moose" presidential campaign, to direct the candidate's press relations. Although Durstine respected Woodrow Wilson, from whom he had taken classes at Princeton, and liked Taft personally, he admired Roosevelt greatly and threw himself into the job. He supervised a staff of about twenty-five workers in one of the first modern political publicity campaigns.

After Roosevelt's defeat in the election, Durstine turned to an advertising career that was to span half a century. He worked at first for Calkins and Holden, then in 1914 became secretary-treasurer of an agency that he founded with James Berrien. Four years later Berrien-Durstine was dissolved and Durstine joined forces with Bruce Barton, a magazine editor, and Alex F. Osborn, a Buffalo advertising executive. Barton, Durstine, and Osborn began with only $10,000 of borrowed capital, but it flourished during advertising's boom years of the 1920's. One of the first to recognize the potential of radio as an advertising medium, Durstine persuaded his agency to establish the industry's first radio department in 1926. He realized that successful radio advertising and programming had to take into account the medium's distinctive characteristics, and not simply employ newspaper and magazine techniques and strategies.

In 1928 Barton, Durstine, and Osborne merged with the long-established George Batten Company. Upon its formation, Batten, Barton, Durstine and Osborn (BBDO) had 113 clients and 600 employees. In its first year of operation, it handled $32.6 million of advertising. Durstine's first position with BBDO was vice-president and general manager. Although he preferred copywriting to agency administration, he was increasingly called upon to do the latter, especially after he assumed the agency's presidency in 1936.

Although less widely known than Barton, Durstine was a leading spokesman for the advertising business during the 1920's. He wrote a rather slapdash textbook on copywriting, *Making Advertisements and Making Them Pay* (1920) and a collection of essays and sketches, *This Advertising Business* (1928). His articles appeared frequently in business publications and general-interest magazines. Following travels to the Soviet Union, Germany, and Austria, Durstine wrote *Red Thunder* (1934). After his first marriage ended in divorce in 1932, he married Virginia Gardiner on August 30 of that year. They had one son.

In April 1939, Durstine resigned from BBDO. Three months later he announced the opening of Roy S. Durstine, Inc. He explained that he wanted to spend more time creating advertisements and less time handling managerial tasks. This agency, which he headed until his death, stressed personal attention to small and medium-size clients.

Durstine was willing to concede that some advertising, such as paid testimonials from nonusers, was deceptive, and that some campaigns showed poor taste; he nevertheless was a vigorous defender of advertising's social role and of the agency system. At times the tone of his writings bordered on flippancy, but he approached his craft with great seriousness. A job applicant at BBDO who happened to refer to "the advertising game" would soon be ushered to the door. As president of the American Association of Advertising Agencies in 1925–1926, Durstine persuaded President Calvin Coolidge to speak to the organization and drafted a speech in which Coolidge proclaimed that "advertising ministers to the spiritual side of trade."

Durstine's fundamental economic and political conservatism was balanced by a degree of open-mindedness and willingness to innovate. Although a 1933 profile described him as "complex, aloof, mysterious," James Rorty, a radical critic of advertising, found him honorable and fair. Durstine's long-term Republican allegiance did not prevent him from early enthusiasm about the New Deal, although Franklin Roosevelt's "court packing" scheme of 1937 alienated him.

In addition to his pioneering work in radio advertising, Durstine joined with Barton in 1935 to persuade U.S. Steel to present its messages to the public in institutional advertising. In 1962 the last advertisement he prepared was an appeal for advertisers to use a group of black-owned newspapers. Durstine was, in short, able to combine his loyalty to American advertising with an awareness of social change. He died in New York City.

[There apparently are no collections of Durstine's papers. A few references to him can be found in the James Rorty Papers, Special Collections, University of Oregon Library, Eugene. Durstine's reminiscences, recorded in 1949, are in the Columbia University Oral History Collection. They concentrate on his early political work.

A brief biographical sketch is "Tiger Man," *Advertising and Selling*, Jan. 19, 1933. Obituaries appeared in the *New York Times*, Nov. 29, 1962; *Advertising Age*, Dec. 3, 1962; and *Printers' Ink*, Dec. 7, 1962. A special issue of the *BBDO Newsletter* (1966) has material on the agency's growth and some references to Durstine's role.]

DANIEL A. POPE

DWORSHAK, HENRY CLARENCE (Aug. 29, 1894–July 23, 1962), publisher, and U.S. congressman and senator, was born in Duluth, Minn., the son of Henry Dworshak, a printer, and of Julia Ohotto. He was educated in the Duluth public schools and began learning the printer's trade at age fifteen. During World War I he served in France as sergeant in the Fourth Antiaircraft Machine Gun Battalion.

On Dec. 31, 1917, Dworshak married Georgia Belle Lowe; they had four sons. He managed the Northwest Printers' Supply Company in Duluth from 1920 to 1924 and also worked on several local newspapers. He moved to Burley, Idaho, in 1924 and became owner and publisher of the *Burley Bulletin*, which over the next twenty years gave him wide political coverage and influence.

In 1938 Dworshak was elected to the U.S. House of Representatives as a Republican. He served four terms (1939–1947), during which he became known as a champion of conservation, reclamation, and government economy. Like most conservative Republicans he was a staunch isolationist. In 1939 Dworshak supported a bill to "take the profits out of war" by imposing a 75 to 90 percent tax on certain incomes in excess of $50,000 a year; he voted for the mandatory arms embargo in the Neutrality Act of 1939; and he voted against the Selective Service Act in 1940, against passage of the Lend-Lease Act in 1941, and against extending the Reciprocal Trade Agreements Act.

On domestic issues Dworshak's voting record was anti-New Deal. As a member of the House Appropriations Committee, he voted against adding $100 million to the work relief programs in 1939 and against increasing the Civilian Conservation Corps's budget by $50 million in 1940. He opposed farm parity payments, federal regulation of prices, and increased funds for rural electrification.

Dworshak was elected to the Senate in 1946 to fill the unexpired term of the late John Thomas, but was defeated for reelection in 1948 by Idaho Supreme Court Justice Bert H. Miller. Miller died a year later, and Dworshak, appointed to fill the vacancy, won the 1950 election to complete Miller's term. In 1954 he defeated Glen H. Taylor, who had the support of the liberals, for a full term, and was reelected in 1960.

After the war Dworshak continued to be isolationist and economy-minded, and became a leader of the conservative bloc in the Senate. He opposed passage of the Greek-Turkish aid bill (1947) and the Marshall Plan (1948). On the Senate Appropriations Committee he staunchly opposed what he called "Socialist spending," working to trim and limit government expenditures. He backed Republican efforts in 1947 to reduce income taxes and suggested slicing $100 million from the War Department civil functions bill.

In the early 1950's Dworshak was frequently linked with Senator Joseph R. McCarthy of Wisconsin. In 1953 both voted against confirmation of Charles E. Bohlen as ambassador to the Soviet Union, although Bohlen was a career diplomat and a leading authority on that country. (By 1959 Dworshak had revised his opinion. When Bohlen was being considered as special adviser on Soviet affairs to Secretary of State Christian A. Herter, Dworshak was quoted as saying, "If Mr. Herter wants him, he's entitled to have him.")

In 1954, when Senator McCarthy stepped down from chairmanship of the Senate Permanent Investigations Subcommittee during the Army-McCarthy hearings, he appointed Dworshak to take his place. Dworshak usually favored

McCarthy in the hearings, and with three other Republican members of the subcommittee signed the majority report clearing McCarthy of charges that he had exerted personal pressure on the army in order to secure favors for Private G. David Schine. When the Senate subsequently voted, 67–22, to censure McCarthy, Dworshak voted with the minority.

In the Senate Dworshak spoke out on regional issues, backing the appointment of a westerner as secretary of the interior in 1948 and becoming embroiled in the controversial Hell's Canyon project during the 1950's. Idaho Democrats chose to make the Hell's Canyon project a major issue in the 1954 election, endorsing a plan to use federal funds to build a 600-foot concrete dam on the Snake River near the Oregon border. Dworshak and other Idaho Republicans opposed a federally financed high dam but favored the use of private capital for power development. They supported the Idaho Power Company plan to build three low-level dams on the river. Nevertheless, Dworshak generally advocated close cooperation between the states and the federal government in developing and managing the nation's natural resources.

Dworshak died in Washington, D.C. He won respect from friend and foe alike for his integrity and kindness. A political opponent once stated, "His was a friendly, humble, homey manner, yet always dignified, courteous and always businesslike." In 1963 Congress enacted legislation changing the name of the Bruces Eddy Dam and Reservoir in Idaho to the Dworshak Dam and Reservoir.

[Dworshak's papers are at the Idaho Historical Society, Boise. There is no full-length biography. See Robert S. Allen and William V. Shannon, *The Truman Merry-Go-Round* (1950). For statements by political opponents, see *Congressional Record* (House), July 24, 1962. An obituary is in the *New York Times*, July 24, 1962.]

DARLIS A. MILLER

EDDY, MANTON SPRAGUE (May 16, 1892–Apr. 10, 1962), army officer, was born in Chicago, Ill., the son of George Manton Eddy, an insurance broker, and Martha Bishop Sprague. After receiving his early education in the Chicago public schools, Eddy graduated from the Shattuck Military School in Faribault, Minn., in 1913. Uncertain whether he wanted a military career, he went to work for a casualty insurance company in Indiana. By 1916 his doubts were resolved, and he accepted a commission as a second lieutenant of infantry in the regular army. The next year, after completing the First Provisional Officers Course at the Army Service Schools, Fort Leavenworth, Kans., he was promoted to captain.

In April 1918, Eddy went to France with the Fourth Infantry Division. As commander of a machine gun company, he saw action in the Aisne-Marne offensive and in August was wounded during an operation on the Vesle River. He recovered in time to participate in the Meuse-Argonne offensive, and finished the war as a battalion commander. Eddy was promoted to the temporary rank of major in November 1918 and served with the American occupation force in Germany until the summer of 1919, when he returned to the United States.

In the period between the two world wars, Eddy held assignments in which he gained recognition as an outstanding military educator. Reverting to his permanent grade of captain in 1920, he completed the Company Officers Course at the Infantry School, Fort Benning, Ga., in 1921. On Nov. 23, 1921, Eddy married Mamie Peabody Buttolph; they had one daughter.

Eddy remained at the Infantry School until 1925, attached first to the Infantry Board and then to the demonstration regiment. In August 1925 he was sent to the Riverside Military Academy, Gainesville, Ga., where he served as a professor of military science and tactics. Returning to the Infantry School in 1929, he completed the advanced course in 1930. Two years of regimental and staff duty in Hawaii followed.

From 1932 to 1934, Eddy attended the Command and General Staff School at Fort Leavenworth, and from 1934 to 1939 he was an instructor in tactics at the school. After assignments as a regimental and a staff officer, he was promoted to the temporary rank of brigadier general in March 1942 and was appointed assistant commander of the Ninth Infantry Division.

During World War II, Eddy was a field commander in the European theater. He was elevated to the command of the Ninth Infantry Division in June 1942 and led the division through the North Africa, Sicily, and Normandy campaigns. Under his direction the Ninth Infantry emerged as a first-rate combat unit, and General Dwight D. Eisenhower, supreme commander of the Allied Expeditionary Force, rated it as one of his two best divisions. Lieutenant General George S. Patton later wrote that Eddy probably commanded larger groups of combat troops in that theater longer than any other general.

In August 1944, Eddy was assigned command of the XII Corps, which was attached to Patton's Third Army. Showing "tactical deftness," he played a major role in the rapid advance of the Third Army across France to the Siegfried Line, the Lorraine campaign, the crossing of the Rhine River, and the drive into the heartland of Germany. Eventually the months of combat strain exacted their toll, and in April 1945 illness forced Eddy to return to the United States.

In 1946–1947, following his recovery, Eddy served successively as commander of the Third Service Command, deputy commander of the Second Army, and chief of information in the Office of the Chief of Staff. In 1948 he was named commandant of the Command and General Staff College and director of the Army Educational System. In these positions he oversaw major changes in the curriculum and teaching methods at Fort Leavenworth and the reestablishment of the Army War College. In June 1950, Eddy was appointed deputy commander in chief of the European Command and six months later was given command of the reactivated Seventh Army. After two years in this post he was named commander in chief of the U.S. Armed Forces in Europe. During this stint he superintended the buildup of a force of more than 200,000 for the North Atlantic Treaty Organization. Eddy retired in 1953 with the rank of lieutenant general and returned to Columbus, Ga., where he was involved in business and civic affairs.

Eddy's military reputation rests upon his service during World War II. A burly, amiable man who looked more like a teacher than a soldier, he was never a "dugout" general. Organizing his headquarters in a fashion that resembled the German practice, he kept his deputy commander at the command post to make emergency decisions and supervise the staff, so that he would be free to be "right up at the front where it was hot." He was awarded the Distinguished Service Cross for "repeated acts" of "extraordinary heroism" during the capture of Cherbourg from the Germans in June 1944, and by the end of the war he had earned four of the five highest American decorations for bravery. Notwithstanding his personal bravery, Eddy was a cautious commander. He performed classic maneuvers and, as General Omar Bradley, one of his wartime superiors, recalled, counted "his steps carefully before he took them." They usually took the form of sweeping, well-prepared end runs around the flanks of the enemy rather than frontal attacks. Eddy's conservatism often irritated the hard-driving Patton, but the men serving under him appreciated his ability to win battles with a minimum of casualties. Eddy stands out as one of the most reliable and battle-tested army commanders in the European theater. He died at Fort Benning, Ga.

[Sources in the series U.S. Army in World War II include Martin Blumenson, *Breakout and Pursuit* (1961); Hugh M. Cole, *The Lorraine Campaign* (1950) and *The Ardennes: Battle of the Bulge* (1965); Gordon Harrison, *Cross-Channel Attack* (1951); George F. Howe, *Northwest Africa: Seizing the Initiative in the West* (1957); Charles B. MacDonald, *The Last Offensive* (1973); and Howard M. Smyth and Albert N. Garland, *Sicily and the Surrender of Italy* (1965). See also Omar Bradley, *A Soldier's Story* (1951); George Dyer, *XII Corps: Spearhead of Patton's Third Army* (1947); George S. Patton, *War as I Knew It* (1947); and Ernie Pyle, *Brave Men* (1944). An obituary is in *New York Times*, Apr. 11, 1962.]

JOHN KENNEDY OHL

EICHELBERGER, ROBERT LAWRENCE (Mar. 9, 1886–Sept. 26, 1961), army officer, was born in Urbana, Ohio, the son of George Maley Eichelberger, an attorney, and of Emma Ring. He grew up on a farm near Urbana, and after graduating from Urbana High School, entered Ohio State University in 1903. Two years later he left to attend the United States Military Academy, from which he graduated in 1909.

Assigned as a second lieutenant to the Tenth Infantry Regiment at Fort Benjamin Harrison, Ind., Eichelberger stayed with the regiment when it was transferred to San Antonio and then to the Panama Canal Zone in 1911. While in Panama he met Emma Gudger, whom he married on Apr. 3, 1913; they had no children.

After returning to the United States in 1915, Eichelberger undertook various assignments before being named operations officer of the Eighth Division in July 1918. Several thousand of the division's fittest men, Eichelberger among them, were soon ordered to Vladivostok to protect American interests in Siberia during the Russian Civil War. Already a (temporary) major under the accelerated system of promotion in effect during wartime, Eichelberger served as assistant chief of staff and subsequently as chief intelligence officer for General William S. Graves, commander of the troops. With the termination of the American intervention in 1920, he remained in military intelligence, traveling extensively in Japan and China before returning to the United States in 1921.

During the next two decades Eichelberger held desk jobs in intelligence and later in the adjutant general's office, to which he transferred because promotion in it was more rapid during peacetime. Considered to have leadership potential, he was assigned in 1925 to the Command and General Staff School at Fort Leavenworth, Kans.; he completed the course with distinction in 1926 and remained as an instructor until 1929, when he enrolled at the Army War College. After graduating in 1930, he spent a year on duty at the War Department, followed by three years as adjutant general at West Point. Promoted to lieutenant colonel in 1934, Eichelberger was detailed to the War Department in 1935 as secretary to the General Staff. In this capacity he impressed two successive chiefs of staff: Generals Douglas MacArthur and Malin Craig. The latter counseled him that he should be in the field in case of war, and in 1937 Eichelberger transferred back to the infantry.

Promoted to (temporary) brigadier general in 1940 and named superintendent of West Point, Eichelberger requested a field command shortly after Pearl Harbor. He was put in charge of the Seventy-seventh Infantry Division. Eichelberger's success in training this recently organized division led to his elevation to commander of I Corps, which he was to lead in the planned invasion of French North Africa. But when the need arose for a capable corps commander in the Southwest Pacific in August 1942, Eichelberger and his staff were ordered there.

In late November, some three months after his arrival in Australia, Eichelberger was summoned to the headquarters of the Southwest Pacific's commanding officer, General Douglas MacArthur, and told that an American division was bogged down in a bitter struggle to seize Buna, on the north coast of Papua, New Guinea. Alarmed at the decline of morale among the disease-ridden troops there, MacArthur, in oft-quoted words, instructed Eichelberger to take command of the Americans at Buna (Australian forces also played a major role there) and seize it, or "don't come back alive." Eichelberger's forces had the situation well in hand by the start of January 1943, gaining the war's first offensive victory against Japanese ground forces. His energetic leadership became known as a model for successful command on the corps level and was studied in the postwar curriculum at Leavenworth.

Despite his success at Buna, Eichelberger was unable to get another combat assignment for a full year; an officer senior to him received the commands he desired. MacArthur relegated Eichelberger to training duties and refused to consent to his transfer to the European Theater, where, as a lieutenant general, he could have had command of an American army. In 1944 and 1945, however, more opportunities opened for leaders at the corps and army levels. Eichelberger was given corps commands at Hollandia and Biak, both in New Guinea, and subsequently was named commander of the newly organized Eighth Army, elements of which participated in the campaign to liberate Manila and in a series of amphibious operations that reconquered Mindanao and other islands in the central and southern Philippines. Throughout these campaigns Eichelberger insisted on seeing combat conditions for himself; on his periodic visits to the front he wore his three-star insignia despite the fact they made him an obvious target for Japanese snipers. He explained that he wanted his troops to know that "I'm here going through it with them."

His record in New Guinea and the Philippines earned Eichelberger leadership of the Eighth Army in the assault on the main Japanese island of Honshu that was tentatively scheduled for March 1946. But the war ended before the invasion of Japan had to be undertaken, and his main role there was as commander of the army of occupation, a position he held from Jan. 1, 1946, until his retirement in 1948. Promotion to the rank of general came in 1954 as a belated honor for Eichelberger and several other lieutenant generals of comparable wartime distinction. He retired in Asheville, N.C., where he died.

Although he is not as widely known as some of his wartime contemporaries, such as his friend and West Point classmate George Patton, who commanded armies in the European Theater, Eichelberger's leadership throughout World War II was a model of consistency in increasingly responsible positions. A master of logistics, he gave painstaking attention to detail and succeeded in maintaining the morale of his troops in the debilitating conditions of jungle warfare.

[Eichelberger's letters are at the Duke University Library. His memoirs, *Our Jungle Road to Tokyo* (1950), were first serialized in the *Saturday Evening Post* (1949). Jay Luvaas, ed., *Dear Miss Em* (1972), is a selection of letters from Eichelberger to his wife. On his role in World War II, see Robert Ross Smith, *The Approach to the Philippines* (1953); Samuel Milner, *Victory in Papua* (1957); Robert Ross Smith, *Triumph in the Philippines* (1963); Lida Mayo, *Bloody Buna* (1974); D. Clayton James, *The Years of MacArthur, 1941–1945*, vol. II (1975); General Walter Krueger, *From Down Under to Nippon* (1953).

Also see William S. Graves, *America's Siberian Adventure* (1931). A detailed obituary is in the *New York Times*, Sept. 27, 1961.]

LLOYD J. GRAYBAR

EISENHART, LUTHER PFAHLER (Jan. 13, 1876–Oct. 28, 1965), mathematician, was born in York, Pa., the son of Charles Augustus Eisenhart, a dentist and inventor, and Emma Catherine Pfahler. He received an A.B. from Gettysburg College in 1896, and a Ph.D. in mathematics from Johns Hopkins University in 1900. After graduating from Johns Hopkins, Eisenhart joined the faculty of Princeton University, where he remained until his retirement in 1945.

Eisenhart was one of the original group of "preceptors" set up at Princeton by Woodrow Wilson in 1905. He rose rapidly in the academic ranks, becoming a full professor in 1909, when only thirty-three. On Aug. 17, 1908, Eisenhart married Anna Maria Dandridge Mitchell. She died in 1913, after the birth of their only child. On June 1, 1918, he married Katharine Riely Schmidt. They had two daughters. In 1923 Eisenhart designed one of Princeton's major educational reforms, the four-course plan of study. The plan emphasized independent work, encouraging students, as much as possible, to educate themselves. Eisenhart was dean of the faculty from 1925 to 1933 and dean of the graduate school from 1933 to 1945. In 1929 he succeeded Henry Burchard Fine as chairman of the department of mathematics. From 1929 to 1945 he was also chairman of the university's committee on scientific research.

Eisenhart will be principally remembered as an expositor of the new differential geometry, to which Albert Einstein was insisting the world pay attention. That geometry, later including what came to be known as tensor analysis or absolute differential calculus, had its beginnings in the mid-nineteenth century in the work of Karl Friedrich Gauss and Georg Friedrich Bernhard Riemann. Eisenhart compiled much of the earlier work and its continuing development by Gregorio Ricci-Curbastro, Tullio Levi-Civita, and many others, making it more accessible in an important series of textbooks. He also wrote scientific papers that contributed to the development of the subject. In particular his work supported Einstein's application of this mathematics to the problems of physics, both in the Special Theory of Relativity, and later in the General Theory. Eisenhart's most important original contribution was the notion of the invariant theory of the group space of an r-param-

eter çontinuous group. This was later developed by Élie Joseph Cartan and Jan Arnoldus Schouten and achieved an enduring place in modern differential geometry.

Eisenhart's first textbook, *Differential Geometry* (1909), established his fame worldwide. It made available some of the methods of Gaston Darboux and Ernesto Cesàro, Gauss's use of differential forms to analyze the properties of curved surfaces, and the generalization of this by Riemann to curved spaces of any dimension. Other important research textbooks were: *Transformations of Surfaces* (1923); *Riemannian Geometry* (1926); and *Non-Riemannian Geometry* (1927). These books gave an account of the development of intrinsic differential geometry and its application to the world of physics, including, in particular, major contributions made by Luigi Bianchi, Eugenio Beltrami, Elwin Bruno Christoffel, Ricci-Curbastro, and Levi-Civita. Most important of these was the concept of infinitesimal parallel displacement formulated by Levi-Civita in 1917. *Continuous Groups of Transformations* (1933) owes its main substance to Eisenhart's own work. He also wrote two introductory textbooks, *Coordinate Geometry* (1939) and *Introduction to Differential Geometry* (1940), employing the methods of tensor analysis and the absolute calculus that had come into prominence through the development of differential geometry. *The Educational Process* (1945) is an account of his long experience and contact with students.

Eisenhart died in Princeton, N.J.

[See the article on Eisenhart and an extensive bibliography in the *Dictionary of Scientific Biography, IV* (1971). Eisenhart's obituary is in the *New York Times*, Oct. 29, 1965.]

DOUGLAS R. CROSBY

EKLUND, CARL ROBERT (Jan. 27, 1909– Nov. 4, 1962), ornithologist and Antarctic explorer, was born in Tomahawk, Wis., the son of John Eklund and Maria Olsson. His father, a Swedish immigrant, was a carpenter and builder. Eklund attended the Tomahawk public schools, then enrolled at Carleton College, from which he received the B.A. in 1932. While at Carleton he earned all-Midwest Conference honors in football as an end.

In 1933 Eklund began twenty-nine years of government service by accepting a position as a forestry foreman in Shenandoah National Park. He became a graduate fellow at the Oregon State College Cooperative Wildlife Research Unit in 1936; two years later he received an

M.S. there. In 1937 Eklund joined the Department of the Interior Fish and Wildlife Service, initially working as a biologist at the Seney National Wildlife Refuge in Michigan (1937–1938). On Oct. 5, 1939, he married Harriet San Giovanni; they had two daughters.

Eklund first traveled to Antarctica in 1939–1941, as one of the scientists attached to the U.S. Antarctic Service (Admiral Richard E. Byrd's third expedition). A central purpose of this undertaking was to strengthen American claims to the region, and in pursuit of this goal Eklund and Finn Ronne made one of the most important land treks in Antarctic history. In the course of an eighty-four-day journey by dogsled, which included travel through what Ronne termed "the most dangerous crevassed area that . . . can ever be encountered in Antarctica," they covered 1,264 miles. They mapped 350 miles of coastline, discovered a group of islands in King George VI Sound (now known as the Eklund Islands), ascertained that Alexander I Land is an island, and plotted the position, based on sun sights, of some 320 peaks and nunataks.

After the United States entered World War II, Eklund's polar experience led to his being assigned to the Arctic Section of the Army Air Force. He served in Greenland and Canada, and was instrumental in the magnetic surveying of Labrador and Baffin Island. Eklund also offered expert advice on cold-weather equipment. He was discharged with the rank of major, and returned to the Fish and Wildlife Service. Eklund served for two years in the Office of River Basin Studies in Portland, Oreg., and for five years as officer in charge of the Wildlife Section, first in Chicago and then in Washington, D.C. While in Washington he began studies that led to a Ph.D. from the University of Maryland (1959). In 1955–1956 he was assistant regional director of the Fish and Wildlife Service in Atlanta, Ga.

The International Geophysical Year of 1957–1958 offered Eklund the opportunity for a second trip to Antarctica, and he accepted the post of scientific leader of the Wilkes Station. During 1957–1958 he conducted intensive research, and his findings formed the crux of his dissertation as well as his most important contribution to science. In particular, Eklund studied the skua and other Antarctic birds, banding many of them and learning a great deal about the survival of wildlife in regions of bitter cold. He measured the temperature of incubating eggs of the Adélie penguin by means of a transistorized thermometer inserted in an egg, and he also closely observed the habits of seals. These researches brought Eklund an international reputation as a scientist, as did several articles and the monograph *Antarctic Fauna and Some of Its Problems* (1956). In 1959 he was a founder and first president of the Antarctican Society, and from his return to the United States in 1958 until his death he was a member of the Committee on Polar Research of the National Academy of Sciences and chief of the Polar and Arctic Branch of the Army Research Office.

Eklund lectured widely in his final years, and in 1962 he served as the official representative of the National Academy of Sciences at an international meeting in Paris. During this period he also was a member of the Panel on Biology and Medical Science of the National Academy of Sciences. He died in Philadelphia, of a heart attack.

[Eklund's personal papers are held by the U.S. National Archives and Records Service, Center for Polar Archives, Washington, D.C. He was coauthor of *Antarctica During the IGY* (1961). Also see Walter Sullivan, *Quest for a Continent* (1957).

Obituaries are in the *New York Times*, Nov. 5, 1962, and *Nature*, Jan. 5, 1963.]

JAMES A. CASADA

ELIOT, T(HOMAS) S(TEARNS) (Sept. 26, 1888–Jan. 4, 1965), poet, was born in St. Louis, Mo., the son of Henry Ware Eliot, a manufacturer of bricks, and of Charlotte Champe Stearns, a volunteer social worker and an amateur writer. At Smith Academy, the preparatory department of Washington University at St. Louis (which had been founded by his paternal grandfather), Eliot began his study of classical and modern languages. Somewhat shy, he was more given to solitary reading than to playing with friends. His family summered in a large seaside house in Gloucester, Mass., and he enjoyed sailing the New England coast. Memories of those holidays appear in several of his mature poems. He contributed short stories and verse to the *Smith Academy Record,* and on graduation in 1905 he was selected class poet. After a year at Milton Academy in Milton, Mass., Eliot entered Harvard College in 1906.

Even as a student, Eliot had the bearing characteristic of his later years. His Harvard classmate Conrad Aiken remembered him as "a singularly attractive, tall and rather dapper young man with a somewhat Lamian smile." Bertrand Russell, whose graduate seminar he attended, described him as "ultra-civilized, . . . very well dressed and polished with manners of the finest Etonian type." Fifty years later, in its obituary notice, the London *Times* echoed those early descriptions: "In public, Eliot, a stooping, sombre-clad figure, appeared to be shy and retiring, formal in his manner, which was courtly and attentive, but detached." With friends, though, Eliot could enjoy banter and jokes. In verses written in 1933, he wittily depicted himself thus: "How unpleasant to meet Mr. Eliot!/ With his features of clerical cut,/And his brow so grim/And his mouth so prim/And his conversation so nicely/Restricted to What Precisely/And If and Perhaps and But."

As an undergraduate, Eliot continued his study of languages and also took courses in history, philosophy, and literature. In an effort to overcome his inhibitions he joined various social clubs and, briefly, took boxing lessons. In several poems published in the *Harvard Advocate,* of which he became an editor, Eliot followed the fashions of late-nineteenth-century English verse. But in 1908 he discovered the French symbolist poets, especially Jules Laforgue, and his poetry soon reflected his appreciation of their lively rhythms, natural diction, and ironic detachment.

Although his academic record was not brilliant, Eliot completed the undergraduate studies in three years and devoted the fourth to an M.A. in comparative literature. He was powerfully impressed by the teaching of Irving Babbitt and the poetry of Dante. Babbitt's incisive criticism of modern life and thought confirmed Eliot's native anti-romanticism and sanctioned the appreciation of suprapersonal authority that informed his later literary, social, and religious thought. Dante's poetry offered a model of precise diction and clear visual imagery; he was, Eliot said later, "the most persistent and deepest influence upon my own verse."

In 1910–1911, while studying French literature and philosophy at the Sorbonne, Eliot wrote the first of his mature poems, "Portrait of a Lady" and "The Love Song of J. Alfred Prufrock," dramatic monologues whose helpless narrators' bewilderment and erotic frustration became themes of his verse for the next decade. Back at Harvard in 1911, he put poetry largely aside and, preparing for an academic career, enrolled as a graduate student in philosophy. In addition to the classics of Western philosophy, he studied Eastern languages and thought, primitive religions, anthropology, and mysticism. His eclectic learning was evident in his later verse.

In June 1914, Eliot went to Europe on a Sheldon Traveling Fellowship; save for a brief visit in August 1915, he did not return to America for eighteen years. After a summer course in Marburg, Germany, Eliot arrived at Merton College, Oxford, where he wrote his dissertation, which was completed in 1916 and was warmly praised by his Harvard supervisors. Owing to the difficulty of travel during World War I, he did not return to Harvard for his oral examination, and the Ph.D. was never conferred. In 1964, Eliot published the dissertation, *Knowledge and Experience in the Philosophy of F. H. Bradley,* remarking, "I do not pretend to understand it." It was by then, he said, only "a curiosity of biographical interest, which shows . . . how closely my own prose style was formed on that of Bradley." Several critics, though, have found Bradley's idealism to be central to Eliot's poetry and criticism.

During his fellowship year in England, Eliot's life took several important turns. On June 26, 1915, he married Vivien (sometimes Vivienne) Haigh-Wood, whom he had met that April in Oxford. The daughter of a British portrait painter, she was intelligent and vivacious, but physically frail and subject to obscure but persistent neuroses. Almost from the beginning the marriage was a failure—a burden Eliot bore until her death in 1947 at a London hospital for the emotionally disturbed. The marriage did, however, tie Eliot to England when otherwise he might have heeded his parents' advice that he return to America to pursue the academic career he had come to find less and less attractive.

In the fall of 1914, Eliot met Ezra Pound in London; that meeting was also influential. Impressed when Eliot showed him "Prufrock," Pound sent the poem to Harriet Monroe, editor of *Poetry,* and acclaimed Eliot as "the only American I know of who has made what I call adequate preparation for writing." Pound urged Eliot to concentrate on poetry rather than philosophy, and introduced him to English literary circles, and generously offered various other kinds of support. Eliot again began writing poems.

The appearance of "Prufrock" (1915) was soon followed by the publication in avant-garde little magazines of other bitterly ironic poems that captured in strikingly original free-verse forms the squalor of urban settings and the sterility of life without faith or purpose. To please his parents, who had little confidence in his prospects as a poet, and to retain the option of an academic career, Eliot also wrote more than a dozen technical essays and reviews for philosophical journals. At the same time he was teaching in London grammar schools and undertaking a number of appointments as university extension lecturer in order to support himself and his ailing wife.

In March 1917, weary of schoolmastering, Eliot took a job in the colonial and foreign department of Lloyds Bank, where for the next eight years he held increasingly responsible positions involving foreign exchange, postwar reparations, and international trade. His essays in the *Egoist*, of which he was appointed assistant editor in 1917, and the publication of his first volume of poetry, *Prufrock and Other Observations* (1917), brought Eliot to the attention of the Bloomsbury Group. He became a close friend of Leonard and Virginia Woolf, and his next book of poems was handprinted by the Woolfs at their Hogarth Press. In 1917 he was commissioned, at Pound's suggestion, to write a brief, unsigned appreciation of *Ezra Pound: His Metric and Poetry* (1918) for publication in America.

Eliot's attempts to enlist in the United States Army had been frustrated by a medically disqualifying hernia and government delays in approving his application for the intelligence service. Thus, remaining in London during the war, he continued to write poems, including several in French and a number in witty, learned quatrains, which appeared in *Poems* (1919) and *Ara Vos Prec* (1920). "Gerontion" is the most important poem of this period. In it the reveries of an old man, meditating on his experiences and awaiting a sign of the redemption that would give them meaning, yield Eliot's characteristic early themes of erotic failure and spiritual longing; its variety of rhythm and elliptical syntax anticipate his future work.

While winning recognition as a poet, Eliot was also gaining respect as a critic. Essays and reviews that had originally appeared in some of the leading journals of the day were gathered in *The Sacred Wood* (1920). He later remarked that the spirited writing in this brief volume was "workshop criticism," the effort of a young poet to prepare an audience for the kind of poetry he was writing and to recommend as models such writers as he himself had found useful. Along with incisive "essays of appreciation" (on Elizabethan dramatists and Dante), Eliot included several polemical "essays of generalization" iconoclastically challenging the premises of prevailing Georgian literary taste. The most famous, "Tradition and the Individual Talent," advanced an "impersonal" theory of poetry and insisted that contemporary poetry should reflect a "historical sense" of the entire Western literary tradition.

Even in this earliest criticism Eliot spoke with a tone of authority that belied his youth, his still-modest standing, and his personal diffidence. Due partly to that tone, his criticism was influential in revolutionizing critical theory and practice, especially in universities. To his surprise and later embarrassment, terms like "objective correlative" and "dissociation of sensibility" soon enjoyed wide currency; Eliot's insistence upon the self-sufficiency of the work of art became a central tenet of the New Criticism.

The strain of establishing a literary reputation while holding down a full-time job at the bank and caring for his wife told on Eliot's health, both physical and emotional. In October 1921 he went to Margate for rest and consultation with a specialist in nervous disorders. A month later he left for Lausanne, Switzerland, where he spent six weeks in psychiatric treatment. While there he completed a draft of a poem he had been mulling over for several years. In Paris, on his way back to London, he presented the draft to Pound, who, Eliot later said, turned "a jumble of good and bad passages into a poem."

Like James Joyce's novel *Ulysses* (1922), Eliot's poem "The Waste Land" (1922) revolutionized English literature in demonstrating new possibilities of traditional genres. In a 1923 review of *Ulysses*, Eliot pointed to Joyce's use of myth to manipulate "a continuous parallel between contemporaneity and antiquity. . . . It is simply a way of controlling, of ordering, of giving a shape and a significance to the immense panorama of futility and anarchy which is contemporary history." Using the symbolism of fertility myths that he believed form the basis of the Christian Grail legend, Eliot unified a series of vividly drawn vignettes that portrayed the banality of life, the sterility of sex, and the isolation of the individual in a ruined civilization desperately awaiting relief from spiritual drought. Both in its numerous literary and historical allusions and in its variety of sound and rhythm, the poem was the most complete expression of Eliot's decade of poetic experimentation.

"The Waste Land" appeared first in the (American) *Dial* and the (English) *Criterion*. Several months later it was published separately with extensive annotation added by Eliot to fill some blank pages in the book. From the beginning the poem was both praised and condemned for its allusiveness, its fragmentary form, and its apocalyptic tone. Probably the most widely discussed of all modern poems, it has become a central document of literary modernism because of its technical innovation and its expression of postwar disillusionment.

The October 1922 issue of the *Criterion*, in which the poem first appeared, also marked the beginning of Eliot's editorship of that new literary review. For seventeen years the *Criterion* provided a forum for the systematic exploration of literary and social issues of concern to Eliot. An admiring, although never large, readership found in its pages essays and imaginative works by many of Europe's most distinguished writers and thinkers. Eliot's selection of contributors (many of whom came together for monthly *Criterion* dinners) and his regular editorial "Commentaries" reflected the steady evolution of Eliot's interests from literary matters to religious and social affairs.

When it lost the support of Lady Rothermere, its founding benefactor, in 1925, the journal was taken up by the new publishing house of Faber and Gwyer (later Faber and Faber). That same year Eliot had left Lloyds Bank to join Faber, which hired him both for his business experience and for his ability to attract promising young writers. Eventually appointed a director, Eliot remained active in the firm until his death and was responsible for the publication of much of the most important literature of that period. "An artist needs to live a commonplace life if he is to get his work done," Eliot remarked. As a publisher he enjoyed the steady income and flexibility of schedule that permitted him to pursue his writing.

During the mid-1920's Eliot published in the *Criterion* parts of two poems: "The Hollow Men" (1925), whose total despair went beyond even the pessimism of "The Waste Land," and the unfinished "Sweeney Agonistes" (1932), his earliest effort in verse drama, which reflected a long-standing interest in the British music hall. He also published there his translations of the work of various French contributors and a number of book reviews, including several of detective novels. But his most important critical essays of the period appeared, unsigned, in the *Times Literary Supplement;* some were collected in *Homage to John Dryden* (1924) and others in *For Lancelot Andrewes* (1928).

In the preface to the latter, Eliot made the startling announcement of his conversion to Anglo-Catholicism. Since 1926 he had regularly attended morning communion, and in June 1927—several months before renouncing his American citizenship to become a British subject—he had been baptized and confirmed in the Church of England. Drawn to its Catholic wing by its emphasis on tradition, authority, and

the role of aesthetic values in worship, the modernist poet of despair shortly became a trusted church warden and an earnest participant in informal discussion groups that met to explore the implication of Christian faith for contemporary affairs.

To many readers Eliot became a lost leader; his conversion, a betrayal. Edmund Wilson found it "sadly symptomatic of the feeble condition of modern literary people, of their unwillingness or incapacity to confront the realities about them." To the reviewer for the *Times Literary Supplement*, Eliot had "abdicated from his high position" in rejecting "modernism for medievalism." In fact, Eliot had exchanged his prestige as a skeptical, avant-garde modernist for a different kind of standing as an Establishment figure and spokesman for religious and social Toryism.

His new religious commitment was evident in the writing that followed his conversion. In Christmas poems like "Journey of the Magi" (1927) and "A Song for Simeon" (1928), and in short, brilliantly lyric poems collected as *Ash Wednesday* (1930), Eliot drew upon the traditions and language of the Church to portray the struggle of the new Christian to accept the consequences of religious belief and discipline. In appreciative essays on writers like Lancelot Andrewes (1926), Archbishop Bramhall (1927), Dante (1929), and Blaise Pascal (1931), he recalled the intellectual and artistic heritage of Christianity. And in *Thoughts After Lambeth* (1931), B.B.C. broadcast talks titled "The Modern Dilemma" (1932), and numerous contributions to religious and secular periodicals, he reflected his concern for Anglican affairs and the Church's role in the world. The appearance of much of this writing in *Selected Essays* (1932) demonstrated the evolution of Eliot's critical interests since *The Sacred Wood*, his previous major collection.

A convert to Christianity when many of his contemporaries were embracing the politics of the Left, Eliot said, "Anyone who has been moving among intellectual circles and comes to the Church, may experience an odd and rather exhilarating feeling of isolation." For Eliot communism and fascism were equally unsatisfactory, in that neither accepted Christian values. Britain seemed hardly more principled. "The world is trying the experiment of attempting to form a civilized but non-Christian mentality," he wrote in 1931. "The experiment will fail." As he said in 1933, he held a belief, "what in the eyes of the world must be a desperate belief, that a Christian world-order, *the* Christian world-order, is ultimately the only one which, from any point of view, will work." In a series of lectures published as *The Idea of a Christian Society* (1939), Eliot attacked secular liberalism and outlined the structure of a society founded on explicitly religious principles. Here, as in most of his Christian sociology, his approach was more hortatory than specific—an earnest tract for the times rather than a recipe for feasible social reform.

The changed literary perspective resulting from his conversion was evident in two series of lectures delivered in America in 1932 and 1933. In University of Virginia talks published as *After Strange Gods: A Primer of Modern Heresy* (1934), Eliot spoke as a moralist whose censorious approach to contemporary literature fulfilled his new principle that "literary criticism should be completed by criticism from a definite ethical and theological standpoint." As Charles Eliot Norton professor at Harvard, he showed his broader interest in the place of poetry and the poet in a larger social context. At the end of those lectures, published as *The Use of Poetry and the Use of Criticism* (1933), he remarked: "Every poet would like . . . to be able to think he had some direct social utility. . . . The ideal medium for poetry . . . , and the most direct means of social 'usefulness' for poetry, is the theatre." Eliot would shortly act upon that belief.

His marriage having proved an intolerable burden, Eliot had instructed his attorney to proceed with a legal separation while he was in America. When he returned to England in June 1933, he became a paying guest in the presbytery of his London church. Along with the Oxford and Cambridge Club, where he took many of his meals, his small room there was to be his home for the next seven years.

Soon Eliot was asked to write a pageant play as part of a campaign for funds to support the construction of churches in the London suburbs. Happy to combine his long-standing interest in poetic drama, his sense of the social utility of the theater, and service to the Church, he accepted. Depicting various episodes in the history of the Church, *The Rock* (1934) was well received during its two-week run at Sadler's Wells Theatre. It was the first of Eliot's many collaborative efforts with the director E. Martin Browne. A commission to write for the 1935 Canterbury Festival soon followed. *Murder in the Cathedral,* an account of St. Thomas à Becket's martyrdom in 1170, was performed at Canterbury Cathedral and then enjoyed success on the stage. It has remained the most popular

of Eliot's plays. *The Family Reunion* (1939), a tale of sin and expiation that is an effort to translate the Oresteia into Christian terms and a contemporary setting, was less successful. Although the stylized chorus proved obtrusive and the characters were insufficiently realized, this first of his plays written expressly for the popular stage represented another of Eliot's efforts to share his Christian vision with a wide, largely secular audience.

Eliot next turned to the completion of *Four Quartets* (1943), his last major nondramatic poetry and, for many, the greatest achievement of his career. The first of the *Quartets,* "Burnt Norton," had begun from passages deleted from *Murder in the Cathedral* and first appeared in *Collected Poems* (1936). The others were "East Coker" (1940), "The Dry Salvages" (1941), and "Little Gidding" (1942). Each is independently intelligible; as a group, though, they loosely follow musical form in developing themes and images presented in the first. Technically brilliant in their use of various verse forms, these serenely lyrical poems are by turns philosophical, religious, autobiographical, and (in their discussion of poetry itself) critical. Meditating on the relation of the chaotic flux of "sad waste time" to the timelessness of eternity, the poems show the redemption of time by the gift of the Incarnation.and by the timeless moments of illumination of which human history is a pattern.

Like many other Londoners, Eliot sought refuge in the suburbs during the bombing of the city in World War II. He stayed a few days each week in the Russell Square offices of Faber and Faber, where he spent the night as a fire watcher. After the war he returned to the city and began an eleven-year tenancy in the London flat of John Hayward, a wealthy bibliophile and man of letters. Eliot had known Hayward since the 1930's, and while writing the *Quartets* he had sent him drafts for his suggestions. Because he was so shy and reserved, Eliot had few intimate friends; Hayward was one of them.

After the death of William Butler Yeats in 1939, Eliot was unquestionably the foremost living poet writing in English, and he was increasingly in demand as a speaker on literary topics. His essays were now written for the lecture platform rather than the literary reviews. "The Frontiers of Criticism" (1956) was delivered before an audience of 13,000 at the University of Minnesota. A number of his essays from the late 1940's and early 1950's were collected in a book entitled *On Poetry and Poets* (1957). The iconoclasm and strident moralizing of his earlier criticism were here replaced by a mellow wisdom. In essays like "Poetry and Drama" (1951) and "The Three Voices of Poetry" (1953), Eliot combined literary theory with reflections on his own poetic practice. In "Milton II" (1947) he retracted many of the charges leveled in his influential attack on that great poet eleven years before. And in essays on Yeats (1940), Johnson (1944), Virgil (1951), and Goethe (1955), he paid tribute to his predecessors. Tributes to Eliot were being paid as well: In 1948 he was awarded the Nobel Prize for literature and the British Order of Merit.

Eliot continued to write on social and religious topics. *Reunion by Destruction* (1943) examined a proposal for Church union in South India. *Notes Toward the Definition of Culture* (1948) considered the necessary preconditions for a flourishing culture and the interrelationship of religion and culture. The University of Chicago lectures titled "The Aims of Education" offered a review of issues in educational theory. Abstracted from workaday realities and lacking both the dogmatism and the sense of impending crisis of his earlier social and religious criticism, such later work is of interest less for sustained argument than for the example it offers of an earnest man of letters venturing into fields generally the province of specialists.

More fruitful was Eliot's resumption, after the war, of writing for the theater. As his poetic output became slight, verse drama engaged the greatest part of his creative effort. Artistically and commercially *The Cocktail Party* (1949) was the most successful of his plays written for the popular stage. Like the earlier plays it contrasted characters of limited spiritual awareness with others whose greater consciousness calls them away to fulfill their destiny. Now, though, the Christian basis of the play was only implicit; the classical source was thoroughly assimilated into the action of this drawing-room comedy; and the verse was so unobtrusive as to be subliminal. In the two plays that followed, *The Confidential Clerk* (1953) and *The Elder Statesman* (1958), Eliot further accommodated himself to the conventions of the naturalistic stage. Focusing now on ordinary people rather than the spiritually elite, these plays quietly urge the importance of honesty with self and others, the necessity of understanding and forgiveness, and the healing power of love.

By then, after many years of loneliness and guilt over the failure of his first marriage, Eliot had come to enjoy such love. On Jan. 10, 1957, ten years after the death of his first wife, he married Esmé Valerie Fletcher, then thirty years old, who since 1949 had been his private

secretary at Faber and Faber. His touching poem "To My Wife" (1959) reveals the personal fulfillment he enjoyed in his final years. After Eliot's death in London, a memorial stone was placed in the Poets' Corner, Westminster Abbey. His body was cremated and his ashes were buried in the parish church at East Coker, the Somerset village from which his ancestors had emigrated to America in the seventeenth century. His epitaph asks: "Of your charity/pray for the repose/of the soul of/Thomas Stearns Eliot/Poet."

[Much of Eliot's correspondence is being collected by his wife for a forthcoming edition of his letters. Important collections of Eliot letters are in the Humanities Research Library of the University of Texas, the libraries of the University of Chicago, Northwestern University, the University of Virginia, and Yale University, the Houghton Library at Harvard University (which also has material dating from Eliot's years at Harvard), the Princeton University Library, and the New York Public Library (which has both letters and the revised manuscript of "The Waste Land"). John Hayward's collection of Eliot's papers, including drafts of the *Four Quartets,* is in the library of King's College, Cambridge.

Eliot expressly asked that there be no authorized biography of him, but see Hugh Kenner, *The Invisible Poet: T. S. Eliot* (1959); Herbert Howarth, *Notes on Some Figures Behind T. S. Eliot* (1964); Allen Tate, ed., *T. S. Eliot: The Man and His Work* (1966); Russell Kirk, *Eliot and His Age* (1971); Bernard Bergonzi, *T. S. Eliot* (1972); Thomas S. Matthews, *Great Tom* (1974); Stephen Spender, *T. S. Eliot* (1975); Lyndall Gordon, *Eliot's Early Years* (1977); A. D. Moody, *Thomas Stearns Eliot: Poet* (1979). Two memoirs should be used with caution: William Turner Levy and Victor Scherle, *Affectionately, T. S. Eliot* (1968) and Robert Sencourt, *T. S. Eliot: A Memoir* (1971).

On the composition of some of Eliot's most important works, see E. Martin Browne, *The Making of T. S. Eliot's Plays* (1969); Valerie Eliot, ed., *The Waste Land* (1971); and Helen L. Gardner, *The Composition of Four Quartets* (1978). Studies of various aspects of his career include F. O. Matthiessen, *The Achievement of T. S. Eliot* (1939); Helen L. Gardner, *The Art of T. S. Eliot* (1949); D. E. S. Maxwell, *The Poetry of T. S. Eliot* (1955); Grover C. Smith, *T. S. Eliot's Poetry and Plays: A Study in Sources and Meanings* (1956); D. E. Jones, *The Plays of T. S. Eliot* (1960); Carol H. Smith, *T. S. Eliot's Dramatic Theory and Practice* (1963); Graham Martin, ed., *Eliot in Perspective* (1970); Roger Kojecký, *T. S. Eliot's Social Criticism* (1972); John D. Margolis, *T. S. Eliot's Intellectual Development, 1922–1939* (1972); Elizabeth W. Schneider, *T. S. Eliot: The Pattern in the Carpet* (1975); and David Newton-DeMolina, ed., *The Literary Criticism of T. S. Eliot* (1977).

Also see Donald C. Gallup, *T. S. Eliot: A Bibliography* (rev. ed., 1969). Obituaries are in *Obituaries from the* (London) *Times, 1961–1970* (1975); and in the *New York Times,* Jan. 5, 1965.]
                                                JOHN D. MARGOLIS

ELVEHJEM, CONRAD ARNOLD (May 27, 1901–July 27, 1962), biochemist and educator, was born at McFarland, Wis., the son of Ole Johnson Elvehjem and Christine Lewis, Norwegian immigrants who operated a family farm. After graduation from Stoughton High School in 1919, he entered the University of Wisconsin in Madison, where he spent the rest of his life as student, professor, dean, and president. In 1923, after completing the B.S. in agricultural chemistry, he continued his studies under E. B. Hart and received the Ph.D. in 1927. His dissertation dealt with the calcium and phosphorus requirements of lactating animals. On June 30, 1926, Elvehjem married Constance Waltz; they had two children.

Two years before completing his doctorate, Elvehjem became an instructor in agricultural chemistry. For the next several years he was associated with Hart, Harry Steenbock, and J. Waddell in research on nutritional anemia in young animals on a whole milk diet. The study revealed the role of copper in hemoglobin regeneration. In 1929–1930, Elvehjem was a National Research Council fellow at Cambridge, where he studied catalytic oxidation in the laboratory of F. G. Hopkins.

Returning to Wisconsin as assistant professor, Elvehjem conducted research that resulted in rapid promotion; he became full professor in 1936. He not only continued to study copper and iron in nutritional anemia but also undertook broad-ranging studies dealing with trace nutrients, both minerals and vitamins. His laboratory conducted pioneering studies on manganese, zinc, and cobalt, as well as on vitamins of the B complex.

In the mid-1930's Elvehjem became interested in nutritional control of pellagra. He used dogs as experimental animals because Joseph Goldberger had shown earlier that canine blacktongue was equivalent to pellagra in human beings. Elvehjem and his associates studied liver extract and, by 1937, had developed a concentrate from it that cured blacktongue in dogs. Recalling that the German biochemist Otto Warburg had isolated a new coenzyme, Elvehjem and R. J. Madden, D. W. Wooley, and F. M. Strong fed Warburg's coenzyme to one group of animals and their concentrate to another. Both cured blacktongue. The active antipellagra substance was nicotinic acid (now known as niacin). Clinicians elsewhere soon proved that it was a curative for human pellagra. Elvehjem later demonstrated that diets high in corn were particularly likely to cause pellagra because the tryptophan content of corn proteins is lower than that of other cereals. Tryptophan was found to have a role in niacin formation.

Elvehjem's laboratory later contributed heavily to the understanding of folic acid in nutrition and of the role of metabolic enzymes. He generated extensive studies of nutritional deficiencies (of pantothenic acid and of vitamin B_6) in chickens. When specific vitamins became available as pure chemicals, he utilized them in experimental rations in order to study particular deficiency symptoms uncomplicated by multiple deficiencies, the bane of earlier students of deficiency diseases.

Elvehjem's work was characterized by concern for both the fundamental and the practical. He had a strong desire to know the exact nature of the chemicals responsible for specific metabolic phenomena. At the same time he never excluded consideration of these factors—vitamins and minerals—in the nutrition of farm animals and of human beings. He supported the move to supplement flour and bread with vitamins and minerals at the beginning of World War II, and his laboratory produced numerous evaluations of the nutrient content of foods, especially meat and milk products.

With the retirement of Hart in 1944, Elvehjem became chairman of the department of agricultural chemistry (now biochemistry). Two years later he took on the added duties of dean of the graduate school, carrying both administrative posts while continuing his research in biochemistry. He was able to hold the three positions successfully because he was a hard-driving, no-nonsense person who expected similar performance from students, associates, and employees. He was prone to survey a problem quickly and arrive at a decision without delay. Many associates considered Elvehjem cold and humorless, but those who knew him well found him to be a warm person with a sense of humor.

During the postwar years enrollment was exploding at Wisconsin. Research expanded as funding of projects improved and as new problems arose to be solved. As chairman and dean Elvehjem played a significant role in the university's rapid growth. Because of his stature as a scientist he was also involved in nutritional problems on the national level. He was a member of the National Academy of Sciences and served on boards of the National Research

Council, particularly the Food and Nutrition Board. Elvehjem also lectured widely. During these years his laboratory continued to produce a steady stream of graduating students and publications.

In 1958, Elvehjem was appointed president of the University of Wisconsin. In that office he sought to develop balanced strength, encouraging scholarly expansion in the humanities and social sciences while maintaining the natural sciences. His presidency was fraught with serious problems: a branch of the university was being organized at Milwaukee; other schools were seriously raiding Wisconsin's faculty; and a troublesome deanship crisis had to be resolved in the Medical School. He died at Madison, Wis.

[Elvehjem's papers are in the archives at the University of Wisconsin. The biochemistry department has a complete set of his more than 800 published papers. The only published bibliographies of his works, although incomplete, are in J. C. Poggendorff, *Biographisch-Literarisches Handwörterbuch zur Geschichte der exacten Wissenschaften*, vol. 6, part 1, and vol. 76, part 2; and the listings in the author indexes of *Chemical Abstracts;* the biochemistry department holds a mimeographed list. Also see Robert Eskew, "Elvehjem of Wisconsin," *Let's See* magazine, Sept. 1961; A. J. Ihde, "Conrad A. Elvehjem" in, W. D. Miles, ed., *American Chemists and Chemical Engineers* (1976); and "Memorial Resolution of the Faculty of the University of Wisconsin on the Death of Conrad Arnold Elvehjem," mimeographed document 1549, Oct. 1, 1962.

Obituaries appeared in the Madison, Wis., *Capital Times,* and *Milwaukee Journal* on July 27, 1962; and the Madison *Wisconsin State Journal* and the *New York Times* on July 28, 1962.]

AARON J. IHDE

ENGLE, CLAIR WILLIAM WALTER (Sept. 21, 1911–July 30, 1964), U.S. congressman and senator, was born in Bakersfield, Calif., the son of Fred Jewell Engle and Carita Alta Keeran. A sometime cattle rancher, attorney, schoolteacher, and railroader, Fred Engle moved his family to northern California in 1913. His bitter and protracted struggle with large power companies over water rights apparently made a deep impression on his son, and may well have influenced Clair Engle's later political career. Engle attended the Red Bluff, Calif., public schools, Chico Junior College (1928–1930), and Hastings College of Law of the University of California. On Jan. 12, 1933, while still a student, he married Hazel Burney Sheldon; they had one daughter.

In 1933, Engle received the LL.B. from Hastings, passed the bar, returned to Tehama

County, and immediately plunged into local politics. He was elected Tehama County district attorney in 1934, and first won statewide attention in 1940, when he prosecuted a highly publicized homicide case in an adjoining county at the request of California Attorney General Earl Warren. Following a successful race for the state senate in 1942, Engle won a special election to the United States House of Representatives from California's second district in 1943. An avid outdoorsman, he loved this rugged, sprawling, sparsely populated district that encompassed a third of the state. He piloted his own airplane while visiting constituents and maintaining his political fences. Shortly after his first marriage ended in divorce, Engle married Lucretia Caldwell Hibner on Dec. 4, 1948.

An exceptionally vigorous and colorful campaigner and an agile cloakroom politician, Engle, a Democrat, spent fifteen years in the House promoting state and regional interests. He criticized federal officials for "coddling" Japanese and Japanese-Americans during World War II, voted for the Submerged Lands Act in 1953, sponsored legislation to help the domestic mining industry, and emerged as a forceful advocate of statehood for Alaska and Hawaii. From his positions on the Public Lands Committee and the Interior and Insular Affairs Committee (which he chaired from 1955 to 1959), Engle devoted himself to water, land, and reclamation issues, all of great concern to his district and state. He won enactment of the Saline Water Act (1952) to finance research into the conversion of salt water to fresh, and he was responsible for several major additions to the Central Valley project in California, including the American River Development, the Trinity River and San Luis projects, and a system of canals in the Sacramento River valley.

His promotion of the Central Valley project involved Engle in elaborate intrigue over funding for competing reclamation-irrigation undertakings elsewhere in the country. He blocked the Central Arizona project in 1952 because it threatened California's water supply, and he slowed the Hell's Canyon project in Idaho. By his adept support of several Rocky Mountain water projects he won vital votes for his own Trinity River legislation.

At the same time Engle emerged as a leader among congressional liberals advocating federal power development rather than the Eisenhower administration's "partnership" approach, which involved private power utilities. In two searing battles with the administration, Engle's public power forces won on the Trinity River project, but lost to the "partnership" advocates on Hell's Canyon.

Engle capitalized on a liberal Democratic trend to defeat Governor Goodwin Knight for a United States Senate seat in 1958. While still attempting to protect his state's large defense and aircraft industries through his position on the Senate Armed Services Committee, Engle operated on a somewhat broader stage than in the House. During the campaign he proposed an expanded Middle East regional development authority, and in 1959 urged a rethinking of American policy toward China. He criticized the Eisenhower defense posture, and called for unification of the Air Force, Army, and Navy as a means of promoting efficiency. He also opposed the multilateral Antarctica Treaty involving the United States and the Soviet Union in 1960.

Responding to a larger liberal constituency, Engle renounced his earlier support for the Taft-Hartley Labor Act and called for an end to "right-to-work" laws, enactment of effective civil rights legislation, aid to education, and federal support for medical care for the aged. Expressing deep concern for the environment, he fought for the Wilderness Act of 1964 and sponsored legislation creating the Point Reyes National Seashore to prevent dangerous development of the coastline in Marin County, Calif. He also urged clean-air legislation and a delay in the construction of atomic power plants in California earthquake zones. In 1961, Americans for Democratic Action gave Engle's voting record 100-percent approval.

Because Engle was on friendly terms with both the Lyndon Johnson–Sam Rayburn congressional forces and the Kennedy White House (having been mentioned as a possible vice-presidential running mate for Kennedy in 1960), some observers thought that he might find a place on the national ticket in the 1960's or 1970's. But, striken by brain cancer, Engle underwent repeated surgeries in 1963 and 1964 and was left partially paralyzed. In June 1964, one month prior to his death in Washington, D.C., he voted from a wheelchair for the Civil Rights Act.

[The Clair Engle Papers are divided between the Tehama County Library, Red Bluff, Calif., and the California State Archives in Sacramento. See Stephen Paul Sayles, "Clair Engle and his Political Development in Tehama County, 1911–1944," *California Historical Quarterly*, Winter 1975; and his "Clair Engle and the Politics of California Reclamation, 1943–1960" (Ph.D. diss., University of New Mexico, 1978). Also see Paul F. Healy, "Wildcat in Washington," *Saturday Evening Post*, Mar. 12, 1955.

Obituaries are in the *New York Times* and *San Francisco Chronicle*, July 31, 1964.]

WILLIAM HOWARD MOORE

ERLANGER, JOSEPH (Jan. 5, 1874–Dec. 5, 1965), physiologist, was born in San Francisco, Calif., the son of Herman Erlanger, a merchant, and of Sarah Galinger, both immigrants from southern Germany. He was the only one of their seven children who sought an education beyond high school. As a child he spent much time dissecting animals and plants—an activity that led his older sister to nickname him "Doc." In 1889 Erlanger enrolled in San Francisco Boys' High School (which, despite its name, was co-educational), and in 1891 he passed the entrance examination of the University of California, where he enrolled in the College of Chemistry to prepare for a career in medicine. As a senior, while studying vertebrate embryology, he performed his first experimental investigation—a study of the development of the eggs of the newt *Amblystoma.*

In 1895 Erlanger received the B.S., and that fall he enrolled in the newly created medical school of the Johns Hopkins University. He received the M.D. in 1899, graduating second in his class. His performance brought him an internship (1899–1900) at Johns Hopkins under the supervision of William Osler, the preeminent clinician of the day.

While a medical student, Erlanger's appetite for experimental research became insatiable. During the summer between his first and second years, he worked in Lewellys Barker's histological laboratory, where he helped identify, in the spinal cord of rabbits, the location of the anterior horn cells that innervated a particular voluntary muscle. The following summer he studied in dogs the amount of small intestine that could safely be excised surgically without interfering with absorptive functions; this work resulted in his first publication, "A Study of the Metabolism in Dogs with Shortened Small Intestines" (1901).

Following his internship, Erlanger accepted an assistantship at Johns Hopkins under the experimental physiologist William H. Howell.

Erlanger had acquired his scientific education entirely in America, his only study abroad having occurred during the summer of 1902, when he interrupted an extended European vacation to spend six weeks in the biochemistry laboratory of the University of Strassburg. His formal preparation contrasted markedly with that of his teachers at Johns Hopkins, who had obtained their scientific training in Germany.

As an assistant in physiology, Erlanger undertook a number of important investigations. In 1904 he devised and constructed an improved sphygmomanometer, an instrument for measuring the blood pressure. His instrument was easier to use than any existing such device, since it could determine the blood pressure in the upper arm. In 1904 Erlanger utilized this apparatus to study the relationship of blood flow to orthostatic albuminuria (the appearance of protein in the urine when a person stands). He demonstrated that the appearance of albumin in the urine of patients affected with this condition related much more closely to the pulse pressure (the difference between the systolic and diastolic blood pressures) than to the mean arterial blood pressure.

In another major project Erlanger studied the conduction of electrical impulses in the heart. Using cardiac surgery on dogs and a special clamp he designed that could reversibly apply carefully graded pressure, Erlanger discovered that electrical conduction between the auricles and ventricles of the heart occurred through a particular anatomic pathway known as the bundle of His. He also showed that impaired conduction through the bundle of His ("heart block") was responsible for the clinical syndrome of Stokes-Adams attacks (fainting episodes with slow pulse).

These investigations brought Erlanger recognition as a physiologist of the first rank and, in 1906, appointment as the first professor of physiology at the University of Wisconsin Medical School. On June 21, 1906, he married Aimée Hirstel. They had three children.

At Wisconsin, Erlanger hoped to equip and staff a modern laboratory of physiology. His efforts were frustrated by the lack of funds. In 1910 he accepted the professorship of physiology at the recently reorganized and well-endowed Washington University School of Medicine in St. Louis. There, with adequate financial backing, he built one of the world's premiere departments of physiology. At Washington University, Erlanger also continued his researches in cardiovascular physiology. During World War I he developed a solution of glucose and gum acacia for the treatment of wound shock. This preparation, used by the U.S. Army in France, was the first example of treatment with artificial serum containing high-molecular-weight polymers. He also conducted sophisticated studies that elucidated the origin of the sounds of Korotkoff, which are heard through the stethoscope while measuring blood pressure.

In 1921 Erlanger's interest shifted to neurophysiology. Much of his work in this area was done in collaboration with Herbert Gasser, a colleague at Washington University. Prior to 1920 very little was known about the electrophysiology of nerves because the electrical impulses they transmit are so weak and of such short duration that no one had been able to measure them accurately. In 1920 Gasser devised an amplifier that magnified these impulses about 100,000 times. The following year Erlanger and Gasser developed a device that could record the amplified impulse: the cathode-ray oscilloscope. Using this instrument, they made fundamental observations concerning the conduction of impulses through peripheral nerves. Their most important discovery was that the velocity of impulse conduction is directly proportional to the diameter of the nerve fiber—that is, that large nerve fibers transmit impulses more rapidly than smaller ones. For this discovery they shared the Nobel Prize in Medicine or Physiology in 1944.

The significance of Erlanger for American science goes far beyond the specific discovery that brought him the Nobel Prize. The cathode-ray oscilloscope that he and Gasser developed made possible the modern field of neurophysiology and served as the central instrument of the new discipline. Erlanger was also part of that generation of American scientists that was wresting leadership of the scientific world from Europe.

Erlanger was chairman of the physiology department at Washington University, an officer of the American Physiological Society (president, 1926–1929), and a member of the National Academy of Sciences. A man of strong personality and highly independent in his social, religious, and political views, he was a person of few words, who spoke only when he had something to say. His greatest recreational pleasure came from mountain climbing. Erlanger died in St. Louis.

[The Joseph Erlanger Papers, in the Washington University Medical School Archives, are described in Robert G. Frank, Jr., ". . . The Joseph Erlanger Collection at Washington University School of Medicine, St. Louis," *Journal of the History of Biology*, 1979. His writings include "A Study of the Metabolism in Dogs with Shortened Intestines," *American Journal of Physiology*, 1901; *Electrical Signs of Nervous Activity* (1937), written with Herbert Gasser; "A Physiologist Reminisces," *Annual Review of Physiology*, 1964. Also see Hallowell Davis, "Joseph Erlanger," *Biographical Memoirs. National Academy of of Sciences*, 1970. Oral history interviews with Erlanger, conducted by Estelle Brodman shortly before his death, are in Washington University Medical School Archives. An obituary is in the *New York Times*, Dec. 7, 1965.]

KENNETH M. LUDMERER

EVERS, MEDGAR WILEY (July 2, 1925–June 12, 1963), civil rights leader, was born in Decatur, Miss., the son of James Evers, a businessman, and Jessie Wright. He attended Decatur Consolidated School and Newton High School, and in 1943 entered the army, seeing service in the Normandy invasion and the French campaign. After the war Evers attended Alcorn Agricultural and Mechanical College in Lorman, Miss., and received a bachelor's degree in business administration in 1952. Following graduation he worked for a few years as an insurance salesman. On Dec. 24, 1951, Evers married Myrlie Beasley, whom he had met in college. They had three children.

In 1952, Evers joined the National Association for the Advancement of Colored People (NAACP). Two years later he became its field secretary in Mississippi, the organization's only paid position in the state. He worked vigorously establishing local chapters.

Evers' life was molded and subsequently destroyed by the bigotry and injustice that Mississippi society then routinely meted out to blacks. When he was fourteen, he witnessed the lynching of one of his father's friends, who had been accused of insulting a white woman. The image of this event never left him, and throughout his life he tried to overcome the racial system of his native state.

Not long after his graduation from Alcorn, Evers failed in an attempt to register at the University of Mississippi; in 1962 he aided James Meredith in his successful accomplishment of the same act. In 1957, Evers vainly protested to the Federal Communications Commission regarding the refusal of a Jackson, Miss., television station to allow him equal time to answer racial statements broadcast by white politicians. The following year he was arrested for sitting in a "white" bus seat in Meridian, Miss., and in 1960 was sentenced to thirty days in jail and fined $100 for criticizing an earlier conviction of another black. This sentence was eventually overturned by the Mississippi Supreme Court. In 1961, Evers applauded a defendant in a trial involving sit-down demonstrations, and was beaten by a court policeman. He became heavily involved in the civil rights movement in Jackson in 1962 and 1963, advocating the appointment of black policemen and the establishment of a biracial committee to study black-white relations in the city.

During his tenure as NAACP field secretary, Evers gained a reputation as a quiet, reasonable, and effective organizer who believed that blacks should rid themselves of their sense of inferiority and seek equality through voting and economic boycotts. Despite this attitude he was consistently the target of white hostility, which increased significantly by 1963 as a result of his work in Jackson. He received many threatening phone calls and death threats. He soon taught his children to duck and cover whenever they heard any strange noise outside, and he often commented on the possibility of violence to him and his family.

The fulfillment of this prophecy came shortly. On June 2, 1963, a firebomb was thrown into the carport of his Jackson home. Then, in the early hours of June 12, when Evers returned home from an NAACP function, he was shot and killed by an assassin while stepping out of his car.

Evers instantly became both a national figure and a martyr of the civil rights movement. The murder came at a time of increasing confrontation over the issue of black rights, a day after two black students were finally admitted to the University of Alabama over the obstruction of Governor George Wallace, and only hours after President John F. Kennedy's "moral crisis" speech defending the blacks' right to full citizenship. His death was a vivid example of white extremist reaction to black demands, and it gave support to those blacks who were beginning to claim that nonviolence was a dangerous folly. A major riot in Jackson was narrowly averted after Evers' funeral. Racial tension throughout the South intensified.

Most white Americans were also shocked by Evers' murder. The crime speeded the passage of civil rights legislation in Congress, and generally confirmed the involvement of the federal government in the cause of racial equality. It energized black political activism in Mississippi. Evers' brother, Charles, assumed the role of NAACP field secretary in Mississippi and organized boycotts, demonstrations, and voter registration drives.

Evers was buried at Arlington National Cemetery with full military honors. In death he had focused the attention of the nation on the problems that he had fought to solve during his life. The man who was later accused of Evers' murder, Byron de la Beckwith, was freed after two mistrials in which all-white juries could not decide on his guilt or innocence.

[Evers' feelings on life in Mississippi were published in *Ebony*, Sept. 1963. Much information on Evers' life can be found in articles that appeared 1957–1963 in *Time, Newsweek, Life,* and the *Saturday Evening Post.* Also see Benjamin Muse, *Ten Years of Prelude* (1964); James W. Silver, *Mississippi: The Closed Society* (1966); David L. Lewis, *King: A Biography* (1970); Jack Bass and Walter DeVries, *The Transformation of Southern Politics* (1976); Frank T. Read and Lucy S. McGough, *Let Them Be Judged* (1978). The *New York Times,* June 13, 1963, contains an obituary, a description of the events surrounding the murder, and background material.]

ERIC JARVIS

FAIRLESS, BENJAMIN F. (May 3, 1890–Jan. 1, 1962), industrialist, was born Benjamin Franklin Williams, at Pigeon Run, Ohio, near Massillon, the son of David Dean Williams, a coal miner, and Ruth Woolley. Because his mother was injured when Williams was two years old, he went to live with her sister Sarah and her husband, Jacob Fairless, a grocer in nearby Justus, Ohio. Although he remained close to his parents, he continued to live with his aunt and uncle, became known as Ben Fairless, and at age five was legally adopted. In 1907 he graduated valedictorian of a class of eight from Justus three-year high school. He then took courses at the College of Wooster to complete a fourth year of high school and enrolled at Ohio Northern University in 1909. Four years later he received a civil engineering degree.

Fairless worked from the age of five, selling newspapers, mowing lawns, caring for horses, and doing farm work. To finance his schooling at Wooster, he taught school at Riverdale (1907), Rockville (1908), and Navarre, Ohio (1909). This part-time work and a loan paid for his college education. In 1912, Fairless married Jane Blanche Trubey; they had one son.

After graduation Fairless worked as a surveyor for the Wheeling and Lake Erie Railroad. In 1914, while going to Massillon to watch the assembling of Coxey's second army of the unemployed for a march to Washington, he saw a steel mill under construction. Getting off the trolley, he applied for a job and was hired on the spot. The Central Steel Company kept him on after the plant was built, making him mill superintendent, then general superintendent, and finally, in 1921, vice-president in charge of operations. In 1926, the firm merged with the Central Furnace Company and the United Alloy Steel Corporation to form the United Alloy Steel Corporation. Fairless became vice-president and general manager and, two years later,

president. When the Republic Steel Corporation absorbed United Alloy Steel in 1930, Fairless was made executive vice-president of that company.

In 1935, Fairless faced a major career decision: to become president of Republic Steel or president of the Carnegie-Illinois Steel Corporation—a subsidiary of United States Steel. He accepted the latter post and two years later succeeded William A. Irvin as president and chief administrative officer of United States Steel. In 1952 Fairless became chairman of the board and chief executive officer, a position that he held until 1955. In retirement he remained a member of the board of directors and until his death was president of the American Iron and Steel Institute.

Under Fairless' leadership United States Steel enjoyed swelling profits, particularly between 1945 and 1955. Fairless plowed some of this income into plant expansion and modernization. In 1945 he authorized explorations in Venezuela for new sources of ore, and within a decade the Cerro Bolívar mines were shipping eight million tons of ore each year to the United States. Meanwhile, to process the Venezuelan ore into steel, United States Steel constructed a huge modern facility at Morrisville, N.J. The new Fairless Works added 1.8 million tons to the corporation's capacity. Overall, between 1938 and 1955, United States Steel increased its output 35 percent.

Fairless was an effective defender of bigness in the steel industry. He branded critics of concentration "Calamity Johns suffering from a midget complex—they think small." "No one," he once observed, "has yet invented an accordion-pleated steel plant that will contract conveniently under the glowering eye of the Department of Justice, and then expand obligingly in times of national peril."

During Fairless' tenure major steel strikes occurred in 1942, 1946, 1949, and 1952. Although he vigorously contested union demands, he usually was obliged to concede both higher wages and such other demands as a closed shop for employees in the "captive mines" owned by United States Steel, noncontributing worker pensions and welfare benefits, and a modified closed shop for all steelworkers. Fairless often complained of having to battle the unions and the federal government simultaneously. The strikes of 1946 and 1952, for example, came at times when the government controlled prices. Although Fairless was willing to grant part of the wage demands of the United Steel Workers of America (USWA), he argued that he could not do so unless the government allowed substantial price increases. In both instances the government, after much resistance, yielded.

At the close of the fifty-four-day strike of 1952, which President Harry Truman tried to forestall by seizing the companies, Fairless concluded that there must be a better way of dealing with labor. The celebrated "Ben and Dave" tours of United States Steel's mills followed. Fairless and David McDonald, president of the USWA, mingled with workers, radiating goodwill and a spirit of mutual conciliation. No important strikes took place during the balance of Fairless' career.

These labor policies illustrate negative aspects of equalizing the power of big business and big labor: when the two disagree, the resulting protracted strikes hurt the public as much as or more than the principals; when they agree, costly wage increases are simply passed along to the consumer in the form of higher prices.

On Oct. 14, 1944, two years after the death of Fairless' first wife, he married his son's mother-in-law, Hazel Hatfield Sproul. They were divorced on Dec. 20, 1961, twelve days before his death. Fairless died at Ligonier, Pa.

[See Benjamin F. Fairless, *It Could Happen Only in the U.S.* (1957); Howard Templeton Hill, Jr., "Benjamin F. Fairless: Spokesman for Industry With Particular Reference to his Main Lines of Argument" (Ph.D. diss., The Pennsylvania State University, 1957); and Richard William Nagle, "Collective Bargaining in Basic Steel and the Federal Government, 1945–1960" (Ph.D. diss., The Pennsylvania State University, 1978). Other sources include "Managers of Steel," *Fortune*, Mar. 1940; and obituary notices, Jan. 2, 1962, in the *New York Times, Pittsburgh Post Gazette, Pittsburgh Press,* and *Washington Post.*]
                                        GERALD G. EGGERT

FARNUM, FRANKLYN (June 5, 1878[?]– July 4, 1961), silent film actor, was born in Boston, Mass. He confided to an interviewer that his name was really William Franklyn Smith but that with advice he had changed his last name to Farnum and added his own middle name to form a more glamorous stage name. Farnum left school when he was twelve to help support his poverty-stricken family. A Protestant minister who heard him singing as he shoveled snow gave him a place in his church choir and sponsored his singing lessons. Farnum began his professional career singing at local smokers, and before the turn of the century was appearing as a chorus boy in musicals. He was reported to have made his debut as a principal as understudy to Walter Lawrence in *Sultan of Sula* at the Tremont Theater in Boston when he was seventeen. He soon became a leading man in the Nixon-Zimmerman Company, which sent out road shows and maintained theaters in Philadelphia and New York.

Farnum first appeared on Broadway in *The Dollar Princess* (1909). Next came *Madame Sherry,* an Otto Harbach-Karl Hoschna production that was one of the most famous pre-World War I operettas (1910), and *The Sunshine Girl,* with Julia Sanderson (1912). Victor Herbert's *The Only Girl* (1914) was Farnum's last Broadway vehicle.

His Broadway experience won Farnum parts in early three-reel movies produced in New York City; he was billed as Smiling Franklyn Farnum. In 1914 he went to Hollywood to appear with Ruth Stonehouse in *Love Never Dies.* Farnum played romantic leading men "bearing the Farnum brand of smiles and tears" in several one- and two-reel films for Triangle, Bluebird, and Metro. Tall, lean, and broad-shouldered, he had a special flair, particularly in roles calling for period costumes. He was described as being far handsomer off screen than on, and as having a special magnetism and warmth that the camera could not capture. In *The Clock* (1917), a five-reel comedy, he introduced a comic element into his adventure roles, modeled after the style of Douglas Fairbanks. This comic manner was at its best in *The Fighting Grin* (1918).

Farnum played Silent Joe in a mystery-western serial, *Vanishing Trails* (1920), and co-starred with Helen Holmes in *Battling Brewster* (1924). But his real popularity was as a hero in such westerns as *The Struggle* (1920), *The Fighting Stranger* and *The Galloping Devil* (1921), *So This Is Arizona* (1922), *The Firebrand* (1923), *A Two-Fisted Tenderfoot* (1924), and *The Gambling Fool* (1925). Although he had never ridden a horse or tried stunt work until he went to Hollywood, his name came to have the kind of magic that was associated with Tom Mix and William S. Hart. Farnum's appeal was not diminished by the similarity of his name to that of two brothers, William and Dustin Farnum, who were famous western stars of the period.

In 1928, at the height of his popularity as a western star, Farnum made a triumphant return to Boston to star in *Come Back to Erin,* a comedy-drama. Reviewers complimented him on his attractive tenor voice and his "delightfully intimate personality."

Farnum played in 150 films before the introduction of sound changed the direction of his
career. The number of productions was reduced as major studios made the transition,
and he was no longer sought for starring roles.
He quickly adapted to work as an extra, often
for independent companies. This reversal did
not make Farnum bitter: "I have no false
pride. There are people who say 'I won't work
extra,' but they're only kidding themselves.
You have to stay active and keep vindicating
yourself."

During the next twenty years Farnum appeared as henchmen, villains, and other characters in dozens of films, including *Three
Rogues* (1931), with Victor McLaglen and Fay
Wray; *Leftover Ladies* (1931); *Mark of the Spur*
and *The Texas Bad Man* (1932); *Powdersmoke
Range*, with Harey Carey and Hoot Gibson
(1936); *In Early Arizona* (1938); *Saddle Leather
Law* (1944); *Dear Wife* (1950); *My Friend Irma*
(1949); *All About Eve* (1950); *Sunset Boulevard*
(1950); *Lemon Drop Kid* (1951); *With a Song
in My Heart* (1952); and *Casanova's Big Night*,
with Bob Hope (1954). In 1956 he appeared in
Top Secret Affair, his 1,100th film.

Farnum was elected president of the Screen
Extras Guild in 1956. At the formal celebration
of his eightieth birthday in 1958, he was presented with a gold life-membership card. He
resigned as president of the union in January
1959, stating: "I feel that younger blood is
needed in the presidency in the approaching
contract negotiations." He retired from film
work in 1960.

Farnum was married to Edith Goodwin, who
died in 1959. Their daughter Geraldine was also
an actress. Farnum died in Los Angeles.

[Clipping files are available at the New York Public
Library Theater Collection, Lincoln Center, and the
National Film Information Service of the Academy
of Motion Picture Arts and Sciences. Also see Doris
Delvigne, "From Plain Bill Smith to Franklyn Far-
num," *Motion Picture Magazine*, Apr. 1919; Kalton
Lahue, *Continued Next Week* (1964); Ernest N.
Corneau, *The Hall of Fame of Western Film Stars*
(1969); John T. Weaver, comp., *Twenty Years of
Silents, 1908–1928* (1971); Arthur F. McClure and
Ken D. Jones, *Heroes, Heavies and Sagebrush* (1972);
George N. Fenin and William K. Everson, *The West-
erns: From Silents to the Seventies* (1977). Obituaries
are in the *Los Angeles Times* and *Mirror*, July 5,
1961, and the *New York Times* and *Herald Tribune*,
July 6, 1961.]

ELIZABETH R. NELSON

FATHER DIVINE. See DIVINE, FATHER.

**FAULKNER (FALKNER), WILLIAM
CUTHBERT** (Sept. 25, 1897–July 6, 1962),
writer, was born in New Albany, Miss., the son
of Murry Cuthbert Falkner, a railroad employee, and of Maud Butler. When he was a
little more than a year old, his parents moved to
Ripley, Miss., where his great-grandfather, Colonel William Clark Falkner, principal developer
of the Gulf and Chicago Railroad, had lived.
Just before Falkner's fifth birthday the family
moved to Oxford, seat of Lafayette County,
Miss., and home of his grandfather, John Wesley Thompson Falkner. One of the town's most
prominent citizens, he helped establish Murry
Falkner in a series of businesses.

In Oxford, Falkner absorbed regional and
family lore that later enriched his fiction: prewar
plantation history; local fighting in the War Between the States; and the career of his great-
grandfather, "The Old Colonel," who had
fought with distinction at the battle of First
Manassas, raised a regiment of Partisan Rangers, prospered as a blockade runner, and after
the war transformed the Ripley Railroad Company into the Gulf and Chicago. He also wrote
several books, including the popular romance
The White Rose of Memphis. As a schoolboy
William Falkner told his teacher, "I want to be
a writer like my great-granddaddy."

Falkner entered the first grade in 1905 and
showed himself bright enough to advance to the
third grade at the beginning of the next year.
Now called Billy, he was the leader of his three
brothers in games and occasional devilment, and
a loving and usually obedient son. By eighth
grade Falkner was finding school boring and
truancy attractive. Drawing and writing stories
and poems was far more absorbing than class
assignments. Maud Falkner, believing in his talent, had encouraged her son's reading. By late
1915 Falkner had dropped out of school.

In the summer of 1914, he had shown his
poetry to Phil Stone, an older friend. Stone
talked modern literature to Falkner and loaned
him books in vicarious satisfaction of his own
strong literary bent and plunged into the nurturing of Falkner's talent. Falkner went bear hunting at Stone's father's camp and worked briefly
and unhappily at his grandfather's bank.

The recipient of many of Falkner's poems
was Lida Estelle Oldham, a neighbor and university coed, but his dream of a life with her
vanished when his lack of a profession and her
family's pressure resulted in her marriage to
Cornell Franklin, a lawyer, in April 1918.

Early that month Falkner had gone to stay
with Stone in New Haven. He found a job as a

ledger clerk with the Winchester Repeating Arms Company. After unsuccessful attempts to enlist for flight training in the U.S. Army (he could not meet height and weight requirements), he was accepted by the Royal Air Force-Canada. Convinced he had to pass as British, he had invented an English background for himself and changed the spelling of his name to Faulkner. In July 1918 he began training but was discharged in December. He had not flown, but he had absorbed lore that would prove useful in his fiction.

Faulkner returned home to a life of footloose roaming. His first published writing, a long pastoral poem, "L'Apres-Midi d'un Faune," appeared in the *New Republic* on Aug. 6, 1919, but further publication in national magazines eluded him for more than ten years. His outlets for poetry were now the *Oxford Eagle* and the university newspaper, *The Mississippian*. Over the next two years Faulkner published essays and reviews in the latter reflecting poetic tastes formed on Algernon Swinburne, A. E. Housman, and John Keats, and moderns such as Conrad Aiken and T. S. Eliot. In the fall of 1919 he entered the University of Mississippi as a special student. Although he did well in French and Spanish, he seemed more interested in The Marionettes, a drama club for which he wrote an unproduced experimental play. He was probably glad to use a university crackdown on fraternities (he was a Sigma Alpha Epsilon) as an excuse for withdrawing in November 1920. He now passed the time writing, doing odd jobs, and acting as assistant scoutmaster.

In the fall of 1921, Faulkner accepted Mississippi writer Stark Young's invitation to visit him in New York City. There he worked as a bookstore clerk for Elizabeth Prall and tried unsuccessfully to place his work with New York editors. He returned home in December to become postmaster at the university, a job he performed unhappily and inefficiently until late 1924. He resigned after charges were brought by the postal inspector, including the correct allegation that he had worked on his own writing during business hours. In December of that year he published *The Marble Faun*, a cycle of pastoral poems, after Phil Stone had supplied the $400 that the Four Seas Company charged for the first edition. Reviews and sales were scanty. Fire destroyed most of the copies, helping ultimately to make the book a collector's item.

Planning an extended stay in Europe, Faulkner paused in New Orleans to visit Elizabeth Prall, now married to the writer Sherwood Anderson. The stay lengthened as Anderson en-

couraged Faulkner, who plunged into various kinds of work: stories and sketches for the *New Orleans Times-Picayune* and *The Double Dealer*, more poetry, and a novel he called *Mayday*. On Anderson's recommendation Faulkner sent it to Anderson's publisher and sailed for Europe on July 7 with architect and artist William Spratling. The two made their way from Genoa to Paris and settled on the Left Bank. By early September, when Spratling left for home, Faulkner was well into another novel, called *Elmer*. Although he still wrote poems, he had realized that his true métier was fiction, and *Elmer* showed the way he was experimenting with impressionistic, symbolic writing. He stored up more material on a short trip to England, and on walking tours in France, before he sailed for home in early December.

Faulkner's novel *Mayday*, renamed *Soldiers' Pay*, was published in 1926. Although it was a rather derivative postwar wasteland story (that drew on his frustrated hopes as an RAF cadet and his brother Jack's experience as a wounded Marine), its verbal virtuosity and creative exuberance earned rather good notices for a first novel. He had earlier returned to New Orleans and moved in with Spratling. He wrote an introduction to a book of Spratling's drawings called *Sherwood Anderson and Other Famous Creoles*, which appeared in December 1926. Done in a spirit of fun, the book nonetheless offended Anderson and helped drive a wedge between him and Faulkner.

Anderson's hurt could only have been deepened with the appearance of *Mosquitoes* (1927), in which Anderson was caricatured, it seemed to some, as the writer Dawson Fairchild. Dealing with dilettantes and littérateurs in the manner of Aldous Huxley, the book again showed Faulkner's versatility and fertility, but it fared less well than *Soldiers' Pay*.

Anderson had advised Faulkner to mine his native Mississippi material. This he had done when he put aside a tale of a rapacious rural tribe called Snopes, in a fragment entitled "Father Abraham," (which he later used as a basis for his Snopes trilogy), and concentrated instead on a long chronicle-style novel named *Flags in the Dust*. The novel traced the Sartoris family, whose towering figure, Colonel John Sartoris, was based on Colonel William C. Falkner. Faulkner's publisher, Horace Liveright, rejected it. The much-revised text was rejected approximately a dozen times before Harcourt, Brace published it in a simpler form as *Sartoris* (1929).

Faulkner's emotional life had grown as complicated as his literary fortunes. For more than half a dozen years Estelle Oldham Franklin had returned periodically to Mississippi. Her marriage had not gone well, and gradually her relationship with her former sweetheart acquired a renewed, if altered, intensity. She divorced Franklin, and married Faulkner on June 20, 1929.

Early in 1928, Faulkner, despairing over the rejection of *Flags in the Dust,* had decided to write for himself, and not for any publisher's list. He began a novel first called *Twilight* that consisted of three first-person narratives (brothers: an idiot, a psychotic, and a neurotic) and a final narrative in the third person, all four focusing on their beautiful and tragic sister, Caddy Compson, and her doomed family. A spectacular novel employing stream of consciousness, mythic and biblical references, and a dense texture of symbolism, it reminded some readers of James Joyce and others of Feodor Dostoevsky. For those who had followed Faulkner's work, it represented a quantum leap forward. Harcourt, Brace refused the novel, but Harrison Smith took it for his new firm of Jonathan Cape and Harrison Smith and published it as *The Sound and The Fury* (1929). Although it is chief among Faulkner's masterpieces, it did not sell.

By the spring of 1930, Faulkner had begun to crack the national magazine market with stories such as "A Rose for Emily." He aimed for the *Saturday Evening Post* but placed his work where he could, for his income was modest and unpredictable. He took a night job at the university power plant to supplement his income, and it was there that he wrote what he called a tour de force, entitled *As I Lay Dying* (1930). This time there were fifty-nine interior monologues as no fewer than fifteen narrators related events in the sickness, death, and burial journey of Addie Bundren as her family took her from their farm to the family plot in Jefferson, seat of Yoknapatawpha County. The brilliantly imaginative tale, in which spoken words were recorded with fidelity to dialect while inner thoughts were rendered with poetic virtuosity, was seen variously as a study of the capacity for heroism in ordinary folk or a bleak rendering of a bizarre world bereft of meaning. Faulkner was now transmuting his "little postage stamp of native soil" into his "apocryphal county"—a process like that accomplished by Honoré de Balzac, a writer he admired and with whom he would be compared.

By now Faulkner had achieved a voice that was uniquely his own. But his books still did not sell well enough to support him, his wife, his two

stepchildren, and the servants he gradually acquired, some as virtually inherited family dependents.

Always a man with a particular affinity for children, an inveterate maker of fairy stories and teller of tales, he was close to his stepchildren. He and his wife had a daughter in January 1931, but she lived for only nine days. Her death was one of the two greatest traumas of Faulkner's life. Ironically, his first commercial success came the next month with the publication of *Sanctuary.* Faulkner always said that he had written this novel to make money. He had begun it more than two years before, its bald outline taken from a tale he had heard in a nightclub of a girl raped with a blunt object by an impotent gangster and then sequestered in a brothel. He would say it was the most "horrific" story he could think of. Faulkner had always enjoyed murder mysteries, and he apparently conceived of this as a kind of three-in-one: a spectacular mystery-detective-gangster story, a commercially successful novel, and a work of art that would mirror the corruption of society at large in the lives of a limited number of people from different strata of society.

When Harrison Smith received the typescript, he shelved it for fear of prosecution. Later, with the increasing financial pressure brought on by the Great Depression, he had it set in type and sent the galleys to a surprised Faulkner, who was now horrified at what he called the cheap approach he had employed in treating his material. At Smith's insistence he agreed to publication, but only after extensive revisions. It was one of his most powerful books, but the horrors were unrelieved, often nearly side by side with some of his funniest and most poetically evocative writing. Unfortunately, Cape and Smith went into receivership before Faulkner could get $6,000 due him.

Sanctuary was a watershed book that led to a watershed year. Other publishers began to approach Faulkner. He caught Hollywood's eye, and in early May 1932 he signed with Metro-Goldwyn-Mayer (MGM) as a contract writer. He worked intermittently as a scenarist over the next twenty-two years, mostly for MGM, Twentieth Century-Fox, and Warner Brothers.

Faulkner's screenwriting earnings (as distinct from sales of his fiction to film makers) came to about $150,000. It was money he desperately needed, but he resented having to go to California to work in a medium he never regarded as his. All of Faulkner's direct male ancestors had been heavy drinkers, and from his late teens he had been no exception. Hollywood exacerbated this tendency (as did personal troubles and the exhaustion following the completion of a book). Although he could drink moderately and even abstain when he chose, for the rest of his life Faulkner was a "binge" drinker whose bouts were often protracted and could constitute the equivalent of at least one serious illness every year.

In 1932 the new firm of Harrison Smith and Robert Haas published *Light in August*, a long, powerful novel of social tensions in Yoknapatawpha County. Although dense-textured, it was not as difficult as *The Sound and the Fury*. It was experimental in a different way, contrapuntally telling the story of Lena Grove, a pregnant country girl seeking her lover, and Joe Christmas, a man who thinks he is part black and who meets his destiny through a fatal involvement with Joanna Burden, a spinster of abolitionist lineage, one of several characters isolated from the community by the strength of the past and their own psychodynamics. By now Faulkner had a national, if limited, audience; and though the power of the novel enhanced his standing with some, to others it was further evidence of his difficulty and propensity for violence and perversion. His reputation was higher in France, where he was regarded by critics as a modern master.

By early 1933 a new force had entered Faulkner's life. With some of the Hollywood money he bought an airplane and began taking flying lessons. Now he could live out some of the dreams that had led to the wounded-aviator pose he had assumed in New Orleans. A greater change in his life came with the birth of a daughter in June. His devotion to his craft sometimes seemed to make him oblivious to his family, but his love for his child was a constant all his life.

Although he published *A Green Bough*, his last book of verse, in 1933, and *Doctor Martino and Other Stories* in 1934, Faulkner took time for hunting and occasional flying. A trip to the dedication of New Orleans' Shushan Airport in 1934 gave him the material for *Pylon*, a novel of rootless barnstorming aviators published in 1935. Flying left its mark on his life in a different fashion that November. Faulkner gave his plane to his brother Dean, a commercial aviator. When Dean was killed in a crash, Faulkner blamed himself and suffered nightmares and feelings of guilt for years. He felt responsible for his brother's wife and the child she was expecting, as well as for his widowed mother. Financial responsibilities forced a return to Hollywood that December. The separation

necessitated by his assignment at Twentieth Century-Fox exacerbated another problem that had been developing for some time. Estelle Faulkner found the pressure of financial need and the inconvenience of living in an antebellum home without plumbing or electricity difficult. Faulkner was often withdrawn and devoted to his work; she was a social woman with expensive tastes and little of the social activity she enjoyed. She drank too, and her problem was often as acute as her husband's. Faulkner began an affair with a studio secretary that continued intermittently for nearly thirty years. It was not his only one.

But even through his grief and scriptwriting Faulkner continued work on the long, complex, and often intractable novel he had called *Dark House*. After two short-story treatments of the material, he had approached the story of Thomas Sutpen within a dialectical framework provided by Quentin Compson, the second narrator in *The Sound and the Fury*, and his Harvard roommate Shreve McCannon. Faulkner said it was the story of a man who wanted sons and got too many of them. A self-made man who denied a part-black son because he did not fit the princely line he wanted to found, Sutpen brought about his own destruction and that of his line by his denial of human worth and dignity. An enormous body of criticism grew up about the novel. It was seen as an allegory of the South, as an exploration of the problem of how one can "know" history, and as an intricate psychological study of "the human heart in conflict with itself." To some critics this was his crowning masterwork. Published as *Absalom, Absalom!* (1936) by Random House (which had absorbed Smith and Haas), it further enhanced Faulkner's reputation but again failed to provide the financial security he hoped for.

Faulkner was still eking out a precarious existence with film work and short stories. He collected a group of the latter, reshaping and adding to them to form a Civil War novel called *The Unvanquished* (1938). It brought $25,000 from MGM (more than either "Turn About" or *Sanctuary*) but it was never filmed. Faulkner bought a farm. He named it Greenfield Farm and installed his brother John and his family on it. Although his future assertions that he was "just a farmer" were reminiscent of his posing as wounded aviator and bohemian writer, Greenfield Farm satisfied a need he often felt.

In 1939, Faulkner was elected to the National Institute of Arts and Letters, but *The Wild Palms*, which came out in January, was received with the usual mixture of admiration and puzzlement. Technically it was another daring experiment. The contrapuntal stories of a convict disillusioned with love and anxious to return to the prison from which flood waters have temporarily released him, and a doctor who sacrifices career and liberty for love, were separated in time by ten years and in geography (at times) by half a continent. At once a critique of heedless romantic love and an evocation of the nuclear family, it was another novel that sold but modestly. Faulkner next collected another group of magazine stories, reshaped them, and added to them to make *The Hamlet* (1940).

Set in Frenchman's Bend, the novel mixed outrageous parody and bucolic comedy with the starkest treatment of soulless avarice as Flem Snopes conquered and prepared to move on to Jefferson. The structure was primarily chronological and the narration principally third-person, but Faulkner's exuberant rhetoric and mythic consciousness enriched the novel in a characteristic way. It revealed part of the essence of his gift: a self-styled "failed poet," he employed a rich poetic sensibility and technique in the service of prose fiction that was both realistic and symbolic.

Distracted more than ever by debts, Faulkner tried to change publishers. When America entered World War II, he sought a commission, without success. He had gathered stories that formed a narrative of the relations between black and white families in Yoknapatawpha County from slavery times to the present. The magazine versions had been, in the main, comic. He deepened them with compassion and a sense of the tragic realities of the South's racial dilemma. Rewriting material, Faulkner created a segment called "The Bear" that was essentially a novella. It described Ike McCaslin's growth and consecration to the big woods and his rejection of his family's plantation, built on the injustice of slavery. A ritual and mythic story, "The Bear" treated man's relation to nature and his depredations, dramatized in the story of the legendary bear Old Ben; the great dog Lion, who was finally able to bring it to bay; and the men, principally Sam Fathers (part Chickasaw king, part black slave), who would bring about Ben's inevitable death. Entitled *Go Down, Moses,* the book was published in May 1942, not quite lost in the furor of the war.

By mid-1942, Faulkner was back in Hollywood, struggling with various stories for several directors, doing his best as "script doctor" for Howard Hawks, who knew how to use Faulkner's fertility of invention. He hoped that a film partnership with Hawks would provide

financial independence, but the project failed. With two other men he worked at a film treatment of an old idea: the reappearance of Christ and the repeated sacrifice in which he would become the Great War's Unknown Soldier. Desperately committed to the idea, he found it intractable. Only when Random House promised to advance money so he could write it in Mississippi, as a novel, was he able to leave California, in September 1945. Malcolm Cowley's edition of *The Portable Faulkner* for Viking Press brought his work renewed interest the next year, but his progress on the war novel he called *Who?* was painfully slow.

The dam was about to break. Turning from the big book to what he thought would be a short mystery story, Faulkner wrote *Intruder in the Dust* (1948), the tale of a black man jailed for murder who is aided in his struggle for exoneration by two adolescent boys and a courageous spinster. In the novel's growth it also became the story of the white boy's introduction to maturity and a commentary on racial prejudice that showed Faulkner's increasing awareness of and concern about contemporary tensions in the South. The screen rights were sold to MGM, and the book made money for Random House. At the age of fifty-one Faulkner had finally achieved financial security. On Nov. 23, 1948, he was elected to the American Academy of Arts and Letters.

It was obviously a logical time for Random House to plan publication of Faulkner's short stories. In November 1949, *Knight's Gambit,* a series of cases solved by county attorney Gavin Stevens, who resembled Phil Stone in some ways and Faulkner in others, appeared. In August 1950, *Collected Stories of William Faulkner,* a massive volume that showed his range and mastery in this form, was brought out. In May 1950 the American Academy had awarded him the Howells Medal for Fiction. That November he received the 1949 Nobel Prize for literature. His plea that he was a farmer who needed to stay home with his crops availed him nothing. He gave in to family and governmental pressure, and after a desperate drinking bout he shakily boarded the plane for Stockholm with his daughter. His short acceptance speech on Dec. 10, 1950, seemed uncharacteristically optimistic to some: Man would not only endure, he said, he would prevail. But the speech enunciated the virtues his work had celebrated for a quarter of a century, and became the most quoted of all Nobel Prize speeches.

Still withdrawn and usually shy and taciturn, Faulkner was now a public man. The next half-dozen years were filled with activities and honors. In 1951 he received the National Book Award for *Collected Stories* and the French Legion of Honor. He completed *Requiem for a Nun*, a play within a novel, that followed the life of Temple Drake in the years after her experiences in *Sanctuary*. In it he confronted again the problem of the human capacity for evil but concentrated as well on attempts to atone for that capacity and to find faith.

Faulkner had worked intermittently on the novel begun in Hollywood, now called *A Fable*, and though it was nearing completion, he broke off work on it in late 1953 when Howard Hawks asked his help on a picture to be filmed in Egypt. He went there by way of Europe, and it was early spring before the job was completed and he could return to the United States. *A Fable* (1954) was a massive retelling of Christ's passion and death, set in the French army during the mutinies late in World War I. He called it his "magnum opus," but it was also, he said, the only one of his books to derive from an idea. It won the 1954 National Book Award for fiction and the Pulitzer Prize.

In spite of his continuing preference for privacy, Faulkner reluctantly embarked on a series of cultural missions out of a sense of patriotism: an International Writers' Conference in August 1954 in Brazil, and a State Department trip in 1955 that took him to Japan, the Philippines, Italy, France, England, and Iceland. In 1956 he worked in the People-to-People Program, and six months later in 1957 he undertook a State Department mission to Greece. His last such trip came in 1961, a fortnight in Venezuela.

Faulkner became intensely concerned with the civil rights crisis in the mid-1950's, writing and speaking in an attempt to avert violence and establish a position for political moderates. He was writer-in-residence at the University of Virginia in 1957 and 1958.

During these years Faulkner completed the Snopes trilogy with *The Town* (1957) and *The Mansion* (1959). These novels traced the ascendancy of Flem Snopes in Jefferson, marked by his assumption of the presidency of what had been Colonel Sartoris's bank, but they also showed a faith in human possibility as lawyer Gavin Stevens and sewing-machine salesman V. K. Ratliff struggled against Snopes and Snopesism. Both novels used relays of first-person narrators, but the storytelling was not as complex as that in earlier works. Although *The Town* showed a falling off in power, much of the recapitulative *The Mansion* displayed the strength and beauty of Faulkner's best work. His last novel was *The Reivers*, published in June 1962. It was a mellow, retrospective, first-person tale with autobiographical elements, the story of a boy's loss of innocence and initiation into the adult world.

In April 1962, Faulkner and his family visited the U.S. Military Academy at West Point. The next month he went to New York to accept the Gold Medal for Fiction of the National Institute of Arts and Letters. It had not been an easy year for him. An injury-prone horseman who in his career had suffered a fractured collarbone, ribs, and vertebrae, he had been reinjured in a fall in January. At Oxford, in mid-June, he was thrown once more. He treated himself until finally his family took him to a small private hospital in Byhalia, Miss., where he died of a heart attack.

[The largest and most important collection of Faulkner materials is in the University of Virginia Library. Other collections are at the University of Texas, the New York Public Library, the University of Mississippi, and Yale University. Writings by Faulkner not noted in the text are *Big Woods* (1955); *William Faulkner: Early Prose and Poetry*, ed. Carvel Collins (1962); *The Wishing Tree* (1964); *Essays, Speeches and Public Letters by William Faulkner*, ed. James B. Meriwether (1965); *William Faulkner: New Orleans Sketches*, ed. Carvel Collins (1968); *Mayday*, ed. Carvel Collins (1976); *The Marionettes*, ed. Noel Polk (1978); *Uncollected Stories of William Faulkner*, ed. Joseph Blotner (1979). For bibliographical and textual information see James B. Meriwether, *The Literary Career of William Faulkner*, rev. ed. (1971). Faulkner's comments on his life and work are in *William Faulkner in the University*, ed. Frederick L. Gwynn and Joseph Blotner (1959); *Faulkner at West Point*, ed. Joseph L. Fant and Robert Ashley (1964); *Lion in the Garden*, ed. James B. Meriwether and Michael Millgate (1968).

Memoirs of Faulkner include John B. Cullen and Floyd C. Watkins, *Old Times in the Faulkner Country* (1961); John Faulkner, *My Brother Bill* (1963); *William Faulkner of Oxford*, ed. James W. Webb and A. Wigfall Green (1965); Murry C. Falkner, *The Falkners of Mississippi* (1967); Meta Carpenter Wilde and Ori Borsten, *A Loving Gentleman* (1976). Biographical and autobiographical material is in Joseph Blotner, *Faulkner*, 2 vols. (1974); *Selected Letters of William Faulkner*, ed. Joseph Blotner (1977).

Faulkner criticism includes Olga Vickery, *The Novels of William Faulkner* (1959); Cleanth Brooks, *William Faulkner: The Yoknapatawpha Country* (1963); Michael Millgate, *The Achievement of William Faulkner* (1966); *William Faulkner: Four Decades of Criticism*, ed. Linda Welshimer Wagner (1973); Warren Beck, *Faulkner: Essays* (1976); Cleanth Brooks, *William Faulkner: Toward Yoknapatawpha and Beyond* (1978). Also see Calvin S.

Brown, *A Glossary of Faulkner's South* (1976). Obituaries are in *Obituaries from the* (London) *Times 1961–1970* (1975) and in the *New York Times,* July 7, 1962.]

JOSEPH BLOTNER

FAUSET, JESSIE REDMON (Apr. 27, 1882 [?]–Apr. 30, 1961), writer, teacher, and editor, was born in Camden County, N.J., the daughter of Redmon Fauset, an African-Methodist-Episcopal minister, and of Annie Seamon. She attended Philadelphia public schools, where she was the only black in her class, and was the first black woman admitted to Cornell University. She graduated in 1905, probably the first black woman to win Phi Beta Kappa honors. In 1919, Fauset received an M.A. from the University of Pennsylvania. She lived briefly in Paris, studying French at the Sorbonne and the Alliance Française. Later she continued her study of French at Columbia University.

Fauset first taught Latin and French at Douglass High School in Baltimore and then until 1919 at Dunbar High School in Washington, D.C.; later she taught at a Harlem junior high school and DeWitt Clinton High School (1927–1944) in New York City. In 1919 she accepted W. E. B. Du Bois' invitation to join the staff of the *Crisis,* the official publication of the National Association for the Advancement of Colored People (NAACP), as literary editor. In 1926 she relinquished this position and became a contributing editor. During this period she also worked as literary editor, and then managing editor, of *The Brownies' Book,* a monthly magazine for black children created by Du Bois. In 1929 she married Herbert E. Harris, an insurance agent and businessman. They had no children.

Fauset's novels, *There Is Confusion* (1924), *Plum Bun* (1928), *The Chinaberry Tree* (1931), and *Comedy: American Style* (1933), although widely read, were not best-sellers. Her upper middle-class background, her brilliant college career, her teaching, and her distinguished service on the staff of the *Crisis* placed her in the mainstream of the new black literature of the 1920's and 1930's. Fauset was an integral figure in the Harlem Renaissance. As editor of the *Crisis* she encouraged many young black writers and published their work for the first time. She also wrote many poems, short stories, articles, reviews, and essays and translated French West Indian poets. One of her best-known articles was the perceptive report in the *Crisis* on the second Pan-African Congress, which met in London, Brussels, and Paris in 1921. She attended these historic meetings as a delegate.

Although generally regarded as a minor writer, Fauset was one of the main black novelists to depict middle-class black society during the 1920's and 1930's. Like Walter White and Nella Larsen (with whom she is often compared), she represented the majority position of the black writers of the period. Her novels used themes such as "passing," miscegenation, the pressure of American racial prejudice, lynching, racial pride, the belief that hard work and superior achievement would eventually win equality, and loyalty to country despite differences and unfairness.

Many of the incidents and characters in Fauset's novels are based on actual persons and occurrences. Her style is stiff and self-conscious; her plots and subplots, complicated, unconvincing, and melodramatic. She overused coincidence in her story development, and at times her dialogue is stilted and wooden. Yet she succeeded in creating some memorable female characters and provided the reading public with a truthful picture of black urban bourgeois society that whites rarely saw or even knew existed. Robert Bone described Fauset's novels as "uniformly sophomoric, trivial and dull," but another critic, William Stanley Braithwaite, compared her novels of prim and virtuous Negro middle-class manners and morals with the works of Jane Austen.

Fauset's first novel, *There Is Confusion,* is probably her most representative. Its themes include the importance of heredity and genealogy, education, financial success, respectable social standing, and creative and artistic expression. *Plum Bun* deals with a black girl passing as white, her eventual acceptance of her race, and her return to the black community, and *The Chinaberry Tree* presents an intimate picture of a small black community in New Jersey and the narrow-mindedness of blacks toward a beautiful mulatto woman. In her last novel, *Comedy: American Style,* Fauset again dealt with "passing," in a family where the mother's obsession with white identity is so great that she destroys her children, her husband—and herself.

The best-known of Fauset's many poems, which mostly appeared in anthologies, are "La Vie C'est la Vie," "Noblesse Oblige," "Words! Words!," "Rondeau," "Christmas Eve in France," and "Oriflamme," a poem about the black evangelist Sojourner Truth. In a few words she could combine feeling and state of mind with a pictorial scene, as in "Dusk":

Twin stars through my purpling pane,
   The shriveling husk
Of a yellowing moon on the wane—
   And the dusk.

Fauset's best-known essay, "The Gift of Laughter" (1925), discusses the stereotype of the black as a comic character in the American theater.

Fauset's career reflects the basic problem of black intellectuals of her day who had been assimilated into white society and had oriented their art and writing to white opinion. In her novels she presents the bitter facts of racial injustice and prejudice in so respectable and genteel a way that modern critics would likely accuse her of lacking soul.

In 1949, Fauset was visiting professor at Hampton Institute. She also taught writing and French at Tuskegee Institute. In her spare time she lectured on black writers and traveled extensively. As a leader of the black literati, Fauset held many cultural gatherings at her home in Harlem, where distinguished figures of both races gathered. She died in Philadelphia.

[A collection of Fauset manuscript material, including letters, may be found at the Moorland-Springarn Research Center, Harvard University. A good source of information is Carolyn Wedin Sylvander, *Jessie Redmon Fauset, Black American Writer* (1981). For critical material see Robert A. Bone, *The Negro Novel in America* (rev. ed., 1965); Hugh M. Gloster, *Negro Voices in American Fiction* (repr. 1965); Robert Hemenway, ed., *The Black Novelist* (1970); Arna Bontemps, ed., *The Harlem Renaissance Remembered* (1972); and Margaret Perry, *Silence to the Drums* (1976).
Also see Marion L. Starkey, "Jessie Fauset," *Southern Workman*, May 1932; William Stanley Braithwaite, "The Novels of Jessie Fauset," *Opportunity*, Jan. 1934; and Abby Arthur Johnson, "Literary Midwife: Jessie Redmon Fauset and the Harlem Renaissance," *Phylon*, June 1978. An obituary is in the *New York Times*, May 3, 1961.]
MARY SUE DILLIARD SCHUSKY

FAY, FRANCIS ANTHONY ("FRANK") (Nov. 17, 1897–Sept. 25, 1961), vaudevillian actor, was born in San Francisco, Calif., the son of William Fay and Molly Tynan, both performers. He first appeared before the footlights in Chicago at the age of four, when his father carried him on stage in *Quo Vadis?*; two years later he played the teddy bear in *Babes in Toyland*. His first role on Broadway was as Stephen in *The Redemption of David Corson* (1906).

Fay attended school in New York City but ended his formal education with the fifth grade. He then worked in Shakespearean companies before turning to vaudeville. For awhile he teamed with Gerald Griffin as a singer and later joined Johnny Dyer in a comedy act. Along the way, he married and divorced Lee Buchanan, a singer.

In 1917 Fay began working as a single performer. Appearing in formal attire, he treated his audiences to witty, sophisticated satirical humor. After landing a part in the Broadway musical *Girl o'Mine* (1918), he performed in *The Passing Show of 1918* (1918), *Oh, What a Girl!* (1919), and *Jim Jam Jems* (1920). On Apr. 12, 1917, Fay married Frances White, a well-known singer, but the marriage lasted less than six months.

In 1922 Fay wrote, produced, and starred in *Frank Fay's Fables*, a musical that received poor reviews. He then returned to performing in *Pinwheel* (1922) and *Artists and Models* (1923). In 1924 he was back in vaudeville, where he became a hit as the master of ceremonies of shows at the Palace Theater. By 1926 he had broken the record for number of performances at the Palace.

In 1926 Fay wrote and produced an unsuccessful play, *The Smart Alec*, that cost him a considerable amount of his own funds. The next year he played in the musical *Harry Delmar's Revels*. Then, on Aug. 26, 1928, he married Barbara Stanwyck, a young actress. (A Roman Catholic, Fay later had his earlier marriages annulled so that they could be remarried by a priest.)

Fay and Stanwyck moved to Hollywood in 1929, when he began to make movies. His first motion picture was *Show of Shows* (1929), a musical revue. His first starring role as an actor was in *Under a Texas Moon* (1930), a box office success. Fay went on to leads in *The Matrimonial Bed* (1930), *Bright Lights* (1931), *God's Gift to Women* (1931), and *A Fool's Advice* (1932), none of which was well-received by the public.

In 1933, Stanwyck, now an established star, joined with Fay in producing the stage revue *Tattle Tales*, written by Fay and Nick Copeland. This show, like Fay's earlier productions, folded quickly. In 1935 he starred in another mediocre movie, *Stars Over Broadway*. That same year, Fay and Stanwyck were divorced, the split complicated by widely publicized legal battles over the division of their property and the custody of their adopted son.

In the wake of his marital and professional difficulties, Fay, known for his heavy drinking, drank even more, and many considered him an alcoholic. Nonetheless, he struggled to regain his stature in show business, and a chance to do so came in radio. Following successful appearances on the Rudy Vallee program, Fay began his own radio show in 1936. During its four-month run millions of listeners became acquainted with his technique of reciting lyrics of popular songs, then making satirical comments on them.

During the late 1930's and 1940's, Fay appeared in the movies *Nothing Sacred* (1937), *Meet the Mayor* (1938), *I Want a Divorce* (1940), *They Knew What They Wanted* (1940), *A Wac in His Life* (1940), and *Spotlight Scandals* (1943). On stage, he appeared in *Frank Fay Vaudeville* (1939), *New Priorities of 1943* (1943), and *Laugh Time* (1943). He also worked in nightclubs.

A big break came for Fay in 1944, when he was selected to play the eccentric alcoholic Elwood P. Dowd in the Broadway production of *Harvey.* Both the play and his performance were tremendous successes.

In 1945 Fay published *How to Be Poor,* a collection of humorous stories. In that year he became embroiled in a political controversy. After remarks critical of the Catholic Church were made at a rally for Spanish refugees, Fay asserted that some of the actors involved with the event were pro-communists. The dispute came before the National Council of Actors' Equity, which censured Fay. He then took the matter before the membership of the organization, only to have the censure upheld.

Fay wrote and produced the musical *If You Please* in 1950, experiencing yet another disappointment. In 1951 he acted in three movies: *Love Nest, Stage From Blue River,* and *When Worlds Collide.* Thereafter, he limited himself to nightclub and television appearances. He died in Santa Monica, Calif.

[Material on Fay and his career is in the Billy Rose Theatre Collection in the Library and Museum of the Performing Arts, the New York Public Library at Lincoln Center. See Frank Buxton and Bill Owen, *The Big Broadcast 1920–1950* (1976); "Frank Fay Returns," *New York Times,* Oct. 27, 1957; Roger D. Kinkle, ed., *The Complete Encyclopedia of Popular Music and Jazz 1900–1950* (1974); John T. Weaver, comp., *Forty Years of Screen Credits 1929–1969* (1970); and Maurice Zolotow, "Frank Fay," *Life,* Jan. 8, 1945, and *No People Like Show People* (1951). Obituaries are in the *New York Times,* Sept. 27, 1961; and *Variety,* Sept. 27, 1961.]

THOMAS BURNELL COLBERT

FAZENDA, LOUISE MARIE (June 17, 1896–Apr. 17, 1962), film comedienne, was born in West Lafayette, Ind., the daughter of Joseph Altamar Fazenda and Nelda Schilling. Her father, born in Mexico, was apparently of mixed Italian, French, and Portuguese parentage. Her mother was a native of Chicago. Louise grew up in Los Angeles, where her father opened a grocery store. At an early age she worked after school and during vacations to supplement the family income. After graduation from Los Angeles High School in 1913, she became an extra at Universal Studios. Her versatility soon led to offers of minor roles, and she became a member of Universal's "Joker" comedy unit. In 1915 she signed a contract with Mack Sennett's Keystone Company.

Fazenda's rise at Keystone was remarkable. By 1917, *Motion Picture* called her the "star comedienne of Mack Sennett's aggregation, and perhaps the most popular 'slap-stick' actress" in Hollywood. Lacking the glamour of Sennett's highly publicized "bathing beauties," she proved more durable than any of them. Her appearance on the screen belied her natural good looks. She wore outlandish clothes and used ludicrous makeup; her hair was drawn back severely from her brow. She generally had either a woebegone or a blank expression. Sennett once said that just by making an appearance on the screen, Fazenda "could get a laugh, or at least a smile, from everybody." Her athletic ability and talent for improvisation were important assets in working for Sennett, whose films relied heavily upon fast and zany physical activity and horseplay for comic effects. Among her more notable Keystone films were *Are Waitresses Safe?* (1917), with Ben Turpin; *The Kitchen Lady* (1918), the first of many movies in which she appeared in pigtails, gingham dress, and long pantalettes; and *Down on the Farm* (1920), her first five-reel motion picture.

Leaving the Keystone Company in 1920, Fazenda sought unsuccessfully to obtain financial backing to produce her own films. For a time in 1921 and 1922, she toured the country with a vaudeville company. She returned to Hollywood in 1922 and resumed her movie career, primarily as a supporting actress in comedy films. Although she signed a long-term contract with Warner Brothers in 1924, she made films for other studios as well. Her memorable roles in the late era of silent films included Mabel Munroe in *The Gold Diggers* (1923), "Sweetie" in *Bobbed Hair* (1925), and the title role in *Tillie's Punctured Romance* (1928).

A shrewd businesswoman, Fazenda invested her screen earnings wisely, particularly in real estate. She avoided the Hollywood social lime-light, and remained close to her parents. Her first marriage was to film director Noel Mason Smith on Mar. 7, 1917; they had no children. They separated six years later, and she obtained a divorce on the grounds of desertion in 1926. She married Hal B. Wallis, then director of publicity for Warner Brothers, on Nov. 24, 1927; they had one son.

Fazenda easily made the transition from silent films to talkies in *The Terror* (1928). During the next five years she appeared in approximately thirty films, playing mainly eccentric comedy roles although occasionally performing in melodramas and musicals. She first sang on screen in *The Desert Song* (1929). By the mid-1930's her career was becoming less important to her, particularly after the birth of her son in 1933. That same year her husband became executive producer for Warner Brothers, and Fazenda was content to devote more attention to her private roles of wife and mother. While not abandoning her career, she curtailed her screen activities. She had star billing in *The Winning Ticket* (1935) for Metro-Goldwyn-Mayer and in *Swing Your Lady* (1938) for Warner's, but she mainly played minor character parts. Her last appearance, as a servant in Warner's *The Old Maid* (1939), was a straight dramatic role.

Fazenda left the screen with no regrets. She often remarked that moviemaking had become an impersonal and none too benign industry; she preferred the spontaneity and camaraderie of the early Hollywood years. After 1939 she spent her time cooking, hooking rugs, and supervising the agricultural enterprises of the San Fernando Valley ranch, where she and her family lived. She also devoted much time to charitable and benevolent endeavors.

In her retirement Fazenda's circle of friends consisted largely of neighbors. She was warm-hearted, generous, and unpretentious, but she could also be moody and at times quick to anger and slow to forgive. She died at Hollywood, Calif.

[The year of Fazenda's birth is usually given as 1895, but her birth certificate, in the Tippecanoe County, Ind., Health Dept., and her death certificate, in the Los Angeles County Registrar-Recorder Dept., both give 1896. Obituaries are in *Los Angeles Times* and *New York Times*, Apr. 18, 1962, and *Lafayette* (Ind.) *Journal and Courier*, Apr. 19, 1962. Further information on Fazenda's career is in the clipping files of the Academy of Motion Picture Arts and Sciences and Tippecanoe County Historical Association. For listing of articles, see Mel Shuster,

comp., *Motion Picture Performers* (1971) and supp. (1976). Additional information was provided by Louise Fazenda's son, Brent Wallis of San Francisco.]

EDWIN A. MILES

FEARING, KENNETH FLEXNER (July 28, 1902–June 26, 1961), poet and novelist, was born in Oak Park, Ill., the son of Henry L. Fearing, a corporation lawyer, and Olive Flexner. He attended the Oak Park public schools and the University of Illinois, and graduated from the University of Wisconsin with a B.A. in 1924. At Wisconsin he wrote for and edited the *Wisconsin Literary Magazine.*

Before and during his college years Fearing worked as a salesman, a millhand, and a reporter. Determined to earn his living as a writer, he moved to New York City shortly after graduation and began writing under pseudonyms for pulps like *Telling Tales* and *Captain Billy's Whiz Bang.*

The *Double Dealer* accepted Fearing's first professional work published under his own name, two poems. Most of his early verse appeared in minor publications, but with a friend's help he was successful in placing some work in the *New Yorker* and in *Poetry.*

Between 1929 and 1936 Fearing's work appeared primarily in *New Masses, Partisan Review,* and *Menorah Journal.* These journals were allied with the American Communist party, and the poems Fearing published in them have been called "proletarian." From 1930 to 1933 Fearing was a contributing editor of *New Masses,* writing movie and book reviews. In 1935–1936 he was a member of the editorial board of *Partisan Review.* Fearing's first book, *Angel Arms* (1929), contained sixteen poems on the rigors of city life. Leftist novelist Edward Dahlberg raised funds to publish Fearing's second collection, *Poems* (1935), as the first volume in a series by proletarian poets.

Horace Gregory considered Fearing's work of this period one of the cornerstones of "beat" poetry, but the poet Kenneth Rexroth has denied that Fearing's verse had any influence on the "beat" generation. Whatever the influence of his early writing, Fearing's life-style was colorful enough to cause at least three novelists to model characters on him: W. L. River, in *The Death of a Young Man* (1927); Margery Latimer, in *This Is My Body* (1930); and Albert Halper, in *Union Square* (1933).

In 1938 Fearing issued *Dead Reckoning,* followed two years later by *Collected Poems,* which included sixty-nine of the seventy-eight selections from his first three books and twenty new verses.

Fearing published a novel, *The Hospital*, in 1939, rapidly following it with two psychological thrillers, *The Dagger of the Mind* (1941) and *Clark Gifford's Body* (1942). During the 1940's his poetry appeared regularly in the *New Yorker*. He published another collection of poems, *Afternoon of a Pawnbroker*, in 1943. Fearing's most popular novel, *The Big Clock* (1946), a murder mystery, was made into a movie starring Ray Milland and Maureen O'Sullivan in 1948. In the same year he issued his last collection of poems, *Stranger at Coney Island* (1948).

The remainder of Fearing's career was devoted to commercial work and fiction. He wrote the novel *John Barry* (1947) with Donald Friede and H. Bedford-Jones, publishing their work under the pseudonym Donald F. Bedford. Three other novels, *The Loneliest Girl in the World* (1951), *The Generous Heart* (1954), and *The Crozart Story* (1960), appeared under his own name.

A final collection of Fearing's verse appeared in 1956. The title, *New and Selected Poems*, was something of a misnomer, for only four of the poems were new. An introductory essay, "Reading, Writing, and the Rackets," was sharply critical of McCarthyism. Fearing expected that the essay would prompt an investigation of his past and spark new interest in his writing, but it did not. In spite of the essay and in spite of the fact that the book was nominated for a National Book Award, sales were sluggish.

Over the years Fearing received several awards. He was given Guggenheim fellowships in 1936 and 1939. *Poetry* awarded him the Guarantor's prize for "Three Poems" (1940), and in 1944 the American Academy of Arts and Letters awarded him $1,000 "in recognition of his creative work in literature."

Fearing's poetry, always aimed at deepening social consciousness, is marked by a robust style and a satirical outlook. Many of the poems use bold images to shock the reader into an awareness of the surroundings, a technique incorporated in titles like "A Dollar's Worth of Blood," "Lunch With the Sole Survivor," and "The Juke-Box Spoke and the Juke-Box Said," as well as in the poetic lines themselves. Horace Gregory has maintained that Fearing's genius lay in transforming the shockers of tabloid journalism into genuine literary art. William Rose Benet, denying that Fearing made any unique contribution to poetry, has argued that his work was imitative of Carl Sandburg's without being either as coherent or as liberating.

Fearing married Rachel Meltzer in 1933; they had one son. The marriage ended in divorce, and in 1945 he married Nan Lurie, a painter. They separated in 1958. Fearing died in New York City.

[Small collections of Fearing manuscripts and letters are at the Butler Library of Columbia University, the poetry collection of the Lockwood Memorial Library at the State University of New York at Buffalo, and the Archive of Contemporary History at the University of Wyoming, Laramie. *The Collected Poems of Kenneth Fearing* (1977) is a photographic reproduction of the 1940 edition. See Horace Gregory and Marya Zaturensha, "The Critical Realism of Kenneth Fearing," in their *History of American Poetry, 1900–1940* (1942); Charles Humboldt, "The Voice Persisted Until Death," *Trace*, Summer 1962; Sy Kahn, "Kenneth Fearing and the Twentieth Century Blues," in Warren French, ed., *The Thirties* (1967); James Perkins, "An American Rhapsody: The Poetry of Kenneth Fearing (Ph.D. diss., University of Tennessee, 1972; and Macha Rosenthal, "The Meaning of Kenneth Fearing's Poetry," *Poetry*, July 1944, and "Chief Poets of the American Depression" (Ph.D. diss., New York University, 1949). Obituaries are in the *New York Times*, June 27, 1961; *Time*, July 7, 1961; *Publishers Weekly*, July 24, 1961.]

DAVID O. TOMLINSON

FEJOS, PAUL (Jan. 24, 1897–Apr. 23, 1963), film director and anthropologist, was born in Budapest, Hungary, the son of Desiré Emery Fejos, an aristocrat, and of Aurora Novélly. His father died when Fejos was two, and the family lived with his granduncle. During World War I (1917–1919), he served in the Hungarian cavalry and the air service. In 1921 he received the M.D. from the Royal Hungarian Medical University in Budapest. Fejos had studied medicine to please his family, but never practiced. While in medical school he directed films for Mobil Studios. In 1921–1923 he staged plays and operas in Budapest and Paris.

In 1923, Fejos moved to New York City. After doing odd jobs he became a research technician at the Rockefeller Institute for Medical Research. In 1926, wishing to resume his career in motion pictures, he moved to Hollywood. His first film there, *The Last Moment* (1928), produced on a budget of $5,000, won critical praise for its technical virtuosity. He directed several films for Universal Studios, including *Lonesome* (1928) and *The Last Performance* (1929), which employed advanced cinematic technique in rapid montage effects and in the use of crowds. For the film *Broadway* (1929) Fejos and his cameraman invented an overhead steel camera crane that greatly increased the mobility of the sound camera. In 1930 he directed German and French versions of *Big House* for Metro-Goldwyn-Mayer. That year he became an American citizen.

Fejos returned to Europe in 1931. He directed films in France (1931), Hungary (1932), Austria (1933), and Denmark (1934–1935). In 1936, he made a number of ethnographic films of the people of Madagascar and the Seychelles islands for Nordisk Film of Denmark. From 1937 to 1939 he directed ethnographic documentary films in Indonesia and eastern Asia for Swedish Film Industry. He wrote and produced *A Handful of Rice* (1940), a film made in northern Siam about the Maio people. In the course of his work, he became a self-taught anthropologist and ethnographer.

During his Asian expeditions Fejos met Axel Wenner-Gren and began a relationship that was to move his career into new channels. In December 1939 he led an expedition to Peru under the sponsorship of Wenner-Gren, for the purpose of studying and photographing the Mashco Indians in the upper Amazon Basin. This project was aborted; instead, in 1940–1941, Fejos explored the site of the Inca city of Phuyu Pata Marka and other Inca ruins. The expedition made topographic surveys and mapped thirty-six square kilometers in the Cordillera Vilcabamba. Five of the largest ruins were cleared of vegetation and mapped. Five smaller sites were studied for land-surface information. Fejos published his findings in *Archaeological Explorations in the Cordillera Vilcabamba, Southeastern Peru* (1944).

On the Peruvian expeditions Fejos also studied the Yagua Indians, who were among the least-known of the lowland Peruvian tribes. His report appeared as *Ethnography of the Yagua* (1943). His cinematic experience produced a new field technique in ethnography when he filmed the Yaguas reenacting a clan migration to another living site, an event that occurred only once in a generation.

In 1941, Wenner-Gren had established the Viking Fund in New York City to support anthropological research, with Fejos as director of research. The fund became the Wenner-Gren Foundation for Anthropological Research in 1951 under Fejos, who served as president from 1955 to 1963. He affected the development of anthropology through the research projects supported by the foundation. Fejos was a humanist in his approach to anthropology, and stressed the study of man as the goal of the discipline. The conference "Ceramics and Man" (1961) typified his view, concentrating on the relation-

ship between people and the artifacts they create.

Fejos constantly emphasized the need for worldwide communication among scholars, and lent foundation support to international conferences and to the establishment of the journal *Current Anthropology*. His stress on communication included interdisciplinary exchange between anthropology and other fields, both scientific and humanistic. In 1947 he brought together researchers in paleoanthropology and geophysics, at a Viking Fund conference in New York City, to discuss and develop the use of carbon 14 for dating fossil remains. He supported an interdisciplinary conference at Princeton in 1952 on the human role in change on the face of the earth.

Through the Wenner-Gren Foundation, Fejos supported a program for the creation of plastic casts of ancient skulls and bones for study. These models were much more accurate than plaster casts, and made rare museum specimens available to schools as teaching tools.

During 1943–1963, Fejos was consulting professor of anthropology at Stanford University, where he taught in the Far Eastern Area and Language Program (1943–1944). He was a professorial lecturer in anthropology at Yale University in 1949–1951, and also taught at Columbia and Fordham. He stressed the importance of photography as an anthropological tool. In 1954, Fejos served as president of the New York Academy of Sciences.

Fejos' marriages to Mara Jankowsky (1921), Mimosa Pfalz (1925), Inga Arvad (1936), and Marianne Arden (1942) all ended in divorce (1924, 1929, 1942, and 1957). In November 1958 he married Lita Binns. Fejos had no children. He died in New York City.

[Fejos' publications are listed in John W. Dodds, "Eulogy for Paul Fejos," *Current Anthropology*, Oct. 1963. Life and work, with portrait, are described in John W. Dodds, *The Several Lives of Paul Fejos* (1973). For film productions see the unpublished lists at the Wenner-Gren Foundation: "Paul Fejos' Filmography" and "General Information about Some of Paul Fejos' Films." "Paul Fejos and His Film Career," at the Wenner-Gren Foundation, lists articles about Fejos. An obituary is in the *New York Times*, Apr. 24, 1963.]

ADELE HAST

FERGUSON, MIRIAM AMANDA WALLACE (June 13, 1875–June 25, 1961), governor of Texas, was born in Bell County, Tex., the daughter of Joseph Lapsley Wallace and Eliza Garrison. Her father, one of the landed gentry of Bell County, prospered in the land and cattle business. After early education by a tutor, Miriam attended Salado College and Baylor Female College. On Dec. 31, 1899, she married James Edward Ferguson; they had two daughters.

James Ferguson subsequently became a prosperous lawyer, farmer, and banker. While they were living in Temple, Tex., he became active in civil affairs; Miriam devoted herself to home and family. In 1914 he was elected governor of Texas, and was reelected in 1916. A controversy developed over his handling of finances during his second term, and in 1917 he was impeached, convicted of misusing state funds and other irregularities, and removed from office. He was also barred by law from holding office in the future. After he failed to have this restriction lifted, Miriam Ferguson entered the political arena.

Although neither Ferguson had fought for women's suffrage, Miriam entered the 1924 race for governor of Texas, primarily to see her husband vindicated. It was generally believed that he would be the real governor if she was elected. Yet contemporary writers, although depicting Miriam as an unassuming individual, a "quiet sort of woman," noted that she had a mind of her own and generally accomplished what she set out to do. Her daughter Ouida later wrote that her mother was "the most positive and strongest minded woman I have ever known."

During the campaign James Ferguson filled most of the speaking engagements, but they frequently campaigned together. Miriam Ferguson traveled the length and breadth of Texas, making a special appeal to "the mothers, sisters, and wives of Texas to help clear her family's name." A newspaper man—for brevity—originated the nickname "Ma," substituting initials for Miriam Amanda. The campaign quickly produced such catchy slogans as "Me for Ma" and "Two Governors for the Price of One." By using folksy tactics the Fergusons won strong support in rural areas and in small towns.

The Ferguson campaign centered, in addition to the call to vindicate Jim's name, on promises to reduce state spending and an all-out attack on the Ku Klux Klan, which both Fergusons opposed. Many voters saw in the campaign a chance to break the Klan's grip in Texas, and the Texas Klan suffered a crushing defeat. In the Democratic primary Ferguson came in second to Judge Felix D. Robertson, the Klan-supported candidate, but she defeated him by 100,-000 votes in the runoff. Although the Klan switched its support to the Republican candidate, she easily won the general election.

As a first-term governor Ferguson was unable to meet her campaign promises to reduce government spending, and failed in efforts to enact gasoline and tobacco taxes to build highways and aid education. She was successful in securing a law prohibiting the wearing of masks in public (directed at the Ku Klux Klan) and an "amnesty bill" restoring Jim Ferguson's civil and political rights (later declared unconstitutional by the Texas Supreme Court). In line with other campaign promises, Ferguson made liberal use of the pardoning power, granting an average of 100 pardons a month. Critics were scandalized, claiming pardons were for sale, but the governor justified her actions on humanitarian grounds, pointing to injustices in the legal system. Critics also charged that there was graft in the State Highway Commission, claiming that contracts were given without competitive bidding to friends of commissioners. Jim Ferguson was one of the three appointed by his wife to the commission. Governor Ferguson ordered an investigation, but the Highway Commission episode brought much bad publicity.

Ferguson sought renomination as governor in 1926 and in 1930, but in each instance was defeated in the primary. She was reelected in 1932, in the depths of the Great Depression. The state was on the verge of bankruptcy, but one observer stated that the Fergusons "met the challenges of the depression in a progressive manner." Ferguson proclaimed a Texas bank holiday on Mar. 3, 1933, anticipating by two days President Franklin D. Roosevelt's national bank holiday. She strongly supported Roosevelt's New Deal legislation and took advantage of federal programs. She also approved a "bread bond" issue of $20 million to purchase food and clothing for the poor. To deal with overproduction in the oil industry, Ferguson pushed a severance tax of two cents per barrel of oil through the Texas legislature, but failed to secure a sales tax or a corporate income tax. She also resumed her controversial policy of pardoning large numbers of convicts.

In 1940 Ferguson again ran for governor, this time on a platform calling for, among other items, pensions to citizens over age sixty-five and state and federal aid to tenant farmers. But she finished fourth in the Democratic primary. After her husband's death in 1944, she retired to Austin, Tex., where she died.

The key to the success of the Fergusons was their identification with common people. The masses believed that "Ma" and "Pa" Ferguson were for them. Indeed as governor, Miriam Ferguson consistently made herself available to the public, seeing anyone who came to her office. Believed by many to be merely a stand-in for her disbarred husband, Miriam Ferguson nevertheless had the strength of character to make her imprint on Texas politics.

[Ferguson's official papers are deposited in the Texas State Archives in Austin. See Jack Lynn Calbert, "James Edward and Miriam Amanda Ferguson: The 'Ma' and 'Pa' of Texas Politics" (Ph.D. diss., Indiana University, 1968); and Ouida Ferguson Nalle, *The Fergusons of Texas or "Two Governors for the Price of One"* (1946). Also see Charles C. Alexander, *The Ku Klux Klan in the Southwest* (1965); George Norris Green, *The Establishment in Texas Politics, the Primitive Years, 1938–1957* (1979); and Seth McKay, *Texas Politics, 1906–1944* (1952). An obituary is in the *New York Times,* June 26, 1961.]

DARLIS A. MILLER

FIELD, MARSHALL, IV (June 15, 1916– Sept. 18, 1965), publisher, was born in New York City, the son of Marshall Field III and Evelyn Marshall. A great-grandson of the founder of Chicago's Marshall Field and Company department store, he was heir to one of America's largest family fortunes. He was educated at the Fay School in Southboro, Mass., and St. Paul's in Concord, N.H. A good student, he entered Harvard in 1934 to study English literature. During the summer of his freshman year, he shoveled slag in a steel mill, using the name "Mike Farly" to avoid being recognized as a rich man's son. He received the B.A. in 1938. On June 20 of that year he married Joanne Bass, daughter of Robert P. Bass, a former governor of New Hampshire. They had two children.

Field then studied law at the University of Virginia and received the LL.B. in June 1941, having been chosen class president and editor of the law review. Shortly after graduation, he was admitted to the Illinois bar and clerked briefly for Judge A. M. Dobie of the Fourth U.S. Circuit Court of Appeals. Field had intended to clerk for U.S. Supreme Court Justice J. Stanley Reed, but following the United States' entry into World War II, he promptly enlisted in the navy.

Desiring sea duty, Field resigned his initial commission as an ensign and attended a ninety-day midshipman's school at Northwestern University, Evanston, Ill. He was recommissioned an ensign in June 1942 and was shipped to the Pacific. From August 1942 to October 1944, Field participated in twelve major naval engagements. As a gunnery officer on the U.S.S. *Enterprise,* he was wounded twice during the Battle of Santa Cruz (Oct. 26, 1942). He was awarded the Purple Heart and the Silver Star and was discharged with the rank of lieutenant commander in 1945.

After the war Field abandoned his law career and joined the staff of the *Chicago Sun* (founded, edited, and published by his father) as a truck driver's assistant in the circulation department. From 1946 to 1949, he worked successively in the advertising, promotion, administration, production, and editorial departments, also serving briefly in the paper's Washington and London bureaus. Two years after joining the *Sun,* Field became assistant editor.

In August 1947, Marshall Field III bought the *Chicago Times,* an evening tabloid. In October the *Sun* became a tabloid, too, and in February 1948, the papers were merged to form the Chicago *Sun-Times.* In October 1949, Field was appointed assistant publisher and associate editor of the new *Sun-Times.* A year later, when his father retired, Field became editor-publisher. In July 1947 Field was divorced from his first wife, and on May 12, 1950, he married Katherine Woodruff. They had three children.

Ambitious to challenge Colonel Robert R. McCormick's domination of Chicago journalism, Field broke ground in 1955 for a $21-million building large enough to house two newspapers. He also began negotiations to purchase the *Chicago American,* but the attempt was not successful.

For some six months after his father's death in November 1956 Field suffered from a nervous breakdown. But in 1957, he opened the new *Sun-Times* plant and resumed active management of the newspaper and of Field Enterprises, of which he was now president. He sold Field Enterprises' interest in Simon and Schuster and in Pocket Books, and reorganized Quarrie Publications (publishers of the *World Book* and *Child Craft* encyclopedias) as a wholly owned subsidiary, Field Enterprises Educational Corporation. In 1958 he sold *Parade,* a Sunday supplement, to John Hay Whitney for a reported $10 million. He used that money and a bank loan, to buy the *Chicago Daily News,* an afternoon newspaper, from John S. Knight for $24 million. The deal was announced in January 1959, and the *Daily News* became part of Field Enterprises soon after—as did the Manistique (Mich.) Pulp and Paper Company. Manistique used an exclusive flotation process that recycled deinked waste paper.

With these and other innovations, Field expanded and increased the profit of the communications network that he had inherited. He also changed its political stance. Marshall Field

III had been an ardent New Deal liberal who had endorsed Adlai Stevenson for president in 1952. However, Marshall Field IV and the *Sun-Times* endorsed Dwight David Eisenhower. "I'm a liberal conservative," he said, and both the *Sun-Times* and *Daily News* reflected their publisher's centrist Republican attitudes and respect for journalistic decorum.

On Aug. 13, 1963, Katherine Woodruff divorced Field, and on July 7, 1964, he married Julia Lynne Templeton. They had one daughter. Field died in Chicago.

[See John W. Tebbel, *The Marshall Fields: A Study in Wealth* (1947); Franklin L. Mott, *American Journalism: A History 1690–1960*, 3rd ed. (1962); and Stephen Becker, *Marshall Field III: A Biography* (1964). Magazine articles include "The Challenger," *Time*, Jan. 20, 1961; "Challenger in Chicago," *Newsweek*, Apr. 20, 1959; "Coming Up," *Time*, Sept. 30, 1946; "The Joust," *Time*, Jan. 11, 1963; "Marsh Moves In," *Time*, Nov. 14, 1949; "Then There Were Two," *Newsweek*, Jan. 19, 1959; and "We're In This As a Public Service," *Printer's Ink*, Aug. 26, 1960. Obituaries appeared in the *Chicago Tribune* and *Washington Post*, Sept. 19, 1965; the *New York Times*, Sept. 20, 1965; *Editor and Publisher*, Sept. 25, 1965; *Publishers Weekly*, Sept. 27, 1965; and *Time*, Oct. 1, 1965.]

NANCY L. STEFFEN

FISCHER, RUTH (1895–Mar. 15, 1961), writer and ex-Communist activist, was born Elfriede Eisler in Leipzig, Germany, the daughter of Rudolph Eisler and of Marie Edith Fischer. She was raised in Vienna, where her father was on the philosophy faculty of the University of Vienna. She was the sister of the modernist composer Hanns Eisler and of Gerhart Eisler, who was active in Communist politics in Weimar Germany during the 1920's, China in 1929–1930, the United States during the 1940's, and the German Democratic Republic after 1949.

Assuming her mother's maiden name at some time during her career, "Ruth Fischer" first joined the Austrian Social Democratic party while a student at the University of Vienna during World War I. She broke with the party over its nationalities policy and became a charter member of the Austrian Communist party in November 1918. In 1919, she moved to Berlin, which she believed to be the real center of revolutionary struggle in Europe. She was elected chairman of the Berlin branch of the German Communist party in November 1921 and attended the Fourth World Congress of the Comintern in 1922. She was elected a Communist

delegate to the German Reichstag in 1924 (serving on the Foreign Affairs Committee), and was a member of the Comintern Presidium from 1924 to 1926.

As a leader of the "Left Opposition," in 1925–1926 Fischer dissented from the more conservative and Russian orientation of the German party, the Comintern, and the Soviet party led by Stalin. She identified with the Zinoviev-Bukharin-Trotsky "bloc" (although in 1924 she had vilified Trotsky and his policies). She lived in Moscow from August 1925 to June 1926 (she claimed to have been detained at Stalin's orders but stayed at the Lux Hotel, which was the official residence for Comintern members). Upon her return to Berlin she denounced the 1926 treaty concluded between the Soviet Union and Germany and also the more conservative thrust of Soviet foreign policy.

Although expelled from the German Communist party in July 1926, Fischer retained her Reichstag seat and with four other expellées formed the Independent German Communist party. In December 1926 she returned to Moscow, where her expulsion was reviewed and eventually reaffirmed. In 1927 she unsuccessfully attempted to form an international conference of Left Communists, in effect an anti-Stalinist bloc among European Communists. (During the Moscow purge trials of 1936, Fischer was tried in absentia on the charge of conspiring on Trotsky's order to assassinate Stalin in 1933.)

After the Nazi seizure of power, Fischer fled to Paris and eventually became a French citizen. There, in 1933, she met and renewed personal and political relations with Trotsky. After the fall of France, she fled to Lisbon and in April 1941 immigrated to the United States. (She became a United States citizen in 1947.) An emotional anti-Stalinist, she began and edited a newsletter, *The Network* (1944–1945), subsequently renamed *The Russian State Party* (1946–1947), in which she identified a number of individuals, including her brother Gerhart Eisler, as Soviet agents in the United States. In November 1946, she published an article in the *American Mercury* (reprinted by the *Reader's Digest*) claiming that the leaders of the East German Socialist Unity party were Soviet agents.

That same month, in testimony before the House Committee on Un-American Activities (HUAC), the ex-Communist Louis Budenz publicly identified Gerhart Eisler as "equivalent to a representative of the Communist International" to the United States Communist party and "as the power behind the throne." The Committee subpoenaed Eisler to testify on Feb. 6, 1947, and the resultant hearings focused on his entry into the United States on a fraudulent passport. Eisler, however, refused to be sworn in by the committee unless first allowed to read a prepared statement. He was later indicted and convicted for contempt of Congress and for passport fraud.

Ruth Fischer did testify on February 6. She denounced her brother Gerhart as "a most dangerous terrorist" and further impugned the loyalty of her other brother, Hanns, who was later subpoenaed and also cited for contempt by HUAC. In May 1949, Fischer further developed these charges before a Senate Subcommittee, emphasizing the need to revise existing immigration laws to make it more difficult for Communist "agents" to enter the United States.

In 1948, Fischer published a lengthy monograph, *Stalin and German Communism*. The book contains considerable biographical detail, but is limited to her German years and admittedly biased. She claimed to be working on a sequel study of Comintern activities in Europe but never published it. In 1958 she did publish in German a study of post-Stalin reform efforts surveying the period 1953–1958. It is unclear how she supported her research and writing. In her 1947 HUAC testimony, she claimed to be "writing for" Harvard University Press and, in her 1949 Senate Subcommittee testimony, to be "working under the auspices of Widener Library of Harvard University." She died in Paris.

[There is no scholarly biography of Fischer. The obituaries in the *New York Times*, Mar. 16, 1961, *Time*, Mar. 24, 1961, and *Newsweek*, Mar. 27, 1961, are either sketchy or contain numerous factual errors. The standard scholarly studies of German politics either do not even discuss Fischer or rely predominantly on her generally descriptive but tendentious study (cited above). The only available, if not always reliable, accounts of her American activities are the hearings and reports of congressional anti-Communist committees. See, particularly, U.S. House, Committee on Un-American Activities, *Hearings on Gerhart Eisler: Investigation of Un-American Activities in the United States*, 80th Cong., 1st sess., 1947; *Annual Report for the Year 1949*, Mar. 15, 1950; and U.S. Senate, Committee on the Judiciary, Subcommittee on Immigration and Naturalization, *Hearings on Communist Activities among Aliens and National Groups*, 81st Cong., 1st sess., 1949. See also Fischer's "Stalin's German Agents," *American Mercury*, Nov. 1946; and *Die Umformung der Sowjetgesellschaft* (1958). For a contrasting account of Gerhart Eisler's role in the United States,

see Joseph Starobin, *American Communism in Crisis, 1943–1957* (1972), 304–305.]

ATHAN THEOHARIS

FISHER, ALFRED J. (1892–Oct. 9, 1963) and **CHARLES T.** (Feb. 16, 1880–Aug. 8, 1963), carriage and automobile body builders, were born in Norwalk and Sandusky, Ohio, respectively, the sons of Lawrence Fisher, a builder of carriages and wagons. They were trained as blacksmiths and as carriage builders by their father.

Charles for a time was a traveling carriage builder. He worked at the C. R. and J. C. Wilson Carriage Company in Detroit (1901–1902), then went to the Chauncey Thomas Company in Boston, but returned to Wilson in 1904, where his older brother, Fred, was superintendent. At this time foresighted carriage manufacturers were turning to the growing market for automobile bodies. Fred and Charles Fisher were aware of this trend, but they realized that an automobile body had to be more than a carriage body with minor adaptations. It had to be capable of carrying passengers in comfort while withstanding the stresses created by a power-driven vehicle operating at higher speeds than a horse-powered carriage could reach. This would demand ingenuity in design and high quality in craftsmanship.

For this purpose Fred, Charles, and an uncle, Albert Fisher, organized the Fisher Body Company in 1908 to manufacture automobile bodies. The capital was $50,000, of which $30,000 was paid in. One of their early customers was the Herreshoff Motor Company, a builder of luxury cars, and through this association Louis Mendelssohn of Herreshoff and his cousin Aaron Mendelson joined the firm, becoming treasurer and secretary and providing additional financing. Meanwhile, Albert Fisher left the firm and became a truck manufacturer.

The success of the Fisher Body Company was due to the fact that its management saw the possibilities in a well-designed, closed automobile body at a time when even luxury automobiles were predominantly touring cars that provided minimal protection from the weather. The brothers had the technical proficiency to design and build closed bodies in attractive styles and with the strength and resiliency required for use in power-driven vehicles. In 1910 an order from Cadillac for 150 bodies, the first big order for closed car bodies by an American manufacturer, secured Fisher Body's position. At the end of that year the company was reorganized as the Fisher Closed Body Company, to emphasize the specialization. Growth was rapid, and in 1916 the Fisher Body Corporation was formed with a capitalization of $8 million.

Meanwhile, the other brothers were brought into the company. Alfred, who had engineering talent, came to Detroit in 1914. In a short time he was made chief engineer of Fisher Body, a position he held until he retired in 1945. There was a definite specialization of function among three of the brothers: Charles was the administrator, Fred the design innovator, and Alfred the engineer.

During this period of its growth, Fisher Body followed the example of Henry Ford in seeking profit through increased output and lower unit costs. To this end it pioneered in the development of interchangeable body parts. It was a distinct feat to be able to combine this technique with a level of craftsmanship that made "Body by Fisher" a hallmark of quality. Indeed, the company for some time had a problem because many automobile manufacturers charged prices for closed cars that exceeded what the Fishers believed was justified by the cost of their bodies. Some consideration was therefore given to making their own cars. It was probably just as well that this step was never taken, given the high rate of attrition in the automobile industry. The skills that made the Fisher brothers brilliantly successful automobile body builders were not necessarily transferable to the making and selling of complete motor vehicles.

In 1919, General Motors bought a 60 percent interest in Fisher for $27.6 million, $5.8 million in cash and the rest in five-year notes. This move was part of the General Motors expansion program launched by William C. Durant when, with Du Pont support, he became president of General Motors in 1916. Durant had known the Fishers since their Norwalk days, when they had done work for the Durant-Dort Carriage Company, but that association was probably a minor element in his decision. The Fisher Body Corporation was easily the most attractive of the body-building firms to a man who wanted a self-contained automotive empire, and it was one of the sounder acquisitions Durant made for General Motors. For the Fishers it was a good bargain. Their company was the world's largest manufacturer of automobile bodies, which was very gratifying so long as they had a market commensurate with their productive capacity. If General Motors had acquired a competing body company or started its own, Fisher might have been in trouble. The only feasible alternative purchaser of Fisher bodies in the quantity the company needed was the Ford Motor Com-

pany, and Ford in 1919 was completely committed to the Model T, hardly a promising candidate for "Body by Fisher."

The deal with General Motors gave the Fishers an assured market. General Motors agreed to buy all its automobile bodies from Fisher for ten years. Management of the Fisher Body Corporation was left in the hands of the Fisher brothers. This arrangement lasted until 1926, when Alfred P. Sloan's reorganization of General Motors had been worked out and was in operation. As part of the change Charles Fisher had become a vice-president of General Motors in 1924; he withdrew from active management of the Fisher Body Corporation. Two years later, General Motors acquired all the remaining stock of Fisher Body by an exchange of stock, one share of General Motors for one-and-a-half shares of Fisher, and Fisher Body became the Fisher Body Division of General Motors. There was still Fisher management: Edward F. Fisher as vice-president in charge of production and Alfred as vice-president in charge of engineering.

Charles Fisher stayed with General Motors until 1934, when he resigned to become president of the family investment firm, Fisher and Company. The family fortunes allegedly suffered heavy losses in the 1929 stock market crash but were rebuilt under Charles's management. Fisher and Company had extensive real estate investments in Detroit, including the Fisher and New Center Buildings. At the time of Charles's death, Fisher and Company was estimated to be worth between $500 million and $1 billion, and there were individual family holdings as well. Charles Fisher had a personal investment firm of which he was president, Prime Securities Company.

Charles Fisher married Sarah Wilhelmina Kramer; they had five children. He and his wife were unostentatiously philanthropic, with a particular interest in foundling and orphaned children. They gave a wing to the Providence Hospital in Detroit for the care of foundling infants and established the Sarah Fisher Home for orphaned children. Charles's principal hobby was the breeding and running of racehorses, for which he had a thoroughbred stable in Kentucky. He died in Detroit.

Alfred J. Fisher married Alma Crisp; they also had five children. He died in Detroit.

[See Arthur Pound, *The Turning Wheel* (1934); Bernard A. Weisberger, *The Dream Maker: William C. Durant, Founder of General Motors* (1979). Obituaries are in *New York Times*, Aug. 9 and Oct. 10,

1963; *Detroit Free Press,* Aug. 10, 1963; *Detroit News,* Oct. 10, 1963.]

JOHN B. RAE

FITZGERALD, ALICE LOUISE FLOR-ENCE (Mar. 13, 1875–Nov. 10, 1962), nurse and international health care administrator, was born in Florence, Italy, the daughter of Charles H. Fitzgerald and Alice Riggs Lawrdson. Her parents had become enamored of Europe on their honeymoon and settled there permanently. Independently wealthy, they employed private tutors to educate their children in Italian, German, French, and English. Fitzgerald also attended the Convent of the Sacred Heart in Florence and, later, a finishing school in Germany.

Following her debut in Baltimore at the age of nineteen, Fitzgerald announced her intention to pursue a career as a nurse. She never married. When she reached the mandatory age of twenty-five she was accepted by the Johns Hopkins Hospital Nurses Training School, but her mother's illness caused a two-year postponement of her enrollment. Although Fitzgerald's education was interrupted by trips to Italy to care for her mother and by her own sickness from overwork, she graduated in 1906 and remained on the Johns Hopkins staff through 1908.

While visiting her parents in Italy in 1908, Fitzgerald volunteered for duty in the aftermath of the earthquake at Messina, Sicily. Initially viewed with suspicion by the Italian doctors who were not accustomed to trained nurses, she was eventually recognized—the government conferred upon her the Italian Red Cross Disaster Relief Medal.

Fitzgerald resumed her position at Johns Hopkins, becoming head nurse in 1910. During 1911–1912 she served as head nurse of the operating rooms at New York's Bellevue Hospital and reorganized the nursing service there. In 1912 she became superintendent of nurses at Wilkes Barre City Hospital in Pennsylvania. A similar position at Robert W. Long Hospital in Indianapolis in 1915 enabled her to introduce public health nursing in Indiana; she conducted a pioneering public relations campaign to explain the role of visiting nurses in homes, schools, and factories.

In 1916 Fitzgerald became director of student health at Dana Hall in Wellesley, Mass. Later that year she was selected to be the Edith Cavell Memorial Nurse with the British army during World War I (the position, funded by a Boston committee, was designed to commemorate the British nurse executed by the Germans in Belgium). Fitzgerald served in a general hospital at Boulogne, France, and at makeshift medical facilities in tents on the Somme front. In his poem, "The Merciful Hand," Vachel Lindsay praised her work:

> Your fine white hand is Heaven's gift
> To cure the wide world, stricken sore,
> Bleeding at the breast and head,
> Tearing at its wounds once more.

After transferring to the American Red Cross in 1917, Fitzgerald established a hospital at Rimini, Italy. As supervisor of nurses and nurses' aides assigned to the hundred military hospitals of the French Service de Santé in 1918, she cared for wounded Americans. Appointed Chief Nurse of the American Red Cross for Europe on May 10, 1919, she surveyed nursing in Poland. After she became director of nursing of the League of Red Cross Societies in Geneva on Nov. 17, 1919, she established nursing schools in Czechoslovakia and Yugoslavia. In 1920 she helped create an International Public Health Nursing Course in England, which attracted students from many countries.

In 1922, working for the International Health Board of the Rockefeller Foundation, Fitzgerald surveyed nursing in the Philippines. As adviser to Philippine Governor General Leonard Wood, she upgraded nursing standards and established a nurses' training facility to provide care for the mountain people. She introduced public health nursing courses at the University of the Philippines (previously, island nurses had to travel to the United States for advanced studies).

In 1926 Fitzgerald did survey work for the Rockefeller Foundation in Hawaii, China, Japan, Singapore, and Thailand (then Siam), where she established a nursing school in Bangkok. During her stay in Thailand she said of her profession: "Nursing has developed best in countries where the medical profession is most up to date, where it has outgrown its fear of a rival in 'nurses' and where it has encouraged cooperation, collaboration and partnership through appreciation of what it means."

Fitzgerald returned to the United States in 1929, having circumnavigated the globe in her effort to publicize modern nursing. She was director of nursing at Polyclinic Hospital in New York from 1931 to 1937. Then she became director of the nurses' residence at a private psychiatric hospital, Sheppard-Pratt in Baltimore. She retired in 1948.

Fitzgerald spent her last years at the Peabody Home in the Bronx, N.Y., where she died. In an interview conducted several years before her death, she said: "I have had a lovely life. I was so happy in my work in all those countries that I never took a vacation. Work was recreation. . . ."

[Fitzgerald's reports on her work in the Far East and her correspondence with officials of the Rockefeller Foundation are preserved at the Rockefeller Archive Center in Pocantico Hills, N.Y. Her "personnel" folder is available at the headquarters of the American National Red Cross in Washington, D.C.

Articles by Fitzgerald in the *Red Cross Courier* include "Strengthening the New Bond of Nurse Fellowship," Sept. 1, 1925; "Seeing Japan in Light of Social Work and Nursing," Feb. 15, 1927; and "Siam, the Essentially Joyful Country," Jan. 15, 1929.

The following books contain information about Fitzgerald's work: Lavinia Dock, *History of American Red Cross Nursing* (1922); Portia Kernodle, *The Red Cross in Action* (1949); Foster Rhea Dulles, *The American Red Cross* (1950); and Iris Noble's juvenile biography, *Nurse Around the World: Alice Fitzgerald* (1964). Obituaries appeared in *New York Times*, Nov. 11, 1962, and *Washington Post*, Nov. 13, 1962.]

MARILYN E. WEIGOLD

FLYNN, ELIZABETH GURLEY (Aug. 7, 1890–Sept. 5, 1964), labor organizer, civil libertarian, suffragette, and political leader, was born in Concord, N.H., the daughter of Thomas Flynn, a granite worker and civil engineer, and Annie Gurley, a tailor. Her parents were working-class intellectuals with traditions of radicalism.

While still at Morris High School in the Bronx, Flynn was closely affiliated with the socialist movement and, shortly thereafter, in 1906, joined the recently formed Industrial Workers of the World (IWW). Emerging as a leading orator and organizer of the IWW, she left high school in 1907 and became a full-time political worker. In January 1908, on a speaking trip to Duluth, she met and married Jack A. Jones, a miner and labor activist. The marriage was not a success and they soon separated, before the birth of their son. They did not obtain a divorce until 1920.

After her son was born, Flynn traveled throughout the United States, speaking and organizing. For the next decade she was involved in many of the historic strikes of that period, including the textile strikes in Paterson (1913) and Passaic (1926), N.J., and in Lawrence, Mass. (1912). Flynn was particularly well known for her leadership in the free speech fights con-

ducted by the IWW workers. Virtually all the prominent labor and radical leaders of the period, such as Bill Haywood, Eugene V. Debs and William Z. Foster, were friends or at least associates of Flynn.

Flynn's friend Joe Hill, the Utah labor martyr, wrote his famous song, "The Rebel Girl," to her while in prison. She was one of the small but bright galaxy of women leaders who stirred millions to join the struggles for women's suffrage, peace, the rights of labor, civil liberties, and socialism.

With the entry of the United States into World War I, Flynn's focus of activity shifted to defense of those arrested for opposing the war. She became a key leader in these civil liberties battles. She was prominent in the fight to free California labor organizers Thomas J. Mooney and Warren K. Billings and in the massive campaign to save Sacco and Vanzetti.

In 1920 Flynn was a founder of the American Civil Liberties Union (ACLU) and was a member of its board of directors until 1940. With the outbreak of World War II, the ACLU was beset with tensions arising from the conflict and centering around their attitude toward Communists and the Communist party. In February 1940 the ACLU board and national committee adopted a resolution stating that it was "inappropriate for any person to serve on the governing committees of the Union or its staff, who is a member of any political organization which supports totalitarian dictatorship in any country, or who by his public declarations indicates his support of such a principle." Although technically this purge resolution applied to Nazis, its main thrust was against members of the Communist party and sympathizers with the Soviet Union. The resolution brought into effect "guilt by association," a principle that the ACLU had always opposed. This violation of civil liberties by the Civil Liberties Union created a great furor among liberals, radicals, and civil libertarians. It also served as a model for trade unions, civic organizations, and governmental committees which eventually joined the nationwide anti-Communist witch-hunt.

Flynn had become a member of the Communist Party of the United States of America in 1937. She so informed the ACLU board before being reelected in 1939 for a three-year term. Since she defied the purge resolution, on May 7, 1940, a special meeting was called to consider her expulsion. After long and often acrimonious discussion, she was expelled by a vote of ten to nine. The national committee soon ratified this action.

The ACLU expulsion did not affect Flynn's strenuous work in the Communist party. For the last twenty-five years of her life she fought on behalf of her liberal and leftist causes within the framework of the party. She became a member of its leading committees and in 1961 its first woman chairman, a post she held until her death. Along with other party leaders, she was prosecuted (1951) and convicted (1953) under the Smith Act of 1940 during the era of McCarthyite repression, for conspiring to teach, and to advocate, the overthrow of the United States government. She was imprisoned from January 1955 to May 1957 in Alderson Prison, W.Va.

Meanwhile, many members of the Civil Liberties Union opposed the Flynn expulsion. (A contribution to the opposition was the publishing of the verbatim manuscript of *The Trial of Elizabeth Gurley Flynn by the American Civil Liberties Union* by Corliss Lamont in 1968.) Finally, in April 1978, a group led by George Slaff, a prominent attorney and president of the Southern California Civil Liberties Union was able to persuade the board to rescind posthumously Flynn's expulsion.

In August 1964 Flynn made her first visit to the Soviet Union; she died in Moscow. Her battle with the ACLU and her crusading activities as a Communist made her a national figure in the perennial struggle for a better America and a warless world.

[Flynn wrote popular pamphlets such as *Women in the War* (1942); *Coal Miners and the War* (1942); *Horizons of the Future for a Socialist America* (1950); *Communists and the People* (1953); *I Speak My Own Piece: Autobiography of "The Rebel Girl"* (1955); and *The Alderson Story* (1963). Her obituary appeared on the front page of the *New York Times*, Sept. 6, 1964.]

CORLISS LAMONT

FLYNN, JOHN THOMAS (Oct. 25, 1882– Apr. 13, 1964), journalist and political commentator, was born in Bladensburg, Md., the son of John Flynn, a lawyer, and Margaret O'Donnell. He attended local public schools and Catholic schools in New York City before entering Georgetown University. He earned an LL.B. there in 1902 but did not follow his father into law. On Apr. 7, 1910, Flynn married Alice Bell; they had two sons.

Flynn was a press officer for the German embassy before World War I and a reporter for the *New Haven Register* during the war, and later city editor. In the early 1920's he became both city editor and managing editor of the *New York Globe*. When the paper folded in 1923, he turned to free-lance work.

Only in middle age did Flynn step into national political debate as a columnist, lecturer, and broadcaster. He was forty-seven when his first book was published. But his short career of political commentary was too long for many of Flynn's one-time allies. His column in the *New Republic*, "Other People's Money," was dropped in 1940, when the editors concluded that Flynn had strayed from both economic affairs and liberalism. Franklin D. Roosevelt, whom Flynn had supported in 1932, proposed in 1939 that Flynn "should be barred hereafter from the column of any presentable daily paper, monthly magazine or national quarterly. . . ." When Flynn turned to the far right after World War II, his conservative readers and editors again found the drift of his ideas maddening.

In the early 1930's Flynn was a liberal. He urged stricter regulation of the securities market, enlarged public works budgets, antitrust prosecutions, and income redistribution. But the National Industrial Recovery Act of 1933 marked Flynn's apostasy from the New Deal. He argued that the National Recovery Administration, which it established, encouraged corporate control of American society and the death of competitive markets. His articles reminded Americans that under Roosevelt mass unemployment continued, the national debt grew, and Wall Street maintained its shady practices. Flynn did support reformers in Congress: he was an adviser to the Senate Committee on Banking and Currency in the investigation of the New York Stock Exchange (1933–1934) and an economic consultant to the Special Senate Committee Investigating the Munitions Industry (1934–1935). In 1936 he campaigned for Norman Thomas, the Socialist party candidate for president. Flynn's historical research and his observations of bureaucrats and capitalists led him to conclude that America was on "the march toward the Fascist society. . . ."

Fascism abroad, Flynn argued, was no reason for Americans to take up arms. As an Irishman who had been moved by the anti-imperialist protest at the turn of the century, he blamed Britain and France for the threat to peace. He condemned the appeasement policy toward Germany but concluded that the United States was not threatened by the military power of the Axis. After 1939 he crusaded against American intervention in the war, and in 1940 he became chairman of the New York chapter of the America First Committee.

Both in public and in private Flynn denounced anti-Semitism within that diverse organization. For him, racial hatred was neither the heart of fascism nor a sufficient reason to fight the Axis. *As We Go Marching* (1944) was one of the few books published during World War II to break with the consensus of support. Flynn believed that mobilization caused America to move toward facism: "At this moment, in the midst of the war, we have a very close approach to national socialism." Before the end of the war, Flynn published his claims that American intervention was part of a conspiracy: President Roosevelt, he said, had provoked the attack on Pearl Harbor and cynically exploited the disaster.

Flynn's conclusions often differed so sharply from those of his contemporaries because he took little account of the events that guided their thought. He wrote little about the stock market crash of 1929 (in his first book, *Investment Trusts Gone Wrong!* [1930], he did not mention the event in the first hundred pages). He wrote about the danger of Roosevelt's program and personality, not Hitler's or Stalin's. He said little about the noneconomic policies of totalitarian states.

In the 1940's Flynn glimpsed threats to freedom that few Americans could see: the growth in power of the Federal Bureau of Investigation and the blacklisting that was practiced, he said, by liberals. What was truly remarkable about Flynn's support for Senator Joseph R. McCarthy in the early 1950's was that he was able to join such a broad political movement. (Flynn broke with McCarthy in 1956 only because the senator supported Britain and France during the Suez Crisis.)

Flynn's view of power combined the intellectual agility of his Jesuit education with, on occasion, the cynicism of many newspaper editors. He could celebrate loyalty while he scoffed at patriotic conceits. Leaders without a political philosophy, or with an overreaching one, earned his scorn—Franklin D. Roosevelt and John Foster Dulles, for example. After World War II, Flynn agreed with the right that American interests abroad had been sold out by a conspiracy on the left, but he thought that freedom would be lost if conservatives built a state powerful enough to fight communism around the world. His cautionary lectures to his allies on the right amounted to a critique of anti-Communist foreign policy; and many of his warnings, especially his denunciations of American aid to the French in Vietnam, anticipated voices on the left in the 1960's.

However warmly Flynn may be embraced as a prophet, he should not be ranked among the best journalists of his generation. He was a good deal more familiar with the New York Public Library (where he did prodigious research) than with the citizens and statesmen he criticized. He began as an investigator of economic life, but over the years the "workers" and "bureaucrats" and "communists" and "imperialists" became abstractions in his work. In fourteen books on contemporary affairs, Flynn rarely claimed to have talked with the leading figures of the day. When Roosevelt asked for a private meeting to discuss Flynn's economic ideas, the journalist refused.

As a polemicist Flynn was, perhaps, aided by his lack of interest in personality. A rousing public speaker, he was at the same time self-effacing; he did not brag or bluster, and could charge a person with treason in a perfectly courteous manner. Roosevelt was the only man in public life who caused Flynn to attempt character assassination. "He is without mercy, justice or fairness," the *New York Times* said of Flynn's 1940 biography of Roosevelt, "yet he is neither spiteful nor venomous." Flynn battled ideas, not the Americans who believed them.

Flynn died at Amityville, N.Y.

[In addition to his column for the *New Republic*, Flynn wrote about 250 articles, fourteen books, and numerous pamphlets. The books include *Country Squire in the White House* (1940); *As We Go Marching* (1944); and *The Roosevelt Myth* (1948). Flynn's correspondence and manuscripts, including drafts of his radio broadcasts, are at the University of Oregon Library, Eugene. Studies of Flynn's politics are Richard C. Frey, Jr., "John T. Flynn and the United States in Crisis, 1928–1950" (Ph.D. diss.)University of Oregon at Eugene, 1969); Ronald Radosh, *Prophets on the Right: Profiles of Conservative Critics of American Globalism* (1975); and Michele Flynn Stenehjem, *An American First, John T. Flynn and the America First Committee* (1976). See also Bruce Bliven, *Fifty Million Words Later* (1970); and "John T. Flynn, RIP," *National Review*, May 5, 1964. An obituary is in the *New York Times*, Apr. 14, 1964.]

THOMAS C. LEONARD

FOLKS, HOMER (Feb. 18, 1867–Feb. 13, 1963), child welfare worker, welfare administrator, and public health crusader, was born in Hanover, Mich., the son of James Folks, a farmer, and of Esther Woodliff. He attended the local schools and then entered Albion College at Albion, Mich. Unable to decide between a ministerial and a teaching career when he graduated in 1889, Folks enrolled at Harvard for a year of further study. There he fell under the influence of Francis G. Peabody, "Harvard's theologian of the social gospel," and George Herbert Palmer, a professor of philosophy whose courses on ethics emphasized self-sacrifice and service to humanity.

Searching for a meaningful way to satisfy a sense of responsibility and service instilled in him by both his parents and his teachers, and eager to experience the real world, where he could do things rather than merely talk about them, Folks found social service irresistible. A life of practical helpfulness to the needy, he concluded, would give him more satisfaction than the church or the classroom. After graduating from Harvard in 1890, Folks was offered a job in Philadelphia, as general superintendant of the Children's Aid Society of Pennsylvania. He quickly accepted the position.

Almost immediately after joining the Children's Aid Society, Folks helped revolutionize the care of needy children in the United States by successfully experimenting in the home care of delinquent children as well as the orphaned and neglected. On Dec. 22, 1891, he married his college sweetheart, Maud Beard. They had three daughters.

In February 1893, Folks was called to New York City as executive secretary of the New York State Charities Aid Association (SCAA), created in 1872 by concerned citizens to keep vigil over the state's public welfare institutions and to "bring about such reforms . . . as might be in accordance with the most enlightened views of Christianity, Science, and Philanthropy." He headed that organization for the next half-century and more—with the exception of 1902–1903, when he served as commissioner of public charities of New York City, and 1917–1918, when he was director of the Department of Civil Affairs of the American Red Cross in France. His career has been unmatched in American social welfare history.

Initially Folks's efforts with the SCAA consisted of carrying on his earlier work with needy children, particularly the placing and boarding out of dependent and delinquent youngsters. Before long, though, he became convinced that the preventive rather than the ameliorative approach to child care was wisest. He discovered that in most cases dependency and delinquency among needy children resulted from the breakdown of family life, which in turn was caused by poverty. He felt that poverty was not rooted in personal failure, as was widely believed, but in social and economic conditions, especially sickness, invalidism, and the premature death of the family breadwinner. Certain then that health and welfare were inseparable, Folks saw the

need for child welfare workers to concern themselves not merely with the protection of children but with the safety and security of their parents as well. He stressed the importance of maintaining the family in its entirety by preventing, as much as possible, distress resulting from various social and economic hazards, particularly disease. In doing so he played an exceedingly important role in the early twentieth-century public health movement.

As New York City commissioner of public charities, Folks founded the nation's first municipal tuberculosis hospital. He served on the New York Charity Organization Society's Committee on the Prevention of Tuberculosis, which in 1903 conducted the first comprehensive analysis of the "white plague" in the United States. A year later he helped to create the National Association for the Study and Prevention of Tuberculosis. He served on its board of trustees for many years and in 1912 was elected its president, the first layman to hold that position. Finally, and perhaps most importantly, through the SCAA he conducted an anti-tuberculosis campaign that led to the enactment of laws governing the reporting and treatment of all cases and the building of public institutions that made New York a model in that regard.

Folks was not only in the forefront of these social reforms. He was instrumental in the establishment of juvenile courts in New York State and in 1907 was responsible for the creation of the nation's first state probation commission, which he chaired for the next ten years. The commission established an effective system of probation in New York and elsewhere, and brought skillful and well-trained personnel into the field. Folks also was one of the founders, and subsequently chairman (1935–1944), of the National Child Labor Committee, which led the fight to eliminate that evil.

Folks was the presiding officer at the historic 1909 White House Conference on Dependent Children, which gave rise to the U.S. Children's Bureau three years later and established the practice, still maintained, of calling decennial White House conferences on children. He was among the nation's earliest social workers to favor widows' pensions, and he played a prominent role in their introduction in New York State in 1915. He was involved in the creation, in 1909, of the American Association for the Study and Prevention of Infant Mortality, a body he served as president in 1915. Elected president of the National Conference of Social Work in 1911 and in 1923, he was the only person in that organization's history to serve two terms.

In 1913 Folks drafted a bill that was considered "the most important landmark in the history of state health administration in the United States" since the creation of the first state health department in 1869. Its most important feature was establishment of the nation's first state Public Health Council, a small, expert administrative body with quasi-legislative power that in effect took public health administration out of politics in New York State. During 1913–1955, when Folks served as vice-chairman, the council reorganized the state's Health Department, making it the most progressive such body in the nation. In 1930 Folks was secretary of a public health commission created by Governor Franklin D. Roosevelt to study the ways to improve the state's health laws and institutions. A decade later he chaired yet another such commission, created by Governor Herbert H. Lehman, this time to study ways to curtail the rate of increase in the population of the state's mental institutions.

By 1940, Folks had become somewhat of a legend in his own time. He planned to retire in May 1942, but World War II intervened. He remained on the job until November 1946, when he suffered a slight stroke. In February 1947, fifty-four years after he joined the New York State Charities Aid Association, this "statesman of the public good" finally retired. He died in Riverdale, N.Y.

Folks's life of selfless devotion to the helpless and the ill was eloquently summed up in a citation for "distinguished service in the advancement of social justice" awarded to him in 1940 by the (Theodore) Roosevelt Memorial Association:

A dreamer, he [Folks] has dreamed not of power, but of mercy; a crusader, he has gloried not the sword but the flaming heart; a statesman and a man of action, he has brought to his own and other lands not destruction and heartbreak but healing and new horizons. . . .

[The Homer Folks Papers are at the Columbia University School of Social Work in New York City; the New York State Charities Aid Association's papers are in that organization's offices in New York City. Folks also contributed to the Columbia University Oral History Project at the Columbia University Library. His books are *The Care of Destitute, Neglected and Delinquent Children* (1902); *The Human Costs of the War* (1920); *Public Health and Welfare: The Citizens' Responsibility* (1958), ed. Savel Zimand. Also see Anna Liebowitz, "Homer Folks: A Study of His Professional Growth in Terms of His

Contributions to Social Work and the Milieu in Which He Developed" (Master's thesis, New York School of Social Work, 1950); and Walter I. Trattner, *Homer Folks: Pioneer in Social Welfare* (1968). The best brief account of Folks's life and accomplishments is in the introduction to Folks's *Public Health and Welfare*. An obituary is in the *New York Times*, Feb. 14, 1963.]

WALTER I. TRATTNER

FORD, GUY STANTON (May 9, 1873–Dec. 29, 1962), editor and educator, was born in Liberty Corners, Wis., the son of Thomas D. Ford, a physician, and of Helen Elizabeth Shumway, a schoolteacher. When Ford was ten, the family moved to Plainfield, Iowa. He was educated in the Plainfield public schools, early displaying a bent toward a career as an educator. At twelve Ford passed examinations for a teacher's first-grade certificate. In 1888 he entered the preparatory department of Upper Iowa University at Fayette and, after attaining sophomore standing, taught in a one-room school in Bremer County (1891–1892). He entered the University of Wisconsin in 1892, having been accepted with many conditions due to his haphazard preparation for the school's requirements.

On the Madison campus Ford studied with the frontier historian Frederick Jackson Turner and the economist Richard T. Ely, and had as his adviser the medieval specialist Charles H. Haskins. Each of these professors had great influence upon his subsequent career. After graduating with the B.Litt. in 1895, Ford was superintendent of schools in Grand Rapids, Wis., for three years. He then returned to the University of Wisconsin as a graduate student. In 1899–1900, he studied at the University of Berlin, and subsequently enrolled at Columbia University, where his dissertation, *Hanover and Prussia, 1795–1803: A Study in Neutrality*, brought him a Ph.D. in 1903. In this work, based on materials in German and British archives, Ford skillfully traced the development and failure of the idea of neutrality in Prussian history.

In 1901 Ford had accepted appointment as instructor in history at Yale University, where he remained for five years, and then left to assume a newly created professorship in modern European history at the University of Illinois. He married Grace Victoria Ellis on Sept. 6, 1907; they had two children.

Ford was offered the dual posts of chairman of the history department and dean of the graduate school at the University of Minnesota in 1913. It was a dynamic era when Minnesota, under President George E. Vincent, was being transformed into a great state university. During Ford's quarter-century as dean, the graduate school grew from 175 students to 3,300. He built up the history department by bringing to Minnesota promising scholars and teachers, including some former colleagues from Illinois. Having a wide circle of acquaintances in the academic world and a gift for recognizing rising scholars, Ford raised the level of intellectual life not only in the university and the state, but also in the nation. At the university he developed the library, dispensed grants with an eye to cooperative research, and fostered the university press. He was responsible for making the Mayo Clinic a part of the graduate school, with a stress on specialized training beyond the M.D. degree. During most of these years, Ford taught an undergraduate course on modern Europe to classes as large as 700 students. He also offered graduate seminars in Prussian history.

Ford soon achieved a national reputation and received many job offers. In 1915, when he was appointed to the Executive Council of the American Historical Association, he began an influential relationship with that organization. After the United States entered World War I, George Creel, chairman of the Committee on Public Information, persuaded him to come to Washington, D.C. From May 1917 to January 1919 Ford served there as director of civic and educational publications for the committee. Before he left this position, he was appointed to the American Historical Association's Special Committee on History and Education for Citizenship in the Schools. In 1920 he became a member of the association's board of editors; he served as chairman of that board from 1921 to 1927. He was on the association's Commission for Investigation of Social Studies in the Schools in 1929. Ford's second book, *Stein and the Era of Reform in Prussia, 1807–1815* (1922), stressed Stein's agrarian reforms and became a standard study.

But it was as an "academic statesman" and editor that Ford chiefly made his mark. When his teacher Turner became president of the American Historical Association, Ford edited *Essays in American History: Dedicated to Frederick Jackson Turner* (1910). In 1922 he became editor-in-chief of *Compton's Pictured Encyclopedia;* he was also editor of Harper's Historical Series. A volume of essays produced under his editorship, *Dictatorship in the Modern World* (1935), was widely read.

With a "winking shrewdness and good temper," Ford directed his talents, not without be-

nefit to the University of Minnesota, to some of the nation's great intellectual institutions. In the Association of American Universities he wielded great influence. From 1923 to 1940 he was a member of the Social Science Research Council, which he served for three years as vice-chairman, managing at last to give the American Historical Association official representation in that body.

The Laura Spelman Rockefeller Foundation, of which he was a staff member, sent Ford to Germany in 1924 to study postwar university needs in the social sciences. The following year he became a member of the Guggenheim Foundation's advisory council. He was also a director of the National Bureau of Economic Research for a number of years. In 1930 he was named to study the aims, organization, and policies of Brown University; the report of the survey committee was published by Brown.

Ford was offered the presidency of the University of Texas in 1924, but he declined. In 1931–1932 and in 1937–1938 he served as acting president of the University of Minnesota, and in 1938 was appointed president. In the same year he served as president of the American Historical Association. His presidential address, "Some Suggestions to Americans," affirmed his creed: "If history has any lessons to teach, the supreme one is that of ceaseless change within human society and in mankind's relation to his physical environment." Also in 1938, colleagues presented Ford with a volume of his writings, *On and off the Campus.*

Ford retired from the university presidency in 1941. Later that year he was named by the American Historical Association to the combined offices of executive secretary, editor of the association, and managing editor of the *American Historical Review.* Because of the entrance of the United States into World War II, the 1941 meeting of the association was canceled and the inflow of contributions temporarily shrank. But with his wonted enterprise Ford continued to bring out the *Review* during the war and concluded twelve years of editorship in his eightieth year, during the hysteria created by Senator Joseph McCarthy. In his valedictory Ford said, "The only intolerance that befits a democracy is the intolerance of the intolerant whether of the right or the left."

Following his retirement, Ford lived in Washington, D.C., where he died.

[A voluminous collection of Ford's papers is in the University of Minnesota archives; it includes personal papers (1885–1963), papers of the Graduate School

(1913–1938), papers of the president's office (1931–1932, 1937–1941), and a transcript of his interview for the Columbia University Oral History Program. The records pertaining to the American Historical Association during his years as executive secretary are in the Library of Congress. The best biographical sketch is George E. Vincent's introduction to *On and off the Campus* (1938). See also *American Historical Review*, Apr. 1963, and Theodore C. Blegen, *Minnesota: A History of the State* (1963). Obituaries are in the *Washington Post* and *Minneapolis Tribune*, Dec. 30, 1962.]

JAMES A. RAWLEY

FOSTER, WILLIAM Z. (Feb. 25, 1881–Sept. 1, 1961), Communist leader and labor organizer, was born in Taunton, Mass., the son of James Foster, an Irish nationalist, and Elizabeth McLaughlin. When Foster was six, the family moved to the slums of Philadelphia, where his father worked as a carriage washer and livery stableman. The family's poverty forced Foster to leave school at the age of ten and take a job in 1891 as a sculptor's assistant. After three years he quit, and for the next twenty-three years he traveled restlessly across the American industrial landscape, toiling in Philadelphia type foundries, in Pennsylvania fertilizer plants, in Florida lumber camps, on New York trolley cars, on British merchant ships, in northwestern farms, sawmills, and metal mines, and in Chicago rail yards.

While acquiring this education in the harsh realities of American working-class life, Foster began immersing himself in the political and economic movements that responded to those conditions. Abandoning his youthful attraction to William Jennings Bryan's free silver movement, as well as his father's Irish nationalism and his mother's Catholicism, he joined the Socialist party (SP) in 1901 and began his sixty-year commitment to revolutionary trade unionism and socialism. Although that commitment was steadfast, his attachment to a particular movement was not. In 1909 Foster and other members of the SP's left wing in the state of Washington split from the party and launched the short-lived Wage Workers party. But Foster soon shifted from political to trade-union radicalism by joining the Industrial Workers of the World (IWW) during the Spokane free-speech fight.

Foster's membership in the IWW also proved brief. In 1910 he left the Pacific Northwest and spent thirteen months in Europe studying radical and union movements. Impressed by the French syndicalist tactic of "boring from within" existing unions, he returned to the United States in 1911 and campaigned to persuade the IWW to abandon its independent, "dual unionist" stance and work within the American Federation of Labor (AFL). With the failure of his efforts, Foster resigned from the IWW in 1912 and began to "bore from within" the AFL by joining the Brotherhood of Railway Carmen. At the same time he founded the Syndicalist League of North America (SLNA), with himself as unpaid national secretary, in order to mobilize radical unionists within other AFL craft unions. The early recruits to this new movement included a number of anarchists. He married one of them, Russian-born Esther Abramowitz, on Mar. 23, 1912. Under the influence of anarchist ideas and comrades, Foster became an anarcho-syndicalist, believing that a revolution would come solely through the economic struggles of unions, strikes, and sabotage.

The SLNA never exceeded 2,000 members during its two years of operation (1912–1914); the Independent Trade Union Educational League, which Foster founded in 1915, proved even less successful. It was largely an organization of Chicago union militants who believed that trade unions would inevitably turn to "the overthrow of capitalism." Although Foster would later criticize this policy as "right opportunism," it was the basis of his most notable successes as a labor leader.

In 1915, Foster, then working in the Swift's car shops in the Chicago stockyards, was elected business agent of the Chicago District Council of the Railway Carmen. In this position he gained both organizing experience and influence in the Chicago labor movement. In 1917 he was able to win the Chicago Federation of Labor's support for an effort to organize packinghouse workers. As secretary of the Stockyards Labor Council, Foster brilliantly led an organizing campaign that increased union membership tenfold. As a result the packinghouse workers won the eight-hour day and other benefits through federal arbitration.

Having thus gained the confidence of AFL leaders, Foster in 1918 moved on to the even more ambitious task of organizing the steel industry. Again he was spectacularly successful; nearly 100,000 steelworkers had joined the union by the spring of 1919. But the strike of 365,000 steelworkers that fall proved much less successful. In the postwar "red scare" atmosphere, Foster's radicalism became a major issue in the strike. Although he repudiated many of his previous radical positions in testimony before the Senate Investigating Committee, the red-baiting proved crucial in the eventual defeat of the strike.

Despite the ultimate failure of the steel organizing drive, Foster's work as leader of the packinghouse and steel campaigns received almost universal praise. Even his longtime political opponent James P. Cannon admitted that "no one but Foster, with his executive and organizing skill, his craftiness, his patience and his driving energy, could have organized the steelworkers on such a scale and led them in a great strike."

The defeat of the steel strike ended Foster's immediate hopes for transforming the AFL into a revolutionary labor movement and left him at a crossroads. He decided to return to the rail yards to build left-wing unionism as a rank-and-filer. But, finding himself blacklisted, he was forced to turn to full-time organizing. In November 1920 he formed the Trade Union Education League (TUEL), another left-wing organization devoted to industrial unionism and working within AFL unions. Although the American Communist party, which had been formed in 1919 out of the left wing of the Socialist party, disdained Foster's approach, the Soviet Communists showed much greater interest. In 1921 the RILU (a Moscow-centered "international" of revolutionary trade unions) invited him to attend its Moscow convention, at which it designated the TUEL as its American affiliate.

Foster, who had been gradually moving away from antipolitical syndicalism, spent three and a half months in Moscow, studying Soviet society and the Communist movement. Pleased by the attention paid to the TUEL and the Russian support for "boring from within" the AFL, and impressed by the results of the Russian Revolution, Foster joined the American Communist party in 1921. Although he did not join the party until two years after its creation, he devoted the next forty years to the Communist movement and to insuring that he would never again be absent from what he called his "proper place in the ranks of the revolutionary Communist International."

For the first two years, Foster kept his party membership secret, so that it would not interfere with his trade union work. Initially his organizational talents won significant results; the TUEL gained the support of numerous AFL unions for the principle of industrial unionism. But by 1924, under attack from the leadership of the AFL and in the atmosphere of Coolidge "prosperity," the TUEL found itself, as even Foster later conceded, in "relative isolation from the masses."

Just as Foster's trade union efforts were faltering, so were his efforts to win ascendancy within the American Communist party (known as the Workers Party of America from 1922 to 1929). Although his loose faction of the party—dominated by such Chicago-centered, American-born trade unionists as James P. Cannon, Earl Browder, and himself—often had the support of the majority of party members, they lacked the crucial backing of the Communist International (Comintern). In 1929, Josef Stalin intervened on behalf of the Foster group, but for Foster the triumph was ambiguous. Criticized by Stalin for too energetically fighting the factional battles of the 1920's, he was gradually pushed aside in favor of the less well-known and seemingly more tractable Earl Browder, who had previously been little more than Foster's "errand boy." To add insult to injury, Foster was told to administer the party's new policy of creating independent unions outside the AFL, an approach that he had fought since 1911. Abandoning this longtime opposition to "dual unionism," Foster became secretary of the new federation—the Trade Union Unity League (TUUL)—formed in 1929 as a center for organizing independent, revolutionary, industrial unions.

Although Foster had been denied the top leadership post in the party, he remained its best-known and most popular public figure. Tall, slight, partially bald, and with what literary critic Edmund Wilson described as "a small mobile Irish mouth and a plebeian Irish lantern jaw," Foster was a soft-spoken but effective orator. To many American radicals he became a legendary and heroic figure—the "embodiment of the American working class, the living confirmation of the historic mission of the proletariat." He was the party's presidential candidate in 1924, 1928, and 1932. The last campaign, in which he garnered 102,785 votes, was his most successful, but personally the most costly. Although run-down from years of overwork, Foster undertook a grueling campaign tour. In September 1932 he collapsed from a heart attack. Only after three years of recuperation could he again make even a ten-minute speech.

When Foster returned to active party life, he found Browder solidly entrenched as party secretary, and himself relegated to the largely honorary post of party chairman. He continued to give advice, particularly on labor questions, but for the most part he was confined to "literary" activities. His articles appeared almost monthly in the party's theoretical magazine, *The Communist*, in the late 1930's and early 1940's.

An activist, not a writer or theoretician, in both temperament and talent, Foster grew increasingly frustrated over Browder's dominance and his own limited role in party affairs. Political disagreements reinforced Foster's personal bitterness. While Browder had championed close cooperation with the Roosevelt administration in pursuit of the antifascist "popular front" of the late 1930's and of wartime national unity, Foster remained suspicious and critical of such alliances.

In May 1944, Browder took his coalition policy to the logical extreme of dissolving the Communist party, replacing it with the "nonpartisan" and "educational" Communist Political Association, and declaring, "Capitalism and Socialism have begun to find the way to peaceful coexistence and collaboration in the same world." Such visions of class harmony were anathema to the more "fundamentalist" Foster. Despite these sharp disagreements, Foster publicly supported Browder's policy, became a vice-president of the new association, and even presided over the expulsion of a party official who refused to accept the new line.

Foster finally felt vindicated when, in April 1945, French Communist leader Jacques Duclos, with the apparent support of Soviet leaders, published an article attacking Browder for "opportunist illusions." Within months the American party repudiated Browder, reestablished the Communist party, and turned over leadership to Foster. Despite continued ill health he led an often vicious purge of all remnants of "Browderism." Some of Foster's policies were modified by the more pragmatic Eugene Dennis, the party secretary during the postwar years.

Tragically for Foster, he had achieved dominance of the American party only to watch it collapse. Although his own sectarianism probably encouraged this decline, a more important problem facing the party was cold-war-era repression. In 1948 the government indicted twelve top party leaders under the Smith Act for advocating the overthrow of the American government by "force and violence." Following their conviction in October 1949, the government successfully prosecuted secondary party leaders all over the country. The party, now even more firmly under the leadership of Foster, who had escaped trial and imprisonment because of his heart condition, aided the process of party disintegration by sending thousands of trusted members "underground" to evade further anticipated governmental attacks.

Such actions accorded with Foster's apocalyptic "five minutes to midnight" line, which predicted impending economic depression, domestic fascism, and international war. This crisis, he argued, would propel the American working class to a revolution under Communist party leadership.

But the cataclysmic clash between capitalism and socialism anticipated by Foster never materialized. Instead, postwar prosperity continued, domestic repression gradually diminished, and the cold war began to thaw. Even more important, at the Twentieth Party Congress in 1956, Nikita Khrushchev revealed the crimes of the Stalin years. In these circumstances the American party met in April 1956 to assess the party's decline over the past decade. Such reflections, notes historian and former party member Joseph Starobin, "inevitably cast doubt on the competence of Foster as ideologue and leader." In effect, the report of party secretary Dennis, *The Communists Take a New Look,* which was approved with only Foster dissenting, repudiated the leadership Foster had given to the party since 1945.

Despite some initial hesitation Foster counterattacked forcefully until a serious stroke sidelined him in October 1957. Earlier that year he had been pushed out of his position as party chairman and made chairman emeritus. But he ultimately won a pyrrhic victory as most of his strongest opponents—centered around *Daily Worker* editor John Gates—left the party in 1957 and 1958. Still, one of those who remained in the party complained privately that Foster had "become very rigid and inflexible on tactical and personnel questions and is intensely subjective and bitter." Thus, in the last four years of his life Foster had the ambiguous status of ignored, but honored, party elder statesmen.

Foster died in Moscow, where he had gone for medical treatment, and was honored by a state funeral in Red Square. Both his life and his legacy were riddled with ironies: hostile to intellectuals and insecure over his lack of education, he spent many years as a party theorist; an extremely talented labor organizer, he failed to demonstrate those talents as a leader in his own party; personally rooted in the realities of American working-class life, he increasingly seemed to lose touch with those realities.

[There are no manuscript collections relating primarily to Foster, but the FBI has about 11,000 pages of documents on him. His two autobiographies are *From Bryan to Stalin* (1937) and *Pages from a Worker's Life* (1939). His other major books include

The Great Steel Strike and Its Lessons (1920); *Toward a Soviet America* (1932); *Twilight of World Capitalism* (1949); *History of the Communist Party of the United States* (1952). A complete bibliography of his writings as a Communist is in Joel Seidman, ed., *Communism in the United States: A Bibliography* (1969). On his early career see U.S. Senate Committee on Labor and Education, *Investigation of Strike in the Steel Industry* (1919); David Brody, *The Butcher Workmen* (1964) and *Labor in Crisis* (1965); Melvyn Dubofsky, *We Shall Be All* (1969).

On his role as party leader see Theodore Draper, *The Roots of American Communism* (1957); Elizabeth Gurley Flynn, *Labor's Own William Z. Foster* (1949); Irving Howe and Lewis Coser, *The American Communist Party* (1957); David Shannon, *The Decline of American Communism* (1959); Theodore Draper, *American Communism and Soviet Russia* (1960); Joseph Starobin, *American Communism in Crisis* (1972); Philip J. Jaffe, *The Rise and Fall of American Communism* (1975); James Weinstein, *Ambiguous Legacy* (1975); Bert Cochran, *Labor and Communism* (1977); Maurice Isserman, "Peat Bog Soldiers: The American Communist Party During the Second World War" (Ph.D. diss., University of Rochester, 1979).

Reminiscences of former comrades include Benjamin Gitlow, *The Whole of Their Lives* (1948); James Cannon, *The First Ten Years of American Communism* (1962); George Charney, *A Long Journey* (1968); Al Richmond, *A Long View from the Left* (1972); Peggy Dennis, *The Autobiography of an American Communist* (1977). Also see Edmund Wilson, *American Jitters* (1932).

An obituary is in the *New York Times*, Sept. 2, 1961.]

ROY ROSENZWEIG

FOX, FONTAINE TALBOT, JR. (June 4, 1884–Aug. 9, 1964), cartoonist, was born in Louisville, Ky., the son of Fontaine Talbot Fox and Mary Pitkin Barton. Both his father and paternal grandfather were judges. Upon graduation from high school in Louisville, he was hired as a reporter and part-time cartoonist by the *Louisville Herald*. With a perceptive eye for the local scene, Fox poked fun, in homely, unstylized drawings, at Louisville's Brook Street trolley line, which was known for its haphazard schedule and failure to run during foul weather. The drawings became so popular with readers that Fox continued to draw a weekly cartoon even after he left the paper to attend Indiana University in 1904. The work indirectly reinforced his interest in railroads, since he had to stay up to put his cartoons on a train that left Bloomington at 1:10 A.M. He sent the cartoons to Louisville by train, according to one account, because they "were too large to put into first-class mail boxes."

His preoccupation with cartooning was responsible for his indifference to his studies, Fox later said, so he left the university in 1906 to return to the *Herald* as a full-time cartoonist. In 1907 he moved to the *Louisville Times*, for which he worked until 1911. From 1911 to 1915 he was a cartoonist for the *Chicago Post*. On Apr. 22, 1915, he married Edith Elizabeth Hinz; they had two daughters.

Afterward Fox sold his work to feature syndicates until his retirement in 1955. His cartoons were handled by the Wheeler Syndicate from 1915 to 1921, the McNaught Syndicate from 1921 to 1926 and 1942 to 1949, and the Bell Syndicate from 1926 to 1942 and 1949 to 1955. Fox was one of the few cartoonists of that day to own his own copyright.

Known mainly for his witty comic strip "Toonerville Folks," which traced its origins to his early trolley sketches, Fox produced a lively and inventive commentary on the people and places along the tracks of a mythical trolley line that went from rural environs through suburbs into a large city. At the height of its popularity, "Toonerville Folks," which centered on the rickety "Toonerville Trolley" with its nameless skipper and a twisted current collector, appeared in more than 200 daily newspapers with circulations in the millions.

Fox's outlandish, rustic characters were followed by readers as if they were actual people—like actors in movie serials and radio or television soap operas. They were so easily recognized that Fox could drop them in and out of the strip for weeks or months without using their names yet be entirely sure that the readers would know who they were when they reappeared.

Fox based his characters on people he had known as a boy. In addition to the Skipper they included the Terrible Tempered Mr. Bang (said to be based on his father), Aunt Eppie Hogg (the fattest woman in three counties), Suitcase Simpson, Powerful Katrinka (who sometimes single-handedly hoisted the wayward trolley back on its tracks), and Mickey (Himself) McGuire (a little tough guy). Mickey McGuire was so popular that a child actor named Joe Yule, Jr., tried to cash in on the name's public acceptance. He used it until Fox went to court and proved that he owned the copyright on the character. The actor subsequently changed his stage name to Mickey Rooney.

The Toonerville strip began in 1915 as a daily gag cartoon distributed by the Wheeler Syndicate. The trolley first appeared in the strip in 1916, and the various characters were added in the 1920's and 1930's, when the cartoon was most popular. Toy replicas of the trolley were manufactured, and Educational Pictures produced *Toonerville Comedies by Fontaine Fox.* Books of Fox's collected strips also were published. Although the trolley line was based on the Louisville system and on one in Pelham Manor, N.Y., several other cities claimed to have inspired Fox's creation.

It was the gentle, comedic style of the drawing and the antics of the "Toonerville Folks" that most charmed and amused readers. To William C. Murrell, historian of American graphic humor, the Fox characters played "boisterously and humorously upon the whole gamut of human ambitions and passions from childhood to old age." They were "part and parcel of the daily lives and laughter of thousands in every section of the country."

Fox poked fun at life-as-usual and such varied issues as spring tonic and the country store. Cartoonists like W. T. Webster (creator of Caspar Milquetoast) and Clare A. Briggs (creator of "When a Feller Needs a Friend") also worked in this tradition. The genre of comic art produced by Fox and his contemporaries was truly a product of American culture. Its themes reflected a nation suffering the growing pains caused by the shift from an agrarian to an urban society. Fox was among the earliest comic observers of suburbia, although the suburbia he viewed had little in common with the sprawling communities that grew up after World War II.

Ironically, Fox decided to bring his strip up to date in 1953 by removing the trolley from the strip and replacing it with a gas-driven bus. Three months before his retirement in 1955, he restored the trolley to the strip—readying it, he said, for its final run. At his death the *New York Times* estimated that he had earned more than $2 million from the cartoons.

In 1939, Fox briefly visited the European war zone and wrote a series of humorous articles about his "escape" for the *New York Sun.* During World War II he was a member of the War Department's Division of Pictorial Publicity while continuing to draw the strip. Active in New York City social affairs, Fox was also an accomplished golfer. He died in Greenwich, Conn.

[Fox's work is collected in *Toonerville Folks* (1973). Early books by Fox include *Fontaine Fox's Funny Folk* (1917); *Fontaine Fox's Cartoons,* (1918); and *Toonerville Trolley and Other Cartoons* (1921). American cartooning is discussed in Everette E. Dennis and Melvin L. Dennis, "One Hundred Years of Political Cartooning," *Journalism History,* Spring 1974. An obituary is in the *New York Times,* Aug. 10, 1964.]

EVERETTE E. DENNIS

FRANCK, JAMES (Aug. 26, 1882–May 21, 1964), physicist, was born in Hamburg, Germany, the son of Jacob Franck, a banker, and Rebecca Drucker, both descendants of Sephardic Jewish families. Franck's father wanted his son to study law, but from childhood on Franck was intrigued by natural phenomena and by age thirteen had already decided to become a physicist. After graduating from the Wilhelm Gymnasium in Hamburg, he began university studies at Heidelberg in 1901. He transferred in 1902 to Berlin, where the university physics colloquium run by such professors as Max Planck, Heinrich Rubens, and Emil Warburg made a lasting impression on him. In 1906, he completed his Ph.D. under Warburg with a study of ion mobilities. On Dec. 23, 1907, he married Ingrid Josephson, a Swedish pianist; they had two daughters.

As a postdoctoral assistant to Rubens, Franck conducted research on collisions between electrons and atoms of the inert gases. He found the collisions to be mainly elastic, that is, without loss of kinetic energy. In 1911, he attained university lecturer status as *Privatdozent.* With a younger colleague, Gustav Hertz, he engaged in a thorough study of collisions. The study culminated in the discovery of excitation potentials. The Franck-Hertz experiments, for which both men shared a 1925 Nobel Prize, demonstrated conclusively the transfer of kinetic energy to light energy in discrete quanta. Franck and Hertz thus provided experimental verification of the quantum theory, yielding a new way to measure Planck's constant and presenting in effect the first decisive proof of the quantized energy levels postulated by Niels Bohr.

Following the eruption of World War I, Franck served first as a volunteer and then as an officer in the German army, but in 1916 a severe polyneuritis caused his reassignment to noncombat duty. He served for the rest of the war in Fritz Haber's gas warfare research project in the Kaiser Wilhelm Institute for Physical Chemistry in Berlin-Dahlem. After the war he remained for two more years at Haber's institute.

In 1920, Franck accepted an offer to become professor of physics and director of the Second Physical Institute at the University of Göttingen, where he joined the theoretical physicist Max Born and experimentalist R. W. Pohl.

Franck and Born were bound by common interests and ties dating back to student days in Heidelberg, and their close relationship enhanced the spirit of cooperation that marked the most productive years of the quantum mechanics revolution. Franck trained a generation of fine experimentalists and helped guide many of the best theoreticians of the 1920's.

During these years, his interest widened to include collisions between atoms as well as physical properties of molecules. Particularly significant was his 1925 concept that neither the momenta nor the position of atomic nuclei change appreciably during an electronic transition: given quantum theoretical treatment by the American Edward Condon, the Franck-Condon principle remains fundamental in describing the intensity distribution of absorption and flourescence spectra for simple molecules. By 1933, Franck's research had led to an interest in the process by which light quanta are converted into chemical energy during photosynthesis.

The Göttingen atmosphere, however, was shattered by Hitler's coming to power. Despite contrary advice from colleagues and friends, Franck resigned his chair on Apr. 17, 1933, to protest the regime's racial policies. He labored to find positions abroad for those who were dismissed and left Göttingen himself on Nov. 27, 1933. After visiting professorships at Johns Hopkins University and at Bohr's institute in Copenhagen, he became professor of physical chemistry at Johns Hopkins in 1935. In 1938, he was named professor of physical chemistry at the University of Chicago, where support from the Samuel Fels Fund enabled him to continue his research in photosynthesis. He became a naturalized citizen in 1941.

In December 1942 Franck was put in charge of the chemistry division of the Manhattan Project's Metallurgical Laboratory. He took the post only after he was assured the right, toward completion of the project, to express any reservations he might have to the highest policy-making levels of government. He thus came to chair a committee formed in 1945 to assess the social and political implications of atomic weapons. The result was the "Franck Report" (June 11, 1945), which counseled against the use of atomic bombs on Japanese cities, warned of an arms race with the Soviet Union, and advocated international control of nuclear weapons. The document went unheeded by the United States government, but many young researchers soon echoed its tone when they lobbied against military control of atomic energy. The Franck Report became a symbol of the social responsibility of concerned scientists.

Meanwhile, Franck resumed photosynthesis research. Over the years, his group contributed actively to the field, and his theoretical arguments helped biologists realize that they would have to reconcile biological observation with the principles of atomic and molecular physics. He received the Rumford Medal of the American Academy of Arts and Sciences in 1955 for this work. Although his theories at the biochemical level in photosynthesis have not generally been accepted, his contributions to the understanding of energy transfer at the quantum mechanical physical level have been lasting.

After the war, Franck also encouraged reconciliation with Germany, holding that scientists should not repeat the Weimar error of isolation from politics if they wanted to see a democratic and peaceful Germany created. His wife had died in 1942, and on June 29, 1946, he married German-born Hertha Sponer, a physicist at Duke University who had been one of his assistants in Göttingen. In 1951, Franck was awarded the Planck Medal, and in 1953 he received honorary citizenship from the city of Göttingen, where he died during a visit.

[Franck's papers are in the special collections department of the Regenstein Library at the University of Chicago. Other letters and an extensive oral history interview are included in the collections housed in various locations of the Archive for History of Quantum Physics. Franck was coauthor, with Pascual Jordan, of *Anregung von Quantensprüngen durch Stösse* (1926), which summed up his most important work to that time. A bibliography of his more than 160 publications is included in the best exposition to date of Franck's career: Heinrich Kuhn, "James Franck," *Biographical Memoirs of Fellows of the Royal Society*, 11 (1965), 53–74. See also Alan Beyerchen, *Scientists Under Hitler* (1977); Roderick Clayton, *Molecular Physics in Photosynthesis* (1965); and Alice Kimball Smith, *A Peril and a Hope* (1965). An obituary is in the *New York Times*, May 22, 1964.]

ALAN BEYERCHEN

FRANKFURTER, ALFRED MORITZ (Oct. 4, 1906–May 12, 1965), art critic and connoisseur, was born in Chicago, Ill. Educated at Princeton and at the Institute for Art History in Berlin, he informally continued his studies at Bernard Berenson's villa, "I Tatti," in Florence. Upon returning to the United States in 1927, he joined the periodical *International Studio* as an art critic, soon moving on to *The Antiquarian* and to *Fine Arts* as editor from 1929 to 1934.

He then was a free-lance writer until he joined *Art News* as editor in 1936, and for the next twenty-nine years made that publication pecuiarly his own.

Frankfurter married three times and was the father of three children. His third wife, Eleanor Munroe, had been on the staff of *Art News*.

Frankfurter served on the Executive Committee of the 1939 New York World's Fair and was policy control chief for psychological warfare, overseas branch, of the Office of War Information (1942–1945). For his work in the latter he was awarded the Legion of Merit. He was director of the American pavilion at the Venice Biennale International Exposition of 1948, for which he was awarded the Order of Merit by the Italian government. The French government made him a Chevalier of the Legion of Honor for his services to French art. He served on the board of the Clark Art Museum at Williamstown, Mass., and informally advised many other notable art collectors.

A plump, warm-eyed, and stubborn-jawed bulldog of a person (in his Savile Row clothes, Legion of Honor ribbon in the buttonhole), Frankfurter bustled, barked, and cajoled by turns. During working hours he sought good art and good writing on the subject. After hours he would go considerable distances to find good wines, victuals, and conversation.

Editorially, Frankfurter favored giving a fair shake to out-of-fashion art forms, at the same time condemning stick-in-the-mud art policies. He spoke up for quality as against quantity in art collections and exhibitions. In his efforts to preserve architectural landmarks and prevent such faceless new constructions as the New York Coliseum, he battled officialdom—especially as represented by New York City Parks Commissioner Robert Moses. Elitist by temperament, Frankfurter regarded artists as an unsung elite to be defended.

He gave his deputy (and successor) Thomas B. Hess full scope to promote contemporary movements such as abstract expressionism, which he himself found less than exciting. The Frankfurter-Hess team made *Art News* an important publication in its time—an era when most Americans regarded art as if it were a sissified and somehow fraudulent game.

Frankfurter was not writing, editing, or publishing for the ages, and he knew it. Yet, the sometimes obscure appreciations and occasional thunderclaps that emanated from his magazine were taken very seriously by those who cared about such things. One reason for this was the high quality of the European contributors

whom Frankfurter recruited. He brought Georges Salles, Jean Cassou, André Malraux, Kenneth Clark, Philip Hendy, John Pope-Hennesy, and Cyril Connolly to public notice in the United States. His American list was not much less distinguished, for it included Henry McBride, Robert Beverly Hale, Agnes Mongan, Walter Pach, Aline Saarinen, John Rewald, and Elaine de Kooning.

Frankfurter understood how to receive, and also how to give, delight, not just in art but in people as well, and in the "good things of life." No mere austere ambition haunted Frankfurter. He carved no considerable niche in American culture. What he did accomplish was to radiate a generally sunny and even fructifying influence.

While visiting Jerusalem for the inaugural ceremonies of the Israel Museum, Frankfurter died suddenly. In accordance with his final wish, his remains were interred in the Lutheran cemetery at Jerusalem. The consensus at his funeral was that, friendship apart, the world had lost a particularly cogent, congenial, and chivalrous champion in the cause of art.

[See *New York Times,* May 13, 1965; *Art News,* Summer 1965; *Art News,* Sept. 1965, "Letters" column; *American Artist,* Sept. 1965.]

ALEXANDER ELIOT

FRANKFURTER, FELIX (Nov. 15, 1882– Feb. 22, 1965), legal scholar and Supreme Court justice, was born in Vienna, Austria, the son of Leopold Frankfurter, a rabbinical student-turned-businessman, and of Emma Winter. A paternal uncle was chief librarian of the University of Vienna. Not prospering in business, Leopold Frankfurter brought the family to New York City in 1894; there he became a linen merchant. His naturalization in 1898 conferred citizenship on his children.

Felix Frankfurter was enrolled in P.S. 25, where he began his lifelong love affair with the English language and nourished his patriotic ardor; at his graduation two years later he recited William Pitt's speech on America. He attributed his prowess in speech to a Miss Hogan, who forbade his classmates to speak to him in German. Much of Frankfurter's proficiency and his zest for the written and spoken word were doubtless developed by frequenting the reading rooms of the Cooper Union and neighboring libraries, attending lectures and debates, and haunting the tea shops and coffeehouses for the freedom and excitement of talk. He completed a combined high school and college course at the College of the City of New York, receiving the B.A. in 1902.

After a year as a clerk in the tenement house department of the New York City government, Frankfurter entered Harvard Law School in 1903. The discipline and power of legal studies, the eminence of the faculty, and the impressive backgrounds of the students at first made his diminutive stature—less than five feet, five inches—seem to him symbolic of his status. But when he led his class at the end of his first year, his self-doubts were dispelled. At Harvard, Frankfurter developed a remarkable circle of friends. For a time his roommate was Morris Raphael Cohen, a graduate student in philosophy. Other friends were Emory Buckner, later an admired United States attorney in New York, and Grenville Clark, who became a leader of the New York bar and a pioneer in the movement for world government.

Following graduation in 1906, Frankfurter became an associate in the New York City law firm of Hornblower, Byrne, Miller and Potter, which reputedly had never employed a Jewish lawyer. Shortly thereafter he joined the office of the United States attorney, where he worked under Henry L. Stimson. It was a fateful decision; from it sprang a lifelong immersion in federal law and public affairs, and a commitment to the scrupulous standards of law enforcement that the austere Stimson insisted upon. Frankfurter's work involved largely antitrust and criminal law, as well as the legal problems of immigrants. In fact he served as a general assistant to Stimson, and when the latter resigned to run for governor of New York in 1910, Frankfurter went with him on the campaign trail. Stimson lost the election, but then became secretary of war in President William Howard Taft's cabinet. He appointed Frankfurter legal officer of the Bureau of Insular Affairs, having jurisdiction over American territorial possessions, but treated him as a confidant in handling broader War Department concerns.

Frankfurter remained in the War Department after Woodrow Wilson became president in 1913, though his duties fell far short of his energies and interests. He became a pillar of the House of Truth (so named by Justice Oliver Wendell Holmes), a bachelor residence that was a center of intellectual ferment in the early days of Wilson's "New Freedom." He was one of the first contributing editors of the *New Republic* and an intimate of a circle of literary and political commentators that included Francis Hackett, Herbert Croly, and Walter Lippmann. At that time Frankfurter also became a devoted

friend of two men who, with Stimson, were the most decisive influences in his professional life: Justice Holmes and Louis D. Brandeis, the "people's attorney" of Boston.

The Washington experience was an apprenticeship, and when a call came from Harvard in 1914 to become the first Byrne Professor of Administrative Law, he accepted, entering on a teaching career of twenty-five years, interrupted by a wartime leave in 1917–1920. Bringing his characteristic zest and love of dialectic to his teaching, he expanded the traditional classroom approach (a logical critique within the confines of appellate opinions) to encompass a study of full records of cases, briefs of counsel, biographies of judges, and the interplay of legislative, administrative, and judicial interventions—in short, a holistic view of the legal process. Each year he selected a law clerk for Justice Holmes and, after Brandeis became a Supreme Court justice in 1916, for him as well.

Frankfurter's subjects were weighted on the procedural side: administrative law, federal courts, and public utilities. In each field he produced an innovative casebook for teaching purposes. In addition, he wrote, with James M. Landis, *The Business of the Supreme Court* (1927), a historical account of the procedures and functions of that tribunal, and with Nathan Greene, *The Labor Injunction* (1930), a study of the use and abuse of that weapon in labor disputes. His concern for right procedures was reflected in his service during World War I. In 1917 he was commissioned a major in the judge advocate's department of the army, and appointed secretary and counsel to the President's Mediation Commission, which dealt with labor stoppages in war industries. He investigated the Bisbee deportations, in which more than 1,000 striking copper miners were carried by a force of vigilantes across the Arizona border into New Mexico. Frankfurter's report was strongly critical of the managers of the companies who planned the reprisal against the strikers; but it also pointed out that the strike itself was unjustified and that the basic need was for an orderly, impartial system of adjudication of grievances. Such a system was established by the Mediation Commission.

On instructions from President Wilson, Frankfurter also investigated the Mooney-Billings case in San Francisco, which involved the conviction of radical labor leaders for planting a bomb that killed many people at a Preparedness Day parade in 1916. His report (1918) asserted "ground for disquietude" in "the atmosphere surrounding the prosecution and trial of the case," and recommended that the president use his good offices with the governor of California to secure a new trial. Mooney's death sentence was commuted, and in 1939, Mooney and Billings were finally pardoned. In 1918 Frankfurter was given broader responsibilities as chairman of the interdepartmental War Labor Policies Board, where one of his colleagues was Franklin D. Roosevelt, an assistant secretary of the navy.

After the war Frankfurter became one of the original members of the American Civil Liberties Union. He was appointed by Federal Judge George W. Anderson of Boston to assist in the defense of aliens arrested and held for deportation in a series of episodes that were the product of postwar hysteria. Virtually all of those held were ultimately released. This experience, together with the Bisbee and Mooney-Billings controversies, identified Frankfurter in many minds with radical political and social causes; in fact it was his respect for history, tradition, and received values that impelled him to join the battle on behalf of those whom he saw as victims of a miscarriage of justice.

In this spirit Frankfurter entered the most notable of these causes, the case of Nicola Sacco and Bartolomeo Vanzetti. The two Italian immigrants, who were philosophical anarchists, had been convicted of murder during a payroll robbery after a trial in which the defendants' radical beliefs were, in Frankfurter's words, "raked fore and aft" with extreme prejudice to their case. He was never formally counsel in the case, but energetically assisted the defense at the appellate stage. He published an extensive article in the *Atlantic Monthly* in March 1927, and later expanded it into the book *The Case of Sacco and Vanzetti* (1927). Both works analyzed the evidence; sharply criticized the conduct of the trial judge, Webster Thayer, and the prosecutor; and urged a new trial for the defendants. A commission appointed by Governor Alvin Fuller to review the case supported the conduct of the trial, and the two defendants were executed.

In 1932, Governor Joseph B. Ely stirred the embers of that painful drama by nominating Frankfurter for a seat on the Supreme Judicial Court of Massachusetts. The nomination came as a surprise to the nominee, who was not attracted to the position. Nevertheless, the opposition to the nomination led him to delay his declination until there was assurance that he could be confirmed.

While at Harvard, Frankfurter's relationship with Brandeis was extremely close. When the latter was named to the Supreme Court in 1916,

Frankfurter succeeded to the responsibility of arguing two important cases before that Court: *Bunting* v. *Oregon* (243 U.S. 246 [1917]) and *Stettler* v. *O'Hara* (243 U.S. 629 [1917]). In the former he successfully argued on behalf of the validity of maximum-hours-of-labor legislation; in the latter an equally divided court let stand a decision upholding minimum-wage laws for women.

Justice Brandeis maintained his active interest in Zionist affairs, a subject not likely to come before the Supreme Court, and Frankfurter frequently served as his spokesman. In 1919 Frankfurter was at the Paris Peace Conference seeking to persuade European Zionists to adopt Brandeis' program of social justice as the basis of a mandate for Palestine. One result was a letter from Prince Faisal, chief of the Arab delegation, giving assurances that Jews would "receive a hearty welcome home." In April 1931 Frankfurter published "The Palestine Situation Restated" in *Foreign Affairs*. He charged that British policy was deviating from the principles of the Balfour Declaration of 1917. His belief in the Zionist cause was qualified, he acknowledged, by a dislike of nationalism, and his critical attitude toward Britain was mitigated by his immense admiration for that country.

Frankfurter's relationship with Brandeis was by no means confined to Zionist matters. The published letters of Brandeis (5 vols., 1971–1978) reveal a flow of suggestions for articles, books, studies, and appointments to office—and, indeed, financial subventions to enable Frankfurter to meet the expenses involved in his research and writing.

On Dec. 20, 1919, Frankfurter married Marian Denman, the daughter of a Congregational minister. The civil ceremony was performed by Benjamin N. Cardozo of the New York Court of Appeals in the chambers of Federal Judge Learned Hand. Their courtship had been a protracted one, owing to the coolness of their families to a marriage outside the faith. Marian Frankfurter served, her husband proudly proclaimed, as his literary critic. With Gardner Jackson she edited *The Letters of Sacco and Vanzetti* (1928). The Frankfurters had no children.

When Franklin D. Roosevelt was elected president in 1932, it was widely assumed that Frankfurter would have a place in the administration. When Roosevelt became governor of New York in 1928, he had sought Frankfurter's counsel, particularly concerning the regulation of public utilities. Roosevelt did offer Frankfurter the solicitor generalship, which he declined. Many of his friends were disappointed, feeling that the solicitor generalship would be a springboard to the Supreme Court.

Frankfurter spent the academic year 1933–1934 at Balliol College, Oxford, as Eastman Visiting Professor. It was perhaps the most idyllic year of his life. The impact of his vibrant personality is conveyed by Isaiah Berlin, then a young don, in "Felix Frankfurter at Oxford" (in Berlin's *Personal Impressions* [1981]):

> He was the centre, the life and soul of a circle of eager and delighted human beings, exuberant, endlessly appreciative, delighting in every manifestation of intelligence, imagination or life. . . . No wonder that even the most frozen monsters in our midst responded to him and, in spite of themselves, found themselves on terms of both respect and affection with him. Only the vainest, and those most "alienated" (a term then not in common use) from their fellow men, remained unaffected by his peculiar type of vitality or positively resented it.

The New Deal excited Frankfurter's sympathies and evoked a stream of encouragement and advice to President Roosevelt. In the summer of 1935 he was for several weeks a resident guest at the White House. His counsel was directed less at the early emergency measures of economic recovery than at the subsequent proposals for reconstruction and reform, notably in the areas of securities regulation, labor legislation, and unemployment insurance. For the drafting of legislation covering securities, stock exchanges, and public utility holding companies, Frankfurter enlisted the services of his protégés Benjamin V. Cohen, Thomas G. Corcoran, and James M. Landis. He recognized that much of the new legislation faced a formidable threat from a hostile majority of the Supreme Court, and he counseled a temporizing litigation tactic. But this was not always possible, and by the end of 1936 the National Industrial Recovery Act, the Agricultural Adjustment Act, the Bituminous Coal Act, the Railroad Retirement Act, the Frazier-Lemke Farm Bankruptcy Act, and state minimum wage laws had all been declared unconstitutional by the Supreme Court.

President Roosevelt's response, the Court reorganization bill presented to Congress in February 1937, took Frankfurter by surprise, and placed him in an awkward position. The disorder—a Supreme Court majority that identified its own social and economic philosophy with the mandate of the Constitution—that provoked the plan was real enough, and he had long fought it. But the proposed remedy—the appointment of an additional justice for every member of the Court over the age of seventy who refused to retire (up to a total of fifteen)—was disturbing. It could not fail to offend Brandeis, then in his eighty-first year, and it threatened the principle of judicial independence. Above all, the plan aimed at a false target, the supposed inefficiency of the Supreme Court, when what was needed was a thorough education of the judges, the bar, and the public regarding the Court's misbehavior.

Frankfurter resolved his predicament by public silence while furnishing the president with material sharply critical of the Supreme Court's record in reviewing social legislation. Privately he took the position that it was more important to expose the Court's misdeeds than to pass immediate judgment on the remedy. His formula was to "tell the truth about the Court for a good stretch of time and then I don't care what remedy you propose or oppose," as he wrote to Learned Hand.

When Justice Cardozo died in 1938, there was widespread belief that, as he had been the rightful inheritor of the place left by Holmes, his rightful successor would be Frankfurter. A poll conducted in the autumn of 1938 showed that he was the choice of five times as many lawyers as any other individual; his appointment was also urged by the faculties of leading law schools. He was nominated on Jan. 5, 1939. While his nomination was pending, he was invited to appear before the Senate Judiciary Committee. He did so, although expressing regret that the committee was departing from an almost unbroken practice of refraining from summoning a Supreme Court nominee. Despite Frankfurter's expressed misgivings about the propriety of a judicial nominee's supplementing his past record by present declarations, the procedure in his case has become the prevailing practice. The nomination was reported favorably without dissent, and was confirmed unanimously by the Senate on January 17. Frankfurter took his seat on January 30.

The Supreme Court to which Frankfurter came was entering a new phase. The issue of governmental power over the economy was essentially settled. The "fighting issues" would center increasingly on claims of civil rights and civil liberties. For the vindication of basic rights of participation and fair procedure, Frankfurter found ample safeguard in the Constitution: in its broad guarantees of equal protection and due process, and in the specific provisions of the Bill of Rights. He worked closely with Chief Justice Earl Warren to secure a unanimous decision outlawing racial segregation in public schools (*Brown* v. *Board of Education of Topeka*, 347 U.S. 483 [1954], 349 U.S. 294 [1955]), and he strongly expounded the doctrine of the rule of law in conflicts of this kind (*Cooper* v. *Aaron*, 358 U.S. 1, 20 [1958]). Giving reality to the Fifteenth Amendment's enfranchising of black citizens, he wrote: "The Amendment nullifies sophisticated as well as simple-minded modes of discrimination" (*Lane* v. *Wilson*, 307 U.S. 268, 275 [1939]; also *Terry* v. *Adams*, 345 U.S. 461 [1953]; and *Gomillion* v. *Lightfoot*, 364 U.S. 339 [1960]).

Condemning the summary procedure whereby the attorney general designated organized groups as Communist, Frankfurter wrote: "The heart of the matter is that democracy implies respect for the elementary rights of man, however suspect or unworthy; a democratic government must therefore practice fairness; and fairness can scarcely be obtained by secret, one-sided determination of facts decisive of rights" (*Joint Anti-Fascist Refugee Committee* v. *McGrath*, 341 U.S. 123, 149, 170 [1951]). He drew upon the Supreme Court's supervisory powers over the lower federal courts to require exclusion of confessions extracted during excessively long preliminary detention (*McNabb* v. *United States*, 318 U.S. 332 [1943]; *Mallory* v. *United States*, 354 U.S. 449 [1957]). No one was more exacting in enforcing the requirements of a search warrant upon federal officers (*Harris* v. *United States*, 331 U.S. 145, 155 [1947], dissent). He wrote feelingly on the meaning of academic freedom, specifically the immunity of the college classroom from governmental intrusion (*Sweezy* v. *New Hampshire*, 354 U.S. 234, 255 [1957]).

But for Frankfurter as a judge there was no single supreme simplicity, however noble its aspect. To rely on the judges for the maintenance of national ideals seemed to him to be ultimately enervating. From Holmes and Brandeis he derived the teaching of judicial self-restraint, and from Brandeis he learned the cognate lesson of the complexity of issues in the pattern of litigation: among them, standing to sue, federalism, justiciability, the scope and contours of a decree. Whether, as critics have suggested, Frankfurter's mentors would have developed a fully principled escape from these constraints in the vindication of basic human rights, as some of their utterances suggested, can only be conjectured; for Frankfurter the question raises the more general problem of discipleship. To him,

at any rate, the melancholy experience of judicial policymaking in the pre-1937 period remained relevant; and if in resisting the advances of some of his colleagues, Frankfurter placed himself in an uncongenial position, he did so to counter what he regarded as a too freewheeling, stimulus-response approach to judging.

Having written the Supreme Court's opinion sustaining the compulsory flag salute in public schools, over the objection of Jehovah's Witnesses that for them it was a profanation (*Minersville School District* v. *Gobitis*, 310 U.S. 586 [1940]), Frankfurter stoutly maintained his position in dissent when a majority of the Court overruled that decision (*West Virginia State Board of Education* v. *Barnette*, 319 U.S. 624, 646 [1943]). He joined in the decision upholding the Smith Act, which declared it unlawful to organize a party that taught or advocated violent overthrow of the government, though he disavowed belief in the wisdom or efficacy of such a law (*Dennis et al.* v. *United States*, 341 U.S. 494, 517 [1951]). He protested that the Court was entering a "political thicket" when it held that grossly unequal voting districts in a state violated the equal-protection guarantee of the Fourteenth Amendment (*Baker* v. *Carr*, 369 U.S. 186, 266 [1962], dissent).

During his years on the bench, Frankfurter kept up his correspondence with an extraordinary range of friends. A volume of his essays, published in 1956 under the title *Of Law and Men* includes memorials on such diverse figures as Alfred E. Smith and Alfred North Whitehead, Harold J. Laski and Lord Lothian, John Dewey and Thomas Mann. His gift of appreciation, warm and uninhibited, when directed toward his law clerks and other young friends more than matched his demanding expectations of them.

While Frankfurter was not, as were John Marshall and Holmes and Brandeis, an originator of transforming thought, he was a centrally influential figure in law and government. His immense energy, both intellectual and physical; the intensity of his caring for people and ideas; his unabashed reverence for the institutions of America and its heroes; and his learning carried with exuberance ignited the wide circle he reached, and left his imprint on them.

In April 1962, Frankfurter suffered a stroke, from which he never fully recovered, and on August 28 of that year he retired from the Court. In 1963 he was awarded the Presidential Medal of Freedom. He died in Washington. Shortly before his death Frankfurter made plans for a simple funeral service. Although he had not been a practicing Jew, he asked that the Hebrew prayer for the dead (Kaddish) be recited. "I came into the world a Jew," he said, "and . . . I want to leave it as a Jew." Because some of the assemblage would not understand the prayer, he suggested that it be explained, perhaps compared with the Catholic Magnificat. He would be a teacher to the end—and beyond.

[Frankfurter's general correspondence is at the Library of Congress; his Supreme Court papers are at the Harvard Law School library. Among his nontechnical writings not mentioned in the text are *Mr. Justice Brandeis and the Constitution* (1931); and *Mr. Justice Holmes and the Supreme Court* (1938, 1961). Collections of his writings include *Law and Politics*, edited by Archibald MacLeish and Edward F. Prichard (1939); *Of Law and Men*, edited by Philip Elman (1956); and *Of Law and Life and Other Things that Matter*, edited by Philip Kurland (1965). A perceptive biographical essay, sympathetic but not uncritical, is in Joseph P. Lash, *From the Diaries of Felix Frankfurter* (1975). Other biographies are Helen Thomas, *Felix Frankfurter* (1960); Liva Baker, *Felix Frankfurter* (1969); and Harry N. Hirsch, *The Enigma of Felix Frankfurter* (1981). Relations with Roosevelt are shown in Max Freedman, ed., *Roosevelt and Frankfurter* (1968). Also see Louis L. Jaffe, "The Judicial Universe of Mr. Justice Frankfurter," *Harvard Law Review*, Jan. 1949; Paul A. Freund, "Mr. Justice Frankfurter," *University of Chicago Law Review*, Winter 1959; Wallace Mendelson, ed., *Felix Frankfurter: A Tribute* (1964), and *Felix Frankfurter: The Judge* (1964); Joseph L. Rauh, "Felix Frankfurter: Civil Libertarian," *Harvard Civil Rights–Civil Liberties Law Review*, Nov. 1976; David W. Levy and Bruce A. Murphy, "Preserving the Progressive Spirit in a Conservative Time: The Joint Reform Efforts of Justice Brandeis and Professor Felix Frankfurter, 1916–1933," *Michigan Law Review*, Aug. 1980. Conversations with Frankfurter are recorded in the Columbia University Oral History collection, and are published in Harlan Phillips, ed., *Felix Frankfurter Reminisces* (1960). Memorial proceedings in the Supreme Court are contained in U.S. Reports 382:xix–xlvi (1965). An obituary is in the *New York Times*, Feb. 23, 1965.]

PAUL A. FREUND

FRAZIER, EDWARD FRANKLIN (Sept. 24, 1894–May 17, 1962), sociologist and educator, was born in Baltimore, Md., the son of James Edward Frazier, a bank messenger, and of Mary E. Clark, who occasionally did domestic work. He attended elementary and secondary school in Baltimore, and received a diploma from Baltimore High School in 1912.

Frazier's family life was characterized by a high degree of discipline. His father, who had taught himself to read and write, was the dominant family figure. He instilled in his children a respect for formal education, in order that they might escape the kind of manual work he had to do.

James Frazier died in an accident when Franklin was thirteen. His mother therefore had to work as a domestic servant in order to support the family. Young Frazier worked part-time as a common laborer and, as the oldest child, assumed some responsibility for his siblings.

Upon graduating from high school, Frazier received a scholarship to Howard University. Although he had to work in order to supplement his scholarship, he completed the classical curriculum in the required four years, and was graduated with honors in 1916. After graduation he was an instructor of mathematics in the high school division of the Tuskegee Institute (1916–1917). He next taught English and history at Saint Paul's Normal and Industrial School, Lawrenceville, Va., for a year. In 1919–1920 he taught French and mathematics at Baltimore High School.

In 1919, Frazier began graduate work in sociology at Clark University, and received the M.A. in 1920. He credited Professor Frank Hankins with having introduced him to the possibility of utilizing sociological theory for objective analysis of social problems. During 1920–1921, Frazier was a research fellow at the New York School of Social Work. The following academic year he was a fellow of the American-Scandinavian Foundation, conducting a study of the Danish folk high schools.

Upon his return to the United States in 1922, Frazier became the director of the summer session at Livingstone College, Salisbury, N.C. On Sept. 14, 1922, he married Marie Ellen Brown, a teacher. They had no children.

In the fall of 1922, Frazier became professor of social science at Morehouse College, in Atlanta, Ga. Later he added the duty of director of the Atlanta University School of Social Work, an institution he helped to establish for the training of black social workers. Frazier's performance in these dual roles and his writings on sociological subjects marked the emergence of a promising academic career. This was suddenly interrupted by publication of "The Pathology of Race Prejudice" (*Forum*, June 1927). His views on white prejudices led to threats of violence, and he was forced to leave Atlanta.

Frazier then became a research fellow in the Department of Sociology at the University of Chicago. After two academic years (1927–1929) as a doctoral student, he accepted a position as lecturer in sociology at Fisk University, Nashville, Tenn. He received the doctorate in 1931, and subsequently became research professor of sociology. In 1934 Frazier joined the faculty at Howard University as professor and head of the Department of Sociology. He remained at Howard until his death.

Frazier's major research interests dealt with the black family and race relations. For him these areas were related. He studied the family as a social work unit; the family's contribution to the adjustment of its members; and the impact of urbanization upon family organization. Frazier's dissertation, *The Negro Family in Chicago* (1932), analyzed the variations found in black family organization and behavior in different areas of the city. It was regarded by students in the field as making a distinctive contribution by combining the case study and ecological methods in the study of family behavior. His interest in free blacks resulted in the publication of *The Free Negro Family* (1932).

The Negro Family in the United States (1939) was Frazier's definitive contribution to the subject. It is regarded as a "natural history" of the black family, analyzing the forces that influenced black family life over time. It gives attention to the influence of the African background, slavery, the experiences of the American plantation system, the Emancipation and Reconstruction period, and the impact of large-scale urbanization.

Frazier was interested in race relations in the United States and in the effects of such phenomena as slavery, prejudice, and discrimination upon black community life and personality. His *Black Bourgeoisie* (1957) analyzed the distortions that occurred in black life as a consequence of blacks' marginal status in the American society. The black middle class represented an attenuated group, lacking a firm basis in the economic order. This marginality and the extreme isolation that characterized black community life resulted in a set of values that varied from those of the white middle class. According to Frazier, the black middle class was more interested in conspicuous consumption and display than in production and savings; thus, it imitated the behavior of an upper class that possessed leisure and wealth.

Frazier's interest in race relations was not restricted to the United States. He investigated racial interaction and family life in Brazil and the Caribbean as a Guggenheim fellow in 1939. For most of his professional life he maintained an interest in European-African relationships. The social, economic, and political consequences of the impact of European expansion

upon African and Asiatic peoples was the subject of his *Race and Culture Contacts in the Modern World* (1957).

Frazier received many academic honors. He also was elected president of the District of Columbia Sociological Society, the Eastern Sociological Society, and the American Sociological Society (now American Sociological Association). In the last post (1948) he became the first black to be elected an official of a national professional association. At the time of his death he was vice-president of the African Studies Association.

In addition to his contribution as a teacher and researcher, Frazier had two significant nonacademic assignments. In 1935 he was appointed director of the Mayor's Commission on Conditions in Harlem, which investigated the social and economic conditions related to the Harlem riots of that year. From 1951 to 1953, he was chief of the Division of Applied Social Sciences of the United Nations Educational, Scientific, and Cultural Organization.

Frazier also taught, usually on a part-time basis, at Sarah Lawrence College, the New York School of Social Work, New York University, the University of California at Berkeley, and Carleton College (Minnesota). He died at Washington, D.C.

[Frazier's writings not cited in the text include "Durham: Capital of the Black Middle Class," in Alain Locke, ed., *The New Negro*, (1925); "The Negro Family in Bahia, Brazil," *American Sociological Review*, Aug. 1942; *The Negro in the United States* (1949); "The Failure of the Negro Intellectual," Feb. 1962; and *The Negro Church in America* (1963). See "E. Franklin Frazier 1894–   ," in Howard W. Odum, *American Sociology* (1951); Arthur P. Davis, "E. Franklin Frazier 1894–1962: A Profile," *Journal of Negro Education*, Fall 1962; G. Franklin Edwards, ed., *E. Franklin Frazier on Race Relations* (1968); "E. Franklin Frazier," in James Blackwell and Morris Janowitz, eds., *Black Sociologists* (1974); and "E. Franklin Frazier: Race, Education and Community," in Robert K. Merton and Matilda W. Riley, eds., *Sociological Traditions from Generation to Generation* (1980). Also see Grace E. Henderson, "The Life and Works of E. Franklin Frazier" (Ph.D. diss., University of Virginia, 1978); and Dale R. Vlaser, "The Social Thought of E. Franklin Frazier" (Ph.D. diss., University of Iowa, 1978). An obituary is in the *New York Times*, May 22, 1962.]

G. FRANKLIN EDWARDS

FREED, ALAN J. (Dec. 15, 1921–Jan. 20, 1965), a nationally known disc jockey, called the "Father of Rock 'n' Roll," was born in Johnstown, Pa., the son of Charles Freed, a clothing store clerk, and of Maude Freed. He grew up in Salem, Ohio. While he was studying mechanical engineering at Ohio State University, from which he received the B.S. in 1943, he played trombone and led his own band, The Sultans of Swing, named after a famous Harlem band. Following graduation and two years in the U.S. Army, he began his radio career in 1945 on WKST in New Castle, Pa., playing classical music.

In 1947, Freed moved to WAKR in Akron, Ohio, where he hosted a radio program "Request Review." For about six months in 1950, he hosted a television dance show on the Cleveland station WXEL. He then returned to radio and took a job at WJW in Cleveland, playing classical music.

Through his association with a local record store owner, Leo Mintz, Freed launched a new show, "The Moon Dog Rock 'n' Roll Party," in June 1951. It would change the course of American popular music. While visiting Mintz's record store, Freed noted the popularity of black "rhythm and blues" records with white youths. In the music trade rhythm and blues records were known as "race" records because they were sold mostly to jukebox operators in black neighborhoods. Freed began to follow his evening classical music show with the music that he called "rock 'n' roll." Actually, Freed did not invent the term "rock 'n' roll"—it is of blues origin and was used as a euphemism for fornication—but he deserves full credit for naming the new music and popularizing the term.

Freed's show was carried by stations outside Cleveland, and he soon received national attention. He added to his fame when, beginning in 1952, he staged his "Big Beat" all-black-talent rock 'n' roll shows at the Cleveland Arena and at movie theaters in other cities during school holidays. Whenever the slim, youthful announcer walked on stage, usually wearing a loud, checkered sports jacket, he was greeted with a shrieking welcome akin to that given the Beatles nearly a decade later.

In 1954, Freed moved to WINS in New York, where "Alan Freed's Rock 'n' Roll Party" occupied the key 6:30–11 P.M. spot Monday through Saturday. His fame exploded. He had roles in four movies: *Rock Around the Clock* and *Don't Knock the Rock* (1956), *Rock, Rock, Rock* (1957), and *Go Johnny Go* (1959). He also shared writers' credits on a number of records, including the hits "Sincerely" and "Maybelline," although these credits were probably gifts to insure their being played on the air.

Freed defended rock music and its fans against charges of immorality and juvenile delinquency, and answered criticisms of rock music with charges of racial bias. He favored playing black artists because of their basic contribution to rock, and refused to play white artists who made "cover" records of black originals, regardless of the cover record's sales and popularity.

In 1957, Freed hosted a "Rock 'n' Roll Party" on CBS-TV that became controversial because it was sponsored by Camel cigarettes, which was trying to capture the teen-age market, and because the camera caught a black singer dancing with a white girl. Freed's "Big Beat" stage shows were banned in many cities because of a riot following a show at Boston in 1958. Freed was charged with inciting to riot and anarchy. He fought the charges for two years, at an estimated cost of $30,000, before they were dropped.

In July 1958, Freed filed for bankruptcy, claiming his liabilities exceeded his assets by $50,000. Feeling that WINS had failed to support him against the Boston charges, he quit the station and moved to WABC in New York. He also hosted a dance party on New York's WNEW-TV. In the fall of 1959, rumors about a "payola" scandal surfaced. ("Payola" meant accepting money or favors in return for playing a particular record on the air.) WABC asked Freed to sign a statement denying he had ever taken payola. He refused, and was fired. He later signed a similar statement for WNEW-TV, but his dance show was dropped.

The payola scandal wrecked Freed's professional life. After losing his New York shows, he held a daytime job with KDAY in Los Angeles, but his career took a depressing downward dip. In 1960, Freed was charged with accepting $30,650 in payola from six record companies. He always denied taking direct bribes, and said he accepted gifts only when he played records he was sure would be hits anyway. Nevertheless, in 1962, while at radio station WQAM in Miami, Freed pleaded guilty to two charges of commercial bribery. He was given a six-month suspended sentence and fined $300; five other charges were dropped.

His career shattered, Freed moved to Palm Springs, Calif., where he spent the last years of his life. In 1963 he told reporters that he was bankrupt. The following March he was indicted for evading $37,920 in income taxes stemming largely from payola payments received between 1957 and 1959.

Through October 1964, Freed played jazz records on radio station KNOB in Los Angeles.

Shortly thereafter he was taken ill with uremia, and died in Palm Springs. He was one of radio's most vibrant personalities, and he brought an excitement to disc jockey programming that was little known before him.

Freed was married three times. His first marriage was to Betty Lou Bean; they had two children. After divorcing his first wife, he married Jacqueline McCoy; they had two children. The marriage also ended in divorce. His third wife's name was Inga.

[See Arnold Shaw, *The Rockin' '50s* (1974). Obituaries are in the *New York Times* and *New York Herald Tribune,* Jan. 21, 1965, and in *Billboard,* Jan. 30, 1965.]

JOSEPH P. McKERNS

FREEMAN, JOSEPH (Oct. 7, 1897–Aug. 9, 1965), poet, radical journalist, publicist, and novelist, was born in the province of Poltava in the Ukraine, the son of Isaac Freeman, a merchant, and Stella Lvovitch. Both his grandfathers were rabbis. When he was seven, the Freeman family came to the United States and settled in the Williamsburg district of Brooklyn, N.Y. In a few years, Isaac Freeman became a prosperous builder and real estate dealer. Joseph's troubled boyhood—memories of anti-Jewish violence in the Ukraine and the initial poverty of the family after the arrival in the United States—instilled in him an awareness of injustice and confirmed somber aspects of his Jewish heritage. As a teen-ager he considered himself a socialist; he was familiar with the writings of Lincoln Steffens and Upton Sinclair, and was ready to repudiate the life-style and politics of his father.

In 1916 Freeman entered Columbia University, where his interests in literature and politics were stimulated by Charles A. Beard, John Erskine, Raymond Weave, and H. W. L. Dana, and by his college friends, Kenneth Burke and Matthew Josephson. Freeman headed the varsity debating team and graduated in 1919.

Freeman's first job was on the editorial staff of Harper and Brothers. He became a naturalized citizen in 1920 and in July of that year went to Europe. Deciding to become a journalist, he took a job as Paris correspondent of the *Chicago Tribune.* During this period he also wrote and published poetry. Attracted to the private realm of the poet, he was at the same time increasingly committed to the hopeful expectations of a world socialist revolution. World War I, he later said, strengthened his belief that "only Socialism could save mankind from barbarism."

After working for a short time as London correspondent for the *Chicago Tribune* and New York *Daily News,* Freeman returned to the United States in 1921 and joined the editorial staff of the *Liberator.* The *Liberator* had been founded by Max Eastman in 1918 after its predecessor, the *Masses,* was suspended under the threat of government suppression for "interference with military enlistment." Freeman, an avid reader of the *Masses* as a youth, greatly admired the writings of Eastman, Floyd Dell, and John Reed, as well as the cartoons of Art Young.

Throughout his life Freeman sought to fuse and master two strong but conflicting impulses: the urge to try to create a just society, requiring direct political action; and the urge to liberate the individual from society, which he believed was the role of the poet and the artist. In his writings for the *Liberator* from 1920 to 1924 Freeman tried to reconcile his love of romantic poetry and art with his concern about unemployment, poverty, and injustice. Ultimately, though, he turned out to be "more of a poet than a revolutionary," according to his friend Granville Hicks.

The *Liberator,* embracing Marxist doctrine, was turned over to the American Communist party in 1924 and merged with other Communist publications. In 1926 Freeman and Michael Gold, the party's leading literary lights, revived the *Masses* as the *New Masses.* During the twenty years of its existence the *New Masses* adhered to the Communist party line, although Freeman in 1936 denied that Communists financed it. In 1924 Freeman began working as publicity director for the American Civil Liberties Union, and the following year joined the staff of Tass, the Soviet news agency. He worked off and on for Tass until 1931, continuing to write poetry and Marxist literary criticism. "For a long time," Freeman said later, "Michael Gold and I were the only literary critics in the United States attempting to evaluate art and literature by revolutionary standards."

On his first book, *Dollar Diplomacy: A Study in American Imperialism* (1925), Freeman collaborated with Scott Nearing, an independent radical. The work, which was also published in Germany, Mexico, and Russia, was described by R. L. Duffus in the *New York Times* (Nov. 8, 1925) as "a handbook for propagandists against 'Imperialism' . . . full of carefully selected ammunition."

Late in 1926, Freeman worked his way to the Soviet Union on a freighter and took a job at the office of the Comintern as a translator. His transformation from a romantic rebel to a committed revolutionary progressed rapidly. He was depressed, however, by the conflicts in the party after the expulsion of Leon Trotsky, and dispirited by the unprincipled career-hunting he saw. But he did not lose faith in Communism.

In the spring of 1927, Freeman spent several months in Gemany. Returning to the United States, he worked for Tass and taught journalism and literature to workers' classes in New York City. In 1929 he was Tass correspondent in Mexico. He collaborated with Joshua Kunitz and Louis Lozowick in *Voices of October* (1930), a study of Soviet art, literature, and films. Freeman contributed substantial sections on films, music, and literature.

In 1932 Freeman married Charmion von Wiegand, a painter and art critic. They had no children.

Freeman's book *The Soviet Worker* (1932) dealt with the social, cultural, and economic status of labor in the Soviet Union. The work collated important printed material, much of which was in Russian. Earlier, Freeman worked in Hollywood for MGM with Russian novelist Boris Pilnyak on a script called *Soviet*, but the film was never produced. During the early 1930's he was active as a writer in explicating Marxist ideas and formulating the principles governing the creation of proletarian literature. He wrote an excellent critical introduction to *Proletarian Literature in the United States* (1935), a book edited by Granville Hicks, Michael Gold, Joseph North, and others. Freeman argued that even the poet expresses "a class reality" and that "all art is class-conditioned." At the first American Writers Congress (April 1935), he urged writers to voice their sympathy with the proletarian revolution. He had been a co-founder of the *Partisan Review* in 1934 and in the first issue of the magazine was listed as a member of the editorial board and as the contributor of four poems.

Freeman's ardent adherence to the Soviet Union as "the living test of our faith in the socialist revolution" caused him to defend Stalin and the Moscow Trials (1936–1938) after many American intellectuals—his early idol Max Eastman among them—had retreated from Communism.

While working on the preface to a projected volume of his poems, Freeman decided to write his autobiography. *An American Testament: A Narrative of Rebels and Romantics* (1936) was Freeman's outstanding literary achievement, an extremely interesting and informative book. Freeman tried "to explain how a man living in modern times arrives at the viewpoint known as Communism." Theodore Draper called the book "one of the few Communist human documents worth preserving." In a perceptive review Malcolm Cowley found that Freeman accurately and movingly revealed his essential position in the radical movement—"that of a translator and intermediary—one who explained to artists the ways of radical politicians, and explained to radical politicians the feeding and fighting and mating habits of the queer unfeathered birds that nested in the arts." However, Freeman's measured words of praise for Trotsky in the book greatly displeased Russian Communists as well as Stalinists in the United States. As a result he was, on orders from Moscow, expelled from the party.

In 1937 Freeman left New York City and settled in the foothills of the Catskills, at Accord, N.Y. For fifteen years he had dedicated himself to the cause of Communism but now that part of his life was over. He had not been able to resolve the problems of being at the same time a zealot and a critic, a poet and a politician. By late 1939 all of his connections with left-wing publications and organizations were severed. At the end of the period of Freeman's life recounted in *An American Testament* (the spring of 1926, when he was 29), he judged his own career thus far to have been "a mass of disconnected, contradictory actions and beliefs." The fragmentations and contradictions continued during the remainder of his life.

Freeman did free-lance writing after 1937 and went back for a time to his old post as publicity director of the American Civil Liberties Union (1940–1942). He wrote more poetry and tried his hand as a novelist. *Never Call Retreat* (1943) was described by *New York Times* reviewer Stanley Young as "powerful and filled with dramatic action and color . . . the characters fully realized and memorable." *The Long Pursuit* (1947), a comic, hard-boiled story based on Freeman's experiences with a USO unit touring Germany after V-E Day, won little critical acclaim.

From 1943 to 1945 he worked on the basic plan for the *Information Please Almanac,* an annual compendium of facts and statistics. Henry Luce commissioned him to write a 30,000-word article on twenty-five years of the Russian Revolution and then liked the completed work so much he had it printed as a pamphlet and mailed to all the members of Congress. Freeman was subsequently invited to work for *Time.* He was willing to do so, but he was "screened" by Whittaker Chambers, whom he had met in 1928 and worked with on the staff of the *New Masses*. Chambers made it clear to Luce that he did not want his former colleague on the staff of *Time*, and Freeman was not hired. In 1948 Freeman joined the staff of Edward L. Bernays' public relations firm.

Freeman was a genial person. Granville Hicks, who thought his friend's diverse interests kept him from achieving the lofty reputation to which he was entitled, described Freeman as "massive, dark, and careless of his appearance." Floyd Dell said he was "one of the most interesting talkers in the world, and a friend of whom I was very fond from the first meeting."

Freeman died in New York City.

[The Joseph Freeman papers are deposited in the Columbia University Library. On Freeman and his career, see Louis Kronenberger, "Making of a Communist," *Nation*, Oct. 24, 1936; Malcolm Cowley, "Unfinished Symphony," *New Republic*, Oct. 28, 1936; James T. Farrell, *A Note on Literary Criticism* (1936), Chapter 10; Stanley J. Kunitz and Howard Haycraft, eds., *Twentieth Century Authors* (1942; and First Supp., 1955); Harry R. Warfel, *American Novelists of Today* (1951); Walter B. Rideout, *The Radical Novel in the United States 1900–1954* (1956); Theodore Draper, *The Roots of American Communism* (1957); Daniel Aaron, *Writers on the Left* (1961), a brilliant examination of left-wing writers in the United States from 1912 to the early 1940's with extensive treatment of Freeman; Granville Hicks, *Part of the Truth* (1965); Daniel Bell, *Marxian Socialism in the United States* (1967); and Kent M. Beck, "The Odyssey of Joseph Freeman," *Historian*, Nov. 1974, an appraisal in depth. Obituaries appeared in the *New York Times*, Aug. 11, 1965, and in *Publishers Weekly*, Sept. 6, 1965.]

WILLIAM McCANN

FROST, ROBERT LEE (Mar. 26, 1874–Jan. 29, 1963), poet, was born in San Francisco, Calif., the son of William Prescott Frost, Jr., a hard-drinking newspaperman and dabbler in politics, and of Isabelle Moodie. Following her husband's death in 1885, Frost's mother went with her children to Salem, N.H., where she began teaching school. She tended to coddle her son, filling him with tales of heroism and indulging his lack of discipline, aversion to work, and dislike of school. (These character traits later plagued Frost, especially during the first twenty years of his marriage, when he was hard-pressed to earn a living.) Despite his relative lack of formal preparation, Frost passed the entrance examinations for Lawrence (Mass.) High School and matriculated in September 1888.

His high school years were a turning point. Fascinated by classical languages, science, and especially by the poetry in Francis Turner Palgrave's *The Golden Treasury of the Best Songs and Lyrical Poems in the English Language*, Frost earned a reputation as a serious student and promising writer. His first poem, "La Noche Triste," a ballad inspired by W. H. Prescott's *The Conquest of Mexico*, was published in the Lawrence High School *Bulletin* in April 1890. Frost was later editor of the *Bulletin*, to which he contributed editorials and other poems. When he graduated in June 1892, he was the class poet and covaledictorian with Elinor Miriam White, whom he would soon marry. Although the official wedding date was Dec. 19, 1895, evidence suggests that Frost and Elinor so feared the separation to be caused by his plans to enter Dartmouth and hers to attend St. Lawrence University that they conducted their own marriage ceremony in the summer of 1892.

Frost entered Dartmouth in September 1892 with financial aid from his grandfather and a scholarship from the college. He did not complete the first semester. Using the excuse that his mother needed help in her private school at Methuen, Mass., but in truth jealous of Elinor's life at St. Lawrence and afraid that she would be attracted to other men, he returned to Methuen, where he taught for a short while, and then worked in the Arlington Mill in Lawrence. Frost was unable to accept criticism of any kind from any source, and he blamed Elinor for his failure to complete his studies at Dartmouth. Although he could not hold any job for long, he was convinced that all would be well if Elinor would leave school and join him at home. Her refusal, plus his jealousy of her intellect, were the beginnings of a tension that persisted in their marriage until her death (March 21, 1938). The tension also affected the subject and tone of Frost's poetry. Later poems such as "Bereft" and "The Subverted Flower" touch on the domestic strain of this period.

Frost taught school in Salem, N.H., during the spring term of 1894. In March, the New York *Independent* accepted "My Butterfly: An Elegy." Appearing in the Nov. 8, 1894, issue, it was Frost's first professionally published poem. The bibliographical importance of "My Butterfly" is matched by its personal significance. The $15 that he received as payment convinced him that he could make his living as an author. Resentful of Elinor's college career, self-deceived about his lack of direction, and blind to his many faults, he continued his efforts to persuade Elinor to join him. Partly to celebrate the success of "My Butterfly," and partly to prove his potential as a writer, Frost, in March 1894, privately printed five of his poems in a two-copy edition that he called *Twilight*. He traveled to St. Lawrence to present a copy to Elinor, but when she did not respond in the manner he had anticipated, he destroyed his copy (the remaining one is in the Clifton Waller Barrett Library of the University of Virginia) and embarked on one of the most astonishing journeys of his life: a three-week trip to the Dismal Swamp of Virginia made in the fall of 1894 in the vain hope that his serious injury or violent death would punish Elinor for the wrongs he had doubtless imagined but nevertheless believed.

Frost survived this trip uninjured and returned to Lawrence, where he worked as a reporter for the *Sentinel* and the *Daily American*. He spent the spring of 1895 teaching in his mother's school. After his marriage to Elinor in December 1895, he published "The Birds Do Thus" in the *Independent* (Aug. 20, 1896). The first of the Frosts' six children was born in September. During 1896 and 1897 Frost and Elinor made their living by teaching, but their marriage was strained by her silences and his self-centeredness. Frost continued to publish poems that he later judged unworthy of collecting. In September 1897 he entered Harvard as a special student. Although he considered his time at Harvard a significant influence on his career because of his study of classical languages and his introduction to the philosophy of William James, Frost followed his usual pattern and withdrew from the university in March 1899 without receiving a degree. Suffering from severe bouts of hay fever and shocked by the death of his first child in July 1900—a tragedy that increased the pressure on his less than ideal marriage—Frost received financial help from his grandfather, which he would never acknowledge, and moved to a farm in Derry, N.H. They stayed there until September 1909.

The Derry years were among the most artistically creative of Frost's life, for he wrote most of the poems that appeared in his first two books. Yet during his first years there he had to cope with periods of suicidal depression. His mother died in 1900, and his grandfather the following year. Although his grandfather left him the Derry farm and an annuity, Frost had lost the two people who had supported him in various ways during the multiple failures of his life. By 1905 he had four children under six but no income save what he could earn from his chickens and the annuity—about $500 a year. However small, the annuity provided the financial margin he needed to write poetry. Wracked by vindictiveness toward those he believed

thwarted him, and probably by guilt over his laziness and ill treatment of his wife, he used his art to order his despair, to provide, as he would write in later years, a "momentary stay against confusion." In September 1906, Frost began teaching full-time at the nearby Pinkerton Academy, a position he kept until the summer of 1911. He moved to Derry Village in September 1909 and two years later to Plymouth, N.H., where he began teaching at the normal school. He sold the Derry farm in November 1911.

Frost's years as a teacher were by and large successful. He introduced unstructured classes and modern literature, notably the plays of William Butler Yeats. Although he placed such well-regarded poems as "The Tuft of Flowers" and "Into Mine Own" in obscure magazines, no one knew of his extraordinary experiments with blank verse in poems of the first rank that remained unread and unpublished. Like Ezra Pound, T. S. Eliot, and other American poets of the era, Frost was discouraged by conservative editors who favored the rhythms and rhymes of Victorian poetry. And like Pound and Eliot, he left America.

In September 1912, Frost took his family to England. Not only did he escape an atmosphere that encouraged his depression, but he was lucky enough to meet other writers who hoped to change the course of poetry: Pound, Yeats, Edward Thomas, Wilfred Gibson, Lascelles Abercrombie, Harold Monro. Now nearly forty years old, Frost had finally found people who cared about the arts as he did.

All of Frost's mature poetry up to this time had been written in the relative isolation of rural New England. The only opinions he had received of watershed poems written before 1912 (poems such as "The Death of the Hired Man," "An Old Man's Winter Night," "The Subverted Flower," and the sonnets "Hyla Brook" and "The Oven Bird") came from friends who did not understand or editors who did not care. The sojourn in England gave him the opportunity to discuss the innovations in what was then called "the new poetry" and to begin searching for a publisher.

Frost did not have to search for long. David Nutt, a London firm, published *A Boy's Will* (1913) and the extraordinary *North of Boston* (1914). The poems in *A Boy's Will* are short lyrics, many of them love poems for Elinor. Although a few have the inversions and poetic language associated with nineteenth-century poetry, others, such as "Mowing" and "Storm Fear," indicate the experiments with voice tone and colloquial diction that distinguish

Frost's great poetry. The lyrics are arranged to chronicle a boy's maturation from idealism and self-centeredness to a realization of love and an acceptance of loss. In the first edition Frost included prose glosses for all but two of the thirty-two poems. Although these often provide an ironic perspective upon the immature boy, they were omitted from later reprints.

The English Georgian poets with whom Frost associated were excited about *A Boy's Will*, but it was Ezra Pound who listened through the traces of old-fashioned diction and heard the rhythms of a genuinely new poet. Pound said later that he had "hammered" Frost's "stuff" into the journal *Poetry* by writing appreciative reviews. Pound was especially impressed by *North of Boston.*

He had reason to be. In 1914, *North of Boston* was so different from contemporary poetry that it baffled readers as perspicacious as Ford Madox Ford. Many critics called poems such as "Home Burial" and "The Death of the Hired Man" free verse, but Ford realized that there was a meter, although he did not know how to define it. Brimming with an enthusiasm equal to Pound's, he described some of the lines in "Mending Wall" as a "truly bewildering achievement." Ford's reaction was typical. Readers were unprepared for narrative poems that used "sentence sounds," Frost's term for the merger of free-flowing colloquial speech rhythms and the regularity of unrhymed iambic pentameter. These variations with blank verse are Frost's greatest contribution to American prosody. Although often misread as gentle portraits of rural values, many of the poems in *North of Boston* reflect the defeat, the shattering of communication, and the struggle to find order amid the losses that Frost continued to experience.

When Frost and his family returned to America in February 1915, he was heralded as a leading voice of the modern poetic renaissance. Editors who had rejected his work now requested the same poems; Henry Holt, the New York publisher, decided to publish his books; and Tufts University invited him to be the Phi Beta Kappa poet for 1915. Still jealous of the success of other poets and bitter toward those who disagreed with him, Frost carefully constructed a mask of the gentle farmer-poet. This pose endeared him to a public that found his poetry more accessible than the work of his major contemporaries. Even his strained marriage was publicized as ideal.

Frost played the role for all it was worth. The mask hid the man and helped the poet. For Frost was a survivor, a man of incredible determination who used his art to order his sense of chaos. After two decades of neglect, he understandably relished the adulation. In 1916, Harvard named him Phi Beta Kappa poet; the National Institute of Arts and Letters elected him to membership; and Holt published *Mountain Interval.*

Frost was generally disappointed with the form of *Mountain Interval* because he had not been given time to arrange the poems with his usual concern for organization, but the book included some of his best and most popular poems, among them "The Road Not Taken" and "Birches." Although not as dark a collection as *North of Boston,* many of these poems illustrate the barriers among men and between man and nature that Frost accepted as a constant predicament. "An Old Man's Winter Night" and "The Hill Wife" are excellent examples.

By this time Frost's popularity was so sustained that he began what he later called "barding around"—accepting invitations to read and to teach at various colleges—for instance, at Amherst (1917–1920, 1923–1925, 1926–1938) and at the University of Michigan (1921–1923, 1925–1926). Amherst awarded Frost the first of his forty-four honorary degrees in 1918. He won the first of his four Pulitzer Prizes for *New Hampshire* (1923). This collection and *West-Running Brook* (1928) were his two major books in the 1920's. Although the title poem of *New Hampshire* illustrates Frost's continued interest in blank-verse narratives, the great poems in these two collections are the short lyrics that combine dramatic tension and the ambiguities of nature imagery to communicate a dark world view. "Fire and Ice," "Stopping by Woods on a Snowy Evening," "To Earthward," and "Acquainted with the Night" echo the sentiment, expressed in "West-Running Brook," that existence is "The universal cataract of death/That spends to nothingness" and that can be resisted only by man's determination to create form.

In 1930, Frost received another Pulitzer Prize for *Collected Poems* (1930) and was elected to the American Academy of Arts and Letters. He won the Russell Loines Poetry Prize in 1931 and was named Phi Beta Kappa poet at Columbia University in 1932 and Charles Eliot Norton professor of poetry at Harvard in 1936. His only new volume of poetry published in the 1930's, *A Further Range* (1936), won the Pulitzer Prize.

But despite the awards and acclaim, the 1930's was a decade wracked by personal tragedy for Frost. His daughter Marjorie died from puerperal fever in 1934, and his wife died of a heart attack in 1938, refusing to permit Frost to enter her sickroom. His son Carol committed suicide in 1940. In addition, *A Further Range* was the first of his books to be attacked by such influential critics as Newton Arvin, Rolfe Humphries, and R. P. Blackmur. Published in the Great Depression, with fascism on the rise and World War II on the horizon, the collection infuriated readers who believed that Frost's conservatism, as expressed in "A Lone Striker," "Build Soil," and the famous "Two Tramps in Mud Time," indicated his selfish refusal to address serious problems. Never again did Frost enjoy the nearly unanimous approval of literary critics.

Yet what finally matters is not political persuasion but poetic genius, and Frost showed that he had not lost his art in "Desert Places," "Neither Out Far Nor in Deep," and "Design," lyrics that again illustrate the fear and uncertainty that were often at the core of his life. Although critical opinion split, honors continued to increase. In 1939, Frost was awarded the Gold Medal for Poetry of the National Institute and was appointed Ralph Waldo Emerson fellow in poetry at Harvard; in 1940 he was Phi Beta Kappa poet at Tufts; in 1941 he won the gold medal of the Poetry Society of America and was Phi Beta Kappa poet at Harvard and at William and Mary. In 1942 he published *A Witness Tree,* the last of his books to win the Pulitzer Prize. The severe attacks of guilt and depression that Frost suffered following the tragedies of the 1930's, especially the death of his wife, spurred his thoughts of suicide. But with the help of Kathleen Morrison, to whom *A Witness Tree* is dedicated, he again displayed his tenacity, his refusal to be beaten down by any death but his own. Some of his finest poems appeared in *A Witness Tree,* especially the dark lyrics "The Most of It," "November," and "All Revelation." In "The Silken Tent" and "The Subverted Flower," which he refused to publish until after Elinor's death, he provides oblique and contrasting views of his forty-two-year marriage.

From 1943 to 1949, Frost was George Ticknor fellow at Dartmouth. During these years he published two book-length blank-verse narratives about man's puzzling relationship with God, *A Masque of Reason* (1945) and *A Masque of Mercy* (1947), and his eighth collection, *Steeple Bush* (1947), which revealed a decided falling off of artistic power. Frost was now seventy-three years old. Although *Steeple Bush* includes the great "Directive," a major poem by any standard, too many of the lyrics seem writ-

ten more to display Frost's conservative skepticism than to continue his probes into the human dilemma.

In his last years Frost was the most admired American poet of the century. The mask of the gentle bard of the nation had held firm, and most readers were blind to the sense of fear beneath the surfaces of his poems. He was given a lifetime appointment as Simpson lecturer at Amherst in 1949, saluted by the United States Senate in 1950, and appointed consultant in poetry in the Library of Congress in 1958. Probably his greatest popular triumphs came in 1961, when he read "The Gift Outright" at the inauguration of President John F. Kennedy, and in 1962, when President Kennedy presented him with the Congressional Medal and sent him on a goodwill tour of Russia. Frost's ill-considered public remarks after the tour misrepresented both President Kennedy and Premier Nikita Khrushchev, and the president never again received him.

Frost's last book, *In the Clearing* (1962), contains two important poems: "For John F. Kennedy His Inauguration" and "Kitty Hawk," a musing on the relationship between the material and the spiritual. In early January 1963, Frost was awarded the prestigious Bollingen Prize in poetry. Some three weeks later he died in Boston.

The shock at the details of Frost's personal life, which were not published until after his death, was an overreaction to the revelation that the poet was not the white-haired, grandfatherly bard of the nation. Even Bernard DeVoto's rebuke of Frost as a "good poet but a bad man" is too simple. One cannot accept the poet and dismiss the man without being unjust to both. The revelations of Frost's jealousy, selfishness, and spite were shocking primarily because they did not square with the image that the poet had carefully nurtured and the public had gratefully believed. Frost was neither a hateful man nor a saint. Perhaps he had more than his share of serious flaws, but he was also generous and strong. Frost was finally an artist of the first rank, a poet who achieved what he called "the utmost of ambition" and lodged many poems in American literature where "they will be hard to get rid of."

[Significant collections of Frost's material are in the Clifton Waller Barrett Library of the University of Virginia; the Jones Library at Amherst, Mass.; and the Dartmouth College Library, N.H. Frost's letters are collected in Margaret Bartlett Anderson, *Robert Frost and John Bartlett* (1963); Louis Untermeyer, ed., *The Letters of Robert Frost to Louis Untermeyer* (1963); Lawrance Thompson, ed., *Selected Letters of Robert Frost* (1964); and Arnold Grade, ed., *Family Letters of Robert and Elinor Frost* (1972). A selection of essays is in Hyde Cox and Edward Connery Lathem, eds., *Selected Prose of Robert Frost* (1966); his interviews are in Edward Connery Lathem, ed., *Interviews with Robert Frost* (1966). The official biography is Lawrance Thompson, *Robert Frost: The Early Years, 1874–1915* (1966); ... *The Years of Triumph, 1915–1938* (1970); ... *The Later Years, 1938–1963* (1976), with R. H. Winnick.

Bibliographical sources include W. B. Shubrick Clymer and Charles R. Green, *Robert Frost: A Bibliography* (1937); Donald J. Greiner, *Checklist to Robert Frost* (1969); Joan St. C. Crane, *Robert Frost: A Descriptive Catalogue of Books and Manuscripts in the Clifton Waller Barrett Library University of Virginia* (1974); Frank and Melissa Christensen Lentricchia, *Robert Frost: A Bibliography, 1913–1974* (1976); and Donald J. Greiner, in *First Printings of American Authors*, vol. I (1977).

Studies include Lawrance R. Thompson, *Fire and Ice* (1942); Reginald L. Cook, *The Dimensions of Robert Frost* (1959); John F. Lynen, *The Pastoral Art of Robert Frost* (1960); George W. Nitchie, *Human Values in the Poetry of Robert Frost* (1960); Reuben A. Brower, *The Poetry of Robert Frost* (1963); James Radcliffe Squires, *The Major Themes of Robert Frost* (1963); Donald J. Greiner, *Robert Frost: The Poet and His Critics* (1974); Frank Lentricchia, *Robert Frost: Modern Poetics and the Landscapes of Self* (1975); Richard Poirier, *Robert Frost: The Work of Knowing* (1977). The most comprehensive collection of essays about Frost is Jac Tharpe, ed., *Frost: Centennial Essays*, 3 vols. (1974–1978). Obituaries are in *Obituaries from the Times 1961–1970* (1975).]

DONALD J. GREINER

FUNK, WILFRED JOHN (Mar. 20, 1883–June 1, 1965), publisher and lexicographer, was born in Brooklyn, N.Y., the son of Isaac Kauffman Funk, one of the founders of the publishing firm of Funk and Wagnalls, and of Helen Gertrude Thompson.

In 1909, following graduation with a B. Litt. from Princeton University, where he had been an English major and class poet, Funk joined the family company. His first job was selling *The Jewish Encyclopedia* in New York City. He also prepared advertising copy and directed the firm's educational department. After his father's death in April 1912, Funk became secretary of Funk and Wagnalls. He moved up to the vice-presidency two years later, and in 1925 he became president, remaining in that position until 1940. He married Eleanor McNeal Hawkins on July 29, 1915; they had four children.

While working in publishing, Funk also wrote poetry. His light verse appeared regularly in

magazines after 1927. Six volumes of his poems, including two later collections, were published. The first of them was *Manhattans, Bronxes and Queens* (1931). In 1933 he won the Cora Smith Gould Poetry Prize, awarded by *Bozart and Contemporary Verse*, a magazine published at Oglethorpe University, in Atlanta, Ga., for a poem entitled "The Surgeon."

In March 1936, Funk took over the editorship of *Literary Digest*, which Funk and Wagnalls had founded in 1890. The magazine's circulation had been falling for several years because of the Great Depression and competition from newer weekly magazines, particularly *Time*. Funk continued the efforts begun earlier to revive the magazine, but although he tried to make it more like its competition, he was unable to arrest the circulation decline.

As editor, he oversaw the 1936 *Literary Digest* presidential straw poll, which reported the Republican challenger, Alfred M. Landon, to be far ahead of incumbent President Franklin D. Roosevelt. Since beginning its straw polls in 1916, the *Digest* had earned a reputation for accuracy, particularly in presidential election polls. Its 1936 experience has been cited as a classic example of bad polling technique. Professional pollsters have been especially critical of the *Digest*'s method of mass mailings of ballots to persons whose names were selected from various sources, including telephone books and its own subscription rolls.

Although the 1936 poll is often cited as the major reason for the magazine's demise in 1938, it was only the last blow to an already tottering publication. Funk served as editor until June 1937, when the magazine was purchased by, and merged with, the *Review of Reviews*. It ceased publication in February 1938. Funk used money from the 1937 sale to start new publishing ventures: Kingsway Press, Yourself Publications, Your Health Publications, and Publications Management. He was president and director of each company and editorial director of the magazines they established, the first of which was *Your Life* (1937), a pocket-size magazine devoted to self-improvement. In April 1940, Funk resigned as president of Funk and Wagnalls to start Wilfred Funk, Inc., a book publishing firm. One of its first books was John F. Kennedy's *Why England Slept* (1940). Funk sold his interest in the firm to Funk and Wagnalls in 1954, and in 1961 he divested himself of his other publishing interests.

Funk was best known for his books and articles on vocabulary improvement and etymology and for other works exemplifying "his taste for whimsical research," as one reviewer noted of his first published prose volume, *So You Think It's New* (1937). After his death at Montclair, N.J., *Time* wrote: "Wilfred J. Funk was born to words. He reveled in them, ranked them and made a small fortune from them." His work, *Time* observed, "made the entire nation self-conscious about its vocabulary," and he was "a tireless missionary for the English language." He viewed the language as living and evolving, "formed by everyday usage."

Over the years Funk periodically announced lists that, the *New York Times* wrote, "became cultural conversation pieces." They included the ten most overused words (*okay, terrific, lousy, racket, definitely, gal, honey, swell, contact, impact*); the ten most beautiful words (*dawn, hush, lullaby, murmuring, tranquil, mist, luminous, chimes, golden, melody*); and a 204-word vocabulary of a pet dog. With Norman Lewis, Funk wrote *30 Days to a More Powerful Vocabulary* (1942), which remained a top seller among vocabulary-building books for many years. From 1946 until his death he also wrote a popular *Reader's Digest* monthly feature, "It Pays to Increase Your Word Power." In the preface to his *Word Origins and Their Romantic Stories* (1950), Funk wrote: "I wish that the reader might be encouraged to walk among words as I do, like Alice in Wonderland, amazed at the marvels they hold."

[In addition to those mentioned in the text, Funk's books include *When the Merry-Go-Round Breaks Down* (1938); *If You Drink* (1940); and *The Way to Vocabulary Power and Culture* (1946). See also "Rimes and Dictionaries," *Publishers Weekly,* July 25, 1931; Frank Luther Mott, *A History of American Magazines 1885–1905* (1957); Theodore Peterson, *Magazines in the Twentieth Century* (2nd ed.; 1964); and "Words That Sizzled," *Time,* June 11, 1965. An obituary is in the *New York Times,* June 2, 1965.]

RONALD S. MARMARELLI

GAITHER, HORACE ROWAN, JR. (Nov. 23, 1909–Apr. 7, 1961), lawyer and foundation executive, was born in Natchez, Miss., the son of Horace Rowan Gaither, a banker, and Marguerite Chamberlain. Shortly after his birth the family moved to Portland, Oreg., where the senior Gaither began his banking career. He later became a bank examiner in Kansas City, Mo., and in 1919 moved to San Francisco.

Gaither was educated in the public schools of Piedmont, Calif. After frequently listening to his father testing Boy Scouts for merit badges, he was able to qualify as an Eagle Scout at the age of twelve. He was graduated from Piedmont

High School in 1926 and, with the B.A., from the University of California at Berkeley in 1929. On July 18, 1931, Gaither married Charlotte Cameron Castle, whom he had known since high school. They had two sons. In 1933, Gaither graduated from the University of California Law School, tied for first in his class. He then spent three years in Washington, D.C., working for the Farm Credit Administration. Next he joined the San Francisco law firm of Cooley, Crowley, and Supple. While practicing over the ensuing five years, he also taught law at Berkeley night school.

The entry of the United States into World War II was a watershed in Gaither's professional life. After Pearl Harbor he offered a course in "war law" at Berkeley, which attracted the attention of Monroe Deutsch, dean of the undergraduate college. Upon the death of the assistant director of the Massachusetts Institute of Technology (MIT) Radiation Laboratory in 1942, Deutsch proposed Gaither as a successor, and Gaither was shortly thereafter appointed to this position. Until 1945, although not a scientist, he participated in both the planning and operation of the laboratory. His colleagues were Lee DuBridge, Alfred Loomis, Ernest O. Lawrence, Luis Alvarez, Karl Compton, Vannevar Bush, and James Killian. It is revealing of Gaither's personality and his way of working that all these men remained his friends for life. His abilities in program planning and his skill in helping others to reach a consensus, even on matters in which he was a layman, won Gaither the respect of scientists.

In 1948, Karl Compton, a trustee of the Ford Foundation, persuaded Henry Ford II to put Gaither in charge of a study group that was to prepare a program and policy for the foundation, which was then about to receive the bequests of Henry and Edsel Ford. The trustees wanted the study group "to take stock of our existing knowledge, institutions, and techniques in order to locate the areas where the problems are most important and where additional efforts toward their solution are most needed."

"Problems," in contradistinction to "needs," was a key word, and such an approach suited Gaither's temperament. He showed great breadth of interest in social policy (there were only one natural scientist and one physician on his advisory committee), assuming that science and health already were adequately financed. Social policy, based on social science and management, was the field in which the real possibilities might emerge. In September 1950 the trustees accepted Gaither's report. The Ford

Foundation was to engage in solving problems of world peace, democracy, the economy, education, and the scientific study of human behavior.

Gaither's work with the Ford Foundation and organized philanthropy preoccupied him for the rest of his career. In March 1951, at first on a part-time basis, Gaither accepted the post of associate director of the Ford Foundation, with primary responsibility for the Behavioral Sciences Program. The other associate directors were Robert M. Hutchins of the University of Chicago, Milton Katz of Harvard, and Chester A. Davis, a longtime administrator of government programs in agriculture. Paul Hoffman, president of the foundation, wanted activists, and he got them. But almost immediately serious and systematic friction developed among the officers. When Hoffman took leave of absence in 1952 to campaign for Dwight Eisenhower, Henry Ford was forced to assume the title of acting president, and he became very aware of the internal tensions. He was also being plagued by complaints from Ford Motor Company officials over some of the more cavalier Ford Foundation pronouncements. Hoffman was forced to resign in February 1953. Gaither was named acting president of the foundation and given the mandate to move its headquarters from Pasadena, Calif., to New York City. In September he was elected president, and he quickly turned away from Hoffman's style of staffing. His officers were less in the public eye and more amenable to administrative discipline. Gaither was preeminently a generalist at a time when generalists were in particular demand. Even his abilities as an administrator were largely confined to helping others reach a consensus. His way of conducting a meeting was to let the participants talk until (he hoped) a consensus emerged. He rarely made decisions himself. Every stage of his career in the Ford Foundation revealed this pattern of operation.

In 1954, against great opposition and in a charged atmosphere of personal rivalries, Gaither and a member of his new team, William McPeak, pushed through lump-sum grants to the Fund for the Advancement of Education and the Fund for Adult Education that were terminal in everything but their labels. Gaither, characteristically, acted as a mediator, while McPeak did the arguing and paid the personal price. The Fund for the Advancement of Education ultimately was merged into the Ford Foundation, but so was its president, Clarence Faust, who was given McPeak's job as vice-president for education.

Before this occurred, though, Gaither and McPeak had invested hundreds of millions in programs to raise faculty salaries. They also set up the National Merit Scholarship Corporation and the Council on Library Resources, and put a new and permanent base under the American Council of Learned Societies' program supporting postdoctoral scholars. The groundwork for a national expansion of the Woodrow Wilson graduate fellowship program also was laid.

Gaither moved the Ford Foundation toward a more responsible set of budgeting decisions. During a period of congressional attacks (Representatives Eugene Cox and Carroll Reece) on the foundation, Gaither muted much of the "static" directed at Henry Ford from Ford Motor Company executives. He kept them informed about what the foundation was doing, something Hoffman, Hutchins, and Katz had either neglected or disdained to do.

It is difficult to say how much Gaither's hold on the presidency of the Ford Foundation was weakened by his frequent choice of conciliation over decisiveness. Donald K. David, vice-chairman of the board of trustees, had supported Gaither's appointment in 1953, but by 1956 he decided that Gaither's usefulness had ended. He moved his own office into the Ford Foundation, and became a de facto layer between the president and the board. A few months later Gaither was elevated to chairman of the board, and the search for a new president was initiated. In 1958, Gaither became ill. He remained a trustee but gave up the chairmanship to John J. McCloy.

During his career at the Ford Foundation, Gaither continued to be concerned with scientific development and the applications of technology and the social sciences to national security. When the RAND Corporation was established at Santa Monica, Calif., in 1946, Gaither became a trustee, as well as secretary and general counsel. He was chairman of the board between 1948 and 1959.

The ambiguous position of RAND, somewhere between the private sector, the military, and the aerospace industry, steadily brought the institution into controversy, although chiefly after Gaither's death. But one venture into national security policies during Gaither's lifetime proved controversial from the start. In April 1957, MIT president James Killian told President Eisenhower that Gaither was the man to organize a security resources panel to be established by the Science Advisory Committee, pursuant to an action by the National Security Council.

Entitled "Deterrence and Survival in the Nuclear Age," the report of the panel called for a massive fallout shelter program, for both "wide-area" and "point" defense against missiles, and for an improvement of the breadth and depth of the strategic nuclear weapons arsenal. Appearing within weeks after the Soviet launching of Sputnik, the report failed to discuss arms control and warned, for the first time, of the danger of a missile gap: "The evidence clearly indicates an increasing threat which may become critical in 1959 or early 1960."

The Eisenhower administration kept the Gaither Committee report classified, and did not endorse or implement it. Gaither commented: "I believe it will remain a secret until it is obsolete, then it will no longer be news." Declassified in 1973, the report was published in 1976 by the Joint (Congressional) Committee on Defense Production. In transmitting it Senator William Proxmire of Wisconsin said: "Few documents have had as great an influence on American strategic thinking in the modern era as the Gaither Committee Report of 1957."

Gaither died in Boston. He had exerted only nominal control over Ford Foundation affairs since 1956, but without his efforts the foundation in its first decade would not have contributed to making organized philanthropy a profession.

[Report of the Study for the Ford Foundation on Policy and Program (1950) was the work of several hands, but Gaither took responsibility for the whole. The Gaither Committee report appeared as Deterrence and Survival in the Nuclear Age (1976), and a number of Gaither's speeches were published by the Ford Foundation between 1954 and 1958. No published study devoted to Gaither exists, but see Waldemar Nielsen, The Big Foundations (1972); Dwight Macdonald, "The Ford Foundation," in The New Yorker, Nov. 26, 1955; "Men of the Ford Foundation," Fortune (Dec. 1951); and "World's Biggest Helping Hand," Saturday Evening Post, Nov. 27, 1954. The obituary appeared in New York Times on Apr. 8, 1961.]

W. McNeil Lowry

GALLI-CURCI, AMELITA (Nov. 18, 1882–Nov. 26, 1963), opera singer, was born in Milan, Italy, the daughter of Enrico Galli, a well-to-do businessman and banker, and Enrichetta Bellisoni. The family was musical: her paternal grandfather had been an opera conductor, and her paternal grandmother, a well-known opera singer. Amelita showed talent at an early age. She began the study of piano at five, receiving her general education at the International Insti-

tute (1895–1901) and the Liceo Alessandro Manzoni (1901–1905). She became proficient in German, French, Spanish, and English.

At sixteen Galli-Curci graduated from the Milan Conservatory, winning a gold medal in piano. But the composer Pietro Mascagni, a family friend, advised her to cultivate her voice. Not satisfied with any teacher she knew, she undertook to teach herself. (She claimed to have learned voice production by listening to the birds.) After reading many books, Galli-Curci based her technique on the writings of Manuel Vicente Garcia and Lilli Lehmann. In 1906 she auditioned for Vogherd, an impresario in southern Italy who was looking for an inexpensive prima donna to sing Gilda, and made her debut in Rigoletto at Trani on December 26 of that year. Her success was encouraging. At Trani she met the Curci brothers—Luigi, a painter, and Gennaro, an operatic basso and pianist. She married Luigi, who had become the Marchese di Simeri, on Feb. 24, 1908; they had no children.

Galli-Curci's official debut took place in Rome, at the Teatro Costanzi, on Apr. 20, 1908, in Bizet's Don Procopio. In 1910 she went to Buenos Aires for a season directed by Leopoldo Mugnone. Another soprano sang the leads, but one day when she was indisposed, Galli-Curci stepped in as Gilda, winning a real success. Engagements followed in various Italian cities, in South America again, in Spain, and in Russia. In 1915 she was back in Buenos Aires, this time singing with Enrico Caruso. An engagement in Havana and a tour of Central America followed.

In 1916, stopping over in New York, Galli-Curci met the vocal teacher William Thorner, who had heard her in Italy. He introduced her to Cleofonte Campanini, director of the Chicago Opera Association. (Rumors that she had been turned down by Giulio Gatti-Casazza, general manager of the Metropolitan Opera House, were vigorously denied.) Campanini engaged her for two performances at $300 each, but after hearing the dress rehearsal he extended her contract through the season at $1,000 a performance. After her debut this was increased to $1,500.

Galli-Curci's sensational debut in Chicago as Gilda on Nov. 18, 1916, made operatic history. Critics with long memories looked back to Adelina Patti and Jenny Lind for comparable performances. This single performance established her as the reigning coloratura singer of her time, and she triumphantly met the test in subsequent performances.

Even before her American debut Galli-Curci was making records for the Victor Talking Machine Company, and the first of them established her, along with Caruso, on the best-seller lists. She did not perform in New York until Jan. 28, 1918, when she sang the title role in *Dinorah* with the Chicago Opera Association. Not surprisingly the critics were guarded in their praise. Richard Aldrich of the *New York Times* hailed "the completest and most beautiful voice of any woman singer at the present time," but other reviewers noted that other singers had displayed more dazzling coloratura. One critic declared that she sang flat, but Gennaro Curci, who claimed to have been her coach, insisted that it was a matter of tone production: "Mme. Galli-Curci has a true ear; she knows when she flats."

In 1918, Galli-Curci separated from her husband, and was divorced on Jan. 6, 1920. On Jan. 15, 1921, the year she became an American citizen, she married Homer Samuels, her accompanist. They had no children. She made her Metropolitan Opera debut, as Violetta in *La Traviata*, on Nov. 14, 1921. Although that performance was disappointing, she remained a popular member of the company for nine seasons. For the first two she was also a member of the Chicago company, but she left it in a dispute over which opera was to open the 1924 season; her last performance was on Jan. 4, 1924. In 1930 she canceled her contract with the Metropolitan, declaring that opera was dead, its audiences diminishing because it was out of date. That same year she embarked on a tour of Europe, but soon broke it off because of illness. For several years she had been suffering from a goiter that interfered with her breath support. After a tour of South America, South Africa, and India (1934–1935), she underwent surgery in 1936 and tried a comeback as a lyric soprano, making her new debut at Chicago as Mimi in *La Bohème*, on Nov. 24, 1936. Although her audience welcomed her back warmly, critics were frank; after a few more appearances she retired to California. In her California years Galli-Curci read a great deal, notably the works of Emanuel Swedenborg, and became interested in Indian philosophies. After her husband's death in 1956, she spent much of her time painting. She died at La Jolla, Calif.

Early on, Galli-Curci developed an interest in American songs, although her recital programs, like those of other prima donnas, were a mixture of styles and languages, from coloratura arias to simple ballads. She spoke of the song repertory as musically superior to opera, but rarely ventured into the field of lieder. She sang only four times on the radio, the first two occasions on behalf of Victor Records.

Galli-Curci professed never to read reviews of her singing, declaring that she knew when it was good or bad. Her voice was notable for one of its type, being perfectly even over a range of two and a half octaves, from B-flat to F in alt. The ease with which she tossed off pyrotechnics, especially high staccato arpeggios, was unique, as was her fluid legato in the lower register. These talents can still be heard on her numerous recordings, but she owed part of her appeal to personal attractiveness and a gracious manner. Although she could move audiences to tears by singing "Home, Sweet Home," she never sentimentalized. The effects she achieved were purely vocal.

[Galli-Curci wrote "My Career as a Prima Donna and How It Developed," *Musical Observer*, May 1919. Also see Charles E. Wagner, *Seeing Stars* (1940); C. E. LeMassena, *Galli-Curci's Life of Song* (1945); Mary F. Watkins, "Aftermath," *Opera News*, Apr. 25, 1949; John Freestone, "Collector's Corner," *Gramophone*, July 1953; Max de Schauensee, "Violetta Assoluta," *Opera News*, Oct. 27, 1954. An obituary appeared in the *New York Times*, Nov. 27, 1963.]

PHILIP LIESON MILLER

GARIS, HOWARD ROGER (Apr. 25, 1873–Nov. 5, 1962), journalist and creator of the Uncle Wiggily stories, was born in Binghamton, N.Y., the son of Simeon H. Garis, a railroad telegrapher, and Ellen A. Kimball. Because his father was frequently transferred, Garis' early education was often interrupted. During his family's stay in Syracuse, he walked through the freight yards with his father and learned to read from the words printed on the boxcars. Soon he became an avid reader, with a special fondness for the *Arabian Nights* and the tales of Hans Christian Andersen.

Around the age of sixteen, Garis was rebuffed by a young girl he admired. From that experience came his first novel, "A World Without Women." He sent the 400-page manuscript to Harper's, but it was rejected. Even so, he hoped to become a writer. Such aspirations were not well received by his practical father, who promptly sent him off to study mechanical engineering at Stevens Institute of Technology in Hoboken, N.J.

Unsuccessful at Stevens, Garis left at about the age of nineteen and turned to writing magazine articles. After many rejections, he sold his first story to *Happenchance* for $9. In 1894 his father's death forced him to secure regular employment in order to support himself, his mother, and his two sisters. For $7 a week and board, he found work at a weekly called *The Sunnyside*, an undertakers' publication. Soon he moved on, trying one job after another until he began writing for *Town Talk*, a weekly owned by Thomas Burke, city editor for the *Newark Evening News*. This was his first break, for it led to a personal connection with Burke and then, when he was twenty-three, to a job as a cub reporter for the *News*. He married Lillian C. McNamara, a society editor for the *News*, on Apr. 26, 1900; they had two children. For more than fifty years Garis was a reporter and special writer for the *News*, although his tenure was punctuated by "retirements" that allowed him to pursue his other writing interests.

During off hours at the *News*, Garis began to write and sell stories to such magazines as *Companion* and *Argosy*. In 1902, J. S. Ogilvie published his historical novel, *With Force and Arms: A Tale of Love and Salem Witchcraft*, which sold fewer than 5,000 copies and earned him no royalties. Two years later Lippincott published his first children's book, *Isle of Black Fire*.

Around 1905, Garis accepted an offer from Edward M. Stratemeyer to write for the Stratemeyer syndicate. Stratemeyer provided plot outlines and established pen names for writers of children's books. With his active imagination and his ability to write a 35,000-word book in about a week, Garis began turning out the "Motor Boys" books under the pseudonym Clarence Young. These books focused on the romance and danger of the recently invented automobile.

With the success of the "Motor Boys," Garis went on to write about the young inventor Tom Swift. All the Swift books were published under the pseudonym Victor Appleton, and Garis wrote many of them. A 1910 Grosset and Dunlap advertisement sums up the spirit and intent of the Swift series:

Every youngster is filled with the marvels of invention displayed in motor cars, motor boats, submarine boats and airships. It is the purpose of these spirited tales to convey . . . the wonderful advances in land and sea locomotion. Stories like these impress themselves on the youthful memory—cling to it like a burr—and their reading is productive only of good.

The Swift books sold in tens of thousands, but Garis received no royalties, only a fixed stipend of $125 per book. He seemed content with this

arrangement, as was his wife, who also worked for the Stratemeyer syndicate. Together they wrote some of the "Bobbsey Twins" books. For Garis this marked the beginning of a prolific career in juvenile writing, a career that would produce more than 700 children's books (many written under pseudonyms) and more than 15,000 stories concerning his most famous creation, Uncle Wiggily.

Garis created Uncle Wiggily in 1910, when Edward M. Scudder, owner and publisher of the *Newark Evening News*, asked him to write a daily children's column for the paper. While on a walk after Scudder's request, Garis crossed paths with a rabbit that had long, wiggly ears. At that moment he conceived of Uncle Wiggily, the gentleman rabbit with the striped rheumatism crutch and the silk top hat. In the stories Uncle Wiggily engages in everyday adventures and constantly outsmarts the "Skillery-scallery" alligator and other villains. Each Uncle Wiggily story ends with the promise of another: "And if the gold fish doesn't try to flip out of its bowl and go to sleep in the canary bird's cage, pretty soon we'll have another Uncle Wiggily story." The first Uncle Wiggily story was published in the *News* on Jan. 30, 1910. The stories, read by children and adults alike, became quickly popular and were nationally syndicated. Garis wrote six Uncle Wiggily stories every week for more than fifty years.

Like Uncle Wiggily, Garis was an optimist; when any adversity threatened, he would simply say, "Oh hum suz-duz and a basket of carrots— let's not worry." In 1950 Garis and his wife moved to Amherst, Mass., to live with their son, Roger. He continued to write his Uncle Wiggily stories until his death at Amherst.

Although many of Garis's children's books follow simplistic plot lines and introduce flat characters, they nevertheless convey a sense of adventure and excitement. His Uncle Wiggily stories manage to rise above his other works because they present memorable and innocently humanized animal characters in a fantasy world with distinctly amusing qualities.

[See George H. Douglas, "Howard R. Garis and the World of Uncle Wiggily," *Journal of Popular Culture*, 1974–1975. The best biographical source is Roger Garis, *My Father Was Uncle Wiggily* (1966). An accurate obituary is in the *New York Times*, Nov. 6, 1962.]

PHILIP LUTHER

GASSER, HERBERT SPENCER (July 5, 1888–May 11, 1963), physiologist, was born in Platteville, Wis., the son of Herman Gasser, a physician, and of Jane Elizabeth Griswold. His father named him for the British philosopher Herbert Spencer, whose writings he admired. Young Gasser received his secondary education at the State Normal School in Platteville. An avid reader, he pursued a variety of hobbies, including music, furniture building, and photography.

Upon his graduation in 1907, Gasser entered the University of Wisconsin, where his academic interests became focused on zoology. After completing undergraduate requirements in only two years, he took courses in the newly organized medical school. There he studied physiology with Joseph Erlanger and pharmacology with Arthur S. Loevenhart. In 1911, although still a student, Gasser was appointed instructor in physiology. Since the University of Wisconsin offered only preclinical medical education in those years, Gasser transferred to Johns Hopkins in 1913 to complete his training. After receiving his M.D. in 1915, he returned to the University of Wisconsin as instructor in pharmacology.

Gasser's primary interest, however, was physiology. In 1916, his former teacher Erlanger invited him to join the Department of Physiology, which he was organizing at Washington University, St. Louis. Following the outbreak of World War I, Gasser and Erlanger began studying the relationship between trauma-induced blood loss and shock; they published eight papers on various aspects of this topic. At the request of Loevenhart, in the summer of 1918 Gasser joined the Armed Forces Chemical Warfare Service in Washington, D.C.; as a pharmacologist he conducted research on gas agents for military use. After the armistice he returned to Washington University.

Gasser then initiated the series of investigations that would distinguish him as one of the world's leading neurophysiologists. With a classmate from Johns Hopkins, H. Sidney Newcomer, an expert in physics, he devised a vacuum tube amplifier, which he coupled to a string galvanometer to record the progression of electrical impulses along the nerve. In 1921 they published the first amplified recording, from the phrenic nerve, of the action potentials that collectively constitute the nerve impulse. But Gasser realized that the method employed was not sufficiently sensitive to achieve undistorted results.

Erlanger then joined Gasser in an attempt to display, on the face of a cathode-ray tube, the amplified nerve activity in mixed nerve trunks. This was made possible with an oscillograph provided by the Western Electric Company. In 1922 they published these pathbreaking oscillograph recordings; included were the first clear representations of nerve-action potentials. Erlanger and Gasser demonstrated that each spike in the recorded waveforms was actually composed of individual spikes reflecting electrical activity within many individual nerve fibers. Their ability to bring recent advances in electronics and physics to bear ingeniously on questions in physiology opened the way to a series of critically important discoveries concerning nerve structure and function.

Gasser's research in neurophysiology was interrupted in 1921 when he accepted an appointment as professor of pharmacology at Washington University. Shortly afterward, Abraham Flexner, author of the renowned Carnegie Foundation report *Medical Education in the United States and Canada* (1910), visited Washington University to review its progress in establishing a full-time medical faculty. Upon seeing Gasser, then only thirty-two years old, tall and slight, Flexner reportedly asked the dean, "What are you doing, making freshmen professors?" But Flexner arranged for Gasser to spend two years abroad (1923–1925) on a grant from the Rockefeller Foundation as part of a program to improve the quality of American medical education. Gasser studied in London, Munich, and Paris, working to refine his language and laboratory skills.

Upon Gasser's return to St. Louis in 1925, he and Erlanger continued their research on the electrophysiology of nerves. They broke down the nerve trunk into its component fibers to study their variegated characteristics through the use of the cathode-ray oscillograph. Next they identified distinct types of nerve fibers which they classified in three groups—A, B, and C—depending on the rate at which they conducted electrical impulses. "A" fibers were the fastest conducting nerves, carrying messages to the voluntary muscles as well as sensory impulses occasioned by tactile stimulation and pressure. The intermediate "B" fibers transmitted impulses to and from the viscera. The slowest conductors, the "C" fibers, conveyed pain sensation. Gasser and Erlanger proved that the speed of conduction corresponded to the diameter of the nerve; "A" fibers were the widest, "C" fibers the most slender. With these dramatic discoveries, the modern categorization of nerve fibers had begun.

In 1931 Gasser was was appointed professor of physiology at Cornell Medical College in New York. The appointment finally enabled him to combine research and teaching in his field of interest. At Cornell, he conducted further research into the phases of nerve impulse activity, identifying a short-duration spike, an after-potential during which the nerve was especially excitable, and a period during which excitability was depressed. He became one of the world's leading experts in electro-physiology, and scientists frequently visited his laboratory to consult with him, particularly on problems of technique.

Gasser left Cornell in 1935 to assume the directorship of the Rockefeller Institute, a position which many researchers considered to be the most prestigious in American science. He succeeded the pathologist Simon Flexner, who had directed the institute since its inception in 1903. The appointment came as a surprise to many in the research community as the institute had in the past devoted most of its resources to the study of infectious diseases. Gasser made no sudden changes, but the appointment of a physiologist marked a shift in the institute's agenda. Gasser explained to a somewhat concerned John D. Rockefeller, Jr., that substantial progress had been made in the conquest of infectious diseases, and that degenerative diseases of the organs demanded greater attention. Although Gasser had initially been reluctant to take the position because he considered himself an investigator rather than an administrator, the institute flourished under his leadership, attracting a number of outstanding young researchers. His wide-ranging knowledge of science and his insistence on intellectual rigor in research commanded the respect of his colleagues.

In 1936, Gasser joined Erlanger at the University of Pennsylvania, where they received honorary degrees and reviewed their pioneering studies in electrophysiology in a series of lectures. These lectures were published as *Electrical Signs of Nervous Activity* (1937), a classic in the field of neurophysiology. Their contributions to an understanding of "the highly differentiated functions of single nerve fibers" were recognized in 1944, when they were awarded the Nobel Prize. Gasser devoted his prize money to research.

Although Gasser retired from the directorship of the Rockefeller Institute in 1953, he continued to do research in electrophysiology. Convinced that the best time to pursue a scientific problem was before it became a vogue, or after all investigators had left it, Gasser returned to issues that remained unsettled in his early work. Always quick to employ new techniques,

he now used the electron microscope to examine nerve fibers.

Throughout his career Gasser was totally devoted to his work. He published over one hundred scientific papers. He never married. Soft-spoken and modest, he was troubled by poor health throughout his life, especially migraine headaches. He died in New York City.

[A brief autobiography with a complete bibliography of Gasser's scientific writings is in *Experimental Neurology*, Supplement I (1964). Some of his most important articles appeared in *American Journal of Physiology*: "Physiological Action Currents in the Phrenic Nerve," Aug. 1921; "A Study of Action Currents of Nerve with the Cathode Ray Oscillograph," Nov. 1922; "The Compound Nature of the Action Current of Nerve as Disclosed by the Cathode Ray Oscillograph," Nov. 1924; and "The Role Played by the Sizes of the Constituent Fibers of a Nerve Trunk in Determining the Form of its Action Potential Wave," May 1927. An obituary is in the *New York Times*, May 13, 1963.]

ALLAN M. BRANDT

GAXTON, WILLIAM (Dec. 2, 1893–Feb. 2, 1963), stage and film actor, was born Arturo Antonio Gaxiola in San Francisco, Calif., the son of John Gaxiola, a saddlemaker, and Cecelia Hill. He was a seventh-generation Californian. Arturo attended Boone Military Academy and Lowell High School in San Francisco, and for approximately two years studied at the University of California at Berkeley. At the age of eighteen he assumed his professional name of William Gaxton.

Gaxton's first stage "appearance" was in *The Count of Monte Cristo*, in which he was one of the young men who crawled under a canvas on stage in order to simulate the movement of waves. This unheralded beginning was made while he was a student at the University of California.

His actual debut on the stage was in vaudeville; he and a partner had a song-and-dance act in 1915. The following year he appeared with Anna Laughlin, and in the same year, as a single, he followed Douglas Fairbanks in the lead role in the sketch "A Regular Business Man."

Gaxton served in the navy as an enlisted man during World War I. He was stationed at Pelham Park, N.Y., with his more famous friend Humphrey Bogart. Following his tour of duty, he made the movie *The Old Army Game* with W. C. Fields. On Oct. 17, 1918, Gaxton married Madeline Cameron, a musical-comedy actress and a member of the Cameron Sisters dance team in the 1930's. They had no children.

Gaxton made what is generally considered his first adult appearance on the regular stage in *The Music Box Revue* on Oct. 23, 1922. During 1925 he toured in *Betty Lee*, and in 1925 and 1926 he appeared in *All for You*, followed in 1926 and 1927 by appearances in *Miss Happiness*.

In November 1927 Gaxton opened as Martin in *A Connecticut Yankee*, a musical adaptation of Mark Twain's novel. This performance made him a star. The day after the opening his name was placed above that of the play. Two years later Gaxton was a smashing success as Peter Forbes in *Fifty Million Frenchmen*. He returned to the vaudeville stage briefly in 1930, and in 1931 was again in the legitimate theater as John P. Wintergreen in the musical *Of Thee I Sing*, a hit that ran into 1932. In October 1933 Gaxton once more appeared as Wintergreen, this time in *Let 'Em Eat Cake*. In 1931 he teamed up with Victor Moore in an association that lasted nearly a decade.

In November 1934 Gaxton played Billy Crocker in *Anything Goes*, a production that brought together Ethel Merman, Victor Moore, and Gaxton. His long list of subsequent stage roles included Leopold in *White Horse Inn* (1936), Buckley Joyce Thomas in *Leave It to Me* (1938), Jim Taylor in *Louisiana Purchase* (1940), Dick Live Eye in *Hollywood Pinafore* (1945), and Frank Jordan in *Nellie Bly* (1946).

In the early 1930's, when the Palace Theatre (the most famous of all vaudeville houses) was about to close, Gaxton and Lou Holtz, a comedian, were asked to pool their talents to try to save the famous institution. They formed a variety show that increased the theater's income tenfold. When Holtz was called away after eight weeks, Gaxton and Jack Benny carried on for two additional weeks. The Palace was saved.

It took considerable pressure from a number of movie moguls to get Gaxton before the cameras. He carved himself a modest niche in films but never abandoned the stage. Among his successful pictures were *Stepping Along* (1926), *It's the Old Army Game* (1926), *Fifty Million Frenchmen* (1931), *Silent Partners* (1932), and *Their Big Moment*, sometimes called *Afterwards* (1934). Gaxton played in two Gregory Ratoff musicals, *Something to Shout About* (1942) and *Tropicana* (1944). In 1943 he appeared with Lucille Ball in *Best Foot Forward*.

When Billy Gaxton—as he was known on Broadway during those years—played Joe Davis in the movie *Billy Rose's Diamond Horseshoe* (1945), it was said that he fit the lead character so well that he was actually playing himself. In the movie Gaxton was surrounded by a cast of luminaries from musical comedy: Betty Grable, Dick Haymes, Beatrice Kay, and Phil Silvers.

For the years 1936–1939, 1952–1953, and 1957–1962, Gaxton was shepherd (president) of the Lambs, a New York theatrical club. He was also a trustee of the Actor's Fund and a vice-president of Parfums Charbert, a perfume manufacturing company.

A handsome man, five feet, nine inches tall, with dark hair and dark eyes, Gaxton played golf and tennis, and enjoyed watching baseball, football, boxing, and wrestling. Most of his leisure time was spent on his Connecticut farm, where he raised chickens and swans.

Gaxton's last performance was in the June 24, 1961, Guy Lombardo production of *Paradise Island*, costarring Arthur Treacher, presented at Jones Beach, N.Y. He died in New York City.

[Obituaries are in *New York Times* and *San Francisco Chronicle*, Feb. 4, 1963.]

NORMAN E. TUTOROW

GEORGE, GRACE (Dec. 25, 1879–May 19, 1961), actress, theater manager, translator, and adapter, was born Grace Doughtery in Brooklyn, N.Y., the daughter of George Doughtery and Ellen Kinney. She attended the Convent of Notre Dame in Fort Lee, N.J., which she later called a training school for the stage: "In the convent we had what they called monthly 'rehearsals,' when every girl played the piano or spoke a piece or gave a little play. More than that, we had to write our own plays!" She changed her name in 1892 for professional reasons, taking the name George because it was her father's first name. In 1894, George made her debut in *The New Boy*, a farce. She next spent several years with road companies, making her first important New York appearance as Juliette in *The Turtle* (Sept. 3, 1898). She was small and fragile, with blond hair and blue eyes.

George married the producer William Aloysius Brady on Jan. 8, 1899; they had one son, who also became a producer. William Brady had been a sports promoter and manager of the prizefighter James J. Corbett.

George appeared as Adelle in *The Countess Chiffon* in 1900. In the same year she played the title role in *Mlle. Fifi* and Honoria in *Her Majesty, the Girl Queen of Nordenmark*. She appeared in *Pretty Peggy* in 1903. Her greatest success came in 1907, when she played Cyprienne ("the first of my parts that I really liked") in Victorien Sardou's *Divorçons*. It opened in New York in April, and in London in

June, with Frank Worthing playing opposite her. Forrest Izard said in *Heroines of the Modern Stage* (1915): "The effect produced by them remains one of the memorable incidents of American acting." George had another fine role as Lady Teazle in *The School for Scandal* (1909). In 1911 she opened the Playhouse, built by her husband, as Kitty Constable in *Sauce for the Goose*. In the same year she played Beatrice in *Much Ado About Nothing* at Detroit.

George presented a repertory season (1915–1916) at the Playhouse, serving as manager as well as acting. Guthrie McClintic was her stage manager. She had the title role in George Bernard Shaw's *Major Barbara*—the first time the play was performed in the United States (1915). It had been very difficult to get production rights from Shaw. According to George, "He saw me in *Divorçons* in London, and I suppose he didn't think I was the type. When Mr. Brady cabled and insisted that he wanted the play very much for me, Mr. Shaw wired back: 'The Bradys are surely the play boy and girl of the Western World.'" The reviews were superb. George also starred as Lady Cicely Waynflete in Shaw's *Captain Brassbound's Conversion* (1916).

George was also a translator. *The Nest* (1922) was her adaptation of *Les noces d'argent,* by Paul Geraldy. She starred as Gerry (she often appeared in plays she adapted) in *She Had to Know*, adapted from Geraldy's *Si je voulais.* Heywood Broun, reviewing it for the *New York World* (Feb. 3, 1925), remarked, "There is never any skimpiness in the playing of Grace George." McClintic observed that even when doing a revival, George rehearsed as if it were a new play. Brady often came to rehearsals (and gave his suggestions in a loud voice). George always acknowledged how much the "dean of American theatrical producers" had helped her career, but she also helped his. Casting was her great strength. She recommended Helen Hayes for the part of Maggie in *What Every Woman Knows* (1926), a play Brady had purchased for his wife. Much earlier, she had "discovered" Douglas Fairbanks.

George showed her skill as a director in *The First Mrs. Fraser* (1929), which ran for 352 performances. Brooks Atkinson praised her directing: she had "searched the play for every humor." Some also considered it her finest performance as an actress. George once remarked that "the fascination of comedy is the immediate response you get. You know just how your audience feels." She added that "a person must have an instinct for comedy. You can learn

other forms of acting, but nobody can teach you to see what's funny."

George starred with Alice Brady, her stepdaughter, in *Mademoiselle* (1932) and as Mary Herries in *Kind Lady* (1935). She also played Linda Lessing in *Matrimony Pfd.* (1936), a play she and James Forbes adapted from the French. She appeared as Nell Carter in *Spring Again* (1941). Her only movie, *Johnny Come Lately* (1943), costarred James Cagney.

In 1949, George played Mother Hildebrand in *The Velvet Glove*. Appearing with her were Walter Hampden and her granddaughter, Barbara Brady. Her last appearance was in *The Constant Wife* (1951), staged by McClintic, in which she starred with Katharine Cornell. George was awarded the Delia Austrian Medal by the Drama League of New York and the Medal for Good Speech by the American Academy of Arts and Letters in 1950. She died in New York City.

[George's translation of *The Nest* appears in *The Best Plays of 1921–1922.* There is an extensive clipping file on her in the Theater Collection at the New York Public Library of the Performing Arts at Lincoln Center, which also has scrapbooks donated by William Brady. His book, *Showman* (1937), tells about George's ability to find new talent. Also see Guthrie McClintic, *Me and Kit* (1955). Obituaries are in the *New York Times* and *New York Herald Tribune,* May 20, 1961.]

RALPH KIRSHNER

GESELL, ARNOLD LUCIUS (June 21, 1880–May 29, 1961), pediatric psychologist, was born in Alma, Wis., the son of Gerhard Gesell, a photographer, and Christine Giesen, a schoolteacher. After graduation from high school in 1896, he took the teacher's training course at the Stevens Point, Wis., Normal School, and then, for a short time, taught at the high school in that town. In 1903 he obtained the B.Ph. at the University of Wisconsin. His thesis was on "Higher Education in Ohio and Wisconsin." Soon afterward he became principal of the Chippewa Falls (Wis.) High School, where he came under the influence of Joseph Jastrow, professor of psychology at the University of Wisconsin. Jastrow induced him to enroll at Clark University at Worcester, Mass., where he studied the new field of child psychology under G. Stanley Hall and obtained the Ph.D. in 1906.

Following his doctorate, Gesell taught at the State Normal School in Los Angeles, Calif. On Feb. 18, 1909, he married Beatrice Chandler; they had two children. In the summer of 1909 he visited the Pennsylvania Training School for Feeble Minded Children, the country's first psychologic clinic. During this time he spent several weeks at the Vineland (N.J.) Training School, where Henry H. Goddard was investigating Binet tests in feebleminded children. This marked the beginning of Gesell's interest in mentally retarded children. Later he conducted summer courses with Goddard at New York University, training teachers of defective children. In 1910 Gesell enrolled at the University of Wisconsin to study anatomy. The next year he obtained an appointment in the Department of Education at Yale University and at the same time he matriculated at the Yale Medical School. The dean of the medical school, George Blumer, provided Gesell with space in the New Haven dispensary to study retarded children, and in 1911 the Clinic for Child Development at Yale was founded.

In 1915 Gesell received the M.D. and was appointed professor of child hygiene at the Yale Medical School. For the next four years he also served as school psychologist for the Connecticut State Board of Education, identifying handicapped children and devising individual programs for them. In 1918 he made a survey of student mentality in the elementary schools of New Haven. Dissatisfied with the numerical methods of mental tests as measurements of intelligence, he instituted his own normative studies on the assessment of mental development in childhood.

In 1924, Gesell initiated the use of cinematography in evaluating infant development. He obtained voluminous pictorial records of infant behavior from birth throughout early childhood and up to the age of ten. He and his co-workers were able to determine normal ranges of child development as well as behavioral patterns from these records. A remarkable stream of publications resulted, important not only to the world of scientific psychology but also to the general public because of the light shed on the rearing of children. In 1925 Gesell established the photographic library of the Yale Films of Child Development; and the next year he founded a child guidance clinic, where in 1930 he devised a one-way observation dome for recording infant behavior by camera. *The Mental Growth of the Pre-school Child* (1925) contained 200 action pictures, and the great acclaim it earned, along with many of his subsequent books which were especially popular for parental guidance, brought Gesell much-needed support for his work. His *Atlas of Infant Behavior* (1934) was illustrated with 3,200 action photographs.

From 1928 to 1948 Gesell was attending pediatrician at the New Haven Hospital. After retiring in 1948 he served as director of the Yale Child Vision Research Project until 1950. In that year the Gesell Institute of Child Development, which superseded the Yale Clinic of Child Development, was founded in his honor.

Gesell was a proud and self-confident man, tall and well built, outstanding in a group by his distinguished carriage and dignity. His chief recreations were sailing and the study of biographies. He died in New Haven, Conn.

Few practical results had been achieved in the assessment of the mental development of infancy until Gesell began his studies. He was able to ascertain the normal growth and development of human behavior in association with the various stages of neurologic maturation. He clung to the concept that behavior develops along structural lines dependent on organic development of the nervous system so that patterns can be predicted as well as measured. As the organic mind grows, behavioral patterns are developed; environment influences the behavior but does not generate its progressive steps in development. Thus he brought out the fact that growth and development are both part of a cycle of morphogenetic events characteristic of living organisms. He developed practical applications, with a neat system of psychological testing, that were widely adopted in the education of young children. Insisting that child development belongs in the province of clinical pediatrics, child psychiatry, and child neurology, he exerted a decided impact on the practice of medicine.

[Gesell's papers are at the Library of Congress Medical Collection in Washington, D.C. His works not cited in the text include *Exceptional Children and Public School Policy* (1921); *The Pre-school Child from the Standpoint of Public Hygiene and Education* (1923); *Infancy and Human Growth* (1928); *Infant Behavior: Its Genesis and Growth* (1934), written with Helen Thompson; *Feeding Behavior of Infants* (1937), written with Frances L. Ilg; *Developmental Diagnosis* (1941); *Infant and Child in the Culture of Today* (1943), written with Frances L. Ilg; *How a Baby Grows* (1945); and *Youth: The Years from Ten to Sixteen* (1956), written with Frances L. Ilg and Louise B. Ames.

On his life and work, see Louise B. Ames, "Arnold Gesell: 'Behavior Has Shape,'" *Science*, July 28, 1961; Walter R. Miles, "Arnold Gesell," *Biographical Memoirs of the National Academy of Sciences*, vol. 37 (1964); Rachel S. Ball, "The Gesell Developmental Schedules," *Journal of Abnormal Child Psychology*, May 3, 1977; and the obituaries in the *New York Times*, May 30, 1961; *Journal of the American*

Medical Association, vol. 177, 1961; and Hilda Knoblock, "In Memoriam: Arnold Gesell 1880–1961," *American Journal of Psychiatry,* vol. 118, 1961–1962.]

SAMUEL X. RADBILL

GIBBS, ARTHUR HAMILTON (Mar. 9, 1888–May 24, 1964), author, was born in London, England, the son of Henry James Gibbs, a departmental chief of the board of education, and Helen Hamilton. The youngest member of a large family, he was sent in 1901 to the Collège de St. Malo in Brittany. There, as he said later, he became "a French boy in a French uniform, with brass buttons and a peaked cap, thinking, fighting, eating, smoking—all in French." He acquired a command of the language and a knowledge of French life that later served him well as an author. After returning to England in 1905, Gibbs worked with a firm of assayers and refiners of precious metals.

From 1907 to 1909 he studied at St. Johns College, Oxford, where he had been sent by his brother Cosmo Hamilton (Gibbs), playwright and novelist. Another brother, Philip Gibbs, a journalist and novelist, encouraged him to write, although the family wanted him to become a barrister. At Oxford Gibbs wrote for *Isis,* the varsity paper, and helped start the *Tuesday Review,* a successful weekly that occasionally printed special articles by well-known contributors. Gibbs contributed a series of light satirical sketches that made up his first book, *The Compleat Oxford Man* (1911). He also rowed on the college crew and was an amateur boxer.

After publishing his first novel, *Cheadle and Son* (1912), Gibbs came to the United States and Canada to play a small role in his brother Cosmo's play *The Blindness of Virtue.* He left the play in Chicago and returned to New York City to join his brother, who urged him to resume writing.

Gibbs wrote two more novels before World War I—*The Hour of Conflict* (1913) and *The Persistent Lovers* (1914). When the war began, Gibbs returned to England, joined the Twenty-first Lancers as a trooper, and fought in Flanders before transferring to the Royal Field Artillery. He was trained in gunnery and then served in the abortive Serbian campaign and in Egypt. He next fought in France, where he was gassed. In 1918 he was awarded the Military Cross and discharged with the rank of major. His war experiences were described in *Gun Fodder* (1919), a realistic, revealing memoir, permeated with bitterness and disillusionment as to the motives for which the war was fought. The *New York Times* reviewer found Gibbs's description of the British retreat from the Marne "as vividly graphic as any bit of personal narrative of the war that we have read."

After the war, Gibbs returned to the United States and on Apr. 12, 1919, married Jeannette Phillips, a lawyer and writer. They had no children. The couple moved to a farm near Lakeville, Mass. Gibbs liked being a country gentleman and resided for the rest of his life at Lakeville, although he and his wife traveled extensively. He became a United States citizen in 1931. "I like the bigness of the country," Gibbs said. "It has breathing spaces."

Gibbs published fourteen novels, all well received by a large reading public. At least four were best-sellers: *Soundings* (1925), *Labels* (1926), *Harness* (1928), and *Chances* (1930). But scant attention was given to his work by literary critics. *Labels,* a dramatic story of life in a middle-class English home after World War I, was well wrought and interesting, but Robert Wolf, reviewing it in the *New Republic,* wrote, "The fact that Mr. Gibbs's morals are good, and that he is on the side of the angels in this argument, will not keep his book from being a best seller, nor save it from its abject and pervasive mediocrity." This reaction was fairly typical of serious critics.

Gibbs nevertheless had an easy, rapid, and highly readable style, and he drew effectively, if often with undiluted sentimentality, upon his war experiences and his familiarity with France and French customs. In the novel *Way of Life* (1947) he sympathetically dealt with the problems of a young American paratrooper and an English girl in World War II. Riley Hughes described the book in *Commonweal* as "a not very perceptive love story meant for magazine appearance among the refrigerator ads." One of his last works, *One Touch of France* (1953), a creditable book of verse, was a moving memoir of his life in France as student and soldier. His last novel, *Obedience to the Moon* (1956), was a somewhat tired but warm and fanciful love story. Gibbs's pretensions to lasting literary recognition probably rest more substantially upon his book of World War I memoirs, *Gun Fodder,* than upon his numerous novels, popular as they were.

Gibbs had a dry British humor. Swarthy, handsome, and of athletic build, he was an accomplished swimmer, golfer, and tennis player. To the end of his life he was active physically. He was giving a golf lesson at a Lakeville club when he collapsed of a heart attack. He died shortly thereafter in a Boston hospital.

[In addition to the books cited, Gibbs wrote *Row-landson's Oxford* (1912), *Bluebottles* (1920), a small book of poetry, *Undertow* (1932), *Rivers Glide On* (1934), *The Need We Have* (1936), *The Young Prince* (1937), and *A Half Inch of Candle* (1939). On his life and career see Cosmo Hamilton, *Unwritten History* (1924), and *People Worth Talking About* (1933); and Philip Gibbs, *Adventures in Journalism* (1923), and his introduction to A. Hamilton Gibbs, *Gun Fodder* (1919). An obituary appeared in the *New York Times* on May 26, 1964.]

WILLIAM McCANN

GIBSON, EDMUND RICHARD ("HOOT") (Aug. 6, 1892–Aug. 23, 1962), cowboy and motion picture actor, was born in Tekamah, Nebr., the son of Hyram Gibson, a grocery store operator who also ran a small ranch, and Ida Belle Richards. He acquired the nickname "Hoot" as a youth because of his fondness for hunting owls on the nearby Sioux Indian Reservation. While there is little information about his early years it is clear that he learned to ride on his father's ranch and had left Tekamah by the time he was fourteen. He worked as a cowboy throughout the West, eventually driving horses from Nevada to the San Fernando Valley of California. He also participated in Wild West shows and rodeos.

Along with many other cowboys, Gibson was drawn into the emerging film industry as a stunt rider. At the end of one of the horse drives to California he was offered $20 a week, plus $2.50 for each fall from his horse, by one of the film companies operating in the San Fernando Valley. Gibson's first screen appearance was in *Shotgun Jones* (1911). For the next few years he alternated appearances in rodeos and Wild West shows with work in movies made at Universal's San Fernando Valley ranch—which was complete with an Indian Village and a bunkhouse for the actors and cowboys.

Gibson was part of a group of men whose way of life was destroyed as the open range was closed and the long cattle drives ended. They gravitated to Wild West shows, rodeos, and to the movies—moving from one to the other much as they had once moved from ranch to ranch. In 1912 Gibson won the gold belt as World's All-Around Cowboy Champion at the Pendleton, Oreg., Round-Up, a measure of the real skills he brought to his film work. In 1915 he toured Australia with a Wild West show. After the United States entered World War I he served in the Fourth Division in France. He then returned to California and began to appear more regularly in films but attracted little attention.

Gibson's break came in 1920 when Carl Laemmle, head of Universal Pictures, selected John Ford, the younger brother of a Universal director, to direct a series of five-reel Westerns, and Gibson, who had been part of Universal's cast of extras and stuntmen off and on since 1910, to star in them. The first of these was *Action* (1921). The two men made three pictures together in rapid order and were launched on their successful careers. Gibson and Ford shared an apartment in Hollywood while making these pictures and became lifelong friends. On Apr. 25, 1922, Gibson married singer Helen Johnson; they had one daughter and were divorced in 1927.

Gibson's career reached its peak between 1925 and 1930. He was earning an average of $14,500 a week and making up to eight films a year, nearly all of which were Westerns, including several serials—*Long, Long Trail* (1929), *Lariat Kid* (1929), *Mounted Stranger* (1930)—with titles that left little doubt as to what they were about. In all he made 200 silent and seventy-five talking pictures. He lived on the grand scale of Hollywood stars of his generation. Most of the estimated $6 million he earned was spent on fast cars, airplanes, a ranch in Nevada, and several marriages and divorces. In June 1930 he married actress Sally Eilers; they were divorced in August 1933.

Two months earlier Gibson survived an airplane crash during a match race against fellow cowboy star Ken Maynard. As he was being carried from the wreckage of his biplane, he grinned and told his rescuers, "You can't kill me." Many feared his film career would be ended by the serious injuries he suffered, but despite a permanent limp he returned to the screen in 1935. In 1941 he married rodeo performer and singer Dorothy Dunstan.

In 1944 Gibson retired from motion pictures. He lived on his ranch in Nevada, which he had named the "D-4-C." He tried to operate it as a dude ranch without success, at least in part because, as a friend noted, he played the role of host better than that of landlord. In the early 1950's he turned to television as host of a live cowboy show on a Los Angeles station. Following the show's short run he became the greeter at the Last Frontier Hotel in Las Vegas, where he lived until his final illness.

During his retirement Gibson made occasional film appearances, the most notable of which was as a blacksmith in John Ford's *The Horse Soldiers* (1959). When the company gathered in Natchez, Miss., for location shooting, the headline of the local paper revealed

Gibson's enduring popularity. Although the cast included John Wayne and William Holden, the *Natchez Times* proclaimed, "Filming Starts. Hoot Gibson, Others Arrive."

Gibson was among the most popular stars of Westerns, and probably only Tom Mix enjoyed greater popularity. His pictures captured a vanishing way of life that Gibson knew well. The hard-riding, hard-fighting character he played on screen was not far from the kind of person he was off the screen.

[See Cecilia Ager, "Then and Now," *New York Times Magazine,* Sept. 20, 1959; "Hard-Riding Hoot," *Newsweek,* Sept. 3, 1962; and Ray Stuart, comp., *Immortals of the Screen* (1965); Helen Gibson, "In Very Early Days Screen Acting Was Often a Matter of Guts," *Films in Review,* Jan. 1968; and Buck Rainey, "Hoot Gibson, Cowboy, 1892–1960," *Films in Review,* Oct.1978. An obituary appeared in the *New York Times,* Aug. 24, 1962.]

WILLIAM H. MULLIGAN, JR.

GILBERT, ALFRED CARLTON (Feb. 15, 1884–Jan. 24, 1961), inventor and manufacturer of toys, was born in Salem, Oreg., the son of Frank Newton Gilbert and of Charlotte Ann Hovenden. In his youth Gilbert was devoted to competitive athletics, but his career grew out of his invention of the Erector Set, a construction kit for children, from which he developed a number of successful instructional toys.

Frank Gilbert, a banker, moved his family in 1894 to Moscow, Idaho. There, in a gym that he and his two brothers built, young Gilbert began the athletic career that became his first vocation. He was skilled in gymnastics, wrestling, boxing, and track and field.

When Gilbert was sixteen, the family returned to Oregon, where he was enrolled in the Tualatin Academy, the preparatory school of Pacific University, in Forest Grove, near Portland. In the next four years he added football to his athletic repertoire, and became captain of the college track team. He won prizes for wrestling, and was reported by the *Portland Oregonian* to have broken the world pull-up record by chinning himself forty times.

After a summer working on a farm to help pay his expenses, Gilbert entered Yale to study medicine in the fall of 1904, "my hands calloused and my muscles . . . like iron," he recalled, "but I looked with wonder at the splendid physiques of some of the athletes I saw in the big gymnasium . . . ." In 1908, the year before he received the M.D. at Yale, he set a new record (12 feet, 7.75 inches) for the pole vault, at the Olympic trials in Philadelphia. That summer he tied for

the Olympic championship in London with a 12-foot, 2-inch vault. His interest in the pole vault continued: he coached at Yale in the late 1920's and wrote the article on pole vaulting in the fourteenth edition of the *Encyclopaedia Britannica.* On Sept. 19, 1908, after his Olympic success, Gilbert married Mary Thompson; they had three children.

Gilbert studied medicine because it seemed to him the best preparation for an athletic director; he had no interest in a medical practice. When he graduated, he and John Petrie formed the Mysto Manufacturing Company, which produced kits for sleight-of-hand performers. (Sleight of hand had been another of Gilbert's many interests; he had earned money as a magician while a student at Yale.) The Mysto Manufacturing Company was not an unqualified success. Retail stores hesitated to carry magic kits because they thought most of the potential buyers could not perform the tricks. Gilbert opened a store in New York City in 1910, assigning one of the magicians he had engaged as salesmen to manage it. The next year he opened similar stores in Philadelphia and Chicago, but in 1911 the company's net profit (Gilbert reported later) was only $360.

En route to visit his store in New York, Gilbert became fascinated by the construction of power lines for the electrification of the New York, New Haven, and Hartford Railroad, on which he was riding. Watching crews assemble the network of girders to support trolley wires gave him the idea on which his toymaking business was built. Gilbert made cardboard designs for plates and girders, and sketched axles, pulleys, and the other parts that would make the Erector Set "the world's greatest construction toy for boys." A New Haven toolmaker made working models in steel, and the Mysto Manufacturing Company entered a new era.

Within five years, renamed the A. C. Gilbert Company, it was a million-dollar enterprise. "If the idea appealed to me," Gilbert reasoned, "I figured it would appeal to a lot of other kids." He also recalled with pleasure that the famed Bailey bridge, developed by the Allied forces during World War II, was based on a scale model built with an Erector Set.

With Erector firmly established, Gilbert went on to produce a number of other instructional toys, and a series of books to go with them: for example, *Meteorology* (1920), *Magnetic Fun and Facts* (1920), *Coin Tricks for Boys* (1920), *Chemical Magic* (1920), *Carpentry for Boys* (1920), *Handkerchief Tricks* (1920), *Sound Experiments* (1920), *Mineralogy for Boys*

(1922), *Knots and Splices* (1920), and *75 Electrical Toys and Tricks.* (1932)

In 1929, on the advice of his bankers, Gilbert sold a 49 percent interest in the company for $1.25 million, which he invested conservatively and therefore was able to survive the stock market crash. In later years, however, occasional tensions with his stockholders apparently made him wonder whether he should have sold any of his stock. In 1938, Gilbert acquired the American Flyer Company, redesigned its train models, and added another successful line to the Gilbert catalog. In 1956 he turned over the presidency to his son and became chairman of the board. Thereafter he spent much time at Paradise, his 600-acre estate near Hamden, Conn.

Gilbert was founding president, in 1916, of the Toy Manufacturers' Association of U.S.A., Incorporated, and a member of the Association of Amateur Athletes of America. He died in Boston.

[Gilbert's writings include "Do What You Like, but Do It Better than the Other Fellow," *American Mercury,* Jan. 1924; and a reminiscence, with Marshall McClintock, *The Man Who Lived in Paradise* (1954). Also see John Bainbridge, "Profile: American Boy," *New Yorker,* Dec. 20, 1952, and "Toy King," *Life,* Nov. 18, 1946. An obituary is in *New York Times,* Jan. 25, 1961.]

DAVID WINSTON HERON

GILDERSLEEVE, VIRGINIA CROCHERON (Oct. 3, 1877–July 7, 1965), college dean, was born in New York City, the daughter of Henry Alger Gildersleeve, a judge, and of Virginia Crocheron. She grew up in comfortable circumstances. "We were not 'in society' exactly," she later wrote, "we were professional people." She never married, and lived with her parents until their deaths in 1923. Gildersleeve graduated from the Brearley School in New York City in 1895, then entered Barnard College, the undergraduate women's college within Columbia University. Her teachers included James Harvey Robinson, Franklin Giddings, and Nicholas Murray Butler. She graduated with the B.A. in 1899, first in her class and president of it.

A graduate fellowship and the lack of alternative plans kept Gildersleeve at Columbia, first as an M.A. student in medieval history and then as a doctoral candidate in English literature. She began teaching at Barnard in 1904, and by 1908, when she received the Ph.D. for her dissertation "Government Regulation of Elizabethan Drama," she held a regular appointment in the Columbia English department and was teaching at the graduate level. Two years later, with her prospects for securing a permanent place at Columbia seemingly bright (she always insisted that she detected no prejudice against female professors among her male colleagues), Gildersleeve was asked by Columbia's president, Nicholas Murray Butler, to set aside her promising scholarly career and become dean of Barnard College. Initially she was dubious about Butler's motives in recommending her, at age thirty-three, to replace Laura Gill, who saw Barnard's independence threatened by Columbia at every turn. But she accepted the offer and assumed the post in 1911.

During her thirty-six years as dean, Barnard's relations with Columbia were close and cordial, in large part because Gildersleeve consulted regularly with President Butler, and also because she so penetrated the administrative command structure of Columbia that she was able to keep most proposals prejudicial to Barnard from surfacing. The college's finances were also improved during the 1920's; Barnard survived the Great Depression with only a modest retrenchment. Under Gildersleeve the Barnard faculty provided instruction for a growing number of profession-motivated undergraduate women and contributed significantly to the scholarly standing of Columbia. In some quarters she was criticized for her practice of hiring mostly women for junior faculty positions, while reserving most senior positions, which required Columbia approval, for men from outside. "Perhaps this was discrimination against women," she later allowed, "but it was, I am sure, for the good of the college as a whole." Hers was the feminism of the institutional insider.

Early in her deanship Gildersleeve escaped what she called the "hen with one chicken" outlook by venturing into public affairs. During World War I she coordinated activities of several women's war work organizations, including the Women's Land Army. She spoke on behalf of the League to Enforce Peace and, later, for the League of Nations Association. In 1919, with Bryn Mawr president Martha Carey Thomas, she helped organize the International Federation of University Women, through which she came to know many of Europe's most accomplished women. Among them was Caroline Spurgeon, professor of English at the University of London, with whom she spent her summers in England throughout the interwar years.

Gildersleeve was involved during the 1920's with several American Protestant educational efforts in the Middle East; in the process she became an anti-Zionist. She opposed the creation of Israel after World War II as "contrary to the national interests, military, strategic and commercial, as well as to common sense." Such outspokenness offended some of Barnard's Jewish trustees, just as her campaigning for Al Smith and for Franklin D. Roosevelt must have put off some of the college's Republican benefactors.

Her internationalism was not of the pacifist variety. In 1940, incensed by the German air assault on her beloved England, Gildersleeve joined the Committee to Defend America by Aiding the Allies. With American entry into World War II, she helped bring a women's naval reserve, the WAVES, into being. In February 1945 she was appointed by President Roosevelt as one of six American delegates—the only woman—to the conference to draft the Charter of the United Nations. Both at the preliminary meetings of the American delegation at Dumbarton Oaks and in San Francisco, Gildersleeve, as conspicuous for her elaborate hats and startling dark eyes as for her gender, influenced both the phrasing of the charter's preamble and the substance of what became UNESCO.

Having broached the subject of retirement in 1941, only to be rebuffed by the seventy-nine-year-old Butler, Gildersleeve secured her release from the Barnard trustees in 1946. She and Elizabeth Reynard, a Barnard English instructor with whom she had worked in connection with the WAVES and who had accompanied her to San Francisco, then took up residence in Bedford, N.Y., where she wrote her memoirs, *Many a Good Crusade* (1954), and a collection of magazine articles entitled *A Hoard for Winter* (1962). After the death of her companion in 1962, Gildersleeve entered a nursing home in Centerville, Mass., where she died. She might have, she wrote in retirement, combined her more-than-ample responsibilities as an academic administrator with gardening or breeding terriers, but chose instead "to have lived fully in the main events of my times, making some effort to grapple with our most vital problems."

[Gildersleeve's papers are in Special Collections, Columbia University. See Annie Nathan Meyer, *Barnard Beginnings* (1935); Alice Duer Miller, *Barnard College: The First Fifty Years* (1939); and Robert A. Divine, *Second Chance* (1967). An obituary is in the *New York Times*, July 9, 1965.]

ROBERT A. McCAUGHEY

GIRDLER, TOM MERCER (May 19, 1877–Feb. 4, 1965), industrialist, was born in Silver Creek Township, Clark County, Ind., the son of Lewis Girdler, manager of the family cement mill, and Elizabeth T. Mercer. After an education in one-room country schools, Girdler attended Manual Training High School, Louisville, Ky. (1893–1897) and earned a mechanical engineering degree at Lehigh University (1897–1901).

After one year in England as sales engineer for the Buffalo Forge Company, Girdler began his fifty-four-year career in the American steel industry. His first jobs were minor managerial posts with the Oliver Iron and Steel Company of Pittsburgh (1902–1905) and the Colorado Fuel and Iron Company at Pueblo, Colo. (1905–1907). On Nov. 4, 1903, Girdler married Mary Elizabeth Hayes; they had four children.

In 1907 Girdler became rolling mill superintendent of the Atlantic Steel Company of Atlanta and from 1908 until 1914 was general manager of the firm. The next fifteen years he spent with Jones and Laughlin Steel of Pittsburgh, becoming general superintendent of its Aliquippa works in 1920, general manager of the company in 1924, a director and vice-president in charge of operations in 1926, and president in 1928. Joining forces with Cleveland financier Cyrus Eaton in 1929, he helped to organize the Republic Steel Corporation, becoming chairman of the board and chief executive officer in 1930. This depression-born firm, smaller only than United States Steel and Bethlehem Steel, lost more than $31 million by 1935. Under Girdler's leadership it became a major producer of light alloys, and between 1936 and 1943 realized profits in excess of $87 million.

Following the death of his first wife in 1917, Girdler entered into a brief second marriage with Clara Astley on Aug. 5, 1918. She divorced him on March 26, 1924. On April 26 that same year, Girdler married Lillian Compton Snowden.

Initially an enthusiast for President Franklin D. Roosevelt's National Industrial Recovery Act (NIRA), which encouraged businessmen to work together to restrict output and to maintain prices, Girdler broke with Roosevelt over New Deal labor policy. To comply with the NIRA's requirement that employers bargain collectively with their employees, Republic (and many other firms) set up employee representation plans. Enactment of the Wagner Act (1935) angered Girdler because it outlawed such organizations and promoted regular unions, especially the Committee for Industrial

Organizations (CIO). In November 1937, *Fortune* quoted him as saying: "I won't have a contract, verbal or written, with an irresponsible, racketeering, violent, communistic body like the CIO, and until they pass a law making me do it, I am not going to do it."

The early successes of the Steel Workers' Organizing Committee (SWOC)—a CIO affiliate that became the United Steel Workers of America in 1942—soon produced a confrontation. U.S. Steel had surrendered to SWOC without a fight in March 1937. Jones and Laughlin, following a thirty-six-hour strike at the Aliquippa plant, capitulated in mid-May. Republic and other independents held out, arguing that their employees did not want to join the union. SWOC's leaders, Girdler charged, had no interest in wages, hours, or working conditions—only in closed-shop contracts that would force workers into the union and the automatic checkoff that would require companies to collect dues for the union from employees' paychecks.

Girdler's firm stance contributed to his election on May 27, 1937, to a two-year term as president of the American Iron and Steel Institute. Three days later the "Memorial Day Massacre" occurred outside the gates of Republic's South Chicago works. Between 1,000 and 2,500 demonstrators (men, women, and children) attempted to set up a massive picket line around the plant. Chicago police, employing unusual brutality, scattered them, killing ten and injuring scores as they fled. Sporadic violence continued for months at Republic plants in Michigan and Ohio and at other nonunion steel mills. But victory in the "Little Steel" strike proved short-lived. To secure wartime government contracts, the companies bowed to a 1942 War Labor Board order calling for certification elections, which the union won.

In December 1941, Girdler, still in charge at Republic, became chairman of the board and chief executive officer of two aircraft corporations, Vultee and Consolidated. Under his direction these companies, which merged in 1943, adapted assembly-line techniques to the mass production of airplanes. Two of their products, the PBY Flying Boat and the B-24 Liberator bomber, contributed significantly to victory in World War II. On Nov. 28, 1942, Girdler's third wife divorced him. Five days later (Dec. 2, 1942), he married his secretary, Helen R. Brennan.

After the war, Girdler directed expansion at Republic Steel, building new facilities and swelling payrolls to 70,000 employees. When he retired in 1956, Republic's most profitable year,

he took up the breeding and racing of horses. He died at Easton, Md.

Throughout his career Girdler gloried in power, in being "boss." "You can't relax authority and hope to keep it," he wrote in his autobiography, "neither in a home, a schoolroom, on a ship, in a factory, or a country." On his first job as a foreman he beat a worker for defying an order, then had the man discharged. The beating, he insisted, was essential to maintaining his authority. The theme rings through his autobiography: "I ran that steel plant; I was its captain." The company town of Aliquippa, he admitted, was "a benevolent dictatorship" where he was "unofficial caliph," "a sort of political boss . . . without responsibility to 'the people.' " Once he reached the top, Girdler delegated full authority to trusted assistants, held them entirely responsible, then "left them alone to do their job." Forced by law to deal with labor unions, Girdler was not happy; "the boss is no longer boss," he complained.

[Addresses by Girdler are in *Yearbook of the American Iron and Steel Institute, 1934, 1935, 1953.* He wrote *Boot Straps, the Autobiography of Tom M. Girdler,* in collaboration with Boyden Sparkes (1943). Also see *Fortune,* Dec. 1935 and Sept. 1942. Obituaries are in the *Cleveland Plain Dealer, New York Times,* and *Washington Post,* Feb. 5, 1965.]

GERALD G. EGGERT

GITLOW, BENJAMIN (Dec. 22, 1891–July 19, 1965), radical politician and author, was born in Elizabethport, N.J., and raised in New York City. His parents, Louis Albert Gitlow and Katherine Golman, emigrated from Russia in 1888 and worked in the New York garment industry. They became socialists, Kate Gitlow gaining prominence as a Socialist party organizer. Later she became one of the "matriarchs" of the Communist party.

After graduating from Stuyvesant High School, Gitlow held various jobs, but these always took secondary importance to his political activities. In 1909 he followed his parents into the Socialist party, and eight years later (1917) he was elected to the New York Assembly. He served only one term.

Captivated by the Bolshevik Revolution in Russia, Gitlow joined the left-wing faction of the Socialist party in 1918 and a year later helped organize the Communist Labor party, one of two Communist parties organized in the United States that year. That November, at the height of the "red scare," he was arrested in a massive raid by New York officials against radical organizations. Because he was the first Communist tried under the state's Criminal Anarchy Act, Gitlow's case received widespread publicity. In 1925 the Supreme Court upheld his conviction in *Gitlow* v. *New York* (268 U.S. 652), a landmark First Amendment decision. Gitlow was in and out of prison from 1920 to 1925, serving a total of three years. On Dec. 11, 1924, he married Badana Zeitlin; they had one son. On the first anniversary of his marriage, Governor Al Smith pardoned Gitlow, stating that he had served sufficient time for a "political" crime.

Gitlow's trial and imprisonment brought him much notoriety in radical circles. The Communist party kept his name before the public and presented him as its candidate for mayor of New York City and for Congress while he was in Sing Sing Prison. In 1924 and in 1928 the party nominated him as its vice-presidential candidate on a ticket headed by William Z. Foster. Throughout the 1920's Gitlow remained near the top of the Communist party hierarchy and was honored by Moscow with an appointment to the Presidium, the permanent governing body of the Executive Committee of the Communist International.

Despite his prominence and popularity, Gitlow fell victim to the machinations of Josef Stalin and in 1929 was expelled from the party. With Jay Lovestone, Bertram Wolfe, and several others who had been expelled, he organized the Communist Party, U.S.A. (Majority Group), but it had little impact. Throughout most of the 1930's he wandered from one radical organization to another and even rejoined the Socialist party for a while. Gitlow became increasingly disillusioned not only with Communism but also with radical politics in general. Bitterness toward his former comrades, the rise of fascism in Europe, and the Hitler-Stalin nonaggression pact led him to a strong anti-Communist position by the end of the decade.

The first public pronouncement of Gitlow's new position came in September 1939, when he testified before the House Committee on Un-American Activities. He followed this with the publication of *I Confess: The Truth About American Communism* (1940). In both his testimony and his writing he claimed that American Communists were controlled and directed by the Soviet Union, and that their primary purpose was to undermine American institutions for the benefit of Moscow.

Gitlow's allegations were generally ignored during World War II, for the United States and the Soviet Union joined as allies to defeat Hitler. Shortly after the war, however, he and several other former Communists gained the public's attention. Their portrayal of a massive Communist conspiracy that threatened American life and society found favor with both conservative politicians and a frustrated public bewildered by the successes of Communism in eastern Europe and Asia.

Gitlow now found himself in demand both as a witness and as a public speaker. During the late 1940's and the early 1950's he testified at numerous congressional hearings and at state and federal trials. He lectured around the country, and wrote books and articles on Communism. Along with Whittaker Chambers, Louis Budenz, Elizabeth Bentley, and John Lautner he became one of the most important ex-Communist witnesses in the nation.

By the mid-1950's the intense anti-Communist crusade had run its course. The government ceased to pay former Communists for their testimony at hearings and trials. Lecture fees and royalties on the subject of Communism were no longer forthcoming. In the decade before his death, Gitlow continued as a free-lance lecturer and writer, but he did not find it a lucrative endeavor. He died in Crompond, N.Y.

Throughout his later years Gitlow remained interested in politics, but his warnings about the dangers facing the United States and his recommendations for action were accepted by only the most conservative Americans. Still, his impact both upon the Communist party in the 1920's and upon the anti-Communist effort of the 1940's and 1950's was considerable. As one of the founders and leaders of the Communist party, he helped shape its direction and character during its formative years. Later, as an anti-Communist, he helped influence American attitudes that contributed to the cold war.

Gitlow never felt comfortable with mainstream American political liberalism. As a radical he rejected it as too shallow to challenge capitalism and rescue the working class from the bondage of wage slavery. Later, as a conservative, he equated liberalism with radicalism, and believed that it was undermining American institutions and laying the foundation for a revolution.

[The Gitlow manuscript collection is divided between the J. Murrey Atkins Library at the University of North Carolina, Charlotte, and the Hoover Institution on War, Revolution and Peace at Stanford University. The pamphlets he wrote as a Communist leader include *The Question of Disarmament* (1921); *Some Plain Words on Communist Unity* (1932); and

America for the People (1933). An important work as an anti-Communist is *The Whole of Their Lives* (1948). Also see Theodore Draper, *The Roots of American Communism* (1957); and Harold Josephson, "The Dynamics of Repression: New York During the Red Scare," *Mid-America*, Oct. 1977. An obituary is in the *New York Times*, July 20, 1965.]

HAROLD JOSEPHSON

GOODMAN, LOUIS EARL (Jan. 2, 1892–Sept. 15, 1961), federal judge, was born in Lemoore, Calif., the son of Joseph Goodman, a clerk, and Emma Neustadt. While he was a child, the family moved to San Francisco. After graduating from Wilson High School there, he attended the University of California at Berkeley, from which he received the B.A. in 1913. Two years later he was awarded a law degree by Hastings College of Law (he had been admitted to the California bar the previous year) and began to practice in San Francisco. On June 27, 1917, he married Carolyn Verona Nathan; they had one daughter.

In 1930, Goodman formed a partnership with Louis Brownstone, a younger man who had just passed the bar examination. Gradually Goodman became known as a power in local Democratic politics. In 1942, Franklin D. Roosevelt named Goodman a judge of the District Court for the Northern District of California.

The importance of the Northern District of California (Southern Division) arose not only from the commercial and maritime activities in the San Francisco Bay area but also from the heavy immigration through the port and the presence of Alcatraz and San Quentin prisons. Reflecting the character of the region, Goodman's written opinions often concerned citizenship and admiralty matters. His admiralty rulings are not exceptionally distinguished, although he showed a distinct preference for helping aggrieved sailors. His opinion in *Tadayasu Abo* v. *Clark* (77 Fed. Supp. 806 [1948]) held that the renunciation of American citizenship by certain native-born Americans of Japanese ancestry while in detention camps during World War II was invalid. He ruled that pressures from other inmates and from the government led to conditions in the camps that were so oppressive as to destroy the voluntary nature of the surrender of citizenship. Although the scope of the decision was lessened on appeal (186 Fed. Reptr. 2nd 766 [9th Cir., 1951]), Goodman's opinion brought into question a sordid policy in which two future Supreme Court justices (Tom Clark and Earl Warren) had played a part.

In 1951, Goodman ruled that Henry Miller's sexually explicit but serious works *Tropic of*

Cancer and *Tropic of Capricorn* could not be legally imported. He chided the attorney for the American Civil Liberties Union who appeared in support of Miller's works for confusing "civil liberties" with "license and obscenity." (See *United States* v. *Two Obscene Books*, 92 Fed. Supp. 934 [1950] and 99 Fed. Supp. 760 [1951].)

Two years later Goodman ordered a grand jury to ignore certain evidence in an investigation of Internal Revenue Service corruption, introduced by an assistant U.S. attorney, unless the evidence had been cleared with the chief attorney (12 Fed. Rules Decisions 496 [1953]). Subsequent investigation by a congressional committee resulted in the issuing of a subpoena to Goodman. He refused to testify on the basis of the doctrine of separation of powers. The committee, suspecting his reasoning might be legally correct, did not pursue the matter.

In 1955, the federal government asked Goodman to revoke the naturalization of Harry Bridges, the leader of the International Longshoremen's Union. To do so, the government had to prove that Bridges had been a Communist at some time during a ten-year period prior to his becoming a citizen. But Goodman found the government's evidence too unreliable for so drastic an action (*United States* v. *Bridges*, 133 Fed. Supp. 638 [1955]).

On Mar. 1, 1958, Goodman became chief judge. As chief judge he built a new courthouse dubbed "Goodman's Towers" and persuaded the White House to add associate judges to the court. The Caryl Chessman case brought Goodman to national prominence. Chessman had been convicted in 1948 in state court of a series of robberies and kidnappings, and sentenced to death. While an appeal was pending, the court reporter, who used a peculiar transcription system, died. Chessman contended that the state then willfully selected an incompetent transcriber. In 1955 Chessman sought a new hearing from Goodman, claiming that he had been deprived of due process by the state, and thus was entitled to habeas corpus (*In re Chessman*, 128 Fed. Supp. 600 [1955], rev. per curiam 350 U.S. 3 [1955]).

Goodman had publicly criticized some of the habeas corpus petitions filed before his court by prison inmates as dilatory (see "The Use and Abuse of the Writ of Habeas Corpus," 7 Fed. Rules Decisions, 313 [1947]), explaining his decision to uphold the state court despite two Supreme Court rulings ordering him to grant Chessman a wide review of the questioned proceedings (*In re Chessman*, 128 Fed. Supp. 600

[1955], rev. per curiam 350 U.S. 3 [1955], *Chessman* v. *Teets,* 138 Fed. Supp. 761 [1956] rev. 354 U.S. 156 [1957]). After hearing Chessman for the third time, Goodman again upheld the essential accuracy of the transcript and fairness of the proceedings, but suggested "extrajudicially" that Chessman might be granted clemency because the prisoner had been on Death Row for thirteen years. Goodman thus echoed the contentions of many throughout the world who believed Chessman was being cruelly treated because of his long incarceration. But the Court of Appeals criticized Goodman for abandoning his judicial role and upheld the conviction (*Chessman* v. *Dickson,* 275 Fed. Reptr. 2nd, 604 9th Cir. [1960]). After eight reprieves, on May 3, 1960, as Chessman was being led to the gas chamber, his attorneys were making one more argument before Goodman, whose own life had been threatened because of the case. Goodman granted a stay of execution for one hour, but Chessman was in the gas chamber by the time officials at San Quentin received notice.

Goodman died in Palo Alto, Calif. He had been a voice for fairness and mercy for the immigrant and the seaman. He believed in letting the law work without undue emphasis on procedure. His decision on the Miller books, although criticized by the artistic community and eventually overruled, was designed to protect the American society that he treasured. Some will argue that Goodman missed a chance to rectify a major injustice when he failed to give the fullest constitutional scope of review to Chessman's pleas.

[A total of 180 of Goodman's written opinions are in *Federal Supplement,* vols. 47–193 (1942–1961). Also see William M. Kunstler, *Beyond a Reasonable Doubt?* (1961); E. R. Hutchison, *Tropic of Cancer on Trial* (1968); and Charles P. Larrowe, *Harry Bridges: The Rise and Fall of Radical Labor in the United States* (1972). Obituaries are in the *New York Times, San Francisco Examiner,* and *San Francisco Chronicle,* Sept. 16, 1961.]

JOHN DAVID HEALY

GOODYEAR, ANSON CONGER (June 20, 1877–Apr. 23, 1964), industrialist and art collector, was born in Buffalo, N.Y., the son of Charles Waterhouse Goodyear and Ella Conger. The family was wealthy and socially prominent. Goodyear followed a traditional route: Yale (B.A., 1899), marriage to Mary Martha Forman, daughter of a Buffalo banker, on June 29, 1904, and four children. After graduating from Yale he returned to Buffalo to join his father and uncle, who were lumber manufacturers.

The business expanded over the years to include related industries—railroads to transport the logs and companies to process the by-products of lumber mills—and Goodyear assumed an active role in almost all its phases. He became a vice-president of the Goodyear Lumber Company in 1907 and president of both the Norwich and Goodyear Lumber Companies when his father died in 1911. In 1920 he assumed the presidency of one of the country's largest lumber enterprises, the Great Southern Lumber Company, which operated from Bogalusa, La., until 1938, when the depletion of its lumber supply (despite belated attempts at reforestation) forced the company to close.

Subsidiaries of the Great Southern Lumber Company, which Goodyear headed, included the Bogalusa Turpentine Company and the Bogalusa Paper Company. Bogalusa Paper supplied the material for the fiberboard corrugated boxes manufactured in St. Louis, Mo., by Robert Gaylord. The two companies merged in 1937 to become the Gaylord Container Corporation. Goodyear was chairman of the board until 1952, when Gaylord Container merged with the Crown Zellerbach Corporation.

From 1907 to 1910, Goodyear served as vice-president of the Buffalo and Susquehanna Railroad, which serviced the Goodyear Lumber Company. From 1920 to 1930 he was president of the New Orleans Great Northern Railroad Company, which he organized to bring logs to New Orleans from the hundreds of acres that the Great Southern Lumber Company controlled in Louisiana and Mississippi. In 1930 he merged this line with Gulf, Mobile, and Northern, in which he also had considerable holdings; and this became the Gulf, Mobile, and Ohio Railroad, which ran from Chicago to New Orleans. Goodyear served as chairman of the board from 1940 to 1951 and as chairman of its executive committee from 1931 until his death. From 1928 through 1930 Goodyear's Bogalusa concern also flirted with the idea of transporting logs from the West Coast to be processed at the Great Southern Lumber Company, and he became president of a fleet of ships known as the Redwood Line. When nothing came of the idea he merged Redwood with Swayne and Hoyt, and was chairman of the board from 1930 until the fleet ceased operating in 1942.

Goodyear was a surprising man. Solid in appearance, with a perpetual iron-gray crew cut, he had a bulldog set to his jaw that only hinted at a neurotic temper that plagued him all his life. He was a military man—a colonel in the army in World War I, and a brigadier general in the National Guard during World War II. He preferred to be addressed as "General." But he had a brilliant eye for art, fine furniture, and silver, and this connoisseurship marked him as unique in his time and lifted him above even his substantial success in business.

In 1912 Goodyear succeeded his father as a director of the Buffalo Academy of Fine Arts. He changed the academy from a collection of academic works (concentrating on the Barbizon and Hudson River schools) to one of the nation's premier modern-art museums. He founded the Fellows for Life Fund in 1926, contributions from which helped the gallery acquire works by Paul Gauguin, Augustus John, August Rodin, Jacob Epstein, Constantin Brancusi, Georg Kolbe, Edgar Degas, Paul Cézanne, and Henri Matisse. Goodyear was particularly interested in sculpture, and exhibitions of Aristide Maillol, Rodin, Epstein, Charles Despiau, Gaston Lachaise, and Isamu Noguchi, among others, were brought to Buffalo under his leadership. The museum, however, was not ready for Picasso, and when Goodyear supported the purchase of *La Toilette* from the John Quinn estate for $5,000 in 1925, his fellow directors kept the painting as a fait accompli but chose not to reelect Goodyear to the board when his term expired in 1928.

The incident coincided with Goodyear's separation from his wife (whom he subsequently divorced in 1942), and he left Buffalo for New York City. One of the few people he knew in New York was Katherine Cornell, an old Buffalo friend whose plays he helped produce. His circle widened in 1929 when he was invited to lunch at Abby Aldrich Rockefeller's home (the artist Walt Kuhn later claimed it was at his suggestion). Goodyear emerged as the president of the nascent Museum of Modern Art.

Goodyear served as its active and opinionated president until 1939. He remained on its board of directors and acquisitions committee, but his commitment to the museum weakened progressively as his taste became increasingly conservative. In 1931 he believed that the museum's collection should have the fluidity of a river; in 1952 he left the acquisitions committee because it approved the purchase of a Mark Rothko painting. He remained a trustee of the museum, however, until his death. On Nov. 10, 1950, Goodyear married Enide Cobb Bliss, widow of Cornelius Bliss.

Goodyear's own collection, a brilliant assemblage of late-nineteenth- and early-twentieth-century art, included paintings by Giacoma Balla, Cézanne, Jean Baptiste Camille Corot, Salvador Dali, Honoré Daumier, Degas, André Derain,. Gauguin, John, Walt Kuhn, Roger de La Fresnaye, Fernand Léger, Matisse, Amedeo Modigliani, Jules Pascin, Camille Pissarro, Henri de Toulouse-Lautrec, and Vincent van Gogh; and sculptures by Alexander Calder, Degas, Despiau, Raymond Duchamp-Villon, Epstein, Kolbe, Wilhelm Lehmbruck, Maillol, and Noguchi.

After Goodyear died in Old Westbury, N.Y., the trustees of the Museum of Modern Art expected that most of his collection would be bequeathed to the museum. They were bitterly disappointed. The bulk (more than 300 items) went to the Buffalo Museum of Fine Arts. Goodyear stipulated, however, that Buffalo could keep the works only for a limited time, after which they were to be sold and the money channeled into the A. Conger Goodyear Fund for the benefit of the Museum's Albright-Knox Gallery. Buffalo was eventually forced to buy back many of the masterpieces that Goodyear had donated.

[Goodyear wrote "Messieurs, the Art of America," *New York Times*, May 22, 1938; *The Museum of Modern Art—The First Ten Years* (1943); and "The Future of the Creative Arts: A Symposium as Part of the Niagara Frontier," *University of Buffalo Studies*, Feb. 1952. Obituaries appeared in the *New York Times*, Apr. 24, 1964; *Time*, May 1, 1964; and *Newsweek*, May 4, 1964.]

HELAINE MESSER

GRAFF, EVERETT DWIGHT (Aug. 7, 1885–Mar. 11, 1964), steel company executive, book collector, and philanthropist, was born in Clarinda, Iowa, the son of Valentine Graff, the proprietor of a successful clothing and dry-goods business and a state legislator, and of Nancy Elizabeth Fairley.

After attending public schools in Clarinda, Graff entered Lake Forest College in Illinois, from which he graduated in 1906. He then joined Joseph T. Ryerson and Son, a steel company, with which he remained for his entire business career, being named president in 1937. In 1935, Ryerson merged with Inland Steel Company, becoming a wholly owned subsidiary of Inland. Graff was a director of both Ryerson and Inland until his retirement in 1952.

Graff married Verde Alice Clark on Nov. 19, 1918; they had three children. Their home contained works of art and a major collection of Western Americana. These two interests led Graff to serve as trustee and president of both the Art Institute of Chicago (1954–1958) and the Newberry Library (1952–1964).

Graff would probably be remembered only by his family and friends were it not for a passion for books that resulted in the establishment of the Everett D. Graff Collection of Western Americana at the Newberry Library. As a book collector he had high standards. While he relied heavily, especially at first, on the great Americana book dealer Wright Howes, his acquisition files are a roster of Americana dealers from coast to coast.

Between 1940 and 1950, while still engaged in the steel business, Graff took brief book-hunting trips with Howes. They sought books in Illinois and Iowa, as far south as Mexico, and in the Pacific Northwest. Howes frequently placed advance advertisements in local newspapers along the way so the book dealer and book collector could pursue their respective interests. Reflecting on his association with Graff, Howes said:

> Most western collectors have been satisfied with trying to cover some *one* phase of this fascinating subject—overland narratives, the fur trade, the cattle trade—or some *one* state, some *one* region. . . . The insatiable curiosity and interest of the collector we are discussing was content with nothing less than the uncompromising aspiration of covering the *whole.* He has tried to assemble every basic and significant printed source relating to every important event, every phase of human activity, in all the vast interior regions of the United States—throughout the entire sweep of its pioneer and earlier periods. . . .

Howes's judgment of Graff was shared by the rare-book specialist Colton Storm, who called Graff "one of the finest book collectors I have ever known." The Western historian Ray Allen Billington agreed with Howes and Storm, concluding that, with the addition of the Graff Collection, "the Newberry Library, already rich by virtue of the [Edward Everett] Ayer Collection, joins the very front rank among depositories specializing in Western history. . . ."

Graff's contribution to the Newberry was not limited to his bequests of his collection and of a fund to maintain it. He used his leverage to further the general interests of the library as well. Under his leadership the Newberry declined an invitation to merge with the University of Chicago; thus it remained independent and on Chicago's Near North Side. It was also under his leadership that the library, in 1959–1962, modernized its facilities, adding air-conditioning and fireproofing to protect the collections. Full of energy and of plans for the library, at age seventy-eight, Graff continued his activities even after a serious stroke. He died in Rome, en route home from Greece. Until his death he worked with Colton Storm on the catalog of his collection, which was published in 1968. .

[The Everett D. Graff Papers, which include extensive correspondence concerning his collection, fragments of genealogies on both the paternal and the maternal sides, a brief start of an autobiography, and seven typescript journals of book-hunting trips with Wright Howes, are in the Newberry Library. Articles by S. P. (Stanley Pargellis), Colton Storm, and Ray Allen Billington dealing with Graff and the collection are in *The Newberry Library Bulletin,* Dec. 1960. See also Colton Storm, ed., *A Catalogue of the Everett D. Graff Collection of Western Americana* (1968).]
                                    LAWRENCE W. TOWNER

GRAHAM, PHILIP LESLIE (July 18, 1915–Aug. 3, 1963), journalist and publisher, was born in Terry, S.D., the son of Ernest R. Graham, and of Florence Morris. When he was six, his family moved to Dade County, Fla., where his father engaged in farming and cattle raising, and served as a state senator and state roads commissioner.

After graduating from the University of Florida in 1936, Graham drove a truck for his father's dairy for several months. Then he entered Harvard Law School, where he was president of the *Law Review.* He graduated in 1939 and became a Supreme Court law clerk, first to Justice Stanley Reed and then to Justice Felix Frankfurter.

In 1941, Graham was an attorney for the Office of Emergency Management and then for the Lend-Lease Administration. After joining the Army Air Corps as a private in 1942, he won a commission. During the war he helped to decipher the Japanese military codes and was an adviser to General George C. Kenney in the Philippine campaign. When discharged in 1945 he held the rank of major and had won the Legion of Merit.

On June 5, 1940, while Graham was still a law clerk, he married Katharine Meyer, a daughter of Eugene and Agnes Ernst Meyer, owners of the *Washington Post.* They had four children. Graham's marriage into this journalistic family changed the direction of his career. Eugene Meyer induced him to give up plans to enter politics and join the *Post* organization. Graham became associate publisher on Jan. 1, 1946.

Six months later Meyer was named the first president of the International Bank for Reconstruction and Development, and the full burden of directing the *Post* fell upon Graham. When Meyer returned to the *Post* after completing organization of the World Bank in six months, Graham continued the day-to-day direction of the paper as publisher, and Meyer became chairman of the board. In July 1948, Meyer transferred the voting stock of the newspaper to Philip and Katharine Graham.

In his early years as publisher of the *Post*, Graham was under constant pressure to maintain the pace his father-in-law had set. Meyer had purchased the *Post* in 1933 through a bankruptcy sale and sustained it through nine years of huge losses, while circulation and advertising were gradually increased. During the war small profits were realized; but when Graham took over, the physical plant was inadequate, the staff undermanned and underpaid, and the paper in intense competition with three other Washington dailies. Knowing that financial success was essential to continued progress, Graham launched a broad-gauged campaign to upgrade every department.

For this task he was well qualified despite his relative youth. A keen mind and a friendly disposition won him ready acceptance in the composing room no less than in the editorial and business departments. Eager and dynamic, Graham charmed his associates into moving forward with him. He brought in James Russell Wiggins as managing editor and worked with him for complete and unbiased coverage of the news. John W. Sweeterman, the new business manager, proved to be competent, hard-working, and resourceful. Under prodding from Graham, Meyer purchased radio station WTOP, and later a television station that became WTOP-TV. Both proved to be profitable investments, and this led to the purchase of additional broadcasting facilities.

The *Post* set up a committee of eminent citizens to prevent its sale under any circumstances that might detract from its devotion to the public interest. Graham was also the moving spirit behind a stock-option plan for the company's business and editorial executives. Later he instituted a profit-sharing arrangement for employees and induced the Meyers to give $500,000 worth of nonvoting stock in the Washington Post Company to 711 employees and circulation contractors.

When the *Post* moved into a new building in 1950, Graham wrote in a special supplement that the paper was "grounded in its local community, wedded to the traditions of our country, fixed with a love of liberty, capable of indigna-

tion over injustice and aware of the destiny and responsibility of America as a world leader." In the furor over communism that bedeviled the 1950's, he repeatedly argued, in articles, editorials, and speeches, for sanity, fairness, and respect for facts.

The great opportunity for the *Post* came in 1954, when Graham and Meyer purchased the *Washington Times-Herald* from Robert R. McCormick of the *Chicago Tribune*, thus bringing about probably the most successful merger in modern American journalism. The circulation of the *Post* was almost doubled. It suddenly vaulted into the position of Washington's leading newspaper and to ninth place among the great morning dailies of the country. In the years that followed, it grew rapidly in circulation, advertising, and journalistic influence in national affairs. In 1961, Graham bought *Newsweek* magazine.

Graham's standing as a publisher was notably enhanced when his close friend Senator John F. Kennedy was elected president in 1960 and a still closer friend, Lyndon B. Johnson, became vice-president. At the Democratic National Convention in Los Angeles, Graham had helped to persuade Kennedy to offer the vice-presidential nomination to Johnson. With these two friends occupying the highest offices in the land, Graham's great journalistic influence appeared to be at its height.

Then came tragedy. As early as 1957 a siege of acute depression had sent him to Glen Welby, his Virginia farm, for several months of recuperation. After he returned to Washington, brilliant exploits were interspersed with manic-depressive spells. By the early 1960's these had brought him into conflict with President Kennedy, his associates at the *Post*, his wife, and many others. His erratic behavior led to three separate commitments to a psychiatric institution in Rockville, Md., two of them voluntary. On Aug. 3, 1963, having obtained permission to go to Glen Welby with his wife, he ended his life with a shotgun.

[Manuscripts of Graham's speeches and clippings of his articles, editorials, and news articles are in the *Washington Post* library. See "Guest at Breakfast," *Time*, Apr. 16, 1956; Alfred Friendly, "A Career of Eloquence Reflects Philip Graham," *Washington Post*, "Outlook" sec., Aug. 11, 1963; and Don Irwin, "Philip Graham of the Washington Post," *New York Herald Tribune*, Mar. 5, 1961. Also see Benjamin C. Bradlee, *Conversations with Kennedy* (1975); Merlo J. Pusey, *Eugene Meyer* (1974); Chalmers M. Roberts, *The Washington Post: The First 100 Years* (1977); Arthur M. Schlesinger, Jr., *A Thousand Days*

(1965); and Theodore H. White, *The Making of the President 1960* (1961).]

MERLO J. PUSEY

GRAINGER, GEORGE PERCY (July 8, 1882–Feb. 20, 1961), composer and pianist, was born in North Brighton, Melbourne, Australia, the son of John Harry Grainger, an architect, engineer, and amateur singer and painter who complicated the family's early years through his fondness for alcohol and women, and of Rosa Annie Aldrich.

Grainger began the study of piano with his mother, then became a pupil of Louis Pabst at the Melbourne Conservatory. By age ten he was concertizing. In 1895 Rose Grainger left her husband and took Percy to Germany to continue his education. She was an ambitious and dominating mother. In deference to her, Grainger later changed his name to Percy Aldridge Grainger. Until her suicide in 1922, mother and son were seldom separated; she was his business manager and the rigid protector of his personal life. Grainger's idiosyncrasies and fascination with sado-masochism, most particularly self-flagellation, can probably be traced to his over-protective and harsh mother and weak father.

From 1895 to 1901, Grainger studied piano with James Kwast and composition with Iwan Knorr at Dr. Hoch'schen Conservatory in Frankfurt. He later briefly studied piano with Ferruccio Busoni in Berlin. He was lauded for his ability as a pianist, yet his professors severely criticized his attempts at composition. Among Grainger's classmates and friends were the composers Roger Quilter, Henry Balfour Gardiner, Norman O'Neill, and Cyril Scott. This "Frankfurt Group" championed one another's careers throughout their professional lives.

Grainger began his concert career at London in 1901 and was soon among the ranking pianists. Yet he disliked performing, and devoted most of his energies to composing. Nearly all his significant music, distinct from his popular settings, was sketched or conceived before he was thirty. But, anticipating rejection, he made no early attempts to bring his music before the public.

Between 1905 and 1907, Grainger collected a large body of folk tunes from the English countryside. He later expanded his collecting to Scotland, Denmark, the Faeroe Islands, and Polynesia. He was the first to collect English folk songs with the Edison wax-cylinder phonograph, his transcriptions uniquely noting the rhythmic, dialectal, and linear variations among the singers. Initially controversial, this work stands today as a scholarly contribution to folk-song literature. Grainger's later instrumental and choral arrangements of some of these songs became the basis for his popularity, but they are not characteristic of his compositional style.

When, in 1912, the Balfour Gardiner Choral and Orchestral Concerts brought Grainger his first public success as a composer, he allowed some of his music to be published. Following the criticism of his music at Frankfurt, he had rebelled against "all things non-English." Eschewing the traditional Italian directions, he inserted English terms in his scores, such as "louden lots," "glassily," "bumpingly," and "hold till blown." Although critics ridiculed this eccentricity, by 1915 his compositions for orchestra were the most frequently performed in London of all British composers.

In 1914 Grainger immigrated to the United States, where he spent the rest of his life. In 1918, while serving as a musician in the army, he became an American citizen. The setting of "Country Gardens," which he had "dished up" for a World War I bond drive, made his name a household word.

On Aug. 9, 1928, before more than 20,000 people at the Hollywood Bowl, Grainger married Swedish-born Ella Viola Ström during the intermission of a concert at which he performed both as soloist and as conductor. They had no children. In 1932 Grainger was appointed associate professor and chairman of New York University's Department of Music. The position lasted one year. "I'm not against education," he later remarked. "It's harmless." Beginning in 1935, the Graingers worked at building a museum in Melbourne, Australia, to house his personal papers and mementos. Grainger held strong ties to Australia and, despite his American citizenship, pointedly described himself as an Australian composer.

Grainger craved vigorous daily exercise, and his hurried pace led to his being dubbed "the running pianist." He spurned tobacco, liquor, and meat, and he slept little and irregularly. He was slight of build but muscular, with a shock of unruly orange-red hair. His habits and public statements were not a commitment to conventional behavior. Grainger would often hike between concerts dressed in army fatigues and regarded blue-eyed composers as being superior. He openly decried the gaudy trappings of civilization and spoke of the harmonium as his favorite instrument. The public and his colleagues regarded him as eccentric.

During his years in America, Grainger remained active as a concert pianist. World tours took him to Australia, Europe, and Africa. His interest in bands, stimulated by his army service, led to the composition of wind pieces that greatly influenced the burgeoning American band movement. The more important of these include "Irish Tune from County Derry" (1918), "Children's March" (1919), "Shepherd's Hey" (1918), and the famous "Lincolnshire Posy" (1937), based on folk songs of the English singers who "had sung so sweetly to me."

Among Grainger's unusual pieces are "Random Round" (1913), perhaps the earliest composed music based on aleatory principles, and "The Warriors" (1916), which called for a gargantuan professional orchestra utilizing three conductors and combinations of pianos in threes. Yet another, "Tribute to Foster" (1916), requested the members of its chorus to rub their fingers across rims of water glasses to produce an ethereal accompaniment to their voices.

Additional experiments include Grainger's attempts to achieve what he called "free music." This "beatless music" was his youthful vision of music lacking emphatic beats, with gliding intervals, greater dissonance, and independence of lines. It occupied him throughout his life. In 1944 he joined with Burnett Cross, a young scientist, to develop an apparatus that would produce his "free music" by reading a composer's graphic notations. "My free music is very different to the new kind of music from France and Germany that I have heard and liked very much," Grainger wrote in 1958. "Mine is an extension of existing (normal) music, not a repudiation of it."

Grainger's most popular works are foursquare and diatonic, and exhibit a generous feeling for melodic line. Yet he also composed the most impractical, complex pieces conventional notation would allow. These received little acknowledgment during his lifetime.

Conceptually, Grainger was ahead of his time, but his bizarre behavior detracted from achievements that foreshadowed contemporary techniques. Not all his claims to musical innovations are defensible. Nevertheless, his reputation as a piano virtuoso and composer of pleasant pieces in a congenial vein is but one aspect of his complex musical personality. Grainger died in White Plains, N.Y. He is buried at Adelaide, Australia.

[Grainger manuscript materials are in the Grainger Collection, Library of Congress, and the Grainger Museum, Melbourne, Australia. His published writings include "Collecting with the Phonograph," *Journal of the Folk-Song Society,* May 1908; and "The Impress of Personality in Unwritten Music," *Musical Quarterly,* July 1915. Also see Teresa Balough, *A Complete Catalogue of the Works of Percy Grainger* (1975); John Bird, *Percy Grainger* (1976); Richard Franko Goldman, "Percy Grainger's 'Free Music,'" *Juilliard Review,* Fall 1955; Sparre Olsen, *Percy Grainger,* trans. Bent Vanberg (1963); Thomas C. Slattery, "The Wind Music of Percy A. Grainger" (Ph.D. diss., University of Iowa, 1967), and *Percy Grainger—The Inveterate Innovator* (1974). An obituary appeared in *Musical America,* April, 1961.]

THOMAS C. SLATTERY

GRANT, HARRY JOHNSTON (Sept. 15, 1881–July 12, 1963), newspaper executive, was born in Chillicothe, Mo., the son of Benjamin Thomas Grant, a horse dealer and equestrian, and Ida Belle Johnston. When Grant was fifteen, his father committed suicide. His mother went to work as a dance teacher; Grant quit school and became a railway messenger, earning $5 a week. He spent six years working for railroads and in stockyards, rising from mail clerk to ticket clerk. In 1900 he quit to become a bookkeeper and cattle checker at the East St. Louis branch of Swift and Company.

By saving his money and studying at night, Grant was able to enter Harvard as a special student in 1903. After one year his money ran out, and he returned to St. Louis to try to start a mail order company. The plan failed because he could not raise enough capital.

Grant then took a job as a roofing salesman. He returned to Harvard in 1905 and struggled through his sophomore year, studying mining and geology and working part-time as advertising salesman for student publications. At the end of the year he gave up trying to get a degree and moved to New York City, where he and a Japanese friend attempted to set up an export-import business.

When that did not succeed, Grant found a job with the N. W. Ayer and Son advertising agency, where he worked from 1906 to 1909. One of his early accounts was Rubberset Brush Company. The firm hired him in 1909 and sent him to London as its British representative.

Grant lived in England for several years. There he met Dorothy Glyde Cook, a wealthy American; they were married on July 6, 1910. They had one daughter. Late in 1910, Grant met a British capitalist who wanted to develop the rayon industry in the United States. Grant was named manager of what became the American Viscose Company in Marcus Hook, Pa. Although the business prospered, Grant left it in 1912. After a brief period back in England, he joined the New York advertising firm of O'Mara and Ormsbee in 1913. Shortly thereafter he became vice-president of the firm, in charge of its Chicago office.

One of Grant's clients was the daily *Milwaukee Journal.* In 1916, Lucius W. Nieman, the owner of the *Journal,* hired Grant as advertising manager of the paper. Grant proceeded to reorganize the advertising department, substantially increasing the advertising volume of the *Journal.* In 1919 he bought one-fifth of the Journal Company stock from Judge J. E. Dodge and George P. Miller, the *Journal's* legal adviser. In three years Grant had become vice-president and treasurer of the Journal Company, a stockholder, one of the three directors, and publisher.

In 1919 the *Journal* won the Pulitzer Prize for its editorial support of intervention in World War I on the side of the Allies, a stand that reduced its popularity among the large German population in Milwaukee. Grant nevertheless stuck to his principles, stressing the importance of editorial freedom. "We don't trade with politicians," he said. "We don't make commitments. We must have freedom, freedom, freedom—not to be willful or bigoted or swellheaded or to give us delusions of grandeur, but so the *Journal* can act entirely as it sees best for the community."

Grant avoided making public appearances and took no part in direct handling of the news. Under his leadership the *Journal* achieved the largest circulation in Wisconsin. For several years it carried more advertising than any other publication in the world (51 million lines in 1953). The paper was a leader in using new methods of printing and photography.

Shortly after Nieman's death in 1935, Grant succeeded him as president and editor of the *Journal.* Three years later he gave up both titles and became chairman of the board. Thereafter he spent half the year in Milwaukee and the other half in Miami Beach.

Grant initiated his unit holders plan after Nieman's death. He wanted the *Journal* to be free to report the news without being tied to any outside interests, and to provide security for its employees. When Nieman died, he held 1,100 of the *Journal's* 2,000 shares. His will directed that his stock should not be sold to the highest bidder, but to those willing to carry out the established ideals and principles of the *Journal.*

Moses L. Annenberg, owner of the *Philadelphia Inquirer,* offered to buy the stock at $4,250 per share. Grant declined financial backing to buy the stock for himself and, as a representative of the Journal Company, offered to buy the stock for $3,500 a share. The trustees and County Judge Michael S. Sheridan ruled that the Journal Company would best carry out the intent of Nieman's will. Under Grant's plan shares of company stock are held in trust; employees who wish to sell their shares must sell them back to the trust. Thereby all stock is kept within the company. The first 25 percent of company stock was acquired by employees in 1937, and by Grant's death the employees owned 75 percent of the stock. By 1980, employees owned 90 percent of the stock, with Grant's daughter, wife of Journal board chairman Donald Abert, owing the rest.

Grant was director of the Associated Press in 1940 and 1941, a member of the American Society of Newspaper Editors and of the Milwaukee Art Institute. The national professional society of journalists, Sigma Delta Chi, elected Grant one of its first three honorary fellows in 1948. He died in Milwaukee, Wis.

[See also "The Fair Lady of Milwaukee," *Time,* Feb. 1, 1954, an anecdotal account of Grant as the man behind the success of the *Milwaukee Journal;* Will C. Conrad, et al., *The Milwaukee Journal* (1964), which includes history of *Journal* and biographical information with specific references to Grant; Emery Edwin, *The Press and America* (1972), with a brief statement about Grant and the *Milwaukee Journal;* and Grant's obituary in the *Milwaukee Journal,* July 13, 1963.]

WILLIAM A. HACHTEN

GRAVES, ALVIN CUSHMAN (Nov. 4, 1909–July 29, 1965), nuclear physicist, was born in Washington, D.C., the son of Herbert Cornelius Graves, chief of the Division of Hydrography and Topography in the Coast and Geodetic Survey, and of Clara Edith Walter, a teacher at the Spencerian Business College in Washington. His father died when Graves was ten, and his mother took a job with the Bureau of the Census. He went to live with an aunt and uncle in Washington Grove, Md. In 1924 Graves returned to Washington and completed high school. He studied electrical engineering at the University of Virginia (1927–1931), then did graduate work in engineering at Massachusetts Institute of Technology (1932) and in physics at the University of Chicago (1935–1939), where he received the Ph.D. Graves married Elizabeth Boykin Riddle, a graduate student in physics at the University of Chicago, on Sept. 27, 1937; they had three children. His wife received the Ph.D. in 1940.

In 1939, Graves became an instructor in physics at the University of Texas, where he started a program of cosmic ray research. He was joined in this work by his wife. In 1941 he was promoted to assistant professor, and the following year to associate professor.

Soon after the United States entered World War II, Graves was asked by Professor Arthur Compton to return to Chicago, to work on the development of nuclear reactors for the production of plutonium. At Chicago he participated in the work that demonstrated the feasibility of a nuclear-fission chain reaction. Then he worked with the small group of scientists who built the first nuclear reactor, located under the football stands on the Chicago campus. At the time the reactor first went critical, Graves and two others were standing on top of it with bottles of cadmium sulfate to pour into the reactor if the controls failed. Fortunately they worked perfectly.

After the demonstration that a nuclear reactor could be built and controlled, Graves worked on the design and construction of the nuclear weapons that would be made from the reactor-produced plutonium rather than on the engineering and construction of the production reactors. In April 1943 he and his wife arrived in Los Alamos, N.Mex., where he worked first on nuclear physics measurements necessary for design of the bomb, then on properties of metals at very high temperature and pressure that were required for the design. At the first nuclear weapon test in July 1945, the Graveses measured the effects of the explosion.

In 1946 Graves was observing a demonstration of the assembly of fissionable material when the assembly accidentally became supercritical. One participant was killed by nuclear radiation, and Graves received a very large exposure. After a serious illness he returned to work with nuclear weapons. In 1948 he was deputy scientific director for the first weapons test series conducted by the Atomic Energy Commission (AEC) at Eniwetok atoll in the Pacific Ocean. Following the 1948 test series and until his death Graves was chief scientist on nearly every nuclear weapons test conducted by the United States. During this time he was also head of the nuclear weapons testing division of the Los Alamos Scientific Laboratory and influential in the technical direction of the laboratory. His specific responsibilities included, in addition to nuclear weapons testing, the testing of reactors for nuclear rocket propulsion and detection of foreign weapons tests. He also headed such research activities as solar eclipse expeditions and radio-

chemical research that led to discovery of new transuranic elements.

Graves served on advisory panels to government agencies, including the Committee of Senior Reviewers of the AEC and the Army Science Advisory Panel. Among his honors were the U.S. Air Force Civilian Service Award (1951), the U.S. Army Certificate of Achievement (1954), the Federal Civil Defense Administration Distinguished Service Award (1955), and the Department of Defense Medal for Distinguished Service (1965). He died at Del Norte, Colo.

[A brief, informal autobiography and other documents are at the Los Alamos National Laboratory, Records Management, Los Alamos, N.Mex. His writings include *Miscellaneous Physical and Chemical Techniques,* ed. with Darol K. Froman (1952); "The Challenge to Religious Leaders in the Utilization of Nuclear Energy," in *Proceedings of the Fifth Military Chaplains' Nuclear Symposium* (1965). Obituaries are in the *New York Times,* July 30, 1965; *The Atom,* Aug. 1965; *Nature,* Sept. 18, 1965.]

BENJAMIN C. DIVEN

GRAY, GLEN ("SPIKE") (June 7, 1900–Aug. 23, 1963), saxophonist and orchestra leader, was born Glen Gray Knoblauch in Metamora, Ill., the son of Lurdie C. Knoblauch, musician and clerk in the family store, and Agnes Cunningham Gray. At an early age he learned to play several woodwind instruments, but it was on the saxophone that he made his reputation as a musician. After graduating from Roanoke (Illinois) High School, he attended the American Conservatory of Music in Chicago and also studied music at Illinois Wesleyan University.

For a time in the early 1920's Gray had his own group, Spike's Jazz Band, in which his sister played the piano. In 1924 he joined the Orange Blossom Band, a part of Jean Goldkette's Detroit-based musical organization. When he began his professional career in music, Gray legally changed his surname.

The Orange Blossoms contracted to play at the Casa Loma Hotel in Toronto, Canada. When the nightclub there failed to open, the band took the name, went on tour, and in 1929 arrived in New York City, where it became known as the Casa Loma Orchestra, Incorporated, with Gray as the company president. He continued to play in the saxophone section while violinist Mel Jenssen fronted the band until 1937. When Jenssen left, Gray became the leader.

The Casa Loma Orchestra's chief arranger from 1930 to 1935 was guitarist Gene Gifford, who was largely responsible for the band's style. His arrangements helped set the characteristic musical expression of the Swing Era: danceable rhythms on slow numbers and riff-based up-tempo tunes. Gifford also composed the band's theme song, "Smoke Rings."

The first major booking for the Casa Lomans in New York City was at the Roseland Ballroom. In the late summer of 1931 they went to Atlantic City, and after an extensive tour of the Middle West returned to the Glen Island Casino in New Rochelle, N.Y., in 1933, for the first of several regular summer appearances there. In the autumn of that year the orchestra moved to the Essex House in New York City, the start of many performances in that location. Also in 1933 it was hired for the "Camel Caravan," the first radio series to feature a swing band.

In the autumn of 1935, the group appeared at the Paramount Theater in New York City, inaugurating its famous stage-band policy. Shortly thereafter the Casa Lomans began a long engagement at the Rainbow Room atop Radio City. These and other performances, including some at the Terrace Room of the Hotel New Yorker, helped to build and maintain the orchestra's wide acceptance by both college students and the general public. Early in 1937 the Casa Lomans left New York on a tour of the West that eventually took them to the Palomar Ballroom in Los Angeles. At this time they were hired to play for the "Burns and Allen Radio Show" (1938).

Thus, by the time the group was ten years old, it was one of the nation's leading dance bands, having placed in the *Metronome* popularity polls in 1937 and 1940, in the swing and sweet band categories, and having won the *Down Beat* poll as the dance band favorite in 1938. It also enjoyed a large and steady sale of phonograph records. Probably its best-known records were "No Name Jive," "Casa Loma Stomp," and the band's theme song. Among the stars who recorded with the band were trumpeter Louis Armstrong, vocalists Mildred Bailey, Connie Boswell, and Lee Wiley, pianist Frankie Carle, and pianist-composer Hoagy Carmichael.

At the height of their popularity, the Casa Lomans played in the nation's major movie theaters and dance halls, on college campuses, and in the motion pictures *Time out for Rhythm* (1941) and *Gals, Inc.* (1943). During the early 1940's the group retained its public favor, but according to critics, its musical performance level declined because key members left.

The Casa Loma Orchestra Corporation was dissolved in 1942, but Gray continued to lead the orchestra until 1950, when he retired. In 1956 he began supervising recording sessions that featured the original Casa Loma sound and a series of tributes to the big bands of the 1930's performed by outstanding studio musicians. This project was so successful that Gray was asked to make public appearances with his own group. He refused to do so, preferring to spend his time in semiretirement with his wife, Marion Douglass, and their son. He died at Plymouth, Mass.

Gray was handsome, tall, dignified, and a fine musician. These qualities, coupled with his excellent business ability, helped lead the Casa Lomans to success. More than any other single orchestra, they set the stage for the big band era.

[See Leo Walker, *The Wonderful Era of the Great Dance Bands* (1964); George T. Simon, *The Big Bands* (1967), and *Simon Says: The Sights and Sounds of the Swing Era, 1935–1955* (1971); Albert McCarthy, *The Dance Band Era* (1971); and *The Big Band Almanac* (1978). Information on 78 rpm recordings is in Brian Rust, *The American Dance Band Discography, 1917–1942* (1975); and *Jazz Records, 1897–1942* (1978). Obituaries are in *New York Times*, Aug. 25, 1963, and *Newsweek*, Sept. 2, 1963. Representative LP recordings are "Glen Gray and the Original Casa Loma Orchestra's Greatest Hits" (MCA-122; 78 rpm reissues); "Casa Loma in Hi Fi" (Capitol W-747); "Sounds of the Great Casa Loma Band" (Capitol T-1588).]

BARRETT G. POTTER

GREEN, WILLIAM JOSEPH, JR. (Mar. 5, 1910–Dec. 21, 1963), U.S. congressman, was born in Philadelphia, Pa., the son of William Joseph Green, a saloon keeper, and Annie Theresa Duffy, both Irish immigrants. Green graduated from St. Joseph's Preparatory School but left St. Joseph's College after two years (1930–1931) to enter politics. His family was Irish-Catholic Republican, but he became a Democrat in 1932 under the influence of Franklin Delano Roosevelt and the New Deal.

During the 1930's Green held several government positions, including insurance examiner for the Commonwealth of Pennsylvania and U.S. chief deputy marshall. He also operated a small insurance business in a desultory fashion. "My business," he said, "is politics, not insurance."

On Sept. 25, 1937, Green married his childhood sweetheart, Mary E. Kelly; they had six children. From March to December 1944 Green served in the army as a private in the

Quartermaster Corps. While in the army he ran for Congress, and although barred by military regulations from campaigning, he won easily. In 1946, however, he lost his seat to Republican George W. Sarbacher, Jr. In 1948, Green was reelected and served until his death. For ten of those years he was also chairman of Philadelphia's Democratic Committee.

In 1951, the stocky, pink-faced Green ("Bill" or "Billy" to the public, "Willie" to his friends) shaped a Democratic coalition comprising ward politicians and Philadelphia blue bloods such as Richardson Dilworth and Joseph S. Clark. The coalition became what the *New York Times* called "one of the nation's most powerful political machines." Green was a two-fisted disciplinarian in party matters but resented the term "boss," preferring instead "chairman of the board." At the 1956 Democratic National Convention, Green's support was crucial to Adlai Stevenson's winning the presidential nomination from Averell Harriman. His loyalty to the party was legendary. In the 1960 presidential election, his Philadelphia organization delivered a 331,000 majority for John F. Kennedy. As a result, Green became a close friend of Kennedy.

In Congress, Green led Philadelphia's six-representative delegation. He served first on the Armed Services Committee of the House and later on the Committee on Ways and Means, where he was able to control important committee assignments. AFL-CIO officials called Green "one of labor's staunchest champions."

In 1956, a federal grand jury indicted Green on charges of conspiracy to defraud the government by accepting a bribe from a contractor who was to build an Army Signal Corps depot in Tobyhanna, Pa. Green was acquitted by a federal jury in Lewisburg, Pa. In December 1963 Green was stricken with a gall bladder ailment while on his way to the funeral of ex-Governor Herbert H. Lehman of New York. He died after a brief illness. Three thousand mourners attended his funeral, including President Lyndon B. Johnson and Senator Robert F. Kennedy. His son and namesake succeeded him in Congress and in 1980 became mayor of Philadelphia.

[See the *Washington Star*, Feb. 16, 1949; *New York Times*, Oct. 4, 1958; *Philadelphia Bulletin*, Sept. 6, 1961; *Washington Post*, Dec. 10, 1963; *Washington Star*, Dec. 21, 1963; *Philadelphia Daily News*, Dec. 21, 1963; *New York Times*, Dec. 22, 1963; *Washington Post*, Dec. 22, 1963; *Philadelphia Inquirer*, Dec. 25, 1963; *Congressional Record*

(House), Jan. 1964; and *Biographical Directory of the American Congress, 1774–1971* (1971).]

JOHN T. GALVIN

GREW, JOSEPH CLARK (May 27, 1880–May 25, 1965), diplomat and author, was born in Boston, Mass., the son of Edward Sturgis Grew, a wool merchant and banker, and of Annie Crawford Clark. The family was one of wealth and prominence, not of the very top rank in Boston society but moving easily among and related to the Sturgises, Parkmans, and Wigglesworths. Grew was also a distant cousin of J. P. Morgan.

Grew attended the Groton School (1892–1898) and Harvard (1898–1902), from which he received the B.A. As was usual for young men of his class, he then took a tour abroad, longer and ranging farther afield than most. In Amoy, China, he shot a tiger, a feat that later convinced Theodore Roosevelt to approve Grew's appointment to the diplomatic service.

After his return Grew tried to secure a position in a Boston publishing house, but failed. A year later the public-service consciousness cultivated at Groton and Harvard and his wanderlust pushed him into a diplomatic career. Because of a hearing impairment he was initially rejected for a consular post when he was mistakenly thought to be nearly deaf, but he then received an appointment to Cairo in 1904. In 1906 he was one of the last to receive a transfer from the consular service to the foreign service as the new system of competitive exams was introduced by President Theodore Roosevelt.

On Oct. 7, 1905, Grew returned to the United States to marry Alice de Vermandois Perry, a descendant of Commodore Oliver Perry. Later in his career this connection was to serve him well, for she had spent her youth in Japan, knew the language, and provided entrees to Japanese society unusual for a Western diplomat. The Grews had four daughters.

After a brief return to Egypt, Grew was assigned to Mexico City, where he served as a third secretary in 1906, and to Moscow in 1907. He was promoted to second secretary when he moved to Berlin in 1908, became first secretary at Vienna in 1911–1912, and returned to Berlin in 1912. Grew went home on leave in that year, and after Woodrow Wilson was elected president, he called on Franklin D. Roosevelt and other old Groton and Harvard friends who were Democrats to use their influence to prevent him from being a victim of the spoils system.

In 1918, Grew was appointed secretary to the United States Commission to the Versailles

Peace Conference. He had charge of arrangements for the Peace Commission, a position that brought him the equivalent of the rank of minister. In this post he was buffeted by the factions contending for control of the American delegation. His ability to solve problems by tact and finesse helped save him. After the peace conference, Grew achieved the promotion that insured his career—he became minister to Denmark in April 1920.

Grew proved his mettle as a negotiator at the Lausanne Conference on Near Eastern Affairs (1922–1923), at which he skillfully thwarted British attempts to have things their way, especially concerning oil concessions from Turkey. His role was remembered in 1927 when he became ambassador to Turkey and was warmly welcomed there. In the interim he returned to Washington as undersecretary of state to Frank Kellogg. His major task was to supervise the restructuring of the foreign service authorized in the Rogers Act of 1924.

Grew and Kellogg did not get along well, so Grew leaped at the opportunity to become ambassador to Turkey. From that post he moved to Japan in 1932. He was the first career foreign service officer to be made ambassador to a major nation. Tokyo was Grew's last overseas assignment. He hoped to become the peacemaker for Asia, turning Japan away from its course of conquest. This ambition was not realized, in part because events prevented it and because he did not have the right temperament to bring off such a coup.

Grew tried desperately during his decade in Japan to explain the Americans to the Japanese and the Japanese to the Americans. He lectured the Japanese Foreign Office on the need for restraint while attempting at the same time to convince Franklin D. Roosevelt and Secretary of State Cordell Hull to provide Japan with some economic elbow room. After 1937 he confronted an ever-growing animosity in Washington toward Japanese violations of the treaty structure on which America based its Eastern policy. After 1939, Stanley K. Hornbeck, adviser on Far Eastern affairs to Secretary Hull, discounted Grew's advice, judging it a form of appeasement.

Grew made a last-ditch effort to avoid war by encouraging President Roosevelt to meet with Prince Fumumaro Konoye, the Japanese prime minister, to talk out the differences separating the two powers. This failed in part because Hull thought the Japanese were stalling; Hornbeck advised him that such a meeting could come to no good end. Grew was convinced that the failure to pursue these talks brought on the attack on Pearl Harbor and that Washington had failed him in his efforts to preserve the peace.

After he was repatriated in 1942, Grew became special assistant to Secretary Hull. In 1944 he was made director of the Far Eastern Affairs Division, and from December 1944 to August 1945 he served again as undersecretary of state. In this capacity he expressed his long-standing anti-Bolshevik conviction concerning dealings with the Russians. He also worked to prevent the use of the atomic bomb against Japan, to preserve the position of the emperor, and to prevent unconditional surrender, which he was sure would promote fanatic resistance by the Japanese. After his retirement Grew served on many boards and commissions, some of a semiofficial nature. He died at Manchester-by-the-Sea, Mass.

[Grew's papers are in the Houghton Library at Harvard. Materials dealing with his career are also in the Department of State records in the National Archives in Washington, D.C., and in the Roosevelt Papers at the Franklin Delano Roosevelt Library, Hyde Park, N.Y. Grew's writings include *Sport and Travel in the Far East* (1910); *Ten Years in Japan* (1944); *Turbulent Era*, ed. Walter Johnson, assisted by Nancy Harvison Hooker, 2 vols. (1952). Also see Edward M. Bennett, "Joseph C. Grew: The Diplomacy of Pacification," in *Diplomats in Crisis*, ed. Richard Dean Burns and Edward M. Bennett (1974); Waldo H. Heinrichs, Jr., *American Ambassador: Joseph C. Grew . . .* (1966). There is significant material in the Columbia University Oral History Project dealing with Grew and his diplomacy. Obituaries are in *New York Times* and *Washington Post*, May 27, 1965.]

EDWARD BENNETT

GRISWOLD, ALFRED WHITNEY (Oct. 27, 1906–Apr. 19, 1963), scholar and university president, was born in Morristown, N.J., the son of Harold Ely Griswold, an insurance broker, and Elsie Montgomery Whitney. After receiving his secondary education at the Peck School in Morristown and at the Hotchkiss School in Lakeville, Conn., Griswold entered Yale University in 1925, preparatory to a career as a writer or journalist. As an undergraduate he achieved an excellent academic record, wrote regular columns and light verse for the *Yale Daily News*, and served as managing editor of the *Yale Record*. He was also one of the founders of a literary society called the "Mountain." In 1929 he received the B.A. in English.

Griswold accepted a position as a clerk for a Wall Street brokerage firm in the summer of 1929. But the financial world did not attract him, and and he returned to Yale in the fall to teach freshman English while doing graduate work in the English department. In the summer of 1930, after his marriage on June 10 to Mary Morgan Brooks, with whom he had four children, he studied in Germany. Upon resuming his graduate program in the fall, he switched to the history department and completed his Ph.D. in 1933.

Later that year Griswold became an instructor in history at Yale, but his rise through the academic ranks was not meteoric. In 1935 he was appointed research assistant in international relations; in 1938, after the publication of his first book, he was promoted to assistant professor in government and international relations; in 1942 he was named associate professor of history; and in 1947 he became professor of history.

A popular figure on campus, Griswold gained a reputation as an outstanding lecturer who spiced his material with amusing anecdotes and the mimicry of historical personalities. He did most of his scholarly writing during the 1930's and 1940's. His first publication, an article on the New Thought movement of the early twentieth century, entitled "New Thought: A Cult of Success," appeared in the *American Journal of Sociology* in November 1934. It had been a part of his doctoral dissertation. Over the next decade Griswold's work focused mainly on United States foreign relations. In articles for scholarly journals and learned magazines and in *The Far Eastern Policy of the United States* (1938) he examined American policy toward Eastern Asia. He saw this policy as inherently flawed because a variety of uncontrollable factors undermined its main thrust, which was support of the Open Door in China. During World War II Griswold wrote essays on German expansionism and on other aspects of German history. By the end of the war his main interest was in the wellsprings of American democracy, and his attention shifted to study of Thomas Jefferson and the United States agrarian tradition. In 1948 he published *Farming and Democracy*.

During World War II Griswold served as director of the Foreign Area and Language Curriculum of the Army Specialized Training Program and as director of the Army Civil Affairs Training School at Yale, handling both assignments skillfully. But he had not prepared himself for administrative work and had no great interest in it. Thus it came as a great surprise to him and to his associates when in February 1950 the Yale Corporation appointed him the sixteenth president of the university.

Despite his lack of experience, Griswold was a successful university president. Yale was running an annual deficit of $450,000 when he assumed office, and faculty salaries, especially in the lower ranks, were meager. Within ten years he had tripled the university's endowment and doubled faculty salaries. He was a stout defender of academic freedom and a vigorous opponent of loyalty oaths. The only loyalty worth anything, he argued, was one that "survives curiosity and withstands criticism and doubt." During the McCarthy era he delivered ringing declarations in favor of civil liberties: "Books won't burn," he often stated.

Alarmed at contemporary trends, Griswold deplored the emphasis on sports at major universities and assailed the national traffic in athletic scholarships as "one of the greatest educational swindles ever perpetrated on American youth." As a teacher and scholar who knew what was pedogogically sound, he attacked the "service station" concept of higher education wherein colleges and universities hastened to offer whatever courses outside pressure groups urged upon them. He also believed that teachers' colleges did a miserable job. He often referred to the paucity of resources spent on the nation's secondary schools and their deficient academic programs as a national scandal.

If Griswold's scholarship manifested painstaking research, his administrative work reflected concern for quality over numbers and for the liberal arts tradition over technological instruction. An anachronism in an era of the managerial administrator, he was the quintessential humanist and, in the words of one Yale undergraduate, "an awful good man." He died in New Haven, Conn.

[In addition to works mentioned in the text, Griswold wrote *Essays on Education* (1954); *In the University Tradition* (1957); and *Liberal Education and the Democratic Ideal* (1959); and numerous periodical articles. Articles on Griswold appeared in *Time*, Feb. 20, 1950, and June 11, 1951; in *Newsweek*, June 11, 1951. Obituaries are in the *New York Times*, Apr. 20, 1963, and *Life*, May 3, 1963.]

RUSSELL D. BUHITE

GRUNDY, JOSEPH RIDGWAY (Jan. 13, 1863–Mar. 3, 1961), business leader and senator, was born in Camden, N.J., the son of Mary Ridgway and William Hulme Grundy, a woolen mill owner. Grundy grew up in a financially secure Quaker home in Bristol, Pa. He attended private and public schools and studied at the Secondary Division of Swarthmore College for two years (1877–1879) before he entered

Swarthmore College as a freshman in 1879. After one year, he went to Europe for a grand tour. Upon his return, he worked for his father, starting at the lowest level and learning the family business of manufacturing woolen goods.

While taking on greater responsibilities in the business, Grundy began to assist his father in lobbying for a high tariff. When his father died in 1893, Grundy became head of the woolen mills and principal stockholder of the Farmers National Bank in Bristol. He inherited approximately $1 million, which he had increased to $18 million by the time of his death. He never married.

Grundy was the Bucks County Republican leader for Senator Boies Penrose, and he also served on the Bristol borough council. In 1909 he founded the Pennsylvania Manufacturers' Association (PMA), an organization of small manufacturers intent on combating the growing power of reform groups, and became its first president. With the primary goal to maintain the status quo, the PMA tried to influence the Pennsylvania legislature through campaign contributions and lobbying efforts. The capital stock tax-exemption and laws covering child labor, female labor, and wages and hours were Grundy's chief concerns.

Grundy's rise to national importance began with his participation in the selection of Warren G. Harding as the 1920 Republican presidential nominee at the Blackstone Hotel in Chicago. In 1924, Grundy was responsible for raising $800,-000 for the Coolidge campaign. His abilities as a fundraiser and lobbyist made him a major figure among the Republican politicians in Pennsylvania. After the death of Penrose in 1921, Grundy was one of a handful of Republican leaders who took charge of the party.

In the 1926 Pennsylvania elections, Grundy's choice for governor, John S. Fisher, won the Republican nomination and was elected in November. But Philadelphia's "boss," William S. Vare, defeated Grundy's favorite, the incumbent senator George Wharton Pepper, and Governor Gifford Pinchot in the Republican senatorial primary, and easily won the November election. Vare, however, was refused his seat in the Senate, pending an investigation into charges of campaign corruption and vote fraud. The then-astronomical sum of $300,000 was raised by the PMA in support of Fisher and Pepper.

Grundy fought hard for a high-tariff plank in the 1928 Republican party platform, and in 1929 he persistently lobbied for fulfillment of that pledge. The Smoot-Hawley Tariff (1930)

raised duties on most manufactured goods. Although not its author, Grundy was so closely associated with the bill that it was commonly referred to as the Grundy Tariff.

As the nation's best-known lobbyist, Grundy was called to testify before the Lobby Investigating Committee of the United States Senate in late 1929. His appearance before that committee gave him an opportunity to present his views on tariffs, taxation, and the importance of manufacturing. His frank, hard-hitting, often tactless testimony displayed his beliefs as well as his charm, and it won him praise in numerous editorials. When Vare was denied his Senate seat in December 1929, Governor Fisher appointed Grundy to the vacancy that had existed since 1927.

Grundy's stay in the Senate was short. He was defeated in the 1930 Republican primary by Secretary of Labor James J. Davis, an ally of the Mellon family in Pittsburgh. Grundy had expected full Republican support when he accepted Fisher's offer, but Vare gave his support to Davis, while the Mellon forces backed Grundy only halfheartedly.

Grundy's loss to Davis demonstrated that the PMA was not as powerful as had been thought. Thereafter, Grundy's prominence as a national figure declined. His role in state politics, however, increased during the 1930's. With Grundy's help, Gifford Pinchot won a second term as governor in 1930. With the Democrats in power in Pennsylvania after the 1934 elections, the death of Vare in 1935, and the weakening of the Mellon influence in Pittsburgh, Grundy became the undisputed Republican leader. Ironically it was a time when the Republicans in Pennsylvania were at their lowest point in seventy years. After the 1936 elections, Grundy began to share party control with Joseph N. Pew, a wealthy Philadelphia oilman.

The Republican party regained control of state politics in 1938 and stayed in power for sixteen years, but Grundy was less involved and had less control than in the past. In 1947 he retired as president of the PMA Executive Committee. That year Governor James H. Duff openly attacked Grundy's leadership. In 1950 Duff won the Republican primary for senator and carried his gubernatorial running-mate to victory over Grundy's choices. During the rest of his life, Grundy contented himself with civic and philanthropic activities. He was very generous to his hometown of Bristol. He spent his last years in Nassau in the Bahamas, where he died.

Grundy's greatest accomplishment was the founding and fostering of the PMA, the largest political interest group of its kind in the United States. Its methods of influencing legislation became the model for other interest groups, especially labor organizations. Grundy's views on the tariff were influential, but his conception of world trade was based on nineteenth-century conditions.

Grundy was an excellent businessman who represented well-defined economic, political, and social viewpoints. Originally seen as "conservative," "Grundyism" came to mean "reactionary." Grundy's personal opposition to all change other than a return to the ways of the late nineteenth century earned him many opponents. As a business leader, Grundy was a success; as a politician and public figure, he was not.

[There is not much original material about Grundy. The largest amount of information is in the PMA's files in Philadelphia, mostly on Grundy as leader of the PMA, with only a few items concerning his political work and tariff activities, and a few printed versions of his speeches. His testimony before the Senate Lobby Investigating Committee is available through the Senate.

The most complete and scholarly examination of Grundy's career is J. Roffe Wike, *The Pennsylvania Manufacturers' Association* (1960). Less scholarly but more biographical is Ann Hawkes Hutton, *The Pennsylvanian: Joseph R. Grundy* (1962).

Two unpublished undergraduate theses of note are Samuel Humes, "The Role of G.O.P. Leadership in the Keystone State" (Williams College, 1952); and R. Bruce Brumbaugh, "The Grundy Movement in Pennsylvania" (Princeton University, 1953). *Time* covered Grundy's career closely and accurately from 1940 to 1950; and an excellent account of leadership in Pennsylvania during Grundy's time is Herman Lowe's "Pennsylvania: Bossed Cornucopia," in Robert S. Allen, ed., *Our Sovereign State* (1949). An obituary appeared in *New York Times* on Mar. 4, 1961.]

ALFRED L. MORGAN

GUINZBURG, HAROLD KLEINERT (Dec. 13, 1899–Oct. 18, 1961), publisher, was born in New York City, the son of Henry Aaron Guinzburg, a businessman and philanthropist, and Leonie Kleinert. The family was well-to-do and cultured. Guinzburg received his early education in New York and in 1917 entered Harvard University, from which he obtained a B.A. in 1921.

After working briefly as a reporter in Bridgeport, Conn., and as a correspondent for the Boston *Evening Transcript,* Guinzburg studied law at Columbia Law School (1922–1926). He found the prospect of a legal career progressively less appealing and was influenced by a friend, Richard Leo Simon, to try publishing instead.

In 1924 Guinzburg worked for Simon and Schuster; but he soon resolved, with what he later called "the over-optimism of youth," to establish his own publishing firm. On Dec. 24, 1923, he married Alice Reizenstein; they had two children.

On Mar. 1, 1925, Guinzburg and George S. Oppenheimer, who had been advertising manager at Alfred A. Knopf, founded the Viking Press, Inc., with a capital of about $50,000. They had planned to call their venture the Half Moon Press until Rockwell Kent designed a colophon for them that more closely resembled a Viking vessel than Henry Hudson's flagship. The Viking image provided an effective symbol for the firm's announced policy: "to stand for enterprise, adventure, and exploration in the publishing field."

On Aug. 1, 1925, Guinzburg and Oppenheimer secured a backlist of impressive titles by merging with the veteran publisher Benjamin W. Huebsch, whose authors included James Joyce, D. H. Lawrence, and Sherwood Anderson. Huebsch became vice-president and editor in chief at Viking, while Guinzburg served as president and Oppenheimer as secretary and treasurer. The first Viking book list appeared in the fall of 1925 and included William Ellery Leonard's *Two Lives,* James Weldon Johnson's *The Book of American Negro Spirituals,* and translated works of Joseph Arthur de Gobineau and Johan August Strindberg. Through Huebsch's extensive contacts with European authors, the press acquired a substantial number of foreign works. Books such as Arnold Zweig's *The Case of Sergeant Grischa* (1928), Stefan Zweig's *Marie Antoniette* (1933), and Franz Werfel's *The Song of Bernadette* (1942) proved very popular with American readers. An English novel published by Viking, Sylvia Townsend Warner's *Lolly Willowes* (1926), was chosen by the newly established Book-of-the-Month Club as its initial offering.

In November 1926 Guinzburg founded a rival book club, the Literary Guild of America, in collaboration with Samuel Craig. The Guild was patterned after the successful German book clubs that had developed after World War I to supply an impoverished public with cheap reading material. It proposed to cut production and distribution costs through the large-scale purchase of books at discount rates and their sale to club members through the mails. Carl Van Doren was appointed to select the Guild's offerings, and the club's first book—Heywood Broun and Margaret Leech's *Anthony Comstock*—was distributed in March 1927. Angry protests from publishers and booksellers caused Guinzburg to tone down his advertising the following year and to permit booksellers to handle Guild subscriptions on a commission basis. With these modifications the Guild prospered, reaching 41,226 members with its twelfth selection. As Guinzburg began to have second thoughts concerning the potentially harmful effects of mass merchandising upon publishing standards, he gradually relinquished his interest in the Guild. In 1929 Nelson Doubleday bought 49 percent of the club's stock, and five years later Guinzburg sold the rest to him for $380,000. The Literary Guild thereafter became an extension of Doubleday's publishing empire.

Despite the depression of the 1930's, Viking expanded its publications by adding a juvenile department in 1933 under the direction of May Massee. Her discriminating taste in children's literature produced a distinguished juvenile list that included Munro Leaf's best seller *The Story of Ferdinand* (1936). Another valuable addition to the staff was Pascal Covici of Covici-Friede, who took a position as senior editor at Viking when his own publishing house failed in 1938. Covici brought along his most important author, John Steinbeck, whose *Grapes of Wrath* was published the following year. Other notable American writers published by Viking in the 1930's were Erskine Caldwell, Dorothy Parker, Albert Halper, and Alexander Woollcott.

During World War II Guinzburg worked for the Office of War Information (OWI), which he joined in January 1942. His duties involved the recruitment of personnel and the setting up of programs for OWI offices in friendly and neutral countries. In 1943 he became chief of the agency's Domestic Bureau of Publications and the following year he went to London as director of the London Publications Division. Under his direction almost half a million leaflets, books, magazines, and other informational materials were printed for distribution in the liberated areas of Europe. He returned to Viking in December 1944, but continued to serve as a general publishing consultant to the OWI until the end of the war.

One enduring by-product of the wartime experience was the creation of Viking's Portable Library, a series of compact anthologies designed for servicemen. The first volume, Alexander Woollcott's *As You Were* (1943), proved so popular that the Viking editors continued to publish the selected writings of prominent authors in a "portable" format. In the 1950's Guinzburg authorized a paperback edition of many titles in the series. He also helped to launch Compass Books, paperback reprints of serious modern works taken largely from Viking backlists, in 1956. Each of these series sold well.

A member of the American Civil Liberties Union, Guinzburg defended freedom of the press against the conformist pressures of the cold-war era. "Not only must man be allowed to say what he wishes," he argued in an influential Windsor Lecture delivered at the University of Illinois in 1952, "but . . . those who control the limited channels for reaching the public have an obligation to present both sides of controversial issues." To insure the continued production of significant books in an age of mass marketing, Guinzburg advocated a more responsible publishing code, the expansion of the public library system, and the inculcation of sound reading habits in young people through more innovative teaching in schools and colleges. He served as president of the American Book Publishers Council from 1956 to 1958, and remained the active head of Viking until his death in New York City.

[Guinzburg's unpublished letters are in the Benjamin W. Huebsch Papers, Library of Congress. His 1952 lecture at the University of Illinois, "Free Press, Free Enterprise, and Diversity," was published in Guinzburg, Robert W. Frase, and Theodore Waller, *Books and the Mass Market* (1953). For further discussion of Guinzburg's reform proposals, see his "Book Publishing: A Dubious Utopia," *Saturday Review of Literature*, May 26, 1951, and "Educate Students so They Want to Read," *Wilson Library Bulletin*, Feb. 1957. For details of his wartime work for the OWI, see "Take a Bow," *Publishers Weekly*, Feb. 3, 1945.]

MAXWELL BLOOMFIELD

GUNNISON, FOSTER (June 9, 1896–Oct. 19, 1961), entrepreneur in the prefabricated housing industry, was born in Brooklyn, N.Y., the son of Herbert Foster Gunnison, publisher of the *Brooklyn Eagle,* and of Alice May. Educated mainly in Brooklyn public schools, Gunnison finished secondary school at Culver Military Academy, Culver, Ind. He then entered St. Lawrence University, Canton, N.Y., from which he graduated in 1918. Gunnison next studied at the United States Naval Academy and in 1919 was commissioned as an ensign. He served a two-year tour of duty in the Mediterranean and resigned his commission in 1921. On Apr. 13, 1918, he married Caroline McAllaster; they had one son.

From 1921 to 1923, Gunnison worked for Edward John Noble, the manufacturer of the

Life Saver candy at Port Chester, N.Y. In 1923, determined to create a business for himself, Gunnison entered a partnership in a small company that designed and built electric lighting fixtures. Cox, Nostrand and Gunnison became a leading firm in the lighting of major Art Deco buildings in New York, including the Empire State Building, the Waldorf-Astoria Hotel, the Chrysler Building, and Rockefeller Center. The company attracted national attention with the creation of a huge chandelier (twenty-five feet in diameter, six tons in weight, with 400 floodlights) for the Center Theater in Rockefeller Center, and received much praise for the design and effects of its other fixtures.

Gunnison became steeped in the ideas and ideology of the Art Deco movement, which despite its various modes of development claimed above all to come to terms with and to express fully the meaning, values, and materials of what had become known simply as the Machine. A trip to Europe in the 1920's and extensive contact with Beaux Arts–trained architects provided Gunnison with the assurance that both art and architecture were developing in concert with modern technology rather than being threatened by it.

With its emphasis on technology, the Art Deco movement provided Gunnison with the vision of a machine-based housing industry, rather than one depending on craftsmen working on single structures. Prefabrication of houses, he argued, would bring the full benefits of mass-production technology to a backward industry and provide a new level of abundance for society.

With the support and advice of Owen D. Young, chairman of the General Electric Company, Gunnison moved from the design and production of lighting fixtures to houses. Young was a friend of the family who had been helped through St. Lawrence University by Gunnison's uncle, president of that school. Like Gunnison, he was a member of Beta Theta Pi fraternity; and Gunnison used this fraternal bond to approach Young and convince him of the promise of prefabrication. In 1934 Gunnison founded Houses, Inc., a company created to stimulate research, construction, management, and financing in prefabricated housing.

Houses, Inc., was affiliated with two important companies: National Houses, which made steel-frame, steel-panel buildings; and American Houses, producer of the Motohome, which was constructed of steel-frame, asbestos cement panels. Houses, Inc. extensively promoted the Motohome. Its invitation to the opening exhibition of the Motohome called it "the prefabricated house that comes complete with food in the kitchen." In April 1935, President Franklin D. Roosevelt's mother untied a ribbon wrapped around a cellophane-packaged Motohome at Wanamaker's department store in New York. Gunnison also promoted the Motohome by holding open houses.

As the result of internal dispute, chiefly personality conflicts, Gunnison divested himself of Houses, Inc., in late 1935 and soon formed his own company, Gunnison Magic Homes, in New Albany, Ind. He hoped, according to a trade publication, to make it "the General Motors of the homebuilding field." Adapting a waterproof plywood, stressed-skin panel developed by the U.S. Forest Products Laboratory, the company became one of the best-known manufacturers in the prefabrication industry. Gunnison recruited production experts from the automobile industry and, according to *Architectural Forum*, "perfected prefabrication on a true mass-production, assembly line basis." In 1944 he reported an output of 600 houses per month.

Gunnison sought to emulate not only the automobile industry's production methods but also its marketing strategy. While other prefabricators sought to build entire subdivisions or villages, he developed and adhered to a retail merchandising system based upon the dealership. Like automobile dealers, Gunnison house dealers offered individual customers various home models, a year-long warranty, and a complete line of maintenance services. His particular contribution to the prefabrication of houses, therefore, resulted from his recognition that "to provide a continuous flow of orders . . . becomes the most important problem of all. Thus, upon the method of distribution and sales used, depends the ultimate success or failure of the industry as a whole and each company within it."

In 1944 Gunnison's company, known since 1937 as Gunnison Housing Corporation, became a subsidiary of United States Steel Corporation under the name Gunnison Homes. Gunnison remained as president of the company until 1950 and was a director until 1953. The company was then renamed United States Steel Homes. It was phased out in 1974.

Gunnison was one of the creators in 1942 of the Prefabricated Homes Manufacturing Institute. In recognition of his contributions to prefabrication, the National Association of Home Builders elected him to its Hall of Fame, calling him the Father of Prefab. Others have called him the Henry Ford of Housing.

In 1949 Gunnison's first marriage ended in divorce, and on Oct. 24, 1950, he married Mary Moore. They had one daughter. He died in St. Petersburg, Fla.

[Some manuscripts related to Gunnison Homes are in the records of the Albert Farwell Bemis Foundation, MIT, Archives and Special Collections, Cambridge, Mass. Gunnison's work on prefabrication is documented in Alfred Bruce and Harold Sandbank, *A History of Prefabrication* (1944); and Burnham Kelly, *The Prefabrication of Houses* (1951). For his earlier work on electric lighting design, see Alan Balfour, *Rockefeller Center: Architecture as Theater* (1978); and Carol Herselle Krinsky, *Rockefeller Center* (1978). An obituary is in the *New York Times*, Oct. 20, 1961.]

DAVID A. HOUNSHELL

HACKETT, FRANCIS (Jan. 21, 1883–Apr. 24, 1962), literary critic, editor, and novelist, was born in Kilkenny, Ireland, the son of John Byrne Hackett and Bridget Doheny. Hackett's father held hospital appointments in Kilkenny, and served as medical officer to the Urban District Council and as coroner. His mother, the daughter of a farmer, was intimidated by the aristocratic pretensions of her husband's family. As a boy, Hackett learned to appreciate both the folk culture of the farm and literary culture, and to distrust privileged groups.

Hackett's father, a fervent supporter of Charles Stewart Parnell, imparted a special form of Parnellism to his son, who was raised in an intensely Catholic family setting but learned to resent the church's denunciation of Parnell. When Parnell died in 1891, Hackett had a martyr to remember.

Hackett first studied with the nuns and then with the Christian Brothers in Kilkenny. He attended a prestigious Jesuit secondary school, Clongowes Wood College, from 1897 to 1900. There he went through a period of religious zeal but also began to resent rote learning and the school's acceptance of pro-British and upper-class values. He read widely in late nineteenth-century British and American literature. At seventeen he matriculated in the Royal University but left without a degree.

In 1901, convinced that Ireland was ruled by two alien masters (the British and the Catholic Church), that the Irish people did not have sufficient nationalist feelings, and that his family and town were unable to provide him with additional education or a career, Hackett sailed to the United States. He arrived in New York on October 6. A myopic, chunky youth wearing a pince-nez, he was passionately against the British, imperialism, and the Catholic Church, and passionately for Ireland, literature, and a girl he had known in Ireland. While job hunting he published articles in Standish O'Grady's *All Ireland Review*, Arthur Griffith's *United Irishman*, and Samuel Richardson's American magazine, *The Gael.* Early in 1902 he found a job as a clerk and apprentice in the law firm of Philbin, Beekman and Menken. Next he worked as an office boy under Frank Griffin in the advertising department of *Cosmopolitan* magazine, and then he sold book cloth at Holliston Mills and helped John Quinn establish an Irish literary society. Griffin hired Hackett as assistant paymaster in a sea-going prep school venture on the S.S. *Pennsylvania.* When the school failed, Hackett was rejected for enlistment by the American navy and was thus blocked in his second attempt to escape confining jobs and see the world. He secured employment in December 1904 with the Chicago and Alton Railroad as a clerk in the waybill department.

Irish connections in Chicago introduced Hackett to the Little Room, a nest of genteel culture in the brawling city. There he met the city's leading cultural figures. He resigned from the railroad and wrote a brief series on the life of the clerk for *The Reader.* In preparation for the series he worked in the stockyards and the basement of Marshall Field's wholesale house and as a cub reporter on William Randolph Hearst's *Chicago American.* When the *American* editors discovered that Hackett exaggerated stories and could not wrench photographs, they fired him. Early in 1906, Hackett reviewed books for Tiffany Blake, literary editor of the *Chicago Evening Post,* and then secured a job on the *Post* writing reviews, editorials, and feature articles. In mid-1906, Hackett moved into Hull House, where for a year he taught English to Russian immigrants. His acquaintance with Jane Addams and familiarity with books by her, Thorstein Veblen, William James, and the British Fabians lent an intensely democratic and culturally radical cast to Hackett's reviews. Yet he also enjoyed Chicago's cultured, affluent youth.

On Blake's departure in 1908, the *Post*'s managing editor, Leigh Reilly, made Hackett literary editor and then, in March 1909, editor of the *Post*'s new literary supplement, the *Friday Literary Review.* Hackett and his associate Floyd Dell made this review the first sustained voice in America to support literary realism and cultural radicalism. Hackett attacked Chicago's genteel and commercial cultures, racism, and the subordination of women, and praised writers such as H. G. Wells, E. M. Forster, Walt Whitman, Robert Herrick, Jane Addams, and Herbert Croly.

In 1911, Hackett resigned from the *Post,* claiming that he wanted to write a novel. He spent the winter on a farm near Madison, Wis., then visited his sick father in Ireland, and subsequently served as Quinn's secretary at the 1912 Democratic convention in Baltimore. The experience killed the friendship between Hackett and Quinn, a political chieftain for Thomas Fortune Ryan at the convention.

In 1913, Croly invited Hackett to New York City to join him, Walter Lippmann, and Walter Weyl in the creation of the *New Republic.* The magazine began publication in 1914. In his post as literary editor, Hackett vigorously supported the cultural radicals, the new literary realists, cultural pluralism, and an inclusive democracy. He was fiercely independent, and grew stubbornly resistant to policies favored by Croly and Lippmann. They were disturbed by Hackett's intense Irish nationalism, but the real division came over issues involving World War I, the Versailles Treaty, and the League of Nations.

On Sept. 5, 1918, Hackett married Signe Kirstine Toksvig, a *New Republic* editor who had been born in Denmark. In 1922 he resigned from the *New Republic,* moved to Europe, and began a long career as a free-lance writer. He wrote briefly for the S. S. McClure syndicate, produced a serialized book on Ireland for the *New York World,* and, in 1922–1923, wrote a column, "The Rolling Stone," for the *World's* famous Op-Ed page. In his essays he supported the League of Nations, praised Hull House, and paid tribute to Denmark. He also wrote travel material and literary essays. In 1924 he began writing popular histories, the first of which was a study of Henry VIII (1929).

In 1927, Hackett returned to the United States for a brief visit. Prosperous from 1929 to 1937, he moved to Ireland and bought a country home. But when the Irish censored *Green Lion,* his autobiographical novel, in 1936, he and his wife regretfully moved to Denmark the following year. When he and his wife fled Denmark in 1940, to escape the Nazi threat, Hackett published *I Chose Denmark,* a moving autobiographical volume praising small democratic countries and folk and cooperative cultures, and attacking imperialism of all kinds. In 1941 he wrote *What "Mein Kampf" Means to America,* an attack on appeasement. He entered into lawsuits with Alexander Korda (1935) and with Maxwell Anderson (1949) over their alleged plagiarism of his studies of Henry VIII and Anne

Boleyn. Hackett received a substantial settlement from Korda; but he and Anderson soon withdrew their suits against one another.

From 1939 until the early 1950's Hackett and his wife lived in the United States. He wrote literary reviews and essays for the *New Republic* (1937, 1956), the *New York Times* (1944–1945), the *American Mercury* (1944), and many other magazines. In April 1948 he became a citizen of the United States. By the early 1950's the Hacketts lived mostly in Denmark on very little income. Old friends such as Felix Frankfurter and Benjamin W. Huebsch helped Hackett secure literary work and foundation support. He died in Virum, Denmark.

[Hackett's correspondence is in the collections of prominent literary figures such as H. L. Mencken. There are large holdings in the Felix Frankfurter and Benjamin W. Huebsch collections at the Library of Congress and in the possession of Signe Toksvig. His books include criticism: *Horizons* (1918), *The Invisible Censor* (1921), and *On Judging Books* (1947); studies of Ireland: *Ireland: A Study in Nationalism* (1918), *The Story of the Irish Nation* (1922); popular histories: *Francis the First* (1935), *Queen Anne Boleyn* (1938); novels: *That Nice Young Couple* (1924), *The Senator's Last Night* (1943); and the autobiography edited by Signe Toksvig, *American Rainbow* (1971). See Philip Littell, "F. H.," *New Republic,* Oct. 12, 1918; James Delehanty, "The Green Lion: In Memoriam Francis Hackett (1883–1962)," *Kilkenny Magazine,* Summer 1962; George A. Test, "Francis Hackett: Literary Radical Without Portfolio," *Midcontinent American Studies Journal,* Fall 1964; Charles Angoff, "Francis Hackett," in *The Tone of the Twenties* (1966). Also see Hyland Packard, "Critic as Witness: Francis Hackett and His America, 1883–1914" (Ph.D. diss., Louisiana State University, 1970), and "From Kilkenny: The Background of an Intellectual Immigrant," *Eire-Ireland,* Fall 1975. An obituary is in *New York Times,* Apr. 26, 1962.]

HYLAND PACKARD

HAGEDORN, HERMANN LUDWIG GEBHARD (July 18, 1882–July 27, 1964), poet, novelist, and biographer, was born on Staten Island, N.Y., the son of Hermann Hagedorn and Anna Schwedler. His father, who emigrated from Germany in 1866, was a founding member of the New York Cotton Exchange. Despite losing two of three fortunes he made, he supported his wife and children in relative affluence in a succession of rented houses in Brooklyn. He adhered strongly to German culture and tradition, insisting that only German be spoken at home and taking the family to Germany for frequent long visits. Hermann, the last-born, did not learn to speak English until he was enrolled in a private school at age five. He later attended Bedford Academy, Brooklyn Polytechnic Institute, and, from 1898 to 1901, the Hill School in Pottstown, Penn., where winning the mile race in an important track meet bolstered his self-confidence and gave him the sense of becoming a part of the American social fabric.

Consenting to his father's desire that he enter business, Hagedorn became an office boy at Bliss, Fabyan, and Company in 1901 and took business courses. But he felt unsuited to such work and in 1903 welcomed a chance to write for a literary magazine, *The Reader*. That fall he entered Harvard, where he was active in campus journalism and was elected to Phi Beta Kappa. For the 1907 commencement, at which he received the A.B., he composed the class poem, "A Troop of the Guard," a striking work that was widely reprinted. On June 6, 1908, after travel in Europe and study during the winter semester (1907–1908) at the University of Berlin, Hagedorn married his fiancée of long standing, Dorothy Oakley. They had three children.

In 1909 Hagedorn accepted a position at Harvard as instructor of English literature and assistant to Professor Barrett Wendell. But he left in 1911 to devote full time to writing. He had issued his first book in 1908, *The Woman of Corinth, A Tale in Verse*; now he tried his hand at fiction with *Faces in the Dawn* and at drama with *Makers of Magic*, both completed in 1914. In 1916 Hagedorn and three friends formed the Vigilantes with the purpose of stimulating patriotic sentiment among young Americans.

After the United States entered World War I, Hagedorn wrote *Where Do You Stand?* (1918), an appeal to his fellow Americans of German extraction. It drew praise but also censure: upper-crust German families charged him with betrayal of his heritage, while super-patriots accused him of disloyalty to the United States. The war also caused a deep and tragic division of his own German-American relatives, which he movingly reported in *The Hyphenated Family* (1960), his last major book and one of his finest.

By 1918 Hagedorn's casual acquaintance with Theodore Roosevelt had ripened into close friendship. Hagedorn viewed the Rough Rider as a paragon of Americanism. After Roosevelt died in 1919, he worked tirelessly to confirm his greatness and to perpetuate his memory. As the moving force of the Roosevelt Memorial Association (later renamed the Theodore Roosevelt Association), he assembled the nation's first

presidential library, now housed at Harvard. Hagedorn wrote *The Boys' Life of Theodore Roosevelt* (1918), which Roosevelt asked him to prepare; *The Rough Riders*, (1927); and many volumes of edited collections of Roosevelt's speeches and writings. His most popular work was *The Roosevelt Family of Sagamore Hill*, a 1954 best seller. He also led campaigns to restore and establish as national shrines both Sagamore Hill, at Oyster Bay, Long Island, and Roosevelt's Manhattan birthplace; he helped to create a fitting memorial in Washington, D.C., and to celebrate in 1958 the centennial of Roosevelt's birth.

Interest in Roosevelt did not preempt other work. Hagedorn continued to publish poetry and substantial biographies of General Leonard Wood (1931), Albert Schweitzer (1947), the mining magnate William Boyce Thompson (1935), Robert Brookings of the Brookings Institute (1936), and Edwin Arlington Robinson (1938), whose close friend he became while serving on the board of the Edward MacDowell Association. Capacity for friendship was one of Hagedorn's conspicuous traits.

Hagedorn was tall, strikingly handsome, and gregarious albeit somewhat reserved. A religious experience in 1933 broadened his concern for humanity at large and altered the style and nature of his poetry, which displayed thereafter fewer heroics and more spirituality. Hagedorn and his wife eventually settled in Santa Barbara, Calif. Never one to consider retiring, he had just begun a biography of his friend Walking Buffalo, a Stony Indian chief, when he died of heart failure at the wheel of his car, after passing a driver's examination.

[Hagedorn collections can be found in the Beinecke Library, Yale University, including the bulk of manuscripts; MS Division, Library of Congress; Arents Research Library, Syracuse University; and the papers of Dorothea Hagedorn Parfit, Santa Barbara. Other collections are in the libraries of Colby College, University of Southern California, University of Pennsylvania, Columbia University; Theodore Roosevelt Association; American Academy and Institute of Arts and Letters; and the Theodore Roosevelt Collection, Harvard. Biographical and critical material can be found in the twenty-fifth and fiftieth anniversary reports, Harvard class of 1907; John A. Gable, "The Life and Work of Hermann Hagedorn," *Theodore Roosevelt Association Journal*, Fall 1977; Alan R. Havig, "Presidential Images . . . ," *American Quarterly*, Fall 1978; and Phyllis Keller, *States of Being: German-American Intellectuals and the First World War* (1979). Hagedorn's obituary appears in the *New York Times*, July 28, 1964.]

WILLIAM PEIRCE RANDEL

HALE, FREDERICK (Oct. 7, 1874–Sept. 28, 1963), U.S. senator, was born in Detroit, Mich., the son of Eugene Hale and Mary Douglas Chandler. His father represented Maine in the United States Senate from 1881 to 1911, and his maternal grandfather, Zachariah Chandler, was secretary of the interior under President Ulysses Grant and a senator from Michigan (1879). Hale attended Lawrenceville (1889–1890) and Groton (1891–1892) preparatory schools and received the B.A. degree from Harvard in 1896. He then attended Columbia University Law School (1896–1897). After leaving Columbia, he read law for two years in the Portland, Maine, office of an uncle, Clarence Hale, and was admitted to the Maine bar in 1899. In 1902 he formed a law partnership in Portland with Arthur F. Belcher. After Belcher's death he entered the partnership of Verrill, Hale and Booth.

Hale served one term (1905–1906) in the lower house of the Maine legislature, then was defeated for reelection. From 1912 to 1918 he was Maine's Republican national committeeman. In 1916, as the first United States senator from Maine chosen by popular vote, he began a career in the Senate that lasted until his retirement in 1941. He served on the Rules, Appropriations, and Naval Affairs committees, and was chairman of the latter for nine years and briefly chairman of the Appropriations Committee. Hale was noted for his strong advocacy of a large navy. He firmly believed that "preparedness is cheaper than war." He counted naval strength on a comparative basis, however, and voted for the naval arms limitation treaties proposed by the Washington Arms Conference of 1921–1922 In his early years in the Senate he supported the woman suffrage amendment and the Lodge reservations to the League of Nations covenant.

In 1931 Hale joined other senators who unsuccessfully opposed the London treaty for naval limitation. By this time he concluded that the ratio offered was less satisfactory than the one in 1922, and that the pact would "hamstring and hogtie" the United States. His strenuous objections to the Coolidge and Hoover economy cuts in naval construction finally resulted in a cruiser-building program. In 1925 Hale told President Calvin Coolidge that the American fleet was all but helpless in the Pacific because of inadequate bases, and he worked for the strengthening of Pearl Harbor. Throughout the 1920's and 1930's he tended toward isolationism, voting in 1933 against extending diplomatic recognition to the Soviet Union. By 1939, however, he was warning that strong aid to Great Britain was essential to American safety.

Hale disliked publicity and viewed speechmaking with distaste. Nevertheless, as chairman of the Naval Affairs Committee he made the key speeches on naval legislation. Both in Maine and in Washington, he was respected for his honesty and integrity. "If Hale says so, it's so," a colleague reportedly remarked. He attempted to protect the interests of his constituents, on one occasion almost single-handedly leading, and winning, a fight to remove the tariff on commercial fertilizers in order to aid Maine potato growers. Yet he refused either to make campaign promises or to engage in congressional "logrolling." In 1936 he refused to vote for the huge expenditures for the Passamaquoddy tidal power project that would have been located in his state.

Hale was reserved and outwardly crusty, but those close to him recognized the wit, humor, and kindness that lay beneath the forbidding exterior. Once, on a hunting trip in Alaska, he was charged by a bear and forced to kill it. Upon discovering that the bear had left three small cubs, he wrapped them up, carried them by train across the country, and presented them to the Washington Zoo. Throughout the trip he bottle-fed the cubs every two hours, and named one of them Portland, after his hometown.

The fact that he was unmarried occasionally posed political problems for Hale. In 1922 his opponent, Howard Davies, raised the issue of the family man versus the bachelor. During the campaign hecklers shouted at Hale: "Get married! Get married!" He also deeply resented being called "Washington's most eligible bachelor."

During the 1930's Hale consistently opposed New Deal spending policies. He voted against President Franklin D. Roosevelt's "court-packing plan" and contended that the New Deal attitude toward business retarded economic recovery. On the questionnaire sent him for the Fiftieth Anniversary Report of the Harvard Class of 1896, Hale wrote that his most enduring satisfactions in life were "1. That the people of my State elected me to four terms in the U.S. Senate. 2. That fifty-six years of my life were spent *not* under the New Deal."

In retirement Hale led an active life, golfing, fishing, and hunting. In 1943 he accepted the chairmanship of the Red Cross War Fund campaign for the Greater Portland area. At the close of World War II, he became vice-president of the Navy League of the United States, which sought to inform the country of the importance of maintaining an adequate navy. He warned that the "pacifists of this country would undoubtedly seek . . . to cut down our navy," as they had after World War I. Hale died in Portland, Maine.

[Hale's papers are at Syracuse University. Some of his more noted speeches are in *Congressional Digest,* Jan. 1929; June 1930; Apr. 1934. Also see "Chairman of Republican City Committee," *Portland* (Maine) *Times,* Nov. 29, 1903; *Sprague's Journal of Maine History,* June 1920; "No 'Hale of Maine' in the U. S. Senate After Jan. 3," *Portland* (Maine) *Sunday Telegram,* Dec. 29, 1940; *Fiftieth Anniversary Report, Harvard Class of 1896* (1946); and *Portland* (Maine) *Press Herald,* July 11, 1945; Oct. 11, 1963; Nov. 2, 1963. Obituaries are in the *Boston Sunday Herald, Portland Sunday Telegram, Boston Sunday Globe,* and the *New York Times,* Sept. 29, 1963.]

MELBA PORTER HAY

HAMILTON, EDITH (Aug. 12, 1867–May 31, 1963), teacher, classicist, and author, was born in Dresden, Germany, where her parents were visiting, the daughter of Montgomery Hamilton, a Fort Wayne, Ind., businessman, and of Gertrude Pond. Edith's childhood was spent in Fort Wayne. Her father was devoted to classic literature, and she began to study Latin and Greek with him at an early age. She learned German from servants and a Lutheran tutor, developing an ever-deeper interest in languages and in literature. She attended Miss Porter's School at Farmington, Conn., and Bryn Mawr College, where she earned an A.B. and an A.M. in 1894 and was a Bryn Mawr fellow in Latin in 1894–1895.

Hamilton received a Bryn Mawr European Fellowship in 1895; she then spent a year at the universities of Leipzig and Munich with her younger sister, Alice Hamilton, a physician. The first women even admitted to Munich, they observed German society from an unusual vantage point. Hamilton became headmistress of the Bryn Mawr School in Baltimore, Md., in 1896, where she taught until 1922 when she resigned and moved to New York City to devote full time to classical studies. By that time, she had built the Bryn Mawr School into a leading academic center from its early failure as the nation's first women's college-preparatory school.

Hamilton was encouraged to write by a new circle of literary friends that included Edith J. R. Isaacs, a founder of *Theatre Arts Monthly;* Rosamond Gilder and Dorothea McCollester, editors of *Theatre Arts Monthly;* and Elling Aannestad, an editor with W. W. Norton and Company. She published her first popular article, "Tragedy," at the age of 59 in *Theatre Arts Monthly.* This and seven other articles from the same magazine were expanded into her first book, *The Greek Way* (1930; revised, expanded, and reissued as *The Great Age of Greek Literature,* 1942).

The Greek Way was immediately acclaimed as the work of a major author with a fresh style and program. Her later works are marked by the same individualism, her ideas based almost entirely upon critical knowledge of the original-language sources, with little attention to later interpretations. Her style is varied and flowing, highly polished but slightly embellished, reminding one much of the style of Walter Pater but lacking his coldness. Her style is restrained romantic, with more interest in philosophy than in morality. Her second book, *The Roman Way* (1932), is a colder picture of a less fertile and admirable culture, but contains no overt judgments.

The Prophets of Israel (1936), Hamilton's first venture into the biblical field, is a study of the Old Testment from three contradictory viewpoints: orthodoxy, higher criticism, and mythopoeia. Although hard to evaluate against the body of Old Testament literature, it is an exciting account of her own knowledge of the texts. *Mythology* (1942) shows the same conflicts in Greek and Roman myth, and *Witness to the Truth* (1948), a study of the New Testament, cuts through and ignores almost all later commentary, being based almost entirely upon Greek texts. Christian ideology seems refreshed in her personalized view of the Messiah. *Spokesmen for God* (1949) revised and enlarged her *Prophets of Israel,* also dealing with the first five books of the Bible.

Hamilton's long apprenticeship to classical studies led to a late maturity of ten books, thirty popular articles, and four translations. Despite her social poise and polished lecture style, she was a very private person, the great events of her life being intellectual ones. She received many honors, the most gratifying of which was the Golden Cross of the Order of Benefaction, presented by King Paul of Greece on the stage of the ancient theater of Herodes Atticus at Athens in 1957.

Hamilton finished each writing project quickly and left little unpublished material at her death in Washington, D.C. Her translation of Euripides' *Trojan Women* was then in press and was published on almost the same day as Jean-Paul Sartre's French rendering of the same play. These two different translations, each grand in its own manner, seek some common ground in antique texts for the differing thoughts of our age.

As a scholar, Hamilton was accustomed to reading rather than to translating, and in her fresh approach to the classics she brought a revival of learning for modern readers. She carried a new sense of ancient literature into modern life. Her achievements and ideas inspired many women to new ideals of self-achievement.

[A collection of Hamilton's personal papers is in the Schlesinger Library, Radcliffe College; scholarly papers and reviews were gathered and published with an interpretative biographical prologue as *The Ever Present Past* (1964). Works by Hamilton not mentioned in the text include *Three Greek Plays* (1937), *Introduction to Plutarch* (1951), *The Echo of Greece* (1957), and *Collected Dialogues of Plato,* edited with Huntington Cairns (1961). Also see Alice Hamilton, *Exploring the Dangerous Trades,* an autobiography by Hamilton's sister; and Doris Fielding Reid, *Edith Hamilton: An Intimate Portrait* (1967), an authoritative source. Obituaries appeared in *Publishers Weekly,* June 1963; the *New York Times,* June 1, 1963; *Time,* June 7, 1963; and *Newsweek,* June 10, 1963.]

JOHN WITTHOFT

HAMMETT, SAMUEL DASHIELL (May 27, 1894–Jan. 10, 1961), writer, was born in St. Mary's County, Md., the son of Richard T. Hammett, a farmer and politician, and Annie Bond Dashiell. Hammett's only schooling was at Baltimore Polytechnic Institute, which he left at fourteen after less than one year. He then worked sporadically at odd jobs, including stints as freight clerk, stevedore, and railroad employee. At twenty he joined the Pinkerton National Detective Agency; his assignments ranged across the country and introduced him to the world of crime. In 1918–1919 he served in the Ambulance Corps and was stationed near Baltimore. He contracted tuberculosis, the first of a series of pulmonary illnesses which eventually caused his death. In 1920–1921, while being treated for tuberculosis in hospitals on the West Coast, he met a nurse, Josephine A. Dolan, whom he married on Dec. 27, 1920. The union produced two daughters but was not close; on occasion the two lived apart. They separated in 1927 and were divorced in 1937.

In 1921 Hammett was employed by the Pinkerton branch in San Francisco, a city he called home for the next eight years. After a few months he quit the agency. Fearing that ill health would cut his life short and driven by a desire to write, he retreated to a cheap single room and wrote verses and sketches.

During 1922–1926, part of his support came from producing advertising copy for a local jeweler.

Hammett now began to draw from his experiences with Pinkerton and the low life of San Francisco. In late 1922 he began to be published in the *Smart Set* and other journals, including *Black Mask,* a popular pulp-fiction magazine. In October 1923 *Black Mask* printed the first of many stories about the Continental Op, the prototype of the hard-boiled investigator most often associated with his work.

Between 1922 and 1934 Hammett produced over seventy short crime tales and was acknowledged as a master of the form. By 1927 he had also begun to develop serials in *Black Mask,* which he later published as novels. The first, featuring the Continental Op, were *Red Harvest* and *The Dain Curse* (both 1929). In 1930 he introduced Sam Spade in *The Maltese Falcon;* Ned Beaumont appeared in *The Glass Key* (1931), and Nick and Nora Charles in *The Thin Man* (1934).

Hammett had moved to New York City in 1929 but soon settled in Hollywood to work on film scripts. He continued to live in the self-destructive pattern set in the 1920's: periods of concentrated work were interspersed with bouts of drinking, womanizing, gambling, and reckless spending. In November 1930 he met Lillian Hellman, then in film work and later a noted playwright. Their affair was stormy and punctuated by periods of living apart and by the taking of other lovers; but it lasted until Hammett's death.

Hammett's career was meteoric and lucrative; but by 1934 most of his creative energy was spent. The decline was signalized by his next project, the story for a syndicated comic strip, *Secret Agent X-9.* He continued to do movie work, the most important of which was his screenplay for *Watch on the Rhine* (1943), based on Hellman's play. But political interests —especially the antifascism which engaged many writers of the time—were now occupying much of Hammett's time. He became a Marxist and by 1937 had joined the Communist party. His left-wing associations would bring him much trouble, but although often critical of party policies, he never wavered in his commitment. Through frequent reprintings of his work, Hammett's name remained well known after 1934. His reputation was also enhanced by the film versions of a number of his stories, most notably *The Thin Man* (1934), its several sequels, and *The Maltese Falcon* (1941), with Humphrey Bogart.

In September 1942 Hammett, at forty-eight, enlisted in the Army Signal Corps. He was stationed in the Aleutians, where he edited a paper and wrote the text of a pamphlet, *The Battle of the Aleutians* (1944). He was discharged in September 1945.

Although Hammett developed three radio shows based on his fictional characters, in the postwar years he devoted most of his energy to politics. He became an official of the Civil Rights Congress (considered subversive by the attorney general) and taught at the Jefferson School of Social Sciences in New York City (1946–1947). In 1951 he was haled before the New York State Supreme Court as a trustee of the bail bond fund of the Civil Rights Congress. He refused to testify, was convicted for contempt of court, and was imprisoned from July to December 1951. In April 1953 he appeared before Senator Joseph McCarthy's Subcommittee on Investigations. His increasing notoriety put him on the Hollywood blacklist, and his income began to shrink. The final blow was a judgment against him by the Internal Revenue Service for back taxes of over $140,000; his earnings were attached for the rest of his life. He had given up drinking in 1948 after a doctor's warning, but his pulmonary ailments now left him physically debilitated. From 1956 on he was cared for by Lillian Hellman; he eventually developed lung cancer and died in New York City.

Hammett is generally credited with initiating the hard-boiled school of detective fiction and with changing the crime novel from an intellectual puzzle to a drama involving realistic characters from the dark underside of life. His tight-lipped dialogue and his spare scene setting were often imitated. As his rival Raymond Chandler commented, "Hammett took murder out of the Venetian vase and dropped it into the alley. . . . . Hammett gave murder back to the kind of people that commit it for reasons, not just to provide a corpse; and with the means at hand, not with hand-wrought duelling pistols, curare, and tropical fish." Most importantly, Hammett created a hero for his times: the incorruptible private eye who confronts the corrupt world of depression and gangsterism; the tough-skinned romantic who combats evil with the weapons of evil; the proletarian knight who fights for the good society in which criminals must be made to pay for their acts.

[Of the many editions of Hammett's work, two collections are notable: *The Big Knockover* (1966), with preface by Lillian Hellman, includes Hammett's unfinished autobiography "Tulip"; and *The Conti-* *nental Op* (1974), with an essay by Steven Marcus. For biographical and critical materials, see David Madden, ed., *Tough Guy Writers of the Thirties* (1968); William F. Nolan, *Dashiell Hammett: A Casebook* (1969); Julian Symons, *Mortal Consequences* (1972); Joseph N. Gores, *Hammett* (1975). Personal reminiscences are in Dorothy Gardiner and Kathrine S. Walker, eds., *Raymond Chandler Speaking* (1962) and Lillian Hellman's three volumes: *An Unfinished Woman* (1969); *Pentimento* (1973); *Scoundrel Time* (1976). A comprehensive guide to Hammett's work in all fields, including his many book reviews, is Richard Layman, *Dashiell Hammett: A Descriptive Bibliography* (1979), which contains a portrait. An obituary appeared in the *New York Times* on Jan. 11, 1961.]

JOSEPH V. RIDGELY

HAND, LEARNED (Jan. 27, 1872–Aug. 18, 1961), jurist, was born in Albany, N.Y., the son of Samuel Hand and Lydia Coit Learned. His father, two uncles, and grandfather Augustus C. Hand, were lawyers. Samuel Hand was a leading appellate advocate in Albany, an adviser to Democratic governors, and briefly a judge of the state's highest court. He died when Learned Hand was fourteen. The early death of his successful, cultivated, but remote father left Learned Hand with an inspiring but anxiety-producing model for emulation.

Christened Billings Learned Hand, in accordance with the Learned family's tradition of using maiden surnames as given names, Hand found the name too formidable. At college he called himself B. Learned Hand. When he graduated from law school in 1896, he dropped the first name entirely. Throughout his life, however, close friends called him "B," shortened from his early nicknames of "Bunny" and "Buck" rather than from "Billings."

Hand was an obedient, bookish boy. At Albany Academy he viewed himself as an outsider, uninterested in military drills and too poorly coordinated for most sports. His major delights came from reading and from vacations in Elizabethtown, where he could hike with his cousin, Augustus N. Hand, a lifelong friend and longtime colleague on the bench.

New horizons of intellectual excitement and independence opened for Hand when he entered Harvard College in 1889. He quickly moved from the traditional courses in mathematics and the classics to the richer fare offered by F. W. Taussig in economics, Charles Eliot Norton in art history, and the stimulating teachers of Harvard's golden age in philosophy: Josiah Royce, William James, and George Santayana. His questioning mind blossomed. By the end of his college years, he found himself incapable of adhering to the religious beliefs of his childhood. Hand became a skeptic and an agnostic, although he was envious of people like his cousin Augustus who could find inner peace in religion.

Hand received his B.A. in 1893 and seriously considered pursuing graduate work in philosophy. But family pressures prevailed and he entered Harvard Law School, which was then in its golden age. Dean Christopher C. Langdell's case method of instruction reigned, and Hand found its sharply honed dialectics especially congenial. He developed a lasting admiration for the great teachers then at the law school—John Chipman Gray, James Barr Ames, and James Bradley Thayer. Thayer's advocacy of judicial self-restraint in the review of legislation exerted a very strong influence on Hand. He was persuaded that law could be a challenging intellectual calling, not merely a trade. Of these teachers he said at the end of his Oliver Wendell Holmes Lectures in 1958: "From them I learned that it was as craftsmen that we get our satisfactions and our pay. In the universe of truth they lived by the sword; they asked no quarter of absolutes and they gave none." (His Holmes lectures were published that year as *The Bill of Rights.*)

At law school, as at college, Hand was an outstanding student, yet he could not quell the feeling that he was an uncouth outsider. He was not asked to join the top rung of clubs on a campus permeated with social snobbery. Awareness that he was not considered one of the suave "swells" rankled for the rest of his life.

After graduation in 1896 Hand returned to Albany, acceding to his mother's expectations and to his own doubts about his aptitude for success at the bar. From 1897 to 1902 he practiced with Marcus T. Hun, a civic-minded lawyer. Hand found Albany intellectually and professionally confining. His practice offered only occasional stimulation—a few civic reform efforts and some part-time teaching at Albany Law School. By 1900, his mind unchallenged and progress at the bar disappointing, Hand was seeking wider horizons.

In the fall of 1902 Hand moved to New York City. His marriage to Frances Amelia Fincke of Utica helped prompt the move. His wife, a Bryn Mawr graduate, self-confident and poised, possessed the social graces Hand thought he lacked, and her calmness assuaged Hand's lifelong proclivity to moodiness. They were married on Dec. 6, 1902, and had three daughters.

The move to New York did not produce success as a practitioner, but it did provide more

intellectual challenges and, ultimately, a change in Hand's career. In his eagerness to escape Albany, he had accepted a position in 1902 as managing clerk in the firm of Zabriskie, Burrill and Murray. After two years he became a partner in Gould and Wilkie, where he practiced until 1909. Hand spent most of his time with uninspiring work for clients garnered by his seniors. He disliked law practice: his work was competent, but he did not think he was good at it.

New York offered other sources of satisfaction. Groups of lawyers and intellectuals gathered to discuss topics beyond the immediate concerns of getting clients and winning lawsuits. Hand also participated in civic reform and wrote articles for legal periodicals. His most important piece appeared in the *Harvard Law Review* in 1908 and reflected Thayer's teachings. It attacked the Supreme Court's approach in *Lochner* v. *New York* (1905), a decision which invalidated a law limiting the hours of bakers and which inaugurated three decades of judicial limitations on reform legislation.

Hand's involvement in New York's intellectual circles led to his career on the bench. After an unsuccessful try at a federal judgeship in 1907, he was named a district judge in New York by President William Howard Taft in 1909. His youth and lack of political connections would ordinarily have barred Hand from consideration for judicial appointment. But Taft, with the advice of his attorney general, George W. Wickersham, was seeking to improve the caliber of the federal bench. The strong recommendation of New York reformer and lawyer Charles C. Burlingham led to Hand's selection.

During his first decade on the bench, Hand continued to participate in public affairs. It was Hand who first brought to Theodore Roosevelt's attention Herbert Croly's influential book, *The Promise of American Life* (1909). Hand had long abandoned his Democratic forebears' belief that concentrations of economic power had to be broken up. Instead, he was drawn to the Croly-Roosevelt view that, although bigness was inevitable, governmental power could curb the excesses of concentrated wealth.

Hand was an enthusiastic supporter of the 1912 Bull Moose campaign of the Roosevelt Progressives. In 1913 he permitted his name to be used as a Progressive candidate for a seat on the highest state court in New York. Moreover, he participated in discussions with Croly, Walter Lippmann, and others which led to the founding of the *New Republic* magazine in 1914. He was a contributor to its pages in its early years. But after World War I, he concluded that his position precluded extrajudicial involvements in controversial issues.

In 1924 Hand was named to the Court of Appeals for the Second Circuit. At that time, the Second Circuit—covering New York, Connecticut, and Vermont—was the leading intermediate appellate court in the nation, especially on commercial and maritime problems. He served as chief judge of that court from 1939 until retirement from regular service in 1951. And he continued to carry a heavy workload on that court for the rest of his life.

Hand is widely regarded as one of the foremost American judges of the twentieth century. Although he never sat on the Supreme Court, very few justices have matched his achievements. His fifty-two-year tenure on the federal bench is unequaled in the twentieth century. He wrote about 3,000 opinions, in every area of law, from common law to statutory interpretation and constitutional adjudication, from patents and copyrights and maritime law to contracts, torts, commercial law, and administrative law.

For decades, many viewed Hand as a potential Supreme Court Justice. As early as 1923, Justice Oliver Wendell Holmes placed Hand on his ideal Supreme Court. During the Old Guard Republican administrations of the 1920's, ex-President Taft, while Chief Justice, used his influence to block consideration of Hand. (Taft had not forgotten Hand's participation in the Progressive movement.) In the early 1940's Franklin D. Roosevelt resisted appeals to name Hand to the highest bench. This time, age rather than political independence was the primary barrier.

Hand's national reputation grew quickly within the legal profession. From the founding of the American Law Institute in 1923, Hand played a leading role in the preparation of the institute's restatements of the law and model statutes. But his major influence stems from his published opinions. Lawyers and judges typically cite precedents only by case name; rarely do they identify the judge who wrote the decision. But no American judge has been more often invoked as a weighty authority in lawyers' briefs and scholars' treatises and judicial opinions than Learned Hand.

Most of Hand's contributions to the clarification and evolution of legal doctrine pertain to problems of private law and statutory interpretation. Yet he was also an important voice in constitutional theory, although few constitutional cases came before his courts. In his Holmes Lectures three years before his death, he questioned the judicial enforceability of the Bill of Rights. These lectures were an extreme restatement of Hand's criticism of the *Lochner* philosophy. He opposed willful judges ready to set aside the majority's wishes on the basis of personal values; he did not wish to be ruled by a "bevy of Platonic Guardians" in judicial robes.

On and off the bench, Hand demonstrated his deep commitment to free expression. Probably his greatest constitutional contribution was his controversial decision *Masses Publishing Co.* v. *Patten* (1917). Hand's ruling protected the mailing of antiwar materials in the midst of a national atmosphere hostile to dissent. His *Masses* opinion shielded all speech falling short of "direct incitement" to illegal action. In 1919 the Supreme Court made its first effort to delineate the contours of the First Amendment and refused to go as far as *Masses* had. Instead, *Schenck* v. *United States* (1919) launched the "clear and present danger" test, under which the protection of speech turned on a guess about its probable impact. In a rare disagreement with his one judicial idol, Oliver Wendell Holmes, Hand criticized Holmes's *Schenck* approach as an inadequate bulwark against majoritarian passions.

The Supreme Court adhered to Holmes's standard for decades and Hand assumed that his *Masses* approach had failed. But in 1969, Hand's approach, combined with the best elements of Holmes's, became the modern standard for First Amendment protection: *Brandenburg* v. *Ohio* (1969).

Hand is equally well known for recasting and, many believe, diluting the "clear and present danger" test by affirming convictions of the Communist leaders in *U.S.* v. *Dennis* (1950). This ruling reflected not only Hand's mounting skepticism about judicial protection of fundamental rights, but also his consistent obedience to Supreme Court pronouncements. Privately, Hand remained convinced even in the 1950's that his *Masses* approach offered better protection to dissenters.

During the last two decades of his life, Hand's renown spread from the profession to the general public. Attention mounted with the widespread reprinting of his brief, moving 1944 speech. Its central passage begins: "The spirit of liberty is the spirit which is not too sure that it is right." The publication of his extrajudicial addresses in 1952 added to the public acclaim.

For much of the public, Hand's reputation rests on his unusual name, his eloquent style, the length and productivity of his judicial service, and his physiognomy, marked by bushy eyebrows and square, strong features. But his main achievements stem, as Judge Henry Friendly has said, from "the great way in which he dealt with a multitude of little cases." Hand's performance is probably the best demonstration in American judicial history of the capability to act in accordance with the modest yet creative model of judging—a model that contrasts with the activist, instrumental one associated with judges such as Earl Warren and William O. Douglas. Hand's record shows that disinterestedness and lack of crusading zeal need not condemn judges to intellectual impotence. His decisions were not noted for dramatic overturning of majoritarian sentiments, but rather for his craftsmanlike performance of the more modest task of operating creatively within the confines set by the political branches. By probing the underlying questions beneath the surface of words, by rejecting glib formulations, suspecting absolutes, and striving for orderly sense amidst the chaos of received legal wisdoms, he was truly innovative within the areas he thought legitimately open to judicial choice.

The qualities central to this modest model of judging—open-mindedness, impartiality, skepticism, restless probing—came naturally to Hand. Reflectiveness, questioning, intolerance of absolutes, relentless searching for answers despite an abiding conviction that there were no permanent ones: those traits were ingrained by the time Hand became a judge. He remained intellectually engaged, always ready to reexamine assumptions. He was philosopher and humanist as well as judge. To social acquaintances, he was a gregarious, joyful companion; to his daughters, he was a warm, playful father. Yet there was also a darker element of anxiety and melancholy in Hand. The public portraits depict him as a magisterial, serene figure; he viewed himself as driven and beset by self-doubt. Hand never ceased questioning the worth of his work and the justifiability of the mounting applause. But his doubts did not produce intellectual paralysis. The skeptical judge persevered, willing to act on the basis of provisional hypotheses.

Hand's unmatched capacity to behave in accordance with the prescriptions of the modest model was not wholly a conscious deduction from the theory of judicial self-restraint instilled by Thayer. It was in large part a product of Hand's temper and personality. The doubting, open-minded human being could not help but act that way as a judge.

Hand's contributions go beyond the permanent imprint of his decisions on the fabric of the law. His major legacy lies in his demonstration that wise, detached, open-minded judging is within human reach.

Hand died in New York City.

[A detailed inventory by Erika C. Chadbourn accompanies Hand's papers—primarily comprised of varied, personal correspondence—that are on deposit at the Harvard Law School Library. Gerald Gunther's forthcoming biography of Hand will be the first to rely on this collection.

Selected extrajudicial writings by Hand are "Due Process of Law and the Eight-Hour Day," *Harvard Law Review,* May 1908; *The Spirit of Liberty: Papers and Addresses of Learned Hand,* edited by Irving Dilliard (1952; 3rd ed., 1960); and *The Art and Craft of Judging: The Decisions of Judge Learned Hand,* edited by Hershel Shanks (1968). A Hand bibliography by Ernest H. Breuer was published in 1946 by the New York State Library.

See also Philip Hamburger, "The Great Judge," *Life,* Nov. 4, 1946; articles evaluating the judge's work on the occasion of his seventy-fifth birthday in the *Harvard Law Review,* Feb. 1947; Richard L. Hough, "Judge Learned Hand—Master Craftsman of the Law" (Ph.D. diss., University of California, Los Angeles, 1957); Jerome N. Frank, "Some Reflections on Judge Learned Hand," *University of Chicago Law Review,* Summer 1957; *Proceedings of a Special Session of the United States Court of Appeals for the Second Circuit* in vol. 264 of the Federal Reporter, 2d series, 1959; Marvin Schick, *Learned Hand's Court* (1970); Kathryn P. Griffith, *Judge Learned Hand and the Role of the Federal Judiciary* (1973); Michael A. Kahn, "The Politics of the Appointment Process: An Analysis of Why Learned Hand Was Never Appointed to the Supreme Court," *Stanford Law Review,* Jan. 1973; Gerald Gunther, "Learned Hand and the Origins of Modern First Amendment Doctrine: Some Fragments of History," *Stanford Law Review,* Feb. 1975; and G. Edward White, *The American Judicial Tradition: Profiles of Leading American Judges* (1976).]

GERALD GUNTHER

HANSBERRY, LORRAINE VIVIAN (May 19, 1930–Jan. 12, 1965), playwright, was born in Chicago, Ill., the daughter of Carl Augustus Hansberry and Nannie Perry. Her father was a realtor whose landmark suit to overturn the restrictive covenants that barred blacks from white neighborhoods was argued successfully before the Supreme Court in 1940. His commitment to equality and his active involvement with the National Association for the Advancement of Colored People made a firm impression on Lorraine, who experienced both verbal and physical threats as a result of her parents' courage. She graduated from Englewood High School in Chicago in 1948 and for two years attended the University of Wisconsin, where her interests in art and writing were complemented by courses in dramatic literature and stage design.

Hansberry was dissatisfied with college, and after a summer of art studies at Roosevelt University in Chicago, she moved to New York City in August 1950. There she renewed her acquaintance with Paul Robeson, who, along with such celebrities as Walter White and Jesse Owens, had visited her Chicago home. Louis Burnham, editor of Robeson's radical monthly magazine *Freedom*, invited her to become a reporter; and within a short time she was involved in the civil rights struggle. In 1951 she was a member of the delegation that petitioned Governor of Mississippi Fielding L. Wright on behalf of alleged rapist Willie McGee, and a year later she represented Robeson at the Intercontinental Peace Congress in Montevideo, Uruguay.

By 1953 Hansberry was an associate editor of *Freedom*. In that year she resigned her position to pursue a playwriting career. On June 20, 1953, she married Robert Nemiroff, a writer and a graduate student at New York University. They had no children. For the next three years she worked at a variety of part-time jobs, studied African history under W. E. B. Du Bois, and wrote plays. In 1957 she completed the manuscript for *A Raisin in the Sun*, which opened on Broadway in March 1959 and was an immediate hit.

The success of *A Raisin in the Sun* (which ran for 530 performances and made Sidney Poitier a star) thrust Hansberry into national prominence. She was the first black woman to have her work produced on Broadway, and when the play won the Drama Critics' Circle Award, she was the youngest American and the first black to receive that prestigious prize. In a nation about to enter a turbulent decade of racial strife, Hansberry was hailed as a fresh and courageous voice; her public speaking skills and wide knowledge of African culture seemed to be ideal qualifications for the role.

But Hansberry's plays were also an expression of her commitment, and sometimes people balked at her honesty. In 1960 the National Broadcasting Company commissioned her to write a television drama about slavery as part of its commemoration of the Civil War, but network executives considered *The Drinking Gourd* too controversial, and the project was discontinued. (The play was subsequently published in 1972.) Similar difficulties pervaded her attempts to write an expanded screenplay of *Raisin* for Columbia. (A version close to the stage play was

finally approved and won a Cannes Festival prize in 1961.) In the meantime she worked on new plays—*Les Blancs* (1966), *The Sign in Sidney Brustein's Window* (1964)—and continued her political activities. She raised funds for the Student Non-Violent Coordinating Committee and wrote the text for a photobook called *The Movement* (1964). In 1963 she joined with James Baldwin and others in a historic meeting with Attorney General Robert Kennedy to persuade him to play a more active role in protecting civil rights workers in the South. She was tireless in her commitment to human rights, but her health was not good. She was often fatigued and ill. In the summer of 1963 she was operated on twice for cancer. In March 1964 she and Nemiroff were divorced.

As the civil rights conflict intensified and the cries of black power and white supremecy threatened civil war, she struggled to maintain her radical position. At the Town Hall debate in New York City on June 15, 1964, between black artists and liberal whites, she argued for a militant commitment to the black cause but denounced the concept of racial hatred. It was a position that was difficult to maintain and easily misunderstood.

The opening of *The Sign in Sidney Brustein's Window* in 1964 did not ease the tensions. Some were shocked that the author of *A Raisin in the Sun* had turned to the white intelligentsia of Greenwich Village for her subject matter. *Brustein*, which advocates a radical commitment to a just cause, was greeted with mixed reactions and was kept open only by the herculean efforts of Hansberry's friends, who now realized that she was dying. Her projected plays about Mary Wollstonecraft and Toussaint L'Ouverture were never finished. *Brustein*, after 101 performances, was closed the night she died in New York City.

Nemiroff assembled many of her notes, letters, and scenes into an informal autobiography, *To Be Young, Gifted and Black*, which was adapted for an off-Broadway production in 1969. But Hansberry is best remembered for *A Raisin in the Sun*, which did so much for black artists in the American theater. For a time it was fashionable in some circles to denounce the play for its domineering mother figure and its apparent happy ending. But Hansberry insisted that moving into the white neighborhood was only the beginning of the struggle. The passage of time has vindicated her view. *A Raisin in the Sun* proved to be a landmark in the emerging struggle for both human and artistic freedom, a precursor in a revolution in black arts and theater, which Hansberry acutely foretold but did not live to see.

[The Hansberry Papers are controlled by Robert Nemiroff, who has compiled a detailed bibliography for *Freedomways* (1979). This special issue also contains eighteen articles by distinguished artists and critics about various aspects of Hansberry's life and career. *To Be Young, Gifted and Black* (1970) is an excellent autobiographical source but must not be confused with the dramatic adaptation of the work of the same name. The only biography, Catherine Scheader's *They Found a Way: Lorraine Hansberry* (1978), contains several good photographs but is written for young readers. *Raisin,* the musical version of *A Raisin in the Sun* that won a Tony Award in 1974, is available from Samuel French, as is *Les Blancs,* which was completed by Nemiroff. Other pieces about Hansberry include Lucille Banta, "Lorraine Hansberry," *American Dialogue,* May–June 1965; and Nat Hentoff, "They Fought—They Fought!" *New York Times,* May 25, 1969. An excellent film, *Lorraine Hansberry: The Black Experience in the Creation of Drama,* is available from Films for the Humanities, Princeton, N.J., and *Lorraine Hansberry Speaks Out* about art, theater and the black revolution is on Caedmon Records (1972).

Hansberry's obituary appeared in the *New York Herald Tribune,* Jan. 13, 1965.]

BARRY WITHAM

HARD, WILLIAM (Sept. 15, 1878–Jan. 30, 1962), journalist, was born in Painted Post, N. Y., the son of Clark Pettengill Hard, a Methodist minister, and Lydia E. van Someren. When he was four, he went with his parents to India, where they were missionaries. He attended Philander Smith Institute in Mussoorie, India, and the University College in London, England, before returning to the United States to enroll at Northwestern University. After receiving a B.A. in history in 1900, he received a fellowship at Northwestern and lectured there in medieval history for one year.

In 1901 Hard moved to the Northwestern University Settlement House in Chicago as head resident. He wrote on local reform issues for the settlement house's monthly newsletter. His professional journalism career began in 1902 when he was hired as an editorial writer by the *Chicago Tribune,* a job he held until 1905. On Nov. 3, 1903, he married Anne Nyhan Scribner, an editor for the *Chicago Post.* They had two children, both of whom followed their parents into careers in journalism.

Hard's involvement in the settlement house movement influenced his early journalism. Like many of his colleagues, he developed strong sympathies for urban workers and ties to the

organized labor movement. In 1903 he was a resident at Hull House. His first magazine article was published in the *Commons* in October 1903, and the following year he worked with Ernest Poole on an article on the stockyards strike for the August 13 issue of *Outlook.* Recalling their association, Poole described Hard as "a brilliant witty dark little man who was later to win such a name as a writer. . . ." Hard also served briefly in 1905 and 1906 as assistant to Joseph Medill Patterson, public works commissioner, in Chicago in a reform administration.

In 1905 and 1906 Hard's articles on reformers, reform issues, and workingmen appeared with increasing frequency in such magazines as *Outlook, World To-Day, Saturday Evening Post,* and *American.* He soon began a productive association with *Everybody's Magazine* and its publisher, Erman J. Ridgway, that continued through 1916. After working as Chicago editor of *Ridgway's Weekly,* which first appeared in late 1906 and folded early in 1907, Hard began muckraking for *Everybody's* in 1907, writing on unsafe conditions in industry. In January 1908, the magazine ran his "De Kid Wot Works at Night," a journey through the night world of the Chicago newsboy and messenger boy. Hard later claimed that the article was influential in the passage of protective child labor laws in Illinois.

From 1908 to 1914, Hard wrote four major series of articles for *Everybody's* and *Delineator* on the social, economic, political, and legal issues related to modern woman's role, status, and problems. Throughout this period, Hard continued writing articles for numerous other public affairs journals and general-circulation magazines, pursuing the free-lance career that was to continue over three decades.

After 1914, his attention was directed almost exclusively to national and international political and economic issues. Working out of Washington, D.C., he was a correspondent first for the *Metropolitan,* then for the *New Republic.* He was a weekly contributor to the latter from 1917 through 1920, and one writer has described him as "perhaps the most vivid reporter *The New Republic* ever had, [one whose] spare and racy style approximated the first true 'reportage' in America." During the immediate postwar years he was actively involved in the fight against the League of Nations and the debate over Bolshevik Russia, both in print and privately. Hard's long friendship with Raymond Robins, which dated from their Chicago settlement worker days, led to the publication of *Raymond Robins' Own Story* (1920), Hard's account of Robins' eighteen-month experience as an observer in Russia. At the time, a colleague recalled later, Hard was "a man of about forty, small of stature, [who] carried on his slight body a head with a magnificent dome and a face out of a gallery of Rembrandts."

During the 1920's, Hard wrote the "Weekly Washington Letter" for the *Nation* (1923–1925), and articles for *Asia, Collier's, Century,* and *Review of Reviews,* among others, and supplied newspapers with Washington correspondence through his own Hard News Service and David Lawrence's Consolidated News Service. He was an early supporter of Herbert Hoover and wrote a campaign biography, *Who's Hoover?,* in 1928. After the election, Hard was a member of Hoover's "Medicine-Ball Cabinet," which gathered at 7 A.M. six days a week on the south grounds of the White House to throw the ball around.

The coming of radio brought a new career for Hard, and by 1929 he was a regular correspondent and commentator for the National Broadcasting Corporation (NBC). In January 1930 he provided daily summaries from the London Naval Arms Conference, participating in the first regular international broadcasts. Between 1930 and 1935, Hard, with his resonant baritone voice, broadcast weekly reports and interviews from Washington, daily summaries from the 1932 Republican Convention in Chicago, and coverage of international conferences and events from Geneva, London, and Berlin.

By 1936 he had become an outspoken critic of the New Deal, and in July of that year he began a schedule of daily fifteen-minute commentaries on the presidential campaign, under the sponsorship of the Republicans. Each night, the *Literary Digest* observed, "Republicans sat comfortably beside their radios and nodded in agreement while William Hard riddled this or that foible of the New Deal." In February 1937 he was appointed executive assistant to the chairman of the Republican National Committee, and served as secretary of the Republican Program Committee until he resigned his party posts in October 1938, saying he wished to return to "independent political journalism." In the following year, he began writing regularly for *Reader's Digest,* and he was a roving editor for the magazine until his death in New Canaan, Conn.

Writing in 1942 of Hard's long career as "an interpreter of the feverish chronicle of the present," Alva S. Johnston, a fellow *Reader's Digest* editor, said Hard "practices journalism with the historian's freedom from narrowness and preju-

dice." This quality of journalistic integrity that characterized Hard's work was widely acknowledged among his colleagues, as was his brilliance as a writer. To them he was, as *Everybody's Magazine* stated, "the man who can put drama even into figures and without distorting the figures, [who] adds to his uncommon qualities as an investigator the gifts of clear and convincing statement, good humor, and imagination based on facts rather than on rainbows." His career in public-affairs journalism was productive and consistent, although his associations with various sides of public issues were usually short-lived. The reason, said Johnston, was that he was "a cause man, not an organization man. . . . He has been a real free-lance—free, and a lance at every evil he has seen."

[Manuscript collections of Hard are available at Wyoming's Archive of Contemporary History, which includes a voluminous quantity of correspondence and notes; and the Seeley G. Mudd Manuscript Library at Princeton, which has Hard's files for a planned book on the League of Nations fight.

Hard's magazine articles provide a valuable perspective on the man and his times. Nearly all are indexed in *Reader's Guide to Periodical Literature.* Aside from *Raymond Robins' Own Story* (1920) and *Who's Hoover?* (1928), his books consist of reprints of magazine series: *Injured in the Course of Duty* (1910) contains his muckraking articles for *Everybody's* on industrial safety; *The Women of To-Morrow* (1912), which had appeared in *Everybody's*; and *How the English Take the War* (1917), which contains articles from *Metropolitan.*

The following contain observations on or assessments of Hard's career, his work, or his personality: Upton Sinclair, *The Brass Check* (1920); Geoff Conklin, ed., *The New Republic Anthology, 1915–1935* (1936); Ernest Poole, *The Bridge* (1940); Arthur and Ila Weinberg, eds., *The Muckrakers* (1961), which also contains his best muckraking articles; Louis Filler, *The Muckrakers* (1976); and Isaac Don Levine, *Eyewitness to History* (1973). Frank Luther Mott, *A History of American Magazines,* 5 vols. (1938–1968), mentions Hard frequently.

Complete obituaries appeared in the *New York Times* and *Chicago Tribune,* both Feb. 1, 1962.]

RONALD S. MARMARELLI

HARDWICKE, CEDRIC WEBSTER (Feb. 19, 1893–Aug. 6, 1964), stage and film actor, was born in Lye, Stourbridge, Worcestershire, England, the son of Edwin Webster Hardwicke, a physician, and Jessie Masterson. His interest in the stage was apparent by 1905, when he "produced" *The Merchant of Venice* in the family kitchen and played the role of Antonio. Two years later, in another home performance, Hardwicke assumed the title role in

Hamlet. After graduating from Bridgnorth School in Salop, he studied at the Royal Academy of Dramatic Art in London. He made his professional debut as Brother John in *The Monk and the Woman* (1912), and later that year was appointed general understudy for productions at His Majesty's Theatre.

The following year Hardwicke toured the provinces, South Africa, and Rhodesia, playing Shakespearean roles with F. R. Benson's Northern Company. He returned to London to play in the Old Vic Company's productions of *Macbeth* and *Hamlet.* In 1914 Hardwicke served with the British army in France and, as a captain in the judge advocate's office, at the war's end was assigned to work on legal problems resulting from the British army's presence in Europe. He had the distinction of being the last British officer to leave the war zone officially, in October 1921.

In January 1922, Hardwicke joined Barry Jackson's Birmingham Repertory Theatre, which was notable for giving first productions of George Bernard Shaw's plays. That year Hardwicke played what he later described as his favorite Shavian role, Captain Shotover in *Heartbreak House.* Later in 1922 he played the He-Ancient in *Back to Methuselah,* and in 1924 his first popular success, the seventy-year-old Churdles Ash in *The Farmer's Wife.* The following year Hardwicke played Caesar in Shaw's *Caesar and Cleopatra.* He went on to play Iago in *Othello* (1925), Richard Varwell in *Yellow Sands* (1926), and Sir Peter Teazle in *The School for Scandal* (1928), among other roles.

During these years he cultivated a close friendship with Shaw, who became, according to Hardwicke, "a sort of godfather to me." Shaw supervised the first productions of many of his plays, and it was their close relationship that enabled Hardwicke to play King Magnus in the first production of *The Apple Cart* (1929) at the Malvern Festival. The play proved to be such a success that it was brought to London for a nine-month run. This led to a number of subsequent long runs for Hardwicke, including the 1930–1931 production of *The Barretts of Wimpole Street,* in which he played Edward Moulton-Barrett.

Hardwicke embarked on a parallel career in films during this period, but this path proved to be less successful. His first film appearance was in *Nelson* (1926), and was followed by his starring in *The Dreyfus Case* (1931). In the next six years Hardwicke made fourteen motion pictures, including *Rome Express* (1932), *Nell Gwynn* (1934), and *Bella Donna* (1935). In ad-

dition to his work on the stage and in film, Hardwicke published the first volume of his autobiography, *Let's Pretend* (1932). Meanwhile, his stage credits included *For Services Rendered* (1932), a revival of *Heartbreak House* (1932), *Too True to Be Good* (1932), and *The Late Christopher Bean* (1933). Later in 1933 he directed *Laburnum Grove.* On Jan. 1, 1934, he was knighted for his achievements.

Ironically, shortly after receiving this honor, Hardwicke began to turn his attention toward the United States, and in 1935 made his American film debut in *Becky Sharp.* Later that year he appeared in *Les Miserables.* Hardwicke returned to England to appear as Prince Mikail in the play *Tovarich* (1935), and then directed a revival of *The Apple Cart.* He returned to the United States for his New York stage debut in the comedy *Promise* (1936). This play and the next one in which Hardwicke appeared, *The Amazing Doctor Clitterhouse* (1937), were failures. He had his first American stage triumph as Canon Skerritt in *Shadow and Substance* (1938). This performance brought him the Delia Austrian Medal of the New York Drama League.

During the next few years Hardwicke channeled most of his energy to Hollywood. Between 1937 and 1940 he made seven films, including *Green Light* (1937), *Stanley and Livingstone* (1939), *The Hunchback of Notre Dame* (1939), and *Victory* (1940). According to film historian David Thomson, Hardwicke's film career "soon lost shape" when his studio, Radio Keith-Orpheum (RKO), "loaned him out at random." He subsequently appeared in such films as *The Invisible Man Returns* (1940), Alfred Hitchcock's *Suspicion* (1941), the western *Sundown* (1941), and *The Ghost of Frankenstein* (1942).

During World War II, Hardwicke organized the British actors living in Hollywood to produce the propaganda film *Forever and a Day* (1943), in which he played a leading part. After appearing in *The Moon Is Down* (1943), *Wilson* (1944), *Wing and a Prayer* (1944), and *The Keys of the Kingdom* (1944), he returned to England to act in the play *The House on the Bridge.* In 1945 he toured France, the Netherlands, and Belgium in a revival of *Yellow Sands* for the Entertainments National Service Association.

After the war Hardwicke returned to the United States, dividing his time between New York and Hollywood. In New York he directed *Pygmalion* (1946) and *An Inspector Calls* (1947). In addition he played Creon in *Anti-*

gone (1946). Of this performance John Mason Brown wrote: "His Creon is all intellect . . . glacial, immobile, and commanding." In 1948 Hardwicke returned to the Old Vic to appear in three plays. Then he was back in Hollywood to film *A Connecticut Yankee in King Arthur's Court* (1949), with Bing Crosby and William Bendix. Hardwicke's King Arthur was heralded as "a keen satirical interpretation." In addition to making more films both in America and in England during the 1940's, Hardwicke had one of his great successes on Broadway with a revival of *Caesar and Cleopatra* (1949). He directed the production as well as playing Caesar.

In 1951, Hardwicke appeared with Agnes Moorehead, Charles Boyer, and Charles Laughton in a reading, without costumes or sets, of Shaw's *Don Juan in Hell.* His performance as the Statue may well have been his finest work. The company toured the United States extensively after its New York run. Hardwicke's film career was increasingly undistinguished, however. One critic complained that he "made whatever he was offered."

Hardwicke made his television debut in 1956, re-creating his role of Caesar in the National Broadcasting Company (NBC) production of *Caesar and Cleopatra.* In 1959, after a number of small roles on the New York stage and in road productions, he had a major success on Broadway in *A Majority of One,* in which he played Koichi Asano, the Japanese suitor of a Brooklyn widow. In 1961 he appeared in the television series "Mrs. G. Goes to College," and published his second volume of autobiography, *A Victorian in Orbit.* His last two movies were *Five Weeks in a Balloon* (1962) and *The Pumpkin Eater* (1964). Early in 1963, Hardwicke directed *A Wilde Evening with Shaw.* He made his last stage appearance, as Mr. Bagot in a revival of *Too True to Be Good,* in New York City, where he died.

Hardwicke was married twice. His first wife was the English actress Helena Pickard, whom he wed on Jan. 8, 1928; they had one son. They were divorced in May 1950, and on July 27, 1950, he married the American actress Mary Scott. They had one son, and were divorced in 1961.

[Obituaries are in the *New York Times, New York Herald Tribune,* and London *Times,* Aug. 7, 1964. See also *Films in Review, 1965–1969* (1972).]

FRANCIS J. BOSHA

HARRIS, JULIAN LA ROSE (June 21, 1874–Feb. 9, 1963), journalist and publisher,

was born in Savannah, Ga., the son of Joel Chandler Harris, a journalist and author, and Esther La Rose. He spent his childhood in Atlanta, Ga., where his father worked on the *Atlanta Constitution.* His formal schooling was limited to the West End Academy and one year at the Gordon Military Institute in Atlanta (1889–1890). In 1890–1891 he attended Frères Maristes Academy in St. Ephrem d'Upton, Quebec, to study French. His father instilled in him a love of reading, a belief in sectional reconciliation, racial tolerance, and decency toward others. From an early age Harris saw himself as a crusader for human rights.

Harris early decided on journalism as a career. At the age of eighteen he joined the *Atlanta Constitution* as a reporter. Desiring experience with a larger metropolitan daily, he spent a six-month leave of absence in 1896 with the *Chicago-Times Herald,* where he was assistant to the Sunday editor. Back to the *Constitution* in the fall of 1896, he rose through the ranks and became managing editor in 1900, a position he held four years. In 1904–1905, Harris served as news editor of the *Atlanta Daily News,* a short and unrewarding association for him. He and his father launched a new southern-based periodical, *Uncle Remus's the Home Magazine,* which first appeared in June 1907. The publication was intended as a mouthpiece for Joel Chandler Harris' ideas about sectional and racial reconciliation in order to bring the South into the mainstream of twentieth-century American life. When the elder Harris died suddenly in July 1908, Julian Harris assumed the position of editor and general manager.

Uncle Remus's was only modestly successful. It attracted few superior writers and remained largely an innocuous organ for middle-class consumption, rarely addressing itself to the original goals of Joel Chandler Harris. Financial problems led to its demise in 1913.

On Oct. 26, 1897, Harris married Julia Florida Collier, the daughter of a prominent Atlanta family. She became his professional associate as well as a writer and journalist in her own right. They had two sons, both of whom died in childhood.

In the 1912 presidential campaign Harris supported the Progressive party of Theodore Roosevelt, long a friend of the Harris family. Harris was one of Roosevelt's few important southern backers. Harris spent the World War I years in France as editor of the *New York Herald* Paris edition. With the United States' entrance into the war, Harris served as a commanding first lieutenant (1917) and a captain of the military intelligence division of the army (1918). He returned to the *Herald* as assistant managing editor in January 1919, rising to chief European correspondent in April 1919 and to general manager the following January.

In 1920 Harris achieved a lifelong ambition of buying into a newspaper of his own, the Columbus, Ga., *Enquirer-Sun.* By 1922 he was sole owner and editor. His paper fearlessly battled the Ku Klux Klan in Georgia, attacked lynching and advocated justice for blacks (although within a segregated society), supported the teaching of evolution, worked for more efficient and responsive state and local government, urged greater support for Georgia's public schools, and supported free speech and civil liberties. The *Enquirer-Sun* brought news of the best books, music, and art to its somewhat provincial Columbus readers. In 1926 the *Enquirer-Sun* was awarded the Pulitzer Prize for Meritorious Public Service.

Despite this achievement, financial stability remained elusive for the *Enquirer-Sun.* Each controversial crusade brought a temporary loss of readers and advertisers. The business side of the paper was run carelessly, and in 1929 Harris had to sell it. Shortly thereafter he resigned because the new owner, J. M. Stein, interfered with editorial policy.

Harris returned to the *Atlanta Constitution* in 1930, where he spent five years as news director, advertising director, and book review editor. His last major position was as executive editor of the Chattanooga *Times* from 1935 to 1942. This was largely an administrative position. Upon his retirement from the Chattanooga *Times* in 1942, he became a southern correspondent for the *New York Times,* a part-time position that he held for three years. A long retirement followed in Atlanta, where he died.

Associates of Harris believed he could have been more influential than he was. The *Enquirer-Sun* was unquestionably a quality newspaper, but Harris wrote above the heads of most residents of Columbus, a cotton mill town. A persistent compulsion to emerge from the shadow of his more famous father and carve his own niche in the world often made his journalism more pugnacious than it needed to be. "Julian made too many enemies without giving any of the sores time to heal. He was caustic in his criticism of those who differed with him," commented a fellow editor.

Yet Harris' strengths outweighed these deficiencies. He was one of a small band of liberal southern journalists of the 1920's who exhorted their region to cast aside the shackles of ignorance and to fight intolerance and injustice. His battles against the Ku Klux Klan required a degree of courage that few other southern editors or public figures exhibited. He deserves as much credit as any single man for some diminution of the Klan in Georgia. His goal was to make his state and the American South the humane and tolerant land he always believed it could be.

[For more information, see the Julian La Rose Harris Collection, Special Collections Division, Emory University Library.

Writings about Harris by William F. Mugleston include "Fruitful and Disastrous Years" (Ph.D. diss., University of Georgia, 1972); "The Perils of Southern Publishing: A History of *Uncle Remus's Magazine,*" *Journalism Quarterly,* Fall 1975; "Julian Harris, the Georgia Press, and the Ku Klux Klan," *Georgia Historical Quarterly,* Fall 1975; and "A Georgia Editor Looks at the 1920's," *Atlanta Historical Journal,* Spring 1978. See also Arnold Shankman, "Julian Harris and the Negro," *Phylon,* Dec. 1974; and "Julian Harris and the Ku Klux Klan," *Mississippi Quarterly,* Spring 1975. An obituary appears in the *Atlanta Constitution,* Feb. 11, 1963.]

WILLIAM F. MUGLESTON

HART, MOSS (Oct. 24, 1904–Dec. 20, 1961), playwright, was born in the Bronx, N.Y., the son of Barnett Hart and Lillian Solomon, both of English parentage. As a boy he did not feel close to either parent. He resented his father's inability to support the family. Skilled as a cigar roller, Barnett Hart was reduced to occasional odd jobs once cigar-making was mechanized. Lillian Hart was so loaded with household work that she had no time to display maternal love. As Moss admitted in his remarkable autobiography, *Act One* (1959), he actually disliked her.

Home was an apartment that the family shared with live-in boarders, the major source of income. They were also crowded by the presence of Lillian's father, Solomon, and her sister Kate. Their constant bickering made everyone unhappy; yet these two misfits won Moss's love and were major influences on him. Grandfather Solomon, autocratic and demanding, took great delight in having Hart, at age five or six, recite passages of prose or poetry. Aunt Kate, conspicuously eccentric in dress and behavior, and very poor, occasionally managed to take Moss to plays. To her he owed his lifelong love for the theater. No less enduring was his memory of early deprivation. "Poverty," he wrote in *Act One,* "was always a living and evil thing for me." At age twelve he worked part time in a music store and thus began to contribute to the family budget.

Hart's schooling ended with the seventh grade in the summer of 1919, when at the age of fourteen he took a full-time job as storage vault clerk for A. L. Neuberger Furs in lower Manhattan. It was tedious and unpleasant. But shortly before his seventeenth birthday, Hart's dreams of theatrical work came true when he became an office boy for Augustus Pitou, a manager of touring theatrical companies. Reading plays submitted to Pitou prompted Hart to submit one himself, under an assumed name. Billed as *The Beloved Bandit*, it failed miserably when tried out in Rochester and Chicago in 1923, costing Pitou $45,000 and Hart his job.

Hart next tried acting, but found only a single role, that of Smithers in a revival of *The Emperor Jones.* Then for six years he alternated between work as a director of little theater groups and as social director at summer resorts on the Borscht Circuit in the Catskills. He also continued to write plays, about one a year, with serious themes. They were all rejected and never saw production, but writing them was useful practice. The experience of directing was of even greater value. At one agent's suggestion, Hart reluctantly turned to comedy; and early in 1930 he wrote the first version of *Once in a Lifetime.* It dealt with the panic in Hollywood when sound was added to moving pictures and the eclipse actors faced if they could not speak well. Dore Schary, a little theater colleague, advised Hart to show the work to several producers, one of whom, Sam Harris, arranged for Hart's collaboration with George S. Kaufman. Weeks of tedious rewriting at Kaufman's residence ended with tryouts in Atlantic City and Brooklyn in the late spring of 1930. Audiences and critics were equally unresponsive. But after more revision during the summer, the play opened on Broadway in September. It was an instant hit.

Transformed overnight to a celebrity and finally assured of an ample income, Hart at once moved his family into a suite at the Ansonia Hotel. Soon after, he rented a town house. He became notorious for spending money freely, and friends ruefully spoke of him as "Gold-plated Hart." For example, he impulsively purchased a run-down farm in Bucks County, Pa., near Kaufman's country home. The renovations and additions needed to make it suitable for Hart's lavish style of entertainment caused great trouble but provided the theme for his 1940 comedy *George Washington Slept Here.*

In 1932 Hart wrote the books for Irving Berlin's *Face the Music* (1932) and *As Thousands Cheer* (1933). In the course of a round-the-world cruise, Cole Porter and Hart worked together on *Jubilee* (1933). But most of his plays prior to 1941 were cowritten with Kaufman, with variable success. *Merrily We Roll Along* (1934), a serious portrayal of a young playwright spoiled by success; *I'd Rather Be Right* (1937) and *The American Way* (1939), both with political overtones; and *George Washington Slept Here* (1940) all did well but fell short of being smash hits. Two big hits were *You Can't Take It with You* (1936), which portrayed the zany behavior of the Vanderhof and Sycamore families and was awarded the 1937 Pulitzer Prize for Drama, and *The Man Who Came to Dinner* (1939), suggested by the irascible behavior of the critic Alexander Woollcott.

On the eve of World War II, an ill-defined sense of dissatisfaction prompted Hart, with the approval of a psychiatrist, to sever the tie with Kaufman, who reluctantly agreed it would be in Hart's best interest. The brief exposure to psychoanalysis provided a theme for Hart's *Lady in the Dark* (1941). Rejection of his application for a navy commission, on the ground of "lack of education," was a disappointment, but it was followed by a request from General Henry H. ("Hap") Arnold for a play about the Army Air Force. Hart went through basic training with the rank of private and, for the sake of authenticity, logged about 20,000 miles of flight. His play, *Winged Victory* (1943), was a double contribution to the war effort. It bolstered pride in American fliers, and Hart turned over his proceeds from the film version, more than a million dollars, to the Army Emergency Relief Fund.

On Aug. 10, 1946, Hart married the actress Kitty Carlisle; they had two children. Their marriage was one of the happiest in theatrical history. But domesticity did not lessen his driving activity. In addition to more plays—*Christopher Blake* (1946), *Light Up the Sky* (1948), and *The Climate of Eden* (1952)—he wrote numerous screenplays, including *Frankie and Johnnie* (1935); *Hans Christian Andersen* (1952); *A Star Is Born* (1954); and the Oscar-winning *Gentleman's Agreement* (1947). He also resumed his old role of director. A great admirer of George Bernard Shaw, his directing of *My Fair Lady* (1956), a musical based on Shaw's *Pygmalion*, was superb, "making the difference between a splendid musical play and a classic," according to critic Brooks Atkinson. In 1960 he again met success directing the musical *Camelot.*

Without abandoning his lavish spending or his joy of living, Hart in this period developed a new seriousness. As an officer of the Dramatists Guild and the Authors League, he sought better working conditions for all theater people. During the Joseph McCarthy years he strongly opposed all forms of blacklisting. His final contribution to the American stage was his informal mediation of the Broadway actors' strike of 1960.

Not to work in the theater would have been a denial of life for Hart. In what may have been his last letter, he wrote that he was "still charmed and fascinated by the amusement racket," and signed himself "Huckleberry Hart." He disregarded the warning of two heart attacks; and while hard at work on a new play at his home in Palm Springs, Calif., a third attack ended his career.

[The Wisconsin Center for Film and Theater Research, in Madison, houses the Moss Hart Papers. This collection includes the bulk of correspondence, 1922–1962, manuscripts and typescripts of plays and screenplays, editions of published works (including *Act One*), scrapbooks of photographs, memorabilia, and awards, miscellaneous nondramatic writings, and family records. Minor holdings are at Columbia University, Library of Congress, and the University of Iowa.

Bibliographical and critical material is in Brooks Atkinson, introduction to *Six Plays by Kaufman and Hart* (1942); *On Stage: Selected Theatre Reviews from the New York Times 1920–70* (1973); Scott Meredith, *George S. Kaufman and His Friends* (1974); and the obituary in the *New York Times*, Dec. 21, 1961.]

WILLIAM PEIRCE RANDEL

HATCH, CARL A. (Nov. 27, 1889–Sept. 15, 1963), senator and federal district judge, was born in Kirwin, Kans., the son of Harley Atwood Hatch and Esther Shannon Ryan. Near the turn of the century, the family moved to Eldorado, a booming railroad town in southwest Oklahoma. Harley Hatch operated a store in Eldorado, and Hatch worked there while finishing his secondary education. After completing high school he became a reporter for the weekly *Eldorado Courier*. For a brief period he and a friend owned the newspaper.

Restless, Hatch decided at age twenty to go to law school. He entered Cumberland University in Lebanon, Tenn., and received his degree in 1912. He then returned to Eldorado to practice law. On Sept. 2, 1913, he married Ruth Caviness; they had two children.

Hatch moved from Eldorado to Clovis, N.Mex., in 1916. Once he became established as a lawyer he purchased a cattle ranch. A Democratic party stalwart, he served as an assistant state attorney general (1917–1918), a state dis-

trict judge (1923–1929), a collector of internal revenue, and chairman of the Democratic state committee.

Hatch was appointed a United States senator in October 1933, when Sam G. Bratton resigned. In 1934 Hatch was elected to complete the remainder of Bratton's term. He was reelected in 1936 and 1942. As a senator, Hatch was a comfortable ally of presidents Franklin D. Roosevelt and Harry Truman. He was most interested in farm and labor legislation. Hatch advocated higher minimum wages and legislation that would compel arbitration in key-industry disputes. He also strongly advocated antiracketeering investigations and specific legislation against certain activities on the part of union officials. Hatch supported appropriations for the National Park Service and numerous Interior Department reclamation projects. During his last term he engaged Senator Wayne Morse of Oregon in a series of debates and discussions concerning oil leases on federal lands and indiscriminate "pork barrel" reclamation projects. In these instances Hatch tended to favor the forces of exploitation.

Hatch was an avowed supporter of a bipartisan foreign policy. In 1943 he was instrumental, along with Lister Hill of Alabama, Joseph Ball of Minnesota, and Harold Burton of Ohio, in committing the Senate to participation in a postwar international organization. He was especially influential as a supporter of Truman during the debates on the Truman Doctrine and the Marshall Plan. A believer in reciprocal trade, he favored strong economic and political alliances. Truman considered Hatch to be one of his most loyal and dependable supporters.

Hatch is best remembered as the author of the Hatch Acts of 1939 and 1940. He was deeply concerned about rumors that federal relief recipients, especially Works Progress Administration employees, were being asked to contribute to political campaigns. He succeeded in pushing through legislation for cleaner elections. His goal was to prevent what he called "pernicious political activity." The 1939 Hatch Act prohibited all but top-level federal officials from engaging in political activity. It also forbade parties to solicit funds from any employee of a public-works relief project. The second act extended the provisions of the law to any state employee whose salary was paid in part by federal funds, and attempted to limit the annual expenditures of any national party or committee to $3 million. Individuals were limited to maximum contributions of $5,000. In 1942 an amendment was passed that assured teachers the right to participate in political activities. Another provision, added in 1944, forbade the government to disseminate political literature among the members of the armed forces.

It was Hatch's hope that this legislation would curb the influence of special interests, regardless of whether they were governmental, corporate, or labor. But by 1946 Hatch admitted that the Hatch Act was a failure, especially the provisions on limiting campaign expenditures. Through numerous loopholes and questionable accounting techniques, political expenditures had soared far beyond the legislative limit. By the end of his Senate tenure, Hatch was advocating full disclosure of all contributors and the amount each person donated. But it was not until after the Watergate scandal that clarifying legislation was passed.

Following Hatch's retirement from the Senate in 1949, Truman appointed him to a federal district judgeship in Albuquerque, where he served until early 1963. Five months after retirement as a judge, Hatch died at Albuquerque.

[There are no Hatch papers on deposit at the New Mexico Archives, the University of New Mexico, or the Library of Congress. There are significant Hatch collections at the Roosevelt and Truman presidential libraries and at the AFL-CIO Library in Washington, D.C. Most references in secondary accounts are concerned with the Hatch Act. David L. Porter, "Senator Carl Hatch and the Hatch Act of 1939," *New Mexico Historical Review*, April 1973, is the best detailed account of a specific aspect of Hatch's life. A complete obituary is in the *New York Times*, Sept. 16, 1963.]

F. ROSS PETERSON

HATLO, JIMMY (Sept. 1, 1898–Dec. 1, 1963), cartoonist, was born James Cecil Hatlow in Providence, R.I., the son of James Melbourne Hatlow, a printer who had emigrated from the Orkney Islands, and of Isabelle Putnam. Hatlo's father was totally deaf and Jimmy learned to communicate with him in sign language. This ability later aided him in his work; he could make his characters communicate a telling message with a few gestures.

In 1899 James Hatlow moved his family to Los Angeles, where he became a headline setter for the *Los Angeles Times*. After one year of high school, young Hatlow joined his father at the *Times* as a printer's devil. Three years later he moved into the art department, his real interest, but the limited chances for advancement prompted him to leave the paper and go into publicity work. His accounts included Mack Sennett and several automobile companies.

Hatlo's career in publicity was a short one. In 1918 he moved to San Francisco, where he became an automobile editor, first for the *Bulletin* and then for the *Call.* He continued to draw, turning out occasional editorial cartoons, and in 1921 he became the sports cartoonist, producing a strip called "Swineskin Gulch."

In 1928, Hatlo was asked to dash off something to fill a blank space on the comics page of the *Call.* The result—"They'll Do It Every Time"—was immediately successful, and by 1935 had become nationally syndicated, eventually running in some 800 papers. The cartoon featured such people as J. P. Bigdome, everybody's pompous boss; Henry Tremblechin, the much-put-upon office worker; any number of drunks called Lushwell; Phootkiss the yes-man; Bloodstone the credit manager; Mothwallet the skinflint; and other immediately recognizable characters bearing such names as Lugbolt, Fescue, and Iguana.

"They'll Do It Every Time" was drawn in two panels. In the first, Bigdome might be accepting the chairmanship of a fund-raising drive. In the second, he is, of course, handing over all the work to the harried Tremblechin. Hatlo also pointed out the little day-to-day humiliations that we all suffer. In one cartoon, "Cashlow gets the red-carpet treatment when he goes in to cash a check all by himself." (The teller declares that Mr. Cashlow never needs any identification at *this* bank.) In the second panel, "Today he went in with a customer he'd like to impress . . . so he runs into Sourpuss, the new teller." (Cashlow is, of course, asked to provide every conceivable type of identification, even a birth certificate.)

Hatlo got most of his ideas from readers, and he always acknowledged his source in a small box in the corner, labeled "Thanx and tip of the Hatlo hat to . . .," followed by the person's name and complete address. He received aid from other sources as well—in the form of assistants who did most of the finished drawings. Tommy Thompson, who drew in exactly the same style as Hatlo, refined his sketches and then forwarded them to Bob Dunn in New York for further work. Dunn was the chief artist for "Little Iodine," an offspring of "They'll Do It Every Time." Iodine, the daughter of Henry Tremblechin, was born in 1943.

Many of Hatlo's characters had little balloons above their heads showing what they were really thinking. A restaurant cook, for example, might be imagining obnoxious customers being boiled alive in a large cauldron. These repressed revenges, which sometimes carried the caption

327

"the urge to kill," became the basis of a new strip called "Hatlo's Inferno." In one memorable cartoon, inveterate revolving-door shovers were depicted with their feet nailed to the outer edges of a rapidly spinning giant turntable, with the devil himself at the controls. In hundreds of similar cartoons, Hatlo consigned such boors to their own particular hell.

Hatlo's drawings are characterized by a wealth of detail—one might say they border on the busy. There are many secondary characters, and most of them have a great deal to say about the central figures in the drawings—all of it withering and all of it funny. Hatlo admitted that he borrowed from the style of T. A. ("Tad") Dorgan, the creator of a strip called "Indoor Sports." In turn, Hatlo's influence can be seen in such strips as "Right Around Home" and "There Oughta Be a Law." Many of the titles of these strips entered the language as everyday expressions.

After his first wife, Fern Johnson, had died, Hatlo married Eleanor Dollard on May 29, 1937. They had one son. He spent at least four months of the year in New York City "so as not to stagnate." A quick-tempered man, Hatlo resembled some of the irritable characters in his work. One friend remarked that no one could "wreck a dinner party faster than Jimmy." He also apparently inspired loyalty and hard work in his associates and friends. After his death at his home, "Wit's End," in Pebble Beach, Calif., his cartoons were continued by Dunn and two collaborators.

[The Museum of Cartoon Art, Port Chester, N.Y., has a small collection of the original artwork for "They'll Do It Every Time." Hatlo's *Jimmy Hatlo's Office Party* (1959) contains more than 100 cartoons. Also see Jack Alexander, "He Needles the Human Race," *Saturday Evening Post*, Nov. 3, 1951; Stephen Becker, *Comic Art in America* (1959); Jerry Robinson, *The Comics* (1974); Maurice Horn, ed., *World Encyclopedia of Comics* (1976). An obituary is in the *New York Times*, Dec. 2, 1963.]

MARSHALL DE BRUHL

HAWLEY, PAUL RAMSEY (Jan. 31, 1891–Nov. 24, 1965), physician and army officer, was born in West College Corner, Ind., the son of William Harry Hawley, a doctor, and Sabina Cora Ramsey. After attending local schools Hawley entered Indiana University at Bloomington, but proved so indifferent a student that he flunked out after his sophomore year. Three A's in medical courses over the summer got him reinstated, and he earned the B.A. in 1912. Following in his father's and grandfather's foot-

steps, he went on to the University of Cincinnati, where he received the M.D. in 1914. On Dec. 20, 1915, after internship at General Hospital in Cincinnati, Hawley married Frances Katherine Gilliland, a dietician. They had two children.

Succumbing to a yen for adventure, Hawley accepted a first lieutenant's commission as a reserve officer in the Army Medical Corps in August 1916. That October he began an army career that spanned almost thirty years. After completing basic training at the Army Medical School in February 1917, and two short assignments at Fort Thomas and Camp Taylor, Ky., Hawley (now a major) went to France in June 1918 as a surgeon with the 334th Infantry Regiment.

In the 1920's and 1930's Hawley saw service in various army medical jobs. From January 1925 to April 1927 he was a surgeon and medical inspector in the Philippines and a surgeon with the Nicaragua Canal Survey of 1929–1931. Although opportunities for promotion came slowly—he did not become lieutenant colonel until 1937—those for schooling did not. Hawley attended the advanced course at the Army Medical School in 1921, received a Ph.D. in public health from Johns Hopkins in 1923, and studied at the Command and General Staff School (1934–1936) and the Army War College (1938–1939).

A few months before Pearl Harbor, Hawley, now a colonel, was sent to England as a special observer. In January 1942 he became chief surgeon for the Army Air Forces there. Promoted to brigadier general in September 1942 and to major general in February 1944, he helped organize medical support for the invasion of France. After D-Day he was named chief surgeon of the European Theatre. Not only did Hawley efficiently direct a huge organization of medical personnel, but he also showed solicitous regard for the quarter-million sick and wounded under his jurisdiction. He insisted on air evacuation whenever possible and on hospital ships rather than ordinary transports until the U-boat threat subsided.

Upon Hawley's retirement in June 1946, General Omar Bradley, then head of the Veterans Administration (VA), named him chief medical director of the organization. During his tenure in this post, Hawley completely revitalized what had been called "the backwash of American medicine." Alternately cajoling and threatening both Congress and the American Medical Association (AMA)—the one by threatening to resign and the other by raising

328

the specter of socialized medicine—he secured their cooperation in his program. Appropriations and numbers of doctors, specialists, nurses, and hospitals all increased. Red tape was slashed; training was improved; patient load was increased. To secure the finest physicians Hawley cut VA doctors free of the civil service and paid them more. When Hawley left the agency to become chief executive officer of the Blue Cross and Blue Shield Commission in April 1948, there were physician-residency programs at thirty-two VA hospitals and a functioning outpatient clinic program using local physicians nationwide—both innovations. A $500 million construction program had also been authorized. On Mar. 1, 1950, Hawley became director of the American College of Surgeons, a post he held until he retired in 1961. Honed by his battles with politicians and bureaucrats, and possessing a streak of natural combativeness, Hawley used his position to expose abuses in the medical profession. He gained nationwide attention in 1953 by denouncing unnecessary surgery, exorbitant fees, and the practices of "fee splitting" (kickbacks from specialists for referrals) and "ghost surgery" (operations performed by doctors other than the specialists whom patients expected). Some segments of the AMA, deploring the notoriety resulting from the charges, attempted to censure Hawley at the 1953 convention, but failed.

Hawley continued to travel and speak widely throughout the 1950's, constantly urging members of his profession to keep their own house in order. He opposed national health insurance but was a firm advocate of voluntary, nonprofit health insurance plans. He also favored strict licensing of surgeons and more extensive accreditation of hospitals as ways of insuring the highest quality of medical care for patients.

Of his father and grandfather Hawley once said: "To them medicine was never a business. It was a profession to which they were called, like a minister of the gospel." It was his creed too. Ever the plain-spoken country doctor, Hawley never outgrew "the atmosphere of responsibility to the patient" in which he was raised. After being divorced in 1951, Hawley married Lydia W. Wright on Nov. 24, 1951. He died in Washington, D.C.

[A substantial collection of Hawley's personal and professional papers is at the U.S. Army Military History Institute, Carlisle Barracks, Pa. Hawley wrote extensively for professional journals, and a nearly complete bibliography is at the U.S. Army Center for Military History in Washington, D.C. On his World War II career, see Morris Fishbein, ed., *Doctors at War* (1945); and U.S. Army, *Medical Department in World War II* (Administrative series), 5 vols. (1963–1975). Also see *Collier's,* May 11, 1946; *Saturday Evening Post,* Oct. 4, 1947; *Congressional Digest,* Mar. 1949; *Vital Speeches,* May 1, 1949; *U.S. News and World Report,* Feb. 20, 1953; *Newsweek,* Aug. 5, 1957. The files of the American College of Surgeons in Chicago also contain helpful information. An obituary is in the *New York Times,* Nov. 26, 1965.]

THOMAS E. SCHOTT

HAYES, CARLTON JOSEPH HUNTLEY (May 16, 1882–Sept. 3, 1964), historian and ambassador to Spain in World War II, was born at Jericho Farm in Afton, N.Y., the son of Philetus Arthur Hayes and Permilia Mary Huntley. "In Afton," he wrote later, "five generations of both paternal and maternal ancestors lived and are buried. Here is my true home, along the gently flowing Susquehanna and the smiling wooded hills." Hayes enrolled as a student at Columbia University in 1900, beginning a career at Columbia that lasted for fifty years. "I spent seven years listening to other people and forty-three years with other people listening to me." He received a B.A. in 1904, an M.A. in 1905, and a Ph.D. in 1909 with a dissertation on "Sources Relating to the Germanic Invasions." He was assistant professor (1910–1915), associate professor (1915–1919), professor (1919–1935), and Seth Low Professor of History (1935–1950). He was also visiting professor at California (1917, 1923), Johns Hopkins (1930), and Stanford (1941).

Hayes served as a captain in the Army Military Intelligence Division of the General Staff (1918–1919) and was a major in the Officers' Reserve Corps (1918–1933). On Sept. 18, 1920, he married Mary Evelyn Carroll; they had two children.

At Columbia Hayes rose to fame as teacher, textbook writer, and pioneer specialist in the history of modern nationalism. His lectures were among the most popular on campus. One student commented that "Hayes brought history from textbook abstractions to an experience lived and a problem to be faced." Tall, baldish, and sharp-featured, Hayes presented his material with the skill of a great actor. Looking out into space over the heads of his audience, he would boom out several impeccably chiseled sentences, pause, and then resume in either mildly whispered phrases or a shouting tone. He made shrewd use of sarcasm and irony. Although aware of socioeconomic trends, he took special pleasure in a biographical approach. In describing the courtly manners of Louis XIV, for example, he would pause and dramatically draw a handkerchief from the sleeve of his coat jacket. On occasion he would wrap his double-breasted coat around himself and become Metternich, Talleyrand, Disraeli, or Bismarck. This kind of dynamism made him a campus legend.

Hayes's advanced seminar on modern nationalism, offered in the Graduate School, won international fame as the finest and most productive study group of its kind, and doctoral candidates regarded acceptance to it as a special honor. Among the steady flow of dissertations supervised by Hayes were those by Robert R. Ergang (Germany), Beatrice Hyslop (France), John H. Wuorinen (Finland), and Oscar I. Janowsky (national minorities).

Nationalism was Hayes's central interest throughout his career, and he pursued the subject with unflagging zeal. Along with Hans Kohn and Boyd C. Shafer he was a pioneer in its study. His works are regarded as classics, notably *Essays on Nationalism* (1926), *France, A Nation of Patriots* (1930), *The Historical Evolution of Modern Nationalism* (1931), and *Nationalism: A Religion* (1960). His style was described by the critic Lewis Gannett as reflecting "an easy learning and grace granted few historians."

According to Hayes, nationalism moved from an originally positive to negative form, from "blessing to curse," going through several stages in its development: humanitarian, Jacobin, traditional, liberal, and integral—from a liberal tone during Metternich's time to a dynastic conservatism in the Bismarck era to a tragic descent into aggression and expansion in the twentieth century.

Hayes also wrote *British Social Politics* (1913), an outline of the growing trend toward state action for the solution of social problems. In *A Generation of Materialism, 1871–1900* (1941) he concluded that materialism "has brought us to the status of clogs in an economic machine, to fascism and communism, essentially the same tyrannies, and finally to the threat of the atomic bomb and threat of total destruction." Hayes's highly successful textbook, *Political and Social History of Modern Europe* (1916), was reprinted many times, and, together with *Modern and Contemporary European History* (1919) by his close friend Jacob Salwyn Schapiro, virtually monopolized the college history textbook market for years.

In 1924 Hayes was received into the Catholic Church, which he saw as a spiritual and antinationalistic force. Thereafter he became a leading Catholic layman. He was a cofounder of the National Association of Christians and Jews and was its Catholic cochairman from 1928 to 1946. In 1946 he was awarded the Laetare Medal by the University of Notre Dame, given annually to the most distinguished American Catholic.

Throughout his career Hayes was the subject of controversy. He enjoyed some of it: he was fond of showing a half-page caricature of himself in a Hearst newspaper as an "iconoclast." But in October 1927 he was deeply troubled when the National Americanization Committee of the Veterans of Foreign Wars charged that *Modern History* (1923), a high-school textbook he had written with Parker T. Moon, was pro-British. Three years later the New York City Board of Education removed the book from its permitted list of textbooks after a Staten Island minister and a local school board called it pro-Catholic and un-American. Hayes and Moon were defended by educational and civic groups, but their book was not restored to the approved list.

Despite his abhorrence of dictatorship, Hayes spoke out in favor of Generalissimo Francisco Franco, chief of the Spanish state. In April 1942 President Franklin D. Roosevelt, concerned about the possibility of Spain's intervention in World War II on the side of the Axis, appointed Hayes ambassador to Spain. The appointment was criticized by liberals who accused Hayes of hypocrisy in attacking Hitler and Mussolini but supporting Franco's "equally reprehensible dictatorship." The *New York Times*, on the other hand, reacted favorably in an editorial of Apr. 4, 1942:

As an uncompromising historian [Hayes] has the perspective to relate the present to the past in a country with deep roots in history. As an uncompromising enemy of the totalitarian system, he will be able to make the mind of democracy felt in the wavering margins of the Axis-dominated countries. As a Catholic who has done yeoman's work to break down intolerance in the inter-faith committee of Protestants, Catholics, and Jews, he will bring a special comprehension to the religious problems that are fundamental to the understanding not only of Spain but of all Latin America.

As ambassador, Hayes found Franco entangled in a knotty political situation. The Axis was making every possible effort to push Spain into the war, but the Spanish dictator had to face the possibility of an Allied victory that would leave Spain isolated. In addition, the Spanish people had little appetite for further conflict. Hayes regarded it as his prime duty to strengthen Spain's resolve to keep out of the war. Hayes remained in Spain as ambassador until January 1945. He worked effectively to discourage the sale of Spanish minerals and chemicals to the Axis. At the same time he urged that extensive American aid be given to Spain.

In 1945 Hayes published *Wartime Mission in Spain*, a personal record of his service as envoy. He argued that he had influenced Franco against overt entrance into the war and that the Falange, the only political party allowed in Spain, had exercised less influence on Franco than many people believed. Critics accused Hayes of being influenced by his religion to paint a more favorable picture of Catholic Spain than the facts warranted, "an inexcusable lapse for the objective historian."

In 1950 Hayes retired to his Jericho Farm in Afton. He continued to write and kept himself busy as a self-described "dirt farmer." He died at Jericho Farm.

[Hayes's papers are in the Columbia University Library Manuscript Division. In addition to his major works cited in the text, Hayes published *These Eventful Years* (1924); *Essays in Intellectual History* (1929); *A Quarter Century of Learning* (1931); *The United States and Spain* (1951); *Modern Europe to 1870* (1953); *Christianity and Western Civilization* (1954); *Contemporary Europe Since 1870* (1958); and *History of Western Civilization* (1962). He was the editor of *Social and Economic Studies of Post-War France* (1929–1930). Beginning with "The War of the Nations," *Political Science Quarterly*, Dec. 1914, he was the author of many scholarly articles and book reviews. He also served as a member of the editorial council of *Commonweal*.

On Hayes and his career see the excellent unpublished dissertation by Arthur Joseph Hughes, "Carlton J. H. Hayes: Teacher and Historian" (Columbia University, 1970); Howard W. Hintz and Bernard D. N. Grebanier, eds. *Modern American Vistas* (1940); and "Professor Hayes to Madrid," *Commonweal*, Apr. 17, 1942. Obituaries are in the *New York Times* and *New York Herald-Tribune*, Sept. 4, 1964; and *American Historical Review*, Jan. 1965.]

LOUIS L. SNYDER

HECHT, BEN (Feb. 28, 1894–Apr. 18, 1964), journalist, writer, playwright, and screenwriter, was born on New York City's Lower East Side, the son of Joseph Hecht, a tailor and later a dress designer, and Sarah Swernofsky. He attended Broome Street Grammar School before the family moved to Racine, Wis., where he graduated from high school. In 1910, having spent only three days at the University of Wis-

consin, he quit and went to Chicago, where he got a job on the *Chicago Journal*. In 1914 he joined the *Chicago Daily News*, assumed a newsman's cynicism, and soon established a reputation as an imaginative, often outrageous reporter and the best writer on Chicago in the city. As a newspaperman he saw himself as unique, an outsider; as a Jew he struggled all his life with his identity. In November 1915 he married Marie Armstrong, a reporter on the *Chicago Journal;* they had one daughter.

Sent to Berlin as a foreign correspondent in 1918, Hecht filed excellent columns on the ferment and chaos of post–World War I Germany. Having discovered dadaism in Europe, he returned to Chicago in 1920 and became part of the Chicago Renaissance. He railed against the tradition and morality of what H. L. Mencken (one of his idols) called the "booboisie" and extolled individualism, experimentation, and liberation. He wrote *Erik Dorn* (1921), his first and best novel; *A Thousand and One Afternoons in Chicago* (1922), a collection of his columns; *Gargoyles* (1922); a play *The Egotist* (1922); *The Florentine Dagger* (1923); *Fantazius Mallare* (1922), a novel that was banned as obscene; and *Humpty Dumpty* (1924). Together with Kenneth Sawyer Goodmen he also wrote a number of short plays; and in 1917 he collaborated with Maxwell Bodenheim in writing plays. In 1923 Hecht founded the *Chicago Literary Times*, a short-lived publication which folded in June 1924. During this most productive and original period of his life, Hecht described, according to Harry Hansen, "the conglomerate mob life of a big industrial city."

In 1924 Hecht moved to New York City and the following year he and his wife were divorced. He then married Rose Caylor, also a reporter; they had one daughter. Not long after coming to New York, Hecht began work with Charles MacArthur on *The Front Page*, which opened on Broadway on Aug. 14, 1928. The play was based on Hecht's knowledge of the older crime scene in Chicago before the Al Capone era, on his relationship with Dion O'Banion, an Italian North Side gangster, and on the frantic, florid, tough journalism of that period. A successful, tautly written drama, it remains the best-known work of both men.

Hecht was equally adept as a screenwriter. Beginning with an original eighteen-page story from which the film *Underworld* (1927) was shot, he wrote or collaborated on some seventy films, including *The Front Page* (1931), *Scarface* (1932), *Twentieth Century* (1934), *Wuthering Heights* (1939), *His Girl Friday* (1940),

Spellbound (1945), *Notorious* (1946), *Monkey Business* (1952), and *A Farewell to Arms* (1958). Hecht became one of the most skillful and highly paid screenwriters.

In *A Jew in Love* (1931), Hecht described the leading character, Jo Boshere, as a "dark-skinned little Jew with a vulturous and moody face." Boshere, a successful publisher who played the market, appears to have sprung from Hecht's own insecurities. In 1939, reacting to the Nazi Holocaust, Hecht leaped to the defense of Zionism. He wrote columns praising Yiddish writers, was disappointed with Jews who suffered "racial amnesia," and put on pageants such as *A Flag is Born* (1946), which applauded the anti-British terrorist underground in Palestine. After Hecht congratulated the terrorists in a New York *Herald Tribune* advertisement in 1947, Great Britain boycotted his films and books; the boycott was relaxed in 1952.

Hecht also wrote several hundred short stories and columns. Many of his columns are gathered in *A Thousand and One Afternoons in Chicago* and *1001 Afternoons in New York* (1941); most of his best stories are in *Broken Necks* (1924), *The Champion from Far Away* (1931), *The Collected Stories of Ben Hecht* (1945), and *A Treasury of Ben Hecht* (1959). His autobiographies, *A Child of the Century* (1954), which revealed as much by what was left out as by what was included, described the Chicago he had known, and *Gaily Gaily* (1963) were best sellers. He admitted frankly: "Although I am known here and there as a writer not without wit and fecundity, the information is a bit spotty and I can rely little on reader snobbery."

In his last years Hecht was as productive as ever. The quality of his literary work declined but his screen scripts improved. "We were all fools to have left Chicago," he wrote of the roots he had severed in his biography of Charles MacArthur, *Charlie* (1957).

When Hecht died in New York City, the Chicago *Daily News* called him a "One Man Fiction Factory" and the *New York Times* obituary described him as having had "a genuine instinct for the cinema and a commanding talent for film dialogue." He was an author who drew on rich reserves of wit, rhetoric, and fantasy—as well as upon an "impassioned religious preoccupation." Whether or not he ever achieved his full potential, his writing breathed vitality and gusto. As Saul Bellow remarked: "If he is occasionally slick, he is also independent, forthright and original. Among the pussy-cats who write of social issues today he roars like an old-fashioned lion." Doug Fetherling wrote that Hecht brought to American writing a picture of the missing link between hero and antihero and infused intelligence into the popular culture, making it more meaningful and important.

[A collection of Hecht's papers may be found at the Newberry Library, Chicago. The best sources on Hecht are Ronald M. Roberts, "The Novels of Ben Hecht" (Ph.D. diss., Baylor University, 1970); Doug Fetherling, *The Five Lives of Ben Hecht* (1977), an insightful, analytical biography; and Jeffrey Martin, "The Screenplays of Ben Hecht" (Ph.D. diss., Indiana University, 1978). All three have valuable bibliographies.

Among the most helpful periodical and book articles are Harry Hansen, *Midwest Portraits* (1923), possibly the best book on the Chicago Renaissance; Donald Friede, *The Mechanical Angel* (1948); Elia Kazan, "Writers and Motion Pictures," *Atlantic Monthly*, Apr. 1957; Leslie Fiedler, "Genesis: The American Jewish Novel through the Twenties," *Midstream*, Summer 1958; Joseph Waldmeir, "Novelists of Two Wars," *Nation*, Nov. 1, 1958; Leslie Fiedler, "The Breakthrough: The American Jewish Novelist and the Fictional Image of the Jew," *Midstream*, Winter 1958; Peter M. Jack's discussion of Hecht's early fiction in Malcolm Cowley, ed., *After the Genteel Tradition* (1964); Allen Guttmann, "The Conversion of the Jews," *Wisconsin Studies in Contemporary Literature*, Summer 1965; Abe Ravitz, "Ballyhoo, Gargoyles, and Firecrackers: Ben Hecht's Aesthetic Calliope," *Journal of Popular Culture*, Summer 1967; Stephen Fuller, "Ben Hecht: A Sampler," *Film Comment*, Winter 1970–1971; Harold Rosenberg, "Man as Anti-Semite," in his *Discovering the Present* (1973); and Fred Guiles, *Hanging on in Paradise* (1975), an excellent study of Hollywood's screenwriters with a significant emphasis on Hecht and MacArthur.]

DANIEL WALDEN

HEINEMAN, DANIEL WEBSTER ("DANNIE") (Nov. 23, 1872–Jan. 31, 1962), engineer and industrialist, was born in Charlotte, N.C., the son of James Heineman, who was in the chewing-tobacco business, and of Minna Hertz, who had been born in Germany. In 1880, after his father's death, he moved with his mother to Germany, where he studied electrical engineering—then a new subject—at the Technical College of Hannover. Following graduation in 1895, he joined the Union-Elektrizitäts-Gesellschaft, a Berlin company affiliated with General Electric. For the next ten years he directed the conversion from horse to electric power of the tramways of Naples, Koblenz, Liège, and Brussels, and from hydraulic to electric power of the funicular on Mt. Vesuvius. In

1905, Heineman became managing director of the Belgian firm Société Financière de Transports et d'Enterprises Industrielle (SOFINA). He remained its chief executive for fifty years. Heineman married Hettie Meyer. They had three children.

When Heineman joined SOFINA, it had only two other employees; by the beginning of World War II it had either built or taken over the tramways and electrical systems of Bilbao, Buenos Aires, Constantinople, Bangkok, Barcelona, and Lisbon, among other places, and with its subsidiaries employed 40,000 people. SOFINA was recognized as one of the corporate giants of electrical equipment, and Heineman as one of the human giants in that field.

Heineman was a businessman in the high European style. He was generally acknowledged to be basically a builder rather than a financial manipulator, and some of his former colleagues have even insisted that he was uninterested in money. According to his son James, he was "in awe of men who could create." He liked to discuss politics, writing, or music in his office before getting down to work. Outside his office he was known as a humanitarian and collector of rare books and manuscripts. During World War I he helped to found the Commission for Belgian Relief, which was later headed by Herbert Hoover.

Heineman's book and manuscript collection, begun about 1905, has been described by Frederick B. Adams, Jr., former director of the Pierpont Morgan Library in New York (where the collection is now housed), as "not large, but a well-chosen cabinet. It is especially strong in French and German literature of the eighteenth and nineteenth centuries and in musical manuscripts, and his collections of Mozart, Goethe, Heine, Rousseau, Napoleon, and Maupassant would hold the status of national treasures in Germany or France."

Heineman returned to the United States as a refugee during World War II and continued to direct the operations of SOFINA from New York City. After 1945 he divided his time between Europe and the United States. At this time he bore, and was amused by, a fairly striking physical resemblance to J. Pierpont Morgan.

It is ironic, in light of the generally nonpredatory character of Heineman's business career, that the last important episode in it should have been a decades-long battle with the Spaniard Juan March, a onetime tobacco smuggler and financial freebooter. In 1948, March—with significant help from the Franco government, which owed him favors for huge financial ad-

vances made early in the Spanish Civil War—undertook to seize control, by fraudulent means, of Barcelona Traction, Light and Power Company, a leading SOFINA holding that supplied most of the electric power of Catalonia. Through a series of Machiavellian maneuvers aided by complaisant decisions of the Spanish courts, March, by the time of Heineman's retirement in 1955, had drawn a net around the company. Heineman's successors at SOFINA carried the matter to the International Court of Justice at The Hague, which heard pleadings for eleven years and in 1970—eight years after the death of both of the original principals in the dispute—decided that it lacked jurisdiction and thus let Barcelona Traction go to March's successors by default. It was a real-life international thriller, a legal-financial war in the grand style, into which Heineman had been forced against his will and temperament. He died in New York City.

[A catalog of Heineman's book and manuscript collection was published by the Pierpont Morgan Library in 1963. Heineman wrote *Outline of a New Europe* (1930). Information on Heineman is in an article on Juan March, "Annals of Finance" by John Brooks, *New Yorker,* May 28, 1979. An obituary is in the *New York Times,* Feb. 2, 1962.]

JOHN BROOKS

HEMINGWAY, ERNEST MILLER (July 21, 1899–July 2, 1961), novelist and short-story writer, was born in the Chicago suburb of Oak Park, Ill., the son of Clarence Edmonds Hemingway, a physician, and of Grace Hall, a music teacher. Both his grandfathers had fought in the Civil War—Ernest Hall in the First Iowa Volunteer Cavalry and Anson Hemingway in the Illinois Infantry—a fact in which Hemingway took great pride. The family spent winters in Oak Park, where Hemingway was a kind of Tom Sawyer, and summers in the lake country near Petoskey, Mich., where he went barefoot, wearing suspenders and a straw hat like a veritable Huckleberry Finn.

Hemingway's parents were devout Congregationalists. He was a choirboy and president of the Christian Endeavor Society, and seems to have been a tractable and imaginative child, physically strong and handsome, mentally alert and adventurous. His mother encouraged Hemingway's marked impulse toward creativity, and his father provided an early grounding in nature lore and woodsmanship. Although Hemingway later pretended that his youth had been wild and rebellious, it was in fact wholly normal, religious, middle-class, polite, fairly well-to-do, and—apart from a few adolescent pranks—reasonably chaste and subdued.

The first notable change in his way of life occurred in October 1917, when Hemingway started work as cub reporter for the *Kansas City Star* in Missouri, his graduation from Oak Park High School having ended his formal education. He stayed at the *Star* for six months, haunting the city hospitals and police stations, learning the trade to which he would later return, and reveling in his first experience of living away from home.

A far greater adventure lay ahead. Prevented from enlisting in the armed forces by a congenital eyesight deficiency, Hemingway volunteered to drive ambulances for the American Red Cross in Italy. On June 4, 1918, he reached Schio, near Milan, and began transporting Italian wounded from the mountain front to base hospitals. When Austrian pressure started to mount on the lower Piave River front, Hemingway left Schio to become *tenente* in charge of a Red Cross canteen in the village of Fossalta, carrying cigarettes and chocolate to the Italian soldiers entrenched along the western riverbank. These activities ended abruptly on the night of July 8, when an Austrian trench mortar made a direct hit on the dugout where he was at work. Hemingway was severely wounded in the legs and feet by metal fragments. He behaved admirably, even heroically, carrying a dying companion to the rear.

After five days in a field hospital near Mestre, Hemingway was taken to the Red Cross Hospital in Milan. There he spent the summer and fall, recovering from his wounds and falling in love with Agnes von Kurowsky, an American nurse. These experiences, suitably fictionalized, gave him the substance not only for *A Farewell to Arms*, one of his best novels, but also for several noteworthy short stories. Apart from brief furloughs at Stresa and Treviso, and a holiday in Taormina, Sicily, he remained in Milan until he sailed for home on Jan. 4, 1919.

For nearly three years after the war, Hemingway stayed in the Middle West, often expressing a nostalgic desire to renew his association with the more sophisticated civilization of Europe. The most severe blow of the spring of 1919 was a letter of rejection from Agnes, who had fallen in love with an Italian officer. Hemingway assuaged his wounded feelings with a healthy summer at the family cottage in Michigan, and in the fall he rented a room in nearby Petoskey, where he began to write serious fiction. In January 1920 he went to Toronto as paid companion to Ralph Conable, Jr., the son of the head of the Canadian branch of F. W. Woolworths. Before his return in May, he had managed to secure a part-time job as feature writer for the *Toronto Star*. That summer he revisited Michigan. In the fall he moved to Chicago, where he began to work as subeditor of the *Cooperative Commonwealth*, a trade journal for a national cooperative society. He also wrote as many poems and stories as time permitted.

In Chicago Hemingway met and soon fell in love with Elizabeth Hadley Richardson, who came from St. Louis and was eager to share his plans for returning to Italy. Also in Chicago, in the spring of 1921, he met Sherwood Anderson, who had recently visited Paris, extolled its virtues as a literary center, and offered to write letters of introduction for Hemingway to deliver to such famous American expatriates as Ezra Pound and Gertrude Stein. About three months after Hemingway and Hadley were married on Sept. 3, 1921, they sailed for France, where Hemingway began work as foreign correspondent for the *Toronto Star*.

The Hemingways' first residence in Paris was a rather grubby walk-up apartment on the Montagne Ste. Geneviève in the Latin Quarter. In the intervals between Hemingway's newspaper assignments, the couple began to discover the joys of European life: vacationing in Switzerland; hiking over the Pass of St. Bernard in knee-deep snow; visiting Milan, where Hemingway interviewed Mussolini; paying a call at Schio; and making a sentimental journey to the site of his wounding at Fossalta. In September 1922, Hemingway went to Constantinople to cover the Greco-Turkish war. On his return the following month he wrote two short stories, "Up in Michigan" and "My Old Man." He covered the Lausanne Peace Conference for the *Star* but also secretly filed stories for William Randolph Hearst's International News Service to supplement his meager income. When Hadley left Paris to join him in Lausanne, she carried a valise containing all but two of Hemingway's manuscripts. It was stolen en route, a seemingly irreplaceable loss. They shook off the ugly memory with a skiing holiday near Montreux, a walking tour with the Pounds in Italy, and a visit to Cortina d'Ampezzo. There Hemingway composed half a dozen miniature short stories that appeared in *The Little Review* (April 1923). It was his first substantial European publication. After an interval of reporting in the Ruhr valley, Hemingway rejoined Hadley at Cortina, where he wrote "Out of Season," the most mature story he had done to that time. He now had three stories and ten poems, which he submitted to Robert McAlmon for publication in a slender volume that appeared in the fall of 1923.

In May 1923 Hemingway visited Spain for the first time, in the company of McAlmon and an American newspaperman, William Bird. Bird had taken over as a hobby an ancient hand-press on the Quai d'Anjou. He named it the Three Mountains Press, and in March 1924 published Hemingway's second book, *In Our Time*, which contained the six miniatures that had appeared in the *Little Review* and twelve others laboriously composed that summer.

In July 1923 Hemingway also discovered the annual *feria* at Pamplona, Spain, where Hadley, between bullfights, stitched baby clothes for the child they were expecting in the fall. In mid-August 1923 they left Europe so that Hemingway could earn a regular salary as daily reporter for the *Toronto Star*. But they could hardly wait until the baby, a boy, was old enough to go back to France. Toronto struck them as hidebound and provincial, and Hemingway quarreled repeatedly with Harry Hindmarsh, his city editor. He was, moreover, convinced that he must abandon newspaper work in order to get on with serious fiction.

They returned to Paris in 1924 and rented a spacious apartment at 113 rue Notre Dame des Champs, near the Luxembourg Garden. Ford Madox Ford had just begun publication of the *Transatlantic Review*, and Hemingway, eager to secure an outlet for his work, became subeditor and columnist for the magazine, which brought out three of his stories before ceasing publication in January 1925. The *Little Review* took another story; and a German magazine, *Der Querschnitt*, issued four of his more scabrous poems, so that he could now say with some justification that his reputation was becoming international.

In July 1924 the Hemingways returned to the Pamplona fiesta, accompanied by John Dos Passos and a young Irish officer, Eric Dorman-Smith, both of whom Hemingway had first met in Italy in 1918. Also present were his two "publishers," McAlmon and Bird, and the American humorist Donald Ogden Stewart. After the fiesta they all made a fishing trip to Burguete in the Pyrenees, where Hemingway absorbed the atmosphere and scenery that would eventually emerge in his first novel, *The Sun Also Rises*.

Despite his small successes in Paris and Berlin, American magazines had remained impervious to Hemingway's repeated attempts to gain acceptance. But Edmund Wilson's laudatory review of the two Paris chapbooks in the October 1924 *Dial* encouraged Hemingway to think that an American publisher might consider a collection of his short stories. His new friend Harold Loeb, editor of *Broom*, introduced him to the Paris agent for Horace Liveright of the New York house of Boni and Liveright. Prospects seemed bright enough to enable the Hemingways to take a working holiday at Schruns in the Austrian Vorarlberg. He was skiing in the Alps when a cable informed him of the acceptance of his book *In Our Time*, containing fourteen short stories interfoliated with the miniatures from the *In Our Time* published in Paris. Liveright rejected "Up in Michigan" as too outspoken on sex, so Hemingway promptly wrote a substitute, "The Battler." This was among the best of the half-dozen Nick Adams stories, which gave the book the incipient flavor of a bildungsroman, carrying Nick from boyhood to young manhood.

The year 1925 was a lucky one. The gregarious Hemingway rapidly enlarged his corps of acquaintances, both literary and otherwise, cementing friendships with Scott and Zelda Fitzgerald, Archibald and Ada MacLeish, Gerald and Sara Murphy, Guy and Mary Hickok, the *Vogue* fashion editor Pauline Pfeiffer, and Lady Duff Twysden, estranged wife of a British baronet. In the spring he spent many hours helping Ernest Walsh start a new magazine, *This Quarter*, which paid him liberally for "Big Two-Hearted River" and "The Undefeated," his longest stories to date. In the summer came the famous visit to Pamplona. The group that assembled under Hemingway's captaincy included Duff Twysden, Harold Loeb, and Don Stewart. The bullfighter Cayetano Ordóñez performed admirably and even heroically. The stage was now set for the development of *The Sun Also Rises*. By Hemingway's own account, he began the novel in Valencia on his twenty-sixth birthday and finished the first draft in about six weeks, close to the moral and emotional atmosphere of the memorable fiesta. The effort exhausted him, and he put the book aside for revision that winter in Schruns.

But he was now confident enough to attempt yet another book. During a single week in November, he composed a satirical jeu d'esprit called *The Torrents of Spring*. The title was from Turgenev, but the locale was Petoskey, Mich., and the victim was Sherwood Anderson, of whose most recent novel, *Dark Laughter*, the book was a sustained and sometimes amusing parody. Hemingway sent it off to Liveright, who wanted *The Sun Also Rises* but summarily rejected this attack on one of his leading authors, thus freeing Hemingway from his contractual obligations a mere thirteen weeks after the appearance of the New York edition of *In Our Time.*

In February 1926, Hemingway made a hasty trip to New York, returning with the news that Maxwell Perkins of Charles Scribner's Sons had agreed to publish both *The Torrents of Spring* and *The Sun Also Rises.* He was exuberant at the change of publisher but remorseful over an incipient change in his marital status, for he had fallen in love with Pauline Pfeiffer and his five-year marriage rapidly approached dissolution. Shortly before *The Torrents of Spring* appeared in May, Hemingway went alone to Madrid. On rejoining his wife and son at Juan-les-Pins, he showed the carbon of *The Sun Also Rises* to Fitzgerald, who strongly urged alterations in the text. Hemingway deleted the first fifteen pages of his typescript, advised Perkins of the change, and vainly sought to gather up the shards of his crumbling marriage. Pauline and the Murphys accompanied Hemingway and Hadley to Pamplona in July. In August the Hemingways returned to Paris and agreed to set up separate residences. Their divorce became final in January 1927.

The Sun Also Rises had appeared Oct. 22, 1926, to considerable acclaim, and the sales momentum continued well into the new year. American magazines were now clamoring for stories, and Perkins suggested a new collection for the coming fall. With Pauline and her sister Virginia, Hemingway spent most of the winter in Gstaad, Switzerland, skiing and writing on alternate days. In March 1927 he and Guy Hickok toured fascist Italy, a journey eliciting a series of sketches that Hemingway ironically called "Che Ti Dice La Patria." Along with "The Killers," "Fifty Grand," "The Undefeated," and other stories, it appeared that October in *Men Without Women.*

On May 10, 1927, Hemingway and Pauline Pfeiffer were married in Paris. They honeymooned at Grau du Roi in the south of France and spent the summer in Spain. In the spring of 1928 they moved to the United States, because Pauline wished to bear her first child—it was to be a son—on American soil. The site they chose was Key West, Fla., where Hemingway could indulge his love of fishing and at the same time get forward with a new novel, *A Farewell to Arms.* He finished it in January 1929, soon after his father committed suicide. In February Perkins carried the completed typescript from Key West to New York, and *Scribner's Magazine* paid $16,000 for serialization rights. In April,

flushed with success, Hemingway moved his family to Paris, where they remained, except for a summer in Spain, until early January 1930.

Back in Florida, Hemingway began work on a book about the Spanish bullfight, as he had been yearning to do since 1925. Despite the stock market crash and the deepening Great Depression, sales of *A Farewell to Arms* had been brisk, and its critical reception excellent, so he could afford to experiment with two nonfiction books: the bible of the bullfight and another, still amorphous in his mind, about big-game hunting in Kenya and Tanganyika, where he longed to go on safari. To escape the humidity of Key West, Hemingway resolved to spend the summer and fall at the dude ranch of Lawrence Nordquist in Clark's Fork Valley, Wyo., an ideal place for fishing, hunting, and writing.

The motor trip home had hardly begun on November 1 when Hemingway broke his right arm in a road accident and had to spend seven weeks at St. Vincent's Hospital in Billings, Mont. All through the spring of 1931 he wrestled with the frustrations of slow healing and disappointment over the postponement of the African trip, yet he managed to move forward with the bullfight book. To update his knowledge he and his family went to Spain that summer, leaving in May and returning in the fall for the birth of Pauline's second child. Their last act before sailing was the purchase of a large house at 907 Whitehead Street in Key West, with funds provided by Pauline's wealthy uncle, G. A. Pfeiffer.

The Hemingways moved into the new house on Dec. 19, 1931, a month after the birth of their second son. Three weeks later *Death in the Afternoon* was finished. Hemingway had now discovered the pleasures of marlin fishing off Cuba, and was assembling short stories for a third collection. In the typical hurly-burly of his life in these years, he saw *Death in the Afternoon* through the press, drove back to Nordquist's ranch for another hunting season, and came home in late October, only to leave almost immediately to spend Thanksgiving and Christmas with Pauline's family in Arkansas.

Amid all these arrivals and departures, the mixed critical reception of *Death in the Afternoon* seemed a relatively minor event. Hemingway entered 1933 determined to renew his reputation as a writer of fiction. *Winner Take Nothing* was the title of his third collection of stories. Sending the typescript off to Perkins, he said that it represented the next fourteen chapters in his secret program to make a picture of the whole world, or at least as much of it as he had seen.

At last it was time for Africa and the sight of a new continent. Hemingway's friend Charles Thompson and Pauline were his companions, and Philip Percival his professional hunter. Although Hemingway contracted an acute case of amoebic dysentery, the safari otherwise went beautifully. At home in April 1934, he began a nonfiction narrative, built like a novel, that appeared in 1935 as *Green Hills of Africa.* No less absorbing was the delivery in May of his new cabin cruiser, *Pilar,* which he called a "fishing machine" par excellence, and used for relaxation from his writing.

For a year Hemingway had been contributing journalistic articles to a new magazine, *Esquire,* by which, intentionally or not, he projected an image of, himself as a man's man—tough, profane, and resilient—and perhaps the leading outdoor playboy of the Western literary world. This image was partly responsible for the adverse reviews of *Green Hills of Africa.* He sullenly complained that he could bring out a *Hamlet* tomorrow, only to have "the critics" pick away at it like vultures. Half defiantly he took up fishing from the *Pilar* at Bimini in the Bahamas—esteemed by the wealthy sportsmen who frequented those waters, yet aware of his true brotherhood with the common man. Out of his position between these extremes emerged two excellent short stories, "The Snows of Kilimanjaro" and "The Short Happy Life of Francis Macomber," in which Hemingway self-righteously attacked his new acquaintances among the rich while seeking to vindicate his personal philosophy of courage and durability. Another product of the same dilemma was the novel *To Have and Have Not* (1937), which dramatized his fraternal admiration for a Key West desperado named Harry Morgan, driven outside the law and at last to his death by the inexorable thrust of Great Depression economics.

The outbreak of the Spanish Civil War in July 1936 drew Hemingway's attention back to the European country he loved best. As an antifascist of long standing, he allied himself with the Loyalists. When he sailed for Spain in February 1937, under contract to the North American Newspaper Alliance (NANA), he was accompanied by Sidney Franklin, the bullfighter from Brooklyn, of whose exploits he had long been an admirer, and Martha Gellhorn, an attractive writer whom he had befriended the preceding December and who shared his support of the Loyalist cause.

Apart from feature stories for NANA, Hemingway's first business was the preparation of a propaganda film, *The Spanish Earth,* on which he worked with Dos Passos, Joris Ivens, and John Ferno. In June 1937 he addressed the Second American Writers' Congress in New York, and spent part of the summer raising money to buy ambulances for the Loyalists. The next result of his Spanish experience was *The Fifth Column,* a melodrama of counterespionage in besieged Madrid, composed there during his second visit in the fall of 1937. His developing love affair with Martha Gellhorn was now becoming apparent to his closest friends. The break with Pauline was imminent when Hemingway returned to Spain for the third time in March 1938, and more or less complete when he came home in May. He stayed in Key West long enough to read proof on *The Fifth Column and the First Forty-Nine Stories,* a collected edition issued in October, and then made one final visit to Barcelona before taking leave of Spain for a fifteen-year interval.

By the spring of 1939, Hemingway was already deep in the novel he would call *For Whom the Bell Tolls.* On April 10 he went to Cuba and was joined there by Martha Gellhorn, who had leased a large house, La Finca Vigía, on a hilltop in the village of San Francisco de Paula, some twelve miles from Havana. Hemingway bought the house in 1940, and it became a fairly permanent home for the rest of his life. In August he paid a last visit to the Nordquist ranch and then left for Sun Valley, a new resort among the Sawtooth Mountains of Idaho. There and in Cuba, while Martha came and went on journalistic assignments, he moved on with the novel that was taking shape as the indubitable masterpiece of the second half of his writing life.

Long awaited, eagerly read, sold to the films for $100,000, *For Whom the Bell Tolls* was the most successful of Hemingway's books through 1940. His divorce from Pauline became final on Nov. 4, 1940, and on Nov. 21 he married Martha. In January 1941 he set off with Martha to Hong Kong to report on the Sino-Japanese War for the newspaper *PM.*

The war in Europe, which Hemingway had been predicting ever since the rise of Hitler, was now in progress. Between May 1942 and May 1944 he busied himself with setting up a counterespionage organization in Cuba (which was heavily infiltrated with agents from Nazi Germany) and supervising the adaptation of his beloved *Pilar* to serve as a Q-boat against German submarines preying on Allied shipping in the Caribbean. Martha continued her career in journalism and urged Hemingway to do likewise. In mid-May 1944 he capitulated, flying to England to report for *Collier's* on the activities of the Royal Air Force.

Hemingway had scarcely settled down in London when, after a night of wassail, a motor accident in the blackout caused him to be hospitalized with a severe concussion. Martha was so indignant over his roistering in wartime that he sought solace in a love affair with Mary Welsh, an American journalist for *Time-Life*. Owing to his injuries, he was unable to go ashore in France during the D-Day invasion, though he crossed the English Channel with the flotilla.

Except for a week's stay in Cherbourg, Hemingway remained in England until mid-July, after which he attached himself to the 4th Infantry Division and the 22nd Infantry Regiment under Colonel Charles T. Lanham, with whom he formed a lasting friendship. In the drive to liberate Paris in August he was in nominal command of a small group of Free French guerrillas. Having entered Paris on Aug. 25, 1944, he settled into the Ritz Hotel, where Mary Welsh soon joined him. During the autumn campaigns he often returned to Lanham's regiment as it pursued the enemy across Belgium and Germany. Early in March 1945, Hemingway flew homeward having arranged for Mary Welsh to join him at La Finca Vigía as soon as she had initiated divorce proceedings against her husband. His marriage to Martha ended in divorce that December, and he and Mary were married at Havana on Mar. 14, 1946.

Except for *Men at War*, a large anthology that he edited with an introduction in 1942, Hemingway had written almost nothing since 1939–1940. Now he began a retrospective novel, "The Garden of Eden" (unpublished), in which he drew on his memories of his first two wives in France and Spain before the Spanish Civil War. Yet it was not until early 1949, at Cortina d'Ampezzo, that he at last regained his stride as a novelist. Once again his subject was love and war. This time, though, the war was engaged through the memories of an American colonel, Richard Cantwell, who had fought in the European theater in both 1918 and 1944. The "love interest" was provided by a Venetian girl, aged nineteen, as Hemingway had been at the time of his being wounded at Fossalta. The fictional Renata was partly modeled on Adriana Ivancich, a young Venetian with whom he had lately established a strictly Platonic friendship. Renata is made to listen sympathetically to Cantwell's bitter reminiscences of two world wars before he dies of a heart attack at the end of the book.

Across the River and into the Trees (1950) found little approbation among the reviewers who found it garrulous, pretentious, tired, like a parody of his former style. Two years later Hemingway regained his reputation with *The Old Man and the Sea*, a novella based on a true story he had heard fifteen years before from his Cuban boatman, Carlos Gutiérrez. The book forms part of a much longer novel, *Islands in the Stream* (1970), on which he had begun work before undertaking *Across the River*. Hemingway set forth the tale of old Santiago and his battle with the giant marlin as a kind of universal fable: one man alone, locked in a struggle with a worthy adversary, losing his prize to marauding sharks on the long voyage home but winning the Pyrrhic victory of having carried on against great odds with courage and endurance, the two qualities of mind and heart that Hemingway most revered.

This novella, which earned Hemingway a Pulitzer Prize in 1953, perfectly embodied his most profound discovery in aesthetics, the ability to achieve what he called "the fifth dimension." It incorporated the other four, yet rose beyond them into a symbolic realm that partook of the nature of mythology. With little taste for the abstract or the theoretical, Hemingway always insisted upon grounding his aesthetic in empirical data. Yet he knew that mere reportage is flat and that the writer must invent from the whole range of his experience in order to attain the roundness and depth of verisimilitude, a quality "truer than truth." His new friend, the art historian and critic Bernard Berenson, delighted him by saying of the tale of Santiago: "No real artist symbolizes or allegorizes—and Hemingway is a real artist—but every real work of art exhales symbols and allegories. So does this short but not small masterpiece."

Two retrospective journeys in 1953–1954 took the Hemingways to Spain and Africa. In Spain he discovered the matador Antonio Ordóñez, son of the man who had served as model for the bullfighter Pedro Romero in *The Sun Also Rises*. In Africa he went on safari with Philip Percival, his old friend from 1933. Afterward the Hemingways were making a pleasure flight over Uganda when successive plane crashes on January 23 (Murchison Falls) and 24 (Butiaba) left him with a concussion and severe internal injuries from which he was still recovering on his return to Havana in June. He had long and secretly coveted the Nobel Prize; but when he won it in 1954, he was too ill to attend the Stockholm ceremonies. Instead he wrote an acceptance speech to be read by John Cabot, the American ambassador.

The ensuing years were dogged by recurrent illness, at first physical, centering in the liver and kidneys, and at last mental, with severe paranoid symptoms beginning about June 1960. Much of 1955 was devoted to a sprawling account of the recent African adventure, posthumously excerpted by *Sports Illustrated* in 1971–1972. On Sept. 17, 1955, Hemingway made his will, naming his wife as sole heir and literary executrix. He helped cameramen secure fishing footage for a film version of *The Old Man and the Sea* but spent the final weeks of the year in bed. A trip to Peru in April 1956 provided more fishing sequences for the film and seemed temporarily to restore his health, but he fell ill again in Spain while following the exploits of Ordóñez and was still ailing on his return to Cuba in January 1957. That summer he collaborated with Archibald MacLeish, Robert Frost, and T. S. Eliot in trying to secure Ezra Pound's release from a Washington, D.C., mental hospital.

In the fall and winter of 1957–1958, Hemingway summoned energy to push forward with a series of sketches on his life in Paris in 1921–1926. Eventually named *A Moveable Feast* (1964), and constituting in effect a belated *apologia pro vita sua*, the book was by far the best work of his later life. In 1958–1959 he took it with him to Ketchum, Idaho, where he bought a two-story chalet overlooking the Big Wood River and, across the valley, the cemetery where he would be buried.

The Castro revolution, which Hemingway favored, was about to change the quality of life in Cuba. The house in Ketchum and the subsequent rental of a New York apartment were Hemingway's defenses against the possible loss of his Cuban home. But he spent little time in either place. From May to October 1959 he was in Spain gathering material on the rivalry between Ordóñez and Luís Miguel Dominguín. Working desperately against time, he completed a book-length typescript called "The Dangerous Summer," of which *Life* published excerpts in the fall of 1960. The effort, however, helped to push him to the brink of a mental breakdown.

Following an abortive trip to Spain, Hemingway was hospitalized in Rochester, Minn., from Nov. 30, 1960, to Jan. 22, 1961, and again from Apr. 25 to June 26, subjected both times to electric shock therapy. He had been long determined to take his own life, and he accomplished his purpose with a double-barreled shotgun in the foyer of the house at Ketchum at seven on the Sunday morning of July 2, bringing to an end a brilliant career that had lasted forty years.

Hemingway's influence has been vast and pervasive, both in his lifetime and posthumously. Young and middle-aged writers, native and foreign, have repeatedly and publicly testified to the effects of his work upon their own. They have recognized the importance of his prose style, his handling of dialogue, his narrative methods, his skill in the portrayal of character, his love of the outdoors, and his magical ability with scenery and setting. Many of them have shared in what the Nobel Prize citation called his "manly love of danger and adventure" and his "natural admiration for every individual who fights the good fight in a world of reality overshadowed by violence and death."

Detractors have little damaged either Hemingway's influence or his reputation. His books, on which he lavished his best powers, continue to sell in quantity and to be read by new generations both in the United States and abroad. In 1978 his publisher Charles Scribner, Jr., asserted that Hemingway and Fitzgerald were still his top-selling authors, each of them accounting for several hundred thousand copies each year, and therefore reaching millions of readers. This above all was the fate Hemingway hoped for.

[Hemingway's papers are widely scattered but the chief collection is at the John F. Kennedy Library in Boston.

The principal biography is Carlos Baker, *Ernest Hemingway: A Life Story* (1969); see also Gregory H. Hemingway, *Papa: A Personal Memoir* (1976); and Mary Hemingway, *How It Was* (1976). The major bibliography is Audre Hanneman, *Ernest Hemingway: A Comprehensive Bibliography* (1967; supp., 1975); see also Philip Young and Charles W. Mann, comps., *The Hemingway Manuscripts: An Inventory* (1969). Posthumous publications include William White, ed., *By-Line* (1967); *The Fifth Column and Four Stories of the Spanish Civil War* (1969); *Islands in the Stream* (1970); Philip Young, ed., *The Nick Adams Stories* (1972); Carlos Baker, ed., *Ernest Hemingway: Selected Letters 1917–1961* (1981).

Among critical studies are Carlos Baker, *Hemingway: The Writer as Artist* (1952; 4th ed., rev., 1973); Philip Young, *Ernest Hemingway: A Reconsideration* (1952; second ed. 1966); Earl Rovit, *Ernest Hemingway* (1963); Sheridan Baker, *Ernest Hemingway* (1967); Richard Hovey, *Hemingway: The Inward Terrain* (1968); Robert O. Stephens, *Hemingway's Non-Fiction* (1968); Jackson J. Benson, *Hemingway* (1969); Emily S. Watts, *Hemingway and the Arts* (1971); Sheldon Grebstein, *Hemingway's Craft* (1973); Michael S. Reynolds, *Hemingway's First War* (1976); and Scott Donaldson, *By Force of Will* (1977).]

CARLOS BAKER

HENCH, PHILIP SHOWALTER (Feb. 28, 1896–Mar. 30, 1965), physician and rheumatologist, was born in Pittsburgh, Pa., the son of Jacob Bixler Hench and Clara John Showalter. His father was a schoolteacher and classics scholar. After receiving preparatory-school education at the Shadyside Academy and the University School, both in Pittsburgh, Hench enrolled at Lafayette College in Easton, Pa. He received his B.A. in 1916. He next entered medical school at the University of Pittsburgh. While a student there, Hench enlisted as a private in the Army Medical Corps (1917), but was transferred to the Enlisted Reserve Corps to finish his medical training. He received the M.D. degree in 1920. After a year's internship at Saint Francis Hospital in Pittsburgh, Hench became a fellow in medicine at the Mayo Graduate School of Medicine of the University of Minnesota at Rochester, Minn. In 1925 he was appointed a member of the staff of the Mayo Clinic, and in 1926 he became a consultant in the division of medicine and head of the new section on rheumatic diseases of the clinic.

Hench's compelling interest was the study of patients with rheumatic disease. In 1925, in a report of 320 cases of arthritis, he declared that "each arthritic patient is a problem for research of the most intensive kind." He retained this belief throughout his medical career.

On July 14, 1927, Hench married Mary Genevieve Kahler, daughter of John Henry Kahler, the Mayos' friend who had developed the Kahler Corporation's hospitals and hotels to serve the patients and physicians of the Mayo Clinic. They had four children.

In 1928, Hench was appointed instructor in the Mayo Graduate School of Medicine, University of Minnesota at Rochester. Between October 1928 and May 1929, he studied with Ludwig Aschoff at the University of Freiburg, and with Friedrich von Müller at the Ludwig-Maximilians University, Munich.

Returning to Mayo, Hench devoted himself to helping his rheumatic patients by using all time-tested methods of therapy available and by teaching them how best to help themselves. The attention to the concerns and ideas of his patients enabled Hench to make, in 1929, an important observation on the analgesic effect of jaundice on rheumatoid arthritis. His lifelong effort to understand and control this phenomenon began at that time. His experiments centered on the induction of jaundice by various techniques. He carried out extensive studies of the clinical use of uricosuric agents in treatment of gout.

Hench was an American pioneer in the diagnosis and treatment of gout in its various manifestations. In 1936 he wrote that only one of four or five cases of gout were correctly diagnosed, and it was the suspicion of gout, not the disease, that had disappeared. He urged American physicians to have a new awareness of gout and diagnose it correctly, because "a group of patients who are suffering needlessly will be restored to a large measure of comfort and contentment."

One of Hench's important contributions to American rheumatology was his role during 1932–1948 in compiling and editing the annual *Rheumatism Review* of the American Rheumatism Association, the first issue of which appeared in 1935. This exhaustive coverage of the English and American literature did much to give form and direction to the field.

By 1940 Hench had become a commanding figure in his specialty. He always seemed to be unaware of his speech handicap, a cleft palate, which would have hindered a less determined man. His concentrated interest in the clinical and investigative aspects of rheumatic diseases, combined with his abilities as a teacher, lecturer, and author, brought an unpopular field of medical practice into prominence. He established that chronic rheumatism and arthritis were among the most severe medical problems in the world. Hench was a founder of the American Rheumatism Association, and he also took part in organizing Ligue International Contre le Rheumatisme. He was president of the American Rheumatism Association in 1940–1941.

In August 1942, Hench was commissioned a lieutenant colonel in the Army Medical Corps. He served as chief of the Medical Service at Camp Carson, Colo., and then as chief of the Medical Service and director of the Army Rheumatism Center at the Army and Navy General Hospital at Hot Springs, Ark. He was deactivated in January 1946 with the rank of colonel. In 1947 he was made a professor at the Mayo Graduate School.

In the mid-1930's, Hench discussed his postulation that there was an "antirheumatic substance X," which could cause dramatic remission of the symptoms of rheumatoid arthritis, with the famous biochemist Edward C. Kendall. Kendall's laboratory had been a center for isolation and chemical identification of the hormones of the adrenal cortex since 1930. "Compound E" of the Kendall group of compounds had been found to be biologically active in muscle-work test in late 1935. Three years later its chemical name had been determined to be 17-hydroxy-11-dehydrocorticosterone. By 1941,

Hench and Kendall had decided to test Compound E for a possible effect on rheumatoid arthritis, as soon as a sufficient amount became available for clinical investigation.

In 1948, Hench and his associates, Charles H. Slocumb and Howard F. Polley, began their studies of the effects of 17-hydroxy-11-dehydrocorticosterone (cortisone) and the adrenocorticotropic hormone (ACTH) of the anterior lobe of the pituitary body in rheumatoid arthritis. Compound E was given to a patient with rheumatoid arthritis in September 1948. Great precautions were taken to prevent premature publicity about this mysterious "Substance H," the term used during first hospital tests. The physicians were soon convinced of the antirheumatic action of Compound E. Preliminary results were presented in April 1949 at the regular scientific meeting of the staff of the Mayo Clinic. The undesirable effects as well as the desirable ones were described. Cortisone, an acronym devised by Hench in 1949 from *corticosterone* rapidly assumed great importance as a therapeutic agent.

In 1950, Hench, Kendall, and Tadeus Reichstein of Switzerland were awarded the Nobel Prize in physiology or medicine for "discoveries in the hormones of the adrenal cortex, their structure and biological effects." Many more honors followed.

Hench became senior consultant of the Mayo Clinic in 1953. He retired from the clinic and the Mayo Graduate School of Medicine in 1957. He died at St. Ann's Bay, Jamaica, while on vacation.

Hench's motivation and effort are exemplified in his axiom: "Medical truth must be put to work, it must serve." If it had not been for his ebullience, tenacity, boldness, and ability, the great therapeutic comfort of cortisone would certainly have been delayed or it might never have been achieved.

[Hench's papers and letters are in the Archives of the Mayo Clinic, Rochester, Minn. His articles include "The Systemic Nature of Chronic Infectious Arthritis," *Atlantic Medical Journal*, Apr. 1925; "Analgesia Accompanying Hepatitis and Jaundice in Cases of Chronic Arthritis, Fibrositis and Sciatic Pain," *Proceedings of Staff Meetings of the Mayo Clinic*, July 12, 1933; "The Present Status of the Problem of 'Rheumatism'," *Annals of Internal Medicine*, Apr. 1935, with W. Bauer, A. Fletcher, D. Ghrist, F. Hall, P. White; "The Diagnosis of Gout and Gouty Arthritis," *Journal of Laboratory and Clinical Medicine*, Oct. 1936; "The Effect of a Hormone of the Adrenal Cortex (17-hydroxy-11-dehydrocorticosterone: Compound E) and of Pituitary Adrenocorticotropic Hormone on Rheumatoid Arthritis. Preliminary Report," *Proceedings of Staff Meetings of the Mayo Clinic*, Apr. 13, 1949, with E. C. Kendall, C. H. Slocumb, H. F. Polley. Also see H. F. Polley and C. H. Slocumb, "Behind the Scenes with Cortisone and ACTH," *Mayo Clinic Proceedings*, Aug. 1976. Obituaries include J. Eckman, *Lancet*, May 1965; C. H. Slocumb, *Arthritis and Rheumatism*, Aug. 1965; R. G. Sprague, *Transactions of the Association of American Physicians*, 1965. The *New York Times* obituary appeared on Apr. 1, 1965.]
RUTH MANN

HERSEY, EVELYN WEEKS (Dec. 9, 1897–Nov. 3, 1963), a social worker, was born in New Bedford, Mass., the daughter of Charles Francis Hersey, a Congregational minister who was director of a settlement house, and of Sarah Dow Weeks. The settlement house where she grew up served immigrant groups who worked in the textile mills.

Hersey attended the public schools of New Bedford through the tenth grade, then transferred to Northfield Seminary, graduating in 1915. She received the B.A. from Mount Holyoke College in 1919. Upon graduation she entered the National Young Women's Christian Association (YWCA) training school for a course in religious education. Almost twenty years of employment with the YWCA followed. In Trenton, N.J. (1919–1920), and Lowell, Mass. (1920–1922), Hersey supervised club work. Her next job, as executive secretary of the International Institute of the Baltimore YWCA, focused upon helping first- and second-generation immigrant women solve problems of cultural adjustment.

In 1927, Hersey took a one-year course at the Pennsylvania School of Social Work in Philadelphia, receiving a certificate in 1928. During the 1930's she took additional courses at the Pennsylvania School and received the M.S.W. degree in 1938.

Following receipt of her social work certificate in 1928, Hersey accepted a position as executive secretary of the YWCA International Institute of Philadelphia. For the next eleven years she supervised a bilingual staff engaged in casework and group work. During the Great Depression she worked closely with other community agencies and with the Works Progress Administration and the National Youth Administration. She mastered immigration law, and, convinced that the International Institute should serve families rather than women exclusively, she led a movement for separation from the YWCA that succeeded in establishing the institutes as independent organizations.

From 1939 to 1943 Hersey was service director of the American Committee for Christian Refugees in New York City. The committee assisted refugees from Germany and Italy, helping them to relocate and find employment in the United States.

In 1943 Hersey was appointed special assistant to the United States commissioner of immigration and naturalization in Philadelphia. With a staff of 180, she was responsible for developing community services, such as health, education, and recreation, in the civilian internment camps established for enemy aliens. After the war she assisted in deportation of internees.

In 1947 Hersey was appointed a foreign service reserve officer, with the title social welfare attaché, and was assigned to the American embassy at New Delhi, India, the following year. This position was abolished in 1952, but she was soon employed as social welfare adviser by the International Cooperation Administration. She worked in India until 1958, when she left to become a United Nations social welfare adviser in Turkey.

The position of social welfare attaché was new, two such jobs having been set up by the Department of State to improve government knowledge of social conditions and problems and of progress in social welfare in relation to political and economic stability in foreign countries. A person of tremendous energy, essentially optimistic, and a careful observer and reporter, Hersey was exceptionally well qualified for these duties in India. The core of the job, as she saw it, was to interpret Indian social conditions to the embassy and, when requested, to report to Indians about social problems and programs in the United States. To this end she traveled more than 700,000 miles, visiting the villages as well as all the principal cities. She established important contacts, particularly among women leaders and social workers, that were highly valued by the embassy.

Although Hersey was a firm supporter of the American aid program, she consistently emphasized how hard the Indians were working to help themselves. In her work with the International Cooperation Administration, she contributed significantly to social-work education in India, both through professional guidance and by raising money. Never one to impose her ideas on others, however, she regarded social work in India as developing out of the country's own social and psychological heritage.

Hersey's work in Turkey followed the same lines as in India, but her tour of duty was interrupted by a malignancy that required surgery.

Upon her return to the United States in 1960, she carried out a study for the National Federation of Settlements and Neighborhood Houses, then worked for about a year as executive director of the San Francisco International Institute.

Hersey, who never married, died in Milton, Vt. The Indian government sent its consul from New York to speak at her funeral. Subsequently the School of Social Work at New Delhi named a room in her honor.

[Frances Hersey Waldo, North Ferrisburg, Vt., has materials concerning her sister, Evelyn Hersey. Other materials are in the Williston Memorial Library, Mount Holyoke College; in the records of the International Conference of Social Work, the Social Welfare History Archives, University of Minnesota; files 845.40/1–45 and 845.40/123, State Department records, National Archives. Hersey's only publication of any length is "The Future of Voluntary and Private Welfare Agencies in India" (June 1955), in the library of the Department of Health and Human Services, Washington, D.C.

See also Delia Kuhn, "For Pioneering Services," *Foreign Service Journal,* Sept. 1963; Mrs. Robert M. (Helen Peck) Moore, "My Most Unforgettable Friend," *New Jersey State Federation of Women's Clubs* magazine, ca. 1964 (copy in Waldo collection); Ruth W. Page, "Widely-Travelled Evelyn Hersey . . .," *The Suburban List* (Essex Junction, Vt.), May 9, 1963.

An obituary is in the *New York Times,* Nov. 4, 1963.]

BLANCHE D. COLL

HERTZ, JOHN DANIEL (Apr. 10, 1879–Oct. 8, 1961), transportation executive and financier, was born in Ruttka, a village north of Budapest, now Czechoslovakia, the son of Jacob Hertz and Katie Schlessinger. In 1884 his parents, desperately poor, migrated to Chicago. Hertz ran away from home at eleven because of school problems and parental discipline. He paid the weekly fees to live in a Chicago waifs' home by working as a newsboy. His father found him and he returned home briefly, but he had no more formal schooling beyond the fifth grade.

For a while Hertz drove a livery wagon, then delivered information from sporting events to the *Chicago Record.* About 1895 he began writing sports news, a task he had to learn from scratch because he knew little of writing. Hertz was paid at space rates, and he turned in so much material that he earned more than regular staff reporters. He was also interested in athletics and often visited local gymnasiums. He fought in several exhibition boxing matches, but not being of championship caliber, he became a manager of two professional fighters, while continuing his sports writing. His job ended a year after the *Record* merged with the *Herald.*

A friend suggested in 1900 that Hertz sell automobiles. Hertz decided that selling cars was not much different from writing about sports, but his commissions the first year were about half of what he had earned as a sportswriter. His second and third years as an automobile salesman saw commissions rise tenfold. His technique was to promise to provide assistance for stranded customers at any hour of the day or night and to help them obtain necessary repairs.

Another turning point in Hertz's career was his purchase of an automobile agency partnership. His aggressive salesmanship made the business profitable. A third turning point came with his decision to use the cars traded in for a chauffeured livery business. This "ride-for-hire" business quickly became the most profitable part of the partnership. When drivers went out on strike over their conditions of employment, Hertz examined their grievances and broke the strike by his willingness to provide more for his men than they could through their own efforts.

Hertz traveled to Europe to investigate metropolitan motor livery services. His findings led him to change taxi operations from a luxury business to one providing comfort without luxury at a lower price. In 1915 he organized the Yellow Cab Company of Chicago, the nation's first dependable taxicab service. Because of a "chance reading of a scientific journal detailing color tests," Hertz selected a shade of orange-yellow for his taxis as most visible and most impressive. Yellow Cab expanded quickly to more than a thousand other American cities, and Hertz became a millionaire while still in his thirties.

Hertz married Frances L. Kesner on July 3, 1903; they had three children. As his wealth increased, Hertz, who enjoyed horseback riding, bought land northwest of Chicago, near Cary. He established the family home and stables there. Eventually this 1,800-acre property became one of the largest thoroughbred establishments in the country, with more than 100 horses on the grounds. Hertz's colors of yellow silks, black circle on sleeves, and yellow cap began to show up at many race tracks. Outstanding horses from these stables and from the family's stud farm near Paris, Ky., were Anita Peabody, Reigh Count, Count Fleet, and Count Turf. Hertz helped to organize the club that purchased Arlington Park, near Chicago.

After Hertz learned how to operate taxicab companies, he began to build cabs. He organized the Chicago Motor Coach Company in 1922 to operate motor buses, and in 1924 he organized the Hertz Drive-Ur-Self Corporation, which he later sold to General Motors. In the 1920's the Fifth Avenue Coach Company of New York merged with the Chicago Coach Company to form Omnibus Corporation of America, and the Yellow Cab Manufacturing Company became the Yellow Truck and Coach Manufacturing Company, a division of General Motors. At this high point in his career, in 1929, Hertz retired with a large fortune. He became a director of Paramount-Publix Corporation in 1931, and for two years he was chairman of the firm's finance committee. In 1934 he became a partner in the investment banking firm of Lehman Brothers. The Hertz Corporation was formed in 1954.

The Fannie and John Hertz Engineering Scholarship Fund was created to assist 100 students for a year. This and his financial service during wartime brought Hertz the Department of Defense Medal for Distinguished Public Service, the department's highest civilian award in 1958. He died in Los Angeles, Calif.

[Short articles by Hertz appeared in *Illustrated World*, Jan. 1923, and in *Saturday Evening Post*, June 4, 1927. See also *The Racing Memoirs of John Hertz as Told to Evan Shipman* (1954). Hertz's wife collaborated in a three-part story in *Saturday Evening Post*, Apr. 9, Apr. 23, and May 7, 1932. Accounts of his business activity can be found in *Current Opinion*, Jan. 1925; *American Magazine*, Aug. 1925; *Business Week*, Nov. 7, 1935; *Time*, Nov. 18, 1935; *Fortune*, Feb. 1936; *Nation*, July 9, 1960. An obituary is in *New York Times*, Oct. 10, 1961.]

HOMER E. SOCOLOFSKY

HESS, VICTOR FRANZ (June 24, 1883– Dec. 17, 1964), physicist, was born in Schloss Waldstein, Styria, Austria, son of Vinzenz Hess, forester to the Prince of Oettingen-Wallerstein, and Serafine Grossbauer-Waldstätt. He studied at the gymnasium in Graz, graduating in 1901, and was trained in physics and mathematics at the University of Graz, receiving the Ph.D. in 1906. After more advanced study in Graz, Hess became a physics instructor at the Vienna Veterinary College. In 1910 he was appointed chief assistant to the director of the Institute for Radium Research at the University of Vienna, and a year later he was named associate professor.

Around the turn of the century many scientists were puzzled by background radiation which was often detected by their instruments in sealed containers and which spoiled their experiments. Research by Theodor Wulf and A. W. Gockel before 1910 suggested possible extraterrestrial sources rather than solar or terrestrial ones.

Hess took up this problem in 1911, combining a knowledge of scientific instrumentation with the daring of the experimenter. He made ten adventuresome balloon ascents, including five at night, collecting data with instruments in hermetically sealed chambers. He concluded that after an initial decrease in the level of radiation to a height of 1000 meters the emissions increased at greater elevations. For example, the radiation at 5,000 meters was several times that of sea level. These experiments indicated that the same levels of radiation penetrated the atmosphere at all hours of the day and night. Even during a solar eclipse, radiation remained constant. Hess deduced that the radiation had a cosmic and not a solar or terrestrial origin. To gather conclusive proof he began extended research by collecting data at a mountaintop station near Innsbruck, which he personally equipped with instruments.

World War I halted experimentation. Hess served as head of an X-ray department of a military hospital in Vienna from 1915 to the end of the war. On Sept. 6, 1920, he married Mary Bertha Warner Breisky, a native of Hungary. They had no children. In 1920 the University of Graz appointed Hess associate professor. He took a leave of absence in 1921 to become chief physicist and director of research for the United States Radium Corporation and to act as a consultant for the Bureau of Mines, Department of the Interior.

Hess returned to Graz in 1923 as full professor and became dean of the faculty in 1929. At this time research on the origin and dimension of extraterrestrial radiation was being intensified throughout the scientific world. In 1925 Robert A. Millikan named such emissions "cosmic rays." Hess, a leader in this field, accepted the post as head of radiation research at the University of Innsbruck. He founded several new data collection stations in the Alps.

In the interwar period Hess wrote *The Electrical Conductivity of the Atmosphere and Its Causes* (1928), *Ionization Balance of the Atmosphere* (1933), and a number of important papers. These works confirmed his earlier research and established him as a leading world physicist. In addition, he verified that sunspot activity had no effect on cosmic radiation and claimed proof for variation in radiation based on differing latitudes.

In 1936 Hess shared the Nobel Prize in phys-

ics with Carl D. Anderson. Hess's work laid the groundwork for Anderson's discovery of the positive electron, or positron.

Although a Nobel laureate, Hess did not escape the scrutiny of Nazi officials after the annexation of Austria to Germany in 1938. In 1938 he was dismissed from the post at Graz because his wife was Jewish. Hess, a devout Catholic, and his wife fled to Switzerland after a warning from a Gestapo officer that they were about to be sent to a detention camp. In 1938, Fordham University offered a full professorship to Hess and he accepted. He became an American citizen in 1944.

During World War II Hess continued radiation research and taught meteorology to army students at Fordham. After the development of the atomic bomb, he became more interested in the biological impact of nuclear energy (he himself lost a thumb because of an accident while handling radium). In 1946 he and a colleague, Paul Luger, conducted the first tests for radioactive fallout in the United States. Four years later Hess joined an Air Force radiation research program. He warned that nuclear and biological scientists had insufficient data on the long-range effects of radiation, and he urged an end to testing of nuclear weapons until more information was available.

Hess, who spoke English with a slight German accent, enjoyed teaching at Fordham. In 1955 his wife died. A few months later he married Elizabeth M. Hoenke; they had no children. Retiring with emeritus status from Fordham in 1956, he continued limited research activities. He died in Mount Vernon, N.Y.

[Victor Francis Hess's papers are in the Fordham University Archives. See also Robert A. Millikan, "Award of the Nobel Prize in Physics to Victor F. Hess and Carl D. Anderson," *Scientific Monthly*, Jan. 1937; Obituaries appeared in *New York Times* on Dec. 19, 1964; and in *Nature* on July 24, 1965).]

WILLIAM E. ELLIS

HIGH, STANLEY HOFLUND (Dec. 30, 1895–Feb. 3, 1961), writer and editor, was born in Chicago, Ill., the son of the Reverend Frank Albert High and Julia Hoflund. High described his father as "a hard-working, small-town preacher who seldom wore a long coat and never a long face but who believed devoutly that he was called of God to help men and women to a more abundant life." High spent his boyhood in a number of small Nebraska and Wyoming towns where his father served. He graduated from high school in Douglas, Wyo., in 1913 and then entered Nebraska Wesleyan University, in Lincoln, Nebr.

After receiving an A.B. in 1917, he worked briefly as a correspondent for Wyoming newspapers before being commissioned a second lieutenant in the United States Army. He was an aviator in World War I. In 1919 he served with the Relief and Reconstruction of Europe Commission and later that year went to China with an education study commission for the Methodist Mission to China. Upon his return in 1920, he entered the Boston University School of Theology, from which he received an S.T.B. in 1923. On June 8, 1923, High married Dorothy Brown Cutler; they had three children.

The career that High was beginning during this period was described in 1932 by the *Christian Century* as that of "a sort of Christian war correspondent, going to and fro over the earth wherever the fighting was fiercest—not necessarily the actual clash of arms but the conflict of cultures and the struggles of faith." In 1921 and 1922 High wrote articles on Asia for *Travel* magazine and published his first book, *China's Place in the Sun* (1922). He also joined the staff of the *Christian Science Monitor* as a special correspondent, writing on Europe and the Soviet Union. Working closely with the Epworth League, a Methodist youth group, High organized conferences and activities of student religious groups. His second book, *The Revolt of Youth* (1923), dealt with the struggles and aspirations of youth around the world, one of his chief concerns in the 1920's. The book was dedicated to Frank Mason North, corresponding secretary and later secretary-counsel of the Methodist Episcopal Board of Foreign Missions, which High joined as assistant secretary in 1924. He accompanied North on several trips throughout Europe, Africa, and Asia. These trips and his other earlier overseas work for the *Monitor* supplied him with material for *Europe Turns the Corner* (1925) and numerous magazine articles on international affairs for such journals as *Outlook*, the *Christian Century*, *Methodist Review*, *Nation*, and *Asia*. He also lectured frequently on international affairs.

High was described by a *New York Times* writer in 1927 as a leading "voice of the younger generation in the Prohibition movement." His was a moderate voice, calling for the "Drys" to make a reasoned case for their cause to youth and the general public without damning all who drank. His association with Dry leader Daniel A. Poling led in 1928 to his becoming a member of the staff of Poling's *Christian Herald*, first as an associate editor, then as editor. He resigned in

June 1931 (though he continued for many years as a contributing editor) to start a Dry daily newspaper in New York City. It was to be a general newspaper, not a propaganda sheet, that would give full coverage to world news and have a progressive editorial line while also devoting more space than existing papers to news of interest to Prohibitionists. The effort failed and High moved on to other work. From 1932 to 1935 he worked in radio as a current events lecturer specializing in religion news and comment for the National Broadcasting Company (NBC).

By this time, High was attending a Presbyterian Church. Although never ordained, he often served as a lay minister and guest speaker. One of his appearances was in 1932 at the First Congregational Church in Stamford, Conn., which was without a pastor. Urged to remain as the church's pastor, High did for more than two years. He was also active in later years in various committees of the National Council of Churches.

Meanwhile, his magazine career continued. A regular contributor to *Literary Digest* in 1933 and 1934, he did a series of eight articles for the magazine in 1933 on events in Hitler's Germany, following a trip there.

Although High had supported Herbert Hoover in the 1932 presidential election, he began in 1934 to support the New Deal. In 1935 he became an unofficial adviser to President Franklin D. Roosevelt. In February 1936, NBC was asked by the president to release High from his duties as manager of talks so he could work in Roosevelt's reelection campaign. He served as one of Roosevelt's top four speechwriters and as executive director of the Good Neighbor League, an organization financed by the Democrats to attract and organize independent voters. He was identified variously as "Apostle for the New Deal" and the "Democrats' St. Paul" because of his religious background and his past Republican activity. Samuel Rosenman, with whom High worked on drafting the Democratic platform and Roosevelt's acceptance speech, described him as "an excellent writer and a very congenial collaborator [who] had a happy facility of expression and phrasemaking."

High's departure from the White House staff and Roosevelt's favor was announced by the White House in February 1937 after the *Saturday Evening Post* declared that High's article "Whose Party Is It?" would appear in its February 6 issue. Its billing of him as "one of the President's close advisors," along with the nature of the article's disclosures of White House plans to purge the Democratic party, displeased

345

the president. "Unfortunately," Rosenman wrote later, "Stanley was a professional writer and could not resist the temptation to write for publication on current public affairs. . . . So after what I thought was too short a stay, Stanley was withdrawn from that group." Later that year, High published a series of articles on the Roosevelt presidency in *Harper's*, which described him in its column on contributors as "a friendly but detached critic" of the president. These were expanded into a book, *Roosevelt—and Then?* (1937).

In 1940, High supported Wendell Willkie for president. He was also active in 1944 and 1948 in Thomas Dewey's presidential campaigns and in 1952 was an adviser and speechwriter for Dwight D. Eisenhower.

Reader's Digest, for whom he had regularly written since 1936, appointed him roving editor in June 1941 and senior editor in May 1952. He wrote almost exclusively for the *Digest* until his death, covering domestic politics, international affairs, and religion. In 1954, he met evangelist Billy Graham while on assignment for *Reader's Digest*. Two years and several articles later, his biography of Graham was published. He died in New York City.

High was an activist as both public affairs journalist and lay churchman, careers that he usually pursued in tandem. Although often controversial, he was highly regarded among associates and contemporaries as being, as *Current History* stated in September 1938, "one of the most competent observers and interpreters of the national scene."

[Correspondence and other papers of the Good Neighbor League, which High headed in 1936, are at the Franklin Delano Roosevelt Library, Hyde Park, N.Y. There are some 400 items covering the period 1935–1937. High's magazine articles (1921–1960) provide a valuable perspective on the man and his times. In addition to works mentioned by title in the text, his books include *A Waking World: Christianity Among the Non-White Races* (1928); *The Church in Politics* (1930); *The New Crisis in the Far East* (1932); and *Billy Graham: The Personal Story of the Man, His Message, and His Wisdom* (1956). Useful articles on his work for Roosevelt are Silas Bent, "Apostle for the New Deal," *Nation's Business,* Nov. 1936; and Mary Scribner, "Introducing Stanley High," *Today,* Oct. 3, 1936. His role in the White House and the Good Neighbor League is described in Charles Michelson, *The Ghost Talks* (1944); and Samuel I. Rosenman, *Working With Roosevelt* (1952). Also useful is Ralph L. Roy, *Communism and the Churches* (1960). A complete obituary appeared in the *New York Times,* Feb. 4, 1961.]

RONALD S. MARMARELLI

HILLYER, ROBERT SILLIMAN (June 3, 1895–Dec. 24, 1961), poet and critic, was born in East Orange, N.J., the son of James Rankin Hillyer and Lillian Stanley Smith. He was educated at the Kent School (Conn.) and received his B.A. cum laude from Harvard in 1917. He won the undergraduate Garrison Prize for poetry in 1916 and in February of that year published a poem, "To a Scarlatti Passepied," in the *New Republic.* In 1917 he published his first volume of poetry, *Sonnets and Other Lyrics,* verses in the Elizabethan tradition.

Upon graduation Hillyer joined the American Field Service for ambulance duty with the French army, for which he was awarded the Verdun Medal. Then, transferring to the American army, he served as a courier at the Peace Conference. He was discharged a first lieutenant in 1919, whereupon he joined the Harvard English faculty as an instructor. During 1920–1921 he studied in Copenhagen as a fellow of the American-Scandinavian Foundation. In 1926 he became assistant professor at Trinity College and in 1928 he returned to Harvard as associate professor. In 1937 he became Boylston Professor of Rhetoric and Oratory and retained the chair until his retirement in 1945.

Hillyer published seven volumes of verse, beginning with *The Five Books of Youth* (1920) and *Alchemy* (1920) and including *Collected Verse* (1933), for which he received the Pulitzer Prize. He also published three novels, *The Happy Episode* (1927), *Riverhead* (1932), and *My Heart for Hostage* (1942), all of them delicately written, slightly plotted, and autobiographical. In 1922, with S. Foster Damon and Oluf Friis he published *A Book of Danish Verse.* His *First Principles of Verse* (1938) became a popular textbook.

Later critics have described Hillyer as a poet who was in, but not of, his time. He remained a lifelong member of the traditional poetry establishment, a poet whose works were rooted in the great tradition of English sixteenth-century verse. In 1942 he became chancellor of the Academy of American Poets, and in 1949 and 1951–1953 he was president of the Poetry Society of America. He was Phi Beta Kappa Poet at Tufts (1924), Harvard (1929), Columbia (1936), Harvard (1936), William and Mary (1938), and Goucher (1940), and he was elected to the National Institute of Arts and Letters and the American Academy of Arts and Sciences.

Hillyer was married three times, first to Dorothy Stewart Mott in 1917, then to Dorothy Hancock Tilton on July 1, 1926. Both marriages ended in divorce. On Sept. 3, 1953, he married Jeanne Hinternesch Duplaix. He had one son, born of the second marriage. After his retirement from Harvard to write and to sail his sloop *Gloriana* (named for Elizabeth I), he was visiting professor of English at Kenyon College from 1948 to 1951 and H. Fletcher Brown Professor of English Literature at the University of Delaware from 1952 until his death, in Delaware.

Hillyer was a Republican, an Episcopalian, and a highly civilized man. As a poet he found his subject matter in what he considered the eternal verities of love, death, and honor. He wrote with restraint and saw himself as a spokesman for human dignity. Unfriendly critics insisted that he was a prisoner of the form and ideas of a dead tradition, insensitive to the social issues of the modern world. During the 1930's he came under attack by left-wing critics for his refusal to man the political and social barricades and to celebrate the proletariat.

Hillyer refused to reply to such charges. He spent increasing amounts of time in "those moments of contemplation more than ever necessary to a conservative and religious poet in a radical and blasphemous age." Yet, he was shocked and offended by the announcement in 1949 of the Bollingen Prize in Poetry by the Library of Congress to Ezra Pound for his *Pisan Cantos*. Pound had been indicted for treason after World War II for his wartime broadcasts in support of the Axis. Hillyer declared that "it is by my authority as a citizen that I protest. A scandalous thing has been done in the name of my Library of Congress!"

In his published essay on the subject, "Treason's Strange Fruit," in the *Saturday Review of Literature* for June 11, 1949, he mounted an attack on the award (named after Carl Jung's Swiss home), on Jung's early Nazi sympathies, on Pound's anti-Semitism, and on the *Cantos*, "so disordered as to make the award seem like a hoax." He declared Pound's poems to be "vehicles of contempt for America, Fascism, anti-Semitism, and, in the prize-winning 'Pisan Cantos' themselves, ruthless mockery of our Christian war dead." He concluded with an attack upon the Bollingen jury made up of Fellows of the Library of Congress in American Letters, and especially upon T. S. Eliot, like Pound an expatriate American and, according to Hillyer, an anti-Semite and the possessor of "a stranglehold on American poetry through the so-called 'new criticism.'"

While the controversy raged amid congressional demands for an investigation, Hillyer followed the attack on the award to Pound with an attack the following week on "Poetry's New Priesthood" in the *Saturday Review of Literature*. Focusing on Eliot and the new criticism as elements "sufficiently stagnant to serve as a breeding place for influences so unwholesome as to permit the award to Pound," he denounced the tendency of the modernists to "stuff their text with oddments chosen from other writers without quotation marks or explanation" and their subsequent movement into "semantics and private unintelligibility."

Hillyer concluded the article with the statement that "an uncompromising assault on the new estheticism is long overdue." He carried on the attack in "The Crisis in American Poetry" in *The American Mercury* (January 1950), attacking "the school of Eliot as characterized by stagnation and obscurity." His charges triggered the most vociferous poetic debate since the emergence of Walt Whitman. Hillyer's was the first serious questioning of the modernists, and it marked the beginning of the decline of the new criticism that had overthrown Marxist criticism with its own doctrinaire aestheticism. Hillyer did, however, see hope for the future in the works of such younger poets as Louis Simpson.

In his last years Hillyer published *The Death of Captain Nemo* (1949), a narrative poem described by Peter Viereck as "part of our twentieth-century addition to the continuous stream of English literature"; *The Suburb by the Sea* (1952); *The Relic and Other Poems* (1957); *In Pursuit of Poetry* (1960), a collection of critical essays; and *Collected Poems* (1961). These last works demonstrate Hillyer's nature as a poet and a man and reveal his commitment to his craft, to his origins, and to his faith in man's ultimate triumph. Although not a great poet, it would be an oversimplification to dismiss him as academic, snobbish, trite, or sentimental, as critics both of the left and of the modernist persuasion have done. His work is minor but true. It is quiet and reserved, but it is significant in its lovely simplicity, in the strength of its underlying faith, and in its affirmation of the human spirit. Hillyer was a poet in the tradition that began with Chaucer, and his verse is worthy of recognition for its place in that continuing tradition.

[Other collections of verse include *The Hills Give Promise* (1923), *The Halt in the Garden* (1925), *The Seventh Hill* (1928), *The Gates of the Compass* (1930), *A Letter to Robert Frost and Others* (1937), *In Time of Mistrust* (1939), and *Poems for Music, 1917–1947* (1949). There is no biographical or critical study of Hillyer. Brief essays on his life and work include W. R. Benét, "Round About Parnassus," *Sat-*

urday Review of Literature, Jan. 6, 1934; R. Holden, "Pence of Persistence," Poetry, Nov. 1934; Christopher Lazare, "Dead Letters," Nation, Nov. 13, 1937; W. T. Scott, "An Unfashionable Poet," New Republic, Nov. 4, 1940; Peter Viereck, "Parnassus Divided," Atlantic Monthly, Oct. 1949; Sara Henderson Hay, "Mysterious Islander in East Indies," Saturday Review of Literature, Sept. 17, 1949. His obituary appears in the New York Times, Dec. 25, 1961.]

DAVID D. ANDERSON

HOAN, DANIEL WEBSTER (Mar. 12, 1881–June 11, 1961), public official and Socialist and Democratic party leader, was born in Waukesha, Wis., the son of Daniel Webster Horan (he dropped the "r" from the family name) and Margaret Augusta Hood. His parents were divorced in 1888, but his father imbued Hoan with his radical views on religion, politics, and economics. Hoan quit public school in the sixth grade and worked as a cook in Milwaukee and Chicago. He had already embraced socialism before returning to school and entering the University of Wisconsin as a preparatory student in 1901. Upon graduation with a B.A. in 1905 he became a clerk in the law office of Stedman and Soelke.

Admitted to the bar in 1908, he moved to Milwaukee at the invitation of Milwaukee's Social-Democratic leaders. On Oct. 9, 1909, Hoan married Agnes Bernice Magner; they had two children. After helping draft a workmen's compensation bill, he reluctantly ran for city attorney and won narrowly in the April 1910 Social-Democratic sweep that made Emil Seidel mayor.

As attorney, Hoan and his competent nonsocialist assistants moved aggressively, in the courts and before the Railroad Commission, against public utilities and railroads on fares, services, and other franchise obligations. These experiences, related in his book, The Failure of Regulation (1914), confirmed Hoan's belief in public ownership. He also investigated tax assessments and won parity with union contracts for city employees. Mayor Seidel lost his bid for reelection to a fusion candidate in 1912, but in 1914 Hoan was reelected as city attorney by 374 votes in the city's first nonpartisan election. Two years later, running for mayor on a reform platform, he defeated incumbent Republican Gerhard Bading by 1,657 votes. Hoan was narrowly reelected in 1918 and 1920 (for a four-year term); he increased his margins in 1924, 1928, and 1932 (to 63 percent); and he won more modestly in 1936 (54 percent).

Hoan was an unorthodox but indefatigable and effective campaigner. Tall and spare, his arms flailing, he condemned the "special interests." He always urged the election of other Socialists and valued the local party organization and the daily Milwaukee Leader of "boss" Victor L. Berger. But after 1916 the Socialists controlled the Common Council only twice and briefly, with nonpartisan help. They rarely elected any other citywide officials.

World War I complicated Hoan's early years as mayor. Milwaukee was predominantly German, and the Socialist party was opposed to war on principle. Hoan privately regretted the national party's antiwar St. Louis platform. Recognizing the force of nationalism and patriotism, he scrupulously fulfilled his legal obligations to administer draft registration and the other local defense efforts of the Wilson administration. But while the federal government prosecuted and persecuted Berger and the Leader, Hoan tried to protect civil liberties. At war's end he launched an aggressive attack on the rising cost of living through municipal marketing and on the housing shortage through a consortium that financed and built 105 low-cost cooperative housing units, known as Garden Homes.

At first handicapped by a hostile council and a "weak mayor" charter, Hoan gradually gained control of the government by his administrative skill. He supported the merit system, and was constructive and practical rather than revolutionary. He fostered professional administration, planning, zoning, and city beautification, and expanded public services, centralized purchasing, and pay-as-you-go municipal financing. His "sewer socialism" was derided by eastern Socialists, but he strengthened the water utility with sewage treatment and water filtration systems, and built municipal port facilities. However, the voters twice defeated referenda to acquire the electric utility.

Hoan forged a close alliance with organized labor, bringing its leaders into the governing process and neutralizing the police in labor disputes. His experiences are described in City Government: The Record of the Milwaukee Experiment (1936), published when he was dean of American reform mayors in what many considered America's best-governed city.

World War I and the Russian Revolution had shattered American Socialism in 1919. Hoan's hopes to broaden the party in the early 1920's collapsed with the La Follette fiasco of 1924. Berger's death in 1929, climaxing a severe party decline, forced Hoan to assume local leadership and rescue the Leader. Despairing of the faction-ridden national party, he led the Social-

ists via the Farmer-Labor-Progressive Federation to the La Follette Progressive ballot without dissolving the Socialist organization. The
combination worked in 1936 but fell apart in
1938. Hoan finally concluded that a workers
party was contrary to American traditions. By
1940 little was left of the idealistic, disciplined,
optimistic movement that had launched Hoan's
thirty years of public office, and on April 2 mayoral candidate Carl F. Zeidler, a handsome,
youthful assistant city attorney running a media
campaign, upset Hoan by 12,159 votes.

Hoan then accepted a federal appointment,
drifted from the Socialists, and in 1944 joined
the Democratic party. As candidate for governor in 1944 and 1946, he was defeated, but he
revived and liberalized the Wisconsin Democrats. A compulsive campaigner, he also ran unsuccessfully for both mayor and Congress in
1948, for the Senate in 1950, and for state senate in 1952.

Hoan's wife died in 1941. On Apr. 8, 1944,
he married Gladys Arthur Townsend, a divorced
Indiana schoolteacher. She died in 1952. Thereafter Hoan limited his public activities to his
long-standing promotion of Milwaukee's port
and the St. Lawrence seaway.

Hoan had the folksy touch of a professional
joiner and booster. He was frugal, sometimes
brusque and biting, often profane. His long tenure as mayor of Milwaukee was primarily a reflection of his devotion to public service and
administrative skill.

[The Milwaukee County Historical Center and the
Milwaukee Public Library share Hoan's public and
personal papers; the Socialist Party of America collec-
tion at Duke University (also on microfilm) supple-
ments these local resources. Edward S. Kerstein, *Mil-
waukee's All-American Mayor: Portrait of Daniel
Webster Hoan* (1966), is authorized and uncritical
but benefits from personal acquaintance and interviews. Also see Robert C. Reinders, "Daniel W.
Hoan and the Milwaukee Socialist Party During the
First World War," *Wisconsin Magazine of History*,
Autumn 1952; Floyd J. Stachowski, "The Political
Career of Daniel Webster Hoan" (Ph.D. diss.,
Northwestern University, 1967); Reinders, "The
Early Career of Daniel W. Hoan; A Study of Socialism in the Progressive Era" (M.A. thesis, University
of Notre Dame, 1949); and Frederick I. Olson, "The
Milwaukee Socialists, 1897–1941" (Ph.D. diss., Harvard University, 1952) are basic studies with valuable
bibliographies. See also *Time*, Apr. 6, 1936. The *Milwaukee Journal* (including an obituary, June 12,
1961) and the *Milwaukee Leader* (1911–1939) provide contrasting viewpoints on Hoan and the Socialists.]

FREDERICK I. OLSON

HOBBY, WILLIAM PETTUS (Mar. 26,
1878–June 7, 1964), governor of Texas, editor
and publisher, was born in Moscow, Tex., the
son of Edwin M. Hobby and Eudora Adeline
Pettus. The family moved to Livingston, Tex.,
in 1879, when Edwin Hobby won election as
district judge, and William attended school
there.

In 1893 the family moved to Houston. After
two years of high school Hobby received his
parents' permission to leave school and accept a
job as circulation clerk with the *Houston Post.*
His obvious interest in and aptitude for newspaper work earned him the financial column assignment in 1901. Hobby also became active in
Democratic politics. He organized a young
Democratic club and in 1904 became secretary
of the state Democratic party's executive committee. He was promoted to the city editorship
of the *Post*, and in 1905 became managing editor.

In 1907 Hobby became publisher and half-
owner of the floundering *Beaumont Enterprise.*
Local Beaumont businessmen subscribed to the
remainder of the stock, hoping to keep the
town's only newspaper in operation. Hobby immediately launched a drive to make Beaumont
a deepwater port. He filled the pages of the
Enterprise with editorials and articles on the
subject, worked closely with Congressman Samuel Bronson Cooper, and made frequent visits to
Washington to help secure federal permission
and funding for the project.

In 1914, while visiting Dallas, Hobby was
asked to run for lieutenant governor of Texas.
Hobby had never sought public office but agreed
to run. He was elected in November and reelected in 1916. On May 15, 1915, Hobby married Willie Cooper, daughter of Congressman
Cooper. In that year Hobby was elected president of the Texas Associated Press Managing
Editors Association.

In 1916 James E. Ferguson was elected governor of Texas; but in August 1917 the Texas
House of Representatives impeached him on
twenty-one counts. In September the state senate convicted Ferguson on approximately half of
these counts. He resigned one day before the
decision was announced. Hobby had assumed
Ferguson's duties on Aug. 24, 1917, the day
after Ferguson's impeachment.

Upon Ferguson's resignation, Hobby set out
to restore confidence in the governor's office.
His quiet nature and soft-spoken but firm actions quickly did so. After the United States
entered World War I, Texas became the major
center of training for military recruits. Although

personally opposed to Prohibition, Hobby got the legislature to stop the sale of alcohol within ten miles of military posts, which made 90 percent of Texas "dry." Hobby felt that valuable grains should not be used for alcohol during the war.

During the Ferguson administration the legislature had created a highway department; Hobby appointed its first effective administrators and helped get Texas drivers "out of the mud." He completed the Ferguson program of aid to education by sustaining state funding, and he secured passage and implementation of a constitutional amendment to provide free textbooks to the public schools. Hobby also helped bring oil and gas under the regulation of the Texas Railroad Commission, and he worked determinedly for political reform. His recommendations resulted in the 1918 revision of the state primary laws. Hobby persuaded the legislature and the Democratic party to permit women to vote in the 1918 primary for the first time, and he organized support for ratification by Texas of the Nineteenth Amendment. In 1918 Hobby was elected governor, defeating Ferguson by the largest majority ever achieved up to that time.

In 1921 Hobby returned to Beaumont and the publication of the *Enterprise.* He bought a competitor, the *Beaumont Journal,* publishing both in a morning-evening tandem considered innovative. In administrative matters the papers were the same; in editorial policy they frequently differed. In 1924 Hobby returned to the *Houston Post* as president, and in 1939 he acquired ownership as well as control, including its radio and eventually its television affiliates.

After Willie Hobby's death in 1929, Hobby married Oveta Culp of Houston in February 1931. (During World War II she commanded the Women's Army Corps, and in 1953 she became the first secretary of the Department of Health, Education and Welfare.) They had two children. Hobby died in Houston.

[The Department of Archives of the University of Texas and the Texas State Archives, both in Austin, contain papers relating to Hobby's public career. See James A. Clark with Weldon Hart, *The Tactful Texan: A Biography of Governor Will Hobby* (1958), the only book-length study; and "William Pettus Hobby," in Eldon S. Branda, ed., *The Handbook of Texas* (1976), written by Hobby's son. An obituary appeared in the *Houston Post,* June 8, 1964.]

ARCHIE P. MCDONALD

HODES, HENRY IRVING (Mar. 19, 1899– Feb. 14, 1962), soldier, was born in Washington, D.C., the son of Harry Ketcham Hodes and

Mary Sophie Shaw. Around 1900 his father moved his medical practice to Houston, Tex., where the family lived until Hodes completed high school in 1918. He entered the U.S. Military Academy in June 1918, and graduated from the accelerated wartime course on July 2, 1920. Although commissioned a second lieutenant in the infantry, Hodes soon joined the cavalry and graduated from the Cavalry School at Fort Riley, Kans., in 1921. He deeply loved the horse cavalry, and was an accomplished polo player and a prize-winning rider in equestrian competitions. On July 9, 1925, he married Laura Celeste Taylor; they had three children.

Advancement came slowly during the years of routine peacetime duty at a series of western posts and a tour in the Philippines. Hodes was promoted to captain in August 1935, and a year later entered the Command and General Staff School, from which he graduated in 1937. Besides being a highly capable troop commander, Hodes became an able staff officer. In 1939, still a captain, he was ordered to the Army War College, which was the customary preparation for promotion. Upon graduation in June 1940, he was immediately assigned to the War Department General Staff. War brought quick promotions, and after he became colonel, Hodes established the troop movements section, theater group, of the Operations Division in April 1942, earning the Legion of Merit for his work during the next two years.

Anxious for a combat command, Hodes won assignment to England in January 1944 to command the 112th Infantry Regiment. This was a National Guard regiment unready for combat, and Hodes established a rigorous training program. The 112th went into action on July 23 as part of the 28th Infantry Division, and was soon in the stiff fighting of the breakout from Normandy. Hodes was a leader who kept close to the front line, and on August 7 he was wounded, though not seriously.

On Aug. 29, 1944, Hodes led his regiment down the Champs Élysées in the famed parade through liberated Paris. His regimental command ended suddenly in the Luxembourg Ardennes on September 19, when he was severely wounded and evacuated to the United States. For the rest of his career Hodes always proudly wore the Combat Infantryman's Badge he earned in 1944.

After recuperating from his wounds, Hodes returned to Washington in January 1945 as a brigadier general and assistant deputy chief of staff. He remained until August 1947, working on the shift of forces to the Pacific and the problems of postwar reorganization, and earning his first Distinguished Service Medal. After duty as chief of staff of the Fourth Army in Texas, he was ordered to Japan in April 1949, as assistant commander of the 1st Cavalry Division and later of the 7th Infantry Division.

When the Korean War began, the 7th Division lost many of its best men to other units, and had to be rebuilt hurriedly to be able to follow the Marines at the Inchon landing in September 1950. Hodes personally led the assault that crossed the Han River and captured Nam San, the high ground overlooking Seoul. By November, Hodes was on the banks of the Yalu River, and he again distinguished himself during the difficult retreat in the face of large Chinese forces. In January 1951 he became deputy chief of staff of the Eighth Army, and a month later he was promoted to major general. For five frustrating months (July–December) Hodes also served as chief army representative at the armistice negotiations. In October 1951 he was promoted to deputy army commander, and when relieved as negotiator, he commanded the 24th Infantry Division for six weeks, until the division moved to Japan.

For the next two years Hodes was commandant of the Command and General Staff College at Fort Leavenworth, Kans. In March 1954 he went to Germany, where he held posts of increasing responsibility for five years, commanding the VII Corps and then the Seventh Army, and becoming a lieutenant general in August 1954.

From May 1956 until March 1959, Hodes was commander in chief of the U.S. Army in Europe, with the rank of general. He again emphasized training, with frequent surprise visits to troops on maneuvers. He was less successful in his efforts to bring more American ground troops to Europe, a policy not in line with the fiscal or military priorities of the Eisenhower administration.

Hodes enjoyed the social as well as the military aspects of high command, making special efforts to maintain good relations with both civilian and military authorities in Germany. Upon his retirement he was honored with the first postwar *Grosser Zapfenstreich*, the traditional torchlight retreat parade.

Sometimes known as "Hammering Hank" in Korea, Hodes excelled in both staff and command assignments. He was very much a product of the army system, and his career was marked by consistent, solid achievement rather than any single outstanding event. As Brigadier General M. N. Huston recalled, Hodes was "a fearless forthright leader, always conspicuous on the battlefield, with a flare for instilling confidence" among his troops. Hodes's major decorations include three awards of the Distinguished Service Medal, the Legion of Merit twice, the Silver Star for both Normandy and Korea, the British Distinguished Service Order, and the Korean Order of Military Merit, Taiguk. Hodes died in San Antonio, Tex.

[Hodes left very little correspondence or other papers, but many scrapbooks. All are in the possession of his son, Colonel John T. Hodes, of Killeen, Tex. The outline of Hodes's career can be followed in official army histories, particularly Ray S. Cline, *Washington Command Post: The Operations Division* (1951); Roy E. Appleman, *South to the Naktong, North to the Yalu* (1961); and Martin Blumenson, *Breakout and Pursuit* (1961). Also see William H. Vatcher, Jr., *Panmunjom: The Story of the Korean Military Armistice Negotiations* (1958); M. M. Drachkovitch and Allan E. Goodman, eds., *Negotiating While Fighting: The Diary of Admiral C. Turner Joy at the Korean Armistice Conference* (1978).]

PATRICK J. FURLONG

HODGE, JOHN REED (June 12, 1893– Nov. 12, 1963), army officer dubbed by reporters "the Patton of the Pacific," was born in Golconda, Ill., the son of John Hardin Hodge and Melissa Caroline Steagall. He attended Southern Illinois Teachers College in 1912– 1913, and the University of Illinois in 1917. Following the entry of the United States into World War I, Hodge enrolled in Officers Training School at Ft. Sheridan, Ill., in May 1917 and won his regular army commission as second lieutenant of infantry in October. On Oct. 6, 1917, he married Lydia Gillespie Parsons; they had one daughter. He sailed for France a few months after his marriage, attended the Army Signal School at Langres, and served with the 61st Infantry Regiment during the St. Mihiel and Meuse-Argonne offensives in the summer of 1918, rising to the temporary rank of captain. He remained in Europe until August 1919.

Hodge attained the permanent rank of captain in July 1921, major in August 1935, and lieutenant colonel in 1940. He served as ROTC professor of military science and tactics at Mississippi Agricultural and Mechanical College, with the Civilian Conservation Corps, and in command and staff positions at various posts, including Schofield Barracks, Hawaii, alternating with tours at the Infantry School, Ft. Benning, Ga.; the Chemical Warfare School, Edgewood Arsenal, Md.; the Command and General Staff School at Ft. Leavenworth, Kans.; the

Army War College, Washington, D.C.; and the Air Corps Tactical School, Maxwell Field, Ala. When war broke out in Europe in late 1939, he was on duty with the War Department General Staff in Washington.

In February 1941, Hodge became G-3, and later chief of staff of the VII Corps. Immediately after Pearl Harbor he accompanied the corps to the West Coast, was made assistant commander of the 25th Division in Hawaii, and in December 1942 moved with the division to reinforce hard-pressed American forces on Guadalcanal. He distinguished himself as an aggressive front-line commander in the actions of January–February 1943 that consolidated the American hold on the island.

Hodge was now marked for higher command. In July 1943, as a major general, he received his first divisional command with the Americal Division. The following month Lieutenant General Millard Harmon, commanding army forces in the Pacific Theater, gave him temporary command of the 43d Division, then heavily engaged on New Georgia; Harmon considered him "the best division commander I have in the area for this particular job." By the first week of August the division had mopped up the last opposition in its sector.

In January 1944, while leading the Americal Division on Bougainville in the northern Solomons, Hodge was wounded. During July he served on the Buckner Board, which investigated the relief of Major General Ralph Smith, commander of the 27th Division, by Marine Lieutenant General Holland Smith during the Marianas campaign. The board's report, which found the relief unjustified, was an episode in a widely publicized controversy ("Smith vs. Smith") that caused serious interservice animosity in the Pacific, with repercussions in the Washington high command.

In April 1944, Hodge had been given command of the newly formed XXIV Corps, which in September was assigned to the Sixth Army under Lieutenant General Walter Krueger, assembling for the invasion of the Philippines. The invasion began on October 20–22 with successful landings on Leyte. From then until Christmas, Hodge's corps was almost continuously engaged in a slow, grueling advance across the southern part of the island, which ended only with the virtual extermination of the Japanese defenders. During the campaign Hodge often flew low-altitude missions over combat areas in a small liaison observation aircraft. He narrowly escaped death when a shell fragment from a nearby ammunition dump hit by an enemy bomb ripped through the tent in which he was sleeping.

Early in 1945 Hodge reassembled and loaded his corps for the invasion of Okinawa. The XXIV Corps, now part of Lieutenant General Simon Buckner's Tenth Army, landed on Okinawa on April 1, taking over the southern sector. The ensuing three-month campaign was one of the bloodiest of the Pacific war. Japanese forces were nearly exterminated, losing an estimated 110,000 dead and 7,400 prisoners. The XXIV Corps suffered battle casualties of 4,400 killed and almost 18,000 wounded. Hodge was made a lieutenant general. During the war Hodge was awarded the Legion of Merit, the Distinguished Service Medal with two oak leaf clusters, and the Air Medal.

Following Japan's collapse, Hodge was designated by General Douglas MacArthur to receive the surrender of Japanese forces in southern Korea and to occupy and administer the country south of the thirty-eighth parallel. (Soviet forces were already in control to the north.) Elements of the XXIV Corps entered South Korea early in September.

The next three years were a trying period. Hodge's efforts to implement United States policy, based on a supposed agreement with Moscow to work toward an interim four-power (United States, Soviet Union, China, Great Britain) trusteeship over all Korea and early full independence, were blocked by the Soviets on the joint American-Soviet commission in Korea. The Soviet propaganda fostered the belief that the Americans, under the guise of trusteeship, wanted to delay Korean independence indefinitely. Hodge became a prime target of anti-American attacks by the nationalists led by Dr. Syngman Rhee. Communist-inspired riots in the fall of 1946 seemed to herald an attempted "liberation" of South Korea by the Communist north.

In October 1947 the United States finally recommended to the United Nations that UN-supervised elections be held in both zones before Mar. 31, 1948, as a prelude to formation of a national Korean government. Although the Soviet Union and North Korea refused to cooperate, elections were held in the south on May 10, 1948, resulting in the establishment on August 15 of a republic with Dr. Rhee as president, and termination of the military occupation. Hodge, in view of his differences with Rhee, recommended that he be relieved, and left for home that same month.

In the next few years Hodge held several assignments, including that of chief of army field forces. He retired in June 1953 with the rank of full general. He died at Washington, D.C.

[See Roy A. Appleman et al., *Okinawa, the Last Battle* (1948); M. Hamlin Cannon, *Leyte, the Return to the Philippines* (1960); Philip A. Crowl, *Campaign in the Marianas* (1960); Stanley L. Falk, *Decision at Leyte* (1966); John Miller, Jr., *Guadalcanal, the First Offensive* (1949); and *Cartwheel, the Reduction of Rabaul* (1959);
An obituary is in the *New York Times*, Nov. 13, 1963.]

RICHARD M. LEIGHTON

HOLBROOK, STEWART HALL (Aug. 22, 1893–Sept. 3, 1964), journalist and historian, was born at Newport, Vt., the son of Jesse William Holbrook, a businessman and logger, and Kate Stewart. He went to school in Newport and Lemington, Vt., and attended Colebrook (N.H.) Academy.

From his early years the forests and rivers of New England and the Pacific Northwest captured Holbrook's imagination. He recalled how every spring as a boy he awakened to the roar of the great loggers' drive down the Connecticut River. "You threw off the heavy quilt and went to the window; and you saw what every boy waited to see in April—the rushing, churning Connecticut River filled with spruce and fir. Yes, the drive was a-comin' down."

At eighteen Holbrook moved West, where he worked for the *Winnipeg Telegram;* joined a stock company and toured the western provinces of Canada with a troupe that included Boris Karloff, a lifelong friend; and played semiprofessional baseball. Holbrook returned to Vermont in 1914 and worked as a logger until he entered the army. During World War I he saw service in France, becoming a first sergeant in the 303rd Field Artillery and winning two battle stars.

Returning in 1919 to logging on the Connecticut River, Holbrook met woods boss "Jigger" Jones, whom he later wrote about in his first book, *Holy Old Mackinaw* (1938). A year later, "wearing the only derby hat in British Columbia," he arrived in Victoria, soon taking up the job of "cheater" (timekeeper) in a logging camp. At this time he began contributing articles and essays to magazines. In 1923 he joined the staff of a trade magazine, *Lumber News*, in Portland, Oreg., serving as editor from 1926 to 1934. From 1930 to 1937 he was a feature writer for the *Portland Oregonian*. On June 12, 1924, he married Katherine Stanton Gill.

In 1934 Holbrook resigned his editorship to concentrate on free-lance writing. Beginning in 1938 he published more than thirty books, and the number of his articles defies enumeration because he used pseudonyms. He once contributed to eleven consecutive issues of *Century* magazine. He also wrote for the *New Yorker,* the *New York Times,* the *New York Herald Tribune,* the *Saturday Evening Post, American Mercury, American Heritage,* and *American Forests.*

During two years of temporary residence in Cambridge, Mass. (1942–1944), Holbrook lectured at Harvard and Boston University. Committed to the conservation movement, during World War II he devoted his summers to directing a program to fight fires with the Division of Forestry in the state of Washington; he also headed the new "Keep Washington Green" program, whose success extended the movement across the nation. After the death of his first wife, he married Sybil Walker of Portland, a writer, on May 1, 1948. They had two children.

Holbrook wrote for both adults and young readers; his favorite subjects were forests and rivers; heroes of the West, industry, and wars; and popular customs. H. L. Mencken gave him encouragement, and his first check for an article was for $5 from Harold Ross, who later became editor of the *New Yorker. Holy Old Mackinaw: A Natural History of the American Lumberjack* (1938) established his reputation and was the forerunner of a number of books on loggers and forests. *Lost Men of American History,* published in 1946, with an introduction by Allan Nevins, won wide notice. Anecdotal in style, the book was unorthodox and fresh, treating themes such as the introduction of the log cabin by the Swedes (not the English) and describing obscure persons like Christopher Ludwick and Lorenzo Coffin. A reviewer for the *Mississippi Valley Historical Review,* after making customary academic caveats, acknowledged that " even specialists in United States history will find much that is new in it." Its success impelled him to write further on matters other than forests and the lumber industry. The following year Holbrook brought out a popular and durable work, *The Story of American Railroads.*

In 1950 Holbrook published *The Yankee Exodus: An Account of Migration from New England.* More than his other books it bore earmarks of scholarship—investigation of town, county, and state histories, and familiarity with specialized research. In superabundant detail, citing over 2,000 names, with emphasis upon personality and story, he recounted the movement of Yankees from New England to the Pacific from the eighteenth century to the twentieth century—a migration of which he was a part. Writing with the belief that the Yankee's role in settling the nation had been ignored, he concentrated on the "older stock" that moved not to the eastern cities or the South but to the West.

From 1946 until his death Holbrook published one or more books and about four articles a year. *The Age of the Moguls* (1953) led Doubleday's Mainstream of America series, to which he also contributed *Dreamers of the American Dream* (1957). *James J. Hill* (1955) was a volume in Knopf's Great Lives in Brief series. For Rinehart's Rivers of America series he wrote *The Columbia* (1956). In 1962 Holbrook became general editor of a series on historic American and Canadian forts projected by Prentice-Hall.

Unlike many free-lance writers, Holbrook made a comfortable living. Advances on *The Age of the Moguls* amounted to $6,000; royalties of $31,683 were paid him in 1954. His unsuccessful effort in 1961 to reduce his income taxes by invoking the "spreadback" provision of the Internal Revenue code (spreading back a large royalty payment over the years of writing) elicited attention and sympathy.

Late in his career Holbrook invented "Mr. Otis," a "primitive-modern painter" who stealthily painted in Holbrook's attic study while the writer was away. In 1958 *Mr. Otis,* a book of paintings, with an introduction by Stewart H. Holbrook was published. In 1963 Holbrook's writings on forests brought him an award from American Forest Products Industries, Inc.

Holbrook wrote with gusto, humor, and flavor, turning up neglected places and people, with historical intuition, and telling a good story. Untrained in scholarship, he never engaged in extensive research, grasped the complexities of historical forces, or displayed the depth of understanding that makes a great historian. But his prolific writings made history pleasurable and interesting for a generation of Americans. He died in Portland, Oreg.

[The Holbrook manuscripts (1904–1964) at the University of Washington Library include his correspondence and diary. In addition to the books mentioned in the text he wrote *Iron Brew: A Century of American Ore and Steel* (1939); *Burning an Empire: The Story of American Forest Fires* (1943); *Machines of Plenty: Pioneering in American Agriculture* (1955); and *The Old Post Road: The Story of Boston Post*

Road (1962). See also James B. Craig, "The Man Who Wrote like an Angel," *American Forests,* Oct. 1964. There are autobiographical fragments scattered in his writings, especially *Far Corner* (1952). Obituaries are in *New York Times,* Sept. 4, 1964; and *Publishers Weekly,* Sept. 21, 1964.]

JAMES A. RAWLEY

HOLLIDAY, JUDY (June 21, 1921–June 7, 1965), actress, was born Judith G. Tuvim in New York City, the daughter of Abraham Tuvim, a journalist and fund raiser for Jewish and social organizations, and of Helen Gollomb, a piano teacher at the Henry Street Settlement. At the age of six, her parents separated. An unusually brilliant child with a 172 I.Q., Tuvim described herself as "one of those obnoxious children who read *War and Peace,* Schnitzler and Molière."

After graduating from the Julia Richman High School in New York City in 1938, she hoped to attend Yale Drama School but was too young for admission. She went to work in the summer of 1938 as a switchboard operator at Orson Welles's Mercury Theater. Later that year, Max Gordon, owner of a Greenwich Village nightclub, offered her a chance to demonstrate her talent as a scriptwriter and lyricist. Tuvim contacted a group of performers she had met while vacationing at an upstate resort who called themselves "Six and Company." Among them was an unknown pianist, Leonard Bernstein, and lyricists Betty Comden and Adolph Green. The group renamed themselves "The Revuers," and as Lee Israel comments, "with her immense, fawnlike eyes and her brown hair piled up, Judy's talent for comedy was quickly perceived." The Revuers subsequently appeared for thirty-two weeks on an NBC radio program. With Judy Tuvim's career burgeoning, she adopted a new name, Judy Holliday (*tuvim* is the Hebrew word for holiday). In 1943 The Revuers left for Hollywood, but to their disappointment the major studios were more interested in the girl with "the natural gift of comedy," than in the group.

Holliday finally accepted a seven-year contract with Twentieth Century-Fox in 1944 but insisted that The Revuers appear in her first film, *Greenwich Village.* It was a box-office failure. Unhappy with the beginnings of her film career, Holliday did not enjoy her stay in Hollywood. After appearing in *Winged Victory* (1944) and *Something for the Boys* (1944), she was released from her contract and returned to New York. In March 1945, she starred on Broadway in *Kiss Them for Me,* playing the first of her many dumb but good-natured characters. Her performance won her the Clarence Derwent Award as the best supporting actress of the year.

In early February 1946 Jean Arthur's misfortune came to be Holliday's biggest break. Three days before Garson Kanin's stage comedy *Born Yesterday* was scheduled to open in Philadelphia, Arthur was forced to leave the cast due to illness. Holliday auditioned for the role of Billie Dawn and learned it in three days. The play opened on Feb. 4, 1946, to rave reviews and Holliday then played Billie Dawn for three years. Garson Kanin remembers her as a "tremendously rare combination of intellect and instinct. And a girl of principle, and of deep social feeling."

In 1948 the screen rights to *Born Yesterday* were purchased by Columbia Pictures. As a movie, *Born Yesterday* (1950) brought Holliday an Academy Award for best actress. Gloria Swanson, a nominee for the Oscar for her performance that year in *Sunset Boulevard,* congratulated Holliday saying, "My dear, couldn't you have waited? You have so much ahead of you—so many years. This was my only chance." On Jan. 4, 1948, Holliday married David Oppenheim, a clarinetist. They had one child, but were divorced in 1957.

Holliday's other screen credits included *The Marrying Kind* (1952), about a blue-collar couple facing divorce. The remaining films for Columbia were all tailor-made for the roles she played best. George Morris commented that she could "switch from comedy to tragedy with a mere inflection in her voice: a mixture of dumb blonde, naivete, N.Y. savvy was her strongest instrument."

Holliday's career was threatened in 1952 when she was subpoenaed, along with many other performers, by a Senate subcommittee investigating subversive influences in the performing arts. As Lee Israel comments, "In the context of the 1950's when guilt was historic and by association . . . she had plenty to be frightened of." Certain facets in her life lead to such conclusions. Many of the performers at the Mercury Theater were labeled "radicals," and she had been a signer of an advertisement that appeared on Dec. 1, 1948, calling upon the film industry to revoke its Communist blacklist. Holliday stated to the subcommittee: "I am not a member of any organization that is listed by the Attorney General as subversive. In any instance where I lent my name in the past, it was certainly without knowledge that such an organization was subversive." But certain allegations

could not be denied. "Irresponsible and slightly more than that—stupid," was Holliday's self-description of her association with these groups.

As a result of the hearings Holliday was blacklisted by television for ten years. She was still able to star in films, such as *It Should Happen to You* (1954), *Phffft* (1954), *The Solid Gold Cadillac* (1956), in which she played a shrewd, inexperienced businesswoman, and *Full of Life* (1957). In 1956 she starred on Broadway as Ella Peterson in *Bells Are Ringing* and received an Antoinette Perry Award for her performance. She recreated the role four-years later in the film version.

In 1960, during the pre-Broadway tryout of *Laurette,* in which she played her first dramatic role, Holliday developed a voice problem that prevented her from projecting her voice beyond the first few rows of the theater. The show was forced to close, and the problem was subsequently diagnosed as throat cancer. Holliday was unable to perform again with the exception of a brief run in the musical *Hot Spot* (1963). At that time, she was involved in an intense relationship with jazz saxophonist Gerry Mulligan. After five years of struggle with her illness, Holliday died in New York City.

Judy Holliday's career was paradoxical. Although gifted with intelligence and humor, she consistently portrayed inarticulate nitwits. Gene Lees, who remembered her comedic ability, remarked that "had she lived, Judy Holliday would be, without question, one of our major dramatic actresses."

[Clippings on Holliday may be found in the Clarence Derwent and Kesslere collections of the New York Public Library. On Holliday's career see Winthrop Sargeant, "Dumb Blonde in Hollywood," *Life,* Feb. 13, 1950; and "Judy Holliday," *Life,* Apr. 2, 1951. Also see Jerry Tallmer, "Judy: A Girl to Remember," the *New York Post,* June 8, 1965; Lee Israel, "Judy Holliday," *Ms.,* Dec. 1976; Gene Lees, "Judy Remembered," *High Fidelity and Musical America,* Jan. 1977. Obituaries appeared in the *New York Post, New York Daily News, New York Times,* and *New York Herald Tribune* on June 8, 1965.]

HELEN STRITZLER AND LINDA LA SALA

HOLMES, JOHN HAYNES (Nov. 29, 1879–Apr. 3, 1964), minister and social reformer, was born in Philadelphia, Pa., the son of Marcus Morton Holmes, a furniture salesman, and Alice Fanny Haynes. The family moved to New England in 1884, eventually settling in Malden, Mass., where Holmes attended public elementary and high schools.

In 1898, Holmes entered Harvard University,

where he studied history with Albert Bushnell Hart and philosophy with George Herbert Palmer. Completing the required work in three years, he received the B.A. in 1902. Thereafter he entered Harvard Divinity School, where he studied social ethics with Francis Greenwood Peabody. In 1904, he received the Bachelor of Sacred Theology. After graduation he was ordained to the ministry of the American Unitarian Association and called to the Third Religious Society of Dorchester, Mass. On June 27, 1904, he married Madeleine Hosmer Baker; they had two children.

In Dorchester, Holmes was influenced by the works of Edward Bellamy, Henry George, Henry Demarest Lloyd, and Walter Rauschenbusch. When he was called to New York as pastor of the prestigious Church of the Messiah in 1907, he began a radical social ministry. The following year he joined with like-minded clergymen to found the Unitarian Fellowship for Social Justice.

Holmes understood socialism as "political Christianity." With his friend Rabbi Stephen S. Wise, he signed the call to organize the National Association for the Advancement of Colored People (NAACP) in 1909; he was national vice-president of the NAACP for more than fifty years. In 1912, Holmes outlined his understanding of the social gospel in *The Revolutionary Function of the Modern Church.* His quest for political alternatives led him to Theodore Roosevelt's Progressive party.

When World War I broke out in 1914, Holmes began organizing peace forces in America. He was active in both the American Union Against Militarism and the Fellowship of Reconciliation. In *New Wars for Old* (1916) he argued for radical nonresistance to force.

After the United States entered the war, Holmes worked for the protection of dissenters' rights. He helped organize the American Civil Liberties Union and led pleas for the release of Eugene V. Debs from federal prison. The near unanimous support of the war effort by the American Unitarian Association had alienated Holmes from the denomination. In 1919, influenced by Josiah Royce's idea of the "beloved community," he severed his ties with the Unitarians and persuaded his congregation to change its name to the Community Church of New York. The change was a self-conscious repudiation of particularistic Christianity in favor of the religion of democracy.

In the 1920's Holmes was an ardent prohibitionist, an advocate of striking workers, and one of those who appealed to spare the lives of

Nicola Sacco and Gaetano Vanzetti. Although not a supporter of the League of Nations, he placed great hopes in the movement to outlaw war. He supported Robert La Follette's Progressive party candidacy for president in 1924 and Norman Thomas' Socialist presidential campaigns in 1928 and subsequent years.

The Community Church became increasingly reflective of the pluralistic character of New York City. The congregation included people of thirty-four nationalities and all of the major religious traditions. From 1929 to 1938, Holmes chaired the New York City Civic Affairs Committee, which exposed corruption in the administration of Mayor James Walker. Encouraged by Rabbi Wise, he toured the Near East and, in *Palestine Today and Tomorrow* (1929), presented a powerful argument for Zionism.

On a trip to England in September 1931, Holmes met Mohandas Gandhi and subsequently became the leading American proponent of Gandhi's nonviolent philosophy. He led early public protests against Adolf Hitler in 1933. Although at first a sympathetic interpreter of the Soviet experiment following visits to Russia in 1922 and 1931, Holmes rejected the Soviet regime because of Stalinist excesses in 1935. His play, *If This Be Treason,* which celebrated the promise of pacifism, had a Broadway run of six weeks in 1935, but critics were scornful of its artless moralism.

Shortly after becoming chairman of the board of directors of the American Civil Liberties Union in 1939, Holmes cast the tie-breaking vote to oust Elizabeth Gurley Flynn, a Communist, from its membership. Increasingly disturbed by the events that led to World War II, he was nonetheless willing to lose many of his liberal friends by holding on to his principles of pacifism throughout the war. Horrified by America's "sin" in dropping the atomic bomb, he was convinced that human nature was not to be trusted with such destructive power. He advocated world government as a curb on the clash of national interests.

Holmes's last major trip abroad was to India in 1947, to meet Gandhi again. After the Indian leader was assassinated, Holmes began work on *My Gandhi* (1953). In 1949 he retired from the ministry. A year later Parkinson's disease began to sap his strength. Nevertheless, he continued to preach once a month until 1959 and was still capable of righteous wrath. Holmes indignantly rejected allegations by the House Un-American Activities Committee in 1953 that he and Rabbi Wise had collaborated with Communists to infiltrate American churches. His autobiography, *I Speak for Myself* (1959), won the Ainsfield-Wolf Award in race relations in 1960. Also in 1960 he resumed his affiliation with the Unitarian/Universalist Association.

Although confined to a wheelchair, as late as 1963 Holmes joined in a protest against the repression of Buddhism in South Vietnam. When he died in New York City, a *Christian Century* editor said: "We sorely need prophets of his ilk today and we will need them in the days to come."

Holmes was a man of many parts. For twenty-five years (1921–1946) he edited *Unity* magazine and also contributed to many other periodicals. Although he published more than twenty books, Holmes thought he was not a success as a writer because he wrote on too many different subjects to excel in any one of them. For over fifty years this pacifist fought for his vision of freedom and social justice. Finally, Holmes will be remembered as a preacher. Tall, lean, and distinguished, he assaulted his audience with an opening rush of words and held its attention with a prophetic fervor reminiscent of Savonarola. He was, said Rabbi Wise, "the unmatched prince of the pulpit."

[Holmes's papers are in the Library of Congress and the Andover-Harvard Theological Library at Harvard University. Besides those mentioned above, Holmes's more important books include *Religion for Today* (1917); *The Life and Letters of Robert Collyer,* 2 vols. (1917); *New Churches for Old* (1922); *Rethinking Religion* (1938); *The Collected Hymns of John Haynes Holmes* (1960); and *A Summons unto Men,* ed. by Carl H. Voss (1971).

See also Edgar Dewitt Jones, *American Preachers of To-day* (1933); Wallace P. Rusterholtz, *American Heretics and Saints* (1938); Robert H. Budrie, "An Examination of the Religious Presuppositions and the Ethical and Social Concerns of John Haynes Holmes as Revealed in His Writings" (Ph.D. diss., Union Theological Seminary, 1956); and Carl H. Voss, *Rabbi and Minister: The Friendship of Stephen S. Wise and John Haynes Holmes* (1964). Obituaries appeared in *New York Times,* Apr. 4 and 6, 1964; *Newsweek,* Apr. 13, 1964; and *Christian Century,* Apr. 22, 1964.]

RALPH E. LUKER

HOOVER, HERBERT CLARK (Aug. 10, 1874–Oct. 20, 1964), mining engineer, public administrator, and thirty-first president of the United States (the first president born west of the Mississippi), was born in West Branch, Iowa, the son of Jesse Hoover, an ambitious blacksmith and dealer in farm implements, and of Hulda Minthorn. Jesse Hoover died of heart

trouble in 1880. After her husband's death Hulda Hoover turned increasingly to religious work among the Quakers, an endeavor that frequently took her away from home. In 1884, after returning from a revival meeting, she died of pneumonia, possibly complicated by typhoid fever.

The influence of rural midwestern Quakerism can be seen throughout Hoover's life. His dress was plain; his demeanor, often blunt. He believed in education and the rational working out of problems and was drawn to the ideals of peace, economy, and simplicity and to improving the living conditions of Indians, prisoners, and blacks. The bustling economy of West Branch in the 1870's impressed Hoover with the importance of the business community. An element of prudishness also was present in the town, exhibiting itself in support of prohibition and blue laws, and distaste for the theater. The characteristic Quaker traits of self-reliance and individualism were also in his character.

In November 1885, Hoover boarded the train for Oregon, where he was to live with his uncle and aunt, John and Laura Minthorn, an educated couple who ran a preparatory school in Newberg. He attended their school for about three years. His uncle was as much attracted to the promising economic future of the Oregon fruit lands as to his strict educational and moral work. Soon he had Hoover working for his Oregon Land Company in nearby Salem and attending business school at night. Hoover displayed a flair for business; he also grew to love fishing in the mountain streams. Using a small inheritance left by his mother, he was able to enter the first class at Stanford University in 1891. Ill-prepared for college, he attended summer classes in Palo Alto.

At Stanford, Hoover majored in geology. During the summers he worked for the U.S. Geological Survey. At the university he was elected treasurer of the student body, and soon put the accounts in good order. He also showed great skill at business, starting paper routes and a laundry service. He transferred this acumen to university service by turning athletic events into profitable enterprises. At Stanford he met another geology major, Lou Henry, daughter of a Monterey banker. Married on Feb. 10, 1899, they had two sons.

After graduating from Stanford in May 1895, Hoover worked as a day laborer in California mines. He soon attracted the attention of senior mining men, who gave him more responsible jobs. In March 1897, having received good recommendations from his California mentors, he went to London to work for the firm of Bewick, Moreing, which sent him to western Australia as a mine "scout." Hoover found gold, particularly in one mine, the Sons of Gwalia, which he had puffed in telegrams to London. Fortunately for both Hoover and the firm, the mine became one of Australia's richest. He also excelled in developing new technologies for the economical mining of gold.

In 1899, after his success in Australia, Hoover was sent to China as chief engineer for the Chinese Engineering and Mining Company. He discovered no substantial gold, but immensely rich coal deposits in Chihli Province near the port of Ch'in-wang-tao. He also found himself in the midst of the Boxer Rebellion of 1900. At the same time that he helped to organize relief activities in the foreign settlement of Tientsin, he managed to extract a trustee deed to the coal properties from a Chinese official, Chang Yen-mao, ostensibly to prevent them from being taken over by the Russians. After the rebellion had run its course, Hoover and his wife took the deed to London, where he was rewarded with a partnership in the firm.

During the next fourteen years Hoover developed mining interests all over the world and spent a sizable portion of his time visiting likely sites. He was both a businessman and engineer, his business judgment all the sharper thanks to his knowledge of drifts and leads, rock formations, and metallurgy. His biggest finds were silver, lead, and zinc in Burma, zinc in Australia, and, just before the outbreak of World War I, copper and petroleum in Russia.

From 1908, Hoover worked on his own. He was known as a "doctor of sick mines," and specialized in bringing their finances into good order. He accumulated some $4 million by 1913. Hoover also was drawn to public service, and labored on such projects as the Panama Pacific Exposition at San Francisco (1915).

In the early years of the twentieth century, Hoover lived principally in London. He wrote articles on both the technical and the financial aspects of mining, and also supervised the editing and translation from the Latin of a massive sixteenth-century treatise on mining, De re metallica (1912). More important, in terms of his social thought, was the publication in 1909 of Principles of Mining. This textbook, used for decades in mining schools, revealed Hoover's thinking on capital and labor. He endorsed collective bargaining, the eight-hour day, and the importance of safety in mines; he denounced "reactionary capitalists" and "academic economists" who, he claimed, stood in the way of

reform. Hoover also tried to improve professional standards among mining engineers. He financed the publication of new mining journals, such as Mining Magazine, and eventually assumed high offices in professional mining organizations, including president of the American Institute of Mining and Metallurgical Engineers. All this was done not without a measure of self-interest, for, especially in London, he lacked the currency of family and proper breeding.

By 1914, at the age of forty, Hoover was seeking new worlds to conquer. His professional standing and his work on the American Citizens Relief Committee made him a logical choice to head the Commission for Relief in Belgium (CRB) after the outbreak of World War I. The CRB had the delicate job of feeding the Belgians, whose country had been overrun by the German army. For more than two years Hoover arbitrated between the warring parties and managed, largely through voluntary contributions and a shrewd manipulation of public opinion, to organize the feeding of some 9 million people. The operation was extended to 2 million more in northern France during the spring of 1915. All this was accomplished despite personality conflicts between Hoover and his volunteers, on the one hand, and various Belgian, German, and British officials, on the other. Hoover's capacity for work and his stubborn insistence on getting his own way prevailed. He so impressed President Woodrow Wilson that after the United States entered the war, he was appointed food administrator in Washington, D.C. (1917).

In this post Hoover emphasized voluntary conservation of food and fuel so that America could feed its soldiers and the Allies. Patriotic Americans flocked to Washington to work for the man now known as the Great Engineer. These volunteers enabled Hoover to circumvent the civil service and carry out his work free from the control of Congress.

The Food Administration used the CRB and certain of Hoover's prewar business organizations as its paradigms. The prevention of waste was its keynote. Hoover introduced the concept of standard sizes for packages. Although he condemned price fixing, with the cooperation of the Lever Food Control Act (August 1917) he in effect set the long-term price of wheat, inimical as price controls were to his philosophy. "War is a losing business—an economic degeneration," he wrote. He meant that it required some compromise of ideals.

Hoover worked closely with experts from the

businesses the government had to deal with. This gave the millers and packers considerable influence, but Hoover's purpose was to standardize business practices and prices. This foreshadowed the trade association movement of the 1920's, which he supported. Nevertheless, when his approach failed to curb excessive profits, Hoover began to advocate a wartime excess-profits tax.

Hoover caused a damaging political problem for Wilson and the Democrats by limiting the price of wheat while allowing that of cotton to soar, yet it must be said that he was faced with enormous problems. He had to stimulate production, prevent prices from soaring, and at the same time be prepared to dispose of tremendous surpluses should the war come to a sudden end. What saved him was postwar "relief." Hoover seized upon war-ravaged Europe's needs to solve America's problem of overstock, and persuaded Congress to make $100 million in credits available to the Allies. Hoover was appointed chairman of the Inter-Allied Food Council in Paris after the war, and soon took on a multitude of new duties. He served as director general of the American Relief Administration—both the public agency and the private one that succeeded it in July 1919. He was also economic director of the Supreme Economic Council, personal adviser to President Wilson at the Versailles Peace Conference, and chairman of the European Coal Council. The economic reorganization of Europe proceeded in considerable part under Hoover's direction while the peace negotiations dragged on. His importance can be overestimated because of the dramatic nature of his work, but certainly no other person did as much to restore European capitalism to some measure of well-being. By opposing European control of relief, he kept tight rein on the distribution of food and other supplies.

Hoover applied all his tactical skills to the problems at hand. He rushed shiploads of food to European ports. He worked to clear the rivers and railroads so as to get food to where it was needed. He supervised the rebuilding of communications and brought in medicines to prevent or eradicate disease. Hoover went ahead with many feeding operations, without any guarantee that governments would take formal responsibility for American loans. Where necessary he engaged in barter to supply food.

Did Hoover use food for political purposes? Specifically, did he withhold it from Bolshevist regimes in eastern Europe? Certainly he despised the new Russian government, and had employed the rhetoric of anti-Bolshevism to get

what he wanted from Congress. But his most open threat to withhold food was not directed against the Bolsheviks; rather, it came about in an effort to unseat the reactionary Hapsburg monarch, Archduke Joseph of Hungary.

Hoover took a moderate position on the need of the United States to fight Bolshevism in Europe; many Americans in Paris advocated a more active policy. He sometimes urged an aggressive policy, and sometimes not. If his actions toward the Bolsheviks in Hungary and elsewhere are taken as a gauge of his thinking, he had no clear aim. To Wilson he urged patience in dealing with Bolshevism, and he fiercely opposed taking military action against Russia.

Hoover was at his best in advocating food for Germany, which many of the Allies opposed immediately after the war. He argued fiercely against the Allied blockade of Germany. When it was temporarily lifted in March 1919, Hoover sent in food that had not yet been paid for. Later that year he cooperated with the American Friends Service Committee in supplying food to German children. He also worked through the American press to make the relief operations in Germany more acceptable at home.

During the Russian famine in 1921–1923, Hoover, now secretary of commerce, again helped to save the lives of millions. Despite Soviet suspicions he supervised the shipment of food to the Soviet Union without any political strings attached. Thus, American generosity may have saved the Soviet state, and Hoover received effusive thanks from the Moscow government.

When Hoover returned to the United States in September 1919, his mind was filled with plans for social reconstruction. He wrote extensively for magazines, taking a progressive, individualistic line in a time of reaction. His ideas —service to the community and equality of opportunity—reached fruition in *American Individualism* (1922). Hoover opposed sharp class differences and counseled a Jeffersonian meritocracy. He had an optimistic belief in moral and scientific progress, including greater efficiency to cope with poverty and unemployment, and he opposed the suppression of civil liberties or the use of laissez-faire dogma to restrict equal opportunity for all individuals to develop fully. Hard work, intelligence, and character should determine a person's place in the world. Business opportunity brought out the best in people. Greed could be curbed by government. Hoover asked for "pioneers" to probe "continents of human welfare of which we have penetrated only the coastal plain." He refused to accept the popular belief of 1919 that "Reds" were responsible for America's problems.

Hoover preferred a gradualist approach to change. He got an opportunity to exercise leadership when Wilson appointed him vice-chairman of the Second Industrial Conference, which convened in December 1919. He urged a federal employment service, a home loan bank, and a fairer distribution of profits between capital and labor. The conference, in a report written chiefly by Hoover, endorsed a minimum wage law, equal pay for men and women, the prevention of child labor, a forty-eight-hour week, better housing, and insurance plans.

Hoover, then, was a typical American progressive of that day. A few supporters energetically promoted his candidacy for the Republican presidential nomination in 1920. Although he refused to campaign, Hoover spoke vigorously for the League of Nations and, when Warren Harding was nominated, pushed him hard in a pro-League direction. Ultimately he blamed the Democrats for making the League a partisan issue, and attacked the Wilson administration as "reactionary."

Somewhat reluctantly, at the urging of Secretary of State Charles Evans Hughes, Hoover accepted the position of secretary of commerce in the Harding administration. In that post he tried to apply what he saw as the lessons of the war era: self-regulation, coordination and provision of information, and the use of experts and volunteers to promote "cooperative capitalism."

Hoover's principal device for accomplishing his goals, both as commerce secretary and later as president, was to organize national conferences. These gatherings were attended by leaders of concerned constituencies. The conferences amassed information and disseminated ideas. Sometimes they drew up legislative proposals, usually for local levels of government. Those who attended were expected to return home and publicize the results of the conference. The conferences functioned like Quaker meetings, reaching consensus without coercion.

Hoover's first important conference, held in the middle of the depression of 1920–1922, concerned unemployment. It suggested government-financed public works projects, the maintenance of wages, and the expansion of the U.S. Employment Service. Only a few of the recommendations, such as road building, were enacted by Congress, but the educational effects were important. Private sources funded important studies, such as *Recent Economic Changes in the United States* (1928).

Much of Hoover's efforts during the 1920's concerned farming and labor problems. He pushed cooperative marketing schemes to aid the agricultural economy. But, due to a problem of personalities, he could not work effectively with Secretary of Agriculture Henry C. Wallace, who died in 1924. Then Congress' enactment of the McNary-Haugen Bill, which Hoover, with the president's support, opposed for its encouragement of agricultural surplus, stymied his efforts. His ideas did not get a trial until the Agricultural Marketing Act was passed in 1929.

In labor matters Hoover's main success was, with the cooperation of President Harding and private groups, to embarrass the steel industry into abandoning the twelve-hour day in 1923. Less successful was his attempt to bring stability to the soft-coal industry. The Jacksonville Agreement of 1924 extended wage agreements until 1927, when the influence of nonunion mines brought chaos to the industry.

Among Hoover's major domestic accomplishments as commerce secretary was the Colorado River Commission. He persuaded the various states concerned to build a major dam, and deserves as much credit as Congressman Phil Swing of California for the Boulder Canyon Project Act of 1928. He also spearheaded efforts for a St. Lawrence seaway, which Congress blocked.

Hoover expanded the activities of his department in every direction. He encouraged the trade association movement, which some denounced as a price-fixing scheme. His Bureau of Foreign and Domestic Commerce sought new markets abroad, working diligently in behalf of American business and farming interests. He fought foreign "monopolies" of raw materials, such as rubber, as detrimental to American consumers. He also worked on commissions to settle foreign debts, and was noteworthy for his generous treatment of Germany. (The foreign debt problem, like so many others, culminated during Hoover's presidency.)

Hoover began his campaign for the Republican presidential nomination indirectly, by supervising relief efforts in the Mississippi flood of 1927. His trips to the devastated areas to organize and direct the feeding, clothing, and housing of displaced families received wide coverage in the national press. The engineer was also in prominence: Hoover made recommendations on how to avoid similar disasters in the future. Nothing could have better reminded the country of the skills of the Great Engineer and Humanitarian. When President Calvin Coolidge announced that he would not run, Hoover allowed his name to be entered in the primaries. Volunteers who had worked with him during the war placed his name on the ballot in various state primaries, only three of which he lost to favorite sons. He won the nomination at the Republican National Convention at Kansas City in June, and chose Senator Charles Curtis of Kansas as his running mate.

The campaign between Hoover and the Democratic nominee, Governor Alfred E. Smith of New York, both avoided and centered on the issues of Smith's Roman Catholicism and Prohibition. Recent studies have emphasized the importance of religion in the campaign. No doubt there were considerable defections from the Democratic party because of Smith's Catholicism, particularly in the South. The New Yorker's candidacy gave a temporary spur to the Ku Klux Klan. Smith himself attempted to ignore the issue. Hoover denounced religious prejudice on more than one occasion, but whether he spoke out often enough and loudly enough remains in dispute. On Prohibition Hoover was intentionally ambiguous; he made the statement, often misquoted, that it was an "experiment noble in motive" and "far-reaching in purpose." Smith favored repeal.

During the campaign Hoover's major theme was the abolition of poverty through greater productivity. He advanced plans for the aid of depressed agriculture, for regional waterpower projects, and for building highways. On the tariff and war debt issues he took a conservative position, responding to the dominant constituencies in his party and to what he perceived as the weight of public opinion. Toward the end of the campaign, Hoover seemed to resort to a near-"demagogic" attack on Smith, accusing him of favoring state socialism. In the election he received 21,392,000 popular votes to Smith's 15,-016,000, and 444 electoral votes to the New Yorker's 87. Hoover's victory resulted from the appeal of prosperity and his own effective campaign uniting disparate Republicans, while Smith failed to build a broader progressive alignment beyond the growing base of northern white ethnics and immigrants. After the election Hoover went on a goodwill tour of eleven Latin American countries.

Only some of Hoover's cabinet choices reflected his progressive aims, most notably Ray Lyman Wilbur as secretary of the interior. Most of his appointees were good administrators. Henry L. Stimson accepted the key post of secretary of state after Charles Evans Hughes and Harlan Fiske Stone had declined the position.

William D. Mitchell, a Democrat, became attorney general. Andrew Mellon, a Republican party favorite, stayed on as secretary of the Treasury and became ambassador to Great Britain two years later.

The first eight months of the Hoover presidency exhibited a distinct reformist character. How much of a progressive record Hoover would have made had good times continued is impossible to say. But the record is strong in civil rights, conservation, Indian welfare, and prison reform. The first major White House conference dealt with child welfare. Some 2,500 delegates gathered in 1930 and contributed toward a report published in thirty-five volumes. A 1931 conference on housing brought 3,700 registrants and resulted in another multivolume report. Similar conferences met and made recommendations in the areas of education, conservation, and waterpower. The appointment of the Wickersham Committee to study law enforcement resulted in a mass of equivocations pleasing no one.

One of Hoover's most important achievements was the passage of the Agricultural Marketing Act of June 1929, which set up a $500 million revolving fund to encourage farm cooperatives. The new Federal Farm Board had the power to enter the commodities market indirectly and to make loans to farm organizations in order to sustain prices. The board was the first government agency to react to the Great Depression. We "turned the Board into a depression remedy," Hoover observed in his *Memoirs*. The board bolstered the prices of wheat, cotton, and several other crops for months after the stock market had crashed. The business community became angry over its activities on the Chicago Board of Trade, and although it continued to function, lack of congressional appropriations hindered its effectiveness after 1931.

Hoover had repeatedly complained of stock market speculation during the 1920's, warning that Federal Reserve policies were encouraging it. He was ignored, and by the time of his presidency there was little to be done to check it that would not risk collapse. Having sold most of his own holdings, Hoover felt constrained to take minor actions and make grim complaints about the situation on Wall Street.

Yet, after the market crashed in October 1929, Hoover was quick to take both symbolic and concrete actions to reassure the country. Beginning on November 19 he met for five days with leaders of business, finance, agriculture, and labor. In this Conference for Continued Industrial Progress he recommended avoiding strikes and no wage cuts until the cost of living fell, a sharing of work where practicable, and employers providing relief where needed. Hoover asked Congress for more money for public works, and he urged state governors to expedite projects already under way. But he spent most of his energies on trying to revive business rather than on unemployment and relief.

Judging from Hoover's willingness slowly to encourage a more active government role against the Great Depression, we may conclude that he was capable—as he later claimed —of most of the "uncoercive" reforms of the New Deal. When the stock market had made a substantial recovery in the winter of 1930, he erred in drawing parallels with the deep but short-lived depression of 1920–1922. By 1932, if not before, Hoover was aware that voluntary organizations could not handle relief needs. The Reconstruction Finance Corporation (RFC) of January 1932, his major legislation against the Great Depression, concentrated on helping bankers and industrialists, pouring vast sums into failing concerns. But it also made substantial grants to the states for relief. Hoover continued to speak against direct federal relief, but by 1932 he had in fact accepted the concept.

There is considerable debate among historians about Hoover's responsibility for the government's slow response to problems of relief. Hoover remained impressed with the basic soundness of the American economy; at the same time, he had little faith in the ability of Congress to cope with crisis situations. Despite the preponderance of conservative thinking in Congress, Hoover was often singled out as insensitive to the needy. His remark, as late as December 1930, that liberal senators were "playing politics at the expense of human misery" did not help matters.

Hoover's relief efforts in the war era indicated that people would help their neighbors in hard times. Voluntary relief, he believed, worked more efficiently than bureaucratic government programs. He feared that the subsidy seekers would drain the government treasury; he also wanted to preserve the work ethic. He believed that individual initiative could have as its object not merely personal greed but also acts of sharing. His biographer David Burner remarks: "Few sentimental liberals could have had a more naive expectation about human conflict."

In the fall of 1930, long before the RFC began to direct its monies toward relief, Hoover had established the President's Emergency Committee on Employment (PECE). Created partly in response to a serious agricultural drought, PECE was directed by Colonel Arthur Woods, who became disappointed with Hoover's sporadic concern for the poor. The subsequent President's Organization on Unemployment Relief (POUR) was directed by Walter S. Gifford. Sometimes his own worst enemy, Hoover said that unemployment was exaggerated, while at the same time he was trying to raise money among the wealthy to alleviate such bad conditions.

Hoover's worst problem was the American banking system, whose needs he sought to address through the RFC. Thousands of banks had failed by 1932. By then, weighty international problems had complicated and intensified the banking crisis. Hoover had not helped the international situation by signing the Smoot-Hawley Tariff Act of 1930. It raised many tariff schedules beyond the point where foreign countries could trade with the United States in order to repay war debts. The inevitable crisis came late in 1931, when Hoover was forced to call an eighteen-month moratorium on the repayment of these debts. The European economy had collapsed in 1931, driving Britain off the gold standard. Hoover then persuaded Senator Carter Glass to sponsor an omnibus banking bill to free up credit. In the meantime he directed his loathing at "short sellers," like Joseph Kennedy and Bernard Baruch, whose activities appeared to drive stock prices downward.

In foreign affairs Hoover sought to improve relations with Latin America and to encourage international disarmament. Unfortunately, despite the successful London Naval Disarmament Conference of 1930, the World Disarmament Conference at Geneva (1932) ended inconclusively; no nation appeared to know how to disarm or what weapons to do away with. Hoover wanted to abolish offensive, but not defensive, weapons; military advisers claimed not to understand the difference. The Japanese invasion of Manchuria in 1931 led to the Stimson, or Hoover-Stimson, Doctrine. Hoover wished to cast "the searchlight of public opinion" on the Japanese; the doctrine declared a more firm refusal to recognize any government established contrary to the Kellogg-Briand Peace Pact. But Hoover believed that the Japanese would ultimately be swallowed up on the mainland of Asia, and he would not consider military intervention there.

As the Great Depression worsened, Hoover came to believe that many of the nation's problems had originated abroad. The seeds of European collapse had, perhaps, been sown at Versailles, he said. Yet, at best it is debatable whether American policy helped or hindered Europe. Both the high tariff and the public hard line on war debts drained the economies of European allies, and thus may have contributed to collapse in Austria and Germany. The debt moratorium of June 1931 was a step in the right direction, but Hoover's meeting with France's Premier Pierre Laval—patterned on an earlier, more successful one with Britain's Prime Minister Ramsey MacDonald—failed to secure cooperation.

Then came a dramatic event that insured Hoover's exit from the White House. In the spring of 1932, unemployed veterans and their families flocked to Washington to lobby for early payment of a bonus due in 1945. They lived in abandoned buildings and shantytowns that were then springing up within many cities. When General Douglas MacArthur went beyond Hoover's orders and ejected the demonstrators from their main camp, Hoover remained silent. The veterans became refugees, and the federal government seemed heartless and cruel. Hoover, the great humanitarian, received the blame. The incident helped assure victory for the Democratic candidate, Franklin D. Roosevelt, in the 1932 presidential campaign.

The Great Depression turned what had been assets for Hoover in 1928 into liabilities in 1932. His career in relief was now an embarrassment. His 1932 campaign speeches were dull and pessimistic; Roosevelt's evoked hope. An angry mob met Hoover in Detroit, and in Madison Square Garden few responded to his poetic warning about the results of free trade: "the grass will grow in the streets of a hundred cities, a thousand towns; the weeds will overrun the fields of millions of farms . . . churches and schoolhouses will decay." As the campaign progressed, the economy worsened. As prosperity had been the overriding issue in 1928, so depression was the issue in 1932. Hoover lost by 22,-810,000 to 15,759,000 popular votes; 472 electoral votes went to Roosevelt, and only 59 to Hoover.

The "interregnum" between Hoover's defeat in early November and Roosevelt's assumption of office the following March was so nearly disastrous that it contributed to passage of the Twentieth Amendment, setting the inauguration of a president in January. The economy continued to sink, while Hoover bickered with a president-elect who seemed unwilling to place the national interest above personal politics. A banking crisis developed just before Roosevelt's inauguration, and thanks only to the similar economic policies of their subordinates was complete collapse averted. Hoover left the White House a lonely and bitter figure, shunned by many former friends.

Moving first to Palo Alto and, in 1934, to the Waldorf Astoria Hotel in New York City, Hoover remained silent during the first year of the new administration. In 1934 he published *The Challenge to Liberty,* a book warning of the threat of fascism within the New Deal. The theme was continued in *Addresses Upon the American Road,* published in eight volumes between 1936 and 1961.

In his postpresidential years Hoover tended toward isolationism, or at least nonintervention militarily. He opposed American entry in World War II until Pearl Harbor. After the war, he favored the withdrawal of American forces from Europe. Hoover told President Harry S. Truman that he had "no patience with people who formulated politics in respect to other nations 'short of war.' They always lead to war." The United States position "should be to persuade, hold up our banner of what we thought was right and let it go at that." His urgent anti-Communism obscured a commitment to peaceful coexistence. Later, he opposed United States military participation in both Korea and Vietnam. Nonetheless, at the request of Truman, Hoover served an advisory role in post–World War II relief, undertaking the coordination of world food supplies for thirty-eight countries from March to June 1946 and a study of the economic situation of Germany and Austria in 1947.

Under presidents Truman and Dwight D. Eisenhower, Hoover also headed the Hoover Commissions to reorganize and streamline the federal government. The first of the two commissions to reorganize the federal bureaucracy (1947–1949) was generally effective; the second (1953–1955) was largely ignored owing to its markedly conservative recommendations. Both of these commissions and Hoover's advisory role on post–World War II relief enhanced his reputation as an elder statesman.

Hoover's last years were spent productively. He wrote a work on the life of Woodrow Wilson (1958) and chronicled American relief activities in the four-volume *An American Epic* (1959–1964). His health remained relatively good, although his gall bladder was removed in 1962. Declaring that a sound doctor must be opposed to exercise and in favor of tobacco, he survived until the age of ninety, dying at New York City. His best-known memorial—aside from the Herbert Hoover Presidential Library at West Branch, Iowa—is the scholarly Hoover Institution on War, Revolution, and Peace at Stanford, Calif.

[The Herbert Hoover Presidential Library and Museum at West Branch, Iowa, is the most extensive repository of personal and official papers and published works; materials are also in Library of Congress collections, the National Archives, and the Hoover Institution on War, Revolution, and Peace at Stanford University. Interpretive addresses and scholarly articles are in J. Joseph Huthmacher and Warren I. Susman, eds., *Herbert Hoover and the Crisis of American Capitalism* (1973); and Martin Fausold and George Mazuzan, eds., *The Hoover Presidency* (1974).

In addition to works mentioned in the text, Hoover published *American Ideals Versus the New Deal* (1936); *America's First Crusade* (1942); two books written with Hugh Gibson, *The Problems of Lasting Peace* (1942) and *The Basis of Lasting Peace* (1945); and *The Memoirs of Herbert Hoover*, 3 vols. (1951–1952). Collections are William Starr Myers, ed., *The State Papers and Other Public Writings of Herbert Hoover*, 2 vols. (1934); and Ray Lyman Wilbur and Arthur Mastic Hyde, eds., *The Hoover Policies* (1937).

Biographies and scholarly works include Will Irwin, *Herbert Hoover: A Reminiscent Biography* (1928); Herbert Corey, *The Truth About Hoover* (1932); Eugene Lyons, *Our Unknown Ex-President* (1948), rev. as *Herbert Hoover: A Biography* (1964); Harold Wolfe, *Herbert Hoover: Public Servant and Leader of the Loyal Opposition* (1956); Carol Green Wilson, *Herbert Hoover: A Challenge for Today* (1968); Joan Hoff Wilson, *Herbert Hoover: Forgotten Progressive* (1975); and David Burner, *Herbert Hoover: A Public Life* (1979).

Specialized works include Joseph Brandes, *Herbert Hoover and Economic Diplomacy* (1962; repr. 1975); Albert U. Romasco, *The Poverty of Abundance* (1965); Gene Smith, *The Shattered Dream* (1970); Craig Lloyd, *Aggressive Introvert* (1973); and James S. Olson, *Herbert Hoover and the RFC* (1977). A scholarly article is Ellis W. Hawley, "Herbert Hoover, the Commerce Secretariat and the Vision of an 'Associative State,' 1921–1928," *Journal of American History*, June 1974.]

JOSEPH BRANDES

HORNSBY, ROGERS (Apr. 27, 1896–Jan. 5, 1963), professional baseball player, was born in Winters, Tex., the son of Edward Hornsby and Mary Dallas Rogers. His father, a rancher, died when Rogers was two years old. The family then moved to a farm near Austin. When he was five, they moved again, to Fort Worth. The first plaything Hornsby remembered was a baseball; in time, the game became the main thing he lived for. As a young boy he starred on the

sandlots around Fort Worth. By the time he was fifteen he was playing semiprofessional ball in Dallas. Hornsby's brother Everett, meanwhile, was signed as a pitcher with Dallas in the Texas League. He obtained for Hornsby, then just eighteen, a tryout as a shortstop. Dallas sent him first to Tyler in the East Texas League and then to Hugo, Okla., in the Class D Texas-Oklahoma League. Shortly afterward that club was dissolved, and Hornsby was sold to the Denison, Tex., team of the Western Association for $125.

During the 1915 season, the second team of the St. Louis Cardinals played an exhibition game against Denison. Bob Connery, a Cardinal scout, quickly spotted Hornsby's talent and at mid-season bought his contract for $500. When Hornsby joined the Cardinals on Sept. 10, 1915, he was regarded as a glove, not a bat. In eighteen games of the waning season he hit .246. The manager of the Cardinals, Miller Huggins, considered Hornsby too slight (he weighed 135 pounds) to hit big-league pitching. Huggins commented one day that he would have to farm him out until he grew heavier and more muscular. Hornsby, naïvely taking the statement literally, spent the winter pitching hay and lugging milk cans on his uncle's farm. On a diet of cream and steak he filled out his lean five-foot, eleven-inch frame. The following spring he reported for training weighing 165 pounds, still about ten pounds lighter than he would be in his prime.

Huggins switched Hornsby from shortstop to the other infield positions before finally concluding that he performed best at second base. Huggins also persuaded Hornsby to cease choking up on his bat and taught him to stand in the rear left corner of the batter's box with his feet fairly close together. Years later a fellow player recalled that while a rookie with Denison, Hornsby had lamented as he went around the league, "Won't somebody teach me how to hit?" He asked the question no longer.

Hornsby's extraordinary eyesight—his eyes were variously described as hazel or cold blue steel in color—gave him an enormous advantage. He maintained he could follow a pitch so well that he could see the bat and ball come together when he made contact. His superb reflexes enabled him to step into the pitch he wanted with a smooth, level stroke. The story was told again and again of the pitcher who, facing Hornsby one day, criticized the umpire's call of the first pitch, insisting it was a strike. The umpire responded quickly: "When you get the ball into the strike zone, Mr. Hornsby will let you know."

In his twenty-three years in the big leagues Hornsby led the National League in batting seven times—six years in a row. Three times he hit over .400, reaching .424 in 1924—a figure that remains the modern major-league record. In the five seasons from 1921 to 1925 Hornsby's average was .402. He was clearly the greatest right-handed hitter baseball had ever known. His lifetime average, after twenty-four years of playing, was .358, exceeded only by Ty Cobb's .367. In his career Hornsby batted 1,579 runs, a total surpassed at the time he retired by only five other players—Babe Ruth, Ty Cobb, Lou Gehrig, Al Simmons, and Goose Goslin. Hornsby led the National League in home runs in 1922 with 42 and in 1925 with 39, and he was the Most Valuable Player in 1925 and 1929. Dubbed by sportswriters "the Rajah," he was as commanding—and as hard and icy personally—as an Oriental potentate.

Hornsby's first wife, Sarah, divorced him in 1923, and on Feb. 29, 1924, he married Jeannette Pennington Hine. He had one son from the first marriage and another son from the second one. The second marriage ended in divorce, and on Jan. 27, 1957, he married Marjorie Bernice Frederick.

In June 1925 Sam Breadon, owner of the Cardinals, removed Branch Rickey as manager and replaced him with Hornsby. Under Hornsby's taut leadership, the following year this fourth-place team won the league pennant and defeated the New York Yankees in the World Series. Hornsby, a perfectionist, demanded a full measure of performance from his players. Many of them felt the often cruel lash of his tongue. He also spoke candidly and often caustically to his employers. A salary dispute with Breadon, whom he embarrassed in front of the team, led to Breadon's trading Hornsby to the New York Giants in December 1926—even as the cheers of victory were still ringing in the streets of St. Louis.

As a Giant, Hornsby sometimes served as acting manager, and it appeared that he was being groomed to take over for John McGraw, then contemplating retirement. But Hornsby's abrasive way with players and management led to his being traded to the Boston Braves before the 1928 season began. That year he led the league in hitting, .387, but his high salary was a burden to the team. So he was traded again, this time to the Chicago Cubs—for five players and $200,000. In 1929 Hornsby hit .380 as the Cubs won the pennant. But the Philadelphia Athletics rolled over the Cubs in the World Series, and Hornsby struck out eight times.

When Joe McCarthy resigned in September 1930 as the Cubs' manager in anticipation of taking the reins of the Yankees, Hornsby was appointed in his place. The team finished third in 1931. Hornsby looked forward to winning with it in 1932; but his blunt talk to the owner —Bill Veeck this time—amid rumors that he was betting on the horses and pressuring his players to make up his losses, cost him his job. He signed with the Cardinals once more in October 1932, but now his playing skills were fading. In July 1933 the Cardinals released him so that he could become manager of the St. Louis Browns in the American League. Under his leadership—he played only occasionally—the team remained mired in the second division. Yet when the Browns dropped Hornsby in July 1937, it was again a consequence of his betting on horse races. Earlier, when the commissioner of baseball had asked him to stay away from the racetrack, Hornsby had told him to go to hell. Hornsby excused his zeal for the thoroughbreds: "I don't smoke, I don't drink. I don't read much nor go to the movies. I must have some relaxation."

Baseball was all that Hornsby really knew or cared about. He bounced from job to job as coach and playing manager in the minor leagues, winding up with Fort Worth in the Texas League, which folded as World War II began. Subsequently he managed a team in the short-lived Mexican League. In 1942 he was elected to baseball's Hall of Fame at Cooperstown, N.Y.

Hornsby won championships in 1950 with Beaumont in the Texas League and the following year with Seattle in the Pacific Coast League. As a result of these successes the Browns brought him back to the big leagues as their manager in October 1951. But they dropped him early the following season. The harassed players delightedly sent the owner— perhaps at his instigation—a huge silver trophy inscribed to him in appreciation "for the greatest play since the Emancipation Proclamation." The next month the Cincinnati Reds signed Hornsby as manager. He remained with them only briefly. In 1955 the city of Chicago hired him to create an athletic training program for boys. He had patience with youngsters. He once said: "Any ball player that don't sign autographs for little kids ain't an American. He's a Communist." Major-leaguers he managed were at the top of the baseball ladder, and he expected top performance from them, including cheating if necessary. His motto as manager was: "Do anything you can get away with."

The big leagues continued to summon him. He was a coach with the Cubs in 1958–1959; and in 1962 the newly created New York Mets took him on as a batting coach.

A stormy petrel, he seemed eternally angry— off the field as well as on it. To a congressional subcommittee investigating baseball in 1957 he sent a long unsolicited letter denouncing the baseball draft arrangements and urging a drastic curtailment of the system of farm clubs. Hornsby readily allowed that he was not a mixer or an interesting companion. He was provincial and arrogant and apparently deeply prejudiced against Jews and blacks. He refused to take Social Security payments when he became eligible for them, with the same vehemence with which he had refused to endorse whiskey, beer, or cigarettes for money in his playing days. When he died in Chicago, a step-daughter honored his request that there be no flowers at the funeral. She explained readily: "He didn't like flowers."

[The statistics of Hornsby's career are in *The Baseball Encyclopedia* (1969). Details may be found in the files of the *New York Times*. Memorabilia and newspaper clippings are in the National Baseball Hall of Fame, Cooperstown, N.Y. Hornsby wrote two autobiographies: *My Kind of Baseball*, edited by J. Roy Stockton (1953), and, with Bill Surface, *My War with Baseball* (1962). Good summaries of his accomplishments, including anecdotes, are in Arthur Daley, *Kings of the Home Run* (1962); Lee Allen and Tom Meany, *Kings of the Diamond* (1965); and John Devaney, *The Greatest Cardinals of Them All* (1968). Judicious evaluations are Red Smith, in the *New York Herald Tribune*, Jan. 8, 1963; and Bill Surface, in the *Saturday Evening Post*, June 15, 1963. See also the obituary in the *New York Times*, Jan. 7, 1963.]

HENRY F. GRAFF

HORST, LOUIS (Jan. 12, 1884–Jan. 23, 1964), musician and dance educator, was born in Kansas City, Mo., the son of Conrad Horst, a musician, and of Carolina Nickell. His parents had immigrated to the United States from Germany in 1882. Ten years later, when Conrad Horst joined the San Francisco Symphony as a trumpet player, the family moved from Bethlehem, Pa., to San Francisco.

In a German-speaking household, music offered enlightenment, discipline, and a way of life that was to become the root of Horst's contribution to dance. As a child he studied violin with John Josephs and John Marquand. After graduating from public school he studied piano with Samuel Fleischman. By the time he was eighteen Horst had joined the musician's union. He supported himself as a pianist in dance halls and

gambling houses, specializing in ragtime. As a pit musician at the Columbia Theater, he played the violin for musical productions and the piano for dramatic shows. He also worked with a concert trio and accompanied violinists and singers, among them Nathan Firestone and Berniece Pasquale. On Nov. 29, 1909, he married Bessie (Betty) Cunningham. They separated a few years later but were never divorced. They had no children.

In 1915 the famous Denishawn Company, founded by Ruth St. Denis and Ted Shawn, came to San Francisco on a Pacific Coast tour, and Horst was asked to join as accompanist and later made his debut as musical director. When the Denishawn School opened in Los Angeles that year, Horst was named head of the music department. The school subsequently attracted such students as Martha Graham in 1916, Doris Humphrey in 1917, and Charles Weidman in 1919.

In collaboration with St. Denis, Horst began to analyze the relationship of music to dance with experiments in musical visualizations. The school formed a "synchoric orchestra" of dancers patterned after a symphonic orchestra, and this influenced a trend toward a more abstract dance form, which was later developed by Doris Humphrey. Throughout this period, Horst continued to study composition.

After ten years with Denishawn, Horst resigned. He went to Vienna to study composition at the Conservatory of Music but, disillusioned by the dominant classical traditions there, returned to New York seven months later to join Martha Graham. Beginning with her first New York City concert in 1926, Louis Horst served as Graham's accompanist, musical director, composer, and adviser. Their close artistic liaison endured until 1948. Horst encouraged Graham's artistic growth from the Denishawn-influenced Debussyian studies of her first concerts to explorations of more dramatic materials. These resulted in penetrating dance statements such as *Heretic* (1929) and *Lamentation* (1930).

Horst also served as accompanist and musical director for Helen Tamiris (1927–1930) and for Doris Humphrey and Charles Weidman (1927–1932), as well as for Agnes de Mille, Ruth Page, Hans Wiener, Michio Ito, Adolph Bolm, Edward Strawbridge, Harald Kreutzberg, and others.

In 1932 Horst wrote incidental music for a production of Sophocles' *Electra*, and in 1935 for the Broadway production of *Noah* by André Obey. Between 1944 and 1953 he wrote five scores for documentary films. Horst's most successful compositions were *Primitive Mysteries* (1931), *Celebration* (1934), *Frontier* (1935), and *El Penitente* (1940), done in collaboration with Graham.

Horst began teaching at the Neighborhood Playhouse in 1928 (and continued until his death), where he developed a course entitled Pre-Classic Forms. At the same time, he became music director for the Perry-Mansfield School of Theatre, continuing there for five years and returning again in 1946.

From 1934 to 1942 Horst taught Pre-Classic Forms and developed Modern Dance Forms and Music Composition for Dance at the Bennington School of Dance. His discerning eye and constant moral support to dance artists gave him unique insight into dance as an art form. He became respected as an educator and mentor in this seminal period of American dance history.

Horst taught at Sarah Lawrence College (1932–1940), at Teachers College, Columbia University (1938–1941), at Mills College (1939), and at Barnard College (1943; 1950–1951). He also taught at the American Dance Festival, formerly at Bennington College and later at Connecticut College (1948–1964), and the Juilliard School (1951–1964), institutions that became leaders in developing modern dance. In 1955 Horst received a Capezio Award.

Seeing a need for a critical review publication in dance, Horst founded the *Dance Observer* in 1934. He was managing editor and a major contributor to that periodical until his death. His role as a theoretician of dance composition also influenced his teaching methods. He attempted to give students a sense of discipline and an understanding of style through their handling of movement. Aesthetic awareness was a first priority, to be followed by personal artistic statement with freedom of scope and originality in style.

Horst's *Pre-Classic Dance Forms* (1937) was the first text to draw upon musical knowledge for formal principles of choreography. To make it possible for dancers to explore content in dance, he developed a course of study that analyzed the components of modern art in movement studies exploring time, force, and space in relation to other art forms. He drew upon art history for source material and focused on studies in style and content based on experiences of modern life. His *Modern Dance Forms in Relation to Other Modern Arts*, with Caroll Russell, was published in 1961. He died in New York City.

[The Dance Collection, Lincoln Center Library for the Performing Arts, New York City, has scrapbooks of articles and clippings; manuscript sources include Ted Dalbottom, "Louis Horst" (M.A. thesis, Teachers College, Columbia University, 1968); and Esther Pease, "Louis Horst" (Ph.D. diss., University of Michigan, 1953). See also Robert Sabin, "Louis Horst and Modern Dance in America," *Dance Observer*, Feb., Mar., Apr., 1953. An anniversary article by Allen Hughes appeared in the *New York Times*, Jan. 12, 1964.]

JANET SOARES

HOUDRY, EUGENE JULES (Apr. 18, 1892–July 18, 1962), inventor and industrialist, was born in Domont, France, the son of Jules Houdry and Emilie Thais Julie Lemaire. His father was a wealthy structural steel manufacturer. Intending to join his father's business, Houdry studied mechanical engineering at the École des Arts et Métiers in Paris. In 1911 he received the French government's gold medal for the highest scholastic attainment in his class. After graduation he began as an engineer with his father's firm, soon becoming the junior partner of Houdry and Son. During World War I, Houdry served as a lieutenant in the French tank corps. He was seriously wounded in the battle of Juvincourt (1917), and for his actions won the Croix de Guerre and became a chevalier of the Legion of Honor.

After the war Houdry resumed his engineering career. By the early 1920's he was a director of several industrial companies, one of which manufactured automobile parts. Houdry had been an avid automobile racing fan for more than a decade, and his association with the manufacture of automobile parts served to further his interest in improving the performance of automobile engines. He pursued this interest in 1922 by coming to the United States to see the Indianapolis 500 and to visit the Ford Motor Company plant in Detroit. After returning to France, Houdry married Genevieve Marie Quilleret on July 1, 1922. They had two sons.

World War I proved to the French government the need to develop an indigenous supply of automotive fuel. Although France lacked significant oil deposits, oil shale and bituminous coal existed in abundance. In December 1922, the government invited Houdry to participate in laboratory experiments aimed at the synthetic production of oil from these sources. He accepted the assignment, and in early 1923 organized a research syndicate to investigate the possibilities of producing gasoline from lignite by means of a catalytic process. After two years of research and experimentation, Houdry developed a successful catalytic process. It proved a commercial failure, however, since synthetic oils could not be produced at costs competitive with oils made from crude petroleum.

Houdry's experience with catalytic research led him to abandon his career in the steel industry. In 1925 he expanded his work in catalysis to the transformation of crude petroleum into automotive fuel. In April 1927, after months of diligent laboratory work, Houdry discovered a method of catalytically "cracking" low-grade crude oil into high-test gasoline.

Although his laboratory and pilot plant results attracted the attention of several oil companies, Houdry was unable to find the financial support needed to expand to full commercial production. Backing was finally given by an American refiner, the Vacuum Oil Company, which brought Houdry to the United States in 1930 for further development of his catalytic cracking process. In the following year he became president and director of research of the newly formed Houdry Process Corporation, in which Vacuum Oil held one-third interest in the patents and ideas. Houdry sold another one-third interest in his corporation to the Sun Oil Company in 1934. The Houdry Process Corporation put its first catalytic cracking unit in operation at the Socony-Vacuum refinery in Paulsboro, N.J., in 1936. Its first commercial unit came on stream at Sun Oil's Marcus Hook, Pa., refinery in the following year.

Houdry's catalytic cracking process revolutionized the art of making gasoline. It enabled refining companies to produce twice as much high-quality gasoline per barrel of crude oil as simple distillation. Moreover, it allowed the utilization of even the poorest grades of crude oil. Within a decade catalytic cracking became the standard process for petroleum refining companies worldwide.

With the outbreak of World War II in 1939, the French government invited Houdry to visit France in order to assist in the production of high-octane aviation gasoline. His patented catalytic cracking process offered the only feasible way to produce large quantities of aviation gasoline. Within a year fourteen Houdry process plants were producing aviation fuel in the United States for France and Great Britain. By 1942, 90 percent of all aviation gasoline produced in the United States was catalytically cracked.

After the Nazis overran France, Houdry again came to the aid of his native land. In June 1940 he founded France Forever, to generate American support for the cause of the Free French under General Charles de Gaulle. Houdry became an American citizen in January 1942, and further directed his research activities to aiding the Allied cause. His most important contribution during the war was his development of a single-step butane dehydrogenation process—a cayalytic method for producing synthetic rubber.

In 1943 a special division of the Houdry Process Corporation was formed to investigate some of the chemical problems important to cancer research. As a result of this research, Houdry became convinced that the large increase in lung cancer was due primarily to the carcinogenic hydrocarbons emitted into the atmosphere by the growing number of automobiles and industrial activities. Finding that he was unable to devote all his efforts to this endeavor at the Houdry Process Corporation, he left in 1948. In the following year he formed another company, Oxy-Catalyst, to develop oxidation catalysts for the elimination of carbon monoxide and unburned hydrocarbons from industry and automobile exhausts. His most successful development was a catalytic muffler that was granted a patent in 1962.

Up to the time of his death at Upper Darby, Pa., Houdry continued to combine his expertise in catalysis with his concern for health matters. By analogy, he saw the human body as a sophisticated catalytic converter. As with industrial converters, he believed that additional oxygen was highly beneficial to the aged human body. He therefore invented an ozone converter to increase the oxygen content in the air during sleeping hours, reasoning that this would increase longevity.

Houdry's pioneering contributions in catalysis led many in the chemical and petroleum industries to refer to him as "Mr. Catalysis." He was an indefatigable worker; with more than 100 patents in his name, he was one of the most prolific inventors of his time. In the laboratory he was a brilliant organizer and motivator of people. In addition, he had the rare ability to go beyond the inventive stage to develop his ideas commercially. He represented, as well as anyone in the twentieth century, that social type for which the United States had become so well known in the previous century: the heroic inventor.

[Houdry's scientific papers are in the Manuscript Division of the Library of Congress. Articles on his career include "Eugene J. Houdry," *Chemical and Engineering News*, Nov. 8, 1948; "Man of the Month: Eugene J. Houdry," *Chemical Engineering*,

Oct. 1953; "Houdry—Round-the-Clock Researcher," *Chemical and Engineering News,* Jan. 12, 1959; "Eugene J. Houdry," *Chemical and Engineering News,* Mar. 26, 1962. Obituaries are in the *New York Times,* July 19, 1962; *Chemical and Engineering News,* July 30, 1962; *Chemistry and Industry,* Oct. 27, 1962.]

JEFFREY K. STINE

HOWARD, ROY WILSON (Jan. 1, 1883–Nov. 20, 1964), newspaper executive, was born in the Ohio village of Gano, on the edge of Cincinnati, the son of William A. Howard, a railroad brakeman, and of Elizabeth Wilson. The family tended a gate on the Dayton pike, and the tollhouse was Roy Howard's birthplace. When he was a small boy his family moved to Indianapolis, where the undersized but energetic youth worked at odd jobs while attending public school. From carrying papers he advanced to school correspondent for the *Indianapolis News.* On graduation from the Manual Training High School in 1902 he became a cub reporter on the *News* at $8 a week.

The early death of his father from tuberculosis made Roy the family breadwinner, a thrift-inducing experience that influenced the rest of his life. In succession he was sports editor of the *Indianapolis Star,* assistant telegraph editor of the *St. Louis Post-Dispatch,* and news editor of the *Cincinnati Post,* on which he made his first connection with the Edward W. Scripps newspaper organization. This led to his assignment in 1906 as a Scripps-McRae news service correspondent in New York City, where he was also manager of the Publishers' Press Association. In 1907 those two services and the Pacific Coast Scripps news organization were joined under Scripps's control to form the United Press Association, with Howard as general manager and vice-president.

Howard first met E. W. Scripps in 1908, when the death of United Press president John Vandercook put Howard temporarily in full charge. Scripps described the young man as "a striking individual . . . a large speaking countenance and eyes that appear to be windows for a rather unusual intellect. His manner was forceful, and the reverse from modest. . . . There was ambition, self-respect, and forcefulness oozing out of every pore. However, so completely and exuberantly frank was he that it was impossible for me to feel any resentment on account of his cheek." On June 14, 1909, Howard married Margaret Rohe, a newspaperwoman, in London. They had two children.

While working for Scripps, Howard, tireless and ambitious, soon vaulted to new heights in management. To expand the United Press he traveled widely in 1916–1917 in South America, Europe, and the Orient. He handpicked correspondents and brought more newspapers into the spreading network. He cultivated notables in many countries and fields—business, government, and diplomacy.

Howard gave detailed personal attention to the coverage of World War I. Indeed, on Nov. 7, 1918, in Brest, France, he was the central figure in the dispatch announcing prematurely that an armistice had been signed. His own explanation was that Admiral Henry Braid Wilson, commander of American naval forces in France, had given him a copy of what Wilson thought was an official announcement of the war's end. The dispatch had originated in Paris, and Wilson had facilitated its passage through the censor to New York, from where the United Press had flashed it around the world. The signing occurred four days later.

Contending that any alert reporter would have done what he did, Howard did not allow the incident to depress him or his organization. Nor did Scripps hold it against him. In 1921 Howard was advanced to chairman of the board, and in 1922 the Scripps-McRae organization was renamed Scripps-Howard. Howard then changed his main interest from the United Press, which under his direction had grown to 780 clients, to management of the newspaper group. The number of dailies in the organization rose to more than thirty, but ranged generally between thirteen when Scripps died (1926) to twenty-five under Howard.

Now more than ever, entry into New York City with a daily was Howard's goal. He achieved it in February 1927 with the purchase of the *New York Telegram* through William T. Dewart from the Frank Munsey estate.

Then, in February 1931, he bought the *New York World* for $5 million. Dropping the morning and Sunday editions, Howard merged the *Evening World* with the *Telegram.* In 1933 the *World-Telegram* received the Pulitzer Prize for meritorious public service. When Howard acquired the *New York Sun* in January 1950, he renamed the newspaper the *World-Telegram and Sun.* Thus Howard joined the last of the journalistic ventures in New York of Dana, Pulitzer, and Munsey.

Howard had his ups and downs with various Scripps-Howard notables, like Heywood Broun, Eleanor Roosevelt, Westbrook Pegler, Rollin Kirby, and Lowell Mellett.

In 1928, when Heywood Broun was discharged from the *New York World* for "disloyalty"—having assailed supporters of Massachusetts legalism who advocated executing Sacco and Vanzetti—Howard welcomed the free-swinging columnist to the *Telegram.* But Broun broke away in December 1939, when Howard advised him that any "unsatisfactory" columns not revised by Broun would be omitted from the *World-Telegram.* That year political cartoonist Kirby had moved to the *New York Post* rather than "support a point of view which seemed many times to be unfair." Generally Howard agreed with Pegler's anti-Roosevelt, antilabor positions but sought to regulate their frequency: Pegler therefore signed with Hearst in August 1944.

Howard's personnel troubles reflected his own conservative trend as well as the Scripps-Howard group's changing political preferences. Its liberal, crusading newspapers had provided Robert La Follette's Progressive party with its chief journalistic backing in the 1924 presidential election, but endorsed Hoover against Smith in 1928. Although the papers supported Roosevelt enthusiastically in 1932 and 1936, they opposed him in 1940 and thereafter were largely Republican. Howard had his professional standards, as when he employed the Scripps *Rocky Mountain News* in the 1920's to battle against Frederick G. Bonfils, publisher of the *Denver Post,* in a range of matters including the Teapot Dome scandal. A quarter century later he stood unshakably against the American Newspaper Guild, the union of news and editorial employees.

Regarding himself as a working news reporter, Howard took pride in his headline-making interviews with Lloyd-George, Emperor Hirohito, and Joseph Stalin. As an executive, he tried hard to win Newton D. Baker the presidential nomination at the Democratic convention in 1932, and eight years later he entertained his Republican choice, Wendell L. Willkie, aboard his yacht. Alert to change, he promoted the transmission of news pictures by wire in the mid-1920's, pioneered in extending news service to radio stations, and spurred the Newspaper Enterprise Association (NEA), an affiliate, into becoming the largest newspaper feature syndicate.

A dapper dresser, regularly attired in eye-catching checks and stripes, Howard was an easy mixer, who told Hoosier-twang stories and tossed out verbal hot shots in a Park Avenue office furnished with oriental antiques. His son, Jack Rohe Howard succeeded him as Scripps-Howard president in 1953. Howard's half-century career contributed significantly to journalism's development, growth, and change. He died in New York City.

[See Gilson Gardner, *Lusty Scripps* (1932); Negley D. Cochran, *W. W. Scripps* (1933); Webb Miller, *I Found No Peace* (1936); "Roy Howard: Super Reporter," *Literary Digest,* Mar. 14, 1936; "New Job for Roy Howard's No-Man," *ibid.,* June 27, 1936; "Hawkins for Howard," *Time,* June 29, 1936; Forrest Davis, "Press Lord," *Saturday Evening Post,* Mar. 12, 1938; George Seldes, "Roy Howard and His Papers," *New Republic,* July 27, 1938; George Seldes, *Lords of the Press* (1938); Robert Bendiner and J. A. Wechsler, "From Scripps to Howard," *Nation,* May 13 and 20, 1939; "Thou Art the Man!" *Time,* Sept. 2, 1940; A. J. Liebling, "Publisher," *New Yorker,* Aug. 2, 9, 16, and 23, 1941; Frank L. Mott, *American Journalism* (1941); Leland Stowe, "Roy Howard: Newspaper Napoleon," *Look,* May 30, 1944; Charles R. McCabe, ed., *Damned Old Crank* (1951); Kenneth Stewart and John Tebbel, *Makers of Modern Journalism* (1952); Jonathan Daniels, *They Will Be Heard* (1965); and Edwin Emery and Michael Emery, *The Press and America,* 4th ed. (1978). An obituary is in the *New York Times,* Nov. 21, 1964.]

IRVING DILLIARD

HUBBARD, BERNARD ROSECRANS (Nov. 24, 1888–May 28, 1962), Jesuit priest, explorer, photographer, and lecturer, was born in San Francisco, Calif., the son of George Milton Hubbard, a professor at St. Ignatius College, and Catherine Cornelia Wilder. Although very small at birth and susceptible to childhood ailments, Hubbard was an active youngster with a keen interest in the outdoors. The family moved to Santa Cruz, Calif., when he was six, and four years later to the Big Basin Redwood area, fifty miles south of San Francisco. There he devoted his spare time to roaming with gun, camera, and dog.

After attending secondary school at St. Ignatius College in San Francisco (1898–1906), Hubbard completed two years at Santa Clara College. In 1908 he became a member of the Jesuit order. He spent his vacations in scenic regions, including Yosemite Valley and the Grand Canyon. His interest was turning toward viewing spectacular geological landscapes.

Hubbard received his Jesuit training at Los Gatos, Calif. (A.B., 1913), Los Angeles College (1913–1918), and Gonzaga University in Spokane, Wash. (M.A., 1921). He then attended Ignatius College at Innsbruck, Austria, from 1921 to 1925. "As a youngster," he wrote later, "I was always in great difficulty because I was always arguing with my teachers. . . . I decided the only way for me to succeed was to go somewhere where I didn't know the language well enough to argue." In Austria he "devoted more than his spare time to probing and photographing the alpine peaks and glaciers of the Austrian Tyrol." The local people dubbed him *gletscher Pfarrer* ("Glacier Priest"), and this became his lifelong sobriquet.

In 1925 Hubbard studied at St. Andrew-on-Hudson, N.Y., and the following summer transferred to the University of Santa Clara, where he taught geology, Greek, and German.

Apparently drawn by the spectacular scenery of Alaska, then largely unexplored, Hubbard set out in the summer of 1927 to see Mendenhall and Taku glaciers, accompanied by athletic college students. In succeeding summers he explored the previously unknown interior mountains of Kodiak Island, and visited the Valley of Ten Thousand Smokes near Mt. Katmai and Aniakchak peak in the Aleutians, before and during its dramatic eruption of 1931. He served as guide in the Taku River area in 1929 for a United States Coast and Geodetic Survey triangulation team. Alone in 1931 Hubbard traveled by dogsled 1,600 miles from the interior of Alaska to the Bering Sea. In 1932 he and others made the first winter ascent of Mt. Katmai. In 1934, for the National Geographic Society, he mapped Alaskan areas altered by recent eruptions.

Hubbard spent the winter months of 1937–1938 isolated with 200 Eskimos on King Island off Seward Peninsula. He studied their language and customs, and during the following spring and summer he traveled by boat to Eskimo settlements along Alaska's northern coast to determine whether these widely separated people spoke the same basic language. He concluded that they did.

Viewing the spectacular was Hubbard's preference, and he documented his Alaskan expeditions well. He accumulated, by his own estimate, "over one million feet of standard sized film and over one hundred thousand still pictures of the terrain." He presented these photographs in lectures, in educational films and travel shorts, and in magazine articles. He also wrote two books on his Alaskan adventures: *Mush, You Malemutes!* (1932) and *Cradle of the Storms* (1935).

Hubbard was a colorful lecturer who, in his prime, delivered 275 lectures in eight months. The public responded to the drama of his flying close over an erupting volcano, scaling mountains, and devoutly performing daily mass in the wilderness. Proceeds from his lectures supported

his continuing trips to Alaska and contributed to the scattered Jesuit missions there. Alaskans appreciated his role as their volunteer ambassador. Because of the public's enthusiasm, the University of Santa Clara released Hubbard from teaching in 1930, so that he could devote full time to lecturing, writing, and further trips to Alaska.

For his intimate knowledge of traveling the terrain of Alaska, Hubbard was called upon by American military forces during World War II. He summarized for them his fourteen expeditions, provided his vast film footage and photographs, turned in reports on Bering Sea weather, and advised on arctic clothing and survival techniques. He offered to the army his own specially bred Arctic dogs, and he served as an auxiliary chaplain to the military forces in the Aleutians.

Hubbard's trips to Alaska after World War II were less strenuous, but he continued to lead students to scenic points in summers until the mid-1950's, when his traveling was interrupted by a series of strokes. He died at Santa Clara.

Hubbard's scientific expertise as a geologist was not great, but he put little-known Alaska on the map for the general public and accumulated a valuable photographic record of its terrain.

[Hubbard's papers are at the archives of the University of Santa Clara, and at the Jesuit Provincial Archives in Los Gatos, Calif.; among them are a fifty-page· autobiography and several unpublished memorials. His photographic collection is preserved at the University of Santa Clara. In addition to his books, "A World Inside a Mountain," *National Geographic*, Sept. 1931, is a good example of Hubbard's vivid writing and photography. See also Arthur D. Spearman, "Bernard R. Hubbard, S.J." in *Woodstock Letters* (1965).]

ELIZABETH NOBLE SHOR

HUBBARD, WYNANT DAVIS (Aug. 28, 1900–Dec. 9, 1961), naturalist, author, and expert on Africa, was born in Kansas City, Mo., the son of Charles Hubbard and Alice Field. His early education in England and Switzerland reflected the family's fondness for travel. World War I interrupted Hubbard's European studies but enabled him to work on cruises organized by the medical missionary Wilfred T. Grenfell along the Labrador coast in the summers of 1917–1919. This experience sharply whetted his wanderlust and sense of adventure.

Meanwhile, Hubbard completed his high school education at Milton Academy in Massachusetts (1918) and then enrolled at Harvard University. Although he did not earn a degree, his studies in geology under Vilhjalmur Stefansson were of considerable importance to his subsequent activities. He also earned some renown as a tackle on Harvard's undefeated football teams of 1919 and 1920. Hubbard spent the summers of his college years traveling and prospecting for gold and silver in Ontario. In 1921 he married Margaret Carson and left Harvard to become a prospector for asbestos mines in Quebec. In connection with this work he was offered a position as a consulting engineer for a mining consortium in British Central Africa. His acceptance of the job in 1922 marked the beginning of a lifelong love affair with that continent.

The engineering job fell through as a result of postwar economic fluctuations, but Hubbard stayed on in Africa as a professional hunter who specialized in obtaining live specimens for zoos. In this capacity he traveled widely in southern Africa and came to know the region so well that he was eventually recognized as one of America's leading authorities on Africa.

The Hubbards' first son had been born in Canada, and a second son was born shortly after they reached the African interior. A daughter was born to the couple after they returned to the United States following their second African venture in 1925–1926. The death by drowning of the elder son at Provincetown, South Africa, in 1925 led to the publication of the first of Hubbard's many works on African wildlife. *Wild Animals: A White Man's Conquest of Jungle Beasts* (1925) was essentially a compilation of stories, most of which had previously appeared in newspapers, scientific journals, or popular publications. In addition to being a memorial to his son, the book was—as Hubbard wrote—a "contribution towards a better understanding by outsiders of a part of Africa's life."

By the time of his return to the United States in mid-1925, Hubbard clearly had become enamored of Africa and its people. He devoted most of the rest of his life either to travel on the continent or to undertakings based on his African experiences. After the publication of *Wild Animals* he was asked by National Pictures Company to lead an expedition in Africa that was to produce a film on wild animals. The 1925–1926 undertaking eventually led to the release of two films, *Adventures in Africa* and *Untamed Africa.* But because of injuries inflicted by a lion and differences with producers, Hubbard did not receive the profits, which he had hoped to use in creating a research station in Northern Rhodesia. During the long period of convalescence from his wounds he wrote a second book, *Bong'kwe* (1930), and a number of articles.

About that time Hubbard inherited a sizable fortune, and he decided to build a research station at Ibamba. He had been divorced from Margaret Carson about 1927, and the following year he married Isabella Menzies; they had one son. His teen-age wife joined him in his enthusiastic plans. Their aim was to conduct a ten-year experiment in crossbreeding cattle and wild water buffalo in order to produce a strain that could resist the ravages of diseases carried by the tsetse fly. They also envisioned their station as a scientific outpost that others conducting research in Africa could utilize without charge.

This ambitious enterprise (1929–1935) proved beyond Hubbard's resources, and by 1932 he was publishing letters in the *New York Times,* pleading for donations to continue his work. Sufficient funds were not forthcoming, and by the mid-1930's he had returned to New York. In 1935 the Italian campaign in Ethiopia offered Hubbard an opportunity to return to Africa, and he covered the conflict as a war correspondent. He was sharply critical of the Italians, both in his dispatches and in *Fiasco in Ethiopia* (1936), but despite his antipathy to Mussolini and his followers, he remained convinced that white rule was essential to African development. Indeed, this was the vital element in the advice he offered as an unofficial but respected consultant on Africa to American presidents from Calvin Coolidge to Franklin D. Roosevelt.

After his coverage of the war in Ethiopia, Hubbard was involved in various enterprises over the next decade. These included the presidency of the Africa Company, an exporting firm (1938–1939); involvement in the import and export of minerals through the Matavic Corporation and the El Ghedem Mining Corporation; and service to the United States government on overseas agricultural development. During World War II, Hubbard served in G-2 in antisubmarine warfare and intelligence.

On June 10, 1950, Hubbard married Loyala Bradley Lee. His final years were spent in semiretirement in Florida, where he continued to write regularly for adventure magazines. In his last years he completed two books, *Wild Animal Hunter* (1958) and *Ibamba* (1962). He died in Miami, Fla.

[The bulk of Hubbard's papers apparently remain in family hands. In addition to the books mentioned in text, he wrote *The Thousandth Frog* (1934). Margaret Carson wrote *No One to Blame: An African Adventure* (1934). All these books contain autobiographical information, and collectively they constitute the most important source on Hubbard. An obituary is in the *New York Times,* Dec. 10, 1961.]

JAMES A. CASADA

HUEBNER, SOLOMON STEPHEN (Mar. 6, 1882–July 17, 1964), insurance teacher and writer, was born in Manitowoc, Wis., the son of Frederick August Huebner, a major landholder, and Wilhelmina Dicke. He was brought up on a farm, and benefited from his rural upbringing. His scholastic and leadership abilities were early displayed at Two Rivers High School, from which he graduated as valedictorian in 1898. He then attended the University of Wisconsin at Madison, receiving the Bachelor of Letters in 1902 and a Master of Letters in 1903. He then earned a Ph.D. in economics at the University of Pennsylvania in 1905. His doctoral dissertation was on marine insurance. Huebner married Ethel Elizabeth Mudie, a Canadian teacher, on June 24, 1908. They had four children.

At the time Huebner was completing his Ph.D., the Wharton School of Finance and Commerce of the University of Pennsylvania was one of only three collegiate schools of business in the United States. The classical economists at most universities did not take kindly to courses in applied economics. Huebner's talent for innovation was evident at an early stage of his career. Wharton had no courses on insurance. Strongly impressed with the notion that insurance was a branch of applied economics, Huebner persuaded the provost to let him give a course in that subject. In 1904 he became the first instructor of insurance and the stock exchange at a salary of $500 a year. Two years later he was appointed assistant professor of insurance and commerce, and professor in 1908. In 1913, when an insurance department was established, he became its chairman. Huebner remained at the Wharton School until his retirement in 1953. He taught an estimated 75,000 students, to whom he was known as "Sunny Sol" because of his mild manner and pleasant disposition.

Huebner wrote twelve textbooks on various aspects of insurance. These were widely used in colleges and universities. He also was editor or coeditor of fifteen works on insurance and related fields. His "Human Life Value Concept," explained in detail in *The Economics of Life Insurance* (1944), was employed by generations of insurance agents and field underwriters. Insurance instructors and professors in American colleges also spread the concept in their courses.

A man of great vigor, Huebner helped to es-

tablish such institutions as The American College of Life Underwriters in Bryn Mawr, Pa. (1927), which originated the chartered life underwriter (C.L.U.) and master of science in financial service degrees; the American Association of University Teachers of Insurance, later the American Risk and Insurance Association (1932); and the American Institute for Property and Liability Underwriters (1942). Through his speeches and articles he influenced the public with respect to the need for and choice of insurance plans. Huebner was also an adviser to congressional committees, the War Department, the Department of Commerce, and the Civil Aeronautics Board. During his frequent travels abroad he spread the Human Life Value Concept among insurance academicians and insurance professionals in Europe, Asia, and South America, as well as in Canada and Mexico.

Huebner died in Merion Station, Pa.

Widely known as the Father of Life Insurance Education and a teacher who changed an industry, he never sold a dollar's worth of insurance himself. Nevertheless, he left an indelible imprint on the insurance industry and on many of its basic institutions.

[Huebner's best-known work is *The Economics of Life Insurance* (3rd ed., 1959). Also see David McCahan, "Solomon Stephen Huebner—World's Foremost Insurance Educator," *Life Association News,* July 1940; David McCahan and D. W. Gregg, "A Collection of Huebnerian Philosophy," *Journal of the American Society of Chartered Life Underwriters,* June 1952; Mildred F. Stone, *The Teacher Who Changed an Industry: A Biography of Dr. Solomon S. Huebner* (1960), and *A Calling and Its College: A History of the American College of Life Underwriters* (1963).]

HARRIS PROSCHANSKY

HUEBSCH, BENJAMIN W. (Mar. 21, 1876–Aug. 7, 1964), publisher, was born in New York City, the son of Adolph Huebsch, a rabbi, and Julia Links. Much of Huebsch's education came from tutoring by his uncle Samuel. His interest in music began early; in the 1890's he studied the violin with Sam Franko (who secured for him a position for the 1898–1899 season as a music critic with the *Sun*). His father died when he was eight, and five years later Huebsch began to prepare himself for a business career by attending the Packard School of Business. After several months he took a job with the New York Engraving and Printing Company and in June 1890 became an apprentice lithographer with Joseph Frank and Sons, where he remained for three and a half years. By this time his older brother Daniel was running a small printing firm with their uncle Samuel. During the late 1890's D. A. Huebsch and Company developed as its specialty the production of engagement books and diaries, advertising and distributing them nationally. After joining the firm, Huebsch became particularly involved in the promotional side of the business.

A turning point came in 1900, when Edward Howard Griggs asked the Huebsch firm to distribute as well as print his book *The New Humanism,* for which he had not been able to find a publisher. Huebsch agreed, as he later recalled, "without the slightest knowledge of what publishing implied." Griggs was apparently pleased with the result, for over the next several years Huebsch brought out more of his work. In this way Huebsch gradually became a book publisher. By then his uncle was no longer with the firm; and when his brother left to pursue doctoral studies, Huebsch sold the printing equipment and then announced on Apr. 15, 1901, the change in the firm name to B. W. Huebsch. He continued for a few years as a contracting printer and marketed the yearbooks for two decades. But by late 1905 he was publishing books by authors other than Griggs, and in 1906 he attracted attention at the American Booksellers Association convention by distributing copies of one of his publications of that year, Gelett Burgess' *Are You a Bromide?,* in a special jacket by Burgess that satirized dust-jacket advertising and first used the word "blurb" to describe it.

The direction Huebsch's firm would take became evident early. By World War I it had published Maxim Gorky, Gerhart Hauptmann, Hermann Sudermann, and August Strindberg; poetry by James Oppenheim, Horace Traubel, and William Ellery Leonard; and discussions of social questions by John Spargo, Ellen Key, André Tridon, and H. G. Wells. The firm became known for translations of European works, books on socialism, psychoanalysis, and little theater, and literature by the kind of new and experimental writers whom the more established publishers hesitated to publish. Even as the firm grew, it continued to bear the stamp of Huebsch's personality: he published what he personally liked, and he had a hand in every aspect of the business, writing some of the advertising and deciding on the physical appearance of the books. (His abilities as a book designer recall his early aptitude for art and the course he took at the Cooper Union Art School.)

The distinction of the firm's output over the next decade is indicated by the names of some of its authors: Van Wyck Brooks, George Jean Nathan, James Joyce (four books, one preceding its English publication), D. H. Lawrence, Thorstein Veblen, Sherwood Anderson, and Randolph Bourne. From March 1920 to March 1924 Huebsch also published the *Freeman,* a weekly journal of "radical" political and literary opinion financed by Helen Swift Neilson and maintained on a high level throughout its brief but illustrious life. On Sept. 14, 1920, Huebsch married Alfhild Lamm; they had two sons. By 1925 Huebsch's device of the seven-branched candlestick had appeared on some 400 books and had come to stand for an exceptional publishing achievement.

In that year the Huebsch imprint came to an end, and Huebsch's impact on American publishing from then on was exercised through the Viking Press. Harold K. Guinzburg and George S. Oppenheimer, founders of the Viking Press, had not yet issued a book when, on Aug. 1, 1925, they acquired the Huebsch firm. The merger was mutually advantageous, for it improved Huebsch's financial position and provided Viking with an impressive backlist. Huebsch became vice-president of Viking and headed the editorial department. Marshall A. Best, who had joined Huebsch shortly before the merger, also played an important role in the new firm.

Although Huebsch lost a few writers over the years who felt that he had not adequately promoted their work, for the most part his authors were extraordinarily loyal. James Joyce, for instance, inserted a clause in his 1931 Viking contract allowing him to follow Huebsch, should Huebsch leave the firm. The quality of the Viking lists over four decades was strongly influenced by the personal attachments that Huebsch inspired. In addition to the authors who went with him to Viking, he brought in many others (among them Harold Laski and Stefan Zweig) through his wide acquaintance and his regular trips to Europe. He was active until his death in London while on a business trip.

Huebsch was one of the great elder statesmen of American publishing during his last two decades. In addition to his record as a publisher and the breadth and humanity of his interests, he worked unselfishly on behalf of the book world and the cause of freedom of expression. From his early days he wrote and spoke frequently on the need for greater cooperation among all concerned with book distribution. He championed the idea of a national book center, with a permanent cooperative exhibition displaying books from all publishers, and he advocated courses of study for booksellers. It was at a meeting of publishers in 1919 that he first advanced the plan that led to the formation of the National Association of Book Publishers. Among other activities, he was a member of Henry Ford's Peace Expedition in 1915–1916 (editing a daily paper aboard ship), a member of the original committee (1920) of the American Civil Liberties Union (he remained treasurer for over thirty years), and the representative of the book industry on the United States National Committee for UNESCO (1949–1950). His kindness, generosity, and fair-mindedness were proverbial. He regarded publishing as a way of life, and his idealistic approach was reflected in a 1936 speech in which he described the publisher's function as "comparable in dignity with that of the ideal teacher." "There is no business," he said, "which demands more constant adherence to a high standard than that of publishing books."

[The bulk of Huebsch's papers are housed in the Manuscript Division of the Library of Congress and are briefly described in the Library's *Information Bulletin,* Aug. 31, 1964. Other papers can be found in The Newberry Library and the university libraries at Buffalo (SUNY), Harvard, Texas, and Yale. Huebsch contributed numerous articles to *Publishers Weekly,* other book journals, and the *Freeman,* 1920–1924; and he published a translation of Stefan Zweig's *The Royal Game* (1944). Some of his most revealing writings are "Reflections on Publishing," *Publishers Weekly,* Apr. 25, 1936; "Footnotes to a Publisher's Life," *Colophon,* new series 2 (1936–1937), and his Bowker Lecture, *Busman's Holiday* (1959). The fullest study of Huebsch's publishing activities through 1925 is Ann McCullough, "A History of B. W. Huebsch, Publisher" (Ph.D. diss., University of Wisconsin, 1979), which has as an appendix a memoir of the later years by Marshall A. Best.
    Also see *B. W. Huebsch, 1876–1964: A Record of a Meeting of His Friends at the Grolier Club, New York City, on December 9, 1964* (1964); G. T. Tanselle, "In Memoriam: B. W. Huebsch," *Antiquarian Bookman,* Aug. 30, 1965; Charles A. Madison, *Book Publishing in America* (1966), and *Irving to Irving* (1974); John Tebbel, *A History of Book Publishing in the United States,* III (1978); and James Gilreath, "The Benjamin Huebsch Imprint," *Papers of the Bibliographical Society of America,* 73 (1979). Obituary notices appeared in the *New York Times,* Aug. 8, 1964, and in *Publishers Weekly,* Aug. 17, 1964.
    For more information see the series of interviews by Louis Starr (1954 and 1955) and the Marshall A. Best material in the Oral History Office of Columbia University Library. (Also at Columbia are several hundred books from Huebsch's library and some of his correspondence.)]

                                   G. THOMAS TANSELLE

HUPP, LOUIS GORHAM (Nov. 13, 1872– Dec. 10, 1961), automobile pioneer, was born in Kalamazoo, Mich., the son of Charles Jasper Hupp, an assistant general freight agent for the Michigan Central Railroad, and Anne M. Klinger. Hupp attended public school in Kalamazoo and high school in Detroit. He then entered the University of Michigan and graduated in 1895 from its school of engineering.
    His first job was as a commercial agent for the Michigan Central Railroad in Grand Rapids, where he met and married Lillian K. Hazlewood on Oct. 28, 1905. They had two sons. After a time Hupp left the railroad and formed the Hupp-Turner Machine Company in Detroit. In 1908 Hupp's younger brother, Robert Craig Hupp, started the Hupp Motor Car Company; the two firms were merged later that year. The first Hupp automobile exhibition model was demonstrated at the Detroit Automobile Show in 1908. The 1909 Hupmobile, described as the "smallest and best little car ever marketed in America at anything like the money," was a four-cylinder, twenty-horsepower vehicle that sold for $750.
    In 1912 the Hupp brothers began producing the RCH automobile (named after the younger Hupp) by a separate company, the RCH Corporation. In 1915 the Hupp Motor Car Company was reincorporated in Virginia as the Hupp Motor Car Corporation, but manufacturing continued in Michigan. In 1916 Hupp started the Tribune Motor Car Company but, with American intervention in World War I looming, closed shop after only three cars were produced.
    An extremely popular car in the boom years of the 1920's, the Hupmobile had a distinctive "Hupmobile blue" body with black fenders and running board. While not known for speed, the car was durable, simply constructed, and innovative in design. It was easily identified by the uncommonly tall filler necks on the radiator and by the unusual fan-shaped tail lamps. In 1923, some 38,000 new Hupmobiles were produced and more than 117,000 were in service. The latter figure is an indication of the durability of the vehicle, which typically lasted longer than the six-year average life span of other American automobiles.
    The Hupp Motor Car Corporation thrived and by 1924 occupied more than four million square feet of floor space, including a factory for gear and machine work in Jackson, Mich.; a body-building plant in Racine, Wis.; a shipping plant in Windsor, Ontario; and the Detroit Auto Specialties Company, a stamping concern.

In 1925 the Hupp company produced 129,000 cars, which placed it among the top ten American automobile producers.

In the early 1920's Hupp also became involved in residential real estate development. He formed the Hupp Farms Corporation and the West Maple Road Corporation and developed Bloomfield Village, west of Birmingham, Mich.

Like all other automobile-manufacturing concerns, the Hupp firm had difficulty maintaining production and sales levels during the Great Depression. In a futile attempt to reverse the sales decline, Hupp produced a series of radically designed "aerodynamic" models in 1934 and 1935. These cars featured windshields that were divided into three parts and headlights that were built into the side of the hood. In August 1938 Hupp acquired from the Auburn Automobile Company dies, tools, and patterns that enabled him to imitate the design of the 1937 Cord. But sales continued to slump, and the last Hupmobile was built in 1941.

Hupp volunteered for government service at the outbreak of World War II and was appointed an examiner with the Office of Defense Transportation at Detroit in 1942, where he served for the duration of the war. After the war he continued to invest in real estate development. Hupp died in Detroit.

Hupp and his brother Robert Craig were in the vanguard of early American automobile entrepreneurship. The Hupmobile was an imaginative, attractive, and popular vehicle that deserves a place in American automobile history beside the products of Henry Ford and the Olds brothers.

[The Hupmobile is discussed in Joseph F. Clymer, *Treasury of Early American Automobiles, 1877–1925* (1950); Tad Burness, *Cars of the Early Twenties* (1968); and Stephen W. Sears, *The American Heritage History of the Automobile in America* (1977). *Detroit Saturday Night*, Sept. 16, 1911, contains a profile of Robert Craig Hupp and the brothers' pioneer automobile days. Obituaries appeared in the *New York Times* and *Chicago Daily Tribune*, Dec. 12, 1961.]

STEPHEN D. BODAYLA

HURLEY, PATRICK JAY (Jan. 8, 1883–July 30, 1963), lawyer and diplomat, was born in Choctaw Nation territory near the present community of Lehigh, Okla., the son of Pierce O'Neil Hurley, sharecropper and later a coal digger, and Mary Kelly. He spent his early life in coal mining and farming communities in Indian Territory, where his father struggled to eke out a living. When Hurley was eleven, his father got him a job as an air trapper in a coal mine. Thereafter he was virtually self-supporting, spending most of his adolescent years working in the mines or as a ranch hand.

In 1897, Hurley enrolled in the night school of Thomas Golightly, a Scots day laborer-turned-educator. Rudimentary as his classes were, Golightly exerted profound influence on Hurley by encouraging him to develop his intellectual ability. Benjamin F. Smallwood, a Choctaw chief who befriended Hurley and lent him books, was another major influence on the youth. So was his mother, a gentle and refined woman whose attention to him was not matched by her blustering and ill-tempered husband.

Aside from the brief period in night school, Hurley had received no formal education until he was seventeen. Then, through the intervention of a friend, he enrolled in Indian University, a Baptist school for Indians (later Bacone College) at Muskogee, Okla. He completed his elementary school, high school, and college work at Indian University—a university in name only—in five years, and received the B.A. in 1905.

Hurley then took a position as a clerk in the Indian Service at Muskogee, a job that allowed him time to study. The reading of the law books of a local attorney stimulated him to become a lawyer. In 1907 he went to Washington, D.C., hoping to attend one of the law schools there. He was unsuccessful in his attempts to enroll at Georgetown and George Washington, but finally was accepted at National University. Working at part-time jobs during the day, Hurley attended night classes. He received the LL.B. in 1908.

Hurley then moved to Tulsa, Okla., and began a career in law and business that would enrich him financially, involve him in politics, and eventually catapult him into national prominence. From 1911 until 1917 he was national attorney for the Choctaws, a position that involved working with the Oklahoma congressional delegation as well as with political leaders from other states. In 1917, after serving with the Oklahoma National Guard, he accepted a commission in the army and served in 1918 with American forces in France. On Dec. 5, 1919, he married Ruth Wilson, daughter of Admiral Henry B. Wilson, commander of the Atlantic Fleet. They had four children.

In the 1920's Hurley increased his personal wealth through his law practice and real estate investments. He became active in the Republican party, the minority party in Oklahoma. In 1928 he helped carry Oklahoma for Herbert Hoover and was rewarded with appointment as assistant secretary of war in the new administration. The secretary, James W. Good, died in November 1929, and Hoover named Hurley to succeed him. As secretary of war, Hurley dealt directly with the march on Washington by the Bonus Expeditionary Force in 1932 and with Philippine independence, both of which he opposed vigorously.

After the defeat of Hoover in 1932, Hurley spent much of his time in Washington, D.C., revitalizing his law practice and recovering the financial losses he had suffered in the collapse of the real estate market. During this period he became acquainted with President Franklin D. Roosevelt, who was attracted to Hurley partly because Hurley's Republicanism, tinctured with some of the ideas of the Populist-Progressive reform movement, allowed him to support elements of the New Deal.

It was in diplomacy that Hurley made his most significant mark on American history. As a private emissary for the Sinclair Oil Company in 1940, he negotiated a settlement of its claims with the government of Mexico. This agreement broke an impasse that had followed the Mexican expropriation of American oil properties in 1938 and impelled the four other American oil companies to negotiate a general claims agreement with the Mexican government.

After the beginning of World War II, Hurley, who had been a colonel in the reserves since World War I, was promoted to brigadier general. In January 1942, President Roosevelt appointed him to the southwest Pacific to break the blockade of Bataan and get supplies to General Douglas MacArthur, an assignment impossible to carry out successfully because of Japanese control of the region. Hurley next became United States minister to New Zealand. He did not want the post, which he occupied only from April to August 1942. Later in 1942, Roosevelt sent him on a "good will" trip to the Soviet Union, where Hurley conferred with Joseph Stalin and visited battlefields. In 1943 and early 1944 Hurley made fact-finding tours of the Middle East. In November 1943 he attended the Teheran Conference, where he drafted the Declaration on Iran, which pledged the United States, Great Britain, and the Soviet Union to maintain the independence, sovereignty, and territorial integrity of the country.

In 1944, Roosevelt dispatched Hurley as a special envoy to China to try to compose differences between General Joseph Stilwell and

Chiang Kai-shek, and to mediate a settlement between the Chinese Communists and Chiang's Kuomintang. In November 1944 Hurley became ambassador to China. Roosevelt's objectives were to improve the Nationalists' military capability and to create a strong, stable, and non-Communist post-war China. Hurley's assignment involved using a Soviet promise not to support the Chinese Communists as leverage in securing an arrangement subsuming the Communists within Chiang's government. He failed to resolve the Stilwell-Chiang dispute and, although he worked for nearly a year, also failed to get an agreement between the Nationalists and Communists (this task was probably beyond the competence of any American official). In November 1945 he angrily submitted his resignation, charging that his efforts had been undermined by a group of disputatious and disloyal foreign service officers in China.

After the war Hurley became a crusading anti-Communist and was among the first to attack the China policy of the Truman administration. He never again held an important public position. Hurley died at Santa Fe, N.Mex.

Always brash, bombastic, and possessed of an oversized ego, Hurley displayed only his negative qualities during his latter years. Consequently his career is difficult to assess dispassionately. It is easy to underestimate his abilities and achievements. A gregarious man with a retentive mind and good communicative skills, he had notable success in his business and legal careers. His accomplishments as a statesman, however, were small.

[The Patrick J. Hurley Papers are deposited in the Western History Collection, University of Oklahoma Library. See also Parker La Moore, *"Pat" Hurley: The Story of an American* (1932); Don Lohbeck, *Patrick J. Hurley* (1956); and Russell D. Buhite, *Patrick J. Hurley and American Foreign Policy* (1973). An obituary appeared in *New York Times* on July 31, 1963.]
                                    RUSSELL D. BUHITE

HUSING, EDWARD BRITT ("TED") (Nov. 27, 1901–Aug. 10, 1962), radio announcer, was born in the Bronx, N.Y., the son of Henry Frederick Husing and Bertha Hecht. His immigrant parents moved frequently as his father's jobs as headwaiter and club steward changed, and Husing received a spotty education in the New York City and suburban public schools of Johnstown and Gloversville, N.Y. Stuyvesant High School suspended him from several athletic teams for scholastic deficiency, and as a teenager he disappeared twice on unannounced hitchhiking trips to Missouri and Florida, adventures that tested his parents' "abundant love" for him. He held numerous short-term jobs. Underage and using an assumed name and false birth certificate, Husing served in the New York National Guard during World War I. He was working as a payroll clerk for a hosiery firm when he married Helen Gelderman on June 8, 1924. They had one daughter, and were divorced in 1934.

In 1924 Husing joined the infant broadcasting industry as an announcer for the Radio Corporation of America stations WJY-WJZ in New York City. Although only a high school graduate, Husing claimed that he held a degree from Harvard University; such brashness and a superior audition won him the job over 600 other applicants. With WJY-WJZ, which in 1926 became a part of the new National Broadcasting Company (NBC), Husing became one of the pioneers of broadcasting. He developed his skills while working with such important announcers as Milton Cross, Norman Brokenshire, and Major J. Andrew White. White was particularly influential in shaping Husing's career: he introduced him to sports announcing, the aspect of programming with which he became most identified. His first sports broadcast was the Penn-Cornell football game in November 1925.

To better prepare himself for sports announcing, Husing played during the 1920's for the Prescotts, a semiprofessional football team in New York. Two of his teammates, Les Quailey and Jimmy Dolan, later became his play-by-play broadcasting partners. But sports events occupied only part of Husing's varied schedule. In the day prior to narrow specialization in radio Husing was a complete announcer, covering special events and introducing dance bands, among other duties.

In 1927 Husing resigned from NBC and worked briefly for stations WBET in Boston and WHN in New York. On Dec. 25, 1927, he joined the Columbia Broadcasting System (CBS). Within two years both he and the new network had become established successes, and his role in placing the network on a sound footing was recognized by President William S. Paley. Husing covered aviator Floyd Bennett's funeral, the 1928 and 1932 Democratic conventions, and presidential candidate Herbert Hoover's acceptance speech in California in 1928. He became the network's "name" sports broadcaster, covering polo, tennis, college football (including Army-Navy, Army-Notre Dame), the World Series, the Kentucky Derby,

the Orange Bowl games, and the 1932 summer Olympic games in Los Angeles. To facilitate their football broadcasts Husing and Quailey developed the electric annunciator. (Quailey, using binoculars to identify player's numbers, pressed buttons on a board that caused lights, corresponding to the player's numbers, to light up on Husing's board. This device allowed Husing to deliver a smooth play-by-play account of the game.)

Husing also participated in prime-time entertainment programming during the late 1920's and early 1930's. He was the announcer on the Eddie Cantor and Ethel Merman shows, and played a role in bringing such entertainers as Rudy Vallee, Paul Whiteman, Bing Crosby, and Guy Lombardo to radio.

Blunt and outspoken on the air as well as off, Husing created controversy. When he characterized the performance of Harvard quarterback Barry Wood as "putrid" in the 1931 Dartmouth game, he was banned from the university's sports events for two years. He was prohibited from broadcasting baseball after he criticized the umpires in the 1934 World Series.

After quitting CBS in 1946 because of a salary dispute, Husing worked briefly for WCAU in Philadelphia. Later that year he made a major career transition and became a disc jockey for station WHN in New York. "Ted Husing's Bandstand," which continued into the 1950's, symbolized a format that radio would increasingly rely on in its competition with television. Husing's annual income reached $250,000, nearly ten times what his salary had been at CBS. During the late 1940's and early 1950's Husing continued to broadcast sports events, including a season of the professional football Baltimore Colts.

Although Husing was a professional success, both he and his associates judged his personal life a failure. Among the "victims of my brashness, discourteousness, and thoughtlessness," he wrote in his second autobiography, was his first wife. Neglecting his marriage as he obsessively pursued recognition and acclaim, Husing spent more time in New York nightclubs than at home. Husing married Frances Sizer on Apr. 28, 1936, but the marriage lasted only until August of that year. On Apr. 21, 1944, he married Iris Lemerise; they were divorced in 1958. By his third marriage he had one son. In 1954 illness left him partially paralyzed and blinded. He died in Pasadena, Calif.

[Husing wrote two autobiographies: *The Years Before the Mike* (1935) and, with Cy Rice, *My Eyes Are in My Heart* (1959). See also Julian Bach, Jr., "Hold 'Em Husing!" *Literary Digest,* Nov. 6, 1937; Red Barber, *The Broadcasters* (1970); *New York Times,* Oct. 7, 1945; "Thank You, Mr. Husing!" *Time,* Nov. 11, 1946; *Newsweek,* Dec. 10, 1956.

Obituaries are in the *New York Times* and *New York Herald Tribune,* both Aug. 11, 1962.]

ALAN HAVIG

HUTTON, EDWARD FRANCIS (Sept. 7, 1875–July 11, 1962), stockbroker and business executive, was born in New York City, the son of James Laws Hutton, a farmer. He left public school at fifteen and worked briefly as a "grease monkey" in Kingston, N.Y. He then resumed his schooling at the New York Latin School and Public School 69, where he became friendly with Bernard Baruch, an older classmate. Later he attended Trinity Chapel School.

In 1892, Hutton took a job as a mail boy for a Wall Street mortgage company at $5 per week. He was fired after a year for taking an unauthorized vacation. His next position was as a writer of checks for Manhattan Trust Company. His poor penmanship reportedly led the firm's president, John I. Waterbury, to recommend that he go to night school to improve his handwriting. Offended, Hutton resigned. He learned shorthand at night at Packer's Business College and privately studied finance and economics as well.

In 1895 Hutton helped form, and became a partner in, Harris, Hutton and Company, stockbrokers. The firm reportedly purchased membership in the old Consolidated Stock Exchange (which dealt exclusively in odd lots) for $375. When the firm was dissolved in 1901, Hutton persuaded his uncle, William E. Hutton, of Cincinnati, to open a New York City branch of his brokerage firm. He became the resident partner and a member of the New York Stock Exchange.

Hutton organized his own brokerage house, E. F. Hutton and Company, in 1904. He was senior partner until 1921 and a special partner from then until his death. The business grew rapidly, and at one point held memberships in the New York, American, Pacific Coast, Midwest, Boston, Salt Lake City, and New Orleans stock exchanges, and in eighteen commodity exchanges. It was the first firm to operate a securities wire to the West Coast.

Hutton married Blanche Horton, who died in 1918. Their son died two years later. On July 7, 1920, he married Marjorie Merriweather Post Close, daughter and heir of Charles W. Post, founder of Postum Cereal Company. They had one daughter, who became the actress Dina Merrill.

At the request of Colby M. Chester, Postum's treasurer, Hutton took a leave of absence from his brokerage firm and joined the cereal manufacturer in 1921. He was elected the unsalaried chairman of the board of directors in April 1923. With Chester, who became president, Hutton revitalized the company and brought about the merger of fifteen food and grocery manufacturing companies. The Postum name was changed to General Foods Corporation in 1929. Hutton's marriage to Marjorie Post Close ended in divorce in August 1935, and he resigned as chairman of General Foods. In 1936 he married Dorothy Dear Metzger.

A lifelong Republican, Hutton was a staunch supporter of President Herbert Hoover. In the early New Deal years he was strongly critical of the Roosevelt administration, and in November 1935 attracted nationwide attention by calling upon American industry to "gang up" against the administration. He later modified this position somewhat, claiming that his attitude toward the New Deal had become less hostile.

Hutton was an enthusiastic proponent of Americanism and the free-enterprise system, and an opponent of communism. He took out full-page newspaper advertisements to promote patriotism, advance constitutional government, sing the praises of capitalism, and combat communism. An October 1947 ad in the *New York Times* read in part: "Please, God, as a prayer, may we never accept any foreign 'ism'— totalitarianism, collectivism—for Americanism." From 1953 to 1960 Hutton wrote a syndicated column, "Think It Through," for the *New York Herald Tribune* and some sixty other newspapers. The column voiced objection to government "meddling" in American business. It was his consistent theme that the federal government was becoming too big and too paternalistic.

In 1949 Hutton founded the Freedoms Foundation (at Valley Forge, Pa.), which was dedicated to maintaining the "indivisible political and economic freedoms" inherent in the Constitution and the Bill of Rights. The foundation gives awards to organizations and individuals who promote patriotic ideals. The Wall Street American Legion post awarded Hutton the Bill of Rights Gold Medal in 1949, in recognition of his patriotic efforts.

At various times Hutton was chairman and director of Zonite Products and director of Chrysler, Manufacturers Trust, and Coca-Cola. He was a yachtsman and owned a series of sailing vessels, including one more than 300 feet in length and with a crew of 70. He died at Westbury, N.Y.

[A profile with considerable biographical information appeared in the *New Yorker*, July 26, 1958. A very detailed obituary is in the *New York Times*, July 12, 1962.]

STEPHEN D. BODAYLA

HUXLEY, ALDOUS LEONARD (July 26, 1894–Nov. 22, 1963), writer, was born at Laleham, Sussex, England, the son of Leonard Huxley, a schoolmaster, and of Julia Arnold. His grandfather was the biologist and author Thomas Henry Huxley, affectionately known as Darwin's Bulldog. Huxley's great-grandfather was Thomas Arnold, the renowned headmaster of Rugby School, and his great-uncle was the poet and essayist Matthew Arnold.

Huxley was first educated at Laleham's Field, a school established and run by his mother, and subsequently at Eton and Balliol College, Oxford, from which he graduated with first-class honors in English in 1916.

His childhood and youth were overshadowed by three tragedies: In 1908 his mother died of cancer; in the spring of 1911 he contracted keratitis punctata, at Eton, was virtually blind for eighteen months, and never wholly recovered his sight; in August 1914 he was deeply affected by the suicide of his elder brother Trevenen. The loss of his sight meant that Huxley could not pursue a career in the exact sciences, where his other brother, Julian, born in 1887, was to win great distinction. Instead he became a writer.

In 1916, Huxley published a volume of poetry, *The Burning Wheel. Crome Yellow*, his first novel, appeared in 1921. From a purely literary point of view it is still considered by some critics to be his best work, but *Antic Hay* (1923) and *Those Barren Leaves* (1925) established him as the novelist who best expressed the mood of the 1920's in England. Both are novels of disillusionment, shot through with the recollected horror and futility of World War I. Both present characters who have lost all belief in God, society, or morality. Both are extremely witty, ironically insisting that human knowledge is incapable of solving human problems. Huxley's skepticism reached its peak with *Jesting Pilate* (1926), his account of a trip around the world made in 1925–1926.

In *Point Counter Point* (1928), a roman à clef in which the character of Mark Rampion is based upon D. H. Lawrence, Huxley tried to put forward a more defiantly optimistic and humanist standpoint. He was a great admirer of Lawrence, and enthusiastically endorsed his doctrine of "Life Worship," both in the favorable presentation of Rampion in *Point Counter Point* and in the volumes of essays entitled *Proper Studies* (1927) and *Do What You Will* (1929). The violence and the pessimism about human relationships that characterize the plot of *Point Counter Point* nevertheless belie this official optimism, and recur in Huxley's best-known work, *Brave New World* (1932).

The action of his "Utopian fantasy" takes place in A.D. 2520, designated by Huxley as A.F. (After Ford) 632. Man's control over the environment, exemplified by the triumphs of industrial technology, has extended to biology. Genetic engineering and Pavlovian conditioning ensure that society has exactly the number and types of human beings it needs. "Soma" drugs and constantly available sex ensure happiness for all in a world from which suffering and disease have been banished. But this scientific paradise can exist only by eradicating everything that makes human beings human: affection for children, responsibility for parents, love, art, literature, religion.

Although Huxley's marriage to Maria Nys, a Belgian woman whom he had married on July 10, 1919, was outwardly stable, there were problems. He had extramarital affairs, and later acknowledged that he had been an inadequate father to their son. The publication of *Eyeless in Gaza* (1936) marked the beginning of Huxley's attempt to solve his personal and philosophical problems through religious mysticism. The long essay *Ends and Means* (1937) signaled his conversion to pacifism. In April 1937, announcing that "Europe is no place for a pacifist," he moved to the United States. He worked temporarily in Hollywood, where in 1940 he adapted *The Life of Eve Curie* and *Pride and Prejudice* for Metro-Goldwyn-Mayer.

Huxley's bitterly satirical novel on longevity, *After Many a Summer Dies the Swan* (1939), revealed a growing tendency to use fiction as a medium for preaching mysticism. He improved his sight by applying the Bates method of eye training, and described the results in *The Art of Seeing* (1942). *Time Must Have a Stop* (1944) contained an ambitious attempt to depict the state of mind of a typically "attached" human being immediately after death, and foreshadowed the more systematic exposition of mystical doctrine in *The Perennial Philosophy* (1945). *Ape and Essence* (1948) depicted the horrors of a civilization given over to systematic devil worship as the only way to make sense of human experience after a devastating atomic war. It was matched in horror by a historical reconstruction of the obscene sadism of seventeenth-century witch hunting in *The Devils of Loudun* (1952).

Although a convert to mysticism, Huxley had not had a mystical experience until his first experiment in taking mescalin in May 1953, under the direction of Dr. Humphry Osmond. *The Doors of Perception* (1954) analyzed this experience, and may have contributed to the development of the Californian drug culture of the 1960's.

In February 1955, Maria Huxley died of cancer, and on Mar. 19, 1956, Huxley married the violinist Laura Archera. *Brave New World Revisited* (1958) and the fantasy *Island* (1962) showed Huxley continuing to use essays and fiction to preach the virtues of mysticism, pacifism, nonattachment, and the correct use of consciousness-enhancing drugs. Huxley's lectures on the role and purpose of science drew large audiences on American college campuses in 1961 and 1962. There is a marked contrast between this later role as a fashionable guru and the brilliantly iconoclastic Huxley of the 1930's and 1940's. He died in Los Angeles, Calif.

Huxley's reputation as a writer declined as his apparent faith in the ability of human beings to improve their lot through mysticism and unorthodox science increased. He had a surprising ability to foresake his earlier skepticism for a touchingly naïve belief in the virtues of LSD, pacifism, vegetarianism, the Bates method of eye training, the views of F. Matthias Alexander, and the psychophysiology of Dr. William Sheldon. A consistently gentle, courteous, and civilized person in his private life, his books are full of murder, torture, whippings, amputations, abortions, maimings, war, persecution, and betrayal.

[The standard biography is Sybille Bedford, *Aldous Huxley* (1974). Also see Grover Smith, ed., *Letters of Aldous Huxley* (1969); and Claire J. Eschelbach and Joyce L. Shober, *Aldous Huxley: A Bibliography, 1916–1959* (1961) and *A Supplementary Listing, 1914–1964* (1972). An obituary is in the *New York Times*, Nov. 24, 1963.]

P. M. W. THODY

IDE, JOHN JAY (June 26, 1892–Jan. 12, 1962), aeronautical consultant and author, was born at Narragansett Pier, R.I., the son of George Elmore Ide, a rear admiral in the United States Navy, and Alexandra Louise Bruen.

Ide attended private schools in New York City, graduating from the Browning School for Boys in 1909. He received a Certificate of Architecture at Columbia University in 1913 and did one year of postgraduate study at the Ecole des Beaux Arts in Paris. He worked as an architect with Harrie T. Lindeberg in New York City, 1916–1917, and during the winter of 1920–1921.

In 1917, Ide joined the Naval Reserve Flying Corps and later went on to head the Technical Data Section (Aircraft) in the Bureau of Construction and Repair. He spent the summer of 1920 in Europe on assignment from the Office of Naval Intelligence to assess aeronautical developments in England, France, Belgium, and Italy.

Ide returned briefly to architecture following his release from the Navy in September 1920, but his interest in aviation proved irresistible. When the National Advisory Committee for Aeronautics (NACA)—created by Congress in 1915 to coordinate, promote, and conduct scientific research into all phases of aeronautics —sought a replacement for their technical representative in Europe, Ide was selected for the expertise he had acquired.

Attached in 1921 to the American embassy in Paris, Ide proved ideal for the post. He was a consummate diplomat, managing to appease the military attachés who had secured the recall of his predecessor while at the same time he replaced them as the primary source of information for technical developments in European aviation. Ide traveled all over Europe, visiting aeronautical research facilities, touring aircraft and engine factories, and purchasing foreign equipment and publications for NACA.

Ide served as a bridge between the American and European aeronautical communities for nearly twenty years. His social prominence and his appreciation of French art and food facilitated access to the highest governmental circles. NACA technical reports, not otherwise available for foreign distribution, reached Europe through Ide. In turn, he kept NACA and other interested agencies apprised of the latest foreign advances. His reports circulated widely, and they were appreciated. "I consider these documents," wrote aeronautical expert Edward P. Warner in 1923, "the most important of any descriptive material which ever came to my desk."

In addition to gathering technological intelligence, Ide often represented the United States at conferences for the formulation of laws and regulations to govern international civil aviation. An acknowledged expert in this field, he delivered in 1935 the James Jackson Cabot lecture at Norwich University on "International Aeronautical Organizations and the Control of Air Navigation."

Ide returned to the United States and married Dora Browning Donner, member of an affluent Philadelphia family, on Feb. 12, 1940. They had no children.

Recalled to active duty with the navy in November 1940, Ide took charge of the Foreign Intelligence Branch in the Bureau of Aeronautics. From 1943 to 1945 he served on the staff of the commander of the United States Naval Forces in Europe as a technical air intelligence officer. His final military assignment, as captain, was Assistant Naval Attaché for Air at the embassy in London from August 1945 to November 1946.

Ide's interest in the international aspects of aviation continued during the postwar period. He served in 1947 as a delegate to the Anglo-American Air Conference, and he held the post of vice-president of the International Aeronautic Federation in 1948–1950.

Ide was reappointed NACA technical representative in Europe in 1949. Although he resigned the following year, Ide remained a consultant to NACA until 1958. Ide devoted his last years to the history of architecture, publishing a number of articles on the subject. He died in New York City.

[Ide's reports and a small collection of personal material are incorporated in the records of the National Advisory Committee for Aeronautics at the National Archives. The best account of NACA, including mention of Ide's role in the organization, is Alex Roland, *Research by Committee: A History of the National Advisory Committee for Aeronautics, 1915–1958* (1981). Ide's technical articles appeared frequently in aeronautical journals during the interwar years.

An obituary appeared in the *New York Times*, Jan. 13, 1962.]

WILLIAM M. LEARY

IVES, IRVING MCNEIL (Jan. 24, 1896–Feb. 24, 1962), U.S. senator, was born in Bainbridge, N.Y., the son of George Albert Ives and Lucy Keeler. He attended public schools in Bainbridge and Oneonta, then entered Hamilton College. In 1917 he enlisted in the army and saw action in the Meuse-Argonne offensive and at St. Mihiel. Discharged as a first lieutenant, Ives returned to college and graduated with the B.A. in 1920. He married Elizabeth Minette Skinner on Oct. 23, 1920; they had one son. For the next three years Ives worked as a bank clerk for Guaranty Trust Company in Brooklyn, N.Y.

In 1923, he returned upstate to Norwich and took a position with Manufacturers Trust Company. Ten years later he established his own insurance firm in Norwich.

Meanwhile, Ives became active in Republican politics. In 1930 he helped topple the leadership of the Chenango County Republican organization and, in the process, was elected to the first of eight terms in the New York Assembly. He soon demonstrated a keen understanding of the nuances and subtleties of government. When a group of young legislators revolted against the Assembly leadership in 1935, they chose Ives as speaker. After a year he stepped down to become majority leader, a position he held for the rest of his tenure in Albany. Through his progressive leadership Ives did much to move the New York Republican party beyond the rigid dogma of Old Guard conservatism.

As chairman of the Joint Legislative Committee on Industrial and Labor Conditions, Ives rewrote New York's labor-relations act and pushed through such measures as increased unemployment benefits, improved workmen's compensation, and an amendment that established the Department of Commerce. His chief accomplishment, however, was drafting and sponsoring a 1945 law prohibiting racial, religious, or ethnic discrimination in employment. Described by *Business Week* as "the nation's first State economic equality law," it became a model for fair-employment laws in other states.

Bitter over Governor Thomas E. Dewey's refusal to support him for the Republican nomination for the U.S. Senate in 1944, Ives left the Assembly a year later and became dean of the New York State School of Industrial and Labor Relations at Cornell University. But at the urging of Republican legislative leaders, Dewey slated Ives for the Senate in 1946. In what was considered an upset, Ives soundly defeated former Governor Herbert Lehman in the election.

Ives's first wife died in 1947. On July 12, 1948, he married Marion Mead Crain, who had been his secretary. In the Senate Ives stood with Republican liberals on most issues. After leading the coalition that defeated Robert A. Taft's 1947 amendment to restrict industrywide collective bargaining, Ives voted for the final version of the Taft-Hartley Labor Act, noting that Taft had made substantial revisions. He generally backed President Harry Truman's foreign policy, including the Marshall Plan and Truman Doctrine, but in 1950 he introduced a resolution calling for the dismissal of Secretary of State Dean Acheson on the grounds of his Far

Eastern policies. Following the 1949 Communist triumph in China, Ives contended that Acheson had lost the confidence of the American public.

Ives deplored the red-baiting methods of Senator Joseph R. McCarthy, and in June 1950 he joined seven Republican colleagues in signing a "Declaration of Conscience" against what would become known as McCarthyism. In December 1954 he voted for McCarthy's censure.

One of the first senators to endorse Dwight D. Eisenhower for the presidency in 1952, Ives advised him on labor issues during the campaign. In 1953 he took a prominent part in shaping the administration's labor policy. Yet he expressed frustration that Eisenhower was giving short shrift to liberal Republicans. In December 1953, Ives wrote: ". . . there has been too great a tendency to appease and placate the reactionaries and isolationists in our party." On social welfare issues, especially public housing and civil rights, he felt the administration did not go far enough. Nevertheless, he was a staunch supporter of Eisenhower's foreign, economic, and fiscal policies.

Ives won reelection to the Senate in 1952 by a record plurality of 1.3 million votes. Two years later, Averell Harriman defeated him for the governorship by slightly more than 11,000 votes in one of the closest races in New York's history. Returning to the Senate, Ives helped establish the Senate Select Committee on Improper Activities in the Labor or Management Field. The committee was headed by John L. McClellan with Ives as vice-chairman and Robert F. Kennedy as counsel. Ives and John F. Kennedy were cosponsors of a 1958 labor reform bill that would have required union officials to guarantee regular elections with secret ballots and to file financial reports with the Department of Labor. Endorsed by the AFL-CIO, the bill passed the Senate but was defeated in the House. A second Kennedy-Ives bill, which required public disclosure of pension and welfare funds, was enacted into law.

Because of ill health Ives reluctantly declined to seek a third term in 1958. Following his retirement he lived in Norwich, N.Y., where he died. He was a man of considerable wit and intelligence. A hard worker who kept himself well-informed on a range of issues, Ives was especially skillful in committee and caucus work. Although a lackluster speaker, he came to be effective in floor debate through careful preparation and homespun charm.

In describing his political philosophy, Ives once observed that he sought "to improve the world—not reform it." Although he sponsored progressive legislation, there were definite limits to his liberalism. On his election to the Senate, Ives was regarded as a potential party leader. But he proved to be too liberal for the mostly conservative Senate Republicans and never achieved power and prominence.

[Ives's papers are at Cornell University. The Thomas E. Dewey papers at the University of Rochester and the Herbert Lehman Oral History Project at Columbia University also contain useful materials. The *New York Times* and *Chicago Tribune* libraries have extensive files of clippings about Ives. See also Warren Moscow, *Politics in the Empire State* (1948); Allan Nevins, *Herbert H. Lehman and His Era* (1963); Gary W. Reichard, *The Reaffirmation of Republicanism* (1975); and Arthur M. Schlesinger, Jr., *Robert F. Kennedy and His Times* (1978). The *New York Times* obituary appeared on Feb. 25, 1962.]

STEVE NEAL

JACKSON, CHARLES DOUGLAS (Mar. 16, 1902–Sept. 18, 1964), journalist and diplomat, was born in New York City, the son of Carl David Jackson, a marble importer, and Eda F. Strauss. Part of his elementary schooling was in Switzerland. After attending the Hill School in Pottstown, Pa. (1915–1920), he entered Princeton University, where he majored in French and literature, and rowed on the crew. Jackson graduated with the B.A. in 1924. His father's death in that year kept him from carrying out his intention to teach French. He took over the family business, which failed during the Great Depression.

In 1931, Jackson offered his talent and enthusiasm to Henry R. Luce, head of the fledgling news weekly *Time*. Granting that he had no experience in journalism, he believed that he could be "a worthwhile assistant" to Luce, who was impressed enough to hire him. Jackson was connected with the Luce publishing organization for the rest of his life. Soon after the start of *Life* in late 1936, Jackson was named its general manager (1937). His exuberant personality and his skill at development and promotion brought him election to the vice-presidency of Time, Inc., in 1940. Five years later, after service in World War II, Jackson was made managing director of Time-Life International, in charge of all the company's news collection and publishing activities outside the continental United States.

In 1949, Jackson was named publisher of *Fortune*. From vice-president in charge of general management in 1954, he moved in 1959 to the office of administrative vice-president, from which he supervised the varied publishing efforts of Time-Life International, *Fortune,* and two new magazines, *Architectural Forum* and *House and Home.* His last official post was publisher of *Life,* which he held from 1960 until his death.

Jackson's many posts in the Luce empire reflected his frequent leaves of absence to devote himself to public service. His staff set up the "Fun and Games Committee of the C. D. Jackson Hello and Goodbye Society" to send him off and welcome him back. He organized the Council for Democracy (1940), to counter isolationist opinion, and then went on a special mission to Turkey for the State Department and the Bureau of Economic Warfare (1942). Holding the position of special assistant American ambassador, his purpose was to retain access to Turkish chrome, although the American contract with the Turkish government had expired and German agents had moved in. Jackson was remarkably resourceful in offsetting the Nazis' efforts to monopolize the greatly needed chrome.

Jackson had barely completed his Turkish assignment when, in 1943, he went to Allied headquarters for North Africa, Sicily, and Italy, for the Office of War Information. As deputy chief of the Psychological Warfare Branch, he was associated with Brigadier General Robert A. McClure, intelligence officer on the staff of Lieutenant General Dwight D. Eisenhower. McClure took Jackson with him to London early in 1944, to help organize the Psychological Warfare Division (PWD) of Supreme Headquarters Allied Expeditionary Force, preparatory to the invasion of France.

The PWD planned and executed propaganda and related activities during combat and devised de-Nazified information control programs to be used in the Allied zones in Germany after the conclusion of hostilities. This meant the preparation and distribution of leaflets to influence enemy troops and civilians, the broadcasting of appeals and announcements, and cooperation with the French underground. It also required the training of units equipped to take charge of a militarily licensed "clean" press, theater, music, and films. For his contributions Jackson was presented with the France's Legion of Honor.

Jackson returned to Time, Inc., in 1945. Six years later he became president of the National Committee for a Free Europe and again went to Europe, to establish radio broadcasting to Czechoslovakia and other Iron Curtain countries.

As a consequence of their wartime contacts, Jackson became an influential adviser in Eisenhower's 1952 campaign for the presidency, writing speeches and recommending strategies. Eisenhower credited Jackson with proposing that, as Republican nominee, he pledge to the public, "I will go to Korea." Jackson was special assistant to the president in 1953–1954 and accompanied him to the Bermuda three-power and Berlin four-power conferences. He had a major part in the preparation of Eisenhower's "Atoms for Peace" address to the United Nations (UN) in 1953, and later he prepared White House notes for Soviet Premier Nikita Khrushchev's visit. Even after returning to *Time,* he was a member of the American delegation to the UN in 1954. He was also an organizer of the International Executive Service Corps, which sought to show businessmen that both international affairs and trade held opportunities for them if they informed themselves on international policies and activities. Jackson's managerial duties left little time for writing, but he did prepare articles occasionally on his overseas trips: an example is "Bold Outpost Off China (Quemoy)," which appeared in *Life,* Nov. 2, 1962.

Jackson was also involved in civic, social, educational, and musical causes and organizations. He served on the boards of the Metropolitan Opera Association, the Lincoln Center for the Performing Arts, the Boston Symphony, the Carnegie Corporation of New York, the United Negro College Fund, and Project Hope.

Tall, handsome, buoyant, and devoted to precise use of words to reflect clear thinking, Jackson relished life and shared his enjoyment with those around him. He took flying lessons and earned a private pilot's license. He and his wife, Grace Bristed, whom he had married on Sept. 12, 1931, often entertained their guests by playing piano duets.

Jackson died in New York City. "C. D." was well described as "an amalgam of two continents, bringing together Old World grace and New World enthusiasm." Yet he could be blunt and even hard, as when he unsuccessfully urged Eisenhower to confront directly Senator Joseph R. McCarthy and his unsupported charges against government employees.

[Jackson's papers are in the Eisenhower Library, Abilene, Kans. Materials from Luce publications are in the Time, Inc., archives. Information on Jackson may be found in the Seeley G. Mudd Manuscript Collection, Princeton University. See Robert T. Elson, *Time, Inc.: The Intimate History of a Publishing Enterprise, 1923–1941,* I (1968), and *The World* of *Time Inc., 1941–1960,* II (1971). Also see Harry C. Butcher, *My Three Years with Eisenhower* (1946); Irving Dilliard, *The Development of a Free Press in Germany* (1949); Daniel Lerner, *Psychological Warfare Against Nazi Germany* (1949); Michael Balfour, *Propaganda in War* (1979); William S. Paley, *As It Happened* (1979); and Allen Yarnell, "Eisenhower and McCarthy," *Presidential Studies Quarterly,* Winter 1980. An obituary is in the *New York Times,* Sept. 20, 1964.]

IRVING DILLIARD

JACKSON, SHIRLEY HARDIE (Dec. 14, 1919–Aug. 8, 1965), novelist and short-story writer, was born in San Francisco, Calif., the daughter of Leslie Hardie Jackson, a lithographer, and of Geraldine Maxwell Bugbee. During her early years the Jacksons were moderately well-to-do. The family moved to Burlingame, a suburb of San Francisco, in 1923, and to Rochester, N.Y., in 1933. Jackson graduated from Brighton High School in 1934, then enrolled at the University of Rochester. A tendency to pudginess and a consequent anxiety about being personally unattractive had troubled her since childhood and provided a psychological basis for her feeling that she was an outsider. In 1936 Jackson withdrew from the university and spent the next year at home, in an autodidactic literary apprenticeship. During this period, and in her subsequent three years at Syracuse University, from which she received the B.A. in 1940, she became a meticulous and disciplined writer.

On June 3, 1940, Jackson married a classmate, Stanley Edgar Hyman, who became a noted literary critic. They had four children. The couple moved to New York City in 1940, when Stanley Hyman accepted a position as an editorial assistant on the *New Republic.* In 1945, when he was appointed to the Bennington College faculty, they moved to North Bennington, Vt.

Jackson was treated by a psychiatrist for some years to counteract symptoms of social withdrawal. She suffered from a sense of personal isolation, insecurities about the affection and loyalty of friends, and recurrent anxiety and depression. In her work she consistently identified with the underdog, and attacked racial and ethnic prejudice as well as the smug, gratuitous cruelty of the insiders in any group toward outsiders. For example, her first major publication, "After You, My Dear Alphonse" (*New Yorker,* Jan. 16, 1943), was a short story describing the inability of a middle-aged white liberal to overcome her stereotypical ideas about Afro-American culture. Her first novel, *The Road Through*

the *Wall* (1948), was a tale about a closed society that displayed anti-Semitic attitudes and class prejudice.

The story that made Jackson's reputation, "The Lottery" (*New Yorker,* June 26, 1948), illustrates the same concerns in its depiction of the cruelty and brutality of humanity in the mass and the insensitivity of individuals to the sufferings of society's victims. It is a stark, cold tale depicting a timeless community in which a scapegoat is annually selected by lot from the entire population of the village as a human sacrifice to insure an abundant corn crop. The story aroused a storm of protest and indignation from readers who could not grasp its meaning or considered it morally perverse. Critical reaction, though, was unequivocal. "The Lottery" rapidly became a standard selection for anthologies, a model of the technique of the short story. It was adapted for television in 1952, made into a ballet, and rendered in dramatic form in 1953. Jackson was most gratified by the reaction of the South African government, which banned the story, thus exhibiting a clear understanding of the author's intention.

Jackson was a master of the understated psychological horror tale, but at the same time she was a comedic genius who wryly depicted the humorous aspects of everyday family life. The bulk of her comic work is anecdotal. It appeared originally as sketches and short stories in popular magazines—*Good Housekeeping, Woman's Day, Collier's*—and was subsequently collected in *Life Among the Savages* (1953) and *Raising Demons* (1957). She considered this part of her work secondary, but it sold well and provided the financial security that allowed her to pursue more serious writing.

This division of Jackson's work is somewhat artificial. It obscures the similarities between the genres of comedy and suspense-terror. Irony, peripeteia, the element of surprise, the importance of emotional atmosphere and mood, the controlled rhythm of the tale, and the precise timing of episode are common to both. They are central to Jackson's fictional technique and provide the structural and tonal unity of her work.

Thematically, the major focus of Jackson's work stresses the psychological dimension of experience (especially the disintegration of personality and psychic alienation) and the stark isolation of the individual. Her major strengths lie in her extraordinary gift for storytelling, her masterly ability to evoke mood and to dissect character almost clinically. Her style is taut and spare, her descriptions matter-of-fact, and her prose seldom metaphorical. Since much of her work has a psychological dimension, it contains few descriptions of overt action. Setting is of relatively minor importance; it is the interior landscape of the mind that is all-important.

The people in Jackson's fictional world are often emotionally frigid; they find it difficult (and potentially dangerous) to relate to others. They appear unfeeling: they have no love affairs, no religious feelings. Indeed, with the exception of a cold-blooded hatred and malevolence, the characters seem to experience no passion at all. They are coldly cerebral, psychologically self-absorbed.

The most notable of Jackson's characters are, almost without exception, women. The best of them are sensitive, self-aware, and strong, which distinguishes them from the cold insensitivity of most of her characters and more particularly from her male characters, who are weak, ineffectual, and fatuous. There is a powerful feminist tendency in her fiction that most critics have overlooked. Certainly a feminist perspective informs the stories that deal with the frustrated ambitions of "career girls" and the loneliness of single, independent-minded women (such as Elizabeth Style in "Elizabeth" [1949]). In the unfinished novel "Come Along with Me" (1965), Jackson seemed to be moving further in the direction of a feminist fiction. The book deals with a middle-aged woman who feels confined and ill-defined by her marriage; more than anything she is starved for experience. When her husband dies, she begins life anew, moving to another city, inventing a new name for herself, and even trying her hand at shoplifting.

Both critical and popular reactions to Jackson's work were largely positive. Although she declined all offers to teach full time, she was regularly involved with the Marlboro and Cummington fiction conferences and the Breadloaf Writers' Conference. Her stories were frequently anthologized, and four were selected as among the best American short stories of the year ("Summer People," 1951; "One Ordinary Day with Peanuts," 1955; "Birthday Party," 1964; "The Bus," 1966). Her popular appeal is attested to by the fact that two of her short stories and two of her novels were dramatized. Two films were made from her novels: *Lizzie* (1957), based on *The Bird's Nest* (1954), and *The Haunting* (1963), an adaptation of *The Haunting of Hill House* (1959).

While Jackson's popularity with a mass audience rests primarily upon her comic domestic chronicles and the superficial suspense of her more serious fiction, her critical reputation is based on her depiction of the darker side of the human soul and her probing psychological portraits of loneliness, emotional disaffection, and chronic dissociation. She held out no false hope for humanity. In *The Sundial* (1958), as a select group of people withdraws to the stately mansion they believe is to shelter them from the holocaust that will usher in a new world, one of them says: "You all want the whole world to be changed so you will be different. But I don't suppose people get changed any by just a new world. And anyway that world isn't any more real than this one."

In the face of that world of appearance and form, where malevolence seems to be the only vital force, Jackson suggests that humanity must continue to try to define its own reality, to find out who the individual is even if one cannot know why, and to strive to survive with dignity. Her vision is a fitting one for an age marked by genocide, nuclear proliferation, chronic alienation, and universal paranoia. It is the vision of a moralist, a critic of insensitivity and cruelty. And, in the long run, it is upon this universal ethical concern that her literary stature will rest.

Jackson died of heart failure at North Bennington, Vt.

[Jackson's papers, along with her watercolors and pencil and ink drawings, are at the Library of Congress. In addition to the novels mentioned in the text, she published *Hangsaman* (1951) and *We Have Always Lived in the Castle* (1962). Her short stories were collected in *The Lottery* (1949); Stanley Edgar Hyman, ed., *The Magic of Shirley Jackson*, (1966); and Stanley Edgar Hyman, ed., *Come Along with Me* (1968). A critical analysis is Lenemaja Friedman, *Shirley Jackson* (1975). Bibliographic works are Robert S. Phillips, "Shirley Jackson: A Checklist," *Bibliographic Society of America Papers*, Jan. 1962, and "Shirley Jackson: A Chronology and a Supplementary Checklist," *Bibliographic Society of America Papers*, Apr. 1966. Also see Harvey Breit, "Talk with Miss Jackson," *New York Times*, June 26, 1949; and Stanley Edgar Hyman, "Shirley Jackson, 1919–1965," *Saturday Evening Post*, Dec. 18, 1965. Obituaries appeared in the *New York Times*, Aug. 10, 1965; *Newsweek*, Aug. 23, 1965; and *Publishers Weekly*, Aug. 23, 1965.]

Louis J. Kern

JACKSON, WILLIAM ALEXANDER (July 25, 1905–Oct. 18, 1964), bibliographer and librarian, was born in Bellows Falls, Vt., the son of Charles Wilfred Jackson, a Baptist clergyman, and of Alice Mary Fleming. He grew up in Pasadena, Calif., and graduated from South Pasadena High School in 1922. His next-door neighbor was Dr. George Watson Cole, the first head of the Huntington Library, who was then engaged in organizing and cataloging the library's collection preparatory to its opening. Cole introduced him to the Huntington collection and aided the first steps in his bibliographical education. From then on, Jackson's vocation was clear and unswerving, and his natural ability quickly impressed seasoned professionals in the field of rare books.

Cole advised Jackson to attend Williams College, where Alfred Clark Chapin had just placed his choice collection of some 12,000 volumes, mainly in English literature. Jackson entered Williams in 1923 and soon was working up to eight hours a day in the Chapin Library, assisting its librarian, Lucy Eugenia Osborne, an important influence on him. He was thus able to earn his way through college while engaging in what was, for him, the most congenial of occupations.

By the end of his freshman year, Jackson had devised a style and plan for the bibliographical catalog of the Chapin collection. He worked on it intensively through the summer of 1925. In 1926 his parents helped finance his first trip to Europe so that he could check his work against libraries there. Aboard ship he met his future wife, Dorothy Judd. In the same year A. W. Polland and G. R. Redgrave published *A Short-Title Catalogue of Books Printed in England . . . 1475–1640,* the key to the books Jackson loved most and the bibliographical tool he was to spend the rest of his life revising and enlarging. He immediately began annotating his own interleaved copy of the *S.T.C.,* as it is familiarly known.

Jackson's work on the Chapin catalog continued after his graduation from Williams in 1927. By November 1928 he had described the approximately 1,500 early English books in the collection, and specimen pages had been set in type. On Aug. 28, 1929, Jackson married Dorothy Judd; they had one son. The couple first settled in Altadena, Calif., where Jackson did more work at the Huntington Library, then moved to New Haven, Conn.

In 1930 financial difficulties caused Chapin to cancel further work on his catalog. It was never published. Jackson gave up his pursuit of a Ph.D. at Yale, which was prepared to accept the catalog as his dissertation. He went to work for Carl H. Pforzheimer, Sr., in New York City, preparing a bibliographical catalog of Pforzheimer's magnificent library of English literature. Seven years of concentrated work, one of them in England, brought the Pforz-

heimer catalog to page proofs. It was not published until 1940, but long before then its scholarship, which Jackson made freely available, had established his reputation as the leading bibliographer of his generation on both sides of the Atlantic.

In 1937 Keyes DeWitt Metcalf, director of the Harvard University Library, recruited Jackson as assistant college librarian and associate professor of bibliography. His responsibilities were to enlist support for the development of the research collections of the library, to teach, and to assist and encourage faculty use of the library. He succeeded brilliantly. Within three years plans were being drawn for the Houghton Library, the first modern building in the United States scientifically designed for the proper housing of rare books and manuscripts. Jackson pioneered in the collecting of American literary archives while pursuing other primary research materials, written and printed, with vigor and success. Use of the collection increased, and the courses he developed attracted many promising students.

Meantime, Jackson's own scholarship did not flag. In 1957 he published his edition of *Records of the Court of the Stationers' Company, 1602–1640.* Amid a spate of articles on all phases of books and bibliography, he continued his revision of the *S.T.C.* Unfortunately he did not live to see its completion. The first portion of it to be printed did not appear until 1976, completed by his last assistant, Katharine F. Pantzer. Like the Pforzheimer catalog, it has a place among the standard works of bibliography.

Tall, handsome, and assured, Jackson made a deep and lasting impression upon colleagues and acquaintances. His work as librarian and in the many professional societies to which he belonged was a major force in shaping collection development and bibliographical research in England and America in the twentieth century. Jackson died in Cambridge, Mass.

[The fullest account of Jackson's life and career is in the introduction to W. H. Bond, ed., *Records of a Bibliographer: Selected Papers of William Alexander Jackson* (1967), together with a checklist of his published works. An account of his personal reference collection is in James E. Walsh, "The Librarian's Library," *Book Collector,* Winter 1965, and Spring 1966.]

W. H. Bond

JAEGER, WERNER WILHELM (July 30, 1888–Oct. 19, 1961), classicist, was born at Lobberich, Niederrhein, Prussia, the son of Karl August Jaeger, a businessman, and Helene

Birschel. The family was Lutheran. At the age of eight he began Latin; at thirteen, Greek at the local Catholic gymnasium (now the Werner Jaeger Gymnasium). While still a schoolboy he was attracted to "a history of the Greek mind," his interest in ideas disciplined by a rigorous historical conscience.

After a summer semester at Marburg (1907), Jaeger transferred to the Friedrich-Wilhelms University in Berlin (1907–1911), where he studied under Hermann Diels, Adolf Lasson, Eduard Norden, Johannes Vahlen, and Ulrich von Wilamowitz-Moellendorff. The last won him for classical philology. His Berlin dissertation was *Studien zur Entstehungsgeschichte der Metaphysik des Aristoteles* (1912). Jaeger argued that the *Metaphysics* was not a systematic book but a collection of lectures. From this grew *Aristoteles, Grundlegung einer Geschichte seiner Entwicklung* (1923; in English, *Aristotle: Fundamentals of the History of His Development*, [1934]), which perceived Aristotle's intellectual development as a gradual distancing from his teacher and colleague Plato. Jaeger's *Habilitationsschrift, Nemesios von Emesa,* studies in Neoplatonism and Posidonius, appeared in 1914.

On Mar. 28, 1914, he married Theodora Dammholz; they had three children. Later that year Jaeger assumed the chair of classical philology at the University of Basel, once held by Friedrich Nietzsche. The next year he went to Christian-Albrechts University in Kiel, where he became a colleague of Eduard Fraenkel, Felix Jacoby, and Julius Stenzel. At the suggestion of Wilamowitz, Jaeger began his most enduring work, the critical edition of Gregory of Nyssa; the first two volumes appeared in 1921.

The most important event in Jaeger's career occurred on Mar. 12, 1921, when he was invited to succeed Wilamowitz at Berlin. Ability, diplomacy, and unexpected luck (he was fourth on the list) won him this position. His period of greatest influence coincided with his tenure of the chair (1921–1936). Among his students were Viktor Pöschl, Wolfgang Schadewaldt, and Friedrich Solmsen.

Alarmed at the decline of Greek and Latin, Jaeger fought to restore classical humanism to the center of German intellectual life. This struggle became known as the Third Humanism. As part of the effort, in 1925 he founded two journals, *Die Antike,* which he edited until 1936, and *Gnomon,* which was edited by his student Richard Harder. In the former, directed at the educated laity, Jaeger and his followers argued that many Greek ideals had an impor-

tant bearing on modern life. He also founded Neue Philologische Untersuchungen (1926–1937), a monograph series in which his better students published their dissertations.

The great document of the Third Humanism remains Jaeger's *Paideia,* a history of the Greek mind from Homer through Plato. The first volume appeared in Berlin in 1934. In a courageous review Bruno Snell drew attention to *Paideia*'s dangers: emphasis on heroism, victory, elitism, the passionate rhetoric, and the implicit exhortation to imitate the Greeks could be twisted by romanticism and rabid nationalism. In fact, some of Jaeger's outstanding students became supporters, if not ideologists, of National Socialism. Jaeger of course was no more responsible for this than Socrates was for Alcibiades, Critias, and Plato.

After a divorce from his first wife, Jaeger married Ruth Heinitz, a Jew, on Dec. 29, 1931. They had one daughter. With the rise of National Socialism the Jaegers left Germany. In 1934 Jaeger became Sather Professor at the University of California at Berkeley. There he delivered lectures that were published as *Demosthenes: The Origin and Growth of His Policy* (1938). In 1936, Jaeger moved to the University of Chicago, to fill the chair of Paul Shorey, and in 1939 to Harvard. In 1943, he became a naturalized citizen. He retired in 1960.

Jaeger wrote sadly in 1960 that to learn what classical scholarship was like in a culture where classical humanism did not exist, one must visit America. Classics were not an intellectual force in the United States, and American students could not compare with his German ones. Most colleagues seemed to Jaeger well-intentioned dilettantes.

While in the United States, Jaeger produced three volumes of *Paideia,* translated into English by Gilbert Highet (1939–1944), *The Theology of the Early Greek Philosophers* (1947), the Oxford edition of Aristotle's *Metaphysics* (1957), *Scripta Minora* (1960), and *Early Christianity and Greek Paideia* (1961). There was also steady publication of volumes of Gregory of Nyssa by Jaeger and his associates.

During Jaeger's lifetime *Paideia* was thought to be his great achievement. But his abstract, almost homiletic, approach now seems dated. The volumes are rarely read by scholars today. Contrarily, his work on Aristotle, although challenged (especially by Hans von Arnim and H. F. Cherniss), changed all subsequent historical study of the philosopher. The undertaking least known to classicists, the edition of Gregory of Nyssa, because of its exactitude, objectivity, and scope, remains standard and exemplary.

Jaeger's American students found him a serene, gentle sage, withdrawn from the arena, with a twinkle in his eye and ever encouraging the deserving. They never imagined the brilliant zealot and organizer who had dominated German classics of the 1920's. Jaeger died in Boston.

[Jaeger's papers are at the Houghton Library, Harvard University; his personal library is at the Center for Hellenic Studies, Washington, D.C. Valuable biographical material is in Jaeger, *Five Essays,* translated by Adele M. Fiske, R.S.C.J. (1966). The only adequate, though selective, biography is Wolfgang Schadewaldt, *Gedenkrede auf Werner Jaeger 1888–1961* (1963), repub. in Schadewaldt's *Hellas und Hesperien,* second ed. (1970). Obituaries appeared in *New York Times,* Oct. 20, 1961, and in *Gnomon* (1962). See also William M. Calder III, "The Correspondence of Ulrich von Wilamowitz-Moellendorff with Werner Jaeger," *Harvard Studies in Classical Philology* (1978); Volker Losemann, "Nationalsozialismus und Antike," *Historische Perspektiven* (1977); and Bruno Snell, *Gesammelte Schriften* (1966), pp. 32–54.]

WILLIAM M. CALDER III

JANNEY, RUSSELL DIXON (Apr. 14, 1885–July 14, 1963), author and theatrical producer, was born in Wilmington, Ohio, the son of Reynold Janney, a high school teacher, and of Ella Dixon. Shortly after his birth the family moved to Chillicothe, Ohio, where his father was high school principal. In 1894 they settled in Keene, N. H., where the elder Janney opened a bicycle manufacturing business. Janney attended school in Keene, saw a number of professional touring companies—Keene was a popular stopover between Boston and Montreal—and began writing song lyrics and short sketches as preparation for a theatrical career.

Janney continued his writing "hobby" at Yale, and by the time of his graduation in 1906 he had written and produced several plays for his college fraternity. After graduation Janney apparently married Edith Cramer, a musical comedy actress; they were subsequently divorced. (There is little information about her or the marriage.) Their son, William Janney, became a successful radio and motion picture actor.

In 1907 Janney went to London, where he sought to establish himself as a theatrical press agent and free-lance writer. He studied commercial play production with George Edwardes and wrote publicity features for the producer Sir Herbert Beerbohm Tree.

After returning to the United States in 1910, Janney gained further experience by managing stock companies in Milwaukee and Indianapolis in association with Stuart Walker. He also published short stories in *Smart Set* and wrote sketches for the *Ziegfeld Follies.* In 1916 Janney and Walker presented a series of plays in New York City under the name of the Portmanteau Theater, but after a road tour Janney was forced back into publicity to recover his losses.

In 1918 Janney and Walker produced a successful adaptation of Booth Tarkington's *Seventeen* in New York City. Three productions followed—*June Love* (1921), *Marjolaine* (1922), and *Sancho Panza* (1923)—but it was not until 1925 that Janney emerged as a significant producer with the success of *The Vagabond King,* which was based on Justin Huntly McCarthy's play about the dashing French poet François Villon.

The Vagabond King was written by Janney and Brian Hooker, with music by Rudolf Friml. It became one of the biggest musical hits of the decade. By 1928 it had been produced in England and Australia and had grossed over $4 million. Janney's original New York production ran for 511 performances.

The success of *The Vagabond King* enabled Janney to divide his time between producing and writing. He backed *Ballyhoo* (1927), *White Eagle* (1927), and *The O'Flynn* (1934). After the death of his longtime friend and business associate, Olga Treskoff, he began working on a novel about his experiences as a press agent and advance man. The result was *Miracle of the Bells* (1946), a sentimental and hopelessly romantic account of the funeral of a beautiful young actress (Olga Treskovna). *Time* called it "one of the worst" novels ever written, but it became a best seller. By 1950 it had sold 700,000 copies and generated, according to Janney, 10,000 letters to the author. As a result of the publicity surrounding *Miracle of the Bells,* Janney undertook a nationwide speaking tour in 1946 sponsored by the National Conference of Christians and Jews. He lectured on brotherhood and racial and religious tolerance (popular themes in the novel) in thirty-five American cities.

Some of his statements came back to haunt Janney when he was selected as the final juror in the 1949 trial of eleven Communist leaders in New York City. Determined to challenge the legality of the Smith Act (1940) and the jury selection process, lawyers for Gus Hall, Benjamin Davis, and other defendants prolonged this trial for 169 days. In the emotional and often

389

chaotic atmosphere, prosecution witness former Communist Herbert Philbrick emerged as a national celebrity (his testimony became the basis for the popular television series *I Led Three Lives*). Meanwhile, Janney was repeatedly denounced in the press for earlier speeches in which he had condemned Communism for breeding intolerance. Despite the controversy Judge Harold Medina refused to remove Janney from the jury, which ultimately convicted the defendants of conspiring to advocate the violent overthrow of the United States government.

Always a private person, Janney was stung by the publicity. His verse drama, *The Vision of Red O'Shea* (1949), was not well received, nor was his second novel, *So Long as Love Remembers* (1953). But he retained his sense of humor and lived his last years comfortably, in seclusion with his cats. He died in New York City, remembered more for a single novel than for the numerous theatrical ventures that had been his lifework.

[There is little published information about Janney. See Murray Schumach, "Francois Villon's Alter Ego," *New York Times*, July 18, 1943; and the *New Yorker*, Apr. 30, 1949. An obituary is in the *New York Times*, July 15, 1963.]

BARRY B. WITHAM

JARRELL, RANDALL (May 6, 1914–Oct. 14, 1965), writer and teacher, was born in Nashville, Tenn., the son of Owen Jarrell and Anna Campbell. The family moved in late 1914 to Long Beach, Calif., where his father worked as a photographer's assistant. The divorce of his parents left him in Hollywood for a time, in the care of his paternal grandparents and great-grandmother. They appear in his poem "The Lost World" (1963) as Mama, Pop, and Dandeen, and an aura of myth and make-believe dating from this stay colors his ensuing vision. The poems "In Those Days," "The Elementary Scene," and "Windows," from *The Woman at the Washington Zoo* (1960), describe his reluctant return to Nashville in late 1926 and his attendance at Tarbox Elementary School and Hume-Fogg High School (1928–1931).

Jarrell took a series of part-time jobs, the most significant of which was posing for the Ganymede of the Nashville Parthenon. His free time was spent mainly in the library, at the backboards of tennis courts, or writing alone in his room. In 1935 he graduated from Vanderbilt University with a B.S. degree, having concentrated in psychology and English. Four years later Jarrell received an M.A. from Vanderbilt.

His thesis was "Implicit Generalization in [A.E.] Housman." Already he had received a poetry prize from the *Southern Review* (1936) and had begun teaching at Kenyon College (1937–1939), where John Crowe Ransom was one of his colleagues and where the poet Robert Lowell and the fiction writer Peter Taylor were among his students.

Jarrell moved in 1939 to the University of Texas, where he taught English. On June 1, 1940, he married Mackie Langham; they had no children. He subsequently left the university to serve in the U.S. Army Air Force (1942–1946). During these years he contributed to *Five Young American Poets* (1940) and published two volumes of poetry, *Blood for a Stranger* (1942) and *Little Friend, Little Friend* (1945). The prewar poems are characterized by the sense of loneliness, inadvertent pain, and malingering guilt that combine and deepen with his military experiences into pathos and the horror of war.

Jarrell also began at this time to publish critical essays and reviews that helped turn American poetry from abstract issues to the concrete legacies of Darwin, Freud, and Marx. He felt that these issues needed to be faced, though, not necessarily accepted. (Jarrell made much of the coincidence that he and Freud were born on the same day of the same month, though Freud was born in 1856. Art became "the union of a wish and a truth" or "a wish modified by a truth." Work as acting literary editor of the *Nation* and a teaching post at Sarah Lawrence College (1946–1947) followed his release from service. His time at Sarah Lawrence afforded Jarrell many of the experiences described brilliantly in his only novel, *Pictures from an Institution* (1954).

In 1946 Jarrell received a Guggenheim fellowship and the John Peale Bishop Memorial Prize for his poem "The Märchen." The following year he accepted a teaching post at the Woman's College of the University of North Carolina (later the University of North Carolina at Greensboro), which he held until his death. He took leaves of absence to teach at Princeton University (1951–1952) and the University of Illinois at Urbana (1953), and to serve as consultant in poetry to the Library of Congress (1956–1958) and Phi Beta Kappa visiting scholar (1964–1965). Jarrell also taught at the Salzburg Seminar in American Civilization during the summer of 1948 and the Indiana School of Letters (1952), and he served as Elliston lecturer at the University of Cincinnati (1958–1965).

Losses (1948) consolidated Jarrell's gains as a

war poet. It was followed by *The Seven-League Crutches* (1951) and a collection of critical essays, *Poetry and the Age* (1953), which established his reputation as a critic. On Nov. 8, 1952, eight days after his divorce from Mackie, he married Mary Eloise von Schrader; they had no children. His *Selected Poems* (1955) increased Jarrell's reputation as a poet of childhood, war, and literature, and *The Woman at the Washington Zoo* earned him a National Book Award (1961). A second book of essays, *A Sad Heart at the Supermarket* (1962), and a last collection of poems, *The Lost World* (1965), followed.

Jarrell served as poetry critic for the *Partisan Review* (1949–1951) and the *Yale Review* (1955–1957), and was a member of the editorial board of the *American Scholar* (1957–1965). He published children's books—*The Gingerbread Rabbit* (1963), *The Bat Poet* (1964), *The Animal Family* (1965)—and translations—*The Golden Bird and Other Fairy Tales of the Brothers Grimm* (1962), *The Rabbit Catcher and Other Fairy Tales of Ludwig Bechstein* (1962), and Anton Chekhov's *The Three Sisters* (produced in 1964; published in 1969). Posthumous works include *The Complete Poems* (1969) and *The Third Book of Criticism* (1969); a children's tale, *Fly by Night* (1976); and translations of *Snow White and the Seven Dwarfs* (1972), *The Juniper Tree and Other Tales from Grimm* (1973), and Goethe's *Faust, Part I* (1976).

Jarrell was struck and killed by an automobile in Chapel Hill, N.C., several months after recovering from a nervous breakdown. His death was thought at first to be a suicide, but was later ruled accidental.

[The Berg Collection at the New York Public Library, the Walter Clinton Jackson Library of the University of North Carolina at Greensboro, and the Beinecke Rare Book and Manuscript Library at Yale University are the major repositories of Jarrell's manuscripts and letters. No authorized biography has yet appeared. On his poetry see Suzanne Ferguson, *The Poetry of Randall Jarrell* (1971); M. L. Rosenthal, *Randall Jarrell* (1972); Helen Hagenbüchle, *The Black Goddess* (1975). Also see Charles M. Adams, comp., *Randall Jarrell: A Bibliography* (1958), supplemented in *Analects*, Spring 1961; and Robert Lowell, Peter Taylor, and Robert Penn Warren, eds., *Randall Jarrell: 1914–1965*, (1967). An obituary is in the *New York Times*, Oct. 15, 1965.]

JEROME MAZZARO

JEFFERS, JOHN ROBINSON (Jan. 10, 1887–Jan. 20, 1962), poet, was born in Pittsburgh, Pa., the son of the Reverend Dr. William Hamilton Jeffers and Annie Robinson Tuttle. The Reverend Dr. Jeffers was a Presbyterian minister who, at the time of his son's birth, held the chair of Old Testament Literature and Exegesis at Western Theological Seminary.

Jeffers received his first training in languages, principally Latin, from his father, who rewarded each accomplishment with a heavier work load. Soon, however, the youth was attending private schools in Europe and in America, changing schools frequently at his parents' whim. By the age of twelve, he had mastered Latin, could read Greek, and could speak French and German fluently.

Jeffers entered the University of Western Pennsylvania in 1902 but transferred to Occidental College when his family moved to California in 1903. He completed his B.A. at Occidental in 1905 and enrolled in the University of Southern California that fall to do graduate work in literature. After a year's study, he spent a summer with his family in Switzerland and took courses at the University of Zurich. Abandoning the formal study of literature, Jeffers enrolled in 1907 at the University of Southern California Medical School, remaining there through the summer of 1910. He then studied forestry at the University of Washington from the fall of 1910 through the following spring.

At the University of Southern California, Jeffers had met Una Lindsay Call Kuster, the wife of a prominent attorney. Their casual friendship grew into a love that both felt was unwise to pursue. Jeffers' move to Washington and his accompanying change of professional plans came, in part, from an effort to end the relationship. Neither this effort nor a trip Una took alone to Europe worked. She sought a divorce, and in August 1913 she and Jeffers were married. They had three children; a girl who died in infancy and twin boys.

Jeffers was already writing verse at the age of eleven. In college and graduate school he contributed regularly to student publications and wrote poems for Una and for other women. In 1912 he used part of a $9,500 legacy to publish his first book, *Flagons and Apples*. The poems were traditional in form and conception, as were those in the commercially published *Californians* (1916). Neither book occasioned any literary stir.

The issues involved in the entrance of the United States into World War I, the birth of the twins, and the construction of Tor House, the home he built on the rugged slopes outside Carmel, Calif., all affected Jeffers' poetic vision. His third book, *Tamar and Other Poems* (1924), contained work even the poet himself called "singular." Critics praised it in newspapers and magazines with national audiences. When the privately printed edition was exhausted, Boni and Liveright brought out *Roan Stallion, Tamar and Other Poems* (1925) to the accompaniment of critical predictions that Jeffers would be one of the greatest poets of the age.

In these long narratives and short, philosophical verses Jeffers revealed an unusual stance toward humanity. Man, he seemed to declare, is not the center of the universe. His philosophy, labeled inhumanism, has been seen as an extension of the ideas of Nietzsche and Spengler. Jeffers saw civilization toppling and the human race moving toward annihilation. The world, he maintained, would be better off if these things did happen.

Jeffers' *The Women at Point Sur* (1927) caused some critical retrenchment. The poem was long and, in spite of its violence, dull. *Cawdor and Other Poems* (1928) and *Dear Judas and Other Poems* (1929) were, however, highly praised, although orthodox Christians objected to *Dear Judas*'s presentation of Christ as a traitor who misled men into seeking love rather than annihilation. *Thurso's Landing and Other Poems* (1932) and *Give Your Heart to the Hawks and Other Poems* (1933) gave further boosts to Jeffers' poetic stature.

Subsequent volumes, *Solstice and Other Poems* (1935), *Such Counsels You Gave to Me* (1937), and *Be Angry at the Sun* (1941), lacked the verve and excitement of the earlier work. Jeffers became bored with his writing, and when he began to write about his boredom, his critical reputation faltered. His popular reputation remained strong, however. The publication of *The Selected Poetry of Robinson Jeffers* (1938) and a triumphal reading tour of eastern colleges and universities in 1941 attest to the fact.

Jeffers' reputation waned in the mid-1940's, as he continued to preach the wisdom of isolationism, which he had advocated in the 1930's. During World War II that idea lost its popular appeal; to many Americans it seemed almost treasonous. When *The Double Axe and Other Poems* (1948) was published, the United States was still awash in the feelings engendered by the war, and the publisher, Random House, included a prefatory note denouncing Jeffers' political views. Although the book was not well received, the reception was not entirely the result of Jeffers' politics. The poems were not considered to be among his best.

Reviews of Jeffers' *Medea* (1946), an adaptation of Euripides' play, were mixed, but a stage version ran for the full 1947–1948 season on Broadway, with Judith Anderson in the title role. Two other Jeffers dramatic poems were produced as plays in New York, *Dear Judas* in 1947 and *The Tower Beyond Tragedy* in 1950. Neither enjoyed the success of *Medea*.

Jeffers' last volume of poetry, *Hungerfield and Other Poems* (1954), contained, in the title work, a kind of dedication to the memory of Una Jeffers, who had died in 1950. Thereafter he wrote little. In his last years his reputation recovered somewhat from the slump it had suffered following World War II. He died at his home near Carmel, Calif.

[The largest collections of Jeffers manuscripts and materials are in the Humanities Research Center at the University of Texas and in the libraries at Occidental College, the University of California, and Yale University. See also *The Selected Letters of Robinson Jeffers, 1887–1962* (1968).

Other books of criticism and poetry by Jeffers are *Poetry, Gongorism, and a Thousand Years* (1949), *Themes in My Poems* (1956), and the posthumous *The Beginning and the End and Other Poems* (1963).

A Bibliography of the Works of Robinson Jeffers (1933) by Sydney S. Alberts is incomplete; it has been supplemented by William Nolte, *The Merrill Checklist of Robinson Jeffers* (1970).

Louis Adamic, *Robinson Jeffers* (1929); Melba Bennett, *Robinson Jeffers and the Sea* (1936) and *The Stone Mason of Tor House* (1966); and Edith Greenan, *Of Una Jeffers* (1939), are helpful but not authoritative.

Books about Jeffers' career include Robert J. Brophy, *Robinson Jeffers* (1973); Arthur B. Coffin, *Robinson Jeffers* (1971); and Radcliffe Squires, *The Loyalties of Robinson Jeffers* (1956). *The Robinson Jeffers Newsletter* is devoted to Jeffers' life and writing.

An obituary appeared in the *New York Times* on Jan. 22, 1962.]

DAVID O. TOMLINSON

JEMISON, ALICE MAE LEE (Oct. 9, 1901–Mar. 6, 1964), American Indian journalist and activist, was born at Silver Creek, N.Y., just off the Cattaraugus Indian Reservation of the Seneca nation. Daniel A. Lee, her Cherokee father, a cabinetmaker by trade, and Elnora E. Seneca, her Seneca mother, were both graduates of Hampton Institute. She considered herself Seneca since she was raised by her mother and her relatives at Cattaraugus. Born into the matrilineal society of the Senecas, with its ancient traditions of women's behind-the-scenes political participation, she had the self-assurance that became the cornerstone of her later political crusades. Jemison's conservative Seneca background, with its strong suspicions of all non-

Indian governmental authority, combined with the right-of-center political attitudes of western New York, and its historic distrust of Washington-directed policies, to mold her into a leading Indian opponent of the New Deal.

Poverty plagued Jemison and her family throughout much of their lives. Although her goal had been to become an attorney, her formal education was limited because of family financial exigencies. She graduated from Silver Creek High School in 1919, and on December 6 of that year she married Le Verne Leonard Jemison, a Seneca steelworker; they had two children. The marriage ended in separation in December 1928. From that time on, because of severe economic pressures, Jemison worked at various jobs to support her children and her mother: beautician, Bureau of the Census employee, clerk, confectionary store manager, dressmaker, factory worker, farmer, free-lance journalist, housekeeper, paralegal researcher, peddler, political lobbyist, practical nurse, secretary, and theater usher.

The Clothilde Marchand murder case in Buffalo in 1930 was a major turning point in Jemison's life. Working closely with Seneca President Ray Jimerson and attorney Robert Galloway, she helped coordinate the legal defense of the two Indian women accused of the crime. Despite the strong anti-Indian feelings of the period, the women were eventually released from jail, largely through the defense team's efforts. During the trial Jemison wrote columns for the Buffalo newspapers, criticizing the prejudicial publicity, countering racial stereotypic portrayals of Indians, and appealing for even-handed justice for the accused.

The success of these articles led to Jemison's journalistic career. She later wrote a series of syndicated columns for the North American Newspaper Alliance from 1932 to 1934 and edited *The First American,* a newsletter she published in Washington from 1937 to 1940 and 1953 to 1955.

Jemison became increasingly active in the political and economic concerns of American Indians. Disturbed by the terrible conditions of life on her reservation and throughout Indian America, she advocated the abolition of the Bureau of Indian Affairs, which she accused of neither working for nor protecting Indians. She preached the sanctity of Indian treaty rights, especially the guarantees expressed in the Iroquois treaty of Canandaigua (1794), which she affirmed could not be unilaterally abrogated by non-Indian policy makers. She was influenced by the writings and ideas of Dr. Carlos Mon-

tezuma, the noted Pan-Indian leader, who had urged the abolition of the Bureau of Indian Affairs because of its overly bureaucratic nature and historic failures.

In 1934, Jemison was appointed by the tribal council of the Seneca to lobby in Washington for the Beiter bill, which would guarantee Seneca jurisdiction over fishing and hunting on their reservations. When the Beiter bill was vetoed by President Franklin D. Roosevelt in 1935, she was hired as a lobbyist by Joseph Bruner, an Oklahoma Creek who was president of the American Indian Federation. Jemison worked for this anti–New Deal organization until 1939, appearing at more congressional hearings during this era than any other Indian. Throughout the mid- and late 1930's she urged the removal of Commissioner of Indian Affairs John Collier, the abolition of the Bureau of Indian Affairs, and repeal of the Indian Reorganization Act. She accused Collier of wasting taxpayers' funds, excessive experimenting with Indian education, tampering with existing tribal political structures, pushing through authoritarian measures in the bureau's herd-reduction program among the Navajos, and general administrative incompetence.

Jemison, in testimony and in *The First American,* advocated the causes of Sioux who questioned the legality of the Indian Reorganization Act referendum, Cherokees who opposed the construction of the Blue Ridge Parkway through their reservation in North Carolina, and California Indians who sought the recognition of treaty rights and redress for injustices to their ancestors.

Throughout the 1930's she accused Interior Department personnel of being Communist and anti-Christian, and thus won support from the far right, including the Daughters of the American Revolution and William Dudley Pelley, the extremist leader of the Silver Shirts of America. Her unremitting war against the Bureau of Indian Affairs led her to appear in 1938 and 1940 before hearings of the House Committee on Un-American Activities.

Although her activism primarily centered on nationwide Indian concerns, by 1938 federal officials were portraying Jemison as an Indian Nazi. This false charge was heightened, in the view of the American public, by her strong opposition to the Selective Training and Service Act of 1940. Nevertheless, she passed every loyalty check made by the Federal Bureau of Investigation and was able to secure government employment in the Bureau of the Census during World War II.

After the war Jemison again called for the abolition of the Bureau of Indian Affairs. In spite of repeated governmental harassment for her past activism, she reestablished her newsletter, *The First American.* The ultimate irony of her career was that her fervent work over three decades for Indian self-determination was distorted by the congressional establishment of the 1950's through the policy of termination (the policy of removing the bureau's role in administering Indian programs by ending the separate legal status of Indians guaranteed by treaties). It had the opposite effect on Indians from what she had envisioned.

Jemison was foremost a Seneca woman, a political disciple of Montezuma, an evangelical abolitionist, an individual, who, until her death in Washington, D.C., had complete faith in Indian peoples to rule themselves. Her militancy presaged much of the Red Power movement of the late 1960's and 1970's. Although she lived in Washington for thirty years, she remained close to her Seneca heritage by keeping abreast of tribal concerns.

[Jemison's correspondence is in the Bureau of Indian Affairs Central Classified Files, 1907–1939, and Office File of Commissioner John Collier, Record Group 75, National Archives; further information is in FBI file released Aug. 17, 1978, under Freedom of Information and Privacy Act #60, 431; and *The First American.*

See also Laurence M. Hauptman, "Alice Jemison: Seneca Political Activist, 1901–1964," *Indian Historian,* Summer 1979; Kenneth Philp, *John Collier's Crusade for Indian Reform, 1920–1954* (1977).

An obituary notice is in the *Buffalo Evening News,* Mar. 10, 1964.]

LAURENCE M. HAUPTMAN

JENSEN, PETER LAURITS (May 16, 1886–Oct. 25, 1961), pioneer in radio and electronics, was born near Stubbekobing on the island of Falster, Denmark, the son of Lods Ole Jensen and Hansine Petersen. His father was a navigator who piloted vessels through the waters between Falster and Lolland, and it was expected that Peter would follow family tradition by becoming a sailor. But a teacher noted his outstanding potential and urged that he receive an education that could lead to a university degree. After preliminary schooling in Moseby, Jensen went to a secondary school in Norre Alslev and at age sixteen passed the entrance examination for the University of Copenhagen. A university education was prevented by his father's death in 1901, which compelled him to help support his family by working for a lumber firm. His employer convinced him and his mother that he should seek larger opportunities befitting his talents. Lemvig Fog, a Danish engineer-entrepreneur, also took an interest in the lad, and in 1903 Jensen went to Copenhagen to become an apprentice in the laboratory of radio pioneer Valdemar Poulsen.

Poulsen had just developed an improved transmitter for generating continuous radio waves by means of an arc that burned in an atmosphere of hydrogen in a strong transverse magnetic field. It was a temperamental device, and Jensen gained Poulsen's confidence by becoming adept at regulating it. Advancing to the rank of assistant, he became involved in Poulsen's efforts to broadcast the human voice rather than telegraphic impulses. In 1906 Jensen made an important breakthrough by linking a microphone and a transmitter circuit as a sending apparatus and connecting a crystal detector to a grounded telegraph ticker as a receiver. While Poulsen's engineers developed the new method, Jensen experimented with various applications, including broadcasting recorded music to ships at sea.

In 1909 Poulsen sold his American patent rights to a California enterprise, the Poulsen Wireless Telephone and Telegraph Company, which subsequently reorganized as the Federal Telegraph Company and became an important pioneer in American radio. With a fellow mechanic, Carl Albertus, Jensen went to California to install the Poulsen equipment. There he met Edwin Pridham, an electrical engineering graduate of Stanford University who taught him English and became his close friend and collaborator. The reorganization that produced Federal Telegraph left Jensen and Pridham jobless. After an unsuccessful attempt to secure patent rights from Poulsen, they obtained financial backing from California industrialist Richard O'Connor, and established their own research firm, the Commercial Wireless and Development Company. During the next few years, in a small bungalow on the outskirts of Napa, Calif., they developed the first dynamic horn loudspeaker, which they named the Magnavox ("Great Voice"). It utilized a coil of copper wire situated in an electromagnetic field and attached to the diaphragm of a sound reproducer.

A vast improvement over previous speakers, the new device was first demonstrated in public at a football game in San Francisco in 1915. Subsequent demonstrations before a large crowd at the San Francisco Civic Center on Christmas Eve, 1915, and at the dedication of a new municipal auditorium shortly thereafter were so successful that additional capital was obtained from Frank M. Steers of the Sonora Phonograph Company of California. This led to the establishment of the Magnavox Company by 1917. Steers and O'Connor were executives in the firm, and Jensen and Pridham were its chief engineers.

During World War I, Jensen and Pridham developed an "antinoise microphone" that made the human voice audible over the roar of an airplane engine. Adopted by the U.S. Navy for use in the Curtiss NC-4 flying boat, it enabled crew members to communicate with one another during the navy's pioneering transatlantic flight from Newfoundland to Lisbon in May 1919. Magnavox also won national acclaim for a public address system for destroyers and battleships that Jensen and Pridham invented. But the company achieved its greatest recognition on Sept. 19, 1919, when President Woodrow Wilson addressed a crowd of approximately 50,-000 people at San Diego Stadium from a glass-enclosed platform built to protect him from the elements. Speaking in a normal tone of voice, Wilson was heard distinctly by the throng with the aid of two Magnavox loudspeakers.

In the 1920's Magnavox continued to build public address systems. It also moved into the production of phonographs and home radio sets. Meanwhile, Jensen, now famous, visited Denmark and demonstrated his speaker system in a ceremony at Copenhagen. But after returning to the United States, he broke with other Magnavox executives over policy matters and resigned from the firm (1925). In 1927 he founded the Jensen Radio Manufacturing Company, originally headquartered in Oakland, Calif., but soon moved to Chicago. There, with the aid of engineer Hugh Knowles, Jensen worked intensively to eliminate distortion and improve fidelity in sound reproduction.

In 1943 disputes with financial backers led once more to his resignation from a firm of his own creation; he subsequently founded Jensen Industries to manufacture phonograph needles. During World War II, he served as chief consultant to the U.S. War Production Board's radio and radar division. In 1956, Jensen was knighted by the king of Denmark for his achievements. He also received honors from the American Institute of Radio Engineers and the Audio Engineering Society.

Jensen married Vivian Steves in 1912; they had four children. The marriage ended in divorce in 1927, and he married Malvena Oppliger in 1929; they had one child.

Jensen died in Western Springs, Ill. His career was succinctly characterized by an obituary in *Journal of the Audio Engineering Society:* "Of the many men who distinguished themselves in the early years of audio engineering, Peter Jensen was undoubtedly one of the most creative and productive. His inventions, experiments and sound systems were the heralds of today's high fidelity industry."

[Jensen wrote *En verdenskendt Dansker, Jensen, hottalerens opfinder: En selvbiografi* (1948), also available in English as *The Great Voice* (1974). Also see Glenn D. Kittler, "Forgotten Man of Sound," *Coronet,* May, 1954; Jane Morgan, *Electronics in the West: The First Fifty Years* (1967), and articles in *Kraks blaa bog* (1949, 1961) and *Dansk Biografisk Leksikon* (1937). An obituary is in the *Journal of the Audio Engineering Society,* Jan. 1962.]

W. DAVID LEWIS

JOHNSON, HAROLD OGDEN ("CHIC") See OLSEN, JOHN SIGVARD ("OLE") AND JOHNSON, HAROLD.

JOHNSON, WENDELL ANDREW LEROY (Apr. 16, 1906–Aug. 29, 1965), psychologist and educator, was born on a farm near Roxbury, Kans., the son of Andrew Robert Johnson, a successful wheat farmer and cattleman, and of Mary Helena Tarnstrom.

He graduated from Roxbury High School in 1924. Then he attended McPherson College for two years before enrolling at the University of Iowa, where he received the B.A. (1928), the M.A. (1929), and the Ph.D. (1931). From 1931 until his death, Johnson was a member of the University of Iowa faculty. He married Edna Bockwoldt on May 31, 1929; they had two children.

From 1943 to 1955 Johnson directed the program in speech pathology and audiology at Iowa. In large measure the stature and reputation that have been achieved by the University of Iowa as a leading center for the study of speech and hearing disorders are due to his leadership and influence. He relinquished his administrative duties in 1955, following a heart attack, but was able to continue work for another ten years.

Johnson was an inspiring teacher, a diligent researcher, and a prolific writer. Because he was himself a stutterer, it was not surprising that his primary research interests centered on this problem. A highly original and imaginative thinker, he produced more than 130 research, clinical, and theoretical papers that established him as one of the foremost authorities on stuttering.

His research was capped by the publication of three books: *Stuttering in Children and Adults* (1955), *The Onset of Stuttering* (1959), and *Stuttering and What You Can Do About It* (1961). He was editor and coauthor of two widely used textbooks: *Speech Handicapped Children* (1948) and *Diagnostic Methods in Speech Pathology* (1963).

His major contribution to the knowledge about stuttering resulted from his untiring research and clinical investigation of the onset and development of stuttering. He established the rationale, supported by data, that disfluencies in children's speech are normal. He established the relationship between critical listeners' reactions to the child's disfluent speech and the subsequent reaction of tensing and struggling by the child in his effort to speak "better." His interaction theory of stuttering resulted. He posited that a stuttering problem develops when the child begins to react to his own disfluent speech by trying to prevent speaking disfluently. The more a child tries to prevent speech disfluencies, the more difficulty he experiences in speaking. This develops into a continuing spiral of distress.

A scholarly interest of Johnson's parallel to that of stuttering was general semantics. His observations and thinking concerning the way in which human behavior is molded by uncritical habits in the use and interpretation of language contributed substantially to his theoretical formulations concerning the nature of stuttering and also led him to develop a broad interest in problems of interpersonal communication. Writings in this field included *People in Quandaries* (1946) and *Your Most Enchanted Listener* (1956).

Because of his interests in rehabilitation and communication problems, Johnson was a member of numerous scholarly and professional societies. He was a fellow of the American Psychological Association and a diplomate in clinical and abnormal psychology of the American Board of Examiners in Professional Psychology. He served as president of the International Society for General Semantics from 1945 to 1947. Other affiliations included the American Association for the Advancement of Science, the Speech Association of America, the International Society for Logopedics and Phoniatrics, the National Society for Crippled Children and Adults, and the International Society for Rehabilitation of the Disabled. His closest professional identification, though, was with the American Speech and Hearing Association, of which he was a fellow and president (1950).

Johnson edited its *Journal of Speech and Hearing Disorders* (1943–1948) and was chairman of its Publications Board (1959–1962).

In later years Johnson was a consultant to a number of government agencies, including the U.S. Office of Education, the National Institute of Neurological Diseases and Blindness, the Office of Vocational Rehabilitation, Walter Reed Army Hospital, and the Veterans Administration. Until precarious health required him to curtail his activities, he was in constant demand as a lecturer and consultant by industrial groups concerned with problems of interpersonal communication, as well as by colleges and universities.

The personal qualities that brought Johnson the esteem and affection of most who knew him can scarcely be inventoried. He had an unfailing interest in the accomplishments of others, tolerance for opposing viewpoints, and a rich sense of humor coupled with original wit. Above all he had a deep compassion for people and their problems.

Johnson died in Iowa City.

[Johnson's papers, manuscripts, correspondence, and reprints of articles are in the Archives of the State Historical Society, Iowa City. A collection of his research and clinical articles and books is in the Wendell Johnson Memorial Library, All India Institute of Speech and Hearing, University of Mysore, South India. An obituary is in the *New York Times*, Aug. 31, 1965.]

DEAN E. WILLIAMS

JOHNSTON, ERIC ALLEN (Dec. 21, 1896–Aug. 22, 1963), businessman and motion picture executive, was born in Washington, D.C., the son of Bertram Allen Johnston, a pharmacist, and of Ida Fazio Ballinger. Because of his father's failing health, the family moved first to Marysville, Mont., then to Spokane, Wash. Shortly after the move his father died. Young Johnston, raised in what he called "genteel poverty," sold newspapers and did other part-time work. He graduated from Port North Central High School in Spokane in 1913. With encouragement from an uncle, he studied law at the University of Washington, earning an LL.B. in 1917. After graduation he attended officers' candidate school, and was commissioned a marine second lieutenant in 1917.

Johnston might have remained in the Marine Corps had he not sustained a head injury while serving as an assistant naval attaché at Peking, China, in 1921. He received an honorable discharge in 1922 and returned to Spokane, where he sold vacuum cleaners door to door. Johnston married Ina Harriet Hughes on Oct. 22, 1922. They had two daughters.

In 1923 Johnston and a friend bought an electrical manufacturing and wholesale concern, renaming it the Brown-Johnston Company. A decade later the company had split into the Columbia Electrical and Manufacturing Company and the Brown-Johnston Company, respectively the largest electrical contracting company and the largest electrical manufacturer in the Northwest. Johnston was president of both firms.

Tall, handsome, energetic, and genial, Johnston was known as an excellent orator. These qualities help explain his business success and his rise to a position of power in the U.S. Chamber of Commerce in the 1930's and 1940's. He was elected president of the Spokane chapter in 1931, became a national director in 1934 and vice-president in 1941, and was elected president in 1942—the youngest person to hold that office. Johnston was reelected to the Chamber of Commerce presidency each year thereafter, until he stepped down in 1946.

His presidential candidacy was originally supported by a liberal faction in the typically conservative Chamber of Commerce. Ideologically, Johnston was a centrist who stoutly defended capitalism but also urged management and labor to work together. His own companies had a profit-sharing plan whereby one-quarter of the profits were distributed to employees. Shortly after his election as Chamber of Commerce president, Johnston met with President Franklin D. Roosevelt and then arranged for a White House gathering of American Federation of Labor, Congress of Industrial Organizations, and National Association of Manufacturers representatives, which worked out a no-strike pledge of unity during World War II.

Although Johnston lost his only campaign for political office when he ran as Republican candidate for the U.S. Senate in 1940, he served in various capacities in the Roosevelt, Truman, and Eisenhower administrations. He was chairman of the U.S. Commission on Inter-American Development (1943) and a member of the advisory committee of the Economic Cooperation Administration (1948). In 1955 President Dwight Eisenhower sent him on a diplomatic mission to the Middle East.

In 1945 Johnston became president of the Motion Picture Association of America (MPAA), a self-regulating, policy-making body of the industry that had as members almost all the Hollywood studio heads. In this post he worked particularly hard at encouraging the distribution of American films abroad. In line with his belief in international economic development through capitalist enterprise, he believed that the export of American films "helps us create a market for American goods and it conveys American ideas and ideals." As president of the MPAA during a period when domestic movie attendance dropped by more than half, Johnston sought to expand the international market for American films and to discourage other countries from imposing import quotas on them.

One of the biggest crises Johnston faced as head of the MPAA came during the 1947 House Un-American Activities Committee (HUAC) investigation of Communist influence in Hollywood. In the beginning he told the press that the producers had no desire to "defend or shield" members of the Communist party. After the first of the "Hollywood Ten," the screenwriter John Howard Lawson, testified, Johnston told HUAC (Oct. 27, 1947) that he welcomed the committee's attempt to expose Communists. The "Waldorf Statement," drafted in New York City by members of the MPAA in the face of political and economic pressure, and read by Johnston in November 1947, paved the way for the blacklisting of film industry employees who refused to cooperate with HUAC. The blacklist lasted throughout the 1950's and into the 1960's.

In his professional activities, his numerous speeches and articles, and his two books— *America Unlimited* (1944) and *We're All in It* (1948)—Johnston revealed himself to be an ebullient and cogent spokesman for the American consensus of the 1940's and 1950's. If he was more liberal toward organized labor than many businessmen, he was also firmly convinced that America was strong because "our economy is sparked by competition and we thrive on expanding markets." From these principles stemmed his belief in cooperation between labor and management; his desire to expand America's role in the export of movies, technology, and scientific know-how; and his postwar anti-Communism. Johnston is best characterized as a man of considerable business and managerial talents and a tireless spokesman for and defender of the motion picture industry during its painful economic decline in the late 1940's and 1950's. He died in Washington, D.C.

[There is no definitive biography of Johnston. His life is profiled in B. C. Forbes, ed., *America's Fifty*

Foremost Business Leaders (1948). An obituary is in the *New York Times*, Aug. 23, 1963.]
                          CHARLES J. MALAND

JOHNSTON, OLIN DEWITT TAL-MADGE (Nov. 18, 1896–Apr. 18, 1965), governor and U.S. senator, was born near Honea Path, S.C., the son of Edward Andrew Johnston and Leila Webb, tenant farmers and textile workers. He attended Barker's Creek public school and, at age eleven, began work in a textile mill. After attending high school irregularly, in 1914 he entered the Textile Industrial Institute in nearby Spartanburg, receiving a high school equivalency diploma with honors in 1915. He then entered Wofford College. When the United States declared war on Germany in 1917, he joined the army and became a sergeant in the 117th Engineer Regiment of the Forty-Second Division—later named "the Rainbow Division"—commanded by General Douglas MacArthur. This unit saw much combat action in France in 1918. In June 1919, Johnston was discharged with a regimental citation for bravery under fire. He returned to Wofford, from which he graduated with the B.A. in 1921.

Johnston then entered the University of South Carolina, financing his schooling by operating a boardinghouse and a suit-pressing service. He received the M.A. in rural economics in 1923 and the LL.B. in 1924. He then opened an office in Spartanburg. On Dec. 28, 1924, he married Gladys Elizabeth Atkinson; they had three children.

Johnston's desire for a political career had been kindled by a term in the South Carolina House of Representatives while in law school (1923–1924), as the representative of Anderson County. In 1927 he was elected to the same body as representative from more populous Spartanburg County. He served until 1930, building on his experience in textile mills and his friendships with workers to develop a labor following that became the core of his political organization. While in the legislature he constantly championed bills to improve working conditions. As his legal business grew, he opened a law office in Columbia, S.C., where he handled cases for workers.

Johnston strongly opposed the issuance of state bonds to finance the highway program then being pushed by the representatives from the larger cities and by the state highway commission. His rural constituents saw no benefit from such roads. In 1930 he entered the Democratic primary as a gubernatorial candidate but lost by about 1,000 votes.

Johnston blamed his defeat on the Highway Commission. In 1934 he won the gubernatorial primary by a wide majority (which was tantamount to election in one-party South Carolina). After taking office he interpreted his victory as a mandate to declare war on the Commission. Johnston proclaimed the operation of the state highway system to be in a "state of insurrection," and surrounded the capitol with guards armed with machine guns. But the South Carolina Supreme Court and the legislature failed to back him, and Johnston had to withdraw his proclamation.

Unable to succeed himself as governor, Johnston waited four years, ran again in 1942, and won. While governor he supported virtually all of President Franklin D. Roosevelt's New Deal reforms. At the state level he achieved tax-exemption for small homes and farms, a seven-month state-financed school term, a forty-hour workweek for textile workers, and other class legislation.

During Johnston's second term the U.S. Supreme Court upheld the right of blacks to vote in primaries (*Smith* v. *Allwright,* 321 U.S. 649 [1944]). He thereupon called a special session of the legislature to repeal all legislation relating to primary elections. Despite Johnston's and the legislature's efforts to make the Democratic party a segregated political club, the Supreme Court prevented them from doing so.

In 1938 Johnston ran for the U.S. Senate against incumbent Ellison D. ("Cotton Ed") Smith. He lost, but in 1944 he defeated Smith. In the Senate, Johnston continued to support labor legislation, such as increases in the minimum wage, and to oppose civil rights legislation, such as the Fair Employment Practices Commission and the bill outlawing the poll tax. He objected to President Harry Truman's civil rights stand and opposed Truman as party leader. Yet in 1948 he refused to join the Dixiecrat party, headed by South Carolina Governor J. Strom Thurmond.

In the 1950 Senate race Johnston defeated Thurmond largely because he convinced the voters that he could serve their interests better as a Democrat than as a Dixiecrat. In that term and two following ones he epitomized the ambivalent position that moderate or progressive southern legislators were forced to assume in order to continue in office. On the one hand he professed extreme racist and segregationist positions and opposed all legislation that might lead to legal or social equality for blacks. On the other hand he supported legislation designed to benefit the poor, the laborers, and the small business people. Thus Johnston voted for federal aid to education, food price subsidies, and a department of public welfare. He generally opposed foreign aid programs, including the Marshall Plan (1947), on the ground of economy. He early joined the extremists of the right in their anti-Communist crusade, and on one occasion advocated atomic war on Russia.

Johnston won election for the fourth time in 1962 over Governor Ernest F. Hollings, carrying all but one of the state's forty-six counties. He died in Columbia, S.C.

[Johnston's papers are in the Caroliniana Collection of the University of South Carolina. No adequate biography of Johnston has been written, but see John E. Huss, *Senator for the South* (1961); Anthony Berry Miller, "Palmetto Politician: The Early Political Career of Olin D. Johnston, 1896–1945" (Ph.D. diss., University of North Carolina, 1976). Also see Sally Edwards, *South Carolina* (1968); Roy Glashan, comp., *American Governors and Gubernatorial Elections, 1775–1978* (1979); and George C. Rogers, Jr., *A South Carolina Chronology, 1497–1970* (1973). An obituary is in the *New York Times*, Apr. 19, 1965.]

BENNETT H. WALL

JONES, BENJAMIN ALLYN (Dec. 31, 1882–June 13, 1961), horse breeder and trainer, was born in Parnell, Mo., the son of Horace Jones, a cattle rancher and banker, and Julia Allyn, a teacher. The elder Jones, who owned 9,000 acres and several small businesses, had founded the small northwestern Missouri town of Parnell after traveling from Iowa in a covered wagon. His leading economic and social position was an important factor in the early career of Jones, who spent his youth around horses and Sunday afternoon races at a small track on the ranch.

Jones left the local two-room schoolhouse to enroll briefly at Wentworth Military Academy, Missouri Wesleyan College, and the Colorado State College of Agriculture. He spent one year at Colorado and left in 1902 with a permanent limp, the result of a football injury. He returned to Parnell, where his father tried unsuccessfully to interest him in a banking career.

In 1903 Jones married Etta McLaughlin; they had two children. His father gave Jones 500 acres and enough money to purchase a stallion and brood mares to start a business of breeding and racing thoroughbred horses. While his wife kept the books and raised the children, Jones began to race his horses at fairs and small tracks throughout the Midwest and South. He made regular stops in Fort Worth, Tex., Tulsa, Okla.,

Lewiston, Idaho, Salt Lake City, Utah, Butte, Mont., and Oklahoma City. In 1909 he saddled his first winner at an established track, Errant Lady, collecting a purse of $200. That year he began racing during the winter in Juárez, Mexico, and continued for two more winters.

By 1914 Jones was well on his way as a breeder and trainer. His Jones Stock Farm housed the stallions Blues and Harrigan and thirty-two mares, and accounted for fourteen wins totaling $3,470 in that year. He extended his racing to New Orleans in 1915, and two years later added more prestige to his farm with the purchase of Seth, a stallion that sired numerous colts selling for $800 to $8,000 each. But he was still in the "bush leagues" of racing.

Jones graduated to the Chicago circuit around 1925, and for the remainder of the decade was consistently one of the top ten breeders in terms of races won. Among his horses were offspring of Seth: Dolly Seth, Seth's Hope, Senator Seth, General Seth, Colonel Seth, and on down to Private Seth. Whereas his major competitors had large operations and several employees, Jones campaigned independently and earned considerable money in small amounts through hard work, much travel, and perseverance. He always claimed that his major reason for success was simply that he worked harder than anyone else.

Jones discontinued his breeding farm in 1930 and two years later began training for Herbert M. Woolf, a Kansas City clothing merchant, at his Woolford Farm. During his tenure with Woolf, he trained thirteen stakes winners and won more than a half million dollars. In 1938, his last complete year at Woolford, he trained Lawrin, winner at Hialeah, the Flamingo, the Hollywood Trial Stakes, a special invitational race at Hollywood Park for $40,000, and the Kentucky Derby. Eddie Arcaro rode Lawrin in the Derby, beginning an awesome combination of trainer and jockey that continued for at least fourteen years.

In August 1939, Warren Wright, owner of Calumet Farm in Lexington, Ky., who was impressed with Lawrin's victory over his own horse Bull Lea in the Derby, hired Jones as his head trainer. This was the start of twenty-two years with the same employer and a career that included almost continual top national honors for both Jones and Calumet Farm.

In 1940, his first complete year with Calumet, the farm placed third among money-winning owners. A Calumet two-year-old, Whirlaway, was the nation's top money winner with $77,275 and victories in seven out of sixteen starts. The next year Whirlaway ran a record time of 2:01 2/5 for the one-and-one-quarter-mile Kentucky Derby with Eddie Arcaro aboard —a record not broken until 1962—and went on to win the coveted Triple Crown. "Mr. Long-tail," as Whirlaway was affectionately called, was named Horse of the Year, after being known as a problem horse. Jones corrected Whirlaway's tendency to swing out by using a one-eyed blinker. He handled the high-strung horse with kindness and patience instead of punishment.

Jones was the leading trainer in 1941. With only thirty-five horses racing, Calumet Farm earned $475,091, to place first in money won. In 1942 Whirlaway set a new track record at Aqueduct for one and one-eighth miles at 1:49 2/5, and another in the Massachusetts Handicap at 1:48 1/5. Upon his retirement in 1944 Whirlaway had won a record $561,161.

When Whirlaway retired, Jones had other horses to carry the Calumet colors of devil's red and blue. In 1944 Pensive won the Kentucky Derby and the Preakness, but lost the Belmont by half a length. That same year Twilight Tear (or "Suzie," as she was called by Jones) was voted Horse of the Year, the first time a filly was chosen, after she won eleven races in a row. Armed, another Jones-trained horse, also did exceptionally well in 1944. The large brown gelding placed in all but one of his eighteen starts, won eleven, equaled or broke four track records, and won $288,725. In 1945 Pot O'Luck placed second in the Kentucky Derby. By 1946 Armed had earned $342,875 to become the world's richest gelding. In 1947 he won $376,325 and was named Horse of the Year. Upon his death in 1962, he had amassed winnings of $817,475.

Jones became Calumet Farm's general manager in 1947, relinquishing some of his training duties to his son "Jimmy." That year Calumet raced in two divisions, and horses and trainers were interchangeable. Jones and his son, known as the "Jones boys," each earned a $12,000 salary plus 5 percent of the winnings. Their tireless efforts on both the eastern and the western circuits had much to do with Calumet Farm's becoming the first million-dollar owner in 1947, with winnings totaling $1,402,436.

A two-year-old named Citation contributed greatly to this success. In that same year Faultless placed third in the Kentucky Derby. Only losing one race in twenty starts, Citation won the Triple Crown and was unanimously named Horse of the Year in 1948. With the Derby victory, Jones's fourth, jockey Arcaro broke Isaac Murphy's long-standing record of winning

three Derbies. Another Jones-trained horse, Coaltown, placed second in the same race. As further examples of what made Jones and Calumet Farm a great team, that same day Citation won $91,870 in the Preakness at Baltimore, and two other Calumet horses, Faultless and Fervent, ran one and two in New York for $75,300 —a total of $167,170 in Calumet earnings for one day of racing.

In 1949, when Ponder became Jones's fifth Kentucky Derby winner, Jones surpassed the training record of "Derby Dick" Thompson. Wistful won the National Filly Triple Crown that year and, ending the best decade in racing history for any trainer, Citation became the first thoroughbred millionaire with winnings of $1,085,760.

In 1950 Warren Wright's widow, Lucille Parker Wright, took control of Calumet. Two years later she married Rear Admiral Gene Markey. Jones continued to train for the Markeys, and in 1952 Eddie Arcaro rode Hill Gail to his fifth Derby victory, the sixth for Jones. Real Delight, another Calumet and Jones horse, won the National Filly Triple Crown that year. During 1953 and 1954 Calumet raced only on western tracks, but moved east again in 1955. In 1956 Fabius won the Preakness and finished second in the Kentucky Derby.

The following year, because of failing health, Ben Jones unofficially retired. The *American Racing Manual* credited him with having trained the winners of 1,528 races and with earning $4,703,326 from 1914 to 1953. His son went on to win the Kentucky Derby in 1957 with Iron Liege and again the following year with Tim Tam. During this period Jones still worked at Calumet in an advisory capacity and spent some time with young horses in Hialeah, Fla. He officially retired in 1960.

"Plain Ben" Jones was five feet, ten-and-a-half inches tall and stocky, with a bulldog jaw. He was kind and folksy, and moved in a quiet yet bustling manner. He was usually found sitting astride a pony, following and watching his horses. A firm believer in "natural speed," he trained only those horses whose endurance he could improve. He did nothing "by the book." Jones relied on patience and diligence, holding and talking to horses for hours while they fed on fresh grass. Each horse had a personality, he said, so he had to learn how to treat each one. Where a horse was concerned, nothing was too much trouble or too trivial to engage his complete attention.

All of Jones's horses went through numerous rituals of becoming familiar with the track, crowds, and the starting gate. One of the most vocal critics of excessive weights, Jones sometimes withdrew his horses when they were assigned too much. Probably his outstanding skill was his genius at getting a horse ready for one big race, usually his favorite, the Kentucky Derby. In addition to his direct work with each horse, Jones was a tireless student of racing, often sitting up half the night studying condition and stakes books.

During Jones's tenure at Calumet Farm, the stable topped the money-winning owners' list eleven times, was second four times, and third two times. During the same years, Calumet was the leading breeder according to amount of money won fourteen times, eleven years in succession. Overall, while Jones was at Calumet, the farm bred forty-five horses that won $100,000 or more, another world record. Five of those horses—Armed, Bewitch, Citation, Twilight Tear, and Whirlaway—were named to the National Museum of Racing Hall of Fame at Saratoga, N.Y. As, of course, was Jones himself. He died at Lexington, Ky.

[See "Whirlaway, Year's Best Horse," *Life*, June 23, 1941; Hambla Bauer, "Plain Ben Jones," *Saturday Evening Post*, June 16, 1945; "Ben, Eddie, and Co.," *Newsweek*, May 10, 1948; "Calumet's Best. Citation," *Life*, June 7, 1948; Hambla Bauer, "Boss of Calumet Farms," *Saturday Evening Post*, Sept. 11, 1948; "Life Visits Calumet Farms," *Life*, Nov. 1, 1948; "My Old Kentucky Jones; Kentucky Derby," *Time*, May 16, 1949; "Devil Red and Plain Ben," *Time*, May 30, 1949.
Jones's records are in *Arlington Park 50th Anniversary Year* (1977); Margaret B. Glass, *The Calumet Story* (1979); William H. P. Robertson, *The History of Thoroughbred Racing in America* (1964).
Obituaries are in the *New York Times*, June 14, 1961; *The Blood-Horse*, June 17, 1961; *The Thoroughbred Record*, June 17, 1961; *Time*, June 23, 1961; *Newsweek*, June 26, 1961.]

JACK W. BERRYMAN

JONES, JOHN PRICE (Aug. 12, 1877–Dec. 23, 1964), journalist and fund raiser, was born in Latrobe, Pa., the son of David F. Jones and Leah Price. His father was a coal mine foreman, and Jones showed an early determination not to follow that occupation. Through odd jobs and a $150 loan, he managed to enroll at Phillips Exeter Academy in Exeter, N.H., in 1895. He graduated in 1898 and entered Harvard College, where he supported himself as a correspondent for several newspapers. Before completing the B.A. degree in 1902, Jones became private secretary to Samuel L. Powers, a Republican congressman from Massachusetts. After graduation

and a brief trip abroad, he worked as a reporter for three New York papers: the *Globe* (1903–1905), the *Press* (1905–1912), and the *Sun* (1912–1917). In 1917 he left journalism and took a job with the H. K. McCann advertising agency.

World War I changed the pattern of Jones's life. He won notice early in 1917 with *America Entangled*, a lurid account of German spying and the sinking of the *Lusitania*. Far more important was his work for the Liberty Loan Committee of New York (1917–1919). In this work he displayed a systematic attention to detail and a flair for publicity.

Early in 1919 Thomas W. Lamont hired Jones as general manager of the Harvard Endowment Fund. At Harvard, Jones applied the lessons he had learned while selling liberty bonds, and within a year had raised the unprecedented sum of $14.2 million. The Harvard campaign marked a new era in financing higher education, both in the dollar goal and in the tightly organized fund-raising organization. In the words of his longtime colleague Robert F. Duncan, Jones was "the right man in the right place at the right time." Jones and some associates from Harvard moved to New York City, and on Nov. 23, 1919, incorporated the John Price Jones Corporation.

While fund raising always predominated, Jones also sought business in public relations. The firm's purpose, he wrote in 1921, was "to originate and promote an idea." "Think it out first," he advised, "then write. After that it probably won't need much talking over." Jones was an awkward public speaker, and never personally asked for a donation. He was an avid memo writer who required daily and weekly reports from his staff. He supervised employees closely and demanded facts, not guesses. One longtime associate remembered "his livid and furious eloquence when anyone used in his presence the very word 'assume.' "

The John Price Jones Corporation made a profit from its first year. Jones and a staff that numbered more than 100 by the mid-1920's perfected the techniques for raising money for colleges, hospitals, and other causes. Jones stressed carefully written plans, explicit goals, recruitment of effective volunteer workers, and a quota system to identify potential donors and the amounts they would be asked to contribute. He insisted on large print for brochures, arguing that rich people tend to be elderly and to wear glasses. Despite his newspaper experience Jones did not write easily, but he was a demanding critic. Books issued in his name were written largely by staff members under his close supervision. He viewed fund raising as a new profession and worked to establish high standards and professional ethics. The firm's library became the nation's finest collection on philanthropy.

During the early years of the Great Depression, Jones organized relief drives in Baltimore, Philadelphia, and New York City that raised nearly $79 million. During World War II he played a major part in both United Service Organizations (USO) and Red Cross campaigns. In 1945–1947 he made the American Cancer Society into a leading medical appeal. There were occasional charges that the Jones organization asked for excessively high fees and used high-pressure appeals to obtain contributions. Actually the fees rarely exceeded 3 percent of the amount raised.

In private Jones was quiet and gentle, but with his employees he could be gruff. They remembered modest pay and hard work, but generous help when in need. Many who moved on to high positions elsewhere regarded Jones as the great teacher of fund-raising techniques. When he sold control of the company in 1955 and retired, he had managed campaigns that raised a total of $836,380,351.

Jones married Frieda B. Suppes on Dec. 5, 1905; they had no children. Jones had few interests beyond his business and a love for the outdoors and regular physical exercise. His loyalties were to Phillips Exeter, Harvard, and the Republican party. In his later years he lived on a farm in Bucks County, Pa.; he died in Philadelphia. A fund raiser to the last, he left his considerable estate ultimately to Phillips Exeter and Harvard.

[There are no personal papers, but the Baker Library at Harvard has more than 700 volumes of the John Price Jones Corporation papers as well as its library. Jones and Paul M. Hollister published *The German Secret Service in America* (1918); of the later works in his name, *The Techniques to Win in Fund Raising* (1934) is most nearly in his own words. There is a sketch in the *New Yorker*, Sept. 23, 1943. "John Price Jones, 1877–1964," is a brief memoir by his friend Robert F. Duncan and was issued by the John Price Jones Corporation. Also see Merle Curti and Roderick Nash, *Philanthropy in the Shaping of American Higher Education* (1965); Scott M. Cutlip, *Fund Raising in the United States* (1965). An obituary is in the *New York Times*, Dec. 24, 1964.]
PATRICK J. FURLONG

JONES, RICHARD FOSTER (July 7, 1886–Sept. 12, 1965), educator, was born in Salado, Tex., the son of Dr. Samuel Jackson Jones and Charlotte Hallaran. In 1890 his father founded in Salado, and became principal of, the Thomas Arnold High School, so named "in grateful appreciation of the character and work of the great master of Rugby, who made the men who made England." The curriculum was largely classical. His mother helped in the coeducational enterprise, founding the Elizabeth Barrett Browning Literary Society for girls, and holding open house every Friday night for boys.

Jones entered his father's school in 1899 and was graduated in 1902 with a classical diploma. He entered the University of Texas in 1903, majoring in Greek, Latin, and mathematics. After receiving the bachelor's degree in 1907, he returned to Salado to teach mathematics and Latin in his father's school until he registered for graduate study at Columbia University in 1909. There he majored in Greek, English, and comparative literature under the tutelage of Brander Matthews, Joel E. Spingarn, Ashley Thorndike, and William P. Trent. He earned his master's degree within one year; but before he received his doctorate he taught again at the Thomas Arnold High School (1912–1913) and served four years (1914–1918) as an instructor in English at Western Reserve University. He returned to Columbia in 1918 for the conferral of his doctorate, taught there for one year, and in 1919 moved to Washington University in St. Louis as an assistant professor. He rose rapidly up the academic ladder to a professorship (1925), and for the next decade and a half vigorously pursued his scholarly interest in seventeenth- and eighteenth-century English literature and thought.

In 1941 Jones was appointed dean of the graduate school at Washington University, an office he held until 1945. During World War II he served as administrator of the Army Specialized Training Program for Foreign Language and Area Study. In 1945 he became executive head of the Department of English at Stanford University. This post, in which he served until 1951, he considered the crown of his academic career. During his tenure he was instrumental in founding the Stanford Creative Writing Center, and under his leadership the Department of English gained wide recognition for the scholarly achievements of its faculty. He retired from teaching in 1952.

On Dec. 26, 1914, Jones married Lucile Law, an English teacher. They had no children. The two worked as a team and were often seen in the great libraries of England and America, compiling and sifting notes that later served as materials for books. Jones's first book was his doctoral dissertation, *Lewis Theobald* (1919), published by Columbia University Press. In it he not only removed from that eighteenth-century editor the stigma of dullness with which Alexander Pope had branded him in *The Dunciad;* he demonstrated that Theobald was scientific in his editorial methods—indeed, something of a forerunner of modern editorial practices. In 1929 Jones published two textbooks: *Seventeenth-Century Literature* and *Eighteenth-Century Literature;* and in 1937 he edited selections from the works of Sir Francis Bacon.

These editorial activities were ancillary to his interest in the history of ideas, to which he gave early expression (1930–1932) in a number of seminal articles. Conveniently collected in *The Seventeenth Century* (1951), a publication honoring his scholarly achievements, these articles argue that the scientific method trumpeted by Bacon and espoused by the "Bacon-faced generation," more than rhetorical imperatives, was responsible for the rise of a nominalistic, utilitarian prose, stripped of metaphor and trope. This position brought him into controversy with scholars who contended for the primacy of rhetorical traditions in the formation of prose styles.

In 1936 Jones published *Ancients and Moderns: A Study of the Background of the "Battle of the Books."* This book—an expansion of an earlier monograph (1920)—soon became a classic and appeared, with minor changes, in a second edition in 1961, bearing a subtitle more accurately descriptive of its contents: *A Study of the Rise of the Scientific Movement in Seventeenth-Century England.* Jones climaxed his scholarly career with *The Triumph of the English Language* (1953), in which he presented a history of ideas concerning the English tongue from 1476 to 1660. This was his fullest expression of a discipline to which he rendered such high service. He was not only an explorer of ideas; he meticulously mapped out the terrain over which he had traveled.

During his long academic career, Jones wrote numerous articles and reviews on a wide variety of subjects. He also was active in the Modern Language Association, the American Association of University Professors, and the Philological Association of the Pacific Coast. Jones died in Menlo Park, Calif.

[See files in Department of English, Stanford University, and the Stanford University Archives, file SC 118, boxes 1 and 2. See also George W. Tyler, *The History of Bell County* [Texas] (1936); Kate E.

White, *Charlotte Hallaran Jones: A Sketch* (1905). Obituaries appeared in the Palo Alto *Times,* Sept. 13, 1965, and the *New York Times,* Sept. 15, 1965.]
GEORGE F. SENSABAUGH

JONES, LINDLEY ARMSTRONG ("SPIKE") (Dec. 14, 1911–May 1, 1965), drummer, bandleader, composer, and comedian, was born in Long Beach, Calif., the son of Lindley M. Jones, a station agent and telegrapher for the Southern Pacific Railroad, and of Ada Armstrong. At eleven, when the family lived in Calexico, Calif., Spike, as he was called, was given his first set of drums. Soon he was the drummer and leader of a four-piece band. When the family returned to Long Beach, he became drum major of the ninety-piece high school band. Once again he organized his own group, Spike Jones and His Five Tacks. At Chaffee Junior College in Long Beach he improved his drumming skills through two years of music study.

Jones's ambition was to be a timpani player in a symphony orchestra. But at hand were drumming jobs at clubs and night spots. From these he moved into the popular dance bands of Everett Hoagland and Earl Burtnett. By 1937, Jones was a staff drummer at Hollywood radio and recording studios. He held the drum spot in John Scott Trotter's orchestra on the radio show "Kraft Music Hall," starring Bing Crosby. To make the most of a union rule that barred musicians from working on radio for more than two hours a week unless producers asked for them specifically, he generated a demand for his talents by offering unusual extras: tuned cowbells, doorbells, and auto horns; washboards; pistols; and an anvil and iron mallets. Thereafter he worked on a number of important radio shows: Al Jolson, Burns and Allen, Fibber McGee and Molly, Bob Burns, the "Chase and Sanborn Hour."

Radio-show bands played music restricted by time and commercial limitations. With equally bored fellow musicians Jones began holding weekly play-the-way-you-feel sessions, from which emerged raucous spoofs of the tunes they played for a living. Victor Records signed the men to a contract, but nothing much happened until July 1942, when they recorded a number that Jones had written for a Donald Duck cartoon, "Der Fuehrer's Face." Its explosive insults and ripe "Bronx cheers" (from a rubber razzer), aimed at Adolf Hitler, spoke for the whole country during World War II. It sold 1.5 million copies and set Spike Jones and His City Slickers on a course of musical satire and slapstick that made him a millionaire and made millions of Americans and fans overseas laugh at a time when laughs were hard to come by.

Between radio commitments, the City Slickers toured and turned out a succession of recordings that have become satiric classics, such as "Chloe," "Liebestraum," and "William Tell Overture." "Cocktails for Two," which featured an entire chorus of hiccups, became such a big jukebox hit that Victor reportedly made 150,000 pressings with the song on both sides, so that when one side wore out, the record could be flipped over to the fresh side. In December 1942, Jones was voted King of Corn in *Down Beat*'s annual band poll. He snatched the crown from its long-time wearer, Guy Lombardo, and held it through the decade.

Moviegoers soon experienced the Jones musical havoc. Beginning with *Thank Your Lucky Stars* (1943), Spike Jones and His City Slickers made a movie each year for the next four years: *Meet the People* (1944), *Bring on the Girls* (1945), *Breakfast in Hollywood* (1946), and *Variety Girl* (1947). When they were cast as shipyard workers in *Meet the People,* Jones quipped, "A natural. My boys are riveters and blacksmiths at heart!"

After the addition of saws, auto pumps, toy whistles, sirens, fire bells, kitchen utensils, small cannon, and a "birdophone" to his arsenal, Jones set off on tour in July 1946 with a two-hour extravaganza, *Musical Depreciation Revue.* He prophesied that it would set music back 1,000 years. Tours expanded, props proliferated: an octave of Flitguns tuned to E-flat, a "crashophone" for breaking glass, a goat that allegedly bleated in the key of C, and a skunk (well trained). The revue's harpist calmly knitted while the mayhem raged around her. (Estimates of the length of her knitting over a four-year period vary from thirty-five feet to ninety feet). On July 18, 1948, Jones married Helen Greco, a singer with his band who was known professionally as Helen Grayco. They had three children. He had a daughter by his previous marriage to Patricia Ann Middleton, who was also a singer.

Many people thought Jones's music chaotic improvisation. In fact, it was meticulously planned and thoroughly rehearsed. In the 1950's Jones and the band appeared in only one movie, *Fireman, Save My Child* (1954), but found another made-to-order medium: television. "The Spike Jones Show" was first televised in 1951, with subsequent telecasts in 1954, 1957, 1958 (as the "Club Oasis" show), 1960, and 1961. But with the 1960's came radical changes in musical styles and tastes. Jones found the current songs impossible to satirize: "In their original form they are already the funniest renditions ever heard," he said. He abandoned comedy and turned to making records in a fairly straight Dixieland style. But with his cowbells, crashophone, Flit guns, and birdophone silenced, life in music was not the same. He died of emphysema in Los Angeles.

[A file of clippings on Jones is in the Lincoln Center Library for the Performing Arts. See Brian Rust and Albert J. McCarthy, *The Dance Band Era* (1972); and George T. Simon, *The Best of the Music Makers* (1979) and *The Big Bands* (rev. and enl. 1979). An obituary is in the *New York Times,* May 2, 1965.]

AMY LEE

JORDAN, VIRGIL JUSTIN (June 3, 1892– Apr. 28, 1965), economist, was born at Olean, N.Y., the son of James Ernest Jordan and Lillian May Conrad. After boyhood on the family farm near Cuba, N.Y., he worked his way through the College of the City of New York with jobs in butcher shops and as mechanic's helper. He graduated with the B.S., cum laude, in 1912. He had majored in economics and physics, and pursued the former in graduate work at the University of Wisconsin in 1912. The following year Jordan studied at Columbia and Cambridge universities, and in 1914 at Stuttgart, Germany. The outbreak of World War I compelled him to return to the United States without receiving a degree. He professed himself most influenced by Richard T. Ely, A. C. Pigou, and William G. Sumner, only the last of whom espoused the individualist economics that became his passion.

From 1914 to 1920, Jordan was an associate editor of *Everybody's Magazine.* He joined the staff of the National Industrial Conference Board as editor of its publications in 1920, serving also as chief economist from 1924 to 1929. The Conference Board, organized in 1916 by leading business associations in order to share management experience and conduct industrial research, had expanded its activities under the guiding hand of the engineer Magnus W. Alexander during a period of notable prosperity. Under this influence Jordan left the Conference Board in 1929 to become economist on the new magazine *Business Week.* After Alexander died, Jordan became the Conference Board's president on Jan. 1, 1933.

In the depth of the Great Depression, Jordan confronted grievously altered conditions. The economic collapse had reduced the Conference Board's membership, finances, and staff. The board organized a group of executives who gathered weekly, says the official history, "to study and try to find some means of stimulating business recovery." But the group "was unable to agree on solutions to the many problems raised."

Impotence became humiliation, in Jordan's view, under the rescue efforts of President Franklin Roosevelt's New Deal. Nevertheless, he buckled to with his customary energy, and in the next years restored staff and salaries, expanded research, published a new business outlook periodical (*Conference Board Business Survey*), and issued two series of memorandums on foreign and domestic affairs. The board drew leading professors into its Economic Advisory Council, organized symposiums of specialists, and fostered gatherings of the general membership. Newly established government agencies to assist the economy were assessed at round-table and dinner meetings.

One such conference in May 1937, when Roosevelt had been persuaded to relax government "pump priming" and trust to resumption of business initiative, found Jordan in an expansive mood. He complimented his hearers, "a great group of able, earnest, experienced and public-spirited men . . . joined in a common effort to promote the prosperity, security and progress of the American people by . . . strengthening the operation of the enterprise organization upon which it is based." He lamented that the last four years had produced "a new, strange, unfamiliar and unfriendly world in which we live and labor today. . . ." After a passing reference to the masses' "eternal yearning for the golden age of plenty, without end, without effort, and without obligation," he satirized the popular notion that "the state and its prestidigitators provide the magical all-powerful . . . agency which alone can manipulate the Aladdin's lamp of science and play the horn of plenty." Instead, he would celebrate "the individual human personality, whose energies have been the source of all creative power, whose accomplishments have been the standard of all values, and whose development has been the end object of all sound economic, social and political institutions."

This was six months before the recession of 1937, which plunged Jordan deeper into the pessimism that had become his trademark. To a critic of his gloomy forecasts he replied, "I don't mind at all that you find the opinions I express . . . distasteful. I do myself. In fact they make me quite ill at times because I take them so seriously."

Besides many articles, Jordan wrote *The Inter-Ally Debt and the United States* (1925) and *The Agricultural Problem in the United States* (1926). He was cited at Rutgers with the LL.D. for "strengthening the economic foundations upon which our social structure is erected," but as a Rutgers trustee he urged dropping a liberal lecturer in economics. Jordan was tall and "shaggily handsome," with brown hair and blue eyes. In 1914 he married Viola Scott Baxter; they had three children. After their divorce he married Gertrude Bascom Darwin in 1928. His chief recreation was playing the piano.

In the demanding years of World War II and reconversion, Jordan's well-chosen staff continued to serve the needs of the great segment of American business represented on the Conference Board. His own statements, however, became more vehemently condemnatory of governmental intrusion into the economy. The board took pains to distinguish Jordan's personal bias from policy of the organization, as did Jordan himself. His *Manifesto for the Atomic Age* (1946) foresaw the dissolving of all social values, and is best viewed as an intentional extravaganza.

In 1948, his health and judgment impaired, Jordan resigned from the presidency of the Conference Board with the title of chancellor, a nominal connection he maintained for fifteen years. In retirement he lived in Southern Pines, N.C. There a nurse found Jordan and his wife, who had both been ill, dead in a suicide pact.

[See *Let There Be Light; the Conference Board's 50 Years of Service* (1966). An obituary is in the *New York Times*, Apr. 30, 1965. Private information.]

BROADUS MITCHELL

KALMUS, HERBERT THOMAS (Nov. 9, 1881–July 11, 1963), and **KALMUS, NATALIE MABELLE DUNFEE** (1883–Nov. 15, 1965), inventors. Herbert Kalmus was born in Chelsea, Mass., the son of Benjamin G. Kalmus and Ada Isabella Gurney, both professional musicians. He attended English High School in Boston and studied classical piano until injury of his fingers while playing baseball compelled him to give up hope of being a concert pianist. Weakness in Latin prevented him from going to an Ivy League college, so he turned to the Massachusetts Institute of Technology (MIT).

On July 23, 1902, Kalmus married Natalie Mabelle Dunfee. She was born in Norfolk, Va., the daughter of George Kayser Dunfee. She attended Stetson University in DeLand, Fla., the Boston School of Art, and the Curry School of

Expressionism (also in Boston). Following graduation with a B.S. in 1904, Herbert became principal and part owner of University School in San Francisco. He sold his interest one year before the devastating earthquake of 1906, and returned to MIT for further study. He received the Ph.D. in 1906 after study on an MIT fellowship at the universities of Berlin and Zurich. His dissertation was published as *Electrical Conductivity and Viscosity of Some Fused Electrolytes* (1906). Natalie Kalmus studied art at Zurich while her husband was at the university.

They then returned to Boston, where Herbert became an instructor in physics at MIT and, later, associate in the research department (1907–1910). Next, he went to Queens University, Kingston, Ontario, as professor of physics and subsequently of electrochemistry and metallurgy. He also was director of an electrochemistry and metallurgy research laboratory for the Canadian government. Kalmus' studies in the industrial uses of cobalt led to the discovery of abrasives that were equivalents of Alundrum and Carborundum. For these he was awarded patents, and formed a private corporation, Exolon, to manufacture them. He was vice-president, treasurer, and president of this enterprise from 1915 to 1925.

As early as 1912, Kalmus had established himself as both aggressive entrepreneur and dynamic inventor by forming a consulting engineering firm with former classmate Daniel Comstock and W. Burton Westcott, a mechanical genius. He was president of this firm, and of American Protein Company of Boston, until 1925.

A decisive turn in his career came when William Coolidge of the United States Shoe Machinery Company brought Kalmus' consultants the Vanascope, a machine designed to take the flicker out of motion pictures. The inventors wanted an investment of $1 million; Kalmus advised against the project, but remarked that venture capital might be more useful in making motion pictures in color. Coolidge returned a year later to inquire further into the idea of color movies, and Kalmus commented: "The boys have some ideas." The Technicolor Motion Picture Corporation (taking its name from Kalmus' alma mater) was formed in 1915, with Kalmus' consulting firm as an equal partner.

The first laboratory, in a railway car in Boston, developed the Technicolor process. It had a British forebear in the Kinemacolor process patented by George Albert Smith and Charles Urban in 1906. This two-color process, using orange-red and blue-green, had failed commercially in 1911 because of bad color resolution. Another worker

in the field, Louis Dufay, had begun work on an additive color film in 1910, but it did not come on the market until 1930—after Eastman Kodak had come out with a sixteen-millimeter film that it called Koda Color (a film entirely different from its present Kodacolor).

Kalmus and his partners separated when his investors saw little promise in the new company. He recognized the necessity of bringing out a completed film. He therefore moved the railway-car laboratory to Jacksonville, Fla., where he produced *The Gulf Between* in 1917. The film used for this picture, though superior to the Kinemacolor process, was still limited to two colors and required great dexterity on the part of the projectionist and a large amount of light. After carefully assessing the picture at the Klaus and Erlanger Theatre in Buffalo, N.Y., Kalmus determined to give up the additive process and develop a new subtractive film.

Aiding Kalmus in the search for a good color film was his wife, who was often called the codeveloper of Technicolor because of her efforts on behalf of both production and promotion of color films. She was a strikingly beautiful woman with brilliant red hair, and her beauty and coloring made her an invaluable scientific model in the development of color motion pictures. Natalie Kalmus had an integral role in the development of the Technicolor process. Credited with being a top color expert, she was placed in charge of color control on all productions (sets, clothing, makeup, lighting, editing consultation). Her name alone appeared on all Technicolor motion pictures until 1948, when, following a bitter suit against her former husband to gain half of the company's profits, Kalmus ordered her name struck from association with the company.

The Kalmuses were divorced secretly in 1921, but their work made them inseparable. Natalie settled for $7,500 yearly alimony and a position with the company that brought her $24,000 annually plus expenses. The problems surrounding their personal lives never intruded on the Kalmuses' dedication to finding a workable color motion picture process. With his rejection of the additive process, Herbert and his team turned to perfecting a subtractive method of reproducing color prints in the laboratory.

But again money was the problem. The failure of *The Gulf Between* to attract the movie industry's interest turned Kalmus to private investors, such as William Travers Jerome, former New York City district attorney, a trial lawyer, and a hobbyist with a complete machine shop in his study. Jerome in turn attracted money from the Childs brothers, who owned the company that manufactured Bon Ami cleanser, and this brought in Albert W. Erickson and Harrison McCann, advertising executives. They encouraged investment by Albert W. Hawkes of Congoleum floor coverings and John McHugh, a banker. The group was completed by the addition of movie executives Marcus Loew and Joseph N. Schenck, and a stock issue of 150,000 shares at $8 per share quickly brought in the backing needed to perfect the film. Kalmus retained a half interest.

In 1922 the Kalmus two-color process was used in *Toll of the Sea*. It proved a success, grossing more than $250,000. Still experimenting, Kalmus accepted Schenck's offer of the use of his studio to make a version of *Madame Butterfly* starring Anna May Wong. Distributed by Metro, the film made some money, but Hollywood was still not convinced. The technology of producing even black-and-white film was still unsophisticated. With color, actors had to work under brilliant, hot lighting. Further, the heavier print made after joining two films and having color emulsions added in the final print caused cupping as the film threaded through projectors. In 1923, Jesse Lasky of Famous Players Studios gambled on a Kalmus film called *The Wanderer in Wasteland*, with dismal results. Douglas Fairbanks starred in *The Black Pirate* (1926), which also failed to make money. Kalmus, feeling that an extravaganza was needed, persuaded Everett Childs to put up money to make *The Viking* (1929), which was sold to Metro at cost. Again success was not forthcoming.

The redoubtable Kalmus then reorganized his operations, dividing his company into teams of engineers, scientists, and designers to work on a three-color process. One of his men, J. A. Ball, invented a three-strip camera, and Leonard Troland produced a new film. Another team, led by Gerald Ritchett and John Clark, developed a dye-transfer method for print production. New investors provided more money, which in turn attracted the interest of the movie magnate Jack Warner, who in 1929 made *Gold Diggers of Broadway*, using the two-color process. This film grossed $3.5 million, and Technicolor arrived. Kalmus was able now to push on with the three-color idea, solving problems by what he termed an "osmotic oozing to perfection." Meanwhile, he followed *Gold Diggers* with *On with the Show* (1929), the first talking pictures in Technicolor.

Having moved his operations to Hollywood in 1927, Kalmus now had the funds needed to continue his work. In 1932, Walt Disney tested the three-color technology in an animated short, *Flowers and Trees*, which was followed in 1933 and 1934 by the animated films *The Three Little Pigs* and *The Big Bad Wolf*. The first use of the process for live action came in 1933 in the short subject *La Cucaracha*. Kalmus signed a contract with Pioneer Pictures to produce eight pictures. In all, he sold 11 million feet of picture prints in 1934. In 1935 his process was completed and displayed in the David O. Selznick film *Becky Sharp*. This milestone in cinematography was the first true color film, the quality of which has stood the test of time. Indeed, cinematographers, directors, and film scientists concerned with the fading shown by more recent color films have turned back to study Kalmus' original works, which have retained their hues extremely well.

In 1937, Walt Disney produced his enormously successful *Snow White and the Seven Dwarfs* in Technicolor, and assured the future of the new process. With the release of *Gone with the Wind* (1939), Technicolor laid the base for Kalmus' exclusive control of color motion-picture production of extravaganzas, which were very important for the film industry after World War II, when black-and-white television threatened the motion picture business.

In the late 1940's Natalie Kalmus brought suit against her former husband, seeking half of his assets. She declared herself to be both business partner and sharer of his homes in Bel Air, Calif., and in Centerville, Mass. She cited her work as director of color control and the fact that her name alone appeared on finished Technicolor films. Herbert Kalmus had allowed friends and associates to presume that they were still married, and Natalie declared that a large cash, alimony, and pension agreement signed in 1946 was evidence that they were still man and wife at that time. She also named as corespondents five Jane Does, but the court held that her 1921 divorce was irrefutable. She tried to have the divorce vacated, but was unsuccessful. Kalmus ended Natalie's association with the company in 1948. She received a pension of $11,000 a year. After the court decision, Kalmus married a newspaper columnist, Eleanore King, on Sept. 6, 1949. Kalmus had no children by either marriage.

Throughout his career, the quiet Kalmus stayed in the background but kept tight control over his company, Technicolor Incorporated, which by 1949 was free of debt, owned a $7 million plant, and did $20 million a year in business. He hired a press agent, Margaret Ettinger, who had the odd—for Hollywood—duty of keeping his name out of newspapers and magazines. He avoided his former wife (who shared his home until her court action) and surrounded himself with young, stylish women and associates who indulged his fondness for table tennis and croquet. He controlled all Technicolor equipment, limiting the number of cameras to fewer than thirty, never selling them, and hiring his crews to film companies. One of his team, Leonard Troland, invented a new monopack film that allowed more location filming.

Eventually companies such as Ansco-Agfa, Trucolor, and Cinecolor, which used films made by General Aniline and Film and by Eastman Kodak, competed in the color film market, but Kalmus' hold on the business was so complete that the Justice Department brought an antitrust suit against his company in August 1947. This suit, coupled with that brought by his wife, vexed Kalmus greatly. His response to the government was that the "only great knowledge we have is know-how, and you can't break up know-how by court order." Eastman Kodak was charged as a coconspirator, but no resolution was forthcoming and the Kalmus company turned more to the less expensive Eastman film technology in the late 1960's. The only existing Technicolor film processing line existing in the 1970's was one in Peking, China.

Filmmakers and motion picture companies began to rebel against the costly Technicolor process and its exclusive controls even though the process was still the finest in terms of the preservation of color integrity. In the 1980's color film, 85 percent of which was made by Eastman Kodak, could be preserved only in refrigerated, humidity-free vaults or by making extra prints using the original Technicolor process of color separation negatives (making three black-and-white prints of a film on which are recorded images in the three primary colors).

Kalmus retained his control of Technicolor and its subsidiaries until 1959, when he retired. He served on the board of directors of the Stanford Research Institute from 1953 until his death. He invented an ultraviolet lamp to treat tubercular growths and collaborated on the development of a galvanometer to measure mental and emotional stress. For his personal use Kalmus built a teeter-totter cot to improve his circulation. In retirement he liked to entertain, using these occasions to conduct private screenings of new films. A "scientific" horseplayer, he also enjoyed betting on table tennis, croquet, and golf. He died in Los Angeles.

Natalie Kalmus, who had described her role in the development of motion pictures as "play-ing ringmaster to the rainbow," moved to the East Coast after her retirement in 1948. She had proved to be an indomitable aide to Kalmus, working as scriptwriter, color and makeup consultant to filmmakers, and the first woman color cinematographer. In the last ten years that she worked for the company, she traveled an average of 40,000 miles a year to supervise camera setups and stage sets and to resolve contractural arrangements between the company and the studios.

The vitality of Natalie Kalmus' work sustained her in her curious domestic relationship of her divorce until it became evident that Kalmus intended to remarry. Following her retirement, she lived a quiet life. She died in Boston, Mass.

Despite the major achievement of Herbert Kalmus and his associates, they never received any award from the industry at large. He gained recognition in 1938 from the Society of Motion Picture Engineers and a citation from the National Office of Scientific Research and Development in 1945 for his technical advice during the war. Part of the reason, certainly, was his unyielding control of his operations. His exclusive authority over all equipment, including camera crews and lighting, and even aspects of the script, certainly intruded on the studios' management of their affairs. And his prices were high. The average cost per final print foot charged by the company in 1947 was 6.22 cents. More than 222 million feet of film were printed by Technicolor in that year.

[Herbert Kalmus' writings include *Researches on Cobalt and Cobalt Alloys Conducted at Queen's University, Kingston, Ontario, for the Mines Branch of the Department of Mines* (1913–1916); "Technicolor Adventures in Cinemaland," *Journal of the Society of Motion Picture Engineers,* Dec. 1938; and *Mr. Technicolor* (1949), a short book now virtually unavailable. There are no biographical treatments of Herbert Kalmus of any length, but see Frank J. Taylor, "Mr. Technicolor," *Saturday Evening Post,* Oct. 22, 1949, and Fred E. Basten, *Glorious Technicolor* (1980). Obituaries are in the *New York Times* and *Los Angeles Times,* July 12, 1963. Independent references to Natalie Kalmus are nonexistent except in her obituary in the *New York Times,* Nov. 18, 1965.]

JACK J. CARDOSO

KALTENBORN, HANS VON (July 9, 1878–June 14, 1965), radio news commentator, was born in Milwaukee, Wis., the son of Baron Rudolph von Kaltenborn-Stachau and of Bettie Wessels, a teacher of German who died giving birth to her son. Kaltenborn's father apparently never recovered from this tragedy; he could neither hold a job nor curb his drinking. Repeated frustrations appear to have caused him to exaggerate the glories of his past and the grandeur of his Old World background. In part, Kaltenborn's personal development can be considered an attempt to compensate for his father's failures and to redeem his Germanic heritage. Moreover, his professional career seemed to reflect a sustained effort to resolve the tensions between Europe and America.

Kaltenborn left school at fourteen. Thereafter his experiences included clerking in his father's building supply store in Merrill, Wis. (1893–1898), working for the *Merrill Advocate,* and serving as a soldier and newspaper reporter during the Spanish-American War. Kaltenborn's unit never left Alabama, but he sharpened his journalistic skills by writing accounts of camp life. This time away from home also aroused his interest in travel, an interest that would become his passion. After being discharged, Kaltenborn toured in the United States, returned briefly to Merrill as city editor of the *Advocate,* and, in 1900, was appointed the paper's foreign correspondent. For eighteen months he bicycled around England, France, and Germany, broadening his outlook and deepening his commitment to journalism.

Returning to the United States in 1902, Kaltenborn took a job at the *Brooklyn Eagle* as a night reporter. Promotions came quickly; after slightly more than a year he was covering City Hall. Yet each step brought a greater awareness of the deficiencies in his formal education. After three years with the *Eagle,* he applied successfully for admission to Harvard.

Kaltenborn entered Harvard in 1905 as a special student. He graduated cum laude in 1909, majoring in political science. He excelled in public speaking and founded a club to encourage campus discussion of international relations. He continued writing as a staff member of the Harvard *Illustrated,* and contributed pieces on Brooklyn students at Harvard to the *Eagle.*

After several profitable months tutoring John Jacob Astor's son, Vincent, for Harvard, Kaltenborn resumed his position with the *Eagle* in 1910. He married Baroness Olga von Nordenflycht, daughter of a German diplomat, on Sept. 14, 1910. They had two children.

Kaltenborn was associated with the *Eagle* until 1930, and during this time he concentrated increasingly on foreign affairs. He began to use the new medium of radio for analyzing news stories, and came to be known as H. V. Kaltenborn. Suspected of being pro-German during World War I, he dropped the "von," and by the early 1920's was signing his *Eagle* articles simply with initials.

Kaltenborn's radio career stemmed from the reputation he enjoyed as a lecturer on current events. His talks were so popular that the *Eagle* arranged to have one broadcast over a local station. On Apr. 4, 1922, New York listeners heard him analyze a coal strike—probably the first editorial analysis in the history of broadcast journalism. Soon he was regularly airing his daily columns and had established an authoritative image that formed his trademark in the years after 1930, when he joined the Columbia Broadcasting System (CBS) as a full-time commentator.

Over the next quarter-century, millions of Americans became familiar with the "Suave Voice of Doom." They instantly recognized Kaltenborn's pompous, affected manner of speech. They knew his topics would be timely, and his forceful treatment of them often controversial. Kaltenborn could be wrong—as President Harry Truman delighted in pointing out by imitating the commentator's predictions of Thomas Dewey's victory long after the polls had closed on election night 1948. Nevertheless, when he paused in his rapid-fire delivery to announce some "ee-pawk-ul" turning point, the audience was inclined to believe him.

The most resounding demonstration of his influence occurred during the Munich crisis of 1938. Between September 10 and 30, Kaltenborn made 102 broadcasts. Sustained by sandwiches and coffee brought to him by his wife, and napping intermittently on a cot set up in the network's New York studio, he was on the air around the clock. His preparation for this was ideal: he knew foreign languages and never used a script. The moment a German or French speech came over his shortwave receiver, he would translate it while giving his interpretation. Listeners had a sense of being in direct contact with a historic event, an impression enhanced by Kaltenborn's previous interviews with Adolf Hitler, Benito Mussolini, Edouard Daladier, and Neville Chamberlain. Twenty days of virtual nonstop reporting left him groggy, but the ordeal also had made his name a household word. He was hired by the National Broadcasting Corporation (NBC) in the spring of 1940.

Kaltenborn remained a national fixture until the mid-1950's. Then, with the advent of television, he fell victim to changing conditions in broadcast journalism. The style that had proved so effective on radio was not convincing in the person of a seventy-five-year-old man who, *Time* said, looked like a "prosperous professor." Although in 1958 he served as temporary host of the "Today Show," his regular broadcasts ended in 1955. The last decade of Kaltenborn's life was spent quietly among family and friends in Stony Brook, N.Y., and New York City, where he died.

[The Kaltenborn Manuscript Collection is at the State Historical Society of Wisconsin, Madison. His autobiography is *Fifty Fabulous Years 1900–1950: A Personal Review* (1950).

See also David Gillis Clark, "The Dean of Commentators: A Biography of H. V. Kaltenborn" (Ph.D. diss., University of Wisconsin, 1965); David Holbrook Culbert, *News for Everyman: Radio and Foreign Affairs in Thirties America* (1976).

Also see "Radio: Combination for Comment," *Time,* Oct. 10, 1938; "Kaltenborn, Hans von," *Harvard Class of 1909 Fiftieth Anniversary Report* (1959).

An obituary is in the *New York Times,* June 15, 1965.]

J. Kirkpatrick Flack

KÁRMÁN, THEODORE (TODOR) VON (May 11, 1881–May 7, 1963), physicist, engineer, and applied mathematician, was born in Budapest, Hungary, the son of Maurice (Mór) Kármán and Helen Konn. He attributed his interest in science to both his mother, the descendant of a sixteenth-century mathematician at the imperial court of Prague who created the world's first mechanical robot, and his father, a professor of education who encouraged curiosity and stressed the value of understanding above mere observation. All the Kármán children were first taught at home by a private tutor and each other; their father wrote primers and fairy tales for them.

Kármán entered the Minta, a model gymnasium organized according to the elder Kármán's ideas, at age nine. He won the Eötvös Prize for mathematics and scientific reasoning, a success he attributed to his father's stress on principles of thinking rather than memorization. He also was deeply influenced by Henri Poincaré's ideas, later collected as *Science and Hypothesis,* from which he gained the views that science is primarily a classification of experiences and that a correct physical law is one that explains the maximum number of observations without contradiction.

In 1898, Kármán entered the Palatine Joseph Polytechnic. Although the science taught there suffered from an emphasis on the trades, he was able to benefit from courses such as that in descriptive geometry. When he was stimulated by Donat Banki to do creative thinking about a problem involving the clattering of valves at certain engine speeds, he felt drawn toward an engineering career. After graduating in 1902, Kármán served for a year in the Austro-Hungarian army and then was assistant to Banki at the Palatine Joseph for three years. Banki's additional position as consultant to a local machine manufacturing company enabled Kármán to develop a deep appreciation of and interest in practical engine design.

His investigation of the phenomenon of buckling of loaded columns so impressed Kármán's father that he convinced his son to resign his position at the Palatine Joseph in order to pursue graduate study in theoretical engineering at a foreign university. Kármán obtained a two-year fellowship from the Hungarian Academy of Sciences and studied with Ludwig Prandtl at the University of Göttingen.

From Prandtl, who is often called the "father of aerodynamics," Kármán learned the method of abstracting the basic physical elements of a complex process and analyzing it with simplified methods of mathematics. He completed his doctoral dissertation on buckling phenomena under Prandtl in 1908 then spent a semester at the Sorbonne, at g lectures by Marie Curie and others.

While in Paris, Kár nessed a two-kilometer airplane flight. E improve airplane safety and airplane engi returned to Göttingen (where he be rivatdocent), and tested Zeppelin airship the wind tunnel being constructed there 09–1912). Working closely with Prandtl and randtl's colleagues, Kármán became thorough versed in aeronautics, fluid mechanics, and hydrodynamics.

In 1911, Kármán produced what is probably his best-known theory. He became intrigued by the appearance of unceasing-pressure fluctuations in the flow of a fluid past a right circular cylinder, noting that the fluctuations could not be eliminated by any combination of redesign or remachining of the apparatus. All symmetrical approaches to the problem were unstable, and any small pressure deviations would increase until the flow pattern was destroyed. Kármán therefore tried an unsymmetrical solution; much to his surprise, he found a stable solution consisting of two trails of oppositely turning and alternately occurring vortices shed by the cylinder, much like street lights on opposite sides of the street.

The ensuing theory, known as the Kármán theory of vortex streets, was verified by numerous experimental tests. It was found to have application to a wide range of physical situations: the wake behind a moving body, the drag forces of such moving objects as racing cars and airplanes, the oscillations of tall, thin structures in moderate winds, and the explanation for the vibrations that caused the collapse of the Tacoma Narrows suspension bridge in 1940.

Another of Kármán's accomplishments during this period was a paper on the specific heats of solids that he wrote with Max Born (1912). Their theory, although published shortly after a similar theory by Peter Debye, has more recently been recognized as more comprehensive and accurate than the simpler Debye theory.

Since there was no professorial vacancy at Göttingen, Kármán accepted the chair of applied mechanics at the mining academy in Selmeczbánya, Hungary (now Banká Stiavnica, Czechoslovakia), in the fall of 1912. Finding little equipment and poorly motivated students there, he returned almost immediately to Göttingen, where Felix Klein set about finding him a more suitable position. Kármán accepted the chair of aeronautics and mechanics at the Technische Hochschule in Aachen, Germany, in February 1913; he stayed there, with an interruption during World War I, until 1929. During his five years in the Austro-Hungarian army and air force (1914–1919), Kármán worked on such projects as a wind tunnel to test propellers and helicopters with two counterrotating propellers.

After the war Kármán transformed Aachen into a leading aeronautical research center. He also served as consultant for such leading German aircraft builders as Hugo Junkers, Ernst Heinkel, A. H. G. Fokker, and Ferdinand von Zeppelin. In 1921 his mother and sister came to live with him in Aachen. He never married.

In 1926–1927, Kármán lectured and was a consultant for aeronautical experts in the United States and Japan. He visited the United States for a second time in 1928, and was finally persuaded to join Robert A. Millikan at the California Institute of Technology as director of the Guggenheim Aeronautical Laboratory (1930–1949) and director of research of the Guggenheim Airship Institute. He retained his position at Aachen, spending his summers there, until the Nazis forced him to resign in 1933. He became a United States citizen in 1936.

At Cal Tech, Kármán worked in such diverse areas as instability problems in the DC-1 airplane, control problems in the telescope at Mt. Palomar, the shape of turbine blades that would increase the efficiency of electric generators and

jet engines, the pumping and piping of water to the city of Los Angeles, and ways to avoid the cracking of gigantic dams such as the Grand Coulee. He also became interested in rocket propulsion and flight.

In the late 1930's Kármán was drawn increasingly into governmental and industrial circles as consultant and adviser. He and several colleagues formed Aerojet Engineering Corporation in 1942 to design, test, and manufacture jet-assisted takeoff rockets for airplanes. After Kármán and his friends had sold their stock in it, the company was renamed Aerojet-General Corporation and became one of the largest rocket and space conglomerates in the country.

After the war Kármán chaired the Scientific Advisory Group which wrote the the influential report concerning the future of the U.S. Air Force, *Toward New Horizons,* as well as the companion volume, *Science: The Key to Air Supremacy.* He was instrumental in establishing the RAND corporation in 1948, and in 1952 helped establish the Advisory Group for Aeronautical Research and Development as a part of the North Atlantic Treaty Organization (NATO). He also played a significant role in founding and giving direction to the American space program in the 1950's and 1960's through organizations such as the Jet Propulsion Laboratory. In the midst of all this official activity, Kármán continued to publish technical articles. He died at Aachen, not quite three months after having received the first U.S. National Medal of Science.

Although Kármán was an internationalist, he had no qualms about serving the military establishments of Austria-Hungary, Germany, the United States, and NATO. His apparent belief that politics should not interfere with simple facts was shown in his willingness to testify on behalf of the Nazi-controlled Junkers firm during its patent infringement claims against American aircraft companies in the 1930's (Kármán was Jewish), and in his stand against a congressional investigating committee when his colleague and former student Hsue-shen Tsien was accused of Communist ties during the 1950's.

[The definitive collection of Kármán's published articles is *Collected Works of Dr. Theodore von Kármán,* 4 vols. (1956); an additional volume covering 1952–1963 was published in 1975. His technical books are *General Aerodynamic Theory,* 2 vols. (1924), with J. M. Burgers; *Mathematical Methods in Engineering* (1940), with M. A. Biot; *Aerodynamics* (1954); and *From Low-Speed Aerodynamics to As-*

tronautics (1961). His autobiography is *The Wind and Beyond* (1967), with Lee Edson. Also see California Institute of Technology, *Theodore von Kármán Anniversary Volume* (1941). An obituary is in the *New York Times*, May 8, 1963.]

RICHARD K. GEHRENBECK

KAUFMAN, GEORGE S. (Nov. 16, 1889–June 2, 1961), playwright, director, screenwriter, and essayist, was born in Pittsburgh, Pa., the son of Joseph Kaufman and Henrietta Myers. The middle initial "S" stood for nothing and was added to his name by Kaufman when he began to write for publication in 1909. The Kaufman family was much less affluent than others in their circle. Joseph Kaufman went from job to job, losing interest in, or being discharged from, one position after another. From 1900 to 1905 he owned his own tool steel plant in nearby New Castle but was unable to make a success of it.

Kaufman attended local public schools and graduated from Pittsburgh Central High in 1907. Encouraged by his rabbi, he acted with a student group. In collaboration with a friend, Irving Pichel (later a Hollywood actor and director of note), he wrote a play. These activities left him permanently stagestruck. Although he studied law briefly in 1907 at Western University of Pennsylvania (now the University of Pittsburgh), his hopes lay in the theater. Practical considerations, however, made him accept various jobs, including work for a surveying team, as an office clerk and, from 1909 to 1912, as a salesman for the Columbia Ribbon Company of Paterson, N. J., for which his father had become a plant manager in 1909.

In Paterson, Kaufman began to send contributions to the popular newspaper column "Always in Good Humor," which Franklin P. Adams wrote for the New York *Evening Mail.* He signed them with the initials "G. S. K." Adams was asked by the publisher Frank Munsey to choose from among the many young writers contributing to the column and to suggest someone who could provide a daily humor column for the *Washington Times.* He recommended Kaufman. From late 1912 to late 1913 Kaufman held the job. His employment came to an end when Munsey, visiting the paper's offices, saw him for the first time and, recognizing that he was a Jew, dismissed him for that reason alone. It was a brush against anti-Semitism that Kaufman never forgot.

Kaufman then moved to New York City, which remained his home for the rest of his life. In 1913 Adams began to write his column for

the *New York Tribune* and the next year secured Kaufman a post there as a reporter. In 1915 Kaufman became humor columnist for the *Evening Mail.* Dismissed after six months when the paper changed hands, he returned to the *Tribune* as a reporter in the drama department. In September 1917 he accepted a similar post at the *New York Times* and shortly thereafter was promoted to drama editor. He remained at the *Times* until August 1930, long after he had become one of Broadway's most popular playwrights. On Mar. 15, 1917, he married Beatrice Bakrow, of Rochester, N.Y.

Throughout his years as a ribbon salesman, columnist, and reporter, Kaufman strove to secure a place for himself in the theater. In 1910 he had enrolled in the Alveine School of Dramatic Art in New York. In 1914 and 1915 he took courses in playwriting and the study of modern drama at Columbia. His first break came in the 1917–1918 season when the producer George C. Tyler asked him to revise a comedy about a jewel thief by Larry Evans and Walter C. Percival. Titled *Someone in the House,* this play opened on September 9, 1918, after many months of rewriting. It was Kaufman's first Broadway credit. Although not a success, the production initiated a working relationship between Kaufman and Tyler that continued through 1922.

In November 1918 Kaufman and his wife suffered a grave disappointment when Beatrice was delivered of a stillborn child. This event altered the course of their lives; thereafter they formed other romantic attachments, although never intending to conceal them from each other and never contemplating divorce. In 1925 they adopted an infant girl.

After a second unsuccessful "doctoring" effort for Tyler, Kaufman formed a writing partnership with another young theatrical journalist, Marc Connelly, who had already done some work in the professional theater. From 1921 through 1924, Broadway witnessed the opening of five plays and two musical comedies by the pair, as well as some revues to which they made contributions. Most of these productions were hits, including the first, *Dulcy* (1921), a vehicle for Lynn Fontanne. The collaborations, in which Kaufman and Connelly fully exploited their gift for comedy, were acclaimed for their wisecracking wit and broadside attacks on big business. Usually, the protagonist was a naive young man whose success and happiness depended upon the aid of a young woman with considerably more sense than he possessed. The few touches of warmth in the plays were added by Connelly, for Kaufman discovered very early that he had no talent for or interest in sentimental dialogue.

Busy as Kaufman was, he found time on most weekdays for a leisurely lunch at the Algonquin Hotel, whose proprietor, Frank Case, had established a special table in the hotel's Rose Room as a meeting-place for journalistic and theatrical wits. Through the 1920's the Algonquin Round Table was famed for its "Vicious Circle," which included Kaufman, Connelly, Adams, Dorothy Parker, Robert Benchley, Robert E. Sherwood, Heywood Broun, and Alexander Woollcott, along with other writers and many Broadway performers. The noontime quips of these celebrities became the stuff of newspaper columns the nation over, as did reports of their cutthroat games of poker and croquet.

An occasional luncher at the Round Table was the novelist Edna Ferber. After some years, Kaufman realized that his collaborator Connelly did not spend as much time as he at work; Kaufman then formed a writing relationship with Ferber. He preferred the give and take of collaboration to creating plots and dialogue by himself. His first play with Ferber, *Minick* (1924), was not a success, but of the six plays that they wrote together, *The Royal Family* (1927) and *Dinner at Eight* (1932) were among his most highly acclaimed. Unlike Kaufman, Ferber could compose poignant scenes when the plot called for them. The dynastic family and its social and financial fortunes were of keen interest to her, and most of the Kaufman-Ferber plays concerned that subject.

Kaufman's only major noncollaborative work was *The Butter and Egg Man* (1925), a satirical comedy about a Broadway producer who is sadly, though comically, lacking in both morals and money. Also that year he wrote *The Cocoanuts*, a musical comedy for the Marx Brothers; this established him as an expert on material for the zany comedians. Although the musical was credited to Kaufman alone, the journalist Morrie Ryskind helped him with it. Over the next ten years Kaufman and Ryskind worked together on six more projects, including two additional scripts for the Marx Brothers, *Animal Crackers* (1928) and the film *A Night at the Opera* (1935), and the Pulitzer-Prize winning musical *Of Thee I Sing* (1931). Apart from the Marx Brothers comedies, the Kaufman-Ryskind collaborations spoofed American politics, with special attention to the executive branch of government. It was Ryskind, more than Kaufman, who took a passionate interest in politics, but Kaufman as a lifelong liberal was to become a

firm supporter of Franklin D. Roosevelt and Fiorello La Guardia.

After abortive efforts to direct two of his plays in the mid-1920's, Kaufman was persuaded by producer Jed Harris to direct the Ben Hecht–Charles MacArthur comedy *The Front Page* in 1928. Both the play and his direction were highly praised. Thereafter, he staged all but two of his own plays, as well as many by other authors.

In the late 1920's and early 1930's the list of Kaufman's collaborators included Ring Lardner (*June Moon*, 1929), Woollcott (*The Channel Road*, 1929; *The Dark Tower*, 1933), and Sherwood (*Roman Scandals*, film, 1933). But of all the men and women with whom he ever wrote, Moss Hart was his favorite. In 1930 Hart had written a satirical comedy about Hollywood that the producer Sam H. Harris thought needed the Kaufman touch. This play, *Once in a Lifetime* (1930), was the first of eight collaborations between them. Among the others were the Pulitzer Prize-winning *You Can't Take It with You* (1936) and *The Man Who Came to Dinner* (1939). Hart shared Kaufman's gift for creating glittering comic lines that spoofed contemporary preoccupations and for developing bustling activity on stage.

A shy, quirky, aloof man, and so hypochondriacal that he declined to shake hands with anyone lest he be contaminated by germs, Kaufman had few intimates. But Hart quickly became one of the few. After the opening of their first play, they were in touch with each other virtually every day for the rest of Kaufman's life. It was a severe wrench to Kaufman when, after ten years of their writing association, Hart decided that he must compose plays on his own. Thereafter, neither wrote for the stage with such success.

In 1936 Kaufman's name was in the headlines when it was discovered that he had had a prolonged affair with the screen actress Mary Astor. However, neither Kaufman's career nor his marriage was shaken by the scandal. The harshest blow ever to befall Kaufman occurred in August 1945, when Beatrice died. It was only work, both as playwright and director, that revived his spirits. On May 26, 1949, he married the English actress Leueen MacGrath. This marriage ended in divorce in 1957.

In 1950 Kaufman directed, to great acclaim, the musical production *Guys and Dolls*. This was one of the peaks of his long career. Soon afterward he suffered a series of debilitating illnesses. They lessened his strength, but did not curb his urge to work. In his last years he wrote with several new collaborators. Among them were Leueen MacGrath, with whom he worked on three productions, including the hit musical *Silk Stockings* (1955), and Howard Teichmann, with whom he wrote *The Solid Gold Cadillac* (1953), a long-running comedy. In 1957 he directed Peter Ustinov's *Romanoff and Juliet;* this was his last production. He died in New York City.

Although Kaufman was one of the most successful and prolific playwrights of his time, with more than forty plays to his credit, he did not think that the popularity of his works would outlast his lifetime. Time has proved him wrong, for many of the comedies have become classics of the American repertory.

[Kaufman kept very few letters written to him and did not make copies of those that he wrote. (Nor did he date his letters.) Some of his letters to Moss Hart are in the collection of Wisconsin Center for Theater Research at Madison, and those to Woollcott are in the Harvard University Theater Collection. Others are widely scattered. Typescripts of his plays may be found at the Library of Congress, the Theater Collection of the New York Public Library, the Princeton University Theater Collection, the Walter Hampden Library of The Players (New York), and the Wisconsin Center for Theater Research. The standard biography is Malcolm Goldstein, *George S. Kaufman: His Life, His Theater* (1979). See also Howard Teichmann, *George S. Kaufman: An Intimate Portrait* (1972); and Scott Meredith, *George S. Kaufman and His Friends* (1974). The *New York Times* obituary appeared on June 3, 1961.]

MALCOLM GOLDSTEIN

KEARNS, JACK (Aug. 17, 1882–July 7, 1963), boxing promoter, was born John Leo McKernan in Waterloo, Mich., the son of Phillip McKernan, a journalist, and Frances Hoff. He attended public schools in Waterloo, but left school before the age of fourteen. He drifted to Alaska during the Klondike gold rush. He never became a prospector, preferring employment in the saloons of Nome, White Horse, and Dawson. Kearns's first association with boxing may have occurred in Alaska, where he met Tex Rickard, who later became the famous boxing promoter.

By the time he was eighteen, Kearns had drifted to Montana and then to Seattle, where he tried out for a baseball club as a pitcher. While waiting for a contract with the club, he turned to boxing and changed his name to Jack Kearns. He fought sixty-seven professional bouts, competing in the lightweight and welterweight divisions. He was knocked out in 1901 by Honey Mellody, who became welterweight

champion in 1906. Kearns soon recognized his pugilistic shortcomings and turned to the management of other boxers.

Kearns's first prominence as a promoter came when he took a group of American boxers to Australia. After his return to the United States in 1917 he became a national sports personality as the manager of Jack Dempsey. Accounts of his early life may have been colored in retrospect by the flamboyance of his career after his association with Dempsey. Many incidents attributed to him may or may not have been true. It is extremely difficult to separate fact from fiction, partly because of Kearns himself—he was a master storyteller—and partly because of the boxing milieu, where flamboyance, stretching the truth, and excessive promotionalism were and are the normal way of life. In any case, Kearns was one of the most important and successful managers in the history of boxing. Until the 1970's his fighters earned more revenue than those of any other manager in the history of boxing.

Kearns managed six world champions, four of whom have been elected to *The Ring*'s Hall of Fame. They are Jack (William Harrison) Dempsey, heavyweight champion, 1919–1926; Mickey Walker, welterweight champion, 1922–1926, and middleweight champion, 1926–1931; Jackie Fields (Jacob Finkelstein), welterweight champion, 1929–1930; Benny Leonard (Benjamin Leiner), lightweight champion, 1917–1924; Joey Maxim (Joey Berardinelli), light-heavyweight champion, 1950–1952; and Archie Moore (Archibald Wright), light-heavyweight champion, 1952–1961.

Kearns was at the center of the "Golden Age" of boxing in the 1920's. Jack Dempsey began fighting in Utah and Colorado mining camps about 1912. Kearns, who became his manager in 1917, taught him how to box and how to use the left hook, which became Dempsey's most feared punch. After Dempsey won the heavyweight title from Jess Willard in 1919, Kearns began to cash in on Dempsey's popularity. He was Dempsey's manager in boxing's first two million-dollar gates, against Georges Carpentier and Luis Firpo. Nat Fleischer, editor of *The Ring*, credited Kearns with inventing the art of modern ballyhoo, the type of publicity designed to draw crowds to fights. After Dempsey married Estelle Taylor, a movie actress, he and Kearns parted company, but not as friends. Kearns unsuccessfully sued Dempsey for part of the proceeds from Dempsey's two losing matches with Gene Tunney. He never really forgave Dempsey; a year before Kearns died he finished writing his memoirs, *The Million Dollar Gate* (with the assistance of Oscar Fraley), in which he revived a long-standing rumor of foul play in Dempsey's fight with Willard. Kearns claimed that Dempsey floored Willard seven times in the first round because his gloves were loaded. Dempsey denied this, and most boxing authorities discount Kearns's story.

After the 1920's Kearns faded into obscurity. He claimed to have lost about half a million dollars on the stock market, but was still able to leave an occasional $50 tip for a waiter. When Mickey Walker lost his middleweight crown in 1931 because he was no longer able to make the 160-pound weight limit, Kearns was left without a champion. No longer was he able to enjoy the life of a high roller, backing lavish all-night parties at speakeasys such as Texas Guinan's and the Hotsy Totsy Club.

After being involved in a number of enterprises, none of them very successful, Kearns revived his boxing career in the 1950's as manager of Joey Maxim and Archie Moore. By this time he was known as "the Doc," because of his skills in patching facial cuts and abrasions suffered by his charges.

Kearns married Lillian Kansler on May 26, 1932; they had two sons, and were divorced in 1948. He died in Miami, Fla. When Jack Dempsey was told of Kearns's death, he said, "We had a lot of laughs together."

[Kearns's memoir is *The Million Dollar Gate* (1966), written with Oscar Fraley. Information on boxers and boxing is in *Ring Record Book* and the records section of *The Ring* magazine, located in Madison Square Garden.

Obituaries are in the *New York Times* and *Miami Herald*, July 8, 1963.]

HENRY SEYMOUR MARKS

KEFAUVER, (CAREY) ESTES (July 26, 1903–Aug. 10, 1963), lawyer and U.S. senator, was born on a farm near Madisonville, Tenn., the son of Robert Cooke Kefauver, a dairyman and hardware merchant, and of Phredonia Estes. Kefauver attended local schools, and in 1924 received a B.A. from the University of Tennessee, where he had been an outstanding athlete and student leader. After teaching high school at Hot Springs, Ark., for a year, he worked his way through Yale University Law School, which awarded him an LL.B. in 1927.

Kefauver then began practicing law in Chattanooga, where he soon became a successful corporate and banking lawyer. On Aug. 8, 1935, he married Nancy Patterson Pigott, the daughter of shipbuilder Sir Stephen Pigott; they had three daughters and adopted a son.

Active in a variety of civic endeavors in Chattanooga, Kefauver emerged as a leader of a movement devoted to reforming government in Hamilton County. In January 1939 he became state commissioner of finance and taxation. He resigned that position in May to enter a special election for Congress. Running as a New Deal Democrat, he was elected and took his seat in September.

Kefauver served on the House Judiciary Committee and on the Select Committee on Small Business, where he gained a reputation as an antimonopolist. He sponsored legislation to allow Cabinet members to answer questions on the House floor. He took liberal positions on the Tennessee Valley Authority (TVA) and, remarkable for a southerner at that time, on labor, civil rights, and civil liberties. Kefauver distinguished himself as a vigorous advocate of congressional reform. Besides supporting the Legislative Reorganization Act of 1946, he urged that the powers of committee chairmen should be limited; that representatives should be elected to four-year terms; that their staffs should be larger; that House votes should be cast electrically; that the District of Columbia should be represented in the House; that lobbyists should be restricted; that filibusters should be curbed; and that treaties should be ratified by a majority vote of both chambers of Congress. He cogently discussed these and other recommendations in his best-selling book *A Twentieth-Century Congress* (1947), written with Jack Levin.

In 1947 Kefauver decided to run for the Senate. Five years earlier he had started opposing Tennessee's political machine, which represented an alliance between Senator Kenneth McKellar and Memphis Mayor Edward H. Crump. Running for the Senate in 1948, Kefauver directly challenged the machine. In a heated campaign Crump declared that Kefauver was controlled by radical forces and was as deceptive as a pet coon. Kefauver replied, "I may be a pet coon, but I 'ain't' Mr. Crump's pet coon." After this exchange he took to wearing a coonskin cap, which was his campaign symbol for years. In the primary he defeated the incumbent, Senator Arthur T. ("Tom") Stewart, and Crump's candidate, Judge John A. Mitchell. Winning the primary helped destroy the power of the McKellar-Crump organization and made Kefauver widely known as an antiboss crusader. In the November election he easily bested former Republican National Committee chairman B. Carroll Reece.

In the Senate, Kefauver early established a

reputation for diligence and integrity. He served on the Armed Forces, Judiciary, and Appropriations committees. He was known for being liberal, though independent-minded, on antitrust, labor, civil rights, and civil liberties issues as well as on foreign policy. In 1950 he seized the limelight as chairman of a special committee to investigate crime, which grew out of a resolution he had sponsored. By 1951 the Kefauver Committee's exhaustive investigations and adept use of television coverage had made the public sensitive to the dangers of organized crime, spurred prosecutions, and made Kefauver a national figure.

Kefauver declared his candidacy for the 1952 Democratic presidential nomination. He benefited from his Lincolnesque personality and from revelations of corruption in President Harry Truman's administration. Although he lacked a large campaign fund and significant organizational support, he effectively contested almost all of the Democratic primary elections. The result was that before the 1952 Democratic National Convention met, he had the largest number of committed delegates and was the most popular Democrat in the public opinion polls. The nomination was not to be his, however; his independence had incurred the enmity of President Truman, urban political organizations, most southern delegates, and even many liberals. This pointed up Kefauver's dilemma in his campaigns for president in 1952 and 1956: his independent liberalism and personality, which made him popular with so many voters, made too many elements in the Democratic party suspicious of him.

Between 1952 and 1956, Kefauver was a frequent but fair critic of Dwight D. Eisenhower's Republican administration. He was instrumental in defending the TVA against the administration's attempts to weaken it. Kefauver also kept in the public eye through his well-publicized investigations, as chairman of the Senate Subcommittee on Juvenile Delinquency, of violence and sex in movies, television, and publications. He was reelected to the Senate in 1954.

Kefauver again sought the Democratic presidential nomination in 1956, but he was unable to vanquish Adlai E. Stevenson, the party's 1952 nominee, in the primary elections. He withdrew from the contest on the eve of the convention and endorsed Stevenson, who went on to be nominated for president. In an open convention fight, however, Kefauver defeated Senator John F. Kennedy of Massachusetts for the vice-presidential nomination. Kefauver was a strenuous campaigner, but he and Stevenson were unable to prevent President Eisenhower from being handily reelected.

Kefauver spent the remainder of his years in the Senate—he was returned to office again in 1960—as the model of a diligent, responsible legislator. As chairman of the Constitutional Amendments Subcommittee, he helped launch the Twenty-fourth Amendment, which abolished the poll tax. More prominently, as chairman of the Antitrust and Monopoly Subcommittee, he conducted exhaustive investigations into monopolistic practices, particularly into the artificial maintenance of prices. Most significant were the subcommittee's inquiries into administered prices as affected by organized labor and the drug, automobile, and steel industries. He also steered the Kefauver-Harris Drug Safety Act through Congress in 1962.

The body of laws that Kefauver sponsored was small, but he was influential, in debate and committee, in shaping legislation on both foreign and domestic policy. It was in his investigative efforts, however, that he was outstanding, especially in calling the public's attention to important issues. Moreover, if his political and personal independence kept him from gaining greater power in government or in his party, he represented political integrity and incorruptibility for large numbers of Americans. Kefauver died in Bethesda, Md.

[Kefauver's papers are at the University of Tennessee, Knoxville. Books by him not mentioned in the text include *Crime in America* (1951) and *In a Few Hands* (1965), written with Irene Till. See Joseph Bruce Gorman, *Kefauver* (1971), and Charles L. Fontenay, *Estes Kefauver: A Biography* (1980). Also see James B. Gardner, "Political Leadership in a Period of Transition" (Ph.D. diss., Vanderbilt University, 1978); Richard E. McFadyen, "Estes Kefauver and the Drug Industry" (Ph.D. diss., Emory University, 1973); and William H. Moore, "The Kefauver Committee and the Politics of Crime" (Ph.D. diss., University of Texas, 1971). An obituary is in the *New York Times*, Aug. 11, 1963.]

DONALD R. McCOY

KELLAND, CLARENCE BUDINGTON (July 11, 1881–Feb. 18, 1964), novelist, was born in Portland, Mich., the son of Thomas Kelland, an English weaver who emigrated to the United States shortly before the Civil War, and Margaret Budington, the proprietor of a millinery shop. He spent his early years in the idyllic environment of small-town America. His maternal grandmother, the family housekeeper, bore the major responsibility for raising Kelland. Her permissive, worldly philosophy tempered the strict, moralistic Congregational precepts of his mother. From his upbringing Kelland derived the primary values that shaped his life: a strong sense of right and wrong, an aversion to indolence, and a warm interest in and generous love of people.

In 1891 the family moved to Detroit, where Kelland attended private schools and received an LL.B. from Detroit College of Law in 1902. He practiced law briefly, but soon turned to journalism, becoming a reporter for the *Detroit News* (1903). He worked his way up from night police reporter to Sunday editor. In 1907 he left the *News* to become principal of the Sprague Correspondence School of Law. That same year he married Betty Caroline Smith of Ludington, Mich. They had two sons.

It was as editor of the *American Boy* (1907–1915) that Kelland began his literary endeavors in earnest. His first novel, *Mark Tidd, His Adventures and Strategies* (1913), was the first of nine juveniles featuring this rotund hero. During World War I (1918) Kelland served as director of overseas publicity for the YMCA.

In the early 1920's Kelland produced the Catty Atkins books, a series of five juvenile adventure novels: *Catty Atkins* (1920); *Catty Atkins, Riverman* (1921); *Catty Atkins, Sailorman* (1922); *Catty Atkins, Financier* (1923); and *Catty Atkins, Bandmaster* (1924). By the late 1920's he had made a fortune in royalties. He invested heavily in the Bank of New Hampstead at Port Washington, Long Island, and when the bank failed during the Great Depression, Kelland lost everything. He recovered by publishing dozens of short stories (chiefly in the *American Magazine*) and two novels featuring his most popular creation, the wily cracker-barrel philosopher Scattergood Baines.

Scattergood, first created in 1915, was the embodiment of the American folk character. He was not only the character who boosted Kelland to prosperity but the archetypal figure who dominated his most appealing work, whether he was called *Efficiency Edgar* (his first avatar, 1920), Mark Tidd, or Mr. Deeds.

A writer as productive as Kelland (sixty novels and two hundred short stories between 1913 and 1960), whose longer works were usually serialized (most appeared in the *Saturday Evening Post*), normally produces formula books. Kelland was no exception. His protagonist, personifying innocence and solid small-town virtue, is faced with a predicament, a challenge to his traditional values. He resolves the difficulty, usually in some shrewd but kindly way, and good triumphs over evil. The emotional appeal of Kelland's work, like that of the contemporary illustrator Norman Rockwell, was thus to the values of an America cherished in the nostalgic heart of the populist tradition. He depicted a simple, preindustrial America "before speed came into the world—as the serpent came into Eden—and destroyed tranquility forever."

Thematically Kelland's work was remarkably diverse. He wrote about high finance and family dynasties of the wealthy (the Van Horn trilogy, 1930–1934), crusading lawyers (*The Hidden Spring*, 1915), epic historical figures (*Merchant of Valor*, 1947), college life and professorial vagaries (*Skin Deep*, 1939), the southwestern frontier (*Tombstone*, 1953), northern lumber camps (*Sudden Jim*, 1916), crime and detection (*Death Keeps a Secret*, 1953), and romance (*Heart on Her Sleeve*, 1943). Several of his works were made into films: *Speak Easily* (1932), starring Buster Keaton; *Mr. Deeds Goes to Town* (1936), directed by Frank Capra and starring Gary Cooper and Jean Arthur; and *Strike Me Pink* (1936), adapted from *Dreamland* (1935).

Kelland became interested in politics in the 1930's, when his belief in virtue, hard work, and innate shrewdness led him to attack the New Deal. By 1940 he was recognized as a conservative Republican leader, serving as national committeeman from Arizona (1940–1956) and chairman of the Executive and Publicity Committee of the party (1942). In 1944 he endorsed the paranoiac vision of World War II, blaming Franklin D. Roosevelt for the tragedy of Pearl Harbor. Kelland's conservatism was also evidenced by his opposition to Eisenhower's appointment of Earl Warren as chief justice of the Supreme Court and his paternal attitude toward Senator Barry Goldwater, whom he considered his political protégé.

Kelland was deeply involved in many business ventures: cattle ranching (Broken Diamond K Ranch near Phoenix and Rancho Santa Marita, Yavapai County, Ariz.), agriculture (Scattergood Date Gardens, Scottsdale, Ariz.), and publishing. He was vice-president and director of Phoenix Newspapers, Incorporated, and publisher of the *Arizona Republic* and the *Phoenix Gazette*. Kelland died in Scottsdale, Ariz.

Kelland's impact on American popular culture was essentially normative. His emphasis on old-fashioned values and on character provided the link between his literary and political activities. Like Horatio Alger, Kelland addressed an audience disoriented and shocked by contemporary life. He sought "to satisfy the homely, decent emotions and to give pleasure to the millions." His readers' response was duly sentimental; like the audiences of the orator Carnavon (*Thirty Pieces of Silver*, 1913), "in obedience to his genius they swayed with laughter, rewarded his pathos with tears, [and] gasped at the daring of his climaxes." That those climaxes were often predictable, that his pathos sometimes descended to the bathetic, and that the emotive content of his works did not range beyond the cozy confines of the average person's expectancy merely testified to Kelland's astute assessment of the tastes of the mass audience for popular light fiction.

[The major collections of manuscript material by or about Kelland are in the University of Michigan Historical Collections; the I. Robert Kriendler Collection of Typescripts, Manuscripts, and Autographed Volumes of Contemporary Authors, Alexander Library, Rutgers University; and the Collected Papers of George Horace Lorrimer in the Historical Society of Pennsylvania Collections.

Kelland's other important works include *Mark Tidd in the Backwoods* (1914); *Mark Tidd in Business* (1915); *Mark Tidd's Citadel* (1916); *Mark Tidd, Editor* (1917); *Mark Tidd, Manufacturer* (1918); *Scattergood Baines* (1921); *Mark Tidd in Italy* (1925); *Mark Tidd in Egypt* (1926); *Mark Tidd in Sicily* (1928); the Van Horn trilogy: *Hard Money* (1930), *Gold* (1931), and *Jealous House* (1934); *Star Rising* (1938); *Scattergood Baines Pulls the Strings* (1939); *Scattergood Baines Returns* (1940); *Land of the Torreones* (1946); *The Red Baron of Arizona* (1947); and *Murder Makes an Entrance* (1955).

The most useful biographical works are Kelland's "The Happiest Days of My Life," *Saturday Evening Post*, Oct. 14, 1950, and the introduction to *Scattergood Baines;* Robert Van Gelder, "A Talk with Clarence Budington Kelland," *New York Times Book Review*, Apr. 27, 1941; and the transcript of tape-recorded autobiographical memoirs in the Biographical Oral History Collection, 1948–1968, Columbia University Library. See also the substantial clipping collection and a prepared biographical sketch in the Associated Press News Library in New York.

Obituaries appeared in the *New York Times*, Feb. 19, 1964; and the *Arizona Republic*, Feb. 19, 1964.]

LOUIS J. KERN

KENNEDY, JOHN FITZGERALD (May 29, 1917–Nov. 22, 1963), thirty-fifth president of the United States, was born in Brookline, Mass., the son of Joseph Patrick Kennedy and Rose Fitzgerald. His grandfathers, Patrick Joseph Kennedy and John Francis Fitzgerald, had been successful both in business and politics. His great-grandparents had come to the United States as immigrants from Ireland.

Kennedy was the second son in a spirited and closely knit family that eventually numbered four sons and five daughters. In 1927 the elder Kennedy, a talented Wall Street promoter and corporate reorganizer, moved the family to Riverdale, an affluent area of New York City. An early supporter of Franklin D. Roosevelt for the Democratic presidential nomination in 1932, Joseph P. Kennedy served Roosevelt ably as first chairman of the Securities and Exchange Commission (1934–1935), as chairman of the Maritime Commission (1937–1938), and, more controversially, as ambassador to Great Britain (1938–1940).

Despite the claims of business and public affairs, his children remained the center of Joseph Kennedy's life. Ambitious for himself, he was even more ambitious for them. During frequent absences his concern pursued them in admonitory letters. His wife was his staunch ally. The parental insistence on self-improvement, competition, and victory became legendary. "We don't want any losers around here," the father used to tell his children.

There was equal parental pressure for intellectual development. The dinner table was a family seminar. Kennedy, who knew the world of moneymaking too well to be impressed by it, forbade the discussion of business at table. He instructed his children that their duty lay in public service. Although highly opinionated, the elder Kennedy cared less that his sons adopt his opinions than that they learn how to defend their own. "I grew up in a very strict house," John Kennedy later told an interviewer, "and one where . . . there were no free riders, and everyone was expected to do, give their best to what they did. . . . There was a constant drive for us for self-improvement."

Thin and somewhat frail as a boy, Kennedy spent much of his childhood sick in bed, surrounded by books. Scarlet fever, appendicitis, bronchitis, measles, whooping cough, parotitis, hives, jaundice, and later a back injury sustained while playing football at Harvard dogged his early years. Although an omnivorous reader, he was casual and unconcerned as a student. He first attended public school and then the Dexter School in Brookline, later the Riverdale Country Day School in Riverdale, N.Y. In 1930 he entered the Canterbury School in New Milford, Conn., his only experience in a Catholic school, but left because of illness. The next year he followed his older brother, Joseph, to Choate, also in Connecticut, where, although voted "most likely to succeed," he graduated sixty-fourth in a class of 112.

After illness forced him to drop out of the

London School of Economics, and later Princeton, Kennedy entered Harvard in the fall of 1936. At first sports engaged him more than studies. Then European travel, and especially his father's appointment to London, excited an interest in world affairs. He concentrated in government, worked diligently in his last two years, and graduated cum laude in 1940.

His senior honors essay, a study of Great Britain's appeasement policy, was published under the title *Why England Slept* (1940), a brash play on Winston Churchill's *While England Slept* (1938). The book was notable for its dispassionate tone in a highly impassioned time. Considering it "shortsighted" to blame England's plight on "one man or one group of men's blindness," Kennedy laid stress on impersonal forces arising from the nature of democracy and capitalism. The reviews were favorable, and the book was briefly a best-seller.

After a few months at Stanford Business School, Kennedy traveled through Latin America. In 1941 he tried to enlist in the armed forces. Rejected by the army because of his back trouble, he pulled strings and managed to get into the navy three months before Pearl Harbor. He longed for sea duty, more strings were pulled, and in 1942 he was assigned to motor torpedo boat training. By the spring of 1943, Lieutenant (junior grade) Kennedy was in command of his own PT boat in the South Pacific.

On Aug. 2, 1943, the Japanese destroyer *Amagiri* rammed Kennedy's PT-109 in Blackett Strait, west of New Georgia in the Solomon Islands. Kennedy and his crew were plunged into waters aflame with burning gasoline. Kennedy's courageous feat of towing one of the crew to safety by gripping the end of the life jacket belt in his teeth, and his resourcefulness until rescue came were later celebrated by John Hersey in a *New Yorker* article. Kennedy himself minimized the event. In later years, asked how he had become a war hero, he replied, "It was involuntary. They sank my boat."

The incident reactivated Kennedy's back injury. He also contracted malaria, was invalided home in December 1943, and spent some months in a naval hospital, where a disc operation failed to cure his spinal trouble. Malaria recurred in later years and contributed to chronic insufficiency in the functioning of his adrenal glands, an ailment known popularly but imprecisely as Addison's disease (strictly speaking, Addison's disease implies tubercular glands) and correctible by steroids such as cortisone. "At least one-half of the days he spent on this earth," his brother Robert wrote after his death,

"were days of intense physical pain"—pain undergone with notable absence of complaint.

Demobilized in January 1945, Kennedy contemplated a career in journalism. But, after Joseph, Jr., was killed in the war in 1944, his father looked to the second son to carry the family banner into politics. In 1946 John sought the Democratic nomination for Congress in the eleventh Massachusetts district. Still gaunt from wartime sickness, he was stiff and shy as a speaker. But his diligent campaigning, his war record, and his father's money won him the nomination. In November he was elected to the 80th Congress.

In his three terms in the House, Kennedy took a consistent liberal line on social and economic issues. In foreign affairs he supported the Truman Doctrine and the Marshall Plan, but denounced the Truman administration in 1949 for failing to save the Nationalist regime in China. A trip to Asia in 1951, however, persuaded him that "Communism cannot be met effectively by merely the force of arms." The United States seemed "too ready to buttress an inequitable status quo," aligning itself "with the 'haves' and regarding the action of the 'have-nots' as not merely the effort to cure injustice but as something sinister and subversive."

Skeptical of party and parliamentary rituals, Kennedy was something of an outsider in the House. His colleagues regarded him as intelligent but detached, insouciant, and something of a playboy. Kennedy could not wait to move on, and in 1952 he ran for the Senate. He defeated the incumbent, Henry Cabot Lodge, Jr., by 70,737 votes. On Sept. 12, 1953, he married Jacqueline Lee Bouvier; they had two children.

In the Senate, Kennedy pursued his interests in social and economic policy. While remaining a resourceful advocate of Massachusetts interests, he displayed independence by voting, over strong local opposition, for the St. Lawrence Seaway in 1954. In 1958 and 1959 he managed the battle for labor reform legislation. His record was less impressive in regard to Senator Joseph McCarthy, whose demagogic allegations about Communist subversion in government were finding popular sustenance in the frustrations of the Korean War. Although he never endorsed McCarthy or supported his projects, family friendships with McCarthy and the prejudices of his constituents led him to remain aloof from anti-McCarthyism. As the movement to censure McCarthy gathered force in July 1954, Kennedy prepared a speech in support of censure, but on narrow grounds. By the time the censure resolution came before the

Senate in November, he was gravely sick in a New York hospital, could not vote, and did not ask to be paired.

For months the pain in Kennedy's back had been acute. During the spring and summer of 1954 he was on crutches, and in October he underwent a double spinal fusion operation. The shock of surgery on his adrenal insufficiency brought him close to death. Twice he received last rites. Later Kennedy doubted that the operation was necessary.

Restless during a long convalescence, he began work, with research assistance, on a series of sketches of American politicians who had risked their careers in the cause of principle. The result was *Profiles in Courage* (1956). "A man does what he must," Kennedy wrote, "— in spite of personal consequences, in spite of obstacles and dangers and pressures—and that is the basis of all human morality." Critics, recalling Kennedy and McCarthyism, suggested that the author himself had shown more profile than courage. But the book was popular history of high order, and it received the Pulitzer Prize for biography in 1957.

In foreign policy Kennedy saw the cold war not as a religious but as a power conflict. He was an incisive critic of the policies of Secretary of State John Foster Dulles. He opposed American military intervention in Indochina in 1954, advocated the independence of Algeria as well as of Vietnam, and challenged Dulles' proposition that Third World neutralism was "immoral."

Kennedy was not a major Senate figure. He held himself apart from his colleagues, both on and off the floor. He was richer, better educated, and better read than most, and was more contained and more ambitious. To many observers he seemed to be biding his time until the opportunity arose for the next move up the greasy pole. A strong supporter of Adlai Stevenson's renomination as candidate for president in 1956, Kennedy sought the vice presidential nomination but lost to Estes Kefauver.

Kennedy soon began planning for the presidential nomination in 1960. Buoyed by his reelection to the Senate in 1958 with an unprecedented margin of 874,608 votes, he spoke extensively around the country in 1959 and declared his candidacy on Jan. 2, 1960. Conventional politicians held his youth, his Roman Catholic religion, and his independence against him; but these could be assets too. He eliminated one senatorial rival, Hubert Humphrey of Minnesota, by winning the Wisconsin and West Virginia primaries, and overcame later challenges by Lyndon Johnson of Texas, the

Senate majority leader, and by Adlai Stevenson at the Democratic National Convention in Los Angeles. Nominated on the first ballot, he made a pro forma offer of the vice-presidential nomination to Johnson, hoping thereby to propitiate southern Democrats. Johnson's quick acceptance surprised him, and he failed in an effort to persuade the Texan to withdraw.

"We stand today on the edge of a new frontier," Kennedy said in accepting the nomination. ". . . The times demand invention, innovation, imagination, decision." The United States, he contended in the campaign, was falling behind both in competing internationally with the Soviet Union and in meeting national goals of economic growth and social progress. Decline could be reversed only by vigorous presidential leadership to "get the country moving again."

Kennedy had outlined his own conception of the presidency in a speech in January 1960. The "revolutionary sixties," Kennedy said, ". . . demand that the president place himself in the very thick of the fight," that he "exercise the fullest powers of his office—all that are specified and some that are not," and that he "reopen the channels of communication between the world of thought and the seat of power."

The 1960 campaign was marked by a striking innovation in American politics—four televised "debates" in which Kennedy and Vice-President Richard M. Nixon, the Republican candidate, responded to questions asked by panels of reporters. At least 70 million people saw the first debate. Kennedy's poise and command in these encounters destroyed the Republican argument that he was too young and inexperienced for the presidency. He met the religious issue head-on in an appearance before the Houston Ministers Association. Economic recession and spreading unemployment also told against Nixon.

Voter turnout in November was 64 percent of the electorate, the highest since 1908. Kennedy won the popular vote, the closest since 1888, by only 119,057 out of 68.3 million votes cast. With nearly 200,000 votes going to minor-party candidates, he received 49.7 percent of the total. The margin in the electoral college was more decisive—303 for Kennedy to 219 for Nixon, with 15 southern votes for Senator Harry F. Byrd of Virginia.

On Jan. 20, 1961, the youngest man ever elected president took over from the oldest man to that time to hold the office. Kennedy was also the first Roman Catholic president and the first president born in the twentieth century. His cabinet included Dean Rusk, who had served in the Truman State Department, as secretary of state; Douglas Dillon, who had served in the Eisenhower administration, as secretary of the Treasury; Robert McNamara, a former professor at Harvard Business School and later president of the Ford Motor Company, as secretary of defense; Adlai Stevenson as ambassador to the United Nations; Arthur Goldberg, an eminent labor lawyer, later a Supreme Court justice, as secretary of labor; and his brother and most trusted associate, Robert Kennedy, as attorney general.

Kennedy gave his inaugural address—with the memorable injunction, "And so, my fellow Americans, ask not what your country can do for you; ask what you can do for your country"— under the shadow of a truculent speech, delivered a fortnight earlier in Moscow, in which Nikita Khrushchev had predicted the imminent triumph of communism through Soviet support of "national liberation wars" in the Third World. Kennedy responded hyperbolically in his inaugural: "Let every nation know . . . that we shall pay any price, bear any burden, meet any hardship, support any friend, oppose any foe, in order to assure the survival and the success of liberty." At the same time, Kennedy condemned the arms race, asked to "bring the absolute power to destroy other nations under the absolute control of all nations," emphasized that "civility is not a sign of weakness," and declared: "Let us never negotiate out of fear, but let us never fear to negotiate."

This mingling of themes suggests the way in which Kennedy was a transitional figure in American foreign policy. Despite his inaugural extravagance, he had an acute sense of the limitations of American power. Nine months after the inaugural he called on the American people to "face the fact that the United States is neither omnipotent nor omniscient—that we are only 6 percent of the world's population—that we cannot impose our will upon the other 94 percent of mankind—that we cannot right every wrong or reverse each adversity—and that therefore there cannot be an American solution to every world problem."

Kennedy thus had no illusions about a pax Americana. But, if there could be no American solution to every world problem, he did not think there could be a Russian solution either. Agreeing with Khrushchev that the Third World might provide the decisive battleground between democracy and communism, he hoped to encourage the developing countries of Latin America, Asia, and Africa to turn to democratic methods in their quest for independence and growth. The foreign assistance program now concentrated on economic rather than on military aid. The Peace Corps—an undertaking especially close to Kennedy's heart and placed under the direction of his brother-in-law Sargent Shriver—channeled the idealism of individual Americans into face-to-face cooperation in the developing countries. An expanded Food for Peace program under George S. McGovern used the American agricultural surplus to foster development in emergent nations.

The pattern was clearest in the Alliance for Progress, a program designed to use American economic aid to advance development and democracy in the western hemisphere. "Those who make peaceful revolution impossible," Kennedy told the Latin American diplomatic corps, "will make violent revolution inevitable." To the dismay of both North American business and Latin American oligarchies, the Alliance called for economic planning and structural change within a democratic framework. Fidel Castro of Cuba grudgingly called it "a politically wise concept put forth to hold back the time of revolution . . . a very intelligent strategy."

The Alliance for Progress was accompanied by a determined effort to reinforce liberal democracy in Latin America. When a military coup nullified a presidential election in Peru in 1962, Kennedy suspended relations until the junta pledged new elections. His dramatically successful visits to Venezuela, Colombia, Mexico, and Central America enabled the United States for a season to recover its popularity of Good Neighbor days. No president since Roosevelt had shown such interest in the hemisphere.

The problem remained, as Washington saw it, of protecting the fragile democratization process against Communist disruption. Cuba, which Castro had taken into the Soviet camp, was already becoming a base for subversion in Latin America. In 1960 President Dwight Eisenhower had directed the Central Intelligence Agency (CIA) to train a force of anti-Castro Cubans for the mission of overthrowing Castro. In 1961 Kennedy, facing the choice of disbanding this group or permitting it to invade the homeland, let the expedition go ahead. On Apr. 17, 1961, about 1400 Cubans landed at the Bahía de Cochinas (Bay of Pigs) in southern Cuba. In three days of fighting, all were captured or killed, Kennedy declining to escalate the situation by sending in American troops. The affair was that rarity, a perfect failure, and to the world and to many Americans, it was an indefensible exercise in intervention. Remarking wryly that victory has a hundred fathers and defeat is an orphan, Kennedy accepted full responsibility. He acquired a lasting skepticism about the CIA and the Joint Chiefs of Staff, and reorganized his foreign policy process to make sure that nothing like the Bay of Pigs could happen again.

At Kennedy's instruction the CIA now undertook small-scale covert operations intended to encourage resistance and sabotage in Cuba. The CIA also continued to attempt the assassination of Castro, a project that had begun in the Eisenhower administration, when the agency had enlisted the collaboration of notorious gangsters, and that was to persist well into the Johnson administration. There is no evidence that any of the three presidents authorized or approved the CIA's assassination plots. CIA officials did not even disclose the plots to John McCone, whom Kennedy appointed CIA director after the Bay of Pigs. In late 1963, while the CIA was still trying to murder Castro, Kennedy initiated secret negotiations looking to the normalization of relations with the Castro regime.

In 1961 Cuba seemed only the most menacing example of Communist subversion and guerrilla action in the Third World. For a brief period Kennedy thought remedy lay in the new gospel of "counterinsurgency." Counterinsurgency schools were established, and elite counterinsurgency units, like the Green Berets, were formed. In theory, counterinsurgency was to combine military derring-do with social reform. In practice the reform component was seldom pressed. The counterinsurgency enthusiasm primarily nourished the American belief in the United States capacity and right to intervene in foreign lands.

Southeast Asia presented particularly troubling problems. Kennedy successfully negotiated with Moscow in 1961–1962 for the neutralization of Laos; but in neighboring Vietnam, where the Saigon government of Ngo Dinh Diem was under assault by Communist Vietcong guerrillas, he increased the number of American military advisers. While believing the United States "overcommitted" in Southeast Asia, he nevertheless feared that the "loss" of South Vietnam would have adverse political consequences at home and abroad. On occasion he even endorsed Eisenhower's "domino theory," saying that American withdrawal "would mean a collapse not only of South Vietnam but of Southeast Asia." By 1962 American helicopters and personnel were taking a limited part in the fighting. At the end of 1963 there were 16,732 military advisers in Vietnam, and 73 Americans had been killed in combat.

At the same time, Kennedy consistently op-

posed Pentagon recommendations for the dispatch of American combat units. Sending in troops, he remarked, was "like taking a drink. The effect wears off, and you have to take another." Aware that lack of popular support was a central cause of Diem's difficulties, Kennedy urged the regime to broaden its base through political and economic reform. Diem disdained such advice. The Vietcong continued to gain.

Kennedy had already begun to look for a way out. In July 1962 he instructed the Pentagon to prepare a plan for American disengagement by the end of 1965. Publicly he said of the South Vietnamese in September 1963, "It is their war. They are the ones who have to win it or lose it." In October he announced the withdrawal of 1,000 advisers, enjoining McNamara to "tell them that means all the helicopter pilots too."

In the meantime, Diem's repressions had led his generals to plot his overthrow. A message from Washington (later characterized by Kennedy as a "major mistake") informed the generals that the United States would not block a spontaneous military revolt. Kennedy allowed the situation to drift, and intensified reform pressures on the Diem government. On November 1 the generals deposed and murdered Diem.

The evidence is fairly conclusive that Kennedy had determined to end American participation after the 1964 election if the South Vietnamese could not win "their war" for themselves. But he never said this publicly, lest the prospect undermine the Saigon regime. While he had drawn the line at combat units and heavy bombing and had pushed through a withdrawal plan, he had also steadily enlarged the American role in the war, had left on the public record the impression of a major American stake in the defense of South Vietnam, and had retained advisers who favored an all-out commitment. Thus he bequeathed to his successor a contradictory legacy.

The point, as Kennedy saw it, of such border operations as stopping Cuban subversion in Latin America and Communist guerrilla action in Southeast Asia was to secure the stability of the existing world balance. His broad idea, which he set forth to Khrushchev at a summit meeting in Vienna in June 1961, was that each superpower should abstain from initiatives that, by upsetting the rough balance into which the postwar world had settled, might invite miscalculation and compel reaction by the other. Khrushchev, doubtless mistaking Kennedy's restraint at the Bay of Pigs for weakness, brusquely rejected the proposal for a global standstill and threatened to conclude a peace treaty with East

Germany that would extinguish Western rights in West Berlin. Kennedy replied that so drastic a change in the balance of power was unacceptable. Khrushchev said that if America wanted war over Berlin, there was nothing the Soviet Union could do about it. Kennedy commented, "It will be a cold winter."

Kennedy had already discarded the Eisenhower strategy of relying on nuclear weapons to deter both local and general war. He substituted the doctrine of "flexible response"—the diversification of military force so that the level of reaction could be graduated to meet the level of threat.

This shift, with the consequent enlargement of the American capability for limited war, was intended primarily to enable the West to respond to Soviet aggression in Europe without immediate recourse to nuclear weapons. A fateful side effect was to create forces that could be used in "brush-fire" wars in the Third World. In addition, Kennedy had called for a buildup of long-range nuclear missiles, because it was thought that in this field Russia was pulling ahead. By the time in 1961 that reconnaissance satellites and espionage disproved the "missile gap," an American missile buildup was under way. This buildup was more than American security required, and it compelled Khrushchev to worry about his own missile gap.

Upon returning from Vienna after Khrushchev's threat about Berlin, Kennedy called up 150,000 reservists and announced a program—which led to an ugly outburst of near-panic and which he soon regretted—of fallout shelters for protection against nuclear attack. On August 13 the East Germans put up the Berlin Wall, thereby stemming an embarrassing flow of refugees into West Berlin.

Khrushchev postponed the treaty with East Germany, but did not abandon his goal of driving the West out of Berlin. In the summer of 1962 he decided to establish Soviet nuclear missile bases in Cuba—an unprecedented step for the Russians, who had never before placed their missiles in another country. The missiles would give Moscow a potent bargaining counter when it chose to reopen the Berlin question. By making shorter-range missiles effective against American targets, they would increase Soviet first-strike capacity by half. They would also deal America a shattering political blow by showing the Soviet capacity to penetrate the heart of the American sphere of influence. "Our missiles," Khrushchev declared in his memoirs, "would have equalized . . . 'the balance of power.'"

Kennedy had warned the Soviet Union not to send offensive weapons to Cuba; Khrushchev repeatedly denied he had any such intention. On Oct. 14, 1962, a U-2 overflight found indisputable evidence that Khrushchev had lied. Kennedy quickly decided that, one way or another, the Soviet missiles had to be removed from Cuba. For six days he and his close advisers debated how best to get them out. One faction, led by Dean Acheson, Truman's secretary of state now back as an adviser, and by the Joint Chiefs of Staff, advocated a surprise air attack on the bases. The other, led by Robert Kennedy and McNamara, sharply opposed this course on moral and practical grounds. Naval quarantine, this group contended, would both show the American determination to get the missiles out and allow Moscow time to pull back. Kennedy announced the second course in a speech to the nation on October 22.

The days that followed were more tense than any since World War II. Work continued on the missile bases. An American invasion force massed in Florida. Soviet ships with more missiles steamed toward Cuba. Finally, after indescribable suspense, Soviet ships began to turn back. "We're eyeball to eyeball," said Secretary Rusk, "and I think the other fellow just blinked."

On October 26, Kennedy received an eloquent letter from Khrushchev expatiating on the horror of nuclear war and offering to remove the missiles if the United States would end the quarantine and agree not to invade Cuba. On the following morning a second Khrushchev letter proposed an entirely different trade: the Soviet missiles in Cuba for American nuclear missiles in Turkey. Robert Kennedy recommended that his brother ignore the second letter and accept the first. The president followed this advice, but also offered the Soviet ambassador in Washington secret assurances that the Turkish missiles would be removed within four to five months.

The crisis was over. Critics later argued that Kennedy, by insisting on the removal of the missiles, brought the world needlessly to the edge of nuclear war. But, as Khrushchev said later, "It would have been preposterous for us to unleash a war against the United States." The acceptance of the missiles would have convulsed American politics and made any movement toward détente impossible.

Kennedy's greatest hope was to stop the arms race. General and complete disarmament, he had told the United Nations in September 1961, was "a practical matter of life and death." After the missile crisis, impressed by Khrushchev's letter about the nuclear terror, Kennedy hoped he had made the point he had tried to make in Vienna—that neither side dare tamper carelessly with the explosive international equilibrium. He therefore resumed his quest for a test-ban treaty. In a speech at American University in June 1963, he called on Americans as well as Russians to rethink the cold war. Both sides, he said, were "caught up in a vicious and dangerous cycle in which suspicion on one side breeds suspicion on the other, and new weapons beget counterweapons."

In the summer of 1963, the United States, Soviet Union, and Great Britain agreed on a treaty outlawing nuclear tests in the atmosphere, in outer space, and underwater. In September the Senate gave its consent, 80–19. "One of the ironic things," Kennedy mused that year, ". . . is that Mr. Khrushchev and I occupy approximately the same political positions inside our governments. He would like to prevent a nuclear war but is under severe pressure from his hard-line crowd, which interprets every move in that direction as appeasement. I've got similar problems. . . . The hard-liners in the Soviet Union and the United States feed on one another." "I had no cause for regret once Kennedy became President," Khrushchev subsequently wrote in his memoirs. "It quickly became clear that he understood better than Eisenhower that an improvement in relations was the only rational course."

In the longer run Kennedy's vision was of what he called a "world of diversity"—a world of nations various in institutions, ideologies, and creeds—"where, within a framework of international cooperation, every country can solve its own problems according to its own traditions and ideals." Communism could be one element in this pluralistic world, but diversity, he argued, was incompatible with the Marxist dogma that all societies passed through the same historic stages to the same single destination. In his American University speech he summed up his policy in a conscious revision of Wilson's famous line: "If we cannot now end our differences, at least we can help make the world safe for diversity."

The competition between the superpowers produced at least one benign by-product. In April 1961 the Russians put the first astronaut into space orbit. On May 25, 1961, Kennedy committed the United States "to achieving the goal, before this decade is out, of landing a man on the moon and returning him safely to earth." Beating Russia to the moon was not Kennedy's essential interest. At Vienna in 1961, and again at the United Nations in 1963, he suggested that Americans and Russians go to the moon together. He was responding to the newest of new frontiers. On July 20, 1969, six months before Kennedy's deadline, earthlings walked on the moon for the first time.

In domestic policy Kennedy proceeded with circumspection. He had been elected by a thin popular margin and was confronted in the House of Representatives by the coalition of Republicans and southern Democrats that had frustrated social legislation since 1938. The 1962 congressional election strengthened his popular mandate but did not significantly improve his parliamentary situation. His proposals for federal aid to education and for medical care for the elderly encountered stubborn congressional resistance.

The administration pursued steadily expansionist economic policies: in 1962 the investment credit and liberalized depreciation allowances; in 1963 the proposal of income tax reduction, enacted in 1964. These Keynesian measures fostered the longest peacetime growth of the American economy since World War II, with an average annual increase in the gross national product of 5.6 percent. Unemployment declined from 8.1 percent of the labor force when Kennedy became president to 5.2 percent in 1964.

Prices remained stable, in part because of "wage-price guideposts" designed to keep wage increases within the limit of advances in productivity. In 1962, after the Steelworkers Union accepted a noninflationary contract on the expectation that the steel companies would forgo a price increase, United States Steel raised its prices. Kennedy reacted with anger and, through a variety of "hard-ball" pressures, forced the corporation to retract its action. The episode, and especially Kennedy's reported remark—"My father always told me that all businessmen were sons-of-bitches, but I never believed it till now"—provoked business criticism of the administration reminiscent of the Roosevelt years.

While fiscal stimulus increased aggregate employment, it did not directly address the condition of millions of demoralized and inarticulate Americans who in many cases had inherited their poverty and accepted it as a permanent condition. Kennedy had already begun to attack the "culture of poverty" through the Area Redevelopment Act of 1961 and through programs directed at the development of Appalachia. In 1963 he concluded that if structural poverty was to be relieved, general tax reduction required a counterpart program for those too poor to pay income taxes. The planning set in motion in 1963 led to the "war on poverty" of later years.

A particular concern of Kennedy's, enthusiastically shared by his wife, was to give the arts a place of honor. He invited Robert Frost to read a poem at his inauguration, and a distinguished group of writers, painters, and musicians attended the ceremonies. White House dinners celebrated artistic achievement. Kennedy appointed a special consultant on the arts, whose recommendations led to the establishment of the National Endowments for the Arts and for the Humanities. The Kennedys also took the lead in the preservation and restoration of historic Washington. "I look forward," he said, "to an America which will not be afraid of grace and beauty . . . which will reward achievement in the arts as we reward achievement in business or statecraft."

Kennedy's most signal domestic achievement lay in the field of racial justice. As senator he had supported civil rights legislation, although without great personal commitment. As president he began by concentrating on executive rather than legislative action, with Attorney General Robert Kennedy as his chief agent. Challenged by "freedom riders" defying segregation in interstate bus terminals, the attorney general found ways to end segregation in interstate transportation. In October 1962 the Kennedys sent federal troops into Oxford, Miss., to protect a black student's right, assured him by the courts, to attend the University of Mississippi. A riot resulted in two deaths, but James Meredith was successfully registered, and graduated the next year. After much hesitation Kennedy, in November 1962, issued an executive order ending discrimination in housing supported by federal loans and guarantees. He established the President's Committee on Equal Employment Opportunity to end discrimination by federal contractors. The Department of Justice worked to secure blacks the right to vote, and the administration appointed an unprecedented number of blacks to public office.

But the moral dynamism of the civil rights cause outstripped the actions of the administration. Civil rights workers in the South suffered harassment, beatings, imprisonment, and even death in their effort to win black Americans their constitutional rights. As black discontent grew, so did white resistance. In April 1963, when Martin Luther King, Jr., began a campaign to end discrimination in Birmingham, Ala., the police assailed King's marchers with fire hoses, electric cattle prods, and growling police dogs. In June, Governor George Wallace of Alabama tried to block the admission of two black students to the state university, but folded under federal pressure. That night Kennedy went on television to pronounce the civil rights question "a moral issue . . . as old as the Scriptures and . . . as clear as the American Constitution," and to commit the nation to the proposition "that race has no place in American life or law." With that speech he launched a fight for new and sweeping civil rights legislation.

Kennedy's proposals provoked bitter reactions. Opponents denounced the civil rights bill as of Communist inspiration, and claimed that Martin Luther King, Jr., was under Communist discipline. Confident that surveillance would demonstrate King's innocence, Robert Kennedy acceded to FBI requests that King's phone be tapped. The civil rights struggle drove Kennedy down in the polls from an overwhelming 76 percent approval in January 1963 to 59 percent in November. The Kennedys organized a vast educational effort in support of the bill; in August, King led the March on Washington; and in the fall the bill began to make progress through Congress.

Looking back in the autumn of 1963, Kennedy told his brother that he was dissatisfied with the amount of time he had given to foreign affairs, although he had seen no choice: "each day was a new crisis." He expected that, like Theodore Roosevelt, he would get his domestic mandate in his second term.

On Nov. 22, 1963, while riding with his wife in an open car through Dallas, Tex., Kennedy was shot and killed. A commission appointed by his successor, Lyndon Johnson, and chaired by Chief Justice Earl Warren concluded that the murderer was Lee Harvey Oswald acting on his own. The Warren Commission had operated under severe pressure to bring in a report without delay. Both the CIA and the FBI withheld information vital to its inquiries. Various conspiracy theories arose, and in 1979 a House select committee concluded, on the basis of acoustical evidence, that more than one person was implicated in the assassination. The Warren Commission investigation was unquestionably inadequate. Whether a more adequate investigation would have produced a different conclusion remained a field of controversy.

In the years after his death, Kennedy's place in history became a subject of contention. Revisionist historians portrayed him as a rigid and embattled "cold warrior"; others found this an unpersuasive assessment in the light of the movement toward détente after the missile crisis and, indeed, in the light of Khrushchev's testimony. Some scholars, noting his limited legislative success, dismissed his leadership in domestic affairs as more style than substance; others, pointing to his narrow margins of support in Congress, argued that the perseverance with which he addressed such issues as civil rights, aid to education, tax reduction, and Medicare laid the groundwork for legislation in the next administration. The idea of the Kennedy presidency as "Camelot," a romantic fancy arising in the wave of grief after his death and one that he would most probably have derided, lost luster with allegations, often exaggerated, about Kennedy's private life.

Certainly Kennedy inherited difficult problems at home and abroad, and had too little time and parliamentary leverage to do as much about them as he keenly wished. Nonetheless, his directness and openness of mind; his faith in reasoned discussion; his ironic, often self-mocking wit; and his generous vision of American possibilities broke a crust that had settled over American society in the 1950's. He communicated not only an insistence on personal excellence but also a skepticism about conventional ideas and institutions. His message was that the old cold war was played out, that the United States had vital ties of sympathy and interest with the emerging world, that at home the nation was callous toward its old, its poor, and its nonwhite minorities, that it was neglectful of the values of art and the intellect, and that politics (in a phrase he cherished from John Buchan's *Pilgrim's Way*) was "the greatest and most honorable adventure." His high standards for the country encouraged an immense discharge of critical energy throughout American society.

Kennedy greatly enjoyed the presidency, was a virtuoso at press conferences, and could be a compelling orator on public occasions. Personally reserved, he was a man of courtesy and charm who inspired deep loyalty among his associates. He could also be impatient and, on occasion, arbitrary. But he was by nature a conciliator, always hopeful that differences could be rationally worked out, whether with the governors of Mississippi and Alabama, the president of United States Steel, or Khrushchev. He came to be loved in the black community, and he was the first president since Franklin D. Roosevelt who had anything to say to the young. Abroad he was widely perceived, like Roosevelt and Wilson before him, as a carrier of American idealism and as a friend of humanity. He once

described himself as an "idealist without illusions"; and his hope, in which to a measure he succeeded, was to release resources of idealism he felt had been too long repressed in the national life.

[Kennedy's papers are at the John F. Kennedy Library, Boston. The library also contains papers of leading figures in the Kennedy administration, oral history interviews with Kennedy associates, and audiovisual materials. Kennedy edited and contributed a sketch to *As We Remember Joe* (1945), a volume of reminiscences of his older brother. Collections of speeches are John W. Gardner, ed., *To Turn the Tide* (1962); Allan Nevins, ed., *The Burden and the Glory* (1964), and *The Strategy of Peace* (1960). Official publications are *The Speeches of Senator John F. Kennedy: Presidential Campaign of 1960*, Senate Report 994 (1961); *The Joint Appearances of Senator John F. Kennedy and Vice President Richard M. Nixon*, Senate Report 994 (1961); *Public Papers of the Presidents of the United States: John F. Kennedy, 1961, 1962, 1963* (1962–1964); *John Fitzgerald Kennedy: A Compendium of Speeches, Statements, and Remarks . . . in . . . Congress . . .*, Senate Document no. 79 (1964).

For Kennedy's prepresidential career, see James MacGregor Burns, *John Kennedy: A Political Profile* (1960); Herbert S. Parmet, *Jack: The Struggles of John F. Kennedy* (1980); Rose Fitzgerald Kennedy, *Times to Remember* (1974), an illuminating maternal memoir; Theodore H. White, *The Making of the President, 1960* (1961).

For Kennedy in World War II, see John Hersey, "Survival," *New Yorker*, June 17, 1944; Robert J. Donovan, *PT 109* (1961); Paul B. Fay, Jr., *The Pleasure of His Company* (1966); Clay Blair, Jr., and Joan Blair, *The Search for JFK* (1976). Kennedy's medical history is discussed in James A. Nicholas, Charles L. Busstein, et al., "Management of Adrenocortical Insufficiency During Surgery," *Archive of Surgery*, Nov. 1955; Janet Travell, *Office Hours* (1968).

Memoirs by White House associates are Arthur M. Schlesinger, Jr., *A Thousand Days* (1965) and *Robert Kennedy and His Times* (1978); Theodore C. Sorensen, *Kennedy* (1965) and *The Kennedy Legacy* (1969); Kenneth P. O'Donnell and David F. Powers with Joseph W. McCarthy, *"Johnny, We Hardly Knew Ye"* (1972); Pierre Salinger, *With Kennedy* (1966); Walt W. Rostow, *The Diffusion of Power* (1972). Lawrence F. O'Brien *No Final Victories* (1974).

On foreign policy, see Robert F. Kennedy, *Thirteen Days* (1969); Roger Hilsman, *To Move a Nation* (1967); Chester Bowles, *Promises to Keep* (1971); Maxwell Taylor, *Swords and Ploughshares* (1972); J. K. Galbraith, *Ambassador's Journal* (1969); John Bartlow Martin, *Overtaken by Events* (1966); Abba P. Schwartz, *The Open Society* (1968). Special studies include Haynes Johnson, *The Bay of Pigs* (1964); Peter Wyden, *Bay of Pigs: The Untold Story* (1979); Graham T. Allison, *Essence of Decision*

(1970); Norman Cousins, *The Improbable Triumvirate* (1972); R. M. Slusser, *The Berlin Crisis of 1961* (1973); Douglas S. Blaufarb, *The Counterinsurgency Era* (1977); Alain C. Enthoven and K. W. Smith, *How Much Is Enough?* (1971); David Nunnerley, *President Kennedy and Britain* (1972); Jerome Levinson and Juan de Onis, *The Alliance That Lost Its Way* (1970); Arthur M. Schlesinger, Jr., "The Alliance for Progress: A Retrospective," in R. G. Hellman and H. J. Rosenbaum, eds., *Latin America* (1975).

On Vietnam, consult John Galloway, ed., *The Kennedys and Vietnam* (1971); Chester Cooper, *The Lost Crusade* (1970); F. M. Kail, *What Washington Said* (1973); Leslie H. Gelb with R. K. Betts, *The Irony of Vietnam* (1979); and, for documentation, *The Pentagon Papers*, Senator Mike Gravel, ed., 4 vols. (1971).

Assessments by foreign leaders are in Harold Macmillan, *At the End of the Day* (1973); Charles de Gaulle, *Memoirs of Hope* (1971); N. S. Khrushchev, *Khrushchev Remembers* (1970) and *Khrushchev Remembers: The Last Testament* (1974).

In domestic policy special studies include Carl M. Brauer, *John F. Kennedy and the Second Reconstruction* (1977); Walter Lord, *The Past That Would Not Die* (1965); J. F. Heath, *John F. Kennedy and the Business Community* (1969); Victor Navasky, *Kennedy Justice* (1971); Grant McConnell, *Steel and the Presidency* (1963); Walter Heller, *New Dimensions of Political Economy* (1966); W. J. Barber, "The Kennedy Years: Purposeful Pedagogy," in Craufurd D. Goodwin, ed., *Exhortation and Controls* (1975); James L. Sundquist, *Politics and Policy* (1968); Lawrence H. Fuchs, *John F. Kennedy and American Catholicism* (1967).

Journalistic impressions of Kennedy in action are in Benjamin C. Bradlee, *Conversations with Kennedy* (1975); William Manchester, *Portrait of a President* (1962); Hugh Sidey, *John F. Kennedy, President* (1963); Tom Wicker, *Kennedy Without Tears* (1964) and *JFK and LBJ* (1968).

On Kennedy's assassination, see E. A. Glikes and Paul Schwaber, eds., *Of Poetry and Power* (1964); William Manchester, *The Death of a President* (1967); and Anthony Summers, *Conspiracy* (1980).

Condemnatory accounts of the Kennedy presidency include Henry Fairlie, *The Kennedy Promise* (1973); Bruce Miroff, *Pragmatic Illusions* (1976); Louise FitzSimons, *The Kennedy Doctrine* (1972); R. J. Walton, *Cold War and Counter-Revolution* (1972); Victor Lasky, *J.F.K.: The Man and the Myth* (1963).

James T. Crown, *The Kennedy Literature* (1969), is reasonably complete to its date, but much has come out since then.

ARTHUR M. SCHLESINGER, JR.

KENYON, JOSEPHINE HEMENWAY (May 10, 1880–Jan. 10, 1965), pediatrician, was born in Auburn, N.Y., the daughter of Charles Carroll Hemenway, a Presbyterian minister, and of Ida Shackelford. When Kenyon was eleven, the family moved to Glasgow, Mo., where her father became president of Pritchett College, a small, nonsectarian institution. Kenyon later attended the college, receiving a B.A. in 1898 and an M.A. the following year. Interested in a career in medicine, she spent a year at Bryn Mawr College (1899–1900), studying biology, before entering the Johns Hopkins University Medical School in 1900.

At Johns Hopkins, Kenyon studied under such distinguished faculty members as William Henry Welch, William Osler, William S. Halsted, and Howard Kelly. She was one of three women in the class of 1904, which included forty-two men, and was among the earliest women graduates of the school.

After receiving the M.D., Kenyon remained in Baltimore for another year, serving as a house medical officer at the Johns Hopkins University Hospital. She then moved to New York City to serve a residency in pediatrics at Babies Hospital, one of the first institutions in the United States dedicated solely to the care of infants and children. Kenyon worked there until 1911, under the noted pediatrician Luther Emmett Holt, chief of the hospital. Holt later called her "the best man I ever had on my staff." Her training completed, Kenyon established a private practice in New York City. On Sept. 7, 1911, she married James Henry Kenyon, a neurosurgeon. They had two daughters.

Kenyon began a twenty-four-year association with Columbia University Teachers College in 1913, when she was appointed to teach child care and social hygiene. A pioneer in the field of sex education, she directed the national Young Women's Christian Association (YWCA) lecture program for women and girls during World War I. These lectures presented by the Social Morality Committee addressed issues of sexual hygiene and morality, emphasizing proper deportment in relations with soldiers. After the war Kenyon became supervisor of health work for the YWCA, which sponsored health programs for women. In September 1919 she helped to organize the first International Conference of Women Doctors, which discussed questions of health, psychology, prenatal and child care, and aspects of sexual morality. Although Kenyon left the YWCA in 1921, she remained active in church-related health work throughout her career, serving as a member of the Presbyterian Mission Board.

In 1923 Kenyon established the Health and Happiness Club for *Good Housekeeping* magazine. Initially reluctant to take the position because professional ethics forbade physicians to seek publicity, she eventually agreed, citing her interest in health education. Under the auspices of the club, Kenyon wrote eight letters, one each month, to pregnant women, counseling them on prenatal care and preparations for motherhood. This series was followed by a second one that advised mothers on such topics as feeding, growth and development, and toilet training during the baby's first year. These letters proved so popular that Kenyon became a regular columnist for *Good Housekeeping* in 1924. She contributed an article on child care each month, offering advice on a wide range of subjects, including nutrition, recreation, and psychology.

Kenyon published a comprehensive guide to pregnancy and the care of young children, *Healthy Babies Are Happy Babies*, in 1934. By 1951 the book had gone through five editions and nineteen printings, and had been translated into five languages. The popularity of the book stemmed from its common-sense style, as well as from the trend to seek expert advice on questions of family life and child rearing.

Kenyon's advice to mothers reflected the shift in the first half of the twentieth century from a rigid approach to a more indulgent, permissive attitude toward child rearing. Kenyon's early writings in the 1920's suggested maintaining a strict timetable for feeding infants, but by 1940 she argued for "demand feeding" and greater flexibility. She also revised her early stringent views of toilet-training procedures that insisted on starting in the child's fourth or fifth week, and advocated a more relaxed approach. Influenced by the development of theories of personality, Kenyon emphasized in her later writings the need for the infant to feel a sense of security and love—"mothering"—an attitude that earlier advice had suggested could spoil the child. She provided mothers with considerable information on childhood diseases and emotional problems, but she nevertheless recommended frequent visits to a family physician. Although she maintained an active private practice, it was for her writings on child rearing that she achieved prominence.

In 1945 Kenyon retired from practice, but continued to write for *Good Housekeeping* until 1952. She moved in 1950 to Boulder, Colo., where she died.

[See Christopher Brooks, "She's Helped to Raise a Million Babies," *Good Housekeeping*, May 1940. An obituary is in the *New York Times*, Jan. 11, 1965.]
ALLAN M. BRANDT

KERR, ROBERT SAMUEL (Sept. 11, 1896–Jan. 1, 1963), oil executive, governor, and U.S. senator, was born in the Chickasaw Nation, Indian Territory, near the present town of Ada, Okla., the son of William Samuel Kerr, a hardworking and ambitious pioneer and tenant farmer, and of Margaret Eloda Wright. Having inherited his parents' religious and political convictions, Kerr joined the Baptist Church in 1905, and he taught a Sunday school class regularly while governor and senator. Kerr kept his boyhood pledge not to drink alcohol, and his command of Scripture was prodigious.

Kerr attended Ada public schools, and after graduating from high school taught in a country school. With his meager salary he financed a two-year correspondence course from East Central Normal School that brought a degree in 1911. Later he studied law for a year at the University of Oklahoma. Kerr was commissioned a second lieutenant during World War I, but did not see combat. He married Reba Shelton on Dec. 5, 1919, and settled down as a wholesale produce merchant in Ada.

The early 1920's were years of personal tragedy for Kerr. Twin daughters died at birth in 1920; fire destroyed his business in 1921; and his wife and baby son died in childbirth in February 1924. Alone, grieving, and deeply in debt, he turned to work for solace. Although Kerr had established a law partnership with a prominent judge in 1922, a law career was not his goal. Early in life he told his father he wanted three things: a family, a million dollars, and the governorship of Oklahoma, in that order. On Dec. 26, 1925, he married Grayce Breene; they had four children. After several years of accepting shares in oil drilling leases in exchange for his legal services, Kerr gave up his law practice. In 1929 he and his brother-in-law established the Anderson-Kerr Drilling Company. Six years later he began a long and profitable collaboration with Phillips Petroleum Company that led to his association with geologist Dean A. McGee and the eventual establishment of Kerr-McGee Oil Industries.

Concurrent with his business ventures Kerr strengthened his ties within the Democratic party at the state and national levels, contributing generously to Democratic candidates. In 1931 he was appointed a special justice of the Oklahoma Supreme Court. Four years later Governor Ernest Marland appointed Kerr to the Unofficial Pardon and Parole Board. He was elected to the Democratic National Committee in 1940, and proved to be an effective fund raiser.

Kerr was elected governor of Oklahoma in 1942. His margin of victory was slim, a reflection of the strength of anti–New Deal and isolationist sentiment in the state. Two years later he was keynote speaker at the Democratic National Convention, where he helped shape the strategy that won Harry S. Truman the vice-presidential nomination. As Oklahoma's chief executive he stabilized the state's finances and worked to develop a diversified industrial base. But his chief contribution was to introduce a sense of dignity and maturity into state government. He presided over the demise of Oklahoma's turbulent era of "Wild West" politics.

Kerr was elected to the United States Senate in 1948. In Washington he joined an exceptional group of freshman Democratic senators: Paul Douglas, Estes Kefauver, Hubert Humphrey, Clinton P. Anderson, and Lyndon Baines Johnson. These men influenced virtually every national issue of the 1950's and 1960's. In the Senate, Kerr allied with powerful southern committee chairmen. He became the protégé of Richard Russell of Georgia. Realizing that the path to influence was effective committee work, Kerr first used the Public Works Committee as his Senate power base. But before the end of his first term, he had secured seats on the Senate Finance Committee and on the Democratic Policy Committee.

In 1950 Kerr led the congressional forces trying to exempt independent oil and gas producers from Federal Power Commission regulation. Ironically, these events which earned him recognition as a possible presidential contender in 1952, explained a major part of his failure to receive the Democratic nomination. Thereafter he could never shed the stereotype that he was a parochial, special-interest politician. He therefore resolved to exploit the image. Denied the presidency, he became a power in the Senate. He concentrated on legislation to benefit Oklahoma, such as water development, but he also worked on national issues, such as broadening Social Security coverage and the development of the manned space program.

Kerr became chairman of the powerful Aeronautical and Space Sciences Committee in 1961. He was indispensable in the enactment of the Kennedy administration's moon program, and was also a kind of "shadow leader" for Kennedy's crucial trade and tax legislation. Kerr's emergence in 1962 as the only man in Congress who was a powerful legislative force in his own right occurred because of a peculiar combination of weakened congressional leadership, a politically unattractive leg-

islation program and the Oklahoman's own institutional power and dominating personality. On Dec. 16, 1962, after a busy legislation session and a strenuous congressional campaign, Kerr suffered a mild heart attack. He died in Washington, D.C.

Kerr's power within the Senate developed in the late 1950's and matured only in the two years before his death. He was an individual rather than an institutional power. His greatest asset was his undoctrinaire approach to politics. Faced with a legislative problem, he was remarkably free of preconceived ideas, a quality that enhanced his role as the legislative broker for the Kennedy administration. Depending on the circumstances, he was a protectionist or a free-trader, a free spender or an economy advocate, an enthusiastic champion of the large corporation or a compassionate solicitor for the aged pensioner or the abandoned child. Such flexibility did not mean that he was devoid of a political philosophy. His was a materialistic view: the federal government's proper role was funding and expanding the economy through political action in order to widen and stabilize the social system in which individuals made their way. Like so many American politicians, Kerr talked Jeffersonian rhetoric while practicing Hamiltonian principles.

In his mature years Kerr's single-minded purpose was to regenerate Oklahoma, to restore the vigor and confidence of territorial days that the hard times of the Great Depression had beaten down. In doing so, he added to his own wealth, but that was not his basic motive. Business was a diversion; riches, the pleasing result. Politics was his passion.

[The Robert Samuel Kerr Papers, in the Western History Collections at the University of Oklahoma, consist of public and private papers dating from 1943 to 1963. There is no complete biography of Kerr. See John S. Ezell, *Innovations in Energy: The Story of Kerr-McGee* (1979); Anne Hodges Morgan, *Robert S. Kerr: The Senate Years* (1977). An obituary is in the *New York Times*, Jan. 2, 1963.]

ANNE HODGES MORGAN

KERR, SOPHIE (Aug. 23, 1880–Feb. 6, 1965), writer, was born in Denton, Md., the daughter of Jonathan Williams Kerr, a nurseryman, and Amanda Catherine Sisk. In 1898 she received the B.A. from Hood College in Maryland. One year later she sold her first short story to *Country Gentleman*. In 1901 she earned an M.A. from the University of Vermont.

Kerr began newspaper work as an editor of

the women's page of the *Pittsburgh Chronicle-Telegraph.* Shortly thereafter she edited the women's Sunday supplement of the *Pittsburgh Gazette-Times.* She continued to write short stories, many of which were published by *Woman's Home Companion* of which she later became managing editor.

On Sept. 6, 1904, Kerr married John D. Underwood, a civil engineer. They were divorced in 1908, and she never remarried. For many years following the divorce she continued to write under the name Sophie Kerr Underwood. Sometime during the 1940's she resumed writing under her maiden name.

In 1917 Kerr published her first novel, *The Blue Envelope,* which dealt with a young girl unwillingly involved in a spy ring. Thereafter she wrote twenty-two novels and several hundred short stories. Much of Kerr's magazine writing—mainly for *Ladies' Home Journal, Collier's,* and *Saturday Evening Post*—mixed suspense and humor with romantic love. A skillful writer, she used plots typical of fiction in women's magazines and won a large and devoted audience.

In 1922 Kerr published *One Thing Is Certain,* a novel about a young woman whose marriage is destroyed by domestic and religious conflict. *Mareea-Maria* (1929), a novel about a farmer who marries an Italian girl (to his mother's dismay), is set in the backwater country of her native Maryland. *Girl into Woman* (1932), the story of a young woman who runs away from her domineering father to marry a rough and unprincipled mechanic, stands apart from Kerr's other work because it contains little humor. The type of light humor most readers expected is exemplified by the headnote to her 1949 novel, *As Tall as Pride*: "The human and animal characters of this book are entirely fictitious and any similarity to actual people, cats or horses is purely coincidental."

Kerr collaborated with Anna Steese Richardson on a play, *Big-Hearted Herbert,* which was produced in 1934. It was, one critic said, "good clean fun, laid on with a steam-shovel." Her love for good food led her to write the narrative sections for a cookbook (written with June Platt) entitled *The Best I Ever Ate* (1953). She died in New York City.

Kerr's writing did not touch upon enduring themes that broaden, deepen, or sharpen a reader's sense of human experience. But her fiction did provide readers with a satisfying escape from the everyday world. On these terms her writing was polished, professional, and memorable for its humorous interludes.

[Kerr's writings not mentioned in the text include *The Golden Block* (1918); *The See Saw* (1919); *Painted Meadows* (1920); *Confetti: A Book of Short Stories* (1927); *Tigers Is Only Cats* (1929); *In for a Penny* (1931); *Stay Out of My Life* (1933); *Miss J Looks On* (1935); *There's Only One* (1936); *The Beautiful Woman* (1940); *Curtain Going Up* (1940); *Michael's Girl* (1942); *Jenny Devlin* (1943); *Love Story Incidental* (1946); *The Sound of Petticoats* (1948); and *Wife's Eye View* (1947). An obituary is in the *New York Times,* Feb. 8, 1965.]

PHILIP LUTHER

KEY, VALDIMER ORLANDO, JR. (Mar. 13, 1908–Oct. 4, 1963), educator and political scientist, was born in Austin, Tex., the son of Valdimir [*sic*] Orlando Key and Olive Terry. He grew up in Lamesa, Tex., where his father, a lawyer, prepared abstracts of deeds and acquired substantial land holdings. The family had a comfortable income, but was by no means wealthy.

By about age fifteen, Key, in his father's judgment, had exhausted the local educational resources. Accordingly, he went off to McMurry College in Abilene, Tex., to complete the last two years of high school and first year of college. In 1926 he transferred to the University of Texas at Austin, where he earned the B.A. in 1929 and the M.A. in political science in 1930. Key then entered the University of Chicago, a leading center for study in political science. Charles E. Merriam, then at the height of his distinguished career, was responsible for much of its innovative reputation. He stressed careful research using the actual data of political activity, and he impressed upon his students the need to move beyond the descriptive and legalistic political science of the period.

Merriam's influence, and the atmosphere in Chicago's political science department, bred in Key a single-minded devotion to systematic political analysis. He became one of the leaders of the "behavioral movement" in political studies. His dissertation, which he completed under Merriam's direction, was titled "The Techniques of Political Graft in the United States" (1934).

In the fall of 1934 Key went to the University of California at Los Angeles as a lecturer in political science; he was appointed an instructor in 1935. On Oct. 27, 1934, he married Luella Gettys, a fellow student at Chicago, who also had a doctorate in political science. They had no children.

In 1936 Key went to Washington, D.C., where he was first a staff member of the Committee on Public Administration of the Social

Science Research Council (1936–1937), and then a research technician for the National Resources Planning Board (1937–1938). In this period his interests were in public administration—as were those of Merriam, who was serving on the President's Committee on Administrative Management.

Key's scholarly output had begun with three published articles before he left Chicago. While he was in California another half-dozen pieces appeared. Up to 1937 his work usually centered on state and local government and political corruption. The years in Washington brought a change in focus, and a series of articles on federal grants in aid to the states.

In 1938 Key went to Johns Hopkins University. He was promoted to associate professor in 1940 and to full professor in 1946, and served as department chairman from 1947 until 1949. His years at Hopkins were interrupted by service with the Bureau of the Budget (1942–1945).

About 1940 Key's interest began to shift from public administration to politics and political behavior. In 1939 he and W. W. Crouch completed *The Initiative and the Referendum in California*. Three years later he published a monograph on federal grant legislation, the essay "Politics and Administration" (in a volume edited by Leonard D. White), and his extraordinarily successful textbook, *Politics, Parties and Pressure Groups*.

The encyclopedic thoroughness of *Politics* makes it clear that Key's interest in political organization and behavior had been long-standing. The book also showed his concern to use results from systematic research in a comprehensive, cogent, and sophisticated discussion of the phenomena involved.

Key's production of scholarly articles declined somewhat during the rest of the 1940's, partly because of his wartime service in Washington but also because of the effort he was devoting to the centerpiece of his scholarly career, *Southern Politics in State and Nation*, published in 1949. The book showed a masterful use of all the techniques available to the political scientist, from quantitative analysis through description and shrewd judgment. It won a Woodrow Wilson Foundation Award.

Thereafter, with few exceptions, Key's published works related to parties, politics, and political behavior. In 1949 he left Johns Hopkins for Yale, where he became Alfred Cowles Professor of Government and department chairman. He went to Harvard in 1951 and remained there until his death. He served briefly as department chairman (1953–1954) and was Jonathan

Trumbull Professor of American History and Government.

Key's principal publications during the remainder of his career included *A Primer of Statistics for Political Scientists* (1954), which emphasized his concern with mathematical analysis of political data; the seminal article "A Theory of Critical Elections" (1955); and *American State Politics: An Introduction* (1956), in which he pursued some of the lines of inquiry of *Southern Politics* and developed some new approaches. In the 1960's there appeared *Public Opinion and American Democracy* (1961) and *The Responsible Electorate* (1966). The former has been called "the most searching study of the relations of public opinion to the American political process yet to appear." The latter showed again, in brief compass, Key's unique ability to analyze and extract meaning from data.

Key's devotion to scholarship was very nearly all-consuming, but it was not selfish. He served as consultant to governmental units on levels from the national to the local, and on the boards and committees of scholarly foundations. In 1958 the American Political Science Association elected him its president. In October 1961, President John Kennedy appointed him to the President's Commission on Campaign Costs, which reported in 1962.

Key was always ready to assist colleagues and students. His most often cited personal qualities were his modesty, unpretentiousness, openness to people, and concern for others. He died at Brookline, Mass.

[Works by Key not mentioned in the text include *The Administration of Federal Grants to States* (1937); *The Problem of Local Legislation in Maryland* (Maryland State Planning Commission, 1940); *Problems in Long-Term Municipal Fiscal Policy with Respect to Norfolk, Virginia* (National Resources Planning Board, Dec. 1941); *The Matching Requirements in Federal Grant Legislation in Relation to Variations in State Fiscal Capacity* (Social Security Board, Feb. 1942); *A Report on the Maryland State Planning Commission* (Maryland State Planning Commission, 1958); *Financing Presidential Campaigns* (Report of the President's Commission on Campaign Costs, Apr. 1962). An obituary is in the *New York Times*, Oct. 5, 1963.]

ELMER E. CORNWELL, JR.

KIDDER, ALFRED VINCENT (Oct. 29, 1885–June 11, 1963), archaeologist, was born in Marquette, Mich., the son of Alfred Kidder, a mining engineer, and of Kate Dalliba. During his boyhood, the family moved to Cambridge, Mass., where Kidder attended the Browne and

Nichols School until 1901. He spent 1901–1903 at La Villa school in Ouchy, Switzerland, and then attended the Noble and Greenough School in Boston (1903–1904). He received an A.B. from Harvard in 1908, an M.A. in 1912, and a Ph.D. in 1914.

As an undergraduate, Kidder spent the summer of 1907 working on an archaeological survey in the southwestern United States. This experience led him to decide to become an archaeologist. He spent the following summer in Utah, working for the Archaeological Institute of America; this work resulted in his first published archaeological report, "Explorations in Southeastern Utah in 1908," *American Journal of Archaeology* (1910). On Sept. 6, 1910, Kidder married Madeleine Appleton, who became his co-worker; they had five children.

Concurrent with graduate studies, Kidder continued his southwestern fieldwork. During 1910 and 1912–1914, he was the Austin teaching fellow in the Harvard Department of Anthropology, and in 1914 he was curator of North American archaeology at the Harvard Peabody Museum.

In his Ph.D. thesis on southwestern ceramics (1914), Kidder formulated a new methodology. Until then, pottery specimens had been seen as relics of an undifferentiated past. In his work relics became expressions of different times and places that provided a coherent history. His "Pottery of the Pajarito Plateau and of Some Adjacent Regions in New Mexico" (1915) showed the careful organization and precise presentation of detail that characterized all his major publications.

During 1914–1915, Kidder collaborated with Samuel J. Guernsey in fieldwork in the "basketmaker" caves in northeastern Arizona. Their resulting publication, *Archaeological Explorations in Northeastern Arizona* (1919), is a landmark in southwestern archaeology; the cultural distinctions described remain the foundation of archaeological chronology of the southwestern United States.

Kidder's southwestern interests came to fruition when he became director of a major excavation program at the pueblo ruin of Pecos in New Mexico, sponsored by the Peabody Foundation of Phillips Academy (1915–1929). The Pecos project, the first systematic large-scale stratigraphic operation in American archaeology, resulted in the first archaeological area synthesis of the modern type in the American hemispheres.

Another important result was the First Pecos Conference in Southwestern Archaeology, called by Kidder in 1927. It became an annual event after that date. The conference established a system of culture classification that is still in use. The Pecos excavations were interrupted during World War I, when Kidder served in France with the American Expeditionary Forces (1917–1919). He was awarded the Legion of Honor by the French government.

In 1926 Kidder became research associate of the Carnegie Institution of Washington, D.C., and one year later was placed in charge of all archaeological activities of the institution. In 1929 he became head of the division of historical research. For the rest of his career, he planned and participated in archaeological research in the Maya region of southern Mexico and northern Central America, including fieldwork in the Guatemala highlands. The excavations of the Maya project provided data that form the chronological frame of Mayan archaeological studies.

Strongly humanistic in approach, Kidder directed studies in various areas of Mayan cultural history: ethnology, physical anthropology, medicine, linguistics, history, environmental studies, as well as archaeology. He later felt that this general approach to pre-Columbian Mayan cultural history was his most significant contribution to anthropology. At the outset of these studies Kidder participated in an air survey of the Maya region. Accompanied by Colonel and Mrs. Charles A. Lindbergh and other staff, he conducted a reconnaissance that revealed hitherto undiscovered Mayan ruins, thus demonstrating the value of the airplane for observation of archaeological sites.

Kidder served on the faculty of the Peabody Museum at Harvard from 1939 to 1951. He was involved in the creation of the Society for American Archaeology in 1935 and served as president two years later. He was also president of the American Anthropological Association in 1942 and a principal founder of the Institute of Andean Research in the early 1930's.

After retiring from the Carnegie Institution in 1950 Kidder remained active. In 1951 he taught at the University of California at Berkeley and later participated in seminars in archaeology at Harvard.

Kidder was the foremost American archaeologist of his time. More than any other contemporary, he was responsible for transforming archaeology in the western hemisphere from antiquarianism, with stress on collecting specimens for museums, to a systematic discipline acquiring data on past civilizations. A prolific worker, Kidder published over 200 articles and books.

Kidder was the first recipient of the Viking Fund Medal for archaeology (1946). In 1950, the American Anthropological Association established the Alfred V. Kidder award for achievement in southwestern or middle American archaeology. The Guatemalan government honored him with the Order of the Quetzal (1955), and the University of Pennsylvania gave him the Drexel Medal for Archaeology (1958).

Kidder's knowledge of American archaeology was enormous. Never dogmatic, he listened willingly to others and reacted with wisdom and perception. He died in Cambridge, Mass.

[See Richard B. Woodbury, *Alfred V. Kidder* (1973); Gordon R. Willey, "Alfred Vincent Kidder," *National Academy of Sciences. Biographical Memoirs,* 39 (1967); and Robert Wauchope, "Alfred Vincent Kidder, 1885–1963," *American Antiquity,* Oct. 1965, with a complete bibliography of Kidder's writings. Kidder's *Excavations at Kaminaljuyú, Guatemala* (1946), with Jesse D. Jennings and Edwin M. Shook, is the introductory text to Maya highland archaeology. An obituary is in the *New York Times,* June 15, 1963.]

ADELE HAST

KILGALLEN, DOROTHY MAE (July 3, 1913–Nov. 8, 1965), newspaperwoman, television and radio personality, was born in Chicago, Ill., the daughter of James Lawrence Kilgallen, a newspaperman, and Mary Jane ("Mae") Ahern. Kilgallen and her protective Irish-Catholic family lived in Laramie, Wyo., and Indianapolis, Ind., before returning to Chicago when she was six. They moved to Brooklyn, N.Y., in 1923. Kilgallen attended public school and graduated from Erasmus Hall High School in Brooklyn in 1930. Following her freshman year (1930–1931) at the College of New Rochelle, she took a summer job at William Randolph Hearst's New York *Evening Journal.* Her father, she later said, "never suggested that I follow in his footsteps. But the footsteps were there, and what other way could I have gone?"

By the time she was twenty, Kilgallen had a by-line familiar to *Journal* readers. She had a flair for particulars, coupled with a breathless innocence reinforced by the persistent rumor that she was "convent bred." Following in the Hearst sob sister tradition, murders became her speciality. After covering the trial of Bruno Richard Hauptmann, the convicted kidnapper of the son of Charles Lindbergh, Kilgallen, looking "exactly like Minnie Mouse," raced around the world in 1936 on commercial airlines in a contest with two other reporters. She came in second, taking twenty-four days, but "finished first in acclaim and publicity" and instantly became a celebrity.

Sent to Hollywood to capitalize on her new renown, Kilgallen collaborated on a screenplay (*Fly Away Baby,* 1937) based on her recent race, wrote a gossip column, played a bit part in a film (*Sinner Take All,* 1936), but failed to impress the movie kingdom. When she was called back to New York in 1937, she concentrated on social occasions and began participating in news events. While single-handedly covering the coronation of George VI for her paper, Kilgallen became for her readers part of the ceremony. Her tendency to mingle with the people she wrote about became more pronounced in 1938 when she took over the syndicated gossip column "The Voice of Broadway," in the *Journal-American* (the two papers had merged in July 1937). Becoming a personality in her own right, she promoted her friends and "discoveries," while lacing celebrity gossip with "odd tidbits of inconsequential information," "dark hints of international espionage," and shockingly malicious comments. Kilgallen, who had intense feeling for popular music, mingled easily with black musicians at a time when society was still largely segregated. She was among the first to entertain cafe musicians with established society and show people.

On Apr. 6, 1940, she married Richard Tompkins Kollmar, an actor whose ancestor Daniel D. Tompkins had been governor of New York and vice-president of the United States. In 1945 they began "Breakfast with Dorothy and Dick," a radio program in which they detailed their glamorous lives, criticized small-town America, preached right-of-center political views, and praised their sponsors' products. Their three children often joined them on this popular show, which continued until 1963.

In 1950 Kilgallen became the "most visible and celebrated journalist of her time" when the Columbia Broadcasting System picked her for "What's My Line?"—a television program on which panelists guessed the occupations of guests. Kilgallen, an avid, intensely competitive player of parlor games, was a superb choice. Witty, combative, often tactless, and always determined to win, she remained on the show the rest of her life. While helping it capture 10 million weekly viewers, she doubled (raising to 146 by 1965) the number of newspapers carrying her "Voice of Broadway" column.

Kilgallen was slim and of medium height with a high forehead, small chin, and ready smile. She had dark curly hair, blue eyes, and a Dresden-doll complexion. She nearly always wore or carried white gloves, which emphasized her femininity in a predominantly masculine trade.

Kilgallen was called "a newspaperman in a $500 dress." Four times she was included among the world's ten best-dressed women. With each choice assignment from the Hearst chain she proved her ability both to report and to make news. "Dorothy Kilgallen . . . Astounded By Verdict," the *Journal-American* headlined in 1954 when Dr. Samuel Sheppard was convicted of slaying his wife. While covering Elizabeth II's coronation in 1953, Kilgallen wore a dress nearly as elaborate as the queen's and reported Elizabeth's 1957 visit to the United States from a limousine that became part of the queen's procession. This caused a disgruntled fellow newspaperwoman to remark, "There goes the queen covering the queen." During the Khrushchevs' 1959 visit, Kilgallen outraged many Americans when, amidst a barrage of derogatory comments, she likened Nina Khrushchev's suit to "a home-made slip cover on a sofa." Some people admired Kilgallen and others detested her, but nearly everyone read her. She covered events with "a dash of color, a pinch of moral indignation, a soupçon of understanding and two tablespoons of malice."

Kilgallen had become a bigger celebrity than many of the people she wrote about but preferred being called what her own paper called her, "a reporter's reporter." She had tremendous energy and the "eagerness of a cub reporter." She befriended many obscure people; frequently they were Irish—policemen, washroom attendants, court officials, jury members, and even accused criminals. They in turn were fiercely loyal to her and sometimes gave her information for stories. After covering Jack Ruby's trial for murdering Lee Harvey Oswald, President John F. Kennedy's assassin, Kilgallen published Ruby's Warren Commission testimony a month before it was made public. Although the Dallas *Times-Herald* shared this scoop with her, she, as usual, got most of the publicity.

Kilgallen died in her Manhattan home from a combination of barbiturates and alcohol, and since neither was ingested in massive quantity, her death was termed accidental. The *Journal-American*, according her a courtesy she had often denied others, said little about the circumstances of her death. Kilgallen died in her prime. Ten thousand people filed past her casket and crowds stopped traffic outside St. Vincent Ferrer Roman Catholic Church, where James Kilgallen wept aloud for his "little girl."

[More than seventy of Kilgallen's personal scrapbooks are at the Billy Rose Theatre Collection, the New York Public Library at Lincoln Center.

Some of Kilgallen's newspaper pieces are compiled in her *Girl Around the World* (1936) and *Murder One* (1967).

The most complete source on Kilgallen's life is Lee Israel, *Kilgallen* (1979). Israel's suggestion that Kilgallen was murdered because she was trying to secure the facts about the assassination of John F. Kennedy is not substantiated. David Gelman et al., "The Dorothy Kilgallen Story," *New York Post*, Apr. 20–May 1, 1960, is a critical ten-part overview of Kilgallen's career. Her early press years are covered in Ishbel Ross, *Ladies of the Press* (1936), her whole newspaper career in John Jakes, *Great Women Reporters* (1969), and her special place on television in Gilbert Fates, *What's My Line? The Inside History of TV's Most Famous Panel Show* (1978).

Among the numerous articles written about her are Ernest Lehman, "24 Glittering Hours with Dorothy Kilgallen," *Cosmopolitan*, Sept. 1950; "Columnists" and "Reporters," *Time*, Oct. 25, 1963, and Nov. 19, 1965; and "Reports on Ruby Distress Inquiry," *New York Times*, Aug. 19, 1964. Obituaries and reports on her funeral and autopsy are in the *Journal-American*, Nov. 8, 1965; and the *New York Times*, Nov. 9, 12, and 16, 1965.]

OLIVE HOOGENBOOM

KILPATRICK, WILLIAM HEARD (Nov. 20, 1871–Feb. 13, 1965), educator and theorist and philosopher of education, was born in White Plains, Ga., the son of James Hines Kilpatrick, a Baptist minister, and of Edna Perrin Heard, a teacher. As a child he learned to appreciate the folkways and traditions of the rural South. Following an earthquake and the death of two sisters from typhoid when he was fourteen, Kilpatrick was called to the Baptist faith by an itinerant revivalist minister. But in spite of encouragement from his father, he felt no call to the ministry.

From 1888 to 1891, Kilpatrick studied at Mercer University, a Baptist school at Macon, Ga., where he earned the B.A. (1891) and the M.A. (1892). After a year at Johns Hopkins University studying mathematics, he taught and was principal in Georgia public schools (1892–1894; 1896–1897). In these posts he did away with report cards and pupil punishment. In 1897, following more training at Johns Hopkins, Kilpatrick returned to Mercer as professor of mathematics. On Dec. 27, 1898, he married Marie Beman Guyton; they had three children.

In 1904 Kilpatrick became acting president of Mercer. Two years later, though, he had to resign when his religious ideas proved unacceptable to the institution's trustees. He next taught school for a year in Columbus, Ohio, then studied under John Dewey at Teachers College, Columbia University, from 1907 through 1909. He was granted the Ph.D. by Columbia in 1912. His first wife died in May 1907, and on Nov. 26, 1908, Kilpatrick married Margaret Manigault Pinckney.

Kilpatrick's teaching career at Columbia began in 1909, with his appointment as instructor of the philosophy of education at Teachers College. Rejecting the lecture method in favor of group discussions (some with as many as 650 students), Kilpatrick became known as a superb teacher. Over the years more than 35,000 students took his courses, and the *New York Post*, having totaled the fees paid the university by his students in one summer session, labeled him the "Million Dollar Professor."

Kilpatrick rejected the existing educational system, in which the teacher functioned as an authority figure communicating an existing body of knowledge to passive students. In his ideal classroom, students and teachers worked together, cooperatively, learning what at that moment proved useful, and learning it not through the "dire compulsion" of grades and examinations but through "whole-hearted purposeful activity proceeding in a social environment" (the "project method," as Kilpatrick called it in an essay in the 1918 *Teachers College Record*).

Scholars usually have seen Kilpatrick as a popularizer of Dewey's theories. Surely he was influenced by Dewey's experimentalism—his rejection of unquestioned authority and absolutes. On the other hand, Dewey did not share Kilpatrick's intense dislike of the fixed curriculum or his passionate advocacy of pupil-centered learning. Moreover, the focus on intellectual derivatives has obscured the historical origins of Kilpatrick's ideas.

According to Kilpatrick, progressive education was essential for two reasons, each grounded in an interpretation of history. First, it was essential to progress. Kilpatrick argued that science had made the future so unpredictable that authoritarian educational methods—methods functional in a predictable, pre-industrial society—had to be discarded in favor of a system that encouraged openness and adaptability to new ideas.

The second function of progressive education was to construct a new system of morality. This new morality had become necessary because older "external" systems of authority—including religion, the family, and the community (in short, the familiar institutions of his youth)—had deteriorated under the pressures of industri-

alization and urbanization. Its application seemed especially vital in the decade after 1917, when Kilpatrick observed a "moral crisis" reflected in the scandals of President Warren Harding's administration, racketeering, the emancipation of women, and other phenomena. The schools would contribute to a resolution of the moral crisis by facilitating the shift from external authority to internal authority.

The frequent criticism that Kilpatrick was advocating a self-indulgent permissiveness is off the mark. Through group discussion and other tools of progressive education, he sought to produce responsible citizens adept at "self control" and (in the Great Depression) sympathetic to and capable of democratic social planning.

Kilpatrick's growing stature as an educator created new arenas in which he could apply his theories. In 1923 he became involved in the creation of Bennington College and later (1931–1938) chaired that school's Board of Trustees. He helped found *Social Frontier*, a journal of progressive education, in 1934. After retiring from Columbia in 1938, Kilpatrick served as president of the New York Urban League (1941–1951) and as chairman of the Bureau of Intercultural Education (1940–1951), American Youth for World Youth (1946–1951), and the Board of Directors of the League for Industrial Democracy. His second wife died in November 1938, and Kilpatrick married Marion Y. Ostrander on May 8, 1940. He died in New York City.

Although progressive education was never wholeheartedly accepted in the United States, its influence was substantial in the "activity movement" of the 1930's and again in the 1960's. Kilpatrick also had an impact on education elsewhere, especially in Great Britain. Of his methods, group discussion has been the most widely adopted. Kilpatrick's most important theoretical contribution was to emphasize that all education, in any subject matter, is education in attitude and behavior. He used that theory to build a new democratic structure of authority centered in the classroom. In this general sense his legacy can be found in social work, recreation, psychotherapy, child rearing, and industrial relations.

[After 1904, Kilpatrick kept a detailed diary that, with scrapbooks and other materials, will be available in 1985 at Teachers College Library, Special Collections Department, Columbia University. Kilpatrick's 14 books and 375 articles are listed in "Writings of William Heard Kilpatrick," *Studies in Philosophy and Education*, Nov. 1961. Among the most important are *Foundations of Method* (1925); *Education for a Changing Civilization* (1926); *Education and the Social Crisis* (1932); *The Educational Frontier* (1933); *Group Education for a Democracy* (1940); and *Philosophy of Education* (1951). See also Samuel Tenenbaum, *William Heard Kilpatrick* (1951); John L. Childs, *American Pragmatism and Education* (1956); Ernst Papanek, "William Heard Kilpatrick's International Influence: Teacher of World's Teachers," *Progressive Education*, Mar. 1957; Lawrence A. Cremin, *The Transformation of the School* (1961); Charles Frankel, "Appearance and Reality in Kilpatrick's Philosophy," *Teachers College Record*, Jan. 1965; and Leslie R. Perry, ed., *Bertrand Russell, A. S. Neill, Homer Lane, W. H. Kilpatrick: Four Progressive Educators* (1967). *Educational Theory*, Jan. 1966, is a memorial issue. An obituary is in the *New York Times*, Feb. 14, 1965. An oral history memoir is on file at the Columbia University Archives, Division of Special Collections, Butler Library.]

WILLIAM GRAEBNER

KING, ALEXANDER (Nov. 13, 1900–Nov. 17, 1965), author, illustrator, editor, and raconteur, was born Alexander Konig in Vienna, Austria, the only child of Karl Gabriel Konig, a research chemist, and of Malvine Breuer. After being expelled from grammar school for "unaccountable conduct," King, of Jewish ancestry, was sent to a Jesuit school for boys in Vienna. In 1913, his parents immigrated to New York City, where King went to public schools on Manhattan's Lower East Side. (He also claimed that he attended Cooper Union and the Sorbonne.)

At an early age, King began to draw, and at seventeen he found work as a cartoonist on *The Big Stick*, a humorous Jewish weekly paper. In 1920 he became a naturalized citizen. He did sketches for the Socialist newspaper *Call*, and he sold a few covers to *Smart Set*, encouraged in his work by the editors, H. L. Mencken and George Jean Nathan. King also painted, and the first exhibition of his painting was in publisher Horace Liveright's office. Hired by Liveright to do book illustrations, he earned a reputation as a competent and versatile artist. By 1930 he had illustrated more than fifty books, many of them limited editions of classics. He did a number of special editions of Eugene O'Neill's plays.

For nearly twenty-five years (1930–1955), King ceased drawing and painting altogether. During this period, he edited an erratically published magazine *Americana* (1932–1933). He was the first in the United States to publish the drawings of George Grosz, whose work he admired and imitated. He served for a time as managing editor of *Stage* magazine, and as an

assistant editor of *Vanity Fair*. From 1937 to 1940 he was an associate editor of *Life*, where he was reputed to be an "idea" man. He turned out an occasional magazine article in these years, including a profile of Rose O'Neill, the illustrator and inventor of the Kewpie Doll, for the *New Yorker*, Nov. 24, 1934.

In 1945 King took morphine to relieve persistent kidney stone pains. He became addicted. For nine years he struggled against the addiction, spending fourteen months at the Federal narcotics hospital in Lexington, Ky. Eventually, he was cured. He vividly described the drug addict's subculture in his memoirs.

King was known to his friends as a gifted but erratic man, disarmingly gentle in appearance, who spoke five languages, wrote plays (none notably successful), and painted. He published his first book, *Mine Enemy Grows Older*, in 1958. But he had received no appreciable public recognition until his explosive appearance on the Jack Paar television show on Jan. 2, 1959. He captivated the audience. Witty, sardonic, and irreverent, he delivered an incessant flow of commentary on art, life, sex, drugs, women, literature, and other topics engaging his interest. "He was the greatest conversationalist I ever met," said Paar, who described his guest as "a frail but fierce little man with the air of a delinquent leprechaun." King later had his own show, "Alex in Wonderland," on a New York City television station. Critic John Lardner, who was not greatly impressed, found King "so fluent as to make what he says implausible. His talk abounds in bon mots and other meaty observations that were uttered to him personally, he tells you, by famous men, most of them now extinct."

When King first appeared on the Paar show, *Mine Enemy Grows Older* had sold about 6,500 copies. The following week it sold 26,000. Ultimately, it sold more than 175,000. The book was described accurately as "less autobiography than memoirs, less memoirs than a series of impressionistic self-portraits and wildly hilarious anecdotes done so vividly, with such zest and animal bounce, that the book all but leaps in your hands." It was quickly followed by three more books of reminiscences—*May This House Be Safe from Tigers* (1960), *I Should Have Kissed Her More* (1961), and *Is There a Life After Birth?* (1963). There was a recession of spontaneity and quality in the succeeding books and an increase of raunchiness, pumped-up flamboyance, and petulant misanthropy; however, all sold well.

In 1960 King brought out *Alexander King*

Presents Peter Altenberg's Evocations of Love. Altenberg was an obscure Viennese journalist whose meditations and little stories were delightful reading. King translated, introduced, and illustrated a selection of Altenberg's work. He deserves credit for salvaging from oblivion some excellent writing.

King was married four times—for twenty years to his first wife, Nettie, with whom he had two sons. His fourth wife, Margie Lou Swet, whom he married on Feb. 23, 1953, was a young singer who often appeared on his television shows. Among King's numerous dislikes were advertising ("a soggy over-ripe fungus"), abstract painting, millionaires, *Life* magazine, the *New Yorker,* the evangelist Billy Graham, and Ernest Hemingway. People generally, King said, were "adenoidal baboons" caught in "life's erratically operated sausage machine." Of modern times he said: "We had our century and muffed it. We put Coca Cola in Old Vienna. It couldn't be sadder."

In precarious health much of his life (suffering from kidney disease, peptic ulcers, and hypertension), King died in New York City shortly after a television appearance promoting his just-published book, *Rich Man, Poor Man, Freud and Fruit* (1965).

[The four volumes of King's memoirs amusingly reveal his personality, contain important autobiographical facts, and colorfully portray the background of his life and work; but they are laced with exaggerations and fictitious episodes and do not, as he admitted, give a reliable, well-rounded account of his life. Not cited in the text is King's *The Great Ker-Plunk* (1962), about the adventures of a musically talented seal. On King and his career, see "Jack Paar's Pet Imp," *Newsweek,* Feb. 23, 1959; Lewis Nichols, "On and Out of Books," *New York Times Book Review,* Mar. 15, 1959; John Lardner, "Air Channel Thirteen at Night," *New Yorker,* May 9, 1959; Hugh G. Foster, "TV's Greatest Talker," *Holiday,* Nov. 1959; and Jack Paar, *My Saber Is Bent* (1961). Informative book reviews are in *Newsweek,* Nov. 24, 1958; Mar. 18, 1963; Nov. 15, 1965; and *Time,* Mar. 14, 1960. Obituaries are in the *New York Times* and the *New York Herald Tribune,* both Nov. 17, 1965; and *Publishers Weekly,* Nov. 29, 1965.]

WILLIAM McCANN

KIRK, ALAN GOODRICH (Oct. 30, 1888– Oct. 15, 1963), naval officer and diplomat, was born in Philadelphia, Pa., the son of William Thomson Kirk, a successful wholesale grocer, and Harriet Goodrich. He attended preparatory school in Beverly, N.J., and decided upon a naval career after visiting vessels under the command of his uncle, Rear Admiral Caspar F. Goodrich. His father, a Democrat, secured him an appointment to the United States Naval Academy through a New Jersey Congressman, and Kirk enrolled with the class of 1909.

Nicknamed "Hoboken Bill" by his classmates, Kirk excelled in scholarship. Stocky, with blond hair, freckles, and "dancing" blue eyes, he was described variously throughout his career as poker-faced, personable, jaunty, handsome, brilliant, fiery, stoic, and a chain smoker. An avid reader, he especially loved poetry. All these traits made him well-suited for staff and diplomatic roles in and out of the navy.

After shipboard assignments as a junior gunnery officer with the Atlantic and Asiatic fleets, Kirk spent World War I (1916–1919) as proof and experimental officer at the Naval Proving Ground, Dahlgren, Va. His work included testing depth charges for use against German U-boats. At that time, gunnery was regarded as the key to advancement in the navy. Kirk served at the Bureau of Ordnance during 1922–1924 and as gunnery officer on the battleship *Maryland* (1924–1926). From 1926 to 1928, he was fleet gunnery officer of the Scouting Fleet. Subsequently he became commanding officer of the destroyer *Schenck* (1931–1932) and executive officer of the battleship *West Virginia* (1932–1933). On Sept. 19, 1918, Kirk married Lydia Selden Chapin, daughter of a navy captain; they had three children.

Kirk's education in the political realm began in May 1920 with his assignment as executive officer and navigator of the presidential yacht *Mayflower.* He saw little of Woodrow Wilson but a great deal of Warren G. Harding before being detached in October 1921. He was a student at the Naval War College, Newport, R.I., during 1928–1929 and a staff member there for the following two years. From 1933 to 1936 he was assistant director of the ships movements division in the Office of the Chief of Naval Operations, and with the rank of commander he commanded the cruiser *Milwaukee* for several months thereafter. More staff duty followed with his assignment to Admiral Claude C. Bloch, commander first of the Battle Force and then of the United States Fleet (1937–1939).

Now a captain, Kirk received his first diplomatic assignment in June 1939 as naval attaché at the American embassy in London under Ambassador Joseph P. Kennedy. In the early stages of World War II, Kirk was busy transferring American refugees home and adjudicating British seizures of American contraband, at the same time quietly obtaining technical data on British weapons as Anglo-American cooperation grew.

Returning to Washington late in 1940, Kirk served as director of Naval Intelligence from March to October 1941, then commanded convoy escorts and amphibious forces in the Atlantic. In November 1941 he was promoted to rear admiral. He returned to the London embassy in March 1942, with the additional duty of chief of staff to the commander of United States naval forces in Europe, Admiral Harold R. Stark. Kirk was very popular with the British government and military officials, and he carried out his duties with great aplomb until the beginning of 1943.

Admiral Kirk headed the Atlantic Fleet's Amphibious Force from February to October 1943. He led Task Force 85 in the successful assault on Scoglitti, Sicily, in July. That November he returned to England as commander of the American naval forces preparing for the D-Day landings in France. During the assault on the Normandy beaches in June 1944, Kirk flew his flag from the cruiser *Augusta* as commander of the United States Naval Task Force. He also led the capture of Cherbourg in July. Two months later he took command of all United States naval forces in France. His chief jobs were to keep supplies flowing to the army on the continent and to provide amphibious craft for important river crossings. With Germany's defeat, Kirk was advanced to the rank of vice admiral in July 1945. The following month he was assigned to duty on the navy's General Board in Washington.

On Mar. 1, 1946, upon his appointment as United States ambassador to Belgium and minister to Luxembourg, Kirk retired from the navy with the rank of full admiral. While on this assignment he also served as United States representative on the United Nations Special Committee on the Balkans. He left Belgium in April 1949 to become ambassador to the Soviet Union; he arrived in Moscow in June. Although Kirk traveled extensively throughout the Soviet Union, cold war passions made his tenure there generally barren, and he met with Premier Josef Stalin only once and was received officially at the Kremlin only twice during his two years and three months as ambassador. His wife published a book on their experiences in Russia, *Postmarked Moscow* (1952).

Kirk emerged from his ambassadorship to the Soviet Union a devoted enemy of Communism, and in February 1952 he took over chairmanship of the American Committee for the Libera-

tion of the Peoples of Russia and of its Radio Liberation, which beamed broadcasts behind the Iron Curtain. That August he also became director of the Psychological Strategy Board, which sought to counter Communist propaganda. From 1955 to 1959 he was unsalaried chairman of the New York State Civil Defense Commission. In addition to his directorships of several American companies, in 1961 Kirk became president of the Belgo-American Corporation, which had holdings in the secessionist province of Katanga. He undertook several unofficial missions for President John F. Kennedy during the Congo crisis, using his Belgian connections of fifteen years before. Appointed ambassador to Nationalist China in May 1962 by President Kennedy, Kirk was forced to resign the following April due to ill health. He died in New York City.

[The few papers that Kirk left are deposited with the Naval Historical Foundation at the Library of Congress. On his life see the obituaries in the *New York Times* and the *Washington Post*, Oct. 16, 1963; the Naval Historical Center's unpublished outline; and Clark G. Reynolds, *Famous American Admirals* (1978). Samuel Eliot Morison, *Sicily-Salerno-Anzio* (1954) and *The Invasion of France and Germany* (1957), cover Kirk's wartime combat experiences in some depth.]

CLARK G. REYNOLDS

KLINE, FRANZ JOSEF (May 23, 1910–May 13, 1962), painter, was born in Wilkes Barre, Pa., the son of Anthony Kline and Anne Rowe. Anthony Kline, a tavern keeper, committed suicide when his son was seven. Subsequently Anne Kline practiced nursing in order to support the younger children, while Franz and his older brother lived at the Episcopal Church Home in Jonestown, Pa. In 1919 Franz entered Girard College in Philadelphia, a tuition-free trade school for fatherless boys; there he studied carpentry and blacksmithing. He remained there until 1925, although his mother married Ambrose Snyder, a foreman for the Lehigh Valley Railroad, in 1920 and moved to Lehighton, Pa.

Kline began Lehighton High School in 1926. An average student, he soon displayed artistic talent. He was president of the Art Club in his sophomore year and contributed many drawings, cartoons, and lettering to the school yearbook. Although only about five feet seven inches tall, he was an outstanding athlete, participating in football, baseball, and basketball. In maturity, his strength and energy complemented his artistic aptitude, producing a very sensitive but "athletic" art, characterized by the critic Harold Rosenberg as "Action Painting."

After graduation from high school, Kline attended Boston University for one year, where the painter Henry Hensche (for whom Kline later named a painting) was among his teachers. He also attended classes at the Boston Art Students League, specializing in cartooning and illustration. Kline had intended to continue his art education in Paris but instead went to London. He studied traditional drawing and painting at Heatherley's Art School during 1936 and 1937.

In January of 1937, a month before leaving England, Kline met Elizabeth V. Parsons, a model in Frederic Whitings' drawing class at Heatherley's. Three years older than Franz, she had studied ballet and danced professionally. Dance subjects recur in Kline's later work, and it is possible that her interests affected his progression from the academic and illustrative to freer and more gestural experimentation.

Back in the United States in 1938, Kline worked as a window display designer—first with Oppenheim Collins in Buffalo, N.Y., and then with Arnold Constable in New York City. Elizabeth Parsons arrived in America at the end of the year, and they were married on Dec. 5, 1938. They had no children. From her arrival until the mid-1940's Kline's life was emotionally and economically a struggle. Elizabeth was frequently institutionalized, as she would be until a few years before Kline's death. Kline lived in and near Greenwich Village, supporting himself mostly by quick portrait sketches, murals, lettering, and other bar decorations. During the 1939 World's Fair he worked as a sidewalk portrait artist. He exhibited at the Washington Square art show in 1939, met the painter Earl Kerkam who was also showing, and won a small prize. His talent was recognized by the set designer Cleon Throckmorton and by the illustrator Henry Raleigh, for whom he later did some "ghost" work.

Kline showed for the first time in 1942 at the National Academy's Annual Exhibition in New York City, where he won in the following two years the S. J. Wallace Truman Prize for painters under thirty-five, both times for realistic paintings. These exhibitions led to purchases by Dr. and Mrs. Theodore J. Edlich, Jr., and Mr. and Mrs. I. David Orr, his principal and virtually only patrons during these years. Kline began to meet some of the artists who, like him, would make their reputations after World War II— Conrad Marca-Relli, John Ferren, Willem de Kooning, Peter Agostini, and Jackson Pollock.

By the mid-1940's Kline's work, particularly his drawing, was becoming freer and more selective in its emphasis. In 1946 he painted his first completely abstract work, *The Dancer,* and in the following three years, while still doing some figurative work, he began a series of black-and-white paintings containing the bold, gestural brush work of his mature style. Kline was probably encouraged in this direction by De Kooning, who had his first one-man show at the Egan Gallery in 1948, and by Philip Guston and Bradley Walker Tomlin, who both had recently become abstractionists.

In 1950 Kline "came up from underground" and was recognized by uptown galleries. At the Kootz Gallery his work was part of the exhibition "Black or White: Paintings by European and American Artists," including De Kooning, Adolph Gottlieb, Piet Mondrian, Picasso, Tomlin, and Robert Motherwell. Later in the year, at the same gallery, a drawing of Kline's was selected by the critic Clement Greenberg for a "New Talent" exhibition. And still later in 1950, he had his first one-man show at the Egan Gallery. Simultaneously, Sidney Janis paired him with the better known French painter Pierre Soulages in an exhibition called "Young Painters in U.S. and France."

For his remaining years, Kline's bold, slashing drawings and paintings were among the most familiar images produced by the artists of his generation. Along with Pollock and De Kooning he was a quintessential "Action Painter" or "Abstract Expressionist." His work, like theirs, seemed to extend beyond the picture frame, bursting with energy and a sense of endless space—a painting form called "American-Type Painting" by Greenberg in 1955, and "The New American Painting" in an important exhibition at the Museum of Modern Art in 1958.

Kline had one-man shows at Egan (1951 and 1954) and Janis (1956, 1958, 1960, 1961, and 1963), and was included in frequent group exhibitions at galleries and museums. These culminated in the selection of ten of his paintings —along with work by Philip Guston and Hans Hofmann and the sculptor Theodore Roszak— for the 1960 Venice Biennial Exhibition of Modern Art. There, Kline showed works ranging from *Nijinsky* (1950) to the sixteen-foot-wide *1960 New Year's Eve Night Wall* (1960) and won the Italian Ministry of Public Instruction Prize.

Although the Museum of Modern Art had acquired Kline's *Chief* (1950) in 1952 and the Whitney Museum of American Art *Mahoning* (1956), another representative work, in 1957,

American abstract artists were still showing to each other rather than selling to a wide public. To support himself Kline taught at Black Mountain College, N.C. (1952), Pratt Institute (1953), and Philadelphia Museum School of Art (1954). Only after Pollock's death in 1956 did the public begin to acquire American abstract expressionist paintings, allowing Kline to enjoy the economic rewards commensurate with his critical recognition.

In 1961 Kline entered Johns Hopkins Hospital for tests which revealed chronic rheumatic heart trouble. He was put on a strict regimen that he characteristically ignored. As Motherwell said, "He could not take care of himself! It would have meant another existence." Kline died in New York City after two major heart attacks.

[There are no substantial biographies or monographs on Kline, but April Kingsley is writing a monograph for Harry Abrams, publisher. See Fielding Dawson, *An Emotional Memoir of Franz Kline* (1967); Robert Goodnough, "Kline Paints a Picture," *Art News*, Dec. 1952; Frank O'Hara, "Franz Kline Talking," *Evergreen Review*, Autumn 1958 (reprinted in his *Art Chronicles 1954–66*); and David Sylvester's 1960 "Interview with Franz Kline," *Living Art*, Spring 1963. Harry F. Gaugh's *Franz Kline: The Color Abstractions* (1979), The Phillips Collection, Washington, D.C., contains the most detailed chronology, but some of the information therein has been superseded. Catalogs of Kline's exhibitions present an adequate, though far from definitive, record of his work. Of note are the Whitney Museum, *The New Decade* (1955), edited by John I. H. Baur, which contains a brief statement by Kline; Museum of Modern Art, *12 Americans* (1956), edited by Dorothy C. Miller, which contains part of a previously unpublished foreword by Elaine de Kooning; the Sidney Janis Gallery catalogues of 1960, 1961, and the memorial exhibition of 1963; John Gordon, *Franz Kline 1910–1962*, Whitney Museum, 1968, the first major retrospective exhibition; David McKee, *Franz Kline* (1975), contains a good selection of drawings in the Kline estate.

Kline also appears briefly in *Sketchbook No. 1: Three Americans* (1960), a film by Robert Snyder and the editors of *Time*. More important, Mrs. E. Ross Zogbaum, Kline's closest friend from 1957 until his death and subsequently the executrix of his estate, has prepared an audio-visual slide show, taken from frames of films made in Provincetown in 1960 as well as from photographs of his early and later work, thus presenting his development as an artist.]

B. H. FRIEDMAN

KNAUTH, OSWALD WHITMAN (June 3, 1887–July 13, 1962), economist and businessman, was born in New York City, the son of Percival Knauth, a banker, and of Mary Iles Whitman. After private schooling he entered Harvard, graduating with an A.B. in 1909. For a single day he attended law school, and for one term was a theology student, but neither discipline challenged him. Unburdened with financial problems—his father was the American representative of the international banking house of Knauth, Nachod and Kuhne—Knauth experimented in several fields. He worked until 1910 for American Bank Note Company (which manufactured playing cards), then entered Columbia University, where he earned a doctorate in 1913 under the direction of economist E. R. A. Seligman. In 1914, he published *Policy of the United States Toward Industrial Monopoly.* Next he served as an instructor and assistant professor of economics at Princeton (1913–1916) and ventured into journalism for two years, as an editorial writer for the *New York Evening Post.* On Sept. 29, 1911, Knauth married Anna Dixwell Clements. They had three sons.

In World War I, Knauth served in France as a first lieutenant in the 106th Field Artillery, receiving the Distinguished Service Medal for gallantry in action. After the war he wrote on economics for periodicals such as the *Dial* and the *Nation.* He also was a founder of the National Bureau of Economic Research, of which he was a staff member (1919–1922) and, subsequently, director and president. During this period he collaborated on *Income in the United States* (1921), a pioneering analysis widely used by researchers. In 1923, Knauth published *Distribution of Income by States.*

The failure of his father's banking firm forced Knauth to search for more remunerative employment, and in 1922 he accepted a position as an economist with R. H. Macy and Company. For the next decade he distinguished himself less as an economist and more as a businessman. With a keen eye for merchandising, he reorganized several departments and recruited college graduates for training in retailing. After serving as executive vice-president, treasurer, director, and merchandising counsel, he retired from Macy's in early 1934. He spent most of the next year on his schooner in the Caribbean.

In April 1935, New York City's mayor, Fiorello La Guardia, appointed Knauth the city's director of emergency relief, a much-criticized program to which he applied his organizational skills. The position was short-lived because the federal government initiated work relief in the same year. From 1936 to 1943, Knauth was president of Associated Dry Goods Corporation, which controlled eight department stores. During World War II he became a consultant to the quartermaster general (1942–1943) and Army Supply Forces (1942–1944), as well as an assistant director of the statistics division of the War Production Board (1942).

Knauth returned to teaching in 1948, when he accepted a position at Columbia; he remained there until 1954. He also continued his more formal scholarship in economics. In 1948, he completed *Managerial Enterprise: Its Growth and Methods of Operation.* His last book, *Business Practices, Trade Position, and Competition,* appeared in 1956. These works, as well as his articles published in scholarly journals, were conspicuous for their nonacademic style and the insights of a practicing businessman. The publications received a mixed reception from academic reviewers.

Knauth's basic message was that the classical economics of Adam Smith and David Ricardo did not correspond to reality in twentieth-century America. Yet government policy, he maintained, was often geared to the classical model—for instance, in antitrust laws and suits. What was needed, therefore, was the development of a new theory that recognized the merits and shortcomings of large corporations, and the necessity to understand the dynamic quality of the production and marketing system that actually existed, especially in retail sales contexts.

"Trade advantage," Knauth wrote in *Political Science Quarterly,* "is coterminous with organized production and distribution; and large organizations could not exist without the permanence and stability which these trade advantages afford. . . . The power which trade advantage brings can be abused. It yields opportunity for anti-social prices and restrictions. On the other hand, it can be used beneficently, for lower price and increased quality. We are groping toward a scheme of things which will enhance the beneficence of great organization and minimize its abuse. This is neither socialism nor free enterprise; it is neither competition nor monopoly. . . . A new concept for social judgment must be found."

Other than his fondness for sailing, little is known about Knauth's private life or his activities after he left Columbia in 1954. He died in Beaufort, S.C.

[In addition to his books and their reviews, the best source on Knauth is the *New York Times,* especially Apr. 8 and 28, 1935. Also see his articles in *Political Science Quarterly,* Dec. 1915, June 1916, Dec. 1945; and his review essay in *Southern Economic Journal,*

July 1960. An obituary is in the *New York Times,* July 14, 1962.]

THOMAS V. DiBACCO

KOCH, VIVIENNE (1911–Nov. 29, 1961), critic and novelist, was born in New York City, the daughter of John Desider Koch, a manufacturing jeweler, and of Helen Karman. Both her parents were Hungarian immigrants—her father from an urban, intellectual background, her mother from a rural background. As a child Koch learned Hungarian from her grandparents and German from her nurse. She attended New York City public schools, showing special ability in dramatics, debating, and writing.

In 1928, Koch enrolled at New York University's Washington Square College, majoring in drama. But what she later called "the shabby intellectual content of courses in the theatre" turned her away from drama to literature and philosophy. After receiving the B.A. in 1932, she earned an M.A. in comparative literature at Columbia University (1933). Her thesis explored Anton Chekhov's influence on James Joyce. Koch then made substantial progress toward a Ph.D. (which she never completed) at Columbia (1933–1934), at the University of Maryland (1943–1944), and again at Columbia (1945–1947).

In the mid 1930's the need for a job diverted her from literature to social work in Harlem. "My innocence was a blessing and I sailed blithely into marijuana dens, . . . brothels, and dingy-hall bedrooms," she later recalled. Although the experience was generally a profitable one, at the end of three years her initial innocence had been tempered by a street-wise realism.

In 1935, Koch married the poet Norman Macleod; three years later she began her teaching career as a speech instructor at Mount Holyoke College at South Hadley, Mass. In 1939 she returned to social work, only to leave it after two years, when "the [philosophical] inadequacies . . . of case work . . . and the undemocratic political pressures of my professional setting conflicted too monstrously with my human and intellectual values."

Koch began to write literary criticism about 1944, while a teaching assistant at the University of Maryland. From 1945 to 1948 she was an instructor at Columbia University. In 1947 she began a ten-year association with New York University's Division of General Studies and the Washington Square College English department; she taught courses on Joyce, William Butler Yeats, and other twentieth-century writers.

During this time she also founded, and for a time was president of, New York University's Poetry Center, where American and British poets and critics gave readings and lectures. In the summer of 1950, Koch was a lecturer at the Breadloaf School of English in Middlebury, Vt., and during the winter of 1954 she was a visiting professor at the Salzburg Seminar in American Studies. During this period she was also a guest lecturer at Johns Hopkins, Rutgers, Yale, and other universities.

After her divorce from Macleod in 1946, Koch went to England and France for six months to do research on a Juliette Fisher Andrews fellowship. A Rockefeller fellowship supported another year (1949–1950) in England, France, and Italy. During her time abroad, she developed friendships with such British literary figures as T. S. Eliot, Edith Sitwell, Dylan Thomas, and Herbert Read. At home she knew Allen Tate, John Crowe Ransom, Marianne Moore, and William Carlos Williams.

The period 1944–1954 was a prolific one for Koch as a critic. Besides publishing extensively in scholarly journals, she wrote *William Carlos Williams* (1950) and *W. B. Yeats: The Tragic Phase* (1951). Her stay in Austria teaching American literature at the Salzburg Seminar in American Studies prompted her to shift from criticism to fiction. The result was *Change of Love* (1960), an intricate, urban novel of character and intrigue based on her experiences at Salzburg. In 1955 Koch married John F. Day, vice-president of news at CBS. The marriage provided her with domestic and financial security. She had no children with either of her husbands.

More than anything else, Koch was an insightful critic of poetry. Writing under the influence of New Criticism, which with its sophisticated practice and complicated theory drew distinct lines between the poem and the poet, she found and explicated the points where the lines crossed, lucidly illuminating both poet and poem. Her critical writing alone qualifies her as a minor but important contributor to American scholarship during the 1940's and 1950's. Koch died of cancer in New York City.

[Many of Koch's manuscripts and papers are in the hands of her brother, Professor Sigmund Koch, at Boston University. He provided much of the information included in this article. Her articles include "The Influence of Ibsen on James Joyce," *PMLA*, Sept. 1945; "The Poetry of John Crowe Ransom," *Sewanee Review*, Autumn 1950; and "A True Voice," *Kenyon Review*, Winter 1954. An obituary is in the *New York Times*, Nov. 30, 1961.]

                                        PHILIP LUTHER

KOVACS, ERNIE (Jan. 23, 1919–Jan. 13, 1962), television comedian, was born in Trenton, N.J., the son of Andrew J. Kovacs, a Hungarian-born policeman and restaurant owner, and Mary Chebonick. Kovacs' father, a bootlegger during Prohibition, once hired an organ grinder to perform before the Trenton police chief's home at three in the morning. In high school, the young Kovacs showed much intellectual promise but was indifferent to studying. He displayed an enthusiasm for dramatics, especially after appearing in a school production of *The Pirates of Penzance*. From 1935 to 1937 he was a student at the New York School of Theater.

In 1937 Kovacs joined a theater troupe on Long Island. He was the stereotypical, starving actor (a condition accentuated by his penchant for good cigars and poker games). Long hours on stage and over cards and an inadequate diet led to an attack of pleurisy and pneumonia that brought him near death. He spent three years in sanatoriums. Released in 1941, Kovacs established his own theatrical company in Trenton. After the company failed, putting him heavily in debt, he abandoned the stage for soda jerking in drugstores.

In late 1941 Kovacs got a job as an announcer with a Trenton radio station. His satires of commercials and newscasts, as well as a variety of sensational stunts, soon ingratiated him to listeners. He also wrote a column for the *Trentonian* (1945–1951). In 1945 he married Bette Wilcox. They had two children. His wife deserted him soon after their second child's birth in 1949, and they were divorced in November 1952.

In 1949 Kovacs became the host of a cooking show on WPTZ, a Philadelphia television station, where he applied his irreverent radio style to garner a large following. WPTZ soon signed him to host two more programs, one of which was an early-morning open-ended variety show. Regular commercial telecasting had only recently begun, and the newness of the medium allowed him to experiment freely. Kovacs used this morning program, telecast live, to try visual gags. He used a banana with a zipper peel, caused a wavy effect on the camera with a can of sterno, and once had the regular pianist dress as a janitor. Kovacs developed stock characters that he later played over network TV such as Percy Dovetonsils, an effete poet reader of absurdist poetry. The program enjoyed unexpectedly good ratings.

Within two years of his Philadelphia debut, Kovacs transferred his antics to network television, when the National Broadcasting Company

(NBC) hired him to do two programs in 1951 and 1952. These efforts commanded a small but resolute band of viewers and drew the attention of Harriet Van Horne, TV reviewer for the New York *World-Telegram and Sun*, who repeatedly recommended Kovacs' programs.

Good critical notices and generally poor ratings characterized the balance of Kovacs' career in television. Despite repeated opportunities over NBC and other networks between 1951 and 1957, his programs did not win large audiences, and successive networks canceled his programs. Undaunted, Kovacs developed new routines, such as the Nairobi Trio, a group of musicians costumed as apes, and Miklos Molnar, a Hungarian chef given to various states of inebriation.

On Sept. 12, 1954, he married Edie Adams, a singer who had appeared on his second NBC program, "Ernie in Kovacsland" (1951). They had one child.

Kovacs was unpretentious and as friendly with members of TV production units as he was with leading performers. Well read and familiar with classical music, Kovacs wrote routines replete with clever literary and musical allusions. But most characteristic of Kovacs was his personal extravagance; he spent money wildly on himself, his family, and his productions. At his death, he was deeply in debt.

On Jan. 19, 1957, Kovacs scored perhaps his greatest personal triumph with a half-hour special program, "Eugene," over NBC. He portrayed a sort of Chaplinesque Everyman in a series of sketches. The whole program was in mime form, which was unprecedented for television. Partly because of that uniqueness and because it followed a disastrously received special by comedian Jerry Lewis, Kovacs' "Eugene" was extravagantly praised by critics. One of them judged Kovacs to be "the only comic of any magnitude begot by television."

Soon afterward Kovacs temporarily quit TV to write fiction and star in films. The move followed a decline in audience demand for TV comedy and Kovacs' own exhaustion from work in the medium. His novel *Zoomar* (1957) was a parody of network television and received mixed notices. So too, did most of Kovacs' films, in which he never enjoyed the autonomy granted him in television. Furthermore, his appearance (*Time* called him "a sort of Clark Gable with fangs") relegated him to supporting roles. Nevertheless, Kovacs was a performer of considerable range. His best film performance was as a sadistic police captain in *Our Man in Havana* (1960).

Kovacs returned to television in October 1959 as host of the American Broadcasting Company's quiz program "Take a Good Look" (1959–1961) and a retrospective on early motion pictures, "Silents Please" (1961). In 1961 Kovacs began producing and starring in a group of comedy specials sponsored by Dutch Masters, a cigar manufacturer. Dutch Masters gave him complete freedom, and the programs mark the culmination of his career. Each one mixed the satire, technical craftsmanship, and visual creativity of his earlier ventures. Kovacs even produced and starred in the commercials. Soon after completing his last Dutch Masters special, Kovacs was killed when he lost control of his automobile and struck a telephone pole.

Kovacs' humor was not wholly original: he admitted that older comedians like W. C. Fields, Fred Allen, Buster Keaton, and the Marx Brothers, as well as Spike Jones, the bandleader, and the motion picture cartoons of the 1930's all influenced him. But unlike the great TV comedians of the early 1950's, Kovacs did not simply transfer styles derived in vaudeville or radio to television. He aimed for new approaches to comedy that could exploit the medium's possibilities, experimenting with purely visual gags and mastering videotape processes. Kovacs himself, not an anonymous staff of gag writers, wrote his material, usually composed at the last minute, and most often aiming for cutting satire and black comedy.

[Kovacs' papers, scripts, and the recordings of many of his original television programs are at the University of California at Los Angeles archives. David Walley, *Nothing in Moderation; A Biography of Ernie Kovacs* (1975), is carefully researched and quite admiring. Also helpful are the extensive clipping files at the Performing Arts Library of the New York Public Library, Lincoln Center.]

JAMES L. BAUGHMAN

KREISLER, FRITZ (Feb. 2, 1875–Jan. 29, 1962), violinist and composer, was born in Vienna, Austria, the son of Samuel Severin Kreisler, a physician, and Anna Kreisler. Like many musical prodigies he responded to music before he could read: at three he winced at wrong notes played by his father's amateur string quartet and constructed his own instrument from cigar box and shoestrings. At four he was given a miniature violin and first instruction by Jacques Auber, concertmaster of the Ring Theater.

Kreisler broke records by his admittance to the Vienna Conservatory at the age of seven; no student younger than ten had previously attended. He studied harmony and composition with Anton Bruckner and violin with Joseph

Hellmesberger, Jr. He taught himself to play the piano, quickly memorizing accompaniments to the standard violin literature and gaining such facility that Ignace Paderewski was later to say, "I'd be starving if Kreisler had taken up the piano." In 1884 the youth made his first public appearance, sponsored by the Conservatory.

Paris Conservatoire, the core of musical education of that time, saw Kreisler as a student in 1885; his instructor was Joseph Massart, and his tutor in composition Léo Delibes. He graduated in 1887 with the Premier Grand Prix in violin and the Premier Premier Prix ranking him above the prizewinners in every instrumental field. At the age of twelve he had completed his formal musical education.

Kreisler's career unfolded with startling speed. In 1888 he shared an American tour with the pianistic giant Moritz Rosenthal. He made his orchestral debuts in Boston with Walter Damrosch and in New York under the baton of Anton Seidl. During these American appearances he learned English, for his linguistic talents paralleled his musical ones; he eventually spoke eight languages fluently.

Kreisler returned to Vienna in 1890 to complete his academic education. After two years at the Piaristen Gymnasium he entered the Medical School of the University of Vienna but abandoned that profession in 1894 for music. In 1895 he produced his first two cadenzas, both for the Beethoven Violin Concerto. In Vienna, Johannes Brahms was numbered among his coffeehouse friends, and the two often played Brahms's chamber compositions. The critic Eduard Hanslick wrote of Kreisler's debut with the Vienna Philharmonic on Jan. 23, 1898, "He now faces the Vienna concert public as a finished master." A critic at his Berlin debut the next year hailed him as "Paganini redivivus."

In May 1901, returning from what had become his annual American tour, Kreisler met Mrs. Harriet Lies Woerz, an American divorcée to whom he proposed marriage. They had two civil weddings, in the United States in November 1902 and in London in 1903; and in 1947, brought back to their Catholic faith by Bishop Fulton J. Sheen, they renewed their vows in a Roman Catholic rite. They had no children.

In the decade before World War I, Kreisler maintained enormous concert schedules, playing as many as 260 engagements a year. He loved to perform but loathed practicing; "technique is a matter of the brain," he maintained. Rachmaninoff, a close friend, contended that because Kreisler played so much he never needed to practice. His practice habits—or

rather their lack—were part of Kreisler's excuse for never accepting students; he felt that his example would be harmful for pupils who needed constant and consistent exercise.

Before World War I, Kreisler appeared in programs with Enrico Caruso, Geraldine Farrar, and Josef Hofmann; he played chamber music with Harold Bauer, Pablo Casals, and Ferruccio Busoni; and he composed a cadenza for the Brahms Violin Concerto and began to write in archaic style small pieces that he ascribed to composers such as Padre Martini and Antonio Vivaldi.

In early 1914 Kreisler joined the Imperial and Royal Austro-Hungarian Army. Wounded in combat, he was discharged and returned to New York in November 1914. From his experience he produced a small book entitled *Four Weeks in the Trenches* (1915), which is interesting chiefly as an illumination of his humanitarian feelings.

At first his career did not suffer from anti-German sentiment, but when the United States entered the conflict in 1917 many of his engagements were canceled. He played no public recitals until 1919 and made a stunning comeback in England, but it was not until 1924 that he could once again play in Paris. During his withdrawal from the concert stage he wrote an operetta, *Apple Blossoms,* which opened on Broadway in October 1919 to rave reviews. Among the cast were Fred and Adele Astaire. Kreisler produced two other works in this genre: *Sissy,* staged in Vienna in 1932, and *Rhapsody,* produced in New York in 1944.

Kreisler was initially reluctant to make recordings, fearing that it would interfere with attendance at his concerts; but he later found that his audiences increased. Although he is believed to have been the first to record an entire violin concerto, his biggest public was attracted to his series of one-disc instrumental miniatures. He also made Ampico piano rolls of his own transcriptions and piano accompaniments to violin pieces.

Before Kreisler's South American and Balkan tours of 1935 he revealed that compositions published under the title "Classic Manuscripts" —works allegedly transcribed by Kreisler from holographs "found in a monastery" and attributed to such composers as Gaetano Pugnani, Antonio Vivaldi, and Louis Couperin, pieces that had been played in concert for years—were Kreisler's own works. The small teapot of the musical world was tempest-tossed. Before the weather cleared the eminent English biographer and critic Ernest Newman had railed at

Kreisler's duplicity in print. The virtuoso, although more gently, rebutted in kind. Olin Downes, music critic of the *New York Times,* and American musicians in general were considerably less disturbed, accepting it as a gentle joke on themselves. No musicologist or critic had previously questioned publicly the authenticity of these pieces, which had become a useful and popular segment of the string repertoire.

Kreisler built a magnificent home in Berlin in 1924, but in 1933 he refused to play in Germany until artists of any nationality or religion were permitted to appear there. The sale and broadcast of his music was banned, and by 1938 he had become a French citizen. In September 1939 the Kreislers made the United States their permanent home, and Kreisler became a naturalized citizen on May 28, 1943.

In the mid-1920's, disdaining radio performances by musicians, Kreisler had said, "I do not like the idea of being turned on and off like electric light or hot water." But on July 17, 1944, he played the first of five broadcasts for the Bell Telephone Hour, averring that an audience with access to concerts curtailed by wartime schedules could now hear his playing. He continued to appear yearly on the "Great Artists Series" for Bell, and his last public performance was broadcast on Mar. 6, 1950. He had previously said farewell to his concert constituency at Carnegie Hall on Nov. 1, 1947.

Kreisler had owned and sold many Guarneri and Stradivari violins, all of which he had played in public. "In the matter of violins," he declared, "I am and always will be polygamous." He gave one of his Guarneris and a Tourte bow, as well as holograph manuscripts of the Brahms Violin Concerto and the Chausson *Poème* for Violin and Orchestra, to the Library of Congress. The rest of his collection of incunabulae, rare books, and manuscripts was auctioned for charity in January 1949.

After 1950 Kreisler limited his appearances to benefits in support of the Harriet and Fritz Kreisler Fund for the education of young musicians. He died in New York City, leaving a legacy of some 200 original works, transcriptions, and arrangements.

[Louis P. Lochner, *Fritz Kreisler* (1950), contains a wealth of information but is contradictory on several matters of fact. See also Franz Farga, *Violins and Violinists* (1950). The New York Public Library Music Collection at Lincoln Center has a clipping file for the years 1888–1962. The obituary appeared in the *New York Times* on Jan. 30, 1962.]

SAUL BRAVERMAN

KUYKENDALL, RALPH SIMPSON (Apr. 12, 1885–May 9, 1963), historian, was born at Linden, Calif., the son of John Wesley Kuykendall, a Methodist clergyman, and of Marilla Persis Pierce, whose parents were Methodist missionaries in India. The five California schools he attended marked the frequent changes in his father's pastorates. Growing up in a parsonage instilled in Kuykendall a strong sense of morality, a compassionate spirit, and the value of hard work.

In 1910, Kuykendall was granted a B.A. degree by the College of the Pacific. After a year at Stanford University, he worked as a journalist in Florida (1912–1916). Then he turned to history, inventorying county archives during two years with the California Historical Survey Commission. In 1918 Kuykendall received an M.A. from the University of California at Berkeley; his thesis was titled "History of Early California Journalism." On Aug. 11, 1919, he married Edith Clare Kelly; they had two sons.

Kuykendall spent the academic years 1919–1921 at Berkeley, working on a doctorate. He was next awarded a fellowship for research on Spanish voyages to the Pacific Coast, which enabled him to work in Spanish archives in 1921–1922. While in Seville he was invited by the recently constituted Hawaiian Historical Commission to become its executive secretary. He accepted reluctantly, and arrived with his wife at Honolulu on June 19, 1922.

Kuykendall's initial responsibility was to prepare a textbook on Hawaiian history for the elementary schools. Herbert E. Gregory, director of the Bernice Pauahi Bishop Museum, provided three introductory chapters on Hawaii's prehistory. Kuykendall composed the remainder. To minimize the controversies emphasized in earlier Hawaiian histories, he focused each chapter on "some person, some event, or some clearly defined line of development." By stressing both Hawaii's foreign relations and its domestic society, he avoided the polemic aspect of island history. The volume, *A History of Hawaii* (1926), replaced William DeWitt Alexander's *A Brief History of the Hawaiian People* (1891).

In 1923 the territorial legislature authorized the Historical Commission to produce a history of Hawaii's role in World War I. Kuykendall, assisted by Lorin Tarr Gill, took on the task. *Hawaii in the World War* (1928) was a detailed account of military and civilian involvement.

The commission was also directed in 1923 to publish "a revised history of the Hawaiian people." In writing it Kuykendall searched extensively outside the islands in governmental archives and private collections. He visited depositories in North America on three occasions. Investigators were employed to copy diplomatic correspondence in Washington, London, Paris, and Mexico City. More than 8,000 pages of material were gathered from agencies outside Hawaii.

Meanwhile, Kuykendall created a comprehensive file of references to local sources as well as to the documents secured abroad. By mid-1932 he had systematically examined the evidence covering the reigns of the first three Hawaiian kings. The Great Depression intervened, though, and the legislature abolished the Historical Commission. Its functions were shifted to the University of Hawaii.

Kuykendall had offered courses in Hawaiian and Pacific history at the university since 1923, and had attained the rank of assistant professor in 1930. He labored steadily on the general history, and in 1938 published its first volume, *The Hawaiian Kingdom, 1778–1854: Foundation and Transformation.* Stressing politics, diplomacy, culture, and economics, its coverage extended through the reign of Kamehameha III. In 1938 Kuykendall was also promoted to associate professor.

During World War II, Kuykendall chaired a committee that directed the Hawaii War Records Depository, a project of the university to document the islanders' part in the war. He was made a full professor in 1949, and retired the next year. *The Hawaiian Kingdom, 1854–1874: Twenty Critical Years* appeared in 1953.

In retirement, Kuykendall continued his research and writing. He died in Tucson, Ariz., leaving unfinished the final chapter of his volume on Kalakaua and Liliuokalani. His colleague Charles H. Hunter completed *The Hawaiian Kingdom, 1874–1893: The Kalakaua Dynasty* (1967).

Kuykendall spent four decades immersed in the study of Hawaiian history. His three classic volumes on the Hawaiian monarchy are his monument.

[Kuykendall's research papers are at the University of Hawaii Library; his personal papers are in the possession of his son, Delman Leur Kuykendall, Berkeley, Calif. His published writings include [*Biennial*] *Report,* Hawaiian Historical Commission, for 1922, 1924, 1926, 1928 (1923–1929); *Hawaiian Diplomatic Correspondence* (1926); *The Hawaiian Islands: Papers Read During the Captain Cook Sesquicentennial* (1930), ed. with A. P. Taylor; and *Hawaii: A History from Polynesian Kingdom to American Commonwealth* (1948), written with A. G. Day. For complete bibliography, see D. L. Kuykendall and C. H. Hunter,

"The Publications of Ralph S. Kuykendall," *Hawaiian Journal of History,* 1968. Also see Michiko Kodama, "Ralph Simpson Kuykendall, Hawaiian Historian" (unpublished, in the Archives of Hawaii); and A. G. Day, *Books about Hawaii* (1977). Obituaries are in the *Honolulu Star-Bulletin,* May 12, 1963; *American Historical Review,* Oct. 1963; and *72d Annual Report,* Hawaiian Historical Society (1964). An editorial is in the *Honolulu Advertiser,* May 21, 1963.]

CHESTER RAYMOND YOUNG

LADD, ALAN WALBRIDGE (Sept. 3, 1913–Jan. 29, 1964), film actor, was born in Hot Springs, Ark., the son of Alan Ladd, an accountant, and of Ina Rawley. His father died in 1917. Three years later, his mother remarried and the family moved to California, living first in Alhambra and then in North Hollywood. Ladd attended public schools, working after class as a newsboy, a drugstore clerk, and a lifeguard among other jobs. While attending North Hollywood High School, he was the West Coast diving champion (1931) and had a major role in the school play, *The Mikado* (1933). This performance attracted the attention of talent scouts from Universal Studios, which had begun a program to train young actors. But within a few weeks of beginning the class, the studio let go Ladd and a fellow "discovery," Tyrone Power.

Ladd obtained a job in the advertising department of the *San Fernando Valley Sun-Record.* He soon worked his way up to advertising manager at $35 a week. Acting had become Ladd's goal, though, and he took a job at Warner Brothers as a grip. He spent two years rigging lights on catwalks, where, he recalled, "I never did see much of what went on below." After a bad fall, Ladd decided to try acting again and enrolled in the Ben Bard School of Acting. But the training led to no film contracts. In late October 1936 he married Marjorie Jane Harrold. They had one son, named for his father, who later became a noted film executive.

Radio proved Ladd's road to success. After occasional assignments on several Los Angeles–area stations, he landed a job at KFWB in 1936. As the station's lone resident actor, Ladd averaged almost twenty programs a week, doing everything from dramatic portrayals to newscasting. When scripts demanded it, he would take two parts, which forced him to train his speaking voice to have the flexibility that was to become one of his trademarks.

A program on which he played an elderly man and his son provided the break that brought

Ladd to the screen and stardom. Listening to the broadcast, Sue Carol (born Evelyn Lederer), a former screen star and then an actor's agent, thought the two actors, not knowing that Ladd was performing both roles, might have screen potential. Under her guidance, Ladd's screen career began to develop.

In July 1941, Ladd was divorced from his wife, and on Mar. 15, 1942, he married Sue Carol; their children David and Alana became film actors. By then, Ladd had appeared in several "B" pictures, beginning with *Rulers of the Sea* (1939), *Beasts of Berlin* (1939), and *Captain Caution* (1940). He also remained active in radio, appearing with Bette Davis on two occasions.

In 1942, Ladd played major film roles in *Joan of Paris* for RKO and *This Gun For Hire* for Paramount. The latter film made him a star. His murderous but strangely appealing image became the prototype of a new cinematic character, the tough guy who was young, handsome, and sensitive, yet cold and unreachable. The glint of his eye and his inscrutable manner created a flood of fan mail.

In January 1943, following leading roles in *The Glass Key* and *Lucky Jordan* (both 1942), Ladd joined the army. He served until November, when he was discharged with the rank of corporal, because of a double hernia. The same year, Ladd headed a national poll as the most popular male star.

In the following years, Ladd starred in a long list of movies for Paramount, including *Two Years Before the Mast* (1946), *The Blue Dahlia* (1946), *O.S.S.* (1946), *The Great Gatsby* (1949), *Captain Carey, U.S.A.* (1950), *Branded* (1951), and *Botany Bay* (1953). In *Shane* (1953), directed by George Stevens, he had probably his most remembered role: a mysterious stranger who helps a turn-of-the-century farming family ward off a land grab by a group of villainous cattlemen. The hard-riding, quick-shooting Shane personified all strong, silent western heroes, larger than life, a man feared by men and loved by women and children.

After leaving Paramount, Ladd played in *The Iron Mistress* (1952), *The McConnell Story* (1955), *Boy on a Dolphin* (1957), and *All the Young Men* (1960), among other films at several studios. In 1963, he returned to Paramount and appeared in the multi-million-dollar production of *The Carpetbaggers* (1964), drawing rave reviews for his performance as Nevada Smith, destined to be his final portrayal.

Ladd founded and was president of his own film company, Jaguar Productions, for which he produced and starred in four pictures. He was also president of Ladd Enterprises, which was involved in real estate and oil development.

In 1962, Ladd shot himself in the chest, according to official accounts, while cleaning a gun. He died two years later in Palm Springs, Calif., at least in part as the result of the combined effects of alcohol and sleeping pills.

[A biography is Beverly Linet, *Ladd* (1979). Also see Sue Carol, "The Making of Alan Ladd," in Walter Wagner, ed., *You Must Remember This* (1975). An obituary is in the *New York Times*, Jan. 30, 1964.]
                                    LAWRENCE H. SUID

LAFARGE, JOHN (Feb. 13, 1880–Nov. 24, 1963), clergyman, editor, and author, was born in Newport, R.I., the tenth and youngest child of John LaFarge and Margaret Mason Perry. His father, a Roman Catholic and son of a French immigrant, was a celebrated artist and writer. His mother, an Episcopalian convert to Catholicism, was the granddaughter of Oliver Hazard Perry. Born into the social and intellectual elite of New England, LaFarge was educated in the public schools of Newport and, later, by private tutors in New York City. He was a precocious and introspective youth, and a voracious reader with a talent for music and a facility for languages. By the age of twelve he had decided to become a priest.

On the advice of Theodore Roosevelt, a family friend, LaFarge decided against Columbia and Georgetown and entered Harvard in 1897. In preparation for the priesthood, he majored in Latin and Greek, studied Semitic languages, and pursued advanced work in piano and organ. Harvard, though, was a disappointment to LaFarge. He found his professors narrow and uninspiring, and the university indifferent to religion and lacking in pastoral care for Catholic students. After receiving his B.A. in 1901, he sailed for Europe to pursue theological studies at the University of Innsbruck, Austria. In Europe he traveled extensively, and became fluent in German, as well as French and Latin. In January 1905 he decided to become a Jesuit. He was ordained in the university church in Innsbruck in July 1905 and entered the Jesuit novitiate at St. Andrew-on-Hudson in Poughkeepsie, N.Y., the following November. He taught humanities briefly in 1907 at Canisius College, Buffalo, N.Y., and in 1908 at Loyola College, Baltimore. He then studied scholastic philosophy at Woodstock College in Maryland, receiving an M.A. in 1910. But the demands of graduate work proved too strenuous for his fragile constitution, and in late 1910 he reluctantly abandoned the prospect of an academic career. In hope of recovering his health, he accepted assignment to pastoral work.

In September 1911, after eight months as a chaplain in hospitals and penal institutions in New York City, LaFarge was transferred to the Jesuit missions in southern Maryland. For the next fifteen years (except in 1917–1918, when he served his Jesuit tertianship at St. Andrew-on-Hudson) he served rural parishes in St. Mary's County, at the Church of St. Aloysius in Leonardtown, and after September 1915, at St. Inigoes Manor, near St. Mary's City. Confronted for the first time with the problems of rural life, racial discrimination, and the poverty and neglect of black people, LaFarge became preoccupied with the question of racism. Increasingly active in attempts to improve race relations, he saw his early efforts come to fruition in October 1924 with the founding of the Cardinal Gibbons Institute, a black secondary school near Ridge, Md. This was the first national Catholic project on behalf of black education and a precursor of the Catholic interracial movement.

In August 1926 LaFarge returned to New York City to become an associate editor of *America*, the influential Jesuit weekly magazine, which he served for the rest of his life, including a period as executive editor (1942–1944) and editor in chief (1944–1948). An accomplished linguist (familiar with Polish, Russian, and Slovak) and a prolific writer, he covered a broad range of subjects in his articles and editorials but devoted special attention to racial problems, the liturgical arts, Slavic affairs, rural life, European events, and communism. Prominent in the National Catholic Rural Life Conference, the Liturgical Arts Society, the Catholic Association for International Peace, and a host of other organizations, he was especially active in those devoted to the betterment of race relations. For a time he worked closely with the Federated Colored Catholics, and he was instrumental in founding the Catholic Laymen's Union of New York (1928) and the Catholic Interracial Council of New York (1934), which served as a model for the establishment of similar councils in other cities. By the time his most important book, *Interracial Justice* (1937), was published, La-Farge had become the leading American Catholic spokesman on the race question. While in Europe in 1938 he was asked by Pope Pius XI to draft an encyclical on racism. For three months in Paris LaFarge and two Jesuit colleagues labored in secret on the draft, but because of the death of the pope soon afterward, the encyclical was never issued.

LaFarge was tall and slightly stooped in appearance, gentle and conciliatory in manner, optimistic in outlook, and moderate and practical in action. He was fiercely dedicated to the institutional church and to the papacy. He was also a social reformer and a pioneer in the field of race relations, and his patient and persistent efforts on behalf of the rights of black Americans helped to prepare the way for the achievements of the civil rights movement of later years. In addition to his work as a journalist, LaFarge wrote ten books, including a delightful autobiography, *The Manner Is Ordinary* (1954). He died in New York City at Campion House, the editorial headquarters of *America*, where he had lived for thirty-seven years.

[The major manuscript collections are the John LaFarge Papers, New-York Historical Society, New York City; and the John LaFarge Papers, Woodstock College Archives Special Collections Division, Georgetown University Library, Washington, D.C. LaFarge's published works include *The Jesuits in Modern Times* (1928); *The Race Question and the Negro* (1943); *No Postponement* (1950); *The Catholic Viewpoint on Race Relations* (1956); *A John La-Farge Reader*, edited by Thurston N. Davis and Joseph Small (1956); *A Report on the American Jesuits*, with photographs by Margaret Bourke-White (1956); *An American Amen* (1958); and *Reflections on Growing Old* (1963). A scholarly biography of LaFarge is badly needed. The best study to date is Marilyn Wenzke Nickels, "The Federated Colored Catholics" (Ph.D. diss., Catholic University, 1975), which covers LaFarge's career through 1932. Edward S. Stanton, "John La-Farge's Understanding of the Unifying Mission of the Church (Ph.D. diss., Saint Paul University, Ottawa, Canada, 1972) is helpful on the development of LaFarge's thought and on his role in drafting the papal encyclical. The best brief accounts of LaFarge's life are Glenn D. Kittler, "The Manner Was Extraordinary," in *The Wings of Eagles* (1966); and Edward S. Stanton, "The Manner Was Extraordinary," *America*, Nov. 24, 1973. An important article on an interesting aspect of LaFarge's career is John Whitney Evans, "John LaFarge, *America*, and the Newman Movement," *Catholic Historical Review*, Oct. 1978. George K. Hunton, "Father John LaFarge: Priest and Jesuit, 1905–1955," *America*, Nov. 12, 1955, is a warm appreciation by a close associate. Popular accounts appear in *Time*, July 27, 1942, and Mar. 3, 1952. Obituaries are in the *New York Times*, Nov. 25, 1963, and *America*, Dec. 7, 1963.]

                                          ROBERT A. HOHNER

LA FARGE, OLIVER HAZARD PERRY (Dec. 19, 1901–Aug. 2, 1963), author and anthropologist, was born in New York City, the son of Christopher Grant La Farge and Florence Bayard Lockwood. La Farge spent his childhood in Rhode Island. His architect father inspired an interest in the arts, and as a woodsman he initiated La Farge's lifelong interest in American Indians.

La Farge graduated from Groton in 1920, then entered Harvard, where he edited the *Advocate,* worked on the *Lampoon,* and rowed on the varsity crew for two years. He also became interested in anthropology, and after graduating in 1924 he participated in his third expedition for Harvard to Navajo country. That fall he began graduate work at Harvard, but left in 1925 to accept a position as assistant in ethnology at Tulane University.

While working as a linguist and ethnologist, La Farge wrote fiction. His first commercial short story appeared in *The Dial* in 1927, the year that he and Frans Blom published *Tribes and Temples,* an ethnology of Guatemalan Indians. He began *Laughing Boy,* the novel that was to make him famous, at this time. La Farge returned to Harvard in 1929 to complete a master's degree in anthropology, then accepted a research associateship at the University of Pennsylvania museum (1929–1931).

Laughing Boy, which appeared in 1929, was awarded a Pulitzer Prize, and his short story "Haunted Ground" won the O. Henry Memorial Prize in 1930. La Farge's career as an author was firmly established. He settled in New York City to follow an expensive, leisurely life that his autobiography records with regret. In 1931, La Farge completed his second novel, *Sparks Fly Upward,* a story of romance and revolution set in Central America. It marks a turn toward a more liberal outlook coinciding with his becoming a director of the Eastern Association on Indian Affairs in 1930.

Continuing his ethnological work as a research associate in anthropology at Columbia University (1931–1933), La Farge led a Columbia expedition to Guatemala in 1932. His research centered on the Mayan calendar and its associated ritual. Interest in the practical politics of Indian affairs balanced this scholarly pursuit. La Farge became president of the Eastern Association on Indian Affairs (1933–1937), increased its membership, and changed its name to the National Association on Indian Affairs. After differences between it and the American Indian Defense Association were reconciled, the two merged into the Association on American Indian Affairs in 1937, with La Farge as president. Except for service in the army during World War II, he held this post until his death.

La Farge married Wanden E. Mathews on Sept. 28, 1929; they had two children. The marriage ended in divorce in 1937. During the 1930's, a period La Farge regarded as wasted, he published *The Year Bearer's People* (1931), an ethnology written with Douglas Byers; *Long Pennant* (1933), a novel about the War of 1812; and *All the Young Men* (1935), a collection of his short stories. In 1937 *The Enemy Gods,* a novel that La Farge liked more than *Laughing Boy,* appeared.

La Farge often visited the Southwest but retained a base in New York, where he worked on Indian affairs and taught writing at Columbia University (1936–1941). On Oct. 14, 1939, he married Consuelo Otille Cabeza de Baca; they had one son. During the next two years he compiled two influential books about the conditions of contemporary Indians: *As Long as the Grass Shall Grow* (1940) and *The Changing Indian* (1942). In 1942 La Farge joined the U.S. Army and was commissioned in its Air Transport Command. He served as its historian and wrote a popular history, *The Eagle in the Egg* (1949). Several short stories about his wartime experiences appeared in *War Below Zero* (1944), written with Bernt Balchen and Corey Ford. He was discharged with the rank of lieutenant colonel.

La Farge's autobiography, *Raw Material,* was published in 1945. In 1948 he resumed presidency of the Association on American Indian Affairs, sometimes working with the commissioner of Indian affairs and at other times strongly opposing his policies. He lived with his wife's family in Santa Fe, where he wrote a weekly column for the *New Mexican.* Selections from these newspaper columns were published in *Santa Fe* (1959) and *The Man with the Calabash Pipe* (1966). In 1951 La Farge wrote *The White Shell Cross,* a dance drama, following it with the juvenile books *Cochise of Arizona* (1953) and *The Mother Ditch* (1955). He also assembled *A Pictorial History of the American Indian* (1956).

La Farge often differed sharply with the Truman administration over Indian affairs. His wife's family campaigned for Dwight D. Eisenhower in 1952, but within a year of Eisenhower's election La Farge engaged in a bitter struggle with his administration. Previously La Farge's concerns had been mostly for southwestern Indians; he now became the champion of the Indian cause nationwide. He opposed Eisenhower's "termination policy," an attempt to end all special rights of Indians. Advocacy of such rights made La Farge a protector of Indian education, health care, and certain legal rights. In joining Indians in their opposition to the policy, La Farge truly became the "Indian Man" (a childhood nickname).

A heavy smoker, La Farge experienced increasing difficulty in breathing. After several treatments he died in Albuquerque of a collapsed lung.

[La Farge's literary work is evaluated in Everett A. Gillis, *Oliver La Farge* (1967). Biographies are D'Arcy McNickle, *Indian Man* (1971), and T. M. Pearce, *Oliver La Farge* (1972). An obituary is in the *New York Times,* Aug. 3, 1963.]

ERNEST L. SCHUSKY

LA FOLLETTE, PHILIP FOX (May 8, 1897–Aug. 18, 1965), governor of Wisconsin, was born in Madison, Wis., the son of Robert Marion La Follette, Sr., governor, senator, and United States presidential candidate, and Belle Case. That he was the son of a famous public man was, by his own account, the controlling influence in his public life. As a boy he participated in the family councils and was affected by the controversies that swirled about "Fighting Bob" La Follette. The experience provided a rarely matched political education.

La Follette attended public schools in Madison and in 1915 entered the University of Wisconsin. In 1918 he enrolled in the Reserve Officers Training program, was commissioned as second lieutenant, but did not go overseas. After the war he returned to the University of Wisconsin, from which he received his B.A. in 1919 and the LL.B. in 1922. As a student he helped in political campaigns for Progressive Republicans and in 1924 participated in his father's bid for the presidency on an Independent Progressive ticket.

With the death of the elder La Follette in 1925, La Follette's older brother, Robert M. La Follette, Jr., sought his father's Senate seat. Philip organized and managed the campaign, and "Young Bob" won election to the Senate, a position he would hold for twenty-two years.

Philip La Follette married Isabel Bacon of Salt Lake City on Apr. 14, 1923; they had three children. In 1924 he was elected district attorney of Dane County but after one term (1925–1927) returned to private law practice and a part-time lectureship at the University of Wisconsin Law School. In 1930 La Follette challenged incumbent Walter J. Kohler for the Republican gubernatorial nomination, winning by more than 100,000 votes. He easily won the general election, pledging the aid of the state in combating the growing depression. Observers

commented that he had inherited "Old Bob's" political sense, oratorical ability, style, and zest for campaigning—more so than his older brother.

With the legislature split between progressives and conservatives, La Follette saw much of his program defeated. He did push through a new labor code that encouraged collective bargaining and, in a special session, secured the enactment of the first comprehensive unemployment insurance law in any state. Many of his proposals bore an obvious resemblance to later New Deal measures.

The year 1932 was a bad one for incumbents, and La Follette lost the Republican primary to ex-Governor Kohler, who in turn lost to Democrat Albert Schmedeman. Two years later, the Wisconsin progressives, led by La Follette and his brother, broke with the state Republicans and formed the Progressive Party of Wisconsin. On this ticket La Follette won reelection to the governorship but his program was again blocked by a hostile state senate. The chief legislative casualty was the defeat of a comprehensive public works and relief bill that would have made Wisconsin unique in having its own work relief program distinct from the federal Works Project Administration (WPA), despite the promise of $100 million in federal funds.

Reelected by a large majority in 1936, La Follette pushed through a comprehensive program, described by some as a "Little New Deal." Like his father, he made use of the "Wisconsin Idea," bringing such specialists as David Lilienthal and John R. Commons into his administration to help formulate policy. But his support of the ouster of University of Wisconsin President Glenn Frank in 1937, whose relations with the university community had soured, gained him additional enemies. Some denounced him as a dictator who ignored the principles of academic freedom.

The Progressive party had been highly successful in Wisconsin, and La Follette reasoned that it was time to extend its principles to the national scene. Anticipating that the Democratic party would shift to the right and that Roosevelt would retire after two terms, he launched the National Progressives of America (NPA) in a great mass meeting at Madison on Apr. 28, 1938. He described the movement as not a third party but an organization that was certain to become the party of the future. His choice of a symbol, a cross in a circle on a white background, was unfortunate. He interpreted it as "Abundance with Freedom." Critics, conscious of the symbolism accompanying the rise of dictators in Europe, derided it as a "circumcised swastika."

Few progressive leaders endorsed the new party and, contrary to expectations, Roosevelt did not retire in 1940. Further, La Follette attempted to organize the NPA nationwide in 1938 and run for a fourth term as governor at the same time. As a result, he lost the election by a large margin to conservative businessman Julius P. Heil.

La Follette spent much of the next three years trying to keep America out of war, making numerous speeches for the America First Committee. But after Pearl Harbor, he reenlisted in the army. He spent most of the war serving on the staff of General Douglas MacArthur in the South Pacific, rising to the rank of lieutenant colonel.

The war killed the NPA, and in 1946 the La Follette brothers disbanded the Progressive Party of Wisconsin and returned to the Republicans. After his brother's narrow loss in the Republican primary that year to Joseph R. McCarthy, La Follette described the decision to dissolve the Progressive party as a "political blunder . . . of the first order."

After the war La Follette practiced law in Madison. In 1948 he supported the unsuccessful bid of General MacArthur for the Republican nomination, and in 1952 he backed General Dwight D. Eisenhower. He served as a director of the Hazeltine Corporation in New York and for the years 1955 to 1959 was president of this electronics company. After his return to Madison in 1959, he resumed the practice of law and engaged in writing until his death, in Madison.

[La Follette's papers are in the State Historical Society of Wisconsin at Madison. His own account of his career is found in *Adventure in Politics,* edited by Donald Young (1970). The family history is chronicled in Belle Case La Follette and Fola La Follette, *Robert M. La Follette, June 14, 1855–June 18, 1925* (1953). An account of his governorship is in Robert C. Nesbit, *Wisconsin: A History* (1973). Special topics are discussed in Donald R. McCoy, "The National Progressives of America, 1938," *Mississippi Valley Historical Review,* June 1957; and Daniel Nelson, "The Origins of Unemployment Insurance in Wisconsin," *Wisconsin Magazine of History,* Winter, 1967–1968. See also the obituary notice, *New York Times,* Aug. 19, 1965.]

ROBERT S. MAXWELL

LAMBEAU, EARL LOUIS ("CURLY") (Apr. 9, 1898–June 1, 1965), football player, coach, and founder of the Green Bay Packers, was born in Green Bay, Wis., the son of Marcel and Mary Lambeau. His father was a contractor. Lambeau attended Whitney Grammar School and Green Bay East High School, from which he graduated in 1918. Football was Lambeau's consuming passion since his youth. In 1916 he led Green Bay's East High School to a 7–0 victory over its arch rival, West High. The next year he became the unofficial coach of East's team after the regular coach entered the armed forces.

Lambeau received a football scholarship to Notre Dame University in 1918, Knute Rockne's first year as coach there. As a freshman he played first-string fullback. After the end of the season he came down with tonsillitis and missed six weeks of school. He went home to Green Bay and began to work for the Indian Packing Company. He never returned to college.

In 1919, Lambeau and several men with whom he had played football in high school, plus a few former college players from the Green Bay area, organized a semiprofessional team. The team was named the Packers after the Indian Packing Company, which contributed $500 for uniforms and allowed the team to use its grounds for practice. Lambeau served as the coach, general manager, personnel director, ticket manager, captain, and runner and passer. "We just wanted to play for the love of football," he later recalled. "We agreed to split any money we got and each man was to pay for his own doctor bills." Lambeau made $16.75 that first year. The team won ten of eleven games against other semiprofessional teams in the Wisconsin area.

In 1921 the Packers entered the American Professional Football Association, the forerunner of the National Football League (NFL). During the early 1920's Lambeau was also coach of Green Bay's East High football team. One of his players, Jim Crowley, later became one of the fabled "Four Horsemen" of Notre Dame.

From 1922 through 1928 the Packers won forty-six games, lost twenty-three, and tied eleven. The team's success was due in large part to Lambeau's imaginative and demanding coaching. He was the first professional coach to hold practice daily. He was also one of the first to show game films at practice. At a time when other teams passed sparingly or not at all, Lambeau made passing an integral part of the Packers' offense. Because of this emphasis the Packers were generally the most interesting and exciting team to watch in the NFL.

Lambeau was a shrewd judge of talent during a period when professional teams did not have extensive scouting systems. He frequently signed future stars who had been passed over by other teams for being too short or too light. Ruthless, temperamental, and a perfectionist, Lambeau drove his players unmercifully. But he also stressed the importance of "enthusiasm," and the Packers came to be known as "the pro team with the college spirit."

In 1929 the Packers won the first of three consecutive league championships, a feat not duplicated until 1965, 1966, and 1967 under Vince Lombardi's coaching. Although the Packers continued to have winning seasons after 1931, they did not win another league championship until 1936. In 1938 they lost the title game to the New York Giants. The next year the Packers thrashed the Giants 27–0 for Lambeau's fifth league championship. In 1944 the Packers again defeated the Giants in the title game.

The fortunes of the Packers declined precipitously after World War II. The 1948 team won only three games; the 1949 team, only two—the worst record in Packers history. Not being a wealthy franchise, the Packers were unable to compete for players with the All-America Conference. Lambeau was no longer willing to devote all his time to coaching. He spent long periods on a ranch he had purchased in southern California and began to associate with movie personalities. Critics back in Green Bay began calling him "the Earl of Hollywood."

His lack of success on the field exacerbated Lambeau's relations with the Packers' executive committee. During the 1920's and 1930's he had had complete power to determine club policies, hire and fire personnel, and negotiate salaries. After the war, though, the executive committee became increasingly disturbed by Lambeau's high operating expenses, his long absences from Green Bay, the decline in home attendance, and the team's poor record. Lambeau wanted very much to be named the Packers' president, but the executive committee, instead of expanding his authority, stripped him in 1947 of much of his power. Differences over policy soon led to bitter clashes between Lambeau and key members of the committee. He resigned briefly during the 1949 season, returned to coaching, and then was given a new two-year contract in December 1949. But the new contract did not restore any of his former powers and contained a clause requiring him to spend more time in Green Bay.

In February 1950 Lambeau resigned from the Packers to become coach and vice-president of the Chicago Cardinals. Thus ended the longest

uninterrupted coaching tenure in professional football history.

During Lambeau's two seasons in Chicago, the Cardinals won only eight games and lost sixteen. Under fire from management, he resigned in December 1951. He accused the Cardinals' front office of second-guessing him and undermining his authority, while management charged he had lost control over his players and assistants.

The next season Lambeau became head coach of the Washington Redskins. The team won only four games while losing eight. In 1953, however, the Redskins won six games, lost five, and tied one. Lambeau seemingly was building a title contender. The season had been marred by serious quarrels between Lambeau and several players, resulting in the defection to Canadian football of defensive end Gene Brito and quarterback Eddie Le Baron. The loss of Le Baron, "the Little General," was a factor in the decisive losses suffered by the Redskins during the 1954 exhibition season to the Los Angeles Rams and the San Francisco 49ers. George Preston Marshall, the owner of the Redskins, was incensed by these two defeats, and concluded that there had been a complete breakdown of team discipline. Confronting each other in the lobby of the Senator Hotel in Sacramento, Calif., after the 49er game, Marshall and Lambeau engaged in a shouting, pushing, and shoving match. Marshall fired Lambeau on the spot.

Lambeau never coached another professional football team, but he did coach the College All-Stars in their 1955, 1956, and 1957 games with the professional champions. His overall professional coaching record was 236 victories, 111 losses, and 23 ties. He won seven divisional titles and six championships, more than any other coach.

By now wealthy because of prudent real estate investments, Lambeau spent his remaining years in comfort on his California ranch. He remained an avid Packers fan, and passed much of his free time fishing and playing golf. In 1963 he was one of the seventeen charter members elected to the Pro Football Hall of Fame in Canton, Ohio. He died at Sturgeon Bay, Wis. After his death Green Bay's City Stadium was renamed Lambeau Field.

[Roger Treat, *The Encyclopedia of Football*, 14th ed. (1976), contains Lambeau's won-lost record. Arthur Daley's articles in the *New York Times*, Feb. 12, 1950, and Dec. 28, 1951, discuss Lambeau's personality. His years in Green Bay are recounted in Chuck Johnson, *The Green Bay Packers* (1961); Herbert

Warren Wind, "The Sporting Scene: Packerland," *New Yorker*, Dec. 8, 1962; Lloyd Larson, *Milwaukee Sentinel*, June 3, 1965. Lambeau's tenure in Washington is covered by Morris A. Beale, *The Redskins, 1937–1958* (1959); Lewis F. Atchison, *Washington Evening Star*, June 3, 1965; and David Slattery, *The Washington Redskins, a Pictorial History* (1977). The obituary is in the *New York Times*, June 2, 1965.]

EDWARD S. SHAPIRO

LANDIS, JAMES McCAULEY (Sept. 25, 1899–July 30, 1964), law professor and federal administrator, was born in Tokyo, Japan, the son of the Reverend Henry Mohr Landis and Emma Marie Stiefler. He spent his early years at the Meiji Gakuin missionary compound, where his parents were teachers. At the age of thirteen he sailed alone to the United States to continue his education.

A phenomenally bright student, Landis led his classes at the Mercersburg Academy, Mercersburg, Pa., in 1916 and at Princeton in 1921. He won a scholarship to Harvard Law School, where he came under the tutelage of Felix Frankfurter. After graduation in 1924, he remained for a year as Frankfurter's research fellow while earning the S.J.D. (1925). Together they published a number of articles on law and politics and *The Business of the Supreme Court* (1927). In 1925, Frankfurter arranged for Landis to clerk for Supreme Court Justice Louis D. Brandeis. Landis married Stella Galloway McGehee on Aug. 28, 1926; they had two daughters.

In 1926 Landis was appointed to the Harvard law faculty. Academic advancement came rapidly, aided by Frankfurter's prodigious backstage efforts. At the age of twenty-nine Landis became Harvard's first professor of legislation. His pioneering work in the field formed the basis for his influential article "Statutes and the Sources of Law," in *Harvard Legal Essays . . .* (1934).

At the onset of the New Deal, Landis joined Frankfurter, Benjamin Cohen, and Thomas Corcoran in drafting legislation to establish federal regulation of the sale of stocks. His grasp of regulatory and financial policy led President Franklin D. Roosevelt to appoint him to the Federal Trade Commission in 1933 and to the new Securities and Exchange Commission (SEC) in 1934. The next year Landis succeeded Joseph P. Kennedy as chairman of the SEC. A careful administrator with a talent for mastering technical detail, Landis pursued a policy of reconciliation with Wall Street. His conciliatory approach won the support of bankers and brokers for the SEC, but his accomplishments were soon overshadowed by the more activist program of the next chairman, William O. Douglas, who succeeded in winning exchange self-regulation under SEC supervision.

Landis resigned from the SEC in 1937 and returned to Harvard as the youngest dean in the law school's history. He endorsed Roosevelt's "Court packing" plan and served as trial examiner in the Harry Bridges deportation hearings. His continued association with the New Deal raised protests from conservative alumni, but the faculty regarded Landis highly and his tenure was an "era of good feeling" after the stormy deanship of Roscoe Pound. As dean he shifted the curriculum from an emphasis on the common law to the needs of public administration.

In 1938, Landis' Storrs lectures at Yale were published as *The Administrative Process*. It was his most important book. Drawing on his New Deal experiences, he presented an optimistic prognosis of the federal regulatory commissions, with their combination of legislative, judicial, and administrative powers. He saw them as a means of preventing both monopoly and socialism, and of making capitalism "live up to its pretensions."

After Pearl Harbor, Roosevelt appointed Landis director of the Office of Civilian Defense, an organization left foundering by Fiorello La Guardia, the previous director. Landis campaigned strenuously for air raid protection and for an ambitious "block plan" to organize all nonmilitary volunteer activity. In 1943, seeking a post closer to "the fighting front," he became economic minister to the Middle East. Representing the United States at the Anglo-American Supply Centre in Cairo, Landis identified with Arab nationalism and opposed British colonial policy.

In 1945, Landis returned to Harvard, but his years of federal service had left him dissatisfied with academic life, and the collapse of his marriage had alienated him from his colleagues. After an unhappy year he resigned as both dean and professor to accept President Harry Truman's offer of the Civil Aeronautics Board (CAB) chairmanship.

At the CAB, Landis became a proponent of a more flexible response to airline regulation, calling for experimentation with nonscheduled and all-cargo service. He also led the opposition to Pan American Airways' "chosen instrument" plan to combine all American overseas flights into a single line. Such policies won Landis the enmity of the larger passenger lines, which lobbied against his reappointment as chairman. In December 1947, despite earlier promises to the contrary, Truman removed Landis from the CAB.

Caught off guard by the dismissal, Landis turned for help to Joseph P. Kennedy. Kennedy took him on as adviser to Kennedy Enterprises, an amorphous assignment that involved him in myriad Kennedy family business and political ventures over the next decade. Landis also rebuilt his life after his divorce in October 1947. He married Dorothy Purdy Brown on July 3, 1948. They had no children. In 1948 and 1949 he took the bar examinations for the first time and opened a law practice specializing in regulatory cases. Eventually his association with the Kennedys led to his return to federal service as special assistant to President John F. Kennedy.

Landis' report to President-Elect Kennedy in 1960 stimulated the New Frontier's program of regulatory reform and reorganization. Although several of his proposals suffered defeat in Congress, the bulk of the program was established. The reforms strengthened the chairmen and streamlined the work of the independent commissions. Landis' resignation from the Kennedy administration came unexpectedly in September 1961, after he was named corespondent in a divorce suit.

By then Landis had fallen into deeper trouble. In his compulsion for professional achievement, he had allowed his private life to fall into disarray. He was verging on alcoholism; he was more than five years delinquent with his federal taxes; and the Internal Revenue Service had discovered the omission. Although Landis paid his back taxes and penalties, he was indicted, convicted, and sentenced to thirty days in prison. He spent his term in the hospital. Upon his release he was suspended from law practice. Shortly afterward he drowned accidentally in the pool at his home in Harrison, N.Y.

From the New Deal to the New Frontier, James Landis was the leading theorist and staunchest defender of federal regulation. "The administrative process is, in essence, our generation's answer to the inadequacy of the judicial and legislative process," he wrote, and "our effort to find an answer to those inadequacies by some other method than merely increasing executive power." In the independent commissions he believed the nation had found the basic mechanism for policing and promoting private enterprise in the public interest. It was a cause to which he devoted himself obsessively, mindless of the personal consequences.

[The James M. Landis papers, in the Library of Congress, contain the bulk of Landis' correspondence, speeches, and articles. Smaller but also useful Landis collections are at the Harvard Law School Library, Harvard Archives, and John F. Kennedy Library. Much of his official correspondence remains in the files of the Franklin D. Roosevelt and Harry S. Truman libraries, the Securities and Exchange Commission, and in the Office of Civilian Defense and Civil Aeronautics Board papers at the National Archives. The Felix Frankfurter papers, Library of Congress, are an important supplementary collection. The only full biography is Donald A. Ritchie, *James M. Landis* (1980). Also see "The Legend of Landis," *Fortune*, August 1934; the memorial edition of the *Harvard Law Review*, Winter 1964; and Arthur E. Sutherland, *The Law at Harvard* (1967). Landis gave a lengthy oral history to the Columbia University Oral History Collection shortly before his death. An obituary appeared in *New York Times* on July 31, 1964.]

DONALD A. RITCHIE

LANG, LUCY FOX ROBINS (1884–Jan. 26, 1962), labor activist, was born in Kiev, Russia, the daughter of Moshe Fox and Surtze Broche. Her father, a silversmith, immigrated to the United States to avoid military service in Russia but returned to bring his wife and children to America. Lucy Fox was nine years old when she arrived in New York City. She and her father soon moved to Chicago, where he worked in a picture frame factory and she became a tobacco stripper. After work she attended night school.

Although influenced by Jane Addams, Fox identified at an early age with the anarchist movement. In 1901 she met Bob Robins, a bookkeeper-salesman with strong anarchist sympathies. They were married in 1905, but true to their radical principles, they considered the union a "trial marriage." The Robinses moved to New York City, where they bought a cigar store. During the next twelve years they moved in radical circles in both New York and California. In New York they met the fiery anarchist "Red Emma" Goldman, and Lucy formed a lifelong friendship with her.

In San Francisco the Robinses opened a restaurant, the St. Helena Vegetarian Cafe, which became a gathering place for West Coast radicals and labor activists. While in San Francisco they briefly parted, according to the terms of their marriage contract, which called for a separation after five years. Their arrangement attracted the attention of the press, which denounced it as a "veil to cover the shame of free love." The Robinses soon reunited, though, and moved to the socialist utopian settlement of Home Colony on Puget Sound, in Washington. When they tired of this experiment in communal living, they went to Seattle, San Francisco, Los Angeles, New York, Montgomery, Ala., and finally back to San Francisco. Some of this traveling was done in their innovative motor home, "The Adventurer."

About 1917, Robins began to organize support among workers and radicals for the Tom Mooney Defense Committee. This work brought her under the personal and political influence of Samuel Gompers, president of the American Federation of Labor (AFL). She was initially hostile to Gompers, accepting the judgment of many radicals who saw him as a class collaborationist, but soon began to consider Gompers a true friend of labor. Robins' shift from radical left-wing politics to the pragmatism of the AFL was so abrupt that it calls for some speculation as to her motives. One possible explanation is that her radicalism was youthful romanticism; her conversion to trade unionism, the manifestation of greater maturity. Another explanation is that Robins simply passed from her husband's influence to the protective paternalism of Gompers.

Both explanations fail to take into account Robins' sincere commitment to furthering the cause of the American worker. This commitment can be traced to her own work experience as well as to her exposure to political thinkers. She recognized Gompers' political power as a force for the benefit of American labor. She was also attracted to his warm, if crusty, personality.

Gompers, in turn, felt that Robins bridged the distance between the radical and conservative poles of the working population. He said in his autobiography: "Of the services given, none was more remarkable than that of Lucy Robins, who gave up everything to establish a better understanding between radicals and the labor movement."

In 1919, Robins worked to secure amnesty for political prisoners, including conscientious objectors and the Socialist leader Eugene V. Debs. She greeted Debs upon his release from prison in 1921 and accompanied him to Washington, D.C. Debs said of "dear comrade Lucy": "Never was a soul more consecrated to a task than she to the liberation of her imprisoned comrades. She is so thoroughly in earnest and so tirelessly active that she feels the imprisonment as if it seared her body as it does her sympathetic spirit."

In 1922, Robins organized a relief campaign among the United Mine Workers and the United Hebrew Trades to help striking miners. In subsequent years she was active in the Sacco-Vanzetti case and investigated labor conditions

for the AFL in Europe and the southern United States. As her involvement with the AFL grew, so did her estrangement from her husband. He left the United States to settle in Russia but soon returned, disillusioned. They were divorced about 1920.

Although Gompers repeatedly proposed marriage to Robins following the death of his wife, she declined the offer and their relationship remained a platonic one. About 1932 she married Harry Lang, a longtime friend and staff writer for the *Jewish Daily Forward.* She remained active in labor causes until her death at Los Angeles.

[Lang's autobiography is *Tomorrow Is Beautiful* (1948). She also wrote *War Shadows* (1922). An obituary is in the *New York Times,* Jan. 26, 1962.]

ANN SCHOFIELD

LANGE, DOROTHEA (May 25, 1895–Oct. 11, 1965), photographer, was born Dorothea Margaretta Nutzhorn in Hoboken, N.J., the daughter of Heinrich (later Henry) Martin Nutzhorn, a lawyer, and Joanna (later Joan) Caroline Lange, a librarian and later a court investigator. Lange adopted her mother's maiden surname in 1918. She contracted polio when she was seven, an experience which left her with a limp and which she credited with being the most important event of her early life. After her parents' marriage broke up in 1912, Lange attended P.S. 62 on the Lower East Side of New York City, where her mother had secured a job. An outsider in an alien immigrant environment, Lange began her habit of observing the life about her, a trait which marked her later photography.

Four years at Wadleigh High School (1909–1913) and a short stint at the New York Training School for Teachers completed her formal education. By then Lange had resolved to become a photographer, although she had never held a camera or taken a picture. In 1913 she apprenticed herself to the photographer Arnold Genthe, who gave Lange a camera and taught her techniques of candid camera work and portraiture. Lange next went to work for a succession of photographers in order to acquire different types of experience. In 1917–1918 she took a course in photography at Columbia University with Clarence H. White, who believed photography should make a clear statement of its own rather than attempt to duplicate the painter's brush. When the course ended, Lange purchased a camera and two lenses, and taught herself developing and printing techniques in a darkroom converted from an old chicken coop.

Lange then decided to work her way around the world, living by her new trade; but upon arriving in San Francisco in 1918, she and a friend were robbed of all their money. Financial necessity forced her to take a job in a photo-finishing shop, and she remained in the city. Through her work and a camera club she joined, Lange made many friends, one of whom financed her in opening a portrait studio the following year. On Mar. 21, 1920, she married Maynard Dixon, an artist twenty years her senior. They had two sons.

Lange became a popular and successful portrait photographer. She thought of herself mainly as a "tradesman," a competent professional. Moreover, after her children were born, the greater part of her energies went into nurturing the career of her husband and caring for their sons.

Lange accompanied Dixon on several of his painting expeditions into the Southwest. There she photographed outdoors, but was dissatisfied with both the quantity and the quality of her work. In 1929, on a trip into the back country of California, Lange began taking pictures of people that had the feel of what were later called documentary photographs. She realized that what she had to do was "concentrate upon people, only people, all kinds of people."

The onset of the Great Depression had a dual effect on Lange: her portrait business dwindled and the suffering she saw led her to take her camera out of the studio to record it. On her first day in the streets, she took one of her best-known pictures, "White Angel Bread Line." It showed an unemployed man turned away from his fellows awaiting a handout, his mouth grim, folded hands surrounding a cup resting on the rail in front of him in a parody of prayer. For many this photograph epitomized the human cost of the depression. During the following year Lange photographed picket lines, a May Day march, a turbulent maritime strike, and other manifestations of social injustice, all the while continuing her portrait business to help support her family. In the summer of 1934, her documentary photographs were exhibited at Willard Van Dyke's gallery in Oakland.

Lange decided to focus exclusively upon documentary photography, and agreed to work with the economist Paul Schuster Taylor on the problem of displaced farm laborers then streaming into California. The State Emergency Relief Administration employed her as a "clerk-steno," and she and Taylor went into the field to study the migrant families in southern California. "I had to get my camera to register the things about those people that were more important than how poor they were," she recalled, "their pride, their strength, their spirit." Her photographs and Taylor's report resulted in the construction of two migrant labor camps in the area. The pair continued to work as a team for the Rural Rehabilitation Division of the Federal Emergency Relief Administration (FERA). Their marriages had been foundering, and Taylor and Lange divorced their spouses and were married on Dec. 6, 1935.

When the agency was merged into the Resettlement Administration, and then the Farm Security Administration (FSA) in 1937, Lange went to work for Roy Stryker's Historical Section, along with such other photographers as Walker Evans, Ben Shahn, Arthur Rothstein, and Carl Mydans. In 1936, on her way back from her first field trip for the Resettlement Administration, she stopped on impulse in a pea-pickers' camp. There she took what became her best-known photograph, "Migrant Mother." The modern-day Madonna, prematurely aged, with a baby on her lap and two children nestled against her shoulders, stares past the photographer, her face shrouded with anxiety, an indictment of society.

During the following years Lange took many field trips for the FSA throughout the West, East, and South, photographing migrant workers and tenant farmers. In 1939 she and Taylor collaborated on *An American Exodus*, a book about migrant workers. The previous year the poet Archibald MacLeish had used many of Lange's photographs to illustrate his long poem about "stranded" people, *The Land of the Free*. (Lange's FSA photographs accounted for almost half of those in the Museum of Modern Art's 1962 show of the agency's work, "The Bitter Years." One critic wrote of those photographs, "The symptoms of the depression are clearly set forth and through them we can better understand the tragic events of those times. She made intimate contact with the victims. . . . Nothing about [her pictures] was contrived or artificial; her warmth was so contagious that her subjects were virtually unaffected by the presence of the camera.")

Although Lange's subjects were inherently victims, Paré Lorentz observed that they "stand straight and look you in the eye. They have the simple dignity of people who have leaned against the wind, and worked in the sun, and owned their own land." On her darkroom door Lange had posted words of Francis Bacon that shaped her work: "The contemplation of things as they are, without substitution or imposture, without error or confusion, is in itself a nobler thing than a whole harvest of invention."

In March 1941, Lange became the first woman to receive a Guggenheim grant for photography. She resigned the fellowship after America entered World War II, and in April 1942 joined the staff of the War Relocation Authority to photograph the evacuation and internment of Japanese Americans. Her pictures later formed the core of an exhibition and book about the relocation, *Executive Order 9066* (1973).

 After the war chronic illness limited Lange's work. Nevertheless, she taught ocassionally, and in 1952 she assisted Edward Steichen in the preparation of the Museum of Modern Art's "Family of Man" exhibit (1955). She also photographed new migrants to California for *Life* magazine (1956–1957) and completed a long-term project, the book (and later exhibit) *Dorothea Lange Looks at the American Country Woman* (1967). She spent much of the last two years of her life preparing for the 1966 retrospective exhibition of her work at the Museum of Modern Art, the first such exhibit given a woman photographer, and only the sixth one-person show of any photographer. Lange died in Berkeley, three months before the show opened.

[Lange's notebooks and travel journals, as well as a collection of negatives and prints, are in the Prints and Photographs Division of the Oakland Museum; the Prints and Photographs Division of the Library of Congress has the most complete set of her FSA photographs, including caption material, and the notebooks kept on her 1935 field trips. Portfolios of her work include "Death of a Valley," *Aperture*, vol. 8, no. 3 (1960), with Pirkle Jones; *Dorothea Lange* (1966); and Therese T. Heyman, *Celebrating a Collection* (1978). Biographies are Milton Meltzer, *Dorothea Lange* (1978), and Karen Becker Ohrn, *Dorothea Lange and the Documentary Tradition* (1980). In 1960–1961, Lange recorded an oral history, on file at the Bancroft Library, University of California at Berkeley (a copy of the transcript is available at the Museum of Modern Art in New York City). Also see Paul Taylor's oral history (1975), at Berkeley. During her last two years, Lange participated in the making of two films about her work produced by the KOED Film Unit of San Francisco for the National Television and Radio Center, *Under the Trees* and *The Closer for Me.* An obituary is in the *New York Times*, Oct. 14, 1965.]

SYDNEY STAHL WEINBERG

LANGNER, LAWRENCE (May 30, 1890– Dec. 26, 1962), chartered patent agent, playwright, and theatrical producer, was born in Swansea, South Wales, the son of Braham Langner, a businessman, and of Cecile Mendola. After attending grammar schools in Swansea and in Margate, England, he took a job as junior clerk for J. Bannister Howard, theater manager and operator of provincial road companies. Shocked at finding her thirteen-year-old son surrounded by chorus girls, Langner's mother arranged a less provocative apprenticeship to Wallace Cranston Fairweather, a chartered patent agent.

Langner passed the examination of the British Chartered Institute of Patent Agents in 1910 and advanced rapidly. Sent to New York to represent his London firm in January 1911, he found his expertise in British and European patent law was a rare asset in the United States. By 1913 he had set up his own firm, and later founded the firm of Langner, Parry, Card, and Langner with his brother Herbert. During World War I, Langner was consultant on munitions patents to the Army Ordnance Department. Naturalized in 1917, he served on the advisory council that prepared the patent sections of the Treaty of Versailles. He was executive secretary of the National Advisory Council to the Committee on Patents of the House of Representatives in 1939–1945. He was also one of the organizers of the National Inventors Council of the Department of Commerce, serving as its secretary from 1940 to 1958.

Langner is far more famous for the career in the theater that he pursued simultaneously with his patent work. In 1914, with friends from among New York's young artists and literati in Greenwich Village, he organized the Washington Square Players, a "little theater" modeled on European independent art theaters and Maurice Browne's Chicago Little Theater. They sought to elevate the New York theater above the farces, melodramas, and "tired businessman" musicals common on Broadway. From February 1915 through April 1918, the Players presented sixty-two one-act plays and six full-length works. Members of the group, Langner among them, wrote a number of the short plays. Others were written by the young Eugene O'Neill, Susan Glaspell, and such European authors as Leonid Andreyev and George Bernard Shaw.

On Nov. 25, 1915, Langner married a Texas-born singer, Estelle Roege; they had one daughter. American entry into World War I ended the Players as an organization, but many of the people involved appeared again in the programs of Langner's postwar Theatre Guild. Shortly after the Armistice, Langner, actress Helen Westley, and designer Rollo Peters, after many discussions with other Washington Square Players alumni, drew up a short policy statement for a "professional" art theater aiming "to produce plays of artistic merit not ordinarily produced by the commercial managers." The Theatre Guild began its long and influential career on Apr. 19, 1919, with the opening of *Bonds of Interest* by Nobel Prize winner Jacinto Benavente. After Langner's first marriage ended in divorce in 1923, he married in 1924 actress Armina Marshall, who later became a producer in association with him and in her own right. They had one son.

An organization unique in American theater history, the Theatre Guild came to be regarded by many as the world's major art theater, and from the beginning Langner was one of its prime movers. It was he who negotiated its agreements with Shaw, "the backbone of the Guild in the early days." Langner's international patent business gave him contacts with major British and European playwrights, and the Theatre Guild introduced American audiences to many of the major new foreign plays, as well as to works by O'Neill, Maxwell Anderson, and other Americans.

Langner and the Theatre Guild succeeded so well in proving that serious dramatic art could succeed on Broadway that commercial managements began to compete for the better plays. Langner was a strong believer in the artistic advantages of a company of actors playing in repertory instead of the single-play long-run system, and he influenced the Theatre Guild in its experiments, beginning in the 1926–1927 season, with a company of actors doing several plays. Instead of the complex system of changing the program daily, which was traditional in repertory, he suggested weekly changes, the same cast alternating two plays for a week at a time. Using this system, the Theatre Guild achieved its greatest period of artistic and financial success, producing fourteen successive hit plays between April 1926 and October 1928, a record never surpassed in the New York theater. Its brilliant acting company was led by Alfred Lunt, Lynn Fontanne, Helen Westley, and Dudley Digges, and featured an impressive number of actors who later became stage and film stars.

The Theatre Guild's subscription lists in several major cities grew until finally it was no longer possible to handle both the repertory system and touring effectively, so the acting company was abandoned in 1931. The indefatigable

Langner then founded the New York Repertory Company (1931–1933) and built the Westport Country Playhouse in 1932. He operated both with his wife while continuing to work with the Theatre Guild. (The Langner family continues to operate the playhouse.) As administrator of Theatre Guild productions with Theresa Helburn, Langner supervised production of more than 200 plays, including *Strange Interlude* (1928), *Mourning Becomes Electra* (1931), *Mary of Scotland* (1933), *Porgy and Bess* (1935), *Oklahoma!* (1943), *Carousel* (1945), *Come Back, Little Sheba* (1950), *Saint Joan* (1951), *Picnic* (1953), and *Bells Are Ringing* (1956).

From 1945 to 1954, Langner worked on "Theatre Guild on the Air," the radio drama series for which Armina Marshall was executive producer; he produced television plays with Marshall and Helburn, 1947–1953, and later with Helburn and H. William Fitelson for "The U.S. Steel Hour," 1953–1955. These were the Theatre Guild's contributions to the "golden age" of television drama. He founded the American Shakespeare Festival Theater and Academy (1950), opening its new theater at Stratford, Conn., July 12, 1955. He continued to be active in theater and television production until his death in New York City.

The life and achievements of Langner focus attention on the pivotal role played in the theater by creative producer-organizers. His importance in the history of the American theater is assured by his central role in the founding and operation of the Theatre Guild, which, despite its later conservatism, remains unmatched in the boldness of its early vision and in its achievements. It was the closest thing to an American national theater the country has yet seen, and it almost certainly ranks as the most important American theater institution of modern times. Langner's idealism, persistence, and creative organizational skill can thus be said to have made the largest individual contribution to the development of a mature, artistic theater in the United States in the first half of the twentieth century.

[Langner's papers are at the Beinecke Library at Yale University. *The Magic Curtain* is Langner's autobiography. He also wrote *Outline of Foreign Trade Mark Practice* (1923), with Herbert Langner; *The Importance of Wearing Clothes* (1959); *The Play's the Thing* (1960); and *G.B.S. and the Lunatic* (1963). A brief obituary is in the *New York Times*, Apr. 1, 1963 (delayed by newspaper strike).]

DANIEL S. KREMPEL

LANHAM, FREDERICK GARLAND ("FRITZ") (Jan. 3, 1880–July 31, 1965), lawyer and U.S. congressman, was born in Weatherford, Tex., the son of Samuel Willis Tucker Lanham and Sarah Beona Meng. His father was a district attorney, later U.S. congressman (1882–1892, 1896–1903), and governor of Texas (1903–1907). A relative nicknamed Lanham "Fritz," and he used that name throughout his life. He attended school in Washington, D.C., and graduated from Weatherford College in 1897. After attending Vanderbilt University for a year, he entered the University of Texas, where he was the first editor of the *Texan*, the student newspaper. After receiving the B.A. in 1900, Lanham served as his father's secretary in 1901–1902, and entered the University of Texas Law School in 1903. Later he was the first editor of the *Alcalde*, the university's alumni magazine. (He remained active in alumni affairs, and was president of the Ex-Students Association in 1949–1950.) On Oct. 27, 1908, Lanham married Beaulah Rowe.

During his father's last year as governor, Lanham again was his private secretary, and had to give up his formal law studies. He subsequently worked as an actor, reporter, and banker in Weatherford. Admitted to the bar in 1909 after passing the bar exam, he established a law practice in Weatherford with Ben G. Oneal. In 1917 he moved to Fort Worth, where he became a district attorney. He ran successfully on the Democratic party ticket for Congress in 1919 after a vacancy occurred in the Twelfth District, and was reelected thirteen times, serving until 1947.

Since Fort Worth had the only helium plant in the nation, Lanham lobbied hard in the 1920's for government support of production of the gas and for the dirigible industry. He cooperated with Chief Justice William Howard Taft on the plans for a new Supreme Court building as a member on the Public Buildings and Grounds Committee, and he established expertise in patent matters through his membership on the House Committee on Patents.

After the death of his first wife in 1930, Lanham married Hazel Head on Nov. 17, 1931. Both marriages were childless.

As his seniority increased, Lanham distinguished himself primarily through his set speeches. He was remembered as "a wizard with words," and his annual speeches about Texas independence and the battle of San Jacinto became staples of House oratory. He found the New Deal increasingly unacceptable, and warned in 1938 that "the Government cannot afford to employ vast numbers of people indefinitely." As World War II approached, he denounced the German-American Bund and criticized "the activities of un-American workers whose destructive schemes are planned by dictatorial direction from abroad."

In 1939, Lanham became chairman of the Public Buildings and Grounds Committee, a post that gave him greater legislative importance. Several acts relating to domestic policy in wartime bore his name. The Lanham Defense Housing Act (1940) provided dwellings near military bases and defense plants as the nation's war machine expanded. The Lanham Community Facilities Act (1941) sought to ease the burdens that the expansion of defense installations imposed on local governments by providing for housing, water supplies, sewage, and welfare facilities. The law made available federal funds to support day-care centers for mothers working in defense industries. Although the law bore his name because he was chairman of the committee, Lanham did not approve of actual government construction of such centers in 1943, and attempted to block appropriations to build them.

Lanham was similarly conservative in his opposition to appropriations for a fair employment practices committee. To him, its tendency to "promote centralized and bureaucratic regimentation" outweighed its contribution to racial justice. His most noteworthy wartime act beyond his congressional duties was his defense of President Franklin D. Roosevelt's sons in 1943 against Republican charges that they were shirking their duty. The president sent him a letter of thanks.

As a member of the Patents Committee, Lanham devoted much of his energy to revision and reform of national policy on trademarks. The Lanham Act (1947) gave business substantive property rights in trademarks registered with the government. The measure pleased the business community. In 1946, Secretary of Commerce Henry Wallace had called Lanham and another committee member, Frank Boykin of Alabama, "ignorant prostitutes" because of their deference to business. Lanham's friends argued that the law "brought order out of what had been chaos in trademark law and regulation."

Lanham did not seek reelection in 1946. It was time, he thought, to "let a new man tackle the postwar problems." In retirement he was a lobbyist for the Trinity Improvement Association of Texas (seeking federal floodway funds), the National Patent Council, and the American

Fair Trade Council. In 1963, failing health brought him back to Austin, where he died.

Lanham was bald and thickset in later life. His associates recalled his courtly manner and soft-spoken demeanor. He shaped patent legislation himself, but the interesting social legislation that bore his name arose from the initiatives of others. Lanham served during a time when Texans were influential in the House of Representatives, but he does not belong with John Nance Garner and Sam Rayburn in the front rank of the Lone Star legislators of the 1920's and 1930's.

[No Lanham papers appear to have survived, but there are personal letters in the papers of his law partner, Ben G. Oneal, at the University of Texas at Austin. The William Howard Taft Papers, Library of Congress; the Franklin D. Roosevelt Library, Hyde Park, N.Y.; and the Morris Sheppard Papers and Martin M. Crane Papers, University of Texas at Austin, have manuscript materials on Lanham. Lanham's writings include "A Revised Work," *University of Texas Literary Magazine,* Dec. 1900; *Putting Troy in a Sack* (1916); and "Helium: Texas Wonder Gas," *Bunker's Monthly,* Mar. 1928. The Barker Texas History Center, University of Texas at Austin, has a good collection of clippings on Lanham. See also "Who's Who at Texas: Fritz G. Lanham," *The Alcalde,* Nov. 1916; G. A. Holland, *History of Parker County and the Double Log Cabin* (1937); and Escal F. Duke, "The Life and Political Career of Fritz G. Lanham" (M.A. thesis, University of Texas at Austin, 1941). On his career see Donald S. Howard, "The Lanham Act in Operation," *Survey,* Feb. 1943; Neil Borden, "The New Trade-Mark Law," *Harvard Business Review,* Spring 1947; William H. Chafe, *The American Woman* (1972); and John M. Blum, ed., *The Price of Vision: The Diary of Henry A. Wallace, 1942–1946* (1973). Obituaries are in the *Austin Statesman,* Aug. 2, 1965; *Summer Texan* and *New York Times,* Aug. 3, 1965.]

LEWIS L. GOULD

LAUGHTON, CHARLES (July 1, 1899–Dec. 15, 1962) actor, was born in Scarborough, Yorkshire, England, the son of Robert Laughton and Elizabeth Conlon, hotelkeepers. He attended a convent school, then Stonyhurst College, a Jesuit school. Enlisting as a private in 1918, he took part in a bayonet attack at Vimy Ridge, and was gassed shortly before the Armistice. His parents then sent him to work and to learn hotel management at Claridge's, London. Fascinated with acting since childhood, Laughton spent most of his earnings on theater; he especially admired the stylish elegance of Sir Gerald du Maurier. Later, managing the family hotels, he began acting with the Scarborough Amateur Dramatic Society. Enthusiastic press notices encouraged

him to return to London in 1924 to study at the Royal Academy of Dramatic Art.

In 1926 Theodore Komisarjevsky, one of his teachers, gave Laughton his first professional role, Osip in Nikolai Gogol's *The Government Inspector.* After a series of short runs in supporting parts Laughton had his first major success in 1927 in the title role of *Prohack,* a play based on Arnold Bennett's novel. Playing his secretary was Elsa Lanchester, an established young actress. By the time *Prohack* closed in 1928, they were in love and on Feb. 10, 1929, they married. Their relationship based on deep mutual understanding and affection lasted until Laughton's death, despite the discovery of his homosexuality within the first year of their marriage.

In February 1928 the *Times* of London found Laughton "revoltingly brilliant" as a sadistic villain in *A Man with Red Hair.* His success as Agatha Christie's Hercule Poirot in *Alibi* (1928) seemed to assure him of a solid future.

Laughton had another hit in a role specially written for him by Edgar Wallace, a Capone-like gangster in *On the Spot* (1930). By this time he was a leading London star. The guilt-ridden murderer in Jeffrey Dell's *Payment Deferred* was his best stage role, and Gilbert Miller brought Laughton with it to New York in 1931. Although well received, this and the New York version of *Alibi* did not repeat their London success.

Besieged by Hollywood offers, Laughton refused to sign the usual long-term commitments with no control of choice of parts. But when Jesse Lasky made an attractive short-term offer, the Laughtons went to Hollywood. Among Laughton's early films were *The Old Dark House* (1932), *The Island of Lost Souls* (1932), *Payment Deferred* (1932), *If I Had a Million* (1932), *The Devil and the Deep* (1932), and Cecil B. De Mille's *The Sign of the Cross* (1932), in which, despite De Mille's strong objections, he portrayed Nero as a ridiculous, posturing homosexual.

Such audacity was to be typical of Laughton's entire career. He had an affinity for characters of misfits, outsiders, and physical or mental cripples, and he was quickly typed by Hollywood for such roles. To avoid repetition, he found ways of adding unusual facets and ambiguities—even his darkest villains managed to get the audience's sympathy or understanding. In his film roles and his own life Laughton refused narrow limits. He never gave up the stage and eventually made important contributions to the American theater.

The Laughtons returned to England, joining

Alexander Korda in his attempt to create a truly independent film industry in Britain. Korda's *The Private Life of Henry VIII* (1933) earned Laughton an Academy Award and international stardom. Returning to the stage for the 1933–1934 season, the Laughtons worked for minimum wages with the Old Vic company. Directed by Tyrone Guthrie, they acted in plays by Anton Chekhov, William Congreve, and Shakespeare. As Angelo in *Measure For Measure* (another ambiguous villain), Laughton was admired for the way he "revealed the overwhelming of a formidable talent by the senses."

Laughton's films after the Old Vic season showed a marked improvement in the expertise with which he used voice and language. The Hollywood films *The Barretts of Wimpole Street* (1934), *Les Miserables, Ruggles of Red Gap,* and *Mutiny on the Bounty* (all 1935), as well as Korda's British *Rembrandt* (1937), show Laughton at the zenith of his film career. Korda's most ambitious project, the Robert Graves *I, Claudius,* was never completed, but a 1969 BBC-TV film, *The Epic That Never Was,* used the 1937 footage to document Laughton's perfectionist agonies as he groped for the character of the misfit emperor.

Laughton next formed his own film company with Erich Pommer and John Maxwell. Mayflower Films produced *Vessel of Wrath* (American title *The Beachcomber*), 1937; *St. Martin's Lane* (American title *Sidewalks of London*), 1938; and *Jamaica Inn,* 1939. Only the first paid its costs, and the company was dissolved.

Laughton returned to Hollywood to play the most extreme of his deformed outsiders, *The Hunchback of Notre Dame* (1939). His many films of the early 1940's have little distinction, although some contributed to the war effort. Laughton was an effective salesman of war bonds and also did readings of the Bible and other literature for hospitalized servicemen, an activity that later grew into a new career.

From 1943 to 1946 Laughton worked with playwright Bertolt Brecht on an English version of Brecht's *Galileo.* In August 1947 Laughton played this part to Los Angeles audiences seething with the political turmoil created by the House Committee on Un-American Activities investigations of Hollywood. (Brecht fled to East Germany before the play opened its short New York run.) Laughton's best film roles of this period were the "hanging judge" of *The Paradine Case* (1947) and the murderous tycoon of *The Big Clock* (1948).

In 1950 the Laughtons became United States citizens. That year Laughton formed a partnership with agent-impresario Paul Gregory, who booked him into colleges and concert halls across the country with a one-man show of his readings. Gregory then suggested that a group of actors present a more complex form of platform reading. Under Laughton's direction, the First Drama Quartet—Agnes Moorehead, Charles Boyer, Sir Cedric Hardwicke, and Laughton himself—toured every part of America (1951–1952), brilliantly presenting *Don Juan in Hell* from George Bernard Shaw's *Man and Superman.* Laughton then directed Steven Vincent Benét's *John Brown's Body,* with Tyrone Power, Raymond Massey, Judith Anderson, and a large supporting cast and chorus. These productions stimulated tremendous national interest in such platform presentations.

Directing became the main interest for Laughton, although he continued to make money from film acting. He took over and drastically reshaped *The Caine Mutiny Court-Martial* and made it a Broadway and national success in 1954. The only film he directed, *The Night of The Hunter* (1955), is considered by some to be a small masterpiece of American cinema. In 1956 he staged and acted in a scenically innovative production of *Major Barbara.*

In 1957 both Laughton and Lanchester were nominated for Academy Awards for *Witness for the Prosecution;* they went to London to appear in Jane Arden's play *The Party,* and after Laughton's brief appearance on location for *Spartacus,* went to Stratford-upon-Avon to rehearse for the next Shakespeare Festival. Although fellow actors found his interpretations unusually interesting, Laughton was crushed by negative press reviews of his *King Lear* and Bottom in *Midsummer Night's Dream,* and these may have aggravated his already failing health. He suffered a heart attack and nervous breakdown in 1959.

Laughton's last screen role was in *Advise and Consent* (1962). Ill during the shooting, he poured a vicious intensity into his acting of the homosexual-hating bigot Senator Seab Cooley. But, with his usual complex interpretation of character, he also deliberately played upon Cooley's southern warmth and charm, and thus made his behavior in the later scenes more revolting by contrast.

Laughton continued his reading tours to the very end of his strength. The fifty-two films he made in his thirty-three years as a film star are a very fragmentary record of a complex life spent in relentless pursuit of excellence in the art he loved. He died in Hollywood, Calif.

[*Tell Me a Story* (1957) and *The Fabulous Country* (1962) are Laughton's two anthologies of readings. Elsa Lanchester's *Charles Laughton and I* (1938) is the earliest biography. Kurt Deutsch Singer's *The Laughton Story* (1954) derives information from the Lanchester book and from research of periodicals, and brings the story into the 1950's with some biases that reflect the cold war era. The best biography is Charles Higham, *Charles Laughton: An Intimate Biography* (1976), written with Elsa Lanchester's close cooperation and using Laughton's and her papers. See William C. Young, *Famous Actors and Actresses on the American Stage* (1975), for quotations of reviews and memoirs of Laughton's stage performances that are not readily available. The *New York Times* obituary appeared on Dec. 17, 1962.]

DANIEL S. KREMPEL

LAUREL, STAN (June 16, 1890–Feb. 23, 1965), vaudeville and screen comedian, was born Arthur Stanley Jefferson in Ulverston, Lancashire, England, the son of Arthur J. Jefferson, an actor-producer, and Madge Metcalfe, an actress in her husband's companies. Jefferson, an ingenious truant, attended various grammar schools in the north of England, and after 1905, when the family settled in Glasgow, Scotland, he sometimes attended the Ruther Glen School and Queen's Park Academy. Arthur Jefferson, realizing that his son had little interest in schooling, soon brought him into the family business as a box-office manager.

Young Jefferson spent much of his free time backstage with the performers, especially the comedians. He idolized music hall clown Dan Leno, but his early models were the "boy comedians" of the day—Laddie Cliff, Boy Glen, and Nipper Lane—who sang, danced, and told jokes. In 1906 he persuaded Albert E. Pickard, a local showman, to let him do a comedy routine at Pickard's Museum Music Hall in Glasgow. Appearing in baggy pants and comic wig, he told borrowed jokes used by other performers— and a few of his own—and did a song written for him by a musician friend.

In 1907, Jefferson joined Levy and Cardwell's Juvenile Pantomimes, a touring company, in *Sleeping Beauty.* The next season he did a music hall routine and understudied in one of his father's productions. Later he appeared briefly in a play, *Alone in the World*, before joining the famous Fred Karno vaudeville troupe in 1910. He performed in Karno's classic "Mumming Birds" sketch, considered the greatest ensemble act in British vaudeville. He played various other roles and understudied Charlie Chaplin, the troupe's leading comedian.

Working for Karno was the best possible training for an ambitious young music hall performer like Jefferson. He came to America with Karno in September 1910 but, dissatisfied with his salary, left the show in 1911. During the return trip to England, he worked up an original comedy routine for himself and Arthur Dandoe, another refugee from Karno. Entitled "The Rum 'Uns from Rome," the fast-paced, brilliantly timed slapstick number was a great success in London music halls. The act established Jefferson's reputation as a gag writer. In an era when a single classic routine could sustain a career for years, he seemed assured of his place in the theater. Unfortunately, the act broke up. Unable to find a suitable partner for "Rum 'Uns," Jefferson dropped the routine. He took engagements where he could find them, in England and on the Continent, until rejoining Karno for another American tour in 1912–1913.

This time the show folded when Charlie Chaplin, the headliner, accepted an offer to star in American films. Jefferson decided to remain in the United States, too. He teamed briefly with Edgar Hurley and his wife as The Three Comiques. They began in small midwestern theaters. Rechristened Hurley, Stan, and Wren, the team played the Keith circuit and, as The Keystone Trio, toured the prestigious Orpheum circuit. The highlight of their routine was Stan's imitation of Chaplin. The act eventually disbanded because Hurley resented Jefferson's success.

Jefferson quickly formed The Stan Jefferson Trio, which soon gave way to a new act and a new identity. His partner was Mae Charlotte Dahlberg, a young singer-dancer from Australia. Known in vaudeville as Stan and Mae Laurel, they were together for ten stormy years, long enough for Mae to claim common-law wife status. Early in their partnership—probably early in 1917—Mae chose the name under which Jefferson became famous.

Laurel's film career began inauspiciously. His first movie, *Nuts in May* (1917), showed promise, but was not widely distributed. Another early film, *Lucky Dog* (1917), was notable only because Oliver Hardy, Laurel's future partner, was in the cast. In 1918 he signed with Universal Studios to play a rube, Hickory Hiram, in a series of forgettable comedies. He was in several Hal Roach productions for Pathé; appeared in support of Larry Semon, Vitagraph's popular but limited comedian; and made a series of movie parodies for G. M. ("Broncho Billy") Anderson's company.

During this period Laurel combined occasional film work with steady bookings in vaudeville. But with his pantomime experience and a talent for creating gags, he was a natural for silent-screen comedy. Independent producer Joe Rock recognized Laurel's potential and launched him in a series of comedies in the early 1920's. By the mid-1920's Laurel was well established, with scores of pictures to his credit. But he had not achieved great popularity, perhaps because he had not developed a recognizable screen persona, as Chaplin, Harry Langdon, and Harold Lloyd had done.

In 1926, Hal Roach hired Laurel again, this time as a writer, gagman, and director. Assuming his days as a performer were over, Laurel was eager to get on with his new assignment. But the studio prevailed on him to appear in *Get 'Em Young* (1926) as a substitute for an injured member of the cast (who, incidentally, was Oliver Hardy). Thereafter, at the studio's insistence, Laurel remained in front of the camera, although he continued to create gags and supervise production for most of his films. He was, by all accounts, the creative force in his successful partnership with Oliver Hardy.

Beginning with *Slipping Wives* (1927), Laurel regularly appeared on screen with Hardy, but the two were not yet a team—they were merely all-purpose clowns in Roach's large stable of comedians. In 1927, the producer decided to issue a series of Laurel and Hardy comedies. *Putting Pants on Philip* (1927), the team's first starring vehicle, although not the first to be released, was not typical of their work together. They were not pals, nor did they use their own names, as in their later films. Still missing were the bowler hats, Hardy's bangs and his "takes" for the camera, as well as such Laurel hallmarks as the unevenly cropped hair and his head-scratching, eye-blinking bewilderment.

But the unique humor of Laurel and Hardy was not simply the comedy of makeup and mannerism. Nor did it depend entirely upon the amusing physical contrast between the scrawny Laurel and the rotund Hardy. It required the artful blending of style and characterization. To achieve this happy chemistry, Laurel progressively dropped the music-hall acrobatics, derivative clowning, and aggressiveness of his earlier performances. He became, as critic Walter Kerr noted, the childlike "stand-in-the-corner booby," taking his lead from the officious, but equally dim-witted, Hardy.

Several classic Laurel and Hardy elements are visible in *Battle of the Century* (1927), including the first of Laurel's many brilliantly contrived incremental disasters. Novelist Henry Miller proclaimed *Battle* "the greatest comic film ever

made." It culminates in an unforgettable pie-throwing sequence involving scores of passersby and hundreds of pies. This episode typified the inept pair's disruptive, antisocial impact. Innocents with a childish instinct for instant retribution, they brought out the worst in everybody. "Stan and Ollie," wrote film historian Gerald Mast, "can convert a group of normal people into a mass of pie-slingers, shin-kickers, and pants-pullers."

Laurel and Hardy quickly gained favor with exhibitors and the public. Their partnership lasted through approximately one hundred comedies, including twenty-seven feature films, over the next twenty-five years. Among their most popular films were *Two Tars* (1928), *Big Business* (1929), *Brats* (1930), *The Music Box* (1932, Academy Award for Best Comedy Short Subject), *Babes in Toyland* (1934), *The Bohemian Girl* (1936), and *A Chump at Oxford* (1940). Unlike other silent clowns, the team managed a successful transition to the sound era. But Laurel regretted Hal Roach's decision to cast them in feature-length pictures. "We should have stayed in the short-film category," he told his biographer. "You've got to settle for a single basic story . . . and then work out all the comedy that's there—and then let it alone. But you can't take a whole, long series of things we do and stick them all together in eight reels and expect to get a well-balanced picture out of it."

In general, Laurel and Hardy were well served by their association with Roach. They broke with him in 1940, though, seeking greater artistic freedom. They established their own production company, but made no pictures. Instead, they did a stage tour in 1940–1941. Later in the 1940's Laurel and Hardy returned to the screen in several films made at Metro-Goldwyn-Mayer and Twentieth Century-Fox, where Laurel had little creative control over scripts or production. These pictures were uninventive and justifiably unpopular.

In 1947, Laurel and Hardy toured British music halls and in 1951 they completed their last film together, *Robinson Crusoe-Land,* a disastrous low-budget European production. Thereafter they worked sporadically in vaudeville. During the 1950's television resurrected their early comedies. Laurel and Hardy hoped to capitalize on their renewed popularity by making a new series of pictures, but Hardy suffered a stroke that forced cancellation of the project. Hardy died in 1957, and Laurel, unwilling to perform without his partner, retired.

During his long career, private life had held

few attractions for Laurel. He was a compulsive worker who always gave priority to his craft. Indeed, the long, painstaking rehearsals and the extra hours on the set may have provided a necessary distraction from a string of ill-advised marriages. A mild-mannered, courteous man, Laurel had "a marrying complex" (in the words of one of his wives) and a penchant for domineering women. The strain of misogyny that feminist critics find in his comedy may be attributable to his unhappy domestic circumstances. In their pictures Stan and Ollie are forever in league against their shrewish wives. It is perhaps significant that Laurel's partnership with Hardy lasted longer than many of his marriages.

Laurel's relationship with vaudeville partner Mae Dahlberg ended when she obstructed his early movie career. To keep her away from the studio, Stan's producer paid her to return to Australia. (In 1937 Dahlberg sued Laurel for alimony and property rights on the basis of her claimed status as common-law wife. The case was settled out of court.) On Aug. 23, 1926, shortly after Mae's departure, Laurel married Vitagraph ingenue Lois Neilson; they had two children. They were divorced in 1935, after a separation. In April 1934, before his divorce decree was issued, Laurel married Virginia Ruth Rogers in Mexico. (A legal ceremony in Arizona was performed in September 1935.) They were divorced in 1937 but remarried in 1941. In the interim Laurel had married (Jan. 1, 1938) and divorced (1940) Vera Ivanova Shuvalova, a Russian singer-dancer, known professionally as Illeana. His second marriage to Virginia Rogers ended in divorce in 1946. On April 14, 1946, he married Ida Kataeva Raphael, a concert singer and movie actress.

Laurel retired to Santa Monica, Calif., where he spent many hours discussing comedy with younger comedians. He frequently expressed admiration for the work of Jack Benny, Jerry Lewis, Dick Van Dyke, and Jack Paar, but detested most "stand-up" comedians and untalented television masters of ceremonies.

Retirement did not preclude continued recognition of Laurel's achievements. In 1961 the Academy of Motion Picture Arts and Sciences awarded him a special Oscar. Two years later he received a similar award from the Screen Actors Guild. He died in Santa Monica.

[John McCabe, *Mr. Laurel and Mr. Hardy* (1961; reprt. 1966), and *The Comedy World of Stan Laurel* (1974), present a full account of Laurel's life and career. Also see William K. Everson, *The Films of Laurel and Hardy* (1967); Charles Barr, *Laurel and Hardy* (1968); and Richard J. Anobile, ed., *"A Fine Mess!"* (1975). The best critical treatments of Laurel's approach to comedy and his on-screen relationship with Hardy are Gerald Mast, *The Comic Mind* (1973), and Walter Kerr, *The Silent Clowns* (1975). Molly Haskell, *From Reverence to Rape* (1974), examines misogyny in the Laurel and Hardy comedies. An obituary is in the *New York Times*, Feb. 24, 1965.]

WILLIAM HUGHES

LEBRUN, FEDERICO ("RICO") (Dec. 10, 1900–May 9, 1964), painter, muralist, and sculptor, was born in Naples, Italy, the son of Edoardo Lebrun, a railroad official, and of Assunta Carione. After graduating from the National Technical School of Naples in 1914, Lebrun spent the next three years at the city's National Technical Institute preparing for a career in finance. He spent the last year of World War I in the Italian army, then, with two years remaining in his term of military service, he transferred to the navy. Meanwhile, in part through assignments in military drafting, his interest in art was developing. While still in uniform he began attending night classes at the Naples Academy of Fine Arts, where he remained as a student until 1922.

Among his instructors and peers impressionism was very much a prevailing vogue. But Lebrun found the Italian adaptations of this style "ill-suited" for expressing the "carnal" texture of his Neapolitan surroundings. In seeking a foundation for his art, he reached back to the baroque traditions of the seventeenth century, which he felt best captured the human passions and teeming movement of his native city. Years later, after his style had undergone many drastic changes, he claimed that in his abiding concern for portraying the vitality of the human spirit, he had remained faithful to the essence of baroque outlook.

In 1922, Lebrun became a designer for a manufacturer of stained glass. Two years later his firm sent him to America to manage its factory in Springfield, Ill. When his contract with the Italian concern expired in 1925, Lebrun moved to New York City to work in commercial art. Shortly after his arrival there he married Portia Novello, a commercial artist. They had no children. Within a few years Lebrun had become one of the most highly paid magazine illustrators of the day, his work appearing in many publications including *Vogue, Harper's Bazaar,* and the *New Yorker.* But in the early 1930's, increasingly disturbed with the transitory nature of periodical art, he decided to give up this lucrative endeavor in favor of purely "creative" art.

In 1933, after an extended period of study in Italy, Lebrun established his own studio in New York City. Two years later, on the strength of his proposal for a mural on the history of mining, he was awarded a Guggenheim fellowship. Although the grant was renewed the next year, the mural never went beyond the preliminary stages. Simultaneously Lebrun was working on a commission from the Works Progress Administration for a mural in the New York City Post Office annex. But two years of disagreements with his supervisors resulted in abandonment of the undertaking. In 1938, following the dissolution of his marriage (1937), Lebrun moved to Santa Barbara, Calif., where he joined the faculty of Chouinard Art Institute. He became a United States citizen in 1939, and the following year he married Elaine Leonard Corbino. They had no children. These changes in circumstance marked the beginning of his most productive years.

Lebrun's professional evolution defies convenient classification. Embracing both traditional and modern concepts of art, and in the end equally at ease with both, he drew inspiration from quarters as diverse as the Italian baroque masters, Paul Cézanne, and Pablo Picasso. From the powerful realism that characterized the drawings of his first one-man exhibitions of the early 1940's, his art had by the decade's end become a mixture of abstraction and expressionism. Nevertheless, Lebrun never entirely forsook realistic forms, and in his later years he periodically worked out inventive "revisions" of the works of Goya.

By 1947, in an effort to retrieve life's positive meanings after the death of his second wife (1946), Lebrun began his "Crucifixion cycle." For some three years he devoted himself almost entirely to variant portrayals of Christ's martyrdom. The exhibition of this phase of his work in 1950, at the Los Angeles County Museum of Art and the de Young Museum in San Francisco, won him an international reputation.

On July 19, 1948, Lebrun married Constance Johnson Hovey, and shortly thereafter adopted her son by a previous marriage. In 1951 he was appointed director of the Jepson Art Institute in Los Angeles, where he had been teaching since 1947. In the early 1950's he also taught at the Instituto Allende in Mexico. There a new vividness of light and color entered his work, and he began to experiment in collage. On his return to California, Lebrun embarked on a series of drawings and paintings depicting the horrors of the Nazi concentration camps. His thematic concern was not so much man's cruelty to man as the indomitability of the human spirit.

Among the greatest achievements of Lebrun's final period was his mural portrayal of Genesis for Pomona College in California. With this work, one critic claimed, the artist had come closer than ever before to achieving an "essential synthesis of intent and accomplishment." The success of this venture proved something of a catalyst; and in Lebrun's subsequent work, mainly graphic interpretations of literary images from Dante, Herman Melville, and Bertolt Brecht, the unity of purpose and expression reached still greater heights.

Throughout his career Lebrun remained indefatigably adventurous. In the two years before his death, he began experimenting in sculpture. Immediately at home in this medium, he worked with amazing rapidity. The thirty-odd figures in wax and bronze left at his death are considered to be among his most impressive work. Lebrun died in Malibu, Calif.

[Examples of Lebrun's work can be found in many museums, including the Museum of Modern Art and the Whitney Museum of American Art, both in New York City, and the Museum of Fine Arts, Boston. The most extensive collections of his paintings, drawings, and sculptures are located at the Santa Barbara (Calif.) Museum of Art and the Los Angeles County Museum of Art.

Lebrun's papers are in the Archives of American Art, Smithsonian Institution, Washington, D.C. His commentary on his work can be found in *Rico Lebrun Drawings* (1961). The most complete biography is Henry Seldis, *Rico Lebrun* (1968). Also see Donald Bear, "Rico Lebrun," *Pacific Art Review*, Winter 1941–1942; "Lebrun Paints a Picture," *Art News*, Dec. 1950; and Selden Rodman, "Conversation with Rico Lebrun," *Art in America*, Fall 1956. An obituary is in the *New York Times*, May 11, 1964.]

FREDERICK VOSS

LEHMAN, ADELE LEWISOHN (May 17, 1882–Aug. 11, 1965), philanthropist, art collector, and painter, was born in New York City, the daughter of Adolph Lewisohn, financier, philanthropist, and art collector, and of Emma M. Cahn. Adolph Lewisohn had come to the United States in 1867 from Hamburg, Germany, as the representative of his father's business, which dealt in wool, bristles, horsehair, and ornamental feathers. In 1879 he branched out into the metal industry; with two of his brothers he bought a copper mine in Butte, Mont. By 1899 he and others had formed a smelting trust, the American Smelting and Refining Company.

Adele Lewisohn was sent to the Anne Brown

School, and for one year (1900) attended Barnard College. (In 1957 she gave $1 million to the college.) On Nov. 25, 1901, she married Arthur Lehman, an investment banker and brother of Herbert Lehman, the future governor of, and U.S. senator from, New York State. They had three daughters.

Living in an age and coming from a background where philanthropy was regarded as a duty, Lehman readily accepted the obligations expected of one of her social position. In her philanthropic activities she had the example of her husband, who was one of the founders of the Federation for Jewish Philanthropies and its second president. For many years she held the office of "honorary" vice-president of the women's division of the federation, furthering its program and activities through raising funds and arranging elaborate functions.

In addition Lehman was a member of the board of directors of the New York Service for Orthopedically Handicapped. The service ran Oakhurst, a summer camp. It also maintained a sheltered workshop for crippled girls where they were taught manual skills, and a pilot program for children of nursery school age who were afflicted by cerebral palsy. A free school was maintained in order to demonstrate that children with cerebral palsy were educable.

Lehman had a pronounced interest in art in all its forms. An ardent collector, she started with pre-fourteenth-century Italian primitives and went on to acquire contemporary masters. The Lehmans were aided in their collecting by family friend Paul J. Sachs of the Fogg Museum, but they were also influenced by dealers and other connoisseurs. Many of their acquisitions later became part of museum collections, principally those of the Metropolitan Museum of Art in New York, which received twenty-four works of art consisting of tapestries, paintings, and sculptures, and the Fogg Museum, which received seven. The National Gallery received a portrait of Benjamin Franklin by Jean Baptiste Greuze. The bequests to the Metropolitan consisted of nine tapestries, two della Robbia reliefs, and thirteen paintings, which included two large works by Francesco Guardi.

After the death of her husband in 1936, Lehman shifted her interests from predominantly cultural concerns. As a young woman she had actively participated in the woman suffrage movement. She became interested in the League of Women Voters, serving as vice-president in 1945. She also was elected to the board of directors of the Philharmonic-Symphony Society of New York two years later.

In 1954 Lehman turned her thoughts to a project that would perpetuate the memory of her husband. The result was the Arthur Lehman Counselling Service for people who were in need of psychiatric help, but did not want charity. For modest fees therapy was administered by professional personnel to people beset by personal, marital, or family troubles.

Although her formative years had come in the nineteenth century, Lehman combined the characteristics of the nineteenth-century woman and the twentieth-century woman who was stirred by the currents of her time. She was an accomplished horsewoman and an excellent tennis player. She is said to have won thirty-eight cups.

After a heart attack in 1947, Lehman's interest centered on creative work, and henceforth she immersed herself in painting still lifes, floral pieces, and landscapes. She died at Purchase, N.Y.

[See Stephen Birmingham, *Our Crowd* (1967). An obituary notice appeared in the *New York Times*, Aug. 12, 1965.]

CECYLE S. NEIDLE

LEHMAN, HERBERT HENRY (Mar. 28, 1878–Dec. 5, 1963), investment banker, governor of New York, U.S. senator, and director of the United Nations Relief and Rehabilitation Administration, was born in New York City, the son of Mayer Lehman, a cotton merchant, and of Babette Newgass. Growing up in an affluent and "forward-looking" German Reform-Jewish community, Lehman attended Dr. Julius Sachs's Collegiate Institute and Williams College (B.A., 1899). After graduation he went to work for the J. Spencer Turner Company, cotton manufacturers with ties to his family's firm. He became a vice-president and treasurer, and in 1908 he left to join Lehman Brothers, which had been transformed, largely by his brother Arthur, from a cotton-brokerage firm into an important investment banking house. On Apr. 28, 1910, he married Edith Louise Altschul, whose father was head of the New York branch of Lazard Frères, a Paris-based investment banking house. They had three children.

Like many members of New York's German-Jewish elite, Lehman devoted much time to public and community service. By the turn of the century he had begun a lifelong association with the Henry Street Settlement. At the outbreak of World War I, he helped found the Joint Distribution Committee, which collected and disbursed funds for the relief of Jews in

Europe and Palestine. Shortly after American entry into the war, Lehman volunteered as a civilian textile-procurement specialist in the Navy Department, where he met Franklin Delano Roosevelt. In September 1917, as a captain in the army, he was stationed in Washington, D.C. He was a textile procurer, a contract adjuster, and finally a member of the War Claims Board. He resigned from the army in June 1919 with the rank of colonel, the title of address he preferred until he became governor.

In the 1920's Lehman became a supporter of and made significant financial contributions to the political fortunes of Alfred E. Smith. In 1924, Smith appointed him to a garment industry mediation committee, which was his first association with organized labor. After Smith won the Democratic nomination for the presidency in 1928, Lehman became chairman of the Finance Committee of the Democratic National Committee. Later that year he was nominated for lieutenant governor on a ticket headed by Franklin D. Roosevelt. Although the Democratic state election victory that year is often credited to Lehman's attraction for Jewish voters, the fact is that Roosevelt's opponent, Albert Ottinger, was Jewish and Lehman's narrow margin of victory—14,000 votes of more than 4 million cast—was only a little more than half of Roosevelt's.

Part of the reason for Lehman's nomination was Roosevelt's insistence that his lieutenant governor be someone who could run the state during his absences, and in fact Lehman had much more to do with the mechanics of state government than do most lieutenant governors. Roosevelt once called him "my good right arm." After a successful reelection campaign in 1930, Lehman was a "natural" as a Democratic candidate for governor in 1932 when Roosevelt ran for president. He was elected by a large majority.

Lehman served four terms as governor, being elected for two-year terms in 1932, 1934, and 1936, and for the first four-year term in 1938. His first two victories were with margins of over 800,000 votes, his third by more than 500,000 votes. Only in 1938, when he ran against Thomas E. Dewey, did he win by a relatively narrow margin—64,000 votes. Lehman was never a colorful campaigner, but he radiated a stolid, honest respectability. Perhaps in an era in which New Yorkers had Roosevelt in Washington and Fiorello La Guardia in New York City, they needed someone quieter in Albany.

As governor, Lehman presided over an impressive "Little New Deal" combined with relatively orthodox fiscal policy. He turned a fiscal 1933 deficit of $90 million into a surplus of $6 million by 1938. With the onset of prosperity after the outbreak of war, he put through a 25 percent reduction in the state income tax. His most impressive reforms came in the area of labor legislation, the regulation of public utilities (although, as with his two Democratic predecessors, his proposals for public power development on the St. Lawrence were not enacted), and in his appointments, which rarely smacked of partisan politics.

In national politics Lehman supported the New Deal, except during the "court packing" controversy in 1937, when his public letter opposing Roosevelt's plan clouded relations between Albany and Washington for a while. In this matter Lehman may have been guided by his intellectually more gifted brother, Irving, who was then serving on the New York Court of Appeals. (When Irving Lehman was elected chief judge in 1940, New York, for the only time in its history, had brothers heading both the executive and the judicial branches of its government.)

In international affairs Lehman was an interventionist. He expressed his concern for the fate of European Jewry relatively early. A few days before the end of his fourth term in December 1942, he resigned as governor to accept appointment as director of the newly created Office of Foreign Relief and Rehabilitation Operations in the State Department. When the United Nations Relief and Rehabilitation Administration (UNRRA) came into being in November 1943, Lehman was, as the chief American official concerned with relief, elected its first director. After more than four years of work in refugee relief and many accomplishments and frustrations, Lehman resigned in March 1946. Although he gave "failing health" as the reason, it is probable that President Harry Truman's appointment of former President Herbert Hoover to survey food needs in Europe, made without consulting Lehman, was the proximate cause.

In any event Lehman's health did not prevent him from running for the U.S. Senate in November 1946. He suffered his only electoral defeat, losing to Republican Irving M. Ives by 250,000 votes even though he ran almost 400,000 votes stronger than the head of the ticket. Three years later he defeated John Foster Dulles, who had an interim appointment, in a special election for the other Senate seat for New York, which had been held by Robert F. Wagner. He was reelected to a full term in 1950.

In the Senate, Lehman never belonged to the

"club," and initiated no significant legislation. He supported most Fair Deal measures but opposed compulsory health insurance and the Brannan Plan for agriculture. He was one of the earliest politicians to speak out against Senator Joseph R. McCarthy and McCarthyism, and was a chief spokesman for liberalized immigration legislation. By the end of his term in 1957, he was one of the few visible ties to the early New Deal still prominent in American politics.

Even in retirement Lehman lived a full public life. An article written for his eightieth birthday speaks of his dictating to relays of secretaries in order to answer his daily correspondence. In 1959, with Eleanor Roosevelt and Thomas K. Finletter, he commenced a campaign to destroy "bossism" in New York politics. He died in New York City, on the eve of receiving the Presidential Medal of Freedom. Its citation is, perhaps, his best epitaph: "Citizen and Statesman, he has used wisdom and compassion as the tools of government and has made politics the highest form of public service."

[Lehman's papers are at Columbia University; the memoir in the Oral History Collections, Columbia University, is unsatisfactory. His gubernatorial career may be followed in his *Public Papers*, 10 vols. (1934–1946). Books on Lehman include Allan Nevins, *Herbert H. Lehman and His Era* (1963), and Robert P. Ingalls, *Herbert H. Lehman and New York's Little New Deal* (1975). Magazine articles are Jewel Bellush, "Roosevelt's Good Right Arm: Lieutenant Governor Herbert H. Lehman," *New York History*, Oct. 1960; Russell Owen, "The Man Behind the 'Little New Deal,'" *New York Times Magazine*, Mar. 15, 1936; Hickman Powell, "Profiles: The Governor," *New Yorker*, May 2 and 9, 1936; S. J. Woolf, "Lehman Outlines His Social Philosophy," *New York Times Magazine*, Aug. 9, 1936; Barbara Ward, "Lehman at 80: Young Elder Statesman," *New York Times Magazine*, Mar. 23, 1958. Also see William M. Wiecek, "The Place of Chief Judge Irving Lehman in American Constitutional Development," *American Jewish Historical Quarterly*, Mar. 1971, which contains useful material about the brothers' relationship, and David M. Ellis, et al., *A History of New York State* (rev. ed., 1967). An obituary is in the *New York Times*, Dec. 6, 1963.]

ROGER DANIELS

LEONTY, METROPOLITAN (Aug. 8, 1876–May 14, 1965), primate of the Russian Orthodox Eastern Church of America and metropolitan of all America and Canada, was born Leonid Ieronimovich Turkevich at Kremenets, in the Volhynian region of Russia. His parents were Ieronim Iosifovich Turkevich, archpriest in Kremenets and assistant to the inspector of

the Volhynian Theological Seminary, and Anna Antonovna Ivanitskaia. His mother died in 1879, leaving young Turkevich and his two brothers to a rigorous upbringing by their father.

Turkevich attended elementary and intermediate schools in Kremenets, then completed his secondary education and theological studies at the Volhynian Theological Seminary (1889–1895) and the Kiev Theological Academy (1896–1900). After graduation he was given a series of lay assignments, including a teaching position in Kursk, in central Russia, and duties as assistant to the inspector of the theological seminary at Ekaterinoslav (now Dnepropetrovsk), in the Ukraine. In 1905, Turkevich was ordained at the monastery of Pochayev and married the daughter of another priest, Anna Olimpievna Chervinskaia (Anna Chervinsky). They had five children. Also in 1905, Leonid began his pastoral career as his father's successor as parish priest in Kremenets.

In 1906, Leonid was selected by Archbishop Tikhon of the American diocese of the Russian Orthodox Church to be the dean (rector) of the first Russian Orthodox theological seminary in the United States, in Minneapolis, Minn. In 1912 the seminary was transferred to Tenafly, N.J., and three years later Leonid was appointed dean and archpriest of St. Nicholas Cathedral in New York City. He spent 1917–1918 in Russia, as the representative of the North American eparchy to the All-Russian Synod. Upon his return, by way of Siberia and Japan, he found that his church had been taken over by the "Renovated" faction of the Russian Orthodox Church, which was sympathetic to the Soviet regime. As a result, in 1926 Leonid moved his seat to what is now the Cathedral of the Holy Virgin Protection in New York City.

In 1933, taking the monastic name of Leonty, he was consecrated bishop of Chicago and Minneapolis. He was raised to archbishop of New York and ruling bishop of the Council of Bishops in 1945. Following the death of Metropolitan Theophilus, the Eighth All-American Synod (the churchwide assembly of clergymen and laymen) unanimously elected him the new metropolitan on Dec. 6, 1950.

Leonty thus became the head of the largest and oldest of the three branches of Russian Orthodoxy in the United States. He was the spiritual leader of some 750,000 members of the church organized in some 400 parishes in the United States, Canada, South America, and Japan. He was also president of St. Vladimir's Theological Seminary in Crestwood (Tuckahoe), N.Y.

Leonty devoted sixty years of his life to theological, especially biblical, scholarship and to the educational and administrative demands of his church. From 1914 on, he edited a number of newspapers and periodicals, including *American Orthodox Herald*, the *World*, and *Our Path*, contributing many articles to them and to other Russian- and English-language religious publications. He was particularly preoccupied with the problems of Orthodoxy in America, increasingly distinct linguistically and ethnically from its Russian parent, and with its own peculiar mission. Recognizing the American church's great need for missionaries, Leonty nevertheless insisted that American priests be given a rigorous theological education, so that they might be scholars and intellectuals as well. He was sensitive to the need to have English used as the language of instruction and pedagogical literature, and was willing to make adjustments in the church to accommodate students who were not of Russian origin. But he was determined to maintain the "Russian" character of the church as long as possible.

Leonty showed the same ability to couple faithfulness to tradition with receptivity to change in his approach to the problems posed for the American church by the Bolshevik Revolution of 1917. Deprived of material support from Russia, he had to find the means to make his church self-supporting financially. Equally important, after 1923, he had to counter the attempt of the Soviet-backed "Living Church" to extend its influence and control to America. Adamantly opposed to any compromise with the Soviet regime and with Communist ideology, Leonty insisted on the complete autonomy of the American church, and gave it its own independent administrative structure. At the same time he emphasized the continuing love and loyalty of the American "daughter" for her spiritual and historical "mother," now unable to express and execute her own will. He was a skillful and resolute leader of the Russian Orthodox Church in America during a period of crisis and transition. He died in Syosset, N.Y.

[A representative example of Leonty's contributions to periodicals is "Theological Education in America," *St. Vladimir's Seminary Quarterly*, Summer 1965, an abbreviated English translation of a piece that originally appeared, in Russian, in the *Russian Orthodox American Messenger* (1913). Selections from his "messages" and "salutations" are in the memorial volume published (in Russian) by the Russian Orthodox Church in America, *The Life and Work of the Most Reverend Metropolitan Leonty* (1969). The most knowledgeable obituary is "A Life of Service," *St. Vladimir's Seminary Quarterly*, Summer 1965; briefer obituaries are in the *New York Times*, May 15, 1965, and *Newsweek*, May 21, 1965.]

JOSEPH FREDERICK ZACEK

LEVITT, ABRAHAM (July 1, 1880–Aug. 20, 1962), lawyer and contractor, was born in the Williamsburg section of Brooklyn, the son of Louis Levitt, a rabbi who emigrated from Russia, and Nellie Levitt, who was born in Austria-Germany. The family was poor. Abraham left school at the age of ten to do odd jobs, but he was an avid reader and attended meetings of literary and social clubs. He passed a New York State Regents examination to gain entrance to New York University Law School when twenty. While at New York University he wrote a successful study guide on real estate law for fellow students. In 1902 he received his LL.B., and in 1903 he was admitted to the New York State Bar. He practiced real estate law in New York City until 1929.

Levitt married Pauline A. Biederman on Jan. 9, 1906. They had two sons, William Jaird and Alfred Stuart. The family's home environment was described as "argumentative"—Levitt discussed with his sons such diverse subjects as baseball and art. Both sons attended New York University, but neither obtained a degree.

In 1929 Levitt founded the construction firm of Levitt and Sons. William, who was made president of the firm, brought to the post entrepreneurial drive, salesmanship, and organizational abilities; Alfred, as vice-president, contributed the house and community designs that were the hallmarks of the firm in its heyday, the two decades following World War II. Levitt, as chairman of the board, supplied legal know-how, a philosophical outlook, and the maturity necessary for a stable company. Although most of the publicity about the firm focused on William's role, Levitt maintained that William would not have succeeded without Alfred, nor Alfred without William. The Levitt and Sons' reputation was inextricably linked to the contributions of the three principals.

During the 1930's the firm profitably custombuilt about 2,500 houses, mainly in Rockville Centre and Manhasset, in Nassau County, N.Y. Characterized as "one of the best-known homebuilding firms in the New York district," Levitt and Sons in 1942 won federal contracts to build houses for workers and military personnel near Norfolk, Va. Of some 2,300 houses built, the second set of 757 units, for naval officers, was the more successful. Norfolk provided an opportunity for the firm to experiment with its ideas to simplify and standardize the house building process.

National and international fame came from the construction of Levittown, N.Y., after World War II. Levitt, president of the firm during William's absence as a World War II officer, talked as early as October 1944 of planning a community of 6,000 low-priced homes. Contracts already were being executed for land and equipment. Between 1947 and 1951, the Levitts built 17,447 four- and five-bedroom houses fully equipped with appliances in an area of 7.3 square miles that cut across five postal districts on Long Island. Completely landscaped, "Cape-Cod-type" houses were originally rented for $65 a month, and later sold for around $8,500; "Ranch-type" houses sold for less than $10,000. Variety was obtained by employing standardized floor plans with a series of different facades, and by placing the houses at different distances from the curbs on winding streets. Greens containing stores, playgrounds, and swimming pools were strategically placed throughout the development.

Although the community suffered growing pains, Levittown is considered a masterful building achievement. Similar communities were later built by the firm in Pennsylvania, New Jersey, Florida, Puerto Rico, and in Israel and France. By 1962 the firm had built more than 100,000 houses. After the deaths of Abraham Levitt and Alfred, William sold the company in 1968 to the International Telephone and Telegraph Company for a reputed $92 million.

The Levitt house-community building revolution was based on well designed, functional, and attractive communities; standardized interiors behind a variety of exterior facades; rationalized construction incorporating precut and some preassembled components, which reduced the need for on-site skilled labor; subcontracting on an incentive basis; utilization of power-driven tools; direct purchasing from manufacturers; and integration of the firm through wholly owned subsidiaries from raw materials production through sales.

This approach brought the Levitts into conflict with local building codes, marketing systems, and collective bargaining agreements. Their revolution, however, was not a social revolution. They built for "Caucasians," and maintained a "white only" policy as long as it remained legal to do so. Their defense was that they would not be able to sell homes if they diverged from local discriminatory mores.

When the courts struck down these policies nationally, Levitt and Sons employed educational and sociological techniques to prepare their communities for racial integration.

Levitt was responsible for the landscaping of these large building projects. In addition to the planning and supervising, he conferred with residents about the maintenance of the grounds. His company brochure, *The Care of Your Lawn and Landscaping*, was followed by an article, "Fruit Is Fine For Little Gardens" (*American Home*, January 1950). His weekly column in the *Levittown Tribune*, "Chats on Gardening" (begun in 1948), emphasized order, cleanliness, floral beauty, and open space for an aesthetically pleasing community as well as the maintenance of property values. Clauses governing these elements were incorporated into Levitt and Sons' rental and sales contracts. Alfred asserted that "almost everything we have learned about improving the appearance of our communities, we have learned from Father. Every social idea this company had was the result of Father's pressing and persuading."

Levitt was a knowledgeable and effective businessman. His associates recall him as gentle, kind, friendly, and generous. His philanthropies included the Levitt Foundation (created by him and his sons in 1946); the United Jewish Appeal, which honored Levitt and his sons in May 1952; and the Albert Einstein College of Medicine of Yeshiva University, where he served as the first chairman (1955) and honorary chairman (1956–1962). The Levittown, Long Island, community erected a plaque (sculpted by Julio Kilenyi) in his honor on Oct. 28, 1951.

Levitt lived out his last years in Great Neck, N.Y., and died at the North Shore Hospital.

[There is no biography of Abraham Levitt. Boyden Sparkes's *Saturday Evening Post* article, "They'll Build Neighborhoods, Not Houses" (Oct. 1944), contains the longest interview with him published. Of architectural interest are the articles on Levitt houses in *Architectural Forum* (May 1947, Apr. 1949, and Apr. 1950). For a study of Levittown, N.Y., see Harold L. Wattel, "Levittown, a Suburban Community," in William Dobriner, *The Suburban Community* (1958), and for a study of Levittown, N.J., see Herbert J. Gans, *The Levittowners* (1967). The latter has an excellent bibliography. The Levittown, N.Y., Public Library maintains a Levittown Collection and has published Joseph E. Spagnoli's *Levittown, New York: An Annotated Bibliography, 1947–1972*. The most complete obituary is in the *New York Times*, Aug. 21, 1962, with a minor correction on Sept. 5, 1962.]

HAROLD WATTEL

LEWIS, CLARENCE IRVING (Apr. 12, 1883–Feb. 3, 1964), philosopher and educator, was born in Stoneham, Mass., the son of Irving Lewis, and Hannah Carlyn Dearth. Even in old age he thought of himself as an "up-country New England Yankee," by inheritance as well as in temperament. His father, a shoe-maker, lost his job when he participated in a local strike, was blacklisted for defending trade unionism, and found work elsewhere only after years of poverty. Lewis acquired from his father a lively interest in the social problems of the day, and from his mother the conviction that by hard work he could overcome the financial difficulties of obtaining a college education.

But the person who was the most powerful single influence in Lewis's intellectual development was an elderly woman he met at the age of fifteen while working in New Hampshire during the summer. She encouraged his skeptical questioning of the orthodoxies as well as his thoughtful answers to the puzzles of the universe.

When Lewis entered Harvard in 1903 he was already strongly bent on philosophy. William James and Josiah Royce were among his teachers and both left permanent marks on his thought. Royce became and remained his ideal of a philosopher, even though he could not subscribe to Royce's metaphysical idealism. Lewis was awarded the A.B. in 1906. After serving as instructor in English at the University of Colorado (1906–1908), he returned to Harvard. He obtained the Ph.D. in philosophy in 1910 with a dissertation entitled "The Place of Intuition in Knowledge." The next year he assisted Royce in his graduate courses in logic. In 1911 Lewis moved to the University of California in Berkeley, first as instructor in philosophy, then as assistant professor (1914–1920). He then returned to Harvard, where he remained until his retirement as Edgar Pierce Professor of Philosophy Emeritus in 1953. Lewis married Mabel Maxwell Graves on Jan. 1, 1907; they had four children. He received many honors. He was elected president of the American Philosophical Association, where he subsequently delivered the Carus Lectures.

Lewis' central philosophical concern was with questions bearing on the validity and the justification of claims to knowledge. He made significant contributions to logic, the theory of knowledge, and ethics—in that order. His interest in logic was first aroused by Royce, who put into his hands the first volume of Alfred North Whitehead and Bertrand Russell's *Principia*

Mathematica shortly after its publication in 1910.

From the beginning Lewis was troubled by the fact that the logical calculus constructed in that book does not codify any of the relations between the connotations (or meanings) of terms and statements. It is wholly extensional, building on the notion of "material implication" and proving such "paradoxical" theorems as that a false proposition materially implies any proposition. To remedy what he believed to be a serious defect in the system of material implication, Lewis constructed a calculus of what he called "strict implication," with the help of such modal terms as "necessary" and "possible," in which those paradoxical theorems do not occur. He was then faced with the novel questions of whether there can be alternative systems of deductive logic, and, if so, how the validity of any one of them is to be determined. His answer to the first question was in the affirmative. In answering the second, he used the central idea of what he later called his "conceptualistic pragmatism." He maintained that purely logical considerations do not suffice for deciding between alternative logical systems. Pragmatic factors such as the purpose for which a system is adopted and its effectiveness in achieving that purpose must be taken into account. Such considerations, he acknowledged, had been stressed by James and Royce. The results of these logical investigations were published in Lewis' *Survey of Symbolic Logic* (1918) and in corrected and enlarged form in *Symbolic Logic* (1932), which he wrote in collaboration with C. H. Langford.

Even during his preoccupation with the construction of formal logical calculi, Lewis was primarily concerned with the import of logic for the theory of knowledge and other philosophical questions. His main problem in reflecting on epistemology was to identify the components that go into the making of empirical knowledge, and to analyze how, in achieving it, the data given in sense experience are related to the conceptual structures which the mind contributes. His solution of the problem is contained in his *Mind and the World-Order* (1929). It is a development of the conceptualistic pragmatism that had opened important doors for him in the philosophy of logic. In developing it he was influenced not only by the voluntarism of James and Royce, and Kant's emphasis on the mind's activity in knowing, but also by the unpublished writings of Charles Peirce, the founder of pragmatism, which he read in the Harvard Library.

The substance of Lewis' views in *Mind and the World-Order* is that the content of what is given in sense experience is independent of the mind and unalterable by it, but that the mind can construct alternative conceptual modes for dealing with the given. The data of sense do not supply their own conceptual interpretation, any more than the earth's surface determines which type of geometry is to be used in describing it. Just as different types of geometry can be devised for representing spatial objects, between which a choice must be made in the light of pragmatic considerations, so more generally alternative conceptual schemas of interpreting what is given can be constructed, and the decision to adopt one mode of interpretation rather than another must also be made in the light of such considerations. Accordingly, knowledge of an object does not consist in our having a mere presentation of it, but in the implicit prediction that a trait manifested in one presentation of the object is followed by certain other traits in subsequent presentations of the object. Unlike the given, which is neither true nor false, all empirical truth is only probable.

Lewis looked upon ethics as the most important part of philosophy, and on concluding his logical and epistemological studies he gave his entire attention to that subject. He sought to show that valuations and ethical judgments are verifiable or falsifiable, and are a species of empirical knowledge. Without abandoning his naturalistic outlook, he therefore rejected as unfounded the widespread skepticism concerning the possibility of objective moral propositions. His Carus Lectures, *An Analysis of Knowledge and Valuation* (1946), restated in the first two of three parts his theory of knowledge with much fresh detail and new emphases, and offered in the final part a careful account of the nature of values and valuations. According to Lewis, directly experienced satisfactions or dissatisfactions correspond to the given experiential data of scientific inquiry. On the other hand, moral judgments predicting what satisfactions or dissatisfactions will probably eventuate from the actions that implement the choices we may make correspond to the hypotheses of science. Although neither moral judgments nor scientific hypotheses are completely verifiable, their probable truth or falsity can be determined objectively.

He subsequently published two small volumes: *The Ground and Nature of the Right* (1955) and *Our Social Inheritance* (1957). In the former he discussed the source and justification of rights and obligations; and in the latter he examined the warrant for moral imperatives and analyzed the nature of justice, among other

important concepts of social philosophy. There is an increasing angle of vision and a more evident orderly unity in the development of Lewis' philosophy.

Lewis died in Menlo Park, Calif.

[The main sources for biographical data are two autobiographical essays: "Logic and Pragmatism" in George P. Adams and William P. Montague, eds., *Contemporary American Philosophy*, II (1930); and "Autobiography" in Paul A. Schilpp, ed., *The Philosophy of C. I. Lewis* (1968), which also contains a bibliography of Lewis' published writings. In addition to the books mentioned in the text, two collections of his papers, some not previously published, are in *Values and Imperatives* (1969) and *Collected Papers* (1970). An exposition and interpretation of his thought is in Elizabeth Flower and Murray G. Murphy, *A History of Philosophy in America*, II (1977). Also see Donald C. Williams' memorial note, *Harvard University Gazette*, Nov. 7, 1964. An obituary appeared in the *New York Times*, Feb. 4, 1964.]
                                                    ERNEST NAGEL

LIEBLING, ABBOTT JOSEPH (Oct. 18, 1904–Dec. 28, 1963), journalist and author, was born in New York City, the son of Joseph Liebling, a well-to-do furrier, and of Anna Slone. He attended New York City schools and entered Dartmouth College in 1920. After being expelled from Dartmouth in 1923 for failure to attend chapel (he later described himself as "an agnostic of Jewish origin"), Liebling enrolled in the School of Journalism at Columbia University. He graduated in 1925 with the B.Litt. and was hired by the sports department of the *New York Times*. After eight months with the *Times*, he was fired because he gave the name "Ignoto" to a basketball referee whose name he did not know.

Liebling went to Paris in 1926 and studied at the Sorbonne. In Paris he learned about French cooking, which engaged his interest and zestful appetite from then on. After returning to the United States in 1927, he was employed by the *Providence Journal* and the *Evening Bulletin* for nearly three years as a reporter and feature writer. ("I oozed prose over every aspect of Rhode Island life.") In 1930 Liebling left because a staff member was fired to make room for an advertiser's son.

He returned to New York, where he worked on the *World Telegram*. After four years with that paper (1931–1935), during which he wrote more than a thousand feature articles, he asked for, and was refused, a raise. He left, and for a while worked on King Features' *Evening Journal Magazine*. On July 28, 1934, Liebling married Ann Beatrice McGinn.

In 1935, Liebling was hired at the *New Yorker* by editor Harold Ross; he remained with the magazine for the rest of his life. In the early years he wrote articles and profiles of such diverse figures as the jockey Eddie Arcaro, Father Divine (in collaboration with St. Clair McKelway), and General George Marshall. His unpretentious and irreverent style of writing and his accurate, even scholarly, reporting pleased Ross, who during the 1930's hired a number of former newspapermen: Alva Johnston; Joseph Mitchell, who became Liebling's close friend; and Meyer Berger. These writers constituted, Liebling said, "a second *New Yorker* generation" after E. B. White, James Thurber, Wolcott Gibbs, and Robert Benchley.

Liebling's first book, *Back Where I Came From* (1938), containing pieces from the *World-Telegram* as well as from the *New Yorker*, describes New York, the only city he preferred to Paris, with amused affection. He knew the town intimately; walked its streets continually; liked the sound of Broadway speech, the sporting talk, and what he called "the side-street New York language."

In October 1939, Liebling was sent to Paris to report the early phases of World War II. His affection for France and French culture, dating from his student days, had never lapsed; but the quality of French cooking, he observed, had declined. In 1940 he returned to New York, and in July 1941 he flew to Britain to cover the activities of the Royal Air Force. When the Japanese attacked Pearl Harbor, Liebling was sailing home on a Norwegian tanker. His account of the voyage, "Westbound Tanker," is one of his many superb pieces of World War II reportage.

Liebling's second book, *Telephone Booth Indian* (1942), focused on the marvels the author found in the half-mile-square area bounded by Sixth and Eighth avenues and by Forty-second and Fifty-third streets. Many readers, including critic Stanley Edgar Hyman, consider it Liebling's best book.

Liebling later covered American air attacks from England, the African campaign, and D-Day. He also followed the U.S. First Infantry Division into northern France, and was in Paris in August 1944, when the city was liberated. Much of his war correspondence for the *New Yorker* is gathered in three books: *The Road Back to Paris* (1944), *Normandy Revisited* (1958), and *Mollie and Other War Pieces* (1964). For his writing about France and the French people he was awarded the Legion of Honor in 1952. In 1949, Liebling divorced his first wife and married Lucille Hill Spectorsky.

After the war Liebling began writing "The Wayward Press," a *New Yorker* department Robert Benchley had originated in the 1930's. A sharp, satiric, and knowledgeable critic, Liebling wittily exposed the vagaries and shortcomings of newspapers and newspapermen. Max Lerner wrote editorials, he said, "like an elephant treading the dead body of a mouse into the floor of its cage." Liebling contended that a large number of competing newspapers presenting various shades of thought were "the country's best defense against being stampeded into barbarism." He deplored the decrease and decline of dailies and the lack of diversity in news sources. "American cities with competing newspapers," he wrote, "will soon be so rare as those with two telephone systems." The first collection of "The Wayward Press" pieces appeared in 1947 with the title *The Wayward Pressman.*

Liebling lived in Chicago in 1948–1949 and had a long-standing feud with Colonel Robert R. McCormick of the *Chicago Tribune.* McCormick and his newspaper were the targets of some of Liebling's sharpest barbs. And his book *Chicago: The Second City* (1952) stirred much controversy. "Chicago after nightfall," he wrote, "is a small city of the rich who have not yet migrated, visitors, and hoodlums, surrounded by a large expanse of juxtaposed dimnesses." Liebling continued to be a critic of the press to the end of his life. At the time of his final illness, he was doing a study of the reaction of southern newspapers to President John Kennedy's assassination.

Prominent among Liebling's many interests were boxing, food, language, the raffish characters who peopled what Harold Ross called New York City's "low life," France, horse racing (Going to a race, he said, "fills the lungs and empties the mind."), and colorful politicians like Earl Long, about whom he wrote an eminently readable study, *The Earl of Lousiana* (1961). An amateur boxer as a youth, Liebling retained a lifelong interest in the sport. His last assignment in sports was the Sonny Liston–Floyd Patterson bout at Las Vegas on July 22, 1963. "There's more fun in boxing," he said, "than in any other game. It's a sanctioned release of hostility."

Liebling was essentially a magazine writer. Nearly all of his fifteen books—seventeen if *They All Sang* (1934) by Edward B. Marks, "as told to Abbott J. Liebling," and *The Most of A. J. Liebling* (1963), an anthology selected by

William Cole, are counted—are made up of *New Yorker* articles, sometimes extensively rewritten. His expanded boxing articles appeared as *The Sweet Science* (1956) and the second collection of "Wayward Press" pieces was *The Press* (1961). In *The Jollity Building* (1962) he wrote again about the sharp-witted characters who scramble for dollars on Broadway: orchestra leaders, song pluggers, bookmakers, theatrical agents, and assorted promoters.

Liebling claimed the four most interesting men he knew were Harold Ross; Raymond Weeks, who taught Romance philology at Columbia; police reporter Max Fischel of the *New York Evening World;* and the great black boxer Sam Langford, who delighted Liebling by saying, "You can sweat out beer and you can sweat out whiskey, but you can't sweat out women."

Liebling celebrated Paris and Parisian cooking in *Between Meals* (1962). In *Mollie and Other War Pieces,* as in his earlier books, his writing was, as the critic Joseph Epstein said, "urbane without cuteness, skeptical without sourness, and witty in a way that was at bottom serious."

After his second marriage ended in divorce in 1959, Liebling married on Apr. 3 of that year the novelist Jean Stafford. He had no children with any of his wives.

Although in his later years he was overweight and nearsighted, and had chronic gout, he still reacted to life with gusto. Brendan Gill, his *New Yorker* colleague for many years, said Liebling looked "like some eighteenth century Franciscan monk, with a big belly, a bald pate, and small lively eyes behind old-fashioned, thick-lensed glasses. . . . He was sensual and vain and talented and extremely hard-working, and he was just beginning to enjoy the fame he had . . . long waited for when, in 1963 [in New York City], he died."

[In addition to the books mentioned in the text, Liebling's works include *The Republic of Silence* (1947); *Mink and Red Herring* (1949); and *The Honest Rainmaker* (1953). On Liebling and his work, see *Time,* Nov. 10, 1947; Carle Hodge, "A Wayward Pressman Becomes a Critic," *Editor and Publisher,* Aug. 14, 1948; *The Reporter,* Oct. 18, 1956 and Feb. 13, 1964; *Newsweek,* July 25, 1960; *New Republic,* Jan. 29, 1962; *Commonweal,* Jan. 10, 1964; Roy Newquist, ed., *Counterpoint* (1964); Joseph Epstein, "A. J. Liebling—The Minnesota Fats of American Prose," *Book World,* Oct. 10, 1971; Brendan Gill, *Here at the New Yorker* (1975); Gerald Weales, "The Labyrinthian Digression of A. J. Liebling," *Sewanee Review,* Fall 1975; Stanley Edgar Hyman, *The Critic's Credentials* (1978); Nora Sayre, "A. J. Lie-

bling Abroad," *The Nation,* Oct. 7, 1978; and Raymond Sokolov, *Wayward Reporter* (1980). Obituaries are in the *New York Times* and *Herald Tribune,* Dec. 29, 1963; *New Yorker,* Jan. 11, 1964.]

WILLIAM MCCANN

LLEWELLYN, KARL NICKERSON (May 22, 1893–Feb. 13, 1962), legal philosopher and teacher, was born in West Seattle, Wash., the son of William Henry Llewellyn and Janet George. Two years later the family moved to New York City. After graduating from Boys' High School, Llewellyn entered the Realgymnasium in Schwerin, Mecklenburg, Germany, and in 1911 he returned to the United States and enrolled in Yale College. In the summer of 1914 he was studying at the University of Paris when war erupted. A lifelong admirer of German culture, he promptly enlisted in the German Army (78th Prussian Infantry). He was wounded in action near Ypres, and became the only American ever awarded the Iron Cross (second class). Discharged because of the injury, Llewellyn returned to Yale, where he graduated Phi Beta Kappa in 1915. He then entered Yale Law School, where he received the LL.B. (1918) and the J.D. (1920).

Llewellyn began his teaching career while at Yale Law School. After receiving the J.D., he practiced in New York City with Shearman and Sterling, but in 1922 returned to Yale as an assistant professor in the Law School. In 1924, he married Elizabeth Sanford. In 1925, Llewellyn went to Columbia Law School, where he held the Betts professorship of jurisprudence from 1930 until 1951. He married Emma Corstvet in 1933, and Soia Mentschikoff on Oct. 31, 1946. He had no children.

Through most of his career Llewellyn was active in professional affairs, especially the Conference of Commissioners on Uniform State Laws, in which he represented New York State from 1926 to 1951, and of which he was a life member. Through the conference he drafted the Uniform Trust Receipts Act and the Uniform Chattel Mortgage Act. His most important work in this area was the Uniform Commercial Code (UCC). Llewellyn served as reporter beginning in 1944, and is recognized as the code's chief architect. Ultimately the UCC was adopted by forty-nine states. He served on the Commission on the Rights, Liberties and Responsibilities of the American Indian and on the editorial board of the American Law Institute. In 1950 he was president of the Association of American Law Schools.

Llewellyn greatly enjoyed teaching, and his

students responded with affection and admiration. William O. Douglas, a colleague at Columbia, recalled: "There were not many hours in a week when a student was not facing him across a desk stacked so high with books that one could hardly see over the barricade. Students were the spice of his life. His excitement came with the growth of their minds and the flowering of their curiosities. He pushed them to the utmost—teasing, taunting, prodding—flattering, cajoling, scolding."

One of Llewellyn's most popular books, *The Bramble Bush* (1930), consisted of lectures he gave in his course to first-year students, introducing them to the mystery, flavor, and challenge of the law. It went through numerous reprintings, and his wit and humanity, as well as his devotion to the law, were readily apparent in its pages.

Llewellyn started from a firm grounding in traditional commercial law—his first book was *Cases and Materials on the Law of Sales* (1930) —and he retained this interest through his many years of work for uniform commercial codes. But he explored areas far beyond the then-normal boundaries of the law, and he pioneered in cross-disciplinary work. With anthropologist E. A. Hoebel he wrote *The Cheyenne Way* (1941), an examination of where custom and tradition end and formal law begins.

One of Llewellyn's most admired scholarly books was his study of the appellate process, *The Common Law Tradition: Deciding Appeals* (1960). One critic called it "the most emphatically useful work ever written on the subject of common-law appeals." Many lawyers and judges were initially confused by the work, believing that Llewellyn was arguing that judges could intuitively predict four out of five decisions without recourse to complex legal precedents. What Llewellyn did, though, was to examine style and content of numerous state and federal appellate decisions, and find a certain predictability, which he did not disapprove, in most of them.

This analysis derived in large part from the realism school of jurisprudence that Llewellyn and Jerome Frank led in the 1930's. Most of the important essays Llewellyn wrote in this area were collected and published posthumously in *Jurisprudence: Realism, Theory and Practice* (1962). Realism emerged in 1930 as an alternative to the sociological jurisprudence advocated by Roscoe Pound. Applying some of the recent theories of behavioral scientists, Llewellyn distinguished between "paper rules" and "real rules." The former constituted the acknowl-

edged doctrines of the times, what the statute books said the law was; the latter were the real practices of judges and other government officials who made the law flesh and blood. Drawing a great deal upon Oliver Wendell Holmes, Jr.'s interpretation of the common law, Llewellyn and Frank to some extent imposed an amoral context upon judicial decision making. The law, they argued, reflected not the accumulated wisdom and morality of the nation but the active predilections of its magistrates.

Realism enjoyed much popularity in the 1930's, when the Great Depression made a mockery of many social theories based on high and noble motives. The law, the realists seemed to say, is what men in power make of it. With the rise of fascism, critics attacked this new jurisprudence as little different from the amoral "might makes right" of the fascists. In 1940, Llewellyn partly recanted, conceding that ultimately all legal decisions rested on "the fundamental principles of Natural Law."

In 1951, Llewellyn moved to the University of Chicago Law School, where his wife was a member of the faculty, and taught there until his death. He died in Chicago.

[Llewellyn's papers are at the University of Chicago Law School, and are described in William Twining, ed., *The Karl Llewellyn Papers* (1968). See Yale College Class of 1915, *35th Annual Report* (1952). See Yale College Class of 1915, *35th Annual Report* (1952). Obituaries are in the *New York Times*, Feb. 15, 1962; *University of Chicago Law Review* (Summer 1962); and *Yale Law Journal* (April 1962).]

MELVIN I. UROFSKY

LOEWI, OTTO (June 3, 1873–Dec. 25, 1961), neurobiologist and neuropharmacologist, was born in Frankfurt am Main, Germany, the son of Jacob Loewi, a wine merchant, and of Anna Willstädter. He was educated at the Frankfurt City Gymnasium, where the curriculum emphasized Latin (nine years) and Greek (six years). In his autobiographical sketch he wrote that he valued this part of his education because it shaped his attitude toward life and because it taught him to learn without regard for immediate application. He recalled that his grades in physics and mathematics were poor.

Loewi decided that he wanted to study the history of art. His family, dismayed by such an impractical ambition, sent him to study medicine. He entered the University of Strassburg in 1891, but often strayed from his medical studies to attend lectures on German architecture and philosophy. It required a substantial effort at the end of his fourth term to prepare for the first medical examination, and he was grateful for a low pass.

In 1893, Loewi transferred to Munich, where he immersed himself in the music of Richard Wagner and in the art galleries. Medical studies still took second place. In the fall of 1894 he returned to Strassburg. He was required to obtain an attendance signature from Bernard Naunyn, professor of internal medicine, but he arrived after the lecture had begun. Forced to wait, Loewi found himself fascinated with the subject and the next day arrived thirty minutes early to secure a front seat. Suddenly he became deeply interested in experimental medicine. His thesis dealt with the effects of metabolic inhibitors on the isolated frog heart. He received the M.D. in 1896.

Loewi became an assistant in medicine at Strassburg, but after a frustating time tending patients dying of tuberculosis or pneumonia, for which there was no effective treatment, he decided to focus on basic science. In 1898 he was accepted as an assistant to Hans H. Meyer, then professor of pharmacology at Marburg. Loewi's first work there concerned the effects of phlorizin, an inhibitor of glucose uptake, on the kidney. He served as privatdocent in Marburg, 1900–1905.

At that time it was thought that intact proteins were essential in the diet, because animals could not live on a protein-free diet supplemented with an amino acid mixture obtained by the hydrolysis of a single protein. In 1901, Loewi read a paper describing the properties of a tryptic digest of the pancreas, in which the different proteins were broken down into amino acids. He was immediately struck with the idea that animals might survive on the amino acids obtained by breaking down an entire organ.

The experiments were difficult. The digested pancreas was unpalatable, and the dogs had to be coaxed to eat. But it became clear that animals could thrive without intact protein as long as they received an adequate mixture of amino acids. This was a major advance in nutrition and established Loewi's reputation.

In 1904, Meyer was called to the chair of pharmacology in Vienna, and Loewi followed him as an associate professor in 1905. He was studying the response to starvation. It was known that during starvation the liver is rapidly depleted of glycogen. Loewi found that the glycogen was quickly restored when the animal was injected with the hormone epinephrine. These experiments focused his interest on the sympathetic nervous system, since it was known that many of the effects of epinephrine could be mimicked by stimulating sympathetic nerves. The phenomenon was not properly understood because it was generally believed that the nerves acted on the organs they innervated by the flow of electrical currents. Why should a chemical produce similar effects?

In 1907, while vacationing in Switzerland, Loewi met Guida Henrietta Goldschmiedt, daughter of Guido Goldschmiedt, professor of chemistry at Prague. They were married on Apr. 5, 1908; they had four children. In 1909, Loewi accepted the chair of pharmacology in Graz, Austria. The move brought substantial teaching obligations, but he continued work on carbohydrate metabolism and also returned to the study of the effects of drugs on the isolated frog heart.

In 1920, Loewi awoke at 3 A.M. one morning with an idea. He dressed, went to the laboratory, and dissected two frog hearts. Ringer's solution was placed in each heart to keep them alive. The first heart was prepared with a length of the vagus nerve attached. For many years it had been known that stimulating the vagus slows the heartbeat. He stimulated the vagus until the first heart stopped. Immediately he took the Ringer's solution from the first heart and transferred it to the second, which promptly slowed. Loewi concluded that the nerve stimulation released a chemical that could be used to slow the second heart. Soon he and his colleagues had evidence that the chemical, which they first called *Vagusstoff*, was acetylcholine. The idea of chemical transmission across synapses is one of the bases of neurobiology.

Loewi's report of the work was greeted skeptically. In fact, the experiment is remarkably difficult to reproduce. Most species of frog have a high concentration in their hearts of an enzyme that destroys acetylcholine, so none persists long enough to be transferred. Finally, in 1926, Loewi was invited to demonstrate at the International Congress of Physiology in Stockholm. The demonstration worked eighteen times out of eighteen trials on the same pair of hearts. In 1936, Loewi shared the Nobel Prize in Physiology or Medicine with his friend Sir Henry Dale, who had shown that acetylcholine is the transmitter between motor nerve and skeletal muscle.

On Mar. 11, 1938, Loewi was again awakened at 3 A.M., this time by Nazi storm troopers, who took him and his two younger sons to jail, where they joined the other male Jews of Graz. Eventually a bargain was struck. In return for all of his property, including his Nobel award, he and his two sons were allowed to leave Germany. He joined his oldest son and daughter who had been out of Austria at the time of the Anschluss. His wife remained behind, a pauper, until 1941, when she had completed the transfer of a family property in Italy to the German government.

After teaching in Brussels and spending three months in England, Loewi in 1940 accepted a post as research professor of pharmacology at New York University School of Medicine, a position he occupied for the rest of his life. He became a United States citizen in 1946.

In New York, Loewi's circumstances were much reduced, but his spirit was unconquerable. He reflected that if he had stayed in Graz, he would soon have been retired; instead he found himself with an exciting new career. He also resumed experimental work. He usually spent summers at the Marine Biological Station at Woods Hole, Mass., where he especially delighted in talking to the students. After his wife's death in 1958, Loewi rarely left his home, but he was always eager to talk of science, art, the past, the future; to laugh at a favorite story; and to share a glass of kirsch and a macaroon. He died in New York City.

[Loewi's writings include "Über hormonale Übertragbarkeit der Herznervenwirkung," *Pflügers Archiv,* 1921; *From the Workshop of Discovery* (1953); "An Autobiographic Sketch," *Perspectives in Biology and Medicine,* Autumn 1960. Also see F. Lembeck and W. Giere, *Ein Lebensbild in Dokumenten* (1968). An obituary is in the *New York Times,* Dec. 27, 1961.]

WILLIAM VAN DER KLOOT

LONG, PERRIN HAMILTON (Apr. 7, 1899–Dec. 17, 1965), physician, was born in Bryan, Ohio, the son of James Wilkinson Long, a physician, and of Wilhelmina Lillian Kautsky. After graduating from Bryan High School in 1916, he entered the University of Michigan, but left in 1917 to join the American Field Service as an ambulance driver in France. When the United States entered the war, Long enlisted in the army, thus beginning an association with the military forces that continued, with occasional interruptions, throughout a great part of his career. In 1918 he was awarded the Croix de Guerre for bravery in action.

The following year, Long returned to the University of Michigan. On Sept. 6, 1922, he married Elizabeth D. Griswold, also a student at the university; they had two children. In 1924 he received the B.S. and M.D. degrees. He spent the next three years in Boston, the first as a fellow at the Thorndyke Memorial Laboratory and the remainder as an intern and resident physician at the Boston City Hospital. In 1927 he spent several months as a voluntary assistant at the Hygienic Institute in Freiburg, Germany, before joining the staff of the Rockefeller Institute. There, under the aegis of Simon Flexner and Peter Olitski, Long began his work in the field of infectious diseases. In 1929 he joined the faculty of the Johns Hopkins Medical School.

At Johns Hopkins, Long began his pioneering studies with Dr. Eleanor Bliss on the sulfonamide drugs, of which he had learned in England in 1936. He and Bliss reported their preliminary laboratory and clinical findings in the autumn of that year. This report and their subsequent work on the sulfonamides as the first safe and effective antibacterial drugs, which effected a virtual revolution in the management of bacterial infections, brought rapid recognition; in 1940, Long was made professor and chairman of the Department of Preventive Medicine at Johns Hopkins. He also received a number of civic and professional awards.

World War II interrupted Long's academic pursuits. Because of his knowledge of the chemotherapy of infections, he was one of a small group of consultants flown to Pearl Harbor to advise the government on the care of casualties following the Japanese attack on Dec. 7, 1941. He returned to active duty in the army in 1942, and served as a medical consultant in the African and Mediterranean theaters of operation. Long retired from active military service with the rank of colonel and was awarded the Legion of Merit. In recognition of service to the Allies, he received an honorary Order of the British Empire in 1945 and was elected to the Royal College of Physicians the following year. In 1951 he was made a chevalier of the Legion of Honor.

After the war Long returned to Johns Hopkins to teach and to continue his investigations of antimicrobial drugs. In 1951 he became chairman of the Department of Medicine of the newly organized State University of New York Downstate Medical Center in Brooklyn, N.Y. There he turned his energies to teaching and administration, for which he had an extraordinary capacity. He also served in many consultative capacities, working for the National Research Council, the Veterans Administration, the Food and Drug Administration, the Public Health Service, and the U.S. Army, which promoted him to the rank of brigadier general in the reserves. In addition, he was editor of *Medical Times* and *Resident Physician.*

In 1958 a laryngectomy forced temporary curtailment of his activities, but Long was soon back at his busy routine. Although he could communicate well with an artificial larynx, he felt that he had become a less effective teacher. He retired from academic life in 1961, but continued his two editorships. He traveled widely and wrote on both the scientific and the sociological aspects of medicine. He died on Chappaquiddick Island, Mass.

Long was a firm believer in individualism and in accomplishment through hard work. He was one of the new generation of medical academicians who spent their entire careers as teachers and investigators. He possessed both physical and intellectual courage, and never veered from his convictions if he believed them to be right.

[Long's writings include, with E.A. Bliss, "Para-Amino-Benzene-Sulfonamide and Its Derivatives . . . ," *Journal of the American Medical Association,* Jan. 2, 1937, and *The Clinical and Experimental Use of Sulfanilamide, Sulfapyridine and Allied Compounds* (1939); and *A-B-C's of Sulfonamide and Antibiotic Therapy* (1948). On Long's life, see "A Verray Parfit Praktisour," *Medical Times,* June 1966. An obituary in is the *New York Times,* Dec. 18, 1965.

ROBERT AUSTRIAN

LORD, JEREMY. See REDMAN, BENJAMIN RAY.

LORRE, PETER (June 26, 1904–Mar. 23, 1964), film actor, was born Laszlo Lowenstein, in Rosenberg, Hungary, the son of Alvis and Elvira Lowenstein. His father was a prosperous tradesman. In 1908 the family moved to Vienna. After completing his secondary education, Lorre left home at age seventeen to become an actor. He appeared in a number of amateur productions in Vienna, and in 1924 he obtained his first job, in Breslau, Germany. In 1928 he moved to Berlin, where he won roles as young men with serious sexual problems.

Lorre played the lead in director Fritz Lang's film *M* (1931). This film, based on the case of a Düsseldorf child murderer, won worldwide renown for both Lang and Lorre, who made the role of a compulsive murderer frightening, repellent, and, at the conclusion of the film, curiously sympathetic. By turns whining and groveling and indignant, Lorre caught the weakness, desperation, and self-loathing of the character so perfectly that he became more than a villain; indeed, the film's plea that such creatures should be treated with understanding became a dramatically valid one.

Despite his success in *M,* Lorre refused many offers from Hollywood. If he had accepted them, he said in 1934, "after playing villains of

fifty for a year or two I would have been through." Although he was well aware that his short stature, large soft eyes, almost Oriental countenance, and curiously nasal voice and intonations doomed him to character parts, he did not want to be typed. Nor was he interested primarily in money: "Acting, if money is its only object, is childish and undignified work. There must be some higher motive." Although he could not always adhere to his standards, Lorre tried, at least in his younger years, to force producers to give him more challenging roles. He appeared in more than seventy films.

Lorre married Cecilia Lvovsky in 1933. After the release of *M,* he played in films in Germany, Austria, France, and, although his English was not very good, in England, where in 1934 he acted in Alfred Hitchcock's *The Man Who Knew Too Much.* Lorre played one of a band of spies who kidnap a young girl and plan to assassinate a foreign dignitary. He invested his part with a strange, melancholy, and desperate air, an unusual quality in such a melodramatic role. In later years his film parts often reflected his sardonic, witty, debonair, and sarcastic self. Sometimes Lorre played his roles for humor, but at other times he allowed himself to whine in a peculiarly neurotic way. He was capable of depicting the most evil of villains, yet in other films could be cute and lovable. His mannerisms were individual enough to make him the darling of many an impersonator.

Lorre went to America in 1934 when Harry Cohn of Columbia Pictures made an offer that allowed him some artistic freedom. But Columbia had no property for him, and after several months Metro-Goldwyn-Mayer borrowed Lorre for *Mad Love* (1935), directed by Karl Freund in the expressionistic manner. Lorre played a brilliant but sexually unfulfilled plastic surgeon whose only pleasure was to watch an actress be tortured on stage in a Grand Guignol production. He shaved his head for the part and allowed Freund to be merciless with the lighting. Never did Lorre seem more repulsive. His difficult scenes were played with great intensity and conviction and demonstrated, both to audiences and to Hollywood executives, that he was extremely talented. Although the role was not written sympathetically, Lorre gave his part some humanity and pathos. Lorre had accepted the lead in *Mad Love* with the provision that Cohn would allow him to appear as Raskolnikov in *Crime and Punishment* (1935), directed by Josef von Sternberg. He felt that Hollywood was growing up and would accept such serious works. But the film was only moderately successful. Here he once again plays a brilliant but disturbed person. The actor's hair had grown back partially, and he had become thin. He maintained this low weight for almost two decades.

Lorre made *The Secret Agent* for Alfred Hitchcock in England (1936). Upon his return to America, he did some radio work and then appeared in *Crack-Up* (1937). Next he played the Japanese detective Mr. Moto in a series of films. The first of these was released in January 1938, and in that year four additional films were made. Lorre could play many different nationalities; in his long career he appeared as Germans, Hungarians, Russians, Frenchmen, Mexicans, Arabs, and Japanese.

In 1941 Lorre was cast as a strange gentleman crook, along with Sidney Greenstreet, in *The Maltese Falcon*. The contrast of these two continental rogues, the one big and fat and the other small and thin, made good box office. They did for foreign intrigue what Stan Laurel and Oliver Hardy did for comedy. Audiences loved them and they appeared again in *Casablanca* (1942), followed by *Passage to Marseille* (1944), *The Mask of Dimitrios* (1944), *Three Strangers* (1946), and *The Verdict* (1946).

Lorre had always been on the edge of the horror film and in 1940 had joined Bela Lugosi and Boris Karloff in *You'll Find Out*. He starred in *The Face Behind the Mask* (1941) and later returned to the genre in *The Beast with Five Fingers* (1946).

During World War II, Lorre played Nazi and Japanese villains as well as "good guys." In *The Invisible Agent* (1942) he portrayed a Japanese diplomat. In 1943 he appeared as a sadistic jailer in *The Cross of Lorraine*, and the next year he played the alcoholic, semicomic surgeon in *Arsenic and Old Lace*. In *The Mask of Dimitrios* he played a nonvillainous writer.

Lorre was divorced in 1945, and on May 26 of that year he married Kaaren Verne, a former actress. They separated in 1950 and were divorced in 1953. In 1950 Lorre went to Germany to direct himself in a film called *Der Verloren* (*The Lost One*). It is ironic that he might have grown weary of being typecast, yet decided to portray a neurotic killer once again. The film was not a success.

Lorre grew ill, and when he recovered, he suffered from high blood pressure and obesity. His short stature and wide girth made him resemble a malevolent gnome. Indeed, his facial expression became so melancholy that, like a clown, he seemed comical. When he could find work, he no longer played the more elegant parts he had once had.

Lorre married twenty-seven-year-old Annemarie Stoldt on June 23, 1953; they had one daughter. Soon afterward he appeared in John Huston's offbeat comedy *Beat the Devil* (1954). But his career was now quickly fading. He was used by Walt Disney in *20,000 Leagues Under the Sea* (1954) in a minor part. He played an untalented director in *The Buster Keaton Story* (1957) and one of the three Communists in *Silk Stockings* (1957), a musical remake of *Ninotchka*. The vision of a short and rotund Lorre doing a cossack dance on his knees was funny to some people, but sad to those who recalled his immense talent. He played a caricature of his former serious roles in *Tales of Terror* (1962), *The Raven* (1963), and *Comedy of Terrors* (1964). His sense of humor sustained him in these comic-horror productions.

In 1963 Lorre separated from his third wife. He died in Hollywood.

[There is little written information on Lorre. But see Calvin Thomas Beck, *Heroes of the Horrors* (1975); and various articles in *Variety*. An obituary is in the *New York Times*, Mar. 24, 1964.]

ARTHUR LENNIG

LOUIS, MORRIS (Nov. 28, 1912–Sept. 7, 1962), artist, was born Morris Louis Bernstein in Baltimore, Md., the son of Louis Bernstein and Celia Luckman. His father, a Russian immigrant, worked in a factory and later owned a small grocery store. From 1918 to 1929 Louis attended Baltimore public schools and Baltimore City College. Between 1929 and 1933 he studied at the Maryland Institute of Fine and Applied Arts but did not complete his degree.

During 1929–1954, Louis did little that indicated his later greatness as an artist. In the 1930's he took odd jobs and painted in a Baltimore studio. From 1936 to 1940 he lived in New York City. In 1939 he exhibited a piece entitled *Broken Bridge*, at the New York World's Fair, and he was a member of the Works Progress Administration easel-painting project (1937–1940). He dropped the name Bernstein while in New York. In 1940 he returned to Baltimore to paint and teach privately. On July 4, 1947, Louis married Marcella Siegel; they had no children. His work was exhibited along with that of other Maryland artists at the Baltimore Museum of Art each year from 1948 to 1952. In 1952, Louis moved to Washington, D.C., where he took a post as an instructor at the Washington Workshop Center.

The turning point in Louis' career came in 1952, when he became friends with Kenneth

Noland. Noland had studied with Clement Greenberg at Black Mountain College in North Carolina, and he took Louis to New York City to visit Greenberg. There Louis met Helen Frankenthaler and saw her painting *Mountains and Sea* (1952). Both Louis and Noland were impressed with the work. Louis returned to Washington and began working energetically. In January 1954, Greenberg visited Washington and selected three of Louis' new pictures for an exhibit at the Kootz Gallery in New York City. These pieces showed the influence on Louis of Frankenthaler, Jackson Pollock, and Willem de Kooning. That winter, Louis sent nine large canvases to New York City for his first one-man show.

These paintings were called "Veils." Rejecting cubist emphasis on sculptural elements, Louis placed color in an eerie succession of large washes. This experimentation was one of the consequences of his contact with Frankenthaler. According to Michael Fried, "Louis ranks among the supreme masters of color in modern art."

Louis' method of painting was unique. He worked in a small room at home, too small for full extension of his large canvases. One of his "Veils" (*Saraband*, 1959) was more than eight by twelve feet. He therefore began the practice of working on his paintings in sections. (Many times he would cut the unsized canvas after the picture was completed.) In 1948, Louis had begun working with Magna colors (acrylic paints) manufactured by a friend. By 1954 he was staining unprimed and unstretched cotton duck with diluted paint, allowing its flow over the canvas to be controlled by folding and turning the loose fabric.

Louis came to public attention in the late 1950's. His large paintings and daring use of color captured the eye of the viewer. He created a new, more complete and autonomous abstract painting style. His interplay of simplicity and intensity of feeling was remarkable. Reacting against abstract expressionism, Louis became a "color-field painter" by blending subject matter into background.

In November 1957, Louis had a one-man show at Martha Jackson Gallery in New York City after Jackson and Michel Tapié had journeyed to Washington to see Louis' work. Tapié acquired one painting for himself and sent a second to Japan for the Osaka Festival (April 1958). Louis was unhappy about the Martha Jackson Gallery show and later destroyed most of these paintings, returning to earlier themes at the suggestion of Greenberg.

While the chronology of Louis' work is sketchy, it is known that between 1957 and 1959 he painted a new series of "Veils." A set of twenty-three of these were shown in a one-man exhibit at French and Company in New York City in 1959. Louis also exhibited with his students at the Psychiatric Institute, University of Maryland, that year and was praised for his teaching. In 1960, Louis signed a contract with agent Lawrence Rubin. Louis showed five paintings at the London Institute of Contemporary Arts. He also had one-man shows at the Galleria dell' Ariete in Milan, Italy, and at Bennington College, Vermont. In 1961, Louis had a one-man show at Galerie Neufville, Paris, and took part in two London group shows. He held a one-man show at André Emmerich Gallery in New York City in the same year.

Louis shifted from doing "Veils" to "Unfurleds" and "Stripes." During these latter years he paid close attention to the manner in which his paintings were stretched and mounted. He felt that the integrity of his work would be preserved regardless of how the pictures were framed and hung. As a result, his work departed from the conventional horizontal plane that had typified his earlier "Veils."

A perfectionist, Louis was dedicated to his profession. It was not unusual for him to destroy an entire year's output because it did not please him. Years of working in cramped quarters stooped over unstretched canvases took a toll. Louis worked long hours and lived for painting, leaving little time for anything else. He had few friends except painters, and he demanded the same sort of perfection of mind from friends that he demanded of himself. He died in Washington, D.C.

[A microfilm of Louis' papers is in the Archives of American Art, New York, Boston, Washington, D.C., Detroit, and San Francisco. See Guggenheim Museum, *Morris Louis 1912–1962* (1963); Museum of Fine Arts, Boston, *Morris Louis, 1912–1962* (1967); Michael Fried, *Morris Louis* (1970); Arts Council of Great Britain, *Morris Louis* (1974); and Kenworth Moffett, *Morris Louis in the Museum of Fine Arts* (1979). Obituaries are in *Art News*, Oct. 1962, and the *New York Times*, Sept. 8, 1962.]

SPENCER J. MAXCY

LOVEJOY, ARTHUR ONCKEN (Oct. 10, 1873–Dec. 30, 1962), philosopher and historian of ideas, was born in Berlin, Germany, the son of Wallace William Lovejoy, a medical student from Boston, and Sara Agnes Oncken. He was christened Arthur Schauffler Lovejoy, but later changed his middle name to Oncken, in memory of his mother. The family moved to Boston, Mass., in 1874, after Wallace Lovejoy completed his medical studies. In April 1875, Sara Lovejoy died of an accidental self-administered overdose of drugs, and her husband subsequently left medicine for the Protestant Episcopal ministry. Following his marriage to Emmeline Dunton in 1881, he moved his family to Ohio, to New Jersey, and then to Germantown, Pa.

Young Lovejoy graduated from the Germantown Academy in 1891. That year the Lovejoys moved to Oakland, Calif., and he entered the University of California at Berkeley. From the time he took his first philosophy course from George Holmes Howison at Berkeley (1894), philosophy became the focus of his academic career because, he explained, "in studying philosophy a man is not committed to any particular view whatever, beyond a desire for reasonableness and an interest in the history of thought." Although philosophy provided an intellectual alternative to religion, he agreed with his father's injunctions to serve Christ through social service. He helped establish a settlement house in Oakland, beginning an association with the settlement movement that would last for twenty years.

Lovejoy received an A.B. from the University of California in 1895. With his father's reluctant approval, he then entered the Harvard Graduate School, where Josiah Royce and William James were the major influences on his development as a philosopher. He valued Royce's "subtlety, flexibility, [and] open-mindedness," but became increasingly dissatisfied with his absolute idealism. Lovejoy doubted that any absolute could contain all the diversity and development of the actual world. His initial view of James was less favorable, for he considered him "rather disappointing" as a teacher. After leaving Harvard, however, Lovejoy drew from James many of the ideas on time, development, and pluralism central to his own philosophy. In 1897 Lovejoy received an M.A. and in 1898–1899 he studied comparative religions at the Sorbonne. He never completed the Ph.D.

Lovejoy began teaching philosophy at Stanford University in 1899. In 1900–1901 he became involved in the controversy surrounding the dismissal of the economist and sociologist Edward Alsworth Ross. Convinced that academic freedom had been denied Ross, Lovejoy submitted his resignation. He believed academic freedom must be maintained to preserve "the dignity of the teacher's profession [and]

the leadership and social usefulness of the universities."

In the decade after leaving Stanford, Lovejoy taught at Washington University, St. Louis (1901–1907), Columbia University (1907–1908), the University of Missouri at Columbia (1908–1910), and finally Johns Hopkins University, where he remained from 1910 until his retirement in 1938. He never married.

During that decade Lovejoy was deeply involved in settlement work, which he now saw as a "mission of the trained to the untrained." Christian service had, by 1910, become part of the progressive effort to employ the knowledge of the universities in the service of society.

Lovejoy published widely in the history of ideas and in philosophy. Attracted to the history of religious thought, he concentrated on the introduction of ideas about time and development into Judeo-Christian thinking. His studies of European ideas led to his discovery of the long history of evolutionary thought before Charles Darwin. In philosophy Lovejoy was a sharp critic of the pragmatic philosophies of William James and John Dewey. His criticism and his method of careful discrimination of closely related ideas is best exemplified in "The Thirteen Pragmatisms" (*Journal of Philosophy*, 1908). He also continued his attack on philosophies of the absolute by concluding, in 1909, that the eternal was obsolescent.

Following his appointment at Johns Hopkins, Lovejoy devoted more time to research and writing and to his activities in the academic profession, and less to social service. He was instrumental in the formation of the American Association of University Professors (AAUP) in 1915. He served as its first secretary and was its president in 1919. He wrote much of the AAUP's first report on academic freedom and tenure in 1915, and investigated several early cases of alleged infringement of academic freedom.

Lovejoy quickly concluded that Germany threatened American freedom in World War I. As early as 1914 he warned of the German danger in numerous essays. After the United States entered the war in 1917, Lovejoy enthusiastically worked with both the War Department and with private organizations, such as the National Security League and the YMCA. Although sensitive to the misuse of scholarship in war, he nonetheless lent his support to several dubious activities, including the writing of propaganda tracts for the National Security League and the Maryland Council of Defense, designed to sell the war and to rouse hatred of the enemy.

Lovejoy was elected president of the American Philosophical Association (APA) in 1916. In his presidential address, "On Some Conditions of Progress in Philosophical Inquiry," he enunciated key elements of his philosophy. He believed that philosophers should contribute to the settlement of vital issues in human thought by making philosophy more scientific and by developing habits of cooperation to settle philosophic controversies rationally and conclusively.

The 1920's was a decade of scholarship in history and philosophy that led to the publication of Lovejoy's major works, *The Revolt Against Dualism* (1930) and *The Great Chain of Being* (1936). *The Revolt Against Dualism*, originally given as the Carus lectures of the APA in 1928, was Lovejoy's defense of epistemological and psychophysical dualism against a variety of monisms. Epistemological dualism attempted to explain how we know anything. He believed that we lack the capacity for direct knowledge of the world and, hence, that all knowledge is indirect. Indirect knowledge is possible, for ideas mediate between the object as it exists and the perception of the object. Lovejoy also defended psychophysical dualism, which maintained that the world is made up of both material objects and minds, and that neither is to be viewed merely as a manifestation of the other. When this was linked with epistemological dualism, Lovejoy had a coherent account of the universe.

Lovejoy's dualistic views came under attack in the early twentieth century from pragmatists such as John Dewey, the new realists, and others. Lovejoy repeatedly defended dualism against these philosophers, who held that knowledge can be direct or that the world is made of one kind of substance.

In the history of ideas Lovejoy concentrated on eighteenth- and early nineteenth-century thought, especially ideas about evolution, human nature, and the work of the Enlightenment and Romantic thinkers. This work culminated in 1933 in the William James lectures at Harvard, published as *The Great Chain of Being*. Lovejoy discovered three seminal ideas that had provided much of the framework of Western thought since Plato, the ideas of plenitude, continuity, and gradation. By the eighteenth century these ideas had coalesced into the idea of the Great Chain of Being, a chain stretching from God to the lowest creature, in which all the links must be realized and which was characterized by minute gradations between the links.

The chain of being at its most grandiose implied a static conception of the universe, but new discoveries in biology and paleontology in the eighteenth century undermined its permanent and absolute character. By the early nineteenth century, ideas of development and evolution began to replace the chain of being with the idea of becoming. The moral implication of this echoed Lovejoy's early work; the absolute was obsolescent and the world was developing and evolving. *The Great Chain of Being* clearly exemplified Lovejoy's method of tracing the biography of a "unit-idea," a seminal idea in the history of thought. In 1939–1940 he helped establish the *Journal of the History of Ideas* to foster the study of ideas in their historical context.

Lovejoy turned again to public affairs in the 1930's. In 1933 he warned Americans of the danger Hitler posed to world freedom. After retiring from Johns Hopkins in 1938, he became involved in several organizations—the Maryland Committee for Concerted Peace Efforts, the Maryland Committee for Non-Participation in Japanese Aggression, and the Maryland Chapter of the Committee to Defend America by Aiding the Allies—opposed to fascist aggression and favoring American aid to the Allies after the outbreak of war in 1939. During World War II, Lovejoy worked with organizations such as the American Historical Association to foster discussion and rational consideration of political and foreign policy issues. He served on the University of Maryland Board of Regents from 1951 to 1955. He also supported the national efforts to keep Communists from teaching on university faculties, believing that they endangered academic freedom.

Lovejoy continued his scholarship into his eighth decade. He revised two lecture series that were published as *The Reason, the Understanding and Time* (1961) and *Reflections on Human Nature* (1961). In the latter he traced eighteenth-century ideas about human nature and set forth his own ideas on human nature and ethics. He argued that the desire to be praised, the desire for self-esteem, motivated behavior, and he proposed to employ this desire to motivate ethical behavior. Lovejoy pursued his studies even after his sight failed in the late 1950's. He died in Baltimore.

[The Lovejoy Collection, more than 200 boxes of letters and manuscripts, is in the Eisenhower Library of Johns Hopkins University. Books by Lovejoy not mentioned in the text are *Primitivism and Related Ideas in Antiquity* (1935); *Essays in the History of Ideas* (1948); and *The Thirteen Pragmatisms and*

Other Essays (1963). The only full-scale biography is Daniel J. Wilson, *Arthur O. Lovejoy and the Quest for Intelligibility* (1980). Special journal issues are *Journal of the History of Ideas*, Oct. 1948, and *Philosophy and Phenomenological Research*, June 1963. Also see George Boas, "A. O. Lovejoy: Reason-in-Action," *American Scholar*, Autumn 1960; and Lewis S. Feuer, "Arthur O. Lovejoy," *American Scholar*, Summer 1977.]

DANIEL J. WILSON

LOVEJOY, OWEN REED (Sept. 9, 1866– June 29, 1961), minister, propagandist, social worker, and reformer known as the "children's statesman," was born in Jamestown, Mich., a small farming community southwest of Grand Rapids, the son of Hiram Reed Lovejoy and Harriett Helen Robinson. After attending local schools, he was graduated with the B.A. from Albion College in 1891; three years later he received an M.A. there. On June 30, 1892, Lovejoy married Jennie Evalyn Campbell. They had five children, of whom only two sons survived to adulthood.

Lovejoy entered the ministry in 1891, and held pastorates at several Methodist churches in Michigan. In 1898 he was called to the First Congregational Church in Mount Vernon, N.Y. A man of broad interests who had a passionate concern for human rights, he helped organize a Sociological Club that invited noted speakers to its bimonthly meetings to discuss social and industrial problems.

During the anthracite coal strike of 1902, Lovejoy was sent by a group of Mount Vernon citizens to Pennsylvania to observe conditions. Traveling through the strife-torn region, he came to know the miners and their families— their homes, their work, and their problems. He returned to Mount Vernon with a graphic view of the scene and a grave concern about the injustices he had witnessed.

In July 1904, Lovejoy was sent by the newly created National Child Labor Committee (NCLC) to the Pennsylvania coal fields to survey child labor in the breakers. He already knew something of child labor. One of his arms bore the scar of an accident he had suffered as a boy while tending a machine in a Michigan factory, and he had witnessed the evil and its ugly effects during his earlier trip to the Pennsylvania coal-mining region. Nevertheless, his visit to the breakers in 1904 had a profound impact on him. He wrote in one of his later reports:

After I had seen those little boys day after day carrying their lunch pails to the breakers every morning like grown men, bending all day over dusty coal chutes, and finally dragging themselves home in the dark of night, I couldn't think of anything else. Sights like those cling to you. I dreamed about those boys.

As a result, in October 1904, when Lovejoy was asked to give up his comfortable Mount Vernon parish to become one of the NCLC's two paid full-time assistant secretaries, he quickly accepted the offer. He never regretted doing so, for he found in social work a welcome medium for the exercise of his passion for service to humanity that the church apparently did not offer. The NCLC became another pulpit for Lovejoy, especially after 1907, when he became its general secretary and traveled throughout the nation to present the child labor problem to the American people.

Lovejoy's earnestness and zeal were invaluable weapons in the war against child labor, not only in the nation's mines but also in its factories and fields and on its city streets. He was an extremely effective public speaker who also had an unusual ability to discover the facts, interpret them, and present them clearly in writing. In addition, he was an excellent administrator who assembled, and managed to maintain, a large and strong staff of field investigators, legislative agents, board members, and fund raisers. Although child labor had not been entirely eliminated when he resigned as head of the NCLC in 1926—indeed, the nation was in the midst of a bitter and ultimately unsuccessful effort to ratify a proposed child-labor amendment to the Constitution—conditions had improved enormously. Few had equaled his record of achievement with regard to America's exploited youngsters.

Lovejoy was an ardent champion of many other causes. He went to Lawrence, Mass., in 1912 to get a firsthand view of the situation during the famous textile workers' strike. He condemned the use of troops and the suppression of peaceful picketing by the workers in that troubled industrial center. That same year he chaired the National Conference of Charities and Correction's Committee on Standards of Living and Labor, which drafted a platform of minimum social standards for industry; it was incorporated in the 1912 Progressive party platform, and many of the reforms it proposed were enacted during Woodrow Wilson's administration. In recognition of these and numerous other efforts, Lovejoy was elected president of the National Conference of Social Work (NCSW) in 1920.

Lovejoy did not desert the nation's underprivileged children when he left the NCLC in 1926. He remained on the organization's board of trustees and its executive committee, and accepted a full-time position as secretary of the Children's Aid Society of New York, a post he held from 1927 to 1935. In the latter year he became associate director of the American Youth Commission, a private agency established under the auspices of the American Council on Education to formulate plans for the better care and education of American youth. Before retiring in 1939, Lovejoy directed the commission's field studies in Maryland, Indiana, and Texas. The reports of these studies are still considered social documents of major significance.

Jennie Lovejoy died in 1929. In 1937, Lovejoy married Kate Calkins Drake. After his retirement they lived on a farm in Biglerville, Pa., where he died.

A man of abiding faith and hope, Lovejoy believed deeply in the divine purposefulness of life lived in conformity with God's will. Regardless of their formal religious commitment, he had declared in his presidential address before the NCSW in 1920, social workers and reformers were among the devoted—the communion of those who performed good works. Both as a minister of the Gospel for thirteen years and as an advocate of social service and reform for the next thirty-five, Lovejoy spent his life "engaged in a grand conspiracy for the emancipation of the human race," to use his own words.

[There is no collection of Lovejoy's papers, nor is there any full-length study of his life. The NCLC papers, in the Manuscript Division of the Library of Congress, include a great deal of material about and by Lovejoy. So do the committee's annual reports, its periodicals—*Child Labor Bulletin* and *American Child*—and its many other publications, a complete collection of which is at the office of the National Committee on Employment of Youth, New York City. Also see "The New Child Labor Secretary," *Charities and the Commons*, Nov. 2, 1907; *New York Times*, Mar. 5, 1926; *Survey*, July 1939; and Walter I. Trattner, *Crusade for the Children* (1970). An obituary is in the *New York Times*, June 30, 1961.]
WALTER I. TRATTNER

LUCIANO, CHARLES ("LUCKY") (Nov. 11, 1897[?]–Jan. 26, 1962), vice racketeer and leader of organized crime, was born Salvatore Lucania in Lercara Friddi, Sicily, the son of Antonio Lucania and Rosalia Capporelli. His father worked in the sulfur mines. The family came to the United States when Salvatore was

nine and settled on the Lower East Side of Manhattan. He left school at age fourteen, with a fifth-grade education. Because of his constant truancy, in June 1911 he was sent to the Brooklyn Truant School for four months.

In 1914, Lucania began work in a hat factory at a salary of five dollars per week, the only honest job he ever held. After two years he quit and became involved in criminal activities. His first arrest, in June 1916, was for the illegal possession of heroin. He was convicted and served six months at the New York City Penitentiary on Blackwell's Island. Over the next twenty years he was arrested a number of times for various infractions, including illegal possession of heroin, unlawful possession of weapons, and robbery, but he was never convicted.

By 1926, Charles Luciano (after several arrests he had changed the name Salvatore to Charles, and by 1931 Lucania had been changed to Luciano) had reached crime's upper echelons. He had worked for Jack ("Legs") Diamond and was now working for Giuseppe ("Joe the Boss") Masseria, the leader of the Mafia in New York City. He handled bootlegging and hijacking for Masseria. His criminal career almost ended, though, on the night of Oct. 16, 1929, when he was "taken for a ride" by rivals, assaulted, and left for dead on Staten Island. Nevertheless, Luciano survived, and it has generally been assumed that he was given the sobriquet "Lucky" for this accomplishment. He also managed the East Side gangs for Masseria and the numbers racket. He was again involved with narcotics.

At the beginning of the 1930's, the younger men under Masseria were becoming dissatisfied with his Old World ways. Under the direction of Luciano (who was present for the event), "Joe the Boss" was murdered in a Coney Island restaurant on Apr. 15, 1931. A new "boss of all bosses"—Salvatore Maranzaro—appeared, but he could not keep control. On Sept. 10, 1931, Maranzaro was killed on Luciano's orders, and "Charlie Lucky" (as many now called him) became the leader of the New York City Mafia. He took a modernizing approach to Mafia activities. He put the New York Mafia into one family, his own; was willing to work with non-Italian gangsters; maintained and strengthened his association with such racketeers as Louis ("Lepke") Buchalter, Albert Anastasia, Frank Costello, Meyer Lansky, Joe Adonis, "Dutch Schultz," and Abner "Longie" Zwillman. Luciano placed racketeering on a business basis; he helped stop the indiscriminate killing of fellow gangsters; and he was instrumental in establishing the Unione Siciliano, a national Mafia organization.

Luciano was now at the height of his power. With Prohibition at an end, he added prostitution to his rackets. He lived in the Waldorf Towers under the name Charles Ross, wore expensive clothes, drove fast cars, and was seen with beautiful women; in short, he was the epitome of a movieland gangster of the time. His philosophy of life was "I never was a crumb, and if I have to be a crumb, I'd rather be dead." He defined "crumb" as someone "who works and saves and lays his money aside."

In June 1936 this life-style came to an end when, through the efforts of special prosecutor Thomas E. Dewey, Luciano's $12-million-a-year prostitution ring was shattered. He was convicted on sixty-two counts of compulsory prostitution and sentenced to thirty to fifty years in Clinton State Prison at Dannemora, N.Y. While in prison, though, he still wielded power in the underworld. At the beginning of 1946, Dewey, who had been elected governor, commuted Luciano's sentence provided the racketeer was deported to Italy. (Luciano had never become a United States citizen.) His assistance to the war effort was the reason given for the shortening of his sentence. Luciano had apparently passed the word to all waterfront workers in the New York City area to cooperate in preventing sabotage and to report any information about a possible enemy attack. He also seems to have persuaded Sicilian-born Italian-Americans to provide United States military intelligence with data in preparation for the Allied invasion of their homeland. There has been considerable controversy over the value of this assistance, and even whether it was given. The army, navy, and Office of Strategic Services deny receiving any help from him.

In February 1946, Luciano left the United States for Genoa, where he became involved in the Italian black market and the narcotics traffic. In 1951 the Kefauver Committee was told that the flow of heroin from Italy to the United States increased after Luciano was deported. He also kept his connection with organized crime in the United States through couriers who brought messages and cash. At the beginning of 1947, Luciano appeared in Havana, using the name Salvatore Lucania. He patronized the gambling facilities there and apparently met with many leaders of organized crime. When United States narcotics officials learned of his presence there, they put pressure on the Cuban government to deport him. After some resistance the Cuban authorities complied, and Luciano found himself back in Italy. During the ensuing years he lived chiefly in Naples, maintained his American underworld connections, gave handouts to other deportees, and engaged in several legitimate business enterprises, not all of which were financially successful. Until his death, United States narcotics authorities suspected him of heavy involvement in illegal drug traffic.

In November 1949 a Roman newspaper reporter wrote that Luciano had married a dancer, Igea Lissoni, but the couple denied the marriage. Luciano died in Naples.

[For additional material on Luciano's life, see Frederic Sondern, Jr., "Lucky Luciano's New Empire," *Reader's Digest,* Sept. 1951; Emmanuel Perlmutter, "Lucky Luciano's Story," *New York Times,* Feb. 14, 1954, sec. IV; obituary in *New York Times,* Jan. 27, 1962; "Unlucky at Last," *Newsweek,* Feb. 5, 1962; Martin Gosch and Richard Hammer, *The Last Testament of Lucky Luciano* (1974), which contains some errors; Rodney Campbell, *The Luciano Project* (1977). Also see *The Kefauver Committee Report on Organized Crime* (1951); Claire Sterling, "The Boys Who Made Bad," *Reporter,* Oct. 17, 1957; Peter Maas, *The Valachi Papers* (1968); Frederic Sondern, Jr., *Brotherhood of Evil: The Mafia* (1959); Jay Robert Nash, *Bloodletters and Badmen* (1973).]

ALLAN NELSON

LUHAN, MABEL DODGE (Feb. 26, 1879– Aug. 13, 1962), writer and patron of the arts, was born Mabel Ganson in Buffalo, N.Y., the daughter of Charles F. Ganson, an eccentric, nonpracticing lawyer, and Sara McKay Cook, who like her husband came from a rich banking family. Growing up with mismatched parents who had "no happiness to radiate to a solitary child," Mabel Ganson found solace in reading and play with neighborhood children. After attending St. Margaret's School in Buffalo, she spent a semester (1896) at Miss Graham's School in New York City and a summer in Europe (where she determined to "know everything, feel everything, be everything"). She studied a final year at the Chevy Chase School near Washington and "came out" in Buffalo in 1897.

Pressed into a secret marriage by Karl Kellog Evans, a young sportsman, Mabel Ganson remarried him two months later, on Oct. 3, 1900, in a large church wedding. "Always thinking, analyzing, dissecting," she had little in common with Evans, who was killed in a hunting accident before their son was a year old. A year and a half later, in 1904, to terminate an affair Mabel was having with her doctor, her mother sent her and the child off to Europe. On board the steamer she met Edwin S. Dodge, a young Boston architect who had studied at the Ecole des Beaux Arts. They were married on Nov. 4, 1904; they had no children. Remaining in Europe, the Dodges purchased, tastefully renovated, and furnished the Villa Curonia, near Florence, Italy. To their villa came many artists and writers, including André Gide and Gertrude and Leo Stein. Although occasionally depressed and often jealous of the attention given to others, Mabel Dodge attracted people and listened to them in a "fascinating, warm, magnetic and mysterious" way that often helped them formulate their thoughts and express their convictions. Without losing her own identity, she felt that to a remarkable degree she could feel and think as though she were the other person.

Responding to H. G. Wells's advice that she educate her son in America, Mabel Dodge moved in late 1912 to New York City, rented a large, sunny apartment on the edge of Greenwich Village, and had the rooms painted a then unconventional white to accentuate the furnishings she had collected. Shaking off a period of depression with the help of psychoanalysis in 1913, Dodge sought a life apart from her husband, from whom she was divorced in 1916. She helped with the final arrangements for the the Armory Show (a sensational exhibit of postimpressionist art), started holding weekly evening gatherings of bohemians, revolutionaries, and intellectuals, and suggested the Paterson Strike Pageant (a dramatization of the conflict between immigrant silk workers and New Jersey mill owners). Such events brought people together, publicized their causes, and made her a symbol of the avant-garde. A special Armory Show edition of *Arts and Decoration* reprinted Gertrude Stein's "cubist word" *Portrait of Mabel Dodge at the Villa Curonia* with an explanatory article written by Dodge. This prompted readers to search for Mabel Dodge in Stein's *Portrait* just as viewers searched for Marcel Duchamp's nude on the staircase in his celebrated cubist painting.

Dodge's famous evening gatherings were first suggested by Lincoln Steffens to "organize" the "unplanned activity around" her. They formed, he later insisted, "the only successful salon I have . . . seen in America." Besides Steffens, those attending included Walter Lippmann, Carl Van Vechten, Emma Goldman, Margaret Sanger, "Big Bill" Haywood, Max Eastman, Marsden Hartley, and Jo Davidson. While "the winds of promised change whistled and howled

. . . with little bitterness," diverse people traded ideas on announced topics in Dodge's white rooms and stayed for sumptuous midnight suppers.

Linking art and politics, the Paterson Pageant was a theatrical success held at Madison Square Garden on June 7, 1913, involving 2,000 Industrial Workers of the World in a moving reenactment of their strike. For Greenwich Villagers and for the 15,000 mostly working-class spectators who filled Madison Square Garden, it was a memorable rally, but it neither ended the strike nor made money. It displayed Dodge's organizational ability and acquainted her with John Reed, a young journalist who wrote the scenario and directed the production. After the pageant, accompanied by her son and an entourage, she left to summer in Europe, where she and Reed became lovers.

Short and full figured, Dodge was pretty in an unconventional way. She had a Mona Lisa smile that was sometimes followed by a "rippling windy laugh." Her chief quality was her ability to accelerate the atmosphere merely by listening. Besides Reed, who lived with her when they returned to New York City, Dodge had three other ardent admirers in her salon, and half a dozen others were very attached to her. At least eight artists and writers made her the subject of their work.

Realizing she had become a "mythological figure" and tiring of being asked to lend her name to every cause, Dodge spent most of her time after the fall of 1914 at Croton-on-Hudson, where she was a patron of Elizabeth Duncan's dance school. After her affair with Reed ended, she began a romance with Maurice Sterne, a painter, and occupied herself by writing a successful syndicated column for Hearst Publications. On Aug. 18, 1917, she married Sterne and in December joined him in New Mexico, where he had gone to paint the Pueblo Indians. When she visited Taos (which already had a small art colony), Mabel Sterne fell in love with its "gentle vibrating life" and longed to be part of its pueblo. She soon became particularly attracted to Antonio Lujan, an Indian. She and Lujan became a bridge between their cultures. They helped anthropologists and archaeologists gain insights into Pueblo ways and helped Pueblos maintain their rights in an eleven-year struggle over Pueblo lands. In 1922 they brought John Collier, who later became United States Commissioner of Indian affairs, to the Taos Pueblo to inform the Pueblos of the Bursum bill, which had passed the United States Senate. The bill transferred Pueblo land titles to white squatters and outlawed native religious practices. The Pueblos called together the Council of All the New Mexico Pueblos (its second meeting in 242 years). With the Pueblos and their friends united against it, the Bursum bill never became law.

Convinced that D. H. Lawrence could best describe the Pueblos and the area around Taos, Dodge persuaded him and his wife, Frieda, to move there. On Apr. 17, 1923, having obtained a divorce from Sterne, Dodge married Lujan. (She, however, spelled her name with an h.) Except for occasional visits to New York, California, and Mexico, she remained in Taos, living in a large, rambling adobe house, bordering Indian land, and sheltering relics of her past and artifacts of the area. Always a pacesetter (whether it was wearing turbans, decorating in white, being psychoanalyzed, or bobbing her hair), Luhan was soon again surrounded by writers and artists. Robinson Jeffers, Thornton Wilder, Georgia O'Keeffe, and others either occupied one of her half-dozen guest houses or clustered in Taos. Urged by her psychiatrist to keep busy, she assembled her letters and recorded her past. Sampling her remarkably objective story before it was published in four volumes as *Intimate Memories* (1933–1937), Lawrence (who alternated between quarreling with Luhan and being her warm, supportive friend) called it "the most serious 'confession' that ever came out of America." These volumes and the three other books she wrote, including one on Lawrence entitled *Lorenzo in Taos* (1932), give readers the essence of the decades she adorned. At the same time they contain a gallery of vivid and revealing portraits of herself and the complicated, creative people who were her friends. Luhan died in Taos.

[Luhan's papers are located in the Beinecke Rare Book and Manuscript Library, Yale University. Her books, in addition to those mentioned in text, are *Winter in Taos* (1935) and *Taos and Its Artists* (1947). For her full story, see Emily Hahn, *Mabel: A Biography of Mabel Dodge Luhan* (1977), and the obituary in the *New York Times*, Aug. 14, 1962.

See also Muriel Draper, *Music at Midnight* (1929); Mary Austin, *Earth Horizon* (1932); Granville Hicks, *John Reed: The Making of a Revolutionary* (1936); Hutchins Hapgood, *A Victorian in the Modern World* (1939); John Collier, *Indians of the Americas* (1947); Carl Van Vechten, *Fragments From an Unwritten Biography* (1955); Christopher Lasch, *The New Radicalism in America* (1965); Maurice Sterne, *Shadow and Light: The Life, Friends and Opinions of Maurice Sterne* (1965); Justin Kaplan, *Lincoln Steffens* (1974); Louis Rudnick, "The Unexpurgated Self:

A Critical Biography of Mabel Dodge Luhan" (Ph.D. diss., Brown University, 1977; and Robert E. Humphrey *Children of Fantasy: The First Rebels of Greenwich Village* (1978).]

OLIVE HOOGENBOOM

MacARTHUR, DOUGLAS (Jan. 26, 1880– Apr. 5, 1964), army officer, was born in Little Rock, Ark., the son of Arthur MacArthur II, an infantry captain, and Mary Pinkney Hardy, the ambitious, strong-willed daughter of an aristocratic family of Norfolk, Va. An extraordinary influence on MacArthur until her death in 1935, his mother alternately inspired and drove him to superior achievements to uphold the family tradition of distinction set by his brother, Arthur III, a navy captain whose abbreviated career was marked by brilliant service in the war with Spain and World War I; by his father, an outstanding combat leader in the Civil War, the Spanish-American War, and the Philippine insurrection; and by his paternal grandfather, a lieutenant governor (and briefly governor) of Wisconsin and federal judge. MacArthur often attributed his inspiration and success to his family heritage.

After attending the West Texas Military Academy at San Antonio (1893–1897), MacArthur entered the U.S. Military Academy in 1899. His academic record was one of the best ever attained there, and he was first captain of the cadet corps. Upon graduation in 1903, he was commissioned a second lieutenant in the Corps of Engineers.

In the next decade MacArthur served as a junior engineer officer in the Philippines, Wisconsin, Kansas, Michigan, Texas, and Panama; he was also an aide to his father in the Far East and to President Theodore Roosevelt. In addition he attended the Engineer School of Application (1906–1907), in Washington, D.C., receiving a degree in 1908, and worked in the Office of the Chief of Engineers. In 1913–1917, MacArthur was on the general staff of the War Department, with detached-duty assignments on an intelligence mission to Veracruz in 1914 and on public relations work in 1916.

Shortly after the United States entered World War I, MacArthur was promoted to colonel (transferring from engineers to infantry) and appointed chief of staff of the 42nd Infantry ("Rainbow") Division, which was newly organized from National Guard units of twenty-seven states. The division reached France in October 1917, and subsequently saw service in a relatively quiet sector near Baccarat, on the Lorraine front. As chief of staff, MacArthur was well-liked and respected not only by the division's commander, Major General Charles T. Menoher, for his judgment and administrative ability, but also by the soldiers, for his frequent visits to the trenches and his participation in raids. His boldness in battle and his distinctive attire (elegant sweaters, mufflers, and riding crop, but no helmet, gas mask, nor weapon) won him nicknames such as "Beau Brummel" and "D'Artagnan of the AEF."

In the successful Champagne-Marne defensive in July 1918, MacArthur, just promoted to brigadier general, was often found where the combat was fiercest, which prompted Menoher to call him "the bloodiest fighting man in this army." During the Aisne-Marne offensive several weeks later, MacArthur was given command of the 84th Brigade. He performed brilliantly in that operation, as well as in the reduction of the St. Mihiel salient in mid-September and the Meuse-Argonne offensive in late October and early November. He was wounded twice, and refused to leave his post on either occasion; he earned a large number of decorations and citations for his leadership and bravery under fire. Through most of November 1918, MacArthur was division commander. After the armistice he participated in the Rhine occupation, commanding the 84th Brigade in the Ahrweiler district of the American zone. He returned to the United States in April 1919.

In June 1919, MacArthur became superintendent of the U.S. Military Academy. This assignment was accompanied by promotion to the permanent rank of brigadier general; this advanced him above other officers of comparable seniority, many of whom were being reduced to their prewar permanent ranks of colonel or lower. Arriving at West Point at the lowest point in its history, MacArthur inaugurated changes in the tactical, athletic, and disciplinary systems. He also modernized and broadened the curriculum, including the introduction of liberal arts courses; and, despite reactionary faculty and alumni, elevated the school's academic standards. His reforms helped to bring West Point abreast of current pedagogy and made it a pacesetter among the world's military schools.

From 1922 to 1930, MacArthur served two tours of duty in the Philippines, the second as commander of the Philippine Department (1928–1930), and two tours as commander of corps areas in the United States. In 1925 he was promoted to major general, the youngest officer of that rank at the time. The same year MacArthur was also a member of the court-martial that convicted Brigadier General William Mitchell.

In 1928 he headed the U.S. Olympic Committee for the Amsterdam games. He had married Henrietta Louise Cromwell Brooks, a wealthy divorcee, on Feb. 14, 1922; they had no children. Seven years later they were divorced.

President Herbert Hoover appointed MacArthur army chief of staff in November 1930, with the temporary rank of general. Because of the worsening Great Depression, much of his time and energy went toward preserving the army's already meager manpower and matériel. When he left office in October 1935, the army ranked sixteenth in size among the world's armies, with 13,000 officers and 126,000 enlisted men. Although MacArthur's efforts were severely constrained by the fiscal emergency, some of his programs were realized: new mobilization plans were developed; a mobile general headquarters air force was established; and a four-army reorganization improved administrative efficiency. Also, the army-managed Civilian Conservation Corps became one of the most effective work-relief programs of the New Deal under MacArthur's guidance.

As army chief of staff, MacArthur alienated significant elements of the American public by his outspoken criticism of pacifism. In 1931–1932 he observed maneuvers by various European armies, and upon his return spoke out zealously in favor of military preparedness. From the popular viewpoint, MacArthur's period as chief of staff is remembered chiefly for the eviction of the "Bonus Army" of jobless veterans from Washington, D.C., in the summer of 1932. The key decisions on the ouster actually were made by Hoover and Secretary of War Patrick F. Hurley, who, like MacArthur, believed (incorrectly) that the protesters were dominated by Communists. MacArthur's indiscreet conduct and press statements during the crisis produced a lasting image of him as a militarist.

In October 1935, President Franklin D. Roosevelt, at the urging of President Manuel L. Quezon of the new Philippine Commonwealth, appointed MacArthur military adviser to the Philippines. His primary mission was to develop a ten-year program of ground, air, and naval defenses that would deter an enemy from attacking the archipelago. In August 1936, Quezon made him field marshal in the Philippine Army, and in December 1937 MacArthur retired from the U.S. Army to fulfill his Philippine posts. He had married Jean Marie Faircloth on Apr. 30, 1937; they had one son.

For nearly six years MacArthur and his small staff of American officers (including Major

Dwight D. Eisenhower until late 1939) tried to build up effective Filipino military units. But annual goals for recruitment, training, and equipment increasingly fell behind because of inadequate appropriations by the American and Philippine governments. By early 1941 the defense program was lagging badly, yet in his reports to Washington, MacArthur remained optimistic.

When Japanese-American relations sharply deteriorated in July 1941, Roosevelt recalled MacArthur to active duty as commander of U.S. Army forces in the Far East, and federalized the Philippine defense forces as part of his new command. American ground and air reinforcements were allocated for shipment to the islands, but the only important arrivals before the war began were several squadrons of B-17 heavy bombers. Despite belated efforts to mobilize ten Filipino divisions, by early December only about a third of the Philippine Army troops had achieved a minimum level of combat readiness, and even they were poorly armed. MacArthur had held the rank of lieutenant general since July; eleven days after Pearl Harbor he was advanced to full general.

In the stubborn defense of the beleaguered Philippines against the invading Japanese, MacArthur's strategy of delaying actions and coordinated withdrawals of his units into Bataan worked well from December 1941 to January 1942. But his failure to stock food, medical, and other supplies in Bataan for the incoming troops contributed importantly to their declining effectiveness and ultimate capitulation when placed under siege by the Japanese. On Roosevelt's orders MacArthur and his family left the Philippines in March 1942 and went to Australia; Lieutenant General Jonathan M. Wainwright succeeded MacArthur as commander in the Philippines. In early April the Filipino and American troops on Bataan surrendered; a month later Corregidor, the last bastion at the entrance of Manila Bay, fell to the Japanese. Meanwhile, MacArthur was awarded the Medal of Honor, and to the majority of the public in the United States he emerged as the first American hero of the war.

When he arrived in Australia, MacArthur proclaimed, "I shall return" (to the Philippines), setting forth at the outset the determined, aggressive spirit that would characterize his strategy for the rest of the conflict. In mid-April he took command of the Southwest Pacific Area, a newly formed theater in which the principal forces for many months would be Australian. Except for the U.S. Army Air

Force's participation in the battle of the Coral Sea in May, there were no major operations in the theater until late summer. (The time was spent in building up and training Australian and American forces in Australia.)

In the Papuan campaign of July 1942–January 1943, MacArthur's forces, primarily Australian, stopped a Japanese thrust toward Port Moresby. They then counterattacked across the rugged Owen Stanley Mountains, and annihilated the enemy army in battles at Buna, Gona, and Sanananda. The Papuan victory, though, was one of the costliest of the Pacific war in proportion to the Allied forces involved: nearly 9,000 combat casualties (and even more felled by diseases) out of 33,000 troops engaged. After Papua, MacArthur was determined to avert frontal assaults and to bypass enemy strongholds; keeping casualties low weighed heavily in his strategic planning thereafter, and not until the Luzon campaign of 1945 did his forces suffer such high losses again.

In Operation Cartwheel, beginning in June 1943, the advance of MacArthur's Southwest Pacific units along the New Guinea coast was coordinated with amphibious assaults by Admiral William F. Halsey's South Pacific forces in the central Solomons, with both drives aiming toward the capture of Rabaul, the Japanese bastion on eastern New Britain. That summer and autumn MacArthur's Australian and American troops seized Salamaua, Lae, and Finschhafen in the Huon Gulf region, and took Nadzab in an airborne assault which was observed by MacArthur from an accompanying B-17. In December his forces captured Arawe and Cape Gloucester on western New Britain, and Halsey's troops expanded an earlier beachhead on Bougainville in the northern Solomons.

Meanwhile, the Joint Chiefs of Staff had decided that Rabaul was to be bypassed. In response MacArthur, in a bold strategic move, isolated Rabaul with a surprise assault on Los Negros in the Admiralty Islands. Authorities generally regard this as one of the key command decisions of the war against Japan. As was to become his custom in many future landings, MacArthur accompanied the assault force and visited the beachhead on the first day, Feb. 29, 1944. Two weeks later his troops took Manus, which had an excellent deep-water anchorage. Halsey's forces captured Emirau, to the east, thereby completing the encirclement of Rabaul.

Now, with powerful naval support, MacArthur sent General Walter Kreuger's American Sixth Army in a 580-mile leap along the New Guinea coast in April. The expedition bypassed an enemy army near Wewak and took Hollandia, Tanahmerah Bay, and Aitape with relative ease. During May–August 1944, the conquest of Netherlands New Guinea was completed in a well-planned series of amphibious assaults at Wakde, Biak, Noemfoor, Manokwari, and Sansapor. Most of MacArthur's strategic objectives were chosen not only to isolate strong Japanese forces but also to secure air bases (or sites) to extend the valuable air cover provided by General George C. Kenney's Far East Air Forces. Morotai in the Moluccas was seized in mid-September, and the airfields built there became vital in providing air support for later operations in the Philippines.

MacArthur's concern for avoiding heavy casualties was well demonstrated in the operations from Hollandia to Morotai: in ground actions spanning 1,400 miles his forces suffered some 1,600 combat casualties while killing more than 26,000 enemy troops. MacArthur was not reluctant to point out the contrast with the expensive Central Pacific victories of Admiral Chester W. Nimitz' forces—for example, Saipan's capture that summer cost more than 3,400 American lives.

Throughout 1943 and early 1944, MacArthur tried to convince the Joint Chiefs to give priority to his Southwest Pacific axis of advance, but increasingly greater logistical support went to Nimitz' Central Pacific offensive. By the late spring of 1944, the Joint Chiefs were strongly considering halting MacArthur's advance south of Luzon. At the Pearl Harbor conference of July 1944, MacArthur persuaded President Roosevelt and Admiral William D. Leahy, the presidential chief of staff, to back his plan to take Luzon. Finally, in early October, the Joint Chiefs authorized the invasion of Luzon.

In the meantime MacArthur ordered the invasion of Leyte in the central Philippines. On October 20 the Sixth Army secured four beachheads on the island, and subsequently the Japanese poured massive ground and air reinforcements into Leyte. The invasion triggered the huge naval battle for Leyte Gulf that broke the backbone of the Japanese Combined Fleet. MacArthur moved his headquarters to Tacloban, Leyte, in late October, but the conquest of the island was not completed until the spring of 1945.

The slowness of the campaign caused postponements of the invasion for Luzon and, in Nimitz' theater, of Iwo Jima and Okinawa. MacArthur's insistence on retaining elements of the Pacific Fleet in support of his Philippine operations added to the tension that had been growing between his headquarters and Nimitz' on other issues. The absence of unity of command in the Pacific aggravated the competition between the theater commands for men and matériel.

Needing air bases near Luzon for his next major move, MacArthur sent an assault force to Mindoro in mid-December. The troops suffered only light casualties in taking the island, but numerous kamikaze attacks hit the naval support ships and resupply convoys. When MacArthur's invasion of Luzon began on Jan. 9, 1945, the armada of nearly a thousand ships was attacked by kamikazes that sank four ships, severely damaged forty-three others, and narrowly missed the cruiser carrying MacArthur. At Lingayen Gulf beachheads were secured, and 203,000 troops of the Sixth Army went ashore to engage the 270,000-man army of General Tomoyuki Yamashita. The Luzon campaign was by far the largest in the Southwest Pacific war; the capture of Manila alone took nearly a month of costly house-to-house fighting. When the war ended, Yamashita still commanded a force of more than 50,000 soldiers in northern Luzon.

In the spring and summer of 1945, MacArthur sent his other armies south of Luzon, often launching operations without directives from the Joint Chiefs. Lieutenant General Robert L. Eichelberger's American Eighth Army undertook fifty-two amphibious assaults in the central and southern Philippines from February through June. MacArthur planned to use the Eighth Army later to invade Java, while the Sixth Army was to be the main strike force in Operation Olympic, the invasion of the Japanese island of Kyushu scheduled for November. Promoted to general of the army in December 1944, MacArthur commanded all U.S. Army forces in the Pacific beginning in April 1945, and was designated to command ground operations in both Operation Olympic and Operation Coronet, the latter being the invasion of the Japanese island of Honshu set for early 1946.

These operations were made unnecessary by the dropping of the atomic bombs on Japan and the resulting Japanese surrender. Following the end of hostilities, President Harry Truman appointed MacArthur Supreme Commander, Allied Powers (SCAP), to preside over the surrender ceremonies in Tokyo Bay on Sept. 2, 1945, and to command the ensuing Allied occupation of Japan.

MacArthur's administration in Japan was to differ from that of occupied Germany in important respects: the institution of sweeping political, economic, and social reforms; the preservation of the imperial system and the national government after purging the latter's militaristic agencies and personnel; and the almost unilateral control of occupation policymaking by the United States. MacArthur was supposed to be restricted to executing policy, which was to be formulated by the State-War-Navy Coordinating Committee (SWNCC) and the Joint Chiefs for the United States, with ostensible Allied input through the thirteen-nation Far Eastern Commission and the four-power Allied Council for Japan.

The Allied Council was the least effective, being strictly an advisory body in Tokyo whose counsel MacArthur seldom sought or heeded. Of the others, SWNCC was the more significant in establishing the principles and policies for the demilitarization and democratization of Japan. For many reasons, but mainly because of his own aggressive leadership and the complex, often blurred lines of responsibility above him, MacArthur was sometimes able to influence the evolution of occupation policies.

MacArthur's personality and distinctive style of leadership so dominated his headquarters that the Japanese people generally came to view the occupation as personified in his image. To them he seemed to provide strong, inspiring leadership at a time when they had despaired of their old leaders, who had brought the country to ruin. His imperious manner, dignified mien, dramatic flair, dedication to his mission, and firmness combined with empathy for the war-ravaged nation were esteemed by most Japanese. Later they became aware of his shortcomings, especially his vanity and extreme sensitivity to criticism, but, particularly during the early phase of the occupation (1945–1947), MacArthur was successful in projecting an image that made the majority of the Japanese hopeful and cooperative.

The SCAP organization that MacArthur devised was reasonably efficient, but suffered from some of the liabilities typical of any large bureaucracy. In addition to the staff sections normally found in a military-theater headquarters, SCAP included a number of civil sections that paralleled the ministries and bureaus of the Japanese government. The civil sections employed thousands of people, mostly Americans and many with expertise in such fields as law, political science, labor relations, economics, and education. Usually MacArthur issued instructions, called "SCAPINS," to the Japanese government through a central liaison office; in practice his SCAPINS were accepted by Japanese authorities as fiat, especially during the early years of the occupation.

MacArthur's first mission as SCAP was the elimination of militarism. This was accomplished effectively in 1945–1948. Along with the successful administration of a vast repatriation program involving the return of millions of Japanese outside the home islands, he oversaw the demobilization of the Japanese armed forces and the abolition of the navy and war ministries. The Eighth Army, the main occupation force (supplemented by a small Anglo-Australian contingent), proceeded with dispatch to dismantle military installations and destroy war matériel stocks in Japan. The SCAP demilitarization program also included the dissolution of militaristic and supernationalistic societies; the trials of Japanese charged with war crimes; and the purging of more than 200,000 persons in government, business, and education allegedly identified with promoting militarism and aggression during 1931–1945.

MacArthur showed great personal interest in political reforms, in part because they were initiated by the SCAP Government Section of Major General Courtney Whitney, his principal confidant. The outstanding political achievement was the constitution of 1946–1947, which incorporated some of the best features of the British, West European, and American systems. It included liberal provisions on civil rights, universal suffrage, and substitution of the Diet for the emperor as the highest organ of the new government, with sovereign power residing in the will of the people. MacArthur promoted the growth of political parties and trade unions, encouraged frequent elections and greater political participation at the prefectural and local levels, and began ambitious, if not always effective, programs to educate the Japanese in the democratic process. He often expressed pride in the remarkable growth in voting and office holding by Japanese women.

At first optimistic over SCAP's reforms, Japanese socialists and liberals became alienated when MacArthur adopted a tough stance toward radical excesses in 1948–1950. Japanese conservatives came to dominate elective offices and the bureaucracy, and the Japanese government seemed to be aligning the nation with the West in the growing cold war.

Of the many SCAP economic reform efforts, two particularly interested MacArthur and received his strong backing: land reform and *zaibatsu* dissolution. Under the land reform program, which was the boldest of all SCAP initiatives, the system of absentee landlordism was virtually abolished. The government acquired about 5 million acres of arable land for redistribution to peasant farmers at nominal prices. This action resulted in the rapid development of an independent class of landholding peasants. Farm tenancy dropped from 50 percent in 1945 to less than 10 percent in 1951.

MacArthur energetically supported the SCAP Economic and Scientific Section's program (1945–1947) to break up the trusts of the *zaibatsu,* the small group of powerful families that controlled the industrial, transportation, and utilities' combines of Japan. More than eighty *zaibatsu* holding companies were dissolved, and steeply graduated income, inheritance, and corporation taxes were imposed on them. Further deconcentration was planned, but in 1947 directives from Washington abruptly changed the direction of the occupation from reform to recovery, in accord with the new cold war strategy of developing Japan as the principal bulwark to contain the spread of communism in east Asia.

At the start of the occupation, the U.S. government had disclaimed any obligation to provide Japan with assistance for relief and rehabilitation. Mainly because of the persistent demands of MacArthur, though, American shipments of food and fuel were sent to Japan during the unusually severe winter of 1945–1946. Through his continuing efforts the United States ultimately assisted Japan with more than $2 billion worth of relief goods and services during 1945–1951. In addition, the SCAP Public Health and Welfare Section undertook welfare programs that alleviated hunger and suffering, and its massive inoculation drives drastically reduced outbreaks of epidemic diseases.

Although the impact of westernization on Japanese society and culture was accelerated during the "MacArthur era," subsequent developments indicate that SCAP reforms in those areas were not as lasting as in politics and economics. When MacArthur attempted to extend democratization to public education, its implementation at the local level often amounted to the introduction of American educational methodology and administration, as well as American values, which were difficult, if not unfeasible, for the Japanese to adopt. SCAP's development of a wide assortment of American-style junior and state colleges to expand higher education was largely a failure because the new institutions were inadequately funded and could not achieve the level of excellence of the prestigious imperial universities. One of MacArthur's most quixotic plans was to Christianize Japan, but the importation of 10 million Bibles and a large number of missionaries brought few converts to Christianity.

After 1946, MacArthur was also head of the Far East Command, which consisted of all American ground, air, and sea forces in Japan, the Ryukyus, Korea (to 1948), the Philippines, the Marianas, and the Bonins. On July 8, 1950, two weeks after the Korean War erupted, a third concurrent position was added when Truman selected him to be commander in chief of the United Nations Command (UNC). By the time he was able to get sizable American and other United Nations units into action, the North Korean army had captured Seoul and was pushing southward rapidly.

But in the Naktong (or Pusan) perimeter, in the southeast corner of the peninsula, the UNC divisions fought the invaders to a standstill while MacArthur was overseeing a buildup of men and firepower that surpassed the enemy's strength by early September. After personally planning one of the most daring envelopments in military annals, he sent his X Corps in a surprise assault at Inchon, the port near Seoul, on September 15. The North Koreans fell back. Shortly the Eighth Army and South Korean forces broke out of their perimeter and the North Korean retreat turned into a rout. By early October, UNC troops were moving across the 38th Parallel against decreasing resistance.

Supported by a United Nations General Assembly resolution (October 7) calling for the reunification of Korea, MacArthur sent the UNC forces in a dual advance toward the Yalu River, spearheaded by the Eighth Army on the west side of the peninsula and the X Corps on the east. On October 15 he and Truman conferred at Wake Island, mainly about plans for the postwar rehabilitation of Korea, so near did victory seem. Two weeks later, though, UNC troops near the Yalu were attacked by Communist Chinese forces that disengaged and disappeared after ten days of combat. But when MacArthur launched his "end-the-war" offensive in late November, Communist Chinese armies in great strength hit the widely separated UNC forces, driving them back across the 38th Parallel. In January 1951, Lieutenant General Matthew B. Ridgway's Eighth Army undertook a counteroffensive that by early April had advanced into North Korea again.

Meanwhile, tension had been mounting between MacArthur and Truman, whose views differed sharply on the strategic direction of the war and on civil-military relations. From the president's viewpoint MacArthur thwarted the American attempt to negotiate a cease-fire in late March. Also, MacArthur made public his disagreement with Truman's policies, especially in a letter of his that was read in Congress in early April. On Apr. 11, 1951, Truman suddenly relieved him of all of his commands.

MacArthur returned to a hero's welcome in the United States, and on April 19 he addressed a joint session of Congress, where his remarks criticizing the administration were applauded. Public clamor against Truman's action subsided during the Senate hearings in May and June on the general's dismissal, especially after the Joint Chiefs testified that MacArthur's proposals for winning the war had been strategically unsound and might have resulted in a greatly expanded conflict.

In 1944, 1948, and 1952 conservative Republican factions attempted in vain to have MacArthur chosen as the party's presidential candidate. After delivering the keynote address at the Republican National Convention in 1952, he became the chairman of the board of Remington Rand (later Sperry-Rand). Except for occasional speeches, board duties, and a sentimental journey to the Philippines in 1961, MacArthur spent his remaining years in virtual seclusion in New York City. He died at Walter Reed Hospital in Washington, D.C.

Descriptions of MacArthur's personality and character by his contemporaries vary widely because of his complex blend of contradictory traits, his mastery of role taking, and his beliefs that ranged from reactionary to liberal, depending on the issue. In his public image he often appeared vain, aloof, egotistical, and flamboyant, but those who knew him well describe him as a charming, gracious, cultured aristocrat-warrior. It is not likely that anyone will fully probe MacArthur the man, partly because of the unrevealing nature of his personal papers.

MacArthur's career was one of the longest and most controversial of any American military figure, including active service as a general from 1918 to 1951. His genius as a leader was demonstrated most lucidly in his pioneering reforms as West Point superintendent; his bold and imaginative campaigns, with minimum logistical support, during the war against Japan; and, perhaps most important, his enlightened administration of the Japanese occupation. Possessed of monumental gifts and tragic flaws, he fell from power in his collision with Truman in 1950–1951 because of his more serious limitations: his almost paranoid reaction to criticism, his condescension toward superiors that often approached in-

subordination, and his inability to adjust to a strategy of limited warfare.

[MacArthur's personal papers are in the MacArthur Memorial archives, Norfolk, Va., and his official records are in the National Archives and Washington National Records Center; see Vorin E. Whan, Jr., ed., *A Soldier Speaks: Public Papers and Speeches of . . . Douglas MacArthur* (1965). His autobiography is *Reminiscences* (1964). Works by key staff officers include Charles A. Willoughby and John Chamberlain, *MacArthur, 1941–1951* (1954); Courtney Whitney, *MacArthur: His Rendezvous with History* (1956); and Charles A. Willoughby et al., eds., *Reports of General MacArthur*, 4 vols. (1966). Biographies are Frazier Hunt, *The Untold Story of Douglas MacArthur* (1954); Gavin Long, *MacArthur as Military Commander* (1969); D. Clayton James, *The Years of MacArthur*, 2 vols. (1970–1975); and William Manchester, *American Caesar* (1978). Also see Louis Morton, *Strategy and Command: The First Two Years* (1962); William J. Sebald, with Russell Brines, *With MacArthur in Japan* (1965); Jay Luvaas, ed., *Dear Miss Em* (1972); and James F. Schnabel, *Policy and Direction: The First Year* (1972). A long obituary and several articles appeared in the *New York Times*, Apr. 6, 1964.]

D. CLAYTON JAMES

McBRIDE, HENRY (July 25, 1867–Mar. 31, 1962), art journalist, was born in West Chester, Pa. After attending the local public schools, he found employment as a writer and illustrator of seed catalogs published by a local nursery. Having saved $200, he made his way to New York City in 1897. There he studied art under John Ward Stimson (an admirer of William Blake) at the Artists' and Artisans' Institute. McBride later transferred to the Art Students League. He taught himself French in order to pursue his career on summer sketching and walking tours in Europe.

In 1900, McBride felt ready to teach art, and decided to make this contribution to the working class in particular. He therefore inaugurated the art department of the Educational Alliance in New York City. The following year he also accepted the post of director of the School of Industrial Arts at Trenton, N.J., where Abraham Walkowitz, Samuel Halpert, Jo Davidson, and Jacob Epstein were among his students.

Not until 1913 did McBride find his true vocation, art criticism of a dry, subhumorous, and subtle sort. This change in his career occurred, as he later recalled, when he "climbed the two flights of wooden stairs in the old *Sun* building" to join that newspaper's art department (previously dominated by the critic James

Gibbons Huneker and now headed by Samuel Swift). The famous Armory Show of modern art took place in February 1913. Some of the exhibits, such as Marcel Duchamp's *Nude Descending a Staircase,* scandalized the public and received a very bad press, but McBride's unsigned pieces about the exhibition were moderate and informative. Soon afterward Swift resigned from the paper and McBride took full command, having been made, as he put it, "responsible for the activities of about a hundred art galleries." He was to retain this "responsibility" in the New York art world for thirty-seven years.

During and after World War I, McBride, a frequent visitor to Europe, was a brilliant apologist for the School of Paris. While continuing his weekly reviews for the *Sun* he also wrote art essays for the *Dial* (1920–1929) and *Creative Art* (1930–1932). Gertrude Stein, Charles Demuth, Georgia O'Keeffe, Gaston Lachaise, Jules Pascin, Virgil Thomson, Elie Nadelman, and Constantin Brancusi were among his most admired friends.

"It may be an unpleasant fact but it is a fact nonetheless," McBride noted in a *Creative Art* editorial of 1931, "that fifty years hence but a scant half-dozen of our living artists will be remembered with interest . . . and a contemporary critic's task is to be as right as possible about these." McBride more than met this challenge. He was a discriminating appreciator and a deft communicator of all that seems lightest and rarest in modern art.

When the *Sun* merged with the *World Telegram* in 1950, McBride was not kept on. Alfred Frankfurter then hired him to write a monthly column for *Art News.* Until 1955, McBride added luster to that magazine, writing perceptively of such rising painters as Bradley Tomlin, Mark Rothko, and Jackson Pollock, as well as of such old friends as Duchamp and Jean Arp.

Looked after by Max Miltzlaff, his companion for a quarter-century, McBride endured old age philosophically in his sun-filled apartment in New York City, where he died the undisputed dean of American art critics.

[The best of McBride's criticism is in *The Flow of Art* (1975), with introductions by Lincoln Kirstein and Daniel Catton Rich. An obituary is in the *New York Times,* Apr. 1, 1962.]
                                                    ALEXANDER ELIOT

McCARTHY, CHARLES LOUIS (CLEM) (Sept. 9, 1882–June 4, 1962), radio sportscaster, was born in East Bloomfield, N.Y., the son of an Irish-born horse dealer and auctioneer. Because his father traveled extensively, young McCarthy attended schools in a dozen different cities. In 1896 he saw his first Kentucky Derby, and until his fifteenth birthday aspired to be a jockey. After being convinced he was too large for the job, he began his professional career as a handicapper and race reporter for a San Diego newspaper. His constant exposure to horses and racing, and several years of experience as an auctioneer, prepared him for his later career.

In 1927, McCarthy was hired to be the voice on the public address system at Chicago's Arlington Park. There he was able to utilize both his extensive knowledge of horses and racing and the trained voice he had developed during his days as an auctioneer. In 1928 radio station KYW in Chicago hired him to broadcast the first Kentucky Derby ever heard on radio. The following year he joined the National Broadcasting Company (NBC) and began announcing some of the nation's major sporting events, including the Kentucky Derby, the Preakness, and several world championship boxing matches. Also in 1929 he married Vina Smith, a vaudeville actress. They had no children.

By the early 1930's McCarthy's voice was associated with horse racing and boxing events everywhere there were radios, and his announcement "R-r-r-racing fans" became an American institution. With binoculars in one hand and the microphone in the other, McCarthy covered thousands of horse races. He broadcast the Grand National Steeplechase from England; he provided the radio accounts of all the leading races at Saratoga; he broadcast the Meadowbrook polo matches; he was a sports commentator for WMCA in New York; he wrote articles on racing for both dailies and turf publications; he had a syndicated column carried in several newspapers; and he did Pathé newsreels.

McCarthy's command of words and the speed with which he followed the progress of fights and races made him very popular with his listening audience. Probably his two most exciting broadcasts were both aired in 1938: the return bout between Joe Louis and Max Schmeling—"Schmeling is down! Schmeling is down!"—and the duel between War Admiral and Seabiscuit in a "match race"—"They've got 200 yards to come. It's horse against horse, both of 'em driving. . . . Seabiscuit by three! Seabiscuit by three! Seabiscuit is the winner by four lengths, and you never saw such a wild crowd."

Radio listeners appreciated McCarthy's style, which made them feel as if they were actually witnessing the event. He often spent days before a race getting to know horses, trainers, and jockeys. During his career he memorized more than 200 racing colors. This knowledge, along with his "throaty and gravelly machine-gun voice," kept audiences attentive to his every word. McCarthy not only helped sell many radios but also brought the thrill and drama of American sports to more people than ever before.

In May 1939, McCarthy, perhaps remembering his own youth, wrote "So You Want to Be a Jockey" for the *Saturday Evening Post,* the first of several articles for that periodical. He had a reputation for accuracy, but made a memorable blunder in 1947, when he called the wrong winner for the Preakness. After realizing his mistake, McCarthy immediately corrected himself: "All right, we missed, we struck out. Well Babe Ruth struck out, so I might just as well get in famous company."

McCarthy left NBC in 1947 and joined the Columbia Broadcasting System (CBS). His wife, who had been ill with cancer, died in 1949 after draining much of McCarthy's savings for medical treatment. He covered the Kentucky Derby for CBS through 1950, ending his "affair" with Churchill Downs after twenty-three consecutive broadcasts. His last assignments, during the early 1950's, were broadcasts from the meets at Roosevelt Raceway for New York City stations. In May 1957 McCarthy was seriously injured in a car crash. He was awarded $85,000 in a lawsuit, but after all debts were paid, he was left penniless in a nursing home in New York City.

In 1961 several announcers established the Clem McCarthy Fund to help defray his expenses. The William Black Foundation agreed to contribute matching funds. The following year a record, "Clem McCarthy, the Voice of American Sports," was cut at the expense of Riverside Record Company, NBC, and Ed Sullivan, who supplied the introduction and commentary. Proceeds from sales were to go to McCarthy, but he died the following month in New York City.

[Material on McCarthy is scanty, especially concerning his early childhood. The Broadcast Pioneers Library, Washington, D.C., has material relating to McCarthy's announcing career. The best biographical data is in Don Rockwell, ed., *Radio Personalities* (1936); and "Pioneer Announcer: Ill, Forgotten," *New York Times,* Aug. 13, 1961. Also see "Racing: Clem's Derby," *Newsweek,* May 12, 1947; and Bud Greenspan, "The Man Who Blew a Derby," *Sports Illustrated,* May 17, 1971. Obituaries are in the *New York Times,* June 5, 1962; *Sports Illustrated,* June 11, 1962; *Time,* June 15, 1962; *Newsweek,* June 18, 1962.]

JACK W. BERRYMAN

McCLINTIC, GUTHRIE (Aug. 6, 1893–Oct. 29, 1961), theatrical producer and director, was born in Seattle, Wash., the son of Edgar Daggs McClintic, a businessman, and of Ella Florence McClintic. His parents were third cousins. McClintic's interest in the theater began at an early age. As a youth he attended matinee performances of a Seattle stock company. When in high school, he ran away from home to join a traveling repertory company. His parents quickly retrieved him, but a family friend helped convince Edgar McClintic that the theater could be an honorable profession for his son.

In the fall of 1910, McClintic enrolled in the American Academy of Dramatic Arts, in New York City. He graduated in March 1912 and prepared to begin his career as an actor. His first role was in *Oliver Twist,* which was to be presented by a new company throughout Canada. After a dismal start, the company was abandoned by the management in London, Ontario. McClintic next played with a company in Wilmington, Del., where he was fortunate to escape the theater with a few personal possessions when the sheriff seized all property to cover the company's unpaid bills.

McClintic's career seemed headed for oblivion. For a time in 1913 he appeared in a vaudeville act, performing five times a day. But, some fourteen months after his graduation, he calculated that he had worked only twelve weeks. Then an actor from the American Academy suggested that he contact the producer Winthrop Ames, who was casting a new play. McClintic was granted an interview with Ames's director, George F. Platt, who showed no interest and abruptly dismissed him. McClintic felt he had not been treated fairly, and penned an angry letter to Ames. Then he decided not to send it, but three weeks later, while attending a séance, he received a "message" directing him to mail the letter. Subsequently, without ever seeing him, Ames hired McClintic as assistant stage manager for a new play, *Her Own Money,* by Mark Swan. Without an assistant McClintic handled all props and scene changes, memorizing the exact locations so everything could be placed in the dark. The play soon closed, but Ames had been impressed by McClintic's ability and diligence. An association developed that lasted for almost a decade.

In April 1917, when the United States entered World War I, McClintic volunteered for service, but was rejected because of a heart condition. Soon thereafter he was married. He produced his first play during these years (it failed), and also served as a talent scout for Ames. In June 1919 he and his wife separated.

Ames now offered to back a McClintic production. For more than a year McClintic searched for the right play. He found it in A. A. Milne's *The Dover Road*. He also discovered Katharine Cornell, a leading actress in Ames's productions. They were married on Sept. 8, 1921. *Dover Road*, which opened Dec. 23, 1921, ran for thirty-five weeks on Broadway, and was chosen one of the ten best plays of the season.

In the spring of 1925, McClintic directed Katharine Cornell in Michael Arlen's *The Green Hat*, which also starred Leslie Howard. By this time he had developed a method of rehearsal that he would use for the rest of his life. For at least a week, the actors read their parts while seated around a table. Only after this period of reading and dissection would McClintic allow standing rehearsals.

During the 1930's and 1940's McClintic ranked as one of the most successful directors and producers in the United States. He claimed never to have had a serious argument with a playwright, not even with George Bernard Shaw, who was noted for irritability. McClintic produced and directed Shaw's *Candida* (1933, 1937, 1942, 1946), *Saint Joan* (1936), and *The Doctor's Dilemma* (1941). He particularly admired Maxwell Anderson, and was involved in five Anderson plays: *Saturday's Children* (1928), *Winterset* (1935), *High Tor* (1937), *Star Wagon* (1937), and *Key Largo* (1939). Among McClintic's other outstanding productions were Sidney Howard's *Alien Corn* (1933) and *Yellow Jack* (1934), Anton Chekhov's *The Three Sisters* (1942), Somerset Maugham's *The Letter* (1927) and *The Constant Wife* (1951), Noel Coward's *Fallen Angels* (1927), Tennessee Williams' *You Touched Me!* (1945), Robinson Jeffers' *Medea* (1947, 1955), and Mary Chase's *Bernadine* (1952).

Several of the best productions of Shakespeare in the twentieth century were McClintic's work. Late in 1933 he convinced his wife to play the part of Juliet opposite Basil Rathbone's Romeo in a touring version of the tragedy that also starred Orson Welles as Mercutio. During twenty-nine weeks of touring, the company presented *Romeo and Juliet* (thirty-nine times), *Candida* (forty-two times), and the *Barretts of Wimpole Street* (144 times). In her portrayal of

Elizabeth Barrett Browning, Katharine Cornell created her most famous role, to which she frequently returned over the next fifteen years. McClintic tried Shakespeare again in 1936 with *Hamlet*, starring John Gielgud, Judith Anderson, Lillian Gish, and Arthur Byron.

During his lifetime McClintic was involved in more than 100 productions. He directed ninety-four plays, thirty-one of them under his own management. Twenty-eight of his productions featured Katharine Cornell. Among the many outstanding actors and actresses he directed were Leslie Howard, Burgess Meredith, Cedric Hardwicke, Raymond Massey, Ruth Gordon, Ralph Richardson, Edith Evans, Maurice Evans, Laurence Olivier, Paul Muni, Charlton Heston, Julie Harris, Montgomery Clift, José Ferrer, Maureen Stapleton, Marlon Brando, Gregory Peck, and Ethel Barrymore.

After World War II, McClintic was less active. His last production was in 1960, when he and Sol Hurok presented *Dear Liar*, starring Katharine Cornell and Brian Aherne. McClintic died at Sneden's Landing, N.Y. Twenty years earlier, during the production of Shaw's *The Doctor's Dilemma*, he penned his life's credo: "I believe in Will Shakespeare, Bernard Shaw and Katharine Cornell; in the stimulus of a good play, the power of direction, and the magic of the theatre."

[See Katharine Cornell, *I Wanted to Be an Actress* (1938); Guthrie McClintic, *Me and Kit* (1955); and Francis Robinson, "Remembering Mr. McClintic," *New York Times*, Nov. 5, 1961. An obituary is in the *New York Times*, Oct. 30, 1961.]

GERALD THOMPSON

McCRACKEN, JOAN (Dec. 31, 1922–Nov. 1, 1961), actress, singer, and dancer, was born in Philadelphia, Pa., the daughter of Frank McCracken, a sports reporter for the *Philadelphia Evening Ledger*, and of Mary Humes. She was educated at the Harrity School and West Philadelphia High School. When she was ten, her aunt offered to pay for her lessons at the Littlefield Ballet School. The director, Catherine Littlefield, invited McCracken to join the junior group of her company. Shortly thereafter, when Littlefield's newly organized Philadelphia Ballet went to New York City, McCracken received the company's award for her proficiency in their classical repertoire, and the *New York Times* noted her "unusual promise."

During her teen-age years, which she spent with Littlefield's company, McCracken appeared at the Robin Hood Dell and with the

Chicago Civic Opera. In 1937, under the auspices of the International Exposition, she toured Europe with the Littlefield company. She came to regard it as "the luckiest thing that ever happened to me." In 1941, McCracken married Jack Dunphy, an aspiring writer and fellow dancer; they then left the Philadelphia Ballet and hitchhiked to New York with $35 between them.

McCracken first danced in New York as principal ballerina in the corps de ballet of the Radio City Music Hall. In 1942, at the National Theatre, she became a member of Eugene Loring's newly formed Dance Players. That year the *New York Times* dance critic, John Martin, cited her for "her outstanding ability, her comedy playing, and the style and authority of her dancing."

The next season, dancing in Rodgers and Hammerstein's *Oklahoma!*, McCracken converted her chorus role into a success by effortlessly repeating a fall during the "Many a New Day" number. Among the perquisites of her overnight celebrity was billing in the program as "The Girl Who Falls Down."

Shortly afterward Oscar Hammerstein suggested that McCracken prepare for greater opportunities by studying acting. She enrolled in the Neighborhood Playhouse, and a Hollywood screen test brought her a contract to appear in Warner Brothers' *Hollywood Canteen* (1944). Her role was similar to her character in *Oklahoma!*: a cute country bumpkin rebuffed by the boys at a dance contest. Later that year she had the major role of an impish parlor maid in the Theatre Guild's *Bloomer Girl*. She received the 1944–1945 Donaldson Gold Key Award for best supporting performance in a musical.

Returning to Broadway in 1945, McCracken costarred with Mitzi Green in *Billion Dollar Baby*, in which she again played a spunky girl. Her portrayal of a flapper who loves and betrays various men was, as one reviewer phrased it, one of the show's "consolations." She received the 1945–1946 Donaldson Award for her dancing in the show.

In 1947, McCracken joined the Experimental Theatre's production of Charles Laughton's translation of *Galileo* by Bertolt Brecht. She portrayed the daughter who loses her suitor because of the heretical teachings of her father (played by Charles Laughton). Critical response was enthusiastic.

Her 1947 dramatic success was shown not to be a fluke in 1949, when she appeared in Clifford Odets' *The Big Knife*, starring John Garfield. As in *Galileo*, she portrayed a luckless and desperate young woman bullied by the "system." Although the play received mixed reviews, McCracken was cited as "extraordinarily good" and as providing "an inventive performance of quality."

Her career in Hollywood culminated with the 1947 Betty Comden–Adolph Green screen adaptation of the musical *Good News*, in which she costarred with June Allyson. McCracken next turned to television, appearing in such dramatic works as the Theatre Guild's presentation of George Bernard Shaw's *Great Catherine*, with Gertrude Lawrence (1948). She also played the dancing niece in the "Pulitzer Prize Playhouse" production of *You Can't Take It with You*. In 1952 she had her own television series, "Claudia," based on the heroine of Rose Franken's popular short stories about the domestic problems of young newlyweds.

The revue *Dance Me a Song*, according to some, managed to submerge McCracken's "glowing talents." After a divorce from Jack Dunphy in 1951, on Jan. 6, 1953, she married Bob Fosse, another member of the cast of *Dance Me a Song*. They were divorced ten years later.

McCracken's last musical theater performance was in Rodgers and Hammerstein's *Me and Juliet*, in June 1953. After the mid-1950's a heart ailment restricted her to dramatic roles. Following her appearance as the Sphinx in Jean Cocteau's *The Infernal Machine* in 1958, she retired from the stage and spent her last years in seclusion. She died in New York City.

McCracken's comparatively brief career was characterized by a rare versatility. She began her professional life as a ballerina and then achieved success in musical theater, comedy, and drama. Although she was never a star of the first rank, her success may be attributed to the gumption and resiliency beneath her gaminlike charm.

[The Theatre Research Collection of the Library of the Performing Arts in New York City contains correspondence, theater programs, publicity stills, press releases, and obituaries, as well as clippings from the scrapbook collection of Mary Humes McCracken. An obituary is in the *New York Times*, Nov. 2, 1961.]

REUEL K. OLIN

McDONALD, JAMES GROVER (Nov. 29, 1886–Sept. 26, 1964), diplomat, educator, and internationalist, was born in Coldwater, Ohio, the son of Kenneth John McDonald, a hotel manager, and Anna Dietrich. McDonald graduated in 1905 from high school in Albany, Ind., where he met Ruth Stafford, whom he married on Oct. 25, 1915. They had two children.

McDonald worked for a year (1905–1906) in a hotel, then entered Indiana University and received an A.B. in history in 1909 and an M.A. in political science and international relations in 1910. After teaching a year at Indiana University, he attended Harvard University, where he was a teaching fellow in history and international law (1911–1914). After another year teaching history at Indiana University he became a Harvard traveling fellow (1915–1916), studying in France and Spain. He returned to Indiana as assistant professor of history but resigned in 1918 in protest when a faculty member was dismissed because he divorced his wife. McDonald then moved to New York City, where he worked briefly for the Civil Service Reform Association.

With others interested in peace and international relations McDonald formed a study group late in 1918; this became the Foreign Policy Association in 1921. McDonald was its chairman or executive officer from early in 1919 to 1933. The Foreign Policy Association, which sought to present world issues to the American public in an objective way through publications, speakers, and institutes, grew in membership from fifteen to over 12,000 under McDonald's direction. He developed an efficient staff, obtained financial support, spoke and wrote on a wide variety of postwar economic and political issues, and developed extensive personal contacts with public figures in the United States and abroad. He went to Europe nearly every year. In 1932 and again in 1933 he was in Germany, where he saw the rise of the Nazis to power. An interview with Hitler in 1933, which he personally conveyed to President Franklin D. Roosevelt, convinced McDonald of the ruthless character of the new regime.

McDonald lectured extensively. He made an impressive appearance on the platform with his distinguished looks, bronze-gold hair, and slender six-foot, three-inch frame. From 1928 to 1932 he gave weekly radio talks on "The World Today" over the National Broadcasting Company (NBC) network. His addresses, presented with a slight English accent, attracted an extensive radio audience. While McDonald sought to convey to listeners an aura of objectivity, he left no doubt about his personal views. He favored membership of the United States in the World Court and the League of Nations and continually called for the greater participation of the United States in world affairs as the only true safeguard to peace. In the 1930's he insisted

upon an abandonment of economic nationalism.

McDonald publicly expressed his concern over the plight of Jews in Germany and in 1933 he accepted a post under the League of Nations as high commissioner for refugees and as such established a reputation as a champion of minorities. He raised funds and coordinated the efforts of fifteen governments and private organizations in finding homes for over 100,000 refugees fleeing Hitler. In a highly publicized letter of resignation from the League effective Jan. 1, 1936, McDonald castigated the German government for its policy of race extermination and charged the democracies with shirking their responsibilities.

For the next two years McDonald served on the board of editors of the *New York Times,* writing on international affairs. He then became president (1938–1942) of the Brooklyn Institute of Arts and Sciences. He also served as a member of the Board of Education of New York City (1940–1942). He maintained relationships with peace and foreign-policy study groups, serving as vice-chairman of the National Council for the Prevention of War, as trustee of the World Peace Foundation, and as chairman of the Presidential Advisory Committee on Political Refugees (1938–1945). He returned to broadcasting and from 1942 to 1944 presented daily news analyses on the NBC network.

McDonald had long expressed an interest in a homeland for Jews, and in November 1945 he accepted appointment from President Harry S. Truman to the Anglo-American Committee of Inquiry on Palestine. After a visit to the Middle East, the committee recommended in April 1947 that 100,000 Jews be allowed admission to Palestine. While McDonald had not intially favored partition, by 1947 he endorsed that course. With the creation of the state of Israel, Truman, in June 1948, named McDonald as special United States representative. In ensuing months McDonald clarified relations between the two governments, which led to diplomatic recognition on Jan. 31, 1949. He subsequently held the title ambassador extraordinary and plenipotentiary (March 1949–January 1951).

From 1951 to 1961 McDonald served as an adviser to the Development Corporation for Israel and embarked on fund-raising campaigns for several Jewish organizations. He claimed that whatever success in life he achieved was largely attributable to his ability to relate to people; he was also an effective administrator and a hard worker for whatever task confronted him. He died in New York City.

[McDonald's papers are in the Herbert H. Lehman Collection, Columbia University. For pamphlets representative of McDonald's range of interest and his impartial analysis and commentary, see *Europe's Needs* (1921), *Soviet Russia After Ten Years* (1927), *The World Today* (1928), *America's Stake in Europe* (1930), and *Latin America* (1931). Two pamphlets, *The German Refugees and the League of Nations* (1936) and *Where Can the Refugees Go?* (1945), and his book *My Mission in Israel, 1948–1951* (1951), cover his later career. Leonard Dinnerstein, "America, Britain, and Palestine: The Anglo-American Committee of Inquiry and the Displaced Persons, 1945–1946," *Diplomatic History,* Summer 1980, has considerable reference to McDonald. The *New York Times,* Sept. 27, 1964, carried an obituary.]

WARREN F. KUEHL

MacDONALD, JEANETTE ANNA (June 18, 1907–Jan. 14, 1965), singer and actress, was born in Philadelphia, Pa., the daughter of Daniel MacDonald, a building contractor, and of Anna Wright. She attended West Philadelphia School for Girls and a private school in New York City. She first sang in public at the age of three, for a charity benefit, but her early success came as a dancer. She made her professional stage debut in 1921, as a chorus dancer in Ned Wayburn's revue at the Capitol Theater in New York City. At the same time she developed her dancing under the direction of Albertina Rasch and also studied voice. Between engagements she modeled fur coats. A featured role in a Greenwich Village Theater production, *Fantastic Fricasee* (1923), for which MacDonald received good notices, brought her to the attention of an agent for Henry W. Savage, who signed her for a part in *The Magic Ring.* She later appeared, principally on the road, in small parts in the Shubert musical comedies *Night Boat, Irene,* and *Tip Toes.* In 1929, MacDonald was in the Shubert musical comedy *Boom Boom.* Other Broadway musical comedies in which she made song and dance appearances soon followed. They included *Sunny Days; Yes, Yes Yvette;* and *Angela.*

A hard worker with a slim figure, green eyes, and red-gold hair, MacDonald attracted the attention of Hollywood director Ernst Lubitsch, who saw her in *Angela.* He gave her a screen test during the run of the show, but about a year passed before he decided to cast her opposite Maurice Chevalier in *The Love Parade* (1929). Her clear soprano voice and unaffected style immediately impressed both critics and general audiences. There followed leading roles in two other Lubitsch films, *Monte Carlo* (1930) and *One Hour with You* (1931), and in *Love Me Tonight* (1932), a big hit at the box office. In 1934, MacDonald received the starring role in *The Merry Widow,* an adaptation of the Franz Lehar operetta, following intense competition for the part with Grace Moore. That year she also appeared in *The Cat and the Fiddle.*

Following a European concert tour, MacDonald signed a contract with Metro-Goldwyn-Mayer, which was interested in featuring the idealized woman on the screen. Her personality matched the image they wished to project, and they teamed her with Nelson Eddy, a baritone, in a series of films. The first of these pictures was *Naughty Marietta* (1935). MacDonald's manner, diction, and phrasing of such melodies as "Sweet Mystery of Life," "I'm Falling in Love with Someone," and "Italian Street Song" enthralled the public and made her name a household word. The film introduced thousands of people to light opera. In 1936, MacDonald departed from her usual roles to play a dramatic part with Clark Gable in *San Francisco.* Starring with Nelson Eddy, she also made such fanciful films as *Rose Marie* (1936) and *Maytime* (1937). Their repeated appearance together in films led to unfounded reports of a romance that were readily believed by the public.

These rumors were dispelled by MacDonald's marriage to Gene Raymond, a motion picture actor, on June 16, 1937. The event was one of Hollywood's most widely publicized weddings. Thousands crowded the streets outside the church to catch a glimpse of the couple, and it was reported that more than 100 policemen were required to maintain order. During 1937, MacDonald was heard on the Columbia Radio Network on a weekly program, "Vick's Open House." She also made a number of recordings. At this time she acted as her own manager.

MacDonald's first motion picture with Gene Raymond was *Smilin' Through* (1941). According to the critic Bosley Crowther, the story was mawkish and old hat, but her fine voice commanded attention every time she sang. Nevertheless, her manner was regarded as too operatic, her moods too obviously mechanical, and her charm too cosmetically contrived.

With the peak of her popularity in motion pictures passed, MacDonald left filmmaking in 1942 for a concert tour in the United States and abroad. During World War II she frequently gave performances for sick and wounded soldiers. A longtime interest in more demanding singing roles led her to train for opera. On Nov. 4, 1944, she sang Juliet in Gounod's *Romeo and Juliet* before a capacity audience at the Chicago Civic Opera House. She had appeared in

Romeo and Juliet with Ezio Pinza in Montreal and in *Faust* with the Chicago Civic Opera Company. She returned to films briefly in 1947, but thereafter limited her public appearances to occasional guest spots on television and some nightclub performances. MacDonald died in Houston, Tex.

[Materials on MacDonald's career are in the Lester Sweyd Collection and the Chamberlain and Lyman Brown Theatrical Agency Collection, both at the New York Public Library, Lincoln Center. Also see S. Rich, *Jeanette MacDonald, A Pictorial Treasury* (1973); Marjorie Rosen, *Popcorn Venus* (1973); Basil Wright, *The Long View* (1974); J. R. Parish, *The Jeanette MacDonald Story* (1976); L. E. Stein, *Jeanette MacDonald* (1977); and Philip Castanza, *Films of Jeanette MacDonald and Nelson Eddy* (1978). An obituary is in the *New York Times*, Jan. 15, 1965.]
ERNEST A. McKAY

McGRANERY, JAMES PATRICK (July 8, 1895–Dec. 23, 1962), U.S. congressman, federal judge, and U.S. attorney general, was born in Philadelphia, Pa., the son of Patrick McGranery and Bridget Gallagher. He was educated in local Catholic schools, and as a young man worked as a printer. During World War I he served in Europe as an army balloon pilot and as an adjutant with the 111th Infantry. Discharged in 1919, McGranery enrolled in college preparatory courses at the Maher School in Philadelphia. He entered Temple University in 1920. For the next several years he combined his studies with activity in South Philadelphia ward politics.

Well established on the local political scene by the time of his graduation from Temple University Law School and admittance to the bar in 1928, McGranery headed Al Smith's presidential campaign in the city and was elected to a four-year term on the Pennsylvania Democratic Central Committee. Through his participation in Irish-American fraternal societies and Catholic lay groups, he established a successful law practice in which his major clients were the Philadelphia police and firemen's organizations. On Nov. 29, 1939, he married Regina Clark, a prominent Philadelphia attorney; they had three children.

McGranery was an unsuccessful candidate for municipal court clerk (1928), district attorney (1931), and the U.S. House of Representatives (1934). In 1936 he was elected to the House, and was returned in 1938, 1940, and 1942. Like most of his urban Democratic colleagues, McGranery was a consistent supporter of Franklin D. Roosevelt. He was a representative of the

new urban liberals, attuned to the aspirations of the ethnic-religious minorities in the large cities, who provided the strongest and most durable backing for the New Deal and later reform movements. Talented, gregarious, and persuasive, he achieved considerable influence among his fellow congressmen. Although he was a vocal advocate of Irish nationalism, McGranery nonetheless supported Roosevelt's policy of aid to Great Britain before Pearl Harbor and voted for lend-lease in 1941.

When his district was eliminated by reapportionment, McGranery resigned from Congress (November 1943) to become assistant to the attorney general. For the next three years he was the chief administrative officer of the Department of Justice under Francis Biddle and, after May 1945, Tom Clark. Biddle recalled his deputy as "an excellent mixer, with a warm heart and fierce hatred for those whom he considered his enemies." Although he was involved in most of the department's major decisions, McGranery appears to have been bypassed on three sensitive cases under Clark: the *Amerasia* espionage controversy; a sensational vote-fraud scandal in President Harry Truman's home district; and a decision against prosecuting a prominent Kansas City bond dealer on charges of mail fraud.

McGranery was appointed federal judge for the Eastern District of Pennsylvania in October 1946, and quickly established a reputation as a firm jurist. Critics described him as "a highhanded pro-Government man," but Francis Biddle, probably more fairly, characterized him as "fundamentally an advocate, not a judge." In 1949, McGranery refused to allow Earl Chudoff, a U.S. congressman, to represent a client in his court; as employees of the government, he argued, congressmen were barred by law from appearing as defense attorneys in the federal courts. In 1950 he presided over the espionage trial of Harry Gold, upon whom he imposed the maximum sentence of thirty years in prison.

On Apr. 3, 1952, McGranery was appointed attorney general by President Truman. He succeeded J. Howard McGrath, also a prominent Irish Catholic Democrat, who had been forced to resign because of his refusal to cooperate with a special investigator probing scandals within the Department of Justice and the Bureau of Internal Revenue. Because of McGranery's political background and his long-standing friendship with Truman, there were wide expectations that he would conduct a cover-up. Instead, he oversaw a thorough inquiry that led to numerous dismissals and prosecutions. When he left office, the suspicions surrounding his appointment had generally given way to praise for his honesty.

During his brief term as attorney general, McGranery was active in several other areas. He either initiated, or laid the groundwork for, major antitrust cases in oil, steel, detergent manufacturing, the diamond trade, and magazine wholesaling. A militant anti-Communist, he approved Smith Act prosecutions against several important leaders of the American Communist party. He began denaturalization and deportation proceedings against notorious underworld figures. Perhaps McGranery's most important decision was to sanction the presentation of a strong integrationist amicus curiae brief to the Supreme Court in the initial hearing of the school desegregation case *Brown* v. *Board of Education of Topeka* in December 1952. It did much to lay the basis for the decision to overrule the "separate but equal" doctrine.

After the end of the Truman administration, McGranery practiced law in Washington, D.C., and Philadelphia; he made it a policy to avoid lobbying activities and cases to which the government was a party. One of the nation's leading Catholic laymen, he received numerous church awards and was a trustee or advisory board member of several Catholic colleges.

McGranery died in Palm Beach, Fla. His life in many ways exemplified the rise of the Irish-Americans in American society and politics during the twentieth century.

[McGranery's papers are at the Library of Congress. There is no comprehensive account of his life. On his service in the Justice Department, see James Andrew Mayer, "The *s-i-z-z-l-i-n-g* Seat of Herbert Brownell," *American Mercury*, Mar.–Apr. 1953; and Francis Biddle, *In Brief Authority* (1962). On the scandals that led to his appointment as attorney general, see Jules Abels, *The Truman Scandals* (1956); and Alonzo L. Hamby, *Beyond the New Deal* (1973). An obituary is in the *Washington Post*, Dec. 25, 1962. A brief obituary is in the *New York Times*, Apr. 1, 1963 (delayed by newspaper strike).]

ALONZO L. HAMBY

McKECHNIE, WILLIAM BOYD (Aug. 7, 1886–Oct. 29, 1965), baseball manager and member of the Baseball Hall of Fame, was born in Wilkinsburg, Pa., a suburb of Pittsburgh. Raised in a religious home, he was for twenty-six years a member of the choir of the Mifflin Street Methodist Episcopal Church in Wilkinsburg. During his baseball career he received the nickname "Deacon Bill" because of his religious background and clean life. A teetotaler, he was always outwardly unruffled, soft-spoken, righ-

teous, and thoughtful. In 1911, McKechnie married Beryl Bein. They had four children.

McKechnie began his baseball career in 1906 with the Washington, Pa., club in the Pennsylvania-Ohio-Maryland League. He was an adept infielder who covered his territory well, but had difficulty hitting. Fortunately for McKechnie, baseball then was low-scoring and emphasized a player's defensive skills.

McKechnie's undistinguished playing career in the minor and major leagues lasted from 1906 to 1920. He filled all of the infield positions while playing for seven different major-league teams. His major-league playing statistics are the lowest for any nonpitcher in the Hall of Fame: .251 batting average, 8 home runs, 127 stolen bases, 319 runs scored, 86 doubles, 33 triples, and 240 runs batted in.

McKechnie's unique success and his stature as a Hall of Famer are based upon his managerial career. Only Connie Mack, John McGraw, and Bucky Harris served longer as major-league managers. McKechnie guided four National League teams: Pittsburgh Pirates (1922–1926), St. Louis Cardinals (1928–1929), Boston Braves (1930–1937), and Cincinnati Reds (1938–1946). In addition to winning National League pennants with Pittsburgh, St. Louis, and Cincinnati, McKechnie achieved World Series victories with the Pirates and Reds.

McKechnie's initial year as manager of Pittsburgh brought the club its first league championship in sixteen years. In 1925 the Pirates finished eight-and-a-half games ahead of McGraw's New York Giants. The year was capped by a seventh-game World Series triumph over the Washington Senators. Down three games to one in the Series, the Pirates swept the final three games, defeating Hall of Fame pitcher Walter Johnson in the deciding contest. McKechnie attributed his managerial skill to the fine managers under whom he had played, including McGraw, Frank Chance, and George Stallings.

The 1926 season was disastrous for McKechnie and the Pirates. Personal disagreements with club vice-president Fred Clarke divided the players' loyalties, and McKechnie was dismissed at the end of the season. Branch Rickey, general manager of the St. Louis Cardinals, immediately hired McKechnie as a coach for the 1927 season. The following year he became manager and guided the Cardinals to the National League pennant. Unfortunately for the Cardinals, the New York Yankees swept the Series in four games, their second consecutive World Series sweep. Sam Breadon, owner of the Cardinals, blamed McKechnie for the club's poor play in the Series. Before the 1929 season Breadon demoted McKechnie to manager of the Rochester, N.Y., Red Wings, St. Louis' farm club in the International League. But Billy Southworth, the new manager of the Cardinals, was unable to fill McKechnie's shoes. Eighty-eight games into the season, Breadon admitted his mistake and switched McKechnie's and Southworth's managerial assignments. The Cardinals finished a respectable fourth. Breadon's treatment of McKechnie may have led him to consider leaving baseball. In 1929, McKechnie ran unsuccessfully for tax collector of Wilkinsburg.

The Boston Braves were the first beneficiaries of McKechnie's abortive political career. From 1930 to 1937 he brought respectability to a team considered by experts to be the worst in the league. Although never finishing higher than fourth place, the Braves under McKechnie's tutelage stressed defense and pitching. McKechnie was designated "Manager of the Year" in 1937, even though his team finished fifth.

In 1938, McKechnie was hired by Warren Giles, Cincinnati's general manager, to manage the Reds at a salary of $25,000 per season. His nine years with the Reds were the most successful of his managerial career. The Reds won pennants in 1939 and 1940 and the World Series in the latter year. The 1939 pennant was the first Cincinnati league championship in twenty years, but the team lost the World Series to the Yankees in four games. In 1940, after leading the league by twelve games, the Reds bested the Detroit Tigers in a seven-game World Series. Pitchers Bucky Walters and Paul Derringer each won two games, with Derringer winning the deciding game 2–1 in Detroit.

Following his championship season, McKechnie kept Cincinnati in the first division until the Reds finished seventh in 1945 and sixth in 1946, his last year as a major-league manager. His low-key manner and conservative style of play were not appreciated by the Reds' fans. General manager Giles complained that the fans had forced him to fire "the best manager in baseball." McKechnie concluded his baseball career as a coach with the Cleveland Indians and Boston Red Sox of the American League.

McKechnie was the only manager to win pennants with three different teams. His success, with fifteen finishes in the first division in twenty-four years, was due to his thoughtful, calculating leadership. He spurned "snap-dash"

methods and displayed a professorial calm. In May 1944 *Sporting News,* baseball's weekly newspaper, named McKechnie the "most studious" manager in baseball history. A conservative who played the game "by the book," he treated his players with understanding and was sympathetic to their concerns.

McKechnie's special forte was his skill with pitchers. Previous deficiencies would disappear under his tutelage. His stress on defense put a premium on pitching. With the Boston Braves, McKechnie's expertise brought newfound success to pitchers Lou Fette and Jim Turner. Paul Derringer and Johnny Vander Meer of the Cincinnati Reds were considered failures until McKechnie helped turn their careers around. He was one of the first managers to insist upon keeping pitchers in strict rotation. Cleveland's manager Al Lopez thought he "learned more about pitching from Bill McKechnie than from anybody else."

In 1953, McKechnie retired to Bradenton, Fla., where he became a successful produce dealer and land investor. Each spring he visited major-league training centers in Florida, maintaining his interest in the game that had brought him so much success. On July 23, 1962, McKechnie was inducted into the Baseball Hall of Fame in Cooperstown, N.Y. Wet-eyed at the ceremony, he stated simply: "Anything that I have contributed to baseball, I have been repaid today seven times seven." He died in Bradenton.

[Short biographical sketches of McKechnie are in Edwin Pope, *Baseball's Greatest Managers* (1960); Martin Appel and Burt Goldblatt, *Baseball's Best: The Hall of Fame Gallery* (1977). Other aspects of McKechnie's life are profiled in Lee Allen, *The National League Story: The Official History* (1965); Joseph Durso, *Casey: The Life and Legend of Charles Dillon Stengel* (1967); Donald Honig, *Baseball When the Grass Was Real* (1975) and *The Man in the Dugout* (1977). An obituary is in *New York Times,* Oct. 30, 1965.]

DAVID BERNSTEIN

McLEVY, JASPER (Mar. 27, 1878–Nov. 19, 1962), Socialist politician, was born in Bridgeport, Conn., the son of Hugh McLevy and Mary Stewart. His father, a Presbyterian minister, left the clergy upon arrival in America from Scotland in the late 1870's and took up roofing, an occupation that the son entered as an apprentice at age thirteen. Prior to his apprenticeship, Jasper had worked as a helper in a tool factory, having left grammar school because of the family's financial difficulties.

McLevy married his childhood sweetheart, Mary Flynn, in 1915. Three years later she died. On Dec. 10, 1929, he married Vida Stearns. Their marriage was kept secret for nearly five years, during which the couple mostly lived apart while the new Mrs. McLevy cared for her aging father.

As a skilled craftsman, McLevy was active in the labor movement. He joined the American Federation of Labor in 1900 and was vice-president of the Connecticut Federation of Labor. He also was organizer for the Central Labor Council of Bridgeport and of that city's Building Trades Council. He served several terms as international president of the Slate and Tile Roofers Union.

McLevy's initiation into socialism was less influenced by Karl Marx than by Edward Bellamy's *Looking Backward.* He joined the Socialist party on Oct. 11, 1900, becoming a member of Branch 10, Local Bridgeport, along with four others. McLevy ran for his first office, a seat in the Connecticut Assembly, when he was twenty-five. Although defeated, he remained a party activist and a perennial candidate. He was defeated nine times for mayor prior to his victory in 1933. He lost fifteen contests for governor, doing best in 1938, when he was defeated by a relatively small margin.

When McLevy was elected mayor of Bridgeport in 1933, a local newspaper, the Italian-American *L'Aurora,* warned that "the fair name of the City of Bridgeport, as the industrial capital of Connecticut, [was] seriously menaced by the Red Peril." But, as in other cities, such as Milwaukee, Wis.; Schenectady, N.Y.; and Reading, Pa., which elected Socialist administrations during the twentieth century, the advent of Socialism in Bridgeport had anything but revolutionary results. Socialists often came to power in cities when corruption by major-party administrations was uncovered, and, as in McLevy's case, were little different from most progressive reformers. The Bridgeport Socialist platform in 1933 stressed the elimination of waste, inefficiency, and corruption in government; the merit system and civil service; municipal ownership of public utilities; open public meetings of governing boards and commissions; and home rule for the city.

McLevy was proud of having restored the city's credit rating during the Great Depression and of running a tight-fisted administration. His approach to municipal services is usually summed up by the story about his attitude toward snow removal: "The Lord put it there. Let Him take it away." While this comment was probably made by an aide, it symbolizes McLevy's philosophy. Under him the Socialists displayed a great enthusiasm for improving Bridgeport's recreational facilities and shore resorts, curbing pollution, constructing parks, establishing playgrounds, and building esplanades. In 1940, McLevy wrote, "I feel that the American City can be just as much a pleasing picture as a small town." The Bridgeport sewage treatment system far surpassed that of any other Connecticut municipality. One might say that McLevy's administration was a classic example of "sewer socialism."

Businessmen came to trust, and often to depend upon, this frugal Socialist. Sixteen years after McLevy's initial victory, Herman W. Steinkraus, a local business executive who was then president of the U.S. Chamber of Commerce, said, "We have a Socialist Mayor . . . but he never was elected because he was a Socialist. He's a good, honest Scotsman who has handled our money carefully, and we Republicans have put him in office." Not until the end of his mayoral career did business, believing McLevy to be moving too slowly on downtown development, abandon him. An analysis of McLevy's electoral support during 1933–1957 shows that although his early support came from ethnic, working-class districts, by 1957 he was drawing heavily upon upper-income voters. These were often his early supporters who grew old and more affluent with him. In the 1950's McLevy did not get much support from Bridgeport's growing black and Puerto Rican communities.

Over the years McLevy rose to prominence in the Socialist party. By 1936, Norman Thomas saw McLevy, along with Daniel Webster Hoan of Milwaukee, as a viable Socialist presidential candidate, even though Thomas and McLevy were in opposite factions of the party. In the dispute between the old guard and the militants that arose over attitudes toward war, democracy, and cooperation with Communists, McLevy emerged as a leader of the former group. He led the conservative wing of the party when he served as first head of the Social Democratic Federation. In 1950 the party censured him for accepting support from businesswoman Vivian Kellams, labeled a conservative by the Socialists, and for running for governor on a ticket that included Kellams as the senatorial candidate.

Never a radical, McLevy moved to the right through his career in politics. A tireless campaigner, he met voters at factory gates, in city parks, and on the streets of Bridgeport. His weatherbeaten features and reputation for honesty earned the public's trust. The voters of Bridgeport voted not for Socialism, but for McLevy, who imprinted his personality on the local Socialist party and on the city in which he was born and died.

[The McLevy and Schwarzkopf collections at the University of Bridgeport are essential for the study of McLevy's career as mayor. Related materials are in the Socialist Party of America papers at the Duke University Library, Durham, N.C.; the Tamiment Institute Library Collection, New York University; and the Norman Thomas Collection at the New York Public Library. Two helpful official publications are the City of Bridgeport, *Manual* and *Municipal Register.* The *New Leader* magazine provides excellent coverage of the early years of the McLevy administration, and the *Bridgeport Post* and *Telegram* offer daily reports of the city's municipal Socialism. Bruce M. Stave's oral history project concerning the Bridgeport Socialists is on file at the Bishop Room of the Bridgeport Public Library. One of the few scholarly articles dealing with McLevy is Bruce M. Stave, "The Great Depression and Urban Political Continuity: Bridgeport Chooses Socialism," in his *Socialism and the Cities* (1975). An obituary is in the *New York Times,* Nov. 20, 1962.]

BRUCE M. STAVE

MADDEN, OWEN VICTOR ("OWNEY") (June 1892–April 24, 1965), gang leader and racketeer, was born in Liverpool, England. His family immigrated to New York City when he was eleven. He soon became involved in gang warfare and proved adept at using a pipe covered with newspaper, a blackjack, a slingshot, brass knuckles, and a pistol. When he was seventeen he murdered a man, and by the time he was twenty-three, he had killed four more, thereby earning the nickname "Owney the Killer."

At the age of eighteen, Madden became the leader of the Gopher Gang in the Hell's Kitchen area of New York City. As leader he received $200 a day from underlings for planning beatings, robberies, extortions, killings, gang raids, and union beatings. The Gopher headquarters was the Winona Club, a second-floor bistro established by Madden and Tanner Smith.

On the night of Nov. 6, 1912, at the Arbor Dance Hall, Madden was confronted by a group from the Hudson Dusters, the Gophers' chief rivals. In the ensuing shoot-out he fell with at least six bullets in his body. He survived (although his wounds troubled him in later life), but refused to identify his assailants to the police. Before he fully recovered, six of them had been killed.

By 1914, Madden had been arrested at least five times but never convicted of a crime. At the end of the year, though, he was indicted, tried, and convicted of the murder of Patrick ("Little Patsy") Doyle, who had assaulted Tony Romanello, a member of the Madden gang. Madden was sentenced to ten to twenty years in Sing Sing Prison. He was a model prisoner and was praised by warden Lewis E. Lawes as a good influence on other convicts. While in prison he displayed an avid interest in pigeons.

Madden was paroled in January 1923 but found his gang dispersed, some in prison and others in Prohibition mobs. After a brief period as a "troubleshooter" for a taxicab company, he and a partner, William Vincent ("Big Bill") Dwyer, established the Phoenix Brewery, which produced Madden's No. 1 lager, reportedly "the creamiest" beer in New York City. Production eventually reached some 300,000 gallons a day, and a rival characterized Madden as a "good businessman." During this period of his career, he was associated with Dutch Schultz and "Legs" Diamond, and was arrested twice. In December 1923, Madden was accused, with others, of robbing the Liberty Storage Warehouse of 900 cases of whiskey; a month later he was again detained when the police stopped a truck in which he was riding and found stolen liquor. No further action resulted from these arrests.

Madden was also involved with nightclubs, and with Arnold Rothstein owned the Cotton Club in Harlem. He became part of the New York night life along with Mae West and Jimmy Walker. He and his partners owned more than one establishment, and used the services of Joseph Urban, noted architect and theatrical designer, to decorate one of them. Madden also owned three laundries. He apparently lost money on them, and was reported to have said: "I like an investment where you can put your money in this week and pull it out double next week or the next. But these legitimate rackets you've got to wait for your money." Boxing was another of Madden's interests, and with Bill Duffy and George ("Big French") DeMange he owned a large part of the Italian heavyweight Primo Carnera.

In 1932, Madden was employed by Charles Lindbergh to help find his kidnapped son, but he had no success. In July of that year, despite a court fight and a recommendation from Lindbergh to the New York State Parole Board, he was sent back to Sing Sing for parole violation. Again the warden praised him as a model prisoner. Upon his release in July 1933, Madden was employed as a dispatcher by the E. H. Thompson Trucking Company, whose owner was also president of the Champion Coal Company. In 1934 the latter company was charged with fraud in supplying coal to New York City, and Madden's name on the trucking firm's payroll was noted. He subsequently appeared as a witness, but no action was taken against him.

In 1934, Madden's first marriage ended in divorce; the following year he married Agnes Demby and retired to Hot Springs, Ark., supposedly to escape a "contract" on his life. He was in charge of gambling and operated casinos in this spa that became a refuge for gangsters. His wealth at the time of his retirement has been estimated to be $3 million. In his later life Madden became more respectable, and in March 1943 he was granted United States citizenship. He died in Hot Springs.

[See Stanley Walker, *The Night Club Era* (1933); Hank Messick and Burt Goldblatt, *The Mobs and the Mafia* (1972); Hank Messick, *The Beauties and the Beasts* (1973); Jay Robert Nash, *Bloodletters and Badmen* (1973); and Wayne McQuin, ed., *The American Way of Crime* (1976). An obituary is in the *New York Times*, Apr. 24, 1965.]

ALLAN NELSON

MADIGAN, LAVERNE (Sept. 13, 1912–Aug. 21, 1962), administrator and Indian rights advocate, was born in Clifton, N.J., the daughter of George Madigan and Georgia Farrell. Her father, a dentist, died when Madigan was fourteen. Her mother, a dynamic and well-educated woman, became a nurse to support the family. Early on, Madigan demonstrated an interest in politics and liberal causes that reflected her mother's commitment to racial integration and Progressivism.

Madigan was educated in Catholic schools, then enrolled part time at New York University, from which she received the B.A. in classics in 1940 and the M.A. in 1941. Following her marriage to Harold Bordewich on Jan. 26, 1941, Madigan took a job with the War Relocation Authority (WRA) as a relocation officer in New Jersey. This was far from her formal training, but she quickly mastered the skills needed to make her an effective administrator. Furthermore, her concern over the treatment of Japanese Americans in West Coast internment camps during World War II led her to find alternative living arrangements for these citizens in the East. Madigan assisted scores of uprooted families, helping them to integrate into urban communities. She also set up a successful farming cooperative for Japanese Americans in southern New Jersey. Coincidentally,

the WRA was headed by Dillon Myer, who later became commissioner of Indian affairs during the Eisenhower administration—the time when Madigan formally became involved with Indian issues.

In 1945, Madigan left the WRA. Two years later her son was born. She returned to public life in 1949, taking a short-term job as assistant to the director of the American Women's Voluntary Services, a private social welfare agency in New York. She had yet to find a meaningful full-time career.

In 1951, Madigan wrote to Oliver La Farge, the Pulitzer Prize-winning author and a founder of the reform-minded Association on American Indian Affairs (AAIA). Although she had never studied Indians, she wanted to work for the AAIA and thought La Farge would help her. She cited her experiences with the WRA and her interest in minority rights as evidence of her concern for the plight of Indians. Although her credentials and previous work experience made her overqualified for the job, she willingly accepted a position as a "glorified secretary" and administrative assistant. Alexander Lesser, the AAIA's Executive Director, admitted this mismatch in a letter to La Farge. "My only fear in her case is that Madigan's intellectual abilities are too great for the dirty work of the job," he noted. Nevertheless, they hired her in October 1951 at a salary lower than their current secretary.

Madigan, a tiny woman (four feet, eleven inches) with a quick wit and an accompanying temper, had prodigious energy. She easily mastered the association's files, absorbing vast amounts of information regarding Indians— their diverse experiences and problems. She worked late at night and on weekends, and used her vacations to travel to reservations and meet tribal chiefs. Possessing an unusual talent for working with all kinds of people, from the least-educated Indians to professors of anthropology, Madigan somehow got them to do what she wanted. She frequently paid her way to work-related conferences and organized policy seminars for the AAIA and the Bureau of Indian Affairs (BIA). Not surprisingly she advanced rapidly within the association and, only five years after she joined the AAIA, became its executive director.

Madigan put her personal stamp on the association by giving equal attention to the nonpolitical aspects of Indian affairs. During its first three decades the AAIA focused primarily on Indian legal rights and the passage of legislation such as the Indian Claims Commission Act

(1946). Madigan charted several new courses. Her strong interest in education resulted in the establishment of a scholarship fund for Indians wanting a college education. It was the first full-scale private endeavor of its kind.

Madigan used her WRA background to secure funds and conduct a major national study of the 1952 BIA program of voluntary Indian resettlement. This monograph, *The American Indian Relocation Program* (1956), presented a balanced and well-researched picture of federal efforts to aid Indians in finding work and housing in white America. Madigan concluded that the program was neither as good as the BIA claimed nor as bad as its critics suggested. She discovered that 30 percent of the Indians who had left the reservations returned within a year. Many managed to "commute" between jobs in the cities and the family life in Indian country.

Madigan's most important contribution was perhaps her work with Alaskan natives. In particular she gave unstinting support to their land and treaty claims. Historically the AAIA had been interested in Indians of the Plains and the Southwest, but Madigan broadened its perspective on native rights through her "We Shake Hands" program, which brought American Indians together with Alaskan Eskimo and Aleuts for the first time.

Madigan's death at Orleans, Vt., the result of a fall while horseback riding, left many projects unfinished. Prominent among them was a primer for non-Indian children that was to provide "a clearer picture of Indian history," which attested Madigan's unswerving concern for education and the importance of knowing other cultures. Madigan had proved that she could work for Indians and minority rights in a variety of public arenas, but she always emphasized education as the best and most lasting mechanism for improving human relations (as opposed to relying solely on legal remedies).

[Madigan also wrote *We Shake Hands* (1958) and *The Most Independent People* (1959). There are no collections of Madigan's private papers, but the files of the AAIA at Princeton University provide useful data on her professional life. The AAIA published a memorial issue of its newsletter following Madigan's death (Oct. 1962). An obituary is in the *New York Times*, Aug. 23, 1962.]

ALISON BERNSTEIN

MAHLER, HERBERT (Nov. 6, 1890–Aug. 17, 1961), labor organizer and radical, was born in Chatham, Ontario, Canada, where he was raised and educated. He left home in 1910 to find work in the Canadian West. Until 1915 he worked in British Columbia as a riverboat pilot and a logger. He then moved to the United States, where in the state of Washington, in July 1915, he joined the Industrial Workers of the World (IWW) and promptly became involved in strikes on the West Coast. In 1916 and 1917, Mahler served as secretary and organizer for several IWW locals in the Seattle area and was especially active in trying to organize longshoremen and lumber workers.

After the Everett, Wash., "massacre" of November 1916, when state authorities arrested a large group of "Wobblies" and tried them on murder charges, Mahler was secretary-treasurer of the IWW's Everett Defense Committee. Under his direction the committee raised funds, generated publicity, and elicited sympathy for the defendants, all of whom were acquitted in May 1917. While he asserted the innocence of the Everett prisoners, Mahler also threatened the use of sabotage. He once wrote, "It takes money to feed the cats [saboteurs] and it will be them that play the leading role, too."

After the United States entered World War I, Mahler participated in IWW lumber and copper strikes that tied up the production of vital war supplies in Montana, Idaho, and Washington. He also tried to devise an effective, yet legal, antiwar strategy for the "Wobblies." Although he opposed militarism and war as well as conscription, Mahler believed that the IWW could accomplish more through organization of workers and industrial action than through antiwar propaganda and unwise antigovernment activities. "The masters are undoubtedly looking for an opportunity to close down some of our halls," he wrote to another "Wobbly" on Apr. 10, 1917, "and if we do give them an excuse we should be sure to give them a damn good one."

As war hysteria and patriotism swept the United States, Mahler continued to advise caution, informing William D. ("Big Bill") Haywood, the IWW leader, in June and again in August 1917, that "all we can do now is to make the best of a bad situation." But caution did not save Mahler from arrest in September 1917. The federal government indicted him, along with 100 other IWW leaders, in Chicago. He was convicted of three counts of espionage and sedition, and was sentenced in August 1918 to twelve years in prison and a $20,000 fine. He began his sentence at Leavenworth Federal Pententiary on Sept. 7, 1918. Although eligible for parole as early as May 1920, Mahler declined to file for it. He remained in prison until December 1923, when President Calvin Coolidge commuted the sentences of all the Chicago IWW inmates still incarcerated to time served.

After his release Mahler resumed work in the IWW. He functioned through Chicago Branch number 1, and by the end of the 1920's had again become a national leader. He served as secretary of the organization's General Defense Committee, and on Mar. 1, 1931, became general secretary-treasurer, the IWW's highest office. But on Nov. 25, 1932, during the IWW's twentieth national convention, Mahler resigned from the post because of the convention's refusal to support him on two policy issues (nonexpulsion of a suspect member, and failure to provide adequate support for Harlan County, Ky., miners). He made his last official appearance within the organization at its 1934 convention, as a delegate from the General Recruiting Union and an unsuccessful nominee for general secretary-treasurer.

Some time later Mahler moved to New York City, where in 1937 he organized the Kentucky Miners Defense Committee on behalf of four union coal miners serving life sentences for murder as a result of the bloody 1931 Harlan County strike. But generally he remained organizationally inactive until 1948, when he appeared with a small group of IWW pickets at the New York office of the *New Republic* to protest the publication in that magazine of an article that accused the IWW martyr, Joe Hill, of being a common criminal. Mahler died in New York City. He was survived by his wife, the former Bessie Freiberg.

[Some manuscript and personal materials are in the Archives of Labor History and Urban Affairs, Wayne State University, Detroit; the Department of Justice files, Record Group 60; and the pardon attorney's files, National Archives, Washington, D.C. Also see William D. Haywood, *Bill Haywood's Book* (1929); Patrick Renshaw, *The Wobblies* (1967); and Melvyn Dubofsky, *We Shall Be All* (1969). An obituary is in the *New York Times*, Aug. 18, 1961.]

MELVYN DUBOFSKY

MALCOLM X (May 19, 1925–Feb. 21, 1965), black leader, was born Malcolm Little in Omaha, Nebr., the son of Earl Little, a Baptist minister and organizer for Marcus Garvey's Universal Negro Improvement Association, and Louise Little. When his mother was pregnant with him, Ku Klux Klan riders, brandishing shotguns and rifles, galloped up to the family home looking for his father. In 1929 the family moved to East Lansing, Mich., where the Reverend Little was subjected to threats from a local white group known as the Black Legion, who objected to his desire to start a store and to the Garvey philosophy that he advocated.

In 1929 local racists burned down the Little home, forcing the family to move to the outskirts of town. Two years later Malcolm's father was found murdered. Several years later the state welfare agency, over the opposition of Louise Little, placed her children in state institutions and boarding homes because of the family's destitution. She subsequently suffered a mental breakdown, and the court placed her in the state mental hospital at Kalamazoo, where she remained for the next twenty-six years. The mistreatment of his parents, especially his mother, became a source of bitterness to Malcolm Little. Louise Little and her children were casualties of a welfare system that made meager efforts to keep impoverished black families together.

Malcolm was subsequently placed in a foster home and then in a detention home in Mason, Mich., for having placed a tack on his teacher's chair. While at the detention home he made an excellent record at the Mason Junior High School and was elected seventh-grade class president. But his accomplishment only temporarily obscured the racism of this relatively liberal environment. The husband and wife team that ran the detention home often referred to blacks as "niggers." Malcolm's history teacher taught a stereotypic American history replete with happy, ignorant, and lazy slaves and freedmen. His English teacher advised him to take up carpentry, although he was an outstanding student and wished to become a lawyer.

Malcolm grew withdrawn, and following placement in another foster home his official custody was transferred to Boston, where he lived with his half sister after dropping out of the eighth grade. He obtained jobs with a dining-car crew on trains traveling to New York City and as a waiter in a Harlem nightclub.

In New York City, Little began selling and using narcotics, gambling, and steering whites looking for sex in Harlem to the correct locales. During World War II he parlayed his zoot-suit, street-hustler image and the fears of the white psychiatrist at the induction center into a draft exemption. In 1946, after returning to Boston, he was arrested for burglary and sentenced to ten years in prison.

In prison, Little began a process of self-education that enabled him to more than hold his own in intellectual debate with those of far more formal education. Through letters and visits from family members he was introduced into the Lost-Found Nation of Islam (popularly known as the Black Muslims). His eventual conversion to the Nation of Islam resulted in his renunciation of his life-style.

The Nation of Islam held, through its spiritual leader, Elijah Muhammad, that the black race was the first creation of God, or Allah. To the Muslims, whites were the physical and spiritual descendants of the devilish Yacub, a black scientist in rebellion against Allah. This explained the worldwide exploitation of nonwhites and their devotion to non-Islamic religions. Whites, to the Muslims, were "devils" whose evil was manifested in their immorality and racial oppression. The origins of the Muslims can be traced to the early years of the Great Depression, but the movement reached its peak in the mid-1930's, after a schism developed that forced Elijah Muhammad to move to Chicago's Temple Number Two. From Chicago, the Nation of Islam grew into a significant socioreligious movement that eventually established schools, apartment houses, grocery stores, restaurants, and farms for the benefit of American blacks.

Released from prison in 1952, Little quickly entered the Muslim fold and became an effective recruiter. He replaced his family name with an X, as was the custom of the Nation of Islam, which considered last names to be those of white slaveholders. In the summer of 1953, Malcolm X was appointed assistant minister of Detroit's Temple Number One. His effectiveness as an organizer of temples in Boston and Philadelphia and his oratorical skill led to his appointment as minister of Harlem's important Temple Number Seven in June 1954.

From this point, the rise of the Black Muslim movement reflects the rise in popularity of Malcolm X. As the Nation of Islam grew rapidly in the black ghettos it attracted increasing coverage by both the black and white media. Malcolm's column for the *Amsterdam News* was later transferred to the *Los Angeles Herald Dispatch* when Elijah Muhammad began to write a column for the *Amsterdam News.* In 1961 Malcolm founded *Muhammad Speaks,* the official organ of the movement. The appearance of a television documentary on the Nation of Islam, "The Hate That Hate Produced," on the Mike Wallace show in July 1959 further brought the movement to national attention, although many Muslims considered the documentary slanted. On Jan. 14, 1958, Little married Betty X Shabazz. They had six children.

The emerging civil rights movement provided a forum for blacks of varying ideological persuasions. The basic philosophical and tactical

differences between integrationist groups such as the National Association for the Advancement of Colored People (NAACP) and the Congress of Racial Equality (CORE), on the one hand, and nationalistic Muslims, on the other, were quickly manifested. Malcolm X asserted that whites acted devilishly toward blacks because that was their nature. Therefore, it was absurd to believe that racial equality and integration could be achieved. Even more foolish, he insisted, was the tactic of nonviolent confrontation, which often resulted in violence directed at civil rights demonstrators who rejected retaliatory violence or self-defense. Since there was little difference between white liberals and conservatives on the race issue, the only solutions were the return to Africa or the division of the United States into black and white nations.

At a rally on December 1, 1963, Malcolm X referred to President John F. Kennedy's assassination as a case of "the chickens coming home to roost." The hate directed at blacks, he maintained, had spread to the point where it had struck down the president. The white media, which had portrayed Malcolm X as a violent racist fanatic, played up the statement. Elijah Muhammad disassociated the Muslims from the statement and prohibited Malcolm X from speaking publicly for the next ninety days.

As early as 1961, Malcolm had heard rumors that officials surrounding Muhammad were highly critical of him, claiming that he was taking credit for Muhammad's work and trying to take over the Nation of Islam. Malcolm X privately had grown dissatisfied with the Muslim policy of "general nonengagement" from active involvement in confronting racism. Rumors of Elijah Muhammad's sexual involvement with his secretaries further contributed to Malcolm's concern. On Mar. 12, 1964, he announced that "internal differences within the Nation of Islam" forced him to leave the movement. He still, however, believed that Elijah Muhammad's nationalistic analysis of the racial problem was the "most realistic" one. After this break with Muhammad, Malcolm sought to internationalize the Afro-American freedom struggle. He announced the formation of the Muslim Mosque, Incorporated. In April 1964 he left for Mecca.

On his trip he met with important Arab officials and Islamic scholars, who told him that their religion did not make racial distinctions or subscribe to the Yacub demonology taught by the Nation of Islam. In Mecca and throughout the Middle East, he met white Islamic practitioners who appeared to be without racial prejudice. After leaving Mecca, Malcolm visited Beirut, Cairo, Ghana, and Nigeria. In a speech at the University of Ibadan, he emphasized the need for African nations to support a move to bring the United States before the United Nations for violating Afro-American human rights. On his return from Africa, he told a press conference that his experience in the Islamic world had led him to conclude that whites were not inherently racist but, rather, that racial prejudice was a product of Western culture. He subsequently formed the Organization of Afro-American Unity (June 1964) to be modeled on the Organization of African Unity (OAU). He hoped to unify Afro-Americans previously divided in philosophy and tactics and envisioned the possibility of cooperation with progressive white organizations.

During the summer of 1964, Malcolm returned to Africa and was accorded observer status at the heads of states summit conference of the OAU. In his presentation to the conference he asserted that an identity of interest existed between Afro-Americans and African peoples and that each should aid the other's struggle against colonialism and racism. The conference passed a resolution deploring racism in the United States.

After returning to the United States, Malcolm X continued to seek support for bringing the issue of American racism before the World Court and United Nations, to advocate the political and economic control of black communities by Afro-Americans, and to warn against "American dollarism" in Africa. He pointed out that the persistence of racism would lead to racial violence and the need of Afro-American self-defense. He enumerated the connections between Euro-American capitalistic exploitation and racist oppression both in the Third World and America. His willingness to put aside past acrimony with black leaders in order to seek unity proved ineffective amidst the philosophical and tactical differences of integrationists, nationalists, and socialists. The variegated ideological composition of the black community can be seen in the reaction to the post-Mecca Malcolm X, who now called himself El-Hajj Malik El-Shabazz. To some middle-class integrationists, his pilgrimage had transformed him into one of them. Some nationalists were offended by his acceptance of interracial brotherhood. To some Marxists, Malcolm seemed a revolutionary socialist even though his anticapitalistic remarks merely noted the relationship between capitalism and racism, rather than advocating a Marxist solution.

In February 1965, Malcolm X's home was fire-bombed. By this time, he believed that leaders of the Nation of Islam and even more powerful elements within the American government wanted him dead; a week later he was assassinated at the Audubon Ballroom in Harlem. Talmadge Hayer, Norman 3X Butler, and Thomas 15X Johnson were convicted of the killing and given life sentences. Although Butler and Johnson were Black Muslims, the trial did not reveal whether or not the assassins were a part of a conspiracy. Some of Malcolm's critics took the opportunity provided by his death to launch a final attack. Carl Rowan, the first black director of the U.S. Information Agency, attributed his death to feuding between fanatical groups, "neither of them representative of more than a tiny minority of the Negro population of America."

Malcolm X influenced disparate wings of the black movement. The radical faction of the "Black Power" movement accepted his positions on African identification, neocolonialism, black control of the political economy of black communities, and Afro-American self-defense. He also forced civil rights leaders to assume more militant positions, which aided in the passage of civil rights legislation. The enactment of civil rights bills was not his goal; nevertheless, the specter of even wider acceptance of his philosophy haunted white politicians. The historical importance of Malcolm X cannot be derived from these influences or from the numbers in his organization or his fruitless effort to obtain United Nations intervention in the American race problem. Rather, his contribution was his transformation of the consciousness of a generation of Afro-Americans from racially based self-hatred to the racial pride necessary to the struggle for equality.

[The absence of an extensive archival collection of manuscripts increases the value of Malcolm's published writings and speeches. *The Autobiography of Malcolm X* (1965), written with Alex Haley, is extremely important for its treatment of his early life and philosophical transformation. His most memorable speeches are in George Breitman, ed., *Malcolm X Speaks* (1965) and *By Any Means Necessary* (1970); *Two Speeches by Malcolm X* (1965); *Malcolm X on Afro-American History* (1967); and Benjamin Goodman, ed., *The End of White World Supremacy* (1971). Archie Epps, ed., *The Speeches of Malcolm X at Harvard* (1968), contains an extensive introductory essay. *Malcolm X Talks to Young People* (1965) demonstrates Malcolm X's ability as a teacher.

Biographical studies include John Henrik Clarke, *Malcolm X: The Man and His Times* (1969); Peter L. Goldman, *The Death and Life of Malcolm X*

(1973); George Breitman, *The Last Year of Malcolm X* (1967); and Louis Lomax, *To Kill a Black Man* (1968).

Articles on Malcolm's historical importance are Betty Shabazz, "The Legacy of My Husband," *Ebony*, June 1969; Albert Cleage, "The Malcolm X Myth," *Liberator*, June 1967; Robert Penn Warren, "Malcolm X: Mission and Meaning," *Yale Review*, Dec. 1966; and Nat Hentoff, "Odyssey of a Black Man," *Commonweal*, Jan. 28, 1966. On the responsibility for Malcolm's death, see Allan Morrison, "Who Killed Malcolm X?" *Ebony*, Oct. 1965; and Eric Norden, "Who Killed Malcolm X?" *Realist*, Feb. 1967. The *New York Times*, Feb. 22, 1965, has a story on Malcolm X's death.]

LARRY A. GREENE

MALIN, PATRICK MURPHY (May 8, 1903–Dec. 13, 1964), teacher, administrator, and civil libertarian, was born in Joplin, Mo., the son of Hanson Atkins Malin, a banker, and of Ida Elizabeth Murphy. After graduating from Joplin High School in 1920, he entered the University of Pennsylvania, where he received a B.S. degree in economics in 1924. Because of his Quaker background he briefly considered a career in the ministry, but instead became private secretary to Sherwood Eddy of the International Young Men's Christian Association, a position he held until 1929. At the same time, Malin continued part-time graduate studies at Columbia University, first at Union Theological Seminary and Teachers College and then in the economics department. In 1930 he was appointed an instructor of economics at Swarthmore College, where he spent most of his next twenty years, rising to full professor. On June 16, 1928, he married Caroline Cooper Biddle; they had three sons.

During the 1920's and 1930's Malin became involved in a number of organizations and causes, establishing a pattern that would dominate the rest of his life. In 1925 he was made a fellow of the National Council on Religion in Higher Education, later serving as a director (1937–1943) and as president (1939–1943). From 1936 to 1938 he was vice-chairman of the American Friends Service Committee, concerned with administering relief for both sides in the Spanish Civil War. Finally, in order to devote himself to administrative work on a full-time basis, he took an extended leave of absence from Swarthmore College in 1940.

From 1940 until 1942, Malin was director of the International Migration Service, which cared for refugees in Europe and the West Indies. Then, calling himself an independent Democrat, he moved into President Franklin Roosevelt's administration, holding various posts that included associate director of the Export-Import Price Control Office in the Office of Price Administration (OPA) and price executive of the Chemicals and Drugs Branch of the OPA. He was next appointed deputy chief of the Division of Programs and Requirements, Office of Foreign Relief and Rehabilitation Operations, in the State Department. From 1943 to 1947 Malin was also senior American member of the Intergovernmental Committee on Refugees.

Malin's most significant affiliation was his membership in the American Civil Liberties Union (ACLU), which he joined soon after the organization was established in 1920. On Feb. 1, 1950, he was elected its executive director, replacing the founder, Roger N. Baldwin.

As director of the ACLU, Malin proved to be a less dynamic figure than his predecessor. Not surprisingly, given his training, he tended to be more of a cautious administrator. He possessed impeccable credentials, though, and had never had connections with any group that could be considered radical. All these factors were no doubt significant in his selection as director, since by 1950 many in the United States had become increasingly preoccupied with Communist subversion and conspiracy. In this atmosphere the ACLU often experienced difficulties in maintaining its goals, and needed a leader with Malin's temperament and background.

Many within the ACLU believed that the organization had to protect itself from attack by condemning Communist activities and theories and by barring Communists from membership. Malin agreed with the majority of his board of directors on this, and as a result the ACLU continued to prohibit Communist membership and also accepted the necessity for the House Un-American Activities Committee and the Internal Security Act. Usually they disagreed only with tactics of the committee and abuses that resulted. Malin also stated that educational institutions did not violate academic freedom by inquiring whether their teachers belonged to the Communist party. Despite these policies, the ACLU was accused of being a Communist front organization by Senator Joseph McCarthy and the American Legion.

Throughout his term as director (1950–1962), Malin continued to speak and write about violations of civil liberties. He opposed blacklisting, censorship of books and periodicals, loyalty-determination procedures without due process of law, universal military training, anti-contraception laws, legislation aimed against bus boycotts, questions concerning religion on federal censuses, and government wiretapping, with or without a court order. Malin also defended the right of Senator McCarthy to make a political speech on a Seattle television channel in 1954 and the right of the fascist National Renaissance party to disseminate its views. Having taken such stands, Malin was often annoyed by the fact that many people believed he and the ACLU supported the opinions of those they defended. He never shied from becoming embroiled in vigorous debates with such detractors.

In spite of these problems, Malin generally managed to maintain his administrative calm and his sense of humor. He despised both flamboyance and pomposity, and claimed that working for civil liberties was neither dramatic nor romantic, but simply a necessary task that had to be pursued. In this style Malin carefully guided the ACLU through one of its most difficult and troubled periods. And, while some within the ACLU believed that he was too cautious and conservative, there is little doubt that he contributed to its survival and growth. In the process he emerged as one of the nation's leading spokesmen for civil liberties.

Malin retired as ACLU director in February 1962 and became president of Robert College, an American-operated school of 1,600 students in Istanbul, Turkey. In 1964 he returned to New York City, where he died.

[Malin's correspondence as director of the ACLU is in the organization's papers at Princeton University. He published articles expressing his beliefs in the *New Republic*, Aug. 1956, and the *Nation*, Sept. 1956. Articles on Malin are in *Christian Century*, Jan. 1950, and *Survey*, Mar. 1950. On his leadership of the ACLU, see Mary Sperling McAuliffe, *Crisis on the Left* (1978). An obituary is in the *New York Times*, Dec. 14, 1964.]

ERIC JARVIS

MANNES, LEOPOLD DAMROSCH (Dec. 26, 1899–Aug. 11, 1964), pianist, composer, inventor, and music educator, was born in New York City, the son of David Mannes and Clara Damrosch, both of whom were internationally known musicians. David Mannes was a violinist and concertmaster of the New York Symphony Orchestra; Clara Mannes, a pianist, was the daughter of the conductor Leopold Damrosch, and her brothers Walter and Frank were both conductors. David and Clara Mannes jointly founded the Mannes School of Music in 1916.

Leopold Mannes began the study of piano at the age of four and was thoroughly educated in all aspects of music during his formative years.

In addition to his studies at the Riverdale Country School, the Institute of Musical Art (founded in 1904 by his uncle Frank Damrosch and now the Juilliard School of Music) and the Mannes School, he studied piano with Elizabeth Quaile in New York (1908–1909), with Rosario Scalero in New York and Italy (1921–1926), with Berthe Bert in New York (1922–1925), and with Alfred Cortot (1924–1925). He had lessons in music theory from Johannes Schreyer in Switzerland (1910) and in composition from Percy Goetschius in New York (1911–1912). Mannes received a B.A. in music from Harvard in 1920.

After completing his formal education Mannes joined the faculty of his parents' school to teach piano and composition. From 1927 to 1931 he taught at the Institute of Musical Art. His known compositions include *Suite for Two Pianos* (1924); *Three Short Pieces*, for orchestra (1926); two madrigals for chorus (1926); *String Quartet* (1928); and incidental music for a children's performance of Shakespeare's *The Tempest* (1930).

From his youth Mannes experimented with photography and was especially interested in the possibility of producing color photographs. With a classmate, Leopold Godowsky, he set up a small laboratory and began a lifelong association of invention and experimentation. In 1930 the two were persuaded by C. E. Kenneth Mees, director of the laboratories of Eastman Kodak, to come to Rochester, N.Y., and work full-time testing and perfecting their ideas. Their invention of the Kodachrome process of color photography was announced in 1935. Mannes continued to work at the laboratory until 1941, when he returned to music. In that year he also patented a sound track of gold which improved the sound quality of color motion pictures.

As his parents grew older, Mannes increased his commitments to the Mannes School, having become an associate director in 1940. Upon his mother's death in 1948 he assumed the duties of president, while his father continued as a director. Under Leopold's leadership the school became the Mannes College of Music in 1953 and merged with the Chatham Square Music School in 1960. At the time of his death the institution had an enrollment of approximately 630 and offered a five-year program leading to a B.S. in music.

Mannes was particularly interested in chamber music. In 1949 he joined with colleagues Vittorio Brero (violinist) and Luigi Silva (cellist) to form the Mannes Trio. A year later Bronislav

Gimpel replaced Brero, and the name was changed to the Mannes-Gimpel-Silva Trio.

Tall, handsome, urbane, and witty with friends, Mannes retained a particular reticence and sense of propriety concerning the treatment and demeanor of musicians. He was always willing, for example, to serve on juries for student competitions and to participate in honoring outstanding accomplishments. But he objected in 1958 to the idea of a ticker tape parade for Van Cliburn, who had just won the International Tchaikovsky Piano Competition in Moscow, saying that a parade was not the appropriate way to honor such an achievement.

On May 13, 1926, Mannes married Edith Vernon Mann Simonds; they were divorced in 1933. He married Evelyn Sabin on July 16, 1940. They had one daughter. Mannes died at Martha's Vineyard, Mass. He and Leopold Godowsky were about to begin writing their joint memoirs. At the time, the two had just been named to receive the Progress Award of the Royal Photographic Society of London.

Mannes was that rare person who made important contributions in several fields. As a scientist, he was a pioneer in the invention and improvement of techniques of color photography and motion picture production. His work as a musician spanned all fields—composing, performing, teaching—while his long devotion to the Mannes College of Music provided improved opportunities for study for thousands of promising musicians.

[The most detailed source is David Mannes, *Music Is My Faith* (1938). Biographical sketches appear in J. T. H. Mize, ed., *The International Who Is Who in Music*, 5th ed. (1951); and Theodore Baker, ed., *Baker's Biographical Dictionary of Musicians*, 6th ed. (1978). There is an obituary in the *New York Times*, Aug. 12, 1964.]

REBECCA SHEPHERD

MARCOSSON, ISAAC FREDERICK (Sept. 13, 1876–Mar. 14, 1961), journalist and interviewer, was born in Louisville, Ky., the son of Louis and Helen M. Marcosson. His father was a traveling salesman. "By the time I reached the age of fourteen," reads the first sentence of his autobiography, "I knew what I wanted to do once I went to work." He began to gratify his ambition at eighteen, after the lack of money put an end to his education, by going to work for the *Louisville Times*.

Marcosson rose swiftly on the *Times* to assistant city editor and book reviewer; Arthur Krock later recalled that upon entering Louisville journalism in 1910 he heard tales of his energy and advancement. Marcosson also began writing stories and reviews for national magazines; and in 1903, after a dispute with the city editor, he quit and went to New York City, hoping to find a job on a magazine.

Through a slight acquaintance with Walter Hines Page, Marcosson became a staff writer on Page's *World's Work*, a business-oriented monthly. Soon he was writing three articles per issue, two under pseudonyms. At the same time he began his career as a journalistic "lion-hunter," interviewing Theodore Roosevelt and Andrew Carnegie. While on the staff of *World's Work*, Marcosson had married Grace Griffiths, his childhood sweetheart, knowing she was in the last stages of a fatal illness.

In 1907, after a salary dispute, Marcosson joined the staff of the *Saturday Evening Post*, for which he subsequently wrote 124 weekly articles under the general title "Your Savings," as well as other pieces. He commenced the friendly relations with Wall Street figures that led some to deride him as a "Little Brother of the Rich." While working for the *Post*, Marcosson produced his first two books, *How to Invest Your Savings* (1907) and *Autobiography of a Clown* (1910). After three years as an editor at *Munsey's*, he returned to the *Post* in 1913, to begin almost a quarter-century as the foremost interviewer in American journalism.

No American writer, commented the *Bookman* in 1919, received "more varied opportunity" from World War I than Marcosson. Undeterred by fourteen cancellations he secured an interview with David Lloyd George, which not only boosted his reputation but also led to other connections. By the end of the war, Marcosson had interviewed most of the leading Allied figures for the *Post*, gone to Russia (with letters of introduction from Lloyd George) to view the Kerensky government, and published *The Rebirth of Russia* (1917). After the war he went on a lecture tour of the United States, warning against Bolshevism. During the tour, he claimed, his life was threatened twenty-nine times by the Industrial Workers of the World.

Marcosson's interviewing, which depended heavily on contacts and the willingness of his subjects to talk to him, led to a somewhat conservative view of journalism. "When you have played the game straight with a man, and have not had your sense of honor distorted by an impetuous desire to print an exclusive or secure a sensational statement just for the sake of pride or glory, that man will always be your friend," he explained in *Everybody's* in 1921. "Journalism is a high and noble profession and should be employed only as a constructive force. Abuse is what makes it yellow."

During the 1920's and early 1930's Marcosson visited Africa, made several trips to South America, interviewed Sun Yat-sen and other Chinese leaders, and became the first American journalist to interview the emperor of Japan. But his reputation rested mostly on his pieces on European political and industrial leaders. Although he did not interview Adolf Hitler or Joseph Stalin, Marcosson interpreted Leon Trotsky, Benito Mussolini, Paul von Hindenburg, and scores of others for *Post* readers. His departures for and returns from Europe were covered by reporters seeking his impressions.

Marcosson ascribed his 1936 break with the *Post* to editor George Horace Lorimer's conservatism and advancing age. Others have suggested that his long, formal interview style was becoming stale, especially in contrast with the "Profiles" being developed at the *New Yorker*. In any case, Marcosson could afford independence; in 1932, Caroline Freveris, the sister of his friend David Graham Phillips (whose biography he had published in that year), had left him $729,286. On June 8, 1931, Morcosson married Frances Barberey. Shortly after he left the *Post*, she died of cancer.

Marcosson then abandoned other interests for the study of cancer, a disease then seldom mentioned in public. He was elected to the Board of Managers of New York's Memorial Hospital for the Treatment of Cancer and Allied Diseases, and became its first director of public relations. His writings on cancer appeared in *Reader's Digest* and *Woman's Home Companion*.

Through his cancer work Marcosson met Ellen Petts, whom he married on Sept. 1, 1942. She became his assistant and then his successor at Memorial. Later she helped him in the writing of a series of corporate biographies that included *The Romance of the Cash Register* (1945), *Copper Heritage* (1955), and *Anaconda*, (1957).

Marcosson was unquestionably the world's most successful journalistic "headhunter." If, as Vincent Sheean commented, "Mr. Marcosson seldom has anything unexpected to say about his princes and potentates," he was nevertheless a major source of foreign news for the American public, providing careful accounts of significant developments. In John Tebbel's words, Marcosson "imparted a feeling of complete intimacy with his subject," an intimacy with European figures rarely felt by Americans until then. He died in New York City.

[Marcosson's books not mentioned in the text are *Adventures in Interviewing* (1919); *Turbulent Years* (1938); and *Before I Forget* (1959). An article by him is "Everything Is Possible," *Everybody's*, Sept. 1921. Also see John Tebbel, *George Horace Lorimer and the Saturday Evening Post* (1948). An obituary is in the *New York Times*, Mar. 15, 1961.]

DAVID SARASOHN

MARQUIS DE CUEVAS. See DE CUEVAS, MARQUIS.

MARTIN, JOHNNY LEONARD ROOSEVELT ("PEPPER") (Feb. 29, 1904–Mar. 5, 1965), baseball player, was born near Temple, Okla., the son of George Washington Martin, a farmer. When he was six, the family moved to Oklahoma City, where the elder Martin was a house painter and carpenter.

As a youth Martin played both baseball and football. His formal education ended at Irving Junior High in Oklahoma City. He next held a number of jobs as a laborer before joining a semiprofessional baseball team in Guthrie, Okla. His professional career began with Greenville, in the East Texas League, in 1924. His playing skills soon attracted the attention of scout Charley Barrett, who signed him to a contract with the St. Louis Cardinals' Fort Smith, Ark., farm team. Martin married Ruby A. Pope on Nov. 9, 1927; they had three daughters.

In 1928, after he had played for several of the Cardinals' minor-league teams, Martin moved up to the major-league club in St. Louis. He spent most of the season as a pinch runner, then returned to the minor leagues. He came back to stay in 1931. His potential was such that in June the Cardinals traded away their regular center fielder Taylor Douthit, who had played when they won the National League pennant in 1930, and installed Martin in that position.

Martin was five feet, nine inches tall and weighed 170 pounds. He had a weather-beaten face with a hawklike nose and broad, boyish grin. His uniform (which he wore without underwear) was frequently dirty, because he played baseball with joyous abandon, running hard and sliding hard. His exuberant style earned him the nickname "Wild Horse of the Osage."

In 123 games in 1931, Martin hit .300 and batted in 75 runs, but it was that season's World Series against the Philadelphia Athletics that brought his greatest fame. He sparked his team by stealing five bases and setting a new World Series record of twelve base hits in twenty-four times at bat. He was directly responsible for three of the four Cardinal victories that brought the team the championship. Martin electrified fans by his ability to run seemingly at will against Mickey Cochrane, one of baseball's finest catchers. "Red" Smith, then a sportswriter for the *St. Louis Star*, exaggerated only slightly when he wrote, between the fifth and sixth games of the series, that the rest of the Cardinal team had ". . . become merely an indispensable background for the greatest one-man show the baseball world has ever known."

In the years that followed, Martin played sometimes in the outfield and sometimes at third base. In 1934 he was the third baseman when the Cardinals again won the pennant and the World Series, this time against the Detroit Tigers. His rough-and-tumble style (sliding headfirst into bases and often fielding hard-hit balls after stopping them with his chest) typified the play of the "Gashouse Gang," as that year's Cardinal team came to be known.

Off the field Martin was given to zany antics: dropping water-filled paper bags out of windows, driving a midget car in races, playing guitar in the Cardinals' unmelodious "Mudcat Band," and dropping sneezing powder in hotels. Once he and several teammates masqueraded as painters and disrupted a dignified luncheon in Philadelphia. With it all he acquired a reputation as a down-to-earth, generous, good-natured, and honest man.

Martin played for St. Louis through the 1940 season. He then returned to the minor leagues as a player-manager until the World War II manpower shortage brought him back to the Cardinals in 1944. Again the team won the pennant and World Series; during the season he hit .279 in 40 games. In 1945, Martin resumed minor-league managing, and played sporadically through 1947. He made token playing appearances in 1949, 1951, and 1958. As manager of the Miami Sun Sox in 1949, he was suspended for putting his hands on an umpire's throat during an argument.

In 1956, Martin returned to the major leagues for one year as a nonplaying coach (assistant to the manager) of the Chicago Cubs. Although he continued his affiliation with baseball up to the time of his death at McAlester, Okla., he also worked during his last years as a prison athletic director and cattle rancher.

In 1,189 major-league games (not counting World Series and All-Star games), Martin had 1,227 hits in 4,117 times at bat, for an average of .298. He hit 59 home runs, scored 756 runs, and had 501 runs batted in. He stole 146 bases and three times led the National League in that category—26 in 1933, 23 in 1934, and 23 in

1936. His career totals mark him as a good ballplayer but no superstar, and not of Hall of Fame caliber. What set him apart from his contemporaries—what made him an enduring legend in baseball—was that marvelous ten-day period in October 1931 when he dominated the World Series as completely as any player ever has.

[Useful clipping files are at the *St. Louis Post-Dispatch*, *St. Louis Globe-Democrat*, and *Sporting News*. See John Drebinger, "Pepper Martin—Hero of the World's Series," *New York Times*, Oct. 12, 1931; W. C. Heinz, "The Happiest Hooligan of Them All," *True*, Oct. 1959, repr. in Don Congdon, ed., *The Thirties* (1962); "Red" Smith, "Series: Pepper Martin vs. Philadelphia, 1931," in Daniel Okrent, ed., *The Ultimate Baseball Book* (1979); and Bob Broeg, *The Pilot Light and the Gas House Gang* (1980). Obituaries are in the *New York Times*, Mar. 6, 1965, and *Sporting News*, Mar. 20, 1965.]

PAUL STILLWELL

MARX, ADOLF ARTHUR ("HARPO") (Nov. 23, 1893–Sept. 28, 1964), and MARX, LEONARD ("CHICO") (Mar. 22, 1891–Oct. 11, 1961), vaudeville and motion picture performers, together with their brothers Groucho, Gummo, and Zeppo were born in the Yorkville section of New York City, the sons of Samuel Marx and Minna Schoenberg. Their father, who immigrated to the United States from Alsace, worked in New York's Lower East Side as a tailor. Their mother's parents had been entertainers in Germany, and as her sons grew up Minnie Marx devoted a great deal of time to developing and promoting a succession of vaudeville acts involving various members of the family. It was from this constantly changing mix that the Marx Brothers' unique style of comedy emerged.

Neither Chico nor Harpo was involved in the earliest forms of the act, which were musical. One by one the brothers joined Groucho, their mother, aunt, and others, both relatives and nonrelatives, in a succession of musical revue acts that struggled on minor vaudeville circuits. By 1914 the four oldest brothers were the core of a variety act called, aptly enough, the Four Marx Brothers. While on a vaudeville tour the brothers met the manager of a Dennison, Tex., theater who was looking for a comedy act. The sketch that they hastily assembled from memory of other acts—none of the brothers had spent much time in school—was entitled "Fun in Hi Skule—or School Days." It gave free rein to their previously unused improvisational talents, particularly those of Chico, Harpo, and Groucho. The flexible format of the skit incorporated both Chico's piano playing and Harpo's harp playing as well as an endless and energetic assortment of physical gags, outrageous puns, and general ad-libbed mayhem. Despite fines from theater managers and their mother's stern admonitions to control themselves, the act remained volatile: lines changed frequently, the length varied widely, and the large proportion of physical comedy and activity resulted in considerable damage to stage and set. "Fun in Hi Skule" and its successor, "Home Again," gave the brothers their first real success, and, with the assistance of their maternal uncle, Al Shean, of the successful vaudeville team of Gallagher and Shean, they were able to obtain better and better bookings.

World War I temporarily broke up the act as both Gummo and Harpo served in the army. Harpo served overseas for one year with the Seventh Regiment from New York City. After the war Gummo retired from show business and was replaced in the act by the youngest Marx brother, Zeppo. Reunited after the war, the brothers (along with Groucho and Zeppo) toured with a new revue, "Mr. Green's Reception," followed by others, including "On the Mezzanine." Despite their increasing success the brothers became involved in a dispute with the major booking agency, Keith-Albee. A new group, the Shuberts, was trying to challenge the hold of Keith-Albee on the major vaudeville routes, and the Marx Brothers cast their lot with them. While the Shubert challenge ultimately failed, the Marx Brothers act captured the attention of Charles Dillingham, a Broadway musical revue producer and rival of Flo Ziegfeld, who signed the brothers to do a Broadway show. *I'll Say She Is* (1924) received critical acclaim from Ben Hecht, Charles MacArthur, and especially Alexander Woollcott. After a long run on Broadway and a successful tour with the show the brothers were firmly launched. They followed with two more hit shows, *The Cocoanuts* (1925) and *Animal Crackers* (1928).

The introduction of sound greatly expanded the possibilities of motion pictures, and the Marx Brothers took their act to films in 1928. While performing *Animal Crackers* on stage in the evenings they filmed *The Cocoanuts* (1929) for Paramount Pictures by day. A film version of *Animal Crackers* (1930) followed, and their transition to film was nearly complete. Both films enjoyed great success. After a European tour in 1929 and a London stage engagement in *Varieties* in 1930 the team became primarily motion picture performers. The Marx Brothers made three more pictures for Paramount, *Mon-*

key Business (1931), *Horse Feathers* (1932), and *Duck Soup* (1933).

Following *Duck Soup* Zeppo left the team to establish his own business as an agent. Harpo, Chico, and Groucho continued at Metro-Goldwyn-Mayer (MGM), having been attracted to that studio by Irving Thalberg, who believed that if their style of comedy were developed within a motion picture plot the results would be even more successful both artistically and commercially.

The Marx Brothers made five films at MGM: *A Night at the Opera* (1935), *A Day at the Races* (1937), *A Day at the Circus* (1939), *Go West* (1941), and *The Big Store* (1941). During this period they also made *Room Service* for Radio-Keith-Orpheum (RKO; 1938). But Thalberg's idea had not worked out completely. While the first two pictures were first-rate and are part of the canon of classical comedies, the others lacked the freshness and originality that had characterized the Marx Brothers approach to comedy. The marriage of their free-form style and the MGM "formula" for family entertainment was restrictive and somewhat stifling. Following *The Big Store* the team disbanded, and each brother pursued an independent career.

During World War II both Chico and Harpo performed for servicemen and at war bond rallies. Chico organized a traveling band and returned to vaudeville playing the piano and doing dialect skits. Harpo went on stage with parts in short-run revivals of plays, such as Kaufman and Hart's *The Man Who Came to Dinner* (1941), and toured with an orchestra that he had organized. In 1946 the brothers were reunited at United Artists in *A Night in Casablanca* and then appeared in *Love Happy* (1950), their last film, based on a script by Harpo. While Groucho went on to a successful career in television, neither Chico nor Harpo gained the stature as solo performers that they had enjoyed as part of the team.

In writing about their personal lives the brothers devoted great attention to their early years—the many relatives passing through the family flat, their struggle to succeed in vaudeville, their father's skill as a cook and lack of skill as a tailor. But they said little about their adult lives. Chico Marx married Betty Karp, a dancer. They had one daughter and were later divorced. On Aug. 22, 1958, he married Mary De Vithas. After several years of poor health, he died in Hollywood. In addition to the piano, which he had learned to play as a boy, he played the cornet, zither, and violin. He was also an excellent bridge player.

During the team's Broadway years Harpo became part of the Algonquin round table through his friend Alexander Woollcott. On Sept. 26, 1936, he married Susan Fleming, an actress. They adopted four children. Harpo died in Los Angeles.

[Harpo Marx with Rowland Barber, *Harpo Speaks!* (1961); Kyle Crichton, *The Marx Brothers* (1950); Allen Eyles, *The Marx Brothers: Their World of Comedy* (1966); Groucho Marx and Richard Anobile, *The Marx Bros. Scrapbook* (1973); and Paul D. Zimmerman and Burt Goldblatt, *The Marx Brothers at the Movies* (1968).]

WILLIAM H. MULLIGAN, JR.

MASON, MAX (Oct. 26, 1877–Mar. 23, 1961), mathematician and astrophysicist, was born in Madison, Wis., the son of Edwin Cole Mason, a businessman and public accountant, and of Josephine Vroman. He enrolled at the University of Wisconsin, where he was encouraged by Professor Charles Sumner Slichter to study mathematics. As an undergraduate Mason was a star high jumper on the track team. He prized this experience, and remained athletic throughout his life. After graduating from Wisconsin with the B.Litt. (1898), Mason taught for one year at Beloit (Wis.) High School. He next studied for three years at the University of Göttingen, which awarded him the Ph.D. in 1903. Subsequently he taught mathematics for one year at Massachusetts Institute of Technology and for four years at Yale University. On June 16, 1904, Mason married Mary Louise Freeman; they had three children.

In 1908, Mason was appointed professor of mathematics at the University of Wisconsin. After one year he transferred to the physics department as professor of mathematical physics. He remained in this post until 1925. During World War I, he worked on the problem of submarine detection for the Navy. He is credited with inventing the sonar detector. At Madison, Mason and his colleagues tested a crude device on Lake Mendota that worked, but needed much refinement. Since German submarines were wreaking havoc on American ships, Mason and other scientists at the Naval Experiment Station at New London, Conn., worked feverishly to perfect the device, then called the M-V tube. Once it was adapted for seagoing conditions, the decision was made to equip vessels in the war zone with it. Mason went to France to supervise its installation and to instruct crews in its use. In France he found a golf course, and became known as the "crazy American who played golf and solved submarine problems between holes."

After the war Mason returned to the University of Wisconsin to resume his academic career. In 1925 he was named president of the University of Chicago. He believed that endowed universities such as the University of Chicago must be the ones to promote scholarship in the United States because they could restrict their enrollments, have complete freedom from political control, and remain unhampered by popular demands. Mason studied the operation of the university, and stimulated the generosity of donors so that the endowment was increased substantially. During his tenure seven new buildings were provided for. He also arranged for affiliations with the Chicago Lying-in Hospital, the Country Home for Convalescent Crippled Children, the Edward Sanatorium of the Chicago Tuberculosis Institute, and the Home for Destitute Crippled Children. In addition, Mason instituted an undergraduate program in which the first two years were devoted to general education and the second two years to a specific field of interest.

In 1928 the Rockefeller Foundation was in the process of reorganization into five divisions: natural sciences, social sciences, humanities and the arts, medical sciences, and agriculture and forestry. Mason was brought in as director of the Division of Natural Sciences, with assurance that after one year he would be elevated to the presidency of the foundation. The Natural Sciences Division operated projects ranging from the study of the aurora borealis in Alaska to the study of the velocity of light in California. The foundation helped to build a physics research laboratory in Germany as well as the Woods Hole Oceanographic Institute in Massachusetts.

As president of the Rockefeller Foundation, Mason emphasized the importance of both basic research and its application. He insisted that the five divisions be administered as a structural unit aimed at understanding human behavior. In 1936 he wrote: "The search for truth is, as it has always been, the noblest expression of the human spirit. Man's hunger for knowledge about himself, his environment and the forces by which he is surrounded, gives human life its meaning and purpose, and clothes it with final dignity."

Mason retired from the Rockefeller Foundation in 1936. He then joined the California Institute of Technology, where he remained until his final retirement in 1949. As head of the Observatory Council of Cal Tech, Mason oversaw the construction of the 200-inch telescope of the Mount Palomar Observatory, a fitting capstone to his career. The telescope, financed by the Rockefeller Foundation, cost $6 million. The smaller observatory at Mount Wilson, also operated by Cal Tech, had become obsolete, partly because of the interference of the growing amount of background light from the city of Los Angeles. The new telescope was therefore constructed near San Diego, some 160 miles south of the Cal Tech campus. Mason also continued to work for the Navy on antisubmarine devices. As a sideline he developed similar devices for mining companies, to locate ore underground. Following the death of his first wife in 1928, Mason married Helen Schermerhorn Young on Aug. 5, 1938. She died in 1944 and on Nov. 6, 1945, he married Daphne Crane Drake Martin.

Mason's principal scholarly work, written with Warren Weaver, was *The Electromagnetic Field* (1929). It was a synthesis of existing knowledge of the field (with special attention to the work of James Clerk Maxwell and Hendrik Lorentz), which predated but was basic to quantum theory. Mason also published articles on mathematical subjects, including the relation between algebra of matrices and integral equations, differential equations, calculus of variations, existence theorems, oscillation properties, and asymptotic expressions.

Mason died in Claremont, Calif.

[See "The New President of the University of Chicago," *School and Society*, Aug. 29, 1925; Neil M. Clark, "Learn How to Play and You Will Know How to Live," *American Magazine*, June 1926, "President Max Mason and the University of Chicago," *School and Society*, May 19, 1928; and "Mason-Endowed Schools Must Promote Scholarship," *World's Work*, June 1928. An obituary is in the *New York Times*, Mar. 24, 1961.]

DONALD F. TINGLEY

MATTINGLY, GARRETT (May 6, 1900– Dec. 18, 1962), historian, was born in Washington, D.C., the son of Leonard Howard Mattingly, an industrialist and civil servant, and of Ida Roselle Garrett. He attended elementary school in Washington and high school in Kalamazoo, Mich. In World War I he was a sergeant in the 43rd Infantry (1918–1919). After his discharge Mattingly entered Harvard College, from which he received the B.A. in 1923, the M.A. in 1926, and the Ph.D. in 1935. A Sheldon traveling fellowship allowed him to study in Europe in 1922–1924. On June 22, 1928, he married Gertrude McCollum; they

had no children. By then he had begun his teaching career, first at Northwestern University at Evanston, Ill. (1926–1928) and then at Long Island University (1928–1942), where he taught English as well as history.

Mattingly was a product of Harvard's golden years. He studied English with Charles Townsend Copeland and George Lyman Kittredge, and published his first article on a Shakespearean subject. He received more technical training from two great medievalists, Charles Homer Haskins and Charles Howard McIlwain, but above all he was the disciple of Roger Bigelow Merriman—whom he called "the historian of the Spanish Empire" in a tribute published years later. "He taught me," Mattingly remarked privately, "whatever I know of my craft."

Under the influence of Merriman (who himself followed William Hickling Prescott), Mattingly began the study of European diplomatic history, and many years of archival research made him an internationally acknowledged master in this field. In 1937, with the aid of the first of three Guggenheim fellowships, he began intensive study of the manuscript sources in London, Brussels, Florence, Vienna, Paris, and Simancas. The major results were his *Further Supplement to the Letters, Dispatches, and State Papers of Henry VIII* (1940), and, drawing on this, his biography *Catherine of Aragon* (1941).

The second major influence was Mattingly's association with Bernard De Voto, which began in 1926 at Northwestern and lasted until De Voto's death in 1955. "Benny" and "Mat" had not only a lifelong friendship but also a literary collaboration: for Mattingly, De Voto opened up a wider intellectual world and coached him in the art of historical narrative; in return he received professional counsel and virtually a correspondence course in European history for his *The Course of Empire*. Mattingly's first book, *Bernard De Voto, a Preliminary Appraisal* (1938), was an apologetic defense of De Voto from attacks by the "literary left" (notably from Edmund Wilson). The relationship continued during World War II, when Mattingly served in the Naval Reserve (1942–1945), mainly in Washington. "I'm only joining the Navy," he joked to De Voto in 1942, "to boost . . . sales of the Armada book by staking my claim to be an old sea dog and an expert on naval warfare." Already, then, his masterpiece was aweigh.

After the war Mattingly (disappointed, as was De Voto, in his hopes for a Harvard appointment) found a position in the adult program of Cooper Union in New York City, and there perfected his dramatic style of lecturing. In 1947 he accepted an appointment at Columbia University, where he remained for the rest of his life, from 1959 as William R. Shepherd Professor of European History. While teaching his graduate courses, notably "Europe in Transition" and his research seminar, Mattingly completed his last two books. The first was his masterly survey *Renaissance Diplomacy* (1955), based in part on his Harvard dissertation and stemming from an interest going back to his undergraduate Bowdoin Prize essay; the second was his epic narrative, *The Armada* (1959). He had planned the latter as a "quickie" seventeen years before and, in the throes of many revisions, despaired of it as "a bloody, dull book." But critics and book clubs thought differently. So did the Pulitzer Prize committee, which awarded it a special citation in 1960.

Mattingly took a certain facetious pride in being an old-fashioned "literary" historian, concealing, as he wrote in an early stage of unemployment, "the best qualities of Will Durant, Irving Fisher and William Hickling Prescott." Later, in another mood and weary of pompous academic novelties, he classed himself among "the dull, plodding political historians" and wrote a sprightly defense of this neglected genre. Like De Voto, Mattingly had a low tolerance for ideologies of either the right or the left (though he called himself "a socialist without being a communist"), and an even lower one for sociological or theological historians (like Arnold Toynbee).

What he aimed at in his writings and taught his graduate students was "honest historical workmanship with a minimum of bilge and cant." And, despite the extraordinary depth and range of his scholarship, he felt the same way about pretentious erudition as he did about pretentious theories. What he did care about was dramatic effect ("When you get a scene, play it," De Voto had told him), psychological insight, and humor (unleashed most notoriously in his essay on Machiavelli's *Prince* as satire). More than once he said he would have preferred to be a novelist.

The last project Mattingly undertook was to have been an interpretation of the Italian Renaissance—to "redo Burckhardt," as he put it. This was the subject of the course he gave as visiting professor at Oxford in the fall of 1962, but his emphysema cut these lectures short. The foul English winter of that year snuffed out his life before he began his book.

[Mattingly's letters (1927–1955) are in the De Voto Papers in the Stanford University library; De Voto's side of the correspondence is in *The Letters of Bernard De Voto,* ed. Wallace Stegner (1975); other manuscripts are in the Mattingly Papers in the Columbia University Library. His articles include "An Early Nonaggression Pact," *Journal of Modern History,* Mar. 1938; "The Historian of the Spanish Empire," *American Historical Review,* Oct. 1948; "Machiavelli's *Prince*: Political Science or Political Satire," *American Scholar,* Autumn 1958; "Some Revisions of the Political History of the Renaissance," in *The Renaissance,* ed. T. Helton (1961). Also see C. H. Carter, ed., *From the Renaissance to the Counter-Reformation: Essays in Honor of Garrett Mattingly* (1965). An obituary is in the *New York Times,* Dec. 20, 1962 (western ed.).]

DONALD R. KELLEY

MAXWELL, ELSA (May 24, 1883–Nov. 1, 1963), hostess, songwriter, author, and entertainer, was born in Keokuk, Iowa (where her mother was visiting), the daughter of James David Maxwell, an insurance salesman and newspaper columnist, and of Laura Wyman. She was taken as an infant to San Francisco, where she spent her childhood and teens. Because of her father's opposition to formal education, Maxwell had less than two years of structured schooling: a few months in a public school at age eight, and a short period at Miss Denham's private school at age twelve. Her father taught her to read and write and encouraged her to read everything in his library. "I never saw McGuffey's Reader," she wrote years later, "but I was familiar with Browning, Keats and Plato, and I had struggled through Herbert Spencer's philosophy by the time I was eleven."

Maxwell's first experience as a hostess was on her thirteenth birthday, when she borrowed, without permission, the motor launch of a neighbor to take several children on a cruise around San Francisco Harbor. But it was a party to which she was not invited that inspired her career as an international hostess; when she was twelve, her family was left off the guest list of a party given by their neighbor, Senator James Fair, for his daughter, Theresa. The rejection caused Maxwell to decide that she would give great parties to which everyone would want to come. Later, according to some accounts, she seemed to take particular pleasure in snubbing anyone connected with the Fair family.

In 1906, Maxwell joined a traveling Shakespearean repertory company. Her travels took her to New York City, where Harrison Fiske, publisher of the New York *Dramatic Mirror* (for which her father had been West Coast correspondent) helped her get a job as pianist in a nickelodeon. In her nonworking hours she wrote songs and, at age 24, made her first sale, "The Sum of Life" to music publisher Leo Feist, for $10. She met—and composed a song for—vaudeville performer Dorothy Toye, who then took Maxwell on tour to South Africa as her accompanist. In South Africa, Maxwell wrote more songs, and played piano in music halls. She also began what was to become a lifetime occupation: giving parties. From South Africa, Maxwell went to Paris, then London. In the latter city, at the time when Great Britain entered World War I, she wrote "Carry On," a song which was featured in a 1914 musical revue.

By the time she returned to New York City, in 1915, she had penetrated the titled social circle of London and enjoyed a small reputation as a hostess there. In New York, during the war years, she arranged and managed several fundraising events. She also wrote the music and lyrics for Alva E. Belmont's woman suffrage musical, *Melinda and Her Sisters.* This work, which starred Marie Dressler and Marie Doro, was performed at the Waldorf Astoria Theatre in 1916.

The postwar period in Europe provided the ideal climate for Maxwell's decidedly unconventional style of entertaining. She believed that most dinner parties were dull, and that cocktail parties were "ghastly businesses." To be successful a party must include games and have a strong element of surprise. The surprises at her parties ranged from the scavenger hunt (which she claimed to have invented) to providing camels for the return trip to Luxor after a moonlight supper in the Egyptian desert. Murder mystery parties, treasure hunts, and costume events were among her "parties-with-a-difference."

Having positioned herself at the center of the "smart set" with a knack for bringing together members of "high" and "cafe" societies, Maxwell was soon in demand to assure the success of new businesses catering to the rich. She helped establish the Lido at Venice as an international playground by starting a golf club there. She also launched a beach club and restaurant in Monte Carlo and two nightclubs in Paris. By the mid-1930's she was known on both sides of the Atlantic as the "arbiter of international society." Louis Bromfield wrote a play about her—*DeLuxe* (1935)—in which she played herself in a fifteen-performance Broadway run. Cole Porter and Noel Coward wrote songs about her: Porter's, "I'm Dining with Elsa Tonight"; Coward's, "A Marvelous Party."

Maxwell told some of her story in *I Live by My Wits,* serialized in *Harper's Bazaar* (1936). She also wrote *The Life of Barbara Hutton,* serialized in *Cosmopolitan* (1938). In 1938 she moved to Hollywood and appeared in movies: *Elsa Maxwell's Hotel for Women* (1939), *Public Deb No. 1* (1940), and the featurettes *Riding Into Society* (1940) and *The Lady and The Lug* (1940). Maxwell was technical adviser and consultant for the 1943 motion picture *Weekend at the Waldorf.* She also lectured, wrote a syndicated gossip column, and broadcast celebrity news on her radio program, "Elsa Maxwell's Party Line."

Maxwell's autobiography, *My Last 50 Years,* was published in 1943; in 1957, she wrote another, *R.S.V.P—Elsa Maxwell's Own Story.* In the latter year she also shared her party-giving secrets in *How to Do It—or the Lively Art of Entertaining.* A book of anecdotes about celebrities she knew, *The Celebrity Circus,* was published in 1963.

Although Maxwell's abilities provided a substantial living, she did not manage money as well as she managed galas and fetes, and depended on the generosity of wealthy friends for many of her needs. "I have more friends than any living person," she said on her eightieth birthday. "They are my riches."

Maxwell never married, and never settled in a home of her own. She lived instead in hotels, and borrowed others' houses for her parties. Janet Flanner wrote of her, "She has never been any closer to life than the dinner table." Her last public appearance, one week before her death in New York City, was at the April in Paris Ball, an annual event she had founded in 1951.

[An article by Maxwell is "How to Live a Long and Merry Life," *This Week,* May 22, 1960. Also see Janet Flanner, "Elsa Maxwell Profile," *New Yorker,* Nov. 25, 1933; Ishbel Ross, "Life of the Party," *This Week,* May 30, 1937; and Rose Heylbut, "Music, Morale, and Elsa Maxwell," *Etude,* Aug. 1942. Obituaries are in the *New York Times* and *New York Herald Tribune,* Nov. 2, 1963; and *Variety,* Nov. 6, 1963.]

DOROTHY BRIGSTOCK SCHOENFELD

MAYER, OSCAR GOTTFRIED (Mar. 10, 1888–Mar. 5, 1965), meat packer, was born in Chicago, Ill., the son of Oscar Ferdinand Mayer and Louise Christine Greiner, both German immigrants. In 1883 his father established the small Chicago meat market and sausage factory that became Oscar Mayer and Company. (The company has always been a family business.) At the age of six Mayer learned to link sausages, standing on an upturned butter tub to reach the counter. He graduated from Robert Waller High School in Chicago in 1905, and in 1909 from Harvard, where he studied engineering methods that he later put to use in the company. He also developed broad cultural interests at Harvard and wrote for the *Harvard Advocate.*

Beginning as assistant superintendent in 1909, Mayer advanced rapidly in his father's company, becoming secretary, director, and general manager in 1912. He married Elsa Stieglitz on May 10, 1913; they had four children.

From the beginning Mayer concentrated on industrial operations, and under his leadership Oscar Mayer and Company pioneered methods of processing and packaging prepared meats that were adopted throughout the industry. By 1912 he had invented several devices, including a lard-tub washer and a casing flusher, and had introduced the packaging of sausage in cardboard cartons. He also realized that future success depended upon expansion of markets beyond the western Great Lakes area. In 1919 the company acquired a farmers' cooperative packing plant in Madison, Wis., which soon became its biggest operation. Other plants were acquired after World War II in Philadelphia, Los Angeles, and Davenport, Iowa, and in 1961 controlling interest in a Caracas, Venezuela, packing house was purchased.

In 1921 Mayer became vice-president in charge of operations, and in 1928, when his father retired, he succeeded him as president of the firm. At that time the company employed 900 and had annual sales of $21.5 million. By 1955, when Mayer retired as president, the company employed 8,500 and annual sales were $220.2 million. This success was due in large measure to his leadership and his understanding of the implications of new retailing developments. For example, when supermarkets were introduced, Mayer realized that customers were distressed by the loss of the neighborhood butcher, who had advised them on meat selection. He thus saw that the manufacturer would have to replace the butcher, and that a company's success would depend on customers' confidence in easily identified brands. In 1929 the company introduced wieners with a band around every fourth wiener, and in 1944 its engineers developed Kartridg-Pak, a machine that automatically banded wieners. The sausages were then distributed with a strong advertising campaign—"Look for the yellow band on every wiener"—designed to build confidence in "a wiener with a conscience."

Other techniques developed by the company included a linker, which wrapped sausages automatically and twisted them into standard lengths; a stripper, which removed the cooking casing of wieners and made possible the skinless wiener; a tube machine, which encased liver sausage in a plastic tube, pinched each tube to a proper length, and closed it with a metal ring; and the Slice-Pak, which vacuum-packed sliced meats in plastic. All of this equipment was manufactured by subsidiaries of Oscar Mayer and Company, and leased to other meat-packing companies.

Mayer retired as president of the firm in March 1955, but he remained chairman of the board until his death. In 1960 the company introduced a vacuum-sealed package for sausage and wieners after spending six years and $1.5 million to develop it. Such investment was possible because 85 percent of the company's stock was owned by family members and thus more than half the profits could be plowed back into capital expansion and research.

Profit margins are notoriously low in the meat-packing industry. Although Oscar Mayer and Company was ninth in volume among American packers, it was first in profit margin in Mayer's last years. This was largely due to its computerized market research, through which it was able to predict the demand for its products with remarkable accuracy and to pursue its "vacuum policy," which deliberately kept production slightly less than demand in order to eliminate the need to unload "distress merchandise." The company also developed local distribution centers, with refrigeration facilities sufficient to maintain an adequate inventory and with resident sales staffs who were required to maintain prices set by the company.

In 1956, Mayer published *A Plan for Living,* originally an address to Beloit College students, in which he expressed his personal credo: "Lifelong personal development, generous consideration for others, due service to society." His career included extensive involvement in public and philanthropic activities. In 1959 the American Meat Institute honored him for fifty years of service to the industry in which he was one of the great pioneers. He also established and headed the Oscar Mayer Foundation, which aided many medical and educational institutions.

Mayer's career is a record of farsighted and progressive leadership in his industry, a steady willingness to take calculated risks and to accept responsibility for the quality of his product, and a recognition that the success of his company was always related to the welfare of the consumer. He died in Evanston, Ill.

[See "How a Smaller Packer Does Better Than the Giants," *Business Week*, Nov. 22, 1958; "The Meat Packers: To Oscar Mayer's Taste," *Newsweek*, Nov. 14, 1960; *The Link* (Oscar Mayer and Company), Spring 1965; *Oscar Mayer. The Company* (1975). An obituary is in the *New York Times*, Mar. 6, 1965.]

ROBERT L. BERNER

MEAD, JAMES MICHAEL (Dec. 27, 1885–Mar. 15, 1964), U.S. senator, was born in Mount Morris, N.Y., the son of Thomas Mead and Mary Jane Kelly. His father was a section boss for the Lackawanna Railroad, and their home was a shack provided by his employer. In 1890 the family moved to Buffalo, where Mead attended grammar school. He left school at twelve and went to work for the railroad as a water boy. By the time he was twenty, Mead had worked as a lamplighter, spike mauler, track walker, shopman, and switcher. Meanwhile, he attended evening classes at the Caton School of Engineering (1904) and the Buffalo Institute of Technology (1905). He subsequently was employed briefly by the Erie Railroad and later by the Pullman Company in Buffalo and in Florida.

Always a regular Democrat, Mead received a patronage appointment as a member of the Capitol Police Force in Washington, D.C., in 1911. He spent his free time studying law privately and listening to congressional debates. He returned to Buffalo in 1912 and resumed work for the Erie Railroad as a yard switchman. Mead became increasingly active in local Democratic politics, and in 1913 he was elected to the Erie County Board of Supervisors. The following year he won election to the New York State Assembly and to the presidency of his union local. On Aug. 25, 1915, he married Alice Mary Dillon; they had one son.

In 1918 Mead was elected to the U.S. House of Representatives, where he served ten consecutive terms. As a member of the House Post Office and Post Roads Committee, he supported legislation for shorter hours and higher pay for postal workers. He drafted the Mead Air Mail Act and the Forty-Four Hour Week Act for postal employees.

Always sensitive to the needs of labor, Mead supported enlarging the scope of the Locomotive Inspection Act, helped defeat the antistrike provisions of the Cummins-Esch bill, opposed President Herbert Hoover's general sales tax scheme, supported numerous workmen's compensation proposals, called for federal relief aid for the unemployed, and campaigned in support of public works programs. In the 1930's he was a staunch supporter of Franklin D. Roosevelt and the New Deal.

In 1938 Mead was elected to fill the vacancy resulting from the death of Senator Royal S. Copeland. He was reelected to a full term in 1940. In the Senate, too, Mead was a consistent New Dealer. He defended the National Labor Relations Board and opposed cuts in relief appropriations and any legislation aimed at restricting labor. He also supported Roosevelt's foreign policy, including the Neutrality Act, Lend-Lease, and the Selective Service Act.

In 1942, with the support of President Roosevelt, Mead sought the New York Democratic gubernatorial nomination. He was defeated by New York Attorney General John J. Bennett, Jr. (the candidate of New York Democratic party chairman James Farley). During World War II, Mead captured media attention as chairman of the Senate War Investigating Committee, which in 1945 looked into irregularities in the disposal of war surplus and the waste of manpower at defense projects.

In 1946 Mead again ran for governor of New York. He secured the Democratic nomination, but lost the election to Thomas E. Dewey. In November 1949 President Harry S. Truman appointed Mead to the Federal Trade Commission. The following year he was chosen chairman of the commission; he served until 1955, when he resigned. Mead was then named director of the Washington office of the New York State Commerce Department by New York Governor Averell Harriman. It was widely believed that Mead was to promote Harriman's bid for the 1956 Democratic presidential nomination. When Harriman did not receive the nomination, Mead resigned. He purchased an orange grove in Clermont, Fla., which he operated for the rest of his life.

Mead played semiprofessional baseball and football in his youth. He sponsored a softball team in Angola, New York, and was a part owner of the Buffalo professional baseball club. Reportedly shocked by the deaths of many congressional colleagues, Mead provided the impetus for the construction of the congressional gymnasium. He was reportedly considered for the post of commissioner of the All-American Football Conference in 1948.

Gregarious and affable, Mead was popular with his peers. His vote-getting ability is emphasized by the fact that when he moved up to the Senate after ten terms in the House, his district chose a Republican to succeed him. Mead died in Lakeland, Fla.

[See *Time* and *Newsweek*, Aug. 3, 1942. An obituary is in the *New York Times*, Mar. 16, 1964.]
STEPHEN D. BODAYLA

MEIÈRE, MARIE HILDRETH (Sept. 3, 1892–May 2, 1961), muralist, designer of mosaics and architectural decoration, was born in New York City, the daughter of Ernest Meière, a man of independent means, and of Marie Hildreth. Meière's mother had entertained thoughts of becoming a professional artist and in her youth had studied under the painter William Merritt Chase. When Marie exhibited an interest in art, her mother urged her to pursue the career that she herself had forgone in favor of marriage.

In 1911, following Meière's graduation from Convent of the Sacred Heart, mother and daughter embarked for Florence, where the latter studied under the English painter Gordon Carmichael. On her return to New York in 1912, Meière enrolled at the Art Students League. When her family moved to San Francisco in 1913, she continued her studies at the California School of Fine Arts. In 1916, encouraged by actress Margaret Anglin, who had much admired an exhibition of her portrait sketches of actors in costume, Meière moved back to New York to become a theatrical designer. Although she was successful, she was disillusioned when credit for her work on an opera production went to another, and she remained in this occupation only briefly.

Shortly after America's entry into World War I, Meière went to work for the mapmaking division of the U.S. Navy, where she acquired skills in scale drawing, an experience that proved invaluable to her subsequent career. In 1919 she renewed her studies at the New York School of Applied Design for Women and, later, at the Beaux Arts Institute of Design, where her mural designs earned her several first-place medals in student competitions.

Meière's first paid mural commission, a depiction of Norse folktales, was executed for actor Alfred Lunt's home in Wisconsin. In 1922 she met architect Bertram Goodhue, who, though unimpressed with her samples of mural work and building decoration, was taken with her costume sketches. Soon Goodhue was regularly employing Meière to design decorative elements for his buildings. Among her earliest efforts for him were reredos panels in St. Mark's Church, Mt. Kisco, N.Y., and St. Martin's Church, Providence, R.I. A deeply religious Catholic, Meière took particular satisfaction in these church commissions, and for the remainder of her life ecclesiastical design constituted a substantial part of her work.

One of Goodhue's most original accomplishments was the Nebraska State Capitol, constructed in the 1920's. The success of the building's interior owed much to Meière, who designed a large portion of the decoration, including ceiling and floor mosaics, portraying the state's heritage, for the main halls, and tapestry and wall ornamentation for the legislative chambers. This work won a gold medal from the Architectural League of New York in 1928. Also during the 1920's Meière designed the mosaics of painted and gilded gesso for the dome at the new National Academy of Sciences, Washington, D.C.

Meière married Richard A. Goebel on May 3, 1929; they had one daughter. Two years later the marriage was annulled. In 1932 she was hired to do four massive art deco plaques in enameled metal for the exterior of Rockefeller Center's Music Hall. In the following year her mural "Onward Progress of Women," commissioned by the National Council of Women and later given to Smith College, was unveiled at Chicago's Century of Progress.

In 1928 Meière and other artists met in her New York City studio to found the Liturgical Arts Society, for the purpose of fostering interest in church art. In the early 1930's she also directed a mural painting atelier for the Beaux Arts Institute, and in 1935 she chaired the National Society of Mural Painters exhibition at the Grand Central Art Galleries in New York City.

Because Meière's works were meant to complement predetermined architectural settings, the stylistic inspiration for her undertakings came from sources ranging from ancient Roman mosaics and Renaissance frescoes to twentieth-century modernists. To obtain ideas she frequently went abroad to study the decoration of noted buildings. Regardless of whether her designs took traditional or modern forms, she constantly had to adapt their execution to new building technologies. Meière relished this challenge, and experimented tirelessly with new materials and techniques.

For the New York World's Fair of 1939, Meière completed six commissions, one of the largest being the metal relief figures over the entrance of the Education and Science Building. During World War II she served on the Citizens Committee for the Army and Navy, and made it her special concern to supply chaplains with tryptychs for use in their services. In 1946 she became the first woman to sit on the

New York City Municipal Art Commission. Over the next fifteen years, Meière's work included mosaic murals for the Travelers Insurance Building in Hartford, Conn., altar decorations for St. Patrick's Cathedral in New York City, and mosaics for the crypt at the National Cathedral in Washington, D.C. For her contributions in the field of architectural decoration, the American Institute of Architects in 1956 awarded Meière its Fine Arts Medal. When she died in New York City, she was working on dome mosaics for St. Louis Cathedral, St. Louis, Mo.

[Meière's professional and family correspondence, original conceptual drawings of commissions, and photographs of works in finished state are held by her daughter, Mrs. Paxton T. Dunn, of Stamford, Conn. Articles by Meière on her work include "The Question of Decoration," *Architectural Forum,* June 1932. Articles summarizing her life and work are Genevieve Parkhurst, "An Artist Who Happens to Be a Woman," *Pictorial Review,* Sept. 1926; Ernest Watson, "Hildreth Meière," *American Artist,* Sept. 1941. An obituary is in the *New York Times,* May 3, 1961.]
FREDERICK S. VOSS

MEIKLEJOHN, ALEXANDER (Feb. 3, 1872–Dec. 16, 1964), educator and polemicist, was born in Rochdale, England, the son of James Meiklejohn, a textile worker, and Elizabeth France. In 1880 the family immigrated to Pawtucket, R.I. Meiklejohn obtained an A.B. from Brown University in 1893, and an M.A. two years later. In 1897 he received a Ph.D. in philosophy from Cornell University. Returning to Brown as an instructor in philosophy in 1897, Meiklejohn swiftly demonstrated a talent for socratic teaching and a fondness for contest that inclined him to logical disputation and to sports. Skill in both arenas gained him popularity with undergraduates and enabled him to serve effectively. He became dean of students in 1901 and a full professor in 1905. On June 14, 1902, he married Nannine A. LaVilla; they had four children.

In 1912 Meiklejohn was named president of Amherst College, then perhaps at its nadir. In chapel and classroom he was highly appealing to able students. He condemned the emphasis on intercollegiate sports, the equation of education with a tally of course credits, the fragmentation of learning into autonomous departments, and the absence of any unifying sense of purpose. He conceived of college not as a place wherein to acquire substantive knowledge, a concept which he despised, but as a four-year dialogue that would teach the student to think logically. Not

curious about the methods and findings of modern science and the social studies, he remained captive to his narrow training as an idealist in the Kantian tradition.

Distrustful of democratic procedures, Meiklejohn once said to a trustee that if made dictator, he would remake Amherst, and the somnolence of the board enabled him to achieve a measure of autocracy enjoyed by no other president of a New England college. He managed to stop direct communication from individual professors to trustees; but he was unable to prevent faculty participation in personnel or tenure decisions. Never at pains to conceal his contempt for a large part of the faculty, he failed to gain support for his proposal in 1918 to establish a uniform program for the first two years of college, success in which would be the condition for advancement to the junior year.

Until 1921 the trustees fended off the hostility of many professors and alumni. But in that year it was discovered that Meiklejohn had taken college funds for personal use. Restitution of almost nine thousand dollars was required, and he was notified that the board's "confidence was shaken." When it was established in 1922 that he had made deceptive statements to the board about faculty appointments, trust was further eroded. A formal inquiry into the practices of appointment and advancement of teachers at Amherst was instituted by the trustees. In May 1923 their committee reported that reliance on the president had "failed in important respects." A subsequent trustee poll showed that two-thirds of the faculty believed that Meiklejohn should cease to be president. He was advised to resign, which he did on June 19, 1923. Meiklejohn declined the invitation to remain as professor of logic but accepted a leave of absence, with full salary, for the following year.

There is no evidence to support the assertion that Meiklejohn's dismissal rested on disagreement with his theory of education or with his views on issues of public policy. The action of the board constituted, rather, a triumph for faculty participation in governance. But by withholding publication of its findings, the board facilitated acceptance of the legend that academic freedom had been sacrificed. A mass of documents indicate that the trustees wanted no more than a trustworthy president who could inspire the confidence of his faculty.

In 1926 Meiklejohn got a chance to create and staff his own program. The *Century Magazine* had published some of his articles on higher education; and when the editor, Glenn Frank, was made president of the University of

Wisconsin, he asked Meiklejohn to organize an "experimental college." This program was for students in the first two years of the College of Letters and Science. Traditional classes, lectures, and examinations were dispensed with, but the high ratio of teachers to students made abundant association feasible. Demand for admittance to the college was so limited that it was never necessary to select students. After the second year, enrollment dwindled, and in the fourth year the costly program was terminated. Simultaneously, the foundation that had provided Meiklejohn's large salary withdrew its grant to the university. Meiklejohn's first wife died in 1925, and on June 9, 1926, he married Helen Everett. They had no children.

Moving to Berkeley, Calif., in late 1932, Meiklejohn engaged in a short-lived project in adult education. He and a few others founded and ran the San Francisco School of Social Studies. Meiklejohn taught philosophy at the University of Wisconsin one semester in each of the two years 1935–1937. Something of a national celebrity, his skill in the classroom and on the platform brought him occasional appointments as a visiting lecturer or as a speaker whose name would draw an audience.

In the years after World War II Meiklejohn crusaded for the thesis that the First Amendment guarantee of freedom of speech and press should be read literally as an absolute privilege. He died in Berkeley, Calif.

[The principal collection of Meiklejohn's personal papers is at the Wisconsin State Historical Society; his files relating to Amherst College are at Amherst. The archives of Brown, Amherst, Cornell, Dartmouth, Harvard Law School, and the University of Wisconsin have important materials. A bibliography of Meiklejohn's writings to 1941 is in Walker H. Hill, ed., *Learning and Living* (1942). See Meiklejohn's *The Liberal College* (1920); *Freedom and the College* (1923); *Education between Two Worlds* (1942); *Political Freedom: the Constitutional Powers of the People* (1960); and articles in the *Century Magazine*, Sept. 1923, Mar. 1924, and Jan. 1925. On the temper of Meiklejohn's Amherst, the analysis of Walter Lippmann in the New York *World*, June 24, 1923, is informed, perceptive, and balanced. On the Wisconsin venture is George C. Sellery, *Some Ferments at Wisconsin, 1901–1947*, (1960). An obituary appeared in the *New York Times*, Dec. 17, 1964.]

THOMAS LeDuc

MELCHER, FREDERIC GERSHOM (Apr. 12, 1879–Mar. 9, 1963), editor, publisher, and bookseller, was born in Malden, Mass., the son of Edwin Forrest Melcher and Alice Jane Bartlett. When he was four, the family moved to Newton Center, near Boston, where he attended the public schools and graduated from Newton High School in 1895. He took the "Institute course" in preparation for the Massachusetts Institute of Technology, but the death of his father and his own decision not to study engineering led him to look for a job instead. His entry into the book business was accidental. His maternal grandfather, an owner of the Boston property that housed the well-known Estes and Lauriat Bookstore, inquired about an opening there for his grandson. In June 1895, at the age of sixteen, Melcher went to work in Lauriat's mailroom at a salary of $4 a week.

As a boy, books and reading were an important part of Melcher's life. He described himself as "a busy reader of almost anything that came to hand." This interest in books soon took him out of the mailroom and onto Lauriat's selling floor, where he developed a large personal following. His feeling for fine literature and his ability to transmit his own enthusiasm to others were already apparent, and a large measure of his success as a bookseller was attributable to them. When Arnold Bennett's *The Old Wives' Tale* was issued by the George H. Doran Company in 1908, retailers gave it scant attention. But Melcher, excited by the book, urged it on his customers at Lauriat's so successfully that within two weeks he had sold 500 copies and started a sales reaction that swept across the country. Both Bennett and George Doran credited the American success of the book to Melcher. On June 2, 1910, he married Marguerite Fellows; they had five children.

Melcher's work at Lauriat's led him to a broader interest in the book trade. He joined the newly formed Boston Booksellers' League, and in 1912 became its president. As a result of a spirited speech that he gave at the American Booksellers Association convention in New York City in 1911, Melcher was invited to take over W. Kerfoot Stewart's Indianapolis bookstore. In 1913 he and his family moved to Indianapolis, where he served as manager of W. K. Stewart Company for five years. The store became the center of Indiana literary and artistic activity during the height of the Hoosier school of writing, and Melcher came to know Booth Tarkington, Vachel Lindsay, James Whitcomb Riley, George Ade, Meredith Nicholson, and other writers. He both promoted and collected their work. He also met Edwin Grabhorn, who set up his Studio Press in Indianapolis in 1915. They discussed book design and fine printing—subjects that were to have special importance to

Melcher throughout his life. It was also in Indianapolis that Melcher's deep interest in libraries took root, and he began giving the inspirational talks to library groups for which he later became so well known.

In 1918 Melcher joined the R. R. Bowker Company in New York City as vice-president and as an editor of the firm's magazine, *Publishers Weekly.* For the rest of his life, Melcher was associated with Bowker and *Publishers Weekly.* He became president of Bowker in January 1934, shortly after the death of Richard Rogers Bowker. He served in this capacity until 1959, when he became chairman of the board.

As editor of *Publishers Weekly,* Melcher recognized the interdependence of publishers, booksellers, and librarians, and he encouraged each group to help the others. *Publishers Weekly* became an organ for all segments of the book world. Foremost among his concerns throughout his long career at *Publishers Weekly* were the publication of quality children's books and the establishment of library services for children, the dangers of censorship, good bookmaking, United States adherence to international copyright, and professional education for booksellers and publishers.

In 1919 Melcher was an originator with Franklin K. Mathiews, librarian of the Boy Scouts, of Children's Book Week. He was also the originator and donor, beginning in 1922, of the annual Newbery Medal for the most distinguished book for children and, beginning in 1937, of the annual Caldecott Medal for the most distinguished picture book for children. In 1943 Melcher established an annual award for creative publishing named for Mathew Carey and Isaiah Thomas. He was also a founder of the American Booksellers Association's book presentation program for the White House Library. In 1935, with the New York Public Library, he established the R. R. Bowker Memorial Lectures for the study of book publishing.

At the time of his death in Montclair, N.J., the London *Bookseller* proclaimed Melcher "without doubt the greatest all-round bookman the English-speaking world has produced."

[See Mildred C. Smith, ed., *Frederic G. Melcher* (1945); *Top of the News,* Frederic G. Melcher memorial issue, Mar. 1964; Daniel Melcher, "Fred Melcher as I Knew Him," *ALA Bulletin,* Jan. 1967. The most detailed obituary is in *Publishers Weekly,* Mar. 18, 1963. There is also an obituary in the *New York Times* (western ed.), Mar. 11, 1963.]

JEAN PETERS

MELTON, JAMES (Jan. 2, 1904–Apr. 21, 1961), tenor, was born in Moultrie, Ga., the son of James Wilburn Melton, a lumberman and amateur musician, and of Rose Thornton, an organist. Soon after his birth the family moved to Citra, Fla., where Melton attended the public schools and was chorister and soloist in the town church. At the University of Florida, which he entered in 1920 with the intention to study law, he formed and led a dance orchestra and sang with the school band. The president of the university, Albert A. Murphree, became convinced of his talent and urged him to consider a musical career. With this in mind, Melton left the university in his sophomore year to enter the School of Music at the University of Georgia, earning his way by playing the saxophone in the college band. In 1923 Melton transferred to Vanderbilt University in Nashville, Tenn., in order to study singing with Gaetano de Luca. After a year he left Vanderbilt but continued his vocal studies privately with de Luca.

Melton came to New York in 1927 to find a career as a singer. An appearance on a radio program attracted the interest of S. L. (Roxy) Rothafel, manager of the Roxy Theater in New York, who engaged him for the Roxy Gang, which performed weekly over the Columbia Broadcasting System (CBS) radio network. After an engagement with The Revelers, one of the earliest "precision" singing groups on radio, Melton became the singing star of his own radio show, "The Seiberling Singers" (1928). During the next dozen years he was one of radio's most popular singing attractions, starring on such major programs as "The Voice of Firestone," "Sealtest Sunday Night Party," "The Telephone Hour," and "Palmolive Beauty Box Theater." On June 29, 1929, he married Marjorie Louise McClure; they had one daughter.

While working on radio, Melton studied singing with Enrico Rosati. On Apr. 22, 1932, he made his concert debut at Town Hall in New York City. It was received unfavorably by some critics. Refusing to admit defeat, Melton continued his vocal studies in preparation for a career in opera, and his debut took place in Cincinnati, Ohio, on June 28, 1938, as Pinkerton in *Madama Butterfly.* Later that year he appeared with the St. Louis Opera, the San Carlo Opera in New York City, and the Chicago Civic Opera, singing Alfredo in *La Traviata,* Lionel in *Martha,* and Edgardo in *Lucia di Lammermoor.*

Success in opera came with Melton's debut at the Metropolitan Opera on Dec. 7, 1942, as Tamino in *The Magic Flute,* which became his most famous role. The sensitivity of his phrasing, the purity of his vocal texture, and the ease and freshness of his delivery received high praise. Melton remained a principal tenor of the Metropolitan Opera for six seasons, in which time he made sixty-one appearances in New York City and nineteen on tour in seven roles (Tamino, Alfredo, Edgardo, Pinkerton, Don Ottavio in *Don Giovanni*, Wilhelm Meister in *Mignon*, and Des Grieux in *Manon*). Apart from his operatic appearances he was heard frequently in the United States and Canada in recitals and as soloist with symphony orchestras.

Melton starred in the motion pictures *Stars over Broadway* (1935), *Sing Me a Love Song* (1936), *Melody for Two* (1937), and *Ziegfeld Follies* (1946). In 1934 he toured with George Gershwin and the Leo Reisman Orchestra in all-Gershwin concerts. He was the star of the "Ford Festival" on television in 1951. A year before his death in New York City, he toured in Sigmund Romberg's operetta *The Student Prince*. Apart from his singing Melton was famous for his collection of antique automobiles, which was frequently exhibited.

[See *Opera News*, Dec. 7, 1942; *New York Times*, June 17, 1945. An obituary is in the *New York Times*, Apr. 23, 1961.]

DAVID EWEN

MENJOU, ADOLPHE JEAN (Feb. 18, 1890–Oct. 29, 1963), motion picture actor, was born in Pittsburgh, Pa., the son of Jean Adolphe ("Albert") Menjou, who had emigrated from France and become a restaurateur, and Nora Joyce, an immigrant from Ireland. After the birth of a second son in 1891, Menjou's parents opened a restaurant in Pittsburgh. Since both parents worked, the two children were cared for by their paternal grandmother.

When the restaurant failed in 1897, the family moved to Cleveland, where Menjou attended St. Joseph's Seminary, Rockwell Public School, and East High School. He played hookey in high school in order to perform as a supernumerary in the Euclid Avenue Opera House. When his father discovered it, he sent Menjou to the Culver Military Academy for the 1906–1907 term. Wanting him to attend Cornell University and eventually become an engineer, Albert Menjou enrolled his son in the Stiles University Preparatory School in Ithaca, N.Y. In 1908, Menjou began studying engineering at Cornell but soon transferred to the College of Liberal Arts. At the end of his junior year he returned

to Cleveland, where he worked in his father's restaurant.

In 1912 Menjou moved to New York City to become an actor. Since he could not secure steady employment as an actor, he worked on a farm and in a haberdashery, and at other jobs. During this time he obtained some work as an extra at the New York movie studios. He first appeared as a ringmaster in *The Man Behind the Door* (1914), a film produced at the Vitagraph studio. In 1915 he helped his father open a restaurant on Long Island but soon left this venture to look again for acting roles. He got a small part in *A Parisian Romance* (1916) for $100 a week. Later, he played minor roles in a number of films.

When the United States declared war on Germany, Menjou enlisted in the army. He served in an ambulance unit in France in 1918, eventually rising to the rank of captain. After the war he briefly abandoned acting to become production manager in A. J. Van Buren's motion picture company. He found this position unsuitable and traveled to Hollywood in 1920 with his bride, Katherine Tinsley. After several months of disappointment, he eventually obtained a role as a reporter in a Mabel Normand film. He then had minor roles in *The Faith Healer* (1921), *Through the Back Door* (1921), *The Three Musketeers* (1921), *The Sheik* (1921), *The Fast Mail* (1922), *The Eternal Flame* (1922), *Arabian Love* (1922), and *Bella Donna* (1923). His first starring role came in 1923 when he played a wealthy Frenchman in Charlie Chaplin's *A Woman of Paris*. The reviews were laudatory, and job offers subsequently came easily. Menjou's roles in the sophisticated comedies of this period established his image as the suave, well-dressed man with the elegant waxed moustache.

In 1927 Menjou divorced his first wife and married Kathryn Carver. He was earning $7,500 a week, but the new talking pictures put his career in jeopardy. When his contract was not renewed in 1929, Menjou went to Paris and appeared in *Mon Gosse de Père* (1930). In 1930 he returned to Hollywood, where his fluency in various languages allowed him to play in foreign-language films.

The turning point in Menjou's career occurred in 1930 when he replaced an actor who had became seriously ill during the filming of *The Front Page* (1931). His performance as the editor in *The Front Page* earned him an Academy Award nomination. Menjou then acted in *A Farewell to Arms* (1932), *Little Miss Marker* (1934), *Sing, Baby, Sing* (1936), and *A Star is*

Born (1937). In 1933 Menjou divorced his second wife and on August 25, 1934, he married Verree Teasdale; they adopted a son. (Menjou had no children by his two previous marriages.)

During World War II Menjou traveled with the United Service Organizations in England, North Africa, and Sicily, and worked for the Office of War Information, making broadcasts in Italian, French, Russian, Spanish, and German. After the war Menjou played important supporting roles in *State of the Union* (1948), *Man on a Tightrope* (1953), and *Paths of Glory* (1957). He was also the host for *My Favorite Story*, a television series. In 1960 he played a disheveled eccentric in Walt Disney's *Pollyanna*, an unusual role for this debonair actor with the reputation as one of the world's "ten best-dressed men." *Pollyanna* marked the end of Menjou's career; he had appeared in more than two hundred films.

Menjou was a member of the John Birch Society. In 1947 he named alleged Communists in the film industry before the House Committee on Un-American Activities. An active Republican, he enthusiastically supported Richard M. Nixon in his campaign for the presidency in 1960. In 1962 he made his last public appearances as a guest on the Merv Griffin and Johnny Carson television shows. When he died in Beverly Hills, Calif., he was considered to be one of the wealthiest men in Hollywood.

[Menjou's autobiography, *It Took Nine Tailors* (1948), is the best source for his life story. *Reader's Digest*, Feb. 1948, presents a condensed version of the autobiography. See also *Obituaries from the* [London] *Times*, 1961–1970, compiled by Frank C. Roberts (1975); and the *New York Times* obituary, Oct. 30, 1963.]

ALLAN CHAVKIN

MEREDITH, EDNA C. ELLIOTT (Apr. 25, 1879–Jan. 1, 1961), hostess and publisher, was born in Des Moines, Iowa, the daughter of Samuel Mathew Elliott and Adeline Mary Jones. She grew up in Des Moines and attended Iowa State College. On Jan. 8, 1896, when only sixteen, she married Edwin Thomas Meredith, a nineteen-year-old former farm boy who had withdrawn from Highland Park College in Des Moines after one year in order to work with his grandfather in publishing *Farmer's Tribune*, a weekly Populist newspaper. They had two children.

Meredith's grandfather gave the *Tribune* to the young couple as a wedding gift. It was an inauspicious beginning in publishing, for the *Tribune* had only a small circulation and was a consistent money loser. Edwin Meredith changed the paper from a political organ to a magazine of farm information and began a campaign for statewide circulation. He quickly made the journal into a paying venture, but sold it in 1904 in order to concentrate on a new monthly publication, *Successful Farming*, which he founded in 1902. For eight years the new magazine barely remained solvent, but by 1920 it had become one of the most profitable farm magazines in the nation. Its success made possible an additional publishing venture in 1922, a magazine called *Fruit, Garden and Home*. In 1924 the name of the new magazine became *Better Homes and Gardens*. *Successful Farming* and *Better Homes and Gardens* formed the basis for the success of the Meredith Publishing Company (1929), which was to become one of twentieth-century America's most successful media corporations.

In the meantime, Edwin Meredith, with his wife's active support, had become engaged in politics. He was an unsuccessful Democratic candidate for U.S. senator from Iowa in 1914 and for governor in 1916. In 1920 he was appointed secretary of agriculture under President Woodrow Wilson and served in that position during the last year of Wilson's term of office. The Merediths were very popular in Washington, and Edna Meredith acquired fame as an elegant hostess, a fame she had already secured in Des Moines social and Iowa political circles.

A progressive Democrat, Edwin Meredith supported woman suffrage, prohibition, and policies favorable to farmers. He was considered a strong candidate for the Democratic presidential nomination in 1924, when he received 200 votes at the Democratic National Convention. Thereafter Edwin Meredith was a strong supporter of the presidential aspirations of William G. McAdoo in 1924. After McAdoo's withdrawal from the race prior to the 1928 convention, Meredith actively sought the nomination, in an effort to prevent the nomination of Al Smith, whom he felt to be neither "dry" nor sound in his agricultural policies. During the 1928 campaign, Edna Meredith received national attention as a potential first lady. She was described by Frances Parkinson Keyes as "a dainty, exquisite little lady," well-dressed and having the qualities of simplicity, sweetness, and strength. According to *Woman's Home Companion*, she was a perfect hostess whose dominant trait was enthusiasm.

Shortly after Smith received the Democratic nomination, Edwin Meredith died on June 17, 1928, and Edna Meredith took up her husband's opposition to Smith's presidential campaign by supporting Herbert Hoover. She supported Hoover again in 1932, this time out of opposition to Roosevelt and, while remaining a Democrat, formed the nonpartisan National Coalition of Women Supporting Alfred M. Landon for President in 1936. In 1940 she announced, in a telegram to the Republican National Committee, that she would join with other Democrats to support Wendell L. Willkie in his campaign against Roosevelt.

After her husband's death, Edna Meredith inherited a major interest in the Meredith Publishing Company. She served for many years as business manager and, later, as director of the corporation. In 1930 the company inaugurated a book division and published *The Better Homes and Gardens Cookbook.* By 1968 the cookbook had sold more than 12 million copies. For more than thirty years its sales in the United States were exceeded only by the Bible. In 1943 the company brought out the *Better Homes and Gardens Baby Book,* which set a sales record for baby books. In addition to the highly successful book division, the Meredith Corporation continued its success with its two major magazines, *Successful Farming* and *Better Homes and Gardens,* which are among the most profitable magazines published in America in the twentieth century.

In addition to her political and publishing activities, Meredith was known as a philanthropist. Besides donating money to charitable and educational institutions, she started a service club in Des Moines for servicemen (1941) and was later active in the rehabilitation of wounded veterans. She died in Des Moines.

[Articles on Meredith as a potential first lady appeared in *Delineator,* Mar. 1928, and *Woman's Home Companion,* June 1928. On the Meredith Company, see "How Meredith Publishing Builds on a Rich Legacy," *Printer's Ink,* Apr. 28, 1961; Theodore Peterson, *Magazines in the Twentieth Century* (1964); Frank Luther Mott, *A History of American Magazines,* V (1968); "Meredith at 75: Multi-Media Expansion," *Advertising Age,* Oct. 31, 1977; John Tebbel, *A History of Book Publishing in the United States,* III (1978). Obituaries are in the *New York Times,* Jan. 2, 1961, and *Publishers Weekly,* Jan. 30, 1961.]

JERRY L. MILLER

MERRILL, GRETCHEN VAN ZANDT (Nov. 2, 1925–Apr. 15, 1965), figure skater, was born in Boston, Mass., the only child of Abner Scott Merrill, a son of Frank Abner Merrill, founder and senior partner of the private Boston banking firm of Merrill, Oldham and Company,

and Gretchen Van Zandt. Merrill attended Beaver Country Day School in Brookline, Mass. An indifferent student, she was by contrast a natural athlete, always active in competitive sports. She won a diving championship at age four, and before her tenth birthday she had won swimming and tennis championships as well.

Merrill began taking ice skating lessons in 1935. During one of her early lessons she met Sonja Henie, the Norwegian world and Olympic figure skating champion who was on tour in the United States. Watching a characteristic Henie temper tantrum, Merrill decided she could be a successful although untemperamental world-class skater. In 1937 she won the National Novice Ladies Figure Skating Championship. This was followed by a victory in the National Junior Ladies Figure Skating Championship (1938) and two second-place finishes in the National Senior Ladies Figure Skating Championship in 1941 and 1942.

At that time serious figure skaters did not routinely employ gymnastic coaches and choreographers, and Merrill was largely self-taught. She sketched her own routines on paper and practiced them at home in her stocking feet, executing split jumps over the sofa. She trained rigorously from 6:30 A.M. until school began and after school until dinner time. Merrill did have professional instruction, but only after 1941 were these lessons important. In that year she moved to Berkeley, Calif., to train with Maribel Vinson Owen, a former United States champion. There she concentrated on the technical aspects of the sport. She mastered such difficult maneuvers as the loop-change-loop and the bracket-change-bracket. This technical mastery remained the strong point of her performance for years. She also attended the University of California as an extension student, probably as a diversion from her daily routine.

The rigorous training paid off in 1943 when Merrill won the first of six consecutive National Senior Ladies Figure Skating Championships, tying a record held by her coach. Her school figures—those exact tracings on the ice that are at once a mark of agility, concentration, and self-control—enabled her to enter the free-skating portions of championship competitions with comfortable leads over her rivals. Other skaters at times performed more successfully in the free-skating competition, but no one in these years managed to overtake her early lead. This pattern was broken only in 1948 when she won the free-skating portion of the program after finishing second in the school figures.

Merrill was a popular champion. Her shapely

figure, blond hair, and easy manner in interviews captured the public. She was named the best-dressed woman in United States sports in 1945. During World War II she was a popular figure on USO tours. Servicemen called her "Quee-nie." The Massachusetts Horticultural Society named a new white orchid for her after her first seniors championship in 1943. A corsage of these flowers was personally delivered to her by her neighbor Leverett Saltonstall, then governor.

Despite these triumphs, broader success eluded Merrill. She never captured the North American Championship; her best finish was second in 1943. Moreover, the war forced a suspension of international competition, and by the time it resumed in 1948, younger women such as Barbara Ann Scott of Canada were competing. In the 1948 Olympics Merrill finished a disappointing eighth, falling three times in her free-skating program—in part because of her inexperience on outdoor ice. Complaining of exhaustion and overpreparation, she subsequently withdrew from the world championships in February 1948. Although she successfully defended her title in the United States in April 1948, she was hard pressed for the first time in years. The following year she was defeated in her effort to secure her seventh consecutive national title. Thereafter she retired. She never turned professional.

On Jan. 9, 1953, Merrill married William Otis Gay, a stockbroker who was much older than she. The marriage was childless and ended in divorce. Thereafter she lived quietly and alone. She died of unknown but natural causes in Windsor, Conn., where her body lay undiscovered for about a week.

Although short and not spectacular, Merrill's career was noteworthy. At her best she dominated United States women's ice skating as few have. It is unfortunate that the larger events of the century kept her from competing against the best world figure skaters while she was at the peak of her skills.

[Numerous articles about Merrill appeared in the *New York Times* between 1941 and 1948. See also *Time,* Mar. 11, 1946; Oliver Jensen, "Champion Figure Skater," *Life,* Mar. 4, 1946; John Chamberlain, "The Strange World of the Skater," *Harper's,* Feb. 1949. An obituary appeared in the *New York Times* on Apr. 23, 1965.]

CHARLES R. MIDDLETON

MESERVE, FREDERICK HILL (Nov. 1, 1865–June 25, 1962), businessman and collector of historical photographs and Lincolniana, was born in Boston, Mass., the son of William Neal Meserve, a Congregational minister, and of Abigail Burnham Hill. The American Missionary Society sent the family to California, where William Meserve was active in founding several churches between 1868 and 1876. The family then returned to the East for a time and, while his father was pastor of several churches in the Boston area, Meserve completed his secondary education. He studied medicine for a time in Boston, but gave it up to go with his family to Colorado. The vigorous life of an outdoorsman appealed to him, and he spent extensive periods during 1887 and 1888, sometimes alone, atop Pikes Peak as an observer for Harvard University in an experiment to determine an appropriate site for an astronomical observatory.

In 1888 Meserve entered the Massachusetts Institute of Technology. While there he was a reporter for the *Boston Globe and Herald,* writing college news; he also worked part-time for an engineering firm. He left college in 1892, without graduating, to become the western manager for an engineering firm. In 1893 Meserve moved to New York City to join Deering, Milliken, and Company, a textile commission firm. He remained with the firm for the rest of his life, although at one point he held a seat on the New York Stock Exchange with the brokerage firm of Charles W. Turner (1909–1919). On Nov. 6, 1899, Meserve married Edith Turner; they had three children.

Meserve's interest in old photographs began while he was collecting illustrations for a manuscript of his father's Civil War diary. Using income from his business ventures, he became a zealot in collecting photographs and negatives from the period 1850–1900, especially photographs of Lincoln. The collection eventually contained more than 200,000 pieces. The extensive collection of Lincoln photographs was used by Jules Roiné during his work on the Lincoln Centennial Medal and by Victor Brenner, the designer of the head on the Lincoln penny.

In 1911 Meserve had a book entitled *Photographs of Abraham Lincoln* privately printed. In 1917 four sets of a twenty-eight-volume work, *Historical Photographs,* were produced; two more sets were made in 1944. The six extant sets of this work contain several hundred otherwise unpublished photographs of figures from government, education, and entertainment of the last half of the nineteenth century. Carl Sandburg assisted Meserve in the publication of *The Photographs of Abraham Lincoln* (1941).

Through his activity as a collector, Meserve discovered several "lost" photographs of Lincoln and preserved thousands of photographs of public figures that provide a visual record of a segment of American life in the nineteenth century. This collection was generously made available both to professional historians and interested nonspecialists. Meserve died in New York City.

[Biographical information about Meserve is most readily available in a prefatory chapter written by Carl Sandburg in *The Photographs of Abraham Lincoln.* An interview with Meserve is in the Oral History Collection of Columbia University. An obituary is in the *New York Times,* June 26, 1962.]

MICHAEL R. BRADLEY

MEŠTROVIĆ, IVAN (Aug. 15, 1883–Jan. 16, 1962), sculptor, was born in Vrpolje, Croatia, the son of Mate Meštrović and Marte Kurabasa. Shortly after his birth the family returned to Otavice, their home. His father was a poor shepherd and farmer who also did stonemasonry. Since Meštrović did not attend school, his earliest education came from the teachings of his family, in which the Bible and historical ballads played a seminal role. Indeed, Meštrović's father was the only literate villager in Otavice and even had a small library. Meštrović began at an early age to farm and watch the flocks, but he was more interested in carving and produced spoons and other utilitarian things. Figures of friends and animals, Madonnas, and crucifixes soon followed.

In 1898, Meštrović went to Split, where he was apprenticed to Pavle Bilinić, a stonecutter who specialized in memorials and religious items. He distinguished himself, and Alexander Koenig, a Viennese businessman, became his patron; this allowed Meštrović to move in 1899 to Vienna, where he studied with Otto Koenig, a retired professor of sculpture, who helped him to prepare for the entrance examination of the Vienna Academy of Fine Arts. The four years that Meštrović spent at the academy (1900–1904) constituted his only formal training, and even there he was often allowed to follow his own propensities. Perhaps only Otto Wagner, one of his teachers, can be considered a true influence, and that more on Meštrović's architecture than on his sculpture. During this period Meštrović supplemented his meager Yugoslav stipends by sculpting and by producing facsimiles of paintings in museums.

In 1903, Meštrović was accepted as an exhibitor by the Vienna Secession. Karl Wittgenstein purchased *At the Well of Life* and commissioned a number of other pieces. In 1904 Meštrović married Ruža Klein. The proceeds from the Wittgenstein sales financed a trip to Italy and a move to Paris (1907–1909), where his work received favorable comment from Auguste Rodin, who became a good friend. Also at this time Meštrović began work on the monumental Kossovo Temple, a structure that commemorated Serbian nationalism but that was never built. Many of the individual pieces were exhibited in the Vienna Secession in 1909. This was followed by major showings in Zagreb (1910) and at the International Exhibition in Rome (1911), where he was awarded first prize. Meštrović spent much of the time between 1910 and 1914 in Yugoslavia. When World War I forced him into exile, he lived first in Rome and then in London, where in 1915 he exhibited at the Victoria and Albert Museum, a show that had many political overtones. He was, in fact, active in the formation of the Yugoslav Committee on National Liberation. From London he moved to Geneva, and finally to Cannes.

In 1919, Meštrović returned to Zagreb. Here the emphasis of his work shifted from the portraits and religious subjects of his exile to large public monuments—*King Peter I, Indian with Bow* and *Indian with Spear* (1925–1927), and *Gregory, Bishop of Nin* (1926)—and to architectural designs, such as the Račić Memorial Church in Cavtat, which was completed in 1922. Meštrović was strongly nationalistic (a bias frequently reflected in his sculpture). But because he disagreed with current policy, he repeatedly refused government positions—member of the Yugoslav Provisional National Assembly (he served only briefly, in 1919), senator, minister, and even prime minister. He remained in Zagreb until 1942, becoming director of the Zagreb Academy of Fine Arts. In 1923 he married Olga Kesterčanek; they had four children.

In 1924 and 1925, Meštrović visited the United States and exhibited in a number of locations, including the Brooklyn Museum and the Art Institute of Chicago. Beginning in 1933, another major exhibit of his works traveled to Paris, Prague, Munich, Berlin, Vienna, and Graz. During the Italian occupation he refused to cooperate with the oppressors and was arrested by the Gestapo. Eventually he was released and in 1942 he went to Rome (where he began his *Pieta,* among other works), and later to Lausanne and Geneva.

After the war Meštrović refused to live under

Tito's dictatorship in Yugoslavia. He therefore spent some time in Rome, and in 1947 he moved to the United States, where he taught at Syracuse University. Also in 1947 he exhibited at the Metropolitan Museum of Art in New York City; this was the first one-man exhibition ever granted to a living artist by the Metropolitan. After eight years and the completion of many pieces, including *Man and Freedom*, a twenty-four-foot bronze for the Mayo Clinic, Meštrović left Syracuse to become distinguished professor of sculpture at the University of Notre Dame, where he spent the rest of his life, sculpting primarily religious subjects, many of which can be seen on the Notre Dame campus. Neither the 1960 stroke that diminished his sight nor the deaths of his two children could deter him from his work. He continued sculpting until his death in South Bend, Ind. He had become an American citizen in 1954.

Meštrović created folk and national heroes in epic proportions, portraits, religious subjects, and architectural structures in many styles—neoclassical, art nouveau, expressionistic. The effect can be enticing and powerful, or occasionally sentimental. His place in the history of Western art is difficult to ascertain. On the one hand, Rodin believed that "Meštrović was the greatest phenomenon among the sculptors." He was highly praised by the reviewers of his many exhibitions, and the authors of monographs can be adulatory: Laurence Schmeckebier calls him "one of the great personalities of twentieth century art, and indeed . . . one of the great masters in the history of sculpture. . . ." On the other hand, art historians generally ignore him; for example, neither Germain Bazin's *History of World Sculpture* (1968) nor Howard Hibbard's *Masterpieces of Western Sculpture* (1977) mentions Meštrović at all. A tempered evaluation probably lies somewhere between these extremes. His most powerful pieces remind one of Rodin or Gaston Lachaise, but he never ventured into the abstractness of contemporary art. Even the more conservative work of Henry Moore, for example, is extreme compared with Meštrović's most modern pieces. Nonetheless, his finest sculpture is certainly stunning: *The Maiden of Kossovo* (1907, marble) and *The Archers of Domagoj* (1917, plaster) are vibrantly powerful reliefs; the twenty-six-foot *Gregory, Bishop of Nin* (1926, bronze) is awesome; and *Job* (1945, bronze) is an anguished existential cry, reminiscent of Rodin's best work.

[There are public collections of Meštrović's works in Belgrade and in his houses in Zagreb and Split, which are now museums. Notre Dame and Syracuse universities have many Meštrović pieces. See M. Ćurčin, *Ivan Meštrović: A Monograph* (1919), with essays by a number of critics; Christian Brinton, introduction to the catalog *The Meštrović Exhibition* (1924), which is quirky; Harry H. and Estelle S. Hilberry, *The Sculpture of Ivan Meštrović* (1948); Laurence Schmeckebier, *Ivan Meštrović: Sculptor and Patriot* (1959), the most important monograph; Duško Kečkemet, *Ivan Meštrović* (1970); Anthony J. Lauck, Dean A. Porter, et al., *Ivan Meštrović: The Notre Dame Years* (1974), a beautiful catalog. Also see Dorothy Grafly, "Meštrović and Milles," *American Magazine of Art*, May 1932; R. Warnier, "Le Statuaire Ivan Meštrović et son oeuvre," *Revue de l'art*, Mar. 1933; Anthony Lauck, "Ivan Meštrović 1883–1962," *Art Journal*, Spring 1962.]

ROBERT HAUPTMAN

METALIOUS, GRACE (Sept. 8, 1924–Feb. 25, 1964), writer, was born in Manchester, N.H., the daughter of Albert de Repentigny, a pressman, and Laurette Royer. The Repentignys were of French-Canadian descent, and Grace spoke French before she spoke English. Her parents were divorced when Grace was eleven, and she and her sister were brought up by her mother and grandmother.

In 1942, soon after graduating from the local public high school, Grace married George Metalious, a millhand. World War II had just begun, and her husband was soon in the army. She spent the war years working at an air force base. When George Metalious returned from the army, he worked at various jobs until he enrolled at the University of New Hampshire in order to become a schoolteacher. After he graduated, the couple lived a rather precarious and peripatetic existence until he accepted a job as principal at a school in Gilmanton, N.H. By this time they had three children, and Grace had been advised by a physician that another pregnancy could be fatal.

This news was deeply disturbing, and Metalious turned to writing as an alternative form of creativity. Thus was begun, in the winter of 1954, a novel that she called *The Tree and the Blossom* but that in less than two years would appear as *Peyton Place*. When the manuscript was accepted by Messner, a small New York firm, the Metaliouses were living in near poverty and their marriage was virtually finished. Even the well had run dry at the house, called "It'll Do," where they lived in rural New Hampshire.

A young New York editor, Leona Nevler, had recommended Metalious' manuscript to Kathryn Messner during a job interview; her present employer had turned the book down in spite of her strong recommendations. Nevler was asked to edit the book, but Metalious' recalcitrance and reluctance to take any editorial advice immediately led to friction. After one editorial session, Metalious spent the night drinking in a Greenwich Village saloon, and in the early morning went straight to her agent's office to complain. Kathryn Messner then took over the editing of the book. Metalious' discoverer was later paid $1,100 by Messner, whose firm was to make millions from *Peyton Place.*

Peyton Place was published in September 1956, and within a month was on the best-seller lists. It was inevitably seen as an exposé of Gilmanton, a view that was reinforced when George Metalious was fired from his job. It made little difference that he was fired before the book came out. Such a scandal, coupled with reviews that stressed the salacious nature of the work, guaranteed its success. One review in particular, that in *Time* magazine, was instrumental: "Her love scenes are as explicit as love scenes can get without the use of diagrams and tape recorder."

Peyton Place sold 300,000 copies in hardcover and more than 8 million in paperback. On the *New York Times* best-seller list for more than a year, it was denounced by politicians and preachers, and banned in many areas of the country. The book captured the popular imagination, and the term "Peyton Place" became part of the language, used to denote a small town or area with smug, self-satisfied hypocrites who engage in secret and scandalous sexual shenanigans. A successful motion picture and television series were based on the book.

Metalious' personal life did not match her public success. She and her husband separated, and in 1958 she divorced Metalious and married T. J. Martin, a local disc jockey. She confided in a four-part autobiographical series in the tabloid *American Weekly*, "I have found my way safely home." Two years later she divorced Martin and remarried Metalious (although she later denied having done so). By 1963 they had separated again.

Metalious wrote three more books, all of them set in small New England towns, all iconoclastic, sex-ridden treatments of small-town life: *Return to Peyton Place* (1959), rumored to have been partly, if not largely, written by a ghostwriter; *Tight White Collar* (1960); and *No Adam in Eden* (1963). Each was a best seller, in spite of or because of universally bad reviews, although none of them was as successful as her first novel. By the time of her death, her books had sold some 15 million copies.

Metalious was by no means an important writer, although she did have some narrative skill and a certain flair for evoking small-town life. Nowhere are the limits of her modest talent more evident than in the autobiographical pieces she wrote for *American Weekly*, even allowing for her intended audience. The most lasting influence of her books is in the marketing techniques used to promote and sell them and in the legion of similar writers who have followed her. Clever use of reviews and manipulation of publicity could be employed to appeal to, and often create, a mass audience—and thus generate great sums of money. This approach would come to dominate large parts of the American publishing industry.

Grace Metalious died at the age of thirty-nine, of chronic liver disease, in Boston, Mass.

[See Grace Metalious, "Me and 'Peyton Place,' " *American Weekly*, May 18, May 25, June 1, June 8, 1958. A biography is Emily Toth, *Inside Peyton Place* (1981). An obituary is in the *New York Times*, Feb. 26, 1964.]

MARSHALL DE BRUHL

MEYER, ALBERT GREGORY (Mar. 9, 1903–Apr. 9, 1965), cardinal of the Roman Catholic Church, was born in Milwaukee, Wis., the son of Peter James Meyer, a grocer and later a factory foreman, and of Mathilda Thelen. He attended St. Mary's Parochial School, Marquette Academy, and St. Francis Seminary. Having demonstrated his scholastic ability, he was sent by the Archdiocese of Milwaukee to the North American College in Rome to study philosophy for two years and theology for four at the Urbanian College of the Sacred Congregation de Propaganda Fide. Meyer was ordained a priest on July 11, 1926, and received the doctorate of sacred theology a year later. After three more years of graduate work at the Pontifical Biblical Institute in Rome, he was awarded the licentiate's degree in Sacred Scripture in 1930. Meyer was then appointed assistant pastor of a parish in Waukesha, Wis. In 1931 he was named to the faculty of St. Francis Seminary in Milwaukee, and six years later became its rector.

On Feb. 18, 1946, Pope Pius XII appointed Meyer sixth bishop of Superior (a diocese embracing the northwestern part of Wisconsin). He was consecrated by Archbishop Moses E. Kiley in Milwaukee on April 11. During the seven years in which he occupied that see, Meyer held a diocesan synod and regular conferences of the clergy in the deaneries, issued four "Programs of Instructions" to assist his priests in preparing sermons, established the Diocesan Council of Catholic Women (1950), and supervised an extensive building program.

In 1953, after the death of Archbishop Kiley, Meyer was promoted to the metropolitan see of Milwaukee, to lead almost half a million Catholics and nearly a thousand diocesan and religious priests. He was the first native of the archdiocese to become its head. In five years he founded seventeen parishes and five missions, and oversaw the construction of thirty-four churches, seventy-four schools, forty convents, twelve rectories, three hospitals, and one college. Meyer also enlarged and modernized St. Francis Seminary, and fostered organizations for laymen, such as the Serra Club (of which he had been the first chaplain in Milwaukee while he was attached to the seminary), the Holy Name Society, the Archdiocesan Council of Catholic Men, and the Catholic Youth Organization.

In 1956 Meyer was elected to the Administrative Board of the National Catholic Welfare Conference and was named chairman of its Education Department; he retained that post until he was elevated to the cardinalate. He was also president general of the National Catholic Educational Association in 1956–1957. As archbishop of Milwaukee, Meyer was ex officio a member of the board of governors of the Catholic Church Extension Society, in which he took a lively interest, and from 1953 he was a member of the American Board of Catholic Missions.

In September 1958, Meyer was transferred to the metropolitan see of Chicago, succeeding the late Samuel Cardinal Stritch. Chicago was the largest archdiocese in the United States, and Meyer was responsible for the spiritual care of nearly 2 million faithful, including more than 1,200 diocesan and 1,400 religious priests and 8,500 sisters. As the suburban Catholic population was growing rapidly, he established thirty parishes and oversaw the construction of seventy-three churches, sixty-nine elementary schools and eighty-two additions to existing ones, fifteen high schools and six additions to existing ones, forty-one convents, thirty-seven rectories, six hospitals and additions to others, three homes for the aged, and a mausoleum and three interment chapels in the Catholic cemeteries—all in little more than six years.

In 1959 Meyer established the Archidocesan Conservation Council (later called the Office of Urban Affairs), to provide to parishes and institutions the research, planning, and organization necessary for the maintenance of their physical property and conducive to the social welfare of neighborhoods and communities. To help financially distressed parishes he established the Archdiocesan Parish Welfare Fund, which supplemented the parishes' incomes on a cooperative matching basis. He also centralized the banking operations and insurance coverage of the parishes through the chancery office.

After the fire in which ninety-two pupils and three sisters at Our Lady of the Angels Grammar School perished on Dec. 1, 1958, Meyer initiated a program of fire prevention, personal safety, and modernization of buildings in the parochial schools; subsequently he issued detailed regulations designed to improve the personnel and facilities of these schools. In the area of education he devoted particular attention to the founding of high schools. He also built a second day-school seminary on the secondary level, Quigley Preparatory Seminary South, and opened a junior-college division of the major seminary, St. Mary of the Lake, at Niles.

Besides effectively administering the temporal affairs of the archdiocese, Meyer discharged his teaching duty in an enlightened manner. He wrote profound and lengthy pastoral letters and other statements, the most memorable of which was probably his 1964 Lenten pastoral letter, "Ecumenism: The Spirit of Christian Unity," which was designed to prepare the minds of Catholics in the archdiocese for the Second Vatican Council's forthcoming decree on that subject. Further, he advocated the intensive study of the Bible, and wrote the preface to the American edition of the Revised Standard Version adapted for Catholic use.

Meyer promoted equal justice for blacks, and urged his clergy and laity to incorporate black Catholics into all church affairs. He strove to transform black parishes into "mission-centers" with an apostolic program. In May 1958, Meyer testified before the President's Commission on Civil Rights, lamenting the fact that the "new and rapidly increasing Negro middle class" could not freely choose where it would live. He was one of the three cochairmen of the National Conference on Religion and Race, which was held at Chicago in January 1963, and in an address to the assembly he advocated open housing for the entire metropolitan area.

Outside his own archdiocese Meyer instituted the Mission of San Miguelito in the Republic of Panama, staffed it with three priests, and supported it. Under his patronage the Extension Lay Volunteers for Home Missions were organized, and he was permanent chairman of the American Board of Catholic

Missions. When Meyer was made a cardinal, he automatically became a member of the administrative board of the National Catholic Welfare Conference; at various times he was chairman of the Bishops' Committee on the Liturgical Apostolate and of the Bishops' Committee for Migrant Workers.

Meyer was also called upon to share in the work of the Holy See. In the consistory of Dec. 14, 1959, he was created cardinal-priest of the title of St. Cecilia by John XXIII and was appointed to two important congregations: de Propaganda Fide and Seminaries and Universities. In 1962 he was made a member of the Pontifical Commission for Biblical Studies. In June 1963, Meyer took part in the conclave in which Paul VI was elected, and the following November he was added to the Papal Commission for the Revision of the Code of Canon Law. A year later he was attached to the Supreme Congregation of the Holy Office; he was one of the first two cardinals not resident in Rome to become members of that body.

It was during the Second Vatican Council that Meyer's talents were afforded the widest scope. In the initial stage he submitted some thoughtful proposals for the council's agenda. In October 1961, John XXIII appointed him to the Central Preparatory Commission, and he subsequently participated in several of its meetings in Rome. Before the Vatican council convened, Meyer was made a member of the Secretariat de Concilii Negotiis Extra Ordinem (for the extraordinary affairs of the council). When this body was abolished in 1963, he was appointed one of the twelve presidents of the council. After the original draft of a decree "on the sources of revelation" was rejected, he was appointed to the special mixed commission that drew up a new and acceptable one.

Meyer advocated many progressive changes, such as the use of the vernacular languages in the liturgy, recognition of the contributions of contemporary biblical exegesis, and admission in theory and in practice of the collegial nature of the episcopal order. In the name of more than 120 bishops of the United States, whose signatures he had personally solicited, he recommended that binding force be attributed to the collective decisions of national episcopal conferences only in a cautious, reserved manner, and later on behalf of his American colleagues he argued in favor of the proposed declaration on religious liberty. He also espoused an explicit condemnation of all forms of anti-Semitism and a refutation of the charge of deicide against the Jewish people.

On Nov. 19, 1964, the head of the board of presidents of the Second Vatican Council, without consulting Meyer, announced that the scheduled preliminary vote on the scheme on religious liberty would be postponed until the following year. Meyer, accompanied by two other cardinals and backed by nearly a thousand bishops who had signed hastily circulated petitions, immediately protested to the pope, but failed to induce him to reverse the decision. This dramatic effort nevertheless helped to ensure passage of the declaration at the fourth session. By the end of the third session (1964) —the last he attended—Meyer had emerged as the intellectual leader of the American hierarchy and had won the admiration and respect of many bishops of other nationalities. He had addressed the council more often than anyone else from the United States.

After returning to Chicago, Meyer began in January 1965 to suffer the effects of a brain tumor. Despite surgery it caused his death, at Chicago, within a few months.

A tall and robust man, with sparse hair and benign face, Meyer had a placid temperament and simple tastes. He did not have a lively sense of humor, and wasted little time on things unrelated to his office. He tended to be withdrawn; in informal groups he was usually quiet, but on committees and commissions he collaborated with his peers. In spite of his shyness and apparent aloofness, Meyer was genuinely interested in his priests and people. As an administrator he was methodical and orderly, without being coldly impersonal. As a teacher he adhered strictly to Catholic doctrine, but sought deeper insights and fresh applications. In analyzing controverted questions he considered different points of view and obtained expert advice before coming to a conclusion. Though prudent and deliberate by nature, Meyer did not hesitate to act boldly and swiftly when he felt obliged by conscience. In pace with the renewal of the Church which he effectively advanced, his reputation has grown to ever larger proportions in the years following his untimely death.

[The official records of Meyer's episcopate are in the diocesan archives of Superior, Milwaukee, and Chicago. His pastoral letters and other public statements were published in the *Catholic Herald-Citizen* (Milwaukee) and *New World* (Chicago). His personal papers are in the Archives of the Archdiocese of Chicago (at St. Mary of the Lake Seminary, Mundelein, Ill.). His speeches to the Second Vatican Council are in Vincent A. Yzermans, ed., *American Participation in the Second Vatican Council* (1967). A longer biographical sketch is the booklet by George

N. Shuster, *Albert Gregory Cardinal Meyer*, no. 11 in the series The Men Who Make the Council (1964). An obituary is in the *New York Times*, Apr. 10, 1965.]

Robert F. Trisco

MICH, DANIEL DANFORTH (Jan. 8, 1905–Nov. 22, 1965), magazine editor, was born in Minneapolis, Minn., the son of Harry J. Mich and Jean Temple. His father, a mechanic with Pence Automobile Company, started the Mich Automobile Company, an agency, in 1909. Tragedy struck the family that year: Jean Mich's clothes ignited while she was ironing, and young Daniel, then four years old, went for help. By the time he returned with a neighbor, Jean Mich was a mass of flames, and died shortly afterward. She was only twenty-six years old. Two years later Harry Mich married Marie Linehan.

Mich had a lifelong interest in sports and would have liked to become an athlete, but for most of his life he walked with a slight limp that may have been caused in childhood by an unidentified case of polio. As an adult he wore special shoes. When quite young he earned admission to baseball games at Nicollet Park in Minneapolis by helping to drag the infield, hawking peanuts, and sweeping the stands. He was a sportswriter and later the editor of the Central High School (Minneapolis) newspaper. He once commented, "It seems as if there never was a time when I did not know I was going into the newspaper business."

Mich entered the University of Wisconsin in 1922 and soon took a part-time job on the *Wisconsin State Journal* as a sportswriter. He left school in 1924 to become assistant sports editor, and was soon promoted to sports editor. He served as city editor until 1930, when he requested to be switched back to sports editor. From 1930 to 1933, he served as managing editor of the *Muscatine* (Iowa) *Journal*, and from 1933 until 1937 he was managing editor of the *Wisconsin State Journal*. In 1928, Mich married Patricia L. Cavanaugh; they had no children. They were divorced in 1943.

Mich joined *Look* magazine shortly after it was started by Gardner Cowles in 1937. Cowles met Mich during a White House press conference at which he was impressed by the questions Mich asked President Franklin D. Roosevelt. Mich was a member of the editorial staff until about 1942, when he became editorial director. In 1950, he resigned from *Look* to become editorial director at *McCall's*. He returned to *Look* in 1954 as editorial director and vice-president.

He was elected to the board of directors in 1955 and named editor in May 1964.

A pioneer in photojournalism, Mich believed that graphic arts should be used to broaden and deepen the reader's understanding of the news through feature articles. On one occasion a staff member called to tell Mich that a *Life* reporter was on the same assignment. (At that time *Life* published weekly and *Look* every other week.) Mich replied, "Stay there and do it better!" He believed that anything could be improved by cutting, and he frequently told his staff, "Wrap it up . . . leave the reader gasping, laughing, raging or at least pleasantly satisfied." Mich explained his techniques in *Technique of the Picture Story* (1945), written with Edwin Eberman, art director for *Look*, while they were teaching a class at New York University.

Mich liked to take issue with the great and powerful, and he never worried about the furor caused by a hard-hitting article. He explained his philosophy of publishing controversial articles by quoting Dante: "The hottest places in Hell are reserved for those who, in time of great moral crisis, maintain their neutrality."

While managing editor of the *Wisconsin State Journal*, Mich served as president of the fledgling Madison local of the American Newspaper Guild and spearheaded a successful drive for a forty-eight-hour week and a $35 minimum salary. He resigned when the national guild was critical of a managing editor's being a guild member. Mich continued to support efforts to obtain better pay and working conditions, economic and educational opportunities, freedom, women's and civil rights, and freedom of the press. He practiced what he preached, hiring and promoting both women and blacks on the staff of *Look*.

Mich was noted for his abrupt, abrasive, caustic criticism. He had an authoritative voice that carried to every desk in the office. Yet it was his grunt of approval when something pleased him that encouraged staff members to do their best.

On Nov. 4, 1944, Mich married Isabella Taves, entertainment editor of *Look*, in a ceremony at New York's City Hall conducted by Mayor Fiorello La Guardia. He then told her that she could no longer work for *Look*, fearing other staff members might think she was receiving favored treatment. Taves became a full-time free-lance author of articles and books.

At Isabella Taves' urging, Mich wrote an article for *Collier's* (Dec. 7, 1946) called "Roundy Rings the Bell," about Joseph Leo Coughlin, an ungrammatical sports writer on the staff of the *Wisconsin State Journal*, and a short story for

the *American Magazine* (November 1945) entitled "Farewell at the Ritz." But he was too
impatient to write on a regular basis. He was an
editor who was able to improve an author's story
by inserting a key word or deleting an unnecessary word, phrase, or paragraph.

In 1965, Mich suffered from amoebic dysen-
tary in Paris and contracted hepatitis from one
of the blood transfusions. After a nine-month
illness, he died in New York City.

[Articles on Mich are in *Saturday Review of Literature,* Mar. 16, 1946; *Collier's,* Dec. 7, 1946; *Newsweek,* July 17, 1950, and Jan. 11, 1954; *New York
Times,* Sept. 11, 1950, Jan. 6, 1955, Feb. 11, 1958,
Apr. 15, 1959, May 15, 1964; *Look,* May 15, 1964,
and Dec. 28, 1965. Obituaries are in the *New York
Times* and *Wisconsin State Journal,* Nov. 23, 1965.]
                                    JEAN-RAE TURNER

MILLER, DAVID HUNTER (Jan. 2, 1875–
July 21, 1961), businessman, lawyer, diplomat,
editor, and historian, was born in New York City,
the son of Walter Thomas Miller, president of
Walter T. Miller and Company and a founder
and treasurer of the New York Cotton Exchange, and of Christiana Wylie. He was educated at public and private schools in New York
City. After service as a second lieutenant in the
Ninth New York Volunteer Infantry in the summer and fall of 1898, he became a partner in the
family firm. On Apr. 25, 1900, he married Sarah
Whipple Simmons; they had no children.

In 1904 Miller turned to the study and practice of law. In 1910 and 1911, respectively, he
received LL.B. and LL.M. degrees from the
New York Law School; and in 1915, with Gordon Auchincloss as his partner, he established a
law firm in New York. When the nation entered
World War I, Auchincloss, the son-in-law of
Colonel E. M. House, became assistant counselor to the State Department, and Miller participated in departmental affairs. On June 17,
1917, Secretary Robert Lansing named him special assistant with a monthly salary of $1. His
duties primarily involved drafting legal documents for Colonel House.

Miller was an original member of Inquiry, the
group of experts who were to formulate the
American peace program. He was treasurer of
the panel and one of its specialists in international law, although he lacked experience or
training in that field. He contributed to a memorandum on war aims on which the territorial
provisions of President Woodrow Wilson's
Fourteen Points address of January 1918 were
based.

In July 1918, Miller and House presented

Wilson with suggestions for a postwar international organization, and thereafter Miller was
intimately involved in composing the Covenant
of the League of Nations. As technical adviser
to the American delegation in Paris, he was the
chief United States negotiator on details of the
League of Nations' constitution. Miller and Sir
Cecil Hurst drafted a covenant that served as
the basis for deliberations of the Commission on
the League, and it was they who revised the
document into the form that was finally approved on Apr. 28, 1919.

From the beginning Miller agreed with Wilson that the Covenant should be part of the
treaty of peace. He advocated a clause recognizing the Monroe Doctrine that was eventually
added under pressure from the U.S. Senate. He
helped defeat British attempts to tie provisions
for revision of the treaty to the guarantee of
mutual security, but he failed to persuade Wilson that that guarantee should be a negative,
rather than a positive, obligation. Nonetheless,
Miller endorsed the positive guarantee as embodied in the Covenant's controversial Article
X. "The bogey of inconsistency," he later wrote,
"is nothing to me."

Miller participated in discussions in Paris on
various other issues, including an international
labor convention—a project he hoped would
help prevent social revolutions such as the one
in Russia. One of the staunchest opponents of
normalizing relations with the Bolsheviks,
Miller had a hand in planning the Hoover-
Nansen mission that was to distribute humanitarian relief in the Soviet Union while undermining the Soviet regime. William C. Bullitt
referred to Miller as "the blackest reactionary"
in the delegation, blaming him personally for
Wilson's ultimate refusal to recognize the Bolshevik government.

With House, Miller supported Italy's demands for territory on the Adriatic coast, although he acknowledged that the secret treaty
of London of 1915, by which Italy had been
promised such territory as inducement to join
the Allies against Austria-Hungary, had been
invalidated by the Fourteen Points. The issue
contributed to House's alienation from Wilson,
which deepened when the colonel, again with
Miller's support, urged the president to accept
the Lodge reservations in order to secure Senate
approval of the Treaty of Versailles.

Miller returned to Washington in June 1919,
and resigned from the State Department in October. Thereafter he was one of the most vocal
American supporters of the League of Nations
and the Treaty of Versailles. In a newspaper

debate he challenged John Maynard Keynes's conclusions on the economic consequences of the peace. In 1921 he acted as legal adviser to the Weimar government in its unsuccessful claim to all of Upper Silesia following a treaty-mandated plebescite. Two years later he condemned the French and Belgian occupation of the Ruhr Valley as a violation of the terms of the peace settlement.

In 1922, Miller's law firm merged with another whose senior partner was Alton B. Parker, the Democratic candidate for president in 1904. Miller's political activities intensified at about this time. He led the effort in New York to win the 1924 Democratic presidential nomination for William G. McAdoo, and after that failed, he divided his time between partisan and international causes. Coauthor of the American plan that became the Geneva Protocol of 1925, he constantly maintained that the United States could not be disinterested in Europe and that the League of Nations, even without American help, was the best guardian of peace.

In 1929, Miller became editor of treaties in the State Department, a post he accepted at considerable financial sacrifice. The next year he represented Washington at the Nationality Conference in The Hague, and in 1931 he assumed additional duties as historical adviser to the State Department, a post he held until 1938. Miller retired from public life in 1944, having edited eight published volumes of treaties. He died in Washington, D.C.

[Miller's papers are at the Library of Congress; his personnel file for the Peace Commission is in the National Archives, General Records of the American Commission to Negotiate Peace, 1918–1931, file 184.1; additional materials relating to the peace conference are at the Council of Foreign Relations, New York City. Some of his official correspondence, (1917–1919) is in *Papers Relating to the Foreign Relations of the United States, 1919. Paris Peace Conference*, 13 vols. (1942–1947). He wrote "The Making of the League of Nations," in *What Really Happened at Paris*, edited by E. M. House and C. Seymour (1921); much more important are Miller's *My Diary at the Conference of Paris*, 21 vols. (1924); and *The Drafting of the Covenant*, 2 vols. (1928). His other important publications include "The Adriatic Negotiations at Paris," *Atlantic Monthly*, Aug. 1921; *International Relations of Labor* (1921); *The Geneva Protocol* (1925); and *The Peace Pact of Paris* (1928). On his role in Paris, see Robert Lansing, *The Peace Negotiations* (1921); *The Intimate Papers of Col. House*, edited by Charles Seymour, 4 vols. (1926–1928); James T. Shotwell, *At the Paris Peace Conference* (1937); Seth P. Tillman, *Anglo-American Relations at the Paris Peace Conference of 1919* (1961);

and Charles Seymour, *Letters from the Paris Peace Conference*, edited by H. B. Whiteman, Jr., (1965). On the Geneva Protocol, see James T. Shotwell, *War as an Implement of National Policy* (1929), and Harold Josephson, *James T. Shotwell and the Rise of Internationalism in America* (1975). An obituary is in the *New York Times*, July 24, 1961.]

RICHARD A. HARRISON

MILLER, PERRY GILBERT EDDY (Feb. 25, 1905–Dec. 9, 1963), teacher and scholar of American literature and intellectual history, was born in Chicago, Ill., the son of Eben Perry Sturgis Miller, a physician, and of Gertrude Eddy. He grew up in Chicago and spent several summers of his youth in Vermont. Miller attended the Tilton School and Austin High School in Chicago, and in 1922 enrolled at the University of Chicago. He left the university the following year to try his hand at other things. He first went to Colorado, next to New York City, and then abroad. It is not clear now—and it probably was not to him at the time—just what he was seeking in these travels. The theater drew his attention in New York, and for a time he played bit parts in Paterson, N.J. He also performed around New York City with Edward H. Sothern and Julia Marlowe's Shakespeare company.

The stage did not hold Miller for long, and he next took to the sea. His travels, apparently for a time as a seaman, took him to Tampico, Mexico, the Mediterranean, and then to Africa, where he left his ship to work for an oil company in the Belgian Congo. There, he later wrote, he felt the calling to expound what he took to be "the innermost propulsion of the United States. . . ." On returning to the United States in 1926, he resumed his studies at the University of Chicago, where he received the bachelor's degree in 1928 and the doctorate in 1931.

Miller may have felt his first inspiration to study America while unloading drums of case oil in Africa, but his experience in graduate school gave this impulse direction and shape. Several of his teachers attempted to discourage his interest in the American Puritans, which had been stimulated by a reading of John Winthrop's *Journal* and by the conviction that he should begin at the beginning. At least one professor, Percy Holmes Boynton, did not discourage him. In fact, he encouraged Miller to spend the academic year 1930–1931 at Harvard, where Miller took courses with two masters in the field, Kenneth Murdock and Samuel Eliot Morison. On Sept. 12, 1930, Miller married Elizabeth Williams; they had no children.

Orthodoxy in Massachusetts, Miller's doctoral dissertation, was published in 1933. He had begun teaching two years earlier, as a tutor at Harvard's Leverett House. In 1933, with F. O. Matthiessen and Ellery Sedgwick, he began a survey course in American literature, one of the early courses in the field at an American university. Other innovative courses followed, including one on American romanticism that made Miller's reputation as one of Harvard's great teachers.

During the years before World War II, Miller completed the research for *The New England Mind: The Seventeenth Century* (1939). The war interrupted his studies—he joined the U.S. Army in 1942, serving first as a captain and then in the Office of Strategic Services (OSS) as a major until his discharge in 1945. Harvard promoted him to full professor in 1946.

In the years following World War II Miller reached the peak of his powers as a scholar and teacher. For the most part his life resembled— at least on the surface—that of many distinguished academics. He produced outstanding books and articles, and students flocked to his classes and seminars. He won the usual academic honors—and several not so usual, including election to the American Academy of Arts and Sciences and, in 1961, a special award from the American Council of Learned Societies of $10,000, in recognition of the extraordinary quality of his scholarship.

The scholarship included a work edited with Thomas H. Johnson, *The Puritans* (2 vols., 1938), which proved valuable both to advanced scholars and to beginning students; an intellectual biography of Jonathan Edwards (1949); *Roger Williams: His Contribution to the American Tradition* (1953); and *The New England Mind: From Colony to Province* (1953), perhaps his finest work.

Miller's students and friends have described him as a brilliant teacher who demanded much from his students. But he gave good students strong encouragement and took their work seriously. He was no cloistered scholar, too involved with his own work to pay attention to the world around him. Rather, he took an active part in the life of the university and studied the affairs of the world eagerly. Among his interests was the Boston Red Sox baseball team.

Miller offered no facile thesis about either Puritanism or America. Nor did he claim to have a method that would answer questions about American history and literature. He was in certain respects an intellectual historian, a literary critic and historian, and a historian of American culture.

The history of Puritanism obsessed Miller as a young scholar, and it remained of vital interest to him even after he began the study he did not live to complete, *The Life of the Mind in America*. (One volume of this work, *From the Revolution to the Civil War*, was published posthumously in 1965.) His work on Puritanism concentrated on the ideas of the Puritans, who, he argued, had come to America on a great mission—the completion of the Protestant Reformation for the instruction of Europe. They would define the character of the true church organization and the nature of a truly holy society. Explaining what happened to the Puritans' understanding of their mission—their "errand into the wilderness," as they said—led Miller to write some of the most searching history of the twentieth century. In the process he opened up new subjects for study—Ramist logic, typology, and the covenant theology—and revived several old ones—revivalism, and the contributions to America of Roger Williams, Jonathan Edwards, and Solomon Stoddard.

Miller's studies of the nineteenth century were not so systematic, nor were they so profound or brilliant. But his introduction to Thoreau's "Lost Journal," published as *Consciousness in Concord* (1958), forced literary scholars to think anew about American romanticism, and *The Transcendentalists* (1950), which he edited, called attention to secondary figures among the transcendentalists.

Miller died in Cambridge, Mass. His influence on scholars and students is ultimately indefinable. But among his greatest achievements was the setting of a standard for others and inspiring them to try to live up to it.

[Among Miller's important works not mentioned in the text are *Jonathan Edwards: Images or Shadows of Divine Things* (1948); *Errand into the Wilderness* (1956); *The Raven and the Whale* (1956); *Nature's Nation* (1967). For further details about Miller's life and work, see Robert Middlekauff, "Perry Miller," in Marcus Cunliffe and Robin W. Winks, eds., *Pastmasters: Some Essays on American Historians* (1969); and *Harvard Review*, Winter–Spring 1964. An obituary is in the *New York Times*, Dec. 10, 1963.]

ROBERT MIDDLEKAUFF

MILLS, CHARLES WRIGHT (Aug. 28, 1916–Mar. 20, 1962), sociologist and social critic, was born in Waco, Tex., the son of Charles Grover Mills and Frances Ursula Wright. His father was a drummer for an insurance company in the early 1920's, a position that kept him on the road much of the time. Mills grew up under his doting mother's strong Catholic influence. His childhood was not an especially happy one: "I never had a circle of friends. . . . There was for me no 'gang,' no 'parties.'" He lived in Waco until he was seven, but moved frequently thereafter: Fort Worth, Wichita Falls, Dallas, and Sherman, Tex. He attended both public and parochial schools, regularly earning a reputation as a poor student, a rebel, and a loner.

Until 1934, Mills remained an indifferent student. Then, suddenly, he took up reading and began the lifelong habit of keeping a journal. His notebooks were filled with personal recollections, quotations, ideas for further research, and rough drafts of sections of essays and books. Mills attended Texas A and M University, in 1934–1935, then transferred to the University of Texas at Austin, where he earned a B.A. in 1938 and an M.A. in philosophy in 1939. From Texas he went to the University of Wisconsin, where he studied under Hans Gerth, receiving a Ph.D. in sociology in 1942.

Mills apparently was ambivalent about marriage; although divorced three times, he was never unmarried for long. He married Dorothy Helen Smith in 1937. They were divorced three years later, but remarried in 1941. They had one daughter. After a second divorce from Dorothy Smith on July 9, 1947, Mills married Ruth Harper the following day. They had one daughter. Mills and Ruth Harper were divorced in May 1959, and on June 11 of that year he married Gloria (Yaroslava) Surmach. They had one son.

Mills spent his adult life in an institution that he regarded with mixed emotions: the academy. He was an associate professor of sociology at the University of Maryland from 1941 until 1945. After a year (1945–1946) as a Guggenheim fellow, he was associated with Columbia University for the rest of his life, initially as director of the Labor Research Division of the Bureau of Applied Social Research (1945–1948), and then as assistant professor (1946–1950), associate professor (1950–1956), and professor of sociology (1956–1962). Mills also held visiting appointments at the University of Chicago (1949), Brandeis University (1953), and the University of Copenhagen (1956–1957).

At Columbia, Mills quickly became a figure of controversy in both academic sociology and leftist intellectual circles. His mature work was a sustained, many-sided attempt to understand the historical present, to pursue large historical, political, and moral questions in the light of a central goal: "the presumptuous control by reason of man's fate."

For Mills the sociological imagination represented the most comprehensive mode of social vision in the twentieth century. It does not focus exclusively on what he called "the personal troubles of milieu," which "occur within the character of the individual and within the range of his immediate relations with others." Nor does it merely illuminate "the public issues of social structure," which "have to do with the organization of many milieux into the institutions of an historical society as a whole." Rather, the sociological imagination entails a comprehensive effort to "grasp history and biography and the relations between the two within society." Beyond this, it is a form of self-consciousness, a way of defining oneself both as a character and as an actor in the historical present.

Mills's main theoretical investigations of American society led him toward despair as the sociological imagination brought the realities of the cold war into focus. Rather than succumb to this mood, though, he continued to search for ways out of the national and international impasse. A man without a party, a movement, or a received ideology, Mills worked alone, cutting against the grain of what he considered the smug "American celebration" that devitalized radical intellectual life in the 1950's. He was thrown back on the formidable strengths of his personality—moral vision, courage, determination—and the tools of his craft: reason and historical-sociological analysis. As Ralph Miliband observed, Mills was "a man on his own, with both the strength and also the weakness which go with that solitude. He was on the Left, but not of the Left, a deliberately lone guerrilla, not a regular soldier. He was highly organized, but unwilling to be organized, with self-discipline the only discipline he could tolerate."

Because of his restless energy and compelling presence, Mills was easily turned into a hero by admiring students, a man larger than life. But if he possessed (and cultivated) heroic virtues, he also displayed large defects. Although his faults and merits have been debated since his death, no clear portrait emerges; he was a tissue of contradictions, a complex man. As Harvey Swados remarked, Mills was "egomaniacal and brooding, hearty and homeless, driven by a demon of discontent and ambition, with faith only in the therapy of creative work, whether intellectual or physical. . . . In all of his writing, as in his lecturing and his public stance, and indeed in his private existence, it was the blending of these forces that gave his work and life its ineluctable impact, its sense of a powerful mind and a forceful personality at grips not only with the petty and the ephemeral but with the profoundly important questions."

In the welter of conflicting recollections, Mills's intellectual seriousness stands out. His intellectual thrust in the late 1940's and 1950's reflects a systematic attempt to make an "adequate statement" about what he considered a tragic separation of knowledge and moral vision from power in America. His studies of the major echelons of American society—*The New Men of Power* (1948), a portrait of labor leaders; *White Collar* (1951), an analysis of the new middle classes; and *The Power Elite* (1956), an examination of interlocking corporate, political, and military elites—form parts of an overall effort to understand the American "present as history and the future as responsibility."

From about 1956 until his death, Mills sought fresh perspectives on American—and global—dilemmas, moving in several directions with striking speed and characteristic determination. On the domestic front (and in the Western world generally) he continued his search for new levers of change that would combine knowledge and moral vision with power in order to enlarge the scope of human freedom. Having given up on traditional agencies of change, Mills turned to intellectuals and to the young. He challenged his academic peers in *The Sociological Imagination* (1959), and encouraged young radicals in his widely circulated "Letter to the New Left" (1960). At the same time he broadened the scope of his study, exchanging an earlier preoccupation with American themes for a concern with the major global drifts of the epoch: socialism in advanced Communist nations and revolutionary upheavals in the developing world.

Mills operated in more than one intellectual theater during this period. His expanding interests required extensive travel and reading in new fields. And his sense of urgency, based on the accelerating tempo of historical change, its global interconnectedness, and the threat of a nuclear catastrophe, persuaded him to communicate his developing outlook immediately—and impatiently—to a wide audience. Hence his public image was of a free-swinging polemicist, the author of *The Causes of World War III* (1958) and *Listen, Yankee: The Revolution in Cuba* (1960). Simultaneously, though, he was undertaking an ambitious venture in sociological theory, a "six- to nine-volume comparative study of the world range of present-day social structures."

Mills did not live to realize this ambition. A tireless worker like his father, he developed a heart condition that led to his death in West Nyack, N.Y. His legacy is that of a loner: he left no political party, no doctrine, no school of thought. But he did produce a coherent body of work that is still widely read. He kept alive a tradition of native American radicalism in the nonradical 1950's. And he inspired part of a new generation of sociologists to take seriously the challenges and responsibilities of intellectuals.

[A collection of Mills's papers is deposited at the University of Texas, Austin. A complete bibliography of Mills's writings is in Irving Horowitz, ed., *Power, Politics, and People* (1963). Also see Paul Sweezy, "Power Elite or Ruling Class?" *Monthly Review*, Sept. 1956; Herbert Aptheker, *The World of C. Wright Mills* (1960); Ralph Miliband, "C. Wright Mills," *Monthly Review*, Sept. 1962; Harvey Swados, *A Radical's America* (1962); G. William Domhoff and Hoyt B. Ballard, comps., *C. Wright Mills and the Power Elite* (1968); Richard Gillam, "The Intellectual as Rebel: C. Wright Mills. . . ." (M.A. thesis, Columbia University, 1969); Freddy Perlman, *The Incoherence of the Intellectual* (1970); Peter Clecak, *Radical Paradoxes* (1973); and Howard Press, *C. Wright Mills* (1978). The first volume of what promises to be the definitive biography—Richard Gillam, *C. Wright Mills: A Life in Work*—is scheduled for publication in 1983. An obituary is in the *New York Times*, Mar. 21, 1962.]

PETER CLECAK

MINTON, SHERMAN (Oct. 20, 1890–Apr. 9, 1965), U.S. Supreme Court justice, and U.S. senator, was born on a farm near Georgetown, Ind., the son of John Evan Minton, a farmer, and of Emma Livers. The family later moved to nearby New Albany, where he attended high school. At Indiana University Minton was both an honor student and a varsity athlete, excelling in football and baseball. He graduated with the LL.B. in 1915, ranking first in a class that included Wendell L. Willkie and Paul V. McNutt. He next went to Yale University on a scholarship. He helped organize the Yale University Legal Aid Society, and received the LL.M. in 1916. Tall, broad-shouldered, and handsome, he was called "Shay" Minton from his college days on.

Minton opened a law practice in New Albany. On Aug. 11, 1917, he married Gertrude Gurtz; they had three children. He served as a captain in the Motor Transport Corps in World War I (1917–1919), much of the time in France. After returning to New Albany, he resumed his law practice.

Minton's first public position, to which he

was appointed by Governor Paul McNutt in 1933, was as counselor of the Indiana Public Service Commission. Notably successful in opposing utility rate increases, he quickly attracted public favor. He liked the combination of law and politics so much that he ran successfully for U.S. senator on the Democratic ticket in 1934.

Although he had had a thoroughly conservative upbringing and legal practice, Minton vigorously supported the New Deal. "Sure, I'm a New Dealer," he said. "I'd be ashamed to be an Old Dealer." His staunch support of White House measures and his skill in floor debate brought him unusual attention for a freshman senator. He was an internationalist representing a generally isolationist constituency. In 1935 he took the lead in organizing a successful attack on a Huey Long filibuster. He also chaired a special committee that exposed the extent of lobbying pressure and tactics in Washington. While doing all this, Minton rose to Democratic whip and assistant majority leader. He was a delegate to the Democratic national conventions in 1936 and in 1940.

No senator was a more indefatigable backer of the Roosevelt administration in its battle with the Supreme Court over the constitutionality of New Deal legislation. Minton even proposed that seven justices be required to hold a federal statute unconstitutional. When Franklin D. Roosevelt introduced his "court-packing" bill in 1937, Minton was so central to the White House cause that he was strongly considered for the first Supreme Court appointment that Roosevelt was called on to make. But the post went to Senator Hugo L. Black.

In 1940 Minton lost his bid for reelection when presidential candidate Wendell L. Willkie led the Republican ticket to victory in Indiana. In January 1941, Roosevelt put Minton on his staff as an administrative assistant with special responsibility for liaison to military agencies. An instance of Minton's careful attention to issues that would benefit Roosevelt was his effective backing of Senator Harry Truman's resolution to "investigate defense activities" during World War II. He saw an investigation under Truman's control as a way to keep the inquiry in "friendly hands," since Republican senators sought to exploit it.

In May 1941 Roosevelt appointed Minton to the Seventh Circuit of the U.S. Court of Appeals, covering Indiana, Illinois, and Wisconsin. During the following eight years, Minton participated in important cases involving national corporations in restraint of trade, price discrimination, and intimidation of employees. He sus-

tained the Taft-Hartley Act's requirement of anti-Communist affidavits from union officials.

President Harry S. Truman elevated Minton to the Supreme Court on Sept. 15, 1949, to replace Wiley B. Rutledge, an outstanding liberal. The choice provoked much discussion. Interior Secretary Harold L. Ickes was sure that Minton would join Black and William O. Douglas, and thus strengthen "the liberal minority." As a justice-designate, Minton declined to appear before a Senate committee because he held that the legislative and judicial branches had their separate areas of responsibility. However, he made it clear that he would tend to give Congress "leeway."

Shortly before being elevated to the Supreme Court, Minton had written in the *Indiana Law Journal* what appeared to be his acceptance of Justice Black's strong support of the constitutional rights of the accused in a capital punishment case: "Why the Court goes part of the way but not all the way with Justice Black is, to say the least, illogical." Despite this seeming declaration of position, Minton and Justice Tom C. Clark (appointed only one month before Minton) joined Chief Justice Frederick M. Vinson and associate justices Stanley F. Reed, Felix Frankfurter, and Harold H. Burton in deciding many important cases based on the invocation of constitutional guarantees of civil liberties. These involved Bill of Rights provisions concerning freedoms of speech, press, assembly, and petition; separation of church and state; protections against double jeopardy, forced testimony against oneself, and unreasonable searches; and other fundamental reliances of the individual citizen, such as due process of law.

This new alignment swung the Supreme Court back from its strong pro–Bill of Rights record of the 1940's to almost the opposite stance in the early 1950's. It sorely disappointed civil libertarians, but Minton regarded himself as completely consistent. He held that as a senator he was a member of the legislative branch of the federal government, which spoke the popular will on public issues. But as a justice of the Supreme Court he considered his mission to be to deal with the application of legislative and executive authority, and not with whether that application was either sound or desirable.

Within three months Minton was the central judicial figure in a hard-fought controversy that brought him, the Supreme Court, and the Truman administration widespread criticism. In an unusual 4–3 ruling he held that, notwithstanding the War Brides Act of 1945, the attorney general had the authority to bar the admission of the German wife of an honorably discharged veteran, presumably as a security risk, without a hearing (*United States ex rel. Knauff* v. *Shaughnessy*, 338 U.S. 537 [1950]). The Minton opinion kept Ellen Knauff on Ellis Island for months while the Immigration Service sought unsuccessfully to return her to Germany. Eventually, thanks in part to strong editorial backing and other public support, the Immigration Service reversed its position and she was admitted and became a citizen.

Also in 1950, Minton wrote the majority opinion in *United States* v. *Rabinowitz* (339 U.S. 56), which permitted court reliance on evidence obtained in an unauthorized search. This decision expressly overruled the precedent case, *Trupiano* v. *United States* (334 U.S. 699 [1948]). This led Justice Frankfurter to make one of his sharpest judicial statements: that the Supreme Court "ought not reinforce needlessly the instabilities of our day by giving fair ground for the belief that Law is the expression of chance—for instance, of unexpected changes in the Court's composition and the contingencies in the choice of successors." Minton's Rabinowitz opinion was reversed in *Chimel* v. *California* (395 U.S. 752 [1969]).

Another Minton majority opinion that was both denounced and applauded came in the academic freedom case of *Adler* v. *Board of Education of the City of New York* (342 U.S. 485 [1952]). It held that a teacher's membership in a state-prohibited organization could be a proper test of loyalty, and hence of fitness to teach. Minton generally supported governmental actions aimed at "subversive" connections, as shown in *Dennis et al.* v. *United States* (341 U.S. 494 [1951]). But he did dissent on occasion, as in *Feiner* v. *New York* (340 U.S. 315 [1951]), which involved the conviction of an arrested street speaker.

Minton was closely aligned with Chief Justice Vinson, notably on racial discrimination and religious-freedom issues. In *Barrows* v. *Jackson* (346 U.S. 249 [1953]) he wrote the decision ruling racially restrictive covenants in the sale of California property unconstitutional under the Fourteenth Amendment. In *Terry* v. *Adams* (345 U.S. 461 [1953]) he refused to join in finding unconstitutional the deliberate prepri-mary racial discrimination applied by the Jaybird Democratic Association in a Texas county. He asserted his disgust for the "unworthy" Jaybird "scheme," but based his concern on what the Supreme Court "says is state action" under the Fifteenth Amendment.

Almost from the start of his Supreme Court

tenure, Minton suffered from pernicious anemia. During his last term he was forced to walk with a cane. After Vinson was succeeded in the chief justiceship by Earl Warren in 1953, Minton became less influential. He resigned on Oct. 15, 1956, and returned to New Albany.

Although the Supreme Court experience did provide satisfactions, on the whole it was largely disappointing for Minton. At the age of seventy, when asked about the "most exciting period" of his life, he told the press that it was the New Deal era: "We were in a revolution and I was close to the throne." He died in New Albany.

[Minton destroyed many of his papers, but some of his Supreme Court records are in the Truman Library, Independence, Mo. See Irving Dilliard, "Truman Reshapes the Supreme Court," *Atlantic Monthly*, Dec. 1949; George Braden, "Mr. Justice Minton and the Truman Bloc," *Indiana Law Journal*, Winter 1951; C. H. Pritchett, *Civil Liberties and the Vinson Court* (1954); Bernard Schwartz, "The Supreme Court: Constitutional Revolution in Retrospect," *Indiana Law Journal*, Fall 1958; Harry L. Wallace, "Mr. Justice Minton—Hoosier Justice on the Supreme Court," *Indiana Law Journal*, Winter and Spring 1959; C. H. Pritchett, *Congress Versus the Supreme Court* (1961); Walter F. Murphy, *Congress and the Court* (1962); Richard Kirkendall, "Sherman Minton," in Leon Friedman and Fred Israel, ed., *Justices of the United States Supreme Court*, (1969); David Atkinson: "Justice Sherman Minton and the Balance of Liberty," *Indiana Law Journal*, Fall 1974; "Sherman Minton and Behavior Patterns Inside the Supreme Court," *Northwestern University Law Review*, Nov.–Dec. 1974; "From New Deal Liberal to Supreme Court Conservative," *Washington University Law Quarterly*, Spring 1975; "Opinion Writing on the Supreme Court, 1949–1956," *Temple Law Quarterly*, Fall 1975; "Justice Sherman Minton and the Protection of Minority Rights," *Washington and Lee Law Review*, Winter 1977; Irving Dilliard, "Change on the Supreme Court," in Ronald K. L. Collins, ed., *Constitutional Government in America* (1980). An obituary is in the *New York Times*, Apr. 10, 1965.]

IRVING DILLIARD

MITCHELL, JAMES PAUL (Nov. 12, 1900–Oct. 19, 1964), businessman and secretary of labor, was born in Elizabeth, N.J., the son of Peter J. Mitchell, an editor of trade-union journals, and Anna C. Driscoll, an early member of the Retail Clerks Union. Mitchell attended St. Patrick's School and Battin High School in Elizabeth. After his graduation in 1917 he became a clerk in the butter and egg store where he had worked since the age of twelve, following the death of his father.

Mitchell became a small-scale entrepreneur

in 1919 when he opened a grocery store, followed by a second one in 1921. On Jan. 22, 1923, he married Isabelle Nulton; they had one daughter. Both of his stores failed in the business recession of 1923. For the following eighteen years he worked to pay off all his creditors, holding a series of jobs including lumber salesman, truck driver, and door-to-door coal salesman.

In 1929, Mitchell embarked on a career in industrial relations and personnel administration with the Western Electric Company in Kearny, N.J.; having joined the firm in 1926 as an expediter, he gravitated into the personnel department. From 1932 to 1936 he served as Emergency Relief Administration director in Union County, N.J. He returned to Western Electric in 1936 as supervisor of training. In 1938 he became director of the industrial relations department of the New York City Works Progress Administration (WPA).

Mitchell's work with the WPA introduced him to Colonel Brehon Somervell, director of the WPA in New York City. In 1940, Somervell, then chief of the Construction Division of the Army Quartermaster Corps, brought Mitchell to Washington, D.C., to handle labor relations for the army's vast construction program. After the Army Service Forces were formed, Mitchell served as director of its Industrial Personnel Division (1942–1945), with responsibility for personnel management of approximately 1 million civilian employees of the army and for overseeing labor-management relations in all the army's construction work. For this work he received the Exceptional Service Award in 1944. He also served on the National Building Trades Stabilization Board from 1941 to 1945, and in 1948 was a member of the personnel advisory board of the Hoover Commission on the Reorganization of the Executive Branch.

Following the war Mitchell returned to private industry as director of personnel and industrial relations at R. H. Macy and Company (1945–1947) and as vice-president in charge of labor relations and operations at Bloomingdale Brothers (1947–1953). He served simultaneously as chairman of the employee relations committee of the National Retail Dry Goods Association, as a member of the executive committee of the National Civil Service League, and as chairman of the executive committee of the Retail Labor Standards Association of New York. He was also a member of the Personnel Advisory Board of the Hoover Commission in 1948.

Although a Democrat, Mitchell supported Dwight Eisenhower in the 1952 election and became a Republican soon afterward. In May 1953, President Dwight Eisenhower appointed Mitchell assistant secretary of the army for manpower and reserve forces affairs. Mitchell accepted the position of secretary of labor on Oct. 8, 1953, following the resignation of Martin Durkin, who had served only eight months in office. He immediately changed the administrative structure and techniques of the department so as to increase its efficiency in line with recommendations made by the Hoover Commission. He strengthened and expanded programs that directed national attention to manpower problems of the technological revolution and provided help to special groups, such as older workers and migrant farm workers. He served as cochairman of the President's Committee on Government Contracts (Vice-President Richard M. Nixon was chairman), which provided leadership in the government's program to eliminate discrimination in employment. He chaired the President's Commission on Migratory Labor. The causes of migrant workers and equal employment opportunity were among his major concerns. He fought against heavy opposition in order to better the lives of migrant workers. Journalist and editor Harry Hamilton called Mitchell the "social conscience of the Republican party," and he was widely regarded as a liberalizing influence in the Eisenhower administration.

Under Mitchell the Department of Labor maintained excellent relations with both organized labor and management. The AFL-CIO gave Mitchell a testimonial dinner in 1960, just before his leaving office. Some liberal Republicans and labor leaders made an abortive attempt to secure him the Republican vice-presidential nomination in 1960.

Major legislative achievements under Mitchell included amendment of the Fair Labor Standards Act to increase the minimum wage; an act providing temporary additional benefits during the 1958 recession; legislation providing permanent unemployment insurance programs for federal civilian employees and former servicemen; and passage of the Landrum-Griffin Act (1959), guarding against corruption and abuse of power and trust in labor-management relations. During Mitchell's tenure unemployment insurance was extended to cover an additional 4 million workers (it was the first extension since passage of the act).

After leaving the Labor Department, Mitchell served as chairman of the Railroad Retirement Board and ran unsuccessfully for governor of New Jersey in 1961. Following his defeat, he accepted a position as a consultant and director of industrial relations of the Crown Zellerbach Corporation, moving to vice-president for industrial relations and senior vice-president for corporate relations in 1962. Mitchell died of heart failure while on business in New York City.

Mitchell had a distinguished career in both private industry and public service. Many of those who knew Mitchell thought of him as the beau ideal of the pragmatic, twentieth-century man, a union of humanistic ideals and superb technical reality. As a result of his service, he received over forty major awards, honors, and citations. The apex of his career was in the labor portfolio, and whether he was the best secretary of labor the nation ever had, as AFL-CIO chieftan George Meany—not one to ascribe praise to the Eisenhower administration—once said, is open to debate. A more cogent accolade was offered after his death by another former secretary of labor, Arthur Goldberg, who said, "The burden of a Secretary of Labor is a heavy one, yet he bore it always with a warm regard for all of the people who served him, and whom he served. His contribution to his nation was an enduring one, both in what he accomplished and in the way he accomplished it."

[See U.S. Department of Labor, Correspondence files of the secretary of labor, 1953–1961, National Archives record group 174; U.S. Department of Labor, Labor Press Service news releases, 1953–1964; U.S. Department of Labor, *Annual Report of the Secretary of Labor*, 1953–1961; Henry P. Guzda, "James Mitchell: A Biography," in files of U.S. Department of Labor, Historian's Office; and obituaries in *New York Times*, Oct. 20, 1964, and *America*, Oct. 31, 1964.]

HENRY P. GUZDA

MITCHELL, THOMAS GREGORY (July 11, 1892–Dec. 17, 1962), actor, playwright, and director, was born in Elizabeth, N.J., the son of James Mitchell, a furniture store proprietor and mortician, and Mary Donnelly. Both parents were born in Ireland. He was the youngest of seven children and often in the spotlight, a fact that may have had some bearing on his career. Mitchell attended St. Patrick's High School in Elizabeth, where he played the role of Cardinal Richelieu in his graduation play. When he was seventeen he wrote a monologue based on the life of the English boy poet Thomas Chatterton, which he performed in New Jersey vaudeville houses for three weeks.

After graduating from high school in 1909,

Mitchell got a job as a reporter on the *Elizabeth Daily Journal*. However, within two weeks the paper was forced to publish five retractions; the errors were traced to Mitchell's uncontrollable desire to dramatize the commonplace in the news. He then worked for papers in Baltimore, Washington, D.C., and Pittsburgh. The assignment to review a play in Youngstown, Ohio, supposedly was a decisive factor in Mitchell's choice of career. After writing the reviews, he submitted his resignation.

In 1912 Mitchell made his first professional stage appearance in New York City with the Ben Greet Players from Stratford-on-Avon. Alongside Tyrone Power, Sr., he played Trinculo in *The Tempest*. From 1914 to 1916 he appeared with Charles Coburn's touring Shakespeare company, performing in at least fifty roles. He also worked in stock in Denver, Omaha, and Springfield, Mass. Mitchell held no regard for theories or "methods" of acting. "An actor who thinks," he wrote in 1961, "is a dead duck." He rejected the concept of "living" a part. An author's words to him were analagous to a composer's notes and he preferred to play a part as a pianist would play the piano. He tried to create an illusion and always act with the enthusiasm of an amateur. He did not view acting as an art but regarded it along with writing and directing as work. One of his most valuable professional assets was a remarkable ability to commit to memory as he read, grasping paragraphs at a time. He was also versatile in dialect. On the subject of playwrighting, he maintained that any violation of a man-made law is a legitimate subject for comedy; of a law of nature, a legitimate subject for tragedy.

Mitchell had roles in a host of Broadway productions including Tony in *Under Sentence* (1916), Christopher Mahon in *The Playboy of the Western World* (1921), Willy Loman in *Death of a Salesman* (1949 and 1950), and Rollie Evans in *Cut of the Axe* (1960).

In 1936 Mitchell went to Hollywood. He was first under contract to Columbia and then with Samuel Goldwyn. After 1940 he free-lanced. He appeared in sixty films, including *Adventure in Manhattan* (1936), *Lost Horizon* (1937), *Stagecoach* (1939), *Gone With the Wind* (1939), *The Outlaw* (1943), and *Pocketful of Miracles* (1961).

Mitchell also appeared on radio and television. On television he was in "The O'Henry Playhouse" and the series, "Mayor of the Town" and "Glencannon." (The latter, adapted from the Guy Gilpatric magazine stories, had Mitchell in the title role of chief engineer of a freighter.) He was coauthor of *Glory Hallelujah* with Bert Bloch in 1925, and with Floyd Dell of *Little Accident* in 1928 and *Cloudy with Showers* in 1932. He directed *Nightstick, Fly Away Home, Something Gay, Forsaking All Others,* and *At Home Abroad,* and worked as a play doctor for David Belasco and the Shubert Brothers. He served as a councillor of Actors Equity Association for two terms, 1933–1938 and 1953–1958.

Awards came to Mitchell for his performances in every medium, attesting to his consummate professionalism. Although he was probably most famous for his screen portrayal of Scarlett O'Hara's father in *Gone with the Wind,* he won an "Oscar" as Best Supporting Actor for his portrayal of an alcoholic doctor in *Stagecoach* (1939). He had been nominated for an Academy Award the preceding year for a similar role in *The Hurricane.* For his TV work he received an "Emmy" as the best actor of the year in 1952. In 1953 he won the Antoinette Perry "Tony" Award for the best performance by a male actor in a musical, Dr. Downer in *Hazel Flagg,* for which he also received the Donaldson Prize as best actor of the year. He received the Roi Cooper Megrue playwrighting prize for the comedy *Little Accident* (1928).

Mitchell was chunkily built, had a dimpled, ruddy round face, a button-nose, blue eyes, shaggy eyebrows, a full mouth, and brownish hair. Offstage he was usually informal, rumpled and cheerful.

Mitchell married Anne Stuart Brewer (whom he called Susan) on June 5, 1916. They had one child but were divorced in 1936. In 1937 he married Rachel Hartzell, an actress from Philadelphia. This marriage also ended in divorce, and Mitchell remarried Anne on June 30, 1941. During World War I Mitchell served in the army as a private. Mitchell died in Beverly Hills, Calif.

[A clipping file on Mitchell and bound copies of the typescripts of the plays Mitchell wrote with Floyd Dell are in the Billy Rose Collection of the Research Library of the Performing Arts of the New York Public Library at Lincoln Center. The Academy of Motion Picture Arts and Sciences in Beverly Hills, Calif., contains a biographical clipping file. A list of Mitchell's more than sixty television appearances will be found in James Robert Parish, *Actors' Television Credits, 1950–1972* (1973). An obituary appeared in the *New York Times,* Dec. 18, 1962.]

MARTIN TORODASH

MONROE, MARILYN (June 1, 1926–Aug. 5, 1962), actress, was born Norma Jean Mort-

ensen in Los Angeles, Calif., the daughter of Gladys Monroe Baker, a film technician who had been married to, and soon deserted by, Edward Mortensen, a mechanic. (According to Fred Guiles, Norma Jean's natural father was C. Stanley Gifford, an employee of the studio where her mother worked.) Young Monroe used the name Baker during her childhood.

Gladys Baker, frequently institutionalized for mental illness, was unable to raise her daughter. As a result Norma Jean spent her early years in a succession of foster homes and in an orphanage. She was an indifferent student except for some aptitude in English; at Van Nuys High School she tried out for dramatics only to be turned down. Like many adolescents she was stagestruck and star-struck. Although the events of her youth have been blurred by lurid press agentry and hagiography, it is generally accepted that she was fascinated by her own appearance, which she could enhance by an early talent for makeup and a sexual allure that she was able to radiate at will.

On June 19, 1942, Norma Jean Baker married James Edward Dougherty, an aircraft production worker five years her senior. When he went into the merchant marine in World War II, she supported herself by working at a defense plant and by part-time modeling. She became a cover girl for such wartime ephemera as *Laff, Peek,* and *See,* and under the sponsorship of the photographer André de Diennes she appeared on the pages of *U.S. Camera, Pageant,* and *Parade.* After divorcing Dougherty in 1946, Norma Jean cut her hair short and had it bleached, acquired an agent, and changed her name to Marilyn Monroe. She was given a screen test by Twentieth Century-Fox that led to her first contract.

As a Fox starlet Monroe posed for "cheesecake" and bathing suit stills and appeared briefly in the films *Scudda-Hoo! Scudda-Hay!* (1948), from which her scenes were cut, and *Dangerous Year* (1948). When her contract with Fox expired, she was chosen by Harry Cohn, head of Columbia Pictures, to play a full-length role in *Ladies of the Chorus* (1949) that included dancing and the songs "Every Baby Needs a Da Da Daddy" and "Anyone Can Tell." The film was unsuccessful at the box office, but during its production Monroe acquired a dramatic coach, Natasha Lytess, and began the development that eventually led her to the Actors Studio.

For a year Monroe could not find film work and supported herself through modeling. One of the photos, a full-length shot of her in the nude, was taken by Tom Kelley and sold as a calendar picture, which soon provided the critical twist to her career. After playing two minor roles in 1950, she won a small part in John Huston's *The Asphalt Jungle* (1950). Darryl Zanuck was persuaded to give her a new contract at Fox, and a run of minor roles in undistinguished films followed. But her sensuous presence, the wiggle in her walk, and her little-girl voice became popular with moviegoers.

During the filming of *Clash by Night* (1952) it became nationally known that the lovely blonde whose form graced a calendar hung in bars, locker rooms, and garages across the country was Marilyn Monroe. What could have destroyed a promising career was turned by Monroe and Fox press agents into a triumph. (She did it, she said, to earn her keep while out of work.) The photograph brought her to the brink of stardom.

Niagara (1953) gained Monroe the approval of critics who had been reserving judgment. She was cast immediately to play with Jane Russell and Charles Coburn in *Gentlemen Prefer Blondes* (1953). After nineteen films she had finally attained the height of Hollywood achievement, her own dressing room.

The recognition that Monroe was a comedienne of high quality never erased her image of a love goddess. But, as Norman Mailer has pointed out, her artistry consisted in the touch of self-satire that accompanied her coquetry, on stage and off. *How to Marry a Millionaire* (1953) was a film in which three models (Monroe, Betty Grable, and Lauren Bacall) shared a penthouse and schemed to marry wealthy men. The premiere of this film in Hollywood was mobbed by crowds of admirers chanting, "Marilyn . . . Marilyn."

On Jan. 14, 1954, after a well-publicized courtship, Monroe married Joseph Paul (Joe) Di Maggio, the retired "Yankee Clipper" of professional baseball. The marriage, brief and stormy, ended in divorce in October. As a publicity stunt for her film *The Seven Year Itch* (1955), Monroe had been photographed in a low-cut white dress while standing over a sidewalk grating with the updraft billowing her skirt around her thighs. The picture was enlarged to sixty feet in height as an advertisement for the film. Billy Wilder, the director of *The Seven Year Itch*, offered one explanation for the extraordinary effectiveness of her photographed image: her "flesh impact." He observed, "Flesh impact is rare. Three I remember who had it were Clara Bow, Jean Harlow and Rita Hayworth. Such girls have flesh which photographs like flesh. You feel you can reach out and touch it."

During the late 1950's Monroe discovered a world beyond that of the Hollywood studios. She studied with Lee and Paula Strasberg and then entered their Actors Studio in New York City. On June 29, 1956, she married Arthur Miller, one of the preeminent playwrights of the period and, after a short preparation in the basics of Judaism, converted to her husband's faith. She was encouraged by the Strasbergs to become a serious actress and to cultivate the "Method" of internalizing roles.

A succession of highly popular films followed: *Bus Stop* (1956), *The Prince and the Showgirl* (1957), in which she played opposite Laurence Olivier, *Some Like it Hot* (1959), and *Let's Make Love* (1960). *Bus Stop* was a particular achievement, for Monroe played the part of Cherie, a saloon singer who struggles through an amateurish rendition of "That Old Black Magic." The film's mixture of comic high jinks and simple sentiment gave flashes of insight into the essential Norma Jean–Marilyn that broke through ordinary distinctions between life and art.

In the midst of Monroe's success, symptoms of personal deterioration became increasingly evident. Her insomnia and addiction to sleeping drugs, her reliance on psychiatric support, and her tardiness on the set were the outward signs of deep problems probably caused by her childhood years of loneliness, the pressures put upon her by the studios and the press, and the way she was exploited by her close associates. Her insatiable ambition also contributed to her decline.

The filming in 1960 of *The Misfits*, the script of which was written for her and then constantly revised on location by Arthur Miller, was by all accounts a dismal affair. The shooting was greatly protracted by her absences and lateness, as well as her inability to perform during many sessions. That the final result was a modest success was a tribute to the director John Huston and the rest of cast—Clark Gable, Montgomery Clift, and Eli Wallach—more than to the star whose vehicle it was supposed to have been. Gable died twelve days after *The Misfits* was completed, an event that disturbed Monroe considerably. She obtained a divorce from Arthur Miller two months later.

A brief period of confinement in a mental hospital was followed by an abortive effort to do another film for Fox. Ironically titled *Something's Got to Give*, it brought about her dismissal by the studio because she had appeared for only twelve days of the first month of shooting. In 1962 Monroe was reinstated to finish the film, but was discovered dead in her Brentwood, Calif., home before shooting resumed. The autopsy showed a lethal amount of barbiturates in her system.

Joe Di Maggio made the funeral arrangements. Lee Strasberg, in his eulogy, spoke for her public when he said, "She had a luminous quality—a combination of wistfulness, radiance, yearning, that set her apart and yet made everyone wish to be part of it, to share in the childlike naïveté which was at once so shy and yet so vibrant."

[Reliable information on Monroe is in Fred Guiles, *Norma Jean* (1969), the factual base for Norman Mailer, *Marilyn* (1973). Photocopies of vital documents are in Robert F. Slatzer, *The Life and Curious Death of Marilyn Monroe* (1974). Also see Maurice Zolotow, *Marilyn Monroe* (1960); and Edwin P. Hoyt, *Marilyn, the Tragic Venus* (1965). An obituary is in the *New York Times*, Aug. 6, 1962.]

ALBERT F. McLEAN

MONTAGUE, GILBERT HOLLAND (May 27, 1880–Feb. 4, 1961), lawyer and book collector, was born in Springfield, Mass., the son of Dwight Billings Montague and Sarah Helen Perry. He received the B.A. from Harvard College in 1901 and the M.A. in 1902. He then entered the Harvard Law School, from which he graduated in 1904. While in law school he also was an instructor in economics at Harvard College. (Franklin D. Roosevelt was one of his students.) On Oct. 3, 1907, he married Amy Angell Collier; they had no children.

Montague moved to New York upon completing his legal studies, and worked for Simpson, Thatcher and Bartlett for six years; from 1906 to 1908 he also clerked for Justice James A. Blanchard of the New York Supreme Court. Between 1908 and 1910, in addition to practicing law, he was a special deputy attorney general prosecuting election frauds. From 1906 to 1917, Montague taught a course on the law of engineering contracts at Brooklyn Polytechnic Institute.

In 1910 Montague opened his own office, and quickly established himself as one of the nation's leading practitioners in the relatively new field of antitrust law. Nearly all the major oil companies, as well as other large firms threatened by action under the Sherman and Clayton acts, engaged him as counsel. Montague not only acted for his clients in the courtroom and congressional and regulatory hearings but also wielded his pen to win a more liberal governmental attitude toward business monopolies. He wrote more than a half-dozen books on trusts, business, and the law, including *Rise and Progress of the Standard Oil Company* (1903), *Trusts of Today* (1904), and *Business Competition and the Law* (1917), as well as numerous articles in popular newspapers and journals, all defending business against federal antimonopoly rules and policies. During the latter part of his professional career, Montague often appeared before congressional investigating committees, invited by conservative senators and representatives to testify on the dangers of governmental interference with business. Montague was a firm believer in free competition, and opposed the government's interference with the market.

During Republican administrations Montague served as an adviser to several executive agencies and departments, especially Treasury and Justice. In 1953 Herbert Brownell, Jr., appointed him to the Attorney General's Commission to Study Antitrust Laws. Two years later the group submitted a 405-page report, most of it written by Montague, calling for less governmental restriction on private enterprise. The numerous bar association panels he chaired provided another forum for Montague's views. These included the American Bar Association's Antitrust Division, the Committee on Monopolies and Restraints of Trade, and the Committee on the Federal Trade Commission.

Montague's probusiness sentiments would have been of little import had he not also been a highly competent attorney, an expert in a new and rapidly developing area of great importance to businessmen. His ability brought him large fees that allowed him to indulge the passion of collecting books and manuscripts.

By the early 1950's Montague's personal library held more than 15,000 books and more than 20,000 pamphlets. He also collected manuscripts, many of which he donated to Harvard libraries. These included a fourteenth-century copy of the Magna Charta, eighteenth-century volumes of the Abbé de St.-Pierre, materials of the Austrian poet and dramatist Hugo von Hofmannsthal, and more than 900 items of Emily Dickinson. This last collection, which Montague donated to Harvard in 1950, allowed scholars to answer a number of questions about Dickinson's life, including her mysterious love affair. Montague had a special interest in Dickinson, who was a collateral relative, and was considered by many an expert on her writings.

After his wife's death in 1941, Montague made many charitable gifts in her memory. He maintained their summer home, Beaulieu, in Seal Harbor, Me., as she had planned it, and did the same with the gardens behind his New York City home, where he died.

[See Harvard College, Class of 1901, *Twenty-fifth and Fiftieth Anniversary Reports* (1926, 1951); New York Bar Association, *1962 Memorial Book*; Boston *Globe*, May 31, 1950. An obituary is in the *New York Times*, Feb. 6, 1961.]

MELVIN I. UROFSKY

MONTEUX, PIERRE BENJAMIN (Apr. 4, 1875–July 1, 1964), orchestra conductor, was born in Paris, the son of Gustave Élie Monteux, a shoe salesman, and of Clémence Brisac, a piano teacher. At the age of six, he expressed the desire to study violin. A cousin, Félix Bloch, gave him lessons for a year and then entrusted him to Jules Dambé, conductor at the Opéra Comique. At the age of nine, Monteux was one of ten accepted by the Conservatoire National de Paris from among 200 applicants. At the conservatory he studied harmony with Jules Garcin and Albert Lavignac, composition with Charles Lenepveu, and violin with Jean Pierre Maurin and Henri Berthelier.

In 1896, Monteux graduated from the conservatory with a first prize in violin. He had already made his first public appearance, with a string quartet. He earned extra money by playing second violin at the Folies Bergères. Excelling on the viola, he also played in the orchestras of the Opéra Comique and the Société des Concerts Colonne. Within the Colonne orchestra Monteux rose from concertmaster to conductor (after seventeen years as assistant conductor). In addition, he played with, or conducted the orchestras at the casinos in Étretat and Dieppe. As violist he played in the 1902 premiere of Claude Debussy's *Pelléas et Mélisande*.

By 1911, Monteux was finding musical fulfillment as a conductor rather than as an instrumentalist, and he organized his own series, known as the Concerts Berlioz, at the Casino de Paris. During the years immediately preceding World War I, he was guest conductor of the Paris Opéra, the Opéra Comique, Covent Garden, and orchestras in London, Berlin, Budapest, and Vienna. In February 1914 he formed the Société des Concerts Populaires (otherwise known as the Concerts Monteux) at the Casino de Paris. One of his motives for creating these series was to offer contemporary composers public performances of their orchestral works.

At one of his 1911 concerts at the Casino de Paris, Monteux's conducting skills so impressed Sergei Diaghilev that he engaged Monteux as principal conductor for his Ballet Russe. From 1911 through 1914, and again in 1916 and 1924, Monteux conducted many performances of Diaghilev's company. This musical associa-

tion earned him growing fame. He conducted the world premieres of *Petrouchka* (June 13, 1911), *Daphnis et Chloé* (June 8, 1912), *Le Sacre du Printemps* (May 29, 1913), and *Le Rossignol* (May 26, 1914).

The premiere of *Sacre du Printemps*, at the Théâtre des Champs-Élysées in Paris, was one of the most violent events in music history; most of the audience divided into fiercely pro- and anti-Stravinsky factions. They resorted to shouts and hisses, as well as to blows. Yet Monteux persevered until the final curtain. Stravinsky, who was in the audience, admired his steady, "crocodile" nervelessness. Monteux became an integral part of this milestone in musical development, along with Stravinsky, Diaghilev, and Waslaw Nijinsky. A subsequent London performance under Monteux received a less heated reaction.

Monteux continued touring with Diaghilev's company until 1914. He enjoyed his work with the Ballet Russe more for the sake of the new music than for the ballet art form. On a few occasions he lost his temper and once handed in his resignation over a dispute with Stravinsky. But he was rarely given to temperamental outbursts. He remained grateful to Diaghilev for entrusting him with so many musical responsibilities. For their part the dancers appreciated Monteux's dependable beat.

Monteux was a private in the Thirty-fifth Territorial Infantry of the French Army from August 1914 to September 1916. He fought at Rheims, Verdun, Soissons, and the Argonne. As part of a propaganda effort, Diaghilev planned to have his company tour the United States in the fall of 1916; the French War Ministry allowed Monteux to accompany the group. In the summer of 1917, he gave his first concert in the United States as a symphonic conductor, with the New York Civic Orchestra. He then signed a three-year contract with the Metropolitan Opera, debuting with *Faust* on Nov. 17, 1917. At the Metropolitan his primary responsibility was directing the French repertoire, as well as several American premieres of French and Russian works, such as Nicolai Rimsky-Korsakov's *Le Coq d'Or* (Jan. 20, 1919). With Enrico Caruso and Louise Homer he shared the opening of the 1918–1919 season with *Samson et Dalila*.

The Met's general manager, Giulio Gatti-Casazza, released Monteux from the final year of his contract when the opportunity arose for him to become conductor of the Boston Symphony Orchestra. The years with the Boston Symphony were rather difficult. In the spring of

1920, the orchestra struck, and a number of the players left to form a union. Monteux formed a new orchestra of superior quality. He offered his audiences a mixture of the classics and contemporary works, which became his customary concert programming. Many of the American and world premieres that he conducted, though frequently applauded by the critics, were not always appreciated by the Boston public. But at least he was helping to educate listeners to the new harmonies and musical ideas.

On Nov. 15, 1923, the tenor Roland Hayes appeared with the Boston Symphony, the first time that a black soloist performed with a symphony orchestra in the United States. Thirty-two years later Hayes was among the musicians who greeted Monteux during his eightieth birthday gala given by the Boston Symphony.

Monteux returned to Europe and in 1924 did more work with Diaghilev. That same year he began an extremely popular ten-year association as coconductor with Willem Mengelberg and Bruno Walter of the Concertgebouw Orchestra of Amsterdam. In Amsterdam he also organized the Wagner Society. He also founded and served as conductor and music director of the Orchestre Symphonique de Paris (1929–1938). When the orchestra toured Germany in 1932, it was the first French orchestra to appear there since 1914. In 1932, Monteux founded the École Monteux in Paris.

In 1928, Monteux had conducted the Philadelphia Orchestra during Leopold Stokowski's leave of absence. As in Boston, the public did not appreciate the unobtrusive Monteux as much as the critics did. Monteux vowed not to return again to the United States, where the "star-crazy" audiences cared only for "slim, well-tailored conductors."

Monteux finally returned to the United States—to San Francisco, where orchestra and audience spontaneously adored him and adopted him as one of their own. From 1936 to 1952, he was principal conductor and musical director of the San Francisco Symphony. He vigorously reshaped the orchestra by nourishing a high quality of musicianship and formulating special program series and festivals for an audience of all ages and interests. In 1947 the group made a fifty-three-city tour of the United States and Canada. It became recognized as the best orchestra on the West Coast and one of the best in the country. In 1941, Monteux established a summer school for young conductors at his home in Hancock, Maine. He became a United States citizen in 1942.

He returned to the Boston Symphony to guest conduct with his friend Charles Munch during the American and European tours (1952–1953, 1956). He also returned to the Metropolitan Opera in 1954 for two more seasons. On Sept. 28, 1954, he made his debut, conducting *Manon*, at the San Francisco Opera.

In 1961, at the age of eighty-five, Monteux accepted the permanent position of principal conductor of the London Symphony. He continued a rigorous schedule of concerts, tours, and recordings. On Apr. 1, 1964, he fell from the podium while conducting Maurice Ravel's *Pavane for a Dead Princess*, but quickly recovered and concluded the program. Although he appeared afterward in Amsterdam, Tel Aviv, and London, it became clear that he was seriously ill, and he was rushed him home to Maine, where he died.

Many critics believe that Monteux was not accorded the public acclaim to which his conducting skills and musical knowledge entitled him. Some blame this on his calm personality, some on his "Santa Claus" appearance and his unpretentious and undramatic conducting style. Yet he radiated a certain fatherly warmth to audiences, musicians, and critics. To many he was respected as "Le Maître" and loved as "Papa" and "Pierre." His professional knowledge was extremely broad; he excelled in the music of Brahms and Beethoven, as well as in that of the modern composers. He helped to promote such contemporary masters as Igor Stravinsky, Sergei Prokofiev, Arthur Honegger, Charles Griffes, Ralph Vaughan Williams, Ottorino Respighi, Maurice Ravel, Claude Debussy, and Darius Milhaud. He favored minimal baton movements and avoided histrionics. In his "Rules for Young Conductors" he warned conductors never to conduct for the audience and always to have the greatest respect for the instrumentalists.

Monteux was married three times. His first wife was a pianist from Bordeaux; his second, Germaine Benedictus, was the mother of his three children. He married Doris Gerald Hodgkins on Sept. 26, 1928. Monteux's background was Jewish, but he converted to Catholicism. The spiritual side of his life was most important to him.

[Many of Monteux's personal scores (with notes) from his early conducting period in Europe were destroyed during the German occupation. The New York Public Library has a copy of one of his compositions, "Deux piécettes pour flute, hautbois, clarinette, basson, trompette et batterie" (1922). His writings include "Are We 'Star-Crazy'?," *Literary Digest,* May 26, 1928; and "Music," *Theatre Arts,* Fall 1948, as told to Alan Kayes, repr. of 1923 article. An incomplete but extensive discography is Richard Freed, "The Monteux Legacy," *Saturday Review of Literature,* Aug. 22, 1964. Also see the biography by Doris Monteux, *It's All in the Music* (1965); David Ewen, *Dictators of the Baton* (1943), and Charles O'Connell, *The Other Side of the Record* (1947). Information on Monteux's early years with the Boston Symphony is in H. Earle Johnson, *Symphony Hall, Boston* (1950). A portion of Roland Hayes's tribute to Monteux on the conductor's eightieth birthday appeared in *Musical America,* May 1955. Obituaries are in the *New York Times,* July 2, 1964; *Newsweek,* July 13, 1964; *Musical America,* Sept. 1964; Kurt Herbert Adler, *Opera News,* Sept. 26, 1964; and *Obituaries from the* [London] *Times 1961–1970* (1975).]

MADELINE SAPIENZA

MOORE, ANNE CARROLL (July 12, 1871– Jan. 20, 1961), librarian, was born in Limerick, Maine, the daughter of Luther Sanborn Moore and Sarah Hidden Barker. Anne (she was christened Annie) was preceded by two sisters, who had died, and by seven brothers. As favorite in the family, she had a special closeness to her father, a lawyer, who had served as president of the state senate. Upon graduation in 1891 from Bradford Academy, a two-year college in Massachusetts, she began studying law under her father's instruction.

Luther Moore died on Jan. 12, 1892, and his wife died two days later, which ended Moore's interest in the law. During the next few years, while helping a widowed brother care for his children, she decided to be a librarian. She enrolled in the Pratt Institute Library School in Brooklyn, N.Y., in September 1895. At Pratt she was influenced by the lectures of Caroline M. Hewins, a librarian from the Hartford Public Library, who had compiled the first children's book list for the American Library Association. Hewins became Moore's lifetime mentor.

Moore finished library school in June 1896. In the fall of that year, the director of the school, Mary Wright Plummer, offered her the position of children's librarian in the Pratt Institute Free Library. Moore began work early in 1897 and soon discovered her unbounded love for children, although she would never have any herself. She never married.

During the next ten years she displayed astounding energy. She innovated programs that became common in public libraries throughout the United States. Particularly significant was her initiation of storytelling and poetry readings for children.

Through her many papers at library conventions, articles in journals, and lectures to library schools, Moore deeply influenced the first generation of children's librarians. In 1900 she organized a special division for them in the American Library Association. In 1903 she published *A List of Books Recommended for a Children's Library,* which resulted from directing a summer library workshop for the Iowa Library Commission.

About the same time, Moore began to vacation in Europe, chiefly to meet foreign authors and illustrators of children's books, such as Beatrix Potter and Leonard Leslie Brooke, whose work she helped to popularize in the United States. While abroad, she sought to persuade European librarians of the value of children's reading rooms. It was through her influence that Stockholm opened the first European children's library in 1911.

On Sept. 1, 1906, the New York Public Library hired Moore as its superintendent of work with children. Her major responsibilities were to build children's collections in the burgeoning branches of the system and to hire and direct children's librarians. She insisted there should be no restrictions on children as library patrons. She stressed exhibits and festivities to coax children into reading. Literary art, not moral suasion, should be the criterion for book selection. It was, she believed, the obligation of the children's librarians to work to improve the quality of young people's literature.

Moore considered most children's books of the time false, owing to their one-dimensional characters and their stock plots that repressed reality, fancy, and humor, and extolled the sentimental, the heroic, and the saccharine. She weeded out Sunday-school literature and mediocre, contrived serial novels, replacing them with such books as *The Scarlet Letter* and *Tom Sawyer.* She coordinated her efforts with the schools but insisted that the library be a refuge for self-discovery and not overly tied to the school curricula. Moore retired from her position in the New York Public Library in 1941. She died in New York City.

Although frail in appearance and usually carrying a doll called Nicholas, which she manipulated to the delight of children, Moore spoke and acted in a decisive manner. An example of her fiber was her defense of Leo Max Frank in 1915, when he was facing execution in an Atlanta, Ga., prison. As a child, Frank had used Pratt Library; because of this and her correspondence with him, Moore was convinced of his innocence. She visited him in prison before he was lynched. Moore's greatest contribution is her promotion of quality children's literature. She herself wrote two children's novels, *Nicholas: A Manhattan Christmas Story* (1924) and *Nicholas and the Golden Goose* (1932). From 1919 until her death, she reviewed juvenile works for the *Bookman,* New York *Herald Review, Chicago Sun,* and *Horn Book.* Those reviews, most of which are compiled in books, are the first sustained criticism of children's books that encourage the writing and publishing of such works.

[Moore's correspondence with Leo Max Frank is preserved with his papers (1914–1915), housed in the American Jewish Archives, Cincinnati, Ohio.

Three major papers delineating Moore's philosophy are "Story-telling in The New York Public Library," *Bulletin of the American Library Association,* Sept. 1909; "Library Visits to Public Schools," *The Relationship Between the Library and the Public Schools* (1914), edited by Arthur E. Bostwick; and "Children, Libraries and the Love of Reading," *Annals,* American Academy of Political and Social Science, Sept. 1916. Compilations of her book reviews and literary criticism are in *Roads to Childhood* (1920), *New Roads to Childhood* (1923), *Cross-roads to Childhood* (1926), and *My Roads to Childhood* (1939). Three collections of Moore's reviews for the New York *Herald Review* are *The Three Owls* (1927, 1928, 1931).

A succinct overview of Moore's ideas, work, and background, is found in her articles: "The Creation and Criticism of Children's Books: A Retrospect and a Forecast," *Bulletin of the American Library Association,* Sept. 1934; "Children and Book Famine," *Saturday Review of Literature,* Mar. 13, 1937; and "Autobiographical Sketch," in *The Junior Book of Authors* (1951), edited by Stanley J. Kunitz and Howard Haycraft.

Two library science theses are Nancy Meade Akers, "Anne Carroll Moore: A Study of Her Work with Children's Libraries and Literature" (Pratt Institute Library School, 1951); A. M. Poor, "Anne Carroll Moore: The Velvet Glove of Librarianship" (Southern Connecticut State College, 1966). In 1956 the New York Public Library released a festschrift in Moore's honor titled *Reading Without Boundaries: Essays Presented to Anne Carroll Moore,* edited by Frances Lander Spain.

See also Mabel William, "Anne Carroll Moore," *Bulletin of Bibliography,* May–Aug. 1946; Carolyn Sherwin Bailey, "Story-hour Girl" in *A Candle for Your Cake* (1952); Aylesa Forsee, "Librarian from Limerick" in *Women Who Reached for Tomorrow* (1960); Eleanor Estes et al., "Tribute to Anne Carroll Moore," *Top of the News,* Dec. 1961; Frances Clarke Sayers *Anne Carroll Moore; A Biography* (1972). The *New York Times* obituary appeared on Jan. 21, 1961.]

DAVID JOHN MYCUE

MOORE, VICTOR FREDERICK (Feb. 24, 1876–July 23, 1962), actor, was born in Hammonton, N.J., the son of Orville E. Moore and Sarah A. Davis. He gravitated early to the theater; at the age of ten he was carrying a banner for the Minstrel Brothers. At sixteen, after his family moved to Boston, he made his professional debut in *Babes in the Woods.* After playing bit parts in New York and Philadelphia as well as in road shows, he paid another actor $125 for the use of a skit involving a vaudeville team, "Change Your Act, or Back to the Woods." It became Moore's own vehicle to stardom. The act was seen and its star recommended to George M. Cohan, who put Moore into two of his plays, *Forty-Five Minutes from Broadway* (1906) and *The Talk of New York* (1907).

Moore married Emma N. Helwig (Littlefield) on June 23, 1902. They had three children. Moore's first starring role was as a crook in Owen Davis' farce, *Easy Come, Easy Go* (1925). His flair for appearing both wistful and pathetic caught the attention of George S. Kaufman, who cast Moore as Alexander Throttlebottom, the ineffectual but lovable vice-president in Ira and George Gershwin's *Of Thee I Sing* (1931). In this show, which instilled fresh sophistication into the American musical theater, Moore received his greatest acclaim. At once wide-eyed and self-effacing, bumbling and apologetic, his portrayal not only provoked laughter but also added warmth to the political satire. Moore's comic timing had been perfected in vaudeville and, enriched with the air of innocent charm, endowed the part with such fullness that Throttlebottom became better known than many actual vice-presidents. When Moore visited the Senate after his theatrical triumph, he passed himself off as Vice-President Throttlebottom to lawmakers who relished the joke.

None of Moore's later roles equaled the impact of this performance, but he continued to appear with distinction—especially in musical comedies. His special gift was for playing politicians, returning to the stage as Throttlebottom in a sequel to *Of Thee I Sing* entitled *Let 'Em Eat Cake* (1933). With the Great Depression cutting deeper, the sequel's satire was sharper; but Moore's bewildered and unsteady character continued to receive delighted notices. In Cole Porter's *Anything Goes* (1934), he played Public Enemy Number 13, disguised as a parson aboard an ocean liner bound for Europe. In Porter's *Leave It to Me* (1938), Moore played the American ambassador to Russia, Alonzo P. ("Stinky") Goodhue, whose only desire is to return home to Topeka. This inept innocent kicks the Nazi ambassador and shoots a Soviet counterrevolutionary in an undiplomatic attempt to get recalled from his post. Only after his transparently noble deed— proposing a united Europe—is there sufficient provocation for dismissal. In *Louisiana Purchase* (1940), a musical comedy about political corruption, Moore's performance as Senator Loganberry led John Mason Brown of the *New York Post* to observe that, while Moore tended to confine himself to the same kind of roles, a change in the American form of government would almost be preferable to a change in Moore's comic persona.

Moore in fact extended his range somewhat more fully than Brown's whimsical praise indicated. His subsidiary career in Hollywood, which began in 1915, was more varied than the depiction of politicians. He made five films for Samuel Goldwyn in the 1930's. But in Hollywood too his specialty remained comedy, including his final two films, *We're Not Married* (1952) and *The Seven Year Itch* (1955).

Moore gave one of his most droll and memorable performances as Gramps in Paul Osborn's Broadway drama, *On Borrowed Time* (1938). His skill in the most minor variations of inflection and gesture and the wayward charm that he displayed won him the best actor award of the New York Drama Critics Circle when the drama was revived in 1953. Moore also appeared in *Hollywood Pinafore* (1945) and *Nelly Bly* (1946).

Emma Moore died in 1934 and on Jan. 16, 1942, Moore married a ballerina, Shirley Paige. They had no children.

Moore's last stage appearance was in a revival of *Carousel* at New York's City Center in 1957. In a musical pervaded with the presence of death, he played the heavenly Starkeeper, an eerie figure graced, in his interpretation, with gentleness and benevolence. The aged vaudeville clown had proved himself to be a very respectable character actor.

Moore relied on economy of means to achieve his comic effects, getting attention by seeming not to seek it. His girth, popeyed naïveté, and constant awareness of misery were the theatrical attributes he chose to emphasize in generating laughter—although they prevented him from expanding his repertoire to include romance or tragedy. But within his range, Moore achieved unusual believability. Too ill to play Throttlebottom in a revival of *Of Thee I Sing*, Moore died in an actors' home in East Islip, N.Y.

[Brief assessments of Moore's performances are in John Mason Brown, *Broadway in Review* (1940); and in J. Brooks Atkinson and Albert Hirschfeld, *The Lively Years, 1920–1973* (1973). Atkinson's *New York Times* reviews of the plays in which Moore starred are indispensable. Obituary notices are in the *New York Times*, July 24, 1962 ; and in *Variety*, July 25, 1962.]

STEPHEN J. WHITFIELD

MORAN, EUGENE FRANCIS (Mar. 24, 1872–Apr. 13, 1961), tugboat and shipping industry executive, was born in Brooklyn, N.Y., the son of Michael Moran, founder of what became the Moran Towing and Transportation Company, and of Margaret Haggerty. Few boys, however bright and industrious and however prosperous their parents, stayed in school past the eighth grade in the 1880's, and Moran was no exception. He had never liked school, and the excitement of the towboatman's life (his father had first engaged in towing barges on the Hudson River between New York City and Albany) was further heightened by his father's growing prominence in the rough-and-ready business of tugboating and by his older brother Dick's outstanding success as boatman and pilot in New York's booming harbor. Apart from the elements of practical navigation, moreover, the chief requirement for a tugboatman then, as now, was an intimate knowledge of the harbor, the tides, and the currents, which can be learned nowhere but on the job. Moran was determined to be a boatman and served during the summer of 1886 as second deckhand on the *M. Moran*. His service consisted in large measure of helping the cook, but by summer's end he was adept at heaving lines, tying knots, and similar elementary chores—and still determined to be a boatman.

But his father had other ideas. "You're not heavy enough in the stern to work on tugboats," he said, although it is clear that of his five sons he had picked Eugene to succeed him as head of the business. In 1887 he got Eugene a job at $60 a week with the Lancashire Fire Insurance Company, where he could learn the intricacies of marine insurance. In 1889 Moran joined the family firm.

Well before the end of the nineteenth century, the steam revolution was complete, and the ships that tugboatmen were called upon to maneuver were increasing in size, complexity, and cost. Tugs, too, became larger, and by the end of the century the Moran Company was operating a large fleet of them in New York and other major harbors of the United States. The skyscraper building boom and the construction of such major improvements as subways, which transformed New York after 1898, brought added business for the towing firms. Hauling of barges and lighters (the latter vital to the interchange of freight between the numerous railroads whose tracks ended at waterside on the Hudson, the East, and the Harlem rivers and New York Bay) and of scows loaded with garbage or excavation rubble became important tows. "There's more city bottom land out there now than on Manhattan Island," Moran liked to say, referring to the spot in Lower New York Bay where rubble was dumped.

By the turn of the century it was apparent that the thirty-foot channels through which ships made their way across the sandbar that lay athwart the entrance to New York Harbor were no longer deep enough. Moran was active in encouraging the federal government to dredge the channels. As a member (and for fifty years chairman) of the Committee on Rivers, Harbors and Piers of the Maritime Association of the Port of New York, he kept up the pressure on the U.S. Army Corps of Engineers until the Hudson had been dredged to a depth of forty feet, shore to shore, as far north as Fiftieth Street, to give the city the most convenient passenger liner piers in the world.

Like the true seafaring man he was, Moran talked more about the sea than about his personal life: his autobiography, *Tugboat*, consists almost entirely of yarns about record-breaking tows; loads of remarkable size, shape, and bulk; dreadful explosions and fires on the piers; daring rescues at sea; and thrilling dashes to the scene of fast-breaking news with intrepid reporters like Richard Harding Davis. But most of Moran's career was spent in the demanding, dangerous, but ultimately prosaic work of keeping things in motion in the world's busiest port. As he grew older, Moran watched with regret as fewer and fewer people, especially the young, seemed to be aware of the great body of water that had brought New York to first rank among the cities of the world. The tubes and tunnels that were dug beneath the Hudson after 1900 quickly made the ferries that plied between New Jersey and Manhattan obsolete. The passing of the great liners, which were quickly eclipsed by jet airplanes after 1960, soon made such landmarks as the Narrows between Upper and Lower New York Bays and even the Statue of Liberty unknown to all but a few.

On Nov. 10, 1897, Moran married Julia Claire Browne; they had six children. After his father died in 1906, Moran assumed the presi-

dency of the family firm. In the same year he moved the office from South Street to 17 Battery Place, where the dispatchers could shout orders direct to crews from a balcony of the Whitehall Building. In 1930 he became chairman of the board. In 1898 the company's gross revenues had been $125,000; by 1944 they exceeded $8 million. After more than a decade of development and testing of diesel power plants, the Moran company took delivery of its first diesel-electric tug in 1936. Four years later Moran yielded the presidency of the company to a nephew, Edmond J. Moran.

Moran served during World War I as a lieutenant commander in the U.S. Naval Reserve. He served the Port of New York Authority as its chairman from 1942 to 1959. By then he had received all the honors that the maritime organizations operating in the Port of New York had to bestow and also served as a member of the New York Transit Authority. A prominent Roman Catholic layman, he was a lieutenant commander of the Knights of Malta. He died in Palm Beach, Fla.

[Moran wrote *Famous Harbors of the World* (1953), a children's book; and *Tugboat* (1956), with Louis Reed. An obituary is in the *New York Times*, Apr. 14, 1961.]

ALBRO MARTIN

MOREHEAD, JOHN MOTLEY (Nov. 3, 1870–Jan. 7, 1965), chemical engineer, inventor, industrialist, and philanthropist, was born in Spray, N.C., the son of James Turner Morehead, an industrialist and financier, and of Mary Elizabeth Connally. He graduated from the University of North Carolina at Chapel Hill in 1891, with a B.S. in chemical engineering. He immediately became a chemist for the Willson Aluminum Company, which his father and T. L. Willson had founded at Spray, hoping to exploit a new process for the production of aluminum. There he installed one of the first electric-arc furnaces in the United States.

On May 2, 1892, while operating the arc furnace, Morehead stumbled onto the first large-scale commercial means of producing calcium carbide. He later said, "I didn't know it was calcium carbide. Calcium carbide had never existed. I got a lump of this stuff [slaked lime and tar] about the size of a coconut, and when we put it in water, it gave off clouds of smoke. I didn't have any gas-analyzing equipment, so I sent a piece down here [Chapel Hill] to Dr. F. P. Venable [head of the chemistry department], and he analyzed the gas and said it was acetylene gas. I analyzed and found we had calcium carbide."

In 1892 there was no market for calcium carbide. The company failed, and Morehead's father sent him to a New York bank, where he worked briefly. He then went to Westinghouse Electric in Pittsburgh, and graduated from the firm's expert's course in 1895. The next year Westinghouse placed him with Consolidated Traction Company of New Jersey.

In 1894, Morehead's father and Willson had taken jars of carbide to New York City and had interested "some New York capital" in forming the Electro Gas Company to exploit carbide and to promote acetylene for city and home lighting. (Acetylene gas had been a laboratory curiosity for fifty years.) They sold all except the chemical rights to calcium carbide for some cash and stock. Willson Aluminum then turned to experimenting with the electro-smelting of ferro-chrome and ferro-silicon.

In 1897, Morehead joined American Calcium Carbide Interest as construction engineer, bringing his scientific and engineering expertise to supervising the building of plants for the manufacture of calcium carbide, the source of acetylene gas in foreign countries and in the United States. In 1899 he designed an apparatus for analyzing gases, and in 1900 his book *Analysis of Industrial Gases* was published.

The Peoples Gas, Light and Coke Company, one of the American Carbide interests, had taken over Electro Gas in 1898 and had formed Union Carbide. In 1902, Morehead, still engineer for American Carbide, became chief chemist and engineer of tests for Peoples, and moved to Chicago. There he was designing and erecting engineer in charge of technical research and development of new processes, especially in specifications, tests, and inspections in gas, steam, and electrical equipment. In 1906, Union Carbide bought out his father's electro alloys business. In 1910 he completed the course in oxyacetylene welding and cutting at the Imperial School for Machine Building in Cologne, Germany.

Morehead married Genevieve Margaret Birkhoff on July 3, 1915; they had no children. When the United States entered World War I, he was commissioned a major and detailed to the War Industries Board as chief of the Industrial Gases and Gas Products Section under Bernard Baruch. Upon demobilization he moved to Rye, N.Y., in order to be closer to the Union Carbide office, which had moved there in 1917.

Morehead was mayor of Rye from 1925 to 1930. In the latter year President Herbert C. Hoover appointed him minister to Sweden upon the advocacy of the senators of North Carolina, although they were Democrats and Morehead a staunch Republican. Both Hoover and Morehead had been headquartered in Washington during World War I, and were engineers with international reputations. Moorehead was a popular emissary with the Swedish nation, praising their engineering accomplishments and giving financial support for various projects. In 1930 he received the Linné Gold Medal from the Royal Swedish Academy of Sciences, usually awarded to botanists and nature preservers.

In April 1933, Morehead returned from Sweden to Rye and to Union Carbide, where he resumed his duties as consultant engineer, traveling to plants in Europe and the United States and "interpreting the old world to the new." After his wife died in April 1945, Morehead created the John Motley Morehead Foundation at the University of North Carolina, which was to establish the Morehead Scholars Program, patterned after the Rhodes Scholars, and to finance the Morehead Building with a planetarium and Genevieve B. Morehead Memorial Art Gallery. The Morehead Foundation's chief purpose, however, was to promote excellence at the University of North Carolina campus at Chapel Hill. Established in 1951, the undergraduate awards and the graduate fellowships were to be granted solely on the basis of merit; qualities of character, leadership, and a desire to serve the university and fellow students were the criteria.

On May 11, 1948, Morehead married Leila Duckworth Houghton. A year later he presented the completed Morehead Building to the University of North Carolina. In 1961 he added 50,000 shares of Union Carbide Stock to the foundation.

Other benefactions in North Carolina were the Morehead Stadium and Chimes at the Tri-City High School, Leaksville-Spray-Draper, and endowment of the Morehead Hospital in Rockingham County.

In 1964, Morehead planned, had built, and gave to Rye, N.Y., a new city hall that was dedicated on December 5. Morehead listened to the dedication ceremonies on the radio, because he had suffered a broken hip while hurrying from his office to catch a train for Rye. He died in Rye a month later, a major stockholder in Union Carbide; the bulk of his estate was left to the Morehead Foundation.

A contemporary said, "John Motley Morehead was a man who knew what he wanted and was persistent in securing it." His life exemplified his philosophy, expressed at the annual dinners for the graduating Morehead Scholars, many of whom called him "Uncle Mot." "Work," he said, "is the main road to success." Of his fortune he said, "Money doesn't bring happiness, but it helps to quiet nerves."

[Morehead's writing and speeches include *The Morehead Family of North Carolina and Virginia* (1921); "James Turner Morehead, Pioneer in American Industry" (1922); "Heritage, Dreams, and Fulfillment of the Life and Services of Gov. John Motley Morehead of North Carolina" (1952); and *That's That* (1959). Also see Trustees of the Morehead Foundation, *John M. Morehead, a Biographical Sketch* (1954); Union Carbide, "John Motley Morehead, a Retired Union Carbide Executive" (July 23, 1963); William S. Powell, *The First State University* (1972); and Louis Round Wilson, "The Saga of the Morehead-Patterson Bell Tower," in *Historical Sketches*, 1976. An obituary is in the *New York Times*, Jan. 8, 1965.]

ADA P. HAYLOR

MORRISON, DELESSEPS STORY (Jan. 18, 1912–May 22, 1964), public official and diplomat, was born in New Roads, La., the son of Jacob Haight Morrison, a lawyer, and of Anita Olivier. Morrison, who was called "Chep" throughout his life, graduated from Poydras Academy, a Catholic school, in 1928, from Louisiana State University in 1932, and from its law school in 1934. He worked briefly for the National Recovery Administration (1934–1935), before forming a law partnership in New Orleans with Hale Boggs, a future congressman.

But Morrison and Boggs practiced little law. Instead, they assumed leadership of the city's forces opposed to the state administration, dominated by Huey Long and his family. Morrison successfully campaigned in 1940 for the Louisiana House of Representatives. In Baton Rouge he was floor leader for Governor Sam Houston Jones's administration and supported civil service and voting machine legislation. In 1941, before completing his term, he joined the Army Transportation Corps as a first lieutenant. He rose to the rank of colonel, mainly through his work as a staff officer in Europe. On Oct. 3, 1942, Morrison married Corrine Waterman; they had three children.

In 1944, Morrison was reelected to the Louisiana House of Representatives while still in Europe. He returned home the following year and entered the 1946 New Orleans mayoralty primary against the incumbent, Robert S. Maestri, who had been a close friend of Huey Long. Over the years Maestri had pushed the physical rehabilitation of the city, but had done little to

halt the open vice that shocked many members of the community. Morrison attacked prostitution, gambling, and the failure of Maestri to maintain city services during his two terms. Many groups previously uninvolved in political campaigns rallied behind Morrison. He defeated Maestri by 4,372 votes.

Morrison won four terms as mayor. In part his success was tied to his ability to establish a loyal political organization, the Crescent City Democratic Association (CCDA), which controlled municipal patronage, took responsibility for day-to-day decisions in the local wards, and made sure its members voted on Election Day. Morrison also established a record as a progressive, energetic leader. He stressed efficiency and economy in city operations and expanded public services. During his administration streets were repaired and a civic center and a railroad terminal were built. He promoted international trade for New Orleans, often making well-publicized visits to Latin America.

Morrison's public image was so secure that he survived charges of corruption in the police department. New Orleanians knew that prostitutes, bookmakers, and gamblers paid the police money for protection. In the 1920's former mayor Martin Behrman had dismissed a similar situation by explaining, "You might make prostitution illegal, but you can't make it unpopular." But these activities embarrassed Morrison politically. He became embroiled in a bitter controversy with his police chief, Adair Watters, over cleaning up the department. Eventually the chief resigned, but there were claims that Morrison had accepted campaign contributions from New Orleans underworld elements.

Morrison paid little attention to race relations, believing that the city's blacks preferred separation. Consequently there were no blacks in the CCDA and no blacks held important city jobs. City actions and programs were tailored to fit segregation. For example, when black leaders sought to use a "for whites only" city golf course, Morrison had the city council appropriate money for a golf course for blacks. During the school desegregation crisis of the 1960's, Morrison blamed the media for exaggerating the local difficulties, contending that the presence of the media, especially television, encouraged violence.

Despite his success as leader of the reform faction in New Orleans, Morrison failed to win election as governor in 1955, 1959, and 1963. He was never able to overcome his urban image to win the support of rural Louisianians. In campaigns outside of New Orleans, Governor Earl

Long (Huey's brother) and his successors delighted rural audiences with verbal characterizations of Morrison. Long often called the mayor "Dellasoups" or "deLesseps Storeytelling" or "Make-up Morrison."

Morrison's only victory over Earl Long came in 1950, two years after the state legislature passed almost 200 bills severely curtailing the powers of the New Orleans city government. In the "rape of New Orleans," as commentators called it, the governor took control of the city's port, reduced revenue by more than $5 million, and enlarged the City Commission so as to weaken Morrison's power. The mayor responded by leading protest marches in Baton Rouge and New Orleans. He successfully organized a campaign against several of Long's proposed constitutional amendments. Later, when Russell Long, Huey's son, sought to win his first full term as a U.S. senator, Earl Long found himself forced to negotiate for the support of the CCDA. Russell Long won his election, and the legislature, at a subsequent session, returned many of Morrison's powers and much of the city's revenues. Earl Long never again tried to subject Morrison to punitive legislation.

Unable to seek a fifth term because amendments to the city charter limited the mayor to two consecutive terms, in 1961 Morrison accepted appointment as ambassador to the Organization of American States. After less than two years of service he returned to Louisiana to undertake his third and final gubernatorial campaign. Less than six months later he died in a plane crash at Ciudad Victoria, Mexico.

[Morrison's correspondence is at the Howard-Tilton Memorial Library, Tulane University, and in the City Archives, New Orleans Public Library. Morrison wrote, *Latin American Mission*, edited by Gerold Frank (1965). Also see Edward F. Haas, *DeLesseps S. Morrison and the Image of Reform* (1974); and Joseph B. Parker, *The Morrison Era* (1974). An obituary is in the *New York Times*, May 24, 1964.]

J. PAUL LESLIE

MOSES, ANNA MARY ROBERTSON ("GRANDMA") (Sept. 7, 1860–Dec. 13, 1961), folk painter, was born near Greenwich, N.Y., the daughter of Russell King Robertson, a farmer, and of Margaret Shannahan. One of ten children, she left home at age twelve to work as a hired girl. She worked for several families, cooking, cleaning, gardening, ironing, and tending invalids. She married Thomas Salmon Moses, a hired man, on Nov. 9, 1887. They took a wedding trip to North Carolina, where they were to be caretakers on a horse ranch, but set-

tled instead on a 600-acre dairy farm in the Shenandoah Valley. There, in addition to farm chores, Moses churned and sold up to 160 pounds of butter a week and made hand-sliced potato chips, which she traded for groceries. Between 1888 and 1903 she had ten children, five of whom survived.

In 1905 the family returned to New York, settling on a dairy farm in the Hoosick Valley. Moses continued her vigorous farm routine until, at age seventy, she finally found herself "too old for farm work and too young to retire." With free time at her disposal for the first time in her life, she began making woolen embroideries that she called "worsted pictures." But arthritis in her hands made needlework uncomfortable, and in 1938 her sister Celestia suggested that painting might be "better and faster." With house paint and canvas left from repair of a farm machine cover, Moses began to paint.

She soon settled into a system. Canvas was discarded in favor of more substantial Masonite, which Moses coated with three coats of flat white paint so that she wouldn't "have to put on so much expensive color paint." No picture was begun until a frame was ready for it and the Masonite sawed to fit. She worked in her farmhouse bedroom, copying postcards and painting imaginary scenes of a rural America that was already disappearing.

Moses began exhibiting her pictures at a Hoosick Falls, N.Y., drugstore in 1938 with the hope of earning a bit of extra money. One of her first customers, who bought four paintings from the drugstore and all ten that she had on hand at the farm, was Louis J. Caldor, an engineer and antiques collector. By chance the pictures in Caldor's collection came to the attention of Otto Kallir, a New York art dealer and recent émigré from Vienna, who was interested in folk art. He recognized Moses' talent at once. In October 1940, Kallir mounted the first New York exhibition of Moses' work, calling it "What a Farmwife Painted."

The day before the opening, an unsigned article in the *New York Herald Tribune* conferred upon the artist a public identity that became a cornerstone of her popularity: "Grandma Moses." Other publications picked up the name, and eventually millions of people were unaware that she had any other.

The charm, nostalgia, strong sense of design, and luminous color characteristic of Moses' paintings, together with the esteem for the "primitive" in art that peaked in the 1940's, brought her immediate commercial success.

Under Kallir's guidance a corporation was established, Grandma Moses Properties, which copyrighted her pictures, trademarked her name, and sold reproduction rights to companies such as Hallmark, which in ten years sold 35 million Grandma Moses greeting cards.

Although suddenly a celebrity at age eighty, Moses remained steadfast in her habits. She stored her paint in empty coffee cans; her brushes, never discarded until worn to a nub, were soaked in cold cream jars. To save paint, she produced her paintings in series, using the same blue for several skies and the same green for all the foliage. "This way," she explained, "your paints don't dry up on you." Generally she would paint the landscapes first and afterward "put in the boys and the cows." "I can start a batch of five on a Monday and have them finished off on a Saturday," she said at age eighty-eight.

During her two-decade career, Moses "finished off" more than 1,500 paintings, each full of painstaking detail. Kallir bought her entire output, holding back the weaker efforts and exhibiting the works he judged most successful. Between 1941 and 1961, Moses' paintings were shown in hundreds of individual and group exhibitions all over the United States.

Moses' innocent, sentimental, and optimistic outlook seemed quintessentially American. Vividly rendered scenes such as *Sugaring Off, Candle Dip Day, White Christmas,* and *Applebutter Making at the Dudley Place* struck a deep chord in urban America's nostalgia for the "good old days." In 1949 President Harry Truman presented Moses with a Women's National Press Club Award "for extraordinary achievement," and in 1955 President Dwight D. Eisenhower's cabinet commissioned her to paint his Gettysburg home from photographs as its gift to him.

Moses was a matter-of-fact, unsentimental woman. If she had not started painting, she said, she "would have raised chickens. I would never sit back in a rocking chair waiting for someone to help me." Softening her straightforwardness was a rather sly sense of humor that crept into her paintings in amusing narrative details.

As an artist Moses was perhaps more appreciated in Europe than in America. Between 1950 and 1956 fifteen solo exhibitions of her work were held in major European cities. Reviewing a show in Paris, the European edition of the *New York Herald Tribune* concluded, "Though naive in the best sense of the word, she is by no means a primitive. What strikes one is the sophistication with which she achieves certain effects. Her landscapes have depth, and

the farawayness of distant blue mountains is beautifully conveyed. In *Shenandoah Valley* the landscape is composed of varied tones, while the river is rendered as a flat sheet of blue-gray which Whistler might have envied. . . ." The *Wiener Zeitung* reported that, entering a Grandma Moses exhibition, "Something magical begins to happen . . . when confronted with the originals for the first time, one is happily surprised. What delicacy of color gradation . . . one is amazed at . . . the manner in which depth of a landscape is captured on the flat picture surface and by the color values of rolling hills in the blue distance. What great landscape painters consciously composed, Grandma Moses 'knew' from inborn sensitivity without knowledge of perspective and color. . . ."

When Moses died at age 101 in Hoosick Falls, N.Y., her death was front-page news in both Europe and America. Her career had no parallel in the history of modern art, and her worldwide popularity upheld her observation that, in her own childhood, "people enjoyed life more in their way . . . they don't take time to be happy nowadays."

[Moses' paintings are in the collections of the Museum of Modern Art and the Metropolitan Museum of Art, New York City; the Minneapolis Institute of Arts; the William Rockhill Nelson Gallery, Kansas City, Mo.; the Phillips Gallery, Washington, D.C.; the Phoenix Art Museum; and the Bennington Museum, Bennington, Vt. See Otto Kallir, ed., *Grandma Moses: My Life's History* (1952); Otto Kallir, *Grandma Moses* (1973); Don Wharton, "The Incredible Career of Grandma Moses," *Readers' Digest,* Sept. 1967. An obituary is in the *New York Times,* Dec. 14, 1961.]

PATRICIA FAILING

MOTLEY, WILLARD FRANCIS (July 14, 1909–Mar. 4, 1965), novelist, was born in Chicago, Ill., the son of Florence Motley. He was reared as if his mother were his sister and as if her parents—Archibald John Motley and Mary Frederica Huff—were his parents. He sometimes gave his year of birth as 1912. The Motleys were one of the few black families in their neighborhood. Archibald Motley worked as a Pullman porter on the New York–Chicago "Wolverine."

From December 1922 through January 1924, as the first "Bud Billiken," Motley edited and wrote a children's column in the *Chicago Defender.* In 1930, the year after his graduation from Englewood High School, he sought fame and adventure by riding a bicycle from Chicago to New York. The following years were spent largely in odd jobs and unsuccessful efforts to have his stories printed. In 1936 and 1938 he traveled by automobile to the West Coast. These two trips provided material for "Adventures and Misadventures of a Fool," several chapters of which appeared as articles in *Commonweal* and various travel magazines.

In 1939, Motley moved to the Chicago slums. His writing was encouraged by Alexander Saxton, who was then completing his first novel, *Grand Crossing*. With Saxton, Motley founded and edited *Hull-House Magazine* (1939–1940), to which he contributed sketches of slum neighborhoods. From 1940 through 1942 he was employed by the WPA Writers' Project, for which he conducted housing surveys in Chicago's Little Sicily and wrote civil defense material with novelist Jack Conroy, who became a lifelong friend.

Motley's experiences in the slums resulted in his first novel, *Knock on Any Door*. Begun in 1940, it had grown to about 600,000 words when it was submitted to, and rejected by, Harper's in 1943. It was accepted by Macmillan after extensive cutting and revision (to about 237,000 words), but was then rejected as still too long and too sexually explicit. It was finally accepted by Appleton-Century and published in 1947.

The novel remained on the *New York Times* best-seller list for ten months. It was praised— for example, by Charles Lee in the *New York Times Book Review* (May 4, 1947)—for its "powerful, although rude, vitality," and Motley was called "an extraordinary and powerful new naturalistic talent." In 1949, Columbia Pictures released a motion picture version starring Humphrey Bogart. *Knock* follows the life of Nick Romano from acolyte to convicted murderer in the electric chair. The novel and Motley's writing of it set a pattern for his later work. Its characters were based on Motley himself and his acquaintances; it was composed after extensive research; it was heavily revised at the insistence of publishers; and it revealed Motley's brand of naturalism, combining detailed observation with sometimes mawkish sentimentality.

Motley's second novel, *We Fished All Night* (1951), written with the support of Newberry and Rosenwald fellowships, contains three intermittently intersecting plots showing the tragic aftermath of World War II in the lives of a would-be politician, a labor organizer, and a poet. Reviewers called it amateurish, full of clichés, repetitive, and flawed by emotion undisciplined by observation.

It was followed by *Let No Man Write My Epitaph* (1958), which continues *Knock* by portraying Nick's bastard son by a drug-addicted prostitute. Consisting in part of material previously cut from *Knock* and revealing more of Motley's sentimentality and less of his descriptive power, the novel is generally considered his least successful artistically. Reviewing it in the *Nation* (Aug. 16, 1958), Nelson Algren, who probably thought it invaded the territory of his *Man with the Golden Arm*, called it "a syrup that pours too slowly." But it sold fairly well and was made into a movie by Columbia Pictures (1960).

In September 1951, Motley left the United States for a proposed two-month trip to Mexico. He stayed there, except for occasional trips back to the United States, for the rest of his life. He lived on the outskirts of Mexico City until 1961, then bought a house near Cuernavaca, where he was often visited by friends, artists, and writers. Motley's generosity, the poor sales of his books, and the attachment of his income by the Internal Revenue Service combined to make his financial situation difficult. An account of his life in Mexico entitled "My House Is Your House" and a novel-length work entitled "Remember Me to Mama" were both rejected by publishers, although several sections of "My House" appeared in *Rogue*. Motley, who never married, adopted Sergio López, a Mexican boy, as his son. He died in Mexico City.

In 1966, G. P. Putnam's Sons published Motley's last novel, *Let Noon Be Fair*, which chronicles the corruption of a Mexican fishing village by tourism and which received largely unfavorable reviews that called it sensational, superficial, and sentimental.

Thus, after the success of *Knock*, Motley's reputation declined. He was seen by academic critics as a naturalist-come-lately who produced popular fiction. And he benefited little from the increased attention given black writers in the 1960's, since his novels dealt only tangentially with questions of race. (One of his few published works dealing explicitly with race is the short story "The Almost White Boy," which did not appear until 1963 in *Soon, One Morning*, although it was written in 1940.) When *Time* (May 17, 1963) ran a cover story on James Baldwin, Motley wrote a letter to the editor (June 7, 1963) accusing Baldwin of being a "professional Negro." He expanded on his integrationist views in the *Chicago Sun-Times* (Aug. 11, 1963). While not denying the racial oppression in America, which accounted in part for his moving to Mexico, he reiterated his lifelong belief that "people are just people."

In the 1970's Motley began receiving more critical and scholarly attention, as a writer who combined a desire for social reform with a sometimes experimental literary technique. It is likely, as Robert Fleming says, that Motley will "never be ranked with the principal writers of the twentieth century" but that he will remain an important figure in the history of the American novel.

[A large group of Motley's papers, mostly letters dated 1957–1963, is described by Jerome Klinkowitz, James Giles, and John T. O'Brien in "The Willard Motley Papers at the University of Wisconsin," *Resources for American Literary Study*, Autumn 1972. The bulk of his manuscripts, including letters, diaries, notes, photographs, wire recordings, and published and unpublished works, is described by Craig Abbott and Kay Van Mol in "The Willard Motley Papers at Northern Illinois University," *Resources for American Literary Study*, Spring 1977. Jerome Klinkowitz has edited *The Diaries of Willard Motley* (1979). The best biographical and critical study is Robert E. Fleming, *Willard Motley* (1978), which includes a bibliography of works by and about Motley.]

CRAIG ABBOTT

MOTT, FRANK LUTHER (Apr. 4, 1886– Oct. 23, 1964), journalist, author, and educator, was born in What Cheer, Iowa, the son of David Charles Mott and Mary E. Tipton. Members of both families were Quakers. Mott's father was a farmer, schoolteacher, and publisher of the What Cheer *Patriot*, where Mott acquired the virus of printer's ink. He learned to set type by hand when he was eleven. He worked for his father at various weekly newspapers in Iowa, and one in Oklahoma. After graduating from the Indianola, Iowa, High School in 1903, he enrolled in Simpson College there. Three years later he transferred to the University of Chicago, where he received a Ph.B. in 1907. The same year he also received a B.A. from Simpson College. On Oct. 7, 1910, he married Vera Hortense Ingram; they had one daughter.

In 1914 Mott purchased the Grand Junction (Iowa) *Globe*, but after three years he decided to make teaching his career. He sold the newspaper and enrolled at Columbia University, New York City, where he earned his M.A. in 1919 and his Ph.D. in 1924. He was an assistant professor of English at Simpson College (1919–1921) and an assistant professor at the University of Iowa (1921–1925), where he was also coeditor (1925–1933) of the *Midland* magazine, a literary publication.

In 1927 Mott was offered the position of dean of the University of Washington, which prompted the University of Iowa to appoint him director of its School of Journalism that year. In 1929 he was elected president of the American Association of Schools and Departments of Journalism, and from 1930 to 1934 he edited the *Journalism Quarterly*. He collaborated with Ralph Casey of the University of Minnesota in editing *Interpretations of Journalism* (1937).

During this period Mott worked on his monumental *History of American Magazines*. The first volume was published by Appleton in 1930. The second and third volumes, published by the Harvard University Press in 1938, won Mott the Pulitzer Prize for history in 1939. The fourth volume, *A History of American Magazines, 1885–1905* (1957), which won the Bancroft Prize of Columbia University in 1958, is an authoritative work and is probably Mott's most significant contribution to American journalism history. The fifth volume was published posthumously in 1968.

Mott also edited *Headlining America* (1937–1940), a collection of the best newspaper stories of the year. His *American Journalism: A History 1690–1940* appeared in 1941. A year later, when the University of Missouri decided to upgrade the research program of its School of Journalism, Mott was named dean. After World War II he obtained a seven months leave of absence to serve as an "expert in journalism training" at the Biarritz American University in France. In April 1947 he served in a similar post in Japan.

After his retirement in 1951, Mott founded, with Paul Fisher, the Press of the Crippled Turtle. Under the heading *Oldtime Comments on Journalism*, the first issue appeared in January 1953. Ten issues, each limited to 250 copies, appeared from 1953 to 1960.

Mott's prolific writing amazed all who knew him. Asked how he could accomplish so much, he replied: "I never play bridge." He wrote many short stories and one novel. The *Saturday Evening Post* published his short story "The Phantom Flivver" on Jan. 28, 1950. *Time Enough: Essays in Autobiography* appeared in 1962.

Mott was primarily a researcher and writer. As head of the journalism schools, he left the administration largely to others. He died in Columbia, Mo.

[More than 2,000 file folders containing correspondence, diaries, and other private papers, as well as seventy-two printed volumes, are in the State Historical Society of Missouri in Columbia. Additional material is held in the archives of the University of Iowa. See Max Lawrence Marshall, "Frank Luther Mott: Journalism Educator" (Ph.D. diss., University of Missouri School of Journalism, 1975); and articles in *Saturday Review of Literature,* May 6, 1939; *Publishers Weekly,* May 6, 1939; Files of Des Moines, Iowa, *Register Tribune,* May 15, and Mar. 2, 1939. Obituaries are in the *New York Times,* Oct. 24, 1964, and *Editor and Publisher,* Oct. 31, 1964.]

CHARLES C. CLAYTON

MURPHY, GERALD CLERY (Mar. 25, 1888–Oct. 17, 1964), painter, businessman, and patron of the arts, was born in Boston, Mass., the son of Patrick Francis Murphy, who in the 1890's established the Mark Cross Company, a fashionable leather-goods and import store, and of Anna Elizabeth Ryan. Murphy spent five years working for the family company following his graduation from Yale in 1912, but he soon acquired a distaste for the conventional business life and decided in 1918, following a short stint in the U.S. Signal Corps, to study at the Harvard School of Landscape Architecture. He married Sara Sherman Wiborg on Dec. 30, 1915; they had three children. Murphy's wife joined in his determination to renounce the prescribed success of their secure family backgrounds— both families were cosmopolitan and moneyed.

When Murphy completed his two-year landscape program, he and his family went in early 1921 to England, where he studied the celebrated formal gardens. Then they traveled to France, where they chose to live. Like other expatriates of the day, they had decided that only in France were the arts alive. Murphy found the artistic fervor of Paris in the 1920's so engaging, in fact, that he forgot landscaping and began a nine-year career as a painter. He and Sara helped to paint sets for Serge Diaghilev's Ballets Russes in Paris, and they studied art under one of Diaghilev's designers, Natalia Goncharova. When Fernand Léger commissioned Murphy in 1923 to create an "American" ballet for the Ballets Suédois, a Swedish company performing in Paris, Murphy collaborated with another Yale man, Cole Porter, on *Within the Quota,* a short ballet that won acclaim both in Paris and later on a two-month tour of America. Its lively tunes and Murphy's story line and stage sets—huge backdrops bearing a collage of newspaper headlines—satirized an immigrant's stereotypical impressions of America.

Murphy had completed three paintings by 1924, and when the Salon des Indépendants in Paris exhibited *Razor* (1923), *Boatdeck, Cunarder* (1924), and *Engine Room* (1924), Léger

hailed him as "the only *American* painter in Paris." Murphy described his own style as a merger between the real and the abstract. He hoped to "digest" real objects, he said, "along with purely abstract forms and re-present them." His admiration for the exactitude of the fifteenth-century painter Piero della Francesca inspired him to render everyday objects in large scale with meticulous precision. He set up studios in Paris and on the French Riviera, where he worked on his canvases with painstaking slowness, sometimes at the rate of only one painting a year. Some contemporary artists and critics dismissed Murphy's work as that of a wealthy dilettante, but as art critic Rudi Blesh has recognized, his semi-abstract canvases were "so complex in design, so meticulous in craft, and (some of them) so heroic in size (one is ten feet wide and over seventeen feet high) that their production could not have been without protracted or concentrated labor."

During 1923 and 1924 the Murphys renovated a villa in Cap d'Antibes on the French Riviera that soon became the gathering spot for prominent writers and artists. They developed what became close and lifelong relationships with F. Scott Fitzgerald, John Dos Passos, Archibald MacLeish, and Ernest Hemingway. The Murphys had a profound influence on these writers, inspiring such works as MacLeish's "Sketch for a Portrait of Mme. G—— M——" and "American Letter, for Gerald Murphy," and Fitzgerald's *Tender Is the Night,* in which the main characters of Dick and Nicole Diver were patterned after Gerald and Sara Murphy as Fitzgerald knew them in France.

Throughout the latter half of the 1920's Murphy continued to exhibit at the Salon des Indépendants: *Watch* and *Doves* in 1925, *Roulement à Billes* and *Bibliothèque* in 1926, *Wasp and Pear* in 1927, and *Cocktail* in 1928. His final painting, *Portrait* (1929), a starkly segmented collage that bore precise images of his foot, three thumbprints, and one enlarged eye, foreshadowed the personal fragmentation of his life during the 1930's. Murphy had to return, reluctantly, to New York in 1933 to rescue the Mark Cross Company from bankruptcy, and his two sons died of illness in 1935 and 1937.

In 1929, when his younger son, Patrick, contracted the tuberculosis that killed him eight years later, Murphy devoted himself to the boy's struggle for health and put aside painting forever. He said later that he was not happy until he had begun painting and never entirely happy after he was "obliged to give it up."

Murphy's role as "a kind of minor literary

figure" or as a patron of artists tended later to overshadow his real importance as an artist— one who, as MacLeish said, "painted some of the most innovative canvases of those years." When the Galerie Bernheim-Jeune exhibited most of his works in 1936, it brought Murphy some of the recognition due him as an artist, but he had taken up the Mark Cross Company as his personal burden, and he never put it down again. Although he cleared the company of debt during the 1930's and made it a thriving concern during the 1940's and 1950's, he never found the work congenial, and was happy to retire in 1956. Murphy felt heartened to learn prior to his death in East Hampton, N.Y., that his few works had experienced a renaissance of sorts.

The Dallas Museum for Contemporary Arts exhibited five of Murphy's paintings in a 1960 show called "American Genius in Review," and art critics Rudi Blesh and Douglas MacAgy began to discuss his paintings, which brought him to the attention of the Museum of Modern Art in New York City. In 1964 the museum acquired *Wasp and Pear* from MacLeish, and from April 9 to May 19, 1974, the museum staged a one-man show of Murphy's surviving works: *Watch, Razor, Doves, Bibliothèque, Cocktail, Wasp and Pear.* Critics such as Hayden Herrara saw Murphy as "an astonishingly original, witty and prophetic painter" whose paintings "show an assimilation of French painting—Synthetic Cubism, Purism and Léger —and his transformation of these influences into a distinctive style" which was peculiarly American. As MacLeish said, the "canvasses continued their labor of establishing Gerald Murphy as what he really was and always had been, a painter of his time."

[Murphy's correspondence with F. Scott Fitzgerald, Ernest Hemingway, John Dos Passos, and Archibald MacLeish is housed in the main manuscript holdings of these authors at Princeton University, the John F. Kennedy Library, the University of Virginia, and the Library of Congress, respectively. The only letters to Murphy presently published are in Andrew Turnbull, ed., *The Letters of F. Scott Fitzgerald* (1963); and in Townsend Ludington, ed., *The Fourteenth Chronicle: Letters and Diaries of John Dos Passos* (1973). Several of Murphy's letters to Fitzgerald are in Linda Patterson Miller, " 'As a Friend You Have Never Failed Me' . . .," *Journal of Modern Literature,* Sept. 1976. The only concentrated study of Murphy's life and art is Calvin Tomkins, *Living Well Is the Best Revenge* (1971). Biographies and reminiscences that mention Murphy are Andrew Turnbull, *Scott Fitzgerald* (1962); John Dos Passos, *The Best Times*

(1966); Carlos Baker, *Ernest Hemingway: A Life Story* (1969); Nancy Milford, *Zelda* (1970); Archibald MacLeish, *Riders on the Earth* (1978). See also Rudi Blesh, *Modern Art USA* (1956); Hayden Herrera, "Gerald Murphy, An Amurikin in Paris," *Art in America,* Sept.–Oct. 1974. An obituary is in the *New York Times,* Oct. 18, 1964.]

LINDA PATTERSON MILLER

MURRAY, JAMES EDWARD (May 3, 1876–Mar. 23, 1961), U.S. senator, was born near St. Thomas, Ontario, Canada, the son of Andrew James Murray, a farmer and railroad worker, and Anna Mary Cooley. His parents had emigrated in 1874 from County Clare, Ireland, and had settled on a farm near St. Thomas. Murray attended schools in St. Thomas and worked in the dining service at the railroad depot there. After his father died in 1885, his uncle James Andrew Murray of Butte, Mont., supported the family. The uncle was wealthy, owning mines in several western states and in South Africa, as well as public utilities and real estate in the Pacific states. Murray graduated in 1897 from St. Jerome's College in Berlin (now Kitchener), Ontario, and moved to Butte. He then entered New York University, where he received LL.B. and LL.M. degrees in 1900 and 1901, respectively. He became a naturalized citizen at that time.

In 1901, Murray returned to Butte, where his uncle helped him establish a law practice. Along with his uncle he specialized in mining law, and he often clashed with the powerful Anaconda Company. He was president of the U.S. Building and Loan Association and vice-president of the Monidah Trust Corporation of Butte. On June 28, 1905, Murray married Viola Edna Horgan; they had six sons. Soft-spoken, gentle, and modest, he became very wealthy in 1921 when he inherited much of his uncle's estate. An advocate of Irish independence, he was president of the American Association for Recognition of the Irish Republic.

In the 1930's Murray became influential in Montana politics. With the exception of serving from 1906 to 1908 as county attorney of Silver Bow County and in 1920 as a delegate to the Democratic National Convention, he had concentrated on building a successful law practice in Butte. After attending the 1932 Democratic National Convention, he campaigned vigorously for the election of Franklin D. Roosevelt as president. In 1933, Roosevelt rewarded him with appointment as chairman of the State Advisory Board of the Public Works Administration.

Murray sought the Democratic nomination

for the United States Senate seat left vacant by the death of Thomas J. Walsh. Governor John Erickson, a conservative Democrat sympathetic to the Anaconda Company, resigned and was appointed by his successor, Frank H. Cooney, to the Senate pending an election. This maneuver provoked widespread controversy within the state Democratic party, and Murray was persuaded to challenge Erickson in the 1934 primary. Although not well known outside Butte and much less experienced politically, he narrowly defeated Erickson. After a lively campaign defending the New Deal, he easily won the Senate seat.

Murray was reelected in 1936, 1942, 1948, and 1954. He barely defeated Republican Wellington Rankin in 1942. In this contest Senator Burton K. Wheeler's state Democratic party organization did not support him. Wheeler had disagreed with Murray over President Franklin D. Roosevelt's policies. In 1954, Murray narrowly defeated Republican Congressman Wesley D'Ewart, after opponents accused him of having Communist connections.

Murray supported most of Roosevelt's domestic policies. Although remaining silent on the Supreme Court reorganization plan, he endorsed the Wagner, Social Security, and Fair Labor Standards acts and executive reorganization. He was an isolationist until the outbreak of World War II, opposing United States entry into the World Court and other Roosevelt foreign policies. But after September 1939 he regularly aligned himself with the internationalists. Murray voted to repeal the arms embargo and in favor of lend-lease, but opposed the Selective Service Act of 1940.

In 1940–1946, Murray served as chairman of the Senate Special Committee to Study and Survey Problems of Small Business Enterprises. Its investigations disclosed that the federal government awarded nearly all defense production contracts to large businesses. Murray figured prominently in reconversion legislation terminating war contracts and disposing of surplus property.

Murray promoted a number of far-reaching economic and social welfare measures. He cosponsored the Employment Act of 1946, establishing the principle that the government should guarantee every employable American a job and creating the Council of Economic Advisers. He was coauthor of comprehensive legislation to extend social security, broaden old-age and unemployment benefits, and provide federal medical and hospital insurance for all workers and their families. Although Congress did not enact national health insurance, it eventually approved hospital construction and federal aid for medical students. During the early 1950's Murray introduced the nation's first Medicare bill.

In 1945, Murray became chairman of the Senate Committee on Education and Labor. Sympathetic to organized labor, he opposed the Taft-Hartley Act and directed an unsuccessful effort to repeal the measure. During the 1940's and 1950's he sponsored several bills for federal aid to education.

In 1951, Murray was involved in the Reconstruction Finance Corporation (RFC) scandal. The luxury Sorrento Hotel in Miami Beach, Fla., had applied to the RFC for a $1 million loan to pay off mounting debts. Republican Senator Wallace Bennett, a member of the subcommittee on banking investigating the scandal, charged that Murray had used his personal and political influence to obtain the loan. In a letter to RFC chairman Harley Hise, dated Oct. 24, 1949, Murray had suggested that the loan application warranted "further action" and that the RFC had been established to provide this type of relief. Murray considered the letter a routine inquiry made at the request of constituents and others. Murray's son James, a Washington attorney, received a fee of $21,000 for this and other cases. A second son, Charles, Murray's administrative assistant, attended a conference between the attorney for the Sorrento Hotel and RFC director Walter Dunham two days before the loan was granted.

Western issues naturally interested Murray. In 1944–1945 he urged creation of a Missouri Valley Authority patterned after the Tennessee Valley Authority. Although Congress rejected this plan, it adopted the Pick-Sloan Plan for comprehensive development of the Missouri Valley. Murray eventually was chairman of the Interior and Insular Affairs Committees and of the Western Conference of Democratic Senators. Besides coauthoring the first national wilderness bills, he favored establishment of a Point Four program for American Indians. Murray supported unsuccessful attempts to secure legislation authorizing the government to build, operate, and finance a huge dam and hydroelectric plant at Hell's Canyon on the Snake River in Idaho. The administration of President Dwight D. Eisenhower opposed this legislation as wasteful, preferring that private interests develop electric power. To Murray's dismay, the Federal Power Commission in 1955 permitted a private firm, the Idaho Power Company, to build three smaller dams.

Murray originally intended to seek another term in 1960. By this time he was the second oldest member of the Senate, and family and friends convinced him that he could not be re-elected. He therefore retired. Murray died in Butte, Mont.

[Murray's papers are at the University of Montana Library. See Michael P. Malone, "Montana Politics and the New Deal," *Montana*, Winter 1971; Donald E. Spritzer, "Senators in Conflict," *Montana*, Spring 1973. An obituary is in *New York Times*, Mar. 24, 1961.]

DAVID L. PORTER

MURRAY, MAE (May 10, 1889–Mar. 23, 1965), dancer and movie actress known as "The Girl With Bee-stung Lips," was born Marie Adrienne Koening in Portsmouth, Va. Her parents were immigrants, her mother from Belgium and her father from Austria. (Later she stated that her father had been Irish and her mother Italian.) Her father was an artist who died when Murray was four years old. After his death her mother returned to Europe, and she was sent to New York City, where she lived with her grandmother and attended convent schools. (She later stated that she had been brought up by "my great-grandmother who left me in convents all over Europe while she traveled.") When she was nine Murray was placed in a boarding school near Chicago. At thirteen she ran away from this school and went to Chicago, where she was hired as a dancer by a touring show company.

In 1906 she appeared for the first time as Mae Murray, in a Gus Edwards revue. Her first stage appearance that gained her some renown occurred two years later, in the *Ziegfeld Follies of 1908*. Also in 1908 she married William Schwenker, Jr., son of a millionaire broker. The marriage was dissolved within a year.

During this period of dance crazes, Murray danced in cafes and ballrooms in New York City, and even went to Paris to learn new dances such as the tango. After she performed in the cabaret show at the Sans Souci nightclub (1913–1914), she became something of a celebrity in New York. It was at the Sans Souci that Irving Berlin saw her dance and asked her to substitute for Irene Castle in his first hit, *Watch Your Step* (1914).

Murray led the hectic life of a professional dancer. Her frequent partner was an aspiring actor named Rudolph Valentino. When she was featured in the *Ziegfeld Follies of 1915*, Adolph Zukor signed Murray to a film contract with

Lasky Feature Play Company. Her film debut was in *To Have and to Hold* (1916). Although her costar was Wallace Reid, a popular leading man of the day, her performance was not highly regarded. After she had made three more films, Zukor put director Robert Z. Leonard in charge of her films. Under his guidance Murray developed the techniques necessary for successful silent-screen acting. They made five films for Paramount that proved successful, both critically and financially. Leonard established Murray as the epitome of the "glamorous" female film star and, in a few years, raised her weekly salary from $1,200 to $10,000. In 1916 she married socialite Jay O'Brien under bizarre and controversial circumstances. According to Jane Ardmore, O'Brien had Murray kidnapped from the set of the *Primrose Ring* and taken to Pasadena, where she was forced, at gunpoint, to marry him. Murray claimed she later escaped from the wedding banquet at the Alexandria Hotel and went into hiding with the assistance of Robert Leonard and Cecil B. De Mille. The local newspapers, however, carried stories saying that Murray wed O'Brien between scenes of *The Mormon Maid* at the Lasky studio. The marriage was dissolved after a short time.

In 1917, Murray and Leonard organized their own production company, Bluebird, at Universal Studios. They made ten features for Universal, including two in which she appeared with Rudolph Valentino. In June 1918, Murray and Leonard were married. They moved to New York City, and in the ensuing years she made six films for Pathé and Paramount. This period represented the peak of Murray's development as a dramatic actress.

The Leonards then formed a new production company, Tiffany, in association with Metro. During the next two years Murray starred in eight films made under this agreement. These movies heightened her popularity so greatly that Louis B. Mayer, head of Metro production, acknowledged that she was the company's top star.

Murray and Leonard were divorced in 1925. In that year she appeared in Metro-Goldwyn-Mayer's (MGM) *The Merry Widow* under the direction of Erich von Stroheim. The flighty and capricious Murray clashed constantly with the egotistical von Stroheim during the filming. Mayer and Irving Thalberg mediated almost daily between them in order to complete the film. Eventually the studio had to edit von Stroheim's ninety reels of film to ten. The finished product was an enormous success, and probably Murray's best screen performance. When she began to work on her next film, *The Masked*

Bride, she was an egotistical prima donna, demanding and receiving unheard-of privileges, including the replacement of director Josef von Sternberg by William Cabanne halfway through production.

In 1926, Murray married David Mdivani, who was known as a Georgian prince. They had one son. A year after her marriage, she walked out on her MGM contract in order to live in Europe. Mayer thereupon blacklisted her in the Hollywood film industry. The princely life-style of the Mdivanis depleted Murray's fortune in two years. By 1930 she was bankrupt. She attempted a remake of one of her earlier successes, *Peacock Alley* (1922), but the film was a financial disaster. She made two more films—*Bachelor Apartment* and *High Stakes* (both 1931)—then faded from public awareness.

Murray's sense of her own importance, though, remained enormous, and she became a caricature of the once glamorous personality Mae Murray. In 1933 she was divorced from Mdivani. She lost custody of her son, Koran, who later refused to acknowledge her as his mother.

During the 1930's Murray worked in radio, vaudeville, and road-show dance revues. In 1941 she appeared in the stage production *Billy Rose's Cavalcade of the Silent Screen,* but her demands and tantrums led to her dismissal. She lived thereafter in Hollywood, in greatly reduced circumstances, and the Motion Picture Relief Fund assumed management of her financial affairs. In 1964 she was found, ill and destitute, in a St. Louis Salvation Army shelter, believing herself to be in New York City. She died in Woodland Hills, Calif.

Murray was a romantic who sought to create an air of mystery around herself. In 1959, after her biography, *The Self-Enchanted,* had been published, she invaded libraries and bookstores throughout Los Angeles to blot out in individual books the record of her true name. She was completely preoccupied with her extravagant sense of stardom, which continued to increase even as her popularity waned. "You don't have to keep making movies to remain a star," she claimed. "Once you become a star, you are always a star." After viewing the deluded, faded movie queen in *Sunset Boulevard,* she is reported to have said, "None of us floozies was ever that nuts."

[A biography is Jane Ardmore, *The Self-Enchanted: Mae Murray—Image of an Era* (1959). Also see Richard Schickel, *The Stars* (1962); and Ray Stuart, *Immortals of the Screen* (1965). Obituaries are in the *New York Times,* Mar. 24, 1965; *Time,* Apr. 2, 1965; and D. Bodeen, "Mae Murray, 1889–1965," *Films in Review,* vol. 26, 1975.]

JOHN M. HEFTON

MURRAY, THOMAS EDWARD (June 20, 1891–May 26, 1961), engineer, business executive, and public official, was born in Albany, N.Y., the son of Thomas Edward Murray and Catherine Bradley. His father, a contemporary of Thomas A. Edison, had, like Edison, risen from humble origins to become a well-known inventor of devices used in the electric utility industry. In the early 1900's the elder Murray was sent to Brooklyn to purchase existing electrical generating facilities in the New York metropolitan area; he later organized the Brooklyn and New York Edison companies and served as an official of those companies until 1928.

Raised in a devout Roman Catholic family and educated in Catholic schools in Albany, Brooklyn, and New York City, Murray received a bachelor's degree in mechanical engineering from the Sheffield Scientific School at Yale University in 1911. He then worked for two years as an engineer with the New York Edison Company before joining his father's firm, the Metropolitan Engineering Company, which manufactured various products invented by both father and son.

During World War I, Murray was instrumental in developing welding techniques that greatly simplified the manufacture of mortar shells. After the war he applied the same skills to the manufacture of radiators for heating systems and rear-axle housings for automobiles. On Jan. 4, 1917, he married Marie Brady. They had eleven children. Following his father's death in 1929, Murray became president of Metropolitan Engineering and the Murray Manufacturing Company. A prolific inventor like his father, he was awarded more than 200 patents on electrical and welding devices.

Murray entered public life in 1932, when he was appointed the federal receiver of the bankrupt Interborough Rapid Transit Company and of the Manhattan Railway Company. For the next nine years he was engrossed in the complex legal and financial problems related to transforming these privately owned mass-transit companies into a single metropolitan system. Murray's unquestioned integrity, hardheaded business acumen, and financial independence made it possible for him to serve for almost a decade in a thankless position of public trust without becoming mired in the morass of local politics and labor strife that plagued the New

York metropolitan area during the Great Depression. His ability to win the respect of labor leaders like John L. Lewis and Philip Murray led to his appointment to the New York study commission on the bus strike in 1941 and as trustee of the United Mine Workers' health and welfare fund in 1947. During World War II, Murray concentrated his energies on war production contracts held by the Metropolitan Engineering and Murray companies.

In March 1950 President Harry S. Truman named Murray a member of the U.S. Atomic Energy Commission (AEC). The first engineer to be appointed to the AEC, Murray took up his new duties in Washington at a time of rising anti-Soviet sentiments during the cold war. He firmly supported the Truman administration's efforts to strengthen national defenses, and took the lead in advocating a rapid expansion of the AEC's facilities for producing fissionable materials and nuclear weapons. Murray helped accelerate research on the hydrogen bomb and championed the development of nuclear propulsion systems for submarines, warships, and military aircraft.

With the election of President Dwight Eisenhower in 1953, Murray became a lonely but strident voice of dissent on the AEC, now under the leadership of Lewis L. Strauss. Challenging Strauss and the Republican administration on many issues, he opposed the Dixon-Yates contract (1954), which he saw as a partisan and unwarranted use of the AEC's authority to attack the public power movement in the United States. He pushed through the construction of the first full-scale nuclear power plant as a federal project, over the determined opposition of the electric utility industry, and in 1956 urged Congress to authorize construction of 2 million kilowatts of nuclear power capacity in the United States and abroad by 1960.

Although Murray supported the objectives of Eisenhower's Atoms for Peace plan, he closely allied himself during most of the two Eisenhower administrations with the powerful Joint Committee on Atomic Energy in Congress, which was dominated by the Democrats. For years an outspoken opponent of Strauss and the Eisenhower administration, he was not reappointed to the AEC when his term expired in June 1957. As a consultant to the joint committee, he continued his fight for federal funds to develop both military and civilian uses of atomic energy.

Murray's advocacy of vigorous development of nuclear technology was grounded in his religious convictions and economic philosophy. In addresses at Catholic colleges and universities in the 1950's, he described the cold war as an ideological struggle against atheistic Communism. Nuclear technology was a divine gift that the nation had a moral duty to develop, not only to counter the threat of Soviet aggression but also to demonstrate the superiority of a democratic, capitalistic society. Troubled as a practicing Christian by the inhumanity and potential horrors of nuclear warfare, he became increasingly concerned after 1954 that the unrestricted use of very large thermonuclear weapons would destroy civilization. While insisting on the need to develop, test, and produce tactical nuclear weapons, Murray became a firm advocate of a test ban on multimegaton nuclear weapons, a cause he continued to espouse until his death in New York City.

[Some personal papers relating to Murray's business career and to his service on the AEC are held by his family. The files of the AEC, now in the Historian's Office, U.S. Department of Energy, Washington, D.C., contain extensive information on Murray's career as a member of the AEC. The Historian's Office also has a file of Murray's speeches on the atomic energy program. Some materials on Murray are in the records of the Joint Committee on Atomic Energy, now available for research in the National Archives in Washington. Murray wrote *Nuclear Policy for War and Peace* (1960). An obituary is in the *New York Times,* May 27, 1961.]

RICHARD G. HEWLETT

MURROW, EDWARD (EGBERT) ROSCOE (Apr. 25, 1908–Apr. 27, 1965), news and public affairs broadcaster, was born on a farm outside Greensboro, N.C., the son of Roscoe C. Murrow and Ethel Lamb. The family moved in 1913 to Blanchard, Wash., where the father became a logging-locomotive engineer. Egbert, as Murrow had been christened, worked as a farmhand while still in school, spent 1925–1926 in the lumber camps, and in 1926 began to spend summers as a compassman in the timber camps of the Olympic Peninsula. There he shortened his name to Ed, which became Edward in college. He grew up with a background of rough frontierism, strikes and labor violence instigated by the Industrial Workers of the World, and conflict over free speech, trade union organization, and legislative reform.

At Edison High School, which he attended from 1922 to 1925, Murrow was student body president and a member of the regional championship debating team. He continued his debating at Washington State College at Pullman (1926–1930), where he was also drawn to dramatics, to the country's first college course in radio broadcasting, and to the student movement. He became cadet colonel in the Reserve Officers Training Corps and was graduated in 1930 with a B.A. in speech. Having been elected president of the National Student Federation (NSF) in 1929, Murrow moved to New York City after graduation to lead that organization for two years. He spoke on college campuses, arranged student travel and exchange with foreign universities, and attended conventions in the United States and Europe. He also obtained speakers for the Columbia Broadcasting System's (CBS) "University of the Air" program. En route to an NSF conference in New Orleans, Murrow met Janet Huntington Brewster, a delegate from Mount Holyoke College. Married on Oct. 27, 1934, they had one son.

In 1932, Murrow had become assistant director of the Institute of International Education. His student activity suddenly broadened into a cultural rescue operation, bringing scholars from Germany to the United States. He also traveled in Europe, witnessing the advance of Nazism.

In 1935, Murrow was named "director of talks" for the 100-station CBS radio network, and in 1937 he was sent abroad as European director for CBS to transmit special events to America, beginning with the coronation of Britain's King George VI. "Special events" included sports, music festivals, and national ceremonial occasions as well as political speeches and talks by literary luminaries.

Hitler's annexation of Austria in March 1938 marked American radio's coming of age as a swift, reliable, and direct journalistic medium. It also began Murrow's rise to fame. Despite his lack of formal news training, his eyewitness reports of Hitler's arrival in Vienna and its consequences vividly established the forceful Murrow style: crisp yet measured, full of detail and personal impression. The occasion also inaugurated the "news roundup." Murrow arranged live transmissions from London, Paris, Berlin, Vienna, and Washington on the same program. This led to the creation of a full-time foreign news staff, men chosen by Murrow for their reportorial skills, not for quality of voice, including William L. Shirer, Eric Sevareid, and Howard K. Smith.

Austria's annexation was followed by the Munich crisis of September 1938, with its fateful diplomatic conferences and Hitler's ranting speeches. Americans stayed up all night, listening to round-the-clock radio bulletins and analyses, as well as an innovation: the correspondents' round table of conversation between four or more linked cities.

Radio thus changed the nature of news. It was no longer the chronicling of what had already happened, by the print media, in language meant for reading. It had become the communication of what was happening at that very moment, in the more informal spoken language.

Murrow, from street and rooftop, described the aerial Battle of Britain and the German blitz against London. "This . . . is London," his cadenced opening, was heard against the sounds of actual air-raid sirens, antiaircraft guns, and falling bombs. His accounts of bomber raids on Germany, of visits to airfields, air-raid shelters, and training camps, of journeys on a minesweeper and in ambulances brought some of the realities of war into American living rooms. One of the most memorable was his report of the U.S. Army's liberation of the Buchenwald concentration camp. Janet Murrow also broadcast regularly from London on home-front subjects.

Back in the United States, Murrow found himself in the midst of the emerging cold war. A de facto alliance had been replaced by mutual suspicion as the Russians consolidated their hold on eastern Europe in the name of security and the United States embarked on a policy of containment by the strengthening of western Europe.

From 1946 to 1947, Murrow was a CBS vice-president and director of public affairs. As partisan dissension replaced American wartime unity, Murrow, with a nightly radio broadcast of news and commentary, became increasingly concerned with civil liberties, congressional hearings on the "Communist conspiracy," and East-West relations. As an advocate of the widest expression of views and an opponent of the growing tendency to self-censorship in the broadcasting industry—which reached its peak in the blacklisting of actors, producers, and correspondents deemed "controversial"—Murrow made his program the nation's most authoritative and esteemed. His belief in the mass media as an educative force rather than a purely commercial enterprise caused continuing differences with the values and practices of the industry.

From radio Murrow moved to television. In addition to his familiar voice, he became identified by his saturnine good looks, grave mien, and ever-present cigarette. A weekly radio program, "Hear It Now," produced in partnership with Fred W. Friendly, became "See It Now" on television in 1951. It was the most informative and probing, as well as the most provocative, assay of American problems, policies, and personalities to be broadcast.

The stormiest and most disputatious program on this series was broadcast Mar. 9, 1954. Murrow's attack on Senator Joseph R. McCarthy of Wisconsin allowed McCarthy to undo himself by the cumulative effect of shots of his speeches, remarks, and hectoring of witnesses before his committee.

Employing the method of "the little picture" as the microcosm of large situations, "See It Now" broadcast many programs, both lauded and criticized, from all parts of the world. Subjects included Africa on the eve of decolonization, the Suez war, the Budapest uprising, the Korean War, presidential politics, nuclear testing and missilery, cigarettes and cancer, school desegregation, and various aspects of the Bill of Rights. Murrow interviewed Jawaharlal Nehru, Gamal Abdel Nasser, David Ben-Gurion, Marshal Tito, and Chou En-lai.

For many Americans "See It Now" served as the conscience of broadcasting, but it was also a frequent target of attack and was accused of encouraging dissent. Murrow himself was often referred to by detractors as "Old Gloom and Doom." A versifier wrote: "No one's brow furrows/Like Edward R. Murrow's."

A quite different Murrow television program, "Person to Person" (1953–1959), made weekly "visits" to the homes of celebrities. And his "Small World" (1958–1960), an occasional presentation, used simultaneous filming and telephone conversations to give a global reach to Murrow's conversations with the famous.

Network reductions in news and documentary broadcasting, the curtailing and eventual abandonment of "See It Now" (1958) in favor of entertainment programs with higher audience ratings, and Murrow's increasing disaffection with the industry led to his departure from broadcasting. In October 1958, in a speech before the Radio and Television News Directors Association in Chicago, he castigated the networks for fostering "decadence, escapism, and insulation from the realities of the world in which we live."

The most honored man in American broadcasting resigned to join the incoming Kennedy administration in January 1961 as director of the U.S. Information Agency. He served for nearly three years, seeking to disseminate the American "image" abroad with realistic candor. Lung cancer forced his retirement in January 1964. He died at Pawling, N.Y.

[The Murrow Papers are at the Fletcher School of Law and Diplomacy, Tufts University. Murrow's *This Is London* (1941) contains transcripts of broadcasts of the Battle of Britain. Also see Eric Sevareid, *Not So Wild a Dream* (1946); Edward Bliss, Jr., ed., *In Search of Light* (1967); Fred W. Friendly, *Due to Circumstances Beyond Our Control* (1967); Alexander Kendrick, *Prime Time* (1969); Erik Barnouw, *The Golden Web* (1968) and *The Image Empire* (1970). An obituary is in the *New York Times,* Apr. 28, 1965.]

ALEXANDER KENDRICK

MUZZEY, DAVID SAVILLE (Oct. 9, 1870–Apr. 14, 1965), historian and educator, was born in Lexington, Mass., the son of David W. Muzzey, a real estate broker, and of Annie W. Saville. He attended the Boston Latin School and entered Harvard in 1889. After graduation in 1893, he taught mathematics at Robert College in Constantinople until 1894. He then returned to the United States and enrolled at Union Theological Seminary, from which he obtained a B.D. in 1897. Subsequently he studied at the University of Berlin (1897–1898) under Adolf von Harnack and Herman Gencke and at the Sorbonne (1898–1899). It was during these years that he turned away from formal religion as a field of study and as a matter of personal commitment, taking up history and ethical culture instead. He married Ina Jeannette Bullis on Sept. 20, 1900; they had two children.

In 1900 Muzzey had become associated with the Ethical Culture School in New York City, and maintained an interest in that society for many years, both as a teacher of Latin and Greek (1900–1903) and as a director. He joined the faculty at Columbia in 1905, teaching first at Barnard. Simultaneously, he pursued graduate work in history and received a Ph.D. in 1907. He became a member of the graduate faculty in 1923.

Muzzey lectured widely on ethical culture and consistently expressed the view that the future of mankind lay in the development of moral qualities. Accordingly he considered moral qualities necessary for an understanding of history. His stress on the importance of the individual, even in his general treatments of the American past, made the place of morality and right conduct a recurring point of reference.

In 1927, Muzzey was a member of an educational mission sent to Rumania by the Carnegie Endowment; ten years later he was Carnegie lecturer at the universities of Prague, Paris, and Edinburgh. In 1938 he was named the first holder of the Gouverneur Morris chair of American history at Columbia. He retired two years later. After his first wife died in 1934, Muzzey married J. Emilie Young on June 23, 1937.

Muzzey also lectured at the University of Chicago (1907), the University of California at Los Angeles and at Berkeley, and the University of London. He served as a member of the editorial board of *American Observer*, a weekly for high school teachers of American history, from 1914, and as an advisory editor of *Current History* from 1937 to 1945. He died in Yonkers, N.Y.

Muzzey wrote a number of books on ethical culture, among them *Spiritual Heroes* (1902), *The Spiritual Franciscans* (1907), and *Ethics as a Religion* (1951). In all of these he advocated humanistic idealism as a substitute for supernatural theology. But it was as the author of American-history textbooks for secondary schools and colleges that Muzzey made his mark and created a stir.

Particularly controversial was his high school text. Originally published in 1911 as *An American History* and later issued in 1939 under the title *History of Our Country*, it was one of the first such books to offer a realistic account of aspects of American history surrounded by legends. As a consequence Muzzey was often attacked as un-American. One complaint was based on the fact that only a single line had been given to the exploits of John Paul Jones. Others protested his descriptions of graft and corruption in Congress. He told one interviewer that he received letters every day, some challenging him to a duel, because his book had been insufficiently respectful of George Washington or Robert E. Lee or the Supreme Court.

After World War I, Muzzey was accused of being pro-British, which earned him the hostility of Mayor William Thompson of Chicago and the National Society of the Sons of the American Revolution. The Hearst papers carried cartoons depicting the foundations of a schoolhouse being gnawed away by a large rat labeled "Dr. Muzzey." Throughout such attacks he maintained his sense of humor and perspective.

Muzzey's college text, *The United States of America* (1924), narrowly escaped the label of history as past politics, but was a solid narrative nonetheless. The theme was the development of American democracy as it varied in size and direction, with steady attention to the rise of American nationalism. It was an account with a full cast of characters, some highly visible leaders and others obscure, but all with important parts to play. Muzzey explained that he sought "to give vividness to his narration by emphasizing the personality of the outstanding figures of the period (who, after all, make the history) and

letting them tell the story to a considerable extent in their own words." His text also attempted to assess the new economic and social forces affecting the United States in the industrial era.

In addition to his highly successful texts, Muzzey wrote biographies of Thomas Jefferson and James G. Blaine. The former, *Thomas Jefferson* (1918), was brief, impartial, but limited in interpretation. Jefferson's work as a political organizer and his image as a party man were especially emphasized. In *James G. Blaine: A Political Idol of Other Days* (1934) Muzzey returned to political biography, but on a more ambitious scale. His life of Blaine was a thorough exploration of one of the political "movers and shakers" of the Gilded Age, based on a full range of primary source material, vivid in narration and measured in judgments. Giving his subject a "faithful delineation" and seeking "neither to establish nor demolish any preconceived thesis," Muzzey concluded that the key to Blaine's successes and his failures was his party loyalty. The book received honorable mention by the Pulitzer Prize Board in 1935.

[The Columbiana Collection and the Rare Book and Manuscript Collection at Columbia University both contain primary material relating to Muzzey. Also useful are the *Fifth* and *Eighth Reports of the Class of 1893*, Harvard University Archives. An obituary is in the *New York Times*, Apr. 15, 1965.]

DAVID H. BURTON

NELSON, MARJORIE MAXINE (Dec. 24, 1909–Nov. 28, 1962), research anatomist and nutritional biochemist, was born in Kansas City, Mo., the daughter of Aubrey Orville Nelson, a manager for Swift and Company, and of Maude Mintz. Fascinated by science from an early age, she entered Whitman College in Walla Walla, Wash., in 1927, graduating in 1931 with an A.B. in chemistry. She then studied organic chemistry at the University of Washington at Seattle, from which she received a master's degree in 1936. Nelson's budding interest in chemical problems in biology next took her to the Institute of Experimental Biology (IEB) at the University of California in Berkeley, where in 1938 she became a research assistant to Herbert M. Evans and started her lifelong research on the role of various vitamins in reproduction and development.

After receiving the Ph.D. in 1944, Nelson remained on the large interdisciplinary research staff of the IEB, first as a research fellow, then as a research associate, and assistant and associate research biochemist. In 1958 the IEB was dismantled and the personnel were divided between the Department of Anatomy and Physiology on the Berkeley campus and the Department of Anatomy at the University of California Medical School in San Francisco. Although Nelson moved her laboratory to San Francisco, she retained the title of lecturer in both departments.

Nelson was extremely shy and suffered from a progressive loss of hearing. Despite her handicap, which she largely ignored, she was a lucid lecturer. She was a pedagogue in the best sense of the word. Her greatest ambition and pride was to be a good mentor, a role in which she obviously succeeded. Several of her students went on to head academic departments, a fact that highlights the irony that Nelson herself never had a professorial position. She never married.

Beginning in 1945, Nelson published a steady stream of more than 100 original research papers. Throughout her career she did most of her own laboratory work, which required her to be superbly organized, thorough, and persistent.

Much of Nelson's research dealt with the growth, reproduction, and lactation of rats maintained on purified diets. Using rats, she systematically determined the effect on the growth, maturation, and reproduction of nutritional deficiencies in the various B vitamins, protein, and a number of minerals. After eliminating any possible deleterious contributions by the genetic condition of the mother, she carefully cataloged the effects of specific deficiencies on the developing fetus. It was in this area that she made her greatest contribution. In 1950, Nelson discovered marked skeletal abnormalities in the fetuses of rats when the mother was deficient in folic acid, thus confirming and amplifying for another vitamin the already known teratogenic effect of vitamin A deficiency in pregnancy. Later she determined the teratogenic effects of other B vitamin and mineral deficiencies and those of low-protein diets.

Nelson thus demonstrated that there are limits to the well-known ability of the maternal organism to deplete itself in order to protect the fetus from the effects of malnutrition, a fact of the greatest importance for undernourished human populations. Most important, she further established that each nutritional factor is needed for a specific critical period in fetal development, and that even the most transitory deficiency can be highly teratogenic if it occurs at a critical time.

By feeding rats diets deficient in protein, minerals, or specific vitamins on the corresponding critical days of gestation, Nelson and her associates were able to experimentally produce in rats all types of birth defects known in humans. Her extensive nutritional data, together with data of others on teratogenic effects produced by toxic agents, such as viruses, demonstrated that birth defects were primarily nongenetic, although genetic factors might influence the outcome of exposure to a teratogenic substance.

In collaboration with H. M. Evans and his associates, Nelson attempted to use the experimental teratologies to pinpoint the biochemical reactions critical for any given step in embryogenesis. Thus, by determining whether certain metabolites, including hormones, could protect the fetus, conclusions could be drawn about the type of proteins or enzymes involved in that step. This is a difficult problem, and this work, although extensive, was not brought to full fruition. But she did show the interrelation between hormonal balance and nutritional requirements.

Nelson's work played a significant role in the burgeoning interest, starting in the early 1950's, in the effect of environmental factors, including nutrition, on fetal development. She was a charter member of the Teratology Society, its secretary-treasurer from 1960 to 1962, and its president-elect when she died in San Francisco.

[Important papers by Nelson are "Pteroylglutamic Acid and Reproduction in the Rat," *Journal of Nutrition*, 1949, with H. M. Evans; "Skeletal Abnormalities in the Rat Fetus Resulting from Pteroylglutamic ("Folic") Acid Deficiency During Gestations," *Anatomical Record*, 1950, with C. W. Ashing; "Mammalian Fetal Development and Antimetabolites," in *Antimetabolites and Cancer* (1955); "Congenital Defects and Nutrition," *Drug Trade News*, 1957; "Production of Congenital Anomalies in Mammals by Maternal Dietary Deficiencies," *Pediatrics*, 1957; "Effects of Hormone Imbalances on Dietary Requirements," *Vitamins and Hormones*, 1960, with J. Meites. Her curriculum vitae and complete list of publications are on file at the Department of Anatomy, University of California, San Francisco. A brief obituary is in the *New York Times*, Dec. 1, 1962.]

I. D. RAACKE

NELSON, NELS CHRISTIAN (Apr. 9, 1875–March 5, 1964), anthropologist, was born near Fredericia, Jutland, Denmark, the son of Soren Nelson, a farmer, and of Anne Kirstine Larsdatter. He received his early education by attending school during seasonal furloughs from farm chores. In 1892 he went to the United States and worked on his uncle's farm in Minnesota to repay the cost of his steerage ticket to New York. In order to continue his education, Nelson hired himself out to a farmer near Marshall, Minn., where he completed grammar and high school in five and one-half years, graduating in 1901.

Nelson worked his way to California by tending stock for a family moving there. In California he drove a six-mule team and then joined a hog-butchering crew until he had accumulated enough money to enroll in Stanford University (1901). There he began his studies in philosophy, but he transferred in 1903 to the University of California at Berkeley, where he received the B.L. in 1907 and the M.L. in the following year.

In 1906 Nelson accompanied a friend on an archaeological expedition in California. Immediately afterward he decided to become an anthropologist and commenced studies in that field. His research in the prehistoric archaeology of American Indians in the Southwest began while he was a student. In 1908 Nelson became field assistant with the U.S. Geological Survey. From 1909 to 1912 he served as assistant curator at the Museum of Anthropology at the University of California at Berkeley and was instructor in anthropology in 1910–1912. On Dec. 25, 1911, he married Ethelyn G. Field; they had no children.

In California, Nelson had worked under the anthropologist Pliny E. Goddard. Goddard brought Nelson to New York City in 1912 as assistant curator of prehistoric archaeology at the American Museum of Natural History. In the next years he took part in extensive excavations in the Castillo cave in Spain and at other European sites. He also continued his work in the United States, especially the Southwest, where he made his most notable contributions to archaeology. One of his important excavations was of the Pueblo ruins of the Galisteo Basin in New Mexico. He also investigated Mammoth Cave and its vicinity in Kentucky, as well as sites in Missouri and Florida.

In 1921 Nelson was appointed associate curator of North American archaeology at the American Museum, and two years later became associate curator of archaeology. He was archaeologist on the Central Asiatic Expedition of the American Museum, an interdisciplinary project led by Roy Chapman Andrews (1925–1927). That project took Nelson to sites in the Gobi Desert in Mongolia as well as to Szechwan and Yunnan provinces in China. During the winters, when excavation was halted, he sailed the Ch'ang Chiang (Yangtze) River, exploring

caves along the banks and surveying valleys of tributaries.

Between 1928 and his retirement in 1943, Nelson was curator of prehistoric archaeology at the American Museum, and in that position he was responsible for all the archaeological halls. His last field trip in 1941 took him to caves on the Crow Indian reservation in Montana. In 1943 he was named curator emeritus. Nelson died in New York City.

Nelson was one of a small group of archaeologists who, early in the twentieth century, developed scientific standards of modern archaeology. He was a pioneer in the use of stratigraphic techniques in southwestern archaeology. The stratigraphic method of excavation, now standard procedure, is based on the theory that artifacts are found in chronological layers, with the oldest stage of a culture represented in the layer furthest below the surface.

Through archaeology Nelson verified the hypothesis of age and area propounded by paleontologists and ethnologists. The premise is that human culture diffuses outward from a center of origin. Prehistoric pottery, found in great quantity in the Southwest, was a highly suitable test artifact, since it was the one most subject to change. Wherever Nelson excavated an apparent center for new ceramic design, he obtained sample framents from each stratum to chart the chronological evolution of styles. Shallow diggings at various distances from the center in several directions revealed a horizontal evolution of the same styles, showing the later emergence in distant areas of styles found at the center. These findings illustrated the outward spread of culture. Once Nelson had verified the principle of age and area, ethnologists applied it to hemispheres as well as to particular cultures.

Nelson published numerous articles in scientific journals and books, as well as in popular periodicals. He served as president of the American Ethnological Society and the Society for American Archaeology. He was vice-president of the New York Academy of Sciences and of the American Association for the Advancement of Science.

A quiet man devoted to his profession, Nelson was held in high esteem by his colleagues. Walter Granger, paleontologist on the Central Asiatic Expedition, said of him, "If I were going out on a desert island where I would have to be satisfied with the company of only one man, I'd choose him. The most wonderful thing about him, I think, is that he knows when to talk and when to keep quiet, and that is an art few people ever learn."

[Nelson's principal publications through 1938 are listed in Library of the American Museum of Natural History, *Research Catalogue: Authors,* IX (1977); the first was "Shellmounds of the San Francisco Bay Region," *University of California Publications in American Archaeology and Ethnology,* 1909. On his life and work, see D. R. Barton, "Mud, Stones, and History," *Natural History,* May 1941. Obituaries are in an unpublished American Museum of Natural History press release, "Nels C. Nelson, Prominent Archaeologist, Dies in New York City," Mar. 5, 1964; and the *New York Times,* Mar. 6, 1964.]

ADELE HAST

NEYLAND, ROBERT REESE, JR. (Feb. 17, 1892–Mar. 28, 1962), football coach and army officer, was born in Greenville, Tex., the son of Robert Reese, a lawyer, and of Pauline Lewis. His father wanted him to become a lawyer, but Neyland (usually pronounced Nā´land, although he claimed it should be Knee´land) later said that he was too shy to speak in public and therefore chose to become an engineer instead. After graduating from high school in Greenville, he attended Burleson College (1909–1910) and Texas A and M (1910–1911) before receiving an appointment in 1912 to the U.S. Military Academy. Neyland did not make the varsity football team as a plebe and could not play during his sophomore year because of his involvement in a hazing incident. But he played end on the 1914 and 1915 teams, became the heavyweight boxing champion of the academy, and excelled in baseball as a pitcher. His overall baseball record of thirty-five victories and five losses, twenty straight wins, and four victories over Navy brought him bonus offers from John McGraw of the New York Giants, Connie Mack of the Philadelphia Athletics, and other teams.

Neyland chose instead to pursue a military career, and upon graduation in 1916 he served with the Army Corps of Engineers along the Mexican border before going overseas with the Allied Expeditionary Force in 1917. After brief service in France he returned home in 1918 to become a training officer. In 1920 he entered Massachusetts Institute of Technology, from which he received the B.S. in civil engineering in 1921. Neyland then returned to West Point as an aide to the superintendent, General Douglas MacArthur, whom he later called "unquestionably the greatest officer and man I ever knew." He also was assistant coach in baseball, boxing, and football. He married Ada ("Peggy") Fitch on July 26, 1923. They had two sons.

It was a time of change in curriculum and athletics at West Point, but within a few years the "old guard" had beaten back the challenges to tradition and MacArthur had moved on. Neyland, in turn, decided to try coaching and in 1925 accepted a job with the University of Tennessee to head its Reserve Officers Training Corps (ROTC) program and to help upgrade its weak football program. By 1926 Neyland was head coach, and over the next nine years he developed teams that won seventy-five games and lost only twelve. He also continued to teach in the ROTC program until 1931 and, as a regular-army officer, he worked on what was later to become the Norris Dam.

In 1935 Neyland was assigned to serve with the Corps of Engineers in Panama. Unhappy with the post, he resigned from the army in 1936 and returned to coaching at Tennessee. He soon recruited an outstanding team that won thirty-three straight regular-season games. It held regular-season opponents scoreless in 1939 and brought national recognition to Tennessee. The team also played in several post-season bowl games. Ironically, although he helped give such games status, Neyland's teams had little success in them.

Neyland was recalled to active duty in 1941 and had various stateside assignments (including an unhappy time as coach of an Army All-Star football team) before he went overseas. Perhaps his most important assignment was as port officer for Calcutta, where he facilitated the movement of supplies in the China-Burma-India theater and developed a program of competitive athletics to maintain morale among Indian and American workers. He retired from the army in 1946 as a brigadier general.

When he returned to Tennessee in 1946, Neyland found conditions changed. It was an era of wide-open, T-formation, and free-substitution football. But he refused to change his system, retaining the older single-wing offense and requiring his athletes to play both offense and defense. Alumni displeasure and declining fortunes (Tennessee was 9–9–2 in 1947–1948) brought family pressure to retire. Instead, Neyland grudgingly accepted the free-substitution rule and led Tennessee to a 36–6–2 record in 1949–1952. The 1951 team was generally accepted as the best in the nation. But, never altering his views of what he called "rat-race football," Neyland worked quietly behind the scenes in 1953 as a member (and eventually chairman) of the NCAA Football Rules Committee to eliminate the free-substitution rule. The decision for elimination was later modified.

Plagued by a liver and kidney ailment that ultimately took his life, Neyland retired from coaching in 1953. He spent his remaining years as athletic director at Tennessee. He died in New Orleans and was buried in Knoxville.

Neyland was voted into the Helms Foundation Hall of Fame in 1956 and was given the Amos Alonzo Stagg Award by the American Football Coaches Association in 1955. His legacy at Tennessee included 173 wins, 31 losses, 12 ties, 6 won or shared conference championships, and national recognition to Tennessee as a football power. An expanded football stadium was renamed in his honor.

Neyland received many offers to coach at other schools, but Tennessee made sure he never left Knoxville. The success of his teams brought prestige to the university and increased revenues to support his expanding athletic program. With the support of the university administration and an active athletic council, Neyland was a quiet but forceful leader on campus. Yet there were claims that his priorities held back development of other parts of the university.

Neyland's contributions to football were legion. He developed a number of All-American players and took pride in the many alumni who went into coaching. All aspects of the game were subject to his detailed examination. He developed effective recruiting techniques and took good care of the athletes through financial support, separate dormitories, improved training facilities, and tutoring services. He experimented with improved helmets, lighter padding, "tearaway jerseys," "low cut" shoes, and even a cover for the football field. Neyland was one of the first to use films of both his team's and future opponents' performances for training purposes. Early in his career he introduced the press-box observer (legend has it he originally stood on an upper floor of a nearby building) in direct phone communication with the coach on the bench.

Neyland was often called the greatest defensive coach in the country. Although he eschewed what were later called "specialty teams," his players were drilled in the timing and execution of punts, kickoffs, and kick-return strategies. Once he tried to write down his rules for football; characteristically he could come up with only four offensive principles while listing twenty different guidelines for the defense.

Committed to the simple, power football of his brand of the single wing, Neyland's offensive teams relied on nearly perfect execution of a limited number of running plays, occasional pass patterns, and crisp blocking. He stressed meticulous planning to take advantage of opponents' mistakes and the importance of mental as well as physical preparation for the game. Although he was a powerful presence in the locker room, Neyland claimed that last-minute histrionics by coaches probably did more harm than good. He did not attend clinics, lecture, or write about football, yet he freely shared his knowledge with contemporaries who sought him out.

Neyland had little time for "public relations." He refused to be interviewed on radio or television, made few public appearances, and discouraged attempts to write about his career. As a consequence he was not well known nationally and seemed to the public to be aloof, self-assured, and something of a tyrant. Neyland's military background was always present in his bearing, his delegation of authority to subordinates (and expectations of their accomplishments), and his drillmaster preparation of his teams. His players both feared and respected him and in later years spoke with affection of his demands for discipline, hard work, and commitment to the team. He kept his professional duties separate from his private life, where he was to his close friends the genial host, the conversationalist, and an avid bridge player and fisherman.

Neyland was one of a small group who made football coaching and athletic administration respected professions and who gave organization and national scope to what had been a more casual game dominated by a few eastern and midwestern universities.

[Because of his passion for privacy, there is limited material on Neyland. Some information may be found in the files of the Sports Information Office, University of Tennessee. Also see Neyland's article in the *Saturday Evening Post*, Nov. 17, 1951; and Tom Siler, *Tennessee: Football's Greatest Dynasty* (1960) and *Tennessee's Dazzling Decade, 1960–1970* (1970). An obituary is in the *New York Times*, Mar. 29, 1962.]

DANIEL R. GILBERT

NICHOLSON, SETH BARNES (Nov. 12, 1891–July 2, 1963), astronomer, was born in Springfield, Ill., the son of William Franklin Nicholson, a school principal and farmer, and of Martha Ames. Although encouraged to study science by his father, who had a master's degree in geology, he did not become intensely interested in astronomy until he entered Drake University in Des Moines, Iowa, in 1908. He studied astronomy with D. W. Morehouse, best known for his 1908 discovery of the exceptionally bright comet that bears his name. As an undergraduate Nicholson devoted his research time to comets and minor planets. In 1911 he and a fellow astronomy student, Alma Stotts, published a report of the computed orbit of the minor planet Ekard, discovered in 1909. Nicholson also was a physics instructor during his senior year.

Nicholson graduated from Drake in 1912 and then was appointed a fellow in the graduate program in astronomy at the University of California at Berkeley. Alma Stotts entered the program at the same time, and they were married on May 29, 1913. They had three children. Beginning in the fall of 1913, Nicholson was instructor in astronomy at Berkeley for two years. He received the Ph.D. in 1915.

In 1914, while serving as an assistant at the Lick Observatory, Nicholson was directed to observe the recently discovered eighth satellite of Jupiter. He took an unusually long exposure of Jupiter VIII to insure a superior photographic plate, and discovered yet another Jovian satellite at approximately the same distance from the planet. Calculating the orbital characteristics of Jupiter IX provided Nicholson with his doctoral dissertation. In 1938 he again observed Jupiter (this time with the 100-inch Mt. Wilson telescope) in an attempt to reconfirm the discoveries of the nine known moons. Upon developing his large collection of plates, he discovered two new satellites, raising the total to eleven. In 1951, while observing Jupiter X, he discovered a twelfth moon, thus becoming, with Galileo, one of the two astronomers to have discovered four Jovian satellites.

After completing his doctorate Nicholson joined the staff of the Mt. Wilson Observatory. Because this facility was devoted primarily to solar research during its early years, much of his work focused on the sun. Working with George Ellery Hale and other solar astronomers, he conducted long-term studies of solar spectra and surface features, providing an excellent record of sunspots and other solar phenomena. Later, with Harlow Shapley, Nicholson investigated the spectral patterns of Cepheid variables and collaborated with Walter Baade and Edwin Hubble in similar studies of several spiral galaxies. These observations added significant weight to the concept of spiral nebulae as "island universes."

During the 1920's and 1930's Nicholson labored with Edison Pettit to adapt the vacuum thermocouple to measure temperatures of astronomical bodies. They used their new technique to establish the lower temperature of sunspots (compared with the solar surface), the low density of the Martian atmosphere, and the high surface temperature of Mercury. They also made extensive measurements of the rapid changes in the moon's surface temperatures during lunar eclipses, providing significant information about its surface and subsurface structure.

Although primarily a research scientist, Nicholson was active in the dissemination of astronomical knowledge. Between 1911 and 1963 he published 267 articles in scientific periodicals. He often lectured at the University of California during the summer and, after his retirement in 1957, served as western coordinator for the visiting professors program of the National Science Foundation and American Astronomical Association. He was always in demand as a speaker because of his rare ability to present recent astronomical discoveries in a manner comprehensible to laymen.

Nicholson served two terms as president of the Astronomical Society of the Pacific (1935, 1960) and edited its *Publications* from 1940 to 1955. He was chairman of the astronomy section of the American Association for the Advancement of Science in 1944 and a member of the International Astronomical Union. In 1937 he was elected to the National Academy of Sciences.

In June 1963 the Astronomical Society of the Pacific awarded Nicholson the Catherine Bruce Gold Medal for his many achievements. Although severely ill at the time, he listened to the award ceremonies via a special telephone link between the San Diego meeting and his hospital room in Los Angeles, where he died.

[Nicholson's most important articles include "Discovery, Observations and Orbit of the Ninth Satellite of Jupiter," *Lick Observatory Bulletin*, Feb. 1915; "The Application of Vacuum Thermocouples to Problems in Astrophysics," *Astrophysical Journal*, Nov. 1922, with Edison Pettit; "The Satellites of Jupiter," *Publications of the Astronomical Society of the Pacific*, Apr. 1939; "Short-Period Fluctuation in Solar Activity," *Astronomical Journal*, June 1955. A good biographical sketch, with a complete bibliography, is Paul Herget, "Seth Barnes Nicholson," *Biographical Memoirs. National Academy of Sciences*, 1971. An obituary is in the *New York Times*, July 3, 1963.]

GEORGE ERNEST WEBB

NIEBUHR, HELMUT RICHARD (Sept. 3, 1894–July 5, 1962), theologian and educator, was born in Wright City, Mo., the son of Gustav Niebuhr, a minister in the German Evangelical Synod of North America, and of Lydia Hosto, the daughter of a German pastor. His sister Hulda was for many years professor of Christian education at McCormick Theological

Seminary in Chicago and his brother Reinhold was professor of applied Christianity at Union Theological Seminary in New York City.

The Niebuhr home combined German culture, Protestant faith, and a desire to enter wholeheartedly into American life. Art, music, and literature were emphasized, along with theological discussion and daily Bible readings (often in Greek and Hebrew). In addition to this intellectual milieu, the parents cultivated a deep sense of moral and religious responsibility in their children. Thus it was no surprise when Niebuhr chose to follow his father and brother into the ministry of the German Evangelical Church.

In 1908, Niebuhr enrolled at Elmhurst College, his denomination's school near Chicago. He received a B.A. in 1912, and went on to graduate from Eden Theological Seminary at Webster Groves, Mo., in 1915. He then worked briefly for the local newspaper in Lincoln, Ill. In 1916 he was ordained and for two years was the pastor of the Walnut Park Evangelical Church, St. Louis. While serving there Niebuhr took an M.A. in history at Washington University (1917). In 1919, he returned to Eden Seminary as a teacher of theology and ethics. On June 9, 1920, he married Florence Marie Mittendorff; they had two children.

During the summer of 1921, Niebuhr studied at the University of Chicago, where he was influenced by George Herbert Mead's social philosophy and psychology. His desire for further academic work was strong, and he returned to full-time study of theology at Yale Divinity School in 1922. He obtained a B.D. (1923) and a Ph.D. (1924) at Yale, while serving a Congregational church in Clinton, Conn. After receiving the Ph.D., Niebuhr became president of Elmhurst College for three years, helping the institution to receive full accreditation during his tenure.

In 1927, Niebuhr again returned to the faculty of Eden Seminary. There he wrote *The Social Sources of Denominationalism* (1929), the first of the major works on which his reputation rests. This book emerged from Niebuhr's doctoral dissertation, "Ernst Troeltsch's Philosophy of Religion." Appropriating Troeltsch's focus on historical relativity and cultural conditioning, Niebuhr argued that sociological factors were more decisive than doctrinal principles in accounting for the variety of denominations in America. The study also displayed the theological method that would govern Niebuhr's thought: a combination of careful historical analysis, critical exploration of alternative ways

to formulate issues, and creative synthesis leading to an original view.

Niebuhr's multidisciplinary approach to theology, incorporating insights from history, sociology, psychology, and philosophy, was one of his most innovative contributions to religious thought, but in the early 1930's his theological position was still in the making. Although attracted to Troeltsch and other German liberal theologians, particularly as their thinking resonated in the Social Gospel movement, Niebuhr sensed that such views were overly optimistic and lacking in theological depth. A 1930 sabbatical in Germany gave him time to develop these intuitions by studying the work of Karl Barth and Paul Tillich. The latter thinker became especially significant for him, and Niebuhr introduced Tillich's thought to American readers by translating *Die religiöse Lage der Gegenwart* (*The Religious Situation*) in 1932.

Upon completing his doctorate in 1924, Niebuhr had been asked to teach at Yale Divinity School. Now, as he returned from Europe, Yale made another offer, this time of an associate professorship of Christian ethics. He accepted for the fall semester of 1931. An admired mentor, Niebuhr was promoted to professor in 1938 and to the Sterling professorship of theology and Christian ethics in 1954.

Niebuhr was a dedicated churchman. Thus, if *The Social Sources of Denominationalism* held that compromise characterized the church's relation to the world, the sequels to that work increasingly emphasized the church's unique role within society. For instance, in collaboration with Wilhelm Pauck and Francis P. Miller, Niebuhr published *The Church Against the World* (1935). This work cautioned the church against domination by capitalism, nationalism, and shallow humanism. More important, *The Kingdom of God in America* (1937) reassessed Niebuhr's earlier treatment of American Protestantism.

Without relaxing his belief that social forces are crucial in accounting for denominational variety, the latter book focused on the theological convictions that had stimulated religious fervor in America. Specifically, Niebuhr found that a fundamental theme, "the kingdom of God," not only proved indispensable for explaining religious pluralism in American life but also revealed important elements of unity within the diversity.

Puritan views dominated early theology in America, Niebuhr argued. The Puritan vision of the kingdom of God emphasized divine sovereignty, but that emphasis went into eclipse in the nineteenth century as a more evangelical mood equated the kingdom with the reign of Christ. Even more recently, Niebuhr asserted, the Social Gospel had promoted a third vision in which the kingdom of God would arrive on earth through transformation of society.

Blending cultural analysis and theological construction, Niebuhr observed that each of these motifs had energized America's religious life for a time. But their vitality waned, and stagnation followed. The problem, Niebuhr believed, was to keep these three sound theological themes from becoming separate and isolated. By holding them together in a dialectical tension, Christianity would always be in ferment and on the move.

Continuing on from a perspective that stressed culture's influence on Christianity to one that underscored the impact of Christian theology on society, Niebuhr's next major effort was *The Meaning of Revelation* (1941). In it he advanced the thesis that history, the context of revelation, must be viewed in two ways. As external, history is a process open to objective study. Within this viewpoint there will be no revelation. Considered as internal, though, history is experienced as personal. Christians relate to the biblical tradition in that spirit. They testify that its illumination gives meaning to their lives and to all of history. The Christian community's experience of God in Christ, Niebuhr proclaimed, reveals the relativistic qualities of human existence. In doing so, that same experience drives home the conviction that an encounter with the absolute God, who invites human trust and devotion, has occurred.

During World War II Niebuhr plunged into deep depression. But after the war came *Christ and Culture* (1951), probably the most widely read of his books. It describes five different relationships between human civilization and the lordship of Christ. First, the view that a Christian should simply stand against culture is opposed by the claim that a Christian should accommodate to culture's ways. Between these two extremes Niebuhr located three mediating positions. One entails a synthesis that affirms both Christ and culture in such a way that Christ stands above culture as source and norm for all the good that civilization seeks. Another option leaves Christ and culture in a paradoxical relationship. This dualistic version of Christianity accentuates Martin Luther's teaching that the Christian is both justified and sinful. Moreover, the world is fallen and under judgment, yet God sustains the Christian in and through it. The last position described by Niebuhr, conver-

sionist Christianity, was the one he advocated. Christ is pictured as transforming culture. Ongoing interaction between God and humanity, Niebuhr believed, can redirect history. The world is redeemable.

Niebuhr's analysis implied that the church and theological education needed transformation; but he was also convinced that those cultural institutions were vital for a creative redirecting of history. Thus, in 1954–1955, Niebuhr coordinated a study of theological education in Canada and the United States. Joining with Daniel Day Williams to edit the results, Niebuhr published *The Ministry in Historical Perspectives* (1956). It was followed by *The Purpose of the Church and Its Ministry* (1956), which reemphasized Niebuhr's view that theology deals not with God in isolation but with the relations between God and human beings, and by *The Advancement of Theological Education* (1957), written with Williams and James M. Gustafson.

Throughout the 1950's Niebuhr studied the nature of human faith. From his many lectures he developed a large manuscript entitled "Faith on Earth: Essays on Human Confidence and Loyalty." A portion of this work, along with some previous essays, appeared in 1960 as *Radical Monotheism and Western Culture*, the last book Niebuhr published.

This volume argued that polytheism and henotheism are humanity's natural religious persuasions. That is, human existence entails both loyalty and trust, but typically we honor diffuse and competing "gods" or we concentrate on some single finite cause or goal, bestowing upon it an ultimate concern that it neither deserves nor can sustain. In place of these dangerous natural tendencies, Niebuhr urged a radically monotheistic faith. Its vision of a God who is infinite in power, value, and love, he affirmed, not only legitimately fills humanity's yearnings for community and meaning but also keeps those yearnings within a perspective that checks fanaticism, idolatry, and stagnation.

The faith of radical monotheism would be indispensable in forming the "fitting response" that Niebuhr defended in his last years as he elaborated his understanding of Christian ethics. His comprehensive study of ethics was never completed, but glimpses of it are available in *The Responsible Self* (posthumously published in 1963), which contains Niebuhr's Robertson lectures at the University of Glasgow (1960) and his Earl lectures at the Pacific School of Religion (1962). Christian responsibility, Niebuhr argued, should be understood less in terms of "the good" or "the right" and more as a "fitting response" to God. This response requires making choices based on fallible interpretations of complex social circumstances. But in the midst of our existential ambiguity, Niebuhr showed, there are basic patterns that ought to guide decisions about what God desires from us in particular situations. Niebuhr died unexpectedly in Greenfield, Mass.

Niebuhr taught and wrote in the heyday of twentieth-century theology. Karl Barth, Paul Tillich, Emil Brunner, Rudolf Bultmann, and his own brother Reinhold were his contemporaries. Perhaps he was not their equal in every respect, but he certainly deserves to be classed with them. Drawing skillfully on such thinkers as Søren Kierkegaard, Friedrich Schleiermacher, and Josiah Royce, Niebuhr added social-science insights to produce a distinctive theological outlook.

If Niebuhr stressed a confessional stance that is less in vogue now than in his own day, his theology also emphasized perpetual reformation as a guiding principle. He would let no one forget that Christianity existed within society, and he remains one of the most perceptive analysts of American religious history. His evaluation of Christianity in the United States convinced him that Christian faith everywhere had to keep attuned to the God who could free it from cultural enslavement. To the degree that Christian communities made the "fitting response," they could spark a transformation that would bring the world closer to the kingdom of God. Thus, if adjectives such as existential, confessional, relativistic, and cultural are necessary for describing Niebuhr's religious thought, no less accurate are terms such as theocentric, communal, ethical, and universalistic.

Niebuhr will not be remembered for any theological system, but that fact does not detract from his continuing relevance; his greatest contribution may have been his way of doing theology. His style moves back and forth, between society and human encounters with the ultimate, in a spirit that seeks to turn rigidity into openness, misplaced absoluteness into creative relativity, and the vicissitudes of history into movements of responsible faith.

[Among the best studies of Niebuhr's life and thought are Clyde A. Holbrook, "H. Richard Niebuhr," in *A Handbook of Christian Theologians*, edited by Martin E. Marty and Dean G. Peerman (1965); John D. Godsey, *The Promise of H. Richard Niebuhr* (1970); James W. Fowler, *To See the Kingdom* (1974); and Lonnie D. Kliever, *H. Richard Niebuhr* (1977). Books that place Niebuhr within twentieth-century Protestant theology and American religious thought, respectively, are John B. Cobb, Jr., *Living Options in Protestant Theology* (1962); and Frederick Sontag and John K. Roth, *The American Religious Experience* (1972). Helpful bibliographical information can be found in Paul Ramsey, ed., *Faith and Ethics: The Theology of H. Richard Niebuhr* (1957). An obituary is in the *New York Times*, July 6, 1962.]

JOHN K. ROTH

NORDEN, CARL LUKAS (Apr. 23, 1880–June 15, 1965), mechanical engineer and inventor, was born in Semarang, Java, the son of Edward Norden, a prosperous merchant, and Cornelia Gersen. When Norden was five, his father died, and his mother returned with the family to the Netherlands. Norden received his primary education at Nijmegen and Apeldoorn, and from 1893 to 1896 attended the Royal Art Academy at Dresden, Germany. Since his family had already undertaken the support of his older brother's art career, Norden decided that his pursuit of a similar path would be a financial burden. Therefore, in 1897 he apprenticed himself to an instrument maker in Zurich, Switzerland. In 1900 he entered the Federal Institute of Technology in Zurich and graduated four years later with a degree in mechanical engineering.

Recognizing America's congenial climate for engineers and inventors, Norden emigrated in 1904, shortly after his graduation. On Apr. 11, 1907, he married Else Fehring, daughter of a well-to-do German businessman. They had two children. Norden worked at first for two Brooklyn manufacturers, H. R. Worthington Pump and Machine Works, and J. H. Lidgerwood Manufacturing Company, a producer of mine hoists. It was at the latter firm that Norden probably met Lidgerwood subcontractor Elmer Sperry, an established inventor and engineer. In 1911, Sperry offered Norden a job on the research and development staff of Sperry Gyroscope Company.

Norden and Sperry maintained a productive, if somewhat stormy, professional relationship for four years—Norden was twenty years Sperry's junior—and was partial to smoking what Sperry labeled "those vile black cigars." Norden resigned several times from Sperry Gyroscope, only to return the following morning to his work on gyrostabilizers as if nothing out of the ordinary had occurred. While associated with Sperry, his research helped to bring the gyroscope from an embryonic stage of development to a reliability sufficient for naval use.

Norden considered Sperry's offer of a $25-a-week raise in recognition of this effort to be an insult. He resigned permanently in 1915 and set up his own company. Nevertheless, he continued to work as a paid consultant with Sperry on naval gyrostabilizer assignments until 1917, despite continuous disagreement with Sperry over who should have patent rights to the stabilizer.

From 1918 through the end of World War II, Norden worked closely with the U.S. Navy. Initially he concentrated on designing a stable gun platform and a radio-controlled aircraft to serve as a prototype for a flying bomb. The aircraft was to be launched by catapult. It would shed its wings during flight and be transformed into a guided missile with Norden-designed radio controls. Although this device ultimately reached the practical stage, the military never used it in combat because officials considered it an inhuman and undiscriminating weapon against civilian populations. Its controls, though, served as the forerunner of an automatic pilot mechanism that became an integral part of the Norden bombsight used during World War II.

After World War I, the Naval Bureau of Ordnance asked Norden to design a device for dropping bombs from aircraft onto moving ships. Norden started work on it in 1921. Two years later, he took on a partner, Theodore H. Barth, a former army colonel trained in chemical warfare techniques. Together Norden and Barth formed Carl L. Norden, Inc. in 1928, with Barth as president and Norden as consultant. The assistant research chief of the Naval Bureau of Ordnance, Captain Frederick I. Entwhistle, joined Norden and Barth shortly after the company's establishment. All three men participated in the bombsight design and shared patent rights.

While Norden worked at a drawing board—often in Zurich—Barth assembled most of the models in his New York City apartment. Carl L. Norden, Inc., produced its first bombsight in 1927. The first models were not particularly accurate, but by 1931 the Mark XV had been developed. It would remain essentially unchanged throughout World War II.

The Norden bombsight has been called one of the two major secret weapons of the American effort in World War II. Unlike the Manhattan Project, which was kept secret even from most government and military officials, the bombsight's existence was known to most Americans, although until 1944 practically no one outside the military had even seen a picture of the device and its design remained a closely guarded secret. The plant that produced bombsights required 350 guards at all times. Two personal bodyguards accompanied Norden constantly, and bombardiers who operated the ninety-pound instrument took an oath to destroy it if they were captured.

The bombsight could place a bomb inside a 100-foot circle from an altitude of two miles. Bombardiers boasted that they could hit a pickle barrel from 10,000 feet. The sight combined an optical device, a gyroscope, and a computer. It required the bombardier to make only three manual adjustments—for the bomb's weight, and the plane's altitude and speed—after which he would line up the target through the sight. The autopilot kept the plane on course and the bombs released automatically. Earlier Norden designs of the gyrostabilizer corrected for the plane's drift, maintained altitude once set, and adjusted for aircraft control and speed changes.

Norden had developed his bombsight for the navy but, ironically, that military branch never used it. Naval bombing occurred at low altitudes and the Norden bombsight was impractical below 1,800 feet. The Army Air Corps, though, used the device extensively in raids over Germany and in the atomic attacks against Japan. Its reliability allowed daytime precision bombing missions, considered a more humane form of military activity than the nighttime saturation bombing practiced by British and German forces. Nicknamed "the football" by European Theater bombardiers and "the blue ox" (from the Paul Bunyan legend) by Pacific Theater bombardiers, the 2,000-part bombsights cost $10,000 each during the war. By the mid-1960's they were selling for about $25 at surplus stores.

Norden designed numerous other military devices. He developed catapults and arresting gears for the World War II aircraft carriers *Lexington* and *Saratoga*, the first hydraulically controlled aircraft landing gears, and a device that linked his bombsight with an automatic pilot, leaving crew members free to watch for enemy fighters while over target areas.

After World War II Carl L. Norden, Inc., became Norden Laboratories Corporation, a research and development firm. In 1951 the company established Norden Instruments, Inc., as a production subsidiary. Norden and Barth became less active in company affairs, Norden retiring to Switzerland and Barth to Cape Cod, Mass. (In 1955 Norden Laboratories merged with Ketay Instrument Company; three years later this company was acquired by United Aircraft and renamed the Norden Division.)

Norden considered himself a designer rather than an inventor. He had an active interest in painting, especially the works of seventeenth-century Dutch masters. Believing that one did not have the right to change the citizenship to which one was born, he remained a Dutch citizen and an active member of the Netherlands Club of New York City. A Swedenborgian in religious views, he became a trustee of the Swedenborg Foundation of New York City.

Norden preferred a cloistered existence. Despite his significant public role he eschewed public appearances, making a rare exception in November 1944 to accept the Holley Medal of the American Society of Mechanical Engineers, given in recognition of "great and unique engineering genius." He revealed in his acceptance speech that all his patent rights for models and designs had been turned over to the United States government for $1 each. Norden died in Zurich, Switzerland.

[Norden's son, Carl F. Norden, has a substantial collection of letters exchanged between his father and his business partner, Theodore Barth. The General Services Administration, National Archives and Records Service, has Bureau of Ordnance Record Group 74, which contains materials on Norden and the bombsight development in 1920–1943. The Office of the Secretary of the Navy, General Services Administration, National Archives and Records Service, and the Naval Historical Center of the Washington Navy Yard have information on Norden, the bombsight, and pertinent government organizations. Articles on Norden's inventions are referenced in *Applied Science and Technology Index* and in *Engineering Index.* Also see Thomas Parke Hughes, *Elmer Sperry: Inventor and Engineer* (1971). An obituary is in the *New York Times,* June 16, 1965.]

CANDICE DALRYMPLE

OBERHOLSER, HARRY CHURCH (June 25, 1870–Dec. 25, 1963), ornithologist, was born in Brooklyn, N.Y., the son of Jacob Oberholser, a dry-goods merchant, and Lavera Church. After attending local schools he entered Columbia University in 1888, but was compelled to withdraw in 1891 because of poor health. His parents had moved to Wooster, Ohio, and Oberholser clerked in his father's dry-goods store there until 1895. That year he was appointed an ornithological clerk in the Division of Economic Ornithology of the U.S. Department of Agriculture, beginning a forty-six-year government career. In 1896 this agency became the Bureau of Biological Survey, and in 1939 it was combined with the U.S. Fish Commission to form the Fish and Wildlife Service in the Department of the Interior.

For the first fifteen years Oberholser worked under C. Hart Merriam, a major American authority on the speciation and geographical distribution of birds and mammals. Oberholser's principal duties entailed the identification of thousands of birds sent to the bureau. Soon he was being called as an expert witness to identify parts of birds from feathers or bones being used as evidence in trials for alleged violation of federal game laws.

In matters of classification, Oberholser was a dedicated "splitter"—one who based differences between subspecies of birds on very fine physical distinctions—long after "lumping" (the grouping of birds in much broader categories) had come into vogue. No mean authority on nomenclature, Merriam once said that Oberholser thought himself "God, Jesus Christ and the Holy Trinity when it comes to identifying birds."

During his career Oberholser was responsible for reporting 11 new families and subfamilies of birds, 99 new genera and subgenera, and 560 new species and subspecies. His scientific papers totaled nearly 900. He belonged to forty scientific and conservation organizations in various parts of the world.

Most of Oberholser's fieldwork was done between 1895 and 1903, principally in the West. His lifelong interest in Texas bird life began with a biological reconnaissance of the state that he made in 1900 with Vernon Bailey. A persistent stomach disorder ended Oberholser's career in the field, although he later made brief field investigations in several eastern and midwestern states (1917–1926). He was appointed assistant biologist for the Biological Survey in 1914, biologist in 1924, and senior biologist in 1928.

Oberholser received the B.A. and M.S. from George Washington University in 1914 and the Ph.D. in 1916. He married Mary Forrest Smith on June 30, 1914. They had no children. From 1904 until 1910 he spent his summers in North Carolina as professor of zoology at the Biltmore Forest Summer School. From 1920 to 1935 he held a similar post in the graduate program at American University.

Oberholser produced a 3-million-word monograph on the birds of Texas that remained unpublished at his death. A much-cut version of this work, *The Bird Life of Texas,* edited by Edgar B. Kincaid, Jr., and others, appeared in 1974. *Bird Life of Louisiana* (1938) was the most important work Oberholser published during his lifetime.

Oberholser's retirement from government service in 1941 was delayed for a year beyond the statutory age of seventy so that he could finish his Texas bird manuscript. He then became curator of ornithology at the Cleveland Museum of Natural History, where he served until 1947. He died in Cleveland.

Oberholser was a dedicated worker who insisted on a high output from his subordinates and maintained exacting standards of performance. While often interested in the work being done by colleagues, he frequently seemed chary about sharing what he knew with others. Nevertheless, he was capable of taking considerable time with younger workers when they faced serious problems.

[Oberholser's papers, chiefly correspondence from the period 1920–1947, are in the Manuscript Division of the Library of Congress. A number of letters from Oberholser to Witmer Stone (1894–1937) are at the Academy of Natural Sciences of Philadelphia. Other Oberholser materials are in the American Ornithologists Union records, also at the Academy of Natural Sciences of Philadelphia. Some of Oberholser's correspondence and research notes, and biographical sketches relative to his careers with the Biological Survey and Cleveland Museum of Natural History, are in the Western Reserve Historical Society collections, Cleveland, which also contain a file of Oberholser's published articles. A small group of materials dealing with Oberholser is included in the American Ornithologists Union Collection, Smithsonian Institution Archives. Candid impressions of Oberholser and other Biological Survey personnel are in the Waldo Lee McAtee Papers in the Manuscript Division of the Library of Congress. For accounts of Oberholser, see the *New York Times* obituary, Dec. 26, 1963; and John W. Aldrich, "In Memoriam: Harry Church Oberholser," *Auk,* Jan. 1968.]

KEIR B. STERLING

O'BRIEN, WILLIS HAROLD (Mar. 2, 1886– Nov. 8, 1962), pioneer stop-action film animator, was born in Oakland, Calif., the son of William Henry O'Brien and Minnie Gregg. His father directed a military academy and was assistant district attorney in Oakland, but fell on hard times early in O'Brien's life. At thirteen O'Brien quit school, left home, and pursued a succession of occupations for the next four years: hand on chicken and cattle ranches, trapper, wilderness guide, and bartender.

At age seventeen, while working as a draftsman, O'Brien became interested in cartooning. Eventually he worked as a sports cartoonist for the *San Francisco Daily News.* Covering boxing for the paper, he developed an intense interest in the sport, and embarked on a brief career as a professional boxer. He lost his first major fight, quit the ring, and began working for the South-

ern Pacific Railroad. He quickly became unhappy with this job, and finally settled down to work for a stonecutter in San Francisco. His major responsibility was modeling fireplaces in clay; stonecutters later used his models to create fireplaces of marble.

O'Brien, always restless, began modeling small clay prizefighters. The relatively new art of the cinema fascinated O'Brien, and he started to study conventional animation techniques, which consisted of drawing series of individual pictures. He came to believe that a more realistic effect would be achieved if the films could be produced by using pliable, miniature figures of clay over wood framing. He began work on a test film using a small clay dinosaur and a "caveman." For this one-minute film O'Brien exposed each frame individually and then slightly altered the position of each model, achieving the cinematic illusion of movement.

Herman Wobber, who exhibited films in San Francisco, heard of the experiment and advanced O'Brien $5,000 to develop a longer film for commercial distribution. O'Brien worked for more than two months on the film, *The Dinosaur and the Missing Link,* and late in 1915 Wobber began the search for a distributor. Eventually the five-minute film was purchased by the Edison Company, and O'Brien went to New York to produce additional films for Edison's "Conquest Programs." Forming Manikin Films, he worked for Edison from 1916 until late 1917, when the Edison firm was sold. Although his association with Edison was brief, O'Brien gained valuable experience, handling virtually every creative and technical element of the seven films he produced there.

O'Brien returned to Oakland and married Hazel Ruth Collette late in 1917. They had two sons. Shortly after his marriage O'Brien collaborated with producer Herbert M. Dawley on a lengthy film, *The Ghost of Slumber Mountain* (1919). The film earned $100,000 against costs of only $3,000, and represented a significant advance for O'Brien. The dinosaurs created for the project were the most lifelike he had ever produced. The partnership was brief, though, for upon completion of the film Dawley attempted to claim complete credit. Worse, he obtained patent rights to the processes and models O'Brien had created—but O'Brien later demonstrated his ownership of the stop-action techniques.

O'Brien began to look for new projects and soon met Watterson Rothacker, a producer of advertising films who had secured rights to Arthur Conan Doyle's *The Lost World.* The pair sold the idea to First National Pictures. Realizing that production of the film would be a major project beyond the capabilities of a single animator, the two assembled a crew that included Marcel Delgado, Ralph Hammeras, and Arthur Edeson. The film was released in 1925 and was an enormous success. *The Lost World* combined animation and live action, a process that O'Brien had helped to develop at Edison, and the film is still considered a cinema landmark.

After two projects fell through—one was an animated version of *Frankenstein*—O'Brien left First National and went to Radio-Keith-Orpheum (RKO) in 1929. He was just in time to begin work with directors Merian C. Cooper and Ernest B. Schoedsack on a major and spectacular film about a giant ape, eventually entitled *King Kong* (1933). O'Brien's special-effects work achieved unprecedented realism by combining actors and animated miniatures. The models he designed had mechanisms that allowed them to "breathe," and the several "Kongs" used in the picture exhibited remarkably anthropomorphic mannerisms and facial expressions.

O'Brien undoubtedly would have garnered an Academy Award for special effects, but the category was not recognized during this era. He was finally honored with an Oscar for his work on *Mighty Joe Young* (1949), another film about a great ape.

The release of *King Kong* was the high point of O'Brien's career. His personal and professional lives became a series of tragedies and disappointments shortly thereafter. On Oct. 7, 1933, while O'Brien was arguing with Schoedsack and Cooper over the production of *Son of Kong* (1933), his wife, from whom he was estranged, shot and killed their sons and attempted suicide. She had been suffering from tuberculosis and cancer, and after her failed suicide she remained in the hospital for more than a year before dying on Nov. 16, 1934. O'Brien married Dolly Darlyne Prenett the next day.

After *King Kong* O'Brien worked on numerous films but never again enjoyed the complete freedom he had been given on that picture. He developed several film stories and worked without credit on a few films, including *This Is Cinerama* (1952) and a remake of *The Lost World* (1960). The latter was a major disappointment because the producers elected to use live lizards and miniature sets rather than the more expensive animation process. O'Brien was signed to assist in the animated sequences of *It's A Mad, Mad, Mad, Mad World* (1963), but

soon discovered that he had no real work to do. The producers wanted only the prestige of his name. He died at Hollywood, Calif., while the film was in production, and was not credited.

While a few others had used stop-action before O'Brien (Georges Méliès worked with the process prior to 1900), he is credited with developing the technique to an unequaled level of realism. He also worked with and greatly influenced several young special-effects artists who later made major contributions to the art, notably Marcel Delgado, Linwood Dunn, and the widely acclaimed Ray Harryhausen.

[See "Monsters in Miniature," *American Magazine*, Oct. 1950; Don Shay, "Willis O'Brien: Creator of the Impossible," *Focus on Film*, Autumn 1973; Orville Goldner and George Turner, *The Making of King Kong* (1975); and "Miniature Effects Shots," in Ronald Gottesman and Harry Geduld, eds., *The Girl in the Hairy Paw* (1976). Less reliable sources are a special section on O'Brien in *Famous Monsters of Filmland*, Apr. 1963; and E. K. Everett, "Willis O'-Brien, the Man Who Loved Dinosaurs," *Classic Film Collector*, Summer 1974. An obituary is in *New York Times*, Nov. 12, 1962.]

CHRISTOPHER D. GEIST

O'CALLAHAN, JOSEPH TIMOTHY (May 14, 1905–Mar. 18, 1964), clergyman, educator, and war hero, was born in Roxbury, Mass., the son of Cornelius J. O'Callahan, a produce dealer, and Alice Casey. He attended St. Mary's parochial school in Cambridge, Mass., and Boston College High School. In July 1922, O'Callahan entered the Society of Jesus at the novitiate of St. Andrew-on-Hudson at Poughkeepsie, N.Y., and two years later pronounced his first vows; he took his final vows in August 1939.

In 1926, O'Callahan was transferred to Weston (Mass.) College, where he completed his philosophical studies and received an M.A. in 1929. Until 1931 he taught physics and mathematics at Boston College and then returned to Weston College to study theology. In June 1934 he was ordained, and the following year he was a tertian at St. Robert's Hall in Pomfret Center, Conn.

In the fall of 1936, O'Callahan enrolled at Georgetown University to study mathematics, but before earning a degree he was reassigned to Weston College to teach cosmology. In 1938 he went to Holy Cross College in Worcester, Mass., to teach mathematics and physics. By 1940 he was head of the mathematics department.

Following the outbreak of World War II, O'Callahan decided to leave Holy Cross for navy service, and in August 1940 he was commissioned a lieutenant, junior grade, in the Navy Chaplain Corps. For the next eighteen months he taught calculus at the Naval Air Station at Pensacola, Fla. In April 1942, O'Callahan finally received the sea duty he had sought when he entered the navy. He was assigned to the aircraft carrier *Ranger*, and for two and a half years he was the Roman Catholic chaplain on the ship during its extensive service in the naval war against Germany.

In December 1944, O'Callahan, then a lieutenant commander, was sent to Ford Island, Pearl Harbor, pending a new assignment. Shortly afterward he was ordered to sea as a chaplain on the aircraft carrier *Franklin*, part of Task Force 58, which was striking airfields on the Japanese mainland and protecting the invasion force converging on Okinawa. On the morning of Mar. 19, 1945, the *Franklin* was launching its planes when it was attacked by a Japanese dive bomber. Two 550-pound semi-armor-piercing bombs hit the carrier. They set off a chain reaction of explosions among the fully gassed and armed planes on the flight and hangar decks, turning the ship into a floating ammunition dump in the process of blowing up. Fed by thousands of gallons of aviation gasoline, flames swept the length of the ship, and tons of exploding bombs and rockets threatened to tear it apart. It seemed only a matter of minutes before the raging flames would reach a magazine and blow the ship sky high.

O'Callahan was in the wardroom when the bombs hit the *Franklin*. He immediately made his way through the spreading fire to the flight deck, where he helped corpsmen attend to the wounded and performed his priestly functions. One of the more famous photographs from the war features O'Callahan administering the last rites to an injured sailor amid the billowing smoke. Without regard for his own safety, O'Callahan organized and led firefighting crews into the inferno on the flight deck, directed the jettisoning of live ammunition and the flooding of a shell magazine, and manned a hose to cool armed bombs rolling on the listing deck. All the time searing, suffocating smoke was forcing those around him to fall back, gasping.

Throughout the desperate struggle to save the stricken ship, O'Callahan, who had been wounded by shrapnel, inspired crew members with his courage and profound faith in the face of almost certain death. He was a calming influence on those terrified by the incessant explosions. In the belief that "if you were with Father O'Callahan you were safe," the men rallied to his calls for assistance in fighting the fires and rescuing the wounded. Although the *Franklin* suffered 724 killed and 265 wounded, the efforts of O'Callahan and others to save it were successful. For his actions O'Callahan was awarded the Congressional Medal of Honor.

When the *Franklin* limped back to the United States in May 1945, O'Callahan was received as a national hero. Numerous articles about his exploits appeared in newspapers and magazines, and Georgetown University awarded him an honorary doctorate. After the war O'Callahan served as a chaplain on the aircraft carrier *Franklin D. Roosevelt*. He was released from the navy in November 1946, with the rank of commander.

O'Callahan returned to Holy Cross to teach philosophy, but poor health plagued him. He suffered a severe stroke in December 1949 that left him an invalid. Unable to resume teaching, he prepared his best-selling book, *I Was Chaplain on the Franklin*. It was published in 1956, the same year the motion picture *Battle Stations*, depicting his life, was released. O'Callahan continued to live in the Jesuit community at Holy Cross until his death.

O'Callahan was the only Roman Catholic chaplain and only navy chaplain ever awarded the Congressional Medal of Honor, and one of only two noncombatants to receive the nation's highest award for bravery during World War II. Captain Leslie E. Gehres, commander of the *Franklin*, described O'Callahan as "the bravest man I ever knew." But O'Callahan preferred to downplay his courage. "Any priest in like circumstances should do and would do what I did," he modestly declared.

[In addition to *I Was Chaplain on the Franklin*, O'Callahan's writings include articles in religious magazines. Biographical material and clippings are at the College of the Holy Cross and at Georgetown University. Also see Quentin Reynolds, "Chaplain Courageous," *Collier's*, June 23 and 30, 1945. An obituary is in the *New York Times*, Mar. 20, 1964.]

JOHN KENNEDY OHL

O'CONNOR, MARY FLANNERY (Mar. 25, 1925–Aug. 3, 1964), novelist and short story writer, was born in Savannah, Ga., the daughter of Edward Francis O'Connor, Jr., a real-estate broker, and Regina L. Cline. Then known as Mary, she attended St. Vincent and Sacred Heart parochial schools in Savannah until 1938, when Edward O'Connor became ill with disseminated lupus, a disease of the connective tissues, and the family moved to the Cline house in Milledgeville, Ga. The family also acquired the Cline farm, "Andalusia," five miles out of Milledgeville, where O'Connor spent her last years and wrote many of her most successful short stories.

In Milledgeville, O'Connor attended Peabody High School (1938–1942), where she wrote, illustrated books, and maintained a high academic average. In the high school yearbook she declared her hobby to be "collecting rejection slips." Her father died in 1941, and the following year she entered Georgia State College for Women (now Georgia College) in Milledgeville, from which she graduated in 1945 with a B.A. in English and social sciences.

At college O'Connor drew cartoons and made illustrations for the college paper and the yearbook, and edited the literary magazine. She considered herself primarily a cartoonist, submitting several cartoons to the *New Yorker*, which rejected them but encouraged her. She also wrote continuously. After one of her professors submitted several of her stories to the Writers' Workshop at the University of Iowa, she was awarded a Rinehart Fellowship there.

O'Connor was at Iowa from 1945 to 1948, receiving an M.F.A. in literature in 1947. In 1946 she published her first story, "The Geranium," in the summer issue of *Accent*. In 1947 she lived briefly at the writers' colony at Saratoga Springs and then in New York City, where she lived in an apartment hotel, alternately staying with friends in Ridgefield, Conn. In 1950 she fell ill and returned to Georgia.

Between 1946 and 1952, O'Connor published stories and portions of her first novel, *Wise Blood* (1952), in *Accent, Sewanee Review, Tomorrow, Mademoiselle, Partisan Review,* and *New World Writing. Wise Blood* received mixed reviews: praise, largely from academics and Catholic intellectuals, and outrage, from many general reviewers. She felt that both groups misunderstood her work.

In Georgia, O'Connor's illness was diagnosed as disseminated lupus. Seriously ill, she entered Emory Hospital in Atlanta. After her discharge in the spring of 1951, she moved with her mother to "Andalusia," where she remained, except for brief trips and periods of hospitalization, until her death.

During those years O'Connor regularly received honors and awards for her work. "The Life You Save May Be Your Own" was selected for publication in *O. Henry Prize Stories* of 1954. With the exception of 1959–1960, when she was working on her second novel, *The Violent Bear It Away* (1960), her stories appeared regularly in that collection, in *The Best American Short Stories,* and in *Prize Stories.* Her work was widely translated. In 1954–1955 she received a *Kenyon Review* fellowship in fiction, in 1957 a grant from the National Institute of Arts and Letters, and in 1959 a grant from the Ford Foundation. In 1957, 1963, and 1965 her stories won first prize in the annual O. Henry Memorial Awards.

Although her illness grew worse, O'Connor corresponded widely and traveled—on crutches after 1955—to lecture, give readings, and attend writers' conferences. In 1959 she and her mother visited Lourdes and Rome, and her condition seemed to have stabilized. In early 1964 a benign abdominal tumor was removed, but the operation accelerated the development of her lupus. She died in Milledgeville.

O'Connor's substantial literary reputation is based upon the two novels and her short stories, collected in *A Good Man Is Hard To Find* (1955), *Everything That Rises Must Converge* (1965), and *The Complete Stories* (1971). Her stories appear in many anthologies. Nevertheless, her work is difficult to assess, and much current interpretation is based upon the fact that she has become the focal point of a cultlike group of Catholic and women critics.

O'Connor was a devout Catholic and a gifted regional writer, and both strains dominate her fiction. But few of her characters are Catholic; rather, they are cast in the fundamentalist Protestant mode of the South. Her work has been described as "southern gothic," and she has been called "a Roman Catholic Erskine Caldwell," but neither description is adequate. Her work is in the grotesque tradition that has extended in American literature from Edgar Allan Poe through Sherwood Anderson to William Faulkner, with all of whom she has affinities. On several occasions she described herself as indebted to Nathaniel Hawthorne, "with less reliance on allegory." O'Connor's characters, like many of Hawthorne's, are, in the words of critic Caroline Gordon, "lost in that abyss which opens for man when he sets up as God."

In her best work O'Connor's perspectives become clear: the examination of the fundamentalist mentality and the cult of amoral modernism from the oldest of Christian perspectives. Her characters are often violent, arrogant, or stupid; they are products of their social and moral environment; and they are seekers after an often twisted vision of a salvation beyond fulfillment. They are steeped in the manners and mores of the rural South, and they speak in its idioms. O'Connor approaches them not as stock figures in a morality play—although her works have been called that—but as human beings caught up in a world beyond understanding that they desperately try to control.

Conscious of her critical identity as a Catholic writer and as a southern regionalist, O'Connor addressed herself to both identities. Of the former she wrote, "When people have told me that because I am a Catholic, I cannot be an artist, I have had to reply, ruefully, that because I am a Catholic I cannot afford to be less than an artist." Of the latter she wrote, "To know oneself is to know one's region. It is also to know the world, and it is also, paradoxically, a form of exile from that world."

O'Connor was indeed an artist, but she was not a major writer. Perhaps, had she lived, she would have attained the maturity to which her work was pointing. But her vision was limited, as was the range of her work, and she will remain an interesting and important but minor writer.

[O'Connor's manuscripts and many letters, as well as memorabilia, are in Georgia College Library, Milledgeville.

Additional works are Robert and Sally Fitzgerald, eds., *Mystery and Manners* (1969); Sally Fitzgerald, ed., *The Habit of Being: Letters* (1979). Quotations and selections from her essays, letters, lectures, interviews, and a bibliography appear in Melvin J. Friedman and Lewis A. Lawson, eds., *The Added Dimension* (1966). No biography of O'Connor has yet appeared, but important biographical material appears in the introduction by Robert Fitzgerald to *Everything That Rises Must Converge* (1965) and in Stanley Edgar Hyman, *Flannery O'Connor* (1966). Other works about her include Robert Drake, *Flannery O'Connor* (1966); Carter W. Martin, *The True Country* (1969); Sister Kathleen Feely, *Flannery O'Connor: Voice of the Peacock* (1972); Martha Stephens, *The Question of Flannery O'Connor* (1973). *Esprit*, Winter 1964, is a memorial issue containing comments by many writers and scholars.]

DAVID D. ANDERSON

ODETS, CLIFFORD (July 18, 1906–Aug. 14, 1963), dramatist, film-script writer, and actor was born in Philadelphia, Pa., the son of Louis Odets, a Russian-born printer, and of Pearl Geisinger, an Austrian immigrant. When Clifford was two years old his father moved his family to the Bronx in New York City, where Odets was raised in a lower-middle-class milieu. He attended local public schools and Morris High School but, failing several subjects, he quit at the age of seventeen to seek a writing career.

Odets supported himself initially by acting jobs in radio and with Harry Kemp's Poet's Theatre and Mae Desmond's Stock Company,

and understudying Spencer Tracy in the thirty-seven-performance run of *Conflict* (1929). He then joined a junior acting company of the Theatre Guild in 1929 and enjoyed a brief career appearing in minor roles in *Marco Millions, R.U.R.*, and *Midnight*. A founding member of the Group Theatre in 1931, Odets appeared as an actor in several of its productions, including *Night Over Taos* (1932), *Men in White* (1933), and as Dr. Benjamin in his own *Waiting for Lefty* (1935). The Group Theatre's ensemble acting system and its collective ideology contributed to Odets' brief association with the Communist party in 1934 and strongly influenced Odets' first plays, *I Got the Blues* (an early draft of *Awake and Sing!*) and *Waiting for Lefty*. Odets wrote the latter play in three days in a hotel room in 1935. Upon its enthusiastic reception, Odets revised *Awake and Sing!*, which soon opened to both critical and popular acclaim. By December 1935 two further dramas, *Till the Day I Die* and *Paradise Lost*, had appeared.

Odets' New York success led to the first of his three periods in Hollywood as a screenwriter (1936–1938, 1943–1947, 1955–1961). On Jan. 8, 1937, he married Luise Rainer; their troubled marriage ended in divorce in May 1940. Odets' second marriage, to Bette Grayson, on May 14, 1943, produced two children and ended in divorce in November 1951.

Odets' major screenplay during his first period in Hollywood was *The General Died at Dawn* (1936), a story of the Chinese Revolution directed by Lewis Milestone and remembered mainly for journalist Frank Nugent's legendary *Herald Tribune* review, "Odets, Where Is Thy Sting?"

Odets' other plays for the Group Theatre were *Golden Boy* (1937), *Rocket to the Moon* (1938), and *Night Music* (1940). After the Group's demise, Odets wrote *Clash by Night* (1941); its poor reception prompted his second Hollywood stay, made most memorable by his adaptation of the Richard Llewellyn novel *None But the Lonely Heart*, which he both wrote and directed (1944).

Odets wrote only three more plays: *The Big Knife* (1949), *The Country Girl* (1950), and *The Flowering Peach* (1954). In April 1952 he testified before the House Committee on Un-American Activities (HUAC) concerning his association with the Communist party in 1934–1935, perhaps motivated by his fear that *The Country Girl* would not be made into a film unless he did so. He admitted his party membership and informed HUAC of his mock-heroic journey to Cuba in 1935 with a band of writers and union officials ostensibly investigating the plight of labor under the Batista-Mendieta regime, and of the group's prompt arrest and immediate return to New York. That event, together with the party's increasing pressure on Odets to write only agitprop plays, prompted the dramatist to abandon the party shortly thereafter.

By his own account Odets began several more plays after 1954, but none was completed. He received the Award of Merit Medal for Drama in 1961 from the American Academy of Arts and Letters. Whether or not a guilty conscience over his having devoted many years of his career to screenwriting caused an artistic decline is uncertain. (Odets tended after gaining fame in 1935 to tell many interviewers his story, often varying the facts to suit the circumstance.) Harold Clurman, the most dependable source of biographical information in the absence of an authorized biography, recalls that Odets was troubled by his ambivalence between material and artistic success to the day he died, and termed this condition Odets' "(American) tragedy."

Odets' early acclaim—which has tended to stereotype his achievement as exclusively sociological in theme—was not merely the result of the social issues to be found in the plays. As Clurman put it, "Odets' writing is a personal creation, essentially lyric, in which vulgarity, tenderness, energy, humor, and a headlong idealism are commingled." While Odets is certainly important historically for his proletarian plays, even these early dramas are distinguished by his concern with individual loneliness in the modern world and the saving energy of ordinary people that allows an existential struggle toward dignity and moral value.

Especially undervalued is Odets' skill as a tragic dramatist. In a country not renowned for tragic plays, Odets produced *Golden Boy* and *Clash by Night*, which employ the conventions of melodrama to reveal the individual's propensity for self-delusion and isolation from the human community. These plays stand with such dramas as Eugene O'Neill's *Desire Under the Elms*, Maxwell Anderson's *Winterset*, and Tennessee Williams' *Orpheus Descending* in their examination of the spiritual consequences of self-determined inaction. Odets' problem drama, *Paradise Lost*, is perhaps the best American play in this genre and his most subtle in both structure and characterization. In Pike's question to the well-intentioned but passive Leo Gordon, ". . . who then are we with our si-

lence?" lies Odets' most powerful denunciation of the American dream. Its force stems not from a Marxist perspective but a more universally humanistic one.

Despite an occasional strained incident or overblown line, Odets revealed a fine comic gift in *Rocket to the Moon*, *Night Music*, and *The Flowering Peach*, as well as a sympathetic understanding for human folly. Detective A. L. Rosenberger, an especially fine characterization, is Odets' best romantic philosopher; his "Everything remains to be seen" guides *Night Music* to the highest rank of American expressionistic comedy.

Because of his skill in a variety of dramatic types, a hard-edged urban poetic style that was influential upon Tennessee Williams, Arthur Miller, and Paddy Chayefsky, his lyrical presentation of ordinary people searching for self-fulfillment and self-transcendence, and what Clurman terms his "radical humanism," Odets belongs, if below O'Neill, in the second rank of American playwrights.

[*The Flowering Peach*, never published in complete form, is in typescript at the Theatre Collection, New York Public Library. Works by Odets not mentioned in the text include typescripts of *I Got the Blues* and *The Silent Partner*, and continuity scripts of the filmplays *Deadline at Dawn* (1936), *The Story on Page One* (1960), and *Wild in the Country* (1961), all in the Library of Congress.

Harold Cantor, *Clifford Odets: Playwright-Poet* (1978), contains a relatively complete bibliography and surveys the plays thematically. Harold Clurman, *The Fervent Years* (1945), is a sprightly history of the Group Theatre and Odets' early career. Clurman's "Found: A 'Lost' Play by Odets," *New York Times*, Apr. 30, 1972, is helpful on Odets' later years. The first volume of a two-volume work, Margaret Brenman-Gibson, *Clifford Odets: American Playwright*, will be published in 1981. Frank R. Cunningham, "Clifford Odets," in A. Walton Litz, ed., *American Writers, Supp. II* (1981), critically reevaluates Odets' entire canon. Michael J. Mendelsohn, *Clifford Odets: Humane Dramatist* (1969); Edward Murray, *Clifford Odets: The Thirties and After* (1968); and Gerald Weales, *Clifford Odets: Playwright* (1971), are important critical studies. An obituary appeared in the *New York Times*, Sept. 3, 1963.]

FRANK R. CUNNINGHAM

O'DWYER, WILLIAM (July 11, 1890–Nov. 24, 1964), lawyer, politician, and mayor of New York City, was born in Bohola, County Mayo, Ireland, the son of Patrick O'Dwyer and Bridget McNicholas, both of whom were schoolteachers. One of eleven children, O'Dwyer received his early education in his father's class. He then studied at St. Nathays College in Roscommon,

Ireland. From 1907 to 1910 he attended the Jesuit University of Salamanca in Spain with the intention of becoming a priest, but left three years short of graduation. Because of his rejection of the priesthood, which he considered a reproach to his parents, he decided not to return to Ireland.

O'Dwyer arrived in New York in June 1910, reputedly with only $23.35 in his pocket. For the next seven years he worked as a grocery clerk, a deckhand on a freighter, a fireman on a Hudson River boat, a hod carrier and plasterer (long enough to get a union card), and a bartender at the Vanderbilt Hotel. He married Catherine M. Lenihan, a telephone operator whom he had met at the Vanderbilt, on Aug. 3, 1916. They had no children.

O'Dwyer became a United States citizen in 1916. The next year he joined the New York City police force. At that time he began to study law in the evening at Fordham University Law School. He received an LL.B. in 1923 and was admitted to the New York Bar. In 1924 he became head of the legal bureau of the New York City Police Department, but resigned a year later to become a clerk in a law office. In 1926 he opened a private law practice with city alderman George J. Joyce.

In his spare time O'Dwyer was a sports promoter, bringing Irish soccer teams to New York City. This put him in contact with Mrs. William Randolph Hearst, who introduced him to Joseph V. McKee, president of the Board of Aldermen and later acting mayor of New York. On Dec. 7, 1932, Acting-Mayor McKee appointed O'Dwyer a city magistrate.

As city magistrate, O'Dwyer took a special interest in juvenile delinquents, and in 1933 Mayor Fiorello LaGuardia appointed him presiding judge of an experimental adolescent court in Brooklyn. Favorable publicity led Governor Herbert H. Lehman to appoint him to the unexpired term of judge in the County Court of Kings County in 1937. The following year the squarely-built, black-haired, blue-eyed O'Dwyer won election to a fourteen-year term. In 1939 he resigned to run for district attorney of Kings County. He was elected in 1940.

O'Dwyer's term as district attorney got off to a dubious start. He had promised to remain independent of political bosses, but of his first forty appointments, thirty-three came from lists supplied by Democratic district leaders. An in-progress investigation into the Brooklyn waterfront racketeering unions controlled by mobster Albert Anastasia was dropped. But his work as special prosecutor of an underworld execution

squad to which fifty-six homicides had been traced won him national attention. Working with his assistant, Burton B. Turkus, O'Dwyer connected eighty-five homicides in New York City and one thousand throughout the country to the ring, which was dubbed by the press "Murder, Inc." The ring was smashed and seven members were sent to the electric chair. As a result of this work, O'Dwyer received the Democratic nomination for mayor of New York in 1941. But he was unable to defeat the popular incumbent, Fiorello LaGuardia.

The moment he heard the news of the Japanese attack on Pearl Harbor, O'Dwyer telegraphed President Franklin D. Roosevelt, offering his services. He was commissioned a major. After filling several posts within the United States and advancing to the rank of brigadier general in 1944, he was chosen by Roosevelt as chief of the Economic Section of the Allied Commission, and was sent to Italy to represent the Foreign Economic Administration, with the rank of minister and the status of personal representative of the president.

In 1945, O'Dwyer again ran for mayor. Despite a campaign in which his district attorneyship was described as "a rotten mess" and accusations of gangland connections were made, he was elected by the widest margin ever enjoyed by a mayor of New York. In 1946 his wife, who had become increasingly debilitated by Parkinson's disease, died. On Dec. 20, 1949, after a highly publicized courtship, he married Elizabeth Sloan Simpson, a former model and a divorcée. They had no children.

In 1949, O'Dwyer was reelected mayor. In December of that year Brooklyn district attorney Miles F. McDonald launched a probe into gambling and police corruption. O'Dwyer's obvious opposition to the probe shocked the public. Twelve days after being sworn in as mayor, and as the scandal grew, O'Dwyer left for Florida, suffering from nervous exhaustion and a viral infection. After Bronx boss and national Democratic committeeman Edward J. Flynn had rushed to Washington to confer with President Harry Truman, it was announced in August 1950 that O'Dwyer had been nominated as American ambassador to Mexico.

On Sept. 1, 1950, O'Dwyer resigned as mayor of New York. Before doing so, he handed out $125,000 in raises to close friends on the city payroll. To deputy fire commissioner James J. Moran, who was known as the mayor's alter ego, went a $15,000-a-year lifetime appointment as commissioner of water supply.

Soon afterward, an investigation of Brooklyn

bookmaker Harry Gross disclosed that Moran had solicited funds for O'Dwyer's election from all the bookies in town. The Gross case helped set the stage for the New York sessions of the Senate Crime Committee, headed by Senator Estes Kefauver of Tennessee. In the spring of 1951 the Kefauver Committee began televised hearings in New York City. O'Dwyer flew from Mexico City to appear before the committee on Mar. 19, 1951. His opening statement was a rambling account of his life and his accomplishments as mayor. Senator Charles W. Tobey of New Hampshire interrupted this monologue, and his searing cross-examination lasted two days. As a result, although no charges of wrongdoing were made, it became apparent that O'Dwyer had had dealings with criminal elements, in particular racketeer Frank Costello. The Kefauver Commission's report stated:

A single pattern of conduct emerges from O'Dwyer's official activities in regard to gambling and water-front rackets, murders, and police corruption, from his days as district attorney through his term as mayor. No matter what the motivation of his choice, action or inaction, it often seemed to result favorably for men suspected of being high up in the rackets. . . .

After publication of the Kefauver report, O'Dwyer returned to Mexico and resumed his duties as ambassador. But the hearings had ruined his political career, and the president was faced with demands for his recall. With the election of the Republican Eisenhower administration, O'Dwyer resigned as ambassador on Dec. 6, 1952. That same day his wife left him, and they were soon divorced.

O'Dwyer remained in Mexico City as a consultant to the law firm of O'Dwyer, Bernstein and Correa. He became involved in various schemes, including a process to change salt water into fresh water and a patent to preserve meat by radiation. He also helped finance a motion picture on Mexico. In 1960 he returned to New York City, where he died.

O'Dwyer was the stereotype of the affable Irish politician. His meteoric rise in New York politics was due as much to hard work as to an uncanny sense of political timing and a thorough understanding of machine politics. Although controversial, his administration of New York City showed many accomplishments. He helped to bring the United Nations headquarters to the city, reorganized the welfare department, created a traffic department, established a smoke-control bureau, and set up a manage-

ment survey committee. His selection of Robert Moses as New York City construction coordinator made O'Dwyer's administration pivotal in the physical development of New York. As the Kefauver Committee report stated: "It would be unfair to give the impression that the matters in which this committee is interested give anything like a complete picture of O'Dwyer's accomplishments in public office."

[O'Dwyer's papers and correspondence are in the William Stiles Bennet Papers, Syracuse State Library; William H. Allen Papers, Institute for Public Service, New York City; James P. O'Brien Papers, New York Public Library. Records of his years as district attorney and mayor are in the New York City municipal archives. The Oral History Collection at Columbia University has an autobiographical interview. Although there is no biography, many works have chapters on him and his administration: Allan Nevins and John A. Krout, *The Greater City* (1948); Norton Mockridge and Robert H. Prall, *The Big Fix* (1954); Philip Hamburger, *Mayor Watching and Other Pleasures* (1958); Edward Robb Ellis, *The Epic of New York City* (1966); Alfred Connable and Edward Silverfarb, *Tigers of Tammany* (1967); Warren Moscow, *What Have You Done for Me Lately?* (1967) and *The Last of the Big-Time Bosses* (1971); Robert A. Caro, *The Power Broker* (1974). Burton B. Turkus and Sid Feder, *Murder, Inc.* (1951), provides information on O'Dwyer's role in the case. An obituary is in the *New York Times*, Nov. 25, 1964.]

DAVID WILLIAM VOORHEES

OLDS, IRVING SANDS (Jan. 22, 1887– Mar. 4, 1963), lawyer and corporation executive, was born in Erie, Pa., the son of Clark Olds, an admiralty lawyer, and of Livia Elizabeth Keator. Raised in a family of wealth, Olds, upon his graduation from the Erie Public High School in 1903, was sent to Yale College, from which he received the B.A. in 1907, and then to the Harvard Law School. He graduated near the top of his law class in 1910 and received one of the prize law clerk positions, being assigned to Justice Oliver Wendell Holmes, Jr.

In August 1911, Olds joined the New York law firm of White and Case. His first important legal assignment was to serve as counsel for the export department of J. P. Morgan and Company (1915–1917). Although a member of Squadron A of the New York National Guard, Olds was not called to active military service when the United States entered World War I. He was instead appointed as counsel to the purchasing department of the British War Mission. Later in the war he served as special assistant to Edward R. Stettinius, Sr., in Washington, D.C., when Stettinius became surveyor general of supplies for the War Department. On Oct. 13, 1917, Olds married Evelyn Foster, a painter of some renown. They had no children.

After the war Olds returned to White and Case as a partner. (He became a partner on Jan. 1, 1917.) Soon his expertise in corporate affairs, particularly in the reorganization and administration of corporate enterprises, was widely recognized on Wall Street. In 1936 he was elected to the board of directors and the finance committee of the U.S. Steel Corporation. His success as special counsel for that corporation in dealing with the Temporary National Economic Committee's inquiry into monopoly in the steel industry was hailed by *Fortune* magazine as "a model of how Big Business could defend its right to a profit and still be solicitous of the public interest."

When the chairman of the board of U.S. Steel, Edward R. Stettinius, Jr., following the example set by his father in World War I, left business to serve the government as a member of the National Defense Committee in 1940, Olds was chosen to succeed him. His election as chairman of the board was a clear signal that the days of Andrew Carnegie, Henry Clay Frick, and Elbert Gary had passed for the steel industry. Olds and the president of the company, Benjamin Fairless, were recognized throughout the industry as part of the "young guard" of bright, articulate, and soft-spoken corporate executives who knew that big labor and big government were as much of a reality as big business and must be treated with finesse, understanding, and compromise.

During the twelve years of his chairmanship, Olds's skill in dealing with both labor and government was fully tested. These were years of total war and postwar reconstruction, perhaps the most dramatic and significant period in the history of U.S. Steel. The company greatly expanded its own facilities, and built and operated for the government the Geneva Steel Works, its first major steel production center on the West Coast. By working its facilities at more than 100 percent of capacity, U.S. Steel broke all previous production records. Within one year after Pearl Harbor, U.S. Steel alone was turning out more steel than the Axis powers combined. By the end of 1943, Olds could proudly announce that his company had made 60 million tons of steel since the beginning of America's all-out defense effort in 1940 and that its new shipbuilding yard at Port Newark, N.J., was building one new destroyer every five days. Profits during the war years also reached an all-time high, and a great part of these earnings were used for an expan-

sion program that approached the billion-dollar mark.

Victory over Germany and Japan meant no diminution in the demand for steel. In spite of severe postwar labor strife in the steel and coal industries, production exceeded the records set during the war. In the spring of 1947, Olds negotiated a strike settlement with Philip Murray of the United Steel Workers of America that granted a fifteen-cent hourly wage increase and provided for severance pay and paid vacations for workers. It also stipulated that company and union representatives would meet regularly to discuss labor-management problems. The 1947 settlement set an industrywide pattern for labor negotiations.

The Korean War placed new pressure on steel production. Olds became increasingly critical of the demands of both government and labor, vigorously resisting President Harry S. Truman's proposal for new wage and price controls and labor's demands for a guaranteed annual wage. Through his frequent speeches and articles in popular journals, the increasingly conservative Olds became a leading spokesman for the deregulation of industry.

Having reached the mandatory retirement age of sixty-five in 1952, Olds resigned as chairman of the board, ironically at the moment when Truman seized all of the strikebound steel mills of the nation for the federal government, an action that Olds regarded as the first step toward socialism.

Although he remained a director of U.S. Steel until 1960, after his retirement as chairman and particularly after the death of his wife in 1957, Olds turned most of his energy and interest toward fund raising for the New York Public Library, the Metropolitan Opera Association, the Lincoln Center project, and especially his two favorite educational institutions, Cooper Union and Yale University. In 1952, with Frank W. Abrams of Standard Oil of New Jersey and Alfred P. Sloan, Jr., of General Motors, Olds founded the Council for Financial Aid to Education, to encourage corporate giving to private colleges and universities.

Olds's last business venture came in 1960, when he agreed to serve as one of three voting trustees of the huge block of Trans World Airlines (TWA) stock that Howard Hughes and the Hughes Tool Company owned, in order to save that airline from bankruptcy. Olds, over Hughes's protests, succeeded in completely reorganizing the directorship of TWA. He resigned as trustee because of ill health in 1962. He died in New York City.

[There is no collection of Olds's papers, nor is there a biography. His business papers are in the archives of U.S. Steel in Pittsburgh, but are inaccessible to scholars. Olds wrote two books on U.S. naval history: *United States Navy, 1776–1815* (1942) and *Bits and Pieces of American History as Told by a Collection of American Naval and Other Historical Prints and Paintings* (1951). An obituary is in the *New York Times*, Mar. 5, 1963.]

JOSEPH FRAZIER WALL

OLSEN, JOHN SIGVARD ("OLE") (Nov. 6, 1892–Jan. 26, 1963), and **JOHNSON, HAROLD OGDEN ("CHIC")** (Mar. 5, 1891– Feb. 26, 1962), comedians, were partners for nearly fifty years in vaudeville, Broadway shows, movies, radio, nightclubs, and television. Olsen, son of Gustave and Catherine Olsen, was born in Peru, Ind., and reared in Wasbash, Ill. Johnson was born in Englewood, Ill. Both were locally educated and attended Northwestern University; Olsen graduated in 1912.

There are several versions of the story of their meeting (1914); probably it occurred in the office of a musical publisher in Chicago while both were looking for new material. Olsen was the violin-playing member of the College Four quartet, then in need of a piano player. He and Johnson recognized each other's "genius" immediately (as they recalled); Johnson, a ragtime piano player who soon joined the quartet, displayed "the most powerful right hand" Olsen had "ever heard on a piano." Johnson was impressed by Olsen's yellow high-button shoes and his ability to imitate a busy signal on the telephone; "I had to have him for a partner," he stated. Both had hoped for careers as serious musicians (Olsen was inspired by the Czech violinist Jan Kubelik and Johnson by Ignace Paderewski), but they developed an act featuring violin, piano, ventriloquism, and harmony. Early hecklers were never ignored; interruptions were incorporated into the act.

Their slow acceptance in vaudeville encouraged Olsen and Johnson to crash "Mike Fritzel's Frolics," a floorshow at a Chicago club. Their act was popular, and gained momentum at the Majestic Theater in Milwaukee; the team, billed as Two Likeable Lads Loaded With Laughs, subsequently played the Keith, Pantages, and Orpheum circuits. In 1925 they toured England and Australia in *Tip Toes* and *Tell Me More,* and the next year they starred in *Monkey Business* in Los Angeles, the first review of their own. Although they had engagements at the Palace in New York City, they confined their vaudeville tours to the West because Orpheum acts seeking to become established in the East had to take a cut in salary. In 1933 Olsen and Johnson made their Broadway debut, replacing Jack Haley and Sid Silvers, in the musical comedy *Take a Chance* (a move panned by John Mason Brown because they didn't "know when to let enough alone"). They bought 50 percent of the stock in the show and toured with it successfully.

When the large vaudeville circuits began to disintegrate, Olsen and Johnson started one-night stands throughout the South and parts of the West. Their *Surprise Party* on tour provided the basic concept for their most famous show, *Hellzapoppin.* At Buckeye, Ariz., Olsen and Johnson came upon the name *Helzapoppin* [sic], used for the Fiesta del Sol, and adopted the name for a review made up of material from the "unit" shows they had opened in Fort Wayne, Ind., and Denver, Colo. With Lee Shubert's backing, sets and costumes from previous musicals, and a budget estimated between $15,000 and $25,000, the show opened at the Forty-sixth Street Theater in New York City on Sept. 22, 1938. The critics, used to more sophisticated fare, were not enthusiastic: Richard Watts, Jr., of the *Herald Tribune* complained that Olsen and Johnson had "confused noise with humor"; John Anderson of the *Journal* called the show "vulgar and unaesthetic"; Brooks Atkinson of the *Times* saw it as "loud, low and funny." But the public, prompted by Walter Winchell's enthusiastic plugging of the show, lined up at the box office. Sellout crowds forced a move first to the Winter Garden Theater, then to the Majestic.

The production convulsed audiences with its zany antics. Some of the jokes were directed at the audience; stagehands would force air under the skirts of women seated in the orchestra; a plant delivered during the performance grew into a tree by the finale; tickets for other shows were hawked; shots were fired from offstage. *Hellzapoppin*'s first anniversary found former Governor Al Smith dancing in the aisles, and the the show was declared practically "a national institution" by the *Brooklyn Eagle*. It ran for more than 1,400 performances before closing on Dec. 17, 1941. The show returned the partners an enormous profit.

Hellzapoppin's success prompted imitations such as *Hellzafire* (1940, enjoined from continuing when Olsen and Johnson sued the owners and principals, preventing the use of such a similar title) and further Olsen and Johnson productions: *Sons o' Fun* (1941), *Laffing Room Only* (1944), *Funzapoppin* (1949), and *Pardon Our*

French (1950). A proposed skating show had to be canceled, but in 1959 *Hellzasplashin,* an aquatic variation, opened at Flushing Meadow Park, New York City. *Hellzapoppin* became a successful movie (1941), although the *Times* reviewer called it "mostly . . . a jerky sequence of third-rate gags punctuated by gunfire."

Crazy House (1943), *Ghost Catchers* (1944), and *See My Lawyer* (1945) followed, all variations on "the same old pie-slinging and seltzer-squirting routines," according to the *Times.* Actually, Olsen and Johnson had begun their movie careers before *Hellzapoppin* fame; they had appeared in *Oh Sailor Behave!* (1930), *Gold Dust Gertie* (1931), and *Fifty Million Frenchmen* (1931), among other films.

During the late 1930's they began their radio career, introduced by crooner Rudy Vallee, and presented "Comedy News" on WABC, but they achieved only limited success. Either their material was too "corny" for a sophisticated metropolitan audience (as *Variety* said) or, more likely, the shows suffered from the absence of visual, slapstick appeal. Olsen and Johnson realized that television was the "big theatrical business of the future," and were delighted to be signed by NBC as a summer replacement for Milton Berle (1949). They appeared in "Fireball Fun for All" (1949–1950) and "All Star Revue" (1951). Although their work served as an inspiration for such later shows as "Laugh In," the team's spontaneity was restricted by the confinement of television camera positions.

In 1956 Olsen and Johnson resumed their nightclub career at the Latin Quarter in New York City. They could still provoke laughs, but the novelty was gone. They had also appeared at the Canadian National Exhibition in Ottawa and Toronto, drawing record crowds in 1948 and 1949. Their gross was $400,000 weekly in 1949.

Johnson married Catherine Creed in 1918; they had two daughters. She was the woman who shouted for Oscar in *Hellzapoppin* and was the supervisor of props stored at the Johnson farm. Her act, Six Peaches and a Pair, played the Pantages circuit with Olsen and Johnson. Olsen married Eileen O'Dare in 1913; they had three children.

"Which one of you mugs is Johnson?" a running gag often repeated by the comedians, was adopted from early heckling. The two, in fact, were easily distinguishable; Olsen was tall and slim. Johnson had thinning red hair, and was short and stocky. He liked to hunt and fish, and although he had an "oxlike" endurance, was often concerned with his health. He was the more private of the two, preferring a quiet life with his family on a 1,000-acre farm, Winter Garden, at Carmel, N.Y. Both were gregarious, and frequently appeared at Rotary, Lions, Elks, and Kiwanis luncheons or smokers. They welcomed hundreds of out-of-towners in their dressing rooms after performances.

Olsen was too restless to be hospitalized after a car accident in which he broke his right thigh (November 1950). Although he was temporarily replaced in *Pardon Our French,* he still hobbled through some scenes on crutches and "appeared" as an offstage voice. Olsen became interested in the Moral Rearmament Movement in the 1950's, prompted by his daughter's involvement, and appeared in *Vanishing Island,* sponsored by the group. Olsen and Johnson's last appearance as a team was in *Hellzasplashin.*

After Johnson's death Olsen recalled that they had had disagreements but no real fights. Each supplied something the other lacked. They had entertained three presidents—Woodrow Wilson, Franklin Roosevelt, and Harry Truman—and had been received by Pope Pius XII. They were honorary members of dozens of fellowship clubs, and were made "Doctors of Pun and Hilarity" by the College of the City of New York (1939). Their motto, frequently restated, was "Only belly laughs count," and they would accept as a compliment the criticism that they did not know the meaning of "subtle."

Johnson died in Las Vegas, Nev.; Olsen, in Albuquerque, N.M. They are buried together in the Palm Mausoleum in Las Vegas.

[Clippings are in the New York Public Library Theater Collection at Lincoln Center. Olsen and Johnson are the subject of profiles in the *New Yorker,* Jan. 28, 1939, and July 9, 1949. Johnson's obituary is in the *New York Times,* Feb. 28, 1962; Olsen's, in the *New York Times,* Apr. 1, 1963 (delay caused by newspaper strike).]

ELIZABETH R. NELSON

O'MAHONEY, JOSEPH CHRISTOPHER (Nov. 5, 1884–Dec. 1, 1962), journalist and U.S. senator, was born in Chelsea, Mass., the son of Denis O'Mahoney, a furrier, and Elizabeth Sheehan. His parents were Irish immigrants. Although a staunch Catholic, O'Mahoney was educated at the Cambridge Latin School and attended Columbia University (1905–1907).

From 1907 to 1917, O'Mahoney was a newspaper reporter and editor. He settled in Colorado in 1908. On June 11, 1913, he married Agnes Veronica O'Leary; they had no children but raised three nephews. He was a Roosevelt

Progressive in 1912, but became a Democrat by 1916.

In 1916, O'Mahoney went to Wyoming to become the city editor of Democratic Governor John B. Kendrick's *Cheyenne State Leader.* When Kendrick entered the United States Senate in 1917, O'Mahoney became his executive secretary. While in Washington he studied law at night and received the LL.B. degree from Georgetown University in 1920. He then returned to Cheyenne to practice law. O'Mahoney remained active in politics, managing Kendrick's campaign for reelection in 1922, serving as vice-chairman of the Democratic State Committee from 1922 to 1930, representing Wyoming in 1925–1926 at the Conference on Uniform State Laws, and being a member of the Democratic National Committee from 1929 to 1934. O'Mahoney played a prominent role, as a national convention delegate, in drafting the 1932 Democratic platform, and he served as vice-chairman of the Democratic national campaign committee that year. His efforts were rewarded in March 1933 when he was appointed first assistant postmaster general of the United States.

When Kendrick died in 1933, O'Mahoney was appointed to fill the vacant seat. He was elected to the Senate in his own right in 1934 and was reelected in 1940 and 1946. Republican Governor Frank A. Barrett defeated him in 1952, but O'Mahoney was elected in 1954 to take the place of the late Senator Lester C. Hunt. O'Mahoney suffered a stroke in 1959 and retired from public office in 1961.

Early in his Senate service O'Mahoney emerged as an influential legislator, known for his thoroughness, articulateness, and warmth. His major Senate assignments were to the Appropriations, Judiciary, and Interior committees, the last of which he served as chairman from 1949 to 1952. He was noted for his trenchant, though courteous, interrogations.

O'Mahoney had the reputation of being a New Deal reformer, but, showing his Progressive antecedents, he was an independent-minded one. Largely because he opposed arbitrary power in any form, he took a prominent part in defeating President Franklin D. Roosevelt's 1937 proposal to reorganize the federal judiciary. O'Mahoney was also critical of the growth of bureaucratic power, and he opposed the development of a Missouri Valley Authority, wartime limitations on salaries, and an anti–poll tax bill, which embodied an idea he thought should be formulated as a constitutional amendment. Not surprisingly, he favored majority in-stead of two-thirds ratification of treaties, anti-strike legislation during World War II, and strict regulation of American participation in cartels. In 1945, O'Mahoney introduced a resolution for an international agreement to ban the use of the atomic bomb. He was a zealous defender of Wyoming's interests, especially regarding cattle, land reclamation, oil, tariffs, and wool, and he was known as a conservationist.

O'Mahoney's greatest impact was as a crusading antimonopolist. In the Senate he introduced the resolution that established the Temporary National Economic Committee (TNEC), with six members from Congress and six from the executive branch of government. He served as chairman of the TNEC during its investigations (1938–1941) of monopoly and concentration of wealth and their effects on employment, technology, business methods, and the economy in general. From this investigation came O'Mahoney's proposals for national charters for corporations engaged in interstate commerce; stricter enforcement of antitrust laws; revision of tax laws in order to encourage new and small businesses; and a national conference of representatives of agriculture, business, consumers, and labor to set an agenda on goals for the nation's economy. The work of the TNEC underlay part of the Fair Deal program of President Harry S. Truman.

O'Mahoney himself spent much of the rest of his time in the Senate trying to restrict monopolies, reform insurance companies, and develop better governmental instruments to deal with economic problems. This last was particularly seen in his cosponsorship of the Employment Act of 1946. Of special importance in this legislation was the establishment of the congressional Joint Economic Committee, of which O'Mahoney served as chairman for three congresses, and the Council of Economic Advisers.

In addition to further antimonopolistic endeavors, during the 1950's O'Mahoney was noted for his work in supporting the admission of Alaska and Hawaii as states and, as chairman of the Defense Appropriations Subcommittee, in financing American involvement in the Korean War. He was also a leader in the successful opposition to the confirmation of Lewis Strauss as secretary of commerce in 1959. O'Mahoney died in Bethesda, Md.

[O'Mahoney's papers are at the Western History Research Center of the University of Wyoming. Scholarly works are Frank Alan Coombs, "Joseph Christopher O'Mahoney: The New Deal Years" (Ph.

D. diss., University of Illinois at Urbana-Champaign, 1968); Gene M. Gressley, "Joseph C. O'Mahoney, FDR, and the Supreme Court," *Pacific Historical Review,* May 1971. There is an O'Mahoney transcript in the Oral History Collection of Columbia University. An obituary is in *New York Times,* Dec. 2, 1962.]

DONALD R. McCOY

ORRY-KELLY (Dec. 31, 1897–Feb. 26, 1964), fashion designer, was born Orry George Kelly in Kiama, Australia, the son of William George Kelly and Florence Evalean Purdue. His early interest in drawing and painting was encouraged by his mother, who enrolled him in art classes while he was still very young. Another strong interest, acting, was not encouraged. On completing his schooling, he deferred to his mother's wishes and accepted employment in a bank. His banking career lasted only eight months, coming to an end when he joined a traveling company of the musical comedy *Irene.*

In 1923, Kelly went to New York City to pursue an acting career. Unable to find acting jobs, he supported himself by painting murals in private residences, restaurants, and nightclubs, sketching nightclub patrons, painting silk shawls, and, with his neighbor and friend Cary Grant, creating hand-blocked neckties. His nightclub murals, seen by Julian Johnstone, a 20th Century-Fox executive, led to a job with that film company, illustrating titles for silent movies.

By the late 1920's Kelly was back in the theater—as a designer of sets and costumes. Actresses Ethel Barrymore and Judith Anderson were among those who wore his costumes. Katherine Hepburn was costumed by Kelly for *Death Takes a Holiday,* her Broadway debut.

The 1929 stock market crash cut short Kelly's Broadway designing career. A few ventures into the nightclub business proved unsuccessful, and he left New York to design for the St. Louis Opera Company. From St. Louis he went to Reno, Nev., where he decorated a nightclub, and then to Hollywood, where Cary Grant, also newly arrived, helped him by showing some of his sketches to executives at Warner Brothers.

The studio had just signed contracts with two famous actresses, Kay Francis and Ruth Chatterton, and was without a designer to create costumes for these important stars. Kelly was hired, and was put under contract as Orry-Kelly. The hyphenization of his first and last names was thought by studio executives to conjure a more exotic designer image than plain "Mr. Kelly" could.

Orry-Kelly's first picture, *The Rich Are Al-*

ways with Us, (1932), starred Ruth Chatterton and featured Bette Davis. The designer was closely associated with Davis for well over a decade. She referred to him as her "right hand" and counted on his designs to help her create the characterizations that made her a top-ranking star. In 1944, when Orry-Kelly was no longer employed at Warner Brothers on a contract basis, Davis insisted that he be hired as her designer for *Mr. Skeffington.* His work on this assignment was called his "finest achievement in characterization."

For Davis, as for Kay Francis, Ruth Chatterton, Ingrid Bergman, Marilyn Monroe, Marion Davies, and other stars, Orry-Kelly created costumes that defined their roles, camouflaged figure problems, and accurately reflected the fashions of historical periods. When designing for modern-dress pictures, he leaned toward simplicity and untheatrical fashion. "Screen clothes must not interfere with the action," he said. "It's better to underdress your people than let their clothes get in the way."

This underdressing approach was not only suitable to Orry-Kelly's job as movie costume designer; it also resulted in the widespread popularity of his designs. Copies of his screen designs were sold to department stores with the approval of the studio. Russeks 5th Avenue advertised them as "Screenlight Fashions." One design—a jumper for Ingrid Bergman in *Casablanca* (1942)—was such a success it prompted him to ". . . wish I had a dime for every time that's been copied." The dropped-waistline silhouette was another popular style of the 1940's attributed to Orry-Kelly. His views were frequently reported by fashion writers, and during the 1930's his byline appeared on a syndicated newspaper fashion column, "Hollywood Parade."

Orry-Kelly, who became a naturalized United States citizen in 1934, was inducted into the army in 1942. He returned to Warner Brothers after his army service but a series of disagreements led to his being fired. He worked there again only on special assignments—*Mr. Skeffington,* as noted, and, in 1958, the wardrobe for Rosalind Russell in *Auntie Mame.* In a *New York Herald Tribune* review of the latter movie, critic Paul V. Beckley wrote, "Miss Russell's swirling, satirical characterization is helped immensely by the dazzling costumes of Orry-Kelly."

From Warner Brothers, Orry-Kelly went to 20th Century-Fox. Later, he worked for Universal Pictures and for Metro-Goldwyn-Mayer, where he was one of three designers for the musical *An American in Paris*. He and the others, Walter Plunkett and Irene Sharaff, won Academy Awards for the picture's costumes. He also received Academy Awards for his costumes in the 1957 film *Les Girls* and the 1959 film *Some Like It Hot*.

Orry-Kelly's interest in fine art continued throughout his life. He often painted during his off-work hours, and in 1952 a showing of his work, sponsored by Mrs. Oscar Hammerstein II, was presented in New York City.

Orry-Kelly, described by his colleague Walter Plunkett as "the greatest of the Hollywood designers," never married. He was at work on the picture *Kiss Me, Stupid* at the time of his death in Hollywood, Calif.

[See Elizabeth Burris-Meyer, *This Is Fashion* (1943); Diana Vreeland, *Romantic and Glamorous Hollywood Design* (1974); David Chierichetti, *Hollywood Costume Design* (1976); Elizabeth Leese, *Costume Design in the Movies* (1977); Dale McConathy with Diana Vreeland, *Hollywood Costume* (1976). Obituaries are in *New York Times*, Feb. 27, 1964, and *New York Herald Tribune*, Feb. 28, 1964.]

DOROTHY BRIGSTOCK SCHOENFELD

OSTERHOUT, WINTHROP JOHN VAN-LEUVEN (Aug. 2, 1871–Apr. 9, 1964), physiologist, was born in Brooklyn, N.Y., the son of the Reverend John Vanleuven Osterhout and Annie Loranthe Beman. His father was a Baptist minister in poor communities in Massachusetts and Rhode Island. Osterhout attended Brown University, where he received the B.A. in 1893 and the M.A. in 1894. From 1893 to 1895 he was an instructor at Brown and at Woods Hole, Mass. (1894–1895).

Osterhout's interest in biology blossomed in 1892 after he attended a summer course in botany at Woods Hole. The scientists he met there who influenced his research included William A. Setchell and Jacques Loeb. He did further scientific study at Brown University, Bonn University (1895–1896, under the plant cytologist Eduard Strasburger), and the University of California at Berkeley, where he completed work for the Ph.D. under Setchell in 1899. On June 17, 1899, he married Anna Maria Landstrom; they had two daughters.

During the seven years Osterhout spent with Loeb at Berkeley, he turned from studies of morphology and cytology to physiology and physical chemistry. Among his early discoveries was the fact that plants require sodium, which previously had been believed essential only to animals. Employing green, blue, brown, and red algae as his test subjects, Osterhout discovered

in 1912 that the chief functions of sodium in plants include maintenance of osmotic pressure and suppression of the toxic action of other salts.

Osterhout was a talented lecturer who used showmanship effectively. He published an excellent textbook, *Experiments with Plants* (1905), in which he described simple but ingenious class exercises using seeds, corks, lamps, local plants, and other easily obtainable materials. Emphasis was placed on improvisation to understand an experiment's implications. The book was illustrated by Luther Burbank, whom Osterhout knew, and was translated into Dutch and Russian. For his advanced students Osterhout offered some of the earliest practical courses in biochemistry.

Osterhout left Berkeley to accept an assistant professorship at Harvard in 1909. In Cambridge his research interests widened. He studied mathematics and chemistry and their application to botany.

Osterhout devised a system of determining the osmotic pressure of a cell by measuring the electrical resistance of the living tissue. A weak current was passed through the tissue and recorded with a Wheatstone bridge. This procedure made use of an organism not previously used in research, the *Laminaria*, or kelp. Osterhout's studies were summarized in a series of Lowell lectures presented in Boston in 1922 and published as *Injury, Recovery and Death in Relation to Conductivity and Permeability* (1923).

Loeb and Osterhout founded the *Journal General of Physiology* in 1918. Osterhout remained an editor of the journal for forty-five years. The journal became the primary vehicle for publication of his students' and his own research.

In 1924, Osterhout accepted the post as head of the division of general physiology left vacant by Loeb's death at the Rockefeller Institute. The next decade was the most productive of his career. He published many papers, some in collaboration with E. S. Harris and S. E. Hill, extending his work on electrical measurements and the effects of salts. Osterhout used ingenious models to explain the penetration of electrolytes into cells. An important concept that emerged from these studies was that of "carrier molecules," used to describe cellular permeability.

By the age of sixty illness had begun to limit Osterhout's activities. He suffered from glaucoma, which eventually resulted in blindness, and he had a heart attack in 1933. In the same year he and his first wife were divorced, and on February 27 he married Marian Irwin, who worked with him in the laboratory. Assisted by technicians, she carried out research under Osterhout's direction for more than two decades.

Osterhout was elected to the National Academy of Sciences in 1919. He died in New York City.

[The American Philosophical Society Library in Philadelphia has five boxes of Osterhout material containing 750 pieces and 80 photographs from 1894 to 1961; the library has prepared an inventory of this collection. The Rockefeller Archive Center, North Tarrytown, N.Y., holds five folders of Osterhout's papers and two folders of material relating to Marian I. Osterhout. Books besides those mentioned in the text are *The Nature of Life* (1923) and *Some Fundamental Problems of Cellular Physiology* (1927). See L. R. Blinks's piece in *Biographical Memoirs: National Academy of Sciences* (1974). An obituary notice is in *New York Times*, Apr. 10, 1964.]

AUDREY B. DAVIS

OSWALD, LEE HARVEY (Oct. 18, 1939–Nov. 24, 1963), assassin of President John F. Kennedy, was born in New Orleans, La., the son of Robert E. Lee Oswald, an insurance premium collector, and of Marguerite Claverie. Two months before Oswald was born, his father died of a heart attack. He was raised by a mother who alternately neglected and overprotected him. He grew up to be an unstable, violence-prone malcontent. Although Oswald was intelligent, he had dyslexia, a reading problem. In 1945 his mother married Edwin A. Ekdahl, an electrical engineer; they were divorced in 1948. Because of his mother's frequent moves, by age ten Oswald had attended six schools.

In 1952, Oswald and his mother moved to New York City to live with her son by her first marriage, John Pic, Jr., who was in the U.S. Coast Guard. After Oswald threatened Pic's wife with a knife, he and his mother, who always defended his behavior, however aberrant, moved out. Because he was repeatedly truant, school officials sent him to the New York City Youth House, where he was judged in need of psychiatric treatment.

Released from Youth House, Oswald was placed on probation for truancy by the Juvenile Court. While in New York, Oswald read Communist literature and talked of joining the Communist party. At sixteen, unable to join the Marines, he refused to seek the counseling of the Big Brothers as required by his probation officer. He and his mother thereupon moved to New Orleans. When he turned seventeen, Oswald enlisted in the Marines even though still in the tenth grade.

After a year's service, hazing by fellow Marines for being a loner led Oswald to wound himself with a .22-caliber derringer he had bought from a mail-order firm. He was convicted in summary courts-martial for failing to register a weapon and for using profanity to a noncommissioned officer. For the first offense Oswald was sentenced to twenty days at hard labor, loss of pay, and demotion to private. The second offense cost him more pay and twenty-eight days at hard labor. As a trainee he qualified for the sharpshooter rating, the second highest of the ranks, but he fell to marksman, the lowest qualifying rating. He never held a rank higher than private first class.

While stationed in Japan, Oswald studied Russian and enjoyed being called "Oswaldovitch." On Sept. 11, 1959, he received a hardship discharge so that he could care for his mother. He stayed with her in Fort Worth and then left for Europe on September 20. He visited France, England, and Finland, and in mid-October went to Moscow, where, on October 31, he told Richard E. Snyder, the United States consul, that he wanted to renounce his citizenship. After attempting suicide, he turned in his passport to the American embassy and became a stateless person. The Soviet government thereupon sent him to Minsk, where he worked as a metalworker at the Belorussian Radio and Television Plant.

On Apr. 30, 1961, Oswald married Marina Alexandrovna Medvedeva. In June 1962 they traveled to the United States with their infant daughter, and settled in Fort Worth, Tex. They often fought, and separated for a brief time.

Early in 1963, Oswald began to behave erratically and became secretive. That March the family moved to Dallas, where he built a tiny private office in their apartment. Under the alias of A. Hidell, he purchased a Mannlicher-Carcano rifle by mail and equipped it with a telescopic sight. On April 10 he used it in a failed attempt to assassinate Major General Edwin A. Walker, an outspoken rightist. He was never apprehended for this crime; it was only later ballistic evidence that connected this assassination attempt to Oswald.

Two weeks later the Oswalds moved to New Orleans, where he organized a chapter of the Fair Play for Cuba Committee and was arrested for fighting with three anti-Castro Cuban exiles. On September 23, Oswald arranged for his wife, who was pregnant, to move with Ruth Paine, a Quaker friend, to Irving, about ten miles from Dallas. Two days later he went to Mexico City in an unsuccessful attempt to arrange a trip to the Soviet Union via Cuba. To avoid being traced by the Federal Bureau of Investigation, which had been attempting to question him following his trip to Mexico City, Oswald moved to Dallas and took the alias O. H. Lee. Wesley Frazier, the brother of Ruth Paine's neighbor Linnie Mae Randal, worked at the Texas School Book Depository and helped Oswald, at Marina's urging, find a job there. Shortly afterward his second daughter was born.

On Nov. 21, 1963, Oswald visited the Paines' home with Frazier, and the next day went to work with his rifle wrapped in paper. At 12:30 P.M., Nov. 22, 1963, from a window on the sixth floor of the Texas School Book Depository, he shot and killed President John F. Kennedy and wounded Governor John B. Connally. Oswald fled the depository. At approximately 1:15 P.M. he shot and killed Dallas Patrolman J. D. Tippit and ducked into the Texas Theater, where he was captured by the police.

On November 24, as Dallas Police were transferring Oswald from the city jail to the Dallas County jail, Jack Ruby, a Dallas nightclub operator, shot and killed him.

[The records of the Warren Commission are in the National Archives. Official publications on the assassination are *Report of the President's Commission on the Assassination of President John F. Kennedy* (1964); *Hearings Before the President's Commission on the Assassination of President Kennedy*, 26 vols. (1964); and *Findings of the Select Committee on Assassinations in the Assassination of President John F. Kennedy* (1979). Writings on the conspiracy theory include Peter Dale Scott et al., *The Assassinations* (1976); and Edward Jay Epstein, *Legend: The Secret World of Lee Harvey Oswald* (1978). The best biography of Oswald is Priscilla Johnson McMillan, *Marina and Lee* (1977). Also see Jean Stafford, *A Mother in History* (1966); Robert Oswald with Myrick and Barbara Land, *Lee* (1967); James F. Kirkman et al., *Assassination and Political Violence* (1970); and David W. Belin, "The Case Against a Conspiracy," *New York Times Magazine*, July 15, 1979. There is information on Oswald in *New York Times*, Nov. 25 and 26, 1963.]

JAMES P. JOHNSON

OTIS, ARTHUR SINTON (July 28, 1886–Jan. 1, 1964), psychologist and author, was born in Denver, Colo., the son of George Frank Otis and Margaretta Jane Sinton. He entered Stanford University to study civil engineering, but after two years switched to psychology. He received a B.A. in 1910, an M.A. in 1915, and a Ph.D. in 1920, all from Stanford. Otis married Jennie Theresa Minnick on June 15, 1919; they

had no children. He had one stepson by his second marriage to Edna Farmer Jackson.

While working toward his doctorate, Otis experimented with intelligence tests administered to groups and helped devise the psychological tests used during World War I. In 1917 he was assigned to the Army Sanitary Corps before becoming director of research in the psychological division of the Surgeon General's Office in Washington, D.C. After the war he returned briefly to Stanford as an instructor. In 1921, he became editor of tests and mathematics at the World Book Company, a post he held for twenty-five years.

Otis' reputation rests upon his development, publication, administration, and revision of the various forms of the Otis Group Intelligence Scale. Almost completed when the United States entered World War I, it made an indispensable contribution to the Army Alpha Test that was administered to nearly 2 million men drafted into the U.S. Army. Otis' test received an enthusiastic reception when published in 1918. The test has six levels from kindergarten through college, consisting of nonverbal and verbal items, and alternate forms. Nonverbal items ask the respondent to mark from a set of four pictures—for example, rabbit, chicken, turkey, duck—the one that does not belong with the others. Users are warned that the test is not designed to measure innate learning potential and are advised to be especially cautious in interpreting the results from respondents with unusual backgrounds. Lewis M. Terman, the psychologist responsible for the American revision of the Binet individual intelligence test, wrote of it: "The Otis Group Intelligence Scale was the first scientifically grounded and satisfactory scale for testing subjects in groups, and it probably comes as near testing raw 'brain power' as any system of tests yet devised. It is a necessity in schools, industries, armies, or any other institution or situation in which the mental ability of human beings is a factor for consideration." Its success and that of its modified forms, the Otis Self-Administering Tests of Mental Ability (1922) and the Otis Classification Test (1923), was unprecedented in the history of American schoolbook publishing. It continued to be used, but by 1963 the *Sixth Mental Measurements Yearbook* described it as "both antiquated and inadequate." By the time of the publication of the *Seventh . . . Yearbook*, the test had been revised with the aid of Roger Lennon.

During World War II Otis was a psychological consultant to the Navy Bureau of Aeronautics. From 1945 to 1948 he was a psychological and aerodynamics consultant for the Civil Aeronautics Administration. In an age of specialists, Otis was a generalist. As an undergraduate he composed the fight song for the football team; in 1954 he wrote a musical comedy, *Love Among the Stars.* In the same year he published *Reducing Traffic Congestion* and *Financing Highway Improvement.* Among his other books are *Statistical Method in Educational Measurement* (1925), *Modern Plane Geometry* (1926), *Child Accounting Practice* (1927), *Modern Solid Geometry* (1928), *Modern School Arithmetics* (1929), *The First Number Book* (1939), and *Primary Arithmetic Through Experience* (1939). During the war Otis wrote *Elements of Aeronautics* (1941), scripts for the Bray-Otis Aviation Series of educational motion pictures (1943), and *The Airplane Power Plant* (1944). A reporter once wrote of him: "He's master of all trades, jack of none."

Otis was athletic and adventurous. In 1934 he wrote an article on the handling of a glider. After retiring in 1948 he took flying lessons, obtained a pilot's license, bought a plane, and flew from Florida to California and back. A lifelong tennis player, he won several tournaments, including a St. Petersburg senior doubles championship.

In retirement Otis' interests took several more radical turns. In 1948 he and D. R. Brimhall published an article in the *Journal of Applied Psychology,* on the voting of congressmen, which concluded: "To a marked degree, the future voting of an individual congressman can be predicted from his past record." In 1957 Otis published *The Conceptual Framework of the Einstein Theory of Relativity: Is It Valid?,* followed by *Added Revenue Without Burden: A New Plan of Taxation* (1958). The latter advocated a 50 percent tax only on increases in the rental value of property, a significant revision of the original single-tax proposal of Henry George.

Otis died in St. Petersburg, Fla.

[Otis' publications are listed in the text. An obituary is in the *New York Times,* Jan. 2, 1964.]
HENRY C. SMITH

OWEN, STEPHEN JOSEPH (Apr. 21, 1898–May 17, 1964), football coach, was born on the family homestead near Cleo Springs, Okla., the son of James Rufus Owen and Isabella Doak. His father had claimed the quarter section of rolling land when the Cherokee Strip of Indian Territory first opened to settlers; his mother had been the area's first schoolteacher, holding class in a tent.

Owen did not play organized football at grammar school or at the Aline, Okla., High School, from which he graduated in 1916. America's entry into World War I led him to enroll in the Student Army Training Corps (SATC) at Phillips University in nearby Enid, Okla., where he began his career in football. Already six feet tall and weighing 220 pounds, Owen was discovered in the fall of 1918 by coach Johnny Maulbetsch, a recent All-American at Michigan. Maulbetsch coached Owen in the tackle position, at which he started that season. After the war the SATC quickly disbanded, and Owen enrolled as a regular student at Phillips. In this way he managed to play five seasons of college football, not an uncommon occurrence in those days.

With a major in education and physical education, Owen graduated in 1924. He had acquired a football philosophy from Maulbetsch, who had stressed the fundamentals of blocking and tackling and the primacy of sound defense. Using this simple approach, Maulbetsch had guided Phillips to an undefeated season in 1919, including a 10–0 victory over Texas. Owen later molded his own teams along the same lines; they were noted more for preventing than for scoring points.

During the 1924 and 1925 seasons Owen was a tackle for the Kansas City Cowboys in the National Football League (NFL). After the 1925 season he sought to supplement his meager salary by playing exhibition games. One such series brought him to West Palm Beach, Fla., where he impressed Dr. Harry A. March, a member of the New York Giants organization. March soon convinced Giants owner Tim Mara to purchase Owen's contract for $500. Thus, the 1926 season marked the beginning of Owen's long career with New York.

Owen captained the 1927 Giants team, which won the NFL championship through stingy defense, allowing only twenty points in twelve games. His own superlative play at tackle placed him on unofficial "all-league" teams for 1926 and 1927. The pivotal year in Owen's career proved to be 1930. Late in the season head coach Leroy Andrews departed, and the Giants appointed quarterback Benny Friedman and tackle Steve Owen as player-coaches for the concluding games. Owen remained the Giants' coach for twenty-three years.

In 1931 Owen became permanent head coach, but continued to play through the 1933 season. His relationship with the Giants and the

Mara family was personal, a rarity in the uncertain occupation of coaching. Each year his employment was extended by a handshake rather than a written contract.

Owen's record justified his long tenure as coach. In 1933 he led his team into the first "world championship" of the newly divided NFL. The Giants lost to the Chicago Bears 23–21, but revenge came the following year in the legendary "sneakers game," Dec. 9, 1934. The Giants and the Bears, again division champions, met on a frozen Polo Grounds. Concerned about his players' footing, Owen hurriedly procured basketball shoes at Manhattan College. Losing 10–3 at halftime, nine Giants traded cleats for sneakers, and the superior traction enabled them to dominate the second half and win handily, 30–13.

The championship was followed closely by Owen's engagement to Miriam Virginia Sweeny, sister of the Giants' team physician. Married on Nov. 25, 1935, they had no children.

Owen's Giants teams captured additional Eastern Division championships in 1935, 1938, 1939, 1941, 1944, and 1946. His 1938 squad went on to defeat Green Bay for his second NFL championship. Extremely popular with his fellow coaches and with reporters (who affectionately referred to him as "Stout Steve"), Owen pioneered a number of influential coaching strategies. His A formation, a single wing with backfield and unbalanced line strengths set at opposite sides of the center, carried the team to success in 1938 and 1939. His 1949 experiment in platooning ushered in the era of the "one-way" performer. The "umbrella" defense, designed in 1950 to stop the passing attack of Otto Graham and the Cleveland Browns, presaged the 4–3–3 defensive alignment that prevailed in professional football for the next quarter-century.

But Owen's emphasis on defense, a simple offense, and field goals set him distinctly apart from the desires of Giants fans in the early 1950's. A 3–9 season in 1953 led to his resignation as head coach. He left with a lifetime NFL record of 151–100–17. After briefly holding a front-office position with the Giants, he became an assistant coach at Baylor University.

Owen returned to the NFL in 1956–1957 as line coach with the Philadelphia Eagles. In 1958 he joined the staff of the Toronto Argonauts in the Canadian Football League and late in the next season was appointed head coach. During the 1960 season Owen moved to Calgary, again as head coach. He completed his time in Canada by leading the Saskatchewan team during the 1961 and 1962 seasons.

The following year Owen guided the Syracuse Stormers of the United Football League. Late in 1963 the Giants rehired him as a scout. He died in Oneida, N.Y. In 1966 he was elected to the Pro Football Hall of Fame.

[Material on Owen's life is being collected at the Pro Football Hall of Fame, Canton, Ohio, and at the Office of Sports Information, Phillips University, Enid, Okla. Owen wrote *My Kind of Football* (1952) with Joe King. He also contributed to Frank Graham, "Steve Owen: The Man Behind the Giants," *Sport*, Dec. 1947; Charles Dexter, "*Sport*'s Tape-Recorder Lets You Hear Steve Owen," *Sport*, Jan. 1953. A sketch of his life is in George Sullivan, *Pro Football's All-Time Greats* (1968). See also these columns by Arthur Daley in the *New York Times*: Dec. 18, 1934; Nov. 26, 1935; Jan. 22, 1941; May 13 (sec. III) and Sept. 11, 1945; Oct. 13, 1948; Nov. 22, 1950; Dec. 11 and Dec. 13, 1953 (sec. V). Obituaries are in the *New York Times, New York Herald Tribune,* and *New York Daily News,* May 18, 1964.]

STEPHEN HARDY

OXNAM, GARFIELD BROMLEY (Aug. 14, 1891–Mar. 12, 1963), Methodist bishop, author, and social reformer, was born in Sonora, Calif., the son of Thomas Henry Oxnam, a mining engineer, and of Mary Ann (Mamie) Jobe. He began his elementary education at Delamar, Nev., and entered Los Angeles High School in 1905. Forced to leave school by his father's ill health and the panic of 1907, Oxnam worked briefly and completed a year of business school before entering the University of Southern California in 1909. While there, he attended lectures by Alexander Berkman and Eugene V. Debs and read American labor history.

After graduating with the B.A. in 1913, Oxnam entered Boston University, where he studied with the radical social ethicist Harry F. Ward. After his marriage to Ruth Fisher, the daughter of a wealthy California oilman, on Aug. 19, 1914, he received the B.S.T. from Boston in 1915 and did further study at Harvard University and Massachusetts Institute of Technology. The Oxnams had three children.

In 1916, Oxnam was ordained in the Methodist Episcopal Church and began his ministry at Poplar, Calif. A year later he moved to the Church of All Nations in Los Angeles, where he served as pastor until 1927. He taught social ethics at the University of Southern California from 1919 to 1923, when his first book, *The Social Principles of Jesus,* was published.

Oxnam traveled extensively throughout his

career. He visited the Soviet Union with an American delegation in 1926 and published *Russian Impressions* the following year. In 1928, after serving for a year as professor of practical theology and city church at Boston University's School of Theology, he was named president of DePauw University, Greencastle, Ind. His tolerance of dancing and abolition of compulsory military training quickly won the approval of students and the enmity of the American Legion. As secretary of the World Peace Commission and a member of the Methodist Federation for Social Service, Oxnam became a leading spokesman for his denomination's progressives. Frightened that Methodists had turned "socialistic," Elizabeth Dilling accused him of being a key agent in her *Red Network* (1934). Nevertheless, Oxnam served three times as a delegate to quadrennial General Conferences of the Methodist Episcopal Church and in 1936 was elected a bishop and assigned to Omaha, Neb. Three years later he was reassigned to Boston.

Although an early advocate of American intervention in World War II, Oxnam worked to protect the rights of conscientious objectors throughout the war. In *The Ethical Ideals of Jesus in a Changing World* (1941) he commented upon the social creed that he had long espoused: the solidarity of the human race, the supremacy of the common good, and equal rights for all. He insisted that people, not things, are the goal of social living; that cooperation, not selfish competition, is the law of progress; and that love, not force, is the social bond. In 1941, Oxnam convened an exploratory conference on the bases of a just and lasting peace, and in 1943 he launched a crusade for a new world order, developing public support for a strong world peace organization at the end of the war. Yet, with two sons in uniform, he defended Allied bombing policy in Europe as a means to ending the war quickly.

While in Boston, Oxnam persuaded William Cardinal O'Connell to join him in a denunciation of anti-Semitism, but after his move to New York City in 1944, he engaged the Roman Catholic hierarchy in battle over other issues. He attacked the denial of religious liberty in Spain, Colombia, and Argentina; opposed federal aid to parochial schools; and led Protestant opposition to the appointment of an American emissary to the Vatican after World War II.

When Oxnam helped to found Protestants and Other Americans United for the Separation of Church and State in 1948, Francis Cardinal Spellman and Archbishop Richard Cushing

charged him with "unhooded and refined klansmanship." Nevertheless, he became a leader in postwar Protestant ecumenism. He served as president of the Federal Council of Churches from 1944 to 1946, was one of six founding presidents of the World Council of Churches from 1948 to 1954, and presided at the organization of the National Council of Churches in 1950.

In 1952, when Oxnam had become bishop of Washington, D.C., the leadership of the House Un-American Activities Committee was threatening an investigation of Communist infiltration of American churches. When Oxnam questioned the competence of the committee's "vermillion vigilantes," Representative Donald Jackson charged that he was "to the Communist front what Man O'War was to thoroughbred horse racing" and that he "served God on Sunday and the Communist front for the balance of the week."

Oxnam appeared before the committee on July 21, 1953, to demand that it clear its files of unsubstantiated charges against him and to challenge the constitutionality of methods used to discredit patriotic Americans. He forced the committee to acknowledge that it had no evidence of Communist sympathy against him, thus striking a crucial blow against McCarthyism. In *I Protest* (1954), Oxnam expanded upon his objections to the committee's methods.

A stocky, square-jawed man with a powerful voice, who looked and dressed like a businessman, Oxnam sometimes irritated corporate executives by his defense of labor's interests. He might well have been remembered as the extraordinarily able administrator that he was, but his challenge to the House Un-American Activities Committee etched him on the memory of his generation as a man determined to defend American civil liberties. Oxnam remained active until 1960, when the effects of Parkinson's disease forced his retirement. He died in White Plains, N.Y.

[Collections of Oxnam's papers are at the Library of Congress (the largest); Wesley Theological Seminary, Washington, D.C.; and Rose Memorial Library, Drew University. His more important books include *Youth and the New America* (1928); *Facing the Future Unafraid* (1944); *Preaching in a Revolutionary Age* (1944); *Labor in Tomorrow's World* (1945); *Personalities in Social Reform* (1950); *The Church and Contemporary Change* (1950); *On This Rock* (1951); and *A Testament of Faith* (1958). There is no biography of Oxnam. Two dissertations that focus on his attitude toward Communism and his confrontation with HUAC are David E. Gillingham, "The Politics of Piety: G. Bromley Oxnam and the Un-American Activities Committee" (Princeton University, 1967); and William C. Logan, "Bishop G. Bromley Oxnam: A Study of His Views on Communism and of the Consequences of These Views" (Wesley Theological Seminary, 1968). Also see Bruce Catton, "Witness for Decency," *Nation*, Aug. 1, 1953; H. E. Frey, "Bishop Oxnam's Challenge," *Christian Century*, Aug. 5, 1953; Reinhold Niebuhr, "Communism and the Clergy," *Christian Century*, Aug. 19, 1953; and Ralph Lord Roy, *Communism and the Churches* (1960). Obituaries are in the *New York Times*, Mar. 16, 1963 (western ed.), and, abbreviated, Apr. 1, 1963 (because of newspaper strike); and *Time*, Mar. 22, 1963.]

RALPH E. LUKER

PAPANICOLAOU, GEORGE NICHOLAS (May 13, 1883–Feb. 19, 1962), anatomist and oncologist who developed the Papanicolaou smear ("Pap" test), a means of cancer diagnosis, was born in Kyme, Greece, the son of Nicholas Papanicolaou, a physician, and of Mary Kritsoutas. He received his early schooling in Kyme, and at age eleven was sent to Athens for further education. He received the M.D. degree in 1904 from the University of Athens and then served as an assistant surgeon in the Greek army until 1906. After practicing for one year with his father, Papanicolaou did postgraduate work in biology at the universities of Jena, Freiburg, and Munich. The last awarded him the Ph.D. in zoology in 1910. He then returned to Greece, where he married Mary Mavroyeni, the daughter of an army officer, on Sept. 25, 1910. They had no children.

Because opportunities for scientific investigation in Greece were limited, Papanicolaou set out for Paris with his wife, who became his lifelong career associate. En route he visited the Oceanographic Institute of Monaco, where, after an unexpected offer of a staff position, he remained for a year as a physiologist. During the Second Balkan War he again served in the Medical Corps of the Greek army (1912–1913). He and his wife then immigrated to the United States, arriving at New York City on Oct. 19, 1913, without definite plans.

Through the influence of Thomas Hunt Morgan, professor of experimental zoology at Columbia University, Papanicolaou obtained a part-time position as assistant in the Department of Pathology and Bacteriology at New York Hospital. In September 1914 he was appointed assistant and research biologist in anatomy at the Cornell Medical College under Charles R. Stockard. Mary Papanicolaou was soon given a job as her husband's technician.

In 1917, Stockard invited Papanicolaou to collaborate in his work in experimental genetics. At that time great interest was focused on the role of chromosomes in the determination of sex. Papanicolaou began work in this area, using the ovum of the guinea pig. He established the correlation of the cytology of vaginal smears with ovarian and uterine cycles. This work resulted in a paper (1917) by Papanicolaou and Stockard that described the cellular changes observable in vaginal epithelium during the estrous cycle. Their technique became a standard method for studying the sexual (estrous) cycle in other laboratory animals and influenced subsequent work in endocrinology and sexual physiology. Its application in the mouse as an assay of follicular hormone resulted ultimately in the first isolation of a sex hormone, estrogen.

In 1923, Papanicolaou extended his studies to humans by undertaking a systematic study of the cytology of human vaginal secretions in an effort to learn whether comparable vaginal cellular changes occur in women in association with the menstrual cycle. His first observation of distinctive neoplastic cells in the vaginal fluid of a woman with cancer of the cervix gave Papanicolaou what he later described as "one of the most thrilling experiences in my scientific career," and led to redirection of his work.

At this point Papanicolaou focused on careful cytologic study of specimens obtained from women with cancer of the uterus and with other diseases of the reproductive tract. In 1928 his observations, entitled "New Cancer Diagnosis," were presented at the Third Race Betterment Conference and were published later that year. He predicted the application of this technique to the diagnosis of cancer not only of the female reproductive system but also of other organ systems.

For several years Papanicolaou's results were not generally accepted by the medical community, and in 1932 he turned his attention to other problems. For the next five or six years he investigated the effects of various hormones on reproductive cells. In 1939, he began collaboration with Herbert F. Traut, a gynecologist who was convinced of the value of cytologic methodology. They accumulated an enormous amount of data that was published as *Diagnosis of Uterine Cancer by the Vaginal Smear* (1943). Acceptance of the findings followed, and the method was widely acclaimed. Superficial lesions could now be detected in their incipient, preinvasive phase, before the appearance of any symptoms. Papanicolaou later referred to his discovery as an example of serendipity; his early objectives were totally unrelated to cancer detection.

The Papanicolaou smear soon achieved wide application as a routine screening technique. This was followed by a sharp reduction in the death rate from cancer of the uterus and of the cervix. Interest in this diagnostic method has spread rapidly throughout the world since 1947, when the first course in exfoliative cytology was offered at Papanicolaou's laboratory in New York City. The principal value of the test lies in cancer screening, but it is also applied to the prediction of cancer radiosensitivity, the evaluation of the effectiveness of radiotherapy, and the detection of recurrence after treatment. Papanicolaou's work is among the most important in the field of cancer in modern times.

Papanicolaou rose to the rank of professor of clinical anatomy at Cornell University in 1924, and became emeritus in 1949. An indefatigable worker, he is said never to have taken a vacation. He received many honors for his scientific contributions, including the Amory (1948), Borden (1948), Lasker (1950), Wien (1953), Modern Medicine (1954), Bertner (1955), and Passano (1956) awards; the Honor Award of the American Cancer Society (1952); and the Royal Order of Phoenix, presented to him in 1953 by King Paul of Greece. In 1973 Greece, and in 1978 the United States, issued commemorative postage stamps in his honor.

In November 1961, Papanicolaou became director of the Miami Cancer Institute. He died in Miami three months later. The institute was then renamed the Papanicolaou Cancer Research Institute.

[Papanicolaou's writings include "The Existence of a Typical Oestrous Cycle in the Guinea-Pig—with a Study of Its Histological and Physiological Changes," *American Journal of Anatomy*, Sept. 1917, with C. R. Stockard; "New Cancer Diagnosis," in *Proceedings. Third Race Betterment Conference, January 2–6, 1928* (1928); and *Atlas of Exfoliative Cytology* (1954). For information on Papanicolaou's life, see Irena Koprowska, "George N. Papanicolaou—As We Knew Him," *Acta Cytologica*, Sept.–Oct. 1977; and R.C. Swan, "George N. Papanicolaou," *Anatomical Record*, 1962. An obituary is in the *New York Times*, Feb. 20, 1962.]

HARRIS D. RILEY, JR.

PATE, MAURICE (Oct. 14, 1894–Jan. 19, 1965), businessman and United Nations official, was born in Pender, Nebr., the son of Richard Ellsworth Pate, president of the town bank, and of Rachel M. Davis. When he was three, the family moved to Denver, Colo., where his father bought a large furniture store and represented several eastern steel companies. After attending Denver public schools, Pate entered Princeton University, from which he graduated in 1915 with a B.S. He spent the next few months in Hartley, Iowa, working in his uncle's bank.

Dissuaded by his parents from following his impulse to join the Canadian army, Pate secured a position with Herbert Hoover's Committee for Relief in Belgium in April 1916. He went overseas and, after the United States entered the war, served in France with the Twenty-ninth Engineering Regiment. He next rejoined Hoover's commission, now the American Relief Administration, and in February 1919 took charge of a program feeding Polish children.

Pate worked for this organization until it ceased operations in 1922. Fond of Poland by now and having many Polish friends, he remained there. From 1922 to 1927 he was an executive for Standard Oil of New Jersey. Next he ran his own import firm and represented several English and American banks in Warsaw. In 1927, Pate married Jadwiga Monkowska; they were amicably divorced in 1937.

From 1935 to 1939, Pate lived and worked in New York City as an investment banker and director of several business firms. Within a few hours after Germany's invasion of Poland on Sept. 1, 1939, he was in Washington, D.C., volunteering to do whatever he could for Poland. With Herbert Hoover's backing he was named president of the Commission for Polish Relief. After Pearl Harbor he joined the American Red Cross as director of relief to Allied prisoners of war. Pate's administrative acumen, together with the worldwide political contacts he had built up over the years, enabled him to secure safe passage for $170 million worth of relief supplies through war zones in Europe and the Far East.

Although he had intended to return to private business after the war, Pate did not hesitate to accompany Hoover when he undertook a world food survey at President Harry S. Truman's request in 1946. He was appalled by the condition of children in war-ravaged Europe. The Pate-Hoover report to Truman and a subsequent White House initiative helped spur the United Nations General Assembly to establish its International Children's Emergency Fund (UNICEF) in December 1946. The following month Pate was appointed UNICEF's first executive director, a post he held for the rest of his life.

Under Pate's direction UNICEF grew into one of the United Nations' most successful or-

599

ganizations. At first UNICEF concentrated on providing short-term emergency aid—food, clothing, medicine—for the countries of central and eastern Europe. But by 1950 it had shifted its focus to the worldwide problem of chronic starvation and disease among children. In 1953 the United Nations General Assembly made UNICEF a "continuing" agency. Thereafter, UNICEF steadily increased the scope of its operations: in 1965 the agency had 551 long-term programs under way that provided benefits for more than 55 million children in 116 countries.

Although UNICEF responded promptly to floods, storms, epidemics, and other emergencies, its more typical operations aimed at eradicating chronic nutritional deficiencies in children's diets throughout the developing world. It shipped millions of pounds of skim milk to these countries and established more than 130 dairies worldwide. Working closely with the Food and Agriculture Organization and the World Health Organization, UNICEF also helped develop new sources of protein-rich foods: fish, cottonseed, and peanut flours, and soybean products. During the 1950's the agency achieved notable progress in its campaign to eradicate malaria and other diseases.

A quiet and self-effacing leader, yet always pragmatic, Pate was adroit at securing support from both political parties in the United States (always UNICEF's largest contributor) and from foreign governments as well. He was an excellent fund-raiser: during his tenure the number of nations pledging contributions to UNICEF rose from 35 in 1953 to 118 a decade later. Although he wrote little and spoke in public only infrequently, Pate traveled extensively on behalf of the agency. He was one of the first westerners allowed into Hungary after the October Revolution in 1956; within hours emergency relief plans for Budapest had been drawn up. Pate also personally organized relief efforts in Leopoldville during the Congo crisis of 1960.

Also in 1960, Pate refused to allow his nomination for the Nobel Peace Prize. The honor, he said, belonged to UNICEF, not to an individual. The gesture typified the man; he was a selfless team player. On Oct. 31, 1961, he married Martha B. Lucas, an educational administrator. He died in New York City. Ironically, Pate never had children of his own.

[Papers and other materials relating to Pate's work with UNICEF are in the United Nations archives. The most helpful biographical piece is in the *New Yorker*, Dec. 2, 1961. *United Nations Bulletin* and *United Nations Review* during the period of Pate's

career with UNICEF both contain information. Obituaries are in the *New York Times* and *New York Herald Tribune*, Jan. 20, 1965.]

THOMAS E. SCHOTT

PATRI, ANGELO (Nov. 27, 1876–Sept. 13, 1965), educator and columnist, was born in Piaggine, Salerno province, Italy, the son of Nicola Petraglia and Carmela Conte. In 1881 the family immigrated to the United States. His childhood was spent in Little Italy in New York City, an environment similar to that of his native land. He was taught to read and write at home, and did not go to school until he was eleven. His father, a construction laborer who was barely literate, passed on to his son a rich oral tradition. He told him fables and stories with such moral impact that the telling of stories as a teaching strategy became the hallmark of Patri's work as teacher, principal, and syndicated newspaper columnist.

Patri learned English on the street. In time the family moved out of Little Italy, and he became conscious of his otherness. Afterward, he reflected, the change of environment made him "forget, indeed to undervalue, the worth of my people." He was ashamed because his parents did not look or speak like Americans.

Despite these negative evaluations Patri had a strong sense of self-worth. His mother hoped he would become a priest, but he wanted to become a doctor. This dream was put aside when his father suffered an accident and could not work. Patri, who had graduated from the City College of New York in 1897, became a teacher in 1898.

After two difficult and depressing years of teaching in New York City public schools, Patri went to Columbia University for further study. Reading John Dewey's *Ethical Principles* altered his views on teaching. He exchanged the notion of discipline ("You made pupils do what you wanted; you must be the master") for the concept of conduct ("The sacredness of the child's individuality must be the moving passion of the teacher"). With an M.A. (1904) in hand, Patri experienced new pleasure and greater freedom in his teaching. After meeting some opposition to his ideas, he found a more congenial principal who encouraged him with these words: "Children grow because of their contact with you, the best that you know and feel."

From 1908 to 1913, Patri was principal of Public School No. 4 in New York City. Establishing the school of his dreams was not easy. To replace an imposed discipline with a real discipline is a long, slow process. He tried to move his teachers away from the routine treatment of the basics and toward subjects that held emotional values and that promoted creative learning. The central idea behind Patri's work was that of service. How could he, the teachers, and the school best serve the children, the parents, and the community? Patri was instrumental in developing a closer understanding between teachers and parents and in gaining the participation of parents in school activities. "Socializing the school means humanizing the teacher," he said. It was during this principalship, in 1910, that he married Dorothy Caterson, a teacher in the school.

Patri seems to have been the first native of Italy to become a public school principal in the United States. From 1913 until his retirement in 1944, he was principal of Paul Hoffman Junior High School in the Bronx, New York City. There he continued and extended his philosophy in liberal education. He took a special interest in gifted children.

Patri's work extended beyond the teaching and administrative duties of his school. He presented his ideas to a wide audience through radio talks, books, and his syndicated column, "Our Children." Although he and his wife had no children of their own, Patri wrote prolifically about children. Many of his columns were collected into books. Besides his publications on education and child rearing, he wrote several books for children.

Patri's autobiography, *A Schoolmaster of the Great City* (1917), is the account of a poor immigrant lad whose dream of service finds fulfillment in the public school establishment. The story is simple and direct, much like the tales his father told him as a child. The story of Patri's Americanization is essentially that the child is an important influence in the assimilation of the parents (indeed, Patri served as his father's teacher in helping him to gain citizenship). This work was reprinted several times and translated into five languages.

Patri's books on child guidance include *Child Training* (1922), *Talks to Mothers* (1923), *Silver Lining and Common Sense* (1924), *School and Home* (1925), *The Problems of Childhood* (1926), *What Have You Got to Give?* (1926), *The Questioning Child, and Other Essays* (1931), *Your Child* (1931), *The Parent's Daily Counselor* (1940), *The Book of Knowledge* (1940), *Your Children in Wartime* (1943), and *How to Help Your Child Grow Up* (1948). He also edited a periodical, *Youth Today* (1938–1941), which contained reading material for young adults. His books for children include

White Patch (1911), *Pinocchio in Africa* (1911), *The Spirit of America* (1924), *Pinocchio in America* (1928), *Pinocchio's Visit to America* (1929), *The Adventures of Pinocchio* (1930), and *Biondino, an Italian Reader* (1951). He died in Danbury, Conn.

[No collection of correspondence has been located. Patri's master's thesis, "Educational Forces Outside the School from the Viewpoint of an Educational Administrator" (1904), is at Columbia University Library. See Ida M. Tarbell, "The Man Who Discovers Children," *Collier's*, Sept. 16, 1922; Dorothy Canfield Fisher, "Angelo Patri's Public School," *Reader's Digest*, June 1940; Sidney M. Katz, "Beloved Teacher," *Education Digest*, May 1947; Olga Peragallo, *Italian-American Authors and Their Contribution to American Literature* (1949). Italian sources include Lombardo Radice, "Patri," *Pedagogia de apostoli e di operai* (1936), and Prezzolini, "Angelo Patri," *Gazzetta del Popolo*, Dec. 19, 1934. Obituaries are in *New York Times*, Sept. 14, 1965, and *Time*, Sept. 24, 1965.]

JACOB L. SUSSKIND

PATRICK, EDWIN HILL ("TED") (Sept. 3, 1901–Mar. 11, 1964), magazine editor, was born in Rutherford, N.J., the son of John Hill Patrick, a creditman, and of Rita Alyea, whom he credited with nourishing his appreciation for haute cuisine and for introducing him to the delights of New York City's fine restaurants. Virtually nothing is known of Patrick's early life or educational background. He came to editing by way of journalism and writing advertising copy. He began by covering sports for a local newspaper. In 1928 he entered advertising as a copywriter with Young and Rubicam, and was promoted to associate copy director in 1936. He married Vera Yereance on Feb. 11, 1929. They had no children.

In the mid-1930's Patrick was writing for World Peaceways, an organization of American businesses, publishers, and advertisers seeking to promote peace. During the fall of 1935 World Peaceways launched a series of radio broadcasts, "To Arms for Peace," as part of a larger campaign that included material in mass magazines prepared by artists and writers from Bruce Barton's agency and Young and Rubicam. Among Patrick's most moving contributions was the caption for a picture of a skeleton wearing a helmet: "Cornfed kid from the West."

After war broke out, Patrick joined the graphics section of the Office of War Information, serving from 1942 until 1944, when he became director (and subsequently vice-president) of printed word copy at Compton Advertising.

Two years later he accepted an editorial position with the Curtis Publishing Company, which had just launched *Holiday*.

In 1946, Curtis was very successful, thanks mainly to the *Saturday Evening Post* and *Ladies' Home Journal*, which in October of that year had a greater advertising volume than any magazine in history. By contrast, *Holiday* got off to a floundering start; after half a dozen issues the venture appeared doomed. The company decided to change editors. Patrick took over with the September issue, and *Holiday's* course began to straighten. Under his direction the magazine reached impressive circulation totals and became consistently profitable.

Patrick's mark could be found in four principal aspects of *Holiday*. First, he attracted top authors by paying handsomely for articles. Writers such as John Steinbeck, Denis Brogan, William Golding, V. S. Pritchett, Robert Graves, Santha Rama Rau, and Jacques Barzun enhanced the magazine's literary stature. Patrick published *Westward Ha!*, the humorous "world report" of S. J. Perelman and caricaturist Al Hirschfeld, in twelve installments between April 1947 and May 1948. High-quality visual material constituted a second priority. *Holiday* published the photographs of Arnold Newman and Henri Cartier-Bresson. Third, Patrick sought depth by devoting "special issues" to single countries. Finally, *Holiday* served as a vehicle for Patrick's beliefs about the necessity for international understanding. "In this complex world we live in today," he wrote in 1963, "everybody is traveling and we try to tell them about this world from an international, intellectual point of view."

Patrick had definite ideas about the editor's role in communications, and he expressed them frequently and unequivocally. In a 1959 speech at the eastern meeting of the American Association of Advertising Agencies, he called his colleagues to task for being "entranced by the mechanics of communications rather than the simple fact of communicating. We allow ourselves to get mired in research . . . when we ought to be thinking about, and completely absorbed with, human beings, or better yet, a human being." He also demanded independence for editors: "The difference [between advertising and editing] is that an editor is left more to his own devices. He doesn't have a client—that's the biggest difference in the world. Your only client is the reader, and for that reason you can go directly to him." These guiding principles throughout Patrick's tenure at *Holiday* were central to a dispute over his editorial authority that erupted during the early 1960's.

In 1962, with its other magazines struggling, Curtis lost almost $19 million. Company officials desperately sought ways of limiting costs and checking further declines; these included cutting *Holiday's* promotion budget and reducing its print order. It was rumored that Clay Blair, Jr., editor in chief of the *Saturday Evening Post*, would control the content of all Curtis magazines.

Patrick responded publicly. "It's taken a lot of hard work and seventeen years to build *Holiday* into the magazine it is today," he fumed in a *Newsweek* interview. "This is a twenty-four hour a day job. No one can tell me that he can edit the *Post* from nine to eleven, the *Ladies' Home Journal* from twelve to two, and *Holiday* from three to five and still do any justice to them. This type of editing would be the kiss of death for *Holiday*." Blair then issued an unqualified endorsement of *Holiday* and its editor, stating categorically that there would be no interference.

Honors and distinctions that followed this vote of confidence showed the respect Patrick had attained among his peers. In September 1963 he was elected chairman of the American Society of Magazine Editors, a group dedicated to strengthening the influence of magazines as sources of information and ideas. That fall he also was chosen a director of the Magazine Publishers Association. In "An Open Letter to Ted Patrick," which took up the entire back page of the *New York Times* (Jan. 20, 1964), his colleagues applauded the substance of his work and the success of his publications, closing with "You have pursued excellence, and you have achieved it. You are a great editor."

Patrick's passions were gourmet cooking and visiting foreign lands. He was a member of the Confrérie des Chevaliers du Tastevin and of other gastronomical orders. He wrote critiques of great dining places throughout the United States and abroad, and was instrumental in the institution of *Holiday's* restaurant ratings. Patrick died in New York City.

[Correspondence of Patrick's is in the David Ogilvy Papers, Manuscript Division, Library of Congress (access restricted to researchers with written permission from Mr. Ogilvy or his heirs until Jan. 8, 1990). Patrick also wrote *The Thinking Man's Dog* (1964) and, with Silas Spitzer, *Great Restaurants of America* (1960). Also see "Marketing: Curtis Counts Its Chips," *Business Week*, Sept. 28, 1946; "Grolier Gastronomy," *New Yorker*, Feb. 25, 1961; and "Press: Holiday Life," *News-*

week, July 1, 1963. Obituaries appeared in the *New York Times,* Mar. 12, 1964, and "Ted Patrick," *Holiday,* May 1964.]

J. KIRKPATRICK FLACK

PATTERSON, ALICIA (Oct. 15, 1906–July 2, 1963), editor and publisher, was born in Chicago, Ill., the daughter of Joseph Medill Patterson and Alice Higinbotham. Her father was the founder and publisher of the tabloid *New York Daily News,* and her paternal grandfather, Robert Wilson Patterson, was editor and publisher of the *Chicago Tribune,* which he took over from his father-in-law, Joseph Medill, the *Tribune's* developer and publisher for forty-four years. Robert R. McCormick, editor and publisher of the *Tribune,* was a cousin, and Eleanor ("Cissy") Medill Patterson, owner of the *Washington Times-Herald,* was an aunt.

With this background Patterson naturally was close to journalistic discussion, decision making, and practice from girlhood. She was twelve when her father left the *Chicago Tribune* to launch the *New York Daily News* (first called the *Illustrated Daily News*). She attended the Foxcroft School in Middleburg, Va., and several other private schools where her short stays were anything but outstanding. After obtaining an overall view of the *Daily News* while working in its promotion department (1927–1928), she became a reporter. But her erroneous use of an incorrect name in an article on a divorce involving prominent people brought a libel suit that halted her newspaper career.

Patterson returned to Chicago, and later in 1928 she married James Simpson, Jr., son of the board chairman of Marshall Field, on a twelve-month "trial basis." At the end of the year, she separated from Simpson (they were divorced in 1930) and became a staff writer for *Liberty* magazine, also owned by her family. Using the nom de plume Agnes Homberg, she wrote articles based on her experiences while working as a department store detective, a magazine seller, and a cashier in a theater. Patterson was also literary critic for the *New York Daily News* (1932–1943).

Patterson's father influenced her in many ways. For example, he persuaded her to share his interest in aviation. By 1931 she was a pioneer woman transport pilot, and she continued to fly until 1942. During this time she established several records for women fliers. Her writing for *Liberty* included articles on how she learned to fly and on her life in the air.

On Dec. 23, 1931, Patterson married Joseph W. Brooks, an All-American football star,

World War I army captain, and insurance man. They had no children. This union, strongly promoted by her father, ended in divorce after seven years. On July 1, 1939, she married Harry F. Guggenheim, a diplomat, business executive, and philanthropist. They had no children. Guggenheim, Patterson later said, "emancipated [her] from purposelessness." But this marriage was so bitterly opposed by her father that an estrangement resulted. The break was hard on both; he had relied on her companionship, and she had been devoted to him: "a wonderful guy —warm, gay and tough."

To prove to her father that a woman could develop and manage a newspaper, Patterson put approximately $70,000 of her husband's money into the acquisition of the defunct *Nassau County Journal,* on Long Island. She renamed it *Newsday,* assembled pages for the first tabloid-size issue in a converted garage in Hempstead, N.Y., and on Sept. 3, 1940, printed the first 15,000 copies on an outmoded press. She surveyed her handiwork and announced, with characteristic self-criticism, "I'm afraid it looks like hell."

The *Newsday* of Alicia Patterson—she always used her maiden name—won quick acceptance. In two years it achieved a circulation of 32,000, and in less than fifteen years the total press run went well above 200,000. After 1949 it was published in Garden City, N.Y.

Much of *Newsday's* success was due to zoned news coverage, achieved through the publication of four separate editions. Also a factor was the emphasis on attractive appearance. The paper's use of three columns instead of the usual tabloid five and its willingness to venture into new page layouts caused *Time* magazine to assert: "*Newsday* looks like no other U.S. daily." In 1952 and in 1955 *Newsday* received the N. W. Ayer and Son award for "excellence in typography, makeup and printing." The 1955 citation emphasized "ease of reading," "balance and harmony of different elements on a page," and "treatment of pages as a unit of design."

Patterson, as fully concerned with content as with form, dug into local problems that were going unexplored. She strongly supported managing editor Alan Hathway's exposure of corruption at racetracks, which brought about the conviction of William De Koning, building trades union leader, for extorting payments from Roosevelt Raceway contractors at Westbury. These articles received the 1954 Pulitzer Prize for "meritorious public service." Patterson's campaigns included such diverse causes as seeking better service on the Long Island Railroad, calling for a low-tuition college for Long Island, and raising funds to purchase the Huntington, N.Y., home of Walt Whitman as a memorial museum.

Editorially, Patterson broke with her isolationist New York and Chicago kin by supporting internationalist positions in foreign affairs. She was generally a Republican, but on Long Island she sometimes supported the Democratic ticket. She called for the recognition of Communist China, denounced Senator Joseph R. McCarthy, and favored moderation in race relations. Patterson said frankly that *Newsday* reflected her temperamental personality "with violent likes and dislikes." Her job, as she saw it, was "to make *Newsday* readable, entertaining, comprehensive, informative, interpretive, lively but still sufficiently serious-minded so that no Long Islander will feel compelled to read any New York City newspaper."

Patterson was active in professional organizations, and did not hesitate to take her ideas to fellow editors and publishers, whom she urged to cover community needs more adequately, as a counter to the competition of television. She died in New York City after a series of operations for a stomach ulcer.

At the time of Patterson's death, *Newsday's* circulation stood at 370,000. She had written in 1960, in the twentieth-anniversary issue: "It is true that we have become prosperous. But prosperity is dangerous, unless you keep it in its place. We want to grow bigger, but far more we want to grow better and wiser and stronger. We want to slay the evil dragons and rescue ladies in distress. We want to keep our ideals always shined up and our courage high. And we want to remember that even the best mousetrap can be improved."

[See Charles Wertenbaker, "The Case of the Hot-Tempered Publisher," *Saturday Evening Post,* May 12, 1951; Kenneth Stewart and John Tebbel, *Makers of Modern Journalism* (1952); "Alicia in Wonderland," *Time,* Sept. 13, 1954; J. W. Tebbel, *An American Dynasty* (repr. 1968); and Edwin Emery and Michael Emery, *The Press and America,* 4th ed. (1978). Obituaries are in the *New York Times* and *Newsday,* July 3, 1963.]

IRVING DILLIARD

PAUL, JOSEPHINE BAY (Aug. 10, 1900–Aug. 6, 1962), investment executive, was born Josephine Holt Perfect in Anamosa, Iowa, the daughter of Otis Lincoln Perfect, a realtor, and of Tirzah Holt. When she was six, the family moved to Brooklyn, N.Y. She graduated in 1916 from Brooklyn Heights Seminary, a fashionable finishing school, and then attended Colorado College, in Manitou (1916–1917). She then worked briefly as a secretary.

Perfect's abilities as a businesswoman were early evidenced when she and her younger sister, Tirzah, ran a flourishing greeting card business in Brooklyn (1928–1933). Tirzah was responsible for the design work while Josephine traveled as far as the Midwest as sales manager. During this period she revitalized the moribund Junior League of Brooklyn and made it solvent enough to pay off its outstanding debts.

On Aug. 30, 1942, Perfect married her long-time employer Charles Ulrick Bay, a wealthy Norwegian-American broker and investor. Perfect and Bay had been constant companions since about 1923, and Bay's mother had frequently traveled with them. From 1946 to 1953, Bay was United States ambassador to Norway. While living in Norway, the Bays adopted three children.

In 1955 the Tennessee Transmission Company purchased Bay's interest in Bay Petroleum for approximately $20 million.

After her husband's death on Dec. 31, 1955, Josephine Bay assumed many of his directorships and became chairman of the executive committee of the American Export Lines, representing a third of the common shares. She had been a member of the board of directors since May 18, 1955, and was the first woman to control a major steamship company in the United States. She at once set about reorganizing the firm.

On Dec. 1, 1956, Bay was named president and chairman of the board of A. M. Kidder, of which her husband had been a partner, thus becoming the first woman to head a member firm of the New York Stock Exchange. For months following the death of Charles Bay, there had been doubts on Wall Street as to the future of the ninety-two-year-old firm. Bay said that her husband would have wanted her to carry on the family tradition in A. M. Kidder, so she insisted on succeeding him. Her determination, she said, was part of a "wave of the future," a woman's crusade for equality with men:

When women are fully entrusted with estates —not in the role of mere passive coupon-clippers, but as active investment owners— our economy will be more vibrant and more venturesome in areas where increasing capital is our constant need. I am hopeful that in my new responsibilities I can help make some of these things come true.

On Jan. 1, 1959, Bay married Capton Michael Paul, an oil operator and investment banker. Continuing her career as a businesswoman, Josephine Bay Paul became a director of the Connecticut Railway and Lighting Company, of the American Foundation of Religion and Psychiatry, and of General Foods.

In 1956 the Associated Press named Paul woman of the year in business. On Mar. 15, 1957, she was awarded the Commander's Cross of the Order of St. Olaf by Norway for humanitarian services in that country while her first husband was United States ambassador. In May 1962, President John F. Kennedy named her to the advisory committee of the National Cultural Center.

Paul and both her husbands were known for their generous gifts to charitable, educational, and cultural institutions. Her first husband established the Charles Ulrick and Josephine Bay Foundation (1950), to further medical research and education. In 1958 she gave four tapestries, valued at $18,000, to Fairleigh Dickenson University. In November 1962, in memory of his wife, Capton Paul donated $100,000 to the National Cultural Center, the largest gift made to it to that time.

One of Paul's favorite avocations was horse racing. She owned fifteen horses, including Idun, the champion filly of 1957. She once remarked that she was interested in horse racing only as a hobby but that keeping a bad horse was just as expensive as keeping a good one.

Paul moved in the highest echelons of society. She entertained Princess Astrid of Norway in her Palm Beach, Fla., mansion and Adlai Stevenson at her home on Oslo Fjord, Norway, and she turned her Palm Beach mansion over to President and Mrs. Kennedy for the Christmas season of 1961. She also had residences at Palm Springs and Pacific Palisades, Calif., and in upper New York state, as well as in New York City.

Paul's philosophy of business was straightforward and simple. Her object, she said, was to make money and to spend it well. Money well spent created wealth for others. She died in New York City.

[See *Newsweek*, Dec. 3, 1956; *Business Week*, Feb. 23, 1957; and *Forbes*, Apr. 1, 1957. Also see the *New York Times*, Oct. 18, 1956, Feb. 26, 1959, Dec. 25, 1961, and the obituary, Aug. 7, 1962.]
NORMAN E. TUTOROW

PEATTIE, DONALD CULROSS (June 21, 1898–Nov. 16, 1964), popularizer of natural science and history, was born in Chicago, the son of Robert Burns Peattie, who worked on the *Chicago Tribune*, and of Elia Amanda Wilkinson, a literary critic and novelist. He grew up in Windsor Park, a Chicago suburb on the South Shore, surrounded by books and Pre-Raphaelite furnishings. The home was always full of guests, conversation, and laughter.

Donald was a delicate child who had difficulties in Chicago schools, so his mother took him to Tryon, in the Great Smokies of western North Carolina. Away from books and with little companionship, he had time to become interested in nature. In the summer of 1913 he joined his brother and three other college boys in a hiking tour of England and France.

Encouraged by his family, Peattie began to write. With his future wife he set type for his first work, *Blown Leaves* (1916), at University High School. He subsequently attended the University of Chicago (1916–1918), majoring in French.

After his freshman year Peattie tried reporting, but quit after two weeks on the *Tribune*. Meanwhile, his "scrawny and bronchitic body" had been rejected for military service. When his parents moved to New York City in 1918, Peattie joined them and became a reader for the publisher George H. Doran. The inside view of bookmaking that he obtained was invaluable later, but he was miserable as a sideliner in wartime and uncertain of his career. He took refuge in the stimulating city's culture and in lone birdwatching walks and botanizing. A visit to the Bronx Botanical Garden, where the staff encouraged him to use the herbarium, led Peattie to quit his job and start training to be a scientific botanist. He spent the summer of 1919 on the southern Appalachian Trail, and entered Harvard that fall. His first scientific work was *Flora of the Tryon Region* (1928–1931).

Peattie received the B.A. in 1922 and won that year's Witter Bynner Poetry Prize. He then worked for two years under David Fairchild in the Bureau of Foreign Seed and Plant Introduction in Washington, D.C. On May 22, 1923, he married Louise Heegaard Redfield. They had four children. After his *Cargoes and Harvest* (1926), an economic botany, the Peatties collaborated on three books.

In 1924, Peattie left the routines of plant identification and distribution to become a freelance writer. He had a column on the seasons in the *Washington Star* in 1925–1934 (briefly revived in the *Chicago Daily News*). He wrote the biographies of many naturalists for the *Dictionary of American Biography*, and numerous magazine articles. But his life was darkened by sickness and debt. In 1928 his wife's mother provided the couple with the money to escape to Paris.

Their daughter sickened on shipboard and died soon after they reached Paris. The Peatties gradually recovered from this shock on the Riviera, first at Vence, then at Nice, and finally at Menton. Here they both wrote fiction, his wife more successfully, including *Sons of the Martian* (1932), *Port of Call* (1932), and *A Wife to Caliban* (1934). By the time their money ran out, late in 1933, Peattie had disciplined his imagination and acquired a world-historical perspective. His impressionistic history of Vence (1930) was republished in America as *Immortal Village* (1945). The American edition borrowed from the Peatties' summary of their European years, *The Happy Kingdom* (1935).

After returning from France, Peattie lived in Illinois. Through the Field Museum, which had published his scientific study of the Indiana dunes, *Flora of the Indiana Dunes* (1930), he obtained potboiler assignments. In the spring of 1934 he started what became *Almanac for Moderns* (1935) on the pattern of his newspaper column. Next came *Green Laurels* (1936), a collection of lives of naturalists; *A Book of Hours* (1937); and *A Prairie Grove* (1938), an "ecological novel" repeating the pattern of his Vence study and using his wife's family archives. Peattie received Guggenheim fellowships during 1936–1938, to do a study of Robert Owen's community at New Harmony, Ind. The results appeared in the *Reader's Digest* (November 1942) and in a chapter of *Journey into America* (1943). By this time he had established a wide readership for his mixture of history, biography, and description of nature.

In 1937 the Peatties moved to Santa Barbara, Calif. Already a frequent contributor to the *Reader's Digest*, Peattie became its roving editor in 1943. In the last decade of his life he suffered general deterioration from liver dysfunction and diabetes, which affected the spontaneity of his style. His wife bore an increasing share of the burden of his work, for their marriage was an unusually close partnership. Only two of his projected four volumes on the trees of North America appeared (1948, 1950), and no major works were published after *The Rainbow Book of Nature* (1957), for children.

Peattie's style, sometimes turgid, sentimental, and vague, at best joined the humanism of the artist with the precision of the scientist. His forte was to evoke the locality in depth and the person in brief—fitting ideas, feelings, and the natural and historical environment into a compact essay. "I work with the facts," he once said, "and lift them where they sing."

[Peattie's papers, including a biographical sketch by his son Noel, are at the University of California at Santa Barbara. An autobiographical work is *Flowering Earth* (1939). See his wife's sketch in *Wilson Library Bulletin*, Feb. 1936; Joseph Wood Krutch, "Communion with Her Visible Forms," *Nation*, Apr. 24, 1937; his brother Roderick's autobiography, *Incurable Romantic* (1941); and Kimmis Hendrick, "The Peatties Talk About Writing," *Christian Science Monitor Magazine*, Sept. 23, 1950. Obituaries are in the *New York Times*, Nov. 17, 1964; and *Publishers Weekly*, Nov. 30, 1964.]

T. D. Seymour Bassett

PEPPER, GEORGE WHARTON (Mar. 16, 1867–May 24, 1961), lawyer and U.S. senator, was born in Philadelphia, Pa., the son of George Pepper, a physician, and of Hitty Markoe Wharton. His father died when Pepper was five. Pepper was taught at home, first by his mother and later by a tutor, because poor eyesight prevented him from attending school.

In 1883, Pepper entered the University of Pennsylvania. His eyesight had vastly improved, and he enthusiastically participated in athletics, drama, and the school paper. After receiving the B.A., first in his class, in 1887, he entered the University of Pennsylvania Law School. He worked for the law firm of Biddle and Ward while in school and graduated, again first in his class, in 1889. On Nov. 25, 1890, he married Charlotte Root Fisher, daughter of a Yale professor; they had three children.

Over the next twenty-one years Pepper developed an increasingly successful private law practice while also teaching at the University of Pennsylvania and editing and writing legal material. After four years as a teaching fellow, he became Biddle Professor of Law in 1893. With William Draper Lewis he produced the *Digest of Decisions and Encyclopaedia of Pennsylvania Law, 1754–1898* (1898–1906).

By 1892 Pepper had abandoned his early affiliation with the Democratic party, and he remained a loyal Republican thereafter. Because of his expanding private practice, he resigned his faculty position in 1910. That year he was counsel to Chief Forester Gifford Pinchot during the investigation of Secretary of the Interior Richard Ballinger's administration of coal lands in Alaska and the dismissal of Pinchot for criticizing him. Pepper's first involvement in a national political event won him praise, but the political nature of the controversy disturbed him.

During World War I, Pepper served as chairman of the Pennsylvania Council of National Defense. After the war he was a leading opponent of the Versailles Treaty and of American entry into the League of Nations. He felt it was wrong to threaten use of military force to preserve the status quo and thought the treaty too harsh toward the Central Powers.

After Senator Boies Penrose died on Dec. 31, 1921, Pennsylvania Governor William C. Sproul appointed Pepper to his seat. Pepper had earlier declined to serve on the U.S. Circuit Court of Appeals and to run for mayor of Philadelphia. But Sproul's promise to support him in the 1922 special election for the remaining four years of Penrose's term led him to accept. On Jan. 9, 1922, he was sworn in as Pennsylvania's junior senator. The contrast between Penrose, the last and most powerful of Pennsylvania's Republican "bosses," and Pepper, a reform-minded Republican, was significant and upsetting to most members of the Pennsylvania Republican organization, but Pepper won the Republican primary handily in May. Later in 1922 he helped mediate settlement of a strike by anthracite coal workers, which aided him in winning the November election.

During his five years as senator, Pepper served on the Military Affairs, Naval Affairs, and Foreign Relations committees, and he was chairman of the committees on Banking and Currency and the Library of Congress. He was called upon by the U.S. Supreme Court to argue the congressional side in *Myers* v. *United States* (272 U.S. 52 [1926]), involving the right of the president to remove a postmaster without the approval of Congress.

Pepper lost the 1926 Republican senatorial primary, an expensive and bitterly contested campaign, to Philadelphia "boss" William S. Vare in a three-way race that included Governor Gifford Pinchot. Although Pepper, who had the backing of the Andrew Mellon and Joseph Grundy forces, easily outdistanced Pinchot and won in sixty-two of the state's sixty-seven counties, Vare's huge lead in Philadelphia and the backing of antiprohibitionists won him the nomination.

But Vare's election was marked by controversy. Campaign expenses and vote-fraud charges were investigated by the U.S. Senate after the primary and again after Vare's victory in the general election. Nearly $2 million had been spent on behalf of the ticket of Pepper and gubernatorial candidate John S. Fisher, and Vare's primary-campaign expenditures were even larger. Vare was barred from taking his Senate seat because of excessive campaign expenditures, so in 1929, Governor Fisher appointed Grundy, one of his strongest backers, to the vacant seat.

Pepper resumed his law practice. In 1936 he represented the defendants in *United States* v. *Butler* (297 U.S. 1 [1936]), the Supreme Court case that resulted in the invalidation of the Agricultural Adjustment Act. He published his autobiography, *Philadelphia Lawyer*, in 1944, and he continued to practice law and to serve professional organizations into his eighties. He died in Devon, Pa.

Pepper was a many-talented man, representative of the finest conservative thinking, the personification of "respectable" Philadelphia. An excellent lawyer, he based his opposition to the League of Nations and to the New Deal on principle, not petty partisan advantage.

[Pepper's papers are in the Van Pelt Library of the University of Pennsylvania. His writings include *The Way* (1909); *A Voice from the Crowd* (1915); *In the Senate* (1930); and *Family Quarrels* (1931). On his work in the anthracite strike, see Robert H. Zieger, "Senator George Wharton Pepper and Labor Issues in the 1920s," *Labor History*, Spring 1968; and "Pennsylvania Coal and Politics: The Anthracite Strike of 1925–1926," *Pennsylvania Magazine of History and Biography*, Apr. 1969. Also see Frank R. Kent, "Pinchot *vs.* Pepper *vs.* Vare," *Nation*, Apr. 14, 1926, and Samuel J. Astorino, "The Contested Senate Election of William Scott Vare," *Pennsylvania History*, Apr. 1961. An obituary is in the *New York Times*, May 25, 1961.]

ALFRED L. MORGAN

PERKINS, FRANCES (Apr. 10, 1880–May 14, 1965), labor reformer and secretary of labor, was born Fannie Coralie Perkins in Boston, Mass., the daughter of Fred W. Perkins and Susan E. Bean. Both parents came from Maine, and they maintained family ties that were important in Perkins' upbringing. Until late in life she returned regularly to the Perkins homestead in Newcastle, Maine. In 1882, the family moved to Worcester, Mass., where Fred Perkins established a successful wholesale and retail stationery business.

After graduating from Worcester Classical High School in 1898, Perkins entered Mount Holyoke College, from which she received the B.A. in 1902. In her senior year, she became active in the National Consumers' League, which sought to abolish child labor and the sweatshop system. A speech by Florence Kelley, the crusading general secretary, deeply affected her and, she later remarked, "first opened my mind to the necessity for and the possibility of the work which became my vocation."

Lacking experience for the job she sought (a family visitor with the Charity Organization Society in New York City), Perkins taught at girls' schools in New England and, from 1904 to 1907, at the fashionable Ferry Hall in Lake Forest, Ill. She spent vacations and weekends at The Commons and Hull House in Chicago. This settlement-house work both confirmed her commitment to social service and enabled her to become executive secretary of the Philadelphia Research and Protective Association, formed in 1907 to curb the exploitation of young girls arriving in the city.

After taking courses with the economist Simon N. Patten at the University of Pennsylvania, Perkins won a fellowship in 1909 to the New York School of Philanthropy. Part of a team making a social survey of Hell's Kitchen, she studied malnutrition among the children of that slum district and offered her findings as her master's thesis in 1910 at Columbia University. Meanwhile, in April 1910, Perkins became executive secretary of the New York City Consumers' League. This job placed her at the center of the American social-justice movement and in regular contact with Florence Kelley, Paul U. Kellogg, and other national leaders. Perkins became an expert on sanitary regulation of bakeries and on fire prevention in factories. She acted also as the league's lobbyist in Albany. Largely through her unflagging efforts the legislature passed the league's fifty-four-hour bill for women and children in 1912. That battle was her baptism in politics. She learned the mysteries of the legislative process (including the uses of compromise) and discovered the part that machine politicians could play in social reform. She also found a lifelong friend, the young Tammany leader of the assembly, Alfred E. Smith.

In May 1912, Perkins became executive secretary of the Committee on Safety of the City of New York, a citizens' group created in the wake of the Triangle Shirtwaist fire of Mar. 25, 1911. (She lived nearby and had watched the factory girls leaping to their deaths from the flaming building.) Her job was to act as the committee's representative before the New York Factory Investigating Commission. For three years she worked closely with Al Smith, Robert F. Wagner, and other commissioners, and played an instrumental part in shaping the historic recommendations for modern state regulation of industrial and labor conditions. Perkins emerged an acknowledged expert in the field, trusted and respected by the urban liberals

who would recast America's social policies over the next decades. Her work with the Factory Commission, among whose members was Samuel Gompers, reconfirmed her conviction that social legislation rather than trade unionism held out the primary hope for ameliorating the lives of working people.

On Sept. 26, 1913, Perkins married Paul Caldwell Wilson, an expert on municipal administration. Breaking with convention, she retained her maiden name. When the Committee on Safety concluded its work in 1917, she did not seek another salaried position, preferring a voluntary post with an aid program for expectant mothers. In 1915, Perkins had had a child who died in infancy and, the following year, a daughter who survived. Her choice, so she thought, was for family at the expense of career. In 1918 her husband, an important member of the reform administration of Mayor John Purroy Mitchel (1914–1917), suffered a mental breakdown, possibly brought on by a gold-stock speculation that cost him his fortune. Financial need dictated that Perkins resume her career. At this point a second decisive event occurred. In 1918, Al Smith was elected governor of New York. He invited Perkins to become an industrial commissioner, one of the governing members of the state labor department.

Much of Perkins' work on the Industrial Commission was an extension, on a larger scale, of her earlier professional activities. In her first term she reinvigorated the factory inspection and workmen's compensation divisions and, after Smith regained the governorship in 1923, she devoted herself to drafting regulations and hearing compensation cases as a member (1923–1926), and as chairman (1926–1929), of the reorganized Industrial Board. She also helped to advance the labor legislation that characterized the Smith governorship.

Perkins received her first taste of labor-management mediation in the summer of 1919, when she scored a notable success in settling a violent strike of copper workers in Rome, N.Y. She also found herself drawn into party politics. She had regarded her work as nonpartisan, if not nonpolitical, but as a policy-making member of the Smith administration and its ranking female representative, she was expected to be an active partisan. (Smith lectured her sternly when he learned that she was not even a registered Democrat.) In succeeding years Perkins became a seasoned political operative, a fixture at Democratic conventions, and a highly effective campaigner for Smith.

After Franklin D. Roosevelt was elected governor of New York in 1928, he shifted Perkins to the position of industrial commissioner, which gave her the responsibility, unprecedented for a woman, for administering the state labor department. She became an adviser on whose judgment and good sense Roosevelt soon came to rely. The onset of the Great Depression expanded her role, especially in matters related to unemployment. Perkins emphasized the importance of reliable job statistics (and gained national prominence for criticisms of the Hoover administration's optimistic reports), expanded the state's employment agencies, and, most important, made herself an expert on unemployment insurance. Hers was a crucial influence in the evolution of Roosevelt's administration into the model of vigorous state response to the economic crisis that was the launching pad for Roosevelt's campaign for the presidency in 1932.

After the election Roosevelt appointed Perkins his secretary of labor. She was reluctant to take the post, which she felt ought to go to a trade unionist. Moreover, her husband's mental illness had recently grown worse. But the call to service was compelling, both for what might be accomplished in the way of social reform and for what her appointment might mean for American women.

Ever since joining Al Smith's administration in 1919, Perkins had been acutely aware of her pioneering role. She dressed carefully for her new post—simple black dress, white bow, small tricorn hat. The costume became a trademark in later years. "Many good and intelligent women do dress in ways that are very attractive and pretty," she once remarked, "but don't particularly invite confidence in their common sense, integrity or sense of justice." She was determined to be taken seriously, even if she had to act a prematurely maternal role.

Perkins also took pains to shield her personal life from public scrutiny, partly out of a deep sense of privacy and reticence, partly because of painful family circumstances, but also in the hope of discouraging trivializing attention to her as a woman. She always treated with equanimity the slights she received on social occasions. No woman could have proceeded more carefully into the man's world of government and politics. The question of how to address the first woman cabinet member was aptly solved by Speaker-elect Henry T. Rainey of the House of Representatives: Madame Secretary.

Perkins moved vigorously to revive the somnolent Department of Labor. (As her first task she sought the elimination of the cockroaches infesting her own office.) She cleaned out the corrupt Bureau of Immigration, strengthened the statistical, conciliation, and job-placement services, and created the Division of Labor Standards to provide guidance for state labor departments. She built up a strong staff that, for the first time, made the department an important locus of legislative and policy planning.

Perkins spent much of her time as one of the shapers of the New Deal. Such a role defies easy assessment, given the complex nature of policymaking within the Roosevelt administration. Her proposed amendments to the Black-Connery thirty-hour bill in 1933 provoked a harsh response that left her isolated in the discussions that led to the National Industrial Recovery Act. On the other hand, she gave Roosevelt wise counsel about separating public works from industrial regulation in administering the law, and she participated actively in trying to resolve the thorny labor-management disputes arising out of Section 7(a), which asserted the right of workers to organize and engage in collective bargaining. Perkins played a crucial role in achieving the Social Security Act (1935) and the Fair Labor Standards Act (1938), cornerstone measures that brought to fruition her long-standing belief in social insurance, wage-and-hour regulation, and the abolition of child labor. But she was unsympathetic to the National Labor Relations Act (1935) because of its exclusive focus on the protection of organizing and bargaining rights.

Perkins' relations with the labor movement, while they warmed up, always remained distant. Nonetheless, of all Roosevelt's advisers she probably had the most realistic grasp of the industrial conflicts that rocked the country during the mid-1930's. It was primarily her restraining hand that prevented foolhardy federal intervention in the brief San Francisco general strike of 1934.

The hysteria accompanying the San Francisco strike gave rise to rumors linking Perkins to Harry Bridges, the radical leader of the longshoremen whose strike had precipitated the general strike. She became the object of a persistent whispering campaign, anti-Semitic in tone despite her Anglo-Saxon antecedents, that she had Communist sympathies. When she postponed deportation hearings for Bridges in 1938 on technical grounds, the House Un-American Activities Committee launched a campaign to impeach Perkins. The House tabled the impeachment resolution after receiving a unanimous report from the Judiciary Committee, but the incident impaired her political effectiveness.

After Roosevelt's election to a third term in 1940, Perkins would have preferred to resign. Nothing better revealed the personal role she played within the New Deal than Roosevelt's plea that she stay on: "I know who you are, what you are, what you'll do, what you won't do. You know me. You see lots of things that most people don't see. You keep me guarded against a lot of things no new man walking in here would protect me from." Perkins' formal responsibilities did not, however, expand with the coming of the war. To deal with wartime matters, Roosevelt chose to create temporary agencies apart from the cabinet departments, and Perkins found herself confined largely to routine duties.

During the war she helped protect labor standards, and she vigorously defended her department's cost-of-living index—crucial in wartime wage-setting—against charges that it discriminated against labor. After serving in the transitional period for President Harry Truman, Perkins resigned on July 1, 1945. She had been secretary of labor for more than twelve years.

An intense and energetic woman, Perkins was not ready to retire at sixty-five. She had little money and heavy family expenses. Her first project, undertaken reluctantly, was to publish a memoir (Howard Taubman did the actual writing) of Roosevelt. *The Roosevelt I Knew* (1946), a warm and perceptive account, was an instant success and an enduring contribution to Roosevelt scholarship. From 1946 to 1953, Perkins served on the U.S. Civil Service Commission. Following the death of her husband in December 1952, she became freer to travel and began to lecture at universities across the country. A talk at Cornell in May 1955 led to an invitation to serve as a visiting professor at the School of Industrial and Labor Relations in 1957. The appointment was renewed annually, and in 1960 she became a guest in residence at Telluride, a men's living unit. Despite her failing eyesight, she participated vigorously in the campus intellectual life, imparting a rich sense of recent history to her students and receiving in return their enlivening curiosity and enthusiasm. This communion across the generations, lasting almost until her death in New York City, was a fitting close to a life full of endeavor and achievement.

[Perkins left portions of her personal papers to Columbia University (the largest collection), Radcliffe College (mainly the years 1933–1945), Connecticut College, the Roosevelt Library at Hyde Park, N.Y., Mount Holyoke College (mainly on her college associations), and Cornell University (on the last years primarily). A comprehensive oral history, recorded in 1951–1955, is at Columbia University. Other manuscript collections include the Department of Labor records at the National Archives, the papers of Roosevelt and other New Deal figures in the Roosevelt Library at Hyde Park, and the papers of Paul U. Kellogg, University of Minnesota; Clara M. Beyer, Radcliffe College; Charles E. Wyzanski, Harvard Law School; and John B. Andrews, Cornell University. George Martin, *Madame Secretary* (1976), is a full biography. An obituary is in the *New York Times,* May 15, 1965.]

DAVID BRODY

PERKINS, MARION (1908–Dec. 17, 1961), sculptor, was born in Marche, Ark. He lived briefly in Charme, Ark., and, after his parents died, he moved to Chicago, where he was raised by an aunt, Doris Padrone. He attended Wendell Phillips High School for three years, but had to leave to find employment. He worked as janitor, dishwasher, and postal worker, and during the Great Depression he sold newspapers on Chicago's South Side.

In the late 1930's Perkins enrolled in a Works Progress Adminstration (WPA) playwright course. By this time he was carving likenesses of friends and relatives in soap. Peter Pollack, the director of the Community Art Center, Division of Illinois Art Project (WPA), recognized his potential and introduced him to Simon ("Sy") Gordon, then teaching at the South Side Community Art Center. Gordon instructed Perkins in the use of clay models, molds, and the mallet and chisel. (Other than this instruction Perkins was primarily self-taught.)

Perkins' artistic career spanned the period from the late 1930's until his death. Exhibitions of his work were held at the Art Institute of Chicago, Howard University (Washington, D.C.), Hull House (Chicago), Xavier University (New Orleans), Rockford College (Illinois), and the Du Sable Museum of African American History (Chicago).

Although an avid student of Western sculpture from Greek times to the present, Perkins, a black, was most inspired by the art forms of Africa. He was an exponent of black pride through art. His most famous piece, *Man of Sorrows* (1950), demonstrates the difference between his work and other sculptures done during the 1950's. Most sculptors of that day carved animated figures to convey motion. His *Man of Sorrows* is a stationary unshaven head. In this powerful depiction of a black Christ, Perkins conveyed the suffering experienced by his people at the hands of white society.

Perkins' other works also reflect his interest in

black themes. Among his numerous sculptures are *John Henry* (1943), *Ethiopia Awaking* (1948), and *Jean Baptiste Point du Sable* (which appeared on the cover of the Autumn 1963 issue of the Illinois State Historical Society's *Journal*). He wanted to carve a statue of Frederick Douglass, but he died before he could complete it.

Perkins received several awards, including the Robert Rice Jenkins Prize (1948), the Julius Rosenwald Fellowship (1948), and the Pauline Palmer Purchase Prize (1951). The fellowship was particularly valuable because it allowed him to go to New York City, where he visited museums and discussed his work with other artists. Perkins was never able to support himself through his art, so he had to continue working as a freight handler even after he had gained fame from his sculpting. He had to search out buildings being demolished in order to acquire the limestone and other stone he needed for his art.

Perkins firmly believed that everyone could understand and appreciate art, and he actively encouraged art in the Chicago black community. With several other artists he was a driving force in promoting the South Side Community Art Center, the first art institution in the city's black community. He also was a founder of the Lake Meadows Art Fair, a Chicago street fair that displayed the work of black artists.

Several sources claim that Perkins taught at Jackson State College in Mississippi, where another Chicago black artist, Lawrence Jones, was head of the art department. Perhaps Perkins participated in a workshop there, but no records exist to validate this supposition. Jones has no recollection of Perkins teaching at the school. Perkins presented a lecture at the first Black Artists Conference at Atlanta University; it was published as *Problems of the Black Artist* in 1971. After his death his friends established the Marion Perkins Memorial Foundation to encourage art education for blacks.

Art experts count Perkins among the leading black artists of the twentieth century. When he died, the art critic of the *Chicago Daily News* called him "an artist of great integrity," particularly "noted for his expressive portraits." Art historian Cedric Dover referred to him as one of "the more conscious social realists" among black artists.

Perkins and his wife, Eva, had three sons. He died of cancer in Chicago.

[There is very little material available on Perkins and his life. The Ryerson and Burnham libraries of the Art Institute of Chicago have a file containing a few miscellaneous notes and clippings on him. *Ebony,* Oct. 1951, discusses his inability to make a living from his art. A sketch is in Russell L. Adams, *Great Negroes Past and Present* (1963). *Chicago Defender,* Feb. 17, 1979, contains an evaluation of his work. Obituaries are in the *Chicago Daily News,* Dec. 20, 1961; and *New York Times,* Dec. 21, 1961.]
                                    JOHN F. MARSZALEK

PERRY, PETTIS (Jan. 4, 1897–July 24, 1965), Communist party functionary, was born on a tenant farm near Marion, Ala., to sharecropper parents. In 1907 he began working in the cotton fields for his uncle, Stokes King; seven years later he hired out as a farmhand to a plantation owner. After a dispute with this man, Perry left the rural South in 1915, seeking industrial employment in Tuscaloosa and Birmingham, Ala. At about the same time, while in prison in Birmingham for a curfew violation, he witnessed the death by flogging of a fellow black convict.

This event, combined with earlier experiences of economic deprivation and racial prejudice, led Perry to leave the South in 1917. From then until 1924, he drifted, riding freight trains and episodically taking menial jobs in thirty-five different states. In 1924 he "settled" in California, working during winters at a cottonseed mill in Los Angeles and in the spring and summer on farms in the Imperial Valley. While employed in Los Angeles, Perry learned in 1932, through a Communist activist, of the Communist party's defense efforts on behalf of the "Scottsboro boys," black youths arrested in Alabama and charged with raping two white girls. He joined the party's International Labor Defense (ILD) Committee in April 1932, and devoted all of his time to soliciting signatures for petitions and selling subscriptions to the ILD newspaper. Eventually he headed the Los Angeles chapter of the ILD. In September 1932 he joined the Communist party.

Barely literate when he left the South, because of the limited educational opportunities available to black Alabamans—he had five years of schooling, ninety days per year—Perry educated himself by reading the *Communist Manifesto* and *Capital.* He also became an avid student of black history and subscribed to the *Journal of Negro History.* A devoted Communist, he rose steadily from local section to district committee leader, and was a Communist candidate for state and federal offices.

In 1948, Perry moved to New York City to head the Communist party's National Negro Work Commission, and in 1950 he was appointed head of the party's Farm Commission.

His article in the Communist periodical *Political Affairs*, "Destroy the Virus of White Chauvinism" (October 1949), initiated a demoralizing intraparty campaign against the alleged "white chauvinism" of some of its members and sympathizers.

In 1950, Perry was elected an alternate member of the Communist party's National Committee. With the imprisonment or underground status of National Committee members following the Supreme Court's ruling in *Dennis* v. *United States*, Perry, William Z. Foster, and Elizabeth Gurley Flynn formed the party's official ruling triumvirate. In the interim, though, he and eleven other "second-string" Communist leaders in New York City were arrested on June 20, 1951, under provisions of the Smith Act. Because of the statute of limitations and because Perry had not been a prominent leader of the Communist party until 1950, his indictment was limited to his having attended Communist party meetings.

Perry's trial began on Apr. 15, 1952, in federal district court in New York City before Judge Edward Dimock. Perry acted as his own counsel during the 263-day trial and also served on the committee to formulate Communist strategy for the trial. On Jan. 22, 1953, after deliberating for seven days, the jury handed down a guilty verdict. Offered the choice of imprisonment or deportation to the Soviet Union, Perry responded: "I intend to stay in the United States. I was born and raised here and that's where I intend to stay." He was sentenced to three years in prison and fined $5,000.

Perry and the other defendants appealed the verdict. On Jan. 10, 1955, the Supreme Court denied certiorari and on February 28 denied the second defense motion for a rehearing. That May the federal district court in New York City denied another motion by Perry and ten co-defendants for a new trial and the setting aside of their conviction on the ground of false testimony by one of the government witnesses (the court granted a new trial to the other two defendants).

Because his conviction predated the Supreme Court's revision of the Dennis decision in 1957 in *Yates* v. *United States* (354 U.S. 298), Perry was among the 29 Communists, out of the 141 indicted under the Smith Act, to serve a prison sentence. After his release he resumed an active role in Communist activities. Perry, who was married and had three sons, died in Moscow while receiving medical treatment for a severe lung ailment and chronic heart disease.

Despite his "black proletarian" background,

Perry never succeeded in recruiting a mass black following for the Communist party. Even his "white chauvinist" campaign, which unfairly castigated many party members, did not serve to make the Communist party more attractive to blacks. A relatively unsophisticated militant, Perry was thrust into a leadership role more because the Communist party's leadership had been immobilized by the Smith Act prosecutions than because of his own organizational and leadership abilities.

[There is no scholarly biography of Perry, and memoirs of Communist officials and the scholarly studies of the American Communist party only sketchily describe his role and background. For biographical details, see a partisan pamphlet published by the Self-Defense Committee of the 17 Smith Act Victims, Richard Owen Boyer, *Pettis Perry: The Story of a Working Class Leader* (1952). Memoirs of Communists and codefendants include George Charney, *A Long Journey* (1968); Joseph Starobin, *American Communism in Crisis 1943–1957* (1972); and Elizabeth Gurley Flynn, *The Rebel Girl* (1973). Scholarly studies are Irving Howe and Lewis Coser, *The American Communist Party* (repr. 1974); and David Shannon, *The Decline of American Communism* (repr. 1971). Also see "Post-Dennis Prosecutions Under the Smith Act," *Indiana Law Journal*, Fall 1955; Robert Mollan, "Smith Act Prosecutions: The Effect of the Dennis and Yates Decisions," *University of Pittsburgh Law Review*, June 1965; and Michael Belknap, *Cold War Political Justice* (1977). An obituary is in the *New York Times*, July 28, 1965.]

ATHAN THEOHARIS

PETERKIN, JULIA MOOD (Oct. 31, 1880– Aug. 10, 1961), writer, was born in Laurens County, S.C., the daughter of Julius Andrew Mood and Alma Archer. Her mother died shortly after Julia's birth. Reared by her father, a country physician, and by the black nurse, or "Mauma," she was brought up within two cultures: that of the Southern white elite and that of the richly folkloric black community. Julius Mood, a cultivated man, was the key influence in her life. From her nurse she learned the dialect, customs, and superstitions of the Gullah blacks, a "perfect" stock with "tall straight bodies, and high heads filled with sense," as she described them in a novel.

Raised in a country where, as she saw it, "the earth's richness and the sun's warmth make living an easy thing," Mood developed a strong consciousness of place, coupled with an independent nature. When she was fourteen, her father sent her and her sister to Columbia College in the state capital. But within a year the two rebellious girls were dismissed. Undaunted, their father immediately enrolled them in Converse College at nearby Spartanburg. In 1896, Mood received the bachelor's degree and then remained in college for another year to earn a master's degree.

At seventeen, Mood became a teacher in a one-room school with fewer than ten pupils at Fort Motte, a farming settlement some twenty miles from Columbia that was dominated by the Peterkin family of Lang Syne Plantation. In 1903 she married William George Peterkin, heir to the plantation. A tall, attractive woman, she was expected to assume immediately the role of plantation mistress, which implied cultural refinement, social responsibility, and management of a family operation employing between 400 and 500 Gullah blacks. For the next seventeen years, Peterkin learned farming, raised her son, traveled, and led an active social life as member of patriotic, genealogical, and cultural societies. Energetic as well as creative, she experimented with horticulture and aviculture and sought artistic outlet in fancy needlework.

Misfortune struck about 1920, when illness permanently incapacitated her husband, and Peterkin was forced to take complete charge of the estate. First a livestock epidemic, and then the death of the foreman, threatened to ruin the plantation. But, supported emotionally by her father and sustained by her resilience, she brought the plantation through this series of crises.

In 1921, partly as therapy and partly in response to the encouragement of her piano teacher, Dr. Henry Bellamann, Peterkin began to write sketches of plantation life. Through Bellamann she was introduced to Carl Sandburg, who suggested that Peterkin submit these sketches to H. L. Mencken. This chance introduction into the literary world resulted in the publication of one sketch in Mencken's magazine, Smart Set, and fourteen sketches in Emily Clark's literary magazine, the Reviewer. What Peterkin called her "crude, really stark plantation sketches" soon attracted the attention of James Branch Cabell, Joel Spingarn, Alfred A. Knopf, Harriet Monroe, and Alfred Harcourt.

Peterkin's first book, Green Thursday (1924), was a collection of sketches and short stories. Her first novel, a tragedy entitled Black April (1927), won wide acclaim and made Peterkin a leader in the southern literary renaissance. Her best novel, the comedy Scarlet Sister Mary (1928), won a Pulitzer Prize. More than 1 million copies of Scarlet Sister Mary were sold, in English and in translation. Her reputation thus

established, Peterkin continued with Bright Skin (1932) and Roll, Jordan, Roll (1933). But thereafter, until her husband died in 1939, she devoted herself to the increasingly difficult management of Lang Syne. World War II, her failing health, and severe droughts in the early 1950's troubled her last years. She died at Orangeburg, S.C.

As part of the American literary scene between the world wars, Peterkin was compared with such writers as William Faulkner and Katherine Anne Porter. But her literary vision lacked sustaining power, and with the passage of time her works were relegated to the categories of local color and southern regional writing. They were gradually rediscovered in the 1960's and 1970's by folklorists, sociologists, and cultural historians. Black April and Scarlet Sister Mary, in particular, warrant attention as richly textured descriptions of Gullah life and culture within the context of universal or archetypal human experience. Neither a white southern nor a black apologist in these novels, Peterkin experimented with a narrative structure that yields to succeeding episodes in what she perceived as a purposive human drama, the "patient struggle with fate." Carried along by Peterkin's strong feelings, the novels lack a clear ordering principle. Perhaps this deficiency, in the end, curtailed her career and has separated her works from those of such contemporaries as William Faulkner and Willa Cather.

[A manuscript of Scarlet Sister Mary is available at Converse College, Spartanburg, S.C.; letters are in the H. L. Mencken Collection, New York Public Library and in the Lilly Collection at Bobbs-Merrill. See Collected Short Stories of Julia Peterkin, edited by Frank Durham (1970). A critical biography, Thomas H. Landess, Julia Peterkin (1976), lists other important secondary sources, principally Marilyn Price Maddox, "The Life and Works of Julia Mood Peterkin" (M.A. thesis, University of Georgia, 1956); Lenna Vera Morrow, "Folklore in the Writings of Julia Peterkin" (M.A. thesis, University of South Carolina, 1963); and Louis L. Henry, "Julia Peterkin: A Biographical and Critical Study" (Ph.D. diss., Florida State University, 1965). An obituary is in the New York Times, Aug. 11, 1961.]

GLEN E. LICH

PETRI, ANGELO (Sept. 5, 1883–Oct. 4, 1961), vintner and businessman, was born in Marseilles, France, the son of Raffaello Petri and Rosina Bertolucci, natives of Lucca, Italy. Although he did not arrive in the United States until 1895, his father had established the first Petri Wine Company in the San Joaquin Valley of California as early as 1886 and was the proprietor of the Toscano, a small residential hotel in the North Beach section of San Francisco. At the same time his uncle, Amadeo Petri, had set up a back-room cigar business in the same section of town, manufacturing Italian-style, twisted, fermented cigars called *toscani*.

Shortly after completing his elementary education in the late 1890's, Petri went to work in his uncle Amadeo's cigar business. He recognized it as a business with a guaranteed future, because he experienced the response from the community firsthand in his door-to-door sales to local shops. On Apr. 28, 1907, he married Amelia Guidi; they had two sons.

Petri became president of the Petri Cigar Company in 1912. Under his leadership and with the use of advertising, the Marca Petri cigars became known nationally, especially in the Italian areas of the larger cities. By the mid-1920's the company was the largest cigar manufacturing company west of Chicago (including Hawaii, where sales were high because of the similarity between the Italian and the Filipino native cigars). During these peak years, when some 50 million cigars were produced and the business grossed as much as $300,000 annually, Petri expanded to produce American-type, machine-made cigars.

Petri's father's wine company had begun as a purely local business. But, just as Marca Petri cigars gained popularity in Italian communities elsewhere, so Marca Petri wine was sold in bulk as far away as New York City and Detroit. In 1916 Petri's father and his partners purchased a vineyard in the San Joaquin Valley, at Alba Station, Escalon. But the Eighteenth Amendment, prohibiting the sale of wine or liquor, went into effect in January 1920—apparently sealing the fate of Petri Wine.

During Prohibition, Petri concentrated on his growing cigar business, but retained his part ownership of the Alba Grape and Fruit Company, which sold grapes to eastern markets for home winemaking. The grapes were varieties that could travel cross-country with the least spoilage. The availability of these less expensive, thick-skinned grapes contributed to the popularity of sweet (as opposed to dry) table wine, and this was the type of wine that Petri eventually was able to provide.

In 1933 the Eighteenth Amendment was repealed, and Petri saw the golden opportunity in the wine business. He abandoned the manufacture of American-type cigars and sold twenty-two cigar-making machines to raise capital that he used to revive the family wine business. With those funds he acquired wineries all over Napa County. He sold his wine in bulk to bottlers, who resold it under their own names.

Petri's younger son, Louis, was in medical school when he fell in love with Flori Cella, the daughter of the head of the Roma Wine Company, a competitor of Petri Wine. Although Petri wanted Louis to become a doctor, he knew his son would work for Roma if Petri refused to employ him. After the wedding on July 21, 1935, Petri hired Louis as a wine-barrel washer at $75 a month, thus displaying his disappointment while accepting the inevitable. To his credit, he soon recognized Louis' flair for marketing. He named him general manager in 1937, vice-president in 1940, and president in 1944. In the same year Petri's elder son, Albert, became president of Petri Cigars, a subsidiary of Petri Wine. After 1944, Angelo Petri acted mainly in an advisory capacity as chairman of the board.

The steady growth of Petri Wine in the 1930's mirrored the tremendous increase in annual wine consumption in the United States, which jumped from 38 million gallons in 1934 to 104 million gallons by 1941. Three-quarters of this wine was produced in California. The Petri brand name on the label and effective advertising on the "Sherlock Holmes" radio show, a "first" in the wine business, were responsible for bringing the company a significant share of the market. In 1949, Petri Wine acquired K. Arakelian, at Madera, Calif., the second largest winery in the nation, for $3.25 million. At this time the firm was renamed United Vintners. In 1951, with Petri's blessing, Louis took the revolutionary step of organizing about 300 San Joaquin Valley farmers into the Allied Grape Growers Cooperative. He sold the Petri Vineyards to the growers in exchange for the guarantee of the exclusive right to buy their crops. The Italian Swiss Colony label was acquired in 1953, and by 1954, United Vintners was the largest wine-marketing organization in the world. With sales of $41.5 million, the firm produced approximately 22 percent of all domestic wines consumed in the United States.

Petri, a director of the Bank of America (1932–1956), was decorated by the Italian government in 1954 for his aid to needy children during World War II. He retired in 1956 because of ill health and died in San Francisco. Seven years after his death, United Vintners was acquired by the Heublein Company for $33 million.

Using modern merchandising methods, Angelo Petri created a viable wine business in the post-Prohibition era. Because of the strong foundation laid by him, his son was able to build the wine empire that made the Petri name famous.

[There is no biography nor autobiography of Angelo Petri. A 1969 interview with Louis Petri by Ruth Teiser, "The Petri Family in the Wine Industry," is available at the Regional Oral History Office of the Bancroft Library, University of California, Berkeley. See Gerald Adams, "Louis Petri," *San Francisco Examiner*, May 23, 1965; Philip M. Wagner, *Grapes into Wine* (1976); and Leon Adams, *The Wines of America* (1978). Obituaries are in *San Francisco Chronicle* and *New York Times*, Oct. 5, 1961. Also see Louis Petri's obituary, *San Francisco Chronicle*, Apr. 8, 1980.]

BARBARA McCARTHY CROFTON

PEW, JOSEPH NEWTON, JR. (Nov. 12, 1886–Apr. 9, 1963), industrialist and political leader, was born in Pittsburgh, Pa., the son of Joseph Newton Pew, founder of the Sun Oil Company, and of Mary Catherine Anderson. He attended Shadyside Academy in Pittsburgh and the Haverford School. He graduated in 1908 from Cornell University with a degree in mechanical engineering and a collection of trophies won as captain of the track team and as intercollegiate hammer-throwing champion.

After graduation Pew entered the family business. Until 1914 he worked in the oil fields of Illinois, West Virginia, and Venezuela. He had a major role in the development, in 1916 and after, of the Sun Shipbuilding and Dry Dock Company at Chester, Pa., a wholly owned but independently managed subsidiary of Sun Oil Company established largely to build oil tankers (and thus lower transportation costs). On Sept. 23, 1916, Pew married Alberta Caven Hensel; they had five children.

In 1931, when it was decided to build a pipeline to move gasoline from the Sun Oil refinery at Marcus Hook, Pa., to markets in the Great Lakes region, Pew was entrusted with the task of laying the pipes. He demonstrated his finesse in negotiations by securing more than 1,000 permits to cross highways, 183 to cross railroads, and 34 to cross rivers and canals, and about 1,000 easements on property from landowners.

Pew followed his older brother, John Howard Pew, as president and board chairman of Sun Shipbuilding in 1917, and was vice-president of the parent company from 1912 until his brother retired in 1947; he was then named chairman of the board of Sun Oil. Among his contributions to marketing were the use of blue in the company's Blue Sunoco gasoline, and the "custom-blending" pump that delivered gasoline in nine different octane ratings. For oil exploration Pew devised a gyroscopic instrument, patented in 1926, that measured the angle and direction of deviation in oil wells, thus aiding in the achievement of record drilling depths. This deep drilling added substantially to proven oil and gas reserves.

Outside the oil industry Pew was best known for his political activities as a behind-the-scenes strategist of the conservative wing of the Republican party. He was a vigorous and articulate opponent of government interference with market forces, especially the price-fixing clause in the National Recovery Administration's petroleum code. Asserting that "price-fixing is an evil, wicked thing," Pew led a successful fight against the provision. The experience convinced him that the free economy was in danger, and that the salvation of individual freedom required a change in government. Rebuilding the Republican party after its losses during the early 1930's became the main interest of his later years.

In 1935, Pew bought *Farm Journal*, which he merged with *Farmer's Wife* as a means of communicating with the rural voters; later he added *Pathfinder*, another periodical with a large rural circulation. With other members of the Pew family, he acquired a controlling interest in the Chilton Press, which published a number of trade magazines read by businessmen, and the *Philadelphia Evening Ledger*.

Pew's massive contributions to Republican campaign funds gave him a major role in party affairs. Yet the results of his shaking up the party were disappointing to opponents of the New Deal. A Democrat was elected mayor of Philadelphia in 1935. The competent but colorless Republican candidate, Alfred M. Landon, lost the presidential race in 1936. But in 1938 the Republicans elected Arthur H. James, a judge from the coal region, governor of Pennsylvania with an expenditure of $1.2 million, 20 percent of which was contributed by the Pews.

In 1939–1940 the Pew forces supported Governor James as a candidate for president, with Robert A. Taft of Ohio as their second choice. "The Republican party," Pew declared in May 1940, "stands today where the Continental Army stood at Valley Forge, and if Haym Salomon and Robert Morris could empty their purses to keep that army alive, so can we."

At the Republican National Convention in June 1940, as the support for Wendell W. Willkie mounted and the galleries chanted "We want Willkie," Pew refused to release the Pennsylvania delegation to Willkie. He was for

James, he said, until "the bitter end—if I am there alone." Willkie was nominated without help from Pennsylvania. In 1944, though, Pew was an effective leader of the "stop Willkie" forces, and Willkie withdrew from the race.

"Throughout these bleak years," Joe Martin, former Speaker of the House of Representatives and former Republican National Committee chairman, wrote, "I could, fortunately, still count on financial support from . . . Joseph N. Pew, Jr. of Pennsylvania . . . he has given millions . . . his contributions kept coming in. Without them the party might have utterly dried up. . . ." Yet, Martin added, "In all the years I have known him . . . he has never asked me for a single favor." Pew never sought or held any public office, although he was regularly a Pennsylvania delegate to the Republican National Convention. The only business organization in which he was active, aside from Sun Oil, was the American Petroleum Institute, which he served as a director and member of the executive committee. Pew's attachment to conservative Republican ideology never wavered, nor did his disdain for what he termed the "isms," which included the social and economic programs of the New Deal. "Any pretext will do," he said in 1952, "when there is a desire on the part of Government to control business."

Pew's portrait appeared on the cover of *Time* magazine on May 6, 1940. He died in Philadelphia, one of the wealthiest men in America and one of the most fixed in his economic and social views.

[Pew's place in the history of the Sun Oil Company, the Pew family, and its fortunes is treated in *Fortune*, Feb. 1941; *New York Times*, Oct. 28, 1957, and Oct. 10, 1971; *Time*, Apr. 19, 1963; *Philadelphia Magazine*, Sept. 1975; and Dan Rothenberg, "Pew Family: The Sun Gods," in *Business People in the News*, edited by Barbara Nykoruk (1976). On Pew's political activities, see *Time*, May 6, 1940; *Yale Review*, Sept. 1940; *New Republic*, May 8, 1944; Donald Bruce Johnson, *The Republican Party and Wendell Willkie* (1960); and Joe Martin, *My First Fifty Years in Politics* (1960). Obituaries are in the *Philadelphia Inquirer* and *New York Times*, Apr. 10, 1963.]

GERALD CARSON

PFISTER, ALFRED (Sept. 3, 1880–Apr. 3, 1964), chemical manufacturer, was born in Zurich, Switzerland, the son of Jean Pfister and Elise Gloor. After education in the Zurich public schools, he enrolled at the turn of the century in the Chemical Institute of the University of Basel, where he studied with Jules Piccard and C. F. R. Fichter. Basel was a center for the production of dyestuffs and pharmaceuticals, and the Chemical Institute had grown rapidly during the 1880's and 1890's. Its graduates joined such local firms as Ciba, Geigy, and Sandoz. Research was closely linked to local industrial problems, with Piccard and Rudolf Nietzki concentrating on organic dyes and Fichter on electrochemistry. Pfister drew on both research traditions within the institute for his dissertation on the effects of double-bond placement on the conductivity of solutions of pentenoic and hexenoic acids (1903).

After receiving the Ph.D., Pfister obtained a job in Basel at Hoffmann-La Roche, a pharmaceutical company. On Sept. 10, 1906, he married Paula Rebmann. The Pfisters decided to immigrate to the United States soon afterward. They had three children.

At the time, chemists, engineers, and other technical experts with European training were widely sought by American manufacturers and American branches of European firms. Although Pfister's reasons for leaving Switzerland are unclear, his chemistry degree and industrial experience in Basel provided excellent credentials. By 1908 he was working for Nolde and Horst, a hosiery dyeing company in Reading, Pa. Another Reading company, the Spring Valley Dye Works, lured him away from Nolde and Horst in 1910 to become its general manager. Pfister remained with Spring Valley until 1914, when he took a position as research chemist and general manager with Jacques Wolf and Company, a chemical firm in Passaic, N.J.

Passaic is near Paterson, a major center for the manufacture of silk and other fabrics. Wolf and Company was one of many firms that prospered by supplying textile manufacturers in the area with dyestuffs and other process chemicals. Pfister must have demonstrated considerable business acumen in his new job, for he became president and treasurer of the company in 1918, positions he held until 1932.

Although he had moved from research into management, the contacts Pfister made as a member of the American Chemical Society and as a charter member of the American Association of Textile Chemists and Colorists undoubtedly helped him to keep abreast of progress in dye chemistry. Under his direction, Jacques Wolf and Company developed new lines of textile chemicals and captured a share of the lucrative American market for synthetic organic chemicals that had been dominated by German and Swiss firms before World War I.

Despite the Great Depression, Pfister decided in 1932 to start his own firm in Ridgefield, N.J. Initially he marketed a line of dye intermediates, but the company soon branched into the production of other organic intermediates and specialty chemicals for use in bactericides, fungicides, and cancer chemotherapy. During World War II, the Pfister Chemical Company was among a group of manufacturers that provided the Chemical Warfare Service with napalm, an aluminum soap of naphthenic and palmitic acids that converts gasoline into a thick jelly for use in incendiary weapons.

Pfister became a naturalized United States citizen in December 1913, but he remained proud of his Swiss heritage. In 1930 he became president of the *Amerikanische-Schweizer Zeitung,* a German-language weekly published in New York City. This journal was designed to foster pride in Swiss culture among the large community of Swiss-Americans in the New York metropolitan area. In addition to his publishing endeavors, Pfister supported the Pestalozzi Foundation, a Swiss organization that provided education and social opportunities for disadvantaged youth.

Pfister died in New York City. He had retained the presidency of his company until his death; it remains among the many small but significant specialty firms in the American chemical industry.

[Pfister's doctoral dissertation is *I. Elektrolytisches Leitvermögen der Penten- und Hexensäuren, und II. Ueber einige neue Derivate dieser Säuren* (1903). His results were incorporated in two papers published with C. F. R. Fichter: "Leitfähigkeitsmessungen an ungesättigten Säuren," *Annalen der Chemie,* Apr. 1904; and "Zur Kenntnis der Penten- und Hexensäuren," *Berichte der Deutschen Chemischen Gesellschaft,* May, 28, 1904. An obituary is in the *New York Times,* Apr. 7, 1964.]

JEFFREY L. STURCHIO

PHILLIPS, HARRY IRVING (Nov. 26, 1889–Mar. 15, 1965), journalist, was born in New Haven, Conn., the son of Charles Richard Phillips and Charlotte Ann Stannard Johnson. His father, industrious but poor, worked at odd jobs. Phillips was educated in the local public schools but had no opportunity to go to college.

In his adolescent years Phillips had various odd jobs. According to John Chamberlain, he got his start in journalism in 1906. While driving a grocery wagon (a job he disliked intensely), he passed the office of the *New Haven Register.* Impulsively he stopped, tied the horse to a hitching post, and applied for a job as a reporter. The *Register* needed a cub reporter, so he

started work immediately. Chamberlain ends his account by observing: "A day or two later an irate greengrocer came looking for his horse; he found him where Phillips had left him, starving and thirsty."

Phillips' rise in the world of New Haven journalism was spectacular. By 1912 he was managing editor of the *Register.* At this time, as he described it, his chief ambition was to become a cartoonist. He subsequently illustrated several of his Private Purkey books.

On Feb. 8, 1916, Phillips married Mary Irene Gallagher; they had no children. With that added responsibility and filled with confidence, he joined the staff of the *New York Tribune* in 1917. "I figured that I could run a New York sheet with my eyes shut," he later recalled. "And after a few weeks in the editorial room of the *Tribune* the bosses of that paper must have concluded this was exactly what I was doing."

Fired from the *Tribune,* Phillips wandered into a job at the *New York Globe* as a copy boy for $40 a week, much less than he had earned in New Haven. He was unwilling to accept that situation for long, so when, one afternoon, he realized that the *Globe* had no columnist, he wrote a column satirizing the day's news and left it on the city editor's desk. Next day the piece appeared on the editorial page, and he was asked to write a daily column. Phillips "leaped at the opening; in fact, leap is not the verb." After several months of writing a column as a side to his regular work, he became a full-fledged columnist. Syndication followed in 1918.

By the time the *Globe* was sold to the *New York Sun* in 1923, Phillips was a star columnist. The *New York World* lured him away, but an injunction forced him to return to the *Sun.* Written with a gentle and compassionate touch more typical of rural cracker-barrel philosophers than the sophisticated cynicism of New York columnists, his column, "Sun Dial," became a mainstay of the *Sun.* He remained with the paper until it was absorbed by the *New York World Telegram* in 1950.

Phillips never took himself very seriously, although he certainly considered his work as more than mere escapist humor. He was a staunch Republican, and his character Elmer Twitchell reflected his sentiments. According to his obituary in the *New York Times,* Phillips "seldom or never referred to 'the American way,' but it was in that pasture that he pitched his tent." An admitted hater of New York City and what he considered New Yorkers represented in American life, he labeled the New Deal a "New York abomination," filled with "reformers, agitators and fix-it-alls"—all bad words in his lexicon.

Other evils, in Phillips' opinion, were the national debt, government questionnaires, income taxes, fireside chats, and Eleanor Roosevelt. These and other subjects were broached through the characters of Elmer Twitchell, Ima Dodo, Shudda Haddim, the Garble Sisters, Senator Dumm, Representative Dummer, and Pettigrew the Penguin. In the 1930's his columns presented his beliefs that "this country is not nearly as bad off as it thinks, and that if the Government got off its neck prosperity would return so fast that it would be necessary to bank the curves"; that "all you have a right to demand of Congress is the spring vegetable seeds"; and that work does not mean "worrying over the salary, hours or housing arrangements."

During this period before World War II, Phillips wrote radio sketches, skits for Broadway musicals and reviews, and several books: *The Globe Trotter* (1924), *The Foolish Question Book* (1927), *Calvin Coolidge* (1933), and *On White or Rye* (1941). His wife died in 1938, and on November 26 of that year he married Cecilia Carney. They had one son.

During World War II, Phillips introduced "Private Oscar Purkey, the perennial rookie . . . an indigenous American, the good-humored, wise-cracking, grousing, sometimes naive, sometimes extremely wise, person who is flocking to training camps. . . ." Before Pearl Harbor, Private Purkey was not very enthusiastic about the war situation, for his creator shared Charles Lindbergh's isolationist views. But after Pearl Harbor all that changed. Purkey could hardly control his eagerness to get at the enemy, especially the Japanese.

Phillips periodically published the Purkey columns: *The Private Papers of Private Purkey* (1941), *Private Purkey in Love and War* (1942), *All-Out Arlene* (1943), and *Private Purkey's Private Peace* (1945). At the time the Purkey books met with some commercial and critical success, but they were quickly forgotten. In 1942, John Chamberlain described Purkey as the "prototype of the serio-comic, lovable, and thoroughly honest-to-goodness American soldier—[he] is a character of parts, and it is not unlikely that he will be remembered long after the present war is over." Phillips played an important part in convincing Americans that they could get on with the task of winning the war while remaining humane and kind.

After the war Phillips continued to write columns for the *Sun* and then for the Bell-McClure Syndicate. He received awards from the Catholic Institute of the Press (1953) and the Valley Forge Association. He was especially pleased with the latter, feeling that it represented a just reward for his years of fighting for wider application of the values of rural America.

Phillips was by all accounts as much a character in his habits and behavior as Private Purkey was. His close friend John Kieran once joked that "Phillips is full of ideas, most of them quite strange." Kieran also observed, "It is altogether likely that the trials of Private Purkey in war are but a subconscious reflection of the vicissitudes of Colonel Phillips in peace."

Phillips was recuperating from a broken hip when he died in Milford, Conn. His last column was written the day before his death.

[No manuscript sources exist. John Chamberlain's book review in the *New York Times,* June 20, 1942, deals with the Private Purkey books and is a good source for comments. John Kieran's foreword to *Private Purkey in Love and War* (1942) is also a valuable source of information. An obituary is in the *New York Times,* Mar. 16, 1965.]

WILLIAM F. STEIRER, JR.

PICCARD, JEAN FELIX (Jan. 28, 1884–Jan. 28, 1963), organic chemist and aeronautical engineer, was born in Basel, Switzerland, the son of Jules Piccard, the head of the Department of Chemistry at the University of Basel, and of Helene Haltenhoff. Jean Piccard and his identical twin, Auguste, entered the University of Basel in 1902 and then transferred to the Swiss Institute of Technology in Zurich, where both received baccalaureate degrees in 1907 and D. Sc. degrees. Jean Piccard's doctorate, completed in 1909, was in organic chemistry; his brother's was in physics. Piccard did postdoctoral work at the University of Munich from 1910 to 1914, when he was appointed privatdocent. When Germany invaded Belgium, he resigned and returned to Switzerland, where he became a privatdocent at the University of Lausanne.

In 1916 Piccard accepted a position as assistant professor in chemistry at the University of Chicago, receiving a leave of absence from Lausanne. Besides teaching, he conducted research on gas mask construction, studying the ability of filters to absorb toxic gases. In 1918 he became associate professor and met Jeannette Ridlon, daughter of a Chicago surgeon, whom he married on Aug. 19, 1919. They had three children.

Although prospects at Chicago seemed bright, Piccard's leave from Lausanne expired and he felt an obligation to return to Switzerland. He remained in Lausanne from 1919 to

1926, but was not happy there. His position as *professeur extraordinaire* of organic chemistry did not develop into the permanent professorship that he had expected, and by 1921 he was seeking an opportunity to return to the United States. In 1926 he secured a research appointment at the Massachusetts Institute of Technology, which he retained until 1929. Meanwhile, in 1927, he accepted a consultantship with the Hercules Powder Company that grew into a full-time position, in 1929, as head of the chemical service department at the company's experiment station at Kenvil, N.J., and later at Wilmington, Del. He became an American citizen in 1931.

Because of the Great Depression the chemical research staff of Hercules Powder was reduced repeatedly and the department was eliminated in 1932. Like many others, Piccard was unemployed. Gradually, his efforts to reestablish himself professionally shifted to another field.

Inspired by their boyhood reading of Jules Verne, Jean and Auguste Piccard had long been interested in the scientific use of balloons. In 1913 they had made a sixteen-hour flight in Switzerland, recording the density and temperature of the gas in the balloon. Auguste Piccard, a physicist in Belgium, later designed a balloon with an airtight aluminum gondola to enable him to study cosmic rays in the stratosphere. In 1931 and 1932 he made ascents of over 50,000 feet, opening a new field for scientific exploration. The brothers discussed further plans and designed a new balloon, using Auguste's basic ideas and Jean's innovations.

Jean Piccard became a research associate with the Bartol Research Foundation of the Franklin Institute of Philadelphia, in Swarthmore, Pa., where William F. G. Swann was developing a center for the study of cosmic rays; Swann and Robert A. Millikan designed instruments for Piccard's high-altitude cosmic-ray measurements. On Oct. 23, 1934, with his wife piloting the balloon, he ascended over 57,000 feet, returning with data on radiation at various levels that were turned over to others for analysis. The Piccards had not set an altitude record—a navy team using the same balloon had gone to 61,000 feet the year before—but they had made significant contributions to science.

From then on, Piccard devoted his attention primarily to balloons. In 1936 he joined the Department of Aeronautical Engineering at the University of Minnesota. He became professor the following year and continued to work after his retirement in 1952.

Piccard contributed in many ways to the ad-

vance of ballooning. In the 1934 flight he used electrically triggered blasting caps, with which he had worked at the powder company, to sever the mooring ropes and to release ballast from containers outside the sealed gondola. This was the first use of such devices in controlling balloons, and the procedure was later applied in other aspects of flight, such as detaching the balloon from the gondola at the instant of landing.

To lighten balloons and increase their altitude and lifting capacity, Piccard and Thomas H. Johnson began to experiment with plastic at the Bartol Institute in 1935. The following year, at the University of Minnesota, he and John D. Akerman launched an unmanned seventeen-foot cellophane balloon that carried its load of scientific instruments to Arkansas after a ten-hour flight. Especially after World War II, when plastic sheeting of greater flexibility and toughness became available, this type of material became widely used. Piccard also compared the behavior of groups of smaller balloons to that of single larger balloons. In 1937 a cluster of 98 five- and seven-foot balloons, which he called the "Pleiades," carried him in an open gondola to a height of 10,000 feet, with Jeannette Piccard directing the ground crew at the launching. The Piccards planned another stratospheric ascent, using a cluster of larger balloons to lift their gondola to 100,000 feet. Much of the developmental work was finished, but for lack of financial support this "Helios" project was not completed.

Piccard and his students experimented with balloons of different shapes and various types of equipment. In 1946–1947 they developed the prototype of the "Skyhook" balloons used by the navy for meteorological research. During the next decade more than 2,000 of these balloons were launched in many parts of the world, collecting data at altitudes of twenty miles and more, and contributing to the "flying saucer" excitement of that period. Piccard's work also produced a number of devices such as a frost-resistant window for balloon gondolas and airplanes and a balloon gas valve with a metal screen to prevent explosions of the hydrogen that were sometimes caused by sparks from static electricity. He obtained patents on inventions ranging from blasting caps to an X-ray-transparent plaster for use in surgical casts. He published approximately seventy-five papers and translated Einstein's "Physics and Reality" into English for the *Journal of the Franklin Institute* (March 1936). During the summer of 1945 he worked with the U. S. Army Air Document

Research Center in London, interviewing Germans in regard to aeronautical technology.

Piccard continued to be involved in high-altitude flight research as late as 1962, when he discussed problems of astronauts in pressurized suits with Robert Gilruth, a former student who was then the director of the NASA Space Center at Houston. He died in Minneapolis.

[The Piccard Family Papers at the Library of Congress comprise 106 boxes of correspondence, clippings, and publications. The Piccard Balloon Collection at the University of Minnesota brings together material on the history of balloons, including some Piccard papers and photographs. The scientific careers of the Piccard twins have been celebrated in a number of children's books, such as Alan Honour, *Ten Miles High, Two Miles Deep* (1957). There are obituary notices in the *New York Times*, Jan. 29, 1963; and *Nature*, July 20, 1963.]

MAURICE M. VANCE

PITTS, ZASU (Jan. 3, 1898–June 7, 1963), actress, was born in Parsons, Kans. She was named after her mother's sisters, Eliza and Susan, ZaSu being the last syllable of one name and the first of the other. When ZaSu was an infant the Pitts family moved to Santa Cruz, Calif. She attended the public schools of that city. Like many young women whose coming of age coincided with the emergence of the American movie industry, she was a movie-struck girl. Encouraged by family friends who were impressed by her uncommon talent for mimicry, Pitts hoped to find a job in motion pictures.

Her chance came unexpectedly in 1917, when Mary Pickford traveled to northern California to film *Rebecca of Sunnybrook Farm.* Hired as an extra for the circus sequence, Pitts followed the company to Hollywood. Screenwriter Frances Marion later recalled the young actress's first appearance at Paramount studios, looking for work: "She was about fifteen and looked like a trapped little animal. Her eyes were enormous in a small pinched face and her hands waved as if she were trying to catch invisible butterflies on the wing. I watched this pathetic wisp of a girl with astonishment and compassion." On the basis of Marion's recommendation, Mary Pickford selected Pitts to appear opposite her in *The Little Princess* (1917).

The unique personal traits that had caught the attention of Marion and Pickford were hallmarks of ZaSu Pitts's screen image for nearly half a century, and she used her fragile appearance, fluttering hands, wide-eyed countenance, and wistful demeanor to good effect in comedy, melodrama, and tragedy.

Pitts began her career as an ingenue but quickly established herself as a comedienne. During the 1920's, however, she played a full range of roles. She reached the pinnacle of her art under the direction of Erich von Stroheim in two classics, *Greed* (1924) and *The Wedding March* (1928). Film historian Herman Weinberg has called her work in those films "two of the most beautiful performances ever given by an actress in the annals of the screen."

For ZaSu Pitts the 1920's were the most creative years and an important period in her private life. On July 23, 1920, she married Los Angeles sportsman and boxing promoter Thomas Gallery. They had one child. They separated in 1926 and were divorced in 1932. On Oct. 8, 1933, she secretly married John E. Woodall, a real estate broker. They had no children.

Pitts balanced her many comedies with occasional serious roles, but the birth of the talkies irrevocably tilted her career toward comedy. Although her high-pitched, cracking voice, "exactly the kind of voice her fans had imagined, fluttery like her hands," proved unsuitable for heavy drama, it was perfect for comedy, and Pitts had a string of comedy hits in 1929 and 1930. But when she returned to serious drama as Lew Ayres's bereaved mother in *All Quiet on the Western Front* (1930) her mere appearance evoked laughter from preview audiences. Director Lewis Milestone had to reshoot her scenes using another actress, Beryl Mercer.

Pitts subsequently confined herself to comic roles, although her work in Ernst Lubitsch's *The Man I Killed* (1932) was a noteworthy exception. She starred with Thelma Todd in sixteen comedy shorts between 1931 and 1933. In features she often teamed with comic actors Slim Summerville, Lucien Littlefield, and James Gleason.

Always in demand, but increasingly the victim of studio typecasting, Pitts played a succession of nervous telephone operators, doleful maids, talkative tourists, dim-witted nurses, and confused receptionists, usually in low-budget films. However, as the frontier maid who marries the perfect English gentleman's gentleman (Charles Laughton) in *Ruggles of Red Gap* (1935), she momentarily managed to shatter the stereotype with a memorable comic performance.

From 1954 to 1963 Pitts appeared frequently on television. She played familiar comedy types on dramatic anthology programs, including "General Electric Theatre," "Kraft Television Theatre," and "Screen Director's Playhouse." She was best known to television audiences, though, as a regular on "The Gale Storm Show: Oh Susanna" (1956–1960), a popular situation comedy. She also appeared in two Broadway shows, *Ramshackle Inn* (1944) and *The Bat* (1953), both undistinguished and short-lived comedy-mysteries.

ZaSu Pitts died in Los Angeles. Most movie-goers remembered her as the personification of feminine futility, but to those who had witnessed the full range of her talents she meant much more. As von Stroheim observed, "One looks at ZaSu Pitts and sees pathos, even tragedy, and a wistfulness that craves for something she has never had or hopes to have. Yet she is one of the happiest and most contented women I have ever known."

[There is no biography of ZaSu Pitts. Robert Windeler describes her entry into films in *Sweetheart: The Story of Mary Pickford* (1974). Frances Marion offers a more detailed, firsthand account in her autobiography, *Off with Their Heads!* (1972). The concept of the "movie-struck girl" is delineated by Robert Sklar in *Movie-Made America* (1975). Leonard Maltin catalogs the Thelma Todd–ZaSu Pitts comedies in *The Great Movie Shorts* (1972). *The New York Times Film Reviews, 1913–1968*, 6 vols. (1970), reprints reviews of many of her films (1922–1963). Her television appearances are listed in James Robert Parish, *Actors' Television Credits* (1973). An obituary is in the *New York Times*, June 8, 1963.]

WILLIAM HUGHES

PLATH, SYLVIA (Oct. 27, 1932–Feb. 11, 1963), poet, was born in Boston, Mass., the daughter of Otto Emil Plath, professor of biology at Boston University and an authority on the bumblebee, and Aurelia Schober. She grew up in Winthrop, Mass., but after her father died in 1940, the family moved to Wellesley, Mass. Plath later said that the first nine years of her life "sealed themselves off like a ship in a bottle." Her father's death and her seaside childhood form the subject of many of her poems.

Plath graduated from Gamaliel Bradford High School in 1950 and won a scholarship to Smith College, from which she graduated in 1955 with an A.B. in English. At Smith she published poems and short stories in the college literary magazine as well as in national periodicals. Despite this success and a very good academic record, she suffered her first nervous breakdown during this time. In the summer of 1953, after serving as guest editor for *Mademoiselle*'s special college issue, Plath, exhausted and discouraged about her general ability, returned home, entered into a period of severe depression, and attempted suicide. She was rescued,

recovered, and spent some months in McLean Hospital, Belmont, Mass., undergoing psychiatric treatment before returning to college the following winter. These experiences form the material for her autobiographical novel, *The Bell Jar* (London, 1963; New York, 1971), first published under the pseudonym Victoria Lucas.

After graduating from Smith, Plath won a Fulbright Scholarship to Newnham College, Cambridge University, where she spent two years. She earned a B.A. in 1957, submitting forty-three poems as Part II of the Cambridge tripos. Although only six of these poems were included in the 1960 English edition of her first published volume, *The Colossus* (New York, 1962), this manuscript reveals her preoccupation with extreme psychic states and the spirit world.

During her first year at Newnham, Plath met the English poet Ted Hughes. They were married June 16, 1956. They came to the United States in 1957 so that Plath could accept an appointment in the English Department at Smith. But after one year, finding that she had little time for her poetry, Plath abandoned teaching and devoted herself entirely to writing. The following year, Plath and Hughes moved to Boston, where she attended Robert Lowell's seminar in poetry. There she met Anne Sexton. Sexton, Lowell and Plath are often grouped together as a school of confessional poets because of their common treatment of nervous disorders, domestic difficulties, and mental breakdowns.

In the fall of 1959, Plath received a fellowship to Yaddo, the writers' colony in Saratoga Springs, N.Y., where she completed the poems for *Colossus*. Her acquaintance with Lowell and Sexton, her reading of African folktales and the poetry of Theodore Roethke, as well as the new practice of meditations to inspire poems (which she undertook at Yaddo under Hughes's influence) encouraged her to break away from the set forms and technical exercises of her earliest work. She was thus able to deal more openly and freely with the dark underworld of her own dreams, torments, and psychic stress.

Plath and Hughes returned to England at the end of 1959. Their first child was born in 1960. Although Plath won both the Cheltenham Festival Award and a Eugene F. Saxton Fellowship for writing in 1961, this period was difficult; in the winter of 1961 she had a miscarriage and an appendectomy. The couple moved from London to Devon in September 1961, and Plath settled into a country life, becoming a beekeeper, attending the local church, and learning to ride a horse. Although she suffered from severe writing blocks during this time, she worked relentlessly on her poetry, attempting to expand her range of subjects to include her experiences as a hospital patient, a mother, and a beekeeper. Plath had her second child in January 1962. In the late summer of 1962, she was separated from Hughes, and in December she moved with her children back to London to live in an apartment once inhabited by Yeats at Fitzroy Road. There she committed suicide.

In the few months between her separation from Hughes and her death, Plath wrote most of the poetry for which she is best known. Hughes collected the poems and published them in a series of volumes starting with the most powerful, *Ariel* (London, 1965; New York, 1966). Plath's suicide, combined with the subjects of her poems (the extreme psychic states of hatred, revenge, desolation, and disorder) and the brute power of her poetic voice, has forced an equation between her life and her work that has endowed both with an unfortunate notoriety. Plath became a legend, high priestess of the death cult, and the unhappy end of her life became a judgment on her poems. "Poetry of this order is a murderous art," A. Alvarez has argued, and Robert Lowell claimed, "Her art's immortality is life's disintegration." Although evaluations such as these gradually give way to closer analysis of the poems, Plath remains a controversial figure. She wrote about vengeful female figures who rise up to "eat men," about a daughter's hatred and spite for her father, about the death-dealers that haunted her; but she also dealt with the joys of birthing, a mother's love and anxiety, a transcendent female identity. Her power as a poet who manipulated her own most terrifying experiences and created the myth of woman as creator-destroyer continues to attract critical analysis.

[In addition to works mentioned in the text, major collections of Plath's poems are *Crossing the Water* (1971) and *Winter Trees* (London, 1971; New York, 1972); her prose includes *Letters Home: Correspondence 1950–1963* (1975), edited by Aurelia Schober Plath, and a collection of short stories, *Johnny Panic and the Bible of Dreams* (1979).

Critical-biographical studies are Nancy Hunter Steiner, *A Closer Look at Ariel* (1973); Edward Butscher, *Sylvia Plath: Method and Madness* (1976); and David Holbrook, *Sylvia Plath: Poetry and Existence* (1976). Critical comments on all or part of her work may be found in Charles Newman, ed., *The Art of Sylvia Plath* (1970); Judith Kroll, *Chapters in a Mythology: The Poetry of Sylvia Plath* (1976); and Margaret Dickie Uroff, *Sylvia Plath and Ted Hughes*

(1979). Cameron Northouse and Thomas P. Walsh, *Sylvia Plath and Anne Sexton: A Reference Guide* (1974), provides a bibliographic listing of works on and by Plath.]

MARGARET DICKIE UROFF

PORTER, COLE (June 9, 1891–Oct. 15, 1964), composer and lyricist, was born in Peru, Ind., the son of Samuel Fenwick Porter, a druggist, and Kate Cole, the daughter of James Omar Cole, a wealthy landholder. Under the shadow of his father-in-law's wealth and power, Samuel Porter never emerged as a figure of consequence, even in his own household. Adding to marital tensions was the death in quick succession of two infants, prior to Cole's birth. Porter's mother hovered so protectively over him that his father quickly faded into the background as a parent. There was so little interaction between father and son that Porter claimed that he remembered little about his father.

Porter was denied nothing as a child. He had his own Shetland pony, a private tutor for French lessons, and dance instruction. He began the study of violin and piano at the age of six and was also encouraged to compose. When he was ten, Porter wrote a piano piece, "Song of the Birds," which he dedicated to his mother. The following year, he wrote another "bird" piece for piano, "Bobolink Waltz," which his mother published at her own expense and distributed to friends and relatives as an example of Porter's talent.

From 1905 to 1909 Porter attended Worcester Academy, a boy's school in Massachusetts that emphasized the classics. An honor student, he graduated valedictorian of his class. As a reward for this honor, he was sent on a European holiday that summer by his grandfather. He then entered Yale University, where—contrary to his fine record at Worcester—he did not do well in his studies. He belonged to nearly every club on campus. He also wrote more than 300 songs at Yale. Many of them are now lost but some—"Bingo Eli Yale," "Bull Dog," and "Eli" —have become Yale classics. Porter also wrote the scores and lyrics for four musical comedies that were performed by Yale students: *Cora, And the Villain Still Pursued Her, The Pot of Gold,* and *The Kaleidoscope.*

After graduating with a B.A. in 1913, Porter entered Harvard Law School, in response to his grandfather's wishes that he become a lawyer. But after one year he gave up law to concentrate on songwriting. His first Broadway musical, *See America First* (1916), closed after only fifteen performances. The following year, shortly after the United States entered World War I, Porter went to France. Although he claimed that he had joined the French Foreign Legion and served in the French army, these claims were false. While in France he met and courted Linda Lee Thomas, a wealthy American divorcée, eight years his senior and a leading social figure in Paris. They were married on Dec. 18, 1919, and soon set a pattern of great social activity—giving numerous parties and traveling extensively, both together and separately. The marriage was childless.

Prior to his marriage, Porter already had to his credit a hit song, "Old-Fashioned Garden," from *Hitchy-Koo of 1919*, a Broadway revue. After his marriage, some of his songs, like "I'm in Love Again" and "Two Little Babes in the Wood," from *The Greenwich Village Follies* (1924), did rather well. But it was not until 1928 that he achieved his first major hit with "Let's Do It, Let's Fall in Love," written for the Broadway musical *Paris*. Like so many of his songs, "Let's Do It" elegantly combines graceful melody and rhyming ingenuity with a mixture of sexual innuendos, offbeat humor, colloquialisms, and topicality.

After "Let's Do It," hit songs came regularly from Porter's pen: "What Is This Thing Called Love?" (from *Wake Up and Dream*, 1929), "You Do Something to Me" (from *Fifty Million Frenchmen*, 1929), "Love for Sale" (from *The New Yorkers*, 1930), "Night and Day" (from *Gay Divorcée*, 1932), "Blow, Gabriel, Blow," "I Get a Kick out of You," "Anything Goes," "All Through the Night," and "You're the Top" (all from *Anything Goes*, 1934). By the mid-1930's Porter's songs had become internationally famous.

Porter also became active in Hollywood, and wrote the scores for the films *Born to Dance* (1936) and *Rosalie* (1937). Shortly after working on the latter film, he injured his legs so severely in a horseback-riding accident that there was a strong possibility they would have to be amputated. Doctors were able to stave off amputation with numerous painful operations that enabled him to walk with the aid of braces and a cane.

Despite the accident, Porter quickly resumed his songwriting career, writing the scores for the Broadway shows *Leave It to Me* (1938), *Du Barry Was a Lady* (1939), *Panama Hattie* (1940), *Let's Face It!* (1941), *Something for the Boys* (1943), *Mexican Hayride* (1944), and *Kiss Me, Kate* (1948). During this period he also wrote the scores for the films *Broadway Melody of 1940*, *You'll Never Get Rich* (1941), *Some-*

thing to Shout About (1943), and *The Pirate* (1948). His own life was portrayed on the screen in the far-from-accurate *Night and Day* (1946), with Cary Grant playing the lead.

In the 1950's he wrote the scores for such Broadway musicals as *Can-Can* (1953) and *Silk Stockings* (1955) and for the films *High Society* (1956) and *Les Girls* (1957).

In April 1958 Porter's long struggle to save his legs ended when osteomyelitis made it necessary to amputate his right leg close to the hip. Unable to adjust to the amputation, he stopped writing songs. His health steadily declined. He died in Santa Monica, Calif.

Porter's influence on popular music and the American musical theater was enormous and long-lasting. His lyrics in particular set new standards of invention, craftsmanship, and sophistication. Once attuned to them, the public was no longer willing to settle for the mundane—prevalent for so long in popular music.

[Personal documents, memorabilia, manuscripts, and scores are at Yale University and the Porter archives in Peru, Ind. A fairly comprehensive but selected bibliography is in Charles Schwartz, *Cole Porter: A Biography* (1977). Two other books should be noted: George Eells, *The Life That Late He Led* (1967); and Robert Kimball, *Cole* (1971).]

CHARLES SCHWARTZ

POTTER, CHARLES FRANCIS (Oct. 28, 1885–Oct. 4, 1962), clergyman, was born in Marlboro, Mass., the son of Charles Henry Potter, a shoe factory worker, and of Flora Ellen Lincoln. In childhood and youth his outlook was evangelical and orthodox, and the ministry was his obvious and unquestioned vocation. Enrolled in Sunday school at the age of eighteen months, he was memorizing Bible passages at the age of two and a half, and at three he was preaching to his parents.

Potter was first licensed to preach at the age of seventeen. That same year (1903) he entered Bucknell University, but he spent his sophomore year (1904–1905) at Brown. He received the B.A. from Bucknell in 1907. He received an M.A. from Bucknell in 1916. On June 25, 1908, he married Clara Adelaide Cook; they had three sons.

After being ordained at the Central Avenue Baptist Church in Dover, N.H., in 1908, Potter served student pastorates there and at Mattapan, Mass., while attending Newton Theological Seminary (B.D., 1913; S.T.M., 1916). He also eked out a meager living by selling aluminum cookware door to door.

After serving parishes in Edmonton, Alberta, and in Marlboro and Wellesley Hills, Mass., Potter was called in 1919 to the West Side Unitarian Church in New York City, where he launched a successful building program. By that time he had left his Baptist orthodoxy far behind him, and in the fundamentalist-modernist conflict of the 1920's he emerged as a leading advocate on the modernist side. A series of radio debates in 1924 with John Roach Straton, the formidable pastor of the Calvary Baptist Church in Manhattan, on evolution, the Virgin Birth, the infallibility of the Bible, the divinity of Christ, and the Second Coming, was as inconclusive as most such exchanges; the judges awarded two of the debates to Potter and two to Stratton. This "media event" brought Potter to national attention. In 1925 he figured in the famous "monkey trial" of *Tennessee* v. *John Thomas Scopes* as a Bible expert for the defense, furnishing Clarence Darrow with some of the biblical inconsistencies and logical contradictions that Darrow used to badger William Jennings Bryan on the witness stand.

By that time Potter was raising in his sermons questions like "Is the God Idea Essential to Religion?," thereby moving beyond the theology of most of his modernist colleagues. He resigned the West Side Unitarian pastorate in 1925 and spent two years as professor of comparative religion at Antioch College. He returned to the ministry in New York City in 1927, as pastor of the (Universalist) Church of the Divine Paternity. There he aligned himself with the Social Gospel movement of American Protestantism. Rejecting the widely held view that the church ought not to meddle in politics, Potter argued in 1928 that it would be right for churchpeople to oppose a candidate who professed any religious belief that unfitted him for public office. The following year he published the first of his fifteen books, *The Story of Religion*. This was a collection of biographical sketches of major religious leaders of the world.

Like many clergymen, both liberal and conservative, Potter was uncomfortable in the ministerial role. He once compared life to a football game being fought on the field while the preacher remained in the stands, explaining the game to the ladies. Perhaps this ambivalence, even more than the heterodox theological views that displeased some of his church's trustees, caused Potter to resign from the ministry in 1929. He then founded the First Humanist Society of New York, whose advisory board included, at various times, such notables as Julian Huxley, John Dewey, Albert Einstein, Thomas

Mann, and Harry Elmer Barnes. The new organization, Potter declared, would have neither clergy, nor creed, nor baptisms, nor prayers; brides would no longer be given away, "because women are properties in their own rights."

This brand of humanism, scientific and antisupernatural, was not to be confused with the literary humanism professed by Irving Babbitt and Paul Elmer More, whom Potter accused of seeking "decorum rather than progress." But, like some other American religious leaders who have taken the plunge into radicalism, Potter somewhat hedged his bets. In *Beyond the Senses* (1940) he argued that thought transference and clairvoyance, which he believed had been scientifically proved, gave sounder reasons for belief in personal survival after death than did traditional religion.

Potter campaigned against capital punishment and was an early and continuing advocate of birth control. In 1938 he founded the Euthanasia Society of America; twenty years later it claimed 40,000 members. The renewed theological debate that was prompted by the discovery in the 1940's of the Dead Sea Scrolls moved Potter to write *The Lost Years of Jesus Revealed* (1958), a book with the thesis that the founder of Christianity had spent his youth in a Dead Sea ascetic community from which he had derived most of his ideas. Potter also had a folklorist's interest in the origins of children's tongue twisters; *Tongue Tanglers*, one of several of his books on the subject, was in press at the time of his death in New York City.

[Potter's autobiography, *The Preacher and I* (1951), is informative, but his judgments about people with whom he disagreed must be taken with great caution; for a contrasting view of his debates with Straton, see H. H. Straton, *Christian Century*, May 7, 1952. Potter's writings, in addition to those mentioned in the text, include *Humanism, a New Religion* (1930); *Humanizing Religion* (1933); "My First Funeral," *Reader's Digest*, July 1940; and *The Great Religious Leaders* (1958), a revision of *Story of Religion*. An obituary is in the *New York Times*, Oct. 5, 1962.]

PAUL A. CARTER

POUND, (NATHAN) ROSCOE (Oct. 27, 1870–July 1, 1964), law professor, jurist, and botanist, was born in Lincoln, Nebr., the son of Judge Stephen Bosworth Pound and Laura Biddlecome. His life merits the adjective "remarkable," both for its length and its breadth of accomplishment and for its curious twists and turns. The Pound household was affluent and dedicated to learning: from the age of three, when he learned to read, Pound's phenomenal capacity to absorb and remember information was apparent.

At age six Pound was taught German by his mother, a former schoolteacher; at fourteen he entered the University of Nebraska. His proposed course of study was classics, but he quickly developed an interest in botany and, after 1886, concentrated on that subject. After graduating from Nebraska in 1888 and reading law in his father's law office that summer, Pound enrolled at Nebraska as a graduate student in botany.

Law and botany warred for Pound's favor after 1888, with botany winning at first. He found the apprenticeship system of learning law —in which one read treatises such as William Blackstone's *Commentaries* and Thomas Cooley's *Constitutional Limitations*—boring to a fault, and he found Charles E. Bessey's botany laboratory and its companion seminar fascinating. His first article, "Ash Rust in 1888," appeared in the *American Naturalist* that year.

Judge Pound, reconciled to his son's dissatisfaction with the apprenticeship system of legal education, proposed to send him to Harvard Law School for the 1889–1890 academic year. Roscoe reluctantly agreed, largely because of the distinguished botanists in Cambridge and Boston. He resolved to stay at Harvard for only one year, and did so. His "textbook ideas" of education were nonetheless "shaken," he wrote to his mother, by the Socratic teaching methods at Harvard, and he eventually endorsed studying law through the reading of individual appellate cases. Members of the Harvard faculty also attracted him, especially John Chipman Gray and William A. Keener.

Pound gave as his principal reason for returning to Nebraska his desire to assist his father in the latter's law practice, which he began to do in the summer of 1890. He simultaneously enrolled as a graduate student in botany and, with other students, began an extensive survey of the vegetation in Nebraska. This work formed the basis of his doctoral dissertation, eventually published (with F. E. Clements), on *Phytogeography of Nebraska* (1898). One reviewer called the dissertation "the pioneer work of its kind." Pound's methodology assumed that botanists studied growing organisms in the process of changing and was thus a deviation from the "taxonomic" approach to botany. Pound also assumed that the ultimate goal of botany was workable classification systems. Both of these assumptions carried over into his legal scholarship, although in the 1890's he was far from a self-conscious jurist.

The decade after 1890 was an exceptionally busy time for Pound. He practiced law in Lincoln, doing both trial and appellate litigation; he taught Roman law in the Latin department of the University of Nebraska and was an assistant professor at the College of Law, teaching pleading, jurisprudence, and criminal law; he served as an intermediate appellate judge (called a commissioner) on the Nebraska Supreme Court; he helped modernize the Nebraska State Bar Association; he campaigned vigorously for William McKinley in the 1896 and 1900 presidential campaigns. (Pound's politics, at the time, were those of a "standpat" Republican; he bitterly denounced William Jennings Bryan and the Populists and complained about those who would "reform for the sake of reform.") In 1899, after a four-year engagement, Pound married Grace Gerrard. Their two children died at birth. With all of these activities, botany became crowded out; Pound never returned to it.

Pound's appointment as dean of the Nebraska College of Law in 1903 marked a turning point in his professional life. At thirty-three his experience, although diverse, had been essentially regional; in the next decade he became a national figure. Three factors combined to elevate Pound to national prominence: the channeling of his energies into a single vocation, teaching law; his renewed acquaintance with the writings of German legal scholars; and his fusion of scholarship and "progressive" law reform.

Nebraska was a small and unpretentious law school when Pound became dean, and although he resigned from the Nebraska Supreme Court Commission to take the post, he continued to practice law. In 1905 he sought to leave the deanship to go into practice on a full-time basis, but was persuaded to stay on. Despite the relative modesty of the position, Pound found that it stimulated him to rethink his commitment to academic law and to devote more time to fusing his intellectual curiosity and his concern for practical affairs. He proceeded to explore two seemingly disparate subjects and to link them in a theory of professional training.

One subject was jurisprudence, especially comparative jurisprudence. Pound turned to John Austin, Friedrich Karl von Savigny, and, especially, Rudolf von Jhering, whose work eventually led him to develop a theory of "sociological jurisprudence," stressing the dependency of legal rules on changing social conditions. Another subject was procedure: Pound sought to develop a philosophy of procedure by which local rules were seen as embodiments of fundamental features of social organizations. Pound had, one of his biographers said, "a strange way of . . . making difficult and elevated spheres of [legal] thought . . . at one with the law as a practicing lawyer knows it"; he also was personally committed to this fusion of theory and practice.

Out of this work came Pound's famous 1906 address at the annual meeting of the American Bar Association, "The Causes of Popular Dissatisfaction with the Administration of Justice," which launched his national career. The address was a curious blend of traditional criticisms of the legal profession (Pound found lawyers captives of commercial interests and more interested in "beat[ing] the law" than in being honorable) and prescient suggestions for reform. Most significant of those suggestions was Pound's claim that the American system of justice lacked a comprehensive social philosophy at a time when a new social consciousness had emerged in American society. While Pound did not explicitly endorse social reform, he did call for procedural reforms of the legal system and suggested that several substantive common-law doctrines were outmoded.

John H. Wigmore, dean of Northwestern University Law School, who listened to Pound's address, felt that "the white flame of Progress [had been] kindled" by Pound's proposals. Six months later (1907) Wigmore offered Pound a post on the Northwestern faculty that included a sharply reduced teaching load. Pound accepted with enthusiasm. Within two years after going to Northwestern, he had published two of his most famous articles, "Mechanical Jurisprudence" in the *Columbia Law Review* and "Liberty of Contract" in the *Yale Law Journal,* and had received offers from the law schools at Wisconsin, Yale, and the University of Chicago. In accepting Chicago's offer he turned down a Northwestern counteroffer of $7,500 per year, the highest salary then paid to any law professor in the country. But he did not remain long at Chicago; in 1910 he accepted the Story professorship at Harvard. His rise was one of the most meteoric in the history of academic law.

Pound's ability to link abstract inquiries about jurisprudence with concrete proposals for professional reform does much to explain his success. His scholarship between 1905 and 1910 combined forays into comparative jurisprudence with specific recommendations for change. He exposed the ossification or irrelevance of current doctrine, the mechanical quality of judicial decision-making, and the artificialities of procedure. At one level Pound ranged through the ancient

treatise writers; at another, he spoke on practical issues to the bar associations. He was, at this phase of his life, the model of a "modern" jurist.

After 1910, Pound began, gradually, to make his philosophy of professional reform more explicit, and the tenor of his writing changed from largely critical to largely expository. His approach, embodied in the phrases "sociological jurisprudence" and "social engineering," both complemented his earlier work and expanded upon it. By 1916, Pound was regarded as the creator and architect of an approach to common-law decision-making that favored, as he put it, "the adjustment of [legal] principles and doctrines to the human conditions they are to govern." The approach, with its emphasis on flexible responses to changing social and economic conditions and on the ordering of affairs by professional and political elites, was unmistakably "progressive" and avowedly "pragmatic." It was thus perfectly compatible with the advanced intellectual and political thought of the times. By 1916, when Harvard appointed him dean, Pound was the best-known law professor in the nation.

Yet Pound's appointment as dean of Harvard Law School served as a powerful check to his creative energies. During the twenty years of his deanship, he continued to publish at an extraordinary rate; some of his best-known work, such as *Interpretations of Legal History* (1923) and *Law and Morals* (1924), dates from this period. But his scholarship had become repetitious and synthetic, and as time went on, he came to see himself as a defender of the traditional patterns of common-law decision-making and of certainty and predictability in jurisprudence.

At the same time Pound, after identifying himself as a vigorous defender of academic freedom, social reform, and "progressive" legislation in the early years of his deanship, reverted to the cautious social attitudes of his youth. He declined to speak out on public issues and cultivated alumni who were anti-Communist and anti-Semitic. He accepted an honorary degree from the University of Berlin in 1934 and even made flattering remarks about Hitler. Pound also opposed curriculum reform and experimental research programs seeking to integrate law with social sciences. He rejected the Realist movement in legal education, which had borrowed from his own work, and the New Deal, which he referred to as the "service state."

Pound's first wife died in 1928, and he was so shaken by her death that he took a two-year leave of absence from Harvard. On June 30, 1931, Pound married Lucy Berry Miller, with whom he was to live until her death in 1959, when he was in his ninetieth year.

By his retirement from the deanship at Harvard in 1936, Pound had, ironically, become a defender of the "old" ways—creative common-law judging, a "traditional" curriculum, universal moral values, and a largely practical approach to legal education—against advocates of legislative and administrative power, interdisciplinary curricula, moral relativism, and a "university" model for law schools. This role was ironic in two respects: it transformed Pound's language from that of the reformer to that of the reactionary without much change in the content of the language, and it helped assure Pound's success as an administrator. In terms of money raised, buildings built, faculty and student body growth, and solid relations with the bar and alumni, Pound's deanship at Harvard was notable. But by 1936 the dean who had presided over this "progress" had lost his scholarly standing.

Exhausted and embittered by internal dissensions in the last years of his deanship (the dissensions centered on proposed changes in the curriculum that he resisted), Pound gave up the deanship in 1936 to become Harvard's first university professor (1937–1947). He lived for twenty-eight more years and wrote for most of that time. In addition to his scholarly efforts, he spent two years in China as an adviser to Chiang Kai-shek's government, was a regular contributor to debate on public issues involving the legal profession, and was a full-time law professor at the University of California, Los Angeles, from 1949 to 1953. In 1959 his five-volume work *Jurisprudence* appeared, and three years later he organized and contributed to a festschrift for Austin W. Scott, who had come to Harvard Law School the same year as Pound. In 1967 a last article of his appeared, posthumously, in the *Valparaiso Law Review*.

The physical and intellectual capacities that Pound maintained almost until his death were offset by the peculiar evolution of his ideas. After 1948 he endorsed ideas and attitudes that he had seemingly considered and rejected earlier. One by one the features of sociological jurisprudence were cast off: administrative agencies became a threat to private enterprise; the social sciences, alien subjects; comparative scholarship and politics, a threat to the American way of life; academic freedom, an invitation for Communism to flourish in universities; a philosophy of life based on social consciousness, the emblem of the bureaucratic and totalitarian "service state." The same person who had defended Zechariah Chafee, Jr., Felix Frankfurter, and other "radicals" on the Harvard faculty in the 1920's became a vigorous proponent of loyalty oaths for teachers in the 1950's. By the time of Pound's death even the Eisenhower administration was too "welfare-minded" for his taste.

Throughout the changes and controversy in his professional life Pound's personality remained roughly constant. In print he was, for most of his life, vigorous in expression but moderate in tone; in person he was blunt, abrupt, and relatively humorless, but approachable and unpretentious; in power he was autocratic and dogmatic. Despite his international reputation and his fluency in German, French, and Italian, he was not a cosmopolite; his avocational pursuits included American politics, American sports, and Cole Porter.

To students Pound appeared gruff and exacting, if lacking in pretension. He was not a markedly successful teacher, but he did inspire a few students, one of whom, Paul Sayre, published an affectionate biography of Pound in 1948. Pound used the Socratic method in class, but not as an exercise to outwit or to humiliate students. His classroom technique was to focus on the practical features of a case, reaching its theoretical significance only as an afterthought. He did not suffer fools gladly, and he did not believe that undergraduate law students could master the complexities of jurisprudence; his model curriculum reserved legal history, legal philosophy, and jurisprudence for graduate seminars, exposing undergraduates only to traditional common-law courses.

In his graduate seminars Pound debated issues of historiography and methodology, but in a strikingly matter-of-fact fashion. On one occasion, in response to a student's comment that his scholarship stopped well short of formulating a coherent philosophical position, Pound said, "I don't take to the philosophical pattern," since "I don't want to give myself over to any idea." He simply tried, he said, "to look at the actual claims that are made and then evaluate them in terms of our way of life as nearly as [I] can understand it."

Despite his straightforwardness, bluntness, and disinclination to engage in speculative conversation, Pound was not dispassionate as a teacher or a colleague. He loved debate and was regularly provoked to respond to critics in print; he rigidly maintained views on legal education in the face of sharp opposition. As a teacher he tried to be an inspirational, authoritative force; as a dean he tried to cultivate alumni and at the same time dominate his faculty.

Pound had a passion for eating, which made

him overweight for most of his adult life, although he ran daily until his sixties and walked twelve miles to and from work until his eighties. He shunned an overcoat in cold weather, believing that the body's adjustment to variations of temperature was a form of healthful exercise. Normally he worked ten hours a day, five days a week, plus a few hours on the weekends. He planned his schedule carefully and followed a regular routine. He remained physically and mentally alert until the very end of his life, dying in Cambridge, Mass., at the age of ninety-four.

One is struck by two remarkable dissonances in Pound's life. Despite the overpowering quantity and breadth of his scholarship, almost none of it has contemporary stature. When one retraces Pound's steps, one finds abundant and occasionally penetrating insights, but they seem spotted throughout a surface narrative, producing a curiously synthetic effect. Despite his prodigious memory and his remarkable capacities for assimilation and organization, Pound almost deliberately declined to plumb issues to their depth. One thus confronts the paradox of a scholar who for a time can be said to have bestridden his profession like a colossus but who was so disinclined to probe beyond a certain point that one cannot find much of enduring value in his work.

The second dissonance in Pound's life comes from the interplay of his intellectual assumptions—that civilization constantly changes and that law needs to adapt itself continually to such changes—with the intellectual history of his own career. All the while that Pound was announcing that social and legal thought needed to be fluid, his own thought was becoming increasingly rigid. Imagining how a personage from history might react to contemporary affairs may be a fascinating exercise, but one rarely has the opportunity to see such a phenomenon occur. In Pound's case it did occur: a man whose thought matured from 1905 to the 1920's lived long enough and was articulate enough to comment on the New Deal, the Fair Deal, and the Eisenhower years. In those comments he revealed that his thinking had virtually not moved; as social conditions changed, his perspective gradually shifted from progressive to reactionary. Pound could not, and almost intentionally would not, practice the intellectual lessons he had preached. His life is as much a tale of opportunities lost and reflections prematurely cut off as one of staggering achievements.

[There are collections of Roscoe Pound Papers at the Harvard Law School Library and the Nebraska State Historical Society. See Paul Sayre, *The Life of Roscoe Pound* (1948); Arthur E. Sutherland, "One Man in His Time," *Harvard Law Review* (Nov. 1964), and *The Law at Harvard* (1967); David Wigdor, *Roscoe Pound* (1974); and Joel Seligman, *The High Citadel* (1978). An obituary is in the *New York Times*, July 2, 1964.]

G. Edward White

POWELL, RICHARD EWING ("DICK") (Nov. 14, 1904–Jan. 2, 1963), actor, was born in Mountain View, Ark., the son of Ewing Powell and Sallie Thompson. The family moved to Little Rock in 1914, where Powell first gained attention as a singer. While in his teens he sang in church choirs, at National Guard shows, with a local orchestra, and started his own band called the Peter Pan. In addition to many singing appearances during his high school years, Powell also worked for a grocery store, a soda fountain, and a power company.

Following graduation from high school in 1921, Powell studied for a year at Little Rock College, where he also played baritone horn in the band. He left college to work for a telephone company emptying telephone coin boxes. During his free time he sang frequently at town theaters. At this time, he married M. Maund, a model. They had no children. His wife, however, did not like being married to an entertainer, and a divorce soon followed. Shortly thereafter Powell sang with the traveling Royal Peacock Band throughout Kentucky, Ohio, Illinois, and Indiana. His next job was as a banjoist and singer for Charlie Davis' orchestra in Indianapolis. He also played the cornet, clarinet, saxophone, and piano and supplemented his income by appearing in nightclubs and by operating a ballroom, where he became a popular master of ceremonies.

Powell's big break came in 1930 when he was offered a position as singer, comedian, and master of ceremonies for the Warner Brothers' Stanley Theatre in Pittsburgh. In the next three years he gained increasing notice as a singer on the theater circuit and on radio. In 1932 he appeared in the Warner Brothers musical film *Blessed Event*, and after its warm reception by the public, he was immediately signed to a long-term contract. This was the first of more than thirty musicals he made for Warner Brothers and several other studios. He also appeared regularly as a radio singer in the CBS series "Hollywood Hotel."

The handsome, curly-haired tenor became the epitome of the actor-singer in the Warner musicals of the 1930's. He starred in *42nd Street* (1933), *Gold Diggers of 1933* (1933), *Wonder*

Bar (1934), *20 Million Sweethearts* (1934), *Gold Diggers of 1935* (1935), and *Broadway Gondolier* (1935). On Sept. 19, 1936, Powell married actress Joan Blondell; they had one daughter. He continued in musicals, playing the now familiar role of eternal juvenile and singing glamor boy. His films include *Colleen* (1936), *Gold Diggers of 1937* (1936), *The Singing Marine* (1937), *On the Avenue* (1937), *Hard to Get* (1938), *Going Places* (1939), and *Christmas in July* (1940).

By 1940 Powell was tired of musicals. As he put it: "I made four or five of those things a year—and always the same stupid story." He wanted to appear in more dramatic roles, but when he did not receive them, he bought his release from his Warner contract in 1940. He returned to his film work in 1941 and made *Model Wife* (1941) and *In the Navy* (1941). The films of the mid-1940's—such as *Happy Go Lucky* (1943), *True to Life* (1943), and *Meet the People* (1944)—included some comedy and even a few serious scenes.

In 1945 Powell played a tough and cynical private detective in *Murder, My Sweet.* The film received high critical acclaim; one reviewer wrote: "Dick Powell plays the detective as he has never played any other role before." Further praise came for his dramatic roles in *Cornered* (1945), *Johnny O'Clock* (1947), *To the Ends of the Earth* (1948), and *Rogues' Regiment* (1948). Perhaps his finest screen performance was in the 1948 melodrama *Pitfall.* For instance, the novelist John O'Hara had the highest praise for Powell's performance: "Dick Powell . . . sang his way to fame and fortune, and ultimately achieved artistry as a middle-class insurance man in *Pitfall.*" Following his divorce from Joan Blondell, in 1944, on Aug. 19, 1945, Powell married the actress June Allyson. they adopted a daughter and had one son. But it proved to be an off-again, on-again type marriage.

In the 1950's Powell's career took a new turn. He began to direct and produce films, including *Split Second* (1953), *The Conqueror* (1956), *The Enemy Below* (1957), and *The Hunters* (1958). In addition, he founded the successful Four Star Television company. It produced many popular series, including his own "Dick Powell Show." He died in Hollywood.

Powell's versatility has assured him a place among Hollywood's legends. He was a noted singer, fine actor, brilliant director and producer, and later a prominent television personality. He worked very hard and seemed to gain mastery at everything he attempted.

[Competent biographies of Powell are contained in David Thompson, *A Biographical Dictionary of Film* (1976), David Ragan, *Who's Who in Hollywood, 1900–1976* (1976), and John M. Smith and Tim Cawkwell, *The World Encyclopedia of the Film* (1972). Some good glimpses into Powell's family life are in June Allyson, "Let's Be Frank about Me," *Saturday Evening Post,* Dec. 14, 21, 1957; and Marie Torre, "The Much-Mended Marriage of Dick Powell and June Allyson," *McCalls,* June 1962. See the obituary in the *New York Times,* Jan. 4, 1963. A good assessment of his work is in John O'Hara, "Egos and Actors," *Holiday,* Oct. 1966.]

J. MICHAEL QUILL

PRESCOTT, SAMUEL CATE (Apr. 5, 1872–Mar. 20, 1962), bacteriologist, was born in rural South Hampton, N.H., the son of Samuel Melcher Prescott, a farmer and blacksmith, and Mary Emily Cate. After attending public school in South Hampton and the Sanborn Seminary in Kingston, N.H., Prescott entered Massachusetts Institute of Technology (MIT) in 1890. There he took courses in the nation's first industrial biology department and was inspired by the brilliant teaching of William T. Sedgwick. Sedgwick's *Principles of Sanitary Science and Public Health* (1902) helped crystallize public sentiment in many American urban communities of the need for better sanitation facilities.

Prescott graduated in 1894 with the S.B. degree. After serving for fifteen months as chemist at the Worcester, Mass., Sewage Purification Works, Prescott joined Sedgwick's department as assistant and rose through the faculty ranks, becoming professor in 1914, head of the Department of Biology and Public Health in 1922, and dean of science in 1932. Prescott was married on June 30, 1910, to Alice Durgin Chase, daughter of a manufacturer of wood products. They had three children.

Long before Prescott launched his career, certain methods of food preservation had been known of, notably the use of salt, ice, and drying. Prescott belonged to the first generation of professional specialized scientists and engineers who successfully applied the principles of modern science and technology to food preservation. Spurred on by gloomy Malthusian predictions that the earth's food supply would be inadequate in an increasingly urbanized, overpopulated twentieth-century world, he devoted his career to food preservation. Becoming a bacteriologist when that science was barely twenty years old, Prescott made many pioneering discoveries.

Prescott's most important contribution was

the discovery of the definitive scientific method for making canned food entirely sanitary. In 1810 Nicholas Appert, a Frenchman, published the results of his technique of boiling glass jars of food. By the 1890's scientists understood, following Louis Pasteur's discoveries, that microorganisms probably caused deterioration of canned food. Yet canners continued to believe that the introduction of oxygen into cans caused food spoilage; and they tried to perfect a vacuum seal. In 1894, Harry L. Russell of the University of Wisconsin was the first bacteriologist to demonstrate that microorganisms, not oxygen, spoiled canned food; but his findings remained buried in an obscure university extension bulletin for years. Between 1895 and 1897 Prescott and W. Lyman Underwood conducted a series of exhaustive experiments on the presence of microorganisms in canned clams, lobsters, and corn. They showed conclusively that boiling canned food for ten minutes at 250 degrees Fahrenheit killed all microorganisms and rendered the food sanitary. They were concerned with the wholesomeness and attractiveness of the foods, not their nutritional value. Prescott and Underwood disseminated their findings widely, thus gaining wide recognition for their work.

In succeeding years Prescott devoted his efforts to many different kinds of bacteriological researches. A recurrent interest of his was the fermentation process. He founded the Boston Biochemical Laboratory in 1904. There he and his associates worked on many practical bacteriological problems of preservation. Prescott believed that food scientists should have close ties to private industry, keeping enterpreneurs abreast of the latest knowledge. Between 1914 and 1917 Prescott directed a laboratory for the United Fruit Company in Port Limon, Costa Rica, where he worked on bacteriological analysis of local soils and crop diseases. As major in the sanitary corps of the army (1918–1919), he served as chief of the United States Department of Agriculture's dehydration division. He directed vital studies of food dehydration for the war effort. Under his direction significant advances were made in the variety of foods that could be preserved.

When Prescott became dean of science at MIT in 1932, his research did not cease. He continued to work on microorganic fermentation but did not venture into new fields, such as refrigeration, which, especially after Clarence Birdseye organized his company in 1929, dramatically changed the character of the food industry.

By the late 1930's Prescott had become increasingly optimistic that food science and technology might be able to surmount the problems of overpopulation. He shifted his attention somewhat in the 1940's to industrial microbiology, studying substances other than foods. Prescott retired from his post of dean of science at MIT in 1942. He served as consultant to the federal government during World War II and to a variety of corporations in the food industry. Prescott died in Boston.

Prescott was not a seminal thinker whose theories revolutionized an entire field. But he was a pioneer who took the established precepts and paradigms of science and applied them to practical problems. His considerable talent and the academic professionalization of science and technology in America after the 1870's allowed him to do such work.

[Prescott's publications are too voluminous and scattered to list here. His seminal articles on canning with W. Lyman Underwood are "Micro-Organisms and Sterilizing Processes in the Canning Inndustry," *Technology Quarterly and Proceedings of the Society of Arts* (1897); "Contributions to Our Knowledge of Micro-organisms and Sterilizing Processes in the Canning Industries, II. The Souring of Canned Corn," *Technology Quarterly and Proceedings of the Society of Arts* (1898); and "Contributions to Our Knowledge of Micro-Organisms and Sterilizing Processes in the Canning Industries," *Science*, Nov. 26, 1897. Chief among other important publications are with Charles-Edward Amory Winslow, *Elements of Water Bacteriology, with Special Reference to Sanitary Water Analysis* (1904); with Bernard E. Proctor, *Food Technology* (1937); and with Cecil Gordon Dunn, *Industrial Microbiology* (1940). Prescott's historical recollections and views can be found in his "Food Conservation," in P. Ravenel Mazÿk, ed., *A Half Century of Public Health. Jubilee Historical Volume of the American Public Health Association* (1921); "Purpose of the Food Technology Conference," *Food Research* (1938); "Beginnings of the History of the Institute of Food Technologists," *Food Technology*, Aug. 1950; and his book *When M.I.T. Was "Boston Tech"* (1904). Secondary literature on Prescott includes Edward F. Keuchel, "Science, Technology and Food Preservation: The Introduction of Bacteriology to the American Canning Industry," in Burton J. Williams, ed., *Essays in American History in Honor of James C. Malin* (1973). See also Samuel Goldblith's articles: "Science and Technology of Thermal Processing," *Food Technology*, Dec. 1971 and Jan. 1972; and "Thermal Processing in Retrospect and Prospect," *Food Technology*, 1976. An obituary of Prescott appeared in the *New York Times*, Mar. 21, 1962.]

HAMILTON CRAVENS

PRICE, GEORGE EDWARD MC-CREADY (Aug. 26, 1870–Jan. 24, 1963), fundamentalist advocate and geologist, was born in Havelock, New Brunswick, the son of George Marshall Price, a farmer and mill operator, and of Susan McCready. Within two years of his father's death in 1882, Price, his mother, and his younger brother joined the Seventh-day Adventist Church. Following his marriage on Dec. 15, 1887, to Amelia A. Nason, an Adventist colporteur twelve years his senior, Price and his wife sold religious books in eastern Canada. They had three children.

From 1891 to 1893, Price studied at Battle Creek College in Michigan, and during 1896–1897 he completed a teacher training course at the Provincial Normal School of New Brunswick. In 1897, he taught at a small high school in Tracadie, New Brunswick. He tried unsuccessfully, in 1903–1904, to run a Seventh-day Adventist high school, Farmington Industrial Academy, in Nova Scotia. After brief stays in New York City, Washington, D.C., and Oakland and Los Angeles, Calif., he settled in 1906 in Loma Linda, Calif., where he taught nursing and medical students in the newly opened College of Medical Evangelists. In 1912, the college granted him a B.A. in recognition of his previous work. In 1918, Pacific Union College awarded him an honorary M.A., which Price used on virtually all his publications thereafter.

Price subsequently taught at other Adventist institutions: San Fernando Academy (1912–1913); Lodi Academy (1914–1920); Pacific Union College (1920–1922); Union College, Nebraska (1922–1924); Stanborough Missionary College, England (1924–1928), where he was president during 1927–1928; Emmanuel Missionary College, Berrien, Mich. (1929–1933); and Walla Walla College (1933–1938). He often taught courses in religion as well as in geology, and during his last decade in the classroom he held the title professor of philosophy and geology.

For most of his adult life Price led a spirited crusade against evolution, writing more than two dozen books and hundreds of articles advocating the "new catastrophism." He first developed an interest in the subject in the late 1890's, when a physician in Tracadie challenged the creationist views held by Seventh-day Adventists. The progressive nature of the fossil record nearly convinced Price of the truth of evolution, but reading Seventh-day Adventist founding prophetess Ellen G. White's *Patriarchs and Prophets* (1890), which Price believed to be divinely inspired, persuaded him that the Noachian Flood explained all. "The one simple postulate that there was a universal Flood clears up beautifully every major problem in the supposed conflict between modern science and modern Christianity," he later wrote.

In 1923, Price published *The New Geology*, his most comprehensive and systematic book. In it he stated his "great *law of comformable stratigraphic sequences . . .* by all odds the most important law ever formulated with reference to the order in which the strata occur." According to this law, *"Any kind of fossiliferous beds whatever, 'young' or 'old,' may be found occuring [sic] conformably on any other fossiliferous beds, 'older' or 'younger.'"*

Despite attacks from the scientific establishment, Price's influence among fundamentalists grew steadily. By the mid-1920's the editor of *Science* could accurately describe him as "the principal scientific authority of the Fundamentalists," and his byline was appearing in a broad spectrum of religious periodicals, from *Moody Monthly* to *Catholic World.*

On the eve of the Scopes trial in 1925, William Jennings Bryan invited Price to assist the prosecution as an expert witness. Because Price was then teaching in England, he could not accept. During the trial, when Bryan named Price as one of the two scientists he respected, Clarence Darrow remarked, "Every scientist in this country knows [he] is a mountebank and a pretender and not a geologist at all." That same year Price debated Joseph McCabe, a prominent evolutionist, at Queen's Hall in London, and received the Langhorne-Orchard Prize of the conservative Victoria Institute for the essay "Revelation and Evolution."

By the late 1930's Price realized that he was fighting for a lost cause. Public interest was declining, and even his former students were beginning to defect. When Harold W. Clark began promoting his own theory of flood geology in the 1940's, Price charged him with heresy and denounced his views in *Theories of Satanic Origin* (n.d.). Although his intemperate attacks on Clark and others damaged his reputation, Price continued to work in creationist circles.

Early in 1938, during a period of intense theological turmoil at Walla Walla College, he collapsed and remained in a coma for two days. At the end of the school year he retired. Also in 1938 he helped organize the Deluge Geology Society, which between 1941 and 1945 published the *Bulletin of Deluge Geology and Related Science,* of which Price was coeditor. In October 1954, his first wife died, and in April

1957 Price married Florence Bresee. He died in Loma Linda, Calif.

As Price's critics frequently noted, his greatest weakness was a lack of any formal training or field experience in geology. He was, though, a voracious reader of geological literature, an armchair scientist who self-consciously minimized the importance of higher education and firsthand knowledge. For decades he remained the most influential scientific authority in the fundamentalist camp. As one evangelical observed in 1950, Price's ideas had "grown and infiltrated the greater portion of fundamental Christianity in America."

[Price's papers are at Andrews University, Berrien Springs, Mich. The index of Seventh-day Adventist periodicals is in the SDA Room, Columbia Union College (Takoma Park, Md.) Library, lists 235 of his articles. Price's autobiographical writings include "Some Early Experiences with Evolutionary Geology," *Bulletin of Deluge Geology*, Nov. 1941; "Crusader for Creation," *Signs of the Times*, July 17, 1956; and "I'd Have an Aim," *Advent Review and Sabbath Herald*, Feb. 16, 1961. A biography is Harold W. Clark, *Crusader for Creation* (1966). Critical assessments include J. Laurence Kulp, "Deluge Geology," *Journal of the American Scientific Affiliation*, no. 1, 1950; Martin Gardner, *Fads and Fallacies in the Name of Science* (1957); Ronald L. Numbers, "'Sciences of Satanic Origin': Adventist Attitudes Toward Evolutionary Biology and Geology," *Spectrum*, Jan. 1979.]

RONALD L. NUMBERS

PROFACI, JOSEPH (Oct. 2, 1897–June 7, 1962), organized crime leader, was born in Villabati, a village in the Castellammare section of Sicily. In 1920 he was convicted of forgery and spent a year in prison at Palermo. He came to the United States in 1921 with Vincent Mangano, who later became a New York City crime boss; in 1927 he was naturalized.

By 1928, Profaci was connected with Charles ("Lucky") Luciano. On December 6 of that year he was present at a meeting in Cleveland, Ohio, of twenty-one leaders of organized crime, including his brother-in-law, Joseph Magliocco, and Vito Genovese. By 1929, Profaci controlled crime in Staten Island and had become a subdon in Salvatore Maranzano's organization.

When the "Castellammare war" broke out between Maranzano and Joe ("The Boss") Masseria in 1930, both Profaci and Joseph Bonanno, a friend from Villabati, sided with Maranzano. Later, as "boss of bosses," he made them heads of two of New York City's five crime families, sharing power in Brooklyn. Profaci retained this position for the rest of his

life. In 1931 he became a member of the national commission of organized crime, which was established by Luciano and included two other New Yorkers, Mangano and Bonnano, as well as Al Capone from Chicago and Frank Milano from Cleveland.

Profaci used mob money acquired from the numbers, narcotics, and prostitution to set up approximately twenty legitimate businesses. He became the largest importer of olive oil and tomato paste in the United States and acquired the nickname "Olive Oil King." He supposedly used this business as a front for numbers and drug smuggling. In 1956 the federal government fined Profaci $4,000 for adulterating his olive oil. During the 1950's his business interests also included the United Uniform Corporation, G. and P. Coal Company, and the Carmella Mia Packing Company; in addition he infiltrated the construction industry and union labor.

In 1953, Profaci was indicted by a federal grand jury for defrauding the government of $88,547 in unpaid taxes for the years 1946–1949. This indictment was in addition to earlier proceedings against the Brooklyn boss to collect more than $2 million in back taxes, owed since 1938, but the government was unable to obtain any money because his properties were controlled by relatives through second mortgages.

During the 1940's and 1950's Profaci continued to meet with other leaders of organized crime. In December 1946 he went to Havana to meet with "Lucky" Luciano, and in November 1957 he was one of the sixty-five men who met at the home of Joseph Barbara at Apalachin, N.Y.; when the police appeared, he was among those apprehended. He later testified before a New York State investigating commission that he and his companions were on their way to meet with business clients when their driver took a wrong turn. Finding themselves near Apalachin, they decided to visit Barbara, who had been ill.

Along with twenty others, Profaci was convicted of obstructing justice for not revealing the real nature of the meeting. He was found guilty and sentenced to five years in prison, but the conviction was overturned upon appeal. In 1958 a Brooklyn federal court judge revoked Profaci's citizenship on the ground that he had not revealed his arrests in Sicily when applying, but an appeals court later reversed this decision.

Profaci was married to Ninfa Magliocco; of their six children, two daughters married into other crime families. Besides a home in Brooklyn, Profaci owned an estate in Hightstown, N.J., and a home in Miami, Fla. It has been estimated that over a twenty-five-year period the revenue from his Brooklyn rackets amounted to between $100 million and $200 million. The Kefauver committee ranked Profaci as the third most important leader of organized crime in the nation, behind Vito Genovese and Vincent Mangano.

In 1959, Profaci had to deal with a revolt in his organization by the Gallo-Giorelli faction. The immediate issue was the failure of this group to obtain a share of the gambling interests of Frank ("Frankie Shots") Abbatemarco, whom they had killed on Profaci's orders. But there were other causes of the revolt. The younger group resented their boss's old-fashioned ways, such as collecting monthly dues and insisting that a large percentage of the profits from all rackets be given to him. Such practices had ceased in other organizations throughout the country. Nepotism was another issue.

The Gallos made their move after the Apalachin conviction of Profaci. They kidnapped five of his top men, including his brother and brother-in-law. Profaci was supposed to be taken, but managed to escape. The five were released after negotiations in which it was agreed that the Gallo-Giorelli demands were to be considered in a fair manner. On Aug. 20, 1961, an unsuccessful attempt was made on the life of "Larry" Gallo, and the Gallos were forced to barricade themselves in two houses in south Brooklyn. During the ensuing months both sides suffered casualties. The "war" was still going on when Profaci died in Bay Shore, N.Y.

[See Peter Maas, *The Valachi Papers* (1968); Donald R. Cressey, *Theft of the Nation* (1969); Edward Reid, *The Anatomy of Organized Crime in America* (1969); Ralph Salerno and John S. Tompkins, *The Crime Confederation* (1969); State of New York, *Interim Report of the Joint Legislative Committee on Government Operations on the Gangland Meeting in Apalachin, New York* (1958); and Humbert S. Nelli, *The Business of Crime* (1976). An obituary is in the *New York Times*, June 8, 1962.]

ALLAN NELSON

PUTNAM, NINA WILCOX (Nov. 28, 1885–Mar. 8, 1962), author, was born in New Haven, Conn., the daughter of Marrion Wilcox, an assistant professor of English at Yale who later followed an erratic career as an editor and author, and of Eleanor Patricia Sanchez. It was a family of wealth and high social position. Her father's family was descended from John Wilcox, a signer of the Hartford Charter. Her maternal grandfather was a Spanish count who owned a plantation in Puerto Rico. But both family fortunes declined rapidly during her childhood, and her immediate family descended from wealth to shabby gentility, with some periods of near poverty.

Wilcox was educated at home, partly by a governess but mainly by reading in her father's extensive library. Her father counted Rudyard Kipling, Robert Louis Stevenson, and Nathaniel Hawthorne's son Julian among his friends. Frederic Remington, Theodore Roosevelt, and other figures from the arts and politics were guests in the Wilcox home; Nina's childhood efforts at fiction were read and commented on by William Dean Howells.

Unfortunately, Wilcox's father had little talent for making money or holding a steady job. When she was fifteen, he went to South America for two years on an unsuccessful exploration expedition. She was forced to take a job as a milliner to support her mother and younger sister. Although the job was kept a secret so the family's social standing would not be jeopardized, Wilcox took such pride in her earning power that she gave up the job with great reluctance after her father's return.

Wilcox's career as a professional writer began in 1907 with the acceptance of a short story by *Ainslee's* magazine. Shortly afterward, on Oct. 5, 1907, she married Robert Faulkner Putnam of the publishing family; they had one son. From this time on, she had continuing success as a popular author. In her early career Nina Putnam wrote serious romances, but late in 1915 she turned to high comedy and in 1917 to colloquial humor, introducing her most popular character, Marie La Tour, a movie actress given to slang and humorous mishaps. Her first Marie La Tour story was also her first story to be accepted by the *Saturday Evening Post*, in which she then published regularly for two decades. By 1930 she could state that of approximately 950 manuscripts she had written for publication, all but two had been published, bringing her a total of nearly $1 million.

Putnam published twenty-two books over a period of thirty-two years. Among them are *In Search of Arcady* (1912), *The Impossible Boy* (1913), *Orthodoxy* (1915), *When the Highbrow Joined the Outfit* (1917), *Esmeralda* (1918), *Sunny Bunny* (1918), *Winkle, Twinkle, and Lollypop* (1918), *West Broadway* (1921), *Tomorrow We Diet* (1922), *Say It with Bricks* (1923), *The Making of an American Humorist* (1929), *Paris Love* (1931), *The Inner Voice* (1940), and *Lynn, Cover Girl* (1950). These works include historical romances, a play about religion, children's books, comic novels, and collections of colloquial humor about husbands and dieting. Putnam also wrote more than 1,000 short stories and many movie scenarios. Among the twelve of her short stories that were made into movies are "Sitting Pretty" (1933) and "A Lady's Profession" (1933). From 1928 to 1938 she wrote a humorous syndicated column, "I and George," for the North American Newspaper Alliance.

A highly self-reliant person (none of her works appeared in any Putnam publication), Putnam was an early advocate of women's rights. Her most publicized effort came in 1912. Convinced that the women's clothing of the time was both uncomfortable and unhygienic, she designed and wore a wardrobe of loose-fitting, one-piece dresses that slipped over her head, all made of washable fabrics. She also dispensed with a corset and reduced the number of her undergarments from half a dozen to one. "I had abandoned all the nonsensical clap-trap of dress with which women unconsciously symbolized their bondage," she wrote in her autobiography. For months she received attention in the national press, most of it shocked ridicule. Her designs, though, presaged the future of women's clothing.

Putnam married four times. Her first husband died of influenza in 1918. She married Robert J. Sanderson, a businessman, on Nov. 4, 1919; they were subsequently divorced. On Sept. 12, 1931, she married Arthur James Ogle, a Florida real estate man; they were divorced in 1932. Her last marriage, on July 16, 1933, was to Christian Eliot.

In spite of her extensive acquaintance with Greenwich Village radicals prior to World War I, Putnam was a lifelong and ardent Republican. Much of her most popular work was written in an effort to strengthen American patriotism. Although her writing achieved great commercial success, it has never received serious critical attention or acclaim. At the time of her death, none of her books was in print. Putnam died in Cuernavaca, Mexico, where she had spent the last years of her life.

[The primary source on Putnam's life is her autobiography, *Laughing Through* (1930). This work is somewhat unreliable—for example, she incorrectly indicated in one place that she was born in 1884, and in another suggested the year was 1888—and covers her life only to 1919. Also see the obituary in the *New York Times*, Mar. 9, 1962.]

J. L. MILLER

RAYBURN, SAMUEL TALIAFERRO ("SAM") (Jan. 6, 1882–Nov. 16, 1961), Democratic party leader and Speaker of the House of Representatives, was born in Roane County, Tenn. In 1887 the Rayburns moved to Texas, settling on a small farm near Flag Springs. Rayburn's upbringing gave him a lifelong devotion to the classic values of southern agrarianism. His father, William Marion Rayburn, a Confederate veteran, passed along an idolization of Robert E. Lee and a romantic devotion to the Lost Cause. Both his father and his mother, Martha Clementine Waller Rayburn, were Primitive (Hard-Shell) Baptists, who taught him the faith in hard work and personal integrity generally associated with evangelical Protestantism. His own experiences as a young farm boy left him with an abiding belief in the dignity of manual labor and the essential virtue of agricultural life.

In 1900 Rayburn enrolled at the Mayo Normal School (now East Texas State University) at Commerce, Tex. His father had given him the family savings—$25—to provide a start. Working his way through college, he graduated in 1903 with a B.S. in education. He was then a schoolteacher at Dial, Tex. (1903–1905), and Lannius, Tex. (1905–1906). Long determined to pursue a political career, he won election to the state House of Representatives in 1906. For the next two years, he combined his legislative work with law classes at the University of Texas; in 1908 he passed the state bar examinations. Winning quick recognition for his talent, political shrewdness, and amiability, he was elected Speaker of the Texas House in 1911. He substantially strengthened the office by securing assent to a codification of its powers. In 1912 he won election to the U.S. House of Representatives.

Rayburn was a typical southern progressive of the period—devoted to free trade, an advocate of aid to farmers, a believer in states' rights, a prohibitionist, relatively indifferent to urban problems and organized labor, intensely suspicious of big business, and hostile toward concentrated wealth. Backed by prominent Texas congressmen, he secured appointment to the Committee on Interstate and Foreign Commerce, his primary committee assignment until his election as Speaker in 1940. His first important legislative proposal, eventually incorporated into the Esch-Cummins Act of 1920, was a bill to regulate railroad securities.

Gregarious and hardworking, Rayburn won friends and respect from both parties and all sections. His career was especially enhanced by his friendship with the leader of the Texas

House delegation, John Nance Garner. Rayburn was Garner's closest adviser by the time the latter served as Speaker of the House (1931–1933). He was Garner's campaign manager during his unsuccessful bid for the presidency in 1932 and a confidant during his two terms as vice-president (1933–1941). Garner in turn promoted Rayburn's advancement at every opportunity.

On Oct. 15, 1927, Rayburn married Metze Jones, the sister of a fellow Texas congressman, Marvin Jones. They were divorced less than three months later. Thereafter, he lived as a confirmed bachelor.

During the 1920's Rayburn was a leading congressional critic of Republican "normalcy." Along with Garner he represented the southern and western wings of the Democratic party and was not identified with the rising tide of urban liberalism for which Alfred E. Smith was a spokesman. When the Democrats regained control of the House in the 1930 elections, he became chairman of the Commerce Committee.

During the New Deal, Rayburn forged a close working relationship with Franklin D. Roosevelt that he maintained even after Vice-President Garner fell out with the administration. Rayburn's egalitarianism and sympathy with the common man impelled him toward support of Roosevelt's program. His deep party loyalty overrode his doubts about such matters as the effort to pack the Supreme Court, the White House refusal to denounce the sitdown strikes of 1937, and the abortive party "purge" of 1938.

Rayburn helped develop and pilot through Congress some of the most significant legislation of the New Deal. The Securities Act of 1933 and the Securities Exchange Act of 1934 established strong federal oversight of the stock and bond markets. The Public Utility Holding Company Act of 1935 stringently restricted concentration in the electric utility industry. Rayburn took special pride in his sponsorship of the Rural Electrification Act of 1936, which established the Rural Electrification Administration as a permanent agency of the federal government.

Rayburn was candidate for Speaker with Garner's backing in 1934 but lost to Joseph Byrns of Tennessee. After Byrns's death in mid-1936, Rayburn conceded the Speakership to William Bankhead of Alabama, the House majority leader. Contesting instead for Bankhead's old post, he defeated John J. O'Connor of New York, the anti–New Deal chairman of the Rules Committee. After Bankhead's death in September 1940, Rayburn was elected Speaker and held

the post without challenge in every Democratic-controlled Congress for the rest of his life.

Rayburn's position in Texas politics was more tenuous. A reliable defender of the oil and gas producers, especially the smaller operators, he received scant appreciation for his efforts. He was disgruntled by the way the oilmen increasingly embraced Republican conservatism; they in turn found him too close to the New Deal. In 1944 the right-wing "Texas Regular" Democrats nearly succeeded in an effort to defeat Rayburn in the Democratic primary; he won with only 55.7 percent of the popular vote.

By the 1940's Rayburn was out of tune with the changing character of Texas life. He had grown to maturity in a state oriented toward the production of cotton and cattle and in a populistic environment of small towns and small farms, suspicious of the world of large business and finance. By the end of World War II, cotton-and-cattle Texas had given way to oil-and-aircraft Texas. The new men of power had no use for the old populist tradition. Never an important influence in state politics after his first election to Congress, Rayburn increasingly was only a revered symbol in the Texas Democratic party. His major accomplishment within the state was negative—he staved off periodic attempts to enlarge and urbanize his compact, rural congressional district.

Although he customarily spent his vacations on his Texas ranch and seems never to have traveled abroad, Rayburn was among the foremost supporters of the internationalist-interventionist foreign policies of Roosevelt, Truman, and Eisenhower. His work was especially critical in obtaining passage by one vote of legislation to extend the military service terms of draftees in August 1941. After Pearl Harbor, he was a dependable backer of World War II. An equally reliable supporter of the cold war under Roosevelt's successors, he seems to have assumed that the United States was obligated to maintain a strong, perhaps dominant, role in world affairs. Accepting both the concept of presidential leadership in diplomacy and the philosophy of a bipartisan foreign policy, he supported the initiatives of Eisenhower as well as those of Truman and Kennedy.

In many respects, Rayburn was more comfortable with the moderate conservatism of Eisenhower in domestic affairs than with Truman's Fair Deal or Kennedy's New Frontier. In 1949, it is true, he helped obtain a change in the House rules designed to prevent a blockage of Truman's proposals by a hostile Rules Committee; and in 1961 he put all his prestige behind the Kennedy administration effort to pack the still obstreperous rules panel. Still, just as he had not joined the swing to the right in Texas politics, he never became a full participant in the movement to urban liberalism within the national Democratic party.

Never expressing his reservations in public, never criticizing a Democratic president, he remained cool toward organized labor, northern minority groups, and the consumerist-oriented liberalism of the urban middle classes. His most widely perceived break with the Truman administration occurred when Truman vetoed the Kerr Natural Gas Deregulation Bill of 1949, an episode that dramatized the president's choice of the cheap-energy liberalism of the North over the market-pricing demands of the energy-producing Southwest.

Rayburn was a quiet opponent of civil rights measures for most of his career. As a young politician, he had indulged in occasional race baiting, but one doubts that he ever did so with much conviction. Like many southern moderates of his time, he harbored a genuinely parental attitude toward blacks, talked of their slow but steady progress in American life, and doubted the efficacy of forced legislative or judicial solutions to a complex, emotional problem. In 1957 and 1960, he finally lent his active support to civil rights legislation designed to facilitate exercise of the right to vote.

During the 1950's Rayburn and his one-time protégé, Senate Democratic Leader Lyndon B. Johnson, worked as a team with substantial control of the Congress. Together they guided the Democrats on Capitol Hill, a majority in both houses during the last six years of the Eisenhower presidency. They hoped to establish a record that would bring Johnson the Democratic presidential nomination. Although Johnson was the ambitious, dynamic force, it was Rayburn, in the opinion of many observers, who was the dominant partner. His long-established style of leadership in the House had largely established a model for Johnson's politics of consensus and accommodation. They committed the Democratic party to a policy of "moderation" that fit both the requirements of their home constituency and what they perceived as the national mood. In practice, this entailed a general acceptance of Eisenhower's foreign policy, a refusal to press for major new social welfare proposals, and a posture vis-à-vis the Republican administration that was fundamentally unaggressive.

The ultimate outcome was unsatisfactory. Rayburn admired Eisenhower as a general but had little respect for him as a politician. Increasingly, he resented the president's military brusqueness and seeming lack of appreciation for his support. The Rayburn-Johnson approach also drew heavy fire from liberal Democrats, organized as the Democratic Advisory Council (DAC) with the blessing of the party's national chairman, Paul Butler. During Eisenhower's second term, the DAC periodically clashed with Rayburn and Johnson; in the process, it contributed to a wide public belief that they were do-nothing conservatives. In 1960 Johnson was easily defeated for the presidential nomination by John F. Kennedy, a DAC-style liberal. Although Rayburn advised against it, Johnson accepted the vice-presidential nomination.

Rayburn worked for Kennedy in the 1960 campaign as he had worked for every Democratic presidential nominee during his career. He was especially vehement in condemning the use of Catholicism as an issue, just as he had been during the Al Smith campaign in 1928. After Kennedy's victory, Rayburn threw every ounce of his prestige behind a barely successful effort to enlarge, and thus liberalize, the House Rules Committee. The outcome, a 217–212 victory, demonstrated the tight ideological divisions in the House and Rayburn's tenuous hold on the Democrats, despite their pervasive affection and respect for him.

This was the last major struggle of his political life. By mid-1961, he was in perceptibly failing health. On August 31 he left Washington for Texas, where his illness was diagnosed as cancer. He died in Bonham, Tex.

A Jeffersonian Democrat in political philosophy and personal life, Rayburn believed deeply in the virtues of simple living and popular government. Preferring to think of himself as a common man, he early dropped his middle name, Taliaferro (pronounced "Tolliver"), and informally shortened his first name to Sam. By the time he became Speaker, he was widely known as "Mr. Sam," a sobriquet in which he gloried. A plain-living gentleman farmer, he spent most of his time when away from Washington on his farm near Bonham. He was an accomplished breeder of dairy and beef cattle. On the porch of his spacious home he maintained a dozen or so rocking chairs for friends, neighbors, and constituents. In Washington he lived with equal simplicity. In 1956, he joined and was baptized into the Primitive Baptist Church of nearby Tioga, Tex.

Rayburn's prestige and authority in the House of Representatives rested upon his devotion to the institution, his personal qualities, and his accommodationist style of politics. He was vocal and consistent in his assertions that there could be no higher honor than leadership of what he considered the "popular branch" of the national government; he was quick to resent any reference to his branch of the Congress as the "lower house."

As if to compensate for his own lack of children, he acted as a father figure to many young congressmen, including Lyndon Johnson, with whose father he had served in the Texas legislature. Those whom he favored with invitations for drinks and conversation with the House leadership in his Capitol hideaway won instant status and advanced as rapidly as the mores of the Congress allowed.

Perhaps the best-known of Rayburn's aphorisms for neophyte congressmen was, "If you want to get along, go along." It reflected his own distaste for ideological politics and personal conflict. Only on rare occasions, such as the Selective Service extension controversy of 1941 and the Rules Committee fight of 1961, did he resort to even a semblance of arm twisting. He was an intuitive moderate, tolerant to the viewpoints of others and convinced that slow progress was the best type of social or political change. He saw few issues as nonnegotiable. For years House Republican Leader Joseph W. Martin of Massachusetts was one of his dearest friends; within the Democratic party he was closest to liberal-leaning but nonideological "border state" centrists such as Fred Vinson and Alben Barkley of Kentucky or Harry S. Truman of Missouri. In the estimate of Richard Bolling, one of his most notable protégés, his reliance upon the respect and affection of his colleagues led him to eschew any attempt to strengthen the Speakership as an institution; consequently, it was weaker at his death than at his accession to it twenty-one years earlier.

Rayburn served as Speaker of the House for over seventeen years, more than twice as long as the previous record holder, Henry Clay; he was a continuous member of the House longer than any other person in history. His high repute, however, rested on his personal qualities as a democrat and a commonsensical moderate who represented the best values of an earlier, simpler time.

[Rayburn's papers are at the Sam Rayburn Library, Bonham, Tex. H. G. Dulaney et al., *Speak, Mr. Speaker* (1978), is a collection of excerpts from Rayburn's writings, speeches, and interviews. C. Dwight Dorough, *Mr. Sam* (1962), is an admiring, authoritative, and scholarly biography by a longtime friend.

Booth Mooney, *Roosevelt and Rayburn: A Political Partnership* (1971), and Alfred Steinberg, *Sam Rayburn: A Biography* (1975), are useful works by veteran political journalists. Valton J. Young, *The Speaker's Agent* (1956), is an account of Rayburn's agricultural interests by his county extension agent.

Richard W. Bolling, *Power in the House* (1968), contains an assessment of Rayburn's leadership. Neil MacNeil, *Forge of Democracy* (1963), has numerous references to Rayburn and includes a blow-by-blow account of the 1961 Rules Committee fight. Of the Ph.D. dissertations on Rayburn, Dwayne Lee Little, "The Political Leadership of Speaker Sam Rayburn, 1940–1961" (University of Cincinnati, 1970), is perhaps the most analytical; but see also Kenneth Dewey Hairgrove, "Sam Rayburn: Congressional Leader, 1940–1952" (Texas Tech University, 1974); and Alexander Graham Shanks, "Sam Rayburn and the New Deal" (University of North Carolina, 1964).

There are extensive obituaries in the *New York Times* and *Washington Post*, Nov. 17, 1961.]

ALONZO L. HAMBY

REDMAN, BEN RAY (Feb. 21, 1896–Aug. 1, 1961), who sometimes used the pseudonym Jeremy Lord, author, editor, and critic, was born in Brooklyn, N. Y., the son of Walter Herman Redman, a lumber importer-exporter, and of Violet Platt. He was educated at the New York Military Academy and the Pawling School before entering Columbia University in 1914.

In 1915 Redman abandoned his studies to enlist in the British army. He received training in Desoranto, Canada, and in Scotland. Commissioned in 1917 as first lieutenant, he served until 1919 with the Royal Flying Corps as a scout pilot attached to the Seventy-ninth Squadron of the British Expeditionary Forces assigned to Ypres, Belgium. On one mission behind the German lines, Redman's plane was damaged by enemy fire. He made it back and crash-landed but not without some injury: he retained a scar above his lip. Redman's air exploits formed the basis for one of his earliest fictional works, *Down in Flames* (1930), a set of war stories.

After the war Redman returned to New York City to begin his career. On Mar. 7, 1923, he married Amabel Jenks. They had no children. From the start Redman was involved in all aspects of the writer's trade. From 1922 to 1929, he was literary editor of the *Spur*. In 1923, he was the managing editor of *Travel* and from 1924 to 1926 was editorial and advertising manager for G. P. Putnam and Sons. While with Putnam, Redman met Frieda Inescourt, an actress working as publicity director for the house. In 1926 he divorced his wife and on Jan. 31, 1926, married Inescourt. They had no children.

Throughout his life Redman was a prolific and

diverse free-lance writer. The mainstay of his
output always lay in his reviews, which represent
a substantial body of work (one bibliography lists
over 200). The first ones appeared in "Old Wine
in New Bottles," a regular column edited by
Redman, 1926–1937, in the Sunday edition of
the *New York Herald-Tribune*, which reviewed
new editions of established literary works.

Redman's most noteworthy association was
with the *Saturday Review of Literature*. He was
close to the magazine's founders, who began
publishing his reviews in 1925, shortly after the
magazine's inception. The last one appeared
only two months before his death.

In the mid-1930's Redman moved to Los Angeles. The move enabled his wife to pursue her
acting career in motion pictures. For a time, he
also worked with the cinema, from 1936 to 1938
as executive assistant to Charles R. Rogers of
Universal Pictures, and again in 1942 as a scenario writer for 20th Century-Fox. One script
from this period was *School for Saboteurs*, written in collaboration with Michael Jacoby. But
Redman's association with the movie industry
was not very satisfactory. He felt unhappy, according to his sister, because of the low level of
work demanded of him.

Besides his reviews and relatively unsuccessful
script writing, Redman engaged in practically
every conceivable form of free-lance writing. He
composed short stories, a volume of poetry entitled *Masquerade* (1923), as well as a number of
poems for magazines and anthologies. He also
wrote several book-length mysteries, including
The Bannerman Case (1935) and *Sixty-Nine
Diamonds* (1940). For these books he assumed
the pen name Jeremy Lord.

Redman wrote much of his fiction for the
general reader. He directed his nonfiction works
toward a relatively more discriminating audience and at times toward a very specialized one.
His several translations, primarily from French
but also from Italian, reveal an affinity for European authors. His book reviews also reflect his
interest in continental writers, as does his anthology *The Portable Voltaire* (1949). One of
Redman's most ambitious works was his biography of the American poet *Edwin Arlington
Robinson* (1926). Redman's nonfiction, which
includes articles published in *College English*, a
small academic journal, suggests that, although
he wrote to earn a living, he could be motivated
by purely intellectual as well as commercial interests. Norman Cousins, a companion at the
Saturday Review, noted that Redman "was in
every sense an authentic book man" who "was
in the old literary tradition, which is to say, at

home most of all in the field of belles lettres."
Redman's dress and deportment were those of
a sophisticated literary man. Cousins described
him as "elegantly mannered and attired, born
for a part in a Noel Coward play." Redman's
death was sudden. He suffered in his last years
from periods of severe depression. In Hollywood, he became depressed one evening over
world problems and took sleeping pills, ending
his life.

Redman's greatest contribution was as a reviewer. He was witness to many of the major
writers of the first half of the twentieth century,
such as T. S. Eliot, Ernest Hemingway, and
William Faulkner. That so many of his reviews
appeared in the influential *Saturday Review*,
and over a period of more than thirty-five years,
suggests the extensive and persistent influence
that he exerted on American literary taste.

[Unpublished war poems are in the possession of
Edythe Redman Brunet. Other works include translations of Jean Giraudoux's *Suzanne and the Pacific*
(1923), Joseph A. Gobineau's *The Golden Flower*
(1924), and Abel Chevalley's *The Modern English
Novel* (1925); his nonfiction includes *Louis Bromfield and His Books* (1928?), *The Oxford University
Press, New York, 1896–1946* (1946), and an edition
of Thomas Love Peacock's novels, *The Pleasures of
Peacock* (1947).

Although incomplete, the best bibliography of
Redman's works appears in *Literary Writings in
America: A Bibliography* (1977). Obituaries are in
the *New York Times*, Aug. 3, 1961; and *Saturday
Review*, Aug. 19, 1961.]

                                LENNET J. DAIGLE

REECE, BRAZILLA CARROLL (Dec. 22,
1889–Mar. 19, 1961), businessman and U.S.
congressman, was born in Johnson County,
Tenn., one of thirteen children of John Isaac
Reece and Sarah Maples. He was raised on his
parents' farm and educated at Carson-Newman
College at Jefferson City, Tenn., from which he
graduated in 1914 with a B.A.

After serving as a high school principal for a
year, Reece attended New York University
(NYU), from which he took a master's degree in
economics and finance in 1916. He taught at
the university in 1916–1917, then enlisted in
the army and was soon commissioned an infantry lieutenant. He saw much front-line service
with the American Expeditionary Force, and in
one particularly arduous campaign he took command of his battalion. He was wounded in action and was decorated for gallantry with the
Distinguished Service Cross, the Distinguished
Service Medal, and the Croix de Guerre.

Reece studied at the University of London in 1918–1919 and then became director of NYU's School of Commerce, Accounts, and Finance. In 1920 he returned to Tennessee, where he became associated with a family business and ran successfully for election as a Republican to the U.S. House of Representatives. He had studied enough law at NYU to pass soon afterward the bar examination in his home state. On Oct. 30, 1923, he married Louise Despard Goff, the daughter of a government official, Guy D. Goff, who was elected to the Senate from West Virginia in 1924. They had one daughter.

Upon his election to the House of Representatives in 1920, Reece was its youngest member. He served as a congressman from eastern Tennessee until he was defeated in 1930. Two years later, he recovered his seat. In 1946 he declined to run again because of his election as chairman of the Republican National Committee. He ran unsuccessfully for the Senate against Estes Kefauver in 1948; in 1950 he regained his old seat in the House, which he held until his death.

Reece developed the reputation of being a calm and steady legislator. Diligent and conservative, he emerged as one of the leading critics of the Franklin D. Roosevelt and Harry S. Truman administrations. He introduced little legislation, but contributed to the writing and enactment of many bills. As a member of the Interstate Commerce Committee and the Temporary National Economic Committee, Reece was influential in the formulation of legislation dealing with securities, stock exchanges, communications, public power, interstate commerce, food, and drugs. He consistently supported naval development as a member of the Military Affairs Committee. He fought the involvement of the United States into World War II, opposing, among other things, conscription and lend-lease legislation. Reece was also involved in the movements to restrict labor unions and to investigate Communism; he opposed rent and price controls and was critical of increasing federal expenditures. Yet he supported anti–poll tax and antilynching measures and was instrumental in securing the establishment of the Great Smoky Mountains National Park and the Andrew Johnson National Monument.

In 1954 Reece was chairman of a special House committee that issued a controversial report chastising several large foundations for "directly supporting subversion," promoting "socialism and collectivist ideas," and dodging taxes on large fortunes. He was also a stalwart member of the House Rules Committee, and

his last days in Congress were devoted to opposing attempts to enlarge and thereby dilute the power of that committee. On foreign affairs, Reece was especially concerned with American relations with Germany and the use of law to settle disputes between East and West in Europe.

Reece reached his greatest national prominence through his work in connection with Republican politics. He was frequently a delegate to Republican national conventions, and in 1939 he was elected Republican national committeeman from Tennessee, a post that he held until his death. By 1946 he was considered to be the leading Republican politician in the South. That year, as a leader of the Republican faction headed by Senator Robert A. Taft, Reece was a candidate for the chairmanship of the Republican National Committee. He was elected after three hotly contested ballots. Criticized for his factionalism, he declared, "As chairman, I am not anybody's man." A vigorous chairman, he asserted that the 1946 elections were a "fight basically between communism and republicanism," the most important fight that Republicans had faced since 1860. His political leadership was significant in the election of the Republican Eightieth Congress, the first since 1929–1931, and in the development of his party's strength for the 1948 campaign. Reece served as the Republican National Committee chairman until after the nomination of Thomas E. Dewey for president in June 1948.

Over the years, Reece became affiliated with a number of banks in Tennessee, serving as president of four by the 1950's; he became publisher in 1950 of the Bristol (Tenn.) *Herald Courier*. Usually considered a man of integrity, intelligence, and broad interests, Reece was an archtypical conservative and nationalist throughout his long political career. He died in Bethesda, Md.

[A small collection of Reece's papers is in the University Archives of East Tennessee State University. Reece wrote two posthumously published works: *The Courageous Commoner: A Biography of Andrew Johnson* (1962); and *Peace Through Law: A Basis for an East-West Settlement in Europe* (1965). See also *Biographical Directory of the American Congress, 1774–1971* (1971); and the obituary notice in the *New York Times*, Mar. 20, 1961.]

DONALD R. McCOY

REINER, FRITZ (Dec. 19, 1888–Nov. 15, 1963), conductor, was born in Budapest, Hungary, the son of Ignác Reiner, a businessman, and of Vilma Pollak. His mother's interest in music provided him with his first contact with that art. Fascinated by seeing his first opera, *Lucia di Lammermoor*, at age six, he expressed the desire to study piano. Three years later, he was playing Wagner's *Tannhäuser* Overture from memory, and in 1897 he performed as piano soloist in Mozart's *Coronation* Concerto. He attended the Budapest Academy of Music (1898–1908), where he studied with Béla Bartók, Hans Koessler, and István Thomán. He also studied law at the University of Budapest in compliance with his father's wishes, but after the latter's death in 1909, he dedicated himself to music.

After graduating from the academy, Reiner became a coach at the Budapest Komische Oper (1909), where the following year he found himself conducting, at the last minute, a performance of Bizet's *Carmen*. In 1910 he became conductor at the Landestheater in Laibach (now Ljubljana, Yugoslavia), conducting Smetana's *Dalibor;* he also directed Laibach's Grand Symphony Concerts. The following year, he began a three-year stay with the Budapest Volksoper, where he conducted one of the first *Parsifal* performances legally permitted outside of Bayreuth and the Budapest premiere of *The Jewels of the Madonna* by Wolf-Ferrari. He then moved to Dresden, where, from 1914 to 1921, he directed the Saxon State Orchestra. He was also selected as Kapellmeister. During this period he also conducted in Berlin, Hamburg, Vienna, and Rome. His experience at Dresden had offered him the opportunity to conduct his first *Ring*, meet Richard Strauss, and attend Berlin and Leipzig performances conducted by Arthur Nikisch. Reiner usually referred to Nikisch, as well as to the Hungarian composer, Leo Weiner, as great influences on his career.

In 1921 Reiner left Dresden to undertake engagements in Rome and Barcelona. The following year he became director of the Cincinnati Symphony Orchestra, a post he held until 1930. In 1928 he became an American citizen. On Apr. 23, 1930, shortly after divorcing his first wife, Berta Gardini Gerster, he married a Cincinnati actress, Carlotta Irwin.

In 1931 Reiner joined the faculty of the Curtis Institute of Music as head of the orchestra and opera departments (1931–1941). He taught advanced students, conducted the institute's orchestra, and supervised certain activities of the Philadelphia Academy of Music. He conducted the premiere of Menotti's *Amelia Goes to the Ball* (1937). During the 1934–1935 season of the Philadelphia Grand Opera, Reiner conducted five out of ten productions. He was still

occupied with various foreign commitments and participated in the 1936–1937 opera festivities at Covent Garden in honor of King Edward VIII's coronation. There he led Kirsten Flagstad's London debut as Isolde. Reiner was also associated with the Wagner performances (with Flagstad and Lauritz Melchior) at the San Francisco Opera (1936–1938).

In 1938 Reiner became conductor and music director of the Pittsburgh Symphony and arranged its first recording contract in 1941 with Columbia. He resigned from the Pittsburgh Symphony over some financial disputes in 1948 and became a conductor at the Metropolitan Opera, where he made a spectacular debut conducting Ljuba Welitsch in a historic performance of Strauss's *Salome* on Feb. 4, 1949. At the Metropolitan he conducted 113 performances of twelve operas with many of the most outstanding artists of the day. In addition to the celebrated *Salome*, certain of his *Tristan und Isolde* and *Der Rosenkavalier* performances were landmarks. Reiner conducted Flagstad's first postwar appearance at the Met (Jan. 22, 1951) and the Met premiere of Stravinsky's *The Rake's Progress* (Feb. 14, 1953). Though many critics and musicians sometimes felt that Reiner was more proficient as an operatic rather than a symphonic conductor, he used to say that when he was working on an opera, he wished he were conducting a concert and vice versa.

After five years at the Met, Reiner returned to the concert hall podium as conductor of the Chicago Symphony Orchestra (1953–1962). Here, as he had previously in Cincinnati and Pittsburgh, Reiner improved and perfected the quality of the orchestra and planned programs that offered both the traditional classics and modern works (though rarely any twelve-tone pieces, which he considered mere mathematics). His activities as guest conductor continued (including conducting at the opening performances of the Vienna Staatsoper in 1955).

Reiner made the Chicago Symphony one of the leading American orchestras. Unfortunately, a major controversy arose in February 1959, when he announced his decision to cancel the proposed State Department arrangements for the Chicago Symphony to tour western and eastern Europe—the most extensive tour ever planned for an American orchestra up to that time. Reiner's public reasons for the decision stressed the intensity of the touring schedule, and he promised to arrange for a future tour. Some say that Reiner's heart problems affected the decision to cancel the projected tour (he had a heart attack in 1960). In any event, he resigned from the orchestra in 1962. He died in New York City.

Reiner was always the dedicated and thorough musician. Music was his life, and he exemplified the extremely high standards that he always stressed in classes and interviews. He believed that the conductor must have an overall understanding of theory, harmony, counterpoint, and composition (he himself composed a string quartet and songs) as well as a perceptive appreciation of other art forms. According to Reiner, the conductor should be able to play the piano and transpose any score or musical arrangement, and he should rarely need to verbalize his intentions to the orchestra, even when facing it for the first time—the conductor's eyes should help express the mood he wishes to convey.

Reiner's contributions include his individualized method of transmitting the best of certain European conducting methods, especially in regard to opera; his supreme musicianship and attention to detail that upgraded the quality of his orchestras; his programming and recording of prominent classical works, in addition to contemporary ones by such composers as Bartók, Hindemith, Kodály, Rolf Liebermann, Gian Francesco Malipiero, Milhaud, Prokofiev, Schoenberg, Richard Strauss, and Stravinsky, as well as Bernstein, Gershwin, Gould, Daniel Mason, Menotti, Piston, and William Schuman.

Reiner was known for his tempestuous temper during rehearsals and a distant attitude toward members of the orchestras. Yet this formidable public image was forgotten as soon as his almost motionless figure stood before his audience and he revealed to both audience and musicians alike his superior skills and compelling dedication as a conductor.

[Reiner expressed his basic ideas on conducting in "The Secrets of the Conductor" (an interview by Rose Heylbut), *Etude*, July 1936; and "The Technique of Conducting," *ibid.*, Oct. 1951. Some other interesting interview material appears in Jay S. Harrison, "Return of Reiner," *Musical America*, Oct. 1963; and Raymond Ericson, "Varied Agenda for Fritz Reiner," *New York Times*, Aug. 5, 1962, sec. II, p. 7. Roger Dettmer, "Fritz Reiner, 1888–1963," *Musical America*, Dec. 1963; and Cesar Saerchinger, "Fritz Reiner—Perpetual Prodigy," *Saturday Review of Literature*, May 31, 1952. On Reiner's development as a conductor and his conducting style, see David Ewen, *Dictators of the Baton* (1948); Boris Goldowsky, *My Road to Opera* (1979), which contains extensive accounts of Reiner's activities at Curtis; and Irving Kolodin, *The Metro-*

politan Opera, 1883–1966 (1966). For the Chicago period, see Martin Mayer, "Dr. Reiner's Orchestra," *High Fidelity*, Feb. 1960; and Philip Hart, "Reiner in Chicago," *High Fidelity*, Apr. 1964, which includes an extensive list of recordings.

Obituaries are in the *New York Times*, Nov. 16, 1963; Irving Kolodin, "Fritz Reiner: In Memoriam," *Saturday Review of Literature*, Dec. 28, 1963, especially informative on the 1930's and 1940's; and *Opera*, Jan. 1964.]

MADELINE SAPIENZA

RESOR, STANLEY BURNET (Apr. 30, 1879–Oct. 29, 1962), advertising executive, was born in Cincinnati, Ohio, the son of Isaac Burnet Resor and Mary Wilson Brown. His family owned a stove manufacturing firm, but it passed from family control while Resor was a student at Yale.

After graduating in 1901 with a B.A., Resor went to Europe on a cattle boat. Upon his return, he worked briefly as a bank clerk and as a salesman. In 1904, he joined the Proctor and Collier Advertising Agency in Cincinnati. Four years later, he became manager of the Cincinnati office of the New York–based J. Walter Thompson Company. With him were his older brother, Walter, and Helen Lansdowne, a talented copywriter. In 1912, Resor moved to Thompson's New York headquarters as vice-president and general manager. On Mar. 6, 1917, he married Helen Lansdowne; they had three children.

In 1916, J. Walter Thompson, who had owned the agency since 1878, decided to retire, in part because he believed the advertising business was nearing the limits of its potential. With several associates, Resor purchased the firm for $500,000. He became its largest stockholder and president and held the post until 1955, continuing as chairman of the board until 1961.

During Resor's presidency, J. Walter Thompson became the largest advertising agency in the world. Its billings (the volume of the advertising it placed) grew from about $3 million in 1916 to more than $370 million when Resor retired in 1961. By then the firm employed about 6,225 people and maintained offices in more than twenty foreign countries.

Resor's success at J. Walter Thompson was not based on his copywriting talents or ability to charm clients. Indeed, one associate described him as "one of the least articulate men alive." He never enunciated a clear theory of advertising and never imposed a distinctive style on his agency. His chief accomplishment was to make advertising part of broader marketing strategies. He built an organization in which attention to details of technique combined with concentration on the fundamental purpose of selling the client's products.

At Yale, Resor had read the English historian Henry Thomas Buckle, whose works convinced him that human behavior in the aggregate was scientifically predictable. Buckle became required reading for Thompson executives. Resor relied heavily on market research and the compilation of statistical data. As early as 1912, the agency published a volume of demographic information, *Population and Its Distribution*; under Resor, the study was periodically revised and reissued. Similarly, in 1939, Resor established the J. Walter Thompson consumer panel to provide a continuing source of data on consumer buying preferences.

Resor disliked the term "advertising agency" and was glad that those words did not appear in the company's name. Indeed, during his administration, J. Walter Thompson became more than the creator and distributor of advertisements. It offered advice and assistance on marketing activities ranging from the development of new products to corporate public relations. John B. Watson, the behaviorist psychologist, became a vice-president in 1924, and Arno H. Johnson held the position of senior economist for several years.

Persuaded that advertising could be made scientific, Resor also hoped to make the industry professional. J. Walter Thompson firmly refused to solicit new clients by preparing potential advertising campaigns for them, because Resor felt that doing so would divert resources from the agency's current accounts. Furthermore, such presentations would lack the knowledge of a company's marketing needs that a good agency required. Resor also refused to let Thompson handle distilled liquor accounts. Although he usually shunned advertising conferences and rarely gave public speeches, he served as president of the American Association of Advertising Agencies in 1923–1924 and received the Gold Medal Award as Advertising Man of the Year for 1948 from *Advertising and Selling* magazine.

Despite Thompson's growth, Resor tried to keep the agency's structure uncomplicated. Reportedly, when he was shown a proposed organization chart, he simply erased all the lines connecting the boxes. For each brand that Thompson advertised, an account representative handled all relations with the client and shared responsibility with a group head who supervised the copywriters and artists working on the account. The loose structure was comple-

mented by an open-door policy for top executives. Yet the demand for precision and the conservative styles of the firm's leaders produced an atmosphere described as "severely informal."

Many of the pioneers of twentieth-century advertising, from Albert Lasker to David Ogilvy, have been noted for their distinctive, if not flamboyant, personalities. Resor, on the other hand, was scarcely more colorful than the gray suits he favored. However, by his emphasis on the soberly businesslike aspects of advertising, he did as much as anyone to put the advertising industry in the mainstream of the modern American economy. He died in New York City.

[There are no collections of Resor's papers and no significant published autobiographical sources. Useful information can be found in "This Man Resor," *Advertising and Selling*, Nov. 25, 1931; "J. Walter Thompson's Company," *Fortune*, Nov. 1947; Martin Mayer, *Madison Avenue, USA* (1958); James Playstead Wood, "A Pioneer in Marketing: Stanley Resor," *Journal of Marketing*, Oct. 1961; and "Advertising Loses a Titan As Resor Dies," *Advertising Age*, Nov. 5, 1962. *Advertising Age*, Dec. 7, 1964, sec. 2, is devoted to the centennial of the J. Walter Thompson Company; the archives at the firm's New York headquarters contain files of these and other published materials on Resor. An obituary is in the *New York Times*, Oct. 30, 1962.]

DANIEL A. POPE

REYNOLDS, QUENTIN JAMES (Apr. 11, 1902–Mar. 17, 1965), author and war correspondent, was born in Bronx, N.Y., the son of James J. Reynolds, a public school principal, and Katherine Mahoney. The Reynoldses soon moved to Brooklyn, where Quentin grew up in comfortable middle-class surroundings. His mother introduced him to the theater, his father took him to sporting events, and he discovered the delights of vaudeville on his own. Following graduation from Manual Training High School in 1919 and a brief stint as a merchant seaman, he enrolled at Brown University. He was an outstanding athlete at Brown, participating in football, boxing, and swimming. After receiving his Ph.B. in 1924, he drifted from job to job, including a season of professional football and a short tenure as a night school instructor.

Largely at his father's urging, Reynolds began attending evening classes at Brooklyn Law School in 1928. But by the time he received his LL.B. in 1931, he had already decided upon a journalism career. He was a reporter, rewrite man, and eventually a sports columnist for the *New York Evening World*. When that paper merged with the *Telegram*, he was hired in early

1931 as a sportswriter for the newly formed New York *World-Telegram*, but within a few months he was again looking for work, the victim of an economy drive. With assistance from Heywood Broun and Damon Runyon, he then obtained a job with the International News Service (INS). By early 1933 Reynolds was the INS feature writer in Berlin, where he developed a strong dislike for the Third Reich. When his article on German youth under international socialism resulted in a job offer from *Collier's*, Reynolds returned to New York.

Reynolds settled easily into a routine at *Collier's*. A remarkably prolific writer who admitted that he knew the agonies of advanced literary creativity "only by hearsay," he contributed 384 articles and short stories to the magazine in fifteen years. He wrote about everything from race horses to rhumba dances, and about everyone from Joe Louis to Fulgencio Batista. Much of what he produced during the 1930's, he later recalled, was "easy to read—easy to forget." But he consoled himself with the fact that he was well paid and thus able to have "an awfully good time." A burly redhead, who stood over six feet and weighed about 250 pounds, Reynolds was hearty, hard-drinking, gregarious, and a big spender who became a conspicuous man-about-tables at such New York night spots as the Stork Club, Club 21, and El Morocco. On Mar. 30, 1942, he married Virginia Peine, an actress. They had no children and were divorced in 1960.

In March 1940 *Collier's* sent Reynolds to cover the war in Europe. Denied accreditation to the German army because of his writings of 1933, he went to France just in time to report on the French collapse and surrender. Retreating to England, Reynolds quickly came to admire the spirit of the British people under fire. His eyewitness accounts of the Battle of Britain were filled with stories of people unconquered and undiscouraged. *The Wounded Don't Cry* (1941)—the first of seven books he wrote during the war—was based on his articles for *Collier's*. It became a best seller. Reynolds' radio broadcasts for the British Broadcasting Company, his narrations for two famous British film documentaries—*London Can Take It* (1940), and *Christmas Under Fire* (1941)—and several successful lecture tours in the United States, also helped establish his reputation as one of America's leading war correspondents. World War II was the big story of Reynolds' career, and he told it in vivid and dramatic language. Whether aboard a destroyer supporting the raid on Dieppe, or on fighting fronts in North Africa, Italy, or the

southwest Pacific, he repeatedly risked his life to cover the combat. His bravery under fire won him the admiration of leaders such as Dwight D. Eisenhower and Winston Churchill.

Although Reynolds continued to write at his usual prolific pace after the war—producing on the average a book a year for the next two decades—he got more publicity for his involvements in a major literary hoax and a celebrated libel trial. DeWitt Wallace, publisher of *Reader's Digest*, asked Reynolds in 1952 to prepare a work on George DuPre, a Canadian who claimed to have served as a British secret agent in France and Germany during the war. Working with what his detractors charged was a typical disdain for in-depth research, Reynolds hurriedly produced a book based largely on interviews with DuPre. *The Man Who Wouldn't Talk* (1953) appeared in condensed form in the November 1953 *Reader's Digest*. Within weeks, however, DuPre was exposed as an imposter and an embarrassed Reynolds had to concede that he had been duped.

In 1949, Hearst columnist Westbrook Pegler lambasted Reynolds' war record, calling the writer "yellow" and describing him as "an absentee war correspondent" lacking in "guts." Reynolds responded by hiring the noted lawyer Louis Nizer and suing Pegler and the Hearst papers for libel. Nearly five years later, a Federal jury in New York awarded Reynolds $175,001, reportedly the largest libel judgment ever made to date in this country. Nizer's description of the suit in his *My Life in Court* (1961) was the basis for Henry Denker's Broadway play, *A Case of Libel* (1963).

After being stricken by abdominal cancer in Manila, where he had gone to prepare a biography of Philippine President Diosdado Macapagal, Reynolds died at Travis Air Force Base in California.

[Reynolds' autobiography, *By Quentin Reynolds* (1963), is devoted largely to his experiences during World War II; "The Story of an Extraordinary Literary Hoax," *Reader's Digest*, Jan. 1954, describes DuPre's fabrication. There is a lengthy obituary in the *New York Times*, Mar. 18, 1965, and a shorter one in *Publishers Weekly*, Mar. 29, 1965.]

PETER L. PETERSEN

REYNOLDS, ROBERT RICE (June 18, 1884–Feb. 13, 1963), U.S. senator, was born in Asheville, N.C., the son of William Taswell Reynolds, a businessman and clerk of the Superior Court of Buncombe County, and Mamie Spears. In 1906 Reynolds received a B.A. from the University of North Carolina, and the following two years he attended the university's law school, but he did not receive a law degree. His next years were filled with travel and adventure abroad, as described by him in *Wanderlust* (1913) and *Gypsy Trails* (1925), and several motion picture travelogues.

On Jan. 19, 1910, he married Fanny Menge Jackson; they had two children. She died in 1913. Marriages to Mary Bland in August 1914 and Denise D'Arcy in 1920 ended in divorce. His union with Mary Bland produced one child. On Feb. 27, 1931, he married Ziegfeld Follies dancer Eva Grady. She died in 1937, and on Oct. 9, 1941, Reynolds married Evalyn Washington (Beale) McLean, daughter of the wealthy Evalyn Walsh McLean. They had one daughter.

In 1909 Reynolds began practicing law in Asheville and within a year was elected prosecuting attorney for the state's Fifteenth Judicial District, a post he held until 1914. He campaigned unsuccessfully for the Democratic party's nomination for lieutenant governor in 1924 and for U.S. senator in 1926. In 1932, however, he was elected senator, defeating Cameron Morrison.

Reynolds portrayed himself as a man of the people fighting against "the interests." His techniques included wearing a ragged suit and driving all over the state in a broken-down Ford. He would often hold up a jar of caviar before his audience and intone: "This here jar ain't a jar of squirrel shot; it's fish eggs. Friends, it pains me to tell you that Cam Morrison eats fish eggs . . . and Red Russian fish eggs at that. . . . Now, fellow citizens, let me ask you, do you want a senator who ain't too high and mighty to eat good old North Carolina hen eggs or don't you?" Reynolds won the Democratic nomination and the general election handily. Not without reason was he known as "Buncombe Bob" Reynolds.

During his thirteen years in the Senate (1932–1945), Reynolds was an advocate of immigration restriction. He opposed America's entry into World War II but, in general, was a supporter of New Deal domestic legislation. He introduced bills to cut immigration quotas drastically, to register aliens, and to deport criminal aliens. To his depression-impoverished constituents, who were 99 percent native-born white Anglo-Saxons, Reynolds argued that foreigners were occupying jobs and consuming relief monies that rightfully belonged to Americans.

In 1939 Reynolds created the Vindicators Association, whose goals included: "1. Keep America out of war; 2. Register and fingerprint all aliens; 3. Stop immigration for the next ten years; 4. Deport all criminal and undesirable aliens; 5. Banish all foreign 'isms.' " The organization's newspaper, *American Vindicator* (April 1939–December 1942), railed against Communists, Jews, and to a lesser extent Nazis.

Complementing Reynolds' restrictionist views on immigrants were his unilateralist concepts of American foreign relations. In the late 1930's he was a prominent exception among southern senators, most of whom backed President Franklin D. Roosevelt's increasingly activist foreign policy. He voted consistently with midwestern Republicans in favor of the neutrality legislation of the 1930's. More in step with his southern colleagues, however, was Reynolds' advocacy of defense spending. His noninterventionist views, the sometimes anti-Semitic tone of the *Vindicator*, and his praise of Gerald L. K. Smith inspired some in the press to call him the "Tarheel Führer."

After Pearl Harbor, Reynolds supported the war effort, but on questions of postwar international cooperation he clung stubbornly to his unilateralist concepts. In 1944, realizing that his views on foreign affairs were poles apart from those of his constituents, he did not run for reelection. He ended his political career by supporting Gerald L. K. Smith. His 1950 bid to regain his Senate seat failed utterly. He returned to his home on Reynolds Mountain, near Asheville, where he raised Brahman cattle. He died in Asheville.

A colorful if uninfluential member of the Senate, Reynolds was always a maverick, best remembered as a political showman whose nimble wit and flamboyant style distinguished him from his more conservative colleagues.

[There is no significant collection of Reynolds' papers; some of his correspondence may be found among the Oliver Max Gardner and Frank Porter Graham Papers, University of North Carolina at Chapel Hill. The most complete study is Julian M. Pleasants, "The Senatorial Career of Robert Rice Reynolds" (Ph.D. diss., University of North Carolina, 1971). See also Burke Davis, "Senator Bob Reynolds: Retrospective View," *Harper's*, Mar. 1944; *Raleigh News and Observer*, July 17, 1932, Aug. 24 and Sept. 7, 1941; *Greensboro Daily News*, Dec. 4, 1932; and obituaries in the *Asheville Citizen*, Feb. 14, 1963, *Washington Post*, Feb. 14, 1963, and *New York Times*, Feb. 15, 1963.]

DAVID R. KEPLEY

RICKETTS, CLAUDE VERNON (Feb. 23, 1906–July 6, 1964), naval officer, was born in

Greene County, Mo., the son of Gilbert Luther Ricketts and Sarah Bertha Smith. He was raised in that state and in Kansas, and attended the Naval Academy Preparatory School in Bainbridge, Md., for one year before entering the U.S. Naval Academy (1925), where he was a varsity boxer and football player. He graduated in the upper third of the class of 1929.

Following a year at sea as a signal officer on the aircraft carrier *Lexington*, Ricketts married Margery Bernice Corn on May 15, 1930; their two sons also became naval officers. After six months on the Battle Fleet staff of Admiral Frank H. Schofield, Ricketts spent eight years in naval aviation. He received his pilot's wings in February 1932 and then flew scout planes from the cruiser *Cincinnati*, fighters from the *Lexington*, and patrol planes from Coco Solo in the Canal Zone. He also taught at the Pensacola naval air training center.

After a year at the General Line postgraduate school at Annapolis (1936–1937), Ricketts became executive officer of the destroyer-minesweeper *Sicard* in the Pacific near Hawaii (1938–1940). As assistant gunnery officer of the *West Virginia*, he counterflooded that battleship and thus prevented it from capsizing after being struck by aerial torpedoes during the Japanese attack at Pearl Harbor on Dec. 7, 1941. Two months later he transferred to the battleship *Maryland*. Ricketts participated in South Pacific patrols until assigned in September 1943 to the staff of Admiral Harry W. Hill, commander of Amphibious Group Two of the Fifth Amphibious Force. He took part in the capture of the Gilbert, Marshall, and Marianas islands and of Iwo Jima and Okinawa (1943–1945) and in the occupation of Japan. He was relieved in October 1945 and sent to the Army and Navy Staff College with the rank of captain.

After a year as a student at the Naval War College, Ricketts remained as an instructor (1947–1949). He then commanded the attack cargo ship *Alshain* in the Pacific (1949–1950) and later the heavy cruiser *St. Paul* (1954–1955), flagship of the Seventh Fleet during the Quemoy crisis.

Widely respected for his keen mind, Ricketts returned to key administrative posts with the Atlantic Fleet amphibious forces (1950–1952), in the office of the chief of naval operations as head of the Amphibious Warfare Branch (1952–1954), and in the Strategic Plans Division (1955–1957, 1958–1961), during the last year as its head. Promoted to rear admiral at the beginning of 1956, he commanded a destroyer flotilla in the Atlantic (1957–1958) and, with

the rank of vice admiral, the Second Fleet and Atlantic Strike Fleet (1961).

Ricketts was promoted to full admiral in September 1961. Two months later he became vice chief of naval operations, in which capacity he experimented with the concept of a multinational nuclear force of ships manned by crews of the several nationalities of the North Atlantic Treaty Organization, first using the destroyer *Biddle*. He died at Bethesda, Md. The *Biddle* was then renamed the *Claude V. Ricketts*, an unusual gesture that testified to his popularity in the navy.

[A mimeographed biographical sketch is at the Naval Historical Center, Washington Naval Yard, Washington, D.C. His exploits at Pearl Harbor are covered in Homer N. Wallin, *Pearl Harbor* (1968). An obituary is in the *New York Times*, July 7, 1964.]
CLARK G. REYNOLDS

RICKEY, WESLEY BRANCH (Dec. 20, 1881–Dec. 9, 1965), major-league baseball executive, was born on a farm near Lucasville, Ohio, the son of Jacob Franklin Rickey and Emily Brown. Both parents being pious Methodists, they named him after the sect's founder, John Wesley, and imbued him with a dedication to work and learning. They also exacted his pledge never to drink, swear, or profane the Sabbath. Except for smoking, Rickey kept this pledge even when it hampered his baseball career.

Although the family was cash poor, the farm afforded all necessities. Although the elder Rickey was a taskmaster to his sons, he also encouraged their love of sports. Upon completing grammar school in 1900, Rickey passed the West Point entrance examination, but inadequate schooling barred his entry.

Rickey then taught for two years at a rural Ohio school, filling his free time with independent study and baseball. Using his savings to enroll at Ohio Wesleyan University, he excelled as a student and won letters in three sports. He earned money by serving as baseball coach and athletic director. After graduating with a B.Litt. in 1904, Rickey taught philosophy and law and coached at Allegheny College, Delaware (Ohio) College, and Ohio Wesleyan University. In 1906 he received a B.A. from Ohio Wesleyan, and on June 1 of that year he married Jane Moulton. The following year he enrolled in the law school at the University of Michigan, where he served as baseball coach. He received the LL.B. in 1911.

Meanwhile, the short, scholarly-looking Rickey also pursued a professional baseball career. In July 1904 he was signed as a catcher by the Cincinnati Reds, having spent the summers of 1903 and 1904 in the minors. Hampered by injuries and by his opposition to playing on Sunday, he was dropped by the Reds and acquired by the St. Louis Browns. He played occasionally with the Browns and in 1907 was traded to the New York Highlanders, where poor performance and a case of tuberculosis ended his playing career. Rickey spent part of 1908–1909 in a sanatorium. By then he was hard pressed to support his wife and, after 1913, six children. After receiving his law degree, he was advised to move west for his health. He settled in Boise, Idaho, was admitted to the bar—and lost his only case.

At this point Rickey's reputation as a baseball coach opened the door to his lifelong career as a baseball executive. In 1913 he became executive assistant to the owner of the Browns. That year he also managed the team. Seeking a way of obtaining promising players at low cost, he concluded a working agreement with a minor-league team that guaranteed him a supply of young players. This plan revived the farm system and enabled the Browns to compete with wealthy rivals in recruiting players.

A dispute with a new owner ended Rickey's tenure with the Browns in 1916. He then became manager and president of the St. Louis Cardinals of the National League. It was a risky move, for Rickey had to mortgage his house to raise $5,000 as his part of the team's purchase price. And no sooner was he installed than he entered the Chemical Warfare Service as a major.

Returning to civilian life in 1919, Rickey received a three-year contract for $15,000 a year with the promise that he would receive a percentage from the sale of any player. That year Rickey purchased a pitcher for the team—the last time during his twenty-five-year tenure as executive that the Cardinals purchased a major-league player. Henceforth, Rickey recruited and developed all of the Cardinal players.

In the 1920's Rickey built a network of minor-league farm clubs. Although attacked by Commissioner Kenesaw Mountain Landis, who decried the scheme as injurious to the minors, Rickey defended it vigorously. When all other clubs joined in the farm system movement, Landis was forced to yield. In 1938, though, Landis struck a blow at Rickey's organization when he declared eighty of Rickey's players free agents.

But no major-league rival matched the productivity of the Cardinal farm chain. By 1940, Rickey had over thirty teams in the chain, and by devices like tryout camps and innovative scouting, teaching, and evaluation techniques, he almost cornered the market in young players.

Rickey managed the Cardinals until 1925, never very successfully. He was replaced that year at the behest of Sam Breadon, who had replaced him as executive vice-president. Between 1926 and 1942 the Cardinals won six pennants and four World Series titles, all credited to Rickey's innovation.

Throughout Rickey's executive tenure the Cardinals enjoyed a talent surplus that Rickey turned to profit by shrewd sales and trades that won him the reputation of baseball's canniest dealer. But his growing rich from his percentage of player sales led the envious Breadon to dismiss him in 1942.

Rickey's reputation landed him the post of president and general manager of the Brooklyn Dodgers. In 1945, with Walter O'Malley and John Smith, he became a co-owner. Assisted by his son, Rickey built a superb Dodger farm system. Applying his maxim that "in quantity there is quality," Rickey's scouts turned to Latin Americans and American blacks in their search for young talent.

Moved by profit as much as by altruism, arguing that "it's right, it's profitable," Rickey won public support for admitting blacks to major-league baseball. In October 1945 he selected Jackie Robinson as a test case and counseled him on meeting the bigoted attacks that followed. After Robinson had become a star, Rickey quickly added other black players whose abilities helped launch the great Dodger dynasty of the postwar era. For this achievement Rickey was acclaimed "baseball's emancipator."

But Rickey's Dodger career was brief. His successes incurred the hostility of co-owner O'Malley, who first ousted Rickey from his presidency and then forced him to sell his stock, which Rickey did in a clever coup that netted him an estimated $850,000 profit.

Still, it was a disheartened Rickey who accepted a five-year contract as executive vice-president of the Pittsburgh Pirates, a lackluster club. Now a septuagenerian, he once more applied his formula of mass recruiting. But progress was slow. In his five years with them, the Pirates foundered, and in 1955 Rickey was dropped. Yet in 1960 his maturing players won the World Series for Pittsburgh.

His reputation as baseball's greatest innovator was secure, but in 1959 Rickey forced still another innovation on the baseball establishment. Concerned over the rising popularity of professional football and baseball's declining image, Rickey accepted the presidency of the Continental League, a rival major-league venture that promised to bring major-league baseball to new urban regions. Although the league failed, it forced tradition-bound major-league executives to meet its challenge by taking in franchises selected by Continental planners. Thus, Rickey forced major-league baseball to undertake continental expansion, which by 1979 resulted in a total of twenty-six major-league teams.

Following this venture, Rickey briefly served as adviser to the Cardinals, but dissension forced him out in 1964. Now eighty-three years old and disconsolate over the death of his only son, he wondered if baseball was "worth a man's whole life." He was delivering one of his frequent speeches on the game, at his induction to the Missouri Sports Hall of Fame, when he suffered a heart seizure and died in Columbia, Mo. In 1967, Rickey was voted into the Baseball Hall of Fame at Cooperstown, N.Y.

[The Rickey Archives are housed in the Library of Congress. Insights into Rickey's baseball philosophy are in his *American Diamond* (1965), written with Robert Riger. Useful popular biographies include Arthur Mann, *Branch Rickey* (1957); David Lipman, *Mr. Baseball* (1966). Rickey's testimony before a congressional committee inquiring into baseball is useful: U.S. House of Representatives, *Professional Team Sports*, Report no. 2002 to accompany H.R. 95, 82nd Congress, sess. 2 (1952). Rickey's impact on baseball is assayed in David Q. Voigt, *American Baseball*, II (1970). An obituary is in the *New York Times*, Dec. 10, 1965.]

DAVID VOIGT

RIEGGER, WALLINGFORD (Apr. 29, 1885–Apr. 2, 1961), composer, was born in Albany, Ga., the son of Constantin Riegger, owner of a lumber mill, and Ida Wallingford. Both parents were excellent amateur musicians, and music was a continuous presence in the household. When Wallingford was three, the family moved to Indianapolis, where, a few years later, he began studying violin and harmony. In 1900 the family came to New York City, where Wallingford shifted from violin to cello so that the family might have a string quartet.

After graduating from high school in 1904, Riegger entered Cornell University on a scholarship but remained there only a year. Having decided to devote himself solely to music, he enrolled in the Institute of Musical Art (now the Juilliard School of Music) in New York, specializing in cello with Alwin Schroeder and studying composition with Percy Goetschius. In 1907 he became a member of the institute's first graduation class. For the next three years he studied

in Berlin at the Hochschule für Musik with Robert Hausmann (cello) and privately with Anton Hekking (cello) and Edgar Stillman Kelley, an American composer (composition). In 1910 Riegger made his conducting debut with the Blüthner Orchestra in Berlin, directing the concert from memory, at that time an unusual practice.

In 1910 Riegger returned to the United States, and on June 13 he married a high-school acquaintance, Rose Schramm. He earned his living playing the cello in the St. Paul (Minnesota) Symphony and in theater orchestras. He returned to Germany in 1913 and became a year later assistant conductor at the State Theater in Würzburg. He also conducted opera performances in Königsberg (1915–1916) and symphony concerts with the Blüthner Orchestra in Berlin (1916–1917).

Three days before America's entry into World War I, Riegger returned to the United States with his wife and two daughters. From 1918 to 1922 he was a member of the department of theory and cello at Drake University in Des Moines and in 1924–1925 at the Institute of Musical Art.

Riegger's first mature composition was a Trio in B minor (1920), which received the Paderewski Prize, as well as the Society for Publication of American Music Award. It was first performed on Mar. 21, 1930, in New York. *La Belle Dame sans Merci*, his setting of Keats's ballad for four solo voices and chamber orchestra (1923), was the first composition by a native American to receive the Elizabeth Sprague Coolidge Award; it was successfully introduced at the Coolidge Festival in Pittsfield, Mass., on Sept. 19, 1924. In the works of this period, Riegger assumed a conservative posture. His music was occasionally romantic, occasionally impressionistic, utilizing traditional harmonic and melodic procedures within formal structures.

Riegger soon broke with conservatism to embrace atonality, first with the *Rhapsody for Orchestra* (1925), introduced by the New York Philharmonic under Erich Kleiber on Oct. 29, 1931. Riegger gained notoriety with some segments of his audience and almost unqualified approbation from his colleagues for his *Study in Sonority*, for ten violins or multiples thereof (1927), given its first professional performance by the Philadelphia Orchestra under Leopold Stokowski on Mar. 30, 1929. This is a totally atonal composition.

From atonality, Riegger went on to the twelve-tone system—one of the earliest Americans to do so. He used a partly twelve-tone idiom in *Dichotomy* (1932), for chamber orchestra, first performed in Berlin on Mar. 10, 1932, and totally in the String Quartet No. 1 (1938–1939) and *Duos for Three Woodwinds* (1943). Although he was partial to such baroque and polyphonic techniques as the canon, fugue, and passacaglia, and to such classical structures as the symphony, the concerto, and the variation form, Riegger's music from then on was austerely atonal and sometimes twelve-tonal.

From 1926 to 1928 Riegger was on the faculty of Ithaca Conservatory in New York. In 1928 he returned to New York City, where he made his home for the remainder of his life. There he held various teaching posts, most significantly from 1936 at the Metropolitan Music School, of which he ultimately became president. In New York, Riegger channeled some of his creativity into scores for dance works choreographed by Martha Graham, Hanya Holm, Doris Humphrey, and Charles Weidman. His most significant contribution, however, was to concert music, for which he was highly esteemed by composers, who regarded him as a master. The general public remained for the most part apathetic. Some recognition came with his Symphony No. 3 (1946–1947), commissioned by the Alice M. Ditson Fund, which received the New York Music Critics Circle Award following its premiere in New York on May 16, 1946. Tributes and performances of major works in many parts of the United States commemorated his seventy-fifth birthday in 1960. Just before his death, in New York City, the morning after brain surgery, Riegger received the Brandeis Creative Arts Award from Brandeis University.

[See Joseph Machlis, *Introduction to Contemporary Music* (1961); Virgil Thomson, *American Music Since 1910* (1971), John Vinton, ed., *Dictionary of Contemporary Music* (1971); R. F. Goldman, "Wallingford Riegger," *Hi-Fi/Stereo Review*, Apr. 1968; Henry Cowell, "Wallingford Riegger," *Musical America*, Dec. 1, 1948; and R. F. Goldman, "The Music of W. Riegger," *Musical Quarterly*, Jan. 1950. There is an obituary in the *New York Times*, Apr. 3, 1961.]

DAVID EWEN

RIVERS, THOMAS MILTON (Sept. 3, 1888–May 12, 1962), physician and virologist, was born in Jonesboro, Ga., the son of Alonzo Burrel Rivers, a farmer and businessman, and of Mary Martha Coleman. He graduated with a B.A. from Emory College in 1909 and was admitted that year to the Johns Hopkins Medical School. Rivers was physically strong and had led gymnastic classes in college, but during his second year in medical school he developed a weakness of the left hand that was diagnosed as an often fatal neuromuscular degeneration. After leaving medical school he went to the Panama Canal Zone and became a laboratory assistant at San Tomás hospital. However, his illness ceased to progress and he returned to Johns Hopkins in 1912. He received the M.D. in 1915.

After a year's internship at Johns Hopkins, Rivers became assistant resident in pediatrics. In 1918 he was commissioned first lieutenant in the army medical corps and was attached to a special unit investigating an outbreak of pneumonia at an army post. In 1919 he returned to Johns Hopkins to do research in bacteriology. Three years later he was invited to join the hospital staff of the Rockefeller Institute for Medical Research (now Rockefeller University) in New York City to head the infectious disease ward and conduct research on viral diseases. He married Teresa Jacobina Riefle on Aug. 5, 1922; they had no children.

Beginning his studies on viral disease, then a new field of research, Rivers made valuable observations on the latency of certain pathogenic viruses and on passive immunity induced by viral infection. In 1926 he announced that viruses, unlike most bacteria, are obligate parasites: their reproduction depends upon living cells of the host. This fundamental principle has since been firmly established but was then contrary to findings of his chief, Simon Flexner, and his colleague, Hideyo Noguchi. Rivers' stubborn insistence on this point of difference between bacteria and viruses did much to establish virology as a separate division of microbiology. In 1928 he published an article in which he clearly described for the first time the major pathological effects of virus infection, namely cell necrosis and cell proliferation. In 1928 he edited *Filterable Viruses*, summarizing current knowledge about virus infections.

In 1929 a dangerous disease, psittacosis ("parrot fever"), appeared in New York and California. It was so contagious, especially among public-health laboratory workers, that research on its cause was abandoned everywhere except at the Rockefeller Institute. Rivers studied this disease with two young colleagues, George P. Berry and Francis F. Schwentker, both of whom became seriously ill. An experienced clinician as well as laboratory experimenter, Rivers made the first thorough clinical studies of several other rare viral diseases, including "louping ill" of sheep, Rift Valley fever, and lymphocytic choriomeningitis. His work and that of the men who gathered around him made the Rockefeller Institute in the 1930's and 1940's a leading center of virus research. Rivers was promoted in 1927 to full membership in the Rockefeller Institute. In 1937, when Rufus Cole retired from the directorship of the hospital, Rivers succeeded him. A dozen of the leading virologists of the next generation were trained by Rivers.

A kindly man, Rivers was sympathetic with patients and totally without pretense. But as a scientist he was opinionated and pugnacious. His prodigious memory and sharp tongue made him a formidable adversary in debate. In the controversies that surrounded early attempts to produce a vaccine against poliomyelitis he was a fierce opponent of unsafe procedures. When the National Foundation for Infantile Paralysis was organized in 1933 he became chairman of its committee on research. He was later chairman of the foundation's vaccine advisory committee, which conducted the clinical trials of Jonas Salk's vaccine. Rivers was a member of the New York City Board of Health and took an active part in organizing the Public Health Research Institute of the City of New York.

In 1943 the surgeon general of the navy called Rivers to discuss the problems of infection faced by the armed forces in the Pacific area. Subsequently, Rivers directed the formation of Naval Medical Research Unit Number 2, made up largely of Rockefeller Institute physicians and scientists. The unit conducted an antimalaria program in Peleliu and Okinawa, fought an epidemic of paratyphoid fever on Okinawa, and battled hookworm on Guam. Rivers was awarded the Legion of Merit for this work. He retired from the Naval Reserve Medical Corps with the rank of rear admiral.

After returning to the Rockefeller Institute, Rivers edited *Viral and Rickettsial Infections of Man* (1948). In 1953, when Detlev W. Bronk became president of the Rockefeller Institute, Rivers was appointed vice-president, retaining his directorship of the hospital. After retiring from the institute in 1956, he joined the National Foundation as medical director. In 1958 he became vice-president for medical affairs and held the post until his death, in New York City. Rivers was a member of the National Academy of Sciences and the American Philosophical Society, and served as president of several national professional societies in his field.

[See Rivers' article "General Aspects of Pathological Conditions Caused by Filterable Viruses," *American Journal of Pathology*, 4 (1928). Also see the memoir by Frank L. Horsfall, Jr., in *Biographical Memoirs*

of the National Academy of Sciences, vol. 38 (1965); Saul Benison, *Tom Rivers, Reflections on a Life in Medicine* (1967); and George W. Corner, *A History of the Rockefeller Institute* (1964). An obituary appeared in the *New York Times*, May 13, 1962, and a brief but frank obituary notice by Frank E. Shope, in the *Journal of Bacteriology*, Sept. 1962.]
                                    GEORGE W. CORNER

ROBINSON, CLAUDE EVERETT (Mar. 22, 1900–Aug. 7, 1961), public opinion research specialist, was born in Portland, Oreg., the son of Reuben Franklin Robinson, a teacher, and of Emilie Ellen Hallock. He attended public schools and then served as a private first class in the Army Medical Corps during World War I, before going to sea briefly as a merchant seaman. In 1920 Robinson returned to Oregon and enrolled in the University of Oregon, from which he received an A.B. in 1924. While an undergraduate, he worked during the summer as a fire lookout in the Cascade National Forest. In 1925 he received an M.A. in sociology from Columbia University. On Oct. 6, 1927, he married Elizabeth Manning, daughter of an Oregon attorney. They had two sons.

In 1932 Robinson received a Ph.D. from Columbia. His doctoral dissertation, *Straw Votes: A Study of Political Predictions* (1932), examined the *Literary Digest* presidential poll of 1928 and is still regarded as a classic. This study inaugurated a lifelong interest in public attitude testing; Robinson probably predates George Gallup as the first American to conceive of the idea of a public opinion research service for newspapers. He was unable to market the concept, however.

Beginning in 1933 Robinson worked for several Wall Street firms as a statistician. In 1936 he became associate director of Gallup's American Institute of Public Opinion at Princeton, founded in 1935 to conduct national polls on questions of political and social interest.

Robinson and Gallup were pioneers in the area of scientific public opinion research. They believed that their polls were accurate representations of the opinions of the entire nation, although their conclusions were based on a minute sample of the national population. Their method was to interview a limited number of persons (usually 3,000) of specific categories (age, income, sex, political persuasion, occupation). The number in each category was calculated to reflect the proportion of each group in the population. The institute drafted the questions to be asked, gathered the responses, and organized and marketed the resulting data. In 1936 the prestigious *Literary Digest* poll predicted the election of Alfred M. Landon. Gallup and Robinson accurately anticipated Franklin D. Roosevelt's reelection.

Robinson quickly gained recognition in the field. In 1937 he wrote the two-part "Recent Developments in the Straw Poll Field" for the *Public Opinion Quarterly*. In 1938, reportedly with the assistance and encouragement of Gallup, he formed the Opinion Research Corporation (ORC), also based at Princeton. He served as president until 1957 and as chairman of the board until 1960. ORC undertook market and public attitude studies for scores of corporations and trade associations.

In 1943 Robinson began the *Public Opinion Index for Industry*, a detailed monthly survey of industry that was distributed chiefly to executives among his clientele companies. As senior editor Robinson published more than 200 comprehensive analyses of research findings focusing on such topics as automation, inadequacy of college training in economics, productivity, lobbying, and foreign competition.

In 1948, with Gallup, Robinson founded Gallup and Robinson, an advertising research company. Throughout the 1940's and 1950's he wrote numerous articles of interest to American businessmen. In 1956 he created Princeton Research Park, a seventy-five-acre real estate development, and founded there the Princeton Panel, a center where businessmen could study the American capitalist system. He also directed Mirror of America, a research laboratory at Hopewell, N.J.

In 1960 Robinson retired from ORC but remained as chairman of its finance committee. That year, Robinson, a lifelong Republican, served as research counselor to presidential candidate Richard M. Nixon. In retirement he wrote *Understanding Profits* (1961) and engaged in farming in New Jersey. He died in New York City.

Robinson was in the vanguard of the development of scientific public opinion research and reporting. It is mere chance that the name Gallup has become identified nationwide with polling, while Robinson's is much less known.

[See "Researcher Claude Robinson: He Helps Management Set Policies," *Printers' Ink*, Aug. 1, 1958; and the obituary notices in *Public Opinion Quarterly*, Winter 1961; and the *New York Times*, Aug. 8, 1961.]

STEPHEN D. BODAYLA

ROBINSON, HENRY MORTON (Sept. 7, 1898–Jan. 13, 1961), author, was born in Boston, Mass., the eldest of eleven children of Henry Morton Robinson and Ellen Flynn. His father, a businessman, later moved the family to Malden, a Boston suburb, where Robinson graduated from high school in 1917.

Robinson served the next twenty-two months on subchasers and as a rifle instructor, acquiring an "unextinguishable enthusiasm for boats and small arms." In 1919, he entered Columbia University, where he took part in the dramatic and literary life and became known as Rondo because, as editor of the campus literary magazine, *Varsity*, he demonstrated a fondness for the French verse form the rondeau. Robinson said it was his "good fortune to be first a student and later a colleague of John Erskine during those exciting years when he was launching the Great Books program." Robinson joined Boar's Head, Erskine's undergraduate poetry society, and became president of Philolexian, a debating society. Recalling his college years, he later wrote: "If I were to have a college of my own,/ The only subjects in the catalog would be athletics and poetry./ For they are the only things that matter,/ And as Socrates pointed out in his ideal prospectus,/ They include everything else anyway."

In his senior year Robinson wrote his first book, *Children of Morningside* (1924), a verse novel. At graduation in 1923, he was awarded the Moncrieff Proudfit fellowship in letters, which enabled him to take an M.A. in 1924. His thesis on Alan Seeger's poetry won the James S. O'Neal Poetry Prize. Robinson taught at Columbia for the next three years and, during that time, wrote his second book, *John Erskine: A Modern Acteon* (1928).

While teaching at Columbia, Robinson edited *Contemporary Verse* (1925–1927) and contributed to three literary journals, *Century*, *Bookman*, and *North American Review*. On Oct. 18, 1926, he married Gertrude Ludwig; they had three children. Until 1935, Robinson "barely supported" himself and his growing family by selling stories, articles, and poems to national magazines. *Buck Fever* (1929), a collection of verse, including two long narrative poems, won Conrad Aiken's praise. *Stout Cortez, a Biography of the Spanish Conquest* (1931) received mixed reviews. Also in 1931 he was selected as Columbia's Phi Beta Kappa poet.

From 1935 to 1945, Robinson held three editorial positions with the *Reader's Digest*. He published the nonfiction *Science Versus Crime* (1935); a verse volume, *Second Wisdom* (1937); and a defense of the free-enterprise system, *Pri-*

vate Virtue, Public Good (1938). He was particularly proud of the nonfiction *Fantastic Interim* (1943), an "outspoken" account of American "manners, morals and business during the '20s and '30s."

A five-year collaboration with mythologist Joseph Campbell, then a professor at Sarah Lawrence College, led to *A Skeleton Key to Finnegans Wake* (1944). Although still valuable, this full-length commentary on James Joyce's longest and most difficult work has been superseded to some extent by later scholarship.

Robinson's novels include *The Perfect Round* (1945), *The Great Snow* (1947), *The Cardinal* (1950), and *Water of Life* (1960). *The Cardinal*, based in part on the life and career of Boston's William Cardinal O'Connell, took Robinson to the heights of popular and critical success, although some Catholic critics viewed it dimly. It sold 1.5 million copies and was translated into a dozen languages. His last book of verse, *The Enchanted Grindstone and Other Poems* (1952), is an account in poetry of his childhood.

Robinson's later years were spent in Woodstock, N.Y., with his second wife, Vivian Wyndham, whom he had married on July 11, 1953. (He and his first wife had been divorced.) He was a trustee of the Woodstock Public Library and avidly pursued the sports of sailing and falconry. He died in New York City of complications resulting from an accidental scalding at the Columbia University Club.

Although Robinson was, as one critic said, "a natural born poet," he is remembered for the versatility he displayed as a teacher, editor, critic, essayist, scholar, historian, biographer, novelist, and journalist. In all of these endeavors his work, though small in quantity, was excellent in quality.

[An obituary is in the *New York Times*, Jan. 14, 1961.]

CLARENCE ANDREWS

ROBINSON-SMITH, GERTRUDE (July 13, 1881–Oct. 22, 1963), civic worker and music patron, was born in Mamaroneck, N.Y., the daughter of Charles Robinson-Smith, a corporation lawyer and financier, who added the name "Robinson" to his too common patronymic of "Smith," and of Jeannie Porter Steele, a prominent socialite who could trace her ancestry back to John Steele, general in the Revolutionary War, and to Richard Mather, early settler of Massachusetts. Robinson-Smith was educated at the Packer Collegiate Institute

in Brooklyn and at the Brearley School in New York. She fell in love with a French aviator, who died in a plane crash, and subsequently she never married. Through her upbringing, she was made conscious that civic work was the vocation, duty, and privilege of well-to-do families. An early undertaking was her work for the Vacation Saving Stamp Fund, which became the American Woman's Association, of which she was president from 1911 to 1928. During World War I, she associated herself with Edith Wharton in the war-relief effort, and together they raised $70,000 for surgical motor units to be sent to France. After visiting the front lines and flying over the combat zone, Robinson-Smith created the Ice Flotilla Committee, which raised $100,000 for ice-making machines needed by advance field hospitals. For these contributions she was awarded the French Legion of Honor.

In 1922, with the assistance of Anne Morgan, Robinson-Smith raised $8 million dollars to buy land in New York City for a clubhouse for businesswomen. The Great Depression thwarted completion of this project, and the building became the Henry Hudson Hotel. Always interested in French culture and arts, Smith was later instrumental in organizing the French Theater at the Barbizon Plaza Hotel in New York, which remained active from 1937 until World War II.

During World War I, Robinson-Smith's father had bought a 115-acre estate in Glendale, near Stockbridge, Mass., which became the family summer home. This locale was to have much bearing on her most important undertaking. In a corner of her father's estate Robinson-Smith built her own cottage, which she named "The Residence." In this house took place many of the negotiations leading to the founding of Tanglewood. In May 1934 the conductor and composer Henry Kimball Hadley was looking for a suitable place to give summer concerts. A correspondent of the *Springfield Republican* suggested that he speak to Robinson-Smith, who promised to help. Rounding up a committee of sixty-four residents of Stockbridge and the vicinity, she formed the Berkshire Symphony Festival, Inc., of which she was president until 1955. Two months later, on Aug. 23, 1934, the first of three concerts was given in a large horse-show ring in a farm situated between Lenox and Stockbridge. The orchestra, conducted by Hadley, was made up of sixty-five members of the New York Philharmonic Orchestra. The festival drew altogether 5,000 people and ended with only a small deficit.

The following summer Robinson-Smith enlarged and improved the festival. "It is high time that America has its own Salzburg," she said. A larger orchestra, comprising eighty-five players from the New York Philharmonic and other orchestras, was engaged, and a huge tent was rented. Admission prices were raised. The governors of Massachusetts and Rhode Island attended the opening concert, and the festival drew an audience of 9,000.

At this point Hadley, whose choice of repertoire had been criticized and who was in poor health, resigned. The festival committee decided that instead of annually hiring musicians, they would engage an entire well-established orchestra. They approached the Boston Symphony Orchestra's manager, George E. Judd, and Robinson-Smith herself spoke to Serge Koussevitzky, the orchestra's conductor. Envisioning the opportunity to found a music center and school, Koussevitzky agreed to bring the entire Boston Symphony Orchestra to Stockbridge for the 1936 summer season. The site, however, had to be changed, and Margaret Emerson offered the use of her 500-acre estate "Holmwood," situated between Stockbridge and Lenox. A larger tent was rented, and the third festival took place under Koussevitzky's direction with much broader press coverage.

Koussevitzky soon sought to expand the festival by establishing a school, for which a building would have to be erected. The search for a permanent site was unexpectedly solved when Mrs. Gorham Brooks made a gift of her estate "Tanglewood" to Koussevitzky, who in turn offered it to the Boston Symphony Orchestra. Foreseeing a loss of control by the Berkshire Symphony Festival Committee, Robinson-Smith raised objections. After much discussion, a contract was drawn up between the Boston Symphony Orchestra and the festival committee, giving the latter the right to manage the concerts on the Tanglewood estate, provided that the committee cover the cost of building and maintaining a "suitable structure."

The 1937 festival again took place under a tent, at Tanglewood. During the opening concert (which was broadcast for the first time) a thunderstorm broke out; the tent leaked and musicians and audience were drenched. Jumping at the opportunity, Smith told the audience during intermission: "This storm has proven conclusively the need for a shed. We must raise $100,000 to build it." Within a few minutes $30,000 had been pledged. A follow-up campaign raised enough funds to erect the shed, which was dedicated on June 16, 1938. In 1940 the Berkshire Music Center opened. Other am-

bitious projects were undertaken by Koussevitzky, such as the building of a theater–concert hall.

The outbreak of World War II created many difficulties for the festival, and Robinson-Smith became concerned about its fate. Pressure was being applied to have the Boston Symphony placed in charge of all activities at Tanglewood. Although Robinson-Smith fought bitterly to keep the festival under the control of the organization that she had created, in 1945 ownership of the shed and management of the summer concerts were transferred to the Boston Symphony Orchestra. The Berkshire Symphony Festival Committee was dissolved in 1955.

Robinson-Smith never lost interest in Tanglewood, nor was it forgotten that she had been responsible for its creation. A plaque apposed on the north end of the shed reads: "In gratitude to the trustees and friends of the Berkshire Symphony Festival for their promotion of music in the Berkshires under the leadership of Gertrude Robinson-Smith and for the gift of this shed." On her eightieth birthday, she was the guest of honor at a special concert conducted by Charles Munch, conductor of the orchestra at that time.

A few months before her death, Robinson-Smith was appointed to the advisory committee of the National Culture Center in Washington, D.C. She also worked on her autobiography, but it was never published. Although not a musician, she knew and entertained the greatest composers, conductors, and soloists of her time. She died in New York City.

[The Landowska Center at Lakeville, Conn., has unpublished correspondence between Robinson-Smith and Wanda Landowska. See Herbert Kupferberg, *Tanglewood* (1976). An obituary notice is in the *New York Times*, Oct. 23, 1963.]

DENISE RESTOUT

ROETHKE, THEODORE HUEBNER (May 25, 1908–Aug. 1, 1963), poet and teacher, was born in Saginaw, Mich., the son of Otto Theodore Roethke (pronounced "ret-kē"), a commercial flower grower, and of Helen Marie Huebner. The poet's grandfather, Wilhelm Roethke, had been chief forester on the East Prussian estate of Bismarck's sister. Otto Roethke described his forebears as "poop-arse aristocrats," a phrase that his son was fond of quoting. Theodore himself liked to joke about his "Prussian" background and nature. Wilhelm Roethke had immigrated to America in 1872, settled in Saginaw, and set up a truck-farming and then a greenhouse business. Otto, Theodore's father, became the flower specialist. He had a strong influence on his son: somewhat of an early object of filial resentments, but increasingly a person to be lived up to, propitiated, idealized in memory, and invested with a symbolic significance that had metaphysical implications. Roethke early developed a feeling for flowers and for natural objects and phenomena. His knowledge of growing things was equaled by his knowledge of birds. He played in the greenhouse and in the field behind it, and both places had a lasting impact on his poetic sensibility. In them he discovered literal themes and symbolic meanings, concrete and transcendental realities that are distinctive elements of his work.

Although six feet two and about 220 pounds in adult life, Roethke was a thin, undersized boy, susceptible to illnesses and developing the hypochondriacal tendencies that always plagued him. Nevertheless, he often walked the mile and a half to school four times a day. A shy and diffident boy, he would never have much social ease. His parents were undemonstrative but devoted. Helen Roethke, who had been a seamstress, ran a well-organized household: cleanliness, good meals and clothes, such annual rites as butchering and making sauerkraut, and family picnics and rides on the interurban trolley line. Roethke was christened in the Presbyterian church and went to services until he left for college. Roethke often spent summers in Saginaw until his marriage.

Despite a good home life in an attractive setting, Roethke considered his early years unhappy. He may have felt out of things because he was not an athlete or school leader. A pall was probably cast over prior experience by successive disasters in his fifteenth year. Otto Roethke quarreled with his brother and business partner, Charles. The greenhouse was sold in October 1922, and in February 1923 Charles Roethke committed suicide. Otto, ill with cancer, endured great suffering before dying in April 1923. Roethke's whole world must have seemed wiped out, and what was gone acquired a significance and imaginative appeal (notably the Edenic connotations of the greenhouse and the field) that would surface long afterward in his most distinctive work.

In high school Roethke made top grades and read voraciously, but also joined an illegal fraternity dominated by football players, did some drinking, and had dealings with bootleggers. At sixteen he joined the local country club, the Canoe Club, where he made his first contacts with the well-to-do and became a good and furiously competitive tennis player—but one not always scrupulous, according to fellow players. His physical condition improved and made possible his subsequent energetic life. In 1925 he got a job in a pickle factory that he held for half a dozen summers.

Roethke was the first member of his family to attend a university. He wanted to study at Harvard, but his mother thought it too distant, so he enrolled at the University of Michigan, from which he graduated summa cum laude in 1929. He made Phi Beta Kappa and claimed, questionably, membership in Kappa Beta Phi, the underground drinking fraternity. He sported a costly raccoon coat and claimed to be an intimate of "roaring boys." There is no evidence that he knew underworld figures, but he began to romanticize them; in his later-life fantasies about the "mob," some events were attributed to the Ann Arbor period. He admired François Villon, the poet as criminal; criminality symbolized the power that he could publicly joke about wanting.

After a term at the University of Michigan Law School, Roethke transferred in 1930 to the graduate school. After two terms of studying English, he spent the 1930–1931 academic year at Harvard. He received the M.A. from Michigan in 1936.

Roethke's real source of power was the writing and public reading of poetry, and brilliant teaching. He discovered these talents in his twenties. At first he thought he would be a prose writer (in adult life he constantly referred, not always jocosely, to the fact that his high school freshman speech on the Red Cross was translated into twenty-six languages), but he was reading poetry, especially that of Elinor Wylie. He published some mediocre verses in *The Harp*, a little magazine, in 1930, but his first significant publications were in *Commonweal* (1931) and the *New Republic* and the *Sewanee Review* (1932).

Roethke left Harvard in 1931 for a post at Lafayette College. There he began to build his extraordinary reputation as a teacher. Roethke was the rare literary artist who is also an unstinting teacher. He was a conscientious planner of methods and procedures, a prodigal provider of study materials, an intense and spirited performer in the classroom, and a rigorous and generous critic of student verse. He was informal, candid, slangy, vehement, but never without essential dignity and seriousness. In addition to teaching, he coached the Lafayette tennis team (1932–1935) and directed public relations (1934–1935). At the same time, he made headway as a poet, publishing in such diverse journals as *Poetry*, the *Saturday Review of Literature*, the *Nation*, the *Atlantic Monthly*, and *Adelphi* (London). He established lifelong friendships with Rolfe Humphries, Stanley Kunitz, and Louise Bogan, who often acted as shrewd critics of his work.

Roethke taught for about half the 1935 fall term at Michigan State College. There he and the Canadian poet A. J. M. Smith became friends. That November he suffered the first attack of the manic-depressive disorder that afflicted him periodically. In his "high" phase he gave vent to fantasies of entrepreneurial achievement, became irresponsible, and needed institutional care. The disability might last from one to six months. He once claimed that, in search of a deeper reality, he had induced his first attack; apparently such a belief is often held by manic-depressives. Roethke probably came to accept the disease as a part of himself, but he did undergo treatment by a series of psychiatrists, mostly in Seattle, Wash. From one of these, he said at the time, he had learned enough to prevent any recurrence of the disorder. In later years he could jest, sometimes uproariously, about his periods of illness. During these he always kept writing, but a sign of recovery was improvement both in his work and in his judgment of it.

After about a month in the Mercywood Sanitarium at Ann Arbor, Roethke returned to Saginaw. Michigan State did not reappoint him. In the fall of 1936 he began teaching at Pennsylvania State College; he was instructor in 1936–1939 and assistant professor in 1939–1943. During World War II he was declared unfit for service by his draft board.

At Penn State, Roethke formed the second of his long friendships with devoted women—potential wives and semimaternal listeners and helpers. (The first had been Mary Kunkel, daughter of a biology professor at Lafayette.) Kitty Stokes, a librarian at Penn State, gave him many kinds of help, including the typing of his poems. From then until the end of his life he averaged about ten new poems a year, the number fluctuating with the state of his health. His work appeared in some thirty American publications (including the *New York Times*, the *New Yorker*, the *Atlantic*, *Harpers*, the *Sewanee Review*, the *Hudson Review*, the *Yale Review*, and the *American Scholar*) and a dozen European ones.

Roethke's first volume, *Open House*, appeared in 1941. There are a few phrasal and imagistic hints of his mature style ("the waking is slow," "a suddenness of trees," "bitter snow," "the fields stretch . . . far and close"), and "The Premonition" ("Walking this field . . . Close to the heels of my father") anticipates a major theme. But mostly these poems are exercises in traditional styles (from doggerel and ballad to Hudibrastic and epigrammatic), forms, and rhymes (quatrains and couplets), rhythms (including anapestic), and even a certain neoclassical way of introducing objects and scenes, and applying them in comparisons and analogies. *Open House* was praised in reviews by W. H. Auden, Bogan, Humphries, John Holmes, and Yvor Winters.

Roethke began several years of teaching at Bennington College in April 1943. Here he came to know Kenneth Burke (who later wrote a key essay on him). With the college's emphasis on the arts and creativity, Roethke reached a new peak in teaching, and the students felt "awe," as one of them, Beatrice O'Connell (later Mrs. Roethke), put it. Along with the intensity of his teaching, he was experiencing the strain of finding a new poetic material and style. The combination may have contributed to his second major manic episode late in 1945. At Albany General Hospital he was given a terrifying electric-shock treatment and then had a slow convalescence. He spent most of 1946 in Saginaw, on a Guggenheim fellowship. In the fall of 1947, Roethke went to the University of Washington as associate professor, where he would teach the rest of his life. He was promoted to professor in 1948, and given the title poet in residence in 1962. His great reputation as a teacher attracted students from all over the country.

Roethke produced his major work while at Washington. *The Lost Son and Other Poems* (1949) brought together many poems in the new manner that he had been developing since 1945. For the rest of his poetic life, Roethke's basic supply depot was the Saginaw greenhouse and field, with many growing and living things presented vividly, often in paradox, and explored as vehicles of mood and feeling, including a quest for metaphysical reality. Traditional metrical and stanzaic forms yielded to a rich experimentation in rhythms, line lengths, and groupings; logical, discursive statement alternated with striking and often cryptic series of images, repeatedly in a paratactic juxtaposition within and between blunt, end-stopped lines, all this sometimes alternating with fluent nonsense-rhyme quatrains.

In "The Lost Son" Roethke introduced the long poem, or "sequence," ranging between 50 and 175 lines, which was a continuing feature of his work. The new style continued, with elaborations and variations, in *Praise to the End!* (1951) and *The Waking* (1953). In the former the shorter poems are marked by some of Roethke's boldest ventures into a frequently surrealistic chaos of verbal, sensory, and grammatical derangements, intermingled with multiple sound effects. The antilogical spurting of associative and intuitive meaning is partly modified by a more syntactic ordering of materials in the three sequence poems in *Praise to the End!*, and even in some of the shorter lyrics in *The Waking*, which contains the moving "Elegy for Jane" and the very fine villanelle "The Waking." Here, too, notably in the meditative "Four for Sir John Davies," appears the influence of William Butler Yeats that is much commented on, and sometimes regretted as not assimilated and utilized profitably in the evolution of Roethke's style.

Roethke held Guggenheim fellowships in 1945 and 1950, was at the Yaddo Writers' Colony (where he became a friend of the Catholic writer James F. Powers and of Robert Lowell, whom he felt to be his chief rival for the American laureateship) in 1947 and 1950, and received the Tietjens Prize in 1947. The 1950's, however, was the major period of awards and recognition. Chief of these was the Pulitzer Prize for *The Waking* (1953). Others were the top *Poetry Magazine* award and the Levinson Prize in 1951; the American Academy of Arts and Letters award in 1952; the Bollingen Prize in 1958; the National Book Award in 1959; the Edna St. Vincent Millay Award in 1959; the Longview Award in 1960; and the Shelley Award in 1962. Roethke held a Fulbright lectureship in Italy in 1955–1956 and Ford Foundation fellowships in 1952–1953 and 1959–1961.

In December 1952, Roethke met in New York Beatrice Heath O'Connell, who had been a student of his at Bennington. They were married on Jan. 3, 1953, with W. H. Auden and Louise Bogan as attendants. In March they began a two-month honeymoon at Auden's villa on the island of Ischia. They went on to Paris, Geneva, and London, where Roethke did a broadcast for the BBC.

"Love Poems" occupied more than one-third of *Words for the Wind* (1958). Some use Roethke's old storehouses of material—greenhouse, field, and small-animal kingdom. They are often allusive, inquiring, and questing; gnomic elements, technical shocks (especially imagistic), and playfulness prevent sentimental

effects. But Roethke reveals his greatest ease in, and mastery of, the form in the shorter, mainly celebrative "Love Poems" that make up about one-sixth of *The Far Field* (1964). A few pages of *Words for the Wind* and all of *I Am! Says the Lamb* (1961) are devoted to humorous verses, nonsense verses, and poems for children; here Roethke gives full range to the talent for the playful and zany that often crops up in serious poems. *Party at the Zoo* (1963), published a few weeks before his death, was a book for children.

Two sequences, "The Dying Man" and "Meditations of an Old Woman," make up a third of *Words for the Wind*, and "North American Sequence" accounts for about a third of *The Far Field*. In these longer poems, as well as in the thirty shorter poems in *The Far Field*, there is a continued, loving evocation of flowers, growing things, and small beings. He now makes frequent use of western scenes; of the language of the journey, especially "out of the self"; of problems of body and soul, flesh and spirit; of such symbols as "the edge," "beyond," and "light" in many manifestations; and of the eternal and the divine. The struggle toward insights borders on, or partakes of, mystical experience. There are also continuing elements of the pure song to which Roethke had a devotion rare among moderns.

During the 1950's Roethke did considerable reading in philosophy and theology. The Roethkes traveled periodically in Europe. In 1960, shepherded by the Irish poet Richard Murphy, they spent some time on Inishbofin, an island off the west coast of Ireland, a visit that ended when Roethke went into another manic period. From October 1960 to March 1961, the Roethkes were in England, where Roethke did readings, broadcasts, and recordings. For years he did readings throughout United States. Students at San Francisco State College collected most of the money needed to make a film about Roethke, *In a Dark Time* (1963). Roethke was often slightly "high" during his last year, but was still teaching. He died on Bainbridge Island, just west of Seattle.

[Roethke's papers are in the University of Washington Library. Also valuable are the Allan Seager Papers, Bancroft Library, University of California at Berkeley. Bibliographies include James R. McLeod, *Theodore Roethke: A Manuscript Checklist* (1971) and *Theodore Roethke: A Bibliography* (1973); and Keith R. Moul, *Theodore Roethke's Career: An Annotated Bibliography* (1977). The published poems were gathered in *The Collected Poems of Theodore Roethke* (1966). Other collections are *On the Poet and His Craft: Selected Prose of Theodore Roethke*

(1965), edited by Ralph J. Mills, Jr.; *Selected Letters of Theodore Roethke* (1968), edited by Ralph J. Mills, Jr.; and *Straw for the Fire: From the Notebooks of Theodore Roethke* (1972), selected and arranged by David Wagoner. Allan Seager, *The Glass House* (1968), is a biographical study. Also see Arnold Stein, ed., *Theodore Roethke: Essays on the Poetry* (1965); Karl Malkoff, *Theodore Roethke* (1966); Richard A. Blessing, *Theodore Roethke's Dynamic Vision* (1974); Rosemary Sullivan, *Theodore Roethke* (1975); Jenijoy La Belle, *The Echoing Wood of Theodore Roethke* (1976); and Harry Williams, *The Edge Is What I Have* (1976). An obituary is in the *New York Times*, Aug. 2, 1963.]

ROBERT B. HEILMAN

ROMBAUER, IRMA LOUISE (Oct. 30, 1877–Oct. 14, 1962), cookbook author, was born in St. Louis, Mo., the daughter of Hugo Maximilian von Starkloff, a physician, and of Emma Kuhlmann. In 1889 she accompanied her parents to Europe, where her father served as American consul in Bremen, Germany. Reared, as she once put it, "to be a 'young lady,'" she attended fashionable boarding schools in Lausanne and Geneva, became fluent in French and German, and spent much time traveling, going to the opera, visiting galleries, and writing letters—"all utterly delightful," she recalled, "and almost useless from a practical standpoint."

In 1894 the family returned to St. Louis. For several years Irma studied drawing and painting at the School of Fine Arts of Washington University. After a brief romance with the novelist Booth Tarkington, she married Edgar Rombauer, a lawyer, on Oct. 14, 1899. They had three children.

For the next thirty years Rombauer devoted herself to the roles of wife, mother, and hostess. As a bride she was admittedly even more "ignorant, helpless and awkward" around the kitchen than the average upper-middle-class woman of her generation. But memories of many wonderful meals in Europe and at family gatherings made her dissatisfied with the dreary, antiseptic fare prepared by her kitchen help. "In self-defense" Rombauer decided to try her hand at cooking. By trial and error, using recipes and techniques gleaned from relatives and friends, culled from newspapers and books, and pried out of secretive restaurant chefs, she taught herself to cook—but not before she had "placed many a burnt offering upon the altar of matrimony."

With an intellectual rather than an intuitive approach to food, Rombauer took copious notes on her successes and failures, recording the precise weights and measures of ingredients, oven temperatures, and cooking times in a manner similar to that of a scientist. She thereby built up a considerable store of virtually foolproof recipes that she gladly shared with friends and colleagues in the many civic and cultural organizations to which she belonged in St. Louis. In 1922, invited by the First Unitarian Women's Alliance to conduct a cooking class, she mimeographed a collection of seventy-three of her favorites, ranging from borscht to Spanish tripe, for the students.

With her husband, who was active in Republican reform politics (he served for many years as president of the St. Louis Urban League and, for a brief term, as speaker of the city's House of Delegates), Rombauer spent nearly every summer vacation—except in 1925, when they traveled to Europe—in a rustic cabin in Bay View, Mich. There she and the children attended Chautauqua popular education classes while her husband spent his time fishing.

Although the enjoyment of good food constituted an important part of her life, Rombauer was equally enthusiastic about good conversation, gardening, music, and the arts—enthusiasms that often transformed the family dinner into a colloquium on the latest novel or opera. Edgar Rombauer died in 1930, leaving Irma depressed and at loose ends. Partly to fill the void left by his death and partly to meet her children's request for a volume of cookery advice as they prepared to raise families of their own ("I realized," she explained, "they didn't know how to poach an egg"), she began to elaborate upon the handout she had compiled for her cooking class. The result, entitled *The Joy of Cooking*, was printed at her own expense in 1931. It contained more than 500 recipes that ran the gamut from appetizers to desserts and a promise that "inexperienced cooks cannot fail to make successful soufflés, pies, cakes, soups, gravies, etc., if they follow the clear instructions given on these subjects." The book sold fewer than 3,000 copies.

With the help of her daughter, Marion Rombauer Becker, who from the beginning tested and researched many of the dishes, Rombauer soon turned out an expanded manuscript that featured an innovative step-by-step recipe format embedded in a relaxed, humorous commentary about food and drink. "A turnip is not necessarily a depressant," she wrote. "The novice should remember that there are bold mushroom hunters and old mushroom hunters, but no bold old mushroom hunters," she warned.

The enlarged book caught the attention of

Lawrence Chambers, president of Bobbs-Merrill, who frequently dined at the home of Rombauer's Indianapolis relatives. Enchanted as much by the vivacity and wit of the author as by the scope and clarity of her work, he agreed to publish it. The first trade edition of *Joy* appeared in 1936; *Streamlined Cooking*, dealing with impromptu dining done on a potluck basis, followed in 1939. It was incorporated into a 1943 rewriting of *Joy*, a hefty tome that quickly became the best-selling cookbook in publishing history, eclipsing the record formerly held by Fannie Farmer's *Boston Cooking School Cookbook*. A third revision came out in 1946, as did *Cookbook for Boys and Girls*. The fourth edition, *The New Joy of Cooking*, appeared in 1951, with Rombauer's daughter cited as coauthor.

By then *Joy* had grown into a legendary, awesome motherlode of culinary facts. Its 1,000 pages were crammed with 4,000 recipes and 150 explanatory drawings. It covered everything from how to prepare a beaver tail to cooking at high altitudes. Virtually no cook, beginner or experienced, felt secure without one to consult. One eloping bride is reported to have cabled her family: "Am married. Order announcements. Send me a Rombauer cookbook at once." Even skilled French chefs were known to keep sauce-stained copies handy for emergencies, though carefully placed out of sight. Although a few food authorities faulted some of Rombauer's cooking techniques and shortcuts, complaining that they violated established culinary principles, only two buyers of the more than 6 million books sold during the author's lifetime ever took advantage of the publisher's money-back guarantee.

Rombauer loved to travel in search of fresh ideas and original recipes. In 1954, after returning from Mexico, where she found cooks eager to confide their secrets to her but many of their dishes "too hot for comfort," she suffered a stroke and withdrew from active collaboration on the book. Her last years were spent in bed at her St. Louis apartment, which housed a fine collection of American antiques, or at her country cottage in the Ozarks. Rombauer passed her days answering fan mail or thinking of new ways to enliven, yet simplify, old dishes. Under her daughter's direction *Joy* continued to be updated and enlarged, but some of Rombauer's ingratiating personal touch was lost in the process. Yet her larger accomplishment, taking the subject of everyday American home cooking and lifting it from the commonplace to the imaginative, remained. She died in St. Louis.

[Rombauer's personal papers are in the possession of her grandson, Ethan Becker, Cincinnati, Ohio. The best published source is Marion Rombauer Becker's memoir, *Little Acorn* (1966). Useful articles on Rombauer and her cookbook are "One World, One Cookbook," *Time*, Aug. 16, 1943; and Jane Nickerson, "They Wanted to Cook like Mother," *New York Times Book Review*, Aug. 12, 1951. Also see the obituaries in the *New York Times*, Oct. 17, 1962; and *Time*, Oct. 26, 1962.]

JEROME L. STERNSTEIN

ROONEY, PAT (July 4, 1880–Sept. 9, 1962), dancer, actor, vaudeville entertainer, and songwriter, was born in New York City, the son of Patrick James Rooney, a popular singer of Irish character songs, and of Josie Granger, an actress. After Rooney's father died in 1892, Pat Rooney went on the stage with his sister Mattie. Although he occasionally branched into other areas of entertainment, the variety stage dominated his lifelong show business career.

Rooney began in musical comedy in *In Atlantic City*, a show that toured the East in 1897 and 1898. He continued performing in vaudeville and nightclubs as well. He was a song-and-dance man and dance director for numerous Rogers Brothers productions, successful vaudeville farces performed between 1901 and 1907. Following a tour in a popular melodrama, *Daughters of the Poor*, in 1903, he met Marion Bent while dancing in an English pantomime entitled *Mother Goose*. They were married on Apr. 10, 1904, and had one son.

Rooney and Bent formed a memorable vaudeville dance team. They were frequent performers at the Palace Theater and on many other variety entertainment stages throughout the United States. In 1919 Rooney introduced a waltz clog to the tune of "The Daughter of Rosie O'Grady" that identified him throughout his career.

In addition to vaudeville, Rooney and Bent continued performing in musical comedy. Alexander Woollcott wrote of Rooney's performance in *Love Birds* (1921), "Pat Rooney is an amazing phenomenon. Not merely as an indestructible dancer, for he has always been that. But as a permanent youngster. He looks (and behaves) now like one of the younger sophomores at Rutgers. Yet this is set down by one who quite definitely recalls having seen him and Marion Bent in vaudeville fully sixteen years ago. That interval has not altered him in any way at all. Very likely he is ninety and has ten grandchildren in the army." Critics frequently commented on Rooney's youthful appearance and vigor throughout his lifetime.

In 1925 Rooney and Bent starred in *The Daughter of Rosie O'Grady*, a musical developed around the song and already famous Rooney waltz clog; it played in Washington, D.C., Philadelphia, and Baltimore. In 1932 after Bent's retirement, Rooney returned to the Palace Theater to team with Herman Timberg, forming one of the popular Jewish-Irish pairs of vaudeville. Rooney also performed at the Capitol Theatre and Billy Rose's Diamond Horseshoe, assisted on many occasions by his son, Pat Rooney III.

Marion Bent died in 1940. In February 1941, Rooney was forced to declare bankruptcy. His creditors included George M. Cohan, a friend from Rooney's youth, and Bob Hope. On July 21, 1942, he married Helen Rubon Rooney, a dancer and the divorced wife of his son. She died in 1943, and Rooney married Carmen Schaffer on Jan. 21, 1944.

In 1929 Rooney performed a dance routine in *Night Club*, one of the first sound films made in the Astoria Studios, and later appeared in *Variety Time* (1948). He wrote several popular songs, including "You Are the O'Reilly" and "You Be My Ootsie, I'll Be Your Tootsie."

In the stage production of *Guys and Dolls* (1950) Rooney created the role of Arvide Abernathy, the drum-beating missionary whose daughter falls in love with an underworld character. Although a waltz clog was originally planned for Rooney, it seemed out of character and was never performed. Instead Rooney sang "More I Cannot Wish You," which turned into a memorable moment in this landmark musical.

Rooney performed occasional banquet, fund-raising, television, and nightclub dates right up to his death, in New York City.

[Extensive materials documenting Rooney's career are available at the Theater Collection of the New York Public Library. See also Alexander Woollcott, "The Play," *New York Times*, Mar. 16, 1921; John B. Kennedy, "We've Forgotten How to Fight," *Collier's*, May 11, 1929; Gilbert Millstein, "Clean-living Rooney Marches On," *New York Times*, June 29, 1952, sec. II, p. 1; Abe Burrows, "The Making of 'Guys and Dolls,'" *Atlantic Monthly*, Jan. 1980. An obituary is in the *New York Times*, Sept. 11, 1962.]
CRAIG S. LIKNESS

ROOSEVELT, (ANNA) ELEANOR (Oct. 11, 1884–Nov. 7, 1962), humanitarian, United Nations diplomat, and social reformer, was born in New York City. To the extent that there has been a ruling class in the United States she was a member by birth. Her father, Elliott Roosevelt, younger brother of Theodore Roosevelt, was descended from the Oyster Bay Roosevelts. Her mother, Anna Ludlow Hall, was descended from the Livingstons who settled along the upper reaches of the Hudson.

Eleanor grew up among New York's social elite. Yet their social advantages did not shield the family from Elliott's infirmities, especially alcoholism, and Eleanor's mother forced a legal separation, even though by then there were two younger brothers, Elliott, Jr., and Hall. When Anna died of diphtheria in 1892, eight-year-old Eleanor and her brothers were left in the care of Anna's mother, Mrs. Valentine Hall. Elliott, to whom Eleanor was more deeply attached than to her mother, had only visiting rights. A few months later Elliott, Jr., died, and in August 1894 Grandma Hall told Eleanor of her father's death. Her sad comment was, "I did so want to see father once more."

Eleanor was a solemn child with grave blue eyes. Her mother had nicknamed her "Granny" because she was so "old-fashioned." Her sense of responsibility for her little brother Hall, her grandmother, and her aunts seemed paramount. Eleanor spent her winters in Grandma Hall's Thirty-seventh Street brownstone and her summers at Tivoli on the Hudson, amid Livingston and Ludlow kin.

Eleanor attended the fashionable Roser classes, which were held in the mansions of the socially prominent, and she was tutored in French. She saw little of her Oyster Bay relatives, but in 1899 Theodore Roosevelt's sister, "Aunty Bye," had her sent to Allenswood, a finishing school outside London. The headmistress, Mlle Souvestre, was a forceful, brilliant woman, an intimate of writers, politicians, and artists. A special kinship arose between the liberal schoolmistress and the orphaned girl; Eleanor became her traveling companion during holidays and served as her deputy among the girls. Under Souvestre's care, Eleanor's qualities emerged and she left the school in 1902 an acknowledged leader.

Back in New York, Eleanor was not one of society's most beautiful belles, but she was easily one of its most interesting. Eleanor became a Junior League volunteer in an East Side settlement house, teaching dance and literature and learning about the slums. In the midst of these experiences she encountered Franklin D. Roosevelt, a sixth cousin once removed. They fell in love. His mother, Sara Roosevelt, tried to prevent their marriage but succeeded only in delaying it. They were married on Mar. 17, 1905. President Theodore Roosevelt gave away the bride.

Sara Roosevelt did not intend to give up her son; instead she acquired Eleanor, a daughter-in-law who subordinated herself completely, quietly acquiescing in her gift of a town house next to Sara's and with adjoining upper floors. Their domestic arrangements were similarly intertwined at Hyde Park, in Dutchess County, N.Y., and at Campobello Island, in Canada. While Franklin attended Columbia University Law School, Eleanor waited on "Mama." The independence shown in her work with the settlements was stifled. Her energy went into a family life that was dominated by Sara and New York society. She shared the latter's sympathies as well as its prejudices, including a mild anti-Semitism.

Their first child, Anna, was born in 1906. In quick succession she then bore five boys, James (1907); the first Franklin (1909), who died as an infant; Elliott (1910); Franklin, Jr. (1914); and John (1916). She allowed Sara and the governesses to dominate the upbringing of all but the last two.

Politics began to claim Eleanor's husband in 1910 and it drastically influenced her own life. To everyone's surprise he won the state senatorship in Republican Dutchess County. For Eleanor this meant a move to Albany, some participation in capital politics, and some freedom from Sara. To the pleasures and chores of family responsibility, she added frequent attendance at the state legislature.

Eleanor's life shifted again when Franklin, a supporter of Woodrow Wilson, was appointed assistant secretary of the navy in 1913. Socially well connected, with friends in the Teddy Roosevelt and Wilson camps, the Roosevelts moved in Washington's top social circles.

It was not until America's entry into World War I and her assumption of duties with the Red Cross that Eleanor's organizational abilities found a public focus. Qualities of dedication and vitality began to reemerge and gave her a sense of public usefulness that never again left her. The need to make a life for herself outside of her family was implacably reinforced by her discovery of her husband's affair with her social secretary, Lucy Mercer. She offered to divorce him, but he refused, in part because of the pressure of his mother, who controlled the purse-strings, and his own political aspirations. He accepted the alternative that they remain married but that he never again see Lucy Mercer. For Eleanor this personal crisis, combined with a growing radical egalitarianism, effected a major transformation in which the values of tradition and affluence were subordinated to a democratic

ethos to which she remained passionately faithful throughout her life. She began to cultivate women associated with the trade unions, politics, and the successful suffrage movement, to which, incidentally, she had not been a convert.

With the vote, women became more important in politics, and Franklin wanted Eleanor at his side during his active race for the vice-presidency in 1920. For the first time she felt herself a collaborator and during the campaign began to appreciate the qualities of Louis Howe, her husband's secretary, with whom she formed a deep and abiding friendship.

The most searching test of will and values between Eleanor and Sara came with Franklin's polio attack at Campobello in 1921. The disease left his lower limbs useless, and he was urged by Sara to retire to Hyde Park. With the support of Eleanor and Howe, Franklin resisted her. In his determination to remain active in the Democratic party, Eleanor's role as his proxy and surrogate became indispensable.

As part of Eleanor's emancipation she learned to drive, cook, and type. The worst ordeal was speaking in public, but she accepted invitations gamely and meekly submitted to Howe's subsequent critiques. She became active in the League of Women Voters, the Women's Trade Union League, and the Democratic party. While Franklin sought ceaselessly to recover the use of his crippled legs, spending winters first in Florida, then at Warm Springs, Ga., she began to define her identity as a publicist, politician, and organizer, as well as mother. With her friends Nancy Cook and Marion Dickerman, she began a furniture factory at Val-Kill, N. Y., and later started pewter and weaving work. Franklin gave the three women lifetime rights to the Val-Kill land and encouraged them to build a stone house for themselves (1924–1926). Eleanor used it when Franklin was not at Hyde Park. She also helped Marion purchase in 1927 Todhunter, a private school for girls, and took on a three-day teaching schedule there.

When Franklin Roosevelt ran for governor of New York in 1928, Eleanor headed the women's division of the Democratic party. The defeat of Al Smith for the presidency left her despondent despite Franklin's victory. She entered the governor's mansion reluctantly, determined to spend half her time in New York City, Todhunter, and Val-Kill, the other half in Albany. As the state's first lady, she replied to every letter, making increasing use of Malvina C. Thompson, who had worked as her secretary in the Smith headquarters. She became skillful at inspections of state institutions, serving as her husband's surrogate. In the course of these activities she befriended Corporal Earl Miller, a state trooper assigned to the governor's detail, who often accompanied her when she went out alone. Avid for life and new experiences, she encouraged Miller's friendship. He taught her to use a handgun for self-protection and encouraged her to ride and to engage in other outdoor sports. She in turn mothered his romances, and he often stayed with her in New York or Hyde Park.

Despite inner tensions and reticences, Eleanor and Franklin Roosevelt made a good team. Franklin's election as president in 1932 posed again for Eleanor the problem of her own future. Lorena Hickok, a youthful reporter assigned to cover Mrs. Roosevelt, sensed that here was a "reluctant" first lady. The latter, astonished to find herself perceived as an individual and not simply as a cog in Franklin's political machine, opened up to Hickok and they became friends. Hickok later worked for the Democratic party and lived at the White House. Dreading immersion in the White House and the suppression of her hopes to be herself, Eleanor offered to serve as a listening post for her husband and to handle some of his mail. The president-elect turned her aside with the observation that that job was his secretary's responsibility. It was her last effort "to keep in close touch and to feel I had a real job to do."

Nevertheless Eleanor Roosevelt became an activist first lady. Her views and actions, beginning with regular press conferences, restricted to women reporters, became as much a feature of New Deal Washington as her husband's. Seeking to define her own role in relation to Franklin's, she called him the politician, herself the agitator. On some issues she was in advance, but basically they functioned as a team. He was sensitive to the values she espoused while she understood and respected his political necessities.

Eleanor did the things expected of first ladies —preside over mammoth teas, attend receptions, hold state dinners—but she also made speeches that carried her own imprint and took under her wing such New Deal projects as subsistence homesteads, the National Youth Administration, and services that involved women. She was adept on the radio and developed a serpentine skill in raising issues with Franklin. Opponents claimed she exploited the White House. Politicians who feared to attack Roosevelt found her a safer target. She went on serenely doing what her heart commanded and by the end of Roosevelt's first term she shared in

the nationwide endorsement that the 1936 elections constituted.

In 1935, United Features Syndicate persuaded her to write a daily column of four hundred words, "My Day," which initially appeared in sixty newspapers. She employed a lecture agent, took voice lessons, and became a fixture on the lecture circuit as well as the radio. People were interested in the views of the president's wife; but there was interest, too, especially among women and minorities, in the views of Eleanor Roosevelt, a power in her own right.

In 1938 Eleanor dissolved the partnership in Val-Kill Industries and withdrew from active participation in Todhunter. Cook and Dickerman remained in the cottage at Val-Kill, but their relationship with Eleanor became purely formal. Mrs. Roosevelt transformed the factory into a spacious cottage for herself. She also shared a brownstone in Greenwich Village with two old friends, Esther Lape and Elizabeth Reed. Persuaded to try her hand at autobiography, she produced *This Is My Story* (1937), which has become a minor classic.

In the 1930's Eleanor's pacifism yielded to antifascism. She was among the foremost advocates of lifting the arms embargo against Republican forces during the Spanish Civil War. When Madrid fell she said to Leon Henderson, a militant New Dealer and Loyalist supporter, "We should have pushed him harder," and pointed to Franklin.

A spontaneous sympathy with young people, who seemed to be particularly victimized by the Great Depression, caused Eleanor to seek out the American Youth Congress, which despite Communist sympathies and, as it turned out, controls, championed youth objectives in which she believed. She made personal friends of its leaders, invited them to the White House and Hyde Park, obtained a hearing from government agencies for them, and helped them raise their budget. But after the Nazi–Soviet pact she was dismayed to hear most of its leaders denounce the president and take a "Yanks-are-not-coming" posture.

Eleanor's Youth Congress experience, she later said, prepared her to cope with Soviet bloc maneuvers at the United Nations after the war. She supported Franklin's efforts to rearm the nation at the time of the fall of France, but did not favor a third term, fearing it would result in continued congressional stalemate. With the New Deal, she said, "we had bought ourselves time to think." Its measures "helped but did not solve the fundamental problems." But when Franklin did decide to run, she loyally supported his decision and flew to Chicago to help quell a revolt against his selection of Henry Wallace as his running mate.

Eleanor's own desire to serve in the war crisis was fulfilled when the president asked her to become cochairman of the Office of Civilian Defense (OCD). Funded just before Pearl Harbor, the OCD became the whipping boy of Congress and the press. She resigned in February 1942: "I offered a way to get at the President and in wartime it is not politically wise to attack the President," she explained after the war. She advocated a one-world approach to postwar policy. She visited a Britain that was filling up with American troops in the fall of 1942 and journeyed to the South Pacific in 1943 to tour field hospitals and front-line installations. She also managed a vast correspondence with GI's during the war.

Although Eleanor had supported Wallace for renomination as vice-president in 1944, she backed Harry Truman. She accompanied Franklin to Quebec to his second meeting there with Churchill and argued forcefully for the Morgenthau Plan. The more keenly she sensed her political authority, the more vigorously did she argue for liberal policies and appointments. She asked to accompany Franklin to Yalta, but he turned her aside and took Anna, who at her father's request served as his confidential secretary and hostess when her mother was away. At her father's bidding Anna occasionally also welcomed Lucy Mercer Rutherfurd as a dinner guest and did not inform her mother. Eleanor knew on his return that he was tired, but she had often seen him rally in response to political challenges. Others protected him, but she, driven by a knowledge of the many demands for presidential decision, kept after him with proposals and requests. After his death on Apr. 12, 1945, she cabled her sons overseas, "He did his job to the end as he would want you to do."

Eleanor flew to Warm Springs to accompany the president's body back to the White House. There she learned that Mrs. Rutherfurd had been there when the president was stricken. To a friendly reporter who pressed her for an interview, she simply commented, "The story is over."

"He might have been happier with a wife who was completely uncritical," Eleanor wrote later. "That I was never able to be, and he had to find it in some other people. Nevertheless, I think I sometimes acted as a spur, even though the spurring was not always wanted or welcome. I was one of those who served his purposes."

The story, though, was not over. Now standing alone and speaking for herself, Eleanor's public career entered a new phase. She had always wanted her daily column and monthly magazine page to be considered on their merits. "Now I am on my own and hope to write as a newspaperwoman," she said. She left running for political office to her sons, but was pleased to give President Truman, with whom she corresponded freely, her evaluations of the men and women who had served her husband. She pushed hard for women in public jobs, for the continuation of the Fair Employment Practices Committee, and other progressive policies. In December 1945 Truman appointed her one of the five delegates to the first United Nations (UN) General Assembly in London, where she was one of the hardest-working delegates, handling humanitarian, social, and cultural matters in Committee III, addressing public meetings, and mothering the women's group in the UN.

Truman then appointed her to the UN Human Rights Commission, whose first job was to draft an international bill of rights. She spent the summer of 1946 working on *This I Remember*, her account of the Roosevelt presidency. After a minor automobile accident she was fitted with two porcelain teeth, "which will look far better than the rather protruding large teeth which most of the Roosevelts have." She recovered in time to participate in the second General Assembly at Lake Success and to chair the eighteen-member Human Rights Commission.

From the commission's first meeting, she "guided and inspired the work of the UN in the field of human rights." She was the star of the 1948 General Assembly in Paris, where she also addressed the Sorbonne on "The Struggle for the Rights of Man," speaking against the background of the Soviet blockade of Berlin. Subsequently the General Assembly adopted the declaration.

Some members of the UN Secretariat felt that the State Department exploited her for short-term cold war objectives. She was aware of the anti-Soviet slant in American policy and the influence of the military upon it, but she also felt that cooperation had to be a two-way street. Henry Wallace's willingness to deemphasize the hegemonistic thrust of Soviet policy rather than his criticism of America's militarism caused her to break with him. Her formula for working with the Russians was: "Have convictions; Be friendly; Stick to your beliefs as they stick to theirs; Work as hard as they do." After her experience with the Russians in drafting the Declaration of Human Rights, she stated publicly she would "never again" compromise, even on a word. "The Soviets looked on this as evidence of weakness rather than as a gesture of goodwill."

Nevertheless, Eleanor took two trips to the Soviet Union, in 1957 and 1958, and Soviet Premier Nikita Khrushchev visited her in Hyde Park in 1959. She was always ready to meet the Russians halfway; " . . . all of us are going to die together or we are going to learn to live together and if we are to live together we have to talk."

Eleanor's support of birth control and her outspoken opposition to federal aid to parochial schools caused Francis Cardinal Spellman to denounce her as anti-Catholic and for her statements "of discrimination unworthy of an American mother!" She defended herself in a column that ended, "The final judgment, my dear Cardinal Spellman, of the worthiness of all human beings is in the hands of God."

As a UN delegate she vigorously advocated the establishment of a Jewish state. She would have been willing to continue as a delegate during the Eisenhower administration, but the new president accepted her resignation. She then went to work for the American Association for the UN and became an unofficial ambassador at large, visiting the Middle East, Asia, and Europe.

Eleanor remained a political power within the Democratic party until her death. She backed Adlai Stevenson, to whom she was personally devoted, supporting his quest for the presidency in 1952 and 1956, and urging him as a candidate at the 1960 convention. President John F. Kennedy named her to the United States delegation to the UN, and on a visit to the Human Rights Commission she remarked she hoped to see the day when the declaration's principles would be accepted as law. "Then we will have made real steps forward in human rights."

With like-minded Democrats in New York she supported a successful reform effort in the party. To the end of her life she served as honorary chairman of Americans for Democratic Action. After the failure of the Bay of Pigs invasion, of which she disapproved, she agreed to serve on the "Tractors for Freedom" committee. She gave up her forty-year opposition to the Equal Rights Amendment and presided over the Commission on the Status of Women that Kennedy appointed.

There were many changes in Eleanor's personal life after Franklin's death. She transferred ownership of Val-Kill, except for her own cottage, to her son Elliott, who also managed her successful ventures into television and became her literary representative. In April 1953 Mal-

vina Thompson, the secretary and assistant who shared the Val-Kill house with her, died. She was "the person who made life possible for me," she once said.

Another familiar, Earl Miller, after service in World War II, retired to Florida. In 1948 Miller's wife named Eleanor as correspondent in a suit for divorce. A compromise settlement between the Millers resulted in the papers being sealed. Lorena Hickok moved to Hyde Park village, where Eleanor worked with her on *Ladies of Courage* (1954). She was one of several close friends.

In 1960, at age seventy-five, Eleanor was diagnosed as having a-plastic anemia. She recovered sufficiently to go to Europe in February 1962 to do some recordings for Henry Morgenthau III's "Prospects of Mankind." Later in the year her illness flared up again while she worked on her final book, *Tomorrow Is Now* (1963); she made a trip to Campobello for the dedication of the FDR Memorial Bridge. Her evaluation of Franklin had mellowed: "I was never ahead of Franklin in social reform or any of those things," she insisted to reporter Carl Rowan. "I wanted things to happen faster, but Franklin always knew what he wanted."

Eleanor died in New York City, her disease finally diagnosed by a visiting physician as a rare bone-marrow tuberculosis. "I think I am pretty much a fatalist," she had told Edward R. Murrow in 1953. "You have to accept whatever comes and the only important thing is that you meet it with courage and with the best that you have to give."

[Eleanor Roosevelt's papers, including oral histories given by many of her associates, are at the Franklin D. Roosevelt Library, Hyde Park, N.Y. In addition to works mentioned in the text, she wrote *It's Up to the Women* (1933); *The Moral Basis of Democracy* (1940); *India and the Awakening East* (1953); *On My Own* (1958); *You Learn by Living* (1960). She published many of her father's letters in *Hunting Big Game in the Eighties* (1933).

See also James Roosevelt and Sidney Shalett, *Affectionately, F.D.R.* (1959); Lorena Hickok, *Reluctant First Lady* (1962); Joseph P. Lash, *Eleanor and Franklin* (1971), and *Eleanor: The Years Alone* (1972); Elliott Roosevelt and James Brough, *An Untold Story* (1973); Kenneth S. Davis, *Invincible Summer, Based on the Recollections of Marion Dickerman* (1974); James Roosevelt, *My Parents: A Differing View* (1976); and Doris Faber, *The Life of Lorena Hickok* (1980).]

JOSEPH P. LASH

ROWE, LYNWOOD THOMAS (Jan. 11, 1912–Jan. 8, 1961), major-league baseball pitcher, was born in Waco, Tex., the son of Thomas D. Rowe, a circus trapeze performer and railroad man. He grew up in El Dorado, Ark., and attended Hugh Goodwin Elementary School and El Dorado High School, where he was All-State at basketball, football, and baseball, and interscholastic golf champion, before embarking on a career in baseball. In a Church League semipro game he bested his high school coach, Alva Waddell, which prompted a headline in the *El Dorado Daily News:* "Schoolboy Beats Teacher." The nickname "Schoolboy" followed him throughout his career.

In 1932, Rowe was signed by Eddie Goosetree, scout for the Detroit Tigers. In his only minor-league season, at Beaumont of the Texas League, the six-foot, four-inch right-hander compiled a 19–7 record. He joined the Tigers in 1933 and played under Bucky Harris. His first major-league game was a 3–0 shutout of the Chicago White Sox. Rowe finished his first season in the majors with a 7–4 record and a 3.58 earned run average.

The following season proved to be his finest in the major leagues; he led the Tigers from a fifth-place finish to the World Series, the highlight of the season being his sixteen-game winning streak, which tied an American League record shared by Walter Johnson (1912), Joe Wood (1912), and Lefty Grove (1931). On August 29 his attempt to break the record, by recording a seventeenth consecutive victory, brought 33,318 to Shibe Park in Philadelphia. But Rowe lasted only six innings and lost the game. His season record was twenty-four wins and eight losses. In the second game of the World Series against the St. Louis Cardinals, he won in twelve innings and retired twenty-two consecutive batters, a World Series record that stood until New York Yankee Don Larsen's perfect game in 1956. On the morning of the sixth game he showed up with a swollen pitching hand and proceeded to lose the game, 4–3. Throughout the game he was harassed by the Cardinal players because of a statement he had made on a local radio interview. At the end of that radio program, he had asked, "How'm I doin', Edna?" Three days after the World Series, on Oct. 11, 1934, he married Edna Mary Skinner. They had two children.

In 1935, Rowe, with a record of 19–13, again led the Tigers to the World Series and, this time, a world championship. In 1936 he won nineteen games but developed a sore arm that plagued him for the rest of his career. After a dismal season in 1937 and two ineffective starts in April of the following season, he was sent to

Beaumont, Tex. He completed a successful comeback with Detroit in 1940, when he led the American League with a 16–3 record. He also pitched in his third and last World Series, dropping two games to the champion Cincinnati Reds. His career with the Tigers ended in April 1942, when he was sold to the Brooklyn Dodgers for $15,000. After spending most of that season in the minors at Montreal, he was sold to the Philadelphia Phillies. He had a 14–8 record with the Phillies in 1943 and then spent two years in the navy.

After the war Rowe returned to the Phillies for the final four years of his major-league playing career. In 1949 he asked for his release. The following year he played his last baseball game, for the San Diego club of the Pacific Coast League. In 1951 he managed an Eastern League farm club at Williamsport, Pa. During the 1954 and 1955 seasons Rowe served as a pitching coach with Detroit. Beginning in 1957, he was a scout for Detroit in charge of locating talent in Arkansas, Louisiana, Mississippi, and eastern Texas. Rowe died in El Dorado, Ark. His death was reported with front-page headlines in Detroit, where he was considered one of the most popular players in the team's history.

Rowe was extremely superstitious. He carried amulets and talismans, and, although a right-hander, would always pick up his glove with the left hand. His "color" was epitomized by his constant talking to the baseball. Before delivering a pitch, he was known to wrap his fingers around the ball and say to it, "Edna, honey, let's go." He rode an overpowering fastball, a quick-breaking curve, and a change of pace through fifteen seasons in the majors. Much of his success he credited to his confidence in catcher Mickey Cochrane. Rowe's career record included 158 victories and 101 defeats.

[See Frederick Lieb, *The Detroit Tigers* (1946); and Joe Falls, *Detroit Tigers* (1975). Also see David Q. Voigt, *American Baseball*, II (1970). Obituaries are in the *Detroit News, New York Times,* and *Philadelphia Evening News,* Jan. 9, 1961; and *Time,* Jan. 20, 1961.]

DANIEL FRIO

ROYCE, RALPH (June 28, 1890–Aug. 7, 1965), U.S. Air Force officer, test pilot, and civil servant, was born in Marquette, Mich., the son of George Arthur Royce, a bookkeeper, and Katherine Ely.

Following graduation from Hancock (Mich.) High School in 1908, Royce was a part-time reporter on the local newspaper before going to a preparatory school in Findlay, Ohio, for a year in order to qualify for entrance to West Point. He then worked briefly as a laborer prior to entering the U.S. Military Academy in November 1909. He was graduated and commissioned a second lieutenant, and was assigned to the Twenty-sixth Infantry on June 12, 1914, having placed eighty-ninth in a class of 107 that included such luminaries as Carl Spaatz.

Royce served with the Twenty-sixth Infantry in Texas and was also attached to the Eleventh Infantry in Naco, Ariz., until February 1915. He then entered the Signal Corps Aviation School at San Diego, Calif., from which he graduated in May 1916. He was immediately assigned to the First Aero Squadron at Columbus, N. Mex., where he flew the first airplanes used in an American military action as part of the Pershing expedition pursuing Pancho Villa. Royce married Lillian S. Scott on Sept. 18, 1916. They had one son.

With American entry into World War I, Royce assumed command of the First Aero Squadron. In August 1917 he took the squadron to France, where he flew for the First and Third Army Corps at Château-Thierry and during the St.-Mihiel and Meuse-Argonne offensives.

A short, compact man given to colorful language and characterized as "totally fearless," Royce served as an example to his pilots by initiating the first reconnaissance flights directly into the teeth of enemy resistance, taking his squadrons well beyond the enemy lines. His dash and intrepidity won him the Croix de Guerre and promotion to lieutenant colonel by September 1918. It also laid the foundation of his career as one of the creators of a modern air force.

After returning from France in 1919, Royce went to Fort Sam Houston, Tex., as assistant air officer. The following year he was given command of Carlstrom Field, Fla., and two years later he took charge of Brooks Field, Tex. He trained at the Air Corps Tactical School at Langley Field, Va., and graduated from the Command and General Staff School at Fort Leavenworth, Kans., in 1928. As an aggressive and ambitious airman, Royce found the sedentary life of a training officer unappealing, and plunged into the peripatetic pursuit of military reward, leaving little time for family life.

In 1930, Royce took command of the First Pursuit Group at Selfridge Field, Mich., where he personally led a flight of eighteen planes on a test flight to Spokane, Wash., and back in temperatures as low as forty-five degrees below zero. For this "Arctic flight" he was awarded the William MacKay Trophy. He went on to serve the War Department general staff in Washington, D.C., where he attended the Army War College in 1933–1934. Royce was operations officer for a flight to Alaska in the summer of 1934. He then returned to Selfridge as base commander, and in 1937 was sent as air officer to the Philippines, where he spent some time as adviser to the Chinese air force. In 1939 he took command of the Seventh Bombardment Group at Hamilton Field, Calif.

With the coming of World War II, Royce's life changed greatly. In 1941 he became military attaché for air in London, and was promoted to brigadier general. In the following year he was transferred to Australia. In June 1942 he commanded the Northeast Sector of the Allied Air Forces, during which time he planned for the operation that evacuated General Douglas MacArthur from the Philippines. Later that year, Royce led a mission of thirteen bombers from Australia to the Philippines that resulted in the sinking of four transports and the smashing of airstrips and harbors. For this action he received the Distinguished Service Cross.

Royce was next dispatched to Maxwell Field, Ala., as commander, and in the spring of 1943 was given command of the First Air Force at Mitchell Field, N.Y. That September he became commander of the U.S. Air Forces in the Middle East, with headquarters in Cairo. In 1944 he was at Ascot, England, as deputy commander of the Ninth Air Force, which was preparing for the invasion of France. Royce was air officer aboard the cruiser *Augusta* on D day. Upon landing in France a day later, he was made deputy commander of the Allied Air Force and, immediately afterward, commander of the First Provisional Tactical Air Force at Vittel, France, where he served until February 1945. For this service he was awarded the Distinguished Service Cross, the Distinguished Service Medal, the Distinguished Flying Cross, his Second Legion of Merit, and the Legion of Honor commendation.

Royce's final years in the service were spent as commanding general of the Army Air Corps Personnel Distribution Command in Atlantic City, N.J. (later moved to Louisville, Ky.). He retired on a disability pension with the rank of major general on June 30, 1946. His wife had died in 1944, and Royce married on Feb. 9, 1945, Agnes Berges, a former executive of the Savoy-Plaza Hotel in New York, whom he had met when she was a Red Cross volunteer in Cairo, Egypt. Following his retirement, the Royces lived in Coral Gables, Fla. Royce remained in retirement except from Feb. 1, 1948, to Aug. 1, 1949, when he was director of the Department of Economic Development for the state of Michigan. He died at Homestead Air Force Base, Fla.

[References to Royce can be found in vol. 9 (1950) of Cullum's *Biographical Register* of graduates of West Point. The academy's alumni periodical, *Assembly,* for 1965 has a useful piece. The West Point Library has Royce's personnel form, completed when he entered the academy. An obituary is in the *New York Times,* Aug. 11, 1965.]

JACK J. CARDOSO

RUARK, ROBERT CHESTER (Dec. 29, 1915–July 1, 1965), journalist and novelist, was born in Southport, N.C., the son of Robert Chester Ruark, Sr., a bookkeeper, and of Charlotte Adkins, a teacher. While he was still a child the family moved about twenty-five miles north to Wilmington, N.C., where he completed high school at the age of fifteen. But it was in Southport, a small fishing village, that he spent all the time he could with his grandfather Adkins, a retired sea captain. Adkins is affectionately portrayed as the "Old Man" in Ruark's autobiographical novels, *The Old Man and the Boy* (1957) and *The Old Man's Boy Grows Older* (1961).

In the "Author's Note" to *The Old Man and the Boy* Ruark sums up his youth: "Anybody who reads this book is bound to realize that I had a real fine time as a kid."

The Old Man's Boy Grows Older starts with the Old Man's funeral in 1931, when Ruark was about to go to college: "It suddenly occurred to me that I was educated [by the Old Man] before I saw a college. I made up my mind right then that someday I would learn to be a writer and write some of the stuff the Old Man had taught me."

Ruark worked his way through the University of North Carolina, where he also wrote for the *Yackety Yack* and did artwork for the *Carolina Magazine* and the *Buccaneer.* He majored in journalism and graduated in 1935 with a B.A. He then worked as a reporter-editor-subscription seller of the *Hamlet* (N.C.) *News-Messenger* at a salary of ten dollars per week. In 1936 he shipped as an ordinary merchant seaman on the *Sundance* sailing from Savannah to Liverpool and Hamburg. (He had also been an accountant for the WPA.) In 1937 he moved to Washington, D.C., where he became a copyboy for the *Daily News.* He married Virginia Webb on Aug. 12, 1938. They had no children.

At the *Daily News* Ruark rose from copyboy to sportswriter to newswriter to top feature writer and by 1942 to assistant city editor. Ernest Havemann identifies one experience as crucial to his rise: "On Pearl Harbor Day, when Ruark was 25, he was sitting in the press box covering the Washington Redskins. . . . His office . . . gave him the job of rounding up all the editors, reporters and linotype men who were watching the game. . . . He managed to flush out a crew, rushed back to the office to help get out an extra and went to bed two and one-half days later. . . . He was brash, ambitious, cocky, fast and good."

In 1942 Ruark became Washington correspondent for the Newspaper Enterprise Association Service. From 1942 to 1945 he served as an ensign with the navy and for a while was a gunnery officer with Atlantic and Mediterranean convoys. He later saw duty in the Pacific and nearly lost an arm when his jeep overturned in the Solomons. When he recovered, he returned to duty as a press censor.

In 1945 he became the Washington correspondent for the Scripps-Howard Newspaper Alliance, and the following year he became a columnist for the Scripps-Howard Newspapers and United Feature Service in New York. His column was eventually syndicated in 104 newspapers. He also wrote articles and a column for *Field and Stream* magazine.

In 1947 Ruark went to Italy to report on the "sad state" of military personnel there. In the same year his first book, *Grenadine Etching,* appeared. By then, according to *Life,* he was "the most talked-about reporter in the U.S. today."

Ruark was now earning $40,000 a year and living the high life in New York. But he "felt like a complete fraud." In 1950, emulating his hero Ernest Hemingway, he went to East Africa as a hunter. Two of his novels were Book-of-the-Month Club selections: *Something of Value* (1955), on the Mau Mau, and *Uhuru* (1962), both of which resulted from his experiences there. (In the early 1960's, he and his wife acted as guides.)

After 1952 Ruark lived in Spain, England, and Africa. (He said he particularly disliked life in New York.) He made his main home in Palamos, Spain, and had a penthouse in London. He and his wife were divorced a few years before his death.

On Apr. 30, 1965, Ruark discontinued his United Feature Syndicate column; he had written 4,000 columns in twenty years. He died in London.

[Ruark's manuscripts, proofs in various forms, correspondence, scrapbooks, photographs, and miscellaneous items are in the "Robert Chester Ruark Papers: 1942–1965," of the Southern Historical Collection and Manuscripts Department, Wilson Library, University of North Carolina at Chapel Hill (use of this material is restricted). The material is described in Beverly Lake Barge, "A Catalog of the Collected Papers and Manuscripts of Robert C. Ruark" (M.A. thesis, University of North Carolina at Chapel Hill, 1969).

For other biographical information, see "Ruark's Pet Hates Pay Off in Print," *Life*, Oct. 20, 1947; and Ernest Havemann, "Robert Ruark: Brash Country Boy Makes Good as Columnist, Gets Plenty of Caviar," *ibid.*, Nov. 14, 1949; *North Carolina Authors* (1952); and Stuart Rose, ed., *Use Enough Gun* (1966). The major obituary is in the *New York Times*, July 1, 1965; and major sketches by a former teacher and former fellow student are in the *Raleigh* (N.C.) *News and Observer*, July 11, 1965.]

DOUGLAS J. MCMILLAN

RUBINSTEIN, HELENA (Dec. 25, 1870–Apr. 1, 1965), beauty expert and cosmetics manufacturer, was born in Cracow, Poland, the daughter of Horace Rubinstein and Augusta Silberfeld. Her father earned a living by purchasing and reselling eggs and other foodstuffs. The eldest of eight girls, she early assumed a variety of responsibilities at home and in her father's business, experiences that she later said were valuable in the international business world.

Rubinstein attended the public schools of Cracow, and at the age of eighteen she entered the medical school of the University of Cracow. She loved the laboratory work, which later proved helpful in her cosmetics business, but found the sickroom so distasteful that she quit school after two years. At this time she precipitated a serious family crisis by refusing to marry the man her father had chosen for her. Hoping that a change of scenery would help her settle down, her parents consented to her traveling to Queensland, Australia, to live with an uncle. Life on a sheep ranch proved to be disagreeable, and in the late 1890's she accepted a position as governess to a prominent family in Melbourne.

When Madame Rubinstein, as she was to be known professionally throughout her career, left Cracow, she took with her a supply of a special face cream that had long been used by her family. Finding that women in Australia were eager to buy products that would improve their complexions, in 1902 she established the country's first beauty salon in Melbourne. She was swamped with orders for the cream and within a few years had amassed a small fortune from its sale. She subsequently invented and sold a wide

variety of other preparations, marketing at one time as many as 629 different items.

Rubinstein always insisted that the key to her success was not just the products she sold but her emphasis on teaching women how to use them properly. In the early years of the twentieth century she studied with dermatologists in Vienna, Dresden, Berlin, Munich, and Paris, and in 1908 she opened a salon in London, leaving the business in Australia in the hands of two of her sisters. In London she became one of the first to make the use of makeup widely popular. In 1907, she married Edward William Titus, an American journalist; they had two sons. Titus played an important role in developing Helena Rubinstein's advertising campaigns, particularly the emphasis on scientific research. For years, no Helena Rubinstein advertisement appeared without a picture of Rubinstein in her white laboratory coat.

In 1912, Rubinstein opened a third salon, in Paris, and the family lived there until Titus persuaded Rubinstein to move to the United States in 1915. She began to build in New York what was to become a worldwide corporation, opening salons across the country, each staffed by women trained to demonstrate and sell the growing line of beauty products. In the 1920's the business expanded to include salons in Milan, Vienna, Toronto, and Rome.

In 1928 Edward Titus' request for a divorce led Rubinstein to sell a two-thirds interest in her firm for $7.3 million in a dramatic effort to rescue her personal life. The purchasers, Lehman Brothers, a Wall Street banking firm, faced serious difficulty when they tried to convert the company to the production of low-priced cosmetics. As complaints increased, Rubinstein tried to repurchase the business, but her offers were rebuffed until after the stock market crash of 1929, when she was able to buy back controlling interest in the firm for $1.5 million.

During the 1930's the business continued to expand, with increasingly fierce competition between Rubinstein and her arch rival, Elizabeth Arden. In November 1937 she divorced Titus and on June 11, 1938, married Prince Artchil Gourielli-Tchkonia, of Russian Georgia. In the 1940's they established New York's first salon for men.

World War II forced the closing of most Helena Rubinstein salons in Europe, but new ones opened in Rio de Janeiro (1940) and Buenos Aires (1942). Rubinstein contributed to the war effort by donating her services as makeup artist in Hollywood and creating cosmetics for disfigured servicemen. When the war ended, she went immediately to Europe to begin rebuilding her business.

In the 1950's Rubinstein opened salons in Japan, and in 1959 she worked personally in her firm's booth at the American Trade Fair in Moscow. In the same year she concluded an agreement with Israel allowing her to build a cosmetics factory in that country. In return she contributed $250,000 for the construction of the Helena Rubinstein Pavilion of Contemporary Art in Tel Aviv.

Rubinstein was also widely known as a collector of art, jewelry, and antiques. At her death her collections of art and jewelry were each valued at more than $1 million. Her jewelry ranged from priceless gems to costume items purchased at dime stores. Her art collection began with African sculpture, then went on to encompass works by many of the masters of the twentieth century, including Renoir, Picasso, and Degas. These, together with her designer clothing and antiques, were auctioned off after her death. In addition to other wealth, Rubinstein owned as many as seven homes and at the time of her death, in New York City, maintained residences in New York, Paris, London, and Greenwich, Conn.

[Rubinstein wrote *The Art of Feminine Beauty* (1930); *This Way to Beauty* (1936); *Food for Beauty* (1938); *Je suis esthéticienne* (1957); and *My Life for Beauty* (1965), her autobiography. Books on her life include Patrick O'Higgins, *Madame: An Intimate Biography of Helena Rubinstein* (1971), by her personal secretary and traveling companion; and Maxene Fabe, *Beauty Millionaire* (1972). The following articles give perhaps the best comprehensive view: Elaine Brown Keiffer, "Madame Rubinstein, the Little Lady from Krakow," *Life*, July 21, 1941; Richard Carter, "High Priestess of the Beauty Business," *Life*, Mar. 17, 1958; and T. F. James, "Princess of the Beauty Business," *Cosmopolitan*, June 1959. An obituary appeared in the *New York Times*, Apr. 2, 1965.]

REBECCA ANN SHEPHERD

RUDITSKY, BARNEY (Jan. 3, 1898–Oct. 18, 1962), policeman and private detective, was born Barnett Ruditsky in the East End of London, England, the son of Phillip Ruditsky and Blooma Marin. His father was a boot finisher. Little is known about Ruditsky's childhood, and much of his later life remains shadowy. As a child he was taken by his parents to South Africa, back to England, and around 1908 to New York. He grew up on the East Side of Manhattan. In 1916 he served in the U.S. Army on the Mexican border, and during World War I he served in France. After the war he returned to New York and in 1921 joined the New York City police force. On Feb. 18, 1923, Ruditsky married Mollie Feiner; they had one son.

In August 1923, while patrolling in a tough West Side Manhattan district, the slightly built Ruditsky manhandled a large, athletic suspect who resisted arrest. The local magistrate was impressed, Ruditsky was cited for bravery, and the *New York Times* complimented him. In 1924 he was promoted to detective. In 1926 the Ruditskys celebrated their third wedding anniversary at a late-night supper club. On their way home, accompanied by a friend, they spotted a holdup in progress in a confectionery store. Ruditsky drew his pistol and charged into the store to confront two robbers, one of them armed. When the gunman pointed his pistol at Ruditsky, the detective knocked the robber out with the butt of his own weapon. Mollie Ruditsky picked up the robber's gun. The unarmed robber dashed out the door, and as Ruditsky followed, he ordered his wife to guard the disarmed robber. He chased the second robber a block and a half and caught him, much to the surprise of onlookers, who called a police patrol wagon.

In 1928 Ruditsky arrested the "poison ivy" gang in a Turkish bath on Second Street. Shortly thereafter, working with Detective Johnny Broderick, he rounded up the "pear buttons" gang on the West Side. Broderick and Ruditsky became leaders of a special antigangster squad assigned to combat organized crime throughout New York City. Ruditsky fought against such men as Jack ("Legs") Diamond and Arthur ("Dutch Schultz") Flegenheimer. He was responsible for arresting Abe Reles ("Kid Twist"), who was sent to prison but later reemerged to become a key figure in Brooklyn's Murder, Inc.

In 1941 Ruditsky retired after twenty years on the force. During World War II he was an army officer assigned to a unit that guarded prisoners in North Africa. In 1943 he was wounded by shrapnel. After the war Ruditsky became a private detective, and in 1948, following press reports linking him to organized crime, he moved to Los Angeles. There he was a co-owner of Sherry's Cocktail Lounge and Restaurant, a Sunset Strip hangout for underworld figure Mickey Cohen, who in July 1949 narrowly escaped a late-night shotgun assassination in front of the restaurant. During these years Ruditsky was also co-owner of a travel agency with George Jessel and George Raft.

As a private detective for and against Hollywood stars, the most famous and bizarre episode of Ruditsky's career occurred in 1954, when film star Marilyn Monroe was divorcing baseball star Joe Di Maggio. Di Maggio hired Ruditsky to spy on Monroe either, as Di Maggio later claimed, to obtain a reconciliation or to gain evidence that would so besmirch her reputation that she could not collect alimony. According to later testimony, Di Maggio heard that Monroe was spending the night in a borrowed Hollywood apartment; he concluded that his estranged wife had a lover and with the support of Frank Sinatra urged Ruditsky to expose her adultery. Accompanied by several men, one armed with a camera, Ruditsky kicked down the door of the apartment—and amid popping flashbulbs and terrorized shrieks found in bed a lone woman, who was not Monroe. He had broken into the wrong apartment. The "Wrong-Door Raid" became a Hollywood legend, was sensationalized in *Confidential* magazine, and revealed that private detective Ruditsky had no state license. His second wife, Reggie Darryl, died in September 1957 at the age of thirty.

In April 1959 Ruditsky's memoirs of his exploits as a police detective during Prohibition became the basis for an NBC television series, "The Lawless Years." James Gregory played the role of Barney Ruditsky in a show that *Variety* praised for its technical accuracy, its attention to detail, and its ability to capture the spirit of the 1920's. Although the series played for only fifty-two episodes in two seasons, it spurred an imitator, "The Untouchables," which became one of the most popular shows on television. Ruditsky continued as a technical consultant for police and detective movies and television shows. He died in Los Angeles.

[See the *New York Times*, Aug. 15, 1923; Feb. 22, 1926; July 21 and 29, 1949; Feb. 28 and Mar. 2, 1957; *Los Angeles Times*, July 17, 1957; *Variety*, Apr. 22, 1959; and Robert F. Slatzer, *The Life and Curious Death of Marilyn Monroe* (1974). There are obituaries in the *New York Times*, *Los Angeles Times*, and *Los Angeles Herald-Examiner*, Oct. 19, 1962; *Washington Post*, Oct. 20, 1962; and *Variety*, Oct. 24, 1962.]

W. J. RORABAUGH

RUMMEL, JOSEPH FRANCIS (Oct. 14, 1876–Nov. 8, 1964), Roman Catholic archbishop, was born in Steinmauern, Germany, the son of Gustav Rummel and Teresa Bollweber. The family migrated to the United States in 1882, and he became a naturalized citizen with his parents in 1888. His father, at first a self-employed shoemaker, later became an agent for a New York real estate firm. Rummel received a classical education leading to a B.A. degree at St. Anselm's College, Manchester, N.H. (1896). He was drawn to the priesthood and was accepted by Archbishop Michael A. Corrigan of New York City as one of the charter students at the new St. Joseph's Seminary (popularly known as "Dunwoodie"), Yonkers, where he studied philosophy, the humanities, and theology (1896–1899). Seeking a licentiate in theology, he then enrolled as a seminarian at the North American College in Rome. Pietro Cardinal Respighi ordained him in the Basilica of St. John Lateran on May 24, 1902. A year later Rummel earned a doctorate in sacred theology from the Pontifical Urban University.

Rummel served as a curate at St. Joseph's in New York City (1903–1907); as pastor of St. Peter's in Kingston, N.Y. (1907–1915); as vicar forane (dean) of Ulster and Sullivan counties (1912–1915); as pastor of St. Anthony of Padua in the Bronx (1915–1924); and as pastor of St. Joseph of the Holy Family in Harlem (1924–1928). He also held the posts of judge and vice-official of the matrimonial tribunal. He then became executive secretary (1923–1924) of the German Relief Committee, a national agency established to aid the impoverished people, especially destitute children, of his war-ravaged native land. Pope Pius XI named Rummel a papal chamberlain with the title of very reverend monsignor on Apr. 24, 1924. Four years later Pius named Rummel ordinary of Omaha.

Conscientious and methodical, Rummel promptly standardized accounting procedures for the 135 parishes of the Nebraska diocese. In 1930 he launched a successful campaign for funds. His intention was to expand St. James Orphanage and complete St. Cecilia's Cathedral, both in Omaha, but because of the Great Depression much of the money went to relief work within the diocese. Rummel also brought the Sixth National Eucharistic Congress to Omaha (Sept. 23–25, 1930). His meticulous planning made this religious gathering one of the most successful of its kind.

In 1935, Pius XI promoted Rummel to the New Orleans archbishopric. His arrival in Louisiana on May 14, 1935, was a gala occasion. Following a visit to three children's protectories in Marrero, across the Mississippi from New Orleans, port vessels escorted him downriver to the foot of Canal Street while steam whistles blew and ships' bells clanged. After touching city soil and receiving official greetings, the archbishop-designate headed a parade of several thousand men and boys who marched to rousing music through the central business district.

Rummel's dignified presence and poise, combined with his affable manner, his physical stamina, and his deep spirituality, won him the esteem of citizens of all faiths and persuasions in New Orleans. From the outset he committed himself to schedules that took him to all corners of the archdiocese. His jurisdiction as ordinary of the Archdiocese of New Orleans covered some 13,200 square miles in twenty-three southeastern Louisiana parishes (counties). The area included, besides New Orleans with a population of about 600,000, the state capital of Baton Rouge, burgeoning suburbs, growing towns and struggling villages, meandering bayous and marshy hinterlands—all with inhabitants of varied ethnic origins, educational backgrounds, and cultures.

Robust health permitted Rummel to continue liturgical functions and public appearances, to deliver numerous sermons and speeches, to compose pastoral letters, and to maintain a voluminous correspondence until a fall at Baton Rouge in October 1960. By the next spring, although approaching eighty-five, he was again presiding over church functions and directing the affairs of the archdiocese.

Rummel's private secretary has stated that the archbishop personally dictated or wrote every one of the thousands of documents bearing his signature. He rarely used a text or notes in the pulpit or at a lectern; indeed, impaired vision in later life would not allow him to do so.

At crucial times Rummel spoke out on controversial issues, both moral and social. He was a vocal proponent of legislative controls when landlords attempted to exact higher rents during a business recession, and forbade games of chance at church functions, insisting that church support should be motivated by voluntary stewardship. He opposed "right to work" laws introduced in the 1950's by the state legislature. Above all, Rummel was a staunch defender of human rights, especially of racial justice. His strong stand on desegregation, especially as enunciated in the pastoral letters "Blessed Are the Peacemakers" (Mar. 15, 1953) and "The Morality of Racial Segregation" (Feb. 11, 1956), caused an adverse reaction by many white Catholics and by the vast majority of the Louisiana legislators. Rummel was the first Catholic bishop to publicize, through the Archdiocesan School Board, of which he was president, a resolution upholding the U.S. Supreme Court decision in the case of Brown v. Board of Education of Topeka (347 U.S. 483) in May 1954. His stand on racial issues was reinforced in 1958 when his colleagues of the American

hierarchy promulgated a national statement, "Discrimination and the Christian Conscience," declaring, as he had done unequivocally in his diocese, that racial segregation and discrimination are immoral.

The record shows that Rummel continuously used his powers of suasion to prepare whites for the day when segregation would become illegal as well as morally untenable. His position on the matter of social justice surfaced as early as June 1949, with the issuance of the Acta et Decreta Synodi Septimae Novae Aureliae ("Acts and Decrees of the Seventh New Orleans Synod"). Rummel called the synod, presided over it, and personally translated its codification into Latin.

Although he authorized more than $100 million worth of construction—schools, churches, chapels, convents, rectories, hospitals, gymnasiums, seminary buildings, a new chancery, and other structures—Rummel was less a "brick and mortar" bishop than a teacher and prophet. By word and action he sensitized the conscience of Catholics confided to his care. He died in New Orleans.

[Materials on Rummel are in the archives of the Archdiocese of New Orleans and of the Chancery, New Orleans. His library was given to Notre Dame Seminary, New Orleans. See Roger Baudier, The Catholic Church in Louisiana (1939; repr. 1972); and "Archbishop's Silver Jubilee as Ordinary of New Orleans," supp. to Catholic Action of the South, May 15, 1960. Obituaries are in the New Orleans Times-Picayune and New York Times, Nov. 9, 1964.]

HENRY C. BEZOU

SAARINEN, EERO (Aug. 20, 1910–Sept. 1, 1961), architect, was born in Kirkkonummi (Kyrkslätt), Finland, the son of Eliel Saarinen, an architect, and of Loja Gesellius, a sculptor. He was raised with his elder sister Pipsan (Eva Lisa) in the rambling lakeside home and studio Hvitträsk, in which numerous cultural celebrities were entertained: the German art critic Julius Meier-Graefe, Maxim Gorki, Gustav Mahler, the Finnish painter Akseli Gallén-Kallela, the Swedish sculptor Carl Milles, and Jean Sibelius.

Saarinen, who was ambidextrous, drew with amazing facility. He also learned the spirit of moral resolution that the Finns call sisu, a capacity to keep going beyond the limits of energy and expected resources. In 1922 he took first place in a Swedish matchstick design contest. About the same time his father won the $20,000 second prize in the competition for the Chicago Tribune Tower, an award that brought him international recognition. Eliel

Saarinen then moved his family to the United States, settling at Evanston, Ill., in 1923. Until World War II the family returned to Finland every summer.

The elder Saarinen was soon invited to teach at the University of Michigan at Ann Arbor. Among his students were J. Robert F. Swanson, his future son-in-law, and Henry S. Booth, son of George Gough Booth, publisher of the *Detroit Evening News*. Booth was so impressed by what his son told him that he decided to ask Eliel Saarinen to design a group of educational institutions at Cranbrook, his estate in Bloomfield Hills near Detroit. In 1925 the Saarinens moved there after a $12 million foundation had been established to implement the concept.

In some ways Cranbook, a center of high culture and serious environmental thought in the heartland of the United States, was an Americanized version of Hvitträsk. It represented a microcosm of Eliel Saarinen's urban design ideas—perhaps even a partial realization of the propositions laid out in the great scheme for Munkkiniemi-Haaga (Munksnäs-Haga), a new decentralized community for the outskirts of Helsinki (Helsingfors) of 1910–1915, which projected a concept of an ordered total environment. The entire family's creative powers were brought to bear at the Cranbrook complex and the Kingswood School for Girls (1929–1930). Eero Saarinen was responsible for the furniture design. This work was without lasting importance, but its vigorous handling revealed a sculptural inclination that later informed his architecture.

For a time Saarinen seriously intended to become a sculptor, and in 1929 spent a year at the Académie de la Grande Chaumière in Paris. But he finally resolved to become an architect. In 1931 he entered Yale University, then offering a traditional program in the Beaux Arts method. It is likely that the status of Yale and contact with potential clients were among the principal reasons for the decision. By graduating with honors in 1934, Saarinen demonstrated a capacity to work well within a limiting framework, eventually enabling him to combine, in his own career, unorthodox design thinking with allegiance to conservative, moneyed institutional clients.

After graduation Saarinen worked briefly in New York City as a draftsman in the office of Norman Bel Geddes (a connection which led to a meeting with Charles Eames in 1937). He won the Charles O. Matcham fellowship for European travel and spent 1934–1936 visiting the great monuments of the Continent and

Egypt, and undertaking the remodeling of a theater in Helsinki, Finland, with Jarl Eklund.

Upon his return to America, Saarinen joined his father's practice in Bloomfield Hills; he also served as an instructor at Cranbrook (1939–1949). He became a United States citizen in 1940. At his invitation Charles Eames took over the Department of Experimental Design in 1940. Eames and Saarinen then collaborated the same year on the design of furniture using rubber-bonded plywood and metal. The furniture was entered in the Organic Design Competition sponsored by the Museum of Modern Art (1940); they won first prize in the two main categories. World War II postponed exhibition of the entries until 1946—when plywood bonding and construction techniques had advanced sufficiently for the furniture to be put into production by Knoll Associates. Saarinen further developed that design line in 1948 with the "womb chair," also produced by Knoll.

In 1941–1947, Saarinen was a designer in the firm of Saarinen, Swanson and Associates, which included his father, Eliel; his sister, Pipsan; her husband, Robert F. Swanson; and Eero's wife, Lilian Swann, a former Cranbrook student and sculptor whom he had married in 1939 (they had two children). While the influence of his father can be seen in works such as his Kleinhans Music Hall in Buffalo (1938–1940) and the Des Moines Art Center (1944–1948), other works reflect his modern interests: the innovative Crow Island School at Winnetka, Ill. (1939–1941), the A. C. Wermuth House at Fort Wayne, Ind. (1941–1942), and especially the winning design in the Smithsonian Art Gallery competition (1939). The last, never built, was especially controversial as a potential incursion by modernism on the Capitol Mall. Charles Eames, who collaborated on the Smithsonian project, characterized Saarinen's method as a "rigorous analysis of related spatial and practical needs." According to Eames, Saarinen "made 100 studies of each element, picking the best, then he made 100 studies of the combinations of elements, then 100 studies of the combinations of combinations, etc."

This interest in a rational approach perhaps could be seen in the organic furniture, which had moved from craftsmanship to industrial design; Saarinen was attempting a functionalist, economical architecture liberated from pictorial considerations. This evolution was partly inspired by a belief in technology; the stretching of its limits could be seen in a suspension structure for a community center (1941), the PAC (pre-assembled component) house (1943), and an "unfolding house" (1945). In "Serving Suzy," a restaurant proposal of 1944, he introduced a mobile serving unit that came to customers—in some ways a harbinger of his "mobile lounge" concept for Dulles Airport at the end of his career. During World War II, Saarinen served in the Office of Strategic Services. He was also involved in Defense Department housing at Willow Run and Center Line, Mich. a level of professional practice without parallel in the experience of either Saarinen.

Saarinen, Swanson and Associates reorganized in 1947 as Saarinen, Saarinen and Associates, and obtained a commission for the General Motors (GM) Technical Center outside Detroit. The GM complex, originally projected in 1945 as a center rather like Cranbrook, was budgeted at $20 million. The project lapsed for three years, only to resume on the crest of postwar automobile sales, with a projected cost of $100 million for development of a 350-acre site at Warren, Mich.

At this point direction shifted from Eliel Saarinen to his son, who took control of the largest and most opulent commission awarded a modern architect up to that time. The inevitability of such a separation of identities had been foreshadowed earlier in 1948 when father and son had separately entered the Jefferson Westward Expansion Memorial competition. The jury's telegram announcing the first prize award was mistakenly addressed to Eliel. Several days later the error was corrected. Eero Saarinen's gigantic Gateway Arch (St. Louis), a reverse catenary curve in stainless steel 590 feet (eventually 690 feet) tall, stood as the symbol of his arrival. As critic Allan Temko has suggested, "The heir wore his father's crown before the old king's death."

After the death of Eliel Saarinen in 1950, Eero Saarinen had as a partner Joseph N. Lacy, who engaged the Detroit firm of Smith, Hinchman and Gryllis to assure the delivery of full professional services for the GM project. The design firm became Eero Saarinen and Associates, and its staff rose from ten to fifty, and finally to ninety during the course of the GM construction; joining the firm as partner and as chief designer respectively were John Dinkeloo and Kevin Roche.

At GM, Saarinen sought "to base the design on steel—the metal of the automobile . . . and base the construction on the advanced technology of the automobile age." Its aesthetic evoked the subdued modernism of Ludwig Mies van der Rohe. The technical innovations included development of a thin, porcelain-faced "sandwich" panel serving as both exterior skin and interior finish, an extremely thin-shell dome for the styling auditorium, and the use of neoprene "zipper gaskets" for all window glazing, modeled on the system used for installing automobile windshields. Through these new developments Saarinen sought to evoke the spirit of a product "essentially put together, as on an assembly line, out of mass-produced units."

The Finnish quality of *sisu* became the dynamic as the design firm expanded, and Saarinen characterized the working environment as that of constantly being *en charette*. After the GM complex he focused his practice on large-scale undertakings. In 1945, though, he collaborated with Eames on a demonstration house sponsored as Case Study Houses by *California Arts and Architecture,* one of which was built in 1950 for its editor, John Entenza. In 1953, he produced a second house in association with Alexander Girard. Both building plans were basically pinwheels within a square. These were virtually the only residential commissions in Saarinen's career.

Saarinen prepared plans for universities and colleges undergoing postwar expansion. Many involved variations in a curtain-wall aesthetic, such as Noyes House at Vassar College (1954–1958), the law school of the University of Chicago (1956–1960), and the IBM offices at Rochester, Minn. (1956–1959). However these projects may have been related in the use of a thin-skin, technologically produced enclosure, each had particular variations in overall form; Noyes House was a concave curve to complete a campus oval; the law school's faceted profile evoked surrounding Gothic Revival buildings; and IBM's convex curve both eliminated endless corridors and comfortably captured the crest of its hill site.

A break with a more predictable American variation of the modern style was achieved with the Kresge Auditorium and the interdenominational chapel at MIT (1953–1956), comprising two contrasting buildings. The auditorium had a shallow, thin, one-eighth dome with a triangular plan and supported at each point. The chapel had a circular, drumlike cylindrical shape. Saarinen baited those who would place him in the Mies aesthetic by further isolating the auditorium on a circular brick platform and the chapel in a circular sunken moat, then contending that they were more Miesian than were the surface resemblances at GM because of "a consistent structure and a forthright expression of that structure." He was exploring the principle of

671

universal space in the auditorium and the precise definition of pure forms in both.

Saarinen's thirteen-year marriage to Lily Swann ended in divorce in 1953; the following year on February 8 he married art critic Aline Bernstein Louchheim, whose life-style was more compatible with his own. They had one son.

Never committed to the International Style, Saarinen was free in his conceptions. His talent for formal invention and exploration appeared to leave him with little interest in universal vocabularies. His systematic, almost engineer-like insistence on analyzing the nature of a project suggested the possibility of an autonomous architecture for each building, a concept of "the style for the job." Although the 1950's in America could be characterized by a "search for form," Saarinen sought to direct a contemporary technology in a diverse architectural expression within the tradition of the early modern masters. He was committed to the advancement of the symbolic and environmental content of that tradition through the exploration of special architectural vernaculars for each project. Critic Reyner Banham observed, "It was not a style he had to offer . . . since no two functional problems are alike, no stylistically consistent approach could either serve or survive."

Saarinen once observed that the contemporary architecture of the 1950's was word-poor and that he was attempting to "enlarge its alphabet beyond ABC." His method included the spirit of the program, an aim beyond simple pragmatism; in a sense it embodied an updated notion of an associative architecture that would arouse emotions and affect sentiments. This was suggested in the evocation of a village image at Concordia College at Fort Wayne, Ind. (1953–1958), the David S. Ingalls Hockey Rink at Yale (1956–1959), and most clearly in the Trans World Terminal at Idlewild (now Kennedy) Airport (1956–1962), the complex curvilinear forms of which suggested a hovering bird.

One of Saarinen's most controversial projects was the United States Embassy at Grosvenor Square, London (1955–1960), a clearly modern pavilion nonetheless referential to its neo-Georgian context in the use of a portland stone facing. Saarinen's women's dormitories at the University of Pennsylvania (1957–1960) frankly engaged in allusion: figuratively they formed a castle, approached on a metaphorical drawbridge and presenting a tough, compatible image to its dark red-brick Philadelphia context while its interior was bright, delicate, white, and, in extending the allusions, feminine. His Ezra Stiles and Morse colleges at Yale (1958–

1962) evoked a range of associations, most strongly the image of a medieval community of scholars, and the conjunction of the two colleges suggested a townlike quality of public spaces. The CBS Building in New York City, the only tall building and the last design in his practice (1960–1964), suggested, in its solid, dominantly masonry facing a departure from the glass box.

Saarinen's inventiveness characterized much of mainstream architecture not only as a result of his clients and commissions, but also through a string of technical accomplishments extensively used in the 1960's and 1970's. In addition to using structure to give form, as in the realization of the Gateway Arch (1959–1964), or the integrative inclusion of support in his "pedestal" furniture (1958), he evolved thin-skin technology and reduced the curtain wall through a neoprene gasket technique (as mentioned earlier). Saarinen made dramatic use of mirror glass in the Bell Laboratories at Holmdell, N.J. (1957–1962), and self-rusting Cor-Ten steel was employed at Deere and Company, Moline, Ill. (1957–1963). All of these have been used extensively in architectural production since they were introduced.

What is remarkable is that Saarinen's independent work spanned a period of only eleven years. The conception of the Dulles International Airport at Chantilly, Va. (1958–1962), suggested that his approach could lead to a scale beyond the object limits of architecture itself: the perception of arrival in the movement to the terminal; the all-encompassing order of the terminal, whose potential for extension is explicit; and ultimately the detachment from the building itself by virtue of his "mobile lounge" presented a statement of liberation.

Saarinen died at Ann Arbor, Mich., of a brain tumor, within two weeks of the first symptom. Ten of his major design projects were in various stages of construction.

Eero Saarinen not only shared the same birthday as his father but also was engaged in a collaboration overshadowed in large part by Eliel Saarinen's half-century of architectural practice. Although a survey of Eero Saarinen's work after the mid-1930's indicates the gradual synthesis of his more modernist disposition, the recognized period of his independent work is 1950–1961. He did not live to see the completion of any of what are regarded as his major works, but among the Saarinen legacies are the many young architects who shared the milieu of the studio in Bloomfield Hills and were by the late 1970's the leading practitioners in America's professional architectural mainstream.

[Principal archives include the documents file of Kevin Roche–John Dinkeloo and Associates, which also contains scrapbooks and clippings on the various projects. The most complete personal collection is Manuscript Group no. 593 in the Manuscripts and Archives Department, Sterling Memorial Library, Yale University. No authoritative monograph on his work was produced during Saarinen's lifetime. Shortly after his death there appeared Aline B. Saarinen, ed., *Eero Saarinen on His Work* (1962), and Allan Temko, *Eero Saarinen,* Makers of Contemporary Architecture series (1962), both of which suffer from a eulogistic tone. Also see Rupert Spade, *Eero Saarinen,* Masters of Modern Architecture series (1971). Early accounts of his life and practice with his father are found in a book supervised by Saarinen, Albert Christ-Janer, *Eliel Saarinen* (1948; repr. 1979). A forthcoming monograph on Saarinen is being prepared by Peter Papademetriou for the series *GA Architect.* An obituary is in the *New York Times,* Sept. 2, 1961.]

PETER C. PAPADEMETRIOU

SACHS, PAUL JOSEPH (Nov. 24, 1878– Feb. 17, 1965), art educator and philanthropist, was born in New York City, the son of Samuel Sachs and Louisa Goldman, and the scion of bankers and teachers of German origin. He grew up in New York, attending the Collegiate Institute for Boys, presided over by his uncle, Julius Sachs.

In 1900, Sachs graduated from Harvard. Thereupon he joined the New York family firm of Goldman, Sachs and Company, investment bankers, directed by his father and grandfather Goldman. On Jan. 14, 1904, he married Meta Pollak of New York; they had three daughters. In the same year he was elected a partner of Goldman, Sachs.

A banker's career was an easy prediction; but even those who knew Sachs best had not reckoned with his persistent absorbtion with visual art. As a boy, Sachs was captivated by paintings, and he pasted prints from picture catalogs that he had ordered to the walls of his room. Upon reaching his majority he received a tidy sum from his grandfather Goldman; within a week he spent the entire amount on prints. At Harvard he started a print club, where like-minded students could meet to discuss their mutual interest.

In 1912 Sachs joined the visiting committee of the Fogg Art Museum. The director, Edward W. Forbes, had delivered the invitation in person. Clad in his Cantabrigian tweed and carrying a shabby briefcase, Forbes, the artist and professor, the unmistakable idealist and esthete, opened the door to another style of life. This was a turning point in Sachs's career; the lure of art and academe won over Wall Street. In 1915 Sachs was named assistant director of the Fogg Art Museum and joyously moved his family to Cambridge, Mass.

Sachs, the teacher-director, began as a lecturer at Wellesley College in 1916–1917. He rose rapidly in his new milieu. Harvard appointed him assistant professor of Fine Arts (1917), associate professor (1922), and full professor (1927). In 1923 he also became associate director of the Fogg Museum and displayed his mettle as a fund raiser. Sachs and Forbes—"the exuberant mendicants" in A. Lawrence Lowell's phrase—not only devised the plan but raised the money to build the new Fogg Museum, the largest university art museum in the country. It opened in 1928 and was the charge of this unique directorial team for the ensuing twenty years.

Sachs's academic courses were in the field of old-master prints and drawings and the history of French painting. In 1932–1933 Sachs was an exchange professor in France, at Bonn, and at Berlin. However, his most notable contribution as a teacher was his graduate seminar in museum administration, first offered in 1921. Some of his students became directors of the Metropolitan Museum, the Boston Museum of Fine Arts, the National Gallery, the Museum of Modern Art, and about twenty other American museums. The seminar became the model for similar courses in many colleges and universities.

Upon Sachs's retirement as professor in 1948 he assumed a major administrative role in incorporating into the university two international research foundations: Dumbarton Oaks in Washington, D.C., and I Tatti at Settignano, near Florence, Italy. To his earlier publications, *Early Italian Engravings* (1915) and *Drawings in the Fogg Museum* (1940), he added a popular paperback volume, *Great Drawings* (1951), and *Modern Prints and Drawings* (1954).

Sachs was a surprising figure: he was five feet, two inches tall and rather round. A powerful gaze and black eyebrows dominated his countenance. His poise was scholarly, his manner gentlemanly. Although at home in the university environment, he never set aside the banker's dark suit and starched collar, which gave him an air of gravity at odds with his warm and fun-loving nature.

Generosity, curiosity, and gregariousness governed his life. He was generous with his house and library, his counsel, his personal interest in his students, and his influential contacts. Enthusiastic and passionate, Sachs perceived art as a sensual delight. The experience with every work was a personal encounter for him. His students respected his learning but treasured his artistic instinct—the discernment of quality—realizing that its influence was more precious than the academic knowledge he imparted.

As a Harvard professor, Sachs became identified as no other person with the problem of guiding the destinies of American art museums through teaching the principles and practice of their administration. He believed museum directing to be a profession, and he devised the first course of training for it. He was at the same time a brilliant collector of drawings, furnishing inspiration and counsel to two or three generations of his students in the formation of their own collections. As trustee of no less than twenty museums, colleges, and charities, Sachs also had a wide influence.

If, as he so often reminded his pupils, the art museum director's name is written in sand, that of Paul Sachs, the director, will perhaps be no exception. But as a collector his name will be close to immortal through one specific benefaction: the gift to Harvard of one of the greatest collections of drawings in America.

Sachs died in Cambridge, Mass.

[Sachs's papers can be found at the Fogg Art Museum of Harvard University. See also Agnes Mongan, *Drawings in the Fogg Museum of Art* (1940), and *One Hundred Master Drawings* (1949). Perry T. Rathbone, "Paul J. Sachs as Teacher," in *Boston Museum of Fine Arts Bulletin*, vol. 63 (1965), "Friend of the Fogg," *Time*, Jan. 13, 1967. *Lives of Harvard Scholars* (1968). Obituaries are in *Newsweek*, Mar. 1, 1965, and *Art News*, Apr. 1965.]

PERRY T. RATHBONE

SCHILDKRAUT, JOSEPH (Mar. 22, 1896– Jan. 21, 1964), actor, was born in Vienna, Austria, the son of Rudolf Schildkraut, an internationally famous actor, and of Erna Weinstein. From an early age, Schildkraut traveled widely with his father, meeting actors in all parts of Europe and elsewhere. Educated by tutors, he made his stage debut at the age of six in Buenos Aires, playing his father's grandson for one performance. Schildkraut studied the violin and piano at the Imperial Academy of Music in Berlin, but his early love for the theater led him to Albert Basserman, a great character actor of the day, who agreed to coach him. Schildkraut accompanied his father on his first visit to the United States in 1910 to perform in New York. He studied at the American Academy of Dramatic Arts, where Edward G. Robinson, Paul Muni, and William Powell were among his classmates. After graduating in 1913, he ac-

cepted his first professional English-speaking role, the juvenile lead in Russell Janney's production of Edmond Rostand's play, *The Romancers*. Everywhere *The Romancers* played on tour, Schildkraut was singled out for praise by critics.

In 1913, when his father returned to Germany to join Max Reinhardt's company in Berlin, Schildkraut read for Reinhardt, who was impressed by his style and offered him a contract. In October 1913, he opened at the Kammerspielhaus as Jether in *The Prodigal Son*. Still an Austrian citizen (he did not become an American citizen until 1938), Schildkraut served in the Austrian army (1914–1916) in World War I. In 1918 Schildkraut came into his own as an actor in Vienna, appearing in three successive hits: Stephan Zweig's *Jeremiah*, George Kaiser's *The Coral*, and in *Shadow Dance*.

In 1920 Schildkraut returned to New York, where drama critic Kenneth Macgowan arranged a reading for him with the Theatre Guild. Schildkraut was promptly chosen to play the title role in Ferenc Molnar's *Liliom*. This production, costarring Eva Le Gallienne, opened in April 1921 to critical acclaim. Schildkraut's first important movie role was in the D. W. Griffith production *Orphans of the Storm* (1921), with Lillian and Dorothy Gish. On Apr. 7, 1922, during the long run of *Liliom*, he married Elise Bartlett, a young actress. They were divorced in 1931. After starring in the title role of *Peer Gynt* (1923), he left the Theatre Guild to play Benvenuto Cellini in Edwin Justus Mayer's *The Firebrand* (1924).

In 1927 Cecil B. De Mille invited Schildkraut to Hollywood to team with his father in *The King of Kings*. He remained on the West Coast until 1931, managing the Hollywood Playhouse, producing plays, and appearing in such films as *The Forbidden Woman* (1927), *Tenth Avenue* (1928), and *Show Boat* (1929).

Following his father's death in 1930, Schildkraut returned to New York, where he played the title role in a stage revival of *The Affairs of Anatol* (1931). He then went to England and made two films, *Carnival* and *Blue Danube*. In London, Schildkraut met Mary McKay, and they eloped to Vienna, where Schildkraut intended to accept a stage engagement for repertory work. Soon disillusioned with the anti-Semitism around him, Schildkraut returned to New York.

He joined Eva Le Gallienne's Civic Repertory Company in 1932 and appeared in revivals of *Liliom* and *Camille* and in *Alice in Wonderland*. Following the company's collapse in 1933, he starred in Elmer Rice's *Between Two Worlds* (1934).

Movie offers took him back to Hollywood, where he appeared in numerous films including *Cleopatra* (1934), *Viva Villa!* (1934), and *The Crusades* (1935). For his portrayal of Captain Dreyfus in *The Life of Emile Zola* (1937) he won an Academy Award as best supporting actor.

Schildkraut eagerly accepted a part as a Staten Islander in Clifford Odets' *Clash by Night*. Costarring Lee J. Cobb and Tallulah Bankhead, the production opened in New York in December 1941. Schildkraut then worked with his favorite actress, Eva Le Gallienne, in *Uncle Harry* (1942) and a revival of *The Cherry Orchard* (1944).

While under contract with Republic Pictures, he appeared in a series of undistinguished films from 1945 to 1948. In 1951 Broadway beckoned again. Schildkraut played Mr. Dulcimer in *The Green Bay Tree* (1951) and appeared in the New York City Center's production of *Love's Labour's Lost* (1953). He was host of his own television series, "Joseph Schildkraut Presents" (1953–1954), and occasionally starred in the half-hour dramas.

In October 1955, Schildkraut returned to Broadway, giving one of his most memorable performances in *The Diary of Anne Frank*. Winner of several awards, the play ran on Broadway and toured for more than thirty months. In 1958 he re-created his role as Otto Frank for George Stevens' film. In 1962 his wife Mary died, and in 1963 he married Leonora Rogers, a young actress. Schildkraut completed his scenes as Nicodemus in George Stevens' movie *The Greatest Story Ever Told*, three months before his death in New York City.

During his long career Schildkraut appeared in several dozen plays, over sixty films, and more than eighty television productions. He portrayed characters as diverse as a romantic lead or a humble peasant. With an economy of gesture, he could move an audience to laughter or tears. As commentator Critt Davis has noted: "These are the hallmarks of a good character actor and Joseph Schildkraut was one of the best."

[An important autobiographical source is *My Father and I* (1959), as told to Leo Lania. Also see Critt Davis, "Joseph Schildkraut," *Films in Review*, Feb. 1973; Lewis Lewisohn, "The Two Schildkrauts," *Nation*, Feb. 28, 1923; Walter Rigdon, ed., *The Biographical Encyclopaedia and Who's Who of the American Theatre* (1966); Faith Service, "The Genius of Gesture," *Motion Picture Classic*, Sept. 1923;

William C. Young, ed., *Famous Actors and Actresses of the American Stage*, vol. II (1975); "The Mirrors of Stageland: XVIII—Joseph Schildkraut," *Theatre*, April 1923; and the *New York Herald Tribune*, Oct. 12, 1941, and Jan. 18, 1942. Obituaries are in the *New York Times*, Jan. 22, 1964; *Time*, Jan. 31, 1964; and *Newsweek*, Feb. 3, 1964.]

L. MOODY SIMMS, JR.

SCHLESINGER, ARTHUR MAIER (Feb. 27, 1888–Oct. 30, 1965), historian, was born in Xenia, Ohio, the son of Bernhard Schlesinger, a dry-goods store proprietor and fire-insurance agent, and of Katherine Feurle. Xenia was a town in which the Irish, the Germans, and the blacks lived compatibly, if with a degree of self-segregation. Bernhard Schlesinger, only occasionally prosperous in a succession of petit bourgeois occupations, was secretary of the Xenia School Board for almost forty years. Schlesinger attended Ohio State University from 1906 to 1910, where he majored in American history and political science; he was to regret that in both fields pedagogical emphasis was so heavily political-constitutional, diplomatic, and military; early he felt a need for more "anthropology," as he put it. He devoted a very large amount of his time to college journalism.

After receiving the B.A. he pursued graduate work in history at Columbia University; he greatly respected Charles A. Beard and James Harvey Robinson in history, as well as Franklin H. Giddings in sociology and Edwin R. A. Seligman in economics, but he was required to apprentice himself to William A. Dunning and Herbert L. Osgood, whose studies in United States history he found narrowly conceived. After passing his doctoral orals in less than two years, he began work on his dissertation under Osgood, while at the same time teaching at Ohio State (1912–1919). His dissertation, *The Colonial Merchants and the American Revolution* (1917), reflected the rigorous scholarly research demanded by Osgood, as well as some of the suppositions of Beard; it also illustrated Schlesinger's avoidance of polemic and literary pyrotechnics. *The Colonial Merchants* demonstrated that merchants in different colonies reacted differently at different times; few were disinterested, and even fewer disposed to impassivity.

On Sept. 5, 1914, Schlesinger married Elizabeth Bancroft, whom he had met at Ohio State when they were students. They had three sons; one of whom, Arthur Maier Schlesinger, Jr., also became a noted historian.

In 1919 Schlesinger moved to the University of Iowa. Along with fulfilling many of the public speaking and writing responsibilities of a scholar at a state university, he offered what he believed to be the first course in an American college in the "social" and "cultural" aspects of United States history. His collection of essays, *New Viewpoints in American History* (1922), was intended to demonstrate that "the social point of view has become the characteristic mark of the present generation of historians." Successive chapters call the attention of "young scholars" to the importance of immigration and acculturation, the impact of the western movement, the decline of "aristocracy," the role of women, and other "foundations of the modern era."

Dissatisfaction with available textbooks led Schlesinger to collaborate with his Ohio State University colleague Homer C. Hockett on *The Political and Social History of the United States* (1925), a survey several times reissued in various formats and under slightly different titles. They introduced into this textbook a good deal of "social history" as well as "new viewpoints" on political, economic, and constitutional questions.

In 1923 Schlesinger, along with Dixon Ryan Fox, began work on the History of American Life series. Originally to be done in ten volumes in three years, it was eventually concluded in thirteen volumes published over twenty-one years. Schlesinger stated that its purpose was to "free American history from its traditional servitude to party struggles, war and diplomacy" and to direct attention not just to the "highest fruits of American intellectual and spiritual attainment, but also to the interests and tastes of the common man."

From the outset, Schlesinger was not only the moving spirit but the copy editor, cheerleader, critic, and rewrite man of a series that at times exhilarated him, at times struck him as an incubus. One of the better volumes is Schlesinger's own *The Rise of the City* (1933). Anxious not to provide simply a "taxonomy" of facts about the new urban life, Schlesinger followed his own injunction to do more than collect, in the manner of John B. McMaster, or to recount "the quaint and the curious." He tried, rather, to work out what was the "unifying factor of the age." His task was perhaps simplified by the editorial decision to commission Ida M. Tarbell to write the volume *The Nationalizing of Business* (1936), dealing with the same decades (1878–1898) with which Schlesinger was dealing. He was thus able to concentrate on the "habits, abilities, attainments, and conditions that have shaped the social, economic, intellectual, and cultural development of the American people." After prefatory chapters dealing with the atypical experience of the South and West, he devoted the bulk of the volume to demonstrating that "the city was the supreme achievement of the new industrialism." Chapters on women, education, arts and letters, the use of leisure, transportation, the "changing church," as well as "society's wards" expatiated on this theme. Schlesinger was no Pollyanna about the city; both his presuppositions and the evidence he collected led him to note, though not stress, "the darker sides" of America's precipitate urbanization. Since its publication, the work has continued to provide both an agenda of subject areas to be explored further and modest generalizations, which have aroused some polemic, especially from the economic-social Left.

In 1924 Schlesinger moved to Harvard; he was chairman of the Department of History from 1928 to 1931 and then Francis Lee Higginson professor until his retirement in 1954. He was a candid, kind, and sedulous director of graduate students; in 1951 John Higham noted that Schlesinger had supervised an unusually large number of the better dissertations in intellectual history in the past decades. Yet his own inclinations were increasingly toward what might be called "cultural" history; indeed, when his son Arthur joined the faculty at Harvard, he redesignated his course "social and cultural" history, to clarify the distinction.

Schlesinger published two collections of essays, *Paths to the Present* (1949), which includes a version of the address given as president of the American Historical Association (1942) on the Americans' propensity to be "joiners"; and *The American as Reformer* (1950), which includes addresses given in the sometimes sullen post–World War II years celebrating spokesmen for the party of hope. He also published a provocative historical study of American etiquette books, *Learning How to Behave* (1946). After his retirement he published *Prelude to Independence: The Newspaper War on Britain, 1764–1776* (1957). At his death he was at work on what he intended to be a multivolume social history of the United States. The first volume, *The Birth of the Nation*, less "social" than one might have expected, was published posthumously in 1968. His son Arthur edited, with an insightful introductory memoir, a collection of essays, *Nothing Stands Still* (1969).

Schlesinger saw no dichotomy between the life of a professor and that of a citizen. He helped found the Social Science Research Council in 1924 and served as chairman from 1930 to 1933. He was also one of the cofounders in 1928 of the *New England Quarterly.* He helped organize the Institute of Early American History and Culture and the restoration of Colonial Williamsburg. He was a longtime supporter of liberal and labor causes and was the first chairman of Americans for Democratic Action in Massachusetts.

Schlesinger's central importance to the writing of American history lies in his rejection of the unarticulated premises that had constricted much of the writing and teaching of that history to what had been "politically important." Like most United States historians, he was wary of any kind of philosophy of history. Yet, as with many professed empiricists, Schlesinger occasionally yearned for some kind of pattern, regularity, or even "law." Early in his career, he was struck by the "oscillation" in American behavior —especially political behavior—between periods of conservatism and reform. In his many subsequent references to this notion, he often used the term "cycle," stipulated that a "phase" usually lasted twelve to sixteen years, and speculated whether there were not other "laws" in social change; it was a source of wonder to him that while the public was intrigued by this cryptophilosophizing, his fellow historians showed little interest.

As he neared retirement, Schlesinger declared that the historian exerts his widest influence through publications; yet it is arguable that, useful as his many books proved to be, his greatest impact on the profession was as a director of graduate students. Simply by calling their attention to areas of American experience largely ignored by previous historians, he legitimated novel investigations in immigration history, the neighborhood character of city life, religious life and experience (as contrasted to church organization and theology), and science and technology.

Schlesinger was well aware of the emergence of "the new social history"—characterized at once by an often fierce belief in quantification and an explicit commitment to social scientific theory and hypothesis—drawn especially from social psychology and anthropology. To many of the new breed, "Schlesinger's social history" seemed anachronistic. Yet for thirty years it had been a liberating influence among American historians and had provided a kind of agenda of interest, if not a regimen of methods and concepts.

Schlesinger died in Cambridge, Mass.

[The best starting point is Schlesinger's brief autobiography, *In Retrospect: The History of a Historian* (1963), written to amplify an extensive oral history memoir at Columbia University. The memoir itself and some eight boxes of documents and letters are deposited at the Oral History Archive, where they may be consulted with the permission of Arthur M. Schlesinger, Jr. In his introduction to *Nothing Stands Still* (1969), Arthur M. Schlesinger, Jr., has provided the best available short interpretation of his father's whole career.]

ROBERT D. CROSS

SCHOEPPEL, ANDREW FRANK (Nov. 23, 1894–Jan. 21, 1962), lawyer and politician, was born near Claflin, Barton County, Kans., the son of George J. Schoeppel, a grain elevator owner, and of Anna Filip, a seamstress. When he was five, the family moved to a farm in northern Ness County. Andrew attended country schools, graduating from Ransom high school in 1915. He enrolled as a premedical student at the University of Kansas (1916–1918) and then served in the naval aviation corps. In 1922 he received the LL.B. from the University of Nebraska and "honorable mention" on Walter Camp's first All-American football team.

Admitted to the Kansas bar in 1923, Schoeppel began to practice law in Ness City. On June 2, 1924, he married Marie Thomsen; they had no children. The personable six-foot, two-inch Schoeppel became a partner in the law firm of Peters and Schoeppel, which in 1936 became Schoeppel and Smyth. He was well known as a sports official in western Kansas and coached the football team at Fort Hays State College in 1929. He held the offices of city attorney, county attorney, member of the school board and city council, and mayor.

In 1939 Schoeppel was appointed chairman of the Kansas Corporation Commission by Governor Payne Ratner. In this key position, with responsibility for setting rates for public utilities, Schoeppel gained statewide political exposure. He resigned in April 1942 to campaign for the Republican nomination for governor against three better-known Republicans, and won nomination by a margin of 7,000 votes. In the 1942 election he defeated the Democratic candidate by 75,824 votes, carrying 103 of the state's 105 counties. Reelected two years later, he captured a majority in all the counties. His margin of victory was 231,700 votes, the largest of any governor of Kansas to that time.

During his first term Schoeppel stressed economy and "cooperation" between the executive and legislative departments. He offered no legislative program, and the heavily Republican legislature broke into warring factions dominated by local interests. During his second term more of Schoeppel's legislative proposals were implemented. Modernization of school systems and highway building plans were his primary developments. A fair standards labor act, considered punitive by labor unions, was also passed.

Schoeppel was engaged in public controversy at least three times during his terms as governor. Although a state law of 1935 had reimposed capital punishment, no execution had taken place in Kansas since 1870. Schoeppel permitted the first executions. A second issue was his granting clemency to Ronald Finney, convicted in 1933 for embezzling, by bond forgery, almost one-half million dollars from the state. The third controversy involved state prohibition: Kansas had been dry since 1880. When federal agents, late in 1945, seized a large quantity of unlicensed liquor, Schoeppel questioned their good faith because they had not cooperated with Kansas authorities. He launched an investigation and asked the legislative council to assemble information which led to the repeal of prohibition in Kansas in 1949.

Schoeppel left the governorship in 1947 and joined the Wichita law firm of Foulston, Siefkin, Schoeppel, Bartlett and Powers. In 1948 he gained the Republican nomination for U.S. senator. He was elected and reelected in 1954 and 1960, each time by a substantial margin.

During his thirteen years in the Senate, Schoeppel served on the Interstate and Foreign Commerce Committee and at various times on the Appropriations Committee and the Agricultural and Forestry Committee. He was chairman of a surface-transportation subcommittee and he served on a special committee on small business. He was also a member of the Republican Senate Policy Committee. Schoeppel was proud of his association with the Agricultural Trade Development and Assistance Act of 1954, which authorized "the President to use agricultural commodities to improve the foreign relations of the United States and for other purposes."

Continuing to hold outspokenly conservative views, Schoeppel supported Senator Joseph R. McCarthy for a time and backed Senator Robert A. Taft for the Republican presidential nomination in 1952. He spoke in the Senate only rarely; his influence was used in committees and the cloakroom. He died at Bethesda, Md.

[Schoeppel's papers, for both his gubernatorial and his Senate years, are in the Kansas State Historical Society, Topeka. See David Charles Boles, "Andrew Frank Schoeppel, Governor of Kansas, 1943–1947" (M.A. diss., Kansas State University, 1967). Obituaries appeared in the Topeka *Daily Capitol*, Jan. 22, 1961; and Wichita *Beacon*, Jan. 25, 1961.]

HOMER E. SOCOLOFSKY

SCHWIDETZKY, OSCAR OTTO RUDOLF (Dec. 31, 1874–Oct. 11, 1963), medical instrument maker, was born in Konitz, Germany (now Chojnice, Poland), the son of August Schwidetzky and Fredericke Mohnké. At the age of fourteen he began a four-year apprenticeship to Julius Martiny, a maker of surgical and dental instruments in Berlin. He worked with other instrument makers in Berlin, Crefield, and Aix-la-Chapelle, learning orthopedics during this period. After leaving the German army in 1897, he studied sales and marketing by attending night school and reading medical instrument catalogs and medical journals. His skills enabled him, in 1898, to obtain a position as a salesman for the German medical instrument maker Hermann Windler.

In 1900 Schwidetzky immigrated to the United States and settled in New York City, where he improved his English by teaching German at the Berlitz School of Languages. After becoming fluent in English, he became an importer of surgical supplies, including the Bender Ideal bandage, the first elastic bandage made without rubber. Schwidetzky improved this bandage and from it developed the Ace bandage, used where pressure and support are needed. His first wife, whom he married in 1902, died in 1914. They had one son. In May 1916 he married Anna Hasselhuhn: they had no children.

In 1913 Schwidetzky began a lifelong association with the medical instrument firm of Becton, Dickinson and Company, working closely with Andrew W. Fleischer in spearheading research. He became an American citizen in 1917.

Schwidetzky excelled as an inventor of devices designed to provide access to the bloodstream to control and fight disease. With the invention in 1851 of the Pravaz needle by Charles Gabriel Pravaz, the groundwork had been laid for the development of the hypodermic needle. Made of steel with a hard-rubber body, it became the prototype of numerous syringes and needles over the next century. Schwidetzky claimed in 1943 that about 1910 he had made the first glass-barrel and rubber-bulb syringe for a doctor in Seattle. This syringe evolved in 1916 into the Asepto model, produced by the Becton-Dickinson Company, which became the standard syringe for injecting fluids into the genitourinary system.

Another important syringe Schwidetzky promoted was originally designed by Howard Greeley. Modified in World War I, it was used on wounded soldiers to inject morphine tartrate for relief of pain before medical treatment was available. Called the syrette, this unit was produced by the E. R. Squibb and Sons Company.

Schwidetzky understood that the hypodermic needle, which was the only sharp instrument used on conscious patients, had to be constructed to minimize pain during its injection. Refinements (reviewed by Schwidetzky in an article published in 1926) included the fine diameter of the needle, the use of a special instrument called the Titus infusion thermometer to measure the temperature of the solution being injected, and the Luer-Lok syringe, which made it possible to separate the needle from the syringe for hypodermic injections.

As manager and director of research at Becton-Dickinson, Schwidetzky helped develop the caudal needle for the continuous administration of anesthesia into the spinal column. The cooperation between anesthesiologists and manufacturers of syringes and needles fostered by Schwidetzky led to the popularity of syringe anesthesia in the United States. He died in Ramsey, N.J.

Schwidetzky's significance was well stated by Leroy D. Vandam: "Probably at every place throughout this country where there are sick and wounded and suffering persons—some product of his medical skill is relieving pain."

[Among Schwidetzky's writings are "Refinements in Equipment for Parenteral Medication," *Clinical Medicine and Surgery,* Oct. 1926; "History of Needles and Syringes," *Anesthesia and Analgesia,* 1944; and "Hypodermic Needles and Syringes," *Medical Physics,* 1950. Biographical accounts include "Last of the Old Goats," *B-D. World,* vol. 1 (1969); Leroy D. Vandam "On the History of Ideas in Anesthesia," *Current Researches in Anesthesia and Analgesia,* July–Aug. 1976; and obituary notices in the *New York Times,* Oct. 11, 1963, and *Time* Oct. 18, 1963.]

AUDREY B. DAVIS

SCOTT, ALLEN CECIL (Aug. 16, 1882–May 1, 1964), businessman, was born in Omaha, Nebr., the son of William Wilbur Scott, a farmer, and of Elizabeth Johnson, caterer at the local Masonic Temple. He was educated in the Omaha public schools. On Aug. 2, 1905, Scott married Ethel Smith. They had one son. After his wife's death he married Gladys Thornton on May 21, 1921; they had three daughters.

While a railroad inspector, Scott got his start in the tent and awning business by turning over old burlap to an Omaha tent manufacturer.

Within a year he had bought the firm, and he built his Scott Tent and Awning Company into a nationwide firm. This eventually led him, during World War I, to travel to Washington, D.C., with an invention that gave him a claim to fame. In 1918, when the only successful parachutes used by the military, except those of the Germans, were static chutes fixed to the sides of observation balloons and opened by static rip cords, Scott developed the idea of a pilot chute. This was popped out of the individual parachute pack by a spring when the pilot pulled the ripcord; this small chute dragged the main parachute free. A patent granted in 1921 covered the packing of the main chute, the harness and release, and the pilot chute. It became the basic design of all later chutes.

Scott was elected president of the Omaha Chamber of Commerce in 1923. He was known throughout the city for paying for the installation of signs at dangerous intersections warning motorists to be careful because Omaha needed its children. As president of the Omaha Manufacturers Association, he was genial and helpful, quietly doing good deeds of which not even his friends were fully aware. He loved baseball and was president of the Muny Baseball Association for thirteen years. He retired from his firm in 1964, shortly before he died at Omaha.

[The A. C. Scott file, Omaha Public Library, includes photos. An obituary is in the *New York Times,* May 2, 1964.]

ROBIN HIGHAM

SEAGRAVE, GORDON STIFLER (Mar. 18, 1897–Mar. 28, 1965), medical missionary, was born in Rangoon, Burma, the son of Albert Ernest Seagrave, a Baptist missionary, and of Alice Haswell Vinton. When he was twelve, his mother took him and three older sisters to Granville, Ohio, to complete their education. He graduated from the Doane Academy in Granville in 1914 and from Denison University, with a B.A. in biology, in 1917. He then entered the Johns Hopkins University Medical School and served in the Hopkins medical reserve unit during World War I. While working at a camp in Lake Geneva, Wis., during the summers of 1918 and 1919, Seagrave met Marion Grace Morse. They were married on Sept. 11, 1920, and less than three weeks later he was appointed a missionary by the American Baptist Foreign Mission Society. The Seagraves had five children.

After receiving the M.D. in 1921, Seagrave was an intern at Union Memorial Hospital in

Baltimore. In August 1922 the Seagraves sailed from New York City for Rangoon. They arrived at their missionary station headquarters on October 10 and were assigned to the Namkham Hospital in the northeast frontier area of Burma, three miles from China. Seagrave requested this difficult assignment because a family friend, Dr. Robert Harper, was about to retire from Namkham. The first of his family to be a medical missionary, Seagrave considered medicine to be a profession of immediate relevance that allowed him to transcend the American tendency to dwell on the theory of missions, rather than on practical actions within needy societies: "All I wanted was plenty of jungle, and thousands of sick people to treat, preferably with surgery."

The Seagraves found the Namkham Hospital in a shambles. They rebuilt it with indigenous materials and slowly gained the people's confidence. Patients were of five Burmese races (Karen, Kachin, Burmese, Shan, and Chin) and several Chinese tribes from across the border. The major health problems of the frontier states were malaria, goiter, dysentery, syphilis, and gonorrhea. Seagrave learned Shan and Burmese and relearned Karen. He wrote a two-volume nursing textbook in Burmese and thereby gained government accreditation for the nursing school in his hospital. Students of all races, especially the Karen, attended. Throughout his years in Burma the schooling of nurses continued to be one of his most important programs.

In 1928–1929 the Seagraves were in the United States on leave. During the year he attended the New York Postgraduate Medical School at Columbia University for surgical training, visited the Mayo Clinic, and raised funds for supplies. His first book describing his service in Burma, *Waste-Basket Surgery,* was published in 1930. The sequel, *Tales of A Waste-Basket Surgeon* (1938), described his second tour.

Seagrave received the Kaiser-i-Hind Medal for service to India in 1935. This and later service awards resulted from his work ethic. "There is one joy in this world that can be equaled by no other pleasure with which I am acquainted. That is the satisfaction of having too much work to do, and then going ahead and getting it done anyway."

In 1936–1937 the Seagraves took further surgical training at the University of Vienna. When they arrived back in Rangoon in October 1937, they found that Burma had been separated from India by the British and granted limited self-government. But the Japanese invasion of China soon changed Seagrave's work at his isolated border hospital. The vital Burma Road from Lashio to Chunking, China, ran near Namkham. Beginning in November 1938, Seagrave set up and worked part-time in a Chinese hospital at Loiwing, treating American and Chinese workers at an airplane factory. By October 1940, Japanese bombers regularly passed over Namkham. Seagrave's family was evacuated back to the United States, and during the next two years the conflict engulfed him. He worked with the British Liaison Mission to provide medical relief. Soon he ran a 400-bed hospital at Prome in southeast Burma and was responsible for 300 other beds in jungle hospitals along the Burma Road and the Burma-China border.

Following the arrival of General Joseph Stilwell, Seagrave requested a transfer to the U.S. Army Medical Corps. Stilwell had heard of the bespectacled, stocky surgeon of endless energy and commissioned him a major (April 1942). The Seagrave medical unit of twelve nurses, a dentist, and another physician ran the only hospital for the remnants of Chiang Kai-shek's Fifth and Sixth armies. They chose to remain with Stilwell and his band of 114 persons when they retreated across Burma to India. Seagrave received the Purple Heart and promotion to lieutenant colonel in August 1942. The next year he became famous with publication of *Burma Surgeon,* in several versions for separate domestic and military use in the United States. In 1944–1945 the Allies retook Burma, as Seagrave described in *Burma Surgeon Returns* (1946).

After six months' leave in the United States, Seagrave returned to military duty in Burma as chief medical officer of the Shan states for the British Military Administration. He could barely tolerate military or civilian administrative life, but this temporary position permitted him to return to the Namkham area. In March 1946 civilian government was restored.

Seagrave realized that his medical compound would survive in postwar Burma only by changing. He envisioned "not a Baptist hospital alone, but a Christian hospital; a hospital that would appeal to Americans whether church members or not; a hospital above denomination, where Buddhists and animists could come and receive loving care when sick and learn that peace comes only to men of good will." Accordingly, he amicably severed the twenty-six-year relationship with the American Baptist Foreign Mission Society in April 1946. The society retained ownership of the Namkham hospital, but leased it to Seagrave for $1 a year.

In 1946, Seagrave created an umbrella agency, the American Medical Center for Burma Frontier Areas (later the American Medical Center for Burma). From October 1946 to March 1947 and again from November 1947 to April 1948, he made fund-raising lecture tours in the United States. Thus, despite the tenuous political situation in Burma, goodwill, hard work, luck, and private support permitted his work to continue.

But Seagrave's location in the stronghold of the rebellious Karen and Kachin minorities inexorably entangled him in civil war. On Aug. 15, 1950, he was arrested, charged with treason for supporting the Karen rebels, and taken to Rangoon for trial. He remained in jail or under house arrest for fifteen months and was convicted and sentenced to six years of "rigorous imprisonment." During a series of appeals, some witnesses admitted perjury. Seagrave refused to have the charges dismissed on a technicality, and ultimately the High Court of Burma released him on Nov. 14, 1951. In December 1952 his medical buildings reopened.

Seagrave's situation had caused diplomatic and political concern because he was a United States citizen. In 1955 he published *My Hospital in the Hills,* in which he revealed broadened perspectives on missions, religion, and nationalism. From 1959 to 1964 the National Committee of the American Medical Center for Burma (AMCFB) supported his work. In 1961, President John F. Kennedy wrote Seagrave a letter of commendation.

Forty years in rough terrain amid malaria, dysentery, and other diseases finally took their toll. Seagrave died at Namkham hospital and was buried in its compound. In 1965 the Burmese government nationalized his and other major mission hospitals. The AMCFB disbanded, transferring its $150,000 assets to the American Korea Foundation to build a hospital in Seagrave's memory.

[Unpublished materials are available at the American Baptist Foreign Mission Society, Valley Forge, Pa.; the American Baptist Historical Society, Rochester, N.Y.; and the Library of Congress. The contemporary literature on Seagrave includes Peter Kalischer, "He's Still the Burma Surgeon," *Collier's,* Apr. 30, 1954; Sterling Seagrave, "Burma Surgeon's Last Battle," *Saturday Evening Post,* July 3, 1965; "My Most Unforgettable Character," *Reader's Digest,* May 1968; and Sue Mayes Newhall, *The Devil in God's Old Man* (1969). Also see *The Watchman Examiner,* July 30, 1942; Riley Sutherland and

Charles F. Romanus, U.S. Army in World War II series, *Stilwell's Mission to China* (1953), *Stilwell's Command Problems* (1956), and *Time Runs Out in CBI* (1959); and Barbara Tuchman, *Stilwell and the American Experience in China 1911–1945* (1971). On the postwar years, see "Facts Surrounding the Trial of Gordon S. Seagrave in Burma," *U.S. State Department Bulletin,* Feb. 5, 1951; and Frank N. Trager, ed., *Annotated Bibliography of Burma* (1956). An obituary is in the *New York Times,* Mar. 29, 1965.]

JAMES POLK MORRIS

SELZNICK, DAVID O. (May 10, 1902–June 22, 1965), movie producer, was born in Pittsburgh, Pa., the son of Lewis Joseph Selznick, a prosperous jeweler, and of Florence Anna Sachs. In 1910 the family moved to New York City, where Lewis Selznick's business promptly failed. Undaunted, he organized a small motion picture company, and by 1916 films had remade his fortune. The Selznicks moved into a twenty-two-room Park Avenue apartment. Young Selznick attended the Hamilton Institute for Boys (1917–1919) and took extension courses at Columbia University. His prospects for attending Yale University vanished in 1923 with his father's bankruptcy.

Selznick, who added "O." to his name for looks and euphony, produced his first films— "Will He Conquer Dempsey?" of boxer Luis Firpo working out, and another of Rudolph Valentino judging a beauty show—in 1923 for 100 percent profit. Two years later he moved to Hollywood, now clearly the world film capital, where he worked until 1928 for Metro-Goldwyn-Mayer (MGM) as story editor and assistant producer, then for Paramount until 1931 as associate producer. During these years Selznick became known as an effective and profit-making production manager (once producing two low-budget westerns simultaneously for the price of one) and also as an imaginative marketer and perceptive film student. Offered a bonus at Paramount for usable movie titles, he came up with a list of thirty-six, including such marquee attractions as "Love Among the Coeds," "Good Little Chorus Girls," and "Love Among the Rich." Yet he instantly appreciated the genius of Sergei Eisenstein's film *Potemkin* and urged aspiring producers and directors to study it for technique as artists might view a Rubens or a Raphael. His lengthy memorandums on the details of moviemaking were unique. On Apr. 29, 1930, Selznick married Irene Gladys Mayer, daughter of Louis B. Mayer, the head of MGM. They had two children.

During the 1930's Selznick's constant aim

was to produce pictures independently of the studio system, where he felt confined. His first venture was as production chief (1931–1933) of Radio-Keith-Orpheum (RKO) Pictures, a company created at his urging by David Sarnoff, president of Radio Corporation of America. In early 1933, after only fourteen months at RKO, Selznick, partly to satisfy a deathbed wish of his father's, returned to MGM, Hollywood's largest and most prestigious studio and the fiefdom of his father-in-law, where he remained until 1935. Although constrained by finances at RKO and by executive ukase at MGM, he produced many profitable and important pictures, including *Dinner at Eight* (1933), *King Kong* (1933), *Viva Villa!* (1934), *David Copperfield* (1935), *Anna Karenina* (1935), and *A Tale of Two Cities* (1935). He also introduced two great stars: Katharine Hepburn (in *Little Women*, 1933) and Fred Astaire (in *Dancing Lady*, 1933).

In 1936 he finally attained his goal with the formation of Selznick International Studios, the independent company with which, under different names and studio distribution arrangements, he produced the remainder of his pictures.

The films that mark the pinnacle of Selznick's career and include some of the finest in Hollywood history began to appear: *Little Lord Fauntleroy* (1936), *A Star Is Born* (1937), *The Prisoner of Zenda* (1937), *The Adventures of Tom Sawyer* (1938), *Intermezzo* (1939), *Gone With the Wind* (1939), and *Rebecca* (1940). The high point was *Gone With the Wind*, at the time the longest (almost four hours) and costliest ($4 million) movie ever made. The picture was notable for its fidelity to Margaret Mitchell's sprawling novel, its deft use of Technicolor, and its fine casting, especially of Clark Gable as Rhett Butler and of an unknown English actress, Vivien Leigh, as Scarlett O'Hara. The film won ten Academy Awards and grossed many times its cost within a few years. Much of the profit, however, went to MGM for Clark Gable's services and for its service as exclusive distributor.

Selznick garnered eight Academy Award nominations for *A Star Is Born* and another eleven for *Rebecca*. In *Intermezzo* he introduced a brilliant new star, Ingrid Bergman, and in *Rebecca* still another, Joan Fontaine. *Rebecca* marked the Hollywood debut of the noted English director Alfred Hitchcock.

Selznick enjoyed further successes after 1940, including *I'll Be Seeing You* (1945), a compassionate treatment of shellshock; *Spellbound* (1945), directed by Hitchcock; and *The Third*

Man (1950), coproduced with Alexander Korda. But increasingly he wrapped his career around that of actress Jennifer Jones, whom he married on July 13, 1949, after having divorced his first wife; they had one child. Jones (born Phyllis Isley) first appeared for Selznick in *Since You Went Away* (1944) and later in the grandiose western *Duel in the Sun* (1947); a romance, *Portrait of Jennie* (1949); *Beat the Devil* (1954), opposite Humphrey Bogart; and Ernest Hemingway's *A Farewell to Arms* (1958), Selznick's last film. Although the later productions were tasteful and inventive, they seldom equaled the earlier films, either critically or financially.

A muscular, energetic six-footer with bushy brows, Selznick was a formidable presence in Hollywood throughout his career. He interfered far more than most producers in the work of his directors, thus alienating such talents as George Cukor and King Vidor, both of whom quit in the middle of major Selznick projects. Yet his way with performers, particularly young actresses, was often sensitive. Old antagonists recalled him as a tough businessman with streaks of tenderness and loyalty. He gambled heavily (as his father had), was a regular habitué of the Clover Club, a Beverly Hills nightspot, and while still wed to Irene Mayer, hosted weekend parties that were highlights of Hollywood's "golden age."

Unlike his contemporary, producer Darryl F. Zanuck, Selznick was apolitical and did not make socially conscious films. He was aware of the fascist menace in the 1930's, and even while romanticizing the Old South of *Gone With the Wind* he refused to portray the Ku Klux Klan favorably, as D. W. Griffith had done in *Birth of a Nation*. He died in Beverly Hills of a heart attack. The David O. Selznick Golden Laurel Trophy is awarded annually to an outstanding film producer.

[See the collection of "DOS" memorandums in Rudy Behlmer, ed., *Memo from David O. Selznick* (1972). Also see Ronald Bowers, *The Selznick Players* (1976); and Bob Thomas, *Selznick* (1970). Obituary notices appeared in the *Los Angeles Times* and the *New York Times*, June 23, 1965.]

RONALD STORY

SEYMOUR, CHARLES (Jan. 1, 1885–Aug. 11, 1963), diplomat, historian, and university president, was born in New Haven, Conn., the son of Thomas Day Seymour, a classics professor, and of Sarah Hitchcock. After graduating from Hillhouse High School in New Haven, he studied in England at Kings College, Cambridge University, which awarded him a B.A. in modern history in 1904. He then entered Yale College and graduated with a B.A. in 1908. The same year he returned to Cambridge and the following year received an M.A. Subsequent studies at Yale led to a Ph.D. in history in 1911. On May 4 of that year he married Gladys Marion Watkins; they had three children.

Seymour's professional career was tied closely to Yale. He joined the faculty in 1911, became assistant professor four years later, and was promoted to professor in 1918. By that time he had published several significant books. His *Diplomatic Background of the War, 1870–1914* (1916) established his reputation as a diplomatic historian and expert on World War I.

In 1917 Colonel Edward M. House, President Woodrow Wilson's closest adviser, invited him to join the Inquiry, a group of "experts" whose duty it was to prepare background information for the forthcoming peace conference. The following year he served briefly with the State Department. When the war ended, Seymour accompanied President Wilson to the Paris Peace Conference, where he served as chief of the Austro-Hungarian division of the American commission to negotiate peace and as United States delegate on the Rumanian, Yugoslavian, and Czechoslovakian territorial commissions.

Seymour's notes of comments made by President Wilson aboard the *George Washington* provide significant insight into the president's thinking on the eve of the peace conference. Similarly, Seymour's *Letters from the Paris Peace Conference* (1965) give valuable information and an astute analysis of the conference and its work. He became increasingly frustrated and disillusioned as the conference progressed. Convinced that concessions would lead to increased difficulties, he deplored Wilson's failure to stand firmly by the principles enunciated in the Fourteen Points. In the late spring of 1919 Seymour and five other members of the American delegation sent a letter to the president protesting the contemplated accommodation of Italy on the Fiume question.

Following the peace conference, Seymour resumed teaching at Yale, concentrating his research and writing on the diplomatic history of the war and the efforts to establish a lasting peace. In 1922 he was appointed Sterling professor and chairman of the history department.

The following year Colonel House deposited his papers at Yale and asked Seymour to become editor of his "memoirs." The first and second volumes of *The Intimate Papers of Colonel House* were published in 1926; the third and fourth volumes appeared two years later.

In 1927 Seymour was appointed provost of Yale. He enhanced his powers by elevating his new office to the head of the faculty structure, thereby strengthening the authority of the administration. The resulting change amounted to a "new order" which permitted central administrative initiation and review of critical appointments as well as policies and budgets of all branches of the university. Through skillful negotiations with Edward S. Harkness, a leading financial benefactor of the university, Seymour contributed to the realization of an ambitious building program. During this period he also wrote several books designed to correct misconceptions about American diplomacy during the war.

Seymour became president of Yale in 1937. His major contribution was consolidation of the university's internal development. He expanded the curriculum, enhanced the liberal arts program and strengthened the faculty. After the United States entered World War II, Seymour mobilized the campus for war. Most students pursued studies connected with training programs of the army, navy, and air force, or engaged in specialized studies like the Military Intelligence Language Program. At the same time, Seymour accelerated academic programs for civilian students. When the war was over, Seymour made provisions to accommodate large numbers of returning students. Overcrowding strained Yale's facilities, but Seymour insisted on maintaining a high quality of education. Before retiring in 1950 he completed reorganization of the university along divisional lines.

Throughout his presidency Seymour—no doubt because of his background as a historian—made special efforts to induce prominent Americans in various fields to deposit their papers at Yale. Under his leadership Yale expanded its research facilities.

In his emeritus role Seymour resumed his scholarly pursuits. He wrote numerous articles, book reviews, and other papers. He gave priority to his position as curator of the House papers. His last article, "The End of a Friendship" (*American Heritage,* August 1963), dealt with House's version of his "separation" from Wilson and was based on a confidential interview that he had had with the colonel twenty-five years earlier.

In addition to Seymour's influence on Yale, his national importance rests on his contribution as diplomatic historian, especially as interpreter of Colonel House. He maintained that

House had exerted a major influence on President Wilson but as a "diplomatic tactician" rather than as an innovator of policies. Seymour recognized that a definitive study of America's wartime diplomacy had to be based "primarily upon Wilson's own papers, public and private." The number of these documents available to Seymour was limited. Even so, his main conclusions, especially concerning the causes of the war and America's entrance into it, remain sound.

Seymour combined a keen intelligence with a pleasant, warm, and outgoing personality. As he aged, ill health increasingly interfered with his productive capacity. He died in Chatham, Mass.

[The comprehensive collection of Seymour's papers at the Sterling Memorial Library of Yale University is organized in six series and covers his activities as diplomatic historian as well as most aspects of his career at Yale. Official papers connected with his provostship and presidency are at the university archives. A large part of the House-Seymour correspondence is in the Papers of Colonel Edward M. House, at the Sterling Library.

Seymour's books dealing with World War I and its aftermath include *What Really Happened at Paris* (1921); *Woodrow Wilson and the World War* (1921); *American Diplomacy During the World War* (1934); and *American Neutrality, 1914–1917* (1935). Among his books on other subjects are *Electoral Reform in England and Wales* (1915); *Selections from Carlyle* (1915); and *How the World Votes* (1918).

For Seymour's evaluation of House, see "The Role of Colonel House in Wilson's Diplomacy," in Edward H. Buehrig, *Wilson's Foreign Policy in Perspective* (1957). His attitude toward Wilson is found in his "Woodrow Wilson in Perspective," *Foreign Affairs*, Jan. 1956.

Seymour's contribution to Yale is discussed in Reuben A. Holden, *Profiles and Portraits of Yale University Presidents* (1968); George Wilson Pierson, *Yale: College and University 1871–1937*, vols. I–II (1952, 1955); and Brooks M. Kelley, *Yale: A History* (1974). An obituary is in the *New York Times*, Aug. 12, 1963.]

KURT WIMER

SHANNON, FRED ALBERT (Feb. 12, 1893–Feb. 4, 1963), historian and teacher, was born in Sedalia, Mo., the son of Louis Tecumseh Shannon, a tenant farmer, and of Sarah Margaret Sparks. He received a B.A. at Indiana State Teachers College in 1914 and an M.A. at Indiana University in 1918, and took his Ph.D. at the University of Iowa under Arthur Meier Schlesinger in 1924. While a student he taught in grade school and was principal of a high school in Indiana. On Nov. 26, 1914, he married Edna May Jones. They had five children. He began his college teaching at Iowa Wesleyan in 1919, moved to Iowa State Teachers College in 1924, and to Kansas State College of Agriculture in 1926, where he remained until 1939. In that year he joined the Department of History at the University of Illinois, where he taught until retiring in 1961.

Shannon loved teaching. He accepted summer appointments at Ohio State, West Virginia, Missouri, Harvard, Columbia, Wisconsin, Stanford, and South Carolina and a visiting professorship at Williams (1938–1939). He thus obtained a broad perspective on American life and became widely known in the history profession.

Shannon was a rough hewn midwesterner who had a great fund of stories and anecdotes that, combined with his earthy humor, made him an entertaining lecturer. He had little respect for the rich and wellborn in American life and delighted in scorning them and their works. In seminars his "biting criticism and penetrating scholastic demands" kept students on edge and gave them a rigorous training. The logic of his analysis, his critical judgment, and his immense knowledge of bibliography were apparent in everything he wrote. His numerous reviews often stressed the differences between his own interpretations and those of more conservative historians. He devoted much space to pointing out errors, even to alluding ad nauseum to minor mistakes in the spelling of names. As a result he rarely had space to appraise the contributions of a work or to stress the values it might have for other readers.

Shannon's first major work, *The Organization and Administration of the Union Army, 1861–1865* (1928), was a vividly written series of essays dealing with the recruiting, arming, clothing, training, and disciplining of Civil War soldiers. It is a somber story with no heroes or saints—numerous villians seek unconscionable profits and overly ambitious leaders strive for personal victories. The book appeared in the 1920's, when many people were disillusioned with the sordidness of American life, Shannon's work reflected this disillusionment. It was awarded the Justin Winsor Prize of the American Historical Association and the Pulitzer Prize for history.

Shannon's next work was *Economic History of the People of the United States* (1934). It made lavish use of statistics in tables, charts, and graphs. As always his sympathies were with the common man, the debt-ridden farmer, the unorganized worker. He approved of government control of trusts and government efforts to assure that the public lands should not be monopolized by capitalists at the expense of frontier farmers trying to develop their homesteads in the West. Shannon revised this text in 1940 and retitled it *America's Economic Growth.*

In 1939 Arthur M. Schlesinger suggested to the Social Science Research Council, which was engaging in appraising three major books in sociology, economics, and history, that Shannon do the critique of Walter Webb's *The Great Plains.* Shannon must have wondered how he could focus attention on the principles of social science by analyzing *The Great Plains,* which contained little social science. He found Webb's use of geographical terms so elastic as to have little meaning. Perhaps mistakenly, he felt that Webb had commenced with a broad hypothesis and then sought facts to uphold it. He resorted to his usual reviewer's technique of examining the author's use of well-known facts, arguing that they were carelessly introduced and inadequately examined. In short, he made almost a shambles of Webb's book. His critique (1940) was not an appraisal; it was concerned only with errors and misjudgments. Webb was too troubled to reply to the critique, but it was reviewed in the *American Historical Review* by Avery Craven, who was an admirer of Webb's *The Great Plains.* Craven admitted that Webb had used the term "Great Plains" carelessly but called Shannon's critique "a failure from every angle." Shannon struck back by pointing out blunders in Craven's *The Coming of the Civil War* (1942). Rarely have historians resorted to such vituperation as Shannon and Craven did in their resulting correspondence.

Shannon joined Henry David, Harold U. Faulkner, Louis M. Hacker, and Curtis P. Nettels in planning the nine-volume *Economic History of the United States. The Farmer's Last Frontier, Agriculture, 1860–1897* (1945) was the first to appear. These were the years when settlers rushed into the Great Plains following the construction of transcontinental railroads. *The Farmer's Last Frontier* treats pioneering, farm-making, marketing problems, credit relations, economic cycles, and the difficulties that tenants and farm workers faced. His sympathy with the plight of farmers in drought periods permeates the entire work, which is still indispensable for understanding western agricultural history. Shannon's *American Farmers' Movements* (1957) concentrates on the small farmers, whether tenants, squatters, or debt-ridden owners of the land who were overwhelmed by eco-

nomic circumstances and driven to revolt from the time of Bacon's rebellion to the late nineteenth century. His posthumous *The Centennial Years* (1967), which covered American political and economic developments from 1878 to 1895, was a synthesis of his early writings.

Shannon was active in professional organizations, reading papers at meetings, serving on committees, and judging manuscripts. In 1953 he was elected president of the Mississippi Valley Historical Association. He died in Wickenburg, Ariz.

[Shannon's manuscripts, at the archives of the University of Illinois, include a delightfully intimate and personal account of Shannon by Frederick C. Dietz, a long-time colleague. The following papers by Shannon should be noted: "The Homestead Act and the Labor Surplus," *American Historical Review,* July 1936; "A Post Mortem on the Labor-Safety-Valve Theory," *Agricultural History,* Jan. 1945; "The Status of the Midwestern Farmer in 1900," *Mississippi Valley Historical Review,* Dec. 1950; and "Culture and Agriculture in America," *Mississippi Valley Historical Review,* June 1954. A summary of his education, his teaching, and his scholarly publications and a later memorial are in the *Mississippi Valley Historical Review,* June and Sept. 1963. See also Fred W. Kohlmeyer's sketch, *Agricultural History,* Apr. 1963; Robert Huhn amplifies upon it in *The Centennial Years* (1967). Craven's reviews of Shannon's *Appraisal of Walter Prescott Webb's The Great Plains,* and Shannon's review of Craven's *The Coming of the Civil War,* and the resulting correspondence are in *American Historical Review,* Apr. 1942, Apr. 1943, and Oct. 1943. An obituary appeared in the *New York Times,* Feb. 7, 1963.]

PAUL W. GATES

SHEELER, CHARLES R., JR. (July 16, 1883–May 7, 1965), artist and photographer, was born in Philadelphia, Pa., the son of Charles R. Sheeler, a clerk and bookkeeper for a steamship company, and of Mary A. Cunningham. Though far from wealthy, his parents warmly encouraged his decision at the end of high school to become a painter. On advice from the director of the Pennsylvania Academy of the Fine Arts, his professional training began conservatively with a three-year course in commercial design at the Philadelphia School of Industrial Art (1900–1903). One of his teachers there, Herman Diegendesch, allowed Sheeler to use his painting studio on Saturdays, taught him etching, and spoke inspiringly of the famous artists he had known in Munich.

From 1903 to 1906 Sheeler was a student at the Pennsylvania Academy, taking classes with William Merritt Chase, a leading impressionist painter whose dynamic personality and bravura brushwork exerted an irresistible influence. Sheeler was twice able to join Chase's summer classes abroad—in London and Holland in 1904 and in Spain in 1905—where visits to the studios of modern masters and tours of the major museums were combined with creative work.

Also enrolled in Chase's classes at this time was Morton Livingston Schamberg, a recent graduate of the University of Pennsylvania with a degree in architecture, who quickly became a close friend, companion, and important progressive influence on Sheeler. After leaving the Academy, Sheeler spent the summer of 1906 painting in Gloucester, Mass. On his return to Philadelphia he and Schamberg rented a studio together and began submitting their works to annual exhibitions and private dealers.

Late in 1908 Sheeler accompanied his parents on a tour of Europe. In Italy, he discovered the cerebral sense of design underlying early Renaissance fresco and panel painting. Even greater revelations followed in Paris where, during the first six weeks of 1909, Schamberg introduced him to the latest developments in modern art from postimpressionism through fauvism and cubism.

The next few years in Philadelphia were a period of experimentation, but the process of discarding what he had been taught about rapid brushstrokes and getting the subject down in one sitting in favor of more abstract design and arbitrary color did not come easily. Six of Sheeler's works were chosen by Arthur B. Davies for the American section of the Armory Show in New York in 1913, but seeing in one place a large number of recent paintings by Matisse, Derain, Picasso, Braque, and Duchamp decisively influenced Sheeler, like so many other younger American artists, to make his own pictures increasingly abstract, leaving only an occasional hint of natural forms.

In contrast to his artistic aspirations Sheeler made a practical decision in 1912 to become a commercial photographer, specializing in architecture. With a steady source of income, he was able to rent a small house in Bucks County, Pa., near Doylestown, where he and Schamberg could spend weekends working. By 1915 Bucks County barns, the interiors of farmhouses, and early American implements and handicrafts began to appear in his paintings as well as his photographs, their simple, vigorous, geometric shapes taking the place of self-conscious abstractionism.

On one of their frequent trips to New York City, Sheeler and Schamberg met Walter and Louise Arensberg, whose apartment on West Sixty-seventh Street was an epicenter of avant-garde ideas in America. There they discussed art and socialized with a great variety of creative minds, from Marcel Duchamp to William Carlos Williams. After Schamberg's sudden death during the Spanish influenza epidemic of 1918, Sheeler decided, early in 1919, to move permanently to New York.

While working in an art gallery run by Marius De Zayas from 1920 to 1923, he collaborated with Paul Strand on a short film, *Manhatta,* first shown in the summer of 1921 as *New York the Magnificent.* Skyscrapers and elevated railroad tracks appeared in the paintings he worked on during his spare time. Alongside his continuing fascination with the surface textures, planes, and abstract volumes of rural architecture and folk artifacts, these new urban forms were depicted in an increasingly flat, unemotional style, as if to reinforce the clarity of their underlying structure. Critics described Sheeler, together with Charles Demuth, Georgia O'Keeffe, and others, as the "immaculates," but he preferred the term "precisionism."

Sheeler married Katherine Shaffer, also a painter, in 1923. They lived on West Tenth Street, above the Whitney Studio Club, where he helped mount exhibitions, until moving to South Salem, N.Y., in 1927.

One-man shows of his work were held at the Daniel Gallery (1922) and the Whitney Studio Club (1924); but encouraged by Edward Steichen, Sheeler's main occupation from about 1923 to 1932 was commercial photography, especially portraits and fashion plates for the Condé Nast publications *Vanity Fair* and *Vogue.* On commission from the Ford Motor Company in the early fall of 1927, he spent six weeks at the River Rouge Plant, taking thirty-two "portraits of machinery" that further established his reputation. A vacation trip to Europe in 1929 took him to Chartres to photograph the cathedral, to Paris to visit the Louvre and the galleries, and to Germany to see the Deutsche Werkbund "Film und Foto" exhibition in Stuttgart, which included examples of his work.

After a two-year break, Sheeler returned to oil painting, producing pictures such as *Upper Deck* (1929) and several industrial landscapes based on his River Rouge experience. These works brought increasing recognition, including a one-man show at Edith Halpert's Downtown Gallery in 1931.

Katherine Sheeler died in June 1933. On Apr. 2, 1939, he married Musya Sokolova-Isachenko. The publication of Constance Rourke's biography in 1938 and the large retrospective exhibition of his meticulous paintings, prints, conté crayon drawings, and photographs at the Museum of Modern Art in 1939 increased Sheeler's reputation as a major American artist whose images always evince a sense of classical calm through great formal elegance and complete technical mastery.

The last twenty years of Sheeler's creative life were a period of continued growth and change. *Fortune* magazine commissioned a series of six canvases on the theme of "Power" in 1939–1940. From 1942 to 1945 he was photographer-in-residence at the Metropolitan Museum of Art. And two short stints as a resident artist, at Phillips Academy, Andover, Mass., in October 1946 and at the Currier Gallery, Manchester, N.H., in May 1948, marked a notable turning point. He reintroduced hotter colors and began experimenting with simultaneous views, such as double or multiple exposures on a single negative, in his paintings of New England factories. He used glass and even plastic sheets in the process of developing alternative versions of these more complex and openly cubist designs.

During the early 1950's, Sheeler used his camera to investigate and interpret the architecture of Rockefeller Center and the United Nations. He received commissions from the Pabst Brewing Company and United States Steel to photograph their plants in Milwaukee and Pittsburgh, and from General Motors to record its new technical center in Warren, Mich. He suffered a stroke in October 1959 that put an end to his creative work. He died in Dobbs Ferry, N.Y.

[The major collection of Sheeler's papers is in the Archives of American Art, Smithsonian Institution, Washington, D.C., and available on microfilm. Published writings during his lifetime include statements for the catalogs of the Forum Exhibition of Modern American Painters (New York, Mar. 1916) and the retrospective show at the Museum of Modern Art (New York, Oct. 1939); two articles, "Recent Photographs by Alfred Stieglitz," *The Arts*, May 1923, and "Notes on an Exhibition of Greek Art," *ibid.*, Mar. 1925; and an autobiographical manuscript used extensively as the basis for Constance Rourke, *Charles Sheeler: Artist in the American Tradition* (1938; repr. 1969). Transcripts of two taped interviews with Sheeler are also in the Archives of American Art, along with scrapbooks, newspaper clippings, correspondence, and photographs.

A print of the silent movie *Manhatta* is in the collection of the Museum of Modern Art, New York. Three portfolios of Sheeler's photographs were published by the Metropolitan Museum of Art in book form: Susanna Hare and Edith Porada, *The Great*

King, King of Assyria (1945); Nora E. Scott and Charles Sheeler, *Egyptian Statues* (1945); and *Egyptian Statuettes* (1946). See also Martin Friedman, *Charles Sheeler* (1975); and the National Collection of Fine Arts catalog *Charles Sheeler* (1968), containing essays, biographical notes, a complete list of exhibitions, and selected bibliographies. An obituary notice appeared in the *New York Times*, May 8, 1965.]

ELLWOOD C. PARRY III

SHOTWELL, JAMES THOMSON (Aug. 6, 1874–July 15, 1965), historian and internationalist, was born in Strathroy, Ontario, the son of John Blansfield Shotwell, a teacher and small farmer, and of Anne Thomson. He was educated in the local public schools and graduated from the University of Toronto in 1898 with a B.A. in history. He then enrolled in the graduate program at Columbia University, where he established himself as one of the bright stars of the history department and became James Harvey Robinson's outstanding pupil in medieval history. On Aug. 28, 1901, he married Margaret Harvey, who was also a graduate of the University of Toronto. They had two daughters.

In 1903 Shotwell received his Ph.D. His mastery of the "New History," which sought to infuse traditional political and diplomatic history with socioeconomic material and which insisted upon an interdisciplinary approach to the past, led to his appointment in 1905 as adjunct professor of history at Columbia. In 1908 he was promoted to professor. He remained associated with Columbia until his retirement in June 1942 as Bryce Professor Emeritus of the History of International Relations.

In his teaching and writings Shotwell emphasized the impact of science and technology on Western civilization. This theme was prevalent in his famous essay on "History" in the eleventh edition of the *Encyclopaedia Britannica* (1910) and in *The Religious Revolution of To-Day* (1913).

The outbreak of World War I destroyed Shotwell's tranquil world of historical scholarship and college teaching. Increasingly his attention turned to the nature of international conflict and the possibility of its elimination. In April 1917, following America's entry into the war, he helped organize the National Board for Historical Service and became its first chairman. This agency, established in Washington by the nation's leading historians, proposed to explain the war and its implications to the American people. In September 1917 Shotwell accepted a position with the Inquiry, a committee charged with studying the major political, economic, legal, and historical questions that would have to be faced in the peace conference at the end of the war. In 1919 he went with Wilson to Paris as an adviser to the American peace commission. At the Versailles Conference, Shotwell played a minor role, but he did assist in organizing the International Labor Organization.

By the end of the war Shotwell had concluded that future international conflicts could be avoided only through collective security and free trade. Always an activist, he worked in a variety of ways to promote peace and internationalist ideals. Shortly after the war he agreed to edit the massive *Economic and Social History of the World War* for the Carnegie Endowment for International Peace. The project, which took seventeen years, consisted of 152 volumes dealing with the conduct and consequences of the war. In 1924 Shotwell became director of the Carnegie Endowment's Division of Economics and History and used that position to work for United States entry into the League of Nations, the World Court, and the International Labor Organization. In 1927 his suggestion to French Foreign Minister Aristide Briand that the United States and France negotiate a treaty renouncing war as an instrument of national policy led to the Kellogg-Briand Peace Pact, signed the following year by sixty-four nations.

Shotwell combined his activism with scholarly concerns. During the interwar period he wrote extensively on international issues and headed research committees for such organizations as the Institute of Pacific Relations and the Social Science Research Council. In addition, he became the American representative to the League of Nations Committee on Intellectual Cooperation. From 1935 to 1939 he was president of the League of Nations Association.

The savagery of World War II neither surprised Shotwell nor destroyed his optimism. He had long predicted that science and technology would be utilized by the military unless they could be harnessed for peaceful purposes. The war reaffirmed the need to develop a viable international system based on world organization. Shotwell directed his energies to this effort almost as soon as the war began. Along with his colleague Clark Eichelberger, executive director of the League of Nations Association, he established the Commission to Study the Organization of Peace in 1939. The commission produced numerous reports during the war designed to provide a "practical" blueprint for world peace. In addition, Shotwell served on the Advisory Committee on Post-War Foreign Policy, established by Secretary of State Cordell Hull, and in 1945 he became chairman of the

consultants to the American delegation to the United Nations Conference in San Francisco. At the conference he did much to promote the cause of human rights and to strengthen those sections of the United Nations Charter dealing with the social and economic activities of the organization.

Following the war Shotwell continued to promote the cause of liberal internationalism and the United Nations. He strongly backed President Harry S. Truman's activist foreign policy, although he had many reservations about the government's strong anti-Soviet stance. In 1949 he became president of the Carnegie Endowment for International Peace but resigned in 1950 to devote his remaining years to the writing of history. He died in New York City.

Shotwell's dream of a world order based on collective security was doomed to failure. Furthermore, he never fully anticipated that an activist American foreign policy might lead to global interventionism. Still he contributed richly to the American diplomatic experience, not as a policy maker but as the most important and articulate advocate of liberal internationalism and the Wilsonian tradition.

[The most important manuscript collection is Shotwell's papers at Columbia University. The archives of the Carnegie Endowment for International Peace, also at Columbia University, contain useful material. For additional information, see *The Autobiography of James T. Shotwell* (1961) and his "Reminiscences" (1964) in the Oral History Research Office at Columbia University.

A prolific author, Shotwell wrote more than 400 articles, edited some 200 history volumes, and wrote 18 books. Among the most important are *An Introduction to the History of History* (1922); *War as an Instrument of National Policy and Its Renunciation in the Pact of Paris* (1929); *On the Rim of the Abyss* (1936); *What Germany Forgot* (1940); *The Great Decision* (1944); *The United States in History* (1956); *The Long Way to Freedom* (1960); and *The Faith of an Historian and Other Essays* (1964).

Harold Josephson, *James T. Shotwell and the Rise of Internationalism in America* (1975), analyzes his career and offers a useful bibliography of his writings. Also of value are Charles De Benedetti, "James T. Shotwell and the Science of International Politics," *Political Science Quarterly*, June 1974; and "Peace Was His Profession: James T. Shotwell and American Internationalism," in Frank J. Merli and Theodore A. Wilson, eds., *Makers of American Diplomacy*, II (1974). An obituary is in the *New York Times*, July 17, 1965.]

HAROLD JOSEPHSON

SILVER, ABBA HILLEL (Jan. 28, 1893– Nov. 28, 1963), rabbi and Zionist leader, was born in Sirvintus, Lithuania, the son of Moses Silver and Dina Seamon. His father, a rabbi and Hebrew teacher, brought the family to New York City in 1902. After attending public school, Silver studied simultaneously at the University of Cincinnati and the Hebrew Union College, where he was ordained in 1915, the fifth generation of his family to serve in the rabbinate. He occupied his first pulpit, Congregation L'Shem Shamayim, in Wheeling, W. Va., for two years before being called to Tifereth Israel in Cleveland, Ohio, one of the largest Reform congregations in the country. Silver led "The Temple," as it was called, from 1917 until his death. On Jan. 2, 1923, he married Virginia Horkheimer, the daughter of a Wheeling merchant; they had two sons.

As a rabbi, Silver was known as a scholar, a brilliant orator, and a compassionate, if somewhat authoritarian, pastor. He wrote several books on Jewish subjects, including *A History of Messianic Speculation in Israel* (1927), *The Democratic Impulse in Jewish History* (1928), *Religion in a Changing World* (1930), *The World Crisis and Jewish Survival* (1941), *Where Judaism Differed* (1956), and *Moses and the Original Torah* (1961). A collection of his Zionist speeches, *Vision and Victory*, appeared in 1949.

Silver made a striking appearance in the pulpit, always dressed in striped cutaway trousers, starched collar, and black tie. His resonant baritone mesmerized audiences, but not with style alone. He carefully constructed his sermons, often alluding to traditional Jewish sources in history and theology. He did not believe that religion should be easy, and he expected his congregants to be as devoted in their services as he was in his. Yet he also believed that religion should be joyful, and he conducted services with *kavvanah*, a state of intense concentration, devotion, and elevation of spirit.

In his forty-six years at The Temple, Silver gained a reputation as a hard taskmaster, one who dominated officers and laymen and always got his own way. That he had a strong personality is certainly true; and once convinced that he was right, he fought hard to impose his own views. He also took great pains with details; he often knew more about the subject than anyone else, and he abhorred shoddiness. If The Temple was frequently described as a smoothly running machine with Silver at the controls, few of his congregants objected. Moreover, he was an extremely devoted and concerned pastor who went out of his way to help his people. No matter how busy he was, he always returned to

Cleveland every weekend to teach his confirmation class.

Starting in the 1930's, Silver spent more and more time out of the city involved in Zionist affairs. He had first become interested in Jewish nationalism as a boy, founding and leading the Herzl Zion Club on New York's Lower East Side. His natural abilities made him part of the faction aligned with Justice Louis D. Brandeis, which directed American Zionist affairs during World War I, and he walked out with the Brandeis group in the great schism of 1921. Silver and the Americans wanted a Zionist program emphasizing practical work in Palestine, but were defeated by Chaim Weizmann and other European leaders of a politico-religious Zionism. In the 1930's, he gradually began to assume more and important roles in American Zionist and Jewish fund-raising activities.

In 1943 Silver was elected cochairman of the American Zionist Emergency Council with Rabbi Stephen S. Wise. The two men differed significantly over policy. Wise believed that Zionists should trust President Franklin D. Roosevelt and work with his administration, that in the midst of war Jews could not push for special measures. Silver, a Republican, did not share Wise's faith in Roosevelt and often quoted from the Bible: "Put not your trust in princes." He wanted Zionists to pursue a more aggressive policy, calling upon the United States and Great Britain to implement the Balfour Declaration's promise of a Jewish homeland in Palestine.

The fight between the Silver and Wise factions nearly split American Zionism, and Silver resigned from the Emergency Council in December 1944. But growing knowledge of the extent of the Holocaust and of the Roosevelt administration's failure to help persecuted Jews created a groundswell that brought Silver back to power less than a year later.

Beginning in 1945, Silver led a militant American Zionism pressing the Truman administration for action on alleviating the plight of displaced persons and creating a Jewish state. Together with David Ben-Gurion, the leader of Palestinian Jewry, Silver forced the moderate, pro-British Chaim Weizmann out of the presidency of the World Zionist Organization. From 1945 to 1948 American Zionism, under Silver's leadership, orchestrated a complex and effective public relations campaign to convince the American government and people to support Zionist demands for a Jewish state. At the United Nations sessions in the fall of 1947, Silver spoke forcefully as part of the Zionist delegation in presenting the Jewish case to the world body.

Shortly after the establishment of Israel in May 1948, anti-Silver groups forced him out of the Zionist leadership. He had made many enemies by his blunt and often harsh criticisms of colleagues, who were just as tough and unforgiving as he. Moreover, Israeli leaders feared that Silver at the head of a powerful American Zionism would attempt to interfere with policies of the new state.

In the last decade of his life, Silver devoted himself to his congregation, his scholarly studies, and his involvement in numerous civic as well as Jewish activities. He died in Cleveland.

[The Abba Hillel Silver Papers are at the Library of Temple Tifereth Israel, Cleveland; see also the records of the American Zionist Emergency Council in the Zionist Archives and Library, New York; Leon I. Feuer, "Abba Hillel Silver: A Personal Memoir," *American Jewish Archives,* Nov. 1967; and M. I. Urofsky, *We Are One!* (1978). An obituary is in the *New York Times,* Nov. 29, 1963.]

MELVIN I. UROFSKY

SKIDMORE, LOUIS (Apr. 8, 1897–Sept. 27, 1962), architect, was born in Lawrenceburg, Ind., the son of Edgar H. Skidmore and Matilda Matheus. He graduated in 1917 from Bradley Polytechnic Institute (now Bradley University), Peoria, Ill., then joined the Sixteenth Areo Construction Company, U.S. Army, and was sent to England to build airports for the Allied Expeditionary Force. There he and Sergeant Charles R. Strong, a Cincinnati architect, spent weekends studying medieval buildings. After returning to the United States, Skidmore entered the firm of Kruckemeyer and Strong in Cincinnati. His employers encouraged him to undertake advanced architectural studies.

In 1921, Skidmore entered the Massachusetts Institute of Technology (MIT), where he supported himself with scholarships, loans, and funds earned from teaching mechanical drawing. At MIT his drawing ability matured. Ideas that later influenced the nature of his professional practice were nurtured by his design professor, William Emerson, who believed creative imagination was dynamite unless disciplined by structural order and the need for beauty. Skidmore's superior graphic skill stood out among his peers. In the mid-1920's educational ideas of the École des Beaux-Arts in Paris dominated American architectural schools. The seeds of the new architecture of Le Corbusier and Walter Gropius had not yet sprouted in American soil, but one prophet of American functional-

ism, Louis Sullivan, captured Skidmore's imagination.

After completing his studies in 1924, Skidmore entered the office of Maginnis and Walsh in Boston, where he had been working part-time. While there he competed for the Rotch traveling fellowship, awarded for design ability and personality, and won the competition for 1926. With the $3,000 prize Skidmore traveled until 1928 through most of western Europe, Egypt, and Asia Minor, with extended stays at the American Academy in Rome and in the environs of the École des Beaux-Arts in Paris. In Paris he met Eloise Owings, a student at the Parsons School for Designing Women, whom he married on June 14, 1930. They had two sons.

Skidmore extended his tour by traveling to England, where he made measured drawings of cottages and architectural details for Samuel Chamberlain's *Tudor Homes of England* (1929). He returned to Paris in the spring of 1929, at the request of Raymond Hood, to prepare drawings for the Chicago centennial celebration, an event that profoundly influenced the form and direction of his professional career. On his return to the United States, he went to Philadelphia to meet Paul Cret, commissioner of the fair. Learning from Hood that the commission members could not agree on the design of the fair, Skidmore proposed to Cret that he be put in charge, in order to resolve their differences.

Remarkably, that is what happened. Skidmore, a thirty-two-year-old architect without a design of his own yet built, was made chief of design of the fair renamed "A Century of Progress." Despite the Great Depression he succeeded in coordinating the design work to create the first coherent statement of modern architecture in the United States. From Skidmore's point of view, the architecture of the fair was free from the shackles of the past. Economy of construction, the use of new materials or the new use of traditional materials, and an emphasis on the function of a building were characteristics of the new era.

Nathaniel A. Owings, Skidmore's brother-in-law, had joined him at the fair as a development supervisor. They worked closely during the construction period, and independently when Skidmore was given charge of the design division of the exhibits department and Owings assumed the same duties for the concessions department. After the fair closed, they traveled abroad (1935), agreeing to meet in London at the end of the year. In London, Skidmore and Owings pledged to share and share alike, to offer a multidisciplined architectural service competent to design and build structures in the vernacular of their own age, extending the clean, uncluttered tradition pioneered by Le Corbusier, Gropius, and Ludwig Mies van der Rohe.

Skidmore and Owings opened an office in Chicago in January 1936. Through group practice and good design they hoped to establish a volume business, believing that social change, showmanship, and sound economics would prove to commercial clients that economy and aesthetics were not incompatible. Skidmore became director of the Department of Architecture of Armour Institute (now Illinois Institute of Technology) and senior professor of design. He taught only in 1936–1937; after that, work for the American Radiator Company took him to New York City, where he established an office. It was the beginning of the decentralization of practice that became characteristic of the firm. Offices in San Francisco and Portland, Oreg.,were formed later. Skidmore gathered young, bright, and diversified talent around him: Gordon Bunshaft for design, J. Walter Severinghaus for housing, Robert W. Cutler for hospital work, and William S. Brown for prefabrication. The addition of John O. Merrill, architectural engineer, to the Chicago office in 1939 made the Skidmore, Owings and Merrill (SOM) partnership complete.

The SOM partnership was an innovation in architectural practice. The members adopted methods of American business organization to serve commercial clients. They asked for a retainer, a method long used by lawyers, rather than percentage fees of construction costs sought by traditional practitioners. In contrast with other firms, SOM early became both national and decentralized. Its four offices operated autonomously, but joined forces for national and international clients, with movement of specialists and projects among offices. But, most of all, Skidmore established a climate in which creative talent was developed and rewarded with responsibility and professional recognition.

To credit one man with the architectural accomplishments of SOM would be a denial of the firm's basic mode of operation during the first two decades of its practice. Nevertheless, the New York office had the bulk of the work and prestige clients, and Skidmore implemented and gave focus to their projects. He consulted on designs for the 1939 New York World's Fair, using to advantage contacts made in Chicago. Successful design of the New York City pavilion

at the fair resulted in a commission for the Fort Hamilton Veterans' Hospital (1939), which featured a functionalist approach based on the orientation of patient rooms.

During World War II, Skidmore was asked to design the community of Oak Ridge, Tenn., for the Manhattan Project (1942–1945). Experience gained at the fairs proved valuable in solving logistical and organizational problems. By the end of the war the original design for 15,000 inhabitants had been expanded to accommodate 75,000. SOM employed nearly 500 people and had an on-site office at Oak Ridge, headed by Merrill.

Lever House in New York City (1952), a truly collaborative effort of the partnership, broke new ground as a tall, curtain-wall business building, and marked the opening of a new period of skyscraper design. Fittingly, the last design with which Skidmore was associated as an active partner was the commission for the U.S. Air Force Academy at Colorado Springs (1954–1964), which brought to a full circle the architectural career of a corporal in the World War I Areo Service.

Skidmore was awarded the Gold Medal of the American Institute of Architects in 1957. He retired in 1955, but remained a consulting partner until his death at Winter Haven, Fla. To his partners Skidmore was a mystic who reveled in the richness of the twelfth century yet, in all the social, political, and economic changes of the 1930's, had brought together creative talents, new approaches, and modern materials to produce architecture as evocative of the human spirit as were the cathedrals of the Middle Ages.

[Skidmore's drawings are in *Pencil Points*, Oct. 1929, Feb. 1930, Feb. 1931, and Dec. 1931. On the early years and an extensive description of the SOM partnership, see Nathaniel Alexander Owings, *The Spaces in Between* (1973). A critical evaluation of the work of the firm is Ernst Danz, *Architecture of Skidmore, Owings and Merrill, 1950–1962* (1963). Also see *Museum of Modern Art Bulletin*, Fall 1950, a catalog of the exhibition of the works of SOM. The business side of the firm is reviewed in *Business Week*, Dec. 4, 1954; and *Fortune*, Jan. 1958. An obituary is in the *New York Times*, Sept. 29, 1962.]
KENNETH H. CARDWELL

SKOURAS, GEORGE PANAGIOTES (Apr. 23, 1896–Mar. 16, 1964), theater executive, was born in Skourohorion, Greece, the youngest of Panagiotes and Costoula Skouras' ten children. When George Skouras was still quite young, his father died. The family decided that Demetrios, the eldest son, would remain in

Greece and tend the family sheep farm, while Charles, the next oldest son, would attend language school and then immigrate to the United States. In 1907, Charles Skouras settled in St. Louis, Mo., where he was joined by Spyros, the next son, in 1910 and by George in September 1911.

In 1914 the brothers, pooling $4,000 saved from their work as busboys at the Jefferson Hotel, leased and subsequently purchased a nickelodeon, which they named the Olympia Theater. At the Olympia, George sold tickets and guarded the door, a duty that permitted him to meet Julia Ghiglione, whom he married in September 1926. They had two daughters.

In 1919 the three brothers expanded their operations by purchasing other entertainment properties in St. Louis. Within three years they had accumulated facilities worth $1.5 million. They also opened an importing business that sold Greek olives and olive oil produced by brother Demetrios. By 1926 the Skouras chain included thirty-seven St. Louis–area theaters. The seventeen-story, $5 million Ambassador Theater became its flagship house. Charles, the oldest and most business-minded, directed office operations; Spyros, the most gregarious, handled public relations and sales; and George, the most reserved, managed the neighborhood theaters. In their movie "palaces" the brothers introduced on-stage orchestras, high-kicking chorus lines, and Saturday matinees for children.

In April 1926, Demetrios Skouras sued his Americanized brothers, claiming they had denied him his rightful share of the benefits arising from the family's original agreement to share American and Greek incomes equally. But the controversy was never settled because his visa expired before the case reached court. Although the intrafamily squabble subsided, the three brothers' financial problems did not end when Demetrios left the country. After the stock-market crash in 1929, the St. Louis Amusement Company went bankrupt with liabilities of $5,086,410 and assets of $342,462.

Prior to the stock-market crash of 1929, the Skouras brothers sold Skouras Brothers Enterprises to Warner Brothers and after the crash managed to facilitate a merger between Warner-First National Theaters and the Stanley Company of America. The resulting Stanley-Warner Company established Warner Brothers as one of the top theater circuits in the country. When Warners hired the brothers to head different divisions of the company's theater operations, George moved to New York City as general manager for the eastern section.

In 1931, after a series of jobs with different companies, George then became president of a new Skouras Circuit of fifty theaters in the New York City area. Meanwhile, brothers Charles and Spyros filled more lucrative and attractive positions on the West Coast, and Spyros soon became president of Twentieth Century-Fox.

Despite intrafamily conflicts, George Skouras "adopted" Demetrios' son Thanos and supported him through undergraduate and law degrees at American universities. Upon his return to Greece, Thanos was kidnapped and killed by Nazi troops. The Skouras brothers then organized the American Greek War Relief Association. George gathered American and Canadian contributions totaling $150 million. After Pearl Harbor, George enlisted in the Organization of Strategic Services and fulfilled duties in Egypt and occupied Greece, an effort that won him the Bronze Star. Following the war he directed the Animals for Greece drive, which delivered domestic animals, seeds, and farm implements to Greece.

George then reassumed the presidency of Skouras Theatre Corporation, and in 1952 accepted the presidency of the United Artists Theatre Circuit. The following year, acting on behalf of the companies he headed, he filed an $87,960,000 lawsuit against RKO, Warner Brothers Pictures, Paramount Pictures, Universal Pictures, and United Artists Corporation, alleging a conspiracy to monopolize all first-run theaters in the New York City area. In 1958, after most of the companies had settled out of court, United Artists Theatre Circuit absorbed Metropolitan Playhouses, United of California, United Theatres of Texas, Randforce, and others to form a theater circuit with more than 400 houses coast to coast.

Early in the 1950's, when television challenged the entertainment supremacy of motion pictures, studio executives resorted to technological gimmicks like 3-D and Cinerama to woo customers back into the theaters. Spyros Skouras, as head of Twentieth Century-Fox, convinced his studio to acquire the patent for CinemaScope. George thought the trend in motion pictures would be toward the three-hour spectacle, the historical costume drama, and the wide screen. In 1953 he founded Magna Theatre Corporation (later renamed Magna Pictures Corporation). The company's first product, *Oklahoma!* (1955), was shot in Todd-A-O. It displayed all three attributes, but it lost $4 million. Undaunted, George remained as the "unpaid president" of Magna, guiding the enterprise through a lucrative leasing of its Todd-A-O process to Twentieth Century-Fox for the highly profitable *South Pacific* (1958). By 1961 payment of the six-year debentures incurred from the company's *Oklahoma!* disaster left Magna's indebtedness at $1 million. But the company's real problem remained with its expensive rights to Todd-A-O. The licensing fee for the operation was $200,000, a sum that most producers shunned when offered Twentieth Century's CinemaScope process for only $25,000.

In December 1963, after a steady decline in Todd-A-O productions and company profits, Skouras retired as president of Magna Corporation. Legal battles and circuit growth at United Artists Theatre Circuit had not resulted in adequate profits for dissident stockholders, who nearly ousted Skouras in the same month. Within a few months, George had sold his stocks and retired to his New York City, apartment where he died.

A funeral eulogist labeled George Skouras "the quiet one who shunned publicity and kept in the background." His brother Spyros worked with United States presidents and dined with European royalty. George contented himself with the power and rewards of theater operations, the lackluster but crucial end of Hollywood business. From a neighborhood theater in St. Louis to a national headquarters in New York City, George had contributed significantly to the trend toward nationwide corporate enterprise. As an immigrant who rose to prominence within a healthy national economy, he lends credence to mythical stories about success in America. Yet next to other colorful figures in the flamboyant film industry, his laudable accomplishments seem admirably common.

[See Clarence Woodbury, "The Mighty Musketeers of the Movies," *American Magazine,* June 1955. Obituaries are in the *New York Times* and *Film Daily,* Mar. 17, 1964.]

KENNETH R. HEY

SLOAN, HAROLD PAUL (Dec. 12, 1881–May 22, 1961), Methodist clergyman, editor, and author, was born in Westfield, N.J., the son of Theodore Reber Sloan and Miriam B. Hickman. He was brought up in a religious home typical of the late nineteenth century. When he misbehaved, his mother, the daughter of a Methodist minister, read the Bible to him, prayed with him (even instead of physical punishment), and took him to church. At fourteen Sloan joined a Camden, N.J., Methodist church. He studied the Bible closely, reading commentaries and writing essays, and was an active evangelist, preaching to friends and reproving drunks.

This search for religious certainty fell apart during Sloan's years at the University of Pennsylvania and at Crozer and Drew theological seminaries. For a time he became a socialist, defended communism, and denounced Methodism for its emotionalism and negative view of humanity. But he gradually realized he could neither prove the existence of God intellectually nor achieve ethical purity, and while at Drew he experienced the emotions of a salvation experience (an event perhaps associated with an illness that brought him near death). Having resolved his intellectual dilemmas, Sloan established full connection with the New Jersey Conference of the Methodist Episcopal Church in 1906. In 1908, he received a B.D. from Drew. He was ordained in that year.

A tall, imposing figure, Sloan possessed a powerful voice and a quick mind in debate. He quickly rose as a leader, serving seven churches before going to Haddonfield Methodist Church (1924–1933), which became the largest in New Jersey. On Apr. 3, 1909, he married Ethel Beatrice Buckwalter; they had two children.

Within Methodism, Sloan was the principal leader of the fundamentalist defense of the faith. But he was no ordinary fundamentalist. He rejected the term "fundamentalism" in favor of "historic Christianity," asserting that he was defending the "essentials" or "great headlands" of the faith. He disassociated himself from the premillennialism of organized fundamentalism, disavowed biblical literalism, and upheld the legitimacy of higher criticism. While personally rejecting evolution, Sloan conceded that Christianity and evolution were compatible. He believed that the chief problem facing the church was modernism's acceptance of naturalistic and behavioristic philosophy. This philosophy denied man's depravity and need for redemption.

According to Sloan, liberals had converted Jesus' life from one of atonement to one of example; they substituted social reform for personal virtue. Modernists denied Christ's divinity and the inspiration of the Bible. Sloan's chief concern was the danger of these ideas for society. Historic Christianity was for him the "rock of social progress" that since the Reformation had produced the highest achievements of humanity: benevolence, pacifism, abolitionism, mass education, sexual purity, political democracy. Where Christianity weakened, he said, the result was war, crime, greed, dictatorship, communism, and fascism.

New Jersey Methodists, stimulated by Sloan's *The Child and the Church* (1916), charged that behavioristic pedagogy dominated Methodist Sunday-school literature, deemphasizing sin and teaching a salvation of good habits based on the example of Jesus. Following the 1916 Methodist General Conference, Sloan and his supporters expanded their attack to books on the Course of Study, readings designed for ministerial preparation. At the 1920 General Conference, Sloan's forces won several significant victories, the most important being the resolution that books in the course for ministerial students be in "full and hearty accord" with the Articles of Religion, Methodism's chief doctrinal statement. To Sloan's surprise, however, the Commission on Courses of Study then selected fifteen books that seemed in direct opposition to the Articles of Religion.

This seeming insubordination faced Sloan with hard choices. Many warned that he was jeopardizing his career with his obsessive attacks. For a time he vacillated, but eventually he concluded that God had called him to defend the "precious truth of Christianity." In *Historic Christianity and the New Theology* (1922) he detailed the doctrinal errors of the contested books. At the 1924 General Conference, Sloan's forces won victories in committee, but once again objectionable books were chosen for ministerial students. Sloan appeared before the bishops to demand the books' removal, but without success.

In 1925, Sloan became president of the Methodist League for Faith and Life. He launched the magazine *Call to the Colors* (1925–1926), later renamed *Essentialist* (1927–1930). He worked tirelessly, promoting the league, editing copy, and speaking at mass rallies. By 1928 the League had 3,000 members and had distributed 450,000 pieces of literature. Nevertheless, the 1928 General Conference shuffled off to committee the league's 10,000-signature petition protesting liberalism in Courses of Study, theological seminaries, and Sunday-school literature; hooted Sloan off the floor; rejected a strong doctrinal statement; and failed to elect conservative candidates, including Sloan, nominated for positions other than bishop. Thereafter Sloan's attacks grew more and more caustic and personal, especially against Edwin Samuel Lewis of Drew University in *Christ of the Ages* (1928) and against certain schools and pastors in *The Case of Methodism Against Modernism* (1929). Increasingly alienated within Methodism, he moved closer to leaders of the larger fundamentalist movement and accepted positions on the advisory board of the League of Evangelical Students and the faculties of Temple University and the National Bible Institute.

Between 1929 and 1931, Sloan's belligerence moderated. Debts forced the dissolution of the Methodist League for Faith and Life and the merger of the *Essentialist* with *Bible Champion* to form *Christian Faith and Life* in 1931. While Sloan continued as editor until 1933, his editorials lacked the rancor of the past. He declared the controversy was "history" and even praised modernism for its needed emphasis on social service and reexamination of Christian evidences.

Several factors contributed to this change: the humiliation at the 1928 General Conference; a severe illness in 1930 that forced Sloan to reduce his work load and reevaluate his motives; the death, in 1931, of John Alfred Faulkner of Drew, who had secretly been the mind of the movement, advising and encouraging Sloan in confidential letters throughout the 1920's; and the rise of neoorthodoxy within Methodism, which Sloan saw as proof of the victory of the conservative cause.

With Sloan's moderation came a new acceptance within Methodism. He wrote *The Apostle's Creed* (1930); he lectured at Boston and Drew universities and Garrett Theological Seminary, alleged strongholds of liberalism; and he advised church leaders regarding revision of the ritual and hymnal. At the 1932 General Conference, he stood with church leaders in defending the Articles of Religion and the power of the bishops against the liberal Rock River Memorials, which called for removal of constitutional restrictions on Methodist doctrines and thereby subjected the Articles of Religion to General Conference whims. From 1934 to 1936, Sloan served as superintendent of the Camden district, and the 1936 General Conference appointed him editor of Methodism's leading newspaper, the *New York Christian Advocate*, a post he held until 1941.

As editor, Sloan took strong stands on the leading issues of the day. He declared that government must provide food, housing, and employment even if private initiative was sacrificed. He rejected doctrinaire pacifism and urged American preparedness in the face of German and Communist aggression (while also supporting conscientious objection). He denounced racism and supported a General Conference boycott of cities with segregated public accommodations, but he yielded to separate black jurisdictions, partly to mollify the South and partly to secure permanent places of leadership for black Methodists.

From 1941 to 1953, Sloan served as pastor of Wharton Methodist Church in Philadelphia, and after his retirement he was an evangelist for the Philadelphia Annual Conference. During these final twenty years he wrote six more books, all defending Christian orthodoxy and supernaturalism. He died at Camden, N.J.

[The Harold Paul Sloan Collection at Drew University contains 40,000 documents from 1916–1936, but important portions are missing. His writings, in addition to those listed in the text, include *Personality and the Fact of Christ* (1933) and *Eternal Life* (1948). Also see Stewart G. Cole, *The History of Fundamentalism* (1931); and Norman Furniss, *The Fundamentalist Controversy, 1918–1931* (1954), both of which are often inaccurate. Useful dissertations are William J. McCutcheon, "Theology of the Methodist Episcopal Church in the Interwar Period, 1919–1939" (Yale University, 1960); and William Bryant Lewis, "The Role of Harold Paul Sloan and the Methodist League for Faith and Life in the Fundamentalist-Modernist Controversy of the Methodist Episcopal Church" (Vanderbilt University, 1963). An obituary is in the *New York Times*, May 23, 1961.]

BEN PRIMER

SLOANE, ISABEL CLEVES DODGE (Feb. 26, 1896–Mar. 9, 1962), racehorse owner and dog breeder, was born in Detroit, Mich., the daughter of John Francis Dodge, an automobile manufacturer, and of Ivy S. Hawkins. Her mother died in 1901, and in that same year John Dodge and his brother, Horace, started a machine shop that grew rapidly by filling contracts for the automobile manufacturers Ransom Eli Olds and Henry Ford. In 1914 the Dodge Brothers Company began manufacturing its own cars.

Isabel graduated from the Liggett School at Grosse Pointe, Mich., in 1913. When her father died in 1920, his estate was estimated at more than $40 million, of which she inherited more than $7 million. On Feb. 28, 1921, Isabel married George Sloane, a securities broker. They had no children.

The Sloanes lived on an estate in Locust Valley, N.Y.; had an apartment in Manhattan; and also spent time in Palm Beach, Fla. Sloane was active socially, but she did not like publicity and was skeptical of the value of interviews and reporters. She had always liked horses and entered racing through steeplechasing. She bought a jumper named Skyscraper II, which "made me a fan for life by winning his first important start" (the Manly Memorial Steeplechase at Pimlico, Md., in 1924).

But Sloane achieved her greatest fame with flat racers. In 1927 her colt Brooms won the Hopeful Stakes. Her marriage ended in divorce in 1929, and she bought Brookmeade Farm in Upperville, Va., that same year. Sloane supervised every aspect of Thoroughbred activity: workouts, entries, sales, and breeding. She was considered a discriminating and sometimes extravagant buyer at the yearling auctions. It was a long time before Brookmeade Stable had success at breeding, but Flag Pole won the Swift Stakes in 1932.

Sloane liked to bet at the track (where she often entertained lavishly): "I bet small sums, because the interesting thing about betting to me is not the amount of money you can make: it's whether or not you can finish ahead of the book-makers for the day." But she never bet on big races in which her horses were entered.

Sloane was also a successful breeder of dogs. Her Brookmeade Kennels in Syosset, N.Y., did pioneering work with schnauzers and basset hounds. Frank Brumby was the manager. The kennels' first major success came when a schnauzer was judged best in show at Westbury in 1925. At Westminster in 1928, Brookmeade won best of breed in bassets with Walhampton Grappler and in schnauzers with Harno vom Schoenblick. Sloane increased the popularity of schnauzers in the United States—particularly miniature schnauzers, Brookmeade's specialty. One of her greatest contributions was the improvement of breeds by bringing outstanding dogs from Europe.

Okapi, Sloane's favorite horse, won $17,885 in 1932. The next year, Brookmeade Stable was third on the list of money-winning owners, and Inlander was the leading money-winning three-year-old. But 1934 was the best year for Sloane. Brookmeade Stable won more money than any other ($251,138), and for the first time a woman headed the Thoroughbred-owners' list. The Brookmeade colors—white with royal blue cross sashes—seemed to win everything. Cavalcade won the Kentucky Derby and four other stakes. Sloane had bought him for $1,200 as a yearling. His races were especially exciting. He was a slow starter, but after the mile mark he would come on strong. While the opposition was tiring, he would end with a burst of speed to win going away. Sloane said she had many arguments with her trainer Bob Smith about whether Cavalcade or High Quest was their best horse. Smith preferred High Quest, which won the Preakness.

During World War II, Sloane belonged to the American Women's Voluntary Services and was active in the organization's salvage bureau.

She was also involved aiding servicemen and their families, and participated in benefit programs held at racetracks.

The headquarters of Brookmeade Stable was at Belmont Park. Preston Burch, and later his son Elliott, were Sloane's trainers. In 1949, Brookmeade was the breeder of eight stakes winners and Sloane was named the outstanding breeder of the year by the New York Turf Writers Association. She headed the owners' list in 1950, and the next year, as guest of honor at the annual dinner of the Thoroughbred Club of America, she said, "Racing and breeding horses are . . . my hobby, business, my pleasure, and almost my entire life."

In 1952, Sloane reduced the size of her stable and sold her crop of yearlings. In 1955, Brookmeade had an excellent homebred horse, Sailor. Sword Dancer was Horse of the Year in 1959 and, when he was retired, had earned $829,610. In 1960, Bowl of Flowers was the champion two-year-old filly. When Brookmeade-bred Eidolon won the Hutcheson Stakes at Gulfstream Park for another owner in 1962, he was the sixty-third stakes winner Sloane had bred. She died in West Palm Beach, Fla.

[One of the few interviews Sloane gave is in the *New York Times*, Sept. 16, 1934, sec. 3, p. 8. "America's Great Kennels of the Past," *Pure-Bred Dogs— American Kennel Gazette*, June 1965, is about Brookmeade Kennels and Sloane's influence on American dog breeding. Also see John Hervey, *Racing in America: 1922–1936* (1937). Obituaries are in the *New York Times* and *New York Herald Tribune*, Mar. 11, 1962; and *Blood-Horse*, Mar. 17, 1962.]
RALPH KIRSHNER

SMITH, DAVID ROLAND (Mar. 9, 1906– May 23, 1965), sculptor, was born in Decatur, Ind., the son of Harvey Martin Smith, a telephone company engineer and unsuccessful inventor, and of Golda Stoler, a schoolteacher and a devout Methodist, who instilled in him the virtues of discipline and hard work. From earliest childhood he exhibited a passionate craving for independence, sometimes seeking refuge at his grandmother's house from what he regarded as parental oppression. As a boy he tinkered with mechanical objects and was fascinated by trains. Later Smith worked, not very willingly, on weekends and vacations to earn money for his education. He displayed no precocious talent, but at Paulding (Ohio) High School, with vague aspirations toward an artistic career, he took two courses in mechanical drawing and subscribed to a correspondence course in freehand drawing from the Cleveland Art School.

In 1924, Smith entered Ohio University in Athens, Ohio. He spent the following summer working as a welder and riveter at the Studebaker plant in South Bend, Ind., an experience he later invested with much significance for his development as a sculptor in iron and steel. In 1925 he took a job in Washington, D.C., with the Morris Plan Bank, which transferred him to its New York office in 1926. By then Smith was determined to become an artist and, guided by Dorothy Dehner, an art student living at his rooming house, he enrolled at the Art Students League to study under Richard Lahey and John Sloan.

Seeking a more advanced approach to art than that taught by most of the faculty, he gravitated to the modernist painter Jan Matulka. Through other League contacts he met John Graham, a sophisticated artist who expanded his knowledge of School of Paris painting and sculpture as well as such American avant-garde figures as Stuart Davis, Milton Avery, Arshile Gorky, and Jean Xceron. Smith later wrote that Sloan gave him a "feeling of knowing the artist's position as a rebel or as one in revolt against the status quo," but that as a teacher "Matulka was a guy I'd rather give more credit [to] than anyone else." But until their estrangement after 1940, Graham was the major influence on his aesthetic growth.

Smith was tall, burly, enthusiastic, and impressionable. He had immense charm and self-confidence, and worked with sustained, concentrated energy. He also had an erratic, sometimes violent streak that occasionally broke out in uncontrollable rages. A year after they met, Smith and Dorothy Dehner were married, and in 1929 they bought a small farm above Bolton Landing, N.Y., on Lake George, where throughout the 1930's they spent most of their summers.

Smith's first tentative experiments in sculpture were made with coral pieces found on the beach during a trip to the Virgin Islands in 1931. The following year he created wood and metal constructions, and set up a forge in his studio at Bolton Landing. An article in the journal *Cahiers d'art* on the welded sculpture of the Spanish artist Julio González awakened him to the possibilities of working with iron and steel. In 1933, Smith bought welding equipment, and after some unsuccessful attempts to use it in his Brooklyn apartment, he came across a ramshackle waterfront metal shop called the Terminal Iron Works. "Next morning I walked in," he wrote later, "and was met by a big Irishman named Blackburn. 'I'm an artist; I have a welding outfit. I'd like to work here.' 'Hell yes, move in.'" But not until 1935 did he definitely commit himself to sculpture as his chief means of artistic expression.

Like many of his contemporaries, Smith worked on the New Deal art programs. He served as a technical supervisor for the mural division of the Treasury Relief Art Project and later as a sculptor on the Federal Art Project of the Works Progress Administration. He identified with the Left in the ideological struggles of the New York art world, and was active in Artists' Union demonstrations and debates. He was also a vocal advocate of abstract art as the true art of the people.

For Smith the 1930's were essentially a period of intensive experimentation in various sculptural styles derived chiefly from cubism and constructivism. His grasp of sculptural form was apparent from the beginning, and his development was marked by his growing assurance in the use of massive arrangements of planes and solids and of intricately worked constructions, often with clear associative patterns delineating animal and human features as well as landscape and interior settings. Much of his sculpture of the 1930's—and, indeed, throughout his career —uses human or other recognizable references, but very little expresses direct social commentary. An exception is "Medals for Dishonor," a series of bronze medallions produced between 1937 and 1940. Strongly influenced by Pablo Picasso, their symbolic imagery and explicit depictions of the horrors of war and its consequences make a distinct political statement.

The year 1940 marked a turning point in Smith's life. He and his wife took up full-time residence at Bolton Landing, where he built a shop and named it the Terminal Iron Works. He worked as a machinist in Glens Falls and, in 1942, took a welding job in Schenectady at the American Locomotive Company plant, which was making locomotives and tanks for the army. The experience was exhausting, but valuable for its technical training and for expanding his sense of scale.

Smith returned to Bolton Landing in 1944 and built a new house and studio. He began teaching and lecturing at colleges and professional conferences. It was one of his most prolific and inventive periods. His work of that time shows a tendency toward larger pieces and more complex imagery, with an intensely felt and sometimes highly elaborated private symbolism. Two typical examples are *Home of the Welder* (1945) and *The Cathedral* (1950). In the former a domestic setting holds representations of figures and objects—a woman's body, a dog's head, a millstone and chain, a phallic welding torch, a flowering plant. In *The Cathedral,* Smith presents an open structure designed to suggest a church with a symbolic claw, a prostrate man, a coin. In one of his few accounts of the meaning of a work, he pointed out that *The Cathedral* represents a "symbol of power—the state, the church, or any individual's private mansion built at the expense of others."

Some of these pieces have been interpreted as Smith's effort to transform psychic pressures into visual metaphors. Although he abandoned this style in the 1950's, the pressures continued. He and Dorothy Dehner were divorced in 1952, and on Apr. 6, 1953, he married Jean Freas; they had two children. A growing estrangement took place between him and his friends of the 1930's, who were replaced by a new circle of acquaintances, chiefly Robert Motherwell, Clement Greenberg, Helen Frankenthaler, and Kenneth Noland. In 1956 he ended his connection with Marian Willard, his dealer for nearly twenty years.

Never well known to the public, Smith had, by the mid-1950's, achieved a commanding reputation among artists and critics of the avant-garde. The work of the New York School was widely regarded as the most vital art of the postwar years, and a host of new collectors made possible a rapid expansion of the art market. For the first time Smith's sculpture began to sell. The highest form of recognition, a retrospective exhibition at the Museum of Modern Art in New York City, came in 1957. But, despite all this success, Smith's strain of arrogance and harshness grew more pronounced. After his second marriage ended in divorce (1961), he lived alone on his hillside, seeing a few visitors and taking occasional trips to New York City.

Smith's work of this period is characterized by a growing monumentality of scale and form and by greater simplicity and formal plastic design. Figurative elements became less frequent, and there were now more and larger nonobjective arrangements of planes and cursive forms, culminating in the enormous and formidable "Cubi," "Zig," and "Wagon" series, some more than ten feet high and weighing in excess of a ton. To some critics these late works are his crowning achievement. The expansiveness and stylistic organization seen in the massive cubes and cylinders of burnished stainless steel in the "Cubi" series represent a final working out of formal problems encountered as early as the 1930's.

Smith died at the height of his powers when his pickup truck overturned on a road near Bennington, Vt. He left more than 700 pieces, whose complexity and strength make him one of the most significant sculptors in the history of American art.

[Smith's papers are at the Archives of American Art, Smithsonian Institution, which also has several groups of his letters to friends and associates. His works are in the following museums, among others: Hirschhorn Collection, Washington, D.C.; Dallas Museum of Fine Arts; Detroit Institute of Arts; Norton Simon Museum of Art, Pasadena, Calif.; Brooklyn Museum, Guggenheim Museum, Museum of Modern Art, Metropolitan Museum of Art, Whitney Museum, New York City; Baltimore Museum of Art; Art Institute of Chicago; Cincinnati Art Museum; San Francisco Museum of Art. Rosalind Krauss, *Terminal Iron Works* (1971), is an interpretive and rather technical discussion of Smith's aesthetic; her *Sculpture of David Smith* (1977) is a descriptive listing of every known work. Stanley E. Marcus (Ph.D. diss., Columbia University, 1972) thoroughly covers Smith's sculptural technique. *David Smith by David Smith*, edited by Cleve Gray (1968), is a picture book with excerpts from Smith's writings. *David Smith*, edited by Garnett McCoy (1973), is a documentary publication of selected lectures and articles by and about Smith. An obituary is in the *New York Times*, May 25, 1965.]

GARNETT McCOY

SMITH, EDWARD HANSON (Oct. 29, 1889–Oct. 29, 1961), U.S. Coast Guard officer and oceanographer, was born in Vineyard Haven, Mass., the son of Edward Jones Smith, a whaling captain, and of Sarah Elizabeth Pease. He attended Vineyard Haven elementary schools and New Bedford High School. In 1910, after one year at the Massachusetts Institute of Technology, he entered the U.S. Coast Guard Academy (then the U.S. Revenue Cutter Service School) in New London, Conn. He graduated and was commissioned an ensign in 1913. During the next four years Smith served on Coast Guard cutters based in East Coast ports. From August 1917 to January 1919 he was a navigator in the Atlantic Patrol Force on convoy escort duty between England and Gibraltar.

After returning to the United States, Smith served on cutters in Boston and Newport News, Va., on routine patrol duty before being assigned to the cutter *Seneca* in November 1919. When the *Seneca* was assigned to the International Ice Patrol in the North Atlantic in the spring of 1920, Smith served as a scientific observer and navigator.

From this point on, Smith was engaged in research in the Arctic and in the general field of oceanography. He continued with the International Ice Patrol until August 1924. During his off-duty hours he pursued graduate studies at Harvard University and wrote reports based upon his Ice Patrol research. In 1924 he received an M.A. from Harvard. On July 24 of that year he married Isabel Brier; they had three sons.

Smith won a fellowship from the American-Scandinavian Foundation to study oceanography at the Geophysical Institute of Bergen, Norway, from August 1924 to August 1925. He then spent three months at the British Meteorological Office in London, collecting data that proved to be of value to the Coast Guard in its Ice Patrol work.

When Smith returned to the United States and the Ice Patrol in late 1925, he brought back extensive knowledge of modern methods of oceanography and was in a position to put these methods into use. From 1926 to 1928 he was at sea for long periods. When one vessel was returning to port, he often transferred at sea to the patrol ship that replaced it. His friends called him "Iceberg."

From January 1928 to June 1936, Smith was officially assigned to the Coast Guard destroyer force operating against smugglers, but he was able to spend much of his time on detached duty with the Ice Patrol. During the summer of 1928 he commanded the *Marion* expedition to the iceberg-producing areas of the Labrador Sea, Davis Strait, and Baffin Bay, off the west coast of Greenland. This was the most comprehensive oceanographic survey ever made by the United States government. His scientific report on that expedition earned him a Ph.D. from Harvard in 1934.

In July 1931, Smith was the American scientific observer on the six-day, 8,000-mile flight of the *Graf Zeppelin* in the Arctic north of Eurasia. His report on this voyage was published by the American Geographical Society. He was assigned to Alaskan waters in June 1936, and led the rescue of the crew of the U.S.S. *Swallow* from Kanaga Island in February 1938, for which he received a citation from the Navy Department.

As the United States moved closer to war in 1941, Smith was assigned to the Greenland Patrol, first to command the northeast portion but, after October 1941, the entire patrol. In 1942 he was promoted to rear admiral and began to build a fleet of armed trawlers, using Boston fishing boats modified to carry deck guns. In November 1943, Smith was given command of Task Force 24 of the Atlantic Fleet and set up a network of weather and rescue ships across the

North Atlantic to support military flights to England. He also commanded rescue ships during the D-day invasion of France. He was awarded the U.S. Navy's Distinguished Service Medal for his World War II service, and Denmark honored him with the Cross of Danneborg for his work in preventing German occupation of eastern Greenland.

In 1945, Smith became commandant of the Third Coast Guard District (New York) and captain of the port of New York. In 1946 he took on added responsibility for all search and rescue operations in the western North Atlantic. He headed the official inquiry into the loss of the *Constance* in Nantucket Sound in 1949, and his handling of the inquiry became a model for future such investigations.

After his retirement from the Coast Guard in 1950, Smith was director of the Woods Hole (Mass.) Oceanographic Institution until 1956. During his tenure a laboratory of oceanography was built, ships and aircraft were acquired to expand research opportunities, and Woods Hole was accredited as an institution of higher education. From 1956 until his death in Falmouth, Mass., Smith was affiliated with the New York public-relations and fund-raising consultant firm of Marts and Lundy.

[Manuscript records and extensive news clips of Smith's career are in the Archives of the Woods Hole Oceanographic Institution; biographical material is with the U.S. Coast Guard, Washington, D.C.; service records are at the Military Records Center, St. Louis, Missouri. Smith's scientific reports appeared in *U.S. Weather Bureau Monthly Weather Review, U.S. Coast Guard Bulletin, Air-Sea Safety, Geographical Review,* and the *Transactions* of the American Geophysical Union. His major work, *The Marion and General Greene Expeditions to Davis Strait and Labrador Sea under the Direction of the U.S. Coast Guard, 1928–1931–1933–1934–1935: Scientific Results. Part 2. Physical Oceanography,* was published by the Government Printing Office (1937). An obituary is in the *New York Times,* Oct. 31, 1961.]

PETER J. ANDERSON

SMITH, HOMER WILLIAM (Jan. 2, 1895–Mar. 25, 1962), physiologist, was born in Denver, Colo., the son of Albert C. Smith and Margaret E. Jones. He attended high school in Cripple Creek and Denver, and received the B.A. in 1917 from the University of Denver. Smith described his early environment as economically poor but culturally rich.

After graduation, Smith served in the army during World War I, initially in an engineer battalion and subsequently as a chemist under E. K. Marshall, investigating biologic effects of war gases. Following the war he undertook graduate study in physiology at Johns Hopkins University, and in 1921 received the D.Sc.

Smith worked from 1921 to 1923 in the research laboratories of Eli Lilly and Company and then at Harvard University in the laboratory of Walter B. Cannon. In 1925 he became chairman of the Department of Physiology at the University of Virginia. Three years later he was appointed professor of physiology and director of the physiological laboratories at the New York University College of Medicine, positions he held until his retirement in 1961.

Smith's scientific interests gradually moved from physical chemistry and cellular physiology through chemotherapy to chemical physiology of the body fluids. In consequence of these latter studies, he became interested in the kidneys as the organs that control the internal environment, and by the late 1920's he had increasingly narrowed his interests to renal physiology. He went on to investigate phenomena as diverse as evolution, paleontology, the biology of consciousness, and the history of religion.

In 1928, Smith initiated his studies on the African lungfish, describing its biological significance in his philosophical novel *Kamongo* (1932; rev. 1949) and in his book on the evolutionary history of kidney function, *From Fish to Philosopher* (1953). He also published several papers on the comparative renal physiology of other animals. The results of these comparative studies were applied directly to the problems that became central to his later research: the functions of the mammalian (and especially the human) kidney.

Smith played a major role in the development of contemporary knowledge of the kidney and its function. His pioneer studies first involved refinement of the concept of renal clearance. In the 1930's he and A. N. Richards independently discovered that the glomerular filtration rate could be accurately measured by means of inulin, a starch. Smith and his collaborators elucidated the manner in which the kidney "clears" creatinine, urea, mannitol, sodium, and inulin, and subsequently developed the methods for measurement of effective renal blood flow and of tubular mass. He investigated the role of the kidneys in the pathogenesis of hypertension.

Smith's New York laboratory became a center of renal physiology. In it he trained and collaborated with more than 100 clinicians and physiologists, many of whom became leaders in various disciplines. The relationships between his laboratory and various clinical departments were close and mutually beneficial.

Smith somehow found time to accept and discharge many important advisory and consultative responsibilities. He was awarded the Presidential Medal for Merit (1948), the Lasker Award (1948), and the Passano Award (1954) for his research contributions. He also lectured and held visiting professorships at many institutions in the United States and other countries.

Two of Smith's books have had a profound influence in medicine. *The Physiology of the Kidney* (1937) was the first comprehensive English-language study of renal physiology since A. R. Cushny's *The Secretion of the Urine* (1917). His monumental treatise, *The Kidney: Structure and Function in Health and Disease* (1951), definitively surveyed the field of renal physiology and pathology.

Smith was an indefatigable investigator and worker, and an excellent and meticulous writer and editor. It is said that the characteristic that set him apart from his peers was the rapidity and logic with which he could reach the core of an intricate concept. His thorough criticism of the papers of junior associates taught a number of them to write lucidly and logically. He was a voracious reader, not only in the sciences but also in philosophy, religion, art, music, and literature. To him, science and philosophy were never widely separated. In two historical and philosophical volumes, he spelled out his naturalistic humanism: *The End of Illusion* (1935) and *Man and His Gods* (1952). The latter includes an autobiographical account of his Colorado boyhood.

Smith's personal life was not notably happy. His marriage to Carlotta Smith (Sept. 17, 1921) ended in divorce, and his second, to Margaret Wilson (Mar. 19, 1949), with her death. The great joy of his life in later years was his son, born in April 1951. It is said that Smith's way of life, his hopes, and his plans were centered on the boy.

Smith understood how scientific methodology could be brought into the clinic and how clinicians could best be trained in that methodology. He was a creative and precise investigator, a gifted teacher, and a talented writer who exerted a profound influence on contemporary physiologic knowledge. After his death in New York City, a prominent physiologist said, "His death brought to a close what has been aptly termed the Smithian Era of physiology. For over thirty years he had dominated his chosen field in a way that few, if any, have dominated other fields."

[A complete list of Smith's publications is in Herbert Chasis and William Goldring, eds., *Homer William Smith: His Scientific and Literary Achievements* (1965). His last book was *Principles of Renal Physiology* (1956). Also see the memoir by Robert F. Pitts in *Biographical Memoirs. National Academy of Sciences* (1967). An obituary is in the *New York Times,* Mar. 26, 1962.]

HARRIS D. RILEY, JR.

SMITH, HORTON (May 22, 1908–Oct. 15, 1963), professional golfer, was born in Springfield, Mo., the son of Perry H. Smith and Anna Kershner. His father was a successful lawyer-businessman with real estate interests. In 1920 the family purchased a farm near the Springfield Country Club, where Perry Smith was a member and his son annually vied for the junior championship of the club.

Smith attended Missouri State Teachers College at Springfield from 1925 to 1927—he was one of the few professional golfers of this period who had gone to college. But his love of golf led to his decision, apparently against his father's wishes, to leave college and turn professional. He became club pro at the Joplin (Mo.) Country Club in 1927. The following year Smith began his meteoric rise to international recognition. Between November 1928 and December 1929, he won eleven tournaments—the record for a first-year professional—including the French Open. In six other competitions he finished second. This string of victories earned him a spot on the U.S. Ryder Cup team, on which he played for a decade. He continued to do well on the winter circuit of 1929–1930, earning a record $15,500.

Despite his achievements Smith remained soft-spoken and unexcitable. His commitment to golf was complete. He gained the reputation of a genial but reserved man who drank only milk. He became an idol of American sports fans who saw him as a "farm boy" who epitomized the more wholesome aspects of American society.

Smith was the last person to beat Bobby Jones prior to Jones's capture of golf's "grand slam" in 1930. The following year, though, he broke his wrist in an accident. This injury began a slump that lasted until 1934. During this period his interests began to turn toward the organizational aspects of the professional golf tour. He served in 1933 as chairman of the tournament committee of the Professional Golfers' Association (PGA). In this capacity he unsuccessfully recommended that the tournament bureau manager, not the players, be given responsibility for enforcing PGA rules.

Smith returned to his earlier form in 1934, when he won the first Masters Tournament at Augusta, Ga. He repeated as Masters champion in 1936, and continued to win tournaments for the rest of the decade. He was especially dangerous if leading or close to the lead after the third round. Although he never captured a major championship after 1936, he was twice the leading money winner on the PGA tour.

This record was remarkable because Smith's interest and activity were increasingly drawn to tournament business and promotion. He organized players to give speeches in cities where championships were held. He personally wrote to sponsors, thanking them for their support. He also toured for the Spalding sporting goods company after 1935, when he yielded his position as pro at Oak Park Country Club, near Chicago, to his brother Renshaw.

On Oct. 9, 1938, Smith married Barbara Louise Bourne; they had one son. Her father, Alfred S. Bourne, was a member of the August National Golf Club. The separation generated by Smith's career and the war led to estrangement, and they were divorced in 1945.

During World War II, Smith served in Europe as a captain in the Army Air Corps. He apparently saw no action. In 1946 he became pro at the Detroit Golf Club, a position he held until his death. He occasionally entered tournaments, his final victory coming in the Michigan PGA Championship of 1948. Until his death he played annually in the Masters, and was proud that he was the only player from the first field to compete in that event into the 1960's.

Clearly, Smith's interests after the war lay in the business aspects of the PGA. He served as its president from 1951 to 1953. In this capacity he helped to liberalize PGA policy with respect to black players. In 1952 he deftly steered an "approved entry clause" through the tournament committee, a measure that made it possible for black players to compete on the tour.

As the first businesslike president of the PGA, Smith did much to place the organization's affairs on a solid footing. Yet he resisted efforts to exploit television. His view was that regular coverage of tournaments was "too costly, too difficult to schedule, and there was no way to dramatize them effectively."

Smith was instrumental in the revival of the PGA Hall of Fame, to which he was elected in 1958. During his career he won twenty-five tournaments and served as a driving force in the PGA during the critical postwar years. In his lifetime he was not always appreciated by other pros, some of whom felt he was a "chronic manipulator," yet when he died at Detroit, he was counted as extremely influential in the early history of the game.

[Smith's early life is covered in "How Smith of Missouri Showed the French," *Literary Digest,* June 15, 1929; also see "Golf: Even a Shattered Wrist Can't Keep a Good Smith Down," *Newsweek,* Jan. 11, 1936. More general accounts include the following: Tom Flaherty, *The Masters* (1961); Charles Price, *The World of Golf* (1962); *America's Golf Book* (1970); Peter Dobereiner, *The Glorious World of Golf* (1973); and Al Barkow, *Golf's Golden Grind* (1974). An obituary is in the *New York Times,* Oct. 15, 1963.]

CHARLES R. MIDDLETON

SMITH, THOMAS VERNOR (Apr. 26, 1890–May 24, 1964), philosopher, political scientist, and politician, was born in Blanket, Tex., the son of John Robert Smith, a poor farmer who had no more than a third-grade education, and of Mary Elizabeth Graves, who probably had not completed the first grade. His mother died when he was nine years old, and as the oldest son, he was called upon to do a man's work from the age of twelve. His secondary schooling was very limited, but he read avidly and memorized poems, hymns, and whole books of the Bible. This talent for memorization and for recitation later distinguished his public speaking style.

At the age of twenty-three, Smith was admitted to the University of Texas, from which he graduated with the B.A. two years later (1915). While an undergraduate he was a member of the debating team, and soon discovered that he was an effective public speaker and debater. He was appointed professor of English and was head of the English department at Texas Christian University in 1915–1916, and in 1916 received the M.A. in English literature from Texas. In 1916–1917 Smith taught philosophy at Texas Christian. On June 6, 1917, he married Nannie Stewart, his childhood sweetheart. They had two children.

On Sept. 3, 1918, Smith entered the U.S. Army as a private. He was discharged in January 1919. From 1919 to 1921 he was an instructor in philosophy at the University of Texas. In the latter year he entered the graduate program at the University of Chicago, and was appointed instructor in philosophy. His dissertation, "The American Doctrine of Equality," was accepted in 1922 by the philosophy department, and the University of Chicago awarded him a Ph.D. He remained at Chicago for twenty-six years: as dean of the College of Liberal Arts (1923–

1926), as associate dean (1926–1927), and as professor of philosophy (1927–1948).

Smith was a man of great drive and stamina. In addition to his teaching career in philosophy, he was an active politician, an author or editor of a score of books, a poet, a frequent participant in nationally broadcast public-affairs forums such as the University of Chicago Round Table, and a public speaker. He reported in 1956 that for twenty years he had traveled more than 50,000 miles a year in his teaching and lecturing, and that invitations to speak came in almost daily. In 1934 he published three books: *Beyond Conscience, Creative Sceptics,* and *Philosophers Speak for Themselves.*

Also in 1934, Smith was elected to the Illinois State Senate. While in the legislature he drafted a bill creating a legislative council to scrutinize and make recommendations on proposed legislation. He was chairman of the newly created legislative council in 1937–1938. In 1938, Smith was elected a Democratic congressman at large from Illinois. As a congressman he had a generally liberal voting record in support of the policies of the Roosevelt administration. He was not to be reelected.

During World War II, Smith served in the U.S. Army as a lieutenant colonel, and as a colonel from June 1, 1943 to Feb. 28, 1946. He was director of education of the Allied Control Commission in Italy in 1944, and the following year he was director of democratization for German prisoners of war. In 1946, Smith served on the U.S. Education Mission to Japan and, later, to Germany. He left the University of Chicago in 1948 to become Maxwell professor of citizenship and philosophy at the Maxwell Graduate School of Citizenship and Public Affairs at Syracuse University. He retired in 1956.

In his teaching, lecturing, and writing, Smith became known as an able and articulate expounder of democratic principles, and particularly of his idea that the democratic process depends on the willingness of people to compromise when they are in basic disagreement. An emphasis on the process of compromise as the proper way of settling issues is found in many of his books, where the way of doing things takes on special importance. It is suggested in some of his titles: *The Democratic Way of Life* (1926), *The Philosophic Way of Life* (1929), *The Legislative Way of Life* (1940), *The Political Way of Life* (1948), *The Ethics of Compromise and the Art of Containment* (1956).

Smith was optimistic about the future of democracy. The message of faith in democracy,

during the 1930's, when democracy seemed under siege; of faith in reason, when the claims of reason were subject to dispute; and, above all, of faith in the spirit of compromise as the essence of democratic politics characterized his teaching. He died in Hyattsville, Md.

[The chief source on Smith's life is his autobiography, *A Non-Existent Man* (1962). The most complete bibliography of his writings is in Theodore C. Denise and Milton H. Williams, *Retrospect and Prospect on the Retirement of T. V. Smith* (1956). An obituary is in the *New York Times,* May 25, 1964.]

ALAN P. GRIMES

SMITH, WALTER BEDELL (Oct. 5, 1895–Aug. 9, 1961), soldier and diplomat, was born in Indianapolis, Ind., the son of William Long Smith and Ida Frances Bedell, both buyers for the Pettis Dry Goods Company. While still a student at Manual Training High School, Smith decided to enter military service, and in 1910 he enlisted as a private in the Indiana National Guard. He first went on active duty during the 1913 flood in Indianapolis and in 1916 served with the Mexican border expedition. He enrolled briefly at Butler University but had to withdraw because of his father's illness. After working as a mechanic, he was ordered back to active duty during World War I. On July 1, 1917, he married Mary Eleanor (Norrie) Cline; they had no children.

In November 1917, Smith completed the officers' training camp at Fort Benjamin Harrison, Ind., and was commissioned a second lieutenant in the Officers' Reserve Corps. He was assigned to the Thirty-ninth Infantry, Fourth Division, at Camp Greene, N.C., and on Apr. 20, 1918, sailed with the division to France. He fought with the French at Chateau-Thierry and in the third Battle of the Marne. After being wounded by shrapnel, Smith returned to the United States.

Although he was promoted to first lieutenant (as a reserve officer on temporary active duty) in September 1918 and received a commission as first lieutenant in the Regular Army in July 1920, advancement in rank came slowly between the world wars. He was made captain in September 1929 and had to wait nearly ten years before becoming a major.

Smith's assignments during the interwar period equipped him with organizing, administrative, and planning skills crucial to managing modern warfare. He served first in Washington, D.C., with the Bureau of Military Intelligence. From there he went to staff assignments in various posts. In April 1925 he became assistant to the chief coordinator of the Bureau of the Budget and later was deputy chief coordinator and vice-chairman of the Federal Liquidation Board. He was assigned to the Forty-fifth Infantry at Fort William McKinley, in the Philippines, 1929–1931.

Smith graduated from the Infantry School at Fort Benning, Ga., then completed the advanced course in 1932, and remained as an instructor in weapons until August 1933. In 1935 he graduated from the Command and General Staff School at Fort Leavenworth, Kans. After teaching at the Infantry School for a year, he attended the Army War College in Washington, D.C., graduating in June 1937. After graduation he again taught at the Infantry School.

While at the Infantry School, Smith captured the attention of Omar N. Bradley and George C. Marshall. Both men put Smith's name on their lists of future leaders. In October 1939, General Marshall called Smith to Washington to aid him in building up the army. Promotions now came rapidly. Smith became a lieutenant colonel in April 1941, a colonel in August 1941, a brigadier general in February 1942, a major general in December 1942, and a lieutenant general in January 1943.

Marshall made Smith assistant secretary and then, in September 1941, secretary of the General Staff. In this job Smith coordinated the work of staff agencies. The Joint Chiefs of Staff —comprising the military heads of the army, air force, and navy, and a personal representative of the president—was established early in 1942. This group, with the British military leaders, formed the Combined Chiefs of Staff, which formulated the grand strategy of the war. In February 1942 Smith was named secretary of the Joint Chiefs and United States secretary to the Combined Chiefs, posts in which he played a key role in establishing the smooth functioning of the two groups.

In September 1942, Smith joined General Dwight D. Eisenhower as his chief of staff. He served in London while Eisenhower gathered the forces for the cross-Channel invasion and then followed the general during Allied assaults on North Africa in November 1942, on Sicily in July 1943, on Italy in September 1943, and on France in June 1944. After the surrender of Germany in May 1945, Smith remained with Eisenhower until that December.

During this period Smith established his reputation as one of the finest chiefs of staff in history. He often represented Eisenhower at conferences involving the Allied high com-

mand. Some of his important contributions involved his role as a diplomat—he handled the surrender negotiations of Italy, and he helped Eisenhower in the complex negotiations with France.

Although Smith returned from Europe in January 1946 as chief of the Operations and Planning Division of the Joint Chiefs of Staff, President Harry S. Truman appointed him ambassador to Russia (1946–1949) two months later. Smith was a negotiator during the crucial period when relations between the two countries deteriorated into the cold war. He believed that Russia had always been imperialist and that Soviet Russia would continue its expansionist efforts. But he felt that the Soviets wanted to avoid war and that the Communist world was not an impregnable monolith. He argued that the break between Marshal Tito of Yugoslavia and Premier Josef Stalin of Russia was real and that the United States should support Tito and encourage similar defections.

In March 1949, Smith became commander of the First Army, with headquarters at Governors Island, N.Y. In 1951 he received the fourth star of a full general. In the wake of charges of inept intelligence contributing to the outbreak of the Korean War in June 1950, President Truman named him director of the Central Intelligence Agency (CIA). In this position Smith exercised the toughness and administrative skill for which he was noted. He discharged many employees and made structural changes that moved the intelligence community toward greater coordination and centralization. He eliminated outside controls from the covert operations section and merged it with the CIA's covert intelligence-gathering section. He also established a support arm to provide personnel, logistics, and training.

When Eisenhower became president, he moved Smith from the CIA to the State Department as undersecretary. Smith saw himself as "the policy chief of staff" for Secretary of State John Foster Dulles. In May 1954 he was the United States representative to the Geneva Far Eastern Conference, called to discuss the possible reunification of Korea and a settlement of the war in Indochina. He resigned as undersecretary in October 1954 to become vice-chairman of American Machine and Foundry Company, a position he held until his death in Washington, D.C.

Smith was not an initiator of policy—he was always the chief of staff. A careful assessment of his role in formulating or modifying policies has not yet been made. Critics saw him as quick-tempered, harsh, abrupt, and arbitrary. Supporters would probably substitute terms such as "terse" and "exact." Supporters would also point to his personal warmth in relaxed moments.

But, in the estimation of nearly everyone, he was a nearly perfect chief of staff. Army leaders must make decisions upon whose outcome the lives of soldiers and the fate of the nation depend. In order to do this, a commander needs a second self, an assistant who can be, in Eisenhower's phrase, "general manager." The chief of staff coordinates and controls the activities of the staff divisions. Stephen E. Ambrose, in *The Supreme Commander* (1970), summarized Smith's role: "He decided who could see Eisenhower and who could not, handled much of Eisenhower's civil affairs and diplomatic duties, had almost unlimited responsibility and authority in all matters except promotion of officers and operational directives, was the 'no' man in the office, and frequently represented Eisenhower at meetings." Smith's achievements were the more remarkable because he was a "bootstrap" soldier without a college education, let alone a West Point degree.

[The principal manuscript source is the Walter Bedell Smith Collection at the Dwight D. Eisenhower Library, Abilene, Kans. Other important sources are the army theater files in the National Archives and the Washington National Records Center, Suitland, Md. Smith wrote *My Three Years in Moscow* (1949) and *Eisenhower's Six Great Decisions* (1956). There are no books on Smith, and his career must be traced through writings on the World War II and postwar periods. Obituary notices are in the *New York Times* and the *Indianapolis News,* Aug. 10, 1961; and *Time,* August 18, 1961.]

JOSEPH P. HOBBS

SNOW, CARMEL WHITE (Aug. 21, 1887– May 7, 1961), editor and fashion authority, was born in Dalkey, near Dublin, Ireland, the daughter of Peter White, managing director of the Irish Woolen Manufacturing and Export Company, and of Anne Mayne. As honorary secretary of the Irish Industries Association, an organization committed to finding markets for Irish home industries, her father helped arrange for the Irish Village at the World's Columbian Exposition in Chicago (1893). He had made most of the preparations when he died suddenly, a few months before the fair was to open. His wife decided to carry on his work and, leaving her children with relatives, she went to Chicago and supervised the village, a major attraction of the fair. She then opened a shop for Irish handicrafts in Chicago and in 1895 brought Carmel and her sister to America. The girls were educated at a convent in Iowa, a private day school in Chicago, a boarding school in Wisconsin, and a convent in Brussels, Belgium.

By the time White's schooling was completed, her mother had settled in New York City, where she owned a custom dressmaking firm. Young White often worked there as a helper. Occasionally she accompanied her mother on buying trips to the Paris couture collections. She discovered that she had what she later termed a "photographic" eye for fashion details; this was decidedly helpful to her mother in adapting Paris styles for her American customers.

During World War I, White joined the American Red Cross. She served in Paris, where she had charge of all Red Cross female personnel in the city. Her uniforms were made for her by Creed, considered the finest tailor in Paris.

The war over, and still without plans for her future, White drifted back into her mother's dressmaking firm. While preparing for a buying trip to Paris, she was asked by fashion columnist Anne Rittenhouse, who was unable to make the trip that season, to report on the collections for her. Rittenhouse was so pleased with White's meticulous notes that she wrote a letter of introduction for her to Edna Woolman Chase, editor of *Vogue.* White joined *Vogue* in 1921 as an assistant fashion editor.

On Nov. 11, 1926, White married socialite George Palen Snow, an attorney. They had four children: a son who died in infancy, and three daughters. Although she was now leading an active family and social life, Snow's professional responsibilities increased. In 1929 she was made American editor of *Vogue,* and in 1932, she became fashion editor of *Harper's Bazaar,* a move that alienated publisher Condé Nast and others of the *Vogue* staff, but gave her new freedom and opportunity to develop her editorial talents.

Snow immediately set about making *Harper's Bazaar*—as Jessica Daves wrote later—"a fortress of fashion opinion dramatically expressed, dramatically presented, with a reputation for giving fashion photographers their fling." Using the work of photographer Martin Munkacsi, Snow introduced the action fashion picture—of a swimsuit-clad model running on the beach. With Munkacsi and Alexey Brodovitch, whom she hired as art director in 1934, she quickly created a smart new look for the magazine.

Three years after joining *Harper's Bazaar,* Snow was named editor. Under her leadership the magazine became a literary as well as a fashion medium. With such novelists as Virginia Woolf, Eudora Welty, and Colette writing for *Bazaar*, Snow achieved her ambition to make her readers "well-dressed women with well-dressed minds."

Although her editorial scope expanded, Snow never lost her interest in fashion or relinquished her position as a fashion authority. She attended all the Paris showings and is generally credited with bringing the designers Christian Dior and Balenciaga to prominence in the United States. She made the first fashion broadcast from Paris to the United States. An adventurous traveler, she was on one of the earliest passenger flights to Europe, in July 1939.

Her trips to Paris were curtailed during World War II, but she was back there in December 1944, to report on the wartime collections. In appreciation of her helping to revive the French fashion industry, she was awarded the Knight's Cross of the French Legion of Honor in 1949. The Italian government also recognized her efforts on behalf of that country's textile and fashion industries by awarding her the Stella della Solidarietà (Star of Solidarity).

Snow retired in late 1957, but continued as chairman of *Harper's Bazaar*'s editorial board. She also continued to attend the Paris shows. She and her husband moved to a house they had purchased in County Mayo, Ireland, but because the climate was detrimental to her husband's health, they were not able to live there for long, and returned to the United States. In collaboration with Mary Louise Aswell, Snow had just completed work on her memoirs, *The World of Carmel Snow* (1962), when she died in New York City.

[See Edna Woolman Chase, *Always in Vogue* (1954); John Fairchild, *The Fashionable Savages* (1965); Jessica Daves, *Ready-Made Miracle* (1967); and Eleanor Lambert, *World of Fashion—People, Places, Resources* (1976). An obituary is in the *New York Times*, May 9, 1961.]

DOROTHY BRIGSTOCK SCHOENFELD

SOKOLSKY, GEORGE EPHRAIM (Sept. 5, 1893–Dec. 12, 1962), author and consultant to American industry, was born in Utica, N.Y., the son of Solomon Sokolsky and Bertha Rappaport, who had immigrated to the United States in the 1880's from Bialystok, Poland. Solomon Sokolsky, a rabbi, moved the family to New York City shortly after George's birth. Young Sokolsky was raised in the Jewish ghettos

on the East Side and in Harlem, where he claimed to have studied socialism and to have known Emma Goldman and Leon Trotsky.

Following graduation from Bronx High School, Sokolsky studied journalism at Columbia University, but was expelled in 1917 on charges of immoral conduct, either because of his radical political activities or because of an involvement with a young lady whose parents did not approve of him. He immediately left for Russia, where in Petrograd he wrote for the *Russian Daily News*, an English-language newspaper. His experience with the Russian Revolution moderated his fascination with radical ideas and began his movement toward political conservatism. Throughout the rest of his life he remained fearful of all revolutions, the brutality of the mob, the ruthlessness of suppressing the individual to achieve a political ideal.

The reasons for Sokolsky's leaving Russia for China have been variously interpreted. In later life he stated that he was forced to leave because of his criticism of the revolution. Critics contend that his desire to seek a fortune in more promising surroundings may have been the basic motivation. He arrived in Tientsin, China, in March 1918 nearly penniless, and obtained a reporting job on the *North China Star*, an English-language newspaper. Later, in Shanghai, Sokolsky worked with the student leaders of the May Fourth Movement and with members of Sun Yat-sen's Kuomintang. In 1919 he joined the *Shanghai Gazette*, controlled by Sun's party, but gradually moved into the position of promoter of Sun's Nationalist party's views in the Western press. Soon he became manager of the Bureau of Public Information in Shanghai, where his pro-Sun, anti-Japanese propaganda releases worried American officials.

Many suspected that Sokolsky was a Bolshevik agent, but during his time in China he showed a tendency to promote himself more than any ideological or political cause. He wrote for the two major parties contending in China and for several newspapers with conflicting editorial policies, and he advised the student movement while aiding the American Chamber of Commerce in its effort to bypass the student-directed boycott. He attempted in many ways to utilize his knowledge gained in China for financial advantage.

On Oct. 19, 1922, Sokolsky married Rosalind Phang, a Chinese woman born in the West Indies and educated in England. They had one son. The marriage set many barriers between him and the Caucasian community and moved him more into the Chinese social circle. During his last years in China, Sokolsky edited the *Far Eastern Review* (1927–1930) and wrote *Outline of Universal History* (1928).

Sokolsky returned to the United States in 1931. His knowledge of China enabled him to write for some of the nation's leading newspapers, including the *New York Times* and the *New York Herald Tribune.* During the first two years after his return, he wrote more than fifty articles for the *New York Times* and several others for *Atlantic Monthly* and *Christian Century.* He continued as a columnist for the *New York Herald Tribune* until 1940. During the early 1930's he published *The Tinder Box of Asia* (1932) and *Labor's Fight for Power* (1934). His first wife died in 1933, and on May 30, 1935, Sokolsky married Dorothy Fiske. They had two children.

In the 1930's his ideas appealed to many leading industrialists, and Sokolsky became a prominent spokesman for capitalism: "The right to win and use private wealth and to keep and use the benefits that derive from it is part of democracy." He admitted to being a conservative in the major ways of life, a capitalist in his economic thinking, and a rigid constitutionalist in his political thinking. He began broadcasts favoring these positions in 1937, under the sponsorship of the National Association of Manufacturers. In addition to his journalistic work, he was employed as a consultant by Hill and Knowlton and the American Iron and Steel Institute.

In 1940, Sokolsky began writing a column, "These Days," for the *New York Sun.* When the *Sun* ceased publication in 1950, he moved to the Hearst newspaper chain. His strongly conservative columns were distributed by Hearst's King Features to some 331 newspapers. In addition to his column, Sokolsky promoted the cause of political conservatism through speeches and radio appearances. *The American Way of Life* (1939) defended American capitalism against the attacks of consumer interests.

Sokolsky became a close friend and political ally of former president Herbert Hoover, General Douglas MacArthur, and publisher Robert R. McCormick. He strongly supported Senator Joseph McCarthy's anti-Communist crusade in the 1950's and blamed the Truman administration for the triumph of the Chinese Communists. But, to the puzzlement of conservatives, he supported the presidency of John F. Kennedy. The *National Review* commented: "Toward the end he was bemused by the Kennedy Administration, but he must be forgiven, for his weakness was of the most under-standable kind, a long-standing personal friendship with the seductive Kennedy family."

Sokolsky died in New York City, one of the most flamboyant exponents of conservative causes in twentieth-century America. The appellation "Star-Spangled Spieler for Capitalism" accurately describes him.

[The major collections of Sokolsky's papers are at Columbia University and the Hoover Institute at Stanford University. See also *Atlantic Monthly,* Aug. 1933; and Warren I. Cohen, *The China Connection* (1978). An obituary is in the *New York Times,* western ed., Dec. 14, 1962.]

WILLIAM E. AMES

SPAETH, SIGMUND (Apr. 10, 1885–Nov. 11, 1965), musicologist, was born Sigmund Gottfried Spaeth in Philadelphia, Pa., the son of Adolph Spaeth, a Lutheran minister, and of Harriet Reynolds Krauth. One of eleven children, all of whom received a good exposure to music and played the piano, Spaeth also studied the violin. He attended Quaker schools and graduated from Germantown Academy in 1901. He also studied at the Philadelphia Music Academy (1900–1903). In 1905 he graduated with a B.A. from Haverford College, from which he received an M.A. in English the following year.

Between 1906 and 1910, Spaeth studied orchestral and choral music with Philip Mittell and Charles Burnham while pursuing a doctorate in English at Princeton University (where he taught German, 1906–1908). His dissertation was on "Milton's Knowledge of Music: Its Sources and Its Significance in his Works" and he received the Ph.D. in 1910. He was concertmaster of the Princeton University Orchestra (1906–1910) and president of the Princeton Choral Society (1908–1910).

From 1910 to 1912 Spaeth taught English and was director of music at the Asheville School in North Carolina. After a trip to Europe in 1912, he moved to New York City. He rented a small room that had once been O.Henry's and tried to write fiction but found the task financially unproductive and turned to editorial and journalistic endeavors. In 1913, he worked as an assistant editor with the music publishers G. Schirmer (where he also translated songs into English from French, Italian, German, and Russian) and as music editor for the humor magazine *Life.* He also edited *Opera Magazine.* On Jan. 30, 1917, he married Katharine Lane. They had no children.

From 1914 to 1918, Spaeth was music editor for the *New York Evening Mail.* He was a reporter on the sports staff of the *New York Times* (1919–1920) as well as musical correspondent for the *Boston Transcript*. He then became educational director and later promotion manager for the American Piano Company (Ampico) and began his career as a lecturer. From 1928 to 1931, he was managing director of the newly formed Community Concerts Corporation, which, by grouping together certain New York managerial bureaus, hoped to hold back falling concert attendance and rising performing costs. During this time Spaeth wrote numerous articles on music, frequently stressing his analysis of, and concern for, the contemporary American music scene. He also wrote about jazz, barbershop singing, and other popular American music. During his life he published more than thirty books, including anthologies of American music and surveys of the classics and their composers. His *The Common Sense of Music* (1924) and *The Art of Enjoying Music* (1933) were widely read.

Spaeth, an athletic man of imposing stature, became a pioneer radio sportscaster during the 1920's, covering championship tennis, the Rose Bowl, and prizefights. His weekly music program drew thousands of fan letters a week. He also began one of the first radio amateur shows.

In the late 1920's, Spaeth began giving expert court testimony in major music plagiarism cases, usually speaking for the defense. He pointed out that most popular American pieces were derived from classical melodies. His method of revealing these musical sources earned him the title "Tune Detective." He gave demonstrations of this skill on the vaudeville stage, often dressed like Sherlock Holmes.

Spaeth was musical editor for *McCall's Magazine* (1931–1933), *Esquire* (1934), and *Literary Digest* (1937–1938). Between 1935 and 1944, he was president of the National Association of American Composers and Conductors and, around 1937, became dean of the Wurlitzer School of Music. He also composed music. His song "Our New York" was declared the official song of the city by Mayor Fiorello La Guardia in June 1940. During World War II, Spaeth, along with Kate Smith and Gene Autry, helped to organize a collection of records for servicemen. In 1945, he founded the New York Chapter of the Society for the Preservation of Barbershop Quartet Singing in America. He helped make music more available to the blind and was president of the Louis Braille Music Institute (1956–1958).

Forever fascinated with the media (and ultracritical when radio or television failed to try to improve music tastes), Spaeth appeared many times on television. His radio program "At Home With Music" was cited by the Peabody Awards Committee in 1949 and 1950. In 1955, he became editor of the *Music Journal,* a position that he held until his death, in New York City.

Spaeth was the most popular musicologist of his day. His greatest influence was popularizing what most people considered to be "classical" music. He emphasized that music should have a part in everyone's life, that there was a "common sense of music" that everyone has but which people are often timid about discovering. Americans, he believed, had become musically backward. He tried to make his audiences aware of the relation between the "classics" and popular music so that they would lose their initial awe of the former. He made teaching entertaining and entertainment educational. On the lecture circuit, in his writing, and especially on the air as the Tune Detective, Spaeth tried—and largely succeeded—in his massive project of giving the entire nation lessons in music appreciation and in what might now be called musical awareness.

[The Oral History Collection of Columbia University has two memoirs: "The Reminiscences of Sigmund Spaeth" (1951), containing chronology to 1951 and an excellent table of contents and index; and an interview with Robert C. Franklin for the Popular Arts Project (1958).

Spaeth's many articles for *Musician* include "Let Us Cultivate Amateurism in Music!" Oct. 1922; "Creating a New Host of Music Listeners," Nov. 1922; "First Great Listeners; Then Great Performers," Jan. 1923; an interview with Paul Kempf, "How to Convert Our 99 Per Cent Non-Musical Public," May 1924; "Robbing Musical Understanding of Some of Its 'Terrors,' " Sept. 1926; and "Luring Apathetic Americans Into the Concert Auditorium," Sept. 1928. In *Etude* see "A Glance at the Music of Hawaii," Aug. 1937; "The Classical Czar of Tin Pan Alley," Oct. 1942; "Music Teaching as a Profession," Feb. 1951; and "Before Music Lessons Begin," Sept. 1952. See also "Translating to Music," *Musical Quarterly,* Apr. 1915; and "Winning Friends for Opera," *Opera News* Dec. 11, 1965.

Also see Quaintance Eaton's interview with Spaeth, "And Still Champ," *Opera News,* Apr. 10, 1965. Obituaries are in the *New York Herald Tribune* and *New York Times,* Nov. 13, 1965.]

MADELINE SAPIENZA

SPEER, EMMA BAILEY (May 15, 1872– Apr. 25, 1961), association administrator, was born in Pottstown, Pa., the daughter of Charles Lukens Bailey, an ironmaster, and of Emma

Harriet Doll. Raised in comfortable circumstances, she was tutored at home and subsequently attended Miss Stevens School in Philadelphia. She then studied at Bryn Mawr College for two years (1888–1890).

After marrying Robert Elliott Speer on Apr. 20, 1893, Emma accompanied her husband on a round-the-world trip to visit missions. While crossing Persia on horseback, Dr. Speer, who was secretary of the Board of Foreign Missions of the Presbyterian Church, contracted typhoid fever. Fortunately, he recovered. Between 1898 and 1910 Speer had five children but simultaneously was active as a Young Women's Christian Association (YWCA) volunteer. In 1906 she became a charter member of its National Board, and in 1908 she chaired the association's student department. When summoned to the presidency of the National Board of the YWCA in 1915, the unduly modest Speer overcame her misgivings about her lack of preparation for the position. "Nothing is impossible until it is tried," she wrote. She trusted in God to "make up through His infinite resources for my infinite lack."

During World War I, the National Board established the War Work Council, which sent hundreds of its professional staff overseas for emergency war service and administered a war-related budget totaling millions of dollars. Soon after the United States entered the conflict, Speer wrote an article for the *Ladies' Home Journal* in which she called upon American women living near military training camps to organize entertainment for soldiers far from home.

Speer devoted herself to the cause of young women, particularly those who moved to cities in search of employment. Speaking to delegates at the seventh national convention of the YWCA in 1922. She pointed out that "notions of girls derived from Louisa M. Alcott are out of date." The young women of the 1920's were faced with opportunities and challenges unknown to their mothers. Under Speer's leadership the YWCA helped young women cope with a changing world by providing residences, recreation, practical education, and camaraderie. Speer viewed the YWCA as an instrument for transmitting standards and values previously inculcated in the family.

Described by the *Christian Herald* as "mother to 500,000," Speer believed that the American girl was "one of the best products of the race." Having marched with the suffragists, she subscribed to the theory that women were the equal of men and were entitled not only to outward courtesies, which she termed "charm-ing gestures," but also to being taken seriously. "All we want is a chance to contribute our share to the general sum of experience and the good life," she said in 1928.

As president of the National Board of the YWCA, Speer proved to be a superb administrator. She combined several YWCA programs for teen-age girls into the Girl Reserves in 1918. In 1919 the YWCA convened the first International Conference of Women Physicians and organized the National Federation of Business and Professional Women's Clubs. During Speer's presidency, assemblies of students (1920) and of women industrial workers (1922) were sponsored. With major support from the Laura Spelman Rockefeller Memorial Foundation, the National Board also sponsored a conference on the effect of the Great Depression upon female workers (1930).

Although firmly committed to the nation's war effort, Speer was a vocal advocate of the peaceful settlement of international disputes. In a speech at Princeton University in 1928, she advocated American participation in the World Court.

Besides speaking out on international affairs, Speer plunged into the controversial topic of sex education. She provided a foreword to A. Maude Royden's article "The Path of Sanity in Sex," in *Woman's Press,* the monthly magazine of the YWCA. On sexual matters Speer steered a middle course between Victorian and Freudian attitudes. She emphasized the importance of both the physical and the spiritual aspects of marriage, but her observation that "the lasting partnerships in marriage are those in which both give their highest allegiance to God" clearly revealed her priorities. When stepping down as president of the National Board in 1932, Speer underscored the two most important concerns in her life: "Above all, we have been in the Association because it is both a Christian and a woman's movement."

Following her retirement, Speer was named honorary president of the National Board. After stepping down as president, Speer was still active in the YWCA. She served on seven committees during the 1930's, three in the 1940's, and was vice-chairman of the World Service Council until 1950. Although confined to a wheelchair by 1953, she continued to write articles until 1957. She spent her last years at Lakeville, Conn., and died at Bryn Mawr, Pa.

[Speer's official reports and correspondence are in the archives of the National Board of the YWCA, New York City. Additional correspondence is at the

Robert E. Speer Library, Princeton Theological Seminary, and the Rockefeller Archive Center, Pocantico Hills, N.Y. Articles by Speer include "The Boy in Camp and the Girl in Town," *Ladies' Home Journal,* Sept. 1917; "The Most Glorious Job," *Association Monthly,* Aug. 1919; "For a World Court," *Woman's Press,* Jan. 1924; "What Does the Woman Want?" *Woman's Press,* July 1928; and "As It Was in Minneapolis," *Woman's Press,* July 1932.

Also see Samuel D. Fuson, "She Has Faith in the Girl of Today," *Christian Herald,* Apr. 17, 1926; Mary S. Sims, *The First Twenty-Five Years* (1932); Reginald Wheeler, *A Man Sent from God* (1956); and Marion O. Robinson, *Eight Women of the YWCA* (1966). An obituary is in the *New York Times,* Apr. 26, 1961.]

MARILYN E. WEIGOLD

SPEISER, EPHRAIM AVIGDOR (Jan. 24, 1902–June 15, 1965), archaeologist, biblical scholar, and linguist, was born in Skalat, Galicia, a province of Austria-Hungary (now in the Soviet Union), the son of Jonas Speiser and Hannah Greenberg. He graduated in 1919 from the gymnasium of Lemberg (now Lvov), and soon thereafter immigrated to the United States.

Already trilingual (German, Hebrew, and Polish) on arrival, Speiser quickly learned English in the United States. He received an M.A. from the Department of Semitics at the University of Pennsylvania in 1923, and published his master's thesis, *The Hebrew Origin of the First Part of the Book of Wisdom.* He was awarded a Ph.D. by Dropsie College (Philadelphia) in 1924, adding Greek to his language repertoire for his dissertation, "The Pronunciation of Hebrew According to the Transliterations in the Sexapla." He became a naturalized citizen in 1926.

A concurrent Guggenheim fellowship (1926–1928) and professorship at the American School of Oriental Research (ASOR) in Baghdad (1926–1927) launched Speiser's career as an archaeologist and authority on the Sumerian, Akkadian, Babylonian, and Assyrian languages and cultures of ancient Mesopotamia. A field survey of southern Kurdistan led to his discovery of Tepe Gawra. The ASOR and the University of Pennsylvania Museum jointly sponsored excavations there and at nearby Tell Billa (1927–1939), which Speiser partly supervised as field director (1930–1932, 1936–1937). These digs uncovered twenty-four levels and sublevels of habitation; the lower ones, reaching back to about 5,000–3,000 B.C., brought to light major architectural remains and specimens of pottery.

Speiser's seminal contributions to the knowledge of the civilization of ancient Mesopotamia

won speedy recognition. He rose to full professor by 1931, becoming one of the youngest to hold that rank at the University of Pennsylvania. His *Mesopotamian Origins* (1930) focused on the cultural, legal, linguistic, and ethnic structure of society. His analysis in 1932 of the cuneiform tablets found at Nuzi (south of Kirkuk, Iraq) enbled him to reconstruct Akkadian family law as practiced in that locality. Always the synthesizer, Speiser a year later wrote "Ethnic Movements in the Near East in the Second Millennium B.C." (*ASOR,* vol. 13). Interest in the Nuzi dialect sparked his curiosity about its Hurrian element, which resulted in *Introduction to Hurrian* (1941), a feat of linguistic ingenuity. This work was issued in an edition of 100 copies, of which only seven were sold in the first year.

On July 23, 1937, Speiser married Sue Gimbel Dannenbaum; they had two children. In 1943, Speiser took leave to work for the Office of Strategic Services in Washington, D.C., as chief of the Near East section of the Research and Analysis Branch. There he assembled an interdisciplinary team of scholars familiar with the languages and societies of the Near East.

Their weekly and special reports, supervised by Speiser, furnished useful insights into the current and future crises in that region. Speiser participated in the preparation of every report, from the adoption and assignment of the issues for analysis through the editing and proofreading of the final product, bringing to bear skills developed in his editorship of the *Journal of the American Oriental Society.* The output, including an occasional paper of his own on Iraq, bore the stamp of Speiser's insistence on standards of excellence in graceful style without sacrifice of scholarship. The reports from his office were probably the only official ones in wartime Washington that consistently carried footnotes to identify the sources of information.

In *The United States and the Near East* (1947; rev. ed. 1950), written after his return to the University of Pennsylvania, Speiser combined the skills of an ancient historian and an analyst of contemporary affairs to frame guidelines for postwar national policy. Chapter 2, "The Enduring Cultural Factor," encapsulated 5,000 years of the region's history as the context for current assessment. It provides a still meaningful appreciation of the bewildering interplay of past and present among the rival cultures.

Lore, myths, and epics, the comparative study of Semitic morphology, and the idea of history were themes of Speiser's scholarship on ancient Mesopotamia. To these he added a continuing professional concern with biblical studies. He edited and contributed to volume 1 of *World History of the Jewish People*, which was subtitled, *At the Dawn of Civilization* (1964). He also translated into contemporary English, with running commentary, the book of Genesis for the Anchor Bible.

In 1947, Speiser assumed the chairmanship of the Department of Oriental Studies, a post he held until his death. He was a member of the American Philosophical Society and of the advisory board of the Guggenheim Foundation. He also was nonresident director of the ASOR in Baghdad (1932–1946). In addition, Speiser was president of the American Oriental Society (1945), vice-president of the Linguistic Society of America (1942), overseer of the Archaeological School in Jerusalem of the Hebrew Union College (Cincinnati), and fellow of the American Academy of Jewish Research. In 1959 the American Council of Learned Societies awarded him a prize for outstanding scholarly contributions to the humanities, and in 1964 the University of Pennsylvania named him a university professor, in acknowledgment of his range of interdisciplinary activities. Speiser died at Elkins Park, Pa.

[A full list of Speiser's writings is in J. J. Finkelstein and Moshe Greenberg, eds., *Oriental and Biblical Studies: Collected Writings of E. A. Speiser* (1967). An obituary is in the *New York Times*, June 17, 1965.]

J. C. HUREWITZ

SPIER, LESLIE (Dec. 13, 1893–Dec. 3, 1961), anthropologist, was born in New York City, the son of Simon P. Spier and Bertha Adler. His interest in anthropology developed from his work as an engineer for the state of New York in 1912–1913. In the latter year he was assigned to the New Jersey Archaeological and Geological Survey as an assistant anthropologist. His researches during the next three years resulted in a series of papers on the archaeology of the eastern United States. He received a B.S. in engineering from the College of the City of New York in 1915 and then entered the graduate program in anthropology at Columbia University, where he studied under Franz Boas. He received a Ph.D. in 1920.

From 1916 to 1920, Spier was assistant anthropologist at the American Museum of Natural History in New York City. During this period his interest shifted gradually from archaeology and physical anthropology to ethnology. But, following Boasian tradition, he continued throughout his career to be concerned with the broad scope of anthropology—including ethnology, physical anthropology, archaeology, and linguistics.

The institutional focus of American anthropology was changing from government and museum to university at the time Spier received his degree. Spier taught at the University of Washington (1920–1927, 1929–1930), at Yale University (1933–1939), and at the University of New Mexico (1939–1955). He was thus influential in developing anthropology at academic institutions. He also served as editor of *American Anthropologist* (1934–1938) and helped to develop anthropological publication series at the universities where he taught (including the *Southwestern Journal of Anthropology*, 1944–1961).

Like most of Boas' students, Spier was active in fieldwork. Between 1916 and 1935 he was in the field for part of every year. He investigated firsthand the Zuni, Havasupai, Kiowa, Wichita, Caddo, Diegueño, Salish (Flathead), Wishram, Klamath, Maricopa, Okanogon, Mohave, and Modoc Indian tribes. His *Havasupai Ethnography* (1928) served as a model of ethnographic description.

Spier served on the National Research Council Division of Anthropology and Psychology from 1934 to 1937. He was president of the American Anthropological Association in 1943 and vice-president of Section H (anthropology) of the American Association for the Advancement of Science, 1942–1946. He was elected to the National Academy of Sciences and the American Philosophical Society in 1946. He also became a fellow of the American Academy of Arts and Sciences in 1953, and in 1960 he received the prestigious Viking Medal in Anthropology.

Spier's research, ranging over all aspects of the native cultures of North America, cannot be easily summarized. In line with the Boasian tradition, he was interested in using ethnographic data as evidence for unwritten historical events, particularly migrations and tribal contacts. His study *The Sun Dance of the Plains Indians* (1921) remains a classic of the historical method. Although most of the data are based on statistical analysis of trait distributions, Spier's conclusions deal with the integration of cultural traits in particular groups, which makes him a forerunner of the culture and personality focus that developed in American anthropology during the 1920's and 1930's. A concern with culture process and the role of the individual was consistent with the historical reconstructive method. His joint editorship, with A. I. Hallowell and S. S. Newman, of *Language, Culture and Personality* (1941), a volume dedicated to Edward Sapir, is characteristic of this set of concerns.

Spier also was interested in kinship and social organization, a concern shared, among Boas' former students, only by Robert Lowie. Spier was, in sum, both a generalist and a specialist, highly influential in academic anthropology at a crucial period in the development of the discipline. He died in New Mexico.

[Works by Spier not mentioned in the text include *An Outline for a Chronology of Zuñi Ruins* (1917); *Klamath Ethnography* (1930); and *Yuman Tribes of the Gila River* (1933). See Regina Darnell, "Hallowell's Bear Ceremonialism and the Emergence of Boasian Anthropology," *Ethnos*, 1977. An obituary is Harry W. Basehart and W. W. Hill, "Leslie Spier: 1893–1961," *American Anthropologist*, 1965.]
REGNA DARNELL

SPINK, JOHN GEORGE TAYLOR (Nov. 6, 1888–Dec. 7, 1962), baseball publicist, was born in St. Louis, Mo., the son of Charles Claude Spink and Marie Taylor. Two years before his son's birth, Charles Spink had abandoned a homesteading venture to assist his brother Alfred in founding *Sporting News*, a St. Louis-based weekly journal of sporting and theatrical news. Alfred Spink soon left Charles in control of the struggling publication. By concentrating on baseball news, *Sporting News* soon rivaled *New York Clipper* and *Sporting Life* as a leading baseball weekly.

As editor, Charles Spink won local support through his attacks on Chris von der Ahe, the controversial owner of the St. Louis Browns, and national readership through his support of the Players' League in 1890 and his attacks on monopolistic major-league owners during the 1890's. When Spink supported Byron Bancroft Johnson's successful bid for major-league status for the American League in 1903, he gained an important ally.

Taylor Spink spent his early years training to succeed his father as publisher. Since both parents worked on *Sporting News*, his interest was encouraged, and he was permitted to leave high school in the tenth grade to further his apprenticeship. He served stints as office boy, copy boy, writer, and assistant editor.

Spink attained a responsible position with *Sporting News* in 1912, at a time when circulation had fallen to 12,000 a week. Blaming his father's ill-advised support of the interloping Federal League for alienating major league offi-

cials, he tried to contravene that policy. When his father died in 1914, Taylor, who had just married Blanche Keene (on April 15), cut short his honeymoon to assume the editorship. The Spinks had two children.

Reversing his father's policy, Spink ingratiated himself with the baseball establishment by opposing the Federal League "invaders." *Sporting News* circulation improved, while that of *Sporting Life* declined to the point that it ceased publication. For the next two years Spink enjoyed a monopoly of baseball news, but the outbreak of World War I posed a threat to *Sporting News*. When weekly circulation dropped to 5,000, American League president Johnson, a family friend, rewarded Spink's loyalty by buying 150,000 copies each week for distribution to servicemen.

After the war, baseball and *Sporting News* prospered. By working seven days a week, Spink made it indispensable, the "Bible of Baseball," the best source for statistics, box scores, records, and coverage of all levels of professional play. To gather detailed information, Spink deployed an army of correspondents and stringers in every baseball town, tirelessly directing their activities by persistent phone calls and telegrams. As a result, by 1942 *Sporting News*, with its sixteen pages of small type and its colorful headlines, boasted a weekly circulation of 100,000 copies. By then Spink was wealthy, but most of his earnings came from ancillary publications such as *Sporting Goods Dealer*, yearbooks of baseball facts and statistics, and books and pamphlets on various aspects of the game. Among these *The Baseball Register*, first published in 1940, annually sold more than 500,000 copies.

Nevertheless, the heart of Spink's publishing empire was *Sporting News*, which thrived under his fussy leadership. He himself wrote sparingly, delegating even his bylined columns to others. (This was true also of his biography of Judge Kenesaw Mountain Landis.) His strengths were providing imaginative story leads for others to pursue and his martinet style of editorial direction. Unlike his father, Spink supported baseball's status quo, preferring to inform, enlighten, and amuse readers rather than undertake crusades. Both baseball and *Sporting News* profited from national publicity resulting from the awards and trophies he provided.

When World War II brought another circulation crisis, the baseball establishment again subsidized *Sporting News* by distributing 400,000 copies weekly to servicemen. But the postwar rise of rival sports and leisure publications threatened the life of a journal devoted wholly to baseball. Spink adapted by converting *Sporting News* into a lively tabloid and extending its coverage to other professional sports.

After his death at Clayton, Mo., Spink's son became publisher of *Sporting News*. The journal continued to prosper, but inroads from other sporting publications and his lack of an heir prompted him to sell *Sporting News* to the Times Mirror Company in 1977.

[*Judge Landis and Twenty-Five Years of Baseball* (1947), a work attributed to Spink, is the work of ghostwriter Fred Lieb. There is no biography of Spink. C. C. Johnson Spink, *Taylor Spink, the Legend and the Man* (1973), is a compilation of adulatory articles. Also see Stan Frank, "Bible of Baseball," *Saturday Evening Post*, June 20, 1942; and Gerald Holland, "Taylor Spink Is First Class," *Sports Illustrated*, Feb. 27, 1961. Obituaries are in the *New York Times*, Dec. 8, 1962; and *Sporting News*, Dec. 22, 1962.]

DAVID QUENTIN VOIGT

STAGG, AMOS ALONZO (Aug. 16, 1862– Mar. 17, 1965), football coach, was born at West Orange, N.J., the son of Amos Lindsley Stagg and Eunice Pierson. His father was poor and had to supplement his income as a shoemaker by doing general labor. As soon as he was big enough, Stagg helped in these tasks, which included haying the salt meadows of Newark Bay. From his family he learned the work ethic and acquired a strict code of personal morality. He joined the Presbyterian church at seventeen and soon began to aspire to the ministry.

In 1883, Stagg graduated from Orange High School, where the assistant principal, a Yale graduate, urged him to think seriously about going to college. Unable to pass the Yale entrance examinations, he was persuaded by a well-to-do friend to come to Phillips Exeter Academy, which he attended for the spring term of 1884. He was a successful pitcher for the baseball team.

In the fall of 1884, Stagg entered Yale as a freshman. Because Stagg was obliged to earn his way, the Yale experience was a very significant influence on his life, especially the sports values of Walter Camp that prevailed at the time. He pitched Yale to five baseball championships and refused offers from several major-league teams, including one of $4,200 from the New York Nationals. He did not play much football until after receiving the B.A. in 1888, but as a graduate student he played on Yale's undefeated and unscored-on team of 1888. The following year as a student in the Divinity School he was named to the first All-American team as an end.

Stagg came to recognize that his shortcomings as a speaker made the ministry an unrealistic aspiration. At the suggestion of Luther Gulick, he entered the International YMCA College at Springfield, Mass., in the fall of 1890 to study physical education. At that time he coached his first football game. Stagg soon accepted an offer from his former Yale religion professor, William Rainey Harper, to become director of physical culture and athletics at the new University of Chicago, where Harper had become president. Assuming his duties in the fall of 1892, he was the first coach or athletic director to have professorial status and tenure. On Sept. 10, 1894, he married Stella Robertson, a member of the class of 1896 at Chicago. They had three children.

At that time a few eastern colleges virtually monopolized football, but schools in other sections were eager to learn the game. Stagg was in the first wave of player-missionaries who poured out of Yale and, to a lesser extent, Harvard and Princeton, carrying football to the rest of the country. The game gained rapidly in popularity, and by World War I it was the leading intercollegiate sport. The style of the game changed radically during this period. The open, Rugby style gave way to a mass-momentum type of play. When excessive violence threatened football's existence in 1906, there was another change, to a more open running and passing game. No coach turned a more agile or inventive mind to the game during these years than did Stagg.

Experts disagree on the origins of many aspects of college football, but few would argue with the proposition that Stagg was one of the leaders in most phases of the game. He has been credited with creating dozens of plays, formations, and strategies that have become standard; including the T formation and the forward pass. He was noted for his use of deception, by which, in his words, "brains may defeat brawn and the underdog may topple the top dog." Stagg was also responsible for originating the huddle, numbered uniforms, and lighted practice fields. From 1904 he was a member of the Intercollegiate Football Rules Committee. He also served on five American Olympic committees between 1906 and 1932, and coached the middle-distance runners in the 1924 Olympics.

Stagg's inventiveness helps to explain why he was an outstanding coach. He did not recruit extensively, nor did he employ platoons of assistants. But in forty-one years at the University of Chicago, his teams had five undefeated seasons and won six Western Conference (Big Ten) titles; the 1905 team was ranked first in the country. Stagg had the ability to get the most out of limited material and to devise special tactics for special situations. A notable example of the latter skill was the defense he prepared to use against Red Grange and the highly favored Illinois team in 1924. The game ended in a 21–21 tie and brought the last of Stagg's Big Ten titles.

Stagg's coaching style was authoritarian. He permitted no smoking, drinking, or profanity, and required rigorous training. Most of his players accepted this, and both respected and loved the "Old Man," his nickname before he was forty. Several of Stagg's players and assistant coaches, notably Fritz Crisler and Jesse Harper, went on to become successful head coaches. He won approximately 250 games at Chicago, and more than 300 victories in fifty-seven years as a head coach.

Despite his many victories and innovations, it may be argued that Stagg's greatest contribution was in holding up an ideal of what college football could and should be. His concept of the game is best seen in the code of the Order of the C, the first athletic-letter club, which he organized in 1904: a man must be amateur in spirit and act; he must be a gentleman and a sportsman, unwilling to win by cheating or unfair tactics; he must train hard and conscientiously, and willingly make personal sacrifice to produce the best that is in him, then give it freely and loyally to the university; he must have attained distinction as a varsity player or have done good-quality work and performed valuable service to the university over at least two years. Stagg once said that love of country is the closest analogy to the feeling generated by college football.

To Stagg, football was indissolubly tied up with college life; its basis was too purely emotional for it ever to be played successfully by professionals. He was, therefore, adamantly opposed to the emergence of professional football, which he saw as an attempt to exploit the colleges. "The day boys play with one eye on the university and the other on their professional futures," he wrote, "the sport will become a moral liability to the college. . . . Once the game becomes a nursery for professional gladiators, we shall have to plough up our football fields." George Halas, a founder of the National Football League, insists that Stagg revoked the varsity letters of Chicago athletes who turned professional.

Upon reaching Chicago's mandatory retirement age, Stagg became head coach at the College of the Pacific in Stockton, Calif., in 1933. His record there was not impressive—sixty wins, seventy-five losses, and seven ties—although during the war years, with military trainees at the college, he made it one of the strongest teams on the West Coast and was named coach of the year in 1943. He resigned after the 1946 season and became an offensive coach with his son Amos, Jr., at Susquehanna College. He was elected to the Football Hall of Fame in 1951 both as a player and as a coach. In 1953, when Stella Stagg could no longer make the trip to Susquehanna from their home in California, he served as an advisory coach at Stockton Junior College. In September 1960, at age ninety-eight, he finally conceded that it was time to quit.

Stagg's last two decades were notable more for longevity than coaching achievements; it became increasingly remarkable for one so old to remain active in a young man's game. The Grand Old Man, as he was now called, was a living legend by the time of his death at Stockton, Calif. Although neither big-time college football nor professional football evolved in ways that Stagg would have preferred, it is difficult to argue with the conclusion that during his years as a college coach he was the most compelling single force for the tactical growth and ethical elevation of the game.

[A. A. Stagg and W. W. Stout, *Touchdown!* (1927), is Stagg's autobiography. Also see Tim Cohane, *The Yale Football Story* (1951); George W. Pierson, *Yale College: An Educational History, 1871–1921* (1952); Edwin Pope, *Football's Greatest Coaches* (1955); Allison Danzig, *The History of American Football* (1956); Frederick Rudolph, *The American College and University, a History* (1962); and Richard J. Storr, *Harper's University* (1966). An obituary is in the *New York Times*, Mar. 18, 1965.]

HORTON W. EMERSON, JR.

STANDLEY, WILLIAM HARRISON (Dec. 18, 1872–Oct. 25, 1963), naval officer and diplomat, was born in Ukiah, Calif., the son of Jeremiah M. Standley, a sheriff, and of Sarah Charity Clay. He grew up on his father's ranch, where he developed his habits of frank speaking and direct action. At the U.S. Naval Academy at Annapolis, Md., he played football and baseball and graduated in the middle of the class of 1895. Standley spent the mandatory two years at sea, on the cruiser *Olympia* in the Far East, prior to receiving his commission as ensign. On May 28, 1898, he married Evelyn C. Curtis; they had five children.

During the Spanish-American War and Philippine Insurrection, Standley served on the gunboat *Yorktown*, and received a commendation for bravery while leading a scouting party ashore at Baler in April 1899. (Later, in 1915–1916 he commanded the *Yorktown* off Mexico.) After several brief tours of duty ashore and afloat, he went to American Samoa with the rank of lieutenant (1904) for three years. Standley served aboard three vessels in the Pacific before assignment as aide to two commandants at Mare Island, Calif. (1911–1914), and as director of the wartime expansion of the physical plant of the Naval Academy (1916–1919). Success in the latter post won him promotion to captain, command of the battleship *Virginia,* and then assignment as student at the Naval War College, from which he graduated in 1921. He outfitted and brought into commission the airship tender *Wright* (1921).

Standley quickly became a prominent figure in the navy, first as assistant chief of staff to the Battle Fleet commander, Admiral E. W. Eberle (1921–1923), and then as head of the War Plans Division in the Office of the Chief of Naval Operations. After commanding the battleship *California* in the Pacific (1926–1927), he was director of fleet training (1927–1928) and assistant chief of naval operations (1928–1930). Promoted to rear admiral in November 1927 and vice admiral in January 1932, Standley commanded the fleet's destroyers (1930–1931) and its cruisers (1931–1933). After advancing to the rank of full admiral in May 1933, he commanded the Battle Force for only a few weeks before his appointment as chief of naval operations on July 1.

Because of the chronic illness of Secretary Claude A. Swanson, Standley often acted as secretary of the navy. He presided over what he termed a "businessman's navy," his major task being the attempt to convince Congress of the need for modernizing and replacing ships in the midst of the Great Depression. Although generally successful—as shown by the Vinson-Trammel Act (1934)—he failed to persuade Congress or the Roosevelt administration to build the navy up to the treaty strength set at the 1930 London conference. He represented the United States at the naval disarmament conferences at London in 1934–1935. When the Japanese delegates complained about their inferior quota of warships, he defiantly offered to "swap navies" with them and still defeat them.

Standley retired on Jan. 1, 1937, when he reached the statutory retirement age of sixty-four. He helped to run the New York World's Fair in 1939. He remained an outspoken critic of fascist dictators, and in June 1940 he openly advocated a United States declaration of war against Nazi Germany.

In 1939, Standley became naval adviser to President Franklin D. Roosevelt; then naval representative on the Priorities Board of the Office of Production Management; and, in March 1941, having returned to active duty, a member of the Production Planning Board.

Standley's connection with the Soviet Union began when he was U.S. Navy member of the Beaverbrook-Harriman lend-lease mission to that country during the autumn of 1941. After a few weeks with the Roberts Commission investigating the attack on Pearl Harbor, he was appointed United States ambassador to the Soviet Union on Feb. 9, 1942. The Russians admired his firm demeanor and strong support for the second front they wanted so desperately. But the arduous Russian winters, compounded by his seventy years, finally convinced Standley to resign in May 1943, although he did not leave Russia until October. Twelve years later he published a memoir on his ambassadorship that was based on his detailed diary: *Admiral Ambassador to Russia* (1955), written with Rear Admiral Arthur A. Ageton. He served with the Office of Strategic Services from March 1944 until the end of the war.

After the war Standley, a dedicated foe of Communism, joined or supported several right-wing causes, notably the hysterical crusade of Senator Joseph R. McCarthy. While heading a California crime commission in 1948, he blamed the Communists for American labor union troubles. Before and after the war he was a director of Pan American Airways. Standley died at San Diego, Calif.

[Three mimeographed biographical sketches are available at the Naval Historical Center, and Standley's papers are at the Naval Historical Foundation, Library of Congress. See also Clark G. Reynolds, *Famous American Admirals* (1978). Obituaries are in the *New York Times* and the *Washington Post,* Oct. 26, 1963.]

CLARK G. REYNOLDS

STANLEY, HAROLD (Oct. 2, 1885–May 14, 1963), investment banker and securities expert, was born in Great Barrington, Mass., the son of William Stanley and Lila Courtney Wetmore. His father was an inventor for whom the General Electric Company named its Stanley Works at Pittsfield, Mass. Harold Stanley attended the Hotchkiss School in Lakeville, Conn., where he played baseball and hockey. He then entered Yale University, where he was an outstanding hockey player. He graduated with a B.A. in 1908.

After an extended trip to Europe, Stanley was employed by the National Commercial Bank in Albany, N.Y. In 1910 he joined the New York City bond house of J. G. White and Company as assistant treasurer. Four years later he married Edith Thurston; they had no children. In 1915, Stanley joined Guaranty Trust Company, becoming vice-president in charge of the bond department the following year. The department's rapid growth under his management led the bank to establish a subsidiary, the Guaranty Company (with Stanley as president), to handle the securities business.

In the years immediately after World War I, the Guaranty Company underwrote and sold millions of dollars in bonds for government and private organizations. In joint ventures with J. P. Morgan and Company it floated some of the largest bond issues to that time. Stanley attracted Wall Street attention as a leading authority on the bond market.

Impressed by Stanley's expertise, J. P. Morgan, Jr., offered him a partnership in the House of Morgan, where he replaced Dwight Whitney Morrow, who had just resigned to become ambassador to Mexico. When he joined Morgan in January 1928, at age forty-two, Stanley was one of the youngest men ever admitted to a Morgan partnership. He concerned himself primarily with utility financing and investments, and soon was regarded as Morgan's utility expert.

In the early 1930's congressional investigations, spawned by the deepening Great Depression, uncovered numerous instances of negligence and irresponsibility in the practices of the nation's bankers. Pressure for reform resulted in a flurry of new federal banking and securities laws, including the Banking Act of 1933, which required the separation of commercial and investment banking. J. P. Morgan and Company chose to remain a bank of deposit and in June 1934 discontinued underwriting and wholesaling investment securities.

In 1935, William Ewing, Henry S. Morgan, and Stanley, in an arrangement that enjoyed the blessing of the Morgan partners, resigned their partnerships in the firm and organized the independent bond house of Morgan, Stanley and Company, which took over the investment banking business given up by J. P. Morgan and Company. Stanley became the president of the new firm.

As a leading expert in his field, Stanley was frequently called to appear before congressional committees. In 1938 he testified at the Temporary National Economic Committee hearings in opposition to competitive bidding among bond houses in the placement of bonds. At that time he wrote a long and influential memorandum, *Competitive Bidding for New Issues of Corporate Securities,* which argued that competitive bidding resulted in overpriced issues and poorer securities and would drive out the smaller bond houses. Nevertheless, the Securities and Exchange Commission issued a ruling in 1941 requiring competitive, public, sealed bidding for all issues of registered holding companies and their subsidiaries under its jurisdiction.

When Morgan, Stanley and Company reorganized in 1940 from a corporation to a partnership, Stanley became its senior partner. Also in 1940 he led the New York area campaign for the United States Committee for the Care of European Children, a private group devoted to aiding young war refugees. The committee raised $1.5 million under his leadership.

Stanley's wife died in 1934. In January 1939 he married Louise Todd Gilbert, widow of Seymour Parker Gilbert, a former Morgan partner.

Stanley was a principal witness in 1947 when the Justice Department brought antitrust charges under the Sherman Act against seventeen investment banking firms, including Morgan, Stanley, and the Investment Bankers Association. The government failed to demonstrate that monopolistic practices existed in the investment banking business, and the case was dismissed. Judge Harold R. Medina, who presided, paid special tribute to "the absolute integrity of Harold Stanley."

After his retirement in 1955, Stanley remained a limited partner of Morgan, Stanley and Company until his death at Philadelphia.

[Stanley's testimony before the U.S. Temporary National Economic Committee is in that committee's *Investigation of the Concentration of Economic Power: Hearings . . .* (31 pts., 1939–1941). His testimony in the antitrust case is in U.S. District Court, Southern District of New York (civil no. 43-757), *United States of America* v. *Henry S. Morgan, et al.* See also Vincent P. Carosso, *Investment Banking in America* (1970). An obituary is in the *New York Times,* May 15, 1963.]

STEPHEN D. BODAYLA

STEFANSSON, VILHJALMUR (Nov. 3, 1879–Aug. 26, 1962), Arctic explorer, was born at Arnes, Manitoba, Canada, the son of Johann Stefansson and Ingibjorg Johannesdottir, who had emigrated from Iceland in 1877. Christened William, he changed his first name to its Icelandic form Vilhjalmur when an adult. In 1880 a flood caused great property damage around Arnes and claimed numbers of lives, including two Stefansson children. This prompted the family to settle in Dakota Territory outside the small town of Mountain. They engaged in subsistence farming and probably raised some cash crops.

Stefansson went to school infrequently during these years but supplemented his meager education by reading the Bible, Icelandic sagas, and the Icelandic newspaper *Heimskringla.* His father died when Stefansson was a teen-ager, and in order to be less of a burden to his mother, Stefansson went to live with a married sister at Mountain. He soon supported himself by helping his brother Johann in a stock-herding enterprise and by capturing wild horses in Montana and selling them to North Dakota farmers.

In 1898 Stefansson entered the Preparatory Department at the University of North Dakota. But in 1902 he was expelled, allegedly for encouraging students to protest against the administration. (Stefansson denied such activity in his autobiography.) He entered the University of Iowa shortly thereafter and took equivalency examinations in order to graduate in one year (1903).

In 1900 Stefansson met William Wallace Fenn and Samuel Eliot at a conference on religion. They encouraged him to become a Unitarian minister, offering him financial assistance to study theology at Harvard University. When Fenn and Eliot agreed that he could study religion from an anthropological perspective, Stefansson entered Harvard Divinity School in the fall of 1903. At the end of his first year he abandoned theological studies and became a full-time graduate student in anthropology, eventually obtaining his M.A. in 1923. The summers of 1904 and 1905 he went on archaeological expeditions to Iceland for the Peabody Museum of Harvard. In 1905 the Harvard Department of Anthropology selected him as a teaching fellow for the polar regions, especially the Arctic. Ernest de Koven Leffingwell, a geologist, offered him a position as the ethnographer for an Anglo-American polar expedition in April 1906. Stefansson accepted but the expedition was aborted in April 1907 because Leffingwell's ship failed to appear at the appointed spot. Instead he lived with an Eskimo family in a village west of the mouth of the Mackenzie River.

Stefansson went to New York City in the fall of 1907 and met with officials of the American Museum of Natural History, persuading them to finance an Arctic expedition. (At this time he published his first articles about Eskimos in *Harper's.*) With additional support from the Canadian government, the expedition departed

in May 1908. Before it reached Cape Parry the following spring, Stefansson had learned to adequately speak the Eskimo language. He departed from Cape Parry in April 1909 and spent the next three years among the Eskimos of eastern Alaska. In the spring of 1912 he returned to New York City, where he hoped to find backing for another expedition. A Sept. 12, 1912, article in the *Seattle* (Wash.) *Daily Times* stated that Stefansson had discovered "blond Eskimos" who may have been descendents of early European explorers. This caused great controversy, and he became known to many Arctic scholars. He published his findings on blond Eskimos in both the *Literary Digest* and *Scientific American.*

The Canadian government agreed to finance a second expedition. Stefansson divided it into two groups: The first, of which he would be the leader, would explore in the Beaufort Sea, take soundings, look for signs of animal life, and search for undiscovered land—islands of the Canadian archipelago. The other party, led by his friend Rudolph Martin Anderson, an ornithologist, was to do anthropological, zoological, archaeological, and geological research in the vicinity of Coronation Gulf. Both parties left for Alaska in the summer of 1913. Stefansson focused his attention on explorations in the Arctic Ocean—primarily the Beaufort Sea—for the next five years. In 1914 he and two companions lived on the floating ice of the Arctic Ocean for several months and supplemented their limited supplies with polar-bear and seal meat, dispelling the notion that the area had no animal life. While he was at Herschel Island in early 1918, he developed typhoid and pneumonia and did not fully recover until the summer. On his return he was recognized by the Royal Geographical Society, American Geographical Society, National Geographic Society, and Philadelphia Geographic Society.

Stefansson went to England in 1920 and tried to persuade the British to finance another Arctic expedition. The government refused to subsidize his new venture, and Stefansson decided not to undertake any more Arctic expeditions, preferring instead to lecture and write.

His two most influential books, *The Friendly Arctic: The Story of Five Years in Polar Regions* (1921) and *The Northward Course of Empire* (1922), stressed that the Arctic was not a barren land and that transpolar commercial airline travel was feasible. Some explorers, particularly Roald Amundsen, rejected Stefansson's claims, and it was some years before his findings were generally accepted. Stefansson began acquiring materials dealing with polar regions in the early 1920's. The collection, which eventually exceeded fifteen thousand volumes, was sold to Dartmouth College.

On Apr. 10, 1941, he married Evelyn Schwartz Baird; they had no children. During World War II the United States government frequently employed him as a consultant on Arctic matters. In 1951 he moved from New York City, where he had maintained his home and offices for many years, to a Vermont farm. He died in Hanover, N.H.

[Vilhjalmur Stefansson also wrote *My Life with the Eskimo* (1913); *Unsolved Mysteries of the Arctic* (1938); and *Discovery: The Autobiography of Vilhjalmur Stefansson* (1964). See also D. M. Le Bourdais, "Vilhjalmur Stefansson," *New Republic*, July 19, 1922; Earl P. Hanson, "Stefansson: Twenty Years After," *Harper's*, Mar. 1940; and the *New York Times* obituary, Aug. 27, 1962.]

MICHAEL G. SCHENE

STEVENS, DORIS (Oct. 26, 1892–Mar. 22, 1963), suffragist and feminist leader, was born in Omaha, Nebr., the daughter of Henry Hendebourck Stevens and Caroline Koopman. A deeply religious upbringing pointed her toward a career of public service, and upon graduation from Oberlin College in 1911 she began settlement work in Cleveland. Concluding that the dwellings needed more reform than the inhabitants, she asked Cleveland authorities to make her an inspector of tenements. When they offered her only an unsalaried position, she returned to Oberlin to teach (1911–1912). She soon became vice-principal of the Oberlin High School.

Inspired by the British suffragette Sylvia Pankhurst, who spoke in her sociology class, Stevens joined the suffrage crusade. She labored in three unsuccessful state campaigns in Ohio, Michigan, and Montana (1911–1913) and then concluded that only a federal amendment would succeed. She joined Alice Paul and Lucy Burns in Washington, D.C., as a member of the Congressional Union for Woman Suffrage. In 1914 this group withdrew from the National American Woman Suffrage Association in a dispute over money, tactics, and temperament. It became the National Woman's Party (NWP) in 1916 and was responsible for the most dramatic events in the final years of the suffrage campaign.

The NWP sought to embarrass President Woodrow Wilson into endorsing the suffrage amendment. Stevens helped to organize the delegations that harried Wilson. One of the first women arrested for picketing the White House in 1917, she was sentenced to sixty days in the Occoquan Workhouse, but was pardoned after three days. During October and November 1917, while Paul and Burns were imprisoned, Stevens commanded the NWP headquarters and directed the picketing. During a 1919 demonstration in New York City against Wilson, a man wrenched away a banner and knocked her down with a banner pole. After the adoption of the Nineteenth Amendment, she wrote *Jailed for Freedom* (1920) about the militant suffrage effort.

On Dec. 10, 1921, Stevens married Dudley Field Malone, a noted lawyer, whom she had met in 1916. A personal friend of Wilson, Malone had been appointed collector of the Port of New York in 1913. In 1917 Malone became the lawyer for the NWP pickets and in September of that year resigned as collector to protest Wilson's failure to endorse the amendment.

In early 1921 the NWP decided to press for an equal rights amendment. At this time Stevens was in Europe as the companion of the powerful and wealthy backer of the NWP, Mrs. O. H. P. Belmont. From the time they first met in 1914 until Belmont's death in 1932, Stevens sometimes functioned virtually as her personal servant; she made several trips to Europe upon Belmont's summons, wrote most of her speeches and articles in the 1920's, and found her marriage strained by her demands.

Despite his early passion for Stevens (Malone had divorced his first wife to marry her), from the start it was a desperately unhappy marriage. He drank excessively, caroused with other women, and even physically abused Stevens. They were divorced in 1929. On Aug. 31, 1935, she married Jonathan E. Mitchell, a journalist with the New York *World*, whom she had met in 1923. This marriage was a lasting success.

The Equal Rights Amendment (ERA) was introduced in Congress in 1923. Over the next three years the NWP had to battle nearly every other feminist and women's organization, for these groups feared the impact of ERA on legislation designed to protect women. Defeated in the U. S. Congress, the NWP turned to international treaty to press for equal rights. Stevens was on the NWP Executive Committee and chaired its International Relations Committee during 1923–1929. Belmont, who had herself appointed president of the NWP in 1921 (although she resided in France), expected to play a major role in the international effort; but she was too old to do so. Stevens served as her surrogate and deputy so capably, energetically, and brilliantly that she incurred the jealousy of Paul, who was the vice-president from 1921 to 1928.

Stevens led an NWP delegation to Havana, Cuba, in 1928 to lobby for equal rights before the Sixth Pan-American Conference. Her address there was the first made by a woman before any international body to plead for treaty action on women's rights. As a result, the conference created the Inter-American Commission of Women. Stevens was chairman of the commission from 1928 to 1939. The commission investigated the legal status of women in the American republics and presented treaty recommendations to the Pan-American Conferences of 1933 and 1938. Stevens attempted to present a draft of an equal rights treaty to the signers of the Kellogg-Briand Peace Pact in Paris in 1928, but was arrested for disrupting the conference. She spoke on behalf of a treaty for independent nationality for women before the First World Conference for Codification of International Law at The Hague in 1930. She was the first woman to address the Institut de Droit International (1929) and the first woman elected to the American Institute of International Law (replacing Elihu Root) in 1931. In addition, she was a member of the Women's Consultative Committee on Nationality for the League of Nations from 1931 to 1936.

By contributing to the impression that Stevens was not following Belmont's orders, in 1931 Paul undermined Stevens with Belmont, who then unexpectedly dropped Stevens from her will. Eventually there was a power struggle in the NWP, and in 1933 Stevens became a leader of an opposition faction. This faction, which in 1945 objected to the selection of Anita Pollitzer as national chairman, forcefully attempted to seize the NWP headquarters in Washington in 1947. Lawsuits to determine legal control of the NWP followed; Stevens lost her suit in 1947 and resigned from the NWP the following year.

Another blow had come in 1939 when the Roosevelt administration replaced Stevens with Mary Winslow on the Inter-American Commission of Women. Stevens blamed Eleanor Roosevelt for the removal. The action accelerated Stevens' drift toward right-wing politics. She explained that Eleanor Roosevelt had purged her from the commission "for being ungettable for the Commies." She called Winslow a Communist and fed information about Eleanor Roosevelt and Winslow to the vitriolic columnist Westbrook Pegler. She became an ardent champion of Senator Joseph R. McCarthy and his anti-Communist crusade.

In her last years Stevens turned to music. She wrote a number of songs, mostly about growing up on the Plains, and had the pleasure of seeing them performed, recorded, and broadcast on radio in the mid-1950's. She died in New York City.

[The Doris Stevens papers are in the Schlesinger Library at Radcliffe, and the National Woman's Party papers are in the Manuscript Division of the Library of Congress and on microfilm in the University of North Carolina and Lamont (Harvard University) libraries. Stevens wrote various articles for *Forum* (1924, 1926), *Nation* (1926), *American Mercury* (1926), and *Birth Control Review* (1926). An obituary is in the *New York Times*, Mar. 25, 1963.]
J. STANLEY LEMONS

STEVENS, HARRY MOZLEY (June 14, 1855–May 3, 1934), and **STEVENS, FRANK MOZLEY** (Aug. 10, 1880–Jan. 3, 1965), sports concessionaires and caterers. Harry Mozley Stevens was born in London, England. His boyhood education benefited from a well-stocked family library. An assiduous reader, he developed an abiding love of Shakespeare's works. This interest, augmented by a flair for rhetoric, became a part of his personality, which could be characterized as thoughtful, enthusiastic, and convivial, as well as persuasive and ambitious. In 1882 Stevens and his wife, Mary Wragg Stevens, moved to the United States, settling in Niles, Ohio. They came with a daughter and two sons, the youngest being Frank Mozley. Later two more sons were born, and in time all five children joined the father's concessionaire firm.

At Niles, Stevens found work as an iron puddler and within nine months had organized a union and led his fellow workers in a strike. Later, with the assistance of Ohio Senator Joseph Benson Foraker, Stevens became a book salesman. In the meantime both he and Frank Mozley became American citizens. Stevens was still selling books in 1887 when he attended a baseball game in Columbus, Ohio. Dissatisfied with the information on his scorecard, he designed a vastly improved model. For $500 he acquired the concession to sell his scorecards at the Columbus park, an investment he immediately recouped by selling $700 worth of scorecard advertisements. When his scorecards sold well, Stevens obtained other concessions from Tri-State League clubs; and before the year ended he had the scorecard concession for the World Series. Over the next four years "the scorecard man" acquired similar concessions at many major- and minor-league parks, including

Milwaukee, where fans welcomed his German-language version.

"Scorecard Harry" hawked cards with colorful aplomb, reportedly popularizing that oft-repeated cry, "You can't tell the players without a scorecard!" Moving to New York City in 1894, Stevens obtained full concession rights at the Polo Grounds, where he sold scorecards and snack foods to fans of the New York Giants. Shortly after 1900 he revolutionized the diets of fans by offering peanuts, soda pop with straws, and hot dogs as alternatives to the then traditional lemonade and ice cream fare. Stevens' famous "hot dog" was a conversion of the familiar dachshund sausage, which Stevens then swathed with mustard and bundled into rolls. But its immediate and lasting popularity owed to sports cartoonist Thomas A. ("Tad") Dorgan, who depicted it in a famous cartoon and dubbed it by its ever familiar name. As his offerings expanded, Stevens shrewdly acquired his own peanut farm in Virginia.

A favorite of sports fans, players, and sportswriters, Stevens wore the title of "Hot Dog King" with élan. It was said that his was "the loudest voice ever heard in Harlem." As Stevens' growing army of hirelings sold food to fans, he was expanding his concessionaire enterprise into a profitable new catering industry. In the years before World War I he employed hundreds of uniformed workers, whose loyalties he won by his generosity and paternal concern (which included pension benefits). Thus, Stevens could send his "Marching and Chowder Society" far afield to cater to patrons of hotels, indoor shows, exhibitions, and racetracks.

By the 1920's Stevens was famous for his epicurean menus available to the carriage set at such places as the Saratoga Race Track and Madison Square Garden dining rooms. But serving outdoor sports crowds remained his chief concern. When he died in New York City in 1934, Stevens held concessions at the five major-league parks in New York and Boston. By then his enterprise was known as Harry M. Stevens, Inc., having been incorporated in 1925. The New York City–based business used a letterhead proclaiming the scope of its services "From the Hudson to the Rio Grande."

Notwithstanding Stevens' charismatic presence, the firm was run as an integrated family enterprise, with the sons and a son-in-law eventually joining the business. Frank Mozley succeeded his father as president and treasurer of the company. He already had thirty-eight years of experience with the firm, having worked in it since age sixteen. He was a balding, genial man who loved baseball (he was a director of the New York Giants), and under his low-profiled leadership the scope of company operations widened so that letterheads soon read "From Coast to Coast." The firm catered to a variety of shows and public entertainments, yet outdoor sports, including thirty-six racetrack concessions, remained the chief focus. As major-league baseball expanded westward in the 1950's, Stevens men followed. But in the 1960's the firm's baseball concessions dwindled to Shea Stadium in New York and Fenway Park in Boston. Still these were lucrative; ballpark concessions grossed more than ticket sales.

But the scope of Stevens' operations extended far beyond ballparks; 6,000 workers catered to trade shows, conventions, and exhibitions, including all events staged at the New York Coliseum. Expanded operations prompted Stevens to open branch offices in Massachusetts, Pennsylvania, Maryland, California, and Vermont. In 1962 it was estimated that the firm served about 30 million customers: 20 million racetrack patrons, 5 million baseball fans, 4 million convention visitors, and half-a-million football fans.

Without fanfare, but with relentless diligence, Frank Stevens presided over this vast operation for thirty years. It remained a family enterprise. By the 1970's a fourth generation was active in the organization.

On Dec. 28, 1904, Stevens had married Gertrude Honhorst; they had two children. Stevens died at his home in New York City a few months after his retirement.

[There is no published biography of Harry M. Stevens or Frank M. Stevens. Emphasizing the life of Harry M. Stevens are Red Smith, "Peanuts, Popcorn and Friendship," *Sign: National Catholic Magazine,* Mar. 8, 1961; and Gus Steiger, "Strictly a Family Affair," *Columbia: Knights of Columbus Magazine,* Mar. 1965.

Harry M. Stevens, Inc., in New York City, provides materials such as a brochure, "Serving the Action World," and a two-page biographical sketch by Bob Cooke, "The Harry M. Stevens Story." Obituaries include "Harry M. Stevens," *New York Times,* May 4, 1934; and "Frank M. Stevens," *New York Times,* Jan. 4, 1965.]

DAVID Q. VOIGT

STEVENSON, ADLAI EWING, II (Feb. 5, 1900–July 14, 1965), politician and government official, was born in Los Angeles, Calif., the son of Lewis Green Stevenson, a former secretary of state for Illinois, and of Helen Louise Davis. His maternal great-grandfather, Jesse Fell, was a close friend and early supporter of Abraham Lincoln, and his paternal grandfather, Adlai E. Stevenson, was a vice-president of the United States (1893–1897). In 1906 the Stevenson family returned from California to Bloomington, Ill., where Lewis Stevenson managed farms owned by his aunt. Helen Stevenson, a stern disciplinarian, read to her children from the English classics, Greek mythology, the King James version of the Bible, and the works of Hawthorne. Lewis Stevenson traveled frequently, and the son envied his playmates who had close relationships with their fathers. There was considerable tension between his parents, and young Stevenson was often the peacemaker.

As a youth Stevenson had around him the history-makers of his own family, their friends, and the books, written records, and souvenirs of decades of American life. He once observed that as a result of his family's prominence, his horizons were expanded by "meeting famous people." The Stevensons had Sunday dinner regularly at the home of Vice-President Stevenson.

After attending schools in Bloomington, in 1916 he enrolled at the Choate School in Connecticut to prepare for Princeton University, which he entered in 1918. Although he was not an outstanding scholar, he particularly enjoyed history, English, and literature. His greatest satisfaction was the three and a half years writing and editing for the *Daily Princetonian.*

Stevenson's father—regretting his own lack of legal training—insisted that Adlai attend law school. In 1922, after graduating from Princeton, he became a reluctant student at the Harvard Law School. Although he did not fail, at the end of the second year his standing was below the level of his class. In July 1924, Stevenson returned to join the Bloomington *Daily Pantagraph,* which was owned by his mother's family, as managing editor. In 1925 he entered the Northwestern University Law School, spending weekends working on the Bloomington paper. In June of the next year he received his J.D.

After a trip to the Soviet Union, in 1927 Stevenson became a law clerk in the conservative Republican law firm of Cutting, Moore and Sidley in Chicago. He became active in the Chicago Council on Foreign Relations and led a busy social life. On Dec. 1, 1928, he married Ellen Borden, who was from an old Chicago family. Her father inherited wealth, increased it, and then lost it during the Great Depression. They had three sons, one of whom, Adlai E. Stevenson III, served as senator from Illinois from 1970 to 1981. The Stevensons were divorced in 1949.

In July 1933, Stevenson went to Washington to work for the New Deal Agricultural Adjustment Administration. In January 1934, he became chief attorney of the newly created Federal Alcohol Control Administration and rejoined his Chicago law firm in October. In 1935 he was made a partner in the firm. That year he was also elected president of the Chicago Council on Foreign Relations.

Over the next years Stevenson developed a reputation for informed and eloquent speeches. Although his introductions of speakers at the council seemed spontaneous, in fact they had been written and rewritten until every word and sentence satisfied his increasingly exacting standards of style. Indeed, law and making money never interested him as much as public affairs. Between 1934 and 1940, he served on the board of directors of Hull House, the Immigrants' Protective League, the Illinois Children's Home and Aid Society, and the Legislative Voters' League. Among his close friends were Robert M. Hutchins, president of the University of Chicago, and such faculty members as Samuel Harper, Bernadotte E. Schmitt, Quincy Wright, and Jacob Viner. Jane Ward Dick, Stevenson's close friend from the 1920's, recalled in 1966 that "he absorbed from life and people what most people absorb from books."

In June 1940, at the request of William Allen White, editor of the *Emporia* (Kans.) *Gazette,* and chairman of the newly organized Committee to Defend America by Aiding the Allies, Stevenson became chairman of the Chicago chapter. As head of this highly controversial committee, he became acquainted with a wide variety of people and further sharpened his writing and speaking style. Moreover, the experience increased his determination to be more active in public affairs.

In June 1941, Secretary of the Navy Frank Knox appointed Stevenson his principal attorney. During the next three years, Stevenson served as the secretary's speech writer and administrative assistant. He attended important meetings with him, and represented Knox and the navy on various interagency committees. In late 1943 and early 1944, he headed a mission to Sicily and that part of Italy under allied control to study what role the Foreign Economic Administration should play in relief and rehabilitation.

In June 1944, after the death of Secretary Knox, Stevenson returned to Chicago. He tried to purchase control of the *Chicago Daily News* but was outbid. During November and December of that year he traveled to England and

France with his former law associate George W. Ball, then with the Foreign Economic Administration, to study the effects of Allied bombing on the German war effort. In February 1945, Archibald MacLeish, assistant secretary of state for public and cultural relations, lured Stevenson back to Washington. Stevenson became a special assistant to Secretary of State Edward R. Stettinius, Jr. His major task was to improve the public image of the Department of State. MacLeish and Stevenson launched a campaign to rally public support for the Dumbarton Oaks proposals that were the basis for the San Francisco conference on international organization opening in April 1945. In May, Stevenson took charge of the press relations of the United States delegation at the San Francisco conference. The situation had become ludicrous because the delegates—including several potential presidential candidates—refused to allow Stettinius to speak for the delegation. They frequently could not agree on statements to the press. Arthur Krock of the *New York Times* recommended that Stevenson be appointed to brief the press even though the delegation might repudiate his statements. Stevenson performed skillfully and won the respect not only of Stettinius and Republican Senator Arthur H. Vandenberg but of the news people as well.

In September 1945, Stevenson accompanied Stettinius to London as a member of the American delegation to the Preparatory Commission of the United Nations (UN). After Stettinius became ill, Stevenson headed the delegation. He wrote in 1953: "It was the most exacting, interesting and in many ways the most important interval in my life. After almost four years of preoccupation with war, the satisfaction of having a part in the organized search for the conditions and mechanics of peace completed my circle." When the first session of the General Assembly of the UN met in January 1946, Stevenson was appointed senior adviser to the United States delegation. He was an alternate delegate to the second session of the First General Assembly in the fall of 1946 and to the Second General Assembly in 1947, both at Lake Success, N.Y.

Between 1941 and 1947 Stevenson worked at the level of government just below the top, where much of the important work was done. He won the respect of such wartime leaders as President Franklin D. Roosevelt and General George C. Marshall. And he worked closely with many of the people who influenced United States policy in the immediate postwar years, including James F. Byrnes, Senator Vanden-

berg, Robert A. Lovett, John J. McCloy, Dean G. Acheson, and Eleanor Roosevelt.

In 1947 some of Stevenson's Chicago friends tried to win the support of the Cook County Democratic party for his candidacy to the U.S. Senate. Instead, Colonel Jacob M. Arvey, the leader of the Cook County organization, backed Stevenson for the governorship. Stevenson told Arvey that his experience was almost wholly with the federal government and foreign policy. When he asked whether he would be free on patronage appointments, Arvey stated that he would make no recommendations on major appointments but hoped that Stevenson would appoint Democrats to minor positions "if qualified." After thinking the offer over for a few days, Stevenson agreed to run. Arvey wrote in 1966: "I am greatly amused at the stories that Adlai Stevenson was indecisive. He was not a superficial man. He insisted upon knowing everything about his subject. He did not do things impulsively. He did not make impulsive decisions, but wanted to know every facet of a problem before he decided upon action." It was characteristic of Stevenson to worry about a problem, to discuss it. But when he was convinced of a position, he was decisive.

In a tireless, resourceful, and sometimes humorous style, Stevenson waged a vigorous campaign for the Illinois governorship. He focused on trying to reach independents, both Democrats and Republicans. He attacked the corruption, payroll padding, and ties with gambling interests of Governor Dwight H. Green's Republican machine. He promised a responsible government that would serve the public and cope with problems of education, welfare, industrial safety, and roads and highways.

In the campaign, Stevenson established a pattern for his two later presidential campaigns. Although he used speech writers, he seldom delivered their texts without some rewriting. He had the knack of picking speech drafters who knew his ideas and his style. His associates in 1948, and later, complained that he spent far too much time on his writing. While he would nod in agreement, he had too much respect for literary quality, for the use of words in conveying his ideas, to do otherwise. Equally important, he was determined to be his own man, to present the real man, not a myth manufactured by ghosts and public relations manipulation.

Stevenson won the election by 572,067 votes, the largest margin in the history of Illinois. President Truman won the state by only 33,612 votes. Although one house of the Illinois legislature was Republican-controlled during his first two years and both houses in his last two, Stevenson achieved many improvements in state government. These included removing the state police from political patronage; doubling state aid to public schools; improving the state welfare program, with better care and treatment in the state mental institutions; reorganizing state purchasing and improving the budget system; and launching the state's biggest road-rebuilding program. He brought able people into high administrative posts regardless of political affiliation.

As governor, Stevenson was a skillful politician, respectful of the uses of the craft. While he believed in the importance of the party structure, he realized that the party continually had to adapt itself to changing times. He demonstrated that service to the citizens, candor, and a willingness to act responsibly in educating and guiding the people took precedence over service to the party. Through speeches, radio addresses, and correspondence he strove to inform the people about their state government. He was quick to criticize reckless political statements. For example, on Dec. 13, 1951, he said that "'McCarthyism' has become the trademark of a new breed of political demagogue who frightens the people with epithets, carelessly impugns the loyalty of patriotic men and shouts dire forebodings of a treacherous doom for America and all of her cherished institutions."

On June 26, 1951, in vetoing a bill establishing an "antisubversive squad" to police the state, Stevenson wrote: " . . . we must fight traitors with laws. We already have the laws. We must fight falsehood and evil ideas with truth and better ideas. We have them in plenty. But we must not confuse the two. Laws infringing our rights and intimidating unoffending persons without enlarging our security will neither catch subversives nor win converts to our better ideas. And in the long run evil ideas can be counteracted and conquered not by law but only by better ideas."

Early in January 1952, Stevenson announced that he would seek reelection as governor. Three weeks later President Truman asked him to seek the presidential nomination. Stevenson refused, explaining that he wished to be reelected governor to continue his program. His refusal exasperated Truman, who could not conceive of anyone refusing to run with the backing of the incumbent president, and it laid the foundation for their future uneasy relationship.

During the ensuing months, Stevenson was besieged by reporters, government officials, and party leaders. As the convention approached, some party leaders urged him to announce that he would accept the nomination if it were offered him. He was adamant. He said repeatedly: "I want to run for Governor of Illinois—and that's all. And I want to be reelected Governor —and that's all."

Meanwhile a group of Chicagoans formed a Draft Stevenson Committee. But when the Democratic National Convention opened in Chicago in July, many party leaders had given up considering Stevenson. A draft to them required careful planning and a private agreement with the candidate to be drafted. Truman was now supporting Vice-President Alben W. Barkley. On the third ballot, Stevenson was drafted as the nominee because the convention wanted him and nobody else.

Stevenson's acceptance speech revealed what a formidable, literate man he was: "I hope and pray that we Democrats, win or lose, can campaign not as a crusade to exterminate the opposing party, as our opponents seem to prefer, but as a great opportunity to educate and elevate a people whose destiny is leadership, not alone of a rich and prosperous, contented country as in the past, but of a world in ferment. . . . Let's talk sense to the American people. . . . Better we lose the election than mislead the people."

Stevenson then conducted a campaign that raised American political thinking to a high plane. His campaign speeches became best-selling books at home and abroad. James Reston of the *New York Times* wrote that Stevenson "tried to impose his own principles and conscience on American politics," and the historian Henry Steele Commager stated: "He managed by sheer force of intelligence to lift the whole level of public life and discourse, and to infuse American politics with a dignity, a vitality, an excitement it had not known since the early days of the New Deal."

Despite these efforts, Stevenson was overwhelmed in the election by the popular war hero Dwight D. Eisenhower. During the next four years Stevenson prepared himself to serve as president. In March 1953, he left for Asia and the Middle East to observe at first hand the revolt against white, Western colonialism. While on this six-month trip, he wrote articles for *Look* magazine and in 1954 he published *Call to Greatness*.

After Stevenson returned to the United States in August 1953, he devoted himself to rejuvenating the Democratic party. He attracted many young people to the party and played an important role in the successful campaign to elect a Democratic Congress in 1954.

It was at this time that he referred to Vice-President Richard M. Nixon as "the white-collar McCarthy." He observed during the campaign: "There is a great hunger among the people for moral leadership that remains unsatisfied. We have placed too much emphasis on materialism. Most political appeals have been appeals to the belly rather than to the spiritual, the intellectual, the moral and the educational."

On Nov. 15, 1955, Stevenson announced that he would be a candidate for the 1956 Democratic nomination. After several bruising primary battles with Senator Estes Kefauver, he won the nomination. He then took the unprecedented step of calling on the convention to nominate the vice-presidential candidate without dictation from him. Kefauver was chosen following a spirited struggle with Senator John F. Kennedy.

During this second presidential campaign, Stevenson raised issues that the Eisenhower administration had either ignored or handled inadequately. The central issue, he said on Sept. 13, 1956, was "whether America wants to stay on dead center, mired in complacency and cynicism; or whether it wants once more now to move forward." He advocated the suspension of nuclear testing in the atmosphere; reduction of tensions with the Soviet Union; the end of the draft; increased assistance to underdeveloped countries through the UN in order to remove economic development from the cold war; substantial federal assistance to education, to the poor, to the elderly. He spoke of the pressing necessity of improved race relations, and he decried the destruction of natural resources for private profit.

During the campaign and after his defeat, Stevenson was dismayed at the failure of the mass media to probe to any significant degree the challenging issues facing the nation. Moreover, he felt that the Democratic congressional leadership had not produced a substantial record of achievement. As a result, in 1957 he became a prime mover in the founding of the Democratic Advisory Council and in its activities. With the creation of the council, the national party had an effective instrument to issue policy statements.

Stevenson also continued his education by trips to Europe, Africa, the Soviet Union, and Latin America. In addition he was head of his own Chicago law firm and a member of the New York firm of Paul, Weiss, Rifkind, Wharton and Garrison.

After Stevenson's second defeat, he announced he would not be a candidate for the nomination in 1960. As the convention approached, Senator Lyndon B. Johnson tried to persuade Stevenson to join a stop-Kennedy coalition. The Kennedy forces, meanwhile, wanted Stevenson to place the senator in nomination. Stevenson refused both overtures. He remained anchored firmly to his stated public and private position that he would not support any candidate. An attempted draft by such Stevenson supporters as Eleanor Roosevelt and Senator Mike Monroney failed. After the convention, Stevenson campaigned for Kennedy, seeking to reassure those of his supporters who were unhappy with the senator's record.

After Kennedy's victory, Stevenson hoped to be appointed secretary of state; instead, Kennedy offered him the ambassadorship to the UN. Stevenson accepted after Kennedy promised that he would hold cabinet rank and play a key role in policy formulation.

Despite this assurance and a similar assurance from Lyndon Johnson when he succeeded Kennedy, Stevenson had limited influence on Washington decision-making while in the UN post. He wanted the UN to be the center of United States foreign policy, but this concept was not acceptable to Washington. Stevenson ran up against the determined opposition of implacable cold warriors in both the Kennedy and Johnson administrations. People like Stevenson and Chester Bowles (under secretary of state from January to November 1961) failed to persuade the government to rethink the assumptions of the cold war.

Repeated crises, which marked Stevenson's four and a half years at the UN, required almost constant negotiations on his part: the Bay of Pigs; the Cuban missile crisis; the UN forces in the Congo, on Cyprus, on the Egyptian-Israeli border, and in Kashmir; the death of Dag Hammarskjöld followed by the Soviet "troika" proposal (three UN secretaries general); the near bankruptcy of the UN and the impasse over Article 19 of the charter, under which nations that did not pay their assessments were to be deprived of a vote in the General Assembly; the wrangle with Portugal over its unyielding control of African colonies; the question of admitting the People's Republic of China; white racism in Rhodesia and South Africa; and the quest for disarmament.

The Bay of Pigs, among other events, illustrated President Kennedy's failure to consider Stevenson's views. When the decision to invade Cuba was made, Stevenson was not fully informed. As a result, on Apr. 15, 1961, when planes took off from Nicaragua to attack Cuban airfields, Stevenson told the UN they were Cuba's own planes flown by defectors. He presented the Central Intelligence Agency's cover story without knowing it was untrue.

During the Cuban missile crisis in October 1962, he was consulted. At Kennedy's request he became a member of the missile question executive committee. He urged a political—not a military—solution. "Let's not go to an air strike until we have explored the possibilities of peaceful solution," he urged Kennedy. He recommended that the United States should negotiate the removal of *all* foreign bases from Cuba, including the United States base at Guantanamo.

Kennedy, however, decided on a blockade of Cuba, and insisted that the Soviet missiles be removed. At the UN Stevenson negotiated with the Soviet ambassador and the missiles were removed. While these negotiations were taking place, Kennedy read in advance an article by Stewart Alsop and Charles L. Bartlett, "The White House in the Cuban Crisis," *Saturday Evening Post* (Dec. 8, 1962), which quoted the president as telling the authors that "Adlai wanted a Munich." After the article was published, Kennedy denied that he had talked to the two authors.

Although President Johnson exhibited greater respect for Stevenson's views, he also excluded him from key decision-making. An important example was Vietnam. On Aug. 4, 1964, Secretary General of the UN U Thant proposed to Secretary of State Dean Rusk and Stevenson that leaders from Hanoi and Washington talk face to face in an effort to end the fighting. Through the Soviet government, he received a favorable response from Hanoi. In January 1965, Stevenson on his own asked U Thant to find out whether Burma would sponsor a meeting. After Burma agreed, Washington rejected the proposed meeting. U Thant next proposed a seven-nation meeting. Stevenson thought this a good idea and advised Johnson that the United States indicate its "readiness to explore the willingness of the Communists to accept a peaceful solution." This recommendation was unacceptable to the president and the secretary of state. When Stevenson passed on another suggestion from U Thant in July, Rusk told him that negotiation was not the way to end the war. "[We] can do much better than that on the ground," he said. A week later, while in London, Stevenson died of a heart attack.

During the 1950's, Adlai Stevenson became the conscience of American politics, a moral and intellectual leader. In sensitive, witty, and thoughtful speeches he urged Americans to live up to their ideals. National boasting, saber-rattling, and chest-thumping he found nauseating.

After Stevenson's death, Walter Lippmann wondered (*New York Herald Tribune*, July 20, 1965) "whether . . . we shall plunge ourselves into the making of a ramshackle empire in an era when no empire can long survive . . . or . . . as Adlai Stevenson would have done, remain true to our original loyalty, and transcending assertiveness, vulgar ambition, and the seductions of power . . . make this country not only great and free but at peace with its own conscience."

[This article is based largely on *The Papers of Adlai E. Stevenson*, 8 vols. (1972–1979), edited by Walter Johnson. The Stevenson manuscript material is at the Princeton University Library. The papers for his years as governor are at the Illinois State Historical Library. Oral history interviews about Stevenson are at the Columbia University Oral History Collection and at the John F. Kennedy Library, Boston.

See also the introduction Stevenson wrote for *Major Campaign Speeches, 1952* (1953); Walter Johnson, *How We Drafted Adlai Stevenson* (1955); Elizabeth Stevenson Ives with Hildegarde Dolson, *My Brother Adlai* (1956), on his early years; Kenneth S. Davis, *A Prophet in His Own Country: The Triumphs and Defeats of Adlai E. Stevenson* (1957), valuable because of the many interviews with Stevenson, and because Stevenson approved the typescript; *As We Knew Adlai: The Stevenson Story by Twenty-Two Friends* (1966), edited by Edward P. Doyle. John Bartlow Martin, *Adlai Stevenson of Illinois* (1976), and *Adlai Stevenson and the World* (1977), are based on the Stevenson manuscript material.]

WALTER JOHNSON

STRIBLING, THOMAS SIGISMUND (Mar. 4, 1881–July 8, 1965), novelist and short-story writer, was born Thomas Hughes Stribling in Clifton, Tenn., the son of Christopher Columbus Stribling, who ran a small weekly newspaper in Clifton, and of Amelia Annie Waits, who shared equally with her husband in the writing, typesetting, and printing of the newspaper. By 1885 they had sold the paper and opened a general store, where young Stribling was soon put to work. He proved an unwilling helper, preferring to hide under the counter and write stories on wrapping paper.

After schooling in Clifton, Stribling spent a year (1898–1899) at Southern Normal College in Huntington, Tenn., but left in the spring to work for the national census. For a brief period in 1900 he edited the *Clifton News*, happily writing the entire paper himself. At his father's insistence, he went to Florence, Ala., in 1901 to clerk in a law office. During this period Stribling wrote numerous stories, two of which were accepted, without fee, by a Louisville, Ky., magazine. He entered Florence Normal College in the fall of 1901 and graduated in two years. Uncertain about a career, he went to Tuscaloosa, Ala., in 1903 and spent a year teaching high school mathematics. Then he enrolled in the University of Alabama Law School, where he received an LL.B. in 1905. Subsequently he took a position in the law office of Governor Emmet O'Neal in Florence, but quit after eight months.

Still eager to become a writer, Stribling went to work in the office of the *Taylor-Trotwood Magazine* in Nashville, Tenn. There he learned from an acquaintance how to write fiction for Sunday-school magazines. The formula was easy and sufficiently lucrative to allow him to quit his job and go to New Orleans in 1908. He spent four months there, grinding out stories for church publishing houses. "I had at last gone to work at something I liked and I worked . . . beatifically, rapturously," he later explained. Soon he was producing adventure stories for such magazines as *Youth's Companion* and *American Boy.*

Over the next nine years Stribling toured Europe, lived briefly in Philadelphia and Chicago, explored Cuba, Puerto Rico, and the Virgin Islands, and spent six months in Caracas, Venezuela, researching a novel. In 1917 he became a reporter for the *Chattanooga News* and wrote in his spare time *The Cruise of the Dry Dock* (1917), his last juvenile book. Then he worked briefly as a stenographer for the Federal Aviation Bureau in Washington, D.C., and wrote stories for *Adventure Magazine* by night. In 1919 he returned to Clifton. The war was over, he was almost forty, and he wanted to write more-serious fiction.

Stribling conceived a story of a black youth who returns to his Tennessee hill town after graduating from Harvard and discovers how powerless he is to change his community. Titled *Birthright,* the novel was serialized in *Century Magazine* in 1921–1922 and gained wide attention. Despite its artistic limitations, *Birthright* treated racial problems in a serious way; it was one of the first novels by a southerner to do so. Stribling then published several romantic melodramas, based on his South and Central American experiences: *East Is East* (1922), *Fombombo* (1923), and *Red Sand* (1924).

With *Teeftallow* (1926) Stribling returned to his more realistic material, the small southern town and its interracial struggles. Loosely organized around the lynching of a black man, *Teef-tallow* launched a bitter attack on the conventional values of the village. It earned comparison with Sinclair Lewis' *Main Street,* became the first selection of the new Book-of-the-Month Club, and firmly established Stribling's popularity. In 1928 he collaborated with David Wallace on *Rope,* a dramatization of *Teeftallow* which ran on Broadway in 1928. Living in New York and Clifton and summering in Gloucester, Mass., Stribling continued to produce romantic melodramas set in the South (*Bright Metal* in 1928, *The Backwater* in 1930) and in remoter climes (*Strange Moon* and *Clues of the Caribbees,* a series of mystery stories, both in 1929). He remained a bachelor until age forty-nine, when he married Lou Ella Kloss on Aug. 6, 1930; they had no children.

That year he began his most ambitious work, a trilogy imitating John Galsworthy's *The Forsyte Saga* and drawing heavily upon his own family history. This chronicle of the Vaiden family, set in Florence, Ala., extended from the Civil War era (*The Forge,* 1931) to the 1880's (*The Store,* 1932) and to the 1930's (*The Unfinished Cathedral,* 1934). Stribling explained about *The Store,* which won the Pulitzer Prize in 1933, "Every rustic in the Southern hill country believes that if he can get to the nearest village and set up a grocery store, his fortune is made." His final two novels were set in the North: *The Sound Wagon* (1935) satirized big city politics; and *These Bars of Flesh* (1938) attacked urban materialism.

Between 1935 and 1942 Stribling frequently published short stories in the *Saturday Evening Post,* and after 1945 he continued for another decade to write mysteries for *Ellery Queen.* He returned to Clifton permanently in 1959 and died in a rest home in nearby Florence.

Opinions of Stribling's contribution to southern literature vary widely. He has been praised for understanding the problems of blacks and hill men and for his detached "moral sanity and intelligence" (Ernest Bates); but he has been faulted for inadequate craftsmanship and shallow comprehension of issues. Allen Tate found his novels "inferior exercises in sensational journalism," and Robert Penn Warren called them "a strange compound of hick-baiting, snobbery, and humanitarianism." Stribling's most significant achievement, perhaps, was to have treated certain uniquely southern subjects—race relations, the rural village, the Reconstruction period—with an innovative satiric skepticism.

[A lengthy tape-recorded interview made in 1964 is located with the Stribling papers in Clifton, Tenn.

In the early 1920's Stribling wrote a revealing autobiographical sketch that appears in Charles C. Baldwin, *The Men Who Make Our Novels* (1924). Further information on his life may be found in the useful monograph by Wilton Eckley, *T. S. Stribling* (1975). Analysis and criticism of Stribling's novels is in Ernest Bates, *English Journal,* Feb. 1935; Bryom Dickens, *Sewanee Review,* July–Sept. 1934; Allen Tate, *Nation,* June 20, 1934; and Robert Penn Warren, *American Review,* Feb. 1934; reprinted in *Literary Opinion in America,* edited by M. D. Zabel (1937). An obituary is in the *New York Times,* July 9, 1965.]

DEAN FLOWER

STRUVE, OTTO (Aug. 12, 1897–Apr. 6, 1963), astronomer, was born in Kharkov, Russia, the son of Gustav Wilhelm Ludwig Struve, astronomer at the University of Kharkov, and of Elisabeth Struve. His uncle, grandfather, and great-grandfather had all been prominent in German and Russian astronomy. After several years of home tutoring, he attended the Kharkov Gymnasium, graduating in 1914. He then entered Kharkov University, but soon left to enroll in artillery school during World War I. He served on the Turkish front.

In 1918 Struve returned to Kharkov and obtained a first-class degree in astronomy in 1919. He planned to remain at Kharkov as an instructor, but soon returned to military service to fight for the czar during the Russian Revolution. During this period, Struve lost most of his close family, and the few who remained were scattered throughout Europe. He barely escaped with his life in the White Army evacuation to Turkey.

In 1921 Struve received an invitation from Edwin B. Frost, the director of the Yerkes Observatory of the University of Chicago, to work as a spectroscopic assistant. He arrived in the United States on Oct. 7, 1921, and by November was at work at Yerkes, in southern Wisconsin. Directed by Frost, Struve rapidly mastered observing techniques in spectroscopic stellar astronomy and helped to maintain the observatory spectroscopic and photographic programs. He also became a graduate student at the University of Chicago, receiving a Ph.D. in astronomy in 1923. An instructorship at Yerkes came the following year. Struve worked with George van Biesbroeck observing double stars, comets, and asteroids, and so continued the family tradition of contributing to positional astronomy.

But Struve rapidly advanced into modern astrophysics. He quickly grasped the need to apply physics to astronomical problems and keenly felt the inadequacies of Yerkes instrumentation for doing modern high-dispersion spectroscopy. He

was promoted to assistant professor in 1927, the same year he became a United States citizen. He became an associate professor (1930), assistant director (1931), and finally director of Yerkes in 1932, also assuming the editorship of the *Astrophysical Journal,* which he had helped to edit since the late 1920's. In 1925 he married Mary Martha Lanning. They had no children.

By the late 1920's Struve was bringing younger astrophysicists to Yerkes and was pushing for improved instrumentation. But with the Great Depression, the chances of success were slim. Soon after he became director of Yerkes, a university dean suggested that the *Astrophysical Journal* be discontinued. Struve fought to maintain it and to secure funds for a new observing site in the southern Midwest. The president of the university, Robert M. Hutchins, recognized Struve's energy with a small grant, but this was greatly superseded when Struve learned that a Texas banker had left money for the establishment of a Texas observatory. Within a short period, Struve, through Hutchins, drafted a plan whereby the universities of Chicago and Texas would join forces and talents in the construction of a major new facility, the McDonald Observatory, to be equipped with an eighty-two-inch reflector with high-dispersion spectroscopic equipment. While McDonald was under construction (1935–1936) on Mt. Locke in west Texas, Struve gathered a new staff for Yerkes and McDonald consisting of both observational and theoretical astrophysicists—a strong characteristic of the staff for many years.

At this point World War II threatened to undo everything Struve had worked for. Staff members began to leave in 1941, revenues for the *Astrophysical Journal* fell drastically because of the cancellation of foreign subscriptions, and maintenance of the two observatories became extremely difficult. Struve managed to keep the *Journal* alive, and he pushed for the creation of an Office of Scientific Research and Development (OSRD) optical shop at Yerkes in order to retain staff and to insure the viability of the institution during the war. He also cooperated with other observatory directors in securing employment for the many refugee scientists who were coming to the United States. Immediately after the war the Yerkes staff grew to over thirty. It was one of the largest and most dynamic astronomical institutions in the world. In 1947 Struve reorganized this staff, hoping that it would provide him with more research time. But postwar pressures continued, and in 1950 he resigned from Yerkes and McDonald to become chairman of the Department of Astronomy at the University of California at Berkeley. He held this post until 1959, when he became director of the National Radio Astronomy Observatory (NRAO) in West Virginia. Ironically, although Struve had done much to foster the concept of a national facility for astronomy, his tenure at NRAO was not a happy one. He was in poor health and could no longer fully administer an area of astronomy in which he had little background. Still, he aided in the growth of the facility during his three-year tenure, pushing ahead with the construction of major radio telescopes. Ill health forced his retirement in 1962. He died in Berkeley, Calif.

Struve was not only an administrator but a prolific popularizer and profoundly energetic and intuitive researcher. In 1944 he received the Gold Medal of the Royal Astronomical Society of London, the fourth member of the Struve family to be so recognized, for his broadly based research in spectroscopic astrophysics. Among his many projects were his spectroscopic observations of double stars, clarification of the distribution and dynamics of interstellar calcium, use of the Stark effect in line spectra to determine the absolute magnitudes of many hot B-type stars, spectroscopic studies of stellar rotation and of peculiar and irregular variable stars, studies of novae, clarification and expansion of the system of spectral classification, studies of the surface brightness of bright and dark nebulae, and studies of the general radiation of the interstellar medium. To all these areas Struve brought a powerful blend of observational expertise and sensitivity to the application of physical theory. Often he collaborated with theoretical specialists to strengthen the blend. At all times he demonstrated the finest kind of scientific imagination and creativity in the effective use of instrumentation and theory.

In his postwar years, Struve worked on continuing problems in the study of stellar atmospheres, but devoted most of his research energy to the clarification of the spectroscopic properties of periodic intrinsic variables such as Cepheid, RR Lyrae, and Beta Canis Majoris types of stars—all ultra complex spectroscopic problems requiring meticulous attention. Much of his intellectual legacy lies in the fact that he gave such close attention to these complex problems, and thereby produced the observational foundations upon which much of modern stellar astrophysics is based.

[Struve's papers are held at the Yerkes Observatory and at the Bancroft Library, Berkeley. On Struve, see Z. K. Sokolovskaya, *Dictionary of Scientific Biogra-* *phy,* XIII (1976), which provides references to bibliographical and biographical sources; and E. B. Frost, "A Family of Astronomers," *Popular Astronomy,* Nov. 1921.]

D. H. DeVorkin

STUART, JOHN LEIGHTON (June 24, 1876–Sept. 19, 1962), missionary, university president, and ambassador, was born in Hangchow, China, the son of John Linton Stuart and Mary Louisa Horton, Presbyterian missionaries. In 1887 the Stuart family left China to spend a one-year furlough in the United States. John and a younger brother, David, remained in Mobile, Ala., and attended public schools there.

At the age of sixteen Stuart went to Pantops Academy in Charlottesville, Va. He was admitted to the sophomore class at Hampden-Sydney College in 1893 and graduated in 1896. The next three years he taught Latin and Greek at Pantops Academy. He graduated from Union Theological Seminary (Richmond, Va.) in 1902 and was ordained a Presbyterian minister. On Nov. 17, 1904, Stuart married Aline Hardy Rodd; they had one son.

Stuart and his wife arrived in China at the end of 1904 and settled in the Hangchow area. He was professor of New Testament at Nanking Theological Seminary from 1908 to 1919. Hampton-Sidney College awarded him the D.D. degree in 1913. He wrote *Essentials of New Testament Greek* in Chinese (1916) and a *Greek-Chinese-English Dictionary of the New Testament* (1918).

In 1919 Stuart became the first president of Yenching University, which was created by the merger of Peking University and North China Union College. It became the most important private university in China. The first institution of higher education for women in China, North China Union Women's College (largely the work of Luella Miner) soon became part of the new university. Yenching University benefited from ties to Harvard and Princeton and the fund-raising talent of Stuart's friend, Dr. Harry Winters Luce.

Stuart's wife died in June 1926, just before Yenching University moved to a magnificent campus northwest of Peking. During the Nanking affair of 1927 there were revolutionary disorders, but Stuart refused to move his university to Peking, where it could be protected by the American legation. "My sympathies were early aroused against the humiliating terms of foreign treaties and the unfair privileges that the nationals of foreign countries enjoyed—including missionaries." In an article in the *Chinese Recorder*

(1926) Stuart called Chinese nationalism "in the main a thoroughly wholesome tendency." But he did feel there was a foreign threat to China from Japan.

Stuart often returned to the United States to raise funds for Yenching, and on May 1, 1933, he was summoned to the White House by President Franklin D. Roosevelt. Roosevelt "wanted to know what America could do short of war to prevent the Japanese from overrunning the whole of China. "What interested me most," Stuart wrote, "was that in the midst of that frightful depression he was thinking about affairs in faraway China."

After Japan invaded China in 1937 and captured Peking, Stuart refused to fly the flag of the puppet government at Yenching. He tried to protect his students and professors as best he could. When the United States entered World War II, Stuart was interned by the Japanese in a house in Peking. In early 1945 Stuart refused a Japanese offer of release because it did not include two fellow prisoners. He was freed on Aug. 17, 1945, and resumed the presidency of Yenching University until 1946. At a diplomatic reception in Chungking on Sept. 2, 1945, celebrating the end of World War II, Mao Tsetung told Stuart that many Yenching University graduates were working for the Communists at their base in Yenan. Stuart laughed and asked Mao if he thought the students had been well trained.

General George C. Marshall was appointed President Harry S. Truman's special representative to China in November 1945. His mission was to try to end the fighting between Nationalists and Communists and get these bitter enemies to form a coalition government. Marshall brought Stuart into the negotiations because he was highly respected throughout China. Marshall also recommended that Stuart be made American ambassador. Stuart knew many Chinese leaders including Chiang Kai-shek; and while most were Nationalists, in 1946 his appointment as ambassador was acceptable to both factions.

Marshall was recalled from China in January 1947. Thereafter Stuart tried to carry out the sometimes contradictory State Department policies. The United States gave up the unrealistic attempt to get Chiang Kai-shek and Mao Tse-tung to form a coalition government and supported the Nationalist government in its war against the Communists. Despite a huge amount of American aid, the Nationalists lost and the Communists took Peking in January 1949 and Shanghai in May.

In August 1949 the State Department issued a thousand-page explanatory report, later published as the *China White Paper* (1949). Stuart was shocked by its timing (issued even before the Communists had occupied the entire mainland) and contents. He felt it was unsympathetic to Nationalist China. In his memoirs he wrote, "I have felt acutely the irony of my having been my country's Ambassador to China at a time when all that I had previously accomplished in the country to which I was accredited was apparently being destroyed."

Although still officially ambassador to the Republic of China until December 1952, Stuart returned to the United States permanently in 1949. After 1949, he lived in Washington, D.C., with his friend and personal secretary, Philip Fugh, and the latter's family. Fugh had been closer to Stuart than anyone else during his presidency at Yenching University and his ambassadorship. Stuart's memoirs, *Fifty Years in China*, were published in 1954. Kenneth Scott Latourette wrote in the *New York Times Book Review*, "No living American has over so long a period touched the Chinese so helpfully as has John Leighton Stuart." Stuart died in Washington.

[There is manuscript material at the United Board for Christian Higher Education in Asia, New York City, which has the J. Leighton Stuart File, records of Yenching University; at the Historical Foundation of the Presbyterian and Reformed Churches Collections, Montreat, N.C.; and in the State Department Papers, National Archives, which contains material on Stuart's ambassadorship. *The China White Paper* (1949; repr. 1967) contains verbatim many of Stuart's letters to the secretary of state. Stuart's memoirs, *Fifty Years in China* (1954), can be supplemented by his periodical articles, particularly, "Changing Problems of the Christian Colleges in China," *International Review of Missions,* Apr. 1924, and "The Missionary's Chief Task," *Chinese Recorder,* Aug. 1926. Also see Dwight W. Edwards, *Yenching University* (1959); Philip West, *Yenching University and Sino-Western Relations, 1916–1952* (1976); and Yu-ming Shaw, "John Leighton Stuart: The Mind and Life of an American Missionary in China, 1876–1941" (Ph.D. diss, University of Chicago, 1975). Obituaries are in the *New York Times* and *Washington Post,* Sept. 20, 1962.]

RALPH KIRSHNER

STUHLDREHER, HARRY A. (Oct. 14, 1901–Jan. 26, 1965), college football player, coach, and athletic director, was born in Massillon, Ohio, the son of William J. Stuhldreher and Flora Witt. As a child in Massillon, an early hotbed of professional football, he was befriended by his future mentor, Knute Rockne, who coached and played end for the Massillon Tigers. Stuhldreher allegedly carried Rockne's equipment, thus gaining free admission to Tiger games. He attended St. Mary's Grammar School and Massillon High School, quarterbacking the football team there in 1917, 1918, and 1919 under coach Jack Snavely. His high school grades were not good enough for him to enter college directly, so in 1920 he attended Kiski Preparatory School in Pennsylvania. The coach there, Jim Marks, encouraged him to attend Notre Dame, where Rockne had become the football coach.

Stuhldreher played on the Notre Dame freshman team in 1921. (The yet-to-be-named "Four Horsemen" backfield, with him at quarterback and fellow freshmen Elmer Layden, Don Miller, and Jim Crowley at the other back positions, did not play as a unit that year.) The 1921 freshman team did not do very well; it lost to both Lake Forest Academy and the Michigan State freshmen. Stuhldreher, though, caught Rockne's eye. "Even as a freshman," Rockne said, "he was a good, fearless blocker and was mentally sharp." The best blocker but poorest runner of the future "Four Horsemen," Stuhldreher, at five feet, seven inches, and 150–155 pounds, was the smallest.

In 1921 Rockne had begun to experiment with what came to be known as the "Notre Dame shift," a technical innovation that had the running backs change positions immediately before the play began. This concept of backfield "motion" caused a storm of protests from opponents; several amendments to Rule 9, Section 5 —the part of football rules that dealt with restrictions on backfield motion—resulted. Concurrently, Rockne blended new "sleight of hand" and "misdirection" techniques into the quarterback's repertoire, with noticeable success. Stuhldreher later wrote that the "shift" was the key to Notre Dame's offensive success while he was there.

The following year, Stuhldreher, Layden, Miller, and Crowley began to play as a unit. In 1923 sportswriter Grantland Rice, who coined the "Four Horseman" name, first saw them in action. He had chosen to attend the Notre Dame-Army game at Ebbets Field in Brooklyn instead of covering the World Series, and stood at the midfield sideline with Brink Thorne, Yale's 1895 football captain. Stuhldreher led the interference on a left-end sweep that resulted in a twelve-yard gain for Crowley. The backs' momentum carried the four of them out of bounds —directly at and over Rice. "Let's get out of

here," he said. "They're worse than a flock of wild horses on a stampede."

It was not until 1924, though, when Rice, in the Polo Grounds press box this time, watched the backfield march eighty yards in seven plays to key Notre Dame's victory over Army by 13–7, that the name "Four Horsemen" was actually applied to the backfield. In the lead of his article on that game, Rice wrote: "Out from a cold, gray October sky, Four Horsemen rode again. They are known in literature and dramatic lore as famine, fire, pestilence and sudden death, but these are only aliases. Their right names are Stuhldreher, Crowley, Miller and Layden"—a variation on Vicente Blasco Ibáñez' *The Four Horsemen of the Apocalypse.*

Notre Dame did not lose a game in 1924, beating Nebraska—the only team to have beaten it in 1922 and 1923—by 34–6. In that game Stuhldreher threw an eighty-yard touchdown pass to Crowley. The Irish also beat Georgia Tech 40–19, Stuhldreher completing fifteen of nineteen passes, including twelve in a row, for three touchdowns. In the Four Horsemen's only bowl game, Notre Dame defeated Glenn ("Pop") Warner's Stanford squad 27–10 in the Rose Bowl on Jan. 1, 1925. Stuhldreher was named to Walter Camp's 1924 All-America team, the only member of the Four Horsemen to receive that honor. During his four years there, Notre Dame won two national championships, compiled a 26–2–1 record in his three years on the varsity squad, and was undefeated in the fall of 1924. He graduated from Notre Dame in 1924 with a A.B. degree.

In 1925, Stuhldreher became football coach and athletic director at Villanova University. During an eleven-year tenure there he was credited with upgrading the football program while compiling a 65–24–10 record. In 1927 he married Mary McEnery, a movie columnist for the *Philadelphia Ledger* who later wrote an autobiography, *Many a Saturday Afternoon* (1964), about her life as a football coach's wife. They had four sons.

In the spring of 1936, Stuhldreher was appointed head football coach and athletic director at the University of Wisconsin. His teams compiled a record of 45–62–6 through the 1948 season, when he resigned the coaching position under fire but remained as athletic director. On Oct. 23, 1948, Mary Stuhldreher, in response to what she felt was unfair treatment of her husband by some of the local fans, published an article, "Football Fans Aren't Human," in the *Saturday Evening Post.* In 1950 Stuhldreher left Wisconsin to join the industrial relations division of the United States Steel Company in Pittsburgh. He later became assistant to the vice-president and director of community relations and recreational programs for that corporation. He died in Pittsburgh.

[There is no biography of Stuhldreher. Information can be obtained from his file at the International Sports and Games Research Collection (INSPORT) at the University of Notre Dame Library. His writings include *Quarterback Play* (1929); *Knute Rockne* (1931); and *The Blocking Back* (1936), a novel. Also see Grantland Rice, "The Four Horsemen," *Esquire*, Nov. 1945; and *The Four Horsemen of Notre Dame* (1959). An obituary is in the *New York Times*, Jan. 27, 1965.]

MARC ONIGMAN

SUMNERS, HATTON WILLIAM (May 30, 1875–Apr. 19, 1962), lawyer and U.S. congressman, was born on a farm in Boons Hill, Tenn., the son of William A. Sumners, a teacher and farmer, and of Anna Walker. During his childhood Sumners lived in Boons Hill, where his parents operated an academy. He then spent his adolescence on the family's sizable farm. There he became convinced "that we are only responsible for doing our best" with obstacles that "are the gymnastic paraphernalia of Nature."

In 1893 the Sumners family moved to Garland, Tex. Sumners briefly attended Garland High School and then began to read law in the offices of a Dallas firm. Admitted to the bar in 1897, he was elected county attorney in 1900 on an antigambling platform. He was defeated in his bid for reelection in 1902, but regained the office in 1904. Returning to private practice in 1907, Sumners worked as a lobbyist for Texas cotton farmers and the Dallas business community. The resulting political connections enabled him to win election as a congressman-at-large in 1912. He became the Democratic representative from the Fifth Congressional District in 1914 and was reelected every two years until 1946.

In his early years in Congress, Sumners supported the policies of President Woodrow Wilson, though he had qualms about preparedness in 1916 and conscription in 1917. After the war he wrote, "The past four years have been like a nightmare to me." He was named to the Judiciary Committee in 1918, and during the 1920's his congressional career prospered. Friendship with Chief Justice William Howard Taft, who called him the best lawyer in Congress, added to his influence in the selection of candidates for the federal bench. Sumners appeared in four

cases before the Supreme Court as a spokesman for Congress, and he managed impeachment trials of three federal judges between 1926 and 1936. He became chairman of the Judiciary Committee in 1931, when the Democrats regained control of the House, and he assisted Secretary of Labor Frances Perkins when she confronted a Republican-inspired impeachment resolution in 1939.

Sumners considered government bureaucracy a prime danger to the nation. A frequent speaker before bar associations and civic groups, he denounced "this great big, expensive bureaucratic Federal machine." He attributed the Great Depression to the country's having been "on a grand jazz" for a decade. Sumners tolerated the New Deal in its early years and voted for many of President Franklin D. Roosevelt's programs. In 1934 he helped draft a constitution for the Philippine Islands. But by 1935 disagreements over federal anticrime measures had strained relations between Sumners and the White House.

Because of his Judiciary Committee chairmanship, Sumners was a central participant when Roosevelt proposed, in February 1937, to enlarge the membership of the Supreme Court so as to facilitate the appointment of justices more sympathetic to the New Deal. Sumners had introduced legislation in 1935 to make it easier for members of the Supreme Court to retire with full salaries, and he had submitted the bill again in January 1937. Roosevelt's proposal, he thought, was unnecessary and threatened the future of the republic. "Boys, here's where I cash in," he told his colleagues on February 5 as they left the White House after hearing the president outline his court plan. The phrase passed into the historical record as "Boys, here's where I cash in my chips."

Sumners bottled up the "court-packing" bill in his committee and may have helped persuade Justice Willis Van Devanter to retire on May 18, a key setback for the court plan. On July 13 he told the House that the bill was creating havoc and urged that it be dropped. Within a month the administration, seeing inevitable defeat, accepted a mild congressional reform of the judiciary that left the Supreme Court intact. Sumners was not the sole architect of Roosevelt's loss of the court fight, but he helped delay the bill until the forces opposed to packing the Supreme Court could assemble their coalition.

The court battle isolated Sumners from the House leadership, and his influence gradually waned. In March 1941 he said that striking war workers "may have to be sent to the electric chair." Most of his time was spent giving speeches that warned of the loss of state power to the federal government. After a hard-fought reelection race in 1944, arising from his opposition to the president, Sumners retired from politics in 1946 to write and speak about government problems. As director of research at the Southwestern Legal Foundation of Southern Methodist University in Dallas, he wrote *The Private Citizen and His Democracy* (1959). He died in Dallas.

Balding, stoop-shouldered, and round-faced, Sumners "looked less like a Congressman than any man in the House." He never married. His stinginess was legendary on Capitol Hill. He was an effective speaker and a competent legislator with a sense of self-importance nurtured by his rise from youthful poverty.

[Sumners' papers are at the Dallas Historical Society. Aspects of his career are covered in the Woodrow Wilson and William Howard Taft papers at the Library of Congress; in the Roosevelt papers at the Franklin D. Roosevelt Library, Hyde Park, N.Y.; and in the Martin M. Crane Papers, University of Texas at Austin. Sumners wrote and spoke extensively on political issues; "Don't Blame the Bureaucrat," *Reader's Digest*, Sept. 1943, is representative. For biographical data, see Emma Cobb Evans, "Hatton W. Sumners, Congressman," *Holland's Magazine*, Mar. 1935; Raymond Moley and Celeste Jedel, "The Gentleman Who Does Not Yield," *Saturday Evening Post*, May 10, 1941; Lionel V. Patenaude, "Garner, Sumners and Connally: The Defeat of the Roosevelt Court Bill in 1937," *Southwestern Historical Quarterly*, July 1970; Mary Catherine Monroe, "A Day in July: Hatton W. Sumners and the Court Reorganization Plan of 1937" (M.A. thesis, University of Texas at Arlington, 1973); Marvin Jones, *Memoirs* (1973); George Martin, *Madam Secretary: Frances Perkins* (1976); and George N. Green, *The Establishment in Texas Politics* (1979). Obituaries are in the *Dallas Times Herald*, Apr. 19, 1962, and *New York Times*, Apr. 20, 1962.]

LEWIS L. GOULD

SZILARD, LEO (Feb. 11, 1898–May 30, 1964), physicist, was born in Budapest, Hungary, the son of Louis Szilard and Thekla Vidor. Louis Szilard, an engineer, encouraged his son's interest in science. After attending the public schools in Budapest, Szilard entered the Budapest Institute of Technology to study electrical engineering. In 1918 he was drafted into the Austro-Hungarian army and sent to officers' training school. A severe case of influenza ended his military career, and he spent the remainder of the war at home.

In 1919, Szilard went to continue his engineering studies at the Technische Hochschule, Charlottenburg, but soon turned to physics at the University of Berlin, which was then the most important center for work in theoretical physics. Max von Laue, Max Planck, and Albert Einstein directed and encouraged his studies. His dissertation, for which he received the Ph.D. in 1922, established his reputation as one of Europe's leading young physicists. It interpreted the relationship between probability and entropy based on the second law of thermodynamics. With the guidance of Einstein, Szilard contributed a paper in 1929 that became the foundation for information theory and the development of modern computers.

Between the wars Szilard divided his time between the Kaiser Wilhelm Institute and the University of Berlin, demonstrating versatility as both theoretician and engineer. He collaborated with Herman Mark in X-ray crystallography experiments, and with Einstein he developed a pumping system for liquid metals. In 1928, Szilard filed a patent for a prototype cyclotron, or particle accelerator.

Szilard, a Jew, anticipated that Hitler's rise to power would be followed by repression. In 1933, after the Reichstag fire, he fled to Vienna and then to England. Always a political realist, he enlisted the aid of prominent British scientists in finding positions for German-Jewish scientists seeking asylum. He also encouraged Gertrud Weiss, a young medical student, to leave Vienna. Married in 1951, they had no children.

Soon after reaching England, Szilard learned of the discovery of artificial radioactivity by two French physicists; he decided to concentrate his research in the promising field of nuclear physics. He later claimed that H. G. Wells's utopian novel *The World Set Free* influenced his thinking about the promise and peril of nuclear fission. During 1934–1938, at the research facilities of St. Bartholomew's Hospital, and later at the Clarendon Laboratory of Oxford University, Szilard initiated research on the problem of controlling and sustaining an artificial chain reaction. Together with T. A. Chalmers, a young English physicist, he discovered that beryllium emitted slow neutrons if bombarded with gamma radiation from radium. But Szilard determined that beryllium would not sustain a chain reaction.

After a few brief visits to the United States, Szilard moved there permanently in 1938 (he became a naturalized citizen in 1943). Just before his departure three German scientists— Otto Hahn, Fritz Strassmann, and Lise Meitner —demonstrated the fission of uranium (that is, uranium breaks into two parts when it absorbs a neutron). Szilard and other nuclear physicists immediately recognized that neutrons might be emitted during the process and that uranium could sustain a chain reaction. Using the research facilities of Columbia University, Szilard and Walter Zinn proved that in the fission of uranium, two neutrons were discharged for each neutron absorbed. Enrico Fermi, a refugee Italian physicist, independently came to the same conclusion. It immediately became clear to these scientists that a controlled nuclear reaction could become the basis for a bomb of enormous destructive force.

Fermi and Szilard joined forces in the summer of 1939 at Columbia to explore the feasibility of a uranium-water reactor system, but Szilard soon came out in favor of a uranium-graphite matrix. Fermi and Szilard were convinced that nuclear research should proceed with all possible speed and that only direct government support could fund a program of such magnitude. They persuaded Einstein to write a letter to President Franklin D. Roosevelt. Actually, it was Szilard who wrote two draft letters dated Aug. 2, 1939; Einstein chose the longer version. The letter stated, in layman's terms, the probability of developing nuclear weapons and implicitly warned that Germany had already initiated nuclear weapon research. Roosevelt did not appear overly alarmed, but in late October 1939 he appointed the Advisory Committee on Uranium.

In mid-1942 the Manhattan Engineering District, under the direction of General Leslie R. Groves, commenced a top-secret project with the objective of beating the Germans in development of the atomic bomb. Szilard, a leading member of the program, directed most of his energies toward planning a nuclear reactor for large-scale production of plutonium, the material needed for atomic devices.

After moving to the University of Chicago, Fermi and Szilard directed construction of a uranium-graphite reactor. In December 1942 this atomic pile sustained the first controlled nuclear chain reaction. In the later stages of the Manhattan Project, Szilard concentrated his efforts on producing an effective reactor-cooling system. After World War II he and Fermi received patent rights for the world's first nuclear fission reactor.

As the Manhattan Project neared its objective, Szilard, James Frank, and other scientists at the Chicago installation questioned the need for using or further developing nuclear weapons. They reasoned that the war in Europe would soon be won without them. More important, they feared that detonating an atomic bomb would touch off a postwar arms race with Russia. Szilard tried to approach President Roosevelt and then President Harry S. Truman, through presidential aides and Manhattan Project supervisors. When his efforts failed, he again used Einstein's prestige to gain entry to the White House.

The final version of the petition that Szilard presented, the "Frank Report," was signed by more than sixty scientists connected with the Manhattan Project. This paper urged "restraint" on the part of the United States, claiming that the first nation to use the atomic bomb would "bear the responsibility of opening the door to an era of devastation of an unimaginable scale." The petition did not rule out use of the bomb if Japan refused to surrender after being made fully aware of the nuclear consequences. These pleas did not deter Truman from ordering the bombing of Hiroshima and Nagasaki and ushering in the atomic age.

A man of conscience as well as of creativity, Szilard turned in new directions when the war ended. He became less interested in nuclear research and more concerned about control of atomic energy in the postwar world. First, he encouraged civilian control of atomic research and development in the United States. He testified before congressional committees and lobbied for creation of the Atomic Energy Commission. On the international level Szilard tried to persuade Soviet leaders and scientists of the need for arms control. He traveled to the Soviet Union and suggested that Joseph Stalin and Truman exchange information and communications as signs of trust. But the cold war negated most of Szilard's efforts. Only the Pugwash Conferences on Science and World Affairs, a disarmament forum, resulted from his endeavors.

At the height of his career as a nuclear scientist, Szilard abruptly turned to the field of biology. He did advanced work with bacteria and viruses and in bacterial biochemistry with Aaron Novick, a physical chemist. Together they joined the Institute of Radiobiology and Biophysics at the University of Chicago, where they studied mutations and formation of adaptive enzymes. To facilitate research they invented the chemostat, a continuous-flow device that enabled them to control the rate of bacteria growth by regulating one or more of the growth factors. Their experiments indicated that distinct evolutionary changes occurred, causing mutant strains to replace the original bacteria. After the closing of the Institute of Radiobiology and Bio-physics, Szilard contributed theoretical papers on population control, the process of aging, and memory and recall.

In 1959 Szilard entered a New York City hospital with an advanced case of cancer. He refused to allow surgery, but received massive radiation treatments. Remission of the cancer allowed Szilard to dedicate his last years to work for world peace and nuclear disarmament that included organizing the Council for a Livable World, a lobby for peace and control of nuclear weapons, in 1961.

Szilard died of a heart attack at La Jolla, Calif. He had been a resident fellow of the Salk Institute at San Diego. During his last years he received numerous honors, including the Einstein Gold Medal (1958) and the Atoms for Peace Award (1960).

It may appear ironic that the man who was perhaps more responsible for the development of the atomic bomb than any other person became the most outspoken critic of nuclear armament in the scientific community. Szilard, above all, was a man of strong moral convictions and passionate causes. *The Voice of the Dolphins and Other Stories* (1961), a science fiction collection, demonstrated the complexity of his personality. In "The Voice of the Dolphins" he devised an intricate system of arguments for world peace as seen through the wisdom of dolphins who communicate their ideas to some Viennese scientists. Another short piece, "Grand Central Terminal," whimsically details an alien anthropological analysis of coin-operated doors in public restrooms.

As a scientist Szilard combined the intellectual skills of a theoretician with those of an engineer. He proved to be one of the most versatile scientists of this century, blending study in nuclear physics and biology in his long and distinguished career. Yet he was also a man of conscience. No American physicist accepted more responsibility than Szilard for publicizing the dangers of nuclear armaments in the post–World War II era.

[Most of Szilard's important papers, patents, and ideas are included in Bernard T. Feld and Gertrud Weiss Szilard, eds., *The Collected Works of Leo Szilard: Scientific Papers* (1972); and Spencer R. Weart and Gertrud Weiss Szilard, eds., *Leo Szilard: His Version of the Facts*, II (1978). Also see Tristram Coffin, "Leo Szilard: The Conscience of a Scientist," *Holiday*, Feb. 1964. Obituaries are in the *New York Times*, May 31, 1964, and *Bulletin of the Atomic Scientists*, Oct. 1964.]

WILLIAM E. ELLIS

TABER, JOHN (May 5, 1880–Nov. 22, 1965), lawyer and U.S. congressman, was born in Auburn, N.Y., the son of Franklin P. Taber and Mary Parker. After attending the local public schools, he received a B.A. from Yale in 1902. Two years later he graduated from the New York Law School in Albany and was admitted to the New York bar. He then joined his father's law firm of Taber and Brainard in Auburn. In 1918 he opened his own law office and in 1924 went into partnership with Sherman Parker. On Apr. 13, 1929, Taber married his secretary, Gertrude J. Beard; they had one son.

As a young lawyer, Taber joined the Cayuga County Republican Committee, serving as supervisor of Auburn's second ward. He was elected county judge in 1911, a post he held until 1919. He was a delegate to the Republican national conventions of 1920, 1924, and 1936.

Taber began his long congressional career in 1923, when he was elected to the House of Representatives from the thirty-sixth district comprising Cayuga and three (later seven) other counties. Conservative Republican farmers and townsmen dominated this rural district of central New York, and Taber's own conservatism reflected their attitudes on most issues. From 1923 to 1963 he served on the powerful House Appropriations Committee, where he soon became known as a fiscal conservative and a bitter partisan. As the result of Franklin Roosevelt's Democratic landslide of 1932, which toppled senior Republican committee members, Taber became Appropriations' ranking Republican. During the 1930's he was a leading anti–New Dealer. He unsuccessfully assailed "extravagant" unemployment relief allocations, agricultural subsidies, and other Roosevelt programs. Congressional Republicans who refused to compromise with the New Deal, he asserted, were more likely to be reelected. He also opposed the administration's Reciprocal Trade Agreements Act of 1934 and the Naval Appropriations Bill of 1938.

Although Taber voted against the relaxation of the Neutrality Laws and the original lend-lease bill, his isolationism evaporated once the United States entered World War II. He voted for all war appropriations despite his continued criticism of Democratic domestic policy. No one more despised Franklin D. Roosevelt, whom Taber thought to be deceitful and a warmonger.

After the Republican congressional election landslide of 1946 Taber assumed the chairmanship of the Appropriations Committee. He also became the first chairman of the Joint Congressional Committee on the Budget, which made him one of the most influential members of government. His nearly obsessive concern for fiscal conservatism now earned him the ironic epithet "generous John." On the Congress floor his deep, rasping voice thundered against the "excessive" financial requests of President Harry S. Truman's administration. In committee, no appropriation item was too small for scrutiny. His forty-three-member group quickly went to work on President Truman's $37.5 billion budget, with Taber vowing to use a sledgehammer. He recruited a temporary staff of thirty financial experts from the private sector, paying most of them only $15 a day. His committee reduced the budget by several hundred million dollars, the biggest departmental cuts coming from the Interior and State departments. Although Taber failed to reduce federal jobs by 50 percent, enough government employees were fired to justify the expression "Taberizing," meaning dismissal or cutback.

Taber's activities jeopardized Truman's foreign policy in 1947 when he persuaded his committee to cut appropriations to Greece and Turkey by $3 million. He also was responsible for the temporary $1.5 billion reduction in Marshall Plan funding. These decisions came after Taber returned from a European trip, at which time he supposedly quipped that foreigners appeared to be almost as lazy and inefficient as American civil service workers. Despite Taber's postwar isolationist tendencies, he reluctantly supported United States participation in the United Nations and favored loans to Great Britain.

Taber's Appropriations Committee chairmanship terminated when the Democrats regained control of Congress in 1949. By that time he claimed that he had saved the federal government more than $6 billion, a figure Democrats disputed because many of his cuts were soon overturned. If anything, they charged, his actions contributed to the uncertainty of the period. Moreover, liberal critics accused Taber of stopping only projects not in accord with his views.

Taber opposed public housing, prolabor legislation, price and wage controls, and federal grants for school lunches. He voted for a permanent House Un-American Committee, believing that Communists had infiltrated the government, universities, and army. In 1953 he regained the Appropriations Committee chairmanship, which he retained through 1954. Although friendly to President Dwight D. Eisenhower, Taber sometimes found himself at odds

with the administration's centrist policies. He jocularly labeled himself "the worst Republican in Congress." By 1956 Taber appeared to have mellowed, for he urged the Appropriations Committee to propose $335 million more for national defense than the committee favored. He continued to serve in the House until 1963. Two years later he died in an Auburn nursing home.

In his lengthy congressional career, the tall, austere Taber never sponsored any significant legislation. Nor was he known for oratorical or leadership abilities. He assumed the singular role of "watchdog of the Treasury." He won the grudging respect of his colleagues, who viewed him as fair-minded and hardworking. His bluntness and gruff demeanor made him few friends, but he nonetheless showed kindness to those who penetrated the hard exterior. Revealingly, of the seven presidents he knew while a congressman, Taber considered Calvin Coolidge the greatest.

[The John Taber Papers, Cornell University Libraries, are the best primary source. Taber correspondence is also in the William Henry Hill, Richard Brown Scandrett, Jr., and William Irving Myers Papers, Cornell University Libraries. The only lengthy biographical study is Cary Smith Henderson, "Congressman John Taber of Auburn: Politics and Federal Appropriations, 1923–62" (Ph.D. diss., Duke University, 1964). See also H. H. Harris, "Crustiest Crusader: John Taber, Knight of the Shining Meat Ax," *Reporter*, May 26, 1953, and obituaries in the *New York Times*, Nov. 23, 1965, and *Ithaca Journal*, Nov. 22, 1965.]

JAMES GIGLIO

TANSILL, CHARLES CALLAN (Dec. 9, 1890–Nov. 12, 1964), historian, was born in Fredericksburg, Tex., the son of Charles Fiske Tansill, a government telegraph operator, and of May Cordelia Callan. His father was descended from a Virginia Catholic family; his mother was the daughter of Irish immigrants. The family moved to Washington, D.C., where Tansill attended Brookland Public School and the Emerson Institute. He enrolled in the Catholic University of America in 1908 as a scholarship student and received his B.A. degree in history in 1912. After earning his M.A. (1913) and Ph.D. (1915), Tansill taught American history for one year at his alma mater. Then, feeling the need for study at a more prestigious university, he enrolled at Johns Hopkins University. He studied with John H. Latane and received a second Ph.D. in 1918. His dissertation was *The Canadian Reciprocity Treaty of 1854* (1922).

On Feb. 17, 1915, Tansill married Helen C. Parker; they had five children.

Tansill quickly established himself as a productive scholar and a popular teacher. He joined the Department of History at American University in Washington as an assistant professor in 1919 and was promoted to full professor two years later. He proved to be an effective and enthusiastic teacher who took special interest in training graduate students to use the wealth of archival sources in the Washington area. He eventually directed more than fifty doctoral dissertations. During the 1920's, Tansill also served as an adviser on diplomacy to the Senate Foreign Relations Committee and worked in the Legislative Reference Service of the Library of Congress.

Tansill's book *The Purchase of the Danish West Indies* (1932), written while he served as the Albert Shaw Lecturer in Diplomatic History at Johns Hopkins in 1931, examined the history of the American acquisition of the Virgin Islands. *The United States and Santo Domingo, 1798–1873* (1938) was an objective and thorough scholarly study.

In 1938 Tansill emerged as a controversial figure with the publication of his most influential book, *America Goes to War.* This study appeared at a time when revisionist historians such as Harry Elmer Barnes, Charles A. Beard, and Walter Millis were challenging the orthodox view that the United States entered World War I solely to defend its neutral rights. Although Tansill claimed in his preface that he had no thesis to exploit, his book was clearly in the revisionist vein. Assuming that everyone agreed that American entry in the war had been a grave mistake, he sought to explain how that error had come about. Unlike many revisionists, he did not offer a narrow economic interpretation; but his study did include a thorough account of the close economic ties between the United States and the Allies. His major focus was on President Woodrow Wilson's aides, Robert Lansing and Colonel Edward M. House, and he suggested that their strong bias in favor of England led Wilson to adopt policies that ended in war with Germany. The book was well received at the time. Even traditional historians praised its scholarship. Yet some critics argued that Tansill's anti-British bias undercut his claim to objectivity.

America Goes to War marks the high point of Tansill's career; thereafter everything began to go sour. He first encountered difficulty when he gave vent to his intense anti-British and isolationist views. In a radio address in Berlin in 1937, he called Hitler "an inspired leader" and praised the Nazi regime. When he returned to the United States, he was forced to resign his professorship at American University. He was unemployed for the next two years. In 1939 he finally obtained a professorship at Fordham University, where he taught for five years, leaving in 1944 to teach at Georgetown University.

After World War II, Tansill became obsessed with anti-Communism. Serving as an adviser to Senator Joseph McCarthy, he charged Franklin D. Roosevelt and Harry S. Truman with betraying America. In 1952 he published *Back Door to War: The Roosevelt Foreign Policy, 1933–1941,* a polemical book that blamed Roosevelt for Pearl Harbor. The opening sentence revealed his bias: "The main objective in American foreign policy since 1900 has been the preservation of the British Empire." After his retirement from Georgetown University in 1958, Tansill wrote several articles for *American Opinion,* the organ of the John Birch Society. In one of these he called for the impeachment of President John F. Kennedy.

Tansill died in Washington, D.C. His death went unnoticed by the historical profession, which had dismissed him as a right-wing extremist. But he was an able and productive diplomatic historian before he succumbed to his prejudices.

[The main body of Tansill papers is located at the Herbert Hoover Presidential Library, West Branch, Iowa. There is a smaller collection in the Georgetown University Library, Washington, D.C.

In addition to the books cited above, Tansill wrote *The Foreign Policy of Thomas F. Bayard, 1885–1897* (1940); *Canadian-American Relations, 1875–1911* (1943); *The Congressional Career of Thomas Francis Bayard, 1869–1885* (1946); and *America and the Fight for Irish Freedom, 1866–1922* (1957).

The fullest account of Tansill's career appears in Frederick Lewis Honhart III, "Charles Callan Tansill: American Diplomatic Historian" (Ph.D. diss., Case Western Reserve University, 1972). Warren Cohen discusses Tansill's place in revisionist historiography in *The American Revisionists: The Lessons of Intervention in World War I* (1967).]

ROBERT A. DIVINE

TEAGARDEN, WELDON LEO ("JACK") (Aug. 20, 1905–Jan. 15, 1964), trombonist and bandleader, was born in Vernon, Tex., the son of Charles Woodrow Teagarden, a maintenance supervisor in a cottonseed oil mill, and of Helen Giengar, a music teacher and pianist. At the age of five, Teagarden began playing the piano and baritone horn. Two years later his father bought him his first trombone. Because of his still small

735

stature he could not use the orthodox slide positions. He thus developed his own technique, which enabled him to play more rapidly and to achieve certain tones by using his lip rather than the movement of the slide.

Teagarden attended the Vernon grammar and high schools and played in local bands. The music of religious camp meetings held by members of the black community contributed to his unusually deep feeling for the blues style. After his father's death in 1918, Teagarden and his mother played background music in movie theaters. Subsequently, he accepted a job with Cotton Bailey's Band. He was called "Jack" by the leader and thereafter was known by this nickname.

During 1921–1927 Teagarden played with several bands, including pianist Peck Kelley's Bad Boys and Doc Ross' Jazz Bandits. He was with R. J. Marin's Original Southern Trumpeters, when they successfully promoted American jazz in Mexico in 1924. He was featured as the "South's Greatest Trombone Wonder." In 1923 Teagarden married Ora Binyon. They had two sons, but were divorced in 1931.

In 1927 Teagarden moved to New York, where his superior musicianship quickly made him one of the most highly regarded trombonists in white jazz. He exhibited his advanced technique during work with Wingy Manone and the Scranton Sirens. He joined Ben Pollack's Orchestra in 1928, remaining until 1933. During this period he made his recording debut, played in many studio groups, and helped break the racial color-line on records. In September 1931 Teagarden married Clare Manzi.

In 1933 Teagarden was asked by Paul Whiteman to play in his orchestra. He remained with Whiteman until the end of 1938. For a short interval he performed with his brother, Charles (trumpet), and Frankie Trumbauer (saxophone) as the Three T's. In 1934 Teagarden divorced Clare Manzi, and in 1936 he married Edna ("Billie") Coates.

As the Swing Era developed, Whiteman created within his main orchestra a "Swing Wing" featuring Teagarden. The style's popularity induced the trombonist to form "Jack Teagarden and His Orchestra" in 1939, which he led until late 1946. It was musically successful but financially disastrous. The strain of the orchestra business took its toll on yet another marriage. Teagarden was divorced in 1942 and in 1943 married Adeline "Addie" Barriere, who had become his band manager in 1942. They had one son.

In 1941 Teagarden performed in the film

Birth of the Blues with Bing Crosby. He also played in other movies and made many recordings. He toured the country extensively during World War II entertaining the armed forces. And he was featured at the 1944 *Esquire* Jazz Concert, having received the Gold Award in the magazine's Jazz Poll. After breaking up his band, he briefly led a sextet. From 1947 to 1951 he played with Louis Armstrong's All Stars.

Teagarden then appeared with his own All Stars until 1956. Next he spent several months with Ben Pollack, performed at the 1957 Newport Jazz Festival, and led a sextet with Earl Hines, which toured Europe late in the year. From September 1958 to January 1959 he took his own group on a tour of Asia sponsored by the State Department.

Teagarden was elected to a trombone chair in the *Playboy* magazine Jazz Bands in 1957, 1958, and 1960–1963. He performed at the 1963 Monterey Jazz Festival together with his mother, brother Charles, and sister Norma on piano. Teagarden died in New Orleans. His funeral service featured a trombone quartet.

Personally soft-spoken and congenial, Teagarden was noted for his instrumental and vocal renditions of numbers such as "St. James Infirmary" and "Beale Street Blues." He made hundreds of recordings with dozens of well-known musicians. It was largely through his influence that the trombone came to be used for melodic jazz improvisation, not merely for chord basses and "smears" in the traditional New Orleans tailgate style.

Teagarden's distinctive tone and occasional use of a clearly recognizable triplet rhythmic pattern characterized his music. He was also famous for his "glass-and-a-half" technique of replacing the bell of his instrument with a drinking glass, thus giving an unusual sound to his playing. His reputation is perhaps best summarized by the statement that he was a "Musicians' Musician, Trombonists' Trombonist, and Jazzmen's Jazzman," who was "unique in his performing, and a gentleman at all times."

[The best available sources are illustrated bio-discographies by Jay D. Smith and Len Guttridge, *Jack Teagarden: The Story of a Jazz Maverick* (1960), and Howard J. Waters, *Jack Teagarden and His Music, His Career and Recordings* (1960). Richard Hadlock, *Jazz Masters of the Twenties* (1965), devotes a chapter to Teagarden, and information about his appearances in films is in David Meeker, *Jazz in the Movies: A Guide to Jazz Musicians, 1917–1977* (1977). An evaluation of the trombonist's attitudes and communications in jazz is in Charles Smith, Jack Teagarden," *International Musician,* Apr. 1969. An obituary appeared in the *New York Times,* Jan. 16, 1964, and an account of the funeral, Jan. 21. See also the obituary in *Newsweek,* Jan. 27, 1964; and Martin Williams, "In Praise of Jack Teagarden!" in the *Saturday Review,* Mar. 14, 1964.]

BARRETT G. POTTER

TEMPLETON, ALEC ANDREW (July 4, 1910–Mar. 28, 1963), pianist and musical satirist, was born in Cardiff, Wales, the son of Andrew Bryson Templeton and Sarah May Templeton. Although he was blind from birth, Templeton's parents determined to rear their son with two elder daughters as a normal child, and he learned that he was blind at the age of seven from a visitor.

At two, Templeton climbed upon the piano bench to imitate church bells that he had heard. He also corrected the wrong notes in his sister's piano practice. By the age of four he had created his first composition, a lullaby. He began to study the piano with Margaret Humphrey when he was five, taught by ear and touch, and in his first public performance directed a choir of his playmates while accompanying on the piano. Although he studied braille, he learned the music that he performed in concert by listening to phonograph records.

Realizing Templeton's astonishing precocity, his parents sold their farm and moved to London. They secured introductions to prominent English musicians, all of whom forecast a bright future for Templeton. At eleven, he was employed by the British Broadcasting Corporation (BBC) to present a musical program that remained popular with audiences for twelve years. He enrolled at Worcester College, studying organ under Ivor Atkins and learning the art of improvisation from Henry Walford Davies, later Master of the King's Music.

At fifteen, Templeton was invited to play Beethoven's *Emperor* Concerto with the Cardiff Orchestra, and he learned it in four days; at sixteen, he won a piano competition with 8,000 entrants. After four years at the Royal Academy of Music, he earned the licentiate degree in 1931. He further studied at the Royal College of Music (1932–1934), supported by scholarships for composition and piano. He also mastered the violin, organ, and flute, and toured with Henry Wood, Landon Ronald, and Thomas Beecham.

One of Templeton's compositions (he composed by dictating) was awarded a prize by the BBC. He toured Europe with his father during holidays, learning to speak German, French, Spanish, and Italian fluently. His father encouraged his interest in popular music as an emotional safety valve, providing diversionary mental gymnastics.

Templeton made his American debut in 1935, accompanying the Jack Hylton jazz band in a series of radio broadcasts for the Standard Oil Company. He was an immediate success and decided to remain in the United States. At his first public recital, on Mar. 1, 1936, in Chicago's Orchestra Hall, he performed his humorous improvisations for the first time. Templeton's New York debut at Town Hall, on Jan. 23, 1938, was praised highly. After several guest appearances on such radio shows as "The Ford Hour" and "The Bing Crosby Show," he got his own national network radio show, "Alec Templeton Time," in July 1939. He became a naturalized citizen in 1941. A June 21, 1947, *Billboard* review said, "Templeton and his writers do a sprightly job on packaging their half-hour stanzas, mixing in straight and comedy piano, both good; . . . and now more or less standard Templeton routines—the operatic takeoff and the ad-libbed medley, based on audience requests. . . ."

Templeton's fame was earned chiefly from two types of parody: ironic improvisation of operatic themes and on-the-spot creation of melodies based on random notes or songs suggested by his audience. "The Shortest Wagnerian Opera" and "Impression of an Old Fashioned Italian Opera" delighted audiences. Among his most popular parodies were "Bach Goes to Town," "Mozart Matriculates," "Debussy in Dubuque," "Grieg's in the Groove," and "William Do Tell." On Aug. 25, 1940, Templeton married Juliette Barr Vaiani, a concert singer, in Hollywood. They had no children. Templeton's tours of North America, Hawaii, Australia, and New Zealand were phenomenally successful. He appeared with virtually every major symphony orchestra in the United States and was a perennial participant in summer music festivals.

Among his more important compositions are *Concertina Lirico* (1942) and *Gothic Concerto* for piano and orchestra (1954). His work also includes piano exercises and songs, dance tunes, instrumental numbers, a chorale based on the *Venite* psalm, the *Insect Suite, The Pied Piper of Hamelin,* and two string quartets. He composed the scores for two unproduced musical shows, *Dreamboat* and *Sweet Chariot* (based on the life of Anton Dvořák), and the score for the film *Cabbages and Kings.*

Templeton enjoyed demonstrating his collection of music boxes in his home. Although not regarded by critics as a great pianist, his absolute pitch, unusually well developed sense of touch, and prodigiously retentive and accurate musical memory made possible his unique career as composer, concert pianist, and musical satirist. He died in Greenwich, Conn.

[Templeton published *Alec Templeton Piano Course*, 6 vols., edited by Bernard Whitefield (n.d.); *Music for Moderns: Eight Solos for Piano* (1944); *Music Boxes*, as told to Rachael Bail Baumel (1958); and many articles in *Etude*, Jan. 1942–Apr. 1957. For biographical information, see Maurice Dumesnil, "A New Genius Who Does Not See," *Etude*, July 1939; David Ewen, *Living Musicians* (1940); John Tasker Howard, *Our American Music*, 3rd. ed. (1946); Quaintance Eaton, "Alec Templeton: The Wizard of the Sound Waves," *Musical America*, Jan. 25, 1947; and *The World of Music* (1963). Obituary notices are in the *New York Times*, Mar. 29, 1963; *Variety*, Apr. 3, 1963; *Time*, Apr. 5, 1963; and *Newsweek*, Apr. 8, 1963.]

LOUISE HECK-RABI

THOMAS, (JOHN WILLIAM) ELMER (Sept. 8, 1876–Sept. 19, 1965), politician and businessman, was born in Putnam County, near Greencastle, Ind., the son of William Thomas, a small farmer, and of Elizabeth Ewing. After receiving his elementary and secondary education in the public schools, Thomas enrolled in Central Normal College (Danville, Ind.) in 1892 to prepare for teaching. At the normal school he studied law, and to pay his expenses he taught school and worked on various public construction projects. He graduated in 1897 with a teaching certificate and was admitted to the Indiana bar. But instead of practicing law he attended DePauw University, where he received his Ph.B. in 1900.

William Jennings Bryan's spellbinding orations, rural populist appeal, and especially his plea for the free coinage of silver during the 1896 presidential election profoundly influenced Thomas. There were few economic and political opportunities in rural Indiana in 1900; consequently Thomas moved to the Oklahoma Territory. He first settled in Oklahoma City, where he taught English. He was admitted to the Oklahoma bar in 1901. In that year he moved to Lawton to practice law and work for a real estate company. On Sept. 24, 1902, he married Edith Smith, daughter of an influential territorial judge. They had one son. Thomas engaged in land speculation and soon accumulated a sizable amount of property. He developed a profitable resort at Medicine Park, a lake area near Lawton.

In 1907 Thomas, a Democrat, was elected senator to Oklahoma's first legislature. He served four consecutive terms in the senate. After he became chairman of the Appropriations Committee in 1910, his fiscal conservatism, except on the silver question, became evident. He strongly supported financing Oklahoma's infrastructure and educational program on a "pay as you go basis."

By the time he resigned from the senate in 1920 to run unsuccessfully for the United States House of Representatives, Thomas had become a leader in the state Democratic party. In 1922 he won the normally Republican rural and agrarian Sixth District House seat. He spent two undistinguished terms on the Public Lands and Indian Affairs committees, sponsoring several bills on rural electrification and veterans' bonuses. During these years Thomas' monetary theories matured. He saw currency inflation as a panacea for the depressed economic conditions of his farm constitutents. He believed the government should expand the amount of currency in circulation through veterans' bonuses and increased silver purchases. This would stimulate the purchasing of farm surpluses, thereby raising agricultural prices to a competitive level with industry and diminishing the threat of a depression.

Thomas received the support of Oklahoma's powerful Farmer's Union and the Ku Klux Klan in 1926 when he successfully unseated Republican incumbent John William Harreld for the United States Senate. In the Senate he was placed in the Agriculture, Finance, and Indian Affairs committees. He continued to support the interests of farmers and became aligned with southern Democrats and other farm and silver bloc senators who criticized the Calvin Coolidge and Herbert C. Hoover administrations for favoring corporations at the expense of farmers. He easily won a second Senate term in 1932.

Thomas enthusiastically backed most of President Franklin D. Roosevelt's New Deal measures. Through a controversial amendment to the Agricultural Adjustment Act in 1933, Thomas hoped to attack what he felt had caused the Great Depression—deflation—by authorizing the president to inflate the currency by several means, notably the remonetization of silver. Most New Dealers rejected the amendment and it never became law.

Thomas' loyalty to the Roosevelt administration was rewarded in 1938 when the president campaigned for him in a particularly bitter senatorial primary against Gomer Smith. Thomas won that close contest and had no trouble winning another term in 1944. He replaced Ed "Cotton" Smith of South Carolina as Agricultural Committee chairman in 1945. Throughout Thomas' senatorial career no major legislation bore his name. In general he attempted to promote his financial ideas and worked within the Senate and Democratic party structure to protect the interests of farmers and his state.

Internationally, Thomas supported cooperation with other nations, especially in commodity exchanges. But isolationist sentiment in Oklahoma throughout most of the 1930's led him to vote reluctantly for various Neutrality Laws. However, he abruptly changed his position in 1939 when he advocated military preparedness. Ultimately he supported lend-lease.

Throughout World War II Thomas supported Roosevelt's wartime programs except domestic price controls. He felt that price regulations benefited industries at the expense of the farmer. Originally Thomas advocated American participation in the United Nations. But by 1948 he had become disillusioned with the organization and felt it was an ineffective agent to prevent war. He also viewed with alarm Russia's probes into Europe and supported hard-line measures against Communist expansion.

Oklahoma politics had changed by the time of the 1950 Democratic senatorial primary. A. S. ("Mike") Monroney, U.S. representative from Oklahoma City, narrowly defeated Thomas by appealing to rising urban-labor sentiments. After the election Thomas remained in Washington as a lawyer representing various Oklahoma interests, especially oil companies. In 1957 he returned to Lawton, where he devoted considerable time to writing on the money question. He died in Lawton.

[The bulk of Thomas' papers is in the Western History Collection, University of Oklahoma; a small collection is at the Great Plains Historical Association, Lawton. His *Financial Engineering* (1953), *Autobiography of an Enigma* (1965), and "40 Years a Legislator" (unpublished manuscript at the University of Oklahoma) are rambling discourses, almost solely on the silver question, which offer little pertinent information.

Brief biographical sketches are in Rex F. Harlow, *Successful Oklahomans* (1927) and *Oklahoma Leaders* (1928). Eric Manheimer, "The Public Career of Elmer Thomas" (Ph.D. diss., University of Oklahoma, 1952), provides some information but is essentially superficial and laudatory. Good scholarly works on Thomas' political contemporaries are Edward E. Dale and James D. Morrison, *Pioneer Judge: The Life of Robert Lee Williams* (1958); Keith L. Bryant,

Alfalfa Bill Murray (1968); and Anne H. Morgan, *Robert S. Kerr: The Senate Years* (1977). The best obituary is in the Oklahoma City *Daily Oklahoman,* Sept. 20, 1965.]

CHARLES C. HAY III

THOMPSON, DOROTHY (July 9, 1893–Jan. 30, 1961), journalist, was born in Lancaster, N.Y., the daughter of Peter Thompson, a British-born Methodist minister, and of Margaret Grierson. She grew up in upstate New York towns, where her father served. Her mother died in 1901, and two years later Peter Thompson married Eliza Abbott, his church's organist. So poorly did the rebellious Dorothy get along with her dour stepmother that in 1908 she was sent to Chicago to live with her father's sisters. There she enrolled in the Lewis Institute, where she earned high grades and, in 1912, an Associate of Arts degree. She then entered Syracuse University as a junior and graduated with a B.A. in 1914.

While at Syracuse, Thompson became active in the women's suffrage movement. After graduation, she worked out of Buffalo for the New York State Suffrage Association, which successfully campaigned for a state constitutional suffrage amendment. In December 1917 she and a friend, Barbara De Porte, moved to New York City. After briefly holding a dull job at a religious publishing house, Thompson was hired as publicity director for the Social Unit, an urban-poverty program. But she left the project when, by her own account, she fell in love with its administrator, Wilbur Phillips. She and De Porte sailed for Europe in June 1920.

Europe proved to be Thompson's gateway to journalism. She obtained an interview with Terence MacSwiney, the lord mayor of Cork, Ireland, during his fatal hunger strike against British control of Ireland; and later she persuaded the Paris bureau chief of the Philadelphia *Public Ledger* to designate her an unpaid correspondent in Vienna. There she met Marcel Fodor of the *Manchester Guardian,* who became her journalistic mentor. Under his tutelage, she did so well that she was placed on salary. She and Fodor achieved a minor coup in the fall of 1921 by disguising themselves as Red Cross workers to obtain an exclusive interview with the deposed king of Hungary. About this time she met Josef Bard, a Hungarian Jewish intellectual, whom she married in Budapest early in 1922.

Early in 1925 Thompson was named to head the Berlin bureau of the *New York Evening Post* and the *Public Ledger.* Although she was probably the first woman to head a major American news bureau overseas, she dismissed her attainment as "nothing extraordinary." Her marriage did not long survive the move to Berlin. Divorce proceedings began in 1927. That year she met the novelist Sinclair Lewis, then at the crest of his career. After a few weeks of his energetic courtship, she agreed to marry him. In 1928 both of their divorces became final; they were married in London on May 14, after she had resigned from her Berlin post. They had one son.

This marriage interrupted, but did not halt, Thompson's career. She continued to lecture and to write for magazines. In 1931, on assignment from *Cosmopolitan,* she interviewed Adolf Hitler and concluded that he could never take power in Germany—a prediction she repeated in her subsequent book, *"I Saw Hitler!"* (1932). When she returned to Germany in August 1934 she was expelled not only because she had attacked the Nazis' anti-Jewish campaign but because she had belittled Hitler, who was now chancellor.

Back in the United States, the expulsion enhanced her status as a celebrity. Beginning in March 1936 she began a thrice-weekly public-affairs column, "On the Record," published and syndicated by the *New York Herald Tribune.* The column—crisp, outspoken, even strident, but always in the political center—was eventually carried by 170 newspapers. In May 1937 she also began a monthly column for the *Ladies' Home Journal.* Later that year she went on the radio, offering a weekly commentary in a voice that was described as "an intriguing blend of Oxford and Main Street."

Thompson increasingly focused her attention on the threat of Nazism as the international crisis of the late 1930's deepened. In a November 1938 broadcast she brilliantly defended Herschel Grynzspan, the Jewish adolescent whose assassination of a German diplomat in Paris was used by the Nazis as justification for the infamous *Kristallnacht.* In 1939 she created an off-the-air sensation by guffawing loudly at a pro-Nazi rally in Madison Square Garden, New York. After war broke out in Europe in 1939, she attacked American isolationism. She denounced national hero Charles A. Lindbergh for his isolationist views and his contacts with the Hitler regime. Filing from Paris only days before it fell in May 1940, she called for a national-unity ticket in the 1940 election, with President Franklin D. Roosevelt to run with the internationalist Republican Wendell L. Willkie. Roosevelt scoffed at the idea. When Willkie won the Republican nomination, she supported

him, but late in the campaign switched to Roosevelt because, she concluded, the Axis powers wanted his defeat. This caused the Republican *Herald Tribune* to suppress one of her columns and, after the election, to drop her contract. She moved to the Bell Syndicate, and in New York her column subsequently appeared in the *Post.*

Thompson then moved beyond journalism to political activism. Early in 1941 she founded Ring of Freedom, an organization that aimed to put the country on a "war footing." Later that year, Ring of Freedom joined a coalition that created Freedom House, a liberal internationalist organization based in New York City. Thompson was its second president. Late in World War II, she broke with Freedom House on a political issue (her opposition to dismemberment of Germany) and a personal one (Freedom House's preemption of her plan for a memorial to Willkie).

As Thompson's prominence increased—she was sometimes called "the first lady of American journalism"—her marriage to the short-tempered, vain, heavy-drinking Lewis deteriorated. He disliked her public role and accused her of neglecting those close to her. They were divorced in January 1942. Within a year and a half, she met, proposed to, and married Maxim Kopf, an Austrian-Czech painter.

At the end of World War II, Thompson took a position that estranged her from her former constituencies and began what she later called her "decline." After a 1945 visit to Palestine, she supported the case of the Palestinian Arabs and opposed Zionist terrorists. Although she had a long record of support of Jewish causes, she was accused of being anti-Semitic. The New York *Post,* which claimed to speak for the city's Jewish community, dropped her column in March 1947. In 1951 she became head of the anti-Zionist American Friends of the Middle East, which was backed by oil interests and, perhaps unknown to her, by the U.S. Central Intelligence Agency. Not until the Bell Syndicate issued an ultimatum, in 1957, did she leave the Friends organization.

In her final years, Thompson had only a fraction of the influence she had enjoyed in the early 1940's. In 1958 Kopf died and she gave up her column. At sixty-five, she appeared to have lost will and energy. Yet she rallied for an article that her biographer considered her finest—a tribute to Sinclair Lewis that appeared in the *Atlantic Monthly* in November 1960. In December 1960, in poor health, she flew to Lisbon to visit her daughter-in-law, and died there.

[Dorothy Thompson's papers are in the George Arents Research Library of Syracuse University; they contain early chapters of a projected autobiography. Her books not cited above include *The New Russia* (1928); *Dorothy Thompson's Political Guide* (1938); *Refugees: Anarchy or Organization?* (1938); *Let the Record Speak* (1939), a collection of her columns; and *Listen, Hans* (1942), a collection of short-wave broadcasts. The chief biographical study is Marion K. Sanders, *Dorothy Thompson: A Legend in Her Time* (1973). Her marriage to Sinclair Lewis is chronicled in Vincent Sheean, *Dorothy and Red* (1963). Among many magazine profiles, Margaret Case Harriman's "The It Girl," *New Yorker,* Apr. 20 and 27, 1940, is outstanding. Other short treatments are Charles Fisher, *The Columnists* (1944); Irving E. Fang, *Those Radio Commentators!* (1977); and Paul Boyer in *Notable American Women: The Modern Period* (1980). An obituary appeared in the *New York Times,* Feb. 1, 1961.]

JAMES BOYLAN

THORNDIKE, LYNN (July 24, 1882–Dec. 28, 1965), medieval historian and historian of science, was born in Lynn, Mass., the son of Edward Roberts Thorndike, a Methodist clergyman, and of Abbie Brewster Ladd. He was christened Everett Lynn, but later dropped the first name. According to his younger sister Mildred, he was "an exceptionally shy, sensitive, imaginative boy. . . ." After receiving the B.A. from Wesleyan University in 1902, Thorndike entered Columbia University, where he received the M.A. in 1903 and the Ph.D. in 1905.

Nothing shows the single-minded determination of Thorndike's scholarly career more than the fact that his dissertation was titled *The Place of Magic in the Intellectual History of Europe* (1905), and his last book, *Michael Scot* (1965), was concerned with the relationship of Scot's work to astrology, alchemy, and magic. And his masterful eight-volume *A History of Magic and Experimental Science* (1923–1958) fulfilled the promise contained in the title of his dissertation. The dissertation also reflected a dominant influence of his graduate training at Columbia, that of James Harvey Robinson, the exponent of the new "intellectual history."

From 1907 to 1909, Thorndike was an instructor at Northwestern University. He next taught at Western Reserve University until 1924, by which time he had been promoted through the academic ranks to professor. The publication of the first two volumes of *A History of Magic and Experimental Science* in 1923 served notice to the scholarly world of his preeminence in detailed manuscript studies.

In 1924, Thorndike accepted a professorship of history at Columbia University, where his two older brothers already held professorships (Ashley in English literature and Edward Lee in educational psychology). He remained at Columbia for twenty-six years. A virtual cascade of articles and books resulted from Thorndike's research at this university and in many European libraries. That productivity did not cease with his retirement in 1950. He never married.

Thorndike's activity at Columbia was by no means confined to his own research and writing. Many American medievalists were trained in his seminar. His lectures on medieval and early modern intellectual history were mines of detailed fact and novel judgment. In this course (and in many of his publications) he attempted to counterbalance the often derogatory judgments made of medieval thought in comparison with that of the Renaissance.

The greatest debt owed to Thorndike by medievalists is the result of his extraordinary productivity. His *The History of Medieval Europe* (1917; second revision 1949) was, in its earliest form, one of the most popular textbooks in American colleges and universities. In its revised versions it has held its own amid the deluge of more recent textbooks. The third edition represents a balanced account, with emphasis on the classical influence upon the Middle Ages and unusually extensive treatment of the history of science and learning. Also widely circulated was Thorndike's *A Short History of Civilization* (1926; new ed., 1948). It, too, represents something of a "first" in viewing history from a global viewpoint.

But Thorndike's international reputation rests primarily on his contributions to scholarship, and above all on *A History of Magic and Experimental Science.* This is not a twofold history, one of magic and one of science. Rather, it is an attempt to trace the relations between the two. Thorndike's basic thesis was that one of the principal roots of experimental science lies in magic broadly conceived. In a work so packed with facts drawn from manuscript sources, it is difficult to assay his guiding historical beliefs, but Thorndike expressed his general view of history eloquently in his 1955 presidental address to the American Historical Association. The progress made by scientists should be estimated in the context of their period and "according to their own lights," Thorndike argued. He had earlier made this point in *Science and Thought in the Fifteenth Century* (1929; repr. 1963). Also implicit in the *History* is the idea (specifically outlined in "The True Place of Astrology in the History of Science," *Isis,* Sept. 1955) that the only universal "law of nature" prior to Newton's formulation of the law of gravitation was the astrological law of the all-pervading influence of celestial motions on this world.

Regardless of the correctness of its main thesis, the *History* is a work of enormous importance because of the wealth of manuscripts Thorndike consulted. It constitutes a guide to many scientific and magical tracts previously unknown. A similar service is performed by his *A Catalogue of Incipits of Mediaeval Scientific Writings in Latin* (1937; rev. and enl., 1963), compiled with Pearl Kibre. The value of this work is difficult to overestimate, including as it does references to hundreds of scientific treatises and thousands of manuscripts and editions. Its arrangement by incipits rather than by title or author helps in the ready identification of works that often appear in manuscripts without title.

If Thorndike had done nothing but publish the *Catalogue* and his *History,* his primary place in medieval studies would have been assured. But he also published many Latin texts and translations. The first of these, *The Herbal of Rufinus* (1946), prepared with the assistance of Francis S. Benjamin, Jr., contains a wealth of medieval botanical knowledge. It was compiled by the little-known botanist Rufinus, in great part from the main sources available in the thirteenth century.

Thorndike also published two collections of cosmological and meteorological texts, *The Sphere of Sacrobosco and Its Commentators* (1949) and *Latin Treatises on Comets Between 1238 and 1368 A.D.* (1950). Both collections contain mélanges of Latin texts and English translations. Of more general interest to medievalists is Thorndike's *University Records and Life in the Middle Ages* (1944), a judiciously chosen collection of English translations that gives the flavor of medieval university life: the types of courses, the techniques of instruction, and so on.

Thorndike was president of the American Historical Association in 1955. With David Eugene Smith of Columbia and others he helped organize the History of Science Society in 1924, and was its president in 1928–1929. He was also one of the first thirty fellows elected to the Mediaeval Academy of America (1926) after its foundation in 1925. Thorndike died in New York City.

[A detailed bibliography of Thorndike's articles and books to 1952 has been published by Pearl Kibre in *Osiris,* 1954. The principal books of Thorndike's

after that date have been mentioned in the text. An obituary is in *American Philosophical Society Year Book 1967.*]

MARSHALL CLAGETT

THURBER, JAMES GROVER (Dec. 8, 1894–Nov. 2, 1961), writer and cartoonist, was born in Columbus, Ohio, the son of Charles Leander Thurber and Mary Agnes Fisher. Relatives and other Columbus residents would later appear in Thurber's writings as laughable eccentrics in his highly fictionalized *My Life and Hard Times* (1933) or as praiseworthy examples of old-fashioned individualism in his more documented account, *The Thurber Album* (1952).

Actually during Thurber's childhood his father held a succession of clerical or secretarial jobs under various Ohio Republican politicians. As secretary to local Congressman Emmett Tompkins, Charles Thurber moved his family to Falls Church, Va., to be near Washington. In the summer of 1901, during a backyard William Tell bow-and-arrow game with his two brothers, Thurber lost the use of his left eye. The injury was not promptly treated, and the damage eventually spread to the other eye. The cartoons for which he became famous in the 1930's were drawn by a man who was going blind.

The failure of Tompkins to win renomination in 1902 resulted in the family's return to Columbus, where Thurber's flair for art was first noticed by a fourth-grade teacher. In junior high and high schools Thurber did well, graduating with honor from East High in 1913. He entered Ohio State University (OSU) in 1913 but dropped out during his sophomore year. When he returned in 1915 he came under the protection of a fellow student, Elliott Nugent, who helped him into a fraternity and coached him in the social graces.

Nugent and Thurber were later to collaborate in writing and producing a Broadway play, *The Male Animal* (1940). The model for one of the characters was Professor Joseph Villiers Denney, who fought for academic freedom at OSU during their undergraduate years. Another important intellectual influence upon Thurber at OSU was Professor Joseph Russell Taylor, who awakened in Thurber a lifelong affinity for Henry James.

Ineligible for military service in World War I because of his eyesight, Thurber worked as a State Department code clerk, first in Washington and then in Paris (1918–1920). He then began his journalistic career as a reporter on the Columbus *Evening Dispatch* under tough city editor Norman ("Gus") Kuehner. He continued to frequent the OSU campus, writing books and lyrics for college musicals, but he took no degree.

On May 20, 1922, Thurber married Althea Adams, an OSU senior and campus social leader. They had one daughter. People who knew the couple agreed that Althea prompted Thurber to leave Columbus. In 1925 they went to France, where Thurber wrote for the Paris and Riviera editions of the Chicago *Tribune.* He also wrote essays and "casuals," placing some in various American magazines and newspapers.

Financially unable to continue living in France, Thurber came back to the United States in 1926 and went to work for the New York *Evening Post.* In February 1927 he met E. B. White, who introduced him to Harold Ross, editor of the recently founded *New Yorker.* Ross hired Thurber for the magazine's staff. White was Thurber's office mate at the *New Yorker* for several years and was a major force in shaping his literary style. As Thurber later wrote: "The influence I had to fight off in writing was that of Henry James, and the influence that helped me most was that of E. B. White." It was White, also, who first recognized that the drawings Thurber scrawled on office copy paper were potentially publishable cartoons.

In 1929 White and Thurber collaborated on *Is Sex Necessary?,* a parody on the popular psychology books then in vogue. It was illustrated with several Thurber drawings. A book entirely of Thurber cartoons followed, *The Seal in the Bedroom* (1932). Then came the freely invented autobiographical sketches collected as *My Life and Hard Times* (1933). The stories, essays, books, and cartoons that gave James Thurber his reputation as "twentieth-century America's greatest illustrator and humorist" followed in rapid succession. These included "The Secret Life of Walter Mitty" (*New Yorker,* Mar. 18, 1939), *The Last Flower* (1939), *Fables for Our Time* (1940), *My World—and Welcome to It* (1942), and another all-cartoon anthology, *Men, Women, and Dogs* (1943).

Thurber believed he had struck a universal note, asserting for example that "the original of Walter Mitty is every other man I have ever known." Many readers and critics agreed, but these *New Yorker* sketches have lost much of their claim to universality. Thurber's world—except when he was writing about Columbus, Ohio, and, occasionally, France—was an extremely constricted universe of New York cocktail parties and weekends in Connecticut where people joked about the vocabularies of their "colored" maids. His most distinctive invention, the Thurber Woman—that dominant, man-devouring figure who stalks her cowering male prey through so many of the stories and pictures—ranks as one of the most effective of sexist stereotypes. The portrayal of an exploited and oppressed group as if they were actually powerful and dangerous is an ancient satiric device. Thurber denied any prejudice against women, declaring in a letter to Frank Gibney (Oct. 31, 1956) that "my reputation as a woman-hating writer is largely myth and misconception."

Thurber's always rocky marriage to Althea Adams ended in divorce in May 1935, and on June 25, 1935, he married Helen Muriel Wismer, a successful pulp-magazine editor. She straightened out his tangled business affairs and inept household arrangements and thereafter managed them with high competence.

In 1940 Thurber underwent five eye operations, which temporarily checked the deterioration in his sight but left him legally blind. Some have perceived in his literary work thereafter a turn toward greater political commitment, as seen in *Further Fables for Our Time* (1956) and *Lanterns and Lances* (1961). At the same time he turned increasingly toward allegory, legend, and word games. The fairy-tale model with which he had first experimented in *Many Moons* (1943) grew into a number of books of gentle, ironic literary fantasy, typified in *The 13 Clocks* (1950) and *The Wonderful O* (1957). In 1959 Thurber published *The Years With Ross,* a reminiscence of his *New Yorker* mentor. The following year a show based on Thurber's literary sketches and cartoon captions, *A Thurber Carnival,* opened on Broadway, and the author himself acted in one of the episodes for eighty-eight performances. After a rapid decline in health, Thurber died in New York City.

[Thurber manuscripts are in the James Thurber Collection, Ohio State University Library; the Martha Kinney Cooper Ohioana Library, Columbus, Ohio; and in the Beinecke Rare Book and Manuscript Library, Yale University. Lengthy and revealing letters from Thurber are in the E. B. White Papers, Cornell University, and in the Malcolm Cowley Papers, Newberry Library, Chicago. A thorough bibliography of Thurber's published writings and drawings is Edwin T. Bowden, *James Thurber: A Bibliography* (1968), which includes references to foreign translations. Retrospective anthologies are *The Thurber Carnival* (1945), not to be confused with the Broadway revue; and *Thurber Country* (1953). Helen Thurber edited the anthologies, *Credos and Curios* (1962) and *Thurber and Company* (1966).

On Thurber, see Robert E. Morsberger, *James*

Thurber (1964); Charles S. Holmes, ed., *Thurber: A Collection of Critical Essays* (1974), with good critical insights; and Burton Bernstein, *Thurber: A Biography* (1975), the first detailed account of his life.

Notable tributes include E. B. White, *New Yorker,* Nov. 11, 1961; Malcolm Cowley, Peter De Vries, and St. Clair McKelway, "Salute to Thurber," *Saturday Review,* Nov. 25, 1961; and Charles A. Brady, "What Thurber Saw," *Commonweal,* Dec. 8, 1961. Obituaries are in the *New York Times,* Nov. 3, 1961; and *Obituaries from the* [London] *Times 1961–1970* (1975).]

PAUL A. CARTER

TIGERT, JOHN JAMES, IV (Feb. 11, 1882–Jan. 21, 1965), professor, United States commissioner of education, and university president, was born on the campus of Vanderbilt University in Nashville, Tenn., the son of John James Tigert and Amelia McTyeire. His father was a clergyman, religious editor, and bishop of the Methodist Episcopal Church, South; his mother's father, Holland Nimmons McTyeire, was a founder and the first president of Vanderbilt. Compiling an enviable record as a scholar-athlete during his undergraduate years at Vanderbilt, Tigert received a B.A. in 1904 and became the first Rhodes Scholar from Tennessee. He studied at Pembroke College, Oxford, from 1904 to 1907, earning a B.A. in jurisprudence. Oxford awarded him an M.A. in 1915, following the "apprenticeship" of time in a profession required by the university.

Tigert returned to the United States in 1907 to become professor of philosophy and psychology and director of athletics at Central College in Fayette, Mo., a position he held for two years. During this period he met Edith Jackson Bristol, a piano teacher at Howard Payne College. They were married on Aug. 25, 1909, and had two children.

In 1909, Tigert became president of Kentucky Wesleyan College at Winchester, where he served also as player-coach for the boys' basketball team and coach of the girls' basketball team. Disappointed with the level of local and church support for the college, he resigned in 1911 and joined the University of Kentucky faculty as professor of philosophy and psychology. In 1912 he also became director of athletics and coach of the football and girls' basketball teams.

During World War I, Tigert lectured to military personnel in Europe for the Young Men's Christian Association and the Army Educational Corps. A lecture series on community leadership and Americanism for the Radcliffe Chautauqua Company in 1920 caught the attention of leaders in the American Legion.

With the legion's active support, Tigert was appointed United States commissioner of education in 1921, the youngest man to have held that office. Relatively unknown among professional educators, he began his new duties amid charges that he had won the office through political favoritism, but his energy and persuasiveness soon gained him acceptance.

As commissioner, Tigert enjoyed little authority beyond responsibility for collecting and disseminating educational statistics and a general mandate to promote the cause of education. The limitations suited him, for he was opposed to strong federal influence over education. Under his leadership the Bureau of Education's activities remained focused on school surveys, rural education, Americanization, and schooling for native peoples in Alaska, the agency's only direct educational responsibility. In 1923, Tigert accompanied President Warren G. Harding to Alaska, but the trip produced no new education policies for that territory. He involved the Bureau of Education in cosponsoring American Education Week with the American Legion and the National Education Association, but drew strong criticism of the program's militaristic tone from Charles W. Eliot, president emeritus of Harvard, and from the Young Women's Christian Association, the American Association of University Professors, and other groups.

Although Tigert did not expand the Bureau of Education's influence or give it new directions, his failure to do so derived principally from the agency's restricted mandate and the lack of congressional support. In August 1928 he resigned to become president of the University of Florida at Gainesville. He held that office for nineteen years.

Tigert brought a national perspective to the university during the Great Depression, world war, and postwar recovery. His interest in research and advanced studies led to the reorganization of the graduate school and the development of new graduate programs. The university conferred its first Ph.D. degrees in 1934. In an effort to focus attention on relations with Central and South American nations, Tigert created the Institute of Inter-American Affairs. He raised university admission standards, promoted extension programs throughout the state, and added a demonstration school to the College of Education. He also strengthened intercollegiate athletics and supported the development of Reserve Officers Training Corps (ROTC) and military studies. He was instrumental in organizing the Southeastern Athletic Conference and was active in the National Collegiate Athletic Association.

Tigert's most fundamental curriculum innovation came with the creation of the General College, which provided general arts and sciences instruction for all freshmen and sophomores at the university. Reflecting his experience at Oxford, Tigert viewed general education as a prerequisite for both specialized studies and professional training.

Tigert retired in 1947. As an ironic footnote to his career-long dedication to organized college sports, evidence suggests that his resignation resulted in part from Florida Governor Millard F. Caldwell's interference in selecting the university's football coach.

After retiring, Tigert served as one of two Americans on India's Commission on Higher Education and, from 1949 to 1954, as a visiting professor at the University of Miami in Coral Gables, Fla. The University of Florida administration building was named in his honor in 1960, and in 1970 Tigert was inducted into the National Football Hall of Fame. He died at Gainesville, Fla.

Tigert's early career benefited from the respect enjoyed by his father and maternal grandfather, particularly within southern religious circles, but he eventually established a reputation of his own as a lecturer-preacher and author of almost 300 books and articles. He viewed good citizenship as the principal goal of education, and competitive sports, religious conviction, and military training as means to engendering morality and self-discipline among the young. But he also tirelessly promoted high standards of learning. For Tigert, scholarship, not athletics, constituted the university's essential mission, an aim that, he insisted, promised to advance both individual and national well-being.

[The John James Tigert Papers are at the University of Florida Library. In addition to numerous lectures, articles, and reports as commissioner of education and president of the University of Florida, Tigert published *Bishop Holland Nimmons McTyeire* (1955). George Coleman Osborn, *John James Tigert: American Educator* (1974), contains a complete bibliography of Tigert's publications. An obituary is in the *New York Times,* Jan. 22, 1965.]

DONALD R. WARREN

TILLICH, PAUL (Aug. 20, 1886–Oct. 22, 1965), theologian and philosopher, was born Paul Johannes Oskar Tillich in the village of Starzeddel, in the district of Guben in East Prussia, Germany—now a part of Poland. His father, Johannes Tillich, was a Lutheran Pastor

and diocesan superintendent of the Prussian Territorial Church. His mother was Wilhelmina Mathilde Dürselen.

At the humanistic gymnasium in Königsberg-Neumark and then in Berlin, Tillich studied Greek, Latin, and classical culture. He also began the private study of philosophy, especially the works of Immanuel Kant and Johann Gottlieb Fichte. At the gymnasium he faced his first religious crisis in the tension between his Christian faith and the values of classical humanism. With the help of his father he worked out a personal synthesis, which placed him "on the boundary" between the opposing outlooks—a stance that he maintained throughout his life.

Tillich began his theological studies at the University of Berlin in 1904. In addition to theology he avidly read the works of philosopher Friedrich Schelling, whose system became the ontological framework for his whole theological enterprise. The Augustinian tradition that he inherited through Luther, Schelling, and Jakob Boehme accounts for the clearly Neoplatonic elements in his philosophy of religion. At the University of Halle, where he also attended lectures in theology from 1905 to 1907, Tillich came under the influence of Martin Kähler, who inspired him to rethink the doctrine of justification. This project eventually produced the paradoxical Tillichian doctrine that the believer is justified despite his unbelief—*simul justus et dubitans.*

In 1910 Tillich received his doctorate in philosophy from the University of Breslau and in 1912 his licentiate in theology from Halle. For both degrees he wrote dissertations dealing with aspects of Schelling's philosophy of religion. He was ordained a minister of the Evangelical Lutheran Church in Berlin on Aug. 18, 1912, and spent the next two years as an assistant preacher in a working-class section of Berlin. On Sept. 28, 1914, he married Margarethe Wever, only to depart for military service a few days after the marriage.

Following the outbreak of World War I Tillich volunteered to serve in the German army. He performed the duties of a field chaplain on the western front from 1914 to 1918. He received the Iron Cross for courageous service to the wounded and the dying.

The horrors and the suffering of the war created a turning point in Tillich's life. He completely rejected idealist philosophy and the capitalist, bourgeois society that it supported. His theology began to take history and political realities more seriously and to work on the assumption of a universal human estrangement. From this point on, Tillich's theological program had no less a goal than the radical rebuilding and transformation of society.

On the more personal level, Tillich returned from the war to discover that his wife had become pregnant through an affair with a close friend. They were divorced in February 1921. Tillich's own personal life thereafter was unconventional and erratic, marked by unstable erotic liaisons. Neither his second marriage in 1924 nor his anxiety for his career completely contained his Dionysian proclivity.

Between the years 1919 and 1924 Tillich served as privatdozent in theology at the University of Berlin. He gave the first public lecture on his own thought before the Kant Society in Berlin on Apr. 16, 1919. His address, entitled "On the Idea of a Theology of Culture," laid the essential ground plans for his future theological program. It also introduced Tillich's famous dictum: "Religion is the substance of culture; culture is the form of religion."

Tillich's major theological concern during this period was the relationship of the Christian church to the socialist movements of the day. He found the works of Karl Marx to support his own critique of bourgeois Christianity and wrote various studies distinguishing valid aspects of Marx's thought from that which he believed should be rejected.

Amidst the unstable political situation of postwar Germany, Tillich helped found a small but dedicated group of religious socialists called the Kairos Circle. The members shared the hope and expectation that despite the gloomy political picture, a new *kairos* (divine breakthrough) was on the horizon in the form of a religiously grounded socialism. As the group's principal theoretician, Tillich tried to place socialism on sound spiritual and ethical foundations.

In 1924 Tillich accepted an appointment as associate professor of theology at the University of Marburg. On Mar. 22, 1924, he married Hannah Werner Gottschow, who was to become the "companion of his life." They had two children.

At Marburg, Tillich first encountered the growing influence of Karl Barth's neoorthodoxy among his students and began a lifelong debate with that other theological giant. He also struggled with contemporary existentialism, as proposed by his colleagues Rudolf Bultmann and Martin Heidegger. This encounter had lasting impact on his thought.

The years 1925–1929 found Tillich at Dresden, where he had become professor of philoso-

phy and religious studies at the Institute of Technology. His first book, *The Religious Situation,* appeared in 1925 (translated into English in 1932). Its broad cultural sweep was a challenge to the Barthian exclusion of cultural problems from theological investigation. At Dresden, Tillich continued to explore the religious dimension of art, dance, and economics, and began a systematic study of psychoanalysis as a resource for theology.

The climax of Tillich's German career came at the University of Frankfurt, where he accepted the post of professor of philosophy in 1929. His lectures "moved on the boundary line between philosophy and theology," and his political ideas matured in the company of leading social scientists known as the Frankfurt school. In 1933 he published *Die sozialistische Entscheidung* (translated as *The Socialist Decision* in 1977), which attacked both communism and national socialism as forms of "political romanticism," while reaffirming the "socialist principle" as realistic and humanistic. He appealed particularly to the "early Marx" and his Hegelian sources in support of his position.

Tillich had already become unpopular with the Nazis because of his socialist activities and his Jewish friends. But his book provoked the *coup de grâce*—his suspension from the University of Frankfurt on Apr. 13, 1933. In December of the same year, he and his family went into exile in America.

At the age of forty-seven Tillich began a new career in a foreign country. Initially he served as a visiting lecturer in philosophy at Columbia University and visiting professor of theology at Union Theological Seminary. He remained at Union for twenty-two years. At Union Tillich engaged in fruitful dialogue and joint seminars with Columbia philosophers. It was Union, however, which served him as a bridge of communication with Europe and with intellectual life throughout America. He became an American citizen in 1940.

The years at Union saw the publication of some of his most significant English works. *The Protestant Era* (1948) was an excellent collection of essays and lectures representative of Tillich's theology of the German period. *The Courage to Be* (1952) was a concise, tightly argued classic in religious philosophy. It also provided the reader with a penetrating analysis of American culture. Volume I of the *Systematic Theology* (1951) was the first of three that together constitute Tillich's principal contribution to theology. Following his famous "method of correlation," it explores the themes of God and

Revelation as they relate to the very structures of being. The strongly philosophical thrust of the whole *Systematic* results from Tillich's attempt to "correlate" revelatory answers with philosophical questions.

During World War II Tillich continued his political involvement as chairman of the Council for a Democratic Germany and of the Self-Help for Emigrés from Central Europe program. He was also active in the Fellowship of Socialist Christians and gave numerous radio talks to the German people on the Voice of America. In general, though, he saw the period as a "sacred void"—a time of hopeful waiting. His theology became more introspective and existential in focus.

In 1955 Tillich reached the culmination of his academic career with his appointment to Harvard as university professor. He lectured at Harvard on the religious meaning of such diverse disciplines as psychiatry, business, and intellectual history. These years also saw the publication of Volume II of the *Systematic Theology, Existence and the Christ* (1957). This volume proved to be a focus of controversy about the orthodoxy of Tillich's thought. His critics objected that the Christian message becomes submerged in Tillich's ontological system, whereas his supporters defended Volume II as a meaningful reinterpretation of the traditional doctrine of Christ.

Upon his retirement from Harvard in 1962, Tillich began the final stage of his career as the Nuveen Professor of Theology at the University of Chicago Divinity School. As the "distinguished theologian in residence," he maintained a demanding schedule of lecturing and writing. Together with the historian of religion Mircea Eliade, he gave a seminar on religion that became legendary. The third volume of the *Systematic Theology* appeared in 1963. The work, entitled *Life and Spirit*, returned to Tillich's early historical and political themes, but dealt with them in highly abstract terms. Tillich himself was least satisfied with this volume.

Tillich was both a widely sought lecturer and a masterful teacher. He inspired American, English, German, and Japanese audiences with his dramatically delivered lectures on religion and culture. He fascinated students with brilliant discussions of ancient ideas and their relevance for today. But most powerful and moving were his sermons, which might well constitute his greatest achievement. They were primarily directed to those who were alienated from their religious traditions and won him the title "Apostle of the Skeptics."

At the heart of Tillich's system is the ideal notion of "theonomy"—a cultural situation in which religious authoritarianism and secular autonomy are transcended in a genuine freedom grounded in religious depth. Theonomy is only achieved in dialectical struggle with these extremes.

Tillich's biographers agree that the dialectic of theonomy was also an abstract reflection of his personal conflicts with paternal and religious authority. These inner conflicts were embodied both in his professional tension with doctrinal orthodoxy and in his personal difficulties with marital fidelity. Acceptance by the Church and the ultimate reconciliation with his wife were essential to Tillich's own theonomy.

Tillich died at Billings Hospital in Chicago. His ashes were interred in Paul Tillich Park, which he had dedicated in 1963, in the town of New Harmony, Ind.

Tillich's work had significant impact on a variety of disciplines, including philosophy of religion, political theory, art criticism, and existential psychology. Erich Fromm, Rollo May, and Abraham Maslow were indebted to him for key analytic concepts such as "existential anxiety" and the "demonic." He was probably the most famous and celebrated American theologian of the century. Two presidents invited him to the White House. His face appeared on the cover of *Time* magazine, and recent polls indicate that Paul Tillich is the unrivalled "major mentor" of contemporary systematic theologians. Scholarly societies, such as the North American Paul Tillich Society, the German Paul Tillich Gesellschaft, and the French Association Paul Tillich, continue to explore the implications of his thought.

[Tillich's papers, correspondence, and manuscripts are in the Tillich Archives at the Andover-Harvard Divinity School Library, as well as at the Tillich Archives in Göttingen, Germany. A collection of his letters and papers has been published in *Paul Tillich: Ein Lebensbild in Dokumenten* (1980), edited by Renate Albrecht and Margot Hahl. The complete works of Tillich, *Gesammelte Werke*, 14 volumes (1959–1975), are edited by Renate Albrecht. Tillich's autobiographical essays are in *On the Boundary* (1966) and in "Autobiographical Reflections" in Charles W. Kegley and Robert W. Bretall, eds., *The Theology of Paul Tillich* (1964). His *Love, Power and Justice* (1954) is his most significant contribution to the field of ethics. James Luther Adams has translated and edited some of Tillich's important early works in *What Is Religion?* (1969) and *Political Expectation* (1971). Franklin Sherman has translated Tillich's *The Socialist Decision* (1977), which has an excellent introduction by John Stumme. The Tillich sermons have been edited in collections: *The Shaking of the Foundations* (1948), *The New Being* (1955), and *The Eternal Now* (1963).

Secondary literature on Tillich abounds. The standard biography is Wilhelm and Marion Pauck, *Paul Tillich: His Life and Thought,* I (1976). Other important perspectives on his life are Hannah Tillich, *From Time to Time* (1973), and Rollo May, *Paulus: Reminiscences of a Friendship* (1973). Bibliographies are in James L. Adams, *Paul Tillich's Philosophy of Culture, Science and Religion* (1965); Kenan Osborne, *New Being* (1969); Gordon Tait, *The Promise of Tillich* (1971); John Stumme, *Socialism in Theological Perspective* (1978); and Raymond F. Bulman, *A Blueprint for Humanity* (1981). Collections of recent Tillich scholarship have been edited by John J. Carey for the North American Paul Tillich Society in *Tillich Studies: 1975* and *Kairos and Logos* (1978). An obituary is in the *New York Times,* Oct. 23, 1965.]

RAYMOND F. BULMAN

TOBIAS, CHANNING HEGGIE (Feb. 1, 1882–Nov. 5, 1961), civic and religious leader, and YMCA executive, was born in Augusta, Ga., the son of Fair J. Robinson, a coachman, and of Clara Belle Robinson, a domestic worker. He lived with, and was brought up by, a friend of his mother because both his parents had live-in jobs. From 1895 to 1898 Tobias attended Paine College Preparatory Academy and then entered Paine College, from which he received the B.A. in 1902. He continued his education at Drew Theological Seminary, which awarded him the B.D. in 1905. On May 10, 1908, Tobias married Mary C. Pritchard, who had also been a student at Paine; they had two daughters.

In 1900, while still a student at Paine, Tobias was ordained a minister in the Colored Methodist Episcopal Church. After graduating from Drew, he taught Bible literature at Paine College until 1911. In that year he became student secretary of the International Committee of the Young Men's Christian Association (YMCA). His responsibilities involved visiting nearly all the countries of Europe, including the relief areas (1921). Also in 1921 he was a delegate to the Pan-African Congress in Paris.

Tobias rose in the YMCA hierarchy. In 1923 he was named senior secretary of the colored men's department of the organization. Again his job entailed extensive travel—this time throughout Europe, the Near East, and Asia. Some of his impressions were subsequently recorded in the pamphlet *Travel Notes,* which covered the period December 1936–March 1937. Tobias attended the Conference on Race Relations held at Mysore, India, in 1937. While in the country he had a one-hour meeting with Mohandas Gandhi. The experience influenced him profoundly, and he came away ". . . convinced Gandhi is the greatest spiritual leader of our time." He also said that "no teacher has ever made the impression on me as Gandhi because he was the living embodiment of what he taught."

Although the principal focus of Tobias' post in the YMCA was to build a black constituency for the organization, he expanded its scope by serving as a director of Paine College, the National Association for the Advancement of Colored People (NAACP), the Council on Race Relations, the National Council of Churches, and many other groups. His contacts and the prestige of his post made him in great demand as a speaker at commencements and other important public events.

In 1946, Tobias resigned from the YMCA to become the first black director of the Phelps-Stokes Foundation, a post he held until 1953. He traveled extensively in Africa for Phelps-Stokes, visiting Liberia, Sierra Leone, the Gold Coast, Nigeria, and the Belgian Congo. Also in 1946 he was appointed to the Committee on Civil Rights by President Harry S. Truman. Tobias was one of the authors of *To Secure These Rights* (1947), the committee's report, which many consider a major document on the treatment of minority groups and remedial legislation for them. By 1953 he was calling for the end of all racial discrimination by January 1963, the centennial of the Emancipation Proclamation.

Mary Tobias died in 1949. On Mar. 31, 1951, Tobias married Eva Arnold. Shortly after the marriage he was appointed alternate member of the United States delegation to the United Nations. At his confirmation hearings he was asked about affiliations with groups that had been labeled subversive, particularly the Council on African Affairs. His answers apparently were satisfactory, for the Senate Foreign Relations Committee approved his appointment. At the United Nations, when chided by a Communist delegate for his support of American policy even though racial discrimination existed in the country, he replied: "Yes, there are bad laws and racial discrimination in certain American states. But American Negroes are free to protest."

Among Tobias' honors were the Harmon Award for Religious Services (1928), for his work for the YMCA; the Spingarn Medal of the NAACP (1948); and the Lane Bryant Award (1959) of the NAACP. He died in New York City.

[Tobias' speech "Building for Tomorrow's Better Living" (1954) is in *Rhetoric of Racial Revolt,* edited by Roy L. Hill (1964). An account of his life is in Louis Finkelstein, ed., *Thirteen Americans and Their Spiritual Biographies* (1953). An obituary is in the *New York Times,* Nov. 6, 1961.]

EDWARD S. LEWIS

TURKEVICH, LEONID IERONIMO-VICH. See LEONTY, METROPOLITAN.

TURNER, RICHMOND KELLY (May 27, 1885–Feb. 12, 1961), naval officer, was born in East Portland, Oreg., the son of Enoch Turner, a printer, and of Laura Frances Kelly. After being educated mainly in Fresno and Stockton, Calif., schools, he entered the U.S. Naval Academy in 1904. He graduated fifth in the class of 1908 and joined the line of the navy with the rank of passed midshipman. He was commissioned an ensign two years later. On Aug. 3, 1910, Turner married Harriet Sterling; they had no children. At Harriet Turner's request he began using Kelly as his first name.

Upon completion of five years of sea duty in 1913, more than half of it spent on the armored cruiser *West Virginia,* Turner was promoted to lieutenant (junior grade) and was assigned to the Naval Ordnance School. He finished his training in 1916 and spent the following three years in gunnery billets on three different battleships. None of the ships saw combat in World War I. Turner, who had been promoted to (temporary) lieutenant commander in 1917, spent 1919–1922 as ordnance design officer at the naval gun factory in Washington, D.C. He next returned to sea as gunnery officer of the battleship *California* and then as fleet gunnery officer on the staff of Admiral Newton McCully, commander of the Scouting Fleet in the Atlantic.

At this point Turner's career suffered a setback: McCully requested his reassignment, saying he would want the brilliant and efficient, but often tactless, Turner at his side in the event of war—but in the meantime he wanted him elsewhere. Upon his separation from McCully's staff, Turner was put in command of the destroyer *Mervine* (1924–1925). The ship earned high marks for battle efficiency under Turner, who was promoted to commander in 1925.

Turner apparently learned to moderate his outspoken ways, for his career progressed steadily in the next decade. He served from 1925 to 1927 as a section head in the Bureau of Ordnance and then transferred to naval aviation. (He had long been impressed by the combat potential of aircraft.) After earning his pilot's

wings in 1927, he headed the aircraft squadron of the Asiatic Fleet in Manila (1928–1929) and then did a two-year stint as chief of the Plans Division of the Bureau of Aeronautics. In 1931–1932, Turner attended the Geneva Disarmament Conference as adviser on naval aviation matters to the American delegation.

Between December 1932 and June 1934 he was executive officer of the carrier *Saratoga;* he then was named chief of staff to Vice Admiral Henry Butler, commander of the Aircraft Battle Force. From 1935 to 1938, Turner was at the Naval War College (he was promoted to captain in 1935), first as a student in the senior course and subsequently as a faculty member. Although he remained a partisan of air power, he requested a return to the surface fleet and was given command of the heavy cruiser *Astoria* upon completing his tour at the War College.

Turner was ordered to Washington in 1940 to become director of war plans in the Office of Naval Operations, a position he held until early 1942. During this time Turner, who was promoted to rear admiral in January 1941, was in frequent contact with Admiral Harold Stark, chief of naval operations. The possibility of war with Japan was often a topic of discussion between them. Although he at one time believed the Japanese might attack Pearl Harbor, Turner gave no special thought to the likelihood of a surprise attack on the Hawaiian base when he conferred with Stark on the morning of Dec. 7, 1941. When questioned later about the events of December 7, Turner retorted, "Why weren't I and a lot of others smarter than we were? . . . You find out the answers and let me know."

Turner remained in Washington for some six months after the war began, first as director of war plans and then as assistant chief of staff to Admiral Ernest J. King, commander in chief, U.S. Fleet. In July 1942, King ordered him to the Pacific, to head the amphibious forces in the planned attack on Guadalcanal and Tulagi. Turner had no firsthand experience with the landing of troops on enemy-occupied territory, but he soon became a highly successful practitioner of this complex type of warfare, which requires close coordination of naval, air, and ground forces and the maintenance of reliable logistic support for them.

Turner's planning abilities and his aggressive temperament made him an ideal amphibious commander. "If you don't have losses, that means you aren't doing enough," he once said. His own flagship, the *McCawley,* was sunk by a Japanese submarine in 1943. Although Allied forces suffered severe setbacks during the protracted Guadalcanal campaign, particularly at Savo Island (August 1942), where four Allied cruisers were sunk, Turner's reputation for getting the difficult job done survived. He subsequently presided over the invasions of many Japanese-held islands: New Georgia in the Solomons; Makin and Tarawa in the Gilberts; Kwajalein in the Marshalls; Saipan and Guam in the Marianas; Iwo Jima; and Okinawa, where more than 1,000 ships were under his command.

Promoted to vice admiral in 1944 and admiral in 1945, Turner accepted ever greater responsibilities, ending the war as commander of amphibious forces, Pacific Fleet. Samuel Eliot Morison wrote of him: "Schooled by adversity at Guadalcanal and Tarawa, he was not spoiled by success in the Marshalls. He had learned more about [amphibious] warfare than anyone else ever had, or probably ever would."

At the end of the war, Turner was within two years of retirement. He served his final tour (1945–1947) as a member of the Military Staff Committee at the United Nations and then retired to Monterey, Calif., where he died.

[Manuscript material is in the Operational Archives, Naval Historical Center, Washington, D.C. Turner's publications are "The Size of Naval Guns," *Scientific American*, May 20, 1916; "A Fighting Leader for the Fleet," *U.S. Naval Institute Proceedings*, Apr. 1922; and "Gun Defense Against Torpedo Planes," *ibid.*, Oct. 1922, with Lt. Theodore D. Ruddock. Vice Admiral George C. Dyer, *The Amphibians Came to Conquer*, 2 vols. (1972), is a richly detailed biography. Also see Robert Sherrod, *On to Westward: War in the Central Pacific* (1945); Samuel Eliot Morison, *History of United States Naval Operations in World War II*, 4 (1949), 5 (1949), 7 (1951), 8 (1953), and 14 (1960); Roberta Wohlstetter, *Pearl Harbor: Warning and Decision* (1962); and Clark G. Reynolds, *Famous American Admirals* (1978). An obituary is in the *New York Times*, Feb. 14, 1961.]

LLOYD J. GRAYBAR

TYDINGS, MILLARD EVELYN (Apr. 6, 1890–Feb. 9, 1961), lawyer and U.S. senator, was born in Havre de Grace, Md., the son of Millard F. Tydings, a government clerk, and of Mary B. O'Neill. After graduating from Maryland Agricultural College in 1910 with a B.S. in mechanical engineering, he worked for the Baltimore and Ohio Railroad for a year. He then studied law at the University of Maryland, graduating with an LL.B. in 1913. That same year he was admitted to the Maryland bar and opened a law practice in Havre de Grace.

In 1916, Tydings was elected as a Democrat to the Maryland House of Delegates, thus beginning a thirty-five-year career in public life. In that same year he served as a private in the U.S. Army's Mexican border campaign. He was an officer in the Allied Expeditionary Force in World War I, advancing to the rank of lieutenant colonel in the Twenty-ninth Division and participating in the Haute Alsace and Meuse-Argonne offensives. He was awarded the Distinguished Service Medal, the Distinguished Service Cross, and three citations. After the war Tydings returned to public life. From 1920 to 1922 he served as speaker of the Maryland House of Delegates. Then he was elected to the Maryland State Senate, and in 1924 to the U.S. House of Representatives. Two years later he was elected to the U.S. Senate.

During the Great Depression, Tydings rose to prominence as a conservative Democratic opponent of President Franklin D. Roosevelt's New Deal. He voted against unemployment relief, low-cost housing, and such basic New Deal laws as the Agricultural Adjustment Act, the National Industrial Recovery Act, the National Youth Administration, and the Tennessee Valley Authority. He labeled the many New Deal agencies "alphabetical monstrosities," and called constantly for economy in government. At that time he published *The Machine Gunners: Before and After Prohibition* (1930) and *Counter-Attack, a Battle Plan to Defeat the Depression* (1933). He was also an amateur playwright and an accomplished pianist. In 1935 Tydings, long one of Washington's most eligible bachelors, married Eleanor Davies Cheeseborough, daughter of Joseph E. Davies, ambassador to Moscow; they had two children.

Tydings became known as the goad of the Senate, famed for his sharp mind and even sharper tongue. "If I can't vote my sentiments," he said early in his Senate career, "to hell with this job." He bitterly opposed President Roosevelt's plan to reorganize the Supreme Court in 1937. The following year Roosevelt unsuccessfully attempted to "purge" Tydings when the latter sought his third term.

A leader of the southern Democratic–Republican conservative coalition in Congress, Tydings continued to oppose Roosevelt's domestic policies throughout World War II. In 1944 he was easily reelected to the Senate for a fourth term as a self-described strong "states' rights man" and proponent of reducing government spending.

After World War II, Tydings battled for nuclear disarmament. He was one of the ten senators appointed in October 1945 to the Special

Committee on Atomic Energy. "It is up to the United States to find ways of creating friendships between nations to prevent a push-button war that will be over before most people know it began," he said. He advocated disarmament inspection forces "composed largely of Americans," and then added, "I'm not so much interested in sovereignty—I want to survive."

In February 1950, after Republican Senator Joseph R. McCarthy of Wisconsin had charged that Communists in the State Department were shaping American foreign policy, Tydings was named chairman of a special Senate Foreign Relations Committee subcommittee to investigate the allegations. His keen mind and biting wit, so often employed to ridicule the domestic programs of Presidents Roosevelt and Harry S. Truman, were now aimed at the junior senator from Wisconsin. Tydings announced to the Senate in July that there was not "an ounce of truth in Mr. McCarthy's charges," which he labeled "contemptible." He accused McCarthy of perpetrating a hoax on the American public. When McCarthy responded with cries of "whitewash" and an accusation that Tydings was Truman's "whimpering lap dog," Tydings countered with an offer of $5,000 for evidence that would result in the indictment of any of the card-carrying Communists McCarthy claimed were in the State Department.

McCarthy offered no evidence; instead, he actively backed John Marshall Butler's gutter campaign against Tydings' candidacy for a fifth term in 1950. Aided by a faked composite photograph showing Tydings in apparently friendly conversation with former Communist party leader Earl Browder, Butler defeated Tydings. A Senate investigating committee later criticized the "back-street" campaign conducted against Tydings by "non-Maryland outsiders." Tydings won his party's nomination for the Senate in 1956, but withdrew from the race due to poor health. He died at his estate near Havre de Grace, Md.

[The Tydings Papers are at the University of Maryland Library. There is much material on his legislative activities in James T. Patterson, *Congressional Conservatism and the New Deal* (1967). His conflict with McCarthy and his 1950 reelection campaign are treated exhaustively in Robert Griffith, *The Politics of Fear* (1971); and Richard M. Fried, *Men Against McCarthy* (1976). An obituary is in the *New York Times*, Feb. 10, 1961.]

HARVARD SITKOFF

VANCE, ARTHUR CHARLES ("DAZZY") (Mar. 4, 1891–Feb. 16, 1961), baseball pitcher,

was born in Orient, Iowa, the son of A. T. Vance, a farmer, and of Sarah Ritchie. He was raised in rural Nebraska near the Little Creek Community, and graduated from Hastings (Nebr.) High School. (Some people, including Vance's brother, insisted that his name was Clarence Arthur, but birth records in Adair County confirm the telegram that Vance sent to the Baseball Hall of Fame in 1955, in which he requested that the name on his plaque read Arthur Charles.) His famous nickname did not derive from his pitching abilities, as often assumed; rather, it came from a childhood acquaintance who often said, "Ain't that a daisy," pronouncing the last word "dazzy." Vance emulated the older man, and soon neighborhood youngsters called him "Dazzy." In 1916, Vance married Edyth Carmony; they had one daughter.

Vance played baseball with the teams that nearly every rural Nebraska community had. He began his professional career as a pitcher with Superior and Red Cloud in the Nebraska State League in 1912. For eleven years he played for minor-league teams, failing two trials with the New York Yankees and one with the Pittsburgh Pirates. Twice he injured his arm, once severely in 1916, while boxing during the off-season. His lack of control, caused by arm injuries, kept him in the minor leagues until 1922, when he was traded by New Orleans, along with catcher Hank De Berry, to the Brooklyn Robins. Brooklyn wanted only De Berry, but had to take Vance to complete the deal.

Vance did not win his first major-league game until he was thirty-one, but before he hung up his spikes, he had been recognized as the premier pitcher in the National League. He was imposing on the mound. Standing six feet, two inches, and weighing 200 pounds, he used an exaggerated high kick that increased his speed and, with his long, slim arms, gave him a deceptive delivery. His success came as he gained control of his fast- and curveballs. In his rookie season with Brooklyn, Vance won eighteen games. For seven consecutive seasons he led the league in strikeouts, and ended his career with 2,045. He pitched a no-hit game in 1925 and one-hit games in 1923 and 1925. In 1924 he won fifteen consecutive games. Although playing for a habitually second-division team, he won 197 games while losing 140. He retired in 1935 with a 3.24 earned run average.

Vance had his best year in 1924, when he led the league with 28 victories, 262 strikeouts, and a 2.16 earned run average. The National League inaugurated the Most Valuable Player Award that season, and Vance was the first winner. But controversy surrounded the choice, since the St. Louis Cardinals' second baseman, Rogers Hornsby, had set a major-league record by hitting .424 for the season.

Vance used the award and his outstanding season to negotiate a highly publicized three-year, $47,500 contract with Brooklyn owner Charles Ebbetts. Although he experienced one poor season during those three years, Ebbetts signed him for $20,000 when his contract expired in 1928. On the basis of a 22–10 record in 1928, his salary was increased to $25,000 in 1929, making him the highest-paid pitcher in baseball up to that time.

Only twice when Vance was in his prime, in 1924 and 1930, were the Robins (Dodgers) pennant contenders. Otherwise they were a consistent sixth-place team. The team's reputation as a collection of offbeat characters prone to play erratic and remarkably bizarre baseball began with the manager Wilbert Robinson and was enhanced by fun-loving players, most notably Babe Herman and Vance. The most bizarre episode involved a Herman double with the bases loaded. The result was one run and a double play at third base, where Herman, Vance (who had been on second), and Chick Fenster (who had been on first) all ended up. In 1933 Vance, whose effectiveness had declined, was traded to the St. Louis Cardinals. He made a brief relief appearance in the 1934 World Series, playing for the Cardinals. In 1935 Vance returned to Brooklyn, where he pitched one season before retiring. He was elected to the Baseball Hall of Fame in 1955.

Prior to signing his 1924 contract, and as land prices fell from the heights of the Florida land boom, Vance began investing in land on Florida's west coast. Charles Ebbetts advanced Vance funds in 1925, and agreed to serve as trustee for some of his investments. By the time Vance retired, he had extensive real estate holdings in and around Homosassa Springs, Fla. In addition to that property, Vance owned a hotel, fishing camp, woodworking business, gift shop, baseball school, and several small businesses, often run by members of his family. Although he had sold many of his enterprises, he was still an active businessman in Homosassa Springs when he died.

[A file of newspaper clippings on Vance is at the Baseball Hall of Fame in Cooperstown, N.Y. Also see *Saturday Evening Post,* Aug. 20, 1955; Harold Seymour, *Baseball: The Golden Age* (1971); and Lowell Reidenbaugh, *100 Years of National League Baseball*

(1976). An obituary is in the *New York Times,* Feb. 17, 1961.]

HARRY JEBSEN, JR.

VANDERBILT, GLORIA MORGAN (Aug. 23, 1904–Feb. 13, 1965), socialite, was born Gloria Maria Mercedes Morgan in Lucerne, Switzerland, the daughter of Harry Hays Morgan, an American career diplomat, and of Laura Kilpatrick, daughter of a Civil War general and a Chilean aristocrat. Uprooted by their restless mother even more than their father's job demanded, Gloria, called Mercedes as a child, and her identical twin Thelma in a four-year period attended schools in four different countries and languages. Bewildered, stammering misfits, unable to write any of the five languages they spoke, they were enrolled in the spring of 1917 in the Convent of the Sacred Heart in Manhattanville, N.Y., where they remained until June 1920. Seldom able to spend holidays with their family and often mistaken for each other, they seemed to merge into one being with two identical parts; the part that was Thelma always led and the part that was Gloria followed.

After a sojourn in Europe, where the marriage of their older sister Consuelo to Count de Maupas, engineered by their mother, was the social event of the 1920 Paris summer, the twins returned unchaperoned to New York to make their own matches. Renting a small apartment in a Greenwich Village brownstone, they enjoyed a sense of freedom at being their "own masters" and caught the eye of newspaper columnist Maury Paul, who as "Cholly Knickerbocker" chronicled society's activities. Paul dubbed Vanderbilt, who very early exhibited an "exquisite sense of style," "glorious Gloria" of "the magnificent Morgans" and taught her to live her life in print. He was a witness when Reginald Claypoole Vanderbilt, twenty-four years her senior, formally proposed to her, and he advised the couple on "how to handle the press." They were married on Mar. 6, 1923.

Despite dissipation, ill health, a spent fortune, and a daughter from a previous marriage who was the same age as his new bride, "Reggie" Vanderbilt was considered "*the* catch of the social world." His mother, Alice Vanderbilt, honored her new daughter-in-law by having her receive with her at The Breakers in Newport. During a hotel luncheon she spontaneously created "Gloria pearls" by cutting off and giving her a third of a great rope of pearls with the remark, "All Vanderbilt women have pearls." When on Feb. 20, 1924, Vanderbilt gave birth to a daughter, also named Gloria, her sister-in-law Gertrude Vanderbilt Whitney was named godmother, but it was Alice Vanderbilt who held the child at her christening. Vanderbilt, having squandered all of his fortune but $5 million held in trust for his children, was both delighted with his new child and (believing that his wife would be supported after his death by the child's inheritance) freed of his fear that she might be left "a Mrs. Vanderbilt without any money." Gloria Morgan Vanderbilt's unstable mother, insisting on overseeing the baby's care, became part of her household and, siding with the child's overprotective nurse, frequently overruled her daughter. Other Morgan family members lived lavishly on Vanderbilt money both before and after Reginald Vanderbilt's death in 1925.

When Gloria Morgan Vanderbilt's sisters made second marriages nearly as "brilliant" as her first, the three sisters became a favorite newspaper topic. Thelma, who had married enormously wealthy Viscount Marmaduke Furness in 1926, had a five-year affair with the Prince of Wales (later Edward VIII). During these years, Vanderbilt, who was called "the world's most beautiful widow," shared the limelight with her twin. They often appeared, "like matched gems," on either arm of the beaming king-to-be. Cecil Beaton, who photographed the twins in the late 1920's, termed them "as alike as two magnolias" diffusing "hothouse elegance and lacy feminity," and lamented that they had not "been painted by Sargent, with arrogant heads and affected hands."

Although Gloria Morgan Vanderbilt's daughter, who was called "the tiny heiress" and "the world's most expensive tot," shared her mother's life in print, in reality her mother neglected her. A forerunner of the jet set, Vanderbilt in one year lived in six countries and made twelve ocean voyages. While Vanderbilt enjoyed royal weekends and stimulating parties, the child was left with her nurse in hotel rooms or makeshift nursery quarters. Her earliest memory was of her mother "wearing a crystal-spangled white gown, looking more fragile and pale than any moonflower, disappearing down an endless hotel corridor."

When her mother and her child's nurse pressed her, Vanderbilt allowed the child to remain at the Long Island home of Gertrude Vanderbilt Whitney, while she returned to Europe.

In the fall of 1934, during the hysteria following the kidnapping of the infant son of Charles and Anne Morrow Lindbergh, Gloria Morgan Vanderbilt struggled with Gertrude Whitney over custody of ten-year-old Gloria. With Van-

derbilt's mother siding with Whitney, and with her sisters and brother united in her support, the Vanderbilt trial became a seven-week, international soap opera in which Vanderbilt's life and loves were "smeared across the headlines." Vanderbilt was stunned by the verdict, which granted Whitney custody and declared Vanderbilt unfit to mother her child except on weekends and the month of July. Viewing life as "a romance" or "a storybook," she simply waited for someone "to sweep all the bad dreams away."

As usual, Thelma took charge; they spent most of their time together, continuing their restless travel but living principally in Hollywood. To help Vanderbilt supplement the $9,000 annually alloted her by the court, they tried manufacturing dresses, cosmetics, and perfumes, but in the Great Depression years their efforts failed and Vanderbilt was often dependent on her twin's largesse. In her book, *Without Prejudice* (1936), Vanderbilt described her life in what she later called "an age of splendor and extravagance, of great projects and great follies." In 1958 she and Thelma wrote of their past in *Double Exposure*. During these years, Vanderbilt, suffering from glaucoma, was gradually going blind, but Thelma led her with such skill that few people were aware of her handicap.

Vanderbilt's relationship with her daughter, who chose to live with her when she was sixteen, was as rocky as her relationship with her twin was smooth. After reaching her majority, young Gloria on several occasions withheld money from her mother, possibly to make her more aware of her or as punishment for having often ignored her as a child. But before Vanderbilt died following surgery in Los Angeles, she was at peace with her daughter, who—inheriting her name and notoriety—would merge with her in public memory and succeed in areas where she had failed.

[Barbara Goldsmith, *Little Gloria . . . Happy at Last* (1980), contains a well-researched biography of Vanderbilt with numerous photographs. See also Vanderbilt's two books noted above (in which details do not always match) and the obituary and plans for her funeral in the *New York Times*, Feb. 14 and 15, 1965.]

OLIVE HOOGENBOOM

VAN VECHTEN, CARL (June 17, 1880– Dec. 21, 1964), music and dance critic, novelist, and photographer, was born in Cedar Rapids, Iowa, the son of Charles Duane Van Vechten, a banker and insurance agent, and of Ada

Amanda Fitch. The family was middle-class, cultivated, and musical. The Cedar Rapids of his youth became the provincial Maple Valley in *The Tattooed Countess* (1924).

In 1899 Van Vechten entered the University of Chicago. Among his professors were Robert Morss Lovett, William Vaughn Moody, and Robert Herrick. After graduation in 1903 with a Ph.B., he worked for the *Chicago American*, covering spot news, locating photographs, and writing a society column. He moved to New York in 1906 and was commissioned by Theodore Dreiser, then editor of *Broadway* magazine, to write an article on Richard Strauss's opera *Salome*. In November 1906 he became assistant to Richard Aldrich, music critic of the *New York Times*, thus establishing himself as a journalist-critic-essayist in music and the arts.

While in London on his first trip abroad, Van Vechten married Anna Elizabeth Snyder, a long-time acquaintance from Cedar Rapids, in June 1907. They were divorced in 1912. During 1908–1909, he was Paris correspondent for the *New York Times*. Back in New York, he resumed writing music and dance criticism for the *Times* and was, for a brief time in 1913, drama critic for the *New York Press*.

On Oct. 21, 1914, Van Vechten married Fania Marinoff, an actress. This marriage, childless like his first, was a lasting union of colorful, mercurial temperaments that he characterized in his reminiscences taped for the Columbia University Oral History Project (1960) as "a mutual admiration society."

Van Vechten met Mabel Dodge, joined her celebrated salon groups, and was on hand when she galvanized Greenwich Village artists into the Armory Show of January 1913. She arranged his meeting with Gertrude Stein later that year when he was again in Europe. For decades he championed Stein's work with publishers and the public, handled her manuscripts, and acted as her unofficial agent, helping with her lecture tour of the United States in 1934–1935. He served as her literary executor after her death in 1946.

Throughout his life, Van Vechten continued to perform this kind of service for artists whose work he admired and considered neglected. These included experimental composers such as Satie, Schoenberg, and Stravinsky, and a range of colorful performers. His appreciative essays on such figures were collected in *Music After the Great War* (1915), *Music and Bad Manners* (1916), *Interpreters and Interpretations* (1917), *The Merry-Go-Round* (1918), *In the Garret* (1919), and *Red* (1925). Other essays in these

volumes dealt with ragtime, jazz, musical comedy, the blues, and music for the movies. In *Excavations* (1926) he called attention to unusual and overlooked literary figures such as Edgar Saltus, Ronald Firbank, and Ouida. As early as 1921, when it was still neglected, he praised *Moby Dick* as a great novel and called due notice to the later work of Herman Melville.

Van Vechten's first novel, *Peter Whiffle: His Life and Works* (1922), is semiautobiographical, featuring European and New York scenes of which he had been a part. Artists, aesthetes, and intellectuals of the day were its characters, some under their own names, others thinly disguised. In his seven novels Van Vechten presented, with a mock decadence suitable to their decade, a perverse and exotic comedy of manners in which restless sophisticates seek sensation and run from boredom. This is particularly true of the New York novels, *The Blind Bow-Boy* (1923) and *Firecrackers* (1925). The others reflected a number of the era's popular subjects. *Peter Whiffle* capitalized on a post–World War I vogue for continental subjects. *The Tattooed Countess* (1924) fell in with "the revolt from the village." *Spider Boy* (1928) lampooned the movie madness of Hollywood.

Nigger Heaven (1926) dealt with the complex layers of life in Harlem and reflected Van Vechten's role in the Harlem Renaissance of the 1920's. His interest in blacks, their culture, and their art led not only to this controversial novel but also to close friendships with Walter White, James Weldon Johnson, Langston Hughes, and Ethel Waters, and to his private and public philanthropies on behalf of black arts and letters. On the other hand, he was criticized by some, including W.E.B. DuBois and D. H. Lawrence, for exploiting the more sensational elements of Harlem life.

Parties (1930) portrayed frivolous, overextended speakeasy types—among them a couple patterned after Van Vechten's friends F. Scott and Zelda Fitzgerald—at the sobering dawn of the Great Depression. With this book Van Vechten concluded his career as a novelist, although he continued to write personal memoirs, collected in *Sacred and Profane Memories* (1932) and *Fragments from an Unwritten Autobiography* (1955).

In the 1930's Van Vechten turned to photography, long a hobby, producing a wide range of unretouched documentary portraits of both famous and little-known personalities. His first photographic show was included in the "Leica Exhibition" at Bergdorf Goodman in New York City in November 1935.

During World War II, Van Vechten served as a captain at the New York Stage Door Canteen and in other projects of the American Theatre Wing, where he had a wide acquaintance with performing artists. An inveterate collector, he arranged and donated memorial collections from his eclectic interests and voluminous correspondence, most notably to the New York Public Library, Fisk University, and Yale University, which holds his James Weldon Johnson Memorial Collection of Negro Arts and Letters.

Van Vechten continued as a participant in the arts and intellectual life of New York City well into his eighties. He was working in his darkroom up to the day before he died, in New York City.

[The New York Public Library has Van Vechten's manuscripts and correspondence pertaining to his books; general correspondence and special collections are at the Yale University Library. His extensive volume on the lore and literature of cats is *The Tiger in the House* (1920); he also edited a collection of cat tales, *Lords of the Housetops* (1921). Bruce Kellner, *Carl Van Vechten and the Irreverent Decades* (1968), is a detailed, authoritative biography; literary biographies with critical comment on his work are Edward Lueders, *Carl Van Vechten* (1965) and *Carl Van Vechten and the Twenties* (1955). See also Peter D. Marchant, "Carl Van Vechten, Novelist and Critic: A Study in the Metropolitan Comedy of Manners," (M.A. diss., Columbia University, 1954). Collections of special interest are Paul Padgette, ed., *The Dance Writings of Carl Van Vechten* (1975); Saul Mauriber, ed., *Portraits: The Photographs of Carl Van Vechten* (1978); and an anthology of his writings on blacks, Bruce Kellner, ed., *Keep A'Inchin' Along* (1979). An obituary appeared in the *New York Times*, Dec. 22, 1964.]

EDWARD LUEDERS

VARÈSE, EDGARD (Dec. 22, 1883–Nov. 6, 1965), composer, was born in Paris, France, the son of Henri Varèse, an engineer and businessman, and of Blanche-Marie Cortot. Varèse described his father as a "kind of Prussian sergeant, the drill-master type," while he remembered his mother as retiring and frightened of her husband.

Varèse was raised by his mother's family at Le Villars in Burgundy. His father, who had studied at the Polytechnic in Zurich, wanted him to follow in his path and enrolled him at the Polytechnic in Turin when he was nine. Angry at his son's interest in music, Henri locked the piano and hid the key. But Varèse attended events at the Turin conservatory and opera house and, at seventeen, secretly visited Giovanni Bolzoni, director of the conservatory, who gave him his first harmony and counterpoint lessons.

In 1903 Varèse returned to Paris and the following year entered the Schola Cantorum, where he studied with Vincent d'Indy, Albert Roussel, and Charles Bordes. In 1905 he entered the Paris Conservatory, then the Conservatoire de Musique et Déclamation, where he studied under Charles Widor. There he met Suzanne Bing, an acting student, whom he married on Nov. 5, 1907. They had one daughter before they were divorced in 1913.

In 1906 Varèse founded and conducted the Choeur de l'Université Populaire. The following year, on the recommendation of Widor and Jules Massenet, he received the "Première Bourse artistique de la ville de Paris." But he soon became restless and depressed, moods that were to plague him for the rest of his life. Almost immediately he and his wife moved to Berlin, but they returned to Paris frequently.

The first public performance of Varèse's work, a symphonic poem entitled *Bourgogne* in memory of his happy days in Burgundy, took place in Berlin in 1910. Later he not only repudiated *Bourgogne* but also destroyed the score in a rage.

In 1913, with the help of the acoustician René Bertrand, Varèse began to search for new musical resources that would lead the way to a pitchless music. In 1915 he came to the United States with only ninety dollars in his pocket but with letters of reference from important European musicians. To become more American, he dropped the final "d" from his first name but restored it around 1940. He secured the assignment of conducting the Berlioz *Requiem* at the Hippodrome in New York in 1917. In 1919 the New Symphony Orchestra was formed by wealthy music lovers for Varèse. Its purpose was to present new works, but the reaction to the programming was so hostile that after the first concert Varèse was replaced. In January 1922 Varèse married Louise McCutcheon Norton.

The first of Varèse's works that satisfied him was *Amériques* (1921). Written in sonata form, it was Berlioz-like in dimensions and characterized by a new preoccupation with sound. With the help of the composer Carlos Salzedo, he founded the International Composers' Guild (ICG), which held its first concert in Greenwich Village in 1921. Varèse's six years with the ICG were the most productive of his life. He conducted works by the most advanced composers of the time and presented his own new pieces: *Offrandes* (1921), *Hyperprism* (1922), *Octandre* (1923), *Intégrales* (1924), and *Arcana* (1925–

755

1927). When the ICG failed, Varèse made his last attempt to establish an orchestra that would attack neoclassicism and promote experimentation. With the help of several important colleagues, he founded the Pan-American Association of Composers (1928), which held sporadic concerts in Europe, South America, and the United States throughout the 1930's. He became a United States citizen in 1927.

In 1928 Varèse moved back to Paris for four years. Before doing so he began to explore the properties of sound with Harvey Fletcher, an acoustician with the Bell Telephone Laboratories. While in Paris he completed *Ionisation* (1931) for thirty-seven percussion instruments of indefinite pitch. *Ecuatorial* (1934) was the first piece in which he used an electronic instrument, the theremin. After *Density 21.5* for solo flute (1936), Varèse completed nothing for more than a decade. In the late 1930's he became obsessed with the idea of committing suicide. He continued to compose but destroyed everything he wrote.

In 1947 Varèse finished *Etude pour espace* for two pianos, percussion, and mixed chorus, with polyglot words and phrases that bore no relation to one another. After World War II, when he received his first tape recorder, Varèse interpolated taped sounds into an orchestral work, *Déserts*, first performed in 1954 in Paris. It was followed by *Poème électronique*, an eight-minute work of electronic sound, produced for the 1958 Brussels World's Fair. His *Nocturnal*, for soprano, choir, and orchestra, was completed in 1961. *Nuit*, for soprano and chamber group, was unfinished. Varèse died in New York City.

In the 1930's Leopold Stokowski was the only prominent conductor to program Varèse's music. By the 1950's, musicians could more easily cope with its difficulties, and composers were beginning to manipulate volume and density of sound in new ways. The use of electronic instruments, a dream Varèse articulated as early as 1917, had become an accepted and established fact.

[Henry Cowell, "The Music of Edgar Varèse" in *American Composers on American Music* (1933); Henry Cowell, "The Music of Edgar Varèse," *Modern Music*, Jan.–Feb. 1928; Chou Wen-Chung, "Varèse: A Sketch of the Man and His Music," *Musical Quarterly*, Apr. 1966; *Perspectives of New Music*, Spring–Summer 1966; Chou Wen-Chung, "Open Rather Than Unbounded," *Perspectives of New Music*, Fall–Winter 1966; Fernand Ouellette, *Edgard Varèse* (1966); Louise Varèse, *A Looking Glass Diary*, I (1972); Joan Peyser, *Twentieth Century*

Music: The Sense Behind the Sound (1980). An obituary is in the *New York Times*, Nov. 7, 1965.]
                                    JOAN PEYSER

VIERECK, GEORGE SYLVESTER (Dec. 31, 1884–March 18, 1962), writer and propagandist, was born in Munich, Germany, the son of Louis Viereck, a Social Democratic politician, and of Laura Viereck, who were first cousins. His ancestry on both sides was solidly German, a significant detail in understanding his life as a self-proclaimed "stormy petrel." His paternal grandmother was Edwina Viereck, a leading German actress, and according to family legend, his paternal grandfather was Kaiser Wilhelm I (although he was never legally acknowledged as such).

In 1896, Louis Viereck immigrated to the United States, and his wife and son followed one year later. Young Viereck graduated in 1906, with a B.A., from the College of the City of New York, where he was class poet. He then began a lifetime of work on newspapers and magazines, serving as a staff member of *Current Literature* (1906–1915). Simultaneously, he was also a staff member (1907) of his father's German-language magazine *Der deutsche Vorkämpfer* ("The German Pioneer") and, after his father returned to Germany, editor (1911) of the monthly *Rundschau zweier Welten* ("Review of Two Worlds"). When that failed, Viereck became editor of *The Fatherland* (1914), whose masthead motto, "Fair Play for Germany and Austria," suggests the political sympathies Viereck revealed in his early editorial positions.

Viereck's first book of poetry was *Gedichte* (1904); his second volume, in English, was *Nineveh and Other Poems* (1907). His poetry was well received, praised by critics Ludwig Lewisohn and James Huneker. In his characteristically arrogant way Viereck proclaimed himself "one of the leaders of the lyric insurgents . . . inheriting the techniques of Poe and the social conscience of Whitman." His early poems were closest to the works of fin de siècle decadents such as Ernest Dowson, although some of his best work was in the tradition of those earnest Victorians who, like Alfred Lord Tennyson, tried to deal clearly and publicly with current ideas in conventional metrical verse.

But poetry could not contain Viereck's need to engage in political journalism and social controversy. More and more of his energy was directed into these areas, and he especially enjoyed traveling in Europe to report his observations about Continental, particularly German, culture. *Confessions of a Barbarian,* published serially in Reedy's weekly the *Mirror* and collected into a book in 1910, was a witty, shrewd, snobbish report of his jaunts through Germany, comparing its rich and complex civilization with that of provincial America.

After the outbreak of World War I, Viereck functioned increasingly as an apologist for German policies. He claimed his sense of right and his dual loyalties to Germany and America compelled him to defend the land of his birth against the attacks of a hostile and misinformed American press. Perhaps he was driven, too, by a desire to be a spokesman whose voice carried the authority he felt his intelligence and historical acumen should have guaranteed him. Although his wish to keep America out of war and his skepticism toward British propaganda claims were understandable, his comparatively uncritical attitude toward German actions seems less objective.

On Aug. 15, 1915, the *New York World* published information leaked to it by the Treasury Department concerning secret German propaganda efforts in the United States. The story featured a picture of Viereck and correspondence between him and Dr. Heinrich Albert, the former German minister of the interior, who was in America to spend money to aid the German war effort. The evidence in the exposé was circumstantial and subject to varying interpretations, but apparently Viereck had received subsidies from Albert. The government interrogated Viereck in 1918, but did not prosecute him. The public did: a newspaper editor called him a "venom-bloated toad of treason"; a Texas zany periodically sent him checks for a million dollars signed "Wilhelm Hohenzollern"; and in 1918 he was asked to leave the Poetry Society of America (Conrad Aiken, among others, decried this unpoetic request).

Viereck married Margaret Edith Hein on Sept. 30, 1915; they had two sons. After the war he continued his career as a controversial journalist—for example, he opposed the League of Nations because it included neither Germany nor Russia. He also shuttled between Europe and New York City. His interviews with famous figures of the war and the 1920's, some of which were written while he was on assignment for the Hearst papers (1922–1927), are excellent journalistic profiles, partly because of Viereck's intrusive but amusing personality (readers must have wondered sometimes who was interviewing whom) and partly because he was fascinated by, and informed about, the people he interviewed and the ideas that shaped history. He had close relationships with some of them—for instance, his "cousin" the former Kaiser Wilhelm II, George Bernard Shaw, and Sigmund Freud (Viereck became one of Freud's chief popularizers in America during the 1920's). His 1923 interview with Adolf Hitler showed that he possessed a sharp eye for history in the making.

During the early 1930's Viereck met Nazi leaders a number of times. To his son Peter, the strongly antifascist author of *Metapolitics* and other works, he referred to this period as his "Nazi interlude." He willingly defended the Hitler regime and was either drawn or propelled himself into a network of relationships that led to his arrest on Oct. 8, 1941, on a charge of violating the Foreign Agents Registration Act. After a series of trials, convictions, appeals, and reversals he was finally sentenced on July 31, 1943, to one to five years in prison. During his jail term his son George died at Anzio fighting Germans.

Viereck's behavior that led to his arrest and indictment, his relationship to a foreign power with which his country was technically not at war, and the government's prosecution of his case are complicated matters. Viereck was clearly sympathetic to both Nazi Germany and Hitler, especially in the 1930's, but never totally nor uncritically. He was opposed to Nazi anti-Semitism but accepted the official burning of his witty, erotic *My First Two Thousand Years: The Autobiography of the Wandering Jew* (1928), coauthored by Paul Eldridge, by the Nazis in 1933. He also justified the German invasion of Poland as a "drastic countermeasure" triggered by anti-German atrocities. While some of the charges against him seem now extreme—for example, the indictment that he conspired "to undermine the morale of the armed forces"—he was part of Germany's prewar propaganda apparatus and engaged in covert activities of dubious ethical propriety in order to influence American opinion positively toward Nazi Germany. He was a dupe, but not a traitor.

In prison Viereck kept a journal and wrote poetry; the warden at the federal penitentiary in Atlanta could not understand his predilection for sonnets. Released in May 1947, he tried to make money by writing fiction, since the popular journals seemed closed to him. He wrote two novels and an excellent memoir, *Men into Beasts* (1952), which dealt humorously, frankly, and sensitively with his prison years. His later poetry was as technically and politically out of tune with the times as he was in general disfavor; he even had to pay for publishing *The Bank-*

rupt (1955), an elegy lamenting America's use of the atomic bomb and the bankruptcy of Christianity and Western civilization. He spent his final years in South Hadley, Mass., with his son Peter, but remained separated from his wife, from whom he had become estranged during his prison term. He died at Holyoke, Mass.

As a person, Viereck was egotistical, committed, and intense, qualities he carried over to his writing. He graced every form he touched with imaginative flashes, though he achieved greatness in no one of his works, which were generally clever, well crafted, and intellectually stimulating, while lacking aesthetic or philosophic resonance. When not misled into political folly, he was a shrewd, if not deep, thinker.

Viereck's pro-Nazi activities wrecked his reputation and undercut his family life. It is unfortunate that they have dominated accounts of his work, for he was a substantial man of letters. He seems sadly destined to enter history wrapped in the shroud of his disgrace.

[The most important manuscript holdings relating to Viereck are the (Elmer) Gertz manuscripts in the Library of Congress, Manuscripts Division; the Viereck manuscripts in the special collections department of the State University of Iowa Library; Viereck's letters from Kaiser Wilhelm II, in the Harvard University Library; an unpublished autobiography in the personal files of Peter Viereck; and the George S. Viereck papers in the Edward M. House Collection, Yale University Library. Materials relating to Viereck's trial are in the archives of the Federal District Court, Washington, D.C., Criminal Case nos. 68584 and 71674. Viereck's books not mentioned in the text include *The House of the Vampire* (1907); *The Candle and the Flame* (1912); [Theodore] *Roosevelt, a Study in Ambivalence* (1920); *Spreading Germs of Hate* (1930); *My Flesh and Blood* (1931), an autobiography; *The Kaiser on Trial* (1937); and *The Nude in the Mirror* (1953). There is no definitive biography of Viereck, nor any full study of his works, but see Niel M. Johnson, *George Sylvester Viereck, German-American Propagandist* (1972); and Elmer Gertz, *Odyssey of a Barbarian* (1978). An obituary is in the *New York Times*, Mar. 20, 1962.]

JACK B. MOORE

VON KÁRMÁN, THEODORE. See KÁRMÁN, THEODORE (TODOR) VON.

VON WIEGAND, KARL HENRY (Sept. 11, 1874–June 7, 1961), foreign correspondent, was born in Hesse, Germany, into a family of farmers who immigrated to Iowa when he was one year old. He ran away from home at fifteen. He lived briefly in California, where he married Inez Royce; they had four children. Von Wie-

gand began his journalistic career in 1899, while a telegraph operator in Ash Fork, Ariz., working as a local stringer for California newspapers. He soon moved to Los Angeles and then to San Francisco, where he was a reporter for the *San Francisco Examiner*. He went to work for the Associated Press in time to cover the 1906 earthquake. In 1911, Roy Howard hired him away and sent him to Berlin for United Press. Except for brief visits, he never lived in the United States again.

The Turkish-Italian war of 1911 was the first of the twelve wars von Wiegand covered, but it was World War I that made his by-line famous. He managed to reach the scene of the fighting swiftly, and by the end of 1914 had filed dispatches from both the eastern and western fronts. Von Wiegand's journalistic strengths stemmed both from his breathless, smell-of-battle style—"As I write this in the glare of a screened automobile headlight several hundred yards behind the German trenches"—and his extraordinary German connections. On Nov. 20, 1914, he was granted an exclusive interview with Crown Prince Friedrich Wilhelm, a feat that helped United Press gain 103 new clients in one year. For the rest of his life, von Wiegand regaled friends with a quote from the prince that he had not used in the story: "My dear Wiegand, you must tell Papa that we have lost the war. Every time I attempt to tell him, he gets furious at me."

Von Wiegand moved to the Pulitzers' *New York World* in 1915. The next year he broke the story of the German decision to wage unrestricted submarine warfare, and the German ambassador to the United States warned the Foreign Office that William Randolph Hearst "was rather hurt that on Wiegand's account the *World* gets all the important interviews." Such connections, and the resulting stories, fueled rumors that von Wiegand was a German propagandist, although he himself complained bitterly of German censorship. In 1917, when the *World* (whose editorial stance was staunchly anti-German) sent Herbert Bayard Swope to Berlin to balance von Wiegand, the affronted correspondent helped soothe Hearst's feelings by quitting the *World* and going to work for him.

Over the next twenty years, von Wiegand was Hearst's "news generalissimo" on the Continent, acquiring the title chief foreign correspondent of the Hearst newspapers. In the 1920's he flew 1,000 miles, sitting on mail sacks in an open cockpit, to cover the Riff War in Morocco, and reported on civil war in China and rebellion in Syria. On behalf of Hearst, he organized and reported the first round-the-world zeppelin flight in 1929. The trip both reflected and cemented the closeness of his ties with his employer; when the zeppelin reached Los Angeles, Hearst's mistress, Marion Davies, took von Wiegand to her beach house for a few hours' rest. Early in his prominence, he had separated from his wife. He was accompanied on the zeppelin flight by Lady Grace Drummond-Hay, a British correspondent with whom he lived until her death in 1946.

During the 1930's von Wiegand covered wars in China, Ethiopia, and Spain, but he realized that the biggest news was breaking in Berlin. He had first met Adolf Hitler in 1921, and his strong news connections with high Nazis again created rumors about undue friendliness toward his subjects. But both his correspondence and his dispatches reflect a disgust with Nazi attitudes toward Jews. Warning of disaster, he urged the creation of a homeland for German and Austrian Jews in Africa.

Late in 1934, Hearst, adopting a friendlier posture toward Hitler, ordered von Wiegand to move his base to Paris, and placed his dispatches under his personal censorship. Von Wiegand soon returned to Berlin, though, and maintained his news connections—he was one of two reporters inside the Führerhaus when the Munich pact was signed.

After covering the German invasion of France, von Wiegand went to the Orient, expecting the expansion of the war there. At the age of sixty-seven, he stood so close to the Japanese bombs falling on Manila that his eyesight was damaged, and he was virtually blind when he and Drummond-Hay were captured by the Japanese occupying forces. After two weeks in Santo Tomas concentration camp, they were released for medical reasons, and his vision was partially restored by surgery in Shanghai. They returned to the United States in 1943, and by 1944 had gone to Europe to report from Spain.

In 1945, von Wiegand began sounding loudly the anti-Communist views that he and Hearst had long agreed upon, warning: "The war has loosed upon Europe the most powerful imperialistic force since Napoleon—totalitarian, Communist Russia." A Hearst editor later conceded that von Wiegand was "a shade to the right of William McKinley," and von Wiegand's praises of Spain's Francisco Franco and Egypt's Gamal Abdel Nasser eventually embarrassed the home office, which took his dispatches off the wire and air-mailed them to the remaining Hearst newspapers. Nevertheless, he retained the title of

chief foreign correspondent of the Hearst papers, and continued to roam the world until his death in Zurich, Switzerland.

For twenty years, until he was upstaged by the Shirers and the Murrows, von Wiegand was probably the best-known American reporting from Europe, yet he has rapidly been forgotten. One reason is that he never wrote a book; despite numerous publishers' inquiries about his memoirs, he was always interrupted by a war somewhere. Another was probably that he worked for William Randolph Hearst. This made him subject to "the Chief's" impulses, and it shaped his reporting. Von Wiegand "always sees news in terms of scare headlines on pink- or peach-tinted newsprint," observed a journalist in 1933. His reputation has proved to be as evanescent as the headlines.

[Von Wiegand's papers are divided between his daughter, Charmion von Wiegand of New York City, and the Hoover Institute at Stanford University. An interesting sample of his writing, including some autobiography, is "The Sky's the Limit," in Eugene Lyons, ed., *We Cover the World* (1937). A brief contemporary evaluation is in James E. Abbe, "Men of Cablese," *New Outlook*, Dec. 1933. References to von Wiegand appear in memoirs and biographies of fellow journalists such as Bob Considine, *It's All News to Me* (1967); William L. Shirer, *Berlin Diary* (1941); Paul C. Smith, *Personal File* (1964); Herbert L. Matthews, *A World in Revolution* (1971); and E. J. Kahn, Jr., *The World of Swope* (1965). Obituaries are in the *New York Times*, June 8, 1961, and *Time*, June 16, 1961.]

DAVID SARASOHN

WALLACE, HENRY AGARD (Oct. 7, 1888–Nov. 18, 1965), agricultural scientist, editor, cabinet official, vice-president, and presidential candidate, was born on a farm near Orient, Iowa, the son of Henry Cantwell Wallace and Carrie May Brodhead. Both his father and his grandfather, also named Henry Wallace and widely and affectionately known as "Uncle Henry," achieved prominence as agricultural leaders. The family-owned newspaper, *Wallaces' Farmer*, became one of the most influential and prosperous journals in the Midwest soon after it began publication in 1895.

Wallace revered his grandfather, who instilled in him the values and convictions he preached as editor of *Wallaces' Farmer*: the superior virtue of agricultural civilization, the fundamental wisdom of Christian morality as a guide for daily living, the inherent good sense and dignity of common folk, and the need for cooperation and understanding among all peoples.

759

Even as a youngster, Wallace displayed a keen, inquisitive, and serious intellect. At Iowa State College he excelled in subjects relating to agriculture and genetics. He received a B.S. degree in animal husbandry in 1910 and then considered attending graduate school, but decided to study and work independently instead. His first significant achievement was the derivation of statistical correlations to determine a fair price level for farmers raising hogs. He also experimented with various strains of corn and produced the first hybrid corn suitable for commercial use. Later, in 1926, Wallace established the Hi-Bred Corn Company, which pioneered an important new industry and in time provided him with substantial financial returns.

Wallace married Ilo Browne on May 20, 1914; they had three children. He farmed a modest plot of land near Des Moines and did writing and editing for *Wallaces' Farmer*. After "Uncle Henry's" death in 1916, he worked for his father as associate editor of the newspaper. He assumed the editorship in March 1921, when his father became Warren G. Harding's secretary of agriculture.

Midwestern farmers suffered hard times during the 1920's, and Wallace devoted his attention to seeking solutions for their most obvious problem: overproduction. As Wallace had predicted, the end of the war in Europe decreased demand and deflated prices for farm products. Declining foreign markets and a growing surplus of goods triggered a serious depression for American agriculture. Wallace advised farmers to curtail output, suggesting that they treat Europe as if it "were located on another planet" and adjust production to meet domestic needs only.

This appeal for economic self-containment failed to win support, however, and in 1923, Wallace began to advocate an export "dumping" plan that was introduced in Congress as the McNary-Haugen bill. He campaigned vigorously for the bill and was outraged when President Calvin Coolidge vetoed it twice. He was so angry that he abandoned his family's traditional Republicanism and supported Democrat Al Smith in the presidential election of 1928. By 1930 Wallace had decided that the best way to reduce the agricultural surplus was to lower tariff barriers and increase the volume of world trade. He also backed a measure known as the voluntary domestic allotment plan, under which farmers would receive government payments for agreeing to restrict their production.

By that time, the Great Depression had begun, and the condition of farmers had deteri-

orated so seriously that Wallace feared that they might rise up in revolt. He believed that America's failure to assume responsible world leadership during the 1920's and its "selfish ignorance" in tariff and war-debt policies had led to the economic collapse that was engulfing the world. Wallace had little confidence in President Herbert C. Hoover's ability to deal effectively with the depression, and after meeting Franklin D. Roosevelt in August 1932, he became his active backer. Wallace's support in the campaign and his prominence in agriculture led Roosevelt to appoint him secretary of agriculture.

As secretary of agriculture, Wallace concentrated on drafting and securing congressional approval of legislation to assist farmers. On May 12, 1933, Congress passed the Agricultural Adjustment Act, an omnibus measure that gave the secretary of agriculture broad authority to meet the emergency. Wallace moved promptly to shrink the farm surplus by implementing the voluntary domestic allotment plan. For the first time in the nation's history, farmers were eligible to receive support payments for decreasing their output.

The situation was so desperate that Wallace decided to take drastic action where the glut was most serious. Cotton and hog farmers faced dire prospects unless their surpluses were reduced immediately. In the summer of 1933, he authorized paying these farmers for plowing up 10 million acres of growing cotton and for slaughtering 6 million pigs. The spectacle of destroying farm commodities while large numbers of people lacked adequate food and clothing raised a public outcry. Wallace defended the policy as an emergency program made necessary "by almost insane lack of world statesmanship during the period from 1920 to 1932." The Department of Agriculture carried out such draconian measures for reducing output only once, and in later years the domestic allotment plan proceeded in a more orderly fashion.

Systematic production control and acreage reduction, Wallace believed, were only partial solutions to the farm problem. He recommended a "planned middle course" in domestic and international policies. Besides curtailing output, Wallace promoted efforts to find markets abroad for American farm goods, and staunchly supported Secretary of State Cordell Hull's advocacy of reciprocal trade agreements to lower trade barriers and increase world commerce. Wallace maintained that the removal of trade restrictions would greatly benefit farmers, and he never hesitated to complain to the State Department when its negotiations failed to give adequate consideration to agricultural needs.

Wallace believed that the Great Depression was a spiritual as well as an economic crisis. His religious views profoundly influenced his opinions about the causes of the depression and what was necessary to end it. His quest for eternal verities led him far beyond the bounds of conventional organized religion. Wallace dabbled in various unorthodox liturgies and doctrines, and his thinking displayed a prominent strain of mystical idealism. His perceptions of Divinity were more intuitive than cogitative; he believed in the reality of revealed truth through mystical experiences.

Wallace defined religion as "the force which governs the attitude of men in their inmost hearts toward God and toward their fellowmen." He believed that the economic crisis could be overcome only if Americans readjusted their attitudes by subordinating their selfish interests to the general welfare. The trials of the depression provided the opportunity for a spiritual reformation. If selfishness and greed gave way to a commitment to cooperation and social justice, the potential for economic, cultural, and spiritual fulfillment would be limitless.

Wallace maintained that the American people should adhere to the "higher law of cooperation" and recognize that they lived in a spiritually unified world. He urged them to reject "pagan nationalism" and acknowledge the universal brotherhood of man. He never lost hope that a new era of cooperation at home and abroad could be established.

Wallace's efforts to inspire a spiritual reformation inevitably proved futile, but the policies he inaugurated as secretary of agriculture were more successful. Support payments for crop control, soil conservation, food stamp distribution, assistance for tenant farmers, and government-operated warehouses for storing surpluses helped alleviate, though they did not eliminate, the distress of American farmers during the Great Depression. Those programs aroused bitter protests from opponents of government planning and massive intervention in the economy, but they provided the basis for dealing with agricultural problems for decades to come.

In 1940, Roosevelt selected Wallace as his running mate in the upcoming presidential election. Although Wallace was not an intimate adviser, Roosevelt respected his judgment and ability, and hoped that his prominence in the Midwest would help compensate for opposition there to the administration's foreign policies.

But Wallace was not a popular choice with Democratic politicians; the convention nominated him only after an acrimonious floor battle.

Roosevelt's third-term victory in 1940 placed Wallace in elective office for the first and only time in his career. He was an active and highly visible vice-president. Roosevelt sent him on goodwill tours to Mexico in December 1940 and to seven other Latin American nations in 1943. In 1944 he undertook a mission to Soviet Asia, where he was impressed with signs of economic progress, and to China, where he was appalled by Chiang Kai-shek's weakness and unwillingness to make necessary political and economic reforms.

For a time Wallace served as chairman of the Board of Economic Warfare, established shortly before American entry into World War II to initiate and coordinate economic defense programs. Its activities overlapped those of the State and Commerce departments, and quickly enmeshed Wallace in bureaucratic disputes. His differences with Secretary of Commerce Jesse H. Jones over policies and priorities in obtaining strategic materials became so divisive that, in July 1943, Roosevelt reprimanded both men and abolished the Board of Economic Warfare.

Wallace's appeals for responsible American leadership to foster lasting peace and global prosperity in the postwar world commanded wide attention. In speeches and public statements, he urged Americans to help usher in a "century of the common man." Recognizing the forces of change that the war had unleashed, he argued that the United States should provide economic and technical assistance to improve living standards, encourage education, and promote industrialization in underdeveloped areas of the world. Unless hunger, poverty, and ignorance were eradicated, he maintained, the world would continue to suffer upheaval, revolution, and war.

Wallace's vision reflected his belief in the economic and spiritual unity of the world. Modern technology provided ample resources, and the fruits of abundance could be widely distributed through international economic cooperation. The war made a spiritual reformation more essential than ever; a return to world competition, exploitation, and imperialism would generate a new round of depression and war. The century of the common man, Wallace reasoned, required the establishment of a strong, effective world organization and harmonious relations between the United States and the Soviet Union. He insisted that postwar cooperation between the two powers was both possible and necessary to ensure lasting peace.

His pronouncements about postwar policies made Wallace the leading spokesman for liberal opinion in the United States and a target for conservatives. His critics derided his views as "globaloney" and as proof that he was one of the "Post War Dream Boys" who wanted to provide "a quart of milk to every Hottentot." Wallace struck back at his opponents with equal rancor, denouncing them as "American fascists." He feared that selfish interests would lead the United States back to isolationism, incite tensions with the Soviet Union, and destroy his hopes for the postwar world.

Wallace did little to win the support of the elements in the Democratic party that had objected to his vice-presidential nomination in 1940. As the 1944 election approached, these party regulars urged Roosevelt to select another running mate. The president wavered; he assured Wallace that he was his personal choice for vice-president, but also told others that he would be happy to have either Supreme Court Justice William O. Douglas or Senator Harry S. Truman on the ticket.

Roosevelt's tepid endorsement doomed Wallace's chances for renomination, and the Democratic National Convention selected Truman for vice-president.

Wallace was stunned and angered by Roosevelt's behavior, but he campaigned vigorously for the Democratic ticket. He believed that Roosevelt's reelection provided the best hope for implementing his own vision of the postwar world. The president rewarded Wallace's loyalty by naming him secretary of commerce after the election.

Wallace undertook his new duties with customary zeal. He initiated a reorganization of the Commerce Department aimed at giving more assistance to small business. He called for extension of the 1934 Trade Agreements Act as one essential way to promote international economic cooperation and world peace. He remained committed to a "planned middle course" by supporting federal programs to provide full employment and higher standards of living in the United States.

Wallace focused his efforts on the growing tensions between the United States and the Soviet Union. After Roosevelt's death he was deeply concerned that President Truman would repudiate Roosevelt's legacy of conciliation toward Russia. Wallace insisted that the Soviets' suspicion of the West could be dispelled if the United States worked to win their trust. The key

to world peace and stability, he believed, was to achieve international control of atomic weapons. He urged Truman to offer to share with Russia and other nations basic scientific information about atomic energy, though not the technical secrets needed to build atomic bombs.

Throughout the winter of 1945 and spring of 1946, United States–Soviet relations steadily deteriorated. Truman and most Americans became committed to a firm posture toward Russia. Wallace worried about Truman's growing toughness, but still thought the president could be persuaded to take a more accommodating stance. He became increasingly outspoken in calling for American policies to ease tensions with Russia, including economic assistance as well as international control of atomic energy. His efforts culminated, in July 1946, in a twelve-page letter urging President Truman to recognize legitimate Soviet security needs. But Truman believed that firmness toward Russia was the only way to preserve peace and was unmoved by Wallace's arguments. When the commerce secretary aired his views in a speech on Sept. 12, 1946, it created a public uproar and prompted Truman to dismiss him from the cabinet.

Wallace then vowed to "carry on the fight for peace." As editor of the *New Republic,* a position he accepted in October 1946, he sharply criticized Truman's foreign policies. The enunciation of the Truman Doctrine particularly distressed him. Wallace denounced it on the grounds that it undercut the United Nations, unnecessarily antagonized the Soviet Union, and gave military assistance to a corrupt, undemocratic regime in Greece. He accused Truman of "whipping up anti-Communist hysteria" in a futile effort to combat Communism by military means. Wallace insisted that Communism could best be halted by providing economic and technical assistance to raise living standards in underdeveloped and war-torn nations. Initially he guardedly approved the Marshall Plan, but later strongly opposed it because he thought it simply an extension of the Truman Doctrine.

By late 1947, Wallace's views had alienated him from the overwhelming majority of Americans, including most liberals. But he persisted in his lonely dissent. Despite all indications to the contrary, he maintained that the American people, given the opportunity, would rally behind his point of view.

Convinced that there was no significant difference between the existing parties on the vital issues of the day, Wallace announced his independent candidacy for president on Dec. 29, 1947. Not only would his effort help arrest the drift toward war abroad and fascism at home, he believed, but it would also provide the basis for a major new political party. When Wallace began his campaign, he appeared likely to attract enough support to present a serious threat to Truman's chances for reelection in 1948. But he and his Progressive party were soon discredited. The American Communist party endorsed Wallace, and its support alienated many voters. Government officials, the nation's press, and many liberals attacked Wallace as a dupe of Communist machinations. His appeals for Soviet-American understanding were further undermined by the Communist takeover in Czechoslovakia in February 1948 and the Soviet blockade of Berlin in June.

Wallace's shrill rhetoric and dogmatic positions also hurt his cause. His frequent warnings about the dangers of American fascism seemed implausible to Americans growing increasingly alarmed about subversion from the left, not from the right. On election day 1948, Wallace made a dismal showing. He collected only a little more than 2 percent of the total vote.

Wallace retreated to his farm in South Salem, N.Y., after the election. When the Korean War broke out in June 1950, he announced his support for American and United Nations actions to halt the North Korean attack. He did not repudiate his earlier opposition to American cold war policies, however, and maintained that the Korean crisis might never have occurred had his advice been followed. In his last years Wallace returned to pursuits that had fascinated him years before, studying and experimenting in plant genetics. He died in relative obscurity at Danbury, Conn.

[The most important collection of Wallace's personal papers, at the University of Iowa, includes a rich abundance of correspondence and speeches and the original of his diary. Much of the best material in the diary is published in John Morton Blum, ed., *The Price of Vision* (1973). The Library of Congress and the Franklin D. Roosevelt Library house many of Wallace's vice-presidential papers. All three collections are available on microfilm. The National Archives maintains many records, especially for the periods when he was secretary of agriculture and secretary of commerce. A memoir is in the Oral History Collection at Columbia University; a copy is at the University of Iowa.

Wallace's books include *Agricultural Prices* (1920); *New Frontiers* (1934); *America Must Choose* (1934); *Statesmanship and Religion* (1934); *Technology, Corporations, and the General Welfare* (1937); *The Century of the Common Man* (1943); *Democ-*

racy Reborn (1944); *Sixty Million Jobs* (1945); and *Toward World Peace* (1948). Also see Russell Lord, *The Wallaces of Iowa* (1947); Edward L. and Frederick H. Schapsmeier, *Henry A. Wallace of Iowa* (1968) and *Prophet in Politics* (1970); Norman D. Markowitz, *The Rise and Fall of the People's Century* (1973); J. Samuel Walker, *Henry A. Wallace and American Foreign Policy* (1976); and Richard J. Walton, *Henry Wallace, Harry Truman and the Cold War* (1976). On Wallace and the 1948 election, see Karl M. Schmidt, *Henry A. Wallace: Quixotic Crusade, 1948* (1960); Curtis D. MacDougall, *Gideon's Army*, 3 vols. (1965); and Allen Yarnell, *Democrats and Progressives* (1974). An obituary is in the *New York Times*, Nov. 19, 1965.]

J. SAMUEL WALKER

WALLGREN, MON[RAD] C[HARLES] (Apr. 17, 1891–Sept. 18, 1961), U.S. representative and senator, and governor of the state of Washington, was born in Des Moines, Iowa, the son of Oscar Swan Wallgren, a Swedish-born jeweler and watch repairman, and of Carrie Helgeson. In 1894 the family moved to Galveston, Tex., and finally settled in Everett, Wash., in September 1900. Wallgren attended public schools and graduated from high school in Everett in 1909. After studying briefly at Everett Business College, he worked in a hotel in Grays Harbor County before returning to Everett to enter his father's business. He then enrolled at the Washington State School of Optometry in Spokane, graduating in 1914. Thereafter he combined practice as an optometrist with work in the family enterprise. He married Mabel C. Liberty on Sept. 8, 1910; they had no children.

During World War I, Wallgren enlisted as a private in the Coast Artillery. Rising to the rank of second lieutenant, he saw duty at Puget Sound artillery posts. Following his discharge in March 1919, he rejoined the family firm and spent the next thirteen years participating in civic affairs. He also won the National Amateur Balk-Line Billiards Championship in 1929 and later captured the Pacific Northwest 18.2 Balk-Line Championship. The celebrity gained in these events later aided him in his political career.

In 1932, Wallgren ran as a Democrat for the Second Congressional District seat in the House of Representatives. He defeated Linn Hadley, the Republican incumbent, by 18,000 votes. His triumph, unprecedented for the Democrats in that district, was attributed to the popularity of Franklin D. Roosevelt at the head of the Democratic ticket, as well as to Wallgren's appeal and the unpopularity of the Republicans during the Great Depression.

During eight years in the House, Wallgren was a soft-spoken New Dealer and a staunch advocate of public power. His greatest legislative achievement came in 1938, when his bill to create the Olympic National Park in Washington became law after he had thwarted attempts of the lumber interests to defeat the bill. He had interested President Roosevelt in the proposed park, and the latter assisted in the legislative victory.

In September 1940, Wallgren won nomination for the U.S. Senate and in November defeated the Republican candidate, Stephen Chadwick. His tenure began prematurely when, on December 18, he was appointed to fill out the remaining weeks of the term of Lewis B. Schwellenbach, who had resigned to become a federal judge. Wallgren's most impressive work in the Senate began in March 1941, when he joined Senator Harry Truman's special committee investigating national defense contracts. He accompanied Truman on investigative trips and personally uncovered defects in aircraft engines and in Liberty ships. He and Truman became fast friends.

Wallgren resigned his Senate seat in 1944 to run for the governorship of Washington. Although he defeated Arthur B. Langlie, the Republican incumbent, by only 22,000 votes, he proceeded to reverse the conservative policies of his predecessor. Progressive legislation and policies were enacted and adopted during his administration: modernization of the public school system, initiation of a highway safety program that drastically reduced the accident rate, passage of a forest act to check exploitative practices, creation of a model flood disaster plan, and institution of a soil conservation program. Wallgren also signed the nation's most liberal unemployment compensation law, which provided $25 a week for twenty-six weeks to those out of work. In the spring of 1947 he headed a group of western governors who forestalled efforts in Congress to drastically reduce funds for western reclamation and power projects.

In 1948, Langlie defeated Wallgren in his bid for reelection as governor. His political career seemed at an end, but President Truman nominated him to be chairman of the National Security Resources Board. When the Senate Armed Forces Committee refused to recommend confirmation because of Wallgren's lack of experience, Truman reluctantly yielded, only to recommend his friend as chairman of the Federal Power Commission, a post that Wallgren held during 1950 and 1951.

Subsequently, Wallgren and his wife spent their winters in Palm Desert, Calif., where they owned a citrus ranch. Summers were spent in Everett and Olympia, Wash. Wallgren was severely injured in an automobile accident on July 8, 1961, and was confined to a hospital in Olympia, where he died two months later.

[Wallgren's congressional papers are in the Harry S. Truman Library, Independence, Mo., and his gubernatorial papers are in the Washington State Archives, Olympia. On his political career, see Richard L. Neuberger, "Hail Fellow Well Met," *Nation*, Mar. 12, 1949; Willard Shelton, "Presidential Appointment," *Nation*, Feb. 16, 1952; and John Osborne, "Natural Gas and the Authoritarian Liberals," *Fortune*, May 1952. Obituaries are in the *New York Times*, *Daily Olympian*, and *Seattle Post-Intelligencer*, Sept. 19, 1961; also see Ross Cunningham, *Seattle Times*, Sept. 20, 1961.]

GEORGE A. FRYKMAN

WALTER, BRUNO (Sept. 15, 1876–Feb. 17, 1962), symphonic and operatic conductor, was born Bruno Schlesinger in Berlin, Germany, the son of Joseph Schlesinger, bookkeeper for a silk firm, and of Johanna Fernbach.

Schlesinger—he changed his name to Walter around 1897 for professional reasons—attended public schools until the age of fifteen, but from early childhood his principal interest and talent was music. At age six he began piano lessons with his mother, and three years later he enrolled at the Stern Conservatory of Music to pursue advanced study under Alfred Heinrich Ehrlich.

By the age of thirteen, Walter had perfected his piano skills to the point that a concert career seemed imminent. But in 1890 a concert directed by Hans von Bülow so inspired him that he decided to prepare for a conducting career. After three years of intensive study with Robert Radeke, he was engaged by the Cologne Municipal Theater as accompanist-coach for the 1893–1894 opera season. On Mar. 13, 1894, he conducted his first opera, Albert Lortzing's *Der Waffenschmied*.

During the following two seasons Walter assisted Gustav Mahler at the Hamburg Opera. After a year as assistant conductor at the Breslau (now Wrocław, Poland) State Theater, he spent the 1897–1898 season as principal conductor at the Pressburg (now Bratislava, Czechoslovakia) State Theater. From 1898 to 1900, Walter was principal conductor of the Riga State Theater. There he conducted several Mozart and Wagner operas, performed in a number of piano-violin recitals, and led symphonic concerts for the first time.

In 1900, Walter signed a five-year contract as royal Prussian conductor at the Berlin Opera. On May 2, 1901, he married Elsa Wirthschaft, an operatic soprano whose stage name was Korneck, whom he had met at Riga. They had three daughters. Although enjoying his association with Karl Muck and Richard Strauss, Walter chafed at the bureaucratic management of the Berlin Opera. He obtained his release in 1901 in order to become conductor of the Vienna Imperial Opera under Gustav Mahler.

Walter worked closely with Mahler for the next six seasons, and the relationship left an indelible mark upon him. When Mahler departed for America in 1907, Walter remained, under Felix Weingartner and Hans Gregor, until the fall of 1912. During this time he directed Vienna Singakademie programs in 1911 and 1912 and a number of Vienna Philharmonic concerts, in addition to appearing as guest conductor in London, Rome, and Moscow.

On Jan. 1, 1913, Walter became Bavarian general music director and artistic head of the Munich Opera. During the next ten years he conducted both opera and symphony concerts, meanwhile furthering his understanding of Mozart and his music. He resigned this dual position in the fall of 1922, and spent the next three years conducting in Europe and the United States. His American debut occurred on Feb. 15, 1923, with the New York Symphony Orchestra.

During the summer of 1925, Walter made the first of more than a dozen appearances at the Salzburg Music Festival. That fall he became general musical director of the Berlin Municipal (Charlottenburg) Opera. He resigned the post four years later because of repertory and budgetary disagreements.

In late 1929, Walter was installed as director of the Leipzig Gewandhaus Orchestra. This association ended in March 1933, when anti-Semitic municipal authorities forbade him to conduct, on the ground that he threatened "public order and security." Shortly thereafter, Walter was replaced as conductor of a Berlin Philharmonic concert because the Nazi Propaganda Ministry declared him "politically suspicious."

Walter immediately established residence in Austria. During the next three years he conducted extensively in western Europe, Italy, and especially in America, where he directed a substantial number of New York Philharmonic concerts.

In 1936, Walter became principal conductor and artistic adviser of the Vienna State Opera, in which capacity he served until Germany annexed Austria in March 1938. He then settled in Switzerland, where he helped found the Lucerne Festival prior to accepting French citizenship in the fall of 1938. He continued his musical activities in Europe until 1939, when he migrated to the United States.

During the war Walter was guest conductor for the Minneapolis Symphony, the Philadelphia Orchestra, the Hollywood Bowl Orchestra, but mainly for the New York Philharmonic Orchestra; cut his first American recordings; and made his Metropolitan Opera debut on Feb. 14, 1941, directing Beethoven's *Fidelio.* During his ten-season association with the Met Walter conducted 108 performances (thirty-six were of *The Magic Flute*).

After the war Walter frequently visited Europe to conduct, principally in London and Vienna and at the Edinburgh and Salzburg festivals. In America he devoted the bulk of his energy to the New York Philharmonic, for which he was musical adviser and principal conductor from 1947 to 1949. He became an American citizen in 1946.

At the age of eighty, Walter curtailed his concert appearances to record, primarily for Columbia. He was world-renowned for his interpretations of Mozart, Beethoven, Brahms, and especially of Anton Bruckner and Mahler, whose music he constantly championed. Walter shunned dissonance and atonality, which, he said, threatened to "cause the decay of music." He worked assiduously to bring out the "beauty of lyrical feeling" in compositions. Above all, he strove to perform music according to the composer's will, not the conductor's.

Walter excelled in opera. His long apprenticeship in Germany, augmented by years of close association with Mahler, had given him both a full understanding of the human voice and vital experience in the many aspects of dramatic production. He developed an "eye for the musical stage" and was, Lotte Lehmann wrote, "both conductor and stage director at once." Equally important, he realized the orchestra's role was secondary to that of the singers and conducted accordingly.

Modest and introspective, Walter treated his musicians as his equals and viewed his role as that of an educator, not a despot. "The conductor's relation to the orchestra," he stated, "must be tolerant benevolence." Walter died in Beverly Hills, Calif.

[Walter's writings are *Gustav Mahler* (1941); *Theme and Variations* (1946), his autobiography; and *Of Music and Music-Making* (1961). Also of value, but available in German only, are Paul Stefan-Gruenfeldt, *Bruno Walter* (1936); and Lotte Walter Lindt, comp., *Bruno Walter Briefe, 1894–1962* (1969), a collection of letters. There are two recorded conversations with Walter: Columbia BW 80 (1956), in English; and DG 43018 (1958), in German. An obituary is in the *New York Times,* Feb. 18, 1962.]

LOUIS R. THOMAS

WALTER, FRANCIS EUGENE (May 26, 1894–May 31, 1963), U.S. congressman and lawyer, was born in Easton, Pa., the son of Susie E. and Robley D. Walter. He attended Easton schools, and in 1910 entered the Princeton (N.J.) Preparatory School, from which he graduated in 1912. He then spent two years at Lehigh University, two years at George Washington University (B.A.), and three years at Georgetown University Law School (LL.B.). He also served briefly in the Naval Air Force during World War I.

After graduation from Georgetown in 1919, Walter was admitted to the Pennsylvania bar, and returned to Easton to practice. He married May M. Doyle on Dec. 19, 1925; they had two daughters. In 1928 he became Northampton County solicitor and was a delegate to the Democratic National Convention.

Walter won his first of sixteen terms in the U.S. House of Representatives in 1932. During his early years in Congress, he was primarily concerned with local matters, such as obtaining a bridge across the Delaware River near Easton. His first major controversy in Congress was the Logan-Walter bill, requiring judicial review of the regulations issued by New Deal agencies. The bill passed in 1940 but was vetoed by President Franklin D. Roosevelt; the House overrode the veto, but the Senate did not.

Early in 1942, Walter was recalled for six months' active duty in the Navy. In 1947 he was elected chairman of War Veterans in Congress. The previous year he had been coauthor of the McCarran-Walter Act, which required the publication of the rules, regulations, delegations of authority, and other business of federal agencies in the Federal Register. He supported the Marshall Plan for European recovery.

Walter's two specialties throughout the remainder of his congressional service were laws on immigration and investigations of un-American activities. He went to Europe in 1947 as a member of the House Committee on Foreign Aid to investigate European recovery; this led to the House support of the Marshall Plan. In 1949

he returned to inspect the condition of refugees, and in 1950 he sponsored legislation favored by President Harry S. Truman to increase the number of immigrants admitted from European camps for displaced persons. In 1956 he supported efforts to allow additional refugees to enter the United States from Hungary. His best-known role in immigration legislation was the controversial McCarran-Walter Act of 1952. As chairman of the Judiciary Subcommittee on Immigration, Walter backed a law that retained the use of quotas strongly favoring northern European countries and severely limiting the number of immigrants from most others. The number of immigrants allowed under this bill, which was enacted over President Truman's veto, was based on the ratios of foreign-born in the 1920 United States census. President Dwight D. Eisenhower later proposed changing the basis to the 1950 census, but Walter blocked that move. For the last fifteen years of his life, he was in charge of United States immigration laws. Not until two years after his death were the quotas ended.

In 1955, Walter became chairman of the House Un-American Activities Committee, whose purpose was investigation of un-American propaganda and subversion. A staunch anti-Communist, he was not reluctant to issue contempt of Congress citations to witnesses who failed to answer the committee's questions. Walter's search for Communist infiltration covered the fields of entertainment, education, and religion, as well as government. The legality of his actions was usually upheld by the Supreme Court, although the court often criticized the committee's procedures. Walter firmly believed that the Soviet threat after World War II was greater than the Nazi threat had been. He felt that the signs of danger had been ignored before World War II, and was determined not to let that happen again. He even proposed (in a 1949 bill) that American Communists should lose their citizenship.

No congressional committee ever aroused as much debate as the House Un-American Activities Committee. Walter's leadership came at a time when suspicion and fear of the Soviet Union were widespread. He never became a menacing figure like Senator Joseph McCarthy, but he was one of the leading proponents of the theory that there was a dangerous Communist conspiracy within the United States. Unlike McCarthy, he was a member of the congressional establishment. He was skilled in parliamentary maneuvers, and he had considerable influence with his colleagues through his chairmanships of the Immigration and Naturalization Subcommittee (which controlled private immigration bills), the Democratic Caucus, and the Patronage Committee. From these positions of power and respect, Walter was able to withstand attempts to curb the authority of the Un-American Activities Committee or to place it under the Judiciary Committee.

Walter died in Washington, D.C. Although he was often at odds with the Truman and Kennedy administrations on matters of immigration and internal security, he supported the Democratic administrations on economic and social legislation. Because he was most visible in cases involving immigration and un-American activities, he was often perceived as more conservative than he actually was. In general, he was representative of the political establishment of his time.

[Walter's congressional files are in the Lehigh University Library. The records of the House Un-American Activities Committee and the Immigration and Naturalization Subcommittee are in the National Archives. There is no biography of Walter. See Meg Greenfield, "The Melting Pot of Francis E. Walter," *Reporter*, Oct. 26, 1961; and Murray Kempton, "The Lord of the Flies," *New Republic*, June 22, 1963. An obituary is in the *New York Times*, June 1, 1963.]

ALFRED L. MORGAN

WALTON, LESTER AGLAR (Apr. 20, 1882–Oct. 16, 1965), diplomat and journalist, was born in St. Louis, Mo., the son of Benjamin A. Walton, a public school janitor and custodian, and of Ollie May Camphor. After he graduated from the segregated Sumner High School, his father engaged a white tutor to help him pass an examination for a certificate of graduation from a business school. Walton's interest in golf led to his selection as a writer on golf and reporter for the daily *St. Louis Star-Sayings* (1902–1906). Assigned to interview a noted bandmaster at a leading hotel, Walton was directed to use the freight elevator because he was black. He refused and resolutely confronted his editor with the situation. His refusal to yield won him use of the passenger elevator. The experience helped shape his life.

In 1906, Walton left his job and moved to New York City. Attracted to the Negro theater, he first wanted to write plays, but he soon returned to journalism as managing editor of the *New York Age* (1908–1914). On June 29, 1912, he married Gladys Moore; they had two daughters.

Walton wrote drama reviews for the *Age*, which led to his becoming manager of the La-

fayette Theater in Harlem. He was the Lafayette's manager in 1914–1916 and again in 1919–1921, spending the intervening years as managing editor of the *Age*. He took a leave of absence in 1918 to join the party, led by R. R. Moton, that President Woodrow Wilson assigned to inspect and report on the condition and role of black American soldiers in France. The next year he went to Versailles as the *Age's* correspondent at the peace conference.

In 1922, Walton began almost ten years on the *New York World*. A column under his by-line became a feature of the Sunday edition; it dealt with many subjects, including his own observations and reactions in race relations. Notable among his concerns was his campaign, dating back to 1913, for the capitalization of "Negro" in newspaper and magazine articles. In this Walton had the support of the Associated Press. No black had been accorded a place of such prominence in the American press, and his position led to increasing attention to his views and proposals. After a short period on the *New York Herald Tribune* in 1931, Walton returned to the *Age* as associate editor in 1932. During much of this period he was publicity director for the National Negro Business League (1926–1935).

A Democrat at a time when most black leaders were Republican, Walton was in charge of publicity for the black division of the Democratic National Committee during the presidential campaigns of 1924, 1928, and 1932. His impressive political work received the attention of Governor Franklin D. Roosevelt of New York, who after becoming president appointed Walton envoy extraordinary and minister plenipotentiary to Liberia in July 1935.

Walton made Monrovia a site of international negotiations beneficial to the United States and its allies in the conduct of World War II. He spent much of 1937–1939 negotiating treaties between the United States and Liberia on such matters as commerce, navigation, aviation, conciliation, extradition, and consular relations. In 1941 he negotiated an agreement authorizing the landing of American troops on Liberian soil and giving the United States the right to build an air base there. In 1943 he worked out an agreement for the construction of a port in Liberia.

During his long residence Walton traveled throughout Liberia, informing himself intimately on the republic's capabilities and needs. This knowledge led Liberia to choose him as adviser to its delegation to the United Nations in 1948–1949. When Liberia celebrated its centennial as a republic in 1947, the Associated Press assigned Walton to write an extensive feature, "Republic of Liberia Celebrates Full Century of Independence," on the historical and political significance of the occasion, for worldwide distribution. Liberia awarded Walton its highest decoration, the Grand Band, Humane Order of African Redemption.

Back in New York in 1946, Walton served on the Municipal Commission on Intergroup Relations (later Human Rights). When he retired in 1964, a wheelchair victim of arthritis, Mayor Robert F. Wagner described him as "one of New York City's distinguished men ever striving to improve understanding and tolerance . . . always at the heart of a situation with a newspaperman's intuition and a diplomat's dexterity."

A founder of the Negro Actors Guild, Walton was active in the Coordinating Council for Negro Performers. He died in New York City. Among American blacks of his generation, the soft-spoken Walton had few rivals in uncompromising determination when human rights was the issue.

[There is no biography of Walton. The St. Louis *Post-Dispatch* published a recollection entitled "What I Have Lived to See." His writings include "Southern Opinion on the Tuskegee Hospital," *Outlook*, Sept. 5, 1923; "Whitfield: Apostle of Racial Goodwill," *Outlook*, Apr. 9, 1924; "Liberia's New Industrial Development," *Current History*, Apr. 1929; and "Negro Comes Back to the United States Congress," *Current History*, June 1929. Also see M. Cartwright, "Lester A. Walton: Distinguished Diplomat," *Negro History Bulletin*, Oct. 1955; N. Y. City Commission on Intergroup Relations, *COIR News*, Fall 1960; and Walter Christmas, ed., "Negroes in Public Affairs and Government," *Negro Heritage Library* (1966). An obituary is in the *New York Times*, Oct. 19, 1965.]

IRVING DILLIARD

WANER, PAUL GLEE (Apr. 16, 1903–Aug. 29, 1965), baseball player, was born on a farm at Harrah, Okla., the son of Ora Lee Waner and Etta Lenora Beavers. Both parents were members of prosperous farming families who migrated from Germany to Oklahoma during the land rush of 1889. Waner graduated from high school in nearby Oklahoma City in 1921 and then entered State Teachers College at Ada. He remained there for two years. During the summer of 1923, a scout for the San Francisco Seals of the Pacific Coast League persuaded Waner to sign a $500 contract to play baseball.

Waner began his professional career as a pitcher. His success on the mound was short-lived, and arm trouble forced him to become an outfielder. In 1924, his first Coast League season, he hit .356. The following year he hit .401 and had 280 hits, including 75 doubles, a Coast League record. At the end of the season he was purchased by the Pittsburgh Pirates for the then unprecedented sum of $100,000.

Physically, Waner was not imposing. He stood five feet, eight inches tall and never weighed more than 155 pounds. In 1926 a scout for the New York Giants who observed Waner playing his first game in the major leagues reported to John McGraw, the New York Giants' manager: "That little punk don't even know how to put on a uniform." After the Pirates had faced the Giants for the first time that season, McGraw discharged the scout, saying: "That little punk don't know how to put on a uniform but he's removed three of my pitchers with line drives this week. I'm glad you did not scout Christy Mathewson."

During the 1927 season Waner was joined on the team by his younger and even smaller brother, Lloyd. They were nicknamed "Big Poison" and "Little Poison" ("poison" being Brooklynese for "person"). During the World Series, Babe Ruth mockingly commented: "Why they're just kids. If I was that little, I'd be afraid of getting hurt." Although the Yankees won the series in four straight games, the Waner brothers outhit the Yankee sluggers, Ruth and Lou Gehrig, .367 to .357.

Waner was a left-handed hitter. Not known for home-run power—he hit only 112 career four-baggers—he was primarily a line-drive hitter. He became one of the most successful hitters of doubles in the game, smashing fifty in 1928 and sixty-two in 1932. Unlike many players, he did not have a favorite bat. During one game in 1926, he had six straight hits with six different bats.

Waner played twenty seasons of major-league ball, appearing in 2,549 games and compiling a lifetime batting average of .333. He hit better than .300 in twelve consecutive seasons and fourteen overall. He played in four of the first five All-Star games (he failed to get a hit in eight official times at bat). Waner won the National League batting crown in 1927—cracking out 237 hits—with a .380 average, in 1934 with .362, and in 1936 with .373. Overall, he accumulated 3,152 hits, making him one of only fourteen players in the history of the game to collect more than 3,000 hits. In 1927 he was voted the National League's most valuable player.

On June 10, 1927, Waner married Mildred Moore. They had one son. Heavy drinking was a major problem in Waner's career and accounted in part for numerous shifts toward the end of his playing days. In 1940 he was released by Pittsburgh, then played five more seasons as a reserve outfielder and pinch hitter for the Boston Braves, Brooklyn Dodgers, and New York Yankees. A shortage of players during World War II extended his career until he was forty-two.

After leaving the major leagues, Waner moved to Sarasota, Fla., where he operated a batting-practice range. He also served for many years as a part-time batting instructor and coach for the Philadelphia Phillies, St. Louis Cardinals, Boston Red Sox, and Milwaukee Braves. An excellent golfer, he was one of the principal organizers of the National Baseball Players' Golf Tournament in 1934; he won the championship in 1938 after a final-round battle with Babe Ruth. In 1952 he was elected to the Baseball Hall of Fame. He died in Sarasota.

[Scrapbook collections and memorabilia on Waner's professional career are at the Baseball Hall of Fame, Cooperstown, N.Y. An autobiographical account is in Lawrence S. Ritter, *The Glory of Their Times* (1966). Works mentioning Waner are Lee Allen, *One Hundred Years of Baseball* (1950) and *The National League Story* (1961); Lee Allen and Tom Meany, *Kings of the Diamond* (1965); Donald Honig, *Baseball: When the Grass Was Real* (1975); Frank Litsky, *Superstars* (1975); Tom Meany, *Baseball's Greatest Hitters* (1950); Harold Seymour, *Baseball: The Early Years* (1960) and *Baseball: The Golden Age* (1971). Obituaries are in the *New York Times*, Aug. 30, 1965; Arthur Daley, "Artist with a Bat," *New York Times*, Sept. 2, 1965; *Time*, Sept. 10, 1965; *Sporting News*, Sept. 11, 1965; and *Newsweek*, Sept. 13, 1965.]

CHARLES F. HOWLETT

WASHINGTON, DINAH (Aug. 1924–Dec. 14, 1963), singer and pianist, known as "the Queen of the Blues" and "Queen of the Juke-boxes," was born Ruth Jones in Tuscaloosa, Ala. Her birth was not recorded, and different sources give August 8, 22, or 29 as her birthday. Little is known about her father, Ollie Jones. Alice, her mother, was a musician who taught Washington singing and piano. Having moved to Chicago as a child, Washington began playing piano in a South Side Baptist church while attending public school. With her mother as her partner, she later toured the country, singing gospel music in black churches. At the age of fifteen, she won an amateur contest at Chicago's

Regal Theater and performed for a time at several nightclubs. Returning to sacred music in 1940, she became the protégée of Sallie Martin, cofounder of the Gospel Singers Convention and head of the nation's largest black-owned gospel publishing house. During Martin's tours as a vocal soloist, Washington served as her accompanist and later sang lead with the first female gospel group formed by Martin.

Washington's permanent move into popular music occurred in 1942 after she turned from playing piano at the Three Deuces, a Chicago jazz club, to singing at the Garrick Stage Bar. The legendary Billie Holiday, who influenced her style, was singing in the main room when Washington started there. Washington sang for the better part of a year in the upstairs room, where bandleader Lionel Hampton came to hear her on the urging of Joe Glaser, an entertainment executive. From 1943 to May 1945, she sang with the Lionel Hampton band. Authorities differ as to who induced her to change her name during this period from Ruth Jones to Dinah Washington. Some credit Joe Sherman, owner of the Garrick Stage Bar; others, including Lionel Hampton himself, claim that it was Hampton; still others maintain that Joe Glaser was responsible.

While serving as the Hampton band vocalist, Washington made her first recordings, but not with the band. Her disc of "Evil Gal Blues" and "Salty Papa Blues" was released in 1944 on the Keynote label, not Decca to which the Hampton band was signed and which apparently wanted only instrumental recordings from Hampton. With the band, Washington made only "Blowtop Blues." After she left Hampton, she cut twelve sides for Apollo Records. Late in 1946, she signed with manager Ben Bart, who interested Mercury Records, which had taken over the Keynote sides, in recording her.

On Mercury, for whom she recorded until shortly before her death, Washington established herself as the preeminent female rhythm and blues singer of the day. "I like to get inside a tune," she once explained, "and make it mean something more to listeners than just a set of words and a familiar melody. And I can sing anything—anything at all." In a long list of masterful singles and albums, she displayed an artistry that ran the gamut from gospel, jazz, country, and blues to show tunes and pop.

Her more than twenty-five best-selling discs include "Baby Get Lost" (1949), "I'll Never Be Free" (1950), Hank Williams' "Cold, Cold Heart" (1951), "Wheel of Fortune" (1952), "I Don't Hurt Anymore" (1954), "Unforgettable"

(1959), and "This Bitter Earth" (1960). Her biggest hit was a revival of a 1934 ballad, "What a Diff'rence a Day Makes," a song this writer urged her to record in 1959 and that crossed from the rhythm and blues field into mainstream pop. Duet records with fellow Mercury artist Brook Benton also yielded crossover hits in 1960 in "Baby, You've Got What It Takes" and "A Rockin' Good Way." Her two dozen album releases include *Dinah Washington Sings Fats Waller, Swingin' Miss D,* and *Dinah Washington Sings Bessie Smith.*

Critics who caviled about her status as a jazz singer readily acknowledged her as a successor to Bessie Smith in blues. Her 1958 performance at the Newport Jazz Festival was filmed in *Jazz on a Summer's Day.* She toured Europe successfully, and made well-received appearances on British TV. Performing live at the London Palladium, with Queen Elizabeth attending, she announced to the audience, "There is but one heaven, one hell, and one queen, and your Elizabeth is an impostor!"

Washington was imperious, temperamental, and given to tantrums. She was married seven times. Her first husband was John Young, a seventeen-year-old fellow student at Wendell Phillips High School in Chicago. There followed marriages, mostly short-lived, to Walter Buchanan, Raphael Campos, and Eddie Chamblee, a musician. She bore sons to George Jenkins, her husband in 1946–48, and to Robert Grayson, his successor. Her last husband, whom she married in 1963 shortly before her death, was Dick ("Night Train") Lane, backfield star of the Detroit Lions.

Disposed to be plump, Washington went on several crash diets. A combination of reducing pills, alcohol, and sedatives reportedly caused her accidental death, in Detroit, where she had just opened a restaurant.

[Brief biographies and discographies are in Leonard Feather, *Encyclopoedia of Jazz* (1962) and *Illustrated Encyclopedia of Jazz* (1978). Her work as a gospel singer is presented in passing in Tony Heilbut, *The Gospel Sound* (1971) and, as Lionel Hampton's vocalist, in Stanley Dance, *The World of Swing* (1974). Obituaries are in the *New York Times,* Dec. 15, 1963; *Time,* Dec. 20, 1963; *Newsweek,* Dec. 23, 1963; *Down Beat,* Feb. 13, 1964; and *Ebony,* Mar. 1964.]

ARNOLD SHAW

WEBB, WALTER PRESCOTT (Apr. 3, 1888–Mar. 8, 1963), historian, was born in Panola County, Tex., the son of Casner P. Webb and Mary Elizabeth Kyle. When he was four, the family moved to Stephens County. There he experienced the hardships of life in a land deficient in water and trees. The family farm furnished a meager existence, so his father supplemented his income by teaching in one-room country schools, where Webb got his first education.

The books in his father's modest library gave Webb his first glimpse of a different kind of life. He decided to be a writer and earned enough money to complete high school in Ranger, Tex., by teaching in one-room schools. Then, with the help of loans from William E. Hinds, a benefactor he never met, Webb entered the University of Texas in 1909. Always short of funds, he had to interrupt his undergraduate training several times to earn money by teaching high school, which he continued to do after receiving the B.A. from the University of Texas in 1915.

On Sept. 16, 1916, Webb married Jane Elizabeth Oliphant, a former classmate; they had one daughter. While teaching high school history, Webb developed a statewide reputation by introducing the "problem method" (focusing on major events or problems rather than attempting a chronological survey) into classroom instruction. When the history department of the University of Texas needed an instructor to train secondary teachers, it appointed him in 1918. He remained at that university until his death.

In 1920, Webb received the M.A., with a thesis titled "The Texas Rangers in the Mexican War." The history department urged him to go to the University of Chicago for the doctorate. He reluctantly did so in 1922, hoping to complete the residence requirements that academic year. He had the single-minded notion of writing a dissertation on the Texas Rangers and the quaint idea that all his study could be directed toward that end. The faculty suggested that he take preliminary examinations in February 1923 and, not surprisingly, found him insufficiently prepared. His deficiency in medieval history meant a failure on the exams. This cast Webb into the depths of despair, from which he did not emerge for years. He returned to Texas after the 1923 summer session, too embarrassed to inform his colleagues of his failure.

Since the Texas Rangers was his dissertation topic, Webb continued working on it. As he pondered the relationships between the terrain and the Rangers' weapons and enemies, he had a moment of insight that inspired the remainder of his career. He saw that as mounted Rangers fought Indians on the plains, rifles were inadequate. A new weapon—the Colt revolver—had to be devised to enable Rangers to shoot effectively from galloping horses. Webb understood that the environment had demanded a technological innovation. If this were so with weapons, might it not hold true for other technology and institutions?

Webb abandoned work on the Texas Rangers to turn full attention to this arresting idea, and his questioning led to the formulation of the thesis of *The Great Plains* (1931). In this book he argued that American institutions matured in the moist woodlands east of the Mississippi River. When civilization crossed the ninety-eighth meridian, it passed into a land deficient in water, stone, and trees. These shortages caused dramatic alterations in institutions and technology. The environment called forth such things as the Colt revolver, barbed-wire fences, and windmills, and it necessitated changes in laws relating to land and water use, cattle raising, and farming techniques.

Webb's bold ideas immediately caught the attention of professional historians, evoking both high praise and caustic criticism. The book won Columbia University's Loubat Award; and in a poll that Bernard DeVoto conducted for the *Saturday Review of Literature* (Mar. 13, 1937), the responding historians deemed it the most important work published from 1927 through 1936. Whatever the shortcomings of the book, its influence continues as a powerful force in American historiography.

Webb was forty-three when this book was published, and the Texas history department faced a dilemma. He had proved himself an original thinker, but he was just as stubborn as he was original. He would never leave Texas to take the Ph.D., and his career seemed stymied without it. But the department chairman, E. C. Barker, decided that *The Great Plains* would serve as the dissertation, and in 1932, Webb received the doctorate from the University of Texas. The next year he was promoted to professor.

Webb then returned to his first interest, publishing *The Texas Rangers* in 1935. This was the only one of his four major books that rested on traditional archival research. It is an admiring, if not loving, account of the Rangers from their inception through their tracking down Clyde Barrow and Bonnie Parker in 1934. The book glorifies such Ranger captains as Ben McCulloch, Big Foot Wallace, L. H. McNelly, and Frank Hamer. Paramount Pictures bought the movie rights and produced a film in 1936, for the Texas centennial. But, as Webb commented, "The only connection between the

book and the movie was the title." The $8,800 he received enabled him to make real estate investments that made him wealthy.

In 1937, Webb published *Divided We Stand: The Crisis of a Frontierless Democracy,* a passionate indictment of the corporate structures of the Northeast that sapped the economic vitality of the South and West. Webb argued that since the Civil War the Northeast had controlled the nation's wealth through veterans' pensions, protective tariff, and patent monopolies. He made a fervent plea for governmental policies that would insure more equitable distribution of wealth. The book caught the attention of the Justice Department and resulted in some antitrust action. It also contributed to President Franklin D. Roosevelt's labeling of the South as the nation's number one economic problem.

In addition to its immediate impact, *Divided We Stand* led—after a long gestation—to *The Great Frontier* (1952). In the former volume Webb examined the idea of what the end of the physical frontier meant to American democracy. This idea caused him to think about what had happened to the world after its frontier lands were occupied. He hypothesized that the period 1500–1950 had been the Age of the Frontier. During that time the world was divided into the settled area (the Metropolis) and the unsettled lands of the Great Frontier. When medieval European civilization broke its bonds through exploration and settlement, it found vast new riches. The bounty of the Great Frontier represented windfall profits, the like of which the world had never experienced. These enticing riches could be quickly exploited through fur trapping and mining. More lasting wealth through agriculture took longer to accumulate but also added incredible sums to national treasuries. The Metropolis experienced a price revolution and corporate enterprise developed, along with the institutions of democracy, individualism, and religious freedom. The unity of the Middle Ages gave way to the diversity engendered by the Great Frontier.

As important as Webb's striking concepts of the development of modern society during the age of the Great Frontier are the questions he posed concerning the fate of society without the bounty of the Great Frontier. Can those institutions, conceived, nurtured, and developed under one set of conditions, survive their exhaustion? Will democracy, capitalism, and individualism be appreciably modified? Webb chose petroleum as an example of the exploitation of the bounty. What would happen to Western society when this resource was gone? He saw, long before most others, that Americans had grown dependent on cheap petroleum, that they had used this resource profligately, and that a day of reckoning would come sooner rather than later. But few paid any attention in 1952.

Webb's original ideas, presented in persuasive prose, won him the highest honors of his profession. He served as president of the Mississippi Valley Historical Association in 1955 and of the American Historical Association in 1958. In the latter year he also received a $10,000 award from the American Council of Learned Societies for his scholarly contributions and, as if to settle an old debt, an honorary doctorate from the University of Chicago.

In 1960, Webb's wife died. On Dec. 14, 1961, he married Terrell Maverick, widow of Maury Maverick, Sr., the New Deal Congressman. Webb was killed in a car accident while returning to Austin from San Antonio, where he had delivered a speech to retired teachers, "The Confessions of a Texas Bookmaker." Always an exponent of his own ideas, Webb spent his last day characteristically. After the speech he stopped at a bookstore to autograph copies of *Washington Wife* (1963), the diary of Ellen Maury Sladen, which he had edited.

[Materials related to Webb's life and work are in the C. B. Smith collection of Walter Prescott Webb papers in the Texas State Archives, Austin, and the Walter Prescott Webb Papers in the Archives of the University of Texas at Austin. Books dealing with Webb include Ronnie Dugger, ed., *Three Men in Texas* (1967); William A. Owens, *Three Friends* (1969); Necah S. Furman, *Walter Prescott Webb* (1976); Kenneth R. Philp and Elliott West, eds., *Essays on Walter Prescott Webb* (1976); and Gregory M. Tobin, *The Making of a History* (1976). Walter Rundell, Jr., *Walter Prescott Webb*, a pamphlet in the Southwest Writers Series (1970), contains a complete bibliography. Rundell's "Webb at Wisconsin," *Panhandle-Plains Historical Review*, 1977, and "Walter Prescott Webb as Businessman," *The Great Plains Journal*, 1979, deal with aspects of his career. The oral history interview transcript of Mrs. Walter Prescott Webb, in the Lyndon B. Johnson Library at Austin, Tex., deals mostly with Webb's long relationship with Johnson. An obituary is in the *New York Times* (western ed.), Mar. 11, 1963.]

WALTER RUNDELL, JR.

WEBER, MAX (Apr. 18, 1881–Oct. 4, 1961), artist and musician, was born in Bialystok, Russia, the son of Morris Weber, a tailor, and Julia Getz. The name Weber ("weaver") indicates that the family probably came from Germany. His paternal grandfather had gained a reputation as a color chemist in the town, and a granduncle was a famous student of the cabala. Their influence may explain Weber's strong "Russian colorism" and his being rooted in Jewish religion, especially Hasidic traditions. To his biographers he spoke of the impression that Russian folk art had made upon him when he was a child, especially the gay decoration of the wooden synagogues and the rich colors of the icons in Russian churches. In 1891 the family immigrated to the United States and settled in the Williamsburg section of Brooklyn.

Weber entered elementary school and, after graduating, attended Boys High School for one year. He entered Pratt Institute in Brooklyn in the fall of 1898, taking the art and manual-training course for teachers, which encompassed joinery, woodcarving, and clay modeling.

Of fateful importance for Weber were the courses in composition that he took from Arthur Wesley Dow, who had worked with Paul Gauguin at Pont-Aven, Brittany, in 1887. Dow had developed a series of lessons in design, which he taught at Pratt. He treated "art as spatial music," anticipating Wassily Kandinsky's formula. Weber received his diploma from Pratt in June 1900 but continued his studies with Dow on a scholarship for another year.

From 1901 to 1903, Weber taught construction drawing and manual training in public schools in Lynchburg, Va., and at the summer school of the University of Virginia. In 1903 he was made head of the Department of Drawing and Manual Training at the State Normal School, Duluth, Minn.

After he had saved enough money to study in Europe, Weber left New York in September 1905 and entered the Académie Julien in Paris, where he studied under the strict academician Jean Paul Laurens. He hoped to find the new "form" of art as spatial music. He found it in the art of Gauguin and in the East Asian art of the Musée Guimet. The primitive and archaic sculpture collections of the Trocadéro also attracted him.

The sculptors Elie Nadelman and Joseph Brummer (the latter also a member of the Matisse studio and an important dealer in archaic sculpture in New York City) were among Weber's earliest American associates in Paris. In the summer of 1906 he traveled to Spain. His great experience there was encountering the work of El Greco. Like Paul Cézanne and Henri Rousseau, El Greco exerted a lasting influence on Weber's style.

After returning to Paris, Weber became a friend of Jules Flandrin, a pupil of Gustave Moreau. Flandrin was Weber's most important contact with the "school of Paris." He also introduced Weber to Rousseau, who became another intimate friend. (Later, in 1910, shortly after Rousseau's death, Weber organized the first American Rousseau exhibit at the Stieglitz Gallery in New York City.)

Chiefly through Flandrin, Weber also met, in the decisive year 1906, Henri Matisse, Albert Marquet, Maurice Denis, Pablo Picasso, Guillaume Apollinaire, Marie Laurencin, Robert Delaunay, Albert Gleizes, Georges Braque, and Jean Metzinger. Among American painters then working in Paris he associated with Bernard Karfiol and Samuel Halpert. After leaving the Académie Julien, Weber painted from life models without further instruction at Académie Colarossi and Académie de la Grande Chaumière, where Matisse was often seen.

The Cézanne Memorial Exhibition and the organization of the Académie Matisse in 1907 strongly impressed Weber. He had seen Cézanne's work at the Salon d'Automne in 1906, but the great memorial show of 1907 was a revelation. Cézanne's structural discipline most strongly affected Weber's still lifes and landscapes.

In 1907, Weber spent five months in Italy, visiting Florence, Naples, Rome, Pisa, and Venice. There he learned to combine architectural structure with nature in strong, exaggerated colors. Weber studied with Matisse from January 1907 to July 1908. But his art differs from that of Matisse in its almost total rejection of "islamic carpet flatness." The latter's disapproval of Weber's "angellike" worship of Rousseau cooled the relationship between the two.

Weber had an extraordinary talent for meeting the right people at the right time and place. He became the contact between the school of Paris and American modern painting. This role perhaps overshadows Weber's importance as an artist in his own right. He was among the pioneers of cubism and futurism, and was considered by some as responsible for the entry of American art into the mainstream of twentieth-century art. Or, as his earliest biographer, Holger Cahill, put it, "Max Weber has lived the history of Modern Art in America."

After leaving Matisse's class, Weber traveled to Belgium and the Netherlands and resumed painting in Paris. His work in the Salon d'Automne was favorably mentioned in the press. He returned to New York City in January 1909. Weber had his first one-man show at Gallery Haas, in the basement of a picture frame shop. In 1911 he showed at Alfred Stieglitz's Gallery 291, where his paintings were ridiculed by the

critics. An exhibit the following year at the Murray Hill Gallery met a similar fate.

Weber was not represented in the 1913 Armory Show in New York City, which shook the American public into a very reluctant awareness of the existence of cubism and futurism, the styles in which he worked. But he was invited by the English critic Roger Fry to exhibit with the "Grafton group" that year in London. The only other non-English participant was Kandinsky. Weber's *Cubist Poems,* poems inspired by primitive and archaic sculptures and written in the manner of expressionist literature, also appeared at London in 1914. The first showing of his work in an American museum was at the Newark (N.J.) Museum in 1913.

Among Weber's most notable paintings of this period are "Geraniums" (1911); "Rush Hour New York" (1915); and "Chinese Restaurant" (1915). Whereas "Geraniums" is indebted to Cézanne, the two later paintings are done in the style of facet-cubism, but added are the dynamics of life in the American metropolis.

From 1914 to 1918, Weber taught art history and art appreciation at the White School of Photography in New York City. He married Frances Abrams on June 27, 1916. They had two children.

Weber was a very successful teacher at the White School and at the Art Students League, where he taught from 1920 until 1921 and again from 1926 to 1927. During this period he published *Essays on Art* (1916) and much poetry, including *Primitives* (1926), a work inspired by ancient Mexican sculpture. The key to Weber's success as a teacher was his personality. The critic Alfred Werner wrote, "He was a gentle and reflective man of compassion and wit, a musician, an essayist and poet. Music and musicians appear often in his art. A gifted amateur, he entertained in Paris with his tenor voice and played the harmonium in the Matisse studio.

Weber was director of the Society of Independent Artists in 1918–1919, and in 1937 became national chairman of the American Artists Congress. By this time, his art having become less abstract, Weber was firmly established as one of the leaders and defenders of modern art in America. The Museum of Modern Art honored him in 1930 with a retrospective exhibit. No fewer than fifty-three public collections in the United States own his work, as do the "Bazalel" National Art Museum in Jerusalem and the Tel-Aviv Museum, both in Israel. In 1953 he was elected to the American Institute of Arts and Letters. He died in Great Neck, N.Y.

[Some of Weber's papers are in the Archives of American Art, New York City, nos. N.Y. 59-6 through N.Y. 59-10; they include material on the American Artists Congress (1935–1941) and on Rousseau (1942). Among Weber's published graphic works is *Collected Woodcuts* (1965). Biographical information is available in the Oral History Research Offices of Columbia University. Biographies are Holger Cahill, *Max Weber* (1930); and Lloyd Goodrich, *Max Weber* (1949). Exhibition catalogs include Wilhelm Lehmbruck Museum, Duisburg, Germany, *Pariser Begegnungen 1905–14* (1965); University of California at Santa Barbara, "Max Weber: Oils, Gouaches, Pastels, Drawings and Graphic Arts," Feb. 6–Mar. 3, 1968; two from the Bernhard Denenberg Galleries, New York City: "Fifty Years of Paintings by Max Weber," Apr. 15–May 10, 1969, and "Max Weber Early Works on Paper," Apr. 27–May 15, 1971 (with a foreword by Alfred Werner); Detroit Institute of Arts, *Arts and Crafts in Detroit 1906–76* (1976). A good criticism of Weber's works may be found in John Wilmerding, *American Art* (1976). An obituary is in the *New York Times,* Oct. 5, 1961.]

ERNST SCHEYER

WEEMS, TED (Sept. 26, 1901–May 6, 1963), orchestra leader and composer, was born Wilfred Theodore Weymes in Pitcairn, Pa. He first led a band as a pupil at Lincoln Grammar School in Pittsburgh, Pa. The young musicians played mouth organs, combs, and improvised drums commendably enough to receive a penny each from the school principal. When the Weems family moved to Philadelphia, Ted pursued a busy music schedule, playing violin in the West Philadelphia Symphony and trombone in the high school band, where his brother, Art, held forth on trumpet. Before long he was conducting. It was a pattern the brothers maintained through years of dance-band work.

While an engineering student at the University of Pennsylvania, Weems became director of the varsity band and organized a dance orchestra that played for school functions. After playing trombone in Paul Specht's band in the early 1920's, Weems and his brother organized their All-American Band, made up of college musicians. They soon were playing at the Trianon Ballroom in Newark, N.J. Some authorities consider Weems's engagement at the Steel Pier at Atlantic City in July 1923 as his real debut. The band went on the road, playing hotels in major cities, but gravitated to Chicago. There radio broadcasts helped to widen its popularity.

In 1924, Weems married Eleanor Constance Logan; they had one son. That same year the band had a hit record, "Somebody Stole My Gal." Other successes followed: "My Gal Sal," "My Cutie's Due at Two to Two Today,"

"You're the Cream in My Coffee." At dances and in theaters Weems communicated easily with the public, and it responded warmly to the happy, outgoing style of the band. In 1929, back in Chicago after touring the country, the band continued to have good air exposure. The haunting theme "Out of the Night," embellished with gentle whistling, signaled radio listeners that Ted Weems was on. Another hit record, "Piccolo Pete," proved irresistible to eager disc buyers. Besides purveying happy, danceable music, Weems featured entertaining novelty numbers and attractive vocalists such as Parker Gibbs, Red Ingle, Joe "Country" Washburn, and Elmo Tanner, the band's talented whistler. Tenor Art Jarrett was the band's romantic balladeer until early 1931. After his departure Weems kept on the lookout for a replacement. In 1936 he found one: Perry Como. The relaxed Como style, direct descendant of crooner Bing Crosby's, graced the Weems music for six years. Though male vocalists dominated the band, two female singers contributed their share to its popularity: Mary Lee and Marvel Maxwell, who later appeared in films as Marilyn Maxwell.

In the 1930's the Weems band performed on radio with Jack Benny, tenor James Melton, and Fibber McGee and Molly. It was equally busy in the recording studios. Among tunes written by Weems and recorded by the band were "The Martins and the Coys," "The One-Man Band," and a number he wrote with Country Washburn, "Oh, Mon-ah" ("Oh, Mourner" in southern accent). One recording, destined to secure Weems' fame in dance music history, started with a whimper. It was an upbeat, excitingly rhythmic (and quite antiromantic) version of a current romantic ballad, "Heartaches." Released in 1933, it broke no sales records. But when the band recorded it again on a different label in 1938, it zoomed to the million-seller mark.

In December 1942, Weems and his band joined the U.S. Merchant Marine. They were assigned regular duties at Basic Cadet School in San Mateo, Calif., but they were free after 4 P.M. every day. After release from the service, Weems reorganized his band. Prewar "big bands" were disappearing, and disc jockeys were replacing radio "remotes" for promoting bands. In 1947 a disc jockey in Charlotte, N.C., put Weems's 1933 "Heartaches" on his turntable. Victor reissued it; it hit the million-seller ranks; a new generation discovered Ted Weems. The band played on into the 1950's, but the rock 'n' roll craze finally forced Weems to give up. He became a disc jockey, but he still did occasional tours with the band. He died in Tulsa, Okla., "with his boots on" during a tour, doing what he had been doing so engagingly and so well for nearly forty years.

[There is no biography of Weems, but a clipping file on him is in the library at Lincoln Center for the Performing Arts. Also see Brian Rust and Albert J. McCarthy, *The Dance Band Era* (1972); George T. Simon, *The Big Bands* (1974; rev. and enl. 1975) and *The Best of the Music Makers* (1979). An obituary is in the *New York Times*, May 5, 1963.]

AMY LEE

WEIGEL, GUSTAVE (Jan. 15, 1906–Jan. 3, 1964), theologian, was born in Buffalo, N.Y., the son of August Weigel and Louise Leontine Kiefer. His parents, who had immigrated to the United States in 1902 from Alsace, remained un-Americanized throughout their lives. Alsatian was spoken in their simple and frugal home. Weigel attended Catholic primary and secondary schools in Buffalo. During these years he developed special interests in public speaking and writing. In 1922 he entered the Jesuit novitiate at St. Andrew-on-Hudson, near Poughkeepsie, N.Y. There he sought to transcend the limitations of his background through his studies and developed an Oxford-like accent.

Weigel's philosophical and theological studies for the priesthood were done at Woodstock College in Maryland between 1926 and 1934. He became particularly intrigued by epistemology and the quest for "the True" and "the Real" after reading the works of Immanuel Kant and Joseph Maréchal.

Weigel learned to appreciate Platonic and Augustinian epistemologies and became sympathetic to subjectivism, relativism, and the theory of innate ideas. "I need a powerful vision of the truth," he wrote in his diary in 1934. "The truth will make me free but I must see it. Truth can give vision."

Weigel carried out his search for truth in an independent fashion. His need for freedom was expressed in a poem criticizing what he saw as his inadequate theological formation at Woodstock. The "system" attempts to stifle the individual. Therefore, Weigel sought to be linked to it only loosely. He lived, he wrote, "parasitically on the whole and the whole leaves him alone for he is in it but not of it. He has grown big by it. But he never grew into it."

Weigel's impatience with traditional intellectual and spiritual paths was stated clearly in his 1934 diary: "I am making the Spiritual Exercises of St. Ignatius on the basis that they leave the soul in freedom. . . . I use my own ideas in these meditations. . . . I know that the ways taught me years ago are impossible. I shall trust the Spirit." Throughout his life he struggled with the problem of the surrender of his will to authority while preserving his treasured liberty intact.

Weigel pursued graduate studies in dogmatic theology at the Pontifical Gregorian University in Rome between 1935 and 1937. He received the S.T.D. for a dissertation (completed 1937; published 1938) on the fifth-century theologian Faustus of Riez, whose writings during the Semi-Pelagian controversy Weigel had studied at Woodstock. Impatient to get on with something more real, Weigel did not give his research sufficient attention, and his dissertation was lacking in acute theological analysis. It was "history as it ought to have been, not as it was," according to Weigel's friend and colleague John Courtney Murray.

Since his scholarship was not judged totally satisfactory, Weigel was assigned to teach dogmatic theology at the Catholic University of Chile at Santiago. He served there from 1937 to 1948, teaching courses in Christology, soteriology, sacraments, Oriental theology, Thomistic metaphysics, and religious psychology. He was dean of the theological faculty from 1942 to 1948. His teaching style was Socratic, probing students to get them to ask ever deeper questions in search of truth.

With his impressive communicative abilities, disarming frankness, and simplicity, Weigel charmed both Catholics and Protestants in the English and American communities in Santiago. His popularity led to his removal from Chile in 1948; he simply did not fit the confining mold of the Chilean Jesuits. The order's provincial wrote: "The reasons are brief and almost exclusively for fear of that great 'liberty' which you radiate, perhaps innately from your temperament and formation and the lack of adaptation to the many customs and manners of being and working which is ours and which can be dangerous especially because of the influence that your Reverence has due to your great talents and qualities which few others possess."

Weigel returned to the United States in 1948, depressed, bitter, and without direction in his life. But a new impetus came when John Courtney Murray invited him to become the specialist in Protestant theology for *Theological Studies*. With great energy Weigel wrote extensive articles, analyzing the writings of Protestant theologians and Protestant ecclesiastical structures. He became a pioneer in the promotion of ecumenism in the United States.

Weigel became professor of ecclesiology at

Woodstock College in 1949. His theology was quite traditional except for his emphasis on the church as mystery. He stressed that the Roman Catholic Church, as the Mystical Body of Christ, is a divinely instituted society and that the truth of that claim can best be demonstrated by the moral miracle of the church's united and effective existence in the world.

In 1954, Weigel nearly died of complications following surgery for a benign tumor. Afterward his interest in scholarship and teaching declined, and he became an activist in behalf of ecumenism. His ecumenical style was based on his remarkable memory and his magnetic personality. Ecumenism to him meant a kind of conversation between brothers. It was a pursuit of religious truth always coupled with love.

In his ecumenical work Weigel was doctrinally uncompromising. In fact, the position he presented in his course on ecclesiology was fundamentally antithetical to Protestantism. Yet he held that, despite seemingly insuperable differences, he was, in some mysterious and truly real way, at one with his separated brethren. He suggested three possible paths to unity. One was compromise: through give and take, a common basis is agreed upon and all melt into one church. Another was comprehension: certain basic principles are accepted but interpreted differently by various churches. The third was conversion: all churches disband and join one all-embracing church. All of these ways Weigel found wanting. He preferred the path of convergence, in which the churches would move closer and closer to one another. It was this coming together, not the achievement of unity, that was the true purpose of ecumenicism.

Weigel's final contributions centered on the Second Vatican Council (1962–1965). Between 1960 and 1962 he served as a consultant to the Secretariat for the Promotion of Christian Unity. During the council he made three outstanding contributions. First, he was a popular expositor of the purposes of the council to American audiences. Second, he was a member of the U.S. Bishops' Press Panel during the second session of the council in 1963. Third, he was an interpreter for the English-speaking ecumenical observer-delegates to the council.

Weigel was not initially optimistic about the council's chances for achieving serious reforms, but he took new hope from the positive, pastoral, and ecumenical approach of Pope John XXIII. The third session in 1963, under the more curial leadership of Pope Paul VI, revived Weigel's pessimism. He was exhausted by the divisive debates and their meager results, which

were, he said, "not good enough but far better than we deserved."

Weigel was determined not to return for the council's fourth session. Although tired and disenchanted with conciliar processes, he had an abiding confidence that God's Spirit would straighten out any mess that men could make. He died suddenly in New York City.

[Weigel's personal papers are in the Woodstock College Archives, Georgetown University, Washington, D.C. Significant books by Weigel are *A Survey of Protestant Theology in Our Day* (1954); *A Catholic Primer on the Ecumenical Movement* (1957); *Faith and Understanding in America* (1959); *An American Dialogue* (1960), written with Robert McAfee Brown; *Church-State Relations* (1960); *Catholic Theology in Dialogue* (1961); *Churches in North America* (1961); *Knowledge: Its Values and Limits* (1961), edited by Arthur G. Madden; *Religion and the Knowledge of God* (1961), written with Arthur G. Madden; and *The Modern God* (1963). His major articles on ecumenical theology include "Protestant Theological Positions Today," *Theological Studies*, Dec. 1950; "Protestantism as a Catholic Concern," *Theological Studies*, June 1955; and "The Theological Significance of Paul Tillich," *Gregorianum*, 1956. On Weigel, see John Courtney Murray, intro., *One of a Kind: Essays in Tribute to Gustave Weigel* (1967). Also see Sister Olga Neft, O.S.F., "An Annotated Bio-Bibliography of Gustave Weigel, S.J., 1906–1964" (M.S. thesis, Catholic University, 1968); and Patrick W. Collins, "Gustave Weigel: Ecclesiologist and Ecumenist" (Ph.D. diss., Fordham University, 1972). An obituary is in the *New York Times*, Jan. 4, 1964.]

PATRICK W. COLLINS

WELLES, (BENJAMIN) SUMNER (Oct. 14, 1892–Sept. 24, 1961), diplomat, was born in New York City, the son of Benjamin Welles and Frances Swan. The name Sumner reflected a distant relationship to the family of Charles Sumner, the abolitionist senator from Massachusetts. Both parental families were prominent and well-to-do.

Welles attended Groton (1904–1910) and Harvard College (1910–1913), where he majored in architecture and fine arts. When he received the B.A. in 1914, after a year abroad, he had no career plans in mind. His mother's sudden death in 1911 had been a grievous blow, but from her estate he received an income large enough to allow him to live in style. On Apr. 14, 1915, he married Esther Slater, whose family owned the Slater Mills in Webster, Mass. They had two sons.

On the advice of a family friend, Franklin D. Roosevelt, then assistant secretary of the navy,

Welles took the Foreign Service examination in June 1915 and was promptly assigned as third secretary in the embassy at Tokyo. It soon became apparent that he was unusually qualified for a career in diplomacy. He was tall, handsome, elegant, and exceptionally dignified for his age. More important, he was quick-minded and diligent, and had a working knowledge of history and languages. Welles's principal assignment during his two years in Japan was the inspection of camps in which German and Austrian prisoners of war were being held. His diplomacy and reports won him speedy promotions.

In November 1917, Welles became second secretary in Buenos Aires. While most United States diplomats regarded an assignment in Latin America as a waste of time, he viewed Latin America as a neglected area that merited attention and specialization. He soon mastered Spanish and absorbed Latin American history and literature. His work in the embassy, mostly involving commercial problems arising from World War I, earned him another promotion.

In June 1920, Welles was named assistant chief of the Division of Latin American Affairs of the State Department, and in September he became acting chief. It was soon apparent that he aimed to improve the image of the United States in Latin America by lightening the heavy hand of Uncle Sam, especially in the Caribbean. He knew that this could not be accomplished merely by well-meaning restraint; it would require persuasive leadership to develop governments sufficiently stable to permit withdrawal of U.S. Marines from Haiti and the Dominican Republic and to avoid renewed military intervention in turbulent Cuba. The problems Welles faced seemed intractable, and in March 1922, discouraged by the limitations of the career service, he resigned, intending to take up international finance.

Secretary of State Charles Evans Hughes had been impressed by Welles's work, and in July he induced the young man to return with an unusual appointment as commissioner (with the rank of minister) to devise plans for the withdrawal of American troops and the military government from the Dominican Republic. Welles's mission was accomplished in July 1924 with the inauguration of an independent Dominican government. Welles was retained by Hughes and by his successor, Frank B. Kellogg, to assist the Dominicans in solving post-independence problems; but President Calvin Coolidge dismissed Welles early in July 1925. No reason was given, but there may have been a connection with Welles's divorce (1923) and

his marriage on June 27, 1925, to Mathilde Townsend, recently divorced from Senator Peter Gerry of Rhode Island.

Welles spent the next two years writing *Naboth's Vineyard: The Dominican Republic 1844–1924* (1928), the final chapter of which contained a ringing appeal for a more considerate and cooperative policy toward Latin America. The study had a profound effect on Franklin D. Roosevelt, who henceforth regarded Welles as his principal adviser on Latin American affairs.

In early April 1933, President Roosevelt named Welles an assistant secretary of state. In his inaugural address the president had promised that his foreign policy would be that of the "good neighbor," and he was persuaded by Welles to use his Pan-American Day speech (April 12) to spell out this new policy with specific reference to Latin America. The Good Neighbor policy thus came to be associated with the Americas and with Welles as its leading proponent.

Mounting disorders in Cuba put the policy to an immediate test, for a collapse might make another United States intervention unavoidable. On April 21 it was announced that Welles would go to Havana as ambassador, but it was correctly surmised that he would act as a special presidential envoy to mediate a truce between President Gerardo Machado and his opponents. After protracted maneuvering, Machado was supplanted by a broadly representative caretaker government with Dr. Carlos Manuel de Céspedes y Quesada as interim president. Welles was a hero in Havana and Washington until September 5, when Céspedes was overthrown by a coalition of noncommissioned officers and radical students. In view of United States rights under the Platt Amendment and to encourage constitutional stability, Welles recommended the landing of U.S. Marines to maintain the Céspedes government; but Roosevelt and Secretary of State Cordell Hull rejected his advice. Fulgencio Batista emerged as Cuba's strong man, and Welles, dejected, returned to his position as assistant secretary for hemisphere policy. As a result of this experience, Welles negotiated the treaty of May 29, 1934, with Cuba, which abrogated the Platt Amendment.

In 1934, Welles also undertook the negotiation of a treaty with Panama that was designed to rectify some of the inequities of the 1903 Canal Treaty. The new treaty was completed in March 1936, but its beneficial effect in Panama was offset by the reluctance of the U.S. Senate, which took three years to approve it.

In connection with his efforts in 1936 to end the Chaco War between Paraguay and Bolivia, Welles persuaded Roosevelt to call for a special inter-American peace conference at Buenos Aires. Welles assisted Hull at the conference and played a major role in rallying support for a declaration that established the principle of collective consultation should the peace of the Americas be disturbed.

Roosevelt appointed Welles undersecretary of state in 1937, with the grudging assent of Hull, who resented the close relationship between Welles and the president. Hull's relations with Welles deteriorated in succeeding years, as Hull was often ill and Welles, as acting secretary, was increasingly called on by Roosevelt for action or advice.

Following the outbreak of war in Europe, Welles represented the United States at a special inter-American meeting in Panama, at which a neutrality zone was declared around the continent south of Canada. In February and March 1940, Roosevelt sent him on a much-publicized mission to Rome, Berlin, Paris, and London to investigate the possibility of arranging peace before the expected German spring offensive. Since peace was only a remote hope, the more immediate aim of the trip was to lure Mussolini away from Hitler and to demonstrate that the president had not failed to make an effort in behalf of peace.

Welles attended the dramatic meeting of Roosevelt and Winston Churchill off the coast of Newfoundland in August 1941 and assisted in drafting the Atlantic Charter. After the United States became a belligerent, Welles flew to Rio de Janeiro for another special consultative meeting of American foreign ministers (January 1942). All countries except Argentina and Chile favored an immediate break with Japan, Germany, and Italy; but in order to maintain the principle of unanimity, Welles accepted a compromise wording that recommended, but did not declare, a break. Hull was furious, and without waiting to see the results of this decision, he sharply accused Welles of a "sell out." Roosevelt, however, approved the undersecretary's position, and the Hull-Welles breach widened.

Ever since the outbreak of war, Welles had directed the State Department's planning for the peace settlement. After the Rio Conference (1942) Welles intensified these efforts and initiated a speaking campaign to persuade the American people to support a postwar international organization of the United Nations.

In 1943 reports reached Hull of a homosexual incident involving Welles. Although Welles had been intoxicated at the time, Hull made these reports the immediate reason for insisting that the president obtain Welles's resignation, which became effective Sept. 30, 1943.

In retirement Welles wrote and broadcast commentaries on foreign affairs and produced four books combining memoirs and policy analysis. His wife died in August 1949, and on Jan. 8, 1952, he married Harriette Post, a childhood friend. He died at Bernardsville, N.J.

[Welles's personal papers are to be deposited in the Franklin D. Roosevelt Library at Hyde Park, N.Y. His official activities are in the records of the Department of State in the National Archives, Washington, D.C. The department has published a selection of these documents in the form of annual volumes entitled *Foreign Relations of the United States*. Welles's books are *The Time for Decision* (1944); *Where Are We Heading?* (1946); *We Need Not Fail* (1948); and *Seven Decisions That Shaped History* (1950). A useful collection of his speeches is in *The World of the Four Freedoms* (1943). An obituary is in the *New York Times*, Sept. 25, 1961.]

WILLIAM M. FRANKLIN

WELLS, HARRIET SHELDON (1873– Feb. 8, 1961), woman suffragist, was born in Brooklyn, N.Y., the daughter of George Preston Sheldon, president of the Phoenix Fire Insurance Company, and Anne Frances Pendleton. She spent her early life in Greenwich, Conn., and studied languages and music in Europe. On June 21, 1902, she married Thomas Bucklin Wells, of Harper and Brothers, who later became chairman of the corporation's board and editor in chief of *Harper's* magazine.

After her marriage Wells became active in the woman suffrage movement. She served as treasurer of the Woman's Suffrage Party of New York City, and in 1915 she was named chairman of that organization's Woman Voter Subcommittee. A trusted lieutenant of Carrie Chapman Catt, Wells worked to obtain a suffrage amendment to the New York State constitution. She and her associates canvassed homes and factories, and staged publicity-producing rallies and parades.

The leaders of the New York Woman's Suffrage Party sought to dissociate themselves from the militant tactics employed by many zealous suffragists. Wells and others on the organization's executive committee believed that militancy was counterproductive because many people did not discriminate between the moderate branch of the suffrage movement and the more radical one. Wells's efforts met with considerable frustration; not until 1917 did New York State enact woman suffrage.

During her years of intense suffrage activity, Wells also served as a director of the Leslie Woman's Suffrage Committee, a group formed by Catt to handle the legacy of almost $1 million left by Mrs. Frank Leslie to support the suffrage movement. The funds were spent throughout the nation to publicize the suffrage movement by printing and disseminating pro-suffrage speeches and pamphlets.

After woman suffrage was achieved in New York State, Wells began to work for passage of a federal suffrage amendment. Her activities were interrupted by American entry into World War I, during which she and her husband served overseas with the American Red Cross. After her return to the United States, Wells resumed her suffrage activities, working through the New York City and New York State Woman's Suffrage parties. Her greatest moment of glory occurred on Aug. 26, 1920, when she carried a victory banner at the head of a parade to honor Catt upon the enactment of the Nineteenth Amendment to the Constitution. In a sense, Wells, too, was honored by the parade. Although she was more a follower than a leader, it was through local organizing such as she conducted that woman suffrage was finally realized.

In 1931, Wells and her husband moved to France. They remained in Paris after the outbreak of World War II. When the Germans occupied Paris in June 1940, Wells and her husband prepared to return to the United States, but Thomas Wells's health would not permit the trip. He died at the American Hospital in Paris in September 1944. After her husband's death, Wells returned to New York City, where she spent the last sixteen years of her life. She died in New York.

[Little data has been published on Wells. See the obituary notices for Wells and her husband, *New York Times*, Feb. 10, 1961, and Sept. 29, 1944, respectively.]

MARIAN ELIZABETH STROBEL

WHALEN, GROVER ALOYSIUS (June 2, 1886–Apr. 20, 1962), businessman, promoter, and official greeter, was born in New York City, the son of Michael Whalen, a building contractor, and of Esther De Nee. He was educated at Clason Point Military Academy (now La Salle Military Academy), De Witt Clinton High School, Packard Commercial College, and New York Law School, which he was forced to leave

in 1906, because of the death of his father. At that time Whalen took over the family contracting business. On Apr. 23, 1913, he married Anna D. Kelly; they had three children.

The next year Whalen went to work for the Wanamaker Department Store in New York City. The store sponsored the Businessmen's League, devoted to rousing concern for the political, fiscal, and administrative problems that the city faced. Whalen became the organization's secretary.

The Businessmen's League endorsed Democrat John F. ("Red Mike") Hylan for mayor of New York in 1917. Hylan won the election, and soon thereafter named Whalen his secretary. Whalen was retained as a temporarily absentee member of Wanamaker's while in municipal service.

Under Hylan, Whalen served as a member of the New York and New Jersey Bridge-Tunnel Commission from 1919 to 1923. He was the city's commissioner of plants and structures, and chairman of New York's Board of Purchases, from 1919 to 1924. He was general manager of Wanamaker's from 1924 to 1934.

Whalen had been appointed executive vice-chairman of the Mayor's Committee for the Reception of Distinguished Guests in 1919. As such he became the city's official greeter, an unpaid post he held for almost thirty-five years. He set up parades for the returning members of the American Expeditionary Force (AEF) and General John J. Pershing after World War I, and engineered welcoming ceremonies for the Prince of Wales (Whalen thought up the city's first official ticker-tape parade on this occasion), Désiré Cardinal Mercier, the king and queen of the Belgians, Queen Marie of Romania, the swimmer Gertrude Ederle, and Guglielmo Marconi, to mention but a few. Frederick Lewis Allen noted that Whalen was able "to reduce welcoming to a science and raise it to an art." Whalen appreciated the differences between visiting dignitaries and saw to it that the right people were invited for each occasion.

Whalen quickly conceived the idea of bringing his dignitaries from Bowling Green to City Hall at 12:05 P.M., when tens of thousands of workers would be on their lunch hour. These huge crowds made a captive audience, so that even New York's minor guests could feel they were getting a great welcome. The parade for Charles A. Lindbergh after his return from his solo flight to France in 1927 was one of the greatest of the Whalen ceremonies.

In 1928, Mayor James Walker appointed Whalen police commissioner of the city.

Whalen had not wanted the post, but the Wanamaker management persuaded him to take it, guaranteeing him his salary as general manager of the Manhattan store while he headed the police force. He served for a year and a half. Whalen sought to restore the confidence of the citizenry in the police and to improve departmental administration. He founded the Police Academy, had new uniforms designed for the police, and originated a crime-prevention bureau. When he resumed his position at Wanamaker's, many felt that Whalen was the best police commissioner the city had ever had.

In 1933, Whalen became New York administrator for the National Recovery Administration (NRA). He organized the greatest parade ever seen in New York in support of the NRA. In 1934 he left Wanamaker's to join the Schenley Products Corporation as chairman of the board. He was largely responsible for placing the legend "Federal law forbids the reuse or resale of this bottle" on liquor bottles. The new law helped to stabilize the industry and to protect the government's alcohol tax collection. Whalen left Schenley in 1937.

In the mid-1930's Whalen proposed that New York City sponsor a world's fair as a way to revive the fortunes of the city and port. In 1935 a committee, which included Whalen, verified that the Century of Progress Exhibition in Chicago had brought $170 million of new money to the business community of that city.

Whalen was elected president of a nonprofit, private corporation to organize the fair. His salary was about $100,000. The venture was christened "The World of Tomorrow" by Whalen. It was to be an international exposition, celebrating the sesquicentennial of the launching of the American government and the inauguration of President George Washington on Apr. 30, 1789, in New York City.

Whalen, one of the greatest salesmen of his era, went to Europe to sell the idea in 1936. Nations participating in the fair were to be given 3,000 square feet of covered space and 10,000 square feet of uncovered space, rent-free. The participants could purchase more space if they desired. The Soviet Union signed first; its pavilion occupied 100,000 square feet and cost $4 million. Great Britain, France, and Italy were other early major signers.

Enlisting foreign countries was only one item in assuring the fair's success. There was the immense task of transforming 1,216 acres of wasteland into a magnificent exhibition grounds. The North Beach Airport was expanded, the Whitestone Bridge was erected, and new highways in New York and New Jersey were built. Thousands of fair-connected jobs were created.

The fair, with its trylon and perisphere, opened on Apr. 30, 1939. It was a show window for the industrial and scientific advances of the twentieth century. The first regular public television service in the country was inaugurated on April 30 when the National Broadcasting Company (NBC) carried President Roosevelt's opening address live from a platform on the Flushing Meadow fairgrounds.

The World of Tomorrow was continued the next year. It still drew large crowds, but cost too much to run. The World's Fair was the climax of Whalen's long career. In April 1941 he assumed the post of chairman of the board of Coty, a cosmetics manufacturer. He also resumed his volunteer duties as the Mayor's Reception Committee chairman until American entry in World War II. After Pearl Harbor, Whalen was appointed a civilian adviser to Simon B. Buckner, Jr., commanding general of the Alaska Defense Force. In 1943, New York's Mayor Fiorello La Guardia appointed Whalen head of the Civil Defense Volunteers Office. The organization enlisted some 225,000 workers during the war.

The Mayor's Reception Committee was reactivated in 1945, with Whalen as chairman. He prepared suitable ceremonies for the returning veterans as well as for General Dwight D. Eisenhower, Admiral Chester Nimitz, and Winston Churchill. Later he received President Harry Truman, General Douglas MacArthur, and Churchill again (in 1952). In 1948, as part of the city's golden anniversary celebration of the consolidation of the five boroughs into the Greater City of New York, he put on a twenty-eight-day educational exhibition in the Grand Central Palace.

Whalen lost his greeter post to Richard C. Patterson, Jr., in 1953. In 1955 his autobiography, *Mr. New York*, was published. In it were many amusing, nostalgic, and educational stories, but the book revealed very little about the inner workings of the author's mind.

Whalen was elected president of Trans Continental Industries, a Detroit hardware firm, in 1956. The following year he became president of the Fifth Avenue Association. He died in New York City.

[Many of Whalen's papers are in the Archives of the City of New York. There is no definitive biography. The memoirs of Arthur W. Wallander, Frances Perkins, Walter Gellhorn, Claude Wickard, Jeremiah T. Mahoney, and Morris L. Strauss in the Columbia University Oral History Collection mention Whalen. See also material in the Columbia University Manuscript Library. An obituary notice is in the *New York Times*, Apr. 21, 1962.]

THEODORE L. MAYHEW

WHITFIELD, OWEN (Oct. 9, 1892–Aug. 11, 1965), Baptist minister and union organizer, was born in Jamestown, Miss. Little is known of his early life. His parents, former slaves, were sharecroppers. As a young man, Whitfield worked at various jobs in Tennessee and Arkansas, traveling for a while as a tap dancer in a minstrel show. In 1909 he married Zella Brown; they had eleven children. He returned to Mississippi to attend Okolona College (1911–1912), earning money by helping his uncle on a farm.

Whitfield moved to southeastern Missouri in 1923 to sharecrop on a cotton plantation about nine miles from Charleston. He also began preaching about then; by the 1930's he had become pastor of a number of rural churches. In 1937 he joined the Southern Tenant Farmers Union (STFU), which had been organized to try to improve the condition of poor croppers and tenant farmers in the South. STFU attacked the inequities of the New Deal's farm program, specifically the failure of the Agricultural Adjustment Administration (AAA) parity payments to reach croppers. Parity checks were made out to the landlords, who were supposed to share the money with their tenants according to the portion each tenant held in the crop. Many landlords found it easier to evict their croppers and work their land with cheaper day labor. They then could keep the entire check.

STFU activity in southeastern Missouri was slow to start. Its efforts in the early 1930's had been focused on eastern Arkansas, where, as in southeastern Missouri, cotton planting was new and the problems seemed worse than in other parts of the South. A charismatic figure who quickly attracted a large following, Whitfield was responsible for organizing the union in southeastern Missouri. Most of the union contacts were made through the churches. "Take your eyes out of the sky," Whitfield was fond of telling his sharecropper congregation, "because somebody is stealing your bread."

Whitfield did not confine his message to the blacks in his churches; he worked equally hard exhorting the whites in the fields and soon became one of the union's best organizers. His most dramatic effort came in 1939, when he organized a massive roadside protest demonstration in southeastern Missouri. The demonstra-

tion was triggered by mass evictions of croppers and tenant farmers at the end of 1938 because landlords wanted to cheat them of their AAA parity checks. Whitfield decided to use the evictions to dramatize the plight of the homeless cropper by camping along the roadside, in the bitter cold, for several weeks in January. It was an early example of a device that came to be common in the South during the civil rights movement of the 1950's and 1960's.

The publicity from the demonstration won Whitfield an audience with President Franklin D. Roosevelt, but beyond that the strike actually did little to change the conditions of the poor farmers in either southeastern Missouri or the nation. More significantly, the demonstration was responsible for exacerbating a growing struggle within STFU, one that ultimately led to its destruction.

The problems had started in 1937, when the union joined the CIO and became affiliated with the Communist-dominated United Cannery, Agricultural, Packing, and Allied Workers of America (UCAPAWA). Tension grew between the two organizations. It came into the open during the roadside demonstration, when Whitfield turned to UCAPAWA for assistance. Whitfield, who prided himself on his commitment to nonviolence, was not a Communist. "We have a more better [*sic*] and more peaceful way to work out our program and obtain our object," he wrote, "than resorting to violence." But his opposition to Communist methods did not cause him to reject Communist support. On this issue he broke with STFU leaders, who were convinced that he was being lured into the Communist camp.

Further complicating Whitfield's differences with STFU was the issue of race. He had been apprehensive about the union at first, primarily because he felt it was dominated by whites and would do little to help his people, the majority of whom were black. He changed his mind after talking to STFU officials, and soon became enthusiastic about the potential the union held for improving the lot of tenant farmers, both black and white. Actually, STFU was officially biracial, which made it unique among unions in the South in the 1930's. Moreover, STFU seems to have been innocent of any real racial prejudice. But the Communist faction in UCAPAWA charged that STFU was racist, the work of a "sectarian splinter racket of a few whites." Whitfield wisely walked a political tightrope between the two factions, seeking what assistance he could get from each. Although the roadside demonstration did not produce radical changes in farm policy, the federal government did build a housing project in the area to help poor sharecroppers and tenant farmers made homeless by evictions. After the demonstration, Whitfield worked for a while in Chicago with Rev. Claude Williams and the People's Applied Religion, but gradually settled back in southeastern Missouri, where he became the minister of several churches in the area. Whitfield died at Cape Girardeau, Mo.

[Material on Whitfield is in the papers of the STFU, in the Southern Historical Collection at the University of North Carolina, Chapel Hill (now available on microfilm). The most important published source is Louis Cantor, *A Prologue to the Protest Movement* (1969). Donald Grubb, *Cry from the Cotton* (1973), details the union's history. Thad Snow, *From Missouri* (1954), is an account of the 1939 demonstration. Whitfield's role in the demonstration is covered in Cedric Belfrage, "Cotton-Patch Moses," *Harper's*, Nov. 1948; and Louis Cantor, "A Prologue to the Protest Movement: The Missouri Sharecropper Roadside Demonstration of 1939," *Journal of American History*, Mar. 1969. An obituary is in the *New York Times*, Aug. 13, 1965.]

LOUIS CANTOR

WHITNEY, GEORGE (Oct. 9, 1885–July 22, 1963), banker, was born in Boston, Mass., the son of George Whitney, president of the Union National Bank of Boston, and of Elizabeth Whitney. Whitney grew up on Boston's Beacon Hill. He attended Groton School, from which he graduated in 1903, three years after his father's death. His uncle, Edward F. Whitney, a partner in J. P. Morgan and Company, helped him through college. In 1907 he received the B.A. from Harvard. That summer, having long ago set aside childhood dreams of becoming a doctor—"I couldn't afford it and wasn't prepared to make a sacrifice"—he decided to go into business.

Whitney started as a runner in the Boston offices of Kidder, Peabody and Company, one of the country's leading private banking houses. He remained with the firm for two years, gaining experience in deposit and merchant banking, foreign exchange, and underwriting corporate and government securities. He liked the work, and decided to look for wider opportunities in New York City. In August 1909, Whitney joined Redmond and Company, a small Wall Street firm that specialized in retailing foreign public utility issues. A year later, with two other men in their mid-twenties, he helped organize Markoe, Morgan and Whitney, a brokerage house. The new firm's business pros-

pered, and on June 2, 1914, Whitney married Martha Beatrix Bacon; they had four children.

In October 1915, Whitney left his firm to join J. P. Morgan and Company, the preeminent private banking house in the country. He considered the position well worth the sacrifice of giving up his own business. At Morgan's, his first assignment was to help distribute the $500 million Anglo-French loan. The operation gave him his first close experience with underwriting, syndication, and nationwide distribution of a large bond offering, skills he sharpened on subsequent wartime loans for the Allied governments.

Early in January 1915, Great Britain had appointed Morgan and Company its purchasing agents in the United States. Four months later France signed a similar agreement with the firm, which set up a special export department, headed by Edward R. Stettinius, Sr., to deal with the Allies' war business. Whitney worked closely with Stettinius, making certain that funds were always available to pay for the massive war purchases. Late in 1917, because of Whitney's detailed knowledge of Allied finances, Thomas W. Lamont took him to London and Paris to settle the firm's accounts with the British and French governments. While there, Whitney assisted Lamont in his capacity as unofficial confidential adviser to Colonel Edward House, the head of a special American mission struggling to coordinate Anglo-French financial and economic plans with those of the U.S. Treasury.

Impressed by his young associate's knowledge of complex financial questions, Lamont took Whitney with him to Paris in January 1919. Working with Lamont, a representative of the U.S. Treasury at the peace conference, Whitney wrestled with the difficult and controversial problem of determining Germany's reparation payments. This work, together with his experience in war finance, gave him a wide knowledge of both domestic and international banking and business, talents the Morgan partners valued and rewarded. On Dec. 31, 1919, he was made a partner, a position that brought him "tremendous prestige" outside the firm but no change in his work load.

During the 1920's, J. P. Morgan and Company continued to occupy first place among the country's private banks, conducting an extensive domestic and foreign banking and securities business. Whitney worked on several major European reconstruction and currency stabilization loans. In some cases, such as those of Austria (1923), France (1920, 1921, 1924), and

Italy (1925), he helped determine the terms and organize the syndicates that distributed the bonds. In other instances, such as the German (Dawes) loan of 1924, he occupied himself only with syndication and sales. Other foreign government loans with which he was closely involved included the Cuban (1923) and Japanese (1924) offerings.

Whitney devoted much attention to foreign and domestic corporate loans and to other areas of the firm's business. Late in 1920, with Stettinius, he organized the underwriting group that distributed $28 million of General Motors stock for the financially pressed automobile concern, and in 1921 they planned a rescue operation that saved the Guaranty Trust Company from financial embarrassment.

Whitney's experience in financing large enterprises made him a valued adviser to corporate executives, and like other Morgan partners he served as a director or trustee of many major American companies, including General Motors, whose board he joined in 1924. By the time of the 1929 stock market collapse, Whitney was a major leader of the Morgan firm.

The crash and the banking crisis that followed it brought Whitney the public attention he previously had been able to escape. He testified before several congressional committees investigating Wall Street practices in the 1920's; meanwhile, he continued to work quietly and effectively behind the scenes, directing salvage operations that benefited not only his own house but the financial and business communities in general. Early in 1931, Whitney presided over the reorganization of Kidder, Peabody and Company, arranging the necessary loans to keep the firm afloat and advising the new partners during the difficult months of readjustment. The next year, with Lamont, he headed the bankers' group that devised the financial rescue plan that saved New York City from bankruptcy.

The New Deal's banking and securities laws, particularly the 1933 Glass-Steagall Act's provision requiring the separation of commercial and investment banking, forced partnerships like the Morgan firm to choose between deposit banking and the securities business. The Morgan partners opted to remain a commercial bank. Whitney did much to reshape the firm's operations, and when the Morgan firm was incorporated as a commercial bank and trust company, he served as its president and chief executive officer (1940–1950) and then as its board chairman (1950–1955). He resigned as chairman in 1955 but stayed on as a director until

April 1959, when the bank merged with the Guaranty Trust Company to form the Morgan Guaranty Trust Company of New York. He was appointed chairman of the directors' advisory council of this company, a post he held until his death.

Widely respected at home and abroad as a highly knowledgeable, effective, and responsible financier, Whitney suffered the pain and embarrassment of seeing his younger brother, Richard, a five-time president of the New York Stock Exchange, jailed for misappropriation of funds entrusted to him by clients of his brokerage firm. (He was not involved in his brother's activities.)

Whitney was president of the Harvard Board of Overseers (1949–1953). He also served as chairman and director of the John and Mary R. Markle Foundation and as a trustee of both the Alfred P. Sloan Foundation and the Sloan-Kettering Institute for Cancer Research. He was president of Doctors Hospital for sixteen years and a treasurer of the Episcopal Church Foundation. Whitney died in New York City.

[There is no biography of Whitney, nor is there a collection of his private papers open to researchers. His reminiscences, in the Oral History Collection, Columbia University, are the most important primary source. Some of Whitney's work is covered in his testimony before congressional committees, particularly U.S. Senate, Committee on Finance, 72nd Cong., sess. 1, *Sale of Foreign Bonds or Securities in the United States* (4 pts., 1931–1932); U.S. Senate, Committee on Banking and Currency, 72nd Cong., sess. 1, and 73rd Cong., sess. 1 and 2, *Stock Exchange Practices* (7 pts., 1932–1933, 20 pts., 1933–1934); U.S. Senate, Special Committee Investigating the Munitions Industry, 73rd and 74th Congs., sess. 1 and 2, *Munitions Industry* (40 pts., 1935–1943); U.S. Temporary National Economic Committee, *Investigation of Concentration of Economic Power* (31 pts., 1939–1941). Whitney's role as a Morgan partner is discussed in John Brooks, *Once in Golconda* (1960); Vincent P. Carosso, *Investment Banking in America* (1970) and *More Than a Century of Investment Banking* (1979); and John D. Forbes, *Stettinius, Sr., Portrait of a Morgan Partner* (1974). Obituary notices are in the *New York Times* and New York *Herald Tribune,* July 23, 1963.]

VINCENT P. CAROSSO

WIENER, NORBERT (Nov. 26, 1894–Mar. 18, 1964), mathematician, was born in Columbia, Mo., the son of Leo Wiener, a professor of Slavic languages at Harvard, and Bertha Kahn. Norbert was unsuited, in his father's judgment, for a public school education; his father therefore undertook his early education himself.

At the age of nine Norbert entered Ayer (Mass.) High School, from which he graduated two years later. He next enrolled at Tufts College, where he majored in mathematics. He received the B.S. in 1909, when he was not yet fifteen. For his graduate studies Wiener chose philosophy—very much at the urging of his father—working first at Cornell and later at Harvard, where he received the Ph.D. at the age of eighteen. He described the intellectual force-feeding of his early years in *Ex-Prodigy* (1953). Wiener described his father as an exacting teacher, reacting to any erroneous response with ridicule and rage. In the context of Wiener's isolation from all but a handful of children of his own age, this treatment accentuated his feelings of inadequacy. He continued nevertheless to crave his father's praise and approval throughout his life up to the time of his father's death.

The next six years were restless and difficult. Wiener hoped for an academic appointment at Harvard, but none materialized. Harvard did give him a traveling fellowship, which he used at the universities of Cambridge and Göttingen in 1913–1914. At Cambridge he studied with Bertrand Russell. He met G. H. Hardy and J. E. Littlewood, the great Cambridge analysts, and read, at Russell's suggestion, Albert Einstein's papers on Brownian motion and Niels Bohr's on quantum theory. After another year on another traveling fellowship, Wiener became an assistant in the Harvard philosophy department, but no regular appointment ensued. At the suggestion of his father, Wiener applied for and obtained a job as instructor in mathematics at the University of Maine in 1916. He was not happy there. After the entry of the United States into World War I, he worked on ballistics at the Aberdeen Proving Ground in Maryland. In 1919 he obtained an instructorship in mathematics at the Massachusetts Institute of Technology (MIT).

The mathematics department at MIT was not a place of great academic distinction in 1919. Its job, in fact, was primarily to provide engineering students with a basic mathematical competence. Wiener taught twenty hours per week and worked to put the Heaviside calculus (then, as now, widely used in the analysis of electrical circuits) on a more rigorous foundation.

This interest, coupled with two chance events, set Wiener's course in the direction of creative achievements. The first chance event was his acquisition of books belonging to a fellow student who had died. These included books on analysis that introduced him to the Lebesgue integral. The second was a suggestion by I. A. Barnett, another young mathematician, that he investigate the problem of integration in function space. Wiener applied the techniques of the Lebesgue integral to this problem. Having achieved some analytical insights, he sought a physical situation to which those results might apply. He first tried turbulence. When that did not prove fruitful, he tried Brownian motion and discovered therein a vein that he was to mine for the rest of his career.

Wiener's approach to Brownian motion was to consider a statistical ensemble of paths of individual particles, the statistical behavior of the particles themselves being as described by Einstein and Marian Smoluchowski. To describe this ensemble of paths, he devised a construct that he called differential space. He computed the average of some functional over the ensemble of paths and showed that the paths were (almost always) continuous but (almost always) nondifferentiable: the amount and direction of a change in position cannot be predicted with certainty. The power of Wiener's method of analysis lay in its wide applicability to other stochastic processes in physics, electrical engineering, and other branches of science.

In 1924, Wiener was promoted to assistant professor. During the next few years he published papers in potential theory and in the early development of what are now known as Banach spaces. More significantly, he began to work on the problem of "almost periodic" functions, which he approached with his work on Brownian motion as a starting point. An almost periodic function is one that can be described neither by a Fourier series (since it is not periodic) nor by the ordinary Fourier integral (since it has neither beginning nor end). Wiener's 1930 paper "Generalized Harmonic Analysis" was probably his finest contribution. In 1925 he lectured on this topic at Göttingen, where he met Max Born and Werner Heisenberg; in *I Am a Mathematician* (1956) he implied that Heisenberg made use of his harmonic analysis in formulating the uncertainty principle. Wiener returned to Göttingen in 1926 as a Guggenheim fellow. Unfortunately he made important enemies at Göttingen, principally because of his inability to handle political issues, both national and academic. At Göttingen he reformulated and proved certain general Tauberian theorems which had appeared in his work on harmonic analysis. The publication of his work on harmonic analysis (1930) and on the Tauberian theorems (1932) established him as a mathematician of the first rank. MIT promoted him to associate professor in 1929 and to full professor in 1932.

Wiener's mathematical studies during the 1930's included the solution of the Wiener-Hopf equation, the study with R. E. A. C. Paley of the Fourier transform in the complex plane, and work on the ergodic theorem. He spent a good part of his time abroad: in Cambridge, England, during the year 1931–1932, and at Tsing Hua University, Peking, China, in 1935–1936.

After the outbreak of World War II in Europe, Wiener worked on the control of antiaircraft guns. This led him to investigate the problem of estimating the future position of an airplane on the basis of a finite number of (not perfectly accurate) measurements. Wiener attacked the problem through a least-squares procedure and showed that the optimum filter function may be expressed as the solution of a certain integral equation (reminiscent of Wiener-Hopf) involving autocorrelation (signal against signal) and cross correlation (signal against noise) functions. This result was classified at the time; the report in which it appeared was known to communications engineers who read it as the Yellow Peril, from the color of its paper covers and the opacity of its contents. In 1949 it was published as *Extrapolation, Interpolation and Smoothing of Stationary Time Series. With Engineering Applications.* The mainstream of information theory has taken a different, simpler path since then.

For many years Wiener had been convinced that there was a universal applicability of his ideas on prediction theory and control apparatus, some principle that would illuminate such diverse fields as electrical feedback, digital computers, automata, and living organisms. Such was the origin of his book *Cybernetics* (1948), which propelled him to a position of instant fame. It was a best seller. It also stimulated scholarly activities; societies were formed, journals were launched. In retrospect it is hard to understand what all the fuss was about. The book contains little that had not appeared before, and is appallingly written. Cybernetics persists today as a loose conglomeration of disciplines ranging all the way from systems engineering to biophysics, but there is no profession of cyberneticist. Perhaps Wiener's chief contribution was to provide an umbrella under which people working in a number of diverse fields could gather.

On Mar. 26, 1926, Wiener married Margaret Engermann. They had two daughters. Wiener was famous for his eccentricity, and anecdotes about his behavior are still told. He required constant praise and reassurance that he had not lost his touch. He was generous to those he felt needed his help, but never forgave those he felt had slighted him. He wrote a novel under his own name, *The Tempter* (1959), and several detective stories under the name W. Norbert. He died at Stockholm, Sweden.

[Many of Wiener's works are in *Selected Papers of Norbert Wiener* (1964), which also has contributions by Y. W. Lee, N. Levinson, and W. T. Martin. Also see *Bulletin of the American Mathematical Society,* Jan. 1966, an entire issue devoted to Wiener that includes a biography, specialized articles, and a bibliography; and J. Rose, ed., *Survey of Cybernetics: A Tribute to Dr. Norbert Wiener* (1969). An obituary is in the *New York Times,* Mar. 19, 1964.]

C. G. B. GARRETT

WILLEBRANDT, MABEL WALKER

(May 23, 1889–Apr. 6, 1963), educator and assistant attorney general of the United States, was born Mabel Walker near Woodsdale, Kans., the daughter of David William Walker and Myrtle S. Eaton. The family homestead was remote from public schools, and instruction in reading and writing from her parents, both of whom had been teachers, prepared her for schools in Kansas City, Mo., and then at Park College in Parkville, Mo., which she entered at age sixteen. Six years later she was teaching at the high school in Buckley, Mich., and attending Ferris Institute there. On Feb. 7, 1910, she married the high school's principal, A. F. Willebrandt. The couple moved that year to Arizona, where Mabel Willebrandt was graduated from the state normal school at Tempe in 1911. She was next principal of a grammar school at Buena Park, Calif., and then at South Pasadena while attending evening classes at the University of Southern California. After admission to the California bar in 1915; she received the LL.B. in 1916 and the LL.M. in 1917.

The next few years in Los Angeles brought Willebrandt an extraordinary reputation. Although she accepted no criminal cases in her private practice, she volunteered her services as assistant public defender in police courts—the first woman attorney in the country to accept such assignments—where she appeared as defense attorney for more than 2,000 women. She also drafted a law to protect the property rights of married women that was later enacted, became the first woman to serve as a committee chairman for the American Bar Association, and joined the Republican Central Committee for the state of California.

On Aug. 29, 1921, President Warren Harding named Willebrandt assistant attorney general. At the Justice Department she continued to work for women's property rights, but her major responsibilities included the administration of the Bureau of Federal Prisons, the supervision of federal tax cases, and the prosecution of cases arising under the National Prohibition Act, often called the Volstead Act.

As chief prosecutor of the Prohibition law, Willebrandt became the country's most famous woman attorney. By 1925 she had been responsible for the more than 45,000 criminal prosecutions in the federal courts and was arguing for the strict enforcement of the law not only before the Supreme Court but also in public forums across the nation. She said that Prohibition was "a moral crusade under religious leadership, frankly intended to save the people from a habit believed to be the chief cause of crime, poverty and misery." Yet some observers felt that she was motivated more by her principles of respect for all laws than by any desire to advance a moral crusade, that she was more a strict Republican than a strict prohibitionist.

The youngest woman ever to achieve her rank in federal government, Willebrandt had the strong body, the square jaw, and the large eyes and nose that cameras could not flatter. She was regarded as an unusually interesting and intelligent person, of whom it was said that "as an executive she is tireless, as a lawyer she is thorough and as a woman she is charming." She was also a strict and demanding superior, a shrewd political manipulator, and an exciting conversationalist, swift and sharp in repartee. Willebrandt was willing to accept the publicity that came to her as an attorney but resented that which came to her as a woman. She sustained a careful reticence regarding her personal life— the character of her marriage (some sources list her husband's name as Alfred, some as Arthur), the termination of that marriage (her apparent separation around 1916 and divorce in 1924), and her family life later (she had an adopted daughter, Dorothy).

In 1929, Willebrandt published an account of her experiences with the Volstead Act, *The Inside of Prohibition*. In this narrative of corruption, city by city, she praised some local officials while she recorded a spirited critique of others who, she said, promoted alliances among politicians and liquor interests. The book was also her response to charges raised against her during the 1928 presidential campaign, when she had been one of the most outspoken critics of the Democratic candidate, Al Smith of New York. She

had accepted Governor Smith's identification of himself as an opponent of the Volstead Act, and she had attacked him and the "predatory politics" of Tammany Hall. In several speeches she had urged "dry" Protestant ministers to convince the nation that Smith was a threat to the "dry" Constitution. But she had never, she insisted, uttered any sentiment critical of Smith's Roman Catholicism.

It may be that her repeated association of Herbert Hoover with the hope for strict enforcement of Prohibition and her obvious pleasure in public confrontation caused President Hoover to regard Willebrandt as a political liability. In any event, she left the Justice Department on June 2, 1929, returning to private practice in Los Angeles. From 1936 to 1957 she served as counsel to the Screen Directors' Guild. For years she had supposed that her record of devoted public service would sometime bring her a federal judgeship, but this wish was never fulfilled. She died at Riverside, Calif.

[Willebrandt wrote extensively, but scholars have not yet identified any substantial collection of her papers. Short pieces of her correspondence are in the Herbert Hoover Papers at the Hoover Library, West Branch, Iowa, and in the papers of Ernest Hurst Cherrington (of the Anti-Saloon League) at the Ohio Historical Society. Significant contemporary sketches include "The 'First Legal Lady of the Land,' " *Literary Digest*, Mar. 31, 1923; Clyde C. Cooke, "A Portia of the West," *Sunset*, July 1927; H. H. Smith, "Mrs. Willebrandt," *Outlook and Independent*, Oct. 24, 1928. The most careful investigation of Willebrandt's career is in Glenda E. Morrison, "Women's Participation in the 1928 Presidential Campaign" (Ph.D. diss., University of Kansas, 1978). An obituary is in the *New York Times*, Apr. 9, 1963.]

NORMAN H. CLARK

WILLIAMS, AUBREY WILLIS (Aug. 23, 1890–Mar. 3, 1965), social worker, federal official, and civil rights advocate, was born in Springville, Ala., the son of Charles Evans Williams and Eva Taylor, who came from slaveholding families that had been impoversihed by the Civil War. Shortly after Williams' birth, the family moved to Birmingham, where his father ran a blacksmith shop.

Work and religion shaped Williams' early life. Regularly employed from the age of nine, by the time he was twenty-one he had had only one full year of formal education. In Birmingham he saw the post–Civil War South's industrial poverty, and demonstrated an early interest in bettering the lives of the city's laborers, both white and black. Influenced by a preacher who emphasized the Social Gospel, Williams spent

Sundays reading the Bible and playing baseball with industrial workers and their families.

In 1911, Williams entered Maryville College in Tennessee with the intention of becoming a Presbyterian minister. He remained at Maryville for five years and developed an increasing interest in the social sciences. In 1916 he transferred to the University of Cincinnati, but left school the following year to go to Paris as a student representative of the Young Men's Christian Association. Williams was soon caught up in the excitement of World War I and joined the French Foreign Legion, serving until the arrival of American troops led to his reassignment to an American unit. He was wounded in action.

Williams remained in France after the armistice to attend the University of Bordeaux. He returned to the United States in 1919 and resumed his studies at Cincinnati, finally earning the B.A. in 1920. On Dec. 18, 1920, he married Anita Schreck; they had four children.

After spending two years as a church pastor and city recreation director, Williams left Cincinnati to become executive director of the Wisconsin Conference on Social Work in Madison. The conference, which promoted social welfare legislation, drafted laws that made Wisconsin a laboratory in such areas as industrial regulation, workmen's compensation, and unemployment insurance. Williams spent ten years in Madison, gaining a national reputation as an effective proponent of rationally administered public assistance programs.

In 1932, Williams became a field representative for the American Public Welfare Association. His job was to make sure that relief loans from the Reconstruction Finance Corporation actually reached those in need. He proved adept at dealing with local politicians who saw federal relief as a threat. During one foray into Mississippi, he organized what in effect became the country's first statewide work relief program.

In May 1933, Harry Hopkins, the director of the Federal Emergency Relief Administration (FERA), put Williams in charge of FERA's southwestern district. Williams' background, education, temperament, and experience in public welfare made him a fervent New Dealer. Together he and Hopkins began planning for the Civil Works Administration (CWA), the first federally run work relief program.

Williams became a highly visible public advocate of New Deal social welfare policies. As deputy administrator of the CWA and, beginning in 1935, of its successor, the Works Progress Administration, he oversaw the spending of bil-

lions of dollars and helped put large numbers of people to work. He was among the minority of New Dealers who believed that the federal government's responsibility for the well-being of all Americans extended beyond the economic crisis caused by the Great Depression. He was, in short, a passionate liberal whose greatest concern was for the one-third of a nation, as President Franklin D. Roosevelt once put it, that was "ill nourished, ill clad, ill housed." To friends and foes, Williams seemed the archetype of the kind of public servant Roosevelt had brought to Washington. The *Memphis Commercial Appeal*, an anti-Roosevelt newspaper, described him as "a do-gooder among do-gooders . . . in the galaxy of bleeding hearts produced by the Rexford Guy Tugwell School of screwball social planners and uplifters."

Williams' outspoken liberalism made his career stormy. In 1935 his support of striking cotton pickers aroused the ire of Senator Joseph Robinson of Arkansas and almost cost him his job. Williams infuriated conservatives by blaming social injustice on "arrogant aggregates of concentrated economic power." His most controversial action occurred in 1938 when, speaking to a meeting of relief workers, he urged them "to keep our friends in power." This precipitated charges from Republicans that the New Deal sought to buy the votes of the beneficiaries of its relief programs. Republican Congressman Hamilton Fish of New York called Williams "the most dangerous man in the government."

When, in 1935, an executive order created the National Youth Administration (NYA), Williams became its head. His work for the NYA, which aided young people in completing their education by offering them part-time employment, drew him into the orbit of Eleanor Roosevelt, who made the agency one of her pet projects. She and Williams formed a close working relationship and came to admire each other personally. With her support Williams was able to make the NYA particularly responsive to black youths. He made the black educator Mary McLeod Bethune one of his top assistants; under their leadership the NYA won a well-deserved reputation as the most racially enlightened federal agency. Williams repeatedly issued directives to his white state administrators (one of whom was a young Texan named Lyndon Baines Johnson) to find jobs for young blacks. Williams remained head of the NYA until 1943, when Congress refused to renew its appropriations.

By this time Williams was one of America's

most prominent liberals. He became an organizing director for the National Farmers Union and worked with the Southern Conference for Human Welfare (SCHW), a group organized in 1938 to bring New Deal reforms to the South.

In January 1945, President Roosevelt named Williams to head the Rural Electrification Administration, but his appointment came under heavy attack from private utility companies and the American Farm Bureau Federation. The Senate undertook a lengthy investigation of Williams' background and career, during which several senators denounced him for his alleged "Communistic" and "race-mixing" sympathies. Despite the effort of liberals to defend Williams, the Senate voted against his confirmation.

Following the Senate's rejection, Williams returned to the South. He purchased a farm just outside Montgomery, Ala., and bought a monthly publication, *Southern Farmer*. The magazine, the title of which was later changed to *Southern Farm and Home,* proved profitable.

But Williams did not abandon the causes closest to his heart. He stood out as one of the most vigorous white southern spokesman for civil rights and in 1947 became president of the Southern Conference Education Fund (SCEF), an offshoot of SCHW. Under the leadership of Williams and James Dombrowski, SCEF was a small but militantly antisegregationist civil rights organization. It strongly endorsed the 1947 report of President Harry Truman's Committee on Civil Rights, criticized the Dixiecrats, and called for a strong civil rights plank in the 1948 Democratic party platform. In November 1948, Williams personally led an interracial group of about 200 persons on a pilgrimage to Monticello, Thomas Jefferson's Virginia home, and from there demanded the passage of civil rights legislation.

Such activities put Williams very much out of step with the white South's determination to preserve segregation. Not only was he ostracized by Montgomery's white community, but he became the object of political persecution and personal harassment. In March 1954 he and three other white SCEF members were called to testify before the Senate Internal Security Subcommittee, which held hearings in New Orleans that were chaired by Senator James Eastland of Mississippi. Once again Williams was smeared for his alleged Communist leanings. The investigation also led to the decline of his farm journal, which lost advertisers and subscribers after the American Legion conducted a campaign against what it regarded as "Communism in agriculture."

The vituperations heaped upon Williams stiffened his resolve to campaign against segregation and violations of civil liberties. In 1955 he supported the Montgomery bus boycott led by Rev. Martin Luther King, Jr., using his influence to obtain legal aid for the boycotters. Five years later Williams became chairman of the National Committee to Abolish the House Un-American Activities Committee. In 1963, after selling his publishing enterprises, he returned to Washington, D.C., where he died.

[The Aubrey Williams Papers, in the Franklin D. Roosevelt Library, Hyde Park, N.Y., include his unpublished and incomplete autobiography, "A Southern Rebel" (Box 44). Williams' writings include "Twelve Million Unemployed: What Can Be Done," *New York Times Magazine,* Mar. 27, 1938; *Work, Wages and Education* (1940); "Liberal Renaissance from the South?" *New South,* May 1947; and "There Is a Break," *Nation,* Aug. 6, 1949. Much on his career up to 1945 is in U.S. Congress, Senate Committee on Agriculture and Forestry, *Hearings on the Nomination of Aubrey W. Williams to be Administrator, Rural Electrification Administration,* 79th Cong., sess. 1 (1945). Also see Thomas A. Krueger, *And Promises to Keep* (1968); Irwin Klibaner, "The Southern Conference Educational Fund" (Ph.D. diss., University of Wisconsin, 1971); John A. Salmond, "Postscript to the New Deal," *Journal of American History,* Sept. 1974; and Morton Sosna, *In Search of the Silent South* (1977). An obituary is in the *New York Times,* Mar. 5, 1965.]

MORTON SOSNA

WILLIAMS, WILLIAM CARLOS (Sept. 17, 1883–Mar. 4, 1963), poet and physician, was born in Rutherford, N.J., the son of William George Williams, who worked for a company that produced Florida water, and Raquel Hélène Hoheb. His father, born in England, was raised in the West Indies. His mother, born in Puerto Rico, studied painting for three years at the Académie des Beaux Arts in Paris. Spanish was the language most often spoken in the household when Williams was a child.

Williams' paternal grandmother, Emily Dickenson Wellcome, played an important role during his formative years. In "The Wanderer" (1914) she becomes the metamorphosing old queen who baptizes him in the vile Passaic River and provides the source of his strength. In "January Morning" (1917) he dedicates his poetry to her: "All this— / was for you, old woman. / I wanted to write a poem / that you would understand."

Williams' mother lived with him and his family from 1918, when her husband died, until her death in 1949, at the age of 102. To keep her occupied during stretches of illness, Williams collaborated with her on translations of several works, among them Francisco Quevedo's *The Dog and the Fever* (1954), a novel left by Ezra Pound at the Williams' home. In 1959 he published *Yes, Mrs. Williams,* an account of her life interspersed with reminiscences in her own voice.

Williams attended public schools in Rutherford until 1897, when his mother took him and his brother to Europe for two years. He attended the Château de Lancy near Geneva and the Lycée Condorcet in Paris. From 1899 to 1902 he commuted from Rutherford to Horace Mann High School in New York City.

Having settled on a medical career, Williams studied from 1902 to 1906 at the University of Pennsylvania Medical School. There he began what was to be a lifelong literary friendship with Ezra Pound, then an undergraduate, and through Pound met H. D. (Hilda Doolittle). At his rooming house he formed another lasting friendship, with the painter Charles Demuth. (A Williams poem inspired Demuth's 1928 poster painting dedicated to him, *I Saw the Figure 5 in Gold.*)

Williams interned in New York City from 1906 to 1909, first at the old French Hospital and then at the Nursery and Child's Hospital. His first book, a collection of twenty-six poems entitled *Poems,* was printed at his own expense in 1909. Shortly thereafter he studied pediatrics for a year at the University of Leipzig. He also visited Pound in London, where he met William Butler Yeats.

Returning to Rutherford in 1910, Williams started general practice. On Dec. 12, 1912, he married Florence Herman, the Flossie of many of his poems. They had two sons. As a doctor Williams became familiar to his largely middle-class neighbors and to many of the working-class population of the surrounding industrial communities. In 1920 he was named medical inspector of schools in Rutherford, and in 1924 he joined the staff of the Passaic General Hospital as a pediatrician.

Williams' earliest poetic models were John Keats and Walt Whitman. But after publication of "The Wanderer" in *The Egoist* in 1914, he abandoned his youthful imitations and, under the influence of imagism and modern painting, acquired a new attitude toward verse forms and the treatment of subject. Imagism, which he never espoused with Pound's enthusiasm, nevertheless lent a certain authority to his concern for the concrete and commonplace, for a language that is nearly devoid of abstraction

and thus appears to record observations and often to convey the process of perception. Value in the apprehended world, in experience, is acknowledged rather than conferred. The speaker in a Williams poem is drawn by some alembic force to take note of ordinary scene or action and thereby to transform it. Later, in 1927, Williams declared that Alfred North Whitehead's *Science and the Modern World* was a landmark in his career. No doubt he found in the objectivist view—"that things experienced and the cognizant subject enter into the common world on equal terms"—justification for his own aesthetic.

During the second decade of the century, Williams frequented the New York salon of Walter Arensberg and "291," the avant-garde art and photography gallery established by Alfred Stieglitz. From the work of the French postimpressionists and cubists, he gained further support for his own experiments in verse. They offered "release from stereotyped forms, trite subjects."

Williams felt himself at the center of the new, where the visual arts had taken the lead. One of his most astute critics asserts that his writing after the 1913 Armory Show can be described in terms of the three modes of expression articulated by Wassily Kandinsky: impression, improvisation, and composition. Having early considered becoming a painter, Williams thought sight was his strongest sense. He wrote numerous essays on the arts, collected in *A Recognizable Image* (1978). Criticism since the late 1960's has focused much attention on the relationship of his writing to modern painting, particularly cubism.

The startling range of Williams' achievement is evident in his works published in the 1920's. Besides *Kora in Hell: Improvisations* (1920) and *The Great American Novel* (1923), both prose experiments in randomness and discontinuity, there appeared *Spring and All* (1923), his most ambitious and successful early book, which interspersed verse and prose passages; *In the American Grain* (1925), prose studies of figures in American history in which he attempted both to "possess" America through his interpretations and to capture each character in a style "most germane to its sources"; *A Voyage to Pagany* (1928), a novel exploring an American doctor's responses to the cultural milieu of Europe; and *Last Nights of Paris* (1929), a translation with his mother of a novel by Philippe Soupault.

Throughout his career Williams addressed what he believed to be the American writer's

need to discard European precedents. He denounced the urge that T. S. Eliot, Pound, and
other expatriates had answered by emigrating,
and affirmed the primacy of the local and the
American dialect. *The Waste Land* had struck
him "like a sardonic bullet." It was accomplished in craft, he conceded, but foreign to
American life and language. It appeared at a
time when Williams was exhorting writers to
discover new vigor in the American soil, against
the grain of American life if need be. One vehicle for his ideas was *Contact*, a little magazine
he edited with Robert McAlmon and Marsden
Hartley through five issues (1920–1923).

Williams did not turn his back on Europe. In
1924 he and his wife spent six months in
France, where, through Pound and McAlmon,
they associated with James Joyce, Ford Madox
Ford, Gertrude Stein, George Antheil, Soupault, Ernest Hemingway, Kay Boyle, and other
writers and artists. In *Pagany*, dedicated to
Pound and written after his return from a second trip in 1927, the central character must
force himself to resist the pagan allure of the old
cultures and begin his life once more at home.

Although he received little recognition outside the little magazines, in which he published
widely, Williams persevered. He found in the
physics of Albert Einstein and the discoveries of
Marie Curie support for his innovations in verse
and prose. In the spring of 1926 he discussed
Charles Steinmetz's *Four Lectures on Relativity
and Space* (1923) with a young engineer, John
Riordan. With the general relativity theory in
mind, Williams began to construct his own theory of a new poetic meter. Relative measure,
what he was later to call the "variable foot,"
could replace traditional metrics and yet avoid
the formlessness of vers libre; the line would be
relatively fixed, the poet's breath and voice controlling and shaping it according to a beat heard
in units of language. In the *Embodiment of
Knowledge*, notes written between 1928 and
1930 and published posthumously (1974), Williams argued that the poet, not the philosopher
or scientist, must humanize knowledge by emphasizing process, multiformity, and organic
connection instead of deduction and categorization. Fixities led only to disembodied facts.

Although two important collections of his
poems appeared in the 1930's, the first (*Collected Poems, 1921–31*) published in 1934 with
an introduction by Wallace Stevens, Williams'
major writing in this decade was fiction: two
collections of short stories, *The Knife of the
Times and Other Stories* (1932) and *Life Along
the Passaic River* (1938); an experimental novel-

ette, *January* (1932); and *White Mule* (1937),
the first of a trilogy based on his wife's family.
At Pound's urging, Williams met Louis Zukofsky in 1928, and the two became friends and
literary correspondents. *An 'Objectivists' Anthology*, edited by Zukofsky in 1932, included
writing by George Oppen, Carl Rakosi, Zukofsky, and seventeen poems by Williams.
While none of the group desired identity as part
of a movement, clarity of detail and the view of
the poem itself as an object—what Williams
was to refer to as "a machine made of words"
—were aesthetic values they shared, principles
influenced by the emphasis on hard-edged images and the selective realism of photography
and precisionist painting. Direct recording of
observation and speech is equally evident in
Williams' short stories, their subjects often
drawn with unflinching fidelity from his experiences as a doctor.

Williams' epic poem *Paterson* appeared in
five books (1946, 1948, 1949, 1951, 1958).
Based on the quest of a doctor-poet for a re-
deeming language to give meaning to the history and landscape of his environment, and thus
to save his people, the poem centers on the city,
transformed at various points into a mythic
giant reclining on the bank of the Passaic River,
Dr. Paterson, and Noah Faitoute Paterson, a
local hero. It consists of assemblages of lyric
passages, newspaper clippings, details from local
histories and old journals, parts of actual letters
—a literary collage. Following the river from the
falls (whose roar fills the giant's head) to the sea,
the speaker meditates on the welter of experiences, words, and images that have shaped his
life and on the supplying female of daily existence who has fed his imagination. Descent into
the darker recesses of self, toward despair, leads
to reaffirmation. He finds the "Beautiful Thing"
he seeks not in libraries and the past, but in the
fertile, teeming life of Alexander Hamilton's
"great beast," tragically divorced from the richness of experience through the failure of language. Like Marie Curie finally beholding the
glowing radium in her makeshift laboratory, Dr.
Paterson's repeated discovery is "luminous," the
radiant gist.

"Relativity applies to everything, like love, if
it applied to anything in the world," Williams
wrote in 1946. In *Paterson*, as a field of action,
organic unity evolves not from the clear, logical
relationship of all its parts but from the various
motifs and strands of Dr. Paterson's mind. In
this light, Book V, more consistently employing
the triadic form, or "variable foot," and declaring the permanence of art and the female princi-

ple, serves as a summation. The dance to a contrapuntal measure with which it ends is Williams' sure but tragic answer to the meaningless roar.

During the years he was writing *Paterson*, Williams also produced a substantial number of short lyrics; *The Desert Music* (1954), considered one of his finest long poems; *The Autobiography* (1951); *The Build-Up* (1952), the final novel of the Stecher trilogy; and two important plays, *A Dream of Love* (1948) and *Many Loves* (1961). The latter play was produced in New York City by the Living Theatre in 1959. The volume that includes *Pictures from Brueghel* (1962), a series of ten poems based on works by the painter, contains a number of quintessential poems, among them "Asphodel, That Greeny Flower" (1955), a confessional poem addressed to Flossie.

Williams was invited to be poetry consultant to the Library of Congress for 1949–1950, but ill health obliged him to postpone his acceptance. Thereafter, an accusation that he was a Communist sympathizer and the fact of his lifetime friendship with Pound, then incarcerated in a mental hospital after being convicted of treason, led to a government investigation. Although fully cleared in June 1953, the year of his appointment had lapsed and he never assumed the position.

Williams did not fare well with the New Critics and often railed against what he considered the narrow strictures of academics. During the last fifteen years of his life, though, his reputation grew steadily. The publication of *Paterson* attracted critical acclaim. His influence on young poets, among them Robert Lowell, Denise Levertov, Allen Ginsberg, Theodore Roethke, Charles Olson, and Robert Creeley, was extensive. In 1949 he became a fellow of the Library of Congress. Among other honors, he received the first National Book Award for poetry (1950), the Bollingen Prize (1953), and (posthumously) the Pulitzer Prize in poetry (1963). Since his death numerous studies of his writing have appeared, and he is now recognized as a major American poet.

Although a heart ailment and several severe strokes afflicted Williams from 1948 to his death, his late writing possesses mature insight and technical mastery. He died in Rutherford.

[The chief collections of Williams' manuscripts and correspondence are in the American Literature Collection, Beinecke Rare Book and Manuscript Library, Yale University, and in the Poetry Collection of the Lockwood Memorial Library, State University of New York at Buffalo. There are also documents and letters at the University of Texas at Austin, the University of Pennsylvania, and Princeton University. Williams' personal library is housed in the Fairleigh Dickinson University Library, Rutherford, N.J.

Works not mentioned in the text include *The Tempers* (1913); *Al Que Quiere!* (1917); *Sour Grapes* (1921); *An Early Martyr and Other Poems* (1935); *Adam & Eve & The City* (1936); *The Complete Collected Poems of William Carlos Williams 1906–1938* (1938); *In the Money* (1940); *The Broken Span* (1941); *The Wedge* (1944); *Make Light of It* (1950); *The Collected Later Poems* (1950; rev. 1963); *The Collected Earlier Poems* (1951); *The Selected Essays of William Carlos Williams* (1954); *Journey to Love* (1955); *The Farmers' Daughters* (1961).

The standard bibliography is Emily M. Wallace, *A Bibliography of William Carlos Williams* (1968). John C. Thirlwall, ed., *Selected Letters of William Carlos Williams* (1957), is a limited selection from the vast correspondence. Autobiographical reminiscences about his books are in *I Wanted to Write a Poem: The Autobiography of the Works of a Poet* (1958; rev., 1978), edited by Edith Heal. General introductions are Thomas R. Whitaker, *William Carlos Williams* (1968), and James E. Breslin, *William Carlos Williams: An American Artist* (1970). Two important studies of the poet's aesthetic principles are Mike Weaver's seminal *William Carlos Williams: The American Background* (1971) and Sherman Paul's *The Desert Music: A Biography of a Poem* (1968). The authorized biography is Reed Whittemore, *William Carlos Williams: Poet from Jersey* (1975). Since Bram Dijkstra, *The Hieroglyphics of a New Speech* (1969), increasing attention has been accorded Williams' connections with art and artists. Assessments of Williams' poetry in relation to that of his contemporaries are Louis Simpson, *Three on the Tower* (1975), and Hugh Kenner, *A Homemade World* (1975).]

THEODORA R. GRAHAM

WILLISTON, SAMUEL (Sept. 24, 1861–Feb. 18, 1963), lawyer and educator, was born in Cambridge, Mass., the son of Lyman Richards Williston, the head of a private academy, and of Ann Eliza Safford Gale. He received the B.A. from Harvard College in 1882, and after working for a few years as a secretary and then as a teacher, he entered Harvard Law School in 1885. He graduated in 1888, and on Sept. 12, 1889, he married Mary Fairlie Wellman. They had two daughters. After receiving the LL.B., Williston spent a year as clerk to U.S. Supreme Court Justice Horace Gray. He then joined the Boston firm of Hyde, Dickinson and Howe, with which he was affiliated until 1895.

Although Williston practiced law on and off throughout his life, he found its scholarly aspects more appealing than its practice. At Harvard Law School he had compiled an excellent record, winning prizes and serving as a member of the first editorial board of the *Harvard Law Review*. In 1889 his research on state laws proved helpful to the drafters of new constitutions for North Dakota and South Dakota. The following year he accepted an appointment as assistant professor at Harvard Law School. Because of family needs, he continued his practice until he suffered a nervous and physical breakdown in 1895. When he recovered, he discontinued his private work except for occasional cases and devoted himself to teaching and research.

In these areas Williston proved to be one of the most capable and popular men ever to teach at Harvard Law School. He was promoted to professor just before his collapse, to the Weld professorship in 1903, and to the Dane chair in 1919, which he held until his retirement in 1938. Few students who passed through his sales and contracts courses ever forgot the great horse "Dobbin," which figured in countless cases illustrating the finer points of commercial law. An honorary degree from Harvard in 1910 cited him as "brilliant master and keen teacher of the common law, who for a score of years has trained and inspired a generation of lawyers."

Williston's influence extended far beyond Harvard. He wrote or edited eighteen casebooks and more than fifty articles. His five-volume *Law of Contracts* (1920–1922) became the standard text in the field. One scholar called it "the greatest law book of our times." The third edition of his *Law of Sales* (1909) came out in his eighty-fifth year. Other of his treatises covered commercial law, negotiable instruments, bankruptcy, and pleading. Williston's books reflected the qualities of his teaching: balance, the union of scholarly analysis with practical insights, and comprehensive presentation of all salient details.

Williston was active in the movement to promote uniform commercial codes among the various states. He served as Massachusetts commissioner for uniform state laws from 1910 to 1929. In 1901 the Conference of Commissioners on Uniform State Laws chose him to prepare a draft statute covering the law of sales. The first act produced by the conference (on negotiable instruments), speedily adopted by the states, had been a flawed work reflecting the haste in which it had been produced. Williston, working quickly, nonetheless set a high standard and insisted that there be opportunity for review of the draft by law teachers and practicing attorneys. As a result, it was five years before the Uniform Statute on Sales was ready for submission to the states, but it received unanimous praise. Both the code and the method of review became standards against which to measure future efforts.

Williston was responsible for the model statutes on sales, warehouse receipts, bills of lading, and certificates of stock adopted by most states. One estimate held that at least thirty-six states adopted laws he had drawn up. He also played an important role as reporter for the American Law Institute's project on the restatement of the common law and was responsible for the codification and simplification of the commercial law in this undertaking.

Williston's work in commercial law has frequently been compared with that of his predecessor in the Dane chair, Joseph B. Story. Story gave shape to the law received from England, to meet the needs of a dynamic and expanding economy. Williston reshaped the nineteenth-century laws to serve the purposes of a more mature country and economy.

In recognition of his work as teacher and scholar, in 1929 the American Bar Association struck its first gold medal in Williston's honor and awarded it to him "for conspicuous service to American jurisprudence." Williston always referred to the medal as "the greatest honor of my life."

In 1938, Harvard announced that Williston would retire because of age, and the president, James B. Conant, wrote him a routine note: "Your resignation is accepted with regret." Williston, who had not wanted to retire, stormed into Conant's office and delivered an impromptu lecture on the law to the startled president: "A contract consists of an offer and an acceptance. You cannot accept a resignation that has not been tendered." Of course, the university insisted that age must give way to youth. Williston reluctantly stepped down.

Williston's career, though, was far from over. He continued to do research until well past his ninetieth year, and after leaving Harvard he was a visiting professor at the University of Texas and at the Catholic University of America in Washington. During World War II, Williston was called back to Harvard on a part-time basis to help fill teaching ranks depleted by calls to government service. Part-time soon became in effect full-time, and the octogenarian proved he was still an able and popular teacher.

Williston also resumed a more active practice. Throughout his teaching years at Harvard he had always accepted requests from former students that he serve as a consultant on difficult cases dealing with commercial law. Now a former student, Reginald Heber Smith, arranged for Williston to become counsel to Hale and Dorr in Boston. He was given an office and support services at no charge and was free to keep all the fees that came to him. He worked out of this office until failing health in the mid-1950's made it impossible for him to continue. Williston had hoped that he would become Harvard's oldest living alumnus, and he achieved this status, but his physical condition had so deteriorated that it is doubtful that he derived any enjoyment from it. He died in Cambridge, Mass., at the age of 101.

[Williston's autobiography is *Life and Law* (1940). Also see Harvard College Class of 1882, Sixth (1907) and Seventh (1932) *Reports;* the introduction to *Harvard Legal Essays in Honor of Joseph Henry Beale and Samuel Williston* (1934); and R. H. Smith, *In Memoriam Samuel Williston* (1963).]
MELVIN I. UROFSKY

WILSON, CHARLES ERWIN (July 18, 1890–Sept. 26, 1961), automobile executive and secretary of defense, was born in Minerva, Ohio, the son of Thomas Erwin Wilson and Rosalind Unkefer. His father was principal of the Minerva school, and his mother had been a teacher there. According to Wilson, his father, a Welsh immigrant, had been a toolmaker and had organized a union local in Pittsburgh. In 1894 the family moved to Mineral City, Ohio, where Thomas Wilson became a bank cashier. While the family was in Mineral City, two neighbors who were locomotive engineers occasionally allowed Charles to ride in the cab with them, an experience that is alleged to have aroused his enthusiasm for engineering. After the family moved to Pittsburgh in 1904, he graduated from Bellevue High School and then entered the Carnegie Institute of Technology (now Carnegie-Mellon University). He graduated in three years, receiving an E.E. degree in 1909.

Wilson claimed to have followed the family's socialist tradition in college and openly supported Eugene V. Debs for president. For this reason, he said, he could not get a job in engineering when he graduated. He worked as a patternmaker and became business agent of the patternmakers' local. When he was president of General Motors (GM), he kept his framed union card on his desk. His early union experience undoubtedly gave him the perspective that made him a sympathetic negotiator in bargaining with the United Automobile Workers (UAW).

By 1910, Wilson was an engineer for the Westinghouse Electric and Manufacturing Company in Pittsburgh. He became assistant to the brilliant Benjamin G. Lamme, then chief engineer of Westinghouse and considered to be the equal of Charles Steinmetz in electrical engineering.

In 1912, Wilson designed Westinghouse's first starting motor for automobiles, to compete with the motor that Charles F. Kettering had designed for Cadillac at Dayton Engineering Laboratories Company (Delco). His salary at this time was $80 a month, enough for him to marry Jessie Ann Curtis on Sept. 11, 1912. They had six children. In 1916, Wilson was put in charge of all Westinghouse automobile electrical products. During World War I he declined a commission in the army, preferring to work in Washington on the design of electrical equipment for military and naval use.

Wilson's war work had attracted the attention of O. K. Conklin of the Remy Electric Company of Anderson, Ind., a subsidiary of GM. Conklin offered him $250 a month to become chief engineer and sales manager at Remy. In 1921, Wilson was named factory manager, and then general manager. He successfully reorganized the company, and when it was merged with Delco in 1926 as Delco-Remy, he became president. By concentrating all ignition production in Anderson, he saved $5 million a year, but he postponed the removal of these operations from Dayton until he had replaced them with other work, including mass production of fractional-horsepower electric motors.

Wilson returned to Detroit in 1928 as a vice-president of GM, in charge of the accessory-producing subsidiaries. His first achievement in that capacity was to recommend the acquisition of the Allison Engineering Company, the country's leading manufacturer of liquid-cooled aircraft engines. Wilson was also involved in the acquisition of the Packard Electric Company, which became part of Delco-Remy, and of the Winton Engine Company and the Electro-Motive Company, manufacturers of diesel locomotives, which were combined as the Electro-Motive Division of GM. In addition, he had a role in the purchase by GM of minority interests in Bendix Aviation and North American Aviation (now part of Rockwell International).

In 1929, Wilson became vice-president for manufacturing, which gave him, among other things, responsibility for approving any proposal for expansion by a GM division or subsidiary. Subsequently he assumed charge of labor relations. In the strike of 1937, which resulted in the recognition of the UAW by GM, William S. Knudsen, who had just succeeded Alfred P. Sloan as president of the company, told Wilson, "You take care of the labor relations. You've got more patience than I have and you talk more." The concluding phrase applied all too accurately to Wilson, but in this situation his outspokenness seems to have been an asset. He was patient and willing to talk at whatever length was necessary in prolonged bargaining sessions. The settlement he achieved was historic; the acceptance of the UAW by GM meant that the rest of the industry must inevitably follow suit. The open-shop policy that had dominated the automobile industry since its earliest days was ended. Some of Wilson's associates felt that he had conceded too much; they complained that his initials, C. E., meant "Compromise Everything."

Wilson became executive vice-president of GM in 1939, and early in 1941, when Knudsen resigned in order to take charge of defense production, he was appointed president. At this time he acquired the nickname "Engine Charlie," to distinguish him from "Electric Charlie," Charles Edward Wilson, who had just been made president of General Electric. Paradoxically "Engine Charlie" had been educated and had achieved distinction as an electrical engineer, while "Electric Charlie" had risen through accounting and sales and had no formal training in engineering.

Through the war years Wilson supervised the enormous volume of military production turned out by GM: $12 billion worth, including a fourth of the nation's output of tanks and aircraft engines, two-thirds of the heavy trucks, three-fourths of the navy's diesel power plants, and large numbers of naval aircraft. By the end of 1943 every GM war contract was in production and on schedule, and the company was turning out far more than the government had thought possible. Wilson collapsed under the strains of that time. He returned to work in three months, but for the rest of his life he suffered from circulatory problems and headaches.

Wilson was well enough by the end of the war to be a forceful advocate of resuming control of GM's German subsidiary, Adam Opel A.G., which had been taken over by the Nazi government and had passed to the Allied occupation authorities. The property had suffered severe war damage, and with the future of the German economy uncertain, the financial policy committee of GM was dubious about taking Opel back. But Wilson, on the basis of the report of

a special committee that he appointed in 1947, was convinced it should be done. He had the support of Alfred P. Sloan, then chairman of the board, and this was decisive. At the same time (1948), GM sold its holdings in North American Aviation. This step, which Wilson approved, was taken because it was felt that GM, as a major manufacturer of aircraft engines and parts, should not be in the airframe business and, therefore, competing with its own customers.

In 1941, Wilson developed the idea of basing cost-of-living wage adjustments on the National Consumer Price Index, plus an "annual improvement factor," to enable workers to share in increased productivity. These concepts were first applied at GM in the settlement of a strike in 1948. They were subsequently criticized as creating built-in inflationary pressures, but Wilson maintained that they simply protected employees against inflation. The improvement factor was a chronic problem because it was never possible to find an objective way to measure productivity. Wilson also favored the supplementary unemployment benefits plan that was adopted in the automobile industry in 1955.

Wilson was profoundly concerned with problems of management. He believed that the founders of GM had created the structure and constitutional principles and that his generation of management had the task of creating a community. Peter Drucker, who joined GM during World War II as a management consultant, has written, "Insofar as we in the United States have made progress toward income security for employees and toward a self-governing plant community, we owe it largely to Wilson's receptivity to 'heretical' ideas."

When Dwight D. Eisenhower was elected president in 1952, he nominated Wilson as secretary of defense. Up to that time Wilson had not been much in the public eye. The propensity for speaking freely that Knudsen had noted had not caused him trouble. But at the Senate hearings on his nomination, Wilson drew unfavorable publicity when he objected to a requirement that he dispose of his GM stock, estimated to be worth $2.5 million. Later, Senator Robert C. Hendrickson of New Jersey, a Republican, asked him whether, if he had to make a decision that was in the interest of the United States but extremely adverse to GM, he could do it. Wilson's replied, "Yes, sir, I could. I cannot conceive of one because for years I thought what was good for our country was good for General Motors, and vice versa." The last three words allowed critics to reverse what Wilson actually said. They insisted that he had taken the position that what was good for GM was good for the country.

Wilson was confirmed as secretary after he agreed to sell his GM holdings, and he embarked on a stormy four-and-a-half-year term of office. With the Korean War over, the Eisenhower administration wanted to reduce military expenditures. Wilson cut the defense budget by $5 billion and the civilian staff of his department by 40,000, a procedure certain to make him unpopular in the Pentagon. He reversed industrial mobilization policy from a reliance on widespread sources of supply to a concentration on large corporations with high technical skills. In addition, he antagonized part of the military establishment by attempting to curtail conventional forces in favor of reliance on massive nuclear retaliation—the "More Bang for a Buck" policy.

It is not clear whether this policy was Wilson's or Eisenhower's. In any case, Wilson had to take the responsibility. One consequence was a "revolt of the colonels" in 1956, when some Pentagon officers leaked information attacking this strategic doctrine. Wilson responded by having the secretaries of the separate services and the obviously reluctant Joint Chiefs of Staff appear with him at a press conference to dismiss the revolt as limited to a few disgruntled lower-ranking officers.

Wilson also tried to have officers on duty in the Pentagon work in civilian clothes instead of in uniform. This caused another furor, and on this issue he was overruled by the president.

These incidents stamped Wilson as controversial and newsworthy, but none of them compared with a remark that he made at a news conference in Detroit in 1954. He was asked if his department planned to direct defense contracts to high-unemployment communities like Toledo, Ohio. Instead of giving a simple yes or no answer, he replied: "I've got a lot of sympathy for people when sudden change catches them. But I've always liked bird dogs better than kennel-fed dogs myself—you know, one who'll go out and hunt for food rather than sit on his fanny and yell." A predictable outburst of indignation from organized labor and other quarters followed.

Even after he left the government, Wilson continued to be attacked. Lieutenant General James A. Gavin, formerly chief of army research and development, charged him with leaving the nation exposed to nuclear threats from the Soviet Union and with creating a "missile gap," which later proved to be nonexistent. In his last

years Wilson was chairman of the Michigan advisory committee to the U.S. Commission on Civil Rights. He died at his plantation in Norwood, La.

There is a contrast between Wilson's private and public careers. At GM he was a capable industrial statesman; in the Department of Defense he was constantly embroiled in controversy. Wilson seems to have been a reasonably good administrator, carrying out unpopular and possibly erroneous policies that were not necessarily his own. His worst failing was his inability to curb his tongue. He seems never to have realized that the secretary of defense cannot talk in public the way the president of GM can in closed committee meetings or bargaining sessions. On the other hand, Wilson was the victim of misrepresentation. At no time did he use his position as secretary of defense to favor GM. Nor, in spite of the "bird dog" remark, did his record show him to be unsympathetic toward the unfortunate or hostile to labor.

As president of GM, Wilson made considerable progress toward forming the corporate giant into a community. But his attention was diverted by the demands of World War II and the Korean War. At the Pentagon his principal assignment was the unrewarding one of cutting the defense establishment to peacetime proportions, and the record indicates that he did it as well, if as impermanently, as anyone else who has been secretary of defense.

[Excellent evaluations of Wilson as an executive of GM are in Alfred P. Sloan, *My Years with General Motors* (1964); and Peter Drucker, *Adventures of a Bystander* (1979). An obituary is in the *New York Times,* Sept. 27, 1961.]

JOHN B. RAE

WILSON, EDITH BOLLING (Oct. 15, 1872–Dec. 28, 1961), wife of President Woodrow Wilson, was born at Wytheville, Va., one of eleven children of circuit court judge William Holcombe Bolling and Sallie White. The family was part of the southern aristocracy, claiming descent from Pocahontas and John Rolfe, but had little money. Edith was educated mostly at home and had only two years of formal schooling in the late 1880's, at Martha Washington College and Powell's School, both academies in Virginia.

While visiting her sister Gertrude in 1889, Bolling met Norman Galt. After a long courtship they were married in 1896. Several years later Norman Galt became chief owner of his family's jewelry and furnishings business.

In 1908, Norman Galt died, leaving his wife wealthy. With the aid of employees she ran the jewelry business with the proverbial iron hand in the velvet glove. She traveled annually to Europe, often in the company of Alice Gertrude Gordon. In 1915, Gordon was being courted by Dr. Cary Grayson, personal physician to President Woodrow Wilson, whose first wife, Ellen Axson Wilson, had died the previous August. Through Grayson and Gordon, Wilson and Galt met in March 1915. A whirlwind courtship ensued: Wilson's love letters are among the most eloquent in American presidential history. The relationship disturbed Wilson's advisers, including his friend Colonel Edward M. House. Treasury Secretary William Gibbs McAdoo, who was married to one of Wilson's daughters, even used anonymous disparaging letters to attempt to keep the president from marrying Galt so soon after his bereavement. But Wilson appreciated Galt's wit, warmth, and charm. Rejecting all counsel, he and Edith Galt were married on Dec. 18, 1915.

Edith Wilson became one of her husband's most trusted advisers, having access to secret cables and important state papers. In general she acted as a sounding board. They were seldom apart more than a few hours each day. Although the second-marriage issue proved inconsequential, the 1916 election campaign was one of the dirtiest on record, and Edith Wilson suffered from many personal slurs.

When the United States declared war against Germany in 1917, Edith Wilson took a leading role in persuading American women to conserve resources. But she believed her most important task was to care for Wilson and help him to relax. In November 1918, when the armistice was declared, she was one of the few advisers who urged the president to go to Paris to negotiate the peace treaty personally. Wilson's brief illness in Paris during the spring of 1919 increased her role, as she tried to keep the president from exhausting himself. Colonel House felt her influence then to be pernicious, a factor in his break with the president. Later scholarship has disputed this contention.

After Wilson suffered a paralyzing stroke in the fall of 1919, Edith, convinced that he would soon recover and not wishing the government to be taken over by persons hostile to the Versailles Treaty and the League of Nations, acted as a shield for the president. With the backing of Dr. Grayson, she allowed no one to enter his sickroom or to communicate with him, either on paper or in person, without her consent and, most often, her presence.

For several months in late 1919, Edith Wilson took her husband's dictation, relayed his wishes to Cabinet members and other officials, and gave him the latest news.

At the time, and in the years immediately following her husband's death, Edith Wilson was castigated for her role during his illness. It was charged that she was usurping the authority of the presidency. Later evidence, though, shows that she made no policy decisions by herself. But by exercising the power to keep in and keep out, she did affect the workings of the government, in the way that any powerful adviser affects a president's decisions. Wilson's recovery in 1920 was slow and incomplete, but he managed to complete his term. Edith helped dissuade him from attempting to run for a third term. Her counsel was also a major factor in Wilson's refusal to endorse his son-in-law William McAdoo for the nomination.

After leaving the White House in 1921, the Wilsons resided in Washington, and Edith Wilson continued to care for her husband until his death in 1924; thereafter she guarded his papers and historical image with equal zeal. In her later years she kept up her friendships with Herbert Hoover, Bernard Baruch, the Franklin Roosevelts, and others at the center of power. She was an indefatigable world traveler and a mainstay of the Woodrow Wilson Foundation.

That she did not abuse her temporary stewardship in 1919 is a judgment that is only slowly replacing the popular idea that Edith Wilson was the real president at that time. It is incontestable, though, that during the fall and early winter of 1919, she held more power in her hands than any other American woman before or since.

[Edith Wilson's papers became available to scholars at the Library of Congress in 1976. The Galt-Wilson 1915 courtship letters, similarly proscribed, are now appended to the Wilson papers. Her autobiographical *My Memoir* (1939) often obscures as much as it illuminates, and has been contradicted on evidence at many important points. The relationship of the Wilsons is detailed most fully in Tom Shachtman, *Edith and Woodrow* (1981). Earlier biographies include Alden Hatch, *Edith Bolling Wilson, First Lady Extraordinary* (1961); and Ishbel Ross, *Power with Grace* (1975). An obituary is in the *New York Times,* Dec. 29, 1961.]

TOM SHACHTMAN

WILSON, JAMES SOUTHALL (Nov. 12, 1880–June 26, 1963), educator, editor, and author, was born at "Ellerslie," Bacon's Castle, Va., the son of John Wilson and Mary Eliza

Jordan. Both his parents' families owned extensive farms in Tidewater. Two serious eye injuries made it necessary at times for him to be tutored at home, but he graduated from Smithfield High School without undue delay. After a period of working in Norfolk, Wilson entered the College of William and Mary in 1901 and received the B.A. in 1904. An M.A. in English and history from the University of Virginia followed in 1905, and a Ph.D. from Princeton University in 1906.

Wilson was appointed assistant professor of English and history at William and Mary in 1906 and was promoted to professor only two years later.

On Apr. 17, 1911, he married Julia Gardiner Tyler, the daughter of Lyon Gardiner Tyler, long-time president of the College of William and Mary, and the granddaughter of United States President John Tyler. They had two daughters. He served as director of the summer session at William and Mary from 1915 to 1918 and, unusual for one so young, was a member of the Virginia Board of Education from 1915 to 1919.

In September 1919, Wilson became Edgar Allan Poe professor of English at the University of Virginia, a chair he held until his retirement in 1951. In 1937 he was appointed dean of the Graduate School of Arts and Sciences as well as chairman of the Department of English; he held both positions until his retirement. During these years he was also a member of the faculty of the Bread Loaf School of English (1928–1945), where he taught courses on Poe and the novel. Wilson was a member of the Conference of Deans of Southern Graduate Schools (president, 1940), and often represented the University of Virginia in the Association of American Universities. After his retirement he was a visiting professor at Louisiana State University, the University of Mississippi, Davidson College, and Hollins College.

Soon after his arrival at the University of Virginia, Wilson was instrumental in securing for it the John H. Ingram collection of Poe memorabilia. Some years later he suggested to an alumnus the advantage of collecting a comprehensive library of American literature; the result was the Clifton Waller Barrett Library at the university, considered the outstanding one of its kind in the world.

In 1925, Wilson founded the *Virginia Quarterly Review,* of which he was editor until 1930. With the encouragement of the university's president, Edwin Anderson Alderman, he made the *Quarterly* into a national journal of literature and discussion. In the first issue he wrote: "The *Quarterly* hopes to be intelligently entertaining on all sorts of subjects, old and new, and yet retain more than a modicum of old-fashioned courtesy and taste," a description that reflects facets of his own personality. In 1931, acting on an idea that had occurred to him during his editorship, he convened the Convention of Southern Writers, presided over by Ellen Glasgow; the young William Faulkner was one of the participants.

Wilson was dignified, but had a puckish sense of humor and a gentle, compassionate nature. He was a brilliant teacher as well as administrator and editor. His courses on Shakespeare, the novel, but particularly on Poe, were informative and stimulating. Always immaculately dressed, he would enter the classroom radiating vigor, no matter how tiring his day had been. Often using no notes, he lectured with enthusiasm, tempering his instruction with anecdote and allusion. Wilson's almost encyclopedic knowledge of Poe was called on continually, and his guidance appears in at least two biographies, editions of Poe's works and letters, and many dissertations and articles.

Wilson's first scholarly work, *Alexander Wilson: Poet-Naturalist* (1906), based on his Princeton research, exhibited the precise and graceful style that marks his critical writings; in the next year he and a fellow Princetonian, Charles William Kennedy, published "a dramatic poem," *Pausanias,* based on the life of the ill-starred Spartan general. With J. C. Metcalf he edited *The Enchanted Years* (1921), an anthology of contemporary British and American poetry. His works on Poe include *An Appreciation of Edgar Allan Poe* (1923), *Letters of E. A. Poe to George W. Eveleth* (1924), *Facts About Poe* (1926), his edition of Poe's *Tales* (1927), and many essays and reviews.

Wilson died at Charlottesville, Va.

[A large collection of Wilson's papers, both official and private, is in the University of Virginia Library, as are various memorial resolutions. Additional family information has been kindly provided by his daughter, Mrs. Charles M. Davison, Jr.]

IRBY B. CAUTHEN, JR.

WITHERSPOON, ALEXANDER MACLAREN (Oct. 31, 1894–Mar. 4, 1964), educator, was born at Bowling Green, Ky., the son of Thomas Motley Witherspoon, a merchant, and of Angilene Holland. After graduating from Bowling Green High School in 1913, he studied for three years at Ogden College in Bowling

Green and taught English there (1916–1917) before entering Yale University as a senior. He received the B.A. in 1918 and then served in France with the American Expeditionary Forces as a corporal in the artillery. Following his discharge he was an instructor in English (1919–1920) at the Red Cross Institute for the Blind in Baltimore, Md. Witherspoon then returned to Yale, where he was awarded the M.A. in 1921, with an essay on William Vaughn Moody, and the Ph.D. in 1923. His dissertation, *The Influence of Robert Garnier on Elizabethan Drama*, was published in 1924. Two years later he edited *Titus Andronicus* for the Yale edition of Shakespeare.

Appointed an instructor in the Yale department of English in 1923, Witherspoon soon became one of the most inspiring teachers of his time. During a career of nearly forty years, he was especially noted for his courses in the literature of the seventeenth century. Using only a folder of miscellaneous notes, some written on the backs of envelopes, mingled with clippings from periodicals and newspapers, he fascinated generations of undergraduates by relating, with sardonic humor, the works of the Metaphysical poets to the problems of modern life. Despite their apparent casualness, his classes were always skillfully planned and organized. Out of them came his widely used texts *A Book of Seventeenth-Century Prose* (edited with R. P. Tristram Coffin, 1929), *The College Survey of English Literature* (1951), and *Seventeenth-Century Prose and Poetry* (edited with Frank J. Warnke, 1963).

From 1949 until his death, Witherspoon was a member of the board of editors of *The Complete Prose Works of John Milton*, serving as coeditor of volume IV. He was generous with his time in discussing their reading with his students and exacting in correcting their writing. A minor publication, *Common Errors in English and How to Avoid Them* (1943), was an offspring of his scrupulous care.

Though a very private man in some ways, Witherspoon was always a cheerful and convivial companion. In 1938 he was elected to The Club, a small group of distinguished Yale professors, and wrote the story of its first 125 years (1964). He was an original fellow of Berkeley College at Yale. Witherspoon, who never married, died at a nursing home in Hamden, Conn.

[An obituary notice appeared in the *New York Times*, March 5, 1964.]

GORDON S. HAIGHT

WOLFF, KURT AUGUST PAUL (Mar. 3, 1887–Oct. 21, 1963), publisher, was born in Bonn, Germany, the son of Dr. Leonhard Wolff, a professor of music, and of Maria Marx. In 1906 he passed his school-leaving examination at the Königlichen Gymnasium in Marburg, and subsequently studied at the universities of Bonn, Munich, Marburg, and Leipzig. He completed his military service at Darmstadt in a field artillery regiment.

At this stage of his life, Wolff was interested in music, and he had already started to collect books while at the gymnasium. In 1908 he entered his first publishing venture, becoming a silent partner in the Ernst Rowohlt Publishing House. He also edited a number of works, including the *Writings and Letters* of Johann Heinrich Merck and the *Diaries* of Adele Schopenhauer, both published in 1909. In 1912 he became an active partner and invested 90,000 marks in the firm.

In February 1913, Wolff established the Kurt Wolff Verlag in Leipzig, and a month later he acquired a periodical, *Die weissen Blätter*. In October of that year he bought the Hyperion Publishing House. Also during this eventful year, he issued Franz Kafka's first published work, a book of short stories, as well as books by Max Brod, Franz Werfel, and Georg Trakl.

Wolff served as a second lieutenant in the German army during World War I, but was discharged in September 1916 to resume his publishing activities. During this year his firm published, among others, books by Karl Kraus and Arnold Zweig. In 1917 the firm began to specialize in books on modern art. In October 1919 it was moved to Munich, and in 1923, Wolff set up a publishing house in Florence. During the 1920's his establishments published books by Carl Zuckmayer, Adolfo Venturi, Frans Masereel, and many others. By the latter half of the decade 200 titles were being published annually by Wolff's firms. They seem not to have issued any books during 1929, though, and by mid-1930 they had been liquidated. Also in 1930, Wolff's marriage to Elizabeth Merck ended in divorce. The couple, married on Sept. 2, 1909, had two children. On Mar. 27, 1933, Wolff married Helen Mosel. They had one son.

Except for a trip to Berlin in the winter of 1932, Wolff lived in Italy and France during the 1930's. He was in Paris when World War II broke out and was twice detained by the French in a compound for German citizens. He was released from the second confinement on July 28, 1940. He left Paris on Feb. 9, 1941, and arrived in New York City on March 30.

Wolff had friends in the United States, and through their assistance, especially that of Curt von Faber du Faur, he established a publishing firm in 1942. Besides Wolff and von Faber du Faur's stepson, Kyrill Schabert, who became president and sales manager of the company, the investors included friends, especially Lessing J. Rosenwald, former board chairman of Sears, Roebuck and Company. Because the United States was at war with Germany, Wolff did not give his name to the enterprise, but called it Pantheon Books.

The business initially operated out of the Wolffs' apartment. The first work published was Charles Péguy's *Basic Verities* (1943). It was a year in preparation and proved to be a success. Wolff was vice-president and editor of the company, and his policy was to publish "books of fine quality which although not designed for a mass audience would nevertheless appeal to a large number of people." He was interested in "timely" works "of lasting value."

By the spring of 1944, Pantheon had published fifteen books of poetry, art history, fiction, education, and philosophy. Wolff was particularly interested in art books, and among his first publications were two containing the works of Masereel. During the middle and late 1950's, several Pantheon books became best sellers: Anne Morrow Lindbergh's *Gift From the Sea*, Joy Adamson's *Born Free*, Mary Renault's *The King Must Die*, and Boris Pasternak's *Dr. Zhivago*.

The year 1958 was a difficult one for Wolff. He developed heart trouble and became involved in a dispute with his associates at Pantheon. In 1960 he and his wife, who was also an officer of the company, resigned; the following year they arranged with Harcourt, Brace and World to publish Helen and Kurt Wolff Books. *Sunset and Twilight*, based on the diaries of Bernard Berenson, was one of the works published under this arrangement.

Before coming to the United States, Wolff had published such American authors as Sinclair Lewis, John Erskine, and Arthur Kingsley Porter. While with Pantheon, he published many French, Austrian, and German writers not well known in the United States. Among the German-language writers were Stefan George, Hermann Broch, and Günter Grass. Peter du Sautoy characterized Wolff as "the embodiment of all that is best in European culture, a man of wide interests and many enthusiasms, of great taste and discrimination and knowledge." Wolff died in a traffic accident at Ludwigsburg, Germany.

[On Wolff's life, see his *Autoren, Bucher, Abenteuer, Betrachtungen und Erinnerungen eines Verlegers* (1965). Books edited by Wolff include *Briefe und Verse aus Goethes Zeit* (1910); *Frederick Maximilian Klinger, Dramatische Jugendwerke* (1912), with Hans Berendt; *Tausend Jahre deutscher Dichtung*, with Curt von Faber du Faur (1949). Articles by Wolff include "On Franz Kafka," *Twice a Year*, 1942; and "Begegnung mit dem absoluten Erinnerungen an Karl Kraus," *Forum*, June 1956. Letters between Wolff and the authors he published are reproduced in Kurt Wolff, *Briefwechsel eines Verlegers 1911–1963* (1966). Material on his activities in the United States is in "Pantheon Books Expands on First Anniversary," *Publishers Weekly*, Apr. 8, 1944; and "Pantheon in America," *Newsweek*, Dec. 30, 1946. A collection of essays on Wolff is Heinrich Scheffler, ed., *Kurt Wolff 1887–1963* (1963). Obituary notices are in the *New York Times*, Oct. 23, 1963; and *Publishers Weekly*, Oct. 28, 1963.]

ALLAN NELSON

WOLFSON, ERWIN SERVICE (Mar. 27, 1902–June 26, 1962), investment builder and general contractor, was born in Cincinnati, Ohio, the son of Bernard Wolfson, a prosperous manufacturer of men's clothing, and of Rose Service. As a boy he tinkered extensively with radios and cars. When he entered the University of Cincinnati in 1920, he intend to major in engineering, but becoming disenchanted with his original choice, he majored in philosophy.

After graduating in 1924, Wolfson intended to become a teacher, but a vacation in Florida changed the course of his life; there, he was infected by the Florida land-boom fever. After initial successes in building homes, apartment houses, and small office buildings and in real estate speculation, Wolfson lost everything in 1926, when the land bubble burst. He then moved to New York City and was hired by the Abe N. Adelson building organization as an assistant timekeeper for a crew erecting a twenty-eight-story skyscraper on Park Avenue in Manhattan. He stayed with this firm for ten years, during which he directed the construction of more than twenty large commercial structures and became one of its officers and directors.

On Mar. 5, 1936, Wolfson married Rose Fivars; they had two children. In the same year, Wolfson left Adelson and helped organize the Diesel Electric Company, a contracting concern that installed electric plants in commercial buildings, and later the Diesel Construction Company, which engaged in general contracting and investment building. He was vice-president of both firms and in 1952 became their president. (Eventually the former firm was absorbed into the latter.) Wolfson also established the Wolfson Management Corporation to rent space in the buildings erected by Diesel Construction. In a 1957 realignment he became chairman of the board of the construction firm, and in 1959, chairman of the board of Wolfson Management. By 1960 he owned 51 percent of the former and 100 percent of the latter. He was New York City's leading builder.

From 1946 to 1962, Wolfson and his firms were identified, either as principal investor or as general contractor, with the construction of more than sixty major edifices in the New York metropolitan area. These included banks, hotels, department stores, office buildings, and apartment houses. Among his most important projects were those for RKO Pictures, the National Broadcasting Company studios, and Bankers Trust. During his lifetime Wolfson and his firms were responsible for constructing nearly 16 million square feet of office space in New York City. At the time of his death, he was contractor for the fifty-seven-story Americana Hotel, which upon completion became the world's tallest hotel.

The Pan Am Building in midtown Manhattan was the climax of Wolfson's professional career. He conceived the plans for the structure, financed it himself with the aid of British capital after traditional financing methods proved impossible, and had his own contracting firm build it. Wolfson intended it to be the world's largest commercial office building (displacing the Empire State Building), housing more than 25,000 office workers and containing the world's fastest elevators (traveling 1,600 feet per minute). To aid him in creating an aesthetically pleasing "civic monument," he retained the services of the architects Walter Gropius and Pietro Belluschi. The building was completed in 1963, at a cost exceeding $100 million.

In his later years Wolfson assumed civic and social responsibilities. He was generous with his philanthropy, much of it benefiting institutions of higher learning in the United States and Israel. During 1957–1961 he was a member of the Westchester County Parkway Authority and assisted it in charting a reconstruction program for the county's parkway system. In 1961 he was appointed park commissioner for Westchester County.

Despite his reputation as one of the prime forces behind the skyscraper building boom that changed the profile of Manhattan after World War II, Wolfson never studied real estate practice and had no formal training in management or sales. But a continuing reputation for honesty

and dependability made up for these deficiencies. Colleagues and rivals attributed his success to a combination of charm and expert business sense. Once a contract for a skyscraper was signed, Wolfson and his associates could construct it in as short a time as twelve months, from breaking ground to installing tenants.

Wolfson once described his typical working day as "full of deals." He would contact people for secret meetings, negotiate in confidence, discuss large amounts of money, and assume primary responsibility for completing the project on time. "Basically I sell space," he once said. "Tenants don't just come. You have to go out and get them." As implied by Wolfson's words, his field was one of rugged, old-fashioned competition, marked by hard, shrewd bargaining. He amassed a fortune in a line of work that was "no place for the unenterprising or the faint of heart." He died in Purchase, N.Y.

[The most complete account of Wolfson's life is the obituary in the *New York Times,* June 27, 1962. Other biographical details are in *Business Week,* Sept. 10, 1960.]

IRVING KATZ

WOLMAN, LEO (Feb. 24, 1890–Oct. 2, 1961), economist, was born in Baltimore, Md., the son of Morris Wolman, a garment worker, and of Yetta Rosa Wachsman, who had come to the United States from Poland. He received the B.A. from Johns Hopkins University in 1911 and the Ph.D. in 1914. He then was appointed special agent of the National Industrial Relations Commission and began studies of the membership of trade unions that were to occupy him at intervals for many years. Wolman taught economics successively at Hobart College, the University of Michigan, and Johns Hopkins in 1915–1918. After American entry into World War I, he was on the staff of the Council of National Defense and in 1918 became chief of the section of production statistics of the War Industries Board.

Wolman's war service led to his attachment to the mission that negotiated peace at Versailles. His responsibility was to prepare, often on short notice, memoranda on the economies of various dependent countries. Six months' experience convinced him that President Woodrow Wilson had reduced his bargaining power by going to France; he thought Wilson morally firm but politically naïve, as was Wolman himself.

In 1920, Wolman joined the faculty of the New School for Social Research in New York

City. The New School, organized by professors who had had differences with Columbia University, numbered among its lecturers national and international leaders in the social sciences. Wolman first taught statistics and later labor relations. At the same time, he was director of research for the Amalgamated Clothing Workers of America. From 1920 to 1931 he was the close adviser of its president, Sidney Hillman, in establishing unemployment insurance, Amalgamated banks in Chicago and New York, and housing developments in New York. "Great social upheavals," he wrote, "set loose neglected interests and initiate periods of experimentation. Such was the contribution of the World War to the Amalgamated and other labor movements."

Wolman directed publication of *The Clothing Workers of Chicago, 1910–1922* (1922), which recounted the "growth of the workers' rights as free partners in the enterprise of producing clothing." Up to the time of the successful strike in 1910, he wrote, "absolutism had held . . . sway in the tailor shops of Chicago. Since then, it has been forced out of one stronghold after another through the organized power of the workers." Wolman was a director of the Amalgamated banks in 1930–1933 and president of Amalgamated Investors, a labor-owned investment trust.

After lecturing at Harvard in 1930, Wolman became professor of economics in the graduate school of Columbia University. He was also on the staff of the National Bureau of Economic Research, which was committed to fact-finding. Here his publications dealt with union membership. Wolman was known for unobtrusive prompting of his junior associates to avoid overly technical language and to present realities in a straightforward manner.

Wolman became involved with the New Deal less because of his enthusiasm than because of his sense of duty. He was chairman of the Labor Advisory Board and a member of the National Labor Board. When Hugh Johnson, head of the National Recovery Administration, did not crack down on noncomplying automobile manufacturers, Wolman was assigned the troublesome position of chairman and neutral member of the three-man Automobile Labor Board. For more than a year in Detroit he was obliged to substitute skill for authority. In general, he regarded his New Deal colleagues as astute, politically practiced, and—as they themselves admitted—opportunistic.

Wolman surprised and disappointed his former labor associates by becoming increasingly critical of the growing power of unions and of governmental policies regulating labor relations. In 1937 he proposed amendments to the Wagner Act that would forbid the use of certain coercive methods by unions, outlaw strikes against the government, require unions to file financial reports, prevent union contributions to political parties, and assure independent unions equal treatment before the National Labor Relations Board. In January 1947, Wolman repeated these proposals in testimony before the Senate Labor Committee on what became the Taft-Hartley Act. Asserting that increasing governmental favoritism toward labor "was the whole spirit and letter of the labor policy . . . since 1930," he urged that in the interest of equality, proper freedom in dealing with unions must be restored to employers. He condemned industrywide collective bargaining, believing that it produced irresponsible monopoly in the automobile, railroad, coal, iron, and steel industries.

In debate Wolman was informed and positive, but not abrasive. At Columbia he was notably solicitous of his students. His own studies were concerned less with the labor movement than with such matters as wages and the bases of organization. He served on numerous public commissions and academic bodies.

Wolman married Cecil Clark on May 17, 1930; they had one son. His recreations were reading, theatergoing, and music, including near-professional competence as a pianist. He died in New York City.

[No biography on Wolman exists. Wolman's books include *The Boycott in American Trade Unions* (1916; repr. 1971); *The Growth of American Trade Unions, 1880–1923* (1924; repr. 1975), foreword by Wesley C. Mitchell; and *Ebb and Flow in American Trade Unions* (1936). The Oral History Collection of Columbia University contains Wolman's memoir; he is also mentioned in those of Frances Perkins, James P. Warburg, Isidor Lubin, and Lee Pressman, among others. Obituaries appeared in the *New York Times* and *New York Herald-Tribune*, Oct. 3, 1961.]

BROADUS MITCHELL

WONG, ANNA MAY (Jan. 3, 1907–Feb. 3, 1961), actress, was born in Los Angeles, Calif., the daughter of Wong Om-tsing and his wife. She got her start in motion pictures when, in 1919, she was part of a large procession scene in *The Red Lantern*. In 1921 she appeared in some minor scenes in *The First Born* and in *Dinty*. That same year several bigger parts came her way in *Bits of Life* and *Shame*. In 1922, Wong shared in a bit of movie history by appearing in

The Toll of the Sea, the first full-length Technicolor production. Then, in 1924, she came to national attention in the Douglas Fairbanks film *The Thief of Bagdad,* in which she played a Mongol slave girl. After this triumph she appeared in *The Alaskan* (1924) and *Peter Pan* (1924).

At a later time Wong, a beautiful girl with high cheekbones, heavy-lidded eyes, and a full, sensuous mouth, might have become a major star. But during the 1920's and 1930's the accepted rule was that ethnic minorities could not rise above the level of menials or of stock characters of fun or menace. And while they might be cast in bit parts, the major roles calling for black or Oriental characters were played by Caucasians wearing makeup.

Nevertheless, Wong was in great demand for films about China and the Orient, and appeared in many Chinese mystery productions: *Mr. Wu* (1927), *Old San Francisco* (1927), *The Chinese Parrot* (1927), *The Devil Dancer* (1927), *Across to Singapore* (1928), and *Chinatown Charlie* (1928). The practices of the era are illustrated well by *The Crimson City* (1928), in which Wong had a minor role, while the female lead —a Chinese girl—was played by Myrna Loy.

Completely disenchanted with Hollywood, Wong decided to go abroad. Ironically, she found there the fame that her own country had refused to bestow. She did well in Germany, where she appeared in the film *Song* (1928). She worked hard, learning to speak German so well that her voice did not have to be dubbed. More fame and recognition awaited her in England, where in March 1929 she appeared in her first stage play, *The Circle of Chalk,* playing opposite Laurence Olivier. Following this triumph, Wong performed in the British film *Piccadilly* (1929). In 1930 she appeared in the films *Elstree Calling* and *The Flame of Love.* In the latter her language skills enabled her to star not only in the English version of the film but also in the French and German ones. In the autumn of 1930, she moved to Vienna to star in the play *Springtime* (in German), a performance that garnered high praise from Austrian critics.

Wong returned to the United States in 1930 to appear in the Broadway drama *On the Spot.* This play about Chicago racketeering opened on Oct. 29, 1930, and after 167 performances went on an extensive tour. Following this success she was put under contract by Paramount. In 1931, Wong played in a film based on the Fu Manchu stories, *Daughter of the Dragon.* The next year she acted in *Shanghai Express,* playing the treacherous Chinese girl Hui Fei, her most

memorable American movie performance. When the film was completed, she returned to England to play in the Sherlock Holmes film *A Study in Scarlet* (1933), as well as in *Tiger Bay* (1933), *Chu Chin Chow* (1934), and *Java Head* (1934).

Back in Hollywood, Wong starred in *Limehouse Blues* (1934). She then went on an extended tour of Europe, and in 1936 she visited China. Back from these travels, she played in several low-budget features, including *Daughter of Shanghai* (1937), *Dangerous to Know* (1938), *King of Chinatown* (1939), and *Island of Lost Men* (1939). With the coming of World War II, Orientals were in great demand, and she appeared in several undistinguished films, such as *Bombs Over Burma* (1942) and *Lady from Chungking* (1942).

Except for *Impact* (1949) there was no screen work for Wong for a decade after the war. In the 1950's she appeared in a television series, "The Gallery of Mme. Liu," as well as in several dramatic productions on television playhouses. She returned to the screen in 1960 in *Portrait in Black.* Ill health prevented more roles, and she died of a heart attack in Santa Monica, Calif.

Anna May Wong will have a prominent place in the annals of acting because she was the first, and perhaps the only, Chinese actress to become a major box-office attraction. She was an accomplished actress who gained an international reputation against very great odds. A proud, aloof woman, she never married.

[There are no book-length studies of Wong, but an excellent and detailed short account of her career is in James Robert Parish and William T. Leonard, *Hollywood Players: The Thirties* (1976). An obituary is in the *New York Times,* Feb. 4, 1961.]

J. MICHAEL QUILL

WOOLLEY, EDGAR MONTILLION ("MONTY") (Aug. 17, 1888–May 6, 1963), director and actor, was born in New York City, the son of William Edgar Woolley and Jessie Arms, prosperous hotel owners. He spent much of his childhood at the family establishments in Manhattan and Saratoga, where he wore Lord Fauntleroy suits, kept his own ponies, and met Sarah Bernhardt, Lillian Russell, and other luminaries. Although financially indulgent, William Woolley was also a strict Episcopalian who packed his son off, at age twelve, to the Mackenzie School in upstate New York for a dose of education, piety, and discipline.

Woolley entered Yale College in 1907. There he exhibited the dual tendencies of his life. On the one hand, he belonged to a "fast set" that included the sons of wealthy businessmen as well as such creative lights as Cole Porter. Ever the sharp-tongued extrovert, Woolley solidified his social standing by organizing costume parties (including one legendary affair with fifty students dressed as British nobles) and hosting secret champagne bashes at his father's New York City hotel. On the other hand, he played a key role in Yale's first theatrical flowering, acting in serious productions of William Shakespeare and Carlo Goldoni and directing Cole Porter's brilliant froth at the Dramatic Association's smokers.

After graduating in 1911, Woolley studied at Harvard but returned to Yale as drama coach from 1914 to 1917. He encouraged students to write their own plays, and he staged *Tamburlaine* and *Troilus and Cressida* for the first time in America. After serving as an army lieutenant during World War I, he was appointed assistant professor of drama at Yale in 1919. Woolley staged major plays with undergraduate actors and homemade scenery, properties, and costumes. The performances were financially successful and consolidated the university's fragile theatrical tradition. But when Yale established a heavily endowed experimental theater, Professor George P. Baker of Harvard was selected, over campus protests on Woolley's behalf, to direct it. Simultaneously failing to obtain permanent appointment in the English department, which considered him more showman than scholar, Woolley departed for New York City in 1927.

Woolley's post-Yale career was much influenced by his friendship with Cole Porter. His first Broadway success came in 1929, as director of Porter's *Fifty Million Frenchmen.* He directed three other Porter musicals in the next five years; and when his friend went to Hollywood in the mid-1930's, Woolley followed. He appeared in numerous bit parts, including that of a Yale professor in a fictionalized Porter biography, *Night and Day* (1946). His main independent claim to fame resulted from his portrayal of the crusty Sheridan Whiteside in Moss Hart and George S. Kaufman's play *The Man Who Came to Dinner,* a role he performed on Broadway from 1939 to 1941 and in a filmed version in 1942. He received Academy Award nominations for best actor, for *The Pied Piper* (1942), and for best supporting actor, for *Since You Went Away* (1944).

True to form, Woolley was as well known for his socializing as for his theatrical work. During the 1930's his trim beard, "spectacular" personality, and talent for pranks and mimicry gave him entrée to café society from California to Italy. Among his friends were Noel Coward and his companion Jack Wilson; Alexander Woollcott, drama critic and the inspiration for the Sheridan Whiteside role; Elsa Maxwell, professional party giver; Gerald Murphy, after whom F. Scott Fitzgerald drew Dick Diver, the protagonist of *Tender Is the Night*; and, inevitably, Cole Porter. In this extraordinary group, where genius, wit, and wealth mingled inextricably with alcohol, narcotics, and homosexuality, "dear Monty" was the equal of "dear Noel," "dear Elsa," and "dear Cole."

Woolley's stage and film activities declined after World War II, and although he continued to hold flamboyant soirées at his New York hotel suite, ill health forced him to relinquish his place as "Gotham roisterer." He died, unmarried, in Saratoga Springs, N.Y.

Although remembered principally as the "Man Who Came to Dinner," Woolley had a further twofold significance. First, he was a pioneer of university theater and musical comedy in America, thus expanding and enriching the nation's cultural landscape. And he represented a tradition of indulgent, escapist sophistication at odds with the experimental and proletarian styles typical of so much theatrical production between the world wars. This sophisticated tradition has long since proved its resilience and thus the historical importance of such early exemplars as Monty Woolley.

[Brief sketches of Woolley are in the yearbooks of the Yale College class of 1911; and *New Yorker,* Jan. 20, 1940. An obituary is in the *New York Times,* May 7, 1963.]

RONALD STORY

WRATHER, WILLIAM EMBRY (Jan. 20, 1883–Nov. 28, 1963), petroleum geologist and federal official, was born on his maternal grandparents' farm in Meade County, Ky., the son of Richard Anselm Wrather and Glovy Washington Munford. At the age of fifteen he moved to Chicago, to attend high school. At the University of Chicago, from which he received the Ph.B. in 1908, Wrather met Harold Ickes when both were studying law. But Wrather abandoned law for geology at the instigation of one of his teachers, Rollin D. Salisbury, after spending the summer of 1907 in Montana with a field party of the U.S. Geological Survey. When reduced appropriations kept him from rejoining the Survey in 1908, he followed a friend to the oil fields of the Southwest. There he became a scout for the J. M. Guffey Company (soon merged into Gulf Oil). He married Alice Mildred Dolling on Dec. 30, 1910; they had four children.

For Gulf Oil, Wrather leased a number of areas in Texas, on the basis of his geological mapping, that later proved productive. He also initiated the analysis of the deep well at Spur that proved important for the development of oil production in the Permian Basin. But the company's indifference to his reports of structures that promised oil made Wrather impatient. Early in 1916, shortly after he helped found what became the American Association of Petroleum Geologists, he resigned from Gulf to become an independent consultant.

Wrather's search for someone who would act on his geological advice, compensating him with a part interest, led him to Michael L. Benedum, a wildcatter. Their partnership resulted in the discovery of the Desdemona field in September 1918 and the Nigger Creek field in 1926. After the Desdemona boom (1918–1919) Wrather moved to Dallas, where he continued his independent consulting, resisting all suggestions that he form an organization. Benedum's consolidation of his holdings into the Transcontinental Oil Company in 1919 left Wrather, who took his share in cash, with about $1 million.

Beginning in 1919, Wrather's consulting work was largely the valuation of oil properties for both the Internal Revenue Service and investors. In 1926 he established the value of Amerada Petroleum Corporation for Dillon, Read and Company, which financed the purchase of the British minority interest. Ten years later Wrather helped his lifelong friend E. L. De Golyer appraise the Texas Company, which refinanced its debt just before it bought half of Standard Oil's concessions in Bahrain and Saudi Arabia.

Like most petroleum geologists, Wrather supported the running of each oil field as a unit to maximize its producing life, contrary to the wasteful American practice of the time. In 1932–1933 he tried, on behalf of the producing companies, to unitize the Hobbs field in New Mexico, then threatened by flooding. Although unitization failed, Wrather succeeded in stemming the incursion of water. From 1936 to 1938 he helped defend the unitization of the Kettleman Hills field in California against a prolonged legal attack.

His financial independence after 1918 left Wrather free to work in professional organizations and to travel. He was president of the American Association of Petroleum Geologists

in 1922–1923, beginning a program of research that led to three volumes on American oil fields, and of the Society of Economic Geologists in 1934. As president of the American Institute of Mining and Metallurgical Engineers (AIME) in 1948, he began the reorganization that led to autonomy for each of the three major membership groups—mining, metallurgical, and petroleum engineers. He was treasurer of the American Association for the Advancement of Science from 1943 until 1954.

From the time of his first trip to Rumanian oil fields for the Benedum Trees interests in 1925 until illness forced him into a wheelchair in the 1950's, Wrather traveled all over the world. He participated in the International Geological Congresses at Madrid (1926), Pretoria (1929), Washington, D.C. (1933), Moscow (1937), and Algiers (1952). For the Washington congress he organized the trips to the oil fields of the Southwest; at the Algiers congress he led the American delegation.

As one of the most prominent American oil geologists, Wrather was the natural choice of Harold Ickes, then secretary of the interior, for oil referee under the National Recovery Administration. But Wrather declined this and later offers to serve the federal government until after World War II broke out in 1941. Even then he waited until 1942, when a position he wanted was offered: associate chief of the mineral and metals unit of the Board of Economic Warfare, under Alan Bateman, an economic geologist from Yale. In less than a year in this job, Wrather broadened his knowledge, hitherto restricted to petroleum, to all the minerals of commerce.

In 1943, Ickes chose Wrather to be director of the U.S. Geological Survey, the first to be selected from outside the agency since its founding in 1879. Later that year Wrather went to the Middle East as a member of the mission led by De Golyer to evaluate oil resources for the federal government's Petroleum Reserve Corporation; the group reported that the center of oil production would soon shift from the Caribbean to the Persian Gulf.

Wrather maintained the Geological Survey's traditional aloofness from politics, and he left oil geology largely to the American Petroleum Institute. The dislocations of war and its aftermath made major changes feasible. Wrather effected them with minimal friction. Prodded by the Department of the Interior, the Geological Survey moved some activities from Washington to new regional centers in Denver and outside San Francisco. In mapmaking, photogrammetry replaced field mapping and photo-lithography replaced engraving on copper plates. The hitherto separate field investigations of ground-water and surface-water supplies were unified. The settlement begun by Wrather of the long-simmering feud with the Bureau of Mines (once part of the Survey) brought geophysics back to the Geological Survey. When other government departments needed geological work, as did the Atomic Energy Commission in its search for uranium or the navy in its exploration of its Alaskan Petroleum Reserve, Wrather persuaded them to employ the Survey instead of hiring their own geologists. When illness forced his retirement in 1956, Wrather left the Geological Survey a much larger agency than he had found it, yet just as highly regarded for its scientific and technical excellence. He died in Washington, D.C.

[Wrather's official papers as director of the Geological Survey are in Record Group 57 at the National Archives; more than 100 of his personal letters from 1915 to 1956 are in the De Golyer Library, Southern Methodist University, Dallas. A brief biography is in *Supplement to John Fritz Medal Book* (1954). Obituaries are in the *New York Times*, Nov. 30, 1963; J. E. Brantly, *Bulletin of the Geological Society of America*, Apr. 1964; Wallace Pratt, *Bulletin of the American Association of Petroleum Geologists*, Oct. 1964; and Thomas B. Nolan, *Proceedings of the Geological Society of London*, Jan. 21, 1965. Brantly and Pratt list Wrather's publications.

A copy of Wrather's typescript reminiscences is in the Library of the U.S. Geological Survey. The transcript of a 1961 interview with Henry Carlisle is in the Oral History Research Collection at Columbia University; portions were published in *Mining Engineering*, Apr. 1964.]

HAROLD L. BURSTYN

YELLOWLEY, EDWARD CLEMENTS (Aug. 12, 1873–Feb. 8, 1962), federal Prohibition administrator, was born on a plantation near Ridgeland, Miss., the son of James Brownlow Yellowley, a lawyer and planter, and Jessie Perkins. The family, of planting aristocracy, lost most of its wealth in the Civil War. E. C., as he was called, grew up in Mississippi and on a plantation at Greenville, N. C., where he entered a military academy in 1888. Afterward he managed his father's Mississippi plantation. About 1896 he married Mary Helms; she died in 1898. On Dec. 29, 1912, he married Callie H. Gibbons, who died in 1927. Each marriage was childless.

In 1899, Yellowley joined the Internal Revenue Bureau, which was then primarily engaged in catching moonshiners. In 1910 he was pro-moted to agent in charge and served in several cities, including Philadelphia, St. Paul, San Antonio, Nashville, Atlanta, and San Francisco. He was a superb administrator. In 1919, Yellowley was transferred to Washington, D.C., to reorganize the field audit division of the income and estate tax units of the bureau, and in 1920 he became the bureau's regional supervising agent in San Francisco.

In 1921, after the adoption of the Eighteenth Amendment, outlawing the manufacture and sale of alcoholic beverages, Internal Revenue organized a nationwide enforcement unit. Yellowley was placed in charge of special agents who were to be deployed wherever local-level federal Prohibition officials, mostly patronage appointees, were not enforcing the law.

In 1921, Yellowley went to New York City, which he vowed to make a Sahara. Within two months, twenty-six local agents had been dismissed. Yellowley systematized the office and changed the procedures by which physicians could write prescriptions for alcohol for their patients. He arrested rabbis whom he suspected of selling wine to unauthorized persons. As a result of his work, the price of a quart of illegal whiskey rose from $8 to $20. Two of Yellowley's policies were particularly harsh. People who visited hotels or restaurants where liquor was served or brought in by customers were arrested as material witnesses. Still more alarming to businessmen was his insistence that any hotel or restaurant that had two liquor violations be padlocked for one year.

A master of strategy, Yellowley disguised agents as truck drivers, as garment workers, or even as society figures dressed in formal attire. He hired the legendary Izzy Einstein and Moe Smith. He developed a reputation for honesty and incorruptibility at a time when such a reputation in the Prohibition service was almost unique. And he uncovered several scandals. For example, much of the liquor seized in New York City in 1921 was imported. He could not understand how so much alcohol got into the United States until he learned that U.S. Customs routinely admitted liquor upon which the duty had been paid, without notifying the Prohibition Office. In one week raids netted more than $3 million of imported liquor.

From 1923 to 1925, Yellowley and his special agents operated out of Washington, and he visited nearly every state. In 1925 the local units were replaced by regional ones. Yellowley was assigned to San Francisco, but the situation in Chicago was more serious, and he was soon put in charge of the office there. From 1925 to 1930 he applied in Chicago the policies he had used in New York. He even raided the Fish Fan Club, the hangout of Mayor "Big Bill" Thompson. But the city remained largely "wet," for Yellowley was stymied by the power and influence of Al Capone, who had built a crime empire based on bootlegging that was reputed to be making more than $100 million a year. These profits were ensured by threats, thugs, and bribes. Yellowley himself is said to have turned down $250,000. His chief aide, Alexander Jamie, asked agent Eliot Ness to recruit special agents who would be immune to Capone's influence. Thus, the "Untouchables" were born.

In 1930, Yellowley left Prohibition enforcement to become supervisor of liquor permits for the Chicago region. In 1934, after Prohibition had ended, he became the Chicago regional supervisor of Internal Revenue's alcohol tax unit. He designed a system for collecting federal liquor taxes that was a model for the rest of the United States. When he retired in 1946, he was supervising 300 agents.

In his later years Yellowley enjoyed an occasional glass of wine with dinner, but he stated that he had never had a drink during Prohibition. About Prohibition and his enforcement policies, he refused comment except to say, "I believe in all law enforcement. If a law is bad, it should be repealed." He added that he was proud of being called the " 'enforcingest' agent in the lot." He died in Chicago.

[Yellowley is briefly mentioned in Herbert Asbury, *Gem of the Prairie* (1940). Articles on Yellowley and his work appear in *Association Men*, June 1923; *Chicago Daily Journal*, Apr. 5, 1926; *Chicago Daily News*, Mar. 22–23, Dec. 31, 1927; and *Chicago Tribune*, Aug. 11, 1960. Obituaries are in the *Chicago Daily News* and *Chicago's American*, Feb. 8, 1962; *Chicago Sun-Times* and *Chicago Tribune*, Feb. 9, 1962; and the *New York Times*, Feb. 9, 1962.]

W. J. RORABAUGH

YORK, ALVIN CULLUM (Dec. 13, 1887–Sept. 2, 1964), soldier, popularly known as Sergeant York, the most renowned doughboy hero of World War I, was born in Pall Mall, Tenn., one of the eleven children of William York and Mary Brooks. He left school after the third grade to help in his father's blacksmith shop. Although life in the remote Tennessee mountains was hard, York grew to manhood unaware of rustic deprivation. Like many of his contemporaries, he drank, gambled, caroused on Saturday nights, and honed his skill with both rifle and pistol at local turkey shoots.

In 1911, William York died, and Alvin be-

came the main source of family support. Responsibility sobered him somewhat, but Gracie Williams fully changed his life. He saw her often and soon wanted to marry her; but she objected to his life, urged him to change, and introduced him to the Church of Christ and Christian Union. This fundamentalist church captured York's imagination. He gave up the things that "Miss Gracie" hated—"mean drinking, fighting and card flipping"—and finally became a church elder. Above all he accepted his church's emphasis on the Sixth Commandment: "Thou Shalt Not Kill."

When the United States entered World War I in 1917, York was a big, rawboned man over six feet tall who weighed 205 pounds and was in fine health. His draft notice brought consternation to his family, his congregation, and himself. How could he fight? How could he leave the family he supported? His pastor, his mother, and many friends urged him to seek exemption as a conscientious objector. Two appeals for deferment were refused, and York was inducted on Nov. 14, 1917. He reported for training at Camp Gordon, Ga., and was assigned to the Eighty-second (All-American) Division. He had worried about Gracie Williams' reaction to his army service, but just before he left Pall Mall, she agreed to marry him after the war. The business of killing plagued York's conscience. But he hid his concern well and settled into soldiering with skill. "Well, they gave me a gun and, oh my!" he recorded, "that old gun was full of grease, and I had to . . . get that old gun clean, and oh, those were trying hours for a boy like me trying to live for God and do his blessed will."

York earned high repute with his 1903 Springfield rifle; ranges of 200, 300, and even 500 yards were easy to his eye, and positions were all the same to him. Targets with bull's-eyes were fine; when the targets were changed to human silhouettes, he balked, asked to see his company commander, and said, "Sir, I am doing wrong. Practicing to kill people is against my religion." Captain E. C. B. Danforth listened to his earnest marksman, reasoned with him at length about patriotism, but failed to change York's mind. Finally Danforth asked Major George E. Buxton, battalion commander and Bible student, to take up the argument.

A three-day debate raged; chapters, verses, and counterchapters were cited: "He that hath no sword, let him sell his garment, and buy one" (Luke 22:36) and "Think not that I am come to send peace on earth: I am come not to send peace, but a sword" (Matt. 10:34). Finally Buxton sensed the fullness of York's torment and sent him home on leave. Two anguished days on a hill near home brought conviction. York came down the hill and told his family, "I'm going."

The Eighty-second Division went to France at a critical time for the Allies. By May 1918, German strength on the western front had peaked. Allied leaders, fighting to hold the Marne, pressed General John J. Pershing, commanding the American Expeditionary Forces, for infantry and machine gunners. Quickly trained at home, new divisions were rushed abroad, among them the Eighty-second, which arrived while the Germans were driving toward Château-Thierry and Belleau Wood. Pershing refused to commit green troops too early, but the Eighty-second was ready for the major American effort against the St.-Mihiel salient in September 1918. It filtered into the American line in front of St.-Mihiel, took part in reducing the salient, and was then shifted swiftly to a position in the Meuse-Argonne area, where York and his cohorts replaced French troops and waited for attack orders against hilly, well-fortified parts of the Hindenburg Line.

On Sept. 26, 1918, the first phase of the Meuse-Argonne offensive began; it went well in early stages, but finally stalled against bluffs, hills, machine guns, and well-placed artillery. Pershing stopped the attack to regroup.

On Oct. 4, 1918, the second phase of the offensive opened. York's division was pushed toward the eastern edge of the Argonne, and by October 8 had nudged close to Châtel-Chéhéry, a village in the midst of a heavy German defense system. Orders were to take two hills dominating the American advance. "So the morning of the 8th just before daylight," York recalled, "we started for the hill at Châtel Chéhéry. Before we got there it got light and the Germans sent over a heavy barrage and also gas and we put on our gas-masks and just pressed right on through those shells and got to the top of Hill 223 to where we were to start over at 6:10 A.M." York (now a corporal in G Company, 328th Infantry) and his company were to attack another hill and rail point under cover of a barrage. The barrage never came, "and we had to go without one." Once out of cover, York and his comrades encountered heavy German machine-gun fire.

York could see his friends getting picked off quickly. Someone would have to silence the enemy guns. "So 17 of us boys went around on the left flank to see if we couldn't put those guns out of action." Picking their way through underbrush, the detail surprised fifteen or twenty Germans, who surrendered, and the Americans went on toward the flank of an entire German machine-gun battalion. A hasty shot alerted the enemy, who swiveled guns and "fired on us from every direction." Nine of the seventeen doughboys were killed or wounded; York found himself in command of seven men and a good many German prisoners. He noticed that the enemy fire went high, probably to avoid the prisoners, so he crawled to a good spot and sighted "that old gun." Every time a gunner raised his head, York "jes' teched him off." He killed seventeen Germans with seventeen shots.

Enemy officers realized that York was almost alone; a lieutenant and seven men rose out from cover and charged York with fixed bayonets. They made the mistake of attacking in column, and York, out of rifle bullets, picked them off with his pistol. This amazing display of marksmanship overwhelmed a German major near York. Putting his hand on York's shoulder, he said, in English, "Don't shoot any more, and I'll make them surrender." York agreed, the German gave the order, and ninety Germans laid down their arms. His seven surviving buddies joined York in policing the prisoners. The German major, who thought York was one of hundreds, asked how many men he had. "I got aplenty," York snapped, and marched his captives off. He delivered 132 prisoners to his battalion headquarters.

Astounded American officers checked York's story; inspectors found twenty-five dead Germans and thirty-five abandoned machine guns. York suddenly became the classic American hero. He was modest, courteous, abashed by attention, and appreciative of everything, especially being promoted to sergeant on Nov. 1, 1918. He was forever after Sergeant York. General Pershing, always chary with compliments, called York "the greatest civilian soldier of the war," and Marshal Ferdinand Foch told York, "What you did was the greatest thing accomplished by any private soldier of all the armies of Europe." Medals came with the praise. He received the Congressional Medal of Honor, France's Medaille Militaire and Croix de Guerre, and Italy's Croce de Guerra.

York returned home in May 1919 to a New York City ticker-tape parade and a dinner given by the Tennessee Society. Next, escorted by Representative Cordell Hull of Tennessee, York visited Washington. The House of Representatives gave him a standing ovation. A stop at the War Department, a tour of the White House, and a chat with President Woodrow Wilson's secretary, Joseph Tumulty, followed. York was tired. Of reporters he remarked, "I was sorter feeling like a red fox circling when the hounds are after it. They asked me that many questions that I kinder got tied inside my head and wanted to light out and do some hiking." Solicitations for lectures, endorsements, and public appearances were dismissed tersely: "This uniform ain't for sale." He accepted only one reward: a 396-acre farm given by the state of Tennessee. On June 7, 1919, York and Gracie Williams were married by Tennessee's governor, A. H. Roberts; they had seven children.

Although he shunned the limelight, York never shirked duty. He helped found the American Legion and spoke often on defense issues. Increasingly his attention centered on the Alvin C. York Industrial Institute. Ever since his war experience, he had been concerned with fighting ignorance in the Tennessee mountains. With the money he earned through selected appearances and royalties from his memoirs (1928), he established a foundation to build a college and Bible school. In 1941 the film *Sergeant York*, with Gary Cooper in the title role, brought the sergeant more than $200,000, which he gave to the institute.

York's last years were not happy. Despite his stout support of the American way ("Liberty and freedom are so very precious that you do not fight to win them once and stop."), financial troubles dogged him. The Internal Revenue Service demanded more than $170,000 in taxes, which the aging hero resented ("I paid 'em the tax I owed 'em.") and could not pay. Eventually a public subscription, led by Congressman Sam Rayburn, raised $25,000, which was accepted in settlement.

In 1954, York was stricken by a cerebral hemorrhage, from which he never fully recovered; he finally yielded to a wheelchair. His health and destitution attracted the concern of Hallock du Pont of Wilmington, Del., who established a trust fund that paid York $300 a month for the rest of his life. This provided the last comfort for an almost forgotten hero. He died in Nashville, Tenn.

[York's memoirs are *Sergeant York: His Own Life Story and War Diary,* edited by Thomas J. Skeyhill (1928). Also see Sam K. Cowan, *Sergeant York and His People* (1922). An obituary is in the *New York Times,* Sept. 3, 1964.]

FRANK E. VANDIVER

YOUNG, OWEN D. (Oct. 27, 1874–July 11, 1962), lawyer, industrialist, political adviser, and diplomat, was born in Van Hornesville, N.Y., the son of Jacob Smith Young and Ida Brandow. The family's eighty-acre farm provided an ade-

quate living. Young's early life was typical for a nineteenth-century farm boy, with daily work in the fields and education at a one-room schoolhouse and the nearby East Springfield Academy.

Young enrolled at St. Lawrence University (B.A., 1894), where he was a first-rate student and a campus leader. He intended to enter Harvard Law School, but was discouraged by the authorities when he announced that he intended to work part-time. He therefore attended Boston University Law School, from which he graduated in 1896. The same year he entered the law practice of Charles Tyler in Boston. For the next seven years he also taught night classes at Boston University. On June 30, 1898, he married Josephine Sheldon Edmonds. They had five children.

After he became Tyler's partner in 1907, an increasing part of Young's work involved the firm of Stone and Webster, an important company in the electrical industry. This work brought him to the attention of Charles Coffin, the head of the General Electric Company (GE), who convinced him to join that firm as general counsel and vice-president in 1913.

At GE, Young's tasks were to deal with labor problems and to settle patent disputes with competitors in the industry. During World War I he negotiated a settlement of a strike at GE's Lynn, Mass., plant, the last major labor disturbance during his tenure with the company. He dealt with the patent disputes by speeding licensing, cross licensing, and the exchange of patents between electrical companies. Young took an increasing interest in bettering industrial relations within the company and improving GE's image with the public. He was one of the first American industrialists to recognize the need for greater attention to these two areas of corporate life. He served on President Woodrow Wilson's National Industrial Conference in 1919 and 1920 and President Warren Harding's Unemployment Conference of 1921.

In 1919, Young, with the cooperation of the American government and the support of GE, organized and became chairman of the board of the Radio Corporation of America (RCA). The formation of RCA came about as a result of an attempt by the British Marconi Wireless Company to secure exclusive rights to GE's Alexanderson alternator, a radio sending device that revolutionized long-distance wireless communication. Rear Admiral W. H. G. Bullard, representing the U.S. Navy, persuaded Young and GE to discontinue negotiations with British Marconi and form a company powerful enough to meet British competition. Young then founded RCA and negotiated a series of agreements pooling the radio technology of major American companies and dividing the radio equipment and transmission business.

In subsequent years he engineered a series of agreements with foreign companies that divided the world into radio zones and facilitated worldwide wireless communication. The United States became a leader in the field of radio communication, and RCA controlled virtually all radio traffic in the western hemisphere. Young believed that international radio service and broadcasting were important forces for the advancement of civilization and world peace.

In the mid-1920's Young was instrumental in the founding of the National Broadcasting Company, which became a leader in American radio. When a federal court order in 1933 forced him to give up the chairmanship of either RCA or GE, he chose to stay with GE. Leaving RCA was one of the greatest disappointments in his business career.

In 1922, Young became chairman of the board of GE. Partially through Young's influence, Gerard Swope was named president of the corporation. The two men served in their respective posts until 1939 and formed one of the most brilliant and progressive business teams in American corporate history. They fostered labor-management cooperation, improved GE's public image, and increased the firm's production and sales. As advocates of the "new capitalism," they urged closer business-government cooperation and corporate self-regulation under government supervision. In the field of labor relations, the team introduced a plan for profit-sharing, a pension and life-insurance system, and a scheme to provide unemployment insurance for GE employees. Although not all of these plans succeeded, GE's labor relations during the Young-Swope era were generally amicable. As a frequent public speaker and member of many prestigious business organizations, Young established himself as one of the foremost spokesmen of the new capitalism.

Young and Swope transformed GE into a firm strictly concerned with engineering and the production of electrical equipment. Beginning in 1924, they sold GE's utility holdings. The voluntary nature of this divestiture was in keeping with their view that business should be as self-regulating as possible. Another dramatic change at GE during the 1920's and 1930's was the increased emphasis on the production and sale of consumer goods. The firm had been primarily a supplier of capital goods. Young and

Swope put it into the larger electrical appliance field. By 1940 the production of consumer goods accounted for about half of GE's output. Its concentration on the appliance market made the firm a household name and further improved its public image. At the end of the Young-Swope period at GE, the firm employed 67,000 people and did about one-quarter of the nation's electrical business.

During the 1920's, Young became involved in international diplomacy. He was a major spokesman for the Democratic party in foreign affairs. In response to the breakdown of reparations payments and the subsequent collapse of the German economy in 1923, the Allied Reparations Commission appointed two committees of experts to devise a plan to reconstruct Germany's economy and to propose a new formula for the payment of reparations. At Hughes's suggestion, Young and Charles Dawes, a Chicago banker, were appointed to the first committee in December 1923. In early 1924 this group constructed the Dawes Plan. Young was its chief architect and the leader of the American delegation at the Paris meetings of the First Expert Committee.

Drawing upon his business experience, Young skillfully constructed the plan by balancing the various interests at the conference and steering the plan through the committees. The Dawes Plan set forth a formula for the restoration and stabilization of German finances, a temporary solution to the problem of transferring reparations that greatly reduced the yearly payments, and a proposal to raise an international loan for Germany. The reparations experts unanimously accepted the plan on Apr. 9, 1924.

At the London Conference (July–August 1924), Young worked behind the scenes to negotiate a series of compromises that led to the acceptance of the Dawes Plan by the interested governments. He remained in Europe to iron out details and to convince skeptical American bankers to underwrite a sizable loan for Germany. Young was chosen interim agent general for reparations, a post that made him virtually a receiver for the German government. During his short tenure he put the complex Dawes Plan machinery in motion. Later in the fall of 1924, he relinquished the position to Seymour Parker Gilbert, convinced that there was now a "new spirit determined to restore tranquility in Western Europe."

The Dawes Plan helped to restore prosperity in Europe, and created a climate for greater political cooperation among the major powers. But it was only a temporary solution to the reparations problem. The massive influx of private loans into Germany was undermining it. By late 1928, European and American leaders were seeking a final reparations settlement.

Young was appointed chairman of the Second Expert Commission on Reparations on Feb. 9, 1929. He brought the opposing sides together by convincing them, according to Ida Tarbell, that "any settlement was infinitely better than no settlement—'too dear to take, yet too cheap to leave.'" The resulting Young Plan (June 7, 1929) reduced German reparations payments, restricted them to fifty-nine years, and unofficially linked them to the Allied war debts owed to the United States. It also withdrew all economic control agencies from Germany and paved the way for the termination of Allied military occupation of the Rhineland.

Perhaps the most creative feature of the Young Plan was the creation of the Bank for International Settlements (BIS). As a bank for central bankers under business control, the BIS could serve as a clearinghouse for international accounts, facilitate the movement of exchange between central banks, and solve problems inherent in the gold exchange system. Young hoped that the BIS would take the reparations problem out of the sphere of politics and allow business leaders to make the decisions that would eventually eliminate all governmental indebtedness associated with World War I. He believed that the creation of the bank might be "the most construtive job done in our generation."

The Young Plan and the BIS went into operation in May 1930. But the Great Depression soon made the plan unworkable. Although the BIS survived, it was unable to prevent the collapse of the international banking structure.

During the early years of the Great Depression, Young served on President Herbert Hoover's Organization on Unemployment Relief. But he became increasingly impatient with Hoover's resistance to recovery measures he thought important, including federal assistance for the unemployed. In 1932 it was widely speculated that Young would be a Democratic candidate for president, but—not least because of his wife's precarious health—he declined all overtures. He was one of Franklin D. Roosevelt's close advisers during the 1932 campaign.

After Roosevelt's election, Young's relationship with the president-elect began to cool. Roosevelt apparently believed that Young's ties with Wall Street and the public utility industry would be a liability to his administration. Although Young was a candidate for secretary of

state, Roosevelt chose Cordell Hull for the post.

Young took a guarded position on New Deal policies. He praised some programs, but criticized New Deal tendencies toward overcentralization and interference in the business sector. While privately deploring the adversary relationship with labor which the Wagner Act made probable, Young and Swope accepted philosophically the Congress of Industrial Organizations' successful organization of GE's factory workers, and no "sit-down" or other strikes ensued. As a member, and later chairman, of the Federal Reserve Bank of New York (1923–1940), Young was highly critical of the Banking Act of 1935, which he believed might undermine the Federal Reserve System by centralizing too much power in Washington without the checks and balances of the local Federal Reserve banks.

Josephine Young died in 1935, and on Feb. 20, 1937, he married Louise Powis Clark. In 1939, Young retired from GE. After the United States entered World War II, he returned to GE as chairman (1942–1944). He was also chairman of the wartime American Youth Commission—youth being for him a major concern.

In 1947, Young served on President Harry S. Truman's Committee on Foreign Aid, which made recommendations on European relief and reconstruction under the Marshall Plan. The following year he was a member of the Hoover Commission, which studied the organization of the executive branch of government.

Throughout his life Young took a strong interest in education, giving numerous commencement addresses in which he exhorted graduates to appreciate the advantages of learning. As chairman of the New York Temporary Commission on the Need for a State University (1946), he helped to raise the question of the state university system above the realm of partisan politics. Owing in large part to Young's skills as a negotiator and administrator, the final report recommended one of the most far-reaching higher education systems in the nation.

During his last years Young spent much time tending his farm and a citrus grove in Florida. He died at St. Augustine, Fla.

[An extensive collection of Young's papers is in the possession of the Van Hornesville Community Corporation, Van Hornesville, N.Y. A biography of Young is Ida M. Tarbell, *Owen D. Young* (1932). A full-length study by Everett Case and Josephine Young Case, *Owen D. Young and American Enterprise,* is forthcoming. A biographical sketch, "Life of

Owen D. Young," is in *Fortune*, Jan.–Mar. 1931. In the area of foreign policy, see Brady A. Hughes, "Owen D. Young and American Foreign Policy, 1919–1929" (Ph.D. diss., University of Wisconsin, 1969). On his work in reparations, see Stephen A. Shuker, *The End of French Predominance in Europe* (1976), and Melvyn P. Leffler, *The Elusive Quest* (1979). Frank C. Costigliola, "The Other Side of Isolationism," *Journal of American History*, Dec. 1972, discusses Young's contributions to the formation of the BIS. For Young's career at GE, see David Loth, *Swope of GE* (1958); and Kim McQuaid, "Young, Swope, and General Electric's 'New Capitalism,'" *American Journal of Economics and Sociology*, July 1977, and "Competition, Cartelization and the Corporate Ethic," *ibid.*, Oct. 1977. On the formation of RCA, see Michael J. Hogan, *Informal Entente* (1977).

Also see Raymond Moley, *After Seven Years* (1972); and Frank Freidel, *Franklin D. Roosevelt: Launching the New Deal* (1973). An obituary is in the *New York Times*, July 12, 1962.]

JOHN M. CARROLL

YOUNG, STARK (Oct. 11, 1881–Jan. 6, 1963), drama critic, novelist, and playwright, was born in Como, Miss., the son of Alfred Alexander Young, a physician, and of Mary Clark Starks. His mother died when Stark was nine, and the boy was reared primarily by two aunts. In 1895, Dr. Young remarried and moved to Oxford, Miss. Stark was enrolled in the local private school; but its strict discipline proved too much for his sensitive nature, so his father withdrew him from classes after two months. He then attended Union Female College, a Methodist institution that accepted boys as day students. Young showed great intellectual promise, and in 1896 he was accepted as a probationary student at the University of Mississippi. He graduated with the B.A. in 1901 and a year later received the M.A. in English from Columbia University.

Young was enchanted by New York City. After graduating from Columbia, he was hired as a reporter for the *Brooklyn Standard Union*. He found newspaper work unrewarding, so he returned to the South in the spring of 1903 and taught for a year at a military school in Water Valley, Miss. In 1904 he was appointed instructor in English at the University of Mississippi.

Young was well suited for the academic life and was popular with the students. In 1906 he published a verse play, *Guenevere*, and a volume of poems, *The Blind Man at the Window*. The following year he was offered an instructorship in English literature at the University of Texas at Austin. He promptly accepted.

At Texas, Young began to turn his attention from poetry to theater. In 1909 he founded the famed Curtin Club. He not only produced and directed the club's plays but also designed the sets and costumes. Young translated foreign plays that the students presented and occasionally contributed original works. In 1914, while still teaching in Texas, Young founded and edited the *Texas* (later *Southwest*) *Review*. In 1915, in order to be closer to the center of American theater—New York City—he accepted a professorship in English at Amherst College.

During the five years he taught at Amherst, Young published many poems and articles in national magazines and literary journals. His play *At the Shrine* was published in *Theatre Arts Magazine*. He met and befriended the actor Jacob Ben-Ami, the critic Kenneth Macgowan, and the rising young playwright Eugene O'Neill. In 1921, Young resigned from Amherst, abandoning a secure academic career for the doubtful future but personal reward of artistic endeavor in New York City.

The following year Young joined the editorial board of the *New Republic* and became an associate editor of *Theatre Arts Magazine*. In 1923 he directed the Theatre Guild's production of Henri Lenormand's *The Failures*. The next year he became the chief drama critic of the *New York Times*. The pressure of deadlines and a difference of opinion with the publisher, Adolph S. Ochs, caused Young to leave the *Times* and return to the *New Republic* in 1925. That same year the London Stage Society presented his play *The Colonnade*.

Young's first novel, *Heaven Trees*, was published in 1926. It was followed by *The Torches Flare* (1928) and *River House* (1929). The locale of the three novels was the Deep South. All enjoyed good reviews and modest sales.

It was with the publication of *So Red the Rose* that Young achieved widespread acclaim and financial success. It was one of the best-selling novels of 1934, and continued to sell well for almost two decades. A year after publication it was made into a motion picture by Paramount. Unfortunately for Young and Paramount, Margaret Mitchell's *Gone with the Wind* was published in 1936. Mitchell's theme was similar to Young's, and her book soon eclipsed his novel in the public's fancy.

Starting with the death of his friend and mentor Herbert Croly in 1930, Young suffered a series of personal and professional disappointments. As editor in chief of the *New Republic*, Croly believed in the importance of American culture and arts. His successors stressed political coverage at the expense of Young's reviews. He was further anguished by the untimely death of his nephew, Stark Young Robertson, in 1936. His friendship and professional association with Alfred Lunt and Lynn Fontanne soured in 1941 after they failed to produce a play that he had written specially for them.

In 1942, while still employed at the *New Republic*, Young began to dabble in painting. The hobby took more and more of his time as his interest in theater waned. His works were exhibited at the Pennsylvania Academy of Fine Arts in Philadelphia and the Art Institute of Chicago. In 1947, after his reviews were reduced to one column, he resigned from the *New Republic*. He broke all ties with *Theatre Arts* one year later.

Young's activities were severely curtailed in 1959 by a stroke. The last months of his life were spent in a nursing home in Fairfield, Conn., where he died.

Young never married. Although he did not live in the South after 1915, he always identified strongly with southern tradition. In his literature and his life, he strove to discover what elements of the South's tradition might be beneficial to modern life. As his plays and translations attest, he had an uncanny sense of what would work on stage. Young introduced a new style of dramatic criticism. Drawing on his practical experience, erudition, and sensitivity, he illuminated the classics and championed the moderns. His contribution to the flowering of American theater during the 1920's and 1930's was immeasurable.

[Young's correspondence has been collected and edited by John Pilkington as *Stark Young, a Life in the Arts: Letters, 1900–1962*, 2 vols. (1976). Young's memoir, *The Pavilion* (1951), contains a great deal of anecdotal information about his first twenty years. A collection of his criticism is *The Theatre* (1958). Obituaries are in the *New York Times*, Jan. 7, 1963; and *New Republic*, Jan. 26, 1963.]

KEVIN J. MORAN

ZACHARIAS, ELLIS MARK (Jan. 1, 1890–June 28, 1961), naval officer, was born in Jacksonville, Fla., the son of Alron Zacharias, a tobacco grower, and of Theresa Budwig. He graduated from the U.S. Naval Academy in 1912. At the academy he began a lifelong study of Japanese language and culture.

After sea duty during World War I, Zacharias returned to Annapolis for a year's tour as instructor. In 1920 he was assigned to Tokyo as naval attaché, a turning point in his career. During his three years in Japan, he became fluent in the language and met many of the men who later directed Japan's war effort against the United States. Zacharias spent 1924–1926 in the Panama Canal Zone, where he met and married in June 1925 Clara Evans Miller. They had two sons.

In 1928, Zacharias served a short tour in Tokyo as naval attaché, and from 1928 to 1931 he headed the Far East Division of the Office of Naval Intelligence (ONI) in Washington. In 1938–1940 he was intelligence officer of the Eleventh Naval District.

When the Japanese attacked Pearl Harbor on Dec. 7, 1941, Zacharias was at sea commanding the cruiser *Salt Lake City*. His ship returned to Pearl Harbor only hours after the raid ended. During 1942 he participated in the first offensive actions against the Japanese in the Marshalls and at Wake Island. Later that year Zacharias was appointed deputy director of the ONI, and in 1943–1944 he commanded the battleship *New Mexico* in campaigns in the Gilberts, Marshalls, and Marianas. In October 1944 he became chief of staff of the Eleventh Naval District.

The culmination of Zacharias' career was his key role in psychological warfare operations against Japan during the closing months of the war. In August 1942 he had been instrumental in establishing a psychological warfare branch in the ONI. Later he brought his views on Japanese war-weariness and vulnerability to propaganda to the attention of Elmer Davis, head of the Office of War Information; Secretary of the Navy James Forrestal; and Chief of Naval Operations Admiral Ernest J. King. Assigned to Washington in April 1945, he prepared a plan of psychological operations aimed at inducing Japan to surrender unconditionally before the full-scale invasion scheduled for late that year.

Zacharias' views ran counter to the prevailing belief among American leaders that the Japanese were fanatically determined to fight to the finish. He nevertheless won official approval of his plan. On May 8, hours after President Harry S. Truman's announcement of the end of the war in Europe, Zacharias, as the "official spokesman of the U.S. Government," addressed the first of a series of fourteen broadcasts to the Japanese people.

Zacharias was soon caught up in the controversy over the application to Japan of the unconditional surrender formula originally proclaimed by President Franklin D. Roosevelt in January 1943. Truman's announcement on May 8 had stated that there was no intent to exterminate or enslave the Japanese people. Zacharias urged that Japan also be given convincing assurance that the emperor would be spared and the imperial system preserved in some form. Unconditional surrender, he explained in his broadcasts, applied only to the capitulation of the armed forces, not to the peace settlement. His views were shared by some American leaders, including Secretary of War Henry L. Stimson, who recommended that Japan be offered the possibility of a constitutional monarchy under the reigning dynasty. This formula was rejected, though, and Zacharias was not permitted to make any allusion in his broadcasts to the postwar status of the emperor. In an effort to circumvent this restriction, he wrote an unsigned letter to the *Washington Post* suggesting that the Japanese government formally request clarification of American intentions regarding the emperor. The letter was published on July 21 and picked up by Japanese monitors. On July 26, however, the Allied Potsdam Declaration threatened Japan with "prompt and utter destruction" unless its armed forces surrendered at once and unconditionally.

The influence of Zacharias' operations on Japan's surrender is difficult to assess, in light of the dropping of atomic bombs on Hiroshima and Nagasaki on August 6 and 9 and the Soviet declaration of war against Japan on August 8. Japan's civilian leaders, distrusting the Allies and fearing a military coup, vainly staked their last desperate hopes for acceptable peace terms on Soviet good offices, secretly solicited in June. Zacharias later asserted in his autobiographical *Secret Missions* (1946) that on July 24, before Potsdam, the Japanese government had clearly signaled in an official broadcast its readiness to surrender unconditionally on the basis of the Atlantic Charter. A broadcast from Tokyo on August 10, the day of Japan's first formal surrender offer, cited that broadcast and mentioned Zacharias by name. Zacharias was awarded the Legion of Merit for his performance (one of three he received during the war) and retired in 1946 as a rear admiral.

Soon after retiring, Zacharias attracted national attention when, testifying before a congressional committee, he recalled that in March 1941 he had warned Admiral Husband E. Kimmel, then commanding the Pacific Fleet, of the probability that Japan's first war move would be a surprise air attack, on a Sunday morning, against the fleet and its shore installations on Hawaii. Kimmel denied that the incident had occurred. In later years Zacharias advocated an expanded psychological warfare program to combat Communism. During the Korean War he charged that the Soviet Union was conducting germ warfare against United States troops. He died in West Springfield, N.H.

[See Louis Morton, "The Decision to Use the Atomic Bomb (1945)," *Foreign Affairs,* Jan. 1957; Toshikazu Kase, *Journey to the "Missouri"* (1950); and Robert J. C. Butow, *Japan's Decision to Surrender* (1954). An obituary is in the *New York Times,* June 29, 1961.]

RICHARD M. LEIGHTON

ZAHNISER, HOWARD CLINTON (Feb. 25, 1906–May 5, 1964), conservationist and editor, was born in Franklin, Pa., the son of Archibald Howard McElrath Zahniser, a clergyman, and Bertha Belle Newton. He was educated in public schools at Tionesta, Pa., and in 1928 received a B.A. degree from Greenville (Ill.) College. From 1930 to 1931 he did postgraduate work at American University and George Washington University in Washington, D.C.

After college, Zahniser taught English in high school at Greenville. In 1930 he began federal government service as an editorial assistant in the Department of Commerce. From 1931 to 1942 he was employed by the Bureau of Biological Survey, in the Department of Agriculture, and by its successor agency, the Fish and Wildlife Service, in the Department of the Interior. Zahniser served as an editor, writer, and broadcaster on wildlife research, management, and conservation. He was a principal research writer and information officer in the Bureau of Plant Industry, Soils, and Agricultural Engineering, in the Department of Agriculture, from 1942 to 1945. He married Alice Bernita Hayden on Mar. 3, 1936. They had four children.

In 1945, Zahniser became executive secretary (later executive director) of the Wilderness Society and editor of its magazine, *The Living Wilderness,* serving in these capacities until his death. He worked closely with such conservationists as Aldo Leopold and Benton MacKaye. Zahniser was an ardent defender of the preservation of wilderness areas, in the historical tradition of aesthetic and recreation conservationists such as John Muir and Robert Marshall, the latter the principal founder of the Wilderness Society.

This interest was first strongly shown in one of the great conservation controversies of the 1950's, which centered on a proposal for the construction of a dam on the Green River that would have destroyed wilderness features of the Dinosaur National Monument on the Colorado-Utah border. Zahniser was a leader of efforts to defeat the proposal. He wrote speeches opposing the dam that were delivered in the Senate by Richard L. Neuberger, Paul H. Douglas, and Hubert H. Humphrey. His efforts, although resisted by powerful western groups, bore fruit in 1956, when Congress enacted a law prohibiting the construction of a dam in the Dinosaur National Monument.

Zahniser advocated a national wilderness preservation system under which federal natural resource agencies, such as the National Park Service and Forest Service, might be made responsible for preserving wilderness areas under their jurisdiction. He opposed allowing the agencies to continue a permissive policy of preservation by administrative decision. Zahniser began to advocate such a system as early as 1951, and by 1955 he had won the support of the Wilderness Society, the Sierra Club, and other conservation organizations. Soon thereafter he helped to persuade Humphrey and Representative John P. Saylor to introduce bills in Congress for creation of a national wilderness system. The bills, written to a great extent by Zahniser, stipulated that the system should include eighty areas in national forests, forty-eight in national parks and monuments, twenty in national wildlife refuges and ranges, and fifteen on Indian reservations. They created the National Wilderness Council to make recommendations to Congress on administration and possible expansion of the wilderness areas. Numerous hearings on these bills and their various revisions between June 1957 and April 1964 occupied much of Zahniser's time. He made a final appearance at a hearing on Apr. 28, 1964, a week before his death.

Opposition by the forest products, oil, grazing, and mining industries, by professional foresters, and by some government bureaus led Congress to reduce greatly the number of proposed wilderness areas and to eliminate provision for the Wilderness Council. The act was finally signed by President Lyndon Johnson on Sept. 3, 1964. Its passage owed much to Zahniser's zealous efforts.

In addition to the Wilderness Society, Zahniser was active in several other conservation organizations. In 1946 he was one of the organizers of the Natural Resources Council of America, a loose federation of groups concerned about natural resource issues. Later he served as its chairman (1948–1949). He was a member of the Advisory Committee on Conservation to

the Secretary of the Interior from 1951 to 1954, vice-chairman of the Citizens Committee on Natural Resources in 1955, and president of the Thoreau Society in 1957. The Sierra Club made Zahniser an honorary vice-president. He was an essayist and book editor for *Nature* magazine from 1935 to 1959, and he wrote wilderness and wildlife articles for the *Encyclopaedia Britannica.* He died at Hyattsville, Md.

[Principal documentary sources on Zahniser are the records of the Wilderness Society in Washington, D.C., and of the Sierra Club in San Francisco, Calif. Much of his correspondence with federal agencies is among records of the departments of the Interior and of Agriculture in the National Archives Building, Washington, D.C. His efforts to mobilize support for the system are described in Roderick Nash, *Wilderness and the American Mind* (1967). Obituaries are in the *Washington Post* and *New York Times,* May 6, 1964.]

HAROLD T. PINKETT

ZELLERBACH, JAMES DAVID (Jan. 17, 1892–Aug. 3, 1963), industrialist and diplomat, was born in San Francisco, Calif., the son of Isadore Zellerbach, a paper company executive, and of Jennie Baruh. After graduating with a B.A. from the University of California in 1913, he took a trip around the world. He then entered the Zellerbach Corporation, founded by his grandfather, as a counterman. On June 29, 1916, he married Hannah Fuld; they had two children.

In 1928 the Zellerbach Corporation merged with the Crown Williamette Corporation to become Crown Zellerbach, the nation's leading manufacturer of paper and paper products. Zellerbach became president of the new corporation. He succeeded his father as chairman in 1938.

With little labor difficulty over a sustained period of time, Zellerbach came to have a national reputation as a labor expert. In 1945 President Harry S. Truman appointed Zellerbach as the United States employer delegate to the International Labor Organization Conference in Paris. He served as vice chairman of the organization from 1945 to 1948. In 1948 Paul Hoffman, head of the Economic Cooperation Administration (ECA), appointed Zellerbach head of the ECA mission to implement the Marshall Plan in Italy.

After leaving the ECA in 1952, Zellerbach returned to private business activities, which were briefly interrupted in 1953 by duties as alternate United States delegate to the General Assembly of the United Nations. In 1956, President Dwight D. Eisenhower appointed him to succeed Claire Booth Luce as ambassador to Italy. He held the post until the conclusion of the Eisenhower administration. For his activities he was awarded by the Italian government the Decorated Star of Italian Solidarity, First Class (1952); the Commendatore Order of Merit of the Italian Republic (1955); and the Grand Cross of the Order of Merit (1960).

In 1961, Zellerbach returned to San Francisco and his business interests. In addition, he maintained membership in numerous companies, foundations, committees, councils, societies, and clubs. He was active in the symphony and opera associations of San Francisco and was a member of the board of directors of the American Red Cross. He was also a trustee of the Committee for Economic Development, chairman of the National Manpower, a member of the National Conference of Christians and Jews, and a director of the Foreign Policy Associates.

[An obituary appeared in the *New York Times*, Aug. 4, 1963.]

ROBERT J. MITCHELL

INDEX GUIDE

TO THE SUPPLEMENTS

Index Guide to the Supplements

Index Guide to the Supplements

Index Guide to the Supplements

820

Index Guide to the Supplements

Index Guide to the Supplements

822

Index Guide to the Supplements

Index Guide to the Supplements

Index Guide to the Supplements

Index Guide to the Supplements

Index Guide to the Supplements

Index Guide to the Supplements

Index Guide to the Supplements

Index Guide to the Supplements

Index Guide to the Supplements

Index Guide to the Supplements

832

Index Guide to the Supplements

Index Guide to the Supplements

Index Guide to the Supplements

Index Guide to the Supplements

Index Guide to the Supplements

Index Guide to the Supplements

Index Guide to the Supplements

Index Guide to the Supplements

Index Guide to the Supplements

Index Guide to the Supplements

Index Guide to the Supplements

Index Guide to the Supplements

Index Guide to the Supplements

Index Guide to the Supplements

Index Guide to the Supplements

Index Guide to the Supplements

Index Guide to the Supplements

Index Guide to the Supplements

Index Guide to the Supplements

Index Guide to the Supplements

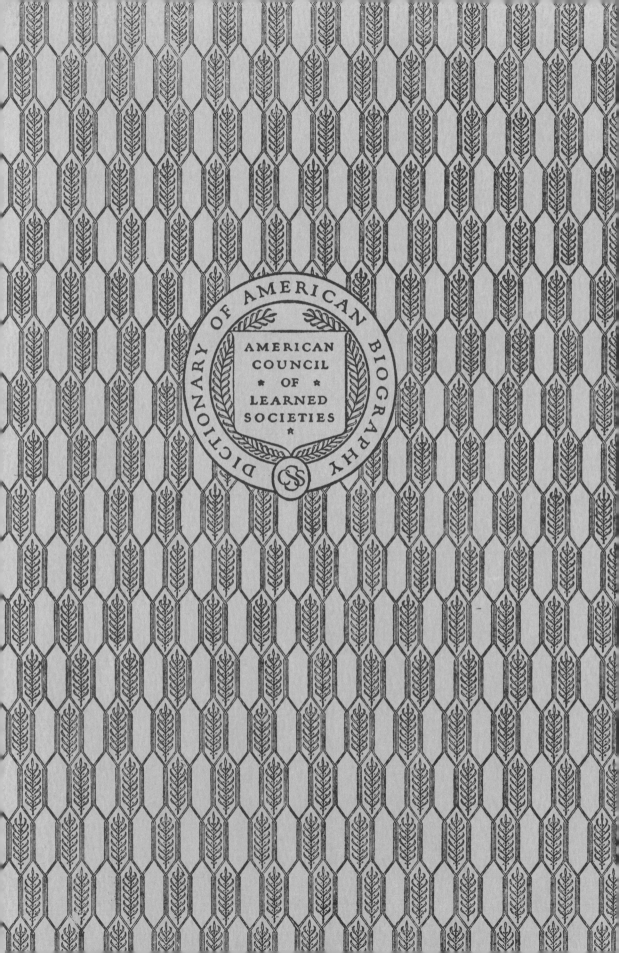